929.409411

Get **more** out of libraries

Please return or renew this item by the last date shown.

You can renew online at www.hants.gov.uk/library

Or by phoning 0845 603 5631

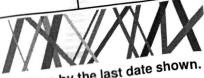

Hampshire
County Council

2/09

The Surnames of Scotland

Their Origin, Meaning, and History

By GEORGE F. BLACK, Ph.D.

BIRLINN

This edition first published in 1999 by
Birlinn Limited
West Newington House
10 Newington Road
Edinburgh EH9 1QS

www.birlinn.co.uk

Reprinted 2004, 2007

ISBN 13: 978 1 87474 483 2
ISBN 10: 1 87474 483 1

British Library Cataloguing-in-Publication Data
A Catalogue record for this book is available from
the British Library

Printed and bound by Antony Rowe Ltd, Chippenham

TO MY WIFE

TO MY DAUGHTERS

MARY AND FLORENCE

AND TO MY SON GEORGE

Preface

THIS work, the result of many years of research, deals with the origin, meaning, and history of several thousand Scottish surnames. It includes, also, a number of early personal names which did not become surnames, but nevertheless have a special interest of their own. The work is not to be considered as genealogical, though doubtless many of the entries and references will be found helpful to those conducting research into family history. As the work is historical and scientific in the treatment of its subject the folklore and fairy tales of family and clan origins are left to be dealt with by other writers with a penchant for that kind of writing. (*See under* Popular Derivations of Surnames.)

The interpretation and history of most Scottish personal names and surnames, it need scarcely be stressed, is of importance as throwing light on the ethnology and genealogy of the people inhabiting the country.

In the case of territorial surnames and surnames of foreign origin I have endeavored as often as possible to record the year or period when they first appear in our records. In the case of a number of surnames, where certain etymologies have been popularly accepted, but which I venture to think are nevertheless erroneous, I have thought it desirable to draw attention to the explanations offered by others in order that readers may not think I have overlooked them when offering my own explanation.

A multiplicity of roots is frequently offered by the amateur etymologist to explain any surname, with the equally obliging intimation that if the reader does not like either of them, there are others which may easily be supplied. In studies of this nature the interpreter must be careful not to be guided merely by sound or by similarity of appearance — the right road to interpretation lying through a diligent search of the historical sources. There are not a few surnames for which as many interpretations are offered as there are authorities, through neglect of this rule.

As in the early days surnames were the exception rather than the rule, it follows that the etymologies of Scottish surnames as in the case of other nations of mixed races, must, in many obscure instances, be a matter of conjecture, especially where the name has not emerged into any degree of prominence in the historical documents of the past.

In some instances, where old forms do not exist or are not known to me, the explanation put forward is more or less of a tentative nature. On the whole, however, where I can give no definite explanation of the name I have preferred to say nothing. It is nearly impossible at times to give a derivation where helping references are not forthcoming, and names of one syllable in general are among the most ancient we have and the hardest to solve.

The head of one of the historically oldest Scottish families (Graham of Menteith) has said that the principal occupation of the ancestors of these families seems to have been the witnessing of charters. He was alluding to the fact that in the charters granted by the kings or great landed barons in Scotland the names of many individuals are appended as witnesses. In the cases of many of our oldest Scottish surnames it can be truly said that if they were not thus recorded by the charter scribes we should not otherwise have known of their early existence.

The fact that many of the names recorded in the work occur only once or twice in the public records should not be taken as evidence that they have died out; they may quite possibly have flourished for generations without becoming sufficiently prominent to break into official notice. There are many surnames still in existence of which we have only late record, but we can be quite certain that they must have been in regular use for generations previously.

Many names explained here have not survived as surnames, but it is never safe to say of any given name that it is extinct. Within recent years some surnames described in public print as no longer existing have brought forth indignant letters of protest from bearers of such names vigorously denying their extinction.

Authority, in almost every case is quoted in support of the statements made, and the key list gives the clue to the authorities quoted. Names of persons and places are often "written otherwise now than they were of old," but the old forms of place names and surnames are given in the forms under which they appear in record. The numerous examples quoted for some surnames illustrate their wide diffusion in place and time.

Upon the author's retirement from the service of The New York Public Library where he had been connected for thirty-five years, the material for this work which had been collected for over forty years was put in order and made ready for publication. On the completion of this task unexpected difficulties were encountered in publication. Publishing houses, recovering from the recent slump in trade, were hesitant to undertake a work which obviously would not be a "best seller," without a financial guarantee. This the author was unable to give, and in discouragement the manuscript was laid aside. In 1939 new hope was born that it would be published in Britain, the logical place for this subject, only to be dashed again upon the outbreak of the world war.

Later the introduction was revised and enlarged, and shown to Mr. Deoch Fulton, editor of the *Bulletin* of The New York Public Library, for his opinion and editorial comment. Realizing its historical value Mr. Fulton made a request to see some of the material on the names. Upon his recommendation, Mr. Franklin F. Hopper, Director of the Library, asked for the author's permission to publish the work in its entirety in the Library's *Bulletin.* This permission was granted, and the first installment appeared in August, 1943.

For much help in reading proofs, verifying obsolete spellings, checking dates, etc., I am indebted to my daughter, Mary Elder Black. I have also to thank Mr. Daniel C. Haskell for his editorial supervision over copy and printed text, and thanks are also due to Mr. Charles M. Farrand for his labor and patience over the galleys.

GEORGE F. BLACK

The new amendments and additions on pages 831–834 have been supplied by Miss Mary Elder Black.

č

Table of Contents

>>>✦<<<

Preface   vii

Introduction   xiii

List of Principal Works Referred to   lix

Abbreviations   lxxii

The Surnames of Scotland   1

Amendments and Additions   831

Glossary of Obsolete Words   835

Introduction

THE USE of fixed surnames or descriptive names appears to have commenced in France about the year 1000, and such names were introduced into Scotland through the Normans a little over one hundred years later, though the custom of using them was by no means common for many years afterward.

William Stewart in his metrical vernacular version of the History of Scotland by Hector Boece[1] says that at a general council held at Forfar in 1061 during the reign of Malcolm Ceannmor (1057–1093) the latter directed his chief subjects, after the custom of other nations, to adopt surnames from their territorial possessions, and there created "The first erlis that euir was in Scotland," and

> "Mony surename also les and moir,
> Wes maid that tyme quhilk wes nocht of befoir.
> As Calder, Lokart, Gordoun, and Setoun,
> Gallowa, Lauder, Wawane, and Libertoun,
> Meldrum, Schaw, Leirmond, and Cargill,
> Stratherne, Rattray, Dundas als thairtill,
> With Cokburne, Mar, and Abircrumby,
> Myretoun, Menzeis, and also Leslie."

And again, he tells, with the future Queen Margaret came

> "Lyndesay, Wallace, Touris, and Lovell,
> Ramsay, Prestoun, Sandelandis, Bisset, Soullis, Maxwell,
> Wardlaw, Giffurd, Maule, Borthuik also,
> Fethikran, Creichtoun, all thir and no mo."

And five of this last lot

> "Come with Edgar out of Vngary."

Sir Thomas Gray in his *Scalacronica*, referring to the return of William the Lion to Scotland after his liberation in 1175, says:

"Wherefore he toke with hym many of the youngger sunnes of the nobyl men of England that bare hym good wylle, and gave them landes

---

[1] *The Buik of the Croniclis of Scotland*, London, 1858, vv. 40,655–40,662; 40,987–40,990. Stewart's editor says Fethikran (Fethirkran) is Fotheringham and Wawane Waugh. In Boece, *Scotorum Historiæ*, Paris, 1575, the corresponding passages are on ff. 256, 258. Father Woulfe suggests (*Sloinnte Gaedheal*, Dublin, 1923, p. xv–xviii) that the great bulk of Irish patronymics became fixed in the eleventh-twelfth centuries, but his conception of "surname" does not tally with the modern definition of the word.

in Scotland of them that were rebelles to hym. These were the names of the gentilmen that he toke with him; Bailliol, Breuse, Soully, Moubray, Saintclere, Hay, Giffard, Ramsey, Laundel, Dysey, Berkeley, Walenge, Boys, Montgomery, Vaulx, Coleville, Fresir, Grame, Gurlay, and dyverse other."[2]

The witnesses to the earliest known Scottish charter, that of Duncan II to the monks of St. Cuthbert of Durham (A. D. 1094), besides the king's brothers, are Accard, Ulf, Eadgar, Hermer, Œlfric, Earnulf, Vinget, Hemming, Toedbold, and Grenton the scriptor, the writer of the charter. The only other name, that of Malcolumb, the king's brother, is Gaelic.[3] Similarly the charter of King Eadgar, brother of Duncan, granting Swintun to the monks of St. Cuthbert of Coldingham, c. 1100, is witnessed by Ælfwin, Oter, Thor the long, Ælfric the steward (pincerna), Algar and Osbern the priests, Cnut, Carl, Ogga,[4] Lesing,[4] Swein, Ulfkill, Ligulf of Babbanburch (= Bamborough), Uhtred son of Eilave, Uniaet white. As in the earlier charter of King Duncan, the only other name, Tigerne, is Gaelic.[5]

The marriage of Malcolm Ceannmor with the Saxon princess Margaret (1068–69) has been commonly stated as the cause of the early immigration of Southrons. "But it had begun earlier, and many concurring causes determined at that time the stream of English colonization towards the Lowlands of Scotland,"[6] and although we have no records during this time of

[2] Quoted in Hailes, Annals of Scotland, 3. ed., v. 1, p. 139 n. Sir Thomas Gray compiled his narrative (c. 1356) in Norman French when he lay for two years a prisoner in Edinburgh Castle, "and beguiled his tedium by studying in the library there." Maxwell, The Early chronicles relating to Scotland, Glasgow, 1912, p. 226.

[3] National manuscripts of Scotland, v. 1, no. 2; Lawrie, Early Scottish charters prior to A. D. 1153, Glasgow, 1905, p. 10.

[4] "Leysing et Oggo Cumbrenses judices" are two of the jurors who gave evidence regarding the lands of the Church of Glasgow, c. 1124. Registrum Episcopatus Glasguensis, p. 5. In reverse order, Oggu, Leising, they are witnesses to King David's great charter of Holyrood. Liber Cartarum Sancte Crucis, p. 6.

[5] Lawrie, Early Scottish charters, p. 17–18. Robertson (Scotland under her early kings, v. 1, p. 286 n.) has pointed out that the witnesses for these two charters having all (with one exception in each) Saxon or Danish names is no proof of the exclusion of the native race from the court and councils. As these charters were most probably written and witnessed at Durham and referred to property in that district, it would be natural that the witnesses should be from the same locality. "The original Scots were no more driven out of the Lowlands by the advance of the Teutons than had the original Franks been driven out of Salic France by the encroachments of the 'Romans.'" Robertson, II, p. 489n.

[6] Innes, Sketches of early Scottish history, Edinburgh, 1861, p. 9. This influx of English people into Scotland with the consequent spread of English customs in the reign of Malcolm III caused

their acquiring lands, "that is probably for the simple reason, that there are no records of the acquisition of lands by laymen earlier than the reign of David."[7] The character of the movement was peculiar. "It was not," says Innes, "the bursting forth of an overcrowded population, seeking more room. The new colonists were what we should call 'of the upper classes' — of Anglian families long settled in Northumbria, and Normans of the highest blood and names. They were men of the sword, above all servile and mechanical employment.[8] They were fit for the society of a court, and many of them became

great opposition on the part of the native population, particularly in the north which showed itself at his death. On Ceannmor's death the throne was seized by Donald Bane, second son of King Duncan I and younger brother of Malcolm. Donald's first action as king was to drive out all those who had formerly been around the court (November, 1093). Duncan II, Malcolm's son by Ingibiorg, with the support of an army of Normans and Englishmen, claimed the throne, but was attacked and defeated by Donald's followers. Peace was however made between the contending parties and Duncan was recognized as king, "but on condition that he would never again introduce into Scotland either Normans or Englishmen, or permit them to give him military service." Mackenzie, *The Ancient kingdom*, 1930, p. 269. This Gaelic opposition persisted because, as William of Coventry, referring to the rebellion under Godfrey, son of Malcolm MacHeth, says, "the later kings of Scots boast of being French [i.e. Normans] in race and in manners, language and culture; and after reducing the Scots [i.e. the Gaels] to utter servitude, they admit only Normans to their friendship and service." *Memorials*, ed. Stubbs, v. 2, p. 206. William the Conqueror in his efforts to crush rebellion in the north of England is said to have left not a single inhabited village between York and Durham. "Those who escaped death fled to the south of Scotland, which was so stocked with English, both men and maidens, that they were to be found in all the farm houses and even in the cottages." Simeon of Durham, *Historia regum*, ed. 1885, v. 2, p. 188. And in the army of William the Lion when he was captured at Alnwick in 1174, says William of Newburgh, were "a great number of English; for the towns and burghs of the Scottish realm are known to be inhabited by English." *Historia Rerum Anglicarum*, Rolls Ser., v. 1, p. 186. It should, however, be noted that Flemings were also included in the term "English," apparently because in the main they seem, as already mentioned, to have come into Scotland through England.

[7] Innes, *Scotland in the middle ages*, 1860, p. 88. By the middle of the twelfth century it is certain that with the exception of Galloway the inhabitants of the southern counties of Scotland were practically English in speech, whatever may have been their proportion of Celtic blood. The Gaelic place names in the Lowlands prove that a people speaking Gaelic formerly possessed the territory but is not evidence as to the continued existence of the Gaelic race there.

[8] This, as M'Kerlie bluntly says, "is a fallacy: it is now becoming better known that the mass of the invading army was composed of the scum of France's adventurers, and, as mentioned by Thierry, were known only by the names of the towns or the districts from whence they came, as St. Quentin, St. Maur, Gascoine, &c. The majority did not even obtain such names, and had none until they were placed in possession of lands taken from some previous proprietor. From the lands so obtained the most of the new settlers called Normans (which in most cases is incorrect), obtained their surnames." *Galloway in ancient and modern times*, Edinburgh, 1891, p. 255. In another work M'Kerlie notes the general belief that to be of Norman descent is a sure mark of nobility, "one of the many popular fallacies which exist as regards past history." *History of lands and their owners in Galloway*, 2. ed., v. 1, p. 126.

the chosen companions of our Princes.[9] The names of the witnesses to the charters of David I and his brothers would prove this without other evidence. It is astonishing with what rapidity these southern colonists spread even to the far north. From Tweed and Solway to Sutherland, the whole arable land may be said to have been held by them. The old native people gave way before them, or took service under the strong-handed strangers.[10] The lands these English settlers acquired, they chose to hold in feudal manner and by written gift of the sovereign; and the little charter with the King's subscribing cross ($+$), or his seal attached, began to be considered necessary to constitute and prove their rights of property. Armed with it, and supported by the law, Norman knight and Saxon thegn[11] set himself to civilize his new acquired property, settled his vil or his town, built himself a house of fence, distributed the lands of his manor among his own followers and the nativi whom he found attached to the soil, either to be cultivated on his own account, or at a fixed 'ferm' on the risk of the tenant."[12]

This preferment given to incomers from the south by Malcolm Ceannmor and his Saxon queen and their immediate successors, placed these favorites in a position that enabled them to have a prominence in public affairs far above that which their numerical strength in the community entitled them to, and was the cause of much discontent among the native population, as witness William of Coventry's remarks quoted later on.

The motley character of the population of Scotland in the twelfth century receives ample recognition in royal charters of the time. Thus the charter

9 In Scotland the Norman came not as a conqueror but as a peaceful citizen, and entered along with those whom he had himself overcome in England. He was soon lost in the mixed nationality of his newest home, but not until he had modified many things in the same way as he had modified things in England. He gave Scotland many of her so-called nobility and three royal families — Balliol, Bruce, and Stewart.

10 We might expect the termination *vil* or *ville* to be much more common looking to the great number of Norman settlers, whose language was undoubtedly French. But the Anglian tongue prevailed, and the *villa Levingi, villa Edulfi, villa Thancardi* of the charters was translated and naturalized as Levingston, Edoluestone (now Eddleston) and Thankerton.

11 One of these Saxon thegns was Thor longus (the 'long') mentioned above as one of the witnesses to the charter by King Eadgar of the lands of Swintun to the monks of St. Cuthbert, c. 1100. Sometime before 1105 King Eadgar bestowed upon him the land of Ædenham (now Ednam), unsettled (*desertam*), and he by his own money cultivated and settled it, built a church and gave it and a ploughgate of land to the same monks for the weal of the soul of King Eadgar, and for the souls of the king's father, his mother, and brothers and sisters, and for the redemption of his own beloved brother Leswin, and for the weal of his own soul and body. Lawrie, *Early Scottish charters*, p. 19. Thor's expression "by his own money" (*mea propria pecunia*) is perhaps the first record of the application of capital to the development of land in Scotland. Between 1107–1117 Thor wrote a letter to his dearest lord, Earl David, commending this grant to the earl's protection, and Earl David confirmed it. *National manuscripts of Scotland*, v. 1, no. 14.

12 Innes, *Sketches of early Scottish history*, p. 10–11; *Origines parochiales Scotiae*, v. 1, p. xxvi.

by Earl David, afterwards David I, founding the abbey of Selkirk (afterwards moved to Kelso), c. 1120, is addressed to "Francis et Anglis et Scottis."[13] His charter of protection, as king, to the priory of Tinmouth, 1138, is addressed to "Francis et Anglis et Scotis et Galwensibus."[14] The original charter to the abbey of Melrose in 1144 is addressed to "Francis et Anglicis et Scottis et Galwensibus," and in addition to the names of the witnesses about the court there are added: "praeterea homines de eadem terra" (besides the men of that land): Gospatric comes, Vlchillus filius Ethestan, Osulfus filius Huctred, Maccus filius Vnwain, Huctredus filius Sioth, Huctredus filius Gospatric, Orm filius Eilas, Eilas filius Gospatric, Edulfus filius Norm[anni], Osolfus filius Ediue, Osulfus filius Elfstan, Robertus Brus meschin, Radulfus filius Turstani, Rogerus nepos Episcopi.[14a] The charter by Malcolm IV to the prior of Coldingham to settle the town of Coldingham with his serfs is witnessed by four officers of state all bearing Norman names.[15] The *Inquisitio* of Earl David, c. 1124, into the possessions of the Church of Glasgow in Cumbria, mentions that after many successors of S. Kentigern were translated to God divers insurrections arose which wasted the whole country and drove the inhabitants into exile. Then came divers tribes of different nations from divers parts and took possession of the foresaid desolate territory, different in race and dissimilar in language. In the charters of Malcolm IV and William the Lion the divers tongues and peoples in Cumbria are addressed "Francis et Anglicis, Scottis, Walensibus et Gaulensibus, et omnibus Ecclesie S. Kentigerni de Glasgu et ejusdem Episcopi parrochianis."[16] In another charter the see of Glasgow is referred to as "the spiritual mother of many nations," a phrase easily understood when the mixed nationality is remembered.

A charter by David, earl of Huntingdon, brother of William the Lion, granting the lands of Leslie in the Garioch to Malcolm, son of Bartholf, between 1171–1199, is addressed "Francis et Englis et Flamingis et Scotis;"[17] and in a confirmation by David II of a charter by Thomas, earl of Mar and the Garioch to John of Mar, canon of Aberdeen, of Cruterystoun in le Garuyauch occurs the clause "vna cum lege Fleminga qui dicitur Fleming lauch."[18]

---

[13] *Liber S. Marie de Calchou*, p. 3.

[14] Lawrie, *Early Scottish charters*, p. 91.

[14a] *Liber S. Marie de Melros*, no. 1.

[15] *National manuscripts of Scotland*, v. 1, no. 31.

[16] *Registrum Episcopatus Glasguensis*, p. 15.

[17] *Collections on shires of Aberdeen and Banff*, p. 547.

[18] *Exchequer Rolls of Scotland*, v. 1, p. lxxxi–lxxxii note.

In the struggle which took place in England between the parties of King Stephen and the Empress Matilda, David I took the part of his sister, and on his return to his own kingdom he was followed by many of her adherents.[19] In the following reign, that of Malcolm IV, David's policy of replacing turbulent and disaffected Gaelic chiefs with his Norman followers was continued, and by the end of the twelfth century the whole arable land may be said to have been held by them. Fordun particularly mentions the fact, possibly with some exaggeration, that in consequence of the rebellious ways of the "nation of the Moravienses" the king "removed them all from the land of their birth, as of old Nebuchadnezzar, king of Babylon, had dealt with the Jews, and scattered them throughout the other districts of Scotland, both beyond the hills and this side thereof, so that not even one native of that land abode there; and he installed therein his own peaceful people."[20]

The decree of Henry II of England in 1155 expelling all Flemings from England doubtless augmented the number of these people in Scotland. Indeed, they may have been invited to come in by Malcolm IV as about this time, as we have already seen, Beroaldus Flandrensis got the lands of Innes in Moray, and Theobaldus Flamaticus got lands (c. 1147–1160) on Douglas Water, etc.[21] Malcolm also confirmed to the canons of St. Andrews the oblations and rents payable to the Church of the Holy Trinity, as well from Scots as French, as well from Flemings as the English living within and without the burgh of St. Andrews.[22] Again, in the fragment of the Life of S. Kentigern[23]

---

[19] Many of these followers, especially younger sons, came from Northamptonshire. Some of them, for example, Bisset, Chisholm, and Fraser, like the contemporary military adventurers in Ireland, became more Gaelic than the Gaels themselves.

[20] *Annals*, iv.

[21] See under the name *Douglas*.

[22] *Liber Cartarum Prioratus Sancti Andree*, p. 194.

According to Jordan de Fantosme Flemings were conspicuous in the army of William the Lion at Alnwick, and John Crab, the Flemish engineer, was a thorn in the flesh of the English during the Scottish War of Independence. See under *Crab*. Mr. John Arnold Fleming in his *Flemish influence in Britain*, Glasgow, 1930, has sought to determine the extent and influence of elements from the Low Countries on the civilization, arts, and fortunes of Great Britain and of Scotland in particular. He describes in detail the influence of the Flemings on the development of the wool industry and the shipping trades, their influence on domestic life, their contributions in printing, painting, glass-making, bell-founding, agriculture, weaving, gardening, and sport. Their influence was particularly strong in Aberdeenshire and Fife, the counties in which they first made their home in Scotland.

Mainardus Flandrensis was appointed the first provost of St. Andrews, c. 1144. *Acts of Parliament of Scotland*, v. 1, p. 75.

[23] "Vita Kentigerni" in *Registrum Episcopatus Glasguensis*, p. lxxxiii–lxxxiv; Forbes, *Lives of S. Ninian and S. Kentigern*, Edinburgh, 1874, p. 131.

it is stated that the great abundance of fish around the Isle of May in the Firth of Forth was such as to induce fishers from all coasts, Angles, Scots, Belgians (i.e. Flemings), and French to resort thither for the sake of the fishing. Doubtless men of all these countries became settlers in and around the east coast about this time. The people of Buckhaven in Fife are said to be descended from natives of the Netherlands whose ship was stranded on the shore about the time of Philip ii of Spain. The family of Wemyss, who possessed the lands, gave them permission to settle and remain. They accordingly settled at Buckhaven, and, says a writer in 1778, "by degrees they acquired our language and adopted our dress, and for these three score years past they have had the character of a sober and sensible and industrious and honest set of people."[24] The fishing community of Newhaven on the southern side of the Firth of Forth is supposed to have in it admixtures of Dutch and Frisian blood, and rarely intermarries with stranger stock. A common surname among them is Flucker, also recorded in Fife as early as 1275.

No surnames appear in the charters of Alexander i (1106-1124), but in the reign of his brother and successor, David i (1124-1153), we find them coming into use. In his charter, as Earl David, before he ascended the throne, founding the abbey of Selkirk, c. 1120, we find Robertus de Brus, Robertus de Umfraville, Galterus de Lyndeseia, etc.[25] In the *Inquisitio* by the same earl referred to above, c. 1124, the names of Gervasius Ridel, Robertus de Burnevilla, Reinald de Muscans, etc., occur among the witnesses.[26] From this time onward we find names mainly territorial derived from possession of land becoming common, though a few are descriptive and some are patronymic.

During the reigns of David i, Malcolm iv, and William the Lion, the inhabitants of the burgh towns were largely English (Anglians) or Flemish, and the surnames of many of these settlers were derived from their trades or occupations. William the Lion granted to Pagan the goldsmith (*aurifaber*) a land in Edinburgh on the south side of St. Giles's church where he settled,[27] and to Henry Bald (Henricus Baldus), another goldsmith, some land in Perth.[28] The same king also granted a toft in Perth to William

---

[24] Quoted by Valentine, *Fifeshire*, 1915, p. 70.

[25] *Liber S. Marie de Calchou*, p. 4.

[26] *Registrum Episcopatus Glasguensis*, p. 5.

[27] *Charters of the priory of Inchcolm*, 1938, p. 5.

[28] *Liber Ecclesie de Scon*, p. 29. Goldsmiths appear to have settled about this period and during the following century in all the principal towns of Scotland. cf. Chalmers, *Caledonia*, v. 1, p. 787.

the helmet-maker, for which he was to render yearly "duos capellas ferri."[29]

Chalmers has noted that "the burgesses and the common people of the towns, who appear in the charters of the twelfth century, are distinguished by English or Flemish names, while the inhabitants of the country, who appear in charters, are distinguished by Gaelic names."[30]

"The burghs of Scotland," says the late George Burnett, Lyon King-of-Arms, "owe much of their prosperity to the large immigration of foreigners which had gone on during the twelfth and thirteenth centuries. The original founders of our towns are supposed to have been in many cases wanderers from Flanders, who brought with them their habits of industry and knowledge of trade and manufactures. Settlers of this description had come in great numbers to England in the reign of Henry i, and spread into the sister country; and when Henry ii drove all foreigners out of his dominions they flocked into Scotland, where a more enlightened policy made them welcome."[31]

The following list of witnesses to the right marches between Stobbo and Hoperewe and Orde is remarkable for the preponderance of Saxon or Old English names contained in it. The document unfortunately affords no

---

[29] *Liber Ecclesie de Scon*, p. 50. William the smith, Alan the tanner, Dernulf the dyer, Dernald the dyer, and William the dyer were all burgesses of Perth (*Liber Ecclesie de Scon*, p. 57; *Cartularies of Balmerino and Lindores*, p. 21–23). It is noteworthy that Perth is still famed for its dyeing industry. Walkelin the brewer (*braciator*) is a charter witness in Angus in the reign of William the Lion (RAA., i. p. 62), and Hugh the lorimer and his heirs had a grant of land in Perth from the same king (*Liber Ecclesie de Scon*, p. 60). Adam the barber was burgess of Dundee (*Cartularies of Balmerino and Lindores*, p. 34), Radulph the merchant, Roger the shoemaker, and Robert the locksmith, were inhabitants of Dumfries during the reign of William the Lion, and William the dyer lived in Kelso during the same reign (*Liber S. Marie de Calchou*, 2, 11, 352). Adam dictus carpentarius held the land of Haldhingleston (Ingliston, Renfrewshire), c. 1260 (*Registrum Monasterii de Passelet*, p. 58), and Nicholas the butcher (*carnifex*) appears in Dumfries c. 1280 (Edgar, *History of Dumfries*, p. 200). Simon the baker was burgess of Berwick (*Registrum S. Marie de Neubotle*, 207), and William the baker and Martin the goldsmith lived in Aberdeen about 1280 (*Registrum Episcopatus Aberdonensis*, v. 2, p. 278, 280).

[30] *Caledonia*, v. 1, p. 779 n. Contrast the Gaelic names of the perambulators of the boundaries of Balfeth in Angus (c. 1204–1211) with the names of the burgesses of Dundee and Aberdeen about the same time. *Liber S. Thome de Aberbrothoc*, p. 60, 85, 96.

[31] *Exchequer Rolls of Scotland*, v. 1, preface, p. lxxxi.
Aberdeen "was already predominantly English speaking in the twelfth century." F. C. Diack, *Scottish Gaelic studies*, v. 1, p. 92. In the earlier records of the city Gaelic names are far from numerous. Indeed the population would seem to have been mainly Teutonic. The first burgess of Inverness on record, c. 1200, is a Norman named Geoffrey Blund. Mackay, *The Celtic element in old Inverness* [1913], p. 12. Rannulfus de Hadintun was one of the first to build a house in King William's new burgh of Glasgow, c. 1177–1199. *Liber Collegii Nostre Domine*, 1846, p. 235.

clue to its date, but Cosmo Innes says the handwriting is at least as old as c. 1200.[32]

Dominus Adam filius Gilberti	Gylis filius Buht aput dunmedler
Dominus Milo corneht	Gillecrist filius Daniel aput glenwhym
Dominus Adam filius Edolfj	Mattheus, Jacobus et Johannes filii Cos-
Johannes Ker uenator aput swhynhope	mungho sacerdotis aput Edolueston
Gillemihhel queschutbrit aput trefquer	Cospatricius romefare
Patricius de hopekeliov	Randulfus de Meggate
Mihhyn brunberd aput corrukes	Adam de seles clericus
Mihhyn filius Edred aput stobbo	Gillecristus filius huttyng aput Currokes
Cristinus heremita de kyngeldores	Gilbertus persona de Kylbevhhoc
Cospatricius heremita de Kylbeuhoc	Gylmor hund apud Dauwic
Padinus filius kercau aput corrukes	Mihhyn senescallus de Dauwic
Gillemur filius kercau aput corrokes	Dudyn de Brouhtune
Cristinus gennan seruiens aput trefquer	Patricius filius Caswale aput stobbo
Gylcolmus faber aput pebbles	Adam et Cosouold filii Muryn aput
Gylmihhel filius Bridoc aput kyngeldures	castrum oliueri

In the instruments of homage preserved in the Tower of London, known as the *Ragman Roll*, which Edward i extorted from the people of Scotland in the course of his military progress throughout the country in the summer of 1296, and later in the parliament held at Berwick in the month of August, are to be found "the largest and most authentic enumeration now extant of the nobility, barons, landowners and burgesses as well as of the clergy of Scotland, prior to the fourteenth century. No part of the public records of Scotland, prior to that era has been preserved, from which any detailed information of the kind might have been derived; and whatever may have been their fate, whether intentionally destroyed, or allowed to perish by mere neglect, certain it is that to these English records of our temporary degradation are we now indebted for the only genuine statistical notices of the kingdom towards the close of the thirteenth century."[33]

---

[32] *Registrum Episcopatus Glasguensis*, p. 89; tabula, p. cxiii n. Gillemihhel queschutbrit evidently represents two individuals: Gillemihhel, "the servant of (S.) Michael." and Queschutbrit, "the servant (Welsh *gwas*) of (S.) Cuthbert."

[33] Thomas Thomson, *Instrumenta publica*, Bannatyne Club ed., p. xiv. Joseph Bain in his Rhind Lectures on *The Edwards in Scotland*, Edinburgh, 1901, p. 27, has called the Ragman Roll the "Libro D'Oro of Scotland," and says "in spite of its degrading origin there are few of our ancient families who are not pleased to point to an ancestor there, or modern who would not rejoice to discover one." Henry Laing calls the instruments "deeds of homage which the power of an unscrupulous King extorted from a distracted people." *Ancient Scottish seals*, Edinburgh, 1866, p. xv. Doubtless many if not most of those who took the oath of fealty to the usurper did so with their tongue in the cheek; at least, let us hope so. An oath of fealty so extorted is worthless.

The era of the War of Independence (c. 1286–1320) was one of remarkable changes of family and property, and many of the ancient families and names of Scotland went down and out altogether. One proof of this incidentally appears in a papal dispensation of 1334 granted to Michael de Werays [? Wemys], knight, and Margaret de Abernetti, to intermarry, they being related in the fourth degree, the letter adds. The dispensation was granted because "owing to the death of so many nobles in the realm of Scotland many of the ladies remain unmarried, or are taken by low-born Englishmen, some of whom are apostates from religion, or already married." *Papal letters*, v. 2, p. 413.

While the bulk of the names recorded in the Ragman Roll are territorial or local, patronymical, and descriptive, the following occupational names are also recorded:[34]

Symon le Glover, Perth	Johan le Mareschal, Roxburgh
Robert le Taillour, Stirling	Johan le Kuere, Fife
Walter the Goldsmith, Roxburgh	Aleyn le Ferur, Berwick
Richard le Forblour, Roxburgh	Thomas le Whright, Lanark
Austin le Mercer, Roxburgh	Thomas le Breuester, Lanark
Rauf le Spicer, Jeddeworth	William le Lardyner
William le Barker, Haddington	John the Porter
Aleyn le Littester, Edinburgh	Johan le Botiler
William le Keu, Edinburgh	Johan le Naper
Aleyn le Barbur, Ayr	Thomas le Moiller
Andrew le Seeler, Peeblesshire	Nicol le Serjaunt

The following list comprises (a) the names of the representatives of the seventeen royal burghs, and (b) the names of the eleven chosen from their number to proceed to Berwick-upon-Tweed to take part in the negotiations for the liberation of David II from his captivity, 1357.[35] The names, says Hill Burton, "may be compared with the many Norman-sounding names we have come across in dealing with the nobility of Scotland."[36]

Alexander Gylyot	Richard de Cadyoch
Adam Tore	John Clerk
John Goldsmyth	of Monros.
of Edinburgh.	John de Burgo
John Mercer	William Sauser
John Gill	of Streuelyn
Robert de [Gatmilke]	John Johnson
of Perth.	William de Saulton
Laurence de Garuok	of Linlithgow
William de Leth	Adam de Haddyngton
John Crab	Adam de Congleton
of Aberdeen.	of Haddyngton.
Master John de Somerville	Symon Potter
Robert Kyd	Peter Waghorn
of Dundee.	of Dunbretane.
Roger Phipille	Patrick Clerk
Thomas Johnson	Patrick Reder
of Inverkeithing.	of Rothirglen.
Richard Hendchyld	Andrew Ade
Richard Skroger	Andrew de Ponfret
of Crail.	of Lanark.
Nicholas, rector of the schools	William de Duncoll
David Comyn	Thomas Lang
of Coupar.	of Dumfries.
Laurence Bell	Nicholas Johnson
Adam de Kirkyntolach	John Williamson
of St. Andrew.	of Peebles.

[34] Bain, *Calendar of documents*, v. 2, p. 193–215.
[35] *Acts of Parliament of Scotland*, v. 1, p. 517.
[36] *History of Scotland*, v. 2, p. 333 n.

The following list is of those appointed to be procurators for the King's ransom:

Alexander Gylyot	John Gill	William de Leth
Adam Tore	Robert de Gatmilk	John Crab
John Goldsmyth	Laurence de Garuok	Master John de Somerville
John Mercer		Robert Kyd

In the following list of names of the burgesses of Stirling who attacked the cruives and fishings of the Abbot and Convent of Cambuskenneth in 1366,[37] ten are derived from trades and five are of local origin:

Robert Raa	Gilbert Faber	Adam Gamilssone
Richard Tector	Thomas Potator	John Witste
Adam Sissor	John Gollane	Thomas de Brigerakis
Robert Foster	Thomas de Ybernia	Robert Carnifex
Wm Ker	John Pelliparius	Thomas Rubiginator
Wm Bemys	Robert Harrow	John de Callenter
Roger Marcator	John Brume	John Tennand

Fifty-six tenants of the lordship of Fermartyne neglected to pay "second tithes" to the bishop of Aberdeen in 1382 and in consequence were placed under excommunication.[38] Of the names in the list no less than twenty-two may be described as patronymics, sixteen are of local origin, six are from trades, and the remainder are of various other origins.

Adam filius Mychael	Robertus Senior	Symon de Balwany
Andreas filius Ricardi	Johannes filius Andree	Willelmus Schany
Andreas filius Mychael	Johannes filius Fallayk	Adam filius Malcolmi
Johannes filius Ricardi	Robertus filius Abraam	Cristinus Seiowrner
Rycardus filius Mychael	Robertus Wynde	Johannes de Molendino
David filius Ricardi	Willelmus Bronnyng	Johannes de Dovrnach
Willelmus filius Ade	Johannes filius Thome	Johannes Freluke
Laurentius Freluf	Walterus de Parco	Adam Gray
Stephanus Freluf	Johannes de Den	Willelmus Mykyl
Johannes filius Roberti	Henricus Burgeis	Willelmus de Dumbrek
Gilbertus de Colmalenene	Fergusius de Pety	Michael de Tubirthach
Johannes Cissor	Thomas filius Andree	Duncanus filius Johannis
Johannes Grefe	Alexander de Rothy	Gilbert de Tulgone
Alanus de Haldawach	Hugo de Molendino	Adam Halde
Thomas Barkar	Willelmus Thyrlstane	Angusius Faber
Johannes filius Roberti	Adam Kerde	Willelmus Scot
Willelmus filius Agy	Johannes filius Ade	Robertus filius Ego
Johannes de Hyl	Johannes filius Jacobi	Robertus filius Cristini
Andreas filius Donni		Willelmus filius Johannis

---

37 *Registrum de Cambuskenneth,* 55; *Acts of Parliament of Scotland,* v. 1, p. 527.
38 *Registrum Episcopatus Aberdonensis,* v. 1, p. 165–166.

Of the following list of names of members of the Guild of Ayr,[39] c. 1431, seventeen may be classed as patronymics, thirteen are of local origin, thirteen are from trades, and three are descriptive.

Hogs McCharry	Will Dixson	William Chere
Morice Glovar	Thom Hacat	Neil Neilsoun
Thom Sourlesoun	Nichol of Fynnyk	Jhon Sadlar
Huchoun Buthman	Jhon Barchar	Adam Lachlin
Thom of Carrik	Jhon Walkar	Newyn McMullane
Patrik McMartyn	Jhon Vazour	Jhon Mour de Sanchar
Patrik Ahar	Adam Mour	James of Cathkert
Gib Lang	Jame Cordinar	Adam of Cunygam
Thom Chepman	Alexr Asloane	Rankyn of Folartoun
Jhon Nicholsoun	Patoun Dugald	John Chamer de Gadyard
Jhon Broun	Alex. Mur	Rankyn Alin
Jhon Bell	Jhon Pantour	John Makyson
Andro Wrycht	Jhon Davisoun	Gilbert Askrik
Jhon Boyman	Jhon Petit	Jhon Lutster
Gib of Askrik	Rolland Proctour	Pattoun Thomsoun
Jhon Listar	Jhon Cambell	Andro Farchair
Jhon Lorimar		Robert Mour de Skeldowy

Patronymics

A large number of Scottish surnames are patronymics, derived in many cases from affectionate or pet diminutives of proper names as Dickson, Robson, Thomson, Watson, Wilson, etc. This custom of naming appears to have commenced with the beginning of the fourteenth century when it became the practice for sons to take their surnames from the Christian names of their fathers.[40] In Latin charters these patronymics were formed from the genitive case of the father's name preceded by the word *filius*, 'son,' as *Stephanus filius Ricardi*. Later *filius* was implied and the name appears simply as *Andreas Mauricii*. Other examples are *Alanus filius Bricii* (1376), *Walterus Bricii* (1409), and *Dugaldus filius Nigelli* and *Dugaldus Nigelli*. It is not always certain, however, whether *filius Davidi* for example, means in the vernacular "son of a man called David" or had been a "Davidson" for several generations.

An interesting instance of the formation of a surname of this type occurs in the *Exchequer Rolls*.[41] In 1428 we have "Jacobus filius Johannis de Holandia et Edome sponse sue;" in 1429 it is "James, son of John of Holland and his wife;" in 1431 this becomes "James Johnson of Holland and Edoma his wife;" and finally we have "Jacobus Johnsoun." Another example occurs in

[39] *Archaeological and historical collections relating to Ayrshire and Galloway*, v. 1, p. 228–229.
[40] Jervise, *Angus and Mearns*, v. 2, p. 166.
[41] *Exchequer Rolls of Scotland*, v. 4, A. D. 1406–1436, p. 436, 471, 506, 541, 575.

1473. In that year the convent of Coupar-Angus let the land of Morton to Thom Soutar and his three sons, called by the names of David Thomson, John Thomson, and Thom Thomson. The father's surname was then dropped and his Christian name with "son" appended became the surname of his descendants.[42] Some patronymics were late in becoming fixed. In Inverness in 1481 there is record of Alexander Donaldson son of Donald Symonson,[43] and in 1511 there is record of a bond of manrent by Doul Ranaldsone son of wmquhile Ronald Alason.[44]

In other cases, again, "son" was dropped and the Christian name of the ancestor alone was adopted as the family surname, as — Andrew, Dick, Edgar, Edward, Henry (Hendry with intrusive d), Martin, Peter, Richard, Sim, Thom, Watt. With some the paternal name appears in the genitive form with "s" representing "son," as Adams, Andrews, Edwards, Richards, etc. Names of this form appear to be mainly of English origin from south of the Border.

Patronymics were not permanent; they changed with each succeeding generation, and it was well into the eighteenth century before the cumbersome system was given up in the Highlands. In Shetland patronymics were very common even in the first half of the nineteenth century, where Magnus Johnson was son of John Magnus, and so alternately for many descents. Gideon Manson, the last man there who exercised the privilege of choosing his own surname, died in Foula in March, 1930. His father's name was James Manson (Magnus's son) and his grandfather was called Magnus Robertson.

Local and Territorial Names

The first people in Scotland to acquire fixed surnames were the nobles and great landowners, who called themselves, or were called by others, after the lands they possessed. Surnames originating in this way are known as territorial, but it does not necessarily follow that every Melville or Somerville is a descendant of the first recorded of these names. All Stewarts were not sib to the king nor are all Campbells sib to the great Mac Cailein. Tenants often took the name of their landlords, e.g. Gordon. Towns and villages and hamlets also gave distinctive appellation to several persons wholly unconnected by blood — to any one, in short, who left one of the towns or villages to reside elsewhere. Formerly lords of baronies and regalities and farmers

---

[42] *Rental book of Cistercian Abbey of Cupar-Angus*, v. 1, p. 191.
[43] Mackintosh, *Invernessiana*, p. 154.
[44] *Spalding Club miscellany*, v. 4, p. 195.

were inclined to magnify their importance and to sign letters and documents with the names of their baronies and farms instead of their Christian names and surnames. The abuse of this style of speech and writing was carried so far that an Act was passed in the Scots parliament in 1672 forbidding the practice and declaring that it was allowed only to noblemen and bishops to subscribe by their titles.

Some of our local names have never travelled beyond the bounds of the place or places which gave them origin, e.g. Barrack, Boyne, etc. Others again have spread over two or three adjoining parishes, and still others have wandered over the entire country, "seeking and finding fresh positions and fresh gains in fresh fields." In many instances in the earlier references it is not always possible to say whether names like John of Renfrew, John of Roxburgh, and Roger of Irvine merely indicates inhabitancy of a particular town or village or is a true surname as undoubtedly such designations did become at a later date. It has been thought best to consider them as true surnames. Many local surnames have been derived from places, the names of not a few of which have not survived, e.g. Dipple. Many of these places were too small to be recorded on the map or have been altered. *De*, again, does not always imply territorial possession but is merely equal to "in." Sometimes it is used in error — thus turning a personal or other name into a local or territorial one.[45] In the bigger towns the burgesses called themselves after the streets they lived in, e.g. Henry de Fishergate, Henry de Cuningstrete, etc.

Names in this work are considered to be of territorial origin when lands or a barony of the same name gave name to the proprietor who had the lands given him by the king; of local origin when they arise from residence in or near a village or town. It should however be remembered that tenants and servants sometimes took, or were given, the name of the manor on which they resided, with or without the territorial "de."

Many of the Scottish surnames are peculiar to certain districts. Thus the oldest surnames in the parish of Liberton, Midlothian, at the end of the eighteenth century, were Veitch, Ewart, Herriot, Tweedie, Peacock, Werock, Gray, Straiton, Richardson, Blaikie, Handyside, Etchison, and Mitchell.[46] At the same period the commonest surnames in the parish of Haddington were Hepburn, Sheriff, Skirvane, Dudgeon, Howdan, Carfrae, and Begbie.[47]

---

[45] "De" popularly supposed to be a sign of aristocratic descent in the Middle Ages more often carried the meaning of 'in,' 'from,' 'at,' Ewen, *A History of the surnames of the British Isles*, p. 175.

[46] *Archaeologia Scotica*, Edinburgh, 1792, v. 1, p. 365.

[47] ibid., p. 49.

The surnames of oldest standing in the parish of Cullen, Banffshire, are Anderson, Coul, Davidson, Finlay, Forsyth, Gardiner, Hay, Ogilvie, Runcie, Simpson, Strahan, and Wright.[48] In the old churchyard of Portlethen, Kincardineshire, most of the tombstones bore the names Laiper, Maine, and Hood, with variants — Leaper, Main. The neighborhood was formerly a prosperous little fishing community which probably accounts for the sameness of the names. In Ferryden, Coulls and Perts predominate, Lorimers in Broughty Ferry, Patons at Usan, Mairs in Portknockie, and Cargills in Arbroath. "Amongst the fisher population" of Nairn "the name of Main is so common that the different families are distinguished by tee names or teetles."[49]

Cant, Hossack, Caogach, Pharoah, Brog, Garve, Strode, Hood, Barrald, Bolloch were names current in Dornoch in the eighteenth century.[50]

Some Aberdeen surnames of the eighteenth century from Register of Indentures are: Crives, Caic, Garvock, Birse, Tilleray, Courage, Kiloh, Cassie, Kemlo, Symmers, Leiper, Mennie, Dauney, Machray, Anson, Catto, Will.

A scoffing saying about Newport in Fife belongs to the time when its whole population consisted of the ferrymen and their families:

> "Take care what you say about neighbours at Newport,
> They are all Uncles and Aunties and Cousins."[51]

This saying would apply to more than one small place.

Official and Trade Surnames

A large number of Scottish surnames are derived from the trade or office of their first bearers. In the earlier instances quoted, it is not always easy to say whether an office or occupation is meant or whether the word has assumed, or — it may be — is in process of assuming, the character of a hereditary surname. It has been thought best to treat such instances as true surnames, as undoubtedly they so become later on. That many of these names derived from trades or professions had become regular surnames is shown by the fact that a trade or profession of quite different character is affixed to the entry.

Numerous offices were hereditary in feudal and in later times. The Stewarts, for example, were at first distinguished by their office alone. The first of the

48 *New statistical account of Banffshire*, p. 331.
49 *Transactions of Inverness Scientific Society*, v. 4, p. 169.
50 ibid., p. 55.
51 Mackay, *A Century of Scottish proverbs and sayings*, Cupar-Fife, 1891, p. 39; Mackay, *History of Fife and Kinross*, Edinburgh, 1896, p. 285.

name in Scotland appears only as Alan, dapifer; his son styled himself Walter Fitz Alan, and his son called himself Alan Fitz-Walter, with the addition of *Senescallus Scotiae*. A retour of the service of Alexander Lindsay as heir of his father, Richard Lindsay, in the shop and office of blacksmith of the lordship of Brechin, dated 29th April 1514, is printed in the *Miscellany of the Spalding Club*, v. 5, p. 291–292.

The Fettercairn charter-chest shows several charters of little tenements surrounding the castle appropriated for the dwelling and support of the retainers of the court, and many of these retained the names of the officers whose appendage they were. Some were named after the pages and palfrey-men, the tirewomen, as well as higher attendants on royalty.[52]

In a few cases it is probable that when some occupations of limited extent which had given rise to certain surnames died out the surname died with them.

In the monastery of Cupar-Angus in 1468 Robert Wrycht and Thomas Wrycht appear as wrights or carpenters; in 1490 Thomas Mason, son of John Mason elder was apprenticed to the mason craft, and John the Mason senior and his son John, were hired in 1485 for five years as masons to the monastery. John Sclater was hired as apprentice *(empticius)* to the trade of tyler; Pattoun Millar leased the Bog-myl within the grange of the Kers in 1492; and in 1497 Alexander Smith was the blacksmith of the abbey.[53] "A family named Porter were for successive generations keepers of the Abbey gate, till the head of the family ultimately obtained the office of porter as an inheritance."[54] So also in the Rental of the Bishop of Dunkeld we have instances of workmen who evidently derived their surnames from their trades: James Smytht, my Lord's smith (1506); Finlay Fischair, fisherman to my Lord of Dunkeld (1506); Bartholomew Sclater, slater to my Lord of Dunkeld (1512); Donald Sawer, carpenter (1512); and Patrick Mason was paid for mason-work in 1512.[55]

Hunting was one of the principal diversions of the kings and nobles in the Middle Ages, and the uncultivated lands were divided into "forests," "parks," "warrens," etc., each under the charge of an officer who in time derived his surname from his office of forester, parker, warrener, woodreeve, woodward, etc. The loss of final -er, a suffix used to form nouns denoting an agent, in

[52] *Registrum Episcopatus Brechinensis*, v. 1, preface, p. xxii.

[53] *Rental book of Cistercian Abbey of Cupar-Angus*, London, 1879, v. 1, p. 241, 304, 305–306, 308, 310.

[54] ibid., introduction, p. xxxiii. See also under surname *Porter*.

[55] *Rentale Dunkeldense*, Edinburgh, 1915, p. 82, 86, 226, 282.

surnames of occupative origin is rare, but we still have examples in Forest, Hunt, Lymburn, and probably in Warren (from warrener).

In the *Edinburgh Marriage Records* of the seventeenth century the following trades are mentioned, many of which at earlier dates gave origin to surnames. Many of these trades are now extinct. The dates within parentheses refer to the year in which I have noted it: Barker (1670), Bower (1614), Cordiner (1684), Coalgrieve (1693), Coriar (1643), Creilman, Craner, Crowdenster (1611), Customer (1670), Feltmaker (1671), Fowler (1698), Glasswright (1655), Glover (1700), Heelmaker (1685), Locksmith (1675), Lorimer (1605), Marakindresser (1638), Mealmaker (1642), Pasment-weaver, Pipemaker (1680), Pewderer and Peutherer, Sediler (1671), Shank-weaver (1652), Shearsmith (1675), Skinner (1698), Sleader, Stabler (1676), Tasker (1677), Vintner (1625), Violer (1680), Walker, Whipman (1618).

Fife surnames derived from trades are: Baxter, Cagger, Colyer, Cordonar, Cutler, Fidlar, Hatmaker, Hornar, Multrar, Plumar, Quarriour, Sclatter, Tailyour, Walcar, etc.

Trade names, it may be noted, are rare among the Gaels, "a plain indication that industry was not their forte." The few trades from which some Gaelic surnames are derived show the circumscribed wants of the community beyond what the skill of each family could supply. Of these trades the most important were the smith, the fuller, and next the tailor.

Nicknames

Contrary to the common view I have found few of our surnames to be derived from nicknames, and my experience in this is confirmed by Ewen. "What on superficial examination," he says, "appear to have been personal epithets are often something entirely different, misunderstanding arising through failure to grasp various processes of corruption, modification, or mutation.

"(i) Supposed nicknames due to failure to recognize archaic and corrupt forms . . . (ii) Supposed nicknames due to failure to recognize language or dialect . . . (iii) Supposed nicknames due to failure to recognize the original application of the description." And he adds: "It is believed that the explanations now offered are sufficient to demonstrate that there is no necessity whatsoever to suppose that names of living creatures given as nicknames have originated any of the modern British surnames. No doubt there are exceptions, and the suggestions now made should not be considered final without proof, but every practical source in a dozen different languages should be thoroughly explored before the origin of a surname is assigned to an alternative epithet. That such by-names were common is admitted, but that they became family names is a different view, the correctness of which should not be rashly assumed." In conclusion Ewen warns us that "having once become obsessed with the idea that surnames are derived from vulgar epithets, discovery of origin becomes easy."[56] "Everything," says the Rev. S. Baring-Gould, "goes to show that we must be very cautious in accepting the face signification of a name that looks and sounds as a nickname."[57]

The late Mr. Joseph Storer Clouston in the course of his studies of Orkney family history could "only find two names which seem very decidedly to have their origin in nicknames. There may very likely be other examples," he says, "but I am convinced that this source is very rare, and that one ought therefore to fall back upon it only when one has been forced upon good grounds to reject every other derivation."[58]

To-names

The great prevalence of certain leading surnames in some small towns and villages led to the use of to-names, "other names," from Old English tō-nama. This condition of affairs has continued to the present day, particularly in the fishing towns and hamlets on the northeast coast, where the fisher-folk might be termed a race apart from the rest of the population. "As they are all descended from a few common ancestors, and have from time immemorial kept themselves distinct from other lowlanders, there are seldom more than two or three surnames in a fish town. There are twenty-five George Cowies in Buckie. The grocers in 'booking' their fisher customers, invariably insert the nick-name or tee-name, and in the case of married men,

[56] Ewen, *A History of the surnames of the British Isles*, p. 326, 332, 336, 337, 341. Mawer gives a list of Old English animal names (*brocc* — Badger, *colt* — Colt, *crawe* — Crow, *bucca* — Goat, *heorot* — Stag, etc.) which he has found in place names, and says that "these names, for the most part, at least, form a very old stratum in English personal nomenclature, and were not in living use at the end of the old English period. They most of them probably go back definitely to heathen times, and there is no evidence that they were given as nicknames, i.e. as additional names supplemental to the names given at birth. They are real personal names, traditional with the race, given at birth with little or no thought of any application of the name to the appearance or disposition of the child." *Modern language review*, v. 14, p. 235–236.

[57] *Family names and their history*, 1913, p. 316.

[58] *Old lore miscellany*, v. 5, p. 63–64. On the other hand Prof. H. C. Wyld is "inclined to believe that if we knew more about Old English and other Old Germanic personal names, and had a thorough analysis according to the nature and origin of all those which are preserved, we should find that, among the English at least, the number of names which were nicknames in origin was considerable." *Modern language review*, 1910, v. 5, p. 290. And quite possibly, one might reasonably suggest, we should find the opposite.

write down the wife's along with the husband's name. Unmarried debtors have the names of their parents inserted with their own. In the town-register of Peterhead, these signatures occur, 'Elizabeth Taylor, spouse to John Thomson, *Souples,*' 'Agnes Farquhar, spouse to W. Findlater, *Stoattie.*'

"In an unsophisticated village the proper names only connect the inhabitants with the external civilization, while the tee-name is, of necessity, the thing for use. It is amusing enough to be permitted to turn over the leaves of a grocer's ledger and see the tee-names as they come up. *Buckie, Beauty, Bam, Biggelugs, Collop, Helldom, the King, the Provost, Rochie, Stoattie, Sillerton, the Smack, Snipe, Snuffers, Toothie, Todlowrie.* Ladies are occasionally found who are gallantly and exquisitely called *the Cutter, the Bear,* etc. Among the twenty-five George Cowies in Buckie there are George Cowie, *doodle,* George Cowie, *carrot,* and George Cowie, *neep.*

"A stranger had occasion to call on a fisherman, living in one of the Buchan fishing villages, of the name of Alexander White. But he was ignorant both of his house and his tee-name. Unfortunately there were many persons of the name in the village. Meeting a girl he asked —

" 'Cou'd you tell me fa'r Sanny Fite lives?'

" 'Filk Sanny Fite?'

" 'Muckle Sanny Fite.'

" 'Filk muckle Sanny Fite?'

" 'Muckle lang Sanny Fite.'

" 'Filk muckle lang Sanny Fite?'

" 'Muckle lang gleyed Sanny Fite,' shouted the stranger.

" 'Oh! It's "Goup-the-lift" ye're seeking,' cried the girl, 'and fat the deevil for dinna ye speer for the man by his richt name at ance?' "[59]

"In a recent roll of voters, confined to male householders, all fishermen, there were in the *quoad sacra* parish of Gardenstown 17 Nicols, 19 Wisemans, 26 Wests, and 68 Watts. Macduff with a few Patersons and Watts, had 17 MacKays and 20 Wests, while in Banff the Woods numbered 27. Two names predominated in Whitehills — Lovie and Watson, numbering respectively 18 and 19.

"Portsoy had 8 Mairs, 11 Piries, and 14 Woods, while in the hamlet of Sandend no fewer than 26 of the heads of fishermen's families belonged to the great family of Smith. Cullen had 33 of the name of Gardiner and 55 of the name of Findlay, while in Portknockie there were 20 Piries, 24 Slaters, 47 Woods, and 84 Mairs, or 175 heads of families of four names. Findochty

[59] *Blackwood's magazine,* Edinburgh, 1842, v. 51, p. 300–301. The article is by Joseph Robertson the historian.

went even one better, for it had 182 fishermen householders with four names between them — Campbell 24, Smith 35, Sutherland 39, and Flett 84. In Buckie, east of the Burn, there were 15 Coulls, 29 Jappys, 69 Murrays, 116 Smiths, and 128 Cowies; while in the western division there were 23 Coulls, 28 Geddeses, and 47 Reids. In Portgordon, there were 21 Coulls, and 32 Reids. The circumstance explains, of course, the habit that is almost universal of having a tee name as well, a name by which the fisherman is more familiarly known than that in which he has been registered. The multiplicity in a small community of instances of the same name makes it not only a convenience but a necessity. How else, among scores of Cowies, of Coulls, of Jappys, Woods, and Slaters, many of them of the same Christian name, is one to differentiate? So accustomed are many of them to be recognised only by what may be called their acquired names, that they are addressed, not by their Christian names, but as Johndie, Saners, Pum, Gyke, Dottie, Smacker, Dumpy, Bosan, Cockie, Bo, and so on."[60]

To-names were also much used on the Border, as they are still to some extent in the West Highlands. Thus in Border records of the sixteenth and seventeenth centuries we find Johannes Irwin vocatus "duk," a Rae known as "red-hede," whilst another is designated "lang Jok." In 1504 there is mention of Robert Ra called "Knewlta," John Ra, the son of Thomas Ra, "in dronokwood," i.e. Dornock wood, and Thomas called "hannay."[61] Robert Oliuere called "Rob with the dog," David Oliuere called "Na-gude Preist," and John Oliuere called "Cageare" are recorded in Jedburgh in the same year.[62] In 1535 we find John Elwald called "Lawis-Johne," John Forrestare called "Schaik-buklar," Thomas Armestrang "Lang Penman," one called "Dikkis Wille," and Symon Armestrang was called "Sym the Larde."[63]

Christian Names

It was a not uncommon practice in the late Middle Ages (fourteenth to sixteenth centuries) for two brothers to have the same Christian name, a custom which has caused much confusion and embarrassment to genealogists in preparing family histories. There were two Davids in the family of the father of Cardinal Beaton, and there are even instances where *three* sons bore the same forename. William de Veteri Ponte, c. 1200, had three sons

[60] Barclay, *Banffshire*, 1922, p. 66, 68. See also Ewen, *A History of the surnames of the British Isles*, p. 331.

[61] *Proceedings of Society of Antiquaries of Scotland*, v. 23, p. 46.

[62] Pitcairn, *Criminal trials of Scotland*, v. 1, p. 104.*

[63] ibid., v. 1, p. *171. For some Galloway to-names see Trotter, *Galloway gossip: The Stewartry*, 1901, p. 413–418.

all named William, distinguished as Willelmus primogenitus, Willelmus medius, and Willelmus junior.[63a] King James v had three illegitimate sons named James, and on 26th February 1531–2 he wrote to Pope Clement vii asking him to declare them eligible to hold ecclesiastical dignities.[64] Under the regulations of the Roman Catholic Church it was allowable to change the baptismal name at confirmation and this apparently was done when it was supposed there was no danger of the selected name dying out.[65] Mr. W. J. Calder Ross mentions finding instances of this duplication of Christian names in families in Caithness, Sutherland, and Inverness-shire. "The reason given for these duplicates," he says, "was the necessity of naming a child after each of its grandparents, and as both of these happened to have the same Christian name, the only way of bestowing the honour and of getting out of the difficulty was by having the double set."[66]

"Christian" names only very gradually came into use. In the excursus upon Christian names in the first volume of his *The Mission and Expansion of Christianity in the First Three Centuries,* London, 1908, Harnack shows that down to the middle of the fourth century Peter and Paul are about the only New Testament names to be met with, while Old Testament names again are also rare. "As the saints, prophets, patriarchs, angels, etc., henceforth took the place of the dethroned gods of paganism, and as the stories of these gods were transformed into stories of the saints, the supersession of mytho-logical names now commenced in real earnest." Theodoret, bishop of Cyrus or Cyrrhus in Syria (fifth century), said that people are to give their children the names of saints and martyrs in order to win them the protection and patronage of these heroes. "The result was a selection of names, varying with the different countries and provinces . . . Withal, haphazard and freedom of choice always played some part in the choice of a name. The Western Church was very backward in adopting Old Testament names, and this continued until the days of Calvinism." Chrysostom at the end of the fourth century exhorted believers to call their children after the saints, so that these

---

[63a] *Liber Cartarum Sancti Crucis,* no. 41.

[64] Dunbar, *Scottish kings,* 1899, p. 238–239.

[65] *Scottish antiquary,* v. 13, p. 20, and references there given.

[66] *Scottish notes and queries,* v. 3, p. 60. Other Scottish examples are given by Ewen, *A History of the surnames of the British Isles,* 1931, p. 403. Ewen also points out that diminutives, apparently of an hypocoristic nature, "served the additional and practical purpose of providing a necessary distinction in days when it was common to bestow the same forename on several sons of one family; thus Guillot was brother of Guillaume de Louviers, 1298, Jehannot was brother of Jehan de Amiens, 1298; on the other hand, two sons of Jehannot (elsewhere Jehan) Hecelin (1297) were both called Jehannot, a sister being Jehannette; and Jehannot was brother of Jehannot Chase-Rat (1299)" (p. 291).

worthies might serve them as examples of virtue. In early Scottish Church record we find ecclesiastics who had adopted Hebrew, Greek, and Latin names upon their ordination, as Abel, Abraham, Adam, Isaac, Solomon, Gregory, Elisaeus, Felix, Hilarius, Laurence, Vedastus, etc. This early use of Hebrew Biblical names, it may be mentioned, has been looked upon by believers in the Anglo-Israel craze as confirmatory of their belief.

The Indo-European Name System

The ancient Indo-European people which imposed its language and culture on the greater part of Europe and on a large part of Asia possessed a common name system which has left traces on most of the languages of Europe and Western Asia, with the exception of Latin, Lithuanian, and perhaps Armenian. These names were made up of two stems or themes welded into one whole according to definite rules of composition. "The elements entering into the ancient personal names might be any of the parts of speech which can be joined together to form intelligible compounds. Thus they might be verbs, adverbs, prepositions, adjectives or nouns." Of the compound names thus formed one element may be restricted exclusively to the beginning and the other to the end of a name, or they may both be placed indifferently at the end or at the beginning. This principle of arbitrary combination was found among the ancient Hindus, Persians, Greeks, Slavs, Celts and Teutons. The number of words used as the stock elements of such compound or full names appears never to have been very great in any one of the branches of the Indo-Europeans.

In prehistoric and proto-historic times these double-stemmed names probably had an intelligible meaning, the elements being put together with due regard to the significance of the separate words, but there seems to have been in historical times no general consciousness of any meaning in the compound names, even when they were formed of words in common use. As a general rule they have properly speaking no meaning at all. Perhaps it would be more proper to say of certain compound names that they are in fact not two *words* joined together but two *names* as in *Earnwulf* ("Eagle-wolf"), *Eofor-wulf* ("Boar-wolf"), *Wolfrhaban* ("Wolf-raven"), etc.

As examples of this principle of name formation we have Sanscrit *Devaçruta* and *Çrutadeva*, Greek *Theodoros* and *Dorotheos*, *Hipparchos* and *Archippos*, Serbian *Dragomil* and *Milodrag*. This reversing of the elements is very common in old Germanic in which we have names like *Wulf-heah — Heah-wulf*, *Wulf-gar — Gar-wulf*, *Helm-wine — Wine-helm*, and other names which mean literally "peace-spear" (Fredegar) or "peace-war" (Fredegunde). Early British also supplies an interesting example in the inscription in Roman characters on the stone at Llandawke near Laugharne, Carmarthenshire, commemorating *Barrivend filivs Vendvbari*, i.e. "Head-white" son of "White-head." [66a]

Names so formed cannot be said to yield the same sense or an equally appropriate sense when the order of the elements is changed, but they might serve as an indication of relationship, as in the system of name-giving that prevailed among the ancient Teutons. Here, as a rule, the first syllable of the name of the parent occurs, perhaps somewhat modified, as the first component of the son's name, especially of the first born. The genealogical tables of early Germanic rulers furnish abundant examples of this: *Theuderic — Theudibert, Gundioc — Gundobad, Gelaris — Gelimer*, etc. Frequently a correspondence of the second compound would show the descent thus: *Genseric — Huneric, Ausprand — Segiprand, Godipert — Reginpert*, etc. Similarly in the Anglo-Saxon genealogies we find *Aelfheah — Aelfweard, Aelfric — Aelfwine, Aelfstan — Heahstan, Sigewulf — Sigebeorht, Wulfstan — Wulfmaer.*

The principle of shortening these double-stemmed names, which were naturally long and cumbersome, obtained from the earliest times of which we have record. Reduced to shorter and more convenient forms for common use they gave rise to names with but a single stem. One evidence of this fact is "that in the great majority of cases where a stem is found in a single-stem name, it is also found in one or more compounds."[67] We have instances of this shortening in English, as Archy and Archie from Archibald, Bert from Herbert, Betty and Liz from Elizabeth, Tim from Timothy, Teddy from Theodore, Will from William, Winnie from Winifred, etc. *Skamandronymus*, the name of the father of the Lesbian poetess Sappho, was sometimes shortened to *Skamandrus* and even to *Skamōn*, and *Mnasidika*, a pupil of Sappho, is addressed in a fragment as *Dika*, and in another place as *Mika*, probably for *M(nasid)ika*.

Old Gaelic personal names appear in two stages. In the first stage which appears to have followed the style of name-giving which belonged to the pre-Celtic inhabitants of Ireland, the formula is no longer two stems or themes welded together, but the first element denotes "servant," "devotee," or "son" of some god or animal, or object or idea, while the second element denoting this is in the genitive case. Examples of this type are *Mog Nuadat* "slave of (the god) Nuada"; *Cu-chulainn* "hound of Culann"; *Cubeathadh*

66a Brash, *Ogham inscribed monuments*, London, 1879, p. 401, pl. xlvi.
67 Stonecipher, *Graeco-Persian names*, New York, p. 9.

"hound of life" (ancestor of the Islay Macbeths); *Cu-duiligh* (in the old Maclean genealogy); *Cusidhe* (whence old clan Consith in Fife); *Fael-chu* "wolf hound"; *Mael-bethadh* "servant of life"; *Maelanfhaidh* "lord of storm" (Maelanfaid of clan Cameron genealogy); *Mugh-ron* "seal's slave" (whence Macmorran).

In the second stage the name, as already mentioned, consists of two stems or themes welded into one. Examples of this stage are *Dumno-* (or *Dubno-*) *vellaunos* "world wielder," now Donald; *Oinogustus* "unique choice one" (in Adamnan, *Vita S. Columbae*, i. 12, *Oingusius*) now Angus; *Vergustus* "super choice one" (in Adamnan, V. C., i. 7, *Forcus*, OBret. *Uorgost*, OW. *Gurgust*, and in the eighth-century inscription on the sculptured stone at St. Vigeans in Angus, again *Forcus*) now Fergus. These spellings point to a period when all these languages were almost one and undivided.

Many old Gaelic personal names were taken from the names of animals remarkable chiefly for their ferocity, strength or swiftness, the wolf and the bear being prominent, and the individuals so named were supposed to possess in an eminent degree the characteristic qualities of these animals. Sometimes these names were taken alone without any change, but more often they were compounded with some other root, or with the diminutive *-an*. Thus we have *art* "bear," whence *Artogenos* "son of Artos"; *bran* "raven" (Bran the voyager), and *bran-chu* "raven-dog" (gen. *mac Branchon*, AFM. 728); *catan* "little cat," "cattie" (whence Catan, Gillecatan, Clan Chattan); *cu* (gen. *con*) (in *Dobarchu* "water-dog," i.e. otter, Mac Dobarcon in *Book of Deer*), *cu mara*, "sea hound, shark," which gives name to Mac Namara; *cuilean* "whelp" (King Cuilean or Culen, 966–971); *ech*, later *each* "horse" (in Eachan and some other names); *fael* "wolf" (with diminutive *-an*, *Faelan* "wolfie," whence *Faolan* — Fillan); *fiach* "raven"; *loarn* "fox" (Loarn of Dalriada, Lorne); *matad, maddad* "hound" (Maddad first known earl of Angus); *mathghamhan* "bear" (Matheson); *os* "fawn" (*Oisin* — Ossian); *sithech* "wolf" (Sithech, a Culdee of Mothel), whence *MacIthich*, Mackeith, and *MacIthichean* its diminutive, now Mackichan.

Color adjectives also enter into the formation of Gaelic names. They occur mostly in combination either as first or second elements in the name, and are sometimes (though rarely) used alone. The most common of these adjectives are: *ciar* "black" (Ciar-an of Clonmacnois. The names of three of his brothers, Cron-an "little tawny," Donn-an "little brown," Odran "little grey," indicate that the family was dark complexioned and were members of a sept of pre-Celtic origin); *dearg* "red"; *dubh* "black" (Duff, king of Scotland;

Dubhsithe "black of peace," whence Macfie or Macphee); *finn* "white," later *fionn* (whence MacFhionnlaigh — Mackinlay); *glas* "grey" (whence Macglashan); *gorm* "blue"; *odhar* "grey" (Odhran); *riabhach* "brindled" (Macgilleriabhach); *ruadh* "red" (Roy, Gilroy).

In Gaeldom, after the introduction of Christianity, a child born on a saint's day was baptized as the *mael* (later *maol*), i.e. the "bald" or "tonsured" servant or devotee of that saint. Hence the large number of old Gaelic personal names of this class compounded with the name of Jesus *(Maol Iosa)*, Mary *(Maol Moire* or *Maol Muire)*, Michael *(Maol Micheil)*, Patrick *(Maol Phadruig)*, etc. *Mael* in early times was confused with *mál* "chief, prince," from Old Celtic *maglos*, seen in *Maelanfaidh* "chief of storm" of the old Cameron genealogy. After the twelfth century *maol* was gradually displaced by *gille* "servant, lad," as in *Gill' Iosa, Gille Bride, Gille Micheil, Gille Phadruig*, etc. The second noun sometimes took the definite article, as *Gille na naoimh* "servant of the saints."

The advisability which existed over great parts of Scotland during many generations of belonging to a large and powerful clan resulted in the assumption of the clan surname of Campbell in Argyll, of Macdonald in the Western Isles and Kintyre, of Mackenzie in the northwest, of Kennedy in the southwest, and so on, by persons who merely lived in these districts, and were of no kindred to the chief to whose clan they attached themselves, or whose protection they claimed, and under whose banner they fought. In like manner the settlement of a powerful southern family within the Highland border was followed by the sudden spread of their name throughout the neighboring glens. The Gordons were hardly settled in Strathbolgy when the whole country around was full of men calling themselves Gordon. This does not mean that the former inhabitants were killed off, but that the native people having themselves no surnames, readily adopted that of their new lords. In some instances we find the adoption of the new name taking place by written band, as in the case of John McAchopich and his sons to Campbell of Cawdor in 1569,[68] and Cosmo Innes states that he has seen petitions of some small clans in the Braes of Angus to be allowed to take the name of *Lyon* and to be counted clansmen of the Strathmores.[69] Many families and small tribes of Breadalbane in the sixteenth century renounced their natural heads, and took Campbell of Glenurquhay for their chief.[69a] To this custom is due the limited number of current Gaelic surnames.

[68] *Thanes of Cawdor*, p. 175–176.
[69] *Concerning some Scotch surnames*, 1860, p. 24.
[69a] *Black Book of Taymouth.*

A great many things were done two, three, or more hundred years ago to "please the lairds," and "changing one's surname was one of these things." It was by this means that Clan Mackenzie was so rapidly enlarged in the sixteenth and seventeenth centuries. Its rapid increase was due to the inclusion of the old native tenants living on the territories acquired by the chiefs from time to time, conciliated, or when needed, coerced, so as to make them good Mackenzie subjects and soldiers. The clan is made up of Mackenzies, Macraes, Murchisons, Maclays, Maclennans, Mathewsons, Macaulays, Morrisons, Macleods, etc.[70]

Another method used by chiefs of clans and heads of landed families to increase the number of followers bearing their name was to bribe poor parents with a "bow o' meal" to substitute in respect of their children the clan surname for their own which was perhaps merely a patronymic and frequently only a tee name. An old Gaelic saying around Beauly illustrative of this is, *Frisealach am boll a mine*, "Frasers of the boll of meal," indicating that some Bissets had changed their name from Bisset to Fraser for that reason. We have records of this among Farquharsons, Forbeses, and Gordons. In the time of Gilbert Cumin, lord of the lands of Glenchearnach, it is said that many of the oppressed people from neighboring districts sought his protection. These he adopted as clansmen by a form of baptism using the stone hen-trough which stood near the castle-door. Cumins so created were called *Cuminich clach nan cearc*, or "Cumins of the hen-trough" to distinguish them from the Cumins of blue blood. For other reasons, also, new names were assumed. In Moray and many other parts of the North persons frequently took the name of another clan without being in any way connected with the chief or his family. An instance of this nature, recorded on a gravestone in Mortlach churchyard in Latin, may be translated thus: "Here lies an honourable man, Robert Farquharson of Lochterlandich who died there on the 5th day of March in the year of our Lord 1446 (or 1546)." This Robert was the son of Farquhar Cuming, but renounced his proper patronymic and called himself after his father's Christian name.[70a]

In the Hebrides, where Gaelic eventually predominated, Norse patronymics were translated into Gaelic, e.g. Norse Goðormsson became Maccodrum, Thorketillsson became Maccorquodale, and Ivarsson became Maciver. Intermarriages and alliances of friendship between the two races became common in the ninth century so that it was usual for Gaelic names to occur in Norse families and Norse names in Gaelic families, e.g. MacThorsteyn

[70] *Proceedings of Society of Antiquaries of Scotland*, v. 14, p. 369.
[70a] *Scottish notes and queries*, June, 1888.

and MacTorfin, though probably the cases in which the husband was a Gael and the wife a Norwegian were exceptional. An instance of such a marriage is recorded in the *Orkneyinga saga* (p. 2) where it is stated that Dungad, the native chieftain in the northeast corner of Caithness, married Gróa, the daughter of a Norwegian Viking, Thorstein the Red, c. 875. The saga of *Egil Skallagrim* (p. 91) states that Olaf the Red was Scots on his father's side, but Danish on his mother's side, and adds that in Northumberland "nearly all the inhabitants were Danish by the father's or mother's side, and many by both." The same happened with Old English, Eadmund filius Gilmichel perambulated the lands of Raith, c. 1206.[71] The following Highland names are all of Norse origin: Gunn, Macaulay (in the northwest), Maccorquodale, Maccotter, Macdougall, Macgorrie, Maciver, Mackettrick, Maclachlan, Macleod, Macmanus, Macranald, Macrurie, Macsorley, Macswan, Macvanish, etc.

"The names of the Galloway clans are not those of the Highlands; or, in instances where they are the same, it is inconceivable that they were offshoots from, say, clans in Badenoch. It cannot well be doubted that there was a silent but steady stream of immigration from Ulster to the opposite coast; and here we have another factor in the mixture of the races which cannot be ignored."[72]

"The use with the Highland prefix 'Mac' of familiar or affectionate diminutives or rendering of Christian names as denoted by the terminal 'ie' seems, as far as my observation goes," says the late Mr. A. M. Mackintosh, "to have been practically confined to Highland districts bordering on the Lowlands and to have obtained only in the case of names borrowed from the Lowlands. Thus, in the Highland fringes of Perthshire, we have McComie, McRichie, McJockie, McJock or McYock, and in Aberdeenshire and Banffshire — both also partly Lowland, are such names as McWillie, McWattie, McRobbie. In some cases the 'Mac' has been gradually dropped, and perhaps an instance of this is the name Michie, found in various parts of the country where Highlands and Lowlands meet. Other names of the class are McAdie, McAndie."[73] Other English and Lowland names with diminutive in -*in* and -*on* in early times were borrowed by the Gaels, and in the Highlands we meet with many — Gibbon (whence MacGibbon), Robin (whence the present-day Macrobin), Paton (whence Macfadyen), Wilkin (whence Maccuilcein — Macwilkin), Rankin (whence Macrankin, now obsolete), Cubbin (from Cuth-

71 *Registrum Abbacie de Aberbrothoc*, v. 1, p. 67.
72 Mackenzie, *The Races of Ireland and Scotland*, 1916, p. 383–384.
73 *Mackintosh families in Glenshee and Glenisla*, Nairn, 1916, p. 38.

bert, whence Maccubin or Maccubbin — a Kirkcudbright name), Michin (from Michael, whence Macmichin and Macmeeking).

After the abortive rebellion of 1745 Gaelic names began to creep into the Lowlands, and their number steadily increased with the passing years. Approximately one-tenth of the population of Edinburgh is said to be of Gaelic origin, and the percentage for Glasgow is vastly higher. At first Highlanders attempted more or less successfully to anglicize their names in order to overcome the Lowland hostility to things Highland,[74] and some Gaelic names have had renderings assigned to them in the most haphazard way.[75] The following

[74] That an antagonism existed to a great extent between the English-speaking Lowlanders and the Gaels beyond the Firth of Forth from early times is shown by the inscription on the old burgh seal of Stirling, 1296. The obverse shows "the bridge of Stirling. On the centre of the bridge, the Crucifixion; the Saviour with the nimbus. On dexter side 3 figures with bows, the foremost bending his bow and barbed arrow towards the Cross. On sinister, 3 figures with lances, the foremost darting his lance towards the Cross. A star and crescent above the limbs of the Cross: *Hic armis bruti Scoti:* stant [north of the Forth]: *hic crvci: tvti*" [south of the Forth]. Bain, *Calendar of documents*, v. 2, p. 186. The continued existence of this antipathy of Lowlanders to Gaels is illustrated by Dunbar's *The Dance of the Sevin Deidly Synnis*. The shouting of a Highland "correnoch" in Hell by a Macfadzane caused such a hubbub among the Gaels there, that

> "The Devill sa devit wes with thair yell,
> That in the deepest pot of hell
> He smorit thame with smuke."

[75] "The English names commonly used as equivalents for certain Gaelic ones must not be considered as exact equivalents. The custom of associating these names," says Dr. Dieckhoff, "seems to have originated at a time when contact between the English and Gaelic speaking section of the population became common, and names roughly resembling each other were introduced for the sake of convenience by those who were acquainted with one of the two languages only." *A Pronouncing dictionary of Scottish Gaelic*, 1932, p. 173. And Alfred Long writing of the mangled forms of Gaelic names such as M'Owl and M'Howl for M'Dowall, says "variations of this type are due to Gaels living in non-Gaelic localities where the unskilled natives fell upon the Highlanders by lip and pen till they hardly knew their own address." *Personal and family names*, Glasgow, 1883, p. 286. In like manner many Irish names are assimilated to English words and names of like sound, the word or name adopted often having no connection in meaning, as *OhEireamhain* to Herdman, *O'Seasenain* to Saxton, *O'Baoghail* to Boyle (also further Englished to Boghill and Hill). An Irish pronunciation of *MacGiolla Eoin* (= Scot. Maclean) is MacAloone and MacLoone, and in the barony of Tirhugh the name is Englished Monday, Munday or Mundy, from the assonance of *luain* 'moon' with (Mac) Aloone. A somewhat similar method was followed by immigrants from the continent of Europe to the United States. Sooner or later after their arrival they modified the spelling of their surnames to bring them into harmony with American names of British origin. Others again, translate their name into some more or less English equivalent. Examples of both methods are illustrated in the following note compiled from Mencken's *The American language* and from other sources: — (1) Anderson covers *Andresen, Andriessen, Andersson,* and *Andersohn.* (2) Black hides German-Jewish *Bloch,* German *Schwartz,* and Yugo-Slav *Cerne.* (3) Bowman hides Pennsylvania-German *Bachmann,* German *Bauman* and *Baumann,* and Swedish *Boman,* and some *Bachmanns* have become Buchanans. (4) Kirk now represents Pennsylvania-German *Kirkeslager.* (4a) Livingstone now hides Pennsylvania-German Loewenstein. (5) Miller takes in German *Mueller,* Greek *Mylonas,* Czech *Mylnář,* Polish *Mielnik,* and Rumanian *Morariu.* (6) Armenian *Tertzagian* is now Taylor, *Hovanesian* and *Ohanesian* is Johnson, *Jamgotvhain* Jamieson, *Bedrosian* Peterson,

are some of the methods employed in changing or concealing Gaelic names: (1) An English or Lowland name is adopted which is similar in sound, e.g. Brodie for Brolachan, Milvain for M'Ilvain (Macilvain), Cochrane for Maceachran, Hatton for (Macil)hatton, Charles for Tearlach, Daniel for Donald, Weir for Macnair and Macamhoir, Livingstone for Maclevy. (2) By translation, Johnston and Johnson for Maciain, Walker for Macnocater, Weaver for Macnider, etc. (3) Another method of concealing (at least partly) the Gaelic origin of a name was by dropping the Mac. In other instances the Mac- instead of being dropped or incorporated was translated into its English equivalent and affixed to the name, as — Donaldson, Davidson, Ferguson, Neilson. The eighth Duke of Argyll refers to this habit of Highlanders dropping one name and assuming another. "During the Military Age," he says, "they did so perpetually when they enlisted under some new chief, and joined some other Clan.[76] In assuming the name of their new associates they kept up that theory of blood-relationship which in nine cases out of ten had no other foundation whatever. Sir Walter Scott tells us that one of his friends, shooting in the North, had a native guide assigned to him under the name of Gordon. But he recognised the man as having served him in a similar capacity some years before in another place under the name of

and *Melkonian* Malcolm. (7) Czech *Mráček* (which means a "small cloud") has become McLoud, and *Vališ* is now Wallace. Other Czech transformations include Brian and O'Brien for *Prujin*, O'Tracy for *Otraska*, O'Shaunnessy for *Očenášek*, and O'Hare for *Zajíc* ("rabbit"). (8) Finnish *Hakomäki* has become Maki and Mackey, *Pitkäjärvi* became Jarvi and now Jarvis, and is also translated Lake. (9) Greek *Christides* has become Christie, *Giannopoulos* Johnson, and John Cameron, a train-robber in 1926, was born *Kamariotis*. (10) Hungarian *Kallay* has become Kelly, *Nyiri* is Neary, *Maklary* McCleary, *Szabó* Taylor, and *Sebes* Speed. (11) Italian *Gallo* is now Galloway, and Jim Flynn, a prize fighter, was born *Andrea Chiariglione*. (12) Jewish *Cohen* is now Cowan and Colquhoun, *Levy* is Lee, *Wolfsohn* Wilson, *Lichtman* and *Lichtenstein* Chandler, *Meilach* King, and *Michil* Mitchell. In addition Jews have freely adopted many good British names as their own, e.g. Ferguson, Gladstone, Howland, Livingston, Macgregor, Morgan, etc. (13) Norwegian *Bruss* has become Bruce, *Knutson* is Newton. (14) Polish *Kucharz* is now Cook, *Tomaszewski* is translated Thompson, *Bartoszewicz* to Barton, and *Chmielewski* (from *chmiel* "hops") Hopson and Hobson. (15) Portuguese *Periera* is now Perry, *Correia* now Curry, *Marques* Marks, *Morais* Morris, *Terra* Terry, and *Laurenço* Lawrence. The Portuguese in the United States have also translated *Ferreira* into Smith, and *Caranguejo* (from *caranguejo* "a crab") to Crabtree. (16) Rumanian *Patrascu* is now Paterson, *Ionescu* is Jones, and *Stanila* Stanley. (17) Swedish *Esbjörn* is Osborn, and *Johansson* is Johnson. (18) Syrian *Maqabba'a* is now McKaba, *Sham'un* now Shannon, *Hurayz* is Harris, *Abbud* Abbot, and *Khouri* (among other forms has also become) Corey. (19) Yugo-Slav *Onlak* has become O'Black, *Podlesnik* Underwood, and *Miklavec* McClautz.

　　In August, 1941, a man with the German name of Schwartz, applied to the Court in New York City for permission to adopt the name of Stewart.

[76] "When a person changes his name to that of some other clan, or powerful chief, he was said to accept the name and clanship *(Ainm 'sa chinneadhas)*." J. G. Campbell in *Celtic waifs and strays*, p. 18.

Macpherson. On asking the man whether he was not the same and whether his name had not then been Macpherson, the composed reply was, 'Yes, but that was when I lived on the other side of the hill.' "[77]

Surnames in the Highlands are of comparatively late date, and in charters and other documents even as late as the first quarter of the eighteenth century we have examples wherein a man is designated by his father's, and not seldom by his father's and grandfather's and great-grandfather's names, as John Roy M'Ean Vc Ewin Vc Dougall Vc Ean, the name of the tenant of Balligrundill, Lismore, in 1585.[78] In 1718 we find (1) Duncan Mcilichristvic Coilvic Cormoid for Duncan Mac Gille Chriosd mhic Dhomhnuill mhic Thormoid, i.e. Duncan son of MacGillechrist son of Duncan son of Norman. (2) John McUnlay keaneir for John Mac Fhionnlaidh mhic Iomhair, i.e. John son of Finlay son of Iver. (3) Malcolm McEanvicvorchay for M. MacIain mhic Mhurchaidh, i.e. M. son of John son of Murdoch. (4) Finlay MacConellvicinish for F. MacDhomhnuill mhic Aonghais, i.e. F. son of Donald son of Angus. In *Argyll Sasines* (v. 1) we find similar names: Sorle Mac Innes VcDonald VcEan diu, Duncan Onneil VcIllespick alias MacCallum, Gorrie McAchan VcAllester VcEan duff, Connacher O'Connacher McEan onnell VcKennich Leich, and Niall McArne VcKewine VcDuncan VcArne. In 1582 there is record of Patrick McDonill glasche Vc ane Vc Neill of Ellanrie.

In clan societies one can enroll as a member if he bears the name under which the society is organized. Thus an individual bearing the name Macdonald may join the Clan Macdonald Society, but how many individuals named Macdonald are really Macdonalds? A present-day John Macdonald may boast of the ancient greatness of that clan when as a matter of fact he may actually be descended from some seventeenth-century Donald Campbell, and therefore the scion of a clan which was the hereditary and deadly enemy of Clan Donald! Previous to the eighteenth century, and even in some cases of much later date, Highland surnames were in a fluid and ever changing state. Thus the old seannachies of Clan Campbell were and still are believed to have been Macewens, whereas it turns out that they were really Macdougals by origin. The Maceachans, again, are said to be of Clan Donald affinity, but it is now known that many are of Maclean origin.

The late Sir James Wilson in a letter published in the *Scotsman*, in December, 1921, on the "Surnames of the people of Crieff," drew attention to the fact often overlooked that "It is to be remembered that a woman when

[77] *Scotland as it was and as it is*, v. 2, p. 18–19.
[78] *Origines parochiales Scotiae*, v. 2, p. 165.

she marries gives up her own surname and adopts that of her husband, and the children are given the surname of their father, not of their mother. It therefore follows that a man's surname generally represents that of his paternal male ancestors, and gives no indication of his maternal ancestors, or of any ancestors from whom he is descended through a female. So that, for instance, when a man has a Celtic surname, it indicates that his paternal ancestors in the male line were of Celtic origin, but he may have in his veins a proportion of Anglo-Saxon blood, which may be large or small. If his father was a pure Celt on both sides, and his mother was a pure Anglo-Saxon, he is himself half Celtic and half Anglo-Saxon, though he bear a Celtic name. If he marries a pure Anglo-Saxon, his children, although they will bear a Celtic name, will have only one-fourth Celtic blood, and so on; so that it is quite possible that a man with a Celtic name may have very little Celtic blood in his veins, and, on the other hand, a man with an Anglo-Saxon name may be almost a pure Celt in blood." This consideration as will readily be seen takes effect both ways. It is evident, therefore, that we can form no just estimate of the Celticity or otherwise of the population from their surnames.

In the author's opinion all Gaelic surnames (there are strictly speaking no longer any patronymics) ought to be written as one word. As a prefix to a name Mac should never be followed by a capital letter. No Macdonald at the present day is son of one called Donald, for the simple reason that Donald here has lost its signification as a personal name, and with "Mac" prefixed has become a different surname. Of course as surnames are personal property a man is quite at liberty to spell and write his name as he pleases and etiquette demands that in writing to an individual we address our letter as our correspondent spells and writes it himself. However in a work like the present some system of standardization has to be adopted. We cannot enter Macdonald under M' in one place, Mc in another, and under Mac in a third, as is done in telephone directories in the United States.

Gregory was of much the same opinion. In his *History of the Western Highlands* he requests (p. 85) the reader to note that "throughout this work, where a patronymic is printed thus — 'MacDonald' — with a capital letter, it indicates that the individual mentioned was really the *Son of Donald* or as the case may be. Where, on the other hand, a patronymic is printed without the capital letter — 'Macdonald' — it is merely a general surname and does not indicate the precise parentage of the individual."

There seems no difficulty in giving Macintyre its correct pronunciation when written this way. We do not say Masintyre. We have also no difficulty in pronouncing the *c* of Macian as hard, and we even have it carried over as *k* in Mackean which is the same name. The interpolation of *k* in Mackintosh, Mackelvie, is an error which has survived from the time when there was no fixed spelling of surnames, and the same applies to the *k* in Mackendrick, Mackinlay, etc. These names are not entitled to the *k*, as that letter forms no part of the name. We might as well retain the *k* in MacKnab — an old spelling of Macnab.

Norman Names

The names introduced into Britain by the Normans are nearly all territorial in origin. The followers of William the Conqueror were a pretty mixed lot, and while some of them brought the names of their castles and villages in Normandy with them, many were adventurers of different nationalities attracted to William's standard by the hope of plunder, and possessing no family or territorial names of their own. Those of them who acquired lands in England were called after their manors, while others took the name of the offices they held or the military titles given to them, and sometimes a younger son of a Norman landowner on receiving a grant of land in his new home dropped his paternal name and adopted that of his newly acquired property.

The names introduced by the Normans were of three kinds: (1) Names of Norse origin which their ancestors had carried into Normandy; (2) Names of Germanic origin, "which the Frankish conquerors had brought across the Rhine and which had ousted the old Celtic and Latin names from France." Examples of this class are Ailward, Archibald, Baldwin, Bernard, Geoffrey, Gervase, Gilbert, Hugh, Lambert, Ralph, Richard, Robert, Roger, and Walter. (3) Biblical names and names of Latin and Greek saints. These names they retained even after they had completely adopted the customs and language of the natives of northern France. Others again, in many instances, adopted French names or had their own names modified or remodeled to suit the French pronunciation, e.g. (a) Humfrid — Humfrey, Winefrith — Winfrey, etc.; (b) by loss of *w*, e.g. Ealdwine — Aldin. After the Norman Conquest not only Normans but Frenchmen and Bretons from other parts of France settled in England, and not a few found their way north into Scotland.

The Anglo-Normans also introduced several diminutive suffixes, viz. *-al*, *-el*, *-et*, *-ett* (mod. Fr. *-ette*), *-ot*, *-at*, *-en*, *-in*, *-oc*, *-on*, *-uc*, and *-cock*. These added to the shortened or "pet" form of the name, give us Martel diminutive of Martin, Benet diminutive of Benedict, Davet diminutive of David, Adamot diminutive of Adam, Dobin diminutive of Dob (Robert), Baldon diminutive of Baldwin, Gibbon diminutive of Gib (Gilbert), Paton diminutive of Patrick, Davoc diminutive of David, Adkin diminutive of Adam, Alcoc (Alcock) diminutive of Alan, etc.

Irish Names of Recent Introduction

From about the year 1820 there has been a fairly constant influx of natives of Ireland into the southwest of Scotland, especially in the shires of Lanark, Renfrew, Ayr, and in Galloway.[79] In the last quarter of the nineteenth century and since, the influx has much increased, and, unfortunately, many of these later incomers are undesirables, being ignorant and densely superstitious. Some of the earlier arrivals, having improved their social standing, from motives of "gentility" says Dr. R. De Brus Trotter, modified the spelling of their surnames in order to conceal their origin. This practice he has humorously dealt with in one of his volumes of *Galloway Gossip*:[80]

"Twa men frae Ireland cam ower to make drains for Col. Andrew McDouall of Logan, for he was a horrid man for improvements, and had hundreds of Irish frainin till him. Yin o' the twa thay ca't O'Toole, an' the ither O'Dowd, and they both married and settled in the Rhinns an' their sons became Mr. Doyle and Mr. Doud. The grandchildren now call themselves McDouall and Dodds . . . Three other Patlanders came over by the names of O'Carrol, McTear, and McGurl, and in consequence of taking this strange complaint [gentility], their grandsons are now known as Mr. Charles, Mr. McIntyre, and Mr. Gourlay . . . Mr. McSweeney's descendants in the same way are now known as Swan, McWheeligan's are called Wales, McNeillage's are named McNeil, Mr. O'Forgan's are all Fergusons, Mr. O'Corcoran has a large family of the name of Cochrane, Mr. McGrimes has a son named Graham, Mr. Duffy's daughter is a Miss Duff, Mr. McSkimming is the father of Mr. Cumming, and so on till you would think no Irishman had ever settled in Galloway . . . Another Irishman of the grand old historical Milesian family of McGillivaddy, now for shortness called Mullivaddy, came over to Wigtown and turned cattle dealer, and he had two sons, and one of them became Mr. McFrederick, and the ither Mr. Mull-Frederick, and the grandsons turned into Fredericks without Mac's, Mull's or anything."

---

[79] The Glasgow Directory records a large percentage of Irish names. See also the chapter on "The Irish immigration" in A. Dewar Gibb's *Scotland in eclipse*, London, 1930, p. 53–62.

[80] *Galloway gossip (Wigtownshire)*, 1877, p. 67–38.

Within recent years there has been a large influx of Polish and Lithuanian miners into Motherwell and neighborhood. They are now said to be dropping their original names and assuming those of their Scottish wives, or they are altering their own so that they have more of a Scottish flavor, — Simski becoming Simpson and Watski becoming Watson, etc.[81] And now the second Great War has largely increased the influx of foreign names into Scotland. The birth and marriage columns of our newspapers frequently record the births of children to Scottish mothers bearing Dutch, Norwegian, or Polish names, or the marriages of Scots women to men with continental surnames, e.g. Bedsiowski, Byjdala, Flakstad, Gucewicz, Janeck, Janowski, Pestereff, Prydz, Soiland, Uruski, etc.

Population Movements

The statement of Fordun already quoted that Malcolm IV removed the rebel nation of Moravians from their territory and scattered them through other districts of Scotland is probably true in part.[82] We have authentic record of such movements or transplantations of greater or lesser extent in later times. Thus at a meeting of the Convention of Royal Burghs in July, 1596: Anent the third article of the 26th Act of the General Convention, "Concerning the inhabiting of the mowth of Lochquhaber and Ileis, thair resolution is that, the said Lochquhaber and Ileis beand maid peciabill, the burrowis sall fynd ane sufficient nvmber to inhabite the samyn."[83]

The peninsula of Kintyre contains many curious surnames, most of which are corrupt forms of Gaelic. Campbeltown was, under the marquis of Argyll, an asylum for persecuted Covenanters of Ayrshire, and there were Lowland Charges in Inveraray as well as in Campbeltown at a time when the whole native population spoke Gaelic. To this source is due the large number of south country surnames found in the peninsula.[84] "The almost complete swamping of Gaelic by Lowland Scots in south Kintyre is due primarily to the big Lowland immigration in the 17th century, from 1640 onwards. There were at least four *big* waves during this century and the inflow has gone on at intervals ever since right down to the 40's and 60's of last century. These immigrants were for the most part 'bien' people and settled, mainly

[81] cf. Ewen, *A History of the surnames of the British Isles*, p. 267.

[82] There is a tradition in Galloway that some of their people took the place of the Moravians displaced c. 1159. Trotter, *Galloway gossip: The Stewartry*, p. 163. But that, as W. C. Mackenzie says, "would be an application of the principle of homoeopathy." *Scottish place names*, London, 1931, p. 294 n.

[83] *Convention of Royal Burghs*, v. 1, p. 493.

[84] cf. Duke of Argyll, *Scotland as it was and as it is*, 1887, v. 1, p. 279–280.

as farmers in the agricultural portions of south Kintyre. They have had a
marked effect both on the character of the local speech and in hastening the
decay of Gaelic. The Lowland Church in Campbeltown was founded as
early as 1654 and the Church Records of Southend Parish show that there
was a Grammar School in Campbeltown in 1656 . . . With nearly three
hundred years of this dominating Lowland element at work in the district
and operating all the time with other causes that brought Gaelic into dis-
repute and threatened its entire extinction, it is surprising that we still have
from five to eight per cent. of Gaelic speakers left."[85]

Migration on a smaller scale is also represented by the following: "Avoch
was originally a Scots settlement in the midst of a Gaelic population. The first
settlers were no doubt boats' crews with their families from further south who
came up in search of good fishing or at the request of local magnates. One of
our contributors, Mr. James Reid, belonged to a fisher family said to have
been brought into the district in the 17th century by Sir George Mackenzie,
known to the Covenanters as the Bluidy Mackingie. His forebear had come
from Dunbar to be the laird of Rosehaugh's official fisherman and the office
remained in the family till the time of our correspondent's father." [86]

Mention may here be made of the belief entertained in various parts of
Scotland that in certain localities there exist descendants of survivors of
shipwrecked mariners of the Spanish Armada of 1588. This belief still prevails
in the East Neuk of Fife, in the Hebrides, in Fair Isle, Shetland, and on the
Solway Firth. Some of the Spaniards, we are told, settled among the people
about Ardrossan in Ayrshire "and left families whose representatives are
still known by their outlandish names and a slight tinge of the dark complexion of Spain."[87] It is much to be regretted that Chambers did not record
some of the "outlandish names" for the benefit of his readers. Of people of
the name Gosman in Anstruther, Fife, it was, and perhaps still is, locally
believed they are descended from Gomez, the admiral of the Armada, or
from Guzman, a Spanish grandee.[88] In Fair Isle, Shetland, the art of knitting
woolen articles of various colors and curious patterns is believed to have
been taught the islanders by 200 Spaniards who escaped from the wreck of
the flagship of the Duke of Medina.[89]

[85] Mr. L. McInnes, Campbeltown, quoted in introduction to the *Scottish national dictionary*, v. 1,
p. xxvii.
[86] *Scottish national dictionary*, introduction, p. xxxvii.
[87] Chambers, *Picture of Scotland*, 1827, v. 1, p. 318.
[88] Mackay, *A History of Fife and Kinross*, 1896, p. 100.
[89] Groome, *Ordnance gazetteer of Scotland*, 1885, s. v. Fair Isle.

Popular Derivations of Surnames

Many a Scottish surname of territorial or local origin has had ascribed to it a derivation altogether different from the truth. These erroneous etymologies are due to that love of the marvelous and romantic to which the uneducated mind is at all times prone.

Thus "once upon a time," to use the language of fairy tales, a body of taxpayers in Glenshee, led by one Andrew Stewart, of Drumforkat, attacked the Campbells, who were the tax-gatherers, defeated them, and cut off the heads of several of the slain. Not long after the Campbells reappeared in the glen "with the intention of capturing the leader, Stewart. He, however, was warned of their approach and took refuge in a neighbouring mill, where he disguised himself by donning the dusty suit of the miller, and, when, in their search, his pursuers reached the mill, he told them there was no such person there but the miller and himself. For this exploit his descendants bore the name of Miller."[90] Similarly the Macbaxters in Glenshira are named from a Macmillan who killed a man, and took refuge in the kitchen of Inveraray Castle from his pursuers. "He exchanged clothes with the cook and set to work in the kitchen kneading barley bannocks . . . from this instance his children received the designation of 'Macbaxter' or son of the baker."[91] Collier, Dalziel, Dinwiddie, Douglas, Erskine, Forbes, Gordon, Guthrie, Leslie, Milligan, Napier, Skene, Turnbull, and many other names have been explained in a similar way.

There is a fondness in the Gaelic mind for quasi and fanciful etymologies in surnames, e.g. Fraser, etc. Prof. Blackie once wrote to a correspondent: "Etymologies are very slippery things, especially in the hands of a half-trained Highlandman," and Bishop Reeves in his edition of Adamnan's Life of Columba (p. 305n), tells us that etymology "without reference to original authorities is an indulgence as dangerous as it is seductive." And Voltaire has said somewhere that etymology in the hands of untrained people is the science where the consonants count for little and the vowels for nothing at all.

Brief mention may be made here of a few of the absurd derivations seriously put forth from time to time of some surnames. Auld from the tail of (Don)ald, Caie "simply the vocative case of Latin name Caius." Carruthers from Carrachers, the men of Carrick, bodyguard of King Robert Bruce in

---

90 Miller, *Tales of a highland parish (Glenshee)*, Perth, 1925, p. 39.

91 Adam, *The Clans, septs, and regiments of the Scottish Highlands*, Edinburgh, 1908, p. 167.

1314. Clephane from Claidheamh-mor (claymore), or more probably a corruption of Mac Ghille-Fhinnain. Cooper from the Latinized form of (S.) Cuthbert, viz. (S.) Coubre, hence "Cupar-Fife" and "Coupar-Angus." Duncan, "king, judge, or noble." Dunn from "old northern" *duna*, thunder. Friseal (Fraser) from Gaelic *frith siol*, "forest tribe or race," Geddes from French word "cadets," the younger branches of a family in landed estates. Govenlock, a Polish rendering of Greek Gowanlock. Gowanlock from Greek "Gounos aloes," a fruitful vineyard. Greenhorn, from a man who used a green drinking cup. Hermiston, "East beautiful town." Keith from the tribe of Chatti mentioned by the Roman historian Tacitus. Larnach from Etruscan *Lar*, "title peculiar to the eldest son," and German *nach*, "near." Lockhart, from Loch-Ard near Ben Lomond (this is Andrew Lang's etymology, but apparently "lifted" from Lower). Lyall, a name assumed by the proprietors of some of the Western Isles. Meldrum, "drummer or drum beater." Middlemass from "middle-mast" of a ship, applied to a tall person (this is the etymology offered by a well-known authority on Scottish place names who ought to have known better). Mitchell from German "Mit schuler" a disciple, literally "with a school." Paxton from Latin *pacis* and Saxon *ton*, meaning "peace town." Rait from Rhaetia, the name of a province of the Roman Empire. Reynolds from Latin *regnator*, "a ruler or king." Rutherford from a battle fought once upon a time between Scots and English. The latter crossed the Tweed at a ford and were driven back with great loss, hence the place name "Rue the ford." Runciman from Ranzaman, a ranchman. Somhairle from Gaelic *soma*, learning and *airle*, advice. Wilkie from British *Gwael-chu=* Irish *Fael-chu*, wolf dog.

Canting arms, or in heraldic phrase, *armes parlantes*, that is, arms allusive to the name, title, or office of the person who bears them, as garvies for Garvie, bells for Bell, "banes" (bones) for Bayne, elephant for Oliphant and Elphinstone, etc., are of no value historically. With many local etymologists and amateur genealogists however, the canting arms are the source of the surname instead of the surname having been (in some cases at least) the inspiration of the arms. "Students of heraldry," says J. H. Round, "are well aware that most of the cherished legends which explain the origin of particular coats-of-arms have been wholly suggested by the arms themselves."[92] Canting arms innumerable are borne by Scottish families, in addition to those above named, as Frasers, Cummings, Blackstocks, Foulises, Provans, Scroggies, etc. Popular etymologies which connect the names of persons with their

---

[92] *Antiquary*, new ser., v. 9, p. 142.

actions is widespread and ancient, and many instances occur in the Old Testament.

Corrupt Spelling of Names

During the Middle Ages the knowledge of the art of writing was confined largely to churchmen, and when they had occasion to record a surname there was no fixed rule of orthography to guide them. They therefore wrote down the names, especially such as were unfamiliar to them, in forms suggested by their sound. Again, the spelling of names of persons and places varied greatly in consequence of some of them being written in Latin, while others appear in Norman-French, and others again in the vernacular. By the end of the fifteenth century the spelling of names in the public records of Scotland appears to have become completely demoralized, and the same name may be found spelled half-a-dozen ways in the same document. This unstable phonetic rendering of proper names continued even into early nineteenth-century time.

Writing before 1666 the Rev. James Fraser remarks that "it is an epidemicall disease to which many ancient surnames are subject, to be ill spelled and variously disguised in writing,"[93] and true it is there was no greater sinner in spreading this disease than Fraser himself! This "epidemicall disease" was also noted by a writer of the sixteenth century who remarks of a contemporary that he

> "vreeitis not veill
> and spellis far var."

The public records of Scotland, as already remarked, especially of the sixteenth and seventeenth centuries, abound with instances where surnames and particularly names of Gaelic origin have been mangled almost (and indeed in some cases) beyond recognition, owing to the ignorance of the notaries and scribes. Instances may be found on almost every page of the *Register of the Privy Council*. "The barbarous jargon into which the low country scriveners reduce Gaelic names," say the authors of *Lays of the Deer Forest*, "is such as often to render them totally unintelligible to any except those otherwise acquainted with the persons and places which they disguised. In some instances the metamorphoses amount to a ludicrous gibberish, grotesque to the eye, and erroneous to the understanding, confounding (unconsciously however) the original word with another of an absurdly different meaning — as Mac O'Neill for MacDhomhnuill (Macdonald) and Macum tosh for Macintosh. But the most amusing series of examples is to

[93] *Chronicles of the Frasers*, Scot. Hist. Soc., 1905, p. 15.

be found in the various gymnastics of the alphabet which it has pleased these Protean scribes to exercise the flexibility of the names 'Moidart' and 'Moidartach,' as 'Mud wort,' 'Midart' and 'Medart' — 'Mowderdache,' 'Mowdertyke' and 'Mowdeworp,' by which last the renowned 'Iain Muidartach' has been transformed into a mole!"[94]

In Shetland personal names have undergone much change chiefly from the mistakes of southern clergymen who have ministered in the islands, and who were anxious to substitute "Christian" names for "heathen" ones, as they deemed those which they found in current use. Thus, Jarm or Bjarmi has become Jerome; Osla or Oslaf has been changed to Ursilla; Salmund is disguised as Simon, but even yet is pronounced Simmund; Thorwald, Tirval, and Taeder have become confused and run into Theodore; while Geirsi, the diminutive of Geirhilda, has assumed the baptismal form of Grisella. Even Haki, the ancient Hakon, has been completely lost in Hercules. In Orkney deeds Mane, Jame, Bere, Reche, Ade, Dawe, appear for Magnus, James, Barne, Richard, Adam, David.

Innumerable errors in the spelling of Scottish place names and surnames also occur in the papal records relating to Scotland.[95] Lastly, in addition to the ingenious perversity of Lowland charter scribes, local peculiarities of pronunciation were also a fruitful source of corruption in the spelling of place names and surnames, e.g., Bauk for Bauchope, Marno for Marnock, Phaup for Fawhope, Pook for Pollock, Rook for Rollock, Wahab for Wauchope, etc.

Letters of Denization to Scots in England

A number of Scots migrated to England in the fifteenth century and obtained letters of denization there. The following is a selection of entries from Bain.[96]

1463. Letters of denization for John Johnston *alias* Jonston, priest and monk, a native of the vill of Jonstone; and also for Laurence Martyn, chaplain, a native of the vill of Jedeworth. 1335.

1463. Letters of denization for Simon Comyn, chaplain, a native of Coldyngham; for John Gray, *alias* Barbour, a native of the city of Edinburgh; and for Alexander Willyamsone, a native of the town of Aberdeen. 1336.

[94] *Lays of the Deer Forest*, v. 2, p. 474. The authors are referring to the *Register of the Privy Council* and to charters of Clan Ronald of Arisaig.

[95] There is a paper on the errors in Scottish names in the papal records in the *Proceedings of the Society of Antiquaries of Scotland*, 1904–5, p. 379–387.

[96] *Calendar of documents relating to Scotland*, v. 4. The numbers at the beginning are the date, and the numbers at the end those of the calendar entries. The number of clerics named is noteworthy. On denizations of Scotsmen in England, 1509–1603, see *The Scottish antiquary*, 1894, v. 8, p. 8–14, 58–61.

1475. Letters of naturalization in favor of Henry Dolas, a native of Arbrodyt (Arbroath); and for William Oughtre *alias* Parker, "taillour," a native of Dundee. 1426.

1480. Forty-six Scotsmen (named) between March and September in this year received letters of denization. 1465.

1481. Letters of naturalization for David Cowle and the heirs of his body begotten or to be begotten. 1468.

1482. Letters of denization for John Borelle *alias* Steward, born in the vill of Morthyngton, and four others. 1473.

1491. Warrant for letters of denization to Robert Amourrey, a native of Scotland; same for John Rede, Scotsman. 1572.

1491. Letters of denization for Sir John Dynham, chaplain, a native of Scotland. 1582.

1492. Letters of denization in favor of Richard Nesbit, priest, a native of Scotland. His petition states to the king that he "hath lede a pouere liffe here within this youre most noble roialme of England by the space of xiiij yeres passed in geting his sustenaunce oonly by the teching of pouere childerne and scolers at scole, and soo yet doth." 1583.

1496. Letters patent naturalizing Alan Vaus, chaplain, a native of Dunfermeyn (Dunfermline), as an Englishman for life. 1625.

1497. Warrant for denization for William Phylpot. 1630.

1498. Letters of denization to John Graunt, with full right to acquire and hold lands. 1645.

Curious Descriptions and Names

Ewen gives a long list of curious descriptions and names recorded in England. The following are a few like names recorded in Scotland.

Adam	Aydrunken, Tyne, 1279
William	Conquergood, Edinburgh, 1665
Johannes	Excommunicatio (LAC., 80)
Andro	Goddiskirk, Edinburgh, 1423
Hastyn	Grontbachelar, Elgin, 1261
Ricardus	Hangpudyng, Glasgow, 1293
Robert	Luggespick, Dumfries, c. 1290
Patrick	Morselmouthe, Newcastle, 1304
John	Oute with the sword, Deer, 1402
Alan	Sorex, St. Andrews, 1298
John	Sowlug, Dunkeld, 1506
William	Spurnecurtoys, Aberdeen, 1274
George	Swynhouse, Over Blainslie, 1575
John	Unkutheman, Newburgh, 1279

Some Letter Changes, Etc.

A. Lowland and General

-all = *aw*, e.g. *Quiggenshall* for *Quhigginshaw*. See also under *-ll*.

-an, -en, -ing, diminutive endings, are sometimes weakened to *-y* or *-ie*.

b is either lost between *ml* or not developed, e.g., *chaumer* for *chamber*, *Chalmers* for *Chambers*. (2) epenthetic after *m*, *Imbrie* (1611) for *Imrie*.

c. Initial *c* and *g* often interchange. *c* and *t* were frequently confused in transcribing mss., e.g. *McGilbochyn* and *McGilbothyn*. About the end of the twelfth century these letters are indistinguishable in mss.

-cen, an OE. diminutive neuter ending, in ME. *-kin*, was freely used to form diminutives of personal names which afterwards became surnames: *Wilekin, Wilkin*, from *William*, whence modern English *Wilkinson*, which again was shortened to *Wilkins*. In the same way we have *Perkin* shortened from *Peterkin*, which with genitive *-s* becomes *Perkins*. Similarly, *Halkin*, whence by phonetic spelling *Hawkin(s)*, from *Hal*, a child's mispronunciation of *Harry* = *Henry*.

ch like *ck* is often dropped at the end of names: *Bullo* — *Bullock*, *Cranno* — *Crannoch*, *Durno* — *Durnoch*, *Marno* — *Marnoch*, *Nimmo* — *Nimmock*, *Rollo* — *Rollock*. Laziness of utterance probably accounts for this.

ck. See under *ch*.

d is often inserted for euphony: *Normand* — *Norman*, *Hendry* — *Henry*, *Maccausland* — *Macauslan*, *Macclelland* — *Macclellan*, *Mackeand* — *Mackean*.

ee. In the Mearns dialect of Glenfarquhar *ee* was used for *o*, as *been*, *steen*, for *bone*, *stone*. So *Beedie* may represent *Bodie*.

-en. See under *-an*.

-ensis is used in Latin to express nationality and locality, e.g., *Flandrensis* "a Fleming," *Glasguensis* "of Glasgow," *Perthensis* "of Perth."

-et, -ett, represent *-head* in surnames derived from place names. See under the names *Blacket, Halket* in the Dictionary.

f and *v* when final are often absorbed by the preceding vowel, e.g. *Shirra* — *sheriff*, *Turra* — *Turriff*. (2) When medial, after a vowel or liquid, *v* is frequently elided: *Purves* pronounced *Purris*, *Steen*, *Steinson* — *Steven* (Stephen), *Stevenson*; *Lennox* — *Levenax*; *Innerleithen* — *Inverleithen*, etc.

g is often vocalized after *o*, the two forming a diphthong, Old English *boga* — Scots *bow*. (2) Sometimes epenthetic after n, *Ewen* — *Ewing*. (3) *g* is also sometimes used for *dge*, *Bridge* — *Brig*. (4) It sometimes interchanges with *j*, *Gocelin* — *Jocelin*.

-ing. See under *-an.*

j. In Caithness initial *j* as in *Jean* is pronounced like *ch* in *chin,* hence *Janet* becomes *Chinnad.*

-ie is the favorite diminutive suffix in Scots. Its origin is uncertain, but it is probably simply the weakened or unstressed form of another common diminutive place name ending — *-in.* cf. *Bidbin* (Book of Deer) — *Biffie, Cragin* — *Craigie, Fethyn* — *Fithie, Seggin* — *Seggie.* It is not found in Old English.

l following *a,* or *o,* or *u* was vocalized and the two letters form a diphthong generally written *au (aw), ou, ow: Baward* — *Balvaird, Cowden* — *Colden, Fawkirk* — *Falkirk, Goudie* — *Goldie, Maltman* — *Matman* (first *a = au*), *Mid Cauther* — *Mid Calder, Rowan (Rowand)* — *Rolland, Water* — *Walter.* (2) *l* before *d* or *t* is silent, and the *d* or *t* is doubled: *Haldane* — *Hadden, Halton (Haltoun)* — *Hatton.* (3) Previous to the year 1600 intrusive *l* was a common way of designating a preceding long vowel, chiefly *a* and *o,* but not sounded: *Chalmeroun* — *Cameron, Colwye* — *Cowie, Culpar* (1499) — *Coupar (Cupar), Haulch* — *Haugh (Hauch).* (4) In the sixteenth century and earlier there was a constant interchange of the liquids *l* and *n* in surnames and in some place names: *Ballantyne* — *Bannatyne, Colville* — *Colvin, Melville* — *Melvin,* etc. In place names we may notice *Dargavell* — *Dargavane* (1376).

-ll final *= w. Quhigginshall* — *Quhigginshaw, Duncoll* — *Duncow.* In old Scots charters it is impossible to distinguish between double *l* and *w* at the end of a word, both being written alike. David Calderwood in his *History of the Kirk of Scotland* as quoted by Rev. L. Maclean-Watt (*Douglas's Æneid,* p. 165–166), when speaking of the Waldenses, says: "Their offspring were called in England *Lollards* . . . and in Scotland *Lowards,* according to our custome, in turning a double *ll* in a German *w,* as when we pronounce *Bow, Pow, Row, Scrow,* for *Boll, Poll, Roll, Scroll.*"

lz, lȝ, ly represent a Middle Scots sound which is supposed to have been identical with *l* mouil*le* in French (dialect). It is often written *lȝ,* in Middle Scots, and hence arose the pronunciation *Dalzell.* See *-zie.*

-man at the end of a surname seems to have three meanings: (1) Ademan, 'servant of Ade (Adam)'; (2) Barnman, 'a worker in a barn, a thresher'; (3) Blythman, 'a man from Blyth.'

n is sometimes epenthetic as in *Messenger, Pottinger. n* liquid represented by *nȝ* in Middle Scots probably approached the sound of French *gn* in *digne.* Later the letters were mistaken for *nz* and a new pronunciation of proper names arose, like *Cockenzie, Mackenzie, Menzies.* The old pronunciation is *Cockenyie* (also *Cockennie*), *Mackingie, Mingies.* See also under *z.*

ng in the middle of a name has a single sound as in singer, e.g. *Sanger*.

p intrusive (epenthesis) occurs in *Campbell, Dempster, Sampson, Simpson, Thompson*. Its insertion is due to the faint explosive sound after *m* before *s*, or the effect of accent falling on the *m*.

quh = *wh*, e.g. *Quigginshall* for *Whigginshaw*, and = *w* in *Macquhat* for *Macwatt, Macqualter* for *Macwalter*.

r more than any other consonant has a tendency to shift (metathesis), i.e., sometimes to precede and sometimes to follow a vowel, e.g. *Bruch* — *Burgh, Glencross* — *Glencorse, Sandris* — *Sanders*. Sometimes it is replaced by *l*: *Plenderguest* for *Prenderguest*.

s. In early charters long *s* and *f* are so much alike as to be frequently mistaken the one for the other.

-s in Williams, etc., is the sign of the genitive "of," the name being the same as *Williamson*. This *-s* is also frequently added to certain names, e.g. *Bowers, Brooks, Chambers*, etc. This added *-s* may be regarded as a vague addition of emphasis, the plural or perhaps the possessive suffix *-s* with all meaning washed out. Dicken or Dickon = "little Dick" or "Dickie" in possessive case Dickens, means "Dicken's son." The fuller forms are Dickenson or Dickinson. Monosyllabic surnames of local origin often add the genitive *-s* after the manner of patronymics, e.g. *Holmes, Yates*. In the great majority of cases it certainly serves to mark descent, taking the place of "son."

sl is sometimes replaced by *scl*, apparently to give greater emphasis to the word, as *Sclater* for *Slater*.

-son is not seldom spelled *-ston*, thus giving a wrong meaning to a name, e.g. *Youngson* and *Youngston*. (2) *-son* is also found added to names of trades: *Clerkson, Grieveson, Smithson, Wrightson*.

-ston, -stone, in some instances appears as *-son*, e.g. *Balderson* for *Balderston, Hilson* for *Hilston*, etc.

-ton is sometimes wrongly spelled *-ston*, q.v.

t accretionary appears in some names: *Deuchart* — *Deuchar, Pinchest* — *Pinches, Makcruteracht* — *Maccruter, Millert* — *Miller, Pendreicht* — *Pendreich*, etc. (2) *t* in mss. is sometimes misread as *c, Murpac* — *Murpat*.

u, v, w are interchangeable in old spellings of surnames and place names. See also under *f* and *v*. *w* is sometimes met with transcribed *ze*, as in *Fawsyde*, which appears as *Fazesyde* (in *Liber Cartarum Sancte Crucis*, p. 11). (2) The Normans seldom used *W* initially, expressing its sound by *Gu*, e.g. *Gulielmus* — *Wilhelmus*.

y intrusive is found in *Sawyer* for *Sawer*.

-*zie* in place names and in surnames is usually pronounced *yee* or *ee*, the 3 being not really a *z* but representing the old *y* or *g*, *Benzie*, *Fingzies*, *Gilzean*, *Menzies*. The sound was something like French *gn*, as in *gagner*. Ninian Winzet, the Roman Catholic opponent of John Knox, wrote his name thus, to-day it is *Wingate*. Lord Kames says somewhere that the sibilating of *z* in *Menzies*, *Mackenzie*, and the like was enough to turn his stomach. The same sound occurs in *Cadzow* (Cadyow), *Colzie* (Coillye), *Culzean* (Cullain), *Ben Chonzie* (Honyie), *Cunzie* (Cunyie), *Dalzell* (Diyell), *Edzell* (Edyell), *Kailzie* (Kailie), *Monzie* (Monee).

B. Gaelic

a. "In Glenlyon, Rannoch, and Badenoch, *a* tends to become *au* before *r* whenever that liquid, whether it be long or short, is followed by *l, n, d, t,* or *s*" . . . as in Macpharlain. C. M. Robertson, *Celtic Review*, v. 3, p. 225. (2) Gaelic *a*, long or short, is often represented in early Scots by *o*, e.g. *Macarcill* (in *Book of Deer*) = *Makorkill* (in Moray). F. C. Diack, *Scottish Gaelic Studies*, v. 1, p. 92.

-*ach* (in Gaulish -*acus*, early Celtic -*acos* "abounding in"). As an adjectival termination it signifies "of or belonging to" or "one of the," e.g. *Domhnullach* "one of the Donalds."

-*ag.* Now a feminine diminutive suffix. (1) with nouns, e.g. *Fearn-aig* "little place of alders;" (2) with adjectives, *Dubh-ag* "little black one," a common streamlet name.

-*an.* This affix like -*oc* was masculine originally. It was most commonly used in forming diminutives in Irish, and the custom was followed in Scots Gaelic. The pronunciation of this diminutive shows that originally it must have had a consonant before it. This consonant we find in the early ogham inscriptions in which occur many names terminating in -*gnos* (genitive -*gni*), e.g. *Giragnos* (later *Geran*, in AFM868), *Maila-gnas* (for older *Mailo-gnos*) whence Mailan. The syllable has the meaning "son of." Examples of the genitive in ogham are *Artagni* (later *Artan*), *Broccagni* (later *Broccan*), *Colomagni* (later *Colman*), *Ercagni* (at Kilgrovane — Macalister, iii, p. 201), *Gattagni* (= Gaithin, father of a king of Leix, AU866), *Grilagni` maqi Scilagni* (= of *Grellan mac Scellan — Book of Leinster*), *Mailagni, Talagni, Ulcogni* (later *Olcan*).

an. The Gaelic definite article. It does not indicate, as some suppose, that the person to whom it is applied, is the head of the clan. No name beginning with Mac should have the definite article before it. Thus used it violates a rule of Gaelic syntax. It is a Gaelic idiom which is still common in connection with certain surnames, and in fact it points out that the name to which it is prefixed, or which it precedes, is *not* a Gaelic one, as *Intolmycht* "the Tolmie," *Intingclarycht* "the Sinclair," etc. The late Macleod of Macleod, I believe, keenly resented the conferring upon him of this dubious distinction. Some Highland chiefs, on the other hand, who have little or no Gaelic, are not averse from being addressed as "The."

c. The *c* of Mac is often flattened to *g* in Galloway and finally succumbs altogether. See further under *Mac* in the dictionary of names.

do. See under *mo.*

e. In Irish (and in Scots Gaelic) *e* of the genitive is often dropped in Englishing of names.

Gil (gille). In old spellings of Gaelic names *Gil* is frequently written *Kil.* Andro M'Gilligain in Ardersier (1613) appears again in 1619 as M'Killigane.

h. The use of this letter to mark the aspiration in Gaelic names no doubt makes many of them look formidable and uncouth, e.g. *Mac Fhionnlaigh* for Mackinlay, and *Mac Dhunnshleibhe* for Mac Anlevy, but it is impossible to print otherwise without special type.

Il', Ill'. In names beginning with *Il' (Ill')* from *Gill'* after Mac the mac is sometimes incorporated as *Macle* or *Mackle* as in Maclehose.

-in. Diminutive ending. See under *-an.* *-in* instead of *-an* appears in *Broicin* and *Matadin.*

k. (1) A letter which does not exist in the Gaelic alphabet but has crept into the Lowland spellings of a number of Gaelic patronymics (Mackerras, Mackinlay, Mackintosh, etc.) and has been retained on the plea that it preserves the pronunciation *c* before *e* or *i* as *k.* (2) An emphatic *k* is often found in sixteenth and seventeenth century spellings of names after Mac, as M'Kwatt for Macwatt. In the Inverness-Dingwall Presbytery records we find this common: McKsoirle for McSorlie, etc. A similar eccentricity is also found in Galloway where we find McKmaster for Macmaster, McKmacken for M'Macken, M'Kmillan for Macmillan. See also under *Mac* in the dictionary of names.

l. There is a tendency to substitute *l* for *r*, e.g. *Griogail* for *Griogair.*

mo. Mo "my" and *do* "thy" were often prefixed to the names of Gaelic saints as terms of endearment or reverence. (This usage is pre-Christian.) At the same time the diminutives *-an, -in,* and *-og* were often postfixed, as *Aed* (later Aodh) with *-an,* Aedan (Aodhan), "little Aed." With *mo* prefixed, in addition we have *Mo-aodh-an* (S. Modan of Rosneath), or with *-og, Mo-aodh-og* "my little Aodh" or "my beloved Aodh."

-oc (later *-og* and *-ag*). This was commonly used in Old Irish in forming diminutives and the custom was followed in Scots Gaelic, but the surviving examples are few in number. (See under *-an.*) *-oc* was masculine originally but now *-ag,* its descendant, is feminine only. From the Old Irish period *-oc,* borrowed at an early stage from Welsh *-awc,* is common in the affectionate forms of names of saints, especially in reduced forms, e.g. *MoChoemoc* from *Coemgin.* Final *-oc* in early mss. has sometimes been misread *-ot.*

ou. In Gaelic border names *ou* is for English *w,* as Macouat for Macwatt.

s. Initial *s* in Gaelic names is eclipsed by *t* of the definite article, as in *Mac an t-saoir* "Macintyre," *Mac an t-sagairt* "Mactaggart."

th. In Gaelic names *th* is often a mere phonetic device for dividing syllables, as *cathag* "jackdaw," pronounced *ca-ag. Latharn* or *Latharna,* Lorne.

List of the Principal Works Referred to

AAB. See: ILLUS.

ABERDEEN. See: ABERDEEN CR.

ABERDEEN CR. The commissariot record of Aberdeen. Register of testaments, 1715–1800. Edinburgh, 1899.

ABOYNE. The records of Aboyne. MCCXXX–MDCLXXXI. Aberdeen, 1894.

ADAM. The clans, septs, and regiments of the Scottish Highlands. By Frank Adam. Edinburgh, 1908.

ADAMNAN. Vita Sancti Columbae. Auctore Adamnano. Edited by Rev. William Reeves. Dublin, 1857.

ADC. Acta Dominorum Concilia, 1478–1495. London, 1839.

AEI. Aberdeen epitaphs and inscriptions; with historical, biographical, genealogical, and antiquarian notes. By J. A. Henderson. Aberdeen, 1907.

AFM. Annals of the kingdom of Ireland by the Four Masters. Edited by John O'Donovan. Dublin, 1848–51. 7 v.

AGNEW. The hereditary sheriffs of Galloway . . . With notes on the early history of the province. By Sir Andrew Agnew. Edinburgh, 1893. 2 v.

ALA. The acts of the lords auditors of causes and complaints. A. D. 1466–1494. London, 1839.

ALC. The acts of the lords of council in civil causes. A. D. 1478–1495. London, 1839.

ALFORD. Records of the meeting of the exercise of Alford MDCLXII–MDCLXXXVIII. Edited by Rev. Thomas Bell. Aberdeen, 1897.

ALHT. Accounts of the lord high treasurer: Compotà thesaurariorum regum Scotorum. 1473–1566. Edinburgh, 1877–1916. 11 v.

ANDERSON. Protocol book (1541–1550) of Herbert Anderson, notary in Dumfries. (In: Dumfriesshire and Galloway Natural History and Antiquarian Society. Transactions. 3. ser. ii. p. 176–224. Dumfries, 1914.)

ANGUS. Memorials of Angus and Mearns. By Andrew Jervise. Rewritten and corrected by Rev. James Gammack. Edinburgh, 1885. 2. ed. 2 v.

ANNALS. Annals of the reigns of Malcolm and William, kings of Scotland. By Sir A. C. Lawrie. Glasgow, 1910.

ANNANDALE. The Annandale family book of the Johnstones. By Sir William Fraser. Edinburgh, 1894. 2 v.

APPIN. The Stewarts of Appin. By J. H. J. Stewart and Duncan Stewart. Edinburgh, 1880.

APS. The acts of the parliaments of Scotland, 1124–1707. London, 1814–75. 12 v. in 13. (v. 12 is index. v. 6 is in two parts.)

ARGYLL. The commissariot record of Argyll. Register of testaments, 1674–1800. Edinburgh, 1902.

ARGYLL INV. The commissariot of Argyll. Register of inventories, 1693–1702. Edinburgh, 1909.

ARGYLL MSS. The manuscripts of the Duke of Argyll. By Sir William Fraser. (Great Britain. Historical Manuscripts Commission. 4th report, p. 470–492; 6th report, p. 606–634. London, 1874–77.)

AS. CHRON. The Anglo-Saxon chronicle. Edited by B. Thorpe. London, 1861. 2 v.

ATHOLE. Report on the charters of the Duke of Athole. (Great Britain. Historical Manuscripts Commission. 7th report, Appendix, p. 703–716. London, 1879.)

ATLAS. The survey atlas of Scotland. By J. G. Bartholomew. Edinburgh, 1912.

AU. Annals of Ulster. Originally compiled down to 1498 and continued to 1604. Dublin, 1887–1901. 4 v.

AYR. Charters of the royal burgh of Ayr. Edinburgh, 1883.

AYR FAM. A genealogical account of the principal families in Ayrshire, more particularly in Cunninghame. By George Robertson. Irvine, 1823–25. 3 v. (v. 2 and 3 include Kyle.)

BAIN. Calendar of documents relating to Scotland preserved in Public Record Office. Edited by Joseph Bain. Edinburgh, 1881–84. 4 v. (Cited by number of document unless page is specially referred to.)

BAMFF. Bamff charters, A. D. 1232–1703, with introduction, biographical summary and notes. Edited by Sir James H. Ramsay. Oxford, 1915.

Principal Works Referred to, continued

BANFF REC. Records of the county of Banff, 1660–1760. Aberdeen, 1922.

BARBER. British family names: their origin and meaning. By Rev. Henry Barber. London, 1903. 2. ed. (Of no value for Scottish names.)

BARDSLEY. A dictionary of English and Welsh surnames. By the late C. W. Bardsley. London, 1901.

BARING-GOULD. Family names and their story. By S. Baring-Gould. New edition. London, 1913.

BB. Am briathrachan beag. By Malcolm Macfarlane. Stirling, n. d.

BBT. The Black book of Taymouth; with other papers from the Breadalbane charter room. Edinburgh, 1855.

BEATON. Some Caithness surnames. By Philologist [Rev. David Beaton]. (In: Wick newspaper, Feb. 2 – April 27, 1911.)

BEATS. The municipal history of the royal burgh of Dundee. [By John Beats.] Dundee, 1873.

BEAULY. The charters of the Priory of Beauly. By Edmund Chisholm Batten. London, 1877.

BIGGAR. Biggar and the house of Fleming. By William Hunter. Edinburgh, 1867.

BINNS. The Binns papers, 1320–1864. Edinburgh, 1936. (Cited by number of document.)

BJÖRKMAN I. Nordische Personennamen in England in alt- und frühmittelenglischen Zeit. Von Erik Björkman. Halle a. S., 1910.

BJÖRKMAN II. Zur englischen Namenkunde. Von Erik Björkman. Halle a. S., 1912.

BM. Bannatyne Club. The Bannatyne miscellany... Edinburgh, 1827–55. 3 v.

BNCH. History of the Berwickshire Naturalists' Club. Alnwick, 1834–1940.

BOEC. Book of the Old Edinburgh Club. Edinburgh, 1908–38. v. 1–22.

BK. ISLAY. The book of Islay: documents illustrating the history of the island. Edinburgh, 1895.

BORDERS. Calendar of letters and papers relating to the affairs of the Borders. 1560–1603. Edinburgh, 1894–96. 2 v.

BRECHIN. The commissariot record of Brechin. Register of testaments. 1576–1800. Edinburgh, 1902.

BUCC. MSS. The manuscripts of the Duke of Buccleuch and Queensberry, preserved at Drumlanrig Castle. London, 1897–1903. 2 v.

BUCHAN. A history of Peebleshire. By James W. Buchan. Glasgow, 1925–27. 3 v.

BUCHANAN. A historical and genealogical essay upon the family and surname of Buchanan. To which is added a brief enquiry into the genealogy and present state of ancient Scottish surnames, and more particularly of the Highland clans. By William Buchanan of Auchmar. Glasgow, 1723. (The Enquiry has separate title page and pagination and is quoted here as Enquiry.)

BURGESSES. Burgesses and guild brethren of Glasgow, 1573–1750. Edinburgh, 1925.

CAB. Collections for a history of the shires of Aberdeen and Banff. Aberdeen, 1843.

CAC. Crossraguel Abbey charters. [Edited by F. C. Hunter-Blair.] Edinburgh, 1886. 2 v.

CAERLAVEROCK. The siege of Carlaverock in the 27th Edward I. A. D. 1300. London, 1828.

CAITHNESS. The commissariot record of Caithness. Register of testaments, 1661–1664. Edinburgh, 1902.

CALDER. A Gaelic grammar... With a chapter on proper and place names. By George Calder. Glasgow, 1923.

CALDWELL. Selections from the family papers preserved at Caldwell. Glasgow, 1854. 3 v. (v. 1 only referred to.)

CALEDONIA. Caledonia; or, An account, historical and topographical, of North Britain. By George Chalmers. London, 1810–24. 3 v.

CAMBUS. Registrum monasterii de Cambuskenneth. A.D. 1147–1535. Edinburgh, 1872.

CAMPBELL. The clan Campbell. Abstracts of entries relating to Campbells in the sheriff court book of Argyll at Inveraray. Edinburgh, 1913. 2 v.

CAMPSIE. The commissariot record of Hamilton and Campsie. Register of testaments, 1564–1800. Edinburgh, 1898.

CANISBAY. Parish registers of Canisbay (Caithness). 1652–1666. Edinburgh, 1914.

CARNWATH. The court book of the barony of Carnwath, 1523–1542. Edinburgh, 1937.

CARRICK. Some account of the ancient earldom of Carric. By Andrew Carrick. Edinburgh, 1857.

CAVERS. Report on the manuscripts of James Douglas of Cavers, by William Fraser. (*In:* Great Britain. Historical Manuscripts Commission. 7th report, Appendix, p. 726–732. London, 1879.)

CAWDOR. The book of the thanes of Cawdor. A series of papers selected from the charter room at Cawdor, 1236–1742. Edinburgh, 1859.

CBBC. Court book of barony of Carnwath, 1523–1542. Edited by W. C. Dickinson. Edinburgh, 1937.

CCPC. Chartulary of the Cistercian Priory of Coldstream. Edited by Rev. Charles Rogers. London, 1879.

CD. The county directory of Scotland. Edinburgh, 1912.

CDE. Charters and other documents relating to the city of Edinburgh, A. D. 1143–1540. Edinburgh, 1871.

CELT. MON. The Celtic monthly. Glasgow, 1893–1917. 25 v.

CELT. REV. The Celtic review. Edinburgh, 1904–16. 10 v.

CG. Carmina Gadelica... By Alexander Carmichael. Edinburgh, 1928. 2 v.

CHALMERS. See: CALEDONIA.

CHANNELKIRK. History of Channelkirk. By Rev. Archibald Allan. Edinburgh, 1890.

CHR. FORT. The chronicle of Fortirgall. (*In:* The Black book of Taymouth. Edinburgh, 1855.)

CHRISTIE. The lairds and lands of Loch Tayside. By John Christie. Aberfeldy, 1892.

CHRON. Short chronicle being chiefly an obituary relating to the Highlands, and compiled early in the sixteenth century. By James Macgregor, Dean of Lismore. (*In:* Archaeologia Scotica. iii, p. 317–328. Edinburgh, 1831.)

CHRON. MAIL. Chronica de Mailros e codice unico in Bibliothesa Cottoniana servato nunc iterum in lucem edita. Edinburgh, 1835.

CHRON. SCOT. Chronicum Scotorum. Edited by William M. Hennessy. London, 1866.

CLAN DONALD. The Clan Donald. By Angus Macdonald and A. Macdonald. Inverness, 1896–1904. 3 v.

CLAN TRADITIONS. Clan traditions and popular tales of the Western Highlands and Islands. By J. G. Campbell. London, 1895.

CLOUSTON. The peoples and surnames of Orkney. By J. S. Clouston. (Orkney Antiquarian Society. Proceedings. v. 2, p. 31–36. Kirkwall, 1924.)

CMN. Carta Monialium de Northberwic... Edinburgh, 1847.
   Appendix II contains 'Transactions in the burgh, being extracts from the Protocol book of Robert Lauder, notary in Northberwic.'

COCKBURN. The house of Cockburn of that ilk and the cadets thereof. By T. H. Cockburn-Hood. Edinburgh, 1888.

COLDINGHAM. Coldingham parish and priory. By A. Thomson. Galashiels, 1908.

COLL. Collectanea de rebus Albanicis, consisting of original papers and documents relating to the history of the Highlands and Islands. Edinburgh, 1847.

COLL. AGAA. Archaeological and historical collections relating to Ayrshire and Galloway. Edinburgh, 1878–99. 10 v.

COLSTON. See: GUILDRY.

COLTNESS COLLECTIONS. Coltness collections, MDCVIII-MDCCCXL. Glasgow: Maitland Club, 1842.

COMMONS. The commons of Argyll. Edited by Duncan Mactavish. Lochgilphead, 1935.

CORBET. Protocol book of Sir William Corbet, 1529–1555. Edinburgh, 1911.

CORSEHILL. Corsehill baron-court book, 1666–1719. (*In:* Ayrshire and Galloway Archaeological Association. Collections. v. 4, p. 65–249.)

CPS. Chronicles of the Picts, Chronicles of the Scots, and other early memorials of Scottish history. Edited by William F. Skene. Edinburgh, 1867.

CR. See: CELT. REV.

CRA. Extracts from the council register of the burgh of Aberdeen. Aberdeen, 1844–45. 2 v. v. 1: 1398–1570; v. 2: 1570–1625.

CRAIL. Register of the Collegiate Church of Crail, Fifeshire... Edited by Rev. Charles Rogers. London, 1877.

CRAW. Chirnside Common. (Reprinted from History of the Berwickshire Naturalists' Club, XXIV.)

Principal Works Referred to, continued

CRAWFURD, *Lives.* The lives and characters of the officers of the crown and of the state in Scotland. By George Crawfurd. Edinburgh, 1726.

CSPS. Calendar of the state papers relating to Scotland... 1547–1603. Edinburgh, 1936.

CSR. Caithness and Sutherland records. Miscellaneous documents. v. 1. London, 1909.

CULLEN. The church and churchyard of Cullen. By William Cramond. Aberdeen, 1883.

CULLODEN. See: MCP.

CUPAR-ANGUS. Rental book of Cupar-Angus ... Edited by Rev. Charles Rogers. London, 1879–80. 2 v.

CWA. Charters and other writs of the royal burgh of Aberdeen. By P. J. Anderson. Aberdeen, 1890.

DALLAS. The history of the family of Dallas. By the late James Dallas. Edinburgh, 1921.

DALRYMPLE. Collections concerning the Scottish history, preceding the death of King David the First... By Sir James Dalrymple. Edinburgh, 1705.

DAUZAT. Les noms de personnes, by Albert Dauzat. Paris, 1932. 4. ed.

DB. Domesday Book.

DBR. The burgh records of Dunfermline, transcribed from the original manuscript volume ...1488–1584. Edited by Erskine Beveridge. Edinburgh, 1917.

DELLQUEST. These names of ours. By A. W. Dellquest. New York [1938].

DICK. Highways and byways in Galloway and Carrick. By Rev. C. H. Dick. London, 1924.

DIECKHOFF. A pronouncing dictionary of Scottish Gaelic... By Henry Cyril Dieckhoff. Edinburgh, 1932.

DIS. See: HIST. DOCS.

DIUR. OCC. A diurnal of remarkable occurrents that have passed within ... Scotland since the death of King James the Fourth till the year M.D.LXXV. Edinburgh, 1833.

DOBIE-PONT. See: PONT.

DONALDSON. Caithness in the 18th century. By John E. Donaldson. Edinburgh, 1938.

DONNER. A brief sketch of the Scottish families in Finland and Sweden. By Otto Donner. Helsingfors, 1884.

DOUGLAS. The Douglas book. By Sir William Fraser. Edinburgh, 1885. 4 v.

DOWDEN. The bishops of Scotland. By John Dowden, D.D. Glasgow, 1912.

DPD. The diocese and presbytery of Dunkeld, 1660–1689. By the late Rev. John Hunter. London, 1917. 2 v.

DRYBURGH. Liber S. Marie de Dryburgh: Registrum cartarum Abbacie Premonstratensis de Dryburgh. Edinburgh, 1847.

DUDGEON. "Macs" in Galloway. [By Patrick Dudgeon.] Edinburgh, 1888.

DUMFRIES. The commissariot record of Dumfries. Register of testaments. 1624–1800. Edinburgh, 1902.

DUNBLANE. The commissariot record of Dunblane. Register of testaments. 1539–1800. Edinburgh, 1903.

DUNFERMLINE. Parish registers of Dunfermline, 1561–1700. Edinburgh, 1911.

DUNKELD. The commissariot record of Dunkeld. Register of testaments. 1682–1800. Edinburgh, 1903.

DURNESS. Parish register of Durness. 1764–1814. Edinburgh, 1911.

DYSART. Notices from local records of Dysart. Glasgow, 1853.

EBR. Extracts from the records of the burgh of Edinburgh, A. D. 1409–1589. Edinburgh, 1869–92. 5 v.

EDGAR. An introduction to the history of Dumfries... By Robert Edgar. Dumfries, 1915. Written c.1746.

EDIN. APP. The register of apprentices of the city of Edinburgh, 1583–1755. Edinburgh, 1906–29.

EDIN. CP. The commissariot record of Edinburgh. Consistorial processes and decreets, 1658–1800. Edinburgh, 1909.

EDINB. MARR. The register of marriages for the parish of Edinburgh. 1595–1750. Edinburgh, 1908–10.

EDINBURGH. The commissariot record of Edinburgh. Register of testaments, 1514–1800. Edinburgh, 1897–99.

EDMONSTONE. The manuscripts of Sir Archibald Edmonstone of Duntreath. (*In:* Great Britain. Historical Manuscripts Commission. Report. v, p. 72–184. Hereford, 1909.)

EGIDII. Registrum cartarum ecclesie Sancti Egidii de Edinburgh . . . 1344–1567. Edinburgh, 1859.

ELGIN. The records of Elgin, 1234–1800. Compiled by William Cramond. Aberdeen, 1903–08. 2 v.

ELPHINSTONE. The Elphinstone family book of the Lords Elphinstone, Balmerino, and Coupar. . . By Sir William Fraser. Edinburgh, 1897. 2 v.

ENQUIRY. *See under* BUCHANAN.

ER. The Exchequer rolls of Scotland. v. 1–23 (1264–1600). Edinburgh, 1878–1908.

ERUS. Early records of the University of St. Andrews. . . Transcribed and edited by James Maitland Anderson. Edinburgh, 1926.

ES. Early sources of Scottish history, A. D. 500 to 1286. Collected and translated by Alan Orr Anderson. Edinburgh, 1922. 2 v.

EWEN. A history of surnames of the British Isles: a concise account of their origin, evolution, etymology, and legal status. By C. L'Estrange Ewen. London, 1931.

FASTI. Fasti ecclesiae Scoticanae. By Rev. Hew Scott. 2. ed. Edinburgh, 1915–28. 7 v.

FB. In famed Breadalbane; the story of the antiquities, lands and people of a Highland district. By William Alexander Gillies. Perth, 1938.

FERMARTYN. The thanage of Fermartyn, including the district commonly called Formartine. . . By Rev. William Temple. Aberdeen, 1894.

FICK. Vergleichendes Wörterbuch. Zweiter Theil von W. Stokes und A. Bezzenberger. Göttingen, 1894.

FISCHER I. The Scot in Germany: being a contribution towards the history of the Scot abroad. By T. A. Fischer, Edinburgh, 1902.

FISCHER II. The Scot in eastern and western Prussia. By T. A. Fischer. Edinburgh, 1903.

FISCHER III. The Scots in Sweden. By T. A. Fischer. Edinburgh, 1907.

FORBES. Place-names of Skye. By A. R. Forbes. Paisley, 1923.

FORBES-LEITH. The Scots men-at-arms and lifeguards in France. . . By Rev. William Forbes-Leith. Edinburgh, 1882. 2 v.

FORDELL. Memorials of the Browns of Fordell, Finmount, and Vicarsgrange. By Robert R. Stodart. Edinburgh, 1887.

FORDUN. Chronicle of the Scottish nation. By John of Fordun. Edinburgh, 1871–72. 2 v.

FORDYCE. The church and churchyard of Fordyce, Banffshire. By William Cramond. Banff, 1886.

FOSTER. Members of parliament, Scotland, including the minor barons. . . 1357–1882. By Joseph Foster. London, 1882.

FRASER. The Aberdonians and other Lowland Scots. By G. M. Fraser. Aberdeen, 1914.

FRIARS. The Aberdeen Friars, Red, Black, White, Grey. Preliminary calendar. Compiled by P. J. Anderson. Aberdeen, 1909.

FRIARS AYR. Charters of the Friars Preachers of Ayr. Edinburgh, 1881.

GAW. Protocol book of Sir Alexander Gaw, 1540–1558. Edinburgh, 1910.

GILLIES. The place-names of Argyll. By H. Cameron Gillies. London, 1906.

GLASGOW. The commissariot record of Glasgow. Register of testaments, 1547–1800. Edinburgh, 1901.

GOOD. Liberton in ancient and modern times. By George Good. Edinburgh, 1893.

GOUDIE. The Celtic and Scandinavian antiquities of Shetland. By Gilbert Goudie. Edinburgh, 1904.

GRAHAM. The manuscripts of Sir John James Graham, of Fintry. (*In:* Great Britain. Historical Manuscripts Commission. Reports on manuscripts in various collections. v, p. 185–275. Hereford, 1909.)

GRANDTULLY. The red book of Grandtully. By Sir William Fraser. Edinburgh, 1868. 2 v.

GRANT. The chiefs of Grant. By Sir William Fraser. Edinburgh, 1883. 3 v.

GREGORSON-CAMPBELL. Superstitions of the Highlands and Islands. By John Gregorson-Campbell. Glasgow, 1900.

GREGORY. History of the Western Highlands and Islands of Scotland, from A. D. 1493 to A. D. 1626. By Donald Gregory. Edinburgh, 1836.

Principal Works Referred to, continued

GROTE. Protocol book of Gilbert Grote. 1552–1573. Edinburgh, 1914.

GUILDRY. The guildry of Edinburgh... By James Colston. Edinburgh, 1887.

GUPPY. Homes of family names in Great Britain. By Henry B. Guppy. London, 1890.

HAILES. The annals of Scotland, from the accession of Malcolm III... to the accession of the house of Stewart... By Sir David Dalrymple of Hailes. Edinburgh, 1819. 3. ed. 3 v.

HAMILTON. The Hamilton papers. Letters and papers illustrating the political relations of England and Scotland in the sixteenth century. Edited by Joseph Bain. Edinburgh, 1890–92. 2 v.

HANNA. The Scotch-Irish; or, The Scot in North Britain, North Ireland, and North America. By Charles A. Hanna. New York, 1902. 2 v.

HARRISON. Surnames of the United Kingdom. By Henry Harrison. London, 1912–1918. 2 v.

HAY. The manuscripts of Robert Mordaunt Hay, of Duns Castle. (*In:* Great Britain. Historical Manuscripts Commission. Reports on manuscripts in various collections. v, p. 1–71. Hereford, 1909.)

HAY, *Arbroath.* History of Arbroath to the present time... By George Hay. Arbroath, 1876.

HE. Bede, Ecclesiastical history of England.

HEIRS. Services of heirs, Roxburghshire, 1636–1847. Edited by John Macleod. Edinburgh, 1934.

HENDERSON. The Norse influence on Celtic Scotland. By George Henderson. Glasgow, 1910.

HEWISON. The Isle of Bute in the olden time. By Rev. James King Hewison. Edinburgh, 1893–95. 2 v.

HIST. DOCS. Documents illustrative of the history of Scotland, from the death of Alexander III, to the accession of Robert Bruce, 1286–1306...edited by Joseph Stevenson. Edinburgh, 1870. 2 v.

HMC. Great Britain. Historical Manuscripts Commission. Reports. London, v. d.

HMON. Highland monthly. Inverness, 1889–93. 5 v.

HOGAN. Onomasticon Goedelicum locorum et tribuum Hiberniae et Scotiae. An index with identifications to the Gaelic names of places and tribes. By Edmund Hogan. Dublin, 1910.

HOLM CULTRAM. The register and records of Holm Cultram. By Francis Grainger and W. G. Collingwood. Kendal, 1929.

HOME. Report on the manuscripts of Col. David Milne Home, of Wedderburn Castle. London, 1902. (Great Britain. Historical Manuscripts Commission.)

HP. Highland papers. Edited by J. R. N. Macphail. Edinburgh, 1914–34. 4 v.

HR. Hundred rolls, 1273. Rotuli hundredorum temp. Henry III — Edward I. London, 1812–18.

HUNTER. Family papers of the Hunters of Hunterston. Edited by M. S. Shaw. Edinburgh, 1925.

IDR. Records of the presbyteries of Inverness and Dingwall. 1643–1688. Edinburgh, 1896.

ILLUS. Illustrations of the topography and antiquities of the shires of Aberdeen and Banff. Aberdeen, 1847–69. 4 v.

INCHAFFRAY. Charters, bulls, and other documents relating to the Abbey of Inchaffray ... Edinburgh, 1908.

INCHCOLM. Charters of the Abbey of Inchcolm. By D. E. Easson and Angus Macdonald. Edinburgh, 1938.

INNES. Concerning some Scotch surnames. By Cosmo Innes. Edinburgh, 1860.

INNES FAM. Ane account of the familie of Innes compiled by Duncan Forbes of Culloden, 1698. With an appendix of charters and notes. Aberdeen, 1864.

INQUIS. Inqvisitionvm ad capellam domini regis retornatarvm, qvae in publicis archivis Scotiae adhvc servantvr, abbreviatio. 1811–16. 3 v.
    Only the retours of general service in the second half of v. 2 are here cited under this head. The retours of special service are cited under RETOURS.

INQUIS. TUT. Inqvisitionvm ad capellam domini regis retornatarvm, qvae in pvblicis archivis Scotiae adhvc servantvr, abbreviatio. 1811–16. 3 v.
    Only the retours of tutory in the latter half of v. 2 are cited under this head. For other retours see under INQUIS. and RETOURS.

INVERCAULD. Records of Invercauld. Edited by Rev. John Grant Michie. Aberdeen, 1901.

INVERNESS. The commissariot record of Inverness. Register of testaments. 1630–1800. Edinburgh, 1902.

INVERNESSIANA. Invernessiana: contributions towards a history of the town...of Inverness. By C. F. Mackintosh. Inverness, 1875.

INVERURIE. Inverurie and the earldom of Garioch. A topographical and historical account of the Garioch...with a genealogical appendix of Garioch families. By Rev. John Davidson. Edinburgh, 1878.

IRVINE. Muniments of the royal burgh of Irvine. Edited by J. S. Dobie. Edinburgh, 1890–91. 2 v.

IRVING. The history of Dumbartonshire, civil, ecclesiastical, and territorial; with genealogical notices of the principal families in the county. By Joseph Irving. Dumbarton, 1860.

ISLES. The commissariot record of the Isles. Register of testaments. 1661–1800. Edinburgh, 1902.

JAMES I. Deeds relating to East Lothian. Transcribed and translated by J. G. Wallace-James. Haddington, 1899.

JAMES II. Charters and writs concerning the royal burgh of Haddington, 1318–1543. Transcribed and translated by J. G. Wallace-James. Haddington, 1895.

JERVISE. Epitaphs and inscriptions from burial grounds and old buildings in the north-east of Scotland... By Andrew Jervise. Edinburgh, 1875–79. 2 v.

JERVISE LL. History and traditions of the land of the Lindsays in Augus and Mearns... Edinburgh, 1882.

JOHNSOUN. Protocol book of Dominus Thomas Johnsoun, 1528–78. Edinburgh, 1917.

JOHNSTON. The Scottish Macs: their derivation and origin. By James B. Johnston. Paisley, 1922.

JUST. REC. Records of the proceedings of the Justiciary Court from 1661 to 1678. Edinburgh, 1905. 2 v.

KEIR. The Stirlings of Keir and their family papers. Edinburgh, 1852.

KEITH. An historical catalogue of the Scottish bishops, down to the year 1688. By the Right Rev. Robert Keith. A new edition...by Rev. M. Russel. Edinburgh, 1824.

KELSO. Liber S. Marie de Calchou; registrum cartarum abbacie Tironensis de Kelso, 1113–1567. Edinburgh, 1846. 2 v.

KILBARCHAN. Index to the register of marriages and baptisms in the parish of Kilbarchan, 1649–1772. Edinburgh, 1912.

KINLOSS. Records of the monastery of Kinloss, with illustrative documents. Edinburgh, 1872.

KIRKCUDBRIGHT. The commissariot record of Kirkcudbright. Executory papers. 1663–1800. Edinburgh, 1903.

LAC. Chartulary of the Abbey of Lindores, 1195–1479. Edited by Rt. Rev. John Dowden. Edinburgh, 1903.

LAING. Calendar of the Laing charters. A. D. 854–1837. Edited by Rev. John Anderson. Edinburgh, 1899.

LAMONT. An inventory of Lamont papers (1231–1897). By Sir Norman Lamont. Edinburgh, 1914.

LANARK. Extracts from the records of the royal burgh of Lanark. With charters and documents. 1150–1722. Glasgow, 1893.

LANARK CR. The commissary record of Lanark. Register of testaments. 1595–1800. Edinburgh, 1903.

LANARK JUSTICES. See: MINUTES.

LANDNÁMABÓK. Landnámabók. Edited by Valdimar Asmundarson. Reykjavik, 1909.

LAUDER. The commissariot record of Lauder. Register of testaments. 1561–1800. Edinburgh, 1903.

LAWRIE. Early Scottish charters prior to A. D. 1153. By Sir Archibald C. Lawrie. Glasgow, 1905.

LCD. Liber collegii Nostre Domine registrum ecclesie B.V. Marie at Anne infra muros civitatis Glasguensis MDXLIX. Glasgow, 1846.

LENNOX. The Lennox. By Sir William Fraser. Edinburgh, 1874. 2 v.

LESLIE. Historical records of the family of Leslie from 1067 to 1868–9... By Charles Leslie. Edinburgh, 1869. 3 v.

LEVENAX. Cartularium comitatus de Levenax ab initio seculi decem tertii usque ad annum 1398. Edinburgh, 1833.

Principal Works Referred to, continued

LIDDESDALE. The history of Liddesdale, Eskdale, Ewesdale, Wauchopedale, and the Debateable Land. Part I. From the twelfth century to 1530. By Robert Bruce Armstrong. Edinburgh, 1883.

LIM. Liber Insule Missarum: Abbacie canonicorum regularium B. Virginis et S. Johannis de Inchaffery registrum vetus. Edinburgh, 1847.

LINDKVIST. Middle-English place-names of Scandinavian origin. By Harold Lindkvist. Uppsala, 1912.

LISMORE. The Dean of Lismore's book. A selection of ancient Gaelic poetry from a manuscript collection made by Sir James M'Gregor. Edinburgh, 1862.

LIVES. Lives of the Lindsays; or, A memoir of the house of Crawford and Balcarres. By Lord Lindsay. London, 1849. 3 v.

LOGIE. Logie. A parish history. By R. M. Fergusson. Paisley, 1905.

LOTH. Chrestomathie bretonne. Première partie. Breton-Armoricain. Par J. Loth. Paris, 1890.

LOWER. Patronymica Britannica, a dictionary of the family names of the United Kingdom. By Mark Anthony Lower. London, 1860.

LSC. Liber cartarum Sancte Crucis... Edinburgh, 1840.

MACBAIN. An etymological dictionary of the Gaelic language. By Alexander Macbain. Stirling, 1911. 2. ed.

MACBAIN I. Early Highland personal names. By Alexander Macbain. (Gaelic Society of Inverness. Transactions. XXII, p. 152–168. Inverness, 1900.)

MACBAIN II. Old Gaelic system of personal names. By A. Macbain. (Gaelic Society of Inverness. Transactions. XX, p. 279–315. Inverness, 1897.)

MACBAIN III. Place names: Highlands and Islands of Scotland. Stirling, 1922.

MACBAIN IV. The study of Highland personal names. By A. Macbain. (Celtic review. II, p. 60–75. Edinburgh, 1906.)

MACBAIN V. Personal names and surnames of the town of Inverness. By A. Macbain. Inverness, 1895.

MACDONALD. Scottish armorial seals. By William Rae Macdonald. Edinburgh, 1904.

MACFARLANE. Genealogical collections concerning families in Scotland, made by Walter Macfarlane, 1750–1751. Edited...by James Toshach Clark. Edinburgh, 1900. 2 v.

MACGREGOR. History of the Clan Gregor. By Amelia Georgiana Murray Macgregor. Edinburgh, 1898–1901. 2 v.

MACKAY. Urquhart and Glenmoriston. By William Mackay. Inverness, 1914. 2. ed.

MACKENZIE. The races of Ireland and Scotland. By W. C. Mackenzie. Paisley [1916].

M'KERLIE. History of the lands and their owners in Galloway. By P. H. M'Kerlie. Edinburgh, 1870–79. 5 v.

M'KERLIE II. History of lands and their owners in Galloway. By P. H. M'Kerlie. New edition. Paisley, 1906. 2 v. No more published.

MACNEILL. Early Irish population groups: their nomenclature, classification, and chronology. By John Macneill. Dublin, 1911. (Royal Irish Academy. Proceedings. v. 29.)

MACNEILL, *Oghams*. Notes on the distribution, history, grammar, and import of the Irish ogham inscriptions. By John Macneill. Dublin, 1909. (Royal Irish Academy. Proceedings. v. 27.)

MACNISH. History of the Clan Neish or Macnish. By David Macnish and William A. Tod. Edinburgh, 1925.

MAIR. Records of the parish of Ellon. By Thomas Mair. Aberdeen, 1876.

MARTIN. A description of the Western Islands of Scotland. By Martin Martin. London, 1716.

MAWER. The place-names of Northumberland and Durham. By Allan Mawer. Cambridge, 1920.

MAY. Records of the Priory of the Isle of May. Edinburgh, 1868.

MCM. Maitland Club miscellany, consisting of original papers and other documents illustrative of the history and literature of Scotland. Edinburgh, 1833–37. 4 v.

MCP. More Culloden papers. Inverness, 1923–30. 5 v.

MELROS. Liber Sancte Marie de Melros... Edinburgh, 1837. 2 v.

METHVEN. The provostry of Methven ... with charters and other documents relating to the provostry. By Thomas Morris. Edinburgh, 1875.

MILL, *Diary*. Diary of the Rev. John Mill, minister of Dunrossness, Sandwick, and Cunningsburgh in Shetland, 1740–1803. Edinburgh, 1889.

MILL, *Plays*. Mediæval plays in Scotland. By Anna Jean Mill. Edinburgh, 1927.

MILNE. The Blackfriars of Perth: the chartulary and papers of their house, edited with introduction by Robert Milne. Edinburgh, 1893.

MINUTES. The minutes of the justices of the peace for Lanarkshire. 1707–1723. Edinburgh, 1931.

MONRO. A description of the Westerne Iles of Scotland called Hybrides. 1549. By Sir Donald Monro. (*In:* Macfarlane, Geographical collections. III, p. 262–302.)

MONTROSE. Report on the muniments of the Duke of Montrose at Buchanan Castle. (*In:* Great Britain. Historical Manuscripts Commission. Second report, p. 165–177.)

MOORE. Manx names; or, The surnames and place-names of the Isle of Man. By A. W. Moore. London, 1903. 2. ed.

MOORE, *Lands*. The lands of the Scottish kings in England... By Margaret F. Moore. London, 1915.

MORAY. The commissariot record of Moray. Register of testaments. 1684–1800. Edinburgh, 1904.

MORAY MSS. Report on the muniments of the ...Earl of Moray. (*In:* Great Britain. Historical Manuscripts Commission. Sixth report, Appendix, p. 634–672. London, 1877.)

MORTON. The monastic annals of Teviotdale; or, The history and antiquities of the abbeys of Jedburgh, Kelso, Melrose, and Dryburgh. By James Morton. Edinburgh, 1832.

MSS. See: NAT. MSS.

MUTHILL. The transcript of the register of baptisms, Muthill, Perthshire, from A. D. 1697 to 1847. Edinburgh, 1887.

NAT. MSS. Facsimiles of national manuscripts of Scotland... Edinburgh, 1867–71. 3 v.

NEILSEN. Old danske Navne samlede af O. Neilsen. [Copenhagen,] 1883.

NEUBOTLE. Registrum S. Marie de Neubotle. Edinburgh, 1849.

NICHOLSON KR. Keltic researches. By E. W. B. Nicholson. London, 1904.

NISBET. A system of heraldry...with suitable examples of armorial figures and achievements of the most considerable surnames and families in Scotland... Edinburgh, 1816. 2 v.

NISBET, *Plates*. Alexander Nisbet's heraldic plates...reproduced with notes...by Andrew Ross and F. J. Grant... Edinburgh, 1892.

NSCM. Miscellany of the New Spalding Club. Aberdeen, 1890–1908. 2 v.

O'DONOVAN. See: AFM.

OLD LORE MISC. Old lore miscellany of Orkney, Shetland, Caithness, and Sutherland. London, 1907–11. 4 v.
   v. 1–2 title reads: Orkney and Shetland miscellany.

OLIPHANTS. The Oliphants in Scotland, with a selection of original documents... Edited by Joseph Anderson. Edinburgh, 1879.

OPPRESSIONS. Oppressions of the sixteenth century in the islands of Orkney and Zetland. By David Balfour. Edinburgh, 1859.

OPS. Origines parochiales Scotiæ: the antiquities, ecclesiastical and territorial of the parishes of Scotland. Edinburgh, 1851–55. 2 v. in 3.

ORKNEY. The commissariot record of Orkney and Shetland. Register of testaments. Part I. Orkney, 1611–1684. Edinburgh, 1904.

OSA. The statistical account of Scotland. By Sir John Sinclair. Edinburgh, 1791–99. 21 v.

OSMISC. Orkney and Shetland miscellany. *See* OLD LORE MISC.

OSR. Orkney and Shetland records. London: Viking Society, 1907–13. 3 v.

OSS. Orkney and Shetland sasines, edited by Henry Paton. London: Viking Society, 1909.
   Cited by number.

PANMURE. Registrum de Panmure. Records of the families of Maule, de Valoniis, Brechin, and Brechin-Barclay. Edinburgh, 1874. 2 v.

PAP. LETT. Calendar of entries in the papal registers relating to Great Britain and Ireland. Papal letters. London, 1893–1933. 12 v.
   v. 1: 1198–1304; v. 2: 1305–42; v. 3: 1342–62; v. 4: 1362–1404; v. 5. 1396–1404; v. 6: 1404–1415; v. 7: 1417–1431; v. 8: 1427–1447; v. 9: 1431–1447; v. 10: 1447–1455; v. 11: 1455–1464; v. 12: 1458–1471. (Quoted by volume and page.)

PAP. PET. Calendar of entries in the papal registers relating to Great Britain and Ireland. Petitions to the Pope. v. 1. A. D. 1342–1419. London, 1896.
   No more published.

Principal Works Referred to, continued

PARISH. Parish lists of Wigtownshire and Minnigaff. 1684. Edinburgh, 1916.

PATERSON. History of the counties of Ayr and Wigtown. By James Paterson. Edinburgh, 1863–66. 3 v. in 5.

PBK. The presbyterie book of Kirkcaldie, 1630–1653. Kirkcaldy, 1900.

PDG. Liber protocollorum diocesis Glasguensis. Edited by Joseph Bain and Charles Rogers. London, 1875. 2 v.

PEDERSEN. Vergleichende Grammatik der keltischen Sprachen. By Holger Pedersen. Göttingen, 1909–13. 2 v.

PEEBLES. Charters and documents...with extracts from the records of the burgh, A. D. 1165–1710. Edinburgh, 1872.

PEEBLES CR. The commissariot records of Peebles. Register of testaments, 1681–99. Edinburgh, 1902.

PITFIRRANE. Inventory of Pitfirrane writs, 1230–1794. Edited by William Angus. Edinburgh, 1932.

PLUSCARDYN. History of the religious house of Pluscardyn... By Rev. S. R. Macphail. Edinburgh, 1881.

POLLOK. Memoirs of the Maxwells of Pollok. By Sir William Fraser. Edinburgh, 1853. 2 v.

POLTALLOCH WRITS. (*In:* The Genealogist, new series, v. 38, 1922, p. 71–77, 135–145, 183–192, London, 1922.)

PONT. Cuninghame topographized by T. Pont, 1804–08. Edited by J. S. Dobie. Glasgow, 1876.

PRESTWICK. Records of the burgh of Prestwick in the sheriffdom of Ayr. 1470–1782. Glasgow, 1834.

PRISONERS. The prisoners of the '45. Edited by Sir Bruce Seton and Mrs. Jean Gordon Arnot. Edinburgh, 1928–29. 3 v.

PROTOCOLS. Abstracts of protocols of the town clerks of Glasgow. Glasgow, 1894–1900. 11 v.
Reference is to number of volume only as each volume contains a full index of names.

PSAS. Proceedings of the Society of Antiquaries of Scotland. Edinburgh, 1851–1938.

PVL. Alphabetical list of electors of the county of Perth, 1832. Perth, 1832.

RAA. Registrorum abbacie de Aberbrothoc. (I) Pars prior, Registrum vetus munimentaque ...1178–1329. (II) Pars altera, Registrum nigrum . . . 1329–56. Edinburgh, 1848–56. 2 v.

RAINE. The history and antiquities of North Durham... By Rev. James Raine. London, 1852.
The Appendix of charters only referred to. These are paged separately from the text and are cited here by number.

RAMAGE. Drumlanrig Castle and the Douglases... By Craufurd Tait Ramage. Dumfries, 1876.

RD. Registrum de Dunfermelyn . . . Edinburgh, 1842.

RDB. Roll of Dumbarton burgesses and guild brethren, 1600–1846. Edinburgh, 1937.

REA. Registrum episcopatus Aberdonensis... Edinburgh, 1845. 2 v.

REB. Registrum episcopatus Brechinensis... Edinburgh, 1856. 2 v.

REBELLS. A list of persons concerned in the rebellion . . . and a supplementary list with evidences to prove the same. Edinburgh, 1890.

REC. INV. Records of Inverness. Edited by William Mackay and H. C. Boyd. Aberdeen, 1911–14. 2 v.

RECORDS. Records of Argyll. Legends, traditions, and recollections of Argyllshire Highlanders... By Lord Archibald Campbell. Edinburgh, 1885.

REDIN. Studies on uncompounded personal names in Old English. By Mats Redin. Uppsala, 1919.

REG. Registrum episcopatus Glasguensis... Edinburgh, 1843. 2 v.

REL. CELT. Reliquiæ Celticæ. Text, papers, and studies in Gaelic literature and philology. By Rev. Alexander Cameron. Inverness, 1892. 2 v.

REM. Registrum episcopatus Moraviensis... Edinburgh, 1832.

RENT. DUNK. Rentale Dunkeldense: being accounts of the bishopric (A. D. 1505–17). Edinburgh, 1915.

RENTAL. Rental book of diocese of Glasgow. 1509–1570. (*In:* Simon. Liber protocollorum. v. 1, p. 41–214.)

RENWICK, *Peebles.* Peebles: burgh and parish in early history. By Robert Renwick. Peebles, 1903.

REO. Records of the earldom of Orkney, 1299–1614. Edited with introduction and notes by J. Storer Clouston. Edinburgh, 1914.

RETOURS. Inqvisitionvm ad capellam domini regis retornatarvm, qvae in pvblicis archivis Scotiae adhvc servantvr, abbreviatio. 1811–16. 3 v.

The retours of special service in v. 1 and in the first half of v. 2 only are cited under this heading, with name of the county and number of entry. The retours of general service are cited under INQUIS., and the retours of tutory under INQUIS. TUT. v. 3 is index.

RHM. Registrum honoris de Morton: a series of ancient charters of the earldom of Morton, with other original papers. Edinburgh, 1853. 2 v.

RMP. Registrum monasterii de Passelet... Passelet, 1877.

RMR. Register of ministers and readers in the Kirk of Scotland... 1574. (In: Wodrow Society miscellany. v. 1. 1844.)

RMS. Registrum magni sigilli regum Scotorum. The register of the great seal of Scotland. v. 1–11 (1306–1668). Edinburgh, 1882–1914.

Cited by volume and number of document.

ROA. Records of old Aberdeen, 1157–1891. Aberdeen, 1899.

ROBERTSON. See: AYR. FAM.

ROLLOK. Protocol book of Sir Robert Rollok. 1534–1552. Edinburgh, 1931.

ROS. Protocol book of Gavin Ros, 1512–1532. Edinburgh, 1908.

ROSE. A genealogical deduction of the family of Rose of Kilravock. Edinburgh, 1848.

ROSG GAIDHLIG. Rosg Gaidhlig. Specimens of Gaelic prose. Edited by William J. Watson. Inverness, 1915.

ROT. SCOT. Rotuli Scotiae in Turri Londinensi et in domo capitulari Westmonasteriensi asservati. 1291–1516. London, 1814–19. 2 v.

ROTHES. The manuscripts of the Countess of Rothes at Leslie House, Fife. (In: Great Britain. Historical Manuscripts Commission. Report no. 4, p. 492–511. London, 1874.)

ROXBURGHE. Report on the muniments of the Duke of Roxburghe at Floors Castle... By Sir William Fraser. (In: Great Britain. Historical Manuscripts Commission. 14th report, Appendix, part 3, p. 1–55. London, 1894.)

RPC. Register of the Privy Council of Scotland. 1. series. v. 1–14 (1545–1625); 2. series. v. 1–8 (1625–1660); 3. series. v. 1–14 (1661–1689). Edinburgh, 1877–1933.

RPSA. Liber cartarum prioratus Sancti Andree in Scotia... Edinburgh, 1841.

RR. Instrumenta publica sive processus super fidelitatibus et homagiis Scotorum domino regi Angliæ factis, A. D. MCCXCI–MCCXCVI. Edinburgh, 1834.

RRM. Selections from the records of the regality of Melrose and from the manuscripts of the Earl of Haddington. Edinburgh, 1914–17. 3 v.

RSCA. Records of the sheriff court of Aberdeenshire. Edited by David Littlejohn. Aberdeen, 1904–07. 3 v.

RSS. Registrum secreti sigillum regum Scotorum. The register of the privy seal of Scotland. v. 1–2 (1488–1542). Edinburgh, 1908–21.

RUG. Munimenta alme Universitatis Glasguensis. Records of the University of Glasgow from its foundation till 1727. Glasgow, 1854. 3 v.

ST. ANDREWS. St. Andrews Kirk Session. Register of the minister, elders, and deacons of the Christian congregation of St. Andrews... 1559–1600. Edinburgh, 1889–90. 2 v.

ST. ANDREWS CR. The commissariot record of St. Andrews. Register of testaments...1549–1800. Edinburgh, 1902.

SASINES. Abstracts of the general register of sasines for Argyll, Bute, and Dumbarton... Collected by Herbert Campbell. Edinburgh, 1934. 2 v.

SBR. Extracts from the records of the royal burgh of Stirling, A. D. 1519–1666. With appendix, A. D. 1295–1666. Glasgow, 1887.

SC. ANN. Scottish annals from English chroniclers A. D. 500 to 1286. By Alan O. Anderson. London, 1908.

SC. ANT. Scottish antiquary. v. 1–17. Edinburgh, 1888–1903.

SC. NAT. See: SCOT. NAT.

SC. PEER. The Scots peerage founded on Wood's edition of Sir Robert Douglas's Peerage of Scotland... Edited by Sir J. Balfour Paul. Edinburgh, 1904–14. 9 v.

SCBF. The sheriff court book of Fife, 1515–1522. Edited by W. C. Dickinson. Edinburgh, 1928.

Principal Works Referred to, continued

SCM. Miscellany of the Spalding Club. Aberdeen, 1841–52. 5 v.

SCOBIE. An old Highland fencible corps. The history of the Reay Fencible Highland Regiment of Foot, or Mackay's Highlanders, 1794–1802... Edinburgh, 1914.

SCON. Liber ecclesie de Scon. Munimenta vetustiora monasterii Sancte Trinitatis de Scon. Edinburgh, 1843.

SCOT. NAT. The Scottish nation; or, The surnames, families... of Scotland. By William Anderson. Edinburgh, 1864. 3 v.

SCOTT. The Pictish nation, its people, and its church. By Rev. Archibald B. Scott. Edinburgh, 1918.

SEALS. Descriptive catalogue of impressions from ancient Scottish seals... From A. D. 1094 to the Commonwealth. By Henry Laing. Edinburgh, 1850.

SEALS. SUPP. Supplemental descriptive catalogue of ancient Scottish seals...from A. D. 1150 to the eighteenth century. By Henry Laing. Edinburgh, 1866.

SEARLE. Onomasticon Anglo-Saxonicum. A list of Anglo-Saxon proper names from the time of Beda to that of King John. By William George Searle. Cambridge, 1897.

SGS. Scottish Gaelic studies. Oxford, 1928–42. 4 v.

SHETLAND. The commissariot record of Orkney and Shetland. Register of testaments. Part II. Shetland, 1611–49. Edinburgh, 1904.

SHR. The Scottish historical review. Glasgow, 1904–28. 25 v.

SHSM. Miscellany of the Scottish Historical Society. Edinburgh, 1893–1933. v. 1–5.

SIMON. Liber protocollorum M. Cuthberti Simonis, A. D. 1499–1513. Also Rental book of diocese of Glasgow, A. D. 1509–1570. Edited by Joseph Bain and Rev. Charles Rogers. London, 1875. 2 v.
Protocols are cited by number.

SKENE, *Highlanders.* The Highlanders of Scotland. By the late William F. Skene. Edited by Alexander Macbain. Stirling, 1902.

SKENE CS. Celtic Scotland: a history of ancient Alban. By W. F. Skene. Edinburgh, 1886–90. 2. ed. 3 v.

SN&Q. Scottish notes and queries. v. 1–12; 2. series. v. 1–8. Aberdeen, 1888–1907. 20 v.

SOLTRE. Registrum domus de Soltre necnon ecclesie collegiate S. Trinitatis prope Edinburgh... Charters of the Hospital of Soltre, of Trinity College, Edinburgh, and other collegiate churches of Mid-Lothian. Edinburgh, 1861.
Contents: (1) Registrum cartarum domus de Soltre, p. 1–54. (2) Registrum ecclesie collegiate Sancti Trinitatis de Edinburgh, p. 55–258. (3) Carte quedam ecclesiarum collegiatarum infra Laudoniam fundatarum, p. 259–332: (a) Ecclesia collegiate Beate Marie Virginis de Campis de Edinburgh, p. 259–272; (b) Ecclesia collegiate de Restalrig, p. 273–292; (c) Ecclesia collegiate de Corstorphine, p. 293–304; (d) Ecclesia collegiate de Creychtoun, p. 302–312; (e) Ecclesia collegiate de Dalketh, p. 313–326; (f) Ecclesia collegiate de Rosslyn, p. 327–332.

SOUTHESK. The manuscripts of the Rt. Hon. James, Earl of Southesk, at Kinnaird Castle. (*In:* Great Britain. Historical Manuscripts Commission. Seventh report, appendix, p. 716–726. London, 1879.)

STEWART. Sketches of the character, manners, and present state of the Highlanders of Scotland... By David Stewart. Edinburgh, 1825. 3. ed.

STIRLING. The commissariot record of Stirling. Register of testaments, 1607–1800. Edinburgh, 1904.

STIRTON. Crathie and Braemar: a history of the united parish. By Rev. John Stirton. Aberdeen, 1925.

STITCHILL. Records of the baron court of Stitchill, 1655–1807. Edinburgh, 1905.

STODART. Scottish arms, being a collection of armorial bearings A. D. 1370–1678, reproduced in facsimile from contemporary manuscripts. With heraldic and genealogical notes. By Robert Riddle Stodart. Edinburgh, 1881. 2 v.
v. 2 containing the text only referred to.

STRATHBLANE. The parish of Strathblane and its inhabitants from early times. By John G. Smith. Glasgow, 1886.

STRATHBOGIE. Extracts from the presbytery book of Strathbogie. A. D. 1631–1654. Aberdeen, 1843.

STRATHENDRICK. Strathendrick and its inhabitants from early times. By John Guthrie Smith. Glasgow, 1896.

STRATHMORE. Report on charters in possession of the Earl of Strathmore and Kinghorn. By Sir William Fraser. (*In:* Great Britain. Historical Manuscripts Commission. 14th report, Appendix, part 3, p. 174–190.)

SWINTON. The Swintons of that ilk and their cadets. [By A. C. Swinton.] Edinburgh, 1883.

TGSI. Transactions of the Gaelic Society of Inverness. Inverness, 1872–1939. v. 1–35.

THEINER. Vetera monumenta Hibernorum et Scotorum historiam illustrantia quae ex Vaticani, Neapolis ac Florentiniae tabulariis, 1216–1547. [Edited by Augustinus Theiner.] Romae, 1864.

THOMSON. Lauder and Lauderdale. By A. Thomson. Galashiels, 1903.

TIGHERNACH. The annals of Tighernach. Edited with translation by Whitley Stokes. (In: Revue celtique. v. 16–18. Paris, 1895–97.)

TORPHICHEN. Register of baptisms, proclamations, marriages, and mortcloth dues contained in the kirk-session records of the parish of Torphichen, 1673–1714. Edinburgh, 1911.

TRIALS. Criminal trials of Scotland, from A. D. 1487 to 1624. Edited by Robert Pitcairn. Edinburgh, 1833. 3 v.

TURRIFF. The war book of Turriff and twelve miles round. Edited by J. Minto Robertson. Turriff, 1926.

URIE. The court book of the barony of Urie in Kincardineshire, 1604–1747. Edited by Rev. D. G. Barron. Edinburgh, 1892.

VEITCH. The history and poetry of the Scottish Border. By John Veitch. Edinburgh, 1893. 2 v.

VIEW. A view of the diocese of Aberdeen. By Rev. Alexander Keith. (In: Collections for a history of the shires of Aberdeen and Banff. Aberdeen, 1843.)

W. I. See: MARTIN.

WADDELL. An old kirk chronicle... By Peter Hately Waddell. Edinburgh, 1893.

WALLACE. The actis and deidis of ... Schir William Wallace. By Henry the Minstrel. Edinburgh, 1899.

WALLACE-CHAMBERS. Life and works of Robert Burns. Edited by William Wallace. Edinburgh: W. & R. Chambers, 1896. 4 v.

WARDEN. Angus or Forfarshire; the land and people, descriptive and historical. By A. J. Warden. Dundee, 1880–85. 5 v.

WARDLAW. Chronicles of the Frasers. The Wardlaw manuscript. By James Fraser. Edited by William Mackay. Edinburgh, 1905.

WATSON I. The history of the Celtic placenames of Scotland. By Prof. W. J. Watson. Edinburgh, 1926.

WATSON II. Personal names. The influence of the saints. By Prof. W. J. Watson. Inverness, 1925.

WATSON III. The Celts (British and Gael) in Dumfries and Galloway. By Prof. W. J. Watson. [Dumfries, 1924.]

WEDD. The compt buik of David Wedderburne, merchant of Dundee, 1587–1630. Edited by A. H. Millar. Edinburgh, 1898.

WEEKLEY. Surnames. By Ernest Weekley. London, 1916.

WEMYSS. Memorials of the family of Wemyss of Wemyss. By Sir William Fraser. Edinburgh, 1888. 3 v.

WETHERHAL. The register of the priory of Wetherhal. Edited with introductory notes by J. E. Prescott. London, 1897.

WIGTOWN. The commissariot record of Wigtown. Testaments. 1700–1800. Edinburgh, 1904.

WILKINS. Concilia Magnae Britanniae et Hiberniae. By David Wilkins. London, 1737. 4 v.

WILL. The Huntly Volunteers. A history of the volunteer movement in Strathbogie from 1798–1808. By William Will. Huntly, 1914.

WINKLER. Friesche naamlijst. Leuuwarden, 1898.

WOULFE. Sloinnte Gaedheal is Gall: Irish names and surnames. By Rev. Patrick Woulfe. Dublin, 1923.

WSCOT. Weekly Scotsman. An Edinburgh newspaper.

WYLD. Universal dictionary of the English language. By Henry Wyld. London, 1934.

WYNTOUN. The original chronicle of Andrew of Wyntoun. Edinburgh: Scottish Text Society, 1903–14. 6 v.

YESTER. Calendar of writs preserved at Yester House, 1166–1503. Edited by Charles C. Harvey. Edinburgh, 1916.

YONGE. History of Christian names. By Charlotte M. Yonge. London, 1863. 2 v. New edition. London, 1884.

ZACHRISON. Notes on some Early English personal names. By R. E. Zachrisson. Uppsala, 1917.

ZCP. Zeitschrift für celtische Philologie.

ZEUSS-EBEL. Grammatica Celtica. I. C. Zeuss & H. Ebel. Berlin, 1871.

Abbreviations

(Other than those detailed above)

AF.	Anglo-French
Bret.	Breton
EG.	Early Gaelic
Fr.	French
G.	Gaelic
Ir.	Irish
L. or Lat.	Latin
LL.	Low Latin
Me.	Middle English
MG.	Middle Gaelic
MIr.	Middle Irish
ML.	Medieval Latin
NF.	Norman French
ODan.	Old Danish
OE.	Old English (Anglo-Saxon)
OF.	Old French
OHG.	Old High German
OIr.	Old Irish
ON.	Old Norse
W.	Welsh

a, ante; c. circa; p, post.

The Surnames of Scotland
Their Origin, Meaning, and History
By George F. Black, Ph. D.

AASIE, Aassie, diminutives of Oswald and Asmund, are now represented in Shetland by Hosea in the surname Hoseason, q.v., pronounced Osieson or Ozieson.

ABBIE. A surname derived from the office or title of lay-abbot of a monastery. In the early Middle Ages the abbot of a monastery usually belonged to a leading family of the district, and in that family the office was hereditary. "In course of time this system gave rise to great abuses; the monastery grew rich in lands, and the energies of the abbot, or some other leading officer, were directed to temporal rather than spiritual management. In fact, latterly, he became a mere layman, holding the abbacy in his family by direct descent, and, delegating his clerical duties to a monk, he himself took to rearing a family in which the monastic lands were hereditary" (Macbain, Scoto-Celtic studies, p. 69). That these 'abbots' were considered as merely laymen is shown, e.g., in the charter by Turpin, bishop of Brechin, referred to below, in which the prior, Bricius, at the time really a clerk, has precedence over Douenaldus (Donald) Abbe. This Douenaldus Abbe de Brechin witnessed a charter by Turpin, bishop of Brechin, c. 1178–1180 (RAA., I, p. 134), and sometime between 1204 and 1211 he gifted the 'Dauach qui vocatur Balegillegrand' to the Abbey of Arbroath, which grant was confirmed by William the Lion (ibid., p. 49, 50). Maurice Abbe of Abireloth or Abereloth appears as witness in charters by Gilchrist, earl of Angus and of John de Mountfort between 1201 and 1214 (ibid., p. 29–32, 47). The family of this Maurice must have taken its origin from the lay abbots of a Celtic monastic foundation near by, "probably established by St. Drostan, with whose name the primitive Christianity of the district is associated" (PSAS., LXV, p. 118). Between 1211 and 1214 Johannes Abbe with the advice and consent of his son Morgund granted to the monks of Abirebroth (Arbroath) permission to take charcoal from 'nemore meo de Edale,' now Edzell (ibid., p. 48). Among the witnesses are 'Morgundo filio meo, Malcolmo fratre, Johanne filio meo.' The same John Abbe and Morgund his son were present at the perambulation of the boundaries of the lands of the Abbey of Arbroath and the barony of Kynblathmond in 1219 (ibid., p. 163). Nicholas Abbe appears as juror on an inquest in 1250 (ibid., p. 190), Simon del Abbeye, Scottish merchant, complained in 1370 of being plundered by English wreckers (Bain, IV, 164), and Arthur Abbay, shipmaster of Carrail in 1613, was probably the father of John Abay, skipper of Carrail in 1635 (Wedd., p. 237; RPC., 2. ser. VI, p. 572).

ABBOT. Alexander Abbot is in record as a witness in Glasgow c. 1290 (REG., p. 200). In the year 1306 Sir John Abbot, dean of Fife and Fothyrrife, was ordered by the bishop to sequestrate the fruits of the provostry of Aberdeen (Bain, II, 1822). Alexander Abbot witnessed an instrument of sasine in Leith in 1548 (Soltre, p. 113), and another Alexander Abbot signed the Band of Dumfries in 1570 (RPC., XIV, p. 66). It is probable that in some instances this name is a shortened translation of Macnab, which in Gaelic means "son of the abbot" (Mac an aba).

Bardsley says that in England Abbot and Abbott are from Abb, diminutive of Abraham with additional diminutive suffix -ot, and that "it is all but certain that the majority of our Abbotts, although bearing a conventual title, are thus descended." As a diminutive of Abraham the name is found in Ireland at least as early as beginning of fourteenth century (Woulfe), but I have found no instance of such use in Scotland.

ABBOTSON. A sept said to be connected with the clan Macnab. If so the name is merely a translation of Macnab, q.v.

ABBOTTOUN. Gilbert Abbottoun in Tippartie, parish of Fordoune, in 1619 (St. Andrews), doubtless derived his surname from the lands of Abbottoun (1625) in Kincardineshire.

ABE. Diminutive of Ebenezer, in Roxburghshire pronounced Ebé.

ABEL, Able. This was a not uncommon personal name in the Middle Ages, derived from the Biblical Abel, Hebrew Hebhel, a name of uncertain meaning, but usually interpreted "breath." Master Abell, clericus regis, was one of the members of a mission sent to England to ask restoration of the earl-

[1]

2

ABEL, ABLE, *continued*

dom of Huntingdon in 1237 (*Bain*, I, 1329). He also appears in documents concerning the Abbey of Kelso in 1235 (*Kelso*, 231, 418), and in 1253 "valuing his own promotion more than the honour of the king or kingdom caused himself to be consecrated bishop by the pope" (*Chron. Mail.*). Nicholas Abel, a Scottish master mariner, was wrecked on the coast of Norfolk in 1388 (*Bain*, IV, 381), Thomas Abel or Abell appears as burgess of Edinburgh in 1387 and 1413 (*Egidii*, p. 23; *Neubotle*, p. 237), and John Abell held land in Aberdeen in 1413 (RMS., I, 943). Robert Abell, chaplain in Brechin, is mentioned in 1512 (RSS., 2440), and William Abel was tenant of Racharral, Kemnay, in 1696 (AEI., p. 23). The name occurs in Dundee towards the latter end of the sixteenth century as Abell, and is found in the parish of Kemnay in 1697 as Ebald (*Inverurie*, p. 426). Thomas Abell was a burgess of Edinburgh in 1430 (*Neubotle*, p. 280), and a John Abell is there also in 1635 (*Edinb. Marr.*). The kindred of John Abell, a celebrated Scottish singer of the reign of Charles II were later known by the name of Eball (*Illus.*, I, p. 57–58). Abill 1633.

ABER. George Aber in Aberdeen 1642 (RSCA., III, p. 2). There is a hamlet of this name in the parish of Kilmaronock, Dumbartonshire.

ABERCHIRDER, ABERKIRDER. From the old barony of Aberkirder in the parish of Marnoch, Banffshire. Johan de Aberkerthe or Aberkerthor of the county of Banff rendered homage in 1296 (*Bain*, II, p. 211). In 1329 provision of a canonry and prebend in Brechin was made to Walter de Abirkerdore and ten years later a dispensation was granted to David de Abirkirhourd to hold a benefice (*Pap. Lett.*, II, p. 288, 544). Vosualdus de Aberkerdor, burgess of Elgin, witnessed a grant to the church of Murray in 1343 (REM., p. 290). Archibald de Aberkerthore forfeited half of the land of Bengouer in West Lothian (*Bain*, III, p. 342), and in 1370 John Aberchirder took part in a murderous assault on John de Gairdvn (*Leslie*, I, p. 71). Sir John of Abyrkerdor resigned the chancellery of Caithness in 1390 (REM., p. 203, 324), David de Aberkerdor, burgess of Donde, witnessed a grant made by Alexander de Moravie of Culbyn and Newtone to another burgess of the same town dated at Scone in 1391 (RMS., I, 834), and in the same year King Robert III confirmed a grant to David de Abirkedor by William Angus, abbot of the monastery of Londoris (ibid., 852). Johannes de Aberkerdor, vicar of Elgyn, appears in several deeds relating to Moray between the years 1388 and 1399 (REM., p. 213, 324, 328, 351), David de Abbukerdor witnessed a resignation by Thomas Strachan of Glenkindy in 1406 (SCM., V, p. 254), and Walter de Abirkerdor possessed a tenement in Dundee in 1442–43 (REB., I, 92; *Charters and writs of Dundee*, p. 20). David Aberkeldor was temporary provost of Dundee in 1463 (RMS., II, 768), and in 1467 George and David Aberkerdo were commissioners to parliament for the same burgh (APS., II, p. 89). David of Aberkirdach was among those who were slain with the earl of Huntly's side in a conflict with the earl of Crawford at the gates of Arbroath in January, 1446 (*A Short chron. of the reign of James the Second*, p. 38), Alexander Abirkeirdour was a follower of Campbell of Lundy in 1529 (RSS., II, 59), Alexander Abirkerdour had precept of a charter of the Legisland in the regality of Kerymure in 1528 (ibid., I, 3989), and in 1531 there is recorded the escheat of Alexander Abirkeirdo in Angus (ibid., II, 1026). Aberkeredoure 1312.

ABERCORN. Of local origin from the village in the parish of the same name in West Lothian. In 1311–1312 there are references to Hugh de Abercorne and William de Abercorne (*Bain*, III, p. 410). Margaret Abercorne, spouse to Robert Frame in Carduis, parish of Torrens is in record in 1564 (*Campsie*). The surname is now very uncommon if not extinct. Abircorne 1510.

ABERCROMBIE, ABERCROMBY. Of territorial origin from the barony, now parish, of the same name in Fife. William de Abercromby of the county of Fife did homage in 1296. His seal bears a boar's head and neck on a wreath, star in base and crescent above, and S' *Will'i de Ab'crumbi* (*Bain*, II, p. 203, 540). As William de Haberchrumbi he was juror on an inquest in the same year which found that Emma la Suchis died seized in demesne in Fife (ibid., p. 216). Johan de Abercromby of the same county also rendered homage in the same year, and in 1305 served on an inquest made at the town of St. John of Perth (ibid., 730, 1670, p. 204). The Abercrombies of that Ilk became extinct in the direct line in the middle of the seventeenth century, and the Abercrombies of Birkenbog are now the representative family of the name. In the lists of the Scots Guards in France the name appears as Abre Commier. Abarcrumby 1552, Abbircrumby 1486, Abbircrummy 1496, Abercrombye, Abercrumie 1556, Abercrummye 1583, Abbyrcrummy, Abhircrummy 1521, Abircrombv 1427, Abircromy 1571, Abircromve 1574, Abircromby 1362, Abircrumbye 1585, Abircrumme 1536, Abircrummy 1491, Abircrumy 1546, Abircumby 1586, Abyrcrummy, Eabercrombie 1639.

ABERDALGY. From Aberdalgie in Perthshire. Thomas Daberdalgyn (i.e. d'Aberdalgyn) of the county of Are rendered homage in 1296 (*Bain*, II, p. 210). In 1312 there is mention of the horse of John de Aberdalgy (ibid., III, p. 425), and between 1315 and 1321 Walter de Abirdalgy had a charter of lands in the burgh of Ayr (RMS., I, 43). Henry of Aberdalgy was burgess of Ayr c. 1340 (*Friars Ayr*, p. 12).

ABERDEEN, ABERDEIN. Of local origin from the burgh of the same name. John of Aberdene, merchant of Aberdeen, was robbed of wool at sea while on a voyage from Aberdeen to St. Omer in 1272 (*Bain*, II, 9), and in 1290 Michael de Abirden held land in Waldefgate in Berwick (*Kelso*, 44). Henry of Aberdeen was clerk to John, king of Scots (*Robert* III) in 1295 (*Bain*, II, 714), John de Abirdene was vicar of Pencatland in 1399 (*Soltre*, p. 55), Helen Aberdein appears in Belhelvies in 1633 (SCM., III, p. 109), and in 1693 there is entry of the marriage of Isobel Aberdeen in Edinburgh (*Edinb. Marr.*). Alexander Aberdein was a merchant in Aberdeen in 1722 (NSCM., II, p. 112), and Jennie W. Aberdein wrote the Life of John Galt, Oxford, 1936.

ABERDOUR. Of local origin from Aberdour in Aberdeenshire or from Aberdour in Fife, or perhaps from both. William Abirdour witnessed a charter by the earl of Huntlie in 1367 (*Aboyne*, p. 13), and another William Abirdour acted as bailie for the Abbey of Arbroath in 1483 (RAA., II, 236). Another William Aberdour admitted burgess of Aberdeen in 1484 appears again in 1508 as a contributor towards repairing the city church (NSCM., I, p. 31; CRA., p. 43, 80). Alexander Abirdour who witnessed the sale of Reidmyr and Quhitriggis in 1487 is probably the Alexander Aberdour who appears as a charter witness in 1500 (REB., II, 144; RAA., II, 409). In 1510 a precept of remission was issued at Banff to two men charged with the murder of William Abirdour alias Jak (RSS., I, 2106). Robert Abirdour in Rothiebirsben appears in 1610 (*Inquis.*, 482), and Gilbert Abirdour in Culquhorsie was on assize in the same year (RSCA., II, p. 61, 134). Abyrdour 1504.

ABERIGH. See under ABRACH.

ABERKIRDER. See under ABERCHIRDER.

ABERLADY. From the village in the parish of the same name in East Lothian. Robertus de Abirlevedi and Henricus his brother are witnesses in an Inchcolm charter, c. 1229–1236 (*Inchcolm*, p. 13). In 1333 William de Aberlady was one of the jurors on an inquisi-

tion made at Aberdeen (REA., I, p. 54), and in 1342, probably the same individual, as William de Aberlefdy, bailie of the burgh of Aberdeen, is witness to "carta Thome Bonere super elimosina Mariote Bonere" (ibid., I, p. 72). In the Register this second entry is wrongly indexed under Aberfeldy, the indexer not being aware that Aberlefdy is an old spelling of the place name Aberlady.

ABERNETHY. "The origin of the Abernethies," says the late Sir James Balfour Paul, "cannot be stated with any certainty." In the twelfth century they appear to have occupied the position of lay abbots of the Culdee Monastery of Abernethy in Strathearn. This would seem to show that they were descended from original native stock and not of Saxon or Norman origin. The first of the Abernethies on record is Hugh, who appears to have died about the middle of the twelfth century (RPSA., p. 130, 132). His son Orm probably succeeded his father as lay abbot. He appears as witness to a charter by Ernulphus or Arnold, bishop of St. Andrews, granted before 1162. He also witnessed a charter of William the Lion (*Scon*, 34). He is the first of the family found bearing the territorial appellation 'de Abernethy.' It is conjectured that he may have given name to the lands of Ormiston (c. 1160, Ormystone), an estate contiguous to that of Salton, East Lothian, with which his descendants became identified in after days, though Orm was not an uncommon name in those early days (see ORMISTON). Between 1189 and 1196 King William the Lion granted the church of Abernethy to the Abbey of Arbroath (RAA., I, p. 25), while about the same time Lawrence, son of Orm de Abirnythy, conveys to the church and monks of Arbroath his whole right "in the advowson of the church of Abernethy" (ibid., p. 35). He retained the land and position of 'dominus' or lord of Abernethy (Skene, CS., II, p. 399). Hugh de Haberinthan is mentioned in a papal mandate to the bishops of St. Andrews and Aberdeen in 1264 (*Pap. Lett.*, I, p. 408). Sir Alexander de Abernethy swore fealty in 1296. His seal bears on the breast of an eagle displayed, a shield charged with a lion rampant, debruised by a ribbon, S' *Alexandri de Abernethi* (*Bain*, II, 751). Abernethies appear in Upper Lauderdale in the thirteenth century, probably as vassals of the de Morevilles. David de Albirnvth appears as vicar of Drisdale in 1320 (REG., p. 229), and c. 1380 William de Abrenythe made a gift of the mill of Ulkeston (now Oxton) to Dryburgh (*Dryburgh*, 259). John of Abrenethy, knight of Scotland, had a safe conduct in England in 1399 (*Bain*, IV, 593), and George Abrnnete, merchant of Scotland, had a similar

ABERNETHY, *continued*

safe conduct in 1465 (ibid., 1358). Among Scots in Prussia in 1644 the name was spelled Abernetti. It became Ebbernet in Sweden. Abernathie 1641, Abernythe 1204, Abirnathie 1596, Abirnethie 1609, Abirnethny 1407, Abirnidhr 1228, Abrenythi and Abrenythie c. 1295, Abrenethyn 1351, Abrenythyn 1338, Aburnethe 1424, Habernethi 1426; also Abernather, Aberneathie, Abirnythy, and Abirnather.

It may here be mentioned that *the* family of Abernethy shared in the "privilege of sanctuary," a privilege which, says Riddell (*Scotch peerage law,* 1833, p. 152), "with us was by no means so common as has been apprehended." In pre-Reformation times certain churches in Scotland and England were set apart to be an asylum for fugitives from justice. Any person who had taken refuge in such a sanctuary was secured against punishment — except the charge were treason or sacrilege — if within the space of forty days he gave signs of repentance, and subjected himself to punishment. By the Act 21 James I (of England) c. xxviii, the privilege of sanctuary for crime was finally abolished. In Scotland all religious sanctuaries were abolished at the Reformation in 1560. The most celebrated of these ecclesiastical sanctuaries were the church of Wedale, now Stow, which treasured what was believed to have been a piece of the true cross brought by King Arthur from the Holy Land; and the church of Lesmahagow, Lanarkshire, fugitives to which had the benefit of the "King's Peace," granted by King David I in addition to the protection of the Church. According to Wyntoun (*Cronykil,* bk. VI, c. XIX) only three persons originally were partakers in such a right: Macduff, Thane of Fife, the Black Priest of Wedale, and the Lord of Abernethy.

ABERNYTE. From the lands of Abernyte in Angus. Sometime between 1200 and 1240 Henry de Abirnyte witnessed the gift of the church of Wemys in Fife to the House of Soltre (*Soltre,* p. 13), and c. 1228 Henry of Abbernith, evidently the same individual, witnessed a charter by Malcolm, seventh earl of Fife (*Laing,* 6; CMN., 9). Phelipp de Abernyd tenant le Roi del counte de Linlescu rendered homage, 1296 (RR). Bain (II, p. 198) has entered him under Abernethy.

ABLE. *See under* ABEL.

ABRACH. In Gaelic the adjective *Abrach,* a contraction of *Abarach,* has the meaning 'of or belonging to Lochaber,' and as a noun, 'a Lochaber man.' A contract of protection and manrent between Collyne Campbell of Glenurquhay and Johne Oyg M'Ane Abrycht of

Glencho in 1563 is on record (BBT., p. 208), and Duncane Abrach M'Gregowre witnessed a Glenurquhay bond of 1584 (ibid., p. 227). John Abroch McDonald alias McEane of Glenco is mentioned in 1617 (RPC., XI, p. 187), and Robin Abroch (Macgregor), described in 1612 as "a clever chief of banditti," was so named from the native place of his father. Sir Thomas Hamilton, Lord Advocate, writing to the king in the following year says that this Robin Abroch "is reported to have bene the most bludie and violent murthourar and oppressour of all that damned race and most terrible to all the honest men of the countrie" (*Coll.,* p. 134). Neil Abrach also occurs in 1773 (*Laing*), and Donald and William Abrach were privates in the Reay Fencibles in 1795 (*Scobie,* p. 371). Aberach or Aberigh Mackays are an old family at Achness, near Loch Naver, Sutherlandshire, descended from Ian Abarach, second son of Angus Du Mackay (d. 1433). In other sixteenth and seventeenth century records spelled Abraich, Abrich, Abrick, and Abrych.

ABRAHAM, ABRAM. The first of these Hebrew names is said to mean 'chief (or father) of a multitude,' and the second 'exalted father,' but the meaning and derivation of both names are uncertain. Bardsley says that Abraham was a popular font-name in England in the thirteenth century, and that "a glance at the London Directory will show that in general Abraham represents the old English stock, and Abrahams the more modern Jewish." Abraham, chaplain of Earl Gilbert of Strathern, a frequent witness in the earl's charters, was probably Abraham, bishop of Dunblane, at a later date. He was son of a priest (*Theiner,* 6). Magister Habraham appears as a charter witness c. 1163–1175 (RPSA., p. 180), and Adam filius Abraham witnessed a charter by Umfridus de Berkeley of the lands of Balfeth to the Abbey of Abirbrothoc c. 1204–1211 (RAA., I, p. 61). Robert filius Abraham in the parish of Fyvv was excommunicated in 1382 (REA., I, p. 165), Thom Abraam appears in Aberdeen, 1408 (CWA., p. 316), Alexander Abraham, chaplain, witnessed a charter to William Peblis in 1491 (*Scon,* p. 201), James Abram, burgess of Inverness, was juror on an assize there in 1591 (OPS., II, p. 670), and George Abrahame or Abram was one of the bailies there, 1641 (*Rec. Inv.,* II, p. 177, 181). The place name 'Abraham' in Lancashire was originally *Eādburge hām,* and was altered in popular speech through a fancied connection with the personal name Abraham. Habram (*Inv. Rec.,* I).

ABRAHAMSON, 'son of ABRAHAM,' q.v. Gilfulain Habrahamson was banished from Perth in 1471 (ER., VIII, p. 56).

ABROCHAN. Nigellus Abroquhen, a student in St. Andrews, 1541 (ERUS., p. 247).

ABSALON. Hebrew 'Abhshālōm, 'father is peace.' A fairly popular font-name in England in the thirteenth century, and not confined to the Jews (Bardsley). Absolon was one of the chaplains of Roxburgh c. 1190 (Kelso, p. 216). A cleric of this name gave origin to MACAUS-LANE, q.v.

ACARSON. See under CARSON.

ACCO. Simoun Ako, beadle of the kirk of Natoun (Newton), 1628 (RPC., 2. ser. II, p. 432). John Acco in Edinburgh, 1688 (Edinb. Marr.). Acca was a common OE. personal name (Searle), and Akko was a Frisian name (Winkler).

ACH. Ach filius Alpini witnesses a charter by Bricius de Ardrossane to Insula Missarum in 1271 (LIM., p. 22). (This charter is also printed in Inchaffray, p. 90.) He also witnessed another charter by the same Bricius in the same year (Inchaffray, p. 92). Ache filius Elpine witnessed a charter by Roger de Mekfen, c. 1370 (ibid., p. 130). "He is not to be confounded with his namesake of a century earlier" (ibid., p. 299). This name seems to have run in the Alpine or Alpin family.

ACHENBRUC. William de Achenbruc witnessed a charter by Muriel de Rothes filia quondam Petri de Pollok granting a mill to the Hospital of S. Nicholas near Bridge of Spe, 1238 (REM., p. 121; Illus., II, p. 286).

ACHESON, AICHESON, AITCHESON, AITCHISON, ATKINSON. These five names all mean 'son of Adam', the first four from the diminutive Atty, and the last from the diminutive Adkin with the d sharpened to t. Johannes filius Ade, custumar of North Berwick in 1384, appears in 1387 as John Atkynsoun, and in following years again as Johannes filius Ade (ER., III, p. 119, 152, 171, etc.). John Atkynsoun is recorded as a forestaller in Aberdeen in 1402 (CRA., p. 385), and William Atkinson was servitor to Sir Symon Glendonwyne in 1408 (Bain, IV, 768). Laing gives the seal of Thomas Atkinson of Bonkyll as bearing on a chevron three buckles and with the legend S' Thomas filius Ade appended to an indenture of 1429 (Seals. Supp., 53; Macdonald, 51). William Atkynson was bedellus in Aberdeen in 1436 (REA., I, p. 234), John Atkinson was admitted burgess of Aberdeen in 1437 and Andrew Atkynson in 1442 (NSCM., I, p. 5, 7), and John Atzinson was vicar of Morton in 1475 (Kelso, 532). Patrick Atzensone was clerk of the diocese of Glasgow in 1479

(Home, 23), William Atyknson, a native of Scotland, had letters of denisation in England in 1480 (Bain, IV, 1462), and George Aczinson in Lanark, who was ordered to "stand under the cownt of the breid irnis" in 1490, appears again in 1498 as George Aczin (Lanark, p. 7, 9). Patrick Atzensone was notary-public in Jedworth, 1500 (PSAS., LIX, p. 102), William Ackynson was a juror in Lanark in 1501 (ibid., p. 11), and from Marc Aichesone who was custumar of the Newhewin of Prestone in 1590 (ER., XXII, p. 89) the haven may have been derived the name of Achesounes hevin (1609), now Morrisons Haven in the parish of Prestonpans. John Achisoune was retoured heir of his father James Achisone of Bodisbek in 1676 (Retours, Dumfries, 281), and Mr. John Echesone was schoolmaster at the village of Killbryde in 1680 (Hunter, p. 64). The name of Magnus Attkinsone, tacksman in Garth in Harray in 1492, may be a misreading of Awkinsone (= Hakon's son, Hauquinus was the Latinized form of Hakon, REO., p. 408). A family of this name was long connected with the Scottish Mint in the fifteenth and sixteenth centuries. James Aitchesoun, 'Maister Cunyear,' was ordered to coin 'babeis' (bawbees) in 1553 (RPC., I, p. 152). Achenson 1525, Acheson 1539, Achesoun 1497, Achesune 1591, Achieson 1673, Achiesoun 1635, Achinsoun 1538, Achisone 1557, Aitchesoune 1610, Aitchysoune 1670, Aschesone 1556, Atchesone 1692, Atchisone 1624, Atyesoun 1540, Atzeson and Etzesone 1531, and (undated) Aichensoun, Aticione, Eticione.

ACHILD. From Achild or Akeld (modern form), a township in the parish of Kirknewton, Northumberland. Robert de Achild witnessed a charter by Roger Maule and Godit, his spouse, to the church of St. Cuthbert of Carram, c. 1200 (SHSM., IV, p. 310).

ACHINCLOCH. John of Achincloch who held lands in Renfrewshire in 1405 (Pollok, I, p. 145) probably derived his surname from Auchencloich near Kilbarchan, Renfrewshire.

ACHINDACHY. From Achindachy in the parish of Keith, Banffshire. Sometime in the first half of the eighteenth century Alexander Achindachy or Achyndachy of that Ilk, chamberlain of Fyvie in 1741, acquired Kincraigie, a patrimony of the Leslies (Leslie; Inverurie, p. 413). William Achyndachy was vintner in North Queensferry in 1774 (St. Andrews).

ACHINFOUR. William de Achinfour had a charter of the land of Achinfour in Galloway from Robert I (RMS., I, App. II, 612).

ACHINLEVYN. Local, probably from Auch-leven, Premnay. Patricius de Achinlevyn, one of the "burgenses rure manentes" in Aberdeen, 1317 (SCM., v, p. 10).

ACHLES. Nicholaus de Achles witnessed a charter of the Priory of St. Andrews, c. 1170 (RPSA., p. 42).

ACHLOCH. Local. Gilbert Achloch held land in Montrose, 1431 (REB., II, 35). There is an Auchlochie in Forfar Retours, 1638.

ACHMOUR. Local. James Achmour appears as witness in Glasgow, 1550 (Protocols, I).

ACHMUTY, AUCHMUTY. Of territorial origin from the lands of the same name in the parish of Markinch, Fife. The first of the name on record appears to be Rotheri de Admulti (as the name was at that time spelled: cf. Auchincraw — Adincraw), who was one of an inquisition held at Berwick in 1296 which found that Elena la Suchis died seized in demesne in the county of Fife of the third part of the lands of Disarde and Strathon (Bain, II, p. 216). David de Admulti de eodem was present at the perambulation of the lands of Gaytmilk in 1466 (RD., p. 355), and John Admowtie, who was member of the town council of Stirling in 1565, appears again in 1576 as John Auchmowty (SBR., p. 280). Florentin Auchmouttie had a lease of a tenth of the lands of Halhill and three parts of Melgum c. 1570 (RD., p. 492), William Auchtmowlty was "prebendar of Strigmertyne" (Strathmartin) in 1584 (Soltre, p. 242), Robert Auchmutie, a barber in Edinburgh, having killed another citizen in a duel in 1600 was executed "for having presumed to take the revenge of a gentleman" (Chambers, Dom. Ann. Scot., I, p. 314). George Auchmowtie of that Ilk is in record in 1602 (Fordell, p. 157), and Alexander and John Auchmutie were among the Scots undertakers granted allotments in Ulster in 1610. A descendant of the family of Auchmuty settled at Brianstown, co. Longford, Ireland, in the first half of the seventeenth century, and this Irish branch is now representative of Auchmuty of that Ilk. James Auchinmowtie was captain of H. M. ship The Thrissell in 1628 (RPC., 2. ser. II, p. 179). Achmoutie 1574, Achmowtie 1630, Admowty 1508, Admuty 1450, Aithmutte 1603, Auchinmoutie 1648, Auchmoty 1585, Auchmoutie 1603, Auchmouthie 1597, Auchmouttie 1583, Auchmowthy 1551, Auchmowthe 1599, Auchmowthye 1555, Auchmuthe 1588, Auchmowtie 1589, Auchmwtie 1580, Auchmutty 1684.

ACHNACH. A shortened form of AUCHINACHIE current in Aberdeenshire. In 1741 Thomas Eachinach obtained a tack of two oxgates of Tomintogle (SN & Q., 2. ser. VII, p. 156), and in 1752 Donald Eachnach was tenant of part of Pitcroy (ibid.). Alexander Achnach, farmer in Cline of Knockandow, in record in 1768 (Moray). Some individuals of this name are said to have changed their name to Grant. Aichnach 1797.

ACHRES. Neuynus (= Nevin) de Achres, a native man of the bishop of Moray, 1364 (REM., p. 161), may have derived his name from Auchries in the parish of Cruden.

ACKINHEVY. Local. Walter de Ackinhevy was juror on inquest at Perth, 1304 (Bain, II, 1592).

A'CULTAN. In Galloway of old. Thomas Acoltane was accused in 1513 for art and part of the forethought oppression done to Sir David Kennedy (Trials, I, p. 95).

ADAIR. The tradition of the foundation of the family of Adair of Dunskey and Kinhilt originating from a fugitive son of Fitzgerald, Earl Desmond of Adair in Ireland, taking as surname his father's estate name seems too hypothetical for belief. Chalmers and others think that Adair is but a different pronunciation of Edzear (z = y) or Edgar. It is a fact that Thomas Edzear or Odeir had a charter of the lands of Kildonan in the Rynes of Galloway from Robert I (RMS., I, App. II, 681). From the Bruce, also, various parties of the same patronymic had grants of land in Dumfries. Richard dictus Edger, for example, had a charter of the "place of Seneschar (Sanquhar) and half the barony thereof" (RMS., I, 27). As Bruce died in 1329, and if Adair and Edzear are the same it is clear that the surname was located in Galloway much earlier than 1388, when the Fitzgerald of Adare is supposed to have acquired the lands. "As a matter of fact ...the name is...simply a form of Edgar, [the] progenitor being probably Edgar, son of Duvenald, a leader at the Battle of the Standard, grandson of Donegal of Morton Castle, a descendant of whom, Robert [sic, Thomas] Edzear had a charter from Robert Bruce of the lands of Kildonan, adjacent to which are those of Kinhilt. In confirmation of this we also find the name Edgar attaching to a hill on his property at Dromore" (Agnew, I, p. 220). In a footnote Agnew adds: "In the Lochnaw charter chest various deeds prove the name Edzear and Adair to have been interchangeable with the Galloway Adairs. In a charter dated 1625 the name is spelled in both forms on the same page." John Adair had a commission for a survey of Scotland in 1681 (RPC., 3. ser. xii, introduction).

ADAM. Bardsley says that "six centuries ago Adam probably ranked as second or third favourite among boys' names throughout England. In the north it attained a most remarkable pre-eminence." It was also a popular name in Scotland. Douglas (*Baronage*, p. 255) absurdly says that a Duncan Adam, who lived in the reign of Robert the Bruce, had four sons, Robert, John, Reginald, and Duncan, and that from them "all the Adams, Macadams, Adamsons, and Adies in Scotland are descended, which sufficiently appears from their carrying the same figures in their armorial bearings." Adam, sub-prior of Melrose became abbot of Cupar, 1189 (*Cupar-Angus*, i, p. xlix). Adam son of Adam was one of the witnesses to the charter by William Bruce to Adam of Carlyle of the lands of Kynemund, c. 1194–1214 (*Annandale*, i, p. 2; Bain, i, 606), and he also witnessed the resignation by Dunegal, son of Udard of a carucate of land in Warmanbie within the same period. Adam became abbot of Newbattle in 1201 (*Chron. Mail.*), and another Adam, a native of Lennox (Levenax), was a monk of great sanctity (ibid.). Duncan filius Ade occurs as witness in a charter gifting the church of Wemyss to the Hospital of Soltre, now Soutra in Midlothian, between 1200–1240 (*Soltre*, p. 14). Sir Ade, a Pope's knight, was vicar of Inverkippe, 1329 (ER., i, p. 209), Andrew Adam was one of the representatives of Lanark in the obligation by the burghs to pay part of the ransom of King James i (APS., i, p. 517), and William, son of Ade de Kydlaw, was a charter witness at Yester, 1374 (*Yester*, p. 26). Robert Adam (1728–1792), architect, and William Adam (1751–1839), politician, were two of the most eminent of the name.

ADAMNAN. This name, celebrated as that of the biographer of S. Columba, is in Gaelic *Adhmhnan* (pronounced Yownan or Yonan), for earlier *Adhamhnan*, early Irish *Adamnán*, Latinized in the seventh century as Adamnanus. A middle Scottish Gaelic form, *Oghomhnan*, also occurs (*Rel. Celt.*, ii, p. 153, 154). Cormac the king-bishop of Cashel in his Glossary explains the name as a diminutive of Adam ('disbecadh anma Adhaimh'), Irish *Ādam*, and this explanation has been generally accepted by scholars. Kuno Meyer, however, has explained it as a pet form in -*an* of the full name *Adomnae*, found in the place name

Ráith Adomnae (*Baile in Scail*, sect. 51). The name really means 'great terror,' from *omon*, *omun*, 'fear,' Welsh *ofn*, old Celtic * *obnos*.

The Annals of Innisfallan in recording the birth of the saint (in 624 A. D.) gives the form Adamnan, and the same in recording his death in 704. The Annals of Ulster in recording his birth spells the name Adomnan. A French version of the Chronicle of the Picts and Scots, compiled at the end of the thirteenth century, after giving the length of the reign of 'Drust fitc Hole' adds 'en soun temps fust Saint Edmonane,' in his time was S. Adamnan. The Latin Life of S. Servanus (14th cent.?) mentions Edheunanus receiving Servanus on his arrival in Scotland, and on the following page the same life spells the saint's name Eudananus. In still another place in the same life the name is spelled Odaudhdanus (CPS., p. 416–417). It also appears as Fidamnan. The aspiration of the *d* and *m* weakened these letters and led to their being finally lost, so that we have such forms as Ownan, Eunan, etc. These secondary forms have led to duplication in the Calendar of Saints. Thus Pope Clement xii sanctioned a mass for 'S. Eunan' for September 7, on which day the Bollandists and Alban Butler have notices of this same fictitious saint (see Reeves, *Adamnan*, p. lxii). Adamnan also appears in Scotland as Theunan and Deunan.

ADAMSON. A not uncommon surname at the present day in Angus, meaning "son of Adam." Adam filius Ade filius Philippi was burgess of Suhtberewick in 1261 (*May*, 36). John Adamsone of the county of Berewyke took the oath of fealty in 1296 (*Bain*, ii, p. 206). Colin, son of Ade, provost of Aberdeen in 1340, appears again in 1349 as Colin Adamson (ER., i, p. 456; *Friars*, 15), and John Adamson (fitz de Adam), a Scot, had a safe conduct to go to Bruges from England in 1433 (*Bain*, iv, 1071). Cuthbert Adamson, a notary public of Glasgow diocese, 1587 (*Poltalloch writs*, p. 75). Sir Harvey Adamson (b. 1854) was formerly lieutenant-governor of Burma. Adamesoune 1595, Ademsoun 1537, Ademson. Addison, q.v., is another form of the name from the diminutive Ade.

ADAN, Aden. These surnames, recorded in the Aberdeen Directory, are derived from the name of the old lands and barony of Auden or Aden in Aberdeenshire (? the Aldin Alenn of the *Book of Deer*). Andrew Aden, weaver in the Spittal bounds of Aberdeen, is in record in 1683 and 1695 (ROA., i, p. 240, 245).

ADD. Jacobus Ad, tenant under the bishop of Glasgow, 1511 (*Rental*). Perhaps meant for Auld, q.v.

ADDIE, ADDY, ADIE, EADIE, EDDIE, EDIE. These names are pet or double diminutives of ADAM, q.v., and were common in Edinburgh and in Aberdeenshire in the seventeenth century. Adam Reid, familiar servitor of King James IV is referred to in 1513 as Ade Rede. William Ade of Inverkeithing rendered homage in 1296 (Bain, II, p. 188), and Andreas Ade is recorded in Edinburgh in 1357. Donald Ade was a presbyter in the diocese of Dunblane in 1465, James Ade was a witness in Linlithgow in 1536 (Johnsoun), and David Aidye (Adye or Ady) and Salomon Ædie were admitted burgesses of Aberdeen in 1591 and 1607 (NSCM., I, p. 81, 96, 105). Payment was made in 1606 "for horss hyir to Dauid Aidye to pas to Strathaquhin" (SCM., V, p. 79), probably the David Aidye who appears as member of council of Aberdeen in 1624 (CRA., p. 393). William Aidy was one of the regents of Marischal College in 1644, and in 1670 it was judicially proven that Alexander Aidy "now in Dantzik, in the kingdome of Polland, who went from this burgh Aberdeen about thretie-thrie yeirs or therby, is the laufull sone of vmquhill David Aidy burgess of the said burgh" (SCM., V, p. 348). Aedie of Moneaght an old family of Aberdeen burgesses. There were also Adies of Newark in Aberdeenshire; and James Adie sat in parliament for Perth in 1596 (Stodart, II, p. 315). George Cardno Adie from New Byth served in the first Great War (Turriff). Adie 1688, Ædie 1688, Aiddie 1613, Aidie 1678, Eddie 1689, Edie 1686; Ade, Adye.

ADDISON. This surname is not uncommon in the eastern counties from Linlithgow to Aberdeen. It means 'son of Addie,' from the diminutive of Adam, and is therefore the same as Adamson. Alicia relict of quondam Johannes filius Ede de Colly granted four acres of land on the north side of the town of Colly in 1367 (SCM., II, p. lxxxix). William Adison was rector of Luss in 1370 (CAC., I, 24; RMP., p. 427), Gilbert filius Ade was a tenant of the Douglases in the barony of Kylboucho in 1376, and Robert filius Ade was another of their tenants in Louchurde in the same year (RHM., I, p. xlvii, xlix). Robert Adyson or Adeson was vicar of Colmonell in 1415 (Ayr, p. 9), Andrew Advson was bailie of the burgh of Invernys in 1430 (ER., IV, p. 515), and King James II confirmed a charter dated 26 August 1436 by Sir William Adesoun, vicar of Lynton (Peebles, p. 206). William Adison leased the mill of Syokis in 1443 (Cupar-Angus, I, p. 128), and Duncan Adeson held land in Stirling in 1449 (REG., 355). Andrew Edisoun in Spittelmylne appears in record in 1580, and in the following year we have David Aydesoun, portioner

of the same place, and John Edisoun of Spittlemylne is mentioned in another document of the same year as John Adesoun (Soltre, p. 144, 145, 109, 110). Laurence Adiesone had a charter of the lands of Pennielandis from the Abbey of Dunfermline in 1611 (RD., p. 504), and John Adieson was a bailie of the burgh of Leith in 1645 (APS., VI, p. 446). Adesone 1594, Adiesone 1636, Adiesoun 1615, Adisoun 1596, Aedieson 1562, Edison 1562, Edisone 1575; Addesoun, Aedesone.

ADDOKESTONE. Probably from the lands of Addokistoun or Adokstoun in the constabulary of Haddington mentioned in the time of David II (RMS., I, App. II, 931). John de Agdokestone of the county of Edinburgh took the oath of fealty in 1296. In the same year, as John de Addokistone, he was juror on an inquisition held on the lands of Robert de Pinkeny. His seal bears a cross patée cantoned with three roses and a crescent, and S' Ioh'is de Acdoknistvn(?) (Bain, II, p. 201, 227, 551). Alexander de Haddokestone forfeited the ten pound land of Addokestone in 1337 (Bain, III, p. 387).

ADDUN. Richard de Addun and Robert de Addun, monks, witnessed a composition anent tithes of Strathvlif, 1239 (REM., p. 87). Nicholas de Eddun, a witness, 1251 (LAC., p. 86). Probably English clerics.

ADDY. See under ADDIE.

ADEMAN. 'The servant of Ade' or Adam. Hew Ademan at Balgillo-mylne, parish of Monifieth, 1599 (St. Andrews). See -man in Introduction.

ADEN. See under ADAN.

ADERSONE. Margaret Adersone in Edinburgh, 1643 (Edinb. Marr.).

ADIE. See under ADDIE.

ADIELL. An Aberdeenshire surname. John Adiel in Auchnagathill, 1632 (RSCA., II, p. 326), and William Adiell in Nether-Brownhill, 1739 (Abd. CR.). Perhaps local from Adziel near Strichen (z = y).

ADIGTON. A complaint was made against Adam de Adigton by the Friars Minor of Berwick, 1332 (Pap. Lett., II, p. 503).

ADINSTON. Adinstoun of that Ilk was an old family which ended in an heiress who married a Hepburn (Nisbet, I, p. 123). There was also a family of Adinston of Carcant in Midlothian (Fordell, p. 192). Perhaps from Adniston, near Macmerry, East Lothian, by metathetic change. Alexander Adinstoun was heir of Henry Adinstoun, "pistor," burgess of Edinburgh in 1618 (*Inquis.*, 793), and John Adingstoun was heir of Thomas Adingstoun, merchant burgess of Edinburgh in 1629 (ibid., 1470). The wife of George Adinstowne in Phanes sued for her services in harvest in 1656 (RRM., I, p. 202). The name is also found in the Edinburgh Marriage Records as Adnestoun (1622) and Adnistoun (1655). The tenement of the late John Adensoun in Linlithgow is mentioned in 1538 (*Johnsoun*), and George Adinston is recorded in Fawnes, 1662 (RRM., II, p. 15). Other old forms of the name are: Adainstoun, Adenston, Adiestoun, Adinstone 1655, Aldinstoune, Adistone, Adningstoun, Adiston (1688).

ADMAGU. John Admagw, shepherd in Clony, Perthshire, 1513 (*Rent. Dunk.*, p. 183). May be local from Auldmad near Dunkeld (Adsometimes = Auld- in place names.)

ADMISTON. Andrew Admistoun or Adamiston, notary in Lauder, Berwickshire, 1638–1642 (RRM., I, p. 94, 136), and James Admistoune in Lauder, 1642 (ibid., p. 94). James Admiston was minister at Sanct Ruikis, 1644 (DPD., I, p. 83). May be for EDMISTON, a variant of EDMONSTON, q.v.

ADNAUCHTAN. Henri de Adnauchtan who witnessed a quit claim of the lands of Drumkarauch in 1260 (RPSA., p. 347) took his name from the lands of Adnauchtan now Naughton near Balmerino, Fife.

ADODDIS. John Adoddis, tenant under the Abbey of Kelso, 1567 (*Kelso*, p. 527).

ADOLIE. John Adolie, late chaplain of Sanct Marie Magdalene de Errot, 1456 (REB., I, 181).

ADOUGAN. Eliseus Adougan, provost of Lincluden, became bishop of Galloway, 1406 (*Dowden*, p. 366–367). John Adowgane was party in an action at law, 1476 (ALA.).

ADUNNALE. Adowell of Dalquhowane, Ayr, is mentioned in 1498 (RMS., II, 2433). Mr. Uchtred Adunnale, to whom a respite was granted to pass in pilgrimage to Sanct Thomas of Canterbery in England, 1507 (RSS., I, 1425), appears as Wchtred Adunnyel de Dalhowane, witness to a charter by Sir James Douglas to the earl of Cassilis, 1520 (CAC., I, 70). Cristine Adumnell is mentioned in the will of Egidia Blair, Lady Row, 1530 (ibid., I, 95). Adonaile 1477, Adouell and Adowell 1508. In RMS., II. index the name appears as Adunnil, Adonyll, Adonaile, Adouell, Adowell de Dalquhowane.

ADZELL. The name till of an old family that survived in Angus till past the middle of the fifteenth century. They were formerly lords of Edzell (or Etzell) and took their surname from their lands of that name in Angus. The last recorded of the name in the direct line is probably John Adzell *de eodem* who was witness of the Laird of Dun's confirmation of the third part of the lands of Baluely (now Balwyllo) in 1451 to Alexander, natural son of the earl of Crawford (SCM., IV, p. 5).

AED, AEDH. One of the most popular of Gaelic names. OG., meaning 'fire,' latinized *Aidus* and *Ædus*. The Aedui, a tribe of Gallia Celtica, were friendly to the Romans (Caesar, B. G., I, 11). Duuenaldus son of Ede (= Aed) was chosen king of the Britons, 943 (CPS., p. 9). Aed Albanach (i.e. 'of Scotland'), a leader of the Dublin Danes, died 942 (AFM.). Comgeall mac Eda was mormaer of Buchan (*Bk. Deer*, II, 1), and Aed was father of Ghgillcomded, witness to a protection by David I to the clerics of Deer, c. 1150 (ibid.). The name of one of the witnesses to a charter of Alexander I to the Abbey of Scone (*Scon*, 14) is spelled *Heth* (= *Aed*) and at first misread as *Beth* was the subject of a good deal of controversy. In some mediæval Latin documents Aedh is rendered *Odo*. Later AODH, q.v.

AENEAS, ENEAS. This Latin-Greek name is frequently used as an English equivalent of the G. forename *Angus*. Gr. *Aineias*, 'praise.'

AFFLECK. This surname is of twofold origin: (1) from the barony of Auchinleck in Ayrshire, and (2) from Affleck in Angus. Richard of Auchinlec was juror on an inquest held in 1263 before the sheriff of Lanark (*Bain*, I, 2677). Nicholas of Haghenlek mentioned in 1292 is probably Nicol de Achithelege of the county of Are who rendered homage in 1296 (*Bain*, II, p. 150, 206). Patrick de Aghleke of Lanarkshire who also rendered homage in 1296 appears again as Patrick de Achenlek, juror on inquest at Lanark in 1303, and is probably the Patrick de Auuynlec who witnessed resignation of the lands of Grenrvg c. 1311 (*Bain*, II, p. 206, 372; *Kelso*, 195). In 1370 the lands of 'le Grevnryg et de le Tathys' were resigned to Kelso Abbey by Adam de Aghynlek (*Kelso*, 514). Thomas of Awqwhvnleke in 1436 witnessed a charter of lands in Peeblesshire (OPS., I, p. 521), Adam Auchinlek had a safe conduct to travel in England in 1451, Andrew Athelek and James Athelek of Scotland petitioned for safe conducts in 1464 (*Bain*, IV, 1232, 1343), and in 1486 William Achlek appears as a friar preacher in Aberdeen (REA., II, p. 300). John of Aghelek

AFFLECK, *continued*

who did homage in 1306 is the first recorded of the Angus family of the name (*Jervise, LL.*, p. 207–208). These Angus Afflecks were hereditary armour bearers to the earls of Crawford (ibid.). John Athlyk was burgess of Inverness in 1499 (*Cawdor*, p. 102). Achinfleck 1536, Achinlek 1443, Achlec 1473, Afflect 1627, Aflek 1563, Athinkel (probably a miscopying) 1414, Athlek 1513, Auchinlech 1605, Auchinlok 1532, Auchlec 1485, Auchlek 1364, Authinlect 1595, Auchynflek 1536, Authinlek 1590, Avthinlect 1610, Awchinlecke 1669, Efflek 1547, Hauchynlek 1505; Achleck, Achtinlek, Achynlek, Aithinleik, Aquinlek 1581, Athinleik, Athinlek, Athynlek, Auchenlek, Auchenleck, Auchinlec, Auchimlek, Auchleck, Auchtlek, Auchynlek, Awchlek.

AFFROOD. James Affrood in Blackshaw, 1733 (*Dumfries*). Most probably of English origin, from the Somerset parish of the name.

AFRICA, AFFRICA. A favorite female name in the twelfth century which continued in use for four or five hundred years later. It is also found at a much earlier date in Ireland: Affrick, abbess of Kildare, died in 739 (*Annals of Clonmacnoise*). Affreka or Affrica, daughter of Duncan, earl of Fife, became the first wife of Harald, earl of Orkney (*Ork. Saga*, p. 88; *Skene*, CS., I, p. 481). Afreka or Affrica, daughter of Fergus, lord of Galloway, married Olaf, king of the Islands, and was mother of Godfrey, king of Man and the Hebrides, who reigned till 1187 (*Early sources*, II, p. 467). Aufrike or Affrica, one of the illegitimate daughters of William the Lion, was married to William de Say (*Foedera*, I, pt. 2, p. 776). Godfrey, king of Man and the Hebrides, married Findguala, daughter of Muirchartach, king of Ireland, and their daughter Affrika was married to John de Courcy (*Chron. Man.*, I, p. 80). Affrica, daughter of Edgar, son of Duuenald of Stranith, granted to the bishop of Glasgow the church of S. Brigide of Wintertonegan in the valley of the Niht (Nithsdale) in 1227 (*REG.*, p. 120). Effrick, daughter of Coline, lord of Carrick, was mother of Coline or Callen More (*HP.*, II, p. 84), and Eafric or Effric neyn Corgitill wrote a poem on the death of her husband MacNeill of Gigha, c. 1470 (*Lismore*, p. 96). Effric Makfatrik had sasine of lands of Killenane in Cowal in 1504 and in 1515 (*ER.*, XII, p. 717, 719), and as Africa Makpatrik is again in record in 1525 as daughter of Duncan Macpatric in Cowal (*RMS*). An Effreta Maclachlan is in record in 1570 (*Poltalloch writs*, p. 144) and Africk McQuhollaster is mentioned in a charter of

wadset of 1571 (*Scrymgeour family docs.*, p. 21). The name appears to have been originally that of a river goddess, *Afraig* (*Aithbrecc*, mod. Gaelic *Aithbreac*, 'somewhat speckled'), the goddess of the (river-)ford. The name survived into the eighteenth century as Effrick = *Oighrig*, and absurdly Englished *Euphemia*!

AGATE. Stephen Agate, a Frenchman, jeweller and goldsmith, trade burgess of Aberdeen, 1696 (*ROA.*, I, p. 246). Bardsley says 'son of Agnes,' from Agg, diminutive Agot. More probably local, "at the gate" (so *Bardsley, Harrison, Lower, Weekley*).

AGNETIS. Johannes de Agnetis, witness in Aberdeen, 1281 (*REA.*, II, p. 279).

AGNEW. This surname is of territorial origin from the Baronie d'Agneaux in the Bocages of Normandy. "A Marquis d'Agneaux still owns portions of the ancestral fiefs, and the Chateau d'Agneaux still overlooks the valley of the Vire" (*Agnew*, I, p. 180). In 1363 the Lochnaw family of the name were appointed hereditary sheriffs of Galloway by King David II and they gradually became great land-owners in the province, holding many estates. An Irish sept, the O'Gnives or O'Gneeves (Irish *O'Gnimh*), hereditary bards to the Clannaboy O'Neils, Englished their name to Agnew, a change which has led some mistakenly to consider the Agnews to be of Irish origin. Agnewe 1610, Aggnew 1512, Agnev 1436, Angnew 1473.

AHANNAY. A form of HANNAY, q.v., still current in Galloway.

AHILLO. Michael Ahillow had precept of confirmation of a charter, 1529 (*RSS.*, II, 613), and in the following year he is again mentioned as Ahillo (*ALHT.*, V, p. 339).

AICKLEY. Individuals of this name are mentioned in Shetland in 1624 (*RPC.*, XIV, p. 735, 736). Isobel Aickla or Acklay in Ronan, Unst, 1629, and Thomas Aickla in Utterbuster, Yell, 1628 (*Shetland*). Andrew Aicklav, portioner of Howgaland, 1627 (*OSS.*, I, 183). Cf. English Ackley.

AIDAN. A diminutive of AED, q.v. Aidan mac Gabran, half Scot, half Briton, was king over the Dalriadic kingdom of Argyll, and died c. 608.

AIKEN, AITKEN, AITKIN, AITKINS, ATKIN, ATKINS. These names are double diminutives of Adam, formed from *Ad* the diminutive of Adam with the diminutive suffix *-kin*(OE.

-cen), and with the *d* sharpened to *t*. These names have been also explained as = little Atty or Arthur, but the preceding origin is the more likely one. John of Akyne ('of' here evidently an error), a Scottish merchant, petitioned for the return of his ship and goods illegally seized in England in 1405 (*Bain*, IV, 712). Andrew Atkin appears as a witness in Aberdeen in 1469 (CRA., p. 406), William Ackin was a witness in Brechin in 1476 (REB., I, 199), Andree Atkyn is recorded in Aberdeen in 1491 (REA., I, p. 329). Aitkane of Dunsleson was declared innocent of part in the detention of King James III in Edinburgh Castle in 1482 (*Lennox*, II, p. 123), Thomas Atkyn possessed a tenement in Glasgow in 1497 (REG., 476), John Eckin was a tenant under the bishop of Aberdeen, 1511 (REA., I, p. 375), and William Atkyn was tenant under the bishop of Glasgow in 1513 (*Rental*), John Ackyne was bailie of Stirling in 1520 (SBR., p. 274), Robert Aykkvne was admitted burgess of Aberdeen in 1539 (NSCM., I, p. 55), and Samuel Atkins was Commissioner of Supply for the city of Edinburgh, 1655 (APS.). Elspeth and James Aitkine in Darnchester took the oath in 1685 (RPC., 3. ser. x, p. 479). Forms of these names are common in the Commissariot Record of Stirling, in the Edinburgh Marriage Record, and in the Records of the Sheriff Court of Aberdeenshire. Paterson says Aitken is an old surname in the parish of Ballantrae (*Ayrshire*, II, p. 87), and in Orkney it is believed to have replaced the Old Norse name Haakon and its derivative Hakonson. Robert Aitken (1734–1832), born in Dalkeith, was commended by resolution of Congress for printing of the Bible in the U. S. As forename: Atkyn de Barr and Atkyn Blake both in Ayr c. 1340 (*Friars Ayr*, p. 15), Atkin Scott in Ettrick, 1456. The oak in the arms of some of the name is merely canting heraldry. The -*s* of Atkins and Aitkins represents 'son,' so these forms are really for ATKINSON, q.v. Ackyn 1521, Ackyne 1524, Aicken 1681, Aickin 1550, Aickine 1674, Aicking 1669, Aikein 1615, Aiken 1689, Aikin 1688, Aikine 1677, Aiking and Aikne 1658, Aitcken 1689, Aitken 1689, Aitkene 1552, Aitkine 1687, Aitkyn 1549, Aitkyne 1658, Aken 1689, Akene 1669, Akin 1693, Akine 1667, Atkine 1667, Aytkine 1669, Aytkyn 1519, Aytkyne 1522; Aikeyne, Aikun, Aikyne, Aukin.

AIKENHEAD, AITKENHEAD. From the old barony of Aikenhead in Lanarkshire. Gilbert de Lakenheued (= Aikenhead with the French definite article L' prefixed) of the county of Lanark rendered homage for his lands in 1296 (*Bain*, II, 808). In 1372 the lands of Akynheuide in the sheriffdom of Lanark were confirmed to John de Maxwell by King Robert II (RMS., I, 450). In the same year Convallus de Akinhead witnessed a grant of the lands of Auchmarr to Walter de Buchanan (*Levenax*, p. 59). (This Convallus evidently has been named after St. Convall, disciple of St. Kentigern, who afterwards became patron saint of the parish of Inchinnan.) William de Akynheued was bailie of the burgh of Rutherglen in 1376 (ER., II, p. 537), and a later William de Akinhede was a notary public in Irvine in 1444 (*Irvine*, I, p. 7). In 1489 remission was granted to three individuals named Akynhed who, with a number of others, held the Castle of Dumbarton against the king (APS., XII, p. 34). So late as 1509 we have mention of a payment to John *of* Akynheyd (LCD., p. 208). The surname, as might be expected, is common in Lanarkshire, particularly around Glasgow. The saintly Leighton is said to have made the following pun on a Lord Provost of Edinburgh of this name, who had "many pimples on his face,"

"If what is said were justly said,
    That's Head of Aiken timber's made,
    His fyrie face had long agoe
    Sett all his head in blazing glow."

(*Coltness Collections*, p. 22)

A quite different version is given in Butler's *Life and letters of Robert Leighton*, p. 55. Aickinhed 1488, Aickinheid 1585, Aikynhead 1513, Akinhed 1501, Akinheid 1506, Akynheid 1521, Akynhede 1450, Akheid 1526, Auchinhead 1513, Aukinhead 1632, Eakinheid 1615. Other forms are: Aikenheid, Aikinheid, Akenhede, and Aitkynheid.

AIKERS. From the farm of Aikers in Swanbister, Orkney. Thome Akirris or Akuris was tacksman of a 6d. land in Tuscarbuster, Swanbuster, in 1492 and 1503 (REO., p. 405, 414). James Aykeris was a witness in Orkney in 1549, and James Aikers and Malcolm Aikers in Swanbister are in record in 1617 (ibid., p. 238, 400). Katherine Aickers in Howbister in Orphir in 1612 (*Orkney*).

AIKMAN. No satisfactory explanation of this name is known. Lower suggested that it was a modification of OE. *Agemund*, Ferguson and Harrison derive it from OE. *Æcemann*, 'oakman' (*æc÷mann*), Sir Herbert Maxwell (*History of Dumfries*, p. 297) finds its origin in OE. *ace manne*, 'an infirm person,' and Dr. Henry Bradley suggested that the first element is perhaps *ac*, and that the name may possibly represent an OE. *ācumann*, which became Acemann by later development, but a form Acemann is not known. The story told of the

AIKMAN, *continued*

officer who had command of the troops besieging Macbeth in Dunsinane Castle ordering his men to march to the attack with branches of oak taken from Birnam Wood, and on that account obtained the name of Aikman, is still an article of faith with some (C. E. Stevens, *Stevens genealogy,* New York, 1904, p. 87–89) though too silly for belief. Alisaundre Akeman of Lanarkshire who rendered homage in 1296 (*Bain,* II, p. 204) is believed to be first of the name recorded in Scotland. His seal shows a fox, with paw raised, looking upwards, and S' *Alexandr' Acman* (ibid., p. 186). The tombs of ten John Aikmans are said to be in Arbroath Abbey, and the surname is also recorded in Orkney in 1575 (*Oppressions,* p. 4). John Hekman was bailie of Montrose in 1400 (*Stodart,* II, p. 404). William Aikman (1682–1731), the portrait painter, sold the family estate in 1707 on leaving Scotland to study in Rome. Akman and Aykman 1505.

AILMER. Emme de Ailmer and Roger de Almere, both of Selkirkshire, rendered homage, 1296. The seal of the latter bears a hunting horn, stringed, and S' *Rogeri d' Alnmer.* As Roger de Aylemer he accounts in 1304 for the ward of Trequair (*Bain,* II, p. 198, 202, 439, 552). Adam Aylmer was a tenant under the earl of Douglas in the vill of Tybris, 1376 (RHM., II, p. 16), and Elizabeth Aimoir appears in Cambuswallace, 1603 (*Dunblane*).

AIMERLAND. Probably from the Aimerland (1602) of *Perth Retours,* no. 106. Henry Aimerland, servitor of James Wishart of Pittarrow, 1629 (RPC., 2. ser. III, p. 209).

AINSLIE, AINSLEE. Most probably from Annesley in Nottinghamshire, England. William de Haneslej who witnessed a charter by Walter, bishop of Glasgow, between 1208–18 (LCD., p. 236) is probably William de Anslee, canon of Glasgow c. 1220 (RMP., p. 1). In 1221 Magister Thomas de Aneslei was one of a number appointed to settle a dispute between the monks of Kelso and the bishop of Glasgow (REG., p. 101; *Kelso,* 230), and Sir Avmer de Aynesley was one of the knights appointed to settle the law of the marches in 1249 (APS., I, p. 413). Two individuals of this name rendered homage in 1296: (1) John le fiz Johan de Anesleye of Roxburghshire, and Johan de Anesleye of Crucfut [? Crawford] of Lanarkshire (*Bain,* II, p. 199, 212). The seal of the former appended to his homage is broken but shows two geese (?) drinking at a fountain and S' *Ioh'is. se.* . . *Ant* (?). Adam de Aynesleye was juror on an inquisition

held at Roxburgh in 1357 (ibid., III, 1641), and John of Aynesley witnessed a grant of the forest of Eteryk to John Kerre in 1358 (*Roxburghe,* p. 8). In 1377 Robert II granted to William de Aynysley a charter of the lands of Dolfynston in the sheriffdom of Roxburgh forfeited by John de Aynysley his father (RMS., I, 592). The lands of Dolphingstoun passed, c. 1500, to the Kers of Cessfurd through marriage of Mark Ker with Marjorie Ainslie, daughter and heiress of John Ainslie. Ralph Aynsle produced a remission for being treasonably associated with Alexander, formerly duke of Rothesay, in 1493 (*Trials,* I, p. *17). John Ainslie, the eminent geographer and land surveyor, was a descendant of the old family, and Robert Ainslie (1766–1838) was a friend and correspondent of Robert Burns. The surname was at one time common in and about Jedburgh, but has now disappeared from there. Anenislie 1598, Ainsley 1689, Ainsloe 1677, Anslie 1567, Anslv 1677, Anysle 1493, Aynisle 1464, Aynsle 1464, Enslie 1685, Henesleis (pl.) 1579.

AIR, AYR, AYRE. (1) Robert Air of Hedreslawe was rentaller of the mill of Hedreslawe in 1281 (*Bain,* II, 196). Johan Ayr of Aytone, Berwickshire, rendered homage, 1296 (ibid., II, p. 206). Thomas Ayre was provost of Kintore, 1331 (ER., I, p. 356), Elyas Ayr witnessed a charter by Robert de Lamberton, 1336 (*Raine,* 230), and in 1401 Richard Ayre made a wadset of part of the lands of Kinnaird to Duthac de Carnegie (*Southesk,* p. 719). Michael Ayr appears as a witness in Brechin, 1450 (REB., II, 83), and the surname of Air subsisted in the parish of Farnell until 1851, when the last of the name (an unmarried woman) died at an advanced age (*Jervise,* LL., p. 239). The lands of William Ayr or Air in the lordship of Dunbar are mentioned in 1522 and again in 1535 (*Home,* p. 32, 35), and the lands of a later William Air in the Merse are mentioned in 1580 (ER., XXI, p. 65). Janet Air in Brechin, 1583, and Patrick Air in Panbryde parish, 1675 (*Brechin*). John Aire in Coldstream, 1780 (*Lauder*). Perhaps same as EYRE, q.v. (2) Of local origin from the royal burgh of Ayr. Reginald of Ayr was clerk in Ayr, 1287 (*Bain,* II, p. 89). Albinus or Aubinus de Are had a charter of "unam obulatam terre que vocatur Cercnokenculrath et Autitigille cum pertinenciis" from Robert I between 1315–21 (RMS., I, 49). Walterus de Are, clericus Glasguensis diocesis, notary public, 1399 (*Pollok,* I, p. 138). Dogall de Are witnessed the sale of a tenement in Glasgow, 1430 (LCD., p. 246). Richard Air was bookbinder in Glasgow, 1432 (REG., p. 335). Cf. EYRE.

AIRD. Of local origin from a place of the name. It may be from Aird near Hurlford, Ayrshire, or from the hamlet of Aird in the parish of Inch, Wigtownshire, more probably from the former. The Airds of Holl and the Airds of Nether Catrine in Ayrshire were ranked as old families. Nicoll Ard and William Ard, followers of the earl of Cassilis, were respited for murder in 1526 (RSS., I, 3386). George Aird was herd in Melrose 1658 (RRM., I, p. 183), William Aird was heir of William Aird of Holl of Neitherburntschellis, 1687 (*Retours, Ayr*, 647). John Aird, merchant in Dundee, 1696 (*Inquis.*, 7669), may be John Aird, maltman in Dundee, 1697 (*Brechin*).

AIRDS. Local. There are several places named Airds, mainly in the south-west. Mr. James Airds was minister of Torryburn, 1686 (RPC., 3. ser. XII, p. 55).

AIRIE. Local, probably from the two and a half mark land of Arie, 1611 (*Retours, Kirkcudbright*, 104). John Airie in Wakemilne, 1685 (RPC., 3. ser. X, p. 197).

AIRKIE. Robert Airkie, servant to Durie of Grange, 1679 (RPC., 3. ser. VI, p. 286).

AIRLAND. Henrie Airland in Strathhendrie possessed the fermes of the land of Fynmouth, 1606 (*Fordell*, p. 159–160).

AIRNES. Bessie Airnes in Glencoubard, 1657 (*Dumfries*). There is an Arness near Fenwick, Ayrshire.

AIRRES. Robert Airres in Siministoun, 1692 (*Peebles CR.*).

AIRSTOUNE. Local. Letters against James Airstoune for defrauding the king's customs, 1524 (*Irvine*, p. 35).

AIRTH. A not very common surname derived from the barony of Airth near Larbert, Stirlingshire. About the year 1200 William de Arthe witnessed a grant to the Abbey of Cambuskenneth (*Cambus.*, 81). Richard Derth (i.e. d'Erth) is mentioned as falconer to the king of Scotland in 1212 (*Bain*, I, 532), and Bain notes in his preface that Airth was a famed breeding place of falcons. Willelmus de Herth witnesses a charter by Maldouen, third earl of Lennox, c. 1248 (*Levenax*, 11). Elena, spouse of Bernard de Erth, laid claim to certain lands in the sheriffdom of Dumbarton in 1271 (RMP., p. 191). Hugh de Erthe, bailiff to Sir John Cumyn in 1291, is probably the Hugh de Erthe, knight, who was taken prisoner in Dunbar Castle in 1296 (*Bain*, II, 532 and p. 178). Marie, widow of Huwe de Erthe of the county of Stirling, and Richard de

Erthe, king's tenant in the county of Edneburk, both rendered homage in 1296 (ibid., p. 201, 214). According to Nisbet's *Heraldry* the family of this Richard de Erthe ended in heirs female. Between 1296 and 1300 William of Erth appears as a charter witness (*Laing*, 18), and in 1331 Thomas de Arth had a dispute with the earl of Mar (APS., I, p. 512). John de Erth witnessed a charter by Robert Steward of Scotland, temp. David II, I, p. 561), W. de Erthe is witness to a confirmation charter of David II 1364 (RMS., I, 187) and Fergus de Erth appears in 1369 (RMS., I, 336). Sir William de Erthe was one of the hostages for King James I in 1423–4 and again in 1426 (*Bain*, IV, 942, 1003). His family ended in three daughters — the eldest Agnes, prior to 1414, married (1) Edward de Brus, second son of Sir Robert Brus of Clackmannan, and (2) an Elphinstone. Remission was granted to a man for the slaughter of John Erth in 1497 (RSS., I, 114), George Arthe of Smetoune and his sons were assaulted in 1537 (*Trials*, I, p. °201), and in 1548 mention is made of cottage lands in Coldingham occupied by David Arth (*Home*, 195). A grant by the late queen to David Arthe, burgess of Cupar, also mentions the lands of George Arthe in 1580 (ER., XXI, p. 100), and in 1601 David Airthe was a member of the town council of Stirling (SBR., p. 283). John Airth is recorded in the Mains of Kincardine in 1617 (*Dunblane*), George Airthe was provost of Cupar in 1628 (RPC., 2. ser. II, p. 178), and as Airthe the surname appears in Tyninghame in the seventeenth century. A pension was paid to Margaret Airth in Edinburgh, 1736 (*Guildry*, p. 157).

AISDAILL. A current form of EASDALE, q. v. James Aisdell in record in Irvine, 1499 (*Simon*, 30). Aisdayle 1507.

AITCHESON, AITCHISON. *See under* ACHESON.

AITH. An Orcadian surname from Aith in the parish of Sandwick. Magnus Aith in record in Naversdaill, Orphir, in 1639 (*Orkney*).

AITKEN, AITKIN, AITKINS. *See under* AIKEN.

AITKENHEAD. *See under* AIKENHEAD.

AITON. A variant of AYTON, q.v.

AIULF. The OE. personal name *Æðe(l)wulf* became *Aiulf* in AF. spelling and pronunciation, and in Latin charters is written *Aiulfus*. Aiulfus or Eyolfus decanus, appears several times as a charter witness in the chartularies of Holyrood, Glasgow, Dunfermline, etc., between 1130–1160 (*Lawrie*, p. 331).

AKINSTALL. Local. Margaret Akinstall in Edinburgh, 1644 (*Edinb. Marr.*).

ALAN, ALLAN, ALLEN. This name in Scotland is of twofold origin: (1) from the Old Gaelic name *Ailéne* (the *Ailenus* of Adamnan, I, 43) or *Ailin*, from *ail* 'rock,' seen in the old name of Dumbarton (*Ail Cluade*, 'rock of the Clyde'). From this source comes *Alwyn*, the name of the first earls of Levenax, early confused with OE. *Aelwin*. (2) from the Breton through NF. *Alan*. Alan or Alain Fergant was one of the leading Bretons who accompanied William the Conqueror to England. The oldest form of the name, on tenth century Breton coins, seems to be *Alamnvs*, though we also find *Alanus* in the same century (*Loth*, p. 83). Alan, king of Brittany, is mentioned in *Brut y Twysogion* under 683. The form *Alamnvs* points to *Alemannus*, the Germanic tribal name, meaning 'all men,' as the source of the personal name. The name became a popular one in Scotland from its occurrence in the family of the Stewards. Alan, son of Waldeve witnessed charters by King David I, 1139 (*Raine*, 19, 20). Alanus, brother of Galfridus Redberd witnessed sale of a tenement in Perth, 1219 (*Scon*, p. 52), and Alanus, capellanus Willelmi Cumyn, comes de Buchan, 1221 (RAA., I, p. 93). Aleyn fitz Maucolum of Berwickshire and John fiz Aleyn, burgess of Montrose, rendered homage, 1296 (*Bain*, II, p. 198, 207). Loughlan le fiz Aleyn, son-in-law of Alexander of Argyll, was received to the king of England's peace in 1301 (ibid., p. 307). Duncan Alowne was admitted burgess of Aberdeen, 1446 (NSCM., I, p. 10). Henry Alane was clerk of accounts of the king's household, 1490. Henry Alane was archdeacon of Dunblane, 1498. Thomas Ailen in Jedburgh, 1641 (RRM., I, p. 89). The Allans of Bute, who appear also in record as Callan, Callen, Macallan, and Maccallan, are properly Macallans. Bearers of the name Allan are permitted by grace of the sartorial fraternity to wear the tartan of Macdonald of Clan Ranald, or, alternatively, that of Clan Macfarlane. Alen, Alene (1565), Allane (1554), Alland, Allone. Cf. ALMAN.

ALANE. Canon Alexander Alane, disciple of Patrick Hamilton, when he fled to the continent had his name changed by Melanchthon to Alesius, i.e. "the wanderer," and from that time forward he was known as Alexander Alesius.

ALARD. Alardus, clericus, charter witness in Angus, c. 1170 (RAA., I, p. 38). Perhaps from *Ealhheard*, a common OE. personal name (*Searle*) or, perhaps better, from *Æðelweard*.

ALASTAIR. From Alasdair the Gaelic form of ALEXANDER, q.v. D in Gaelic is pronounced nearly like *t*, hence the form Alastair.

ALBANACH, i.e. 'of Scotland.' The Annals of the Four Masters under the year 942 record the death of Aed Albanach, a leader of the Dublin Danes. Gillemure Albanach was one of the witnesses to the gift of the church of Torpennoth to the Abbey of Holyrood by Uchtred, son of Fergus and Gunhild his wife before 1165 (LSC., p. 20), and Molcal' Albenach was one of an inquest held at Gerwan (Girvan) in Karrik in 1260 (*Bain*, I, 2674). The epithet is also applied to Irish saints who worked in Scotland (*Watson*, I, p. 322).

ALBERT. An OE. personal name, *Æthelberht*, 'noble bright,' or *Ælebe(o)rht*, 'all bright.' Albertus de Dunde appears in Perth in the reign of Alexander II (*Scon*, p. 62). He may have been the father of Cleopha Alberti, a charter witness in Dundee in 1281 (HP., II, p. 223).

ALBURN. Of local origin from the small place named Alburn in the parish of Markinch, Fife. Henrie Alburne in record in 1640 (*Fordell*, p. 114), Thomas Alburne, plasterer, St. Andrews, c. 1685 (PSAS., LIV, p. 245), and Thomas Alburn appears in the parish of Markinch, 1754 (*St. Andrews*).

ALCOCK. From Al + cock, a double diminutive of ALLAN, q.v. William Alkok, witness in Aberdeen, 1281 (REA., II, p. 279).

ALCORN. Probably from Alchorne, a manor in the parish of Rotherfield in Sussex. A family of this name lived there in the fourteenth century, and Lower (writing in 1860) says "Some of their descendants still resident in that parish have within a generation or two corrupted their name to Allcorn." The mill of Kethyk was leased to John Awldcorn in 1446 (*Cupar-Angus*, I, p. 124), and two years later it was re-let to his son Adam Aldcorn (ibid., p. 127). "Sir" Robert Aldcorne was chaplain in Stirling in 1476 (SBR., p. 259), and John Auldcorne, baker in Glasgow, and Walter Auldcorne, burgess of Elgin, are both mentioned in 1591 (RPC., IV, p. 620, 659). Walter Auldcorne, member of assize of the regality court of Spynie in 1596 (SCM., II, p. 132) may be the aforementioned Elgin burgess. In 1594 Stevin Auldcorne was accused "for wirking on the Sondave" (MCM., I, p. 67), John Aldcorne was indweller in Kelso in 1630 (RPC., 2. ser. III, p. 563), Alexander Auldcorne, messenger, appears in 1634 (ibid., 2. ser. V, p. 621), John Alcoirne was messenger of Gabriel Maxwell during the latter's residence in Daniskine 1635 (*Pollok*, II, p. 257) and in 1649 the wife of "umquhill" John Auldcorne in Lochwinnoch was accused of witchcraft (ibid., 2. ser. VIII, p. 204). Henry Alcorn or Hary Auldcorne was assay-master at the mint, 1687 and 1689 (RPC., 3. ser. XIII, p. xxxvii; XIV, p. 430). The name is also found in the Edinburgh Marriage records as Alcorn (1698), Alcorne (1671), and Auldcorn (1696). It is also found in Castlemilk, Dumfriesshire, and in Kelso in the seventeenth century, and six of the surname are recorded in the Commissariot record of Stirling between 1621 and 1741. Aldycorne 1667.

ALDAN. A personal name from OE. *Ealdwine*, 'old friend,' through the intermediate form Aldwin. Gospatric, son of Alden, was a witness to Earl David's *Inquisitio* concerning the lands of the church of Glasgow, c. 1124 (REG., p. 7). Aldan, brother of Gospatric son of Crin, witnessed Earl Gospatric's gift of Ederham and Nesebite (Nisbet) to the monks of S. Cuthbert, a. 1153 (*Nat. MSS.*, I, 25). Aldanus, cocus, was witness to a charter by Richard, bishop of St. Andrews (*Scon*, p. 27), Gilbert filius Aldin witnessed a confirmation charter by Earl Patrick of Dunbar to the Priory of Coldingham, a. 1232 (CCPC., p 6), and Aldan was owner of the manor of Home, a. 1250 (*Kelso*, 300).

ALDANSTON. Perhaps from the manor of Aldenstone in Cumberland, now Alston. Jurdan de Aldanston was juror on an inquisition held at Berwick on the lands of Lady Elena de la Zuche lying in the sheriffdom of Edinburgh, 1296 (*Bain*, II, p. 215). Andreu de Haldanstone of Edinburghshire rendered homage in the same year. His seal bears an eight-leaved flower and S' *Andree de Haldanistun* (ibid., p. 201, 547). John de Haldanstoun was witness in a document signed at St. Andrews, 1391 (*Wemyss*, II, p. 29). James Haldenstone or de Haldenston, prior of St. Andrews, 1418-43, as Master James of Hawdenston had a safe conduct into England in 1425 (*Bain*, IV, 988). John of Aldynstoun was juror on an inquest on the lands of Gladmor (Gladsmuir), 1430 (*James* II, p. 16). James Aldinstoun of that Ilk was cautioner for Robert, Lord Seytoun, 1586 (RPC., IV, p. 80), and John Aldinstoun was appointed constable for the barony of Broughton, 1633 (ibid., 2. ser. v, p. 83). David Aldinstone who was session clerk of South Leith during the plague of 1645 (PSAS., IV, p. 394) may be the same with David Aldinstoun, reader at Leith, 1657 (*Laing*, 2506). Cf. ALDINSTOUN.

ALDCAMBUS. See *under* OLDCAMBUS.

ALDENGTON. A surname recorded in Annan, Dumfriesshire, 1801. May be from Aldington, a hamlet in Worcestershire.

ALDERSTON. Perhaps from Alderston near Bellshill in the parish of Bothwell, Lanarkshire. There is also an Alderston in the parish of Haddington, East Lothian, and an Alderstone in the parish of Mid Calder, Midlothian. Peter Alderstoune, presbyter in Glasgow, is mentioned in 1544 (LCD., p. 106), and the name is also found in Glasgow at the same period as Alderstoun (1551), Aldirstoune (1552), and Alderstone (1554) (*Protocols*, I). James Alderstoune was minister of Kilmaurs from 1637 to 1642 (*Fasti*, II, p. 178).

ALDIE. From the place of the same name in Strathearn. Thomas Aldie was portioner of Drumbuy in 1676.

ALDINCRAW. See *under* AUCHINCRAW. An old form, Audencraw, perhaps shows NF. influence in the vocalization of the *l*.

ALDINSTOUN. The lands of Aldeneston were held before 1292 by Robert de Veteri Ponte, as in that year 'renunciat A. Regi Scottorum homagium quod ei fecit pro terra de Aldeneston ita quod Rex ipse non teneretur ad warrantiam ejusdem terre' (APS., I, p. 116). An Adam filius Alden is witness to a Kelso charter of 1178 (RAA., I, 2), and in 1329 Willelmus dictus Aldyn was provost of Lanark (ER., I, p. 163). In 1662 the name is spelled Adnistoun.

Aldinstoun, Adinstoun, Auldinstoun, of that Ilk is mentioned in 1546 (*Laing*), and ten years later John Aldinstoun was one of an inquest into Edinburgh's municipal affairs (EBR., 259). Frequent in RAA., II, under various forms. John Aldstone, charter witness, 1498 (RAA., II, 394). Mention of garden of John Hadstone in Arbroath, 1529(?). Haldston, 1532, Aldinston (from estate), 1524. Aldston 1508, Aldstone 1498, Aldynston 1524, Haldstone 1505, Haltanstane 1495. Cf. ALDANSTON.

ALDIRCH. John Aldirch witnessed a writ by Roger Corbet at Langtoun, 1330 (*Laing*, 35).

ALDIS. Probably of territorial origin from the five merk lands of Auldhous of old extent in the parish of Eastwood, Renfrewshire. In 1265 Roger, son of Reginald de Aldhous resigned all claim to the lands of Aldhous which he and his father had held in ferm (RMP., p. 63). In 1284 John de Aldhus, son of Roger, again renounced his right in the court of the Justiciar of Lothian, obtaining a grant of a portion of the lands for the lives of himself and Cristiana his wife (ibid., p. 65, 66).

ALDOCH. Robert Auldhoch or Haldhocht appears as bailie of Edinburgh, 1467–1471 (*Neubotle*, p. 268, 270, 274). He is doubtless the Robert Auldocht, burgess of Edinburgh, 1471, and the Robert Auldoch who held a land in Edinburgh in 1486 (RMS., II, 1035, 1655). Johnne Aldoth in Roxburgh was amerced in 1473 (ALHT., I, p. 11). Thomas Aldoch or Aldocht appears as factour and attourney in Edinburgh, 1473 (*Bain*, IV, p. 407–408). As Thomas Aldock, Scottish merchant, he received a money payment from Edward IV of England, and as Thomas Aldough he had a safe conduct in the same year. In 1474 he appears again as Thomas Aldolf (*Bain*, IV, 1410–1412). Alexander Aldoth was one of the assize on the price of wheat in Edinburgh, 1500 (EBR., 80), and Androw Aldoth was "principall wrycht under the maister of work" there in 1552 (ibid., 342). Aldhoch 1494; Auldhocht.

ALDOWY. The fermes of Ballinab, Islay, granted to Fergus Aldowy for his fee, 1542 (ER., XVII, p. 555). ? shortened from MACILDOWIE.

ALDRED. From OE. E)*Aldred*, 'old (sage) counsel.' Aldredus, rural dean of Teviotdale, witnessed charter to the church of St. John in the Castle of Roxburgh, c. 1128 (REG., 4). Aldred, pistor, witnessed a charter by Roger, bishop elect of St. Andrews, relating to the church of Hadintun, c. 1189–98 (RPSA., p. 153).

ALDRI. William de Aldri witnessed a charter by Thurstan filius Leuing, 1153–65 (LSC., 17). As William de Aldreis he witnessed a charter in the reign of William the Lion (*Melros*). The author of *The Norman people* says from Audrieu or Aldrey near Caen.

ALDROXBURGH. Peter de Aldroxburgh, one of an inquest made at Roxburgh in 1320 (RRM., I, p. xv), derived his name from Old Roxburgh, near Kelso, a place of considerable importance in and before the twelfth century, but now quite extinct.

ALEHOUSE. From the old lands of Ailhous (1602) now Alehouse in the parish of Foveran, Aberdeenshire. Thomas Ailhous was admitted burgess of Aberdeen in 1591 (NSCM., I, p. 82), and James Ailhows or Ailhowse was witness in an Aberdeen witch trial in 1596 (SCM., I, p. 87, 88). George Ailhous, lawful son of the late Arthur Ailhous, of Old Aberdeen, his sister Christian, and his grandfather James, are in record in 1614 (RSCA., II, p. 70). Robert Aillhouss in Auchlochries and George Ailhouss his cautioner appear in 1622 (ibid., II, p. 266). Ailhows and Ailhowse 1597, Elehous 1606.

ALEXANDER. From Greek Ἀλέξανδρος, defender of man. Miss Yonge has pointed out in her *History of Christian names* that nowhere is the name Alexander so thoroughly national as in Scotland, into which country it was introduced by Queen Margaret, wife of King Malcolm Ceannmor, from the Hungarian Court, where she was brought up. "Her third son was the first of the three Alexanders, under whom the country spent her most prosperous days. The death of the last was a signal for the long death-feud between the northern and southern kingdoms, and all the consequent miseries" (I, p. 200, 201). So popular indeed became the name in Scotland that Alexander in its diminutive form "Sandy" is even more the national name than "Donald."

As a surname Alexander is very common on the west coast, where, according to the authors of *Clan Donald*, some of the descendants of Godfrey, second son of Alastair Mor, appear to have settled in the Carrick district of Ayrshire, and several territorial families of Macalexander from this stock were prominent in that region, e.g. the MacAlexanders of Daltupene, Dalreoch, Corsclays, etc. About the end of the seventeenth century they dropped the 'Mac' (*Clan Donald*, III, p. 199). The Alexanders of Menstrie claimed to be connected with the Clan Donald and to be closely allied in blood with the Macallisters of Loup. Gilbert, son of Donald, son of Alastair Mor, got a grant of lands in Stirlingshire in 1330. There is no further trace of this family until the beginning of the sixteenth century, when they are found settled in Clackmannanshire (ibid., III, p. 189). William Alexander was connected with the accounts of the city of Edinburgh in 1435 (ER., IV, p. 663), Robert Alexander was a granger in Feichly and Drummelochy in Strathdon in 1438 (ER., V, p. 56), and the name is of frequent occurrence in the Moray rentals in the first half of the sixteenth century (*Sc. Peer.*, VIII, p. 165). The name was early adopted into Gaelic, appearing as Alaxandair in the Gaelic genealogical manuscript of 1467 (now spelled Alasdair), and as a patronymic it appears as M'*Alasdair*, whence the well-known Macalister, Macallister, etc. Aleckander 1501, Alisandre 1424, Alisschonder 1536, Alschinder 1546, Alschoner 1613, Alschunder 1581, Alshander 1581, Alshunder 1597, Alsinder 1539. The name is said to occur in Hittite as Alakšandu. See also ELSHENER.

ALEXANDERSON. This surname, meaning "son of Alexander," in Latin documents assumes the form "filius Alexandri," as Johannes fil. Alexandri the name of a burgess of Aberdeen in 1317 (SCM., v, p. 10). William Alexanderson and Ade (Adam) Alexanderson were admitted burgesses of the same town in 1443 (NSCM., I, p. 7), and John Alexandri is recorded in Brechin in 1450 (REB., I, 159). William Alexandersoun held the fourth part of the lands of the town of Dunnychthin (Dunnichen) in 1486 (RAA., II, p. 249), John Alexanderson was tenant of part of Litill Pertht, 1495 (Cupar-Angus, I, p. 241), Donald Alexanderson was tenant of Petconnouchty, Ardmanoch, in 1504 (ER., XII, p. 661), and William Alexandersoun was tacksman of Alyth in 1561 (Rent. Dunk., p. 351). Andrew Alexandersoun, a Pope's knight, was a witness in Caithness, 1557 (Laing, 682). The son of Cristina Allistersoun alias Alexandersoun was served heir portioner of his grandfather William Alistersoun alias Alexandersoun in the lands of Lybuster in 1624 (Retours, Caithness, 12). The surname was not uncommon in the fifteenth and sixteenth centuries.

ALEXSONE, 'son of ALEX(ANDER)', q.v. David Alexsone witnessed an instrument of sasine, 1534 (Bamff, p. 64).

ALFORD. Of local origin from the village of the same name in Aberdeenshire.

ALFRED. The OE. personal name Ælfred, meaning 'elf counsel.' The name of Alfred the second prior of Newbattle Abbey, who died in 1179, was usually written Alured and frequently corrupted to Amfridus (Neubotle, intro., p. xv; Chron. Mail., s.a. 1179). He is a frequent witness to privileges granted to the canons of St. Andrews (RPSA.). Alwredus, abbot of Stirling, a. 1158, appears again as Alured (LSC., p. 10, 20).

ALGARUS. From the OE. personal name Ealdgār ("old spear"), or from Ælfgār ("elf spear"). Algarus presbyter attested a grant by King Edgar to the monks of S. Cuthbert of Coldingham, c. 1100 (Nat. MSS., I, 4). Algarus, prior of Durham, c. 1107–24 (ibid., I, 13). The latter appears several times in charters by Alexander I and David I.

ALGEO. "There are several respectable farmers in this parish [Inchinnan] of the name of Algie or Algoe, a name peculiar, it is believed, to this part of the country. In former times a family of this name had considerable estates in Renfrewshire, and were of Italian origin, the first of them having come from Rome, in the suite of one of the Abbots of Paisley. The Algies of Inchinnan are spirited farmers, and the name, along with others in this place frequently flourishes among the prize takers at ploughing matches" (New statistical account, Renfrew, p. 120). Nisbet says the grandson of the Italian immigrant, Peter Algoe, got the lands of Easter Walkinshaw by marrying Marion Morton, heiress thereof, in 1547 (Heraldry, I, p. 266). He was probably the Peter Algeo who was burgess of Paisley in 1550 (Protocols, I.). Robert Algeo, who rendered to Exchequer the account of the bailies of Renfrew in 1585 (ER., xxi, p. 250) is probably Robert Algeo, bailie of the same burgh in 1603 (Laing). John Algeo, tenant of Wattishill in 1591 (RPC., IV, p. 650) may be the John Algeo who was burgess of Paisley in 1603 (Laing). Thomas Algeo was servitor to the countess of Abercorn in 1626 (Lees, Paisley, p. 268), John Algo was heir of William Algeo, portioner of Eister Walkinschawe in 1632 (Inquis., 1903), and Crawfurd says the family failed in the person of John Algeo of Easter-Walkinshaw in the reign of Charles I. John Algeo was a merchant in Aberdeen in 1681 (ROA., I, p. 239), Mr. James Aljo was a writer in Minnigaff in 1684 (RPC., 3. ser. x, p. 242), and William Algeo was town clerk of Queensferry in 1686 (RPC., 3. ser. XII, p. 495–496). The name appears several times in the Campsie Commissariot Record in the seventeenth century. Allgeo 1556, Algow 1768. Cf. AULDJO.

ALICE. A common surname in Dunblane and neighborhood in seventeenth and eighteenth centuries (Dunblane). Robert Alice in Edinburgh, 1637 (Edinb. Marr.). Edward Alise in Dumfries, 1657 (Dumfries), Harie Alice, a Perthshire heritor, 1688 (RPC., 3. ser. XIII, p. 332). John Alice in Foswell, 1749 (Laing), and Jonet Alice in Hilfoot of Castletoune, parish of Muckart, 1764 (Stirling). This may also be a masculine name. "The possibility of appellatives being epicene, that is common to both sexes, is ever present" (Ewen, p. 249).

ALICESONE. Patrick Alicesone of the county of Berewyke rendered homage, 1296 (Bain, II, p. 207). Thomas, son of Alice, burgess of Aberdeen, 1273 (Fraser, p. 11) is probably Thomas filius Alicie, charter witness there, 1281 (REA., II, p. 279) and the Thomas filius Alicie, burgess of Edinburgh, 1294 (ibid., I, p. 35). John Alicie, ground officer in Bucharn, 1487 (SCM., v, p. 236).

ALIE. — Alye in Balronve, 1567 (Laing). John Alie in Edinburgh, 1609 (Edinb. Marr.). John Alie, burgess of Jedburgh, 1634 (RPC., 2. ser. v, p. 285), and William Alie, bailie there, 1646 (APS., VI, p. 589). Kathren Alie witness in Dysart, 1639 (PBK., p. 149). George Allie, tenant of Philiphaugh, married Janet Cleghorn of Galashiels, 1657.

ALISON, ALLISON. (1) usually explained as a metronymic, 'son of Alice,' but more probably it is 'son of ELLIS,' q.v. Lower (s.v. Alison) says: "It may be remarked that the vulgar pronunciation of Ellis in the south is exactly the same as that of the female personal name Alice." (2) In some few cases Alison and Allison may be forms of Allanson. In 1559 a woman Jonet Alysone was also referred to as Jonet Alanesone (*Cupar-Angus*, II, p. 177, 271). (3) On the other hand, with reference to Scottish Alison or Allison, Mr. L. A. Morrison in his *The History of the Alison or Allison family in Europe and America*, Boston, 1893, says that it is "a fact beyond doubt that Alison comes from *Alister* or Alexander, and, further, that the Alisons are offshoots of the famous clan of MacAlister" (p. 4), and that the origin of the name is due to two sons of Alexander MacAlister of Loupe who with some of their followers escaped to the parish of Avondale, Lanarkshire, during the war of Independence, and there later their name was changed from MacAlister to Alison (p. 18). He further states that "the names Alison, Allison, Alinson, Allinson, and of Elison, Ellison, Elissen, Ellysen, are found thus spelled in the early history of some branches of the present Allison family. They are interchangeably mixed. The name was often spelled Ellison and Allison when referring to the same individual" (p. 5). This may have been so in some instances, but the claim as a whole is, I think, too sweeping. Patrick Alissone del counte de Berewyk rendered homage, 1296 (RR). Peter Alesoun was a witness in Brechin, 1490 (REB., II, 134), Thomas Alesoun appears in Lochtoun, Scone, 1586 (*Scon*, p. 232), James Allasone was bailie of Ranfrew, 1688 (RPC., 3. ser. XIII, p. 243), and Gabriel Alason was bailie of the burgh of Dumfries, 1693 (*Retours, Kirkcudbright*, 375). Other early spellings are Alesone 1543, Alesoun 1585, Aliesoune 1616, Aliesone, Allasoune, Allisone, and Elisone 1668, Alizon (in Workman MS.), Allasone 1551, Allasoun 1636, Allasson 1671, Allanson 1551; Aillieson, Alisone, Aleson, Allason, Alleson, Allesoun, Allesoune, Allsoun. (4) Alison as the forename of a woman began to make its appearance about the beginning of the fifteenth century. Miss Yonge (2. ed., p. 405–406) thinks it is from Aloyse (the feminine form of Provençal Aloys), whose correspondence with Abelard was the theme of so much sentiment, and whose fame, brought to Scotland by Scottish Archers in the French service, was the origin of the numerous Alisons found there. The -n probably represents the diminutive ending. Helise Mackcoulogh appears in 1478 (*Sc. Ant.*, III, p. 105). Elison Dalrymple was spouse of Gavin Fullarton, 1514 (*Macfarlane, G. C.*, II, p. 342), Alison Home was prioress of North Berwick, 1524; Alysone or Helysoune Rouche slew her guidson Alexander Cant, burgess of Edinburgh, 1535 (*Diur. Occ.*, p. 19); Allison Allasoune appears in Glasgow, 1554 (*Protocols*, I), and Ellesone Tayis appears in Lanark, 1566 (Mill, *Plays*, p. 262); Elison Begbie jilted the poet Robert Burns. See also ELLISON.

ALLAN. See *under* ALAN.

ALLANACH. Individuals of this name are found in Mar and Strathdon in the sixteenth and seventeenth centuries. They were probably descended from the Macallans of Macfarlane origin who settled in the north of Scotland. It is also said that "all the Allanachs of the Braes of Mar are Stuarts, who came thither from Strathdown" (*Legends of Braes o' Mar*, 1910, p. xiii). Finla Allenoch was tenant on the lands of Innernete in Aberdeenshire in 1588 (RPC., IV, p. 365). William Allanache is mentioned in 1617 (RSCA., II, p. 213), and John Allanach in Delmuickie appears in 1632 (ibid., II, p. 355). William Allanach in Glenmuck was fined for resetting members of the Clan Gregor in 1636 (RPC., 2. ser. VI, p. 216). Alister Alnach in Ledmacoy and Robert Alenach in the Boggach, 1682 (*Invercauld*, p. 263). William Allanach and John Allanach were appointed elders at Strathone in 1686 (*Alford*, p. 375). John Allanock a Moray Jacobite in the '45.

ALLANBY. See *under* ALLENBY.

ALLANSHAW. Most probably from Allanshaws near Stow, Midlothian. Vmfray Alanschaw was summoned in 1479 to answer to parliament for treason and other crimes (APS., II, p. 129). Henry Allanschaw was a witness regarding the multure dues at Duns in 1494 (*Hay*, p. 40), and a payment of oats was made to Peter Allanschaw or Hallandschaw, servant of the late Queen of Scotland, in 1542 (ER., XVII, p. 601). Thomas Ellenschaw witnessed an instrument of sasine in 1578 (*Home*, p. 231), James Allanschaw was "common nolt herd of Eyemouth" in 1649, and Robert Allinshaw was one of a number who attested to the boundaries of Huttsonis Croft in 1651 (ibid., p. 99, 220). James Allanschaw in Fouldaine Mains is in record in 1653, and Alexander Alinshaw in Fouldin 1672 (*Lauder*). Allansha 1696.

ALLANSON. "The son of ALLAN," q.v. Rendered in Latin documents by the genitive Alani. Reginald filius Alani was a burgess of

Aberdeen in 1317 (SCM., v, p. 10). Ada filius Alani occurs in 1326 (ER., I, p. 53), another Ada filius Alani de Dunbretane witnessed a charter by Donald, earl of Lennox after 1334 (*Levenax*, p. 93), and in the reign of Robert I the 20 pound land of Sproustoun was forfeited by John, Thomas, and William filii Alani (RMS., I, App. II, 285). William Aleynsson, a Scots prisoner of war, was discharged from Newgate prison in 1375 (*Bain*, IV, 227), Robert Alanson had a safe conduct to trade in England with Scottish merchandise in 1447 (*Bain*, IV, 1190), Catharine Alanesoun and her father John Alansone of Edinburgh are mentioned in 1459 (REG., p. 412), the house of John Allansone in Leyth is referred to in 1462 (*Soltre*, p. 65), and in the same year "Sir" Alexander Alanesoun, chaplain, appears as a witness in Edinburgh (*Laing*, 147). A payment was made to William Alynson, "Scotte," for his labor in "spying into certain matters touching the king's good" in 1463 (*Bain*, IV, 1333). In the same year safe conducts were granted for Andrew Aleynson and William Aleynson, Scotsmen (ibid., 1338), and in 1471 letters of denisation were issued in favor of Thomas Aleinson, a native of Scotland (ibid., 1399). Bartholomew Alansoun had remission for his part in burning the town of Dunbertane, 1489 (*Lennox*, II, p. 133), and William Alansoun was a friar preacher in St. Andrews in 1545 (*Laing*, 494). A sept of the Macallans (Clan Ranald Macdonalds), are also known as Allansons, from the chief's designation of Mac-'ic-Ailein. Alanesone 1489, Alensone 1582, Allansoune 1545, Allasone 1520.

ALLARDYCE, ALLARDICE, ALLARDES. Of territorial origin from the old barony of Allardice in the parish of Arbuthnott, Kincardineshire. "It is not a very common name, but all who hold it believe in their descent from the old family which was settled for so long a period on the banks of the Bervie Water" (*Genealogical magazine*, VII, p. 296). The estate was sold in 1872 and now forms part of the Arbuthnott estate in the same parish. Nisbet says William the Lion gave charters of lands of Alrethis to a person who assumed that name (*Heraldry*, I, p. 45). Alexander de Allyrdas, who witnessed a charter of the lands of Glack c. 1294 (REA., I, p. 37), is doubtless Alisaundre de Allerdashe of the county of Kincardyn who rendered homage in 1296 (*Bain*, II, p. 209). Walter de Allerdas also rendered homage in the same year (ibid., II, 730). John de Allirdas was a witness in Brechin in 1364 (REB., I, 21), and Thomas de Allirdas had an annual pension of 20s. from the lands of Lytilbarres in 1370 (RMS., I, 306). David

de Allyrdas was scutifer of the duke of Albany in 1413 (RMS., I, 944), Sir James Allirdes was clerk of the king's treasury and archdeacon of Murray in 1478 (*Bain*, IV, 1449), James Alirdes was prebendary of Torbolton in 1491 (REG., 460), and John Allerdes of that Ilk was one of an assize in 1601 (*Trials*, II, p. 36). Among the old people of the locality the name is pronounced "Airdis." Allardes 1543, Allerdash 1296, Allerdes 1481, Allirdasse 1415, Allyrdes 1496, Alyrdes 1443. Other forms are Alerdes, Alerdyce, Alerdice, Alirdes, and Allerdais. It has become Alderdice in Antrim and Armagh. See ARDES.

ALLATHAN. Most probably from the lands of Allathan near New Deer, Aberdeenshire. Andrew Allathin in Meikle Auchredy is in record in 1625 (RSCA., II, p. 281). Auchreddie is also near New Deer.

ALLAWAY. A surname found in Aberdeen, most probably from Alloa in Clackmannanshire, an old spelling of which was Alleway (1359). John Aloway was servitor to King James II in 1440. Elizabeth Alloweius or Aloveius is recorded in Dunfermline in 1549 (DBR., 255), and Marion Alloway in Linlithgow in 1684 (RPC., 3. ser. x, p. 260).

ALLEGATE. Local. John of Allegate was sheriff-substitute of Roxburgh, 1306 (*Bain*, II, 1887).

ALLEIS. James Alleis in Hillhead of Mosstoun and James Aillies in Ald Aberdeen are mentioned in 1663 (RSCA., II, p. 329, 375). Jonet Alise in Hilfoot of Castletoune, parish of Muckhart, 1664 (*Stirling*). Anthony Allies was bailie of Stranraer, 1758 (*Wigtown*).

ALLEN. See under ALAN.

ALLENBY. A Cumberland surname occurring but rarely in Scotland. Sarah Aglionby relict of Richard Lowthian recorded in 1799 (*Dumfries*). Aglionby was the forename of a rector of the High School of Edinburgh, Dr. Aglionby Ross Carson (1780–1850). There is a family of Allanby of Balblair. It is a modification of Aglionby, from *Aguillon+bý-r*, Aguillon's farm. Harrison says the personal name is a nickname, OF. *aguillon* (mod. Fr. *aiguillon*), "goad, spur."

ALLENDRECH. Local. William Allendrech in Dalhande, 1682 (*Invercauld*, p. 264).

ALLERSHAW. Local, perhaps from Allershaw near Abington, Lanarkshire. Peter Allirshaw was "Quenis servand," 1531 (ALHT., v. p. 434). Jonet Allerschaw in Gerchnes, 1540 (RSS., II, 3792).

ALLHUSEN. A rare surname recorded in Perth and in Inverness. ? of recent introduction from England. Weekley (p. 51) says the name seems to represent AF. *al* and the old dat. plur. *husum*, houses?

ALLISON. See *under* ALISON.

ALLISTER. Curtailed from (MAC)ALASTER, q.v. 1615 Alaster.

ALLUM. A curtailed form of MACCALLUM through the form MACALLUM.

ALMAN. From Allemagne the name given to the high ground south of Caen in Normandy, which may have derived its origin from a Teutonic colony (Freeman, *Norman conquest*, II, p. 254). The *S' Roberti d'Alman* is appended to demission of a toft in vill de Coldingham to William de Howburn, 1304, and the *Sigillum Willelmi Alman* is appended to a document of 1355 (*Seals. Supp.*, 36, 37). See ALAN.

ALMOND. A surname recorded in CD., and found in Dalkeith in 1689 (*Laing*). (1) It may be a descendant of OE. personal name *Ealhmund*, a name which appears in the Northumbrian genealogies as *Alchmund* (Sweet, *Oldest English texts*, p. 168). In the absence of intermediate links it is not safe to assume the connection. (2) It might also be from Almond, the river, which gives name to places, Almondbank, etc.

ALPIN, ALPINE. Gallo-Lat. *Alpinus*, W. *Elffin*. In Irish records written Alphin (AU., 693), Alpin (AU., 858), Elphine (*Tighernach*, 622). "Two or three Pictish kings had borne the name of Alpin, the first being on his father's side a Dalriad Scot: but no other instance of it is found among the Dalriad Scots until we come to the father of Kenneth" (*Nicholson*, KR., p. 82). "Whatever the origin of the name (it can have nothing to do with Alba), it has survived into the modern language as Alpan, without a trace of British phonetic development" (Prof. Fraser, SGS., II, p. 199). Alpinus, canon of Dunblane, 1287 (*Inchaffray*, p. 111), was elected to the bishopric after the death of Bishop William in 1296 (*Dowden*, p. 200). Alpin mac Donald was one of the witnesses to a charter of the halfpenny land of the church of Killilan granted to the monks of Paislev, 1295 (RMP., p. 138). Some Ailpin has given name to Rathelpin now Rathelpie in Fife (*Watson* I, p. 237). See ELPHIN and MACALPIN.

ALPITE. Ada de Alpite witnessed a quit-claim of the lands of Drumkarauch, 1260 (RPSA., p. 346).

ALROUNY. James of Alrouny, an Aberdeen merchant, petitioned for restoration of his goods taken by the English at sea, 1438 (*Bain*, IV, 1115).

ALSHIONER. See *under* ELSHENER.

ALSOP. This surname occurs in the Aberdeen Directory, and is most probably of recent introduction from England. From Alsop in the county of Derby.

ALSTON. Most probably from Alston in Cumberland, earlier Aldenstone. A common surname in Glasgow in the eighteenth and nineteenth centuries, and common also in Ayrshire and Lanarkshire. James Auldston in Ravenscraig, 1667, and several Alstounes are mentioned in Campsie Commissariot Record. Dr. Alstoun of Eastend refused the Test, 1684 (RPC., 3. ser. x, p. 291). The name is also found in the Edinburgh Marriage Record as Alstoun and Allstoun. James Alstowne was member of Edinburgh Merchant Company, 1687 (RPC., 3. ser. XIII, p. 154), and John Alston was residenter in Montrose, 1754 (*Brechin*).

ALTON. Robert de Alton juror on inquest held in St. Katherine's chapel, Bavelay, 1280 (*Bain*, IV, 1762). There is a village named Alton in Loudoun parish, but probably the name is from an English Alton.

ALTRILLY. Local. William de Altrilly on inquisition retouring Donald, thane of Calder or Cawdor, 1414 (*Cawdor*, p. 5).

ALUERTUN. Johannes de Aluertun, clerk of Coldingham in 1279 (*Raine*, 229), may have derived his name from Aluretune (now Allerton) in Yorkshire. Robert de Alureton in Perth rendered homage, 1291 (RR).

ALVAH. From the parish of Alvah in Banffshire. George Murdo Alvah from King Edward served in the first Great War (*Turriff*).

ALVES. From Alves in Moray. The surname should be pronounced as one syllable, with *a* sounded long as in alms. Walter de Alvevs was one of an inquisition on the lands of Mefth in 1263 (APS., I; *Bain*, I, 2323). Patrick de Aluays was a chaplain in 1360 (REM., p. 304), and Malcolm de Alues was decanus Cathanensi in 1363 (ibid., p. 313). William Awas was a chaplain, 1464 (RAA., II, 156), and Marjory Awes appears in Inverness, 1481 (*Inv.*, p. 154). Alexander Alves was admitted burgess of Aberdeen in 1406 (NSCM., I, p. 2), and a later Alexander Alwes in Ardewat was juror on an inquisition held at Spynie in 1601 (SCM., II, p. 145). Bessie Alves or Alwas was a witness in Elgin, 1661 (*Rec. Elgin*, I, p. 296–297), and Alexander Alves and David Alves were church elders in the parish of Alves in 1685 (RPC., 3. ser. x, p. 549). William Alves was bailie of Portsburgh before 1724 (*Guildry*, p. 128). A family of this name were lairds of Shipland near Inverness. Alues 1565, Alvess 1678, Aves 1659, Avis 1687.

ALWART. John Aluart was "office bearer," probably procurator of the Scottish Nation in the University of Orleans, 1418 (SHSM., II, p. 101). It probably represents OE. *Ailward*.

ALWAY. John Aulway, a Scots prisoner of war, liberated from custody in the Tower of London in 1413, may be the John Alway, servitor of John Lyouns who received a safe conduct into England in 1417 (*Bain*, IV, 839, 878). The name is probably from the town of Alva (in 1489, Alway) in Stirlingshire.

ALWETH. Siward de Alweth, charter witness, c. 1200 (*Cambus.*, p. 73). Local, from Alva or Alloa. Alloa in 1357 is Alveth, Alva in 1489 is Alweth, and Alvah in Banffshire is Alveth in 1308.

ALWYN. (1) Alwyn in old charters relating to the earldom of Lennox, Latinized Alwynus, is the OG. personal name *Ailin*, found in Adamnan as *Ailenus (Aileni*, gen., lib. I, c. 43). It comes from *ail* 'stone,' found in Al Clud ('rock of the Clyde') the old name of Dumbarton. (2) Alwyn is also the name of a witness who appears frequently between 1128–1152 as Alwyn, Alwin, Alfwyn, Aleuin, Algune, and in Latin as Aluuinus, from OE. *Ælfwine*. As Algune mac Arcill he witnesses a grant by Gartnait and Ete to the monastery of Deer, c. 1131–1132 (*Bk. Deer*, III, 7). He was an east coast, probably Aberdeenshire, potentate, as Dr. Macbain suggests (Skene, *Highlanders*, p. 413). The frequency with which his name is written with 'mac' probably means that he was the son of a resident in Scotland (cf. Thorfinn mac Thore). He appears frequently as a charter witness in the chartularies of Dunfermline, St. Andrews, Kelso, and Dryburgh. For Aluuinus Rennere see RENNARIUS. The name is also found several times between 1175 and 1225. Elwynus was the first known parson of Edzell (*Panmure*, I, p. lii). John Elwyn was burgess of Glasgow, 1564 (*Pollok*, I, p. 300), and an earlier Elvin gave name to ELVINGSTOUN, q.v.

ALYNTON. Local. Magister Petrus de Alyntun (Alinton or Alington), archdeacon of Teviotdale, witnessed a quit-claim of the lands of Eduluestun to the church of Glasgow, 1233 (REG., p. 140), and died in 1242 (*Chron. Mail.*, s.a.). Perhaps from one of the English places named Allington.

ALYTH. Of territorial origin from the barony of the same name, now a parish, in Perthshire, in 1470 spelled Alicht. Thomas de Alyght and Walter Alight were two Scottish prisoners taken in the capture of Dunbar Castle in 1296 and committed, the first to Kenilworth Castle and the other to Tonbridge Castle (*Bain*, II, p. 177, 178). In the same year William Alight of the town of Perth, and Walter de Alight rendered homage for their lands (ibid., II, p. 169, 186, 197).

AMBROSE. William Ambrosij (gen.) was burgess of Glasgow in 1488 (LCD.); and in 1499 a payment of eight bolls of wheat was made to Alexander Ambrose and his wife (ER., XI, p. 144). Alexander Ambroise was minister at Newbotle, 1609 (Pitcairn, *Trials*, III, p. 600). John Ambrose of Graystain was charged with assault in 1628 (RPC., 2. ser. II, p. 615), Jean Ambrois was a resident in Dunkeld in 1675 (DPD., I, p. 197), and four individuals of this name are recorded in Edinburgh in the seventeenth century (*Edinb. Marr.*). The name is from the Greek personal name *Ambrosios*, "immortal, divine," a great favorite in mediæval Europe. In the Latin form Ambrosius it was the name of one of the great fathers of the Latin Church (d. 397 A.D.). See also MACCAMBRIDGE. Ambros 1637. As forename: Ambrose Halyday, 1479.

AMBRUCIUS. Patrick Ambrucius balie of the burgh of Dunbretane, 1365 (ER., II, p. 211).

AMFRAY. A form of (H)UMPHREY, q.v. Thomas Amfray in Aberdeen, 1408 (CWA., p. 316), and John Amphra was admitted burgess there, 1567 (NSCM., I, p. 68).

AMISFIELD. Probably from the lands of Amisfield in Dumfriesshire. James of Amysfeld appears as a witness in Linlithqw in 1472 (*Sc. Ant.*, XVII, p. 117), and there are entries of payments from the mails of Linlithquewschyr of an annual rent to the heirs of James Amisfeld between 1557 and 1594 (ER., XIX, XXI–XXII). Sir John Amisfeld appears as notary public in Dornoch in 1494 (ALA., p. 204). Amisfeild 1590, Hamisfeild 1585. Amisfield in the parish of Haddington, East

AMISFIELD, *continued*

Lothian, was formerly known as Newmills and the name changed to Amisfield only in the first quarter of the eighteenth century when Newmills was purchased by the notorious Col. Charteris and renamed after the ancient home of his ancestors.

AMOURS. Henry Amours, constable of Kinghorn and mair of that quarter of Fife, 1428 (ER., IV, p. 463). Francis Joseph Amours (1841–1910), born in Normandy, was editor of the Scottish Text Society's edition of Wyntoun.

ANCROFT. From Ancroft near Bowden, Northumberland, which early made its way as far north as Aberdeen. Gaufr' de Anecroft witnessed a charter of Patrick, son of Waldeve, fifth earl of Dunbar, to the monks of St. Cuthbert, between 1182–1232 (*Raine*, App., p. 27). William of Anecrofte witnessed a charter by Peter de Morthingtoun, c. 1270 (BNCH., XVI, p. 334), and also a charter of the land of Lambirtoun in 1276 (*Home*, p. 225). The goods of John of Aynecroft, an Aberdeen merchant, were plundered in the wreck of a Seland vessel driven ashore at Kirklee Rode in 1370 (*Bain*, IV, 158). Andrew de Ayncroft who was auditor of accounts in Aberdeen in 1433 may be the Andrew Ayncroft (without the "de") who appears on an inquest in Aberdeen in 1448 (SCM., V, p. 41; CRA., p. 17).

ANCRUM. "For upwards of a century and a half a family, probably sub-tenants and vassals of the see [of Glasgow], derived their surname from the lands of Ancrum" (OPS., I, p. 305). In 1252 John of Alnecromb appears as witness to a charter by Richard Burnard of Farningham to the monks of Melrose (*Melros*, p. 300). In 1296 a writ was issued to the sheriff of Roxburgh, ordering him to restore to Richard de Alnecrum his forfeited lands (*Bain*, II, 832). John de Allyncrum, was Clerk of Register and auditor of accounts in 1358 (ER., I, p. 545). John de Allyncrom, a Scottish merchant, who received in 1361 a safe conduct to England from Edward III (*Rot. Scot.*, I, p. 858–859) is doubtless John of Allyncrum, a prominent burgess of Edinburgh, who, c. 1362, granted his lands of Cragcroke to the Church of St. Giles, Edinburgh (*Laing*, 50). Another John of Alncrum was archdeacon of Teviotdale in 1370 (*Kelso*, 514). In the early years of the fifteenth century William de Alyncrome was abbot of Kelso (*Morton*, p. 90), John Ancrume, James Ancrum, and Michell Ancrum were tenants of the Abbey in 1567

(*Kelso*, p. 523, 528, 530), Elspeth Ancrum appears in Crailing, 1684 (RPC., 3. ser. x, p. 235), and Michaell Ancrum was merchant in Kelso, 1781 (*Heirs*, 406). Alncrom 1426, Ancram 1481, Ancrome 1682, Anckrum 1668.

ANDERSON, 'son of Andrew.' The name is common over a good part of Scotland. David le fiz Andreu, burgess of Peebles, and Duncan fiz Andreu of the county of Dumfries, took the oath of fealty in 1296 (*Bain*, II, p. 197, 210). Henry Androsoun leased part of Balmyle, c. 1443 (*Cupar-Angus*, I, p. 121), and John Andirstoun was commissioner to parliament for Coupar in 1585 (APS., III, 423). The name is sometimes shortened to Andison, which is the spelling in APS. of the name of Michael Anderson of Tushielaw in 1690. John Androsone was burgess of Edinburgh in 1515 (ALHT., V, p. 68). John Andersone in Ridpethe was called Jeanes Johne in 1662 (RRM., II, p. 19). "Anderson's Pills" were a celebrated remedy in Edinburgh, and were made in the Lawnmarket there for over 200 years. James Anderson received a pension for his *Vindication of Scots independence*, 1704. Jhon Enderson was tenant of Stobo in 1529 (*Rental*). The Andersons of Islay are properly MACILLANDRAIS, q.v., who have Englished their name. Andersonne 1582, Andersoun 1509, Andersoune 1582, Andirsoone 1574, Andirsoune 1598, Andreson 1473, Andresoun 1600, Androson 1450, Androsone 1496, Androsoune 1548, Andrson 1505, Endherson 1629, Endirsone 1561, Andersone, Andyrson. See also ANDISON.

ANDIE. A curtailed form of MACANDIE (q.v.), current in Argyllshire.

ANDIRSTON. John de Andirston, prior of Fyvie, 1424, is according to Stodart (II, p. 195) = Anderson. There never were Andersons of that Ilk he says "and certainly the surname does not imply descent from a common ancestor." There seems little doubt, however, that he is the Johannes de Sanctoandrea who was custos of the house (domus) of Fywy in the following year (RAA., II, p. 56). Anderston is occasionally used in our old records for St. Andrews. S. Marie de Anderistona in 1363 is St. Andrews (RMS., I, 167), and in 1394–95 we have record of 'Wilyam Plumer of Tweeddale burgess of Andirstoun', i.e. St. Andrews (RAA., II, 43).

ANDISON, 'son of ANDREW' (q.v.), from the diminutive Andy or Andie. Bartholomew and Galfridus Andisone were tenants of Westirbalbretane in Fife in 1376 (RHM., I, p. lxvi), and Andrew Andison is recorded in Aberdeen,

1408 (CWA., p. 316). Paul Andesoune was hanged in 1558 for stealing a "sorit balsonit horse" (*Trials*, I, p. °400). Andrew Andison appears as a notary public in Selkirk in 1658 and 1666 (RRM., I, p. 199; II, p. 148). See also ANDERSON.

ANDREW. This surname, from the baptismal name Andrew (in Greek *Aindreas*, 'manly') is common in Scotland both as forename and as a surname. Its popularity, no doubt, is due to its being the name of Scotland's patron saint. In the Highlands the name was early adopted appearing in Gaelic as *Aindrea*, with a dialectic form *Anndra* (due probably to Lowland pronunciation of Andrew). Andreas, clericus Moraviensis, in record, a. 1242 (RAA., I, p. 144), Andrew, a monk of Dunfermline, became bishop of Caithness in the reign of David I. [Duncan] fiz Andrew of the county of Dumfries rendered homage in 1296 (*Bain*, II, 810), and John, son of Andree de Huchtirardor (Auchterarder) had a charter of a tenement in Hachtirardor in 1330 (RAA., II, p. 6). John Andree and Adam Andree were present at the perambulation of the boundaries of Kyrknes and Louchor in 1395 (RPSA., p. 3), Wielelmus Andro and Johannes Andro were common councillors of Aberdeen, 1399 (*Guildry*, p. 184), and Malcolm Andree was a tenant of the bishop of Aberdeen in 1511 (REA., I, p. 375). James Andro and Kethrin Andro were 'fylit of picry' (pilfering) in 1488 (*Lanark*, p. 1), Alexander Andree was sergeand in Aberdeen in 1463, Alene Andro had a tack of two oxgangs in Bellady in 1514 (*Cupar-Angus*, I, p. 294), and Magister Alexander Andro was retoured heir in lands in Glasgow in 1605 (*Retours, Lanark*, 53). Androe 1661, Androw 1546.

ANDREWES, ANDREWS, 'son of ANDREW', q.v.

ANDREWSON. "Son of ANDREW," q.v. John Andrewson was admitted burgess of Aberdeen in 1444 (NSCM., I, p. 8). Cuthbert Androsone appears as a witness in Dumfries in 1477 (*Edgar*, p. 227), Jhone Androsone was admitted burgess of Dunfermline "throw resone of his wyf Alesone Bowlyrwell" in 1492 (DBR., 39), and Thomas Androson was admitted burgess of Aberdeen in 1475 (NSCM., I, p. 24). Androssoun 1625. The surname is now very common under the form ANDERSON.

ANDSON. John Andson, provost of Arbroath in 1811 (died 1814), shortened his name from Anderson, "in order the better to distinguish himself from a considerable number of persons of the same name who in his time did business as merchants in Arbroath" (Hay, *Arbroath*, p. 358).

ANECOL. Anakol, a Hebridean viking, "a man of a noble family and hardy," Earl Erland's right-hand man (*raðgjafi*), appears c. 1150 (*OSag.*, p. 154). Anecol witnesses a charter by Gilbert de Strathearn, c. 1200 (LAC., p. 47). As Anechull, Anechul, Anechol, Anecol or Anecholle, thane of Dunning, he appears as witness in other charters by Gilbert, earl of Strathearn, c. 1199–1200 (*Inchaffray*, p. 3, 8, 12, 14, 18). Anekol or Anecol was a witness in a jury trial concerning the lands of Monachkeneran, 1233 (RMP., p. 167). Anakol, an Irish farmer, is mentioned 992 (*Floamanna Saga*, c. 28). See MACANECOL.

ANEWITH. The land of William de Anewith mentioned c. 1220 (*Dryburgh*, 54). He probably derived his name from Anwoth, Kirkcudbrightshire (a. 1200 Anewith).

ANGUS. (1) G. *Aonghas* or *Aonghus*, Ir. *Aonghus*, EIr. *Óengus*, OIr. *Óingus*, W. *Ungust* (*Lib. Landav.*, 201). In Adamnan (V. C., I, 3) the name appears as *Oingusius* (with alternative reading *Oingussius*), the name of the man for whom Columba prophesied a long life and a peaceful end. This last form points to an older °*Oino-gustu-s* 'unique-choice-one.' The first part of the name is the stem of G. *aon* 'one,' the latter part being the same in root (*gu*) as English *choice, choose*. As a forename it is now frequently turned into Æneas, Eneas, and even Ennis. The pronunciation of the name varies considerably in the Gaelic dialects. In South Uist it is Aonas, and Naoghas in Arran, Kintyre, Islay, and Skye.

The first of the name recorded in Scotland was Angus, one of the three sons of Eochaidh, who took possession of Isla and Jura. The name of the Pictish king, Onnust filius Urgust, who died c. 761, is the same. In the different versions of the Pictish and Scots chronicles his name is miswritten Hungus, Denegus, Tenegus, Tenogus, and Tonogus (CPS., p. 150, 173, 201, 286, 301). With the Macdonalds of Islay Angus was a favorite personal name, and it is possible that the Macinneses were a branch of that family. Angus, son of Somerled c. 1150 (*Ork. Saga*, 110). Angus mac Dunec' was one of the perambulators of the lands of Balfeith or Balphe in Angus c. 1204–1211 (RAA., I, p. 60). Anggues 1588.

(2) of local origin from the district of the name. Serlo de Anegus witnessed a composition anent the tithes of Strathvlif in 1229 (REM., p. 87). Eva de Anegos of the county of Forfare rendered homage in 1296 (*Bain*, II, p. 199). William de Anegus was a Scots

ANGUS, *continued*

prisoner taken at Dunbar Castle in 1297, and Edward de Anegous and Laurence of Angus were Scots prisoners taken in the capture of Stirling Castle in 1305 (ibid., II, 877, 1089, 1641, 1644). Michael of Angous, a Scotsman, in 1358, "was foremost at the last capture of the town of Berwick by the Scots, and leapt over the walls the night it was taken" (ibid., IV, p. 6). He may be the Michael of Angus who served on an inquest at Berwick-on-Tweed in 1370 (ibid., IV, 175). William de Angus was abbot of Londoris (Lindores) in 1391 (RMS., I, 852), David Angus witnessed a charter by Archibald, earl of Douglas in 1470 (*Home*, p. 22), John Angus of the convent of Dunfermline is mentioned in 1555 (*Laing*, 633), Andrew Anguis was a beidman in Edinburgh in 1573 (*Soltre*, p. 226), and George Fife Angas, the father and founder of South Australia, was of Scottish descent. Several of the name occur in the Rental Book of the Cistercian Abbey of Cupar-Angus. Angowss 1570, Anguss 1456.

ANGUSSON, 'son of ANGUS,' q.v., but most likely an Englishing of MACANGUS, q.v. Philip Angusie was burgess of Montrose, 1435 (REB., II, 47). John Angusson was tenant of Kethyk c. 1442 (*Cupar-Angus*, I, p. 119), and Thomas Angusson was a witness in Inverness in 1450 (*Invernessiana*, p. 119). William Angusson was admitted burgess of Aberdeen, 1451 (NSCM., I, p. 13), Gilcrist Angusii occupied the lands of Chapeltoun of Buquhadrok in 1475 (SBR., p. 256), and Alexander Angosone is mentioned in Aberdeen in 1493 (CRA., p. 49). Donald Angussoun was concerned in the 'Spulzie of Kilravock' in 1497 (*Rose*, p. 166), John Angussoun was tacksman of Myre, North Sanduik, Orkney, in 1503 (REO., p. 417), and Thomas Angousone was a tenant under the bishop of Aberdeen, 1511 (REA., I, p. 361). In 1510 a warrant was issued for the apprehension of the murderers of Alexander Angusone (RSCA., I, p. 42, 97). William Angusson was tenant of part of Cullychmoir, Delny, in 1539 (ER., XVII, p. 667), Sir William Angussoun was vicar pensionary of Boware, Caithness, 1542 (OPS., II, p. 783), William Angussone was a follower of Murdow McCloyd in his attack on the galley of the laird of Balcomie in 1600 (RPC., XIV, p. cxxiii), and Angus Angussone was burgess of Dornoch in 1630 (OPS., II, p. 644). Angoussoun 1600.

ANISOUN. A metronymic. 'Son of Annie.' George Anisoun indweller in Selkirk, 1590 (RPC., IV, p. 522).

ANKETYN. A variant of ON. *Ásketil*. (For the variation see *Björkman* I, p. 17–19). Anketin, a monk of Glasgow, c. 1175–99 (REG., p. 37). Dominus Anketyn witnessed the gift of three marks of silver annually to the Abbey of Lindores, c. 1232–37 (LAC., p. 94). He may be the dominus Anketill de Foleuille who witnessed gift of a toft in Dundee at the same period (ibid., p. 97). Anketin Malore "who was in the king's service in Scotland" in 1252, appears again as Anketille Malore (*Bain*, I, 1892, 1936). See also ASCELINUS.

ANKRET. A surname recorded in Aberdeen in the seventeenth century. Macfarlane (GC., II, p. 68) has Auket or Aukret, a burgess of Aberdeen, perhaps a miscopying. It may be from *anchoret*, 'a recluse.'

ANNA. Perhaps of local origin. Anna or Annay, a river island, a holm (Roxburgh — *Scot. nat. dict.*). John Anna, indweller in Edinburgh, 1690 (*Edinb. Marr.*).

ANNAL, ANNALL. Jonet Annall at Kippow, parish of Craill, 1550, and one more of the name (*St. Andrews*). David Annall was married in Edinburgh, 1675 (*Edinb. Marr.*). The spelling Annal is found in Orkney. Annal recorded in St. Margaret's Hope 1941. Annell 1589.

ANNAN. (1) From Annan in Dumfriesshire. William de Anand witnessed a grant of two carucates in the fee of Egilfechan to Robert de Brus, 1249 (*Bain*, I, 1793; *Annandale*, I, p. 7), and John de Anand was cleric of William, bishop of Glasgow, 1255 (*Soltre*, p. 34). Walter Danande (for d'Anande) was juror on an inquest held at Dumfries, 1304 (*Bain*, II, p. 412), and Andrew Annan was tailor in Ayr in 1684 (RPC., 3. ser. X, p. 366). (2) A family of this name, prominent in Angus from at least the thirteenth century, derived their name from the lands of Inyaney or Aneny now called Ananias. In old records the place name appears as Annand, Annane, Annanie, Inyaney, Inieneny, Inyoney, Inyanee, Inneane, and Inianey (Jervise, *Memorials*, p. 48). Adam de Anand, canon of Dunkeld, who witnessed charters by Gamelin, bishop of St. Andrews, between 1255–1271 (RPSA., p. 172, 311), is perhaps first of the name recorded. He is probably A. de Anand, rector of Monimail, 1269 (ibid., p. 174). William de Anaund of Forfarshire rendered homage in 1296. His seal bears a boar's head, couped, S'Will' de An . . . (*Bain*, II, p. 199, 552). Henry de Anand was sheriff of Clackmannan, 1328 (ER., I, p. 104). William of Anand one of the assize on the marches of Woodwrae, 1388 (*Bamff*, p. 22), as Willelmus de Anandia was juror on assize in 1389 regarding the mill-lands of Quarelwode in Moray (REM., p. 171). A family of the name was eminent in the municipal history of Dundee (*Wedd.*, p. 80), and other families of the name were in Aberdeenshire (*Fermartyn*, p. 488) and Fife in the fifteenth and sixteenth centuries. The Annands of Angus ended in the middle of the sixteenth century in an heiress who sold the estate to Cardinal Beaton (Jervise, *Land of Lindsays*, p. 173). Thomas Annand, tailor in Perth, 1551 (*Rollok*, 89). Annand 1575.

ANNANDALE, ANNADALE. Of local origin from the district of the name in Dumfriesshire. The name has never been a common one. Elspet Anandel in Nether Tullo, 1657 (*Brechin*). N. Annandale published his *The Faroes and Shetland*, 1905; Thomas Annandale (1838–1907) was senior surgeon, Edinburgh Royal Infirmary, and Dr. Charles Annandale (1843–1915), lexicographer. Old forms are: Annerdaill, Annardale, and (1662) Annandaill.

ANNAT. This surname, found in Dornoch, may be derived from the davoch named Annat in the parish of Kiltarlity, Inverness-shire.

ANNECOMBE. John de Annecombe of Roxburghshire rendered homage, 1296 (*Bain*, II, p. 209).

ANNIESTON. From Annieston in the parish of Covington, Lanarkshire. Symon of Aynestone, of the county of Lanark, swore fealty to Edward I in 1296 (*Bain*, II, p. 213). Anneis de Brus, to whom, about 1180 the right of patronage of the church of Thankerton belonged, is supposed to have given name to the land (*Kelso*, p. 227; OPS., I, p. 143).

ANSDELL. Of recent introduction from England. Probably from Ainsdale, a hamlet in Lancashire.

ANSTIE. Elspeth Anstie in Insharnoch, 1692 (*Moray*), probably derived her surname from one or other of the places named Anstey in England.

ANSTRUTHER. Of territorial origin from the old lands of Anstruther in Fife. William de Candela was possessed of the barony at his death in 1153. His son, also named William, was a beneficiary of Balmerino Abbey sometime after 1165. These de Candelas were of the Norman family of Malherbe, who held the lands of Candel in Dorset *in capite* in the eleventh and twelfth centuries. Henry, son of the second William de Candela, appears to have been the first to assume the territorial designation of Anstruther. As Henricus de Ainestrother he witnessed the gift of fifteen acres of Balmulinauch (Balmerino) to the church of St. Andrews by Adam de Stawell before 1225 (RPSA., p. 272). Gaufridus de Einstrother witnessed a charter of the lands of Ardarie in Fife to the Priory of May by William de Beauier before 1214 (ibid., p. 382). In 1288 Henry de Aynstrother was found heir to his father in the fourth part of the lands of Hethrintone in Tyndale (*Bain*, 340; Moore, *Lands*, p. 84). As Henry de Anstrother or Aynestrothere of Fife he rendered homage in 1296, and in 1304 had his lands in Tyndale restored to him (*Bain*, II, 508, p. 204, 415). William, son of Henry de Aynestrothir gave "tres bothas" in the vill of Aynestrothir to the Abbey of Dryburgh, c. 1320 (*Dryburgh*, p. 16, 251), and an obligation by Cristina relict of Andrew de Aynstrother is recorded in 1336 (*Scon*, 166). The barons of Anstrude of the seigniory of Barry are descended from a David Anstruther, an officer of the Scots Guards of France. Anstrothir 1490, Anstroyer 1585, Anstryuzir 1571, Enstruther 1691; Andstroyer, Anstroder, Ansteruthyr, Anstrother.

ANTENSOUN, 'son of Anton' or Antony. Thomas Antenessoun in Dunrossness, Shetland, 1602 (Mill, *Diary*, p. 180). Peter Antones, beadle in Dysart, 1638 (PBK., p. 135), a variant. Manse Antonsoun is in Coluasetter, 1625, and William Antonioussoun in Sandwick, a witness, 1626 (OSS., I, 118, 159).

ANTHONY. From the Latin personal name *Antonius*, 'inestimable or worthy of praise.' Magister Antonius, a Lombard physician, obtained a grant of the lands of Fulton from Alan senescallus Scotie a. 1204 (RMP., p. 53). Thomas Anthony in Clashbenny, parish of Abirlott, 1607, and eight more are recorded in St. Andrews Commissariot Record, and Isobel Anthonie appears in Edinburgh, 1664 (*Edinb. Marr.*). In Middle Scots this name took the form ANTON, q.v. The *h* is thought to be due to Dutch form Anthonius, also common in mediaeval Latin.

ANTON. A shortened form of the Latin name *Antonius*, meaning 'well-beloved or inestimable.' Anthony is a common mediaeval misspelling. The name was introduced into Britain by the Normans in the French form *Antoine*. Margaret Anton is recorded in Edinburgh in

ANTON, *continued*

1689 *(Edinb. Marr.)*, Christian Antoun in Carpow in 1631 *(Dunblane)*, Katherine Antoun in Clochie, parish of Lethnot, in 1677 *(Brechin)*. John Anton appears in Robiestoun, Aberdeenshire, in 1716 (SCM., IV, p. 172), and John Anton was member of the Huntly Volunteers in 1798 *(Will*, p. 7). As forename: Anton Andersone, Inverness 1623 *(Rec. Inv.*, II, p. 162).

AODH. The later form of AED, q.v. In the late Middle Ages it was mistakenly equated with Teutonic Hugh or Hugo, and in some Latin documents it has been rendered Odo and Odoneus. Latterly it became, as Dr. Macbain remarked, "a mere grunt," e.g. Odo or Y M'Ky (of Stranavern) 1529 (OPS., II, p. 710). Odo or Y Makky in Straithnauern had grant of the forfeited lands of Alexander Suthirland in 1499 (OPS., II, p. 635; RMS., II.). "There are various instances in which two brothers may be found, the one called Aodh and the other Hugh, as, for example, the family of Donald, 1st Lord Reay, where first and third sone were so named respectively" (*Book of Mackay*, p. 5).

APE. Helen Ape in the Regality of Spynie was accused of theft in 1596 (SCM., II, p. 132). *Ape* is the OE. feminine of *Apa*, an ape, and was also a personal name, though perhaps an uncomplimentary one. It was also used as a by-name among the Norsemen, *Api*, fool. As a personal name it is in record in England ante 1066 *(Searle)*. Förstemann considers *Aba*, 'man,' the root of the name. Cf. Björkman, *Zur englischen Namenkunde*, p. 13–14.

APLINDENE. Radulph de Aplindene appears in 1200 *(Melros)*. Robertus de Applingdene in Annandale was forfeited c. 1315 (RMS., I, 93). See *Transactions, Dumfriesshire and Galloway Natural History and Antiquarian Society*, 3. ser. 16, p. 34. Cf. APPLETON.

APPLEBIE. Of local origin from some place of the name in England, perhaps Appleby in Westmorland. Robert de Appilby appears as a witness in 1257 (LSC., p. 80), and John Aplebie, litster, is in record in Edinburgh in 1661 *(Edinb. Marr.)*. James Appleby, merchant in Dumfries, 1798 *(Dumfries)*.

APPLEGARTH. Of local origin from Applegarth near Lockerbie, Dumfriesshire. The *Catholicon Anglicum* defines an "Appellegarth" as *pometum*. William Apilgarth witnessed a grant to Cambuskenneth Abbey c. 1190 *(Cambus.*, p. 80), and Richard of Aplegarth was a hobelar in the garrison of Roxburgh in 1340 *(Bain*, III, 1382).

APPLETON. Probably from Appleton in Yorkshire although there is more than one place of the name in England. Robert de Aplinden or Aplintoune in Annandale was forfeited in the reign of Robert Bruce (RMS., I, p. 520). Robert de Aplinton or Appylton had a charter of land in the burgh of Invernys from Robert II in 1378 (RMS., I, 649, 683), and two years later, as de Apyltoun, he reappears as a burgess and person of consequence in the burgh *(Invernessiana*, p. 79, 80). He is doubtless the Robert of Appyltoun who witnessed a charter by Hugh Fraser, lord of Kynnelle, of land in Angus c. 1390 *(Southesk.* p. 718). Cf. APLINDENE.

AQUHAITH. Of local origin from a place of the name in Aberdeenshire, perhaps Aquhythie near Kenmay or perhaps Auchquhach of *Aberdeen Retours* 1629, no. 214. Andrew Aquhaith, fermorar in Aberdeen, 1625, reappears in 1633 and 1637 as Aquhath and Auquhaith (RSCA., II, p. 287, 364, 447). cf. AQUHARCHE.

AQUHARCHE. Local. Andrew Aquharche in Aberdeen, 1629 (RPC., 2. ser. III, p. 344). cf. AQUHAITH.

AQUHONAN. Local. A contract of marriage between Aquhonam and Agnes Makcalpyn, 1475 (SBR., p. 256). Isobel Aquhynanne in Keith, Banffshire, 1646 *(Strathbogie*, p. 70).

ARBEKIE. Probably from Arbikie in the parish of Lunan in Angus. The seal of Thomas de Arbeke is appended to an instrument of 1453 *(Seals*, 43; *Macdonald*, 36). Alexander Ardbekye of that Ilk (1476) sold an eighth part of his land of Thanistoun in the thanage of Kintore in 1481 *(View*, p. 576; *Inverurie*, p. 120), John Ardbekie in the Spittell is mentioned in 1595, and George Arbekie was juror on an assize in Auld Aberdeen in 1603 (RSCA., I, p. 331; II, p. 25).

ARBIGLAND. From Arbigland in the parish of Kirkbean, Kirkcudbrightshire. Thomas de Arbigland who witnessed a grant of land by Thomas, son of Andrew de Kyrconeuel to the Abbey of Holmcoltram c. 1280–1290 *(Holm-Coltram*, p. 58) is doubtless the Thomas de Erbygland who was juror on an inquisition made at Berwick before the sheriff of Dumfries in August 1296, and who, as de Arbygelande, appears again as juror on an inquisition made at Dumfries in 1304 *(Bain*, II, 824, 1588).

ARBLASTER. A cross-bowman. Probably never became a fixed surname in Scotland. Walter le Arblaster, burgess of Edinburgh, rendered homage in 1296 (*Bain*, II, p. 197).

ARBROATH. From the town of Arbroath in Angus. Adam de Aberbrothoc was rector of the church of Machlin, 1292 (*Bain*, II, p. 146). Patricius de Aberbrothoc had a charter of land in Kircgat, Aberdeen, c. 1311–17 (RAA., I, p. 203). Walter de Abyrbroth was chancellor of the church of Brechin, 1450 (REB., I, p. 132), and Alan Arbroth is in record in Newburgh, 1479 (*Laing*, 153).

ARBUCKLE. Of local origin from Arbuckle in Lanarkshire. John Arnbukle appears as witness in Irvine, 1499 (*Simon*, 18), a later John Arbukile purchased a land in Glasgow, 1511 (*Protocols*, I), and Alexander Arbukill appears as curate of Galston in the same year. Elizabeth Arbucle is recorded in the parish of Carluke in 1624 (*Lanark CR.*). William Arbuckles or Arbucles, merchant in Glasgow, applied to the Privy Council for the job of transporting prisoners (Covenanters) to New England in 1685 (RPC., 3. ser. XI, p. 94). John Arbuckle (1838–1912), philanthropist and sugar refiner, was born in Scotland. Arbuckls 1687, Arbukle 1551, Arbukles 1656, Arnbunkill 1616, Arnbukle 1506.

ARBUTHNOT, ARBUTHNOTT. Of territorial origin from the old barony now the parish of the same name in Kincardineshire. The first of the name in record appears to have been Hugh de Aberbothenoth, who flourished in the reign of William the Lion, and was variously designated 'Dominus' and 'Thanus' de Aberbuthenoth. He obtained his lands from Walter Olifard, son or nephew of Osbert Olifard, sheriff of the Mearns, who died before 1206. In 1206 a dispute between Duncan Aberbuthenoth and the bishop of St. Andrews "super terra de Aberbuthenoth que appellatur Kirktoun" was settled in favor of the bishop (SCM., V, p. 210). Allewinus or Alwinus de Aberbutennauth witnessed two deeds prior to 1241 granted by Christina, daughter of Walter Corbet, in·favor of the Priory of St. Andrews (RPSA., p. 263, 278). Hugh de Abirbuthenoth granted the church of Garuoch to the monastery of Arbroath in 1282 (RAA., I, 314). This Hugh was commonly designated Hugo Blundus or Le Blond from the flaxen color of his hair (*Sc. Peer.*, I, p. 274). Philip de Arbuthnott who succeeded in 1335 (or 1355) appears to have been the first designated *dominus ejusdem*, 'of that Ilk.' In the early part of the eighteenth century the Arbuthnets are described as "the most thriving name" in Peter-

head (CAB., p. 415). The museum in Peterhead was formed by Adam Arbuthnot, merchant there, and bequeathed to the town in 1851. Aberbuthnocht 1443, Arbuthnat 1490, Arbuthnet 1639, Arbuthneth 1583, Arbuthnoth 1513; Aberbuthno.

ARCHEDENISSON, 'son of the arch-dean.' Donald Archedenisson was tenant of Drumnamark, Ardmanoch, in 1504 (ER., XII, p. 661).

ARCHER. This is an English rather than a Scottish surname, and there were few families of the name in Scotland until within a recent period. Patrick le Archer of the county of Are rendered homage in 1296 (*Bain*, II, p. 202), John Archer was vicar of Carrale in 1413 (RPSA., p. 18), and in 1433 there is record of demission of a toft in Portyncrag to Michael Archer (RAA., II, 63). Thomas Archer was treasurer of Brechin in 1439 (REB., I, p. 87), and Jhonne Archar is in record in Scone, 1551 (*Rollok*, 99). The name is also found in Edinburgh in the sixteenth century, and occurs in Haddington in 1543 as Archear. William Archer (1856–1924), dramatic critic and translator of Ibsen, was born in Perth.

ARCHES. Herbert de Arches witnessed a charter of the lands of Lesslyn (Leslie) to Malcolm filius Bartholf c. 1171–99 (CAB., p. 547). Gilbertus de Arches witnessed confirmation of sale of the land of Scrogges to the church of Glasgow c. 1208–13 (REG., p. 76). Perhaps from Arques near Dieppe.

ARCHIBALD. A surname derived from the personal name Archibald, in OE. *Arcebald*, *Arcenbald*, or *Ercenbald*, and doubtfully explained as meaning "right bold," or "holy prince." Archebaldus filius Swani de Forgrunde is mentioned in reign of William the Lion (*Scon*, p. 21). Erchenbaldus, Abbot of Dunfermelyne mentioned c. 1180, appears again in the same record as Arkebaldus and Arkenbaldus (*Scon*, p. 25, 27, 33). Thomas, the brother of Erkenbaldus, witnessed the gift of the church of Kilmaurs to the Abbey of Kelso before 1189 (*Kelso*, 284), and Arkembaldus de Duffus was witness to an agreement between the bishop of Moray and John Byseth concerning the churches of Coneway and Dulbatelauch between 1203–34 (REM., p. 16). Robert Archebalde had a charter of the Hospital of Roxburgh in 1390 from Robert III (RMS., I, 803), and John Archibald was a witness in St. Andrews in 1545 (*Laing*, 494). The OF. form of the personal name is found in Archambaud (earl of Douglas), 1405 (*Bain*, IV, 697). Harrison's explanation of the use of Archibald for Gaelic Gillespie is prob-

ARCHIBALD, *continued*

ably correct: "Archibald was adopted by the Scots as a Lowland equivalent of Gillespie because the -*bald* was mistakenly supposed to mean 'hairless,' 'shaven,' 'servant,' and therefore to be equivalent to Gael. *gille,* 'servant,' 'shaven one,' 'monk' ". Harchbald (earl of Argyll) 1493, Archombaldus 1233, Arkanbaldus 1228, Enkerbaldus a. 1189.

ARCHIBALDSON, 'son of ARCHIBALD,' q.v. Malcolm Erchebaudessone of Peeblesshire rendered homage, 1296 (*Bain*, II, p. 207). Janet Archibauldson in Daltoun 1628 (*Dumfries*).

ARCHIE. A diminutive of ARCHIBALD, q.v. John Archie alias Jamesone in Dalfour (RSCA., II, p. 347). Nisbet says "of that Ilk," but does not say where the place is. As forename: Erche Kinzerd in Kelso, 1567.

ARCHIESON. 'Son of ARCHIE,' the diminutive of Archibald. William Archibald, i.e. Archibald's son, witnessed a grant of the office of derethy of Tarves in 1463 (RAA., II, p. 129). Action was taken against James Archieson in Cleckmae in 1670 (RRM., II, p. 254).

ARD. The family of De Lard (i.e. De Ard or De la Ard) took its name from 'The Aird,' a district in the Vale of Beauly. There are persons of this name still in Rosskeen. In July, 1297, a writer, believed to have been William Fitzwarine, then the constable of Urquhart Castle, wrote to Edward I, stating that John del Ard or de Laarde to whom he was indebted for his personal safety and the lives of his children, had a son, Cristin, who was taken prisoner in Dunbar Castle the year before. The writer begs that this son may be sent to his assistance at Urcharde (Urquhart) as his appearance there would be of great service to the English (*Sc. Peer.*, IV, p. 44–45 – a facsimile of the letter is given in Mackay's *Urquhart and Glenmoriston*, 2. ed., opp. p. 20). The request was not granted, and Cristin remained prisoner until 1302 (*Bain*, II, 1283). Andrew de Ard was a charter witness, 1321 (REA., I, p. 47), and provision of a canonry of Aberdeen was made to David de Lard, 1336 (*Pap. Lett.*, II, p. 535). Godfrey del Arde forfeited a third of Wester Fentone, 1337 (*Bain*, III, p. 387), and in 1342 he forcibly retained the ward and marriage of his heir and daughter Isabella (ER., I, p. 504). John filius Hugonis de Cristino de Ard held land in Inverness, 1361 (REM., p. 306), the lands of Alexander de le Arde are mentioned in 1374 (RMS., I, 600), and in 1536 there is recorded the escheat

of Donald Ard (RSS., II, 2037). Donald Ard was servitor to the bishop of Moray, 1567 (REM., p. 400). The form AIRD also occurs in Ross.

ARDAUCH. Eustace de Ardath who witnessed a charter of part of Auchynlec to Waldeu filius Boydini c. 1160–1180 (*Kelso*, 115), derived his name from the lands of Ardauch which he possessed at the end of the twelfth century. William of Ardauch or Ardach is mentioned in a charter of the land of Fincurrok of the beginning of the thirteenth century (ibid., p. 79–80). In 1266 these lands of Ardauch were resigned by Robert, called Franc' of Lambiniston, the grandson of William, in favor of the Abbot and convent of Kelso (ibid., p. 156). ·

ARDEBETHEY. Lorn de Ardebethey of Perthshire rendered homage in 1296 (*Bain*, II, p. 200). Perhaps from the Ardbeath of Perth Retours, 1616 (no. 236).

ARDENA. Osber or Osbert de Ardena (the -a is merely the Latin ending) witnessed the *Inquisitio* by Earl David as to the extent of the lands of the church of Glasgow, c. 1124 (REG., p. 5), and also David's great charter to Melrose, 1143–44 (*Nat. MSS.*, I, 17). Sir Ralph de Ardena was an envoy of Sir Robert de Brus, earl of Carrik, 1293 (*Bain*, II, p. 158). According to Lower and Bardsley this name is the same as ARDERNE, q.v.

ARDERNE. Sir Alexander de Arderne swore fealty to Edward I at St. Andrews in 1291 (*Bain*, II, 508), and Robert Arderne, merchant of Scotland, petitioned for aid in 1427 (*Bain*, IV, 1014). From Arderne in Cheshire, England, where a family of the name existed early in the thirteenth century.

ARDES. A corruption of ALLARDYCE, q.v. Ardes of that Ilk is recorded but no particulars given (*Macfarlane*, II, p. 82). Andrew Ardes in Aberdeen was bewitched in 1596 (SCM., I, p. 85), John Ardess was messenger in Brechin, 1603 (REB., II, 233), John Ardes appears in Bakiehill, Aberdeenshire, 1620 (RSCA., II, 241), and George Ardese was pedall in Kilconquhar, Fife, 1640.

ARDINCAPLE, ARNCAPLE. Of territorial origin from the barony of Ardincaple in the parish of Row, Dumbartonshire. By the fifteenth century Ardincaple had become an ordinary surname and several individuals of the name appear in record. Morice de Arncappel of the county of Dunbretan rendered homage in 1296. His seal bears a stag's head cabossed, between the antlers a small animal and fleur-de-lys, and S' *Mavric de Arncapil* (*Bain*, II, p. 202, 545). Laing (*Seals. Supp.*, 49) describes an early seal of Mary de Arncaple heraldically identical with this one, and probably "Marie" is a misreading on his part of the name "Mavric." Johannes de Ardenagappill, charter witness in Lennox, c. 1364 (HP., IV, p. 16). Arthur de Ardincapel witnessed a charter by Duncan, eighth earl of Lennox c. 1390 (*Levenax*, p. 77). In 1489 a remission was granted Robert Arnegapill for his part in holding Dumbarton Castle against the King (APS., XII, p. 34), and in the following year John Ardyncapill witnessed an instrument of sasine in favor of Mathew Stevart, son of the earl of Lennox (*Lennox*, II, p. 140). Aulay Arngapill of that Ilk is mentioned in 1513 (RSS., I, 2613), and in 1529 there is recorded the escheat of the goods of Awlane (a miscopying of Awlaue = Aulay) Ardincapill of that Ilk (ibid., II, 341). In the time of King James v Alexander "then the head of the family, took a fancy to call himself Alexander Macaulay of Ardincaple, from a predecessor of his of the name of Aulay, to humour a patronymical designation as being more agreeable to the head of a clan than the designation of Ardincaple of that Ilk" (Nisbet, *Heraldry*, II. Remarks on Ragman Roll, p. 35).

ARDIST. Ada de Ardist who witnessed a charter by Hugo de Nidin of lands in Fife, c. 1204–28, and the gift by Henry Reuel and Margaret his spouse to the prior and canons of St. Andrews in the early part of the thirteenth century (SHSM., IV, p. 312; RPSA., p. 271), derived his name from the lands of Ardist in Balmerino parish, a now forgotten place name. (In RPSA. the name has been miscopied as Ardift.) Alexander de Ardist, another charter witness in Fife appears c. 1245 (RPSA., p. 44, 282, 283, 293). The name of Derlig [= Derling] de Arfdift who witnessed a gift by Duncan, earl of Fife to the nuns of North Berwick a. 1177 (CMN., p. 6) may be a misspelling of Ardist, the long s being misread f). Ardist may have been merely a variation of the name Ardint; or, though less probably, it may have denoted a place so-called in Leuchars parish, and now known as Airdit (Campbell, *Balmerino*, p. 58).

ARDIT. A family of this name failed after three generations. Malcolm, earl of Fife (d. 1266) granted these lands to Johannes de Ardit for homage and service.

ARDLER. From the lands of the same name in the parish of Kettins in Angus. Ingraham Ardler received from King David II a charter of the lands of Baleorie (now Baldowrie), in the sheriffdom of Forfar (RMS., I, App. II, 785). In 1369 John de Ardlere had a charter of all and whole the lands of Ardlere and Baldowry (RMS., I, 344), and in 1384 had an annual rent from the two towns of Kelore (Keilor) (ibid., I, 726).

ARDROSS. From the lands of Ardross near Elie, Fife. Margareta de Ardrosse filia domini Merleswan resigned a land in the tenement of Innergelly, c. 1281 (*Dryburgh*, 13). Ela de Ardros of the county of Fife, an unmarried woman, rendered homage in 1296, and in the same year the sheriff of Fife was directed to restore to her her lands (*Bain*, II, p. 204, 224).

ARDROSSAN. The old family of this name, originally de Barclays, according to the usage of their time took their surname from their new possessions. The family ended in the direct line in Godfrey, about the end of the reign of David II (*Pont.*, p. 58–61). In 1271 Bricius de Ardrossane granted to the Abbey and convent of Insula Missarum (Inchaffray) "sexdecim acras terre citas juxta pontem abbathie ex parte orientali in campo qui vocatur Langflath" (LIM., 21). Sir Fergus of Ardrossan who witnessed a charter by Alexander de Dunhon of the lands of Akencloy Nether, c. 1285 (HMC., 2. Rep., App., p. 166) may be the Fergus de Ardrossan who was granted the barony of Bishoplande near Kirkintogloche by Edward II in 1312 (*Bain*, III, 265). Godfrey de Ardrossan swore fealty to England at Montrose in 1296 (ibid., II, 770). Fergus de Ardrossan and Robert his brother were prisoners in England in 1305 (ibid., II, 1668), and Hugh de Ardrossan late rebel, received back his forfeited lands in the same year (ibid., 1696).

ARDSOUN. Andrew Ardsoun was one of the tenants of Estir Mecra (Easter Micras) in 1539 (ER., XVII, p. 659). Perhaps an Anglicized form of Mac(H)ardy.

ARDUTHIE. From Arduthie or Arduthy in the parish of Fetteresso. John Arduthy, merchant in Leyth, is mentioned in 1554 (EBR., p. 310), and Bessy Arduthy was summoned before the Kirk Session of St. Andrews in 1581 (*St. Andrews*, I, p. 467, 470). The name of Robert Arduthre, who witnessed a grant to the Abbey of Cambuskenneth in 1521 (*Cambus.*, p. 10), is probably from the same source. Thomas Arduthoue of Lungar, Kincardineshire, had a charter of confirmation, 1531 (RSS., II, 1062).

ARDWYKESTONE. Local. Adam de Ardwykestone of Lanarkshire rendered homage, 1296 (*Bain*, II, p. 210).

ARGENT. From Argent or Argentan in France. In an undated charter of the reign of David II the lands of Lethbertsheills forfeited by William Lundie were bestowed upon Adam Argente (RMS., I, App. II, 875), and in April 1370 there is a confirmation by the same king of a charter by Adam de Argent (mis-spelled Salver in the British Museum MS.) to Marjory his spouse of the land of Lethberde schelis with pertinents (RMS., I, 320). By a charter of Robert II dated 19th day of March in the sixth year of the king's reign (1377) the lands of Lethberdschelis with pertinents in the constabulary of Lynlithcu, resigned by Ade de Argent, were bestowed upon Robert, earl of Fife and Meneteth (ibid., I, 571).

ARGENTOCOXOS. 'White hip' (Lat. *coxa*) or 'White foot.' The old British (Pictish) name of the Pictish chief, "husband of the lady whose remarkable conversation with Julia Domna, wife of the emperor Severus, respecting Pictish morals, is summarized in the abridgment of Dion Cassius" (Dion, LXXVI. 16.5).

ARGO. An Aberdeenshire surname. Margaret Argo author of *Janet's choice, a Scots play,* 1921; Dr. G. Emslie Argo died 1931.

ARICARI. A surname found in Aberdeen. It is an abbreviated form of HERRIEGERRIE, which again is a corrupt pronunciation of GARIOCH, q.v.

ARIES. A surname found in the shire of Kirkcudbright. Of local origin from Airies in the parish of Kirkcolm or Airies in parish of Kirkinner. In Timothy Pont's map of Galloway the place names are spelled Aryes and Aries.

ARKLAY, ARKLEY, ARKLIE. A surname in Angus. The old family of the name in the parish of Murroes, Angus, are said to have come from the Lennox country. James Arclay was admitted burgess of Aberdeen, 1595 (NSCM., I, p. 88), and Elizabeth Arkley was married in Edinburgh, 1688 (*Edinb. Marr.*). Patrick Arkley was one of the sheriffs of Edinburgh in last century.

ARKLE. From *Arkil* the Old Danish and Old Swedish form of the Old Norse personal name *Arnketill.* Arkill the seneschal witnessed a grant by Gillemor, son of Gilleconel to the church of Lesmahagow before 1144 (*Kelso,* 187). Henricus filius Arkilli witnessed a charter by Hugh de Normanville of the lands of Kelvesete (Kelfsete in body of the charter) and Faulawe to the Abbey of Melrose in the reign of William the Lion (*Melros,* I, p. 81). A later Arkill was seneschal of Machen,

c. 1249–86 (RHM., I, p. 5), and another Arkil held land near Haddington in the reign of David II (*Lawrie,* p. 149). Malcolm Arkle was admitted burgess of Aberdeen in 1534 (NSCM., I, p. 53), and John Arkill held land in Clackmannane in 1537 (ER., XVII, p. 737). Robert Arkill was occupier of Quhithauch in 1574 (RRM., III, p. 260), Jean Arcle in Knokane is in record in 1590 (RPC., IV, p. 483), and the name occurs in Ayrshire in 1565 as Arkill (*Laing*). The surname is still common in Northumberland. The first Arkill mentioned above may be the individual who gave name to Arkleston near Paisley.

ARMIT. Mariota Armit is recorded in Strogeth, n.d. (*Dunblane*) and George Armitt was shipmaster in St. Andrews, 1751 (*St. Andrews*). Perhaps from ME. *(h)ermite,* 'a hermit.' Cf. English surname ARMITAGE.

ARMOUR. Metonymic for armourer, 'a maker of armour.' In 1297 Adam le Armorere and Gunnore his wife made petition for redress against a distraint by the parson of Forde at Berwick (*Bain,* II, 967), Simon le Armurer or Symon Larmeurer, a Scots prisoner of war from Stirling Castle, is mentioned in 1305 (ibid., 1674), Symon Armour was bailie of Peebles, 1329, and in 1337 John Armurer was one of the garrison of Edinburgh Castle (ibid., III, p. 363). Symon Armourer, bailie of Forfar, 1361 (ER., II, p. 62), may be Simon Armurer who was party to an indenture or agreement with the inhabitants of Montrose, 1372 (*Cupar-Angus,* I, p. 55), and Robert Armorer who was bailie of Lanark in 1490 may be Robert Armerar who held a tenement in Glasgow, 1497 (REG., 496). John Ermar or Ermair, burgess of Perth, was cautioner for the earl of Argyll in 1506 and again in 1510 (*Rent. Dunk.,* p. 197, 216), and John Armar was voter in Monkland, 1519 (*Simon,* 45). Marion Earmour is recorded in the parish of Douglas, 1661 (*Lanark CR.*). Jean Armour (1767–1834) was the wife of Robert Burns, Scotland's national poet. Airmour 1630, Armor 1668, Armore 1508, Armorare 1510, Armowrar 1501, Armwr 1511, Armwre 1562; Armer and Armoure also occur.

ARMOURER. See ARMOUR.

ARMSTRONG. This well-known Border surname – the Norman *Fortenbras* – is an instance of a surname assumed from a personal attribute – strength of arm. The name was not uncommon in the north of England in the latter half of the thirteenth century, and at a later period the Armstrongs were a numerous and warlike clan in Liddesdale and the Debateable Land. Adam Armstrong was pardoned at Carlisle in 1235 for causing the death of another man (*Bain*, I, 1243), and William Armestrangh' served on an inquisition in the same city in 1274 (ibid., II, 24). In 1328 there is entry of payment of the king's debt to William Armestrang, and in 1342 Richard Harmestrang made a loan to King David II at Calais (ER., I, p. 116, 506). Gilbert Armstrong, steward of the household of David II was ambassador to England in 1363 (APS., I, p. 493). Another (?) Gilbert Armestrang, canon of Moray in 1365, appears again as a witness in 1366 (REM., p. 37; REA., II, p. 58). Alexander Armystrang, Geffrai Armestrang, and Davy Armystrang appear as "borowis" for the earl of Douglas's bounds of the West March in 1398 (*Bain*, IV, 512). Armstrong of Gilnockie, a noted freebooter, was executed by James V in 1529, and the injustice of this action formed the theme of several popular ballads. Archie Armstrong was the famous jester of James VI; Kinmont Willie, also celebrated in Border ballads, and Christie's Will, both noted freebooters, were also Armstrongs. Mr. Robert Bruce Armstrong in his *History of Liddesdale* (p. 175) gives twenty-four variants of this name in the singular and twenty-one in the plural. In common speech the name is pronounced Armstrang.

ARNACHE. Robert de Arnache elected a lineator in Aberdeen, 1398 (CRA., p. 374). Perhaps from Arnage near Ellon.

ARNCAPLE. See under ARDINCAPLE.

ARNEIL. This surname found in Glasgow and its neighborhood was common there in the sixteenth century as Arneile (*Protocols*, I) and appears in the Edinburgh Marriage records in 1680 as Arneill. John Arneille is recorded in Coldingham in 1669 (*Lauder*). The name is of local origin from Ardneill in the parish of Kilbride, explained by Timothy Pont as "Ard-Neill or Neil's Knope." Recorded in Dunfermline 1942.

ARNELIGERE. Jhonne Arneligere was one of the signers of the Band of Dumfries, 1570 (RPC., XIV, p. 67). ? a trade name.

ARNKETIL. An ON. personal name. Arnkell is a rare later form, and Arncytel is an OE. form. Archetel occurs in DB. as the name of a landholder at the time of the survey, and the shorter forms Archil, Archel, are very frequent in the list of landholders. The family name Arkle is from this source. Arketillus de Mann-

vers witnessed gift of land of Okelffas to the canons of Holyrood, a. 1214 (LSC., p. 213). Anschetil or Ansketil de Riddel is recorded in last half of twelfth century (*Dalrymple*, p. 348).

ARNOLD. The ME. personal name *Arnald*, OE. *Earnweald*. Aernald (Ernald, Ernold) or Arnold, second abbot of Kelso, was elected bishop of St. Andrews, 1160. William le fiz Arnaud (the French form of the name), king's tenant in counte de Linlescu and Henry le fiz Arnaud del counte de Selkirk rendered homage 1296 (*Bain*, II, p. 201, 203). The seal of the latter shows a hunting-horn, stringed, S' Henrici f' Arnuni (ibid., p. 553). W. Arnold in Saltcoats, 1816.

ARNOT, ARNOTT. From the lands of Arnot in the parish of Portmoak, Kinross-shire. The family was settled there from the middle of the twelfth century (*Fordell*, p. 14), and in 1284 the lands are mentioned as being in possession of Michael de Arnoth. David Arnot of Fyfe rendered homage in 1296 (*Bain*, II, p. 204). The island of Ellenabot in Loch Lomond was confirmed to Matilda de Arnoth c. 1320 (*Levenax*, p. 83). Michael de Arnot, one of the garrison of Edinburgh Castle in 1337 (*Bain*, III, p. 363) may be the Michael de Arnoth mentioned in a letter of David de Manuel relating to the land of Kynglassy in 1340 (RD., p. 225). Henricus de Arnot, knight, attested to the marches of Kyrknes and Louchor in 1395 (RPSA., p. 5). The first of the family of Arnot of Lochrig, in the parish of Stewarton, Ayrshire, was John de Arnot whose name occurs as one of the jury in a cause between the burgh of Irvine and William Fraunces of Stane in 1417 (*Irvine*, I, p. 20). Edward Arnott was repledged to the liberty of the burgh of Irvine in 1472 (ibid., p. 28), and in 1429 the lands of Arnot in the sheriffdom of Fyff were granted to John de Arnutis (RMS., II, 135). John de Arnot, *dominus ejusdem*, occurs in the fifteenth century (RD., p. 301), and David Ernot who appears as archdeacon of Lothian in 1502 (*Bain*, IV, 1691), later became bishop of Galloway (*Dowden*, p. 371). The surname was not uncommon in Edinburgh in the fifteenth and sixteenth centuries, and George Arnot was a merchant burgess there in 1627 (RPC., 2. ser. II, p. 26). Hugo Arnot published a History of Edinburgh in 1816. Arnote 1581, Arnocht, Arnatt.

ARRANTHREW. Of local origin from Renfrew, the popular pronunciation of which is Arrenthrew. Alexander Arranthrew is recorded in the parish of Killallan in 1692 (*Kilbarchan*).

ARRAS, Arres. Johan de Aroz of the county of Dunfres rendered homage in 1296 (*Bain*, II, p. 210), and in 1312 we have mention of the purchase of the horse of Matthew de Arez (ibid., III, p. 427). Adam of Airwis had payment of his fee in 1328 (ER., I). His name occurs several times in the Exchequer Rolls after this date as Aroves, Arowes, Arwys, Arus, and he is mentioned again as Adam de la Arus in 1333 (*Scon*, 164). Alice del Aruys was one of the keepers of the royal wardrobe in 1332 (ER., I). Johannes de Arous, juror on inquisition in lands in Fife, 1300, Johannes de Arous, juror on inquisition on lands in Fife, 1390 (RMS., I, 854), and John Arous (Arowss, Arrouss, or de Arous), archdeacon of Glasgow, was a prominent person in the middle of the fifteenth century. William Arowiss was a monk of Cupar in 1500 (REB., I, p. 220; *Cupar-Angus*, I, p. 93), the house of John Knox in Edinburgh was conveyed to John Arres, barber surgeon, in 1525, and James Arrois and Robert Arroiss were tenants of the Abbot of Newbattle in 1563 (*Neubotle*, p. 326). Janet and Margaret Areiss in the parish of Eccfuird, 1684 (RPC., 3. ser. X, p. 318). Arras in Meigle 1816. More likely to be derived from Airhouse in the parish of Channelkirk, Berwickshire, old spellings of which are Aras (1655), Arreis (1630), Arris (1621), Arras and Arres (1583), than from Arras in France as suggested by Lower. The name of John Arons, a priest of St. Andrews diocese, 1433 (HP., IV, p. 179 n) is most probably a misprint for Arous.

ARRAT. This surname, now somewhat rare, is derived from the lands of the same name near Brechin in Angus. The name is of rare occurrence in Angus although the family continued there as landowners down to the middle of the sixteenth century (*Angus*, II, p. 60). William de Arrade is mentioned c. 1250 (*Panmure*). In 1264 Richard de Arrath possessed the lands of Balnanon or Balnamoon in the parish of Maryton (*Warden*, III, p. 32), and William de Arrade or de Arrath witnessed William de Brechin's foundation charter of the Hospital of Messyndew (Maison Dieu) in Brechin before 1267 (REB., I, p. 7). Johan de Arrac (rightly Arrat) of the county of Anegos rendered homage in 1296. His seal bears a hare blowing a horn, riding on a dog, and S' *Joh'is de Arrat* (*Bain*, II, p. 207, 558). David de Arroth or Arrothe in 1378 sold to Thomas de Rate one-half of the lands of Arroth, held by him of the lords of Brechin (RMS., I, 652, 689). Robert Arrat was a notary and presbyter of St. Andrews diocese in 1473 (SCM., IV, p. 9), George Arrot of that Ilk was escheat in 1528 (RSS., I, 4041, 4106),

and in 1537 was amerciate for absence from an assize (*Trials*, I, p. 180).

ARRES. *See under* ARRAS.

ARROL, Arrell. Of local origin from Errol in Perthshire, one of the old spellings of which was Arroll. John Arrell in Aroquhybeg is recorded in 1556 (*Laing*), and Duncan Errole was minister of Luss in 1590 (*Fasti*, 2. ed., III, p. 333). Thomas Errole in Blairoule was a retainer of Stewart of Ardvorlik in 1592 (RPC., V, p. 28), Thomas Arroll in Arochibeg, Dumbartonshire, and Johnne Arroll in Cashlie, were fined each 20 merks in 1614 for resetting members of the outlawed Clan Gregor (RPC., X, p. 225, 226). Duncan Arrell, cordiner in Drumlegark, was put to the horn along with Macfarlanes of Kepnoch for raiding in 1619 (ibid., XI, p. 589), Bessie Herreall is recorded in Frewche, parish of Glenylla, 1625 (*Brechin*), Duncan Arrell or Arroll, tailor and burgess, and Nicolas Arrile, barber, appear in Edinburgh in 1629 and 1653 (*Edinb. Marr.; Inquis.*, 3853), and John Arrell and William Arrell were burgesses of Stirling in 1646 and 1673 (*Stirling*). Sir William Arrol (1839–1913), engineer and bridge-builder. Arrall 1669.

ARTBRANAN. S. Columba (*Adamnan*, L, 33) baptized a man of this name in Skye, described as chief or captain of the *Geona* cohort. The name is a diminutive of *Artbran*, 'rockraven,' which occurs in the genitive in AU.s.a. 715 as *Artbrain*, for prehistoric Celtic * *Arto-bran-agno-s*. The name is compounded of *Art*, 'stone,' and *bran*, 'raven.'

ARTHUR. G. *Artair*, MG. *Artuir*, EIr. *Artuir*, *Artur*, from OIr. *art*, a 'bear,' W. *arth*. The name may point to early Celtic worship of the bear, whence * *Artogenos*, 'son of Artos,' W. *Arthgen* (SGS., I, p. 11). The name occurs several times, both among the northern and southern Cymry at the close of the sixth and beginning of the seventh centuries (Zimmer, *Nennius Vindicatus*, p. 284). Aedán mao Gabráin, king of Dalriata, whose mother was a British princess, named his eldest son Arthur, "the first Gael, so far as we know, to bear that name" (*Watson* I, p. 129). Arthur of Kyncorth is mentioned 1435 (RAA., II, p. 69). Thomas Harthawr witnessed a commission of bailiary, 1511 (*Panmure*, II, 279). John Airtheor juror on retour of special service in Duns, Berwickshire, 1678 (*Home*, 194). "The fore-name Arthur is common in Shetland now (1879), but I rather think it is only a seventeenth or eighteenth century corrupt form of the Old Northern 'Ottar.' Last century, 'Otto,' or 'Otho,' or 'Ottie' was a frequent forename here; and now no case of it occurs. In our North Isles it has even been Judaised into 'Hosea,' so that 'Otto Ottoson' was transmuted into 'Hosea Hoseason' — so written, but pronounced 'Osie Osieson' " (Arthur Laurenson in letter to Karl Blind, *Nineteenth century*, v, p. 1112). Arcthure 1686, Arthure 1530, Arthwire 1556. Chester Alan Arthur (1830–86), twenty-first president of the United States, was son of a Belfast minister of Scottish descent.

ARTHURLEE, ARTHURLIE. Of local origin from Arthurley in the parish of Neilston, Renfrewshire. Thomas de Arthurlie or Arthurly was vicar of Dalyel in 1362 and rector of Eglisham in 1388 (RMP., p. 144, 337; *Levenax*). A later Thomas de Arthurle witnessed the sale of a tenement in Glasgow in 1418 (LCD., p. 239), and William Arthurle was doctor of decrees (decretorum doctor) in 1469 (RMP., p. 313, 323). In 1478 mention is made of a tenement of quondam Thomas Arthurle in Glasgow (REG., 420), and Jonet Arthorlie had sasine as heir to Arthorlie in 1680.

ARTHURSHULLE. The name of Henry de Arthurshulle of Lanarkshire who rendered homage in 1296 (*Bain*, II, p. 204) may have been derived from the place now known as Arthurshiels near Biggar, Lanarkshire.

ARTHURSON, 'son of ARTHUR,' q.v. Thomas Arthuri (Latin gen.) was a citizen of St. Andrews in 1435 (*Laing*). William Arthurson, witness at Dunbrettan (Dumbarton) in 1427 (HP., II, p. 159) may have been a Macarthur, and so likewise the William Arthurson also in Dumbartonshire in 1467 (APS., II, p. 91a). Arthurson is also a Shetland surname.

ARTLIE. Patrick Artlie and Alexander Artlie were tenants in Nether Dourdie, 1711 (DPD., II, p. 280).

ASCELINUS. Ascelin is a Normanized form of ON. *Ásketil* (later *Askell*), a very early and frequent name. Ascelinus was archidiaconus of Glasgow, c. 1147–50 (REG., 4, 11). Ascelinus, first abbot of Kinloss in Moray died in 1174 (*Chron. Mail.*, s.a.) Acellin, 1159 (*Kelso*, p. 12).

ASHBY. From Ashby in England, "a local name occurring 18 times in the Gazetteer, mostly in the cos. of Lincoln, Leicester, and Northampton." William de Asseby and his son Peter de Asseby had dealings with Dryburgh Abbey concerning the lands of Ingelbriston c. 1200–1203 (*Dryburgh*, p. 160–163). George Ashbie weaver in Edinburgh, 1680 (*Edinb. Marr.*).

ASHENNAN. *See under* SHANNAN.

ASHKIRK. A family of this name were vassals of the bishop of Glasgow in the twelfth century and took their surname from their lands in the barony of the same name in Selkirkshire. Between 1165 and 1182 William the Lion granted to the Church of Glasgow and to Orm de Ashkirke and his heirs certain lands in the neighborhood of Ashkirk within boundaries named, with the liberty of "plowing, sowing, and waynage within the fence that was raised around their deer-parks on the day on which this charter was framed" (REG., p. 28–29). In the reign of Alexander II (1214–1249) a curious family dispute arose respecting the legitimacy of Henry de Eschirche which furnishes the following particulars relating to three generations of the family:

Memorandum anent the brothers Aschirche

"Their first ancestor was named Acolf. This Acolf had two sons. The first born was named Huhtred. This Huhtred had a son also named Huhtred. This second Huhtred begot Richard his true heir. The second son of Acolf was called Orm. Orm begot Adam. Adam begot William. This William begot Henry, to whom it was opponed that he was illegitimate, and Alexander, his younger brother, whose legitimacy was not disputed" (ibid., p. 127). All the individuals here named along with others of the same designation, appear as witnesses in various charters of the twelfth and thirteenth centuries (LAC., p. 28; *Melros*, p. 109, 118, 120, 121, 126, etc.; *Neubotle*, p. 109; REG., p. 28, 46, 65). The dispute concerning Henry's legitimacy was apparently terminated in his favor by a settlement made at Roxburgh according to which he granted to his brother Alexander "the half of the whole fief of Eschirche in all things for his homage and service, to be held of him and his heirs for a reddendo of half the service in all things belonging to half of the same fief of Eschirche" (REG., p. 126). Alexander de Askirke held land of Walter de Ridale in the reign of Alexander II (*Melros*, p. 254), Henry de Askirk had a grant from David II in 1363 of the land of quondam Ade de Glenton in the burgh of Roxburgh (RMS., I, 155), and Gilbert Askyrke or Gib of Askirk was burgess of Are, 1415 and 1438 (*Ayr*, p. 9; *Friars Ayr*, p. 49). Askyrk 1415.

ASHTON. Local. Roger Aschtoun had a pension in 1585 from the fruits of part of the bishopric of Ross (OPS., II, p. 571). Sebastian Ashton, burgess of Linlithgow, 1688 (RPC., 3. ser. XIII, p. 306).

ASKALOK. Apparently for *Ap Scoloc*, 'son of the scholar.' For origin see under SCOLOC. Willelma, widow of Gilbert Askalok of Galloway had a protection in 1291, *sine termino* (*Bain*, II, p. 131). Roland Askeloche and Hector, his son, were jurors on an inquisition made at Berwick, 1296 (ibid., p. 215). The seal of the former bears an open right hand in pale, and S' *Rolandi de Ascole* (ibid., p. 551; *Seals Supp.*, 51). From the reference in Bain's index he would seem to be the same person as Roland MacGachen of the county of Wiggetone who is also recorded as rendering homage in 1296 (ibid., p. 198). Hector Askeloc also rendered homage in the same year (ibid., p. 202). His seal bears a shield with two lions passant in pale, and *Sigillo Hectoris Ascoloc* (ibid., p. 549; *Macdonald*, 50). Roland Ascolog or Magachen granted a charter of lands in the parish of Borgue to Duncan Cambel, c. 1300 (*Sc. Peer.*, I, p. 321). In 1302 Hector was pardoned at the instance of Robert de Bruis, earl of Carric, for causing the death of Cuthbert of Galloway and for other offences (*Bain*, II, 1291). Another of the name, Fergus Askolo, also of Wigtownshire, rendered homage in 1296 (ibid., p. 205).

ASKEBY. Robert de Askeby of the county of Berewyk rendered homage in 1296 (*Bain*, II, p. 206). Perhaps from Asby in Cumberland, in 1226 Askeby.

ASKEY. A curtailed form of MACASKIE, q.v.

ASLOAN. *See under* SLOAN.

ASTIE. John Astie in Dunfermline, 1587 (*Dunfermline*). Bardsley says " 'the son of Anastasia,' from the nickname Anstie, abbreviated to Astie." [?]

ATHERAY. From Airthrey (more correctly Airthrie, in 1317 and 1369 Athray), in the parish of Logie, Stirlingshire. Sir John Athera or Atheray, presbyter of the diocese of Dunblane, 1432 (*HP.*, II, p. 170, 174) is doubtless Sir John Acheray (*t* misread *c*), cleric and notary public, 1443 (*Charter Chest, earl of Wigtown*, p. 6), and Sir John Achra, chaplain and notary public in Argyll, 1450 (*RMS.*, II, 346). As Sir Johannes Athra he was notary public at Allua (Alloa), 1451 (*REA.*, I, p. 259), and as de Atheray, treasurer of Brechin, 1462 (*Cambus.*, 89). A John Atherney, notary in Edinburgh, 1437 (*SCM.*, V, p. 261) may possibly be the same person.

ATHERSTONE. A Fife surname of local origin. There is an Edderston near Peebles and an Adderstoneshiels near Hawick. (*dd = th*).

ATHILMER. John Athilmer, professor of theology in the College of S. Salvator, St. Andrews, 1455 (*RAA.*, II, 104), is perhaps the John Athilmar, clerk of Register in 1467 (*APS.*), provost of the Collegiate Church of S. Salvator, 1468 (*REB.*, II, 111), the Johanne Athilmewe, vicar of Menmer (Menmure) in 1470 (*Wemyss*, II, 98), and the John Achilmar, canon of Brechin in 1474 (*REB.*, I, 198). Jacobus de Achilmere de eodem, in vic. Selkirk, mentioned in 1458 (*RMS.*, II, 664), is the James Athilmere de eodem witness to an inquest concerning the lands of Cranshaws in 1462.

ATHOLL. From the district of the name in Perthshire. Gilbert Atholl and Thomas Atholl were recorded as "quhyt fischeris in Futtie" in 1592, and in 1606, as Gilbert and Thomas Athoill, they were admitted burgesses of Aberdeen (*CRA.*, p. 74; *NSCM.*, I, p. 102). Adam de Athetle who rendered homage at Perth, 1291 (*RR.*), may have derived his name from the district.

ATKIN, ATKINS. *See under* AIKEN.

ATKINSON. *See under* ACHESON.

ATTERSHANK. *See under* ETTERSHANK.

AUCHANESON. An Englishing of MAC-EACHAN, q.v. Charlis Auchaneson and Ferchar Auchaneson were witnesses to a contract of friendship between Dunbar of Westfield and the Clanchattan in 1492 (*Coll.*, p. 86).

AUCHENCRAW, AUCHINCRAW. From the lands now hamlet of Auchencraw in the parish of Coldingham, Berwickshire, locally pronounced Edencraw, and sometimes spelled Adincraw (cf. Auchmoor in Fife, old Admore). In the time of William the Lion the place name was spelled Aldengrawe. Adam de Aldengraue appears as a charter witness in the reign of William the Lion (*Coldingham*, 153), and early in the thirteenth century Michael de Aldengrawe quit claimed to the priory and convent of Coldingham land in the vill of Aldecambus. Many individuals of the name are recorded in Home, *passim*. James of Aldincraw was one of an inquest anent a fishing on the Water of Tweed in 1467 (*RD.*, 461), and Patrick Aldicraw was married in 1491 (*Sc. Ant.*, III, p. 102). About the beginning of the sixteenth century the name began to be shortened to Craw and even sometimes spelled Crow (1648). In 1577 Alexander Auchincraw in Nether Aytoun and Henry Craw, *his son*, appear together as charter witnesses (*Home*,

208). Aldencraw 1298, Aldingcraw 1494, Aldincraw 1498, Aldyncraw 1529, Auchencraw 1510, Audincraw 1476, Awchincraw 1571. See CRAW.

AUCHENHOVE, AUCHINHOVE. There are several small properties of this name in Aberdeenshire from which this surname may have been derived, e.g. near Insch, at Lumphanan, near Grange (Keith), and at Rothie Norman. Dauit Auchnahuf was admitted burgess of Aberdeen in 1462 and James Auchinhuiff in 1598 (NSCM., I, p. 17, 92). James Auchinhuiff, burgess of Aberdeen, and John Auchinhuiff in Cothill of Collistoune, are both mentioned in 1609 (RSCA., II, p. 149, 153).

AUCHENROSS. Anegus de Auchenros was juror on an inquest regarding the lands of Stephen de Blantthyre in 1263 (Bain, I, 2338; APS., I, p. 92). Anegos de Aghenros of the county of Are rendered homage in 1296, as also at the same time did John Haughenros of the county of Elgin (Bain, II, p. 210, 200). John Achinros who witnessed instrument of sasine in favor of James Stevart, son of the earl of Lennox in 1490 (Lennox, II, p. 140), may be the John Atchinrosche who held a tenement in the burgh of Dumbertan in 1495 (REG., p. 491), and the same with John Achinrosch, bailie of the same burgh in 1500 (LCD., p. 204). James Achynros was a charter witness in Glasgow in 1495 (HP., II, p. 195), David Akinros was a charter witness at Dunbretane in 1506 (Lennox, II, p. 182), Katrine Auchinrosch had a respite in 1512 for art and part in the slaughter of Richard Hill (RSS., I, 2436). John Achinros, servitor to M'Lane of Doward, is frequently mentioned in the Calendar of State Papers relating to Scotland, 1589–1603. Akynros 1513, Auchinroche 1520.

AUCHIE. From some small place of the name. William Auchie, minstrall, indweller in Stirling, 1611 (Stirling).

AUCHINACHIE. Of local origin from Auchanachie in the parish of Keith, Banffshire. John Awchanyowche, son and heir of quondam Philip de Auchanyouche, had a charter of the lands of Auchanyouche in the barony of Rothiemay in 1448 (Illus., II, p. 228). William Auchquhennachy of that Ilk appears as juror on an inquest in 1575 (RSCA., p. 219), James Achannachie was servitor to William Meldrum of Moncoffer in 1592 (Innes Familie, p. 161), and Alexander Achynachie is mentioned as present at the battle of Old Earne or Auldearn in 1650 (Strathbogie, p. 121). John Achynachy paid 5 merks for his wife's burial lair in the church of Fordyce in 1697 (Cramond, For-

dyce, p. 54), and in 1703 Alexander Achynachy was compelled to stand before the pulpit and to pay 20s. for an offence committed by him (loc. cit.). Alexander Achynachy was chamberlain of Fyvie before 1740 (Aberdeen), and Sergeant Auchinachie was killed in Flanders in 1915. See also the curtailed form ACHNACH. Achynachi 1650.

AUCHINCLOSS, AUCHINLOSS. From lands of the name in the parish of Kilmarnock. Achinlos of that Ilk an Ayrshire family long extinct. James Auchincloss of that Ilk appears in record in 1493 (ADC.), and again in 1500 as Achinlos of that Ilk (PDG.). James Auchinlos, another of the name, was tenant of Welstoun, Ayr, in 1499 (ER., XI, p. 438), and Felicity (Felicitatis) Achinlos of Adamhill recorded, 1500 (Simon, 12). James Assinlos of that Ilk was one of the jury that tried Adam Colquhoune for murder in 1561–2 (Trials, I, p. 420; Pont., p. 70). There is record in 1592 of a band of caution by James Asloss of that Ilk (RPC., IV, p. 710), and Adam Asloss of that Ilk was cautioner in the testament of Patrick Tran, provost of Irvine, who died in 1611 (Pont., p. 71). James Aslois de eodem succeeded his father in the lands of Aslois in the barony of Kilmarnock in 1616 (Retours. Ayr.). The name is also found in the Edinburgh marriage records in 1679. Hugh Auchincloss (1817–1890) and John Auchincloss, sons of Hugh Auchincloss of Paisley were prominent merchants in New York City. Asloace 1704, Awchinlos 1549.

AUCHINCRAW. See under AUCHENCRAW.

AUCHINLECK. See under AFFLECK.

AUCHINLOSS. See under AUCHINCLOSS.

AUCHINMADE. John Auchinmade was burgess of Irvine in 1465 (Irvine, I, p. 28). He derived his surname from the old 13/4 lands of that name in the parish of Kilwinning, Ayrshire.

AUCHINTORE. Local. James Auchintour occupied part of the land of Glanderstoun in the barony of Renfrew, 1549 (Protocols, I).

AUCHINVOLE. A now uncommon surname derived from Auchinvole in the parish of Kirkintilloch. The name occurs in Edinburgh in 1625 as Achinwall (Edinb. Marr.). Thomas Auchinvale, born in Drumfrochare (an error for Drumtrochar, near Kilsyth) had a birthbrief from the magistrates of Stirling in 1614 on his departing to reside on the continent. He is probably the Thomas Auchinvale who

AUCHINVOLE, *continued*

settled in Elbing in Prussia and died there in 1653. His great-great-grandson, Gottfried Achenwall (d. 1772), was professor of international law at Göttingen (*Fischer* I, p. 228). Alexander Auchinval in the parish of Monyabroch is in record in 1658 (*Stirling*). The name of John Achinwells, servitor to John Miller in Edinburgh in 1636 (RPC., 2. ser. VI, p. 359) is probably from the same source, as likewise that of John Auchtenvallis, clerk in Dunfermline, 1651 (*St. Andrews*).

AUCHMUTY. See *under* ACHMUTY.

AUCHNIEVE. From Auchnieve near Old Meldrum, Aberdeenshire. Walter de Achneve who was admitted burgess of Aberdeen in 1446 was probably the father of Walter de Achneff or Aghneif who was admitted to the same privilege in 1465 and 1476 (NSCM., I, p. 10, 19, 26). Walter Achneve, member of the burgh council in 1481, is mentioned again in 1487 as Wate of Auchnef, burgess of the burgh (CRA., p. 41, 44), and John Achneyve in Aberdeen is mentioned in the same record under the year 1493.

AUCHTER. Perhaps from the small place of the name near Aberfeldy, Perthshire. Michael Ouchtre was dean of the cathedral church of Dunblane, 1422 (*Hay*, 10). William Oughtre alias Parker 'Taillour', a native of Dundee, had letters of denisation in England, 1475 (*Bain*, IV, 1426). John Owchtre was burgess of Perth in 1488 (*Methven*, p. 31), Johnne Uchtir, reidare at Cadder, 1574 (RMR.), and the name occurs in the Glasgow Protocol Books as Wchtyr (1541), Ouchtir and Awchtir (1550), and Ouchter (1551).

AUCHTERARDER. From the town of Auchterarder in Perthshire. Morice de Ughterardoghe of the county of Ughterardour (*sic*) rendered homage in 1296 (*Bain*, II, p. 213). Malcolm of Uchterardore was a charter witness c. 1290 (*Athole*, p. 705), and John, son of Andree de Huchtirardor, had charter of a tenement in Huchtirardor in 1330 (RAA., II, p. 6).

AUCHTERARNE. From lands of this name in Aberdeenshire. Elizabeth and John Ouchterarne were concerned in court proceedings regarding the lands of Ouchterarne in Mar between 1504 and 1508 (RSCA., I, p. 13, 22, 24, 30). Ouchtirarne 1507, Ucheram and Uchterarn 1508.

AUCHTERCRAW. Of local origin. Ninian and Gavine Auchtercraw appear as representatives in law cases, 1519 (EBR., p. 188, 189).

AUCHTERGAVEN. From Auchtergaven in Perthshire. Robert de Oghtergeven of the county of Perth rendered homage in 1296 (*Bain*, II, 809, p. 200, 202). In the last entry his name is wrongly spelled Ostergavene. The seal attached to his homage bears a lion rampant and S' *Roberti de Hvtgavin* (*Macdonald*, 54).

AUCHTERHOUSE. William de Hwuctvruus appears as sheriff of Forfar in 1245 (RAA., I, p. 200), and two years later he witnessed a charter by Alexander II of the lands of Inverlunane in Angus (*Caerlaverock*, II, 405). He may be the Willelmus de hutyrhose (huntyrhoys or Huhtus) who was dominus de Cocpen (*Neubotle*, p. 28, 302, 304).

AUCHTERLESS. From the old barony of the name in Aberdeenshire. Walter de Wictirlys or de Vchtirlys appears as a charter witness between 1204 and 1211 (RAA., I, 33, 74*ter*, 206). Symon de Othyrles or Othirless was a canon of the church of Caithness in 1364 (REA., I, p. 106, 107), and Robert Ouchterless is mentioned in Aberdeen in 1493 (CRA., p. 50).

AUCHTERLONIE, Auchterlony, Ochterlonie, Ochterlony, Ouchterlony. Surnames of old families in Angus, derived from the lands of Auchterlonie near Forfar. John of Othirlony exchanged with Walter, son of Turpin his lands of Othirlony for those of Kenny c. 1226–39 (RAA., I, p. 262–263). Wauter de Oghterloveny of the county of Fyfe who rendered homage in 1296 (*Bain*, II, p. 209) is said in Nisbet to be Auchterlonie of that Ilk. William of Ochterlowny was one of the assize on the marches of Woodwrae in 1388 (*Bamff*, p. 22). Alexander de Uchtirlowny was a charter witness in Perth in 1410 (RMS., I, 927), Thomas de Ochtirlony a charter witness in Dundee in 1430 (HP., II, p. 164), and David Ochterlovnie witnessed an instrument of the procurator of Brechin in 1457 (REB., II, 140). William Auchterlouny de Kellie was sheriff of Forfar in 1514 (SCM., V, p. 291), Eduard Auchtirlonye sat as sheriff-depute at Cupar in 1518 (SCBF., p. 136), and David Auchterlonyng was admitted burgess of Glasgow as servitor to the marquis of Hamilton in 1627 (*Burgesses*). The Ochterlonies of Kintrockat and the Ochterlonies of Pitforthy (in Ayrshire) are descended from the Auchterlonies of Kelly. Auchtirlony 1585, Auchterloney 1672, Aughterlonie 1639, Ochirlony 1512, Ochthorlony 1511, Ochtirlony 1451, Ochtyrlowny 1395, Ouchterlovnie 1454,

Ouchtirlovny 1409, Ouchterlowny 1535, Ouchtirlowny 1502, Oughterlonie 1688, Wchtirlowny 1461, and (undated) Achterlonie, Ouchterlone, Ouchterlonie, Ouchterlony, Ochterlonie, Oughterlonie.

AUCHTERMONY. Pension to Margaret Auchtermony in Edinburgh, 1722 (Guildry, p. 126). Local, probably from Auchtermonzie (now Monzie), pronounced Auchtermonee.

AUCHTERMUCHTY. From Auchtermuchty in Fife. Malcolm de Huctermocdi was one of the jurors on an inquest on lands in Fife in 1296 (Bain, II, p. 216), and Thomas de Hucermickedy or Houctyr Mokedy was a canon of St. Andrews in 1298 (Pap. Lett., I, p. 576).

AUDE. Andrew Aude at Heisseldene, parish of St. Andrews, 1550 (St. Andrews). Cf. Auldie, Audie (1603) in Fife Retours (128).

AUFRASONE, 'son of AUFRAY.' See AUFRAYS. Walter Aufrasone held land in Aberdeen, 1492 (REA., I, p. 329).

AUFRAYS. Thomas Aufrays (Awfrayis, Affrais) recorded in Kintore (Kyntor), 1498 (REA., I, p. 340, 341; II, p. 229). The name is also spelled Anfrays, 1498 (Inverurie, p. 123). Perhaps meant for AMFRAY, q.v.

AUGHENOUL. Patric de Aughenoul was one of the jurors on forfeited lands in Lothian, 1312 (Bain, III, 245), and in the same year John de Aughenoule was one of the garrison of Edinburgh Castle (Bain, III, p. 409).

AULAY. This name is of twofold origin, or rather two names of different origin appear alike in English form. (1) From the OG. personal name Amhalghaidh, pronounced almost as Aulay or Owley. From this comes the Aulay of the family of the old earls of Lennox. In our early records the name has undergone some strange transformations. Amolngnaid, king of Connacht, died between 440–450. From him the district of Torawley (Tir Amolgnado or Amhalghaidh) takes its name. The spelling of Lennox Aulay is very varied and somewhat perplexing in the early records: Amalech, Amelec, Auleth Ameleth, Amelech, Amhlew, Hamelen, and Havel, are some of the forms under which it appears in charters. About 1225 Amelec received from his brother the earl a grant of Faslane and an extensive tract of country on both sides of the Gairloch (Levenax, p. 91, 92). About the same date he granted a salt-pan in his land of Rosneath and wood for repairs to the monks of Paisley (RMP., p. 211). He also gave the same monks all the tracts of nets through the whole of Gairloch for catching salmon and other fish, reserving to himself and his heirs every fourth salmon taken through these tracts (ibid., p. 209–10). As Amelic he also gave the monastery of Paisley the church of Roseneath with all its pertinents, and is a witness in several charters by his brother the earl. This Aulay had a son, also named Aulay, who had two sons, Aulay or Alan de Fasselane and Duncan. Walter de Fasselane, son of Aulay de Fasselane (Levenax, p. 21, 91, 92), was the sole representative of the male line of the house of Lennox, and having married Margaret, countess of Lennox acquired with her its possessions (The Lennox, I, p. 211–13). About the year 1334 we have mention of Anweleth (a miscopying of Auweleth) de Fosselane, and in 1351 of Avileth dominus de Fosselane (Levenax, p. 92, 93), the same person. (2) from ON. Ólafr, which represents ON. Áleifr with nasal a, the n being retained in OE. Anlaf. In early Irish the name appears as Amláib, Álaib, from which comes later G. Amhlaibh, MacAmhlaibh, Macaulay in the Hebrides. See MACAULAY.

AULD. From OE. (e)ald, old. As a personal name Ealda is found in an OE. charter of 765 A. D. Alda occurs in the Liber Vitae of Durham, and Alda cinges gefera ("the king's companion") is in record in a charter of 743 (Birch, Cartularium Saxonicum, 171). Auld was a not uncommon name in Ayrshire from early times. John Alde was servitor of the earl of Carrick in 1284 (Bain, II, 260), and another John Alde was burgess of Perth in 1292 (Milne, p. 5). An agreement was made in 1302 between Nicholas de Haya, dominus de Eroll, and William dictus Ad filius quondam Johannis dictus Ald, burgess of Perth (SCM., II, p. 315). Robert Alde was juror on an inquest held at Berwick in 1315 (Bain, III, 461), Bartholomew Alde was a burgess of Irvine in 1477 (Irvine, 150), and an action was pursued against Johne Auld and others for the wrongous taking of the hay of the Mains of Curmánok in 1488 (ALC., p. 115). John Aulde held a tenement in Glasgow in 1494 (REG., 469), and Robert Awld and William Auld appear in Lanark in 1501 (Lanark, p. 11). Andro Auld was a bonnet maker in Edinburgh in 1532 (EBR., p. 22), and John Auld was commissioner to Parliament for the burgh of Irvine in 1542 (APS., II, p. 410). James Auld in Galdinoch was one of the retainers of Wchtrid McDougall of Frewche in Galloway in 1635 (RPC., 2. ser. v, p. 125), and in the same year John MacAuld in Findret was

AULD, *continued*

charged by John Grant of Ballindalloch with having reset the traitor James Grant and others (ibid., 2. ser. vi, p. 112). Archibald M'Auld, a retainer of Kennedy of Cassilis, was charged in 1635 with armed convocation and riot (ibid., 2. ser. v, p. 509), John Ald was reider at Dysart, 1636 (PBK., p. 92), Andrew Auld in May, Caithness, was a follower of William Sinclair of Mey in 1670 (ibid., 3. ser. iii, p. 194), and William Auld was proprietor in Rothesay in 1689. Auld is also used as one of the Anglicized forms of MacCathail, a name with which it has no connection in root or meaning. Latinized Aldius in Bute in 1507, and in Ireland it appears as Ould.

AULDCHACHTE. Jonet Auldchachte, tenant in Camphell, Cromar, 1539 (ER., xvii, p. 661) may have derived her name from Auldcathers, Fintray, Aberdeenshire.

AULDJO. A current surname but not common. William Awldioy was surety for another, 1518 (EBR., p. 187). Several individuals were charged with 'revising' (ravishing, perhaps 'abducting' is meant) Jonet Aldioye in 1552 (*Trials*, i, p. 421*), and Margaret Auldjoy, wife of an Edinburgh citizen, is in record, 1537 (*Laing*, 415). Peter Aldjeo, advocate, and Claude Algeo, servitor to Claud Hamiltoun in Paisley, are mentioned in 1628, and Thomas Aldgeo was excommunicated in the kirk of Paisley in same year for popery (RPC., 2. ser. iii, p. 327, 344). Aldjo, Aldjoe, Aldjoy, Aljoy, Alljoy. Cf. ALGEO.

AULDMILL. Local. Andrew Auldmale, wright in Edinburgh, 1553 (EBR., ii, p. 351). Edward Auldmill tenant of Mains of Petsligo, 1618 (RSCA., ii, p. 224). James Auldmeill was concerned in an action regarding payment of malt, 1617 (ibid., ii, p. 218). Oldmill (Inverurie) was in 1558 Auldmylne.

AULDNY. John Auldny in Brechin, 1590 (*Wedd.*, p. 152). John Audnie in the Orchard neuk of Wester Elcho, 1639 (*St. Andrews*).

AULDSON. John Auldson a Douglas tenant in the barony of Abirdoure in Fife, 1376 (RHM., i, p. lxv).

AULDTON. Of territorial origin from the lands of Auldton near Hawick, Roxburghshire. Roger de Auldton witnessed a charter by William, lord of Douglas between 1306–29 (RHM., i, p. 13), and in 1329 purchased the privilege of burial for himself and his spouse in the choir of the church of St. James of Roxburgh

(*Kelso*, p. 368). As de Aultoun he was a charter witness c. 1338 (*Dryburgh*, p. 261), and as Roger of Aldtoun he witnessed the grant of the forest of Eteryk to John Kerre in 1358 (*Roxburgh*, p. 8). Thomas of Altoune was Master of the House of Soltre in 1430 (*Soltre*, p. 52).

AULDWARD. Local? Alexander Auldward in Autherb, 1629 (RSCA., ii, p. 313).

AULNOY. Robertus de Alneto witnessed resignation of the lands of Edeluestun to the church of Glasgow, 1233. He is evidently the same with Robertus de Auno who witnessed a second resignation of the same lands in the same year (REG., p. 138, 139). Thomas Alneto gave a charter of the lands of Brunscarth, Dumfriesshire, to Melrose Abbey in 1237 (*Seals*, 93; *Macdonald*, 55). He also, as Thomas de Alneto, witnessed an agreement between the Abbey of Inchaffray and the Hospital of Brackley in 1238 (*Inchaffray*, p. 64). Probably the same with Thomas de Aunou, who appears in the Cumberland Pipe Rolls of 1230–31, and of whose lands in Lincolnshire and Yorkshire an extent was taken in 1246.

AUMBLER. Wauter Aumbler of Roxburghshire rendered homage in 1296 (*Bain*, ii, p. 209). Bardsley says this surname has ramified strongly in Yorkshire, and he explains it as "one who looked after the amblers in his lord's stables; one who taught horses to amble." Among his other duties the ambler broke in horses, i.e. taught them to amble."

AUSTIN. (1) a diminutive of Augustine ('majestic'), the name of the great Father of the Church, Augustinus of Hippo, and of his namesake the first Archbishop of Canterbury. (2) an Englishing of Uisdean (Hùisdean) "one of the many instances in which classical names are utilised to represent Gaelic names of a somewhat similar sound" (HP., i, p. 35n). "The Austins appear first on record as allies and supporters of the Keiths. The name was variously spelt, though in ancient records it was generally begun with Ou or Ow. Of curious interest as showing an early connection between the families is the occurrence in 1587 of the name of Alexander Ousteane, burgess of Edinburgh, as one of the cautioners for George Keith, Earl Marshall, in an action raised against him, by Margaret Erskine, Lady Pitcarie. In the same year Alexander Oisteane, no doubt the same person, was a parliamentary representative of the Burgh of Edinburgh. In 1589 Walter Oustene, a tenant in Lochquhan (a possession of the Keith family), was one of the subscribers to a Bond of Caution imposed on a number of the landed men in the shires of Aberdeen and Kincardine, binding them to keep the peace in the struggles with the Catholic party headed by Huntly" (D. W. Stewart, *Old and rare Scottish tartans*). The Austins of the parish of Fettercairn are said to be of English descent and there during the seventeenth century (Cameron, *History of Fettercairn*, p. 226). John Owstyne was a tenant of earl of Douglas in the barony of Preston, 1376 (RHM., I, p. lxi), Andrew Austyn was prior of Dunfermline, 1448 (RD., p. 309), and in 1503 David Ostien was prebend of Holy Trinity, Edinburgh (*Soltre*, p. 158). John Owstiane was burgess of Edinburgh, 1566 (RPC., I, p. 447), Alexander Oustiane deacon of the southwest quarter of the burgh in 1574 (MCM., I, p. 107), and Alexander Austene tailor there in 1594 (ER., XXII, p. 582). Mary Austine is recorded at Grangeburn, 1676 (*Kirkcudbright*), Agnes Owstine in Reidcastle, 1681 (*Dumfries*), William Oustine of Kirkland, 1699 (*Inquis.*, 8109), and Agnes Austine in Deanstoun, 1755. Austeane 1593, Oistiane 1583, Ostiane 1584, Austein, Ostian, Oustian.

AVAL. John Aval was witness in Brechin, 1458, and a later (?) John Avale witnessed instruments of sasine there between 1497–99 (REB., II, 99, 143, 148). John Awell de Oyne, Aberdeenshire, is in record, 1506 (REA., II, p. 98), and in 1526 mention is made of land of John Awell in Brechin (REB., II, 180). Another John Awell was voter in parish of Qwilton (Coylton), 1513 (*Ros*, 52). Avail 1506.

AVEN. John Aven, merchant in Kirkcaldy, 1747 (*St. Andrews*). William Aven, farmer in Tillynaught, 1761 (*Fordyce*, p. 102).

AVENAUGH. Allaster Avenaugh entered as a pledge for Clan Leane in 1619 (RPC., XIV, p. 583).

AVENEL. A surname, says Anderson, "now scarcely known except in the pages of romance, once borne by high and powerful barons, whose descendants, if any now exist, have long ceased to be called by the name of their progenitors" (*Scot. Nat.*, I, p. 170). The name is territorial, from Avenville in the department of Orne. The first of the name in Scotland was Robertus Avenel who witnessed charters in the reigns of David I, Malcolm IV, and William the Lion. He received from David I grants of Upper and Lower Eskdale, and was a generous benefactor to the Abbey of Melrose, bestowing on the monks of that house a large portion of his lands in Upper Eskdale (*Melros*, 39). Some time after 1175

he became a humble monk in that house and died in 1185: "Obiit Robertus Auenel novicius, familiaris noster, viij idus Martii," and, adds the pious chronicler, "cujus beata anima, semper vivat in gloria" (*Chron. Mailr.*, p. 93). For some eighty years the family was prominent in the history of Scotland. It ended in the direct line in Roger Avenel who died in 1243, and his daughter and heiress married Henry de Graham of Abercorn, into whose hands the Avenel estates passed.

AVENER. William Auyner was notary in Cambuskenneth, 1422 (*Hay*, 10). Elizabeth Awenar was recorded at Dunblane in sixteenth century, and Matthew Aner there in 1543 (*Dunblane*). Thomas Awenar in Raninstreuther, parish of Carstairs, 1564 (*Campsie*). Bardsley says from occupation, 'the avener,' OF. *avenier*, *avener*, 'oat merchant.'

AVERY. Payment was made to Walter Auery, fallen in poverty, 1526 (ALHT., V, p. 306). Michael Awery or Avery was witness in Falkland, 1548 (*Gaw*, 8). John Awerie, portioner of Newtoun, 1596. Martha Avery in Wester Arr, 1766 (*Moray*). Old spellings: Avary, Averie, Awery, Every.

AWLOCHE. That is, an Atholl man (*Athalach*). John Lauchlane Alanson callit John Auchlacht, 1505 (RSS., 1170). John Awloche appears as burgess of Dornoch in 1524 and 1545 (OPS., II, 641), and Patrick Auilloche McGregour (1573) was so named from the district of Atholl whither he fled for protection (*Coll.*, p. 95). Patrick Aulich or Adholach, executed in Edinburgh in 1604, was so named from his having been brought up in Atholl (*Macgregor*, I, p. 100). Athochlach = of Atholl (*Coll.*, p. 56).

AWQUHOLLIE. Mr. John Awquhollie, admitted burgess of Aberdeen in 1575 (NSCM., I, p. 72) probably derived his name from Aucholzie in Glenmuick, Aberdeenshire (z = y).

AYE. A spelling of *Adhamh* (Adam) among the Clan Chattan was *Ay*, which is fairly close to the modern pronunciation. There was also a lost sept of that clan called *Clan Ay*. Ay Mac Bean vic Robert of Tordarroch signed the Clan Chattan Band of 1609 "taking the full burden of his race of Clan Ay," etc. Aye Jonson was spokesman for the jurors on the assize of the marches of Kyrknes and Louchor in 1395 (RPSA., p. 4). Aye M'Ane M'Thomas gave his bond of manrent to George, earl of Huntlie, 1543 (SCM., IV, p. 260). See also EGO.

AYG. Munch (*Chron. Man*, p. 186–187) copies a document in the Vatican dated 20 Sept. 1375 addressed to the bishop of Lismore in favor of "Ayg Mac Petri perpetui vicarij parrochialis ecclesie Sancte Columbe de Kerepol Sodorensis diocesis." With this may be compared the *Eage* of the Mackinnon inscription: *Hec est crux Fingonii abbatis et suorum filiorum Fingonii et Eage.* Cf. *Aytho* and *Eyg* under MACKAY.

AYLEBOT. A family of this name were prominent in Perth in the fourteenth century. John Hailboch, burgess of Perth, is mentioned in 1292 (*Milne*, p. 5). John Aileboth, son of John Ailebot appears there in 1307 (*Inchaffray*, p. 114n), and a horse was purchased from John Ailbot in 1312 (*Bain*, III, p. 428). Michael dictus Aylebot was paid for salmon in 1328 (ER., I, p. 88). John Aylebot, burgess of Perth, received an annuity from the fermes of the town in 1328 (ER., I, p. 88) and is again mentioned in 1333 as John dictus Aylboch, burgess of Perth (*Milne*, p. 25). Aylbet 1329.

AYLIES. William Aeless tenant under the marquis of Huntlie, 1600 (SCM., IV, p. 267). Supplication by Alexander Aylies in Waster Beltie, 1634 (RPC., 2. ser. V, p. 582).

AYR, AYRE. *See under* AIR.

AYSON. *See under* EASON.

AYTON, AYTOUN, AITON. From the lands of Ayton (= the town on the river Eye) in Berwickshire. Steffan, son of Swan de Œitun granted a charter of the lands of Wytefeld to the Priory of Coldingham c. 1170 (*Raine*, 434). Dolfinus de eit' and Hel de eitun were witnesses to a charter by Waltheus, earl of Dunbar, c. 1166 (ibid., 115), and Elya de Eytone and Stephen de Eytona witnessed a charter by Patrick, first earl of Dunbar, c. 1189–99 (ibid., 117). David de Atune appears as witness c. 1220 (CMN., 10). Maurice de Ayton was one of the witnesses to the deed of sale of the serf Adam son of Thurkil to the Prior of Coldingham, c. 1240 (*Raine*, 337), and Robert de Aytoun witnessed a charter by Peter de Morthingtoun c. 1270 (BNCH., XVI, p. 334). William de Evtone of Berwickshire rendered homage in 1296. His seal shows a hare running and S' *Wilelmi de Aiton* (*Bain*, II, p. 207, 553). Henry de Ayton, burgess of Haddington, and Renaud de Eytone of Berwickshire also rendered homage (ibid., p. 197, 207). Matthew de Evton was a Scots prisoner of war in Chester Castle in 1296 (ibid., p. 177). John de Aytoun witnessed a charter of the

land of Nort Lambirtoun in 1300 (*Home*, 225), Mark of Aytoune, Scots merchant of Leith, had a safe conduct to trade in England in 1440 (*Bain*, IV, 1141), Andrew Athone was rector of Spot, 1527 (RAA., II, 656), and Andrew Athoun of Dunmur a witness in 1549 (*Gaw*, 20). Henry Aictoune was a notary public in Glasgow, 1551 (*Protocols*, I), and Alexander Aittine appears in Bonytoune, parish of Marytoune, 1611 (*Brechin*). In the fifteenth century the lands of Ayton passed to George de Home in whose family they continued till 1716 when they were forfeited for rebellion. The surname is found in Fife in the fourteenth century when John Aytoun had a charter of the lands of Over Pittadie. From him come the Aytouns of Inchdairnie. Aetoun 1612, Ætown 1561, Aitone 1650, Aitoun 1547, Aitoune 1607, Aittone 1601, Aittoun 1574, Aittoune 1596, Athone 1557, Atoun 1525, Atoune 1581, Aytonne 1520, Ayttoune 1637.

BAAD. There is a place named Baad near Stirling, and lands of the same name are recorded in Perthshire in 1544 (*Retours*). From the references the former locality seems to have been the parent of the surname. In Aberdeenshire there is a place named Baad (in parish of Peterculter), a Bad (obsolete place name in Cairnie), and Baud (in Birse), all from Gaelic *bad*, a cluster, thicket, and by extension of meaning, a hamlet. Twenty-nine persons named Bad and Baad are recorded in the Commissariot Record of Stirling between 1625 and 1788. John Bad a charter witness, 1498 (RAA., II, 389, 520). John Baid, merchant in Aberdeen, 1541 (SCM., II, p. 33), probably derived his name from one of the Aberdeenshire places so named. Bessie Bad appears in Dunfermline, 1561 (*Dunfermline*), and Alexander Baud witnessed a tack in Kinloss, 1581 (*Laing*, 1028). Caution was found for William Bad in Torriburne, 1591 (RPC., IV, p. 577), John Baid, burgess of Dunfermline, 1661 (*Inquis.*, 4468), David Bade was merchant in Torryburn, 1650 (*Edinb. Marr.*), and David Baud is recorded in Craigie, 1717 (*Brechin*). The name is also found in Culross in 1586 as Baid, and in Dunblane in seventeenth century it occurs as Bad and Baid.

BACHOP. *See under* BAUCHOP.

BACK. Local. Janet Back in Learbarmor, 1683 (*Stirling*), and George Back in Edinburgh, 1689 (RPC., 3. ser. XIII, p. 505).

BACKIE. Thomas Backie, merchant in Thurso, 1756 (*Donaldson*, p. 47). Perhaps local from Backies, a village near Golspie. There is also a Backies near Cullen, Banffshire.

BADBAE. Local, from Badbae in parish of Latheron, Caithness. John Badbae one of Caithness's most celebrated "Men" was noted for his piety.

BADDILEY. Probably from Baddiley in Cheshire. Andrew Badly, monk of Melrose, to study canon law, 1379–80 (RRM., III, p. 173). John Badily, feltmaker in Edinburgh, 1683 (*Edinb. Marr.*).

BADENACH, BADENOCH. These surnames, common in the shires of Aberdeen and Banff, are without doubt derived from the district of Badenoch in Inverness-shire. There were four proprietors of this name in the parish of Inverurie in 1464 (*Inverurie*, p. 119), and the name disappeared from the burgh roll only in the eighteenth century. It was also an old surname in the parish of Oyne. Patricius de Badynach or Badenach, common councillor in Aberdeen, 1435, 1439 (*Guildry*, p. 186), is probably Patrick of Badenoch who witnessed a deed of 1439 relating to land in Aberdeen (REA., I, p. 240), is probably the Patrick Baidyenach who held a land in Aberdeen in 1460 (RAA., II, 134), and two years later served on an assize in the same town (SCM., v, p. 22). Agnes Badienocht held land in Aberdeen c. 1450 (REA., II, p. 298), and Matheus Baydenagh was a notary public in the diocese of Aberdeen in 1473 (RHM., II, 221). John Banzenoch burgess of Enrowre (Inverurie in Gairoch) appears in record in 1541 (REA., I, p. 418), John Bagenoch was commissioner to Parliament for Inverurie in 1621 (APS., IV, p. 594), and Alexander Badonach was a member of Gartly Company of Volunteers in 1798 (*Will*, p 24), and another Alexander Badenoch from King Edward was killed in the first Great War (*Turriff*). Old: Badzenocht, Badzenache, Baidienagh, Bangzie, Baidenach 1464, Badinoch 1669, Badyenoch 1664, Boidyenoch 1513.

BADGER. From the occupation, 'a dealer in corn,' ME. *badger, bager.* Thomas Badger, servant in Inwerweek (Innerwick), 1684 (RPC., 3. ser. x, p. 77).

BADICHEL. Nathaniel Badichel in the old parish of Dumbennan (now Huntly) in 1716 (SCM., IV, p. 169) probably derived his surname from the lands of Badichell in the barony of Phillorthe (Fraserburgh) mentioned in 1637 (*Retours, Aberdeen*, 236).

BADIE, BAWDIE. Jon of Baddy a servant of the tyrant David Menzies in Orknev, 1424 (REO., p. 39). One Baddi, in Randale, was escheat for bloodshed in Kirkyard, 1503 (ibid.,

p. 417). Barbara Baddie in record in Banchory-Devenick, 1598 (*Ecc. Rec. of Aberdeen*). William Bawdie, miller at Nydie milne, 1619, and three more of the name (*St. Andrews CR.*). John Badie, weaver in Newton, died 1745, and was buried in Nenthorn churchyard.

BAGGAT. Adam de Baggat, burgess of Rokesburc in 1235, witnessed letters of dedication of a cemetery in the same year, and in 1237 he appears as sheriff of Rokesburk (*Kelso*, 321, 418, 355). About 1250 he is again referred to as "tunc vicecomit. Teuidalie." He is probably the Ade de Baggat who held part of the lands of Iliuestun in the reign of Alexander II, and as Ade de Baggate a witness in the same reign (*Melros*, p. 231, 232). Cf. BATHGATE.

BAGGEPUTZ. From Bacquepuis in the arrondissement of Evreux, Normandy. A horse was purchased from Johannes de Baggeputz in 1312 (*Bain*, III, p. 427).

BAGNALL. The house of Robert Bagnal in Glasgow was wrecked in 1779 during a riot (Groome, *Gazetteer*, II, p. 116). From Bagnall in parish of Stoke-upon-Trent, Staffordshire.

BAGRA, BAGRIE, BAIGRIE, BEAGRIE, BEGRIE. Of local origin (1) from Balgray in Angus, old record spellings of which are Bagra and Bagro, and (2) from Bagra near Banff. John Bagray was messenger-at-arms in Aberdeen in 1569 (RPC., I, p. 660), may be the John Balgray, notary public, 1577 (RSCA., I, p. 295), and another John Bagray was a baker in Edinburgh in 1625 (*Edinb. Marr.*). A complaint was registered with the Privy Council by John Baigrie in Lufnes, East Lothian, in 1634 (RPC., 2. ser. v, p. 168), and Jean Bagra relict of John Brodie in Portsoy is in record in 1791 (*Aberdeen CR.*). William Watt Bagrie of Ythan served in the first Great War (*Turriff*).

BAIKIE. From the old manor of Baikie in Angus. (See Warden, *Angus*, II, p. 330 ff.). The name seems to have been carried at an early date to Orkney, where the family of Baikie of Tankerness was one of some prominence. John Baikie was bailie of Kirkwall and one of the committee on the war for Orkney in 1643 (APS., VI, p. 56). Thomas Backie was ordained minister for Kirkwall in 1697 (SCM., II, p. 172). Mr. J. S. Clouston, however, says (p. 33) that the name "is once, in 1565, actually found in the form Beaqui, and unless this was a mistake of the scribe (which is unlikely), it is evidently derived from Beaquoy in Birsay. There was certainly a family

BAIKIE, *continued*

of Beaquoy of Beaquoy, and the original odal lands of the Baikies, afterwards of Tankerness, certainly lay in the near neighbourhood." In 1650 there was only one person of the name of Baikie in Wasbister, and in 1739 there were five. Bake 1545, Baickie 1679.

BAILDON, BAYLDON. Most probably from Baildon, the name of a township in the parish of Otley, Yorkshire. Baring-Gould (p. 208) erroneously, I think, says the name is derived from Baladon, a place in Normandy. Patrick Baldon was a priest of the diocese of Ross in 1444 (*Pap. Lett.,* VIII, p. 449). William Baldon appears as perpetual vicar of Inverness, 1536, and Robert Baldon was part tenant in Akinhede, 1565 (REM., p. 438). H. Bellyse Baildon edited an edition of *The Poems of William Dunbar,* Cambridge, 1907. W. Paley Baildon (*Baildon and the Baildons,* I, p. 78–79) gives 57 ways in which his family name has been spelled in recent years and 64 old spellings from records.

BAILEYHEF. Henricus de Baileyhef, chamberlain of Scotland, c. 1223–1245, died at St. James in Spain in 1246 (*Bain,* I, 632). "A large land owner both in England and Scotland, his wife Lora having been one of the heirs of the De Valoniis family. Of his parentage different accounts are given; Bain's *Calendar of documents,* I, no. 632, suggests that he was a son of another Henry who appears in *Foedera* in 1199 as a follower of the Count of Flanders" (*Inchaffray,* p. 275).

BAILLIE, BAILIE, BAILEY. Notwithstanding the "de" attached to the earliest occurrence of this name in Scotland, it is most certainly derived from OF. *bailli,* the bailie or bailiff. The earliest record of the name in Scotland is in 1311–12, when one William de Bailli appears as juror on an inquest concerning forfeited lands in Lothian (*Bain,* III, 245), and in 1315 was one of the witnesses to a charter by John de Graham, lord of Abercorn (RHM., I, 20). This Bailli, says Mr. Bain (III, intro. p. lxiii), is without doubt Baillie of Hoperig, ancestor of the family which acquired and has since been known as of Lambinston or Lamington. "It is curious," he adds, "that nothing seems to be known of the real origin of the family. There is nothing here to favour the Clydesdale tradition that the first of them was a Balliol who changed his name. For Balliol was an existing surname long after this date in Scotland." (It was a popular belief that Baillie was substituted for Balliol on account of the unpopularity of the two kings of

that name.) The Baillies are now divided into many families, the principal branches of which are those of Lamington, Jerviswood, Polkemmet, and Dochfour. The Baillies of Dunain are said to have been founded by Alexander, a younger son of the House of Lamington. Isobel Ballie in the Steall, parish of Moonzie, 1719 (*St. Andrews*). Baile 1728, Bailie 1685, Bailive 1687, Baill 1723, Baille 1642, Baillye 1650, Baillyie 1650, Baillze 1644, Bailvne 1687, Bailze 1545, Bailzea 1650, Bailzie 1679, Ballie 1558, Ballye 1548, Baly 1682, Balye 1574, Balze 1474, Balzie 1621, Baylie 1673, Bayllie 1679, Baylly 1680, Baylze 1522, Baylzie 1668, Beal 1811, Beale 1794; and Bailly, Bailyow, Baleus.

BAILLIES. A variant of English Bayliss (Baylis, Bayless), 'the bailiff's son.' Nancy Nicholson Baillies was married in Glasgow, June, 1941.

BAIN. G. *bàn,* the 'fair'. Thomas Ban, burgess of Perth, 1324 (*Milne,* p. 19). William Bayn tenant in Kethyk, 1467 (*Cupar-Angus,* I, p. 147). Martin Bayne held a tenement in Ayr 1518 (*Friars Ayr,* p. 81). John Bhaine in Kilmaglash, 1675 (*Argyll*). The Bains of Caithness according to the *Book of Mackay* (p. 50) are descended from John Bain, son of Neil Neilson, son of Donald (Mackay) murdered in 1370. Bene and Beine 1597; Baine, Bayin. See also BANE.

BAINES, BAYNES. Alexander Banys had a respite in 1541 for art and part of the slaughter of Schir William Stevinsoune, chaplane, on the Links of Kincrag about nine years before (*Trials,* I, p. °256). This name was not uncommon in St. Andrews in the sixteenth century, and Thomas Banis, a bluegown, is recorded there in 1583. Andrew Beanes, flesher in Edinburgh, 1617 (*Edinb. Marr.*), and another Andrew Baines was locksmith there, 1676 (ibid.). Archibald Beanes, burgess of St. Andrews, 1633 (SCM., III, p. 117), and John Baines in Bogie was charged with deforcement in 1680 (RPC., 3. ser. VI, p. 587). Archibald Beanes, burgess of Aberdeen, 1634 (SCM., III, p. 117). Kathren Beanes recorded in Dysart, 1641, and in 1646 Andrew Beans quarrelled with his wife (PBK., p. 202, 298). James Beans in St. Andrews, 1685 (PSAS., LIV, p. 245). May be from Bains, Baines, or Baynes in arrondissement of Baveux. De Bayns occurs in England, 1263 (*Bardsley*).

BAIRD. This name appears to be territorial in origin. A family "de Bard" or "de Barde" held considerable land in Lanarkshire from the family of de Bigres. Henry de Barde witnessed the gift by Thomas de Haya to the House of Soltre between 1202–28 (*Soltre,* p. 15). In 1228 the great tithes of the land of Richard de Baard lying on the south side of the Auan (Avon) were granted to the monks of Lesmahagow (*Kelso,* 186, 280), and sometime before 1240 Richard Bard (without "de") gave to the same monks the whole land of Little Kyp, a gift confirmed by King Alexander II in 1240 (ibid., 181–82). Robertus Bard was one of the witnesses to the confirmation charter of the churches of Innyrwic and Liggerwod to the monks of Paisley c. 1272–79 (RMP., p. 119). Four individuals of the name rendered homage in 1296: Fergus de Barde of Lanarkshire, from whom may be descended the Bairds of Kipp and Evandale; Nicol Bard and John Bard, also of Lanarkshire; and Duncan Barde of Stirlingshire (*Bain,* II, p. 205–6, 210). The seal of Nicol bears a hare or rabbit to dexter and S' *Nichul Bard;* and the seal of Sir John bears within round tracery, a shield with a cross raguly and *S' Johannis de Barde* (ibid., II, p. 531, 539). Robert Barde who was made prisoner of war in 1315 and ransomed in 1320 (ibid., III, 456, 697), may be the Robert Barde who had a crown charter from Robert I of the barony of Cambusnaythen with pertinents on a reddendo of ten chalders of wheat and ten of barley (RMS., I, 79). He is probably also the Robert of Bard or de Barde, knight, who witnessed resignation of lands in the barony of Drumelzier in 1331 (*Hay,* 9), and appears as sheriff of Lanark in 1329 (ER., I, p. 116, 123). Dovenaldus Bard received a legacy from the Queen, 1328 (ER., I, p. 116), William Barde a Scots prisoner of war was put in irons at Carlisle, 1332 (*Bain,* III, 1074), and Fergus de Bard was a charter witness in Glasgow, 1327 (REG., p. 241). Robert de Barde and his wife appealed in a case against Margaret Fraser, lady of Malkarston, 1369 (APS., I, p. 535). John Bard occurs in an indenture of 1389 (REM., 169), and again ten years later as John de Barde (ibid., 182). Simone Bayard was elected town officer in Aberdeen, 1398 (CRA., p. 375), Thomas Bard de Ordinhuf (Banffshire) was on the assize on the vicarage lands of Abirkerdor, 1492 or 1511 (REM., 203), and in 1526 James V granted to his familiar servitor, William Bard, the lands of Balmaduthy (RMS.). The name is common in the Stirling Commissariot Record between 1607 and 1800, in the Edinburgh Marriage Records, and Paterson (*Ayr,* II, p. 87) says it is an old name in the parish of Ballantrae. Of Baird the son of Terri who granted the church of Anwoth and the chapel of Cardiness to the Abbey of Holywood about the middle of the twelfth century nothing is known, but he must have been a person of importance

in his day. An old prophecy attributed to Thomas the Rhymer says "there shall be an eagle in the craig while there is a Baird in Auchmeddan." John Baird of Kirkintilloch (d. 1891) planned and carried out the construction of New York's elevated railroads on Second and Sixth avenues.

BAIRDIE. William Bardye was burgess of Arbroath, 1560 (*Laing,* 712), and John Bardy rendered to Exchequer the accounts of the bailies of Inverkethin in 1561 (ER., XIX, p. 176). Rob Bardy was made freeman of Arbroath in 1565 (Mill, *Plays,* p. 164), James Bairdi in Dunfermline, 1588 *(Dunfermline),* Helen Bairdye, bedeswoman of St. Leonards, Dunfermline, is recorded in 1618 (*Laing,* 1804), Catharine Bardie in Kinghorn, 1628 *(St. Andrews),* and Walter Bairtie in Baldairdie, parish of Rescobie, 1607 (ibid.). James Bairdie, bailie of Inverkeithing, 1634 (RPC., 2. ser. v, p. 396), may be the James Bardie who was commissioner of supply for the same town in 1655 (APS., VI, p. 840). John Bardie of Selvadge had a commission granted him in 1650 (APS., VI, p. 618), James Beartie in Brechin, 1657 *(Brechin),* William Bairdie in Stirling, 1662 *(Stirling),* Margaret Bairdie in Dunblane, 1682 *(Dunblane),* and James Bairdie, bailie of Linlithgow, 1686 (RPC., 3. ser. XII, p. 492).

BAIRDONE. Thomas Bairdine in Dumfries, 1657 *(Dumfries).* John Bairdone portioner of Clauchan signed the Test, 1684 (RPC., 3. ser. x, p. 226). Most probably intended for BARDONAN, q.v.

BAIRNER. Henrie Bairner had a feu of the lands of Lambhill from the Abbey of Culross, 1587 (PSAS., LX, p. 81). Janet Barner in Dunfermline, 1617, and one more of the name *(St. Andrews).* Robert Bairner was tenant of Lady Dunkintie, 1634 (RPC., 2. ser. v, p. 331), Janet Bairner appears in Edinburgh, 1653 *(Edinb. Marr.),* and Henry of Caltmyln, parish of Saline, 1676 *(Stirling).*

BAIRNSFATHER, BAIRNFATHER. Probably from ON. personal name *Bjarnvardr* (from *Biarnhardr.* The final -*r* is silent). The genitive -*s* was probably introduced through popular etymology. Goods were stolen from John and Adam Barnisfader in Kelshop in 1502 (*Trials,* I, p. 30°), John Barnisfadir in record in Haddington in 1506 (RSS., I, 1288), and Robert Bairnsfather witnessed an instrument of sasine in 1525 (*Home,* 35). Sir James Bairnisfather, a Pope's knight, prebendary of St. Giles, Edinburgh, in 1542 (*Egidii,* p. 254), is mentioned again in 1553 as Sir James Bairn-

BAIRNSFATHER, BAIRNFATHER, continued
isfader, 'prebendar of Sanct Salvators alter'
(EBR., p. 271). Adam Bairnsfather was resident in the parish of Chindilkirk (Channelkirk) in 1563 (Lauder), Robert Bairinfader is mentioned in Over Stitchill in 1590 (RPC., IV, p. 489), and William Bairnsfather is recorded in M'Kestoun in 1687 (Peebles CR.). Bairnesfather 1688.

BAISLER. See under BATCHELOR.

BAIT, BAITH. Probably from the lands named Baith or Bayth in Fife Retours (for Beith). Kath. Bait at Fossoway, 16c. (Dunblane). John Bait witness in Perthshire, 1548, and burgess of Newburgh, Fife, 1549 (Gaw, 7, 24). John Baithe admitted burgess of Aberdeen, 1570 (NSCM., I, p. 69).

BALBIRNIE. An old Fifeshire surname derived from the lands so named in the parish of Markinch. John de Balbrenin or Balbrennin appears as witness to three documents belonging to the latter half of the thirteenth century (RD., 199, 202, 223). Another John de Balbrenny appears in 1312 (Bain, III, p. 429), and Robert de Balbreny was a witness in Brechin in 1364 (REB., I, 20). David de Balbyrny was "mair off ye quarter off Brechine" in 1450, and two years later a safe conduct was issued for James de Balbirny, a Scottish merchant (REB., I, 146; Bain, IV, 1246). Lawrence de Balbyrny was provost of the burgh of Forfar in 1457 (RAA., I, 112), and in 1483 Patrick Balbyrnie of that Ilk (de eodem) was a bailie of Edinburgh. George Balbirnye was serjeant of Dunkeld in 1508, and caution was found for Alexander Balbirnie of Innerrichtie in 1591 (Rent. Dunk., p. 26; RPC., IV, p. 603). Lucres Balbirny is recorded in Brechin in 1622 (Brechin). Anderson (Scot. Nat., I, p. 209) says that about the end of the sixteenth or beginning of the seventeenth century, the lands of Balbirnie were purchased from the Balbirnies, who held them under the earl of Fife, by George Balfour, ancestor of the present Balfour of Balbirnie. Bawbyrny 1477, Bawbrynny 1482.

BALCAIRN. Probably from Balcairn near Blairgowrie. Dugud de Balcairn was witness to a precept of sasine in 1479 (Panmure, II, p. 251).

BALCANQUHALL, BALCANQUHAL. From the lands of the same name in the parish of Strathmiglo, Fife. John Belmacancolle was one of the garrison of Edinburgh Castle on the English side in 1340 (Bain, III, 1323). Richard de Balcanko witnessed resignation by Sir David de Wemyss of certain lands in Fife in 1373 (Wemyss, II, 15), and John de Balmacankow was present at perambulation of the bounds of Kyrknes and Louchor in 1395 (RPSA., p. 3). Walter de Balcancolle was a cleric and notary public of St. Andrews in 1440 (RD., p. 297), and eight years later Thomas de Balcancole appears as burgess of Kirkcaldy (ibid., 424). Henry de Ballincankol had possession of lands of Carmoir "by thatch and turf," 1550, and Walter Ballincankol and Alexander Ballincankol appear in same document (Gaw, 23). Mr. Walter Maccanqueill was on trial before the Assembly in 1575 (MCM., I, p. 120), and Moysie (Memoirs, p. 51, 129, 138), in referring to him spells his name Backanquhale, Balkanquholle, and 'Backanquhell. Walter Ballincanquell was retoured heir of his father Alexander Ballincanquell de eodem in 1624 (Retours, Fife, 342). Anderson (Scot. Nat., I, p. 198) erroneously says "The surname of Balcanquhall seems to have been in course of time changed to Ballingall as more euphonious." Balcancoll 1517, Balcanq[ll] 1640, Balcanquaill 1653, Balcanquo 1639, Balcanquoll 1517, Balganquhill 1642; Ballincankoll. See MACCANQUALL.

BALCASKIE. From the lands of Balcaskie in the parish of Carnbee, Fifeshire. Thomas de Balcaski or Balkasky of the county of Fyfe rendered homage in 1296 (Bain, II, 730 and p. 204). In 1312 mention is made of the horses of John de Balkaski of Roxburgh and of Richard de Balkaski of Dundee (ibid., III, p. 420, 429). Thomas de Balcasky witnessed a donation by Henry de Aynestrother to Dryburgh Abbey c. 1330 (Dryburgh, p. 253). Thomas of Balkasky was rector of Culter in 1388 (Levenax). Provision of a canonry and prebend of Glasgow to William de Balcaska was made in 1332 (Pap. Lett., II, p. 385), and John de Balkasky was chaplain of the Collegiate Church of Dalkeith in 1449 (Soltre, p. 317). Vyl of Balcasky was chosen Brygmaster of Peebles in 1465 (Peebles, p. 154), John Balcasky witnessed an instrument of sasine in 1525 (Home, p. 35), and Martyne Balkesky, burgess of Edinburgh, was charged with using heretical books in 1558 (Trials, I, p. 217–218). The Balcaskies of Balcaskie were succeeded by a family named Strang from whom came Sir Robert Strange, the celebrated engraver. Of old the name was pronounced Bakaske.

BALCATHIE. From the lands of Balcathie in Angus. Between 1180 and 1214 Roger de Balcathin or Balkathyn appears as a charter witness (RAA., I, 58, 63, 25). About the year

1206 he was one of the witnesses to the perambulation of the lands of Rath, and c. 1214 he witnessed a confirmation charter by John de S. Michaele (ibid., I, 82). A later Roger de Balcathen witnessed a charter by Matilda, countess of Angus (ibid., I, 332), in 1254 he witnessed the perambulation of the lands of Conan and Tulloch (ibid., I, 366), and as Roger de Balkathy he witnessed a charter by Richenda filia Vmfridi de Berkelay in 1245 (ibid., I, p. 200). Hutting de Balchathin witnessed a charter by William, son of Bernard of a gift to the church of S. Thomas of Aberbrothoc, c. 1222–1240 (ibid., I, p. 88).

BALCHRISTIE. Johannes de Balcrestin who was one of the jurors on an inquisition apud Muskylburg in 1359 (RD., p. 267), derived his name from the lands of Balchristie in the parish of Newburn, Fife.

BALCOMIE. From the lands of Balcomie in the parish of Crail, Fifeshire. Robert de Balcomie who was constable of Crail in 1297 is probably the Robert de Balcomi who served as juror on an inquest made at Perth in 1305 (Bain, II, 880, 1670). John de Balcolmy was bailie of Crail in 1359 (ER., I, p. 623), and c. 1380 mention is made of the lands of Richard de Balcolmi in the same town (Neubotle, p. 236). Thomas de Balcolmi appears in record in 1429 (RMS., II, 130), James Balcolmy was married in 1492 (Sc. Ant., III, p. 103), and in 1497 Margaret Balcome was fined for disregarding a town ordinance in Aberdeen (CRA., p. 425).

BALCROMBY. Local. Alexander Balcromvy was admitted burgess of Aberdeen, 1472, and John de Balcromby, 1476 (NSCM., I, p. 23, 26).

BALD. This surname has a twofold origin: (1) literally 'the bald,' rendered calvus in Latin charters. (2) Camden the English antiquary says that in his time Bald was a nickname or nurse name for Baldwin (Guppy, p. 25). William calvus in Linton is mentioned in a Peeblesshire charter of 1214–49 (REG., p. 128). Henricus Baldus had a tenement in Perth from William the Lion for reddendo of one pound of pepper yearly, and in 1219 he witnessed a charter of sale of a toft to the Abbey of Scone (Scon, p. 29, 52). Joannes Calvus witnessed division between the lands of the House of Paisley and those of William de Sanchar in 1280 (RMP., p. 228). Henricus Baude, charter witness in Perth in the reign of David II (Scon, p. 126) may have been

a descendant of Henricus Baldus mentioned above. Rychard Bauld was burgess of Edinburgh in 1540 (Irvine, I, p. 46), payment was made to Sir John Bauld "for the annuall of the grammer scole" in 1553 (EBR., p. 272), and James Bald was tenant of the Abbey of Kelso in 1567 (Kelso, p. 519). This surname was not uncommon in Edinburgh and Fife in the seventeenth and following centuries. David Bauld was "capitane of the schip callit The Hoipweill of Carraill" in 1627 (RPC., 2. ser. II, p. 20), and James Bauld, apprentice in Edinburgh, 1666 (Edin. App.) may be James Balld who appears as a cooper in Edinburgh in 1673 (Edinb. Marr.). Belde [= bald] Robin Scot, 1510, is merely a nickname (Trials, I, p. 68*). Baald 1690.

BALDENY. Of local origin, perhaps from Baldinnie (old, Baldinye), Fife. Thomas Baldeny was tenant on lands of Newbattle Abbey, 1563 (Neubotle, p. 326).

BALDERSTON, BALDERSTONE, BALDERTON. From the lands of Balderston in West Lothian, the tún of a man named Baldhere or Bealdhere. William de Baudrestone of the county of Linlescu rendered homage in 1296 (Bain, II, p. 202). George Balderstone was burgess of Linlithgow in 1599 (Laing), and in 1634 Richard Balderstone was charged to appear as a witness in the same town (RPC., 2. ser. v, p. 644). William Baderstoune was a baxter in Falkirk in 1663 (Stirling), and the wife of James Baderstoun in Nidrie was charged with witchcraft in 1628 (RPC., 2. ser. II, p. 444). George Balderston late burgess of Edinburgh, 1731 (Guildry, p. 139). In the seventeenth century the name is also found in Edinburgh records as Balderstoune, Batherstoun, and Batherstain. Balderstoun 1536, Baldirstoun 1530.

BALDIE, BALDY. (1) diminutive of Archibald (Dunbar, Social life in former days, I, p. 10, 12). (2) diminutive of Baldwin. Thomas Baldy was infeft in chaplaincy of S. Ninian's in the parish of Ceres, Fife, 1540 (Macfarlane, II, p. 537), and Elspet Baldy is recorded in Aberdeen, 1555 (CRA., p. 285). William John Baldie was killed in action, 1940. A particular type of fishing boat which came into general use when the fame of Garibaldi (1807–82) was in everybody's mouth was known as 'Baldie' (in Leith) or 'Bauldie' (in Fife) (Scottish national dictionary, s. v. Baldie). See also BAULDIE.

BALDISON, 'son of BALDIE or BALDY,' q.v.

BALDOWIE. Perhaps from Baldovie near Kirriemuir, in Angus. William de Baldowy was a witness in 1455 (RAA., II, 104), Alexander de Baldowy was burgess of Aberdeen in 1464 (ibid., II, 155), and William Baldowy of that Ilk is mentioned in 1470 (ibid., 189). Edward Baldowy appears as chaplain in 1525 (SCM., IV, p. 23), Michael Baldovy, burgess of Montrose, had a precept of remission in 1526 (RSS., I, 3608), and John Baldowy witnessed a precept of sasine at Scone in 1544 (Scon, p. 207). Caution was found in 1591 for Alexander and Andrew Baldavies in Haltoun of Innerarratie (RPC., IV, p. 590). James Baldovye appears as burgess of Dundee in 1594 (St. Andrews), David Baldevi was burgess of Montrose in the same year (Macdonald, 72), and William Baldowie appears as burgess of the same town also in 1594 (Brechin). Balduwy 1474, Baulduvy 1478, Bawduuy and Baudewy 1534.

BALDRANY. Local. William Baldrany had precept of legitimation in 1530 (RSS., II, 666), David Baldranny appears as a witness in Edinburgh in 1531 (Soltre, p. 100), John Baldrany was 'kepar of the Kirk of Feild port' in 1552 (EBR., p. 168), and Thomas Baldranie, a mason, is mentioned in 1584 (Laing).

BALDRED. The OE. personal name Bealdred. Baldred, decanus Laodonie, c. 1235 (LSC., 66). Master Baldred (Bisset) le Scot, one of the commissioners sent to Rome to plead the cause of the independence of Scotland before the Pope, coming from beyond seas to Stirling Castle, had a safe conduct through England in 1306 (Bain, II, p. 495). Boldredus, official domini Sanctiandree, 1282 (Cambus., 3).

BALDRO. Local. Mr. Baldro to leave the country in 1650 under pain of death if he return (APS., VI, p. 580).

BALDWIN. Teut. Baldwin(e, 'bold friend.' A favorite name with the Normans. Baldwin, vicecomes, and Waldeus ejus filius witnessed a grant of the church of Wicestun (now Wiston, Lanarkshire) and its chapel to the Abbey of Kelso, 1153–65 (Kelso, 336).

BALERNO. From the place of the same name near Edinburgh. Thomas de Balhernoc and Walter de Balhernoch were jurors on an inquest held in the chapel of St. Katherine at Bavelay in 1280 (Bain, IV, 1762). Wautier de Balernaghe of the county of Edeneburk rendered homage in 1296. His seal bears a fleur-de-lys and legend S' Walt'i d' Balerah(?)

(Bain, II, p. 201, 546). John Balerno owned a tenement in Edinburgh in 1650 (Laing).

BALFOUR. From the lands or barony of the same name near the junction of the rivers Ore and Leven in the parish of Markinch, Fife. John de Balfure, who appears on an assize in 1304 is the first of the name in record (Bain, II, 1592). (The Ingelram de Balfour, sheriff of Fife, mentioned in Wood's edition of Douglas's Peerage, as appearing in a charter to the monastery of Aberbrothoc was really a Baliol). William de Balfure witnessed a charter by Duncan, earl of Fife between 1331 and 1335 (Laing, 37). Michael de Balfoure who witnessed a confirmation charter by David II to Ysabella de Fyf in 1365 (RMS., I, 221) may be the Michael de Balfwre who was present at the perambulation of the bounds of Kyrknes and Louchor in 1395 (RPSA., p. 5). Over twenty branches of the family of Balfour possessed at one time or another landed property in Fife. The name was originally pronounced with the accent on the last syllable, but Anglified usage has shifted the stress forward to the first. Some of the most prominent of the name are Sir James Balfour (d. 1583), author of Balfour's Practicks; Robert Balfour (c. 1550–1625), philosopher and Greek scholar; Nisbet Balfour (1743–1823), soldier; John Hutton Balfour (1808–1884), botanist; and last but not least, James Arthur Balfour (1848–1930), statesman and philosopher, created Earl Balfour of Whittinghame. Baffour 1545, Balfewer 1715, Balflower 1581, Balfoir 1594, Balfouir 1527, Balfowir 1513, Balfowyr 1524, Balfowr 1530, Baufour 1530, Baufoure 1482, Baulfour 1517, Bawfowre 1510, Bawfowyr 1521, Bawlfowr 1517, Belforde 1591.

BALGAIR. A Galbraith surname. From Balgair near Balfron, Strathendrick.

BALGARNIE. Andrew Balgarny, esquire of Scotland, had a safe conduct into England in 1389 (Bain, IV, 400), and John Balgarno in Dowlaw was a charter witness in 1542 (Laing, 1052). William Bagarna in Lammertoun was a witness in 1584, Peter Bagarno and his wife had charter of a house in Eyemouth in 1600, to which his brother Edmund Bagarno was a witness, and George Bagarnay in Lamarton was a witness in 1631 (Home, p. 215, 228, 230). Balgarnoche 1631 (in Lauder). Margaret Balgarnie was married in Dalkeith, 1939.

BALGARVIE. David Balgarvy was juror on an inquisition made at Arbroath in 1452 (RAA., II, 93). The name probably originated from Balgarvie in the parish of Monimail in Fife.

BALGONIE, BALGOWNIE. From Balgownie in Aberdeenshire. Malcolm Balgowny witnessed a charter of the lands of Glack, 1272 (*Inverurie*, p. 50). As Bal- and Pol- are sometimes interchangeable in place names he again appears as Malcolm de Polgoueny, witness in Aberdeen, 1281 (REA., II, p. 279, 281), as alderman, 1284 (*Friars*, 13), and as Malcolm de Pelgoueni he was provost, 1284–85. He appears again in 1294 as de Polgoueny and de Balgovny (REA., I, p. 35–37). Andrew Polgowny was admitted burgess of Aberdeen, 1409 (CWA., p. 317; NSCM., I, p. 4).

BALGOWAN. There is a small place of this name in Perthshire from which this surname may be derived. William Balgowan was a member of Gartly Company of Volunteers in 1798 (*Will*, p. 23).

BALGREEN. Local. There are places of this name in the shires of Ayr, Renfrew, and Aberdeen. John Balgrein in Haddington, 1680 (*Laing*).

BALHARRIE. From Balharrie in the parish of Alyth, Perthshire. Osbert de Balheri, charter witness, n. d. (*Cupar-Angus*, I, p. 344). John Balharrie is in record in the parish of Glamis in 1674 (*St. Andrews*).

BALINHARD. The old name of the Carnegies, derived from the lands of the name near Arbirlot in Angus. Gocelinus (Jocelin) de Balindard or de Ballendard appears c. 1230 in perambulations connected with the abbeys of Arbroath and Balmerino (RAA., I, p. 197; *Balmerino*, p. 9). As Jocius de Ballendard he witnessed a charter by Henry Reuel and Margaret his spouse (RPSA., p. 271). He was father or grandfather of John de Balinhard, the first authentic ancestor of the family of CARNEGIE, q.v., of Southesk. John de Balinhard sold the lands of Balinhard and acquired the lands of Carnegie in the parish of Carmyllie in Angus. Thomas de Balnehard of Linlithgowshire rendered homage in 1296 (*Bain*, II, p. 211).

BALINMAN. Local. Andrew Balinman at the Mylne of Muckersie, Perthshire, 1652 (*Dunblane*).

BALIOL, BALLIOL. According to the *Dictionnaire des postes* there are thirteen places of the name of Bailleul in northern France. M. de Belleval, author of an account of John Baliol, King of Scotland, says (p. 5) there have been nineteen different families of the name, all of which, except one in Normandy, are extinct (cited in Hodgson, *History of*

Northumberland, VI, p. 15). The family was of Picard, not of Norman origin as widely believed. The family took its name from a small village, Bailleul-en-Vimeu, about six miles south of Abbeville in the department of the Somme. Bernard de Baliol was the first of his name in Scotland. He occurred as witness to numerous charters by David I, from whom he obtained large grants of lands. He endeavored to dissuade David from going to war with England, and fought against him at the battle of the Standard in 1138. Hugh de Baillol witnessed a charter by Ada, mother of William the Lion, to Alexander de St. Martin between 1153–78 (*Laing*, 2), and the same or a succeeding Hugh de Balliol, c. 1200, confirmed an earlier donation by Bernard de Bailliol to the Abbey of Kelso (*Kelso*, 51, 53). Henry de Baylloyl, camerarius domini regis, and Ingraham de Bayllol, appeared in 1225 as charter witnesses (REM., p. 460, 461). Ingeramus de Ballia (Balliol) witnessed a charter by Seyr de Quency, c. 1210 (*Neubotle*, p. 54), and Henry de Baylliol witnessed a charter of King Alexander II to the Abbey of Neubotle in 1241 (ibid., p. 124). In 1295 an annual rent out of the lands of Balliol in France was pledged by John Baliol as "donatio propter nupitas seu dotalicium" on the marriage of his son Edward (APS., I, p. 452). The seal of the competitor (1291) bears a shield charged within an orle and S' Jehan de Baillouel (*Bain*, II, 488). Balyall 1256, Balliole 1293.

BALL. A name of uncertain origin. It may be from *Bæll*, an OE. personal name, which, however, is only known from its existence in place name compounds. There was also an ON. *Balle*. (2) It may be a development from the word 'bold,' (3) a form of BALD, (4) a diminutive of BALDWIN, etc.

BALLACH. *See under* BALLOCH.

BALLANIE. Probably from Balleny near Balerno, Midlothian. James Ballanye in Preston, slain at Langside in 1568 (APS., III, p. 51), is mentioned in following year as James Ballany (*Laing*, 848). Margaret Baleny in Ayttoun was accused of witchcraft in 1629 (RPC., 2. ser. III, p. 290). James Balleny in Newtoune heir of David Balleny in Gilmertoun, 1682 (*Inquis.*, 6350). The surname also occurs in the Edinburgh Marriage Records as Balanie, Ballanie, and Ballenie. Ballaine 1608.

BALLANTINE, BALLANTYNE, BALLINTINE, BALLINYTNE, BALLENDINE. Probably from the lands of Bellenden in the parish of Roberton, Roxburghshire. There is also a Ballinton, Ballintoun or Ballintome mentioned in Stirling

BALLANTINE, Ballantyne, etc., *continued*

Retours. John Ballantyne, Ballentyne or Bellenden, as he is variously known, archdeacon of Moray, was translator of Hector Boece's "History and chronicles of Scotland," and of Livy's Roman history into Scottish. Sir Alexander Ballindin was chaplain and prebendary of the Collegiate Church of Methven, 1563 (*Methven*, p. 55). David Bellenden, cordiner in Maybole, 1630 (RPC., 2. ser. III, p. 624), and another David Ballenden in Parkend appeared in 1642 (*Stirling*). Belindain and Bellanden 1660, Bellanetyn 1493.

BALLARD. From ME. *ballard*, 'baldheaded,' an augmentation of BALD, q.v. Thomas Ballard witnessed charters by William Malvoisine, Bishop of St. Andrews (RAA., I, p. 115, 116, 118).

BALLARDIE. From Ballardie in Fifeshire. James Ballardie was burgess of Dundee in 1611 (*Brechin*), and Thomas Ballardie in Fuird of Pitcur is mentioned in 1622 (*Retours, Forfar*, 144).

BALLENCRIEFF. Symon de Balnecrefe an archer in Livingston pele (= peel) in 1312 (*Bain*, III, p. 411), derived his name from Ballencrieff in West Lothian.

BALLENDINE. *See under* BALLANTINE.

BALLENY. From Balleny near Balerno, Midlothian.

BALLIGALLI. Roger de Balligalli rendered homage at Perth, 1291 (RR.). Perhaps from Balgillo in Angus, which a. 1329 was spelled Balugillachie, Balgillachy in 1369.

BALLINBOUR. Alexander Ballinbour in Wester Telliburries, 1678 (RPC., 3. ser. VI, p. 350).

BALLINDALLOCH. From Ballindalloch in the parish of Balfron, Stirlingshire. William de Balendolaucht was juror on inquisition held at Perth, 1305 (*Bain*, II, p. 456).

BALLINGAL, Ballingall, Ballinghall. From the lands of Ballingall in the parish of Orwell, Kinross-shire. It was a common surname in Newburgh in the middle of the sixteenth century. The seal of John Ballingall or Bangall is attached to a charter of July 1478 (*Macdonald*, 81). William Banegaw was witness, 1545, and Andrew Ballingaw witness in 1551 (*Gaw*, 57, 58). William Ballingall of that Ilk was charged with abiding from the raid of Lauder in 1558 (*Trials*, I, p. *404), and in 1566 William Baingaw of that Ilk was one of an inquest held on the lands of Raith (Fraser, *Melville*, III, p. 113). A payment of £18 was made to Betty Balingual "in respect she is not to be any more troublesome to this city," 1724 (*Guildry*, p. 128). Ballengall 1605, Bangall 1529.

BALLINGRY. From Ballingry near Lochgelly, Fife. Richard de Ballingry was present at the perambulation of the bounds of Kyrknes and Louchor in 1395 (RPSA., p. 3).

BALLINTEW. William Ballintew, burgess of Lauder, 1672 (*Lauder*).

BALLINTINE, Ballintyne. Variants of BALLANTINE, q.v.

BALLIOL. *See under* BALIOL.

BALLOCH, Ballach. From Balloch in Bonhill parish, Dumbartonshire. Donald Balloch appears as a witness, 1476 (RMS., II). Robert Balloch was messenger in Edinburgh, 1598 (*Edinb. Marr.*). William Balloche in Muirhead of Touchgorme, parish of St. Ninians, and William Belloch in the parish of Alloway (Alloa), appear in 1676 (*Stirling*). There was a family of Balloch in the Marnoch district in the end of the eighteenth century. The name appears in the sixteenth century as Bello, Belloch, and Bellocht (*Rent. Dunk.*), and later it became fixed as BULLOCH, q.v.

BALLONE. There were formerly lands of this name in Fife (Liddall, *Place names of Fife and Kinross*). Alan de Ballone was on inquest in Edinburgh, 1402 (*Egidii*, p. 38). Laurence of Ballon, master of the ship 'la Katerine,' of Edinburgh, 1410, may be the Laurence of Ballochyn, master of a vessel of the King of Scots, who had a safe conduct to trade in England, 1424 (*Bain*, IV, 794, 962). Robert Baloun, merchant of Scotland, had a safe conduct into England, 1465 (ibid., 1358).

BALLUNIE. Of local origin from Ballunie in the parish of Kettins, Angus. Thomas of Balewny, schyrreff clerk, was writer of a decreit arbitral anent the marches of Woodwrae, 1388 (*Bamff*, p. 22). Alan Ballowny had part of Kethyk in 1457 (*Cupar-Angus*, I, p. 132), Walter Balwany was tenant in Kethyk in 1511, and Anne Bauvany was a tenant of the Abbot and convent of Cupar-Angus in the same year (ibid., p. 281). Balluny c. 1500, Bawluny 1532.

BALLUSSY. William de Ballussy, canon of Dunkeld, c. 1340 (*Scon*, 167), derived his name from Balhousie (in 1459 Balousse) near Perth.

BALLYGERNAUCH. From Balledgarno or Ballerno a village in the parish of Inchture, Perthshire. Magister Mich. de Ballygernauch witnessed a charter by the Prior of St. Andrews in 1285 (*Neubotle*, 59).

BALMAHARG. From Balmaharg in Fife. John de Balmaharge appears in 1293 (DIS., p. 410), and in the following year as Balnagharg. Malcolm de Balmaharg witnessed a Fife charter of 1315 (HMC., 8. Rep., App., p. 305), and Adam de Balmaharg witnessed a charter of the lands of Nether Cameron, c. 1332 (*Wemyss*, II, p. 12).

BALMAIN. Of local or territorial origin from the lands of Balmain in the parish of Fettercairn. The place name is from the Gaelic *Baile meadhon*, "middle town," and the surname if Englished would be "Middleton." From the scant references in record to this name it is probable that the family became extinct in the main line or that they parted with their patrimonial estate at an early period. In 1553 Patrik Balmeñ took the part of 've mekle devill' in a mediaeval play in Perth (Mill, *Plays*, p. 273), Jon Balmayne received payment of his fee in 1599 (*Fordell*, p. 103), John Balmaine in Leitchill is in record in 1654 (DPD., I, p. 152), and Malcolm Balmean in Hiltoun of Maler was juror on an inquest held at Perth in 1680 (*Oliphants*, p. 276). The town of Balmain, Sydney, N. S. W., was founded by Dr. Balmain, a retired surgeon of the Royal Navy. The lands of Balmain were acquired at an early date by the Ramsays. The English surname Balmain is of quite different origin.

BALMAKIN. From Balmakin near Colinsburgh, Fife. Andreu Balmalkyn of the county of Fife rendered homage in 1296 (*Bain*, II, p. 204), and John de Balmalkyn was juror on an inquest at Carnconane in 1409 (RAA., II, 49).

BALMAKMOLLE. From the old lands of the name now Balmule in the parish of Aberdour, Fife. A decreet arbitral was concluded between Rogerus de Balmakmolle and others and the abbot of Inchcolm, 1233 (*Inchcolm*, p. 13–14). As Rogerus de Balmacmol he is witness in an undated charter of Agnes, granddaughter of Ranulph of Karamund (Cramond) (RD., p. 98). The name of Richard de Balmakemore of the county of Fife, who rendered homage in 1296 (*Bain*, II, p. 204), is probably from the same source.

BALMANNO, Belmanno. Of territorial origin from the old lands of the name in the parish of Marykirk, Kincardineshire. Huwe de Bal-

menaghe of the county of Perth rendered homage in 1296. His seal bears a fox erect, with mitre and pastoral staff, addressing a bird in a tree, S' *Hvgon' de Balmenaih* (*Bain*, II, p. 200, 532). The horse of Adam de Balmanaghe is mentioned in 1312 (*Bain*, III, p. 428), Robert Balmanauch was bailie and burgess of Karale in 1361 (ER., II, p. 61), the land of Gilbert de Balmanow in Crale is mentioned in 1421 (RAA., II, 56), and Robert de Balmannoch is mentioned in a case between the abbeys of Arbroath and Balmerino in 1459 (ibid., 125). Robert de Balmanow or Balmanach was burgess of Dundee in 1447 and 1470 (REB., II, 68; *Laing*, 163), and Robin Balmanoche was auditor of complaints in 1473 (APS., II, p. 103). Jacobus Balmannoch witnessed a lease by George, Abbot of Inchaffray in 1491 (*Inchaffray*, p. xcvii), sasine of the lands of Balmannoche Beth was given to Thomas Balmannoch in 1495 (*Laing*, 221), and in 1556 there is recorded a payment to William Bawmanno (EBR., p. 322). Alexander Balmanno of that Ilk was charged in 1582 with bearing, wearing, and shooting with pistolets (*Trials*, I, p. 100), Adam Balmanno was enrolled burgess of Dundee in 1589 (*Wedd.*, p. 171), in 1627 Peter Balmanno of Carloungie gave a bond of caution (RPC., 2. ser. II, p. 84), and John Balmano was candlemaker in Glasgow, 1684 (RPC., 3. ser. x, p. 274). Bolmanno 1663, Ballmanno.

BALMER. A spice dealer, from Early ME. *balme*, ME. *bawm*(*e* + the agental suffix -*er*. William Balmer in Fallows, 1682 (*Peebles CR.*), Robert Balmer (1787–1844), minister United Secession Church, and Alexander Balmer, laborer at Bridgeward, 1813 (*Heirs*, 601).

BALMIGLO. Robert de Balmiglo witnessed an obligation of 1337 (*Scon*, 166).

BALMOSSIE. From the lands of the same name in the parish of Monifieth in Angus. Alan de Belmosse had a charter from Robert I of some lands in Dundee and a third part of Craigie (RMS., I, App. II, 457), and as Alan de Balmossy he appears as witness to an obligation by John de Dunde in 1321 (HP., II, p. 225). In 1378 the third part of the lands of Craghy, formerly in the possession of Walter de Balmossy were granted to Patrick de Inverpeffre (RMS., I, 655, 687).

BALMYLE. There is a Balmyle near Blairgowrie and another at Meigle. Master Nicol de Balmyl, parson of Calder Comitis of Edinburghshire, rendered homage, 1296 (*Bain*, II, p. 213). Nicolas de Balmile or de Balmyle, canon of and afterwards bishop of Dunblane,

BALMYLE, *continued*

appears as cancellarius Scocie in 1300 (*Inchaffray*, p. 260; *Dowden*, p. 201; RPSA., p. 120). Willelmus de Balmyle was chamberlain of the bishop of St. Andrews "ex parte boreali aque de Forth" in 1395 (RPSA., p. 5). The death of William de Balmyle, rector of Aberbuthenot, was reported in 1429 (*Pap. Lett.*, vm, p. 106). David Balmylis, cotter in Stainhevin, parish of Dynnotar, is in record in 1606 (*St. Andrews*).

BALNABREICH. From Balnabreich near Brechin, Angus. Rogerus de Balnebrech or Balnebrich, rector of the church of Blar, 1313 (RAA., I, p. 291–292) is probably Master Roger de Balnebrich who was rector of Ferrewict in the diocese of St. Andrews in 1332 (*Pap. Lett.*, II, p. 221).

BALNAMOON. *See under* BONNYMAN.

BALNEAVES, BALNAVES. From the lands of Balneaves in the parish of Kinkell, in Angus, which in Latin documents appears as *de villa nativorum*. There is still a small farm near the old place called Balneaves. The old house has long since disappeared, but the site is still marked by three aged trees in a field opposite the manse of Kinkell. Laurence de Balnavis was present at the perambulation of the boundaries of Kyrknes and Louchor in 1395 (RPSA., p. 3). Balnevis of Halhill, Fife, c. 1539, one of the promoters of the Reformation, was described by Knox as "a very learned and pious man." In 1541 Henry Benese (an old form of the name) was on the Justice Ayre at Jedburgh (*Hamilton*, I, p. 74), and in 1587 John Balnaves was scribe to the Assembly of Perth. Many individuals of the name settled in Atholl under the Murrays. The families of Balneaves of Hallhill and of Carnbody were branches of Balneaves of Balneaves. The estate early passed to the Frasers, and Thomas Fraser of Lovat granted a charter of the lands of Balneaves to George, fifth Lord Glammis in 1501. In the first volume of the *Hamilton Papers* we have a wide variety of spellings of this name: Banese 1541, Balnavis, Penneyse, and Pennesse 1542, Bannese, Bennase, Bennese, Bennesse, all in 1543, Bannavis and Balnavis 1556, elsewhere Bannawis 1555, Balnauys 1531, Balneavs 1689, Banavees 1652, Bannevis.

BALNORY. Nigel de Balnory and John de Balnory witnessed a charter by Umfridus de Colquhoune, 1395, and in the same year Sir Nigel de Balnory witnessed a charter by Duncan, earl of Levenax (*Levenax*, p. 65).

BALORMY. Local, from Balormie, near Lossiemouth, Moray. Iohne Balormy of Elgin made a pilgrimage to Quhythirne and was cured at the shrine of S. Ninian (*Legends of the saints*, II, p. 343–344, S. T. S. ed.).

BALQUHIDDER. From Balquhidder in Perthshire, old spellings of which are Bofudder (1526) and in the Book of the Dean of Lismore Bofuddir. The Gaelic pronunciation of the name is *Bo-choidir* (*oi* as short *ao = u* in English hull), and in Rannoch *Bophuidir*. Duncan de Buchfuder appears as a witness in 1284 (LIM., xxxvi), and in 1296 Conon de Bethweder in the county of Perth rendered homage for his lands (*Bain*, II, p. 200). Gylcryst de Boffodyr juror on assize at Perth, 1304 (ibid., p. 414), and Henry de Buchfodyr was juror at Perth, 1305 (*Bain*, II, p. 456).

BALQUHOUNE. Walter Balquhoune in Kirkbride to answer to a charge of violence and robbery, 1592 (RPC., v, p. 28). There is a Balquhyne in Ayr *Retours*, 1622.

BALRAM. From the old land of Balram near Aberdeour in Fife. Nicholas de Balram was witness to a charter of Robert de London, brother of Alexander II (RD., p. 96), and in 1273 a controversy between Simon de Balran, son and heir of John de Balran, and the Priory of Inchcolm was settled (*Inchcolm*, p. 28–29). Matheu de Balran of the county of Fife rendered homage in 1296 (*Bain*, II, p. 209). Matthew Balrain who was admitted a burgess of Aberdeen in 1399 (NSCM., I, p. 1) is mentioned in 1401 as Mathew de Balran (SCM., v, p. 17) and in the following year as Balram. In 1491 there is reference to the land of Wilyam of Balram (DBR., 27), William Balram of that Ilk is mentioned in 1511 (RSS., I, 2185), and David Balram *de eodem* was juror on an inquest held at Cupar in 1516 (SCBF., p. 49). Maister Hercules Balrame witnessed a marriage contract of 1561–2 (*Fordell*, p. 100), James Balrame was retoured heir of William Balrame *de eodem* in 1565. An obligation by Laurance Barram of that Ilk is recorded in 1605 (*Pitfirrane*, 412), and as Laurence Balrahame *de eodem* he was retoured heir of David Balrahame *de eodem* his grandfather in 1619 (*Retours, Fife*, 57, 298). Bawram 1509.

BALRONY. Perhaps from Balrownie near Crathes, Aberdeenshire. Stephen de Balrony was auditor of accounts of Aberdeen in 1433 (SCM., v, p. 41). Robert de Balrony was admitted burgess of Aberdeen in 1439 and Richard de Balrony the same in 1457 (NSCM., I, p. 5, 15). Stephen of Balrony had a charter of a Templar land in the barony of Badfothal in 1450 (Banchory-Devenick, p. 166).

BALSILLIE, BALSELLIE. Of local origin from Balsillie near Leslie in Fife. Andrew Balsillie had a precept of remission granted him in 1536 (RSS., II, 2002), David Bawsilly is recorded in Pursk in 1591 (St. Andrews), John Bassillie was burgess of Perth, 1596 (Inquis., 8434), Bethia Basillie appears in Edinburgh in 1658 and George Barcillie in 1676 (Edinb. Marr.). Bousila 1628. Recorded in Edinburgh 1942.

BALTRODYN. From Baltrodyn or Balantradoch in Midlothian, formerly one of the residences of the Templars. The place name was later changed to Arniston. Walter de Baltrodyn witnessed a composition between the bishop of Aberdeen and the abbot of Lindores in 1259 (REA., I, p. 27). As Walter de Baltrodi (Baltrodin, Baltroddi) he was appointed bishop of Caithness in 1263 (Theiner, 229), and died in 1270. The name of Walter Balrodyn, witness, 1257 (Inverurie, p. 50) is most probably an incorrect spelling of this name. In 1332 reservation was made of a benefice to Adam de Baltrodouch of the diocese of Glasgow (Pap. Lett., II, p. 390). Adam Blancrodock (or Blancrodoke) had a charter of the lands of Craigie and Westmaler in the sheriffdom of Perth from David II (RMS., I, App. II, 1123). In MS. Acta Dominorum Concilii (in MS. in Register House, Edinburgh), the name is spelled Blantrodok.

BALVAIN. Local. Agnes Balvain in Dysart, 1584 (Dysart, p. 40).

BALVAIRD. From the small place of this name in the Fifeshire portion of the parish of Abernethy. Alan Balward appears as vicar of Kalendar in 1530 (Cambus., 182), William Baward was juror on an inquest held at Cupar in 1522 (SCBF., p. 266), Walter Baward appears as burgess of Perth in 1552 (Gaw), and in 1558 Sir Alexander Balward, a Pope's knight, was vicar of Logye (Laing, 688). Caution was found for Elizabeth Balvaird in 1586 (RPC., IV, p. 99), and in 1599 the Tolbuith house with pertinents in Dysart were set to Peter Balvaird (Dysart, p. 25). Agnes Balvaird and her two sisters were retoured heirs portioners of Andrew Balvaird of Glentarkie their father in the vill and lands of Glentarkie in 1647 (Retours, Fife, 713, 714), John Balvaird was minister of Hoy and Gramesay in 1668 (Orkney), and another John Balvaird, of Ballomiln, in the parish of St.

Ninians, is in record in 1767 (Stirling). 1678 Ballvaird; Balvard.

BALWANY. Symon de Balwany in the parish of Fyvie excommunicated in 1382 (REA., I, p. 165). There is a Balvanie or Balvenie near Dufftown, Banffshire.

BALWEARY. From the lands of Balweary near Kirkcaldy in Fife. Richard de Balweri witnessed a quitclaim to the lands of Drumkarauch in 1260 (RPSA., p. 346). Ricardus de Balwery, miles, witnessed a charter by Johannes de Inchesyrith of the gift of a toft in Inchesyrith in the reign of Alexander III (Scon, p. 83). The Scotts became "of Balwearie" only by marriage with the heiress of the estate between 1260 and 1280 (Brown, Michael Scott, p. 9).

BALZARD. Alexander Balzard is recorded at Craill, 1541 (St. Andrews CR.), and Thomas Balzeart in Anstruther, 1592 (ibid.). Cf. Ballonzeard ($z = y$) and Ballyeardis in Fife Retours, 795, 816.

BANBURY. James Banbury, a Scotsman, had a safe conduct into England, 1426 (Bain, IV, 990). Probably from the town of Banbury in Oxfordshire.

BANCHORY. Local. Richard de Bancori quitclaimed land in Dumfriesshire to Robert de Brus in the reign of Alexander II (Bain, I, 1684). For the place name Banchor or Banchory see Watson I, p. 481–482.)

BANE. G. bàn, the 'fair,' white. Malise Bane was juror on an inquest on the lands of Thomas de Cremennane, 1320 (Levenax, p. 82). In 1392 John Bane resigned the five pound land of Langneuton, Yester, East Lothian. The legend on his seal reads: S' Iohis Bnoe (RHM., II, 5; Seals Supp., 79). John Bane was burgess of Edinburgh, 1423 (Egidii, p. 45), and Robert Bane held a tenement in the Flukargait, Dundee, 1442 (Charters and Writs, Dundee, p. 21; REB., I, 92). Master William Bane had a safe conduct to pass through England, 1453 (Bain, IV, 1254). David Bane or Bayn was abbot of Dere (Deer), 1456–1460 (Pap. Lett., XI, p. 344, 585), and abbot of Cupar, 1462–1480. Duncan Bane took part in the second hership of Petty, 1513 (Rose, p. 190), and John Bane, a follower of Donald Gorme of Sleat, had remission for his part in laying waste Trouterness in Sky and Kenlochew in Ross, 1541 (RSS., II, 3943). See also BAIN and BAYNE.

BANIE. Rolland Banie in Cauldsyde, parish of Balmerinoch, appears in 1629, and four more of the name are in the same record (*St. Andrews*). Walter Baynie in Gunnershaw, parish of Dunipeace, 1672 (*Stirling*).

BANKHEAD. There are several small places named Bankhead, but the surname is most probably from Bankhead on the mutual border of the parishes of Kilmarnock and Dreghorn, Ayrshire. Sir William Bankhede was curate to Dame Issabella Wallace, Lady Lowdoune, in 1527 (*Trials*, I, p. 136*). The seal of John Bankhead or Bankheid, eldest son of Peter Bankheid in Bushe, Cunynghame, Ayr, is appended to a charter of 1559 (*Macdonald*, 99). Helen Bankheid is in record in Edinburgh in 1600 (*Edinb. Marr.*), Hugh Bankheid was retoured heir of James Bankheid in Eister Brigend of Kilwinning in 1630 (*Retours, Ayr*, 270), Hew Bankheid was taxed in 1634 for his lands in Perth (RPC., 2. ser. v, p. 588), and another Hugh Bankhead was surgeon in Portnessock, Wigtownshire, in 1764 (*Wigtown*). Peter Bankheid in Corshous, witness in 1609, and John Bankheid indweller at Annanhill in 1680 (*Hunter*, p. 44, 65).

BANKIER. From the old lands of Bankier, now a hamlet, in the parish of Denny, Stirlingshire. John Bankier was innkeeper in Kirkintilloch, 1662 (*Sasines*, 1047), James Bankier was portioner of Davidston in the parish of Calder in 1670 (*Campsie*), and John Banker portioner in Kirkintullock, 1686 (RPC., 3. ser. XII, p. 133).

BANKS. (1) Alexander de Riparia granted a quitclaim of a toft and acre in Tweedmouth in favor of the Abbey of Kelso, c. 1217–27 (*Kelso*, 37). David Banks is recorded in Wester Baldryk, 1573 (*Pitfirrane*, 202), Jonet Banks in Linlithgow, 1684 (RPC., 3. ser. x, p. 262), and in the Edinburgh Marriage Records of seventeenth century the name appears as Banks, Bankes, and Bankis. (2) John Bankis in Kirkwall retoured heir of Alexander Bankis his father, 1648 (*Retours Orkney*, 53) most probably derived his surname from Banks near Kirkwall. The Caithness surname of Banks is also of Orkney origin.

BANNATY. From the small place named Bannaty in the parish of Strathmiglo, Fife. The goods of Thomas Bannaty in Stirlingshire were escheat, 1536 (RSS., II, 2013), and Henry Bannathy was witness in Perthshire, 1549 (*Gaw*, 28). James Bannatie in Cowdoun, parish of Kinross, 1624, and seven more are listed in the Commissariot Record of St. Andrews, 1549–1800.

BANNATYNE. From a place called Bennachtain, the site of which is unknown to me. William de Bennothine witnessed a grant by David Olifard to the Hospital of Soltre between 1153–77 (*Soltre*, p. 4), and Nicolas de Benothyne witnessed a charter by William de Moravia in favor of the same hospital between 1278–94 (ibid., p. 40). Nicol de Benauty of Lanarkshire rendered homage in 1296, and in 1303 he appears as vicegerent of the earl of Carrick (*Bain*, II, p. 213, 372). This Nicolas appears to be the first of the name connected with the West Coast. Johannes de Banauthyn, dominus de Currok (now Corehouse) was a charter witness c. 1354 (*Kelso*, p. 384), and as Johannes de Bennachtyne de le Corrokys resigned the land of Nudre (Niddry) with pertinents in the sheriffdom of Edinburgh, 1362 (RMS., I, 110). In the following year he confirmed the land of Nudre Marescalli to Henry de Nudere (ibid., 143). Richard Bannachtyn, dominus de Corhouse, appears in 1459 (RMS.), and Richard Banauchtyn de Corhouse appears as witness, 1467 (*Neubotle*, p. 263, 314). John Bannatyne of Corhouse in 1662 (RMS.), and Thom of Bannantine of Corhouse, 1684. Sir Richard of Bannochtine of the Corhouse, who flourished c. 1460, sometimes wrote himself 'Bannachty,' and his son is called Sir John Bannatvne. This spelling continued till the time of Charles II, when the proprietor of Corhouse was called indifferently John Bannatyne and John Ballentyne, and his son is described as the son of John Bellenden. Down to recent times the forms Bannatyne and Ballantyne have been used indifferently by brothers of one house, and even by the same individual at different times (*Lower*, p. 17, from information supplied him by Mr. 'F. L. Ballantine Dykes of Whitehaven, Cumberland). The Bannatynes of Bute were followers of both the earl of Argyll and of the Stewarts of Bute, and the laird of Kames, chief of the Bannatynes or MacCamelynes, gave, in 1547, a bond of manrent to Stewart of Bute. Now the Bannatynes are more numerous in Arran than in Bute. Banaghtyn 1304. See MACAOMLINN.

BANNER. Johannes Bannezour witness in Ayr, 1429 (*Ayr*, p. 83). Thomas and Charles Banner, herds in Buchtrig, 1684 (RPC., 3. ser. x, p. 250). Harrison says same as BANNERMAN (q.v.) but?

BANNERMAN. This surname is popularly believed to have been assumed by an ancestor who held the office of standard-bearer to one of the early kings, but I know of no evidence in support of the belief unless it be the romantic story told by Boece of an unnamed standard-bearer of Malcolm Ceannmor or of Alexander I. In the 11th chapter of book xii (in Bellenden's translation) Boece tells us that at a battle on the Spey the banner-man of Malcolm being somewhat of a coward, "trimbland and not passand so pertlie forwart" as the king desired, had the royal banner taken from him and given to Sir Alexander Carron afterwards called Skrymgeour. In the 15th chapter he dates the event in the reign of "Alexander the Feirs." The first authentic reference to the family is in a charter by David II (1368) granting to Dovinaldus Banerman, the king's physician, the lands of the two Clynteys or Clyntreys (Clinterty), and the two Achrinys (now an obsolete place name), namely Watirton and Welton near Aberdeen (RMS., I, 283). In 1373 Alexander Bannerman, son of quondam Donald Bannerman, had a charter "totius terre de Slaty" (REA., I, p. 116), in 1382 was alderman of Aberdeen, and in 1387 he acquired the lands of Elsick from Sir Alexander Fraser of Philorth. He is probably the Alexander Banerman who appears in 1391 as procurator for Adam de Ledhovs, burgess of Aberdeen (RAA., II, p. 40), as a witness in 1396 (REA., II, p. 294) and common councillor of Aberdeen in 1398 (CRA., p. 374). John Banerman was admitted burgess of Aberdeen in 1400 (NSCM., I, p. 1), another John Banarman was a burgess of Berwick in 1467 (RD., 461), Alexander Bannerman of Watertoun was sheriff-depute of Aberdeen from 1498 to 1511 (RSCA., I, p. 440), and Patrick Bannerman was elected provost of Aberdeen in 1715 (CRA., p. 353). Elsick passed out of possession of the family in 1756. Banermain 1548, Bannermane 1665, Bennerman 1663.

BANNOCHIE. A surname in Aberdeenshire. Francis Banackie or Bannachie was one of the petitioners for the formation of the corps of Huntly Volunteers in 1798 (Will, p. 5, 19). Perhaps from Bennochie in parish of Insch.

BANOCK. Marjorie Banock in Wester Kincardine of Culross, 1632 (Dunblane), probably derived her name from Bannock in Stirlingshire.

BANWELL. Adam de Baneuill witnessed a charter by Hugh Malherbe filius Hugonis Malherbe of two bovates in Arbroath, c. 1211–14 (RAA., I, p. 42). Richard de Bannewyll witnessed a quit-claim of lands of Drumkarauch, 1260 (RPSA., p. 347). Probably from Banwell in county Somerset.

BAPTIE. A corruption of Baddeby, from lands of that name which were probably in Berwickshire. Simon de Baddeby had a charter of lands in Lamberton, c. 1270, to which William de Baddeby, tunc constabularius de Berewic, was one of the witnesses (Home, 224; BNCH., XVI, p. 334). William de Baddeby who witnessed a charter by Patrick, earl of Dunbar, c. 1248–89 (Raine, 32) had a confirmation from King Alexander III of "totam terram de Meners cum pertenentiis" (RMS., I, App. I, 95). John de Baddeby and Nicol de Baddeby, both of the county of Berewyk, rendered homage in 1296 (Bain, II, p. 203, 212). Adam de Badby of Lambertone in the county of Berewyke also rendered homage in same year (ibid., p. 206), and in 1300 gave his brother Richard a charter of lands in Nort Lambirtoun (Home, 225). In 1315 an inquisition was made into the lands and fishings of Alexander de Badeby in Paxton and Tweed (Bain, III, 461), and in 1323 Sir Alexander de Baddeby claimed the whole land of Maner in Peeblesshire (APS., I, p. 482; RMS., I, App. I, 96). Nicholas de Badby and Ricardus de Badby appear as charter witnesses in 1325 and 1332 (BNCH., XVI, p. 330, 332). John Badbee had a precept of remission in 1536 (RSS., II, 2033), John Badbe paid iiij lib. for his burgeschip in Haddington, 1539 (Mill, Plays, p. 251). Adam Badby was a witness in Fentounebarnis in 1583 (Laing, 1056), and Robert Baptie was constable of Elstanefurde in 1633 (RPC., 2. ser. v, p. 86). David Baptie apprentice in Edinburgh, 1672 (Edin. App.), John and Thomas Baptie were fined for attending conventicles in 1680 (RPC., 3. ser. VI, p. 426), and Patrick Babtie, son of Patrick Baptie, is in record in 1738 (Fordell).

BARA. Henry de Barue who witnessed a charter concerning the water-course of the mill of Bereford, near Morham, c. 1215 (Neubotle, p. 66), derived his name from the old manor of Bara (in 1327 Barv, Barrw) in the parish of Bara, East Lothian, as likewise most probably did Patricius Baru who witnessed a charter by Walter Cumyn in the reign of Alexander II (Scon, p. 63).

BARBER, BARBOUR. From the occupation of barber, ME. barbour, a barber (and surgeon). Gilbert le Barber or Barbour and Michael le Barber were Scots prisoners taken at Dunbar Castle in 1296 (Bain, II, 742, 801), and Aleyn le Barbur of the county of Are rendered homage in the same year (ibid., p. 205). In 1305 John Barbitonsor [med. Latin form] rendered the accounts for the farm of Mountros (ER.,

BARBER, BARBOUR, continued

I, p. 438). William Barbitonsor had confirmation of a charter of lands in 1317 (REB., II, 5), Robert Bruce granted to Ade Barbitonsor a toft in Moffat with two bovates of land adjoining (RMS., I, 36, 37), and in 1328 there is entry of a payment to Andrew Barber (ER., I, p. 98). In 1329 there is entry of a payment to Ade barbitonsor mentioned in another place as Alanus barber (ibid., p. 178, 214). Robert le Barber forfeited tenements in Borthwyk and Myntowe in 1336 (Bain, III, 321), Philip Barbour granted a charter in favor of his aunt in Aberdeen in 1383 (Friars, p. 20), John Barbour, archdeacon of Aberdeen, author of the "Brus," witnessed an instrument of concord between the bishop of Aberdeen and John de Forbes dominus ejusdem in 1391 (REA., I, p. 189). William Barber is a witness to the document. Robert Barber was presbyter of the diocese of Aberdeen in 1410 (RÉB., I, p. 27), John Barbitonsor of France was admitted burgess of Aberdeen, 1451 (NSCM., I, p. 13) and John Gray alias Barbour, a native of Edinburgh, had letters of denisation in England in 1463 (Bain, IV, 1336). A deliverance was made to Clappertoun Barbour for his fee in 1556 (Kelso, 480), Agnes Barber is recorded in Neither Barleyo in 1677 (Kirkcudbright), and George Barber of Turriff served in the first Great War (Turriff). Barbor 1625, Berbur 1500, Barbere 1365.

BARBITON. William Barbiton (Barbeton, or Berbitoun) had a charter of part of the lands of Kirkborcherwick (or Kirkbothericht) in the barony of Minthow from Robert I (RMS., I, App. II, 134, 135), and Adam Barbiton had a charter of the lands of Bralenawrae or Brakinwra from the same king (ibid., App. II, 150).

BARCHAN. 'Sir' David Barquhan (Barchan or Barrachin) held chaplainries of Sanct Laurent in Dingwall and Arfaill or Ardafaily in Ardmannoch, and was also vicar of Suddy and Kilmowr, 1561–69 (OPS., II, p. 485, 538). Cf. MACGILLEVARQUHANE.

BARCLAY. Of territorial origin probably from the town of Berkeley in Gloucestershire, England. Several individuals of the name are found in Scotland in the twelfth century. Walter de Berchelai or Berkelai held the high office of Chamberlain of Scotland in 1165, was present in curia regis at Lanark in that year, and witnessed several charters of William the Lion, etc. (APS., I, p. 86, 87, 94; REA., I, p. 10, 14). Humfridus de Berkeley witnessed a charter by Bishop Turpin of the church

of Keteryn, c. 1178–98 (REB., II, 257). Robert de Berchelai also appears as a charter witness between 1189 and 1196, and was present in curia regis at Edinburgh (APS., I, p. 88, 94, 388). Fourth in descent from Theobald de Berchelai, who came into Scotland in the reign of David I was Alexander de Berkeley, who married the heiress of Mathers and wrote himself "De Berkeley de Mathers" (Angus, II, p. 144). Walter de Berkelay and Robert de Berkelay witnessed William the Lion's grant of burgh and market to the church of Glasgow c. 1175 (REG., p. 37). Dr. Hay Fleming in his introduction to the St. Andrews Kirk Session Register, says: "A witness named Barclay is mentioned four times, and on each occasion his name is spelt in a different way, Barthlhlat, Barclaytht, Bartclaytht, Barclaitht. Judging from the clerk's attempts to take down his name this witness probably lisped" (p. cv). The Barclays possessed considerable estates in various parts of Aberdeenshire and Banffshire, and were hereditary sheriffs of the latter county. They are also found settled in Ayrshire in beginning of the fifteenth century. Barcklay 1716, Barckly 1685, Barclye 1543, Barcula 1499, Barculay 1548, Barkla 1498, Barkley 1702, Bercla 1499, Berclay 1389, Bercley 1317, Bercula 1505, Berkele 1298, Berkilai and Berklai 1510. Other forms of the name occurring in the Laing Charters are: Barclaye, Barcley, Barklay, and Berklaw.

BARCLET. Most probably an old spelling of BARCLAY which has become a fixed surname (cf. the quotation from Dr. Hay Fleming under BARCLAY). John Barcleyth was retoured heir of James Barcleyth in Cowtray, his father, in the lands of Cowtray, 1600 (Retours, Fife, 87). Agnes Barclet was retoured heir of David Barclet, portioner of Luthrie, 1607, and Margaret Berclit was retoured heir of James Berclit in Boddumcraig, in lands in the barony of Balmerinoch, 1647 (ibid., 187, 705). William Barclett is recorded in the Holmeheid of Pitcairlie, 1632 (Dunblane).

BARD. From G. bàrd, a poet. Simon le Bard, mercator de Scotia, mentioned in 1364 (Rot. Scot., p. 883). Johannes Bard or le Barde was juror in Moray, 1389 and 1398 (REM., p. 200, 212). James the Barde was one of the bailies of Lindsay of Byres for infefting James of Innes in the lands of Aberchirder, 1456. Barde also appears as a surname of several landowners in the district about the same time (Macdonald, Local place names, Huntly, 1887, p. 3). Andro Bard, John Bard, and William Bard, followers of the earl of Cassilis, were respited for murder, 1526 (RSS., I, 3386).

John Bard was tenant of Langmure, Ayrshire, 1552 (*Hunter*, p. 67). Jaspart Bard to be 'harmless and skaithless of all bodelie harme,' 1552 (*Illus.*, III, p. 277–279). In 1529 there is entry of a payment of ten pounds to "Thome the barde" (ALHT., v, p. 385). The name has most probably become lost in BAIRD.

BARDNER. Henry Bardiner, "indweller in Lethe," was executed as a pirate and "sey theiff" in 1526 (APS., II, p. 315), and another Henry Bardnare had a respite for slaughter committed by him in 1529 (RSS., II, 8). The goods of Adam Bardnar in Skamur were escheat in 1541 (ibid., II, 4060). Henry Bairdner of Cultmyln granted a charter 1606 (*Pitfirrane*, 428), William Bardner or Bairdner is in record in Torryburn in 1614 and 1621 (*Laing*, 1707; *St. Andrews*), Robert Bardner, tailor in Carnock, appears in 1622 (*Stirling*), James Bairdner in Kirkcaldy, 1650 (PBK., p. 361), and others of the name are recorded in the parish of Clackmannan in the eighteenth century (*Stirling*).

BARDONAN. Thomas de Bardonan of the county of Dumfries and Patrick de Bardonan rendered homage in 1296. The seal of Patrick bears an eight-rayed figure and S' Patrit de Bardonan (*Bain*, II, p. 198, 210, 558). These two individuals may have been sons of Adam mac Nes (Ade filius Nesonis) of Bardonan, who was killed in the Isle of Man in 1289 (ER., I, p. 35). Bardonan is now Bardannoch near Moniaive.

BARFOOT. Doubtless of local origin. Cf. Barfod near Lochwinnoch, Renfrewshire. Barefoot was also an old spelling of Berford in the territory of Morham. Jock Barefoot, the Careston gillie, was said to have been hanged by Earl Bairdie (d. 1453) for daring to cut a walking-stick from the Covin Tree of Finhaven (Groome, *Gazetteer*). Lady Bairfoot raised an action against George Graham for receipting of a stolen bond, 1664 (*Just. Rec.*, p. 85). Johnne Young, "schipard at Bairfute," in record, 1591 (*Trials*, I, p. 232).

BARGILL or BARGILLY. Thomas of Bargille (Bargylle, Bargilly) "ane vicar ministrand in the queyr of Glasgw," 1477 (REG., p. 458). John Barquhill, witness in Edinburgh, 1539 (*Laing*, 433). The name appears in Glasgow Protocols as Bargilly (1550), Bargille (1554), Bargillye (1551). Thomas Bargille was one of the masons employed in building the tower of Pollok in 1536 (*Pollok*, I, p. 271). Alexander Bargillie in Bogtoun of Calder in record 1669 (*Campsie*).

BARHAM. Johannes Barhame had a brewery in Achmuthy, 1535 (RAA., II, p. 522). Most probably from one or other of the English places so named.

BARHILL. Of local origin from some small place of the name. There is a Barrhill near Lennoxtown, Stirlingshire. John Barhill, notary in Kippen, 1632 (*Dunblane*), and Marjorie Barihill in Castnauchtone, 1636 (ibid.).

BARKELL. Alexander Barkell in Ormistoune was charged with assault, 1679 (RPC., 3. ser. VI, p. 301).

BARKER. From the trade or occupation of 'barker,' an obsolete name for the bark-stripper or rather for the man who prepared the bark for the tanner. Later the word was synonymous with 'tanner.' Patrick Bercar and his son held land in Dunipace c. 1200 (*Cambus.*, p. 108). Alisaundre le Barker, provost of the burgh of Haddington, rendered homage in 1296 (*Bain*, II, p. 197). Richard le Barker of Tyningham, tenant of the bishop of St. Andrews in the county of Edneburk also rendered homage in the same year. His seal bears a cross chequy cantoned with four lions rampant, and S' Richart le Barkier (ibid., p. 205, 555). Thomas Barkar in the parish of Fyvy was excommunicated in 1382 (REA., I, p. 165), William Barcar held a land in Edinburgh in 1400 (*Egidii*, p. 37), and Alexander Barcare was vicar of the parish of Pettinain in 1486 (OPS., I, p. 138). Bercar in 1526, Bercare 1515, Berker.

BARKLAW. Local, or perhaps merely a wrong spelling of BARCLAY. William Barklaw, witness in Linlithgow, 1534 (*Johnsoun*).

BARLAND. Local. George Barland, glover in Perth, 1684, and four others of the name (*St. Andrews*).

BARLAS. James Barles is recorded in West Cultmalundie in 1670 (DPD., I, p. 293), and John Barless was tenant of the mill of Gartly, parish of Foullis, in 1750 (*Dunblane*). The photographs reproduced in Mr. Macdonald's *Scottish armorial seals* (1904) were specially taken for the work by Mr. B. A. Barlas. The name is recorded in Pitlochry, 1940.

BARLOCH. Of local origin from a place of the name. There is a Barloch near Milngavie, Stirlingshire. Caution was found for James Barloche in Blackruthven, Perthshire, 1589 (RPC., IV, p. 350).

BARNCLEUTH. Mungo Barncleuth in the parish of Kirkpatrick-Irongray, 1626 *(Dumfries)*, most probably derived his surname from Barncleuch, near Irongray, Dumfriesshire.

BARNES. From Barnes in the parish of Premnay, Aberdeenshire. Robert of Bernis was a goldsmith in 1465 *(Laing, 154)*, John Barnis witnessed an instrument of sasine in 1496 *(Bamff, p. 37)*, and Alexander Barnis was admitted burgess of Aberdeen in 1524 (NSCM., I, p. 48). Thomas Barnys was notary public in 1536 *(Laing, 404)*, William Barnis granted the chaplainry of the Three Kings of Culane (Cologne) in Dundee, 1588 (REB., II, 362). Alexander Bairins was admitted burgess of Aberdeen, 1575 (RSCA., I, p. 220), Gilbert Bairnis was 'sacristar' there, 1595 (CRA., p. 117), and Mathew Bairnis was admitted burgess of the burgh, 1616 (NSCM., I, p. 117). Euphemia Barns is recorded in Dundee, 1621 *(Brechin)*, and John Barns, skinner in Haddington, was charged with defying the town authorities in 1628 (RPC., 2. ser. II, p. 593). James Barnes was merchant burgess of Edinburgh, 1649 *(Inquis., 3257)*, Jean Barns daughter of deceased William Barns of Belweddocke, 1656 (DPD., II, p. 208), Robert Barnes of Kirkhill, Ayrshire, in record, 1668 *(Corsehill, p. 81)*, John Barns or Barnes was provost of Glasgow, 1687 (RPC., 3. ser. XIII, p. 146, 147), and David Barns was feuar and gardener in Duns, 1766 *(Lauder)*.

BARNET, BARNETT. Popular forms of the personal name Barnard or Bernard. Bardsley says that in England the Cistercian monk, St. Bernard of Clairvaux, gave a great impetus in the thirteenth century to this name, and that "a large number of Bernards sprang up in Furness after the Abbey came under the Bernardine rule." It may also possibly be from the town of Barnet in Hertfordshire. Both forms are current in Scotland, and are also found in the Edinburgh Marriage Records.

BARNETSON. *See under* BARNIESON.

BARNHILL. Of local origin from a small place of the name, perhaps Barnhill near Patna, Ayrshire. A charm was given to Rebecca Barnhill for her son's sake, 1650 *(Pollok, I, p. 354)*.

BARNIE. A current surname in Caithness. Probably from *Bjarni*, 'bear,' a common ON. personal name. Katherine Bernie or Barnie held six acres of land near Cowpargrange in 1558 *(Cupar-Angus, II, p. 169)*.

BARNIESON. This Caithness surname is merely a form of Barnetsoun, which again is "a Scotticised form of the Scandinavian name Bernsten" (Mill, *Diary*, p. lxxxvi). The *t* is not heard in the local pronunciation of the name. In 1576 Bernissoun *(Oppressions, p. 33)*. Anna Barnatsone was charged in 1654 with superstitiously "goeing to St. John's Chappell" in Freswick, Caithness *(Old Lore Misc., v, p. 61)*, and William Barnatson in Kirk, Caithness, appears in record in 1662 *(Caithness, p. 1)*. William Barnesoun, bailie in Quendaill, 1624 (OSS., I, 84).

BARNIGHT. Perhaps from Barneight in parish of Kirkcowan, Galloway. There is also a Barnaight near Mauchline, Ayrshire, and East Barnaigh is near Kilbarchan, Renfrewshire.

BARNMAN. From O. Sc. *barnman*, a worker in a barn, a thresher. Donald Barnman in Diren, Caithness, 1662 *(Caithness)*.

BARNSDALE. Thomas Barnsdaille in Ege, parish of Cortachy, in 1637 *(Brechin)*, probably derived his surname from Barnsdale near St. Ninians, Stirlingshire.

BARNTON. Willelmus de Baryntone and Johannes de Baryntone, jurors on inquest apud Muskylburg in 1359 (RD., p. 267) probably derived their surname from Barnton near Cramond Bridge, Midlothian.

BARNWELL. This surname, of English origin, seems not to have flourished in Scotland. About 1165 Roger de Barneuile witnessed a grant by Serlo, clericus regis, to the Abbey of Kelso *(Kelso, 216)*. Adam de Berneuile witnessed the resignation of Roger, rector of Ellesdene, in 1228 (ibid., 330). Christopher Barnwell appears in Edinburgh in 1665 *(Edinb. Marr.)*. Bardsley says the name is from Barnwall in Northamptonshire.

BARON, BARRON. Baron usually meant one who held his lands from the king by military service, but there are many instances of persons being called barons who held of subject superiors, the "Bissets Barrones" of Lovat for example. In other instances "Barons" were just landowners who had a certain amount of jurisdiction over the populations on their lands. An old surname in Angus. Between 1400–1500 the name appears there as Baron, Baroun, Barrone, Barroun, and Berroun. The name here probably originated from the small baronies attached to the Abbey of Coupar-Angus. Thus the tenant of the barony of Glenisla became Robert Barrone, tenant of Glennvlav, 1508 *(Cupar-Angus, I, p. 265)*, and so throughout all the baronies belonging to the abbey. The name was also common in Edinburgh in the fifteenth-sixteenth centuries. Patrick Baroun was juror on an inquest in Edinburgh, 1428

(RAA., II, 61). A later Patrick Barone, burgess of Edinburgh, who had a grant of the land of Spitalefeld beside Inverkeithing, Fife, from Henry, Abbot of Dunfermline, 1477 (RD., 479), may have been the provost who died c. 1488. Another Patrick Barroun of Spitlefeild witnessed a deed in 1539 (SCM., IV, p. 32). Andrew Baron was present in parliament in 1534 as depute constable (APS., II, p. 337), and James Barroun was dean of guild of Edinburgh, 1555 (Protocols, I). William Barrin in Eistoun, Cromar, 1647 (SCM., III, p. 197). The Frasers of Reelick were known as Mac Barrons = "sons of the baron."

BARONDOUN. Barbour mentions a knight, Sir William de Barondoun, as one of those who fought on Bruce's side at the battle of Methven, 1306. Sir William de Burudun, miles, is witness to a charter by Petrus de Haga to the Abbey of Melrose (Melros) along with Thomas Rimor of Ercildun and others. (Burudun is the spelling given in Russell's Haigs of Bemersyde, p. 463, and in the facsimile of the charter. In Scott's Sir Tristrem, p. xiv, the charter is also given and the name spelled Burndun). Lord Hailes says, who Barondoun was 'I know not' (Annals, II, p. 8). A Roger de Burndon witnessed a charter by Adam de Baddeby in 1300 (Home, 225). It is also possible that the name may be a metathesis of Broundoun. There was a barony of this name which in 1436 was the property of Robert of Haswel (OPS., I, p. 385).

BARR. Of local origin from Barr in Ayrshire or Barr in Renfrewshire, or perhaps from both. The surname is most frequently found at the present day in the district around Glasgow, and is a common surname in the Kilbarchan Commissariot Record. Atkyn de Barr was bailie of Ayr c. 1340 (Friars Ayr, p. 15). John Bar or de Barre was burgess of Edinburgh in 1423 (LSC., p. 227; Egidii, p. 45). Patrick Bar was a witness in Glasgow in 1551, and William Barr 'comburgess' of the same town in 1554 (Protocols, I). Robert Barre, barber in Knockdole, was cited before the Privy Council in 1565 (RPC., I, p. 377), and Alexander Bar was retoured heir of James Bar in Kylesmure, his father, in 1600 (Retours, Ayr, 36). Archibald Bar was burgess of Glasgow in 1612 (Burgesses), and William Barr took the Test in Paisley in 1686 (RPC., 3. ser. XI, p. 496). As Bar, Barr, and Barre the name occurs in the Edinburgh Marriage Records. Sometimes difficult to separate from Barry which also occurs in records as Barre.

BARRACK. From the lands of Barroch or Barrauch in the parish of Bourtie, Aberdeenshire. This surname appears to be confined to the county in which it originated. In 1508 Johnne Barrok was found to be in wrongful occupation of the lands of Auchmaledy (RSCA., I, p. 79). John Barrak in Little Ardo was cautioner for James Barrak, his cousin-german, in 1630, and another John Barrach at the Cobill of Ardlethin is mentioned in 1632 (ibid., II, p. 318, 337). Three brothers named Barrack from Millbrex, Aberdeenshire, fought in the first Great War (Turriff).

BARRIE, BARRY. Of local origin from Barry in Angus. As this surname in old records is sometimes spelled Barre it is liable to be confused with Barr which is also found so spelled. William de Barry was collector of contributions in Gowry sub Yleff in 1360 (ER., II, p. 42). Thomas Barry had a safe conduct into England in 1391 (Bain, IV, 428). Robert de Barre and John de Barre appear in Edinburgh in 1402 and 1411 (Egidii, p. 39, 44), and Suet Barry in Aberdeen, 1408 (CWA., p. 315). Patrick Barre of Scotland had a safe conduct into England, 1405 (Bain, IV, p. 142), John Barry was admitted burgess of Aberdeen, 1408 (NSCM., I), and John de Barry was witness to a charter by John Ramsay, burgess of Montros in 1430 (REB., II, 33). Sir John Barry, a "Pope's knight," mentioned in a disposition of 1435, may be the John Barry who was chaplain of the choir of Brechin in 1456 (ibid., I, 48, 182). Sir Henry Barry, rector of Colas (Collace), had a safe conduct into England in 1468 (Bain, IV, 1382), and was still rector in 1476 (Laing, 169. See also Soltre, p. cxix). Henry Barry was a notary public in Glasgow in 1473 (REG., 400), and Thomas Barry, a native of Scotland, had letters of denisation in England in 1486 (Bain, IV, 1523). Sir John Barry appears as vicar of Dundee in 1495 (REB., II, p. 134), William Barre was clerk of the diocese of St. Andrew in 1496 (Laing, 227), and Andrew Barry was elected for the burghs on the committee of causes in 1526 (APS., II, p. 301). Thomas Barrye, unicorn pursuivant, had his right hand cut off and was banished for forging the regent's signature in 1570 (Stodart, II, p. 405). Wattie Barrie was a tenant of the Abbey of Kelso in 1567 (Kelso, p. 524), John Barry inherited a tenement in the burgh of Dundy (Dundee) in 1617 (Retours, Forfar, 102), and William Barrie was portioner of Galtonside in 1662 (RRM., II, p. 26). The name in the forms Barrie and Barry is common in the Edinburgh Marriage Records of the seventeenth century. There were some Barrie families in Glenmuick under Farquharson of Belladtrach and Gordon of Aboyne, as well as some in Glen Tanar and parish of Aboyne. See BERVIE.

BARROVAD. A stone discovered in the priory church at Whithorn in 1891 bears an inscription in barbarous Latin, probably of the fourth or fifth century A. D. The inscription reads: *Te Dominv[s?] Lavdamvs Latinvs annorv[m] xxxv et filia sva ann[orvm] iv [h]ic si[g]nvm fecerv[n]t nepvs Barrovadi*, "We praise thee Lord, Latinus aged 35 years and his daughter aged 4 (rest) here. The descendant of Barrovados made (this) monument" (Mackenzie, *Scotland: the ancient kingdom*, p. 110). Mr. Francis Diack renders the name "long head" (PSAS., LIX, p. 264). An excellent illustration of the stone from a photograph is given in the Inventory of the Galloway Monuments, p. 164, fig. 109A.

BARROWMAN. A barrowman is defined in the Dictionary of the Old Scottish Tongue as "one who helps to carry a hand-barrow." Heu Reillie was barrow man to Sornbeg, 1686 (RPC., 3. ser. XII, p. 401). The name is spelled Barraman in Workman's MS. William Barrowman or Baroumane had a charter of the lands of Fortrie in the sheriffdom of Banff from David II (RMS., I, App. II, 1033. In the British Museum MS. his name is spelled Borrowman). Alexander Burowmă was a witness in Edinburgh in 1468 (*Neubotle*, 301), Lokky Barrowman was banished from Aberdeen in 1570 (CRA., p. 367), John Barrowman was accused of tumult in Culross, 1686 (RPC., 3. ser. XII, p. 44), William Burrouman appears in Upper Kidston, 1684 (ibid., 3. ser. X, p. 315) and another John Barrowman served on an inquest in Dunfermline in 1705 (*Fordell*, p. 180). The name also appears in the Edinburgh Marriage Records. "There seems to be some confusion between this name, which is sometimes spelt Barram [? Balram] and Baron" (*Stodart*, II, p. 214). J. Barrowman is author of *Scots mining terms*, 1886.

BARRY. See under BARRIE.

BARSKIMMING. This surname, now probably extinct, is derived from the lands of the same name in the parish of Stair, Ayrshire. In 1689 there is an order for the liberation of William Barskimming (APS., IX, App., 12), and in 1697 there is record of the marriage of Helen Barskimming in Edinburgh (*Edinb. Marr.*).

BARSKINE. James Barskine in parish of Newhills, 1739 (*Aberdeen CR.*). Barscone in parish of Buittle, Kirkcudbrightshire, was in 1661 spelled Barskean (*Retours*, 287).

BARTH. A diminutive of BARTHOLOMEW, q.v. William filius Barth, burgess of Edinburgh, 1328 (LSC., 87).

BARTHELS. "Son of Bartle," a diminutive of BARTHOLOMEW. Mary Isobel Barthels died in Edinburgh, 1942. Cf. BARTILL.

BARTHOLOMEW. A widespread personal name in mediaeval England. Of Semitic origin, 'son of the twin' (Assyrian *talimu*, 'twin'). Bartholomew was one of the twelve apostles. Alisaundre Bertholmeu of Edinburghshire rendered homage in 1296 (*Bain*, II, p. 201). Mention is made in 1500 of the lands of John Bertholomei alias Leyis in Glasgow (REG., p. 481). Thomas Barthelmo was kirkmaister of the corporation of baxteris in Edinburgh in 1516 (EBR., p. 160), and Philip Bartilmo is recorded in Grugfute in 1659 (*Retours, Linlithgow*, 200), and in the Edinburgh Marriage Records the name is spelled Bartelmew, Bartilmo, Bartlemo, and Bartilmew. In Strathblane Bartholomew and Barclay were confused in old spelling. As forename we have Bertilmew Rutherfurde 1483 (ALA., p. 98).

Bartholomew is also used as an Anglicizing of *Parlan* (O. Ir. *Partholon*), a name with which it has no connection in origin or meaning. While the Irish name has almost the same sound as that of the apostle Bartholomew in Irish there is no connection between them. Partholon, also written Bartholan, seems to be a compound of *bar* 'sea,' and *tolon* or *tolan*, apparently derived from *tola* 'waves, billows'. "Partholon would thus designate 'one having relation to the waves of the sea.' This is just what we learn from his genealogy, according to which he is sprung from *Baath* (*Leabhar na hUidhre*, p. 1, col. 1, l. 24), whose name also means the sea" (D'Arbois de Jubainville, *The Irish mythological cycle*, Dublin, 1903, p. 14n). The substitution of Bartholomew for Irish Partholon, is, as the late Sir John Rhys says, "probably an instance of a superficial process of translating proper names" (*Rhind Lectures*, Paisley, 1891, p. 45.). He further suggests "that Parlan or Partholon had figured from time immemorial in the family legend of the Gaelic earls of Lennox as a great ancestor, and possibly as a divine personage." Partholon or Parthalon, son of Sear, according to ancient Irish mythology, was the first who took possession of Ireland two hundred and seventy-eight years after the Flood.

BARTIE, BARTY. One of the many diminutives of BARTHOLOMEW, q.v. Robert Barty in Dundee was charged with aiding the English, 1552 (*Beats*, p. 327). John Bairty was burgess of Edinburgh, 1587 (RPC., IV, p. 190). Bailie James Barty was appointed provost of Dunblane, 1938.

BARTILL. This was a surname in Mar, Aberdeenshire, in the seventeenth century. It is a diminutive of BARTHOLOMEW, q.v., through the reduced form Bartilmo. Lower says that in the North of England the feast of S. Bartholomew is called Bartle, and Barthol Fair was an old fair in Kincardine of Neil, held on St. Bartholomew's day (August 24). John Bartill in Cottoun of Kindrokiad is in record in 1600 (*Brechin*), another John Bartill in Balgrummo, parish of Scoonie, in 1616 (*St. Andrews*), William Bartill in Edinburgh in 1668 (*Edinb. Marr.*), and in 1674 Robert Bartle was servitor to John Boyll of Kelburne (*Hunter*, p. 85). As forename: Bartill Laurensoun 1625.

BARTLEMAN. This surname, as shown by the examples quoted, is merely a variant of the name BARTHOLOMEW, q.v. Alisaundre Bertholmeu of the county of Edinburgh rendered homage in 1296 (*Bain*, II, p. 201). In 1343 William Bertylmen rendered to Exchequer the account of the provost (*præpositus*) of Edinburgh (ER., I, p. 521). In the preceding year the same individual, as William Bartholomei, was rewarded for his share in the capture of Edinburgh Castle (ibid., p. 522). A second payment was made to him in 1343 when his name occurs in the form Bertilmen (ibid., p. 522). A fourth spelling of his name occurs in 1368 when he is referred to as "Willelmus Bertillmew in burgo de Edynburgche" (RMS., I, 284). Alexander Bartleman appears in Westhilles, parish of Dunsyre, in 1661 (*Lanark CR.*), another Alexander Bartleman appears in Symningtoune, 1708 (*Lanark Justices*, p. 37). The final *n* is doubtless a miscopying of *u* in the Exchequer Rolls. Bartlmen 1662.

BARTLEMORE. A corruption of BARTHOLOMEW, q.v.

BARTLET. From BARTLE, a diminutive of BARTHOLOMEW + the Fr. diminutive ending –*et*. David Bartlot or Bartlet in Chieburne is mentioned in 1633 (SCM., III, p. 109), Andrew Bartlet was fermorer in Aberdeen, 1643 (ROA., I, p. 232), and David Berthlet appears in Denbug, 1698 (*Inquis.*, 7979).

BARTON. Chalmers (*Dunfermline*, II, p. 307) says that Bartons from Yorkshire came to Scotland after a contest with Edward III, but persons of the name are in Scottish record at an earlier date. Thomas de Bartone of Ayrshire rendered homage in 1296 and had his lands restored to him (*Bain*, II, p. 214, 219). Adam de Bartone of Berwickshire also rendered homage (ibid., p. 206). John de Bertoun was juror on an inquisition at Lanark, 1432 (RAA., II, 65). Robert Barton of Ovirberntoun or Over Barton married the daughter of Moubray of Barnbougle Castle, and was allowed to assume the name of Moubray by Act of Parliament, 10 May, 1527 (APS., II, p. 320). Chalmers (*op. cit.*, p. 456) says other Bartons changed their name to Stedman. William Bartane in Queensferry was charged with assault, 1628 (RPC., 2. ser. II, p. 423), and Adam Bartane was merchant burgess in Edinburgh, 1647 (*Inquis.*, 3360). Robert Bartane of Risk signed the Test in 1684 (RPC., 3. ser. X, p. 227). The death of Sir Andrew Barton, naval commander to James IV is described in an old ballad. In the Edinburgh Marriage Records the name occurs as Bartane, Barten, and Bartoun. Bertane 1550, Berton 1529.

BARTY. See under BARTIE.

BASKEN. James Basken was collector for the shire of Banff, 1653 (*Banff Rec.*, p. 143), and Alexander Basken was apprentice in Edinburgh, 1679 (*Edin. App.*). Nisbet (I) mentions a family Baskin of Ord, but gives no information.

BASS. Andrew de Bas who was one of the jurors in a dispute regarding the Kirketun of Aberbuthenoth in 1206 (SCM., V, p. 212), derived his name from the Bass in Aberdeenshire.

BASSENDEAN. From Bassendean, an ancient parish now incorporated in the parish of Westruther, Berwickshire. The land of John de Bassyndene in the burgh of Haddington is mentioned in 1458 (*Neubotle*, p. 244, 247), and in 1529 there is record of the purchase of brown camlet from James Bassentyne (ALHT., V, p. 309). James Bassantin (d. 1568), astronomer, was son of the laird of Bassendean, and Thomas Bassandyne was printer of the first Bible printed in Scotland (1576–79). The name is of frequent occurrence in the Edinburgh Marriage Records of the sixteenth and seventeenth centuries as Bassandyne, Bassenden, Bassendyne, Bassindean, and Bassinden.

BASSET. From Fr. *bas* 'short,' 'low,' + diminutive –*et*, gave name to a Norman family. Robert Basset or Basseth was a frequent witness to charters by Earl David, and was one of the witnesses to the earl's foundation charter of the monastery of Lundors 1198–99 (LAC., p. 5. See also RAA., I, p. 95). Peter Basset was constable of Lokris (Leuchars) c. 1230 (*Southesk*, p. 717). Families of this name had great possessions in the midland counties of England in thirteenth century. '

BASTARD. Robertus le Bastard witnessed a charter by William the Lion to the Priory of Coldingham (*Raine*, 50). "In Norman times illegitimacy was not regarded with the same contempt as now . . . Robert Bastard appears in Domesd. survey as an important tenant in capite in Devonshire, in which county the family have ever since flourished as great proprietors" (*Lower*).

BASTUMWATHT. Adam de Bastumwatht, charter witness in Fife, c. 1260 (RPSA., p. 108) derived his name from Bassenthwaite near Keswick, Cumberland.

BATCHELOR. (1) Probably from the office of *bacularius* (LL.), corresponding to usher, or (2) from LL. *baccalarius* holder or tenant of a small farm. William Bacheler, burgess of Haddington, rendered homage in 1296 (*Bain*, II, p. 197), and John de Luss is mentioned in 1316 as *bacularius* of Robert I. David Bachetar [error for Bachelar] was serjeant of Forfar in 1472 (*Laing*), Adam Bachiler was "meseinger til our Souerane Lord" in 1476 (SCM., v, p. 25), William Batchler in Bakmure of the Mains of Stradichty, 1598, and four more of the name are recorded in the Commissariot Record of St. Andrews, James Bachlar in Easthills of Carmyllie, 1637 (*Brechin*), and Andrew Batchlar at Craigend of Moncrieff, 1652 (*Dunblane*). In 1665 the name appears disguised as Besler and Beseler (*Jervise*, I, p. 202), and Baisler is the popular pronunciation of the name in Perthshire and Angus. Margaret Baisler was married in Edinburgh in 1668 (*Edinb. Marr.*: the only one of the name here listed), and John Basslour appears in Heughead of Guthrie, 1686 (*Brechin*). Batchelier 1693.

BATCHEN. Local, from the Batchen, near Pluscardyn, Moray. Jonet Botchen was married in Edinburgh, 1688 (*Edinb. Marr.*).

BATE. Local. Walter del Bate of Lanarkshire rendered homage, 1296, and had his lands restored to him (*Bain*, II, p. 209, 219). Petrus de Bate was maris regis in 1415 (*Scon*, p. 168).

BATES, 'son of Bate,' a diminutive of Bartholomew, and so = BATESON. Robert Bates sometime minister of the gospel at Spynie, 1747 (*Moray*).

BATHERSTON. John Batherstoun, cordiner in Falkirk, 1682 (*Stirling*). George Batherstone, feltmaker, burgess of Edinburgh, 1731 (*Guildry*, p. 138). A variant of BALDERSTON, q.v.

BATHGATE. Of local origin from the town of the same name in West Lothian. Master Adam of Baggatte who was buried at Melrose, 1243 (*Chron. Mail.*, s.a.) was most likely the Master Adam de Baggat and 'Sir' Adam de Baggath who witnessed charters (*Melros*, 260, 261, 292). Thomas de Bathket was one of the archers in Edinburgh Castle in 1312 (*Bain*, III, p. 409). The name occurs in the Edinburgh Marriage Records as Bathcat, Bathegat, Bathgait, and Bathgat. Bathget 1405. See also BAGGAT.

BATHIE. Perhaps of local origin from the lands of Bathie in Perthshire mentioned in 1671 (*Retours*, 816). Alexander Bathe witness in Brechin, 1526 (SCM., IV, p. 24). John Bathie petitioned the Privy Council in 1686 (RPC., 3. ser. XIII, p. 42), and John Bathie appears in Dunkeld, 1695 (*Dunkeld*). Recorded in Dundee 1941.

BATT. A diminutive of BARTHOLOMEW, q.v. John Batt in Petdrichie, parish of Glenbervie, 1631 (*Brechin*). See BAIT.

BATTISON. Same as BEATSON, q.v. Five Batisons are recorded in the Commissariot Record of Dunblane in the seventeenth and eighteenth centuries.

BATTLE. The Battles or Batailles probably came from Umfreville, in the canton of St. Mere Eglise, arrondissement of Valognes, department of Manche. Their ancestor was a companion of Robert-cum-Barba, a kinsman of William the Conqueror. Several individuals of this name appear as witnesses in charters by the de Umphravilles in favor of the Abbey of Kelso. Henry Batail witnessed a confirmation by Richard de Vnframuille to Kelso c. 1220 (*Kelso*, 327), and c. 1228 Walter Bataill attested charters by Gilbert de Umfrauille in favor of the same abbey (ibid., 325, 326). Walter Bataile and Henry his son witnessed a charter by William de Umfrauill, c. 1250, and Peter Bataile witnessed a charter of resignation by Roger the rector of the church of Ellesdene in 1228 (ibid., 329, 330). William Bataile witnessed a gift of land to the Hospital of Soltre between 1250–66 (*Soltre*, p. 32). Thomas dictus Batail, son of quondam William Batail, burgess of Berwick, sold his lands in Waldefgate to the Abbey of Kelso c. 1266 (*Kelso*, 47, 48). Johannes de Batalia witnessed a charter by Richard de Laycestria to the Abbey of Inchaffray in 1240 (*Inchaffray*, p. 62), and as Johannes de Labatil he attests another charter by William filius Hawok, c. 1245 (ibid., p. 63). As Johannes de la Batayle he witnessed a grant of a cellar in Perth to the Abbey of Lundors (LAC., p. 74), and as Johannes de Bello and de la Batail he appears as witness in Scone charters of the same period (*Scon*, p. 57, 61, 126). Thomas Bataile rendered homage at Berwick, 1291 (RR.).

BAUCHOP, BAUCHOPE, BACHOP. Believed to be a corruption of **WAUCHOPE**, and said to be found in Falkirk in an old record as *Bauk* (cf. Fawp for Fauhope, Pook for Pollock, and Rook for Rollock). Bachop or Bauchop is common in the Commissariot Record of Stirling in the seventeenth and eighteenth centuries, and eight Bauchops are recorded in the Commissariot Record of Dunblane within the same period. Thomas Bawchok, a chapman, in record, 1591 (*Sc. Ant.*, VI, p. 166), and Patrick Bauhok was "garitur in ye castell" of Stirling, 1589 (ibid., VI, p. 165). William Banchope (for Bauchope) and Robert Banchope witnessed a letter of discharge in Edinburgh, 1595 (SCM., v, p. 204), Robert Bauchop was retoured heir of Robert Bauchop, merchant burgess of Edinburgh, his father, 1604 (*Inquis.*, 170), and Margaret Bawchope was in Edinburgh, 1640 (ibid., 2500). Thomas Bachop or Bachope was treasurer of Stirling in 1622 and 1646 (SBR., p. 156, 190), and William Bauchop, sergeant of Edinburgh, 1630 (*Laing*, 2048).

BAUGERSCHO. John Baugerscho who contributed to church repairs in Aberdeen, 1508 (CRA., p. 79) derived his surname from Balgerscho near Cupar-Angus, Perthshire.

BAULDIE, BAULDY. Diminutives of **ARCHIBALD**, q.v. "O wha hasna heard o' blythe Bauldy Buchanan." Alexander Rodger, *Poems and songs*, 1838, p. 119. See also **BALDIE**.

BAUTIE. Diminutive of **BARTHOLOMEW**, q.v. James Bautie was made burgess freeman of Glasgow in 1576 and John Bawttie in 1607 (*Burgesses*). David Bawty was oistlar in Borthuikscheillis, 1587 (RPC., IV, p. 147), Isobel Bawtie was married in Edinburgh, 1605 (*Edinb. Marr.*) and John Bautie appears in Hauhemmuir of Brechin, 1637 (*Brechin*).

BAWNE. Thomas Bawne admitted burgess of Aberdeen, 1473 (NSCM., I, p. 24). Henry Bavne in Aberdeen, 1493 (CRA., p. 50), and Alexander Bawne, priest there in 1506 (REA., II, p. 96). Agnes Bawin is in Cassindonat, 1593 (*St. Andrews*), and John Bawne in Barnismure, parish of Kilynnie, 1628 (ibid.). Bawin 1584, Bawn 1590. Does not appear to be from Boyne which is spelled differently.

BAXENDINE. Hardly a variant of **BASSENDEAN**, q.v. Perhaps of recent introduction from south of the Border. There is a Baxenden near Blackburn, Lancashire, in 1332 Bakestonden, "the dene by the *tun* of *Bacca*."

BAXTER. This surname comes from the occupation of "bakester," originally a woman that baked, OE. *bæcestre* a female baker. In Middle English the ending *-estre* being unstressed soon lost its final *e*, and *-ster* came to be regarded as an emphatic form of *-er*, and consequently was applied to men as well as women, so that the early Middle English feminine *bakstere* became later Middle English masculine *baxster*. In Latin charters the word or name is rendered *pistor*. Between 1153 and 1177 William pistor witnessed a grant by David Olifard to the Hospital of Soltre (*Soltre*, p. 4), and c. 1188–1202 Aldred pistor was one of the witnesses to a charter of the kirk of Haddington (RPSA., p. 153). Between 1200–1240 Reginald Baxtar witnessed the gift cf the church of Wemys in Fife to Soltre (*Soltre*, p. 13). Geffrei le Baxtere of Lossithe of the county of Forfare took the oath of fealty, 1296 (*Bain*, II, p. 208). Thomas dictus Baxter, burgess of Irvine, made a grant in 1323 for support of a chaplain in the parish church of Irvine (*Irvine*, I, 123), and Hutredus pistor was burgess of Roxburgh, c. 1330 (*Kelso*, p. 369). William Baxtare was a crossbowman in Edinburgh Castle in 1312 (*Bain*, II, p. 409), and Robert Baxter was a town official in Aberdeen in 1398 (CRA., p. 375). Baxter was and still is a common surname in Angus, and as Forfar was a royal residence the first Baxters there may have been the royal bakers. Bacster 1533, Bakster 1467, Baxstar 1505, Baxstair 1506, Baxstare 1531, Baxster 1512.

BAYLDON. See under **BAILDON**.

BAYMAN. John Bayman was taxed for his rent of Easter Bigend, 1634 (RPC., 2. ser. v, p. 587).

BAYNE. Like Bain this name is from G. *bàn*, 'white.' Duncan Bayne, son of Alexander Bayne, burgess of Dingwall, had a grant of the lands of Tulche (Tulloch) and others in 1542 (RMS., III, 2737), and as Duncan Bane of Tullich he witnessed an Inverness charter of the following year (*Laing*, 467). The mill of Kethyk was let to William Bayn in 1469 (*Cupar-Angus*, I, p. 151), Johnne Bavne was tenant in Wall in Tiree in 1541 (ER., XVII, p. 614), Thomas Bayne rendered to Exchequer the accounts of the burgh of Craile in 1558 (ibid., XIX, p. 39), and another Thomas Baynne, baker, was burgess of Edinburgh in 1572 (*Laing*, 874). The name is also found in Edinburgh in 1530 (MCM., II, p. 98), and Ewir Bayne *alias* Quhyte was murdered in Colonsay in 1623 (*Trials*, III, p. 553). By some clan historians the Baynes are reckoned a branch of the Clan Mackay. The name has no connection with English Bayne, a surname of Norman origin. The 'banes' in the arms of the Scottish family are merely canting heraldry. Baine 1611, Bayn 1607.

BAYNES. *See under* BAINES.

BEAGRIE. *See under* BAGRA.

BEAN. G. *Beathán,* a diminutive of *betha* or *beatha* 'life.' See MACBEAN. Bean or Beyn, the name of a saint in the Breviary of Aberdeen (the legendary bishop of Mortlach) is a Scottish form of *Beóán,* a saint of British origin. In the Life of S. Cadroe his name is written alternately Beoanus (*Watson* I, p. 311). There was another Bean (Latinized Beanus), 'magister de Dunblane,' c. 1210 (*Cambus.,* 122), and another Beanus was rector of the church of S. Marie of Arane (Arran), 1357 (RMS., I, 182). A remission was granted to Ferchard Bean in 1428 (*Rose,* p. 126). Adam Bene was witness in Dumfries in 1450 (*Laing,* 129), John Beane is in Minnythill, parish of Dennie, 1675 (*Stirling),* Thomas Been at Miln of Bombie, 1722 (*Kirkcudbright),* and Robert Bean appears in Grayfaulds of Kirkbuddo, 1779 (*Brechin).* The name is found in Edinburgh in seventeenth century as Bean, Beane, and Beaine (*Edinb. Marr.).* (2) The name of Bean, dean of Lismore, afterwards bishop of Argyll or Lismore (1397–1411) is probably to be identified with Benedictus Johannis of the diocese of Argyll, the name a misunderstanding of Bene dictus Johannis = Bene called Mac Ian (*Dowden,* p. 384).

BEANGALL. Isobel Beangall recorded in Sauchie, 1627 (*Stirling).* There is a Bengall near Lockerbie, Dumfriesshire.

BEANSTON. From the old vill and territory of the name in East Lothian. John de Benystoun was juror on lands of Swinton in 1408 (*Swinton,* p. xviii), Jacobus Beinstoun was citizen of St. Andrews in 1540 (*Dysart,* p. 5), Thomas Beinstoun was commissioner to Parliament for Pittenweem in 1579 (APS., III, p. 128), Isobel Beinstoun is recorded in Hornden in 1664 (*Lauder),* and Thomas Beinstone was bailie of Pittinweyme, 1673 (*Inquis.,* 5650). The surname reached the Orkneys where we find John Beinstoun, bailie of Westray in 1617 (REO., p. 402), and Andrew Beinstoun is recorded there in 1640 (MCM., II, p. 211). Beinston 1588, Benistoun 1528, Beynsoune 1596, Beynstoun 1632, and Beanstoun, Beynstoin, and Beynston.

BEAQUOY. An old Orcadian surname. See under BAIKIE.

BEASTOUN. Probably from Beeston near Leeds. James Beastoun, brewer in Edinburgh, 1644 (*Edinb. Marr.).*

BEAT, BEATT, BETT. Most probably diminutives of BARTHOLOMEW, q.v. Andrew Bet and William Bet were burgesses of Edinburgh, 1344. Andrew Bet had a confirmation charter of certain lands and burgages in the burghs of Edvnburghe and Stryvelyne in 1369, and in 1375 he conceded to Cristiane his spouse a tenement in Edinburgh (RMS., I, 323, 625). Thomas Bet, witness in Arbroath, 1466, appears as sub-prior of the monastery, 1482 (RAA., II, p. 155, 184). John Beatt was couper in the parish of Cargill, 1654 (*Dunblane),* Thomas Beat is in record in Peathill, parish of Kettill, 1655, and three more of the name are in the vicinity (*St. Andrews).* William Beet, blacksmith in Aberdeen, 1791 (*Aberdeen CR.).* The origin for the name offered by Mr. J. M. Beatts (SN&Q., XI, p. 156) is too silly for credence.

BEATH. Most probably of local origin from Beath in Fife. Edmund de Beeth witnessed the gift of 10s. annually to the monks of Dunfermline by Gilbert de Cles in 1231 (RD., p. 108), and Malcolmus Beyth witnessed a charter by Maldouen, earl of Leuenauch to the monastery of Arbroath in the same year (RAA., I, p. 94). Donald Bait was servitor to the bishop of Dunkeld in 1508 (*Rent. Dunk.,* p. 85). William Bait is recorded at Kasynbarye, parish of Kinglassie, in 1550, and two more of the name are mentioned (*St. Andrews).* David Bait in Hauchmour of Brechin appears in 1580, and Archibald Baitt in 1657 (*Brechin).* Andrew Bait appears in Knokshynnane in 1491 (RPC., IV, p. 572), and Andrew Bait, brewer (1672), James Beat, tailor (1675), and David Baith, writer (1696), are recorded in Edinburgh (*Edinb. Marr.).* Andrew Baith was constable for the parish of Portmooke, Kinrossshire, in 1633 and 1635 (RPC., 2. ser. v, p. 95; PBK., p. 87).

BEATHAG. This is the feminine of BEATHAN, for which see under BEAN. According to M'Vurich in his Book of Clanranald Beathog was the name of a daughter of Somerled, "a religious woman and a Black Nun. It was she that erected Teampull Chairinis, or the church of Cairinis, in Uist" (*Rel. Celt.,* II, p. 157). According to Martin her tombstone in Iona bears: *Behag Nijn Sorle vic Ilurid Priorissa* (W. I., p. 263). Gillecrist MacNachdan in his grant of the church of Kilmorich, 1247, mentions his wife Bethoc (*Inchaffray,* p. 65). Bethoc, sole daughter of Donald Bane, king of Scotland, was ancestress of John Comyn, lord of Badenoch, a claimant to the Crown in 1291. Bethoc or Beatrice (as Fordun Latinizes the name, IV, 39) was daughter of Malcolm II, and wife of Crinan of Dunkeld,

> "Bethok fayr
>
> . . . .
>
> Scho was to Cryny in hir lyff,
>
> The abbot of Dunkeldenys wiff,"

as Wyntoun tells us (bk. 6, c. 10, ll. 877–880). Another MS. of Wyntoun gives her name as Betow. Richard [? read Rudulph] son of Dunegal and his wife Bethoc gave a ploughgate of land in Rughcestre to the Abbey of Jedburgh (RMS., I, App. I, 94; *Lawrie*, p. 408). From this Bethoc the lands of Rulebethoc, now Bedrule in Roxburghshire, take their name, and Croftbethoc in Cumberland (1200), a now extinct place name, had its origin from another lady of the same name. Dolbethoc ('Bethóc's holme' — Watson) was granted by Gilchrist, earl of Mar to the Culdees of Munimusc (Monymusk) before 1211 (RPSA., p. 371–72). Bethoc was also the name of the wife of Donald Macgilleni of Ross in 1438 (*Pap. Lett.*, IX, p. 12). Bahag Neuyntouchirly held the four merk lands of Torblaren in 1471 (RMS., II, 1044). With *gille-* prefixed it forms Gilbethoc, the name of a witness in an inquest concerning the ownership of the lands of Monachkeneran in 1233 (RMP., p. 167; Innes, *Legal antiquities*, p. 218). The name has been absurdly Englished Sophia! In the seventeenth century usually spelled Baik, Baike, and Beak. Beak Crowbycht was an "vnfre baxter" in Inverness in 1577 (*Rec. Inv.*, p. 258). See GIL-BETHOC.

BEATHEN. John Beathen in Meikleglen, 1685 (*Kirkcudbright*).

BEATON. Two learned families named Macbeth and Beaton or Bethune practised medicine in the Isles in the sixteenth and seventeenth centuries. Their names in the seventeenth and eighteenth centuries became merged in English in the one surname of Beaton. The Macbeths practised in Islay and Mull, and the Beatons in Skye. The first of the Islay family on record is Fercos Macbetha, who witnessed and probably wrote the Gaelic charter of 1408. The family for the next two centuries were official physicians to the Chiefs of Macdonald, from whom they held lands. Gilchristus M'Veig, surrigicus or surgeon in Islay is in record. Fergus M'Baithe in 1609 received from James VI certain lands in Islay in his official capacity as "principalis medici intra bordas Insularum" — chief physician within the bounds of the Isles. His son, John Macbeath, succeeds in 1628 to the lands, but gave them over to the Thane of Cawdor in following year. The words "Leabar Giolla Colaim Meigbethadh" (book of Malcolm Macbeth) are written on one of the Gaelic manuscripts in the National Library of Scotland, glossed in the same hand "Liber Malcolmi Betune" (Mackinnon, *Catalogue of Gaelic manuscripts*, 1912, p. 6, 7). The Mull Beatons or Betons were hereditary physicians to the Macleans of Dowart. In 1572 Hector MacLaine of Dowart granted a charter to Andrew MacDonil Vikinollif (i.e. son of the doctor) and his heirs of the pennyland of Piencross [Pennycross] and Brolas for his skill in the medical art. Martin (p. 254) says that Dr. Beaton was sitting on the upper deck of the "Florida" of the Spanish Armada when it blew up in Tobermory Bay in 1588 and he was thrown a good way off, but lived several years after. Another of the Mull family was Fergus M'Veagh in Pennycross whose medical MS. is now in the library of Edinburgh University. A branch of the family early settled in the Fraser country, and in 1589 it is recorded that they had possessed a davach in Glenconvinth "time out of mind." In 1558, one of them, James Betoun, attended Lord Lovat. He was known "as Tolly-Mullach — *An t-Ollamh Muileach*, the Mull doctor — showing that he was of the noted physicians of that island. The race declined in the Aird, and before the end of the sixteenth century one of them, John M'Klich — John son of the Doctor who kept Lord Lovat's flocks, got into trouble by helping himself to his master's muttons, and was saved from punishment by his wit and skill in archery. By 1622 they probably ceased to practise the healing art" (*Wardlaw*, intro., p. xxxvii-xxxviii). The Beatons of Skye "were real Beatons or Bethunes from Fife, descended from the Lairds of Balfour. A grandson of the fifth laird, Dr. Peter Bethune, settled in Skye about the middle of the sixteenth century. His descendants were numerous, and intermarried with the best families in Skye and the Isles. They are still strong in Skye. The Gaelic of the name is Peutan or Beutan" (Macbain, *Celt. Mon.*, XVII, p. 208). The last of these hereditary physicians came to an end in 1763 in the person of Niel Beaton (*Clan Donald*, III, p. 128). Bittoune 1675.

BEATS, BEATTS. As BEAT, q.v., with genitive -s. John M. Beatts was publisher for a time of *The Dundee Times*, 1855.

BEATSON. The son of Bat or Baty, a diminutive of the scriptural name BARTHOLOMEW. David filius Bety was provost of Linlithgow in 1342 (ER., I, p. 491). The surname ,was not uncommon on the West Marches in the sixteenth and seventeenth centuries, and in the seventeenth century a family of the name acquired lands in Fife. John Batisoun or Batysoune had a charter in 1458 of two mercates and a half of the lands of Dalbeth (Dawech) in the barony of Westir Ker for his services at the battle of Arkenholme (1 May 1455) when the Douglases were overwhelmed (RMS., II, 632). Nicholas Batisoun had a similar grant out of the same lands for his services (ibid., 633), and Robert Batysoune also received a grant of two mark lands of Quhitscheles°for similar services (ER., VI, p. 557). William Beatisoun in Hawick was ordered to be exhibited before the Privy Council in 1627 as a masterless person fit for the wars (RPC., 2. ser. II, p. 85). Baitsone 1683, Beattisoun 1597, Beatisone 1653. Other forms are Batesoun, Batiesoun, Beatisoun, and Betteson; and Armstrong (Liddesdale, p. 184) gives the following plural forms: Batesonis, Batisonis, Batisons, Batsones, Batsons, Battesons, Battissons, Batysonis, Batysonnes, Batysons, Beatisons, and Beatisones. A writer in Notes and queries (13. series, I, p. 287) makes the wild suggestion "that the true derivation is from Old English Pehta, a Pict." BATTISON is another current form of the name.

BEATTIE, BEATTY, BEATY. A well-known Border surname, commonly explained as a metronymic from Beatrice, but really from Bate or Baty, pet or diminutive forms of Bartholomew. (There was, however, a Gilbert fitz Beatrice of the county of Roxburghe who rendered homage for his lands in 1296 (Bain, II, p. 199), but of this name there is no further record). In 1569 "Hew Batie and Johnne Batie enterit plegeis . . . for thame selffis, thair sonnis, men tententis servandis and haill surname of Batesonis" (RPC., II, p. 42). Beatties and Beatsons were fairly numerous in Upper Eskdale, and in Ewesdale, and Wauchopedale. The name is also found in Berwick-on-Tweed as early as 1334 (Rot. Scot., I, p. 275). The surname is also found early in the north, where we find John Betty admitted burgess of Aberdeen in 1473 (NSCM., I, p. 24). Andrew Batie was burgess of Dumfries, 1567 (Edgar, p. 242) and persons of the name of Batie were followers of the earl of Morton in 1585 (APS., III, p. 392). William Baty was burgess of Montrose in 1513 (REB., II, 170), John Bety rendered to Exchequer the accounts of the same burgh in 1558 (ER., XIX, p. 43), John

Baty was prebendary of Lincloudane in 1565 (RRM., III, p. 393), Robert Bettie was burgess in Montrose 1635 (RPC., 2. ser. v, p. 517), and James Batty was officer in Inverness in 1574 (Laing, 907). In the eighteenth century the name was extremely common in the parish of Laurencekirk, "nearly every farm in the parish was at one time or other in the hands of a Beattie" (Fraser, History of Laurencekirk, p. 170). Barbara Beaty and Joneta Bety were retoured heirs portioners of Helene Striveling in the lands of Balcaskie in 1620 (Retours, Fife, 312, 313). There is no evidence to support the theory that this name is from Gael. biadhtach, one who held land on condition of supplying food (biad) to those billeted on him by the chief (AU., II, 128). As forename we find Baty Flessor in Ayr, c. 1340 (Friars Ayr, p. 15), and Batye Muchowray signed the Band of Dumfries in 1570 (RPC., XIV, p. 66). Other old forms are: Baetie, Baitie, Baittie (1567), Baitty, Batye (1579), Baytie, Beatie (1627), Betay (1629), Betie, Bette, Bettie (1629).

BEAUEYR. William de Beaueyr or de Beaueir gifted the lands of Ardarie in Fife to the Priory of May in the reign of William the Lion (RPSA., p. 382; May, pref. p. 15). As William de Beiure he was one of the witnesses to the letter by Alexander II attesting his good faith to Henry III of England, 1244 (Sc. Ann., p. 355). Anderson (op. cit.) suggests that for Beiure we might read Bervie. Cf. BARRY.

BEAUMONT. Of Norman origin from one or other of the many places of the name in France. In Latin charters de Bello Monte. Roger de Bellemont or Beaumont, brother of Robert, fourth earl of Leicester, was chancellor of William the Lion (Scotichronicon, VI, 42). He was consecrated bishop of St. Andrews in 1198, built the castle there, and died in 1202 (Dowden, p. 10–12; Chron. Mail.). Richard de Bello Monte had a grant of the barony of Crail in Fife from Alexander II (charter cited in Bain, II, p. 450). His descendant Isabella de Beaumont, Lady of Vescy, received a grant from Edward I to hold a market on her manor of Karel, 1294, and in 1296 she rendered homage (ibid., 704, 863). Alexander Bevmonde witnessed a charter by the earl of Huntlie, 1367 (Aboyne, p. 31). The surname is not common.

BECC. An old Gaelic personal name from the root seen in Gaelic beuc, 'roar.' Bécc, grandson of Duncan, was slaughtered in 707 A. D. (AU.; Skene, CS., I, p. 273). Dunchad Bécc, 'king of Kintyre,' was victor in the naval battle of Ardde-anesbi fought in 719 A. D. and died in 721 (Tighernach). A diminutive of the name also occurs in *Tighernach* under the year 676, where the death of *Béccán Ruimean,* 'Beccan (of the island) of Rum,' is recorded.

BECK. Of local origin from some small place of the name probably in Dumfriesshire. There is a Beckfoot (a burn mouth) and Beckton in Dumfriesshire. Thomas del Beck was juror on an inquisition in Lochmaben in 1347 (*Bain,* III, 1499), and Thomas de Bek was a tenant of the earl of Douglas in Glenwaldy in the barony of Prestoune, 1376 (RHM., I, p. lxi). John Beck in Balmaclaill (Galloway) found caution for his indemnity in 1627 (RPC., 2. ser. II, p. 69), and John Beck, cordiner at Bridgend of Dumfries in 1683 and six more of the name are recorded in the Dumfries Register of Testaments, 1624–1800. The name is also found in the Commissariot Record of Kirkcudbright in the seventeenth and eighteenth centuries and in the Edinburgh Marriage Records.

BECKETT. An old surname found in the neighborhood of Melrose. It may be an abbreviation of Benedict. Old forms are Becket, Bicket, and Bychat. Harrison says from French Béchet or Béquet, or (2) from residence at the Beck-Head.

BECKIE. Alexander Beckie, shoemaker in Auchtertoul, 1766 (*Moray*).

BECKTON. Local, from Beckton, near Lockerbie, Dumfriesshire. John Bectoune in Tinwald was examined for the Test, 1685 (RPC., 3. ser. XI, p. 435). William Becktoun, merchant in Edinburgh, 1663 (*Edinb. Marr.*). Robert Begtoun in Edinburgh, 1597, and three more of the name there at a later date (ibid.; *Edin. App.*).

BEDDEL. ME. *bedel(l), beddell,* 'beadle,' Old Scots *bedrell.* In Scots the word most commonly means a church officer, town-bellman. Catherin Beddel, brouster in Inverness, 1613 (*Rec. Inv.,* II, p. 103).

BEDDIE, BEEDIE. Probably forms of BEATTIE. In the northeast, in West Angus, and in East Perthshire intervocalic *tt* has become *dd.* Nicoll Beddy appears at Balquharne, 1580 (*Brechin*), David Bedie in Toux, parish of Fetteresso, 1616, and three more of the name are in the Commissariot Record of St. Andrews, John Beddaw, indweller in Edinburgh, 1675 (*Edinb. Marr.*), Thomas Beadie was apprentice in Edinburgh, 1683 (*Edin. App.*), William Beidie appears in Claymires, 1703 (*Banff Rec.,* p. 244), and John Stott Beedie of Gamrie served in the first Great War (*Turriff*).

BEDE. This name is the same as Gaulish *Bed-aios,* Old Bret. *Bedoe* or *Bidoe.* Bede cruthnec ('the Pict'), mormaer of Buchan, bestowed the town of Abbordoboir (Aberdour in Buchan) on the Abbey of Deer (*Bk. Deer,* I, 3, 8). Bede Ferdan of Monachkeneran, who lived in a great house built of twigs (*domo magna fabricata de virgis*) was one of four individuals bound or set apart to receive and entertain all pilgrims repairing to the church of S. Patrick at Kilpatrick, Dumbartonshire. The inquisition of 1233 which gives this information says that he lived sixty years previously, and was slain in defence of the rights of the church (RMP., p. 166–167). Another Beda or Bede, canon of Glasgow, appears in record c. 1175–1207 (LCD., p. 235; RMP., p. 99, 101, 109, 110), and witnessed the gift by Maldowen, son of Alwin, of the church of Kamsi (Campsie) to God and S. Kentigern c. 1208–1214 (REG., p. 88). William filius Bede witnessed the gift of the church of Cadinros to the church of Glasgow by the same earl c. 1208–1233 (REG., p. 93; *Levenax,* p. 14). Another Bede, rector of the church of Muyethe, appears as charter witness in 1284 (LIM., p. xxxvi). Bede the ecclesiastical historian of England is said to have been of Celtic descent.

BEDEFORD. From Bedford in co. Bedford, England. Henricus de Bedeforth witnessed a quitclaim by Johannes, son of Mathew Loremarius of Perth, 1240 (*Scon,* p. 61). W. de Bedeford witnessed a gift to the church of Glasgow, c. 1260 (REG., p. 177).

BEDSON. James Bedson of Glenistowne, 1631, and James Betson, ruling elder in Auchtertule, 1641 (PBK., p. 30, 203). John Bedesoun, constable of the parish of Abircrombie, Fife, 1633 (RPC., 2. ser. v, p. 93). Bedeson 1641. Harrison has Bedson as (1) = Beddoe's son, and (2) for Betson.

BEE. See under BIE.

BEEDIE. See under BEDDIE.

BEEDLES. An old Scots surname, perhaps the possessive of 'Beadle,' from the office. One of this name may have given origin to Biedlieston in parish of Dyce, Aberdeenshire.

BEEN. Harrison says: (1) diminutive of Benedict, or (2) diminutive of Benjamin; and Bardsley says diminutive of Benedict. Margerie Been, sister of James Been, held a tenement in Edinburgh, 1336 (*Bain,* III, p. 346). Thomas Been at the Mill of Bombie, 1722 (*Kirkcudbright*).

BEER. Probably local. Baer, Beer, Bere (OE. *baer(e)*, pasture in wooded districts) is common in place names, simple and compound, in the English Midlands. There is also OE. *bearu*, a wood. William Beir, indweller in the Fischerrawe, 1634 (RPC., 2. ser. v, p. 578). Alexander Bier in Edinburgh, 1680 *(Edinb. Marr.)*. Robert Beer in Linlithgow, 1684 (RPC., 3. ser. x, p. 261). John Beer, farmer, Linkbraeheads, d. 1799 *(Fordyce, p. 91)*.

BEGARNIE. Perhaps a corruption of the Perthshire and Inverness place name Balgarnie. It is a Scots characteristic to clip the prefix Bal in place names to Ba.

BEGBIE. This surname is most probably derived from the lands of Begbie or Baikbie in the constabulary of Haddington. There is also a village named Baikbie in the parish of Roberton, but as the surname is mainly confined to the Lothians the former seems the most likely place of its origin. John Baikbie, tenant in Drumhillis, and William Baikbie in Drem, were cited before the Privy Council in 1566 (RPC., I, p. 444). Baigbie 1609.

BEGG. A personal name descriptive of the original bearer or bearers, from G. *beag*, little, small of stature. Malcol beg filius gilascop witnessed the gift by Maldouen, son of Alwin, earl of Leuenas, of the church of Kamsi (Campsie) to God and S. Kentigern, c. 1208-14 (REG., p. 88). In another (earlier) charter, but of same period, of same church to the same he appears as Malc. filius Gillescop (ibid., p. 87). He may have been a son of Gillescop Galbrath as his name follows immediately that of the latter. His son, Sir Malcolm, was the first to assume the name of DRUMMOND, q.v. Malcolm Beg or Begge, seneschal of Maldoweny, earl of Levenax between 1225 and 1250 (*Kelso*, 222), witnessed a charter by that earl to Stephen de Blantyre, c. 1248 (*Levenax*, p. 36), and also witnessed other charters by the same earl between 1224 and 1250 (ibid., p. 13, 14, 96, 98; RMP., p. 161, 209, 211, 217). He also probably witnessed a charter by Maldowen, third earl of Levenax, before 1270 (*Levenax*, p. 20). Malise Beg was burgess of Stirling before 1300 (*Laing*, 18), Patrick Begge was a hobelar in Edinburgh Castle in 1312 (*Bain*, p. 409), and John Beg was one of the workmen employed in the construction of Cardross Castle in 1329 (ER., I, p. 128). Part of the lands of Parcy was leased to John Beg, son of Gvlglass, in 1463 (*Cupar-Angus*, I, p. 136). Robert Beige was a tenant of the marquis of Huntlie in 1600 (SCM., IV, p. 262). The name is common in the Edinburgh Marriage Records of the sixteenth and seventeenth

centuries. Other old forms are Bege (1574) and Beig.

BEGRIE. A current variant of BAGRIE, q.v.

BEINSONE. James Beinsone, servitor of James Mitchell, minister of Stow, 1624 (RRM., III, p. 380). ? a spelling of BEANSTON, q.v.

BEISDEAN. A colloquialism of GILLEASBUIG (Archibald), as Beisdean bàn, Beisdean Maciain, etc. Spelled Baistain in Uist.

BEITH. Local, most probably from Beith, Ayrshire. The Rev. Dr. Alexander Beith died in 1891 after a ministry of sixty-nine years. His grandson is Major Ian Hay Beith the well-known author.

BELCH. James Belch was tenant in Cowie, parish of St. Ninians, 1735 (*Stirling*). Several persons named Belsh are recorded in Dunblane in seventeenth and eighteenth centuries (*Dunblane*).

BELFIELD. Of local origin from one of the twenty or more small places of the name Bellfield.

BELFORD. Perhaps from Belford near Yetholm, Roxburghshire. James de Beleford, carnifex (butcher) in Berwick, p. 1147 (*Kelso*, 34). Scralvne leased to Ade de Belfurde in 1376 (RHM., I, p. lxvii).

BELFRAGE. A surname of Fife and Kinross-shire which appears to be simply a corruption of BEVERIDGE, q.v., with intrusive l (cf. the spellings Colquhran — Cochrane, Calmeron — Cameron, walter — water). John Belfrage was taken to Sweden in infancy, became burgomaster of Venersborg and was ennobled in 1666. Andrew Belfrage was commissioner to Parliament for Dunfermline, 1681 (APS., VIII, p. 233). Henry Belfradge was heir of James Belfradge, portioner of Netherbaith, his father, 1684 (*Retours, Fife*, 1245). John Belverage, flesher in Dunfermline, 1685 (RPC., 3. ser. x, p. 151). Thomas Belfrage or Beveridge held lands on the foreshore of Lochleven under Sir William Bruce, 1690. The form Belfrage seems to have been dropped in his family after that date as his sons and grandsons are called Beveridge in subsequent records. David Belfrage was treasurer of Culross, 1721 (*Culross and Tulliallan*, II, p. 93), and John Belfrage was merchant there, 1744 (*Dunblane*).

BELGAVEN. Alisaundre de Belgaven of Lanarkshire rendered homage, 1296 (*Bain*, II, p. 212).

BELHAVEN. A rare surname, of local origin from Belhaven, in East Lothian.

BELHELVIE. Of local origin from Belhelvie in Aberdeenshire. William Balhelvy contributed towards the buying of lead for St. Nicholas Church, Aberdeen, in 1500 (CRA., p. 69), and James de Belheluy was witness apud Sconam, 1566 (REM., p. 395).

BELHOUSE. Local. Edward Belhouss was witness in Glasgow, 1521 (LCD., p. 77). Agnes Belhous sold a land in Glasgow, 1551, and Thomas Belhows was witness there, 1552 (Protocols, I). In 1692 there was a tenement in Lanark called Belhouschalmer (Retours, Lanark, 402).

BELJAMBE. Johannes Beleiamb a charter witness, 1248 (RAA., I, p. 171). Farquhar Belcombe who witnessed a charter of Glack in 1272 (Inverurie, p. 50) is probably Sir Farchard Belcambe who witnessed a grant of lands in Aberdeen c. 1294 (REA., I, p. 37). Ferghard Belejaumbe was appointed archdeacon of Caithness by Edward I in 1297 (Bain, II, p. 240). Ferchard Beleiaumbe, bishop of Caithness, witnessed the resignation by Agnes de Morthingtone, of the land of Gillandristone in "le Garviache," 1321 (RMS., I, 84). There is some uncertainty as to the spelling of the bishop's name (Dowden, p. 240). John Belgeam, who had a remission for slaughter committed by him, 1492 (Cawdor, p. 80), may be the John Belgeam "probably some English trooper who had settled in the district, (and) had a considerable croft at Auldearn, known as Belgeam's Croft" (Bain, Nairnshire, 2. ed., 1928, p. 170).

BELL. Three derivations are possible for this name: (1) as a descriptive sobriquet, Peter le Bel ('the handsome,' from OF. bel, handsome, beautiful), found in the English Hundred Rolls; (2) of local origin, as ME. 'John atte Belle' or 'Richard atte Bell' (not uncommon in ME. registers) from the sign of his public house; (3) as a metronymic, "Robert fil. Bell," meaning Robert, the son of Bell or Isabel. 1 and 2 are, I think, the chief parents of the name. John Bell appears as a notary in St. Andrews, 1248 (Pap. Lett., I, p. 245). A family of the name appears to have been hereditarily connected with the church of Dunkeld. Master David Bell was a canon there, 1263 (LIM., p. 77), and William Bell appears as dean, 1329–42 (Pap. Lett., I, p. 301, 557). William Bel, vicar of Lamberton, witnessed a charter to Coldingham Priory, 1271. Adam Belle and Richard Belle of Berwickshire rendered homage, 1296 (Bain, II, p. 206). Thomas Belle was juror on an inquest at Dumfries, 1304 (ibid., p. 412), and Simon

dictus Bell is in Perth in the reign of David II (Scon, p. 125). Thomas dictus Bell, canon of Dunkeld, c. 1340 (ibid., p. 124). Thomas Bell and Alan Bell witnessed confirmation of Snawdoun to the Abbey of Dryburgh, c. 1350 (Dryburgh, 232), Johnne Bell was a witness in St. Andrews, 1463 (CMN., 33), and Henry Bell was a witness in Arbroath, 1528 (Laing, 369). The name was common on the Border for centuries, and the 'Bellis' are included in the list of unruly clans in the West Marches, 1587 (APS., III, p. 466). The Bells of Annandale are said to be descended from Gilbert le fiz Bel, who was deprived of his lands by Edward I (Bain, II, p. 397). Families of the name long predominated in the parish of Middlebie, insomuch that the 'Bells of Middlebie' was a current phrase throughout Dumfriesshire. In the index to REB. the name is confused with the place name Biel. Patrick de Dunbar, dominus de Bele, is indexed under Bell. Robert Bell, born in Scotland, printer of the first edition of Thomas Paine's Common sense, died in Virginia, 1784. Rev. Patrick Bell (1800–1869) was inventor of the reaping-machine and founder of mechanical harvesting. (4) In Islay and Kintyre Bell is used as an Englishing of Mac Illinamhaoil. This is said to have arisen from the marriage of a Macmillan with a Miss Bell, who possessed property, and took her name in English, but continued the old name in Gaelic.

BELLEW. Recorded in Aberdeen, and most probably a late incomer from across the Border. Harrison says from Bellou or Belleau in France, and Lower mentions Belleau, a parish in Lincolnshire. Gilbert de Beleawe witnessed gift of the 'eschalingas i Lambremore' to the church of Kelso by William de Vyerpunt c. 1160 (Kelso, p. 257).

BELLIE. Probably from Bellie in Moray. Robe Bellie, member of bailie court, Stennes, Orkney, 1576 (OSR., I, p. 269). The tenement of the heirs of William Bellie in Brechin is mentioned in 1643 (REB., II, 247), and Margaret Bellie is recorded in Dunrossness, Shetland, in 1648 (Shetland). Mr. John Bellie was schoolmaster of Kinglessie in 1650 (PBK., p. 365), Christian Bellie is recorded in Edinburgh in 1670 (Edinb. Marr.), and James Bellie in Rossie in 1671 (Laing, 2679). Fraser's suggestion (History of Laurencekirk, p. 269) that the name is probably the same as Bailie and Baillie and that "the difference in spelling is not against this supposition, as the three forms applied to the same name during a great part of the seventeenth century," is, I think, unlikely.

BELLINGHAM. From the manor of Bellingham in Northumberland. In 1279 it was stated that the family of Bellingham held their manor of Bellingham, from which they derived their name, by service of being foresters "for time beyond memory" of the king of Scotland's ancestors in the forest of Tynedale (*Bain*, II, p. 52). William de Billingham witnessed a charter of lands in Raynigton to the Abbey of Coldingham in 1275 (*Raine*, 387). The seal of William de Bellingham is appended to an indenture of 1285 (*Seals, Supp.* 93). William de Billingham of the county of Berewyke, perhaps the same person, rendered homage in 1296 (*Bain*, II, p. 206), and Alexander de Belingeham was a Scots prisoner taken in Dunbar Castle, in same year (ibid., p. 177).

BELLMAN. From the occupation of "bellman" or town-crier. Gilbert Belman prope portam de Futye in 1398 (REA., II, p. 213). Philip Belman was amerced in 1505 "for the sellinge of ane apill for ane penny, quhar he micht have sauld thre for ane penny" (CRA., p. 75). Andrew Bellman is in record at the Mylne of Muckarsie in 1653 (*Dunblane*), and Magnus Belman in Caithness in 1663 (*Caithness*). The best known bellman in Scottish history was Dougal Graham (c. 1724–1779), skellat-bellman of Glasgow, author of several popular chapbooks and of "A Full Particular and True Account of the Rebellion in the Years 1745–6," Glasgow, 1746.

BELSCHES, BELSHES. From the barony of the same name in the lordship of Jedburgh, Roxburghshire, which belonged to the monks of Jedburgh. The barony may have been named by some earlier owner from Belasis (so spelled also in 1305) in Northumberland, Bellasis (1345 Belasis) in Durham, or from Bellasis which is near Coulommières in Seine-et-Marne department, France. The seal of Richard de Belchis is appended to his homage of 1296 (*Seals. Supp.*, 86). Alexander Belschis was bailie of Edinburgh, 1530 (EBR., p. 43), John Belcheis of Tofts was commissioner for the Tweed fisheries dispute in 1627 (RPC., 2. ser. II, p. 75), and Alexander Belschellis of Tofts was admitted burgess of Glasgow, gratis, 1631 (*Burgesses*). Alexander Belseis of Tofts was appointed Justice of the Peace for Berwickshire in 1634 (RPC., 2. ser. v, p. 379), and in 1651 Alexander Belsches was one of the Committee of Provisions for the Army (SBR., p. 198). The direct line ended in John Belshes of that Ilk who left four daughters and coheiresses in 1721 (*Stodart*, II, p. 328).

BELTMAKER. From the occupation, a maker of belts and girdles. Walter Beltmakare was burgess of Edinburgh in 1477 (RMS., II,

1308), and Agnes Beltmakar, 'kaikbakstar,' was 'admittit to bak kakis' in Stirling in 1525 (SBR., p. 25).

BELTON. From Belton in the parish of Dunbar, formerly itself an ancient parish. Henry de Beletun granted a charter of his lands of Kingissete (Kingside) to the monks of Melrose, 1231 (*Melros*, p. 195). John de Belton was one of the garrison of Edinburgh Castle in 1312 (*Bain*, III, p. 410).

BELTY. From the lands of Beltie in the parish of Kincardine O'Neil, Aberdeenshire. William Belty in record in Aberdeen, 1489 (CRA., p. 417). Thomas Belty, notary public in barony of ONeill, 1538–1563 (*Laing*, 420; RSCA., I, p. 205).

BEMYS. Perhaps from Beamish in county Durham (in 1449 Bewmys). William Bemys was one of the burgesses of Stirling who attacked the cruives and fishings of the abbot and convent of Cambuskenneth, 1366 (*Cambus.*, 55). See also BEUMYS.

BENDELOW. A surname recorded in Aberdeen. Of Frisian origin from a small place named Bentelo or Benteloo near Delden in Overijssel. Thomas Bendelow, a native of Aberdeen, one of America's pioneer golf architects, died in Chicago, March, 1936.

BENHAM. The lands of Benholm in Angus were anciently held by a family who designated themselves "de Benham," from at least the beginning of the thirteenth century till towards the close of the fourteenth. Master Thomas de Bennum was rector of the schools in Aberdeen in 1262 (RAA., I, p. 193), and a relative, Hugh Bennam or Benhaym, became bishop of Aberdeen ten years after (*Dowden*, p. 106). The family of Hugh de Benhame failed in an heiress, Cristiana, who became the wife of Alan de Lundy (RMS., I, 794), a cadet of the old family of that name.

BENISTON. Thomas Beniston was member of Scots parliament for Pittenweem, 1579 (*Hanna.*, II, p. 483). A Benistounes-thrid is mentioned in Fife *Retours* (1625).

BENJIE. A variant of BENZIE, q.v.

BENNET, BENNETT. Diminutive of Benedict. The fame of S. Benedict (480–543) the patriarch of the Western monks made the name popular. William, Robert, and Hugh Benedictus occur in Normandy c. 1180–95. Benedictus, son of Walter de Sancto Edmundo, witnessed a charter of sale of land in Perth, 1219 (*Scon*, p. 52). Benedict the dean (*decanus*) witnessed the gift of the mill of Wystoun to the Hospital of Soltre in 1249 (*Soltre*, p. 30), John Benet, Scotsman, late an enemy, became liegeman of Henry IV of England, 1402 (*Bain*, IV, 624), and Richard Bennat, chaplain, is mentioned in 1459 (RAA., II, 126). Part of the lands of Williamstoun in the barony of Cardowie was leased to John Bennett, 1563 (LIM., 89), Robert Bennet was one of the first bailies of Culross, 1588, Andrew Bennot witnessed an instrument of resignation in 1527 (*Panmure*, II, 306), and the name was very common in Edinburgh in the seventeenth century. A family of this name in Chesters, were ranked among the 'landit men' of Roxburgh in the early part of the sixteenth century, and the Bennets of Grubbet were at that period an old family in the same county. The form Bennet is more common in Scotland, –ett being the prevailing form south of the Border. Benatte 1651, Bennatt 1574.

BENNIE, BENNY. From Bennie on the east side of the Knock above the village of Braco in Logie-Almond parish (c. 1233 Beny in LAC., p. 244; Laing, *Lindores*, p. 412). Hugh de Benne or Bennef witnessed charters by Gilchrist, earl of Angus, c. 1201–7 (RAA., I, 39, 41, 44, etc.). Hugh filius Hugonis de Benne witnessed a charter by Vmfridus de Berkelay to the Abbey of Arbroath c. 1204–11, and as de Benne or Bennef attested a charter by William filius Bernardi (ibid., 67, 89). James Beny or Bynne was prebendary of Crudane, 1321 (REA., I, p. 47). Adam de Benyn chosen provost of Aberdeen and Simon de Benyn elected bailie, 1399 (*Guildry*, p. 184). William Bynne (entered under Benyng in index), bailie of Aberdeen, 1498 (REA., I, p. 343). Alexander Benne, "dekin of the wobstaris" in Stirling, 1522 (SBR., p. 16). William Bennie in Cottoun of Kynnaber, 1600 (*Brechin*). Thirty-seven Bennies appear in *Stirling Commissariot Record*, 1607–1800. Beney 1516; Benee, Beny.

BENNOCH; BENNY. Malcolm Bennoch was servant to the laird of Barjarg in 1684 (RPC., 3. ser. X, p. 309), and James Bennoche in Bushe, parish of Keir is in record in 1691 (*Dumfries*). James Bennoch in parish of Glencairn was shot for being a Covenanter, 1685 (*Hanna*, II, p. 256, 266). William Bennoch in Shirmurs appears in 1749 (*Kirkcudbright*), and Francis Bennoch was author of *The Storm and other poems*, London, 1841.

BENSON, 'son of Ben,' diminutive of BENNET q.v., or (2) of Benjamin. Patrick Benson was member of parliament for Perth, 1560 (*Hanna*, II, p. 483). Thomas Bensone, clothier in Edinburgh, 1651 (*Edinb. Marr.*).

BENT. Local. There are places so named in the shires of Ayr, Lanark, and Dumbarton.

William Bent, soldier in Edinburgh, 1658 (*Edinb. Marr.*).

BENTON. A name recorded in Aberdeen. Probably of recent introduction from England. There is a parish of the name in Northumberland.

BENVIE. This surname, which still occurs in Angus and in the shires of Kincardine and Perth, is derived from the place of the same name near Dundee. Ysaac de Banevin was one of the jury in a dispute regarding the Kirketun of Aberbuthenoth in 1205 (SCM., V, p. 210), and he also appears with Walter, Prior of St. Andrews, as witness to a charter of the church of Foulis by William Maule of Foulis (RPSA., p. 41). Adam de Banevy or Baneuille (cf. Melvin – Melville), his nephew, appears as witness in charters by the Abbes or hereditary lay abbots of Edzell, Hugh Malherbe, and John de Montfort, between 1204–1214 (RAA., I, 63, 72, etc.). Andrew Benvie in Pitmiddill, parish of Kinnaird, in record, 1598 (*St. Andrews*).

BENZIE, BENZIES. Benzie or Bainzie, with alterations into Badyno, Badenocht, etc., was a common name among Inverurie proprietors in fifteenth and sixteenth centuries (*Inverurie*, p. 50). James Banyeaucht took part in the election of parish clerk of Inverurie, 1536 (ibid., p. 142), and Johnne Baynze at the cross of Inuerowrie appears in 1576 (*Trials*, I, p. 48). Robert Benzie in 1703, one of the elders of the kirk, was charged with conduct amounting to witchcraft (AEI., p. 114). John Bainzie, macer of the Justice Court of Edinburgh, sought payment of his fees, 1686 (RPC., 3. ser. XII, p. 184). Three brothers named Benzie in Marnoch and William Beange from Turriff served in the first Great War (*Turriff*). Old: Bangzie, Banzie, Beingzie.

BEOLLAN. Ir. Beóllán, diminutive of *beul*, 'mouth.' Bjólan was the name of a king of some district in Scotland whose lands were harried by the Norsemen in 886 (*Landnámabók*, II, 11). The name perhaps appears in the cognomen of Helgi Bjóla who went from the Hebrides to Iceland between 874 and 900 (ibid., c. 14). He was son of Ketil Flatnose, and apparently was born in the Hebrides. Beollanus was the father of one of the witnesses to a grant by Ethelred son of Malcolm III to the Keledei of Lochleven, c. 1107 (RPSA., p. 116). About 1222 Beolin the judge witnessed a charter by Randulf de Strathphethain (REB., II, 3). O'Beollan was the family name of Ferchar Mac-in-tagart, created earl of Ross c. 1220.

BERFORD. John de Berford, one of the witnesses to a charter by Roger, bishop elect of St. Andrews relating to the church of Haddinton, c. 1189–1198 (RPSA., p. 153), derived his name from the old place of the name near Morham, East Lothian (c. 1220, vadum de Bereford). Cf. BARFOOT.

BERNARD. A late form of OE. *Beornh(e)ard*, 'warrior brave.' Bernard filius Briani witnessed gift by William de Haya of the land of Ederpoles to the monks of Cupar in the reign of William the Lion (SCM., II, p. 304), and a Bernard was chaplain of Dunkeld in time of Richard, bishop of Dunkeld (RAA., I, p. 149). Adam Bernard of Hiltone, Perthshire, rendered homage, 1296 (*Bain*, II, p. 212); on p. 203 he is named Adam Bernak of Hilton). Bernard, Abbot of Arbroath, chancellor of the kingdom, 1307–1329, is credited with the authorship of the remarkable letter sent to the Pope in 1320 proclaiming the independence of Scotland. Alexander Bernard was cellarer of the Abbey of Cupar Angus, 1492, and James Bernard was tenant of part of Kethyk belonging to the same house, 1495 (*Cupar-Angus*, I, p. 247, 304). James Bernarde, witness in Glasgow, 1551 (*Protocols*, I), and Archibald Bernard is recorded in Harlaw, parish of Wemyss, 1616 (*St. Andrews CR.*).

BERNARDSON, 'son of BERNARD,' q.v. William Berendson (so spelled perhaps through influence of Dutch Berend) who was illegally imprisoned in Orkney in 1424 is recorded again in 1438 as Will Bernardson (REO., p. 44, 71). Roland Bernardsone is also recorded in Orkney in 1640 (MCM., II, p. 211).

BERNER. From the occupation, a 'keeper of the hounds,' from OF. *berner, brenier*. John Berner in Berrydome of Forret, Fife, 1753 (*St. Andrews*). A comparatively late introduction from England.

BERNHAM. From old lands of the name in Berwickshire. In record the name sometimes appears as Bernhame, Beringham, and even Benham, without 'de' preceding it. David de Bernham witnessed a charter of the tithes of the church of Kinghorn to Holyrood, 1204–1214 (LSC., p. 38). David de Bernham, camerarius, witnessed a charter by Alexander II a. 1243, and as de Beringham attested another charter by the same king (*Neubotle*, p. 16, 17). He was also witness to a charter by his brother Robert de Bernham of four shillings a year *ad luminare* to the church of St. Andrews (RPSA., p. 272). David de Bernham, camerarius, was consecrated bishop of St. Andrews 1239–40 (*Dowden*, p. 14). Robertus de Bernham was one of the twelve knights appointed

in 1249 to meet the same number from England to settle the laws of the marches (APS., I, p. 413). Thomas de Berneham witnessed a gift of land to the Hospital of Soltre, 1250–1266 (*Soltre*, p. 32). Mistress Agnes de Bernham, prioress of Berwick, rendered homage, 1291 (RR.).

BERRIDGE. A variant of BEVERIDGE, q.v. current in Fife. John Berrage in Wester Tillochie, parish of Kinross, 1675 (*St. Andrews*), and Helen Berrage in Alloa, 1728 (*Stirling*). Caution was found for John Berrage in Kinglassie, 1686 (RPC., 3. ser. XII, p. 495). John Berrige in Freeland, 1711 (*Dunblane*). John Berridge in Ibrox 1941.

BERRY. The name of an old landed family, 'of Tayfield,' in Fife. In Aberdeen and Angus the name is said to be a variant of BARRIE, q.v. George Berrie, brouster, Inverness, 1613 (*Rec. Inv.*, II, p. 103). In the latter end of the seventeenth century Berries and Berrys were located in Strathdon, under Forbes of Brux, and in the parish of Coldstone under Farquharson of Invercauld. Andrew Berrie, shipmaster in Dundee, 1756 (*Brechin*). Eight of the name in the Edinburgh Marriage Records.

BERRYHILL. Local. There are many places named Berryhill listed in CD., and cf. Berriehill in Fife *Retours*, 1040. The wife of John Beryhill in Aberdeen was convicted by an assize, 1509 (CRA., p. 440). Andrew Berriehill in Gatsyde of Alloway (Alloa), 1620 (*Stirling*), and three more are mentioned in the Commissariot Record. Andrew Berrihill is recorded in Nether-Baith, parish of Dunfermline, 1626 (*St. Andrews*), and Jerome Berriehill in Camps of Carnock, 1646 (*Pitfirrane*, 584), is doubtless Jearome Barryhill in the parish of Dunfermline, 1649 (*St. Andrews*). Jeremiah Berrihill is recorded in Edinburgh, 1669 (*Edinb. Marr.*).

BERSTONE. An Orcadian surname derived from the pennyland of Birstone or Birstane in South Ronaldsay. Thome Birsto was tacksman of Sourquoy in 1502, and John Berston roithman between 1500 and 1522 (REO., p. 399, 413). Johne of Bersto was member of assize of lawting, 1514 (OSR., I, 254), Eduerd Birsten or Byrsto was one of those respited for the slaughter of John, earl of Caithness, at battle of Summerdale, 1529 (RSS., II, 3151; OSR., I, p. 114, 116), and Hugo Berstan was retoured heir of John Berstan in Clettis, his father, in 1678 (*Retours, Orkney*, 121). A pedigree of the family of Berstane of Cletts is given by Clouston (REO., p. 435).

BERTIE. A diminutive of (1) ALBERT, q.v., (2) BERTRAM, q.v. James Bertie in Charletown, 1735 (*Brechin*). As forename: Berte Fala in Kelso, 1567 (*Kelso*, p. 526).

BERTLOTSON, 'son of BERTLOT or BARTLOT,' from BARTLE, a diminutive of BARTHOLOMEW + the Fr. diminutive ending -*ot*. John Bertl'otson held land in Aberdeen in 1436 (REA., I, p. 234), and John Bertlotson was admitted burgess of the same town in 1472 (NSCM., I, p. 23).

BERTOLF. From OHG. *Perahtolf*, "bright wolf." Alexander II confirmed a charter by Maldouen, earl of Levenax to Simon, son of Simon son of Bertolfe of the land of Letterwherling, 1226 (HMC., App. 7 Rep., p. 704). Symon filius Bertolf a. witness, 1208–1233 (RMP., p. 50). Malcolmus filius Bertolfi (RAA., I, p. 65, 66). Normannus filius Bertolfi (loc. cit.). Mentioned under the Norman French form of his name, Malcolmus filius Berthout, c. 1170 (RPSA., p. 42).

BERTRAM. The OE. personal name *Beorhtram*, "shining raven." Johan Bertram, burgess of Inverkeithing, rendered homage, 1296 (*Bain*, II, 819). Walter Bartrem, who had a safe conduct to travel in England in 1464, may be Walter Bertrahame, provost of Edinburgh, 1482 (*Bain*, IV, 1343, 1480). He was also ambassador to France in 1482, and founded two chaplainries in St. Giles (*Stodart*, II, p. 413). Johannes Bertrame had a remission for his share in burning the town of Dunbertane, 1489 (*Lennox*, II, p. 133). Alexander Barthrame was apprentice in Edinburgh, 1667 (*Edin. App.*), and another Alexander Bertram was retoured heir of William Bertram of Neisbitt, 1690 (*Retours, Lanark*, 385). Barthram 1633, Bartram and Bartrim 1632, Bartrum 1625, Bertraham 1493, Bertrahame 1479, Bertrum 1670; Bartherem, Barthrem, Bartrome, Bertrem.

BERVIE. Of local origin from the town of Bervie, Kincardineshire. Gilbert de Berewe made a gift of land in the vill of Berewe to the monks of the Isle of May c. 1250 (RPSA., p. 388). William Bervie was bailie of Kirkcaldy, 1641 (PBK., p. 219), and Agnes Bervie is recorded there, 1685 (RPC., 3. ser. x, p. 146).

BERWICK. This surname is derived from the famous Border town of the same name. Rather curiously the surname is not uncommon at the present day in Fife. John de Berwic was rector of Renfrew in 1295 (*Pap. Lett.*, I, p. 562), and in the year following Geoffry of Berewick, burgess of Roxburgh, rendered

homage (*Bain*, II, 820 and p. 197). Magister Johannes de Beruyc witnessed the gift of half of Litel Gouen to the Hospital of Polmade (Polmadie) in 1320 (REG., p. 229). Patrick de Berwic received a payment from the Exchequer in 1328 (ER., I, p. 98), William de Berwyic was burgess of Aberdeen in 1317 (SCM., v, p. 11), and Robert de Berewick burgess there in 1333 (REA., I, p. 54). Thomas de Berwic, burgess of Edinburgh in 1411 (*Egidii*, p. 44) may be the Thomas of Berwyk who was 'dene of the gilde' of Edinburgh in 1423 (LSC., 113). Thomas Bervic was member of parliament for Edinburgh, 1445 (*Hanna*, II, p. 483). James Berrick workman in Edinburgh in record in 1676 (*Edinb. Marr.*).

BEST. A booth was leased to John Best in Edinburgh, 1457 (EBR., I, p. 17). John Best was a skinner in Edinburgh, 1603 (*Edinb. Marr.* — the only one of the name in this record). Thomas Best was admitted burgess of Aberdeen, 1618 (NSCM., I, p. 120), and Agnes Best is recorded in Jedburgh Forest, 1684 (RPC., 3. ser. x, p. 271). Best occurs in Essex DB. (*Ewen*, p. 63, 64), and Bardsley says it means "'the beast', probably not in an uncomplimentary sense," and cites Richard le Beste in county Cambridge, 1273.

BESYNGHAM. Henry de Besyngham, most probably an Englishman, witnessed a donation to the Hospital of Soltre, c. 1153–77 (*Soltre*, p. 4). There are places named Bassingham in the counties of Norfolk and Lincoln.

BET. Walter Bet, secretary to Duncan Campbell, lord of Lochaw, 1432, was probably a member of the Betoun or Macbeth family, according to the duke of Argyll. A different name from BETT.

BETH. Andrew Beth was landlord of a tenement (*domino capitule*) in Edinburgh, 1380 (*Laing*, 67). Andrew Beth witness in Petcapill, 1591 (RPC., IV, p. 667). Gilbert Beth in 1665 (IDR., p. 312).

BETHAN. A diminutive of BETH, q.v. Bethan de Doul and Kenachy his brother were jurors on inquest at Perth, 1305 (*Bain*, II, p. 456). Bethin filius Constantini was burgess of Aberdeen, 1317 (SCM., v, p. 11), and Bethin filius Jacobi was provost of Banff, 1340 (ER., I, p. 456).

BETHIA. A favorite woman's name among the Edmonstones (*Strathblane*, p. 99). The seal of Bathia Clerk, wife of John Provand, in a Findourie charter, 1593 (*Macdonald*, 436). Bethia Ard in Edinburgh, 1599 (*Edinb. Marr.*).

BETHOC. See under BEATHAG.

BETHUNE. Of territorial origin from the town of the name in the department of Pas de Calais. The name first appears in Scotland between 1165–90 when Robert de Betunia appears as witness in a De Quinci charter (RPSA., p. 354). In old records and charters the name was usually spelled Betun or Beton, and in the sixteenth century it became confused with BEATON, q.v., a name of Gaelic origin. John de Betun, a cleric of the diocese of Dunkeld, witnessed a confirmation charter of the church of Ruthven to the Abbey of Arbroath before 1211 (RAA., I, 216), and David de Betun and John de Betun witnessed a grant of land in the territory of Kerimor to the same house between 1214–26 (ibid., p. 80). Andrew de Byetoine rendered homage at Forfar, 1296, and Sir David de Betune the same at Dundee (Bain, II, 749, 759). Sir Robert de Betune swore fealty at St. Andrews, 1291, and Andrew de Betton of Perthshire rendered homage, 1296 (ibid., II, 508, and p. 200; Macdonald, 127). The seal of Andrew bears a cinque foil in dexter chief and S' Andree de Bettvne. Johannes de Beton was one of an inquest on the marches of Kyrknes and Louchor, 1395 (RPSA., p. 3), Bernard Betown, odaller in Howbister, Orkney, 1492 (REO., p. 406), and William Bettoun of Wosthall was a witness, 1526 (REB., II, 180). The Beatons or Bethunes had lands in Fife and Angus, where their descendants are still to be found. The cardinal and the archbishop are the best known of the family in Scotland. Beathune 1680, Beatoun 1584, Beattone 1604, Bethon 1681, Beton 1546, Betone 1552, Betoun 1547, Betown 1521, Betowne 1524, Betton 1681, Bettune 1292; Beattoun, Betoin.

BETT. This surname today is confined mainly to the shires of Perth and Fife. Andrew Bet and William Bet were burgesses of Edinburgh, 1344. Galfridus filius Betti witnessed a charter by John Skinner, burgess of Inverness, c. 1360 (Grant, III, p. 12), and in 1370 Andrew Bet, a Scottish merchant, complained of being plundered by English wreckers (Bain, IV, 164). Andrew Bet or Beth appears as burgess of Edinburgh, 1368–69–81 (RMS., I, 323; Egidii, p. 1, 22). Walter Bet, rector of Craginche, 1440, appears in 1442 as witness to the foundation charter of the Collegiate Church of Kilmwne (OPS., II, p. 96). Thomas Bet was a monk of Arbroath, 1467 (RAA., II, 174), William Bett qualified as schoolmaster in Kirkcaldy, 1641 (PBK., p. 202), and Hugh Bett was maltman in Edinburgh, 1669 (Edinb. Marr.). Twenty-seven of the name are recorded in the Kirk Session Record of St. Andrews. Harrison says (1) a form of Beat, meaning

blessed, happy, or (2) a diminutive of Beatrice (but?).

BEUGO. A Fife surname. James Bugo, tailor in Edinburgh, 1611 (Edinb. Marr.). Gavin Beugo in the parish of Strabrock, 1683 (Torphichen). John Beugo engraved the portrait for the first Edinburgh edition of Burns's Poems. Bego 1574.

BEUMYS. Hugo de Beumys witnessed a confirmation charter by David de Bernham, bishop of St. Andrews, c. 1239–53 (LAC., p. 68), and another relating to the division of lands of Cullessin and Cardynside (ibid., p. 186). As de Beumes he witnessed an agreement anent the lands of Koneveth, Halton, and Scottiston, 1242 (RAA., I, p. 207). From Beamish (1185 Bewmys) in county Durham. See also BEMYS.

BEVERIDGE. A well-known surname in Fife, where it is pronounced Berridge or Berritch. Mr. Beveridge (Culross and Tulliallan, II, p. 93) says the origin of the name is to be found in 'Beverege,' the name of an island in the Severn referred to by Florence of Worcester as a retreat of the Danes during a revolt of the English. The name, he correctly says, means "Beaver island," from OE. befer or beofer, and ig or ige, island. The earliest mention of the name in Scottish record is in 1302 when Walter Beverage is named as juror on an inquest at St. Andrews (Bain, II, 1350). Henry Beveragh was witness in Paisley, 1504 (RMP., p. 63). A decree against Alexander Baueragh is recorded in 1531 (Cambus., 203), David Beverage was cup-bearer to James V in 1534 (ER., XVI, p. 349), and James Baverage, son of the Queen's midwife, received a payment in 1567 (ibid., XIX, p. 386). Alexander Bavirige was a monk of Culross in middle of sixteenth century (PSAS., LX, p. 93). Robert Beverag indweller in Dysart, 1630 (PBK., p. 14). James Beverage and Andrew Beverage were fined in 1677 for brewing beer of insufficient strength, and a few days later they appeared as James and Andrew Belfarge when they appealed for remission of their fines (RPC., 3. ser. v, p. 198, 199, 202). John Beverich in Houburn-mill, parish of Coldingham, 1724 (Lauder). Balwerage 1667, Baueraige 1603, Baverach and Beuerache 1513, Baverage 1599, Baveraig 1522, Baveredge 1641, Beueradge 1669, Beuradge 1684, Beuerage 1588, Beveraig 1562; Bauerege, Baveriche, Baverych, Bawerage, Bawerege, Bevritch.

BEVERLEY. From the town of Beverley in East Riding of Yorkshire. Nichols de Beverle and Thomas de Beverle, both of Berwick, rendered homage, 1291 (RR.). A horse was purchased from Nicholaus de Beverlaco in 1312 (*Bain*, III, p. 421). Thomas Beverley of Scotland had letters of protection on going abroad in the King of England's service, 1374 (*Bain*, IV, 217). Thomas Beverley, esquire of Scotland, had a safe conduct into England in 1393, and in 1395 there is an entry of payment to Thomas Beverlee, esquire of Scotland (ibid., 458, 468). Alexander Bevirla admitted burgess of Aberdeen, 1485 (NSCM., I, p. 31). Robert Bevyrlay was juror on an inquisition apud Rane, 1418 (REA., I, p. 216). William Beaverlay, trade burgess of Aberdeen, 1640 (ROA., I, p. 232). George Beverly was bailie of Inverury, 1747 (*Aberdeen CR.*), Alexander Beverley, shoemaker in Banchory-Devenick, died in 1829, and Alexander M. Beverley of Turriff was killed in the first Great War (*Turriff*). Baverlay 1689.

BEWS, BEWES. Orcadian surnames. Clouston suggests it has possibly a nickname origin. Adam Bewis in Rendell, 1640 (MCM., II, p. 211). S. Bews, tenant of the Bu or Palace at Orphir.

BEY. A curtailed form of (MAC)BEY, q.v., current in Aberdeenshire.

BIBBERTOUN. Local. Jean Bibbertoun in Edinburgh, 1605 (*Edinb. Marr.*).

BICHART. Agnes Bichart in Dundee, 1628 (*Brechin*). John Bichart, weaver in Edinburgh, 1634 (*Edinb. Marr.*). James Bichart was charged with abstracting multour of corne, 1672 (*Corsehill*, p. 106).

BICKERTON. This surname is of English origin, from Bickerton in Northumberland. There is another Bickerton in the West Riding of Yorkshire. About the year 1200 Richard of Bickirtoune had a grant of lands in Dunypace (*Cambus.*, 83), and in 1266 Sir Richard of Bigirthon witnessed an agreement anent pasturage of the moor of Kellin (*Laing*, 8). Master Eustace of Bikerton was presented to the church of Duglas, Lanarkshire, in 1292 (*Rot. Scot.*, I, p. 7), and in 1296, as Eustace de Bykretone, rector of the church of Hutremokedi (Auchtermuchty), he rendered homage (*Bain*, II, p. 213). John de Bigerton held the castle of Luffenoc' in 1296 (ibid., II, 857), and a payment to Elisabet de Bikertoun by the custumars of Inverkeithing is recorded in 1331

(ER., I, p. 370). Walter de Bykirtoun witnessed a charter by Archibald, earl of Douglas in 1401 (*Swinton*, p. xvii), Valterus de Bekyrtoun, miles, held husband lands in the vill and territory of Elstanfurd in the constabulary of Haddington in 1429 (RMS., II, p. 25), Robert de Bykkirtoune was lord of Lufnois (Luffness) in 1451 (RMS., II, 438), William Bykatone (an error for Bykartone) was vicar of Lochgoyll in 1456 (LCD., p. 180), and John de Bickertone appears as canon of Glasgow and presbyter of Erskyn in 1479 (REG., 422). Marion Bickertoune appears in Largs, parish of Urr, in 1641 (*Dumfries*). Bekartoun 1574, Bekertoun 1530, Bekirtoune 1464, Bekyrton 1456, Bicartoun 1590, Bickartoun 1526, Bickartoune 1647, Bickertown 1688, Bikarton 1525, Bikcartowne 1602, Bikkerstoun 1601, Bikkerstoune 1533, Bikkertoun 1530, Bikyrtoun 1456, Bycartoun, Bykartoun 1549.

BICKET, BICKETT. Local, from Bequet, Bechet, or Le Becquet in Oise. Surety was found for James Bichat in East Teviotdaill, 1569 (RPC., I, p. 661). Peter Bichet, merchant burgess of Edinburgh, 1646 (*Inquis.*, 3126). Isobel Bichet in Lidgertwood, 1664 (*Lauder*). James Bichett in Hareschaw, 1666, and John Bichet in Hareschaw was cautioner for another, 1675 (*Corsehill*, p. 68, 124). Thomas Bickett was herd in Danzielstoune, 1682 (RRM., III, p. 52). Robert Bighet in Kilmarnock, 1688 (RPC., 3. ser. XIII, p. 241). Thomas Bickitt, portioner of Bowden, 1692, and William Bicket, portioner there, 1810 (*Heirs*, 117, 573). Mr. Thomas Bichett minister at Middlebie, 1743 (*Dumfries*).

BIDDESDENE. Robert de Biddesdene of the county of Berewyke rendered homage in 1296 (*Bain*, II, p. 207).

BIDIE. Surgeon-General George Bidie (1832–1914), born at Deskford, Aberdeenshire, discovered the preventative for an insect pest in India which preserved the coffee plantations of that country. Probably a variant of BEEDIE, q.v.

BIDUN. Walter de Bydun witnessed King David's gift of Rindelgros (i.e. Rhind in Perthshire) to the Abbey of Reading c. 1143–47 (*May*, 1). He or a succeeding Walter appears several times as chancellor of Scotland between c. 1165 and 1178, and as a witness to royal charters (*Scon*, 18; *Kelso*, 404; REG., p. 36; REM., p. 454, etc.). A twelfth century pedigree of the family is given in Pipe Roll Society Publications, vol. XXXV, p. xliii.

74

BIE, Bee. A payment was made Stephen le Bee, mariner, 1305 (Bain, п, p. 442). John Be in Hill, Dundee, 1583, and Mage Bie in Blackhall, parish of Lethnot, 1597 (Brechin). Thomas Bie, wobster in Edinburgh, 1604 (Edinb. Marr.). Barbara Bie in Hamnavo, Shetland, 1648 (Shetland). Charles Bee appears in Boreland of Colvend, 1789 (Dumfries), and there are three Bees in Edinburgh Marriage Records. Bee recorded in Edinburgh, 1940. Generally explained as a nickname from the bee (but?).

BIGGAM, Bigham. John de Bigholme, witness in Edinburgh in 1426 (Egidii, p. 49) may be John Bygholme, dean of guild in Edinburgh in 1428 (RMS., п, 116), and the John Bygholme, Scottish merchant, who had a safe conduct into England in 1446 (Bain, iv, 1187). Thomas of Bigholme, Scottish merchant, who had a safe conduct into England in 1453 and 1464 (ibid., iv, 1253, 1347), is perhaps Thomas of Bigholme who was elected magistrate of Edinburgh in 1456 (EBR., i, p. 15). Patric Bigholme had a special respite and protection in 1504 (Trials, i, p. °43), Edward Bigholme held a tenement in Edinburgh in 1554 (Laing, 617), and caution was found for David Biggum in Inverkeithing in 1587 (RPC., p. 170). William Bigholme was heir of Richard Bigholme in Alves in 1622 (Inquis., 1048), Adam Bigholme was witness in Glengirk in 1634 (RPC., 2. ser. v, p. 647), Hector Bigholme is recorded in Auchinbaird of Sauchie, 1640 (Stirling), and Edward Bigholme was admitted schoolmaster of Auchterdirran 1641 (PBK., p. 214). There were 40s. lands of this name in Ayrshire and in Dumfriesshire from either of which the surname may have been derived. Begholme, Bigholm, Bighome, Bigum.

BIGGAR. From the old barony, now the parish of the same name in Lanarkshire. Baldwin de Bigir, who appears as sheriff of Lanark in the reign of Malcolm iv is the first known to bear the territorial designation. Chalmers (i, p. 602, 603; iii, p. 738) identified him with the Baldwin Flam[aticus], who appears as witness in a charter of R[obert?], bishop of St. Andrews, relating to the church of Lohworuora (now Borthwick), c. 1150 (REG., 11), "but for this there is no authority" (OPS., i, p. 134). Between 1147–1160 Balwinus de Digir (Bigir) witnessed the grant by Arnold, Abbot of Kelso, of the lands of Douglas to Theobaldus Flamaticus (Kelso, 107). Sometime after 1170 Baldwin de Bigre, sheriff of Lanark, granted the church of Innyrkyp beyond the moors (ultra mores) to the monks of Paisley (RMP., p. 112). Waldeve, Baldwin's son, was taken prisoner

at Alnwick along with King William the Lion in 1174 (Bain, п, p. 117). In 1228 Hugh the son of Robert de Bygris appears in a grant to St. Machute of Lesmahagow, in which he is styled Hugo de Bvgris filius Roberti filii Waldevi de Bigris (Kelso, 186). Sir Nicolas de Bygir, knight, witnessed a deed dated at Lesmahagow, 1269, and in 1273 appears as "tunc vicecomes de Lanarc" (ibid., 189, 334). He died before 1292, when the marriage of Mary his widow, and the ward and marriage of Marjory and Ada his daughters and heirs parceners, were granted by Edward i to Robert, bishop of Glasgow (Rot. Scot., i, p. 14). The lands and honours appear to have passed into possession of the Flemings, earls of Wigtown, through the marriage of one of these daughters, but the surname continued, probably in younger branches. In 1329–30 Sir Henry de Bygar held the offices of royal chaplain, rector of the church of Bygar, and clerk of livery to the king's household (Chamberlain's Rolls, i, p. 122–4, 168, 192). Walter de Bigare appears as rector of the church of Erole, 1433 (REB., i, p. 58), and Thomas Biggar was reader in Kinghorn, 1621 (MCM., п, p. 46).

BIGGART. Local, probably from Biggart near Lugton, Ayrshire. There is also a Biggarts near Beattock, Dumfriesshire. Math Biggait, tenant of Wattishill, 1591, is indexed under Biggart (RPC., iv, p. 650). Adam Bighart appears in Edinburgh, 1612, and Janet Biggait in 1700 (Edinb. Marr.). Bigard 1607.

BIGGIN, Bigging. Local. There is a Biggins Farm near Mossend, Lanarkshire. John Bigging in Wyneholm, 1682 (Dumfries). In record 1940 (WScot.).

BIGLIE. Local. Stephen Bigly witness in 1392 (Cambus., 76). Laurence Bigli, burgess of Edinburgh, 1411 (Egidii, p. 44), John Biglay was an apprentice there, 1668 (Edin. App.), and John Biglie, bookbinder there, 1680 (Edinb. Marr.).

BILE. A Pictish name. Brude son of Bile, king of Fortriu, defeated Ecfrith, king of Northumbria, at Dunnichen, 685 (ES., i, p. 193), and Beli mac Elphine, king of Dumbarton (Alochluaithe) died in 722 (CPS., p. 74). The name occurs in Irish mythology as that of the father of Mile or Milidh of Spain. Bile is also common in Breton alone or in composition (Loth, p. 110).

BILL. Thomas Bill in Auchingrav, parish of Carnwath, 1667 (Lanark CR.). Robert Bill, wright in Edinburgh, 1668 (Edinb. Marr.). Other two of the name in the same record. Perhaps from 'Bill' a pet form of William.

BILLHOPE. Of local origin from a small place of the name, perhaps Billhope in the parish of Teviothead, Roxburghshire. An old rhyme which celebrates the localities in Liddesdale and Eskdale most noted for game gives prominence to

"Billhope-braes for bucks and raes."

Patrick Bylhope witnessed a declaration dated 1436 (*Home*, p. 20), William Billop appears in Dumfries, 1516, and surety was found in 1569 for James Billop in East Teviotdaill (RPC., I, p. 661).

BILLIE. From the lands of Billie in the parish of Bunkle, Berwickshire. Patrick de Byly of the county of Berewyke rendered homage in 1296. His seal bears the Agnus Dei and S' *Patricii de Billi* (*Bain*, II, p. 202, 552). Complaint was made against John Belly in Polwart in 1563 (RPC., I, p. 245). (2) The following may be from another origin. Robert Billie, town councillor of Perth, 1628 (RPC., 2. ser. II, p. 235). Margaret Billie in Dunrossness, Shetland, 1644 (*Sc. Ant.*, XII, p. 90).

BILLSLAND, BILSLAND. May be from Bellsland (Kilmaurs), or Bellsland (Riccarton) in Ayrshire. John Bellisland, tenant in lands of Drumquhassill near Drymen, 1592 (RPC., V, p. 27). Janet Bilsland is recorded in Edinburgh, 1673 (*Edinb. Marr.*), and Glasgow had a Lord Provost named Bilsland a few years ago.

BILTOUNE. Local. George Biltoune, baron of the barony of Kinneill, 1657 (*Laing*, 2506). Most probably from Bilton in Yorkshire.

BINGALL. Michael Bingall in Stitchill, 1700 (*Stitchill*, p. 145).

BINNEY, BINNIE, BINNING, BINNY. From the old barony of the name in the parish of Uphall, West Lothian, where a family of the name were formerly numerous. The place name Binning in the parish of Whitekirk received its name from the older place in Uphall. William de Binin, prior of Newbattle, was promoted to Crail, 1243 (*Chron. Mail.*). John Binning or de Bynning was infeoffed in lands in Edinburgh which had been forfeited by John Slingisbie in the reign of David II (RMS., I, App. II, 1568). Friar John Benyng was governor of the lands and possessions of the Hospital of St. John of Jerusalem at Torphichen, 1388 (*Bain*, IV, 378). Symon de Bynninge or de Benyn, bailie of Aberdeen, 1396–98 (REA., II, p. 294; CRA., p. 374). It is probably his seal, attached to a document of 1399, which reads S' *Simonis de Beny* (*Macdonald*, 164). He is probably the Symon Benyn selected to be one of the company to accompany the provost of Aberdeen to the battle of Harlaw, 1411 (*Fraser*, p. 20). Alexander Benyn, bailie of Aberdeen, 1408–10, also accompanied the provost to Harlaw (CWA., p. 315; REA., II, p. 275). John de Benyne was a canon regular of Cambuskenneth Abbey, 1403 (*Cambus.*, 167). William de Bening or de Benyne is recorded as possessing a tenement in Edinburgh, 1414–26 (REG., 324; *Egidii*, p. 46). John of Bynnyng, brother of the Hospital of St. John of Jerusalem, is recorded in 1414 and in 1426 (*Bain*, IV, 854; *Egidii*, p. 47). Richard Benyne appears as burgess of Perth, 1458 and 1463 (RAA., I, 120; *Laing*, 151), and Thomas Benyng in Aberdeen, 1468 (REA., I, p. 300). Nicol Bynnyn, cordiner in Edinburgh, 1510 (EBR., 127), and John Bynne was painter there, 1572 (*Laing*, 877). Alexander Bynne held a croft in Aberdeen c. 1550 (REA., II, p. 226), and Sir Robert Bynne was 'cheplane and singar in the quier' there, 1555 (CRA., p. 289). Johannes de Benyne was vicar of Strathardil in reign of James II (*Scon*, p. 89). John Binnie was heir to Elizabeth Binny, 1574 (*Retours, Linlithgow*, 9), and James Binnie in Brigend, parish of Morrowingside (Muiravonside), 1636, and eight more of the name are recorded in the neighborhood (*Stirling*). John Binie was prisoner in Tolbooth of Edinburgh, 1681 (BOEC., VIII, p. 112), and John Binnie of Byrs was heir in lands of Drumcross, etc., 1698 (*Retours, Linlithgow*, 280). The name was common in Edinburgh in seventeenth century (*Edinb. Marr.*). Benieing and Bineing 1686, Benin 1712, Bennie 1614, Benning 1531, Buny 1461, Bynnie 1579, Bynny 1582, Bynnyn 1517, Bynnyne 1533, Bynnyng 1556, Bynnynge 1563; Bining, Binni, Byning, Bynning.

BINNS. From Binns in West Lothian. English (Yorkshire) Binns from another origin.

BIRD. William Bird was admitted burgess of Aberdeen, 1443 (NSCM., I, p. 7), James Burd in Dechmont, 1634 (RPC., 2. ser. V, p. 640), Thomas Burd appears in Shillrige, 1667 (*Stirling*), and John Burd in Avtoune, 1684 (*Lauder*). A popular name (Burd) in Edinburgh in seventeenth century (*Edinb. Marr.*).

BIRGHAM. From the old lordship of Birgham (1098, Brycgham) or Brigham in the parish of Eccles, Berwickshire. The place name is pronounced Birjam. John de Brigeame and others were charged with holding Dunbar Castle against the king in 1479 (APS., II, p. 125). Eliz. Birgen, heir of Adam Birgen in dominio de Birgen, 1590 (*Retours, Berwick*, 489), as Elizabeth Birgem or Birghem

76

BIRGHAM, *continued*
had sasine in 1591 (ER., XXII, p. 453; RPC.,
IV, p. 675). The village of Birgham is of historical interest as having been the place of
two meetings of the Scots and English Commissioners in 1290 to settle the succession to the
Scottish Crown.

BIRKENSHAW. A Renfrewshire surname of
local origin, probably from Birkenshaw in
Lanarkshire.

BIRKMYRE. Of local origin from the old lands
of Birkmyre in Dumfriesshire. Michael of Byrkmyr, a presbyter of the diocese of Glasgow,
1432 (*Laing*, 109), may be the Michael
Birkmyr who witnessed an instrument of
sasine in Dumfries in 1477 (*Edgar*, p. 237).
John of Byrkmyr witnessed a discharge by
John Stewart of Dernlie in 1452 (*Pollok*, I,
p. 173), Alexander Byrkmyr witnessed an indenture in Glasgow in 1485 (LCD., p. 198),
and Andrew Byrkmyr was decanus of Angus
in 1517 (RAA., II, 544). In 1588 George
Birkmyre appeared as cautioner at the Kirk of
Inchynnane for John Stewart of Cassoquhy
(RPC., IV, p. 335; *Methven*, p. 75). William
Birkmyre was burgess freeman of Glasgow by
purchase in 1612 (*Burgesses*), and William
Birkmyre is recorded in Newabbey in 1774
(*Dumfries*).

BIRNIE, BIRNEY. From Birnie in Moray.
James de Brennath (the early form of the
place name), burgess of Elgin, was one of an
inquest concerning the King's garden there
in 1261 (APS., I, p. 99 red). William de Brennath, dictus Tatenel, witnessed the gift by
Hugh Herock, burgess of Elgin, to the church
of Elgin in 1286 (REM., p. 284), and Andrew
de Brenach was clerk to Sir Dovenald, earl
of Mar in 1291 (*Bain*, II, 529). Walter de
Branach was the king's chaplain in Moray,
1360 (REM., p. 304). William de Byrneth,
canon of the church of Moray, appears as a
witness in 1463 (RD., p. 367), Nicholas Birne
was a chaplain in 1514 (*Laing*, 305), and
William Byrny was burgess of Edinburgh in
1558 (ER., XIX, p. 428). Birney 1589, Birny
1568, Birnye 1614, Byrnye 1568.

BIRREL, BIRRELL. John Burell in Newton of
Glendall (Northumberland) had a charter in
1387, and in 1449 Edmund Burell was burgess of Berwick (*Laing*, 76, 127). Andrew
Birrell or Burrell, bailie and burgess of Kirkcaldy, 1540 (*Dysart*, p. 5), appears again
between 1574–1579 (*Laing*, 892, 977). Sir
Andrew Burell, a Pope's knight, held land in
Glasgow, 1549, William Birell was a witness
there, 1550, and Henry Burell sold a tene-

ment there in the following year (*Protocols*,
I). John Birrell is recorded in Gargunnok,
parish of St. Ninian, 1607 (*Stirling*), George
Berrill was portioner of Kinnesswod and Commissioner of Supply for Kinross-shire, 1685
(APS., VIII, p. 468), and James Birrell was
shipmaster in Dundee, 1776 (*Brechin*). Perhaps
simply a variant of BURRELL, q.v.

BIRSE, BIRSS. Of local origin from Birse in
Aberdeenshire. Duncan de Byrss, burgess of
Aberdeen in 1462 reappears in 1469 as Duncan of Birss (SCM., V, p. 23; CRA., p. 406).
Margaret Birse was married in Edinburgh in
1597 (*Edinb. Marr.*), Samuel Birss, writer to
the signet in Edinburgh, was heir to Alexander Birss, tailor burgess of Edinburgh in
1611 (*Inquis.*, 543). James Birse (Briss or
Birce) in Keillsyd was witness in Aberdeen
in 1688 (RPC., 3. ser. XIII, p. 262, 272, 273),
and Robert Birss was shipmaster at Montrose
in 1762 (*Brechin*). John Birss in Dykehead of
Borrowstoun is in record in 1723, and another
John Birse, farmer at Bottomend, Aboyne, died
in 1866.

BISHOP. In 1291 a receipt was granted to
William called 'Bissope' on behalf of Sir
Dovenald, earl of Mar (*Bain*, II, 541). John
Bischope held a land in Edinburgh c. 1426
(*Egidii*, p. 48), and the name is very common in the Edinburgh Marriage Records in
the eighteenth century as Bischop and Bish-
ope. Patrick Bischop was witness in Perth,
1551 (*Rollok*, 88). Mr. James Bischope was
minister at Inverness, 1610 (*Rec. Inv.*, II,
p. 76), James Bishop was guild-brother of
Glasgow by purchase, 1624 (*Burgesses*), and
Francis Bischope was burgess of Inverness
in 1627 (RPC., 2. ser. II, p. 9). Alexander
Bishop in Northbank of Morphie, 1628 (*St.
Andrews*), James Bishop in Whyteside, parish
of Falkirk, 1676 (*Stirling*), and James Bishop in
Linlithgow, 1684 (RPC., 3. ser. X, p. 261).
May have been derived from the character
in the mediæval mystery plays, but Biscop
was also an OE. personal name (*Searle*). Bis-
schop 1547.

BISSET, BISSETT. Sir Thomas Grav in his
Scalacronica (p. 41) states that William the
Lion in 1174, on his return from captivity in
Falaise and in England, brought back young
Englishmen of family to seek their fortune
in the Scottish Court; and among these were
named the "Biseys" (*Maitland Club ed.*, p. 41).
The first of the name recorded in Scotland is
Henricus Byset, who witnessed a charter by
William the Lion granted before 1198 (*Mel-
ros*, I, p. 123). His son, John Byset, who wit-
nessed a charter by Henry de Graham in 1204

(*Neubotle*, 8), was the individual who obtained from the king the grant of lands in the north. In 1226 he had a dispute with Robert, bishop of Ross, anent the patronage of the church of Kyntalargy (REM., p. 332–333). Thomas de Bessat witnessed a Paisley charter a. 1204 (RMP., p. 54), and in 1224 William Bisseth witnessed confirmation by Alexander II of a *yar* super Leven (ibid., p. 214). Walter Biset witnessed a charter by Alexander II concerning the levying of tolls at the Cross of Schedenestun (Shettleston) in 1226 (REG., p. 114), and in 1232 Walter Byseth and William Byset witnessed a charter by Alexander II to Gylandris MacLod in Brechin (REB., I, p. 4). In 1242 the power of the Bissets was brought to a sudden end, though they still continued to be a family of importance. At a tournament held at Haddington in that year Walter Byset, lord of Aboyne, was worsted by the young earl of Atholl. In revenge Byset is stated to have burned the house in which the earl slept, and the earl with it. For this crime Walter Byset and his nephew, John Byset (founder of the Priory of Beauly in 1231), were exiled the kingdom, their property devolving to others of the family. At the desire of Sir William Byset and to free him of suspicion of guilt, Ralph, bishop of Aberdeen excommunicated those who had partaken of the murder of the earl at Haddington:

"The bischope of Abbyrdeyn alssua
He gert cursse denownsse al tha
That gert be art, or part, or swyk,
Gert bryn that tyme the Erl Patrik.
In al the kyrkis hallely
In Abyrdenys dyocysi
Schir Wiljam his processs
Gert be don" (Wyntoun, bk. VII, c. IX.)

A Walter Byset occurs among the witnesses to a charter by Alexander II to the monks of Dunfermline dated 13 January, 1249 (RD., p. 44). In 1251 Walter Biset by an inquest was found seized of the manor of Ulvington at his death, and the information is given that "he died far off in Scotland in a certain island called Araare" (*Bain*, I, 1836). In January of the following year (1252) a pardon was granted to Alan, son of Thomas, earl of Atholl for slaying some of the men of John Biset in Ireland (*Bain*, I, 1865), apparently a continuation of the blood feud. William Bvseth appears as a royal charter witness, 1279 (*Neubotle*, p. 290). The Bissets of Lessendrum are among the oldest families in Aberdeenshire. In 1364 Walter Buset of Lessendrum, as sheriff substitute of Banff, presided at a court held there in which the bishop of Moray obtained a verdict finding that three

men, Robert, Nevin, and Donald were the natives and liege-men of the said bishop and the church of Moray, and his property (REM., p. 161). Jacobus Besat appears as prior of St. Andrews, 1395 (RPSA., p. 2), and Thomas Byssate held a tenement in Glasgow, 1486 (REG., p. 450). Bissets still flourish in Aberdeenshire and Moray. The surname is a personal one, a diminutive of *bis*, OF. for "rock dove." Basok 1583, Beceit 1429, Besack 1677, Besate 1408, Besek 1584, Beset 1362, Biscet 1292, Biseth 1231, Bissait 1529, Bissaite 1468, Bissart 1542, Bissat 1579, Bissate 1543, Bissed 1640, Bissott 1674, Bizet 1686, Byssot 1489. A spelling of 1294, Buset, almost represents the present Gaelic pronunciation, *Buiseid*.

BISSIE. Andrew Bissie in Milntoune of Anstruther, 1592 (*St. Andrews*). David Bissie, heir of Thomas Bissie in Mylnetoun of Pettinweim, 1651 (*Retours, Fife*, 1588).

BISSLAND, BISLAND. A surname found in Glasgow and Stirling. It appeared in Paisley in eighteenth century as Bessland. Thomas Bissland, "Kind Tom o' the Wood," was the subject of an epigram by Tannahill.

BITCHIN. This surname was recorded in Sanquhar and neighborhood in seventeenth and eighteenth centuries (*Dumfriesshire and Galloway Nat. Hist. and Ant. Soc., Trans.*, 3. ser. XIX, p. 118).

BLAAN. Blaan, one of the earliest bishops of Kingarth in Bute, is commemorated in the *Martyrology* of Oengus at August 10: "With a host, sound, of noble birth, well-coloured, fair Bláán of Kingarth." His name is from *blá*, that is yellow, from *°blávo-s*. He is probably also the saint commemorated in the *Calendar* of Gorman as *Bláán buadach Bretan*, "triumphant Bláán of the Britons." He gave name to Kilblane in Southend, Kintyre, and to Dunblane. According to a Bute legend he was mysteriously begotten of a water-sprite (Mackinlay, *Ancient church dedications*, p. 111). Blahan, presbyter of Litun probably Linton in Roxburghshire witnessed a quitclaim by Robert, bishop of St. Andrews, 1127 (*Nat. MSS.*, I, 27). See under MACBLAIN.

BLABER. David Blabir in Aberdeen, 1408 (CWA., p. 317). Simon Blabre was chosen auditor of accounts there in 1433 (SCM., v, p. 41), and was on town council's service in 1442 (CRA., p. 8). David Blabre who was admitted burgess of Aberdeen in 1444 (NSCM., I, p. 8), is doubtless the David Blabyr who had a sasine of a tenement in the Gastraw, 1450 (*Friars*, p. 33), and was a charter witness in the same town in 1464 (RAA., II,

BLABER, *continued*

154). David Blabir was ordered to be ready to enter the king's service in 1476 (SCM., v, p. 25). William Blabir had a remission granted him in 1492 (*Cawdor*, p. 80). William Blaeber in Mekill Fiddes, parish of Arbuthnot, 1626, and two more (*St. Andrews CR.*). Lower says probably from some occupation. Blaber without prefix occurs in the English *Hundred Rolls* (1273), and *Blá-ber* is given as a cognomen in *Islenzkir Annalar*, 1393, but there is probably no connection between the names.

BLACK. "A great difficulty with the Blacknames," says Harrison, "is the impossibility in many cases of deciding whether the etymon is the OE. *blæc, blac,* 'black,' or the OE. *blác,* 'bright,' 'white,' 'pale.' Normally *blæc, blac,* yields 'black,' and *blác* should give 'blake' (or 'bloke'); but the forms are inextricably confused, and the present spelling is often no guide to the pronunciation past or present." Blaecca is a well-known OE. personal name, and Beda says (H. E., II, 16) that the baptism of Blaecca, prefect of the city of Lincoln, and his whole household was the first fruits of the preaching of Paulinus, A. D. 628. In early Scots Latin charters the name is rendered *Niger*. Hugh Niger appears as a charter witness in Angus in 1178 (RAA., I, p. 9), and Radulfus niger, deacon of Lothian, was a charter witness in Fife between 1200–1210 (LAC., p. 131; LSC., p. 38). Robertus Niger, burgess of Elgin, witnessed a composition between Simon, bishop of Moray and Freskyn de Moravia, lord of Duffus, in 1248 (REM., p. 114), Adam the Black was one of the jurors on an inquisition held at Lanark in 1303 (*Bain*, II, 1420), Thomas Blak, a Scots prisoner of war in the Tower of London, was released in 1353 (*Bain*, III, 1568), another Thomas Blak was tenant of Rahill in 1376 (RHM., I, p. lviii), and Laurencius Blac was juror at a court held at "Le Ballocis Hill" near Inverness in 1376–7 (*Innes Familie*, p. 63). Thomas Blac was a witness in 1463 (*Lennox*, II, p. 78), and James Blak and William Blake appear as jurors on an inquest in Lanark in 1498 (*Lanark*, p. 9). The surname was common in St. Andrews and in Prestwick in the fifteenth and sixteenth centuries, and very common in Edinburgh in the seventeenth century. The Clan Lamont Society claims that Blacks were originally Lamonts who changed their name. William Black, the novelist, traced his pedigree to a branch of Clan Lamont who were driven from Lamont territory under a leader called the Black Priest. The surname is also used as an Englishing of Macilduy and Macildowie (G.

M'Ille dhuibh or *Mac Gille dhuibh*, 'son of the black lad'). In Argyllshire it is a translation of Huie, which itself is a much curtailed form of *Mac Gille dhuibh*. Members of the old family of Black of Wateridgemuir, Logie-Buchan, have been burgesses of Aberdeen for at least four hundred and fifty years. Blacke 1682, Blaick 1647, Blayk 1363. See also BLAKE.

BLACKADDER, BLACATER, BLACKATER. From the lands of Blackadder on the stream of the same name in the Merse division of Berwickshire. Blakadir *de eodem* in the earldom of March in 1426. Adam of Blacathathir was one of those sent to conduct the envoys with Princess Cecilia's dower to Edinburgh in 1477 (*Bain*, IV, 1445), and Charles Blakater had a protection and safe conduct to travel in England in 1486 (ibid., IV, 1522). Robert Blackader was bishop of Glasgow at the end of the fifteenth century. Rolland Blaykatter, tenant in the barony of Glasgow in 1521 may be the Roland Blacadyr who appears as sub-dean of Glasgow in 1524 (*Rental; REG.*, 495), and Thomas Blacater was bailie of the Commendator of Coldingham in 1557 (*Home*, p. 206). The name was common in Lanarkshire in the sixteenth century, and the Blacaters or Blackadders of Tulliallan in Perthshire (from which they were dispossessed in 1632) were an offshoot from the Border family. Blacader 1510, Blacadur 1550, Blacadvr 1524, Blackatour 1615, Blackatter 1626, Blackattir 1575, Blackeder 1707, Blacketer 1697, Blaikader 1611, Blakadir 1544, Blakadyr 1503, Blaketter 1542, Blakiter 1563, Blakytar (in Workman's MS.), Blekater 1595. Other old forms of the name are: Blacatar, Blaikater, Blaiketter, Blakatar, and Bleakader.

BLACKBEARD. A by-name, now perhaps obsolete in Scotland. Henry Blakberde witnessed an instrument of sasine of the lands and castle of Temptalloune in 1475 (*Douglas*, III, p. 106), and in 1479 a process was issued against John Blakbeird (perhaps a relative of Henry) and others for holding Dunbar Castle against the king (APS., II, p. 125) Robert Blakberd was one of a jury in 1495 on the retour of the special service of George Hume of Wedderburn as heir of his father (*Home*, p. 27). The surname is also found in Shetland as early as 1602, and the Kirk Session records show that the name was continued in Dunrossness so late as 1777, when the death of Grizel Blackbeard, a pauper, is noted (Mill's *Diary*, p. lxxxix). Colin Blackbeard in Outvo, Shetland, witness, 1623 (OSS., I, 5). Blucbeird 1624. Cf. BROWNBEARD, RED-BEARD, SMIBERT.

BLACKBEID. Thomas Blakbeid witness in Edinburgh, 1522 (EBR., I, p. 208). In index given as Blackboyd.

BLACKBODY. A prisoner named Blackbodie in Edinburgh Castle, 1687 (RPC., 3. ser. XIII, p. xxxvii).

BLACKBURN. From one or other of several small places so named. Willelmus de Blakeburne was witness in 1243 to the ratification of the gift of the church of Lescelvn to Lundors (LAC., p. 90). Robert de Blakeburne of Berwickshire rendered homage in 1296 (Bain, II, p. 206). William de Blakburne appears as Abbot of Cambuskenneth, 1394 (Cambus., 17), John Blacburne was killed by the Armestrangis in 1501 (Trials, I, p. 102*), John Blakborn was tenant in Stobo, 1533 (Rental), and Archimbald Blakburne was burgess of Glasgow, 1550 (Protocols, I). Walter Blaikburne was member of council of Stirling, 1604 (SBR., p. 284), Margaret Blakbairne was married in Edinburgh, 1610 (Edinb. Marr.), and William Blaigburne was bailie of Inverkeithing in 1634 (RPC., 2. ser. V, p. 396). Blakbowrne 1554.

BLACKCRAIG. David Blackcraig was a witness in Edinburgh in 1587 (Laing, 1142). Perhaps from Blackcraig, near Uphall, West Lothian. — Blackcraige, recorded as a resident in the parish of Borgue in 1684 (RPC., 3. ser. IX, p. 567), more probably derived his surname from Blackcraig near Borgue.

BLACKDEAN. From the place of this name in Morebattle parish, Roxburghshire. About the year 1200 Henry de Blachedene witnessed a charter by Cecilia de Molle (Kelso, 148). In 1358 William of Blackdene, son and heir of Christian of Blackdene, granted the forest of Eteryk to John Kerre (HMC., 14. Rep., App. pt. 3, p. 8). In 1560 there is entry of sasine of land in Roxburghshire to James Blaikden (ER., XIX, p. 464). George Blackdoune in Newtone of Coldstreame, 1685 (RPC., 3. ser. X, p. 480).

BLACKETT. Local, from a place of the name (= [at the] Black Head). The old family of Blackett of Durham and Northumberland were originally "de Black Heved" and "Blak-hed" (OE. heafod 'head'). The Scottish Blacketts may derive from the old lands of Blakat or Blackit in Kirkcudbrightshire. Alexander Blakquhit, witness in Irvine, 1499 (Simon, 18). Adam Blackcat (!) was burgess of Perth, 1564 (ER., XIX, p. 69). Dioniss Blackat is recorded in Perth, 1581 (Mill, Plays, p. 280), and Andro Blaikat was burgess there, 1617 (RPC., XI, p. 69). John Blaket was reader at Sanquhar, Dumfriesshire, 1607. Blakatt 1617. See also BLACKWOOD.

BLACKFORD. Local. Paul Blakfurd was accused of manslaughter in Ayrshire, 1509 (Trials, I, p. 62*). There is a Blackford (1662, Blackfuird) in southeast Perthshire.

BLACKHALL. From the lands of Blackhall in the regality of Garioch, Aberdeenshire. William de Blackhall who appears on a jury of inquest retouring William de Tullidaff of Lentush and Rothmaise heir of his father in 1398 is apparently the first of the name recorded. William Blackha is recorded in Cromarty, 1407 (Fraser Mackintosh, Antiq. Notes, 2. ed., p. 216). In 1420 the Blackhalls are mentioned as of that Ilk (de eodem). William Blackhall of that Ilk had a remission in 1499 for slaughter committed by him (Trials, I, p. *100). William Blakhall succeeded his father William Blakhall as coroner and forester in the regality of Gareoche in 1547 (Retours, Aberdeen, 4). The family were hereditary coroners and foresters of the earldom of the Garioch from an early period, probably before the beginning of the fifteenth century. Early in the seventeenth century the family fell into decay and their lands and offices were acquired by the Burnetts who had intermarried with them (Catalogue Exhibition Archaeol. Inst., Edinburgh, 1859, p. 119). Blackhaill 1408, Blaikhall 1531, Blakhal 1467, Blakhale 1504, Blakhaw 1492.

BLACKHOUSE. Of local origin from some small place of the name. There were old lands named Blackhouse in the shires of Berwick, Selkirk, Lanark, and in Fife. Robert Blakhous in Birnie, 1673 (St. Andrews).

BLACKIE. Diminutive of BLACK, q.v. Payment to John Blakye in Clony is recorded in 1506 (Rent. Dunk., p. 160), William Blakye was dompnus in Newbattle Abbey, 1528 (Neubotle, p. 284), and another William Blakie or Blakyie appears in 1547 and 1566 as inhabitant of Leith (Soltre, p. 112, 126). Sir William Blaky was chaplain in Perth, 1545 (Rollok, 33). Andrew Blakie was aid in the Court kitchen, 1589 (ER., XXII, p. 32), David Blakie was burgess of Lanark, 1590 (RPC., IV, p. 525). The surname was common in Edinburgh in the seventeenth century (Edinb. Marr.). Professor John Stuart Blackie (1809–1895) was the best known of the name. Probably confused with BLAIKIE. Blaky 1527.

BLACKLAW. From one or other of several small places named Blacklaw. "The lands of Blaklaw" in the barony of Linton are mentioned in 1476 (ALA.), and there is a Blaklaw "within the parochin and regality of Dumfermling," 1654 (Fife Retours). The seal of Catherine Blaklaw, wife of Robert Strachan, is appended to a document of 1573 (Macdonald, 178). A pension was paid to Janet Blacklaw in Edinburgh, 1733 (Guildry, p. 145).

BLACKLAWS. Of local origin from a place of the name. A Blacklawis is recorded in Forfar Retours (1609). William Blacklawis was vicar of Durris in 1497 (REA., I, p. 339), George Blacklaws is recorded in Cutteshillock, 1680 (Brechin), and Robert Blacklaws was in Birnie, parish of Fordoun, 1683 (St. Andrews).

BLACKLEY. A surname current in Dumfriesshire from some place unknown to me. Perhaps from Blackley in England. Radulphus Blackley was juror on inquest at Berwick, 1321 (Neubotle, p. 155). Mungo Blaikley in Hairtope, parish of Crauford, 1687 (Lanark CR.). Blacklie 1752.

BLACKLOCK. William Blakloche, chaplain in the monastery of Dunfermlyne, appears as charter witness in 1483 (RD., p. 372). Adam Blaiklok of the West Port of Edinburgh was hanged for perjury in 1615 (Trials, III, p. 354), and another Adam Blaiklok was constable of the parish of Kirkpatrick-Juxta, 1617 (RPC., XI, p. 199). Jonet Blaklok was heir of John Blaiklok, burgess of Drumfreis, 1637 (Inquis., 2310), Robert Blaklok in Raehill and John Blaiklock in Harthope, 1638 (ibid., 2386, 2389), and Margaret Blackclock is recorded in Ruckan, 1684 (RPC., 3. ser. x, p. 283). The most prominent of the name was Dr. Thomas Blacklock (1721–1791), the early friend of the poet Burns. Seventeen of the name are recorded in Dumfries Commissariot Record. A familiar Cumberland surname, meaning 'one with black hair,' OE. blaec locc. Blaickloch 1684, Blakloik 1541.

BLACKLUG. Michael Blaklug admitted burgess of Aberdeen, 1457 (NSCM., I, p. 15). Perhaps an early spelling of BLACKLOCK, q.v. Cf. SOWLUG.

BLACKMAN. From the OE. personal name Blaecmon. This name is found in the genealogy of the kings of Bernicia, 765; and in the Durham Liber Vitae in the ninth century. In DB. it occurs as Blackman and Blacheman.

BLACKMANTEL. Petrus Blackmantel rendered homage at Perth, 1291 (RR.).

BLACKRAW. Local. There is a Blackraw near Mid-Calder. Symon Blakra was elected common councillor of Aberdeen, 1435 (Guildry, p. 185).

BLACKRIM. Apparently of local origin from a place unknown to me. William de Blackrim was curate of Kirkintilloch in 1421 (SHSM., II).

BLACKSHAW. Of local origin from some small place of the name. There is a village of the name in Dumfriesshire. John Blackshaw in Hunterstoun, Ayrshire, 1583 (Hunter, p. 31). Some Blackshaws legally changed their name to Black.

BLACKSTOCK. Of local origin from some small place of the name which I cannot find. Blakstok of that Ilk appears in Workman's MS. (date of MS. is c. 1565–1566), but "the name is rarely met with, and no family owning lands of the same name has been met with" (Stodart, II, p. 116). William Blackstok witnessed a notarial instrument of 1517 (Soltre, p. 89), William Blackstock was appointed clerk of court in 1524 (Home, 34), John Blakstok held a tenement in Edinburgh in 1549 (Laing, 553), and one hundred and fifty years later Agnes Blackstock held a tenement in the same city (ibid., 2974). John Blakstok signed the Band of Dumfries in 1570 (RPC., XIV, p. 66), James Blackstok was a tenant of Andrew Hay of Craignethan in 1659 (Diary, p. 11, S.H.S. ed.), John Blackstock was merchant in Dumfries, 1641 (Dumfries), Robert Blackstock was tenant in the barony of Mousewall (Mousewald) in 1673 (PSAS., XXIII, p. 74), and John Blackstocks was burgess of Peebles in 1689 (RPC., 3. ser. XIII, p. 504). David Blackstocks was appointed constable in Littleclyde in 1712 (Minutes, p. 126), William Blackstock was tanner in Minigaff in 1767 (Wigtown), and Robert Blackstock, shoemaker in Dumfries in 1738, and nine more of the name are recorded in the Commissariot Record of Dumfries. According to Gilbert Burns, a Miss Jane Blackstock was the heroine of his brother's 'O Poortith Cauld.'

BLACKSTONE. Local. There are places of this name in Ayrshire and Dumfriesshire, and also in England.

BLACKWATER. An old Aberdeenshire surname derived from the "villa de Blacwatyr" in the barony of Inverugie. Magister Walter de Blacwater, cancellarius Aberdonensi, appears as a charter witness at the end of the thirteenth century (REA., I, p. 37), and in 1317 as burgess of Aberdeen (SCM., v, p. 10). Marjory de Blackwater, spouse of Adam Pyngill, a leading burgess of Aberdeen, made a donation of land for sustentation of a chapel in the church of St. Mary of Aberdeen in 1376 (REA., I, p. 110).

BLACKWOOD. There are lands of this name in Lanarkshire and in Dumfriesshire, and there was an old Ayrshire family of Blackwood, a quo Lord Dufferin. Robert Blakwode, a native of Scotland, to be discharged from prison in London as unjustly arrested, 1384 (Bain, IV, 329). Andrew Blackwud, bailie of Perth in 1532, reappears in 1541 as Andrew Blaket (Milne, p. 116, 151). Adam Blackwood was one of the Privy Council of Mary Queen of Scots. The tenement of Cuthbert Blakwod in Glasgow is mentioned in 1549 (Protocols, I), and Dioniss Blackat was warded for taking part in a mediæval play in Perth in 1581 (Mill, Plays, p. 280). The last of the French Blackwoods in direct line from Adam Blackwood above mentioned was a Mlle. Scholastique de Blackwood, who died an old maid in 1837 (Beveridge, Bibliography of Dunfermline, p. 16). William Blackwood (1776-1834), publisher and founder of Blackwood's magazine. Blaccat 1491, Blacot 1511, Blackat 1489, Blaickwood 1687, Blaikwode 1632, Blaikwood 1666, Blakowd 1545, Blakowid 1546, Blakuod 1549, Blakvod 1545. See also BLACKETT.

BLADDERSTOUNS. Local. Elspet Bladderstouns in Torryburn, Fife, was tried for witchcraft, 1630 (RPC., 2. ser. III, p. 454).

BLAIKIE. Diminutive of BLAKE, q.v. William Blaike in Blainslie, 1605, Patrick Blaikie in Calfhill, 1660, and Thomas Blaikie in Westhouses, 1662 (RRM., I, p. 4, 302; II, p. 3). Robert Blaikie was retoured heir in lands, etc., in the barony of Coldingham, 1634 (Retours, Berwick, 195). Probably confused with BLACKIE. Blakye 1506, Blaiky, Blaikze (z = gutt. y).

BLAIN, BLANE. These surnames, current in the shires of Ayr and Wigtown, are reduced forms of MACBLAIN, q.v. Patrick Blane was provost of the burgh of Wigtown in 1561 (ER., XIX, p. 178), and John Blain had a charter of the half of the ten-mark lands of Meikle-Wig in the parish of Whithorn in 1674 (Laing, 2728). Agnes Blain in the parish of Kirkcudbright, 1684 (RPC., 3. ser. IX, p. 573). The name of BLAHAN, presbyter of Linton, East Lothian,

who witnessed a charter by Robert, bishop of St. Andrews to the monks of St. Cuthbert at Coldingham (Chalmers, II, p. 541) is perhaps the same.

BLAIR. Of territorial origin from one or more of the places of the name. Stephen de Blare was witness to a charter by Dovenald, Abbe de Brechin to the monastery of Arbroath between 1204-1211 (RAA., I, 74 bis). Brice de Blair and Alexander del Blair witnessed an agreement between the burgh of Irvine and Brice de Eglunstone (Eglinton), 1205 (Irvine, I, p. 3). Alexander de Blare witnessed a charter by Fergus, earl of Buchan before 1214 (CAB., p. 408), and also a charter by Randulf de Strethphetham (REB., II, 3). William of Blare who witnessed a charter by Malcolm, seventh earl of Fife (Laing, 8), is probably Sir William de Blar, seneschal of Fife, 1235 (RD., p. 102). Alexander de Blare, miles, witnessed charters by Christina Corbet and her husband in favor of the Priory of St. Andrews, c. 1241 (RPSA., p. 263, 278). David de Blare of Perthshire rendered homage, 1296 (Bain, II, p. 204). Thomas of Blayr of Rodyok had a safe conduct to travel in England, 1460 (Bain, IV, 1311). Bllaer 1688.

BLAKE. From OE. blāc, pale, wan, of complexion. Luce Blake was tenant of land in Waldefgate, Berwick, c. 1266 (Kelso, 47), and Atkyn Blake was a charter witness in Ayr c. 1340 (Friars Ayr, p. 15). Thomas Blaik was a notary in Thornhill in 1627 (RPC., 2. ser. II, p. 27), John Blaik in Upper Cassie and John Blaik in Upper Dumfedling are in record in 1684, and William Bleak in Castlehill in the same year (RPC., 3. ser. x, p. 218, 219). Five of the name are recorded in the Edinburgh Marriage Records. T. Blake, a Scot, was the first Briton to reach the city of Mexico before 1536. See under BLACK.

BLAMIRE. William de la Blamyre mentioned in 1247 (Wetherhal, p. 246) is probably the William de Blamyre who held six acres near Carlyle in 1250 (Bain, I, 1787). A writ was directed to the sheriff of Northumberland in 1304 in favor of Peter de Glynquym, heir of Johanna de Blamyr his mother (ibid., II, p. 415). Susanna Blamire (1747-1794), Cumberland poetess, wrote many popular Scottish pieces. Of local origin from some place of the name, perhaps in Cumberland.

BLANCARD. From OFr. Blanchart, 'whitish' (of complexion). Gillemure mac Blancard a charter witness before 1166 (LSC., p. 20).

BLANCE. A surname found in Shetland. Old forms are Blans and Blanse. The popular tradition is that the bearers of this name are descended from shipwrecked French sailors, and consequently the old forms of the surname have largely given place to Blanch and Blanche, in order to be nearer the supposed original French form. The name of Thomas Blanx in Fetlar occurs in a list of witnesses in 1575. The name is very common in the parish of Delting, and also occurs in Yell (*Old Lore Misc.*, II, p. 138–139). Mathew Blans in Funzie is in record in 1624 (*Shetland*), and Thomas Blance was fined for his tax of Wig in 1633 (RPC., 2. ser. V, p. 563). The name has been also explained as the genitive of BLJAN, an Old Norse personal name (*Old Lore Misc.*, IV, p. 14). See also BLANK.

BLANERNE. From Blanerne or Blanearn in the parish of Bunkle, Berwickshire. Thomas de Blanerne of the county of Berewyke rendered homage in 1296 (*Bain*, II, p. 210). There was an old family of Blenearn of that Ilk.

BLANK. A Caithness surname. The Rev. David Beaton, formerly of Wick, derived it from Fr. *blanc*. Cf. BLANCE.

BLANTYRE. Of territorial origin from the barony of the same name in Lanarkshire. Stephen de Blantyre witnessed a grant to the Abbey of Cambuskenneth c. 1200 (*Cambus.*, 81). About 1248 Maldouny, earl of Levenax granted to Stephen de Blantyr "totam medietatem carucate terre de Kynerine, videlicet illam medietatem in qua ecclesia fundata est, que scotice vocatur Lecheracherach . . . et advocationem dicte ecclesie de Kynherine" (*Levenax*, p. 36). An inquest of mortancestry of Patrick Blantthyre, son of Stephen de Blantthyre, dated 1263, is printed in the Acts of Parliament of Scotland (I, p. 102). Patrick de Blauntire of Stirlingshire rendered homage in 1296. His seal bears a boar passant to sinister, a crab(?) below and serpent(?) above, and S' *Patricii de Blauntir* (*Bain*, II, p. 208, 542). In 1304 a writ was issued to the bishop of Durham to restore to Agnes de Blantyr her dower lands of Norham Liberty (ibid., II, p. 415). Walter de Blanctire is mentioned as a Friar preacher and king's confessor in 1343 (*Pap. Pet.*, p. 33), John of Blanteir, a Scottish merchant, had a safe conduct to enter England in 1426 (*Bain*, IV, 999), and David Blantyre had a gift of the escheat of Alexander Abirkeirdo in Angus in 1531 (RSS., II, 1026). Blantyir 1527.

BLATHO. Territorial. Peter Blatho *de eodem* was juror on inquisition made at Edinburgh, 1506 (RD., p. 377).

BLAW. This surname was formerly common in Fife, but is now believed to be extinct. A family of the name were reckoned among the oldest in the Culross district. "They seem to have come originally from the Low Countries, to judge from their name, which is clearly the same as the Dutch *blauw*, or *blue*" (Beveridge, *Culross and Tulliallan*, II, p. 124). The Blaws are found as lairds of Castlehill, near Culross, in the middle of the sixteenth century, and James or Jacob Blaw was bailie of Culross Abbey in 1565. James Bla had feu of lands of Castlehill from the Abbey of Culross, 1587 (PSAS., LX, p. 80), and in 1686 an allowance was made to Mr. Robert Blaw for his *Vocabules* (grammar), 1686 (RPC., 3. ser. XII, p. 456). John Blaw is mentioned in Lanark (*Dryburgh*, p. 155), Thomas Blaw was dempstar of court, Aberdeen, in 1544 (CRA., p. 212), and the name appears in Edinburgh as Bla (*Edinb. Marr.*). John Blaw was a maker of the celebrated Culross girdles in 1635 (*Sc. Ant.*, VI, p. 114), and a daughter of this family, Margaret Blaw, married Archibald Primrose, and was thus an ancestress of the earls of Rosebery. John Blaw was sent on a mission to the Young Pretender in 1745, and in 1767, during an altercation in a Clackmannan public-house, he fatally stabbed a neighboring farmer. After a trial before Lord Justice-Clerk Miller and Lord Kames he was hanged at Stirling.

BLAWET. Hugh Blowet, herald of Scotland, *alias* 'Brucius heraldus de Scocia,' was confined in the Tower of London, 1401 (*Bain*, IV, 577, 578). William Blawet or Blawat had a safe conduct into England, 1424 (ibid., 961, 964). The name may be derived from Blae Wath near Gosford, Cumberland.

BLAYLOC. A rare name recorded in Annan, 1801. Suggested to be from OE. *blæ* meaning livid or lead-colored hair, but perhaps of local origin. Cf. under BLELLOCK.

BLECKBIE. Adam Bleckbie, residenter in Kelso, 1804 (*Heirs*, 525), derived his name from the lands of Blackbie (now Blegbie) in the parish of Humbie, East Lothian.

BLELLOCK, BLELOCH, BLELLOCH. Of local origin from some small place of the name. There are two places named Blelock in Perthshire (in 1652 Bleloch), and Blelack (in 1657 Bleloch) is a farm name in the parish of Logie-Coldstone, Aberdeenshire. There is also a

Blailoch in Selkirk Retours (1687). Blelloch recorded in Leith 1941.

BLENKHORN. A rare surname in Scotland. Of local origin from Blencarne in the parish of Kirkland, Cumberland. The name of Richard Blauhorne, juror on inquest in Chapel of St. Katherine, Baveley, 1280 (*Bain*, IV, 1792) may be the same with first *n* misread *u*.

BLENKINSOP. Of local origin from Blenkinsop, a township in the parish of Haltwhistle, Northumberland. Roger Blencamshoip or Blencamshape had a charter of lands of Laglene in the sheriffdom of Ayr in the reign of Robert I (RMS., I, App. II, 327). William de Blancanhop was burgess of Are, 1415, and another William Bkemcamhop [*sic*] was burgess there in 1475 (*Ayr*, p. 9, 91).

BLIND. 'Sightless,' ME. *blinde.* Roger Blynde, burgess of Peebles, rendered homage in 1296 (*Bain*, II, p. 198). Simon le Blynde of Peebles held the land of "le Farinhalghe," 1304 (*Bain*, II, p. 428).

BLINDSEIL. A trade name from the occupation of seeling or covering the eyes of falcons used in hawking. From *blind* + OFr. *ciller, siller*, to seal up the eyes of falcons to tame them. The early and principal home of this surname was in Aberdeen, and an old writer states that Blinshall was also "a very Ancient Sirname in Perth. Several persons who bore it were in public offices, as appears from the Charters of the Religious Houses" (quoted in *Sc. Ant.*, I, p. 101). William Blindcele who was concerned in a dispute anent a doublet in Aberdeen in 1398 may be the William Blyndcel who was elected bailie of the burgh in the same year (CRA., p. 371, 374). He may be the William Blyndcele admitted burgess in the following year (NSCM., I, p. 1). Robert Blyndseile was auditor of accounts of Aberdeen in 1433 (SCM., V, p. 41), and Thomas Blyndseil who was juror on an inquest there in 1448 (CRA., p. 17) is probably Thomas Blyndseile who possessed a croft there in 1463 (REA., I, p. 286). Alexander Blyndeseil was bailie of Aberdeen in 1451, and is again referred to in 1464 as burgess (REA., II, p. 297; RAA., II, 154). Robert Blindsele was an assizor in Aberdeen in 1463 (CRA., p. 26) and in 1494 Robert Bliedsell and William Bluidsell (? error for Blindsell) were members of council of the same burgh (*Guildry*, p. 191). Robert Bleyndshelys had a protection and safe conduct to travel into England in 1486 (*Bain*, IV, 1522), Andrew Blinsele was a notary in Edinburgh in 1525 (*Laing*, 351), and Peter Blinsele held the same office in

Methven in 1541. Dauid Blynkskale was hanged for theft in 1530 (*Trials*, I, p. 151*), and Umphridus Blynschelis was a justice depute in 1589 (ibid., I, p. 179). Mr. Umfra Blansells or Blenscheills, advocate, was ordered in 1629 "to remove the haill beggers out of 'his house' at the foote of Leith Wynde" (RPC., 2. ser. III, p. 68). Rev. Mr. Blinshall was minister in Dundee c. 1800. Among the Scots who settled in Prussia the name is found as Blentsczel (1636). Blendseil and Blenseile 1456, Blindsel 1478, Blindschell 1574, Blindzele 1437, Blinschel 1474, Blinschell 1671, Blinseile 1503, Blinseill 1563, Blinsel 1487, Blinsell 1593, Blinshell 1675, Blyndesill 1437, Blvndsel 1469, Blvndzele 1433, Blynschall 1584, Blynsele 1550, and in the seventeenth century Edinburgh Marriage Records it occurs as Blainchill, Blenseill, and Blinsile. The following additional spellings are recorded in *Guildry*: Bliedsell 1477, Bliusdale 1508, Blyndschel 1474, Blyndule 1399.

BLOKKER. From the occupation. Donald the blokker (Dofnaldus blokker) was one of the workmen engaged in the building of Tarbert Castle in 1326 (ER., I, p. 55). In 1302 there are entries of payments of wages to workmen employed on the Castle of Linlithgow (?), and among them are named bloccars or *bloccarii*, who appear to have had to do with the cutting and trimming of wood (*Bain*, IV, p. 365). This definition of blokker is not noted in the *Dictionary of the older Scottish tongue.*

BLOW. Probably a variant of BLAW, q.v. Alexander Blow was servitor to George Preston, 1662 (*Laing*, 2555). Isobel Blow was married in Edinburgh, 1698 (*Edinb. Marr.*).

BLOWER. From occupation. John Blawer was provost of Lanark, 1329 (ER., I, p. 166). Robert Blower was married in Edinburgh, 1658 (*Edinb. Marr.*). The name is also recorded in England, 1273.

BLUE. An Argyllshire surname formerly current in Arran, and a common surname on tombstones in and around Knapdale. From its frequency on the Knapdale tombstones it has been suggested that the original Gorm may have been a Macmillan. It is a translation of MAC GHILLEGHUIRM, q.v. A writer in the *Celtic monthly* (XXIII, p. 207) erroneously suggests that the Blues of Colonsay, Gigha, and Campbeltown are probably descended from the Buies (a quite different name), one of the oldest family names of Jura. Donald Bleu in Torranbeg, 1755 (*Poltalloch Writs*, p. 188).

BLUND. A Norman name common in England and Normandy in the twelfth century, from AN. *blund, blond* (med. Lat. *blundus*), the "blonde." Not from Norse *blundr*, "sleepy," as sometimes explained *(Zachrisson)*. Hugh de Abirbuthenoth, who gifted the church of Garuoch to the monastery of Arbroath in 1292, was commonly designated Hugo Blundus or Le Blond, from the flaxen color of his hair (*Sc. Peer.*, I, p. 274). Sometime before 1200 Rodbert Blundus witnessed a charter by Roger de Quenci (LSC., 36), and Adam Blundus witnessed a confirmation charter by the Chapter of Brechin c. 1212–18 (REB., II, p. 259). John Blund who witnessed a charter by Matilda, countess of Angus, c. 1242–43 (RAA., I, 49) is probably the John Blundus who appears as a charter witness in Brechin in 1267 (REB., I, 8). In 1296 a writ was issued to the sheriff of Edinburgh for behalf of John le Blund of Esseby (*Bain*, II, 832). About 1340 William Blundus witnessed a concession in favor of the monastery of Schon (*Scon*, 167). Geoffrey Blund was the first burgess of Inverness on record c. 1200 (*Rec. Inv.*, I, p. lv) and the name seems to have continued there at least to the sixteenth century as Blunt.

BLUNT. A variant of BLUND, q.v. John le Blunt of Eskeby, Dumfriesshire, rendered homage, 1296 (*Bain*, II, p. 202). James Blunt in Dalscon, 1743, and two more of the name *(Dumfries)*.

BLUNTACH. A rare surname recorded in Moray. Alexander Bluntach, farmer, appears in the parish of Dallas, 1786. Jean Bluntach of Kellas, Moray, married there in 1941.

BLYE. Alan of Blye was attached to the gate of Forfar for stealing a sow, 1296 (*Bain*, II, p. 191). According to Harrison a weak form of BLYTHE, q.v.

BLYTH, BLYTHE. Of territorial origin from the old barony of the same name in the lordship of Lauderdale. The place name still exists as that of an extensive farm. William de Blyth, persone of Chirnesyde, Berwickshire, rendered homage in 1296 (*Bain*, II, p. 207), and in 1302 the seal of Adam de Blyth was appended to an account of goods purchased at Perth (ibid., II, p. 354). James Blyth was burgess of Dundy (Dundee) in 1485 (RHM., I, p. 142), and William Blitht was admitted burgess of Aberdeen in 1488 (NSCM., I, p. 34). Andrew Blyt was admitted burgess, 1524 (ibid., p. 48). Richard Blyth represented Dundee in Parliament in 1567, Cuthbert Blyth was burgess of Edinburgh in 1563 (*Laing*, 757),

Robert Blyth was retoured heir in land of Brounslope, Berwickshire, in 1646 (*Retours, Berwickshire*, 262), and Archibald Blyth appears as baxter in Dysart in 1691 (*Dysart*, p. 54). Blyth was a common name among the Border Gypsies, a late "Queen" being Esther Faa Blyth (d. 12th July, 1883). Blaith and Blith 1684. Other old forms of the name are Blytht and Blythe.

BLYTHMAN. Charlis Blithman was a follower of Campbell of Lundy in 1529 (RSS., II, 59). The tenement of Thomas Blyithman in Glasgow is mentioned in 1552 (*Protocols*, I), John Blythman is in record in Auchenleck in 1626 *(Dumfries)*, and Nicoll Blytheman and John Blythman in Edinburgh in 1698 (*Laing*, 2974). Blythmann 1540. Ewen's suggestion (p. 327, 337) that the name means 'a man from Blyth' in Northumberland, seems reasonable.

BOAG, BOIG. The index to Laing says Boog = Bog = Boig. Perhaps from Boak in the parish of Kirkcolm, although none of the references points in that direction. Weekley (p. 54) suggests Boag is probably a variant of *boak*, a northern form of *balk*, a ridge (as a boundary). Andrew Boog witnessed instrument of sasine, 1550 (*Laing*, 567). David Book, merchant in Edinburgh, 1610 (ibid., 1597), and Thomas Baok, merchant burgess of Stirling, 1622 (*Laing*, 1910). John Book in Thankertoun, 1626, James Boick there, 1636, and William Boak there in 1629 (*Lanark CR.*). Janet Book in the parish of Cadder, 1629 (*Campsie*). Henry Boog in Reddoch, parish of Falkirk, 1643, and other four of the name (*Stirling*), and James Book, maltman in Falkirk, 1652 and three more (ibid.). Henry Buack, burgess of Dundee, 1664 (*Brechin*). The name was common in Edinburgh in the seventeenth century as Boog, and in Torphichen Commissariot Record the name occurs as Boik (1685), Boick (1688), Boack (1697), and Boag (1709), and William Boick was martyred for his religious belief in Glasgow, 1683. David Bock in Bankhead, parish of Morrowingside (= Muiravonside), 1685, and John Bock (otherwise Pock) was change keeper in Denny, 1793 (*Stirling*). Mr. John Boak, doctor of the Grammar School of Perth, 1666, probably was a relative of William Bouok, schoolmaster at Lundy, who was suspended from office "for his scandal in acting a comedie wherin he mad a mock of religious duties and ordinances" in 1668 (DPD., II, p. 225; I, p. 188). Alexander Boak, tanner, burgess of Edinburgh, 1786. The name early made its way to Orkney. Gilbert Boge, witness in Kirkwall, 1523, Magnus Book, juror on assize at Stenness, 1576, Joan Boak, juror there in 1595, and Robert

Boak in Clowstane, a witness, 1613 (OSR., I, p. 269, 220, 278); George Book in Clouston, witness, 1605 (REO., p. 207, 139, 170, 177, 278). Boag 1768, Boock 1608, Böök 1657; Booge. Cf. BOWOK and BOYACK.

BOASE, BOAYS. A Cornish surname. The Boases of Dundee were of Cornish origin. The names are variants of Bowes.

BOATH. From the old lands of Both in Angus (*Retours Forfar*, 154, 385, 449, etc.). Hugh de Boath, grandfather of Hector Boece, progenitor of the Scottish family of Boethius, is said to have acquired the lands of Bal-in-bridget, now Panbride, "along with the heiress in marriage, in reward for his services to David II at the battle of Dupplin in 1332" (*Bamff*, p. 26). Prof. Watson says "Hugh Boece or Bois, Hector Boece's great-grandfather, was baron of Drisdale (Dryfesdale) in Dumfriesshire, and got land in Forfarshire by marriage" (I, p. 521). David Both is recorded in Cottoun of Gardin, 1606 (*St. Andrews*), and William Bothe in Kirkburne of Cortachy, 1633 (*Brechin*). Still current.

BOCLAND. Adam de Bocland who forfeited a tenement in Edinburgh, 1336 (*Bain*, III, p. 345) may have derived his surname from one or other of the English places named Buckland.

BODDEN. Gilbert Boddane witnessed an instrument of sasine at Bordland of Laik, Kirkcudbrightshire, 1552 (*Laing*, 598). John Bodane in Meiklehalf, 1686 (*Kirkcudbright*), and John Boddane and Williame Boddane were recorded as masters of families in the parish of Buittle, 1684 (RPC., 3. ser. IX, p. 569). Suggested to be from Bowden, Roxburgh, but all references are to Kirkcudbright.

BODDIE, BODIE, BODDY. Perhaps from OE. *boda*, messenger. Hugh Body of Roxburghshire rendered homage in 1296 (*Bain*, II, p. 208). Andrew Body was admitted burgess of Aberdeen in 1494, Robert Bawdy in 1548, and Patrick Bodie in 1593 (NSCM., I, p. 37, 61, 84). Mr. Gilbert Bodie "a drunken Orkney asse" was a member of the General Assembly which met at Dundee, 1597–8 (William Scot, *Apological narration*, p. 103), and James Body was heir by conquest of Master Gilbert Bodye, minister of the church of Holme in Orkney, in the vill and lands of Cragquhorthie in the parish of Kinkell, Aberdeenshire, in 1608 (*Retours, Aberdeen*, 118). Patrick Bodie in Pitterheid (? Peterhead) 1633 (SCM., III, p. 102), Andrew Bodie in Dysart, 1645 (PBK., p. 281), and Christian Bodie in Edinburgh, 1647 (*Edinb. Marr.*). The surname is common

in the Aberdeen Poll Book of 1696. James Boddie and Thomas Boddie of Marnoch served in the first Great War (*Turriff*). Guppy (p. 287) has Boddy as a Norfolk surname, and says it occurs in Cambridgeshire, Hunts, and Oxfordshire in thirteenth century.

BOE. A much attenuated form of BULLOCK, q.v. In the sixteenth and seventeenth centuries part of Bonnington near Peebles was held by the Bullos of Bonnington-Bullo. In the public records the name appears as Bo, Boe, Bowie, or Bullo. Barbara Boo in Darnick, 1655, and George Boo or Boe in Dainyeltoune (or Danzielton), 1660 (RRM., I, p. 159, 297; II, p. 84). John Booe took the oath in 1685 (RPC., 3. ser. X, p. 455). Agnes Boe in Symington, Lanarkshire, 1677, and three more are in record there (*Lanark CR.*), and Andrew Boe in Parkhill, 1682 (*Peebles CR.*). William Boa in Easter Glentueing, parish of Crawfordjohn, 1723 (*Lanark CR.*), and Mr. James Boe was schoolmaster at Moffat, Dumfriesshire, 1745 (*Dumfries*).

BOED. Gille filius Boed was one of the witnesses to Earl David's *Inquisitio* concerning the lands of the church of Glasgow a. 1124 (REG., p. 5), and a Gilbert filius Boet is mentioned c. 1155–57 in a charter by Henry II of England as the former owner of the barony of Gillsland in Cumberland (*Sc. Ant.*, XVII, p. 111). "In the Foundation Charter of Lanercost (*Illus. Doc.*, XXIII, *Wetheral Priory*, p. 419), and in a confirmation by Pope Alexander III in 1181 certain lands are described 'per has divisas quas Gille filius Bueth illam melius et plenius in vita sua tenuit,' and, again, 'Dedi autem eis omnem corticem de merremio meo proprio...in boscis meis infra baroniam meam de terra quae fuit Gille filius Bueth'" (*Lawrie*, p. 304). Gylis filius Buht apud Drumedler was one of the witnesses to the *Diuise de Stobbo*, c. 1190 (REG., p. 89).

BOG, BOOG. This surname is found around Coldingham, Berwickshire, and tradition there says the family is of French origin. It is, however, more probably of local origin. There is Bogg near Canonbie, Dumfriesshire, and another in Lanarkshire. Edward Bog, priest of the diocese of St. Andrews and notary public, 1505 (*Bamff*, p. 43). John Bog was retoured heir in lands of Burnhouss and Auchterstown, etc., in Berwickshire, 1546 (*Retours, Berwick*, 1), George Bog was master of the Queen's beer cellar and Alexander Bog janitor of the outer gate in 1563 (ER., XIX, p. 237). Nicolas Bog, witness in Glasgow, 1550 (*Protocols*, I), and another Nicolaus Bog was served heir to his father John Bog in a tenement in Rox-

BOG, Boog, continued

burgh, 1576 (*Retours, Roxburgh*, 329). John Bog and James Bog were jurors on the trial of Barbara Napier in Edinburgh, 1591 (*Scottish Papers*, x, p. 522). John Boig was retoured in lands in the barony of Coldynghame, 1632 (*Retours, Berwick*, 183), and another John Boig in Turriff was admitted burgess of Aberdeen, 1607 (NSCM., I, p. 104). Hugh Boog, writer in Edinburgh, 1683 (*Inquis.*, 6493), George Boog in Klinkhill of Blacklaw, 1713 (*Dunkeld*), and John Bogue of Prestonhaugh, 1790 (*Lauder*). There is also a place named Bog in Roxburghshire (*Retours*, 323) and another place of the name in Perth Retours (228, 451, etc.). Boige 1681, Bwg 1658.

BOGGIE. See under BOGIE.

BOGGS. Local. There is Boggs near Pencaitland, Midlothian. Gilbert Boggis recorded in the parish of Beith, 1559 (*Laing*, 704). Euphaim Boiges was married in Edinburgh, 1601 (*Edinb. Marr.*), and William Boggs is recorded in Mains of Gorthy, 1702 (*Dunblane*).

BOGIE, Boggie. From the lands of Bogie (anciently Bolgyne) in the parish of Abbotshall, Fife. John filius Malcolmi Bolgy was burgess of Aberdeen in 1317 (SCM., v, p. 11). John Bolgy, custumar of Edinburgh, 1327 (ER., I, p. 81). William Bolgy appears as chaplain in Perth in 1455, and John Bolgi was sergeant to the Friars there in 1477 (*Milne*, p. 48, 81). Robert Boggie of Kinnastoune was retoured heir of Robert Boggie of Kinnastoune, his father, in lands in the parish of Leuchars, 1690 (*Retours, Fife*, 1309). Robert Boigie of Kinnistoune, 1691 (*Inquis.*, 7170). Alexander Boggie possessed a garden and house in Dumfries, 1820 (*Dumfriesshire and Galloway Nat. Hist. and Ant. Soc., Trans.*, 3. ser. xxi, p. 37).

BOGLE. Probably from the place named Bowgyhill in the parish of Monkland, Lanarkshire. Margaret Bogyll is recorded in Glasgow, 1487 (LCD., p. 256), and Robert Bogyll or Bogill was rentaller of the lands of Carmyle, 1510 (*Rental*), and voter in Monkland, 1519 (*Simon*, 45). James Bogyl was tenant of the 16s. 8d. land of Carmyle, 1520 (*Rental*). The name is common in the Campsie Commissariot Record. Thomas Bogile or Bogill in Glasgow is mentioned in 1552 and 1558 (*Protocols*, I, x), Merione Bogill was spouse of Thomas Brovne in Wyndvege, 1564 (*Pollok*, I, p. 299), and Robert Bogill was serjeant burgess of Linlithgow, 1583-1599 (*Sc. Ant.*, xi, p. 131; *Laing*, 1381). John Bogill was burgess freeman of

Glasgow, 1575, James Bogil was made burgess as a burgess-heir, 1579 (*Burgesses*), and James Bogell was merchant burgess, Glasgow, 1685 (RPC., 3. ser. x, p. 471). John Bougle at Bougilsholle, Ilasabeth Bogell in Sandiehills, and Archibald Boggell were charged with attending conventicles in 1686 at Daichmonthill (ibid., xii, p. 565). Bogyl, 1510.

BOGLILIE. John de Balglaly was bailie of the burgh of Kingorne in 1428 (ER., iv, p. 463). From Boglilie in the parish of Kirkcaldy, Fife.

BOGRIE. A surname "of respectable standing in the country" around Cruden. Said to be from French Beaugre, the name of a French servant who returned to Scotland with earl Francis of Erroll on the latter being pardoned by King James vi. The servant obtained a farm from his master and gave it the name of Fountainbleau (Pratt, *Buchan*, ed. 1901). The name, however, may be from Bogroy, Cornhill, Banffshire. There is a Bogrie near Kirkcudbright and another near Dunscore, Dumfriesshire. There is a Fountainbleau near Ellon, Aberdeenshire, another near Dundee, and a third near Dumfries.

BOGSIDE. Local, from one of the many small places of the name. Sandy Bogsyde, voter in Monkland, 1519 (*Simon*, 45).

BOGTOWN. Of local origin from one of several small places named Bogton and Bogtown. Anabelle de Bogtowne in Glasgow, 1410 (LCD., p. 238). Meg Bogtoun in Prestonpans was accused of witchcraft, 1590 (*Trials*, I, p. 246).

BOGUE. Never a common surname. Probably local, from Bogue in the parish of Minnigaff, Kirkcudbrightshire. David Bogue (1750–1825), one of the founders of the London Missionary Society, was born in Coldingham, Berwickshire. Cf. BOAG.

BOGWOOD. Probably from Bogwood near Mauchline, Ayrshire. Henry Bogwod charged with forestalling in 1431 (Coll. AGAA., I, p. 227).

BOIG. See under BOAG.

BOILOND. Bernardus de Boilond c. 1150, witnessed a charter of the church of Lohworuora (REG., 11). There was a place and family of this name, perhaps from Boyland in co. Norfolk.

BOITE. Boite or Boete the father of Gruoch, queen of Macbeth, was killed in 1033. Anderson suggests (ES., I, p. 571) the name may

be an Irish form of Bui(t)te of Monaster-
boice (Latinized *Boethius*), which Plummer
(*Vitae Sanct. Hiberniae*, I, p. xxxiv) says
means 'heat.' The gloss on his name has: *Buite.
i. beo, no buite. i. teine*, i. e. living or fire.
Gilbert Buyte was witness in Wigtown, 1484
(RMS., II, 1623).

BOLAM. A surname of recent introduction
from England. From Bolam, a township in
South Northumberland. The De Bolams were
an influential family of the thirteenth century
(*Guppy*, p. 313).

BOLD. From the lands of Bold in the parish
of Traquair, Peeblesshire. In the beginning
of the fifteenth century the lands were occupied by John of Bolden (Buchan, *Peebles*, II,
p. 535). Bridget Bold and two others of the
name appear in the Edinburgh Marriage Register.

BOLE. William Bole was admitted burgess of
Aberdeen, 1508 (NSCM., I, p. 44), and Janet
Bole, 1629, and eight others of the name are
recorded in Edinburgh (*Edinb. Marr.*). Cf.
BOLL. Harrison says "a variant of BULL," and
Lower says a De Bolle is found in the English
Hundred Rolls.

BOLEBEC. From Bolbec in the department
of Seine Inférieure, Normandy. Only three
individuals of this name appear in Scottish
records. Walter de Bolebec witnessed Earl
David's foundation charter of the Abbey of
Selkirk, c. 1120 (*Kelso*), and the confirmation
by Earl Henry of the grant of Ederham and
Nesbit by Gospatrick to the monks of St.
Cuthbert at Coldingham, c. 1141 (*Raine*, App.,
103). He also witnessed King David's gift of a
toft in Berewic to the Priory of May c. 1147–
53 (*May*, 2), and c. 1153–65 he witnessed a
charter by Malcolm IV of "terra Jocelini" to
Neubotle (*Neubotle*, p. 9). As de Bolebech he
witnessed, c. 1150, the charter by Robert,
bishop of St. Andrews granting the church of
Lohworuora (now Borthwick) to Herbert,
bishop of Glasgow (REG., p. 13). William
de Bolbethi witnessed a charter by Waltheus,
earl of Dunbar in 1166 (*Raine*, App. 26).
Dominus Ricardus de Bolbek witnessed a resignation of the lands of Edeluestun to the
Church of Glasgow in 1233 (REG., p. 141).
A genealogy of the English family of the
name is given in J. C. Hodgson's *History of
Northumberland*, v, p. 224, Newcastle-on-
Tyne, 1902.

BOLL. Jehone Boll of Ballachkewin and his
son Jehone Boll were witnesses in Irvine, 1572
(*Irvine*, I, p. 57). John Boll was tenant in
Nether Calsay, 1710, and Thomas Boll is re-
corded in Ancrum, 1784 (*Heirs*, 153, 425).
Cf. BOLE and BOYLE.

BOLT. Hugone Bolte witnesses an Inchcolm
charter c. 1178–1214 (*Inchcolm*, p. 5). It may
be for le Bolt, 'the bold' recorded in England,
1273.

BOLTEBY. William de Bolteby witnessed a
confirmation charter by Patrick, earl of Dunbar of a grant to the Abbey of Melrose c. 1230–
31 (*Wemyss*, II, p. xviii), and as de Boltevy
witnessed a charter of lands to the Priory of
Coldstream a. 1232 (CCPC., p. 20). His name
probably comes from Boltby in Yorkshire, in
DB. *Boltebi* and *Bolteby*.

BOLTON. Probably from Bolton in East Lothian. Adam de Boultone was reeve of Dunfres,
1287 (*Bain*, II, 324). William fiz Geffray de
Boultone del counte de Edeneburk rendered
homage, 1296 (ibid., p. 201). John of Boulton
was employed as a mason at Castle of Linlithgow, 1302 (*Bain*, IV, p. 365), and Robert of
Bolton, a Scot, was released from prison in
Colchester, 1396 (*Bain*, IV, 483). Bessie Bolton
is recorded in Edinburgh, 1640 (*Edinb. Marr.*),
and William Bolton in Burntiland, 1645 (PBK.,
p. 242).

BOMBIE. John de Bundeby or de Bondeby
of the county of Dunfres who rendered homage in 1296 and in the same year served as
juror on an inquest held at Berwick (*Bain*, II,
p. 210, 216) derived his name from Bombie
in the parish of the same name in Kirkcudbrightshire. Andrew Bomby in Ayrshire denounced rebel in 1512 (*Trials*, I, p. *83).

BONACH. Patrick Bonach and George Bonach
in Chastletoune, 1682 (*Invercauld*, p. 264).

BONALLY, BONALLO, BONELLA, BONELLO.
From Bonaly near Colinton in Midlothian.
There was also a place Banaley in Fife, now
obsolete (Liddall, *Place-names of Fife and
Kinross*, p. 23) which might account for the
Fife references. Thomas de Bounavelin was
one of the jurors on an inquest held in the
Chapel of St. Katherine, Bavelay, in 1280
(*Bain*, IV, 1762). William Bonavlay and his
spouse had a charter of part of the lands of
Beyth Bonaylay c. 1570 (RD., p. 470), Robert
Bonalay is recorded in Balcormo, parish of
Largo, in 1637 (*St. Andrews*), John Bonallie in
Weyms, 1641 (PBK., p. 206), James Bonalley,
wheelwright in Edinburgh, is mentioned in
1668 (*Edinb. Marr.*). David Bonallo (1818–
1889) was minister of Ardoch in 1844 and of
Blackford in 1858 (Scott, *Fasti*, II, p. 784–
785). The last two forms are current in Fife.

BONAR, BONNAR, BONNER. Usually described as a descriptive name, 'the gentle, courteous,' from OFr. *bonair*. The name may have reflected the character of the first bearer or bearers but not that of Walter Bonar of 1527. Thomas Boner, charter witness in Aberdeen, 1281 (REA., II, p. 279). William Boner, constable of Kinghorn, 1328 (ER., I, p. 112). Roger Bonere, burgess of Aberdeen, 1342 (REA., I, p. 71). The ship of John Bonere, a Scotsman, was wrecked at Holkham, 1388 (*Bain*, IV, 381). William Bonare, citizen of St. Andrews, who had a charter of a third part of the lands of Balwely, 1451 (SCM., IV, p. 3), may be William Bonare (Bonere, or Bonour) who had safe conducts to travel in England, 1452–53 (*Bain*, IV, 1244, 1246, 1254). Ninian Bonnar of Kelty became man to William, earl of Montrose by a band of manrent, 1507 (HMC., 2. Rep. App., p. 168), and Walter Bonar of Kelty had remission for forethought felony and oppression, 1527 (*Trials*, I, p. *240). Bonar was the name of a Flemish gunner afterwards tenant of a royal farm in Fife (*Sc. Ant.*, IV, p. 114). Charles and Thomas Banner or Bammer were herds in Buchtrig, 1684 (RPC.). In Burke's account of the family of Bonar it is stated that the surname was at one period so numerous in Scotland that no less than thirty-seven different lines of Bonars are to be found upon record, each styled by their territorial designation (*Scot. Nat.*, III, p. 689). Bonarr 1456.

BONBIRY. Local. John de Bonbiry held land in Waldeugate, Berwick, in 1307 (*Kelso*, 43).

BONDINGTON. William de Bondington (d. Nov., 1258), chancellor of the kingdom and bishop of Glasgow, most probably received his surname from the lands of Bondington, now Bonnington, in the parish of Peebles, Peeblesshire, as suggested by Anderson (*Early sources*, II, p. 490). He appears frequently in charters. Alisaundre de Bondingtone, chaplain, of Berwickshire, and Johan de Bondingtone, clerk, of the county of Strivelyn, rendered homage, 1296 (*Bain*, II, p. 206, 208). John of Bonygton, a Scot going abroad, who had letters of protection through England, 1371, may be the John de Bondyngton who was a merchant in the service of the earl of Fife and Menteith, 1383 (ibid., IV, 195, 324). The name appears to be confused with BONNINGTON, q.v.

BONE. This name is common in Ayrshire, and six of the name are recorded in the Edinburgh Marriage Register from 1640. It has been suggested that the name is a variant of Bonar (*Sc. Ant.*, IV, p. 114), but this is improbable. It may be from Fr. *le bon*, 'the good.' A contemporary Scottish family of this name of remarkable genius is composed of Captain David Bone, of the Anchor Line, his brother James Bone, editor of the *Manchester Guardian*, Muirhead Bone the artist, Stephen Bone who did the mural paintings in the Piccadilly Circus Underground Station, and Freda Bone, daughter of Captain David Bone, who also is an artist. The name may be from Bohun, a place near Carentan, in France.

BONELLA, BONELLO. Variants of BONALLY, q.v.

BONNAR, BONNER. See under BONAR.

BONNET. George Bonnet, late box-master of the landmen of Borroustounness, 1688 (*Laing*, 2868). Bonnet is a common French surname.

BONNINGTON. Andrew de Bonynton, burgess of Linlithgow, who died in 1442 (*Analecta Scotica*, I, p. 173), and David Boninton, witness in Lythqw (Linlithgow) in 1444 (*Sc. Ant.*, XVII, p. 115) most probably derived their surnames from Bonnytoun in West Lothian. The name has been confused with BONDINGTON, q.v.

BONNYMAN. This surname is most probably derived from the lands of Balnamoon in the parish of Menmuir in Angus, the local pronunciation of which is given as "Bonnymune." Duncan Bonyman was a mason at Dunkeld in 1514 (*Rent. Dunk.*, p. 295), and George Bonyman was a merchant in Edinburgh in 1590 (*Laing*, 1203). John Bonyman appears as a juror in the regality of Spynie in 1597 (SCM., II, p. 141), Mr. George Bonyman was servitor to Mr. John Hay of Eister Kennet in 1626 (*Fordell*, p. 113), and John Balnamoon of Glasgow was released on signing a bond not to take up arms in 1679 (RPC., 3. ser. VI, p. 296). W. Bonniman was a member of the Huntly Volunteers in 1798 (*Will*, p. 18).

BONTAVERN. Alexander Bontawerne was juror on an inquest at Cupar in 1522 (SCBF., p. 266), and John Bontavern witness in Fife, 1548 (*Gaw*, 40). George Bontaverone is recorded in Wester Kilsleif, parish of Creich, in 1593 (*St. Andrews*), and Thomas Bontaveron in Lethame in the parish of Monymaill in the same year. Other twelve of the name are recorded in *St. Andrews*. David Bontaverone was retoured heir of Thomas Bontaverone, portioner, his father, in 1643 (*Retours, Fife*, 653), and Mariota Bontavorine, spouse to Thomas Alison, is recorded in Dunblane (*Dunblane*). Cf. Holyn de Prontauerin (a place near the Clyde and Nethan), c. 1208–18 (*Kelso*, 103). This name seems to have become BONTHRON, q.v.

BONTEIN. See under BUNTEN.

BONTHRON, BONTHRONE. A surname now mainly confined to Fifeshire. Thomas Bunthorn, portioner of Lelethame in the parish of Monymaill in 1617 (*St. Andrews*). William Bunthorne was witness in Dysart in 1640 (*PBK.*, p. 184), George Buntrone, smith in Edinburgh, is in record in 1644, and James Bontram was a tailor there in 1653 (*Edinb. Marr.*). Margaret Bontrone in Cottoune of Balfarge appears in 1671 (*Dunblane*), Joannes Bonthrone heir of John Bonthrone in Straemiglo in 1680 (*Inquis. Gen.*, 6237), is doubtless John Bontron, baxter in Stramiglo in 1696 (*Dunkeld*). Alexander and Thomas Bonthrone of the parish of Forteviot were among the Scots killed in the first Great War. See BONTAVERN. Bunthorn 1689, Bonthrean 1816.

BONTINE. *See under* BUNTEN.

BONVALET. Explained by Harrison as from Fr. *bon valet*, 'good valet.' Willelmus Bonuaillet was one of the witnesses to a charter by David de Lyndessay c. 1200 (*Neubotle*, p. 103). Ewen (p. 88) mentions William Bonvalest, a tenant in chief, 1086, and (p. 114) one Bonvalet (1230). In the face of these early references Harrison's explanation seems unlikely?

BONVILLE. Of Norman territorial origin. The *Itinéraire de la Normandie* records three places so called – two near Rouen and the third near Yvetot. Adam de Bonuill was present at perambulation of the bounds of Kynblathmund, 1219 (*RAA.*, I, p. 163). John de Boneville had a charter of the lands of Collistoun and two roumes of Ardendrachtis in the lordship of Buchan, 1321 (*CAB.*, p. 379; *RMS.*, I, App. II, 392), and John de Bonevyle is mentioned in 1326 as owner of the land of Blairtoun in the thanedom of Balhelvie, Aberdeenshire (*RMS.*, I, App. II, 414). John de Bonevyle witnessed an obligation by Robert, abbot of Dunfermline, 1326 (*RHM.*, I, p. 34). John de Bona villa was one of the witnesses to the foundation charter of a chapel infra le Garvyach c. 1340 (*REA.*, I, p. 67), and witnessed the grant of the barony of Dalkeith to William de Douglas in 1341 (*RHM.*, II, p. 45). In 1376 Eden Bondvyle held a cotagium in the barony of Kilbochope (ibid., II, p. 16). King Robert III in 1400 granted a charter to John Bonvile, son and heir of John Bonvile of Balhelvy Bonvile of certain lands there (*CAB.*, p. 289). John Bonville, Scottish merchant, had a safe conduct into England, 1475 (*Bain*, IV, 1433).

BOOKLESS, BUGLASS. From the old lands of Booklawes near Melrose, Roxburghshire, spelled Bukelawis in 1606 (*Retours, Roxburghshire*, 43). Robert de Buclesŏ who witnessed a confirmation charter by Richard de Vmfra-

muilla in favor of the Abbey of Kelso, c. 1220, is doubtless the first of the name recorded. John Bewclase, a trustworthy man, witnessed the testament of Alexander Hume of Dunglass in 1423 (*HMC.*, 12 Rep., App. 8, p. 87), and John Bukles witnessed an instrument of sasine in Lothian in 1535 (*Laing*, 398). Letters of Slains were subscribed by Kathrine Bukles in 1589 (*RPC.*, IV, p. 347), Agnes Buckles is recorded in the parish of Livingstone in 1675 (*Torphichen*), and John Bowglase in Overlaskeoch signed the Test in 1684 (*RPC.*, 3. ser. X, p. 226). Other sixteenth century forms of the surname (all in Lothian) are Buccles (1539), Bukeles (1571), Buikles (1584 and 1603), Booklaws (1685). The name is also found in the Edinburgh Marriage Register as Bookles (1618) and Bugloss (1680). Other old forms are: Bucklijs, Buckijlis, Buklijs, Baukle, and Bwikles. James Buglass died in Edinburgh in 1940, and Jessie Buglass of Belhaven in same year.

BOONRAW. A rare surname of local origin, from Boonraw near Hawick, Roxburghshire. The surname is practically confined to its place of origin.

BOOSIE. *See under* BOWSIE.

BOOTH. Of local origin from residence at a booth (ME. *bothe*, a hut or temporary shelter). The surname is found in several parts of Scotland. The ship of Walter de La Bothe, merchant of Aberdene, was plundered at sea by the English near Yarmouth in 1273 (*Bain*, II, 9), and Cristiane "atte bothe" of Berewyk rendered homage in 1296 (ibid., p. 208). Andreas de Botha witnessed a Glassarie charter in Dundee in 1321 (*HP.*, II, p. 225), and Nicholas de Botha was proprietor of a land in Dundee in 1381 (*RMS.*, I, 691). William de Botha witnessed a gift of lands to the Hospital of Soltre, c. 1350–66 (*Soltre*, p. 32).

BORLAND. Of local origin from one or more of the places of the name. There are localities named Borland or Boreland in Dumfriesshire, Galloway, Fife, and Perthshire. Bordland appears to have been equivalent to 'home-farm.' James Bordland witness in Ayrshire, 1513 (*Ros*, 56). Allan Bordlandes was a weaver in Edinburgh in 1609 (*Edinb. Marr.*). In the same record the name also appears as Borland, Bordland, Borelands. Marion Bordland in Righeid, parish of Lesmahago, is recorded in 1625 (*Lanark CR.*), Robert Borlan in Muirton of Balhousie, 1652 (*Dunblane*), and James Bordland in Edelwood, parish of Hamilton, 1661 (*Campsie*). Thomas Borlands was writer in Edinburgh, 1684 (*RPC.*, 3. ser. X, p. 361), and Alexander Borland was a poetical friend of Tannahill.

BORRIE. A Perthshire surname prevalent in Blairgowrie and Dunkeld districts. William Borie in Rusland, 1626 (*Inquis.*, 8566). William Borrie in Claypotts, parish of Little Dunkeld, 1656 (*Dunblane*). Daniel Borrie in Middle Dalguse, 1701 and seven more of the name (*Dunkeld*).

BORROWMAN, BORROMAN. William Borowman held a land in Montrose in 1437 (REB., II, p. 56). John Borowman was one of an inquest to determine the rights of pasturage which the Temple lands had over the adjoining town and territory of Letter in 1461 (*Strathendrick*, p. 222). William Borrowman was a baker in Edinburgh, 1673 (*Edinb. Marr.*), and John Borrowman is recorded in Neather Stewartoune, 1696 (*Inquis.*, 7757). In old Scots a borrowman was a burgess, or burgage tenant.

BORTHWICK. From the old barony of Borthwick along Borthwick Water in the parish of Roberton, Roxburghshire. 'Quondam' Thomas de Borthwic is mentioned in a document of his son William de Borthwic regarding the lands of Middleton in Midlothian in 1368 (APS., I, p. 147). This quondam Thomas de Borthwick had a charter from John of Gordon, lord of that Ilk, of the half lands of Ligertwood near Lauder, between 1357 and 1367 (*Sc. Peer.*, II, p. 94). In 1378 William de Borthwick was owner of the lands of Catcune in Midlothian to which he gave the name of Borthwick after his original lands (Nisbet, *Heraldry*). William de Borthwick had a charter of the lands of Borthwick and Thoftcotys in the sheriffdom of Selkirc in 1410 (RMS., I, 928), probably a restoration of the original lands of the family. In 1424 William of Borthik was one of the auditors of the taxation of burgesses for payment of the ransom of James I (APS., II, p. 5), and in the following year was one of the hostages for the king (*Bain*, IV, 983). George de Borthwike was archdeacon of Glasgow in 1423 (APS., I, p. 227), David Borthik, a Scot of the diocese of St. Andrews, was elected procurator of the Scottish 'nation' in the University of Orleans in 1502 (SHSM., II, p. 95), and Alexander Borthwik was a commissioner for holding parliament in 1505 (APS., II, p. 257). The surname was common in Edinburgh in the sixteenth and seventeenth centuries. It early travelled north, as William Borthwvk appears as bailie of Aberdeen in 1398 (CRA., p. 372) and Patrick Borthwik was admitted burgess of the same town in 1400 (NSCM., I, p. 1). There is no proof for the statement that the family of Borthwick are descended from a Livonian Knight, Andreas Burtick, who was attached to the Court of

Hungary. Barthwick 1679, Boirthuik 1565, Boirthwik 1588, Borchtwik 1488, Bortheik 1510, Borthek 1530, Borthewyk 1411, Borthuic 1430, Borthuicke 1652, Borthuik 1573, Borthuyk 1473, Borthvic 1511, Borthvik 1593, Borthwyke 1408, Borthyk 1516, Bortyk 1575, Brothvik 1506, and (undated) Borthuyke, Borthweke, Borthock.

BOSTON. The Bostons of Gattonside are an old Border family, and their name appears in record as Boustoune and Bowstone. There is a town named Boston in Lincolnshire, but the Scottish name may be of local origin. Bernard Boustoun was one of the witnesses to a charter by Andrew, abbot of Melrose, 1540 (RRM., III, p. 225). Robert Boustoun, tailor in Edinburgh, 1603 (*Laing*, 1459), Janet Bowstoune in Pittincreiffe, parish of Couper, 1619 (*St. Andrews*), John Bowstoune in Mekill Govan, 1628 (*Campsie*), and Helen Boustoun in Smailholme 1634, (*Lauder*). Adam Bowstoune heir of Adam Bowstoune in Mauchlin, 1636 (*Retours, Ayr*, 789), Thomas Bowstoun, portioner of Galtounside (Gattonside), 1662 (RRM., II, p. 29), and Robert Bowstone was examined for the Test in 1685 (RPC., 3. ser. XI, p. 434). Twelve of the name are recorded in the Edinburgh Marriage Register spelled Bowstein, Boustein, Bowstine. Boustain 1649, Boustoune 1652, Bowstain 1650, Bowsting 1643.

BOSWALL, BOSWELL. (1) From a vill near Yvetot, Normandy, or (2) from a place now Beuzeville near Bolbec. The first of the name in Scotland was Robert de Boseuille, who witnessed several charters in the earlier part of the reign of William the Lion, and is said to have held land in Berwickshire (*Inchaffray*, p. 304). He was witness to a charter by Walter de Berkeley to the Abbey of Aberbrothoc c. 1170 and to the king's confirmation of same (RAA., I, 56, 57). Between 1178–80 he witnessed gift by William the Lion of a "salina in Kars" to the same abbey, and last appears c. 1204 when he witnessed grant of a toft in Forfar (ibid., I, 7, 11). Paganus de Bosseuilla before 1200 gave a bovate of land in Edenham to the Abbey of Kelso (*Kelso*, 12). Henry de Boysuill witnessed a charter by John, earl of Huntingdon to Norman, son of Malcolm c. 1225 (*Leslie family*, 1). Walter de Boseville was taken prisoner at Dunbar, 1296, and William de Boseville of Berwickshire and William de Boseville of Roxburghshire rendered homage, in same year. The seal of the latter, the charge of which is identical with that of Robert de Bovville of Ayrshire, a bull's head cabossed, S' Will'i de Boyville (*Bain*, II, p. 176, 197, 199, 207, 208). Noteworthy, too, is the fact that the names are alike spelled 'Boyville.' William de Boswill received payment of money for Sir Alexander de Seton, 1329 (ER., I, p. 184), and Roger de Bosseuvll or Bosvyll was custumar and burgess of Edinburgh, 1368–9 (ER., II, p. 608; *Egidii*, p. 1). Roger de Boswell married Mariota, daughter and co-heiress of Sir William Lochore of that Ilk, about middle of fourteenth century and was first of the family settled in Fife. The pedigree of the family from the time of William the Lion down to Samuel Johnson's bearleader is given in Rogers's *Boswelliana*, 1876. Boisuell 1584, Boisuill and Boiswall 1627, Bosewall 1685, Bossuale 1611, Bosswald 1677, Bosuell 1506, Bosvell 1506, Bosvile 1463, Bosvill 1362, Bosvyle 1395, Boswald 1527, Boswele 1506, Boswille 1363; Bosuele, Bosewell, Bosswell, Boswall, Boswel.

BOTHIE. A local Aberdeenshire surname. Thomas Bothie was admitted burgess of Aberdeen, 1508 (NSCM., I, p. 44), and Gilbert Bothie was defender in a court action, 1595 (RSCA., I, p. 351).

BOTHWELL. From the lordship of Bothwell in Lanarkshire. The place name is derived from a 'weyll' or fishpool in the Clyde, as pointed out by the late Dr. George Neilson (SHR., II, p. 319). William de Bothvile witnessed the grant by Bernard de Hauden to the House of Soltre, c. 1190–1220 (*Soltre*, p. 10). The *Sigill. Ricardi de Boteville* is appended to a document relating to fishings on the Tweed, 1250 (*Seals Supp.*, 124). Roger de Bodevill was juror on an inquisition relating to the lands of Hopkelchoc (now Kailzie) in 1259 (*Bain*, I, 2162; APS., I, p. 98 *red*). Richard de Botheuile was provost of Aberdeen in 1342 (ER., I, p. 180; REA., I, p. 72), and in 1346 a dispensation was granted to Patrick de Bothewill, clerk of the diocese of Glasgow (*Pap. Lett.*, III, p. 113). Thomas de Bothwyl had a conveyance of land in the tenement of Denburn in 1347 (*Friars*, 15), and John de Bothuyle is recorded as a canon of Aberdeen in 1366 (REA., II, p. 58). The name is early found in Orkney, John of Boduel being recorded in a document drawn up at Kirkwall in 1369 (*Diplomatarium Norvegicum*, I, p. 308), Erasmus Bothwell in Whalsey is mentioned in 1576, also Bodwell, elder and younger in Houssetter, Northmavine, Shetland. Richard Bothwell was abbot of Dunfermline in 1449 (RD., 427) and, John Bodvell was fermorar in Aberdeen in 1697 (ROA., I, p. 246). Boduall 1617, Boithuile 1523, Boituile 1528, Boithwell 1592, Bothuile 1484, Bothvile 1435, Bothwill 1398.

BOTHWELLSON, 'son of BOTHWELL,' q.v. Erasmus Bothwelson in Burravo, parish of Northmaving, 1615 (*Shetland*).

BOUCHER. From the occupation, properly one who kills 'bucks' (he-goats), a seller of goat's flesh, eaten by the common folk in the middle ages, ME. *bocher, bouchier* <OFr. *bouchier*. James Boucher, schoolmaster in Garvald, died 1939. See BUTCHER.

BOURHILL. Local. The seal of Laurence Bourhil, sheriff of Lanark in 1456, bears *Sigillum Laurentii de Bourhil* (*Seals*, 127). Andrew Bourhil appears as charter witness in Glasgow, 1481 (LCD., p. 195), and in 1500 there is reference to a tenement belonging to him (REG., 481). Marion Burehill was married in Edinburgh, 1598 (*Edinb. Marr.*).

BOURHILLS. A rare local surname, perhaps from Bourhills, St. Andrews, Fife.

BOURTIE. Robert de Bouerdyn who held a toft in Inueruri (c. 1232–1237) (LAC., p. 22) derived his name from Bourtie in the Garioch, Aberdeenshire.

BOUSIE. *See under* BOWSIE.

BOWAR. A Caithness surname of local origin from Bower (pron. Boor) near Wick.

BOWDEN. From the lands of Bowden in Roxburghshire. "For a period of about two hundred years various persons of the same surname are witnesses to a number of charters [in the chartulary of Kelso]. These are not mentioned as holding lands in the parish, but would appear to have been kindly tenants of the monastery who took their name from the barony. The monks of different periods were in the practice of sub-letting the lands of the barony, and some of the lands, on whatever condition originally let, came at length to be held by the parties in hereditary right" (OPS., I, p. 288). Between c. 1200 and c. 1240 one or more individuals named Richard de Boulden witnessed charters by Cecilia de Molle, Symon Maulverer, etc. (*Kelso*, 148, 151, 157, 194). Master Richard de Bouldone, parson of the parish of Edilstone, rendered homage in 1296 (*Bain*, II, p. 212). William de Bolden was Abbot of Kelso in 1370 (*Morton*, p. 92), and in 1399 we have mention of the tenement of John de Bolden in Westerkelsow (*Kelso*, 522). About 1450 Andrew Boldane was a burgess of Arbroath (RAA., II, 94). The name is also found in Edinburgh in the seventeenth century as Boudoun and Bowdoun (*Edinb. Marr.*).

BOWER. (1) From the old manor of Bower in the parish of Drummelzier, Peeblesshire. Lorence atte Bure of the county of Peebles, and William Oftherebure of the county of Roxburgh rendered homage, 1296. The seal of the latter reads, S' Will' d' Lebvre (Bain, II, p. 200, 207, 533). Adam de Bwr, bailie of Ayr in 1401 (Friars Ayr, p. 37) appears in 1415 as Adam de Bowr or de Bowre, burgess of Are (Ayr, p. 9, 11), and as Adam of Boure burgess of Are, gave an annual rent of 4s. to the Friars Preachers (Friars Ayr, p. 47). (2) A shortening of BOWMAKER, q.v. Before the invention of gunpowder a bowmaker was an honorable and lucrative profession. In Edinburgh the bowmakers in the seventeenth century were known as 'Bowers.' Walter Bower or Bowmaker, abbot of Inchcolme, was continuator of John of Fordun's Scottish Chronicle. The surname is found in Aberdeenshire and in Angus at an early date, and a family of the name were burgesses of Dundee in the seventeenth century (Wedd.). Roger Bower held land at the Cuykstoll, Aberdeen, in 1317 (SCM., v, p. 7), John Bower was a monk of Arbroath in 1387 and Robert Bowar the same in 1425 (RAA., II, 39, 59). John Bouer, procurator in Brechin, 1435, may be John de Bouere de Frertoun, armiger, 1450 (REB., I, 78, 143). Patrick Bowre had a remission for his share in burning the town of Dunbretane in 1489 (APS., XII, p. 34; Lennox, II, p. 132), and Thomas Bower was forfeited for holding Dunbar Castle against the king, 1479 (Stodart, II, p. 415). John Bowyr was tenant in Stobo, 1528 (Rental).

Roger Ascham in his Toxophilus (1545, ed. Arber, p. 83, 84), commenting on Textor's praise of excellence of the Scottish archers, says: "The Scottes surely be good men of warre in theyr own feate as can be: but as for shotinge, they neyther can vse it for any profyte, nor yet wil chalenge it for any prayse ... James Stewart fyrst kyng of that name, at the Parliament holden at Saynt Johnnes towne or Perthie, commaunded vnder payne of a greate forfyte, that euerye Scotte shoulde learne to shote: yet neyther the loue of theyr countrie, the feare of their enemies, the auoydyng of punishment, nor the receyuinge of anye profyte that myght come by it, could make them to be good Archers... Therefore the Scottes them selues proue Textor a lyer, both with authoritie and also daily experience, and by a certaine Prouerbe that they haue amonges them in theyr communication, wherby they gyue the whole prayse of shotynge honestlye to Englysshe men, saying thus: that every Englysshe Archer beareth vnder hys gyrdle, xxiiii. Scottes."

BOWERHOPE. Local. There are places of this name in Roxburghshire and in Selkirkshire. William de Birhope of Roxburghshire rendered homage in 1296 (Bain, II, p. 209). Robert Beirope of that Ilk in 1606 was 'dilatit of airt and pairt of the Steilling of certane ky and oxin... brak up the byre-duris of the said place... and away-tuik furth thairof saxtene ky and oxin with sax horse and meiris' (Trials, II, p. 515), and John Berhope of that Ilk was on the Committee for War in Roxburghshire, 1643 (APS., VI, pt. I, p. 54).

BOWERS. Probably just the same as BOWER (1), q.v. Added s is common in such specific names. Margaret Bouris in Stobo, 1511 (Rental). John Bowers, silk weaver in Edinburgh, 1666 (Edinb. Marr.), and Christian Bowars appears in Bankhead, parish of Tulibole, 1677 (Dunblane).

BOWHILL. A Berwickshire surname of local origin, perhaps from Bowhill, Selkirkshire. Thomas Bowhill, gardener in Kelso, 1763 (Heirs, 343). Bowell 1600. Recorded in Edinburgh 1942.

BOWHOUSE. Of local origin from one of several small places of the name in Ayrshire, Lanarkshire, etc. John Bowhows, 1507 (PDG.). Peter in the Bowhous, mentioned in 1591 (RHM., I, p. 175), apparently had no surname. John Bowhouse in Kirktun of Kilbryde, 1610 (Campsie).

BOWIE. John Boye, alias Bowy, alias Boee, a Scotsman living at Yarmouth, had letters of denisation in England, 1481 (Bain, IV, 1471). John Bowey had remission for holding Dumbarton Castle against the king, 1489 (APS., XII, p. 34; Lennox, II, p. 132). Mariot Bowy appears in Edinburgh, c. 1523 (Soltre, p. 265), and Andrew Bowye was notary public in Scone, 1570 (Scon, p. 212). Hieronomy or Jerome Bowie or Bowy appears as master of the king's wine cellar, 1585–89 (RPC., IV, p. 24; ER., XXII, p. 31), and two years later William Bowie is mentioned as servitor in Edinburgh (Laing, 1212). William Bowie was notary in Lauder, 1606 (RRM., III, p. 370), and Elizabet Boway was charged with being a disorderly person (i.e. non-conforming) in the parish of Carsfern, 1684 (RPC., 3. ser. IX, p. 578). William Bowie was member of Gartly Company of Volunteers, 1798, and another William Bowie member of Drumblade Company, 1804 (Will). The name is very common in the Commissariot Records of Stirling and Dunblane in seventeenth and eighteenth centuries. Bowie of Keithock bear a Sagittarius as crest, but this is merely canting heraldry. Cf. BOE. (2) See under BUIE.

BOWLAND. Robert of Bowland was one of the garrison of Stirling, 1339-40 (*Bain*, III, p. 241). Probably from the township of Bowland in the West Riding of Yorkshire.

BOWMAKER. From the trade or occupation of bow-maker, a maker of bows, a bowyer. In 1343 there is entry of payment for wine for Gislinus boumaker (ER., I, p. 532). In 1376 John Bovmaker was bailie of Haddington (ER., II, p. 535), and in 1395 he was deputy of William Cockburn, bailie of the same burgh (ibid., III, p. 364). In 1396 he appears again as John Bouman, which seems to point to Bower, Bowmaker, and Bowman being the same in meaning. Johannes Bomaker was rector of the parish church of Moncabio (i.e. Monyabroc, the old name of Kilsyth in the deanery of Lennox) in 1422 (*Wyntoun*, I, p. xxxvii, S.T.S. ed.). John Bowmakkare of Cardone gave sasine of half his lands of Cardon to Margaret Menzies in 1557, and in 1558 a commission was issued for the trial of John Bowmaker (ER., XIX, p. 423). The surname is also found in Edinburgh from 1620 (*Edinb. Marr.*), and George Bowmaker of Whitrig was on the War Committee of Berwick in 1648 (APS., VI, pt. II, p. 33).

BOWMAN. Innes (p. 37) says this name means a man in charge of the *bow* or cattle, and in his *Legal antiquities* (p. 266) he defines *bowman* as "a person who farms for a season the tenant's milk-cows, and the pasture to maintain them," and James Macdonald (*Local place names*, p. 126) after referring to Innes's definition says "The sheriff is no doubt strictly correct as to the primary meaning and use of the term, but so far as I have observed, 'bowman' is used in various parts of the country to designate small farmers and occasionally farm servants." I rather think that the name has the same meaning as Bower and Bowmaker. In 1328 Gregory Bovman who rendered to Exchequer the accounts of the sheriff of Aberdeen (ER., I, p. 107) appears as Gregory dictus Bowman in an inquisition in Aberdeen in 1333 (REA., I, p. 54; on p. 53 his name is wrongly spelled Bluman). Gyb Bowman in Aberdeen was charged with being a forestaller in 1402 (CRA., p. 383). Robert Bowman, a follower of the earl of Cassilis, was respited for murder in 1526 (RSS., I, 3386). The surname is common in the West Coast, and is found in Glasgow so early as 1550 (*Protocols*, I), and in Stirling in 1592 (*Sc. Ant.*, VI, p. 167). In 1723 several persons of this name residing in Glenmuick and Glenesk, approached the earl of Strathmore, setting forth that their forbears were truly and really of the surname of Lyon, who had

come out of the shire of Angus on account of some troubles, and assumed the name of Bowman, but being by blood Lyons they now desired to resume their true surname (*Aberdeen Journal Notes and queries*, IV, p. 242). Boman 1504. See BOYMAN.

BOWN. A rare current surname. John Bown, clerk, a native of Scotland, had safe conduct in 1392 (*Bain*, IV, 449). Sibbie Bowne was tenant under the Abbey of Kelso, 1567 (*Kelso*, p. 528). There were lands and barony of Bownne in Berwickshire in 1608 (*Retours*, 75; in 1632 Boun).

BOWOK. George Bowok witnessed a sasine in 1525 (*Home*, 35). Alexander Bowok was chaplain in Linlithgow, 1533 (*Johnsoun*). David Bowk or Bowak, prior of Glenluce, was a charter witness, 1560-1572 (Rusk, *History of parish and abbey of Glenluce*, p. 135, 139). William Bowah was admitted burgess of Aberdeen, 1504 (NSCM., I, p. 42). Cf. BOYACK and BOAG.

BOWSDEN. From Bowsden near Lowick, Northumberland, old spellings of which are Bollesdene (1228), Bollisdun (1239). R[adulf] de Boilestunea witnessed gift of the church of the vill of Leuing to Holyrood, c. 1128 (LSC., p. 11). Radulphus de Boiliston witnessed a charter by Richard, bishop of St. Andrews, c. 1170 (*Scon*, p. 30). The seals of Tomas de Bollesdune and of Radulph Bollesdune are appended to an agreement regarding fishings on the Tweed, 1250 (*Seals Supp.*, 112, 113). The seal of Tome de Bolesdvne is also appended to a confirmation of lands at Bollesden to St. Cuthbert at Durham, and also in the thirteenth century we have a charter by Agnes "filia Margrete de Bollesden" of lands of Bollesden to St. Cuthbert at Durham (ibid., 110, 111).

BOWSIE, BOOSIE, BOUSIE. A surname of local origin from Balhousie in Fife, which appears in seventeenth-century record as Bowsie and Bousay, still the local pronunciation of the place name. The surname was mainly localized in Fife. 'Sir' John Bousie who claimed the chaplaincy of the Trinity of Dysart in 1566 (*Dysart*, p. 33) is probably the Sir John Bowsie who was "chargit to produce his richt of the chaplancie of Ouchtarogill" in 1580 (*Soltre*, p. 236), and the Sir John Bowsie, hospitaller and master of the Hospital of Holy Trinity, Edinburgh, in 1584 (ibid., p. 152). Thomas Bousa, witness in Brechin, 1556 (*Laing*, 648) may be Thomas Bowsye who was notary public in St. Andrews diocese in 1567 (*Laing*, 816), and David Bowsie was commissioner to

94

BOWSIE, Boosie, Bousie, continued
parliament for Crail in 1579 (APS., III, p. 128a). William Bowsie, burgess of Crail, was deprived of the office of bailie in 1567 (RPC., I, p. 578), John Bowsy was a resident there in 1587 (RPC., IV, p. 244), Thomas Bowsie is recorded in Aithray in the parish of Logie in 1615 (Stirling), and Katharine Bousie in Athelstanford, 1688 (Torphichen). Bousy 1567, Bowzie 1657; Bowse, Buse.

BOWTOUN. Henry Bowtoun or Bowtoune, witness in Glasgow, 1504 (Simon, 82, 83), probably derived his surname from Bowton near Ochiltree, Ayrshire. Adam Bowtoun, servitor of the laird of Pitfirrane, 1589 (Laing, 1185).

BOYACK. A Fife surname. Christian Bawak in Kelly, 1583, and eight more of the name are in record (St. Andrews CR.). Thomas Boyack in Murroes, 1614 (ibid.). Bowack was also a common surname in Brechin, and fourteen of the name are recorded there and in the neighborhood between 1576 and 1800 (Brechin). Walter Bowack was burgess there, 1643 (REB., II, 246), John Boyack was burgess there, 1690 (Jervise, I, p. 204), and Barbara Boyck was married in Edinburgh, 1647 (Edinb. Marr.). Cf. Bowok and Boag.

BOYCE, Boyes, Boece. From AF. del Bois, 'in or by the wood,' Latinized in early charters de Bosco. Cf. Fr. Dubois and English Attewood. The s was preserved as a voiceless consonant, and the name rhymes with voice and choice. Hugo Delboys witnessed a confirmation charter by Hugh, bishop of St. Andrews, between 1185–88 (Scon, p. 32). Richard del Bois witnessed a confirmation charter of the fishery in Torduf between 1194–1211 (Holm Cultram, p. 35), and as Richarde de Bosco witnessed resignation of lands in Weremundebi and Anant within the same period (Bain, I, 606). Walterus de Bosco witnessed a charter by Robert de Bruce c. 1190 (Annandale, I, p. 1). Willelmus de Bosch or de Bosco, cancellarius domini regis, appears frequently as witness in the chartularies of Soltre, Glasgow, Kelso, Brechin, and Arbroath between 1189–1222. Gaufridus de Bosco, Humphrey de Bosco, and Thomas de Bosco appear as charter witnesses between 1215–45 (Bain, I, 1682; Neubotle, 27; RMP., p. 89; RD., p. 44). Robert Boys is recorded in Dumfriesshire, c. 1259 (Bain, I, 2176; APS., I, p. 88). Humfridus de Bosco, knight, witnessed a charter by Robert Bruce, earl of Carrick, p. 1271 (Annandale, I, p. 8). Thomas de Boys of Edinburghshire and Patrick fiz Johan de Boys of Lanarkshire rendered homage, 1296 (Bain,

II, p. 201, 213). Humphrey de Boyes, knight, of Dumfriesshire, also rendered homage, 1296. His seal bears the forepart of a monster, tongue protruded, emerging from waves, S' Humfridi de Bosco (ibid., p. 185, 531). James de Bosco of Paris petitioned for a benefice in the gift of the abbot and convent of Holywood in the diocese of St. Andrews, 1345 (Pap. Pet., I, p. 95), and Thomas Boyis was tenant under the earl of Douglas in Garvald, 1376 (RHM., I, p. lviii). John of Bowys, Scots prisoner of war in the Tower of London was liberated, 1413 (Bain, IV, 839), and James of Boys had a safe conduct into England, 1422 (ibid., 914). William of Boyis was witness in St. Andrews, 1435 (Laing, 115), and James de Boyis was bailie of the Abbey of Arbroath, 1446 (RAA., II, 87). Patrick Boyce or Boyiss appears as treasurer of Brechin, 1493 and 1511 (REB., II, 138, 164), and Alexander Bowis is recorded in Mains of Melgond, 1703 (St. Andrews CR.). There was an old family of this name in Panbride. Alexander Boys de Panbrid is in record, 1502 (RAA., II, 427), and Patrick Boys was portioner of Panbrid, 1527 (Panmure, II, 305). Hector Boece, the historian, was of this family. He and his brother Arthur Latinized their name as Boethius, Boetius, Boecius. In the fifteenth century in addition to the spellings already noted the name appears as Bois, Boist, Boiste, Bos, Bost, Boust, Bowes, Boyes, Boyess, Buste; in sixteenth century: Boas, Boeis, Boess, Boice, Boies, Boise, Boiss, Bouse, Bowayse, Boyse, Buse; in seventeenth century: Boes, Boos, Boost, Bows, Boze, Bozse. These forms are found only in Fife or in parishes immediately adjoining, and the name is probably the source of Buist, q.v.

BOYD. This surname may be derived from the name of the island of Bute, in G. Bod. The marquess of Bute in Gaelic is Morair Bhoid. The first Boyds were vassals of De Morevilles in the regality of Largs, and quite possibly may have come in their train from England. Dominus Robertus de Boyd, miles, witnessed a contract between Bryce de Egluntune and the burgh of Irvine in 1205 (Irvine, I, p. 3), and Alan de Bodha appears in Dumfries a. 1214 (Kelso, 11). Robert Boyd is traditionally said to have distinguished himself at the battle of Largs, 1263. He is mentioned in a charter by Sir John Erskine of the lands of Halkhill, 1262 (Sc. Peer., V, p. 137). Walterus de Boht witnessed confirmation of gift of the church of Cragyn to the monastery of Paisley, c. 1272 (RMP., p. 233). Robert Boyt, a tenant under the king, in Ayrshire, rendered homage, 1296. His seal shows a small hawk or pigeon (?) and S' Roberti Boit (Bain, II, p. 202, 534).

As Sir Robert de Boyt he was taken prisoner in 1306, and Duncan Boyd, Scotsman, was hanged in the same year for aiding Bruce (ibid., p. 486, 490). Robertus Boyd, miles, witnessed a charter of the church of Kircmacho a. 1329 (RAA., I, p. 313). Malcolm de Bute was chaplain to Robert III, 1405 (Milne, p. 40). Thomas Boyd was one of the hostages for the king of Scotland in 1425 (Bain, IV, 981, 983), and Will Boyde was a charter witness in Ayr, 1438 (Friars Ayr, p. 49). Johne Boyd was tenant of part of Cowbyr, 1479 (Cupar-Angus, I, p. 230), George Boid was burgess of Irvine, 1500 (Simon, 9), and another George Boid was notary public there, 1572 (Irvine, I, p. 57). The surname was very common in Edinburgh in seventeenth century (Edinb. Marr.). Boid 1545.

BOYLE. This Scottish surname, by many thought to be the same as Irish Boyle (from O'Baoghail, Anglicized as Boghill, Boyle, and even as Hill), is of Norman origin, from Boyville, otherwise Boeville or Beauville, near Caen (Baring-Gould, p. 212). DD de boiu (= David de Boiuil) appears as a witness between 1164–74 (Melros), William de Boyvill was one of an inquisition held at Carlisle, 1280, and in 1291 he was appointed to take the fealty of the bishop of Whitherne, and thereafter with the bishop the fealty of those of all Galloway (Bain, II, p. 59, 124). In 1291 Henry de Boyville was castellan of the castles of Dumfries, Wigtown, and Kirkcudbright, in succession to Sir William de Boyville (ibid., II, 576, 580). Three individuals of this name, probably all related one to another, rendered homage in 1296 (ibid., II, p. 203, 205, 210). In course of time the pronunciation of the name slipped into one syllable, written in 1362 Boyll, 1367 Boyuil, 1482 Boyle, 1500 Boyl, 1560 Boile. Gavin Boyll was prebendary of Abirnethy, 1547 (Rollok, 37). The name is not common anywhere outside of Ayrshire and Wigtownshire, where until recently it was pronounced in common speech as "Bole." Boill 1721, Bowill 13c., Boyell 1625, Boylle 1653.

BOYMAN. An old surname in Ayrshire. Robert Boyman who witnessed a charter in favour of the monastery of Kilwinning, 1357 (RMS., I, 182) may be Robert Boyman, medicus, recorded in the same year (Coll. AGAA., I, p. 169). Adam Boyman and Robert Boyman were burgesses of Irvine, 1418 (Irvine, I, p. 127), Alan Boyman, bailie of Ayr, 1471 (Friars Ayr, p. 54), and John Boyman, witness in Ayr, 1494 (Laing, 220). George Boyman and Alan Boyman were voters in the parish of Qwilton (Coylton), 1513 (Ros, 52), and John Boyman held land in Leith, 1565 (ER., XIX,

p. 285). Lower says "a known corruption of Bowman."

BOYN, BOYNE. From Boyne near Portsoy in Banffshire, an ancient thanedom. Patrick Boyne rendered to Exchequer the accounts of the bailies of the burgh of Forres in 1556 (ER., XIX, p. 11). Catherine Boyne was tenant of the lands of Auchincloich in 1571 (RRM., III, p. 299), Thomas Boyn was one of an inquest in Shetland in 1577 (RPC., II, p. 657), and Alexander Boyne was burgess of Elgin in 1591 (ibid., IV, p. 637). Thomas Boyne in Skallowaybanks, parish of Tingwall, is in record in 1613 (Shetland), James Boyn was merchant in Elgin, 1685 (RPC., 3. ser. X, p. 389), Frank Boyne from Monquhitter was killed in the first Great War, and Francis Boyne and his sister Jean, from Forgue, served in the same war (Turriff). Boynd 1685.

BOYTER. Andrew Boytour was a monk of the monastery of Balmorinach (Balmerino) in 1518, and David Boytour was tenant of the same house in the same year (SCBF., p. 103). Alexander Boyture was enrolled burgess of Dundee, 1553 (Wedd., p. 133), David Boittour recorded at Flisk, 1550 (St. Andrews). James Boytour admitted burgess in 1594 is probably the James Boyter, auditor of Dundee, 1617 (Wedd., p. 279), and father of Thomas Boytour of Pilmor, merchant, admitted burgess in 1626. James Boyter, elder of Nethercliff in Angus, gave a bond of caution in 1627 (RPC., 2. ser. II, p. 71). James Boyter, burgess of Dundee, 1643, and six more of the name are recorded in Brechin Commissariot Record. The editor of the Compt buik of David Wedderburne says (p. 76) this name is of French origin. Boytar 1654, Boytoir 1584, Boytor 1616, Bytor 1594.

BRACK. An old surname on the east coast from Berwick to East Lothian. Jordanus Brac gave a piece of land to the church of S. Mary and S. Kentigern of Lanark c. 1214 (Dryburgh, p. 156). This land was afterwards known as Braxfield, and gave title to the notorious Lord Braxfield, one of the Judges of the Court of Session. In the reign of Robert I Michael Hart had a charter of the lands of Brakysfield which Ade Braks resigned (RMS., I, App. II, 603; OPS., I, p. 121 errs in placing this grant in the reign of William the Lion). In 1511 William Brax and his son, David Brax, had a lease of an eighth part of the Grange of Connan (RAA., II, p. 405), and John Brak is in record in 1522 (Home, 46). Thomas Brack in Mandirstoune, 1673, and four others of the name are in record (Lauder). Thomas Brack in Heittoun, 1690 (Peebles CR.).

BRACK, *continued*

William Brack, portioner of Smaillholme, 1769, and Nicol Brack, millwright in Newtown, 1815 (*Heirs*, 330, 623).

BRACKENRIDGE, BRECKENRIDGE, BREKONRIDGE. These surnames are confined mainly to Lanarkshire and Ayrshire, though occurring in the Edinburgh Marriage Register as far back as 1600 in the forms Brakinrig, Brackenrig, Braikingrig and Braikenrig. The surname is derived from the lands of Brackenrig in the old barony of Avondale in Lanarkshire. The yard of John of Bracanryggis in Glasgow is mentioned in 1454 (LCD., p. 177), Johannes Brakanryg was sergeant of the upper baronie of Renffrew in 1454, and Robart Brakenrig witnessed a letter of reversion in 1504 (*Pollok*, I, p. 175, 224), William Braikinrig in Clevens complained of having been assaulted in 1629 (RPC., 2. ser. III, p. 189), and John Breckinrig is mentioned as a servitor in Lanarkshire in 1634 (*Laing*, 2139). Braickenrig 1662, Brakanrig 1504, Bracanrig 1510, Breakenrig 1679, Breckanrig 1686, Brikinrig 1661.

BRACO. Local, probably from Braco near Strichen, Aberdeenshire. There are other places named Braco in the shires of Angus, Perth, Lanark, Ayr, and Dumfries. John Braco in Miln of Pettie, 1743 (*Aberdeen*).

BRADEN. Perhaps from Ir. *O'Bradáin*, descendant of Bradán, Englished Bradan and Bradden. Robert Braden in Renfrew and William Bredin in Foirhills were charged with opposing a new method of tanning, 1629 (RPC., 2. ser. III, p. 359). Elizabeth Braiding and two other daughters of Robert Braiding were heirs portioners of William Braiding of Litleclock, 1649 (*Retours, Renfrew*, 141). See MACBRADDEN.

BRADFUTE, BRAIDFOOT, BROADFOOT. Evidently of local origin from some lost place name formerly either in Ayrshire or Dumfriesshire. The opposite is Braidhead (Dumfriesshire). The name is almost identical in meaning with the Gaelic place name Bondriech, 'foot of hill place.' Marion Bradfute was the wife of Sir William Wallace. Robert Braidfut was vicar of Dunnyn, 1491 (REG., 460). Mr. William Bredfut was minister of Falkland, 1593 (*St. Andrews*), James Braidfoot, merchant in Edinburgh, 1611 (*Edinb. Marr.*), and James Bredfoot was retoured heir in lands in parish of Dunss, 1678 (*Retours, Berwick*, 397). The surname is common in Lanark Commissariot Record. There was an old Cumberland family of Braidfoot (see *Cumberland and Westmorland Archaeological and Antiquarian Society*

Trans., new ser. XIII). Bradfut 1573, Bradfutt 1566, Breadfoot 1639; Braidfoot, Braidfutt, Breadfotte, Bredfute, Breydfut.

BRADLEY. From the lands of Braidlie in the barony of Hawick, Roxburghshire. John de Bradely rendered homage at Berwick in 1291 (*Bain*, II, 508), and William de Bradeleye of the county of Roxburghe rendered homage in 1296 (ibid., II, p. 199). The seal of William is a curious one, bearing a tree supported by two hares, the dexter one beating a cymbal or drum, the sinister playing a pipe; bird in top, a dog coiled at base, and legend S' *Will'i de Bradeley* (ibid., p. 532). In Argyllshire Bradley has been used as an Anglicized form of O'Brolachan, although the two names have no connection either in root or meaning.

BRADY. Richard Brady witnessed a notarial transumpt in Dundee, 1430 (HP., II, p. 164). Galwanus Brady, presbyter and notary public in Dunblane, 1456 (*Scon*, p. 192). Robert Brady resigned the land of Easter Kennet, 1537 (RSM., III.). Cuthbert Brady is recorded in Berwickshire, 1542 (*Laing*, 459; Laing has other early references to Bradys in Berwickshire). Mongo Bradie was goldsmith in Edinburgh, 1576 (RPC., II, p. 537), Master Thomas Brady was chaplain of the chaplaincy of St. John the Baptist of Helmisdell, 1578 (OPS., II, p. 731), and Thomas Bradie is recorded in Kirk of Bonhill, 1623 (*Sasines*). Elspeth Braidie in Peilwalls, 1682 (*Lauder*) and John Braidie in Law, parish of Carluke, 1667 (*Lanark CR.*). The name is also in Edinburgh in seventeenth century (*Edinb. Marr.*).

BRAES. Local, current in Linlithgow and in Musselburgh. There are places of this name listed in CD.

BRAICK, BRAIK. Recorded in Aberdeenshire. A Robert Braick appeared in Lephinmoir, 1676 (*Argyll*).

BRAID. The name of a family which once possessed extensive territories on the south side of Edinburgh and took their surname from their lands. The first of the name recorded is Henry de Brade, who appears in the middle of the twelfth century as owner of not only the Braid Hills, but also of Blackford Hill, the Plewlands, and Bavelaw. He was sheriff of Edinburgh in the reign of William the Lion (*Neubotle*, 14), and as Henricus de Brade, marescallus, witnessed the gift of a toft in Stirling to the church of Glasgow by William the Lion before 1199 (REG., p. 67). He and his successors were proprietors of the Braids for nearly two hundred years, and with one exception they all used the patronymic Henry.

In the reign of William the Lion, probably about the year 1200, Henry de Brade, sheriff of Edinburgh, was witness to a gift of the church of Boeltun by William de Ueteri ponte, son and heir of William de Ueteri ponte and Emma de Sancto Hylario to the church of the Holy Rood of Castle of Maidens and the canons serving the same (LSC., p. 28). Before 1214 he witnessed a gift by Robert de Lyne to the monks of Neubotle (*Neubotle*, p. 12), and before 1220 he is one of the witnesses to a charter by John de Morham to the same monks (ibid., p. 66). About 1230 the second Henry de Brade granted to the monks of Holyrood the tithes of all his moorland of Pentelands and of his land of Baueley (Bavelaw) for the maintenance of divine service in the chapel of the blessed Katherine in the Pentlands (LSC., p. 45). (This little church is now covered by the waters of the Glencorse reservoir, and the ruins, with the little graveyard, have been on several occasions exposed to view in recent years during times of extreme drought.) In 1231 there is mention of John de Brade, canon of Glasgow, and Radulph de Brade his brother (*Soltre*, p. 29). In 1249 Sir Henry de Brade was one of the twelve Scottish knights appointed to meet a similar number of English knights for the purpose of settling the law of the marches (APS., I, p. 413), and in 1261 he was one of the adjudicators in a dispute having reference to the earldom of Menteith. He was dead before November 1274 (*Bain*, II, 34), and was succeeded by his son, Thomas de Brade, who with his brother, Radulf de Brade, a priest in the Cathedral Church of Glasgow, witnessed confirmation of the gift of the church of Maleuille to Dunfermline in 1255 (RD., 206). Sheep belonging to the king's tenants of the Pentlands often strayed upon the lands of Bavelay in search of better pasturage, and it was the practice of the lord of Braid to refuse to return them unless under a 'punlayn' or fine of 8d. per animal. In 1280 an inquisition was made at the chapel of St. Katherine "which found that for fifty years 'byegone' and more, the king never had right within the bounds of Baveley, which is the lord of Brad's; but the servants of the lords of Brad always took the animals of all the king's farmers in the moor of Pentland and imparked them, and took 'punlayn' whenever they found them within the bounds of Bavelev, and thus all the lords of Brad have ever held that land of Bavelay till the time of Sir William de Sancto Claro, and this because Sir Thomas de Brad demanded 8d. of 'punlayn' from the King's men, as the King's men have taken 8d. from his men" (*Bain*, IV, 1762). Henry de Brade of the county of Edinburgh

rendered homage in 1296. His seal bears a squirrel, with the legend S' *Henrici de Bard* (ibid., II, p. 198, 545). In 1426 the lands of Brade passed into the possession of John de Farle (RMS., II, 75). Helen Braid in Dundee, 1638 (*Brechin*). The surname is now found in Fife and in south-eastern Perthshire as *Bread*, and occurs in the St. Andrews Kirk Session records in the sixteenth century. Braed 1569. Braad, Brad, Bradd, Bred.

BRAIDFOOT. *See under* BRADFUTE.

BRAIDHEAD. Local. John Braidhead in Kirkcaldy, 1580 (*Laing*, 998).

BRAIDWOOD. Of local origin from the lands and later village of the same name in Avondale parish, Lanarkshire. John de Bradwod was one of the jurors on an inquest held in St. Katherine's Chapel, Bavelay, in 1280 (*Bain*, IV, 1762). John Braidwod or Braidwoth and Patrick Braidwot are recorded in 1498 as inhabitants of Vddynston (REG., 478, 479), and Cristine Braydwoyd was tenant in the barony of Glasgow in 1521 (*Rental*). James Braidwood, surgeon, burgess of Glasgow, appears in 1649 (*Inquis.*, 3553). The name also occurs in the Glasgow protocol books as Braidwode (1553) and Braidwod (1550). The founder of the firm of Messrs. Broadwood, piano manufacturers, was born in Cockburnspath in 1732. Other early forms of the name are Breadwood and Braiduode.

BRAIKMAN. John Braikman, tenant in Graden, 1685 (RPC., 3. ser. X, p. 481).

BRAIN. Thomas Brayne of Baldowy, witness in 1462 (*Laing*, 149), and David Brane, artium magister, 1477 (*Cawdor*, p. 63). David Brane, witness in Aberdeen, 1492 (REA., I, p. 331). John Brane signed the Band of Dumfries, 1570 (RPC., XIV, p. 66), Roger Brain in Allegawin, parish of Glenbervie, 1601, and four more of the name are recorded in Brechin Commissariot Record. Katherine Brayn appears in Harvestoun, parish of Kynneff, 1605 (*St. Andrews*), and John Brane in Gleddisholme, 1686 (RPC., 3. ser. XII, p. 406). In RPC., 3. ser. X the name is equated with Brand in the index. It may derive from Brain in Côte-d'Or, or from Braine in Ouse (*Baring-Gould*, p. 256).

BRAINWOOD. Local. Thomas Branewod, 1515 (reference unfortunately lost). Margaret Brainewode in Drumkavell, parish of Cadder, 1636 (*Campsie*).

BRAITHNOCH. From Ir. *Breathnach* (more anciently *Breatnach*), a 'Welshman.' "A descriptive surname applied generically to the early Anglo-Norman invaders who came hither [to Ireland] from Wales" *(Woulfe)*. Robert Braithnoch appears in Auchinhay, parish of Kirkpatrick-Durham, 1641, and Agnes Braithnach in Barjarg, 1677 *(Dumfries)*.

BRAITHWAITE. An English surname. There are two places of the name in Yorkshire and one in Cumberland. The name is found in Edinburgh in the seventeenth century as Breathit and Breathwit *(Edinb. Marr.)*. George Brathwait took the oath in 1684 (RPC., 3. ser. x, p. 455), and Jean Braithwaite appears in Dumfries, 1750 *(Dumfries)*.

BRAKHAUGH. Local. Perhaps from some place in Aberdeenshire. William Brakath was witness to a charter in 1464 (REA., I, p. 287). John Brakahe who was admitted burgess of Aberdeen in 1506 (NSCM., I, p. 43) may be the John Brakhauche who contributed to church repairs in Aberdeen in 1508 (CRA., p. 79). Cf. BRACO.

BRAKIE. David de Brakie had a charter of lands in Angus in 1344 (RAA., II, p. 18). Easter and Wester Braikie or Braky are near Inverkeilor, Montrose.

BRALTOUNE. Local. Thomas Braltoune signed the Band of Dumfries, 1570 (RPC., xIV, p. 66).

BRAMBER. John Brember, burgess of Stirling, 1711, and John Bramber, maltman there, 1749 *(Stirling)*.

BRAMWOOD. Local. Bessie Bramwood in parish of Glenholm, 1684 (RPC., 3. ser. x, p. 299).

BRAN. Gaelic and OIr. *bran*, 'raven,' W. *brān*, 'crow'. A common element in personal and river names. Seven or eight persons named Bran occur in the Breton chartularies, besides diminutives and compounds. Bran was the name of the famous hound of Finn. Bran, son of Aidan was slain in the battle of Circhend (fought probably in the Mearns), c. 598 *(Anderson, ES., I, p. 118)*. Bran, son of Macgillegunnin witnessed the confirmation charter by Christian, bishop of Galloway, of the church of S. Marie and S. Bruoc, of Dunrod to Holyrood between 1154 and 1186 (LSC., p. 20), and Donecan, son of Bran witnessed Earl Gilbert's confirmation of his grants to the Abbey of Inchaffray in 1219 *(Inchaffray, p. 34)*. William Bran at the mill of Carnwath was charged with assault, 1629 (RPC., 2. ser. III, p. 209).

BRANCH. A surname early associated with Aberdeen. Andrea Branche in Aberdeen, 1408 (CWA., p. 316) is most probably the Andrew de Branche mentioned there between 1433–38 (SCM., v, p. 41). Andrew Branch and Matthew Branche were admitted burgesses of Aberdeen, 1474 and 1497 (NSCM., I, p. 24, 38), and Andrew Branche, perhaps he already named, was a councillor there, 1492 (CRA., p. 48). Dene David Brance or Brenche was a monk of Paisley, 1563 *(Trials, I, p. 429)*, James Branche was a witness in Aberdeen, 1571 (SCM., II, p. 38), and Thomas Branch, burgess, died in 1574. John Branche in Wilkeistoun, parish of St. Andrews, 1593, and two more of the name are recorded *(St. Andrews)*. The name occurs in Edinburgh from 1614 onwards as Bransh, Brainch, Brench, Brenche, and Bransche *(Edinb. Marr.)*, and possibly Branische found there in 1599 is but another spelling of the name. Bardsley has 'of Branch,' a hundred in county Wilts.

BRANCHELL. Probably from Branchal near Wishaw, Lanarkshire. There is another Branchal near Bridge of Weir, Renfrewshire. Robert Branchall occupied the twenty merk land of Finnart, 1580 *(Laing, 1004)*. James Branchell, burgess of Dumbarton, 1758 (RDB.). "Branchall Sacrament" was the name given to "the sacrament of the Lord's Supper held by Seceders from the Church of Scotland at Burntshiels in the parish of Kilbarchan about the beginning of the nineteenth century. 'Branchall' is one of the forms of Bryntschelis" (Metcalfe-Jamieson, *Scottish dictionary*, s.v. Branchall). The lands of Bruntchells, the seat, of old times, of Bruntchells of that Ilk, lie towards the south of Ranfurly. John Bruntchells, the last of that race, resigned the lands in favor of William, Lord Semple, 1547 (Craufurd, *Shire of Renfrew*, 1782, pt. II, p. 141).

BRAND. A common OE. personal name, ON. *Brandr*, Old Swed. *Brander*, Old Dan. *Brand*. It was a common name in the Danelaw. "The name Brand in England is usually taken to be of Norse origin, but it may be noted that as early as 1046 we find Bransbury, Hants, as Brandesburh, while Branston, Staffs, is Brantestun, in a charter (Birch, *Cart. Saxonicum*, 978) dated 956" *(Mawer, p. 30)*. Giliane Brand held land in Irvine, 1323 *(Irvine, I, p. 124)*. Thomas Brand was burgess of Edinburgh in 1512 *(Laing, 287)*, and the name was common there in the seventeenth century *(Edinb. Marr.)*. Adam Brand had a charter of lands of Steillend, 1631 *(Pitfirrane, 526)*, William Brand is recorded in Urquhart, 1685 (RPC., 3. ser. x, p. 388), and James Brand was baker in the burgh of Canongate,

Edinburgh, 1700 (*Inquis.*, 8785). The Brands of Redhall or Castle Brand were an old family in Angus. As a forename we have Brande Fide, 1506 (*Cawdor*, p. 118).

BRANDANE. S. Brandan appears to have been the special patron of Bute, for the Butemen were of old called the 'Brandans.' Wyntoun (*Chronicle*, v, p. 317, S.T.S. ed.) mentions 'the Brandanys of But' as followers of Sir John Stewart of Bute.

BRANDER. James Brander in Urquhart signed the Test, 1685 (RPC., 3. ser. x, p. 417). William Brander, member of Huntly Company of Volunteers, 1805 (*Will*, p. 30). Said to be from the occupation — the man who branded the (fish) barrels. The "brand of Aberdeen" passed current through Europe in the fifteenth century. (2) It may also have originated from the trade of brander or grid-iron smith, "a trade which centuries ago was as close a corporation as any to-day."

BRANDON. Helen Brandon in Waltoun, parish of Forfar, 1683 (*St. Andrews*), may have derived from Brandon in Northumberland. There is another Brandon in county Durham.

BRANDSON, 'son of BRAND,' q.v. An Orkney surname, perhaps obsolete. Patre Brandesone in Kirkwall, 1516 (SCM., v, p. 395). Edward Brandisone was retoured heir of his father, Edward Brandisone, sailor in Kirkwall, 1674 (*Retours, Orkney*, 111).

BRANKSTON. The *sigill Wilelmi de Brankist* (= Brankiston) is appended to confirmation (undated) of a charter by Alexander de Bollesden of some lands at Bollesden to St. Cuthbert, Durham (*Seals Supp.*, 130). There are places named Brankston in Lanarkshire, Fife, and Aberdeen.

BRANZEAN. The surname of Branzane occurs early in the sixteenth century in connection with Lochar Moss, when record is made of the theft "apud le redkirk" of horses and cows "extra lochirmoss" from Walter and Matthew Branzane. Branzanes were also during the sixteenth century resident in the royal burgh of Dumfries (PSAS., xxii, p. 45). Three Branzeans are recorded in the Commissariot Record of Dunblane in seventeenth and eighteenth centuries.

BRAOSE. Of territorial origin from the Honour of Braose or Briouse in the Department of Orne, halfway between Domfront and Argentan. Paganus de Braiosa is the only member of the family known to have been connected with Scotland. He appears as witness to King David's charter founding the

Abbey of Selkirk (afterwards removed to Kelso), c. 1120 (*Kelso*, 1), to the inquisition as to the extent of the lands of the church of Glasgow c. 1124 (REG., p. 7), and to the confirmations of Coldingham and other lands to the monks of Durham in 1126 and 1130 (*Raine*, 16, 17). The name has been sometimes confused with Bruce.

BRASH. Possibly a form of BRASS, q.v. A common surname in Strathblane in the eighteenth and nineteenth centuries. John Brash was a stabler in Edinburgh in 1622, and Robert Brash was a gardener there in 1630 (*Edinb. Marr.*). John Brash appears in Wester Craigend, 1657 (*Stirling*), and Adam Brashe in the parish of Campsie, 1664 (*Campsie*). Not from German *Brasch*, which is a pet diminutive of *Ambrosius* (Ambrose).

BRASS. (1) Most probably from Birse, Aberdeenshire, the old spellings of which were Bras (c. 1275) and Brass (1511). (2) There are or were also lands named Bras in Fife. (3) Possibly from Bras in France. William Bres was put in the pillory in Orkney, 1425 (REO., p. 41), and Robert Bras held a tenement in Leith, 1548 (*Soltre*, p. 112). Nicholas de Bras in county Bucks, 1292, and Walter Bras in Salop, 1273. Cf. BRASH.

BRATCHIE. Recorded in Shetland, 1942. A variant of BROTCHIE, q.v.

BRATNEY, BRATNIE. Galloway surnames, from (MAC)BRATNEY, q.v. John Braitney was resident in the parish of Senneck in 1684 (RPC., 3. ser. IX, p. 568).

BRATTON. Either from Bratton in Derby or from Bratton in Wilts. Walter Bratoun appears in Glenbervie, 1558 (*Laing*, 690), Andro Brattoun was reidare at Kirkbeane, Dumfriesshire, 1574 (RMR.), and Jennet Bratton and Robert Bratton were examined for the Test in Tinwald, 1685 (RPC., 3. ser. XI, p. 433). Robert Bratton appears in Dallsible, 1680, and two more of the name are in the same record (*Dumfries*).

BRAY. Local. Perhaps from one or other of the many places called Brae. There are also parishes named Bray in England. Godfredus de Bra, juror on inquisition in Aberdeen, 1400 (REA., I, p. 203). Thomas de Bra, burgess of Dunfermline, 1438–48 (RD., p. 288, 305). Walter de Braa leased part of Camsy c. 1443 (*Cupar-Angus*, I, p. 121). Agnes Bray in Craginche, parish of Kilspindie, 1617 (*St. Andrews*). David Bre in Ledcassie 1691 (ibid.), and Michael Bree, causewayer in Edinburgh (EBR., III, p. 99).

BREAD. A form of BRAID, q.v., current in Fife and southeastern Perthshire. Robert Breid is recorded in Dunfermline in 1568 (*Dunfermline*), and John Bread appears in St. Andrews in 1606 (*St. Andrews*), along with several more of the name.

BREADIE. A form of BRYDIE, q.v. David Breadie, son of David Breadie, burgess of Craill, retoured heir of James Williamson, burgess of the same burgh, 1629 (*Retours, Fife*, 426). John Breadie, burgess of Stirling, 1636 (*Stirling*), John Breidie in Balmean, parish of Largo, 1653 (*St. Andrews CR.*), and William Breadie, elder in the parish of Traquair, 1684 (RPC., 3. ser. x, p. 298).

BREBNER. See under BREMNER.

BRECHIN, BREECHIN, BREICHEN, BRICHAN. Of local origin from the town of Brechin in Angus. Ysaac de Brechyn witnessed a charter by Turpin, bishop of Brechin, between 1178 and 1198 (REB., II, 257), and about 1180 Magister Hugh de Breychiñ witnessed a confirmation by Symon Loccard (*Kelso*, 333). Between 1202 and 1218 Andrea de Brechyn witnessed a confirmation charter by Radulph, bishop of Brechin (REB., II, 256), and the William de Breyhyn, who witnessed a charter by Alexander II in 1234 (LIM., xxix), is probably the William de Brechyne who witnessed a convention between Peter, bishop of Aberdeen, and Alan Hostiarius, c. 1250 (REA., I, p. 17). The seal of John of Bricun (? Brechin) is appended to an indenture of 1285 (*Seals Supp.*, 132). Sir David de Breghyn of Forfarshire rendered homage to England in 1296 (*Bain*, II, p. 199, 209), and in 1320 was executed for treason. Alanus de Brechyn held a tenement in Perth before 1330 (RAA., II, p. 7), Cuthbert de Brechine, decanus, is mentioned in 1410 (REB., I, 27), John Brechine appears as witness in Brechin in 1471 (ibid., I, p. 195), John Breching was burgess of Aberdeen in 1527 (CRA., p. 119), and another John Brechyne was admitted burgess in 1529 (NSCM., I, p. 56). Thomas Brechin and John Brechin were merchants there, 1541 (SCM., II, p. 33). Margaret Breischane in Nether Auchinleiss, parish of Glenyllay, 1595 (*Brechin*). Brechane 1518, Breyhyn 1279.

BRECK. Hugh Brec witnessed Eschina de London's gift of the church of Molle to the Abbey of Kelso, 1185 (*Kelso*, 146). Gilbert Brek, witness in Dumfries, 1506 (*Edgar*, p. 230). Isabel Breck in Edinburgh, 1692 (*Edinb. Marr.*), and William Breck, feuar in Insch, Aberdeenshire, died in 1818.

BRECKENRIDGE. See under BRACKENRIDGE.

BRECKLAY. Most probably of local origin from Braichlie (in 1638, Brakley) in the parish of Glenmuick, Aberdeenshire. Walter Breklay was juror on an inquisition held in Aberdeen in 1457 (RAA., II, 108), and John Breklay was admitted burgess of Aberdeen in 1505 (NSCM., I, p. 43).

BRECNACH. See under BRETNACH.

BREDONE. Probably from Breedon in county Leicester, England. Robertus Bredone, perpetual vicar of Abbirellot, 1464 (RAA., II, p. 134).

BREERETOUNE. Most probably from Brereton in Yorkshire. Thomas Breeretoune (probably an Englishman) was factor for the earl of Dysart, 1702.

BREEZE. Most probably of recent introduction from England, where Breese and Breeze are from Welsh *Ab-Rees*, 'son of Rees (Rhys).'

BREGHOUN. Shortened from MACABHRIUIN, q.v. In 1618 a number of Clan Breghoun were living in and around Laggan. Ferquhar Bryon was tenant of Haynis, Tiree, 1541, and Gilpatrick Bryon was tenant of Corrare, Islay, in the same year (ER., XVII, p. 614, 615).

BREICHEN. See under BRECHIN.

BREIRLAY. John Breirlay in Edinburgh, 1661 (*Edinb. Marr.*), probably derived his surname from Briarley in Yorkshire.

BREKBELL. Sir John Brekbell or Brekebell, chaplain and notary public in Brechin, 1409 (REB., I, 27), is probably John Brekbell, notary public in Perth, 1420 (Patrick, *Councils*, p. 82). Brekbel 1436, Brekevell 1411.

BREKONRIDGE. See under BRACKENRIDGE.

BREMNER, BRIMNER, BRYMNER. The old form was Brabener, 'the Brabander,' i.e. a native of Brabant. In the Caithness pronunciation of the name the medial *b* is sometimes heard. Artificers and traders from the Low Countries of the continent settled in Aberdeenshire and elsewhere on the East Coast at an early date. "The braboner, or webster craft, or weaver trade, holds the eighth place amongst the nine trades" of Dundee (Warden, *Burgh laws of Dundee*, p. 503). The name was common in East Ross, Mar, and Strathdon in the sixteenth century. Walter Brabounare held a tenement in Irvine, Ayrshire, in 1418–26 (*Irvine*, I, 126, 130), and Gerard de Brabancia, medicus, held a tenement in Glasgow, 1486 (REG., p. 450). Agnus Brebner witnessed an Elgin document of 1489 (*Laing*, 235), Alexander Brabanar was tenant of the Twa Half Dawakkis (i.e. davochs), Ardmanoch, 1504 (ER., xii, p. 660), and Thomas Brabnair is mentioned in a precept of 1521 (*Cawdor*, p. 143). Andrew Brabnere was admitted burgess of Aberdeen, 1507 (NSCM., i, p. 44), Patrick Brebner is recorded in Strathdee, 1527, and John Brabonar was tenant of Dalmoloak in 1539 (ER., xvii, p. 671). William Brabner was a 'quhytfischer' in Futtie, 1601 (CRA., p. 217), Dod mcAllistr vic finlay Brembner is in record, 1649 (IDR., p. 367), and James Brimner was servitor to John, earl of Atholl, 1630 (RPC., 2. ser. iii, p. 559). Alexander Brymner, burgess of Stirling, 1775 *(Stirling)*. Brabanere 1565, Brabiner 1595, Brabnar 1550, Braboner 1653, Brabuner 1541, Braymer 1681, Brebener 1641, Breboner 1540, Brember 1685, Brimmer 1760, Brobner 1662; Brabanner, Brabener, Brabin, Braibner, Brebiner, Brebner, Bremner, Brender, Brymer 1681.

BRENOCK. Most probably from Brechnock in Wales, a name introduced into Ireland during the time of the Anglo-Norman invasion, and from there introduced into Galloway. Andrew Brenock and John Brenock in Barnbarroch in record, 1684 (RPC., 3. ser. x, p. 265).

BRENTOUN. Margaret Brentoun in Ellusrigle, parish of Welstoun, 1658 *(Lanark CR.)*. Brendon and Brenton are given by Guppy (p. 105, 461) as Cornish surnames of local origin there.

BRESSACK. A form of PRESSOCK, q.v. Several individuals whose names appear in the *Rental book of Cupar-Angus* as Brisauch, Brisaucht, Bresaucht, Briseacht, Brysaucht, Brischo (1508), Brescho, Bresok (1514), Brysauch, Breschock (1508), and Brasauch were tenants of the Abbey of Cupar-Angus in the fifteenth and sixteenth centuries. Breassauch was the form of the name used by a family or families named Lyon, who changed their name back again to Lyon in July 1731 (*Aberdeen Journal Notes and queries*, iv, p. 242). John Bressak was portioner of Inverarity, 1779 *(Brechin)*.

BRETNACH, i.e. the 'Briton,' modern G. *Breatunnach*. Gilcudbricht Brecnach (i.e. Bretnach, *t* misread as *c*) witnessed a grant by Ranulfus, son of Dunegal to the Hospital of S. Peter of York c. 1124–65 (*Edgar*, p. 217). The name is misspelled or miscopied Gilendonrut in Bain (ii, p. 421). Gillecrist Bretnach witnessed a charter by Duncan, son of Gilbert, son of Fergus of lands in Carric c. 1200 (*Melros*, p. 22). Duncan Bretnaghe of Fife rendered homage in 1296 (*Bain*, ii, p. 214). S. Patrick is called *in Britt*, 'the Briton,' in the *Book of Leinster* (164b15).

BREW. Patrick Brue in Dundee was charged with aiding the English, 1552 (*Beats*, p. 326), and Agnes Brew is recorded in Newcrage, parish of Glenylla, 1688 *(Brechin)*. Perhaps shortened from (MAC)BREW. Brew from Mac-Brew occurs in Isle of Man in 1616 (*Moore*, p. 47).

BREWHOUSE. Johannes del Breuhous, mercator de Scotia (*Rot. Scot.*, i, 892). Robert Brewhous, witness in Perthshire, 1547 (*Gaw*, 9). Archibald Brewhous was burgess freeman of Glasgow in 1578 (*Burgesses*), Robert Brewhouse appears in Kilgrastoune, parish of Dunbarnie, 1625 *(St. Andrews)*, Robert Brewhouse in Bladesheill, 1659 *(Dumfries)*, James Brewhouse in Nether Marytoune, 1681 *(Brechin)*, John Brewhouse in Sproustoune, 1685 *(Peebles CR.)*, and Isobel Brewhouse sometime at Abernethy, 1790 *(Dunkeld)*. The brewhouse, in Latin documents *brasina*, was a pertinent of an estate in land. There is Brewhous of Monikie in Forfar *Retours*, no. 85.

BREWIS. May be (1) from one of the many old spellings of BRUCE, q.v., or (2) a shortened form of BREWHOUSE, q.v.

BREWSTER. From the occupation of 'brewster' or 'brewer.' The feminine suffix *-ster*, as with Baxter, shows that originally it was a woman's occupation. Sir John Skene, in his *De verborum significatione*, defines 'Browsters' as 'wemen quha brewes aill to be sauld.' In mediæval Latin documents the word is rendered *braciator* (a word of Gaulish origin as noted by Pliny, *Hist. Nat.*, xviii, 11, whence French *brasseur*, brewer). Nicholaus, braciator regis (i.e. the king's brewer), was present at the perambulation of lands in 1219 (APS., i, p. 91). Johannes the 'braciator' was one of the 'native men' of the Abbey of Dunfermline in the thirteenth century (RD., 330), and Thomas le Breuester of the forest of Passeley in the county of Lanark rendered homage in 1296 (*Bain*, ii, p. 213). Johannes dictus Brouster held land in Aberdeen in 1382 (RMS., i, 682), Robert Brewester, a Scot, received letters of denisation in England in 1480 (*Bain*, iv, 1465), another Robert Broustar was burgess of Glasgow in 1487 (REG., 449), William Broster held land in Arbroath in 1513 (RAA., ii, 541), Thomas Brouster was curate to Sir John Swinton of that Ilk in 1515, and Duncanus Broustir appears in Murthlac, 1550 (*Illus.*, ii, p. 261). In some instances, particularly in the north, this name is a translation of MACGRUER, q.v. Gillecrist Brouster was one of the sufferers from the hership of Petty in 1502 (*Rose*, p. 176). Broistar 1541, Brostar 1460, Broustar 1528, Broustare 1556, Browistar 1550, Browster 1798, Browstare 1468.

BRIAN, BRIEN, BRYAN. A well-known Breton personal name of common occurrence in Breton records from the ninth century. It is a derivative from some full name compounded with *bri* 'dignity,' 'esteem' (*Loth*, p. 111). The name was introduced into Britain by Bretons who were among the Normans in the invasion of England. Linaldus filius Brian is mentioned in reign of William the Lion (*Kelso*, 13), and Bernard filius Brien granted a carucate in the vill of Hauden to the Abbey of Kelso early in the same reign (ibid., 214). He also appears as a charter witness in two charters to the Abbey (ibid., 226, 274). Berñ fil. Bryen also witnessed a grant to Arbroath Abbey a. 1204 (RAA., I, 11), and Bryen may be the person who gave name to Bryanton near Inverkeillor. Brian fitz Alan rendered homage, 1296 (*Bain*, II, p. 196). Hugh Briane, burgess of Irvine, 1446 (*Irvine*, I, p. 137). John Brian, witness in Kyle, 1549 (*Laing*, 551), and Wille Bryand, 'hyrd,' is mentioned in 1527 (*Prestwick*, p. 52). John Bryan, heir of Andrew Bryan of Natherpark, his father, in 20s. lands of old extent of Natherpark, 1631 (*Retours, Ayr*, 273). William Bryane in Barquhy, heir of William Bryane, his father, in the merklands of Barquhay, 1637 (ibid., 319).

BRICE. See under BRYCE.

BRICHAN. Most probably a variant of BRECHIN, q.v. The Rev. David Brichan, minister of Dyke, died in 1814. His son, James Brodie Brichan (died 1864), was the principal author of *Origines parochiales Scotiæ*, published by the Bannatyne Club, 1851–55.

BRICK. Patrick Brick was commissioner of supply for Glasgow, 1655 (APS., VI, pt. II, p. 840). Joseph Brick, wright in Tollohill, 1790 (*Aberdeen CR.*). A form of BRIGG, q.v.

BRIDAN. Bridanus Breach, Bridanus filius Fergusii, and Bridanus mc Dor, men of the bishop of Moray, had remissions and protections from David II for crimes committed by them, 1363 (REM., p. 164).

BRIDE. A middle Scots form of G. and Ir. *Brighid*. From it comes the diminutive BRIDIE, and see also BRYDE and MACBRIDE.

BRIDGE. Local, from residence near a bridge. John Bridge in Drum, 1658, and John Brig in Drum, 1691 (*Dumfries*). Andrew Bridge in Burns, 1771 (*Kirkcudbright*). Cf. BRIGGS.

BRIDGEFOORD. Local. A surname in Banchory-Devenick, Aberdeen-Kincardine shires (Henderson, *Banchory-Devenick*, p. 313–314). Isobel Brigfuird in Steanhyve (Stonehaven), 1637 (*St. Andrews*).

BRIDIE. See under BRYDIE.

BRIDIN. Brydinus, vicar of Tene (now Tain), was present at Kenedor in Moray at the settlement of a dispute between the bishops of Moray and Ross, 1227 (REM., p. 82). Bridin potanach and Bridi Camb' were two of the assessors of the lands of Dunduff, 1231 (RD., p. 111). Bridinus was son of Bridinus puddyng, a serf of the Abbey of Dunfermline in thirteenth century (ibid., p. 222). Bridin, son of Kolin, son of Anegus the shoemaker did homage to the prior and convent of St. Andrews at Dull, 1264 (RPSA., p. 349). Richard, son of Bridin was burgess of Dundee, 1321 (HP., II, p. 225), and Bridinus called Candelane was bailie of Roxburgh c. 1338 (*Dryburgh*, 313).

BRIDOC. G. *Brideoc*, diminutive of BRIDE, q.v. Bridoc was one of the assize on the boundaries of Stobbo, c. 1190 (REG., p. 89).

BRIDYSON. An Anglicizing of MACBRIDE, q.v. John Bridison was member of an inquest on the lands of Dunmaglass in 1414 (*Cawdor*, p. 5), and a later John Bridyson or Brydison had a tack of part of Kethyk in 1467 (*Cupar-Angus*, I, p. 132, 147).

BRIEN. See under BRIAN.

BRIGERAKIS. Thomas de Brigerakis was one of the burgesses of Stirling who attacked the cruives and fishings of the abbot and convent of Cambuskenneth, 1366 (*Cambus.*, 55). Perhaps = toll collector.

BRIGG. The Scots form of Bridge. Of local origin from residence near a bridge, in Latin documents rendered *ad pontem*. Elena de Bryg held land 'in vico de le Grene,' Aberdeen, in 1382 (RMS., I, 682). Robert Brig had remission for slaughter of Thomas Dunwedy of that Ilk, 1504 (*Trials*, I, p. 40°). Patrick Brig was wricht in Edinburgh, 1508 (EBR., 117), Robene Brig in the towne of Bowdene, 1567 (*Kelso*, p. 519), and Alexander Brig, constable of the parish of Kingsbarns, 1633 (RPC., 2. ser. V, p. 94). Four individuals named Brig were charged with deforcement in Langnewton, 1628 (RPC., 2. ser. II, p. 512), and Andrew Brig, rebel fugitive from justice, and John Brigg in record in Balhassie, 1684 (RPC., 3. ser. X, p. 239, 246).

BRIGGS. Of local origin from one or more of the small places of the name. Throughout the country Brigg is in common speech the pronunciation of Bridge. Duncanus Brigis appears in Murthlac, Banffshire, 1550 (*Illus.*, II, p. 261). Cath. Brigs was married in Edinburgh, 1611 (*Edinb. Marr.*).

BRIGHOLM. John Brigholme, Scots merchant, had a safe conduct to trade in England, 1439 (*Bain*, IV, 1136). Perhaps from Bridge Holm in the North Riding of Yorkshire, in 1301 Brigholme.

BRIGTON. Of local origin from Bridgeton, now included in the city of Glasgow. Richard Brigton of Paisley is mentioned in 1503 (RMP., p. 61), William Brighton in Edinburgh in 1610 (*Edinb. Marr.*), and Elizabeth Brigtoun in Eardhousses, parish of Carnwath, is recorded in 1650 (*Lanark C.R.*).

BRIMER. A surname in Fife, perhaps a variant of BREMNER, q.v.

BRIMNER. *See under* BREMNER.

BRIMS. A Caithness surname of local origin from Brims near Thurso. Janet Brymes in Thurso is mentioned in 1664 (*Caithness*). John Breyme held a tenement in the town of Thurso, 1655 (*Caithness*).

BRINACH. Donald Brinach in Inverchorain, a Seaforth tenant, 1726 (HP., II, p. 336).

BRINTON. Local. Hugh Bryntoun rendered to Exchequer the accounts of the bailies of the burgh of Lanark, 1558 (ER., XIX, p. 43), and David Brentoun, bailie of the same burgh, 1568 (*Laing*, 836), was commissioner to Parliament for Lanark, 1585 (APS., III, p. 374). David Brentoun in Edinburgh, 1610 (*Edinb. Marr.*). Brintoun 1559.

BRISBANE. This name appears to be of Anglo-French origin, from *brise bane*, 'break bone,' i.e. a bone-breaker. Probably the first of the name in Scotland is William Brisbone, whose name occurs in the list of archers sent from Berwick to Roxburgh in 1298 (*Bain*, II, 1019), and who was most probably an Englishman. Thomas Brisbane or de Birsbane had a charter of Litill Rothy in Aberdeenshire from Robert I (RMS., I, App. II, 34). Alanus dictus Brisbane filius quondam Willelmi Brisbane shortly after 1334 obtained a grant from Donald, earl of Lennox of the land called Mucherach in the earldom of Levenax and of the land called Holmedalmartyne (*Levenax*, p. 61). In 1358 there is entry of a payment to Alexander Brysban (ER., I, p. 549), and in 1376 Herthornhill was leased to Thomas Brisbane (RHM., I, p. lxvii). Alan Brysban witnessed a charter of the lands of Ballebrochyr and Lechard, c. 1390–1400 (*Lennox*, II, p. 52). Another Thomas Brysbane, dominus de Latheris, in 1415 witnessed the charter of the barony of Cowie to William de Haya de Erole (SCM., II, p. 321), and in 1417 was present at a perambulation of the lands of Tarwas and Wldny (Udny) (RAA., II, 53). James Birsbane was proprietor of the lands of Reise and Akirgyll in Caithness, 1498 (*Laing*, 235). The surname is found in Aberdeen in 1401 (CRA., p. 382), in Perth, 1409 (REB., I, 26; II, 16), and in Edinburgh from 1610 onwards as Brisbain, Brisbaine, and Brisben (*Edinb. Marr.*). The Brisbanes of Bishoptoun acquired the lands of Killincraig and Goga in the parish of Largs, c. 1400. By a Crown charter, dated 1695, the estate was erected into the barony of Brisbane (*Ayr Fam.*, I, p. 136), which thenceforth became the usual territorial designation of the family, 'Brisbane of Brisbane.' Alexander Bisbane, burgess of Dundee, 1674 (*Brechin*) was doubtless a Brisbane, and so likewise Agnes Bursbean in Colhowis of Dennie, 1622 (*Stirling*). Barsbayne 1561, Birsbain 1696, Birsbaine 1641, Birsben 1684, Brisban 1618, Brisbine 1587.

BRISCOT. James Briscat, tailor, burgess of Glasgow, 1576, and Thomas Briscatt, tailor, burgess in 1594 (*Burgesses*). John Birscat, merchant and burgess freeman of Glasgow, 1614 (ibid.). Patrick Briscot held land in Glasgow, 1588 (*Protocols*, x). Birscatt 1629.

BRITTAN. From Norm. Fr. *le Brit* or *le Bret*, and *le Breton*, a native of Brittany. Hugo Bret witnessed a grant by Earl David for the use of the church of Glasgow a. 1123 (REG., 2), and as Hugo Brit witnessed King David's charter of the lands and liberties of Coldinghamschyr in 1126 (*Raine*, 16). As Hugo Britone or Brittone he also witnessed several other charters between that date and 1153 (*Lawrie*, p. 293). Gaufridus Britt' witnessed a charter by Alan filius Walteri between 1177–99 (RMP., p. 12), and c. 1200 Radulf Bret or Britone witnessed charters by William the Lion and William de Veteri Ponte (LSC., 33, 41, 44). Thomas le Bret witnessed a grant by Hugh Bygris in 1228 (*Kelso*, 186), and Eliz Britun of Berwickshire rendered homage in 1296 (*Bain*, II, p. 207). William Bretone of Linescu, who also rendered homage in 1296, may be William le Bretoun on whose behalf a writ was issued by the sheriff of Edinburgh in the same year (ibid., p. 203, 218). William Brittan from Turriff served in the first Great War (*Turriff*). As Bretagne and Normandy were adjacent provinces it was natural that many Bretons came to England with the Normans. Old Ir. *britt* meant a Bricon, and one of the brethren of Iona in the time of Columba was named Brito, probably indicating that he was a Briton, not a Gael.

BROACH. *See under* BROATCH.

BROADFOOT. An Anglicized spelling of
BRADFUTE, q.v. Agnes Broadfoot in Glengarne,
Dumfriesshire, 1638 (Dumfries). Broadfoott
1687.

BROADWOOD. The English spelling of
BRAIDWOOD, q.v.

BROATCH. A Dumfriesshire surname, of local
origin from Broats in the parish of Kirkpatrick-
Fleming. James Broatch is recorded in Hietae
in 1628 and six others are in the same record
at later dates (Dumfries). Mary Broach is
recorded in Torphichen in 1712 (Torphichen).
BROACH and BROTCH are variants.

BROCAS. Families of the name De Brocas are
found in Guinne and Gascony in the twelfth
and thirteenth centuries. Two places, one probably the oldest in the arrondissement of Mont
de Marsan and canton de Labrit (D'Albret)
and the other in the arrondissement of St.
Sever. John Brocaz had payment in 1338 for
"the safe custody of the marches of Scotland"
(Burrows, Family of Brocas of Beaurepaire,
London, 1886, p. 62). Thomas Brokas had a
remission for his share in burning the town of
Dunbertane in 1489 (Lennox, II, p. 133; APS.,
XII, p. 34). Patrick Brocas, chaplain, is in
record in 1493 (Cambus., 186), James Brokkas
was a witness in Linlithgow in 1532 (Johnsoun), and John Brocass was witness in Glasgow in 1536 (LCD., p. 129), William Brokkus,
smith, was true to his obedience to the queen
in 1562 (RPC., I, p. 216). John Brokkas was
a citizen of Brechin in 1588, Patrick Brokass
was officer there in 1602, and another Patrick
Brokus or Brockhouse appears as doctor of the
Grammar School of Brechin in 1649 and 1660
(REB., II, 227, 232, 247, 249). James Brockhouse was town officer of Brechin in 1660
(ibid., II, 249), George Brockhous was wool-
finer in Edinburgh in 1619 (Edinb. Marr.), and
William Brockhouse in Tamcure, parish of
Falkirk, is recorded in 1633 (Stirling).

BROCEIN. Brocein was one of the witnesses
to the grant by Colbain, mormaer of Buchan
and Eva his wife, to the monastery of Deer,
c. 1131 (Bk. Deer, VI, 25). In the letter of
protection by King David I to the same clerics
(c. 1150) he appears again among the witnesses as Brocin. The name is a diminutive
of brocc, a badger, a common element in Gaelic
personal names in inscriptions, both ogham
and Roman, in southwestern Ireland and in
western Britain.

BROCH. A Caithness surname of local origin
from residence near by the site of an ancient
broch.

BROCK. Local. There is a Brock in East
Renfrewshire. Henry Brok had provision of a
canonry and prebend of Dunkeld in 1328 (Pap.
Lett., II, p. 285). David Broik was tenant of
the croft of Twa Half Dawis [davochs] alias
Petslawis Croft, Ardmanoch, 1504, and Alexander Brok was tenant of the Castletoun, Ardmanoch, in the same year (ER., XII, p. 660–
661). Thomas Broik and Alexander Broik appear as tenants of Casteltoune, Ardmanoch,
1539 (ibid., XVII, p. 680). William Brok was
witness in Glasgow, 1554 (Protocols, I),
Robert Brok appears in Tillearblit, parish of
Naver, 1611 (Brechin), Christian Brock in Dun-
fubert, parish of Edzell, 1625 (St. Andrews),
and Walter Brock, burgess of Glasgow, 1619
(Burgesses). Joannes Brock in parish of Kinkell,
1663 (Retours, Aberdeen, 370). The name
was common in Edinburgh after 1609 (Edinb.
Marr.).

BROCKET. Most probably of local origin from
Brocket near Monkton, Ayrshire. Jhon Brokat,
one of inquest at Carnwath, 1524 (CBBC.,
p. 14). George Broket held land in Irvine,
1540–42 (Irvine, I, p. 169, 200). Isobel Brocket
in Baittanes, parish of Lesmahagow, 1626,
and five more of the name (Lanark CR.).

BROCKIE. Gilbert Broky was 'chantour' of
Brechin, 1411 (REB., I, 32), Robert Broky,
witness in Edinburgh, 1429 (REG., 336),
Archibald Broky in Downe, 1581 (RHM., I,
124), Robert Brockie in Glengairn in sixteenth century, and the surname is found in
Stitchill in 1684 as Brocky (Stitchill, p. 96).
John Broikie, heir of William Broikie, lawful
son of quondam William Broikie in Cartair,
1603 (Inquis. Tut., 29), and three of the name
occur in Edinburgh after 1666 (Edinb. Marr.).
Marianus Brockie, a native of Edinburgh, was
prior of the monastery at Ratisbon. His MS.
collections for a Scottish Monasticon are now
in the library of Blair's R. C. College near
Aberdeen. John M. Brockie of King Edward
served in the first Great War (Turriff). Lower
says that the family of Brockie is of Moray
descent, and that the name is found in REM.,
in 1364, but I do not find it there. REM.,
p. 164 (A. D. 1364) has mention of Bridanus
Breach. Hardly from Bruchtie, Brugtie, or
Brochtie in Forfar Retours (38, 71, 249, 380).
These would give Broughty?

BROCKLEY. Of local origin, perhaps from
Brockley in Kinross-shire. John Brockley in Falkirk, 1680 (Stirling).

BRODIE. Of territorial origin from the barony
of the name in Moray. Michael de Brothie had
a charter from Robert I in 1311 (not in RMS.)

of the lands of Brodie as his father's heir. In 1337 there is mention of the "terra de Brothy domini" (ER., I, p. 441). Thomas de Brothy was juror at a court held at "Le Ballocis Hill" near Inverness 1376–7 (*Family of Innes*, p. 63). John de Brothy appears in 1380 as witness in a matter between the bishop of Moray and Alexander Stewart, lord of Badenoch (REM., p. 187). Thomas Brothi and his son, John Brothy appear in 1386 in a negotiation regarding the vicarage of Dyke of which his younger son, Alexander de Brothi, was vicar (ibid., p. 323), and Johannes Brody *de eodem* or thanus de Brody was witness in an agreement anent the marches of Croy and Kildrummy in 1492 (ibid., p. 236, 238, 241). Adam Brothy, Archibald Brothy, and Alexander Brothy witnessed sealing of sasine of Skelbo in 1487 (OPS., II, p. 646), and Thomas Brodie of that Ilk was juror on an inquest made at Inverness, 1546 (ibid., p. 666). John Brothy, witness at Knokschynnoch, 1512, may be John Brothy, sheriff of Ayr, 1514 (*Ros*, 5, 83). The surname is found in Edinburgh from 1599 onwards (*Edinb. Marr.*), and is also used as an Englishing of the Irish and West Highland name O'BROLOCHAN, q.v. Although the family of Brodie have been "long located in the province of Moray, less is known of their history than of almost any other of similar antiquity. This has been accounted for by the fact that all their papers and charters were destroyed when Brodie House was burnt by Lord Lewis Gordon in 1645. It does not, however, explain entirely the almost entire want of information about them, and it may therefore be presumed that their estate was not large, nor were they much known as having taken a share in public affairs until the middle or close of the sixteenth century, when they somewhat suddenly take a prominent place in the county, and so continue down to our time" (Young, *Parish of Spynie*, Elgin, 1871, p. 328). Broadie 1690, Broddy 1622, Brodve 1546; also Brady, Bridy, Broddie, Brothu, Brydie.

BROG. John Brog, burgess of Abirbrothoc, witnessed an indenture relating to the Abbey of Arbroath, 1394 (RAA., II, 43), and William Broge witnessed a charter by John Ramsav, burgess of Montrose, 1430 (REB., II, 33). Robert Brog was subprior of St. Andrews, 1440 (RD., p. 300), and William Broge was member of the burgh council of Stirling, 1603 (SBR., p. 283). Jonet Brog was heir of dominus Willelmus Brog in 1636 (*Inquis.*, 2216), and the name is also recorded in Edinburgh in 1659 (*Edinb. Marr.*). Stodart (II, p. 106) gives seventeenth century spellings Brog,

Broge, and Broig, and mentions Braug of Mooresk (? Aquhorsk). William Broge was servant to Alexander Stewart of Auchlunchart, 1747 (*Moray*).

BROGAN. An early surname in the parish of Slains, Aberdeenshire, evidently assumed from the lands of Broggan or Brogan, which were held under the Leasks (*Jervise*, II, p. 248). John Brogane was admitted burgess of Aberdeen in 1486 (NSCM., I, p. 32), and Agnes Brogan resigned her two parts of the lands in 1495 (*Buchan Club Trans.*, x, p. 223). Thomas Brogane in Fuirdmouth of Arnage is in record in 1643 (RSCA., III, p. 16).

BROKISMOUTH. Johannes de Brokismouth, juror in Angus, 1322 (RMS., I, App. I, 29) probably derived his surname from Broxmouth near Dunbar (in 1094 Broccesmuthe).

BROKMYR. Local. Alexander Brokmyr was declared innocent of part in detention of King James III in Edinburgh Castle, 1482 (*The Lennox*, II, p. 123).

BROLOCHAN. Duncan Brolochan, merchant in Campbeltown, is in record in 1778 (*Argyll*), and Peter Brelachan had part of the Moil of Kintyre from 1780 to 1789 (*Adam*, p. 469). From O'BROLCHAIN, q.v.

BROOK, BROOKE. The first form recorded in Aberdeen. Thomas Bruke was admitted burgess there in 1483 (NSCM., I, p. 30). Local from residence by a brook.

BROOKS. Practically the same meaning as BROOK, q.v. For -s see under 'Some Letter Changes.' Probably of recent introduction from England.

BROOM. Local. There are places so named near Hawick, and in the shires of Ayr, Dumfries, Clackmannan, and Banff. John Brume was one of the burgesses of Stirling who attacked the cruives and fishings of the abbot and convent of Cambuskenneth, 1366 (*Cambus.*, 55). Marion Brwme resigned a tenement in Glasgow in favor of her kinsman Robert Brwne, 1549 (*Protocols*, I). Five of the name are in the Edinburgh Marriage Register from 1627 onward. William Broom, farmer in Muiravenside, 1771 (*Stirling*). In Galloway the name appears in 1684 as McKbroome.

BROOMFIELD. Local. A common place name in CD. Three persons of the name are recorded in Edinburgh (*Edinb. Marr.*). James Broomfield, tenant in Hiltoun-hill, 1749 (*Lauder*). Bromfield 1655.

BROOMHEAD. Local. There is a Broomhead near Dollar, Clackmannanshire.

BROOMHILL. A common place name in Scotland. Patrick Bromehill, a monk of Glenluce Abbey, 1565 (*Dumfriesshire & Galloway Nat. Hist. & Ant. Soc., Trans.*, 3. ser. xxi, p. 303).

BROOMPARK. Catherin Broompark who is recorded in Woodsyd, Torphichen, in 1676 (*Torphichen*), derived her surname from the small place named Broompark in the parish of Torphichen, West Lothian.

BROOMSIDE. Local, probably from Brumesyid (1648, *Retours, Forfar*, 306). A man was charged with drawing blood from David Brymsyd, 1520, and Johnne Brymsyd and Thomas Brymsyd are mentioned in same record (SCBF., p. 195). John Brumsvd in Dysart, Fife, 1630 (PBK., p. 19), and Robert Broomside was made burgess of Dumbarton as son of a burgess, 1638 (RDB.).

BROSTER. An old spelling of BREWSTER, q.v., which has become a separate surname. D. K. Broster is author of several novels on Scottish themes.

BROTCH. *See under* BROATCH.

BROTCHIE. A surname found in Caithness and Orkney. William Brotchie in Thurso was fined in 1728 for forestalling (*Donaldson*, p. 196).

BROTHERSTONE, BROTHERSTONES. From the lands of Brothirstanys (now Brotherstone) in East Lothian, granted by Malcolm IV to the Hospital of Soutra (*Soltre*, p. 3). Those of the name residing around Gordon, Earlston, and Smailholm, may derive their surname from Brotherstones near St. Boswells. Between 1153 and 1177 Hugh de Brothirstane witnessed a grant by David Olifard to the Hospital of Soltra (*Soltre*, p. 4), and a later Huwe de Britherstanes of the county of Berewyke rendered homage in 1296 (*Bain*, II, p. 206). Thomas Brothirstanis witnessed an instrument of sasine in 1493 (*Laing*, 217), John Brodyrstanis was tenant in the barony of Stobo in 1511 and James Brodirstane was also tenant there in 1537 (*Rental*). Janet Brotherstones appears in Lesuden in 1663 (RRM., II, p. 53), James Brotherstones was minister of Lesmahagow in 1672 (*Fasti*, II, p. 328), and Peter Brotherston of Penicuik was minister of Dysart 1816–1828 (ibid., II, p. 536, 573). The surname is also found in the Edinburgh Marriage Register as early as 1612. The final *s* is dropped in some instances as in Gladstone. *Brother* is an Old West Scandinavian personal name, *Bróðir*, Old Swedish *Brodher*, Old Danish *Brothær*, and OE. *Brothor*. Brodarstaines 1652, Brodirstanis 1561, Brodyrstane 1537.

BROTHERSYDE. Local. William Brothersyde was beheaded in 1532 for the slaughter of Thomas Smythe (*Trials*, I, p. *160).

BROUGH. (1) An old surname in Orkney, derived from either Overbrough or Netherbrough in Harray. Thomas Burgh, witness in Harray, in 1530 may be the Thomas Burcht, witness at the Kirk of Harray in 1557 (REO., p. 108, 211). William Bruche was juror in Harray in 1601 (ibid., p. 174). (2) An old surname in Perthshire, may be from Brough in Yorkshire. Robert Burch (with metathesis of *r*), a frater de Cupro, 1500 (REB., I, 220). John Brugh is recorded in South Kinkell in 1598 (*Dunblane*), Gilbert Brugh in Lethendie in 1683 (DPD., I, p. 487), and Malcolm Brough was a tenant in Glenfender, Athol, in 1705. The surname also occurs as Bruch in the Dunblane Commissariot Record, and is also in the Edinburgh Marriage Register after 1665. Brucht 1506, Brught 1575.

BROUGHTON. Henry Broughton was collector of excise, Stirling, 1763 (*Stirling*). Perhaps from one of the many places of the name in England.

BROUNFIELD, BROWNFIELD. Local. Gilbert Brunfeld was witness to a claim of a third part of Cranshaws, 1453 (*Swinton*, p. xxxix). John Brounfeild and Thomas Brounfeld of the Abbey of Melrose were witnesses in 1535 (RRM., I, p. xv), and Robert Brounfeild was servitor to Mr. John Home in 1610 (ibid., III, p. 378). Stephen Brounfeild made payment from rents of his lands of Grenelawdene in 1563 (ER., XIX, p. 231), and John Brounfeild was retoured heir in lands in Chirnside, 1606 (*Retours, Berwick*, 61). The seal of Andrew Brownfield of Pittilseuch bears the legend *S'Andree Brvnfild* (*Macdonald*, 262). Alexander Brounfeild frater germanus quondam Jacobi Brounfeild de Nether Mains, 1609 (*Inquis. Tut.*, 143). Adam Brounfeild or Brounfield was witness in Kirkwall, 1634 (OSR., I, p. 280). See under HAITLIE for notice of feud with that family.

BROW. Local. John Brow, bailie of Aberdeen, 1362 (REA., I, p. 104). Edward Brow is recorded there, 1546 (CRA., p. 238), and

John Brow in Chapeltown, parish of Bendochy, 1653 (*Dunblane*). Thomson Brow died in Leith 1941.

BROWN. A very common name in Scotland, of more than one origin. (1) Brūn is a common personal name in OE. charters, e. g. Brun, c. 970, Brun bydel ('beadle'), c. 1000 (Kemble, *Codex Diplomaticus*, 981, 1353), etc. The name is from an old adjective meaning 'brown, dark red,' OE. and OHG. brūn, ON. brūnn. The adjective was also borrowed from OHG. into old French and is the source of the French surname Le Brun. A family of this name were the possessors of several estates in Cumberland shortly after the Norman Conquest. Gamel, son of Brun came into possession of Bothel (now Bootle) in the time of Henry I (1100–1135). Gilchrist, son of Bruun witnessed a charter by R. son of Dunegal to the Hospital of S. Peter of York c. 1136 (cited in *Bain*, II, p. 421). Patric Brun witnessed resignation of land of Weremundebi (Warmanbie in Annandale) and Anant between 1194–1214 (*Annandale*, I, p. 3; *Bain*, I, 606). Ricardus Brun witnessed a charter by Ebrardus de Penkathleht (Pencaitland near Edinburgh) to the church of S. Cuthbert of Durham in the reign of William the Lion (*Raine*, 163). Several individuals of this name are recorded in the thirteenth century, but what connection, if any, existed between them is not known. Robert Brune witnessed a gift of land to the Hospital of Soltre c. 1250–1266 (*Soltre*, p. 32). Richard Broun, witness in Irvine, 1260 (*Irvine*, I, p. 5), and another Richard Brun was an assizer in Elgin, of which place he was an inhabitant in 1261. William Brun, who witnessed a charter of Donald, earl of Mar, of the lands of Dorlaw or Dronlaw c. 1279–1294 (SCM., II, p. 313) is probably William Brun, witness in Dundee, 1281 (HP., II, p. 223). Several of this name in the shires of Berwick, Edinburgh, Lanark, and Linlithgow rendered homage, 1296 (*Bain*, II). Joannes Broun who had a grant of the thanage of Formerteine (Fermartyn) from Robert I (RMS., I, App. II, 423) is probably the person who was sheriff of Aberdeen, 1331–1332 (ER., I, p. 24). William "dictus Brune del Borumore" (the Boroughmuir of Edinburgh) granted to John de Raynton a charter of the lands of Kirclambirston c. 1332 (BNCH., XVI, p. 331), and Ricardus Broñ de Otterstoñ attested the marches of Kyrknes and Louchor, 1395 (RPSA., p. 5). Patrick Broun was burgess of Edinburgh, 1405, and John Brown, clerk and notary public there, 1426 (*Egidii*, p. 41, 47). Broun of Hartrie near Biggar is said to have been settled there from about the end of the fourteenth century, and Broun of Colstoun

claim descent from and bear the arms of the ancient royal house of France — three fleur-de-lys. Several individuals of this name from Scotland entered the French military service about the middle of the fifteenth century, and their names are recorded in the muster-rolls as Brom, Bron, Brun, and le Brun (Forbes-Leith, *Scots men at arms in France*). Members of a younger branch of Broun of Colstoun settled in Elsinore, Denmark, and became prominent merchants there. Many of the name Brown in Islay, says the late Hector Maclean, "came to the island from the low country (i. e. Lowlands) within the past century, and have no claim to be considered descendants of the Britheamh Ileach (the Islay Judge)" (*Book of Islay*, p. 19n); and the Browns of Tiree at the present day, says the late Rev. J. Gregorson Campbell, are called *Brunaich*, evidently a word not of native origin, and likely an adaptation of English *Brown* (*Waifs and strays of Celtic tradition*, v. 5, p. 12). (2) From G. *Mac a'bhriuthainn*, from *britheamhain*, the former G. genitive of *britheamh*, 'brehon, breive, judge.' Pat: Mʹ aBriuin is one of the witnesses in the unique Gaelic charter of 1408 (*Bk. Islay*, p. 18). Donald Broune was rector of Lochow, 1539 (*Poltalloch Writs*, p. 184). Robert Abroun is recorded in Aberruthven, 1616 (*Dunblane*), and Niall M'Abrioune was servitor to the laird of Lochnell, 1658. The name of Diorbhorgail Nic a' Bhriuthainn, the royalist poetess and satirist of the Campbells of the beginning of the eighteenth century is Englished Dorothy Brown. Among the many islands on the west coast is one called Elan a Bhriu, 'the judge's isle.' (3) The name is also used as an English rendering of G. M'Ille dhuinn, and possibly of earlier M'Mhaoil dhuinn (see MACILDUIN). Braun 1676, Bron 1446, Brouin 1546, Broun 1320, Broune 1502, Browne 1509, Browyn 1525, Brune 1333, Brwne 1505.

BROWNBEARD. A byname. "Mihhyn brunberd aput corrukes" was one of the witnesses to the right marches of Stobbo, c. 1190 (REG., p. 89), and a payment was made to John, son of William Brunbert, a Galloway hostage, in 1300 (*Bain*, II, 1179; *Hist. Docs.*, II, p. 426). Cf. BLACKBEARD, REDBEARD, and SMIBERT.

BROWNCLERK. John Brownclerk was burgess of Edinburgh in 1423 (LSC., p. 228), and the seal of William Brownclerk, designated as William Clerk, one of the bailies of Edinburgh in 1515, bears Sʹ *Willelmi Bronclerk* (*Macdonald*, 261).

BROWNFIELD. *See under* BROUNFIELD.

BROWNHILL. Local. A common place name in CD. A payment was made to Ade de Brunhill in 1359 (ER., I, p. 608), probably the Ade de Bronhill, burgess of Edinburgh, recorded in 1368 (*Egidii*, p. 1). Adam Brownhill was member of Scots parliament for Edinburgh, 1367 (*Hanna*, II, p. 485). Ade de Brounhill or Bronhil held lands near Edinburgh in 1425–30 (*Soltre*, p. 294; RMS., II, 173). The surname was common in Edinburgh and neighborhood in the late fourteenth and fifteenth centuries as Brounhill, Brounhil, Bronhil, Bronhill, and Bronhyll (*Egidii*). William Brounhill witnessed a notarial transumpt in Angus, 1442 (*Panmure*, II, 233), and Andrew Brounhill was a notary public in Glasgow, 1512 (REG., 490). Magister Andrea Brounhill was a charter witness at Parbrovth, 1529 (RAA., II, p. 501). William Brounhill had a precept of remission in 1536 (RSS., II, 2033), Patrick Brownhill, friar of Glenluce, 1560 (Rusk, *Parish and abbey of Glenluce*, p. 135), and James Brounhill in Stenton took the oath in 1685 (RPC., 3. ser. x, p. 551).

BROWNING. From the OE. personal name *Brüning*, 'son of *Brün*.' John Brwnyng was one of the "burgenses rure manentes" of Aberdeen, 1317 (SCM., v, p. 11), and Sir John Browning was sheriff there in 1328 (ER., I, p. clxxxi, 107). Willelmus Bronnyng in the parish of Fyvy was excommunicated in 1382 (REA., I, p. 165). James Brounin, burgess of Dundee, 1647 (*Brechin*), James Brouning in Spittal, parish of Stanehouse, 1667, and three more are recorded in Lanark Commissariot Record. John Buiening or Brunning in Galloway was hanged for being a Covenanter, 1682 (*Hanna*, II, p. 255, 269). Old spellings are Brening, Brinyng, Brinenge, Brounyng, Bruning, Bruninge, and Brwninge.

BROWNLEA, BROWNLEE, BROWNLIE, BROWNLEES, BRUNLEES. Of local origin, perhaps from Brownlee in Lanarkshire. There is also a Brownlee near Dundonald, Ayrshire. "Wedow" Brounlees was tenant on lands under Newbotle Abbey in 1563 (*Neubotle*, p. 327), Gavin Brwnelie was heir to James Brwnelie in Kinpuntmyln, 1608 (*Retours, Linlithgow*, 58), and Issobell Brounleis was tenant on lands of Kelso Abbey in 1567 (*Kelso*, p. 527). Janet Brownlee or Brownlees is recorded in Ersiltoune, 1653 (*Lauder*), John Brounllves in Chappell, 1659, and James Brounleyis there in 1661 (RRM., I, p. 224, 334). Nathaniel Brounlie in Mauldslie, 1685 (RPC., 3. ser. x, p. 123), and John Brounlie in Toun of Belstaine, parish of Carluke, 1624, and five more are recorded in Lanark Commissariot Record. Sir James Brunlees (1816–1892) was a distinguished engineer. Brownleis 1567, Brunlie 1700; Brounley, Brownley.

BROWNRIGG. Of local origin from some small place of the name. The lands of Alanshaw had as one boundary Burnerig (now Brounrig) in the time of Alan the Steward (*Melros*, p. 69). Margaret Brounrig at Balmaclellan, 1684 (RPC., 3. ser. x, p. 616).

BROWNSIDE. From Brownside in the parish of Neilston, Renfrewshire. The surname was common in Glasgow in the sixteenth century. William Browynsyde held land in Glasgow in 1505 (LCD., p. 259), and George Brounnsyde or Brounnesyde, servitor to William Hegait, Glasgow, 1548–49 (*Protocols*, I), is in record again in 1570 as George Brovnside, apostolic notary (*Pollok*, I, p. 308). John Brounsyde of the monastery of Melrose was a witness in 1574 (RRM., III, p. 251), Hew Brownsyd, bonnetmaker, was admitted burgess of Glasgow as husband of a burgess's daughter in 1601, and Patrick Brownsyd was admitted burgess in 1617 (*Burgesses*). Brounesyde 1549, Brownesvde 1551, Brownesyde 1550, Brownsyde 1505.

BROWNSWALD. Alexander de Brownyswalde, bailie of Glasgow, 1430, and Robert Brownswalde, charter witness there, 1476 (LCD., p. 164, 190, 246).

BRUCE. This surname, so celebrated in the history of Scotland, is of territorial origin, from the Château d'Adam at Brix, between Cherbourg and Valognes, Normandy. The ruins of the extensive fortress built in the eleventh century by Adam de Brus and called after him Château d'Adam yet remain. The first Robert de Brus on record in Britain was probably the leader of the Brus contingent in the army of William the Conqueror in 1066. He appears to have died about the year 1094. A son of this Robert de Brus, known as Robert le Meschin or the cadet, was the first of his family connected with Scotland. A companion of David I at the English court, he received from the "Soir Sanct for the Crown" the grant of Annandale, here printed. This fief he seems to have renounced in favor of his second son (also Robert), just before the battle of the Standard (1138), on the failure of his attempted mediation between King David and the English Barons. He died in 1141.

Owing to the fact that the Bohuns, earls of Essex, held Bruce's Annandale estates for the best part of a century, manv of the early Annandale deeds came to the hands of their successors, the dukes of Lancaster, and are now in the Public Records (Bain, *The Edwards in Scotland, A. D. 1296–1377*, p. 48).

"David by the grace of God King of Scots, to all his barons and men and friends, French and English: greeting. Know that I have given and granted to Robert Brus, Estrahanent [= valley of the Annan], and all the land from the march of Dunegal of Stranit [= valley of the Nith] even to the march of Randulf Meschin. And I will and grant that he hold and have that land and its cattle, well and honourably, with all its customs; to wit, with whatever customs Randulf Meschin had in Carduill and in his land of Cumberland, on whatever day he had them best and most freely. Witnesses: Eustace son of John, and Hugh of Morville, and Alan of Perci, and William of Sumerville, and Berengar Engain, and Randulf of Sules, and William of Morville, and Herui son of Warin, and Oedmund the Chamberlain. At Scone."

This charter conveying the whole of Annandale fills eleven lines of a strip of parchment measuring 6½ by 3¾ inches. It was probably granted about the year 1124–1130. A facsimile of it is given in the *Facsimiles of the national manuscripts of Scotland*, I, no. 19. "The clergy were the only lawyers and the only conveyancers. They wrote concisely, and to the point. Bits of parchment one inch in breadth, and a very few inches in length, were enough to convey great Earldoms and Baronies in the days of David I" (Duke of Argyll, *Scotland as it was and as it is*, 2. ed., p. 41). Even smaller (5¾ by 2¼ inches) is the strip of parchment erecting the Valley of Annandale into a free forest marching with Nithsdale on the one hand the Valley of Clyde on the other, and stretching eastward till it met the Royal Forest of Selkirk. As one of the witnesses to this charter is Walter, son of Alan, the first of the Stewards of Scotland, it was probably granted between 1147 and 1153. The grant of Annandale is as follows:

"David, King of the Scots, to all good men of his whole land, French and English and Galwegians: greeting. Know that I have given and granted to Robert of Brus, in fee and heritage, to him and his heir, the Valley of Anant, in forest, on both sides of the Water of Anant, as the marches are from the forest of Seleschirche [Selkirk] as far as his land extends towards Stradnitt and towards Clud [Clyde], freely and quietly as any other forest of his is best and most freely held. Wherefore I forbid that any one hunt in the aforesaid forest unless by his authority, on pain of forfeiture of ten pounds, or that any one go through the aforesaid forest unless by a straight road marked out. Witnesses: Walter the Chancellor and Hugh of Moreuill and Walter son of Alan and Odendell of Vmfrauill and Walter

of Lindesei and Richard of Moreuill. At Stap[elgo]rtune."

The Swedish family of Bruce, ennobled in 1668, were probably descended from Robert Bruce of Lynmlyne. The name is still pronounced in common speech with a close approach to its original pronunciation —Bris, *i* short as in *is*. Brewc 1591, Brewes 1654, Brewhous 1634, Brewhouse 1530, Briews 1221, Briwes 1239, Broce 1526, Brois 1481, Broise 1456, Broiss 1490, Brose 1504, Brouss 1506, Brouyss 1558, Broyce 1390, Broys 1461, Brovse 1450, Broyss 1506, Brues 1255, Bruice 1673, Bruis 1511, Brus c. 1143, Bruse 1446, Bruss 1488, Bruwes and Bruys 1240, Brwss 1490, Brywes 1254, Bruze 1251; Bruc, Brwce.

BRUDE. ? a title rather than a name. Brude, son of Derile d. 706 (CPS., p. cxxi). Brude mac Bile, re Fortrenn (ibid.). Bred or Brude, son of Dergard 'ultimus rex Pictorum' (RPSA., p. 113). See also *Lawrie*, p. 228 and refs. there. Brude, son of Feredach (*Lawrie*, p. 228). Brude, son of Meilcon (*Lawrie*, p. 221, etc.). See also Scott, *Pictish nation*, index. The name appears in Bede in a more British form, Bridei (Stokes equates it with Eng. *proud*).

BRUNHUS. Robert de Brunhus, tenant of the bishop of St. Andrews in Edinburghshire rendered homage, 1296 (Bain, II, p. 205). The lands of Bromehous near Corstorphine are mentioned in 1626 (*Retours, Edinburgh*, 572).

BRUNLEES. A form of BROWNLEE, q.v.

BRUNSCHAW. David Brunschaw, chaplain, Brechin, 1524 (REB., II, p. 179). Andrew Bruntschaw in Aberdeenshire, 1595 (RSCA., I, p. 329). William Bruncha is in Clunie, 1611, and John Bruncha (Brunchew) was burgess of Fraserburgh, 1620 (ibid., II, p. 167, 242). Marjorie Bruntsha in Skallowaybanks, 1630 (*Shetland*).

BRUNTCHELLS. See under BRANCHELL.

BRUNTFIELD. Local. From Bruntsfield, a former suburb of Edinburgh, now incorporated within the city. Previous to the place taking its present name it was known as Brounisfield (1479, Bronisfeld) from an early owner, Richard Broune of Boroumore, who held the lands in the fourteenth century. Adam Bruntfield fought a duel with James Carmichael in 1597 over the murder of his brother, Stephen Bruntfield, merchant in Edinburgh (Birrel, *Diary*, ed. Dalyell, p. 42). Andrew Bruntfield was heir of James Brounfield of Pittilisheuch, 1600 (*Retours, Berwick*, 18). James Bruntfield was servitor to John Neven of diocese of Orkney, 1625 (OSS., I, 109). James Bruntfield

BRUNTFIELD, *continued*

of Hardaikers was retoured heir of his father in the lands of Hardaikers in the earldom of March, 1633 (*Retours, Berwick*, 190), and Hendreta Bruntfield is in record, 1681 (BOEC., VIII, p. 116). The surname is now probably extinct.

BRUNTON. Local. There is a Brunstane on Brunstane Burn, Midlothian, and there is a village of Brunton in the parish of Criech, Fife. Stodart says Walter of Burntoun held part of Luffness in the reign of Robert III (II, p. 329). John Brountoun was tenant of Aliebank, Selkirkshire, 1558 (ER., XIX, p. 421), James Bruntoun of Calfhill, Roxburghshire, 1660 (RRM., I, p. 285), and James Bruntoun in Boongate of Jedburgh, appears in 1746 (*Heirs*, 211). George Brunton, miscellaneous writer, was born in Edinburgh, 1799. Brentoun and Brountoun 1584, Burnetoune 1504; Brantoun, Brenton, Bromton, Brwntoun. Brunton near Embleton, Northumberland is = Burnton, with metathesis of *r*.

BRUSSOUN. James Brusoune in Balmadiesyde, parish of Creich, 1593 (*St. Andrews*). Henry Brucesoune in Cupar, 1618 (ibid.). John Brussoun retoured heir of Andrew Brussoun sometime burgess in Pittenweym, 1642 (*Retours, Fife*, 623). Thomas Bruisone, burgess of Perth, 1654 (*Dunblane*). Cf. BRYSON.

BRYAN. See under BRIAN.

BRYANTON. From the small place called Bryanton near Inverkeilor, Angus. Robert de Briantoun who leased part of Estirbrekkis in 1478 appears again in Arbroath in 1485 (RAA., II, 203, 261). Andrew Bryantoun, presbyter and notary public of St. Andrews diocese, is in record in 1505 and 1507 (REB., II, 149, 158).

BRYCE, BRICE. From Bricius, a Gaulish saint of the fifth century, nephew of S. Martin of Tours, whom he succeeded in the bishopric there. A common personal name in Scots records at end of twelfth and beginning of thirteenth centuries. Bricius, *judex*, c. 1189–99, witnessed a charter by Laurence, son of Orm de Abernethy (RAA., I, 35), another by Gilbert, earl of Strathern, a. 1198 (LIM., p. xxiv), and between 1204–11 he witnessed a third by William the Lion (RAA., I, 74 *ter*.). Bricius, prior of Brechin, is mentioned c. 1178–98 (REB., II, 270; RAA., I, 75), and another Bricius was chaplain to Matthew, bishop of Aberdeen c. 1180 (REA., I, 11). Bricius, prior of Lesmahago, became bishop of Moray, 1203 (*Dowden*, p. 147). Bricius, persona de Cref, c. 1200–20 appears several times as charter witness (*Scon*, 125; *Laing*, 5; *Inchaf-*

fray, p. 3, 14, 22; LIM., 8, 12, etc.). He is probably the Bricius who as chaplain to Gillecrist, earl of Angus, is witness to several local charters between 1201–07 (RAA., I). Bricius de Dunyn witnessed a charter of confirmation of Fedel c. 1220–44 (LAC., 25), and c. 1260 another Bricius doubtless Brice, abbot of St. Columb, rendered homage, 1296. His seal bears 'In a vessel with one mast and pennon, sails furled, two figures seated, the dexter one mitred, each holding a pastoral staff erect,' *S' abbatis de Insula Sancti Columbi* (Bain, II, p. 197, 542). Brice, abbot of Deer, also rendered homage in the same year. His seal bears the figure of an ecclesiastic standing, pastoral staff in right hand, left on breast, a maniple over his arm, *Sigillum abbatis de Deer* (ibid., p. 197, 542). Richard Brice, burgess and alderman of Stirling, also rendered homage, 1296 (ibid., p. 186, 197). Brice, chaplain to Duncan, earl of Fife, c. 1331–1335, is probably Bricius, dean of Fife and Fothriff, is in record in 1350 (*Cambus.*, 56). Bricius bane attested a charter of lands of Ochterardour, c. 1370 (*Inchaffray*, p. 131). John Bris, elder and younger, followers of the earl of Cassilis, were respited for murder, 1526 (RSS., I, 3386). There was an old Lennox family of Bryce, and John Bryse of Drumquhassell assisted the Macfarlanes in their feud with the Buchanans in 1619. Adam and John Bryce in Braco were resetters of outlawed members of Clan Gregor, 1613 (RPC., XIV, p. 639). As forename we have Brice Strayton in 1480 (*Bain*, IV, 1465), and Bris Duncansoun was member of council of Stirling, 1546 (SBR., p. 277).

BRYDE, BRYDIE, BRIDIE. Dovenald Bryd, burgess of Perth, rendered homage, 1296 (*Bain*, II, p. 197). Malcolm Bridy was a monk of Arbroath, 1451, prior of Fyvie, 1453, and abbot of Arbroath from 1456 to 1470 (RAA., II, 92, 100, and pref. p. x). James Bridy was perpetual vicar of Ennirkelor, 1464 (ibid., 153). William Bridy or Bride was presbyter of St. Andrews diocese, 1508 (REB., II, 161, 162), and another William Bride or Bryde was grieve at Mains of Clunie, 1513 (*Rent. Dunk.*, p. 182, 186). Malcolm Bridve was servant to the bishop of Dunkeld, 1511 (ibid., p. 115), and Thomas Bryde was witness at Lochlevyn, 1546 (*Rollok*, 3). Andrew Brydie appears in Newburgh, 1635 (RPC., 2. ser. v, p. 505). John Bryde, dean of guild of St. Andrews, d. 1636, and his daughter, described as "Onna Briddie, daughter of John Briddie," died in 1648 (PSAS., LXX, p. 72, 77). Rachel Bryd was married in Edinburgh, 1667 (*Edinb. Marr.*), William Brydie, portioner of Dungarthill, had sasine of part of Dulbethie in

1674 (DPD., I, p. 262), and Alexander Brydie was shipmaster in Peterhead, 1753 (CRA.). Brydie is an old surname in the parish of Lochwinnoch, and in modern times the spelling has been changed to Brodie (Tannahill, *Poems*, note by the editor, David Semple, p. 271), and Breadie and Broddie are given as variants of the name in DPD. The name is also recorded in the Commissariot Record of Dunkeld and Muthill.

BRYDEN, BRYDON, BRYDONE. A Border surname which occurs seven times in the Flodden Roll (1513) of the Burgesses of Selkirk. Phelippe de Briden of Roxburghshire rendered homage, 1296 (*Bain*, II, p. 200). John Bridin (Bridyne, or Bridynne) appears as presbyter and notary public in Glasgow, 1527 and 1548 (*Pollok*, I, p. 256; LCD., p. 63). William Brydane, common clerk of Selkirk, 1590 (RPC., IV, p. 481). John Bryddin in Lessuddine, 1662 (RRM., II, p. 45). A pension was paid to Isobel Bryden in Edinburgh, 1730 (*Guildry*, p. 136). Breydon 1710, Broaden and Broadon 1689, Brydin 1590, Brydynne 1536. William Brydonne, 1371 (RMS.). Cf. Briddon, place in Leicestershire and Bredon in Worcestershire.

BRYDON, BRYDONE. See under BRYDEN.

BRYMNER. See under BREMNER.

BRYOT. John Bryot is recorded in 1681, and Thomas Bryot in Endrick, 1707 (*Kirkcudbright*).

BRYSON, 'son of BRICE.' See also BRYCE. A once popular name in Strathclyde. Alanus filius Bricii, tenant of the earl of Douglas in the vill of Prestoun, 1376 (RHM., I, p. lxi). Duncan Briceson was outlawed as part guilty of the slaughter of Walter de Ogilvy, sheriff of the Mearns, 1392 (APS., I, p. 579). Walter Bricii, rector and vicar of the church of Glasfurd, 1409 (RMP., p. 57). William Bryson, Scots prisoner of war liberated from Tower of London, 1413 (*Bain*, IV, 839). Henry Bressoune, bailie of burgh of Perth, 1488 (*Methven*, p. 30). David Brisoun declared innocent of part in detention of King James III in Edinburgh Castle, 1482 (*Lennox*, II, p. 123). Thomas Brysone or Broyson in Newton of Fordve, 1506–09 (*Rent. Dunk.*, p. 48, 53). James Brisoun, witness in Perth, 1546, may be James Brisone, merchant burgess there, 1551 (*Rollok*, 12, 116). Patrick Brisone exempted from process while in French service, 1552 (RPC., VIII, p. 136), and Thomas Bruisone was burgess of Perth, 1654 (*Dunblane*). Brison 1513, Brisoune 1526, Brissoun 1497, Brissoune 1558, Broissoun 1589, Browsoune 1469, Broysoun 1591, Brusone 1469, Bryssoun 1637, Bryssoune 1605. Cf. BRUSSOUN.

BUCCAT. Probably local. There is or was in 1783 a Buchat in the parish of Alyth in Angus, and cf. Buccat-Pottis in *Fife Retours* (928). Silvester Buccat in Over Clony, parish of Blairgowrie, 1675 (*St. Andrews CR.*).

BUCHAN. Of local origin from the district of the name in Aberdeenshire. Ricardus de Buchan was clerk of the bishopric of Aberdeen c. 1207–08 (RAA., I, p. 138), and William de Buchan held land in Aberdeen in 1281 (REA., II, p. 278). Thomas de Boghan of Edinburghshire rendered homage in 1296. His seal bears an eight-rayed figure and S' *Thomae de Bvcan* (*Bain*, II, p. 208, 553). Malcolm and Patrick de Buchane were tenants of the Douglas in the barony of Morton in 1376 (RHM., I, p. lvi). Walter de Bochane or Bucchan, canon of St. Magnus cathedral in 1369 appears as archdeacon of Shetland in 1391 (*Diplomatarium Norvegicum*, I, p. 404; II, p. 402; RMS., I, 824). Richard of Bughwan, a Scot, was illegally arrested at Lowestoff in 1405 (*Bain*, IV, 690), William de Buchane was admitted burgess of Aberdeen in 1436, Thomas and William Bughan in 1477 (NSCM., I, p. 4, 26), and Duncan Buchane was burgess of Abberbrothoc in 1458 (RAA., II, 115). The Buchans of Auchmacoy (Logie-Buchan parish) were one of the principal families of the name. Androw Buchan of Achmakwy was on the assize for settling the boundaries between the lands of St. Peter's Hospital in Old Aberdeen and the neighboring property of the Cottoun in 1446 (REA., I, p. 245). Bicthaine and Bucthaine 1645, Bowchane 1499, Buccam 1515, Bucchaine 1649, Buchtaine 1645, Buquhan 1556.

BUCHANAN. From the district of the name in Stirlingshire. The original name of the Buchanans was MACAUSLAN, q.v. Buchanan of Auchmar (in 1723) says the original patronymic was retained by the eldest cadet when disused by the rest of the clan, but in the old genealogical tree of the Buchanans, of date 1602, the first Buchanan mentioned is "Sir Valtir vat conquest pairt of ye landis frae ye Mauslanis" (*Strathendrick*, p. 284). ('Conquest' is an old Scots law term meaning the acquisition of real property in other ways than by inheritance.) Dominus Absolone de Buchkan witnessed a charter by Malcolm, earl of Lennox to Sir Robert Herthford, precentor of Glasgow, a. 1224 (RMP., p. 217). Alan de Buchanan was one of the witnesses to a charter of lands of Gartechonerane to Malcolm Macedolf c. 1270 (*Levenax*, p. 84). Malcolm de Bougheannan who rendered homage, 1296 (*Bain*, II, p. 205) is probably Malcolm Macabsolon, one of the witnesses to a

112

BUCHANAN, *continued*

charter by Earl Malcolm to Sir John of Luss, 1316. Walter de Buchanan had a grant of Auchmarr in 1373 (*Levenax*, p. 59). Maurice Buchanan, who acted as treasurer to Princess Margaret, wife of the Dauphin of France (afterwards Louis XI) is reputed to have been author of the *Book of Pluscarden*. George Buchanan (1506–82) was a Latin scholar of European fame, and James Buchanan (1791–1868), fifteenth president of the United States was of Scottish ancestry. Among the Pennsylvania Germans Buchanan is used as an Englishing of Buchenhain. Balquhannan 1566, Balquhannen 1553, Bochannane 1627, Boquhannan and Buchquhannan 1536, Boquhennan 1621, Boquhennane 1622, Bowhanan and Bowhannan 1562, Buchquhannane 1526, Buchquannan 1525, Buchunnuch 1662, Bucquannane 1622, Bucquhannane 1492, Buhannane 1588, Buquhannan 1512, Buquhannane 1611.

BUCK. John Buc, a charter witness in Glasgow, 1495 (HP., II, p. 195). Thomas Buk in Dunfermline had a remission in 1508 (*Trials*, I, p. 109*). Alexander Buk was admitted burgess of Aberdeen, 1506, and Duncan Buk in 1560 (NSCM., I, p. 43, 67). Andrew Buk was skipper of the 'Nicolace' of Aberdeen, 1540 (CRA., p. 173), and Andro Buck was burgess there, 1591 (SCM., III, p. 156). Alexander Bucke in Auchorties, 1658 (*Brechin*), and Job Buck was shipmaster in Eyemouth, 1753 (*Lauder*).

BUCKHAM. A current form of BUCKHOLM, q.v.

BUCKHOLM. From the lands of the same name in the parish of Melrose, Roxburghshire. Thome or Thomas Bukum was a tenant of the Abbey of Kelso in the town of Reddene in 1566 and 1567 (*Kelso*, p. 521; RPC., I, p. 484). Euphame Buckam and Isobel Buckholme appear in Edinburgh in 1629 and 1652 (*Edinb. Marr.*), and James Buicam was clerk of the parish of Tyninghame in the seventeenth century (*Waddell*, p. 54). Adam Buckholme of Westlies, 1683 (*Peebles CR.*). Robert Buckham in Westlees, 1772, and John Buckham, tenant in Bedrule, 1790 (*Heirs*, 366, 456).

BUCKIE. Local. There is a hamlet of this name in the parish of Alford, and a town in Rathen parish. Gawin Buckie in Kincaid, parish of Larbert, 1613 (*Stirling*).

BUCKLE. Local. Helen Bukhill appears in Edinburgh, 1605 (*Edinb. Marr.*), and Elizabeth Buckle in Craigneuk, parish of Lanark, 1658 (*Lanark CR.*). James Buckle recorded in Nether Robertland, 1678–1688 (*Corsehill*, p. 150, 177), and Alison Bucle was dispossessed

in 1684 (RPC., 3. ser. X, p. 221). Andrew Buckle, exiled Covenanter, was drowned off Orkney, 1679 (*Hanna*, II, p. 253), and Hugh Buckle was burgh officer of Irvine, 1698 (*Irvine*, II, 66).

BUCKLER. From the occupation, a maker of buckles. Robert Buklar de Athirwicke was charged with forestalling in Aberdeen, 1402 (CRA., p. 385). Helen Buclavr appears in Tullelum, 1512 (*Dunkeld*), and Mr. John Bucler of Kirkland is in record, 1647 (*Inquis.*, 3333). The name is also found in England as Bucklermaker and Bucklesmith. There was a Bucklemakker Wynd in Dundee now stupidly renamed Victoria Street. William Moyses alias Bucklemaker in Hill of Dundei is mentioned in 1615 (*Retours, Forfar*, 83).

BUCKNEY. Probably of local origin. There is a Buckney Burn in Stormont district. Patrick Bucknay, heir of Patrick Bucknav, burgess of Linlithgow, 1680 (*Inquis.*, 6257). Patrick Bucknev in Linlithgow, 1684 (RPC., 3. ser. X, p. 262).

BUDDO. Thomas Buddo is recorded in St. Andrews, Fife, c. 1590, and Effam Buddo in Brounhills, parish of St. Andrews, in 1598 (*St. Andrews CR.*). The name is of local origin from Buddo (Ness) in the parish of St. Andrews.

BUDGATE. Johannes Budet who witnessed a contract between Alexander Doles de Cantra and George Gordone, constable of Baidzenach, in 1542 (*Grant*, III, p. 87), derived his name from Budgate near Cawdor, Nairnshire. John Buddyt appears as a witness in Inverness in 1535 (*Invernessiana*, 209), and John Budeth was burgess there, 1556 (*Rec. Inv.*, I, p. 4). The surname occurs several times in the Records of Inverness as Buddet, Buddit, Buddyth, Buddytht, Budet, and Budzit.

BUDGE. This surname, now somewhat rare, is recorded in Caithness and in Orkney. In a manuscript "Genealogie of the Lairds of Toftinggall," written about 1700, it is stated that "Whence they came or took their name is unknown for the most part, but by common tradition it is affirmed . . . that they are descended of the family of Macdonald, and that the first of this family that came to Caithness fled thither for slaughter, and changed his name from Macdonald to Budge . . . As the Budges had certainly settled in Caithness towards the end of the fifteenth century, their descent from the Macdonalds, and their connection with the county, through Donald Galloch, are not improbable" (Henderson, *Caithness family history*, p. 181–182). Hugh Macdonald, the Sleat seanchaidh, in his *History of the Macdonalds* (HP., I, p. 20), mentions "the Butikes in Caithness, of whom is the Laird of Tolingail," that is, the Budges of Toftingall. The Rev. John Fraser says that in 1438 there were "continual jarres betuix the Benes (Bayns) and Budges and other clans in Cathnes" (*Wardlaw*, p. 103).

The notarial double of a charter granted by 'Henricus de Sancto Claro, Comes Orchadiae,' to —— Budge, of tenements in Wick is undated, but a charter granted by one of the two Henrys, earls of Orkney would carry the Budges back to between 1379, the date of creation of the first Henry St. Clair, as earl of Orkney, and 1420 when the second earl of the name died (*Henderson*, loc. cit.). The first authentic mention of the name, however, is in 1440 when two churchmen of the name appear in record. Magnus Buge appears in that year as canon of Ross, and in 1444 is mentioned as vicar of Tain (*Pap. Lett.*, IX, p. 144, 149). The death of a brother of Magnus, Henry Buge, or de Buge, described as treasurer of Ross, took place at about the same time (ibid., p. 431, 439, 449). John Budge is recorded in Oxsetter, Shetland, 1615 (*Shetland*), and Isobel Buge was married in Edinburgh, 1662 (*Edinb. Marr.*). Budege 1583. Jenner's suggestion (*Cornish grammar*, p. 198) from Welsh Ap Hodge is unlikely.

BUGHT. Wilzame off Buch, burgess of Inverness, had a charter of an acre of land in the Garbreide (Gairbread) in 1449 (*Invernessiana*, p. 117). In 1454 he appears as William de Buyth, in 1455 as de Botha, in 1456 simply as William Buyth, and in 1461 as William Buthe (ibid., p. 126, 131, 132, 140). From the small land called Bught (G. *bog*) near the town of Inverness.

BUGLASS. *See under* BOOKLESS.

BUIE, BOWIE. From the G. adjective *buidhe* 'yellow (or fair) haired.' In Argyllshire curtailed forms of MACILBOWIE, q.v. Bowie was and still is a common name in Jura, and there was a small sept of the name in South Uist. The Bowies of Strathspey are counted followers of the Grants. Mathow Bouie, free burgess brouster in Inverness, 1614 (*Rec. Inv.*, II, p. 123). James Buie in Nether Auchinrivock, 1670 (*Campsie*). John Buy and Donald Buy appear in the Inverness Stent Roll, 1671 (*More Culloden papers*, I, p. 183, 185), and Alexander Buj in Portclare is in record, 1679 (IDR., p. 91). A lykewake was held for Alexander Buie in Elgin, 1737 (*Rec. Elgin*, II, p. 336). Bouwie 1686, Bui 1704.

BUIST. A surname of Fife origin, and confined mainly to the shire. Ernaud and Roger Boiste (or Buiste) are said to occur in Normandy, 1198 (*Mem. Soc. Ant. Norm.*, 15–17), but this is not a probable source of our name. Harrison's etymology (after Jamieson, *Scot. Dict.*) seems to me unlikely. A writer in *Weekly Scotsman* says first record of the name is Peter Buste at Auchtermuchty, 1360, but gives no reference. It may be connected with BOIS and BOYCE, q.v. Laurence Boyst was member of assize at Cupar in 1521 and Andro Boyst is mentioned there in same year (SCBF., p. 192, 222). Cristine Bust, spouse of Andrew Bouman of Vtherogall, is mentioned in 1584 (*Soltre*, p. 153). John Boast was a suspect papist in 1589 (*Scottish Papers*, x, p. 855), and David Boisk is recorded in Carnbenny, 1620 (*Dunblane*). Five of the name, spelled Boist, are in Dunblane Commissariot Record in seventeenth century. Janet Boyst appears in Sherreiftoun, parish of Scone, 1687 (*St. Andrews CR.*), and John Boost in Friertoun, 1697 (*Dunkeld*).

BUITTLE. Of local origin from Buittle in Kirkcudbrightshire. Patrick de Botyl of the county of Dunfres who rendered homage in 1296 appears to be Patrick Mac Gilbochin (q.v.) (*Bain*, II, p. 198, 541, 545). Thomas de Butyl, bachelor of canon law, who petitioned for a benefice in Whithern, 1399 (*Pap. Pet.*, I, p. 574) was the Thomas de Butil (d. 1422), archdeacon of Whitherne, later bishop of Candida Casa (*Dowden*, p. 367–368).

BULGACH. From some small place of the name in the north. Thomas Bulgath (c misread t, a common error) was tenant in part of Cullychmoir, Delny, Ross-shire, 1539 (ER., XVII, p. 667). May nik (i.e. daughter of) William Bulgalch was admitted brouster in Inverness, 1613 (*Rec. Inv.*, II, p. 115), and William Bulgich is in record, 1649 (IDR., p. 369).

BULL. William Bule of Ayrshire rendered homage, 1296 (*Bain*, II, p. 205). Thomas Bull was a tenant in the barony of Newlands, 1376 (RHM., II, p. 16). A payment was made to Robert Bull, a Scottish merchant, 1474 (*Bain*, IV, 1412). John Bule was a witness in Brechin, 1503 (REB., II, 162). John Bull, a pauper, was presented to a bed in the hospital of St. Nicholas and admitted to the privileges of the said hospital as regarded lepers, 1513 (PDG., 637). Another Jhone Buvll rented land in Edingeyth, 1521 (*Rental*). John Bull, burgess of Dundee, 1601, and five others of the name are recorded (*Brechin*). James Bull in Kirkintilloch, 1666 (*Sasines*, 1312), John Bule, tenant in barony of Mousewall (Mouswald), Dumfriesshire, 1673 (PSAS., XXIII, p. 74), and Margaret Bull in Dunning, Perthshire, 1781 (*Dunblane*). Buill 1590.

BULLEN. From Boulogne in France. Aleyn of Bollone appears in Edinburgh, 1394 (*Bain*, IV, 460). The seal of Thomas Bullyn, canon of Glasgow, 1460, bears the legend *Sigillum dñi thome bully* (*Macdonald*, 293). Agnes Bollegna is recorded in Edinburgh, 1612 (*Edinb. Marr.*), and Hew Bollen was goldsmith there, 1649 (ibid.).

BULLERWELL. From the old place of Bullerwell in the parish of Hobkirk, Roxburghshire. Mention is made in 1489 of the land of vmqwhill George Bullirwell in Dunfermline (DBR., 306), and in 1491 Alison Bullirwel resigned a land lying in the Nethirton (ibid., 315). Jhone Androsone was admitted burgess of Dunfermline "throw resone of his wyf Alesone Bowlyrwell" in 1492 (ibid., 39), and Sir John Bullerwale was curate of the church of Arryngrosk in 1527 (*Cambus.*, 22). Six individuals of this name are recorded in the Edinburgh Marriage Register from 1613. James Bullarwall appears as burgess of Selkirk in 1662, and William Bullerwall was burgess of Jedburgh in 1663 (RRM., III, p. 63, 70). Mr. James Bullerwall was schoolmaster at Duns in Berwickshire in 1699 (*Lauder*), Alexander Buleruall in Tolbooth Kirk parish signed the Test, 1685 (RPC., 3. ser. x, p. 456), and George Bullenwell was deacon of shoemakers in Jedburgh, 1756 (*Heirs*, 285).

BULLIE. Perhaps local. John Bully had a special respite and protection in 1504 (*Trials*, I, p. °43). Margaret Bullie at Burnside of Touche, parish of St. Ninians, 1616 (*Stirling*).

BULLION, BULLIONS. These surnames still current in the adjoining shires of Stirling and Perth are of local origin from one or more of the small places of the name. There is a Bullions near Larbert, Stirlingshire, another near Cairneyhill, Dunfermline, and a third near Nemphlar in Lanarkshire. In the parish of Ecclesmachen in West Lothian there is also a mineral spring named Bullion Well (Penny, *Linlithgowshire*, p. 18). These place names are derived from Gaelic (Irish) *bullán*, defined by Joyce as "a round spring well in a rock or rocks. Often applied to an artificial cuplike hollow in a rock which generally contains rain water" (*Irish names of places*, III, p. 152). The -*s* is English plural. Andrew Bulzeons made a renunciation of the third part of the lands of Little Tullibeltane in 1674 (DPD., II, p. 160).

BULLOCH. This surname has nothing to do with the name Bullock, though doubtless the names have been confused in early times. Bulloch is simply Balloch, and practically all of the name come from or originated in the parish of Baldernock, Stirlingshire (SHR., II, p. 191). In old records the form Balloch was almost invariably used until the middle of the eighteenth century. The Ballochs or Bullochs were ranked or included as a sept of the Macdonalds. "The race has not been known much to fame, which is probably the reason that it has been quite overlooked by the genealogists" (SHR., II, p. 191). See also BALLOCH.

BULLOCK. This surname is rare in the north, but was fairly common in the shires of Peebles, Haddington, Linlithgow, and Dumbarton. The name was probably introduced from England, and in the fourteenth century there was "a family of sailors of the name trading between English and Scottish ports" (SHR., II, p. 191). The earliest of the name recorded in Scotland appears to be Adam Bulloc who witnessed an agreement between the abbot and monks of Newbattle and Alexander de Drochyl regarding the marches of Kingside, c. 1250 (*Neubotle*, p. 27). Richard Bulloch was slain in the field of Cambok, 1278 (*Bain*, II, p. 34). Walter Bulloc was juror on an inquest which found that Robert de Pinkeny held the tenement of Balincref in 1296 (ibid., II, 857). William Bulloc was attorney for the provost of Haddington, 1329 (ER., I, p. 164). Another William Bullok, "an ecclesiastic of obscure birth but great military talent was prominent in the early part of the reign of David II, but eventually falling under suspicion was confined in a squalid dungeon in Lochindorb Castle to die of cold and hunger" (ER., I, pref. p. clv), in 1346. Robert Bullock, custumar of Aberdeen, 1358–70 (ER., II) may be the Robert Bullok who witnessed a deed of sale, 1383 (REA., II, p. 284). William Bullok, bailie of Peebles, 1444, appears four years later as William Bullo (*Peebles*, 12, 14). John Bullok, merchant and shipmaster of Aberdeen, is in record 1446–54 (*Bain*, IV, 1194, 1265), and David Bullok was a chaplain in the Abbey of Arbroath, 1464 (RAA., II, p. 142). William Bullow was an apprentice in Edinburgh, 1692 (*Edin. App.*). Bullo or Bullock was the name of an old family in Peeblesshire who were in possession of the lands of Bullo "vulgo nuncupatis Bonningtoun-Bullo" in the sixteenth century (*Retours, Peebles*, 3). This surname has nothing to do with Bulloch, a name of quite different origin.

BULLOUGH. A Perthshire variant of BULLOCH, q.v.

BULLY. William Bully was bailie of Edinburgh, 1403 (EBR., 2). Andrew Bully held a tenement in Irvine, 1418 (*Irvine*, I, p. 126), and Nicolas Bully was burgess of Glasgow, 1425–1433 (LCD., p. 243, 247). Alexander Bulli witnessed a charter by Stephen Flemyng, master of the Hospital of Soltre, 1426 (*Soltre*, p. 52). William Bully was 'commissar of burrows' in 1440 (SCM., v, p. 263), Thomas Bully appears as a churchman in Glasgow, 1463 (RD., 467), and as Sir Thomas Bully was a canon in the cathedral there, 1470 (SBR., p. 255). John Bully was bailie of Stirling, 1511 (*Logie*, I, p. 14).

BULMAN. Stephen Bulman in Longnewtoun, 1662 (RRM., II, p. 44), and Isobel Bulman in Boun Jedburgh, 1686 (*Peebles CR.*). Explained by Bardsley and Harrison as = bull-herd.

BULMER. Perhaps from the parish of the name in the North Riding of Yorkshire which gave name to a family in the twelfth century (*Guppy*). Anketin de Bulemer or Bulmere was one of the witnesses to the letter of David I respecting the consecration of Robert, bishop of St. Andrews, at York, and also to the charter by Thurstin, archbishop of York, on the same subject in 1128 (Haddon and Stubbs, *Councils and ecclesiastical documents*, II, pt. I, p. 215). Johannes de Buloṁ (= Bulomer) witnessed a gift to the church of Glasgow, c. 1260 (REG., p. 177).

BULT. Magnus Bolt, "underfold (under bailiff) in Vawiss," 1510 (REO., p. 86). Magnus Bult, fowd of Brassay, 1612 (MSM., II, p. 166), and William Bult in Sistay in Bressay, 1624 (*Shetland*). Robert Boult in Edinburgh, 1681 (*Edinb. Marr.*). Harrison says "a variant of Bolt for Bold" (?).

BULTIE. Robert Bultie, merchant, admitted burgess of Dundee, 1578 (*Wedd.*, p. 180). Thomas Bultie, residenter in St. Andrews, 1695 (*St. Andrews CR.*).

BUNCH. A surname peculiar to Perth and neighborhood, and found in Perth so early as first half of the fifteenth century. Alexander Bunshe held a land in the burgh in 1444 (*Milne*, p. 30). William Bunch also held land there and John Bunche was witness there c. 1450 (*Scon*, p. 188, 189). Duncan Bunche, vicar of Wystone, was principal regent of the faculty of arts in the "studium" of Glasgow in 1459 (RUG., I, p. 13). William Bunche was abbot of Kilwinning in 1474 (REG., 404), and Alexander Bunsch, a Scottish merchant, received a payment in the same year (*Bain*, IV, 1412). John Bunche was sheriff of Perth in 1505 (*Milne*, p. 14), and Andro Bunch, burgess of Perth in 1508 may be the Andrew Bunche who held a tenement in the same town in 1524 (*Rent. Dunk.*, p. 3; *Scon*, p. 203). Walter Bunchss was a monk of Cupar in 1500

(REB., I, 220), Johannes Bonche or Bounche appears as witness at Scone, 1556 and 1566 (REM., p. 395, 403), Alexander Bunche was witness in Perth, 1546, and Sir Walter Bunsche chaplain there, 1551 (*Rollok*, 42, 86), and the name occurs in Arbroath in 1521 as Bownche (RAA., II, 573). Bunsche 1596, Bwnche 1463.

BUNCLE, BUNKLE. From the lands of that name in the Merse. Adam de Bonekil witnessed a charter by Richard Cumyn granting the church of Lyntun roderic to Kelso c. 1160 (*Kelso*, 274). In 1212 Ranulf de Bonekil was excused from an assize and suits in Cumberland while in the service of the king of Scotland (*Bain*, I, 542). Sir Ranulf de Bonkill was present *in curia regis* at Roxburgh in 1231 (APS., I, p. 408). Four individuals of this name rendered homage in 1296: Johan de Bonekil, Thomas Bonequil, Anneys de Bonkhille, all three of the county of Berewyke, and Alisaundre de Bonkhille of the county of Edinburgh (*Bain*, II, p. 198, 206, 207, 214). The seal of Thomas is a gem, lion's head in profile, open jawed, S' *Thome de Bonkil cleric* (ibid., p. 540), and that of Alisaundre de Bonkhille bears three buckles, shield on a tree of three branches, between two wyverns, S' *Alexand' de Bonkil* (*Macdonald*, 196). James of Boncle was elected bailie of Edinburgh in 1403 (EBR., p. 2), and Adam de Bonkle was burgess there in 1423 (*Egidii*, p. 45). Alexander Boncle held land in Edinburgh in 1467 (*Neubotle*, 299), Robert Bonkill was bailie of Perth in 1514 (OPS., II, p. 662), Sir Eduard de Bouncle was first provost of Trinity College Church in Edinburgh in 1464 (*Macdonald*, 201), and Thomas Bawnikill is recorded as a 'wadsett haver' in 1630 (LIM., p. 107). The portrait of Sir Edward Buncle, provost of Collegiate Church of Edinburgh appears on the Trinity Screen in Holyrood Palace. Bonckle 1632, Bonekille 1217, Bonekulle 1246, Bonkyl 1296, Bonkyll 1426, Bonnequil 1301, Bunkill 1622.

BUNNOCK or BONNOK of Barbour's *Brus*, VII, 451, 492. Nisbet (*Heraldry*, I, p. 100) says the name is same as Binney or Binning.

BUNTEN, BUNTIN, BUNTINE, BUNTING, BUNTON, BONTEIN, BUNTAIN, BONTINE. Macfarlane (II, p. 278) describes Buntine of Ardoch as "a very Antient family in the county of Dumbarton where they Still Remain in Lustre." Most probably a branch of the English Buntings, found in several of the English counties in the thirteenth century. Roger Ortolanus (= Bunting, Lat.) was one of an inquest made at Peebles, 1262 (APS., I, p. 101 *red*). Thomas

BUNTEN, Buntin, Buntine, etc., *continued*

Bunting one of an inquest at Traqueyr in 1274 (*Bain*, II, 34) may be Thomas Buntynge of Peeblesshire who rendered homage in 1296 (ibid., II, p. 207). Finlay Bunting had a charter of the lands of Mylnetelame in the barony of Cardross from Robert III (RMS., I, App. II, 1796). Robert and William Bontyne had remission for their share in burning the town of Dunbertane in 1489 (*Lennox*, II, p. 132), and Nicolas Buntyne witnessed sasine in favor of James, son of the earl of Lennox, 1490 (ibid., II, p. 140). John Buntyne of Ardoch was a follower of the earl of Argyll in 1536 (RSS., II, 2152) and cautioner for Walter Makfarlan in the same year (*Trials*, I, p. *178). John Bountene served on an assize in 1541 (ibid., I, p. 361*), John Bunteyne was burgess of Glasgow, 1580 (*Burgesses*), John Buntene was retoured heir in lands of Ardoch-Buntein, etc., 1605 (*Retours, Dumbarton*, 8), William Buntein was burgess of Stirling, 1614 (*Stirling*), and Margaret Bonetoun is recorded in Quhytrig, parish of Morrounsyd (Muiravonside), 1618 (ibid.), Archibald Bontein was secretary to the "Bluidy Mackenzie." The form Bontein, as spelling of the family name, was adopted by Sir James Bontein in 1782. The Buntings of England, according to Kemble, were an old Anglo-Saxon clan. Buntene 1603, Buntin 1591, Buntyn 1513, Bwntene 1556, Bwnteyne 1563, Buntyng 1452, Bunton.

BUNY. William Buny, Scots merchant, had a safe conduct into England, 1412 (*Bain*, IV, 829). Patrick Buny held land in Linlithqw, 1461 (RAA., II, p. 119), and Henry Buny held a tenement there in 1472 (*Sc. Ant.*, XVII, p. 116).

BUNYIE. David Bunyhe, latimus in Edinburgh, 1517 (*Soltre*, p. 179). John Bunzie, portioner of Newstead, Roxburghshire, 1662, and Robert Bunzie, mason there, 1672 (RRM., II, p. 15; III, p. 85). James Bunvan, mason and portioner of Newstead, 1778 (*Heirs*, 395). Andrew Bunzie, portioner of Newstead, 1812 (ibid., 591). Buinzie 1692, Bunyie 1694.

BUNZEON. Local, from Bunzeon or Bunzion in the parish of Cults. Alexander Bunzeon in Fullartoun, parish of Marytoun, 1635, and three more are in record (*Brechin*).

BURBONE. John Burbone, merchant burgess of Edinburgh, 1642 (*Inquis.*, 2642), Bethia Burbone in Edinburgh, 1658 (*Edinb. Marr.*), and Archibald Burbon of Thridpart, 1684 (RPC., 3. ser. X, p. 324).

BURDON, Burden, Bourdon. Probably from the place now called Burdon in the county of Durham, where a family of the name are found shortly after the Norman Conquest. Thomas Burdun witnessed a charter by Ebrardus de Penkathleht to the church of St. Cuthbert of Durham in the reign of William the Lion (*Raine*, 163). William de Bourdon witnessed a charter of Alexander II to Hugh de Abernethy, c. 1245 (*Nisbet*, I, p. 419). — de Burdon witnessed a charter of Sir Ralph Noble of half the lands of Kenpunt to David Graham. Sir William Burdone swore fealty in 1291, and in 1296 Rogier de Burghdone of Blakeder in Berwickshire and Wautier de Burghdone of Roxburghshire rendered homage (*Bain*, II, p. lix, 199, 203). The seal of the latter bears the legend S' *Walteri de Bordun* (*Macdonald*, 294). In 1337 the manor of Blakeder is mentioned "que fuerunt Roberti de Burghone qui de Rege tenuit in capite" (*Bain*, III, 371). John Burdon, one of the suite of the earl of Angus, had a safe conduct in England, 1357. The Burdons of Perthshire claimed descent from a younger son of the Lamonts of that Ilk (in the reign of Robert III), but no certain proof of connection exists. Burdens are found in possession of Auchingarrich in the parish of Strowan in middle of sixteenth century, and several individuals named Burdon are recorded in the parish of Muthill and district in seventeenth century (*Dunblane*). John Burdoun was minister at Balquhidder, 1574 (RMR.). In Edinburgh the name was recorded as Burdon and Burdoun (*Edinb. Marr.*).

BURESYD. Local, from some small place named Bowersyde or Bowerside. David Buresyd rendered to Exchequer the accounts of the bailies of Anstruther, 1594 (ER., XXII, p. 429).

BURGAN. Thomas Burgane held land in Innerkethin, 1500 (RAA., II, 404), and in the same year John of Burgoun was one of an assize (EBR., 79). Thomas Burgan resigned his share of Ferrihill in 1595 (RD., p. 493), and four years later John Burgan had a charter of a tenement in North Quenesferrie (ibid., p. 495). James Burgane in Northferrie was retoured heir of Peter Burgane, portioner of Ferriehill in three sixteen parts of land of Fairhill in the parish of Dumfermeling, 1634 (*Retours, Fife*, 507). Anthony Burgane appears in Fornaught, 1680 (*Dunblane*), William Burgane in Prendergaist, 1682, and John Burgan in Harcas, 1683 (*Lauder*). George Burgen appears in Edinburgh, 1700, and eleven others of the name Burgen and Burgone are recorded in the Edinburgh Marriage Register.

BURGAR. An Orcadian surname probably derived from Burgar in Evie-Rendall parish, Orkney. Mawnis Burowgar who was tacksman of part of the urislands of Marwick in 1492 (REO., p. 406), is doubtless the Magnus Burgar tacksman of Netherskaile, Marwick, in 1503 (ibid., p. 417). Christopher Burgar and Brandam Burgar were witnesses in 1534 (ibid., p. 217), and James Burgar in Colvasetter, Yell, is recorded in 1627 (*Shetland*). The surname has now been merged in BURGESS. Recorded as Burgher in Inverness, 1942.

BURGESS, BURGES. A burgess was a citizen or freeman of a corporate town or burgh, ME. *burgeys*. Henricus Burgeis in the parish of Fyvy was excommunicated in 1382 (REA., I, p. 165). William Burges was admitted burgess of Aberdeen in 1475 (NSCM., I, p. 25), and Jennet Burgess and John Burgesse were examined for the Test in Tinwald in 1685 (RPC., 3. ser. XI, p. 433). The old Orkney surname of Burgar has become Burgess.

BURGH. Local. "In Scotland the name is limited and never attained to any eminence" (*Scot. Nat.*). Robert de Burghe of Lanarkshire rendered homage in 1296 (*Bain*, II, p. 212). William Burgh witnessed confirmation of a charter by Robert Herys of date 1498 (*Bamff*, p. 39), Gilbert Burgh was a follower of Campbell of Lundy, 1529 (RSS., II, 59), and Malcolm Burghe, a rebel, was rescued from officers of the law in 1630 (RPC., 2. ser. III, p. 560). Four individuals of the name are recorded in the Commissariot Record of Dunkeld. James Burgh (1714–1775), author, born at Madderty, Perthshire.

BURGILLOUNE. Johannes Burgilloune de Saultoune made a gift to the Abbey of Dryburgh, c. 1295 (*Dryburgh*, 254). The Burgullian of Burgundy (*Ewen*, p. 143).

BURGON. About the year 1128 Robert Burgonensis, miles, was accused of rapacity by the monks of St. Serf's island, Loch Leven (RPSA., p. 117, 118). He was a frequent witness to charters in the earlier years of the reign of David I. "M. Merlet suggests that he was the 'Seigneur de Sablé,' 'troisieme fils d'un autre Robert de Bourgignon Seigneur de Sablé qui s'était croisé' en 1096" (*Lawrie*, p. 330).

BURN. Of local origin from residence by or on a burn (ME. *burna*, *burne*, a brook, rill). There are places named Burn in Ayrshire and Lanarkshire, and the surname occurs early in the former shire. About 1280 Adam de Burne granted letters anent the land of New-

ton of Ayr (RMP., p. 71). Adam de Burn was a tenant in the moor of Cavers, 1303 (*Bain*, II, p. 386), and William de Burne was a tenant in the barony of Kilbucho, 1376 (RHM., II, p. 16), and Nicholas de Burn, cleric and notary public in the diocese of Glasgow is in record, 1397 (LSC., 111). William Burne, John Burne, and Thomas Burne were repledged to liberty of burgh of Irvine, 1460 (*Irvine*, I, p. 27). David Burne was a witness in Glasgow, 1497 (LCD., p. 203), Robert Burne a witness there in 1551 (*Protocols*, I), and Alexander Burne was a merchant in Stirling, 1649 (SBR., p. 196). Burn is an old surname in the parish of Larbert, a common one in the Stirling Commissariot Record, and several of the name are also recorded in the Peebles Commissariot Record. About a dozen persons of this name were tenants or dependents of the Abbey of Cupar-Angus, c. 1500 (*Cupar-Angus*).

BURNARD. A form of BERNARD, q.v. John Burnart witnessed a charter by William, lord of Douglas, 1306–29 (RHM., I, p. 13).

BURNBANK. Of local origin from some one of the many small places of this name. John Burnbank in Ballibeg of Rednoche is in record in 1618 (*Dunblane*).

BURNESS. This surname is said to occur in England in early times, but the Scottish Burness is most probably of local origin. Burneshead, Cumberland, was the seat of a family of Burnes up to the reign of Edward I (Burn, *Cumberland*, London, 1777, I, p. 124). Bernes in the parish of Glenbervie before 1329 appears as Bernes and Bernis (RMS., I, App. II, 432, 585). The lands were perhaps those afterwards known as Burnhouse of Kair in the barony of Mondynes and may be the present Burnside of Monboddo (cf. *Jervise*, I, p. 155). A family of the name of Burnes were leaseholders of the lands of Bralinmuir and Bogjordan which form the estate of Inchbreck in the early part of the sixteenth century (ibid.). A Bernys in the barony of Renfrew is mentioned in 1375 (RMS., I, 591) and Bernis in the shire of Dunbertane in 1495 (RMP., p. 405). David Burnis a follower of the earl of Cassilis, was respited for murder, 1526 (RSS., I, 3386), and a later David Burnis was burgess of Ayr, 1587 (*Ayr*, p. 115). Robert Burns's right name was Burness (pron. Bur'ness not Burness'), but because the name was pronounced in Ayrshire as if written Burns, he and his brother Gilbert agreed to drop Burness and assume Burns in April 1786 (*Wallace-Chambers*, I, p. 318). Burnace, Burnasse, Burnice.

118

BURNET, BURNETT. A variant of Burnard from the OE. personal name *Beornheard*. About the year 1200 Roger Burnard made two grants to the monks of Melrose from his lands of Faringdun, one of them being witnessed by his four sons, Gaufrid, Ralph, Walter, and Richard (*Melros*, p. 75, 76). About the same date Gaufridus Burnald is named, and a little later Ralph, designed son and heir of Roger Burnett, witnessed a charter by Stephen de Blar to the monks of Cupar, and between 1208–32 as Radulph Burnard, son and heir of Roger Burnard, he granted the bishop of Glasgow and his successors fuel for their house of Alnecrumbe (now Ancrum) (REG., p. 99, 100). About 1250 Patrick Burnard held lands near Gordon, Berwickshire (*Kelso*, p. 90), and in 1264 Henry Burnet is called 'serviens' of the Justiciary (ER., I, p. 4). William de Farningdon of Roxburgh, probably one of the family, rendered homage, 1296. His seal bears a cross of four pine branches, a cone in dexter base point, S' *Will'i d' Franingdv* (*Bain*, II, p. 199, 532). Alexander Burnard or Burnett went north in the train of Robert I and received charters of lands in the forest of Drum and the barony of Tulliboyll in the sheriffdom of Kincardine (RMS., I, App. II, 429, 433). The Burnets of Barns, who gave name to Burnetland in the parish of Broughton, claimed descent from Robertus de Burneville, time of David I, "but this claim," says Stodart, "hardly seems proved" (II, p. 292). Burnaitt 1578, Burnarde 1369, Burnat 1458, Burnate 1527.

BURNEVILLE. From Burneville in the department of Eure, Normandy. Robert de Burnetuilla was a witness to Earl David's charter founding the Abbey of Selkirk, c. 1120 (*Kelso*, p. 4). (This it may be noted is the only instance in which the letter *t* appears in the name.) As Robert de Burneuilla, he was one of the inquest on the lands belonging to the see of Glasgow, c. 1124 (REG., p. 5), and was also a witness to King David's great charter to the Abbey of Holyrood, c. 1128 (LSC., p. 6). He was also witness to David's confirmation of the rights of the abbot of Holyrood in Heret (Airth), c. 1130 (ibid., p. 8), and to the same king's charter of the church of S. Mary at Berwick to the monks of S. Cuthbert, c. 1130–33 (*Raine*, 18). Another Robert de Burnevilla was one of the hostages for King William the Lion, 1174 (*Annals*, p. 194). A third Robert de Burneuill filius Matildis filie Geroldi de Thanu granted a tenement in Brockesmude (Broxmouth) to the Abbey of Kelso between 1200–14 (*Kelso*, 323). He may be the Robert de Borneuill, vicecomes de Berewic, c. 1190–1200 (*Home*,

224), and witness to charter of a third part of Lambertun (BNCH., XVI, p. 332). Adam de Berneuile witnessed a charter by Roger, rector of the church of Ellesdene, 1228 (*Kelso*, 530). Robert de Burnaville and his son, also named Robert, witness a charter by Patrick, earl of Dunbar before 1233 (*Raine*, 116). Robert de Burneuile appears as witness in Lammermuir c. 1270 (*May*, 23). In ——? lands in the counties of Edinburgh, Berwick, and Roxburgh were restored to Agnes, widow of John de Burneville, who had died about twenty years before. William de Burneton (probably the equivalent of Burnevilla) was mayor of Berwick-on-Tweed, 1333–36. It is probable that the BURNFIELDS, q.v., a one-time numerous family or clan in the Merse, were descended from the de Burnevilles.

BURNFIELD. A family of this name were in the fifteenth century vassals of the bishop of Glasgow, and in the following century were a numerous clan in the Merse. It is probable that they were an offshoot from the family of DE BURNEVILLE, q.v. Members of the family were cited in 1566 for renewing their feud with the Haitlies (RPC., I, p. 451), and in April 1568 the Brunfields or Brownfields bound themselves and their servants under penalty of £1000 Scots, and assured Alexander Hately in Lembden, John in Broomhill, George in Hardlaw, Lawrence in Haliburton, and Leonard, brothers, and Patrick Hately in the Kleyis, their children, household, men, and servants, that they shall be unharmed and unmolested for three years. In 1571 there was a renewal of the feud between William Burnfield of Grenelawdene and his kin and the Haitlies in which Steven Burnfield was killed (RHM., I, p. 69–70).

BURNGATE. Of local origin from some small place of the name. A charge of usury was made against William Burngate in 1670 (*Just. Rec.*, II, p. 30). William Burngait was portioner of the Kirktoun of Douglas, 1677 (*Lanark CR.*).

BURNIE. A Dumfriesshire surname, most probably a shortened form of (MAC)BURNIE, q.v.

BURNKYL. Local. Patton Burnkyl and Thomas Barnkyl were jurors on assize at Cupar, Fife, 1520 (SCBF., p. 192).

BURNLIE. Local. William Burnlie, skipper in Kirkcaldy, 1662 (*St. Andrews CR.*), and David Burnelie sailor there, 1691 (*Inquis.*, 7167).

BURNS. *See under* BURNESS.

BURNSIDE. Of local origin from one or more of the ten or a dozen small places of the name. There are villages named Burnside in the shires of Fife, Nairn, and Kincardine. John Burnesyid was a charter witness in Brechin in 1511 (REB., II, 166), and six of the name are recorded in the Edinburgh Marriage Register. John Burnesyde was member of Scots parliament for Culross, 1650 (Hanna, II, p. 485). Janet Burnsyde recorded in Larbert in 1669 (Stirling) may have derived her name from Burnside in the parish of St. Ninians, Stirlingshire. Jennit Burnsyde raised an action in the baron court of Corsehill in 1673 (Corsehill, p. 110). Burnesyde 1512.

BURR. Burr is an old name in the district of Tarves, Aberdeenshire, and is still pretty general there. Three of the name are in the Aberdeen Poll Book of 1696. Andrew de Burr of Mundole and Culbyn had a remission in 1337, and Andrea Burr was clerk of liberation in 1342 (ER., I, p. 442, 447). Walter Bur or Burre had a charter of an annual rent in the lands of Tyrie and Sefield in the constabulary of Kinghorne from David II (RMS., I, App. II, 1076). Robert Bure was procurator in Glasgow, 1433 (LCD., p. 247), and in 1440–42 a Robert Burr or Bur is mentioned as vicar of Peebles (REG., 344, 346). William Bur was admitted burgess of Aberdeen in 1487 (NSCM., I, p. 33), James Bure was witness in Inverness in 1535 (Invernessiana, p. 209), William Burre was bailie of William Ruthven of Ballindane, 1551 (Rollok, 98), and William S. Burr from Fyvie was killed in the first Great War (Turriff).

BURREL, BURRELL, BURRALL, BURRILL. Probably local from Burrill in North Riding of Yorkshire (in 1282 Burel, Burrell 1568). This name is early found upon the Border, particularly in the East Marches. Henry burel witnessed charter of the church of Pencathlan to the Abbey of Kelso c. 1180 (Kelso, 369). William Bwrel attested a document concerning the land of Cnoc in Renfrew, 1234 (RMP., p. 180). William Burel witnessed gift of land in Ayton to William Scot of Coldingham, c. 1250 (Raine, 202). Alan Burell witnessed a charter by Malcolm, fourth earl of Lennox, 1285 (Levenax, p. 87). John Burelle was one of an inquest at Roxburgh, 1357 (Bain, IV, 1). The lands of Swynset and Raynaldstoune in the sheriffdom of Roxburgh, belonging to Robert Bwrelle were forfeited by him and in 1391 were confirmed to William of Laundelis and Jonet his spouse (RMS., I, 813). Henry Burell was witness in Glasgow, 1477 (REG., p. 462), Andrew Burell, chaplain there, 1504

(Simon, 88), and George Burell bailie there, 1536 (LCD., p. 98). John Borelle alias Steward (born in the vill of Morthyngton) had letters of denisation in England, 1482 (Bain, IV, 1473). John Burell, witness in Fife, 1542 (Laing, 464), Thomas Burrale, baxter in Aberdeen, 1544 (CRA., p. 206), and Alexander Burrell was owner of a saltpan in Kirkcaldy, 1573 (RPC., II, p. 265). John Burel or Burell, a poet, wrote a description of Anne of Denmark's entry into Edinburgh, 1590, preserved in Watson's Collection. The name is common in sixteenth century Glasgow protocols. Burelle (of Tevydale) 1391, Burl 1488, Burrel 1505. See also BIRREL.

BURRIE. Local. Thom Burrie in Dunfermline, 1588 (Dunfermline), and William Burrie, trade burgess of Aberdeen, 1665 (ROA., I, p. 235).

BURROCH. Local. William Burrocht possessed a garden in Perth, 1547 (Rollok, 35), and Henry Burroch was burgess there, 1591 (St. Andrews CR.). Donald Burroch appears in Lurg, parish of Comrie, 1663 (Dunblane). Burrouch 1504, Burroucht 1492.

BURSIE. Robert Bursie was admitted burgess of Dundee, 1582 (Wedd., p. 185). Janet Bursie in Kirriemuir, 1615 (St. Andrews CR.), Alexander Bursie, burgess of Dundee, 1657 (Brechin), and Robert Bursie in Pittenweem, 1773 (St. Andrews CR.).

BURT. The home of this name seems to have been Fife and neighborhood. Robert Burt witnessed a tack by the abbot of Cupar, 1521 (SCM., V, p. 294), and a later Robert Burt in Dundee was charged with aiding the English in 1552 (Beats, p. 326). John Burt, prebendary of Moy, 1545 (REM., p. xxiii), Bessie Burt in Dunfermline, 1590 (Dunfermline). Andrew Burtt was chosen treasurer of Dysart, 1600 (Dysart, p. 26), and another Andrew Burt was notary in Dunkeld, 1649 (Inquis., 3528). John Burt, Alexander Burt, and David Burt are in record in Cassidewglie, 1649 (Fordell, p. 34). Robert Burt, cordiner in Dysart, 1695 (Dysart, p. 55), and Agnes Burt appears in Dunkeld, 1721 (Dunkeld). Eight of the name appear in the Commissariot Record of Dunblane in the seventeenth century. Charles Burt, one of the chief engravers for the U. S. Treasury Department, was born in Edinburgh.

BURWICK. From Burwick in Sandwick, Orknev. Magnus Burvik assisor in Sandwick, 1579 (REO., p. 149). Andrew Burwick recorded in Orkney, 1643 (Dalyell, Darker superstitions of Scotland, p. 266).

BUSBY. From the lands of Busby or Busbie in the parish of Carmunnock, Renfrewshire. In 1330 the office of notary was conferred on David de Busby of the diocese of Glasgow (*Pap. Lett.*, II, p. 312). John Busby or Busseby appears as chaplain to the duke of Albany and as canon of Moray in 1408 and 1411 (*Bain*, IV, 751, 801, 813, 814), and Andro Busby, alderman of Are is in record in 1488 and 1491 (*Ayr*, p. 92; *Friars Ayr*, p. 62). John Busby and Gawin Busbe, followers of the earl of Cassilis, were respited for murder in 1526 (RSS., I, 3386). James Busbie was a bookseller in Edinburgh in 1648 (*Edinb. Marr.*), and John Busby published a report of his mineralogical survey of Caithness in 1815.

BUTCHART. An Anglicized form of Fr. *Bouchard*. A family or families of this name appear as tenants on lands of the Abbey of Cupar-Angus in the fifteenth and sixteenth centuries. William Bowchart had a tack of part of the Grange of Kyncreff in 1450 (*Cupar-Angus*, I, p. 122). In later entries his name appears as Bowehart (for Bowchart 1458), Bouchard, Bouchart and Buschart (1554). David Buchart or Buchert, mason's laborer at Dunkeld, 1512 (*Rent. Dunk.*, p. 125, 131). John Buchart is mentioned in the will of Sir Thomas Maule of Panmure, 1513 (*Panmure*, II, 285). James Buchart, admitted burgess of Dundee, 1608. Nine of the name are recorded in the Edinburgh Marriage Register with spellings Bouchart, Boutcher, Boutchert, Butchard, and Butchart; and there are twelve of the name recorded in Brechin Commissariot Record. There is a Butcharts-land in *Forfar Retours* (425). Buschart or Buchat (1549) also appears as a misspelling of Wishart.

BUTCHER. From OF. *bochier* (Fr. *boucher*), a man who slaughters 'bucks' (he-goats, from OHG. *bocch*). Goat's flesh was a common food on the continent in the Middle Ages. Gilbert Boutcheour, tenant in Craignathro, Angus, was assaulted in 1590, and Robert Boutcher and Richard Boutcher are also mentioned at the same time (*Fordell*, p. 23).

BUTHERNOKE. Gilbert de Buthernoke del counte de Strivelyn rendered homage, 1296 (*Bain*, II, p. 205). From Baldernock in Stirlingshire, Buthirnok c. 1200, Buthernock 1400.

BUTHILL. Local. David Buthill, burgess of Cupar, 1592, and three more of the name in the neighborhood (*St. Andrews CR.*).

BUTHLAW, BUTHLAY, BUTHLEY. Aberdeenshire surnames. Of local origin, perhaps from the Buthlawis (1628) of *Aberdeen Retours*

(209). William Buthlaw, vintner in Aberdeen, 1760 (*Aberdeen CR.*).

BUTHMAN. Perhaps 'one who held a booth.' The name is also found in the English *Hundred Rolls*, 1273. Huchoun Buthman was member of the Guild of Ayr, c. 1431 (*Coll. AGAA.*, I, p. 228).

BUTLER. Originally the servant in charge of the butts or casks of wine, OF. *bouteillier*, in Latin documents rendered *pincerna*. Some of the name in later times may derive from *boteller*, maker of leather bottles, specimens of which are in Scottish museums. Hugo, pincerna, witnessed charters by Richard, bishop of St. Andrews, a. 1173 (RPSA., p. 134–136, 138, 139), and c. 1200–1207 Petrus, pincerna, appears as a witness (LAC., p. 81). Warinus, pincerna of the bishop of Glasgow, witnessed confirmation of the sale of land of Scrogges to the church of Glasgow, 1208–13 (REG., p. 76). Malcolm, pincerna, witnessed a confirmation charter by Alexander II of his father's grant of the right of a fair, etc., to the bishop of Glasgow, c. 1225 (ibid., p. 113). Sir John le Botiler swore fealty in 1291, and in 1296 Johan le Botillier of Cramond, Johan le Botiler of Perthshire, and Sir John called le Botillier all rendered homage. Alisaundre de la Butelerie (= butlery) of Ayrshire also rendered homage in the same year (*Bain*, II, p. 205). The name in Scotland appears to have been ousted by SPENCE.

BUTTAR, BUTTER, BUTTERS. These surnames are common to the shires of Fife and Perth and may be connected with the old name Buttergask, the name of a village in the parish of Ardoch. Butter was the name of an old family in Perthshire where they possessed the lands of Fascally, and the Butters of Gormock were a still older family in the same county. In 1331 we have record of the escheat of Adam Butir (ER., I, p. 356), and in 1360 William Butyr and Patrick Butirr are mentioned as collectors of contributions in Gowrie "super ylef" (ibid., II, p. 41). James Buttir, fisherman, received an ox-hide for making his currok (currach) in 1511 (*Rent. Dunk.*, p. 117). Others of this name are mentioned in the Acts of Parliament and in Laing (Charters), and several individuals named Butter are mentioned in a charter of the lordship of Swinton of date 1656, and Butterlaw Loche, Butterlaw Syke, and Butterlaw Cairne are also named in the same charter (*Swinton*, p. cxciv–cxcv). John Buttyr deponed to the right boundaries of the Monk Myre in 1546 (*Cupar-Angus*, II, p. 4). The name is also recorded in Dunrossness, Shetland, in 1602 but is now extinct there (Mill, *Diary*, p. lxxxix, 187). It is also found in Orkney in the seventeenth century (*Retours, Orkney and Shetland*, 52, 58, etc.). The name is evidently of local origin (cf. under BUTTERCASE), and it occurs frequently in the records of the Diocese and Presbytery of Dunkeld. The Butter road (an old drove road across the Ochils, from Old Gaelic *bóthar*, a road for cattle) is in Kincardineshire.

BUTTERCASE. This surname, which is confined mainly to eastern Perthshire and the adjoining part of Fife, is a softened form of Buttergask, now the name of a village in the parish of Ardoch, Perthshire. Reginald de Buthyrgasse witnessed a Maule charter of 1261 (*Panmure*, II, 85). Johan de Botirgask, one of the king's tenants in Perthshire, rendered homage in 1296 (*Bain*, II, p. 202), and in the same year Walter de Bothergask was among the Scottish prisoners taken in the capture of Dunbar Castle (ibid., II, 742, 873). Shortly after this date Walter de Buthergax agreed to enter the foreign service of the English king (ibid., 942). Ade or Adam de Buthirgask, who is repeatedly mentioned in the first volume of the Exchequer Rolls, granted, as heir of Gilbert de Buthergask, a charter of the lands of Buthyrgaske in favor of the abbot and Abbey of Scone in 1304 (*Scon*, 126). Andrew de Bothirgask, miles, who witnessed a charter by David II in 1344 (*RAA.*, II, 20), was among those killed at the battle of Durham in 1346 (Hailes, *Annals*, II, p. 386). William de Butyrgak was prior of Urchard, now Urquhart, in the middle of the fourteenth century (*Rose*, p. 117), and Mariota de Buthirgask resigned the lands of Camysmychel in 1379 (*Scon*, p. 144). A Butergask *de eodem* is referred to in 1445 (*SCM.*, v, p. 283), and in 1458 mention is made of the land of John de Buthergask *de eodem* in Dundee (*REB.*, I, p. 185, 190). Margaret Buttirgask *de eodem* resigned the lands of Buttirgask in the sheriffdom of Perth in 1507 (*RMS.*, 3100), and Patrick Butergask, vicar of Cortoquhy, was a charter witness in 1514 (*Illus.*, II, p. 45). Buthurgasc 1365.

BUTTERWAIN. John de Boterwange was one of the Scots prisoners of war taken in Dunbar Castle in 1296 (*Bain*, II, 742). In the following year as John Buterwan, he was one of many belonging to the district of Atholl pledged to serve the king of England beyond the seas (ibid., II, 942). James Buttirwambe was bailie of the burgh of Banff in 1323 (*RAA.*, I, p. 223), and fifty years later William Butirwaine was collector of contributions in the

sheriffdom of Perth 'super Ileff' (*ER.*, II, p. 423).

BUTTERWITH. Of English origin from a place of the name (*Harrison*). Margaret Butterwith in Edinburgh, 1673 (*Edinb. Marr.*).

BUY. George Boy, mason at Dunkeld, 1511 (*Rent. Dunk.*, p. 123). Mathow Bouie, brouster in Inverness, and Andrew Bluy (probably an error for Buy) was officer there, 1614 (*Rec. Inv.*, II, p. 123, 124). Donald Buy and Cathrin Buy in Inverness, 1616 (ibid., II, p. 146, 148). Donald Roy Buy in Petnadalloch, parish of Comrie, 1666 (*Dunblane*), and Allan Buy in Linlithgow, 1684 (*RPC.*, 3. ser. x, p. 261). James Buie in Bellavrait, parish of Dollas, 1684 (*Moray*), Katherine Buy in Culcrieff, 1716 (*Dunkeld*), and John Buie was member of Huntly Volunteers, 1801 (*Will*, p. 8). Perhaps from G. *buidhe*, 'yellow,' pronounced 'buy.'

BY. Local. Alicia de By, spouse of quondam William de Chernsyd or Chernysyd, burgess of Berwyk, made a gift of lands to the Hospital of Soltre c. 1250–70, and during the same period mention is made of Robert de By (*Soltre*, p. 31–32). Richard Bye of Aberdeen had a safe conduct to import salmon from Aberdeen to London, 1439 (*Bain*, IV, 1130). Janet Buin in Dunblane, 1657, and Donald Roy By in Petnadalloch, Comrie (*Dunblane*). The name of these last two may be from G. *buidhe*, 'yellow.'

BYRES, BYERS, BUYERS. These names are derived from the old barony of Byres in East Lothian. John de Byres appears as a monk of Neubotle in 1309 (Wilkin, *Concilia*, p. 382). Thome de Byris owned a tenement in Edinburgh in 1392 (*Egidii*, p. 27), and in 1534 Thomas Byrs was admitted burgess of Aberdeen (NSCM., I, p. 53). George Byris and Thomas Byris were successively ministers of Legertwood in Berwickshire from 1593 to 1653. John Byres, an eminent merchant in Edinburgh, treasurer, dean of guild, and provost, died in 1639 (*Stodart*, II, p. 329). Andrew Byers appears as a burgess of Cupar in 1694, and Mr. Thomas Byers was schoolmaster at Melrose in 1690 (RRM., III, p. 113). For centuries the barony was the property of the family of Lindsay and gave title to Lindsay of Byres.

BYTH. From the small place of the name near Turriff, Aberdeenshire. Alexander Byth and his brother, Robert Byth, from Auchterless, served in the first Great War (*Turriff*).

CABLE, CABEL. John Cabell was witness in Brechin, 1464 (REB., II, 103), and Alexander Cabel or Cabell, witness in Aberdeen, 1493–1497 (REA., I, p. 333, 338), may be Alexander Cabell, parson of Banchory-Devenick in 1499 and 1508 (SCM., II, p. 261; REA., I, p. 352). Matilda Cabell occupied land in Brechin, 1508 (REB., II, 160), and George Cabell was convicted in 1527 for importing "ffalse and fforged pennies into the Kingdom" (Trials, I, p. 137*). William Cable was admitted burgess of Dundee, 1561 (Wedd., p. 164).

CADDENHEAD. See under CADENHEAD.

CADDER. From the village of Cadder in the parish of the same name in Lanarkshire. James Cader was juror in Lanark in 1498 (Lanark, p. 9), Thomas Cadder is recorded in Neddir Mosplatt in 1528 (Rental), and George Cadder was witness in Linlithgow in 1536 (Johnsoun).

CADELL, CADDELL. This name is a form of CALDER, q.v. Innes says (p. 45) the northern Cawdors were disguised as Cadells and de Cadella even in old Scots chroniclers, and they have kept that variety permanently in the South. Johne Cawdale, sone and apperand air to James Cawdale of Aslovne, who had a remission in 1536 (Trials, I, p. 248*) is most likely John Calder of Aslowne, 1558, referred to in the same year as John Caddell (ER., XIX, p. 78, 426). Issobell Cattall in Edinburgh, 1530 (MCM., II, p. 105), and John Caldaile in Aberdeen had to find surety in the same year (CRA., p. 138). Hectoure Caddell and Robert Caddel and others made a raid on the lands of Ardwale in Banff, 1600 (RPC., VI, p. 135), and William Cadall was tenant under the marquis of Huntlie in same year (SCM., IV, p. 262). Several of this name appear in Kilmadock parish in seventeenth century (Dunblane), and the name was common in Edinburgh in the sixteenth century (Edinb. Marr.). George Caddell was paid ten pounds Scots of assythment in 1724 (Urie, p. 124). Cadell of Cockenzie is principal family of the name.

CADENHEAD, CADDENHEAD. Of local origin from the head of the Caldon or Cadon Water in the Selkirkshire part of the parish of Stow, and not from De Cadneto or Caisneto as the author of The Norman people says. William de Caldanhed or Caldenhed, a monk of Newbattle, who was treasurer to the Abbey in 1467, is apparently first of the name on record (Neubotle, p. 254). William Caudenhed was a witness in Edinburgh in 1482 (ibid., p. 276). The name appears to have made its way to Aberdeenshire in the sixteenth century, and there

Archibald Cadenheid was "ane of the maisteris of the fische boittis of Futtie" in 1601 (CRA., p. 218). Magnus Caddenheid in Cortance is on record in 1633 (SCM., III, p. 116). The name also appears in Edinburgh in 1677 and 1699 as Caldenhead and Caddonhead (Edinb. Marr.). Cadenhed 1743, Cadinheid 1634, Cadonhed 1675, Caldanhede 1502, Caldenheid 1505, Cattenhead 1626, Caudenhead 1482, Cauldenhed 1494, Cawdinhed 1467, Kaddinheid 1637.

CADGER. From the occupation of 'cadger,' one who carries burdens, a porter, a hawker. Michael Cagger was one of an assize in Dunfermline in 1493 (DBR., 45), and alms were given to the relict of Simon Cagear in Dunkeld in 1511 (Rent. Dunk., p. 114). In 1558 the caggers of Dunkeld furnished candles to the bishop (ibid., p. 360). A serious assault was committed on the widow of John Kaidger in 1612 (RSCA., II, p. 182), and in the same year a burgess of Perth was "decernit in the vrang bluid latting of Thomas Clerk, cagger, in Elgin, in stricking of him with ane greit irone key in the heid" (Rec. Inv., II, p. 98).

CADY. John Cady was a tenant under the earl of Douglas in the barony of Kylbouho, 1376 (RHM., I, p. xlix; II, p. 16), and Thomas Cady was presbyter in Glasgow, 1440 (REG., 344). Peter Cady was burgess of Edinburgh, 1484 (ibid., 435), and three persons named Cadie are in Edinburgh Marriage Register from 1606. John Kady was reidare at Dunsire, 1574 (RMR.), and John Kady and others in Dysart were bound 1577 that they shall not perturb others in the town (Dysart, p. 39). Not likely, I think, to be a reduced form of MACADIE, q.v.

CADZEON. John Cadzeon in Burnsyd of Machany, parish of Blackfuird, appears in 1662, and seven more of the name are recorded in the vicinity (Dunblane).

CADZOW. From the old barony of Cadzow now included in the parish of Hamilton, Lanarkshire. W. de Cadio, canon of Glasgow, is mentioned in 1258 (REG., 208), and as Willelmus de Cadihou he made a gift to the church of Glasgow c. 1260 (ibid., p. 177). William de Cadyow was removed from the King's Council in 1296, and in the same year Adam de Cadiou of the county of Lanark rendered homage (Bain, II, p. 213). Richard de Cadiagh or Kadiagh, messenger, carried letters of Edward I in 1304 (Bain, IV, p. 482–484). Sir John de Cadiou was rector of the church Insule Sancti Braoch (Inchbrayoch) c. 1328 (RAA., I, p. 339). Richard Cadyock was member of Scots parliament for Montrose, 1357 and

Johnne Cadyow the same for Aberdeen, 1440 (*Hanna*, II, p. 485). David de Cadzow (Cadyhow, Caidyoch, Cadiou, Cadzhowe, Cadioch, Cadioche, Cadyoche) appears frequently in record between 1440 and 1463 as precentor, procurator, bailie and canon of Glasgow, rebuilder of the altar of S. Servan in 1446, and rector of the university in 1452 (REG., index; LCD., p. 173, 252). William de Cadeau was clerk of the burgh of Aberdeen in 1436 (REA., I, p. 234), John de Cadyow there to ask forgiveness of the council in 1442 (CRA., p. 7), and William Cadiou was a charter witness in the same town in 1450 (*Illus.*, III, p. 272). Elizat Cadyou was resident in Dysart in 1554 (*Dysart*, p. 23), Master Andrew Cadyhoith, Scottish merchant, had a safe conduct and protection in England in 1486 (*Bain*, IV, 1517), George Caiwdow, a follower of the earl of Cassilis, was respited for murder in 1526 (RSS., I, 3386), and Bessie Kaidzow is recorded in the parish of Carnwath in 1652 (*Lanark CR.*). Cadiow 1487, Cadizo 1424, Cadeyoch and Cadvoch 1453, Cadyhou 1460, Caidzow 1551, Kedzow 1583, Kegzow 1584.

CAIE, CAY. Thomas Cay alias Makcuyk was tenant of Tumbelle in Strathdee, 1539 (ER., XVII, p. 659). William Cay was cautioner for George McConil Reoche, 1602 (*Rec. Inv.*, II, p. 3), and William J. Caie from Forglen served in the first Great War (*Turriff*). The name has been for some time associated with Aberdeen. *Cai* (modern Welsh *Cei*), the name of one of Arthur's chief companions of the Round Table, is borrowed from Latin *Caius (Gaius)*.

CAIG. From (MAC)CAIG, q.v. John Caig and Andrew Caig in the parish of Buittle, 1684 (RPC., 3. ser. IX, p. 570).

CAIL. A surname recorded in Glasgow. Probably shortened from MACKAIL, q.v.

CAIRBRE. From the OIr. personal name *Coirpre*, later *Cairbre*. Spelled *Coirpri* in Lib. Armagh. The church of S. Carpre de Dunescor in Galloway is mentioned in the reign of William the Lion (LSC., p. 214). Carbre Mackan, juror on an inquest held at Gerwan (*Girvan*), 1260 (*Bain*, I, 2674). See MACCAIRBRE.

CAIRD. From G. *ceard*, a craftsman, an artist mechanic, and later a travelling tinker. In an ancient Irish manuscript *cerdd* is glossed by Latin *aerarius* (Zeuss, *Grammatica Celtica*, p. 60), which means 'worker in brass.' Many of the fine old Highland plaid brooches of brass, specimens of which are shown in the

Scottish National Museum of Antiquities in Edinburgh, are believed to be the work of men of this class. Spalding in his *Memorialls* (Aberdeen, 1829) referring to an officer in the regiment of the Master of Forbes says: "This captain's true name was Forbes, but nick-named Kaird, because when he was a boy he served a kaird" (p. 191). Ross also refers to the cairds in his *Helenore* (p. 66):

"What means that coat ye carry on your back?
Ye maun, I ween, unto the Kairds belang."

In connection with the old definition of caird as a worker in brass it is interesting to find the caird in Burns's *Jolly Beggars* say of himself:

"My bonie lass, I work in brass,
A tinkler is my station."

Individuals bearing this name are found in record as early as the thirteenth century. In 1275 Gilfolan Kerd, a mariner in the service of Alexander de Argadia, was with others arrested at Bristol on suspicion of piracy (*Bain*, I, 55). Euġ Makinkerd (here *in* represents G. *an*, 'the') was juror on an inquisition regarding the lands of Inchesturphyn in 13c. (RD., p. 222), and Gregor Makenkerd was to serve Edward I abroad in 1297 (*Bain*, II, 942). Payment was made to Robert Kerd in 1343 for four horseshoes for the king, David II, and for material for his jousting spear (ER., I, p. 528). Adam Kerde in the parish of Fyvy was excommunicated in 1382 (REA., I, p. 165), John Kerde was commissioner of the burgh of Irvine in 1430 (*Irvine*, I, 23), William Kerd is named as a witness in Prestwick in 1446 (*Prestwick*, p. 114), and Robert Kerde was a priest and notary public in the diocese of Glasgow in 1453 (*Scots lore*, p. 272). Gilchrist Mcincaird witnessed a bond of manrent in 1592 (*Coll.*, p. 198), Gillespic MacIncaird is in record in Monyvaird, Perthshire, c. 1602 (RPC., VI, p. 60) and Duncane McIncaird in Glenurcht in 1611 (ibid., IX, p. 140). John Caird in Balledman was fined in 1613 for reset of Clan Gregor (ibid., XIV, p. 635), Angus McInkeard or McInkaird appears at Barawirich or Bartanemireach (? in Perthshire), in 1618 (ibid., XI, p. 415, 486), and David Kaierd died at Carmyllie in 1632 (*Jervise*, I, p. 248). The surname of John Caird, the Tinkler Covenanting preacher of the *Heart of Midlothian* (c. xlvii) infers his descent from a race of ceards. On the West coast this name has been Anglicized by the Norman 'Sinclair,' instead of Tinker or Tinkler. Card 1531, Keeard 1721, Keerd 1726. Cf. MACNOCARD.

CAIRNCROFT. Local. John Cairncroft or Cairnscroft, servant at Bailly Know, 1737 (*Stitchill*, p. 194).

CAIRNCROSS, CARNCROSS. The name appears in Nisbet (by metethesis) as Crynecross. From the lands of the same name in the old barony of Glenesk in Angus. In old charters the name was sometimes Latinized 'Carnea Crux.' Sometime before 1325 Duncan de Caryncros appears as witness in a charter by Henry de Maule, lord of Panmure (*Panmure*, II, 159), and Henri of Carnecors was a charter witness in 1388 (*Bamff*, p. 22). John de Carincors who served on an inquisition made at Forfar in 1438 (RAA., II, p. 545) may be the John de Karyncorss who was one of an inquest made at Brechin in 1450 (REB., II, 79). Thomas Carncors was a burgess of Dundee in 1459 (RAA., II, 129), Nichol Carncorse was a bailie of Edinburgh in 1518 and dean of guild in 1530 (EBR., 174; MCM., II, p. 107). William Carnecors of Colmislie had a grant of the lands of Eister Rarechye in the earldom of Ross in 1550 (RMS., IV, 446), Robert Karnecors was a witness in Ferne in 1545 (*Laing*, 495), and in 1571 sentence of forfeiture was passed against Robert Cairncorse of Clumislie (*Diur. Occ.*, p. 244), probably a son of the forementioned William Carnecors. A 'dour' was 'bocht from Jeillis Cairncorss' in Urie in 1614 (*Urie*, p. 14), and James Carniecroce was bailie of Sanquhar before 1687 (*Dumfries*). This surname is said now to be represented in Cairns and Cross, which have been adopted in its place (*Aberdeen Journal Notes and queries*, II, p. 55). Cairncrose 1658, Cairnecroice and Cairnecroce 1662, Carnecroce 1633, Carnross 1595, Kernecrose 1597.

CAIRNEY. An old surname in Perthshire. A shortened form of CARDENY, q.v. William Cairny had a charter of the land 'vulgo vocata lie gerves aiker,' 1603 (RD., p. 498). Thomas Cairny in West Gormok, 1743 (*Dunkeld*).

CAIRNIE. A common surname in Galloway, shortened from Ir. *MacCearnaigh*, 'son of Cearnach,' victorious (one).

CAIRNS. Of territorial origin from the lands of Cairns in the parish of Mid-Calder, Midlothian. The first of the name recorded is William de Carnys, who appears as a charter witness in 1349 (*Family of Cairns*, p. 4). Though this is the earliest mention of the name in record there must have been many of the surname living at an earlier date, as

in the latter half of the fourteenth century many individuals of the name are mentioned in documents referring to the adjoining counties of Midlothian and West Lothian. In 1363 William de Carnys and his son, Duncan de Carnys, had a charter of the baronies of Esterquytburne and Westirquitburne from David II (RMS., I, 33). Two years later David de Carnys appears as a bailie of Edinburgh (ER., II, p. 208). William de Carnys was constable of Linlithgow Castle and afterwards of the Castle of Edinburgh in 1372 (ibid.). Thomas de Caernis held a land in Edinburgh in 1386 (*Egidii*, p. 23). Many of the name entered the service of the church, as in 1395 there appears Thomas de Karnys, cleric and notary public of the diocese of St. Andrews (RPSA., p. 5), and a William de Karnis, who held the same office in 1406 (ibid., p. 11), in 1431, as vicar of Glamis, founded the altar of St. Fergus in St. Andrews. This William must have lived to a good old age as he is mentioned again as vicar of Glamis in 1455 (*Seals. Supp.*, 155). Alexander de Carnys who witnessed a charter of the lands of Cranshaws in 1401 (*Swinton*, p. xvii) is probably the individual who was provost of Lincluden in 1408. The provost was the first of his name in Galloway, where he accumulated a large amount of land which he bestowed on his nephew John, founder of the Galloway branch of the family. Magister Alexander de Carnys had a safe conduct into England in 1418 (*Bain*, IV, 887). The surname appears in Montrose in 1430 (REB., II, 33), in Arbroath in 1452 (RAA., II, 93), in Glasgow in 1454 (LCD., 175), and in Paisley in 1503 (RMP., p. 61). It was a common name in Edinburgh from the sixteenth century onwards (*Edinb. Marr.*). Cairnis 1403, Carneis 1552, Kairnes 1634, Kairnis 1525, Kayrnis 1578.

CAITHNESS. This surname is not derived from the northern county of the name but is a corruption of Kettins, the name of an old barony in Angus. A canonry in the church of Brechin was conferred on Robert de Kethenis in 1345 (REB., II, 391), and in 1347 Ingram de Ketenis was granted a canonry of Aberdeen. Master Simon of Catnes, clerk, had a safe conduct into England, 1377 (*Bain*, IV, 253), and as Symon de Ketnes (Ketness or Ketenes), canon of Aberdeen, was witness to a number of charters relating to the church of Aberdeen between 1376–86 (REA., I, p. 109, 142, 175). "Ingeram of Ketenis archdein of Dunkeld, sone and air of umquhill Johnne of Ketenis," granted his lands within the town of Kethynnis to our Lady Kirk of Dundee in 1391 (PSAS., XLV, p. 247). John Catnes was admitted burgess of Aberdeen in 1454 and Richard Catnes in 1475 (NSCM., I, p. 14, 25), and John Katness was a laic of Brechin in 1483 (REB., II, 117). Alison Caittins appears in Rottinraw of Panbryde, 1626 (*Brechin*), James Cathnes was 'post' in Aberdeen, 1650 (SCM., V, p. 174), Isobel Caithens appears in Montrose, 1668, John Caithness, burgess of Montrose, 1669, and David Cathnes in Cottertoun of Pitforthie, 1690 (*Brechin*). Mr. James Caithnes, writer in Tolbooth Kirk parish, Edinburgh, 1685 (RPC., 3. ser. X, p. 458), and seven persons of the name are recorded in Edinburgh from 1640 (*Edinb. Marr.*). Caitnes 1647. (2) Robert of Catenesse, Catnesse, or Catnes, servant (*vallettus*) of the earl of Sutherland, who had a safe conduct to return to Scotland in 1362 (*Rot. Scot.*, I, p. 858, 874) may have derived his name from that of the county.

CAKEMUIR. From Cakemuir in Cranston parish, Midlothian. Edulph de Cakmore or Kakmore witnessed grants to the Hospital of Soltre between 1214 and 1240 (*Soltre*, p. 19, 23, 24).

CALABYR. Local. William de Calabyr, canon of Aberdeen, 1360, is doubtless William de Calabre, prebendary of Ellon, 1392 (REA., I, p. 89, 178), who appears many times as charter witness in Aberdeen.

CALBRAITH. A current variant of GALBRAITH, q.v.

CALCOTT. A surname recorded in Caithness, of recent introduction from England. There is a Calcott in Wilts and Calcutt in Warwickshire.

CALDCLEUCH. From Cauldcleugh in the parish of Teviothead, Roxburghshire. John Caldcleuch was retoured heir in lands in the territory of Ugstoun in the bailliary of Lauderdaill in 1602 (*Retours, Berwick*, 29), and James Caldcleughe is recorded in Blainslie in 1662 (RRM., II, p. 4). Thomas Calclewch and William Caldcleuch in Stenton took the oath, 1685 (RPC., 3. ser. X, p. 551). Caildcluiche 1588, Calclithe 1591, Caldclewch 1660, Caldcluiche and Cauldcluiche 1589.

CALDCOTT. Most probably from Coldcoat now Macbiehill in Peeblesshire. There was a manor of Caldcote in Huntingdon forfeited by Bruce in 1304 (*Bain*, II, 1540, 1837), but Peeblesshire Coldcoat seems most likely source of the name. Geoffry de Caldecote witnessed a resignation of lands in Annandale a. 1245 (*Bain*, I, 1682). Galfridus de Caldcot witnessed a charter by James Steward of Scotland in 1294 (RMP., p. 96), as Galfridus de Caldecotes witnessed a charter by Robert de Brus, lord of Annandale in same year (HP., II, p. 130), and as Geffrey de Caldecote of the county of Edeneburk rendered homage in 1296. His seal bears a head in profile and S' Galfridi de Caldecote (Bain, II, p. 201, 546). Robert de Cauldcotys or Caldcotys witnessed a charter of the lands of Lamberton in 1332 (BNCH., XVI, p. 327), and the seal of S' Johannis Caldecot is appended to a charter by John of Caldecotys to William of Caldecotys, his son of the lands of Grayden in the earldom of March c. 1360 (*Seals Supp.*, 157). John de Caldicotys, dominus de Hoton, was a charter witness in 1361 (PSAS., XXIII, p. 30), and the seal of Cristiane de Caldecottis is appended to the renunciation by her of the lands of Grayden and Sympryne in 1424 (*Macdonald*, 310). The seal of John Caldecote of that Ilk, c. 1387, bears the legend S' iohannis caldcotys (ibid., 309). Caldcottis 1459.

CALDER. Hugh de Kaledouer witnessed a charter by William the Lion at Munros (Montrose), c. 1178–98 (RAA., I, 76), and the gift of a toft in Forfar to Willelmus de Haia by the same king (SCM., II, p. 304). In the same reign he granted forty acres in Buthyrgasc to the Abbey of Scone (*Scon*, p. 19), and witnessed a charter by Swan filius Thori (ibid., p. 18). Donald of Calder, lord of that Ilk, acquired half of Dolmaglas (Dunmaglas) in 1419 (*Cawdor*, p. 6–8) from William Meignes, being previously owner of the other half. Farchardus de Caldor was prebendarius de Crechmont, 1461 (REA., II, p. 91), and John Calder, Bute Pursuivant in 1589, appears again in 1591 as John Cadder (ER., XXII, p. 16, 175). Calder and Caddell, Caithness surnames, are from Calder or Cawdor. Calder in Caithness "in its older form of Caldell, is of considerable antiquity, and in the middle of the seventeenth century few names in the county are of more frequent occurrence" (Henderson, *Caithness families*, p. 209). Johannes Cauder in Murthlac, and George Caulder in Petglasse appear in 1550 (*Illus.*, II, p. 261). William Musgrave Calder, U. S. Senator, was grandson of Scots from Aberdeen.

CALDERHEAD. Of local origin from Calderhead a *quoad sacra* parish in the parishes of Shotts and Cambusnethan, Lanarkshire. Agnes Calderhead appears in Edinburgh in 1640 (*Edinb. Marr.*). James Calderheid is recorded in Windie-edge in 1646 (*Inquis.*, 3086), and Alexander Calderhead was Burgher minister at Hawick in 1791.

CALDERWOOD. From the ancient lordship and manor of the same name in Lanarkshire. Isabele de Calrewode of the county of Lanark rendered homage in 1296 (*Bain*, II, p. 213). John de Calderwode witnessed an instrument of sasine in 1456 (*Panmure*, II, 238), Edward de Caldorwud had his pension of 20 marks and a croft of church land assigned to him at Cambuslang in 1458 (REG., 382), and Archibald Caldderwood was vicar of Cadder in 1509 (ibid., 489). David Calderwood (1575–1650), born probably at Dalkeith, was author of the *History of the Kirk of Scotland* (1678). Calderwoods were settled at Dalkeith in 1566 and were numerous in the parish in the seventeenth century (*Coltness collections*, p. 391). A pedigree of the Calderwoods of Polton from c. 1700 is given in the same work, p. 393. Caderwood 1650, Calderuod 1552, Calderuode 1554, Calderuood 1685, Calderwod 1504, Cawdirwood 1509.

CALDOW. Of local origin, perhaps from Caldow near Corsock, Dalbeattie. William Caldow in Nedir Mosplat, 1532 (*Rental*), James Caldow in Biggar, 1643 (*Lanark CR.*), Robert Caldow was an exiled Covenanter from Balmaghie, 1679 (*Hanna*, II, p. 254), William Caldow in Lochenbreck, 1675, and John Caldow there, 1774 (*Kirkcudbright*).

CALDWELL, COLDWELL. Of territorial origin from the lands of the name in Renfrewshire. The old family of the name appears to have ended in the direct line in an heiress in the fifteenth century (*Crawford*). In 1342 there is an entry of the fee of William de Caldwell (ER., I, p. 510). Robert Cauldwell was a merchant in the service of Sir John of Montgomery, 1405 (*Bain*, IV, 697). Hugh de Calde Wel, scutiferus, appears as charter witness, 1419 (LCD., p. 240), Watte Cawdwellis was witness in Dunfermline, 1495 (RD., 320), and Martyne Caldwell, a follower of the earl of Cassilis, was respited for murder, 1526 (RSS., I, 3386). James Caulduoll was presbyter and notary public in Glasgow, 1548 (LCD., p. 63), and Patrick Caldwools is recorded in Cockerhaugh, 1687 (*Peebles CR.*). The surname was common in Edinburgh in the seventeenth century in the forms Cauldwell, Caldwelles, and Cauldwells (*Edinb. Marr.*). In the Records of Invercauld the forms Guildwell and perhaps Camdell occur. John E. Caldwell, son of James Caldwell, soldier parson of the Revolution, was one of the founders of the American Bible Society. Calduall 1688, Caldwellis 1488, Calludwell 1503, Caulduall 1661, Caulduell 1551, Cawldwell 1498. An old local pronunciation of the name was Carwall.

CALGĀCUS. The leader of the Caledonians at the battle of Mons Graupius (commonly spelled Grampius) in A. D. 85, described by Tacitus as "the most distinguished for birth and valour among the chieftains" (*Agricola*, c. 29). The name is a derivative of *calg*, 'a sword,' and Prof. Watson I, (p. 7) gives the meaning of the name as 'Swordsman.' The name is more commonly, though erroneously, written Galgacus. "Historians have done him scant justice; he was of the type and race of Vercingetorix, the hero of Alesia, and, one might add, of Wallace; but though they are both commemorated by statues, he is not" (loc. cit.).

CALLAM, CALLUM. The surname of an old Glenbuchat family, an abbreviation of MALCOLM, q.v. William Callum in Glenbuchat was fined for reset of two outlawed Macgregors in 1636 (RPC., 2. ser. VI, p. 215). There are still people of the name in the parish. Challum 1741. The full form Maolchaluim was used till the seventeenth century.

CALLAN, CALLEN. From (MAC)CALLAN, q.v. Cath. Callan in Little Fandowie, parish of Little Dunkeld, 1653 (*Dunkeld*). Thomas Calland (with accretionary *d*) in Falsyde, parish of Robertoune, 1684, and Alexander Callan in Robertoun, 1687 (*Lanark CR.*). William Callan, elder, in Disdow, 1681, and John Calland of Brockloch, 1756 (*Kirkcudbright*). There is a Bute family named Callan, and some Callens live in Dunoon.

CALLANDER, CALLENDAR, CALLENDER. From the old lands or barony of Callander in Perthshire. Alwyn de Calyntyr witnessed a grant by Maldoueny, earl of Lennox to Stephen de Blantyr c. 1248 (*Levenax*, p. 36). The forename would suggest that the Calvntyrs were a branch of the family of the earls of Levenax. Richard Callender was constable of Stirling Castle in 1282. A later Alewyn de Calantir (Kalentyn) of the county of Stirling, and Sir John de Calentyr, knight, his father rendered homage in 1296 (*Bain*, II, p. 196, 211). From an inquisition of 1303–4 (*Bain*, II, 1457) Alewyn is shown to be the son and nearest 'haire' of Sir John, being twenty-eight years old in that year. John of Calenter witnessed Elphinston charters of c. 1340–41 (*Elphinstone*, I, p. 6; II, p. 221). John de Callender was one of the burgesses of Stirling who attacked the cruives and fishings of the abbot and convent of Cambuskenneth, c. 1366 (*Cambus.*, 55). George Kallender was admitted burgess of Glasgow in 1631 (*Burgesses*). In Scotland this name is undoubtedly of territorial origin and not derived from the occupation of calendering or glossing cloth (Fr. *calendrier*). Callenter 1536.

CALLENDER. See *under* CALLANDER.

CALLEY. A surname recorded in Fife. Probably from (Ma)cauley through an intermediate form. Patrick M'Kalla was apothecary in Cupar, 1688. See MACAULAY.

CALLUM. G. *Calum* for earlier GILLECALUM, q.v. (See also note on p. 831.)

CALMINOCH. Patrick Calminoch in Edraharvie, 1717, and five more of the name in the neighborhood (*Dunkeld*).

CALVERT. Perhaps from the occupation of 'calf herd,' a keeper of calves. An old name in Yorkshire, Calvehird in reign of Edward II (*Guppy*). Johannes Calfhyrd witnessed confirmation of Snadoun to the Abbey of Dryburgh, c. 1350 (*Dryburgh*, 232). William Calwart, notary public in Arbroath, 1467, and another William Cauart in the regality of Arbroath is mentioned, 1535 (RAA., II, 174, 828). John Calward and Thomas Calwart had sasine of lands in Fife, 1563 (ER., XIX, p. 512, 514). Robert Calvart or Cawart was rescued from justice, 1567 (RPC., I, p. 577). John Calwart was retoured heir of John Calwart, portioner of Kingisbarnis his father, 1601 (*Retours, Fife*, 105), and in 1611 another John Calvart was retoured heir of Thomas Calvart his father (ibid., 219). John Cailvairt was burgess of Anstruther, 1628 (ibid., 1404), and Lancelot Cavart appears in Birnok, parish of Lamington, 1669 (*Lanark CR.*).

CALVIE. John Calvy was bailie of Newburgh, 1544 (Laing, *Lindores Abbey*, p. 487), and John Calvie was retoured heir of John Calvie, burgess of Lundoris, his *proavus*, in a croft in the regality of Lundoris (*Retours, Fife*, 681). John Calve had a tack near Newburgh, 1560 (RMS., IV, 2326), and John Calvie was bailie of burgh of Newburghe, 1671 (*Inquis.*, 5474). Cf. CAVIE.

CALZIEMUCK. From lands of this name in Perthshire. In 1502 there is record of "the warde and mariage of Johne Calzemuk, sone and are to umquhile Huchoun Calzemuk, baron of the sammyn" (RSS., I, 790). In 1507 the local name is spelled Kilzemuk (ibid., 1527).

CAM. Perhaps from G. *cam*, 'crooked, oneeyed, or cross-eyed.' Hector Cam, a follower of Donald Gorme of Sleat, had remission in 1541 for his part in laying waste Trouterness in Skye and Kenlochew in Ross (RSS., II,

3943). Finlay Cam, miller at Derboch, 1633 (*Rec. Inv.*, II, p. 173).

CAMACHA. A tribe descended from the Stewarts of Garth, "are called Camachas or Crookshanks, from a bend or deformity in his leg, by which their ancestor was distinguished from others of his name" (*Stewart*, I, p. 27).

CAMBERNON. David de Cambernon and Sir John de Camburnon agree to serve Edward I in France or elsewhere, 1296 (*Bain*, II, p. 242). These two individuals were probably offshoots of the family of Champernwn or Champernowne of Devonshire, who were from the parish of Cambernon in the department of La Manche, Normandy. Is this the origin of Cameron (II)?

CAMBIE. Local. John Cambii was burgess of Dunfermline, 1316 (RD., I). Thomas Camby, servant to William Olyfaunt, had a safe conduct into England, 1425 (*Bain*, IV, 986). James Cambie, tailor in Edinburgh, 1661 (*Edinb. Marr.*).

CAMBO. From the lands of Cambo in the parish of Kingsbarns, Fife. Willelmus de Camboc witnessed the gift of fifteen acres of Balmulinauch (Balmerino) to the church of St. Andrews before 1225 (RPSA., p. 272). Johannes filius Willelmi de Camboc in Caral (Crail), 1288 (RAA., I, p. 270). Walter de Cambok or de Camehou (for Camebou) was warden of the county of Fife in 1294 (*Bain*, II, 701, 708). Johan de Cambhou of Fife, who rendered homage in 1296, was probably Sir John de Cambhou, one of the Scots prisoners summarily executed by the English at Newcastle in 1306. His seal bears a hare or rabbit at foot of tree, bird in top, and S' Johis de Camboc (ibid., p. 204, 485, 549). Thomas de Cambow had from Robert I a charter of the lands of Grosmanstoun in tenement of Crail, and William de Cambow a charter of the lands of Cambow (RMS., I, App. II, 636, 637), and Alexander de Camboch was rector of the church of Ochermukedy (Auchtermuchty) in 1358 (ibid., I, App. I, 141). Sir William de Kambov witnessed a charter by the bishop of St. Andrews in 1327 (LSC., 90).

CAMBUSNETHAN. Alan de Cambusnethane who held land in Edinburgh before 1468 (RD., p. 368, 369) derived his name from the village of Cambusnethan in Lanarkshire.

CAMELYN. Anselm de Camelyn who witnessed a charter by Adam de Morham, p. 1214 (RAA., I, p. 21) derived his name from Camelon in Stirlingshire.

CAMERON. This surname is of twofold origin, — Lowland and Highland. The name of the Camerons of the Lowlands is of territorial origin, from one of three places so named: (1) Cameron near Edinburgh; (2) Cameron in Lennox; (3) Cameron (of old, Camberone), a parish in Fife, the principal if not the only source of the Lowland surname. (1) The Highland clan name, like that of Campbell, is derived from a facial deformity, *cam-shròn*, Gaelic for 'wry' or 'hook nose.' The late Rev. Dr. Joass of Golspie stated that a hooked nose was a characteristic of the old Clan Cameron families (*Celt. Rev.*, I, p. 95). The middle Gaelic genitive form is found in Macvurich as *Camsroin*, while the MS. of 1467 has the form *Gillacamsroin*, and *Camronaich* is the adjectival form found in the Book of the Dean of Lismore. The general hereditary patronymic of the chiefs of the Clan is MacDhomhnuill Duibh, from their ancestor Domhnull Dubh or 'Black Donald.' By writers of the sixteenth and seventeenth centuries "this title is distorted into Macilduy, Macillony, Macgillonay, and a variety of other barbarous corruptions" (*Lays of the Deer Forest*, II, p. 476). "By pressing into the service people who lived south of the Grampians," says the late Dr. Macbain, "and who probably never even visited far Lochaber, historians have sought to give the Clan Cameron the much desired 'lang pedigree.' The first assured chief is Donald Du, c. 1411, from whom the Clan Chief takes his patronymic Dhomhnuill Duibh." The Clan Cameron consisted of three main branches, (1) Macmartins of Letterfinlay (for an account of them see TGSI., XVII, p. 31–45); (2) Macgillonies of Strone; and (3) Macsorlies of Glen-Nevis. Camern 1718, Camron (of Lochyell) 1628. (II) Of the Lowland Camerons the first in record is Adam de Kamerum who witnessed a charter of 'vnum rete super matricem aquam de Thei' (Tay) by David de Haya to the monks of Cupar between 1214–49 (SCM., II, p. 307). Hugh Cambrun, sheriff of Forfare, was one of the perambulators of the marches between the lands of Arbroath Abbey and Kinblethmont, 1219 (RAA., I, 228), and witnessed a charter by Randulf de Strathphetham c. 1222 (REB., II, 3). Johannes Cambron, a witness in Moray, 1233 (REM., 83), may be Sir John Cambrun who witnessed grant of part of the land of Carrecros c. 1239 (*Panmure*, I, p. cliv). Another (?) John Cambron, who witnessed a charter by Alan Hostiarius, 1261 (REA., II, 275), is probably John de Cambrun who is mentioned in 1264 as sheriff of Perth (ER., I, p. 3). David de Cambrun is mentioned in the chartulary of Lindores Abbey in 1266 (LAC., 115). David de Cam-

broun or de Cambernon, one of the Scots prisoners taken in Dunbar Castle, 1296, in the following year undertakes, along with Sir John de Camburnon or Caumbroun, another Scots prisoner of war, to serve in the king of England's army beyond the sea (*Bain*, II, 742, 873, 938, 942). John de Cambron swore fealty in 1291 and in 1296 rendered homage along with Sir John de Cambrun de Balligarnach (ibid., II, p. 124, 169). Sir John de Cambroun served on an inquest at Perth, 1305 (ibid., II, 1689), and John de Cambroun was sheriff there, 1333 (*Milne*, p. 26). Sir Robert Cambron was sheriff of Atholl, 1296 (*Bain*, II, 733). Robert de Caumberen de Ballegligernauch, who is mentioned in 1286 (RAA., I, p. 333) is probably Sir Robert Cambroun of Balnygrenagh of the county of Perth who rendered homage, 1296. His seal bears a shield with three bars within tracery, S' Ro . . . Cambrv' de Balligyrna...lit... (*Bain*, II, p. 178, 199, 548). Robert Cambroun de Balnely, one of the king's tenants in the county of Fife, rendered homage, 1296. His seal is similar to that of Sir Robert Cambroun mentioned above, a shield with three bars, S' Rob'ti Cambrun de Balnel' (*Bain*, II, p. 202, 539). Another (?) Robert Cambron de Balnely of the county of Forfare also rendered homage. His seal bears a heater shield, barry of eight, label of five points, S' Rob' Cambrvn d' Balnegh (*Bain*, II, p. 209, 533). Though classed among Forfarshire barons he is probably of Fife, namely of Balnello, Balulie, or Balmillie (*Angus*, 1861 ed., p. 292–293). Meg Cambrawno de Monymusk was charged with being a forestaller in Aberdeen, 1402 (CRA., p. 385). Johannes de Cameron, presbyter and canon of St. Andrews, who petitioned for office of prior of Lochleven, 1421 (Wyntoun, *Chronicle*, I, p. xxxiv), may be John Cameroun who was prepositus of the Collegiate Church of Linclowdane, 1425 (*Soltre*, p. 295). Another John Cameron appears as burgess of Aberdeen, 1434 (CRA., p. 5). John Camerown leased part of Cowpar Grange c. 1446 and 1453 (*Cupar Angus*, I, p. 124, 129). William Cameroun had a safe conduct to pass through England, 1448 (*Bain*, IV, 1207). James Cameron was a canon regular of Holyrood, 1454, and in following year Thomas Cameron is recorded as rector of the prebendal church of Gowan (Govan) (REG., p. 405). William Cameron, prior of the Abbey of St. Andrewe, had a safe conduct into England, 1470 (*Bain*, IV, 1390). Payment was made to Alan Camron, Scottish merchant, 1474 (ibid., 1412). Dane Camrowne witnessed an indenture in Glasgow, 1485 (LCD., p. 198), and John Camron was procurator in Lanark, 1498 (*Lanark*, p. 10). Robert Camproun held lands in

Perth, 1546 (*Rollok*, 12), and David Camroun, subprior of Blackfriars of Perth, 1543–1549, also appears as Camprone, Camrone, and Campbroun (*Milne*, 64, 68, 73, 79). The name was common in Edinburgh in the seventeenth century (*Edinb. Marr.*). Robert Calmeroune was merchant in Glasgow, 1605. Cambrin 1365, Cambrone 1351, Cameronne 1650, Cammeron 1532, Camphron 1574, Camrowne 1552, Camrun 1598. Cf. CAMBERNON.

CAMES. Radulfus Cames witnessed a charter by Earl David c. 1193–98 (LAC., 11), and about the same date the name is spelled as Kamais and Camais (ibid., 12, 14). The S. *Walteri Cames* is appended to an instrument in Melrose cartulary, c. 1240 (*Seals*, 152). Alison Cames is in Edinburgh, 1616 (*Edinb. Marr.*).

CAMMOCK. John Cammok held an aucht pairt of Corrouchane (Carruchan) in 1557 (M'Dowall, *Lincluden*, p. 111), and there were tenants of that name there as late as 1750. Fergus Cammok in Knockwalloche, 1630 (*Dumfries*). A John Cammok in Cumberland is recorded temp. Henry viii (*Dugdale*, iii, p. 273).

CAMOYS. Walter Camoys, clerk of Robert, bishop of Glasgow is probably the Wautier Cammays, clerk, of Roxburghshire, who rendered homage, 1296 (*Bain*, ii, p. 238, 208). Richard Cambays of Roxburghshire also rendered homage in the same year (ibid., p. 209). Sir Ralph de Camoys of Great Stukeley was one of the adherents of Simon de Montfort in the baron's war (Moore, *Lands*, p. 110). "Camoys, not known anything of before the reign of King John; an interpolation in Roll of Battle Abbey" (*Baring-Gould*, p. 214).

CAMP. Local, from residence at a camp or field. Nicol de Camp, vicaire del eglise de Grenlawe, rendered homage, 1296 (*Bain*, ii, p. 210).

CAMPANIA. De Campania is the Latin form of CHAMPAGNE, q.v. The name is apparently now extinct or disguised beyond recognition. Radulph de Campania witnessed a charter in favor of the Hospital of Soltre between 1214 and 1240 (*Soltre*, p. 18). About 1219 Robert de Campania witnessed a charter by John, earl of Huntingdon, in favor of the Abbey of Arbroath (RAA., i, 84), and about the same date he witnessed another charter by Earl John to Norman filius Malcolm de Lesslyn (CAB., p. 548). Sir Rauf de Campania in 1263 granted the church of Warg (= Borgue) to the canons of Dryburgh (*Dryburgh*, p. 22). Robert de Campania, son and heir of Nicholas

de Campania, remitted and quit claimed to Dervorgilla of Galloway all his lands in Borg held of her *in capite* in 1282 (*Bain*, ii, 212–214). Ralf de Campania served on an inquest made at Berwick in 1296 on lands in Dumfries and also rendered homage in the same year (*Bain*, ii, 730, 824). For later entries see under CHAMPAGNE.

CAMPBELL. G. *Caimbeul*, 'wry (or crooked) mouth,' a name probably applied to some early chief of the clan. Compare the name Gifford, i.e. 'fat cheeks,' and especially Cameron, Gaelic *Camshron*, 'wry nose.' There is also a parallel in the nickname of Earl Einar, Thorfinn's son, a great Norse earl of the Orkneys, who was known as 'wry-mouth,' in ON. *Rangmuðr* (*Ork. Saga*, c. xiv). Henderson suggests the epithet may have been applied by neighboring clans on account of moral if not physical traits (ZCP., iv, p. 270); and a poem by Iain Lom's son speaks of "luchd nam beul fiar" (Sinclair, *Gaelic bards*, iii). No explanation, however, is given why the second element lacks the normal aspiration. The name may simply mean "with arched lips." In a charter of 1447 in *The manuscript history of Craignish*, by Alex Campbell (printed in Scottish History Society, *Publications*, ix, Miscellany, iv) the name Campbell seems then to have been recognized as no more than a nickname. In this charter by the first Lord Campbell he is styled 'Duncan le Cambell,' where *le* is the *lie* so commonly used in Scottish charters to denote that what follows is in the vernacular, and may be translated "as we say," or "so called," or "known as," so this Duncan was Duncan "known as Cambell." The popular but erroneous opinion is that the name is of NF. origin, from de Campobello, 'of the beautiful plain,' but unfortunately for this derivation the earliest forms show no *de*, and the name is always in early records spelled Cambel or Cambell. If the name were of NF. origin the idiom of that language would require the form *de Bello Campo*. This form does occur in early English records and is the origin of the present day surnames Beauchamp and Beecham. Clan tradition represents the Campbells as being originally known as Clann Duibhne or O'Duine from a certain Diarmid O'Duine of Lochow. As the O'Duines, and therefore the Campbells also, were traditionally said to be of the Siol Diarmid, the Fingalian hero who slew the wild boar, it is to be noted that the father of Diarmid was named Fergus *Cerr-beoil*, 'wry-mouth.' This traditional descent is in part corroborated by a charter granted 15 March 1368 by David ii confirming to Archibald

CAMPBELL, *continued*

Campbell of Lochow, son of Colin, all donations, venditions, and impignorations of the lands of Craignish, Melford, Straquhir, and others, with all the liberties of the same as freely as Duncan M'Duine, progenitor of the same Archibald, did enjoy in the barony of Lochow or any other lands belonging to him (*Argyll charters,* p. 477). That O'Duine or Mac Duine was the true Gaelic name of the clan is also shown by Bishop Carswell's dedication of his Gaelic Prayer-Book (1567) to the earl of Argyll: *Do Ghiollaeasbuig Vanduibhne Iarrle Earragaoidheal* . . ., where *Vanduibhne* is *Ua Duine.* Skene says (CS., III, p. 338) that Duncan M'Duine lived in the reign of Alexander II, but there is no historical proof that he did live then. To this day there is no equivalent in Gaelic for "Clan Campbell," the term being always *Chlann O'Duibhne.* On the door-lintel of Carnassarie Castle near Kilmartin is an inscription in Gaelic which reads: *Dia leinn O'Duibhne,* "God with O'Duibhne," i.e. Campbells (Macgibbon and Ross, *Castellated and domestic architecture of Scotland,* IV, p. 321). "The period assigned for their appearance in Argyll [404 A.D.] by genealogical manufacturers merely excite a smile." The "astounding antiquity of the race of Campbell is vouched for by the bards and senachies," authorities "which may be of value in the West Highlands, but nowhere else . . . The 'beautiful' Eva, heiress of O'Dwin existed only in the imagination of some Highland senachie" (Maidment, *Pasquils,* p. 114). A manuscript pedigree of the Campbells of Argyll in the National Museum of Antiquities in Edinburgh traces them to King Arthur, and a MS. of 1550 goes one better by tracing them to "Enos mic Set mic Adaim mic De." The earliest individual of the name Campbell in record is Gillespic Cambel, who held from the Crown the lands of Menstrie and Sauchie in 1263 (ER., I, p. 24), and who is also witness to a charter by Alexander III erecting Newburgh in Fife into a burgh in favor of the monks of Lindores (LAC., 8). Nicholas Cambell witnessed a charter by James the Steward, 1294 (RMP., p. 96). Several Campbells rendered homage for their lands, 1296: Duncan Cambel del Illes, Sir Dovenal Cambel of the county of Dunbretan, Dougal Cambel, Arthur Cambel, and Duncan Cambel of the county of Perth (*Bain,* II, p. 200, 204, 211). Thomas Cambel was one of the Scottish prisoners taken at the capture of Dunbar in the same year (ibid., 742). About 1390 Duncan Campbell dominus de Gaunan witnessed a charter by Duncan, earl of Levenax (*Levenax,* p. 77), and in the same document John Cambel appears as tenant of the same earl in the lands of Drumfad and Kyrkmychel. This Duncan Campbell may have been the individual who first put the *p* in the name under the influence of the Norman theory, but in 1282 we have Nigellus filius Colini Campbell (*Cambus.,* 70) who eight years later is designed Sir Nicholas de Chambelle (*Sc. Peer.,* I, p. 322). Duncan Cambell, son and heir of Colin Cambell, dominus de Ergadie, attested the marches of Kyrknes and Louchor in 1395 (RPSA., p. 5). Sir Duncan Cambell or Cambelle of Lochow, one of the hostages for the ransom of James I in 1423 (Bain, IV, 981, 983), created Lord Campbell in 1445, was the first of the family who took the designation of Argyll in addition to, and sometimes in place of Lochow. He was ancestor of the ducal house of Argyll. From his younger son, Sir Colin Campbell, first of the House of Glenurchay (c. 1400–78), are descended the earls and marquesses of Breadalbane (creations 1677 and 1831–1885); and from the third son of Archibald, second earl of Argyll, who fell at Flodden in 1513, the earls of Cawdor (created 1827). Campbell has been carelessly used as one of the Anglicized forms of the name *Cath-mhaoil,* and this has led some people to imagine that Cathmhaoil is the old Gaelic form of the name. In the same way Cameron has been used as an Anglicizing of Ir. *O'Cumarain* or *O'Cumrain.* Cambal 1545, Cambale 1375, Cambele 1432, Cambelle 1424, Camble 1513, Camille 1451, Cammell 1473, Campbele 1481, Campbill 1617, Campble 1672 (and as late as 1785), Kambail and Kambayl 1448, Kambaile 1394. The Clan Campbell was divided into three septs each bearing a separate name: the Clan Dubhgal Craignish, Clan MacIver of Asknish, and Macarthur of Strachur. Probably they were septs that had separated from the main stem at an early period (Lord Archibald Campbell, *Records of Argyll,* p. 15). Campbell of Barcaldin and Baileveolan, *Sliochd Phara bhig.* Campbell of Cawdor, *Caimbeulaich bhoga Chaladair.* In the northeast for some mysterious reason a pig was sometimes called "Sandy Caumal." The name has become Kumpel in Holland.

CAMPION. Nicholas Champion of Berwick rendered homage, 1291 (RR.), and again as Nicol Campvon of Berwickshire, 1296 (*Bain,* II, p. 206). Simon Campion witnessed a protest dated 1500 (*Cawdor,* p. 106). ME.<OF. *champiun,* a champion, "originally one who took part in a contest, especially in single combat, to defend his own or another's honour, or to uphold a cause" (*Wylde*). The name occurs in English *Hundred Rolls,* 1273, as Campiun, Campyun, Campiown.

CAMPSIE. From the old lands of Campsie in the parish of the same name in Stirlingshire. Finlay de Campsy or de Camsi, son of Robert de Campsy witnessed several charters by Malcolm and Donald, earls of Lennox about the middle of the fourteenth century (*Levenax*, p. 24, 48, 49, 54, 62, 93, 95). About 1350 he had a charter of Balecorrach and other lands from Donald, earl of Lennox (ibid., p. 52). In 1382 mention is made of land of quondam John Campsy in Aberdeen (RMS., I, 682). Ione Campsy was a burgess of Inverness in 1449 (Mackintosh, *Inverness*, p. 117), and Alexander Campsy was declared innocent of part in the detention of King James III in Edinburgh Castle in 1482 (*The Lennox*, II, p. 123). Hugh of Camsy was tenant of lands of Camsy, 1471 (*Cupar-Angus*, I, p. 220). Patrick Campsy was tenant of Petlundy and Hiltoune alias Ballnaknok in 1504 (ER., XII, p. 661), and James Campsie was tenant of Priestfield in 1791 (*Dunblane*).

CANANAICH, NA. A sept of Macphersons in Skye are known by this name. See under MACCHANANAICH.

CANCH. A curtailed form of (MAC)CANCH, from MACANGUS, q.v.

CANDEL. From Candel in Dorset. Henry de Candela was juror on an inquest on the lands of Hopkelchoc in 1259 (APS., I, p. 98 *red*). Thomas de la Chaundel of Peeblesshire rendered homage in 1296. His seal bears a lion rampant to sinister, S' *Thom de Candela* (*Bain*, II, p. 199, 550). Martyn de Chaundel of Edinburghshire also rendered homage in the same year and had his lands restored to him (ibid., p. 206, 218). William de Candyl witnessed a charter by Stephen Flemyng, master of the Hospital of Soltre, 1426 (*Soltre*, p. 52). See also under ANSTRUTHER.

CANDELANE. Bridinus called Candelane, bailie of Roxburgh, c. 1338 (*Dryburgh*, p. 261). The name is a form of Gandelin or Gandelevn, and Prof. Skeat says (*The Tale of Gamelyn*, p. viii-ix) it can hardly be doubted that Gandeleyn in the ballad 'Robeyn and Gandelevn' is a corruption of Gamelyn, from *gamel-ing*, 'son of the old man.'

CANDLISH, CHANDLISH. From MACCANDLISH, q.v. Robert Smith Candlish (1806-73), a great ecclesiastic, was one of the leaders of the "non-intrusion" party, and one of the principal organizers of the Free Church of Scotland. In 1684 the name appears as Candleis and Canleis (*Parish*).

CANDOW. Probably local. There was a Candow Park in Aberdeenshire, c. 1450 (REA., I, p. 246). Hardly likely, I think, at least in every case, to be from G. *ceann dubh*, 'black head.' All the references are to Angus and neighborhood. Tazour Candow, tenant of Wester Drumme, 1474 (*Cupar-Angus*, I, p. 197). Robert Kendo or Kendow, merchant, Dundee, died 1606 (*Wedd.*, p. 113), James Kendow, heir of Robert Kendow, merchant burgess of Dundee, 1621 (*Inquis.*, 982). Robert Kendo, burgess of Dundee, 1622 (*Brechin*).

CANDVANE. A nickname, from G. *ceann bhàn*, 'white head.' The *d* is excrescent after *n*. Patrick Candvane was tenant of part of Camisnakist, Strathdee, in 1539 (ER., XVII, p. 656).

CANMORE. The name given to King Malcolm III (c. 1031-93). G. *Ceannmhór*, 'big headed' (Prof. Watson), "which does not warrant his head being represented abnormally large, as it usually is, in his imaginary portraits" (Dunbar, *Scottish kings*, p. 25).

CANNAN, CANNON. Probably from Ir. *O'Canáin*, descendant of *Canán* (diminutive of *Cano*, a wolf-cub). This surname is found in Kirkcudbrightshire and in part of Dumfriesshire. Fergus Acannane had sasine of lands in the parish of Balmakclellane, 1562 (ER., XIX, p. 499); and John Acannane was retoured heir in lands in the same parish, 1574 (*Retours, Kirkcudbright*, 33). James Acannane and Kilochie and James Acannane in Dumfriesshire were charged with tumult in church, 1607 (RPC., XIV, p. 520); and Gilbert Achannane of Murdochat was one of a number charged with abiding from the raid of the Isle, 1611 (*Trials*, III, p. 118). David Cannane was retoured heir in lands of Slawigdau alias vocatis the Fell, 1624; and James Cannane was recorded heir of James Cannan of Kilochie, 1643 (*Retours, Kirkcudbright*, 160, 223). John Cannan of Guffockland, 1684 (RPC., 3. ser. IX, p. 570). George Cannon (b. c. 1805 at Kirriemuir), general in the Turkish service, was mainly instrumental in producing the Russian discomfiture at Gingevo in 1854.

CANNONHEAD. Local. Cf. Channonbank and Channoniscroft in Berwick Retours. Payment to Ralph Cannonhead in Edenmouth, 1739 (*Stitchill*, p. 196).

CANOCH, CANNOCH. Alexander Canoch, pursuivant, 1529 (ALHT., v, p. 381). John Caneoch in Mylne of Argatie, 1666 (*Dunblane*). Also Caynoch (in Dunblane). Cf. CANONOCH.

132

CANOCHSON. G. *Cathanach* + Eng. *son.*
James Macdonald of Dunyveg and the Glens
was called Cannochsoun after his grandfather,
Sir John Macdonald, surnamed Cathanach,
chief of the Clan Ian Mhor of Islay and Kin-
tyre. Alexander Canochson was Alexander
MacConnell of Dunyveg and the Glens. James
Cannochtson assures the earl of Argyll, 1546
(RPC., I, p. 30). In 1531 Canochsoun and
Caynochsoun.

CANONOCH. Donald Canonoch in Earn,
parish of Port, 1683 *(Dunblane).* Duncan Caynoch in Easter Drummawhance, 1702 *(Muthill).* Nine of this name in seventeenth and
eighteenth centuries *(Dunblane).* An old spelling there is Cayneoch. Cf. CANOCH.

CANT. William Cant and Sithow Cant were
tenants under the Douglases in Telny in the
barony of Aberdoure, Fife, 1376 (RHM., I,
p. lxiv). A writer in the *Scottish antiquary*
(IV) says that the name occurs in the *Exchequer Rolls* in the fifteenth century, and that
the family, by trade dealers in cloth, supplied
the king's household. They were evidently,
he says, Flemings, and are mentioned in connection with Flanders. They obtained land at
Masterton near Dunfermline, which they descendants of the name still possess. A family
of the name early attained prominence in Edinburgh, where the name was common in the
fifteenth and sixteenth centuries. Adam Cant
was bailie there, 1403 (EBR., 2), and James
Cant was chosen dean of guild, 1413 (CDE.,
21). Alexander Cant was provost of Montrose,
1430 (REB., II, 33), and Patrick Kant or
Cant and Thomas Cant, Scottish merchants,
had safe conducts into England, 1426–50–
75 (*Bain,* IV, 990, 1230, 1433). Alan Cant
was rector of the Hospital of Soltre and chancellor of St. Andrews, 1461 (*Soltre,* p. 58).
Henry Cant represented Edinburgh in the
Scottish Parliament from 1473 to 1493 (*Sc.
Ant.,* VII, p. 79). A family of this name were
tenants on lands of the Abbey of Cupar-Angus
(*Cupar-Angus,* I, p. 147, 167). Lands were
leased to Richard Cante in 1485, and two
years later Alexander Cant appears as burgess
of Montrose (RAA., II, 260, 311). Dauyd
Kantt, 'chamurlane in the Kyngis owmuth'
(commission) is in record in Orkney, 1509
(REO., p. 82), and Robert Cant was tenant
under the bishop of Moray, 1565 (REM.,
p. 438). Mr. Andrew Kant was minister at
Pitsligo, 1634 (SCM., III, p. 120). Richard
Kant, the grandfather of Immanuel Kant the
philosopher, was an inn-keeper in Russ and Werden
at Heydekrug, was a native of Scotland
(Heintze-Cascorbi, *Die deutschen Familien
Namen,* 1925, p. 237).

CANTELOU. From Norman *de Cauntelowe*
(Lat. *de Cantulopo*), i.e., of Chantiloup in
Seine-et-Oise. John de Cantelou swore fealty
in 1291 and in 1296 Sir John de Cantelou,
probably the same person, rendered homage
(*Bain,* II, p. 196). Robert de Cauntelou was
constable of Lochmaben Castle in the English
service, 1298 (ibid., p. 270). About the same
time William de Cantilupe served in Scotland
under Edward I, and William de Cantilupe
was at the siege of Caerlaverock (*Stodart,* II,
p. 302).

CANTLEY, CANTLIE. From the Yorkshire
place of the name. Milne's etymology (*Place-
names of Aberdeenshire*) from Gaelic *chuitail*
corrupted into Whitehall and then translated
into Gaelic by *can,* white, and *tulach,* hill, is
nonsense. William Cantuli was admitted burgess of Aberdeen, 1452 (NSCM., I, p. 13), and
William Cantuly or Cantuli held land there
before 1497 (REA., I, pp. 338–339). Andrew
Cantly was admitted burgess in 1508 (NSCM.,
I, p. 43). Master John Cantly or Cantely
appears as archdeacon of St. Andrews, 1524
and 1541. Gilbert Cantlie, witness in Shetland, 1626 (OSS., I, 152). Cantlie 1612.

CANWELL. William Canwell was one of the
tenants of Inveryalder (Invergelder) in 1539
(ER., XVII, p. 659). From G. *Ceannmhaoil,*
'bald head.' Evidently a nickname.

CANYCHT, = 'merchant,' G. *ceannaiche.* Ewen
Canycht was one of the tenants of Balmacaan
at the time of the great raid of 1545 (Mackay,
Urquhart, p. 511). On p. 474 the name is
spelled *Candych.* Molcallum Candyth appears
in the Black Isle, 1500 (*Rose,* p. 169), and
William Candith was tenant in Dalmoloak,
Kynnarde, 1539 (ER., XVII, p. 671). Cf.
M'CANDYCHT.

CAOLISTEN. This is the Gaelicized form of
the surname Kelso in the island of Arran.

CAPLOCHY. Margarete de Caplachy, daughter of quondam Johannes de Caplochy had a
charter of the lands of Caplochy in Fife, resigned by David de Caplochy in 1380 (RMS.,
I, 644).

CAPPAR. Probably from the occupation of
'cap-maker.' The cappers or cap-makers were
a craft-guild in England. John Cappar witnessed an instrument of resignation in Brechin,
1511, and in 1530 mention is made of the
tenement of John Cappar in the same town
(REB., II, 165, 182).

CARA. An old Orcadian surname now probably extinct. From the lands of Cara in South
Ronaldsay. Mawnis (Magnus) Cawra was on

an assize at Kirkwall in 1514 and Cristiane Caro is mentioned in 1563 (REO., p. 87, 114).

CARALDUS. Karaldus or Kereldus who appears as judex or dempster of Angus between 1226 and 1251 (RAA., I, p. 94, 162, 263), was probably Kereld, father of the widow Forveleth, who made a grant of the land of Hachenkerach in Buthehulle (Bonhill) to the church of Glasgow, c. 1270 (REG., p. 145). Matheus Caraldus was one of the canons deputed to elect the bishop of Dunkeld, 1312 (Theiner, 398; Pap. Lett., II, p. 96). The dwelling of Keraldus received the name of Keraldistun, now Caraldston (in local pronunciation, Careston).

CARAN. May be from Carron, Stirlingshire, notwithstanding that the early spellings of the place name are Karun (c. 1200) and Caroun (1208). Wautier de Caran of Fife rendered homage, 1296 (Bain, II, p. 200). Laurence Carran one of an inquest in 1431 (Rose, p. 129). David Carrin, baker in Edinburgh, 1666 (Edinb. Marr.).

CARBARNS. Now a very rare surname. Ninian Carbarnes, cordiner, was burgess of Hamilton in 1625 (Campsie), Thomas Carnbarnis was reidare at Douglas, Lanarkshire, 1574 (RMR.), and Thomas Carbarnes, writer in Hamilton, was retoured heir of James Carbarnes in Hamilton, his father, in 1692 (Retours, Lanark, 399). The surname recorded in Edinburgh, 1940. From the small place called Carbarns near Wishaw, Lanarkshire.

CARBERRY. From the lands of Carberry in the parish of Inveresk, Midlothian. Johannes de Crebarrin filius Gilleberti de Crebarrin made two grants of lands from his territory of Crebarrin, c. 1230, and about the same period Adam filius Patricii de Crebarrin gifted four bovates of his land of Crebarrin to the Abbey of Dunfermelin (RD., p. 102–105). Alexander Crabarri, juror on forfeited estates in Lothian, 1312 (Bain, III, 245). William Carbery, M.A., petitioned for a canonry of Aberdeen, 1406 (Pap. Pet., I, p. 624).

CARD. Probably a variant of CAIRD, q.v. Richard Card, late The Royal Scots, died in Edinburgh, 1941. In 1531 the name Caird appears once as Card.

CARDEAN. From the place of the same name near Meigle, Perthshire. David Cardean died in Airlie in 1662 (Jervise, I, p. 162).

CARDLE. From MACARDLE, q.v.

CARDNEY. From the lands of Cardney near Dunkeld, Perthshire. The Cardenys or Cairdeneys, "an antient family in the county of Pearthshyre," now unknown and forgotten, were at one time extensive landowners in the shire. Mariote de Cardny, "one of King Robert the Second's Mistresses by whom he had many children" (Macfarlane, II, p. 302), had a charter from the king of the two Clyntres, etc., in the sheriffdom of Aberdeen in 1372 (RMS., I, 506). Robert de Cardini, brother of Mariota, was made bishop of Dunkeld and died at a great age in 1436, "et sepultus in Dunkell coram alteri Sancti Niniani" (Chr. Fort., p. 112). Andrew of Cardeny of that Ilk had confirmation of a charter of lands in the sheriffdom of Perth in 1416 (Athole, p. 706), Adam de Cardeny was admitted burgess of Aberdeen in 1443 (NSCM., I, p. 8), and Duncan de Cardny held land of Clathadre in Strathern in 1450 (Oliphants, p. 11). William Cardney first of Foss (or Fossach), married the heiress of Macnair of Foss, and both died in 1452. Duncan Cardeny succeeded, and he and his son, Andro Cardene, figured in a case before the Lords Auditors of Causes and Complaints in 1484. Andrew Cardein of Fos witnessed a retour of Neis Ramsay in the barony of Bamff in 1507 (Bamff, p. 45). He appears to have been the last of the Cardenys of Foss, as soon after the property appears in the possession of the Stewarts. Alexander Cardeny witnessed a charter of Robert Mersar of Inuerpefery in 1454 (LIM., 120), Patrick Cardeny was shepherd of the bishop of Dunkeld in 1511 (Rent. Dunk., p. 68), Sir Andrew Kardny, a Pope's knight, was presented to a chaplaincy in the Collegiate Church of Methven in 1516 (Methven, p. 40), Sir David Cardny is in record as burgess of Perth in 1546 (Dunblane), and Patrick Cardny of Clachladrun in the parish of Foulis in 1618 (ibid.). The name also appears in record as Cairney, Cardany, Carden, Cardenye (1507), Cardine, and Cardoni.

CARDNO. From Cardno in the parish of Fraserburgh, Aberdeenshire. A family of this name were long tenants in Bankhead of Inverallochy (AEI., p. 68).

CARDONESS. Nicholas de Kardes (or Karden, Kardeses, or Culenes) had a long dispute with the abbot of Dundrennan regarding certain lands in the diocese of Whithorn between 1240 and 1250 (ES., II, p. 565 n.). Johan de Kerdernesse and Michael de Cardelnes both of Dumfriesshire, who rendered homage in 1296 (Bain, II, p. 185, 211), derived their name from Cardoness in the parish of Anwoth, Kirkcudbrightshire. Bertram de Kerdones witnessed confirmation of the foundation charter of Sweetheart Abbey, 1359 (Genealogist, new series XVI, p. 218).

CARFRAE. A not very common surname of local origin, either from the lands of Carfrae in the parish of Garvald-Barra, East Lothian, or from the lands of Carfrae in Berwickshire. The name does not occur in any of the old charters or public records. Thomas Carfrae in Wyntoune frater german of quondam John Carfrae in Edmeistoune is recorded in 1635 and also Ninian Carfrae (*Inquis. Tut.*, 524, 525). John Carfrae was author of a volume of poems, *The Pilgrim of sorrow*, published in Edinburgh in 1848. The place name is Welsh *caer fre*, "hill fort."

CARGILL. From the lands of the same name now a parish in East Perthshire. Walter de Kergyl witnessed a quitclaim of the land of Drumkerauch in 1260 (RPSA., p. 346). Bernard de Kergylle received a gift of the lands of Leisington from William de Munificheth in 1283 (*Oliphants*, p. 3). Iwyn de Garghille of the county of Strivelyn and Wauter de Kergille of the county of Perth rendered homage in 1296 (*Bain*, II, p. 205, 212). Bernard de Kergylle had a confirmation charter of the lands of Culmelly and of Ald Culmelly in the barony of Cusseny (Cushnie) in 1374 (RMS., I, 453). William de Kergill granted a charter in favor of the Friars Preachers of Aberdeen in 1401 (*Friars*, 23), and Symon Cargyl held part of Kethyk in 1457 and was tenant of Park of Newbyggyn, 1473 (*Cupar-Angus*, I, p. 132, 185). In 1481 a letter of denisation was issued to John Kergyll, clerk, a Scotsman living in Kent (*Bain*, IV, 1471), and Master Bernard Gargyl resigned the vicarage of the church of Banff in 1497 (RAA., II, 373). Patrick Cargil was a charter witness in 1498 (ibid., II, 394), and Thomas Carnigill, who was appointed "maister of the gramar skwill" in Aberdeen in 1580, is mentioned again in 1585 as Cargill (SCM., II, p. 53, 64). Donald Cargill, a Covenanting preacher, was condemned to death for high treason in July 1681. In the fishing village of Auchmithie, Angus, in 1859, out of a population of 375 persons, 123 bore the surname of Cargill. Cargile 1545.

CARKERY. Margery de Carkery who rendered homage in March 1296 (*Bain*, II, 730) may have derived her name from Carcary near Farnell, Angus.

CARKETTLE. From Carkettle in Midlothian. In Blaeu's Atlas Karkettill is placed on the right bank of the Esk near Roslin. Prof. Watson says "the personal name Catell or Catel was not uncommon among the Britons" (*Watson* I, p. 369). He thinks Caerketton Hill, a summit of the Pentlands, is probably a corruption of the older form. Peter de Karynketil witnessed the sale of a tenement in Gouyrton

in 1317 (*Neubotle*, p. 306), William de Carketill was bailie of Edinburgh in 1403 (EBR., p. 2), Thomas of Carketylle of Scotland had a safe conduct into England in 1439 (*Bain*, IV, 1134), and Adam de Carketill, burgess of Edinburgh, witnessed an instrument of sasine in Glasgow in 1459 (REG., p. 412). Jonet Carkettle was married in 1490 (*Sc. Ant.*, III, p. 103). The surname was common around Edinburgh in the fifteenth and sixteenth centuries. Alexander Carketle was burgess of Edinburgh in 1517 (ALHT., V, p. 104), John Carketill was bailie there in 1536 (Colston, *Trades*, p. 103), Johnne Carkettill of Finglen had a precept of remission in the same year (RSS., II, 2033), and in 1567 he along with John and George, his sons were warded in the Castle of Edinburgh (RPC., I, p. 575). John Carkettle was tenant of Newbattle Abbey in 1563 (*Neubotle*, p. 330), John Carketill in Haddington gave allegiance to the king in 1567 (RPC., I, p. 558), and George Carkettill rendered to Exchequer the accounts of the custumar of Haddingtonshire in 1590 (ER., XXII, p. 93). Adam Carkettill of Nunland in Haddington is in record in 1602 (*Retours, Haddington*, 17), and in the same year Margaret Carkettill was retoured heir of George Carkettill of Eister Munkrig, her father (*Inquis.*, 97). Patrick Carkettill of Markill was heir of Patrick Carkettill of Markill in 1616 (*Retours, Linlithgow*, 93).

CARLAVEROCK. From Caerlaverock in Dumfriesshire. William de Carlaverock was received to the king of England's peace, 1331 (*Bain*, III, 724).

CARLAW, CARLO, CARLOW. Of local origin. James Carlaw in Maruinside (Muiravonside), 1690 (*Torphichen*).

CARLBOLLGY. Local. John of Carlbollgy, a voter in Monkland, 1519 (*Simon*, 45).

CARLE. An Aberdeen surname. John Carle admitted burgess there in 1479 (NSCM., I, p. 28), and Alexander Carll in Castlehill of Drimmor is mentioned 1492 (CAB., p. 382). John Carl or Carle occupied part of lands of Torsopy, Perthshire, 1543 (*Rollok*, 23). Merione Carle, freewoman, "to use the tred of huxter" in Aberdeen, 1640 (ROA., I, p. 232). From ME. *carl(e<OE. ceorl*, husbandman, peasant, 'churl.'

CARLISLE, CARLYLE. From Carlisle in Cumberland. The first of the name who appears in Scotland is Odard de Carlyle, who witnessed a charter by Uchtred, son of Fergus, lord of Galloway, to the Hospital of St. Peter at York between 1158–64 (*Bain*, I, p. 422). He appears to have also held the land of Hoddam as he is described as Odard de Hodelme (cf. HODDAM). Evdone de Karleolo or Eudo de Karliol, c. 1207, was witness to a charter by Eustace de Vescy of 20/- per annum out of the mill of Sprouiston to the Abbey of Kelso (*Kelso*, 208). Robert of Carlyle or of Hodelm, as he is chiefly styled, refers to himself in a plea dated 1199 as being 60 or more years of age (*Bain*, I, 280). His son, Adam of Carlyle, is the first of the name whose connection with Scotland is clearly established (ibid., 2660, and elsewhere in the volume). To Adam de Carleolo the lands of Kynemund were granted by William de Brus who died in 1215 (*Annandale*, I, p. 2; *Bain*, I, 606). Sir William de Carlyle, knight, had charter of a piece of land in Newby, after 1271 (*Annandale*, I, p. 8). Gilberd de [Karlel] of Dumfriesshire rendered homage, 1296. His seal bears a lion, rampant, and *S' Gilb' de Karliolo*(?) (*Bain*, II, p. 210, 531). Beatrice de Karlele of Dumfriesshire also rendered homage, 1296 (ibid., p. 203). William of Carlile was one of the conservators of the truce between Scotland and England, 1451 (*Bain*, IV, 1239). Thomas Carlyle (1795–1881) is perhaps the greatest of the name known. Acairhyll 1577, Cairlell 1635, Carleil 1368, Carleill 1631, Carlele 1592, Carlyll 1682, Carrell 1684.

CARLTON, CHARLTON. Local. There are places named Carleton in the shires of Kirkcudbright, Wigtown, and Ayr, and the surname is common in the north of England. Duncan de Carletone of Ayrshire rendered homage, 1296 (*Bain*, II, p. 205). Johannes de Carletoun had a charter from Robert I of the lands of Dalmakeran in Ayrshire, 1323 (*RMS.*, I, App. I, 63; *Annandale*, I, p. 132). Beatrix de Carletona was wife of William de Eychles, 1371 (*RMS.*, I, 383). In the sixteenth century the Charltons were one of 'the four principal graynes or clans that ruled in North Tyne' (*Guppy*, p. 309).

CARLYLE. See under CARLISLE.

CARMAIG. John Carmag (Carmage, or Karmag), tenant in Adhory, 1464–1476 (*Cupar-Angus*, I, p. 140, etc.). Alexander Caremaig was sheriff of Fife, 1520 (*SCBF.*, p. 174), and part of the lands of Kinclune were leassed to Thomas Carmage and his wife, 1526 (*RAA.*, II, 624). Grissell Carmaig or Carmok is recorded in Brodmuir, 1610 (*Brechin*), John Carmok in Broklhoss, parish of Cortachy, 1637 (ibid.), and George Carmag in Cowie, 1692 (*Inquis.*, 72, 82). Kermag and Kermaig 1525, Kermage 1517.

CARMENT. Local, perhaps from Carmount near Stonehaven, Kincardineshire. James Carment, schoolmaster at Enzie Chapel, died 1812 (Jervise, *Epitaphs*, I, p. 276).

CARMICHAEL. Of territorial origin from the lands and barony of Carmichael in the parish of the same name, Lanarkshire. The lands were long in possession of the family the first of whom in record appears to have been Robert de Carmitely (evidently an error in spelling) who resigned all claim to the patronage of the church of Glegern (now Cleghorn), c. 1220, and about 1250 had a right of lordship in the land of Cleghorn (*Dryburgh*, p. 171). William de Creimechel witnessed a charter by Nessus de Lundors c. 1225 (*LSC.*, p. 51). William de Carmichael is mentioned in a charter of the lands of Poufeigh c. 1350 (*OPS.*, I, p. 151), and Sir John de Carmychell had a charter of the lands of Carmychell between 1374 and 1384 from William, earl of Douglas (*Douglas book*, III, p. 398). John Carmichael of that Ilk is found on an inquest in 1406 (*Memorie of the Somervilles*, I, p. 152), and William de Carmychale, *dominus ejusdem*, appears as witness to a charter granting Thomas de Wardelaw a tenement in St. Andrews, 1410 (*RPSA.*, p. 427). William de Carmychel *de eodem* was one of an inquest at Lanark 1432 (*RAA.*, II, 65), George Carmichael, 'thesaurer' of Glasgow in 1475, was elected bishop late in 1482, but died the following year without having been confirmed (*Dowden*, p. 330), John of Carmichel was an Edinburgh councillor in 1518 (*EBR.*, p. 174), and John Carmychall was younger of that Ilk, 1575 (*RHM.*, I, 83). John Kirkmichael or Carmichael, who escaped the carnage of Verneuil (1424), was at the death of Guy de Pruneley, bishop of Orleans, appointed by the French king to that see in recognition of the great services rendered by Scots in France (Forbes-Leith, *Scots men-at-arms in France*, I, p. 35). He is known in French ecclesiastical history as Jean de St. Michel. In 1429 he founded in his cathedral church a *Messe écossaise*, still maintained, for his countrymen slain at Verneuil, and in the same year he was one of the officiating prelates at the *sacre* of Charles VII at Rheims (*SHSM.*, II, p. 55). The surname is still a common one in Lanarkshire. Carmechele 1517, Carmichaill 1672, Carmichel 1470, Carmichill 1494, Carmigell 1646, Carmighell 1590, Cayrmichell and Cavrmichel 1474, Carmychel 1485, Kermvchell 1497. Carmichael is used as a 'translation' or equivalent of Macgillemichael which "used to be common in Lismore. But many of the tribe have assumed Carmichael in its place — probably under the impression that they were accommodating themselves to a higher civilisation" (*HP.*, IV, p. 176).

CARMONT. Local. There is a Cairnmount in Roxburghshire. The surname is recorded in the Stewartry (five of the name in *Kirkcudbright*). Robert Cairmount in Urr, 1624 and other three recorded in the neighborhood *(Dumfries)*. Samuel Cairmunt who was a member of Scots parliament for Kirkcudbright, 1681 (*Hanna*, II, p. 485), may be Samuel Carmount in Kirkcudbright who signed the Test, 1684 (RPC., 3. ser. x, p. 248), Andrew Carmont, stockmaster there, 1688 *(Kirkcudbright)*, and William Cairmont, merchant in Dumfries, 1689 (RPC., 3. ser. xiv, p. 690).

CARMUIR. From Carmure (Easter and Wester), near Falkirk, Stirlingshire. Alexander de Carmur was juror on assize at Liston in 1459 (*Edmonstone*, p. 80). James Carmure was chaplain in 1518 (EBR., p. 174), and another James Carmure witnessed a notarial instrument of 1530 (SCM., II, p. 185). A third James Carmure was indweller in Edinburgh in 1662 (*Just. Rec.*, I, p. 50).

CARMYLLIE. Of local origin from Carmyllie in Angus. Robert Carmylie, vicar of Ruthwenis, was accused of perjury in 1579 (Wilson, *Memorials of Edinburgh*, 1891, II, p. 298).

CARNABAY. A surname found in Caithness. From Carnaby in the East Riding of Yorkshire.

CARNACHAN, CARNOCHAN, CARNAHAN. Ir. *O'Cearnachain*, 'descendant of Cearnachan,' a diminutive of *cearnach*, 'victorious.' The first form is still a common surname in Galloway. John Acarnechan in Portinkylle a follower of Campbell of Lundy, 1541 (RSS., II, 3666). Six of the name are recorded in Kirkcudbright in seventeenth and eighteenth centuries (*Kirkcudbright*). See MACCARNOCHAN.

CARNBEE. From Carnbee near Pittenweem, Fife. Ricardus de Karnebehyn witnessed gift of lands of Blarkerocch to the church of S. Andrew in first half of thirteenth century (RPSA., p. 277). John Carnbee was admitted burgess of Aberdeen, 1411 (NSCM., I, p. 4), and payment was made in 1528 to "ane honest man callit Stene of Carinbe dowlland in Lowdeane" (SBR., p. 32). The name appears as Carnebe (1553) and Carnebie (1568) in the Glasgow Protocol books.

CARNDUFF. A rare surname of local origin from the lands of Carnduff in the old lordship of Avondale. John Cornduf or Carnduff witnessed charters by Andrew, lord of Avandale in 1524 and 1526 (RMS., III, 1114, 1156). Several individuals of this name are recorded in the Commissariot Record of Glasgow between 1618 and 1688, and William Carneduff

is mentioned in the Commissariot Record of Hamilton in 1671. The name is also found in Edinburgh in 1681 as Cairnduff *(Edinb. Marr.)*. John Carnduff, feuar in Straven (Strathaven), 1684 (RPC., 3. ser. x, p. 76). This name has been given by Scots settlers to a town in southeastern Saskatchewan.

CARNE. James Carne had precept of remission for 'forthocht fellony,' 1493 (RSS., I, 29). Local, probably from one or other of the places so named in England (Cornwall).

CARNEGIE, CARNEGY. Of territorial origin from the old barony of the same name in the parish of Carmyllie, Angus. The old name of the Carnegies of Southesk was DE BALINHARD, q.v. They acquired the lands of Carnegie about 1340 and assumed their surname from them (*Angus*, I, p. 86). Duthac de Carnegy witnessed a deed of sale in Aberdeen, 1383 (REA., II, p. 284), and John Carnegy *de eodem* witnessed a transumpt of 1450 (REB., I, 141). James Carnegie, fifth earl of Southesk, who was present in raising of the "Standard on the Braes of Mar," 1715, was the hero of the song "The Piper o' Dundee," and *Jacobite relics* says Carnegie of Phinhaven was "celebrated as the best flier from the field of Sheriffmuir." Andrew Carnegie (1837–1919), the Scottish-American multi-millionaire, is perhaps the best known of the name. Carnage 1489, Carnagie 1565, Carnagy 1567, Carneaggie 1650, Carneggie 1652, Carnegi 1606, Carnigy 1655, Kernagy 1450; Carinnegi, Carrinegy, Carryneggi.

CARNEIL. From the lands of Carneil near Dunfermline, Fife. Robert de la Kerneille witnessed a charter by William de Haya of the land of Petmulyn in 1171 (RPSA., p. 313). As R de Kerneil he witnessed the charter of the lands of Lesslyn (Leslie) to Malcolm filius Bartholf, c. 1171–99 (CAB., p. 547), and he is probably the Robert de Kernelle who witnessed the grants of Camsv and Altermunin to the Abbey of Kelso c. 1200 (*Kelso*, 226). William de Kerneil was parson of Dunde a. 1214, and Roger de Kerneil was a charter witness about the same date (REB., II, 261; *Panmure*, II, p. 127; SCM., II, p. 305):

CARNEQUHEN. Local. There is a Carnwhin (wh = quh) near Girvan, Ayrshire, and a Carnquhin in Kincardine Retours. In February 1497–98 James, earl of Buchane raised an action against Wilyeame Carnyquhin for "the wrangus occupacione and manuring of the landis of Saltcottis . . . in the schirefdome of Abirdene, pertenyng to the sade James and occupyit be the sade Wilyeame without tak of him be the space of xx yeris . . . and for the wrangus uptaking and withhalding fra him of the malis and proffittis of the sadis landis" (ALC., p. 117). A payment was made to William Carnoquhen, 1552 (EBR., p. 274). William Cairnoquhen and John Cairnoquhen were recorded as masters of families in parish of Buittle, 1684 (RPC., 3. ser. IX, p. 568).

CARNEY, CARNIE, CARNY. Surnames current in the shires of Aberdeen and Banff. Of local origin from Carnie, near Skene, Aberdeenshire. Philip Carny appears in Karale, 1332 (ER., I, p. 414). Oliver Carnie from Turriff served in the first Great War (*Turriff*).

CARNIGILL. Probably from some place of the name in Aberdeenshire. John Carngyll was procurator for Alexander Lyell, 1557, and Thomas Carnegill appears in same record (RSCA., I, p. 150, 152).

CARNOCHAN. Of local origin. There is a Carnochan near Patna, Ayrshire. William Carnochan, burgess of Kirkcudbright, 1667 (*Kirkcudbright*), and another William Carnochin is recorded as resident in the parish of Senneck, 1684 (RPC., 3. ser. IX, p. 569). Kairnochane 1621.

CARNOCK. Walter de Carnoc granted to the monks of Kelso the churches of Trauerflet (Trailflat) and Dumgrey, and his grant was confirmed by William the Lion (*Kelso*, 341). Walter de Carnoc was succeeded by his son Thomas, and he by his son Robert de Carnoc, who in 1266 confirmed the gift of these churches to Kelso (ibid., 342). Thomas de Carnocus, cancellarius, attests a charter by David II, 1341 (*Scon*, p. 111). John Carnuk was a tenant under the bishop of Aberdeen, 1511 (REA., I, p. 368).

CARNWATH. A Lanarkshire surname, either from the old manor of Carnwath or from the village of the same name. Richard Carnewath was writer in Edinburgh in 1522 (*Aboyne*, p. 55), and Thomas Carnewatht witnessed a precept of sasine at Scone in 1544 (*Scon*, p. 207). Carneweth 1504.

CARPENTER. From the occupation of carpenter or joiner. William the Carpenter (*carpentarius*) appears to have been a person of prominence in the latter half of the twelfth century, as he appears as witness to a charter by Malcolm IV to Radulf Frebern in 1153 (SCM., v, p. 242), and to another charter by the same king in favor of the Abbey of Scone c. 1160 (*Scon*, 10). He also witnessed, c. 1171–77, King William's confirmation of the foundation charter of Holyrood (LSC., p. 24). Douenaldus Carpentar witnessed charters by Maldouen, earl of Levenax c. 1250–70 (*Levenax*, p. 20, 98). Adam dictus Carpentarius held Haldhingleston (Auld Inglistoun) c. 1260, and about the same period Laurence Carpentarius is also mentioned (RMP., p. 53, 58, 59). This surname has not flourished in Scotland, its place being taken by the native 'wright,' distinctly a worker in wood.

CARPHIN. Of local origin from Carphin in the parish of Creich, Fife. Recorded in Edinburgh 1942.

CARR. A variant of KER, q.v. In the list of Border chiefs who took 'assurance' of Protector Somerset at Kelso, 1547, the names of all the Border Kers are spelled Car (Patten, *Expidicion into Scotlande*, 1548, in Russell, *Haigs of Bemersyde*, p. 465). John Carre of Cavers appears in 1766, and Alexander Allan Carr published a *History of Coldingham Priory*, 1836. Cuthbert Carre, a Scot, rector of the parish church of Mychyng in Sussex, received letters of denisation in England, 1480 (*Bain*, IV, 1465). A group of families of this name appear in Central Scotland from fifteenth to seventeenth century. Robertus Car, witness in Scon, 1491 (*Scon*, p. 199), James Carr in Carkarie, 1582, and ten more recorded in Brechin and neighborhood between 1576 and 1800 (*Brechin*). Gilbert Care in Laichbert (Larbert), 1608, and four more in the record between 1607 and 1800 (*Stirling*).

CARRACH. Malis Carrach had a grant of the lands of Blarechos in Strathblane, 1398 (*Levenax*). Alexander Macdonald of Keppoch is known in Gaelic legend as Alasdair Carrach, 'Alexander the crafty' (*Mackay*, p. 48). Carrach is also the Gaelicized form of Kerr in Arran (= 'one of the Kerrs').

CARRAILL. William Carreill, reidare at Edrem, 1574 (RMR.). Mr. Matthew Carraill, minister at Edrem and clerk to Presbytery of Chirnsyd, 1642 (*Home*, 219). An old spelling of CRAIL, q.v.

CARRICK. From the district of that name in Ayrshire. Duncan Karryc witnessed a charter by Maldowen, earl of Lennox, a. 1224 (RMP., p. 217). Sir Rolland de Karryk was juror on inquest at Gerwan (Girvan) in 1260 on the marriage contracted between Hector de Carric, knight, son of Sir Hector, and Samuel Mackan's daughter (*Bain*, I, 2674). Mestre Duncan de Carrike of county of Berewyke rendered homage, 1296 (ibid., II, p. 206). Mariota, wife of Nigel de Karrik, daughter of quondam

CARRICK, *continued*

Robert de Rosiue (Rossyth in Fife) sold a third part of the lands of Maisterton to the monks of Newbattle, 1320 (*Neubotle*, p. 41). Her son Robert is mentioned in same charter, and in the following one describes himself as Robertus Nigelli de Karrik (ibid., p. 43). John of Carryk, secretary of David II was appointed one of his envoys to the king of England, 1360 (*Bain*, IV, 59), and may be John de Carrik, canon of Glasgow, 1372 (*Irvine*, I, p. 12). Thomas of Carric, bailie of Are, 1429 (*Ayr*, p. 83). Thomas Carrig to be cautioner for Dame Margaret Howme, 1554 (CMN., 69), and in same year a tenement was granted in feu farm to Beatrix Carrik in Glasgow (*Protocols*, I). William Carrick in Arnmoir, parish of Kippen, 1606 (*Dunblane*), and Agnes Carrick in Unthank, parish of Coulter, 1665 (*Lanark CR.*). Robert Carrick, banker in Glasgow, c. 1820.

CARRIDEN. From the old barony of Carriden in the parish of the same name in West Lothian. Godwin de Careden and Roger de Careden witnessed the gift of a tithe of land of Oggelfast (now Ogleface) to the monks of Holyrood in the reign of William the Lion (LSC., p. 35).

CARRIE. An abbreviated form of MACHARRIE, a Galloway name, q.v.

CARRINGTON. From the lands of Carrington in East Lothian. Wautier de Keringtone, parson of the church of Dunnotre, rendered homage in 1296 (*Bain*, II, p. 214). William Keringtoun appears in 1506 as "unus occupatorum carbofodinarum de Gilmertoun" (*Soltre*, p. 78), and George Keringtoun was retoured heir of Andrew Keringtoun in Nungait, his father, in 1602 (*Retours, Haddington*, 18). Cristian Keringtoune alias *Likkit* in Prestonpans was accused of witchcraft, 1590 (*Trials*, I, p. 246).

CARROCH. Probably from the small place named Carroch near Kirriemuir in Angus. Isobel Carroch in Reddine in 1656 (*Stirling*), and Helen Carrioch in Braco, parish of Muthill, 1663 (*Dunblane*).

CARROL, CARROLL. From the Irish personal name *Cearbhall*. Duncan Carroll in Little Fandowie, 1653 (*Dunblane*). William Carrol and George Carrol served in the first Great War (*Turriff*).

CARRON. From Carron in the parish of Larbert, Stirlingshire. David Carron is recorded at the Pow of Allowey (Alloa) in 1643 (*Stir-*

ling), and William Carroun at the same place in 1644 (*Inquis. Tut.*, 685). John Carrone was burgess of Dundee, 1645 (*Brechin*), and James Carron, burgess of Edinburgh, 1684 (*Inquis.*, 6570).

CARRUBER, CARRUBBER. From the lands of Carriber in West Lothian. Thomas de Caribre, king's tenant in the county of Linlescu, and Phelippe de Carriber of the same county, rendered homage in 1296 (*Bain*, II, p. 201, 205). Andrew de Cariber witnessed a notarial instrument in 1440 (*Cambus.*, 168). William Carribris, a Scots ship owner, who had a safe conduct into England in 1438, may be the William Careberis (Kareberis, Carrebris, Carribris, Carribrys, Carribirs, or Carybbrys), Scottish merchant, who received several safe-conducts into England between 1446 and 1468 (*Bain*, IV, 1110, 1187, 1230, etc.). William de Carribris was bailie of Edinburgh in 1455 (*Cambus.*, 96), and George Carribers was a burgess of Glasgow in 1483 (REG., 394). Joannes Carribber was retoured heir of Robert Carribber *de eodem* in the lands of Carribber in 1574 (*Retours, Linlithgow*, 8). Margaret Caribdis in Edinburgh, 1638 (*Edinb. Marr.*).

CARRUM. From Carham-on-Tweed (c. 1050 Carrum, 1251 Karram). Ranulph de Carrum witnessed a charter by Roger Maule and Godit, his spouse, to the church of S. Cuthbert of Carrum, c. 1200 (SHSM., IV, p. 310).

CARRUTH, CARUTH, CURRUTH. Of local origin from the lands of Carruth in the parish of Kilmalcolm (in 1359 Carreth), Renfrewshire. The surname is mainly confined to the shire. Alexander Corruich(? *ch* error for *th*) witness in Renfrewshire, 1575 (*Laing*, 916). Jean Carruth was charged with attending conventicles in Dalry, 1686 (RPC., 3. ser. XII, p. 355). Several persons named Corruith were burgesses of Dumbarton in seventeenth century (RDB.).

CARRUTHERS. From the lands of Carruthers in the parish of Middlebie, Dumfriesshire, in local speech pronounced Cridders. Henderson (N. I., p. 202) renders the place name "fort of Rydderch, the King Roderc of Adamnan," but Watson more cautiously says "the second part is probably a personal name" (I, p. 368). The family of Carruthers were in the thirteenth century stewards of Annandale under the Bruces. Simon Carruthers, parson of Middlebie, swore fealty to Edward I (HMC., 6. Rep., App., p. 709). About 1320 Thomas, son of John de Carutherys received a charter of the whole lands of Musfald and Appil-tretwayt with pertinents (RMS., I, 92). Sir Nigel de Karrutheris, a cleric, who obtained the rectory of Rivel (Ruthwell) in 1330 (*Pap. Lett.*, II, p. 307) is mentioned again in 1337 and 1351 as Nigel de Carrothorys, canon of Glasgow (ibid., p. 540; RMP., p. 140). In 1340 we find Sir Nigel de Karuther high chamberlain to the Regent (ER., I, p. 458, 462), and in 1344, as Sir Nigel de Carother, he is named as chancellor of Robert Steward of Scotland (*Laing*, 39). A charter was granted at Moysfald in 1361 in favor of John de Carotheris (HMC., 6. Rep., App., p. 710), Simon de Carrutheris witnessed a deed in 1394 (RMP., p. 108), and John of Carrutheris was one of the 'borowis' for the earl of Douglas's bounds of the West March in 1398 (*Bain*, IV, 512). Sym of Carruthers was commissioner for the West Marches in 1429 (ibid., 404), and John Carruthers was keeper of Louchmabane Castle in 1446 (ER., V, p. 284, 521). Alexander Caruderis had sasine of the lands of Glengapp and Gerartgill (Garragill) in 1468 (PSAS., XXIII, p. 38). William de Carrutheris, presbyter of Glasgow in 1460 is probably Schyr Wylyame of Carruderys, persoun of Daltone (LCD., p. 198, 254). The Carruthers were included in the roll of unruly clans in the West Marches in 1587 (APS., III, p. 466). Carrotheris 1361, Carruthris 1375, Carruderes 1572, Carruderis 1537, Carrothvris (in Wyntoun), Carrutheriis 1330, Carruthirs 1398, Carrutheres 1628, Carruthoris 1405, Caruderis 1468, Caruders 1673, Carutheris 1370, Carutherys a. 1329, Caruthris 1370, Caruyeris 1452.

CARSCALLAN. Local. Andrew Carscallan in Mains of Lesmahago, 1638, and one other of the name (*Lanark CR.*).

CARSE, CARSS. Baldricus de Cars held a land in Perth in the reign of Alexander II (*Scon*, p. 57), and Alexander Cars leased part of Kethik in 1478 (*Cupar-Angus*, I, p. 226). James Cars was one of an inquest at Coldingham, 1561 (*Coldingham*, App. v.), and Bessie Kerse is recorded in Edinburgh, 1653 (*Edinb. Marr.*). Patrick Carse in Skaithmure, 1655 (*Lauder*), Richard Kerse in Falconhous, 1656 (*Retours, Linlithgow*, 187), John Carse in Balmure of Plaine, 1661 (*Stirling*), Marcus Carss of Cockpen, 1693 (*Inquis.*, 7344), and John Carss in Riddene, Lanarkshire, 1711 (*Minutes*, p. 115).

CARSLAW. Local. Payment was made in 1548 to William Kerslaw "for the keping of the knok in the yeir" (SBR., p. 53). John Carslaw

in Dunfermline, 1589 (*Dunfermline*), and John Carslaw in Graham, Saltcottis, parish of Falkirk, 1635 (*Stirling*).

CARSON, CORSAN, CORSON. An ancient family in Galloway which ended in the direct line in the reign of James IV. Corsans were provosts of Dumfries for several generations and were also prominent in local affairs of Kirkcudbrightshire. No value need be attached to the tradition of descent from an Italian named Corsini reputed to have been brought to Scotland by Dervorgilla to superintend the building of Sweetheart Abbey. Everything points to native origin. Maurice Acarson, bailiff of Isle of Man, appointed by King Alexander, is the same person as Mauricius Okarefair (*Chron. Lanercost*, p. 64). Sir Robert de Acarson or de Carsan, a cleric, witnessed a charter to Holm Cultram c. 1276 (*Holm Cultram*, p. 58; *Edgar*, p. 198), and may be Robert de Carsan, parson of moiety of the church of Kircandres, Dumfriesshire, who rendered homage, 1296 (*Bain*, II, p. 212). Laughlan, son of Laughlan de Carsan and Dovenald, son of Thomas de Carsan were among some Galloway hostages lodged in Carlisle (*Bain*, II, p. 301). In 1305 John Acarson and others took the castle of Dumfries from its garrison. Morice Acrassane and Gilbert were jurors on an inquisition at Drumfrese, 1367 (RHM., II, p. 64), and Thomas Acarsane was 'minstrall regis,' 1377 (ER., II, p. 586). Thomas a Carsan, deputy to the custumar of Linlithgow, 1373 (ibid., p. 402), had charter of a tenement in Lynlithcu from Robert II, 1374 (RMS., I, 561). Donald Akersan petitioned the Pope in 1394 for a benefice in the gift of the abbot and convent of Holyrood (*Pap. Pet.*, I, p. 619), Michael Acarsan, canon of St. Rynyon (Ninian), had a safe conduct to travel in England, 1445 (*Bain*, IV, 1180), and Patrick Corsen witnessed a notarial instrument in Dumfries, 1453 (*Edgar*, p. 225). Andro Corsane had a respite for his part in 'the birnyn of the hous and place of Dunskay,' 1503 (RSS., I, 933), and Egidia Akersane was wife of Andrew Fullarton of Carntoun, 1531 (ALHT., V, p. 398). Adam Corsan, merchant burgess of Dumfries, is mentioned in 1665 (*Retours, Dumfries*, 252). Kit Carson, the Indian scout, may have been of Scots origin. Joseph Carson, early shipping merchant of Philadelphia, and an earnest supporter of the American Revolution, was born in Scotland. A Kersane 1414, Carsen 1662, Carssane 1645, Kersane 1476.

CARSS. See under CARSE.

CARSTAIRS. From the manor or barony of the same name in the parish of Carstairs (= 1170 Casteltarres, 'Castle of Tarres'). Thomas, son of Adam de Castrotharis was one of an inquest on the land of Pardevinan in Lanark, c. 1259 (APS., I, p. 88 after preface; *Bain*, I, 2175). Petrus de Castellstaris was witness in Abyrbrothok, 1351 (RAA., I, p. 335). Alexander de Castiltarris was vicar of the parish church of Muktone, 1450 (REB., I, 133). Alexander de Castiltaris witnessed an instrument of sasine of the superiority of Pollok, 1486 (*Pollok*, I, p. 192). Thomas Castaris was vicar of Quhalislaw, 1536 (ibid., I, p. 272). The name appears as Kerstairs and Kilstairs in the Brodie *Diaries* (Spalding Club ed.), p. 151, 255. Catrina Kerstaris was wife of William Mane in Perth, 1551 (*Rollok*, 94). Carstaris 1583, Castilcaris 1443; Carstairis, Castares, Crastaris.

CARSWELL. A family of Carsewells, who derived their name from Carsewell in the parish of Neilston, are said to have been settled in Renfrewshire for centuries, but they seldom appear in the public records. (2) There is also a Carswell (in 15. cent., Creswell or Carswell) in the barony of Carnwath, Lanarkshire, and (3) there was a tenement of the same name in the barony of Hassendean, Roxburghshire. Alexander de Cressewell witnessed a charter by Roland of Galloway, son of Vchtred, c. 1200 (*Kelso*, 254). Willelmus de Cressewell was chancellor of Moray, c. 1281–98 (*Grant*, III, p. 7), and Robert de Cressewelle was one of the Scots prisoners of war taken at Dunbar Castle in 1296 (*Bain*, II, 742). Symon de Cresseville of the county of Roxburgh, and David de Cressewelle of Lanarkshire rendered homage in 1296. The seal of the former bears an eight-rayed figure and S' Symonis d' Cresvile (*Bain*, II, p. 199, 212, 550). William de Creswille witnessed a charter by Thomas de Stradeqwhyn in the Mearns in 1351 (RAA., II, 25), and another (?) William Kersseuyle or Cresseuvle had confirmation of a charter of lands in the barony of Roberton in the sheriffdom of Lanark, 1373 (RMS., I, 517). Johannes de Kerswell witnessed a notarial instrument in 1413 (*Pollok*, I, p. 146). In 1561 "ane chenyie of gold" was redeemed in Stirling "for Master Johne Carswele, persone of Kilmertyne" (SBR., p. 79), afterwards the first protestant bishop of the Isles, and translator of the Book of Common Order into Gaelic in 1567. Malcolm Carsuell, constable of Craginche, appears in record in 1572 (OPS., II, p. 100). Catherine Carswell's *Life of Robert Burns* (1931) caused much fluttering in the dovecotes of the poet's admirers. Carsell 1692, Kersewell 1549.

CARTER. From the occupation, a 'carter,' driver of a cart; the headman in the stables on a farm. James Cartare witness in Edinburgh, 1439 (CDE., p. 65). Hob Carter was a tenant on lands of the Abbey of Kelso, 1567 (*Kelso*, p. 527). The Carter brothers (Robert, Peter, and Walter), Scots, were publishers and booksellers in New York in latter half of nineteenth century.

CARVEL. From Carville in Normandy. Roger de la Keruel witnessed a confirmation charter by William the Lion to the Abbey of Aberbrothock c. 1204–1214 (RAA., I, 89*bis*). Thomas Caruel was burgess of Arbroath in 1461 and John Carvale burgess in 1505 (RAA., II, p. 121, 358). Keruel 1483.

CARVER. Most probably from the occupation of wood-carver,

"Ne purtreyour, ne kerver of images"

Chaucer, *The Knightes Tale*, 1.1041.

Payment was made to John Kerver, merchant of Scotland, 1476 (*Bain*, IV, 1443). Symon Karwur bound himself to the Abbey of Dunfermelyn in 1507 "for all and hail the dais of his lyfe that he sall remane and wirk in the abba in the craft of the wryt craft and repare all neidfull werkis of the samyn als far has he hafis knawlege" (RD., p. 361). Robert Carwor witnessed a precept of sasine at Scone, 1544 (*Scon*, p. 207).

CARVIE. Margaret Carvie in Falkland accused of witchcraft, 1661 (Chambers, *Domestic annals of Scotland*, II, p. 279).

CARWOOD. An old family of this name which possessed the lands of Carwood, near Biggar, Lanarkshire, became extinct in the male line c. 1550 (*Biggar*, p. 70). William Carwod of that Ilk was respited in 1526 for "tresonable intercomonyng" with certain "Inglismen and traitouris dueland upoun Levin" (RSS., I, 3474). Margaret Carwood, perhaps the last of her name, was bed-chamber woman to Mary Queen of Scots, and assisted the Queen's escape from Holyrood in 1566. Between 1557 and 1585 there is record of an "assedation to Margrat Carwod pantrice to the Queen of Ye Kirks of Muling and Strathordill" (RD., p. 486). She was afterwards married to John Stewart of Tullymet (Cowan, *Mary Queen of Scots*, I, p. 118, 161). A John Carwood, probably of Scottish descent, was assistant Justice in South Carolina, in 1725. An old spelling was Carvewood.

CASH. This surname, now seldom met with, may be derived from the small place named Cash in the parish of Strathmiglo in Fife. Charles Cash, late bookbinder, Edinburgh, 1734 (*Guildry*, p. 149). See under CASS.

CASKIE. From (MAC)CASKIE, q.v. Alexander Caskie and John Caskie are recorded in Kirktoune in the parish of Stewarton in 1666 (*Corsehill*, p. 69). Patrick Caskie in Home, 1684, and David Casskie or Kasskie, keeper of Canongate Tolbooth, 1686 (RPC., 3. ser. x, p. 250; XII, p. 378), John Caskie recorded in Bridgend, 1688 (*Corsehill*, p. 179). Robert Caskie, flesher burgess of Edinburgh, 1722 (*Guildry*, p. 125).

CASKIN. Andrew Caskin in record in Inverness, 1603, Jean Caiskin there in 1606 (*Rec. Inv.*, II, p. 16, 49). In same record the name appears as Caskyn, Kathkin, and Kathkyne.

CASS. King David I granted to the church of Dunfermline a ploughgate of land in Craigmillar reserving the liferent of the wife of Roger Cass, c. 1130 (RD., p. 11). "Long afterwards there were people of the name of Cass feuars of Monktonhall and other places under the Abbey of Dunfermline" (*Lawrie*, p. 336). John Cass in Dalkeith was summoned before the Privy Council in 1566 (RPC., I, p. 444), and Robert Cas, eldest son of Richard Cas of Fordell and John Cas, notary, are in record in 1610 (*Laing*, 1581). John Cas, butcher in Dalkeith, was heir of James Cas, his father, in 1642 (*Inquis.*, 2688), and Mr. Alexander Case was parson of Pollvart in 1658 (ibid., 4352). As the old family of this name were feuars under the Abbey of Dunfermline their name may have been derived from the lands of Cash in the parish of Strathmiglo.

CASSELS, CASSELLS, CASSILS. Of local origin from some place of the name, perhaps Cassilis (in 1363 Castlis) in the parish of Kirkmichael, Ayrshire. The place name is in plural form, and Skeat has shown that "when three consonants come together the middle one goes; no one pronounces the *t* in castle." Families of this name are said to have been settled in Bo'ness for several generations, but no proof offered. William Cassillis was admitted burgess of Glasgow, 1624 *(Burgesses)*. Thomas Cassellis was in Stanevbyrewood, parish of Lesmahago, 1657, and eight more of the name in the neighborhood are noted (*Lanark CR.*). John Cassillis, writer in Edinburgh, was appointed Islay Herald, 1667, James Cassells of Geattvsyde of Pollmood is in record in same year *(Stirling)*, and Isobell Cassles in Lesmahago parish, 1686 (RPC., 3. ser. XII, p. 337).

CASSIE. William Casse, juror on inquest at Lanark, 1303 (*Bain*, II, 1420). William Cassy was a notary public in Brechin, 1435, and John Cassye and William Cassye were citizens of the burgh in 1531 (REB., II, 54, 184). Andrew Cassy was witness in Aberdeen, 1446 (REA., I, p. 245), another Andrew Cassie was admitted burgess of the burgh. in 1582 (NSCM., I, p. 78), and John Casse, piper, died there, 1583 (SCM., II, p. 55). Andrew Cassie of Quhytstryppis was heir of James Cassie there, his father, 1648 (*Retours, Aberdeen*, 292). Mr. Alexander Casse was parson of Polwart, 1652 (*Lauder*), and John Cassie is recorded in Kirkmill, Ayrshire, 1675 (*Corsehill*, p. 135). The name is also recorded in Edinburgh, 1650 (*Edinb. Marr.*), and William Cassie from Millbrex was killed in the first Great War (*Turriff*). Casie 1795. The name was derived by the late Mr. R. L. Cassie, a good Gaelic scholar, from Ir. *Cathusach*, which may be rendered 'battle-slayer' or 'battle-sustainer.'

CASSINDONISCH. Local. Thomas Cassindonisch was concerned in witchcraft in Ross, 1590 (*Trials*, I, p. 195).

CASSON. A shortened form of (MAC)CASSANE, q.v. Cassen 1684.

CASTLE, CASTEL, CASTELL. Ricardus de Castello is mentioned in a charter by David I, c. 1142 (*Neubotle*, 18). Magister Peter de Castro witnessed a confirmation by Galfridus, bishop of Dunkeld, of the church of Madirnvn (Madderty) and lands of the Abthan of Maddirnyn in 1238 (LIM., 72). Normannus de Castello, burgess of Dundee, witnessed Ysabell de Brus's gift of her messuage of Cragyn near Dundee to the monks of Lundors, c. 1240 (LAC., p. 42). John de Castro, a charter witness in Dundee, 1281 (HP., II, p. 223), Robert Castello admitted burgess of Aberdeen in 1408 (NSCM., I, p. 3), and David Castell, wobster there, 1612 (SCM., v, p. 87).

CASTLELAW. Of local origin from one or more of the many places of the name in the southern counties. William Castellaw was witness at Failfurd, 1504 (*Simon*, 125), and forethought felony was done to Alexander Castellaw, 1532 (*Trials*, I, p. 160°). Alexander Castallaw was bailie of the burgh of Dysart in 1543 (*Dysart*, p. 12). The surname appears in Stirling in 1563 (*Soltre*, p. 126), and James Castellaw was bailie there in 1602 (SBR., p. 103, 283). The name is also found in Edinburgh in 1567 (MCM., II, p. 308). W. Castellaw was minister at Stewarton in 1637, and another William Castellaw was recorded heir

CASTLELAW, *continued*

of William Castlelaw, apothecary burgess of Edinburgh, in 1656 (*Inquis.*, 4167). John Castellaw appears in Templhouse in 1667 (*Corsehill*, p. 75), Alison Castillaw in Fouldine in 1672 (*Lauder*), and Margaret Castlelaw was retoured heir in lands, etc., in the barony of Coldingham in 1692 (*Inquis. Sp.*). Thomas Castellaw, clerk to the Presbytery of Glasgow in 1688 may be the same who was minister of Leswalt, Wigtownshire, in 1715 (*Wigtown*).

CASTRO TERRI. Magister Petro de Castro terri, canon of Dunkeld, witnesses charters by Gilbert, bishop of Dunkeld (RD., p. 78; *Inchcolm*, p. 13) and Clement, bishop of Dunblane, 1234 (*Inchaffray*, p. 53). In 1238–39 he appears as Magister Petrus de Castro Theodorici precentor Dunkeldensis (*Inchcolm*, p. 16; *Inchaffray*, p. 57). Castrum Theodorici is Château Thierry on the Marne, and Castro Terry is an imperfect Latinization of the name.

CASWELL. A variant of CARSWELL, q.v.

CATHAL. G. and MG. *Cathal* (in M'Vurich, Ir. *Cathal* (common from seventh century onwards), O. W. *Catgual*, from °*Katu-valo-s* 'war wielder.' Kathil mac Murchy sealed an inquest made at Dumbarton, 1239 (APS., I, p. 99; *Bain*, I, 2174). The name was early borrowed by the Norsemen and occurs in *Landnámabók* (II, 18) as *Kaðal*. Cathal or Kathel is a common personal name in Assynt at the present day. From this comes MACCALL.

CATHAN. A diminutive of *Catt*, an old Irish personal name, from *catt*, a cat. Cathan or Cattan was an Irish Pict, friend of SS. Comgall and Cainneach, and uncle of S. Blane after whom Dunblane takes its name. He was founder of Kingarth in Bute (*Gillies*, p. 175). Hardly anything is known of him, but his existence is also vouched for by such place names as Kilchattan. Cathan, senex, was juror in an arbitration in Fife, c. 1128 (RPSA., p. 118). Balmacaan means "stead of the sons of Cathan" (*Watson* I, p. 238).

CATHCART. Of territorial origin from the lands of Cathcart in Renfrewshire. The first of the family came to Scotland with Walter fitz Alan, the first of the Stewards, and from his name, Rainald, may like his leader, have been of Breton origin. Rainald appears as witness to a charter by Alan fitz Walter conveying the patronage of the church of Kethcart to the monastery of Paisley c. 1178 (RMP., p. 12). He also witnessed, as Ranulfus de Ketkert, a similar charter by Alan, the son of

Walter in favor of the same house c. 1202–3 (ibid., p. 14). As Reginaldus de Cathekert he witnessed another charter by the same Alan to Robert Croc of the lands of Kellebrid c. 1200 (*Lennox*, II, p. 2). His son, William de Cathkert witnessed a charter whereby Duugallus filius Cristini de Levenax exchanged the lands of Cnoc with the monastery of Paisley for lands near Walkeinschaw in 1234 (RMP., p. 180). William de Kathkerte of the county of Are rendered homage in 1296 (*Bain*, II, p. 205). Sir Alan of Cathcart, an adherent of Bruce, was probably the first to be designated *dominus ejusdem* (in 1336) (LCD., p. 158). Adam Cathcart was heir of Thomas Cathkert in Mylneholme of Auchincreif his father in 1622 (*Retours, Ayr*, 215). The name was originally pronounced Cathcàrt but has now been Anglicized into Càthcart. Kethkert 1451.

CATHER. From Catter or Cather in the parish of Kilmaronock, Dumbartonshire. James Cader, witness at Antermony Wester, 1512 (*Ros*, 20). Agnes Cather recorded in Dennie in 1676, and John Caitter was miller in Larbert in 1682 (*Stirling*). The old earls of Lennox had at one time their residence at Catter. (2) A vocalizing of CALDER, q.v. James Cather (Calder) in Burn was present at Bothwell Brig (Grosart, *Parish of Shotts*, p. 100).

CATHERWOOD. A variant of CALDERWOOD, q.v., with *l* vocalized. James Catherwood in Peacock Bank, 1705 (*Corsehill*, p. 207).

CATHIE. A shortening of MACCATHAY, q.v. Janet Cathie in Dykeside of Foullartoun, 1628 (*Brechin*). Dod Mc ean vic Cathie in Tarradaill an engager on the royalist side, 1649 (IDR., p. 368). Samuel Cathay, spirit dealer, Dumbarton, 1828 (RDB.).

CATHKIN. From the old lands of Catcune now represented by the ruined castle in the parish of Borthwick, Midlothian. Thomas de Catkone of the county of Edeneburk rendered homage in 1296. His seal bears a hawk killing a bird, S' Thome de Cathkwin (?) (*Bain*, II, p. 201, 546). Thomas Cathkin, dempster, is mentioned in 1481 (*Cambus.*, 211), and Andro Cathkin had precept of a letter of gift from the king in 1500 (RSS., I, 544). William Cathtkin was a burgess of Edinburgh in 1514 (*Soltre*, p. 171), and Edward Cathkin was a "buikseller and burgess" of the same city in 1601 (BM., II, p. 229). In 1550 we have record of the revision of four acres of land at Lochbank, near Edinburgh, by Margaret Cathkene or Caethkin, wife of David Kinloch, one of the deacons of trades in Edinburgh (*Seals. Supp.*, 195).

CATHRO. A surname found in Angus, evidently derived from lands of the same name there. Cf. the place name Stracathro. Jacobus Catrow, a charter witness, 1533 (*Inchcolm*, p. 19). William Cathraw was burgess of Perth in 1509 (*Rent. Dunk.*, p. 212), and another William Cathrow was married in Perth in 1562 (*Sc. Ant.*, I, p. 102), David Cathrow was miller in Kethinnis (Kettins) in 1602 (*Trials*, II, p. 388), and Alexander Cathrov died in Glamis in 1643. Helen Cathrow is recorded in Dundee in 1613 (*Brechin*). There is a place Cathrowseat in Forfar Retours, 367, 512.

CATION. See *under* CATTEN. Recorded in Edinburgh, 1942.

CATOR. Perhaps from ME. *cater, catour*, a buyer of provisions, a caterer. Alexander Catour or Caytour held a tenement in Arbroath, 1464, 1466, and Thomas Caytour witnessed letters of sasine, 1467 (RAA., II, 151, 167). Alexander Catour was carter at Dunkeld in 1515 (*Rent. Dunk.*, p. 150).

CATTANACH, CATTENACH. Gaelic *Catanach*, Middle Gaelic plural *Cattanaich* (*Lismore*, p. 100), "belonging to (Clan) Chattan," the *Clann Gillecatan* of the 1467 MS. The clan claims descent from Gillacatain (1467 MS.), "servant of (S.) Catan," whose name denotes "little cat." Individuals of this name were fairly numerous in Braemar, Upper Deeside, and in Strathdon. Thomas Kethirnathie (Kathirnach or Cattanach), a canon of Whithern, was appointed abbot of Fearn in 1407 but was rejected by the canons (Gordon, *Monasticon*, Glasgow, 1868, p. 351; OPS., II, p. 436; *Beauly*, p. 313). Arthur Catanache was attorney in Wadbuster, Shetland, 1623 (OSS., I, 16), James Cattanach was kirk officer of Contane in 1673 (IDR., p. 331), and Robert Catanach was slandered in 1679 (ibid., p. 341). James Catnach (1792–1841) was one of the pioneers in the cause of promoting cheap literature, and established presses at Alnwick, Newcastle, and finally in London. Catanoch 1696, Cattanoch 1737, Cattenoch 1682. In Gaelic individuals of the name are known as Catan, e.g. Iain Catan is Englished as John Cattanoch.

CATTELL, CATTLE. Sharpened forms of CADDEL, q.v.

CATTEN, CATTON. Of local origin from Catton near Allendale, Northumberland. There is also a Caton in Lancashire. The name Cation, found in Fife, is probably a variant. Thomas de Cattone of Perthshire rendered homage, 1296 (*Bain*, II, p. 211). Marion Cattane, spouse of Henry Mansone in Skelberrie, Lunnasting, Shetland, 1635 (*Sc. Ant.*, XII, p. 89).

CATTER. From the lands of Catter or Cather in the extreme north of the parish of Kilmaronock, Dumbartonshire. See also CATHER.

CATTO. A surname confined mainly to the Buchan district of Aberdeenshire. A modulated form of Cattoch, like Bullo from Bulloch, Nimmo from Nimmock, etc. Andrew Cathoch, witness in Aberdeen, 1463 (RAA., II, p. 129). Henrie Cattow in Aberdeen, 1597 (SCM., I, p. 134–137). Andrew Cattache in Artleache, 1633 (SCM., III, p. 124). William Cattoch in Thurso, 1685 (RPC., 3. ser. x, p. 430).

CAULDFIELD, CAULFIELD. Of local origin. There is a Cauldfield near Langholm, Dumfriesshire.

CAULDHAME. There was a family of Caldom or Cauldhame of Blackness. The name is also recorded in Edinburgh Marriage Register as Caldame and Caldum. There is a Caldhame in Marykirk parish, another at Airdrie, and there are several Cauldhames listed in County Directory.

CAULDLAW. From Cauldlaw near Carnwath. Thomas de Cauldlaw or Caldlaw was a tenant of the Douglases in the barony of Kilbochoke (Kilbucho) in 1376 (RHM., II, p. 16), and Wilzam Cauldlaw was tenant of Neddyr Mosplat in 1528 (*Rental*).

CAULVELEY. Richard Caulveley, "grwme of his Ma. privie chalmer," admitted burgess of Aberdeen, 1617 (NSCM., I, p. 118). Probably from Calveley in England.

CAUNCE. A Galloway surname, from (MAC) CANCE, q.v.

CAVELIN. From some place of the name unknown to me. Gilbert of Cavelyn was witness in Lythqw, 1444 (*Sc. Ant.*, XVII, p. 115), and Henry Cavelin, member of the Scots parliament for Linlithgow, 1468 (*Hanna*, II, p. 487), is probably Henry of Caveling a witness there, 1472 (*Sc. Ant.*, XVII, p. 115).

CAVELL. William Cavell of Tulynestyn who appears in 1537 is mentioned again in 1547 and 1558 (REA., II, p. 112, 319; *Aboyne*, p. 95). Most probably here a variant of CABLE, q.v.

CAVENS. From the lands of Cavens in the parish of Kirkbean, Kirkcudbrightshire. John de Cavens is said to have owned Cruggleton Castle in 1421 (*M'Kerlie*, II, p. 387), and Gilbert de Cavans was presented to the church of Kirkinner in 1402 (*Pap. Pet.*, p. 618). Janet Cavens recorded in Hollmyre in 1676 (*Kirkcudbright*) may be the Janet Cavin in Kirkcudbright in 1684 (RPC., 3. ser. x, p. 241). Christian Kaven in Millthird, 1686 (*Kirkcudbright*).

CAVERHILL. The lands of Caverhill in the parish of Manor, Peeblesshire, gave name to the family of Caverhill of that Ilk. Jonete, daughter of John de Caverhille was spouse of William Watsone of Cranystone in 1409 (RMS., I, 930). Thomas de Caverhyl had the lands of Foulleth in the sheriffdom of Peebles confirmed to him in 1427 (RMS., II, 103), and these lands were still in possession of the family in 1559 (Retours, Peebles, 9). John Cavirhill, indweller in Roxburghshire, is recorded in 1489 (Cavers, p. 729), and Thom Cawerhill was tenant of Stobo in 1528 (Rental).

CAVERS. From Cavers in the parish of Bowden, Roxburghshire. William de Caueris was juror on inquest made in Edinburgh in 1402 (Egidii, p. 38). Thomas Caveris was witness in Lythqw in 1444 and 1472 (Sc. Ant., XVII, p. 115, 119), and a later Thomas Caveris was burgess there in 1531 (Johnsoun, 5). William Cavers had a grant of part of land of Mukdrum, 1503, and three years later Dionisius Cavers exchanged part of Mukdrum for other property (RMS., II, 2758, 2985). Dionisius Caweris who held land in Perth, 1535, appears in 1546 as Dionese Cavers, witness there (Rollok, 116, 2). William Cavers was tenant of Neubattle Abbey in 1563 (Neubotle, p. 327).

CAVERTON. From Caverton in the parish of Eckford, Roxburghshire. Alisaundre le fiz Henry de Cavertone of the county of Roxburgh, rendered homage in 1296 (Bain, II, p. 206, 209). There were many 'ferry-loupers' in Orkney and Shetland in the sixteenth and seventeenth centuries from various parts of Scotland, and most probably John Caverton or Cavertoun of Shapinsay, an underling of Robert Stewart, earl of Orkney, in the last quarter of the sixteenth century (REO., p. 134, 155, etc.) was one of them.

CAVIE. James Cavy, reidare at Creich, 1574 (RMR.). Archibald Cavie, servitor to the earl of Sutherland, admitted burgess of Glasgow, 1629 (Burgesses). Christiane Cavy ordered to be banished, 1684, is evidently Christian Cavie, an old woman Conventicler, prisoner in the Tolbooth, Edinburgh, 1687 (RPC., 3. ser. X, p. 251; XIII, p. 134, 479). Cf. CALVIE.

CAW. A curtailed form of (MAC)CAW, q.v. Alexander Caw, writer in Edinburgh, is in record in 1679 (Edinb. Marr.), a pension was paid to Christian Caw in Edinburgh 1741 (Guildry, p. 177), and Sir James Lewis Caw (b. 1864) was Director of the National Gal-

leries of Scotland. Fifteen of this name are in the Commissariot Record of Dunkeld.

CAWART. Herbert Cawart, witness in Dumfries, 1542 (Anderson). Marie Cavart in Little Daltone, 1683 (Dumfries). Thomas Cawart in parish of Monzie, n.d. (Dunblane). There is a Cawartsholme in Dumfries Retours (55).

CAWDOR. This represents the old Lowland pronunciation of northern Calder. It has been suggested, and it is probable, that the displacement of Calder by the false form Cawdor is due, in part at least, to Shakespeare, who in Macbeth adopted the Lowland form of the name.

CAY. See under CAIE.

CAYNES. A Norman territorial name, perhaps from Cahaignes (Eure). Guido de Caynes was one of the witnesses to Earl David's Inquisitio regarding the lands pertaining to the church of Glasgow, c. 1124 (REG., p. 7). The Keynes were a well-known Norman family in Sussex.

CEACHAIRNE, CHEACHARNA. See under MACEACHEARN.

CELESTINE. Late Latin Cœlistinus for a time was used as a Latinization of Gaelic Gillespie.

CELLACH, i.e. "warlike." Cellach, a prince or mormaer of Scotland, was one of those killed in the great battle of Brunanburh in 937 (AFM.). Cellach, provincial king of Moray, was killed c. 950 by Malcolm, Donald's son (CPS., p. 10), and Tighernach records that in 976 Cellach, son of Findguine and Cellach, son of Bard were two mormaers in Scotland. Cf. MACKELLY.

CERES. From the lands or barony of Ceres in Fife, anciently Syras or Syres. The family appears to have been descended from a son of Gillemichael, 3. earl of Fife, d. p. 1133. Adam de Syreis appears frequently as a witness in charters by William the Lion, Earl Duncan, and Robert and Richard, bishops of St. Andrews (Sc. Peer., IV, p. 5). He witnessed King William's charter of the church of Aberrotheven to the Abbey of Inchaffray, c. 1199–1200 (Inchaffray, p. 4), and the same king's charter of Rosin clerac (Rossieclerach) to James de Pert (SCM., II, p. 318). As de Sirais he witnessed a gift by Duncan, earl of Fife, to the nuns of North Berwick, a. 1177 (CMN., 6), between 1189–99 he witnessed grants in favor of Arbroath Abbey (RAA., I, 19, 28), and before 1200, as de Sireis he attested another charter by King William the Lion (LSC., 42). His son and successor, Duncan de Syreis, flourished early in the thirteenth century, and left daughters only, one of whom, Margaret, was married to Michael Scot (RD., 174, 175), ancestor of the family of Scot of Balwearie. Simon of Sireis was falconer of the king of Scotland, 1212 (Bain, I, 532), Alexander de Sireis witnessed a grant by Thomas de Lundin to the nuns of North Berwick, c. 1220 (CMN., 11), and Galfridus Surays witnessed a confirmation by William, earl of Ross, 1263 (REM., p. 279). The goods of John of Syres, merchant of Aberdeen, were plundered in England, 1370 (Bain, IV, 158), William Soreys was on an assize in 1389 regarding the mill-lands of Quarelwode in Moray (REM., p. 171). Robert de Seres was admitted burgess of Dundee, 1408 (Wedd., p. 20n), John Ceras and Robert Ceras were witnesses in Inverness in 1456 (Invernessiana, p. 133), George Seres was cantor in Brechin Cathedral, 1457 (REB., II, 274), and Thomas Seres was bailie of Dundee 1492 (Sc. Ant., VI, p. 23). Patrick Ceras held land in Arbroath, 1505 (RAA., II, 448). Scheres 1447, Serass 1437, Sereys 1260, Suryass (Fam. of Innes, p. 10), Svrais c. 1250; Serras, Seyrus, and Soreys (all three in REM.).

CESSFORD. Of local origin from the hamlet of Cessford in the parish of Eckford, Roxburghshire. Adam Cessfurde was bailie of the burgh of Hawick in 1558 (Wilson, Annals of Hawick, p. 328, 330), Gavin Cesfuird in Westhouses, 1641 (RRM., I, p. 85), Thomas Cesfoord in Tron Kirk parish signed the Test, 1685 (RPC., 3. ser. x, p. 457), and James Cessfoord, tailor in Edinburgh, was heir of George Cessford, writer in Edinburgh in 1699 (Inquis., 8076). Cesfurd 1696, Cessfuird 1671.

CHADBURN. This surname, recorded in Aberdeen, is most probably a recent introduction from England. The name is of local origin from Chadburn in Lancashire.

CHALLONER. A maker of chalons, i.e. coverlets for beds, so named from Châlons-sur-Marne in France, the town where they were first made or where the materials were procured. Robert Chalonar held a tenement in Linlithqw in 1472 and John Chalonare was a witness there in the same year (Sc. Ant., XVII, p. 117, 118). The name of Janet Schalender in Edinburgh, 1647 (Edinb. Marr.), may be the same with intrusive d.

CHALMERS, CHAMBERS. The correct forms are Chalmer and Chamber, from OF. de la chambre, of the chamber: (1) a chamber attendant, (2) of the Treasury chamber (camera), and so metonymic for CHAMBERLAIN, q.v. The spellings with -s are later. When the OF. word was naturalized in Scots it lost b by elision, and received l to safeguard as it were, the length of the preceding vowel, as shown in the pronunciation 'chaamer' or 'chaumer' (Gregory Smith, Specimens of Middle Scots, p. xxiii–iv). Hugh de Camera appears as witness to a charter of David I (RPSA., p. 193), and to charters of Malcolm IV (ibid., p. 197; Cambus., 50). Richard de Camera witnessed two charters of William the Lion (Cambus., 121; RAA., I, 60). Radulfus de Camera and his brother, Herbertus de Camera "are occasional witnesses to charters of William the Lion during the greater part of his reign; but nothing is known of their family or local connections, except that a son of Radulf had an interest in the churches of Campsie and Altermony in the Lennox" (Inchaffray, p. 269). Several persons of the name rendered homage in 1296: (1, 2) Robert de la Chaumbre and William de la Chaumbre of Lanarkshire. The seal of Robert bears a lion rampant, and S' Rob'ti de Camera (Bain, II, p. 204, 544), (3) William de la Chaumbre, bailie and burgess of Peebles, (4, 5) Symon and William of Dumfriesshire, and (6) Wautier of Berwickshire (ibid., p. 198, 204, 206). Willmus de Camera was common councillor in Aberdeen, 1399, and Alexander Chaumir was elected serjeant in 1475 (Guildry, p. 184, 187). James Chamber and Gilbert Chawemere, Scotsmen, had safe conducts into England in 1465–6 (Bain, IV, 1358, 1365). Alexander of Chamowr was "forspekar for the comownis and merchandis" of Aberdeen, 1461 (CRA., p. 22), and in 1474 Gilbert of Chamer (Chamver, or Chadmer) was alderman of the same burgh (ibid., p. 32–33). Robert of Chawmyr witnessed resignation of a feu in Peebles, 1471 (Scots lore, p. 52), and another Robert Chamer was tenant on lands of Polkak, 1472 (Cupar-Angus, I, p. 221). Sir John of Chawmir of Gatgyrth is recorded in 1491 (HMC., 3. Rep., II, p. 391). Thomas Chamer was admitted burgess of Aberdeen, 1521 (NSCM., I, p. 47), and a particate of land was sold to John Chalmyr in Glasgow, 1555 (Protocols). The sounded l in Chalmers is a modern affectation. Chailmers 1692, Chalmair 1575, Chalmbers 1688, Chalmer 1508, Chalmour 1515, Chalmvris 1557, Chamyr 1477, Chaumar 1503, Chaumyr 1502, Chavmyr and Chawmer 1477, Chawmuir 1553, Schambers 1650.

146

CHAMBERLAIN. From the office, OF. *chamberlenc*, Latin *camerarius*. The office of royal chamberlain was one of great responsibility in virtue of the fact that until the reign of James I he managed the king's revenue and was head of the Exchequer. The great nobles, also, had each a chamberlain who looked after his lord's business affairs. John Camerarius witnessed a confirmation charter by William the Lion, c. 1175 (REA., I, p. 9). Walter Camerarius witnessed a charter by Eschina, wife of Walter Fitz Alan, before 1177 (RMP., p. 74). Menzeis Chammerlan appears in Caldystarris, 1532 (*Rental*). The surname was never common in Scottish records.

CHAMBERS. *See under* CHALMERS.

CHAMPAGNE. From Champagne, an ancient government of France. The name was also Latinized de Campania in early charters. Pieres de Chaumpaigne, rector of the church of Kynkel, who rendered homage in 1296 is probably the Pieres de Chaumpaigne of Fifeshire who is recorded as rendering fealty at the same time (*Bain*, II, p. 194, 204). Rauf de Chaumpayne and William de Champaigne, both of the county of Wyggetone, also rendered homage in the same year (ibid., p. 184, 206). In 1306–07 Huwe de Champane, a tenant *in capite* of the king of England, petitioned for 'mitigacioun' of the relief for his lands in Galloway "according to their present value, not the old valuation before the Scottish war, as they have been so wasted thereby, that otherwise he must sell them" (ibid., II, 1984). He appears to have died at this time as very soon after the daughter of Hugh de Chaumpaigne, deceased, was given in marriage in 1306–07, to Dungal MacDouyl, junior in Galloway (ibid., 1905). John Champenay in 1343 had a gift of one hundred shillings from the king (ER., I, p. 535–536), and Johannes Champnay had a remission for his share in burning the toun of Dunbertane in 1489 (APS., XII, p. 34; *Lennox*, II, p. 132). Robert Champane, reidare at Balmaghe, Galloway, 1574 (RMR.). See also CAMPANIA.

CHANCELLOR. From the office of 'chancellor,' either civil or ecclesiastical; an official who kept registers of an order of knighthood, an ecclesiastical judge. An ancient family of this name in Lanarkshire were vassals of the lords of Somerville before 1432. They have possessed Shieldhill and Quothquhan for centuries, but are scarcely mentioned in record. William Chancellor was merchant burgess of Edinburgh, 1681 (*Inquis.*, 6264), and James Chancellor of Scheilhill refused the Test, 1684 (RPC., 3. ser. x, p. 289). Chanslar 1524.

CHANDLER. From ME. *chaundeler*, AF. *chandeler*, OF. *chandelier*, in Latin documents *candelarius*: (1) a maker of candles; (2) the officer who superintended the supply of candles in a household. John the "Candelar" was appointed to bring certain Scottish jewels and writings from Berwick to London in September 1296 (Bain, II, 840). Payments to Alanus candelarius and Bridinus candelarius are recorded in 1329–30 (ER., I, p. 216, 320). The London Livery Company of Tallow Chandlers was incorporated in 1463.

CHANDLISH. Like CANDLISH curtailed from MACCANDLISH, q.v.

CHAPEL. From residence at or office in a chapel, AF. *chapele*, OF. *capele*, Church Lat. *capella*. The office of usher of the king's chapel, that is, Chancery, was hereditary in a family called from the office de Capella, and was attached to a third part of the lands of Craigmillar (Thomson, *The Public records of Scotland*, p. 68). In 1328 there is entry of wages of the boys of William de Capella (ER., I, p. 118). John de Capella possessed Craigmillar after the Craigmillars, and in 1374 the lands were purchased from them again by Sir Simon Preston (Dickson, *Ruined castles of Midlothian*, 1894, p. 69). Little is known of this John de Capella. John Chapell held a tenement in Ayr, 1502 (*Ayr*, p. 97).

CHAPLAIN, CHAPLIN. From the office of 'chaplain' (AF. *chapelein*, Church Latin *capellanus*). Henry the chaplain and Humfrey the chaplain are charter witnesses in reign of Malcolm IV (*Bain*, II, p. 421, 423). John called Chapelayn, burgess of Aberdeen in 1271 (*Fraser*, p. 9). Henry le Chapelevn of Roxburghshire rendered homage, 1296. His seal reads S' *Henrici Capellani* (Bain, II, p. 199, 532). Roger capellanus was custumar of Edinburgh in 1327 (ER., I, p. 82), and Alecia dicta Chapelane filia quondam Ade Chapelane, burgess of Aberdeen, is recorded in 1310 (REA., I, p. 40). Richard Schapillayn or Schapellayn held a burgage in Dundee in 1344 (HP., II, p. 134). John Chapellaune was made guild brother in right of his wife in Edinburgh in 1462 (EBR., 19), and Peter Chaplan or Chaplane was parson of Dennennow (Dunins) in 1526 (SCM., IV, p. 23, 25). Chaplin of Coliston, a Scots family. Richard Chaipland was member of Scots parliament for Haddington, 1644 (*Hanna*, II, p. 487). Chaiplane 1595; Chaeplen, Chaeplin, Cheplene.

CHAPMAN. This surname, found mainly in the Lothians and in Perthshire, is derived from the occupation of 'chapman,' OE. *ceápman*, 'merchant.' It is probable, as Bardsley says, that the early chapman was stationary and dealt in a much larger way than we are now accustomed to suppose. The chapman portrayed in Burns's *Tam o' Shanter* was of a lower grade. The earliest occurrence of the name seems to be in 1296 when a pardon was granted to a man for causing the death of Ralph Chepman in Dundee (*Bain*, II, 839). William Chapman, provost of Aberdeen in 1327 (ER., I, p. 59, 60) is probably the Willelmus dictus Chapman who appears on an inquisition in the same town in 1333 (REA., I, p. 54). Hugh called Chepman held a land in fee in the town of Roxburgh in 1338 (*Dryburgh*, 260, 261), David II granted a charter of the lands of Rotherstoun near Dee to Duncan Chapman (RMS., I, App. II, 1403), and Symon Chepman, a burgess of Lanark in 1359 (ER., I, p. 599), had a confirmation charter from David II of the lands of Banks and of the Brerybankes in Lanark in 1367 (RMS., I, 266). Thomas Chepman, Scottish merchant, complained in 1359 that his ship was captured and sunk by the English during a truce (*Bain*, IV, 23), and Hugh Chaypman, bailie of Stirling in 1387 (ER., III, p. 159) appears in the same record in the following year as Hugh Mercator (= merchant). Donald Chapman, a Scot in Norwich, was arrested in violation of the truce in 1396 (*Bain*, IV, 483), and Finlai Chepman held a land in Irvine in 1426 (*Irvine*, I, 129). To Walter Chepman, merchant burgess of Edinburgh, and Andro Myllar jointly, James IV granted a patent to establish the first printing press in Scotland in 1507 (Dickson-Edmond, *Annals of Scottish printing*, p. 13–22). Chaipman 1492, Chapmane 1484, Cheipman 1600, Chepmane 1526, Chopman 1593, Chopmane 1628, Schapman 1548, Shepman 1367.

CHAPPIE. Magnus Chappie, witness in Shetland, appears again as Magnus Crippie, 1623, and Andrew Chappie was merchant there, 1625 (OSS., I, 1, 128).

CHARLES. From the personal name Charles, Latinized *Carolus*. It is rarely found as a forename before the reign of Charles I. John Charles to compear before the justice in Aberdeen, 1569 (RPC., I, p. 674). Alexander Charles, William Charles, and Oliver Charles in Gairth, Evie, Orkney, 1649 (*Inquis.*, 3538–9). William Charles, barrowman, St. Andrews, c. 1688 (PSAS., LIV, p. 238).

CHARLESON, 'son of CHARLES,' q.v. A Caithness surname. Aychin Carlichsoun was witness to an obligation by the earl of Ross in 1439 (*Cawdor*, p. 16), and in 1494 there is recorded the obit. 'Duncan Charlissoun apud Lochdochord' (*Chr. Fort.*). The 1439 form has been influenced by the Gaelic form of the name Charles (*Teàrlach*).

CHARLIESON. An Anglicizing of MACCAIRLICH and MACKERLICH.

CHARLTON. See under CARLTON.

CHARTERIS, CHARTERS. From Chartres in the department of Eure-et-Loire, France. "The Sirname of Carnatto, which we English Charters, is very ancient with us" (Crawford, *Lives*, p. 19). In the reign of William the Lion, Walter de Carnoto gifted the church of Trauerflet (Trailflat) and the church of Dungrey or Drumereyoch to the Abbey of Kelso (*Kelso*, 13, 334). In 1266 we have a charter confirming this gift which supplies us with the names of four generations: Robert called of Carnoto, knight, son and heir of Thomas de Carnoto, son and heir of Thomas de Carnoto, son and heir of Walcher [i.e. Walther] de Carnoto (ibid., 345). Adam de Carnoto witnessed quitclaim by Richard de Bancori to Robert de Brus of the whole land of Loyerwode (Locharwood), a. 1249 (*Bain*, I, 1684). Thomas de Carnoto who witnessed a charter by Gamelin, bishop of St. Andrews to the Abbey of Lindores, 1259 (LAC., p. 132), may be Thomas de Carnoto, archdeacon of Lothian, who had a dispensation to hold the church of Fetheresath (Fetteresso) in the diocese of St. Andrews, 1262 (*Pap. Lett.*, I, p. 382). Ada de Cartres witnessed the gift of William's vill in Garviach to the Abbey of Lindores c. 1261 (LAC., p. 146). Magister Thomas de Carnoto is mentioned as chancellor in 1290 (ER., I, p. 49). A Charteris had the wardship of Amvsfeild granted him by the Guardians of the Kingdom after the death of Alexander III (ER., I). Robert de Chartres and William de Chartres of Roxburghshire rendered homage, 1296. The seal of Robert bears an eight-rayed figure and S' *Roberti d' Chartris* (*Bain*, II, p. 199, 202, 552). Thomas de Carnoto witnessed a Dumfries charter of 1341 (RHM., II, 48), and Sir Patrick and Thomas de Chartres held land in the vill of Malkarestone before 1361 (*Bain*, IV, 60). Another Thomas de Carnotho was charter witness in 1406–7 (REB., I, 26; II, 16). James Charterhous, a steward of Kelso Abbey at Trailflat, 1556 (*Kelso*, p. 484), and Agnes Charterhouse was in Dundee, 1613 (*Brechin*). Archibald Charterhous rendered to Exchequer the accounts of the bailie of Kintore, 1593 (ER., XXII, p. 340). John Charters was herd at Yetholm, 1790 (*Heirs*, 452). Chairtris and Chairteris 1706, Charteouris 1610, Charteris 1586, Chartirris 1525, Chartrews 1660, Chartris 1455, Chartrous 1546.

CHATTAN, Clan. In G. *Clann Chatain.* See CATHAN. The collective name given to a number of clans united into a confederation in 1609, viz.: Cattanach, Clark, Crerar, Davidson, Farquharson, Gillespie, Gillies, Gow, Macbain, Macbean, Macgillivray, Macintosh, Macphail, Macpherson, Macqueen, Noble, Shaw. The "cat" in the armorial bearings is merely canting heraldry. Some ultra-patriotic clan historians derive the name from the Catti or Chatti (who had their seat in the region of modern Hesse), a tribe of Germany described by Tacitus (*Germania,* xxx, 1).

CHATTO. From the lands of Chatto on the Kale Water in the parish of Hounam, Roxburghshire. William de Chetue witnessed a charter by William de Veteri Ponte, c. 1198–1214 (*Kelso,* 139). Adam de Chatthou witnessed various charters in the reign of William the Lion (*Melros,* 109, 142, etc.), and John, son of Adam de Chatthou appears in a charter in the same reign (ibid., 149). Two charters were attested by Alexander de Chatthou, c. 1225, and in the following year he renounced a claim which he had previously made (*Melros,* 245, 246, 247). He may have been the Alexander de Chattun who was constable of Roxburgh in 1255 (*Kelso,* p. 130). Adam de Chathou of the county of Roxburgh rendered homage in 1296. His seal bears a fleur-de-lys, S' *Ade de Chattov* (*Bain,* II, p. 199, 532). Robert de Chattone also of the county of Roxburgh and William de Chattone, vicar of the church of Ederham of the county of Berewyke rendered homage in the same year (ibid., p. 207, 208). Walron de Chattoun was rector of the church of Jetham (Yetholm) in 1300 (*Kelso,* p. 137), in 1322 Robert I confirmed to John de Chatton certain lands in Roxburghshire (*Melros,* p. 466), Eustace of Chattow witnessed a grant of the Forest of Eteryk to John Kerre in 1358 (*Roxburghe,* p. 9), and three years later he appears as juror at Roxburgh (*Bain,* IV, 62). Thomas de Schatto confirms his cousin's sale of a tenement in Lessydwyn to the monks of Melrose in 1415 (*Melros,* 535–537). Richard Chatto signed an assedation by the convent of Melrose in 1534 (*Melrose,* p. 629), and between 1537 and 1559 several charters of the convent were witnessed by Dein Jhon Chatto (*Dryburgh,* p. 281, 284, etc.). Sir Adam Chatto was subprior of Kelso in 1531 (*Protocols,* I), Richard Chatto was subprior of Melrose in 1540 (RRM., III, p. 225), John Chatu is recorded in Dunfermline in 1572 (*Dunfermline*), and Catherine Chatu in Over Ingievar in 1695 (*Stirling*). Cato 1731.

CHAUMONT. A Norman territorial name from Chaumont in the arrondissement of Argentan,

Normandy. W. de Chamund witnessed a charter by Sayer de Quinci, earl of Winton, of the lands of Duniker to the church of Dunfermline (RD., p. 91). William de Chaumunt attested an agreement between the abbot of Holyrood and Roger de Quinci in 1222 (LSC., p. 49), and Dominus Willelmus de Chamunt (Chaumunt or Chaucmunt) witnessed resignation of the land of Edeluestun to the church of Glasgow in 1233 (REG., p. 138, 139).

CHEAP, CHEAPE. The Cheapes of Sauchie, Stirlingshire, are an old family, and so are the Cheaps of Mawhill near Kinross. William Chaip was merchant burgess of Perth, 1510 (*Rent. Dunk.,* p. 4), Johannes Chaip was chaplain of Scone, 1524 (*Scon,* p. 205), George Chaipe bailie of Linlithgow, 1536 (*Johnsoun*), and Alexander Chaip or Chop held land in Inverbervie, 1616 (*Laing,* 1749). William Cheape in Hillsyde, 1666 (*Stirling*), Anna Cheap in Newtoun of Hountingtour, 1688 (*Dunkeld*), and Mr. Henri Cheap of Ormistoune, 1698 (*Inquis.,* 8000).

CHEAPLAND. Local. William Cheapland, 'nauta,' was retoured heir in part of the lands of Byrehills, St. Andrews, 1699 (*Retours, Fife,* 1422).

CHEINE. A variant of CHEYNE, q.v.

CHELFORD. William de Chelford and John de Chelfurd witnessed a grant of the lands of Swaynystoun to the Hospital of Soltre, c. 1221–38 (*Soltre,* p. 24). In a succeeding charter William appears as "de Schelford." Most probably from Chelford in Cheshire, England.

CHENHOLM. Local, from some small place of the name unknown to me. Mary Chenholm of Chirnside died in 1329.

CHERRY, CHERRIE. Adam Chery who held land in Ayr, 1348, (*Friars Ayr,* p. 17) is doubtless the Ade Chiry who forfeited lands in the sheriffdom of Are in 1368 (RMS., I, 239). Stephen Cherie had confirmation of a charter of the lands of Kinbruin and Badecashe in the barony of Rothienorman, 1380 (*Illus.,* III, p. 552). Johannes Chery was burgess of Ayr, 1415, William Chere, burgess in 1454, and John Chery, bailie of Are, 1460 (*Ayr,* p. 9, 11, 16, 87). William Chere was member of Ayr Guild c. 1431 (*Coll. AGAA.,* I, p. 228). John Churrie, merchant burgess in Glasgow, 1623 (*Burgesses*), William Churrie in Burnefit, parish of Dumfries, 1638 (*Dumfries*), Alexander Chirray appears in Drumwharne of Killearn, 1715 (*Stirling*), and William Cherry was keeper of the toll-bar on the road to Greenock, 1798 (*Campsie*). Chirrie 1649. The surname gave name to Chyrrelands (*Ayr*, 67).

CHERRYLAW. Local. Gavin Chirrilaw, glazier in Edinburgh, 1626 (*Edinb. Marr.*).

CHESSOR. From Cheshire in England, pronounced Chesser, and spelled Chesher and Chessire. Ronald Chessure was admitted burgess of Aberdeen, 1604 (NSCM., I, p. 99), William Chessor was burgess there in 1611 (ROA., I. p. 231), William Chessour and John Chessor in Goullie (or Gullie) appear in 1633 (SCM., III, p. 81, 130), and Edward Chessor appears in same year (ibid., p. 80). Thomas Chesser was witness in Brabuster, 1626 (OSS., I, 158), Frances Chessyre is in record in Edinburgh, 1649 (*Edinb. Marr.*), William Chesser in Aberdeen in 1726 (NSCM., II, p. 116), and George Chessor in Strathrey in 1735 (CRA.). Chessour 1634.

CHEVES. A variant of SHIVAS, q.v.

CHEYNE, CHEINE, CHIENE, CHENEY. Of Norman origin from Quesney near Coutances, a place name meaning 'oak-plantation.' The Scots family is believed to be a branch of the house of Cheyne or Cheyney of Buckinghamshire. Ricardus de Chenai witnessed gift by Hucdredus filius Fergus to the Hospital of St. Peter of York c. 1158–64 (*Edgar*, p. 219). But the earliest of the name in Scotland appears to have been William de Chesne, witness to a charter by William the Lion, a. 1200 (LSC., 33). Some of the early charter writers confused *chene*, 'oak,' with *chien*, 'dog,' and so erroneously Latinized the name *canis*. William le Chen had a protection while in the king of England's service beyond seas, 1230 (*Bain*, I, 1089). There were three Reginalds in succession, all figures of great importance in their day: (1) Reginald, a nephew of John Balliol of Badenoch, sheriff of Kincardine, 1242, in 1267 appointed chamberlain (*camerarius*) of Scotland; (2) Sir Reginald who held the thanage of Fermartyn as 'firmarius' in 1286, and rendered homage in 1296; (3) Reginald the third and last of that name in succession was one of the signers of the barons' letter to the pope, April, 1320. His line ended in two daughters, co-heiresses, Mary and Margaret or Marjory. By the marriage of Mary with John Keith of Inverugy the Keiths obtained a footing in Caithness. Margaret Chein, before 1370, had from David II a charter of the lands of Strathbrok and the half of Cathness (RMS., I, App. II, 1537). Henry le Chen was bishop of Aberdeen for the long period of forty-six years, 1282–1328 (REA., I, p. xxvi–xxviii), and Freskyn de Chen appears as decanus Aber-

donensis, 1321 (ibid., I, p. 47). Sir Reginald de Chen petitioned Edward I in 1305 for two hundred oaks to build his manor of Dufhous (*Bain*, IV, p. 375). The Cheynes of Esselmont are descended from marriage of Janet Marshall, heiress of Essilmonte (end of fourteenth century) to Chene of Straloch. Thomas Chyne appears in Reddene, 1567 (*Kelso*, p. 522), and John Chyine was trade burgess in Aberdeen, 1666, and Gavin Chisnie the same in 1669 (ROA., I, p. 235–236). In the United States the name appears to have become Chinn. Chayne 1600, Cheen 1687, Scheyne 1649.

CHIARAN, CLANN. The Clann Chiaran were a sept of the Grants, and had their seat at Dallachaple in Cromdale (*Shaw*, I, p. 227). The name Ciaran is a personal one from *ciar* 'dusky,' therefore the dusky one. See CIARAN and MACILHERAN.

CHIENE. A variant of CHEYNE, q.v.

CHIESLEY, CHIESLY. Thomas Cheslye is recorded in Caldyrstarris, 1532 (*Rental*), and David Cheislie was witness in Linlithgow, 1534 (*Johnsoun*). Magister John Cheislie was minister of the word of God at Quothquon or Quodquan, Lanarkshire, 1635 and 1653 (*Inquis.*, 2171; *Lanark CR.*). Sir John Cheislie of Kerswall, knight, in record, 1677 (*Retours, Lanark*, 341), and John Cheislie of Carswell was warded in the Canongate Tolbooth, Edinburgh, 1683 (BOEC., VIII, p. 156). Chiesly of Dalry assassinated Sir George Lockhart in 1689, and John Chiesley, a Scottish merchant in London, suggested the establishment of an East India Company in Scotland, 1695. George Cheislie, elder in Elrig, 1652, and other two of the name are recorded in Stirling Commissariot Record. John Chiesley, writer in Edinburgh, 1730 (*Guildry*, p. 137). Cheislay 1649, Cheisle 1525, Chesle and Chesly 1527, Cheyssly 1537, Schesle 1531.

CHILD. From the OE. personal name *Cild*. The "exact sense of the name is uncertain. The singular is used as a title of honour in late OE. times and this is found also throughout the Middle Ages, as in Childe Roland" (Mawer, *The Chief elements used in English place-names*, p. 16). It was synonymous with *enfant* in France. Henricus Child was canon of Scone c. 1275 (*Scon*, p. 85), and James Chyld was canon of Monymusk, 1549 (*View*, p. 180). Robert Cheild, burgess of Dundee, 1564 (RPC., I, p. 276). William Child was dean of guild in Aberdeen, 1829 (*Guildry*, p. 203).

CHILHAM. Roese de Chilham of the county of Rokesburgh who rendered homage in 1296 (*Bain*, II, p. 214) most probably derived his name from Chilham in Kent.

CHIRNSIDE. From the place of this name in Berwickshire. William de Chernysyd is mentioned as holding land c. 1250–1266 (*Soltre*, p. 31), and in the same century we have a charter by Mariote de Chirneside "quondam uxor Ricardi de Reston" of a carucate of land at Remingston to the prior of St. Ebbe, Coldingham (*Seals. Supp.*, 206). Hugh de Chirnesyde who witnessed an agreement between the bishop of St. Andrews and the abbot of Kelso in 1316 (*Kelso*, 310), may be Hugo de Schirnessyd who witnessed an instrument of relaxation of c. 1328 (ibid., p. 370). Laurence de Chernside held land in Edinburgh in 1391 (RMS., I, 855), and John Chirnsyde had a charter of the lands of Fowllerland in the toun of Quhitsome from Robert III (RMS., I, App. II, 1805). John Chyrnesey, chaplain, 'Scocheman,' *alias* Chyrnese *alias* Chirnesyde had a pardon in 1407 (*Bain*, IV, p. 151). David of Chernside is in record in 1448 and again in 1451 (*Bain*, IV, 1207, 1240), and a Chirnsyde of Whitsumlawes appears in a retour of the lands of Vedderburn in 1469 (*Sc. Ant.*, VII, p. 25). John Chernside and David Chernside witnessed an instrument of sasine in 1474 (*Home*, p. 23), and David Chernside was summoned in 1479 to answer to Parliament for treason and other crimes (APS., II, p. 129). Patrick Chernside was admitted burgess of Aberdeen in 1493 (NSCM., I, p. 37; CRA., p. 50), and Robert Chyrnsid of Possil was "commisser of Glesguowe" in 1595 (*Cawdor*, p. 211). William Chirnsyde was the first Reformed minister of the parish of Luss. David Chirnesyde of Posso was on an assize in 1613 (*Trials*, III, p. 250), and another David Chyrnsyde was retoured heir in lands in the barony of Haills in 1662 (*Retours, Berwick*, 288). The name of Bothwell's servant, Archibald Chirnside, appears in record as Chirnseede, Chirneseede, Chirmseede, and Chernsyde (CSPS., x). Chernsid 1478 and 1495, Chernsvd 1476, Chirniesyd 1605, Chyrnsyd 1552, Chyrnsyde and Chyrnesyde 1598.

CHISHOLM, Chisholme. An old Border family deriving their name from the barony of Chisholm in the parish of Roberton, Roxburghshire. The name occurs but seldom in early Scots records. The first of the name recorded is John de Chesehelme, mentioned in a bull of Pope Alexander IV, 1254. John de Chesolm of Berwickshire, and Richard de Chesehelme of Roxburghshire rendered homage in 1296. The seal of the latter bears on a heater shield, a boar's head, couped, contourné, dropping blood, and S' *Ricardi de Cheishelm* (*Bain*, II, p. 199, 207, 531). Inquisition was made in 1315 into the lands and fishings of John

de Cheseholm in Paxton and Tweed (*Bain*, III, 461), and Robert de Chesholm is mentioned in an action against the burgh of Dundee, 1348 (RAA., II, 22). By the middle of the fourteenth century members of the family had made their way to the North, and in 1359 Robert de Chesholme appears as sheriff of Inverness, and an Alexander de Chesseholme is there also (ER., I, p. 569, 570). Robert de Chesholme was custodian of the Castle of Vrchard (ER., II, p. 143), and in 1369 he is mentioned as dominus de Quarelwode in Moray (REM., p. 169). John de Sheshelm was admitted burgess of Aberdeen in 1439 (NSCM., I, p. 5), and three members of the family of Chisholm of Cromlix held the bishopric of Dunblane in the sixteenth century (*Dowden*). In 1499 certain individuals were put to the horn for the slaughter of Harrald of Schlescheme, dwelling in Straglas (OPS., II, p. 527). It is interesting to note that so late as 1512 the territorial form "of Chessam" was still in use in the North (*Cawdor*, p. 126). Weyland Chisholm had his lands of Comer in Strathglass erected into a barony in 1513. John Chesholm of Kinereis in record, 1603 (*Rec. Inv.*, II, p. 14), Walter Chisholm of that Ilk was bailie of regality of Melrose, 1605 (RRM., I, p. 1), and Alexander Cheshom was a private in the Reay Fencibles, 1795 (*Scobie*, p. 371). The Gaelic form of Chisholm is *Siosal*, and collectively the clan is known as An Siosalach. The Highland Chisholms were also sometimes distinguished from the Lowland Chisholms as An Siosalach Glaiseach, the Chisholms of Strathglass. Chehelme 1376, Cheishame 1508, Cheisholme 1626, Chesame 1511, Cheshelme 1480, Cheseim 1527, Chesim 1506, Chesolme 1522, Chesom 1531, Chesome 1511, Chessame 1480, Chisolm 1721, Chisolme 1674, Chisomme 1562, Chissem 1544, Chissolme 1670, Schescheme 1499, Schisholme 1642, Schisolme and Schisome 1675, Shisholme 1650, Schishome 1650, Scvkklaw (for = lam) 1361. In Antrim the name has become Chism.

CHIVAS. A variant of Shivas, q.v.

CHOMBICH. See under Macchombich. The shortened form was a personal name in Breadalbane 150 years and more ago (SN&Q., III, p. 172).

CHREE. There were families of this name in Glenbuchat and Strathdon in the eighteenth century, and the name is still found in Angus. George Cree was schoolmaster at Glenalmond, 1743 (*Dunkeld*).

CHRISTIAN. From the Latin personal name *Christianus*, 'belonging to Christ.' Christianus was the name of a bishop of Candida Casa

(Whithorn) who died at Holm Cultram in 1186 (*Chron. Mail.*). James Christane in Kirkcudbright signs the Test, 1684 (RPC., 3. ser. x, p. 248). See CHRISTIE.

CHRISTIE, CHRISTY. A diminutive of (1) Christian or CRISTINUS, q.v., and (2) perhaps also of CHRISTOPHER. The surname is very common in Fife, which indeed seems to have been an early home of the name. Chrystie was the name of an old Stirling family (see "The Christies and their doings," in *Stirling antiquary*, III, p. 212–214). In a charter dated 13th July 1457, granted by the abbot of Lindores to the burgh of Newburgh, John Chrysty appears as a burgess (Laing, *Newburgh*, p. 479–480). John Chryste was admitted burgess of Aberdeen in 1530 (NSCM., I, 51). Sir Robert Criste, presbyter, witness in Fife, 1547 (*Gaw*, 9). Cristina Criste or Crystie was tenant under the bishop of Moray, 1565 (REM., p. 434). Jhone Cristie was a "burne ledder" (water carrier) in St. Andrews, 1590 (*St. Andrews*, p. 687). Henry Crystie, heir of John Crystie in Leith, 1597 (*Inquis.*, 7). John Crystie had precept of sasine of land in the vill of Stentoune, 1605 (RD., p. 503), and David Crystie was burgess of Dysart, 1624 (*Retours, Fife*, 503). As forename: Cristy de Carvant of Edinburghshire, 1296, also appears as Cristine de Carvan (*Bain*, II, p. 201, 227), Cristie Pairman, 1569 (RPC., I, p. 661). Chrystie 1605, Chrysty 1688, Creste 1612, Criste 1541, Cristy 1476.

CHRISTISON, 'the son of Christopher,' from the diminutive CHRISTIE, q.v. Christy and Chrystinus were used as equivalents of Christopher as a forename (*Milne*). Henry Cristeson held a tenement in Stirling in 1412 (*Cambus.*, 210), Alexander Cristini (Latin gen.), burgess of Brechin in 1436 is probably the Alexander Cristisone or Cristysoun who appears as a witness in the same town in 1446 and 1447 (REB., I, 81, 105, 109; II, 60). In the Scots text he is Alexander Cristysoun and in the notary's Latin note he is Alexandro Cristini. John Crysteson was burgess of Edinburgh in 1450 (EBR., 9), and the surname was common there in the fifteenth and sixteenth centuries. Robert Cristison witnessed a sasine in 1458 (*Neubotle*, p. 246, 248), Alan Cristison was admitted burgess of Aberdeen in 1479 (NSCM., I, p. 28), Alexander Cristesone was member of assize at Cupar in 1521 (SCBF., p. 223), David Criteson was presented to the vicarage of the parish church of Abirkerdor in 1525 (RAA., II, 611); Robert Crystison was a friar of Culross in 1569 (*Laing*, 844),

Donald Cristyson was burgess of Kyrkwaw in 1455 (REO., p. 191), William Cristesoune was fugitive from the law in 1531 (*Trials*, I, p. 155), and Andrew Chrystesone was retoured heir of John Chrystesone his father in lands of Wester Coudlands in the barony of Coudland in 1620 (*Retours, Fife*, 303). "The name was common in the shires of Aberdeen, Kincardine, and Forfar, and was borne by many churchmen" (*Stodart*). Chirstison 1699, Chrysteson 1575, Chrystesone 1532, Chrystesoun 1635, Chrystesoune 1655, Chrystiesone 1643, Cresteson 1529, Crestesone 1522, Crestesoun 1526, Cristessone 1523, Cristesoun 1522, Cristesoune 1523, Cristin 1456, Cristisone 1494, Cristisoun 1526, Crystesone 1588, Crystesoun 1508, Crystisoun 1555, Crystyson 1525.

CHRISTOPHER. Formerly a not uncommon forename in Scotland, but better known under the pet form CHRYSTAL, q.v. Used also as an Englishing of *Gille Chriosda* (Gilchrist).

CHRISTOPHERSON, 'son of Christopher,' and thus = CHRISTISON. Andrew Christopherson is recorded in Setter, Nesting, Shetland, in 1648 (*Sc. Ant.*, XII, p. 90).

CHRYSTAL, CHRYSTALL, CHRISTAL, CRYSTAL, CRYSTALL. Bardsley says this surname is of local origin, but in Scotland it is certainly a diminutive or pet form of CHRISTOPHER, q.v., as shown, for instance, by the name of Christall Murray who appears as depute of the sheriff of Stirling in 1561 (SBR., p. 79). The first form was an old surname in Foveran, and it was not uncommon in Prestwick, Ayrshire, in the fifteenth century. Willi Cristole was a burgess of Prestwick in 1470 (*Prestwick*, p. 1), and in 1474 Charles Cristoll was presented in court and the bailies were asked "to put till enquest to inquir and se gef that he was narrest and apperand air to vmquhill Cristoll Jonsoun" (ibid., p. 25). John Cristall witnessed a charter of land in Rait in 1491 (*Scon*, p. 199), George Cristall of Dysart was a captive among the 'Turks' of Algiers, 1650 (PBK., p. 361), and Thomas Cristell was master of the ship *James of Dundee* in 1567 (RPC., I, p. 544). Chrystell 1657, Cristale 1548, Cristle 1474. As forename: Cristall Knowis 1549 (*Gaw*, 34). See also under MACCRISTAL.

CIARAN. Diminutive of *ciar* 'black, dusky.' See under CHIARAN and MACILHERAN.

CINAED. This name in the genitive (*Cinatha*) is in the *Book of Deer* (II, 11), and is the origin of KENNETH, in English, q.v.

CINNAMOND. A current variant of KINNINMONTH, q.v.

CITHARISTA. From the occupation, player on the cithara. An old name in the parish of Methlick, Aberdeenshire (*Jervise*, II, p. 25). Nicholas Cithariste had a charter of the forfeited lands of Alexander Cruk or Cruiks in the constabulary of Lithgow from Robert the Brus, and Ade Cythariste or Chichariste had a charter of the lands of Balveny and Tolecandalantum in the thanedom of Abrelemno from the same king (RMS., I, App. II, 901, 950). Thomas cithariste who was provost of Rutherglen in 1328 was probably the individual to whom a pension was paid in the following year (ER., I, p. 87, 150). Cf. also HARPER.

CLACHAN. Local, from one or other of the several small places of the name in the shires of Wigtown, Ayr, Perth, Argyll, and Dumbarton.

CLACHAR, CLACHER. From Gaelic *clachair*, a mason. Thomas Clachar in Achiltie was fined in 1613 for resetting outlawed members of Clan Gregor (RPC., XIV, p. 640). John Clachar in Blindgerie is in record in 1661 *(Caithness)*. See also MACCLACHER.

CLACKMANNAN. Of local origin from the village of the name in Clackmannanshire. William de Clackmanayn was burgess of Dunfermline, 1316 (RD., 349).

CLAKKESTON. Robert de Clakkeston, Benedictine prior of Goldingham, 1378 (*Cal. Papal Registers*, III, p. 236), most probably derived his name from Claxton in county Durham.

CLANACHAN, CLANAHAN, CLANOCHAN. Surnames current in Galloway and Arran. Alexander Clannachan in Barrsceoch in 1753 *(Wigtown)*. From (MAC)CLANNACHAN, q.v.

CLAPPERTON. George Clapartoun who appears as subdean of the Chapel Royal of Stirling in 1546 was probably Sir George Clappertoun or Clappertoun who appears between 1558 and 1573 as Provost of the College of Holy Trinity, Edinburgh (*Soltre*, p. 222, 225). Mr. John Clapperton of Neatoune appears in 1655 *(Lauder)*, and Edward Clawpirton in Dinrod in 1688 *(Kirkcudbright)*. Hugh Clapperton (1788-1827), the African explorer, was born at Annan, Dumfriesshire. Clappertone 1680, Clappertoun 1684, Clappertoune 1658.

CLARK, CLARKE, CLERK. Originally a man in a religious order, and later a scholar, a penman, in early charters Latinized *clericus*. Roger clericus held a land between 1174–78 (*Kelso*, 383), and Thomas clericus was one of those appointed in 1246 to determine the right marches of Wester Fedale (LAC., 23). James the clerk was witness to a charter by Richard de Bancori of land in Dumfriesshire, a. 1249 (*Bain*, I, 1684), and Alan clericus was charter witness in Aberdeen, 1281 (REA., II, p. 279). Nine persons named 'le clerk,' rendered homage for their possessions, 1296 (*Bain*, II). In the fourteenth and following centuries the name was quite common throughout the Lowlands and is found in all old Scots charters and public documents, and only after 1400 do we feel certain that the word is truly a surname. John Clerc possessed a tenement in Edinburgh, 1400 (*Egidii*, p. 37), Adam Clark or Clerk was burgess of Dundee, 1406 (REB., I, 25; II, 12), and Hugh Clerk and Alan Clerk were burgesses of Irvine, 1418 (*Irvine*, I, p. 27). John Clerk of Leith, shipmaster, had a safe conduct into England, 1446 (*Bain*, IV, 1186). Robert Clerk took part in the second hership of Petty, 1513 (*Rose*, p. 190), Johannes Clark was prior of Scone, 1524 (*Scon*, p. 204), and Angus the clerk, a follower of Donald Gorme of Sleat, had remission in 1541 for his part in laying waste Trouterness in Sky and Kenlochew in Ross (RSS., II, 3943). Richard Clark, a native of Montrose, became vice-admiral of Sweden and presented a brass chandelier to the parish church of his native town, 1623. Hans Clerck, of a different family, rose to be an admiral in the same service. The name still exists in Sweden and Finland in the form Klerck. The word was borrowed into Gaelic and gave origin to the surname Mac a' chleirich. Claerk 1547. George Rogers Clark (1752–1818), to whom is due the possession of the territory northwest of the Ohio, 1783, was of Scottish descent.

CLARKSON, 'son of the clerk' (i.e. scholar). See CLARK. Thomas Clerkson de Aldane was a forestaller in Aberdeen in 1402 (CRA., p. 383). Simon Clerici (Latin gen.) witnessed an instrument of resignation in Brechin in 1434 (REB., I, 65), and a booth was set to Besse Clerkson in Lanark in 1488 (*Lanark*, p. 1). William Clerkson, chaplain at the altar of the B. V. within the parish church of Lanark in 1500 (RSS.), is mentioned again in 1501 as Sir William Clerksone (*Lanark*, p. 11). John Clarksone was tenant of the bishop of Glasgow in 1513 *(Rental)*, and John Clerksoun and Donald Clerksoun were tenants of Feris, Balcomy, in 1531 (ER., XVII, p. 668). Andro Clerksone had a special respite and protection in 1504 (*Trials*, I, p. 43*), Charles Clerksoun in Leith acknowledged the king's coronation and the regency in 1567 (RPC., I, p. 563), Agnes Clerkson in Dirleton, East Lothian, was executed for witchcraft, 1649 (*Trials*, III, p. 599) and Andrew Clarksone was portioner of Holhouse, parish of Slamannan in 1685 (*Stirling*). Clearkson 1674, Clercsone 1461, Clerksson 1538.

CLARSAIR. G. *Clàrsair*, 'harper.' Eugene Klerscharch, a charter witness in Dundee, 1434, appears in following year as Eugene Klaresthabch (HP., II, p. 175, 177).

CLASON. Probably from Clas, a diminutive of Nicholas. Payment to Johannes Clayson at mandate of chamberlain, 1328 (ER., I, p. 101). Katherine Clasone in Fossoquhy, parish of Logie, 1615 (*Stirling*). James Clasone was prisoner in Canongate Tolbooth, Edinburgh, 1684 (RPC., 3. ser. x, p. 352). Four persons named Clasone are recorded in Coldhome, parish of Logie, in the seventeenth century (*Dunblane*). James Clawson was indweller in Bathgait, 1688 (*Edin. App.*).

CLASS. A Caithness surname, probably from Klaas, Dutch pet form of Nicolaas. See under NICOL.

CLATT. This surname, at one time common in Aberdeenshire, was assumed from the village of Clatt in the parish of the same name there. William de Clatt was a canon of St. Andrews in 1264 (RPSA., p. 349). John Clat or de Clat was prebendary of Cloueth (Clova) in 1434 (REA., I, p. 234), prebendary of Glenberuy in 1448 and in 1453 referred to as a canon of Aberdeen (REB., I, 123, II, 72; RAA., II, 96). Duncan Clat or Duncan de Clat who appears in Aberdeen between 1433 and 1438 (SCM., v, p. 41) is doubtless Doncan of Clat or Dunkan of Glatt, merchant and burgess of Aberdeen, who had safe conducts into England in 1438 and 1439 (Bain, IV, 1114, 1134), nine years after he was appointed on a war committee in the same burgh (REA., I, p. 239; CRA., p. 16), and again appears as a witness in 1451 (REA., II, p. 297). Alan Clat was admitted burgess of Aberdeen in 1449 (NSCM., I, p. 12), and John Clatt was vicar of Banchory-Devenick in 1425 (*Illus.*, III, p. 517).

CLATTI. William of Clatti who witnessed the homage of Andrew, son of Gilmur to the prior of St. Andrews in 1269 (RPSA., p. 349) perhaps derived his name from Clatto in the joint parishes of St. Andrews-Kemback, Fife.

CLAYHILLS. From the lands of Clayhills near Blairgowrie in Perthshire. Robert Clayhills was admitted a burgess of Dundee in 1524 (*Wedd.*, p. 9n), and a family of this name for cen-

turies were prominent merchants and members of the Guildry Incorporation of Dundee. Thomas Clahills took his bachelor's degree at St. Andrews in 1523 and George Clahillis took his in 1526. Andrew Clayhills, admitted minister of Jedburgh by the General Assembly in 1586, took a prominent part in Church affairs (Calderwood, *History*, IV, p. 566, 604, 637, 682, etc.). Robert Clayhills de Baldovie was retoured heir of Robert Clayhills his father in 1633 (*Retours, Forfar*, 216). Thomas Clayhills emigrated to Riga, c. 1639, and became ancestor of "a highly esteemed race of merchants" in the Baltic provinces and Finland (*Donner*, p. 22). Mary Clayhills became the wife of a cavalry-captain, A. S. Lvoff, and her name appears in Russian as Kleigel. The area of the church of Invergowrie is used as a cemetery by the Clayhills family (*Jervise*, I, p. 193). Clayhillis 1552.

CLAYPOLE. Magister Symon de Claypoll who witnessed the gift of the church of Maleuille to the monastery of Dunfermline in 1255 (RD., 206), and two years later appears as Master Simon de Claipol, rector of Insula (St. Mary's Isle) in the diocese of Whithern (*Pap. Lett.*, I, p. 344), was probably a cleric from England. Claypole is a parish in Lincolnshire.

CLEAN. From *Cle'an*, a Gaelic reduced form of *(Mac)Gill' Sheathain* (Maclean). Effie Clean in parish of Borgue, 1684 (RPC., 3. ser. IX, p. 568).

CLEATOUN. Local. Andrew Cleatoun in Magdalan-Cheppell, parish of Brechin, 1622, and four more of the name (*Brechin*).

CLEATT, CLEAT. An old Orcadian surname, from the township of the same name in the parish of St. Ola. Mawnus of Clat was witness to a wadset of date 1447 (REO., p. 190). Cleet is recorded in Jedburgh 1942.

CLEAVE. From (MAC)CLEAVE, 1684.

CLEGHORN. Of local origin from Cleghorn in Lanarkshire. David Cleghorne witnessed a sasine of 1541 (*Home*, 252). James Gleghorne was admitted burgess freeman of Glasgow in 1601 (*Burgesses*), and another James Gleghorne is recorded in Coldingham in 1635 (*Lauder*). The home of the Cleghorns is in the West of Scotland, but a group of families of the name flourished in the parish of Cramond for several generations, and Robert Cleghorn, farmer, at Saughton, near Edinburgh, was a friend of Robert Burns. Clegorne 1651, Gleghorne 1589; Cleggorne.

CLEISH. From Cleish in Fife. Gilbert de Cles was one of an assize of marches in Fife in 1230 (RD., 196), and in the following year made a gift of ten shillings annually to the monks of Dunfermline (ibid., 192). In 1488 there is mention of the land of vmqwhyll Johne of Clech in Dunfermline (DBR., 1).

CLELAND, CLELLAND. This surname is supposed to be derived from lands named Cleland or Kneland in the parish of Dalziel, Lanarkshire. The first of the family in record is said to be Alexander Kneland of that Ilk, temp. Alexander III. He married Margaret, daughter of Adam Wallace of Riccarton, father of the Patriot, and Kneland, a follower of Wallace, is mentioned several times by Henry the Minstrel (Wallace, III, 55, 201, etc.). Anderson (Scot. Nat.) says there are several instances of Cleland of Cleland being called Knieland of that Ilk; thus among the persons who were delated for being art and part of the murder of Darnley were William Kneland of that Ilk and Arthur Kneland of Knowhobbilhill. William Kneland was burgess of Glasgow, 1464 (LCD., p. 182), Gavin Kneland, witness in Linlithgow, 1534 (Johnsoun), and Marjory Kneland appears in Fosh, parish of Monkland, 1546 (Campsie). James Kneland of that Ilk made his will in 1547 (Comm. Rec. of Glasgow), Kneland of Foskane is mentioned in 1557, Gawin Cleland was denounced rebel in 1568 (RPC., I, p. 621), and William Kneland was burgess-freeman of Glasgow, 1574 (Burgesses). The seal of Andrew Cleland, one of the bailies of Edinburgh, 1612, reads S' Andree Kneland (Macdonald, 438). John Cleaveland or Cleland of Garrenshaugh appears in 1686 (RPC., 3. ser. XII, p. 69, 77), and James Cleiland was a merchant in Edinburgh, 1692 (Pitfirrane, 659). The name may be an early corruption of Cleveland. Roger de Clivaland was found in default for not attending an assize at Carlisle, 1278 (Bain, II, p. 34), and Osbern de Clivelond of Lanarkshire rendered homage, 1296 (ibid., p. 212). Clealand 1633, Cleilland 1678, Clayland 1604, Cliland 1687, Coleeland 1685, Kneband (error for Kneland) 1586.

CLEMENT. A personal name from Lat. clemen(t-)s, humane, merciful, through Fr. Clément. S. Clement, according to tradition, was the third bishop of Rome after S. Peter, and died c. 100 A. D. Clement, bishop of Dunblane, elected 1233. William Clement had remission for his part in burning the town of Dunbertane in 1489 (Lennox, II, p. 133). James Clement in parish of Tongland was shot for being a Covenanter, 1685 (Hanna, II, p. 268). Helen Clement is recorded at the Miln of Muckhart

in 1742 (Stirling), and six of the name are in the Commissariot Record of Dunblane.

CLEMISON. Son of Clemmie, a double diminutive of CLEMENT, q.v. John Clemison, workman in Leadhills, 1737 (Lanark).

CLENACHAN, CLENACHAN, CLENOCHAN. See under MACCLANNACHAN.

CLENHILL. Probably from Clennell near Alwinton, Northumberland, which appears in early record as Clenhull (1255) and Clenhill (1346). Thomas de Clenhill, miles, witnessed a charter of the lands of Dolar in the fee of Clackmanan, 1277 (RD., p. 54). He may be the Thomas de Clenhile who received a fee in 1290 (Bain, II, p. 97) and the Thomas de Clenel of Lanarkshire who rendered homage in 1296 (ibid., p. 213).

CLEOPHAS. From the Biblical Cleophas or Clopas (John, XIX, 25). Cleophas, clericus de Dunde, 1202–04 (RAA., I, p. 96). Cleopha Alberti (= son of Albert), charter witness in Dundee, 1281 (HP., II, p. 223).

CLEPHANE. The Clephanes appear to have been an offshoot of an ancient family in England which derived their surname from Clapham in Sussex, where they appear to have been settled shortly after the Conquest. The first of the family in Scotland settled in Lauderdale as a vassal of the Morvilles. Alan de Claphaṁ witnessed a charter by Roland of Galloway, c. 1200 (Kelso, 254), and Walter Clapham witnessed a charter by Thomas de Galwethia to the Abbey of Neubotle, c. 1230 (Neubotle, 27). William de Clopham was one of the Scots prisoners taken at Dunbar in 1296, and Marc de Clapham of Fife rendered homage in the same year. His seal bears a fleur-de-lys, and S' Marci de Clapha (Bain, II, p. 177, 205, 554). Johanne de Clapam witnessed confirmation of Snowdoun to Dryburgh Abbey, c. 1350 (Dryburgh, p. 232), Alan de Clappam witnessed homage of Duncan, 12th earl of Fife to the abbot of Dunfermline, 1316 (RD., 349), and Alexander of Claphame witnessed a charter by Henry St. Clair, earl of Orkney, at Kirkuaw, 1391 (RMS., I, 824; REO., p. 28). John Clephane, dominus de Kerslogy, 1410 (Milne, p. 41), Ricardus Clapehame, canon of Aberdeen, 1451 (RD., p. 327), Margret Clapane was banished the town of Edinburgh in 1529 for "bving of fische to regrait agane" (MCM., II, p. 85), John Clapen was one of the Scottish undertakers granted an allotment in Ulster, 1610 (Ford, Scotch-Irish in America, Princeton, 1915, p. 553), and Adam Clephane was killed in a radical riot in Greenock, 1820 (Williamson, Old Greenock, I, p. 241). Clapain

1527, Clapame 1520, Clepan and Clepon 1661, Cleppin 1698, Cleponne 1574, Claiphame 1465, Claiphane 1489, Clapane 1529, Clapen 1584, Claphaine 1593, Clepan 1563, Clepane 1567, Clepen 1582, Clephame 1460, Clepheane 1637.

CLERACH. G. *cleireach*, a clerk, a writer, but perhaps shortened from MACCHLERY, q.v. Archibald Cleiroche, burgess freeman of Glasgow, 1609 *(Burgesses)*. Thomas Clerach in Balnahegleish (in Mar) fined for reset of Clan Gregor, 1613 (RPC., XIV, p. 632).

CLERIE. Recorded in Galloway, 1684 *(Parish)*. From MACCHLERY, q.v.

CLERIHEW. An Aberdeenshire surname. William Clerihew of Kegge was convicted of profanation of the Lord's day, etc., in 1644 *(Alford*, p. 49, 61), Patrick Clerihew was a church elder at Tullinessell in 1680 (ibid., p. 316), John Clerihev, indweller in the barony of Whitehaugh, is in record in 1686 (SCM., v, p. 235), and Arthur Clarihew in Woodend in Tillienestle in 1731 (CRA.). Clariehew 1687, Clariehue 1775, Clerichue 1799, Clerihewe 1686.

CLERK. *See under* CLARK.

CLERK EGO. John *alias* Clerk Ego or Clerkego was tenant of Innerquhanavit and Innerree, 1539 (ER., XVII, p. 656, 657).

CLEUCH. Of local origin from a place of the name. Cf. Cleuch, Clooch in *Dumfries Retours* (191, 259, 266, etc.). William Clewgh, fuller, in Glasgow, 1505 *(Simon*, 116). Robert Cleuch in Cademuir, 1557 (PSAS., LXXV, p. 114), James Cleuch on assize in Edinburgh, 1567 (MCM., II, p. 308), and William Cleugh, tidewaiter at the port of Dumfries, 1778 *(Dumfries)*.

CLIFTON. From one or other of the several places named Clifton in England. Johannes de Clystona [? for Clyftona] held land in Edinburgh, 1368 (RMS., I, 242), and a later John Clyftoun was burgess there in 1414 (REG., 324). Long s and *f* were frequently confused in transcribing old records.

CLIMIE. Most probably diminutive of CLEMENT, q.v. Two smithies were resigned in favor of George Clemy in Glasgow, 1553 *(Protocols*, I). The name occurs elsewhere in the Protocols. William Climav appears in Achinames, 1652, and Andrew Climie or Cleemy in Lawmarnoch, 1677 *(Kilbarchan)*. Climy 1673.

CLINGAN, CLINGEN. A not uncommon Galloway surname, from (MAC)CLINGAN, q.v. William Clingane in Ladieland, 1658 *(Dumfries)*. Edward Clingzean in Castletoun, 1680 *(Kirkcudbright)*. Alexander Clingane in Kirkcudbright signed the Test, 1684 (RPC., 3. ser. x, p. 248). Clingen 1684.

CLINK. An uncommon surname recorded in Perthshire and still existing in the Fife district *(Sc. Ant.*, IV, p. 114). The writer there says it is Flemish, and that Jan Clink was a magistrate of Ghent in the fifteenth century.

CLINKSKILL, CLINKSCALE, CLINKSCALES. Doubtless of local origin from the "terra cottagia in villa de Coldinghame vocata Clinkskaillis," of 1601 *(Retours, Berwick*, 27), and not from an ancestor, "an energetic tradesman or money changer,"· as suggested by Weekley (p. 258). Walter Clinkscales is recorded in Wedderburn mylne in 1635 and Isobel Clinkscales in Grewldykes in 1675 *(Lauder)*, and Agnes Clinkskell died in 1785 and was buried in Langton Churchyard. Dr. John G. Clinkscales (d. 1941), professor of mathematics at Wofford College, South Carolina, was of Scottish descent.

CLINTERTY. A surname found in Aberdeenshire, derived from the small place of the name in the parish of Newhills.

CLINTON. Most probably in Scotland a shortened form of MACCLINTON, q.v. John Clinton in Laich Lochfergus, 1674 *(Kirkcudbright)*. John Clinton resident in parish of Senneck, 1684 (RPC., 3. ser. IX, p. 569).

CLINTS. Probably from Clints near Stow, Midlothian. Richard Clvntis and John Clyntis to be apprehended, 1566 *(Report on Laing MSS.*, I, p. 17).

CLOACK. Alexander Cloack, gardener to Tannochy, 1685 (RPC., 3. ser. x, p. 542), probably derived his surname from Cloak in the parish of Lumphanan, Aberdeenshire.

CLOCHODERICK. Finlaius de Clourotrich or Clochotrich appears as a charter witness in 1270, and c. 1272 he appears again as Fynlaius de Clouchrocherg (RMP., p. 138, 190, 233). He probably derived his name from Clochoderick in the parish of Kilbarchan so named from the huge isolated rock mass there. For an account of the place name see Watson I (p. 201).

CLOGG. Matheus Cloig was one of the 'appreciatores carnium' (pricers of flesh) in 1403 (EBR., I). John Clog in Dundee was charged with aiding the English in 1552 (*Beats*, p. 327). A tenement was granted in feu farm to Allan Cloge in Glasgow, 1554 (*Protocols*, I). Alexander Clogg in Over Ardwell, 1674, and three others of the name are in the Commissariot Record of Kirkcudbright, 1663–1800. Thomas Cloggis, merchant in Glasgow, 1606.

CLOGIE. Thomas Clogie and Johnne Clogie were charged with tumult in Glasgow, 1606 (RPC., VII, p. 244), Thomas Clogie was burgess freeman of Glasgow, 1609 (*Burgesses*), Jonet Cloggie was spouse to John Luggie in the parish of Monkland, 1624 (*Campsie*), and Thomas Clogie in Crostandie in Elnrick, 1634, and two more of the name are recorded in the Stirling Commissariot Record. Cloggie 1672.

CLOKIE. A shortening of MACLUCKIE, q.v.

CLOSEBURN. From Closeburn in Nithsdale, Dumfriesshire. Ivo, son of Stephen de Killeosberne, Scots prisoner of war, died in Carlisle prison in 1299 (*Bain*, II, 1179).

CLOUDSLIE. James Cloudslie, burgess of Montrose, 1638, and three more of the name are recorded in Brechin Commissariot Record, and John Cloudslie, burgess of Montrose, died in 1658 (*Jervise*, I, p. 222). Perhaps of English origin from Cloudesley, an old surname in Sussex (*Guppy*, p. 383).

CLOUSTON. From the place called Clouston (earlier Cloustath, for N. *Klóstaðr*), in Stenness, Orkney. William Cloustatht, roithman (councilman) in Stenness, 1500 (REO., p. 75), Mawnis of Clustay was one of an inquest at Sabay, 1522, Huchone or Hutcheon Clouchstay and his daughters are mentioned, 1527, and George Clouston of that Ilk in 1607 (ibid., p. 95, 177, 209). Magnus Clousta was witness in Shetland, 1624 (OSS., I, 60). Clistoun and Clisten 1655–1671, Clouchstath 1514, Clouchston 1548, Cloustaith 1503, Cloustan and Cloustane 1626, Cloustone 1574, Cloustoun 1597, Clustane 1551. J. Storer Clouston (1870–   ), antiquary, historian, and novelist.

CLOW. Of local origin from the small place of the name in the parish of Dunning, Perthshire. Lawrence Clow was witness in Perth, 1547 (*Rollok*, 28). Andrew Clow in Pett, parish of Muthill, 1663, and fourteen more of the name from 1610 onward, are recorded in Dunblane Commissariot Record. Andrew Clow, soldier in Edinburgh, 1674 (*Edinb. Marr.*), Laurence Clow in Gillgrastoune (now Kilgraston), 1687 (*Inquis.*, 6874). John Clow, merchant in Crieff, 1717, and three others of the name are in Dunkeld Commissariot Record. A payment was made to Agnes Clow in Edinburgh, 1736 (*Guildry*, p. 156), and Jenny Clow in Edinburgh bore a son to Robert Burns the poet. James Claw, burgess of Culross, 1632 (*Dunblane*), may be another spelling (cf. THAW and THOW).

CLUB, CLUBB. A surname confined almost exclusively to the shire of Aberdeen, and long common in the district of Pitsligo. Patrick Club was one of the 'appreciatores carnium' in Aberdeen in 1398 (CRA., p. 375). William Club was admitted burgess of Aberdeen in 1444 (NSCA., I, p. 9), and Thomas Club held land there in 1451 (ibid., II, p. 297). Sir Andrew Club was chaplain of the browne croice altar in 1475 (CRA., p. 33), and Alexander Club was a witness in the same burgh in 1489 (REA., II, p. 303). David Club held land in Aberdeen about the year 1530 (REA., II, p. 232). John Club or Clwb was bewitched in Aberdeen in 1576 (SCM., I, p. 87), Edward Club was tenant and shoemaker in Dibbieshill in 1696 (*Jervise*, II, p. 401), James Club of Westfield of Airth is recorded in 1757 (*Stirling*), and Andrew Club in Upper Bracco died in 1710 (*Jervise*, II, p. 400).

CLUCKIE. (Wigtown). A shortening of MACLUCKIE, q.v.

CLUGSTON. From the barony of Clugston in the parish of Kirkinner, Wigtownshire. The barony passed by an heiress to the Dunbars of Mochrum. The name is still common in the Stewartry. Sir John de Klogestoun who appears c. 1230–32 (LAC., 73) is probably the John Clugestoun who witnessed a charter by Morgund, son of Abbe, of part of the lands of Carrecros c. 1239 (SHSM., IV, p. 316; *Panmure*, I, p. cliv). Adam de Gloggestone of Edinburghshire rendered homage in 1296 (*Bain*, II, p. 213), and John de Cloggestone was one of the Scots prisoners of war taken in Dunbar Castle in the same year (ibid., 742). John Clugston of that Ilk is in record, 1484, Schir Alexander Clugstone witnessed an obligation by John, earl of Lennox, 1493 (*Pollok*, I, p. 205), William Clougston, provost of Wigtown, died in 1734, Mary Clugston is recorded at Glasserton, 1785 (*Wigtown*), and John Clogston was writer in Kirkcudbright, 1798 (*Kirkcudbright*). The surname occurs several times in the Register of Cupar Angus Abbey, and may be from a place of the same name in the vicinity (?). Thomas de Clogstoun leased part of Aberbotheny, 1448 (*Cupar-Angus*, I, p. 127).

CLUNE. Archibald de Clone, judex, 1337 (ER., I, p. 442). Robert of Clone made payment of a debt due by the earl of Strathern, 1380 (ER., III, p. 37). John de Clune was witness to a notarial instrument, 1426 (*Cambus.*, 90); James Clune was a witness in Fife, 1545 (*Gaw*, 41); and John Clwne was a witness in Glasgow, 1551 (*Protocols*, I). Perhaps from Clune in parish of Birse, Aberdeenshire, though the references are all to Fife and Perthshire. Cf. CLUNY.

CLUNIES, CLUNESS (in Shetland). From the old land of Clunes in Inverness-shire (*Retours*). Archibald de Clunace witnessed a grant of lands in Badenoch in 1338 (SCM., IV, p. 126), and William Clunes possessed a house in Leythe (Leith) in 1462 (CDE., 38; *Soltre*, p. 65). Alexander Clwnes was burgess of Cromarty in 1533 (OPS., II, p. 564), Alexander Cluneis of Culbene was a follower of Ross of Balnagown in 1599 (*Celt. Mon.*, XXIII, p. 60), and William Clunes, burgess of Dornoch, was juror on an inquest held in the tolbooth of Dornoch, 1603 (OPS., II, p. 644), and Alexander Clunes was church beddell at Cawdor, 1685 (RPC., 3. ser. X, p. 550). Individuals of this name settled in Northmavine, Shetland, in the early years of the eighteenth century, and from one of them was descended John Clunies-Ross, who, in 1825, became first chief and proprietor of the Keeling (Cocos) Islands.

CLUNY, CLUNIE. From Clunie in the district of Stormont, Perthshire. William de Clonin witnessed a confirmation charter by Alexander II to the Abbey of Arbroath c. 1214–1218 (RAA., I, 100). The ward of Eugene de Cluny is referred to in 1263 (ER., I, p. 3). William de Cluny of Perthshire rendered homage in 1296, and appears again on an inquest at Perth in 1304 (*Bain*, II, p. 191, 211, 414). Another William de Cluny, chaunteur of Breghyn in the county of Strivelyn, also rendered homage in that year and is mentioned again in 1305 as Sir William de Clony, chaplain to the bishop of Brechin (ibid., p. 208, 455). Adam Cluny of Fifeshire also rendered homage in 1296 (ibid., p. 204), and John de Cloni or de Cloney of Fife was one of the Scots prisoners taken at Dunbar Castle in the same year (ibid., p. 176; IV, p. 358). John Clunie or Clunnie was charged with tumult, 1686 (RPC., 3. ser. XII, p. 81), and Rev. John Clunie (b. 1757) was author of the song "I lo'e na a laddie but ane." Twelve of the name are recorded in the Commissariot Record of Dunblane from 1616 onward. Other old forms are: Clenye, Clwny, Clwnye.

CLURG. A shortened form of (MA)CLURG, q.v. Alexander Clurg in Dereagill, parish of Kirkinner, 1684 (RPC., 3. ser. X, p. 264).

CLUTTON. A surname recorded in Ross. Most probably of recent introduction from England. Bardsley says Clutton in Cheshire is the chief parent of the name.

CLYDE. Local. Villelmus Clide witnessed instrument of sasine to lands of Mauldislee in 1493 (*Pollok*, I, p. 206), William Clyde was admitted burgess of Dundee, 1580 (*Wedd.*, p. 172), and Helen Clyde is recorded in the toun of Belstaine, parish of Carluke, 1665 (*Lanark CR.*).

CLYDESDALE. This surname, as might be expected, is not uncommon in Glasgow. In 1256 Jordan de Cludesdale during a quarrel was struck on the head by John Schaft and instantly killed (*Bain*, I, p. 397). Andrew de Clydesdale, Scottish trumpeter, attended Edward I from Strivelin to Yettham in 1304 (*Bain*, IV, p. 476). A payment was made to John de Clydysdall in 1358 (ER., I, p. 559), and in 1480 John Cliddisdaill, burgess of Edinburgh, had the fourth booth of "the belhouse vnder the stair" (EBR., p. 39). The tenement of George Clyiddisdaile in Glasgow is mentioned in 1550 (*Protocols*, I), William Cliddisdaill was burgess there in 1583 (*Burgesses*), Jonet Clydesdaill appears in Carmyle, parish of Monkland, 1605 (*Campsie*), and Richard Clidsdaill was burgess of Dundee in 1662 (*Brechin*). James Clydesdale was married in Newbattle, 1939. Cliddisdale 1477, Clidisdaile 1552, Clydisdale 1549, Clydsdaill 1631.

CLYDESHEAD. Of local origin from a small place on the Clyde. Thomas Cludisheid was burgess of Renfrew, 1594 (*Campsie*).

CLYNE. From the lands of Clyne in the parish of the same name in Sutherlandshire. Various charters dated between 1350 and 1372 were witnessed by William of Clyne (OPS., II, p. 482), who is probably the William de Clvn, "nobilis vir," who appears in record in 1375 as holding the lands of Cathboll in Tarbat of the bishop of Moray (REM., p. 180–181). Malcolm de Clyne, secretary of the bishop of Orkney in 1390, was also a cleric in Moray (*Diplomatarium Norvegicum*, XVII, p. 932), and petitioned for a benefice in 1394 (CSR., I, p. 177). William of Clyne of that Ilk gave seisin of the earldom of Sutherland to John, the son and apparent heir of John, earl of Sutherland in 1456 (OPS., II, p. 724), and in 1512 William of Clyne of that Ilk witnessed a seisin of the same earldom in favor

CLYNE, *continued*

of John, the son and heir of the deceased Earl John (ibid.). The family appears to have ended in daughters, as in 1518 Adam, earl of Sutherland gave to John Morray of Aberscors for his sons the ward and marriage of Jonet Clyne and of her sister Elizabeth, the daughters and heiresses of William Clyne of Clyne. John Morray disponed the same to one of the Sutherlands who "mareid the hevre of Clyne" (Gordon, *Genealogical history of the Earldom of Sutherland*, 1813, p. 94). Alexander Clyne in Greenland, Caithness, is recorded in 1662 *(Caithness)*. Norval Clyne (1817–1889), man of letters, was perhaps the only prominent bearer of the name in modern times.

CLYNTER. Alexander Clynter in Aberdeen, 1408 (CWA., p. 313), derived his name from Clinter in the parish of Birse, Aberdeenshire.

COALSTON. William Colstan, juror on inquest at Selkirk, 1305 (*Bain*, II, p. 453). ? var. of COLSTON.

COATES, COATS. Variant spellings of COUTTS, q.v. Sir James Coats (b. 1834) and his brother Sir Peter, founders of the great thread mills, were born in Paisley. English Coates is of different origin.

COBB. John Cob in Ardoch appears as witness in 1479 (REB., I, 203), and in 1508 there is mention of land of Malcolm Cob in Brechin (ibid., II, 160). John Cobb, citiner of Brechin in 1629 and thirteen more of the name appear in the Brechin Commissariot Record. Some individual of this name gave name to Cobbisland in Brechin, in record in 1528 (REB., II, 181), and a family of the name contributed to the expense of building the bellhouse at Novar in 1773 (Jervise, *Land of the Lindsays*, 2. ed., p. 133). Bardsley and Harrison say this name is a diminutive of Jacob, but there was also an OE. personal name *Cobba*.

COBBAN. Macbain (v, p. 69) says from Cobban in Lincolnshire, but more probably from the ON. personal name *Kolbein*, in common speech pronounced Cobban, with diminutive Cobbie. Patrick Coben admitted burgess of Aberdeen, 1486 (NSCM., I, p. 32). Andrew Couban or Coban in Muir toune of Corss, 1633–36 (SCM., III, p. 72, 133). The name is also recorded in Fochabers in 1705 as Coban (MCM., III, p. 432). (2) Cobban in Orkney is a contraction for Kolbeinson, Coban and Cobane, 1687. Cobbie Row's Castle in Weir, Orkney, is a corruption of Kolbein Hruga's Castle (*Orkneyinga Saga*, 1873 ed., intro., p. lxxv). Cf. COBBANSON, COLBAN, and COVINGTON.

COBBANSON. A surname of Orkney in the seventeenth century and possibly later. Cobban is a late form of the Old Norse name Kolbeinn. Sigvat Kolbeinson was lawman of Orkney in 1325, and Kolbein Kolbeinson made a conveyance of land in Shetland in 1355 (REO., p. lxxii, 13).

COBLER. Perhaps from the occupation of 'cobbler,' one who cobbles or mends shoes, from 'cobble,' to patch or repair (shoes). Gelis Cobler in Balgour, 1615, and John Cobler in Dalreoch, 1668 *(Dunblane)*.

COBURN. A phonetic variant of COCKBURN, q.v.

COCHET. Nicolas Cochet witnessed a confirmation charter of Maldouenus, third earl of Levenax, a. 1214 (*Levenax*, p. 14; RMP., p. 209), and Robert Cochet of Stirlingshire rendered homage, 1296 (RR.).

COCHNO. From Cochno or Cockno in the parish of Old Kilpatrick, Dumbartonshire. Alan de Quochnay witnessed charters by Malcolm, earl of Levenax of the church of Kilpatrick and certain lands to the monks of Paisley in 1273 (*Levenax*, p. 15, 16), and Johannes de Coknay received a payment for his services, 1331 (ÉR., I, p. 376).

COCHRAN, COCHRANE, COCHREN. Of territorial origin from the five-merk lands of Cochrane (old, Coueran), near Paisley, Renfrewshire. The first of the name in record was Waldeve de Coueran, who witnessed a charter granted in 1262 by Dugal, son of Syfyn (or MacSwein), to Walter Stewart, fifth earl of Menteith, of the lands of Skipnish, Kedeslat, and others in Kintyre (*Red Book of Monteith*). William de Coughran of the county of Lanark rendered homage in 1296 (*Bain*, II, p. 213). John de Coweran witnessed a notarial copy, made in 1346, of a bull of Honorius III in 1219, dealing with the creation of the Abbey of Paisley (RMP., p. 10), and Glosmus de Cowran' in 1369 witnessed a charter by Robert Steward of Scotland (ibid., p. 31). Robertus de Cochrane witnessed a charter by Robert the Steward to Thomas Simple of the land of Cragrossy in Stratherne c. 1360 (REG., p. 275), and John de Cogherane had protection for two years for going on the king of England's service bevond seas in 1370 (*Bain*, IV, 170). In 1415 William of Cochran witnessed a charter of the barony of Cowie to William de Hava de Erole by Robert, duke of Albany (SCM., II, p. 321). Peter de Cochrane appears as a charter witness in 1452 and 1455 (*Milne*, p. 22; *Scon*, 217), and in 1487 a later Petir Couchran witnessed an obligation in favor of the burgh of Prestwick (*Prestwick*, p. 117). Edward of Cochran was declared innocent of part in detention of King James III in Edinburgh Castle in 1482 (*Lennox*, II, p. 123), Analphus Coheren and John Coheren were witnesses in Linlithgow in 1538 (*Johnsoun*), and Dem Coireeren was a resident in Edinburgh in 1529 (MCM., II, p. 88). Cochrane of that Ilk ended in an heiress, Elizabeth, whose husband, Alexander Blair, assumed the surname and arms of Cochrane. Their son was the first peer of the name (*Stodart*, II, p. 59). Adam (p. 142) says that some MacEacherens who removed to the Lowlands adopted the surname of Cochrane to conceal their origin. This has misled some persons into imagining that there is a connection between the names or that Cochrane may be derived from an old spelling of Maceachern (MacKauchern). Cawchrin 1670, Coachrin 1768, Cocheran 1682, Cocherane 1524, Cochrein 1596, Cochren 1503, Cochroume 1622, Cochroune 1623, Coichraine 1549, Coichran 1586, Coichtran 1552, Coichtrane 1555, Colquheran, Colquhran, and Colquhrane 1507 (the 'l' silent in pronunciation), Coucherane 1574, Couchrain 1649. Among the Scots Guards in France the name appeared as Colqueran.

COCK. This name appears in Fife c. 1550 (CMN., xxiv). Alesoun Cock is in Newmyln, 1585, and Cristane Cock had a feu of half the Myln of Dundaff in same year (*Scon*, p. 226, 231). Thomas Cock was church elder in Dysart, 1641 (PBK., p. 209), Patrick Cock, heir of Master Thomas Cock, minister at Sanday, Orkney, his father, (*Retours, Orkney*, 78), and Rev. James Cock was parish minister of Sanday, 1676 (PSAS., LX, p. 408). Thomas Cock was session clerk of Spynie, 1685 (RPC.; 3. ser. x, p. 386), and James Cock was town clerk of Banff, 1690 (*Banff Rec.*, 162). Agnes Cock is in Raveinstruther, parish of Carstairs, 1662, and three others in neighborhood (*Lanark CR.*). As Coke the name is recorded in Comrie parish, 1667 (*Dunblane*), and James Cock, weaver in Locheye (Lochee), d. 1741.

COCKBURN. Of territorial origin from lands so named in the Merse. In the reign of William the Lion (1165–1214) there was a 'Cukoueburn' (i.e. 'Gowk's Burn') in the territory of Clifton, Roxburghshire, pertaining to the Abbey of Melrose (*Melros*, 113). Peter de Cokeburne witnessed the grant of Floria or Fluria to the House of Soltre between 1190 and 1220 (*Soltre*, p. 10). John de Kocbrun, a landowner in Fife, for the weal of his soul and the souls of his ancestors and successors granted to the monastery of Lundors certain

lands beside his vill of Cullessin c. 1250 (LAC., p. 184–185). The marriage of a daughter of Robert de Cokburne, miles, is mentioned in 1266 (ER., I, p. 22), and at about the same date is entry of a fine paid by Robert de Kokeburn in Roxburghshire. It was perhaps the same Robert de Cokeburn who witnessed the resignation of the lands of Langholm in 1281 (RHM., I, 11). Peter de Kokeburne who witnessed the resignation of lands by Hugh de Reuedene in 1285 (*Kelso*, 219), is probably the Peres de Cokeburne who rendered homage in 1296. His seal bears a cock walking, and S' *Petri de Cokeburn* (*Bain*, II, p. 187, 554). Thomas de Cokeburne of the county of Roxburghe also rendered homage in 1296 (ibid., p. 200), William de Cokeburgne, warden of Blantyr Priory, was released of ransom in 1304 (ibid., 1469), and Gilbert de Chockeburn had a charter of land in Popil in East Lothian (*Laing*, 22). Alexander Cokeburne or Cocburn de Langtoun was keeper of the Great Seal in 1390 and 1391 (RMS., I, 824; *Irvine*, I, p. 17). Renatus Cocqueborne was appointed procurator of the Scottish 'Nation' in the University of Orleans in 1504 (SHSM., II, p. 95). Some Cockburns who settled in Danzig (now Gdansk) had their name changed, according to the dialect of the district, into Kabrun (*Fischer* I, p. 60), and Samuel Cockbrun, born 1574, settled in Finland and was known as Cobron. There have been many individuals of distinction of this name in the fields of law, theology, politics, and medicine, of whom may be mentioned John Cockburn of Ormiston (1685–1770), an improver of Scottish agriculture; Alison Cockburn (? 1712–1794), author of one of the two versions of 'The Flowers of the Forest;' Henry Cockburn, Lord Cockburn (1779–1854), judge, politician, and author; and Sir George Cockburn (1772–1853), admiral, who conveyed Napoleon to St. Helena, etc. Defoe in his *Tour* (1725) noted that the pronunciation of the name was, "as commonly express'd, Coburn." The three cocks in the family arms are mere canting heraldry. Caikburni 1589, Cobron 1688, Cocbvrn 14 c., Cogburne 1532, Cokborn 1388, Cokborne 1449, Cokbovrne 1519, Cokbrine 1596, Cokbrown 1548, Cokbrowne 1567, Cokbvrn 1415, Cokbvrne 1637, Cokbwrn 1531, Cowborn 1591, Creburne 1503, Cukburn 1467, Kokburn 1500, Kokburne 1364, Togburn 1502.

COCKER. Alexander Cokker held land in Nudre Marescalli in 1363 (RMS., I, 143), Mathew Cokcar was tenant of Nether Nuntoun in 1478 (*Cupar-Angus*, I, p. 214), and James Cokir, burgess of Edinburgh, was convicted of treason in 1573 (*Diur. Occ.*, p. 335).

COCKER, *continued*

James Cockhart (? for Cocker) was admitted burgess of Glasgow by purchase in 1618 (*Burgesses*), and Thomas Cocker is recorded at Boat of Murthly, 1785 (*Dunkeld*).

COCKERELL. Bernard de Cokerel, doubtless an Englishman, was one of an inquisition held at Perth in 1305 to inquire into the dealings of Michael de Miggel with Sir William le Waleys (*Bain*, II, p. 456).

COCKIE. Thomas Coky was admitted burgess of Aberdeen, 1408 (NSCM., I, p. 3), John Coky was one of the "principal maisteris of the fleshouris craft" in Edinburgh in 1488 (EBR., 54), and Alana Cokkye was one of the assize of wheat and bread in 1495 (ibid., 69). Patrick Cokkie was merchant burgess of Glasgow, 1583 (*Burgesses*).

COCKING. There is a Cocken in county Durham (c. 1138 Coken, which gave rise to a surname) and there is Cocking, a parish in Sussex, from either of which the name may be derived, but the absence of 'de' might seem to rule out a local or territorial origin. Johannes Cokyn is recorded in Perth some time after 1200 (LAC., p. 74). Johannes Cokyn witnessed Richard de Laycestria's two charters to Scone, and another charter to that abbey shows that he was prepositus of Perth in the reign of Alexander II (*Scon*, p. 56, 57, 61). He is most probably the same with Johannes Sokyn who is witness in another charter by Richard de Leycestria of land in Perth to Inchaffray, 1240 (*Inchaffray*, p. 62), and also c. 1245 witnessed a quitclaim of a sum of money to the same house (ibid., p. 63). Symone Kokyn witnessed a concession in favor of the monastery of Schon c. 1340 (*Scon*, p. 125). John Cokyne was rector of Alnecrom (Ancrum) in 1362 (REG., p. 270), and John Coking is recorded in Leadhill, 1665 (*Lanark CR*.). John Cockine, fermourer in Netherkidstoun, 1673 (*Edin. App*.).

COCKLA. Janet Cokla in Logie to find caution, 1596 (*Logie*, I, p. 83). Coklay 1599.

COCKS, Cox. Heruinus Koks witnessed a charter of the lands of Cragyn (Craigie) near Dundee c. 1236–48 (LAC., p. 42). The ancestors of Cox of Invergowrie were originally Cocks or Cock. Duncan Cokkis was shepherd of the flocks of the bishop of Dunkeld, 1511 (*Rent. Dunk*., p. 178), and George Cocks appears in Lenstoune, 1690 (*Dunkeld*).

CODLIN. From the OE. personal name *Codda* + the diminutive suffix -*ling*. Adam Codlin was elected town officer in Aberdeen, 1398 (CRA., p. 375).

COGAN. From Cogan in the diocese of Llandaff, South Wales. Peter Cogan witnessed the gift of an acre of land in Coldingham to the monks of St. Cuthbert, and Robert Cogan witnessed a charter of lands in Ravnigton to the Priory of Coldingham, 1275 (*Raine*, 282, 387). Robert Cogan del counte de Berewyk rendered homage, 1296 (*Bain*, II, p. 203). Robert Cogan (Coggane or Coigin) was schoolmaster at Glencairn, 1684 (RPC., 3. ser. x, p. 309, 570), and Samuel Cogan appears in Glengaber, 1731 (*Dumfries*). Cogan or Coggan is an old west of England name. A John de Cogan of Hunispull, Somerset, in reign of Edward I (HR.), in Cambridgeshire in the thirteenth century (*Guppy*).

COGGESHALL. William de Cogeshale witnessed an East Lothian charter by William the Lion (*James* II, p. 3), and also attested a charter by Malcolm, earl of Fife, c. 1214–26 (RHM., II, 1). He was probably a cleric. From Coggeshall or Cogshall in Essex.

COGHILL. A respelling of the name COGLE, q.v. Families of this name are numerous in Caithness today. Mr. James Henry Coghill in his *The Family of Coghill* (Cambridge, Mass., 1879) erroneously claims that the Caithness Coghills are a branch of the Coghills of Knaresborough in the West Riding of Yorkshire.

COGLE. A surname current in Shetland derived from the lands of Cogle in the parish of Watten, Caithness. Alexander Cogle died in 1630 and was succeeded by his son David. Andrew Cogill in Papastour, parish of Waiss, appears in 1628 (*Shetland*). In Caithness the name is pronounced Go-gl. Later the name was spelled COGHILL, q.v.

COIS. James Cois in Dunfermline, 1561 (*Dunfermline*). Johnne Cois, reidare at Gogar, 1574 (RMR.). Cf. under CASH.

COL. Thomas Col admitted burgess of Aberdeen, 1406 (NSCM., I, p. 2), appears again in 1408 along with William Col (CWA., p. 313). Alan Col witnessed a charter in Ayr, 1438 (*Friars Ayr*, p. 49). Col as a personal name occurs in English coins and charters from the middle of the ninth century.

COLBAN. From the ON. personal name *Kolbeinn* (ODan. *Colben*). A person of this name gave name to COVINGTON, q.v. Colbanus a cleric, 1107–24 (*Nat. MSS*., I, 11, 12). Colban, mormaer of Buchan, made a gift to the monastery of Deer, c. 1150 (*Bk. Deer*). Later, as earl of Buchan he witnessed a confirmation charter to the Abbey of Lindores (LAC., 1), and was witness to a charter by William the

Lion to the Abbey of Arbroath, 1178–82 (RAA., II, p. 535). In Shetland Kolbeinn appears in place name as Cullin, in Cullinsbroch, Bressay *(Jakobsen)*.

COLDEN. From the lands of Cowden near Dalkeith, Midlothian. David Colden who appears as notary in St. Andrews diocese, 1459 (REB., I, 193) may be David Coldane, succentor of Dunkeld, 1492 (REA., II, p. 338). Hugh Colden held tenements in Dalkeith, 1504 (*Soltre*, p. 324), and John Coldene was chancellor of Brechin, 1537 (*Methven*, p. 42). The Rev. Alexander Colden was one of the most eminent ministers of the Revolution settlement. His name appears to have been pronounced Couden or Cowdon. Cadwallader Colden (1688–1778), distinguished as physician, botanist, mathematician, and lieutenant-governor of New York colony for fifteen years, was born in Dalkeith. See also COWDEN.

COLDINGHAM. From the village of Coldingham in the parish of the same name, Berwickshire. Ricardus de Coldingham witnessed a charter by Adam de Lamberton, c. 1190–1200 (BNCH., XVI, p. 332; *Home*, 224). Edithe de Goldingham (an old spelling of the place name), Berwickshire, rendered homage, 1296 (*Bain*, II, p. 203). Robert de Coldingham living in Rainton, county Durham, an excommunicated person, to be arrested, 1313 (*Registrum Palatinum Dunelmense*, I, p. 486).

COLDSTREAM. Barbray Coldstream at the Mylne of Fossuall in the parish of Auchterarder is recorded in 1602 and five more of the name appear in the district *(Dunblane)*. Robert Cauldstreame was a tailor in Edinburgh in 1638 *(Edinb. Marr.)*. John Coldstream wrote a memoir of William Blackie, optician, 1844, and John P. Coldstream wrote on the increase of divorce in Scotland in 1881. Captain Coldstream, surgeon, formerly of Edinburgh, was killed in Peshawar, India, in June 1932. Of local origin from one or other of the places so named.

COLDWELL. An Anglicized form of CALDWELL, q.v.

COLDWELLS. Local, from one of several places of the name. David Coldwalls was bailie of Coldstream, Berwickshire, 1743 *(Lauder)*.

COLES. A Galwegian surname. One of the many forms assumed by the name MACDOWALL, q.v. (2) English Coles is the patronymic form of Cole, diminutive of Nic(h)olas.

COLIN. G. *Cailean*, MG. *Callane* (Dean of Lismore), *Cailin* (1467 MS.), *Colinus* (Latin, 1292). This is a personal name more or less peculiar to the Campbells, the chief being always in G. *MacCailein*. The name has no connection with English and continental Colin (from Nicholas), and it appears, as Dr. Macbain pointed out, to be derived from a dialect form of Cailean prevalent in Menteith and Perthshire in the thirteenth century. 'It is hence the Campbells brought it.' Colanus Mcgilcungill witnessed a charter by Ferkar, earl of Ross, c. 1224–31 (REM., p. 334), and Colyn, ostiarius, witnessed a charter by Alan Ostiarius, earl of Atholl, 1232–33 (RAA., I, p. 91). Colin filius Gilglas (Gilleglas or Gylleglasse) witnessed Atholl charters between 1284–90 (LIM., XXXVI; REM., p. 466–467; *Athole*, p. 705). Colin de Londermer was a charter witness in 1261 (REA., II, p. 275), and Kolinus filius Anegus, sutor, did homage to the prior and convent of St. Andrews at Dull in Atholl, 1264 (RPSA., p. 349). Cf. CULEN. Collen 1646. (2) A double diminutive of Nicholas.

COLINSON, 'son of COLIN,' q.v. Adam Colini and John filius Colini in Aberdeen were accused in 1402 of being forestallers (CRA., p. 383). Willelmus Colini, bailie of Montrose in 1431 (REB., II, 36) is most probably the William Colynson, merchant of Montrose, who had a safe conduct into England for two years in 1439 (*Bain*, IV, 1124). Willelmus Colini appears in Brechin in 1435 (REB., I, 79), David Colini was burgess of Arbroath in 1451 (RAA., II, 92), and Fergus Colini was rector of Kirkbryd in 1472 (REG., p. 420).

COLKITTO, COLLKITTO. Alexander Macdonald, Montrose's lieutenant, is never known in Gaelic as Macdonald, but as MacColla or Coll Ciotach, a designation which accounts for the confusion in which English writers labor in regard to his proper name. In Gaelic *ciotach* has the meaning 'left-handed, cunning.' Spalding *(Troubles)* calls him 'Mac Coll Mac Kittish,' Dr. John Hill Burton (*Hist. of Scotland*, VI, p. 369) thought the name was territorial and writes of him as 'Macdonald of Kolkitto,' and some English writer turned him into 'Colonel Kitto!'

COLL. An OG. personal name. G. and MG. *Colla*, EIr. the same. It is difficult to say what is its precise meaning for the root *col* has several meanings. Colla Uais, semi-legendary king of Ireland, 327–331, is claimed as the great ancestor of the Macdonalds. *Coll*, hazel, was one of the three gods of the *Tuatha De Danann*. From it comes the clan name MACCOLL, q.v. Coll is also an OE. personal name (10. cent.) and is also an English rendering of OSw. personal name *Kollr*.

COLLACE. From the old lands and barony of the same name in Perthshire. The seal of John de Cvlas is appended to a Newbattle charter of 1340 (*Macdonald*, 463), and John de Cullas was portioner of the lands of Menmuir in 1364 (RMS., I, 214). Andrew Colless, merchant in Aberdeen, got a charter of the barony of Kelly from Robert, Lord Marr, 1404 (*Nisbet*, I, p. 103). In 1451 it was charged against Jhone of Cullace of Menmur that he "wrangusly occupeis and manuris certane landis and boundis pertenynge to ye bischop and cheptur of Brechine" (REB., I, 162). Thomas de Collace had a grant of half the foggage, with the vert and venison of the forest of Kilgery in 1488 (*Bamff*, 58). Patrick Culess in Fife is mentioned in 1517 (ALHT., V, p. 102), and Robert Cullace of Balnomone had a lease of certain lands from the Dean and Chapter of Dunkeld in 1550 (*Rent. Dunk.*, p. 350). A brief account of the old family of the name is given by Jervise (*Land of the Lindsays*, 2. ed., p. 312–314). Colace 1690, Coleis 1638, Collaise 1574, Colleis 1651, Colless 1587, Collesse 1621, Cullaiss 1451, and Colese 1574.

COLLANWODE. Thomas de Collanwode had a tenement in Hautwisle, 1279 (*Bain*, II, p. 52). Probably an early form of Collingwood, the name of an ancient Northumberland family that flourished there and in county Durham for centuries.

COLLECESTER. W. de Collecester, canon (probably of Holyrood), witnessed an Inchcolm charter, a. 1199 (*Inchcolm*, p. 7). An Englishman, probably, from Colchester.

COLLEGE, COLLEDGE. Local. There are six places named College in CD. A writer in WScot. said there was a family or families named Colledge resident for many generations at Hawick, Darnick, near Melrose, and Lauder; in Edinburgh for over 200 years and also in Glasgow. "In the west of England any court or group of cottages having a common entrance from the street is called a college, and residence at such a place... probably originated the name" (*Lower*).

COLLIAR. See under COLLIER.

COLLIE, COULLIE (in Fettercairn). Perhaps of local origin from some place in the north rather than from an abbreviated form of Nicholas. Thomas de Colley rendered homage at Kildrummy, Aberdeenshire, 1296 (*Bain*, II, p. 196). William Coly admitted burgess of Aberdeen, 1436, appears c. 1438 as guild brother there (NSCM., I, p. 5; SCM., V, p. 44). Alexander Colly was tenant of Little Perth,

1464 (*Cupar-Angus*, I, p. 139). George Colle in the Kirktoun of Lundy, 1541 (RSS., II, 3666), Robert Collye, tenant under the marquis of Huntlie, 1600 (SCM., IV, p. 285), William Colie, heir of Robert Colie in Dilsco, 1631 (*Inquis.*, 1852), George Colly in Kircock, 1711 (*Dunkeld*). Elizabeth Whyte Collie from Crudie served in the first Great War (*Turriff*). Couley 1720, Coulie 1731, Coullie 1697, Cowllie 1734, Cowly 1713.

COLLIELAW. From the lands of Collielaw near Oxton, Berwickshire. The tofts and crofts of William de Colilawe (now Oxton) are mentioned c. 1208 as landmarks (*Kelso*, p. 202). Thomas, son of William de Collilaw, granted eight acres in the territory of Ulkilstoun to the Abbey of Dryburgh in the thirteenth century (*Dryburgh*, 131). Aleyn de Colilawe of the county of Edneburk rendered homage in 1296, and a writ was issued to the sheriff of Berwick to restore to him his forfeited lands (*Bain*, II, 832, p. 211).

COLLIER, COLLIAR, COLYEAR. The word 'collier' originally meant a charcoal-burner and not, as now, a coal-miner. John Colzear was piper in Dunfermline in 1582 (*Dunfermline*), and another John Coilzear was retoured heir of John Coilzear de Lochgellie his father in 1606 (*Retours, Fife*, 163). Major David Coolyear referred to in 1667 (*Bruces of Airth*, p. xxvi) is doubtless the Major David Robertson alias Collyar in the parish of Tillicoultrie mentioned in 1671 (*Dunblane*). This major may be the person referred to by Macfarlane: "A Robertson a Branch from the family of Strowan Changed his name from Robertson to Collier having got out of Scotland to Holland for a Slaughter in a Collier Ship from Culross to Holland... Settled there and called himself Collier he came to be a Collonell in the Service of the States" (*Macfarlane*, II, p. 314–315). William Coalvear in Craigiewall, 1674 (*Edin. App.*). Colyeer 1679, Colzear 1563.

COLLING. Redin says (p. 46, 166) Colling in DB., and later is a patronymic derived from OE. *Cola*, but the present-day surname is more likely to be from Cole or Colin, a diminutive of Nicholas. Sir Thomas Coling was chaplain in Perth, 1535 (*Rollok*, 34).

COLLISON. May be 'son of Collie,' a diminutive of Nicholas. An old surname in Aberdeenshire, described in 1732 as "one of the chief surnames here of old" (*View*, p. 126). The same writer says that the Collisons of Auchlunies or Auchinlaumes have been there for fifteen generations (ibid., p. 265). They had their burial place in one of the two aisles of S. Nicholas Church, Aberdeen. John Colesoun was burgess of Banff in 1487 (RAA., II, 311), John Colyson, David Colyson, and John Colison were admitted burgesses of Aberdeen in 1449 and 1476 (NSCM., I, p. 12, 25). Robert Colisoun was a presbyter in 1489 and John Colisone was presented to the vicarage of Inverness in 1497 (RAA., II, 323, 388). Schir John Colison or Colleson, subchantar of Ald Aberdeen in 1577 died in 1584 (SCM., II, p. 45; Analecta Scotica, I, p. 283), Duncane Colisone was 'forspekar' of an assize in Aberdeen, 1505 (Mill, Plays, p. 135), and Gilbert Colinsonne or Collisonne appears as burgess of Aberdeen in 1574 and 1591 (CRA., p. 13; SCM., III, p. 156, 157). Thomas Collesoun of Auchlownie was heir of John Collesoune his father in 1623 (Retours, Aberdeen, 182), and Johannes Colliesoune was burgess of Aberdeen in 1674 (Inquis., 5752). Coleson 1518, Collisoun 1511, Collesoune 1574, Colliesone 1674, Collisen 1475, Collisone 1663, Collyson 1502, Collysone 1633.

COLLOW. The Collows of Auchencairn were an old family of Glencairn parish, Dumfriesshire, descended from Peter Collace, who is mentioned in Kelso, 1580. Mr. John Collow was minister of Penpont, c. 1743. William Collow of Auchencairn, 1788 (Dumfries).

COLMAN. Colmán, one of the commonest names in OIr., even before the time of S. Columba (Macneill, Oghams, p. 332), is for earlier Columbán (Rev. celt., XLIV, p. 41). An ogham inscription found at Glanawillan, Cork, reads (MacAlister, III, p. 40): Colomagni avi Ducagni, where Colomagnos (nom.) is a diminutive in -agnos (later reduced to -án) of Colum. The name is a borrowing from Latin columba, 'a dove.' The name was borne by two hundred and eighteen saints, of which ninety-four are commemorated in the Martyrology of Donegal. Later it became Calman. This form was borrowed in Old West Scandinavian, and Kalman the Irishman (irskr) was one of the earliest Norse settlers in Iceland (Landnámabók, 15). William Colman was declared innocent of part in detention of King James III in Edinburgh Castle, 1482 (Lennox, II, p. 123).

COLP, CULP. Of local origin from the small place named Colp near Turriff, Aberdeenshire. Johannes Coup is recorded in Aberdeen, 1408 (CWA., p. 312). A "commone hande bell, with ale proffetis," was granted to William Colp and his son, David Colp in the same town in 1503 (CRA., p. 72), and a payment was made in 1518 to Sir Andrew Cup, evidently a cleric (ibid., p. 95). Local tradition

has it that on the morning of Sir John Cope's arrival at Nairn in 1745 "the wife of a fisherman presented her husband with a son, who in commemoration of the event, was christened John Cope Main. Descendants of this infant are still to be found among the fishing community of Nairn. They still bear the name Main Cope or Coup" (Rampini, A history of Moray and Nairn, p. 214). So much for unveracious local history.

COLQUHOUN. Umfridus de Kilpatrick had a grant of the lands of Colquhoun in Dumbartonshire from Maldouen, earl of Levenax in or before 1241 (Levenax, p. 25). Robert de Colechon, apparently the first to take his surname from the lands, was one of an inquest held at Dumbarton in 1259 (Bain, I, 2174), and again at Dumbarton, as Robert de Culchon in 1271, he was one of the inquest which found that the daughters of the late Finlay of Campsie were the lawful heirs of deceased Dufgall, brother of Maldowen, earl of Levenax (Red book of Menteith, II, p. 218; RMP., p. 191). As Sir Robert of Kylkone, he witnessed a charter by Alexander of Dunhon of the land of Akencloy Nether, c. 1285 (HMC., 2. Rep., App., p. 166), and as Robert de Colquhoune he witnessed a charter by Malcolm, earl of Levenax to Arthur Galbraith, c. 1290 (Levenax, p. 30). Umfrai de Kilwhone, knight of the county of Dunbretan, rendered homage in 1296 (Bain, II, p. 202), as Vmfredus de Kelquon witnessed a confirmation charter by Robert I to Sir John Colquhoun, 1308 (Lennox, II, p. 407). About the middle of the fourteenth century Sir Robert Colquhoun married the heiress of Humphrey of Luss and thus became lord of Colquhoun and Luss. Robert de Colquhoune witnessed a grant of Auchmarr to Walter de Buchanan in 1373 (Levenax, p. 59), John de Culqwon was sheriff of Dunbrettan in 1427 (HP., II, p. 159), Malcolm de Qulchone was a witness in Ayr in 1429 (Ayr, p. 83), and Alexander of Qulchon appears as witness in the same town in 1438 (Friars Ayr, p. 49). In 1497 John Culquhone of Lus sold a half markland in the territory of Innerquhapill occupied by a certain procurator with the staff of S. Mund (cum baculo Sancti Munde) called in Scots 'Deowray' (RMS., II, 2385). Adam Choquoyn was rector of Stobo in 1513 (Rental). Several of this name achieved distinction in Sweden, and descendants of Walter Colquhoun, a sixteenth century cannon-founder still exist there under the names of Cahun, Cahund, Caun, Gaan, Gahn, and Kharun. Hugh Cahun revealed the conspiracy headed by Charles de Manay in September 1574, and lost his life in spite of a promise of pardon (Stodart, II, p. 119). Johan Gottlieb Gahn (1745-1818) was one of the

COLQUHOUN, *continued*

greatest scientists of his day, and Henry Cahun *vulgo* Gahn was physician to the Admiralty of Sweden in 1781. Duncan Ban spells the name in Gaelic *Cothun* (ed. Calder, p. 10, line 6). In the United States it has been shortened to Calhoun (John Caldwell Calhoun, 1782–1850, Vice-President, and champion of States' Rights), and among the Scots Guards of France it became Quohon. In Gaelic the Colquhouns are known as *Mac a' Chounich* or *Macachonnich* (Macfarlane, *Am Briathrachan Beag*, p. 77, says *Mac a' Chombaich*). Cachoune 1592, Cahune 1686, Calquhoun 1689, Calwhone 1329, Colchoun 1744, Colfune 1368, Colhoun 1611, Colhoune 1673, Collequhone c. 1430, Collquhone 1432, Colquhowne 1400, Colqhuen 1521, Colquhyn 1504, Colqwhone and Colqwhoun 1405, Cowquhowne 1541, Culchone 1329, Culchoun 1309, Culquhone 1499, Culquhoun 1574, Culquhoune 1527, Culqwan 1391, Culqwhone 1374, Culqwone 1406, Culwone 1358, Kelquon 1308, Kulwoun 1264. In the United States we have Israel Cohen, *alias* Ian Colquhoun!

COLSON. For 'Coles' son,' from Coles, diminutive of Nic(h)olas + son. In Flemish the name is spelled *Colas-zoone.*

COLSTON. Local. There is Colston near Bishopriggs, Lanarkshire, and Colstoun in East Lothian. Colstane in Aberdeenshire in local speech is a contraction cf Codilstan (in Logie-Codilstane) now Logie-Coldstone. The surname rarely appears in record. Robert Colston, a Scotsman, had a safe conduct in England, 1465 (*Bain*, IV, 1353). James Colston was an Edinburgh magistrate and local historian. Colstine 1731.

COLT. There was a barony of Colt or Cult in Perthshire from which the name may have come. William Culte de Strathawen, Lanarkshire, took the oath of fealty, 1296. John Colti held land in barony of Lastalryk before 1365 (RMS., I, 200), Thomas Colt is mentioned in Perth, 1446 (RAA., II, 362), and John Colt was one of the tenants of Moneydie, 1483. James Colt and Andro Colt appear as witnesses in Perth, 1547 and 1551 (*Rollok*, 43, 75). Andrew Colt was vicar of Redgorton, 1574–91, and Oliver Colt was procurator for the burgh of Irvine, 1590 (*Irvine*, I, p. 63). A succession of Colts were merchant burgesses of Perth in the sixteenth century, and the Colts of Gartsherrie, Lanarkshire, are said to be an offshoot from the Perthshire family.

COLTART, COLTHARD, COLTHART, COLTHERD, COLTHERT, COULTHARD, COULTHART. Explained as from Coltard = Colt herd, OE. *colt + hierde.* Of the Coultharts of Galloway a ridiculous genealogy has been published, in which the family are traced to one Coulthartus, a Roman soldier who fought in the battle of Mons Graupius! The local pronunciation in the Stewartry is Cowtart. Lower says probably from Coudhart, a village in the department of Orne, NE. of Argentan in Normandy. He says the name is no doubt territorial as it is written with "de" in the thirteenth and fourteenth centuries. Alan Colthird witnessed the sealing of an inquest at Berwick anent a fishing on the Tweed in 1467 (RD., p. 359). John Colthird, tailor in Edinburgh, 1619 (*Sasines*, II, 51), John Coltart in Waistwood, 1627 (*Dumfries*), and Jean Colthart or Colthird in Kirkcudbright, 1666 (*Kirkcudbright*). William Cultert and Robert Cultert were residents in the parish of Buittle, 1684 (RPC., 3. ser. IX, p. 570), and James Colthird in Snaipsheid, 1663, and sixteen more of the name are recorded in the Commissariot Record of Lanark. James and Michael Coutart were present at conventicles in 1686 (RPC., 3. ser. XIII, p. 22, 23), James Coulthred was chamberlain of Crawfurdjohn in the same year (ibid., XII, p. 424), and Adam Coutert was witness in Ayr, 1687 (*Ayr*, p. 211).

COLTERJOHN. John the colt-herd, an ancient and uncommon name. Albert Colterjohn died in Edinburgh, 1939.

COLTON. Of local origin probably from one or other of the places named Colton in England. Thomas de Coltoun witnessed a gift by Richard Germyn to the Hospital of Soltre, c. 1235–58 (*Soltre*, p. 26). Ingram de Colton rendered homage at Berwick, 1291 (RR.).

COLTRAN. An old surname in Galloway, but now uncommon. Michael Acoltrain in Wigtown, 1511 (ALHT., IV, p. 160). Patrick Coltrane had sasine of lands of Culmalzie, parish of Kirkinner, 1663 (*M'Kerlie*, I, p. 407), and in 1667 was provost of Wigtown, owner of the lands of Kirwaugh, Culmalzie, and others in the parish of Kirkinner. Andrew Coltran in Barglass, parish of Kirkinner, 1684 (RPC., 3. ser. x, p. 265). William Coltrane who signed letters to the Privy Council, 1688 (ibid., XIII, p. 282), is probably William Coltrane, provost of Wigtown, 1693 and 1709, and the William Cultran one of the commissioners for trade in the Scots Parliament, 1700 (Hume of Crossrig's *Diary*, p. 11). Tradition assigns to the provost of Wigtown a prominent part in the apprehension and drowning of Margaret McLauchlane and Margaret Wilson, the Wigtown martyrs.

COLTROP. Thomas Coltrop, weaver, burgess of Dumbarton, 1818 (RDB.). Probably a variant of Colthrop from Calthrope in England.

COLUMBA. The name of the famous saint of Iona is an early borrowing from Latin *columba*, a pigeon. Adamnan spells the name Columba, Columbanus, Columbus, and Columb. The Irish call him Colum, with *cille*, 'of the churches,' as a distinction. Some Irish writers say he was christened *Crimthann* 'fox,' but was designated Columba by his playmates "on account of his gentleness." Notwithstanding the assertion of Adamnan (V. C., III, 23) Columba was little known on the Continent of Europe, and his name there was associated with superstitious practices against storms, fire, and field rats! The first bishop of Dunkeld (fl. 640) was named Columba. From the common diminutive form Columan or Colman comes the G. personal name *Calum*, from which we have *MacCaluim*, English MACCALLUM, q.v.

COLVILLE. Although there are more than one place named Colleville (= Col's vill or farm) in Normandy the surname is probably from Coleville, a town between Caen and Bayeux in Normandy. The first of the name recorded in Scotland is Philip de Coleuille who witnessed a general confirmation by Malcolm IV of all the donations by his predecessors to the monastery of Dunfermline in or before 1159 (RD., 35), and other charters by Malcolm and William the Lion (APS., I, p. 364; REG., 15), etc. He possessed the baronies of Oxnam and Heiton in Roxburghshire (OPS., I, p. 389), and was a hostage for William the Lion under the treaty of Falaise in 1174 (Bain, I, 139). Thomas de Colevill appears in a perambulation of the marches of Elstaneshalche, 1181 (Melros, p. 111), and is a witness in a number of documents in the last decade of the twelfth century. In a charter of c. 1200 where he styles himself "Thomas de Colevilla cognomento Scot" he grants the land of Kerseban on the Doon to the Abbey of Vaudey in Lincolnshire (Melros, p. 172–173). The seal appended to the charter of Kerseban to the Abbey of Melrose, c. 1223, contains a classic head and the inscription *Thome de Collevilla Scotti* (Seals, 190). Thomas de Colouilla was charged with treason in 1211 (Chron. Mail., s.a.). Ada de Coleuyll gave the lands of Kynnard in Fife to the Abbey and monks of Neubotle in 1241 (Neubotle, p. 169). Thomas de Coleville of Dumfriesshire rendered homage, 1296 (Bain, II, 810). Robert de Collevyll was lord of Oxenham c. 1330 (Kelso, p. 369–370), and Robert de

Colvylle of Scotland for his courage and steady obedience to England was granted an annuity of 20 marks from the customs of Kingston on Hulle, 1358 (Bain, IV, 24). Mr. William Colveil, brother to the laird of Cleish, was admitted burgess of Glasgow, 1630 (Burgesses). Coilwill 16c., Colluyne 1503, Collwell 1541, Coluil 1655, Coluile 1503, Coluill 1512, Colvele 1484, Colvvle 1388, Colvyll 1432, Colweill and Colwell 1542, Colwill 1583, Colwyng 1546.

COLVIN. A vernacular pronunciation of COLVILLE, q.v. Cf. MELVIN – MELVILLE. John Colvin in the parish of Bothkennar, 1680 (Stirling). In the sixteenth century the same person is recorded as Colville and Collwyne (Protocols, II, 106, 108). There was an earlier *Colvin* from OE. *Colwine*, but the Scottish surname is undoubtedly from Colville.

COLYEAR. A form of COLLIER, q.v.

COMBE. Most probably shortened from (MAC)COMB, q.v. A payment was made to Robert Comb, wright in Edinburgh, 1728 (Guildry, p. 168). George Combe (1788–1858), the phrenologist, and his brother Andrew (1797–1847), physician, were two of the most eminent of the name.

COMBICH. "A class of the Stewarts of Appin are called Combich; and in this manner, through nearly all the Clans, tribes, and families in the Highlands" (Stewart, Sketches, I, p. 27). Stewart is referring to such names as Clan Duileach (black-eyes) and the Camachas. The Breadalbane Combachs claim to have come to Lawers from Appin of Stewart (FB., p. 357). See CHOMBICH and MACCOMBICH.

COMBLINE. John Combling, merchant burgess of Kirkcudbright, 1639 (Inquis., 2466), and William Combling in Graing, 1643 (Inquis. Tut., 659). William Combline, a resident in parish of Borgue, 1684 (RPC., 3. ser. IX, p. 567).

COMISKEY, COMISKY, CUMISKY. From (MAC)COMISKEY, q.v. These forms are current in Ayrshire.

COMLOQUOY. Variant of CUMLAQUOY, q.v.

COMMON. A Dumfriesshire surname, probably a variant of CUMMING, q.v. The Comyns possessed large estates in Galloway in the fourteenth century.

COMMONS. A Dumfriesshire surname. Probably same as COMMON, with plural s. In 1659 Comenes.

COMRIE. From the lands of the name in Perthshire, now a parish and village. John Combry, son of John Combry *de eodem* granted a charter of the lands of Combry, Kungart, etc., 1476 (*Oliphants*, p. 34). John de Cumre had a charter in 1447 (RMS., II, 640), and John Comrie in the paroch of Comrie is in record, 1673 (*Edin. App.*). John Comerie in Comerie, 1599 (*Retours, Perth*, 1089). Sixteen of the name are recorded in the Commissariot Record of Dunblane, seventeenth and eighteenth centuries. Some of the proscribed Macgregors settled at Comrie, on the opposite bank of the river from the other inhabitants of the village of Comrie, which name was adopted in lieu of their own (*Adam*, p. 496). Comri and Cumry 1495.

COMYN. See under CUMMING.

CONACHER, CONACHAR. The name of an old Atholl family located about 1600 on the lands of Stewart of Atholl. Probably from the family of O'Conocher of Lorn, who were in the sixteenth and seventeenth centuries physicians to the Campbells of Argyll. See under OCONOCHER.

CONAN. (1) From *Conán*, 'little hound,' an OG. personal name. Adam filius Conani is in record, 1292 (*Nat. MSS.*, I, 74). Conan de Bithweder (Balquhidder) rendered homage, 1296 (RR., p. 128). From the name of Conan de Glenerochy, illegitimate son of Henry, earl of Atholl, comes CUNIESON, CUNISON, CUNNISON, q.v. (2) From the lands of Conan in the Mearns, Kincardineshire. John Conan de Conansythe mentioned in 1387 appears in 1394 as John de Conane dominus de Connansytht (RAA., II, p. 39, 42). William de Conane was perpetual vicar of the church of Aberbrothoc in 1394 (ibid., 42). John de Conan or Conane had a charter of a toft of Kethvk, etc., in Forfar, 1415 (REB., II, 18, 37), Duncan de Conan was juror on inquisition on lands of Tulloch, 1438 (RAA., II, 83), and in 1443 David de Connane or Conane had a grant of the lands of Tempilhill (REB., I, 89). David Conan witnessed an "instrament of sessyn" of the bell of S. Meddan in 1447 (SCM., IV, p. 118), Thomas Connane in Glenbuchet had a remission in 1603 (SCM., IV, p. 159), and Alexander Conand is recorded in Kinharrachie, Ellon, 1640 (*Mair*, p. 86). See under CUNIESON.

CONCHAT. The name of a king in a notitia in the Register of the Priory of St. Andrews (p. 115), probably meant for Donald Bane (1094–97). "Conchat is so written for Donchat . . . the original Mac-Donchat causing

an assimilation of the initial D, just as MacDonnell is often written MacConnell, and when the translator rendered the Mac by filius he left the assimilated Conchat unrestored" (Reeves, *Culdees*, p. 127).

CONCHER. Isabell Concher in Logierait, 1684 (DPD., I, p. 488). From *Conachar*.

CONCHIE. Recorded in Galloway, from Macconchie (1684). Dudgeon (*Macs*, p. 23) says the son of a man of this name signed himself M'Kechnie. See MACCONACHIE.

CONDIE. There was at one time a family of Condie of that Ilk, who derived their name from the lands of Condie, near Forgandenny, Perthshire. John de Conady is in record in Perth in 1414 (RAA., II, 52), John Condy was tenant of Fruchy, Falkland, in 1541 (ER., XVII, p. 723), William Condy witnessed a marriage settlement of 1561 (*Fordell*, p. 100), and James Cundie is in record in Edinburgh in 1595 (*Edinb. Marr.*). David Condie, an Edinburgh man, is recorded in Dunfermline in 1572 (*Dunfermline*), Isobel Condie in Wester Colsie, parish of Abernethy, in 1616 (*Dunblane*), and John Condie in Saughie, parish of Clackmannan, in 1684 (*Stirling*). Henry Condie in Litill Fildie is in record in 1606 (*Fordell*, p. 102), Patrick Condie was warded in the Canongate Tolbooth, Edinburgh, in 1682 (BOEC., VIII, p. 123), and Alexander Condie was a resident in Stirling in 1717 (*Sc. Ant.*, VI, p. 88).

CONEVETHE. Johan de Conevethe, persone del eglise de Alnecrom (Ancrum), rendered homage 1296 (*Bain*, II, p. 210). Probably from Conveth, the old name of the parish of Laurencekirk.

CONGALTON, CONGILTON, CONGLETON. From the old barony of Congalton in the parish of Dirleton, East Lothian. The family, however, may have come from Congilton in Cheshire and given that name to their new possession. The first of the name in record appears to be Robert de Congaltoun who witnessed a charter of Richard de Moreville, granted c. 1182 (in Anderson's *Diplomata*). Walter de Congilton witnessed an agreement between the Abbey of Neubotel and John de Morham (who was a Malherbe), c. 1214–40 (*Neubotle*, 40). He also witnessed a charter of Dryburgh Abbey, c. 1224 (*Dryburgh*, p. 33), a charter by Nesus de Lundors, c. 1225 (LSC., 64), and the charter by Adam, son of Edulph of a part of the manor of Eduluiston to Constantine between 1214–33 (REG., p. 142). As Walter de Kungeltun he attested the donation of Sleparfeld (Slipperfield, West

Linton) to the Abbey of Holyrood between 1214 and 1249 (LSC., p. 212). Wautier de Congeltone and Mabille de Cungiltone, both of the county of Edneburke, rendered homage in 1296 (*Bain*, II, p. 203, 206). In the same year Walter de Congilton and Adam de Congilton appear as jurors on an inquest into the lands of Robert de Pinkeny of Ballencrieff (ibid., 857). John and Gilbert de Congeltoun were jurors on an inquest on the lands of Gladmor in 1430 (*James* II, 16), and John of Congiltoun had a safe conduct into England in 1424 (*Bain*, IV, 963). Henry of Congiltoune was one of the "maloris and occupyoris" of a fishing on the Tweed in 1467 and George of Congiltoune was one of the witnesses (RD., 461), John Congiltoun was "unus occupatorum carbofodinarum de Gilmerton" in 1506 (*Soltre*, p. 78). John Congiltoun was admitted burgess of Aberdeen in 1548 (NSCM., I, p. 61), a yard in the Potterraw of Edinburgh was occupied in 1610 by George Congiltoun (*Laing*, 1584), and in 1673 William Colgingtoun of Colgingtoun was appointed one of the justices of the peace for Haddingtonshire. The family appears to be extinct in the direct line, and some members of the family married heiresses of Richard and Hepburn and assumed these surnames. Another succeeded to the estate of Bethune of Balfour and assumed that name. Old: Cungetun.

CONGHAL. Conghal, son of Donecan, son of Malisius had a grant of the vill of Catherlauenach, called Tulichbardene, from Robert, earl of Stradhern before 1234, in which year the grant was confirmed by Alexander II at Scone (LIM., App., p. xxix). "S. Conall of Dumfriesshire and south-west Scotland generally was a British saint, whose name is properly spelled Congual or Congal" (*Watson* II).

CONGUST. OW. *Cingust*, *°Cunogustus*. *Congus*, Ir., ogham gen. *Cunagussos* Bodfeddan). Welsh *Cingust*, *Cinust*, from *Kuno-gustu-s*. *Fick-Stokes*, p. 84.

CONHEATH. From the old lands of Conheath in the parish of Caerlaverock, Dumfriesshire. Simon of Conehatheam witnessed a charter by Nicholas Corbet of the Hospital in Glendall, Northumberland, c. 1253–80 (*Laing*, 9). Adam de Culenhat de Killosebern made an agreement with the abbot and convent of Kelso regarding the church of Killosebern in 1281 (*Kelso*, 343), and about the same time he had a lease of the tithes of the parish of Closeburn for the yearly sum of 53 marks and a half (ibid., 240). The office of notary public was conferred on John de Kulvehach

(for Kulnehach) of the diocese of Glasgow in 1339 (*Pap. Lett.*, II, p. 546), and he appears again in 1346 as John de Kulnehath (RMP., p. 10). Thomas de Culnehathe 'familiaris regis' David II had a charter from the king of the lands of Keldewod and Bourland in the sheriffdom of Dumfries in 1369 (RMS., I, 307). Payment was made to John of Colnehethe and his men at arms going to Calais on the king of England's service in 1370 (*Bain*, IV, 173). James Conhaith in Pairthet (= Penrith in Cumberland) in 1673 (*Dumfries*) may be James Conheath, tenant in the barony of Mousewall in the same year (PSAS., XXIII, p. 74). Jennet Conhath in Tinwald was examined for the Test in 1685 (RPC., 3. ser. XI, p. 435).

CONING. Coning or Conning, c. 1250. Fergus filius Coning who witnessed a charter by Maldounech, third earl of Levenax (*Levenax*, p. 96), is doubtless Fergus filius Cuning who held land c. 1225–70 (RMP., p. 161). Six Conings are recorded in Wigtownshire in eighteenth century (*Wigtown*), and the name still exists there. In 1684 (*Parish*): Connein, Connin, and Conning. Conaing is an old Irish personal name, perhaps of Norse origin.

CONINGHAM. Variant of CUNNINGHAM. Archebaldus de Coningham attested the marches of Kyrknes and Louchor, 1395 (RPSA., p. 5).

CONKIE. A reduced form of MACCONACHIE, q.v.

CONLAY. Persons of this name in Kintyre derive their name from old *Mac Donnsleibhe* or *Mac Donnshleibhe* > M'Onlave > M'Onlav > MacConlea > Conlay. See DUNSLEVE and MACLAE.

CONN. An old name in Aberdeenshire, where there was a prominent Roman Catholic family of the name, Con or Cone of Auchry, in the parish of Monquhitter. They claimed to be a branch of the Clan Donald (*Archæologia Scotica*, IV, p. 376), the surname being assumed from the traditional name of the Clan, 'Siol Cuin' or 'Con.' They were designated of Auchry before 1539. George Con or Conæus (as his name was Latinized), the Pope's agent at the court of the queen of Charles I (1636–1639), was the most prominent of the name. Alexander Cone in Auchry is mentioned in 1522. The family were driven into exile soon after 1642 (*Aberdeen Jour. Notes and queries*, III, p. 82). In the birth brieve of Gilbert Chalmer, 1650, the Cons or Cones of Auchry are said to be descended from William Con [five generations earlier] "lauchfull sone to

CONN, *continued*
Donald of the Iles and Kyntyr, chief of the Mackdonald" (SCM., v, p. 334). William Conn witnessed the laird of Balfour's bond in 1552 (SCM., IV, p. 222), Thomas Con was a merchant in Glasgow, 1606, and in 1640 there is record of payment to Thomas Con, post, in Aberdeen (SCM., v, p. 156), and John Con, flesher in Edinburgh, is recorded in 1508 (EBR., p. 114). (2) Conn is also an Ayrshire surname, and Dobie suggests that it is an abridgement of PETCON, q.v. Johannes Con, burgess of Irvine, 1499 (*Simon*, 29). Conne 1690.

CONNACHER. Variant of CONACHER, q.v.

CONNAL, CONNELL, CONNEL, CONNALL. Modern for Congal or Congual. The last form is the name of an old West country (Stirlingshire) family. Cuthbert Connell was a voter in the parish of Qwilton (now Coylton), 1513 (*Ros*, 52). Robert Connall was retoured heir of Patrick Connall de Greynghill in parish of Beith, 1647 (*Retours, Ayr*, 414). Cf. GILLECONAL.

CONNOCHIE, CONOCHIE. From MACCONACHIE, q.v. Robert Connoquhie, mariner in Edinburgh, 1619 (*Edinb. Marr.*).

CONNON, CONNAN, CONNEN. G. *Connán*, a diminutive of *Conn*. The first is an old surname in Aberdeenshire and in Banffshire, and there were families of this name in Glenbuchat in the sixteenth and seventeenth centuries. They were followers of the earls of Huntly, and took part in the battle of Glenlivat, 1594. Several Connons from Turriff and neighborhood served in the first Great War (*Turriff*).

CONQUERGOOD. Sir James Conquergud, a cleric, was witness, 1549 (*Gaw*, 26). William Conquergood, cordiner in Edinburgh, 1665 (*Edinb. Marr.*), Agnes Conquergood recorded there in 1672 (ibid.), and there is mention in 1683 of the relict of Patrick Conquergood in the same burgh (BOEC., VIII, p. 152). A name 'not easily explained' (*Lower*). Frank Conquergood died in Edinburgh, 1940.

CONQUEROR. Burgesses of this name 'were very respectable in Perth, and some of them were in public stations and very active in directing the affairs of the Burrow' (Rev. James Scott of Perth, c. 1790, quoted in *Sc. Ant.*, I, p. 100). Diones Concreur, curator of Patrick Scott, 1567 (RPC., I, p. 586) may be Dionysius Conqueror who witnessed confirmation of a charter in Dunkeld, 1603 (*Athole*, p. 716). Dionys Conqueror was member of Scots parliament for Perth, 1579 (*Han-*

na, II, p. 488). John Conqueror in Bankhead of Crumbie, parish of Torrie, 1623 (*Stirling*), and Robert Conqueror of Friartoune was bailie of Perth, 1690 (*Inquis.*, 7014).

CONSTABLE. In the time of the Roman Empire the position of *Comes stabuli*, 'count of the stable,' was an office of dignity. Transferred to the court of the Frankish kings, the title became one word, *Comestabulus*, and after the eighth century was changed to *conestabulus*, as the name of the officer entrusted with the charge of cavalry. By the thirteenth century the title of Constable (OF. *conestable*) was given to the commander of all the forces. In Scotland to the Constable was "entrusted the guard of the king's person and of his dwelling and the maintenance of the king's peace for twelve leagues around the place where he might be in residence, and with the arrest and trial of offenders within this limit" (Mackinnon, *Constitutional history of Scotland*, p. 127). The office was hereditary in the family of Hay of Errol. The surname in Scotland is not common, and is without doubt from the more humble office of town constable or peace officer. Thomas Cunstabil, witness in Lanark, 1490 (*Lanark*, p. 8). Archibald Constable (1774–1827) was first publisher of the Waverley Novels.

CONSTANE. Like Costine another abbreviated form of CONSTANTINE, q.v. Thomas Constane appears in Edinburgh in 1501 (EBR., 91), and Patrick Constyne was witness in Perth, 1544 (*Rollok*, 36).

CONSTANTINE. Constantine, king of Devon and Cornwall in latter half of sixth century, after a wicked life, was 'converted to the Lord.' He then abandoned his throne and became a monk under S. Carthach at Rahin, King's county, Ireland. He afterwards crossed over to Scotland, founded the church of Govan, and suffered martyrdom in Kintyre, where there is a church, Kilchousland, named after him. In Angus he is vulgarly called Cousnan (PSAS., II, p. 189). A Constantine was judex of Strathern, 1189–99 (RAA., I, 35), and Waldeve, fourth earl of Dunbar had a son of the same name. Constantine, abbot of Newbattle resigned his office, 1236 (ES., II, p. 499). See GILLECOSTENTYN.

CONVALL. Ir. *Conmhaol* (from early °*Kunovalos*, 'high mighty' one). Fordun (*Chronica*, III, 29) records S. Convallus, an Irish saint, one of S. Kentigern's principal disciples, renowned for miracles and virtues, whose bones rest buried at Inchinnan near Renfrew. As no boat was available for him to cross the channel from Ireland to Scotland he was miraculously conveyed across upon a large stone now said to be lying within the grounds of Blythswood. Convallus de Akinhead was a charter witness in Dumbartonshire, 1372 (*Levenax*, p. 59), and Convallus de Kelle witnessed an instrument of sasine of the lands of Mernys and Netherpollok in 1454 (*Pollok*, I, p. 176).

COOK, COOKE. A surname derived from the occupation of 'cook,' in Latin documents *cocus*. A very common name in early Scots records. Richard the cook (*cocus*) held land in Berwick after 1147 (*Kelso*, 34) and Jocelin Cocus held land before 1178 (*Neubotle*, 156). Raginaldus the cook witnessed the gift of the church of Cragyn in Kyle to the Abbey of Paisley, a. 1177 (*RMP.*, p. 232). John Coquis witnessed a charter by Eschina de Lundin in favor of Kelso Abbey, c. 1190 (*Kelso*, 147), and about the same period Hamone Cocus attested a charter by John, bishop of Dunkeld (*Inchaffray*, p. 5). Radulphus Cocus witnessed resignation of the lands of Ingilbristoun in 1204 (*Dryburgh*, 163), and Walterus Cocus witnessed excambion of the lands of Dolays Mychel in 1232 (REM., p. 88), and Thomas quocus witnessed a charter by Eggou ruffus of lands to the Priory of May early in the thirteenth century (RPSA., p. 383). There was a family of this name in Fife as early as 1260, when John Cocus de Balcasky and John Cocus and Richard Cocus of Abircrumby witnessed a charter by John de Dundemore to the Priory of the Isle of May (*May*, 29). Walter the cook held land in Brechin in 1267 (REB., I, 5), and Richard Cook, janitor, witnessed a charter in favor of Dunfermline Abbey in 1274 (RD., 207). "Henricus dictus Koc, pistor" (baker), held a croft in Aberdeen in 1281 (REA., II, p. 279), and Roger Cocus de Inuerdouete witnessed a transaction between Serlo de Lascelis and the prior of St. Andrews in 1288 (RPSA., p. 346). Martin, son of Walter Cocus, held land in Irvine in 1323 (*Irvine*, I, p. 123), William Cuk was concerned in a dispute anent a doublet in 1398 (CRA., p. 371), John Cuke was burgess of Edinburgh in 1402 (*Egidii*, p. 39), James Kok resident in Newburgh, Fife in 1479 (LAC., 153), John Cuk a follower of the earl of Cassilis was respited for murder in 1526 (RSS., I, 3386), and George Cuick was merchant burgess of Glasgow in 1645 (*Inquis.*, 3031). Ceuk 1674, Coowk 1686, Cowk 1492, Cuch 1231, Cuik 1566, Cuyk 1540, Cuvke 1519, Cwik 1554, Kewk 1504, Kuyk 1394, and Cwke, Cwyk, Cwyke.

(2) In the eighteenth century the Cooks of Arran were MACCOOK, q.v. The popular explanation is that English 'cook' was borrowed into Gaelic as *cug*, so *Iain a' Cug* is 'John son of Cook.' Neil Cuke, a follower of Donald Gorme of Sleat, had a remission in 1541 for his share in laying waste Trouterness in Skye and Kinlochew in Ross (RSS., II, 3943).

COOPER, COUPAR, COUPER, COWPER. This surname occurs in one form or another in nearly every county of Scotland. The name was in most cases derived from Cupar in Fife, but the occupation of 'cooper' has also contributed to its origin. The earliest record of the name is territorial, when dominus Salomone de Cupir appears as a charter witness in 1245 (RPSA., p. 44, 282). The name, also, is common in early Fife records from the thirteenth to the fifteenth century, additional evidence of its local origin. An instance pointing to the occupation as the source of the name occurs in 1329 when payment to "Alanus cuparius" (i.e. the "cooper") is recorded (ER., I, p. 221). John Cupar held land in Aberdeen, 1281 (REA., II, p. 278). Christian Cowper who held lands in Ravenysden near Berwick in 1275 (*Dryburgh*) may have been a relative of Symon Coupare of Berwickshire who rendered homage in 1296 (*Bain*, II, p. 207). Michael Couper was tenant in vill de Butyll, 1376 (RHM., II, p. lx), and William Coupare had a tenement in Irvine, 1426 (*Irvine*, I, p. 130). Thomas de Cupro, canon of the church of St. Andrews, 1406 (RPSA., p. 10). Patrick Culpar (the *l* is silent), witness in Aberdeen, 1468, appears in 1477 as Cowlpar and his wife as Cowlper (REA., I, p. 300, 212). Finla Couper in Belnakeill, Atholl, was fined for resetting outlawed Macgregors, 1613 (RPC., x, p. 151), Patrick Cowper in Tilliemad, 1634 (SCM., III, p. 134), and Helen Copper in Keltie, 1672 (*Dunblane*). William Cowper, the poet, writing to Mrs. Courtenay, one of his friends says: "While Pitcairne whistles for his family estate in Fifeshire, he will do well if he will sound a few notes for me. I am originally of the same shire, and a family of my name is still there" (*New statistical account*, IX, p. 344). Coupar 1479, Couppar 1662, Cowpar 1500, Cowpare 1512, Cuper 1286.

COPLAND, COPELAND, COUPLAND. Most probably from Coupland in the parish of Kirk Newton, Northumberland. There is, however, a district in Cumberland bearing the same name. William de Copland was one of the witnesses to the gift of Dundas to Helias, son of Huctred, c. 1160 (*Nat. MSS.*, I), Thomas de Coupland held a land in the vill of Greenlaw, c. 1200 (*Kelso*, 78), and about the same time Rodbert de Copland witnessed a charter

COPLAND, COPELAND, COUPLAND, *continued* by Roger de Quenci (LSC., 36). Sampson de Coupland was one of the assessors selected to settle the law of the marches, 1249. Robertus de Coupland witnessed a sale of land in Glasgow, c. 1280–90 (REG., p. 198). Payment was made to Thomas de Coupeland, esquire of Sir Thomas de Multone in 1306 (*Bain*, II, p. 512). John de Coupland was the hero of the battle of Neville's Cross in 1346, when he took David II prisoner. John de Coupland had a charter of the lands of Altonburn c. 1354 (HMC., 14. Rep., App., pt. 3, p. 8). His seal is a shield couché bearing what appears to be a cross, etc., S' *Johis de Coupland* (ibid.). The surname early made its way north and is found in Orkney in 1455, and appears in the Scat Book of Zetland c. 1500. Copland 1488, Coupillande 1456, Cowpelande 1550, Cowpland and Cowpelande 1465.

COPLAY. Perhaps from Copley, a hamlet in the parish of Halifax, Yorkshire. Robert Coplay to be admitted burgess freeman of Glasgow "provided he first marie Jonat, 1. dau. to dec. (lawful daughter to deceased) Robert Stevinsoun, upone whom he is contractit and begottin bairns," 1611 (*Burgesses*).

CORBET, CORBETT. A diminutive of Fr. *corbeau*, a raven. The first Corbet came from Shropshire and settled in Teviotdale under Earl David in the first quarter of the twelfth century. He is said to have obtained the manor of Foghou which he held as a vassal under the earls of Dunbar (*Chalmers*, I, p. 499). Robert Corbet was a witness to the *Inquisitio* of Earl David c. 1124, and to a charter by the earl to Selkirk Abbey (*Kelso*, 4). His son, Walter, acquired the manor of Malcarvestun and other lands in Teviotdale and made grants to the Abbey of Kelso, and gifted the church of Malcaruiston to the same abbey (*Kelso*, 12). Between 1179–89 he witnessed a charter by William the Lion (RMP., p. 89). The seals of Robert Corbet and of Walter Corbet are attached to charters of the lands of Cliftun granted to the Abbey of Melrose, c. 1170 (*Seals*, 202, 203), and the seal of Patrick Corbet, also appended to a Melrose charter of about the same date, bears a tree supported on each side by a lion rampant and in the branches two corbeau (ibid., 201). This device of the raven was afterwards adopted as the armorial bearing of several families of Corbets in Scotland and England. Nicholas Corbet was "in curia regis" at Berwick, 1248 (APS., I, p. 409, 410), and as Nicholas Corbeth he witnessed a charter de warenna de Muskilburg to the monks of Dunfermline,

1249 (RD., p. 44). The Corbets ended in direct line in an heiress, Christiana, who died in 1241 and was buried in the chapter-house of Melrose (*Chron. Mail.*). Rogier Corbet of Roxburghshire rendered homage, 1296. His seal is a gem, "a warrior arming himself, shield at his feet, *Sigillum Rogeri Corbet*" (*Bain*, II, p. 200, 532). Adam Corbet of Berwickshire and Johan Corbet of Roxburghshire also rendered homage in same year (ibid., p. 207, 211). William Corbet was one of an inquest at Roxburgh, 1361 (ibid., IV, 62), and Donald Corbatt had a charter of the lands of Ester Arde from John of Yle, earl of Ross, 1463 (*Clan Donald*, I, p. 539). Till lately a family of Corbet possessed lands in Clydesdale. Corbat 1613, Corbart 1567, Corbert 1562.

CORBIE. Alexander Corbie was retoured heir of Alexander Corbie, his father, in four sixteen parts of the lands of Luthrie, 1615 (*Retours*, Fife, 255). John Corbie, messenger in New Milne in 1676, and seven more of the name are recorded in the Kirkcudbright Commissariot Record in the seventeenth and eighteenth centuries. Perhaps of local origin from Corby in Cumberland.

CORBRIDGE. Alexander de Correbrige, cleric of Alexander III, 1254 (RD., p. 49) doubtless derived his name from Corbridge-on-Tyne (in 1217, Corebrigg). William de Corbridge, monk of Jedburgh, 1296 (*Bain*, II, p. 219).

CORC. Corc or Kork was one of the sons of Alwyn, second earl of Levenax, and appears as witness in one of his father's charters (*Levenax*, p. 98). From him are descended the Leckies of Lecky. See under MACCORC.

CORDINER, CORDWAYNER. From the occupation, 'the cordwainer,' AF. *cordewaner*, the shoemaker who made shoes of goat-skin leather, which came, or was supposed to come, from Cordova in Andalusia, Spain. Thomas Cordonar was admitted burgess of Aberdeen, 1442 (NSCM., I, p. 7), Adam Cordonar witnessed a notarial instrument in Dumfries, 1453 (*Edgar*, p. 225), Robert Cordoner held land in Kyntor, 1498 (REA., I, p. 341), and the goods of John Cordonar in Jedworthe were wasted in 1502 (*Trials*, I, p. 27°). Donald Cordinair in Little Suddie, Avoch, was a tanner in 1620 (RPC., XII, p. 472), John Cordiner in Seater, Caithness, was a follower of Sinclair of Moy, 1670 (ibid., 3. ser. III, p. 194), and Charles Cordiner, Episcopal minister in Banff, published a work on the *Antiquities and scenery of the north of Scotland*, 1780. The Cordiners were erected into a fraternity in Edinburgh 28th July 1349 (Maitland, *Edinburgh*,

p. 305). The name of Radulph Cordwan, a tenant in Perth, c. 1330 (RAA., II, p. 8, 9), may mean that he was a native of Cordova. Cordonnar 1659, Cordownar 1657.

CORE. A surname in Lanarkshire. Said to be French. Spelled Cure in Workman's MS. Henry Cor rendered homage at Elgin, 1296 (Bain, II, p. 195). Clement Cor was bailie of Edinburgh in 1560 (Macdonald, 501). William Cor appears in Newbigging, 1624, and James Cor in Carnwath, 1665 (Lanark CR.). Cf. TOR.

COREHOUSE. From Corehouse in the parish of Lesmahagow, Lanarkshire, the old spelling of which was Corrokys. Jordan de Currokes had a dispute with the bishop of Glasgow anent the lands of Stobhou, c. 1232 (REG., p. 108–110). Elene de Corrokys received a gift in 1266 (ER., I, p. 27), and Reginald de Corrokys resigned his land of Fyncorrokys to the Abbey of Kelso, 1290 (Kelso, p. 165).

CORKRAN, CORKRANE. A Galloway surname. From Ir. O'Corcrain, 'descendant of Corcran.' Hugh Corkran at the Mill of Drummore, 1785 (Wigtown).

CORMACK, CORMICK. Cormac (Cormag) is an old Gaelic personal name occurring in Adamnan (VC., I, c. 6) as Cormacus. From early Celtic *corb-mac "chariot lad" or "charioteer." Modern Cormack may be the shortened form of MacCormaic or MacCormaig, "son of Cormac."

CORMANNO. From Carmunnock in Lanarkshire. The surname probably now extinct. Henry de Cormannok witnessed a charter by Alan filius Walter, 1179–99 (RMP., p. 12), and between 1189–99 another charter by William the Lion (ibid., p. 101). As de Cormanoc he attested gift of a toft in Stirling by the same king to the church of Glasgow between 1189–99 (REG., p. 67), and also witnessed William de Moreuille's charter of Gillemoristun to Edulfus filius Uctredi before 1196 (ibid., p. 40). As de Curmannoc he attested another charter by Alan filius Walteri c. 1202 (RMP., p. 14). Perhaps it was a succeeding Henry de Cormunnoc who witnessed a confirmation charter by Alexander II in 1225 (Levenax, p. 92). Stevene de Cormanoughe of Lanarkshire rendered homage, 1296 (Bain, II, p. 212). Early in the sixteenth century the name appears in Dundee. Sir John Cormanno (Carmannoch, Cormannocht), chaplain in Sounde, is in record 1506–15 (Rent. Dunk., p. 3, 7, 19), Robert Curmannow was burgess in Dundee, 1534 (RMS., III, 1398), James Carmanno and Cristian Carmanow are mentioned there in 1588 and 1589

(Wedd., p. 30, 217), and Gilbert Carmano was burgess there, 1610 (Brechin).

CORMOKSON. An Anglicizing of MACCORMICK, q.v. Donald Cormokeson was master of the Hospital of Saint John of Helmsdale, 1471 (OPS., II, p. 731).

CORNEQUY. Laurence Cornequy tacksman of the one penny scatland of Cornequy in 1492 (REO., p. 407) most probably derived his name from Cornquoy in Paplay.

CORNER. John Coronare 1512, Lion Crovnar 1519, James Crownar 1512. Macbain (v, p. 62) says compare old designations 'de la Corner;' it may sometimes come from coroner, as John le Corner. Harrison says: (1) dweller at an angle or corner of land. (2) hornblower, trumpeter, from Fr. corneur. (3) from coroner, crown officer, e.g. John le Coroner. In HR. it is 'de la Cornere,' also Latinized in angulo.

CORNET. A Sir Milo Corneth otherwise Milone Cornet appears in record about the close of the twelfth century and during the first quarter of the thirteenth he is designated prior of St. Germains in East Lothian. As Dominus Milo Corneth he was witness to the marches of Stobo about 1180 (REG., p. 89). As Milone Cornet he witnessed a grant of the old castle of Forfar by Robert de Quincy to Reginald de Argentine c. 1200 (RPSA., p. 354), and as Milone Coruet he witnessed a grant by Peter de Grame to the Hospital of Soltre between 1190–1238 (Soltre, p. 11). In 1220 he appears again as a witness (LSC., 62). About 1230 he is again a witness in a charter by Ade fil. Edulphi to the Abbey of Neubotle (Neubotle, 25). As Milone Corneth he witnessed a charter granted by Sayerus de Quincy, earl of Winchester, for the souls of King William, R. de Quincy, my father, and R. my son. To this charter the earl appends "the seal of Roger, my son, the only one with me."

CORNFOOT, CORNFUTE. Alexander Cornefutt had a feu charter of a sixteenth part of the lands of Balcrystie c. 1570 (RD., p. 472), and Andrew Corfuit [for Coifuit = Cornfuit] had a charter of confirmation of Balchristie linkis in 1601 (ibid., p. 501). David Corfitt was enrolled burgess of Dundee in 1602 (Wedd., p. 171), and Alexander Cornfut, portioner of Balcristie, was retoured heir of Andro Cornfut, portioner of Balcristie, 'his gudger,' 'in the sixtein pairt of the toune and landis of Balcristie,' 1653 (Retours, Fife, 815). Janet Cornfoot or Corphat was a victim of the witchcraft superstition, being murdered in a horrible manner by the populace of Pittenweem in 1705. Probably a corruption of Cornforth, the name of a place in county Durham.

CORNICK. A Galloway surname. Shortened from (MAC)CORNACK, q.v.

CORNTON. Probably from Cornton near Bridge of Allan, Stirlingshire. John de Corintoun, chaplain, who witnessed charter of the office of coronator of Lennox, 1400 (Levenax, p. 95), is doubtless the Johannes de Corntoun, vicar of Stryvelyne, 1413 (RMS., I, 950). George Cornetoun recorded in Edinburgh, 1493 (CDE., 56), and the seal of Florence Corntoun is appended to sasine of a tenement in Leith, 1554 (Macdonald, 502). Henrie Corntoun, inhabitant of the town of Quhiterne, 1553 (Dumfriesshire and Galloway Nat. Hist. and Ant. Soc., Trans., 3. ser. XXI, p. 302).

CORNWALL. From Cornwall in England. The first of this name in Scotland appears to have been Robert de Cornewall who witnessed a charter by Hugh, bishop of St. Andrews granting the lands of Malar to the abbot and canons of Stirling, c. 1180 (Cambus.). William de Cornhal of Edinburghshire rendered homage, 1296 (Bain, II, p. 201). William de Cornal attested the homage of Duncan, earl of Fife, to Robert de Karal, abbot of Dunfermline, 1316 (RD., p. 236). Mr. Richard Cornell was archdeacon of Dunkeld, 1406, and professor of canon law in University of St. Andrews, 1410 (Tytler, Hist. of Scot., II, p. 43). Sir John Cornwell, vicar of Telvne (Tealing) in Angus, 1450 (Illus., III, p. 135). Johne of Cornewal of Bonhard was killed at Flodden, 1513, and John Cornuell was witness in Crail, 1526 (Crail, p. 39). Nicholas Cornwall of Bonhard was provost of Linlithgow and a commissioner for holding parliament, 1592 (APS., III, p. 527). Archibald Cornwall, town-officer of Edinburgh, was hanged in the city in 1601 for having, at the sale of some sequestrated goods at the Cross, driven a nail into the gibbet standing close by, intending to suspend on it a portrait of the king on a board that was among them, for the purpose of its being better seen, but was dissuaded from doing so by those present. His action was considered by the authorities as lese-majestie. Donald Cornell, heir of Malcolm Cornell, burgess of Perth, 1604 (Inquis., 177). Marie Carnewall in the parish of Logie, 1674 (Dunblane), and Duncan Cornel in Hill of Arnfinlay, parish of Kippen, 1734. Cornwalls were seated at Bonhard early in the fifteenth century, and the direct line ended on the death of Elizabeth, heiress of Bonhard in 1763. Cornale and Cornevale, 1479, Cornewale 1483, Cornwale 1530.

COROTICUS. This name was formerly identified with Ceredig, the name of the Welsh prince who gave name to the county of Cardi-

gan in South Wales. Sir Samuel Ferguson (Patrician documents, xxxii) first pointed out that the individual meant was Ceretic Guletic ('prince'), the ruler of Alcluith or Strathclyde, c. 420–450 A. D., and Prof. Zimmer (Celtic Church, p. 54–55) has proved this conclusively. Muirchu, the biographer of S. Patrick, calls him "Coirthech regem Aloo," king of the rock (Alclwyd). In two passages of S. Patrick's letter to the subjects of Coroticus (c. 2, 15) he applies the epithet 'apostate' (Pictorum apostatarum) to the Picts that were allies of Coroticus. "It is not clear," says Rev. Dr. White, "why they were called 'apostate;' perhaps on account of their having joined Scottic [i.e. Irish] heathen in a raid on Patrick's Scottic Christians; perhaps because of an actual lapse into formal heathenism. In any case," he adds, "it proves that they had once been Christians" (St. Patrick, p. 5). The mission of S. Ninian of Whitherne to the Southern Picts is dated between 394 and 432.

CORQUODALE. See under MACCORQUODALE.

CORRIE. From the lands of Corrie now included in the parish of Hutton-Corrie, Dumfriesshire. Hugh de Corrie witnessed a charter of a fishery in Torduf c. 1194–1211 (Holm Cultram, p. 35), and as de Corri he witnessed resignation of land in Weremundebi and Anant within the same period (Bain, I, 606; Annandale, I, p. 1, 2). Radulph de Corry witnessed a charter by Henry de Grahame a. 1200 (RHM., 3). Walterus de Corri and Nicholas de Corri witnessed a charter by the earl of Carrick c. 1271 (Annandale, I, p. 8), and Nicholas is recorded as steward of Annandale in that year. Walter de Corry or de Corri, cousin and one of the heirs of Helewisa de Levynton, rendered homage to Edward I for his portion of her lands held in capite, 1274 (Bain, II, 21). Nicol de Corry of Dumfriesshire and Sir Walter de Corri rendered homage in 1296 (ibid., p. 194, 206). Adam of Corry, one of the garrison of Loghmaban Castle, had a fiat of protection for one year in 1379 (ibid., IV, 280), and Harbard or Harbarte of Corre was one of the 'borowis' for the earl of Douglas's bounds of the West March in 1398 (ibid., 504). Gilbert of Corry had a charter of the lands of Torduff and Dalbank in 1449 (Annandale, I, p. 13), and Thomas Corry of Keldwood, a follower of the earl of Cassilis, was respited for murder in 1526 (RSS., I, 3386). George Corry was retoured heir of Thomas Corri de Kelwode, Ayr, who was killed at the battle of Fawsyde, 1547 (Retours, Ayr, 2). John Maitland Corrie, archaeologist, died in Dumfries, 1940.

CORRIGALL. An Orcadian surname derived from the old township of the name in Harray. The Corrigalls still hold part of the property from which they derive their surname. Wilyam Corgill was odaller of the 2d. land of Corstath in 1492, and James Corgill was tacksmar. of the 1d. land in How in 1503 (REO., p. 408, 415.) James and Robert Corigilles are mentioned in 1572, and James, Robert, and John are mentioned in 1601 (SHR., XVII, p. 22). James Corrigill in Rendell in 1640 (MCM., II, p. 211).

CORRINI. Duncanus de Corrini who witnessed an instrument of concord between the bishop of Aberdeen and John de Forbes, *dominus ejusdem*, in 1391 (REA., I, p. 189), may have derived his name from Coranie (in common speech Corénnie) in the parish of Cluny, Aberdeenshire.

CORSAN. *See under* CARSON.

CORSAR, CORSER. From the occupation, ME. *corser*, *corsere*, or *courser*, 'a horse dealer.' Agnes Corser was "delaited for bearing ane burden of clothes on the Lordis day," 1661 (*Rec. Elgin*, II, p. 292). David Cosser in Touchgorme, 1663, reappears in 1683 as David Corser in Touchgorme, parish of St. Ninian *(Stirling)*. John A. Corsar from Auchterless was killed in the first Great War *(Turriff)*. The old family of Courser or Corser (Corseir of that Ilk in Workman MS.) have three coursers (running horses) in their arms (*Nisbet*, I, p. 306).

CORSBIE, CORSBY. Metathesis of CROSBIE, q.v. "Of that Ilk" says Nisbet.

CORSCALLANE. Bessie Corscallane in Burnbra in the parish of Hamilton in 1603 (*Campsie*) derived her surname from Carscallan in the parish of Hamilton, Lanarkshire.

CORSE. From *cors* or *corse*, the Scots form of *cross*. See CROSS and CROUCH. Robert Cors or Kors was tenant in Westhorn, 1465–70 (*Cupar-Angus*, I, p. 152, 155), John Cors burgess-freeman of Glasgow, 1601 *(Burgesses)*, Robert Corss in Dysart, 1630 (PBK., p. 20), and James Corss was a mathematician in Edinburgh in latter half of seventeenth century. David Corse Glen was a Glasgow geologist. (2) An old surname in Rousay, from Corse in the parish of St. Ola, Orkney. John of Corss was witness to a disposition made at Kirkwall in 1455 (REO., p. 191).

CORSEHILL. John de Corshill, notary public in Aberdeen in 1366, is probably the John de Corshyll, perpetual vicar of the parish church of Aberkerdor in Moray in 1375 (REA., II, p. 59; RAA., II, 34). He most probably derived his name from one of the places so named in Aberdeenshire.

CORSKIE. From one of the three or more places so named in Aberdeenshire. Symon Corsky perambulated the bounds of Yochry and Achbrady, 1492 (RAA., II, 339). In another copy of the charter he is named Symon Quorsque or Sime of Corsque (REM., p. 246, 248).

CORSLAT. Of local origin, perhaps from Corslat near Castle Semple, Renfrewshire. There is another Corslat near Ochiltree. David Corslat was a witness in Glasgow, 1550 (*Protocols*, I). Corsat 1558.

CORSON. *See under* CARSON.

CORSTON. From Corston in Strathmiglo. The lands of Andrew Corstone are mentioned in 1510 (*Rent. Dunk.*, p. 269). The Corstons, an old Orkney family, may have given their name to the township of Corston in Harray. Magnus of Corstath (the old spelling of the name) was odaller of 2d. land of Corstath in 1492 (REO., p. 408).

CORSTORPHINE, CORSTORPHAN. The name of an old family in Fife, derived from the village and parish of the name in Midlothian (*Macfarlane*, II, p. 201–202). George Corstrophyne was witness in Crail, 1526 (*Crail*, p. 39). George and Thomas Corstorphin in Crail were cited before the Privy Council, 1567 (RPC., I, p. 578), Martin Corstorphine of Balrymonth was heir of Martin Corstorphin, portioner of Byrehillis, 1608 (*Retours, Fife*, 194), Henry Carstorphine was indweller in Hilwall, Shetland, 1624 (OSS., I, 51), and John Corstorphine, portioner in Kingsbarns, died 1767. Carstorphene and Carstorphine 1598, Carstraphen 1660, Carstrophein 1583, Carstrphen 1590, Custorphing 1589; Carstrophen, Carstrphein, Costorphin, Crostrophin, Crostrophyn.

CORTHIE. Local. There is a Corthymuir near Udny, Aberdeenshire. William Corthie of Ellon to appear on the repentance stool in Ellon church, 1627 (*Mair*, p. 72).

COSCRACH. From *cos-carach*, 'victorious' (*Rel. Celt.*, II, p. 604). Coscrach or Coscarach occurs but rarely in Scotland, but is fairly common in Ireland. Drostan mac Cosgreg came from Hi with Colum Cille to Aberdeen .in Buchan according to the legend in the *Book of Deer*. Duuene filius Croscrach witnessed the gift by Alewinus, earl of Leuenax of

COSCRACH, *continued*

the church of Kamsi (Campsie) to God and S. Kentigern, c. 1208–14, and as Duuene filius Coscrach he witnessed another charter relating to the same church by Alewinus, son of Maldouen (REG., p. 87, 88). Donald Coskroch and Neill Coskroch in Kip, parish of Balquhidder, appear in 1663 and 1685 (*Dunblane*). John Coskrie in Strathmoddie, 1799 (*Wigtown*). See also MACCOSKRIE.

COSH. From (MAC)COSH, q.v.

COSKRY. See under MACCOSKRIE.

COSMUNGHO, 'servant of (S.) Mungo,' i.e. Kentigern. Cosmungho, sacerdos, aput Edoluestone (now Eddleston), was father of three of the witnesses to the *Diuise de Stobbo*, c. 1190 (REG., p. 89). *Cos*<W. *gwas* = G. *gille*.

COSOUOLD. "Cosouold filius Muryn aput castrum Oliuerj," was one of the witnesses to the *Diuise de Stobbo*, c. 1190 (REG., p. 89). Prof. Watson suggests that the name should probably be read as Cososuold, "Oswald's servant," a Welsh formation. *Cos* from Welsh *gwas*, 'servant.' From Oswald, the Anglic king killed in battle against Penda, 642 A. D. See GILLASALD.

COSPATRIC. A common personal name in the twelfth century, spelled Gospatric in the *Anglo-Saxon Chronicle*, Cospatricius in Simeon of Durham, Gospatlicus on the tombstone at Durham, and Caius Patricius in Orderic Vitalis (bk. iv, c. 5). In the Life of Edward (1066–74) it is Gaius Patricius (ES., II, p. 39). It means 'servant of Patrick,' from W. *gwas*, 'a youth, servant.' Cospatric frater Dalfin, Cospatric filius Uctred, and Cospatric filius Alden all appear as witnesses to Earl David's *Inquisitio* as to the extent of the lands of the church of Glasgow, c. 1124 (REG., p. 5). Cospatricius romefare (so named from having made the pilgrimage to Rome) and Cospatricius, heremita de Kvlbewhoc, were witnesses to the *Diuise de Stobbo*, c. 1180 (ibid., p. 89). Cospatrick filius Madad witnessed a charter by Fergus, earl of Buchan a. 1214 (CAB., p. 409), and c. 1220 as Cospatric Macmadethyn he had a charter of Stratheyn and Kvndrochet from William Cumyne, earl of Buchan (REA., I, p. 14).

COSSAR, COSSER, COSSART, COUSAR. Probably assimilated forms of CORSAR, q.v. Robert I granted charters to Henry Cosur or Henry dictus Cosure of the lands of Bondvngtone and Bethocrulle (RMS., I, 9, 10). Henry Coceur, son and heir of Henry Coceur of Trebroun,

granted a charter of lands in Over Lamberton in 1332 (BNCH., XVI, p. 326), and in same year as Henry Cosour he appears as charter witness (ibid., p. 330). Adam Cossour was macer (*claviger*) to David II and had from him charter of a bovate of land with pertinents in the tenement of Aymouthe in barony of Coldingham, 1361 (RMS., I, 263). In 1360 he was one of the collectors of contributions from the county of Berwick (ER., II). Henry Cossoure, son of John Cossoure, had charter from Robert II of the lands of Otterburne in the sheriffdom of Berwyk on resignation of his father, 1373 (RMS., I, 472). Adam Cousour who witnessed a notarial instrument dated 1442 is doubtless Adam Cosour, juror on a claim to third part of Cranshaws, 1453 (*Home*, 21; *Swinton*, p. xxxix). Another Adam Cosur, burgess of Stirling, had safe conduct to travel in England, 1453 (*Bain*, IV, 1256). Alexander Cosour, Robert Cosour, and Dugal Cosour were burgesses of Stirling, 1476, and William Cossour was burgess there, 1520 (SBR., p. 6, 259). David Coissoure was sasine witness, 1541 (*Home*, p. 252). The name is Corseir of that Ilk in Workman MS. Coussor, Corsour, Cosouris (pl.).

COSSENS, COSSINS. Cossens of that Ilk, formerly an old family in the parish of Glamis, took their name from the lands of Cossins, about a mile northeast from the Castle of Glamis. They were allied in marriage to the Lyons of Glamis (PSAS., II, p. 248). Johannes Cossynnis apud Dunde had a precept of remission in 1492 (RSS., I, 14). The seal of Thomas Cossynnis is appended to a charter in the Glamis collection of date 1509 (*Seals*, 204; *Macdonald*, 504). David Cossins in Kinclune, 1662, and two more of name (*Brechin*).

COSTENTIN. A family of this name, vassals of the Stewards, were settled near Innerwick, East Lothian, on lands obtained from their superiors. They probably derived their name from Côtentin, an ancient territory in Normandy, forming the larger part of the department of Manche. Robert, Walter, Nigel, and Gaufrid de Costinten or Costentin appear as witnesses in various documents, principally relating to the Abbey of Paisley, between 1165 and 1204 (RMP., p. 6, 15, 74, 232; *Cambus.*, 174; RAA., I, 6; *Bain*, II, p. 421). Nicholas de Costentin granted "una cultura" of his lands of Innvrwic to the monks of Paisley c. 1200 (RMP., p. 116).

COSTERMAN. From the occupation, a 'costerman,' one who sold costards (a kind of apple), or generally a hawker of fruit. Laurence Costerman witnessed an instrument of sasine in Berwickshire, 1571 (*Laing*, 858).

COSTINE. An abbreviation or pet form of CONSTANTINE, q.v. Sir Ralph Costein was witness to a charter c. 1200 to the church of S. Mary in Stirling (Cambus., p. 79). Hew Costine was merchant burgess of Dumfries, 1638–39, and twelve more of the name appear in the same record between 1624–1800 (Dumfries). James Costyne was resident in Edinburgh, 1527 (EBR., 230). Cousteine 1705.

COTTON. Of local origin from one of the many places of the name in Perthshire, Kincardineshire, Angus, and Aberdeenshire. A common place name in Fife in the seventeenth century.

COUBROUGH. A now not very common surname found in Lanarkshire and in Midlothian. It is a shortened form of MACCOUBREY, q.v. David Cowbratht witnessed testament of inventory of Catharine Lauder, 1515 (Swinton, p. xci). The name also occurs as COULBROUGH and COWBROUGH in Stirling, and is an old Strathblane surname (1511, Cowbroch). Euphame Cubrughe in Badow, parish of Calder, 1669 (Campsie). William Cubrugh, a Perthshire heritor, 1688 (RPC., 3. ser. XIII, p. 332). John Couburgh in Balglairosh, parish of St. Ninians, and two more recorded there (Stirling).

COUGHTREY. A Galloway name, curtailed from MACAUGHTRIE, q.v.

COULBROUGH. See under COUBROUGH.

COULL, COWL, COWLE. From Coull in Aberdeenshire. William de Cull was one of the witnesses to a charter by John, earl of Huntington to Norman filius Malcolm of the lands of Lesslyn etc., between 1219–37 (CAB., p. 548). John Cowl possessed a tenement in Glasgow in 1458 (REG., 369), and Sir John Cowill, a cleric, was witness in Aberdeen, 1567 (Aboyne, p. 107). Patrick Coule at Newburgh is mentioned in the Lindores Chartulary in 1479 (LAC., 153). David Cowle, a native of Scotland, had letters of naturalization in England in 1481 (Bain, IV, 1468), and in the same year Alexander Coule was admitted burgess of Aberdeen (NSCM., I, p. 29). The Coulls were formerly a numerous race in Cullen, and among them, John was the most common Christian name:

> "There's Hooker Jock and Souter Jock,
> And cripple Jock the tailyer,
> Jock-o-boy, the Din-o'-Guil,
> And Lang Jock the Jailer."
>
> Cramond, Church and churchyard of Cullen, p. 119.

COULTAR, COULTER, CULTER. From the manor of Coulter in Lanarkshire. Richard of Culter, sheriff of Lanark, appears in record in 1226 (Athole, p. 704). Alexander de Cultre witnessed a grant by Maldoueny, earl of Lennox to Stephen de Blantyr, c. 1248 (Levenax, p. 36). John Coulter in Preistsvde, parish of Cummertrees, 1686 (Dumfries). William Coulter, lord-provost of Edinburgh, died in 1810. (2) Andrew de Cultvr who held land in Aberdeen in 1281 (REA., II, p. 278) doubtless derived his name from the lands of Coulter in Aberdeenshire.

COULTHARD, COULTHART. See under COLTART.

COULTS. A form of COUTTS, q.v.

COUPAR, COUPER. See under COOPER.

COUPLAND. See under COPLAND.

COURTIE. Catharine Courtie in Edinburgh, 1633 (Edinb. Marr.). Patrick Courtie in Loanhead of Lasswade, 1672 (Inquis., 5498).

COURTNEY. Belonging to a place of the name in France. William de Courtney married Ada, daughter of Patrick, earl of Dunbar and obtained with her the lands of Home (Chalmers, Caledonia, I, p. 499). Notwithstanding this early entry the name is most probably of much later introduction. John Courtney and William Courtney were residents in the parish of Senneck, 1684 (RPC., 3. ser. IX, p. 568).

COUSIN. A cousin, kinsman, ME. cosyn, cusyn. Nicholas Cusing admitted burgess of Aberdeen, 1512 (NSCM., I, p. 45), and Andrew Cosin was burgess there, 1527 (CRA., p. 119). A sasine was recorded in favor of James Cousin in Steilend, 1572 (Pitfirrane), Robert Cusing appears in Dunfermline, 1579 (Dunfermline), and the escheat of John Cusigne there is recorded in 1609 (RD., p. 502). Jean Cuseing appears in Auchtertule, 1653 (PBK., p. 390).

COUSLAND. Of local origin from Cousland in the parish of Cranston, Midlothian. Randulphus de Cousland witnessed a charter by Adam, son of Patric de Crebarrin (now Carbery) of land in Muskilburcscyr in the thirteenth century (RD., p. 103). John Cousland appears in Stirling in 1522, and Walter Cousland, member of council there in 1527, appears again in 1531 as bailie of the burgh (SBR., p. 17, 275, 276). Perhaps it was a succeeding Walter Cousland who was custumar of Stirling in 1558 (ER., XIX, p. 38). John Cosland rendered to Exchequer the accounts of the burgh of Dundee in 1559 (ibid., p. 83), and a payment was made to Andro Cowsland in Clony in 1558 (Rent. Dunk., p. 357).

COUSTON. Of local origin from the lands of Couston near Newtyle, Angus. A family of the name held some position in the shires of Clackmannan and Perth in the sixteenth and seventeenth centuries (*Stodart*, II). David Cowston, chaplain in Dundee, died c. 1505. Several Coustons were burgesses of Dundee in the sixteenth century (*Wedd.*, p. 168), Thomas Cowstoun was tenant in the lordship of Dudop (Dudhope), 1562 (ER., XIX, p. 506), and John Costoun rendered to Exchequer the accounts of the baillies of Dundee, 1565 (ibid., p. 297). Alexander Cowistoun was bailie of Leith, 1576 (REO., p. 295). Gilbert Coustoun was retoured heir in lands in Clackmannan, 1605 (*Retours, Clackmannan*, 2, 3), Alexander Coustoun was burgess of Culross in 1611 (*Dunblane*), Alexander Cowstein, weaver in Edinburgh, 1617 (*Edinb. Marr.*), Janet Couston is recorded in Swinton, 1674 (*Lauder*), and Archibald Coustoune was a sailor in Leith, 1678 (*Inquis.*, 6092). Coustine 1679, Coustown 1630, Cowstane 1610.

COUTIE, COUTTIE. From lands which formerly belonged to the Abbey of Coupar-Angus, old spellings of which were Cowte, Cowty, and Cultby. The early form of the place name was Cupermaccultin (1150, RD., p. 74) explained by Watson as 'Cupar of the sons of Ultan' (*Watson* I, p. 238). Euphemia Couttie is recorded in Dundee in 1610 (*Brechin*), and Henry Coutie in Tulliallan c. 1680 (*Dunblane*). In Edinburgh 1941.

COUTTS. Of territorial origin from Cults in Aberdeenshire. A common surname in Upper Deeside. Richard de Cotis appears as a landowner in Elgyn, 1343 (REM., p. 289). In 1392 John de Cowtis and Donald de Cowtis were put to the horn as part guilty of the slaughter of Sir Walter de Ogilvy, sheriff of Angus and others (APS., I, p. 579). The principal family of the name was established in the earldom of Mar, Aberdeenshire, by a Crown charter in 1433, of the lands of Ochtercoull or Auchtercoul in favor of William Coutts, his brother Alexander, their cousin John, and his brother Alexander (*Fordell*). William de Coutis witnessed a deed in Aberdeen, 1434 (CRA., p. 5), Alexander Kowtis was admitted burgess of same burgh, 1470 (NSCM., I, p. 22), and William Cottis was master of the ship *le James* of Scotland, 1473 (*Bain*, IV; 1411). Robertus Coittis was vicar of Dummanv, 1478 (REG., p. 438), Alexander Couts was on an assize of service of James Bonar of Rossie, 1483, and James Coittis was rector of Carstaris, 1525 (REG., 497). Thomas Cowltis was vicar of parish church of Abirkerdowr, 1526 (RAA., II, 635), John Couttis was a "master massoun" of the burgh of Stirling, 1529 (SBR., p. 38), and William Cultis was admitted burgess of Aberdeen, 1531 (NSCM., I, p. 52). Robert Cowtis was retoured heir of John Cowltis of Auchtercoul, his brother-german, 1553 (*Retours, Aberdeen*, 17), and David Coitis possessed a land in Glasgow in the same year (*Protocols*, I). Allan Cowttis witnessed precept of sasine of Dunfermline, 1555 (*Laing*, 633), and Andrew Cowtis was one of the sergeants of the regality of Holyroodhouse, 1583 (*Soltre*, p. 149). Helen Cutis, goodvyf of Carnbarrow, desired relaxation of sentence of excommunication (*Strathbogie*, p. 83). A family of the name settled in Montrose at the close of sixteenth century, when William Coutts became provost of the town. The name was common in Edinburgh in the sixteenth and seventeenth centuries (*Edinb. Marr.*), and the London banking firm of the name is said to have been founded bv a member of the Montrose family. Coittes 1653, Cotis 1477, Cottes 1653, Cottis 1506, Coultis 1466, Couttss 1597, Cowtes 1610, Cowtis 1511, Kowtis 1529; Coutes, Coutys, Cults.

COVENTRY. From the city of the name in the county of Warwick, England. Peter de Coventre rendered homage at Berwick, 1291 (RR.). The earliest bearers of the name in Scotland appear to have been churchmen. Johannes de Couentre was a charter witness in Angus, 1344 (RAA., II, p. 19), and William de Couentre granted anew the church of Inhyrharyte (? Inverharity) in the diocese of St. Andrews the following year (*Pap. Pet.*, I, p. 89). Thomas de Conventre was canon of Caithness, 1348 (CSR., I, p. 127), Walter de Covingtre was decanus of Aberdour, 1426 (RMS., II, 55), and Patrick Cowentre, rector of Garwald in 1509 (LCD., p. 209), is probably the Patrick Covintre, decanus de Restalrig in 1539. William Covintrie is recorded in Kirkwall, 1612 (MCM., II, p. 157), David Coventrie had a charter of a fourth part of Arlarie in Kinross-shire, 1607 (RD., p. 500). Janet Couentrie in Geeven of Tillibodie, 1621, and eight more of the name are recorded in Dunblane Commissariot Record. Cowentrie 1564.

COVERHAM. From Coverham in the North Riding of Yorkshire. A horse was purchased from Willelmus de Coverham, 1312 (*Bain*, III, p. 421).

COVINGTON. From Covington in Lanarkshire, the earliest form of which was Colbaynstoun, i.e. the vill or tun of Colbayn or Colbain, perhaps the Colbanus who was a witness to the charter by Earl David founding the Abbey of Selkirk (afterwards Kelso), c. 1120 (*Kelso*, 1). He is doubtless the ancestor of Thomas de Colbainestun who witnessed a charter by William the Lion confirming certain churches in Dumfriesshire to the see of Glasgow between 1187–89 (REG., p. 65). Thomas de Colbaynstoun witnessed resignation of the lands of Ingilbristoun (later Inglisberrie) in 1204 (*Dryburgh*, 163), and as Thomas de Uilla Colbain witnessed an undated charter by William the Lion to David de Haia, son of William de Haia, of Herol (SCM., II, p. 305). William de Colbaynston between 1202 and 1222 is witness to a charter by Brice, bishop of Moray bestowing the church of Deveth (Daviot) on the cathedral of the Holy Trinity at Spyny (REM., 53). Margaret de Colbanstone and Isabele de Colbanston rendered homage for their possessions in 1296. The seal of Isabel bears the Virgin and Child and S' *Isabelle de Colbanestō*, and that of Margaret bears a device like a shuttle (?) in pale between 3 stars and the legend S' *Margar' d' Colbanst* (*Bain*, II, p. 198, 534, 550). Edmund de Colbenstone of Lanarkshire, probably a relative, also rendered homage in the same year (ibid., p. 213). In 1297 a royal message from Edward I of England was directed to William de Colbeynston and in 1304 Sir John de Colbaynston held the farm of the barony of Colbayneston of the king (*Bain*, II, p. 232, 428).

COW, Cowe. Radulfus Cowe, juror on inquest apud Muskylburg, 1359 (RD., p. 267). Johannes de le Cow, juror at a court held at 'Le Ballocis Hill' near Inverness, 1376 (*Innes Fam.*, p. 63). Robert Cow held a tenement in Ayr, 1490 (*Ayr*, p. 94), Alexander Cow was notary public in Edinburgh, 1504 (*Soltre*, p. 325), and Elizabeth Kow was tenant under the bishop of Aberdeen in Fethirneyr, 1511 (REA., I, p. 365). David Cow was tenant of lands in the Baitschell, 1512 (*Cupar-Angus*, I, p. 286), and Thomas Cowe was accused of part in the murder of Riccio, 1566 (RPC., I, p. 457). Three persons named Cowe and one named Cowy were tenants of Middil Tullbardin, 1565 (REM., p. 442). George Cow was 'post' in Banff, 1740 (*Aberdeen CR.*), and Alexander, James, and Margaret Cow were residents in Kildrummy, 1826–34 (*Aberdeen Jour. N & Q.*, I, p. 127). Lower suggests perhaps local, and mentions John de Cowe in HR., but also says it may be a sobriquet, for both De Cu and Le Cu are in the same record. Cf. Cuie.

COWAN, Cowans, Cowen. Common surnames in Ayrshire, Dumfriesshire, and other Lowland counties. (1) Sometimes explained as from Scots *cowan*, a dry-stone-diker, but I doubt this explanation. (2) It may be a corruption of Colquhoun, the common pronunciation of which is Cohoon. Mr. Alexander Cowan, father of Sir John Cowan of Beeslack is said to have left on record that many of his grandfather's books bore the name of Colquhoun. (3) In the south Highlands the 'Mac' of *Macillechomhghain* disappears from the name and in Argyllshire, e.g. Iain MacCòmhain becomes Iain Còmhan in Gaelic while the English equivalent is Cowan. Couen 1687. The name of James Cowhen, chaplain in North Berwick, 1560 (CMN.) is most likely from another source. There was an old family of Cowane in Stirling (*The Stirling antiquary*, v. 2, p. 168–178). Cowan's Hospital in Stirling was founded in 1639 by John Cowan, a merchant there, for the support of twelve decayed Guild Brethren (Nimmo, *History of Stirlingshire*, 2. ed., I, p. 346).

COWBISTER. Local. Stephen Cowbister in Howe, Orkney, had a precept of sasine in 1565 (REO., p. 283).

COWBROUGH. See under COUBROUGH.

COWDEN. From Cowden in the parish of Dalkeith, Midlothian. There is also a Cowden near Dollar, but Cowden near Dalkeith is more probable source of the name. Joneta Cowden, heir of William Cowden, burgess of Edinburgh, 1595 (*Inquis.*, 4). Hugo Cawdoun on inquest in Edinburgh, 1634 (*Fordell*, p. 119). Katherene Cowdon and Agnes Cowdon in Tinwald were examined for the Test, 1685 (RPC., 3. ser. XI, p. 434), and Patrick Cowdane appears in Traprainlawend, 1689 (*Edin. App.*). See also Colden.

COWEN. See under COWAN.

COWGIL. Perhaps from Cowgill, a hamlet in the West Riding of Yorkshire. Andrew Cowgil in Tron parish signed the Test in 1685 (RPC., 3. ser. X, p. 456).

COWIE. Local, from one or other of places of the name but mainly from the ancient barony of Cowie in Kincardineshire. Herbert de Cowy witnessed a charter by Nicholas de Dumfres in 1394 (SCM., v, p. 251). John Cowy was admitted burgess of Aberdeen, 1505 (NSCM., I, p. 43). Janet Cowie or Cuj was a witch in Elgin, 1646 (*Rec. Elgin*, II, p. 254, 356). A family of the name was long connected with Newburgh, Fife, and John Colwye, bailie of Newburcht is recorded in 1617 (*Wedd.*, p. 139). Alexander Covie in Coschnay was heir of John Covie in Reidmyre, 1642 (*Retours, Kincardine*, 73). In local speech the name is pronounced Cooie or Ku-ie. Calvie 1594, Colvie 1644, Couye 1613, Covy 1668, Cowye 1636.

COWL, COWLE. Surnames recorded in Aberdeen. See under COULL.

COWNIE. Recorded in Aberdeen. In Edinburgh, 1941. Perhaps of local origin.

COWPAR, COWPER. See under COOPER.

CRAB, CRABB. Of Flemish origin. The first of the name of prominence was Paul Crab, in Aberdeen, 1310. His seal bears a chevron between two fleur-de-lis in chief and a crab in base (Macdonald, 506). John Crab, Flemish engineer, came into notice at the siege of Berwick in 1319, when the stones discharged from his crane shattered the roof of the English 'sow.' In answer to a complaint by Edward II of England in that year Robert, count of Flanders, says that if he catches John Crabbe he will punish him on the wheel as he has been banished for murder (Bain, III, 673). Three records of payments to Crab are in ER. (I, p. 64, 81. 398). He received from Robert I the lands of Prescoby, Granden, Auchmolen, and Auchterrony in Aberdeenshire for his services (RMS., I, App. II, 409). He also took part in the siege of Perth, 1332 (ER., I, p. 450). John Crab, perhaps a son, was burgess and custumar of Aberdeen (ER., I, p. 587, 595), and in 1357 was one of those appointed to treat for the ransom of David II (APS., I, p. 517). John Crab witnessed sale of two crofts in Aberdeen to Ade Pyngil, 1362 (REA., I, p. 105, 106). In 1384 John Crab, burgess of Aberdeen, granted a charter in favor of his son, Paul Crab (ibid., II, p. 286), and in 1398 appears as proluctor for William Cuk in same burgh (CRA., p. 371). Craibstone, Newhills, Aberdeenshire (in 1401 Crabistone) derives its name from the engineer. John Crabbe, constable of Berwick, 1331 (Raine, 433), was charter witness at Lamberton, Berwickshire, 1332 (BNCH., XVI, p. 327). Perhaps a different person from Crab of Aberdeen. Crayb 1528.

CRAE. A curtailed form of (MA)CRAE, q.v.

CRAGBARNY. Local, probably from Craigbarnet near Glasgow. Ricardus de Cragbarnv, bailie of Muskylburg (Musselburgh), 1359 (RD., p. 267).

CRAGBAYTH. Local, probably from Craigbea near Ballinluig, Perthshire (th final in certain place names is mute, e.g. Aultbea, Tombea, etc.).William de Cragbavth, a witness in Dumbarton, 1271 (RMP., p. 192).

CRAGDALE. Local. David Cragdale to be kept scatheless, c. 1547 (Gaw, 10a).

CRAGHILT. Of local origin from lands of the name near Dunkeld (Rent. Dunk., index). Thomas de Craghilto was in receipt of alms from the granitar of Dunkeld, 1506–09 (Rent. Dunk., p. 79, 108). Cragilto 1693.

CRAGNASTON. From the old barony of the name (in 1606 Craignestoun) in Kincardineshire. Malcolm de Cragnaston was witness in Kyncardyn, 1434 (HP., IV, p. 238).

CRAHOC. Alan de Crahoc who witnessed a charter by Nesus de Lundors of the mill in Lynton to the monks of Holyrood c. 1225 (LSC., p. 51) derived his name from Crahoc, now Crauchie, in East Lothian.

CRAIB. A surname found in the shires of Aberdeen and Banff. A softened form of CRAB, q.v.

CRAICK. Local, from Craik in Aberdeenshire. William John Craick and Duguid Craick from Turriff served in the first Great War (Turriff).

CRAIG. Local. As the surname occurs in early Scots records in many parts of the country it must have originated from more than one locality. In the fifteenth century there were three families "of that Ilk." The name was also common in Edinburgh in the fifteenth and sixteenth centuries and so elsewhere throughout the Lowlands. Johannes del Crag witnessed a charter by William the Lion, and Robertus de Crag witnessed one in the reign of Alexander II (REG., p. 83, 123). Walter del Crag was an elector in 1278 (Bain, II, 147). Anneys del Crage of Edinburghshire and Johan del Cragge of Lanarkshire rendered homage, 1296 (ibid., p. 209, 213). The land of James del Crag, son and heir of John del Crag, in Ayrshire is mentioned in 1323 (Irvine, I, p. 123). The dramatic intervention of John of the Craig with his band of 300 "played a decisive part in the battle of Culblean on 30th November 1335" (PSAS., LXIV, p. 54). Johannes de Crag, burgess of Aberdeen, had a charter of land in the lordship of Rubyslaw in 1358 (RMS., I, 107), and for two centuries and a half later a family of this name was seated at Craigfintray (afterwards Craigston) Castle near Kildrummie. William de Crag was elected councillor of Aberdeen, 1398 (CRA., p. 374), and Richard de Crag, presbyter and notary public of St. Andrews diocese, 1415, may be the Richard de Crag, vicar of Dundee, 1443 (REG., 325). In 1429 the lands of Estircrag in the barony of North Berwick were granted to Walter de Crag in succession to his father, John Crag (RMS., II, 145). David of Crag, a Red Friar in Aberdeen in 1439, is referred to again in 1442 simply as David Crag (*Friars*, 29, 30). William Craigh, merchant in Culross, 1668 (*Dunblane*). John Craig (1512–1600) was colleague of John Knox.

CRAIGDALLIE. A now very uncommon surname in Perthshire originating from the village of the same name in the Carse of Gowrie. Thomas Craigdallie was appointed Treasurer of Perth in 1731, and a later Thomas Craigdallie was a student in St. Andrews University in 1770. Bailie Adam Craigdallie is one of the characters in Scott's *The Fair maid of Perth*.

CRAIGDUCKIE. Of local origin from the lands of Craigduckie near Dunfermline, Fife.

CRAIGEN. Local. In 1272 the church of Cragyn (now Craigie) in Kyle was confirmed to the monks of Paisley by Thomas de Cragyn, son and heir of John Hose, who had assumed his surname from his lands (RMP., p. 232). He may be the Thomas de Cregeyn del counte de Are who rendered homage in 1296 (*Bain*, II, p. 206). Ade Cragyne who held a tenement in Irvine, 1477 (*Irvine*, I, p. 149), most probably derived his name from the same source. A family of this name in New Pitsligo village were remarkable for their longevity (AEI., p. 47). Christian Craigane was liferenter of Readfurd, 1630 (LIM., p. 110). Patrick Craigen in Burnebray of Gorthie, 1670 (*Dunblane*), and Robert Craigin in the parish of Dumbennan, 1716 (SCM., IV, p. 171). William Craigin was a member of the Huntly Volunteers, 1798 (*Will*, p. 19), and John W. Craigen from King Edward served in the first Great War (*Turriff*). Cf. CRAIGIE.

CRAIGFORTH. Andrew Cragworth or Craggorth, chaplain of the Holyrood altar in Stirling, 1477 (SBR., p. 261), derived his name from Craigforth in the parish of Stirling, Stirlingshire.

CRAIGHALL. Local, from one of the several places of the name, but probably from the lands of Craigie now Craighall in West Lothian. James and Marion Craghall were tenants of Mervenislaw in Jedburgh Forest, 1541 (ER., XVII, p. 702). Bessie Craighall in Ardeth, 1585 (*St. Andrews*, 565).

CRAIGHEAD. Of local origin from one or more of the places of the name. David Craighead appears as a witness in Aberbrothok in 1546 (REG., p. 561). William Craigheid, baxter in Aberdeen, is in record in 1613 (SCM., v, p. 88), and John Craigheid in Fidesbeig in 1633 (ibid., III, p. 95). Craghede 1492.

CRAIGIE. Of local or territorial origin from lands of the name in Ayrshire, West Lothian, Angus, and Perthshire. Johan de Cragyn of Linlithgowshire rendered homage, 1296. His seal bears device of a winged griffin respecting, S' Ioh'is de Cragvli (*Bain*, II, p. 185, 200). Cragvli seems really to be = Craigielea, and Agnew says the property was carried by the heiress to Wallace of Riccarton. Brice de Cragy was burgess of Edinburgh, 1317 (SCM., v, p. 7), and John de Cragy was witness there, 1362 (*Egidii*, p. 8). John de Cragy who obtained charter of the lands of Merchamstom (now Merchiston), Edinburgh, in 1367 (RMS., I, 267) may be the John de Craigie who rendered homage to Robert III in 1371 (APS., I, p. 546b). Alexander de Cragy who was bailie of the Templelands of St. John, 1429 (*Ayr*, p. 83), and Alexander de Cragy who sold the lands of Orchardefelde in 1430 (RMS., II, 180) may be same person. Persons of this name early made their way to Orkney, where John de Krage appears as one of the prominent men in 1427 (*Oppressions*, p. 107), and Craigie of Gearsav were a family of long standing in the islands. Sir William A. Craigie, one of the editors-in-chief of the *Oxford English dictionary* is the best known of the name. Craggy 1700, Cragye 1488, Kraghe 1424. Cf. CRAIGEN.

CRAIGINGELT. Of territorial origin from the lands of that name in Stirlingshire. Thomas Cragyngelt de eodem, 'armiger,' witnessed an instrument of sasine in favor of Cambuskenneth Abbey in 1462 (*Cambus.*, 89), and in 1480 he or a succeeding Thomas Craigingelt became the king's tenant in Blairgib (ER., IX, p. 568). On the death of Thomas Craigingelt de eodem John Craigingelt, probably his son, became tenant of Blairgib in 1499 (ibid., XI, p. 410). Clothing was given to "a woman in Stirling called Craigengelt" in 1531 (ALHT., v, p. 432). John Cragingelt de eodem, who appears as provost of Striveling in 1542 and 1547 (ER., XVII, p. 467; SBR., p. 50), and was present at the king's coronation in 1567 (RPC., I, p. 536), may be the John Craigingailt of that Ilk against whom sentence of forfeiture was passed in 1571 (*Diur. Occ.*, p. 244). John Craggilt who occupied the Coileheuch of Skeauch in the barony of Skeauch in 1541 without paying rent (ER., XVII, p. 712) may be the John Craigingelt who was molested by certain individuals in 1555 and had his left arm cut off (*Trials*, II, p. 157–158). Another John Craggelt was a witness in Culross in 1569 (*Laing*, 844). George Craigingelt, one of the earl of Gowrie's attendants, was tried for his share in the Gowrie conspiracy in the year 1600 and executed

CRAIGINGELT, *continued*

at the market cross of Perth. Patrick Craigengelt was retoured heir of David Craigengelt, his brother, in lands in the barony of Tilliecoultrie, in 1680 (*Retours, Clackmannan*, 47), Charles Craigengelt of Woodside was Commissioner of Supply for Clackmannan in 1696 (APS., x, p. 30), and Captain Craigengelt is one of the characters in Scott's *The Bride of Lammermoor*. Cragingelt 1637.

CRAIGMILE, CRAIGMYLE. Of local origin from Craigmile or Craigmyle in the parish of Kincardine-O'Neil, Aberdeenshire. Elspett Cragmyll found surety for her conduct in 1570 (CRA., p. 369). Margaret Cragmyll is recorded in the parish of Strathauchin in 1593 (*Brechin*), Robert Craigmyll appears in record at the mylne of Mekill Elrick in 1608, and Thomas Craigmyll at the Brigend of Fyvie in 1609 (RSCA., II, p. 140, 142), is probably the Thomas Craigmill admitted burgess of Aberdeen in 1597 (NSCM., I, p. 91). Andrew Craigmyle was fined in 1626 for absence from the wapinschaw (SCM., v, p. 223). There was a family of Craigmile of that Ilk in Kincardine parish, Aberdeenshire, in the eighteenth century.

CRAIGMILLAR. From Craigmillar in the parish of Liberton, Midlothian. William, son of Henry de Cragmilor, in 1253 granted in pure alms a toft of land in Cragmilor which Henry de Edmundistuñ held of him to the Church of Dunfermline. Duncan de Cragmilor is one of the witnesses (RD., p. 114).

CRAIGNISH. Of territorial origin from Craignish in Argyllshire. Dugald Gregyns rendered homage in 1296 (*Bain*, II, p. 187). Some of the earlier generations of Campbell of Craignish (*MacDhughail Chraignis*), known as MacDougall, from their ancestor Dougall Campbell, a younger son of the lord of Lochow, c. 1130 (*Poltalloch Writs*, p. 142), seem to have used this territorial name instead of their Gaelic patronymic. In 1361 the heiress Christina parted with the barony "in her sore distress" to Colin Cambel of Lochow, ancestor of the duke of Argyll. Malcolm de Cragginche is in record, 1432 (HP., IV, p. 200). John M'Kegragnisse witnessed an instrument of sasine of Cragniche to Archibald, earl of Argyll, 1493 (OPS., II, p. 97).

CRAIGO. Of local origin from Craigo near Montrose, Angus. John Cragow appears as tenant in part of Campsy in 1483 and 1494, and John of Crago was tenant of same in 1513 (*Cupar-Angus*, I, p. 237, 242, 290).

CRAIGSHORE. Local. Payment made to John Cragschor, 1529 (*Prestwick*, p. 53).

CRAIGSWALLS. From Craigswalls near Edrom, Berwickshire. James Craigiswallis had a precept of remission in 1536 (RSS., II, 2033).

CRAIGTON. Alexander Cragtoun in North Ferrie of Tay, 1651 (*Brechin*), derived his name from one of the many small places of the name. There are places of this name in Stirling, Angus, Kinross, Aberdeenshire, etc.

CRAIK, CRAKE, CREYK. From Crayke, a village in Yorkshire. An old surname in the Lowlands. Three individuals of the name rendered homage in 1296: Henry de Crake of Dumfriesshire, James de Crake of Selkirkshire, and John de Crak' of Edinburghshire (*Bain*, II, p. 201, 209, 212). The seal of the latter bears a hound running, S' Joh'is de Crake (ibid., p. 547). Adam de Crake was juror on an inquest at Roxburgh, 1303, and Walter de Creyk leased two-thirds of the manor of Blakeder (ibid., 1435; III, p. 37). Thomas Crac, a Scots prisoner of war in the Tower of London, released in 1413 (ibid., IV, 839). Individuals named Crak and Crake were admitted burgesses of Aberdeen, 1458 and 1513 (NSCM., I, p. 16, 45), Andrew Craik witnessed a "letter of sesing of the hold of Dumdurnach," 1453 (CAB., p. 541), and Thomas Creke, a Scot born in Aberdeen, had letters of denisation in England, 1480 (*Bain*, IV, 1465).

CRAIL. From the town of Crail in the parish of the same name in Fife. Reingod de Karel witnessed the gift of the lands of Ardarie to the Priory of May, c. 1200 (RPSA., p. 382). Walter de Karel witnessed a charter by Alexander filius Walteri, the Steward, 1246 (RMP., p. 87), and Adam de Karal was a canon of St. Andrews, 1280 (*Pap. Lett.*, I, p. 462). Richard de Karale was prepositus of Karale, 1330 (ER., I, p. 265), Walter de Carale witnessed a donation by Henry de Aynestrother to the Abbey of Dryburgh, c. 1330 (*Dryburgh*, 252), and Symon de Krael was succentor of Urquhart, 1343 (*Rose*, p. 117). John de Carall had licence to take shipping in the ports of London or Dovorre at pleasure, 1372 (*Bain*, IV, 198), Alexander Crale was camerarius of the Abbey of Arbroath, 1492 (RAA., II, 336), and David Crayl, the notary public of Forfar, 1497 (REB., II, 142), is probably David Carrail or Carraile, sheriff clerk of Forfar, 1513 (*Rent. Dunk.*, p. 23, 139). James Craell, chirurgeon, was admitted burgess of Dundee, 1577 (*Wedd.*, p. 17), and Andrew Creall was chirurgeon there in 1609 (*Brechin*). Crayll 1503.

CRAILING. From Crailing in the parish of the same name in Roxburghshire. Peter de Cralyng witnessed a confirmation charter by John filius Hugh de Reueden c. 1250 (*Kelso*, 508). William de Crelinge, king's tenant in Peeblesshire, rendered homage in 1296, as also did Richard de Creling of Lanarkshire (*Bain*, II, p. 202, 204). Richard of Cralein appears again in record in 1304 (REG., p. 217).

CRAKE. See *under* CRAIK.

CRAM, CRAMB. Surnames of Perthshire and vicinity. Shortened forms of CRAMBIE, q.v. William Cramme, charter witness, 1511 (RAA., II, 520). James Cramb, chaplain in Perth, 1523 (*Milne*, p. 89). Thomas Crame, tailor in Edinburgh, 1610 (*Edinb. Marr.*). Four of the name are recorded in the Commissariot Record of Dunblane from 1700.

CRAMBIE, CRAMMY. Surnames current in Fife. From Crambeth the old spelling of Crombie, a village and ancient parish in Fife now comprehended in the parish of Torryburn. William de Cram'[beth] witnessed a charter by Gilbert, earl of Strathern a. 1198 (LIM., p. xxiv). Gilbert de Crambeth was one of assize of marches in Fife, 1230 (RD., 196), Duncan de Crambyt witnessed quitclaim of land of Drumkerauch, 1260 (RPSA., p. 346), and Matthew de Crombech or Crambeth, canon of Dunkeld, 1283 (*Pap. Lett.*, I, p. 469), afterwards became bishop of Dunkeld (*Dowden*, p. 59–60). Sir Hervy de Crambathe, dean of Dunkeld, rendered homage in 1296. His seal bears the Virgin and Child, etc., and S' *Hervei de Crambeth decani Aberdonen* (*Bain*, II, p. 195, 543). Willelmus de Crambreth witnessed confirmation of a charter by Malise, earl of Strathern, 1360 (*Scon*, p. 136), John Cramby, witness in Perth, 1463 (*Milne*, p. 53), and Andrew Cramby, witness in Edinburgh, 1481 (EBR., 40). John Cramby witnessed a charter by the abbot of Scone to William Peblis, 1491 (*Scon*, p. 201), and Henry Cramby was vicar of Kylspyndy in the same year (loc. cit.). Andrew Cramy, merchant of Scotland, had safe conduct in England, 1473 (*Bain*, IV, 1407), Thomas Crammy was king's tenant in lands in Ardmanoch, 1504 (ER., XII, p. 660), Bartholomew Cramby was burgess of Perth, 1523, and James Crambe had a feu of part of the lands of Lethindey, 1586 (*Scon*, p. 228, 232). The old family of Crambeth of that Ilk are now of Dawhill, Kincardineshire. Thomas Cramby was burgess of Perth c. 1534 (*Rollok*, 35).

CRAMER. See *under* CREAMER.

CRAMINNAN. From the old barony of Craminnan in Stirlingshire. "Cremenan was a small

place above Balfron, and is now no longer in existence" (*Strathendrick*, p. 263). Thomas de Cremenane witnessed charters by Malcolm, earl of Lennox to Arthur Galbraith and to Michael Mackessane, c. 1290 (*Levenax*, p. 30, 43). About the same year he granted the lands of Croyne (now Croy) to Murechauich [Murechanich in the text] filius Kork, grandson of Alwyn, earl of Lennox, and in 1294, as Thomas de Crumenan, he is referred to in an inhibition by the bishop of Glasgow (RMP., p. °203). In 1316 he witnessed a charter by King Robert I in favor of John de Luss (*Levenax*, p. 22). He appears to have died in 1320, as in that year an inquisition was held at the church of Killearn in connection with the feu duties, etc., of the lands of the late Sir Thomas de Cremennane (ibid., p. 81, 82). His family terminated in heiresses (*Inchaffray*, p. 294).

CRAMOND. From the lands, now parish, of Cramond in West Lothian and partly in Midlothian. An early offshoot of the family is found in Angus in the latter half of the thirteenth century, where they were proprietors of Aldbar, and so continued till 1577 (*Jervise LL.*, p. 320). The Crawmounts of Fullarton were an old family in Maryton parish, Angus. Magister William de Caraumund was "clericus de wardropa domini regis" (Alexander III) in 1278 (RD., p. 52, 53). In 1289, as de Cramund, he was clerk of Sir Alexander de Baliol, chamberlain of Scotland, and John de Cramund was escheator of the same Sir Alexander de Baliol north of the Forth in 1292 (*Bain*, II, 374, 599). Laurence de Craumound of Forfarshire and William de Cramund of Edinburghshire rendered homage in 1296. The seal of the latter, a cleric, bears the Virgin and Child, S' *Willelmi de Cramond, clerici* (ibid., p. 199, 211, 551). Lawrens of Cramond was one of assize on the marches of Woodwrae in 1388 (*Bamff*, p. 22), Thomas Cramount, merchant, had a safe conduct to travel in England in 1476 (*Bain*, IV, 1439), and Sir Alexander Cramond of that Ilk is referred to in 1505 as Crabmond, Crabmonde, Crawmonde, and Grammont (*Nisbet*). Cramont 1717, Craumvnde and Crawmonde 1447, Cravmunde 1483, Crawmound 1586, Crawmont 1511. William Cramond (1844–1907) was an industrious and accurate local historian of latter half of nineteenth century.

CRANE, CRAN, CRANN. An OE. personal name. See CRANSTON. In 1261 an inquest found that a man named Crane had held, by gift of King William the Lion, the lands of Inyaney and the office of gate-keeper of the royal castle, and that he never raised an army or gave assistance or did anything else in the

CRANE, CRAN, CRANN, *continued*

world for the said lands, except gate-keeper of our lord the king's castle of Montrose ("Nec dederunt auxilium nec aliquid aliud in mundo pro dicta terra facerunt nisi officium Janue Castri domini Regis de Munros") (APS., I, p. 100). Cran and Crann are current in the shires of Aberdeen, Banff, and Inverness, and Patrick Crane is recorded in Aberdeen in 1398 (CRA., p. 373). Crane is the spelling used by an old family in the parish of Maryton.

The English personal name Crane is commonly said to be from the name of the bird, but we must remember that mediæval epithet names are often something entirely different when properly studied. So many of the beast, bird, and fish names which enter so largely into personal nomenclature belong to a very old stratum, and in fact go back definitely to heathen times, "and there is no evidence that they were given as nicknames. They are real personal names, traditional with the race, given at birth with little or no thought of any application of the name to the appearance or disposition of the child."

CRANEBROUN. Thome de Kranebroun, n.d. (*Seals Supp.*, 240). Macdonald (520) gives the name as Cranburn. There is a Cranborne in Dorsetshire.

CRANNA. A softened form of CRANNACH. Sometime before 1489 Thomas Cranno held the cure of souls in Fyvy. His tombstone there bears the inscription: "Hic jacet Thomas de Cranno, orate pro anima" (*Illus.*, I, p. 496). William Cranna from Turriff served in the first Great War (*Turriff*).

CRANNACH. Of local origin from some place of the name, which in Gaelic signifies "abounding in trees." There are places named Cranna, Crannah, and Crannoch in Banffshire. John Cranok, bishop of Caithness in 1425 (*Bain*, IV, 988), appears again as John de Crannoch, bishop of Brechin, 1429–51 (REB., I, pref. p. ix, x). David de Crannoch, canon of Aberdeen, is mentioned in 1433 (ibid., I, p. 59), and Robert de Crannacht was cantor in Brechin in 1444 (ibid., I, p. 98). His seal is appended to a Brechin document of 1453 (*Seals*, p. 206). Laurence Crennoch, notary public, is in record in 1470 (RAA., II, 186). See also CRANNA.

CRANSTON, CRANSTOUN. From the lands or barony of the name in Midlothian, the 'tūn of Cran or Cren.' Certain individuals of this name are mentioned in early charters but it is not now possible to establish their connection with one another. Elfric de Cranston is one of the witnesses to a charter by William

the Lion to Holyrood (*Dalrymple*, p. 350). Thomas de Cranystoun in the reign of Alexander II made a donation to the hospital of Soltre of some lands lying near Paistoun in East Lothian for the welfare of his own soul and for the souls of his ancestors and successors (*Soltre*, p. 19). Andrew de Cragestone (an error for Cranestone) of Edinburghshire rendered homage, 1296. His seal bears a crane (canting heraldry), S' *Andree de Cranist* (*Bain*, II, p. 199, 550). Another Andrew de Cranstoun, dominus *de eodem*, apparently the first so styled, was dead before 1338 (*Neubotle*, p. 167). Thomas de Cranstoun, provost of Edinburgh, 1423 (*Egidii*, p. 45; LSC., p. 228), may be Thomas of Creinstoun, ambassador of James, king of Scots, 1449 (*Bain*, IV, 1218). William of Cranstoun was one of the conservators of the truce between Scotland and England, 1451 (ibid., 1239). Andrew Crenestoun, witness in Edinburgh, 1515 (*Laing*, 311). Some early Cranstons did their best to live up to their family motto, 'Thou shalt want ere I want,' being notorious reivers. Cranstone 1451, Cranestowne 1641, Craynston 1427, Crenestone (of that Ilk) 1534.

CRARER. See *under* CRERAR.

CRAS. From OF. *cras*, Lat. *crassus*, fat. Ricardus le cras or Ricardus Crassus appears as witness in a Fife charter of the thirteenth century (RD., p. 98, 99).

CRAUFURD, CRAWFORD, CRAWFURD. Of territorial origin from the old barony of Crawford in the Upper Ward of Lanarkshire. John de Craufurd witnessed Abbot Arnold's charter to Theobald Flamaticus of the lands on the Douglas Water c. 1147–60 (*Kelso*, 107). He was probably a stepson of Baldwin de Bigir who also witnessed the charter. Galfridus de Crauford, probably a cleric, appears as witness to charters by Roger, bishop of St. Andrews, between 1188 and 1202 (RPSA., p. 154; *Kelso*, 431). Galfridus de Krauford witnessed the confirmation charter by John, earl of Huntingdoun of the land of Kynalchmund to the Abbey of Arbroath c. 1219 (RAA., I, 84). Helva de Craufurd was a charter witness c. 1203 (*Dryburgh*, 160), and in 1204 Roger, son of John de Crouford, witnessed resignation of the lands of Inglisbristoun (ibid., 163). Sir Reginald de Crauford, who was sheriff of Ayr in the reign of William the Lion (*Melros*, p. 64–66, 71), with William, John, and Adam, his sons, witnessed a grant by Hugh de Bygris, the son of Robert, son of Waldeve de Bigris, to the Abbey of Kelso in 1228 (*Kelso*, p. 153). About the same year Reginald, another son of Sir Reginald de

Craufurde, was parson of the church of Strathavon (ibid., 280). Robert de Crauford witnessed the gift of Parva Kyp to Kelso a. 1240 (ibid., 181), and Roger de Crawford witnessed Eustace de Balliol's charter to Holyrood in 1262 (LSC., 81). Hugh de Craufod and John de Craufurd, Scots, were adherents of Henry III of England in 1255 (Bain, I, 1937). John de Craufurd, who died before 1259, gave land in Glengoner to the Cistercians of Neubotle (Neubotle, 146). Hugh de Craweford, who appears as a witness in Irvine in 1260 (Irvine, I, p. 5), may be the Sir Hugh of Craufurd, knight who held the lands of Draffane in Lesmahagow of the Abbey of Kelso in 1271 (Kelso, p. 364). Reginald de Crauford witnessed a charter by James, Seneschal of Scotland, in 1294 (RMP., p. 96), and in 1296 was appointed sheriff of Ayr, and in the same year rendered homage for his possessions (Bain, II, 739, 808). John de Crauuford and William de Craunford (error for Crauuford) of the county of Are rendered homage in 1296. The seal of the latter bears a fess with indistinct charges between three mullets, and S' Will'i de Cravford (ibid., II, p. 206, 214, 556). The name was early carried to France and is found there in the records of the Scots Guards as Crafort. In the vernacular of Buchan the name is pronounced Crawey. Crafoard 1691, Crafoord 1684, Craford and Crafford, 1464, Crafurd 1646, Crafuirde 1463, Crauffurd 1566, Craufoord 1695, Crauforth 1344, Craufurd 1506, Craufurde 1405, Crawfaird 1640, Crawfeurd 1512, Crawffurd 1623.

CRAW. The surname of an old family in Berwickshire, shortened from Auchencraw, q.v. "Craw of Auchencraw in the Merss, an old family now extinct" (Nisbet). The family was forfeited for their complicity in Mar's Rebellion (1715). Walter Crawe was one of an inquest held at Berwick-on-Tweed, 1370 (Bain, IV, 175). Stephen Craw had a remission for his share in burning the town of Dunbertane, 1489 (Lennox, II, p. 133). John Craw, schoolmaster of Colinton, Midlothian, was deposed in 1655 for brewing and selling 'aile' "near the Kirk and hard by the minister's yate" (Grant, Call of the Pentlands, p. 20). Patrick Craw was retoured heir in lands in the barony of Coldinghame, etc., 1679 (Retours, Berwick, 400). Sixteen persons of the name are recorded in the Commissariot Record of Lauder between 1561–1800. James Hewat Craw (1880–1933) was a distinguished Scottish archaeologist.

CRAWFORD, Crawfurd. See under CRAUFURD.

CRAWSHAW, Crawshay. English surnames of local origin from Crawshaw, a hamlet in Lancashire. Richard Crawshaw in Collionard, 1781 (Aberdeen CR.).

CREAMER, Cramer. From the occupation. Sir John Skene (1681) says: "Ane pedder is called ane merchand or cremer, quha beirs ane pack or creame upon his back" (De verborum significatione). In the Old statistical account (1792) of the parish of Kirkden in Angus, Creamers are described as "persons who go through the parish, and neighbourhood, and buy butter, hens, eggs, &c., mostly for the Dundee market" (v. 2, p. 508).

CREAR, Creer. Variants of Crerar, q.v.

CREE. A surname in Ayrshire and Glasgow. More probably a shortening of (Ma)crae, than from the place name Cree.

CREECH. From Creich in Fifeshire, where a family of this name rented land for several generations. "The parish of Creich, in the northern part of Fifeshire, contains the remains of an ancient castle but there is no trace of any family bearing the name occupying the lands" (Rogers, The Book of Robert Burns, I, p. 129). Douenaldus (i.e. Donald) de Creych, a cleric, was one of the witnesses to a confirmation charter by Walter, son of Alan of the land of Tubermor between 1204 and 1241 (Scon, p. 125). Simon de Crevch who petitioned for a canonry of Moray, 1394 (Pap. Pet., I, p. 620), appears in 1403 as councillor of the earl of Atholl (CSR., I, p. 180). Master Richard Creyche of Scotland, who had a safe conduct into England in 1423 (Bain, IV, 935), is probably Richard de Creich who was rector of the church of Croile (Crail) in the diocese of St. Andrew in 1429 (RMS., II, 137). Andrew Creich is recorded in Dunfermline in 1585 (Dunfermline). John Creych was merchant in Leith, 1544 (Rollok, 36). Issobella Creich and Joneta Creich were heirs portioners of Robert Creich, avus, in a house in the burgh of Newburgh and regality of Lundoris in 1611 (Retours, Fife, 222, 223). William Creech (1745–1815) published the first Edinburgh edition of the Poems of Burns. Craich and Craigh 1686.

CREEVEY. See under CREVIE.

CREGAN. From Ir. MacRiagáin, son of Riagan, or from the form MacCriagáin, where the c of Mac is attracted to the name (Woulfe).

CREIGHTON, A variant of Crichton, q.v.

CRERAR, CRARER. A surname derived from an occupation, G. *criathrar*, generally rendered (the miller's) 'sifter,' but more correctly translated 'sievewright.' It is the name of a small sept at one time fairly numerous in Strathspey and Lochtayside. They are ranked as Mackintoshes and some persons of the name in the United States now call themselves Mackintosh (*Celt. Mon.*, v, p. 279). John McAchrerar had half of Balinlagan, 1541 (FB., p. 356). In 1554 there was complaint of oppression by William Crerar on the tenants of the Abbey of Coupar (SCM., II, p. 215). Individuals of the name are also in record in Glenurquhay in 1594 (BBT.). See also *Celt. Mag.*, VI, p. 38. John Crerar (1827–1889), a Chicago merchant of Scottish parentage, gave that city the sum of two and a half million dollars as an endowment fund for a public library.

CREVIE, CREEVEY. Curtailed forms of MACCREVIE, q.v. Jon Crevey, weaver in the Spittal, Aberdeen, 1674 (ROA., I, p. 237), and Thomas Crevey was minister at Newhills, Aberdeen, in 1694 (SCM., II, p. 166).

CREYK. A form of CRAIK, q.v., current in Moray.

CRIBBS, CRIBBES. A surname of local origin current in Edinburgh. Probably from the place Cribbis near Lauder mentioned in 1637 (*Lauder*). Robert de Cribbes of Linlithgowshire and Robert de Cribbes of Lanarkshire rendered homage in 1296 (*Bain*, II, p. 205, 213).

CRIBLETHEUED. Local, from some obsolete place name near Edinburgh. Nicholaus Cribletheued held a toft near Crebarrin (now Carbery) in the territory of Muskilburcscyr in the thirteenth century (RD., p. 103).

CRICHTON, CRICHTEN, CREIGHTON, CRIGHTON. Of territorial origin from the old barony of Crichton in Midlothian. The old spellings of the barony name are very various, but one, Kreiton, "seems to settle how the name was pronounced" (*Sc. Peer.*, III, p. 52). Turstan de Crectune witnessed King David's great charter to Holyrood, c. 1128 (LSC., p. 6), and Henricus Crictannus witnessed a charter by Roger, bishop elect of St. Andrews, relating to the church of Hadintun, c. 1189–98 (RPSA., p. 153). Thomas de Kreytton or Creitton was a burgess of Berwick c. 1200 (*Neubotle*, 209), and William de Crichton witnessed a grant by Maldoueny, earl of Lennox, to Stephen de Blantyre, c. 1248 (*Levenax*, p. 36). Alisaundre de Creightone of Edinburghshire, and Thomas de Creghtone of Berwickshire rendered homage in 1296 (*Bain*, II, p. 206, 213). William de Kreitton, rector of the church of Kreitton, gave his lands to the Abbey of Newbattle in 1338 (*Neubotle*, 165–167), Robert of Crichtoun was one of the conservators of the truce between Scotland and England in 1451 (*Bain*, IV, 1239), and Alexander Crechtoune appears as a witness in Edinburgh in 1462 (*Neubotle*, 290). Peter de Crechtoun was rector of Kynoule in 1465 (RAA., II, 162), and Margaret Chrightone was examined for the Test in Tinwald in 1685 (RPC., 3. ser. XI, p. 434). Chreichton 1647, Chreichtone 1506, Chrightoune 1643, Chrychtone 1563, Chrychtoune 1595, Crechttoun 1558, Crectoun 1539, Creghtoun 1361, Creichtane 1530, Creichtoun 1536, Creichtoune 1387, Creihton 1320, Creitoun 1537, Creychton 1337, Crevchtone 1544, Creychtoun 1601, Creychtoune 1581, Creyghton 1492, Creyghtoun 1656, Crichtoune 1608, Crightoun 1656, Crychtoun 1576, Crvchtown 1485, Cryttone 1617, Greythorn 1429 (*Bain*, IV, 1032), Kreittoun 1328.

CRIEFF. Of local origin from the town of the name in Perthshire. Symon de Kref, witness in Perth in reign of Alexander II (*Scon*, p. 56).

CRIN. A Pictish king (CPS., p. 397). The name may be from Ir. *crín*, 'dry, withered.' Gospatric filius Crin witnessed a charter by Earl Gospatric in favor of the monks of S. Cuthbert a. 1153 (Nat. MSS., 25). A Bruige (Brude) Urcrin is also given in the list of Pictish kings (CPS., p. 398). Crin or Crina was the name of a moneyer of Cnut (DB.).

CRINAN. Old G. *Crínán*, a diminutive of CRÍN, q.v. Crinan the Thane, hereditary lay abbot of Dunkeld and father of Duncan I, was slain in battle at Dunkeld in 1045.

CRINGLE. A late development of Grimkel (for earlier ON. *Grimketill*). Grimketel held a carucate which later was given to the Abbey of Paisley after 1165 (RMP., p. 5).

CRIPPLE. Katherine Cripple, almswoman at Dunkeld, 1514 (*Rent. Dunk.*, p. 131, 140). Ellen Crippill in Aberdeen, 1517 (CRA., p. 445).

CRIRIE. A shortened form of MACCRIRIE, q.v. Rev. James Cririe (1752–1835), born at New Abbey, became one of the masters of the Edinburgh High School in succession to William Cruickshank, the friend of Burns, and was author of *Scottish scenery: or, Sketches in verse, descriptive of scenes chiefly in the Highlands of Scotland*, London, 1803, which contains an address to Burns.

CRISPIN. A popular personal name in the Middle Ages, from Crispinus, the patron saint of shoemakers, a legendary Roman saint who is said to have suffered martyrdom at Soissons in 287 A. D. Roger Crispin had a charter of the lands of Cnoculeran from Robert Bruce, c. 1218 (*Annandale*, I, p. 5), and Richard Crispin witnessed a charter by Robert de Brus, lord of Annandale, c. 1215–45 (*Bain*, I, 1680). Crispinus, a cleric of Paisley, was a charter witness in 1246 (RMP., p. 89), and Richard Crispin witnessed a charter by Alexander, son of Walter the Steward in 1252 (ibid., p. 91). Elizabeth Cryspyne resigned the lands of Brandriggs in Annandale in 1410 (*Laing*, 90). As forename we have Crispinie Swyne in Dunfermline, 1581, and Crispine or Crispinion Swyne in Dysart, 1641 (PBK., p. 209; *Dunfermline*).

CRISTALL. An old diminutive of CHRISTO-PHER, q.v. Of Christopher Seton who married Christina, sister of Robert I, Blind Harry says "to nayme he hecht gud Cristall off Cetoun" (*Wallace*, VII, 126).

CRISTINUS. A shortened form of CHRISTI-ANUS. A common personal name in the thirteenth century and later. Magister Christianus, a cleric, who witnessed a confirmation charter of Fedale to the monks of Lundors, c. 1220–44, may have been the Cristinus who appears as clerk to Robert, earl of Strathern, c. 1233–44 (LAC., p. 29, 31). Cristinus, judex, witness to a document relating to the regality of Arbroath, 1299 (RAA., I, p. 165). In a bishop's precept for the investment of chaplains in the church of Lochalveth, Moray, in 1333, Dominus Cristinus is named as perpetual vicar of the church (REM., p. 289). Cristinus filius Duncani, a 'man' (serf) of the bishop of Moray, had a remission and protection in 1364 (ibid., p. 164).

CRITCHLEY. A surname recorded in Inverness, doubtless from Critchlow or Chritchlow, some small spot in Lancashire (*Bardsley*).

CROAL, CROALL, CROLE, CROLL. Crole or Croll is the name of a small place near Closeburn, Dumfriesshire, but there is no evidence that the surname comes from it. The name appears in Kincardine and Mearns where Croll has been prevalent for several centuries. It is perhaps from Criél or Crieul near Eu in the department of Seine-Inférieure. Bertram de Criolle was one of the witnesses to grant to Roger de Mumbray, 1251–52, and as de Criovl he witnessed a grant to Robert de Brus, 1252

(*Bain*, I, 1868, 1871). Alexander Criole rendered to Exchequer the account of the feufarmer of Fethircarne, 1559 (ER., XIX, p. 93), David Croill was in Kethik, 1584 (REB., II, 347), and John Croill was retoured heir of John Croill in Auldtoun of Aberdeen, 1642 (*Retours, Aberdeen*, 264). Andrew Croill, portioner of Kettrick, parish of Brechin, 1614, and four more of the name in the district (*Brechin*). Patrick Croyll in Whiteley, 1690 (*Dunkeld*). Crol 1678, Crole 1730, Croole 1493.

CROC. Crôc or Krôk, a personal name whose form throws no light whatever on its being either ON. or OE. Robert Croc, a retainer or vassal of Walter the first High Steward, probably accompanied him from Shropshire where the name of Croc obtained. He usually occurs along with the High Steward of whom he held his lands afterwards called Crookston, and others in Renfrewshire and Ayrshire. Between 1165–73 he witnessed a grant of lands to the church of Paisley (RMP., p. 6), and a. 1177 witnessed a charter by Eschina, wife of the High Steward (ibid., p. 75). In 1180 he received permission to build a chapel for the use of his own family (ibid., p. 18), and between 1189–99 he witnessed the gift by Helias filius Fulberti of the church of Mernes to the monks of Paisley (ibid., p. 100). He also gave the patronage of the church of Neilston to the same monks for the salvation of his soul, and was one of the perambulators of the boundaries of Moniabroc in Stragrif c. 1202 (ibid., p. 13). His seal appended to a charter of the lands of Hungerig to Simon Lindsay, c. 1200, bears three shepherds' crooks contourné (*Macdonald*, 573). Walter Croc, son of Robert Croc, is a charter witness c. 1203 (*Dryburgh*, 160). Alan Croc and Simon Croc are charter witnesses a. 1225 (RMP., p. 209; *Levenax*, p. 14). Symone Croc witnessed a quitclaim in 1244 (*Cambus.*, 171), and the gift of an annuity of ten marks to Arbroath Abbey by Alexander II in 1247 (RAA., I, p. 202). Thomas Crok attested a confirmation by Alexander filius Walteri of her father's gifts to the church of Paisley, 1239 (RMP., p. 225), and as Thomas Croch appears as a charter witness at Forfar, 1251 (RAA., I, p. 162). Robert Cruoc was juror on an inquisition on the lands of Hopkelchoc in 1259 (*Bain*, I, 2162; APS., I, p. 88), and in 1262 was charged with having molested burgesses of Peebles in leading their peats from the moss of Walthamshope, etc. (APS., I, pref., p. 90, 91, 98). With Sir Thomas Croc the direct line of the Crocs seems to have failed about the close of the thirteenth century.

CROCHET. Perhaps the palatal form of CROCKETT, q.v. Robert Crochet of the county of Strivelyn rendered homage, 1296 (*Bain*, II, p. 205). John Crochat held part of Grange of Balgreschach, 1470, and John Curchet was tenant in Grange of Kynecrech, 1472 (*Cupar-Angus*, I, p. 155, 222).

CROCKATT, CROCKET, CROCKETT. Huwe Croket of Kameslank (Cambuslang) and William Croketa of Kylbride, Lanarkshire, rendered homage, 1296. The seal of William bears an eight-rayed figure and S' Will' Crok-itta (*Bain*, II, p. 185, 204, 557). Andrew Crokat was one of the chaplains of Sir James Douglas of Dalkeith and Morton in 1384 and in 1390 one of his executors (RHM.). Walter Crokat was tenant of Brwnty, 1457, and Thomas Crokkat tenant of Girnal Mill of Kincreach, 1483 (*Cupar-Angus*, I, p. 137, 236). Alexander Croket was admitted burgess of Aberdeen, 1521 (NSCM., I, p. 47), Patrick Crockett witness in Glasgow, 1530 (LCD., p. 92), and Andrew Crokat held land of the Abbey of Cupar before 1555 (*Cupar-Angus*, II, p. 120). John Crokat of Erneameny, parish of Crossmichael, was charged with intercommuning with the earl of Morton, 1585. Johnne Crokatis in Rinabir, Dumbarton, 1609 (RPC., VIII, p. 310), Robert Croket in Aber was a Macgregor resetter, 1614 (ibid., x, p. 226), and John Crokkit in Achinkyle was charged with molesting the minister at Inchcallioch and stealing his timber, 1634 (ibid., 2. ser. v, p. 212). Colene Crokat was shipmaster in Dundee, 1614, and there was a wealthy family of this name in Edinburgh in seventeenth century. Bardsley says "the origin is undoubtedly local" but cannot discover the spot. (2) The Galloway family name Crockett is said to be derived from *MacRiocaird*, son of Rickard (Richard).

CROCKER. From the occupation, a maker or seller of crocks, a potter. A commission for the trial of John Crokar in Lanarkshire, 1557 (ER., XIX, p. 417).

CROCKET, CROCKETT. *See under* CROCK-ATT.

CROFT. Local. There are small places of this name in Scotland. Thomas Crofts and David Crofts held land under the Abbey of Aberbrothoc, 1485 (RAA., II, p. 222). Thomas Croftis appears again in 1524 (ibid., p. 442).

CROLE, CROLL. *See under* CROAL.

CROMAR. Of local origin from Cromar in Aberdeenshire. There are still many families of the name living in the district. Thomas Cromar was accused of consulting a sorcerer in 1672 (*Alford*, p. 182), and four persons of the name occur in the Aboyne Poll Book of 1696. Margaret Cromar was scourged in Banff, 1704 (*Annals of Banff*, I, p. 78), and John Cromar was a wright in Aberdeen in 1721 (NSCM., II, p. 107).

CROMARTY. This surname is early found in Orkney, and now appears to be confined solely to South Ronaldsay. It is curiously enough not found in Scotland proper. Manys Cromate, senior, and his son, Manys Cromade, were jurors on an assize of lawting in 1509, and John Cromate and Magnus Cromate were two of those respited for the slaughter of the earl of Caithness in 1539 (RSS., II, 3151). This Orkney form of the surname comes near to the old forms of the place name which shows no second r (1292 Crumbathi). William de Crumbacy, valet to John, earl of Caithness, was granted a safe conduct returning to his lord in 1291 (*Bain*, II, 535). John Crummartie was arbitrator in a land dispute in Orkney, 1567 (OSR., I, p. 162).

CROMB. Alexander Crom (Cromy, or Crome) had his office of tochdoreschip (*tochoderatus*) annulled, 1477 (SCM., IV, p. 135). A bond of manrent was given by Alexander Crome of Inuererane in 1503 binding himself to become a 'lele trew mane and seruande' to the earl of Huntly (SCM., IV, p. 192). He is probably Alexander Crom Makalonnen, whose office of tochdoreship was ordered to be rendered to the kin of Donald Crum Mc Cownane in 1532 (*Trials*, II). Donald Crome Mc Ranald vane had a precept of remission in 1542 (RSS., II, 4454). John Croume appears in Pykertoune of Corstoune, 1610, and Margaret Cromb in Blackburne, 1666 (*Brechin*). Payment made to Patrick Crome in Fife, 1684 (PSAS., LIV, p. 239). Cromb, Crombie, and Crommie are common names in Glenlivet. See under CRUM.

CROMBIE. A surname found mainly in Aberdeenshire, derived from the place Crombie in the parish of Auchterless. The Gaelic *b* is silent, and the local pronunciation as well as most old deeds omit it, e.g. Cromee, Cromy, Cromie, Crommay, and Crumy (PSAS., LXV, p. 430). Robert Crumby, chaplain, witness in Brechin, 1450 and 1464 (REB., I, 138; II, 103). Patrick of Cromby, chaplain of Scotland, had a safe conduct into England, 1423, William of Crumby the same in the following year, and Andrew Cromby, Scottish merchant, the same in 1475 (*Bain*, IV, 928, 970, 1433). David Crommy was admitted burgess of Aberdeen, 1516 (NSCM., I, p. 46), Thomas Crommy, witness in Aberdeen, 1567 (*Aboyne*, p. 107), James Crommy or Crommie, witness in Spynie, 1560–71–84 (REM., p. 409, 410, 422), and Thomas Cromby was writer in Edinburgh, 1618 (SCM., IV, p. 258). Crombye 1566, Cromey 1580, Cromme 1523, Crommie 1536, Crumbee and Crumbie 1688, Crummy 1558.

CROMDALE. From the district, now parish of the name in Moray. John de Croindale (a miscopying of Cromdale), kinsman of the king of Scotland, was granted the church of Torrech (Turriff) in the diocese of Aberdeen in 1345 (*Pap. Pet.*, I, p. 104), and appears again in 1365 as Johannes de Cromdole, doctor of decrees and canon of Ross (RMS., I, 191).

CRON. From Ir. *crón*, saffron, yellow-colored. The name occurs in ogham on a stone found at Brough on Drummin, near Poltalloch, in 1931, a relic doubtless of the Dalriadic settlers in Argyll (PSAS., LXVI, p. 450). A diminutive of the name is CRÓNÁN, thirty saints of this name being in record.

CRONROTHERYK. Gilbert fiz Gregoire de Cronrotheryk and Gotherik fiz Matheu de Cronrotheryk of Lanarkshire rendered homage, 1296 (*Bain*, II, p. 213).

CROOK. From CROC, q.v. Malcolm Crok rendered homage in 1296 (*Bain*, II, p. 169). Robert Cruk of Fingaldestone, Lanarkshire, also rendered homage (ibid., p. 212). A benefice was reserved to Adam Croke of the diocese of St. Andrew, 1329 (*Pap. Lett.*, II, p. 314). John Cruke was a tenant in Garvalde under the Douglas, 1376 (RHM., I, p. lvii). Galfrid Crok held land in the burgh of Crale in 1421 (RAA., II, 56), John Cruik was admitted burgess of Aberdeen, 1503 (NSCM., I, p. 41), payment was made to a 'menstrale' named John Cruke in 1529 (ALHT., v, p. 373), and Peter Croche was witness in Glasgow, 1559 (HP., II, p. 203). Cruak 1636.

CROOKS. John Cruikis, merchant and burgess of Irving, 1635 (*Inquis.*, 2180). John Cruix or Cruiks in Galashiels is in record in 1643 and 1662 (RRM., I, p. 104; II, p. 6), and William Cruikis in Polwart, 1665 (*Lauder*). Alexander Cruicks was retoured heir in lands in the barony of Mounkland, 1692, and James Crukes of Garturk was retoured heir of Alexander Craiks of Garturk, 1698 (*Retours, Lanark*, 405, 440). Ramsev Crooks (1786–1859), fur-trader, described by Black Hawk the Indian chief as "the best pale-face friend the red man ever had," was born in Greenock.

CROOKSHANKS. *See under* CRUICKSHANKS.

CROOKSTON. A very rare surname if still extant. Local, from Crookston in Renfrewshire. See under CROC.

CROPHILL. William de Crophill rendered homage at Perth, 1291 (RR.).

CRORIE. Perhaps shortened from Ir. *MacRuaidhri*, son of Ruaidhri (from ON. *Hrothrekr*). There is, however, a Crurie in Dumfries Retours (212) from which the name may have come.

CROSAR, CROSIER. Persons of this name were early settlers in Liddesdale, and c. 1376 we find "locus Croyser" in the rent-roll of the lordship (Armstrong, *Liddesdale*, p. 181, and App., p. iii). William Crosier, professor of philosophy in the newly founded University of St. Andrews, 1410 (Tytler, *Hist. of Scot.*, 4 v. ed., II, p. 42). William Croyser, a Scotsman at present in Bruges, in Flanders, to have a safe conduct in England in 1429 (*Bain*, IV, 1027), is perhaps Master William Croyser, archdeacon of Teviotdale, who had a safe conduct to travel in England in 1433 (ibid., 1062). James Crosare witnessed a declaration dated 1436 (*Home*, p. 20), and John Crosar witnessed an instrument of sasine of lands and castle of Temptalloune in 1475 (*Douglas*, III, 106). William Croyser held the parish church of Kyrthgunnen (Kirkgunzeon) in 1418, and in 1424 he appears as canon of Dunkeld (*Pap. Lett.*, VII, p. 67, 344). In 1526 the duke of Richmond complained of the doings of the Crosaris and others (ALHT., v, p. 318), and a band against Crosars on the Border is recorded in 1569 (RPC., I, p. 652). William Crosar was witness in 1537 (*Johnsoun*), and John and Thome Crosare were entered before the warden, 1564 (RPC., I, p. 259). The Crosaris are included in the "Roll of the clannis that hes capitanes cheiffis and chiftanes quhome on thai depend oftymes aganis the willis of thair landislordis," 1587. Armstrong (*Liddesdale*, p. 181) gives the following old spellings of this surname: *Singular*: Crosair, Crosar, Crosare, Croser, Crosir, Crosore, Crossar, Crosser, Crossr, Croysar, Croyser, Croyset. *Plural*: Cossyers, Crosares, Crosaris, Croseers, Crosers, Croseys, Crosiers, Crosrs, Crosyers, Crosseres, Croysaris, Croysiers, Croyssyers, Croziers, Cwsers, Grosars, Grossars.

CROSBIE. A surname common in Wigtownshire and Dumfriesshire, and of local or territorial origin from one or other of the places named Crosbie or Corsbie in the shires of Ayr, Kirkcudbright, and Berwick. Iuone de

CROSBIE, *continued*

Crosseby witnessed charter by Robert de Bruys to Arbroath Abbey between 1178–1180 (RAA., I, p. 38), and in 1189, as Ivo de Crossebi, along with Richard de Crossebi, he witnessed an agreement regarding lands in Annandale (*Bain*, I, 197). Iuone de Crossebj and Richard de Crossebj witnessed gift of the church of Moffet, etc., to Church of Glasgow, c. 1187 (REG., p. 64). Robert de Crossebi witnessed resignation of land of Weremundebi and Anant, c. 1194–1214 (*Bain*, I, 606), and a charter of lands in the fee of Pennersaughs within the same period (*Annandale*, I, p. 3). Adam de Crosseby quitclaimed to Sir Robert de Brus lands and holdings in Cumbertres in exchange for a tenement in Gretenhou (Gretna) between 1215–45 (*Bain*, I, 1685). Richard de Crossebi witnessed a charter of lands of Egilfechan c. 1249 (*Annandale*, I, p. 7). Raginald de Crosseby witnessed a charter c. 1280 (LSC., p. 67), and in 1296 rendered homage (*Bain*). John de Crosseby was appointed to the vacant church of S. Mary in the Forest in Selkirk, 1298 (*Bain*, II, 1008). Walterus de Crosby was charter witness at Lamberton in 1332 (BNCH., XVI, p. 327), Robert de Crosby assizer at Lochmaben, 1347 (*Bain*, III, 1499), Thomas de Crosby is recorded in Glasgow, 1440 (REG., 344), and Isabel Corsbie in Dysart, 1593 (*Dysart*, p. 42). Sir James Corsby, cleric, was witness at Inchestuir, 1546 (*Rollok*, 5). Corsbe 1517. The earlier Crosbies were followers or vassals of the Bruces.

CROSS. From residence at or near a wayside crucifix. (See under CROUCH). In English records the name appears as *ad Crucem* and *atte Cross.*

CROSSHILL. Of local origin from one or other of places so named. Johannes de Croshill, cleric of diocese of Glasgow, 1365 (REA., I, p. 113), may have derived his surname from Crosshill near Bishopriggs, Lanarkshire.

CROSSTHWAITE. An English surname of recent introduction. There are places named Crossthwaite in Cumberland, Westmoreland, and Yorkshire.

CROSTONE. Perhaps from Croston, Lancashire. There is, however, a Cross-stone near Broughton, Peeblesshire. Andrew de Crostone of Linlithgowshire rendered homage, 1296. His seal bears a rude cross patee, S' *Andrie Orstvn* (*Bain*, II, p. 201, 534). The seal of Gilbert Crouston, 1573, is described by Macdonald (575).

CROUCH. From residence at or near a roadside cross or crucifix, ME. *crouche.* The surname is more English than Scottish. The word crouch "was applied in general to such crosses as stood at the intersection of two roads . . . and although they have long disappeared, they have left the name of 'cross' and 'crouch' upon many localities, especially in the South of England" (*Lower*). Johannes Crooch witnessed a confirmation charter by Alexander Cumyn, earl of Buchan, to the canons of St. Andrews (RPSA., p. 283). John Cruche was burgess of the Canongate, Edinburgh, 1567 (MCM., II, p. 309). See CORSE.

CROW, CROWE (Caithness). John Crow and Thomas Crow, laics of the diocese of Dunblane, in record, 1470 (*Scon*, p. 194). Magnus Crow, a follower of Walter Ross of Morange, 1596 (RPC., v, p. 304), may have derived his name from Crov, Inverness-shire. James Crow, tailor, received freedom of the burgh of Dysart, 1602 (*Dysart*, p. 43). Alexander Crow in Bogjarg, 1668 (*Brechin*), and Mellis Crow, ferrier in Newton, 1781 (*Kirkcudbright*). The chemical knowledge of James Crow (c. 1800–1859), born in Scotland, vastly improved the methods of distilling whisky and founded the great distilling industry of Kentucky. See also CROY.

CROWAN. James dictus Crwane was one of an inquest in Aberdeenshire, 1333 (REA., I, p. 54). John Crowan was member of an assize in Edinburgh, 1529 (MCM., II, p. 96).

CROWBO. A nickname from Gaelic *crùbach,* 'cripple, lame.' Tailzour Crowbo (i.e. the 'cripple tailor') was one of the tenants on lands in Strathdee in 1527 (*Grant*, III, p. 68). Janet and Cristan, daughters of Gillepadryk Crowbach, are mentioned in Inverness in 1561 (*Rec. Inv.*, I, p. 53), and Beak[=Bethag] Crowbycht was an "unfre baxter" in the same town in 1577 (ibid., p. 258).

CROWDEN. *See under* CRUDEN.

CROWLEY. Current. Lower cites Crowley in county Chester.

CROWNER. Hankin Criouner is recorded in Aberdeen, 1408 (CWA., p. 313), and Lion Crovnar was a voter in Monkland, 1519 (*Simon*, 45). Elizabeth Crownear made a resignation of property in Glasgow in 1554 (*Protocols*, I). Crownar 1567.

In Scotland a crowner was "an officer to whom it belonged to attach all persons, against whom there was an accusation in matters pertaining to the *crown*" (Jamieson, *Scottish dictionary*).

CROY. Most probably from the hamlet of the name in Inverness-shire. John de Croye, clerk in Scotland, had a safe conduct in 1359 (CSR., I, p. 133). Alexander Croye is recorded in Murthlac, 1550 (*Illus.*, II, p. 261), Johnne Croy was a follower of Walter Ross of Morange, 1596 (RPC., V, p. 304), and John Croy was merchant in Dundee, 1694 (*Brechin*). Margaret Croy in Burnsyde of Ballformow, 1652 (*Dunblane*). The name is also found in Shetland.

CRUDEN, CRUDDEN, CROWDEN. From Cruden in the district of Buchan. Marion of Croudane made complaint to the town council of Aberdeen in 1441 (CRA., p. 10), and Thomas Croudane was admitted a burgess of the same town in 1445 (NSCM., I, p. 9). Alexander Cruden (1701–1770) was author of *Concordance of the Old and New Testaments*. The form Crowden is current in Caithness. Other old forms of the surname given by Nisbet are Crowdan, Crowdane, and Crudane.

CRUICKSHANKS, CRUICKSHANK, CRUIKSHANK, CROOKSHANKS. With the possible exception of the first record of this name, which may point to a nickname, I do not think this surname has any connection with bowleggedness or 'crooked shanks.' The earliest spellings of the name, with the one exception noted, are always in the singular. The two counties with which the name is most intimately connected are Kincardine and Aberdeen, and in the former we have the river Cruick rising in the parish of Fearn and joining the North Esk near the Kirk of Stracathro. The word 'Cruick' is found several times in combination in Scots place names, i.e. 'Cruikitheuch' (1564), the 'cruikit aiker' (1585, *Scon*, p. 229), Cruikitheugh (1616), later Cruikhaugh at Inverbervie. 'Shank' is also a common element in Scots place names, either alone or in combination, i.e. Schank (in Midlothian, whence the surname Shank or Schank); Shankend, Shankfoot, etc. In toponymy 'shank' has the meaning of 'projecting point of a hill joining it to the plain.' The surname may thus quite well be of local origin — the shank on the Cruick or the Cruick-shank. Cf. the place name Pitlurg (1232 Petnalurge) from G. *peit na luirge*, 'portion of the shank,' i.e. distinguished by a shank-like strip of land (*Watson* I, p. 412). Cf. Cruiksetter in Shetland, 1623. John Crokeshanks, burgess of Haddington, rendered homage, 1296 (*Bain*, II, p. 197), Christin Crukschank is mentioned in foundation charter of the chapel of Urchany, 1334 (REA., I, p. 59), Cristinus Cru[k]sank was admitted burgess of Aberdeen, 1408 (NSCM., I, p. 3), and John Cru[k]sank was one of the burgesses of Aberdeen selected to accompany the provost to the field of Harlaw, 1411 (*Fraser*, p. 21). Adam Crukshank was vicar of Crovdane (Cruden), 1414 (CAB., p. 381), the mill of Tybardy was leased to David Croyssaynt in 1434 (RAA., II, 70), and in 1452 there is entry of payment to John Cruxschank in Aberdeen (SCM., V, p. 50). John Crukshanke was granted 'the seruice of the keping of the orloge for the yer' in Aberdeen, 1453 (CRA., p. 20). John Cruishank owned a rood of land in the regality of Arbroath, 1535 (RAA., II, 816), Johannes Crushank is recorded in Murthlie, 1550 (*Illus.*, II, p. 261), and John Crewshank cr Crushank was a tailor in Aberdeen, 1688 (RPC., 3. ser. XIII, p. 262, 272). Amos Cruckshank laid the foundation of the famous Sittyon herd of Aberdeen cattle, c. 1840. Isaac Cruikshank (1756?–1811?) caricaturist, was born in Scotland, and his son, George Cruikshank (1789–1856) was born in London. Among Scots settled in Prussia the name appears in 1644 as Kriegschank. Coukschank (an error for Croukschank) 1538, Crewschank 1602, Crokeshank 1483, Crewkschankis 1602, Crookschank 1641, Crookshank 1678, Cruckshanke 1654, Crucshank 1640, Cruickshank 1586, Cruikank (*sic*) and Cruiksank 1600, Cruikschank 1598, Cruischank 1591, Crukeschank 1585, Crukschank 1559, Crukschanke 1463, Crukshaink 1673, Cruykschank 1448, Crwickschanks 1688, Crwikschank and Crwkschank, 1595. In common speech the name is usually pronounced 'Crushak.'

CRUIKLAW. Local. George Cruiklaw, portioner of Nether Ancrum, 1746 (*Heirs*, 212).

CRUM. From MACILCHRUM, q.v. Crum and Crumb were common in Dumbarton in seventeenth and eighteenth centuries (RDB.). Robert Crum in record in Paisley, 1653 (*Kilbarchan*), and Mary Crum was indweller in Whithorn, 1786 (*Wigtown*). Cf. under CROMB.

CRUMME. Perhaps from the lands of Crummy which belonged to the Abbey of Culross. John Crumme was excommunicated under letters of the Official of Lothian, 1532 (*Johnsoun*, p. 9). Patrick Crummy of Cariddin was keeper of the havens of Carriden, 1565 (RPC., I, p. 381), and another Patrick Crümy was summoned in 1592 to answer for certain crimes of treason (APS., III, p. 528).

CRUNZANE. John Crunʒane, canon of Holyrood, 1456 (LSC., p. 165). Janet Crunzean in Ponfeich, parish of Douglas, 1623 (*Lanark CR.*), Thomas Crunzean, hortulanus, burgess of Edinburgh, 1634 (*Inquis.*, 2092). Robert Crungean in Edinburgh, 1688 (*Edinb. Marr.*), may be Robert Cruizean, late deacon of cordiners there, 1723 (*Guildry*, p. 127).

CRYNE. There was a noted family of this name in Aberdeen in the fourteenth and fifteenth centuries, and many of them witnessed charters and made donations to the church of S. Nicholas, Aberdeen. From one of the family is derived the name Cryne's Croft in Futye. The family may have had connection with Cryne in the parish of Kilbucho, Peeblesshire. Laurencius Cryn held land in Aberbrothoc in 1303 (RAA., I, p. 278), and David Cryn appears in Aberdeen, 1317 (SCM., v, p. 12). William Cryn or Cryne appears as burgess of Aberdeen, 1398–1400 (CRA., p. 373; REA., I, p. 205), and is frequently mentioned as a charter witness between 1400–30 (REA., I and II; CAB.; RMS., II, 156; SCM., v, p. 254). William Kryne was admitted burgess of Aberdeen, 1461 (NSCM., I, p. 17). Crynne 1449. (2) Cryne was the name of the father of Gospatric and Aldan (RMS., I, 265, reproducing a twelfth century charter). A different name from CRIN?

CRYSTAL, CRYSTALL. See under CHRYSTAL.

CUBBIE. Perhaps an assimilated form of Cuthbert. Cf. CUBBISON. Robert Cuby, appointed prior of Fyvie, Aberdeenshire, 1460 (Theiner, 430), may be the Robert Cuby, monk of Arbroath, recorded in 1480 (RAA., II, 207). Thomas Cubbie was a tenant under the Abbey of Arbroath, 1567 (ibid., II, pref., p. xxxiv). Cubie 1525. One of this name gave name to Cubbiestoun-Holme, Ayrshire.

CUBBIN, CUBBON. From (MAC)CUBBIN, q.v. Cubbin and Cubbon are mutations of Gibbon, diminutive of Gilbert.

CUBBISON. An old surname in the Stewartry. An Englishing of MACCUBBIN, q.v., or from 'Cubby.' Three persons of the name are in Commissariot Record of Kirkcudbright in eighteenth century, and several Cubbisones were resident in the parish of Carsfern, 1684 (RPC., 3. ser. IX, p. 575).

CUDDIE. A diminutive of Cudbert, the common pronunciation of Cuthbert in the southern counties and north of England. "Cuddy Rig, the Drumfress fuill" of Dunbar's Complaint to the King, aganis Mure, was Cuddy Rigg, "fethelar" in Dumfries in 1506 (Edgar, p. 103). Cuddy Headrigg is one of the characters in Scott's Old Mortality. Cuddy Henderson was pledge for the Borders, 1566 (RPC., I, p. 462).

CUDUILIGH. Cu-duiligh, gen. Con-duiligh or Con-doiligh (Mart. Don. May 16). Cu-duiligh or Con-duiligh is still a Maclean name, and appears in the old genealogies. The Mac-

lean pipers known as Rankins being Clan Duly (see TGSI., XXIX, p. 319).

CUFFIE. Probably reduced from Ir. MacDhuibh, a variant of MacDuibh, 'son of Dubh' ('black'). James Cuffie and Andrew Cuffie, residents in the parish of Senneck, 1684 (RPC., 3. ser. IX, p. 568).

CUIE. Perhaps from ME. for cook, from OFr. (le) keu. William Cwe in Middiltoune was accused of theft in regality of Spynie, 1596 (SCM., II, p. 132). Margaret Cuie in Braco Brae, parish of Grange, 1693, and George Cuie, elder, in Braco of Enzie, 1764 (Moray). James Cuye in Muire, 1703 (Banff Rec., p. 244).

CULBERT. A Fife surname, a variant of Colbert, from OE. Ceólbeorht. William Culbaird at Kowfurd, 1578 (Brechin).

CULBERTSON, 'son of CULBERT', q.v. John Culbertson is recorded in Heittoun in 1686 (Peebles CR.), Marion Culbertson appears in Trabroun in 1746 and Thomas Culbertson was there in 1748 (Lauder).

CULBRECH. Local. Peter Culbrech witnessed a charter by James, earl of Moray, 1539 (Cawdor, p. 164).

CULEN. EG. cuilén, G. cuilean, 'a whelp.' A favorite name with early Scottish kings. The name of 'Cuilen mac Iluilb, ri Alban,' killed 971 (Chron. Scot., p. 218), in the Pictish Chronicle is Latinized caniculus (CPS., p. 10). Culeón, probably the same name, appears in the Book of Deer as that of father of Mal Coluim. See COLIN.

CULLEN. From the burgh of Cullen in the parish of the same name, Banffshire. Henricus de Culane in record, 1340 (ER., I, p. 458). John de Coulane was juror on inquest held apud Rane, 1418 (REA., I, p. 216). John de Culane was elected bailie of Aberdeen, 1440 (CRA., p. 6), Andrew de Culane had a grant of the lands of Knaven in the barony of Kelly, 1444, and Andrew Coleyn or Colen, merchant of Aberdeen, had safe conducts to travel in England, 1438 and 1451 (Bain, IV, 1118, 1234). John of Culane was "abbot of boneacord" in Aberdeen, 1486, and Robert of Cullane was chosen "priour of bonaccord" there in 1497 (Mill, Plays, p. 132, 134). Elene Culan held a land in Glasgow, 1494 (REG., 469). Mr. William Colen was minister in Edinburgh, 1649 (Lamont, Diary, p. 7). John Cullen was appointed Islay Herald in January, 1661. William Cullen, M. D. (1710–1790), was one of the most eminent physicians of his time. (2) The Ayrshire and Galloway Cullens most probably of Irish origin from MACCULLEN, q.v.

CULLETNACHY. Local. James de Culletenachy was one of the "burgenses rure manentes" in Aberdeen, 1317 (SCM., v, p. 10). Jacobus de Culletnachy was juror on an inquiry relating to the boundaries of Ardlogy and Fyvyne, 1335 (RAA., I, p. 311).

CULLOCH. From MACCULLOCH, q.v.

CULP. See under COLP.

CULROSS. From the town of the same name in Perthshire. William de Culros was canon of Inchaffray and vicar of Dunyn, 1381 (Inchaffray, p. 253). William Colneros and John Colneros were Scottish shipmasters in 1473 (Bain, IV, 1407). Stephen Culross was vicar of Fyntra in 1539 (Stirling of Keir, p. 363), and John Culross of Leitgreen is mentioned in 1616 (Dunblane). Sir Stephen Culross, a cleric, was witness in Perthshire, 1548 (Gaw, 7).

CULTER. See under COULTER.

CULTON. Probably a variant of COLTRAN, q.v. Edward Cultan in the parish of Abbey, 1666, and five more of the name are in record (Kirkcudbright).

CULWEN. From Colvend near the mouth of the river Urr, Kirkcudbrightshire, the old spelling of which was Culewen. Gilbert de Culewen witnessed Eustace de Balliol's charter of the church of Hur (Urr) to the Abbey of Holyrood, 1262 (LSC., 81). Adam de Culwenne who witnessed a grant by Thomas, son of Andrew de Kyrconeuel to Holmcultran c. 1280–90 (Holm Cultram, p. 48), may be the Adam de Colwenne who was one of an inquest at Berwick in 1296 (Bain, II, 824). Sir Thomas filius Gilbert de Culwenne attested the bounds of the grange of Kircwynni and the land of Culwen in Kirkgunzeon, 1289, and Adam de Culwenne is another witness (Holm Cultram, p. 88). William de Colven of Dumfriesshire rendered homage in the same year, and Patrick de Collewen was in the king of England's service, 1298 (Bain, II, 810, 989).

CUMINE, CUMMINE. Forms of CUMMING, q.v. John Cummine was a member of the Huntly Volunteers in 1798, and William Cumine was a member of the Drumblade Company in 1804 (Will, p. 19).

CUMISKY. An Irish surname. See MACCOMISKEY.

CUMLAQUOY, COMLOQUOY. Local, from small place of the name in Orkney. Mareoun Cumlaquoy in Birsay accused of witchcraft, 1643 (Dalyell, Darker superstitions, p. 8, 109). John Halcro Comloquoy of Birsay was married in 1942.

CUMMERTREES. From Cummertrees in Dumfriesshire. William de Cumbertrees in 1285 was appointed attorney for two years to Robert Bruce (Bain, II, 281).

CUMMING, CUMMINGS, CUMING, CUMINE, CUMMINE. The once powerful family of Comyn or Cumyn are believed to have come from the town of Comines near Lille on the frontier between France and Belgium, though there is no positive evidence in favor of this view. The name is always written without 'de' in early Scots records. Andrew of Wyntoun's account of the origin of the name is quaint and amusing if not trustworthy. He tells us that of

". . . thre breþer of Normondy,
Faire ȝoung men and rycht ioly,
. . . .
In Scotland baid þe ȝoungest broþer,
William wes his proper name.
Thus duelt he with þe King Williame,
The quhilk saw him a faire persoune;
Forthy in gret effectioun
The king þan had þis ilk man.
For vertu he saw in him þan,
He maid him, for he wes stark and sture,
Kepare of his chalmer dure.
Na langage couth he speke clerely,
Bot his avne langage of Normundy;
Neuerþeles ȝit quhen þat he
Wald opin þe dure to mak entre,
'Cum in, cum in,' þan wald he say,
As he herd oþer bid perfay.
Be þis oiss þai callit him þen
William Cumyn with all men."
                    Wyntoun, book VIII, c. CXXXIX.

The first of the name connected with Scotland is Willelmus Comyn, a churchman, chancellor to David I. He was promoted to the bishopric of Durham by the Empress Matilda, but had many controversies with his clergy. Later he was poisoned by some of their number who mixed poison with the wine of the Sacrament and gave it to him to drink. Richard Cumyn, second of the name in Scotland, made a gift of the church of Lyntun-ruderic (Linton-Roderick) to the Abbey of Kelso for the weal of the souls of Earl Henry (d. 1152) and his own son, John (Kelso, 274). He also witnessed charters by William the Lion after 1165 (REM., 1, 2). By his marriage with Hextilda, granddaughter of Donald Bane, king of Scots, he had a son, William, who became

CUMMING..., *continued*

chancellor and great justiciary of Scotland. William married Marjory, daughter and heiress of Fergus, the last Celtic earl of Buchan between 1211–24, and in right of his wife became earl of Buchan. Through other fortunate marriages the family "obtained, for a time, the earldoms of Angus and Athole, so that, by the middle of the 13th century, there were in Scotland 4 earls, 1 lord, and 32 belted knights of the name of Comyn. Within seventy years afterwards this great house was so utterly overthrown that, in the words of a contemporary chronicle, 'there was no memorial left of it in the land, save the orisons of the monks of Deer' (founded as a Cistercian monastery by William Comyn, earl of Buchan, in 1219)" (Chambers's *Encyclopædia*, s. v. Comyn). Simon Comyn, a native of Coldingham, had letters of denisation in England, 1463 (*Bain*, IV, 1336).

In the time of Gilbert Cumin, lord of the lands of Glenchearnach, it is said that many of the oppressed people from neighboring districts sought his protection. These he adopted as clansmen by a form of baptism using the stone hen-trough which stood near the castle-door. Cumins so created were called *Cuminich-clach-nan-cearc*, or 'Cumins of the hen-trough' to distinguish them from the Cumins of blue blood.

A Gaelic rhyme anent the Cummings runs:

Fhad's bhios maide anns a' choill
Cha bhi Cuimeanach gun fhoill.

(So long as there is a stick in the wood
There will not be a Cumming without
    treachery.)

Which the Cummings have rendered:

Fhad's bhios maide anns a' choill
Cha bhi foill an Cuimeanach.

(So long as there is a stick in the wood
There will not be treachery in a Cumming.)
(*Wardlaw*, p. 68n.)

CUMNOCK. Local, from probably Cumno near Alyth. There is also Cumnock in Ayrshire (Comnocke in 1297). Mathew de Comnoc or Comnok is mentioned in 1329 (ER., ‡. p. 213, 245). Elena Cumnok of Aberdeen in 1411 was described as a 'communis pykar et rebellis' (CRA., p. 4). Nicholaus Cumnok made a gift to the church of Aberdeen in fifteenth century (REA., II, p. 133). Alison Cumno was spouse of Thomas Rechard, 1561 (CMN., 80).

CUMRAY. From Cumrie in the parish of Cairnie, Aberdeenshire. Alexander de Cumray held land in Aberdeen, 1447 (CRA., p. 15). Perhaps now lost in COMRIE, q.v.

CUMSTOUN. Wauter de Cummstun of Dumfriesshire who swore fealty to England in 1296 is probably the Walter de Comestone, juror on an inquisition at Dumfries in 1304 (*Bain*, II, p. 185, 412). Adam de Combistoun was custumar of Kirkcudbrith in 1331 (ER., I, p. 374). The name most probably derived from Cumstoun, Tongland, Kirkcudbrightshire. There is also a Cumstone near Lockerbie, Dumfriesshire.

CUNACH. A surname in Mar in seventeenth century.

CUNIESON, CUNISON, CUNNISON, 'son of Conan,' i.e. Conan de Glenerochy, the illegitimate son of Henry, earl of Atholl. 'The name of Cunnison or MacConich was prevalent in Athole in the fifteenth, sixteenth, and seventeenth centuries; yet not an individual of that name now remains.' All died out without violence or expulsion (Stewart, *Sketches*, 3. ed., I, p. 26). John Cunysoun, baron of Eddradoun, had sasine of the lands of Ardgery in the barony of Eddradoun, in 1474 (RMS.). The 'obitus Johannis Cwnyson de Edderdedowar apud Melyng, qui fuit interfectus per Willelmum Robertson de Strowen ix die mensis Mai anno &c vᶜ desimo' is recorded in the Chronicle of Fortirgall (p. 115). George Cunysoun was apparent of Edderdour, 1595. John Cunieson in Dunkeld had charter of the lands of Fordieshaw, Dunkeld, 1606 (*Athole*, p. 716). Alexander Cunnison, merchant burgess of Hamilton, 1667 (*Campsie*), and Thomas Cunnison in Dunkeld, 1699 (*Dunkeld*). Norman Cunnison was merchant in Campbeltown, 1772 (*Argyll*), and Mr. John Cunyson was minister of Dull.

CUNINGHAM, CUNINGHAME, CUNINGHAM, CUNNINGHAME, CUNNYNGHAME, CUNYNGHAM. Of territorial origin from the northern district of the name in Ayrshire. Now a widespread surname, old families having divided into many branches. Wernebald, a vassal of Hugh de Moreville, obtained the manor and vill of Cunningham from his feudal superior. Robert filius Wernebaldi granted the church of Kilmaurs with half a carucate of land belonging thereto to the monks of Kelso, c. 1170, and the grant was confirmed by his superior, Robert de Moreville, and by Robert, son of Robert, son of Wernebaldus (*Kelso*, 283–285). Robert filius Warnebald (? Robert filius Roberti filii de Warnebald) married Richenda, daughter of Vmfridus de Berkeley, and made a grant to the Abbey of Arbroath, 1228 (RAA., I, 198). Richard de Cunningham appears as witness to charter by Alan, son of Roland, Constable of Scotland, between 1210–33 (*Sc. Peer.*, IV, p. 224). Alexander de Kuningham witnessed the grant of Kirkbride Largs to the nuns of North Berwick, a. 1190 (CMN., 14). Magister William de Cunigham, rector of the church of Kilmaurs, 1246, and dominus William de Cunyngham, 1269, were charter witnesses (*Kelso*, 179, 282). James de Cunyngham who witnessed gift of the church of Largs to church of Paisley c. 1317 (RMP., p. 237), is probably the individual who had a dispensation to remain in marriage with Helen de Catantilly of the diocese of Glasgow (*Pap. Lett.*, I, p. 224). James de Côgheime was canon of Dunkeld, 1375 (*Milne*, p. 36), and Sir William de Conyngham appears as dominus de Kylmawrus, 1370 (*Kelso*, 514). William de Cuningham, vicar of Dundonald, was threatened with excommunication for intruding himself into the administration of the Poor House of Polmadie (domus pauperum de Polmade), 1403 (REG., p. 295). Adam de Cunygam was member of Ayr guild, c. 1431 (Coll. AGAA., I, p. 229). Cunninghams from Ayrshire migrated to Strathblane in middle of sixteenth century, and descendants of Cunninghams of Caprington, Ayrshire, are found settled in Caithness, c. 1624 (Henderson, *Caithness families*, p. 201–208). Johnne Cromyghame was messenger-at-arms in Fife, 1569 (RPC., I, p. 659), and many of the name appear in Edinburgh in the sixteenth and seventeenth centuries. The name was also carried to France at an early period by Scots emigrants and there appears at different dates as (plural) Coninglants, Coigans, Coningans, Cogingands, and Convghans (Burton, *The Scot abroad*, I, p. 81). Chonigham and Conigham 1499, Conighame 1568, Conynghame 1424, Cunigom 1654, Cuninggame 1546, Cunyghame 1548, Cunnyngayme 1580, Cunningghame 1556, Cunygam 1480, Cunnygam 1503, Cunyngaham and Cunyngahame 1476, Cunyngame 1553, Cunynghame and Cwnninghame 1608, Cwnygham 1552, Cwnyghame 1550, Cwnynghame 1615, Kyninghame 1653.

CUNLIFF, Cunliffe. This surname but rarely found in Scotland is of English origin from Cunliffe, a place name in Lancashire, in 1278 Gundeclyf, 'the cliff of Gunnhildr.'

CUNNINGHAM, Cunninghame. See under CUNINGHAM.

CUNNISON. See under CUNIESON.

CUNNYNGHAME, Cunyngham. See under CUNINGHAM.

CURDIE. A shortened form of Mackirdy, q.v. James Curdie (1796–1877), minister of Gigha and Cara, was said to have been a

descendant of Rev. James M'Kirdie, incumbent of Kilmorie in Arran.

CURLE. Perhaps same as English name Curle and Curll, explained as meaning 'curly-headed.' Not likely to be a form of Croall, q.v. Henry Corle of Stevenstone in Conyngham, a Scots prisoner of war in Carlisle, 1305 (*Bain*, II, p. 449). Thomas Kirle, witness in Glasgow, 1500 (LCD., p. 204). James Curle, burgess of Edinburgh, 1557–63 (*Home*, 206; RPC., I, p. 252). David Curll or Curlle appears as reidar at Tarbolton, Ayrshire, 1567/1574 (RMR.). Mark Currell in Roxburgh, 1668 (*Edin. App.*), and Thomas Curle, merchant burgess of Jedburgh, 1748 (*Heirs*, 219).

CURQUHRUNY. Duncan de Curquhruny, juror on inquest at Rane, 1413 (REA., I, p. 214) derived his surname from the old lands of Corquhorny (1641, Culquherny), near Tullynessle, Aberdeenshire.

CURR. Master Walter Curre witnessed an appointment by John, earl of Lennox, 1521 (*Pollok*, I, p. 246).

CURRAN, Currans. Surnames recorded in the shires of Ayr and Wigtown. Most probably from Ir. MacCorráin, 'son of Corran' (diminutive of corradh, a spear).

CURRIE. (1) A variant of Corrie, q.v. Although there is a place named Currie in Midlothian there is no evidence of its having given origin to a surname. Philip de Curry granted the lands of Dalhengun and Bargower in Kyle to the Abbey of Melrose, 1179 (*Seals*, 299). About 1210 Peter de Curri witnessed a charter by Malcolm Loccard (RMP., p. 71), and John Curry of Scotland is mentioned in an Annandale charter, 1238 (*Bain*, I, 1427). Robert de Curri witnessed a Melrose charter of 1243–44 (*Melros*, 191), and Adam de Curry was witness to a charter by Laurence Avenel between 1260–68 (REG., 221). Sir Walter de Curry was appointed keeper of the castles of Wyggeton, Kirkcudbright, and Dumfries by Edward I in 1291 (*Bain*, II, 572). Henry de Curry appears as charter witness c. 1330 (RHM., I, 39), and about the same time he attested a charter by Radulph, lord of Cranystoun to the Hospital of Soltre (*Soltre*, p. 43). He may be the Henry who appears as canon of Glasgow in 1339 (*Pap. Lett.*, II, p. 545) and in 1362 (RMP., p. 144, 239). Walter de Curry took a prominent part in the capture of Edinburgh Castle from the English and was rewarded for the same, 1342 (ER., I, p. clvi, 507). Robertus de Curry was a 'native man' of the bishop of Moray, 1364

CURRIE, continued

(REM., p. 161). Henry Curry was admitted burgess of Aberdeen, 1400 (NSCM., I, p. 1), Edward Curre was tenant in barony of Stobo, 1511 (Rental), and John Curre held a tenement in Glasgow, 1506 (REG., 485). Sir Hugh Currye was Commendator of Strathfillan, 1549 (Statutes Scot. Church, ed. Patrick, p. 88), and Robert Curray was merchant burgess of Edinburgh, 1693 (Inquis., 7326). Cwrry 1528. (2) A modification of MACVURICH, q.v. The minister at Row, Dumbartonshire, 1709–19, was known as Rev. Archibald Currie or M'Currie.

CURRIER. From ME. coriour, curiour, OF. corier, one who dresses or colors tanned leather. According to Innes (p. 27) sometimes shortened to CURRY, q.v.

CURROR. From ME. courour<OF. coreor, 'a runner,' courier. Nicol Corour of Berwickshire rendered homage, 1296 (Bain, II, p. 207), and in 1305 Walter le Corour accounted for the ward of Selkirk in the Forest (ibid., p. 440). William Curour was assizer in Edinburgh, 1402 (Egidii, p. 38). William Curriour, charter witness in Edinburgh, 1425 (RMS., II, 25) may be William Curroure who held lands near Edinburgh in the same year (Soltre, p. 294). William Currour or Courrour, merchant of Scotland, had safe conducts into England, 1408 and 1410 (Bain, IV, 764, 798). Johannes Currour was burgess of Perth, 1440 (RD., p. 297), and John Currour, burgess of Banff, 1487 (RAA., II, 311). John Currour of Logymegil witnessed a retour of service of Neis Ramsay in the barony of Bamff, 1507 (Bamff, p. 45). George Currour was charged with "trublance of the toune" of Aberdeen, 1512 (CRA., p. 443), and William Currour was factor for the abbot of Jedburgh, 1560 (ER., XIX, p. 115). Gyllis Curror in Glenkil, 1626, and four more in the neighborhood are in record (Dumfries). Thomas Curror, heir of Patrick Currer, burgess of Dysart, 1649 (Inquis., 3526).

CURROW. John Currow in Kennokfute, parish of Douglas, 1657, and one other of the name (Lanark CR.). Gilbert Currow in Slaid, 1683, and six others of the name (Dumfries).

CURRUTH. See under CARRUTH.

CURRY. A variant of CURRIE, q.v.

CURSITER. From the lands called Cursetter in the parish of Firth, Orkney. Magnus Cursetter "in that Ilk" had from Earl Robert Stewart a feu charter of the three penny land of Cursetter in 1587, in which he and his predecessors "is and has bein in peacobill possessioun . . . past memorie of man" (OS. Rec., I, p. 209). General George Custer of the United States Army (killed by the Indians in 1876) was believed to have been a son of a Cursetter of Binscarth, who emigrated to the United States (Clouston, A note on an Odal family, p. 136). This however is not so – the general was of German descent, from one Küster, a Hessian soldier paroled after Burgoyne's surrender in 1777. Corsatir 1536, Cursattour 1532, Cursettare 1574.

CURWEN. A surname found in Cumberland, originally the same as CULWEN, q.v. The identity is clearly shown by Border records (cf. Bain, index). Faculty was given the bishop of Glasgow to grant a dispensation to Master Reginald de Cyrwin, the king's clerk, to hold an additional benefice, 1245 (Pap. Lett., I, p. 220).

CUSHNIE, CUSHNEY, CUSHNY. From the place of this name in the parish of Leochel, Aberdeenshire. John Cusne witnessed sasine of third part of Drumflogne, 1508 (Bamff, p. 44), and in 1534 another John Cowsny witnessed sasine by Master Alexander Ramsay (ibid., p. 64). A payment was made to Donald Cousny, an invalid, in 1509 (Rent. Dunk., p. 108). Gavin Cusny was admitted burgess of Aberdeen in 1526 (NSCM., I, p. 50). William Cusne was prebendar of the Collegiate church of Methven in 1549 (Methven, p. 49), Thomas Quishney was admitted burgess of Aberdeen in 1560 (NSCM., I, p. 67), and James Cusnye or Cuschny was reader of Aboyne in 1567 (AEI., p. 118; RMR.). John Cushnie was admitted burgess of Aberdeen in 1606 (NSCM., I, p. 101), payment was made to Patrick Cuschnye in the same burgh in 1629, and four years later John Cuschnie in Culsalmond is mentioned (SCM., v, p. 103; ibid., III, p. 89). Thomas Cushney, "glasior in Aberdein," in record in 1658 (Inquis., 4332). John Cushnie, shipmaster, died in Aberdeen in 1801, the Rev. Alexander Cushny, minister at Oyne died in 1839, and his son, Rev. Alexander Cushny, minister of Rayne, died Father of the Church of Scotland in July 1874 (Fasti, VI).

CUSINE. Gilcrist de Quisine or de la Cusine was a Scots prisoner of war from Stirling Castle, 1305 (Bain, II, p. 449, 451). The name of James Cusing, weaver and portioner of Uddingston, 1753 (Campsie), may be the same.

CUSITHE, 'hound of peace.' From this comes the name of Clan Consithe of Fife: 'Cusidhe a quo Clann Consithe a Bhib' (Skene CS.,

III, p. 481). The clan has not yet been identified. *Cu*, 'hound,' was a term of respect and regard among the early Gaels (cf. Cu Chulainn). In composition it is a complimentary title like 'hero.'

CUSTOMER. From the office of customar or customer, the lessee of burgh customs and dues. John Custumer was witness in Glasgow in 1500 (LCD., p. 204).

CUTELLAR. See under CUTLER.

CUTHBERT. An OE. personal name meaning "bright champion." The popularity of this surname in the Lothians and in the north of England is due to the great saint of Lindisfarne after whom the town of Kirkcudbright was named. A church dedicated to S. Cuthbert in Dryfesdale was granted to Jocelin, bishop of Glasgow in 1174. The common pronunciation of the saint's name over the whole north of England is invariably Cudbert, from which comes the diminutives 'Cuddie' and 'Cuddy.' Paton Cudbert and Thom Cudbert were tenants in the Grange of Kerso in 1466 (*Cupar-Angus*, I, p. 154). Maister Cuthberd Welshe witnessed the laird of Pitfouris band in 1543 (SCM., II, p. 271), a marriage contract between George Cudbert or Cudberth and Jonet Balye is recorded in 1560 (CMN., 77), and James Cuthbert was a charter witness in Brechin in 1566 (REB., II, 212). A family of this name settled in Inverness in the beginning of the fifteenth century and for long after took a prominent part in the civic affairs of the town. Thomas Cuthbert, burgess of Inverness, entered into an obligation to William, earl of Errol in 1455 (SCM., II, p. 211), and John Cutbert was alderman of the town in 1510. Andrew Cutbert held a yard and land in Perth, 1545 (*Rollok*, 4). In 1686 the Scottish Parliament granted warrant to Charles Colbert de Croissy (1625–96), brother of the marquis of Seignelay, for a bore-brieve as a descendant of the Cuthberts of Castlehill, and as a connection of all the more ancient families of Scotland (APS., VIII, p. 611–613; SCM., V, pref. p. 30. In APS. the pedigree for several generations is given). The Cuthberts of Castlehill are styled in Gaelic *Mac Sheorais* (TGSI., XXI, p. 10). John Cudbert charged with 'casual murder' in Brechin, 1650 (PBK., p. 348). As forename: Cubbe Anderson, 1557 (M'Dowell, *Lincluden*, p. 111). Cuttie or Cuthbert Armorer was agent of the earl of Bothwell, 1589 (*Calendar of Scots papers*, x, p. 140, 652). Cutberd 1550, Cuthberd 1587.

CUTHBERTSON, 'son of CUTHBERT,' q.v. Willelmus filius Cuthberti witnessed the gift

of a piece of land to the Abbey of Newbattle (*Neubotle*, p. 235). John Cutbertson is in record in Aberdeen in 1444 (CRA., p. 11), James Cuthberti held land in Forfar in 1453 (RAA., II, 101), and in the same year John Cuthbertson, a Scotsman, had a safe conduct to travel in England (Bain, IV, 1264). James Cuthbertsoun in Dalkeith was cited before the Privy Council 1566 (RPC., I, p. 444), and Archibald Cuthbertsone was summoned to an assize in 1688 (RPC., 3. ser. XIII, p. 235). Cudberson 1608.

CUTHEL, CUTHELL, CUTHILL. Of local origin from Cuthell or Cuthill, a suburb of Prestonpans, East Lothian. Thomas Cuthill and George Cuthill, witnesses, 1536 (*Binns*, 35). Steven Cutle was indweller in Edinburgh in 1696 (*Edinb. Marr.*), and in 1708 the uppermost stories of the tenement of Mrs. Cuthel were damaged by the fire in Edinburgh (Reid, *New lights on old Edinburgh*, p. 93). Cuthill was also a surname in Stirling in the eighteenth century. Lawrence Cuthill, burgess of Dumbarton, 1825 (RDB.).

CUTLER, CUTELLAR. From the occupation of knife-maker (ME. *cutyler, coteler* <OF. *cotelier*). Matthew de [error for le] Coteleir of Berwick rendered homage in 1296 (RR.). A Galloway surname. The Cutlers of Orroland, parish of Rerwick, are said to have obtained the lands from the monks of Dundrennan Abbey in 1437. The local tradition is that the first of the Cutlars who came to the parish was employed in sharpening the tools of the masons engaged in the erection of the abbey [1142], and thereby acquired their name (M'Kerlie, v, p. 104). This is most improbable. There is no mention of the family until 1606 when John Cuitlar was served heir to his father in Oroland (*Retours, Kirkcudbright*, 68). The surname occurs in Aberdeen in 1460 (CRA., p. 405). Hugh Cutlar was repledged to liberty of burgh of Irvine, 1472 (*Irvine*, I, p. 28), and Thomas Cutlar possessed a tenement in Brechin, 1493 (REB., II, 138). Payments were made to Robert Cultellare or Cultelar 'for suordis for turnaving,' in 1503 (*Trials*, I, p. 119*). Henry Cuthleyr possessed a land in Glasgow c. 1540 (LCD., p. 34), John Cuttler was retoured heir of John Cutler, portioner of Auchtermuchtie, his father, 1698 (*Retours, Fife*, 1412), and Mrs. Deborah Cutler of Craigdarroch is recorded in 1796 (*Dumfries*). Cuitlar 1648, Cuthlar 1466, Cutlair 1511, Cutlare 1508.

CYSTER. Henricus dictus Cyser, burgess of Ayr, 1316 (*Ayr*, p. 21), as Henricus dictus Cyster held a land in burgage in Are, c. 1325 (RMS., I, 44).

DABINGWITH. Roger de Dabingwith witnessed a charter by Richard Lupellus, dominus de Hawic, c. 1183 (RPSA., p. 262).

DACKER. From Dakyr, now Dacre, near Penrith, Cumberland. William de Dakyr or Dakre was sheriff of Cumberland, 1278 (Bain, II, p. 34; Moore, Lands, p. 63). Malcolm dictus dakir, sergeand of the burgh of Aberdeen, witnessed a deed of 1434, and is mentioned again five years later as Malcolm Dacre, and in 1447 as M. Dachar (CRA., p. 5, 6, 15). Nicholas Dakyr, probably his son, was sergeand in Aberdeen, 1450 (REA., II, p. 296). Dakkyr 1449. Major G. M. Dacker, R. A., recorded in Edinburgh, 1941.

DAE. Six persons of this name are recorded in the Commissariot Record of Dunblane from 1621. Christian Dea in Carie, 1629 (Dunblane), Andrew Daa, glover in Edinburgh, 1643 (Edinb. Marr.), Robert Dae in Wester Weyms, 1668 (Inquis. Tut., 936), James Dae sometime in Montrose, 1668 (Brechin), and John Dae, notary in Achtergaven, 1712 (Dunkeld).

DAGG. Wille Dag in Strathdee, 1527 (Grant, III, p. 70). It was also a surname in the Debateable Land in sixteenth century, in 1550–52 recorded as Dog (ALHT.), so it may be a form of DOIG, q.v.

DAGLISH. A variant of DALGLEISH, q.v., recorded in Edinburgh, 1942.

DAINTY. Mary Dainty in the parish of Westcather (West Calder), 1686 (RPC., 3. ser. XII, p. 369). Bardsley thinks this name is an imitative doublet of Daintree (= Daventry), the name of a parish in co. Northampton. Cf. DAVENTRY.

DAKERS. John Daikers in Kyndrocat is mentioned in 1589 (REB., II, p. 227). Margaret Dakers in Barrellwall, 1637, and seven more of the name are recorded in the vicinity of Breehin (Brechin). William Dakers, writer in Edinburgh, 1690 (Edin. App.). David Dakers Black published a History of Brechin in 1867.

DALCROSS. From Dalcross near Croy, Inverness-shire. William Dalcors appears as a witness in 1499 (Cawdor, p. 101).

DALE. Local. Johannes de Dale was charter witness at Yester, 1374 (Yester, p. 26), Syme of Daile and Jok of Dail of the Newtoun occur in Ayrshire, 1470 (Prestwick, p. 4, 5), and John Daill in Fouldaine, 1653 (Lauder).

DALGAIRNS, DALGARNS. See under GAIRN and GARDYNE.

DALGARNO. From the lands of Dalgarnock in Dumfriesshire. The old family of Dalgarno of that Ilk, however, were in Aberdeenshire. In 1262 William de Dalgarnoc, rector of Rathen in the diocese of St. Andrews, had a dispensation to hold the church of Aberbrothoc then held by him in commendam (Pap. Lett., I, p. 382). William de Dalgernok, preceptor of David II, was abbot of Kelso, 1329 (REG., p. 245–246). Johannes de Dalgarnok, burgess of Aberbrothoc, 1333 (RAA., II, p. 13) was custumar there in 1359 (ER., I, p. 610). John Dalgarnet, a monk, was a charter witness in 1333 (Pap. Lett.). Johannes de Dalgarnok, burgess of Aberdeen, 1366 (REA., II, p. 61) is probably the same with the laird of Westiressyntoly in Durris (RMS., I, 444). A petition on behalf of John de Dalgernoc, appointed abbot of S. Mary's, Kylwynyn, that he may receive benediction from any Catholic bishop was presented in 1344 (Pap. Pet., I, p. 82), and a John de Dalgernock is mentioned in 1348 as prior of Lesmahagow (SCM., v, p. 246). The goods of Adam de Dalgarnok, an Aberdeen merchant, were plundered by the English in 1370 (Bain, IV, 158, 164). William de Dalgarnok, vicar of Brechin, 1372 (REB., I, 20), and another William de Dalgarnok was dominus de Fyntre, 1400 (CAB., p. 422). Alexander Dalgarno was a canon of the cathedral of Old Machar, Aberdeen, 1386 (REA., I, p. 176), John Dawgarnow was one of an inquest in Aberdeen, 1505 (Illus., III, p. 260), and William Dalgarno de eodem was retoured heir of William Dalgarno de eodem, 1603 (Retours, Aberdeen, 91). Arthur Dalgarne, a talebearer in Kinethmont, 1664 (Alford, p. 46), and John Dalgairn in Edindrack, parish of Gartly, 1688 (Moray). Dalgarnie 1665, Dalgardno 1627, Dalgarnocht 1571, Dalgarnowch 1417, Dilgarno 1623, Dulgarnocht 1599.

DALGETY, DALGETTY. From Dalgety in the parish of the same name in Fife, or from the lands of Dalgety or Delgaty in Aberdeenshire, formerly belonging to a family of that name. There appears also to have been lands of the name in the parish of Brechin, and there is record of a grant in 1594 to Hercules Delgaty of the escheat of the goods of Robert Low in Brechin (REB., II, 368). David Delegate was retoured heir to Margaret Butchert, 1649 (Inquis., 3537). The name has been made famous by Scott's Dugald Dalgetty in A Legend of Montrose. Old spellings are Dalgitie (1672), Daigati.

DALGINCH. Nessus de Dalginge who witnessed a gift by Duncan, earl of Fife, to the nuns of North Berwick, a. 1177 (CMN., 6) derived his name from Dalginch near Markinch, Fife.

DALGLEISH, DALGLIESH, DALGLISH, DAG-LISH. Of territorial origin from the lands of Dalgleish above the sources of Tinna Water in the parish of Ettrick, Selkirkshire. Individuals of this name on the Border figure constantly in the public records as disturbers of the peace. The first form is the most common. Symon de Dalgles in 1407 witnessed a charter by Robert, duke of Albany in favor of John de Hawdene of the lands of Hawdene and Yethame (RMS., I, 912). Simon of Dalgles, probably a son of Symon, was canon and prebend of Askirk in 1448 (REG., 352). Sir William de Dalgles was steward to the bishop of Glasgow in 1452 and afterwards held the same office under the king. John of Dalgles or Dalgleis of that Ilk had a remission in the year 1494, and in 1507 there was another precept of remission to three persons of the name, Ade Dalgleisch in Braidhalch, Thomas Dalglesch, and William Dalglesch (RSS., I, 1484). Ninian Dalgles was prebendary of Bothwell in 1503 (PDG.), John Dalglese was hanged in 1510 for being concerned in the burning of Branxholm and Ancrum and other offences (Trials, I, p. °69), Andrew Dawgles or Dawgleich was tenant of Balbrogy, 1507–10 (Cupar-Angus, I, p. 264, 278). James Daugleich was member of assize at Cupar in 1521 (SCBF., p. 222), and Lawrence Dalgleish was bailie of Dunfermline in 1556. George Dalgleish, confidential servitor of the earl of Bothwell, was hanged and quartered for participation in the murder of Darnley (Trials, III, p. 495). Offshoots of the family early established themselves in Fife and in Perthshire, and the Dalgleishes of Tinnygask in Fife "successfully avoided any distinction." An account of this family (of Tinnygask) by the marquis de Ruvigny and Raineval was published in the Genealogical magazine, v, p. 315–320, London, 1902. Dagleich 1561, Dagleische 1577, Dalgleise 1487, Dalgleiss 1548, Dalglesche 1516, Dalglis 1551, Dalglische 1511, Dalgliss 1644, Daugleis 1519, Dawcleych 1493, Dawgleis 1513, Dawgleish 1561, Dawgleiss 1541.

DALHAM. John de Dalham witnessed a grant of lands in Langtoun to the Hospital of Soltre between 1200–53 (Soltre, p. 14). Probably from Dalham in Suffolk.

DALITH. Walter Dalith and Thomas Dalith agreed to serve Edward I in France or elsewhere, 1297 (Bain, II, p. 242).

DALLACHY, DALLACHIE. Of local origin from Dallachy in the parish of Bellie in Moray, or from Dallochy in the parish of Glass in Aberdeenshire, more probably the latter. Robert Dawloquhy, canon of Moray, who appears in 1484, 1487, and 1494 (RAA., II, p. 211; RMS., II, 1694, 2220) is probably the Robert Dalloquhy de Kynnoir mentioned in 1484 (REM., p. 264, 265). Richard Dallouchquhy appears as a witness in 1534 (RMS., III, 1337). Thomas Daloquhy, clerk and notary public in the diocese of Aberdeen, 1536 (Echt-Forbes charters, p. 255), is probably Thomas Daloquhy, notary in Alford in 1545 (RMS., III, 3115), and the same with Thomas Dalaquhy, notary public in Lesmoir, 1562 (Aboyne, p. 103). Hector Dolloquhy or Dallowquhy was convicted of assault in Aberdeen in 1561, and in 1570 he was banished from the town (CRA., p. 330, 368). Thomas Dalloquhy was "reidar" in Aberdeenshire in 1570, and Gibby Dallachy is said to have been the last person hanged on the Gallow Hill of Keith. Dallonquhy (? Dallouquhy) 1494.

DALLAS. From the old barony of the same name in Moray. The first of the family was Willelmus de Rypeley, an Englishman, who obtained a grant or confirmation of the lands of Dolays Mykel from William the Lion (Dallas, p. 28). Archebaldus de Doleys appears as juror on an inquisition on the lands of Mefth in 1262 (APS., I, p. 101; Bain, I, 2323). William de Doles witnessed a charter by Malcolm de Moravia of the lands of Lamabride to his son, William de Moray c. 1278 (REM., p. 461), and c. 1284 he witnessed another charter as William de Dolays, knight (ibid., p. 462), and in 1286 witnessed the gift by Hugh Herock to the church of Elgin (ibid., p. 221). He is probably the William de Dolays, sheriff of Forres, who appears in 1292 (Bain, II, 597). In 1429 we have mention of the lands of John de Dolas (RMS., II, 124), and six years later William Dolasse appears as procurator in Brechin (REB., I, 78). Henry Dolas, a native of Arbroydt (Arbroath), had letters of denisation in England in 1475 (Bain, IV, 1426), Duncan Dolace was a tenant of the bishop of Aberdeen in 1511 (REA., I, p. 373), and William Dollas and Hew Dollace were tenants of Ballachattrechin in Islay in 1686 (Bk. Islay, p. 497). Dallass 1655, Dallyas 1510, Dolles 1512.

"It has always been supposed, from the name and location of the family, that it was of native Celtic origin, and that it was lineally descended from the Mackintoshes. The more commonly accepted view, however, is that it was a small but independent clan affiliated to Mackintoshes or to Clan Chattan. In Adam's What is my tartan? it is definitely stated that Dallas is dependent upon Mackintosh, and similar statements are to be found elsewhere. The available facts are, however, insufficient

DALLAS, *continued*

to substantiate the idea of dependence. The few notices of the early barons give no indications of close relations with Clan Chattan, and in later times the Dallases are found much more intimately associated with the lairds of Cawdor and Kilravock than with the Mackintoshes. In 1513 Henry Dallas of Cantray joined with the Mackintoshes in what is known as the second heirship of Petty, but his being married to a daughter of John Keir Mackintosh of Rothiemurchus might well account for the part he took in the affair. Again, in a 'contract of appoyntment betwix the Laird of Calder and M'intosche' in 1581, Alexander Dallas of Budgate is mentioned as one of the 'kin' of Lachlan Mackintosh of Dunachten, but he too was married to a Mackintosh, which may account for the relationship. Other instances of kinship or of friendship might be cited in support of the contention that the Dallases were affiliated to Clan Chattan. Dallas of Cantray and some of his kinsmen served with the Mackintosh Regiment on the disastrous field of Culloden, but these facts seem hardly sufficient to establish the position that the Dallases, like the Macgillivrays, Macbeans, Macqueens, and others, were incorporated in the great Celtic Clan Chattan" (*Dallas*, p. 11–12). Dollase 1558.

The *System of Stiles*, by George Dallas, published in 1697, was "the earliest book to bear upon its title-page the name of Dallas."

DALLING. Robert Dawling in Leith accepts the king's coronation, 1567 (RPC., I, p. 563), and Jonet Dauling was heir of Violet Dauling, lawfully born daughter of Robert Dawling, 1637 (*Inquis.*, 2302). James Dawling was member of Scots parliament for South Queensferry, 1639 (*Hanna*, II, p. 490). Jeanna Dawling and Helena Dawling were heirs portioners of James Dawling, burgess of Sowth Queensferrie, their father, 1668 (*Retours, Fife*, 1024; *Retours, Linlithgow*, 221). George Daulling, 'skiper in Queinsferie,' was warded in Canongate Tolbooth, Edinburgh, 1684 (BOEC., IX, p. 117), Mathew Douling, polentarius in Borroustounes, 1691 (*Retours, Linlithgow*, 272), and Thomas Dauling was retoured heir of Thomas Dauling of Leith, in the lands and barony of Cumnock, Ayr, 1695 (*Retours, Ayr*, 686). Probably of English origin from Dalling in Norfolk. Dauline 1643.

DALLISTHOCH. Janet Dallisthoch in the parish of Dowalle (Dull), 1658 (*Dunblane*).

DALMAHOY. From the old barony of the same name in Midlothian. Sir Alexander de Dalmhoy, miles, c. 1295, granted permission to the monks of Newbattle to pass freely through his lands of Dalmhoy (*Neubotle*, p. 165). He and his son, also named Alexander, about the same time appear as witnesses to a charter in favor of that monastery (ibid., p. 161), and as Alisaundre de Dalmahoy of Edinburghshire the father rendered homage in 1296. His seal carries three mullets on a chief, and S' *Alexandri de Dalmihoi* (*Bain*, II, p. 185, 200). Henry de Dalmahoy of Linlithgowshire also rendered homage in 1296 (ibid., p. 205), and Roger Dalmahoy was one of the garrison of Edinburgh Castle in 1339–40 (ibid., III, p. 241). Andrew Dalmahoy was "serjand mare of Edinburgh" in 1522 (ALHT., V, p. 204), Matthew Dalmahoy was a witness in Linlithgow, 1534 (*Johnsoun*), Catharina Dalmahoy recorded in Edinburgh, 1627 (*Retours, Peebles*, 74), and William Dalmahoy was "quartermaster of his Māties troup of gauird" in 1684 (BOEC., IX., p. 152). Damahoy 1528, Dammahoy 1648.

DALMENY. Gilbert de Dunmanyn (the early form of the place name), the king's tenant in the county of Edneburk, rendered homage in 1296. His seal bears a fleur-de-lys and S' *Gilberti Jvvenis*(?) (*Bain*, II, p. 201, 551).

DALOWE. Andrew Dalowe had a safe conduct in 1424 (*Bain*, IV, 963). Probably from Dallow in Yorkshire.

DALREOCH. Andrew of Dalrewach, son of Ysaac Macclibarn, granted a charter of the lands of Dalrewach to Sir William of Murray, c. 1290 (*Athole*, p. 705). From Dalreoch (Dunning, Perthshire) or Dalreioch (Dunkeld).

DALRYMPLE. The first authentic notice of Dalrymples is in the charter of their lands to John Kenedy of Dunure in 1371. The charter embraces three generations, of which Adam de Dalrympil is the first of the name (RMS., I, 381). James of Dalrymple witnessed a charter by Robert, earl of Fife, c. 1390 (*Athole*, p. 706), and John de Dalrympil was provost of Edinburgh in 1392 (*Egidii*, p. 28). Gilbert of Dalrympille, a Scots prisoner of war, was released from the Tower of London in 1413 (*Bain*, IV, 839). John of Dalrymple (Dalrympille, or Dauripill) received safe conducts to travel through England between 1447 and 1459 (ibid., 1207, 1228, 1299), and David Dalrumple, who had a similar safe conduct in 1463 (ibid., 1338) may be the David de Dalrumpyll or Dalrumpil recorded in Edinburgh in 1467 (*Neubotle*, 299). Fergus Dalrumpill, a follower of the earl of Cassilis, was respited for murder in 1526 (RSS., I, 3386). In the muster rolls of the Scots Guards in France the surname appears as de Romple. Dalrimpil 1516, Dalrympill and Dalrympill 1616, Dalrumpill 1541, Darumple 1650 (and also the pronunciation in common speech), Darymple 1426, Dawrumpyl 1532, Derumpill 1529.

DALSWINTON. Richard de Dalswynton, attorney for William Comyn and Isabella, his wife, derived his surname from Dalswinton in the parish of Kirkmahoe, Dumfriesshire.

DALTON. Doubtless from Dalton in Northumberland. Mention was made c. 1315 of certain lands in Roxburgh, Kerton, etc., which had belonged to quondam William de Dalton (RSM., I, 14). William de Dalton was bailie of Aberdeen in 1368 (REA., II, p. 286), Helisei de Dalton was a bailie there, 1396 (ibid., II, p. 294), and Thomas Dalton was admitted burgess of the town in 1409 (NSCM., I, p. 4).

DALWELL. Local? Mr. John Dalwell, minister at Prestonkirk, 1622 (Waddell, p. 59).

DALYELL, DALYIEL, DALZELL, DALZIEL. Of territorial origin from the old barony of Dalziel in Lanarkshire. The names are pronounced as 'Diyell' or simply DL. Some of the name, however, call themselves Dal-yell, some Dalzell, and some Dal-zeel. Rev. Mungo Dalvell, minister of Cranshaws, signed his name Diyell in 1639, in the Memorie of the Somervilles (I, p. 267) it is spelled Deill, and "in the rarer modern form Dalyell we have the purist's protest against the more general Dalziel." In Shetland Dalziel has been substituted for the native Yell (derived from the name of the island of that name). Some of the bearers of the name there write it Deyell or De Yell. The first of the name appears in 1259 when the baron of Daliel served on an inquest (Bain, I, p. 426). He was probably father of Hugh de Dalyhel, sheriff of Lanark in 1288 (ER., I, p. 39, 46). Thomas de Dalielle of the county of Lanark rendered homage in 1296 (Bain, II, p. 212). Safe conducts were granted Sir William Dalyelle and William Dalyelle, his son in 1415 (Bain, IV, 890). The name of William Daliell, witness at Dirleton, 1649, is also spelled Duill (Pitcairn, Trials, III). A famous or infamous individual of this name was General Thomas Dalvell (d. 1685) of the Binns, the "Muscovy Beast who had roasted men." The Dalvells of Binns in West Lothian are the oldest cadet family. James Deell and Hugh Deell were residents in parish of Borgue, 1684 (RPC., 3. ser. IX, p. 566), and James Dyell

was treasurer of burgh of Dumfries, 1689 (ibid., 3. ser. XIV, p. 684). Sir John Graham Dalyell was author of the Darker superstitions of Scotland, 1835. An old Galloway rhyme anent the Dalyells of Glenyae runs (Galloway gossip: Kirkcudbrightshire, p. 279):

"Deil an Da'yell begins wi yae letter; Deil's no gude, and Da'yell's nae better."

The place name is an old Gaelic locative meaning "at the white dale" (Gaelic Dailghil). Daleyhell and Dalevhelle 1397, Daliel and Daliell 1649, Dalliell 1511, Dalyhell 1392, Dalzel 1504, Dalzelle 1390, Danȝhaell 1518, Davȝill 1590, Dyayell 1666, and Froissart spells it Alidiel.

DAMMESONE. In the first half of the thirteenth century mention is made of the lands of Ylistoun formerly belonging to Alan Dammesone (Dryburgh, p. 149). John Dammesone, alderman and burgess of Jeddeworth, and John Dammesone of Over Aytone rendered homage, 1296 (Bain, II, p. 197, 206). Lower (under 'Damson') says "'Dame's son,' but whether the son of Dame, apparently an old Christian name, or 'filius dominae,' I know not." Weekley (p. 193) quotes Geoffrey Dammesune from the English Pipe Rolls and also renders 'dame's son.'

DANCER. From the profession, a dancer. James Dancer, a captive in Argier (Algiers), 1643 (PBK., p. 250). The name occurs in English Hundred Rolls in 1273.

DAND, DANDIE, DANDY. Hypocorisms of ANDREW with prosthetic d. Andrew Kerr, son of the eighth lord of Ferniehurst, who died in 1499, was generally known as 'Dand Kerr.' Dand was common as a Christian name in the south of Scotland in the sixteenth century, and in the list of tenants under the Abbey of Kelso in 1567 we find Dand Howy, Dand Glernet, Dand Lermont, Dand Craige, Dand Stobe, etc. (Kelso, p. 518-532). Andrew alias Dandie Cranston, witness in Edinburgh, 1514 (Ros, 69). In 1642 we have record of Andreas alias Dand Plumbar filius Joannis Plumbar in Kelso (Retours, Berwick, 243), and Andrew alias Dand Greinfeild is recorded in Merton (RRM., I, p. 105). In the beginning of the seventeenth century seven Olivers, all with the forename Andrew or Dand, were distinguished bv the part of the town (Kelso) in which each dwelt.

DANDISON. A south country surname, "son of DAND or DANDIE," q.v.

DANIEL. A surname recorded in Aberdeen. From the Hebrew personal name *Dănyyĕ'l*, "El is my judge," though some scholars think there is connection with Avestan *dănu*, 'wise' or 'wisdom.' Daniel, son of Herleuine, witnessed a charter by Uchtred, son of Fergus, lord of Galloway, c. 1166 (Coll. AGAA., IV, p. 55), and another early individual of the name gave origin to the ancient barony of Danzielstoun in the parish of Kilmalcolm. Walter Daniel had a safe conduct to travel in England, 1424 (*Bain*, IV, 970). John Dangzell [*z = y*] in Dunfermline, 1562 (*Dunfermline*). By the Gaels this name was adopted as an equivalent for Donald.

DANN. From 'Dan,' diminutive of DANIEL, q.v.

DANSKEN, DANSKIN, DANSKINE. This surname meant originally a native of Danzig (now Gdansk), and appears in Scottish record about the beginning of the seventeenth century. John Danskyne was a skinner in Dundee in 1616 (*Wedd.*, p. 278), and Patrik Dansken was constable "landwart of Craill" in 1633 (RPC., 2. ser. v, p. 93). Henry Danskin was one of the contributors to the *Delitiæ poetarum Scotorum*, published in Amsterdam in 1637. George Gladstanes, archbishop of St. Andrews, in a letter to King James VI, refers to him as "Your Maiestie's owne poet and natiue seruant, Mr. Henry Danskene" (*Pollok*, II, p. 71). The surname is also found in Stirling in 1717 (*Sc. Ant.*, VI, p. 88), and there are twelve of this name in the Commissariot Record of Dunblane from 1604 onward. "Gerald Stanley," composer of the "Woodland Whispers" waltzes, was in private life George Dansken. For an account of the early commercial relations between Scotland and Danzig see Fischer's *The Scot in Germany*, part 1. Daniskine 1664.

DANSON, 'son of Dan,' diminutive of DANIEL, q.v. Recorded in Aberdeen, and probably of recent introduction from England. "For several centuries," says Bardsley, "Danson has been a familiar South Cumberland and Furness surname."

DAREL. Gilbert Darel of Peeblesshire rendered homage, 1296 (*Bain*, II, p. 207). Bardsley has the name under *Darrell* but gives no explanation. Harrison says Fr. *Darel* (also later *Dareau*), probably Frankish cognate of OE. personal name *Deór(a)* [?]. *Darel* in English HR.

DARG, DARGE. John Darge possessed a tenement in Northberwyk, 1477 (CMN., 36), and Stephen Darg witnessed a notarial transumpt

of a letter of James III in 1537 to the burgesses of Haddington (*James* II, 21). Andrew Darg admitted burgess of Aberdeen, 1572 (NSCM., I, p. 76), is probably Andrew Dayrg who was elected deacon in 1591 (SCM., II, p. 67). Robert Darge was admitted burgess of Aberdeen, 1612 (NSCM., I, p. 110), Janet Darg appears in Dundee, 1613 (*Brechin*), Duncan Dairge is in record in Balchirnoch, 1620. Mr. Walter Darge was deprived of the liberty of preaching within the presbytery of Fordyce, 1666 (*Alford*, I, p. 86), James Darg, messenger in Edinburgh, 1687 (*Edin. App.*), and Robert Darg, boatman in the Bass, 1689 (RPC., 3. ser. XIII, p. 447). Thomas Dark, 'tyd waiter,' in Aberdeen before 1721 (NSCM., I, p. 107), Alexander Darg is in Gavill, 1743 (*Aberdeen CR.*), and Angus Derg was a Moray Jacobite of the '45. The surname is said to be a common one in Glenlivet. Explained as from G. *dearg*, but with exception of the last entry, this seems unlikely. It is an English surname.

DARGAVELL. From the place of this name in the parish of Erskine, Renfrewshire. John de Dargavell was a tenant of the Douglas in Thornhill, Dumfriesshire, 1376 (RHM., I, p. lvi), and a later John Dargavell was groom at Drumlanrig Castle, c. 1740. Persons of this name are found mostly in Dumfriesshire. The name of Thomas de Dargavane who leased part of Thornhill in Mortoune in 1376 (loc. cit.) is the same with *n* for *l*.

DARGIE. Of local origin from the village of Dargie in the parish of Liff-Benvie in Angus. John Dargie in Hill of Fynnevine, 1613 (*Brechin*). Dargyie 1699.

DARLEITH. The Darleiths of that Ilk derived their name from the barony of Darleith in the parish of Bonhill, Dumbartonshire. A remission was granted to Arthur Darleith in 1489 for holding the Castle of Dumbarton against the king (APS., XII, p. 34). Another Arthur Darleith of that Ilk is in record in 1567 (RPC., I, p. 553), and John Darleyth of that Ilk appears as witness in 1591 (RPC., IV, p. 710). The same or a succeeding John Darleith assisted the Macfarlanes in their feud with the Buchanans in 1619. The lands of Darleith were acquired by the Zuills in 1670.

DARLING. *Dyrling* or *deôrling* was the OE. term used to denote the young noble of a house, perhaps exclusively the eldest son, on whom all expectation rested. Afterwards it became a family name. *Cild* (child) was similarly used (cf. A. S. Chron. a. 1016, 1066). Derlig de Arfdift was a witness a. 1177 (CMN., 7), and Waldevus Darling or Derlyng was a charter witness in Roxburgh c. 1338 (*Dry-*

burgh, 313; BNCH., xxiv, p. 226). Sir John Derlynge was precentor of Caithness in 1368 (OPS., ii, p. 617), John Derling and Andrew Derling were burgesses of Edinburgh in 1381 (*Egidii*, p. 22), and Stevyne Darling, John Darlyng, and Ryn3yn (= Ninian) Darling witnessed resignation of a feu in Peebles in 1471 (*Scots lore*, p. 52). Dem̃ Elen (Dame Elena) Darling or Derlyng, a religious of North Berwick, is in record in 1544 and 1548 (CMN., 60, 65). Mr. Robert Darline was minister at Ews in 1733 (*Dumfries*), and William Darling in Grainyfoord of Grange of Balmaghie is in record in 1752 (*Kirkcudbright*). A family of this name were kindly tenants for many generations under the monks of Melrose, and latterly as tacksmen and feuars. Darleing 1671. Thirteen of the name are recorded in Lauder Commissariot Record.

DARLINGTON. From Darlington in the county of Durham, England. Ada de Derlingtun was precentor of Ross in 1281 (REM., 220), and Johan de Derlingtone, parson of the church of Dunlopy in the county of Forfar, rendered homage in 1296 (*Bain*, ii, p. 211).

DAROCH. A variant of DARROCH, q.v.

DARRIE. Mr. Robert Darrie was minister of Anster, 1606. John Darrie, wright in Hilltoun, 1637 (*Lauder*), and Rachel Darra, witness in Dunbar, 1688 (RPC., 3. ser. xiii, p. 260). Jeams Dary died in 1715 and was buried in Eccles churchyard.

DARROCH, DAROCH, DARRAGH, DURROCH. John Darach was bailie of Stirling in 1406 (ER., iv, p. 26). John Darach de Cruce mentioned in 1445 (*Cambus.*, 214) may be John Darraugh, commissioner for the burgh of Stirling in 1450 (*Ayr*, p. 28). Jonete Daroch is in record in 1458 (RMS., ii, 671), and Mariote Darrauch appears as nurse of the Lady Margaret, second daughter of James ii, 1462 (ER., i, p. cclxxxv). Marion Darroch in Stirling in 1471 protested that she had not given consent to the alienation of an annual rent due to her (*Sc. Ant.*, x, p. 62). Jacobus Darow, notary public, who was a witness in 1477 'apud manierium de Keir' (RMS., ii, 1301), appears again as Jac. Darroch (ibid., 2388), and may be the James Darrow who was notary public in St. Andrews, 1482 (*Cambus.*, 213). William Darroch was witness in Ayr, 1505 (*Friars Ayr*, p. 72). Duncan Darrow was deacon of craft in Stirling, 1522 and 1525 (SBR., p. 24, 275); Alexander Darroch was witness in Edinburgh, 1545 (RMS., iii, 3094); and Ninian Darroicht, Thomas Darroicht, and Robert Darroycht appear in Glasgow in 1550 (*Cambus.*, 214). William Darroch was reidare at Kirk of Mwir, 1574 (RMR.).

Ninian Dorroche, burgess freeman of Glasgow, became a burgess as eldest son of a burgess, 1608 (*Burgesses*). John Darroch was merchant burgess of Glasgow in 1620 (ibid.); M. Darroch was parson of Kilberrie in Kintyre in 1629 (OPS., ii, p. 37); Bertie Derroch was tenant of Caldwell in 1632 (*Caldwell*, i, p. 279); and Alexander Dorrach appears in Falkirk, 1684 (*Moray*). People named Darroch were at one time common in Islay and Jura, and were counted a sept of Clan Donald. (1) The Stirling Darrochs derive from the place named Darroch near Falkirk. (2) The name may also be from adjectival form of a lost *MacDara*, 'son of oak.' Cf. *Macc Dara* in the Book of Armagh. With 'son of oak,' cf. *MacCarthainn*, 'son of Rowan' (tree). See also MacDHUBHDARA. (3) Popular tradition in the West Highlands is that the name is from *Dath riabhach*, a shortening of *Mac 'Ille riabhach*, but this seems doubtful. Darrocht and Darroitch 1550, Darrovcht 1553, Daracht 1506, Darroche 1561, Darrock 1724, Dorrocht 1556 (in Stirling); Darwcht.

DARSIE. From the lands of Dairsie in Fife, now comprehended in the parish of that name. William de Dersy was a monk of the monastery of Aberbrotht in 1427 (REA., i, p. 225). Anderson says the lands were held by the Dairseys of that Ilk under the bishops of St. Andrews, the hereditary offices of bailie and admiral of the regality of St. Andrews being also possessed by them. The family ended in an heiress, Janet de Dairsey, who, marrying a younger son of Learmonth of Ercildoune, Berwickshire, brought to him the lands of Dairsie. About 1590 the name of Darsie is found to occupy a prominent place in the records of the parishes of Easter and Wester Anstruther (*Scottish nation*, ii, p. 21). John Darsie was burgess of Anstruther Wester, 1696 (*Inquis.*, 7659).

DAUN. A form of DON, q.v., from G. *donn*.

DAVENTRY. Johan de Daventre of the county of Edneburk rendered homage in 1296 (*Bain*, ii, p. 209). The feu ferm of a tenement in Leth was granted to Symon de Dayntre in 1351 (*Neubotle*, 274), and William Dayntre is mentioned in Aberdeen in 1402 (CRA., p. 383). Most probably from Daventry, a parish in Northamptonshire, which appears to be pronounced Daintree. Cf. DAINTY.

DAVENY. William Daveny in Aberdeenshire was "dilatit of airt and pairt in cutting and destroving of coirnes," 1613 (*Trials*, iii, p. 259). Probably a form of Daubini or de Aubini or Daubeney, forms of a name of Norman origin, recorded in English *Hundred Rolls*.

DAVID. A personal name from the Hebrew *Dāwidh*, probably meaning "beloved one," though some scholars take it to mean "paternal uncle." Lord Hailes after commenting on the fact that not one of the six sons of Malcolm III received the name of any of the ancient kings of Scotland, but only Anglo-Saxon names evidently chosen by Queen Margaret, says "As David was the youngest, we may conjecture that he was born when Margaret had no hope of more children; and therefore that he received the name of the youngest son of Jesse" (*Annals*, 3. ed., I, p. 47). One of the first professors of the University of Copenhagen (founded 1479) was a Scot, Petrus David de Scotia, D. D., who was elected president of the university no fewer than six times.

DAVIDSON, DAVISON, 'son of DAVID,' q.v. The second form is from the diminutive DAVIE. Johannes filius Davidis was burgess of Perth in 1219 (*Scon*, p. 52), and Adam fiz Dauid of Forfarshire and Johan le fiz David of Berwickshire rendered homage in 1296 (*Bain*, II, p. 206, 208). The seal of the former bears a long-legged bird and S' *Ade filii Davit* (ibid., p. 555). William filius Davidi was provost of Aberdeen in 1340 (ER., I, p. 456), and Adam Davyson, merchant and burgess of Edinburgh, had a safe conduct into England in 1360. Robert Davidson or Robert filius David, elected provost of Aberdeen in 1408, was killed at the battle of Harlaw in 1411, John Davison who held a land in Irvine in 1426 (*Irvine*, I, p. 130) may be the John Davidson, bailie of Are, in 1430 (*Ayr*, p. 85). A distribution of cloth of divers colors was made to Walter Davisoun and his men by command of the king in 1429 (ER., IV, p. 510). Who or what this Walter Davisoun was there is nothing in the record to show. Fynlay Dauison leased Petklochery in 1453 (*Cupar-Angus*, I, p. 129), John Davysone was witness in Linlithgow in 1472 (*Sc. Ant.*, XVII, p. 120), George Davidsone, witness in Peebles 1473 (*Peebles*, 24), and David Davyson, a native of Dundy (Dundee), had letters of denisation in England in 1484 (*Bain*, IV, 1498). Colyn Davidsone witnessed a charter by James Scrimgeour, Constable of Dundee, in 1492 (HP., II, p. 194), Thomas Dauyson was elected bailie of Aberdeen, 1509 (*Guildry*, p. 193), Duncan Dawvsoun was a resident in Stirling in 1566 (*Soltre*, p. 128), and Jok Dauisone was tenant under the Abbey of Kelso in 1567 (*Kelso*, p. 520). The Davidsons of Roxburghshire seem to have formed a small clan in the sixteenth and seventeenth centuries. The chief family seated at Samieston became extinct in 1670 (*Stodart*). Thomas Davidson (b. 1840), born in Deer, Aberdeenshire, devoted his life to the study of the language,

literature, and philosophy of Greece and Italy. In common Gaelic speech this name appears as *Deibhiosdan*. The Davidsons are known as *Clann Dàidh*. Daueson 1550, Dauesoun 1547, Dauiesone 1620, Dauisoun 1513, Dauysone 1490, Daveson 1591, Daviesoune 1653, Davitson 1552, Dawysone 1567.

DAVIE, DAVY. Diminutives of DAVID, q.v. Meg Davy is recorded in Aberdeen, 1408 (CWA., p. 314). The name is found in Strageyth in 1601 (*Dunblane*). Thomas Dawie appears in Eglismaqhene in 1637 (*Brechin*), James Davie in Moshatt, parish of Carnwath, in 1658 (*Lanark CR.*), Jonet Davie was fined for breach of the act against "flyting and scolding" in 1669 (*Corsehill*, p. 88), and Edward Davie was portioner of Torbean in 1676 (*Retours, Linlithgow*, 242). The old family of Grimbister in Grimbister, Orkney, changed their name to Davie, the patronymic of one of the family, and Davies occupy Grimbister at the present day (*Clouston*, p. 35).

DAVIES, 'son of DAVIE,' q.v. Thomas Davies in Altoun, parish of Lesmahago, 1622 (*Lanark CR.*).

DAVISON, 'son of DAVIE,' diminutive of DAVID. See DAVIDSON.

DAVY. *See under* DAVIE.

DAW, DAWE. Diminutives of DAVID, q.v. John Daw was burgess of Haddington in 1426 (*Soltre*, p. 51), and William Daw in Auld Montrose in 1626 and ten more of the name are recorded in the Commissariot Record of Brechin. Andrew Dawe was member of Scots parliament for Crail, 1665 (*Hanna*, II, p. 490).

DAWES, 'son of Daw or Dawe,' a diminutive of DAVID, q.v. Robert Dause in Little Dunkeld, 1657 (*Dunkeld*).

DAWSON. From DAWE, diminutive of DAVID + son. John Daweson was a merchant in the service of Archambaud, earl of Douglas in 1405 (*Bain*, IV, 697). John Dawson is recorded in Kethyk in 1466 (*Cupar-Angus*, I, p. 146), and James Dawson was godson of King James IV (ALHT., I). Duncan Dalsoun (cf. the *l* in Chalmers) was coalman to the king in 1531 (ER., XVI, p. 134), Robert Dausoun was tenant of Westirrossy, Uchtermukty in 1531, and John Dawson and Nicholas Dauson were tenants in Uchtermukty in the same year (ibid., p. 494). David Dason, monk of Beauly, 1541, is Dauid Dauisone in 1568, and Dauid Dauson in 1571 (*Beauly*, p. 220, 256, 268). Jasper Dason and Andrew Dasone appear in Melrose in 1607 and 1699 (RRM., I, p. 40; III, p. 118), Thomas Dasone was bailie of the burgh of Anstruther Wester in 1671 (*Inquis.*, 5415), and Joannes Dasone in Findhorne, 1677 (*Retours, Elgin*, 188). Dawsone 1627. Dawsons were once numerous in Badenoch. Cf. DEAS-SON.

DAY, DEY. From the colloquial Gaelic *Daidh*, 'David.' The Deys are one of the oldest families in the parish of Mortlach, Banffshire. William Dey in Balvany and others made a raid on the lands of Ardwele in Banff in 1600 (RPC., VI, p. 135), and Robert Day in Marhaugh is in record in 1727 (*Dunblane*). Dr. William Dey (d. 1916), a native of Banffshire, was a distinguished student of Aberdeen University, and Agnes Chrystall Dey (1861–1895) was an Aberdeen poetess.

DEACON. From the ecclesiastical office. Walter Dekne, burgess of St. John's town of Perth, had a safe conduct into England for two years, 1291 (*Bain*, II, 535).

DEACONSON, 'son of the deacon.' John Deconson, farmer, Lochmaben, 1374 (*Bain*, IV, p. 49). Duncan Deaconson witnessed a notarial transumpt, 1465 (*Lamont*, p. 19).

DEAN. Of local origin. There is or was a place named Den in the parish of Kildrummy, Aberdeenshire, and Dean in the parish of Kilmarnock, Ayrshire, was an ancient seat of the Boyds, earls of Kilmarnock. Permission was granted in 1345 to Robert de Den, canon of Dunkeld, "for leave to choose his confessor, who shall give him plenary absolution at the hour of death" (*Pap. Pet.*, I, p. 89). Johannes de Den in the parish of Fyvy was excommunicated in 1382 (REA., I, p. 165). In a bond of manrent dated 1703 by William Dean alias Davidson, "miller at the King's Milne (and many other individuals), who and their ancestors, all named Deans, otherwise called Davidsons," acknowledged themselves to be followers, dependents, and kinsmen under and to the lairds of Mackintosh (*Mackintosh muniments*, p. 150). John Dene was burgess of Irvine, 1499 (*Simon*, 1), William Dane, burgess of Are, 1503 (*Friars Ayr*, p. 70), Thomas Deyne held a tenement in Irvine, 1542 (*Irvine*, I, p. 200), John Deyne was a monk of Kilwinning Abbey, 1557. John Dene or Dein in the regality of Kilwinning, 1590 (*Retours, Ayr*, 755), and James Dean, tenant in Chapelgill, 1792 (*Lanark CR.*).

DEANS. This surname was common in the district about Hawick in the sixteenth century in the form Deinis and Deins. A tombstone in the churchyard of Hawick reads:

Heir. lyis. ane. honest. man. iohne.
deinis. quha. vas. tenent. kyndlie.
of. Havik-miln. and. slain. in. debait.
of. his. nichtbovris. geir. the
zeir. of. God. M.D.XL.VI.
(*Sc. Ant.*, I, p. 151)

John Deaness, sclater, was burgess freeman of Glasgow in 1588 (*Burgesses*), and Jacobus Deanes was bailie burgi Vicicanonicorum (i.e. Canongate, Edinburgh) in 1682 (*Inquis.*, 6411). James Deins was a merchant in Glasgow, 1606. Deannes 1608.

DEAS. James Dais is recorded in Dundee, 1611 (*Brechin*), and Mr. John Daes in Huntliewood, 1638 (RRM., I, p. 136). James Daes was minister of the church of Ersiltoune, 1643 (*Inquis.*, 2858). Andrew Daes, stabler, appears in Edinburgh, 1627, and David Daes, tailor there, 1666 (*Edinb. Marr.*). John Deas in Tulloes, parish of Dunnichen, 1683 (*Brechin*). A pension paid to Janet Daes in Edinburgh, 1742 (*Guildry*, p. 180).

DEASSON, DEASON. An Englishing of G. *Macdhai*, son of David. William Deasone in Artlache is mentioned in 1633 (SCM., II, p. 124), Joannes Dasone in Findhorne, heir of John Dasone, his father, 1677 (*Retours, Elgin*, 188), and in 1716 we have record of James Deassoun in the parish of Dumbennan (SCM., IV, p. 170). James Deason was member of Drumblade Company of Volunteers, 1804 (*Will*). There were several Dessons in the parish of Fordyce in middle of nineteenth century (*Fordyce*, p. 89–90). Cf. DAWSON.

DECHMONT. Local, from Dechmont near Uphall, West Lothian. John of Dychtmunt on inquest at Carnwath, 1524 (CBBC., p. 14). See also DICHMOUNT.

DEE. An Aberdeenshire surname. The author of *A View of the diocese of Aberdeen* (p. 76) says: "Dee and Don are two surnames; whether taken from these rivers I know not; though seeing each of them bears a fess, the one waved azure, the other argent on a field vert, it may be thought that such fesses do possibly represent the runnings of these waters." The *View* was written c. 1712.

DEER. Of local origin from Deer (New and Old) in Aberdeenshire. Alloas de Der was one of the "burgenses rure manentes" in Aberdeen in 1317 (SCM., V, p. 10), and Thomas Dere appears as abbot of Kynloc (Kinloss) in 1327 (ER., I, p. 75). John de Dere was

DEER, *continued*

a witness in Brechin in 1445 (REB., I, 103), Thomas Deir or Deyr appears as a notary public in Perth, 1528–32–46 (*Milne*, p. 116, 196; *Rollok*, 21), and Jhone Deir is in record as a trade burgess of Aberdeen in 1617 (ROA., I, p. 231).

DEERNESS. Of local origin from the parish of the same name in Orkney.

DEIRDRE. The spouse of Naoise, and afterwards of Conchubhor Mac Neasa. The name means 'the raging one' (*Pokorny*). Deredere, wife of Cospatric Earl, 1166 (*Annals*, p. 109), gave a portion of the lands of Hirsel to the nuns of Coldstream. It is the Darthula of Macpherson's *Ossian*. Other forms of the name are given as Deirdie, Deiridire, Dearduil, Deurduil, Dearshuil, Diarshula, Deurthula.

DELDAY. An old Orcadian surname from the lands of Deldaill in the parish of Deerness. James Deldall, merchant in Kirkwall, in 1616 (MCM., II, p. 190). Probably extinct.

DEMPSTER. The origin of this surname is found in the office of 'judex' or 'dempster' to the Parliament, shire, or baron-bailie. Until the year 1747 every laird whose land had been erected into a barony was empowered to hold courts for the trial and punishment of certain offenders within his barony; and the dempster was part of his retinue. The name of Haldan de Emester of Perthshire, who rendered homage in 1296 (*Bain*, II, p. 200), is to be read Haldan Deemester. Andrew Dempstar made a gift of his lands of Menmuir to the Priory of Restennot, 1360, and witnessed a Brechin document in 1364 (REB., I, 21). In 1370, as dominus de Keraldstoun, he had a charter of the office of dempster from the Abbot of Arbroath to himself and his heirs (RAA., II, p. 31), and in 1379 the office of judex in parliament and justiciar in courts in the sheriffdom of Forfar was also confirmed to him and his heirs by Robert II (RMS., I, 758). Robert Demster was bailie of Forfar, 1361 (ER., II, p. 62). David Dempster of Careston was one of the perambulators of marches near Arbroath, 1370 (RAA., I, p. 31, 114), Androw Dempstar was on the assize of the marches of Woodwrae, 1388 (*Bamff*, p. 22), and Henry Demstar was one of an inquest made at Edinburgh, 1428 (RAA., II, 61). Matho Dempstar and Andro Dempstar were burgesses of Brechin, 1579 (RPC., III, p. 202), caution was found for Thomas Dempstare of Cushnie, 1585 (ibid., p. 732), Alexander and William Dempstar and other 'broken' Moray men assisted the Macdonalds of Glencoe in a raid in Moray, 1602

(ibid., VI, p. 431), and Bessie Demster is recorded in the parish of Rerrick, 1684 (ibid., 3. ser. IX, p. 573). Thomas Dempster (d. 1625), historian, and George Dempster (1755–1818) of Dunnichen, the agriculturist, were two of the more distinguished of the name. The *Historia Ecclesiastica* of Thomas Dempster has been described as "probably the most untrustworthy book upon Scottish literature ever written" (Geddes, *Bibliography of Middle Scots poets*, p. xvii).

DEMPSTERTON. From the old lands of Dempstartounis (1607) in the barony of Stramiglo, Fife, now Demperston. James de Demstartone was present at perambulation of the marches of Kyrknes and Louchor in 1395 (RPSA., p. 3). Sir John Dempstartoun, a cleric, was witness in Perthshire, 1548 (*Gaw*, 7), Laurence Dempstertoun in Kinrois is mentioned in 1585 (RHM., I, 141), and Robert Demperstoun was portioner of Auchmithie in the sixteenth century. James Dempstertoun in Tillicultrey in 1681 (*Dunblane*).

DENBY. William Danby was chaplain in Glasgow in 1447 (REG., 349), Stephen Denby or Demby held a tenement in Glasgow in 1454 and 1497 (LCD., p. 175; REG., 476), and William Dembeis tenement in the same burgh is mentioned in 1509 (REG., 489). John Denby or Denbye was a notary public in the diocese of Dunblane in 1494 (*Oliphants*, p. 31), and Marion Dembie is recorded in Edinburgh in 1612 (*Edinb. Marr.*). Perhaps from Denby, a village in Yorkshire, or from Danby, a parish in the same county.

DENHOLM, Denham. From the old barony of Denholm, in the parish of Cavers, Roxburghshire. The name may also be from Denholm, a parish in Dumfriesshire, in which county there were landowners of the name in the fifteenth century (*Stodart*), but the first is the more likely source of the name. Guy de Denum of Roxburghshire rendered homage, 1296, and as Guy de Denhom served as juror on inquests at Roxburgh and Dumfries in 1303–4 (*Bain*, II, p. 199, 376, 412). Alan de Denvme purchased the lands of Le Hyllis together with a piece of ground lying on the Maydebane (now Medwyn), 1299 (REG., 253). John of Denum and William of Denum appear in record between 1333–57 (*Rot. Scot.*, I, p. 223, 245, etc.). Rowe Dennum was witness in Lanark, 1488 (*Lanark*, p. 4), Symon Dennum was retoured heir in lands in barony of Carnwath, 1506 (*Retours, Lanark*, 462), and Margaret Dennym appears in Neder Mosplat, 1533 (*Rental*). John Dennholm or Dennhome was ordained commissarie for the army in 1650

(*Irvine*, I, p. 104, 106). William Denholme, portioner of Ersilton, 1662 (RRM., II, p. 29), James Denholme, fermorar in Marsemilne, 1680 (*Inquis.*, 6224), and James Denholm (1772–1818) wrote a history of Glasgow. A pension paid to Margaret Denham in Edinburgh, 1741 (*Guildry*, p. 177). The surname is said to be now unknown in the neighborhood of its origin.

DENMILN. A local surname recorded in Glasgow Directory. There are several small places named Denmill, and there is Denmylne in Fife. See DINMILL.

DENNIS. From the personal name Denis (earlier Denys), the French form of Latin Dionysius. S. Denis, the patron saint of France, was the titular saint of five Scottish fairs. Johannes Dennys was burgess of Aberdeen, 1499 (REA., I, p. 344), James Denis was burgess of Linlithgow, 1536 (*Johnsoun*), and Isobel Denoiss is recorded in Abernethie, 1617 (*Dunblane*). As forename we have: Dionisius Cavers, 1506 (RMS., II, 2985), Dionisius Chalmer, bailie of Newburgh, Fife, 1544 (Laing, *Newburgh*, p. 487), Dioniss Blackat in Perth, 1581 (Mill, *Plays*, p. 280), and Denovis Gilruff in parish of Lesmahago, 1623 (*Lanark CR.*). Dionysius became third prior of Scone, 1140 (*Scon*, pref., p. ix), and Dyonisius was decanus de Anegus in first quarter of thirteenth century (RAA., I, p. 106).

DENNISON. See under DENSON.

DENNISTOUN, DENNISTON. Of territorial origin from the old barony of Danzielstoun in the parish of Kilmalcolm, Renfrewshire. The manor took its name from some man named Daniel, and it bore this name as early as the reign of Malcolm IV (OPS., I, p. 87). The statement of Buchanan of Auchmar that the family sprang from a younger branch of the old earls of Lennox is more than doubtful. Sir Huew de Danielestoun of Lanarkshire rendered homage in 1296. His seal bears a shield, crucilly a fess compony, *S'Hvgonis de Danielst* (*Bain*, II, p. 203, 556). Johannes de Daniellyston who witnessed confirmation of a charter to Jacobus de Lekprewyk of lands in Kyle, 1365 (RMS., I, 204), as John de Daniotson (a miscopying of Daniolston) is designed *dominus ejusdem* in 1369 (RMP., p. 31), and in 1371 was keeper of Dumbarton Castle and a baron of parliament. In the fourteenth century the family held the greater part of the barony of Glencairn in Dumfriesshire, and Robert de Danyelestona, son of John de Danvelestona, had a charter "totam baroniam de Glencarne cum pertinenciis" in the sheriffdom of Dumfries which his father

had resigned in 1370 (RMS., I, 362). Sir John de Danyelstona had a confirmation of all his lands of Mauldisley, etc., in 1373 (ibid., 493), and Johannes de Danveellstoun witnessed a charter of the lands of Duppolle to the Friars Preachers of Ayr, 1381 (*Friars, Ayr*, p. 23). The family ended in the direct line in an heiress, Margaret, "who in 1404 carried the baronies of Glencairn and Kilmarnock to her husband Sir William Cunningham, ancestor of the earls of Glencairn." Robert de Danyelstoun attested a charter of the lands of Myrecairnie and others in Fife c. 1390 (*Wemyss*, II, 27). William Dennestoun was a witness in Linlithgow, 1536 (*Johnsoun*), John Dennilstoun was archdeacon of Dunblane, 1545 (CMN., 61), and Robert Danyelstone, rector of Dysart, 1551 (*Dysart*, p. 20). The daughters of Charles Danielstoun were infeft in the lands of Petliver, 1566 (*Pitfirrane*, 157), and Robert Denniestoun or Danielston was admitted freeman of the Incorporation of Goldsmiths of Edinburgh, 1597 (PSAS., XXV, p. 175). James Denisone, (church) elder in the parochine of Kirkcaldie, 1641 (PBK., p. 210). Daneelstoun 1439, Danielstoun 1513, Danielstone 1552, Dannelstone 1371, Danyelstoune 1500, Danyelstoun 1545, Danzelston 1531, Deneldstoun and Denelstoun 1575, Denestoun 1515, Dennestoune 1622, Dennielstoun 1365, Denzelstoun 1574; Danastoun, Danniestone, Denniestoun, Dinnistoun.

DENNY, DENNEY. The first a common surname in Dumbarton. Of local origin from Denny, a town and parish in Stirlingshire. John of Deny had a safe conduct into England, 1424 (*Bain*, IV, 963), John Dennye was heir of John Dennie, merchant burgess of Glasgow, 1634 (*Inquis.*, 3950), and Peter Denny (1821–1895) was famed as builder of iron steamships.

DENOON. The old family of this name in Ross-shire were descended from Duncan Campbell, one of the Campbells of Lochow, who to escape from justice for certain offences committed by him fled with his brother to the north, where he settled. Both assumed their mother's name of Dunune (Anderson, *Scottish nation*). Mariot Denune was made heir of her brother, John Denune, 1416, and in 1496 Andrew Dunown resigned half of Davidstoun in favor of his son, Alexander Denune (*Macfarlane*, II, p. 35, 8, 360). Johnne Dennoun, who had a 'respitt' for his "treasonable remanent and biding at hame fra our souerane lordis oist and army at Werk," 1529 (RSS., II, 461), may be John Denone of Daveistone who witnessed a notarial instrument at Ferne in 1545 (*Laing*, 495). William Dunnon acquired a third part of Arkboll near Tain, 1535 (RMS., III). Master Thomas Dunnone was

DENOON, *continued*

rector of Kincardine in the north, 1536–66 (OPS., II, p. 411). Donald Denoun of Ferne died February 1540 *(Kal. of Fearn)*. The family were small landowners in Ross-shire in the sixteenth century. Margaret Dunnoven or Denune was heir of William Dunnoven of Pitnelie in Ross, 1574 (*Retours, Ross,* 5, 24). John Denone was heir of Andrew Denone of Catboll-Abbot, his father, in the lands of Catboll-Abbot, 1606, and Andrew Denune was heir of John Denune of Catboll, his father, 1649 (ibid., 20, 100). William Denoin, servitor to James Cuthbert of Drackie, 1617 (*Rec. Inv.,* II, p. 150). Alexander Denune, burgess of Inverness, 1679 (IDR., p. 92), and Alexander Denune, preacher at Pettie, 1683 (ibid., p. 113). John Denone was vicar of Delting in Shetland, 1576. See DUNOON. Dunhoven is an old (1270) spelling of the Argyllshire place name Dunoon, in 1476 Dunnovane. Dennoune 1547, Denoone 1679, Denowne 1536, Denune 1649, Denoome (in Terry, *The Cromwellian Union,* p. 131), Dynnvne 1566; Dunnown, Dunnune.

DENOVAN. From the lands of Denovan in the parish of Dunipace, Stirlingshire. Six individuals of this name appear in the Commissariot Record of Dunblane from 1598 onwards. J. C. Denovan was author of *Ocean rhymes,* printed privately in Edinburgh in 1824. The Finlaus de Donnouen in Bothwell from whom a horse was purchased in 1312 (*Bain,* III, p. 421) may have derived his name from the same place. The local pronunciation of the name is Dunniven.

DENSON. Sir James Macgregor, dean of Lismore or Argyll, a Pope's knight of the end of the fifteenth and beginning of the sixteenth centuries and well-known as the compiler of the collection of Gaelic verse known as the Dean of Lismore's Book, left descendants in Perthshire, who are traced under the patronymic of Macindene or Deneson for some generations after his time (*Archaeologia Scotica,* III, p. 317). He was, however, not the only dean who gave origin to the name. Neil McYndone or McYndayn was tenant of Ballegrogane, Kintyre, in 1505 (ER., XII, p. 698), and John McYndayn McCollef and Macan or Macum (i.e. Malcolm) Mc yndayn appear in record in 1519 (*Cawdor,* p. 131). Martin M'Indayn or M'Indene appears as a witness at Isle of Lochtav in 1552 (BBT., p. 195, 196), and Gregour Denesoun in Stwix, "ane peciabill trew man," was "cruellie murthurit de certane rebellis" in 1565 (*Coll.,* p. 33). Donald M'Coule VcIndeane and Doug-

all Denesoun M'Gregor, 1589, were son and grandson of the dean of Lismore. The name survives as Denson and perhaps as Dennison, though this latter name is more likely to be a shortening of Dennistoun.

DENTON. From the old barony of Denton in Dumfriesshire. Alan de Denton was juror on an inquest held at Gerwan (Girvan) in 1260 (*Bain,* I, 3674). In 1329 Elizabet de Denton received a legacy from the Queen (ER., I, p. 216).

DERBY. From Derby, the capital of the county of that name in England. Stephanus de Dereby was canon of Aberdeen c. 1240 (REA., I, p. 16), and Magister Roger de Derbi, precentor of Aberdeen, c. 1250 (RAA., I, p. 266), appears two years later as canon of Dunkeld (*Scon,* p. 74). A family of this name, probably recent incomers from England, were millers at Cluden Mill, Dumfriesshire, c. 1880.

DERCHESTRE. From some place perhaps in the north of England. Thomas de Derchestre of Berwickshire rendered homage, 1296 (*Bain,* II, p. 207).

DERMID. G. *Diarmid,* MG. *Dermit* (Lismore), *Diarmida* (gen.) in 1467 (Gaelic MS.), MIr. *Diarmait,* OIr. *Diarmuit, Diarmit,* and in Adamnan the name of Columba's faithful attendant is given in Latin as *Diormitius* (V. C., I, 8). Zimmer explained the name as *Dia-ermit,* 'god reverencing,' from *dia* and *ermit* (*are-ment,* 'on-minding'). The true meaning of the name, however, appears to be 'unenvious' (= *di(f)ormit*), from *format,* 'envy' (Pedersen, *Vergleichende Grammatik der keltischen Sprachen,* v. 2, p. 62). "Dormitius filius Cerbulis, totius Scotiae regnatorum" (V. C., I, c. 36), was killed by Aedh Dubh. Diarmaid, the Achilles of Celtic legend, is traditionally said to be buried in Glen Lonain, Argyllshire, the site of his grave being marked by a rude monolith, locally known as *Clach Dhiarmaid.* It is 12½ feet high with a girth of over thirteen feet. It is figured in the *Proceedings* of the Society of Antiquaries of Scotland, LIX, p. 82.

DERNINGTONE. Wauter de Dernyngtone, parson of Parton, Dumfriesshire, rendered homage, 1296 (*Bain,* II, p. 212). Perhaps from Darrington, Yorkshire, in DB. Darnintone and later Dernington.

DERTFORD. Magister Adam de Dertford or de Derteford, canon of Glasgow, witnessed gifts to the church of Glasgow c. 1260–68 (REG., p. 174, 177). An Englishman from Dartford in Kent.

DERVAIL. The English rendering of G. *Diorbhail*, spelled Derval in poem by McGillinduk in Bk. Dean of Lismore. Early Gaelic is *Deirbheile*, meaning 'grief, trouble of mind' (ZCP., VII, p. 303). The name is also Englished Dorothy!

DERVORGILLA. The Latin and better known form of G. *Diorbhorguil*, Ir. *Dearbhforgaill* (*Derb-forgaill* — Meyer). Dervorgilla, daughter of Alan, lord of Galloway, appears on her seal as Dervorgille (*Macdonald*, 1028). On the seal of her charter to Balliol College, Oxford, her name is given as Devorgulla. Fordun spells the name Darworgilla, and in a document of Edward III it appears as Dervorgoyle. Wyntoun refers to Lady Dervorgilla as:

"A bettyr lady than scho wes nane
In all the yle of Mare Britane."

Chronicle, v. 5, p. 263, S. T. S. ed.

Dervorgoyl, widow of Robert Carnot, rendered homage, 1296. Her seal shows a lady holding a shield in her right hand, and a falcon on her left hand, and *Sigill. Derworgoyl d' Crauford* (*Bain*, II, p. 198, 547). The name is sometimes confused with DERVAIL, q.v.

DESK. Probably local, cf. Deskie and Deskford. Agnes Desk in Kilraine in Ross-shire was charged with witchcraft, 1699 (Black, *Witchcraft in Scotland, 1510–1727*, p. 81).

DESSON. An Anglicized form of MACDHÀI, q.v.

DEUCHAR, DEUCHARS. Of territorial origin from the lands of Deuchar in the lordship of Fern or Fearn in Angus. The Deuchars of that Ilk were considered one of the oldest families in the district, and are said to have come into possession of the lands of Deuchar about the year 1230. An imaginative genealogy (*Warden*, III, p. 276) traces the family to the second son of Gilchrist, earl of Angus, but no documentary records of the family exist till 1369 when Sir Alexander Lindsay of Glenesk granted a charter of the lands of Deuhqwhyr to William de Deuhqwhyr *de eodem* as heir to his father (*Jervise LL.*, p. 232). The family were evidently vassals of the Lindsays at that period, and probably, at a still earlier date, of the Montealtos (Mowats). The connection of the Deuchars with the lands ceased in 1819 when the lands were sold and the late owner left Scotland for the colonies (ibid., p. 230). Duchir of that Ilk is mentioned as one of the arbiters in a dispute among neighbors in 1478 (ALC., p. 18), David Duchir, portioner of the lands of Walterstoune is in record, 1535 (REB., II, 186), Robert Dewquhir was a friar of Culross, 1569 (*Laing*, 844), John Dwichair, cordiner in Aberdeen, 1581 (SCM., II, p. 54), and in 1591 there is recorded a band of caution by David Dewchar fiar of that Ilk (RPC., IV, p. 672). Alexander Docher was a writer (lawyer) in Edinburgh, 1686 (RPC., 3. ser. XII, p. 230). Dequhar, Deuchair, Deuchars, Deucharys, Deucher, Deuchor, Deughar, Deugher, Deuquhair, Deuquhar, Deuquhare, Deuquhyre, Dewchare, Dewquhar, Docher, Docker, Doker, Doucher, Doughar, Douquhar, Dowchar, Dowgar, Duchar, Duchre, Duquhar (1570), Duquhare (1713), Dwichair (1581).

DEUCHART. A surname found in Caithness, probably = DEUCHAR with accretionary *t*.

DEVER. Perhaps from Ir. *O'Duibhidhir*, a variant of *O'Dubhuidhir*, descendant of Dubhodhar.

DEWAR. G. *Deoir*, *Deoireach*, in documents Jore (1428), from *deoradh*, a pilgrim, later an official designation which afterwards became a family name. In mediæval times the *deoradh* was the person who had custody of the relic of a saint. An old family of this name in Perthshire were for centuries custodians of the crozier-head of S. Fillan. After travelling to Canada this precious relic of the early Gaelic church is now preserved in the Scottish National Museum of Antiquities in Edinburgh. The name of the Skye family of Maclure, in G. *M'Leora* or *Mac a'Leoir* is for fuller *Mac Gille dheoradha*. See also MACINDEOR and MACJARROW. (2) Of territorial origin from Dewar in the parish of Heriot, Midlothian. Thomas de Deware and Pieres de Dewere of Edinburghshire rendered homage in 1296 (*Bain*, II, p. 208, 209).

DEY. A variant of DAY, q.v.

DEYELL. A form of DALYELL, q.v., current in Shetland. See also under YELL.

DIACK, DYACK. The surname Diack appears for the first time in Aberdeenshire about the close of the seventeenth century, principally about the parish of Logie-Durno. Alexander Diack in Craigsley, 1781 (*Aberdeen CR.*). A tradition among bearers of the name is that the family came from Denmark (Sc. N. & Q., III, p. 29). Sir Alexander Henderson Diack was senior financial commissioner of the Punjab. Mr. Francis C. Diack has published *The Newton Stone and other Pictish inscriptions*, Paisley, 1922, and later studies along the same lines. Said to be an Aberdeenshire form of DICK, but?

DIBBS. A surname recorded in Fife. A contraction of *Dibble*, itself a pet form of Theobald.

DICHMOUNT. Marion Dichmount in Revingstruther, parish of Carstairs, 1626 *(Lanark)* probably derived her surname from Dechmont in the parish of Cambuslang, Lanarkshire. Thomas Dechmone was first recorded schoolmaster in the parish of Shotts, 1650 (Grosart, *Parish of Shotts*, 1880, p. 193). See also DECHMONT.

DICK. A diminutive of RICHARD, q.v. Anderson (*Scot. Nat.*, II, p. 31) errs in saying that William de Dyck was first magistrate of Edinburgh (1296) — the magistrate's name was Dederyk. John Dic, witness in Ayr, 1490 (*Ayr*, p. 94), Wille Dic was 'dekin of the bakstaris' of Stirling, 1526 (SBR., p. 28), John Dyk or Dik was bailie of David, earl of Craufurd in Perthshire, 1547 (*Gaw*, 46), and Alexander Dik was archdean of Glasgow, 1555 (REG., p. 581–582). Sir William Dick of Braid, owner (for his time) of the vast fortune of £226,000 (equal to more than £2,000,000 at the present day), financier of the armies of the Covenant and upholder of the Stewart cause, had his reward by dying of starvation in a debtor's prison in Westminster, 1658. Sir Charles Dick, lineal descendant of Sir William, acting as custodian of the Brighton Museum, renewed application in 1873 for the meagre pension which had been continued under successive sovereigns till 1845 (Wilson, *Memorials of Edinburgh*, II, p. 10).

DICKIE. A diminutive of DICK, q.v. Robert Dikky is recorded in Glasgow in 1504 (*Simon*, 87). Money was given 'Sir' Archibald Dikkie, "for rowelling and gyding of the knok and for lying nychtlie in the tolbuth to rewll and keip the samyne and for helping and support of him to bed clais," 1583 *(Burgesses)*. David Dickie was burgess of Montrose in 1627 *(Brechin)*.

DICKINSON, 'son of Dickin or little Dick.' This surname is more common in England. Dickconsoune 1488. See DICKSON.

DICKMAN. Probably from the occupation, a maker or repairer of dikes, a ditcher. William Dickman in Hawick, 1688 *(Peebles CR.)*.

DICKSON, 'son of DICK,' q.v. A Border surname. Thom or Thomas Dicson was the faithful follower of the Douglas in the surprise and capture of Castle Douglas on Palm Sunday, 1307 (Barbour, *Brus*, IV, Jamieson's ed.). William Dicsoun witnessed a charter by John Skinner, burgess of Inverness, c. 1360 (*Grant*, III, p. 12), and William Dicson or Dicsoun appears as bailie of Aberdeen in 1398 (SCM., v, p. 13; CRA., p. 376). Andrew Dicsoun held

a land in Edinburgh, 1400 (*Egidii*, p. 37), Henry Dikson, Scotsman, had a safe conduct into England in 1426 and William Dicson, Scotsman, had the same in 1445 (*Bain*, IV, 990, 1181), and James Dekyson or Dekysoun was rector of Kirkbutho, 1472, and prebendary of Guthre, 1474 (REB., I, 114; II, 198). Wyll Dekyson, custumar, witnessed resignation of a feu in Peebles, 1471 (*Scots Lore*, p. 52), Patric Dicson de Mersantone granted a charter of land to his son and heir, Robert Dicson, 1472 (BNCH., XXIV, p. 89), and Patrik Diksone, William Diksone, and Thomas Diksone were summoned in 1479 to answer to Parliament for treason and other crimes (APS., II, p. 129). William Dekesoune was charged with the slaughter of George Myddilmest, 1513 (*Trials*, I, p. 87°), the seal of Isobel Dyxsoun is appended to a charter of lands in the town of Yester dated 1527 (*Macdonald*, 643). Bessie Dikesone appears in Dernik, 1606 (RRM., I, p. 11), and John Dichison was shoemaker in Aberdeen, 1721 (NSCM., II, p. 109). Two brothers, Dickson of Montrose, went to Sweden in beginning of nineteenth century, engaged in business and amassed great wealth. A descendant, Oscar Dickson (1823–1897), made many gifts to science, etc., and fitted out Nordenskiöld's Spitzbergen expedition in 1872. Decesovne 1481, Dekeson 1513, Dekisoun 1473, Dekysoun 1457, Dickesoun 1488, Dikesoune 1567, Dikessoune 1567, Dikiesoun 1607, Dikkesone 1505, Dikkyson 1515, Diksonne 1616, Dikyson 1488, Duckieson 1712, Duckison 1724, Dukison 1647, Dyxsoun 1527; Dikesoun, Dikkesoun, Dykesoun.

DIKIN. A double diminutive of RICHARD, q.v., an early form of which is *Dic(c)on*. Dikin, *incisore*, witnessed gift of Okelsfas to the Abbey of Holyrood in reign of William the Lion (LSC., p. 212).

DILDARG. Of local origin from old lands of the name in Angus. Andrew Dilldarg is recorded in Balzordie in 1656 *(Brechin)*, and John Dildarg was schoolmaster of Fern in Angus in 1778 (Jervise, *Land of Lindsays*, p. 428).

DILL. Thomas dictus Dyll witnessed a charter by John Skinner, burgess of Inverness, c. 1360 (*Grant*, III, p. 12), and Marjorie *dicta* Dyll held land in Inuernys, 1361 (REM., p. 305). Still current.

DILLIDAFF. A corruption of TILLIEDAFF, q.v. John Dillidaff was charged with assault and fined "ten pond scotis" in 1668 (*Corsehill*, p. 80), and in 1673 complaint was made by

John Dilliedaff, perhaps the same individual, at Kirktoune in 1673 (ibid., p. 112). Henry Dillidasse (probably a misreading of Dillidaffe) had a feud with Sinclair of Sandwich in the sixteenth century (Mill, *Diary*, p. 117). Dilledaffe 1649, Dillodaffe 1649, Dillydaffe 1657.

DIN. An old Strathblane surname, frequent in Fintry in the seventeenth and eighteenth centuries. Nine of the name are recorded in the Commissariot Record of Dunblane from and after 1664. William Din appears in Cardoroche, parish of Calder, 1627 (*Campsie*), Thomas Din in Glencaple, 1639, and two more in Dumfries Commissariot Record. Thomas Din in Mylne-lands, 1667 (*Lanark CR.*), David Dinn and Roger Dinn in Laight, 1686 (RPC., 3. ser. XII, p. 151), and William Din in Slogenholl, 1693 (*Dunkeld*). Payment to John Din in Edinburgh, 1733 (*Guildry*, p. 146).

DINGWALL. From the lands of Dingwall in Ross. A charter by William, earl of Ross, 1342, is witnessed by John Yonger of Dyngvale; and between 1350–72 another charter by the same earl is witnessed by John called Yong and Thomas, his brother (OPS., II, p. 491). In 1389 William of Dyngwale appears as dean of Aberdeen and Ross (REM., p. 354). Thomas of Dyngvale, canon, is a charter witness, 1451, and in 1463 Thomas the younger of Dingvale had a grant of the lands of Usuy in the earldom of Ross with remainder to his brother, John of Dingvale and his heirs and to the better and more worthy successor of his relatives of the name, in exchange for the third part of Arkboll and the lands of Inchfure, etc. Thomas Dingwell was admitted burgess of Aberdeen, 1548 (NSCM., I, p. 61). Sir John Dingwall, provost of Trinity College, Edinburgh, one of the Senators of the College of Justice, in 1532, had his Edinburgh residence, Dingwall Castle, on the ground now occupied by the buildings at the junction of Waterloo Place and (old) Shakespeare Square. Some severe Latin verses on him by George Buchanan are quoted in Brunton and Haig's *Senators of the College of Justice*, p. 11. He is also the "Sir John Dingwell" or Dungwail whom John Knox accuses of having "according to the charitie of Kirkmen," entertained the wife, and wasted the substance of one Alexander Furrour during the latter's confinement in the Tower of London (*History of the Reformation*, 1790, p. 73). Dingval 1528, Dinguel 1571, Dingvall 1555, Dingvaile and Dingvaille 1460, Dingvell 1567, Dingwell 1506, Dyngwaile 1525.

DINMILL. Local. From Denmill, a small place near Benvie in Angus, in 1750 Dinmill, or Denmill near Guthrie (1640 map). See DEN-MILN.

DINNELL. William Dinnall appears in Inglistoun, parish of Twynholm, 1734 (*Kirkcudbright*), and Archibald Dinnel, merchant in Buyach, 1797 (*Wigtown*).

DINNES. Helen Dynnes in Montrose in 1629 and four more of the name are recorded in Brechin Commissariot Record. Two brothers named Dinnes from Millbrex served in the first Great War (*Turriff*). Duness 1657.

DINNETT. Most probably a variant of DUN-NET, q.v.

DINNIE. This surname is confined principally to Deeside, and may be of local origin. There is a Water of Dinnie which empties into the Dee in the parish of Birse. David Dynnie in Little Margie, a follower of Ross of Pitcalny (RPC., v, p. 31) may have derived his surname from Denoon.

DINNING. A variant of DUNNING, q.v.

DINSMORE. See under DUNMORE.

DINWIDDIE, DINWOODIE, DINSWOODIE. Of territorial origin from the lands or barony of Dinwoodie in the parish of Applegarth, Dumfriesshire. Sir Alan de Dunwidi was seneschal of Annandale in the first quarter of the thirteenth century (Bain, I, 1685), and Adam de Dunwidie witnessed a quit claim of the lands of Weremundebi and Anant c. 1194–1214 (ibid., I, 606). Between 1218 and 1245 Adam de Dunwudhi was witness to a quit claim of land in Annan (ibid., I, 705; *Annandale*, I, p. 6). Aleyn de Dunwvthve of Berwickshire rendered homage in 1296 (Bain, II, p. 206). John de Dunwothy, *dominus ejusdem*, appears as charter witness, 1361 (PSAS., XXIII, p. 30). In 1504 Thomas Dunwedy of that Ilk was slain by the Jardings at his place of Dunwedy, and in 1512 another laird of the name was slain in Edinburgh. In 1504 Robert Dunwedv, son of the laird, was convicted of stouthreif, and Nicolas Dunwedv was hanged for reset of theft (*Trials*, I, p. 40*, 41*). Jean Dinwoodie was examined for the Test in Tinwald, 1685 (RPC., 3. ser. XI, p. 433). Robert Dinwiddie, born in Glasgow in 1693, was governor of Virginia from 1751 to 1758. His recommendation of the annexation of the Ohio vallev secured that great territorv to the United States. This surname is spelled in more than one hundred forms in old Scots records.

DIONYSIUS. See under DENNIS. Dionysus the Greek vine-god appears in hagiology as S. Denis.

DIPPIE. A surname of French origin from the town of Dieppe. From the massacre of St. Bartholomew, 1572, onward through the reigns of Louis XIII and XIV, French Protestants underwent violent and relentless persecution and many fled for refuge to Britain. Among them were the ancestors of the Dippies. Katharine Dippo was married in Edinburgh in 1595, and Hendre Depo in Langshaw is recorded in 1606 (RRM., I, p. 7). Robert Dippie (or Dieppe or Dippe), upholsterer and trunkmaker in Coldtoune, Edinburgh, made a marriage contract in October 1663, his will was proved in 1676, and he was buried in Greyfriars' churchyard. James Dipo died in 1695, and was buried in Earlston churchyard, and Peter Dippie of Chirnside, died in 1881 in his eightyeighth year. See the Border magazine for 1909.

DIPPLE. From the name of an ancient suppressed parish in Moray. Walter de Duppul had a yearly pension of 3 marks from the bishop of Moray in 1328 (Pap. Lett., II, p. 285). The parish was united with Essil in 1743 to form the modern parish of Speymouth. Rev. John Scott (d. 1738), minister of Dipple, emigrated to the American colonies, became minister of Overwharton parish, Stafford county, Virginia, and called his estate there Dipple.

DIREKSON. Probably from Dutch Dierk (for fuller Dietrich) + son. Magnus Direkson in Grutquoy in Walls, 1620 (Shetland).

DIRLAND. From IRELAND, q.v., with the French preposition 'de' coalesced. Johannes Dirlaund, a Scots prisoner of war in Northampton, 1296 (Bain, IV, p. 358). Thomas Dirland of Roxburghshire rendered homage in the same year. His seal bears a fleur-de-lvs and S' Tome de Ybernia (ibid., II, p. 213, 555). William Dirlande, a Scot taken at Stirling Castle was prisoner of war in Newcastle, 1305 (ibid., p. 437, 439).

DIRLETON. From Dirleton in the parish of the same name in East Lothian, old forms of which are Driltone (1288) and Dryltoun (1438). Robert fiz Adam de Dreltone of the county of Edneburk rendered homage in 1296 (Bain, II, p. 209). Symon de Driltona held land in Berwyck before 1324 (RAA., I, p. 220). Robertus de Drilton, 1329 (ER., I, p. 211). Dirleton was an early possession of the family of VAUS who brought the place name from England.

DIRLOWENAN. Nichole Dirlowenan agreed to serve Edward I of England in France or elsewhere, 1297 (Bain, II, p. 243).

DIROM. An old surname in Dumfriesshire, apparently a corruption of DURAND, q.v. Wautier Durand or Durant who held land in Dumfriesshire in thirteenth century may have given name to the parish of Kirkpatrick-Durand, later corrupted to Durham, the change probably influenced by Durham in England. John Dirrin in Kirkpatrick-Fleming, 1657 (Dumfries). Alexander Dirom, wright in Aberdeen, 1725 (NSCM., II, p. 116). General Alexander Dirom (1757–1830) entertained Robert Burns at Cleughead, Dumfriesshire, in 1795. Dirom also appears as surname in Banff in eighteenth century and is still current there. See also DURHAM.

DIRRINGTON. From the lands of Dirrington, near Longformacus, Berwickshire. William de Diuringdon held the lands before 1316 for an annual payment of five shillings with ward and relief (Kelso, p. 465). (The name is misspelled Dunrigdon in Morton's Monastic annals, p. 168.) A moiety of the lands of Derrington were held by Joneta Schaw, heiress of William de Deryngtone, c. 1329–1334 (Kelso, p. 405).

DISHART. A Fife surname. Sir Michael Disert, preceptor of the Augustinian house of S. Anthony, Leith, 1542 (PSAS., LXIV, p. 289). John Dishart in St. Andrews, 1689 (ibid., LIV, p. 242).

DISHINGTON. The surname of a family prominent first in Angus and afterwards in the East Neuk of Fife from the early fourteenth century to the sixteenth century. Through intermarriage the Dishingtons became connected with many prominent Scottish families. The name appears to be derived from Dissington in Northumberland, in OE. Dicing(a)-tūn, the farm or tūn of *Dica or his sons. The name is often familiarly contracted (in pronunciation) to Distin. A couplet of a ballad of unknown date and unknown authorship runs:

"Were you e'er in Crail town,
Saw you there Clerk Dischington."

The first of the name recorded in Scotland appears to be Sir William de Dissingtoun who received from Robert I a charter of the lands of Balglassy in the thanedom of Abirlemenache in Angus (RMS., I, App. I, 78). William de Dyssingtoun witnessed a donation bv Henry de Avnestrother to the Abbev of Dryburgh c. 1330 (Dryburgh, 252). W. de Disscvngtone witnessed a confirmation charter by David II to Ysabelle de Fyf in 1365, and as William de Dissyngton he witnessed another charter in Edinburgh in 1364 (RMS., I, 187, 221). King Robert III granted to Thomas Eshington (= Dishington) a charter of the lands of Tulliwhenland (*Warden*, II, p. 295). Sir William Dysshvngton was a Scots hostage in England in 1427 (*Bain*, IV, 1005), and John of Dyshvnton, Scotsman, had a safe conduct to travel in England in 1447 (ibid., IV, 1201). In 1457 Dischington of Ardross in Fife was one of the assizers in the perambulation of the marches of Easter and Wester Kinghorn, and in 1495 John Dissington of Ardrosse had license to import Scottish goods into England (*Bain*, IV, 1619), and Bessie Dishon was forbidden in 1512 "to set (i.e. to lease) her house, but at sight of the Baillies" of Dysart (*Dysart*, p. 28). A branch of the family of Dishington settled in Orkney about the end of the sixteenth century, and John Dischingtoun appears there as depute of the earl of Orknev at the Castle of Scallowav in 1602 (MCM., II, p. 145), and in 1660 Thomas Dishington was minister at St. Magnus Cathedral. Some Dishingtons also emigrated to Norway and appear there as Dessingtons. Deschentone 1542, Dischingtoun 1550, Dischinton 1567, Dischyntoun 1548, Disscyngton 1365, Dissyngton 1364, Dissyntoun 1387, Dysschingtoun 1329.

DISQUAN. Evidently of local origin. William Disquan in Schilliheid, parish of Roberton, 1621, and one more of the name (*Lanark CR.*).

DISSELDUFF. A curious corruption of TILLIEDAFF through the form DILLIDAFF. Captain John Disselduff, M. C., was presented with a piece of silver plate as a mark of esteem on the occasion of his semi-jubilee as sheriff-clerk depute at Oban in 1930.

DITCHBURN. A rare surname. I have found it only in the Glasgow Directory. Of local origin from Ditchburn in Northumberland. James Ditchburn of Ushaw Moor (Cumberland) was author of *The Deil's reply to Robert Burns*, published in 1793 and now a very rare item.

DIVERTIE, DIVORTY, DOVERTIE. Martin Diverty was vicar of Pettv in 1492 (*Rose*, p. 156). Andrew Durty who appears in record in Aberdeen in 1538 was one of assize on Gypsies in the same burgh in 1540 as Andrew Durtty, and he appears again in 1546 as Andrew Dirty (CRA., p. 153, 167, 238). As Andrew Dwerttv he is recorded again in 1568 (SCM., II, p. 35). John Durtty was admitted burgess of Aberdeen in 1543, John Douerty in 1560, and Gilbert Devertie in 1589 (NSCM., I, p. 58, 67, 69, 81). Agnes Dovartie appears in Aber-

deen, 1594 (CRA., p. 93), and John Dovertie in Ardo, 1633 (SCM., III, p. 118). Thomas Davortie pursued another for debt in 1674 (*Corsehill*, p. 117), James Divertye was at Bridge of Don, 1688 (RPC., 3. ser. XIII, p. 263), and Margaret Doverty was mantua maker in Newburgh, 1784 (*Aberdeen CR.*). Dortve 1596. The name Doraty recorded in Manitoba may be another spelling.

DIVETT. Recorded in Aberdeen. A shortened form of Ir. *MacDaibheid*, son of David.

DIXON. This is the English form of Scottish DICKSON, q.v.

DOAG. *See under* DOIG.

DOAK. A variant of DOIG, q.v. William Dowok in Lones is mentioned in 1623 (*Prestwick*, p. 129). Robert Dook was thesaurer of the burgh of Ayr, 1646 (*Ayr*, p. 161), and James Dock heir of John Dock, "burgis of Air his guidsir brother son," 1654 (*Retours, Ayr*, 464). Robert Doak in Prestwick, 1782.

DOBARCU. *See under* MACDOBARCON.

DOBBIE, DOBIE. The tradition that the first of this name in Scotland came from France in the time of Mary Queen of Scots and that the name is Scotticized from De Bois is erroneous. The surname, which is simply from DOBB, a pet form of ROBERT, with the diminutive suffix -ie, existed in Scotland long before the time of Queen Mary. Thomas Doby, younger, burgess of Peblis, son of Thomas Doby, elder, resigned the feu of his land in 1471 (*Scots Lore*, p. 51). John Dobie was pledge for Nicol Bauld in 1490 (*Lanark*, p. 6), and in the same year William Doby held part of the land of Weitlandsid (ibid., p. 8). Sir Alexander Doby, a Pope's knight, is recorded in Perth in 1506 (*Rent. Dunk.*, p. 197). John Dobv was rector of Ancrum in 1525 (REG., 497), William Doby was witness in Dumfries in 1542 (*Anderson*), an annual-rent of William Dobv in Peebles is recorded in 1557 (ER., XIX, p. 9), and Richard Dobie had charter of the lands of Staniehill in 1608 (RD., p. 503). As forename: Dobi Spendluf in Peebles, 1457 (Renwick, *Peebles*, p. 23). Dobe 1462.

DOBBIN. A diminutive of DOBB, which itself is a pet diminutive of ROBERT.

DOBERVILLE. *See under* OBERVILLE.

DOBIE. *See under* DOBBIE.

DOBIESON, 'son of DOBBIE,' q.v. John Dobysoun was burgess of Lanark in 1429 (HMC., 5. Rep., App., p. 633).

DOBINSON, 'son of DOBBIN,' q.v. William Dobynsoun, juror at Irvine, Ayrshire, 1417 (*Irvine*, I, p. 20). Cf. DOBIESON.

DOBSON, 'son of DOB or DOBB,' a pet diminutive of ROBERT. John Dobsoun was tenant of the abbot of Kelso in 1567 (*Kelso*, p. 520), and John Dobsone is recorded in Selkirk in 1675 (RRM., III, p. 86).

DOCHARD, DOCHART. Of local origin from Dochart in the parish of Killin, Perthshire.

DOCHERDICH. Local. Elspeth Duchartoch in Edinkip, 1663 (*Dunblane*), and John and Don. Docherdich in the parish of Comrie, 1665 (ibid.).

DOCKAR. Surname recorded in Gamrie in seventeenth century. Most probably an early variant of DEUCHAR, q.v.

DOCKRAY. From Dockray, a hamlet near Matterdale in Cumberland.

DOCTOR. Among early Scots charters are notices of hereditary physicians who enjoyed lands in virtue of their office. One of these physicians is favorably noticed in Rymer: "Littera ab Alexandro primogenito Regis Scottorum pro Ade Kercudbright, medico quondam Roberti de Brus, qui contra communem medicorum opinionem ipsum sanitati restituerat," Scone, 3 Julii, 1282 (*Fœdera*, new ed., I, 611). Magister Martin, 'medico meo,' witnessed a charter by William the Lion, before 1214 (RAA., I, 71). As Martin, medicus, he witnessed a grant by Richard filius Michael to the Hospital of Soltre between 1189–1214 (*Soltre*, p. 8). Henry, medicus, witnessed a charter by Hugh, cancellarius regis, to the Abbey of Arbroath, c. 1189–99 (RAA., I, 80), and about the same period witnessed a charter by Hugh, bishop of St. Andrews (RPSA., p. 290).

DODD. Most probably from the OE. personal name *Dodd, Dodda*, given under several forms by Searle. Willelmus Dodde de inuirkethi, who appears as witness in a document of end of thirteenth century (RD., p. 116), as William Dod, burgess of Inverkeithing, rendered homage, 1296 (*Bain*, II, p. 198). There was an ancient clan of this name in North Tyne.

DODDS, DODS. (1) Perhaps local. There were lands of Doddis in the barony of Bowne, Berwickshire, 1610 (*Retours, Berwick*, 92); (2) from 'son of DODD,' q.v., but most probably from (1). Alexander Dodys, servant to Patrick of Dunbarre, had a safe conduct in England, 1425 (*Bain*, IV, 986). In 1469 there is recorded a dispensation in favor of William Doide and Eufrata, daughter of Roderic Hugonis alias Hucheson of the diocese of Caithness empowering them to marry lawfully, they being related within the forbidden degrees. William Doddis, witness in Golspetoure (Golspie tower), 1527 and 1542 (OPS., II, p. 677–678). The Doide or Dodds family were connected with the parish of Golspie until within the last hundred years. They held Golspie tower in the sixteenth century, and it is very likely that the above William Doide was a member of the family. Svmon Dodis or Doddis, canon of the cathedral church of Aberdeen, 1486, is mentioned in 1489 and 1493 as also holding the rectory of Innernothy (REA., I, p. 333; II, p. 299, 302). Robert of Doddys and Archie, his son, 'Englishmen,' were charged by the prior of Canonby (Canonbie, Dumfriesshire), with stealing from the lands of Canonby certain kie, oxen, shepe, and geite (goats) in 1494 (*Bain*, IV, p. 418). James Doddis was prior of the friars preachers, Wigtown, 1558 (ER., XXII, p. 47). James Doddis of Murecleuch, 1661 (RRM., I, p. 341). The name was early carried to France and appears there to this day.

DOE. A current surname, though not common. Charles Do was witness in Perth, 1546, and Cuthbert Do was witness there, 1547 (*Rollok*, 35, 42). Harrison explains the name as a nickname or sign-name from the doe, the female deer, and Bardsley records 'le Do' and 'le Doe' in 1273.

DOEG. See under DOIG.

DOIG, DOAG, DOAK, DOEG. "Dog, Dogg, Doig, the surname of several landed families in the Kilmadok district, is for *Gille Dog*, 'St. Cadoc's servant.' " "From Doc, Dog, Dogg, Doge, Doig, now Doig, Doag, Doak, a surname which appears often on record, almost always in the neighbourhood of...places in which Cadoc was commemorated. . . Alexander Dog was canon of Inchmahome in Menteith in 1491, when he resigned his lands of Auchounbannow to his brother James. In 1532 James Dog of Dunrobin, in Menteith, got the lands of Severie in the parish of Kilmadok. In 1608 we find James Dog of Ballingrew, a place in Menteith. Alexander Graham, of Douchray, writing in 1724, mentions 'Dog of Ballingrew, a family now extinct.' John Dog of Gartincaber, in Menteith, appears in 1583; in 1608 James Dog is styled of Gartincaber. Alexander Dog of Murdestoun, in Menteith, appears in 1559; the family is often mentioned later. In 1620 there is John Dog in Ballindornick in Menteith. In 1615 Mareona Dog is wife of David Mushet of Calyiechatt, in Kilmadock parish. Thomas Dog was in Craigmackerrane, near Perth, in

1645. In 1583 John Dog was servitor of the earl of Gowrie. The following are connected with Forfarshire. In 1500 John Dog was in Wester Lowrie. William Dog, burgess of Dundee and a landed man besides, appears from 1492 to 1513. In 1643 Robert Dog was in Lumlathin. David Dogg or Doig was messenger in Forfar, 1653 to 1667" (Prof. Watson, *Scottish Gaelic studies*, II, p. 10, 11). All the foregoing references, says Prof. Watson, are from RMS. Mr. Alexander Doge was vicar of Dunnychtyne (now Dunnichen) in 1372 (REB., I, 20), and about 1449–50 another Alexander Dog or Doge, probably a descendant, was vicar of the same place (ibid., I, 130; II, 77). Patrick Dog of Kranne in record in the forest of Platane, 1472, and Walter Dog was tenant of Kyncrech, 1478 (*Cupar-Angus*, I, p. 161, 213). James Dog was exempted from process while in French service, 1552 (RPC., VIII, p. 136). There was a burgess family of Doigs in Brechin who held property there in the early part of the sixteenth century (REB.), and some were chief magistrates of the town between 1700 and 1741. William Dog was admitted burgess of Aberdeen in 1457 (NSCM., I, p. 16), Johon Dog, who was burgess of Dundee in 1490 (RAA., II, 326), may be John Dog who appears as witness at Cortachy in 1491 (*Laing*, 379). James Dog is celebrated by the poet Dunbar as "The Wardraipper of Venus boure." Johnne Dog in Scottistoun and James Dog, his son, were followers of Campbell of Lundy in 1529 (RSS., II, 59), and John Doge witnessed an infeftment of lands of Qwchtyreleth in 1533 (*Bamff*, p. 61), Thomas Dog leased part of the lands of Craigmakerane in 1585 (*Scon*, p. 227), and a later Thomas Doig of the same lands is recorded in 1644 (*Inquis.*, 2983). James Dog, feeir of Dunrobin, was a witness at the Doune of Menteith in 1606 (*Coll.*, p. 132), Janet Doog is recorded in Edinburgh in 1647 (*Edinb. Marr.*), John Dock, smith, was burgess of Air, 1654 (*Retours, Ayr*, 464), and Robert Dook, glessenwright (glazier) in Irvine, 1681 (*Irvine*, II, p. 297). Dr. David Doig (1719–1800), rector of Stirling Grammar School, whom Burns met on his Highland tour, contributed articles on Oriental and Classical subjects to the Encyclopædia Britannica.

DOLEPAIN. William Dolopen was one of the witnesses to a deed of the time of Richard, bishop of St. Andrews (1163–68) (RPSA., p. 319). Willelmus dolepenne witnessed a grant by Bernard filius Brien to the Abbey of Kelso, c. 1165–71 (*Kelso*, 214), and c. 1168, as Willelmus de Olepene, he appears again as a charter witness (*Cambus.*, 52). Gilbertus Dolepene witnessed charters concerning the lands

of the churches of Garviach, etc., by Earl David, brother of William the Lion, c. 1200–14 (LAC., p. 10; RAA., I, p. 56). "The form Dolepain probably arises from the phonetic adhesion of the *d* in 'de.' It is doubtless the same witness who appears in no. XI (1195–98) as 'Gilbertus Olepain,' and in no. XII (same date) as 'Gilbertus de Holepen.' We find a 'Willelmus Dolepen,' witnessing a deed of the time of Richard, bishop of St. Andrews" (LAC., p. 236).

DOLFIN. An old English personal name, even before the Norman Conquest. Dolfin, son of Earl Cospatric, was earl of Cumberland c. 1085. Searle records several of the name, and as Dolfinus and Dolfyn it was still a personal name in the fourteenth century. "Dalfin or Dolfin was a name so common that, in the absence of record, conjecture must be fruitless as to the individual from whom the manorial village [Dolphinton] took its appellation" (OPS., I, p. 130). In the early part of the twelfth century the Dolfins swarmed in Cumberland "as thick as leaves on Vallambrosa."

DOLFINESTONE. Reynaud de Dolfinestone of Roxburghshire rendered homage in 1296. His seal bears a monster emerging from sea (?), S' *Reginaldi de Do . . n . on* (*Bain*, II, p. 199, 532). He probably derived his name from Dolphiston in the parish of Oxnam, Roxburghshire. Dolphinton in Lanarkshire (in 1253, Dolfinston) may have been named from Dolfin, son of Gospatric, who appears in the *Inquisitio Davidis* (c. 1124), though "Dalfin, or Dolfin, was a name so common, that, in the absence of record, conjecture must be fruitless as to the individual from whom the manorial village took its appellation" (OPS., I, p. 130).

DOLLAR. Of local origin from the town of Dollar in Clackmannanshire. Matthew de Doler was one of an inquest at Kyrcaldy, 1316 (RD., p. 235), Willielmus de Dolar was charter witness apud Dunfermellyn, 1412 (ibid., p. 280), and Andrew Dollare is in record, 1526 (*Cambus.*, 141). Robert Dollour and James Dollour were burgesses of Kirkintilloch, 1654, and Andrew Dollour was weaver there, 1665 (*Sasines*, 870, 1223). John Dollor was church elder in parish of Logie, 1701 (*Logie*, I, p. 148). Robert Dollar (1844–1932), a native of Falkirk, was a great shipping magnate in the United States, founder of the Dollar Line of steamships.

DOLPATRICK. For Nigellus de Dolpatric, who appears as one of the witnesses to Earl Gilbert's great charter founding the monastery of Inchaffray in 1200, see under LOUTIT.

214

DOMANGART. From *domhan* (earlier *dumno* as in Donald — *Dumno-vall-*) and *gart*, head = 'world head.' The Welsh form is *Dyfnarth*. An early Gaelic personal name several bearers of which are recorded in early Scots annals. Domangart, son of Ness, king of Scotland, died c. 506 A. D. (*Early sources*, I, p. 4). Domingartus or Domangartus, son of Aidan mac Gabhran, was slain in battle "in Saxonia" (i.e. in England) according to Adamnan (*Vita S. Columbae*, I, 9), but according to Tighernach he was slain *i cath Chirchind* (in the battle of Circhend) which was fought in the Mearns, c. 598. Domangart or Domaingart, son of Donald Brecc, was killed c. 673 (*Early sources*, I, p. 182). Domongart, "ferleginn turbruad" (= Turriff) appears as witness in one of the Gaelic entries in the Book of Deer, 1132 (*Bk. Deer*, III, 9, 10).

DOMINGO. From the personal name Domingo, Spanish form of *Dominicus*. Harve Domingo was trumpeter in Aberdeen in 1605 (SCM., V, p. 79). Robert Domingo, journalist in Hawick, retired in 1935 after fifty years service. Cf. SPAIN.

DON, DAUN. Aberdeenshire surnames common in Mar. Matheus Done and Johannes Done were tenants in Strathdee, 1527 (*Grant*, III, p. 68). Don was the surname of a family which formerly possessed the lands of Teith in Monteith, Perthshire. David Done was witness in Glasgow, 1552 (*Protocols*, I), and Rev. George Daun, minister of Insch, Aberdeenshire, died 1821. In old spellings likely to be confused with DUNN. Dwne 1551.

DONACHIE. See under DONNACHIE.

DONAGHY. A curtailed form of *(Mac)donnchaidh*, for which see MACCONACHIE.

DONALD. This is one of the very oldest of our Gaelic personal names, and, from the greatness of Clan Donald, commonly considered as the Highland name pre-eminently. It, however, ranks only second, John being the first. The name has come down to us in two forms, Gaelic and Cymric. The modern Gaelic spelling of the name is Domhnall; in the Gaelic genealogical manuscript of 1467 and in the Gaelic entries in the Book of Deer (c. 1100) it is *Domnall*. The early Gaelic is also *Domnall* (Adamnan, VC, I, 7, *Domnall-us*, with ablative *Domnall*, III, 5). Dunegal (for Old Welsh *Dumngual* or *Dumnagual*) was lord of Stranit (Strath Nith in Dumfriesshire) in 1124, and Gillemor Macdunegal witnessed a charter of lands in Carric in the reign of Alexander II (*Melros*, I, p. 173). The early Welsh form (*Annales Cambriae*, ann. 760) is *Dumnagual*,

later Welsh *Dyfynwal* and *Dyfnwal*. In the *Gododin*, the old Welsh poem on the battle of Cattraeth (A. D. 603) it is *Dyvynwal*. In the Chartulary of Redon, Brittany, written in the eleventh century but dating largely from the ninth, we have the name in the fuller forms *Dumnouuallon* and *Dumuuallon* (*Loth*, p. 38). *Donewaldus*, king of the Britons, died in the reign of Constantine (900–943), and *Duuenaldus*, son of Ede (i.e. Aed) was chosen to succeed him. *Dunegal* was a native chief in the north-east corner of Caithness in early Norse times. The district in which he resided was named Dungalsbae (Dungalsboer) by the Norsemen, and is now Duncansbay.

These early forms of the name all point to early Celtic *Dubno-* or *Dumnovalos*, with the meaning of "world-mighty" or "world wielder," a name probably applied to themselves "by tribal rulers who had an exaggerated sense of their own importance." The first part of the name (*Dumno-*), as the late Sir John Rhys suggested, may mean the smaller world of the tribe before meaning the world in the wider sense (*Celtic Britain*, 3. ed., p. 297).

The earliest record of this name is not found in Britain, where one would naturally expect to find it, but in an inscription at the other end of the Roman empire in Galatia, engraved probably about the year 20 A. D. Suetonius in his life of the Emperor Augustus (B. C. 63 – A. D. 14) says the emperor by his last will desired an abstract of his achievements to be engraved on brazen tablets and placed before his mausoleum. The record was composed by Augustus himself before the year 2 B. C., and probably revised from time to time between that date and 14 A. D., the year of the emperor's death. The tablets perished in the downfall of the imperial city. Fortunately for us the inhabitants of Ancyra in Galatia, the modern Angor or Ankor, obtained from Rome a transcript of the emperor's record, the most important inscription of the Latin empire (the "Queen of Inscriptions," Mommsen the historian calls it), and engraved it with a Greek translation on the wall of a temple which they had erected in their city in honor of the emperor and the city of Rome. The Latin inscription was discovered in 1554 by Buybeeche, a Dutch scholar, and the Greek shortly after. Both inscriptions still exist, but as might be expected after so many years, both are imperfect in places. Fortunately the Greek is perfect in parts where the Latin is imperfect and vice-versa, so that practically the whole record can be read and understood. In this inscription is recorded the name of a British prince or petty king (*regulus*) otherwise almost unknown to history, except from a few of his coins which have been found in the south of

England. In his inscription Augustus says that among those kings who had betaken themselves to him as suppliants was "of the Britons, Dumnobellaunus." This Dumnobellaunus appears to have had dominion over the country of the Cantii (i.e. people of Kent) and later of the Trinobantes, a people who inhabited what is now modern Essex. From this he was expelled by Cunobelinos, the Cymbeline of Shakespeare. Coins of Dumnobellaunus have been found in Kent and in Essex, and on his gold issue his name appears more or less abbreviated as *Dvbno . . ., (Dv)bnovell . . ., Dvbnovilla, (Dvbno)viillavn*, and *Dvbno(vella)vnos* (Evans, *Coins of the ancient Britons*, p. 198–205, pl. iv).

The stem *Dumno-*, root of OIr. *domum*, Gaelic *domhan* "the universe," is common in Gaulish proper names, and *-vellaunos* had the meaning of "prince" or "one who ruled." It occurs also in the OE. title *Bretwalda* and better in the fuller form *Brytenwealda* "ruler of the Britons."

By the time the name "was first written in Gaelic the terminal *-os* had disappeared, the *v* had become vocalized, and the name was written Domnall although sounded Dovnall" (*Celt. Rev.*, vi, p. 3), and in Gaelic it is now written Domhnall. The devocalization of *-ll* final in Domhnall suggested to non-Gaelic ears that a *d* or *t* followed, hence in early Latin records and charters the name is written *Dovenald*, in English Donald, and the caricature *Tonalt*. The same explanation applies to Dougall — Dugald, Tugalt. Donald is sometimes erroneously rendered in English by Daniel. In Benbecula Domhnall is pronounced Domhull (with *mh* silent,) and the assimilation of *n* to *l* gives Doll (cf. Doull Macgilleduf, 1502, *Rose*, p. 176). In Badenoch Domhnall becomes Dò'ul, with nasalized *ò*. Rob Donn, the Gaelic poet, spells the name regularly *Do'll*, gen. *Dho'll*, and with Mac-, *Mac Dho'll*. In the Gaelic entries in the Book of Deer the name occurs three times regularly as Domnall, and in the twelfth and first half of the thirteenth century the spelling of the name (omitting the Latin ending *-us*) occurs as Dofnald, Dofnalt, Douenald, Douunald, Dufenald, Duuenald, and in 1255 Devenold. In the Norse *Orkneyinga Saga* the name occurs as *Dufnjáll*, a form which has probably arisen from confusion with the Norse personal name Njall. In a papal document of 1389 it is spelled Dompraldus. As a forename it is now quite commonly given to boys in England, and it is also becoming a favorite in the United States among non-Scots.

The contribution of Haket Donald for peace was paid to the bailie of Kinross in 1328 (ER., I, p. 103), and in 1398 Robert Donaldus was elected bailie of Aberdeen (CRA., p. 374).

In 1567 Ilene Donald was tenant of "ane quarter land" under the Abbey of Kelso (*Kelso*, p. 520), and George Donnald is in record as a merchant burgess of Jedburgh in 1641 (RRM., I, p. 86). Domh'll Phail (1798–1875) was known as the Shepherd Poet of Badenoch.

DONALDSON. An Englishing of MACDONALD, q.v. Lucas filius Douenaldi de Lumenach (Lennox), a Scots prisoner of war in Berkhamstede, 1296 (*Bain*, IV, p. 358). Henry Donaldson was one of the garrison of Edinburgh Castle in 1339–40 (ibid., III, p. 241). William filius Donaldi was a tenant under Douglas in Moffat, 1376 (RHM., I, p. lxii). Neuen (i.e. Niven) Donaldson was transferred to the jurisdiction of the court of regality of Logy, 1392 (*Grandtully*, I, p. 143). David Donaldson was one of the tenants of Camsy (Campsie) in 1443, and Jak Donaldson leased part of Cowpar Grange in 1453 (*Cupar-Angus*, I, p. 121, 129). The name is found in Aberdeenshire as early as 1419 (REA., II, p. 218), and Donaldsons were important individuals in Strathdee in early sixteenth century. Alexander Donaldson, son of Donald Symonson in Inverness, is in record in 1481 (*Invernessiana*, p. 154). Thomas Donaldson was tenant of Drumnamark, Ardmanoch, 1504 (ER., XII, p. 661), and Patrick Donaldsoun was keeper of the king's wardrobe in 1516 and following years (ALHT., v). Jean Dodson (i.e. Donaldson) in Kinclevin, 1685 (DPD., I, p. 488). Donaldsone 1503, Donaldsoune 1491, Donnaldsone 1695.

DONAN. Adam de Donan or Douan of Lanarkshire and Arthur de Donon of Ayrshire rendered homage in 1296 (RR.). There is a Dowan near Milngavie, Lanarkshire, with which the name may be connected.

DONCHILL. Local? Spulzie was committed upon William Donchill in Glennegas, 1546 (RPC., I, p. 66).

DONDOCH. Euuyn Dondoch was tenant on lands in Strathdee, 1527 (*Grant*, III, p. 68).

DONEWYCE. Thomas de Donewyce who rendered homage at Perth, 1291 (RR.), probably derived his name from Dunwich in co. Suffolk, c. 1175 Dunewiz.

DONGAN. From Ir. *Dongán*, a form of Duncan. William Dongane was repledged to liberty of burgh of Irvine, 1472 (*Irvine*, I, p. 28).

DONNACHIE, DONACHIE, DUNNACHIE. Small septs connected with Clan Robertson of Struan. See under MACCONACHIE. They are said to have adopted these forms of the name of the clan "in order to conceal their identity after the events of 1745" (*Adam*, p. 174).

DONNAN. A Wigtownshire surname, from Ir. O'Donnáin, 'descendant of Donnán,' diminutive of donn, brown, = English 'brownie.' Agnes Donnan in Whithorn, 1798 (Wigtown). See also MACILLDONANE.

DONNAT. John Donnat and Thomas Donnat witnessed a charter of land in Scone, .1491 (Scon, p. 199). David Donnit in Dundee was charged with aiding the English, 1552 (Beats, p. 327). Mark Donat in record in Dunfermline, 1586 (Dunfermline), and- James Donnat in Mourpersie, parish of Kingoldrum, 1679 (Brechin). Margaret Donnat was married in Edinburgh, 1939. Not likely to be from Dunnet, Caithness.

DONNELRIACH. Two of the Bethunes of Skye, Angus and Ewen, held the title of "Donnelriach," i.e. Domhnull Riach or Riabhach. "They were bold, fierce-looking, soldierly men, as well as medical specialists, hence probably the sobriquet" (Celt. Rev., IX, p. 80).

DOORS. A form of DUIRS, q.v.

DORAN. From Ir. O'Deoráin, a shortened form of O'Deóradháin. Deóradhán or Deóraidhin diminutive of deoradh, an exile, stranger (Woulfe). For meaning cf. DEWAR. John Dorrane and Martha Dorrane in Kirkcudbright, 1685 (Kirkcudbright).

DORBBENE. The oldest extant manuscript of Adamnan's Life of Columba was written by Dorbbene, who was elected abbot of Hi in 713. His name means 'tadpole,' Latinized Dorbbeneus.

DORCH. Payment was made for livery for Andro the Dorch, 1526, and in 1529 livery was given to John the Dorch (ALHT., v, p. 312, 383). Perhaps from G. dorch, 'dark,' as in Ir. mac Dorchaidh, MacGorty.

DORDOFE. Johan de Dordofe of the county of Dunfres, who rendered homage in 1296 (Bain, II, p. 206), probably derived his name from Torduff in the parish of Dornock, Dumfriesshire.

DORNOCH. From the town of Dornoch in Sutherland. Adam de Dornocht, acolyte of the diocese of Caithness, is in record in 1328 (Pap. Lett., II, p. 272, 273), and Walter Durnag was a charter witness in Aberdeen in 1450 (REA., II, p. 296).

DORRAT. A surname found in Fife and considered to be a corruption of DORWARD, q.v. John Dorrat was burgess of Brechin in 1753 (Brechin). See also DURRAT.

DORWARD, DURWARD. Several families in Scotland owe their surnames to tenure of office, and of these names so derived Durward is the greatest. Dorward, the form still common round Arbroath, is however, more likely to be derived "from the office of door-ward of the Abbey, than that so many descendants in humble life remain of the great family who had their surname from being Ostiarii Regis" (Neubotle, pref. p. xix). The surnames Porter and Usher (OF. ussher) are from the same office. Between 1208 and 1213 Galfridus, hostiarius of the bishop of Glasgow, witnessed confirmation of the sale of the land of Scrogges to the church of Glasgow (REG., p. 76), and another Galfridus, ostiarius, witnessed a charter by John, bishop of Dunkeld, c. 1199 (Inchaffray, p. 5).

The office of door-ward to the king (in Latin documents, 'hostiarius regis' or 'ostiarius regis') was a very honorable one, and in the beginning of the thirteenth century was hereditary in the powerful family of de Lundin, probably from Lundin in Fifeshire, but their actual origin is unknown. The de Lundins migrated to Aberdeenshire as the result of a prolonged lawsuit between the family and Duncan, earl of Mar, from whom Thomas de Lundin claimed the earldom through his mother, a daughter of Orabilia, countess of Mar, and her first husband, Earl Gilchrist. In this claim the family appears to have had the support of the Scottish kings (William the Lion and Alexander II) who wished to break up the old Gaelic Palatinate of Mar. The dispute was settled about 1228 and resulted in the de Lundins or Durwards obtaining an enormous lordship in the valley of the Dee, the greater portion of the earldom in fact. The first, perhaps, who took his name from the office (c. 1204–11) was Thomas de Lundyn, hostiarius domini regis (RAA., I, 59). His son was Alan Durward, one of the great figures in Scottish history during the thirteenth century. Alan married Marjorie, an illegitimate daughter of Alexander II, and for some time during the minority of Alexander III he was Regent of the kingdom. He died either in 1268 or 1275 (ES., II, p. 674), and his lands were divided among his three daughters. Thomas de [an error for 'le'] Durward was burgess of Arbroath in 1452 (RAA., II; p. 80), and John Durward and William Durward, son of John, held part of Burntown from the Abbey of Arbroath in 1478 (ibid., p. 179). John Durewarde held land in Brechin, 1508 (REB., II, 159), Thomas Durvart was tenant under the bishop of Aberdeen, 1511 (REA., I, p. 372), and Allane Duruart, a follower of the earl of Mar, was charged with resetting outlawed Macgregors, 1636 (RPC., 2. ser. VI, p. 215). Alexander Durwart in Craigendowie, parish of

Navan, 1668, and five more are in record (*Brechin*). Duruard 1504, Durwarde 1501, Durwartt 1541, Durwat 1478.

DORWOOD. A corrupt form of DORWARD, q.v.

DOTCHEOUN. John Dotchitoun (vel Dotchieltoun) was retoured heir to Gilbert Dotchitoun de Dowray, his father, in the 20s. lands of Dowray in 1629 (*Retours, Ayr*, 262). Another John Dotchin of Dowray is in record, 1670 (*Edin. App.*), John Dotchoun was portioner of Corsehill, 1633 (*Retours, Ayr*, 291), and John Dotcheoun was heir of John Dotcheoun of Dowray, his father, in the 20s. land of old extent of Dowray in the parish of Killwyning, 1668 (ibid., 502).

DOTHANE. John Dothane, monk in Kilwinning Abbey, 1532 (LCD., p. 12; *Coll. AGAA.*, I, p. 186). There is a Dothane in Fife.

DOTT. Perhaps a sharpened form of DODD. Henry Doyt is mentioned in 1343 (ER., I, p. 531), and William Dot appears as a witness in St. Andrews in 1475 (*Soltre*, p. 73). Dott 1492, Doit 1506. Ælfric *Dot* is recorded in DB. as 'nomen viri' (*Searle*).

DOUCHALL. Of local origin from Duchal in the parish of Kilmalcolm, Renfrewshire. Alexander Duchall had sasine of lands in Dumbarton in 1561 (ER., XIX, p. 484), and Elizabeth Douchall was retoured heir of Alexander Douchall of Ardochbeg in the earldom of Lennox in 1596 (*Retours, Dumbarton*, 2). Patrick Douchell is recorded in the paroch of Kilmalcom, 1675 (*Edin. App.*), and Patrick Duchal was minister of Logie parish, 1721 (*Logie*, I, p. 157).

DOUGAL, DOUGALL, DUGAL, DUGALD. G. *Dùghall*, MG. *Dowgall, Dubgaill* (gen., 1467 MS.). The OIr. form of the name is *Dubgall*, 'black stranger,' a 'Dane.' With 'Mac' we have MACDOUAL and MACDOUGAL, q.v. Dufgal occurs on a runic stone in the Isle of Man as *Tufcal*, and in the form *Duggall* it is found in Norse *Konunga Sögur* (p. 332). Dufgal filius Mocche, 'senex, justus, et venerabilis,' appears in a complaint by the monks of St. Serf's Island in Loch Leven c. 1128 (RPSA., p. 117). Reeves (*Culdees*, p. 130) says this Dufgal "resembles the old Dubhgall of Scone who is mentioned in the Irish tract on the men of Alba preserved in the Book of Ballymote and in MacFirbis genealogical MS. Old Dubhgall was father of Raingce whose son Aiscdhe was a progenitor of Clann Considhe in Bib" (Fife). But he occurs too high in the pedigree to admit of his being contemporary

with King David, 1124–53. In the Gaelic genealogical MS. of 1467 'Ruingr mc Sean Dubgall' is given as one of the ancestors of the Macleans. Duuegall, brother of Maldouen son of Alwin, earl of Levenax, witnessed the earl's gift of the church of Kamsi (Campsie) to S. Kentigern c. 1208–14, and as Duuegallus he appears c. 1208–33 (REG., p. 88, 93). Dugal, canon of Dunblane, was afterwards bishop (*Inchaffray*, p. 260), and Dugall, thane of Molen, 1261, was one of the inquisition on the king's garden at Elgin and the lands belonging to it (APS., I, p. 101 red). Patrick Dougale was burgess of Ayr, 1415 (*Ayr*, p. 11), and Edward Dougall was witness in Perth c. 1552 (*Rollok*, 114). Fraser (*Wardlaw*, p. 81) spells the name Duellus, and Doul or Dowill appears for Dougal, 1511, in a bond of manrent (SCM., IV, p. 195). The devocalization of -*ll* final suggested to non-Gaelic ears that a *d* or *t* followed, hence the spelling Dugald, and in caricature Tugalt. Dowgal 1527.

DOUGALSON. William Dougalsone or Dugalsone of the county of Lanark rendered homage in 1296. His seal bears device, a fish and the legend S' *Will' f' Dugalli* (Bain, II, p. 204, 186).

DOUGAN. *See under* DUGAN.

DOUGHTY. Perhaps from OE. *dyhtig*, ME. *doughty(e*, valiant. Ricardus Duchti held land in the vill of Traqwayre, 1365 (RMS., I, 202). Thomas Douchtie, 'ane heremeit foundit the cheppill of Lauriet besyid Mussilburgh" in 1533 (*Diur. Occ.*, p. 17). The hermit's name may be a variant of Duthie as it is also found spelled Duthy, Douchtie, and Dughtie (*History of regality of Musselburgh*, p. 95–96). In Wright's *Court hand restored* the name is Latinized *Durentius*.

DOUIE. *See under* DOWIE.

DOUGLAS, DOUGLASS. Of the Douglases, "the great, turbulent, daring, and too often treacherous house," as Lang calls them (*History*, I, p. 236), Hume of Godscroft, the old historian of the family, writing of their origin says "We do not know them in the Fountain but in the Stream; not in the Root, but in the Stock and Stem, for we know not who was the first mean Man that did raise . . . himself above the Vulgar" (*History of the house and race of Douglas*, 1743, pref., p. xiv). Of the sixteenth-century legend of the knight of 770 A.D. who was rewarded with the Clydesdale lands in return for his aid rendered a Scottish king at an opportune time there is not the slightest evidence, and no one nowadays places any dependence in the tale. The statement of

DOUGLAS, Douglass, *continued*

Chalmers (*Caledonia*, I, p. 579) that the Douglases sprang from Theobaldus a Fleming, who obtained a grant of lands on the Douglas Water from the abbot of Kelso is equally discredited. The lands granted by the abbot to Theobald the Fleming (*Theobaldus Flamaticus*) between 1147 and 1160, though on the Douglas Water, were not a part of the ancient territory of Douglas, and "there is no proof nor any probability of William of Douglas of the twelfth century, the undoubted ancestor of the family, being descended of the Fleming who settled on the *opposite* side of his native valley" (Innes, *Sketches*, p. 184). William de Duglas, the first of the family in record, between 1175 and 1199, witnessed a confirmation charter by Jocelin, bishop of Glasgow to the monks of Kelso (*Kelso*, 454), and was a witness to another charter to the canons of Holyrood by William the Lion about the year 1200 (LSC., p. 44). Between 1204 and 1211 William de Duueglas also witnessed a charter by Thomas, son of Thancard, in favor of the Abbey of Arbroath (RAA., I, 99). His son and heir, Archibald (Archabaldus, Archembald, Arkembald, Arkenbald, Erkembald or Erkenbald) de Duueglas appears as a witness to numerous charters in the chartularies of Melrose, Kelso, Newbattle, and Moray. The subsequent history of the Douglases is co-extensive with the history of Scotland. The principal stems are as follows: (1) the old Douglas of Douglasdale (the Black Douglas), illustrious in the War of Independence; (2) the senior cadet branch, the line of Morton, so largely bound up with the fortunes of Mary Queen of Scots; (3) the house of Drumlanrig and Queensberry, which came to its zenith with the "Union Duke;" and (4) that of Angus, the Red Douglas, which, after overthrowing the elder stock at Arkinholm (1455), played much the same part between Scotland and England as its kindred of the Black. In Argyllshire this territorial surname is used as an Englishing of MACLUCAS (MACLUGASH), q.v. Dawgleiss 1540, Dogles 1633, Douglace 1504, Douglase 1429, Dougleische 1583, Dougles 1529, Douglles 1688, Dovglas 1499, Dowglace 1511, Dowglas 1679, Dowglass 1559, Dowglasse 1684, Dufglas 1225, Dulglace 1454, Dulglass 1433, Duueglas 1220, Dwglas 1688, Dwglass 1399. The old pronunciation of the name was Doo-glas, the modern Dug-las. The Hon. Henry Maule alliteratively described Hume of Godscroft's *History* as "full of fables, falsehoods, and errors" (*Panmure*, I, p. lxxiii).

DOULL. A form of *Domhnall*. Cf. Doull Macgilleduf, 1502 (*Rose*, p. 176). In Badenoch

Domhnall becomes *Dò'ul*, with nasalized ó. Rob Donn (*Songs and poems*, Edinburgh, 1899, p. 455) spells the name *Do'll*, with genitive *Dhò'uill*. Iain Mac Dhoil mhic Huistean, of the Assynt Macleods, was the murderer of John Morison, the Lewis judge (*breitheamh*) about the end of the sixteenth century. A family of this name, of Thuster, appear in 1650 and continue to the present time (Henderson, *Caithness family history*, p. 324-325). Johne Duill, brebner, in Inverness, 1606, appears in following year as Dowill (*Rec. Inv.*, I, p. 41, 54). James Doull, elder in Wick, 1623 (*Caithness*), and James Doule was member of Gartly Company of Volunteers, 1798 (*Will*, p. 24). Sir William Patrick Andrew Doull, of the Caithness family, was chairman of the Scinde and Panjab Railway.

DOUNE. Of local origin from the village of Doune in the parish of Kilmadock, Perthshire. Four of this name are recorded in the Commissariot Record of Dunblane. Cf. Down.

DOVARY. Malise de Dovary, juror on inquest made at Perth, 1305 (*Bain*, II, 1670). Michael de Douery witnessed resignation by Sir David de Wemyss of certain lands, 1373 (*Wemyss*, II, p. 15). Sir Walter Dowary alias Robertson was accused of seizing a ship from a Swede, 1567 (RPC., II, p. 589). Perhaps old forms of Durie, q.v.

DOVE, Dow, Dowe. (1) From G. adj. *dubh*, 'black,' pronounced like Scots *doo*, 'pigeon;' (2) an Anglicizing of Maccalman, q.v.; (3) perhaps as a variant of Daw, diminutive of David. Ede Douw held a land in 'vico boreali,' Edinburgh, 1366 (RMS., I, 261; *Egidii*, p. 19), and John Dowe was one of an inquest taken at Berwick-on-Tweed, 1370 (*Bain*, IV, 175). George Dow appears in the Home manuscripts, 1479 (*Home*, 13). Dow is not uncommon in Perthshire appearing there in 1497, when Robert Dow held a land in Perth (RAA., II, 382). Gillaspy Dow was bailze of Troutiones (Trotterness), 1510 (*Trials*, I, p. 111*). Angus, son of John Dubh Macallister, is called Angus John Dowisoun in 1516 (RSS.), and Willzeme Dow is recorded in Strathdee, 1527 (*Grant*, III). Donald Dow was minister of Kilmorack and of other churches, 1574, and William Dove is in Corsehillock, parish of Glass, 1716 (SCM., IV, p. 168). John Dove, landlord of the Whitefoord Arms, Mauchline, was familiarly known as 'Johnie Doo' or 'Johnie Pigeon.' Burns wrote his epitaph.

DOVERTIE. A variant of DIVERTIE.

DOW, Dowe. *See under* DOVE.

DOWAL, DOWALL, DOWELL. G. *Dùghall*, for which see DOUGAL. Symon Dowele was servitor of earl of Douglas, 1408 (*Bain*, IV, 765). Doweill 1503, Dowill 1584.

DOWAN. From the old lands of Dowane (now Greenrig) in the barony of Lesmahagow. Between 1180 and 1203 Osbert, abbot of Kelso, granted to Constantine, son of Gilbert the priest of Lesmahago, the land of Dowane (*Kelso*, p. 77). His son was probably Adam de Dowane, who used the territorial designation. Sometime before 1240 Constantine de Dunan (an error for Duuan) witnessed a charter by Richard Bard of the land of Little Kip (parua Kype) (ibid., p. 150), and c. 1240 Daniel and Robert de Dowan and their wives were in dispute with the abbot of Kelso concerning their lands (ibid., 194). In 1294 Adam de Dowane, son of Daniel de Dowane, resigned his land of Dowane to the Abbey of Kelso for a sum of money (ibid., p. 159). Adam de Dowan of Lanarkshire, who rendered homage in 1296 (*Bain*, II, p. 213), may be the Adam de Dowane, junior, who resigned his claim to land in Dowane in exchange for the land of Hauhtiferdale (*Kelso*, p. 161), and the Adam de Dowan who was juror on an inquest at Lanark in 1303 (*Bain*, II, 1420). Adam of Dowan, the elder, resigned his land of Grenerig in the barony of Lesmahago to the Abbey of Kelso in 1311 (*Kelso*, p. 163), and in 1326 John, son and heir of Adam de Duwan, junior, received the whole land of Aghtvferdale in exchange for the half of Duvan (Dowan), and in the same year he and his heirs were appointed hereditary janitors "ad portam nostram prioratus de Lesmahagw" (ibid., p. 367).

DOWASKARTH. Johannes Dowaskarth was tenant in Dowaskarth, Stennes, Orkney, 1563 (*OSR.*, I, p. 137).

DOWCROW. An old surname in Paplav and Grenewall, Orkney, from the township of that name in Paplay (1502).

DOWDALL. Steyne Dwdaill in Dundalk was burgess freeman of Glasgow, 1596 (*Burgesses*). Bardslev says the name is local, of Dowdale, seemingly a Yorkshire place name.

DOWIE, DOUIE. Most probably shortened from (MACIL)DOWIE, q.v. The name occurs in Macildowie territory. John Mc John Dowy in Boespick and Thomas Mc Allester Dowie in Dalquhalliche were fined for reset of Clan Gregor, 1613 (RPC., XIV, p. 632). Andrew Dowie, indweller in Anstruther, 1697 (*Inquis.*,

7901), and seven Dowies in Dunblane and neighborhood are recorded from 1671 (*Dunblane*).

DOWN. Perhaps of local origin from Doune, Perthshire. Johannes Downe was bailie of Perth in reign of James II (*Scon*, p. 189). Malcolm Downe in Killichasson was fined in 1613 for resetting Clan Gregor (RPC., XIV, p. 634), James Down was merchant burgess in Edinburgh, 1719 (*Guildry*, p. 122), and William Down is recorded in Alnacealich, 1768 (*Durness*). See DOUNE.

DOWNES, DOWNS. Recorded in Glasgow Directory. John Douns in Greenhead to be constable, 1709 (*Minutes*, p. 57). Perhaps from Ir. *O'Dubháin*, 'descendant of Dubhan' (a diminutive of *dubh*, black), which is Englished Down, Downes, etc. (*Woulfe*.)

DOWNIE, DOWNEY. Of territorial origin from the old baronv of Duny or Downie (in 1331 Douney) in the parish of Monikie, Angus. The surname is still common in the district, and there was also an old Stirling family of the name. Downie is also said to be probably one of the oldest names in the parish of Kemnav (AEI., I, p. 24). The first of the name recorded is Duncan de Dunny who witnessed a composition regarding the boundaries between the lands of Tulloes (Tulloch) and Conon in 1254 (RAA., I, p. 325). Jervise's suggestion that the Downies were probably vassals of some lord, as the name is so rarely found in early record, is probably correct (*Jervise LL.*, p. 384). Alexander Downy or Dounv held land of the abbot of Arbroath in 1330 (RAA., II, p. 7, 8), and Mury Dunnv, forestaller in Aberdeen, is mentioned in 1402 (CRA., p. 383). Thomas Downy was burgess of Glasgow in 1550 (*Protocols*, I), and three vears later an annual rent was sold by Peter Downy in the same city (ibid.). James Dewinny was chosen barlaw man in the barony of Urie in 1620 (*Urie*, p. 33), and Isobel Dewnie is recorded in Brechin in 1675 (*Brechin*). A genealogy of the Farquharsons claims that the Dons and Downies are descended from James Farquharson, grandson of the Ferquhard "who was called Don or Doun from his Brown Hair" (*Farquharsons of Invercauld*, p. 4), but as shown above the name was in existence before there was a clan Farquharson. Davenie 1628, Dewinv, Dewnev, and Dewnv 1621, Down 1760, Downe 1619, Downve 1565.

DOWNS. See under DOWNES.

DRAFFAN, DRAFFEN. From the lands of Draffan, near Lesmahagow, Lanarkshire. Between 1160 and 1189 James de Draffan or Drafan appears several times as a charter witness in the chartulary of Kelso. He witnessed a grant of part of ffincurrok to Gilmagu, c. 1160–80, and the charter of part of Auchynlec to Waldeus filius Boydini (*Kelso*, 114, 115). He also witnessed a grant by Radulf de Clere to the Abbey of Kelso, c. 1170, and before 1189 the confirmation by Robert of the charter of his father Robert, son of Warnbald of Kilmaurs, to the same monastery (ibid., 349, 284). Charles Draffan is recorded in Westoun, parish of Douglas, 1650 (*Lanark CR.*), and George Draphan in Lesmahago in 1679 was released from imprisonment on signing a bond not to take up arms (RPC., 3. ser. VI, p. 296). A pension was paid to Mary Draffan in Edinburgh, 1730 (*Guildry*, p. 136). The surname was carried to the New World and given to Draffan farm in Hebron, Nova Scotia. Draffin 1679. Draffen in Edinburgh 1942.

DRAIN. A Kintyre surname, perhaps now obsolete. From Ir. *O'Dreain*, 'descendant of Drean,' a wren. "The M'O'Drains, who were Lairds of Carrin and Drumavoulin are now called Drains. The last of these old lairds was Donald M'O'Dhrain (who) was out in the wars of Montrose" (*Adam*, p. 469).

DRAINIE. Local. There is a town and parish in Moray of this name.

DRAWHILL. This surname, found in Hawick and neighborhood, is most probably a corruption of DROCHIL, q.v.

DRAX. William Drax, prior of Coldingham, 1429 (*Raine*, 153, 638) probably derived his name from Drax or Drakes in Yorkshire.

DREDAN. Thomas Dreden and Ralfe Dredden were tenants on land of the Abbey of Kelso, 1567 (*Kelso*, p. 524, 528). William Dredane, burgess of Mussilburgh, 1647 (*Inquis.*, 3310), and Agnes Dredan and William Dredan of Edmiestoun were warded in the Canongate Tolbooth, Edinburgh, 1682 (BOEC., VIII, p. 135–136). Cf. DRYDEN.

DREGHORN. From the place of this name in the parish of Dreghorn, Ayrshire. William de Dregarn appears as a witness in 1446 (*Prestwick*, p. 114), and another William Dregarne held a tenement in Ayr in 1500 (*Ayr*, p. 95). Adam Dregarne was vicar pensioner of Torboltoune in the same year (*Simon*, 123).

DREM. From Drem in East Lothian. Gilbert de Drem was one of the jurors on an inquisition made at Berwick on the lands of Lady Elena de la Zuche in the sheriffdom of Edinburgh in 1296 (*Bain*, II, 824).

DRENG. The seal of *Patr. Dreng de Remingtune* is appended to an undated confirmation of the lands of Remington to St. Ebb at Coldingham (*Seals Supp.*, 297). In ON. *drengr* means a young unmarried man, lad, fellow. In OE. it occurs only in documents relating to the northern counties, and in Gospatric's charter to his subjects, c. 1072, it seems to indicate a landowner who did not enjoy the full rights of a free man. "On English soil the word came to denote a man holding by a particular form of free tenure, combining services and money payments with a certain measure of military duty" (Mawer, *The chief elements used in English place-names*, p. 23).

DRENNAN, DRINNAN, DRYNAN. These surnames recorded in Galloway and also in the parish of Ballantrae, Ayrshire, are from Ir. *O'Draghnáin*, from *draighneán*, 'blackthorn.' There were many individuals named Drynan and Drynen in the parish of Inch, Wigtownshire, in 1684. Some have changed their name to Drummond.

DREUX. The first of the family of this name in Scotland is said to have come from France in the eighteenth century. Laurence and John settled in Glasgow, where they bought land. Laurence lived at Bogleshole. The family is said to have been of the noble family of the comtes de Dreux, but in *Notes and queries* (12. ser. VI, p. 37) a correspondent stated (erroneously) that that family was extinct at an early date (SN&Q, 3. ser. III, p. 214; IV, p. 132).

DREVER. A surname confined to Orkney and Shetland. Brandy Dravar and John Dravar gave evidence in 1492 how the butter stent was paid in old times, and Nicholas Dravar was witness in Kirkwall, 1562 (REO., p. 408, 270). Jonet Drever was tried for witchcraft in Orkney, 1615 (MCM., II, p. 167), Johne Draver was witness in Kirkwall, 1616 (OSR., I, p. 241), and Alexander Drevar in Fitch, parish of Tingwall, appears in 1630 (*Shetland*). Dreaver 1630.

DREW. A common surname in the Campsie Commissariot Record. Drewe, capellanus, charter witness in reign of Alexander II (*Scon*, p. 62). John Drew and James Drw were tenants of the bishop of Glasgow in 1512, and

Patrick Drw was renter of the land of Badirmonoch in 1517 (Rental). A John Drew is mentioned in 1526 (Cambus., 141), William Drew was a witness in Glasgow in 1552 (Protocols, I) and John Drew, maltman, became burgess freeman in Glasgow in 1577 (Burgesses). John Drew, heir of Patrick Drew in Jaw, 1581 (Retours, Stirling, 353).

DRIMMIE. A rare Perthshire surname from Drimmie in the parish of Rattray. Charles Drymmie was witness at Ragortoun, 1546 (Rollok, 8). Alexander Drimmie, creelman in Stracathrow, is in record in 1628 (Brechin), and William Drimmie was recorded in Montrose in 1676.

DRINKER. Thomas Potator (Latin, a 'drinker') was one of the burgesses of Stirling who attacked the cruives and fishings of the abbot and convent of Cambuskenneth, 1366 (Cambus., 55). Ewen (p. 338) says Drinker is for Drencher, "a tenant by knight's service."

DRINNAN. See under DRENNAN.

DRIPPS. Of local origin from Dripps near Thorntonhall Station, Lanarkshire. In 1648 there is mention of the five merk lands of old extent of Litle Drippis, and the ten pound lands of old extent of Meikle Drippis (Retours, Lanark, 231). John Drippis was burgess of Glasgow, 1549, James Drippis resigned a tenement in Glasgow to Beatrix Duffus in 1562 (Protocols), and John Drippis, tailor, was admitted burgess freeman of Glasgow, 1580 (Burgesses). The surname is recorded in Sanquhar and neighborhood in seventeenth and eighteenth centuries as Drips. William Drips, exiled Covenanter from Mauchlin, was drowned off Orkney, 1679 (Hanna, II, p. 253).

DRIVER. Perhaps from the occupation. Baring-Gould (p. 121) has: "Driver, the driftman; on moors the man employed to sweep together the colts and horses and cattle and sheep sent out on the commons, to a centre where the owners may claim them."

DROCHIL. From the old barony of the same name in Peeblesshire. About 1260 Alexander de Drochyl and Alice, his wife, made an agreement with the abbot and monks of Neubotle anent the marches between the lands of Kynggesside and the abbey lands of Spurlande (Neubotle, p. 27). Alisaundre de Droghkil of the county of Peebles rendered homage for his lands in 1296 (Bain, II, p. 207). William de Drouchilde was a tenant of the Douglases in the barony of Kilbucho in 1376 (RHM.,

II, p. 16). DRAWHILL seems to be a modern form of this name.

DRON. Of local origin from the place of this name in southeast Perthshire. The surname is confined mainly to this part of the shire and the adjoining county of Fife. Laurence Drone "apud molendinum de Exmagirdill" was retoured heir of Laurence Drone, his father, in 1617 (Retours, Fife, 270). The name is common in the Commissariot record of Dunblane from 1621 onwards. Alexander Dron, sailor in Leith, 1677 (Inquis., 6034), and Catharine Dron at Milne of Muckarsie, 1688 (Dunkeld). James Dron in Auchtermochtie, 1670 (Edin. App.).

DRONAN. Margaret Droanann who was charged with being a disorderly person in the parish of Carsfern in 1684 (RPC., 3. ser. IX, p. 577) doubtless derived her name from The Dronnan in the parish of Minigaff, Kirkcudbrightshire. John Dronnan was tenant in Kirklebryde in 1681 (Dumfries), Helen Dronan was a servant in Dumfries in 1687 (RPC., 3. ser. XIII, p. 169), and John Dronnan in Langtone is recorded in 1703 (Kirkcudbright).

DROSTAN. Drostan was the name of the saint to whom the Abbey of Deer was dedicated, and the name also occurs on the St. Vigeans stone (8th century) near Arbroath as Drosten. The name early occurs in a Christian inscription in Cornwall, Drustagni hic iacit Cunomori filius, where Drustagni is genitive of ° Drust-agno-s, 'sprung from Drust.' The Welsh is Drystan in legend, the Tristram of the romances (Anwyl). Drostan's Croft (Croit Mo-Chrostáin for Mo-Dhrostáin) lies immediately west of Balmacaan House. His relics were under the charge of a 'deoir' (see DEWAR) or keeper, who had a croft at Kil St. Ninian (Croit an Deoir) which is mentioned in a rental of 1649 (Mackay, Urquhart and Glenmoriston, 2. ed., p. 326, 337). See also TRISTRAM.

DRUM. Of local origin from Drum in the parish of Drumoak, Aberdeenshire. John de Drum was prebendary of Butirgill, 1372, and another John de Drum was prebendary of Buthirgill in 1449 (REB., I, 20; II, 130). A horse was poinded from Edward Drum in Aberdeen, 1539 (CRA., p. 161), George Drum was trade burgess of Aberdeen, 1600 (ROA., I, p. 234), Isobel Drum appears in the parish of Strichen, 1685 (Brechin), and William Drum in Lonhead of Pitmillen, 1748 (Aberdeen CR.).

DRUMBLEE. Local. Andrew Drumblee was reidar in Mar, Aberdeenshire, 1570 (CAB., p. 230).

DRUMBRECK. From the old lands of the same name in Aberdeenshire. The old spellings of the name waver between Drum-, Dum-, and Dun-. Philip de Dunbrek is in record as deputy to the sheriff of Aberdeen in 1348 (ER., I, p. 542), John de Drumbrek was chancellor of the diocese of Aberdeen in 1360 (REA., I, p. 89), and Willelmus de Dunbrek in the parish of Fyvv was excommunicated in 1382 (REA., I, p. 166). Malcolm de Drumbrec to be a canon of Caithness, 1349 (CSR., I, p. 128), and John de Drumbrek petitioned for a canonry there in 1365 (Pap. Pet., I, p. 507). Philip de Dunbrek, *dominus ejusdem* (apparently the first of the family to be so styled), was present at perambulation of the lands of Tarwas and Wldny in 1417 (RAA., II, 53; *Illus.*, I, p. 344). He appears also to have been bailie on the lands of the Abbey of Arbroath in Aberdeenshire (RAA., II, 123). Laurence of Dunbrok had a safe conduct to return to Scotland in 1425 (Bain, IV, 985). Walter de Drumbrek was elected bailie of Aberdeen in 1440 (CRA., p. 6), Philip of Drumbreck was "ane of the serjiandis" of Aberdeen in 1469 (ibid., p. 409), William Dumbrek was burgess of the same burgh in 1487 (ibid., p. 43), and Philip Dumbreck was chosen sergeant there in 1494 (Guildry, p. 191). John Dunbrek was a monk of Arbroath in 1502 (RAA., II, 425), another John Drumbrek was juror on an inquisition at Aberdeen in 1508 (*Illus.*, III, p. 516), and Elspet Drumbreck renounced her rights in lands in Aberdeenshire in 1512 (RSCA., II, p. 187), William Dunbrek of Ortane (Orton on Spey) was juror on an inquisition in Inverness in 1542 (OPS., II, p. 631), and John Dunbrek was retoured heir of William Dunbrek de Urtane, his father, in 1627 (Retours, Elgin, 45). Katrina Dunbrek had sasine of lands in Shapinsay, Orkney, in 1548 (OSR., I, p. 117), William Dumbraik was servant to Alexander Gordoun of Baldorny in 1592 (Rose, p. 274), Agnes Dumbraik is recorded in Dunnichen in 1728 (Brechin), and William Dunbreak in Mostowie in 1743 (Moray). In 1705 persons of this name are recorded in Fochabers (MCM., III, p. 433). The old family of the name seems to have terminated in the direct line in two co-heiresses, c. 1564.

DRUMDUFF. William de Drumduff was present in 1395 at the perambulation of the boundaries of Kyrknes and Louchor (RPSA., p. 3). The name is of local origin but hardly likely to be from Drumduff in the parish of Eaglesham, Renfrewshire.

DRUMGREUE. Robertus de Drumgreue, charter witness in Fife, c. 1280 (LAC., p. 186).

DRUMMOND. The barony of Drummond wᵤ probably identical with the parish of Drymen, of which name it is but a variant, the final *d* being excrescent. "Persons deriving their designation from the lands of Drummond are frequent witnesses in the early charters of the earls of Levenax; and the family appear to have held various lands in the earldom, as well as offices in the household of the great earls of Levenax, at an early period and until they migrated to the earldom of Stratherne" (OPS., I, p. 38). The first of the name recorded is usually said to be Malcolm, who witnessed charters by Maldouen, third earl of Levenax from 1225 to 1270. This Malcolm was chamberlain to the earl and married Ada, his daughter. Gilbert de Drummyn, chaplain to Alwyn, earl of Levenax, however, witnessed a charter by that earl, c. 1199 (Levenax, p. 12; RMP., p. 157). Malcolm de Drummond or Drumman witnessed a charter by Gillemichell Edolf c. 1270, served on an inquisition at Dumbarton in 1271, and witnessed several charters by Malcolm, fourth earl of Levenax between 1273 and 1290 (Levenax, p. 15, 16, 30, 33, etc.; RMP., p. 191). He also witnessed a charter by Thomas of Munimuske c. 1285 (HMC., 2. Rep., App., p. 166). Malcolm de Drummond or Droman is mentioned in an inhibition by the bishop of Glasgow in 1294 (RMP., p. ° 203), and was among the Scots prisoners taken at Dunbar in 1296 (Bain, II, 742). In 1298 he was confined in Kenilworth Castle and received 4d. a day for his maintenance (ibid., 985). Gilbert de Dromund of the county of Dumbretan rendered homage in 1296. His seal bears two triangles interlaced and S' Gilberti Droman (Bain, II, p. 203, 558). John Drommed was prisoner of war in Wisbeach Castle in 1296, and in the following year he was released on condition that he shall serve the king of England in France (ibid., 178, 940, and p. 242). Johannes de Drominth witnessed a charter by Robert the Steward to Thomas Simple of the lands of Cragrossy in Stratherne c. 1360 (REG., p. 275). Andrew of Dromonde witnessed a papal dispensation by the bishop of Dunblane in 1422 (Hay, p. 10), and Walter Drommwnde was deacon of Dunblane in 1498 (REA., II, p. 306). Little dependence need be placed on the alleged descent from Maurice, son of George, a younger son of Andrew, king of Hungary, who is said to have accompanied Edgar Atheling to England. Dormond 1551, Dormondy 1553, Dreumond 1684, Dromonde 1424, Drommonde 1421, Dromounde 1413, Drommount 1593, Droumound 1559, Drumon 1522, Drumont 1407, Drvmvn 16c., Drumund 1602, Drumunde 1500, Drummownt 1422. See under BEGG.

DRUMSARGARD. William de Drumsyrgarde who served on an inquest held at Berwick in 1296 (*Bain*, II, p. 215) derived his name from the old barony of the name in the parish of Cambuslang, Lanarkshire. Mauricius de Dromsagard, 1312 (ibid., III).

DRUMTOKTY. Mavnys de Drumtokty, witness in Kyncardyn, 1434 (HP., IV, p. 238) derived his name from Drumtochty, Kincardineshire.

DRUST. A common name among the Picts, became in Gaelic Drost (*Watson* I, p. 318). It is common in CPS. index, and corrupt forms are Drest, Derst, Druxst. The Paris MS. of the Pictish Chronicle has a form Drest, which is more suggestive of British philology (SGS., II, p. 198). DROSTAN, q.v., is a diminutive.

DRUSTICC. Daughter of Drust (*Skene CS.*, I, p. 136). Her name is from the same root as her father's, with Ir. fem. substantive diminutive suffix -*icc* (*Zeuss-Ebel*, II, p. 812). She is said in Irish legend to have been a pupil of S. Finnan at Candida Casa, but what happened to her there shows that it 'must have been,' as Lawrie says, 'a poor school of virtue.'

DRYBURGH, DRYBROUGH. From the lands of Dryburgh in the parish of Merton, Berwickshire. The surname is not a very common one. Peter de Dribur witnessed a charter by Walter, son of Alan, c. 1208–18 (RMP., p. 18), and c. 1215 he appears as Magister Peter de Driburght (*Cambus.*, 46). Helen Dryburgh in Wemyss was accused of witchcraft, 1626 (RPC., 2. ser. I, p. 275), and John Dryburgh was servitor to the Lord Sinclair in 1680 (*Dysart*, p. 54). Dribrucht 1550, Driburch 1484.

DRYBURN. Of local origin from some small place of this name. Jonet Dryburne, dwelling in the ville of Potteraw alias Bristo in 1610 (*Laing*, 1584), may have derived her surname from Dryburn near Stow, Midlothian. Robert Dryburn at Abernethie is in record in 1759 (*Dunblane*).

DRYDEN. A writ on behalf of Philip de Dryden was issued to the sheriff of Forfar in 1296 (*Bain*, II, 832). In 1329 payment was made to Henricus de Driden for behalf of the soul of King Robert and in compensation for loss of multure (ER., I, p. 218, 219). Thomas de Driden is mentioned in 1455 as "supprior claustralis monasterii de Abirbrothoc" (RAA., II, 104), and in 1481 Laurence Dridane held a tenement in Stirling (*Cambus.*, 211). Johannes Dridene witnessed a lease by Alexander commendator of Inchaffray, 1521 (*Inchaffray*,

p. xcviii). The name is local. There is Dryden near Roslin, locally pronounced Drayden.

DRYFE. From the lands of Dryfe in Annandale, Dumfriesshire. John and William Dryfe in record in 1530. John Dryffe in Hurlebus, parish of Kirkconnell, 1641 (*Dumfries*). The name of Robert Drieff who held land in East Lothian, c. 1318 (*James* I, p. 10), may be of same origin.

DRYLAW. William de Drilawe of the county of Edneburk rendered homage in 1296. His seal bears a star of six points, S' Will' de Drilav (*Bain*, II, p. 201, 551). In the same year a writ was issued to the sheriff of Edinburgh on behalf of Walter de Drylawe (ibid., p. 218). John de Drylowe or Dryelawe of the county of Stirling also rendered homage in 1296 (ibid., p. 186, 197). Willelmus filius Johannis de Drilaw held land in Strevelin in 1299 (RAA., I, p. 276), and John Drylaw in the parish of Falkirk is in record in 1674 (*Torphichen*). From Drylaw near Davidson's Mains, Midlothian.

DRYMAN. Probably from Drymen, a village and parish in Stirlingshire, old spellings of the place name in Retours being Drymmen, Drimmen, Druman, and Drumind. As the home of the surname, however, is in Ayrshire, the name may really be a form of Drynen. See DRENNAN.

DRYNAN. DRYNEN. *See under* DRENNAN.

DRYSDALE. Of local origin from Dryfesdale, a parish in Annandale, popularly pronounced Drysdale. The dale takes its name from the river Dryfe which flows through it. Gawine Dryfesdale and John Dryfesdale had remission in 1499 (*Trials*, I, p. * 100), "for thare being aganis the Kingis hienes in the battell and feyld committit besyde Striuelin one Sanct Barnabeis day." Thomas Dryisdaill, Ila Herald, was admitted burgess of Aberdeen in 1619 (CRA., p. 364). The surname is common in the Commissariot Record of Dunblane from 1599 onward. Draysdale 1761, Dryisdaill 1574, Drysdaill 1567, Drysdell 1631.

The surname is also common in Fifeshire, especially in the western part of the county, and the following account which has been preserved by representatives of the family explains the adoption of the surname there: "On the twentieth May 1503, We, Thomas, William, and James Douglas, sons of the late departed Thomas Douglas of Brushwood Haugh, in the parish of Drysdale (Dryfesdale) and shire of Dumfries, left our native place for the reason here assigned, viz.: Defending our just and lawful rights against our unjust neighbour,

DRYSDALE, *continued*

Johnston of Greenstonehill, who, being determined to bring water to his mill through our property, and having obtained leave of his friend the King (James IV), began operations on Monday, the 16th May. We prevented him by force. The next day he brought twenty of his vassals to carry on the work. We, with two friends and three servants (eight in all), attacked Johnston with his twenty and in the contest fourteen of his men were killed, along with their base leader. A report of the proceedings was carried to the King, and we were obliged to fly. We took shelter under the shadow of the Ochil Hills in a lonely valley on the river Devon. After having lived there for full two years, we returned home in disguise, but found all our property in possession of Johnston's friends, and a great reward offered for our lives. We, having purchased a small spot called the Haugh of Dollar, and changed our names to the name of our native parish, were clearly in mind to spend the residue of our days under the [h]ope of the Ochils, and with the name of Drysdale to flourish in the lonely valley. The King passed this way with his court on the twelfth June 1506, going from Stirling to Falkland, dined on Haliday's green (an eastern neighbour), but we were not recognised" (*Sc. Ant.*, VIII, p. 158–159).

DUBBER. From the occupation, O. Fr. *doubeur*, 'repairer.' The precise meaning of the term is not known. The company of the Dubbers joined the procession of the York Pageant (*York Mystery Plays*, p. xxvi). Johannes Dubber, a charter witness in Glasgow, c. 1290 (REG., p. 200, 216). In 1329 there are entries of wheat, grain, and corn received from John Dubber (ER., I, p. 129, 132, 179).

DUBHGALL and FIONGALL. These epithets applied to Danes and Norwegians in early Gaelic records cannot refer to complexion or hair as both are fair-haired and of clear complexion. There must have been some other diversity to give rise to the names. Dubh and Finn, says Kendrick, "is usually assumed to be a distinction between dark Danes and fair Norwegians. But it is really a distinction of only dubious ethnological value" (*A History of the Vikings*, 1930, p. 275 n.). The epithets Dugall and Fingall applied by the Gaels to the natives of Norway and Denmark, says Robertson, are "derived probably from some long forgotten distinction in dress or armour rather than from any difference in personal appearance or in nationality . . . The Fingall are sometimes supposed to have been Norwegians

and the Dugall Danes, a fanciful distinction apparently, as Thorsteinn Olaveson was king of the Dugall (AU., 874), and his father Olave was undoubtedly a Norwegian. The Hy Ivar, chiefs of the Dugall, were undoubtedly a Danish race, for the Northmen who slew Elli at York in 867 were Dugall, and known as *Scaldings* or *Skioldingr* of the royal race of Denmark" (*Scotland under her early kings*, v. 1, p. 42, and references there noted).

DUBH-SHUILICH. G. *dubhshuileach*, 'dark eyed.' "A tribe descended from the Stewarts of Garth are Clan Duilach, from their immediate ancestor, who was so denominated from his black eyes" (Stewart, *Sketches*, I, p. 27).

DUBHTOLLARG. The name of Dubhtolargg, "rex Pictorum citra Monoth" (south of the Mounth), who died A. D. 782 (AU.), is a qualified form of TALORC, q.v., literally "Black Talorc."

DUBNI. The eponymus of Clan Campbell is *Duibhne*, whence their name *Clann Duibhne*. *Duibne* is genitive of MIr. *Dubind* or *Dubinn*, a feminine name found in ogham as *Dovvinias* (gen.), later *Dovinia*. The meaning of the name is uncertain. Dubni mac Mal-Colaim was one of the witnesses to a grant to the Abbey of Deer, 1132 (*Bk. Deer*, III, 10).

DUBUCAN. EG. *Dubucán*, 'little black man,' later *Dubhagan*, = Blackie. The modern Anglicized form of the name is DUGAN, q.v. Dubucan filius Indrechtaig, the first recorded mormaer of Angus, died in 938 (CPS., p. 9), and Maelbrigte filius Dubican died c. 970 (ibid., p. 10). MacDubbacin, father of Donald, mormaer of Buchan, occurs in one of the Gaelic entries in the *Book of Deer* (II, 15, 16). "Dufagan comes" is one of the witnesses to the foundation charter of the Abbey of Scone by Alexander I (*Scon*, p. 3), but Lawrie (*Early charters*, p. 280, 285) thinks this charter is a forgery and Dufagan here "a forged name."

DUCAT. Most probably a variant of DUGUID, q.v.

DUCHE. Jonet Duche, indweller in Stirling, 1563 (REB., I, 80). Ewen (p. 144) considers this name = Dutchman (i.e. one from Holland).

DUCTOR. Thom Ducter, tenant in Kemphill, 1474 (*Cupar-Angus*, I, p. 193). Robert Ductor in Duntanloch, 1696 (*Dunkeld*). Robert Douchter, chaplain, Brechin, 1468 (REB., II, 111), perhaps the same name. Not a spelling of DOCTOR.

DUDDING. A rare surname. Most probably from the Dodin who gave name to DUDDINGSTON, q.v. Dudyn de Broughtune was one of the witnesses at the enquiry into the marches of Stobbo c. 1190 (REG., p. 89), and an Alisaundre Dudyn of Peeblesshire rendered homage for his lands in 1296 (*Bain*, II, p. 207). The etymology of *Dud(d)a* or *Dod(d)a* is uncertain and a matter of debate among philologists.

DUDDINGSTON. Of territorial origin from the lands of Duddingston now included within Edinburgh. Malcolm IV confirmed the gift of the lands of Dodin and the lands of Waltheof filius Arnabol to the Abbey of Kelso (*Kelso*, 39). The Dodin here mentioned is doubtless the Dodin de Dodinestun who witnessed a charter by Henry de Simpring of the church of Simpring to Kelso c. 1153-65 (*Kelso*, p. 226), and the Dodin who held a toft 'super Tweda' which William the Lion confirmed to the same abbey, c. 1165-80 (*Kelso*, p. 28). Dudyn de Broughtune who was one of the witnesses at the inquiry into the marches of Stobbo, c. 1190 (REG., p. 89) is perhaps the same person. Shortly before 1200 Hugh de uilla Dodin witnessed a charter by William the Lion (LSC., 33), Richard de Dodinestun witnessed a charter by Herbert, abbot of Kelso, to Thomas filius Reginaldus de Boscho of the land of Esterdodinestun, c. 1219-26 (*Kelso*, p. 197), and about 1230 he witnessed a charter by the second Henry de Brade of the tithes of Baueley (Bavelaw) to the monks of Holyrood (LSC., p. 45). William de Dodingstone, burgess of Edinburgh, was granted freedom from distraint in England for all debts in which he is not principal or guarantee in 1290 (*Bain*, II, 427), and Elayne de Dudingestone of the county of Edinburgh rendered homage for her lands in 1296 (ibid., p. 208). John Dodingstoun or de Dudingstoun had a charter from Robert I of the lands of Pitcorthie in Fife which Richard Syward resigned (RMS., I, App. II, 495), and Stephen Dudingstoune of Sandford was charged in 1558 with abiding from the raid of Lauder (*Trials*, I, p. ° 104).

DUDGEON, 'son of Dodge,' a pet form of RODGER, q.v. John Dugeoun had a precept of remission in 1536 (RSS., II, 2033), and in 1559 there is mention of the late John Duggeoun and of Dionisius Duggeoun, tenant of Oswaldisdeyn in the lordship of Dunbar (ER., XIX, p. 402, 404). David Dudgeon, heir of John Dudgeon, *fabri lignarii* ac burgensis of Edinburgh, 1608 (*Inquis.*, 354). Francis Dudgeon in Halhill on assize, 1688 (RPC., 3. ser.

XIII, p. 245). Patrick Dudgeon published his "*Macs*" *in Galloway*, 1888.

DUDHOPE. From the lands of the same name near Dundee. Captain Adam Dudoip was one of the prisoners taken in the raid of Brechin in 1570 (*Diurnal of remarkable occurrents*, p. 183), and in 1676 Catharine Dudhop was retoured heir of her father, John Dudhop or Didhope, shoemaker in the Canongate of Edinburgh (*Retours, Edinburgh*, 1228; *Cawdor*, p. 321). The name is now probably extinct.

DUFF. As a personal name this is a curtailment of a longer double-stemmed name (cf. *Fionn, Flann*, etc.). The Gaelic is *Dubh*, from older *Dub*. "The family name Duff is merely the adjective *dubh* used epithetically" (*Macbain*). Duncan Duff was witness to a charter of c. 1275 (*Beauly*, p. 57), and in 1292 the lands of another Dunkan Duf and others in Kintyre were erected into the sheriffdom of Kintyre (APS., I, p. 91). In 1341 Brokynus Duff was one of an inquisition on lands in Aberdeen (REA., I, p. 69), and in the following year Machabeus Duff is in record as burgess of Cullen (ibid., I, p. 73). In 1404 Robert Duff and his spouse had a charter of the lands of Maldavit and Baldavy (*Illus.*, II, p. 140). Paul Duff was one of an inquisition in 1414 (*Cawdor*, p. 5), and part of the lands of Twlifergus was let to Donald Duff in 1456 (*Cupar-Angus*, I, p. 136). Andrew Jervise (*Epitaphs*) "having gone carefully into the subject with all the data at his disposal, gave it as his opinion that the connection of the Duffs of Craighead or Muldavit with the ancient earls of Fife is pure assertion, founded on no evidence" (*The Book of Duff*, I, p. 12). Duif 1582.

DUFFERS. Agnes Duffers, spous of Johne Scharp, is in record in 1586 (*Scon*, 233), and David Duffers was bleacher in West Mill of Rattray, 1776 (*Dunkeld*).

DUFFIE. See under MACFEE.

DUFFTOWN. From Dufftown in the parish of Mortlach, Banffshire. John Dufton was a member of the Gartly Company of Volunteers in 1798 (*Will*, p. 23). James Home Dufftown from Ythan Wells served in the first Great War (*Turriff*).

DUFFUS. From the lands of Duffus in Morav. The family of Duffus were of note as early as the thirteenth century when Arkembaldus de Duffus witnessed an agreement between Brice, bishop of Moray (d. 1222) and John Byseth (REM., p. 16). David of Dufis, son

DUFFUS, *continued*

and heir of John Dufis, confirmed to Robert of Holday a tenement within the town of Invercullen, 1330 (*Illus.*, II, p. 336). John de Duffhous or Dufhws who was granted a canonry of Moray in 1347 appears in 1363 as sub chanter (succentor) of Moray (*Pap. Pet.*, I, p. 109; REM., p. 313). David Duffus was admitted burgess of Aberdeen, 1488 (NSCM., I, p. 34), and James Duffes was gardener in Fyvie, 1633 (SCM., III, p. 75).

DUFFY. See under MACFEE.

DUFOC. Dufoc vicecom. de Striueling witnessed King David's charter of Ketlistoun to the Abbey of Stirling c. 1150 (*Cambus.*, 170). Skene identifies him (CS., I, p. 424) with Dufoter de Calatria who witnessed David's charter granting Perdeyc (Partick) to the church of Glasgow c. 1136 (REG., 3).

DUFSCOLOK. Dufscolok de Fetheressau was one of the perambulators of the boundaries of the lands of Balfeith or Belphe in Angus, c. 1204–11 (RAA., I, p. 60).

DUGAL, DUGALD. See under DOUGAL.

DUGAN, DOUGAN (in Wigtownshire). From Ir. *Dubhagán*, diminutive of *Dubh*, black. John Dugan, prisoner of war in the Tower of London liberated, 1413 (*Bain*, IV, 839). Adam Dougane in Udingstoune, parish of Douglas, 1665 *(Lanark CR.)*, Andrew Dougan in Bouochmore, 1677 *(Kirkcudbright)*, and Charles Dugan in Balgirscho, 1773 *(Dunkeld)*. See also DUBUCAN.

DUGUID. A common Aberdeenshire surname. Robert Doget, messenger, carried letters of Edward I to various persons, 1304, and Master Adam Doghete was witness in St. Andrews, 1305 (*Bain*, IV, 482–484, 1807). John Doget, chaplain, 1343 (*Melros*, p. 457). John Dogude, who was bailie of Perth in 1379, as John Dugude departs for Pruvcia (Prussia) in the king's service in 1382 (ER., III, p. 21, 99). The name is found in Dundee in 1470 (SN&Q., I, p. 139), John Dogude was made burgess of Aberdeen, 1479 (NSCM., I, p. 28), and Robert Dogude de Achnahufe is mentioned in 1478 (CRA., p. 408). In 1536 we have a bond of manrent by a later Robert Dugoude of Auchinhuif who signs himself 'Robert Dugud' (SCM., IV, p. 199), a third Robert Dewquhat of Auchinhuif is mentioned in 1607 (RPC.), and in 1675 Francis Duiguid was retoured heir of William Duiguid de Auchinhuiff (*Retours, Aberdeen*, 426). A family of this name were tenants of Ardmore, Udny,

for over a century and a half (AEI., p. 103). John Dugwid was one of the Committee of Provisions for the Army, 1651 (SBR., p. 198), Mr. William Dowcat was portioner of Apletrieleaves, 1664 (RRM., II, p. 88), and Jerome Dugit was prosecuted for riot in 1678 (RPC., 3. ser. v, p. 340). Dogod 1365, Dogud 1541, Doucatt 1680, Dougatt 1613, Ducat 1603, Dugait 1544, Dugat 1669, Dugate 1546, Duged 1597, Dugeit 1597, Duget 1651, Duiged and Duiget 1633.

DUIRS, DURIS, DOORS. Perhaps from Dores near Kettins, Perthshire. There is also Durris in parish of Drumoak, Aberdeenshire. Margaret Dures is recorded in Old Montrose in 1611 and John Dours, cooper there, 1734 *(Brechin)*. Dr. William Duirs, deputy inspector-general of hospitals, died in 1867.

DUKE. David Duce de Montross, witness in Brechin, 1490 (REB., II, 136). John Dooke, smith, burgess of Air, 1655 (*Inquis.*, 4078). Nathaniel Duke of Leathes appears in 1732 and 1763 *(Kirkcudbright; Dumfries)*. *Duc, Duk* is an old Danish personal name *(Nielsen)*, ON. *Dûk-r.*

DULL. From Dull, a village and parish in central Perthshire. Bethan de Doul and Kenachy, his brother, were jurors on inquisition held at Perth before Malise, earl of Stratherne, 1305 (*Bain*, II, p. 456).

DULLOP. Andrew Dullop admitted burgess of Aberdeen, 1483 (NSCM., I, p. 30). ? = Hugh Dulp at Tarbert, 1326 (ER., I, p. 55).

DULY. This name is recorded in Inverness, and Macbain (v, p. 74) says it "may be related to Dulley, which is a French Huguenot family name, originally D'Ully." Hugh Dewly, priest, witnessed instrument of sasine in Perthshire, 1474 (*Athole*, p. 709). John Dullye was juror on an inquisition concerning the common pasture of the tenants of Kirklandbank, 1513 (*Bamff*, p. 47). John Doly of Eschindye, 1506, appears again in 1512 as John Dwlie, and in 1514 as Dulye (*Rent. Dunk.*, p. 88, 185, 277). David Duly in Edinburgh was sentenced to be hung "on ane gebat befor his awin dur" in 1530 for concealing the fact that his wife was ill of the pestilence (MCM., II, p. 107; Lees, *St. Giles*, p. 347).

DUMBART. A surname recorded in Caithness. It may be a form of DUNBAR (sometimes spelled Dum-), with accretionary *t*. The Dunbars of Caithness, an offshoot from the Dunbars of Westfield, are in record there from the middle of the fifteenth century.

DUMBARTON. Of local origin from the town of Dumbarton. Magister Richardus de Dunbretan witnessed a charter by Constantinus de Lochor in 1235 (RD., p. 102), Clement de Dumbertan appears as a witness in Dumbarton in 1271 (RMP., p. 192), and c. 1334 Ada filius Alani de Dunbretane appears in the same role (*Levenax*, p. 93). About 1350 a confirmation charter of the land of Bullul was granted to Robert de Dunbretane (ibid., p. 69), and in 1390 there is mention of another Robert de Dunbrettane et heredibus (RAA., II, 40). Robert de Dunbretayn, cleric at Inuerkethyn, witnessed a charter of 1354 (*Kelso*, p. 385). Alfred Dumbarton is author of *Gypsy life in the Mysore jungle*, London, 1902.

DUMBRETTON. Robertus Dunbredan who witnessed the gift by Huctredus filius Fergus to the Hospital of S. Peter of York, c. 1158–64 (*Edgar*, p. 219) doubtless derived his name from the lands of that name, now Dumbretton, near Kirtlebridge, Dumfriesshire. A later Robert de Dumbredan witnessed a quitclaim by Margaret, wife of Robert de Wathepol, c. 1220 (*Holm Cultram*, p. 11). A third Robert de Dunbretan of the county of Dunfres rendered homage in 1296 (*Bain*, II, p. 206). There is a Drumbreddan in Stoneykirk parish (*Royal Atlas*), but spelled Dumbreddan in the County Directory (1912).

DUMFRIES. Of local origin from the town of Dumfries. William de Dunfres was keeper of the Rolls of Scotland in 1291 (*Bain*, II, 526). Master Alan de Dunfres was appointed chancellor of Scotland in 1296 (ibid., II, 606, 612), and Robert de Dumfries was a monk of Holyrood in 1299 (ibid., II, 1052). Nicholas de Drumfres, tenant of Knockynchangill in 1376 (RHM., I, p. liv) may be the Nicholas de Drumfres, burgess of the same, who erected a chantry in the chapel of St. Nicholas, Dumfries, in 1394 (SCM., v, p. 250). John de Drumfreys "filius et apparens heres Herberti Atkynsoun" is in record in 1460 (LCD., p. 253).

DUMMOCK. Local. Thomas Dummock in Greenhalton, parish of Carnwath, 1630, and two more of the name (*Lanark CR.*).

DUN, DUNN. (1) Of local or territorial origin, perhaps from Dun in Angus. Adam de Dun was elected to the deanery of Moray in 1255 (*Pap. Lett.*, I, p. 325), and William de Dun, perhaps a relative, was dean there in 1268 (REM., p. 279). Patrick de Dun was canon of Glasgow c. 1290 (REG., p. 200), John de Dwne, burgess of Edinburgh, 1428 (RMS., II, 116), and John Dun held a land in Edinburgh before

1467 (*Neubotle*, 299). David Dun appears in Aberdeen in 1442 (CRA., p. 367), Hugh Dun had precept of remission at Abirbrothok, 1492 (RSS., I, 16), Edward Dwn was tenant in Wester Micras (Mecray) in 1539 (ER., XVII, p. 659), William Dyn witness in Perth, 1551 (*Rollok*, 105), and James Dun was a retainer of Stewart of Invermeith, 1579 (RPC., III, p. 126, 155). Charles Dune, dyer, was burgess of Aberdeen before 1673 (*Retours, Aberdeen*, 413). (2) Celtic *donn*, 'brown,' was early naturalized in OE. as *dunn*, 'dun,' 'dingy,' 'brown,' and became an OE. personal name, *Dun, Dunna, Dunne*. Malcolm, son of David Dunne of Conestablestoun, quitclaimed to the bishop of Glasgow the lands of Tor or Windilawes in the territory of Edulfistune between 1260–68 (REG., p. 175). Thomas Dun was hanged at Elgin in 1296 for stealing books and vestments from the church (*Bain*, II, p. 190). Dwn and Dynne 1613.

DUNBAR. From the old lands or barony of Dunbar. The first individuals to use the name were the descendants of Earl Gospatric (of Northumberland, 1067–1072), descendant of Crinan, thane of Dunkeld. The latter's parentage "is not certainly known, but his grandfather was probably Duncan, lay-abbot of Dunkeld, who was killed in 965, and his mother or grandmother may have been a daughter of one of the last kings of the Isles" (*Sc. Peer.*, III, p. 240). John de Dunbar witnessed a gift of land to the Hospital of Soltre c. 1250–66 (*Soltre*, p. 32), Adam of Dunbar, 1269 (*Bain*, I, p. 511), Robert de Dunbar, burgess of Abirbrothoc, 1382 (RAA., II, 38). Robert Dunbarre of Scotland had letters of safe conduct to remain in England for a time in 1398 (*Bain*, IV, 507). James Dunbar, a Scots prisoner of war in Knaresburgh, 1425 (ibid., 981), and another James of Dunbar had a safe conduct into England in 1451 (ibid., 1232). In 1368 the Dunbars acquired the lands of Glenkens and Mochrum (*Agnew*, I, p. 230), and the Dunbars of Caithness, who appear there in the middle of the fifteenth century, are descended from the Dunbars of Westfield. Dounbare 1692, Dumbar 1625, Dumbare 1666.

DUNBARNY. From Dunbarny in Perthshire. Reginaldus de Dunbernyn witnessed an undated charter by Gilbert, earl of Strathern (LAC., p. 47), and Johannes de Dunbernyn witnessed one by Malcolm de Kinspinithin (now Kilspindie) at a later date (ibid., p. 80).

DUNBLANE. From the old town of the name in Perthshire. Laurence of Dunblane, burgess of Stirling, rendered homage in 1296 (*Bain*, II, p. 186, 197).

DUNBRADAN. Local. Reginaldus de Dunbradan had a lease of the lands of Spedalfeilde (now Hospitalfield) near Arbroath in Angus, 1325 (RAA., I, p. 309).

DUNCAN. G. *Donnchad*, MG. (c. 1520) *Duncha*, and in the 1467 Gaelic genealogical MS. it appears in the genitive as *Donnchaid*. The early Irish form *Donnchad* seems to represent early Celtic * *Donno-catu-s*, 'brown warrior,' from *donn* and *cath*. On an ogham stone at Clan Usk near Crickhowel in Wales the name occurs spelled *Dunocatus*, which points to 'fort warrior,' from *dun*, 'fort,' as the meaning of the name. The exact meaning is therefore uncertain. Dunchad, eleventh abbot of Hii (Iona) died in 717 (*Adamnan*, p. 379). Duchad (for Dúchad = Dunchad), abbot of Dunkeld, was killed in the battle of Dorsum Crup (Duncrub in Perthshire) c. 965 (CPS., p. 10). Dunchad mac mec Bead mec Hidid gave the field called Achad-madchor to the Abbey of Deer (*Bk. Deer*, VI, 32), and in the same record we have mention of *Donnachac mac Sithig toesech clenni Morgainn*, 'Duncan Sithech's son, leader of Clan Morgan.' Donchadus, earl of Fife was witness to King David's letter of protection to the clerics of Deer c. 1150 (ibid.). Willelmus filius Dunecan witnessed the gift of Swintun to Hernulf the knight c. 1135 (*Raine*, 12). Dunecanus *comes* witnessed confirmation charter by William the Lion to Jacobus de Pert of lands of Rosin clerac, n.d. (SCM., II, p 318). Willelmus filius Duuecani, c. 1200 (CMN., p. 6) is an error for Dunecani. Dunecan, parson of Duuglas, appears as charter witness between 1240–49 (*Kelso*, p. 163). John Dunkan held a 'waste' in Berwick-on-Tweed in 1367 (*Bain*, IV, 135), and probably John Duncanson or Dunkanson, mayor of Berwick in the same year was his son (ibid., 132, 135). Duncanus 'parvus garcio,' a forestaller in Aberdeen, 1402 (CRA., p. 384). Lieut.-General Jacob Duncan (d. 1685), governor of Fünen, was of Scots parentage. The Clann Donnchaidh (Robertson) derives its name from Fat Duncan (*Donnchadh Reamhar*) de Atholia, chief of the clan in the time of Bruce. In Ireland Donnchadh is Englished 'Denis' by some, and refined to 'Dionysius' and 'Donatus' by others. Docane (for Dōcane) 1516, Dokan (for Dōkan) 1515, Dokcaine 1516, Dunckane 1424, Dunkane 1515, Dwnkane 1527, Dwnken 1707.

DUNCANSON, 'son of DUNCAN,' q.v. Nicholas Donecandonesoune was a Scots prisoner of war taken at Dunbar Castle in 1296 (*Bain*, II, p. 177). William Duncani was burgess of Aberdeen, 1310 (REA., I, p. 40), Colinus filius Duncani witnessed a royal charter of the lands of Dalmakeran c. 1316–18 (*Annandale*, I, p. 132), and John filius Duncani is in record, 1326 (ER., I, p. 57). Gilbert filius Duncani held Park of Mortoun in 1376 (RHM., I, p. liv), John Dunkanson was mayor of Berwick-on-Tweed, 1367 (*Bain*, IV, 135), and Andrew Duncani was present at the perambulation of the bounds of Kyrknes and Louchor, 1395 (RPSA., p. 3). Johannes Duncaneson was juror on inquisition aput Rane in 1413 (REA., I, p. 214), Thomas Dunkesoun was minister of Bowden, 1582 (RPC.), and John Dunkysoun was "ludi-magistro apud Tannadyss," 1603 (REB., II, 233). Janet Dunkesone appears in Weyms, 1630 (PBK., 21), and Andrew Dunckiesone, late minister at Lessudden, 1669 (RRM., III, p. 81), may have been a son of Thomas Dunkesoun mentioned above. Dunkansoun 1625, Dunkeson 1651, Dunkinssone 1652.

DUNCOLL. Probably from the lands now called Duncow (in thirteenth century Duncole) in the parish of Kirkmahoe, Dumfriesshire. William de Duncoll was one of those appointed to treat for the ransom of David II in 1357 (CDE., 6), and Thomas de Duncoll was a tenant of the Douglas in Dalfubill in 1376 (RHM., I, p. lvii).

DUNCURRY. Sir William de Duncurry witnessed sale of a grange to Robert de Brus, lord of Annandale, c. 1215–45 (*Bain*, I, 1681).

DUNDAFE. Robert de Dundafe of the county of Fyfe who rendered homage in 1296 (*Bain*, II, p. 204) most probably derived his name from Dundaff in the parish of St. Ninians, Stirlingshire. There is also a Dunduff near Dunfermline.

DUNDAS, DUNDASS. Of the House of Dundas it has been said that "any prime minister can raise a man to the House of Lords, but it takes seven centuries of Scottish history to make a Dundas of Dundas" (*Dundas of Dundas*, p. xlvi). The Dundases are certainly one of the oldest historical Scottish families in existence, though the dates of the first of the name given in the above work are placed too early. Helias, son of Uctred or Huctred, who obtained the charter of the lands of Dundas in West Lothian from Waldeve, son of Gospatric, most probably in the reign of Malcolm IV or a little later is first of the name recorded. The charter is not dated, a circumstance quite usual in Scottish charters of those early times, but is most probably of the date here assigned. The editor of *Dundas of Dundas* is certainly in error in assigning it to the early years of the twelfth century. Huctred may have been a brother of Waldeve, as a Huctred, son of Gospatric, witnessed King David's charter to the Abbey of Melrose c. 1143–44 (*Melros*, 1), but there is really no evidence to show who he was. It was a very common name at that period. Partial confirmation of the relationship may perhaps be seen in the fact that the earls of Dunbar and the Dundases both carry the lion rampant on their arms. Founding a family connection through arms, however, is always a risky business. The charter of Huctred is given in facsimile in the above work and also in the *National manuscripts of Scotland*, v. 1. Helias de Dundas witnessed the gift by Philip de Mubray to the monks of Dunfermline c. 1202–14 (RD., p. 95), and Saer or Serle de Dundas of the county of Linlescu rendered homage in 1296 (*Bain*, II, p. 202, 213). John de Dundas acquired a charter of the barony of Fingask in Perthshire in 1364–65, and a few years later the lands of Blairmucks in Lanarkshire from Archibald, earl of Douglas. John Dundas of that Ilk was one of the conservators of the three years' truce in 1484 (*Bain*, IV, 1505). Petter Dass (1647–1708), the Norwegian poet, was son of a Scot, Peter Don Dass or Dundas. The lands of Dundas remained in possession of the family till 1875. The Dundases of Virginia are descended from a Scot who emigrated there in 1757.

DUNDEE. Of local origin from the town of Dundee in Angus. Willelmus de Dunde witnessed a charter by Willelmus filius Hawoc, burgess of Perth, c. 1245 (*Inchaffray*, p. 63). He also appears as witness in a Scone charter in the reign of Alexander II (*Scon*, p. 55). Robertus de Dunde, witness in a charter by Malise, earl of Stratherne, 1287 (*Inchaffray*, p. 111). Radulph de Dunde was freed from obligation to Walter, dominus de Venali, burgess of Aberdeen, in 1292 (*Panmure*, II, p. 151). Michael of Dundee, parson of Stubbehoke (Stobo), Rauf de Dunde of Forfarshire, and Master William of Dundee, parson of Alnith (Alyth), rendered homage in 1296 (*Bain*, II, p. 199, 211, 212), and Master Thomas de Dundee was appointed bishop of Ross in 1297 (ibid., p. 240). Magister Johannes de Dunde was a witness in Perth in 1458, and Magister Johannes de Dunde was vicar pensioner of Barre in 1489 (RAA., II, p. 103, 261). The surname seems to have died out early.

DUNDONALD. From Dundonald in Kyle, Ayrshire. Robert de Dundovenald granted to Sir Robert de Brus two carucates in the fee of Egilfechan in 1249 (*Bain*, I, 1793; *Annandale*, I, p. 7).

DUNDOWER. Richard de Dunnydover, witness in Dumbarton, 1271 (RMP., p. 192), as Sir Ricardus de Dunidouir witnessed a sale of land in Glasgow c. 1280–90 (REG., p. 198). Roger de Dundener [for Dundeuer] filius et heres Ricardi de Dundener resigned the lands of Dalmore into the hands of the earl of Levenax c. 1280 (*Levenax*, p. 42). Stephen de Domdouyr, rector of the church of Coneueth, who witnessed a charter by William de Lamburton, bishop of St. Andrews, 1300 (RPSA., p. 120) appears again in 1317 as Stephen de Domdouer, 'camerarius Scotie' (SCM., v, p. 9, 11), though his name does not appear in the ordinary lists of great chamberlains. He was also a canon of the church of Glasgow (REG., p. 220).

DUNDUFF. From the lands of Dunduff near Dunure, Ayrshire. Mathew Dunduffe, heir of William Dunduffe *de eodem* in the lands of Dunduffe, 1580 (*Retours, Ayr*, 720).

DUNFERMLINE. From the town of Dunfermline in Fife. Dovenaldus de Dunfermelyn was wounded in carrying letters from the earl of Carrik in 1304 (*Bain*, IV, 481).

DUNGALSON. William Dugalsone of Lanarkshire rendered homage in 1296 (RR.). A presentation was directed to the bishop of the Isles to give collation to Schir Malcum Dungalson of the chapellanry of Sanct Colme and Sanctt Finlagane in Ilaa in 1503 (RSS., I, 911). Cuthbert Doungalstoun is mentioned in 1538. Roger Dungolsoun, a witness in Dumfries, 1541 (*Anderson*) is most probably Roger Dungalsoun, burgess of Edinburgh, 1564 (*Edgar*, p. 240). Another Roger Dungalsoun, merchant burgess of Edinburgh, appears in 1601 (*Retours, Kirkcudbright*, 50). John Dungallson is recorded in Culmen, 1627 (*Dumfries*), and Florence Dungalson at Conchytoun is in record, 1674 (*Kirkcudbright*).

DUNIPACE. From Dunipace in Stirlingshire. Thomas de Dunipais was one of the witnesses to Adam de Morham's gift of the land of Dunypais to Cambuskenneth Abbey, c. 1200 (*Cambus.*, p. 109). Alexander of Dennipais was a monk of Holyrood in 1299 (*Bain*, II, 1052). John Dunnypase, chaplain, witnessed a charter by the provost of the Collegiate Church of Methven in 1468 (*Methven*, p. 24; REG., 392), a later John de Dunipace was a notary public in 1577 (RHM., II, p. 234); another John Dunipace is recorded in Fokertoun, parish of Lesmahago in 1664 (*Lanark CR.*), and William Dunipace in Crourige to be constable, 1709 (*Minutes*, p. 57).

DUNKELD. Of local origin from Dunkeld in Strathtay, Perthshire. John of Dunkeldyne (an old spelling of the place name) had a safe conduct in England in 1413 (*Bain*, IV, 841).

DUNLAPPIE. Anegus de Dunlopyn who witnessed a charter by Richard de Friuill of the land of Balekelefan to the Abbey of Arbroath c. 1178–80 (RAA., I, 90) derived his name from the lands of that name, now Dunlappie, in the parish of Stracathro in Angus. A horse was purchased from Nigellus de Dounlopy in 1312 (*Bain*, III, p. 420).

DUNLOP. A well-known Ayrshire surname derived from the lands of Dunlop in the district of Cunningham. About the middle of last century the name was locally pronounced Delap or Dulap. The first record of the surname appears to be in 1260 in which year dominus Willelmus de Dunlop is recorded as witness to an indenture between Godfrey de Ross and the burgesses of Irvine (*Irvine*, I, p. 5). The original document does not exist, but a notarial copy was made in 1444. In 1296 Neel Fitz Robert de Dullope (Dunlop) of the county of Are rendered homage, and as Nel de Dunlopp he appears on an inquest held at Berwick on the lands of Lady Elena la Zouch in Conyngham (*Bain*, II, p. 205, 216). Constantyn Dunlop of that Ilk is mentioned in 1496 (*Buccleuch MSS.*). Downlop 1564, Dunlape 1683, Dunlope 1573, Dunloup 1599. In the United States the surname appears as Dunlap. Dalape and Dunlape 1686.

DUNMORE, DUNMUIR, DUNSMORE, DUNSMUIR, DUNSMURE, DINSMORE. From the old lands of Dundemore near Lindores, Fife. The old family kept possession of the lands for a lengthened period, and took the Scottish side in the Wars of Independence (LAC., p. 240). The family appears to have ended in the direct line in an heir-female in the time of David II (*Inchaffray*, p. 286). Henry de Dundemore witnessed a confirmation charter by John, earl of Huntigdoun of land in Kynalchmund to the Abbey of Arbroath c. 1219 (RAA., I, p. 57), and c. 1232–37 he witnessed another charter by the same earl granting the lands of Lundors and of Garuiach to the monks of Lindores (LAC., p. 19). In 1248 he had a controversy with the monks of Lindores concerning the service in the chapel of Dundemor (ibid., p. 69–72), and c. 1250 he attested the gift ·by Alexander, earl of Buchan of one merk of silver annually to the monastery of Arbroath (RAA., I, p. 266). John de Dundemor witnessed letters of protection by Alexander II to the monks of Lesmahagow in 1230 (*Kelso*, 185). As Sir John de Dundemore he was one

of the regents during the minority of Alexander III, and in 1257 he witnessed a grant of the advowson of the church of Cortaky (*Inchaffray*, p. 77). In 1260 he had a controversy with the monks of the Isle of May relative to the lands of Turbrech in Fife (*May*), and in 1266 there is mention of the debt of John de Dundemor to the king (ER., I, p. 31). Patrick de Dundemer of Fifeshire rendered homage in 1296 (*Bain*, II, p. 204), Richard de Dunmore was juror on an inquest at Perth, 1305 (*Bain*, II, 1670), John de Dundemore witnessed a donation by Henry de Aynestrother to the Abbey of Dryburgh, c. 1330 (*Dryburgh*, p. 252), and Stephen de Dunmore in Fife is mentioned in 1406 (RPSA., p. 9). Richard Dunmure appears in Westerguird, 1585 (*Scon*, p. 228), John Dunmuir, notary in Dundee at end of sixteenth century, appears in record as Dunmuir, Dynmour, Dynmur, Dunmur, Dunmure, and Duinmuir (*Wedd.*, p. 77, 88, etc.), John Dinsmure took the Test in Paisley, 1686 (RPC., 3. ser. XI, p. 496), and Alexander Dunmore is recorded in Torphichen, 1688 (*Torphichen*). Dinmuire and Dunmuire 1662, Dinmure 1661, Dynmure 1643. One or more of this name removed to Bally Wattick in Antrim early in the seventeenth century, and from there the family emigrated to Londonderry (now Windham), New Hampshire in 1723. In the United States the name is usually spelled Dinsmore.

DUNNACHIE. See under DONNACHIE.

DUNNET, DUNNATT, DUNNETT. A surname of local origin from the place of the same name in Caithness. The local pronunciation is "Dinnet." Sir Gilbert Dynnocht who was vicar of Ardurnes (Durness) before 1541 (OPS., II, p. 702), as Sir Gilbert Dunnat, vicar of Ra, is recorded as deceased in 1550 (ibid., p. 742). Master John Donat or Dunnat appears as rector of Cannesbe (Canisbay) in 1577 and 1581 (ibid., p. 792). Margaret Dinit appears in Snawburgh, 1648 (*Shetland*), and Katharine Donnat in Holand-Mey appears in 1663 (*Caithness*). Matthew Dunnett and George Dunnett in Gilles, Caithness, to be apprehended as rebels, 1670 (RPC., 3. ser. III, p. 194). Dunet 1700.

DUNNING. From Dunning in Lower Strathearn, Perthshire. The founder of the old family of this name was Anechol, thane of Dunning, who witnessed Earl Gilbert of Stratherne's charter of Madernin (Maderty), c. 1199 (*Inchaffray*, p. 3), and the same earl's foundation charter of Inchaffray in 1200 (ibid., p. 6). He was succeeded by his son, Gillemichel de Dunin who appears in record c. 1208 (ibid., p. 25). Roger de Dunyn, a cleric, was a charter witness c. 1214–49 (*Scon*, p. 57), and B[ricius] de Dunyne or Dunin, steward (senescallus) of Robert, earl of Strathern, appears as a charter witness c. 1226–34 (*Inchaffray*, p. 47, 49, 50). John Donnung was received to the king of England's peace in 1321 (*Bain*, III, 724), Christi Dunyng witnessed a sasine of lands of Tullibody in 1437 (SCM., v, p. 260), Magister Johannes de Donyn was vicar of the church of Perth in 1440 (RD., p. 297), Robert Donyng was seven times provost of Perth, 1472–92, John Dunnyng had remission for his part in burning the town of Dunbertane, 1489 (*Lennox*, II, p. 133), and John Donyng or Dunnyn was bailie of Perth in 1514 (OPS., II, p. 662, 663). John Donyng and James Donyng were witnesses in Perth, 1541 (*Rollok*, 38). Doning 1477, Dwn-nynge 1561, Dynning 1643.

DUNOON. From the lands or barony of Dunoon in Argyllshire. Walter de Dunoun witnessed a confirmation charter of the church of Maleuille to Dunfermline Abbey, 1255 (RD., 206). Alexander Dunon appears in 1265 as holding the lands of Neuyd now Rosneath, Dumbartonshire (ER., I, p. 30). As Alexander de Dunhon he served on an inquest at Dumbarton, 1271 (RMP., p. 191), and c. 1285 he granted a charter of three-quarters of a carucate of Akencloy Nether "which in Scots is called Arachor" (HMC., 2. Rep., App., p. 166). Arthur de Dunnon witnessed a charter by James, steward of Scotland, 1294 (RMP., p. 96), and in 1296 as Arthur de Donon of Ayrshire he rendered homage. His seal is charged with a fesse chequy of 3 tracts, charges in chief obliterated, supported by two lions, S' *Arthuri de Donnovin* (*Bain*, II, p. 208, 558). Huwe de Dunom, persone of the church of Lyberton in Lanarkshire, also rendered homage in same year (ibid., p. 208). John Dunune was notary public, 1442 (*Panmure*, II, 235). Dunnone 1492, Dunnvne 1547. Probably now extinct. See also DENOON.

DUNS, DUNSE. An old Berwickshire family, Dunse of that Ilk, derived their surname from the lands of that name in the shire. Hugh de Duns witnessed the grant of the church of Langtune to the Abbey of Kelso c. 1150 (*Kelso*, 138), and c. 1202–22 Robert de Duns, capellanus, witnessed the gift of the church of Brennath (Birnie in Moray) to the same abbey (ibid., 371). Robert de Douns of the county of Berewyk rendered homage in 1296 (*Bain*, II, p. 208). Nicholas, son of Hugh of Duns, was steward of the earldom of Dunbar c. 1320 (*Laing*, 27), Nicholas filius Michaelis de Duns appears as a charter witness in 1332 (BNCH., XVI, p. 327), and Maliseus de Duns witnessed

a Yester charter of 1374 (*Yester*, p. 26). William de Duns was custodian of the castle of Temptalloun in 1426 (RMS., II, 67), and witnessed a quit claim of the lands of Gladsmure in the following year (*James* II, p. 14). In 1430 Eustachius de Duns was on an assize of the lands of Gladmor (ibid., 16), and in 1443 he was procurator for David of Lauder (HMC., 12. Rep., App. pt. VIII, p. 176). William de Duns, son of quondam William *de eodem*, granted to Walter de Spens a charter of a husband-land in Duns in 1437–8 (ibid., p. 175). Patrick Dunse was a juror on the lands of Swinton in 1500 (*Swinton*, p. lxxii), Thomas Dunce is in record in Netherancrum in 1682 (*Peebles CR.*), and William Dunce, sometime miller at the mill of Airies, is recorded in 1751 (*Wigtown*).

DUNSCORE. From Dunscore in the parish of the same name, Dumfriesshire. Roger de Dunsquier of the county of Dumfries rendered homage in 1296. His seal bears a bird, stars, and foliage in the field, S' *Rob'ti d' Dvnsqyr* (?) (*Bain*, II, 810, p. 531). On p. 210 the name is wrongly given as Drusquem.

DUNSIRE. Of territorial origin from the old barony of Dunsyre in Lanarkshire. John, lord of Dunsyer, son of Adam of Dunsyer, sold to Alan de Denume the land of Le Hyllis in 1299, and Andrew, vicar of Dunsyer, was one of the witnesses to the sale (REG., p. 214, 215). Mariorie de Dunsier of the county of Berewyke rendered homage in 1296 (*Bain*, II, p. 207). Patrick of Donsyer, servant of Andrew Gray, had a safe conduct into England in 1425 (*Bain*, IV, 986). Robert of Dunsyar, Scottish merchant, had a safe conduct to travel in the same country in 1486 (ibid., 1517), Thomas Dunsyre in Ponfeich, parish of Douglas, is recorded in 1623 (*Lanark CR.*), and Andrew Dynsyre, carbonarius in Methill, 1681 (*Inquis. Tut.*, 1061).

DUNSLESONE. An Englishing of Macdunslea (see under MACLAE). John Dunslesoun had remission for his part in burning the town of Dunbertane, 1489 (*Lennox*, II, p. 132), and dominus Walterus Dunslesone was curate of Estvod (Eastwood), 1535 (*Pollok*, I, p. 270). Dunslesoune 1548.

DUNSLEVE. G. *Donnsléibhe* or *Donnshléibhe*, for early Gaelic *Duinslebe*, 'brown of the hill.' An old personal name among the Gaels of Scotland and Ireland, and a favorite forename with the Macquarries of Ulva (Dunslaf 1505, Downsleif 1517). The duke of Argyll has shown that in old Argyll rentals 'd' drops out, and also the 's' by euphonic elision, the name

DUNSLEVE, *continued*

becoming (with Mac-) M'Onlave, M'Dunlave, M'inlay and M'An-lei or M'Onlea which became Maclav. In one document the name Dunslave M'Dunslave is found, clearly showing that the origin of the name lay in a forename (CR., VI, p. 191). Dunslene (for Dunsleue, second u = v) frater Murchardi was one of the witnesses to the confirmation by Walter, earl of Menthet of the gift of the church of Colmanel to the church of Paisley, 1262 (RMP., p. 122). Between 1303–09 James, son of Dunsleph, received a grant of lands in Kintyre from Robert the Bruce for his forensic service of a ship with twenty-six oars with men and victuals pertaining to the same (RMS., I, App. I, 105). Dunslane (for Dunslaue) McNeill is one of the parties to a Macdonleavie bond of 1518. Dunsleve, son of Aedh Alain, through his son Suibhne or Swene was ancestor of the MacSuibhnes or Macewens of Otter, and also the common ancestor of the Lamonts and the Maclachlans (CR., VI, p. 191).

DUNSMORE, DUNSMUIR, DUNSMURE. *See under* DUNMORE.

DUNSTAN. A surname in Fife. Dunstone recorded in Glasgow may be a variant. (1) It may be the common OE. personal name Dunstan *(Searle)*. (2) There is a Dunstane near Lilliesleaf, Roxburghshire. Master William Dunstan held lands in Perth, 1202 (LIM., p. 49), and another William Dunstan of Perth rendered homage, 1291 (RR.).

DUNWALLAUN. Dunwallaun (Dunwallon), king of Strath Clyde (Strathcluyd), visited Rome in 974: "Av ydaeth Dunwallaun brenhin Ystrat Clut y Rufein" *(Brut y Tywysogion,* p. 26). An early Cymric form of DONALD, q.v. Also spelled *Dunguallaun.*

DUNWATERS. A present-day surname created by combining the names Dun and Waters. A Mr. Dun Waters who was one of the proprietors of the *Glasgow Herald* died in Vancouver in December 1939.

DUNWICH. Alexander de Dunewich, merchant of Scotland, was arrested in the port of Lynn, 1225 *(Bain,* I, 907). Perhaps from Dunwich in Sussex (now submerged under the sea).

DUNYFLAT. Robert Dunyflat who witnessed a bond of manrent in 1527 *(Caldwell,* I, p. 62), derived his surname from the five-mark lands of Dunyflatt in the bailiary of Cunningham.

DURAND. An ancient personal name, Latinized *Durandus.* Durandus, vicecomes, perambulated the bounds of Clerchetune (Clerkington, East Lothian), c. 1141 (RPSA., p. 181). Michael, son of Durand, witnessed grant by Thomas, son of Andrew de Kyrconeuel, to the Abbey of Holmcultran, c. 1280–90 *(Holm Cultram,* p. 48). Wautier Durant of Dumfriesshire rendered homage, 1296. His seal bears a squirrel within interlaced squares, S' *Walteri Doraumt (Bain,* II, p. 198, 551). In 1297 there is mention of a royal message to (among others) Walter and John Duraunt (ibid., 884). John Durand witnessed a notarial instrument in Dumfries, 1453 *(Edgar,* p. 225). Malcolm Durande, prebendary of Lochmaben, 1478, appears in 1497 as Malcolm Durans, canon of Glasgow and prebendary of Gowan (Govan) (REG., p. 438, 478, 495). John Durand, notary public, Dumfries, 1506 *(Edgar,* p. 227), probably a son of above John. Robert Durrance, witness in Glasgow, 1519 (LCD., p. 219). Gilbert Durandis was renter of a half-mark land in Carmyle, 1526 *(Rental),* and Thomas Durrane is recorded in Edgartoun, 1679 *(Kirkcudbright).*

DURAY. The surname of an old family in Edzell in Angus derived from the office of 'Dereth.' A writ in the Chartulary of Dunfermline, dated c. 1250, by Robert the abbot, grants the office of 'Dereth,' which, as the title of the deed explains, 'hoc est officium sergiandi' (the office of sergeand), to Symon called Dereth, son of the late Thomas Dereth of Kynglassy (RD., 234). Robert Dereth' de Dunfermelyn carried letters of Edward I to the earl of Menteath, 1304 *(Bain,* IV, p. 480). In 1517 Alexander Dure was a monk of Arbroath (RAA., II, 543). Margaret Dirrow in Puggistoune, parish of Montrose, 1609, and three others of the name are recorded in that neighborhood *(Brechin).* Although the Durays of Durayhill appear in record for the first time so late as in 1644, when John Dirrow of Dirrowhill was appointed "to goe to the presbiterie for . . . competent knowledge to go to the Generall Assemblie which is to be holden at Edinburgh ye 22d Jan. 1645," (Jervise, *Land of the Lindsays,* p. 418), they were evidently then of old standing, as they designated themselves 'of that Ilk.' They were the hereditary dempsters of the lairds of Edzell and they appear also to have had special charge of the bell of St. Laurence. Although they designated themselves as 'of that Ilk' it is evident that their farm of Durayhill on the North Esk took its name from the office. The surname is now probably lost in DURIE, a name which has a quite different origin. Old forms of the name are Dirroc, Dirra, and Durro.

DURHAM. From Durham in the north of England, anciently Ðunhelm or Dunholm. Robertus de Durham was one of twelve Scots knights appointed to settle the laws of the marches in 1249 (APS., I, p. 413). The seal of Walter Durham of Dumfriesshire who rendered homage in 1296 reads S' *Valteri Dwrant* (*Macdonald*, 821). Sir William de Dureame agreed in 1302 to remain sheriff of Peebles till Christmas (*Bain*, II, p. 337). As William de Durem he held land in Hundwalleshope, Peeblesshire, in 1304 (ibid., p. 337). William de Dunolme de Grangia had a grant from Robert I of the land of Monyfothe with the mill, etc. (RMS., I, App. II, 550). Michael Durem de le Grange de Monefuth was one of inquest on the lands of Ouchtirlony, 1457 (RAA., II, 112). Master Thomas of Durame was Dene of Angus, 1479 (*Cupar-Angus*, I, p. 216), vicar of Mathe in 1486 (RAA., II, 298), and is probably the Master Thomas Durhame of the Grange who was on an assize at Forfar in 1495 (ibid., II, 354). Alexander Durhame was argentier to the king and queen, 1565 (RPC., I, p. 419), Francis Durhame was retoured heir in lands in the parish of Lesmahago, 1644 (*Retours, Lanark*, 215), Hew Dirram and his wife were charged with being disorderly persons in the parish of Balmaghie, 1684 (RPC., 3. ser. IX, p. 572), and John Durham is in Dinnins of Balmaghie, 1733 (*Kirkcudbright*). Durehame 1683, Durrame 1567. See DIROM.

DURIE. From the lands of Durie in the parish of Scoonie, Fife. Duncan de Durry witnessed a charter by Malise, earl of Strathern, c. 1258–71 (LIM., XXXIII). John Dury was cleric in St. Andrews diocese, 1464, and Walter Doray was one of the brethren of the Priory of Cupar, 1500 (REB., II, 106; I, 220). Mr. Andrew Dure was presented to the vicarage of Newtyle, 1519 (RAA., II, p. 426), George Dury witnessed a presentation in St. Andrews, 1526 (*Soltre*, p. 97), and Joneta Durye had sasine of lands in Ayrshire, 1564 (ER., XIX, p. 535). Of Andrew Durie or Dury, bishop of Galloway (d. 1558), John Knox says he was 'sometimes called for his filthines Abbot Stottikin' (*Works*, ed. Laing, I, p. 261–262). John Durie, a native of Edinburgh, was author of the *Reformed librarie-keeper*, London, 1650, the first British treatise on library management. Dore 1603, and Latinized Duræus. See DOVARY and DURAY.

DURIS. A Kincardineshire surname. See under DUIRS.

DURISDEER. From the village of Durisdeer in the parish of the same name in Dumfries-

shire. Huwe de Dursdere of Linlithgowshire rendered homage, 1296 (*Bain*, II, p. 205). Andrew de Durisder, proctor of the vicar of Kirkben, 1447 (*Pap. Lett.*, X, p. 280), is doubtless Andrew de Durisder or Durisdere who appears as sub-deacon of the church of Glasgow in 1450 (REG., 359, 360), and as Andrew de Durisdere, dean of Aberdeen in 1453 (*Bain*, IV, 1263). Durrisdur, Dursdeir, Dusdeir.

DURNIE. Recorded in Aberdeen. More probably a variant of DURNO, q.v., than from one or other of the places named Dornie.

DURNO. Of local origin from the village of Durno (Dournach 1257) in the parish of Chapel of Garioch, Aberdeenshire. Johannes de Dovrnach in the parish of Fyvy was excommunicated in 1382 (REA., I, p. 166). George Durno was schoolmaster at Fintray, 1761 (*Aberdeen CR.*), James Durno (1751–1807), a prominent British diplomat, was of Aberdeenshire birth, and Leslie Durno from Fyvie served in the first Great War (*Turriff*).

DURRAN, DURRAND. A Caithness surname from a small place named Durran near Thurso. "The local pronunciation of the name is 'Deeran' which is in accordance with the older spelling" (Rev. D. Beaton). The place name appears in 1605 as Diren and in 1671 as Dirane. Margaret Waters Durran of Caithness died in Edinburgh, 1942.

DURRAT. A surname current in Mar in the seventeenth century. A corruption of DORWARD, q.v. A man was charged in 1620 with hurting Thomas Durart (*Urie*, p. 30). George Durrat was a merchant in Aberdeen in 1724 (CRA.). See also DORRAT.

DURROCH. See under DARROCH.

DURWARD. See under DORWARD.

DUSEY. From G. *Dubhsidhe*. Dusey McFee was tenant of Bar in Islay in 1541 (ER., XVII, p. 616). Dubhsidhe, 'black of peace,' was *fer-léighinn* of Iona in 1164 (AU.). See under MACFEE.

DUSKIE. Elizabeth or Elspeth Duskie in Lyth, Caithness, 1662 (*Caithness*). Cf. Deskie near Ballindalloch, Banffshire, and the stream names Desk and Dusk.

DUST. James Dust in Milnhill of Fardle, 1741 (*Dunkeld*).

DUTCHFIELD. James Dutchfield, late servant to his grace the duke of Atholl, 1765 (*Dunkeld*), was probably an Englishman from Ditchfield in England (probably in Lancashire).

DUTHAC. The Scotticized form of G. *Dubhthach*. The OIr. name is *Dubhthach*, mod. Ir. *Dubhthach*, gen. *Dubhthaigh* as in *Ua Dubhthaigh*, usually Anglicized Duffy or O'Duffy, but rendered Duhig in county Cork, and Dooey, Dowey, and Duhy in Ulster. The Welsh is *Dyfodwg*. The earlier nominative is *Dubthoch* (as in Liber Armagh), and in an ogham inscription at Lamogue, county Waterford, *Dovatuc-eas*. In ON. spelled *Dufthakr*. Dubhthach was arch poet of King Laeghaire, converted by S. Patrick. Dubhthach, coarb (comharba) of Columcille, died 7 October 938. Dubhthach Albanach (i.e. 'of Alba') 'chief soul friend of Ireland and Scotland,' d. 1065 (AU.). Duftach, 'sacerdos,' was one of the witnesses to confirmation of the church of Holy Trinity of Dunkeld to the Abbey of Dunfermline before 1169 (RD., p. 74). He is probably Dustah (*f* misread as long *s*), 'sacerdos et abbas,' probably a Culdee abbot of S. Serf's, who appears as witness to the settlement of a dispute between the Culdees of Lochleven and Robert Burgonensis in the reign of David I (RPSA., p. 118). As forename: Duthacus de Carnegy, 1410 (REB., I, 27). Duthac Ker was burgess of Edinburgh, 1482 (*Neubotle*, 304), and Duthac Rutherfurde was killed, 1495 (*Trials*, I, p. 20*). From S. Duthac comes the Gaelic name of Tain, *Baile Dhu'aich* (*Dhubhthaich*).

DUTHIE. The name may commemorate S. Dubhthach of Tain. It is a shortened Anglicization of *MacGille Dubhthaigh*, "son of the servant of Dubhthach." The Gaelic name of Tain is *Baile Dhubhthaich*, "Dubhthach's town." Marjory Duthe had a tack of Hundclett in Holme, Orkney, 1492 (REO., p. 407). Seven of the name are recorded in Dunblane and neighborhood from 1598 (*Dunblane*). Patrick Duthie is in Insches, parish of Glenbervie, 1612, and four more of the name are in record (*Brechin*). David Duthie appears in Ballbrogie, 1744 (*Dunkeld*), and Alexander Duthie was a planter in Jamaica, 1769. The name is said to be common in Angus and it is also recorded in Banchory-Devenick.

DUVTY. Andrew Duvty was admitted burgess of Aberdeen, 1507, Patrick Dyfwy in 1546, Gilbert Duvy in 1567, and Thomas Duvie in 1620 (NSCM., I, p. 44, 59, 68, 126). Henry Dwithe of Aberdeen was slain at Pinkie in 1547 (SCM., II, p. 34), and Thomas Duwe was elected elder of the kirk in Aberdeen, 1585 (ibid., p. 57) Thomas Duvye was heir masculine of Thomas Duvye, burgess of Aberdeen, 1618 (*Inquis.*, 786), and Elspet Duuie is recorded in Calladrum, 1657 (*Brechin*). William Divie of Marischal College, Aberdeen, 1642, was burgess there in 1659. He was the younger son of Patrick Divvie or Duvie, burgess in 1616. Patrick was the son of Gilbert (burgess 1567), who was the elder son of Patrick Dyfwg, burgess of Aberdeen, 1546.

DYACK. See under DIACK.

DYAT. Hew Dyat, smith in Balgray Mill, Ayrshire, 1669 (*Corsehill*, p. 87). Alexander Dyett or Dyet, councillor in Irvine, 1665 (*Irvine*, II, p. 175), may be Alexander Dyet, merchant burgess of Irvine, 1680 (*Hunter*, p. 64). Robert Dyett, portioner in Meikle Govan, 1772 (RDB.).

DYCE. An old burgess family of Aberdeenshire who derived their name from the lands of Dyce in the parish of the same name. The first of the name recorded appears to have been John de Diss who was admitted burgess of Aberdeen in 1467 (NSCM., I, p. 16). Ranald Diss was a parishioner of Kinkell in 1473 (*Inverurie*, p. 122), and George Dyss was admitted burgess of Aberdeen in 1482 (NSCM., I, p. 30). Other old forms of the surname are Dyes and Dys. An account of the family in the *Thanage of Fermartyn* (p. 678–684). Alexander Dyce (1798–1869), Shakespearian scholar, and William Dyce (1806–1864), founder of the Pre-Raphaelite movement in the English school of painting are the best known.

DYCHTON. Local, probably from Dighton or Deighton in the North Riding of Yorkshire. John de Dychton, subdeacon of Urquhart, 1343 (*Rose*, p. 117).

DYER. From the occupation of *dyer*, one whose trade is to dye cloth, rendered in Latin documents by *tinctor*. Henry tinctor in Dumfriesshire, c. 1259 (*Bain*, I, 2176; APS., I, p. 88), Roger tinctor held land in Aberdeen, 1382 (RMS., I, 682), and John Dyer called 'talp,' was admitted burgess of the same town in 1436 (NSCM., I, p. 4). In Scotland *tinctor* was more commonly rendered LITSTER, q.v.

DYKAR, DYKER. From the occupation, OE. *dicere*, a digger, from *dician*, to make a dyke or bank. This surname is not common and is mainly confined to the northeast. Robert Diker de Elgin was juror on an inquisition concerning the king's garden there in 1261 (APS., I, p. 99 red). James Dyker was admitted burgess of Glasgow gratis in 1631 (*Burgesses*), and four brothers named Dyker from Ythan Wells served in the first Great War (*Turriff*).

DYKE. Macbeth of Dych, juror on an inquisition on the lands of Mefth in 1262 (*Bain*, I, 2323), derived his name from Dyke in Moray. Hugo de Dyke, witness c. 1299–1325 (REM., p. 148), Alexander Dike, witness in Glasgow, 1550 (*Protocols*, I), and Henricus Dik was part tenant in villa de Kynnedour, 1565 (REM., p. 437).

DYKES. This surname is common in the shires of Ayr and Lanark, and is most probably derived from the lands of Dykes in the barony of Avondale or Strathaven. David Dykis was witness in Avondale in 1503 (*Simon*, 63), John Diykis was apprentice mason at Dunkeld in 1512 (*Rent. Dunk.*, p. 123), Hercules Dykis was tenant of the Abbey and convent of Kelso in 1567 (*Kelso*, p. 525), Thomas Dykes is recorded at Jacktoun in the parish of Kilbryde, 1564 (*Campsie*), and Mr. Johne Dykis was minister to ye Kirk of Newbirne in 1606 (RD., p. 503). John Dykes and Andrew Dykes were burgesses of Perth in 1611 (*Inquis.*, 4471; *Inquis. Tut.*, 858), Mungo Dyks was liberated from the Canongate Tolbooth of Edinburgh in 1682 (BOEC., VIII, p. 141), an allowance was made to Mr. Patrick Dykes for his Grammar, 1686 (RPC., 3. ser. XII, p. 456), and William Dyks was writer in Edinburgh in 1687 (RPC., 3. ser. XIII, p. 164). Adam de fossatis (= 'of the ditches') served on an inquisition in 1247 (*Bain*, I, 1716). Dickis and Dikis 1503.

DYNNES. From the personal name Dionysius. John Dynnes or Dioneis, "sword-slipper," admitted burgess of Dundee, 1585 (*Wedd.*, p. 133). Isobel Dynnes in Perth, 1655 (*Dunblane*). Dynes 1597.

DYSART. From the town of Dysart in Fife. Walter and Gaffrid de Dysert are mentioned in an instrument of 1427 by Thomas Maule of Panmure (*Panmure*, II, p. 196). Michael Disard, "sacrista collegiate ecclesie Sancti Trinitatis prope Edinburgh," appears in 1527 (*Soltre*, p. 208). Katherine Dysart, spouse of John Calve in Newburgh, 1560 (RMS., IV, 2326). John Dysart was admitted burgess of Aberdeen in 1569 (NSCM., I, p. 68).

EACHAN. G. *Eachann*, MG. *Eachuinn*, *Eachduinn*, gen. (1467 MS.). The Irish is *Eachdonn* (year 1092), from prehistoric ° *Eqo-donno-s*, 'horse lord,' like *Eachthighearna* (Maceachern), with different termination. The phonetics are against Macvurich's spelling *Eachdhuin*, which is for ° *Each-duine*, 'horse-man,' as explanation (*Macbain*). Achyne mac Nele attested the bounds of the Grange of Kircwynni and the lands of Culwen, 1289 (*Holm Cultram*, p. 88), and Aychyn Carlichsoun witnessed an obligation by Alexander of the Isles, 1439

(*Cawdor*, p. 16). Echdoun Mac Gille eoin is witness to a contract and mutual bond in 1560 (HP., IV, p. 216). Eachann is generally Englished 'Hector' although there is no connection between the names beyond a slight similarity in sound in the first syllable of each. Echine c. 1695. See MACEACHAN.

EADIE. *See under* ADDIE.

EAGLE. There was a Norman family of L'Aigle. Matilda de Aquila, 1129, widow of Robert Mowbray, earl of Northumberland. (2) The name seems also to have been a signname, Gilbert de la Hegle being recorded in Sussex, 1273 (*Bardsley*). Alexander Eagell sometime at Halkhead, 1712 (RUG., III, p. 551).

EAGLESFIELD. The name of a family of considerable prominence in Cumberland in the thirteenth and succeeding centuries. The name is derived from the lands (now village) of Eaglesfield near Cockermouth. Some notes with a pedigree, are given in the *Transactions* of the Cumberland and Westmoreland Archæological Society, new series, XVI, p. 241–247. A writ was issued to John de Eglisfeld in 1307 to levy 60 men from Cockermouth to pursue Robert de Brus (*Bain*, II, 1902). Dorothy Eaglesfield is recorded in Kirkcudbright in 1738 (*Kirkcudbright*).

EAGLESHAM. From the old barony of Eaglesham in Renfrewshire. Dominus Robertus de Heiglssam, chaplain, witnessed a confirmation by Alexander filius Walteri of his father's gifts to the church of Paisley in 1239 (RMP., p. 225). Barthelmeu de Egglesham, chapeleyn, was warden of the New Place of Seneware (Sanquhar) in the county of Dunfres in 1296 (*Bain*, II, p. 206). William de Eglisham, rector of the church of Dunbarny in 1300 (RPSA., p. 120), reappears as William de Egglisham, archdeacon of Lothian in 1316 (*Neubotle*, 147; *Kelso*, 310), and in 1323 as official of St. Andrews (RAA., I, p. 308). Henry de Eglishame was one of an inquest on lands in Aberdeenshire in 1335 (REA., I, p. 61). Thomas Eglishame and Fergus Eglishame, followers of the earl of Cassilis, were respited for murder in 1526 (RSS., I, 3386). Magister George Eglischane, physician to King James VI, was retoured heir to John Eglischane, burgess of Edinburgh, in 1616 (*Inquis.*, 632). In 1626 Dr. George Eglisheim published a curious book entitled *The Fore-Runner of revenge . . . upon the duke of Buckingham for the poysoning of the most potent king, James VI.*" There is an account of the book in Calderwood's *History*, VII, p. 634–638. As Eglesame it is an old surname in the parish of

EAGLESHAM, *continued*

Ballantrae (*Paterson*, II, p. 87), and Hugh Egleshim appears in Knockreavie in 1784 (*Wigtown*). EAGLESON is a variant.

EAGLESON. A variant of EAGLESHAM. John Eagleson was gardener at Culquhae in 1743 (*Kirkcudbright*), David Ecclesom is in record at Culreoch in 1780 (*Wigtown*).

EARLSTON. John Earlstoune, witness in Glasgow, 1553 (*Protocols*), derived his name either from Earlston in Lauderdale, Berwickshire, or Earlston in Kirkcudbrightshire.

EARNESCLEUGH. Archibald de Ernysclucht witnessed confirmation of Snawdoun to Dryburgh c. 1350 (*Dryburgh*, 232). The name is derived from the old lands of Earnescleugh or Ernescleuche in Berwickshire (*Retours*, 62, 71).

EASDAILE, EISDALE, ESDAILE, ISDAILE. Johannes de Esdale witnessed a notarial instrument, 1413 (*Pollok*, I, p. 146). Margaret Eskdale was repledged to liberty of burgh of Irvine, 1472 (*Irvine*, I, p. 28), James Esdaill was burgess there, 1493 (*Macfarlane*, II, p. 341). James Esdale, who held a tenement in Irvine, 1506, is mentioned in 1528 as James Eskdale, burgess of Irvine, and in 1540 as quondam James Esdaill (*Irvine*, I, p. 158, 164, 169). Walter Esdaill was voter in parish of Qwilton (Coylton), 1513 (*Ros*, 52). Rolland Esdaile appears as witness in Glasgow, 1552 (*Protocols*, I). George Esdaile was burgess freeman of Glasgow, 1575, John Aisdaill the same, 1599, and John Esdaill ditto, 1620 (*Burgesses*). George Esdaill was retoured heir of John Esdaill in Muresyd, his father, in lands in parish of Kilwinning, 1643 (*Retours, Ayr*, 373). John Isdaill is recorded in parish of Donyng, 1669 (*Dunblane*), and George Esdaill of Cameron in parish of Bonhill, 1668 (*Sasines*, 1423). Bessie Esdaill was examined for the Test in 1685 (RPC., 3. ser. XI, p. 433). Not likely to be from Easdale in Argyllshire.

EASON, EASSON, ESSON (common in Angus), AYSON. Connected with the Toshes or Toschachs of Glentilt "were the old family called the sons of Adam, first Ayson, latterly Esson" (Fraser-Mackintosh, *Minor septs of Clan Chattan*, p. 179). Aythe filius Thome had a charter c. 1360 from Robert the Steward, afterwards Robert II, of the lands of Fornochtis in Strathearn, and in 1365 he appears as bailie of Stratherne (*Inchaffray*, p. 129). 'Johem aysoñ iuueñe' was one of those outlawed in 1392 as part guilty of the slaughter of Walter de Ogilvy, sheriff of Angus (APS., I, p. 159). A family of Aysons possessed Tulli-

met in Strathtay (*Skene CS.*, III, p. 309; *Athole*, p. 710). Robert Hayeth of Fornocht appears in 1445/6, and the Aysons of Fornocht appear in record down to 1504 when the estate was sold to Lord Drummond (*Inchaffray*, p. 298). Walter Ayson held sasine of a tenement in St. Mary's Aisle, Stirling, 1471 (*Sc. Ant.*, X, p. 62), and John Avsone was witness there, 1481 (*Cambus.*, 212). James Aissoune was mairchand and burgess of Stirling, 1588 (*Sc. Ant.*, VI, p. 144), William Aysoun was member of council there, 1598 (SBR., p. 282), and as Aissone or Aissoune the name occurs seven times in Stirling and vicinity between 1611–64 (*Stirling*). The name also occurs in Dunblane in seventeenth century (*Dunblane*). The land of Alexander Aysone in Dunfermline is mentioned in 1491 (DBR., 314), and in 1494–5 he is referred to as Sande Ason and as Alexander Assone (ibid., p. 51, 62). Some Isons are mentioned in latter half of sixteenth century as resident in and about Wick in Caithness. Alexander Ysoun in Lapok, Caithness, and William Ysoun, his son, were cruelly slain by Sutherlands in 1566 (RPC., I, p. 447). William Ysone, younger, was indweller in Weik, 1622 (ibid., XII, p. 651), and Agnes Isone is recorded in Thurso, 1662 (*Caithness*). Between 1497–99 a man is referred to as Alexander Avisoun, Aysone, and Ayesoun (RSS., I, 111, 113, 375). John Ayson witnessed sasine of lands of Balnacard, 1514 (*Grandtully*, I, p. 48), Robert Aissoun was a notary in Crieff, 1607 (*Laing*, 1526), and Patrick Easone appears at Myln of Cragyven, 1633 (SCM., III, p. 97). John Asson or Easson was member of Scots parliament for St. Andrews, 1681 (*Hanna*, II, p. 482). Aasone 1500, Asone 1498, Aysoune 1515, Ayssoun 1627; Aesone, Aison, Easson.

EASSIE, EASIE, ESSIE. Of territorial origin from the old barony of Eassie or Essie in Angus. Ese or Essie is still a surname in the shire. Hugh de Essi appears as a witness a. 1200 (LSC., 36). Waltyr of Essy had lease of Soutar land of Kethyk, 1476, and was tenant of Coitward, 1479 (*Cupar-Angus*, I, p. 224, 228), Dauid Essee was tenant of part of Tulvangus, 1495 (ibid., I, p. 245), and David Essie of Muirtoun appears as a witness in 1591 (REB., II, 229). Some members of the old baronial family "bore the remarkable Christian name of Brandan or Branden" (Chalmers, *Sculptured monuments of Angus*, pl. xvi). Esse 1505.

EASTNISBET. From East Nisbet, Jedburgh, Roxburghshire. Gilbert de Estnesbyte and Johan le fiz Adam de Estnesbyt rendered homage, 1296 (*Bain*, II, p. 202, 211). See also NISBET.

EASTON. Probably from Easton near Dolphinton, Peeblesshire. There is another Easton near Bathgate, West Lothian. Johannes de Eistoun witnessed a charter by Petrus de Morthingtoun at Lambertoun, c. 1270 (BNCH., XVI, p. 334; *Home*, 225). Andrew Essten in Runningburn, 1663 (*Stitchill*, p. 26), and James Eistone, portioner of Lessudden in same year (RRM., II, p. 52). Eastone 1668, Eastoun 1675, Eastoune 1667, Eiston 1665, Eistoune 1587.

EASTWOOD. From the old barony of the same name in Renfrewshire. Gilisius (Giles) de Estwode, a vassal of the Stewards, witnessed a charter by James the Steward of Scotland in 1294 (RMP., p. 96). In 1296 as Giles or Gyles del Estwode of the county of Lanark he rendered homage for his lands. The seal attached to his homage bears an acorn and leaves and S' *Giliscie de Heesthwit* (*Bain*, II, 812, p. 204). About 1313 as de Estwod he witnessed the grant by the High Steward of the church of Largyss to the monks of Paisley (RMP., p. 237).

EBBOT, 'son of Isabel,' from diminutive Ebb or Ibb + diminutive ending -*et*. Ebote Fentone held land in 1471 (REB., I, 194). James Ebbot in the Ferry, parish of Dundee, 1665 (*Brechin*).

ECCLES, ECLES. Stodart says (II, p. 315) there seems to have been two separate families of this name, one taking their surname from Eccles in Berwickshire, the other from Eccles in Dumfriesshire. Adam de Eccles witnessed a charter by Grim, son of Guido, to the Abbey of Melrose, c. 1170 (*Seals Supp.*, 329). Johan de Eccles of Berwickshire rendered homage in 1296, and Sir Mathew del Ecles of Dumfriesshire was juror in 1304 (*Bain*, II, p. 206, 412). Matthew de Eychles resigned his half of the barony of Ouras in Kincardineshire in favor of Thomas Rate, 1371 (RMS., I, 314, 383). Matthew of Eclys witnessed a charter by Roland Kenedy, lord of Blarechan (Blairquhan), c. 1390 (*Laing*, 72), and Robert de Ecclesia was tenant of the earl of Douglas in Drumcork, 1376 (RHM., I, p. lvi). John Eklis of that Ilk and Mongo Eklis, followers of the earl of Cassilis, were respited for murder in 1526 (RSS., I, 3386). The latter may be the Mungo Ekclis mentioned in a letter of protection by James V in 1530 (RSS., II, 642). Eccles of that Ilk in Dumfriesshire were seated there till after the Reformation (*Stodart*, II, p. 315), and William Eccles was retoured heir of John Eccles de Kildonan, 1668 (*Retours, Ayr*, 556). From the family of Eccles of Kildonan are descended the county Tyrone family of the name. Eickles 1657, Ekillis 1502, Eklys 1362.

ECHLIN. From the lands of Echline in the parish of Dalmeny, West Lothian. Robert de Eghlin and Rauf Doghlvn (? for d'Eghlyn) or Eghlyn of Edinburghshire swore fealty to England in 1296 (*Bain*, II, p. 201, 203). The seal of Robert bears a rude figure of S. Michael overcoming the dragon (?), S' *Radulfi de Echelan*, and the seal of Rauf bears a fleur-de-lys, S' *Radvlfii de Eclin* (ibid., p. 551, 558). A horse was purchased from Johannes de Eghelvn in 1312 (ibid., III, p. 421). John de Hevchlyn had confirmation to him of the lands of Garmylton in 1319 (RHM., I, 22), John de Eychlin, 'tunc senescallus baronie de Coldingham,' was a charter witness in 1332 (BNCH., XVI, p. 327), and Johan de Echlyne was vicar of Kinneff in 1407 (*Stodart*, II, p. 417). William Echeline or Echelyn of St. Andrews diocese was granted the perpetual vicarage of Inchemacbany in the diocese of Aberdeen in 1345 (*Pap. Lett.*, III, p. 94). William Echling of Pittadro is in record in 1457 (RD., 452), and John Echline of Pittadrow, professor of philosophy in St. Leonard's College, St. Andrews, died in 1603.

ECHT. Most probably from the (Kirkton of) Echt in the parish of Echt, Aberdeenshire. The seal of Robert Eicht is appended to an inquisition on the lands of Lumsden in 1444 (*Seals Supp.*, 336; *Macdonald*, 844). The surname also occurs in 1516 and in 1529 as Eycht, Eicht, and Hecht, king's messenger (ALHT., V, p. 97, 98, 380, etc.). The name of John de Echtse, admitted burgess of Aberdeen, 1472 (NSCM., I, p. 23), may be from this as Echt was spelled Hachtis c. 1220.

ECKFORD. From the lands of Eckford near Kelso, Roxburghshire. Alexander de Hecford witnessed a charter by Alan, son of Roland, lord of Galloway, of the lands of Vlfkelyston (now Oxton) to the Abbey of Kelso in 1206 (*Kelso*, p. 202). Geoffrey de Ekkeford received confirmation of a charter of land in the village and territory of Home, c. 1250 (ibid., 508), and Richard le fiz Geffrai de Ekford of the county of Rokesburk rendered homage in 1296 (*Bain*, II, p. 203). Wilzam of Hekfurde was "a clerk of gret wertu" in Glasgow (Wyntoun, *Chronicle*, v. 5, p. 395, S. T. S. ed.). John of Ekford, Scottish merchant, complained in 1358 that goods of great value were carried from the wreck of his ship at Cotum in Clyveland (*Bain*, IV, 26). The name occurs in Edinburgh in 1596 as Aikfurd (*Edinb. Marr.*), and William Eckford was tenant in Keephope in 1765 (*Lauder*). Aikfoord 1686, Eckfoord 1659.

ECLES. *See under* ECCLES.

238

EDDELL. Recorded in Edinburgh, 1940. Probably one of the many variant spellings of the place name Edzell.

EDDIE. A form of EADIE. See under ADDIE.

EDDINGTON. *See under* EDINGTON.

EDDISLAW. Of local origin, probably from an obsolete place name in Edinburghshire. Robert Eddisley, heir of Robert Eddisley in Leswaid, 1619, and James Eddislaw of Dalkeith, 1647 (*Inquis.*, 799, 3361).

EDDLESTON. Edulf filius Uctredi had a charter of the lands of Gillemoristun from William de Moreville before 1189 (REG., p. 40), and thenceforward the lands were known as Edulfstun now Eddleston (in Peeblesshire). From this last form the descendants of Edulf assumed their surname.

EDGAR. From the OE. personal name *Eadgar*, rendered 'happy spear.' Perhaps the first of the name recorded in Scotland is Eadgar, king of Scots, seventh son of Malcolm III, who reigned from 1097–1107. The Edgars of Nithsdale, notwithstanding their OE. name are of Gaelic origin. Other Edgars held lands in Berwickshire of the earls of Dunbar. Edgar, son of Duvenald, son of Dunegal of Stranid (Strath Nith), held extensive lands in Nithsdale during the reign of William the Lion, and his descendants assumed the surname of Edgar. About the year 1200 this Edgar granted the church of Kyllosbern and the church of Mortun in Strehtun to the Abbey of Kelso (*Kelso*, 340, 347). Richard Edgar of Wedderbie, a witness at the second marriage of King Robert Bruce, who possessed the castle and half the barony of Sanchar or Seneschar in Upper Nithsdale during that king's reign (Ross, *Heraldic plates*; RMS., I, 27) is probably Richard Edgar who was sheriff of Dumfries 1329 (ER., I, p. 123), and the Ricardus Edger who witnessed a royal charter of the lands of Dalmakeran, c. 1316–18 (*Annandale*, I, p. 132). Thomas Edzear or Odeir had a charter of the lands of Kildonan in the Rynes from Robert I (RMS., I, App. II, 681). Donald Edzear acquired from David II the captainship of the Clanmacgowin in Nithsdale (ibid., I, App. II, 982), and Richard filius Ricardi dictus Edger had a charter of the land of Kvrckepatric (ibid., I, 94). John Edzer was retoured heir in lands in parish of Colwen (Colvend), 1618 (*Retours, Kirkcudbright*, 139). Aeggar, king of Scots, a. 1189, Edgair 1673, Edgear 1508, Edyear 1591, Edzair 1574, Edzaire 1516,

Edzare 1602, Edzeare 1591, Eger 1686. In the North of Ireland spelled Eager.

EDGELY, EDGLY. Thomas Edgelaw appears in Foulden, Berwickshire, 1653, and Alexander Edgelie there in 1686 (*Lauder*). Thomas Edglaw was witness in the trial of Janet Paistoune for witchcraft in Dalkeith, 1661. Perhaps from Edgelaw in Midlothian.

EDIE. See under ADDIE. Lower says "The Scottish family of Edie appear from armorial evidence to be a branch of the Adamsons, and Nisbet seems to consider the names identical."

EDINBURGH. From the name of the city. Alexander de Edynburgh witnessed a confirmation charter by David, bishop of St. Andrews between 1233 and 1255 (*Soltre*, p. 26; RD., p. 71), and as Alexander de Edenburg he witnessed a charter to the monks of Holyrood in 1240 (LSC., 76). Robertus de Edinbright was canon of Glasgow, 1265 (RAA., I, p. 269), James of Edinburgh, burgess of Edinburgh, rendered homage for his possessions in 1296 (*Bain*, II, p. 197), and in 1328 we have record of a payment to John de Edinburgh (ER., I, p. 101). Other individuals of the name are mentioned in the same volume. Thomas of Edyngburgh, Scots merchant, to be freed from Tower of London, 1396 (*Bain*, IV, 480), John de Edynburgh, burgess of Irvine, witnessed an instrument of sasine there in 1446 (*Irvine*, I, p. 137), and Helen Edinburgh appears in 1499 (PDG.). The surname is now probably extinct.

EDINDEOCHT. Local. There is an Edindiach in the parish of Huntly, Edindiack in the parish of Gartly, and Edyndiach in Keith, Banffshire, William Edyndeach was admitted burgess of Aberdeen, 1499, and Andrew Edindeauch in 1505 (NSCM., I, p. 12, 43). Andrew Edindeocht contributed to church repairs in Aberdeen, 1508 (CRA., p. 79). Robert Edindiaucht who appears in Aberdeen, 1530 (CRA., p. 135), may be Robert Endeocht of Aberdeen whose obit is recorded in 1533 (REA., II, p. 212). Patrick Endeaucht was admitted burgess there in 1526, and Alexander Endeaut in 1529 (NSCM., I, p. 49, 51). David Endeocht who was summoned in an action of spulzie in 1557 is mentioned again as juror on an inquest (RSCA., I, p. 151, 221). He is doubtless the David Indeaucht or Endiaucht who appears as burgess and dean of guild of Aberdeen, 1574 and 1582 (CRA., p. 13, 45), and the David Endiaoche of Aberdeen whose ship was lost in 1577 (SCM., II, p. 47).

EDINGTON, EDDINGTON. From the old barony of the same name in the parish of Chirnside, Berwickshire. Aldanus de Edington and his son Adam successively attested charters granted to the Priory of Coldingham by Waldeve and Patrick, earls of Dunbar, between 1166 and 1189, and Robert of Edington is also among the witnesses to a charter of 1193 (*Raine,* 136, 115, 116, 117, 140, etc.). Adam de Edintun also witnessed a charter by Earl Waldeve to the monks of Melrose of pasture on Lammermuir, c. 1166–1182 (*Frasers of Philorth,* I). John of Edynton in 1290 granted a charter in favor of the Abbey of Neubotle (*Neubotle,* p. 164), and Walter de Edynton, a Scots prisoner of war taken at Dunbar in 1296 and sent to Fotheringay Castle was still prisoner there in 1298 (*Bain,* II, p. 177, 260). The seal of Ricarde de Edington is appended to a document regarding some rights of common c. 1450 (*Seals Supp.,* 333), and the seal of Gilbert of Edington is appended to an inquisition held in the court of Sir Alexander, Lord Home, bailie of Coldingham, in 1453 (ibid., 332). Thomas de Edingtoun *de eodem* is mentioned in a retour of lands of Wedderburn in 1469 (*Sc. Ant.,* VII, p. 25), and Robert de Edingtone is in record in 1478 (*Home,* 17). James Edington and others were summoned for holding the Castle of Dunbar against the king in 1479 (APS., II, p. 125). Richard of Edingtone and Robert of Edingtone witnessed an instrument of sasine in 1478, and Edward Edyngtone witnessed a similar instrument in 1496 (*Home,* 24, 28). Dik Ethingtouñs son was summoned in 1479 to answer to Parliament for treason and other crimes (APS., II, p. 129), and David Edington of that Ilk was one of the Merse proprietors who, in 1567, signed a bond of adherence to James VI as king (Crawford, *Officers of state,* p. 443). Another David Edingtoune was a commander of troops in Sweden under the great Gustavus Adolphus, William Idingtoun was retoured heir in lands in the barony of Coldingham in 1634 (*Retours, Berwick,* 206), Anna Idintoune is recorded in Coldinghame, 1673 (*Lauder*), and Elspit Edentoune died in the Kirktoun of Strickmartin in 1679 (*Jervise,* I, p. 204). The Edingtons of that Ilk sold their lands in 1594 to Sir George Ramsay of Dalhousie. Ethington 1578. Local pronunciation of the name is Ee-din-tun and Ee-thin-tun.

EDMESTON. EDMISTON. Shortened forms of EDMONDSTON, q.v., as shown by the entry "Edmiestoun of Duntreath" in 1681. James Edmestoune of Ballewyn in record in Glasgow in 1550 (*Protocols,* I). Edmistoun 1641, Edmistone 1651.

EDMOND, EDMUND. The OE. personal name *Eádmund.* Aedmund the chamberlain (*camerarius*) witnessed the charter by David I granting Estrahanent (Annandale) to Robert Brus, c. 1124 (*Nat. MSS.,* I, 19). Ædmund filius Forn and Ædmund de faȝeside were witnesses to a charter by Thor, son of Swan, c. 1150 (LSC., p. 11). William Edmen, juror on an inquisition at Stirling in 1598, appears in the following year as William Edmond, bailie of Stirling, and in 1604 as Ednem- (SBR., p. 89, 93, 110). Janet Edmont is recorded in Edinburgh in 1617 (*Edinb. Marr.*). John Philip Edmond was a distinguished Scottish bibliographer.

EDMONDSON, EDMONSON, 'son of EDMOND,' q.v. Laurence filius Aedmundi witnessed a charter by Adam, son of Serlo, of six acres of land of Gorgin (Gorgie), a. 1200 (LSC., 34), and John Edmundson was burgess of Aberdeen in 1406 (*Friars,* 25).

EDMONSTON, EDMONDSTONE, EDMONSTONE, EDMISTON. The Edmondstons take their name from Edmonstone, the tún of Eadmund, near Edinburgh, their original home. The tún may have derived its name from Aedmund filius Forn, one of the witnesses to a charter by Thor filius Swani, c. 1150 (LSC., p. 11). They also settled in later times in Berwickshire and in Lanarkshire on lands to which they gave their name. Henry de Edmundistun who witnessed a charter c. 1200 by Henry de Brade (LSC., 57) is probably the first of the name in record. Henricus de Edmundiston who witnessed a quit claim of land in Swinis Keeth, 1248 (RD., p. 97), may be the same person. William, son and heir of Haldwin of Edmideston, resigned his land of Edmideston in the tenement of Biggar, 1322 (RHM.). John de Edmundston appears in 1368 (RMS., I, 281, etc.). The name was carried to the Shetland Isles c. 1560, and there was a family of Edmondston of Unst, of which the late Mrs. Saxby, the novelist, was a distinguished member. John Edmestoun made burgess freeman of Glasgow, 1612 (*Burgesses*), Ursilla Edmesson in record in Windhouse, 1648 (*Shetland*), and Andrew Edmestoun was notary in Lauder, 1650 (RRM., I, p. 127). Eadmundston 1338, Edemeston 1605, Edmestoune (of that Ilk). See also EDMESTON.

EDNAM. From the old lands or village of Ednam in Roxburghshire. Magister William de Edenam who witnessed a grant to the Abbey of Cambuskenneth c. 1180 (*Cambus.,* 15) is probably Magister William de Edenham who witnessed confirmation of the sale of the land of Scrogges to the church of Glasgow between 1208–13 (REG., p. 76). Robert de

EDNAM, *continued*

Edingham witnessed a gift of two parts of land in the territory of Inuerwyc to Kelso c. 1190 (*Kelso*, p. 213). Stephen de Edynham and William, his father, witnessed the charter by Brice, bishop of Moray of the church of Deveth to Spyny c. 1202–22 (REM., 53). Master William de Edynham, archdeacon of Dunkeld, a charter witness in 1238 (LIM., 72) had possession of the church of Sanchar in 1239 (RMP., p. 226). Richard de Edenham witnessed the gift of Parva Kyp to the Abbey of Kelso a. 1240 (*Kelso*, 181), and in 1258 Robert filius Alani de Edenham witnessed resignation of the lands of Floris in Redden (ibid., 218). Magister William de Edenham who attested a charter by Patrick, first earl of Dunbar (*Raine*, 118) is probably Magister William de Edinham who was a witness c. 1235 (LSC., 67). Robert de Edinham witnessed a confirmation by Philip de Halyburton to Kelso c. 1261 (*Kelso*, 270), and a later Robert de Edenham of Roxburgh rendered homage in 1296 (*Bain*, II, p. 199). Robert de Edenham was one of the garrison of Stirling in 1339–40 (*Bain*, III, p. 241). Individuals of the name early made their way to the north. Robert de Edinham was custumar of Aberdeen in 1340 (ER., I, p. 461), John de Edynham held land in Aberdeenshire in 1342 (REA., I, p. 71), and another John de Edvnhame was a canon of Aberdeen in 1366 (ibid., II, p. 58). In 1368 an agreement was concluded between John de Edynhame, son and heir of Robert de Edynhame, burgess of Aberdeen, and Thomas Lowel (ibid., II, p. 284). Fergus of Edenham had a safe conduct to pass through England in 1372 (*Bain*, IV, 194). Thomas Ednaym (Eddenavm or Ednayme) appears as prebendary of Clat in 1427 and 1434, and as canon of Aberdeen in 1451 (REA., I, p. 227, 234; II, p. 91, 297). Mr. Thomas Edname was admitted burgess of Aberdeen in 1447 (NSCM., I, p. 11), and Andrew Ednem witnessed a lease by George, abbot of Inchaffray in 1491 (*Inchaffray*, p. xcvii). In *St. Andrews* spelled Aidname 1586, Aidnem 1589, and Adnen, Edname, Edneme (see in index). Eddynname c. 1500.

EDNIE. A surname recorded in Fife. Of local origin from Ednie in the parish of St. Fergus, Aberdeenshire. There is also West and North Ednie nearby. Alexander Ednie of that Ilk, 1666 (*Edin. App.*). The name still exists in Edinburgh and Kirkcaldy.

EDOLF. From the common OE. personal name *Ead(w)ulf*, 'blessed wolf.' Edulfus filius Norman witnessed David's great charter to Melrose a. 1153 (*Nat. MSS.*, I, 17). Edulf pre-

positus de Molla a. 1177 (RMP., p. 74). Edulf, son of Vtredi obtained from Richard de Moreuille the lands of Gillemoristun 'que antiquitus uocabatur peniacob' a. 1189 (REG., p. 39), and changed the place name to Edulfestun, later corrupted by vulgar pronunciation to Eddleston. He also got from the same Richard de Moreville some lands in the territory of Lochogow in Lothian where he settled. He was succeeded by his son, Adam, and he by his son, Constantin (*Neubotle*, 33–38). Dominus Adam filius Edolfi was one of the witnesses to the *Diuise de Stobbo*, c. 1190 (REG., p. 89). Adam, son of Edulph, confirmed to Constantine, his son 'pro homagio et servitio suo' a part of his land in the territory of Eduluistun 'que olim vocabatur Peniacob' (ibid., p. 142). Ade filius Edulphi granted a charter to Neubotle Abbey c. 1230 (*Neubotle*, 25), and c. 1245 there is a confirmation charter by 'Constantinus filius Ade filii Edulfi,' among the witnesses to which is 'Constantino filio meo' (ibid., 26).

EDOM. A broad Scots form of Adam, as testified by the well-known ballad "Edom o' Gordon."

EDWARD. From the OE. personal name *Eádweard*, 'happy ward' or 'guardian.' The seal of George Edward, 1441, is described by Macdonald (842). Wattv Edward was tenant of part of the burcht of Kethik, 1504 (*Cupar-Angus*, I, p. 256), Andreas Edwaird in Murthlac, 1550 (*Illus.*, II, p. 262), Thomas Edward, merchant burgess of Linlithgow, 1637 (*Retours, Linlithgow*, 134), and Alexander Edward, writer in Edinburgh, 1688 (*Inquis.*, 6925). John Edward, tanner burgess of Edinburgh, 1722 (*Guildry*, p. 125). The name was early confused with UDARD, q.v., and Peter (*Baronage of Mearns*) says the old name of the family of Edward of Balruddery in Angus was Uduard. Edwart 1634.

EDWARDS, 'son of EDWARD,' q.v.

EDWARDSON, 'son of EDWARD,' q.v. George Edwardson or Edwardeson of Edinburgh who had safe conducts to travel in England in 1486 and 1490 (*Bain*, IV, 1517, 1558) is doubtless the George Edwardsoun, burgess of Edinburgh in 1495 (*Home*, 25; CRA., p. 422), and juror on an inquest at West Reston in the same year (*Home*, 27).

EGARR. A corruption of EDGAR, q.v. Richard Egger was tenant on Newbattle Abbey lands, 1563 (*Neubotle*, p. 330). Jennet Eggar and Margaret Eggar were examined for the Test at Tinwald, 1685 (RPC., 3. ser. XI, p. 433). The name is still current in Dumfries.

EGGLESCLIFFE. John de Egglescliffe, bishop of Glasgow, 1318-22, was an Englishman. He probably derived his name from Egglescliffe, county Durham.

EGLINTON. From the lands of the same name in the Cunningham district of Ayrshire, the 'tûn of Eglun.' Brice de Eglunstone, son of quondam Eglun, dominus de Eglunstone, had a grant of twenty acres of land in feuferme from the burgh of Irvine in 1205 (*Irvine*, I, p. 3). Rauf de Eglyntone of the county of Are rendered homage in 1296. His seal bears a hare in her form, foliage, and S' *Radulfi de Eglintun* (*Bain*, II, p. 205, 549). In the same year he was juror on an inquest held on the lands of Lady Elena la Zuche in Conyngham (ibid., p. 216). Hugh de Eglynton or Eglyntoun appears several times as a charter witness between 1357 and 1372 (REB., I, 16; CAB., p. 539-540; *Irvine*, I, 12; *Inchaffray*, p. 126). "The gude Syr Hew of Eglintoun" is commemorated by Dunbar in his "Lament for the Makaris." William Eglyntoune was a witness in Glasgow in 1550 and 1554 (*Protocols*, I), and Jonet Eglinton in Nethermains, parish of Kilbryde, is in record in 1632 (*Campsie*). The family appears to have ended in the direct line in the latter half of the fourteenth century, when the heiress, Elizabeth, married Sir John Montgomery.

EGO, Eggo. A common surname in Braemar and Cromar in the seventeenth century and earlier, and still found there. The name represents a Gaelic attempt at the name Adam (*Adhamh*), with medial *dh* hardened to g. In the phonetically spelled Fernaig MS. (of date 1688) the name is written 'Ahu,' and in the still earlier manuscript of the Dean of Lismore (c. 1520) it appears as 'Awzoe' (*z* here a guttural *y*). Eggou ruffus made a gift of land to the Priory of May early in the thirteenth century (RPSA., p. 282), and Ego filius Gilberti (for Gillebride) was a serf of the Abbey of Dunfermline in the same century (RD., p. 220). Ego de Strathhathe of Perth rendered homage, 1296 (*Bain*, II, p. 200), and Michel le fiz Ego was one of an inquest in Stirling, 1304 (ibid., p. 381). Ego 'marus' was one of an inquest relating to the Priory of Roustenot (Restennet) in 1322 (RMS., I, App. 1, 29). Ego, son of Fergus, earl of Mar, had confirmation of a charter of land of Huchtirerne (Auchterairn) in Cromarre, 1364 (RMS., I, 191; *Sc. Ant.*, II, p. 10: in Robertson's Index his name is wrongly given as Eugene — RMS., I, App. 2, 1500). Robertus filius Ego in the parish of Tarwas (Tarves) was excommunicated, 1382 (REA., I, p. 166).

Henry Ego and Thomas Ego appear as charter witnesses in Arbroath, 1467 (RAA., II, 174). David Ego was admitted burgess of Aberdeen, 1477, and Andrew Ego, 1498 (NSCM., I, p. 26, 39). Alane Ego held a lease of Bucham in 1477 (*Cupar-Angus*, I, p. 205). Part of the lands of Drumsleed was leased to John Ego and Andrew Ego, his son, 1502 (RAA., II, 429). Merzone Ego is in record in Strathdee, 1527 (*Grant*, III, p. 70). Gilbert Egie in Dysart, 1543, and Thomas Egey, 1565 (*Dysart Rec.*, p. 10, 32). John Ego was one of an assize in the regality of Spynie, 1597 (SCM., II, p. 139). Malcolm Ego, servitor to the Lady Mackintosh, signed the Clan Chattan Band of 1609 as witness, and is frequently mentioned in Mackintosh writs. One of the Mackintosh families was Sliochd Ago vic Lachlan. As forename we have: Ago Lammesone, and Ago McGillequhome, in Strathdee, 1527 (*Grant*, III, p. 70), Ago M'Andoy, 1578, etc. See also AYE.

EGOSON, 'son of Ego,' q.v. Donald Egosone, tenant in Strathdee, 1527 (*Grant*, III, p. 70).

EINARSON, 'son of *Einarr*,' an ON. personal name. Jon Einarson, minister, appears in a Faroese or Shetland document of c. 1407 (REO., p. 29). Manns Enorson in Garth, parish of Tingwall, 1624 (*Shetland*).

EISDALE. A variant of EASDALE, q.v.

ELBOTTLE. Of territorial origin from the place of the same name in the parish of Dirleton, East Lothian. Ivo de Elebotle and Huwe fitz Geffray de Elbotle, both of the county of Edinburgh, rendered homage in 1296. The seal of the former bears the Agnus Dei and the legend S' *Ivonis de Elbotel* (*Bain*, II, p. 201, 547). No further mention of this name appears in record.

ELDER. The 'elder,' signifying the elder of two bearing the same forename. John Eldar or Eldare de Corstorfin was burgess of Edinburgh in 1423 (LSC., p. 227; *Egidii*, p. 44). The surname is also recorded in Aberdeen in 1447 (CRA., p. 15). John Elder, a renegade Scot, urged Henry VIII ('Bagcheeks') to invade Scotland, assuring him of the support of the Highland Clans (*Coll.*, p. 23-32). Andro Elder, reidare at Menmure, 1574 (RMR.). Cf. MACNORAVAICH.

ELDINGSOUN. Umquhill Jacob Eldingsoun held land in Brughe, Unst, 1625 (OSS., I, 137).

ELGE. There was a family of this name in Dundee in the fifteenth century. Thomas Elge was witness there in 1412 (HP., II, p. 152), and James Elge, burgess there, 1427 (*Panmure*, II, 195). In 1443 there is mention of "terris campestribus rudis burgalibus que sunt Nycholaii Elge filii quondam Thomas Elge" in Dundee (REB., I, 93). Patrick Elge alias Eleis, burgess of Montrois, 1596 (*Retours, Perth*, 1083). Janet Eldge is in record in Dunkeld, 1685 (DPD., I, p. 488), and James Ealdge in Fordie, 1693, and two more of the name are in Dunkeld Commissariot Record.

ELGERIK. William of Elgerik of Lanarkshire who rendered homage in 1296 (*Bain*, II, p. 213) derived his name from the lands later known as Elgereth (OPS., I, p. 132).

ELGIN. Of local origin from the town of the same name. Alexander de Elgyn and Augustine de Elgin are witnesses to a charter by Hugh Freskyn c. 1211 (CSR., I, p. 8). Richard de Elgyn appears in Aberdeen in 1317 (SCM., V, p. 12), and in 1328 there is entry of an annuity to William de Elgyn, clerk (ER., I, p. 99).

ELIAS. A favorite personal name in the Middle Ages. From the Hebrew, meaning 'El is Jahweh.' Helias, son of Huctred had a charter of the lands of Dundas from Waldef, son of Cospatric, c. 1180, and Helias of Hadestanden was one of the witnesses (APS., I, p. 82). Helias or Helyas, clericus regis, de Munros, c. 1178–1214 (RAA., I, 1, 9). Helya, canon of Glasgow, 1177–1199 (RMP., p. 99), is probably Helias frater domini Jocelini, bishop of Glasgow, c. 1170 (*Kelso*, 356). Helias, clericus, son of Fulbert (of Pollok) granted the church of Mernes to the monks of Paisley, c. 1189–99 (RMP., p. 100). In the confirmation charter by King William the Lion which follows he is named Helias de Pertheic (Partick). As Elya or Helya, canon of Glasgow, he is a charter witness between 1175–1207 (ibid., p. 109, 110). Helias was parson of Old Rokesburg, c. 1190–1232 (*Kelso*, p. 136; *Melros*, p. 229). Helya de Elmedene witnessed charter by Ebrardus de Penkathleht to the church of St. Cuthbert of Durham in reign of William the Lion (*Raine*, 163). Helia vicarius de Baneth', 1233 (REM., p. 97). A pardon was granted to Elyas de Vaus, 1307 (*Bain*, II, 1919). As forename: Elias Tervett, 1509 (*Trials*, I, p. 110°).

ELIOT, ELIOTT. *See under* ELLIOT.

ELIOTSON, 'son of Eliot' (from Elias + Fr. dimin. *-ot*). Adam Eliotson was juror on inquest at Rane, Aberdeenshire, 1398 (REA., I, p. 202).

ELLEM. From the barony of the same name now incorporated in the parish of Longformacus, Berwickshire. Henry de Ellom of the county of Berewyk rendered homage in 1296, and Adam de Elom was received to the king of England's peace in 1321 (*Bain*, II, p. 203; III, 724). Another Henricus de Ellame is mentioned in 1362 (RMS., I, 137), Richard de Ellum appears as a charter witness in Edinburgh in 1367 (ibid., 265), and Malaseus Ellam was vicar of Forgund in 1463 (CMN., 33). John Ellum de Butterden, who is mentioned in a retour of the lands of Wedderburn in 1469 (*Sc. Ant.*, VII, p. 25) is doubtless the John Elleme against whom a process was issued in 1475 for holding Dunbar Castle against the king (APS., II, p. 125). John of Ellem of Buttirden occurs again in record in 1478 (*Home*, p. 18, 24), and in 1495 there is mention of a David Ellem (ibid., p. 25, 27). John Ellem was retoured heir of Slichthouss in the barony of Bonkle in 1597, and another John Ellem was retoured heir of Peter Ellem in the lands and barony of Butterdene in 1600 (*Retours, Berwickshire*, 14, 19, 58, 95, 493). John Ellem was portioner of Bassindene in 1636 (*Inquis.*, 2207), and Stiphane Ailme was one of a number who attested the bounds of Hattonis Croft, 1651 (*Home*, p. 220). Ellim 1605. Brief accounts of the Ellems of Butterdean are in Thomson's *Coldingham parish and priory* (p. 227–232), and in the *History of the Berwickshire Naturalists' Club* (XIX, p. 355–362).

ELLEN. Alexander Ellen, a Berwickshire laird, in record, 1530 (*Trials*, I, p. 147°). George Ellen recorded in Paxtoun in 1664, and Elspeth Ellain in Aytoun in the following year (*Lauder*) derived their surname from the land of Ellen in Berwickshire (*Retours, Berwick*, 449). Small places named Elleinsyde and Elleinfurde are near by. Elen 1816.

ELLET, probably 'son of Elias' or Ellis, from diminutive Ell + diminutive ending *-et*. Thomas Ellet in Edinburgh, 1604 (*Edinb. Marr.*). Magister John Ellet, advocate, 1643 (*Inquis.*, 2939).

ELLIOT, ELIOT, ELIOTT, ELLIOTT. The early form of this well-known Border name was Elwald or Elwold, for the full OE. *Ælfwald*, and until the end of the fifteenth century the spelling of the name was fairly regular. Elwald and Elwold were common in OE. times and the name continued in use as a Christian name down to the period when surnames became common. It was a common name on the Borders, the original home of the Elliots. The form Elliot is used by the Minto family and most of the others on the Border, and Eliott is used by the family of Stobo. The four forms of the name are thus referred to in an old rhyme:

"The double L and single T
Descend from Minto and Wolflee,
The double T and single L
Mark the old race in Stobs that dwell,
The single L and single T
The Eliots of St. Germains be,
But double T and double L
Who they are, nobody can tell."
— *Annals of a Border Club*, p. 172.

As very often happened in other instances 'Elwald' as a Christian name became extinct, but survived as a surname. One of the earliest and most curious variants of the name was Elwand, which appears as early as 1502 (*Trials*, I, p. 32°). The uniformity in the way of writing this name, which was, as already mentioned, maintained to the end of the fifteenth century, gave way in the sixteenth to a rich variety of spellings, of which Armstrong (*Liddesdale*, I, p. 178) gives no less than seventy examples, a number which really does not exhaust the list. Armstrong's list is reproduced here, with a few additions, as an illustration of the labor and difficulty encountered by one seeking for information on surnames at first hand:

Singular: Ælwold, Allat, Dalliot, Eellot, Eleot (1624), Elewald, Eliot, Eliott, Ellat, Elleot (1655), Ellet, Ellett, Ellette, Elliott, Elliot, Ellioti, Elliswod, Ellot, Ellote (1639), Ellott, Elluat, Ellwald, Ellwod, Ellwodd, Ellwold, Ellwood, Elnuand, Elnwand, Eluand, Eluat (1556), Eluwand, Elvand, Elwaird, Elwald (1561), Elwalde (1494), Elwat, Elwod, Elwold, Elwood, Elwoold, Elyot, Elyoth, Hellwodd, Illot, Ilwand, Eleot, Elwet, Elwett, Elwoode, Helewald.

Plural: Aylewoodes, Aylewoods, Elioats, Eliots, Ellattis, Elliottes, Ellotes, Ellots, Ellottes, Ellottis, Ellotts, Ellwoods, Eluottis (1570), Elwades, Elwaldes, Elwets, Elwaldis, Elwalds, Elwalls, Elwandis, Elwarths, Elwaths, Elwodds, Elwoldis, Elwolds, Elwoodes, Elwoods, Elwoolds, Evlewoodz, Ellyots, Elwatts, Elwottis, Eylwittes.

ELLIS. From ELIAS, q.v., a favorite personal name in the Middle Ages, through OE. *Elis* or *Elys*. The "name was wonderfully popularized throughout western Europe by the Crusaders" (*Bardsley*). John Heles was burgess of Dundee in 1482 (RAA., II, 213). David Elleis was "kevpar of the parroche kirk" of Aberdeen in 1565 (CRA., p. 360), and John Elleiss ap-

pears there in 1522 (ibid., p. 104). Richard Eleis rendered to Exchequer the accounts of the bailies of the burgh of Jedburgh in 1563 (ER., XIX, p. 223), and David Elles was appointed "to teche and leir ony barnis abon sax yeris" in Stirling in 1557 (SBR., p. 71). Andrew Elleis, notary in Kirkwall, 1634 (OSR., I, p. 279), and Alexander Elleis had a charter of lands in Newington in 1639 (BOEC., x, p. 212). Alexander Ealis is recorded in Melrose, 1641, and George Elleis in Darnick, 1662 (RRM., I, p. 87; II, p. 3). Patrick Æles was cordiner in Edinburgh, 1648 (*Edinb. Marr.*), Magister John Eleis of Eleistoune was heir in lands in the lordship of Kilpount, 1686 (*Retours, Lanark*, 261), Andrew Elliss appears in Regorton, 1719 (*Dunkeld*), and Bessie Ellies in Cairnwheep, 1738 (*Moray*). The wife of James Anderson, author of the *Diplomatum Scotiae Thesaurus*, was an Ellies of Elieston or Ellistoune, West Lothian, a family said to be of English origin (*Stodart*). Aeis, Ales, and Aless are given in index to ROA. as forms of Ellis. Eilleis 1677, Eleiss 1685, Eles 1606, Elies 1670.

ELLISON, 'son of ELLIS,' q.v. Rogier Elyssone of Berwickshire rendered homage in 1296 (*Bain*, II, p. 206), William Elysson, Scots prisoner of war, was released from Newgate prison, 1375, and John Elison had a safe conduct into England in 1424 (*Bain*, IV, 227, 970). James Elisone in record in parish of Forteviot, 1654 (*Dunblane*). Schir Alexander Elisoune, chaplane, had a "respitt" for his part in slaughter in 1541 (*Trials*, I, p. ° 257).

ELLISTON. From the lands of Elliston near Bowden, Roxburghshire. John, son of Iliue de Iliuestun or Ylif de Ylifstun, held these lands in the reign of Alexander II, and Laurence Ylifstun is mentioned in 1249 (*Melros*, p. 231, 232, 237). David Elistoun was retoured heir of Henry Elistoun in Kyngarrach, *avi*, in lands of Newbirnetoun in the parish of Newbirne (Newburn) in 1637 (*Retours, Fife*, 543).

ELLON. From the village of Ellon in the parish of the same name, Aberdeenshire. Syme of Ellone contributed towards repair of the church of Aberdeen in 1508 (CRA., p. 79).

ELMSLIE, ELMSLEY, ELMSLY, EMSLIE. A surname now found mainly in Aberdeenshire, and doubtless of English origin. Robert de Elmleghe or de Elmelev of Aberdeenshire rendered homage, 1296 (*Bain*, II, p. 195, 206). William de Elmvsley was one of an inquisition in Aberdeen, 1333 (REA., I, p. 54), and

ELMSLIE, ELMSLEY, ETC., *continued*

Thomas Elmyslie was admitted burgess there, 1498 (NSCM., I, p. 39). William Elmislie was reidare at Ruthven, 1574 (RMR.). Robert Elmslie was in Cultballoch, 1599 *(Dunblane)*, and John Elmislye was tenant of the Dauche (in Inchmarnoche, Banffshire), 1600 (SCM., IV, p. 315). James Emslie of Loanhead first systematically quarried the famous Aberdeen granite between 1715 and 1745 (Watt, *Aberdeen and Banff*, p. 337–338). Robert Elmslie was member of the Huntly Volunteers, 1801 (*Will*, p. 19), and a family named Elmsley were owners of Pitmedden, Dyce, in middle of nineteenth century (AEI., p. 4). Elmeslie 1567, Elmisle 1524, Elmysle 1492, Emslay 1738.

ELPHIN. A variant of ALPIN, q.v. Elphin or Elpin, prior of Inchaffray in first quarter of thirteenth century (LAC., p. 250).

ELPHINSTONE. From the lands of Elphinstone in the parish of Tranent, Midlothian. Elphinstone first appears as a place name in a deed by Alanus de Swinton, c. 1235 (RD., 111, 112), when mention is made of the "homines (serfs) de Elfinistun." This Alanus de Swinton had a son John, and he is probably the John who acquired the Elphinstone lands and so became John of Elphinston. John de Elphinstone witnessed a grant by Roger de Quincy to the monks of Dryburgh of the wood of Gladswood c. 1250 (*Dryburgh*, p. 99). The witnesses to this charter are not recorded in the Bannatyne Club edition of the chartulary, but Crawford, who saw the original chartulary, gives John de Elphinstone as one of them. A later John de Elphinstone rendered homage, 1296. His seal bears a shield charged with a boar's head, etc., and S' *Iohannis de Elphinstun* (Bain, II, 773). Aleyn de Elfinestone of Berwickshire also rendered homage, 1296 (ibid., p. 206). Alexander of Elphinstone (c. 1363–1370) is the earliest of the family known to be styled *dominus ejusdem*. John de Elphinston (d. c. 1340) married Marjorie Erth (now Airth), heiress of Erthbeg, and acquired with her the lands there which formed the nucleus of the barony of Elphinstone in the parish of Airth, Stirlingshire. Port Elphinstone (Inverurie, Aberdeenshire), is named from another branch of the family, Elphinstone of Logie-Elphinstone. Alexander Elphynston and William Elphvnston had protection and safe conduct into England, 1486 (*Bain*, IV, 1522). George Elphistun, saidler in Aberdeen, 1581 (SCM., II, p. 54). Elfinistoun, Elfinvstoun, and Elfvnistoun c. 1370–1390, Elfvneston 1338, Elfynston 1362, Elphestoun 1599, El-phingstoun 1594, Elphingstone 1600, Elphistin 1581, Elphistoun 1521, Elphynstoun 1533, Elphynstoune 1539.

ELRICK. A not uncommon surname in Aberdeenshire and part of Banffshire, of local origin from one or more of the half dozen small places of the name in the former county. Alexander Elrick was concerned in an action about the ownership of corn in 1510 (RSCA., I, p. 40), John and Andrew Elrick are mentioned in the same record in 1574 (I, p. 194, 210), another John Elrik was witness in an Aberdeen witch trial in 1597 (SCM., I, p. 129), Alexander Elrick was sometime in Wester Craigie 1791 (CRA.), and another Alexander Elrick, farmer in Invernettie, was retoured heir to his father in 1803. Isabella Elrick in Banchory-Devenick died in 1873. John Bell Elrick of Cruden was killed in the first Great War *(Turriff)*, and three brothers of the name also from Cruden served in the same war.

ELSHENER, ELSHENAR, ELSHENDER, ALSHIONER. Local or dialectal pronunciations of ALEXANDER, q.v., which have become fixed surnames. Alexander Aleschunder was bailie of Stirling, 1555 (SBR., p. 278), Euphame Elchyneur is in record in Perth, 1561 (*Sc. Ant.*, I, p. 101), and Alexander Elzenour was admitted burgess of Aberdeen, 1574 (NSCM., I, p. 71). Alexander Alshunder of Menstrie in record 1589 (*Sc. Ant.*, VI, p. 164), John Alshenour was accused of theft in Spynie in 1596, and in the following year Katherine Elshenour was burnt for witchcraft in Aberdeen (SCM., II, p. 133, v, p. 68). Archibald Alexshunder or Alschunder appears as bailie and dean of guild in Stirling, 1596 and 1600 (SBR., p. 95, 281, 282). Gilbert Alshenour was warded in the Tolbooth of Aberdeen in 1605 (CRA., p. 267), David Alschunder, merchant burgess of Edinburgh, 1617 (*Inquis.*, 693), and John Alshioner was burgess of Aberdeen, 1633 (SCM., III, p. 117). James Elsheoner in Inverness was described in 1627 as an idle and masterless man (RPC., 2. ser. II, p. 97), and Deacon Elshender, a one-time celebrated worthy of Arbroath (d. 1840), is commemorated in *Poems on various subjects* (p. 69, 137, and notes) by J. S. Sands. Aleschenor 1595, Alschinder 1615, Alschinner 1618, Alschioner 1614, Alschonder and Alschoner 1630, Alshinor 1637, Alshonar 1596, Alshonder 1617, Alshoner 1635, Alshonir 1589, Alshumder 1624, Alzenher 1652, Alzenor and Aschenour 1596, Ashioner 1634, Elchuner 1615, Elshinar 1688, Elshioner 1611, Elshunder 1651, Alshonner, Elsender, Elsher. As forename: Elshie.

ELVINGSTOUN. An old surname recorded in charters relating to the Hospital of Soutra (*Soltre*, index). There is an estate named Elvingston in the parish of Gladsmuir, East Lothian.

ELYOT. Perhaps from Elliot in the parish of Arbirlot in Angus, in 1254 Eloth. Patrick Elyoth, capellanus sancte crucis de Montross, 1437 (REB., II, 56). John Elyot, tenant of Welton of Balbrogi, 1473 (*Cupar-Angus*, I, p. 184).

EMELTOUN. Perhaps from Embleton in Northumberland. Charles Emeltoun recorded in Dunse, 1719 (*Lauder*).

EMM. Alan filius Emme held lands in Dumfries a. 1214 (*Kelso*, 11). Simon filius Emme was witness in Scon in reign of David II (*Scon*, p. 126), Robert Eme was bailie of the burgh of Aberbrothoc, 1394 (RAA., II, 42), and James Eme de Lathame had a charter confirmed to him in 1434 (*Panmure*, II, 197). From a personal name Emma, màsculine as well as feminine?

EMSLIE. A form of ELMSLIE, q.v.

ENDERKELYN. Local. Michael de Enderkelyn of Edinburghshire rendered homage, 1296 (*Bain*, II, p. 211).

ENEAS. See under ÆNEAS.

ENGAINE. The Engaines or Ingaines were Northamptonshire tenants in Domesday, and were most probably of Norman origin. The earldom of Northampton was one of the honors held by David I, and Berengarius Engaine, the first and perhaps only one of his name recorded in Scotland, was doubtless a vassal of that prince and accompanied him to Scotland. Berengarius was one of the witnesses to the *Inquisitio Davidis*, c. 1124 (REG., 1), and to a charter of a carucate of land, etc., to the church of St. John in the Castle of Roxburgh, c. 1128 (ibid., 4). He also witnessed the charter by King David granting Annandale to Robert de Brus, c. 1124 (*Nat. MSS.*, I, 19), witnessed the confirmation by the same king of Coldingham, Oldcambus, etc., to the monks of S. Cuthbert at Durham in 1126 (*Raine*, 15), witnessed the confirmation of the rights of the Priory of Durham to the church of Coldingham c. 1130 (ibid., 16), and was also witness to a charter to the monks of St. Cuthbert at Berwick in 1132 (ibid., 18). As Belingerus Angaine he witnessed two charters by Prince Henry in favor of Eustace Fitz-John, one granted at Seleschurche and the other at Huntendon (Hartshorne, *Feudal*

and military antiquities of Northumberland, II, app., p. cxiv–cxv). He appears to have held lands in Roxburghshire as he made a grant to the monks of Jedburgh of a mark of silver yearly from the mill of Crailing, with two bovates of land, a toft, and a *villein* or bond-servant, and for the support of a chaplain who served in the chapel of the same, he granted other two bovates and other two tofts, one of which was near the church (*Morton*, p. 50). William Engaine, probably of the same family, witnessed the grant by Earl Henry to Holm Cultram (Dugdale, *Monasticon*, v, p. 594). Some notes on the Engaines are given in Round's *Feudal England*, p. 154–156, and a pedigree and additional information in Baker's *Northamptonshire*, 1822–30, I, p. 9.

ENGLISH. From ME. adjective *Englisch*, 'English,' i.e. an Englishman, LL. *Anglicus*. Richard Anglicus appears as witness c. 1220 (CMN., 10), and Reginald and Radulf Anglico attest a charter c. 1330 (RHM., I, p. 39). Thomas Engilsk gave up land he unlawfully bought in Shetland, 1485 (OSR., I, p. 54). Robert English and Samuel English were residents in the parish of Borgue in 1684 (RPC., 3. ser. IX, p. 566). John English, late kirk treasurer, Edinburgh, 1737 (*Guildry*, p. 161).

ENNERKYPE. William of Ennerkype was one of the contractors for building the old house of Drumminor, 1440 (*Jervise*, II, p. 218). Hardly likely to be from Innerkip, Renfrewshire.

ENTERKIN. A rare surname of local origin, from Enterkin, parish of Durrisdeer, Dumfriesshire.

ENYTIYR. Janet Enytiyr in Strathdee in 1527 (*Grant*, III, p. 27). This is not a surname but represents G. *Inghean an t-saoir*, 'the wright's daughter.'

EOCHAID. A common G. name meaning 'yew-warrior,' *Eo-chaid*. It is *Ivacattos* (gen.) in ogham inscription at Colbinstown, county Wicklow, and Latinized *Achaius*. Echodius Find, son of Aidan mac Gabhran, was slain in battle with the Miathi, and Echodius Buide, younger brother of the foregoing, succeeded to the kingdom (*Adamnan*, I, 9). Eochaid, abbot of Lismore, d. c. 637 (Tighernach in ES., I, p. 160).

EOGHANN. G. *Eòghann*. The name comes from OIr. *eo*, a yew-tree, (Macneill, *Oghams*, p. 345), and means 'sprung from yew-tree.' It occurs twice in Adamnan, who mentions Iogenanus (Iogen-anus), brother of King

EOGHANN, *continued*

Aidan (III, 5), and Iogenanus, a presbyter, 'gente Pictum' (II, 9). In later Scots Gaelic and Latin documents the name appears as Eugein, Eugen, Eogain, Heochgain, Heoghan, Heodgen, Avin, Oan, and Ohan, and in Welsh is Owein and Ywein. In the north or northwest it is correctly Englished Evan or Ewan, but in Argyllshire it is erroneously used as equivalent to Hugh. Like some other Gaelic names it arose from tree-worship among the early Gaels.

ERASMUSSON, ERASMUSON. 'son of Erasmus.' Andrew Erasmusson in Sound, Shetland, 1648 (*Sc. Ant.*, XII, p. 90). William Erasmuson in Edinburgh, 1941.

ERC. A very common old Gaelic personal name, possibly of a goddess originally. According to O'Clery it has several meanings. As a man's name Erc, gen. Eirc, appears over a hundred times in the *Book of Leinster*, with a feminine Erca. In an ogham inscription at Rovesmore we find *Maqi Ercias Maqi Faloni*, "of Mac Erce son of Fallon." Erc mac Telt is ultimate ancestor of Clann Maelanfaidh (the old name of Clan Cameron). See ERP.

ERCILDOUN. From the old village of Ercildoun in the Merse, now known as Earlston. Adam de Herceldune witnessed grant of the church of Brennath (now Birnie) to the Abbey of Kelso c. 1202–22 (*Kelso*, 371). "Thomas de Ercildoun filius et heres Thome Rymour de Ercildoun" resigned to the House of Soltre "totam terram meam cum omnibus pertinenciis suis quam in tenemento de Ercildoun," 1294 (*Soltre*, p. 40). Robert of Ercildoun was sued for robbing Henry the forester at Roxburgh, 1295 (*Bain*, II, p. 189). See EARLSTON.

ERIKSON, 'son of Eric' or 'Erik,' from ON. name *Eiríkr*, 'ever powerful.' Laurence Erickson in Breck in Dalting, 1613 (*Shetland*).

ERINOCH. Local. Cf. Drummond-Ernoch in Glenartney, Perthshire. Katherine Erinoche was sister and co-heir of James Erinoche in Easter Craigtoun, 1596 (*Macdonald*, 858). Caution was found for James Eirnoch in the Craig, 1589 (*RPC.*, IV, p. 401). Cf. ERNACH.

ERKLE. John Erkyl and David Erkyl witnessed a retour of service in the lands of Banchy, 1462 (*Grandtully*, I, p. 17). John Erkle, monk of Newbotel, 1482 (*Neubotle*, 304). David Erkill, chaplain of the altar of S. Anne in Linlithgow, 1537 (*Johnsoun*). See ARKLE.

ERNACH. A writ on behalf of Richard Ernaghe was issued to the sheriff of Aberdeen, 1296 (*Bain*, II, 832). Thomas Ernach was burgess of Aberdeen, 1271 (*Fraser*, p. 9), and Thomas Ernach was sergeant of the burgh, 1317 (SCM., V, p. 7). Cf. ERINOCH.

ERNHILL. John de Ernhill was juror on an inquisition made apud Rane in 1418 (REA., I, p. 216). Perhaps from Ernehill, in the parish of Cairnie, now obsolete as a farm name (Macdonald, *Place names of West Aberdeenshire*).

ERP. A common personal name in Pictland. *Erp, Yrp* appears as the name of a Welsh king by itself in *Liber Llandavensis* (p. 72), and also compounded in *Urb-gen* (Nennius), afterwards written *Urien*. The name was borrowed from the Picts by the Norsemen and gave name to the Icelandic family of Erplingi. Erp, son of Meldun, a Scots earl, was captured by the Norsemen, and as a freedman, went to colonize Iceland in the end of the ninth century (*Landnámabók*, II, 16, 17). Erc is the Gaelic equivalent of the name.

ERROLL. Local, probably from Errol in Perthshire. Duncan Erroll, reidare at Inchecalzeoch, 1574 (RMR.). See ARROL.

ERSKINE. Of territorial origin from the barony of the same name in Renfrewshire. Henry de Erskyn who witnessed a confirmation by Alexander II of a grant by Amelec, brother of Maldoven, earl of Lennox, of the church of Rosneath to the Abbey of Paisley in 1225 (RMP., 210), is probably the first of the name in record. John de Irskyne witnessed a donation by Adam *dictus* Carpentarius of the land of Aldhingleston (or Haldhingleston), c. 1260 (ibid., p. 58). Sir John de Ireskin, knight, witnessed a sale of land in Glasgow c. 1280–90 (REG., p. 198). Johan de Irskyn of the county of Lanark rendered homage in 1296. His seal bears a stag's head cabossed, between the antlers a small four-footed animal (lion?) passant to sinister, S' *Johannis de Erkyrn* (?) (*Bain*, II, p. 204, 186). John de Herchyn witnessed a charter by David II to Robert Erskyn "de tertia parte annui redditus de Dunde et Petcarach" in 1359 (REB., I, 15). Robert de Erskyne witnessed an Aberdeen charter of 1361 (REA., I, p. 90), Robert Erschin was canon of Glasgow in 1491 (REG., 460). Rachel Askine in Newstead, 1643 (RRM., I, p. 101), and George Erskine or Askine, tailor in Irvine, 1666 (*Irvine*, II, p. 210). A fifteenth century French spelling of the name is Hasquin, and in the lists of the Scots Guards in France it appears as Assequin. Another French spelling is provided by Voltaire, who in his *Letters* *on the English Nation* wrote it 'Hareskinsl' A common pronunciation in the eighteenth century was Arskine (Fergusson, *Henry Erskine*, p. 405), and a common Scots pronunciation is 'Askin,' which is also the spelling used by Sir James Melville in his *Memoirs* in referring to Arthur Askin, master stabler to the queen. Aersken and Aersk.ne 1637, Aesking 1650, Araskine 1673, Areskin 1696, Areskine 1710, Arskeyne 1645, Arskin 1594, Arskine 1693, Arskyn 1529, Erschine 1506, Ersken 1454, Erskye 1368, Erskynn 1530, Ersskyne 1400, Herskyne and Herchine 1359, Hirskyne 1357, Irskine 1361. Froissart spells the name Aversequin, Auermesquin, and Auernesquin.

ERYNGTONE. Raufe de Eryngtone of Dumfriesshire who rendered homage in 1296 (*Bain*, II, p. 206) most probably derived his surname from Errington, Northumberland.

ESDAILE. See under EASDAILE.

ESHIELS. From the lands of Eshiels in the parish of Peebles. Simon of Escheles was juror on an inquisition held at Peebles in 1305 in connection with the lands of Kailzie in the parish of Traquair (*Bain*, II, p. 451).

ESKDALE. From the district of Eskdale in Dumfriesshire. Robert du Val de Esk of Rokesburk rendered homage, 1296 (*Bain*, II, p. 203). John Eskdale in Nether Dallsible, 1674, and two more of the name are recorded in the Commissariot Record of Dumfries. Cf. EASDAILE.

ESKENDY. From the lands of Essindy or Eschinde (1568) in Perthshire *Retours*, in 1445 Eskyndi (*Grandtully*, I, p. 10). Simon de Eskendy or Eskendi witnessed a quitclaim in Edinburgh, 1278 (RD., p. 52, 53). He is probably the Simon de Estoundy, Scots prisoner taken at Dunbar, 1296, who, as Simon de Hiskendy had letters patent by Edward I to serve abroad, 1297 (*Bain*, II, 742, 942).

ESPLEY. A surname recorded in Glasgow is probably of local origin from Espley near Mitford, Northumberland.

ESPLIN. A corruption of ABSOLOM, q.v. Thomas Esplane, witness in 1500 (*Cawdor*, p. 106), and John Esplene was burgess of Stirling in 1564 (SBR.). Robert Esplein was in Dunfermline, 1567 (*Dunfermline*), and David Espline in Hiltoune of Guthrie, 1583, and eight more are recorded in Brechin Commissariot Record. Janet Espleane was married in Edinburgh, 1610 (*Edinb. Marr.*), Grisel

Hespline in Perth was accused of seeking help from a witch, 1623 (*Chronicle of Perth*, p. 91). William Esplene was cultellar in Stirling, 1652 (SBR., p. 300), and James Esplen appears in Dunfermline, 1653 (Lamont, *Diary*, p. 60). Henry Esplin was a brewer in Cannogait, Edinburgh, 1678 (*Edin. App.*).

ESPY. Johnne Espy was accused of part in the slaughter of Maister Hector Sinclare, parsone of Kilbryde, 1541 (*Trials*, I, p. 256*).

ESSIE. A form of EASSIE, q.v.

ESSLEMONT. From the barony of Esslemont (in 1609 Essilmounthe) in the parish of Ellon, Aberdeenshire. Andrew Esslemont in Newton of Barnyards of Delgaty in record in 1760 (*Aberdeen CR.*). William Esslemont died at Cottoun of Drumminor in 1829 (*Jervise*, II, p. 217), and Alexander Paterson Esslemont of Marnoch was killed in the first Great War (*Turriff*).

ESSLINGTON. Johannes de Esslington who witnessed a charter by Patrick, 3. earl of Dunbar, 1261 (*Raine*, 137) derived his name from Eslington near Whittingham, Northumberland.

ESSON. See under EASON.

ETHERSTONE. John de Etherstone of Roxburghshire who rendered homage in 1296 (*Bain*, II, p. 199) most probably derived his surname from Adderstone (in 1242 Hethereston, 1663 Etherston), near Bamburgh, Northumberland.

ETTALE. Probably from Etwall in England. A surname closely identified with Aberdeen. Walter de Ettale, burgess of Aberdeen in 1362, may be the Walter de Ettale who witnessed a deed of sale in the same burgh in 1383 (REA., I, p. 105; II, p. 284). Nicholaus de Etale held land 'in vico de le grene' in Aberdeen in 1382 (RMS., I, 682), and Johannes de Etal who witnessed an instrument of concord between the bishop of Aberdeen and John de Forbes, *dominus ejusdem*, in 1391 (REA., I, p. 189), may be the John de Etale who granted a writ to the Carmelites of Aberdeen in 1399 (*Friars*, p. 22). William of Etale was bailie of Stirling in 1410 (ER., IV, p. 125), and John Ettale was admitted burgess of Aberdeen in 1440 (CRA., p. 396; NSCM., I, p. 6). William Ettale was chaplain and procurator "pontis de Pulgoveny" (CRA., p. 10), Thomas Ettale was presbyter of the diocese of Aberdeen and notary public in 1461 and 1463 (REA., II, p. 91; RAA., II, 148), and Andrew Ettall was presbyter of Murthlac

ETTALE, *continued*

in 1506 (REA., II, p. 96). John Ettail, chaplain, who witnessed the testament of John Erskine of Dun in 1513 (SCM., IV, p. 12) may be the John Ettell, presbyter of St. Andrews diocese and notary public in 1526 (REB., II, 180).

ETTERSHANK. A surname found in Aberdeenshire. Patrik Ettirshank was juror on an assize in Aberdeen in 1597 (SCM., I, p. 162), and Alexander Attershank is recorded in Curquhattachie in 1623 (RSCA., II, p. 269). John Ettershank appears in Aberdeen in 1650 (SCM., V, p. 170), Alexander Ettershank was deacon convener of trades in the same burgh in 1666 (Bain, *Guilds*, p. 44), and Katherine Atterschank is recorded in Dundee in 1621 (*Brechin*). Weekley (p. 140) says "from dial. *edder*, *etter*, a thin rod used in fence making."

EUIE. James Euie resigned the lands of Letham, 1446 (RAA., II, 87). Robert Euie was one of an inquisition held at Aberbrothoc, 1452, and James Euie held land in Aberbrothoc in the same year (ibid., II, 79).

EUMAN. Probably a variant of OMAN, q.v. Recorded in Edinburgh, 1939.

EUNSON. *See* EWENSON.

EUREWYK. Adam de Eurewyk, burgois de Rokesburgh, rendered homage, 1296 (RR.). Probably an error for INNERWICK, q.v.

EVA. This woman's name is common in early Scottish genealogies, and "in Highland families," says Canon Murdoch, "there is always an Eva, who has to account for things unaccountable" (*The Loyall Dissuasive*, intro., p. xcv). It represents MIr. Aife (*Book of Leinster*, 318c), or Aoife, and in modern Gaelic it is Eubha. Eua, the daughter of Gartnait, was wife of Colban, mormaer of Buchan (*Bk. Deer*, VI, 1). Eva, daughter of Alwyn, second earl of Lennox, was married c. 1217 to Malcolm, son of Duncan, thane of Callendar, from whom sprang the old family of that title (*Sc. Peer.*, v, p. 330). Another Eva was the wife of Robert de Miners (Meyners) in Dunkeld, 1256 (*Theiner*, 186).

EVAN. Variant of EWAN, q.v.

EVANDER. This name is used as an Englishing of IVER and MACIVER, q.v. In classical mythology Evander (more correctly Euander), son of Hermes and Carmentis or Carmenta, led a colony from Pallanteum in Arcadia into Latium and built a city on the Palatine Hill

sixty years before the Trojan war. Ewander Murchieson of Octerteir took the test in Rossshire in 1685 (RPC., 3. ser. XI, p. 417). The name in Greek means "good man."

EVANSON, 'son of EVAN,' q.v. In 1695 an Act of Parliament was passed to allow Evan MacGregor, merchant in Edinburgh, to retain the surname of MacGregor on condition of his children becoming Evanson (APS., IX, p. 355). In an Act anent the Clan Gregor, passed in April 1603 "It wes ordanit that the name of mc gregoure sulde be altogidder abolisched And that the haill persounes of thatt clan suld renunce thair name and tak thame sum vther name And that They nor nane of thair posteritie suld call thame selffis gregor or mc gregoure thairefter vnder payne of deade" (APS., IV, p. 550).

EVE. William le fiz Eve, burgess of Inverkeithing, rendered homage, 1296 (*Bain*, II, p. 198).

EVERLEY. From Everley in the North Riding, Yorkshire. Johannes de Euerlay, canon of Dunkeld, was papal commissioner, 1248 (REA., I, p. 20–21) and also in 1250–51 (LAC., p. 124, 126; *Inchaffray*, p. 154); witness to a charter by Geoffrey, bishop of Dunkeld (RPSA., p. 308). As Johannes de Evirlay or Ewerlay he is a charter witness in Perth in reigns of Alexander II and III (*Scon*, p. 60, 62, 88). He may be Master John de Enerleya (*u* misread *n*), apparently a churchman, who attested a charter to Abbey of Culross, c. 1231 (PSAS., LX, p. 72).

EVINSON. *See under* EWENSON.

EVIOT. Eviot of Balhousie was one of the oldest families connected with Perth and Angus. The history of the name has been obscured by the blunders of transcribers of early charters who almost uniformly mistook the second *u* for *n*. The name is territorial from Eviot in Angus. Willelmus Vniot granted seven acres in the territory of Inueramun to the church of S. Michael of Scone, c. 1190 (*Scon*, p. 36). Willelmus Vniec, perhaps the same person, witnessed a confirmation charter by William the Lion of the land of Ahenepobbel a. 1214 (*Scon*, p. 19). Philip Vuieth witnessed a charter by Hugo de Nidun of lands in Fife, c. 1204–28 (SHSM., IV, p. 312), and as Philip Vnieth witnessed the grant, c. 1211–14, by Swan, son of Thor, to the Abbey of Scon (*Scon*, p. 18). Ricardus uuieth witnessed the gift of a croft by Tristrem to the Abbey of Inchaffray c. 1208 (*Inchaffray*, p. 25), and as Ricardus vnyneth he was one of the witnesses to a charter by Walter, son of Alan, to the monks of Scon in 1233 (*Scon*, p. 91). He may be the Richard Vuyeth (Vuyet, Owyet, or Ouyeth) who witnessed a charter by Ade filius Edulphi and another by Constantine filius Ade fil. Edulphi in favor of the Abbey of Newbattle c. 1230 and c. 1245 (*Neubotle*, p. 19, 21, 26). Richard Vuieth or Vuyeth, perhaps the same person, appears as sheriff of Lanarch c. 1230–35 (*Neubotle*, p. 105, 107), and may be the R. Vinet who witnessed a charter relating to the earldom of Lennox to Maldouen in 1238 (*Levenax*, p. 2). David huniet granted the church of Melginge (Melginch) to the Abbey of Holyrood c. 1230 (LSC., 66), his sons, Alexander and Philip, being among the witnesses. Alexander Uniet who witnessed a grant by Thomas de Lundin, father of Alan Durward, to the nuns of North Berwick, c. 1220 (CMN., 11), may be the Alexander Hunyot who attested a Peeblesshire charter in the reign of Alexander II (REG., p. 128), and the Alexander Hunyeth, sheriff of Lanark in 1264 (ER., I, p. 30). Sir Alexander Huwyet attested a charter by Henry de Graham c. 1230 (HMC., App. to II. Rep., p. 166). Alexander Huuietht or Ouyoth appears as witness in charters relating to the Abbey of Newbattle c. 1240 (*Neubotle*, 144, 146), and Alexander Oviot is mentioned in a mandate directed to the bishops of St. Andrews and Aberdeen in 1264 (*Pap. Lett.*, I, p. 408). William Vnyeth was fined in 1266 (ER., I, p. 27), and Maucolum Wyet of Anegos who rendered homage, 1296 (*Bain*, II, p. 213) was one of the family. In 1296 a writ was issued to the sheriffs of Lanark and Edinburgh in behalf of Richard Ovyot (*Bain*, II, 832), another Richard Ovyot was proprietor of Cassendally in Fife in the reign of David II (RMS., I, 205). David Ovide was burgess of Dundee in 1412 (HP., II, p. 152), and in 1422 a charter was granted by Murdoch, duke of Albany to John Eviot, son and heir of William Eviot, of the lands of Balhousie resigned by the said William. The S *iohannis eviiot* is appended to a charter by John Eviot to his son, Robert Eviot, of all the barony of Balhousie in 1448 (*Macdonald*, 892). Richard Eviot (Eviott, Eveot) is in record in 1461, 1464, and 1484 (*Atholl*, p. 708; *Macdonald*, 893, 894), William Unzet [? Uuzet] appears as witness in Glasgow in 1551 (*Protocols*, I), Margaret Eviot was married in Perth in 1562 (*Sc. Ant.*, I, p. 102), and Colin Eviott of Balhussie became cautioner for the Provost of Methven in 1588 (*Methven*, p. 77). The surname was not uncommon in Perth in the fifteenth and sixteenth centuries, but appears now to be quite extinct (Cowan, *Ancient capital of Scotland*, p. 193–195). Evijot 1567, Eviote 1614, Evyot 1495, Iviot 1698.

EW. From Eu in the department of Seine-Inférieure. Philip de Ew granted to the Hospital of Soltre "unum toftum et duas acras terre proximas illi terre quam Petrus filius Albricti tenuit de Sancta Trinitate de Soltre" before 1233 (*Soltre*, p. 4). He may be the Philip de Ebb (with *w* or *vv* misread *bb*) who attested a charter to the Abbey of Culrose c. 1231 (PSAS., LX, p. 72). See also under Ov.

EWAN, EWEN. G. *Eòghann*, MG. *Eogan* and *Eoghan*, OIr. *Eogán*. In mediæval documents Latinized *Eugenius*. Ewain vicecomes de Scon witnessed King Malcolm's charter to Scon, 1164 (*Scon*, 5), and Douenaldus Ewain perambulated the bounds of Dunpeldre a. 1165 (*Neubotle*, p. 122). Eugene thanus de Rothnoych witnessed a charter by Malcolm de Moravia to his son c. 1178 (REM., p. 461). Ewen, brother of Thomas de Lundyn, a witness in reign of Alexander II. See EOGHANN and MACEWAN.

EWART. The surname of an old family in Galloway, who are said to have come originally from Roxburghshire. Andrew Ewart was treasurer of Kirkcudbright in 1583 (*Ramage*, p. 379). Nigel Ewart was retoured as his grandfather in the lands of Bodisbeg in Annandale in 1607 (*Retours, Dumfries*, 43), and John Ewert was heir of John Ewert in Torris of Keltoun in 1615 (*Retours, Kirkcudbright*, 114). John Eouart died in 1683 and was buried in Foulden churchyard. Thomas Yewart in Tyninghame, 1688 (RPC., 3. ser. XIII, p. 245). The name is of local origin from Ewart near Wooler in Northumberland. The place name appears in 1218 as Ewurthe, in 1255 as Ewrth, 1288 Ewarth, 1579 Eward, and 1589 as Ewertt, from OE. *ea-weorth*, riverenclosure, the place being encircled on three sides by the rivers Glen and Till (Mawer, *Place-names of Northumberland*, p. 79). Euart 1608.

EWEN. See under EWAN.

EWENSON, EUNSON, EVINSON. Anglicized forms of MACEWAN, q.v. Johan Ewynsone, tenant le Roi du counte de Perth rendered homage, 1296 (RR.). John Ewinson held a fold in Auchnalese, c. 1460 (*Cupar-Angus*, I, p. 131), and another John Ewinson was one of an inquest to determine the rights connected with the lands of Latter in 1461 (*Strathendrick*, p. 222). Robert Ewynson was admitted burgess of Aberdeen, 1480 (NSCM., I, p. 28), and Alexander Ewisone was bailie of Stirling, 1503 (SBR., p. 273). Walter Ewinsoun, one of an assize in Stirling, 1522, is probably Walter Ewinsoun of 1525 (ibid., p. 16, 24). John Ewynsoun was a monk of

EWENSON, EUNSON, ETC., *continued*

Culross, middle of sixteenth century (PSAS., LX, p. 93), and Mathew Ewnesoune was witness at Innermeth, 1546 (*Rollok*, 41). William Yewnsoun in Rearwick was on assize in Shetland, 1603 (MCM., II, p. 148), and Magnus Ewinesone or Eunsone is in record in Northwhytefurd or North Wydfoord in 1682 and 1686 (*Retours, Orkney*, 129; OSMisc., II, p. 55).

EWER. Thomas le Ewer rendered homage for his lands in Edinburghshire, 1296. His seal bears a hunting horn and S' *Thome Levver* (*Bain*, II, p. 208, 552). The lands for which he rendered homage were no doubt the 40s. land called Ewer-land, near Cramond, held by Hugh "le Ewer" of the Crown before 1335. In 1505 the lands were in possession of Walter Chepman, burgess of Edinburgh, and Scotland's first printer. The ewer was a servant who supplied guests with washing utensils at meals. The name perhaps now lost in Ure.

EWING. An Anglicized form of EWEN, q.v. John Eving deponed to the right boundaries of the Monk Myre in 1546 (*Cupar-Angus*, II, p. 3). Bartholomew Ewinge was a burgess of Glasgow in 1555 (*Protocols*), and Alexander Ewyne appears in Aberdeen, 1598 (SCM., V, p. 126). George Ewein was schoolmaster of Lauder, 1621 (MCM., II, p. 47). Donald Ewing was retoured heir of William Ewing of Barindroman, Argyllshire, 1636 (*Retours, Argyll*, 57). George Yewing in Loanfoot of Cultamalindie, 1664 (DPD., I, p. 288), and David Yewine in Stirling, 1717 (*Sc. Ant.*, VI, p. 88). Uwing 1679. Other spellings of the name in the Register of Cupar-Angus are Evin, Evyn, Evyng, Ewin, and Ewyn.

EXCOMMUNICATIO. Johanne excommunicatio ('excommunicate John') witnessed a charter by Alan Durward, 1251 (LAC., 80). A nickname based, no doubt, on the man having been at one time excommunicated (ibid., p. 261).

EYRE. Probably from ME. *eire, eyre*<OF. *heir, heyr*, etc., an heir. The names of Henry le Eyer, Adam le Eyr, and William le Eyre are recorded in the English *Hundred Rolls* in 1273. Robert le Eyr of Presfen was charged in 1296 with seizing 966 head of cattle and two chargers belonging to Hugh Dispensar (*Bain*, II, p. 192). Hewe Eyr of Roxburghshire who rendered homage in that year may be the Hugh Eyr who was one of an inquest at Selkirk in 1305 (ibid., p. 199, 453). John Eyr of Mesfennon, of Peeblesshire, who rendered homage may be the John Ayre who held land in Peebles in 1304 (ibid., p. 207,

385). Stevene le fiz Johan Heir of Berwickshire also rendered homage in 1296. His seal bears an eight-rayed figure, S' *Steph'ni Hair* (ibid., p. 207, 555). Stevene Eyr of Eytone who also rendered homage may be the same person (ibid., p. 210). David Ere in the parish of Derray, in 1650 (*Kilbarchan*). Johan Ihre (1707–1780), Swedish philologist, has been claimed as of Scottish descent but on doubtful authority. See also AIR.

EYSTEINN. Eysteinn, i.e. Stein of the Islands, because he lived in the Hebrides. He is the Steinn of *Islendingabók*, c. 12, and the Oistin mac Amlaiph regis Nordmannorun of AU. 874, and was killed in the Hebrides 874 (875, ES., I, p. 350. See also p. 304). The name has nothing to do with Huisdean or UISDEANN, q.v. Dun Eisteann near the Butt of Lewis may have derived its name from him.

FAA, FAW, FALL. Three spellings of one name. Faa is or was a common surname among the Border gypsies (Groome, *Gazetteer*, I, p. 408), and Faw was the spelling of their name in Shetland (MCM., II, p. 164). Sir David Faw was chaplain of Rosemarkie, 1451 (OPS., II, p. 582). Dr. Fae or Falle was principal of Glasgow University in latter quarter of seventeenth century (RPC., 3. ser. XII, p. 522). William. Fall, burgess in Montrose, 1672 (*Brechin*), Robert Faa was late bailie of Melrose, 1692 (RRM., III, p. 114), Robert Fall or Faa was member of Scots parliament for Dunbar, 1693 (*Hanna*, II, p. 493), and Robert Fau, feuar in Coldstream, 1830 (*Heirs*, 736).

FABER. From the occupation of 'wright.' The Latin form of the name has persisted through being set down by clerkly pens instead of the vernacular form. Robertus Faber, burgess of Perth, 1219 (*Scon*, p. 52). Thomas Faber and Cokinus Faber were jurors on an inquest made at Peebles, 1262 (APS., I, p. 101 red). Alan Faber de Thrylstane (Thirlstane) witnessed a confirmation of Snawdoun to Dryburgh, c. 1350 (*Dryburgh*, 232), and a later Alan Faber was admitted burgess of Aberdeen, 1466 (NSCM., I, p. 19).

FADYEN. From (MAC)FADYEN, q.v.

FAED. A Galloway surname. Shortened from (MAC)FEAT, q.v. Thomas Faid was curate of Larg (Lairg) in Sutherland, 1515 (OPS., II, p. 697). John Fead appears at Kirk of Holywood, 1657, and two more are recorded in Dumfriesshire (*Dumfries*). John Faid and William Faid, sons of Duncan Faid in Kirkmahoe, 1686, and Duncan Fied in Newlands in Kirkmaho, 1686 (RPC., 3. ser. XII, p. 405–406). The brothers James, John, and Thomas

Faed were eminent artists. Thomas (1826–1900) painted (Longfellow's) 'Evangeline,' one of the best known of his works. Fade 1685.

FAELAN. *Fáelán* (also *Fóelán*), later *Faolán*, is a reduced form of *Fáelchú*. The root is *fael* 'a wolf' (*faol. i. cu allaidh no mac tire* — O'Clery, 'wild dog,' or 'son of earth'). ffolanus de Leuenauch witnessed instrument of homage by Duncan, earl of Fife to the Abbey of Dunfermline, 1316 (RD., p. 235). Cf. GILFILLAN and MACTYRE.

FAELCHU. Fáelchú, Dorbene's son, received the chair of Columba in 716 (*Tighernach*), and died in 724. The Irish version of Nennius speaks of the race of the Leinster *Fáelchú* or wolf in Ossory, as the fourteenth wonder of Ireland (*Irish Nenn.*, p. 204–205). The men of that race were believed to assume the form and nature of wolves whenever they pleased (Rhys, *Rhind lectures*, p. 37). The Welsh reflex of *Fáelchú* exists only as a poetic name for the sea, *Y Weilgi* 'the wolf.'

FAICHNEY. Duncan Faichnay in Rind, parish of Stragaith, 1592. Individuals named Faichney were numerous in Muthill district in seventeenth and eighteenth centuries (*Muthill*). Mr. James Faichney, minister at St. Martins, 1748, and William Faichney in Cultihildoch, 1774 (*Dunkeld*). William Faichney was minister of Linton in Teviotdale, 1805–54 (*Fasti*, 2. ed., II, p. 77). ffaichney 1721.

FAILBEUS. Eighth abbot of Iona, 669–679 (*Adamnan*, p. 113). He is only twice mentioned by Adamnan. The name *Failbhe* is explained by O'Clery in his *Glossary* by *beodha*, 'lively' (*Revue celtique*, IV, p. 413).

FAILL. A curtailed form of MACPHAIL, q.v. (2) As the name is found on the west coast it may there be local from Fail in Ayrshire. Thomas Faill in Hyndhop, 1683 (*Peebles CR.*).

FAIR. Andro Fair of the Bradhirst, balze deput to John of Craufurd (*Prestwick*, p. 24), and Thomas Fare witnessed an instrument of 1446 (ibid., p. 114). John Faire was presbyter of Glasgow diocese, 1507 (*Friars Ayr*, p. 73), and Isobel Fair in Easter Caldstrem, 1675, and four more of the name are recorded in Lauder Commissariot Record. Margret Fair was charged in Inverness in 1585 with lightly deriding "the law of God and man in committing of the chryme of fornicatioun and adultre" (*Rec. Inv.*, I, p. 299). Farie 1550, Fary 1549, Farye 1551. Lower and Harrison suggest the name is from the adjective *fair* "blond, handsome," and Bardsley says it is of local origin.

FAIRBAIRN. Perhaps a metathesis for Frebern. Stodart seems to infer the same, Fairbairn = Freebairn, and a correspondent of Rev. Robert Wodrow in 1705 spells the name indifferently 'Farbairn' and 'Freebairn' (*Anal. Scot.*, II, p. 17, 21). The name of Bessie Bairebairne in Coldstream, 1685 (RPC., 3. ser. X, p. 478) may be a like mis-spelling. Stephen Fairburn, burgess of Berwick on Tweed, held the hostelry of the abbot and convent of Arbroath in Dundee a. 1327 (RAA., I, p. 315). The name of James Forbrayne who was admitted burgess freeman of Glasgow, 1601 (*Burgesses*), is perhaps an erroneous spelling. Fairbarne 1536, ffairbairne 1646.

FAIRFIELD. Of local origin. A coal-pot and salt-pan were claimed by Alexander Fairfield in Dysart, 1572 (*Dysart*, p. 37). A Fairfields is mentioned in Fife Retours.

FAIRFOWL. John Fairfowl or Fairful was one of the bailies of St. Andrews, 1480 (*Macdonald*, 899). Sir John Ferfulle, chaplain, was witness in Cupar, 1511 (*Laing*, 279), William Fairfull, clerk of Dunkeld diocese, 1550 (ibid., 563), Mr. John Fairfoull or Farfull was schoolmaster in Dunfermline, 1582–85 (*Dunfermline*), and Jonet Fairfull was heir of Andrew Scot in Pettinweyme, 1646 (*Inquis.*, 3169). Alexander Fairfoul, "shoemaker in St. Androes," was retoured heir of Robert Phennesoune "his gudser on the mother syd," 1653 (*Retours, Fife*, 821). Andrew Fairfowl, son of John Fairfowl of Anstruther, was consecrated archbishop of Glasgow, 1662 (Keith, *Bishops*, 1824, p. 265), James Fairfowle was commissary of Brechin, 1686 (*Edinb. Marr.*), and Colin Fairfowl was one of the garrison of Doune in 1715 (HMC., 3. Rep., App., p. 385). Fairefoule and Fairfall 1661, Farefull 1680, and Melville spells the name Fearfull. Ferguson (*Teutonic name system*, p. 93–94) suggests spelling should be Farefowl, with meaning "bird of passage," and compares Summerfugl and Winterfugl.

FAIRGRIEVE. Thomas Feirgrive appears in Bentmylne, 1658, and Gideon Fairgrive in Melrose, 1685 (RRM., I, p. 175; III, p. 106). Feirgreive 1659. See also FORGRAVE.

FAIRHAIR. Probably descriptive, 'with fair hair,' or perhaps more probably a form of FARQUHAR, q.v. Patricius Favrhar, burgess of Perth, 1345 (*Scon*, p. 127). William Favrhair, precentor of Ross, 1407 (*Pap. Pet.*, I, p. 625), and William Farar, capellanus, was charter witness, 1491 (*Scon*, p. 199). Andrew Fairer to stand in sackcloth for quarrelling in time of divine service, 1661 (*Rec. Elgin*, II, p. 293).

FAIRHAUGH. Perhaps from Fairhaugh in Northumberland. Mariore del Fairhalughe of Linlithgowshire rendered homage in 1296. Her seal bears a large fleur-de-lys and S' *Mariore d' Fairalhv* (*Bain*, II, p. 205, 557). Rauf Fayrheych was juror on an inquest made at Berwick on the lands of Lady Elena la Zuche in Conyngham, Ayrshire, 1296 (ibid., p. 216).

FAIRHOLM. Of local origin from Fairholm (*Lanark Retours*, 98), now Farme. A surname in Midlothian for several generations. Janet Fairum was married in Edinburgh, 1604 (*Edinb. Marr.*). Marion Fairholm appears in Overtoun of Quodquen, 1621, and three more of the name are in record in Lanark (*Lanark CR.*). John Fairholm, merchant burgess of Edinburgh, died in 1646 (Douglas, *Peerage*, I, p. 75), and John Ferholme, merchant burgess there in 1655 (*Inquis.*, 3997) may have been his son. George Fairholme, tanner at the West Port of Edinburgh, 1653 (ibid., 3735). Fairholm of Craigiehall an old family in West Lothian. The name has been shortened to FERME, q.v.

FAIRHURST. Of local origin, probably from some place of the name in England.

FAIRIE, FAIRRIE, FARIE. A family named Farie of Farme is said to have been settled in the parish of Rutherglen for about 600 years. A local rhyme says:

"Nae man can tell, nae man has seen
When the Faries haena in Ruglen been."

Rauf Faireye of Ayrshire rendered homage, 1296. His seal bears a wolf or fox, crozier in paw and mitred, preaching to bird in tree, a dog and rabbit, S' *Randulphi Faireye* (*Bain*, II, p. 206, 549). Helen Fairie in Tuedye, parish of Stanehouse, 1623 (*Lanark CR.*), and Cath. Fairie appears in Barcaipell, 1684 (*Kirkcudbright*). Laurencius Fary in Scon, 1523, and William Fairy there, 1586 (*Scon*, p. 203, 231). Fairy 1764.

FAIRLEY. From the barony of Fairley in the parish of Largs. Nisbet (*Heraldry*, II, p. 29) says the family of this name in Ayrshire were descended from Robert de Ross, a branch of the Rosses of Tarbet in Cunningham, proprietors of the lands of Fairley, whence they took their name. The first of the family of whom any notice has been found was William de Fairlie, who was included in a pardon granted by Edward III at Berwick, 1335, for all the crimes committed by him in the war with England (*Rot. Scot.*, I, p. 381). "It is rather remarkable that so few notices of this family are to be found, and that such as exist are of such a disconnected and fragmentary

nature" (*Pont*, p. 137). William Farley was witness in 1368 (*Coll. AGAA.*, II, p. 148). The name also appears in record as Farnley. Allan de Farnley witnessed a charter by Sir Hugh Eglinton, c. 1370 (*Macfarlane*, II, p. 333), and John of Farnle witnessed a sasine of 1446 (*Irvine*, I, p. 137). Wil of Farle of Coupir was commissioner for burgh of Dundee, 1459 (*Ayr*, p. 28). Fairnelie 1527, Farnelie 1524, Farnly *de eodem* 1499, Farnlye *de eodem* 1547. Cf. FAIRIE and FAIRLIE.

FAIRLIE. The family of Fairlie of Braid claimed descent from a natural son of Robert II (*Nisbet*, I, p. 289), and the family arms are appealed to in support of this theory. The claim, however, rests on no very satisfactory evidence and is in conflict with historical records. William Fairlie had a charter from Robert I of the lands of Inuerleith (RMS., I, App. II, 175), and Braid was held by William Fairlie in reign of Robert II, when he resigned the lands of Bavillay (now Bavelaw) to his son John upon the latter's marriage with Elena, a natural daughter of Sir Henry Douglas of Lochleven (RMS., I, 694, 782). "It is plain, therefore, that the royal origin, if true at all, must be thrown back to an earlier date" (*Stodart*, II, p. 183). More probably they are descended from William Fayrly or Fayrley, one of the custumars of Edinburgh, burgess there in 1329, who although unmentioned by either Bower or Wyntoun, seems to have played an important part in the capture of Edinburgh Castle from the English in 1342. In 1329 he advanced a sum to the king (ER., I, p. 166), and in 1331 was clerk to the chamberlain. He is most probably the Fairley who soon after this date appears in possession of Braid in succession to the family of de Braid, and was ancestor of the family of Fairley of Braid, whose representative in later days married the daughter of John Knox. John de Farle, juror on inquest on lands of Swinton in 1408 (*Swinton*, p. xviii), and Thomas de Fayrle or Farle, burgess of Edinburgh, juror in Edinburgh, 1428 (RMS., II, 115; RAA., II, 61). William Farnly, notary public in Dunfermline, 1483 (RD., p. 372), and Johannes de Farnlv *de eodem* in record, 1499 (*Simon*, 72). William Farnelie was appointed sergeant of court in Selkirk, 1524 (*Home*, 35), and Phylpie and Dand Fairlie were tenants under Kelso Abbey, 1567 (*Kelso*, p. 528). In the *Registrum Cartarum Ecclesie Sancti Egidii de Edinburgh* the name appears very frequently in the spellings Fairele, Farinle, Fairle, Fairlie, Fairnlie, Farinlee, Farle, Farnele, Farnlv, Farnlve, Farvinle, Favrle, Favrley, and Ferle. Farnely (of Braid) 1534, Ffarly 1737. See also FAIRLEY.

FAIRLIECREVOCH. A very rare surname, if still in existence, derived from the old ten mark lands of Fairlie-Crivoch (1608) in the bailliary of Cunningham, Ayrshire. The place name also appears as Fairlie-Crevoch (1622), Fairliecreivoche (1628), and Farlie-Crivoch (1667).

FAIRSERVICE. The principal home of this surname appears to have been in Lanarkshire. George Fairservice in Barsteidis, parish of Lesmahagow, 1634, and other thirteen of the name are recorded (Lanark CR.). John Fairservice in Mylneburne, parish of Dalserff, 1629 (Campsie). Agnes Fairservice in Edinburgh, 1640 (Edinb. Marr.).

FAIRWEATHER. John Phairwedder held a land in Perth in the reign of James II (Scon, p. 188), and Christopher Farewethir was serjeant of Linlithgow in 1472 (Sc. Ant., XVII, p. 117). The surname is of considerable antiquity in the Menmuir district. Valter Farwedder, presbyter of Dunkeld, whose name appears in 1547–63 is probably the first of the name in the locality. There were Fairweathers in Blairno in Navar in the early seventeenth century (Jervise, II, p. 340). Walter Fairwedder witnessed a precept of sasine of the lands of Fyndowry in 1558 (REB., II, 280), and Agnes Fairwodder was heir of Robert Fairwodder, merchant burgess of Dundee in 1609 (Inquis., 419). Thomas Fairweather is recorded in Dundee in 1583, and eighteen more of the name appear in the Commissariot Record of Brechin between 1576 and 1800. Thomas Fairwoder was burgess of Dundee in 1634 (Retours, Forfar, 224), and the Devil rebaptized the witch Catherine Skair in Brechin by the name of Isoble Farewedder. Janet Fairweather is recorded in the parish of Olrik in 1664 (Caithness), and John Fairweather of Turriff was killed in the first Great War (Turriff). A fanciful story is told of the origin of the name of the Fairweathers of Angus. This sept, it is said, was a branch of the old tribe of Morrev. The name is said, according to private family tradition, to be derived from 'three brothers' of the ancient Murrevians, who being forced to leave the north, assumed the name, in order to perpetuate the remembrance of their northern descent: — it being written in the Book of Job, ch. XXXVII. 22, 'Fair weather cometh out of the north' (Peter, Baronage of Angus, p. 91). Fairvedder 1609, Fairwadder 1537, Fairwoother 1649, Farveddar 1607. Fairwaddire, Fairweddor, Farewadder, Farweddar.

FAIRWIN. William Fairwin in Cauldlaw, parish of Carnwath, 1624 (Lanark CR.).

FALA, FALLA. From Fala in Midlothian. Radulf Falahe witnessed a charter by Eschina domina de Molle c. 1165–77 (RMP., p. 75). Bartholomew de Faulaw and Samuel de Faulaw were witnesses to a charter in favor of the House of Soltre between 1214 and 1240 (Soltre, p. 19), and Bartholomew appears again within the same period as witness to the confirmation of the land of Swaynystoun (Swanston) to Soltre (ibid., p. 26). Adam de Fawlaw witnessed the grant of a nativus (serf) to the same house between 1235 and 1258 (ibid., p. 26). George de Falow was provost of Edinburgh in 1421 (Seals Supp., 356), and may be the George Falowe, burgess there in 1453 (Rot. Scot.). Another George Falow (Fallawe, Fawlo, Faulo, or Falowe), a Scottish merchant who had warrants of safe conduct to travel in England between 1426 and 1453 is doubtless the George Faulau who was one of the Scottish ambassadors to proclaim the truce within the liberties of Berwick and Roxburgh in 1457 (Bain, IV, 990, 1187, 1230, 1252, 1281, etc.). In 1438 as George of Faulawe, merchant of Scotland, he also had a safe conduct to go to Holland and Zeland to notify the late truce to the Scots there (ibid., 1110). The tenement of George de Faulow or Faulo in Edinburgh is mentioned in 1472 and 1476 (REG., 398, 411). Agnes Fawlaw, wife of Robert Lauder of the Bass, granted an annuity of 10 marks for supporting a chaplain in St. Andrews Kirk, North Berwick, in 1491 (Caledonia, II, p. 517). The seal of William Faula of Wells, Roxburghshire, 1544, reads, S. Wililmi. Favla. de. Vel (Macdonald, 907). Johnne Faulaw and Watt Faulaw were entered before the Privy Council in 1567 (RPC., I, p. 588), and Lard Fala and James Fala were tenants under the Abbey of Kelso in the same year (Kelso, p. 527, 528). David Fala was a maltman in Edinburgh in 1633 (Edinb. Marr.). Faula 1502, Faulowe 1439; Fallo.

FALAY. William Falay in Broughtrige, 1683 (Lauder), John Fallay, cordiner in Kelso, 1686 (Peebles CR.), and John Fallay was portioner of Balbrogie, 1690 and 1697 (Inquis., 7005, 7907).

FALCONER. From the office of 'falconer' (OF. faulconnier<LL. falconarius, one who breeds or trains falcons or hawks for sport). Matheus the falconer (falconarius) is one of the witnesses to a charter by Earl David, c. 1202–3 (LAC., 3). Gulielmus Auceps, i.e. William the falconer, c. 1200, granted certain lands to the kirk of Maringtun or Maryton (RAA., I, 114; Fraser, History of Laurencekirk, p. 36). In the

FALCONER, *continued*

vernacular he may have borne the name Hawker, for while his descendants have retained the name Falconer their estate ('villa eiusdem Willelmi Aucipis') was known as Haukertun or Haukerstun. Robert le Faukener or Fauconer of Kincardyn en Miernes rendered homage at Aberdeen, 1296. His seal bears a falcon killing a small bird and S' *Roberti Faucunur* (*Bain*, ii, p. 182, 209). Gervase or German le Fauconer was one of the Scots prisoners taken at Dunbar in 1296, and was still prisoner in the Castle of Wisbeach, 1307 (ibid., p. 178, 515). Heliscus Faucuner, burgess of Montrose, had a charter of lands in Monros (Montrose), 1350 (REB., ii, 6), and in 1379 there is record of payment made to William Fauconer, Scottish merchant, arrested in Yarmouth (*Bain*, iv, 275). Andrew Faucounere de Lethinvar on inquisition in 1380 in Badenoch (REM., p. 187) is probably Andreas Fawconer, juror on inquest in the episcopal lands of Aldrochty, 1393 (REM., p. 205). William Falconer (1732–1769), sailor and poet, and Hugh Falconer (1808–1865), botanist and palæontologist, are two of the more prominent of the name. Falcener 1793, Falconair 1526, Falknar (of Hakartoun) 1544, Falknor 1574, Fauknar 1468, Favconer 1365, Fawcounar 1459.

FALKIRK. Of local origin from the town of Falkirk in Stirlingshire. The surname is seldom met with.

FALLA. *See under* FALA.

FALLAS. James Fallays at Leidhill (Leadhill) in 1657 and other five of the name (*Lanark CR.*). James Falous in Fingland, 1674 (*Edin. App.*). The name is also recorded in Edinburgh. It may be from Falaise in Normandy, the birthplace of William the Conqueror, *de la Faleyse*, 'of the cliff,' but there is a place named Fallaws in Angus.

FALLASDAILL. An old Dumbartonshire surname. Adam Falovisdale witnessed an instrument of sasine in favor of Mathew Stevart, son of John, earl of Lennox, 1490 (*Lennox*, ii, p. 140), and David Fallusdall was one of the sheriffs of King James. v in the Lennox, 1513 (ibid., ii, p. 208). David Fallisdal was a witness, 1500 (LCD., p. 204), and Thomas Fallusdaill and James Fallusdaill were burgesses of Dunbretan, 1535 (*Pollok*, i, p. 271). Sir David Fallusdell was priest of the diocese of Glasgow and notary public, 1536 (REO., p. 337), James Fallousdaill was reidare at the kirkis of Zell, 1574 (RMR.), and John Fallis-daill was juror on inquest in Kirkwall, 1584 (REO., p. 162). David Fallausdaill, burgess of Dunbarton, 1589, may have been the David Fallisdaill who was slain in the battle of Glenfruin, 1604 (*Trials*, ii, p. 432). Thomas Fallasdaill of Ardochbeg was burgess of Dumbarton, 1619 (*Sasines*, 67), and John Fallusdaill, burgess of Dunbartane, was heir of David Fallusdaill, burgess dicti burgi, 1630 (*Inquis.*, 1595). John ffallowsdale, usher of the grammar school, Inveraray, 1746. Follesdaill 1625.

FAMILTON. Local. The lands of Famylton infra barony de Northberuick in record, 1353 (RMS., i, App. i, 123). James Familton in Home, 1654, and two more of the name near (*Lauder*).

FARAY. From Faray in the island of Walls, Orkney. Henre Fara in Etha (Eday), member of assize in Kirkwall, 1564 (REO., p. 120). Margaret Faray, heir of Henry Faray in Hunclete, 1616 (*Inquis.*, 640).

FARG. Local. Janet Farg in Aberargie, 1629 (*Dunblane*). Aberargie is on the river Farg, near Abernethy, Perthshire.

FARGIE. Mr. Alexander Fargy, member of General Assembly, 1581 (*Logie*, i, p. 20). "Some suppose Fargy to be same as Fergusson. The names Fargy, Fargus, and Fargussone appear in the Presbytery Record, but always as different names. The same names are now Fergie, and Forgie, Fergus, Ferguson, and Fergusson" (ibid., i, p. 20n).

FARIE. *See under* FAIRIE.

FARLAN. A shortened form of (Mac)FARLANE, q.v.

FARLASTONE. Alaster Farlastone of Inchemacrannich and John Farlastone, younger, appeirand of Monnese, of Clan Donachie, subscribe a bond of manrent to their chief, 1612 (SCM., ii, p. 283).

FARMER. This surname in Scotland, at least, does not mean a 'tiller of land,' but one who farmed the revenue, in LL. *firmarius*. Richard Fermarius was juror on inquest at Peebles, 1262 (APS., i, p. 101 red; *Peebles*, 2). Alan Fermour witnessed instrument signed at St. Andrews, 1391 (*Wemyss*, ii, 39). The land of Andrew Fermour in Perth is mentioned, 1458 (RAA., ii, 114), and in the following year William Fermore, presbyter, is in record (ibid., 129). Wilms Fermoir, notary public in Kirkwall, 1580 (OSR., i, p. 199). William Fermour, burgess of Crail, 1619, may be the William Fermor who was active as a notary in Shetland in 1602–03, "when he appears to have been intruded into the office of Fowde i.e. sheriff of Dunrossness, a post never held, except under force, by any one but a resident native" (*Goudie*, p. 213). John Fermour was retoured heir of David Fermour, burgess of Crail, his father, 1643 (*Retours, Fife*, 636). Thomas Fermer in Cottoune, parish of Auchterhouse, 1695 (*Dunkeld*). Cf. William Marnach, fermorer, Aberdeen, 1684 (ROA., I, p. 240). Fermor 1464.

FARNELL. From the lands of Farnell in Angus. Between 1214 and 1246 Duncan de Ferneuel witnessed charters by Malcolm, earl of Angus (RAA., I, 48, 53, and p. 331), and a charter of land in the territory of Kerimor to Arbroath Abbey (ibid., 112). Meg Fernwale is recorded in Aberdeen, 1408 (CWA., p. 312), Alan de Farnyle held land in Edinburgh in 1411 (*Cambus.*, 94), Thomas Farnile or Fernile was a charter witness in the same burgh in 1468 (*Neubotle*, 301, 302), and Patrick Fernyll was hospitaller of Holy Trinity Church, Edinburgh in 1554 (*Soltre*, p. 111).

FARNINGDON. William of Farningdon, who swore fealty to England in 1296, was probably a Burnard as the Burnards were lords of Farningdon. His seal bears a cross of four pine branches, a cone in dexter base point, S' Will'i d' Franingdv (*Bain*, II, p. 199, 532). John Fairingtoun is recorded in Heittoun in 1687 (*Peebles CR.*). The name is derived from Fairnington in Roxburghshire.

FARQUHAR. G. *Fearchar*, MG. *Fearchar* and *Fearchair*, from OG. ° *Ver-car-os*, 'very dear one.' Modern G. is often erroneously written *Fearachar*, and in mediæval records appears in many corrupt forms. Ferchart was the father of Fergus, one of the perambulators of boundaries in a Newbattle charter a. 1178 (*Neubotle*, 156). Farhard, judex de Buchan, witnessed a charter by William Cumyn, earl of Buchan a. 1200 (REA., I, p. 15), and about the same date Malmur mac Hercar, a native or serf, was gifted to the Abbey of Scone (*Scon*, p. 25). Ferkar was earl of Ross, 1224–31 (REM., p. 334), and Macbeth filius Ferchware is in record, 1283 (LIM., 30). Fercardus filius Seth witnessed a composition between Andrew, bishop of Moray, and Walter Cumyn, earl of Mynynteth, 1234, and in another charter of same date he is Fercardus senescallus de Badenoch (REM., p. 99). Pherharchd, judex, who witnessed perambulation of boundaries of lands of Abbey of Arbroath and those of the countess of Buchan, 1251 (RAA., I, p. 162), is probably Ferhare, judex, witness to charter of lands of Ederlarg, about same date (LAC., p. 62). Fercard, late dean of Caithness, was

directed to receive the temporalities of the bishopric of Caithness, 1306 (*Bain*, II, p. 472). The Farquhars of Gilmilnscroft, Kyle Stewart, were seated there at the end of the fourteenth century. Andro Farchare was burgess of Are, 1450 (*Ayr*, p. 27), and a man named Farthquhare was tacksman of Warbuster in parish of St. Ola, 1492 (REO., p. 405). Schir Mathow Farcar, cleric, in Kirkwall, 1514, appears in 1527 as Schir Mathow Farquhar (OSR., I, p. 108, 256). Andrew Ferquhar was burgess of Montrose, 1526 (RSS., I, 3608), another Andro Pharquhair was witness in Kirkwall, 1543 (REO., p. 224), and Johannes Ferchar was tenant in Strathdee, 1527 (*Grant*, III, p. 68). Thomas Forquhair in Gairdie, 1625 (OSS., I, 98). Fairhar 1586, Farair 1550, Farchar 1596, Ferghard and Ferquard 1596, Ferquhar 1633, Feruware c. 1240. Other old forms: Farar, Farahar, Faryar. With 'Mac' it gives MACERCHAR. The name of the earl of Strathern who died in 1171 is spelled Ferteth in three charters by Malcolm IV (*Scon*, p. 8; RD., p. 22, 24). It is Ferthet and Fercheth in two charters between 1160–61, and Ferteth in a third c. 1170–71 (RPSA., p. 129, 132, 144). It is also said to occur as Ferrett, Ferchard, Fereth, Ferthet, and Forthead (*Cupar-Angus*, I, p. 319). In Wyntoun's MS. it is spelled Feretauche and Ferthach (S. T. S. ed., IV, p. 422–423). Ferthed, son of Earl Gilbert of Strathern also appears as witness in his father's charters, c. 1199–1208, as Fertheth, Ferthead, Ferthet, fferthet, Ferquhar, Ferteth, and Fertet (*Inchaffray*, p. 3, 4, 8, 11, 13, 16, 17, 18, 24). See also FARQUHARSON and MACFARQUHAR.

FARQUHARSON, 'son of FARQUHAR,' q.v. As a clan or sept the Farquharsons are descended from Farquhar Macintosh, a grandson of the laird of Macintosh who came to Braemar before 1382 (*Aboyne*, p. 177). Even so late as 1620 the Farquharsons are styled Macintoshes. The Macintoshes seem to have had some claim to the lands of Birse, and in 1382 Ferchard Mcyntoschy was ordained to cease injuring the lands and inhabitants thereof, and to prosecute his claim to them according to law (REA., I, p. 136–137). David Farcharsoun was made burgess and guild brother of Aberdeen, 1440 (CRA., p. 395; NSCM., I, p. 6). Aytho Faurcharsone is mentioned in the will of Alexander Sutherland of Dunbeath, 1456 (*Bann. Misc.*, III, p. 93). Findelav Farcharsone is in Strathdee, 1538 (*Grant*, III, p. 71), and Donald Farquharson in Braemar was appointed keeper of the king's forests of Braemar, etc., 1584 (*Coll.*, p. 189). John Farqrson in Dalhande, 1682 (*Invercauld*, p. 264). Henry Farquharson (d. 1739 or

FARQUHARSON, *continued*

1747), born in Aberdeenshire, was founder of the school of navigation in Moscow, Russia. Farquharson of Invercauld is named in Gaelic *Mac Mhic Fhionnlaigh*, from his descent from Finlay Mor who fell at the battle of Pinkie in 1547. Finlay Mor was said to have been buried in Inveresk churchyard, and the spot was long known as 'the long Highlandman's grave.' The Farquharsons rank as a sept of Clan Chattan. Farchyrson 1560, Faurcharson 1442, Ferquharsoun 1574, ffarquharsone 1664, ffarqrson 1693, Fourcharsoun 1456.

FARQUHART. A current form of FARQUHAR, q.v., with accretionary *t*.

FARRAR. Farrar or Farrer is an old West Riding surname. Its origin is uncertain. Fayrher occurs in Cambridgeshire in thirteenth century, whilst de Ferar or de Ferrar is found in Derbyshire, Devonshire, and Oxfordshire (*Hundred Rolls*) (*Guppy*, p. 427). William Farar, chaplain and charter witness, 1491 (*Scon*, p. 199). Walter Fayrhare was a forestaller in Aberdeen, 1402 (*CRA.*, p. 384). In 1559 John Farar in Inverness "is contentit and he be fundyn slaing salmon on the Vater of Nes to be hangit" (*Rec. Inv.*, I, p. 31). Andreas Farrer is recorded in Orkney, 1562 (ibid., p. 84). The relict of Thomas Fayrhar had lease of part of the town and lands of Craigmakeran, 1585 (*Scon*, p. 226). Cf. under FARQUHAR.

FARRIE, FARRIES. (1) From Ir. *O'Fearghuis*, 'descendant of Fergus.' (2) Local diminutives of FERGUSON, q.v. Robert Farries in Newbigging, 1648 (*Inquis.*, 3461). Agnes Faries was examined for the Test in Tinwald, 1685 (*RPC.*, 3. ser. XI, p. 433). William Fairries, late merchant burgess, 1729 (*Guildry*, p. 139). Eleven of the name are recorded in Dumfries Commissariot Record between 1624 and 1800.

FASKEN, FASKIN. An old surname in the parish of Forgue, Banffshire, derived from the small estate of Farskane near Cullen, locally pronounced Fasken. The estate gave name to the family of Farskin of that Ilk, but since the Reformation the lands have been held by others than the original family. Several persons of the name are buried in Inverkeithny church (*Jervise*, I, p. 274).

FASLANE. The lands of Fasselane were an extensive tract of country on the Gairloch in the earldom of Lennox. The de Fesselanes who derived their name from these lands were descended from Aulay, son of Alwyn, second earl of Levenax. Walter de Fosselane, c. 1285,

is witness to a charter by Duncan M'Churteer (*Laing*, 69). Walter de Fosselane, son and heir of Anweleth (*read* Auweleth) de Fosselane had a charter "totam illam terram que vocatur Tulewyn" (Tilliechewan) in Lennox, c. 1334 (*Levenax*, p. 92), and in 1351 he was made forester "nemorum de Levenax cum officio quod dicitur *tossachiorschip* de Levenax" (ibid., p. 93). About 1350 he witnessed a charter to Robert de Dunbretane, and at the same date a grant by Donald, earl of Levenax to William de Galbraith (ibid., p. 69). In 1370 Walter de Foslane witnessed a royal charter to Maurice de Bouthannane (Buchanan) (RMS., I, 371).

FASSINGTON. (Misspelled Faffington in a couple of entries.) William de Fasingtone of Edinburghshire rendered homage in 1296 (*Bain*, II, p. 201). William de Faffyngton had a grant in 1363 of the lands of Balmady in Fern from Margaret de Abirnythy, countess of Angus (RMS., I, 141), and Margaret de Faffyngton, wife of Patrick de Inverpefre is in record in 1369 (ibid., 321). William de Fassyntoñ is in record in 1406 (RPSA., p. 9), and Richard Fassyntone (Fassintoun on his seal) was one of the bailies of the Canongate of the Monastery of Holyrood of Edinburgh, 1489 (*Macdonald*, 906). Perhaps from a place of the name in England.

FASTFURLANGE. William de Fastfurlange of Roxburghshire rendered homage, 1296 (*Bain*, II, p. 209).

FAULDHOUSE. From the village of Fauldhouse in the parish of Whitburn, West Lothian. John Fauldhouse was a workman at Leadhills, 1734 (*Lanark*).

FAULDS. Local. There are places of this name in the shires of Ayr, Renfrew, Lanark, and Perth, and there were lands of East and West Faulds in the lordship of Dudop or Dudhope near Dundee. John of Fawls of Leith imported salmon into London in 1438 (*Bain*, IV, 1110). Arthur Fauldis held land in Glasgow, 1536 (LCD., p. 98), and Archibald Faullis was merchant burgess there, 1642 (*Inquis.*, 2771). James Faullis in Blacklaw appears in 1666, and Robert Fals, charged with carrying of baggage in 1672, appears again in 1674 as Faules and Fauls (*Corsehill*, p. 86, 105, 113). Robert Fauls was master of a family in the parish of Buittle, 1684 (RPC., 3. ser. IX, p. 570). Cf. FOULDS.

FAWNS. From the lands of Fans or Faunes near Earlston, Berwickshire. Richard de Fawnes, c. 1150–90, gave to his brother David, son of David de Graham, two tofts in Melo-

The Surnames of Scotland 257

stane (Mellerstain) to be held of the said Richard and his heirs. About the year 1200 the same Richard de fauhnes gifted two tofts in Melokeston to the Abbey of Kelso (*Kelso*, p. 104). Ricardus de Faunesse witnessed a confirmation charter by Earl Patrick of Dunbar to the Priory of Coldingham, a. 1232 (CCAC., p. 6). Adam de Faunes, son of deceased Richard de Faunes, gave to the Abbey of Kelso a charter of the two tofts of Melostane which David de Graham, his uncle, held of his brother, c. 1230, and c. 1260 there is recorded a confirmation of the grant of lands of Melocstan previously made by Adam de Fauhnes (*Kelso*, 137). John Fawnies was citiner of Brechin in 1600 and Alexander Fawnis citiner in 1610 (*Brechin*). Patrick Fowns or Phauns, chapman in Thirlstone Miln, 1686 (RPC., 3. ser. xii, p. 369, 375), and William Fawns, chirothecarius, burgess of Brechin, 1691 (*Inquis.*, 7203).

FAWSYDE. Of territorial origin from the lands of Fawsyde in East Lothian. Aedmundus de Faȝeside witnessed the grant of Tranent church to Holyrood Abbey by Thor filius Swani c. 1150 (LSC., p. 11). Alan de Fausyde witnessed a grant by Peter de Grame to the Hospital of Soltre before 1238 (*Soltre*, p. 11), and David de Fauside attested the grant of the lands of Swaynnystoun to the same house before 1238 (ibid., p. 24). William de Fauside was witness to a charter of a carucate of land in Langholme to Herbert Maxwell c. 1270 (RHM., i, p. 7; *Pollok*, i, p. 125). William de Faussyde and Nicol Fausy of Roxburghshire, Rogier de Faussyde of Dumfriesshire, Robert del Fausyde of Edinburghshire, rendered homage, 1296. The seal of Nicol shows a tree of four thick branches and S' *Nichol d' Fawsyde* (*Bain*, ii, p. 198–200, 203, 531). Robert de Faweside was juror on forfeited lands in Lothian, 1312 (ibid., iii, 245), and Roger de Favsyde received payment for his expenses on business to England (ER., i, p. 287). By the middle of the fourteenth century the Fawsydes had extended beyond the Firth of Forth. Falsyde or Fawsyde, described as of that Ilk, held the land of Balmaquien, parish of Marykirk, from at least 1329 to 1371 (*Peter*, p. 93). William de Favside, burgess of Edinburgh, 1392 (*Egidii*, p. 28), and John de Fawside, bailie there, 1425 (RMS., ii, 24). James Fasyde was tenant on lands of Abbey of Kelso, 1567 (*Kelso*, p. 523). Fawsyd 1542; Falsyde, Fausyd, Fauueside.

FAYTHLIE. James de Faythle, burgess of Aberdeen, 1482 (NSCM., i, p. 29) perhaps derived his name from Faichla or Faichlaw, Tarland (*c* in old documents is often misread *t*).

FEA. A surname found in Orkney (1640, MCM., ii, p. 211). Probably derived from the lands of Fea, pronounced Fee-a, near Stove in Sanday. The name is popularly believed to be of Gypsy origin because Faa is a common Gypsy surname in Britain, and several Gypsies of the name (Faw) were indicted for murder in Orkney in 1612. William Phea, juror on assize in Ireland, Orkney, 1595 (OSR., i, p. 220).

FEARGIE. The colloquial form in Angus for FERGUS, q.v.

FEARN, FERN. (1) From Fearn in Rossshire. Sir Andrew Ferne was one of the chaplains of the cathedral church of Dornoch in 1512, Sir Robert Fern or Ferne was curate of Golspie in 1546, and curate of Kylmalie in the same year (OPS., ii, p. 623, 648, 649) and Sir John Ferne, who was presented to the chaplainry of Tain in 1517, is mentioned again in 1543 as Sir John Farny (RMS.), and as Sir John Ferne, chaplain and notary at Lochlevyn, 1546 (*Rollok*, 3). David Fearne of Tarlogie took the Test in 1685 (RPC., 3. ser. xi, p. 417). The Ferns of that Ilk were followers of the earls of Ross. See MACFEAT. (2) From Fearn or Fern in Angus. In 1267 Peter de Ferne witnessed the charter of foundation of the Messyndew (Maison-dieu) at Brechin granted by William de Brechin. John Fern was burgess of Perth in 1432 (HP., ii, p. 170), Christiane de Ferne was disturbed by robbers in 1436 (CRA., p. 392), Robert de Fern and Fynlai de Fern held land in Dundee in 1458 (REB., i, 185), and John Feyrne was presbyter and notary public in St. Andrews diocese in 1567 (RHM., i, p. 27). John of Ferne was charged 'iv merkes, or ellis half a chalder of vitale' for the mill of Ferne, 1488 (ADC., Oct. 25, 1488), and George Ferne was archdeacon of Dunkeld (*Stodart*, ii, p. 316). John Fearn in Wellfoord, 1718 (*Dunkeld*).

FEARNSIDE. A surname recorded in Aberdeenshire. Of local origin.

FEATHERS. A Fifeshire surname of local origin from Fetters in the parish of Leuchars. The *s* is English plural.

FECHIL. Of local origin. There is a Fechil and two places named Fechel in Aberdeenshire. Nicholas Fechil was abbot elect of Inchaffray in 1458, and Laurence Fethil was his procurator in 1461–62 (*Inchaffray*, p. 148, 254). The abbot's name also appears in 1458 as Feyhill (ibid., p. 338).

FEDALE. Simon of Fedale and his son Gillemury were assizors on the marches of Westere Fedale in 1246 (LAC., p. 26). The name is derived from Feddal near Braco, Perthshire.

FEDERATE. From the old barony of Fedderat or Federate in the parish of New Deer, Aberdeenshire. William de Federeth was constable of Roxburgh in 1262 (*Melros*, 294), and William de Fedreth, portioner of Duffhus in 1296 granted four davochs in Strathnavyr to Sir Reginald de Chene (REM., p. 341). William le Fiz William de Federed of the county of Elgyn in Morref rendered homage in 1296 (*Bain*, II, p. 214), and c. 1300 granted a letter in favor of the Abbey of Deer (CAB., p. 189). Magnus of Fetherith was one of those who recommended the marriage of the son of Edward I and the Maid of Norway in 1290 (APS., I, p. 85). William Fedrey or Feddereffe of that Ilk granted the fourth part of Kathness to Ranald Chene, and King David confirmed the grant (RMS., I, App. II, 1317). The de Federeths appear to have ended in an heiress, Helen Fedderesse, in the time of David II (RMS., I, App. II, 1283). The family early intermarried with the Cheynes.

FEE. A curtailed form of (MAC)FEE, q.v.

FELDIE. Johannes Feldew or Feldeu, notary public in Dunfermline, 1419 (RD., p. 282). As presbyter of St. Andrews diocese and vicar of Kilmany, 1413 (RPSA., p. 18) he appears several times in record between that date and 1457 (*Inchcolm*, p. 162–163). Tom Feldie in Dunfermline, 1590 (*Dunfermline*).

FELL. An old surname in Dundee. "The Fells afford an instance of an occupation being hereditary in a family, the earliest recorded of the name i.e. in Dundee being Finlay Fell, butcher, who was admitted burgess on 7th June 1533. The trade descended from father to son for more than a century" (*Wedd.*, p. 115). Robert Fell witnessed an instrument of sasine in 1530 (*Bamff*, p. 58), Andrew Fell was burgess of Dundee in 1611 (*Brechin*), Isobel Fell is recorded in Whinkerstaines in 1653 (*Lauder*), and Ann Fell in Blair Atholle in 1781 (*Dunkeld*). James Fell was mylner at Sandhead Mylne in 1628 (*Dumfries*). The Dundee surname may be a shortened form of 'fellmonger,' a dealer in hides or skins with the hair or wool on. (2) The place name Fell (from Icel. *fell*, 'a fell, wild hill') is common in Cumberland, Westmoreland, and Lancashire, where there were Norse settlements. There is also a Fell near Crocketford, Dumfries, and another near Port William, Wigtownshire.

FEMISTER, FIMISTER, PHEMISTER, PHIMISTER, WHIMSTER. Alexander Feemaister, fisher, had a remission in 1458 "pro capcione filii quondam Alex. Coupland, judicati ad mortem apud Banf in primo itinere tento ibidem per dominum regem" (ER., VI, p. 486). Christiane Phemister in Pettinseit, regality of Spynie, was accused of theft in 1595 (SCM., II, p. 129), and Alexander Fumester was fined 6s.8d. for "playing at the futeball on the Sabboth nicht," 1630 (*Rec. Elgin*, II, p. 215). In 1616 Effie Fumester in Elgin was charged with bidding Agnes Fumester cast strang in the fire so that she might get her heart's desire, apparently a magical ceremony (ibid., II, p. 149). John Phinister in Pitgounie was retoured heir of Thomas Phinister, portioner of Pitgounie his father, in 1654 (*Retours, Elgin*, 99). James Fimister is recorded in Whitehill in 1684 (*Moray*), and Alexander Phimister in Bogside in 1707 (ibid.). Robert Phimister in Netherbyres was rebuked in 1737 "for fiddling and dancing at Alexander Buie's lykewake" (*Rec. Elgin*, II, p. 336), and Alexander Fimister appears as burgess and freeman of Elgin in the last half of the same century (*Jervise*, II, p. 263). The name is derived from the office of 'fee-master' (from OE. *feoh*, cattle, property + *master*), one in charge of the flocks and herds:

"Tirrheus thair fader was *fee maister*, and gyde
Of studis, flokis, bowis; and heyrdis wyde,
As storoure to the king, did kep and ʒime."
Gavin Douglas, *Eneados*,
London, 1553, bk. VII, c. 9.11.21–23.

Melrose Abbey had a fee-master, and the Fiemaisteris-lands in Roxburghshire are mentioned in a retour of 1606 (*Retours, Roxburgh*, 43). In the United States the name is not uncommon as Feamaster, Feamster, Feemster, and Feimster.

FENDE. Jacobus Fende was heir of Magister Johannes Fende, Dumfries, 1587 (*Retours, Dumfries*, 367), and James Fende, probably the same person, was heir of John Fende, advocate, 1588 (*Retours, Stirling*, 360).

FENDER. William Fender, dagmaker in Edinburgh, 1578 (MCM., II, p. 345), and Thomas Fender, 'post' in Aberdeen, 1612 (SCM., V, p. 93). The name also occurs in Nisbet (I, p. 262), but no particulars are given. Falls of Fender and Fenderbridge are near Blair Atholl.

FENTON. The earliest known individual of this name was John de Fenton, sheriff of Forfar in 1261 and following years. Although first appearing in Angus the name has doubtless been derived from the barony of Fenton in East Lothian, held by the Fentons of the lords of Dirleton. Sir William de Fentone sometime before 1270 married Cecilia de Bisset, daughter of Sir John Bisset of Lovat and so acquired the estate of Beaufort (HP., I, p. 210n), and in 1278 it was directed that he receive in the king's court his wife's purparty of her father's lands in Ireland (*Bain*, II, 129). The same Sir William, of the county of Edinburgh, swore fealty to the king of England on July 23, 1291 (ibid., II, p. 124), and performed homage in 1296 (ibid., p. 169). His seal bears on a shield three crescents, two and one, and S' *Domini Wilelmi de Fentun*. Alexander de Fentoun witnessed a donation by Henry de Aynstrother to Dryburgh c. 1330 (*Dryburgh*, p. 252), and in 1362 William de Fenton enriched the old chapel of Baikie, in the parish of Airlie, with a gift of the adjoining lands of Lynros (now Linross) (RMS., I, 99). A later William of Fentoun, lord of that Ilk, acquired the lands of Quodquen in Clydesdale in 1413 (RMS., I, 942), and John de Fentoun is recorded as burgess of Edinburgh in 1426 (*Egidii*, p. 47). Willzame of Fentoun had a lease of the teinds of Cukistoun, 1478 (*Cupar-Angus*, I, p. 217), and Gilbert Fyntone witnessed a sasine in favor of Adam Crechtoun of Ruchtven (Ruthven), 1501 (*Bamff*, p. 39). The Angus Fentons continued in considerable repute till about the middle of the fifteenth century, when they ended in co-heiresses who married, one a Lyndsay and the other William, second son of Halket of Pitfirran (Jervise, *Land of the Lindsays*, p. 355). Their name, however, is still preserved in the district in Fenton Hill, the name of a rising ground near Lindertis. Some notes on the Fentons of the Aird, 1253–1422, are given in the *Celtic magazine*, Inverness, 1887, II, p. 84–90. Fendoun 1528.

FENWICK. From the village of Fenwick in the parish of the same name in Ayrshire. Nicholaus Fynwyk was provost of Ayr in 1313 (*Ayr*, p. 19), and Reginald de Fynwyck or Fynvyk appears as bailie and alderman of the same burgh in 1387 and 1401 (*Friars, Ayr*, p. 37). Robert de ffenwic who witnessed a confirmation charter by de Vmframvilla to the Abbey of Kelso c. 1220 (*Kelso*, 327), and the Border clan of Fenwicks, were most probably kin to the Fenwicks or Fenwykes of Northumberland, who took their name from their ancient castle near Stamfordham. Fenwic 1429. See also FINNICK.

FERADACH. From EG. *Fer-fedach<Fer-fid* (*Ferid*), 'man-wood.' Feradach was a rich man 'who dwelt in the island of Islay' (*Adamnan*,

II, c. 23), and Feradach, abbot of Iona, died 880 (AU.). Brude, son of Feradhach, was king of the Picts (CPS., p. 202), and Feradac mac Malbricin was a witness in the *Book of Deer* (IV, 2).

FERESOUN. A curtailed form of MACPHERSON, q.v. It occasionally represents FERGUSON.

FERGIE. A reduced form of FERGUSON, q.v. Patrick Fergie in Edrintoun-mylne, 1671, and four more in the same record (*Lauder*). In 1508 Fergy.

FERGUS. G. *Fearghus*, MG. *Feargus, Fergus*, OIr. *Fergus* (grandfather of S. Columba). The name is cognate with Cymric *Gwr-gwst*, Old Bret. *Uuorgost*, and Pictish *Forcus*. The Pictish form is also found on the inscribed monument at St. Vigeans in Angus, and the writer of the unique Gaelic charter of 1408 writes it Fercos. In the list of Pictish kings (CPS., p. 7, 8) it is also written Urguist, Wirguist, and Wrguist. It means 'super choice,' from * Ver-gustu-s, the suffix being the same as in the personal name ANGUS, q.v. It is now rare as a surname having been corrupted to Ferries, etc. James Fergus, burgess of Culross, 1582 (*Pitfirrane*, 776). See MACFERRIES and MACKERRAS.

FERGUSHILL. From the lands of this name in the parish of Kilwinning, Ayrshire. The surname is now in all probability extinct. The first record of the name is in 1417 when Robert Fergoushill *de eodem* was one of a jury at Irvine (*Irvine*, I, p. 20). He may be the Robert of Fergishill who witnessed an instrument of sasine in 1420 (*Laing*, 97), appears as burgess of Edinburgh in 1423 (*Egidii*, p. 45), and was appointed legal procurator of Kelso Abbey at the courts of Edinburgh and elsewhere in 1435 (*Kelso*, 528). Walter de Fergushyll witnessed the perambulation of the bounds of Prestwick in 1446 (*Prestwick*, p. 116). The names of George, Robert, and William Forgussillis in Kilbryid are included in an act of deprivation of non-resident burgesses of Irvine in 1595 (*Irvine*, II, p. 38). In the same year a sum of twenty shillings was granted by the town of Aberdeen for the support of Robert Fergushill "burgeis of Irwing pilleit and herreit be the Ireland men" (CRA., p. 110). William Fergushill was bailie of the burgh of Prestwick in 1601 (*Prestwick*, p. 85), and Robert Fergushill was retoured heir of Robert Fergushill *de eodem* in the 7 merks 8 shillings and 8 pence lands of old extent of Fergushill in the lordship of Eglintoun in 1625 (*Retours, Ayr*, 236). The lands were alienated c. 1660. Pont mentions "Fergushill

FERGUSHILL, *continued*

de eodem chieffe of hes name" (p. 15), and the Rev. Robert Wodrow wrote the life of the Rev. John Fergushill (? 1592–1644), minister of Ochiltree. Fergisell 1744, Ferguschill 1542, Forgushil 1547, Furgushill 1685.

FERGUSON, FERGUSSON. An Anglicizing of MACFERGUS, q.v. In the "Roll of þe clannis þat hes capitanes, cheiffis and chiftanes quhome on þay depend," 1587, the Fergussons are classed among the septs of Mar and Atholl (APS., III, p. 466). Auchingassyle was leased to Donald filius Fergucii, 1376 (RHM., I, p. lv). Robert I granted certain lands in Ayrshire to Fergus, son of Fergus, and in 1466 John Fergusson resigned a portion of his estate to Fergus Fergusson [of Kilkerran], his son, and Janet Kennedy, his spouse. Alan Fergusii (the Latin genitive form) was burgess of Glasgow, 1422 (LCD., p. 242). Mychel Fargisone was admitted burgess of Dunfermline, 1499 (DBR., 100). Alexander Feresoun (= Ferguson) was one of the tenants of Estir Mecra (Easter Micras), 1539 (ER., XVII, p. 659). James Fargesoun was put in ward for taking part in a mediæval play in Perth, 1581 (Mill, *Plays*, p. 279). The name is widely scattered and there is no evidence for an original connection of the Atholl, Aberdeenshire and Ayrshire families. Robert Ferguson "the Plotter," Robert Fergusson, the poet, and Adam Ferguson, the historian and philosopher, were among the most eminent persons of the name. Farguesoun 1591, Fargusone 1686, Fargussoun 1551, Fergeson 1577, Fergousone 1501, Fergowsone 1597, Forgusoun 1631.

FERIAR. Alexander Feriar who witnessed a charter by John Ramsay, burgess of Montrose, 1430 (REB., II, 34) is probably Alexander Feryer of Montrose who had a safe conduct into England, 1437 (Bain, IV, 1106). Dominus Peter Feryar was chaplain to John, earl of Lennox in 1490 (Lennox, II, p. 140), Robert Feriar was tenant of Drumnamark, Ardmanoch, 1504 (ER., XII, p. 661), and Eweyne Feriar was a charter witness at Dunbretane, 1506 (Lennox, II, p. 182). Ferar 1435, Ferryar 1588. Cf. FERRIER.

FERME. A shortened form of FAIRHOLM, q.v., in current use. The old lands of Farme are now included within the town of Rutherglen. Row (Hist. Church of Scotland, Wodrow Soc. ed., p. 421) says "Mr. Charles Ferholme (alias Ferme contracte)" was minister at Fraserburgh. Row also spells his name Fairholme, and in 1587 it appears as Pharne (in Edinburgh University Catalogue of graduates). The name has been Latinized Fermaeus.

FERMORY. Local. John de Fermory mentioned in 1395 (RAA., II, 44). John Fermory, juror on inquisition at Arbroath, 1452 (ibid., 93). Gilbert de Fermory, who witnessed an instrument of resignation in Brechin, 1446, appears in following year without 'de' (REB., I, 109; II, 61). Johannes Fermory on inquisition at Abirbrothoc, 1452 (RAA., II, p. 79). In index to RAA. II equated with Fermour.

FERMOUR. The old form of FARMER, q.v., is still known in coast towns in Fife.

FERNIE. From the lands of Fernie in the parish of Monimail, Fife. The name appears in the Workman heraldic MS. as 'Fearnyne of that Ilk.' William de Ferny was juror on an inquest in Fife in 1390 (RMS., I, 854). Robert de Ferny, a charter witness in Perth in 1411 (RMS., I, 933) appears also as Robert de Ferny, *dominus ejusdem*, and witnessed a grant by William Scott of Balwearie in 1410 (Milne, p. 41). A bond of manrent by William of Ferny of that Ilk to Laurence, Lord Oliphant, of date 1472–73 is on record (Oliphants, p. 19), John Farny, witness, 1516 (Binns, 28), and Andrew Fernie of that Ilk was recorded in 1517 (SCBF., p. 73). Payment was made to Alexander Farny in 1561 (ER., XIX, p. 156), Andrew Farny *de eodem* claimed the lands of Ballinbla in the same year (ibid., p. 157), and William Farny of that Ilk rendered to Exchequer his accounts as chamberlain of Fife in 1562 and succeeding years (ibid., p. 184, *et sqq.*).

FERRAR. A surname recorded in Mar. A corrupt form of FERGUSON, q.v.

FERRERS. From Ferrières in Normandy from which place came the English family de Ferrarius. Robert Ferrarius made a gift of land to Newbattle Abbey c. 1150 (Neubotle, p. 4). Matilde Ferers or de Ferers, wife of Richard de London, is mentioned c. 1170 (Dryburgh, 42). Reference is made to the ward of William de Ferrers in Dumfries, 1288 (ER., I, p. 36), and Sir William de Ferrarius, miles, is mentioned several times in reign of Robert I (RMS., I, 4, 53, etc.). In index to RMS., the name is spelled Ferrars, Ferraris, Ferrers, Ferras, Fereres, Ferrariis.

FERRES, FERRIES, FERRIS. From (MAC)-FERRIES, q.v., or simply a corruption of FERGUS, q.v. Old (17th century) spellings are: Feres, Ferres, Phires, Pheres, and Ferries. By local usage in Aberdeenshire Ferris is a contraction of Ferguson (Rev. A. B. Grosart). Ferries also occurs as a diminutive of FARQUHARSON.

FERRIER. (1) From OF. *ferrier* (<Lat. *ferrarius*), a blacksmith, maker of horseshoes. Ferrier of Kintrockat is an old family in Angus. A payment was made in 1301 of tenpence to Henry the Ferrier for iron for the king's use, and fivepence to Walter the Ferrier for the same purpose (*Bain*, II, 1271). The Scottish Ferriers carry horseshoes in their arms, but this may be simply canting heraldry. (2) A second possible derivation is from the occupation of ferryman. Lands originally attached to the ferry between Dumbarton and the point of Cardross parish, where the bridge now stands, called Ferrylands, were in 1512 in possession of Robert Ferrier of Ferrylands. Cf. John Glen, ferrier, at Erskine Boat, 1696 (*Corsehill*, p. 191). Peter Ferryar, maltman, burgess of Glasgow, 1596 (*Burgesses*). Feirier 1615. Susan E. Ferrier, novelist, and Professor James Frederick Ferrier, philosopher, were two of the most prominent of the name. Cf. FERIAR.

FERSITH, FERSITHSON. *See under* FORSYTH.

FERUR. A different formation from FERRIER, q.v. The farrier is one who shoes horses. Radulf Ferur was juror on inquisition on land of Padevinan, 1259 (APS., I, p. 98; *Bain*, I, 2175). Alan le Ferur of Kellawe, Berwickshire, rendered homage, 1296 (*Bain*, II, p. 210), and Henry Ferur of Travirnent was on inquisition held at Berwick in same year (ibid., 824). As Henry le Ferour of Travernent the latter rendered homage, 1296. His seal shows a hammer in pale, S' *Henrici Ferur* (*Bain*, II, p. 203, 546). John le Ferour was received to the English king's peace, 1321 (ibid., III, 724), and Nicholas Ferur witnessed an instrument 'de creatione abbatis,' 1326 (RMP., p. 10). John Ferrour was fined in 1358 (ER., I, p. 559), and a later John Ferrour was curate of Brechin, 1506, 1511 (REB., II, 150, 164). Ferror 1485.

FETRIDGE. Curtailed from (MAC)FETRIDGE, q.v.

FETTERESSO. From Fetteresso in the parish of the same name in Kincardineshire. Dufscolok de Fetheressau was one of the perambulators of the bounds of Balfeth in Angus c. 1204–1211 (RAA., I, 89), and in 1206 Sumerleith de Fetherhesan was one of the jurors in a dispute regarding the Kirketun of Aberbuthenoth (SCM., v, p. 213).

FETTES, FETTIS, FITTIS. Lowrens Fettas witnessed an instrument of resignation in Brechin, 1446 (REB., I, 109). Johnne Fettais was summoned personally in judgment in 1519,

and in 1521 as John Fettas he was in amerciament of court for non comparans (SCBF., p. 153, 218). Alexander Fettes is in Bredfutts gairdin, 1597, and Bessie Fettous in Brechin, 1635 (*Brechin*). Alexander and Andrew Fettes appear in Aberdeenshire, 1603 (RSCA., II, p. 16, 111). William Fettes, grandfather of the founder of Fettes College, Edinburgh, was a native of Laurencekirk, Kincardineshire. Fettes or Fiddes was a surname in the Cabrach in seventeenth century. See FIDDES.

FID. Colynus Fidde (Fydde, or Fyd) was firmarius of Banff, 1327, and between 1330–32 he acted as attorney of the provost of Banff (ER., I, p. 61, 271, 417). Brande Fide on inquest in Nairn, 1506 (*Cawdor*, p. 118).

FIDDES. From the old barony of the name, anciently Futhos or Fothes, in the parish of Foveran, Kincardineshire. Eadmund or Edmund de Fotheis and Alwinus or Aleuin, his son, who witnessed two charters between 1200–07 (RAA., I, 93, 94) are probably the first recorded of the name. Fergus de Fothes, son of John de Fothes, received in 1289 from Alexander Cumyn, earl of Buchan, a charter of the whole tenement of Fothes (*Illus.*, III, p. 112). Payments were made to John Fotis and to Walter de Fothes in 1328–9 (ER., I, p. 93, 237), Eustace de Futhas was collector of contributions in Aberdeenshire, 1373 (*Stodart*, II), and Duncan Futhas and John Futhas were in Aberdeen in 1408 (CWA., p. 316). Andrew de Fothes was *dominus ejusdem* in 1423 (REA., I, p. 219). Duncan of Futhas had charter of a tenement in Kirkwall, Orkney, in 1435, and in 1447 was witness to a wadset of lands there (REO., p. 190, 330). Robert Futhes was admitted burgess of Aberdeen, 1491, and Andrew Futhes in 1498 (NSCM., I, p. 36, 39). Sir David Fudas had a tenement in Lanark, 1488 (*Lanark*, p. 5). Sir William Fudes, another cleric, was chancellor of Caithness, 1524 (OPS., II, p. 619), and Duncan and Gilbert Fuddes were witnesses in Aberdeen, 1597 (SCM., I, p. 135). Elizabeth Fiddes had charter of part of the lands of Waltoune alias Newbiging, 1600 (RD., p. 495). Thomas Fiddes was juror at Dornoch, 1603 (OPS., II, p. 644), and Robert Fiddes was admitted burgess of Aberdeen, 1621 (NSCM., I, p. 127). The surname is still prevalent in its parent district. Fitdeis 1590, Fouthas 1439, Futheis and Futhois 1439.

FIDDISON. William Fiddison in Galloway was hanged for being a Covenanter in 1682 (*Hanna*, II, p. 255, 269).

FIDDLER. From the occupation, a 'fiddler,' from ME. *fytheler(e)*, *fitheler*. In 1496 we have record of a payment of nine shillings "to Bennet the fythelare at the kingis command" (ALHT., I, p. 274). Andrew Fidlar was charged with wrongfully occupying land in Lanark in 1498 (*Lanark*, p. 10), John Fidlar or Fidler was relaxed from the horn for art and part in manslaughter in 1511 (RSCA., I, p. 44), and James Fydlar or Fidlar was one of the mairs of the sheriffdom of Innernes in 1514 (OPS., II, p. 662, 663). Nicoll Fydlair, witness in Shetland, 1525 (Goudie, *Antiquities*, p. 141), Wille Fidlar was fined in 1525 'for the wrangus trublance' of a chaplain in Stirling (SBR., p. 21), Jhoin Fidlair to pay for the teinds of Tronstaye (Tronston), 1565, and John Fidler is recorded in Quholme, Orkney, 1584 (REO., p. 372, 306). Gilbert Fidlar was accused of witchcraft in Aberdeen in 1597 (SCM., I, p. 137), and Meattie Fidler in Belliscampie is mentioned in 1632 (RSCA., II, p. 324). A field called the 'fitheleres flat' is mentioned in a charter c. 1230 (*Inchaffray*, p. 48). Fidlair 1565.

FIDDLETON. From the small place named Fiddleton in Ewes, Dumfriesshire. Archibald of Fiddleton was security for Halbert and Launcelot Glendinning in a court held at Hawick, 1622 (RPC., XIV, p. 688). Agnes Fiddletoune recorded in 1679 (*Kirkcudbright*).

FIDILMOUTH. The goods of John Fodilmuthe (perhaps a misreading), Aberdeen merchant, were plundered in the wreck of his ship at Kirklee Rode, Suffolk, 1370 (*Bain*, IV, 158), and David Fidilmouth (? for Fidilmonth) was admitted burgess of Aberdeen, 1400 (NSCM., I, p. 2). Perhaps from Fidilmonth in the parish of Auchindoir, Aberdeenshire, now Wheedlemont.

FIELDFAIR. Johannes Feldefer held land in Abbirbrothoc, 1461, and Thomas Feldifer, burgess of Dundee, 1498, was his son (RAA., II, p. 121, 196, 318, 358). Richard Feldefair or Feldefer held a tenement in Arbroath in 1483 and in 1505, and in 1498 Thomas Feldifer, burgess of Dundee, son of quondam John Feldefer, is mentioned (RAA., II, p. 196, 318, 358). The land of Margaret Feldefayr also in Arbroath is mentioned in 1524 (ibid., p. 441). Feldefair 1505, Feldefayr 1524.

FIFE, FYFE, FYFFE, PHYFE. From the name of the shire. "The surname of Fife (but a small name now) pretends to be descended of a younger son of Macduff, earl of Fife" (*Nisbet*, I, p. 277). There is no proof of such descent. Ele de Fyfe of the county of Fyfe rendered homage in 1296 (*Bain*, II, p. 204). John de Fyff, charter witness in Aberdeen in 1436, may be the John de Fyff prepositus of Aberdeen in 1451, who appears again as burgess there in 1464 (REA., I, p. 234; II, p. 297; RAA., II, 154). Andrew de Fiffe was perpetual vicar of the parish church of Maryton in 1447 (REB., II, 397). John Fieff, Scottish merchant of Aberdeen, had a safe conduct to trade between Scotland and England in 1453, and Patrick of Fyffe, another Aberdeen merchant, had a similar permit in the following year (*Bain*, IV, 1253, 1265). Sir Patrick of Fyfe was vicar of Aberkerdor in 1462 (SCM., v, p. 286). The surname became Feif and Pfeiff in Sweden where several of the name became prominent. Duncan Phyfe, a Scot, came to the United States about 1784, was a maker of fine furniture equal to that produced by Sheraton, Hipplewhite, and Adams. Fif 1513, Fyif 1608, Fyiff 1647.

FILDAR. John Fyldar was chaplain in the parish church of Soltray, 1511 (*Soltre*, p. 82), payment was made to Andrew Feildar in Aberdeen for "keiping and temporing of thare knok," 1539 (CRA., p. 166), Patrick Fyldar had a lease "de decimis garbalibus de Inueresk" between 1557–85 (RD., p. 492), and Thomas Fyldar was burgess of Haddington, 1575 (*Soltre*, p. 134).

FILDES. An Aberdeen surname. Perhaps of English origin. Bardsley says it is a well-known surname in Lancashire, doubtless arising from the Fylde district, the final *s* probably genitive.

FILDIE. From a small place of the name near Glenfarg, Perthshire. Gilbert Fildie had a lease of the quarter lands of Innerburs in 1585 (*Scon*, p. 228).

FILHOP. William Filhop recorded in 1506 (*Peebles*, 40) may have derived his surname from the 10 pound lands of Phillip (1631) or Phillop (1642) in the barony of Hawick.

FILLAN, FILLANS. Gilbert Fillane alias *McLarne* was servant to James Galbrayth of Kilcrewch, 1567 (RPC., I, p. 615). Robert Phillen in Dunfermline, 1562 (*Dunfermline*), appears as Robert Fillane, burgess there, 1574 (*Pitfirrane*, 207). David Philland in Balseidlocks was heir of Christina Philland, 1605 (*Inquis.*, 212). Robert Fillan was fined for absence at the wapinschaw, 1626 (SCM., v, p. 223). As forename: Phillan Snvpe, 1588; Phillane Morieson, burgess freeman of Glasgow, 1608 (*Burgesses*). James Fillens, sculptor, died 1852. A shortening of GILFILLAN, q.v.

FILSHIE. A surname peculiar to the parish of West Kilpatrick, Dumbartonshire. Most of the lands in the parish belonged to the Abbey of Paisley, but the name does not appear in the rental roll of the tenants dated 1545. At the end of the following century it is frequently mentioned in the parish registers (*Notes and queries*, 8. ser. III, p. 288).

FIMBOGA. Gilbertus fimboga witnessed King David's charter granting Perdeyc (Partick) to the church of Glasgow, 1136 (REG., 3), and Arturus finboga witnessed a charter by Robert, bishop of St. Andrews, granting the church of Lohworuora (afterwards Borthwick) to Herbert, bishop of Glasgow, c. 1150 (ibid., 11).

FIMISTER. *See under* FEMISTER.

FIMMERTON. Of local origin. John Fimmertoun was cordiner in Edinburgh, 1662 (*Edinb. Marr.*), and Janett ffumertoune was "werdet by wryttin warrand" in the Canongate Tolbooth of Edinburgh, 1684 (BOEC., IX, p. 170). There was an article on Janet Fimmerton the Covenanting heroine in the *Scotsman*, June, 1931. There is a Fymmeltoun in Lanark Retours, 473.

FIN, FINN. *Finn* is one of the oldest OE. personal names. Finn occurs in the OE. poem of *Widsiþ* as the name of a king of the north Frisians, and again in *Beowulf* (vv. 1068, 1081, etc.). Björkman I, p. 40, gives Fin, Finn, as a Norse personal name and compares Old West Norse *Finnr*, Old Swedish and Old Danish *Fin*. He also states that although the name is found in England before the Danish period it has always then a more or less mythological character. In DB., it occurs as Fin and *Phin*, but has *danus* or *dacus* (= *danicus*) after it, showing the origin of the bearer. William Fyn of Lanarkshire rendered homage, 1296 (*Bain*, II, p. 204). Soon after the Reformation several persons of the name of Fin or Phin became possessed of the lands of the Abbey of Dunfermline. David Fin resigned his half of the vill and lands of Lymekillis, 1598 (RD., p. 494). Isobel Fynne is recorded in the parish of S. Madois, 1612 (*Dunblane*), and John Fine in Drumlochie, 1667 (ibid.).

FINDARG. Of territorial origin from the old barony of the name in Aberdeenshire. Philip de Phendarg or Fedarg was present at a perambulation of the lands of Tarways (Tarves) in 1236 (*Illus.*, I, p. 337), and as Philip de Feodarg had a grant of the lands of Balcormoch, c. 1242–1249 (SHSM., IV, p. 318). He seems to have been a man of importance in his day and is a frequent charter

witness. From the abbot of Arbroath he received, c. 1250, a charter "terram in territorio de Taruays que vocatur Achathnaneue" (RAA., I, p. 195). Either he or his son seems to have dropped "de Fedarg" and assumed "de Melgedrum" (Meldrum). There is mention in 1462 of the "baronry of Fyndyhark quhilk is now callit Meldrum," which formerly belonged to "the lard that then was callyt Philip de Findark" (RAA., II, 123).

FINDLATER. Of territorial origin from the lands of the name in the parish of Fordyce, Banffshire. Galfridus de Fynleter was juror on an inquest held at Banff in 1342 (REA., I, p. 73). Johanna de Fynletir, wife of Richard de Sancto Claro, resigned to her husband all the land of Fynletir with pertinents in the sheriffdom of Banf in 1366 (RMS., I, 260). Andrew Findlater (1810–1885), a scholar of wide and varied learning, was editor of the first edition of Chambers's Encyclopædia. Also current as FINLATER and FINLATOR.

FINDLAY. The same as FINLAY, q.v., with intrusive *d*.

FINDLUGAN. S. Columba one time while staying in Hinba excommunicated some persecutors of churches, one of whom attacked the saint. Findlugan came between and received the thrust of the spear without being in the slightest degree injured (*Adamnan*, V. C., II, 24). This Findlugan or Finnloga was a disciple and brother of S. Fintan of Dun blesci, county Limerick. He is commemorated in the name of Loch Finlagan, Islay, in which are the isle with the ruins of a chapel of S. Finlagan built by John of Islay, Lord of the Isles (d. 1386). See MACLINLAGAN.

FINDON. From the lands of Findon in the parish of Banchory-Devenick, Deeside. In 1281 Philipp de Findvn is party to a record of the division of the lands of Nvg near Aberdeen (RAA., I, p. 164). As Philip de Fyndon or de Fvndoun of the county of Kincardine rendered homage for his lands in 1296. His seal bears a bald bearded figure, head affronté, above a crescent, and an object(?) protruding from either ear, and S' *Phillippi d' Findun* (*Bain*, II, 730, 818, and p. 201). The lands of Findon appear to have been forfeited as an annuity from their rents was given by Bruce to John Crab, the Flemish engineer who had distinguished himself against the English at Berwick.

FINDRACH. John Findrach appears in Wester Wevms, 1630 (PBK., p. 20). Perhaps from Findrack near Torphins, Aberdeenshire.

FINEGOOD. James Fyndgude, burgess of
Edinburgh, 1473 (CDE., 48). Bardsley has
Finegod (1273), and considers it a personal
name.

FINEMUND. This surname is probably now
extinct in Scotland. The Finemunds were lords
of Cambusnethan in Lanarkshire in the thirteenth century, and were probably of Flemish
origin. They appear in early records about
the same time as their neighbors in that part
of the country, the Flemings of Biggar and
Cumbernauld, to whom they were perhaps
of kin. They were extensive landowners and
made liberal donations to the church. William
de Finemund, lord of the manor of Cambusnethan, granted the church of Cambusnethan to the monks of Kelso before 1153
(Kelso, p. 14), Thomas Finmond appears in
Roxburgh in 1266 (ER., I, p. 29), and Warin
Finemund witnessed a land grant in 1304
(Bain, II, p. 423). Findmond 1264.

FINGALL. G. Fionnghal, sometimes erroneously written Fionnaghal, (1) a Gaelicized
descendant of the Norsemen; (2) a native of
the Hebrides. Latinized Fingallus. Down to
the end of the eighth century Gaill denoted
the foreigners of the southwestern continent.
They were no doubt by that time dark in
hair and complexion. When the first Norsemen — an extremely blond type — appeared
on their shores it seemed natural that the
Irish should call them Finngaill, 'fair foreigners' (Kuno Meyer). Fingall was also used as
a personal name. Fingallus canonicus et sacerdos Candidae Casae, 1235 (Forbes, S. Ninian,
p. lii). James Macpherson made his Fingal
out of Find mac Cumail.

FINGASK. From Fingask in the parish of
Daviot, Aberdeenshire. William de Fingask
and John de Fyngask were burgesses of Aberdeen, 1317 (SCM., v, p. 10, 11). Thomas de
Fingast, canon of Aberdeen and rector of
Forbes, 1329 (Pap. Lett., II, p. 2), as
Thomas de Fyngaske held the deanery of
Brechin and later was appointed to the see of
Caithness, 1343 (Pap. Pet., I, p. 15; Dowden,
p. 243). Johannes de Fyngask or ffyngask
appears on assizes in 1333–35–41 (REA., I,
p. 53, 61, 72), John de Fyngaske was perpetual vicar of Obeyne (Aboyne), 1366 (ibid.,
II, p. 61), and David Fyngask was provost
of Aberdeen, 1333–35, and alderman, 1342
(REA., I, p. 72). William Fingask was admitted burgess of Aberdeen, 1494 (NSCM., I,
p. 37), Sir Henry Fingask was chaplain at
Dunblane, 1547 (Dunblane), and Helen Fingask is recorded there in 1658 (ibid.). William

Fingask or Fingass was member of Scots parliament for Dumfries, 1685 (Hanna, II, p. 493).
Fingas 1676, Fyngasc 1343.

FINGLAND. Of local origin from Fingland in
Dumfriesshire. Thomas of Fyngland, witness
to an obligation by Fergus Graham, c. 1573
(Annandale, I, p. 34). There is also a Fingland
in Peeblesshire.

FINGLASS. A local name. William ffingas or
Finglass appears as bailie in Dumfries in 1679
and 1687, commissioner for Dumfries to the
Convention of Royal Burghs in 1683 and 1685,
and member of parliament for Dumfries in
1685 (Edgar, p. 175, 187, 214; Dumfries).

FINHAVEN. Of local origin from Finhaven
in the parish of Oathlaw in Angus. Jhon Fin-
heaven, post, brought Mr. James Melville,
minister of Kilrenny in Fife, "Psalme buikes
and ballates" from Edinburche in 1570 (Melville, Diary, Bann. Club ed., p. 18). Lyoune
Finewein was denounced rebel and put to the
horn in 1571 (Diur. Occ., p. 239). John
Phinevin was "teicher of the younge childrene"
in Aberdeen in 1583 (CRA., p. 49), and in
1588 there is mention of umquhill John Phane-
vin in the same burgh (SCM., v, p. 115). The
surname was current in the eighteenth
century but is now perhaps extinct.

FINLAISON. A current form of FINLAYSON,
q.v.

FINLATER, FINLATOR. See under FIND-
LATER.

FINLAY, FINLEY, FINDLAY. G. Fionnlagh, less
correctly Fionnladh and Fionnla. In the Gaelic
genealogical MS. of 1467 the name occurs in
the genitive as Finlaeic, and in the Duan
Albanach, an old poetical chronicle of the
kings of Dalriada (c. 1070, though in text
of later date) as Fionnlaoich. In the Book
of Leinster the name of Macbeth's father is
spelled Findlaech (1070), and in Marianus
Scotus (c. 1080, but text of later date) Finn-
loech. In the Norse chronicle known as the
Flateyjarbók his name is spelled Finnleikr,
the name being understood by the Norsemen
as meaning in their language "Finn's game
or sport." The name is generally explained
as 'Fair hero,' from fionn 'white,' 'fair,' and
laoch, 'hero,' OIr. laech (which is borrowed
from Latin laicus). The name has been also
explained as a substitution for or popular rendering of Fionnlugh, earlier Find-lug, meaning
'Fair one of (the god) Lug.' Finlay is a not
uncommon name in early Scots records. Fyn-
layus, clericus, witnessed a charter by Alex-

ander filius Walteri, senescallus, 1246 (RMP., p. 89). Fynlai, 'sutor,' was prepositus (provost) of Stirling, 1327 (ER., I, p. 67). Fyndlaw, thane of Glentilt, leased the lands of Enirvak in 1480 (Cupar-Angus, I, p. 231). Andrew Fyndelai, chaplain of Brechin in 1526, appears again in 1537 as Andrew Finlaius, presbyter of St. Andrews' diocese (REB., II, 180, 192). Robert Finlaw in Leith accepts the king's coronation, 1567 (RPC., I, p. 563). John Phinlaw was retoured heir of James Phinlaw, portioner of Balcristie, his brother-german, in 1629, and Arthur Finlau was retoured heir of Andrew Fynlaw, portioner of Balcrystie in same year (Retours, Fife, 419, 424). John Findlo, burgess of Montrose, died 1639 (Jervise, II, p. 223). Andrew Finlaw in Langton, 1734 (Kirkcudbright). In the Lewis the fairies are, for some unknown reason, called in Gaelic Muinntir Fhionlaidh, 'Finlay's people' (Rev. Malcolm Macphail, Folklore, XI, p. 442). Findlaw 1599, Findlow 1702, Fyndelay 1526, Fyndlae 1594, Fyndllla 1597.

FINLAYSON, FINLAISON. English forms of G. MacFhionnlaigh, 'son of FINLAY,' q.v. Brice Fynlawesone of Netbolge, Stirlingshire, rendered homage in 1296 (Bain, II, p. 205). Duncanus filius Findlai (the Latin form of the name) was one of an inquest held at Banff in 1342 (REA., I, p. 73), and Kessog Findlauson performed like duty at Dunipace in 1426 (Cambus., 87). Andrew Fyndlai (again Latin form) was chaplain in Brechin, 1450 (REB., I, 138). John Finlawsone witnessed an Atholl charter in 1455 (Athole, p. 708), Michal Fynloson was tenant of half of Cragneuydy in 1478 (Cupar-Angus, I, p. 227), Ade Findelasone, tenant of the bishop of Aberdeen in Petglass, 1511, Alexander Findelasone in Inuerquhat in the same year, and John Finlason in Balfaddy (REA., I, p. 369, 374). Thom Findlaisone was presbyter in Dunkeld, 1528 (REB., II, 182), and Robert Fyndlasoun leased the Cruikit aiker called Sanct-augustines land in 1585 (Scon, p. 229). Findleysone 1647, Finlasone 1561, Finlasoun 1620, Finlawsoune 1598, Finlison 1678, Fonlosoun 1585, Finlosoune 1502, Finlsoun 1512, Fyndelosoun 1529, Fyndlosone 1506.

FINN. See under FIN.

FINNAN. Perhaps from Ir. O'Fionnain, descendant of Finnan (diminutive of Fionn, fair). S. Finan of Moville is commemorated at Kirkgunzeon in Galloway and at Kilwinning in Ayrshire. Katherine Finnane recorded in Dumfries, 1681 (Dumfries), Florence Finnan in Trosten, 1780 (Kirkcudbright), and Mr.

James Finnan was minister at Kirkcudbright-Irongray, 1797 (Dumfries). James Finnan was in Colvend (1761) and another James Finnan in Kirkcudbright-Irongray (1775).

FINNICK. Local. Barbare ffinnick in Edinburgh, 1670 (Edinb. Marr.). John Finnick in Redgoall, 1716, and John Finnick, tenant in Coufoord, 1772 (Dunkeld). Cf. (Macnab of) Phinnick, and (in 1671) Phinnickhaugh. Fenwick in Ayrshire is pronounced Finnick (in 1666 Finick). There is also Fenwick near Hawick (in 1615 Fynnick — Retours, Roxburgh, 78). Nichol of Fynnyk recorded in Ayr c. 1431 (Coll. AGAA., I, p. 228), and John Phinnick or Phenick in Cowsland was tried for witchcraft, 1630 (RPC., 2. ser. III, p. 602). See also FENWICK.

FINNIE, FINNEY. Most likely from Ir. O'Fidhne, the name of a Galway family (Woulfe). (2) less likely to be the diminutive of Finn. John Fynne contributed to church repairs in Aberdeen, 1508 (CRA., p. 80), David Fynie was common councillor there, 1509 (Guildry, p. 194), and David Fynne was merchant there, 1541 (SCM., II, p. 33). John Fynne was witness in Glasgow, 1551 (Protocols, I), John Finny, indweller in Brechin, 1578 (Brechin), William Finnie in Waley, witness, 1624 (OSS., I, 86), Thomas Fynnie, burgess of Edinburgh, 1640 (Inquis., 8631), and Margaret Phinne is recorded there in same year (Edinb. Marr.). John Finnie in Drumlochie, 1676 (Dunblane), John Phynnie was cordiner in Edinburgh, 1683 (Edinb. Marr.), and a pension was paid Marion Finnie there, 1741 (Guildry, p. 177). John Finnie, a Midlothian farmer, was one of the first to recognize the importance of chemistry and its application to agriculture, and was instrumental in founding the Agricultural Chemistry Association of Scotland in Edinburgh, 1842. Finney 1552, Phinnie 1631.

FINNIESON. John Fynnysoun was a forestaller in Aberdeen, 1402 (CRA., p. 384), and Bormand Finnysone had a grant of the lands of Blairback and Stouk in Stronwhellen, 1498 (OPS., II, p. 73). Robert Fennison was a merchant in Edinburgh (Nisbet, I, p. 219), and Hugh Fenisoune is recorded in Carpow in the sixteenth century (CRD.). William Fynnesoun was a witness in Glasgow, 1527; John Fenesoun was a witness in Fife, 1545 (Gaw, 41); and Henry Finnisoun appears in Beanislaw, 1663 (Dunblane). John Finnieson was burgess of Culross, 1682 (Edin. App.), and William Finnieson appears in Edinburgh, 1691 (Edinb. Marr.). See also PHENNESONE.

FINNIESTON. From Finnieston, now a part of the city of Glasgow. John Fynnistoun was admitted burgess of Glasgow in 1617 as eldest son of a burgess, and Bartholomew Fynnestoun was admitted burgess in 1621 *(Burgesses)*.

FINNOCK. A surname recorded in Fife, may be a variant of FINNICK, q.v.

FINTRY. Of territorial origin from Fintry, Stirlingshire. Ada de Fyntrif witnessed a charter by Alwin, earl of Levenax, c. 1175–99 *(Levenax,* p. 12; RMP., p. 157). Maldonich, earl of Levenax, c. 1250, granted to Luce (= Luke) "filio magistri Michaelis de Fyntryf clerico meo, pro homagio et servitio suo, illam dimidiam arrachar de Nentbolg que propinquior est terre de Fyntryf" *(Levenax,* p. 34). Gilbert of Fyntreth was burgess of Aberdeen in 1271 *(Fraser,* p. 9).

FIONGALL. *See under* DUBHGALL and FIONGALL.

FIRLINE. Robert Firline recorded at Cladoch, Arran, in 1769 *(Isles),* derived his surname from Feorline on Drumadoon Bay, Arran.

FIRTH. Local. There is a place named Firth near Lilliesleaf, Roxburghshire. Thomas Firth in 1606 *(Home,* 32). Janet Firth in Newbarns of Weitschaw-mure, 1630, and four more of the name *(Lanark CR.).* It is also a current surname in Orkney, from the parish of Firth in Mainland. Nycholl of Fyrtht on inquest at Sabay, 1522, and John Firth, witness in Kirkwall, 1565 (REO., p. 95, 280).

FISH. OE. *Fisc* 'fish,' appears to have been used as a personal name, and Searle records one of the name described as 'liber homo.' William Fysch appears as burgess of Edinburgh in 1423 *(Egidii,* p. 45), and Gilbert Fysche recorded as burgess there in 1483 had a charter of part of the lands of Estir halys in the regality of Mussilburgh in the same year (RD., p. 372). Thomas Fish or Fishe, sometyme mairchand in Glasgow, 1658 *(Inquis.,* 4405), was burgess there in 1669 *(Retours, Lanark,* 311). John Fische, heir of Alexander Fische in Avtoun his father, 1614 *(Retours, Berwick,* 581). Cf. remarks under CRAN.

FISHBURN. An Englishman of this name was lord of Red Castle, Lunan, in 1306 *(Angus,* I, p. 56). Probably from Fishburn in co. Durham. There is also Fishbourne, a parish in co. Sussex.

FISHER. From the occupation, OE. *fiscere,* ME. *fischere,* a fisherman. In Latin charters rendered *piscator.* Robert dominus Piscator,

burgess of Perth, 1292 *(Milne,* p. 5). Michael Fysser who appears in record in 1344 (RMS., I, 196) as bailie of Perth is probably the Michaele Fisser recorded in 1338 *(Keir,* 198). Donald Fyschar witnessed an Atholl charter of 1455 *(Athole,* p. 708), Andro Fischar was admitted burgess of Lanark in 1488 *(Lanark,* p. 4), Constancius Fichar was tenant in barony of Carstairs in 1513 *(Rental),* and Thomas Fyschiar was one of the bailies of Edinburgh in 1603 *(Laing,* 1459). In a number of cases, particularly about Perthshire, this surname is used as an Englishing of MACINESKER, q.v. Malcolm Fisher witnessed a sasine of the lands of Balnacard, 1514 *(Grandtully,* I, p. 48). Feichear 1560, Fischair 1546, Fischare 1509, Fischear 1606; Fyscher.

FISHWICK. Sueinus de Fiswic witnessed a charter by Rodbertus, bishop of St. Andrews in the reign of Malcolm IV (LSC., p. 17). There is a township of this name in Lancashire.

FISKEN, FISKIN. Found in Perth in sixteenth century. Andrew Fiskine, late schoolmaster at Tippermuir, 1721, and Margaret Fiskine in Eastertown of Cultmalundy, 1723 *(Dunkeld),* and Ninian Fisken in Auchterarder, 1778 *(Dunblane).* John Fisken in Grangemouth was married, 1938.

FITCHET. Lower, Bardsley, and Harrison say this name is from "fitchet," a polecat, which seems hardly likely as a surname. Lower also suggests it is perhaps from Montfichett, and also refers to a place near Bayeux called Montfiquet. As Fichet the name is recorded in Suffolk, Cambridgeshire, and Devon in thirteenth century *(Guppy,* p. 131). This surname, first met with in Scotland in Aberdeen six hundred years ago, was not uncommon in Montrose and Perth in the middle of the nineteenth century, and still exists in Dundee. William Fitchet held a land in the Galugat (Gallowgate) of Aberdeen in 1317 (SCM., V, p. 7). Thomas Fichet of Evirenisse (Inverness) and others complained in 1359 that during a truce their vessel was captured and sunk by the English *(Bain,* IV, 23). Richard Fichet was elected councillor of Aberdeen, 1398 (CRA., p. 374). His seal, appended to a document of 1405 bears a chevron between three pea-pods (fitches), and S' *Ricardi fytchet* *(Seals Supp.,* 402). John Fichet, provost of Aberdeen, 1409, appears in following year as bailie of the burgh (NSCM., I, p. 3; REA., II, p. 295). William Fichet 'et uxor' were described as 'communes pikares' (petty thieves) in Aberdeen in 1411 (CRA., p. 4). Nicholas Fechet, servant to the king of Scotland, who had a safe conduct into England in 1424 (*Bain*, IV, 969), may be Nicholas Fichet, burgess of Aberdeen, 1442 (NSCM., I, p. 6). Matthew Fochet (Fichet, or Fychet), alderman of Aberdeen, 1441 (CRA., p. 6), provost in 1442 (NSCM., I, p. 6) and burgess in 1449 (REA., I, p. 254), may be Matheus Fichel (*sic*) who was elected common councillor there, 1475 (*Guildry*, p. 189). John Fichet of the same burgh was ordered to be ready to enter the king's service in 1476 (SCM., V, p. 25), John Fychaitt was merchant there, 1541 (ibid., II, p. 33), Elspet Fitchett is recorded in the parish of Guthrie, 1662 (*Brechin*), and David Fitchet in Windedge, parish of Oathlaw, 1669 (ibid.). Fechait 1475, Fechat 1489.

FITHIE. From the lands of Feithie (now Fithie) in the parish of Farnell, Angus. Duncan de Fethyn witnessed perambulation of the lands of Conan and Tulloch, 1254 (RAA., I, p. 325). Henry of Fythie was one of the commissioners appointed by Robert I to inquire and report what rights and privileges the town of Arbroath had from his predecessors (*Jervise*, I, p. 340), and as Henry de Fethy he witnessed a charter by Walter Shakloc of the third part of the lands of Inieney c. 1328 (RAA., I, p. 339). William de Fethy had a safe conduct c. 1365. Henry de Fethe or de Fethy, who appears as witness and juror at Brechin, 1449–50 (REB., II, p. 79, 201) is probably Henry Fethy de Ballisak who appears in 1464 (RAA., II, p. 142), and in 1483 (*Southesk*, p. 721). George Fethy witnessed a sasine in favor of Adam Crechtoun of Ructhven (Ruthven), 1501 (*Bamff*, p. 39). Walter Fethy appears in Duffus, 1524 (REM., p. 401), and David Fethy or Fithy was amerciated for non-appearance, 1527 (*Trials*, I, p. 137*). Walter Fethe and John Fethe were procurators in St. Andrews, 1546, and William Fethe was procurator for Elizabeth Dischington, lady of Kinkel, 1547 (*Gaw*, 9, 54). A family of this name settled in Dundee, 1517, and long continued burgesses there, and Henry Feithe or Fithie was admitted burgess through the privilege of his father, 1632 (*Wedd.*, p. 77). John Fithie was sergeant of ward of Dundee, 1643 (*Beats*, p. 255), William Feithe was 'reider at the Kirk of Glames,' 1653 (*Inquis.*, 3740), and Magister James Feithie was minister in Peebles, 1691 (ibid., 7185). Henry Futhie or Fithie was member of Scots parliament for Arbroath, 1667 (*Hanna*, II, p. 494).

FITZ. This NF. word signifies 'son,' from Latin *filius* (>Fr. *fils*). The old spelling is usually *fiz*, and another but rarer form is *filtz*. The spelling with *t* was an attempt to preserve the old sound of NF. *z*, which was pronounced *ts*. Like Mac in Gaelic it is prefixed to Norman names to signify descent. A later application of it has been to denote the many natural sons of royalty, as in Fitzclarence, Fitzjames, Fitzroy, Fitzwilliam.

FLAEBARNE. James Flabarne, reidare at Ersiltoun, 1574 (RMR.). Michael Flaebarne, maltman in Ersiltoune, 1645 (RRM., I, p. 111). John Flaebarne, portioner of Ersiltoune, 1651 (ibid., p. 131). Flaebairne 1661.

FLAKEFIELD, FLECKFIELD. From the place named Flakefield in the parish of East Kilbride, Lanarkshire. William Flaikfeilde was burgess of Glasgow in 1562, and the Rev. David Fleckfield was minister of Balfron from 1691 till 1729 (*Strathendrick*, p. 28). David Flaikfield, wobster in Carmyle, parish of Monkland, is in record in 1611 (*Campsie*), and John Flaikfield, wobster, was admitted burgess of Glasgow in 1619 as eldest son of David Flaikfield (*Burgesses*). The story told by Anderson (*Scot. Nat.*, II, p. 218) of the origin of the name is inaccurate as the surname is at least a century older.

FLATAY. From the island of Flottay, Orkney. Thomas Flattay and Jyne Flattay, his daughter, in Holm, 1552 (REO., p. 247).

FLATTISBURY. Robert Flattisbury, reidare at Dumbertane, 1574 (RMR.). Of English local origin?

FLAWS. A surname found only in Orkney and Shetland is of local origin probably from Flawis in South Ronaldsay. James Flawis was tacksman in the urislands of Marwick in 1492 (REO., p. 406), Adam Flawis appears as a juror at Kirkwall in 1509, Magnus Flawis witnessed a charter of confirmation in 1545, and Nicholl Flavis was juror on an assize at Tankerness in 1559 (REO., p. 84, 111, 227). Flais 1624, Flauies 1568, Flawes 1675, Flawys 1580. Other early forms are Flaas, Flaus, and Flause.

FLECK. Perhaps of local origin from Flegg in co. Norfolk. Patryk Flek and others, "cordinaris and barkaris of barkit ledyr," were charged in 1559 with "wrangus brekyne of the statuttis" of Inverness (*Rec. Inv.*, I, p. 36). This surname is also recorded in Edinburgh, 1605 (*Edinb. Marr.*), and in 1650 Andro Flecke was minister of Dundee (Lamont, *Diary*, p. 23). Bessie Fleck in Robertoun, 1657, and eight more of the name (*Lanark CR.*). William Fleck in Humbie was accused of sor-

FLECK, *continued*

cery in 1659 (Dalyell, *Darker superstitions,* p. 275), and Robert Fleck is recorded in Dumfries, 1679 *(Dumfries).* John Fleck of Little Milton, parish of Urr *(M'Kerlie,* v, p. 314).

FLEGEARTH. Ewin Flegearth had a remission for his part in burning the town of Dunbertane, 1489 (*Lennox,* II, p. 133). Perhaps an early spelling of FLETCHER, q.v.

FLEMING, FLEMYNG, FLEEMING. A surname sufficiently indicative of the nationality of its original bearers. In NF. *le Fleming,* Latinized *Flandrensis,* a native of Flanders. Several individuals of the name appear in record in the second half of the twelfth century but the relationship, if any, between them is unknown. Large territories in the Upper Ward of Lanarkshire were later in possession of a family of this name. Their residence was Boghall Castle near Biggar. Theobald the Fleming *(Theobaldus Flamaticus)* had a grant of land on the Douglas Water from the abbot of Kelso between 1147–60 (*Kelso,* 107). Baldwin the Fleming was sheriff of Lanark c. 1150 (REG., 11). Jordan Fleming was taken prisoner at Alnwick along with William the Lion in 1174 (*Bain,* II, p. 117). About 1177 Symone Flamench witnessed a charter by Eschina, wife of Walter the Steward (RMP., p. 75). Ricardus Flammanc witnessed a charter by Robert Bruce c. 1190 (*Annandale,* I, p. 1), and as Flamanc he attested a charter by William Bruce to Adam de Carlyle, c. 1194–1214 (ibid., p. 2). Between 1189–99 William Flandrensis witnessed gift of the church of Gutherin (Guthrie) to the Abbey of Arbroath by William the Lion (RAA., I, 96), and probably within the same dates he witnessed the grant of the lands of Herol (Errol) to David de Haia, son of William de Haia (SCM., II, p. 305). Symon Flandrensis was one of the perambulators of the lands of Kinalchmund between 1211–14 (RAA., I, 83). Adam Flamanke witnessed resignation of lands in Annandale a. 1245 (*Bain,* I, 1682). William fflamang witnessed a grant by Hugh de Bvgris, 1228 (*Kelso,* 186), Bartholomew Flamang attested an agreement between the bishop of Moray and John Bvseth in 1258 (REM., p. 135), and c. 1260 Duncan [note the Gaelic forename] Flandrensi witnessed a donation to the Abbey of Paislev (RMP., p. 58). William le Fleming, knight, of Lanarkshire, rendered homage, 1296. His seal bears a fesse surmounted of a bend, S' Will'i Flandrensis (*Bain,* II, p. 203, 544). Matheus de Flandre witnessed a charter by Herbert de Maxwel to Paisley, c. 1300 (RMP.,

p. 104). James Fleeman or Fleming (1713–1778), was the fool, as part of the establishment of the family of Udny of that Ilk, the last family in Scotland, it is said, to have maintained one. ffleming 1681, fflemyng 1437, Flamyng 1343, Flemen 1539, Flemmayng 1322, Flemmvnge 1427, Flemvn 1511, Fleymen 1652, Fleyming 1645, Flemyne 1512, Flemynge 1424, Flimer 1665, Flymen 1653, Flymyng 1392; Flimimg, Phylemen.

FLESCHAN. Marcus Fleschan in Inverness inhibited from buying meat in the market, 1561 (*Rec. Inv.,* I, p. 60).

FLESHER. From the occupation of 'flesher,' a contraction of ME. *fleschheware,* one who cuts up flesh, a butcher, in Latin charters rendered by *carnifex.* Walter carnifex held land in Dumfries a. 1214 (*Kelso,* 11), and Nicholas carnifex held land in fee in Aberdeen, 1281 (REA., II, p. 278). Laurentius carnifex is in record in Aberdeen, 1317 (SCM., IV, p. 6), William, son of Adam carnifex, appears there in 1398 (CRA., p. 373), and James Fleschewar is also recorded there in 1408 (CWA., p. 313). Robert Flescheware is mentioned in 1445 (*Cambus.,* 214), Thomas Fleshware was one of the bailies of Cupar, 1458 (ER., VI, p. 400), and James Fleschour was burgess of Dundee, 1526. Thomas Flescheour rendered to Exchequer the accounts of the bailies of Cowpare in 1558 (ibid., XIX, p. 40). Robert Flescher, charter witness in Brechin, 1566 (REB., II, 212), and Thomas Fleschour, notary public at Forthar, 1513 (*Laing,* 765). The surname was common in Dundee in the sixteenth century, and there has doubtless been confusion with FLETCHER, q.v. Some Fleshers may really be Fletchers, and *vice versa.* Flescheir 1568, Flescheoure 1570, Fleschour 1500, Fleshour 1629.

FLETCHER. From the occupation, OFr. *flechier,* apparently one who attached the *flèches* or feathers to the arrow-shaft, later 'arrow-maker.' "Though not of old standing in Scotland, the Fletchers were among the most ancient and reputable of the English barons, those of Salton and Inverpeffer being direct descendants of Sir Bernard Fletcher of the county of York" (*Jervise LL.,* p. 348). John Flechvr held a burgage in Roxburgh c. 1338 (*Dryburgh,* p. 263), and Baty Flessor held land in Ayr c. 1340 (*Friars Ayr,* p. 15). Henry Flesher was burgess of Forfar, 1374, Malcolm Fleschar, citizen of Brechin, 1482, Robert Flescher was chaplain there, 1497, and Mr. John Flescheour, vicar of Kirriemuir, 1500 (*Stodart,* II, p. 341). Patrick Flegear, dean of Christianity of Inverness, 1461 (*Invernessiana),* may be Patrick Flegear, chaplain in Arbroath, 1464 (RAA., II, p. 138). Nicholas Flegiar was admitted burgess of Aberdeen, 1464 (NSCM., I, p. 19), and Ewin Flegeare had a remission for holding Dumbarton Castle against the king, 1489 (APS., XII, p. 34). Archibald Flegger, witness in Glasgow, 1539, appears in 1543 as Fleggeour (LCD., p. 121, 127). John Flagear was canon of St. Andrews, 1566 (Laing, 809), and Muldonich Phledgeour was fined in 1613 for reset of Clan Gregor (RPC., XIV, p. 635). Fletcher of Innerpeffer appears in 1631 as Flesher and in 1647 as Flescheour. In the seventeenth century the name became almost hopelessly confused with the name FLESHER, q.v. The following are variant spellings (all in Laing) of the name of Thomas Flesser, clerk of the diocese of St. Andrews and of his son: Flessher 1537, Fleschor 1552, Fletcheour 1539, Flescheoir and Fleschour 1563, Flescher 1589, Flesshour 1552, and Fleschar 1541. Flager 1627, Fledger 1612, Fleger 1609; Flessar, Flesser. See also MAC-LEISTER.

FLETT. An Orcadian surname usually considered to be derived from the place name Flett in the parish of Delting, Shetland. Mr. J. S. Clouston, however, says this name "which occurs several times as a nickname in the Sagas (once being in Orkney), and which is not associated with any land so-called" is a nickname . . . "It is markedly the case with the chief landed families of the later Norse period," he says, "that they can invariably be proved to have owned the property from which they took their name. For this reason alone," he adds, "I would reject a land explanation of Flett, even though there may be (as I think has been stated) a place or places of that name. The family was at one time of such importance that, if they had ever been 'of Flett' we should have evidence of it" (Old Lore Misc., v, p. 64–65).

Kolbein Flæt was one of those who laid charges against David Meyner of Weem in 1427 (Oppressions, p. 110). The name of Ioni Blatto, one of the prominent men of Orkney at the same date (op. cit., p. 109) is considered to be a mis-spelling of Flett. Mawnus Flet, witness in Kirkwall, 1480, and Jhone Fleytt of Hare was member of assize in Orkney, 1509 (OSR., I, p. 53, 252). William Flet of Howbister is mentioned in 1516 (SCM., v, p. 395). George Flett, 'sartor in parochia de Orpher,' was retoured heir of Robert Flett, 'mercator in villa de Kirkuall,' 1665 (Retours, Orkney, 98). Sir John S. Flett, Director of the Geological Survey, is probably the most distinguished bearer of the name in record.

Fflait and Flait 1677, Flete 1506. The Shetland place name Flet is derived by Jakobsen from ON. *flötr,* a strip of arable or grass-land.

FLEX. From the lands of Flex near Hawick. Richard de Flex of the county of Roxburgh rendered homage in 1296. His seal bears a crescent enclosing a star and S' *Ricardi de Flechis*(?) (Bain, II, p. 199, 531). As Richard del Fleckes he was juror on an inquest held at Dumfries in 1304 (ibid., 1588). Alexander of Flex was juror on an inquest at Roxburgh in 1361 (ibid., IV, 62), and in the following year he witnessed a charter to the monks of Coldingham Priory (Raine, 369). Thomas Flex appears as a secular of Elgin cathedral in 1343 (Rose, p. 118), and in 1380 the lands of Flex belonged to Alexander Flex (Bain, IV, p. 85). In 1511 the lands of Flekkis were part of the Douglas of Drumlanrig barony of Hawick (RMS.).

FLINT. Robert Flint, wobster in Aytoun, 1628 (Lauder). John fflint was warded in the Canongate Tolbooth, Edinburgh, 1683 (BOEC., VIII, p. 153), and David Flint was dean of guild in Aberdeen, 1752 (Guildry, p. 203). Bardsley says the surname is common in the Yorkshire Poll Tax of 1379. Not likely, I think, to be local from Flint in Wales, although J. de Flint appears in records of Carnarvon, 1352. Aluuin Flint was an under-tenant in Suffolk, England, in 1086 (Evans, p. 89), and Gottschald (Deutsche Namenkunde) has Flinsch, from MHG. *vlins* 'Kiesel, Feuerstein.'

FLINTHARD. A personal name. Richard Flinthard and Hugh Flinthard were witnesses to a charter by William de Veteri ponte in the reign of William the Lion (LSC., p. 213). The name is also recorded in the English Hundred Rolls.

FLISK. From Flisk near Newburgh, Fife. William de Fliske was one of the witnesses to a division of the lands of Cullessin and Cardynside in the last quarter of the thirteenth century (LAC., p. 186), and Laurence de Flisk of the county of Perth rendered homage for his lands in 1296 (Bain, II, p. 204). John Flesk in Edinburgh, 1686 (Edin. App.).

FLOCK. Andro Flok was on inquest in Carnwath, 1524 (CBBC., p. 14).

FLOCKHART. A development of FLUCKER, q.v. It occurs as Fluckart in Edinburgh, 1679 (Edinb. Marr.). Robert Flockhart, "Daddy Flockhart" (1777–?1857), a street preacher in Edinburgh.

FLORENCE. A masculine personal name, Latin *Florentius*. The fame of Florentius, an Angevin saint, made the name popular among the Normans. The name *Florentius* occurs on one of the early Christian stones at Whithorn, Wigtownshire. Florence, son of Florence III, count of Holland and Ada, granddaughter of David I, was bishop-elect of Glasgow. Florence Wilson (Florentius Volusenus) of Moray was one of the foremost Latin scholars in Europe in the sixteenth century. Alexander Florence, feuar in Old Meldrum, 1777 *(Aberdeen CR.)*. Several of this name from Aberdeenshire served in the first Great War, and John G. Florence from Rothienorman was among the killed *(Turriff)*.

FLOWERS. James Flowers, bonnet maker in Edinburgh, 1630 *(Edinb. Marr.)*. James Floures, servant to the laird of Powrie, 1657 *(Brechin)*. Harrison gives this name as 'son of Flower,' from ME. *floer, flouer,* arrowmaker.

FLUCKER. An old surname in Fife, and a not uncommon one among the fisherfolk of Newhaven near Edinburgh. The name is found in Fife so early as 1275 when John ffloker is mentioned (RD., 320). Dominus Patricius dictus Floker was appointed master and guardian of the Hospital of Polmade (Balmadie) juxta Ruglen, 1316 (REG., p. 223). Michael Fluker was custumar of Inverkethyn, 1359 (ER., I, p. 603), and another Michael Flukar was vicar of the church of Kirkcaldy in 1448 (RD., p. 306). David Flucare held land in Edinburgh, 1486 (RMS., II, 1655), Johannes Flewcare, witness in Avondale, 1503 *(Simon,* 63), and Marcus Flukar was warden of the Friary of Inverkeithing, 1564 (ALHT., XI, p. 314). Katherine Fluccar was spouse of a burgess of Dundee, 1634 *(Brechin)*, and the Nethergate of that burgh was formerly known as the Fluckergate (Flukargait, 1443). Andrew Fluiker was elder in Dysart, 1641 (PBK., p. 209), and Ninian Flooker appears in St. Andrews, 1680 (PSAS., LIV, p. 236). Flukair 1584, Fluckart 1679. Perhaps a metathesis of Frisian Folker or Folcker. See FLOCKHART.

FLYTER. A surname in Aberdeen. James Fliter in Gladhill, Moray, 1708 *(Moray)*.

FOD. Local. There is a North and South Fod in the parish of Dunfermline. John Foyd, tenant of Coupar Grange, 1468 *(Cupar-Angus,* I, p. 142). The boat of Batschele was leased to Ellen of Fovd, 1476 (ibid., I, p. 223). John Fud in Clony, 1512 *(Rent. Dunk.,* p. 183), and Alexander Fod in Ordy, parish of Fynnevine, 1628 *(Brechin)*.

FODDIE. Local. There is a Foodie in the parish of Dairsie. Richard de Fody witnessed confirmation of a charter of the lands of Lethin and Kyninnis, c. 1290 *(Laing,* 15), and in 1304 he was juror on an inquest at Perth *(Bain,* II, 1592). Fode or Foddie was a surname in Oathlaw in beginning of the seventeenth century *(Jervise LL.,* p. 166).

FODDOC. Radulph Foddoc held land "in vico furcarum," Aberdeen, 1281 (REA., II, p. 278).

FODINREY. A variant of FOTHERINGHAM(?), q.v. Robert de Fodinrey, a charter witness in Monorgrund, c. 1230 (LAC., p. 72).

FOGGIE. A current surname, may be a variant of FOGO, or (2) from some small place named Foggie. Cf. Foggieley, Foggiemill, Foggietown, and Foggeyburn, all in Aberdeenshire. The surname was recorded in Edinburgh, 1940.

FOGGO, FOGO. From the lands of Fogo in Berwickshire. Adam de Foghou witnessed the gift by Earl Waldeve to the monks of Melrose of a pasture on Lammermuir c. 1166–82 *(Frasers of Philorth,* I). William de Foghou was abbot of Melrose in 1310 *(Morton,* p. 228), Master Richard of Foggowe, parson of Douglas, had letters of safe conduct through England in 1352 *(Rot. Scot.,* I, p. 746, 752), John de Fogo appears as abbot of Melrose in 1425 (RMS., II, 31) and confessor to King James I in 1436. Robert de Fogo was bachelor of decrees in Glasgow in 1438 (REG., p. 358), Andrew Fogo was member of an assize at Cupar in 1521 (SCBF., p. 223), John Fogow was sub-chanter of Cupar in 1553 *(Cupar-Angus,* II, p. 110), William Fogo was secretary to the archbishop of Glasgow in 1554 *(Protocols,* I), and George Fogo was member of the burgh council of Stirling in 1609 (SBR., p. 286). An action at law was raised against Patrick Fogoe in Bleloch in 1652 (DPD., II, p. 145).

FOLEVILLE. Anketill Foleville witnessed gift of a toft in Dundee to the Abbey of Lundors, c. 1232–37 (LAC., p. 97).

FOLKARD. An OE. personal name from *Folcheard (Folkweard),* later *Folcard,* 'people brave.' Some time before 1218 Henry, abbot of Kelso, granted to Richard, son of Solph, the lands of Folcariston in Lesmahago, as held by his father and ancestors *(Kelso,* p. 78). Adam de Folcartun (see FOLKARDTON), mentioned in 1240, was probably his son. His descendants appear to have dropped the -ton and figure in record as Folkerts or Fokkarts of Fokkartoun till the beginning of the sixteenth century. William Folkard in 1294 witnessed resignation by Adam de Dowane of his land of Dowane in the barony of Lesmahagow (*Kelso*, 192). In 1301 dominus Alexander ffolkard, miles, witnessed resignation by Adam de Dowane, junior, of all his lands in the vill of Dowane (ibid., 193), and c. 1311 he also witnessed a charter of resignation by Adam de Dowane, senior, of his land of Grenryg (ibid., 195). In 1315 there is entry of a claim by Alexander Folkard to ten chalders of meal (ibid., 188), Quintin Folkard had a permit to come to London on his private affairs in 1405 (*Bain*, IV, 696), and John Falkard was master of the ship 'le Katherine' of St. John's town in 1441 (ibid., 1149). The family ended in the direct line in an heiress, Elizabeth Folkart, who became spouse of James Carmichell of Balmady in 1495 (*Kelso*, 553). Patrick Fokert was ambassador to the king of Castile in 1458. Thomas Fowcard, a Scotsman, who petitioned for a safe conduct into England, 1464 (*Bain*, IV, 1343), may have been Thomas Folcart, dean of guild of Edinburgh (*Neubotle*, p. 268), and the Thomas Fokert who sat in parliament for Edinburgh, 1467 (*Foster*, p. 139). John Fokert or Fokart was tenant on the lands of the Abbey of Kelso, 1567 (*Kelso*, p. 524), and in 1574 there is recorded an act in favor of Janet Fokart (RPC., II, p. 719). The name appears as Fokartte in Workman MS. Fockert 1623, Fokhart 1503.

FOLKARDTON. From the old lands of Fokertoun or Folkertoun in the barony of Lesmahago (*Retours, Lanark*, 149, 159). About 1240 Ada de Folcartun witnessed the gift by Richard Bard of the lands of Parva Kype to the Abbey of Kelso (*Kelso*, 181), and as Adam de Folcardistun was juror on an inquisition by the sheriff of Lanark, 1263 (*Bain*, I, 2677). In 1269 William, son of Ada de Folkardston, to avoid pain of excommunication and to deliver the soul of his father from the same, resigned the land called Pollenele (now Poniel, 'Neill's Water') in Lesmahagu to the Abbey of Kelso (*Kelso*, 189).

FOLSTER. A Shetland surname of local origin.

FONCANETT. Charles Foncanett retoured heir of Nicholas Foncanett, burgess of Edinburgh, 1642 (*Retours, Edinburgh*, 886).

FOORD. A form of FORD, q.v.

FOOT. Thomas Fute is recorded in Brechin, 1450 (REB., I, 158), Robert Fut was a tenant under the monks of Cupar-Angus Abbey, c. 1520 (*Cupar-Angus*, I, p. 300), and John Foot appears in Brakywell, 1652 (*Dunblane*). William Fute of Auchlansky in record, 1683

(*Inquis.*, 6489), and several persons named Futt are recorded in Glendevon and Fossoway in the seventeenth and eighteenth centuries (*Dunblane*).

FORBES. From the lands of Forbes in Aberdeenshire. A charter in Wood's edition of Douglas's *Peerage* which says that Alexander, earl of Buchan granted to Fergus, son of John of Forbes, the lands of Forbes has been misread. The name there should read John of Fothes, son of Fergus de Fothes, now Fiddes. Duncan de Forbeys, according to a charter lost since 1730, received a grant of the lands from Alexander III c. 1272. John de Fernbovs who rendered homage, 1296 (*Bain*, II, 730), was probably a Forbes. His name does not occur again. Another John Forbes or Forbees occurs in an English roll of c. 1306 (Palgrave, *Ill. docs.*, p. 312, 314), and a third John de Forbes was *dominus ejusdem*, 1358 (*Illus.*, IV, p. 716). William of Forbace was canon of Aberdeen, 1464 (*Laing*, 152). Annabell Fobess was buried in the Kirk of Dysart, 1589 (*Dysart*, p. 41). B. C. Forbes, financial editor of the *New York Journal of Commerce* and founder of *Forbes' magazine*, a fortnightly for business men, was born in Fedderate, Aberdeenshire. In the French Archer Musterrolls is Thom Fort Bays for Tom Forbes. The old fashion of pronouncing this name was dissyllabic but nowadays the pronunciation is in one syllable. Thomson in his *Autumn* has it dissyllabic:

"The Forbes, too, whom every worth attends."

And Sir Walter Scott in *Marmion* (IV., intro.) has it:

"Scarce had lamented Forbes paid
The tribute to his minstrel's shade."

When the new form first became fashionable it was said that it would "throw Lady Fettes (2 syll.) into Fits," and Keith Leask refers to

". . . unsanctified snobs
That could mangle the sound of a fine
Scottish name
And whittle it down into — Fobbs."

　　　　Interamna Borealis, 1917, p. 98.

Forbas 1505, Forbose 1537, Forebess 1669, Forbss 1695.

FORD, FOORD. Local, from residence by a ford or stream-crossing place. Thomas de Furd was presbyter, diocese of St. Andrews, 1406 (RPSA., p. 11), and William Forde of Scotland had payment for his wages in 1489 (*Bain*, IV, 1551). Adam Furde held the lands of Burnecastell in 1493 (*Laing*, 217), and William

FORD, FOORD, *continued*

Furde of Burncastel witnessed a retour of special service in 1505 (*Home,* 29). George Fuird, 'flescher, indueller in Innernes,' was accused in 1603 of buying 'of quheit plaidis fra unfrie men in the Chanonrie of Ross' (*Rec. Inv.,* II, p. 9). Patrick Fuird in Simprein, 1653, Alexander Foord in Hilton, 1677, and others of the name appear in Lauder Commissariot Record. Isobel Foorde in Pitlandie, parish of Monydie, 1688 (*Dunkeld*), and John Foord in Mosshouses, 1690 (RRM., III, p. 112). Fooourd 1750, Fovrd 1675, Furd 1551, Fwrd 1689.

FORDELL. Perhaps from Fordel in the parish of Dalgety, Fife, or more probably from Fordel in Perthshire. Gregory de Fordale was juror on inquisition at Perth, 1305 (*Bain,* II, p. 456). James Fordell in Cottoun of Stannoquhie, 1601, and John Fordell in Cairncortie, 1665 (*Brechin*).

FORDIE. Local. Bessie Fordie in Aldecambusmilne, 1673 (*Lauder*). There is a vill of Fordie (1664) in *Kincardine Retours* (106).

FORDOUN. From Fordoun in Angus. John de Fordoun witnessed a charter by John Ramsay, burgess of Montrose in 1430 (REB., II, 34), and William Fordoune held land in Brechin in 1500 (REB., I, 217). John of Fordun (died c. 1384) was author of *Chronica Gentis Scotorum,* a history of Scotland down to his own time.

FORDYCE. Of local origin from the lands of Fordyce in the Banffshire parish of the same name. John Fordise was vicar of Athy, 1460, and Johannes Fordys, perhaps the same person, was vicar of Garvok, 1464 (RAA., II, p. 115, 142). The Fordyces were ranked as a sept of the so-called "Clan Forbes." In 1541 there is record of the lands of Tarcastell and Edinquheill in the sheriffdom of Elgin being in the king's hands through decease of Helene Fordyce (ALHT., VIII, p. 9). William Fordyce in Carskellie appears as a charter witness at Rothemay in 1567 (RMS., v, 339), and Johne Foirdyse, saidlar, is in record in Elgin in 1574 (*Elgin,* I, p. 148). Alexander Fordyce was cautioner for Thomas Maitland in Monleyth in 1608, and John Fordyse in Tofthills, parish of Kintor, was under caution to appear when called upon in 1659 (RSCA., II, p. 109; III, p. 58). James and John ffordyce in the parish of Rothemay appear in the valuation roll of 1690 (*Records of county of Banff,* p. 271), and George ffordyce in Achincreive was appointed constable in 1702 (ibid., p. 227).

FOREHOUSE. William Forehouse witnessed an instrument of sasine in the barony of Dirleton in 1438 (*Laing,* 116), and George Fourrous witnessed a similar instrument in 1519 (ibid., 316). David Forros or Fowrus was bailie of Haddington in 1537–39 (*James* II, 21; Mill, *Plays,* p. 250), and George Fourrois was sheriff in Haddington in 1543 (*James* II, p. 41). John Fores who rendered to Exchequer the accounts of the bailies of the burgh of Haddington in 1561 (ER., XIX, p. 176) is probably the John Fourhous, tenant under Newbattle Abbey in 1563 (*Neubotle,* p. 330), and the John Foirhous who appears as provost of the burgh in 1565 (ER., XIX, p. 297). Patrick Forhous was chancellor of Dunblane in 1545 (CMN., 61), John Fourrois was a monk of Melrose in 1569 (RHM., I, 41), and Thomas Forrous was witness at Gullane, 1579 (*Laing,* 979). John Forhous or Forus was member of Scots parliament for Haddington, 1567 (*Hanna,* II, p. 494). From some obsolete place of the name. There is Forehouse near Kilbarchan, but foregoing references all point to an East Coast locality.

FOREMAN, FORMAN. Perhaps from English Forman (13th century), older Formann, Latinized Formannus. Robert Foreman of Edinburghshire rendered homage, 1296. His seal bears a fleur-de-lys and S' *Roberti Porman* (*Bain,* II, p. 208, 555). Adam Forman was scutifer to Archibald, earl of Douglas, 1426 (RMS., II, 84; *Macdonald,* 954). John Forman witnessed sealing of an inquest anent a fishing on the Tweed, 1467 (RD., p. 359), and in 1474 payment was made to John Forman, Scottish merchant (*Bain,* IV, 1412). Schir Johne Forman of Ruthirfurde and Eufame Formane had special respite and protection, 1504 (*Trials,* I, p. °42). Andrew Forman, son of the laird of Hutton in Berwickshire, became archbishop of St. Andrews, 1514, and died in 1521 (*Macdonald,* 955). Martin Forman rendered to Exchequer the accounts of the burgh of Banff, 1562 (ER., XIX, p. 203), and Forman is said to have been quite common in the parish of Rattray at one time. The Poll Book shows four separate householders of the name about 1696 (AEI., p. 83). John Forman, tailor in Hutton, 1743 (*Lauder*).

FOREST, FORREST. (1) From residence near or in a forest; (2) a curtailed form of FORRESTER, q.v. William de Forest was a tenant of the Douglases in the barony of Newlands in 1376, and Hugh de Forest was a Douglas tenant in Drumcorke in the same year (RHM., I, p. lvi; II, p. 16). Morgan de Forest in Aberdeen was charged with being a forestaller in 1402 (CRA., p. 384). Master Thomas de Foresta, licentiate in decrees, was rector of the parish of Soudon (Southdean) in 1404 (*Melros*, p. 486), Stephen de Foresta served on an inquest in Stirling in 1411 (*Scon*, p. 162), and William of Forest was physician to the queen of Scots in 1430 (*Bain*, IV, 1044). Thomas of Forrest and Robert Forest, Scotsmen, had liberty to pass through England in 1453 and 1463 (ibid., IV, 1254, 1338), Thomas of Forest, bailie of St. John, Linlithgow, is recorded in 1472 (*Sc. Ant.*, XVII, p. 118), and Henry Forest, one of the earliest martyrs for the reformed faith in Scotland, was burned in 1533.

FORFAR. Of local origin from the royal burgh of Forfar in Angus. Richard de Forfar witnessed a charter by Richard de Friuill to the Abbey of Arbroath c. 1178–1180 (RAA., I, 90). Ranulf de Forfar was one of the witnesses to a charter by Malcolm, earl of Angus c. 1220 (ibid., p. 331). Roger de Forfar is mentioned c. 1256–64 (LAC., 135), and in 1259 Adam of Forfare was groom of Adam de Liberatione (APS., I, p. 98). John de Forfar was burgess of St. Andrews in 1418 (CMN., 28), and Abraham Forfar was "persewit" for his ferme in 1614 (*Urie*, p. 13). Wylle Forfayr witnessed resignation of a feu in Peebles, 1471 (*Scots Lore*, p. 52). John Forfar is recorded in Dunfermline, 1586 (*Dunfermline*), and Patrick Farfar was admitted burgess of Aberdeen, 1607 (NSCM., I, p. 103). Forfer 1616.

FORGAN. Of local origin from Forgan, a village in the parish of Forgandenny, Fife, the old name of which was Forgrund. Marjory, wife of Walter de fforgrund, burgess of Berwick (post 1147), sold to the Abbey of Kelso an annual rent of two marks, which she derived from a house in Berwick (*Kelso*, 31, 34). Archembaldus de Forgrund was a charter witness in Fife c. 1170–78 (RPSA., p. 41, 265). Families of this name are said to have been for centuries located in the parishes of Cameron, Carnbee, and Kilconquhar. James Berwick Forgan (1852–1924), born in St. Andrews, was president of the First National Bank of Chicago, and a pillar in the American financial world.

FORGIE. (1) may be from Forgie near Montrose. (2) a corruption of Fergie (Fergus), as Forgieson for FERGUSON. Alexander Forgie in Newton Stewart, 1763 (*Wigtown*).

FORGLEN. Of local origin from Forglen in the parish of the same name, Banffshire. "Johannes de Buchania calumpniauit Alexandrum Forglen quod iniuste ab eo duxit sex futhris petarum," 1400 (SCM., v, p. 15).

FORGRAVE, FORGRIEVE. Variants of FAIRGRIEVE, q.v.

FORISKEILL. A dialectic form of THORSKAILL, q.v. Joneta Foriskeill was heir of Thomas Foreskeill, her brother, in the lands of Lumquhatmylne, 1589 (*Retours, Fife*, 1485).

FORK. Robert Fork of Markisworthe was sheriff of Renfrew, 1663 (*Inquis. Tut.*, 889), Gilbert Fork, burgess of Paisley, 1664 (ibid., 905), Robert Fork, writer in Paisley, 1686 (RPC., 3. ser. XII, p. 383), John Fork and Gavin Fork took the Test in Paisley in the same year (ibid., XI, p. 496), and John Fork, minister of Killellan parish, Renfrew, died c. 1730. Perhaps an Englishing of Ir. *O'Gabhalaigh*, 'descendant of Gabhalach,' the name of an old Westmeath family.

FORMOND. Local. From lands of Formond on the Eden, Fife (1567 *Retours, Fife*, 63). David Formond, tenant of Balgrescho, 1507 (*Cupar-Angus*, I, p. 262).

FORN. Forn is one of the assenters to the (? spurious) foundation charter of the Abbey of Scone, c. 1120 (*Scon*, p. 3). He appears as father of Ædmund in a charter by Thor filius Swani, c. 1150 (LSC., p. 11). Fornus, capellanus, is witness to a charter by William Veteri Ponte in reign of William the Lion (ibid., p. 35). The name occurs in OE. charters as *Forna* and *Forne*, and Björkman compares it with Old West Norse *Forni* (I, p. 42), a frequent man's name in Iceland.

FORRES. Of local origin from the royal burgh of Forres in Moray. Alanus de Forays, monk, witnessed a composition anent the tithes of Strathylif at Kynlos, 1229 (REM., p. 87). Master Geoffrey de Forays was canon of Moray, 1328 (*Pap. Lett.*, II, p. 285), William de Fores was archdeacon of Caithness, 1355 (CSR., I, p. 129), and in 1360 there is mention of Oliver de Fores, a canon, who appears again in 1366 as rector of the church of Our Lady in Buchan (REA., I, p. 89; II, p. 61). Nicholaus de fforays granted to the altar of the Holy Cross in the parochial church of Inverness one acre of land, 1363 (PSAS., XLV, p. 200). Eugene de Foress is mentioned in Aberdeen, 1441 (SCM., v, p. 20), and Andrew Forass was friar preacher there in 1486 (REA., II, p. 300). James Forres was citizen of Brechin, 1524 (REB., II, 179), and Alexander Fores was provost of Mary in the Fields, 1554 (*Protocols*, I).

FORREST. *See under* FOREST. Edwin Forrest (1806–1872), actor, was the son of a native of Dumfriesshire.

FORRESTER. From the office of 'forest keeper,' ME. *forester, forster*. Archebaldus Forestar witnessed a grant by Gillemor filius Gilleconel to the church of Lesmahagow a. 1144 (*Kelso*, 187), and c. 1190 the house of William forestarius was one of the boundaries of the lands of the church of Molle (ibid., 147). Marninus Forestarius held lands in the town of Dunipas c. 1200 (*Cambus.*, 81). Robert the forester witnessed a resignation of lands in Annandale a. 1245 (*Bain*, I, 1682), and John le Forester of Berwickshire rendered homage in 1296 (ibid., II, p. 209). Moris le Forester was one of the inquisition on the lands of Sir John de Calentir in 1303–4 (ibid., II, 1457), and William Forrester appears in the muster-roll of the Peel of Linlithgow in 1311–12 (ibid., III). The Forresters of Garden were long one of the most powerful families of Stirlingshire, and persons of the name were prominent in the municipal affairs of Stirling from 1360 to 1654 (Gibson, *Lairds*, p. 157–159). Robert Forrester was bailie of Stirling in 1360. Thomas Frostar was prebendarius of Dulmaok in 1427 (REA., I, p. 227). In Edinburgh a family of the name were among the most ancient representatives of the burgher nobility in the fourteenth century, "not unlike the citizen nobles of Florence and other mediaeval republics." In 1373, before the office of provost was known, Adam Forrester appears as alderman of Edinburgh. In 1376 he acquired the manor of Corstorphine (RMS., I, 604), in the church of which his memorial tablet may yet be read. He was founder of the family of Forrester, Lord Forrester (*Sc. Peer.*, v, p. 80–100). The town house of the family in Edinburgh gave name to Forrester's Wynd, now cleared away. Alexander fforester who witnessed an instrument of sasine in 1711 signs his name 'Alexander Foster' (*Hunter*, p. 70). Forastir (1521), Forester, Forrest, Forrestar, Forstar, Forster, Foryster (1663), Forstare (1428), Fostar; Froster.

FORRET. A surname found in Fifeshire, originating from the lands of Forret in the parish of Logie. In 1248 Symon de Foret was one of the witnesses to a quit claim by John Gallard de Keeth (RD., 170). John Forate *de eodem* was one of an assize in 1466 for clearing the marches of the lands of Gaytmilk belonging to the Abbey of Dunfermline (ibid., 458). Elias Foraete was appraiser of the land of the Hauch and Petconnoquhy, Fife, 1505 (*Wemyss*, II, p. 125). Thomas Forrat was tenant of the land of Borrwfeld in 1520 (*Rental*), and Thomas Forret, vicar of Dollar, one of the earliest martyrs for the reformed doctrine in Scotland, was burned at the stake

in 1538. James Foret was burgess of Glasgow in 1550 (*Protocols*, I), James Forret, portioner of Polduff in 1572 (*Wemyss*, II, p. 206), and John Forret of that Ilk served on an inquest made at Perth in 1579 (*Athole*, p. 715). Andrew Forrett was a cultellar in St. Andrews in 1583, and Mrs. Jean fforat or fforrat was detained a prisoner in the Canongate Tolbooth of Edinburgh in 1684 (BOEC., IX, p. 142, 148). John Forret of Fingask was one of those who took part in the Fife Expedition to the Lewis in 1598 (HP., II, p. 270n), David Forret had a confirmation charter of part of the vill and lands of Drumeldrie in 1606 (RD., p. 498), and in 1694 James Forret was retoured heir of David Forret, portioner of Drummeldrie (*Retours, Fife*, 1358). In the seventeenth century the lands of Forret passed into possession of Sir David Balfour (of the Denmylne family), who, on being appointed a lord of session in 1674 took the title of Lord Forret (*Scot. Nat.*). ffarrett 1559, Forritt 1665.

FORSON. Robert Forsan or Forsane, miller in Newsteid, 1657–62 (RRM., I, p. 141; II, p. 47), may be Robert Forsone, miller in Darnick, 1675 (ibid., III, p. 87). William Forsoun is recorded in Ridpethe, 1662 (ibid., II, p. 5).

FORSYTH. This name appears to be of twofold origin. (1) Local, from some place of the name. William de Fersith, bailie of Edinburgh, 1365, may be William of Forsythe, servant of Aleyn of Bollone of Edinburgh, merchant of Scotland, 1394 (*Bain*, IV, 460). William de Fersith, one of an inquest in Edinburgh, 1402, may be William Fersith (without 'de'), burgess of Edinburgh, 1423 (*Egidii*, p. 38, 45). Thomas of Forsythe in Edinburgh, 1439 (CDE., 26). Robert of Forsythe had a safe conduct in England, 1424 (*Bain*, IV, 970), and another (?) Robert de Forsith was charter witness at Dunottyr, 1426. Thomas de Forsyth who witnessed a precept by Robert dominus de Lyle, 1452 (RMP., p. 250), may be Thomas de Forsith, canon and prebendary of Glasgow, who endowed the altar of Corpus Christi in Glasgow, 1487 (REG., 446, 460). (2) From the old G. personal name Fearsithe, meaning 'man of peace.' Fersithi Mag Uibne, bishop of the two Breifne, died 1464 (AU.). Osbert filius Forsyth had charter of a hundred shilling land in the tenement of Salakhill (now Sauchie), sheriffdom of Stirling, from Robert I c. 1308 (RMS., I, App. I, 40). Robert II made a grant out of the lands of Polmaise-Marischal to Fersith or Forsyth, clerk, who in 1364 rendered to Exchequer the accounts of custumars of Stirling (*Stodart*, II, p. 297; *Cambus.*, 43). Fersyth, claviger, mentioned in 1364; Fersith, constable of Stirling Castle, 1368 (*Stodart*, II, p. 297); and Fersy, son of James, in Inverness, 1405 (*Macbain*). Robert Fersith was burgess of Stirling, 1420 (RAA., II, 55), and as Robert Fersithsoun he rendered to Exchequer the accounts of the bailies of the same town in 1418 (ER., IV, p. 304). Forsythe Toller had the petty customs of Dumbarton, 1428 (ER., IV, p. 462), James Fersith (Forsithe or Forsithsoun) is mentioned in 1446 as servant of the king (ER., V, p. 235), and Forsith Sutor was burgess of Aberdeen, 1451 (NSCM., I, p. 12). Robert faresyth witnessed a charter of Sowlis lands, 1461 (LSC., p. 151); David Forsytht, scutifer, Glasgow, 1471 (REG., 395); William Forsytht, witness in Brechin, 1497 (REB., II, 140); and Thomas Forsitht admitted burgess of Aberdeen, 1498 (NSCM., I, p. 40). Thomas Foresyth was tenant in lands in Ardmanoch, 1504 (ER., XII, p. 650); another Thomas Forsith was presbyter of Glasgow diocese, 1525 (REG., 497); Wille Forsyicht, dempster, Stirling, 1525 (SBR., p. 24); and William Forsith, vicar of Moneky, 1512 (REB., II, 181). By Gaelic speakers the name is sometimes pronounced 'Forsy' (for-sigh). Forseyth 1704, Forsitht 1509, Forsycht 1491.

FORTEITH, FORTEATH. Local, perhaps from Forteith in the Cabrach, West Aberdeenshire. Fortheath recorded in Kirkcaldy 1942.

FORTHIK. A resignation in favor of Robert Forthik is recorded in Glasgow, 1554 (*Protocols*, I), and in 1566 he was tenant of the commons of the Kirk of Glasgow (RPC., I, p. 498). William Forthik, maltman, was burgess freeman of Glasgow, 1579, and Robert Forthik was admitted burgess there in 1613 (*Burgesses*).

FORTRIE. Of local origin. There is a Fortrie near Grange Keith, another at Inverkeithny near Turriff, and a third at King Edward. Alexander Fortre was admitted burgess of Aberdeen, 1552 (NSCM., I, p. 63), John Fortrie was burgess there, 1599 (CRA., p. 178), and John Fortrie was flescher there, 1613 (SCM., V, p. 88).

FORTUNE. From the lands of Fortune in East Lothian, now represented by East and West Fortune. John de Fortun was servant of the abbot of Kelso c. 1200 (*Kelso*, 148). Joce de Fortun witnessed confirmation by Nesus de Lundr of a mill in Lynton, in the reign of Alexander II, 1233 (LSC., p. 51). John de Fortone was one of the Scots prisoners in the Tower of London in 1297 (*Bain*, II, 960). A later John Forton witnessed a retour of special service in 1495 (*Home*, p. 27), and Thomas

Fortoun was tailor and burgess of Edinburgh in 1634 (*Inquis. Tut.*, 504). Robert Fortune (1813–1880), the distinguished botanist and traveller in China, was born in Berwickshire. The surname is not uncommon in the Lothians and in Fife.

FORVELETH. A woman's name. Forveleth, daughter of the late Finlay of Campsie, was found one of the heirs of deceased Dufgall, brother of Maldouen, earl of Lennox, 1271 (*Red. Bk. Menteith*, II, p. 218). Forvelech or Forveleth (*c* and *t* are easily confused in old MSS., as they are much alike in form), daughter of Alwyn, second earl of Levenax, wife of Norrinus de Monnorgund, 1271–73 (RMP., p. 191, 198).

FOSSARD. Alexander Fossarde of Tynningham, tenant of the bishop of Seint Andreu, Edinburghshire, rendered homage in 1296. His seal bears a squirrel and S' *Alexsand' Fosard* (*Bain*, II, p. 205, 544). Richard Fossart or Forshard of Jeddeworthe, Roxburghshire, also rendered homage and had his lands restored to him (ibid., p. 201, 218).

FOSTER, a contracted form of FORRESTER, q.v. Patrick Fostar and John Fostar witnessed an instrument of sasine in 1488 (REG., p. 503), and Alexander fforester who witnessed a sasine of 1711 signed his name 'Alexander Foster' (*Hunter*, p. 70). Fawster 1570.

FOTHAD. Fothadh mac Brain who died A. D. 963 (AU.) was the second of the recorded bishops of the Celtic Church of St. Andrews (Reeves, *Culdees*). Another Fothad, chief bishop of Alba, and last bishop of the Celtic Church of St. Andrews celebrated the marriage of Malcolm III and Margaret in 1069 (Wyntoun, S. T. S. ed., IV, p. 345) and died in 1093 (AU.). In the Register of the Priory of St. Andrews (p. 117) his name is given wrongly as Modach filius Malmykel.

FOTHERGILL. There is a Fothergill and a barony of Fothergill in Perth Retours, now Fortingal. The surname, however, seems to be derived from a place of the name in the North of England. Dr. George Fothergill has published much interesting matter relating to the antiquities of Edinburgh, and incidentally has exploded a few cherished traditions connected therewith.

FOTHERINGHAM, FOTHRINGHAM. From Fotheringham in the parish of Inverarity in Angus. The name is a corruption of ancient Fotheringhay, from the manor and castle of that name in Northamptonshire, which wa

FOTHERINGHAM, FOTHRINGHAM, continued
held in the twelfth century by the royal
family of Scotland as part of the Honour of
Huntingdon (Moore, *The Lands of the Scottish kings in England*, p. 19). The name assumed its present form from the resemblance
of final *ay* to *m* in old records. Dominus Robert
de ffodryngay was witness to a Maule charter
of 1261 (*Panmure*, II, 85). Master Henry of
Fottyngham, presumably an Englishman, was
rector of the church of Taruedal in Ross in
1274 (OPS., II, p. 522). Walter de Fodring-
geye was one of the executors of the will of
Dervorgilla, wife of John de Baliol in 1291
(*Bain*, II, 535). Roger de Foderingeye, vicar
of the church of Kilmor (Kilmuir-Easter) in
the county of Ross, and Huwe de Foderingeye
of the county of Perth rendered homage in
1296 (ibid., II, p. 200, 214). The seal of the
latter bears a stag's head cabossed and S'
Hvgon' de Foderigay. Henry de Foddrynghame
who was deputy (locum tenens) of the sheriff
of Perth in 1358 (ER., I, p. 553) is probably the Henry de Fodrynghay who witnessed a Brechin document in 1364 (REB.,
I, 20). William de Foddrynghame was sheriff
of Banff in 1358 (ER., I, p. 548), Robyn of
Fodryngame was one of the assize on the
marches of Woodwrae in 1388 (*Bamff*, p. 22),
Alexander Forigham (probably for Forigham
= Foringham) appears as a witness in Brechin
in 1464 (REB., II, 103), and Thomas Fod-
ringhame of Poury (now Powrie) was witness
to a charter by John Jardin of Appilgarth in
1476 (*Home*, 23). The Fotheringhams of
Ballindean, Perthshire, are descended from the
family of Powrie in Angus, a race that settled
early in the province and are said to have
derived their descent from Henry de Fodring-
hay who received the lands of Balewny, near
Dundee, from Robert II previous to 1377
(RMS., I, 664). The name early travelled to
Orkney, Richard Fodrungame being recorded
as one of the "lawrikmen" there in 1446
(REO., p. 51). Foddringam 1482, Foderingam
1472, Foderinghame 1511, Fodihervngham
1424, Fodingam 1486, Foderingam 1438, Fod-
ringaym 1450, Fordryngham 1390, Fothergem
1516, Fothrengam 1483, Fothrenghame 1584,
Fothringam 1494, Fothryngam 1450, Foth-
ryngame 1427, Fothrynhame 1531, Fotring-
ham 1565.

FOTHRAY. Duncan Fothray, witness in Kyncardyn, 1434 (HP., IV, p. 238), may have
derived his name from the lands named Fodra
(1636, *Retours, Kincardine*, 67).

FOUBISTER, FOUBESTER. An Orcadian surname from the township of Foubister in the
parish of St. Andrews, Orkney. Hendrie Fow-
buster who was appointed roithman in 1507
(REO., p. 79) may be the Henry Fowbister
in Kirkwall mentioned in 1516 (SCM., V,
p. 395). John ffoubrester or ffoubister, hatt
maker in Leithwynd is in record in 1674
(*Just. Rec.*, II, p. 287–288). Fovbister 1516,
Fowbyster 1570, Fubister 1559.

FOULDEN. From the old lands or barony
of Foulden in Berwickshire. Adam de Fou-
weldene of Hortone of the county of Edeneburk rendered homage in 1296 (*Bain*, II,
p. 201), and Gamelin of Fouleden was
juror on an inquest held before the sheriff of
Berwick in 1300 (ibid., II, 1178). Mathew
Fouldoun, merchant burgess of Jedburgh, 1654
(*Heirs*, 40).

FOULDS, FOWLDS. Most probably variants of
FAULDS, q.v. Andrew Fowls, smith in Wan-
lockhead, 1748 (*Dumfries*). Dr. Trotter (*Galloway gossip: Kirkcudbrightshire*, p. 414)
mentions a man named Andrew Foulles, shoemaker at Kirktoun in 1684, who appears again
in record as Faullis (1688), Faulles (1705),
Fauldis (1708), Fallis (1709), and Foulis
(1696). Cf. FOULIS.

FOULERTON. A form of FULLARTON, q.v.

FOULFORD. From the old lands of Fulford
or Foulfourde "nunc de Woodhouselie vocata"
(1686, *Retours, Edinburgh*, 1301). James de
Foulfourd who made a gift to the altar of
St. James in the paroch kirk of Edinburgh
in the reign of Robert III (RMS., I, App. II,
1882) is probably James de Fulford, burgess
of Edinburgh, 1381 (*Egidii*, p. 22). The
tenement of quondam James de Foulfurde in
Edinburgh is mentioned in 1428 (RMS., II,
116), James of Foulfurd was factor to the earl
of Orkney, 1444 (CRA., p. 13), John Fulford
was mason to the abbot of Cupar-Angus
Abbey c. 1500 (*Cupar-Angus*, I, p. 310), and
another John Foulfurd was prior of the Friars
Carmelites in Aberdeen, 1558 (ER., XIX, p. 41).

FOULIS, FOWLIS. "The surname is doubtless
taken from a locality, and may have arisen
in the neighbourhood of one of the half dozen
places in Scotland called Foulis or Fowlis"
(*Stodart*, II, p. 197). A Reginald de Foulis
witnessed a charter by the High Steward in
the reign of Alexander II. Thor de Foules
witnessed a charter by William Maule of
Foules a. 1260 (RPSA., p. 264). William de
Foulis, perpetual vicar of Kirkis, i.e. Kirktoun
of S. Ninian, Stirling, 1295 (*Cambus.*, 111).
Sir Alan de Foulis, canon of St. Andrews, 1305
(*Bain*, IV, 1807). Master William of Foulevs
who had a safe conduct into England, 1422

(*Bain*, IV, 915) is probably Master William Foulles (Foulls, or Foulys), provost of Bothwell and custodian of the privy seal, 1429–31 (REB., II, 23; *Home*, 19; *Bain*, IV, 1029–32). Thomas de Fowlis was supprior of Abirbrothoc, 1425 (RAA., II, 59), and Alexander Foulis was commissioner to Parliament for Linlithgow, 1469 (APS., II, p. 93). Michael Fowlis, friar preacher in Aberdeen, 1486 (REA., II, p. 300), Andrew Faulis, witness in Glasgow, 1552 (*Protocols*, I), Henry Foulis held land in Linlithgow, 1549 (*Laing*, 552), David Fowllis retoured in lands in barony of Evendaill (Avondale), 1612 (*Retours, Lanark*, 97), and Robert Foulles, advocate, 1633 (ibid., 177). Foulls 1679, Fowlls 1592, Follis 1450, Fawlis 1574. Cf. FOULDS.

FOULZIE. From the lands of Foulzie (in 1549 Fowlsie) in the parish of King Edward. Mr. Gilbert Foulsie, priest of the diocese of Aberdeen, prebend of St. John, 1561, appears in the same record as Foulse (1567), Foulsey (1576), Fowlse (1561), Fowlseye 1574, Fulsee (1574), and Fwilsie (1572) (REO). See also FOWLIE.

FOUNTAIN. Local. There is a Fountain in Midlothian and Fountainhall in East Lothian. Edward Fountain of Loch-hill, sometime master of the revels, n.d. (*Nisbet*, I, p. 219.) There is a Lochhill near Longniddry, East Lothian.

FOVERAN. Of local origin from old lands of the name in the parish of Foveran, Aberdeenshire. Andrew de Fovern was admitted burgess of Aberdeen in 1440 (NSCM., I, p. 6).

FOWAR. Duncan Foware had a remission from James I in 1428 (*Rose*, p. 126). Donald Fouar mc bayne was a charter witness in 1525 (HP., IV, p. 25). Adam Fowar in Mylntoun, 1634 (SCM., III, p. 124). Ewen (p. 261) gives Fower, 'cleaner,' but this is hardly the meaning of this Scottish name. Cf. FOYER.

FOWLER. From the occupation of 'bird catcher,' 'fowler,' in Latin charters rendered *oiselarius*. Dauid oiselarius witnessed a charter by William Wascelyn of the lands of Newetyl to the monks of Lundors, c. 1200 (LAC., p. 39). "Oiselarius . . . may here be an indication of occupation, or, possibly, already an equivalent of the family name, Fowler" (ibid., p. 247). Nicholas dictus Fuler had a charter of lands of Whitsone c. 1315–21 (RMS., I, 8), John Fouler was on an inquest taken at Berwick-on-Tweed, 1370 (*Bain*, IV, 175), and Gilbert Fouler was sheriff of Edinburgh, 1358 (ER., I, p. 564). Andrew Fowlar was admitted burgess of Aberdeen, 1451 (NSCM., I, p. 13), John Folar was tenant

under the bishop of Glasgow, 1513 (*Rental*), and Robert Fouler, portioner of Meikle Allann took the Test in Ross-shire, 1685 (RPC., 3. ser. XI, p. 417). Andrew Foular was made perpetual vicar of the parish church of Arbroath in 1524 (RAA., II, 585), Christiane Fouller in record in Kelso, 1567 (*Kelso*, p. 523), and John Foulier in Robertoun to be constable, 1709 (*Minutes*, p. 57). In 1641 "the towne counsell of . . . Inverness . . . hawing takene to thair considderatione the many bygane miscariages and behaviouris of Donald Foullar, elder, merchand burgis of the said bruch . . . and speaciallie the unreverand, malicious and approbrious spechis utterit and exprest be the said Donald Foullar . . . [had him] censured and punished thairfoir in his persone and guids conforme to the Actis of Parliament" (*Rec. Inv.*, II, p. 208). Foulare and Fowlare 1506, Foweller 1722, Fwler 1571; Foular, Fouler, Foullare.

FOWLIE. Of local origin from the place named Foulzie (z pron. as y) in the parish of King Edward, Aberdeenshire. James Fowlie in Bartholl Chapell, 1741 (*Aberdeen CR.*). Several individuals of the name from Turriff and vicinity served in the first Great War (*Turriff*). See also FOULZIE.

FOWLIS. *See under* FOULIS.

FOWLL. "The landis of wmquhill Johne Fowyll" in Inverness are mentioned in 1559, and in 1561 wmquhill Mald Fowyll there is named (*Rec. Inv.*, I, p. 30, 54). Bardsley and Harrison have this name and explain it as a nickname, 'the fowl.'

FOX. William Fox was tenant in lands of the Abbey of Kelso, 1567 (*Kelso*, p. 528). William Fox in Bogtoune of Dulleward, 1631 (*Brechin*). In England this name has its home in the Midlands. In the Hundred Rolls of the time of Edward I the name occurs in Notts, Worcestershire, and Oxfordshire. Usually considered a nickname, but Lower and Harrison say it may sometimes represent Fowkes or Fawkes.

FOYER. There was an old family of this name, tenants on the lands of Cult Edmonstone in the seventeenth century. In 1682 one of the name was schoolmaster at Duntreath and one of the few Covenanters in Strathblane. In 1716 Cult Edmonstone was bought by James Foyer and the lands were held by his descendants till 1820 (*Strathblane*, p. 81–83).

FRAIL. Peter Frail, burgess of Dumbarton, 1829 (RDB.). Probably from Ir. O'Fearghail, which gives Farrell, Ferrall, Frahill, Fraul.

278

FRAIN. This surname, noted in Aberdeen, is most probably an importation within recent years from Ireland, where it is found as the name of a family of Anglo-Norman descent settled in county Kilkenny. The name is of Norman origin, "de la Freyne," Latinized *de Fraxineto*, "of the ash-tree" (Fr. *frêne*, earlier *fresne*).

FRAME. Several persons of this name are recorded in the Commissariot Records of Campsie and of Lanark. Adam Frame 1495. Arthur Fram, witness in Glasgow, 1551 (*Protocols*, I). Daniel Frame, burgess in Edinburgh, 1642 (*Inquis.*, 2690), William Fram is recorded in parish of Calder, 1679 (*Hanna*, II, p. 252), and William fframe in Mauldslie was warded in the Canongate Tolbooth, Edinburgh, 1683 (BOEC., VIII, p. 155).

FRANCE. A surname recorded in Aberdeen. (1) A native of France. (2) a diminutive of FRANCIS, q.v. James France in Outlacleuch, 1683 (*Lauder*).

FRANCHEAUCHTER. Elspet Francheauchter or Fancheauchter broke "the actis and statutis of this burcht (Inverness) for selling xd. aill," 1569 (*Rec. Inv.*, I, p. 176).

FRANCIS. From AF. *Franceis, Franceys,* 'a Frenchman.' The name Francigena was used in England to denote that a man was not an Englishman or could not prove that he was (Ellis, *Introduction to Domesday Book*, 1833, II, p. 426). A family variously named in record Francigena, le Franceys, le Francaise, or (in Latin) Franciscus, settled in different parts of the North of England and in Scotland. They appear in early documents in connection with the Bruces in Annandale and may have come with them. A family of the name also appeared early in Cunningham but are now long extinct there. Wilelmus Francig' (Francigena) witnessed a confirmation by Jocelin, bishop of Glasgow, c. 1189–99 (RMP., p. 101). William le Franceis witnessed a charter of lands in Maxton in the reign of William the Lion (*Melros*, 81). A. francigena was witness to a charter in the reign of Alexander II (REG., p. 103), and Andrew Frans', perhaps the same person, was witness to a charter by James, Steward of Scotland, to the monastery of Paisley, 1294 (RMP., p. 95). William Francigena held land 'apud Innirwic' in 1246 (ibid., p. 88). Johan Fraunceys of Longa Neuton, Roxburghshire, rendered homage, 1296. His seal bears an eight-raved figure and the legend S' *Iohis Fravnsays* (*Bain*, II, p. 199, 532). William le Fraunceys, constable of Kirketoulagh, 1307 (*Bain*, II, 1962). William Francis guided Randolph up

the rock to the capture of Edinburgh Castle in March, 1314. James Fraunces held land in Irvine, 1323, and in 1417 there was discord between William Fraunces and the same burgh (*Irvine*, I, p. 123, 19). Robert Francess of Stane registered an instrument of protest in 1500 (*Simon*, 5). See also FRENCH.

FRANK. Probably signifying a Frenchman, AF. *Frank*, OF. *Franc*. Timothie Frank in Trabroune, 1677 (*Lauder*). John Frank, burgess of Edinburgh, 1627 (*Retours, Peebles*, 74).

FRANKMAN. A Frenchman, a native of France. Andrew Franckysman was juror on an inquest at Perth, 1304 (*Bain*, IV, p. 414). Hector Frankman was an engager on the royalist side at Kiltearn, 1649 (IDR., p. 160). Ewen (p. 145) has Ric. Frankissheman, Yorks, 1379.

FRASER, FRAZER. The name was originally de Frisselle, de Freseliere, or de Fresel, and Frisale or Frisell is still the common pronunciation in Tweeddale — the first Scots home of the family — and in Lothian. The name then became Fraissier or strawberry bearer, probably from adoption of the flower of the *fraisse*, strawberry, as part of the armorial bearings — a plant abundant in the woods of Neidpath, still however retaining the original name or pronunciation. Sir Simon Frasee, first in record in Scotland, held part of the lands of Keith in East Lothian, called from him Keith Simon. Symon ffraser gave the church of Keith to the Abbey of Kelso c. 1160 (*Kelso*, 13, 85). Gilbert Freser witnessed a charter by Walter Olifard, junior, c. 1210 (SHR., II, p. 175). A later Sir Simon, called "The Scottish Patriot," was a supporter of Sir William Wallace in the struggle for independence. At Roslin in 1302 he defeated three divisions of the English army in one day. By a series of advantageous marriages the Frasers acquired lands in different parts of the country. In 1375 by a marriage with the daughter of William, earl of Ross they acquired Philorth in Buchan which became the chief seat of the family. To the Gaels the chief of the Frasers is known as *MacShimidh* (pron. Mackimmie), "son of Simon." The name has many spellings in record: ffrayser 1293, ffreizer 1667, Fraiser and Fraisser 1659, Frasair 1603, Frassel 1368, Fresal and Fresale 1477, Fresare 1503, Fresell 1494, Fresill 1543, Fresle 1513, Fressair 1556, Fresselve 1296, Fresser 1546, Frevser 1321, Frichell 1284, Friselle 1558, Friser 1304, Frissell 1548, Fryssar 1566, Frysser 1491, Fryssell 1516; Fraseir, Frasser, Fraysser, Fresall, Fresel, Fressell, Freser.

FRATER, Fraiter. By some believed to be from Latin *frater*, a 'brother' or member of a monastic order, and the same in meaning as ME. *frere*. The name, however, is more likely to be from ME. *freytour*, a monastic refectory, and by extension of meaning, keeper of the monastic refectory. It might also be a curtailed form of ME. *fraterer*, superintendent of the *frater*. John Frater was tenant on Abbey lands of Kelso, 1567 (*Kelso*, p. 526). John Frater in Longhauche, 1663, and John Fratter in Roughauch, 1666 (RRM., II, p. 77, 202). George Fraiter, portioner of Langhaugh, 1755 (*Heirs*, 282). Freter 1648.

FRAZER. See *under* FRASER.

FRECKIE. Probably local. Mr. Alexander Macdonald Freckie of Kingussie died 1937.

FREEBAIRN. Robert Freborn or Frebern made a gift of two carucates to the Abbey of Neubotle c. 1150 (*Neubotle*, 3), and p. 1165 he witnessed the grant by Serlo, clericus regis, to the Abbey of Kelso (*Kelso*, 216). About 1153 Radulf Frebern had a grant from Malcolm IV 'terrarum de Rossive et Dunduf' (SCM., V, p. 241). Between 1189–99 Robert de London granted Roger Frebern a charter of Aberdouer, Colestun, Balemacmol and Muntequin (ibid., p. 243). About the same date Walter Frebern witnessed a charter by Hugh, cancellarius regis, to the Abbey of Arbroath (RAA., I, 80), and c. 1200 he witnessed a charter by Henry de Graham (*Neubotle*, 8), and Walter Frebern witnessed a charter by the same Graham to the Abbey of Newbattle (ibid., 7). Robert, son of Robert Freborn, witnessed a charter of the third part of Lambertun c. 1190–1200 (BNCH., XVI, p. 332; *Home*, 224). Roger, son of Robert Frebern, witnessed a charter by David, son of Tructe in favor of Kelso Abbey c. 1200 (*Kelso*, 268), and Robert Frebern appears as witness in a charter by Philip de Valoniis (*Melros*, 140). James Frebarne, witness in Glasgow, 1550 (*Protocols*, I). John Freeburn in Polkem, parish of Livingstone, 1702 (*Lanark CR.*), and Charles Freebain was tacksman of Persabus, Islay, 1780 (*Isles*).

FREELAND. Janet Freeland appears in Aberdalgie, 1657 (*Dunblane*), Lillias Freeland in the parish of Cardross, 1669 (*Campsie*), and John Freeland of Castlecravie in 1766 (*Kirkcudbright*). James Frieland, witness in Bonhill, Dumbartonshire, 1665 (HP., III, p. 34). The name may be from the OE. personal name Frithuland or Freoland, found in the English *Hundred Rolls* (1273) as Frelond.

FREELOVE. From the OE. personal name *Frithulaf*, found in the English *Hundred Rolls*

as Frelove. Laurence Freluf and Stephen Freluf in the parish of Fyvy were excommunicated in 1382 (REA., I, p. 165). Johannes Freluke also in Fyvy, who was excommunicated at same time, is perhaps a misreading (REA., I, p. 166).

FREEMAN. More likely to be from OE. *freomann* (*liber homo*) than from the OE. personal name *Freomund*. Freomann (Freomon) occurs in the *Liber Vitae Dunelmensis*. Jacob Freman del counte de Pebbles rendered homage, 1296 (*Bain*, II, p. 207).

FREEMANSON, 'son of FREEMAN,' q.v. Robert Fremansone, burgess of Jeddeworthe, rendered homage, 1296 (*Bain*, II, p. 197).

FREEVILLE. Richard de Friuille witnessed the gift by William the Lion of the church of Hautwysille in Tyndal to the monastery of Arbroath c. 1178–80 (RAA., I, p. 27), and about the same period he granted the carucate of Balekelefan to the same house (ibid., p. 62). Between 1219 and 1237 Henry de Freville was witness to a charter by John, earl of Huntington to Norman, son of Malcolm of the lands of Lesslyn, etc. (CAB., p. 548.) From Freville between Sante Mere Eglise and Valognes, Normandy. It was the name of a family celebrated both in that duchy and in England (*Lower*).

FRENCH. 'One from France.' In early Scots records this name occurs chiefly in a Latinized form such as Francus, Franciscus, and Francigena. Robert, son of William Franciscus, quitclaimed to Sir Robert de Brus land in Anand (Annan) which the grantee held of him and which the grantee's father formerly held, c. 1218 (*Bain*, I, 705), and Roger, son of William French, quitclaimed lands in Annan for other lands in Moffat, a. 1245 (*Annandale*, I, p. 6). William Franke de Petcokyr is in record, c. 1289 (CCPC.). Six individuals of this name rendered homage in 1296, three in Roxburghshire, two in Edinburghshire, and one in Fifeshire (*Bain*, II, p. 194, 201, 203, 209, 213). Sir Nicholas Franch was curate of the parish church of Strivelin, 1475 (SBR., p. 256). Ade Franx forfeited in the reign of Robert III (RMS., I, App. II, 1921) may be the Adam franche of Scotland who became liegeman to Henry IV of England in 1402 (*Bain*, IV, 606, 638). Robert Franche of Thornvdykis was a Berwickshire laird in 1530 (*Trials*, I, p. 147*). A burgess family of this name in Linlithgow spelled their name: France and Franch (1487), Frans, Franss, and Franche (1535), and Frensch (1538). James France was chaplain at Dunblane in 1558, and there

FRENCH, *continued*

are six more of the name recorded there in the seventeenth century *(Dunblane).* Fransche and Frensche 1580, Fraunch 1584. See also FRAN-CIS.

FRENDRAUGHT. From the barony of Frendraught near Forgue, Aberdeenshire. Michael de Ferendrach witnessed a charter by William the Lion c. 1202 *(Illus.,* I, p. 378) and between 1204 and 1211 he witnessed a grant to the Abbey of Arbroath (RAA., I, 33). In 1226 he witnessed a charter by Alexander II *(Illus.,* II, p. xxi; *Innes Familie,* p. 63). William de Fornindraut was patron of the church of Fornindraut, 1257 *(Pap. Lett.,* I, p. 340). Duncan de Feryndrawcht had a charter of the east davoch of the land of Conynges, c. 1281–1288 *(Grant,* III, p. 6). He is probably Duncan de Ferendraghe or Fernyndrauch, the greatest of the name, who rendered homage in 1296, and in the same year had his lands restored to him *(Bain,* II, 783, 853). The seal attached to his homage is that of Malcolm Frendraught, and bears a shield within round tracery, 3 wolf heads, and S' *Mavcolmi de Frendrav* *(Macdonald,* 1013). A payment was made to Malcolm de Ferindract in 1292 *(Bain,* II, 584). The seal he used shows a lion coiled within a circular tressure of fleur-de-lys, S' *Henrici de Fernindrauth* (ibid., p. 556). Sir Duncan de Ferrindragh appears in 1304–5 as sheriff of Banff and keeper of the forest of Buthyn in 1305 (ibid., p. 442, 462). Marioziota de Ferindrauthe had a dispensation for marriage with James Fraser in 1321, they being within the prohibited degrees of affinity *(Pap. Lett.,* II, p. 217, 299). The family seems to have ended in direct line in Duncan's daughter Margaret (PSAS., 1874), though a Henry de Ferendroch is mentioned in 1404. John Frendracht was a tenant under the monks of Cupar Abbey, 1456 *(Cupar-Angus,* I, p. 137). William de Ferendracht was admitted burgess of Aberdeen, 1468 (NSCM., I, p. 20), and Thomas Frendraucht witnessed an instrument of date 1506 *(Panmure,* II, p. 272). A local pronunciation of the name is 'Frennet' as in the title of the ballad of 'Frennet Hall.' Ferendragh 1305, Frandracht 1495; Feringdraut, Feringdraute.

FRERE, FREER, FRIER. A "friar" or member of one of the mendicant monastic orders, ME. and OF. *frere.* Master William Frere, archdeacon of Lothian, was granted protection in England in 1296 *(Bain,* II, 741). He may be the William Frier, "dictus Frater," professor of canon law in the University of Paris, who was one of the Scottish emissaries at the Papal Court in 1300 (Hailes, *Annals,* I, p. 326). Adam Frere or Frer of the county of Berewyke, who rendered homage in 1296, appears again as juror on an inquest held at Peebles in 1304 *(Bain,* II, p. 207, 377). Freer occurs in a list of the burgesses of Selkirk in 1513–15 and in a list of the inhabitants in Galashiels in 1656 both Frier and Frater are found (Craig Brown, *Selkirkshire,* I, p. 20; II, p. 389). For a notice of the family of Freer, sometime of Essendie, Innernethy, and Woodlands, in Perthshire, see *Miscellanea genealogica et heraldica,* London, 1876, II, p. 70–72. The Gaelic word *frith,* an incantation, is a loan from ON. *frétt,* and the late Dr. Alexander Carmichael erroneously suggested (*Carmina Gadelica,* II, p. 159) that this surname might be a modification of Gaelic *frithir,* augurer, and added that persons bearing the name claim that their progenitors were astrologers to the kings of Scotland! Friar 1688, Freir 1580. See also FRATER.

FRESHIE. Cuthbert Freschie in Burnsyde of Baltersen, 1659 *(Dumfries).*

FRESKYN. Freskyn of Moray is said to have been a Fleming or person of Flemish descent whom David I took north with him and settled in Moray, when he suppressed an insurrection of the natives of that province in 1130. Freskyn held lands of Strabrok in West Lothian but he is nowhere designated 'le Fleming' or 'Flandrensis' as was the custom when Flemings were mentioned in early charters. William, son of Freskyn witnessed the charter by Malcolm IV to Berowald Flandrensis of the land of Innes at Christmas 1160. Between 1165–71 he had a charter from William the Lion of the lands of Strabrok, Duffus, Rosisle, Inchikel, etc. This charter is now missing but was seen and copied by Nisbet (II, App., p. 183). He witnessed several charters between 1187–99, and died c. 1204. Between 1204–11 Hugh Fretheskyn was witness to grant of a church to the Abbey of Arbroath (RAA., I, 33). Fretheskin, 'persona de Dufglas,' witnessed a charter of the church of Brennath [Birnie] to the Abbey of Kelso, c. 1202–12 *(Kelso,* 371). As Friskyne, decanus Moraviensis, he also witnessed a charter by Malcolm, earl of Fife, c. 1214–26 (RHM., II, 1), and as Fertheskyn he appears c. 1218–26 as 'decanus ecclesie Moraviensis' (RAA., I, 79). Freskums de Laundeles of Roxburghshire rendered homage, 1296 *(Bain,* II, p. 200), and Freskyn de Chen was decanus Aberdonensis, 1321 (REA., I, p. 47). Several persons named Friskine occur in the Kirk Session Records of Gask, Perthshire, the first being Andros Friskine who was admitted an elder in 1669, and eight of the name occur in Gask and Findogask in seventeenth century, but the name does not now exist there. James Frisken was portioner of Hutton, 1772 (*Lauder*). Firskin 1727, Fiscam 1725, Frisken seventeenth century.

FRESSELEY. Galfridus de fferseley witnessed confirmation of the gift of the lands of Prendergest to Coldingham Priory in the reign of Alexander II (*Raine*, 73). William de Fresseleye del counte de Fyfe rendered homage 1296. His seal shows an eight-leaved flower, S' Will' Fresele (*Bain*, II, p. 204, 553). Geoffry de Fresseley, an adherent of Balliol, also rendered homage in same year. His lands in Friselay seized at the same time were restored to him in 1304 (ibid., p. 385, 415). Henry de Freslay, dominus de Fourgy, 1295 (*Cambus.*, 5) is doubtless the Henry de Fresseleye of Perthshire who rendered homage in 1296, and served as juror at Perth in 1305 (*Bain*, II, p. 202, 456). He may be the Henricus de Frisshele from whom the English purchased a horse in 1312 (*Bain*, III, p. 428). Henry de Freslay witnessed the homage of Duncan, twelfth earl of Fife to the abbot of Dunfermline, 1316 (RD., 349), and Mariorie de ffreslay quondam relict of dominus Willelmus de ffresley is mentioned in 1337 (*Scon*, p. 123). A family named Friseleye or Fressingleye, a surname which has entirely disappeared, were owners of Duddingston near Edinburgh in the fourteenth century. The name is also spelled Freshelee and Fresheleigh, and the lands appear to have been in Yorkshire.

FREW. This Perthshire surname is derived from some lands in the district of Menteith, locally known as the Fords of Frew or, in English 'the Frews.' Alexander Frew witnessed a bond of friendship in 1581 (*Caldwell*, I, p. 83), David Frew, reader at the Kirk of Dunrossness, 1624 (OSS., I, 49), Robert Frew was portioner in Gattonsyde in 1693 (*Peebles CR.*), a pension was paid to Elizabeth Frew in Edinburgh, 1735 (*Guildry*, p. 151), and James Frew was tenant in Shankhead of Kilsyth in 1795 (*Campsie*). Walter Edwin Frew, a power in the financial world in the United States, was of Scottish parentage.

FRIARMILL. Local. From lands of Friermillin (1654) or Freirmilne (1668) in Fife (*Retours, Fife*, 1040, 1591). Thomas Freremill, juror on inquisition at Cupar, 1552 (SCBF., p. 266).

FRIARTON. From Friarton near St. Martin's, Perthshire. Roger de Frereton, charter witness in 12th century (RPSA., p. 274). Gilbert de ffertoun or frerton was vicar of Rogortun or Rogortuen in 1414 (*Scon*, p. 163, 165), Walter

Freyrton, tenant of part of Denhed, 1510 (*Cupar-Angus*, I, p. 278), and Sir David Freirtoun was vicar pensioner in the Kirk of Alyth in 1534 (*Bamff*, p. 63).

FRIER. "Many friars at the Reformation renounced their vows of chastity, married, and became fathers of families; from one of them descend the Friers of Melrose parish, Roxburgh" (Brockie, *The Family names of the folks of Shields*, 1857). See also under FRERE.

FRIGGE. A surname in Elgin in eighteenth century. John Frigge, merchant in Findhorn, 1759 (*Moray*).

FRISSELL, FRIZELL, FRIZELLE. Old forms of FRASER, q.v., which have become independent surnames. Walter Freselle had a safe conduct into England, 1424 (*Bain*, IV, 963). David Frysaille witnessed resignation of lands of Walle, 1474 (*Home*, p. 220). John Fresall (Fresale, Frezel, or Frezille) was parson of Douglas, 1482 (CDE., 53), dean of Lestalrig and canon of Glasgow, 1491–93 (REG., 460; Bain, IV, 1594, 1596). James Frissal was a dag-maker in 1592 (*Sc. Ant.*, VI, p. 168), Robert Frizell in Tinwald was examined for the Test in 1685 (RPC., 3. ser. XI, p. 435), and Alexander Frizell is recorded in Milhill of Wandale, Lanarkshire, 1734 (*Lanark CR.*).

FRITH. Laurencius del Frith witnessed a charter by Willelmus de Lysuris, c. 1317 (*Neubotle*, p. 304). Bardsley records Richard de la Fryth in county Norfolk, 1273.

FRIZELL, FRIZELLE. See under FRISSELL.

FROG. Frogston in the parish of Liberton, Midlothian, once a small hamlet of which not a vestige now remains, probably derived its name from Alexander Frog who had a grant in 1447 to farm the lands of Straiton with power "to big ane mill" (Good, *Liberton in ancient and modern times*, p. 149). The name of the hamlet survives in Frogston Brae. Mr. John Frog, vicar of Inverkeithing in 1509 (*Inverkeithing*, p. 235) is doubtless the John Frog who witnessed a tack by the abbot of Cupar in 1521 (SCM., v, p. 294). Bessie Froge was tenant of the Terroris Croft within Mussilbrughe schyere in 1561 (RD., p. 430). William Froge, indweller in Edinburgh, 1667 (*Edin. App.*). Lower says a John Frog lived in Oxfordshire in the time of Edward Longshanks.

FROGGET. A surname formerly recorded in Annan (1801), Dumfriesshire, is most probably derived from Froggatt in county Derby, England.

FROOD. Most probably derived from the small place named Frude in the parish of Tweedsmuir, Peeblesshire. A resignation of land in Dumfries in favor of Thomas Frude is recorded in 1544 (*Anderson*), Cuthbert Frud signed the Band of Dumfries in 1570 (RPC., xiv, p. 66), and another Thomas Frude was "reader" in Quhittinghame in 1574 (RMR.). James Frude was witness to an assurance by John Maxwell, earl of Morton, in 1585 (*Annandale*, i, p. 49). Helene Fruid is recorded in Blackshaw in 1628 (*Dumfries*), William Fruid in Harlaw in 1637 (*Lauder*), and Jean Frood or Fruid in Drumalban in 1681 (*Lanark CR.*).

FROST. A surname recorded in Banchory-Devenick, 1819. It occurs in the English *Hundred Rolls*, 1273.

FROSTRAR. Mr. Walter Frostrar, vicar pensioner of Methilowr (Meikleour), 1508 (*Cupar-Angus*, i, p. 273). Christian Frostrar in Dundee and three more, 1640 (*Brechin*).

FROW. The lands of John Frowe and Robert Frowe are mentioned c. 1250–66 (*Soltre*, p. 32). Thomas Frow, juror on inquest at Dawray, 1669 (*Corsehill*, p. 86), and Mathew Frow, merchant in Kilwinning, 1689 (RPC., 3. ser. xiv, p. 445). A shortened form of OE. personal name *Freowine* (*Weekley*, p. 46).

FUDAS. Of local origin from the old lands of Fudass (1491, REA., i, p. 326) which appear to have been near Muir of Rhynie, Aberdeenshire. Lancelot Foudas witnessed a precept of sasine in favor of James Innes of 'yat ilk,' 1468 (*Seals Supp.*, 380; *Macdonald*, 981). Sir William Fudes, a cleric, was presented to the sacristy of the church of St. Duthace of Tane, 1507 (RMS., ii), and in 1516 Stephen Fudis appears as burgess of that town (*Calendar of Fearn*). James Fudas was fined for being absent from the wapinshaw, 1626 (SCM., v, p. 223).

FUGTOUN. Local. James Fugtoun, in Mewhous, Shetland, witness, 1624 (OSS., i, 89).

FUKTOR. G. *fùcadair*, 'fuller (of cloth).' Euerker (? Ivar ciar) and Ade Fouctour, men of the bishop of Moray, had remission and protection in 1363 (REM., p. 164). Katherine Fuktour and "Marsle hyr dotthir" and the relict of — Futtur, were tenants in Strathdee, 1527 (*Grant*, iii, p. 68, 70). "Merzone Ago Mc yfouctouris wif," and Elspet Innyfuktoar are also recorded there in the same year (ibid.). Donald Fuktor was tenant of Swerdale, Balcomy, 1539 (ER., xvii, p. 669), and Thomas Futtor in Murthlac, 1550 (*Illus.*, ii, p. 261).

Finlay Fuccatour appears in Strowane, 1601 (*Dunblane*), Gibboun Fuggatour in Fairlingbrek was fined for resetting Clan Gregor, 1613 (RPC., xiv, p. 643), and Adam Fuckater recorded in Chapel of Glenfroon, 1666 (*Sasines*, 1259) appears again in 1674 as Adam Fugater (*Campsie*). See MACFAKTUR.

FULK. From the Norman personal name *Fulk* (<OHG. *Fulco*). Fulk or Fulco was first abbot of S. Mary at Cupar, 1164, and d. 1170 (ES., ii, p. 252, 268; *Cupar-Angus*, i, p. xlix). He appears as witness c. 1165–70 (RPSA., p. 222–223). Robert Fouk or Fuke, burgess of Perth, rendered homage, 1296 (*Bain*, ii, p. 187, 197).

FULLARTON, FULLERTON, FOULERTON. (1) From the barony of Fullerton in Dundonald parish, Ayrshire, in Latin *de villa aucupis*. Alanus de Fowlertoun who founded and endowed out of his lands a convent of Carmelite or White Friars at Irvine died c. 1280. His son, Adam de Fowlerton, had a charter of the lands of Foullartoun and Gaylis in Kyle Stewart from James the High Steward, c. 1283 (Nisbet, *Plates*, p. 116). A branch of the family settled in Arran, and are said to have had from Bruce a charter of the lands of Kilmichael there in 1307 with the office of coroner. In 1329 there is record of payment of the receipts of Arran by Ade de Foulerton, and also a record of salt under his charge at Glenkill (ER., i, p. 184, 201). Rankin de Fowlartoun, dominus de Corsby, appears in 1429 (*Ayr*, p. 83), Johannes de Foulartoun held a tenement in Glasgow, 1487 (REG., p. 454), and John Fouller or Fullarton was first minister of Sanquhar after the Reformation (*Fasti*, ii, p. 318). (2) In 1327 Robert i granted to Galfridus de Foullertoune the land of Foullertoun in the sheriffdom of Forfar (RMS., i, App. i, 79), with the office of falconer within the sheriffdom. The estate was held by the family for at least 120 years, after which they transferred themselves and their name to the lands in the parish of Meigle still called Fullarton. Stodart (p. 121) says Fullarton of Kinnaber in Angus is a branch of Fullarton of Ayrshire. David de Fowlarton was one of the assize on the marches of Woodwrae, 1388 (*Bamff*, p. 22), William de Foulertoune and Robert de Foulertoune witnessed transumpt of charters, 1450 (REB., i, 141), and Robert Fowlartoun de Dunovn was one of an inquest on lands of Ouchtirlownv, 1457 (RAA., ii, 112). ffowlertoune 1371, ffulartone 1680, Folartoun 1447, Foletoun 1450, Fowlartoune 1532, Fulareton 1432, Fulertoun 1450, Fullarttown 1682, Fullertowne 1679; ffulertoun, Fowillertoun.

FULLEN. Halde Fulane held a land in Aberdeen, 1411 (CRA., p. 387). James Fullen, sometime gardener at Ythan Lodge, 1785 (*Aberdeen CR.*).

FULLER. From the occupation of 'fuller,' ME. *fuller(e)*, a cloth bleacher. In Latin documents *fullo*. Andrew Fullo, tenant in Mikilbrekauch, and John Fullo, tenant in Balgirdane, 1376 (RHM., I, p. lx). Thomas Fullo, burgess of Edinburgh, 1386 (*Egidii*, p. 24). Now perhaps lost in FOWLER.

FULOP. Payment to Fulop, a minstrel, who played before the king, 1397 (ER., III, p. 431). Cf. PHAUP from Fallhope (for Fawhope).

FULSETTER. An Orkney surname of local origin, now probably extinct. Four persons of this name are recorded in the islands between 1612 and 1653 (*Orkney*).

FULSURD. John Fulsurd "ane quhitt freier in Aberdeen," died in 1576 (SCM., II, p. 43). There is a Foulfurd in *Edinburgh Retours* (607, 1301), and the *f* may have been misread as long *s*.

FULTON. From a place in Ayrshire which I am unable to find. There was also an old village of the name in the parish of Bedrule, Roxburghshire. Thomas de Fulton witnessed a donation to the monastery of Paisley, c. 1260, and in 1272 he witnessed a quitclaim of the land of Fulton (RMP., p. 58, 51). Thomas de Fultoun and Alan de Foulton witnessed grants by Malcolm, earl of Levenax to Paisley, 1273 (*Levenax*, p. 15–17; RMP., p. 103). Alan de Fulton appears again in 1284 as witness to a resignation (RMP., p. 65). Henry de Foultone of Lanarkshire rendered homage in 1296 (*Bain*, II, p. 212). Thomas de Fultone, vicar of the church of Imnewyk (Innerwick), and Thomas de Fougheltone of Lanarkshire also rendered homage in same year (ibid., p. 204, 211). Robert Fultoun possessed a tenement in Irvine, 1506 (*Irvine*, I, p. 159), and John Fultoune possessed one in Glasgow, 1554 (*Protocols*, I). Robert Fulton (1765–1815) of Ulster Scots descent was the first successfully to apply steam to navigation in the United States. Ffultoun 1669, Fulltone 1709.

FURBUR. From the occupation of 'furbisher' or 'polisher' of armor, in Latin documents translated *eruginator*. Adam le Furbeur witnessed a grant by Thomas, son of Andrew de Kyrconeuel to Holmcoltran, c. 1280–90 (*Holm Cultram*, p. 48). Richard le Forblour (or Furblur), burgess of Roxburgh, took the oath of fealty to England, 1296 (*Bain*, II, 820 and p. 197). Likewise did Alisaundre Furbur

of Roxburghshire (ibid., p. 211), and Richard le Furbour of the same county. The seal of the latter is a beautiful gem, a figure with rod in left hand, holding a bunch of grapes (?) in right, and S' *Ricardi de*(?) . . . *ebvr* (ibid., p. 199, 532). Between 1327 and 1329 there are several entries of payments to Stephen dictus Fourbour or Forbour (ER., I, p. 80, 98, 211, 244), and in 1343 he rendered to Exchequer the account of the provost of Dundee (ibid., p. 526). In 1344 he appears again as burgess of Dundee (HP., II, p. 134). In 1329 there is entry of a payment of £6.13.4 to William Fourbour in aid of his marriage (ER., I, p. 214). Stephanus Fourbour "tunc maiore de Berwyco" was a charter witness, 1332 (BNCH., XVI, p. 327). Patrick Furbur witnessed a concession in favor of the monastery of Scon, c. 1340 (*Scon*, 167), John Eruginator was burgess of Edinburgh, 1344 (*Egidii*, p. 3), and Thomas Eruginator or Rubiginator who was bailie of Stirling, 1371–2, 1385 (ER., II, p. 387; III, p. 140), may have been Thomas Rubiginator who was one of the burgesses of Stirling who attacked the cruives and fishings of the abbot and convent of Cambuskenneth, 1366 (*Cambus.*, 55). Robert Fourbour was charged with breaking parole in 1358 (*Bain*, IV, 25).

FURDALE. Richard de Furdale of Perthshire who rendered homage, 1296 (*Bain*, II, p. 204) probably derived his name from Fordel in Perthshire.

FURGESON. A surname in Dornoch. A corrupt form of FERGUSON, q.v.

FURMAGE. Robert Furmage held a toft in Dunde c. 1200 (RAA., I, p. 95, 96).

FURRY. Thomas Furry, tenant of Cowbyre, 1463, was tenant in Grange of Balbrogy in Angus, 1468, and James Furry was tenant in Balgreschach, 1473 (*Cupar-Angus*, I, p. 139, 143, 176). Cf. FURUY.

FURUY. John de Furuy, chaplain of the cathedral church of Aberdeen, 1366 (REA., II, p. 61). Cf. FURRY.

FUTHIE. An old Angus surname. Patricius Fothe was 'seruiens episcope Sancti Andree,' 1227 (RAA., I, p. 163). David de Futy or Fothy appears in 1332 and following years as custumar of Aberdeen (ER., I, p. 436, 492), and in 1342 as charter witness (REA., I, p. 72). Laurence de Foty was provost of Aberdeen, 1367–68. He may be the Laurence Foty or de Futy, burgess of Aberdeen, 1390, who appears again in 1403 when he grants a charter to his son, John de Foty, and another in favor of the

FUTHIE, *continued*

Carmelites of Aberdeen (REA., I, p. 189; CAB., p. 423; *Friars*, p. 23), and held land in Aberdeen, 1413 (RMS., I, 943). William Futy was illegally arrested at Lowestoft, 1405 (*Bain*, IV, 690). Patrick Futhie of Futhie's Milne was summoned for treason in 1592 (APS., III, p. 528), James Futhie was indweller in Kirkwall, Orkney, 1612 (MCM., II, p. 157), and another James Futhie was precentor in Dundee, 1655 (*Inquis.*, 3985). Persons of this name were followers of the Ogilvies in the sixteenth and seventeenth centuries. The name sometimes takes the form of Fodie, and perhaps Fode.

FYALL. Of local origin from "terris dominicalibus lie Fyall," in Fife, 1537 (*Retours, Fife*, 29). Kathren Fyell was excommunicated for disobedience in Dysart in 1633 (PBK., 70), and Alexander Fyell appears in St. Monance in 1652 (*Inquis.*, 3707).

FYFE, FYFFE. See under FIFE.

FYNOCHT. Perhaps from Finzeauch in the parish of Keig, Aberdeenshire, with accretionary *t*. William, son of Gilbert de Fynocht, burgess of Aberdeen, 1285 (*Friars*, 13).

FYNROSSY. John de Fynrossy, juror on an inquest at Narn, 1431 (*Rose*, p. 127), derived his surname from Findrassie near Elgin.

FYVIE. From the old lands or barony of Fyvie in Aberdeenshire. Henricus de Fyuin had a lease of the ponds and water of Fyvie in 1266 (ER., I, p. 21). David de Fiuy received money for the Regent in 1340 (ibid., I, p. 462), and a later David Fywe appears as a witness in 1475 (*Soltre*, p. 73). John of Five was witness in Aberdeen, 1446 (REA., I, p. 245), Thomas Fyue was admitted burgess of Aberdeen in 1547 (NSCM., I, p. 59), Robert Fify is recorded as a servitor in Edinburgh in 1566 (*Soltre*, p. 128), and John Fyvie, merchant burgess of Aberdeen in 1698 (ROA., I, p. 246).

GABRIEL. Milton's "Chief of the angelic guards" (*Paradise Lost*, IV, 550). A surname current in Aberdeenshire. From the Hebrew (Dan. VIII, 16), meaning 'man of Ēl.' Frank Gabriel and Edward Gabriel from Turriff served in the first Great War (*Turriff*). As a forename we have Gabriel Gymmill in Edinburgh, 1599 (*Edinb. Marr.*). David Gabriel, a prominent citizen in Aberdeen, died in December, 1939. I have read somewhere that the family of Gabriel of Aberdeen is descended from a Gabriel Grant, but no such person appears in Sir William Fraser's *Chiefs of Grant*.

GACHEN. Grissell Gachine, resident in parish of Borgue, 1684 (RPC., 3. ser. IX, p. 567) may be from (MAC)GACHAN, q.v.

GADIE. May be of local origin from Gadie, Aberdeenshire, but cf. GAUDIE. John Gadie at Milne of Panholls, 1680 (*Dunblane*).

GAIR, GEAR. A descriptive name from G. *gearr*, 'short.' Gair of Nigg was the name of an old family (*Stodart*), and there are still families of this name in Ross and Sutherland. One of the most celebrated of the name was the noted reiver and pirate, spoken of in Gaelic song and story as 'Mac Iain Ghiorr' (CG., II, p. 284). Tarmot Ger had a remission for his part in the hership of Kenlochow and Trouternes in 1541 (RSS., II, 3943). Alexander Gar was charter witness and juror in Dornoch, 1535 and 1545 (OPS., II, p. 639, 641). Alexander Gar in Meikle Terrall was witness to a Denoon of Cadboll charter in 1561. Alexander Gair in Stranarn was a retainer of Macintosh of Dunnachton, Inverness, in 1607. Ewin McVean Gair in Urquhart was fined for resetting Clan Gregor in 1613 (RPC., XIV, p. 629), and John Dow Gair, a Macgregor, was slain at Enzie, 1641. Thomas Gaire, "a chapman that carries a wallett throw the countrey," was made councillor of Cromarty in 1669 (RPC., 3. ser. III). Andrew Gair was tidewaiter in Dundee, 1726 (*Brechin*). The surname Gair in the Shetland Islands may be from the ON. personal name *Geirr*, but it is more likely to have been introduced from the mainland like so many other Orkney and Shetland surnames. Robert Gyre in the parish of Nesting, 1625 (*Shetland*). Hugh Gair was a travelling chapman in Huntly, 1770 (*Aberdeen CR.*), and Iain Dubh Gearr Macgregor was composer of the "Reel of Tulloch" (*Macgregor*, I, p. 193).

GAIRDNER. See under GARDENER.

GAIRDYNE. A form of GARDYNE, q.v.

GAIRN. A shortened form of GARDYNE, q.v., current in Angus. David Garn of Bracculo is in record, 1510 (RAA., II, 503). Thomas Garne was admitted burgess freeman of Glasgow, 1577, at the request of my lord earl Argyle (*Burgesses*), and Mr. Alexander Garne was minister of fforg (Forgue), 1664 (*Just. Rec.*, I, p. 101).

GAIRNER. A form of GARDENER, q.v. Andrew Gairner in Nether Howdoun Mylne, 1663 (*Lauder*). Agnes Garner in Campbeltoun, 1682.

GALASHAN. A corruption of (MAC)GLASHAN, q.v., current in Fife.

GALBRAITH, GALBREATH, CALBRAITH. The 'foreign Briton.' In Gaelic the name is rendered *Mac a Bhreatnaich*, the 'Briton's son' (of Strathclyde). The original Galbraith was most probably one of the British race settled among the Gaels. Gillescop Galbrath witnessed the gift by Maldowen, son of Alwin, earl of Levenax, of the church of Kamsi (Campsie) to God and S. Kentigern, c. 1208–14 (REG., p. 88). In an earlier charter, but within the same period, by Alwin, earl of Levenax of the same church he appears as Gillescop Galbrad 'nepote nostro' (ibid., p. 87). As Gillescop Gallebrad he witnessed a charter by Maldouen, earl of Levenax to Robert Herthford a. 1224 (RMP., p. 217). Maldouen the earl in 1238 granted to William, son of Arthur, son of Galbrat three carucates of land in Lennox, viz. the two Buthernockis and Kyncaith (*Levenax*, p. 30). About 1246 or earlier Gillaspec Galbraith witnessed grant of the lands of Colquhoune to Umfridus de Kilpatrick (ibid., p. 25), and about the same date Earl Maldouen granted to Maurice, son of Gillaspic and Arthur, his son a quarter land in Auchincloich "que jacit propinquior Strochelmakessoc [i.e. Arochelmakessoc] in escambio duarum terrarum, videlicet Thombethy et Letyrmolyn" (ibid., p. 27). Hugh de Galbrath was provost of Aberdeen, 1342 (ER., I, p. 480; REA., I, p. 72); and the name also occurs in Angus, 1506 (RAA., II, p. 368). A number of 'wrychtis' were employed by Sir George Galbrathe in 1494 (ALHT., I, p. 246). James Galbrat was "dekin of the Tailzour crawft" in the burgh of Canongate, Edinburgh, 1554 (LSC., p. 293). Robert Caubraith, a pupil of John Major, may be Robert Galbraith who was rector of Spot in 1534, Lord of Session in 1537, and murdered in 1543. A Gaelic saying of uncertain date ranks Galbraith as the greatest of surnames:

"Bhreatunnach o'n Talla Dheirg,
Uaisle 'shliochd Albann do shloinne."
(Galbraith from the Red Tower,
Noblest of Albannic race, thy pedigree.)

Talla dhearg was probably Dumbarton. Tannahill in his "Kebbuckston Weddin" spells the name Cobreath. Cabreth 1692, Calbraht 1474, Calbreath 1685, Galbrach 1372, Galbrithart 1476, Galbracht 1528, Galbrathe 1440, Galbravt 1592, Galbravtht 1551, Gallbraith 1679, Gallbraithe 1638, Galbrithart 1476, Gawbrath 1464. Collectively the Galbraiths are known in Gaelic as *Clann a' Bhreatannaich*.

GALBREATH. A variant of GALBRAITH, q.v.

GALDIE. A Ross-shire surname. A form of GALLIE, q.v., with intrusive *d*.

GALGACUS. The leader of the Caledonians at the battle of Mons Graupius. See under CALGĀCUS.

GALHUAYES. This curious and unusual name is probably a form of Ghilhazie, often pronounced Gilhayes or Gillies (see GILLIES). The tombstone of George Gilhuayes, 1702, is in Tranent churchyard (PSAS., XLV, p. 148).

GALL. "Strangers to the Gadhelic people were called Gall, and this gave rise to surnames such as Gauld, Gall, and the Lowland Galt" (*Henderson*, p. 59). Gall in the common speech was pronounced 'Gaw.' A rather common surname in Perth and especially in the Muirton of Balhousie during the seventeenth and eighteenth centuries. John Gal was witness to a grant to the Blackfriars of Perth in 1334 (*Milne*, p. 27). William Gaw appears as presbyter in Glasgow, 1397 (LSC., p. 124), and a charge was brought against Robert Gal in Aberdeen, 1399 (CRA., p. 378). James Gaw witnessed a sasine in Perthshire, 1474 (*Athole*, p. 709). Alexander Gaw was chaplain at Finhaven from 1499 to 1513 (ER.), another Alexander Gaw was a notary and kept a protocol book between 1538–58, and Robert Gal was admitted burgess and guild brother of Perth, 1469. Duncan Gaw was admitted burgess of Aberdeen, 1535 (NSCM., I, p. 53), and Duncan Gae of Aberdeen, perhaps the same person, was slain in battle of Pinkie, 1547 (SCM., II, p. 34). James Gaw was witness in Glasgow, 1555 (*Protocols*), and Nicoll Gawe in Dalkeith was summoned before the Privy Council in 1566 (RPC., I, p. 444). Alexander Gaw was minister at Strogeith, and Robert Gaw reidare at Barneweill, 1574 (RMR.). Thomas Gaw was a notary in Perth, 1593 (*Methven*, p. 81). Donald Gaw in Drumnacarrie was fined in 1613 for reset of Clan Gregor (RPC., XIV, p. 632), and Elizabeth alias Bessie Gaw was heir of Andrew Gaw, her brother, in 4d lands of Glenbuk in 1640 (*Retours, Ayr*, 349). Alexander Gall in town of Raithen, 1737 (*Aberdeen CR.*), and another Alexander Gall, farmer in Broomhill of Innes, 1795 (*Moray*). The name of John Gau, translator of *The richt vay to the Kingdome of Heuine*, 1533, was also spelled Gaw and Gall. Gaue 1614, Gauwe 1551; Gawe and Gawy 1510. See GAUL, GAULD.

GALLACHER. An Irish surname of recent introduction. From *Ó Gallchobhair*, 'descendant of Gallchobar,' meaning 'valorous victor,' or 'foreign help' (*Woulfe*). The name is sometimes apocopated *Ó Gallchu*, giving Gallahue.

GALLANT. William Gallant was retoured heir of William Gallant, his father, in the lands of Newnoth, Aberdeenshire, 1655 (*Retours, Aberdeen*, 330). Bardsley has Thomas Galaunt in Surrey, 1273, and says the name means 'the gallant,' but this seems unlikely.

GALLARD. Reginaldus de Galard' witnessed a charter by Adam de Hastengis of the land of Kengildurs to the Abbey of Aberbrothoc, c. 1214–26 (RAA., I, 87). John Galart or Gallard held the land of Keth Sywin or Swinis Keeth, Fife, in 1248, and Reginaldus de Gaillard is mentioned in connection with the land about the same date (RD., p. 96, 97, 106). William Gallard granted a receipt for the Regent, 1341 (ER., I, p. 476). Weekley explains this name as a variant of Gaillard, from AF. *Gallard*, Fr. *gaillard* (merry, lively, etc.). The name is recorded in Cambridgeshire in 1273.

GALLERY. Of local origin from the lands of Gallery (1604 Gallowray, 1638 Gallaraw, 1655 Gallaray) in the parish of Logie-Pert, Angus.

GALLETLY, GELLATLY, GILLATLY, GO-LIGHTLY. William Galithli witnessed a charter by Walter filius Sibald in favor of the Abbey of Arbroath c. 1200–07 (RAA., I, 94). Henry Gellatly, an illegitimate son of William the Lion, of whom little or nothing is known, was grandfather of Patric Galythly, one of the competitors for the Crown in 1291. Patrick Galythly, burgess of Perth, swore fealty to Edward I at Perth in the same year (Bain, II, 508). In 1296 a royal writ was issued to the sheriff of Aberdeen on behalf of Henry Golitheby or Galighly, who rendered homage in that year (ibid., II, p. 210, 218). Ranald Galychtly was burgess of Dundee in 1461 (REB., II, 100), John Galichly of Ebruks sold the temple land of Lethindy in 1472 (*Athole*, p. 709), and in 1480 David Galychtlie was member of an assize in Aberdeen (CRA., p. 410). John Galychtly was tenant of Midil Drome in 1489 (*Cupar-Angus*, v, p. 240), and appears in 1512 as John Galithleis of Mydil Drwme (ibid., I, p. 285). Gilbert Galetly was admitted burgess of Dundee, 1592 (*Wedd.*, p. 175), Agnes Golightlie in West Reston, 1628 (*Lauder*), and Janet Gellatie is recorded in 1683 (*Brechin*). The surname is still common in Perth, Carse of Gowrie, and in Dundee. The variant "Golightly" is explained as "Light-foot; a nickname for a messenger," but as Lower rightly points out, the name has nothing to do with lightness of foot. It "has many forms, to none of which a meaning can well be attached;" but, as he says, "from the termination it is probably local." Alletrie 1700, Gelletlie 1735, Gellitlie 1687, Gellitly 1676.

GALLIE, GALLY. In the Gaelic of Sutherland *Gallaich* is the collective name for the people of Caithness as being foreigners, i.e. (mainly) of Norse origin. On the expulsion of the Gunns from Caithness soon after 1589 many of them found asylum in Ross-shire, chiefly about Tain, and the collective name became their surname. "About the middle of the seventeenth century a Sir John Sinclair, in Caithness, became proprietor of the lands of Culiss and Wester Rarichie. This led to the introduction into the parish of various individuals of the name of Gunn from the boundary that separates Caithness from Sutherland. The people of the parish called them 'na gallaich' (or strangers); and from this arose the name Gallie, which has been for nearly 200 years a common and rather respectable name among the inhabitants. The name is now, however, much on the decrease" (*New statistical account of Ross and Cromarty*). Gallies are therefore reckoned a sept of the Gunns. (2) Gallie is also found as a surname in Ayrshire and the west, with the meaning of 'stranger' (*gallda*). The tenement of Patrick Gallie in Irvine is mentioned in 1426 (*Irvine*, II, p. 130). Donald Gallie appears in Ardroskitill in 1620 (*Sasines*, II, 81), and Finlay Gallie in Iskichragane in 1662 (*Isles*). John Galie (Galy, Gelie, or Gely) in Barmoire, Bute, and his wife were accused of being witches in 1662 (HP., III). The name in Bute was afterwards spelled Gillies. In Ulster Gallie has been softened to Gailey.

GALLIWOOD. Local. Johannes Galliwoode who possessed a tenement in Edinburgh in 1423 (LSC., p. 228) appears in another record in the same year and in 1426 as Johannes de Gallirwode or Gallirvod (*Egidii*, p. 45, 48).

GALLOCH. Probably = GALLIE, q.v. Donald Gromach Gallach mentioned in 1522 (*Cawdor*, p. 144). See under GALL.

GALLON. A surname found in Moray may be a variant of GOLLAN, q.v.

GALLOW. William Gallow in Symington, 1677, and two more of the name (*Lanark CR.*), and Barbaro Gallo in Callans, parish of Biggar, 1689 (ibid.).

GALLOWAY. From the district of the name. Persons bearing this name are early found in other parts of Scotland, a family of the name settled in Dumbartonshire early in the sixteenth century, and others of the name appear early on the East Coast. Thomas de Galwethia, earl of Atholl, made a gift of lands to the Abbey of Neubotle c. 1230 (*Neubotle*, 27), and Michael de Galewath[ia] was a witness about the same time (LAC., 73). John

Galway was master of a ship belonging to Sir John of Mountgomery in 1405 (*Bain*, IV, 697). Gilbert of Galoway was 'familiar' of the abbot of Couper, 1475 (*Cupar-Angus*, I, p. 202), and Jhone of Galloway, tenant of part of Kethik, 1495 (ibid., p. 247). Sande Galowey was guilty of 'twllye' (disturbance) in Lanark, 1488 (*Lanark*, p. 2), and Henry Galloway filius quondam William Galloway of West Weems (or West Mains) is mentioned in 1541 (*Dysart*, p. 7). Pattoun Gallowey had a tack of two acres in Carsegrange, 1550 (*Cupar-Angus*, II, p. 121). John Galloway in Kilmaronok was sued for contempt and deforcement, 1597 (RPC., V, p. 436), and another Galloway, also in Kilmaronok, followed the Macfarlanes in their deadly feud with the Buchanans, 1619 (ibid., XI, p. 554). Caution was found for Robert Galloway in Tullibodie, 1594 (ibid., V, p. 165), Neill Gallouay in Wodstoune was a retainer of the earl of Cassills in Carrick, 1635 (ibid., 2. ser. v, p. 507), William Galloway, shoemaker, was admitted burgess of Aberdeen, 1606 (NSCM., I, p. 103), and Andro Galloway was burgess of Pittinweme, 1654 (*Inquis.*, 3974). Galloay 1506, Gallway 1497, Gallowaye 1485.

GALLY. *See under* GALLIE.

GALRIG. From the old lands of Gallerig or Gallorig in the barony of Pittencrieff, Fife. Alexander Galrik had a charter of half the lands of Sanct Mergratis Stane c. 1570, and in 1607 the same lands are recorded as held by John Galrig (RD., p. 470, 500). John Galrik or Gaulrig is also recorded in Dunfermline in 1583 and 1586 (*Dunfermline*).

GALSTON. Of local origin from the town of Galston in the Kyle district of Ayrshire. In 1473 John of Galstoun accused another of having "wrangwisli strobillit hym," and was himself accused in turn "for the strobillans of the toun" (*Prestwick*, p. 21). Two years later the same individual is indifferently referred to in the same record as "Jok of Gaustoun" and "Jok Gaustoun."

GALT. Variant of GAUL, GAULD, q.v. William Galt, bailie of Perth, 1367 (ER., II, p. 285). John Galt and Alexander Galt were admitted burgesses of Aberdeen, 1437 (NSCM., I, p. 5), and in 1450 there is record of a charter of sale by a burgess Alexander Galt (*Friars*, p. 33). Laurence Galt, priest of the diocese of Glasgow, 1525 (HP., IV, p. 25). Patrick Gow McEan Galt in Torren of Strathdon was fined in 1613 for reset of Clan Gregor (RPC., XIV, p. 631), individuals of the name are recorded in Irvine, 1616 (*Inquis. Tut.*, 228-

230), Robert Galt was retoured heir of Robert Galt in Corsehill-Kilwinning, his father, 1642 (*Retours, Ayr*, 366), and Alexander Galt was pursued for eaten corn and grass, 1674 (*Corsehill*, p. 121). Samuel Gault, a native of Ayrshire, was one of the early Scots settlers in New Hampshire. A son of his was one of Stark's men at Bennington in the Revolution (*State builders of New Hampshire*, 1903, p. 434). John Galt (1779–1839) was a distinguished novelist. Gailt 1689, Gat 1649, Gaut 1649.

GALUHILL. Of local origin from one or other of the many small places of the name (= Gallow Hill). John de Galuhill witnessed a Brechin document in 1364, and in 1448 another John de Galuhill was a witness in the burgh (REB., I, 30, 117). Probably now extinct.

GAMERY. Sir John Gamery, canon of Caithness, 1365 (OPS., II, p. 623) may have derived his surname from Gamrie in Banffshire.

GAMILSON. 'Son of Gammill.' Adam Gamilssone was one of the burgesses of Stirling who attacked the cruives and fishings of the abbot and convent of Cambuskenneth, 1366 (*Cambus.*, 55). See under GEMMELL.

GAMMACK, GAMACK. Probably originally a nickname, from Gaelic *gàmag*, a 'stride.' "Gawmak Molenys wif" was a tenant in Strathdee in 1527 (*Grant*, III, p. 68). 'Molenys' means 'of the mill.' Thomas Gammak was elected burgess of Aberdeen in 1571 (NSCM., I, p. 70), and William Gammock appears as a farmer in Coburty in 1785 (*Aberdeen CR.*). The Rev. James Gammack (1837–1923) was well known as author and editor.

GAMMELL, GAMMILL. *See under* GEMMELL.

GAMMIE. Peter Gammie was member of Drumblade Company of Volunteers, 1804 (*Will*), and two brothers of the name from Turriff served in the first Great War (*Turriff*). Gamie 1816.

GANNOCHAN. Adam Gannoquhe or Gannoquhen, friar, was a charter witness in Glenluce, 1560–72 (Rusk, *History of parish and abbey of Glenluce*, p. 135, 139). A debt was due to Adam Gunochan in Dumfries, 1689 (RPC., 3. ser. XIV, p. 694).

GANSON. A Caithness surname. See under GAUNSON.

GARDEN. A form of GARDYNE, q.v.

GARDENER, GARDINER, GAIRDNER, GARD-NER (most common form). From the occupation of 'gardener,' rendered in Latin charters by *ortolanus*. Rogerus Ortolanus was juror on an inquest in 1296 (*Peebles*, 5). In 1329 there is record of meal delivered to Nicholas Gardener who is again referred to as Nicholas ortolanus (ER., I, p. 128, 130). Gilbert ortolanus is also referred to (p. 130). Robert Gardnar was a notary public in the diocese of Dunblane in 1426 (*Cambus.*, 88), John Gardenar witnessed a precept by Robert dominus de Lyle in 1452 (RMP., p. 250), Richard Garden or Gardenare appears in 1454 and 1458 as vicar of Colmanell (REG., 371, 377), and William Gardennar possessed a garden in Glasgow in 1486 (ibid., p. 450). Alexander Gardnare was burgess of Are in 1503 (*Friars Ayr*, p. 70), and Robert Gardnar was burgess of Linlithgow in 1545 (*Laing*, 493). Gardinar 1511, Gardinare 1507, Gardnard 1566, Gardynar 1430, Gardynnyr 1540, Garner 1545, Gerdnar 1493.

GARDENKIRK. Of local origin probably from Garnkirk in the parish of Cadder, Lanarkshire. Compare the surname Gairn from Gardyne. Johannes Gardinkirk had a remission for his part in holding Dumbarton Castle against the king, 1489 (APS., XII, p. 34; *Lennox*, II, p. 132).

GARDINER. *See under* GARDENER.

GARDNER. *See under* GARDENER.

GARDYNE, GAIRDYNE, GARDINE. From the barony of Gardyne in the parish of Kirkden, Angus, where there was long a family 'of that Ilk.' The name is now common in Arbroath and neighborhood (Hay, *Arbroath*, p. 422), and persons of the name have held lands in Aberdeen, Banff, and Perth for centuries. William Gardeyn of Angus and William du Gardyn of Edinburghshire rendered homage, 1296 (*Bain*, II, p. 208, 209). In the same year a writ was directed to the sheriff of Edinburgh in behalf of Henry de Gardino (ibid., 832). Patrick Gardyne *de eodem* appears as witness, 1450 (REB., I, 141). Maister Gilbert Gardin was minister at Fordice, 1574 (RMR.). Mr. Alexander Gardyne in a letter to Lower states that in the entry of his aunt's death in the parish record she is entered as Margaret Gairden, while his father is entered as David Dalgairns (*Lower*, p. xx–xxi). In the local Angus pronunciation the name is clipped to GAIRN, q.v. Old spellings according to Lower (loc. cit.) are: Garden, Garn, Gardin, Gardne, Garne, Dalgam, Dalgarner, Dalgardns, Dalgardyne, and Dalgarna. Gairdin 1592, Gairdine

1677, Gairdne 1694, Gardin 1508. See also JARDINE.

GARGOWINN. Jonet Gargowinn in the parish of Govane, 1564 (*Campsie*), probably derived her surname from the 16s. lands of Gargowne in the old barony of Uchiltrie, Ayrshire.

GARIOCH, GARRIOCH. Of territorial origin from the lands, now district, of Garioch in Aberdeenshire. Waldevus de Garviacht witnessed a charter by Hugh Freskyn c. 1211 (CSR., I, p. 8). Andrew de Garuiach appears as sheriff of Aberdeen in 1264 and 1266 (ER., I, p. 11, 34). Sir Andrew de Garuiach, probably the same person, witnessed a charter by Alexander Cumyng, earl of Buchan in 1272 (REA., I, p. 34). Adam de Garuiagh of the county of Edinburgh rendered homage for his lands in 1296. His seal bears a fleur-de-lys and the legend S' *Adami de Garviau* (*Bain*, II, p. 201, 546). Andrew de Garviaghe and Sir John de Garviaghe of the county of Aberdene also rendered homage in the same year (ibid., II, p. 195, 203, 207). In 1342 the entry of ward and marriage of the daughter of Sir James de Garuvach was sold to Sir Thomas de Carnato (ER., I, p. 503), and in 1380 Andrew de Garwyach made a grant of lands in the barony of Rothienormond to Stephen Clerk, his son-in-law (*Rothes*, p. 494). William Gariach was admitted burgess of Aberdeen in 1475, another William Gareache in 1486, Thomas Geratht in 1491, and James Gereaucht in 1525 (NSCM., I, p. 24, 32, 36, 48). Jhone Gareok of Home was member of assize, Orkney, 1509 (OSR., I, p. 252). Magnus Gariach was respited for his share in the slaughter of John Erle of Cathnes in 1539 (RSS., II, 3151). William Gareauch was "reidare" at Roscoby in 1574 (*Misc. Wodrow Soc.*, p. 351), George Gareauche was a trade burgess of Aberdeen in 1642 (ROA., I, p. 232), and Alexander Garioch was minister at Cushnie in 1647 (*Strathbogie*, p. 76). Gareach 1492, Gareauche 1490, Gareaucht 1594, Gareautht 1532, Gareoch 1640, Gareoche 1625, Garioche and Gariouch 1663, Garrioch 1570, Garuiock 1598, Garuvach 1342, Garviach 1484, Garwoc c. 1380, Garzeoch 1575, Gerreache 1493. In addition to being current under the forms GERRIE and GERRY this surname has also assumed the extraordinary forms of ARICARI and HERRIEGERRIE, q.v.

GARLAND. (1) From the OE. personal name Gærland; (2) of local origin from some place of the name, *gaer* and *land* are common elements in OE. nomenclature. Joannes de Garlandia (d. 1202), English poet and grammarian, was the probable author of the *Florentius;* (3) in the North of England it is paralleled with Garthland, i.e. "garth land"; (4) Weekley further suggests that the name "may have been taken from the sign of an inn — The Garland in Little East Cheape, some time a brew house (Stow)" (p. 312; cf. *Ewen,* p. 23).

Robert Gerland of Perthshire rendered homage in 1296 (*Bain,* II, p. 204), Thomas Gerland was rector of the church of Banevy, 1321 (HP., II, p. 225), and Gilbert Gerland was bailie of Perth, 1359 (ER., I, p. 618). Thomas Garland was burgess of Linlithgow in 1360 (ER., II, p. 9), and Roger Gerland or Garland was rector of the church of Eglisham, 1368–70 (RMP., p. 329, 427; CAC., I, 24). William Gerland, canon of Caithness, had confirmation of the provision made to him of a canonry in 1379 (*Pap. Lett.,* IV, p. 237–238). Malisius Gerland was one of an assize in 1389 regarding the mill-lands of Quarelwode, Moray (REM., p. 171), Thomas Gerlond had a safe conduct to return to Scotland in 1425 (*Bain,* IV, 985), John Gerlonde was burgess of Glasgow, 1482 (REG., 428), and Elena Garlande, spouse of Robert Broustar, appears also in Glasgow, 1487 (ibid., 454). David Garland in Vindiage, parish of Dunnichen, 1598, and three more of the name are recorded in Brechin Commissariot Record, Andrew Garland in Clarilaw, 1661 (RRM., I, p. 364), and George Garland was changekeeper in Gorbals, 1787 (*Campsie).*

GARMACH. John de Garmach held land in Aberdeen in 1281 (REA., II, p. 279). Thomas Germok was minister of three parishes of Tarves, Fyvie, and Methlick shortly after the Reformation. Robert Garmock, a martyr of the Covenant, was executed October 1681 (Howie, *Scots worthies),* and William Garmack in Old Machar was a Jacobite of the '45.

GARMAN. From OE. personal name *Garmund,* ME. *Garmond.* Alexander Garman, monk of Arbroath, 1465 (RAA., II, 161).

GARMORY. This name is used in the Stewartry as a curtailed form of Montgomery (Frew, *The parish of Urr,* p. 84). Robert Germurie was an inhabitant of the parish of Cross-Michael in 1684 and John Germurie was charged with being a disorderly person there (RPC., 3. ser. IX, p. 574, 582). Garmury is an eighteenth century form (*Kirkcudbright),* and Samuel Garmory is recorded in Drumgans in 1793 (*Dumfries).*

GARNOCK. Local. Johannes Garnoch in Aberdeen, 1408 (CWA., p. 315). John Garnock, smith in East Row, 1656 (*Dunblane)* appears in 1685 as faber ferrarii in Easter Row (*Inquis.,*

6639). Robert Garnock was executed for treason, 1681 (BOEC., VIII, p. 117), and Henry Garnock was minister of Legertwood, 1799–1811.

GARRAWAY, GARROWAY. As there are apparently no references to these names in early Scots records they are probably of modern introduction. Bardsley gives Garraway as of local introduction from Garway, a parish in county Hereford.

GARRET, GARRETT. Forms of the name GERARD, q.v. John Garrot was admitted burgess freeman of Glasgow in 1600 (*Burgesses).*

GARRICK. *See under* GARRIOCK.

GARRIE. A surname in Ayrshire. Perhaps local. There is a Garrie near Stranraer. ? = John Gary in Dundee charged with aiding the English, 1552 (*Beats,* p. 326).

GARRIOCH. *See under* GARIOCH.

GARRIOCK. A surname found in Orkney as early as 1427, in which year Henry Garoch was one of the prominent men in the islands (Balfour, *Oppressions,* p. 108). In 1576 it also occurs there in the forms Garyoch and Garryouche (ibid., p. 45). It also occurs in the west of Shetland and at "The Ness," as GARRICK, and pronounced Gerrik or (with the Norwegian pronunciation of the *j*) Gjerrik. The name is a variant of GARIOCH, q.v., introduced into the islands by some fifteenth-century "ferry-louper" from Aberdeenshire.

GARROCH. Of local origin from Garroch in the parish of Crossmichael or Garroch in the parish of Twynholm. Mary Garroch in parish of Kirkcudbright, 1684 (RPC., 3. ser. IX, p. 573), Margaret Garroch is in record in Whithorn in 1790 (*Wigtown).*

GARROW. A descriptive name, from G. *garbh,* rough, stout, brawny. Donald Gerrow and Johannes Garrow appear as tenants in Strathdee, 1527 (*Grant,* III, p. 68, 70), and Duncan Garro in Dalchorres was fined for reset of members of Clan Gregor, 1613 (RPC., XIV, p. 633). Johne Garrow in Blair, 1624 (*Logie,* I, p. 89). Six persons in the neighborhood of Dunblane are recorded in the Commissariot Record.

GARRUCHEL. From a place of the name in Dumbartonshire, now extinct. Michael de Garuchell witnessed a confirmation charter by Malcolm, fourth earl of Lennox, 1274 (*Levenax,* p. 86). The name of Michael Gartefleith who appears as witness in a charter by Gillemichell filius Edolf to his son, Malcolm (ibid., p. 84) is evidently a miscopying of the name.

GARRUCHEL, *continued*

Eugene de Garchellis, juror on inquest on the lands of Thomas de Cremennane. The territorial designation was apparently dropped for the patronymic MACKESSON, q.v.

GARSCADDAN. From the place of this name near Bearsden, in the parish of New Kilpatrick, Dumbartonshire.

GARSTANG. Bardsley gives this name as of local origin from Garstang, a market town and parish in North Lancashire. There were, however, lands of Gairstange in Dumfriesshire in 1305 (*Bain*, II, 1702), which gave name to Girstenwood there.

GARSTIN. Probably a variant of GARSTANG, q.v.

GARSYDE. Of local origin, probably from some place near the Border (= Garth-side), or, more probably, a recent introduction from England. It is a Yorkshire surname confined mostly to the county (*Guppy*, p. 422).

GARTHGEUERONE. Thomas le fiz Maulolum (? Malcolm) de Garthgeuerone del counte de Strivelyn rendered homage, 1296 (*Bain*, II, p. 205). The name may be for Gartfairn in the parish of Buchanan which appears in the Retours as Gartferrane, Gartfoirine, and Gartforrane.

GARTHWAITE. A Dumfriesshire surname of local origin. Thomas Garthwaite was Thomas Carlyle's tailor in Ecclefechan.

GARTLUGGIE. Of local origin from some small place of the name probably in Stirlingshire now extinct. Robert Gartlugy, cordiner, was admitted burgess freeman of Glasgow, 1575 (*Burgesses*), and Jonet Gartluggie appears in Hiecross, 1596 (*Campsie*).

GARTLY. From the old barony of Garntuly now Gartly in Aberdeenshire. Simon de Garentuly who witnessed an agreement relating to lands in the diocese of Moray in 1229 (REM., p. 26), as Simon de Garentuli witnessed a charter of tofts of Inuerberuyn and Inueruri c. 1232–37 (LAC., p. 22). Andrew de Garyntuly, cleric in the diocese of Moray, 1258 (REM., 122) is probably Andrew de Garentuly, clericus regis Alexander III, in record in 1272 (REA., I, p. 29). Patricius Garntuly in Aberdeen, 1408 (CWA., p. 312), Sir Patrick Garntuly, rector of Glass, 1484, and Master James Grantulie, parson of Glas, 1537 (*Aboyne*, p. 24, 68). John Grantullie, notary in Aberdeen, 1633 (RSCA., II, p. 493). James Gairtlie was chirurgian in Edinburgh in 1627 (*Edinb.*

Marr.), Andrew Gairtlay was stabler in Perth in 1657 (*Dunkeld*), William Cartly was member of Huntly Corps of Volunteers in 1805 (*Will*, p. 30), and two brothers of the name from Auchterless served in the first Great War (*Turriff*). See GRANTULLY.

GARTNAIT. The name of several Pictish kings. Gartnait mac Cannech gave the lands of Petmeccobrig to the Abbey of Deer (*Bk. Deer*, III, 1). Gartnet or Gratney [recte Gartnait], earl of Mar, succeeded to the title in 1297. But little is known of him except that in his father's lifetime he earned the thanks of Edward I for his zeal in supporting the English authority in the north. He is the common ancestor through his son, Donald, and his daughter, Elyne, of all the subsequent earls of Mar. William filius Gartaneti, *pistor*, in Kyrcgat, Aberdeen, is in record, 1317 (SCM., v, p. 11). The exact meaning of the name is not clear. Gartnet and Gartenethe 1297.

GARTSHORE. From the lands of that name in the parish of Kirkintilloch, Dumbartonshire. Gartshores of that Ilk are said to have held the lands since the reign of Alexander II (*Scot. Nat.*). Margaret Gartshore in Auchingeyth is in record in 1591 (*Campsie*), James Garshore minister at Cardross, 1676 (RDB.), and Alexander Garshoar *de eodem*, heir of Alexander Garshore *de eodem* in 1699 (*Inquis.*, 8064). Dr. Maxwell Garthshore (1732–1812), physician accoucheur, was probably the most eminent of his name. Carshore 1681, Gartschore 1478, Garschor 1513, Garschore 1527, Gareshore 1659.

GARVALD. Of local origin from one or more of the places of the name. Magister Robert de Garuald, notary public, who witnessed a charter of the lands of Tubermor and the fishery of Carnis between 1204–41 (*Scon*, p. 92), may have derived his name from Garvald near Denny, and Robert de Garualde, notary public in 1287 (CMN., 23), from Garvald near Dolphinton, Peeblesshire.

GARVAN, GARVEN. From Ir. *O'Garbháin*, 'descendant of Garbhan.' Hew Garvan, tailor, was burgess of Glasgow, 1594, and William Garvane, flesher, was burgess in 1623 (*Burgesses*). Hew Garvene was notary public in Irvine, 1601 (*Irvine*, I, p. 95), and Ninian Garven, heir of Patrick Garven in Dykheid-Eglintoun, 1618 (*Inquis.*, 726) may be the Ninian Garvan who was retoured heir of Hugh Garvan, cleric, burgess of Irvine, his father, 1629 (*Retours*, Ayr, 260). Elizabeth Garveine was retoured heir of Patrick Garveine in Dykeheid-Eglintoun, Ayr, 1649 (*Retours*, Ayr,

433), Hew Garvane and three other Garvanes were jurors on an inquest at Dawray, 1669 (*Corsehill*, p. 86), Thomas Garvan was bailie of the burgh of Air, 1672 (*Inquis.*, 5555), and the surname is found in Edinburgh in 1649 as Garven (*Edinb. Marr.*). Agnes Garvene in Stewarttoune, 1706 (*Corsehill*, p. 211). Garvine 1670.

GARVEY. William Gervie, gardener at Lochwood, 1741 (*Dumfries*). Cf. GARVIE.

GARVIE. Said to be from Gaelic *garbh* "large, harsh," as a nickname, but no proof offered. Most probably a shortening of (MAC)GARVIE, q.v. The Garvies carry three garvies (a species of sprat) in their arms, but such canting heraldry is of no historical value. The arms were registered in Lyon Herald's Office, Edinburgh, before 1723. John Garwy was shepherd in Clony, 1512 (*Rent. Dunk.*, p. 183). Janet Garvie is in Hauchhead of Guthrie in 1613, and three of the name in the same district (*Brechin*). Seven of the name are in the Aberdeen Directory.

GARVOCH, GARVOCK. Of local origin, probably from Garvock in the parish of the same name in Kincardineshire. There is, however, another Garvock in Perthshire (*Retours*). Laurence de Garuok, one of those appointed to treat for the ransom of David II in 1357 (CDE., 6), is probably Laurence Garvock who was provost of Aberdeen in 1365–67. A charter of sale by Malise de Garvok in 1403 is in record (*Friars*, p. 24). George Garvock was portioner of Smiddyhill in 1739 (*Dunkeld*), William Garvock in Dykeside of Towie appears in 1742 (*Aberdeen CR.*), and another William Garvock was a member of the Huntly Company of Volunteers in 1798 (*Will*, p. 19).

GASK. From Gask near Auchterarder, Perthshire. Galfridus de Gaisk who witnessed a confirmation of the gift of a croft by Tristram to the Abbey of Inchaffray, c. 1208 (*Inchaffray*, p. 25), is probably the Galfridus de Gasc mentioned in a perambulation, c. 1230 (LIM., p. xxvii). He was brother of Ricardus de Kenbuc who also appears as witness in the charter of c. 1208, and brother of Ysenda, countess of Earl Gilbert of Strathern (ibid., p. 40). "It is said that by marriage with his heiress the Murrays of Tullibardine obtained the lands of Trinity Gask, which they held for several centuries" (ibid., p. 273). Christian Gask, sergeant in Perth, was a witness there, 1535, and Christopher Gask and Malcolm Gask appear there in 1544 (*Rollok*, 34, 36).

GASKELL. Of local origin from Gaisgill, a hamlet in the county of Westmoreland, England. Thomas Gaskel was one of the witnesses in the dispute concerning the lands of Monachkeneran in 1233 (RMP., p. 167). Samuel Gaskell was tanner at Newton Stewart in 1742 (*Wigtown*).

GASS. John Gass in Tordoch in 1626, and eight others of the name are recorded in the Commissariot Record of Dumfries, 1624–1800. The surname is probably of local origin from the small place named Gasse in the Kirkcudbright Retours (150).

GASTON. An old Roxburghshire surname. David Gastoun in the toun of Lessudden, 1562 (*Lauder*). Hendrie Gastoun, tenant on lands of the Abbey of Kelso, 1567 (*Kelso*, p. 527). David Gaustone or Gaustoune in Lessuddane, 1608, and Thomas Gaston or Gastoune there in 1652 (RRM., I, p. 65, 72). Agnes Gastoun in Melrose was accused of witchcraft in 1650 (ibid., I, p. 220). A form of Gascon, 'a native of Gascony,' and Bardsley mentions a person in the reign of Henry III who is referred to as de Gasconia and de Gaston.

GATEGANG. A surname in the *Liber Vitae Ecclesiae Dunelmensis* (p. 109, 111, 120), explained by Björkman I, p. 47, as from ME. *gate*, 'road, street,' but more likely to be from *gát*, 'goat,' and meaning 'goat-pasture' (Lindkvist, *Middle English place-names of Scandinavian origin*, p. 150). Henricus Categang witnessed a charter by Patrick, earl of Dunbar, in 1261 (*Raine*, 137).

GATES. Patrick Gaittis was minister of Polwarth from 1593 to 1604 (*Fasti*, I, p. 423), and the seal of "Master Patrik Gaittie, minister, vndoutit persone of the perochin and paroche kirk of dunce," 1605 has been described (*Macdonald*, 1020). The legend on his seal reads: S' *Patricii Gait*. Patrick Gaittis and James Gaittis were ministers of Duns from 1582 to 1611 (*Fasti*, I, p. 403), and John Gaittis was minister of Bunkle from 1614 to 1640 (*Fasti*, I, p. 403, 407). John Gaits in Dwns 1686 (RPC., 3. ser. XII, p. 496). Gaitts 1637. The name may be of local origin. Gate (ON. *gata*, a road, and ON. *geit*, goat) is common element in place names on both sides of the Border. Weekley (p. 312) says it may be identical with WAITE, watchman, from OF. *gaite*.

GATHERER. A name of uncertain meaning. "In modern dialect a *Gatherer* works in the harvest fields" (*Weekley*, p. 116). Gadderar of Cowford were an ancient family in Moray

292

GATHERER, *continued*

(Dunbar, *Moray documents*, p. 43). Alexander Gadderar is mentioned in a precept of 1521 (*Cawdor*, p. 143), and Thomas Gaderar was prebendary of Talarisy in 1539 (REM., intro., p. xxiii) and clerk of the diocese of Moray in 1545 (*Laing*, 495). Margret Gaddyrrer was a resident of Inverness in 1556 (*Rec. Inv.*, I, p. 4), and five of the name appear in the Moray Commissariot Record between 1684 and 1800. In 1595 it was ordered that the ale charges of Alexander Gaderer in Spynie be regulated (SCM., II, p. 131), Janett Gaderer in Kinneder was accused of child murder in 1679 (IDR., p. 92), James Gatherer was minister of Old Aberdeen in 1733 (*Aberdeen CR.*), and Adam Geatherer was member of Gartly Company of Volunteers in 1798 (*Will*, p. 24). Gadderare 1556, Gatharar 1546, Gadderer 1672.

GATMILK. From Gatmilk, one of the old "shires" of Fife, now Goatmilk in the parish of Kinglassie. Malcolm de Gatmyelk or Gatemilk, who served as a juror on inquisitions made at Perth in 1304 and 1305 (*Bain*, II, 1592, 1670), may be the Malcolm de Gatemylc, Gathmilk, or Gatmylch, who appears in the Register of Dunfermline in the reign of Robert I (RD., 227, 235, 239, 260). John Gatemylk was one of the witnesses in a dispute between James de Dundas and the abbot of Dunfermline in 1342 (ibid., 262), Robert of Gatmilke was one of those appointed to treat for the ransom of David II in 1357 (*Fœdera*, III, p. 365), and Andreas de Gatmilk was one of the inquest on the marches of Kyrknes and Louchor in 1395 (RPSA., p. 3).

GATT. Patrick Gat is recorded in Dunfermline, 1579 (*Dunfermline*). Mr. James Gat was minister at Graitney (Gretna), 1788 (*Dumfries*), and John Gatt from King Edward and three brothers of the name from Crudie served in the first Great War (*Turriff*). The name may be of local origin. In 1619 there is record in Dumfries Retours of "terris de Kirkpatrick de lie Gaitt" and in 1699 of the lands of Kilpatrick "nuncupatis The Gate" (103, 357). Old spellings of GALT in 1649 are Gat and Gaut. The ON. personal name Geit gave name to Gaits Water in Lancashire.

GAUKROGER. George Gaukroger, farmer and woolstapler in Longniddry. Bardsley, Harrison, and Weekley say the name means 'awkward' or 'clumsy Roger,' but while I do not agree I am unable to suggest another meaning. Bardsley says it is "a Yorkshire name that has ramified strongly, and is found in every local directory."

GAUL, GAULD. An Aberdeenshire surname. From G. *gall*, a Lowlander, a stranger. The *d* is accretionary. Gaul is the less common form of the name. Jacobus Gald and Cristina Gald in Murthlac, 1550 (*Illus.*, II, p. 261, 262). John McAllaster gald in record 1619 (RPC., XII, p. 112). John Gauld in Midtown of Achbegs, 1686 (*Moray*), William Gell, witness at a baptism 1687 (SN&Q., v, 8), and George Gaull in the parish of Glass, 1716 (SCM., IV, p. 168). Robert Gauld, minister at Culsalmond, died in 1786, and James Gauld was member of Huntly Volunteers, 1799 (*Will*, p. 8). Four brothers Gauld from King Edward served in the first Great War as also James Gaul and John Gaul, brothers, from Turriff (*Turriff*). Gald 1766, Gall 1780, Gaull 1816.

Ronald Galda (G. *gallda*, 'pertaining to the Lowlands'), "Ronald the stranger," was so named from having been fostered by his mother's people, the Frasers, at a great distance from Moydert (SCM., IV, p. liv). See also GALL.

GAULDIE. A variant of GALDIE, q.v., recorded in Edinburgh, 1943. James Gauldie in Pitchaish was a Jacobite prisoner of the '45.

GAULT. A variant of GAUL, GAULD, q.v.

GAUNSON, GANSON, GAWENSON. Surnames in Caithness and Shetland. Son of GAVIN (GAVEN), q.v. Alexander Gawensone gave a charter of a tenement of land in Nairn to his brother-german Donald Gawensone, 1563 (*Seals Supp.*, 408). His seal reads: S' *Alexandri Gawieson* (*Macdonald*, 1038).

GAVEN. A Caithness surname, a variant of GAVIN, q.v.

GAVILLOK. Perhaps a curtailed form of GOWANLOCK, q.v. Andrew Gavillok was one of an assize in Edinburgh, 1567 (MCM., II, p. 303), and the name appears again in Edinburgh as Gavelock in 1664 (*Edinb. Marr.*).

GAVIN. Alexander Gavin, indweller in Brechin, 1647, and seven more of the name in neighborhood (*Brechin*). James Gavine, brewer in Potterrow, Edinburgh, 1669 (*Edin. App.*). John Gavin in Chastletoune, 1682 (*Invercauld*, p. 264). Gavin was a favorite forename throughout Strathclyde in past times. It is the Scots form of English *Gawayne*, in French *Gauvain*, from Geoffrey of Monmouth's *Walganus*. In the Welsh Arthurian romances it appears as *Gwalchmei*, the name of the son of Arthur's sister (Rhys, *Arthurian legend*, p. 13). "This ancient British name, Gwalchmai, which signifies Hawk of Battle, is in the French

Romances changed into the not very similar form of Gawain, having first been Latinized into Walganus and Walweyn" (*Mabinogion*, ed. Williams, p. 382). Pokorny (*Die Ursprung der Arthur-Sage*) renders the name 'Falcon of May.' Gavin or Gavine was also a common surname among the gypsies of the Border.

GAW. *See under* GALL.

GAWENSON. *See under* GAUNSON.

GAWIE. John Gawie was "ane of the maisteris of the hospitall" in Stirling, 1600 (SBR., p. 94). Robert Gawy, burgess of Edinburgh, 1606 (*Inquis. Tut.*, 1186), and Thomas Gawie appears in Todlochie, parish of Strathauchine, 1612 (*Brechin*).

GAY. John Gy, chaplain in Dundee, 1452, may be John Gy who appears as presbyter in Brechin, 1458 (REB., I, 156; II, 99). George Gaii was church elder in Dysart in 1641 (PBK., p. 209), and David Gay and Alexander Gay, sailors, were burgesses of the same burgh in 1661 (*Inquis.*, 4465). Janet Gay in Nethertoun of Crawfordjohn in 1682 and five more of the name appear in Lanark Commissariot Record, and William Gay was horse-hirer in Dumfries in 1781 (*Dumfries*). The name is found in England in first half of the twelfth century. It may be a descriptive name, 'light-spirited.' Adam le Gay and Robert le Gay appear in co. Oxford in 1273 (*Bardsley*).

GAYNE. Alexander Gayn or Gayne held land in Glasgow, 1503 (*Simon*, 51). John Gayn was bailie there, 1525 (REG., 497). Jhone Gayne was tenant in Kowkadens, 1521 (*Rental*), Jonet Gayne appears in Glasgow, 1548 (*Protocols*, I), and Robert Gayne was fisherman in Futtie, Aberdeenshire, 1601 (CRA., p. 219).

GAYTON. Of English origin from one or other of several places of the name in England. Geoffrey de Gaytun, burgess of Aberdeen, 1275, as Galfridus dictus de Gaytun, appears as a charter witness there, 1281 (REA., II, p. 279). Philip de Gaydouna and his son, Galfridus de Gaytouna, appear in Aberdeen, 1317 (SCM., v, p. 8.).

GEALS, GEILS. Most probably variants of GILES, q.v. John Geals from Fyvie, Aberdeenshire, was killed in the first Great War. The second form is common to both Aberdeenshire and Dumbartonshire.

GEAR. A Shetland surname. See under GAIR.

GEBBIE. The g is hard. A variant of Gibbie, which is a Scots diminutive of GILBERT, q.v. Four of the name in record in Ayrshire and Lanarkshire (CD.). The George Gebbie publishing firm in Philadelphia issued the complete works of Burns in six volumes in 1898. An Ayrshire family of this name claimed to be descendants of a survivor of the Spanish armada of 1588 (SN&Q., III, p. 31). See GIBBIESON.

GED, GEDD. An old family of this name was Ged of Beldridge near Dunfermline, Fife. Laurence Ged was juror on an inquest at Peebles, 1304 (*Bain*, II, 1436). James Ged was presbyter of St. Andrews diocese, 1536 (RAA., II, 835), and Jhone Ged, dean of Edinburgh, was witness to a tack of the lands of Bowhous near Stirling, 1552 (LSC., p. 158). William Ged was scourged through the streets of Dysart in 1562 for deceiving his neighbors with the horseflesh he sold them (*Dysart*, p. 28), and David Ged, collier, was resident in the same town in 1563 (ibid., p. 30). Thomas Ged was portioner of Fruchy, 1591 (ER., XXII, p. 193), Robert Ged held the mill of Geddis milne, 1608 (RD., p. 503), and William Ged of Baldrig was an elder in the parish of Dunfermline, 1643 (Chalmers, *Dunfermline*, II, p. 315). William Ged (1690–1749) invented stereotyping.

GEDDER. Andrew Geddar was a tenant under the abbot of Cupar-Angus, 1479 (*Cupar-Angus*, I, p. 276). Recorded again in Cairnie, 1696.

GEDDES, GEDDESS. Of territorial origin from the lands of Geddes in Nairnshire, which were in possession of the family of Rose before they obtained Kilravock. The three silver geds hauriant in the family arms are mere canting heraldry. Harrison's definition of the name as a Scots form of Gideon is nonsense. The family of Geddes of Rachan, Peeblesshire, is an offshoot of Geddes of that Ilk (*Nisbet*, I, p. 181). They had a grant of the lands of Ladyurd in the barony of Kirkurd in 1406. Master Matthew of Geddes, a churchman, had a safe conduct into England in 1405 (*Bain*, IV, 710), and was rector of Church of Forest in 1408 (*Annandale*, I, p. 12). A later Matthew Geddas was canon of Aberdeen, 1470 (*Scon*, 223). In 1434 John of Geddes, laird of half of Ladyurd, resigned all that land into the hands of his overlord, Wat Scott, lord of Morthinvyston, who thereupon granted it anew to 'ane honest man William of Geddes' (OPS., I, p. 187). Alexander Geddes was licenciate in theology in Glasgow, 1452 (REG., 373). Matthew Geddis, vicar of Tibbermure, was chaplain and secretary to Bishop Gawin Douglas. William Geddes was killed in 1558 by the Tweedies, and thus began a long feud

GEDDES, GEDDESS, continued

with that family. There is no information about this murder other than an entry in the records of the Privy Council, according to which a respite was granted under the Privy Seal to James Tweedie of Drumelzier [et al.] for the cruel slaughter of William Geddes, son and apparent heir of Charles Geddes of "Cuthil-hall" . . . On 29th December 1592 James Geddes of Glenhigton . . . fell another victim to the treachery of the Tweedies in Edinburgh (*Buchan*, III, p. 282, 283). In the Home charters the name appears as Geddas (1494), Geddess (1522), and Gudhose (1474). Dr. John Geddes (1739–1799), a bishop of the Roman Catholic Church, residing in Edinburgh, was an intimate friend of Robert Burns, the poet, and his brother, Bishop Alexander Geddes (1737–1802) was an eminent Biblical critic, translator, and poet. Geddeis 1624, Gedes 1664.

GEDDIE. A family of this name was long connected with the district of Essie. John Gedy, abbot of Arbroath, was prominently associated with the first formation of a harbor at Arbroath in 1394 (RAA., II, p. 40–42). The agreement between him and the burgesses of the town is "perhaps the most curious and interesting of the records of harbour-making and also of voluntary taxation in Scotland" (ibid., II, p. xviii). John Geddy was servitor to George Buchanan c. 1577 (*Report on Laing MSS.*, I, p. 29). Walter Geddy of St. Andrews appears in 1580 (*Laing*, 1001). Gedde 1680; Geiddy.

GEEKIE, GEIKIE, GEGGIE. From the lands of Gagie in the parish of Murroes. William Geky and Janet Geky had a tack of part of Cowpar Grange in 1453 (*Cupar-Angus*, I, p. 129), and Paton or Patrick Geky appears as one of the Abbey's tenants in 1468 and 1473 (ibid., I, p. 142, 165). Sir Andrew Gagye, a cleric, was master of the place of Gaduane in 1529 (Campbell, *Balmerino*, p. 199), Alison Gagye had a charter of land in Naughton, 1574, from the Commendator of Balmerino (ibid., p. 274), and William Geykye is recorded in Dundee, 1589 (*Wedd.*, p. 180). Janet Geikie was tenant of the Mill of Craig in the parish of Glenilay, 1663, and three more of the name are recorded in the Commissariot Record of Brechin. A family of the name possessed the lands of Baldowery or Baldowrie in the parish of Kettins since the middle of the seventeenth century (*Jervise*, II, pp. 93–94). Sir Archibald Geikie (1835–1924), prince of geologists, and his brother, James Geikie (1839–1915), are the most distinguished of the name. Giekie 1701.

GEIKIE. See under GEEKIE.

GEGGIE. See under GEEKIE.

GEHAN. From Ir. *O'Gaoithín*, descendant of *Gaoithín* (dimin. of *gaoth*, 'wind'). The name is not uncommon in the Stewartry.

GEILS. See under GEALS.

GELCALLON. An action was raised against Gelcallon and others for the wrangous occupying and manuring of the land of Dromore, etc. c. 1480 (*Agnew*, I, p. 285). Agnew explains the name as = Gilla Colm, servant of (S.) Columba.

GELCHACH. Simon or Symon Gelchach was bailie of the burgh of Aberdeen, 1317 (SCM., v, p. 8), and provost of the burgh 1326–29–32–33, and as Symon dictus Gelchach was alderman there, 1333 (REA., I, p. 54). As Simon Gelchauch or Gelsyauch he appears as custumar of the burgh, 1327, 1337 (ER., I, p. 74, 435), and as Gelschach was a witness in 1342 (REA., I, p. 72).

GELLAITRY. Recorded in Edinburgh, 1942. Most probably a variant of GALLETLY, q.v.

GELLAN. Of local origin from Gellan, near Towie, Aberdeenshire. Jeannie Gellan, subject of the poem 'Auld Jeannie's Deathbed,' died 1878 (AEI., p. 25). The surname is also found in Ross.

GELLATLY. See under GALLETLY.

GELLIBRAND, JELLYBRAND. Probably from OE. personal name *Gislbrand*. The first of the name appears to be Laurence Gillibrand, a friend and supporter of Bruce, who was granted a pension of £20 from the lands of Belhelvie, 1309. Laurence Gillibrand, perhaps his son, had a charter from Margaret de Bruis of her right to the lands of Little Morphie, 1345 (*Echt-Forbes family charters*, 1923, p. 31). In the following year, he was among the prisoners taken at battle of Durham (*Hailes*, II, p. 389). In 1355 Sir Laurence Gillibrand had grant from the earl of Mar of 22 pound lands of Echt, and before 1357, as Laurence Gylibrande, he witnessed a charter by Thomas, earl of Mar (CAB., p. 538). He was steward of the queen's household, 1359 (ER., I, p. 618). Laurence Gillebrand or Gilliebrand had charter of the lands of Suthayk in the sheriffdom of Dumfries from David II (RMS., I, App. II, 903). Another Laurence Gillebrande was charter witness in Aberdeen, 1426 (RMS., II, 55). The family gave name to the lands of Gillibrands.

GELLIE. Janet Gellie, heretrix of Braky in Fife at beginning of sixteenth century (*Beauly*, p. 210). John Gellie, parson of Monymusk, 1633 (SCM., III, p. 119). David Gellie, citiner of Brechin, 1635 (*Brechin*), Alexander Gellie, mairchand in Aberdeine, 1653 (*Inquis.*, 3856), and Patrick Gellie, burgess there, 1654 (*Inquis. Tut.*, 810). Gellies in Fordyce were merchants in Poland in 1653 (*Sc. Ant.*, VI, p. 44). Patrick Gellie was retoured heir of Patrick Gellie, merchant burgess of Aberdeen, 1670 (*Retours, Aberdeen*, 397), John Gelly was burgess of Rothesay, 1675, and Ninian Gelly, attorney for Boyle of Kelburne in same year (*Argyll Sasines*, I, p. 245). James Gelly, merchant in Aberdeen, 1733 (NSCM., II), and Janet Gelly is recorded in Borrowmoss, 1743 (*Wigtown*). Places Gelliehill, Gellimuir, and Gelliemylne are in Forfar Retours 306, 508.

GELLION. See *under* GILLEAN.

GELRUTH. A variant of GILRUTH, q.v.

GEMILSTON. William de Gemliston was cleric of the church of S. Nicholas de Worgis (Borgue) in Galloway c. 1150 (*Dryburgh*, p. 50). John de Gemilstoun, son and heir of John de Gemilstoun granted the "ecclesia Sancti Michaeli de Gemilstoun" to the prior and canons of Whithorn, which grant was confirmed to them by Robert I in May 1325 (RMS., I, App. I, 20). Of the Gemils of Gemilstoun "all trace is lost, though the name is not uncommon in Ayrshire" (*Paterson*, II, p. 277). See GEMMELL.

GEMMELL, GEMMILL, GAMMILL, GEMEL, GEMMEL, GEMMIL. From ME. *Gamel*<OWSc. *gamall*, 'the old one,' a common personal name, Latinized *Gamellus*. In Scotland it was a not uncommon name in the southern counties, especially in Ayrshire. Gamel or Gamellus, hostiarius, witnessed charters by Richard, bishop of St. Andrews, a. 1173 (RPSA., p. 134–139; *Scon*, p. 27, etc.), and c. 1189–1198 he witnessed a charter by Roger, bishop elect of St. Andrews relating to the church of Haddington (RPSA., p. 153). Gamellus, clericus, witnessed Lady Eschina de Lundon's gift of Molle to Kelso c. 1190 (*Kelso*, 147), and a toft and croft formerly held by Gamellus was granted to the Hospital of Soltre between 1201–33 (*Soltre*, p. 14). Warin and Gamel, 'norensi servientibus nostris,' were witnesses to a charter by Brice, bishop of Moray of the church of Deveth (Daviot) to Spyny, c. 1202–22 (REM., p. 53). Walter, son of Gamel was one of an assize of marches in Fife in 1230 (RD., 196), William, son of Gamell de Tuinham, gifted the church of Tuenham to the monks of Holyrood about the same time (LSC., 72), and

about 1250 there is mention of a croft in Maxtun which belonged to Gamel, son of Walleve (*Melros*, 302–306). Hugh Gamyl held lands near Langneuton in Roxburghshire c. 1377 (RHM., II, 5), John Gamill was a witness in 1444 (*Cambus.*, 214), Gabriel Gymmill was a cordiner in Edinburgh in 1599 (*Edinb. Marr.*), William Gemmill was retoured heir of John Gemmill, his brother, in Carrik in the same year (*Retours, Ayr*, 24), Andrew Gemmello was burgess of Dundee in 1640, and Dynneiss Gemmello was a skipper in Dundee in 1612 (*Brechin*). John Gemill took the Test in Paisley in 1686 (RPC., 3. ser. XI, p. 496). John Gembell in Aberdeen, 1779. See GEMILSTON. Magister Gamellinus (a diminutive) was cleric of Alexander III, 1254 (RD., p. 49).

GENTLE. Eight of the name Gentle are recorded in Dunblane and neighborhood in seventeenth and eighteenth centuries (*Dunblane*). Bardsley records the name in England in 1273.

GENTLEMAN. Several persons of this name lived in Montrose in the seventeenth century, but the name is now extinct there (SHSM., I, p. 367). William Gentilman in Keig is in record in 1492 (CAB., p. 382), and John Gentleman in Legawin in 1582 and seven others of the name are recorded in the Commissariot Record of Brechin. Several others appear in the Commissariot Record of Dunblane. John Gentilman in Logie was excommunicated in 1624 (*Logie*, I, p. 89). Ann Gentleman is recorded in the parish of Bathgate in 1713 (*Torphichen*), and John Gentleman was shipmaster in Montrose in 1757 (*Brechin*). Weekley (p. 105) says the name is from 'an officer in a household,' and Bardsley has Robert Gentilman in Bedfordshire, 1273.

GENTLES. A current surname.

GEORGE. Weekley says (p. 209) this "is a very rare medieval font name," but "is so common a surname in its unaltered form" that he thinks it must have been derived through the mediaeval popular drama. It was a not uncommon surname in Prestwick in the fifteenth and sixteenth centuries. Archibald George appears as burgess and councillor of Irvine, 1597–1601 (*Inquis. Tut.*, 1275; *Irvine*, I, p. 96).

A country fair called Georgemas Market was formerly held near St. George's Day, April 23, on Sordel Hill, Caithness. Later changed to a monthly tryst while still retaining the name of Georgemas. Sordel Hill came in time to be known as Georgemas Hill, and in 1874 a railway station was erected about a mile or two away, to which the railway company gave the name of Georgemas Junction.

GEORGESON, 'son of GEORGE,' q.v. William Georgeson or Jeorgison was tenant of part of Coupar Grange before 1471 (*Cupar-Angus*, I, p. 148, 159). Robert Georgei (Lat. gen.) was tenant of the bishop of Aberdeen in 1511 (REA., I, p. 362). Alexander Gunn alias Georgeson in Altbraggach appears in record in 1623 (*Adam*, p. 136). James Georgesone appears in the sheriffdom of Orkney, 1700 (*Inquis.*, 8242). The surname is also found in Shetland.

GERARD, GERRARD. Prior Gerard became second abbot of Dryburgh, 1177 (ES., II, p. 297). Henricus filius Gerardi witnessed a charter by Robert Bruce, c. 1190 (*Annandale*, I, p. 1). Alexander Jerard was reader at Drumoak, 1574 (RMR.), and about the same time Thomas Gerart had an interest in Oldquhat, New Deer (*Jervise*, II, p. 227). This is the earliest record of the name in this district. Gerard also appears on the roll of lesser barons of Aberdeenshire, c. 1660, and in 1696 the name was more common in the parish of Aberdour (where it is still current) than in any other place in the county. Sir Thomas Gerard, "gentleman of his Ma[jesty's] privie chalmer," was admitted burgess of Aberdeen, 1617 (NSCM., I, p. 117). James Gyrard is recorded in Ardmelie, 1765, and Peter Gerard in Craigiebrae of Auchintoull, parish of Marnoch, 1773 (*Moray*). Alexander M. Gerrard and George T. Gerrard from Cruden were killed in the first Great War (*Turriff*). The name was introduced into Britain by the Normans from Teutonic *Gerhard* 'spear-power.'

GEREDSON, 'son of GERARD,' q.v. William Geredson was one of those who laid charges against David Meyner of Weem, 1427 (*Oppressions*, p. 110).

GERMAN. From the Norman personal name *Germund*. In early record it interchanges with Gernun. Ricardus Gernun witnessed David's great charter to the Abbey of Melrose, a. 1153 (*Melros*, 1). Richard Germayne granted the church of Lympetlaw to the Hospital of Soltre, c. 1221–31 (*Soltre*, p. 25), and in the reign of Alexander III Richard Germyn or Gernun appears as lord of Lympatlaw (ibid., p. 29). Nicholas, son of German witnessed a sale of land in Glasgow c. 1280–90 (REG., p. 198). A different name from ST. GERMAIN, q.v.

GERMISTON. From the lands of Germiston in the parish of Stenness, Orkney. Hucheoun Garmistath was a witness to the validity of purchases by Earl William in 1503 (REO., p. 416), John Germiston married a daughter of Gibbon Ireland of Ireland, Orkney, before

1573 (*Clouston*), Jhone Garmastoun and his wife appear in Kirkwall, 1574 (OSR., I, p. 267), and Andrew Germestoun is recorded in Harray in 1640 (MCM., II, p. 211). The surname has now quite disappeared from Orkney (*Clouston*). Garmiston 1576.

GERN. Richard Gerin, a charter witness, 1203 (*Dryburgh*, 160), may be Richard Gern who witnessed a charter of the land of Molle between 1225–35 (RMP., p. 77). Gerin might be = Warin or Warren. Cf. GERUN.

GERNALD. Robert Gernald of Fife rendered homage, 1296, and Richard del Gernal was bailiff of Crail in following year (*Bain*, II, p. 204, 231). ? connected with Scots *girnel*, a granary, from OF. *gerner*.

GERRAND. *See under* GERROND.

GERRARD. *See under* GERARD.

GERRAT. A form of GERARD, q.v.

GERRIE, GERRY. Shortened forms of GARIOCH, q.v. Donald Gerrie in Condolick is in record in 1652 (*Dunblane*). A Mr. Gerrie was proprietor of the Daugh of Essie (? 18th century). The name is also found in Thursatter, Caithness, in 1661 (*Caithness*). Peter Gammie Gerrie from Millbrex was killed in the first Great War (*Turriff*).

GERROND, GERRAND. Curtailed forms of (MAC)KERRON, q.v., with accretionary *d*. James Gerron was an inhabitant of Cross-Michael, 1684 (RPC., 3. ser. IX, p. 582) and Margaret Gerran in Livingston, 1738 (*Kirkcudbright*). The name of James Gurran, merchant in Clauchen of Dalry, 1675 (*Kirkcudbright*) is probably from the same source. John Gerrond, the Galloway poet, published his *Poems on several occasions* in 1802.

GERUN. William Gerun, witness to a charter of Henry III of England, 1237 (RPSA., p. 119), is probably identical with Richard Gernon who attests an agreement between Alexander II and Henry III in the same year (*Bain*, I, 1358). Gernon from NF. *guernon*, *grenon* 'moustach' "a real distinction, the Normans being generally clean shaven" (*Ewen*, p. 80). Cf. GERN.

GETGUD. John Getgud held the Templa land within the burgh of Haddington, 155! (HMC., 12. Rep., App. 8, p. 142). Weekley has Getgood which he says is 'commercial,' but in what sense he does not explain.

GEVELESTONE. From the place now known as Gelston in the parish of Kelton, Kirkcudbrightshire. Gelston in Lincolnshire was also early spelled Geuelston. Sir John de Geveliston who witnessed the grant by Thomas, son of Andrew de Kyrconeuel to the Abbey of Holmcoltram, c. 1280–90 (*Holm Cultram*, p. 48), is probably the John de Geueliston who served on an inquest held at Berwick on the lands of Lady Elena la Zuche in Dumfriesshire in 1296 (*Bain*, II, p. 216), and in the same year as John de Gevelestone of the county of Dunfres rendered homage for his lands (ibid., p. 198). His seal bears within round tracery, a shield with three chevrons, and S' *Johis de Geveleston* (ibid., p. 556). Duugal of Gyvelestone, the king of England's valet, received grants of lands in Knapdale and Glenarewyle, 1314–15 (*Bain*, III, p. 80). Gewilhiston 1296.

GHIE. Walter Gie and John Gie were residents in parish of Borgue, 1684 (RPC., 3. ser. IX, p. 568). From Ir. *Mag Aoidh*, 'son of Hugh.'

GIBB. A pet or diminutive form of GILBERT, q.v. Dauid Gyb was member of assize at Cupar in 1521 (SCBF., p. 223), Elizabeth Gib is recorded in Craigmakerane in 1585 (*Scon*, p. 226), and Robert Gib was burgess of Linlithgow in 1622 (*Retours, Linlithgow*, 110). Geib.

GIBBIESON, 'son of Gibbie,' a Scots diminutive of GILBERT, q.v. John Gibiesoun, chorister in Channonry of Ross, 1560 (OPS., II, p. 588). Thomas Gibbison, cordiner in Borrowstounes (Bo'ness) is in record in 1655 (*Inquis.*, 4052). Now doubtless merged in GIBSON. Gibbisone 1622.

GIBBON. A diminutive of GIBB, q.v., + French diminutive suffix -*on*. It was an especial favorite in Perthshire at an early date, hence the sept name MACGIBBON, q.v. As forename we have in 1455 Gebon M'Dowell and Gebon Kennedy (*M'Kerlie*, I, p. 99), and Cybbon M'Callan in Ayr 1476 (*Friars Ayr*, p. 54).

GIBBONS, 'son of GIBBON,' q.v.

GIBBONSON, 'son of GIBBON,' q.v. John Gibbounsoun was juror in Irvine in 1417 (*Irvine*, I, p. 20), and in 1430 and 1435 Patrick Gibbonson or Gibbounsoune, burgess of Glasgow, is mentioned in local record (LCD., p. 165, 251). Roland Gilbunson (for Gibbunson) was tenant of part of Petklochery in 1443, and the lands of Murthly in Atholl were leased to Alexander Gibbunson in 1473 (*Cupar-Angus*, I, p. 169). Angus Gibbonson, son of deceased Donald Gibbonson, broke sasine of the lands of Keilach, Strathearn, in 1468 (*Athole*, p. 709), and Alexander Gybbunson was tenant of Murthly in Athole, c. 1486 (*Cupar-Angus*, I, p. 232). Gibbonesoun 1491.

GIBLING. Recorded in Juniper Green, 1942. Harrison says: Gibb (diminutive of Gilbert), with Fr. double diminutive suffix -*el-in*.

GIBLISTON. From the old lands of Giblistoun (1567) or Gibliestoun (1673), now Gibliston in the parish of Carnbee, Fife. Adam de Gibelotestone or Gibelcoftone (an error for Gibelcostone) of the county of Fyfe rendered homage in 1296. His seal bears the Agnus Dei and S' *Ade Gibeotstv*(?) (*Bain*, II, p. 184, 200). Adam de Gibelotestone of the county of Edneburk also rendered homage in the same year, and in 1304 there is record of the infeftment of Johanna de Giblethiston in Fife (ibid., p. 213, 400). Gibelot (or Gibeot) is a diminutive or pet form of GILBERT, q.v.

GIBSON, 'son of GIB(B), q.v. Johun Gibsoñ surrendered the Castle of Rothesay in 1335 (*Wyntoun*, bk. viii, c. 26), Thomas Gibbeson was charged with breaking of parole in 1358 (*Bain*, IV, 25), John Gybbessone was servitor of William Douglas, one of the hostages of Henry VI in 1425 (*Bain*, IV, 986), and Thome Gibson held land in Dumfries in the same year (RMS., II, 22). Thomas Gibsoun was on assize of lands of Gladmor (Gladsmuir) in 1430 (*James* II, 16), David Gibsone was a charter witness in Glasgow 1451 (REG., 365), and John Gibsoune was chamberlain of that burgh in 1496 (ibid., 472). John Gybson, factor and attorney in 1473 may be the John Gibson, Scottish merchant, who had a safe conduct into England in the same year (*Bain*, IV, p. 286, 408). John Gypsone was tenant of the bishop of Glasgow in 1514 (*Rental*), William Gibsoun witnessed an instrument of sasine in 1525 (*Home*, 35), and David Gibson was bailie of the burgh of Dysart in 1543 (*Dysart*, p. 10). The Gibsons of Caithness and Orkney are mainly of Edinburgh origin, and the Gibsons of Durie date from 1500 and held the lands till 1785. Gipson 1540, Gipsone 1592, Gipsoun 1580, Gybsone 1542, Gybsoun 1486.

GIDDIES. A variant of GEDDES, q.v., current in Fife.

GIFFEN. Of local origin from Giffen in the parish of Beith, Ayrshire. William Giffen was appointed councillor in 1710 (*Corsehill*, p. 245). Sir Robert Giffen (1837–1910), statistician, was born at Strathaven, Lanarkshire.

GIFFORD. A surname derived from the personal appearance of the first bearer, i.e. one fat and rubicund. Roquefort (*Dictionnaire de la langue romane*) defines *Giffarde* as "Joufloue, qui a des grosses joues — servante de cuisine," and Metivier (*Dictionnaire francconormand*) gives *Giffair*, "rire comme un joufflu,"

GIFFORD, *continued*

and adds, "Telle est l'origine de l'illustre famille Normande de *Giffard,* nom repandu tres au dela de cette province [i.e. Jersey, of which M. Metivier was a native] et de nos iles." Du Cange gives *Giffardus,* "ancilla coquina." Sir Hugh Gifford is said to have settled in East Lothian in the reign of David I (i.e. before 1153), but the earliest charter in the family archives at Yester House is one by William the Lion dated 1186 confirming Sir Hugh in possession of estates granted him by Malcolm IV *(Yester).* Hugh Giffard, Walter Giffard, and William Giffard were witnesses to a charter by Countess Ada, to Alexander de St. Martin, c. 1153–77 (*Laing,* 2). Hugh Gifard also witnessed a charter by William the Lion c. 1178–80 (RAA., I, 36), and a charter by Duncan, earl of Fife to the nuns of North Berwick (CMN., 5). William Giffard, "the second of the Giffards of Yester, was witness to numerous royal charters from before 1195 to after 1204; envoy to England in 1200; and alive in 1244" (*Inchaffray,* p. 268). In 1250 a mandate was directed to the bishops of St. Andrews and Dunkeld, at the request of the king of Scotland, to assign to Richard called 'Giffard,' kinsman of the king, who is going to the Holy Land with five knights at his own expense, four hundred marks out of the redemption of Crusaders' vows, and legacies, etc. (*Pap. Lett.,* I, p. 261.) Andreas Giffard was bailie of Aberdeen, 1408, and Willmus Giffard, common councillor, 1435 (*Guildry,* p. 185–186). James Gifhert and Dandie Gifferte were tenants on lands of the Abbey of Kelso, 1563 and 1567 (*Kelso,* p. 325, 523). The village of Gifford in East Lothian was named from the family. Its earlier name was Ystrad (now Yester). In England the G is pronounced soft. Gefard 1660, Gefart 1405, Gefurt, Gifhart, and Gyfhart 1572 (all three spellings in same document), Giffart 1584, Giffert 1405, Goffurd 1296, Gyffarde 1462, Gyffort 1526.

GIGFARTH. W. Gigfarth witness to "carta Regis de decimus redditum et placitorum de Moravia," 1200 (REM., p. 13).

GIGHT. John Gecht was tenant in Balmyle, 1473 (*Cupar-Angus,* I, p. 182), and William Gicht was created dempster of the barony of Urie in 1620 (*Urie,* p. 30). From the place of the name in Aberdeenshire.

GILANDERS. See *under* GILLANDERS.

GILASPISON. See *under* MACGILLESPIE.

GILAVERIANUS. In 1266 the sheriff of Ayr held in his hands the son of Gilaverianus,

a farmer of the Cumbraes, in pledge for a fine of four score cows (ER., I, p. 5).

GILBERT. From the OE. personal name *Gislbe(o)rht,* 'bright hostage.' The early popularity of this name in Scotland was due to its having been taken up as equivalent to GILBRIDE, q.v., a name with which it has no connection either in etymology or meaning. It became a favorite name in the family of the early earls of Strathern, and was a common Christian name in Galloway in the fourteenth century. A payment was made by John filius Gilbert, bailie of Boyet (Bute), in 1329 (ER., I, p. 184). Gilbert or Gilbreid McGloid in Tiree, 1541 (ER., XVII, p. 614). Michael Gilbert was burgess of Glasgow, 1562 (RPC., I, p. 229), and another Michael Gilbert, a rich jeweller, was bailie of Edinburgh, 1588 (*Stodart*). Gilbert is the parent of many other names as Gibb, Gibbon, Gibson, etc.

GILBERTFIELD. Thomas Gylbertfelde who held a tenement in Glasgow before 1487 (REG., p. 454) probably derived his name from Gilbertfield near Cambuslang, Lanarkshire.

GILBERTSON, 'son of GILBERT,' q.v. Johan Gilberdes sone del counte de Pebbles rendered homage, 1296 (*Bain,* II, p. 207). Ambrenes in the barony of Buittle was leased to Gilbert fil. Gilberti in 1376 (RHM., I, p. lix). Johannes Gilberti is mentioned in 1398 (CRA., p. 373), Sir William Gilbertson, a cleric, had lease of part of the church of Glenyleff, 1471 (*Cupar-Angus,* I, p. 219), David Gylbardi appears in 1495 (*Cawdor,* p. 84), and William Gilberti was a witness in Brechin in 1552 (REB., I, 233). Arche Gilbertsone was declared innocent of the detention of King James III in Edinburgh Castle in 1482 (*Lennox,* II, p. 123). Gilbertson is also a Shetland surname.

GILBETHOC. Gilbethoc was a witness in the dispute concerning the ownership of the lands of Monachkeneran in 1233 (RMP., p. 167; Innes, *Legal antiquities,* p. 218). Nothing is known of a S. Bethoc now Beathag (*Watson* II, p. 11). Gillebenthoc, the name of the father of a witness to a charter by Maldoueny, earl of Lennox, of a carucate of Mukraw (*Levenax,* p. 38) is perhaps a miscopying of Gillebeuthoc. Perhaps the saint meant is Begha, the Begu of Bede (*Hist. Eccles.,* IV, 23) commemorated in Kilbucho (c. 1214–49 Kelbechoc).

GILBRIDE. G. *Gille Brighde,* 'S. Bride's servant.' Gilbride or Gillebride was a common name in the middle ages but is now little used. Gilbertus or GILBERT, q.v., was early conceived to be its equivalent and eventually superseded it, e.g., Gilbert or Gilbreid McGloid, a tenant in Tiree, 1541 (ER., xvii, p. 614). Gillbride was the name of the father of Somerled. Gilbryde Macgideride witnessed a charter of the lands of Duueglas (Douglas) to Theobald the Fleming, c. 1147–60 (*Kelso*, 107). Ggillebrite, earl of Angus, one of the witnesses to King David's protection to the clerics of Deer, c. 1150 (*Bk. Deer*) appears c. 1178–98 as Gilbride or Gillebrid (RAA., I, 12, 193). Gillebride, parson of Abirtarf, witnessed the great charter by Bishop Brice "de fundationis canonicorum apud Spyni," c. 1210 (REM., p. 43). Gillebride was one of the jury that made inquiry into the marches of Wester Fedale in Perthshire, 1246 (LAC., p. 26).

GILCHOMEDY. Perhaps from *Gilla-anchoimdedh*, 'the Lord's gillie' (*servus Domini*). Ghgillcomded mac Aed was one of the witnesses to King David's charter of protection to the Abbey of Deer, c. 1150. Gillecondad, son of Gilmychel, along with his brothers Gillemartyne and Gillemichel received from Maldonych, third earl of Lennox a grant of the lands of Bannerad (now Bannachra) and certain islands in Loch Lomond (*Levenax*, p. 25). Gille Homedy of Lanarkshire rendered homage, 1296 (*Bain*, II, p. 213), and in 1379 Gylchomedy, the king's cook, received a payment for marts sent to Bute for the use of the royal household (ER., II, p. 621). John, son of Gilchonedy or Gilchomedy, had a charter of lands of Morintoune in the sheriffdom of Lanark in the reign of David II (RMS., I, App. II, 825). John Gilquhemedy was bailie of Dunbretane sometime before 1476 (ER., viii, p. 395). In 1541 William Douchale and his wife, Helen Gilquhammate had a grant of the lands of Estir Row in the lordship of Menteith (RMS., III, 2438), and in 1546–47 the same Helen Gilquhammatie and her husband granted between them a charter of the lands of Easter Cochnay in the earldom of Lennox (HMC., 8. Rep., App., p. 308). Gilquhomytty 1542.

GILCHRIST. G. *Gille Crìosd*, Mid. G. *Gillacrist*, 'servant of Christ.' The beautiful S. Martin's Cross in Iona was the work of a sculptor of this name: It bears an inscription in Irish characters: *Oroit do Gillacrist doringne t* (-in) *chros sa*, 'a prayer for Gilchrist who made this cross.' The inscription was discovered and deciphered by Prof. R. A. S. Macalister in 1927. Gillecrist mac Fingúni and Gillecrist mac Cormaic are witnesses to Gaelic grants in the Book of Deer before 1132 (*Bk. Deer*, III, 3). Gillecrist mac Gillewinin witnessed the charter by Uchtredus filius Fergusi of the church of Colmanele to the Abbey of Holyrood c. 1165

(LSC., p. 19), and mention is made of the lands of Gilcriste Kide near the river Nethan c. 1180–1203 (*Kelso*, 110). Gillecrist Bretnach (the 'Welshman') witnessed a charter by Duncan, son of Gilbert, son of Fergus, of lands in Carric c. 1200 (*Melros*, I, p. 22), and Gillecrist filius Gillcunil was charter witness in Dumfriesshire in the reign of Alexander II (ibid., I, p. 182). Gilcrist, earl of Mar, c. 1179–1204, disputed the legitimacy of his predecessor, Morgund, and established himself in possession to the exclusion of Morgund's line. What is known of him is chiefly to be gleaned from ecclesiastical sources. He built a priory for the Culdees of Monymusk and endowed them with various churches in Mar. Killecrist, judex de Stethinth (Stranith), who witnessed Edgar's grant of the church of Mortun to Kelso c. 1200, may be the Gillecrist judex who witnessed a charter of the church of Dalgarenoc about the same date (*Kelso*, 347; LSC., p. 44). Gillecristus filius Daniel and Gillecristus filius Huttyng were witnesses to the *Diuise de Stobbo* also about the year 1190 (REG., p. 89). Gillecryst, a serf of the earl of Angus, was one of the perambulators of the lands of Kynblathmund, etc., in 1219 (RAA., I, p. 162), and Gillecrist de lacu ("of the loch") was one of the assessors of the lands of Dunduff in 1231 (RD., p. 111). The name of Gilcrist, earl of Mar is spelled Willicrist in a papal document of 1282 (*Pap. Lett.*, I, p. 476). Patrick Gilcristes sone del counte de Strivelyn and Kilschyn Gilcrist of the county of Perth rendered homage, 1296 (*Bain*, II, p. 200, 208). The seal of the latter bears an eagle displayed and S' *Kilcrist Malbrit* (ibid., p. 532). Adam fiz Gillecrist was juror on an inquisition in Strayavane (Strathaven), Lanarkshire, 1302–03 (ibid., 1343), and in 1304 Gilcrist, son of Brunn and Waldave, son of Gilcrist are witnesses to a grant by R. son of Dunegal of his heritage in Dronfres (ibid., p. 421). The name has been Englished Christopher, and perhaps also as Christie. Note the mixture here of Gaelic and Old English names.

GILCHRISTSON. The Anglicized form of Macgilchrist, q.v. The terminal syllable is sometimes, due to faulty pronunciation, miswritten or misprinted -ton. One Gylkerson held a fifth part of Murthly in Atholl, 1466 (*Cupar-Angus*, I, p. 153). Robert Cilcristsoun was burgess of Glasgow, 1471 (LCD., p. 185), and Johannes Gilchristson alias Mason is recorded there, 1499 (PDG., II, 24). William Gilkerstoun was tenant in Drummaben, Lochaber, 1539 (ER., xvii, p. 682), James Gilcrissoun was a witness in Glasgow, 1551 (*Protocols*, I), and William Gilkersone was also witness there in

GILCHRISTSON, *continued*

1559 (HP., II, p. 203). The name is not uncommon in the protocol books of Glasgow in the latter half of the sixteenth century as Gilcrissoun, Gilcristoun, Gilcristoune, Gilkrisoune, Gilkrisonne, Gilcresoune, etc. Hew Gilcristoune was burgess of Glasgow, 1606, and Andrew Gilchrisoun burgess in 1606, 1620 (*Burgesses*). Hew Gilkerson appears in Hagholm, parish of Lanark, 1624, and thirty-five more of the name appear in the same record (*Lanark CR.*). James Gilkisone who was authorized in 1672 to remove the doors of a house belonging to him if his tenant does not pay the rent due (*Corsehill,* p. 101) may be James Gilkerson, smith in Roughsyde, 1683 (ibid., p. 163). David Gilkerson was warded in the Canongate Tolbooth of Edinburgh, 1683 (BOEC., VIII, p. 155), and John Gilchrist or Gillkrson appears in Carlouk parish, 1686 (RPC., 3. ser. XII, p. 207). James Gilchriest in Hillhouse, witness to an instrument of sasine, 1711, signs his name James Gilkison (*Hunter,* p. 70), and Grizel Gilkison appears in Barnbarrow in 1790 (*Wigtown*). Gilcherson 1681, Kilkerson 1659.

GILCUDBRICHT BRECNACH (for *Bretnach*) witnessed a grant by Ranulfus filius Dunegal, c. 1124–65 (Edgar, *Dumfries,* p. 217). 'The gillie of (S.) Cuthbert of the Britons.' In Bain (II, p. 421) the first name has been wrongly printed Gilendonrut.

GILDAWIE. Alexander Gildawie, builder in Aberdeen, died 1832. Still a rare surname in Banchory-Devenick.

GILENDONRUT. *See under* GILCUDBRICHT BRECNACH.

GILES. From a Greek personal name popular in France in the Middle Ages, rendered Ægidius in Latin, whence Giles. William Gilis gave his land of Mosplat to the church of Lanark c. 1214 (*Dryburgh,* p. 157). Robert Geliss was chaplain, 1527 (*Caldwell,* p. 59), Jhone Gelis was one of an inquest on lands of Gowane (Govan) in the same year (*Pollok,* I, p. 258). Matthew Gellis was burgess of Abernethy, 1615 (*Dunblane*), Andrew Jeeles appears in Home, 1681 (*Lauder*), and John Geills was a wright in Gorballs, 1741 (*Campsie*). The most distinguished of the name was Peter Giles (1860–1935), late Master of Emmanuel College, Cambridge. Geilston in Cardross parish, Dumbartonshire, takes its name from a family named Giles who formerly possessed the place.

GILFILLAN. In G. *Gille Fhaolàin,* 'servant of (S.) Fillan.' O'Clery's Glossary under *Faol*

says ".*i. cu allaidh, no mac tire,*" that is, savage hound or wolf, and Stokes in his glossarial index to the *Felire* of Aengus has *Fael,* s. wolf, whence the diminutive *Faelàn, Foelàn.* Several individuals bearing this name appear in Scots records in the twelfth and thirteenth centuries. In the last quarter of the twelfth century Gillefali Kelde (i.e. a Culdee) witnessed a grant by Turpin, bishop of Brechin, of a toft of Strukatherach to the Abbey of Arbroath (RAA., I, p. 50; REB., II, 270). Gillefalyn held land in Lauderdale, c. 1213–14 (*Kelso,* 201–203). Gilfelan Mac Guostuf witnessed a charter by Maldoune, 3d earl of Levenax, 1217 (*Lennox,* II, p. 401), and about 1213–14 Gilfalyn possessed part of Vlfkelystun, now Oxton, in Lauderdale (*Kelso,* p. 203). Gillefalyn was one of the assize to determine the right marches of Westere Fedale in 1246 (LAC., p. 27), and Gillifelan, dean of Kintyre, is in record a. 1250 (RMS., II, 3136). Gilfolan Kerd (i.e. 'Caird'), a mariner in the service of Alexander de Argadia, was with others arrested at Bristol on suspicion of piracy in 1275 (*Bain,* II, 55). Gille Folan le Rous of Stirlingshire rendered homage for his lands, 1296. His seal bears a boar's head and S' *Gilefevle le Rous* (*Bain,* II, p. 205, 556). Gilfolan was park keeper (*parcarius*) at Cardross, 1329 (ER., I, p. 130), Gilfulan or Gilfulain Habrahamson ('son of Abraham') was banished from Perth in 1471 (ER., VIII, p. 56), and Gilfelan M'Allan was one of a number accused of slaughter at Stirling assizes in 1477. Ewin Gilfillane who had a respite in 1516 for slaughter committed by him (RSS., I, 2780) may be the Ewin Gilfillane who was killed by Donald Androsone in Bordland of Ruslie in the following year (ibid., 2875). Gillefillane M'Laurane was a witness in Glenurquhay, 1559 (BBT., p. 203); and Gillephillane McIlvayne in Ballivoir was fined for resetting a member of Clan Gregor, 1613 (RPC., XIV, p. 638). James Gilfillan, chief justice of Minnesota, was either born in Scotland or was of Scots parentage. Gilphillan and Gillphillan 1686.

GILGERSTONE. Rauf de Gilgerstone of the county of Perth who rendered homage in 1296 (*Bain,* II, p. 202) derived his surname from Kilgraston (in 1625 Gilgerstoun) in the parish of Dunbarny, Perthshire.

GILGOUR. A variant of KILGOUR, q.v. John Gilgour in Ruffle, 1735 (*Dunkeld*).

GILGREWER. Alanus Gilgrewer, son of Patrick Scurfarauch, and Gilcrist Mantauch filius Gilgrewer were 'native men' (serfs) of the Abbey of Dunfermline in the thirteenth century (RD., p. 221).

GILHAGIE. "There were some of this name who were long vassals to the bishops of Glasgow" (*Nisbet*). Thomas Galfagy (? error for Galhagy) and Thomas de Gelghagi, both of Ayrshire, rendered homage, 1296 (*Bain*, II, p. 199, 205). Johannes de Galhagy, juror in Moray, 1398 (*REM.*, p. 212). Thomas Gilhagy who witnessed a sasine of the lands of Mernys and Netherpollok, 1454 (*Pollok*, I, p. 176) may be Schir Thomas de Gilhagi who was vicar of Trailflat in 1466 (*Edgar*, p. 227). Sasine was given to James Gilhage in Glasgow, 1552 (*Protocols*, I), and John Gilhagie was admitted burgess freeman there, 1583 (*Burgesses*). Ringand Gilhagie, servant of Sir John Maxwell of Pollok, 1615 (*Pollok*, II, p. 192), Issobell Gilhagie was heir portioner of Ninian Gilhagie, merchant burgess of Glasgow, 1641 (*Inquis.*, 2559), and John Gilhagie, merchant in Dumfries, 1725 (*Dumfries*). John Galt wrote an historical romance named *Ringan Gilhaize* (1823).

GILHESPY. "The Northumberland form of the Scottish Gillespie" (*Guppy*, p. 314).

GILIVRAY. Shortened from (MAC)GILLIVRAY, q.v.

GILKISON. See under GILCHRISTSON.

GILL. (1) A tradition held by members of the Aberdeen family of this name is that they came originally from Cumberland, where at an early period they owned lands, among others the barony of Gillsland. Gilsland, one of three original baronies in Cumberland, is spelled Gillesland in 1240, and may have been the possession of one Gilli or Gille. Gilli is an old West Scandinavian personal name, borrowed at an earlier period directly from OG. *gilla*, 'a servant,' or from a pet form of one of the numerous G. names in *Gilla-*, as Gillebride, Gillechrist, etc. The abbreviated form was not used by Gaels as a proper name, but such usage originated among the Vikings in the West. The surname is of great antiquity on both sides of the Border. Gille filius Boed was one of the witnesses to Earl David's *Inquisitio* concerning the lands of the church of Glasgow, a. 1124 (REG., p. 5. See further under BOED). This Gille, son of Boed or Boet stands on a pedestal unique, perhaps in Scottish history, as the last Scotic chieftain to hold sway in England against the power of the Norman (*Sc. Ant.*, XVII, p. 111). Gille filius Mercheh was one of the perambulators of the lands of Clerchetune (Clerkington near Edinburgh), c. 1241 (RPSA., p. 181). (2) A second possible and local origin is suggested by the name of Patrick del Gyle (from ON. *geil* or *gil*, 'ravine, cleft') of Peeblesshire who rendered

homage, 1296 (*Bain*, II, p. 208). A payment was made to John Gill of Perth in 1328 (ER., I, p. 88), who appears as alderman there in 1330 (SCM., V, p. 10) and as John Gyl or Gylle is recorded as burgess in 1333 (*Scon*, p. 164–165). He may be the Johannes Gille, dominus de Torsopy, a charter witness in 1366 (RMS., I, 247). Another John Gille, a Scottish merchant in Normandy, received payment for his cargo of barley in 1369 (*Bain*, IV, 151). John Gylle was provost of Perth, 1389 (*Milne*, p. 38), Henry Gyll was burgess of Edinburgh, 1460 (*Ayr*, p. 35), Thomas Gill was miller in Newton Mill, 1658 (RRM., I, p. 183), Bessie Gill appears in Troquier, 1659 (*Dumfries*), and Margaret Gill in Coldon, 1690 (*Dunkeld*).

GILLA-ALDAN. Gilla Aldan was bishop-elect of Candida Casa (Whithorn), c. 1126, and was consecrated in the following year (*Lawrie*, p. 54, 314; *Dowden*, p. 354). He was the first bishop of the see after its re-establishment by Fergus of Galloway.

GILLACHAD. Gillachad witnessed the gift by Huctredus filius Fergus of a carucate and toft in Creveqver (Troqueer) to the Hospital of S. Peter of York, 1158–64 (*Edgar*, p. 219; *Bain*, II, p. 422).

GILLAN, GILLAND. John Gillane sometime in Corslat, Dumbartane, 1656 (*Inquis.*, 4172). James Gillan, member of Huntly Volunteers, 1798 (*Will*, p. 8).

GILLANDERS, GILANDERS. G. *Gilleanndrais* or *Gillaindreis*, 'servant of (S.) Andrew.' A favorite personal name formerly, now a surname. Gillendrias mac Matni was a witness to King David's protection to the clerics of Deer, c. 1150 (*Bk. Deer*). Gilandrias dapifer or steward to Thor filius Swani in the reign of David I (LSC., p. 11). Gillandris filius Oggu was one of the perambulators of the lands of Clerchetune (Clerkington, Midlothian), c. 1141, and in 1152 as Gillandres was witness to a charter by Prince Henry (RPSA., p. 181, 191). Glinn filius Gilandres was one of the witnesses to a charter by Malcolm, second earl of Atholl of the church of Dul to St. Andrews (RPSA., p. 246). Gillanders filius Alfwini (an OE. name) witnessed confirmation charters of Malcolm IV to the Abbey of Scone, c. 1165 (*Scon*, p. 8, 10). In 1206 Duncan of Arbuthnot took possession of Kirktoun of Arbuthnott which belonged to the bishop of St. Andrews, under whom the lands were possessed by vassals named Gillanders (*Warden*, I, p. 254). The Gillanderses of Arbuthnott probably stood in the same relation to the see of St. Andrews as the Gilleserfs of Clackmannan did to the convent of St. Serf. Gillandres Macleod is

GILLANDERS, Gillanders, continued

mentioned in 1227 (APS., I, p. 91), and another Gillandres was one of the assessors of the lands of Dunduff, 1231 (RD., p. 111). Grudach Nickillandris (daughter of Gillanders), "ane excommunicate woman," is mentioned in 1666 (IDR., p. 317). The Rosses in the north are known as Clann Anrias, and Gillanders as a surname is often equivalent to Ross. Some of this name have probably Englished themselves as ANDERSON, q.v. See also MACGILLANDERS. Gilleanris 1467, Gillenders 1816.

GILLAODRAN, described in the Orkneyinga Saga under the year 1159 as "of a great family, but a violent man." He incurred the displeasure of the king of Scots for manslaughter and other violent crimes and fled to the Orkneys, where he committed more manslaughter. He then went to the West coast and was slain in Myrkvifiord, probably Loch Gleann Dubh. In the Icelandic original his name is spelled Gilliodran, which represents modern Gaelic Gille Odhran, 'servant of (S.) Odran.' Maelduin mac Gillaodran "epscop Alban," i.e. bishop of St. Andrews, died 1055 (Tighernach).

GILLATLY. See under GALLETLY.

GILLE. G. gille, Ir. giolla, E. Ir. gilla, signifies a 'youth,' but now generally a servant, 'gillie.' "Hence it happened that families who were devoted to certain saints, took care to call their sons after them, prefixing the word Giolla, intimating that they were to be the servants or devotees of those saints . . . There were very few saints of celebrity, from whose names those of men were not formed by the prefixing of giolla . . . This word was not only prefixed to the names of saints, but also to the name of God, Christ, The Trinity, the Virgin Mary, and some were named from saints in general, as well as from the angels in general . . . But when an adjective, signifying a colour or quality of the mind or body is postfixed to giolla, then it has its ancient signification namely, a youth, a boy, or a man in his bloom, as Giolla-dubh, the black or black-haired youth, Giolla-ruadh, the red-haired youth, &c." (O'Donovan, AFM., III, p. 2–3.) When Mac was prefixed to gille the g was slurred over in order to obviate the harsh sound of the two consonants, hence the forms MacIl- and MacIll-, as in Gill' Sheathain, M'Illeathan, and lastly, simple l for ill. The BBT., among others, shows extraordinary curtailments of this kind: M'Lechrist for M'Ille Chriosd; M'Levorri or Maklivorrie for M'Illemhoire; M'Lehoan for M'Gille Chomghain, S. Comgan; M'Lephadrick for M'Illephadraig;

M'Lecheir for M'Gille-chiar; and Maklinow for M'Gille-naoimh. Indeed l after Mac usually indicates a curtailed gille. Gille itself very commonly disappears from Gaelic names as Calum from Gillecalum, etc., which were originally not used as ordinary names without the prefix of gille or maol. Prof. Zimmer maintained (Göttingische gelehrte Anzeigen, September 1, 1891, p. 184) that the word giolla is not Irish but a loan from ON. gild-r, 'strong, brawny.' Marstrander, however, has clearly shown ('Altirische Personennamen mit gilla,' in Zeitschrift für celtische Philologie, v. 13, p. 1–2) that the word antedates the Norse period.

GILLEAN, GILLEON, GILLIAN, GILZEAN, GELLION (in Inverness). These names are said to be all connected with Clan Maclean, from G. Gill' Eoin, 'servant of (S.) John', once a personal name. Through the imaginary Gillean of the Mackenzie pedigree "a Geraldine descent was provided also for the Macleans. Another descent for both Mackenzies and Macleans is from Gilleoin of the Aird! Sir William Fraser apparently regarded Gilleoin merely as a way of spelling Colin (The Earls of Cromarty, I, p. XV)" (HP., II, p. 6n). In the Isle of Man Gilleon in 1511 is M'Gilleon.

GILLEASALD. Gilleasald Mac Gilleandris witnessed a charter by Roger de Scalebroc of lands in Carrik in the reign of William the Lion (Melros, I, p. 25). As Gilleasald or Gilasald mac Gilleandres he witnessed charters by Duncan, son of Gilbert, son of Fergus, of lands in Carric, c. 1200 (ibid., I, p. 22, 24). Prof. Watson suggests that the name means 'Oswald's servant.' The name of Gilaffald, one of the witnesses to the bounds of the grange of Kircwynni and the land of Culwen in Kirkgunzeon, 1289 (Holm Cultram, p. 88) is probably a miscopying of Gilassald (long ss misread ff). See COSOUOLD.

GILLEBARAN. Gillebaran, chaplain, witnessed an agreement concerning the tithes of Fedal, Beny, and Concragh in 1239 (LAC., p. 59), and about four years earlier he witnessed confirmation of Egglesmagril by the Chapter of Dunblane (ibid., p. 58).

GILLEBARCHANE, 'servant of (S.) Berchan,' a saint of whom but little is known. The old church of Kilberry was dedicated to him and not to S. Finbar as generally understood (Scot. Eccles. Soc. Trans., v, p. 65), and Kilbarchan in Renfrewshire shows his connection with that neighborhood. In 1547 the lands of Stronechreiffiche in the bailiary of Cowall were by Archibald, master of Argyle,

and Earl Archibald, his father, granted to Gillebarchane M'Kerres and his heirs for a certain
annual rent, and in 1551 the same Gillebarchane was seized in the same lands (OPS.,
II, p. 78). See also McGILLEVARQUHANE.

GILLECALLINE. Callin or Callan is an early
saint about whom nothing appears to be known
beyond the fact that the old church of Rogart
in Sutherland was dedicated to him, and that
his fair was formerly held at the same place
(Forbes, Kalendars). He may be the Callin
of the Felire of Oengus at 13 November.
Gillecalline, a priest, is one of the witnesses
to the joint grant by Gartnait and the daughter
of Gillemicel to the church of Deer before
1130 (Bk. Deer, VI, 2). Gilcolyn Slugepah
was one of the witnesses to King David's letter
respecting the consecration of Robert, bishop
of St. Andrews at York in 1128 (Haddan and
Stubbs, Councils, II, p. 215; Lawrie, p. 64 —
in the charter following, by Thurstan, archbishop of York, on the same matter, he appears,
wrongly, as Gille Colman, Slugedt.) Melcallan,
archdeacon of Aberdeen, appears c. 1180.

GILLECALLUM. G. Gille Caluim, 'servant of
Calum,' i.e. Columba. A very popular personal name in the twelfth and thirteenth centuries. Gillecolaim mac Muredig, a witness in
the Book of Deer (III, 10). Gillyeacollom was
the name of an early Sutherland family (Scott,
Pictish nation, p. 384).

GILLECATFAR. Gillecatfar, 'collactaneo
Vchtredi,' i.e. foster brother of Uchtred, witnessed a charter by Uchtred, son of Fergus,
lord of Galloway, of the church of Colmanele
to the monks of Holyrood in the reign of Malcolm IV (LSC., p. 19). He is the Gillecharfar
who witnessed a charter by the same Uchtred,
c. 1166 (Coll. AGAA., IV, p. 55). "The saint
after whom Gillecatfar is named is Welsh,
perhaps Catfarch, an early Welsh saint" (Watson III, p. 16).

GILLECHATTAN. G. Gille Catain, 'servant of
(S.) Catan,' a saint commemorated in Bute,
Luing, Gigha, Colonsay, and at Ardchattan,
and who gave name to Clan Chattan. See also
under CATTANACH and MACGILLECHATTAN.

GILLECOLMAN. 'Servant of (S.) Colman.'
There were 218 saints of this name! Gille
Colman witnessed a declaration by Thurstin,
archbishop of York, regarding the consecration
of the bishop of St. Andrews, 1128 (Haddan
and Stubbs, Councils, II, p. 215).

GILLECOMGHAIN. G. Gille Chomghain, 'S.
Comgan's servant.' Gillacomgan, mormaer of
Moray and fifty of his men were burned to

death in 1032 (AU.). From his name comes
MACILCHOMHGHAIN, q.v.

GILLECONAL. Gillemor, son of Gilleconel,
made a grant to the church of Lesmahagow
a. 1144 (Kelso, 187). Gillioneill (? for Gilli-
coneill), son of Edgar filius Dofnaldi witnessed a charter by his father granting the
church of S. Michael of Dalgarnoc to Edgar's
nephew, Gillibert, in the reign of William the
Lion (LSC., p. 213–214). As. Gylconell fil.
Edgari fil. Dovenaldi he appears as witness
in another charter of the same period (Kelso,
340). Nothing more is known of him. Gilleconel Manthac (the 'stammerer'), 'frater comitis de Carric,' was witness in a dispute
regarding the lands of Monachkeneran, 1223
(RMP., p. 168; Innes, Leg. Ant., p. 219),
and Gillecrist filius Gillcunil was charter witness in Dumfriesshire in the reign of Alexander
II (Melros, I, p. 182). Gilcomgal mac Gilblaan
witnessed a grant by R. son of Dungal [temp.
Malcolm IV?] of his heritage in Dronfres (Dumfries) to the Hospital of S. Peter of York (cited
in Bain, II, p. 421). Gilcomgal would be
'servant of (S.) Comgal,' abbot of Bangor, but
the saint meant is more probably Congal or
Congual, who gave name to Dercongal, later
Holywood, Dumfriesshire.

GILLECOSTENTYN. For Gilleconstentyn,
'servant of (S.) Constantin,' king and martyr,
A. D. 590. According to the Aberdeen Breviary
Constantin was venerated at Dunnechtyn on
the 11th of March. Gillecostentyn who was
one of the assize to determine the right marches
of Westere Fedale in 1246 (LAC., p. 26) is
doubtless the Gillecostentin who served in a
similar capacity in connection with the lands
of Dunduff in 1230 (RD., p. 111). The name
is much altered in Cousland (Kilchousland)
and in the personal name Còiseam (in MAC-
COSHAM).

GILLEDONENG. Gilledoneng, brother of
Gillenein Accoueltan, witnessed a charter in
favor of Melrose Abbey c. 1185 (cited in 1429
in charter in RMS., II, 142). As Gilledoueng,
brother of Gillenem Accoueltan, he witnessed
charter by Roger de Scalebroc of lands in
Carrik in the reign of William the Lion (Melros, I, p. 25.

GILLEDUFF. Cristiane Gilleduffis dochter
was one of the sufferers from the hership of
Petty, 1502 (Rose, p. 177).

GILLE ETHUENY. Gille ethueny was one of
assize to determine the right marches of Westere Fedale, 1246 (LAC., p. 27). The form
indicates that Ethne is here a saint's name,
'Ethne's lad' (Watson I, p. 381).

304

GILLEFIN. Gillebert mac Gillefin witnessed donation of the church of Torpennoth to the Abbey of Holyrood by Uchtred, lord of Galloway, in reign of Malcolm Canmore (LSC., p. 20). Here -*fin* seems to be a short form of *Finnén* (*Watson* I, p. 323n).

GILLEGIRG, 'servant of (S.) Cyricus.' S. Ciric or Cyricus, the martyr of Antioch, was probably the patron saint of Giric, son of Dungal (Donald), king of Scotland, who reigned from 878 to 889. At any rate there was an early cultus of him in Scotland, and St. Cyrus in the Mearns, anciently Egylsgryg or Eglisgyrg, was named from him. The church was in existence in the reign of William the Lion (RPSA., p. 218, 229). Kilegirge (i.e. Gillegirge), son of Malise, earl of Strathearn, witnessed a charter by Ada, daughter of Earl David and wife of Malise the earl, granting to the monks of Lundors a ploughgate of land in the vill of Balemagh, c. 1195–99 (LAC., p. 38). Between 1211 and 1216 mention is made of the land of Ballebelin held by Gillegirg (RPSA., p. 317). In the same document he is again referred to simply as Girg. This is the source of *Greig*, a famous Fifeshire surname. See GIRIC and MALGIRC.

GILLEGLAS. Colin Gilglas or Colin, son of Gilleglas (Gilleglasse, or Gylleglasse) appears as witness in three Atholl charters of 1284 – c. 1290 (REM., p. 446, 447, 470; *Athole*, p. 705). As Colinus filius Gilleglas he is witness in an Inchaffray charter of 1287 (*Inchaffray*, p. 111, 294). A son of one Gvlglass rented part of the lands of Parcy, 1463 (*Cupar-Angus*, I, p. 136). G. *Gille glas*, the 'grey lad.'

GILLEKER. The 'dusky *(ciar)* lad.' Payment was made to Gilleger or Gilegar, stalker, from the fermes of Tulibanquhare, 1461, and following years (ER., VII-VIII). Patrick Gillecor was messenger and sheriff to Rose of Kilravock, 1501 (*Rose*, p. 175), and Adam Gillekeir, tenant of Cally, 1508 (*Cupar-Angus*, I, p. 269). As forename: Gilleker M'Mulich in Strathtay, 1480. See MACGILLECHIAR.

GILLEMACHOI, 'Mo-Choe's lad,' from a saint Mo-Choe (*Watson* I, p. 162). Gillemachoi de Conglud, a serf, "cum liberis suis et tota eius secta que de ratione eum sequi debuerint" were gifted to the church of S. Kentigern in Glasgow by King William the Lion, c. 1180 (REG., p. 32–33).

GILLEMANTHACH. *See under* M'GILLE MHANTAICH.

GILLEMARTIN. The 'servant of Martin,' probably S. Martin of Tours. Gillemartain was

a common Gaelic personal name in mediaeval times, and is especially frequent in the early Cameron genealogies, the Macmartins being one of the original septs of the clan. Gilleroth filius Gillemartin witnessed a grant of lands in Carric in the reign of Alexander II (*Melros*, p. 172). Another Gillemartin was one of the assessors of the lands of Dunduff in 1231 (RD., p. 111). See under MACMARTIN.

GILLEMELOOC, 'Gille of Mo-Luóc' of Lismore. The saint's name is an affectionate diminutive of *Lugaid, Lugaidh*, in Ogham *Lugudeccas* (*Watson* I, p. 292). Gillemelooc witnessed two charters by Orabilis, daughter of Nessus, c. 1200 (RPSA., p. 290–291). Gvllemallouock Macnakeeigelle was a lay thrall or bondman turned over to the possession of the bishop of Moray in 1234 (REM., p. 84). Gillemelnoc (for Gillemeluoc), decanus de Lesmor, was a charter witness in 1251 (RMS., II, 3136, citing an earlier charter), and Gilmelonoc (for Gilmelouoc) was a juror in Fife in the middle of the thirteenth century (RD., p. 222). The saint is commemorated at Kilmaloog in the barony of Renfrew, 1377 (REG., p. 289), and at Dochmalook, 1504 (ER., XII, p. 663).

GILLEMERNOCH. The gillie of (S.) Marnock, i.e. (S.) Ernan, with the honorific *mo* and diminutive ending *og*. Gillemernoch, brother of Gilleasald mac Gilleandris, witnessed a charter by Roger de Scalebroc of lands in Carrik in reign of William the Lion (*Melros*, I, p. 25). Malcolm Gilmornaike or William Gilmernaykie had a grant of the lands of Touris in reign of Robert I (RMS., I, App. II, 682). Gillemernock M'Eane VcConnachie in Leragis, Argyll, 1622, was denounced for not appearing as a witness (RPC., XIII, p. 68).

GILLEMICHAEL. G. *Gille Micheil*, 'servant of (S.) Michael.' Symeon of Durham under the year 1069 refers to a powerful chief 'beyond the Tyne,' i.e. in Scotland, called Gillomichael, that is, he says, the 'Lad of Michael,' by contrariety, for he would have been more justly named 'Lad of the Devil' (quoted in *Sc. Ann.*, p. 89). S. Cuthbert in a vision revealed to one of the clergy of Durham the death and torments of this Gillomichael in Hell (loc. cit.). Eva, daughter of Gillemicel, was one of the grantors of lands to the Abbey of Deer (*Bk. Deer*, III). Gillemichel the earl witnessed Earl David's foundation charter of Selkirk (afterwards removed to Kelso) Abbey, c. 1120 (*Kelso*, 1), and also David's great charter to Holyrood, c. 1123 (LSC., p. 6). Gylmhhel filius Bridoc at Kyngeldures was one of the witnesses to the *Diuise de Stobbo*,

The Surnames of Scotland

305

c. 1190 (REG., p. 89: the digraph *hh* represents the guttural spirant *ch*). Gillemichel was 'persona de Moethel' (Muthill) c. 1200 (*Cambus.*), and the hermitage of Gillemichel 'hermita' was gifted to the monks of Cupar by David de Haya between 1214–49 (SCM., II, p. 307). Gillemychel M^cath of 1232 (REM., p. 88) probably took his name from that of the patron saint of Kilmichael in Moray, and another Gillemichel was a bondman of Richard de Moreville in thirteenth century (APS., I, p. 94). Gillemichel mac Edolf, a juror in Lanarkshire, 1263 (*Bain*, I, 2338) appears in the Lennox chartulary as Gillemichel Makedolf, c. 1260 (*Levenax*, p. 85). As Gillemichell filius Edolf or mac Edolf, c. 1270, he granted 'illam quartariam terre que vocatur Gartchonerane' to his son Malcolm (ibid., p. 83–84). In 1329 there is an entry of payment to Gilmichel hunter, 'pauper' (ER., I, p. 131). Three Gilmichaels were tenants under the bishop of Aberdeen, 1511 (REA., I, p. 367–368). Gilmichel a. 1152, Gyllemechall 1561. See also MAELMICHAEL.

GILLEMOWBAND. A fool of this name was at the Court of James V, and in 1527 received a payment of xxs. (ALHT., V, p. 320). He is also referred to in Lindsay's *Ane Satyre of the Thrie Estatis*, 1.4624.

GILLEMURE. *See under* GILMOUR.

GILLENEF. G. *Gille Naomh* or *Gille nan Naomh*, "servant of the saints." The name is often wrongly spelled in early records. Gillenem M'Colmane witnessed a charter of lands in Carric in favor of Melrose Abbey c. 1180 by Raderic Mac Gillescop (*Melros*, I, p. 29). As Gillenem Accoultan he witnessed another charter by Roger de Scalebroc of lands in Carrik in the reign of William the Lion (ibid., I, p. 25). Patrick Mac gill Nef witnessed the gift of Kyllosbern (Closeburn) to the Abbey of Kelso c. 1200 (*Kelso*, 340). Gillenef, senescallus de Stratheame, witnessed a confirmation charter by Henry, earl of Atholl, c. 1200 (RD., 148). As senescallus his name also appears as Gillenem, Gillenen, Gillenanem, Gillenenam, Gillenanof, Gillenief, Gillenefe, Gillenanemh, Guillinamene, and Gillenes (LIM.; LAC.). Gillenef Mc Gilherf, one of the chief men of the lineage of Clenafren of Wigtown, made peace with the king of England, 1298 (*Bain*, II, p. 253). Gilnef M'Ewin was a witness in Bute, 1491 (ADC., p. 203), Gilnew M'Ilwedy is recorded there, 1506 (RMS., II, 2987), Gillenew McVicar of Auchinbreck appears in 1525 (HP., IV, p. 26), Gilnow Mc-Markische appears in 1541 (ER., XVII, p. 628),

and Gilnow M'Kaill appears in Bute, 1575 (*Retours, Bute*, 7). Gilnive McCavor was a tenant in Islay, 1686 (*Bk. Islay*, p. 497).

GILLEONAIN, 'servant of (S.) ADAMNAN,' q.v. Formerly a Christian name in the Highlands, in the Macdonald family, and first recorded as *Giolla-Adhamhnain*, the name of the father of Somerled of the Isles. It was a favorite name in the Macdonald family, and subsequently passed into the family of Macneil of Barra. Giladuenan filius Dunegal [misprinted Duuegal] witnessed a grant of lands in Carric in the reign of Alexander II (*Melros*, I, p. 172). In another charter of the same period he appears as Gillauenan filius Dunegal (ibid., p. 173). Gilleghanan, son of the late John, Scriptor of Mule [Mull], acolyte, was to be received, if found fit, into the monastery of S. Columba of Hy in 1353 (*Pap. Lett.*, III, p. 490). Gilleownan Makneill in 1427 received from Alexander, lord of the Isles, a charter of the isle of Barra and the lands of Boisdale in South Uist. This charter does not exist in original but is cited in the confirmation to Gilleownan's grandson by King James IV in 1495 (RMS., II, 2287). Gillawnane Mc-Crouder in Comrie was one of the witnesses to a charter to John de Cumre in 1447 (RMS., II, 640). In 1495 there is also mention of a Gilleownan Macpheill, grandson of Gilleownan. Gilliganan McNeill of Barray was one of the councillors of Donald, lord of the Isles in 1545 (*Clan Donald*, I, p. 371). Gillonane McMoy was tenant of Corpolan in Islay, 1541 (ER., XVII, p. 617). In Barra the name was pronounced Gill-Eonan, and Anglicized 'Gallion.' Gillownane M'Neill in Islay, 1686. The MS. of 1467 gives a genealogy of the clan 'Mhic-Gillagamnan' which Skene fancied wrongly to be the Maclennans. Gillewan 1546, Gillewin 1516.

GILLEPATRIC. G. *Gillephadruig*, MG. *Gillapadruig*, 'servant of (S.) Patrick.' A serf named Gillepatric was gifted to the Abbey of Dunfermline by King David c. 1126 (RD., p. 13), Gillepatric mac Impethin is mentioned, 1150 (RD., p. 4), and Gillepatric Macanargus witnessed a Dumfries charter of Alexander II (LSC., p. 59). Gilpatr filius Malbrid, a witness c. 1250, appears again as Gillepatrik Macmalbride in a confirmation charter by Duncan filius Gillemichel Makedolf of land in the Lennox c. 1270 (*Levenax*, p. 85, 91). Gilpatrick Mac Gilbeg was juror on inquest on lands of Mefth, 1262 (APS., I, p. 101; *Bain*, I, 2323). Gillipadrick Mc Rorie, 1656 (IDR., p. 280).

GILLESBIE. From Gillesbie near Lockerbie, Dumfriesshire. Thomas Gillisbe was a Scots prisoner of war in Eccleshall Castle, 1358. Bain (IV, 25) gives his name (? wrongly) as Gibbeson.

GILLESERF, 'S. Serf's gillie.' The 'gilleserfis de Clacmanec,' or servants of S. Serf (SERVANUS, q.v.) are mentioned in a charter by David I, c. 1143, in favor of the Priory of May (*May*, 5). There seems in early times to have been individuals or families attached to churches and were named after the saint, e.g. Gilmodyn, Gilmahessog, Gillafaelan, etc. Killeserf de Rotheuen witnessed a convention between the prior and convent of St. Andrews and Gillemor Scolgo (Scolog) de Tarualont in 1222 (*Illus.*, II, p. 19), and Gilleserf mac Rolf, a bondman (*nativus*), is one of the witnesses in 1231 to a perambulation between the lands of the Abbey of Dunfermline and those of David Durward (RD., p. 111). Lorin Mac Gil serf (*Mac Gille Sheirbh*), probably a personal attendant of the earl of Strathearn, was witness to a charter in 1258 granting Gilmure Gilendes, a nativus, 'cum tota sequela sua,' to the Abbey of Inchaffray (*Inchaffray*, p. 77). Lorin appears as witness in another charter of 1266 as 'lorn Mach gilherve' (ibid., p. 85). In Gilherve we have the aspiration of the *s* of Serf. Gillenef M'Gillherf, one of 'the lineage of Clenafren' in Galloway, made his submission to Edward I of England, 1298 (*Bain*, II, 990).

GILLESON. *See under* GILLIESON.

GILLESPIE. This name is an attempt at the spelling of Gaelic *Gilleasbuig*, the 'bishop's gillie' or 'servant.' Easbuig is a borrowing from Latin *eposcop-us*. The name for some mysterious reason is regarded as the Gaelic equivalent of Archibald, though why this should be is somewhat puzzling. The late Dr. Macbain suggested that the *Arch*, since it appears in arch-bishop may have suggested the correlation of the names, which otherwise have no connection either in sound or roots. Ewan filius Gillaspeck witnessed a charter by Alwin, earl of Levenax, c. 1175–99 (*Levenax*, p. 12). Between 1220 and 1240 Gillescop de Cletheueys (now Clavage in the parish of Dunning) witnessed a confirmation charter of the lands of Fedale (LAC., 25). Gillescop mac camby witnessed a perambulation of the lands of Kinblathmond in 1227 (RAA., I, p. 163). Gillascop senescallus de Karric is mentioned c. 1250 (CMN., 13), and in 1282 we find Gillastop (a miscopying of Gillascop), brother of Gilchrist Magilmore (*Cambus.*, p. 49). In an undated charter of c. 1360 we have Guilleaspos Cambell (SHR., X, p. 34). The surname has invaded Northumberland, appearing there as Gilhespy. Galeaspe 1653, Ghillaspic 1360, Gilaspy 1477, Gilhaspy 1508, Gilispie 1688, Gillaspik 1364, Gillaspy 1528, Gillespey 1541, and Milton spells the name Galasp. Gilasp who witnesses King David's charter to the Abbey of Jedburgh c. 1147–50 (*Lawrie*, p. 152) is most probably an error for Eilaf.

GILLETALARGYN, 'servant of (S.) Talorgan.' See TALORCÁN. Gylletalargyn was one of the witnesses to a "compositio super advocationem ecclesie de Dulbathlach" between the bishop of Moray and John Byseth, c. 1206–1222 (RÉM., p. 60).

GILLETHOMAS. Gyllethomas filius Alise who had a charter of a dauath (davoch) of the land of Kennyn Muchardyn in the territory of Kyncoldrum in 1199 from Henry, abbot of Abirbrothoc (RAA., I, p. 262) is probably Gillethoma filius Malysii, the steward, who witnessed the confirmation by Fergus, son of Earl Gilbert, of the earl's gift of the lands of Rathengothen to the church of Lundors before 1219 (LAC., p. 34). He also witnessed the gift by Earl Gillebertus of lands to the Abbey of Inchaffray in 1219, and confirmation charters by Robert, son of Earl Gilbert, c. 1220–24 (*Inchaffray*, p. 34, 36, 45). He is probably the Gillethomas, one of the assessors of the lands of Dunduff in 1231 (RD., p. 111). Three chapels in Fife (Falkland, Lumquhat, and Seamills) were dedicated to S. Thomas the Apostle.

GILLEWNAN. *See under* GILLEONAIN and MACGILLEWNAN.

GILLIE. A form of GILLIES, q.v.

GILLIES, GILLIS. G. *Gille Iosa*, 'servant of Jesus.' It has displaced the older MALISE, q.v. The name was at one time numerous in Badenoch, and at present is common in the Hebrides. Gillise was one of the witnesses to the charter by King David I to the Abbey of Holyrood c. 1128 (LSC., p. 6), and Vhtred, son of Gilise held land in Lothian c. 1160 (*Laing*, 2). M. filius Gilise witnessed a confirmation charter of Malcolm IV to the Abbey of Scone in 1164 (*Scon*, p. 5), and Gylis, son of Angus the shoemaker (sutor) did homage to the prior and convent of St. Andrews at Dull in 1264 (RPSA., p. 349). Nigel filius Gelyse was tenant in the lands of Dalfibill in 1376 (RHM., I, p. lvii), and John Gyllis rented the Fermeland of Newtoun in 1521 (*Rental*). Some eighteenth century Macphersons who bore Gillies as a forename Englished it as 'Elias' (*Celt. Mon.*, VIII, p. 34). The form Gilhuayes occurs on a tombstone in Tranent churchyard, dated 1702. William

Gillice, farmer in Findtassie, 1799 (*Moray*). Gilleis 1592, Gilies 1692, Gillise 1724, Gilliss 1484. Cf. under GILL.

GILLIESON, GILLESON, GILLISON. 'Gillies' son' or 'son of Gillies.' Janet Gillison is recorded in Three-merk-land, Dumfriesshire, 1625 (*Dumfries*). John Gillesone was retoured heir of Homer Gillisone in the 5/- lands of Burnefute of old extent in the barony of Holywode, 1631, and Robert Gillisone was retoured heir of John Gillisone, his father, 1695 (*Retours, Dumfries*, 147, 343).

GILLILAN, GILLILAND. From G. *Mac Gill' Fhaoláin*, 'son of the servant of (S.) Fillan,' through one of the early forms McGillolane or M'Gillelan, with omission of 'Mac.' There was also an old Irish family of the name *Mac Ghiolla Fhaoláin*, extant at the beginning of the seventeenth century, but which apparently has since died out. The surname at the present time is common in Ulster (where it is of late Scottish origin), mainly in the form Gilliland, but also found as Gelland, Gilelin, Gillan, Gilland, Gilleland, Gillilan, and Guililand. The late Sir Samuel Fergusson, the distinguished Irish poet and scholar, wrote a poem immortalizing one Willy Gilliland, which I have not seen. See MACGILLELANE.

GILLIM. A variant of Gillam, from Guillaume, the French spelling of WILLIAM, q.v. Andrew Gillum in Donyng (Dunning), 1663, and John Gillim there, 1683 (*Dunblane*).

GILLINGHAM. Of recent introduction from England. There are places named Gillingham in the shires of Dorset, Norfolk, and in Kent. Elizabeth Gillinghame at Perth in 1735 (*Dunkeld*).

GILLINVEINE. Gillinveine M'Vretny in Killmaluag, 1723 (*Campbell*, I, p. 188).

GILLIPETER. G. *Gille Pheadair*, 'servant of (S.) Peter.' Gilli-petair mac Donnchaid, a witness in the *Book of Deer* (VI, 32). Apparently the only example of the name. Cf. GILPEDDIR.

GILLIS. *See under* GILLIES.

GILLISON. *See under* GILLIESON.

GILLMOR. A variant of GILMOUR or GILMORE. Second Lieutenant S. J. Gillmor, Royal Scots Fusiliers, died August 1941.

GILLONBY. Henry de Gillonby of the county of Dumfries rendered homage in 1296 (*Bain*, II, p. 206). He probably derived his name from Gillenbie in the parish of Applegarth, Dumfriesshire.

GILLOT. A diminutive of *Guillaume* (French for WILLIAM) — diminutive ending -*ot*. Gillot, a tailor (*cissor*) was bailie of Peebles, 1330 (ER., I, p. 299). Alexander Gyliot was one of those appointed to treat for the ransom of David II in 1357 (CDE.). He is most probably the Alexander Gilyot or Gelyot, deputy of the chamberlain, 1358–59 (ER., I, p. 565, 569, 584), and the Alexander Gilliot (Gilyot, Gillyot, or Guillot) who appears as burgess of Edinburgh between 1362–1368 (*Egidii*).

GILLOUR. G. *Gill' odhar*, 'dun or grey lad.' Gillouir Mack Crain 'liv'd to have kept one hundred and eighty Christmasses in his own house' (*Martin*, p. 234), and died in the reign of Charles I. See under MACCRAIN and MACLIVER.

GILLS. A Caithness surname of local origin from Gills in the parish of Canisbay.

GILMAGU. Ir. *Giolla Mo-Chuda*, 'servant of (S.) Mochuda' (= my Cuda), another name for S. Carthage of Lismore. The saint is commemorated in Scotland in the place names Kirkmahoe, Dumfriesshire, Kilmahoe in Kintyre, and Kilmahew at Cardross, Dumbartonshire. Part of the lands of ffincurrokis were granted to Gilmagu and his heir c. 1160–80 (*Kelso*, 114). In another charter he is mentioned as Gilmagu mac Aldic (ibid., 110), and he is most probably the Gilmalgon (evidently a miscopying of Gilmahagou) mac Kelli, who witnessed Abbot Arnald's gift of the lands of Duueglas (Douglas) to Theobald the Fleming, c. 1150 (ibid., 107). See also MACILHAGGA.

GILMAKALI. Gylmakal,' vicar of Fotherues, was one of the witnesses to the great charter of Bishop Bricius founding the cathedral of Moray at Spyny, c. 1208–15 (REM., p. 43). Between 1224 and 1231 Gilmakali the judge of Caithness ('judex Catanie') witnessed a charter by Ferkar, earl of Ross, to Walter de Moravia of two davochs of land in Ross (ibid., p. 334). *MacCaille*, 'devotee of the veil,' was, according to the legend in the *Liber Hymnorum*, the name of the man who lifted up the veil over Brigit's head when the episcopal order was conferred on her by Bishop Mel (*Lives of the saints from the Book of Lismore*, p. 322–323).

GILMAKESSOC. St. Kessoc was an Irish Pict who labored in the Lennox and was martyred there by the Scots of Dalriada (A. D. 560). He is the patron saint of the parish of Luss. The name Kessoc or Kessan, says Macbain (*Macbain* III, p. 161) is "from 'ces' meaning 'spear' in Gaelic, but what it means in Pictish it

GILMAKESSOC, *continued*

is impossible to say." The place of the saint's burial was marked by Carn-ma-Cheasoig or Cairn of S. Kessog, a large cairn which existed as late as 1796 (OSA., xvii, p. 264; OPS., i, p. 30). Another tradition, equally authentic, says he was martyred abroad, and that, embalmed in sweet herbs, his body was brought for interment to the church of his native place, and that the herbs (*lus* in Gaelic) gave name to the parish. Gilleheshoc filius Johannis de Clechenes was a charter witness c. 1200 (*Cambus.*, p. 217). Gillemakessoc filius Gillemore was witness to a charter of the land of Lus to Maldoun filius Gillemore, c. 1250 (*Levenax*, p. 96), and in 1270 Maurice filius Gilmehesseoch, possibly a son of the preceding, was witness to a charter by Angus, son of Duncan Ferkardi (= Farquhar's son) (RMP., p. 138).

GILMER. A variant of GILMOUR, q.v.

GILMIN. Waldeve, son of Gillemin, was husband of Octreda or Ethreda, daughter of Gospatric, first earl of Dunbar (*Sc. Peer.*, iii, p. 245). Thomas Gilemyn of Heweden (Hauden), a Scotsman, was charged with murder, 1256 (*Bain*, i, 2047), and Gilminus, the tailor is in record, 1343 (*Melros*, p. 456).

GILMODAN, 'servant of (S.) Modan.' S. Modan was patron of Rosneath in Dumbartonshire, and appropriately enough it is there we find individuals bearing his name. *Modan* is from AIDAN, q.v., a diminutive of *Aed*, or rather of the later form of the name, *Aodh*, with the endearing prefix *mo*, 'my.' About the year 1199 Magister Michaele Gilmodyn, 'persona de Neuet' (i.e. Neveth = Rosneveth = Rosneath), is witness to 'carta de Cochnach et aliis terris ecclesie de Kilpatrick' by Alwinus comes de Levenax (RMP., p. 157; *Levenax*, p. 12). 'Gilmothan filius sacriste de Neueth,' c. 1230, witnessed a charter by Heuel' (i.e. Amelec = Aulay), brother of Maldowen, third earl of Lennox, granting a saltpan in his land of Rosneth to the monks of Paisley (RMP., p. 211); and in 1294 John MacGilmothan is mentioned in an inhibition by the bishop of Glasgow (ibid., p. °203). He is probably the John Makelmochan of Dumbartonshire who rendered homage in 1296 (*Bain*, ii, p. 202). His seal bears an eight-rayed flower and the legend 'S' *Johan Gilmotam*' (ibid., p. 544). Adam Malmodan (showing the *maol* prefix) was one of an inquest made at St. Andrews, 1302–3 (ibid., p. 350).

GILMORE. A variant of GILMOUR, q.v.

GILMOUR, GILMER, GILMORE. G. *Gille Moire,* 'servant of (the Virgin) Mary.' Some time between 1133 and 1156 Gilmor, son of Gilander, founded the chapelry of Treverman (now Trierman) in the parish of Walton, Cumberland. The chapel was constructed of wattlework *(capella de virgis),* and on its completion Gilmor appointed his kinsman Gillemore to the chaplaincy (*Victorian history of Cumberland*, ii, p. 17). These names, it may be mentioned, attest the strong Gaelic influence in Cumberland at that period. Gillemor, son of Gilleconel, possessed the lands of Fincurroks in the beginning of the twelfth century (*Kelso*, p. 79), and some time before 1144 'Gillemor filius Gilleconel' granted a half mark of silver to the church of S. Machute in Lesmahagow (*Kelso*, 187). Gillemure Albanach ('the Scot') and Gillemure mac Blancard witnessed the donation of the church of Torpennoth, etc. to Holyrood by Uchtred, lord of Galloway, between 1153–65 (LSC., p. 19, 20). Gillemore vicecomes de Clacmanan witnessed the gift by Malcolm iv of a carucate of land in Melchrethre to the church of St. Andrews (RPSA., p. 197); and Gillemure the deacon witnessed a charter by Symon, bishop of Stratherne (i.e. Dunblane) c. 1190 (*Inchaffray*, p. 1). Gillemur, senescallus Atholie, witnessed a confirmation by Henry, earl of Atholl, c. 1200 (RD., 148), and about 1190 or earlier 'Gylmor hund apud Dauwic' was a witness to the *Diuise de Stobbo* (REG., i, p. 89). Gillemor, son of Anecol, was witness to a charter by Gilbert, earl of Strathearn, between 1211–14 (LAC., p. 47), and another Gillemur held a toft near the lake of Lundin, Fife, c. 1250 (RPSA., p. 263). Gillemore Ruadh who witnessed a charter by Maldouen, earl of Levenax c. 1250 (*Levenax*, p. 98) appears in another charter of 1316 as Gillemoroch. About the same date the patronage of the church of Luss was granted to Gillemore and his father Maldouen, dean of Lennox (*Levenax*, p. 96, 97), and sometime before 1270 Gilmoir, servitor to Maldouen, appears as a charter witness in the Lennox (ibid., p. 20). Gillechad Gillamor witnessed a grant by Huctred, son of Fergus, of a carucate and toft in Creveqver (for Treveqver, i.e. Troqueer) to the Hospital of S. Peter of York, 1304 (*Bain*, ii, p. 422). Thomas Gilmur, indweller in Irwin, 1572 (*Irvine*, i, p. 58). The late Dr. John Milne, by the process of philological gymnastics familiar to readers of his works on place names, says Gilmour is for *Geal mor*, which was originally *Chuit mor*, aspirated, cattle-fold, and *mor* means big. Chuit was corrupted into white, which being regarded as an English name, was turned into Gaelic by *geal*, white! Gilmoure 1661, Gilmure 1598.

GILNEWLAND. Gilnewland McMay in 1541 appears as Gillonane McMoy in the same year, and is evidently the Gilnewland McInay who is recorded as tenant of Mealand, Islay (ER., XVII, p. 617, 620, 641).

GILOCLERY. Gyloclery, father of Morgund, earl of Mar, is Gillocher in a deed of 1171. Perhaps the true form is Gillechleire, 'servant of the clergy.' There is mention in 1290 of the restoration of the earldom of Mar to Morgund M'Gylochery (Bain, II, 465).

GILPATRICK. A Caithness surname. See under GILLEPATRIC.

GILPEDDIR, 'servant of Peter,' from the unaspirated form Peadar. Gilpeddir Mor was one of the crown tenants of Eddergoll in 1480 (Christie, Lairds and lands, p. 84). Gilpeuder (Fraser, p. 10). Cf. GILLIPETER.

GILQUHOME. From MACILWHAM, q.v. John Lech, son of deceased Gilzequhone or Gilquhome, had a grant of lands of Kildauanan in sheriffdom of Bute, 1429 (RMS., II, 123; OPS., II, p. 229). Morgund Gilquhome witnessed sasine of lands and barony of Inuernochy, 1507 (Illus., IV, p. 740). In 1510 an action was raised against Morn Gilquhomson and others in the sheriffdom of Aberdeen for "wrangwis occupacioun" of land (Illus., IV, p. 474).

GILROY. G. Gille ruaidh, 'red (haired) lad.' Ewen Gilry witnessed a deed of resignation of lands in the barony of Drumelzier in 1331 (Hay, p. 9). The hero of the well-known ballad (executed 1638) had his name changed in the low country speech to Gilderoy. See MACILROY.

GILRUTH, GELRUTH. The Gillroid mac Gillemartan of the old Clan Cameron genealogy (1467) is evidently the Gilleroth filius Gillemartin who was witness to a grant of lands in Carric in 1223 (Melros, p. 172). This Gilleroth is probably the Gilroth or Gilrod, aider and abettor of Thomas, the illegitimate son of Alan, lord of Galloway (ES., II, p. 496–498). Gylleroch (t misread as c) of Urquhart witnessed an agreement (compositio) regarding the lands of the church of Urquhart, 1233 (REM., 83). Gilruth (Gylruth or Gilrouth) was burgess of Roxburgh c. 1338 (Dryburgh, p. 261; BNCH., XXIV, p. 226). William Gilruth was one of the burgesses of Aberdeen chosen to accompany the provost to the field of Harlaw, 1411 (Fraser, p. 20). Thomas Gilrebth was admitted burgess of Aberdeen, 1444, and John Gilrutht the same in 1489 (NSCM., I, p. 9, 34), and Duncan Gilrucht contributed to repairs of a church there in 1508 (CRA.,

p. 79). Jhone Gilrowth deponed to the right boundaries of the Monk Myre, 1546 (Cupar-Angus, II, p. 4), and in 1555 is recorded the obit of William Gilrwif in Aberdeen (SCM., I, p. 78). James Gilrwitht was witness in a witch trial in St. Andews, 1575 (St. Andrews, p. 415). Denoyis Gilruff in Over Powneill, parish of Lesmahago, 1623 (Lanark CR.). William Gillreith (Gilreith or Gilrooth) was a farmer in Aberdeen, 1689 (RPC., 3. ser. XIV, p. 665, 666). Gilrooff 1688.

GILRYE. A variant of GILROY, q.v.

GILSTON. From the lands of Gilston in the parish of Newburn, Fife. John de Gilstoun was a witness in 1445 (Cambus., 214). Still a surname.

GILZEAN. G. Gill'Eðin, 'servant of (S.) John.' The z is pronounced y. James Gilzean in Trows, 1696, and four more of the name are recorded in Moray (Moray). Gillzean 1695, Gilzeane 1633. See GILLEAN and MACLEAN.

GIMPSIE. A surname recorded in Galloway. In 1684 Macgimsie (Parish). From Ir. Mac Dhiomasaigh, 'son of Diomasach,' proud, haughty, a rare Ulster surname (Woulfe).

GIRDWOOD. Of local origin from Girdwood at Carnwath, Lanarkshire. James Girdvod was one of an inquest at Carnwath, 1524 (CBBC., p. 14). David Girdwood in Kerse, parish of Carnwath, 1622, and sixteen more are recorded in the Lanark Commissariot Record. Adam Girdwood, shoemaker in Edinburgh, is recorded in 1657 (Edinb. Marr.), Isobel Girdwood in Grinlaw in 1675 (Lauder), and George Girdwood, 'incola de Sauchtone,' was retoured heir of Thomas Girdwood his grandfather in 1677 (Retours, Edinburgh, 1242). Rev. Thomas Girdwood (1802–1861) was Secession minister of Penicuik where he was ordained in 1831. His son and successor, Rev. William Girdwood, succeeded in Penicuik in 1862, and afterwards went out as missionary to Kaffraria. Old: Girdwod, Gyrdvid, Gyrdvod.

GIRIC. King Giric (Gyric, Girig, or Cirig), fourth in succession from Kenneth I, is termed by Pictish Chronicle Ciricius, and elaborated by Fordun (Chronicle, IV, 16) into Gregorius. He is the 'Gregory the Great' of the feudal fabulists and the legendary ancestor of the Macgregors. King Giric probably adopted S. Quiricus or Cyricus, martyr of Antioch, as his patron saint from the resemblance in sound to his own name, which comes from the root seen in G. cir, a comb, crest. Girig is the source of modern GREIG, q.v. See GILLEGIRG. The influence of the Greek Church appears to

GIRIC, *continued*

have reached the east coast of Scotland as early as the first half of the eighth century. It was about that time that S. Andrew displaced Peter as the patron saint of Scotland.

GIRTHRIG. Local. There is a Girtrig near Irvine, Ayrshire. John Girthrig in Redslap, 1712 *(Wigtown)*.

GIRVAN. From Girvan, the name of a parish and town in Ayrshire. Andrew Girvane was custumar of Irvine, 1529, and Sir William Girvan was witness in same year *(Ros, 1018)*. Gyrvane 1556. As Girvin in Edinburgh 1941.

GISBURN. A rare surname in Scotland. Henry de Gyseburn, "frater" (friar), witnessed a composition anent the tithes of Strathylif in 1229 *(REM., p. 87)*. Thomas Gysburne or Gyseburne is recorded in North Berwick in 1561 *(CMN., 80, 81)*, and Margaret Guvsburn in Edinburgh in 1677 *(Edinb. Marr.)*. From Gisburne, a parish near Clitheroe, Yorkshire.

GIVEN, Givens. Thomas Given, miles, witnessed a charter of "vnum rete super matricem aquam de Thei" (Tay) by David de Haya to the monks of Cupre, 1214–49 *(SCM., II, p. 307)*. John Givene in Auchlochane, parish of Lesmahago, 1630 *(Lanark CR.)*, James Given was minister at Blackford, 1655 *(Dunblane)*, William Givane alias Wardlaw in Westerhoill of Craigbarnet, parish of Campsie, 1666 *(Campsie)*, and John Given, tailor in Neilstoune, 1679 *(RPC., 3. ser. VI, p. 297)*. Givaine 1649.

GLACK. From Glack in the parish of Daviot, Aberdeenshire. Alicia de Glak held the lands of Glak in 1381 *(REA., I, p. 135)*.

GLADHOC. Robertus Gladhoc, juror on inquisition at Peebles, 1262 *(APS., I, p. 101 red; Peebles, 5)*.

GLADSTONE, Gladston, Gledstone. From Gledstanes, Lanarkshire, now the name of a farm in the Upper Ward of Clydesdale, about four miles north of Biggar. Herbert de Gledstan or Gledestane of the county of Lanark, who took the oath of fealty to Edward I in 1296 is the first of the name on record. His seal bears an eight-leaved flower, and *S' Herb' d' Gledstan (Bain, II, p. 204, 558)*. William de Gledstanes witnessed a charter by Roger de Auldton, c. 1354 *(Kelso, p. 387)*, and Sir William of Gledstanes, probably the same person, was present at the battle of Poitiers in 1356 *(Fordun, I, p. 377n)*. Andrew de Gledstan was a witness in Brechin in 1364 *(REB.,*

I, 21), Andrew of Gledstanis was arrested in Norwich, England, in violation of the truce in 1396 *(Bain, IV, 483)*, Magister Amere Gledstanys witnessed an instrument of sasine of the lands of Mernys and Nether-pollok in 1454 *(Pollok, I, p. 176)*, Thomas Gledstane was admitted burgess of Aberdeen in 1480 *(NSCM., I, p. 29)*, and in 1488 there was a concord between Stene Lokart and John of Gledstanis *(Lanark, p. 3)*. Sir John Gladstone, father of the late William Ewart Gladstone, on 10th February 1835 obtained the royal license to change his name from Gladstones to Gladstone. The meaning of the name (ME. *glede stan*), is "the stone or rock frequented by the glede" a species of hawk. In the Museum in Hawick is preserved an old Bible which was formerly the property of the Gledstaines of that Ilk *(Memories of Hawick, p. 192)*. Gladistane 1487, Gladstanis 1664, Gladsteanis 1597, Glaidstainis 1634, Glaidstanis 1603, Glaidstouns 1631, Glattstouns 1599, Gledstaines 1649, Gledstains 1649, Gledstand 1504, Glestanis 1505. The name became Gladtsten in Sweden.

GLAISTER. From the old lands of Glaister or Glacester in Angus. The name of the old family was originally 'de Dunde.' Eustace de Glasletter witnessed perambulation of the lands of Conan and Tulloch, 1254 *(RAA., I, 366)*, and Beel de Glacelester witnessed a charter by Cristina de Valoniis c. 1256 *(Panmure, II, 141)*. John de Glasreth filius et heredes quondam domini Radulphi de Dunde had a receipt for ten marks due him in 1312 (ibid., p. 157; HP., II, p. 116). In 1315 as John de Glassereth, lord of that Ilk, he granted to Dugald Cambel and his wife his lands of Knocnagullaran *(OPS., II, p. 45)*. Gilbert de Glassester mentioned in 1368 as *dominus ejusdem (Panmure, II, p. 177)* in 1371 had a grant from David II of the lands of Edderlings, Cambysenew, etc. *(RMS., I, App. II, 1046)*, and as Gilbertus de Glascestre had a grant from Robert II of all the lands of Glacestre and castle of the same in the sheriffdom of Argyll, 1374 *(RMS., I, 461)*. In the first half of the fifteenth century their lands had passed into the possession of the Scrymgeours of Dundee. Murthacus Glastre was admitted burgess of Aberdeen, 1444 *(NSCM., I, p. 8)*, Matthew Glastre was one of an assize there in 1448 *(CRA., p. 401)* and Andrew Glastir the same in 1457 *(RAA., II, 108)*.

GLAMES. Stephen del Glames held lands near Lyntonrothrik, c. 1200 *(RHM., II, 3)*. Perhaps from Glamis in Angus (in 1187 Glammes).

GLANDERSTONE. Of local origin from the old five merk lands of Glanderstoun in the parish of Neilston, Renfrewshire. William filius Johannis de Glanderstone witnessed a notarial instrument in 1412 (*Pollok*, I, p. 146).

GLAS. An old Gaelic personal name found in Dunmaglas, *Dùn Mac Glais*, 'fort of the sons of Glas' (*Watson* I, p. 238). See GLASS.

GLASCORY. From Glascorry, Lethnot, Brechin. John de Glascory appears in Brechin in 1450 (REB., I, 159).

GLASDERCUS. A 'countryman' who questioned S. Columba regarding his son's future (*Adamnan*, I, 16). OIr. *glas derc*, 'grey eyed.'

GLASENWRIGHT. This surname, probably now obsolete in Scotland, is derived from the occupation of 'glazier,' a trade formerly held in honor. In Latin documents it was rendered by *vitrearius*. In 1237 Ricardus vitrearius was one of the witnesses to a charter by Andrew, bishop of Moray (REM., 121). He was, says Cosmo Innes, without doubt one of the persons employed in building the cathedral church of Elgin (ibid., intro., p. xiii). William Vitrearius was one of the temporary bailies of Elgin in 1343, and Thomas Vitruarius was a burgess there in 1363 (REM., p. 313). Johannes Glasinwricht was presbyter of the diocese of Moray in 1406 (RPSA., p. 11), David Glassynwricht, chaplain in Ayr, 1429 (*Ayr*, p. 83); in 1466 a 'carta feodifirmi pro Cudbert Knytheson' was witnessed by John Glasynwryth (*Kelso*, 531), probably the Sir John Glassinwright, sub-prior of 1477 (HMC., 12. Rep., App. 8, p. 122). In 1497 James Glasynwrycht was one of the witnesses to a charter by Roger Weyr de Rogerhill (*Kelso*, 534), George Glaiswrycht was tenant of the Mill of Birnie in 1565 (REM., p. 440), and Margaret Glassinwrecht or Glassinwrycht, probably a descendant of Richard the vitrearius above, is in record in Elgin in 1576 and 1582 (*Elgin*, I, p. 152, 166). Glessinvrycht 1567.

GLASFORD, GLASSFORD, GLASFURD. Late in the thirteenth century the lands of Glasforde in Strathaven, Lanarkshire, were in possession of a family who took their name from the lands. Alexander de Glasfrith was escheator south of the Forth in the English service in 1289–90 (*Bain*, II, p. 100). Roger de Glasford and Aleyn fiz Roger de Glasfrithe or Glasfrethe of the county of Lanark rendered homage in 1296. The seal of Aleyn bears the Agnus Dei and S' *Alani de Glasfrit* (ibid., II, p. 203, 212, 213, 544). About 1300 Sir Alan de Glasfrud witnessed a donation by Herbert de Maxwell (RMP., p. 104), and Master Andrew

de Glasfrith was appointed sequestrator of the provostry of St. Mary's in St. Andrews by William Lamberton, bishop of St. Andrews, in 1306 (*Bain*, II, 1822). Alan de Glasfurth, c. 1317, witnessed a grant of the church of Largis to the monks of Paisley by Walter the High Steward (RMP., p. 237), and near the same date Alan de Glachfrith held the lands of Mucherach in the Lennox (*Levenax*, p. 61). John de Glassrith had an annuity granted him in 1328 (ER., I, p. 115), John of Glasfurde of Welshehawe was servant to James Hamilton in 1425 (*Bain*, IV, 986), Willelmus de Glasfurd witnessed a notarial instrument in 1413 (*Pollok*, I, p. 146), and John Glasfuird in Maxwood was retoured heir of John Duncane in Barnaycht in 1636 (*Retours, Ayr*, 315). The lands of Glasforde were granted to Johannes Sympille, son and heir of Thomas Sympille, by John, earl of Carric, which gift was confirmed by Robert II in 1373 (RMS., I, 490). Glasford 1694. The early forms of the place name point to a Welsh or Gaelic origin (W. *ffridd*, G. *frith*, early loans from OE. *friδ*, forest). Brigadier-General Glassford was chief of police in Washington, D. C., during Hoover's administration.

GLASGOW. From the old burgh now the city of Glasgow. John de Glasgu was chaplain of Gamelin, bishop of St. Andrews in 1258 (RPSA., p. 173), Andrew de Glasgow, escheator in 1289 (ER., I, p. 47), and John of Glasgow appears as a monk of Holyrood in 1299 (*Bain*, II, 1052). Payment was made to John de Glasgu in 1343 for the table of the king's servants (ER., I, p. 531), Alan Glasgw was murdered in 1494 (*Trials*, I, p. 19*), Robert Glasgow was a witness in the burgh in 1554 (*Protocols*, I), and John Glasgow was creditor of Mr. William Cuninghame in 1761 (*Irvine*, I, p. 121). Mac Giolla-Domhnaigh (*Some Anglicised surnames in Ireland*, p. 25) says that this name in Ulster is an Anglicized form of McCluskey (*MacBhloscaidhe*).

GLASHAN. From (MAC)GLASHAN, q.v. The lands of Drumfolaty were let to Glaschen MkGow in 1473 (*Cupar-Angus*, I, p. 205). The name is also found in Peebles in 1506 (*Peebles*, p. 41), Duncan Gleschan was tenant in Drumfallantin, 1512 (*Cupar-Angus*, I, p. 283), and Thomas Glaschen was 'post' in Aberdeen in 1592 (SCM., V, p. 117). Gleschane 1517, Glesthane 1524.

GLASS. Either simply from the adjective *glas*, 'grey,' or a shortened form of *Mac Gille glais* (or *Mac Ghille ghlais*), 'son of the grey lad.' Glass of Ascog in Bute existed as one of the

GLASS, *continued*

families locally called barons from the fifteenth century till recently (*Stodart*, II). In 1506 there is record of a grant of half the lands of Langilculcreich in Bute to Alexander Glass (RMS., II, 2987). The name is also in record in Perth in 1674 (*Methven*, p. 103), and fifteen of the name are recorded in the Commissariot Record of Dunblane from the sixteenth to the eighteenth century. Donald Glasse in Dingwall is mentioned in 1652 (IDR., p. 239), and John Glass was a 'bucher (butcher) in Elgine,' 1674 (ibid., p. 45). The Rev. John Glass, minister of Tealing, was founder of the religious body known as 'Glassites' (later Sandemanians). In a letter to the *Oban Times* some years ago the late Mr. Henry Campbell, an accurate genealogist, says: "I know of at least one case where a small family of Campbells showed every indication of forgetting their surname and settling down as Glass — because an ancestor happened I suppose, to go grey at an early age; and I have little doubt there are persons now labelled as Glass who are really Campbells." See also MACGILLEGLAS. *Glas* is also an old Gaelic personal name, whence Dunmaglas (*Dùn Mac Glais*), 'fort of the sons of Glas' (*Watson* I, p. 238).

GLASSFORD. *See under* GLASFORD.

GLAY. A family of this name in the twelfth century were vassals of the Stewarts. Roger Glai or Roger filius Glaii appears between 1164 and 1177 as witness in charters by Walter filius Alani to the Abbey of Paisley (RMP., p. 86, 87). Between 1175 and 1199 Raañ Corbeht gave to his man ('homini nostro', i.e. serf), William Gley, a plenary toft in Glasgow (REG., p. 37). Between 1207 and 1240 Roger, son of Glay (Glaii or Glayne), probably a son of the before mentioned Roger, appears frequently as a charter witness (RMP., p. 19, 209; LSC., 66; LIM., p. xxix; *Levenax*, p. 14). Rogerus filius Glay witnessed a charter of Alexander II of a fishing in the thanage of Scon in 1234 (*Scon*, p. 41), Willelmus Gley 'tunc prepositus' witnessed the sale of a land in Glasgow c. 1280-90 (REG., p. 198), and William le fiz Gley was appointed keeper of the Castle of Kyrktologhe in 1296 (*Bain*, II, p. 225). John del Glay or del Glaw of the county of Lanark rendered homage in 1296 (ibid., II, 812, and p. 204), and Alexander le fitz Glay was a Scots prisoner of war in Rockingham Castle in 1297 (ibid., 925). The family of Glay ended in an heiress, Isabel, daughter of Sir Roger de Glay, in the reign of David II. Donald Gley in Aberdeen, 1408 (CWA., p. 314).

GLEDLAW. Local. John Gledlaw was burgess of Forfar, 1509 (RAA., II, p. 386). A Gled Burne near Kyncoldrum is mentioned in 1458 (ibid., p. 104).

GLEDSTONE. A rare current form of GLADSTONE, q.v.

GLEGG, GLEIG. The name Glegg, Gleig, or Glyge is traditionally of French origin, but no evidence is produced in support of the statement. Rogers (*Geneal. memoirs of family of Robert Burns*, p. 20) says first of the family of whom we have any authentic record is Adam Glyge mentioned on a tombstone in Marykirk, 1698. But 'Mr. John Glyg, maister of the Grammare Schoole' of Dundee is in record, 1622 (MCM., II, p. 44).

GLEN, GLENN. From the lands of Glen in the parish of Traquair, Peeblesshire. Colban del Glen received a legacy left him by the queen, 1328 (ER., I, p. 116), and in the same year King Robert I. confirmed to Colban del Glen and Anabile his spouse the land of Quilte in the sheriffdom of Peebles (RHM., I, 35). In the following year there is recorded an annuity to Roger del Glen (ER., I, p. 209), probably the Roger del Glen who rendered to Exchequer the accounts of the provost of Peebles at Scone, 1332 (ER., I). Duncan de Glene was a witness in 1368 (*Coll. AGAA.*, II, p. 48). John de Glene witnessed a charter of Longneuton c. 1377 (RHM., II, p. 4), and another John de Glen who witnessed confirmation of the lands of Mircarny in Fife, 1386 (*Wemyss*, II, p. 19) may be the John de Glen who was present at perambulation of the bounds of Kyrknes and Louchor, 1395 (RPSA., p. 5). Margaret de Glen granted the lands of Harlaw and others to Walter Ogilvy of Luntrathin, 1420 (SCM., IV, p. 115), Thomas of Glen had a safe conduct into England, 1422 (*Bain*, IV, 914), and William Glen, armiger, was witness in Paisley, 1452 (RMP., p. 250).

GLENCAIRN. From Glencairn in Nithsdale, Dumfriesshire. Sir Fergutianus de Glenkarn appears as witness in a document of c. 1222 (*Dryburgh*, 62), and as Fergus de Glencarn appears as witness in Dumfries about the same period (LSC., 70).

GLENCAIRNIE. From the old lands of Glencairnie in Moray. Gilbert de Glencarny witnessed a charter by Malise, earl of Strathern, between 1258 and 1271 (LIM., p. xxxiii). About 1278 as Sir Gilbert de Glenchernie (miswritten Glencheruie) he witnessed a charter by Malcolm de Moravia to his son

(REM., p. 461), and between 1281-98 he granted a charter to Duncan of Feryndrawcht of the east davoch of the land of Conynges (*Grant*, III, p. 7). Sir Gilbert de Glynkerny of the county of Elgin rendered homage for his lands in 1296 (*Bain*, II, 808 and p. 211). Malmore de Glencharny had a charter of land in Badenoch, viz. Dalnafert and Kinrorayth in 1338 (SCM., IV, p. 125), and in 1362 Gilbert de Glencharny got a charter from David II of the barony of Glencharny in the sheriffdom of Invernes and county of Moray (RMS., I, 116). The family retained Glencairnie till 1391 when they exchanged it for Fochabers (*Grant*, III). Glenkerni 1307, Glenkerny 1296, Glymcarny 1296.

GLENCORSE. A Dumfriesshire surname derived from the lands of Glencrosh near Moniaive, old spellings of which are Glencros, Glencrosche, Glencrash, and Glencorse. Thomas Glencors, a Scot, born in Anaunt, received letters of denization in England in 1480 (*Bain*, IV, 1465), and Margaret Glencorss was retoured heir of Alexander Glencorss *de eodem*, her grandfather, in 1609 (*Retours, Dumfriesshire*, 65). John Glencors and James Glencors, followers of the earl of Cassilis, were respited for murder in 1526 (RSS., I, 3386). Andro Glencorse in Peirstoune was burnt for poisoning and adultery in 1580, and in the following year John Glencorse of that Ilk was murdered at Gribtoune (*Trials*, I, p. 84; II, p. 507). Jean Glencrose, widow in Dumfries in 1687 (RPC., 3. ser. XIII, p. 169). (2) Johannes, clericus, de Glenkrosch, who witnessed the sale of a tenement in Gouertun in 1317 (*Neubotle*, p. 306), probably derived his name from Glencorse in Midlothian. Glencross 1713.

GLENDAY, GLENDY. A common name in Angus from the district of that name. William Glendy obtained a decree against the earl of Craufurd in 1569 (RPC., I, p. 686). Glendei 1690.

GLENDINNING. From the lands of the name in Westerkirk, Dumfriesshire. Douglas (*Baronage*) states that a charter was granted by John Macgill of that Ilk (*de eodem*) to Adam de Glendonwyn of all his part of the lands and baronies of Clifton and Merbotel in the shire of Roxburgh prior to 1286. In 1313 Sir Adam obtained a discharge of all bygone feu-duties from Archibald Douglas, lord of Galloway, and in 1398 John of Glendonwyne and Symoun of Glendonwyne were two of the 'borowis' for the earl of Douglas's bounds of the West March, and Symon of Glendonwyn was hostage for Archibald, earl of Douglas, 1408 (*Bain*,

IV, 512, 762). William de Glendonwyn was procurator of the Scottish 'Nation' in the University of Orleans in 1408 (SHSM., I, p. 73), and in the same year died Matthew de Glendonwyn, bishop of Glasgow (*Dowden*, p. 317). William de Glendonwyn appears as rector of Crawfurdjon in 1450 and as canon of the church of Glasgow, 1467 (REG., p. 379, 380). Symon of Glendynwyn was one of the conservators of the truce between Scotland and England, 1451 (*Bain*, IV, 1239). Goods were stolen from Bartholomew Glendunwyne, 1504 (*Trials*, I, p. 41°). In 1587 the Glenduningis were named among the unruly clans on the West March (APS., III, p. 466), and in 1599 Robert Glendonying was retoured heir in lands in parish of Balmaghie (*Retours, Kirkcudbright*, 41). Isabel Glindinine appears in Doucat Maines, 1667 (*Lauder*), John Glendinning joined Montrose and in consequence was outlawed and his lands forfeited. The direct line is said to have ended in 1720, but William Glendonwyn of that Ilk is mentioned in 1798 (*Kirkcudbright*). In the north of Ireland the name is spelled Clendinnon. Gladinin (in Froissart), Glendonewyne 1380, Glendoning 1599, Glendonyng 1637, Glendovyn 1492, Glendowyn 1493, Glendunwyn 1488, Glendynwene 1545, Glendynwyng 1530; Glendinan, Glendoinnowing, Glendonning, Glendonwin, Glendounn, Glendouwyn, Glendouwyne, Glendouyn, Glendowyne, Glendverneyn.

GLENDOCHART. From the district of Glendochart in the parish of Killin, Perthshire. John de Glendocher or Glendochir witnessed a charter by Maldoveny, earl of Levenax, 1238 (*Levenax*, p. 13; RMP., p. 161). Malcolm de Glendochyr who witnessed a charter by Malise, earl of Strathern c. 1260 (HMC., 2. Rep., App., p. 166), as Malcolm de Glendochrad is witness again in 1284 (LIM., XXXVI). He is probably the Maucolum de Glendughred or Glindoghride of Perthshire who appears twice as rendering homage in 1296. His seal bears two birds at the foot of a palm tree regardant, S' *Malcolmi de Glen* . . . (*Bain*, II, p. 199, 202, 533). Patrick de Glendoghrad of Perthshire also rendered homage in 1296. His seal bears an eight-raved figure, S' *Pa* . . . *cii de Glendoir*(?) (ibid., p. 200, 531). As Patrick de Glendhouchret he was juror on an· inquisition held at Perth in 1304 (ibid., 1592). Glendochart, says the duke of Argyll, has apparently been thought to have been held previous to 1300 by the Macgregors. This he believes to be erroneous, and that the Glendocharts were of Campbell origin (HP., IV, p. 49).

GLENDY. See *under* GLENDAY.

314

GLENESK. Of territorial origin from the barony of the same name in Angus. The first of the name recorded is John de Glenesk who witnessed a grant by Christian, widow of Sir Peter Maule of Panmure to John Lydl about 1256 (*Panmure*, II, 141). As John de Glenesch, miles, he witnessed c. 1260, the charter of Rossy to Walter de Rossy (RAA., I, p. 336). The same or succeeding John de Glenesk was one of the subscribers to the letter of the community of Scotland to Edward I of England consenting to the marriage of his son Prince Henry to Princess Margaret in 1289 (APS., I, p. 85). Johan de Glennysk and Morgund de Glennesk, both of the county of Forfare, took the oath of fealty in 1296 (*Bain*, II, p. 199). The seal of the latter bears a shield with bend charged with escallops (?), field crusily, and S' *Morgvndi de Glenesk* (ibid., p. 550).

"Who the early Norman or Normanised lords of Glenesk may have been, and whence they came, are questions to which no certain answer can be given. In the most ancient records, from about 1260 onwards, they appear simply under the territorial designation of de Glenesk. That they were a Normanised native family, rather than immigrants, is suggested by the fact that one of them, Morgund de Glenesk, who swore fealty to Edward I at Berwick 28th August, 1296, has a Celtic name. It is not proved, but is exceedingly likely, that these de Glenesks were the descendants of a family named Abbe, of whom Malise, John, Morgund, and Michael are successively on record as disposing of lands in Glenesk early in the thirteenth century. This family almost certainly took its origin from the lay *abs* or abbots of a Celtic monastic foundation, probably established by St. Drostan, with whose name the primitive Christianity of the district is associated. At a later period in the thirteenth century we have records of a family of Stirling or Strivelyn de Glenesk: but whether these were of the same stock as the earlier lords who are styled simply 'of Glenesk,' it does not seem possible now to say. In or about 1357, Catherine Stirling, heiress of Glenesk, married Sir Alexander, third son of Sir David Lindsay of Crawford, and thereby acquired the barony of Glenesk" (Dr. W. Douglas Simpson in PSAS., LXV, p. 117–118).

GLENGAVEL. Marie de Glengavel or Glengevel of the county of Lanark who rendered homage in 1296 (*Bain*, II, p. 204, 206) derived her name from the old lands of Glengavill in the barony of Strathaven. Edwart Glengawell appears in Carnwath, 1534 (CBBC., p. 164).

GLENHOLM. Gillecrist, the son of Daniel at Glenwhym was one of the witnesses to the perambulation of the marches of Stobbo c. 1190 (REG., p. 89). Sir Nicholas de Gleynwim or Glenwim, rector of the church of Yetholm, a Pope's knight, was witness to a charter of the lands of Stobbou c. 1233 (ibid., p. 111, 142). In 1293 Stephen of Glynwhym was appointed guardian of Magduf, the son of Malcolm sometime earl of Fife (*Rot. Scot.*, I, p. 18). Stevene de Glenwhym of the county of Peebles who rendered homage in 1296 (*Bain*, II, p. 207) is probably the same person. He or a later Steven appears a few years afterwards as witness to charters of lands in the neighborhood (*Melros*, p. 319). Peter de Glynquym is recorded in 1304 as heir of Johanna de Blamyr, his mother (*Bain*, II, p. 415), and Robert of Glenquhym had a confirmation of the lands of Wra in the barony of Glenquhym in 1451 (RMS., II, 481). Dene James Glenquhom was a monk of Kelso in 1466 (*Kelso*, p. 424), Joisse Glenquhin was at horn for slaughter in 1495 (*Trials*, I, p. 22*), and James Glenquhum who had a remission for the slaughter of John Halywell in 1535 (RSS., II, 1642) may be the James Glenquhome who appears as a witness in 1557. John Glenwhome is recorded in Symington, Lanarkshire, in 1687, and William Glenholm in Carnwath in 1732 (*Lanark CR.*). From the barony of Glenholm in the parish of the same name, now united with Broughton and Kilbucho.

GLENILEF. John of Glenylef or John Glenylay was tenant of Kemphill, 1474–82 (*Cupar-Angus*, I, p. 193, 233). From Glenylif the old spelling of Glen Isla, Perthshire.

GLENISON. Adam Glenyson was admitted burgess of Aberdeen, 1407 (NSCM., I, p. 2), and Angus Glenison held a tenement "in vico furcarum," there in 1436 (REA., I, p. 234). Angus Glennysone, burgess of Aberdeen, died c. 1500 (ibid., II, p. 203).

GLENMELLON. A charter in favor of John de Glenmalwing or Glenmalyng is dated 1450 (REA., II, p. 296). Murthairus Glenmalin admitted burgess of Aberdeen in 1473 may be the Mordacus Glenmalwyne, burgess there in 1491 (NSCM., I, p. 23; REA., I, p. 328). John Glenmaluin was member of council of Aberdeen in 1484, and John Glenmaluyn is recorded as burgess there in 1487 (CRA., p. 41, 43). The land of Mordacus Glenmalwing, a descendant perhaps of the above-mentioned Murthairus, is mentioned c. 1550 (REA., II, p. 234). Of local origin from Glenmillan in the parish of Lumphanan, or from the Glenmilling of 1699 (*Retours, Aberdeen*).

GLENNEA. Perhaps from Glenae, Amisfield, Dumfriesshire. Christian Glennea in the parish of Govan, 1623 (*Campsie*).

GLENNIE, GLENNY. Of local origin from Gleney or Glennie in Braemar, Aberdeenshire. Glennie is a surname of some antiquity in and about Aberdeen, and both forms of the name were borne by generations of tenant farmers in the districts of both Dee and Don (*Jervise*, II, p. 123). William Gleny had a lawsuit in Aberdeen, 1398–9, with respect to the wool from certain lands (CRA., p. 372; Kennedy, *Annals of Aberdeen*). These lands are still called "Glennie's Parks." Angus Gleny is recorded in Aberdeen, 1408 (CWA., p. 313), and in the following year mass was said in the church for the wife of Angus Glennie. John Glenning was in Kinkell in 1473 (ALA., 24), and Robert Glynne was admitted burgess of Aberdeen, 1554 (NSCM., I, p. 64). James Stuart Stuart-Glennie wrote on *Arthurian localities; their historical origin*, 1869, etc. Glenna 1556, Glennay 1503.

GLENORCHY. From Glenorchy in Lorn, Argyllshire. John de Glenurchwar, Scots prisoner of war taken at Dunbar, 1296 (*Bain*, II, 742) is again mentioned as John Gleniarchwar, and in following year, as John Glenurhard, was liberated to serve the king of England abroad (ibid., 875, 940).

GLESLOGY. From Claslogie an old spelling of Carslogie in parish of Cupar. Robert Gleslogy who witnessed a charter of the lands of Glack, 1272 (*Inverurie*, p. 50) may be Robertus de Glasclogy, charter witness in Aberdeen, 1276 (REA., II, p. 278).

GLESPIE. Perhaps a shortened form of GILLESPIE, q.v. Robertus Glespy in Aberdeen, 1408 (CWA., p. 317). Joannes Glespie in Kilmernok, 1644 (*Retours, Ayr*, 390).

GLOAG. The marriage of Janet Glook in Perth is recorded in 1565 (*Northern notes and queries*, I, p. 165). James Glook in Vindiage, 1612 (*Inquis. Tut.*, 1293). Ninian Gloag in Annatland, 1670 (DPD., I, p. 293), and seventeen persons of the name are recorded in Dunblane and neighborhood from 1662 (*Dunblane*). James Gloak appears in Irvine, Ayrshire, 1700 (*Irvine*, II, p. 317). Gloog 1674.

GLOVER. From the trade or occupation of glove-maker, an important one in the Middle Ages. In Latin documents rendered *cirothecarius*. Henry Cirothecarius, burgess of Perth, swore fealty to Edward I at Perth in 1291 (*Bain*, II, 508), and Simon Glover or le Glovere, burgess of Perth, swore fealty in 1291 and again in 1296 (*Bain*, II, p. 124, 187, 197). Patrick Glovar or Glufar and Michael Glofar were burgesses of Glasgow in 1426 and 1440 (LCD., 245, 251), David Gluur was also a burgess there in 1468 (ibid., 183), and John Gluvar in 1494 (REG., 469). Nicholas Glofar was burgess of Irvine in 1446 (*Irvine*, I, p. 137), John Gluffar was merchant burgess of Linlithgow in 1610 (*Retours, Linlithgow*, 82), and James Glover is recorded in Poucroft in 1668 (*Kirkcudbright*). Catherine Glover is the heroine of Scott's *Fair maid of Perth*. Gl:uer 1504.

GLOWHOLME. Local. Agnes Glaholme in Ormistoune Mains, 1687 (*Peebles CR.*). Andrew Glowholme, indweller in Hutton, 1753 (*Lauder*).

GOAR. An old Orcadian surname. Andrew Gor, tacksman of Pretty, 1490 (REO., p. 409).

GOCELYN. A variant spelling of JOCELIN, q.v.

GODDARD. From the OE. personal name *Gōdheard*, 'god-firm,' ME. *Godard*. Now a rare surname in Scotland. Robert filius Godardi was one of an inquest made at Peebles, 1262 (APS., I, p. 101 red). William Godarde, a charter witness, 1320 (*Inchcolm*, p. 32). Peter Godard, 'bruer,' a Scot, had letters of denization in England, 1480 (*Bain*, IV, 1465). James Godard admitted burgess of Aberdeen, 1493 (NSCM., I, p. 36). Peter Gouderd, feltmaker, burgess of Edinburgh, 1734 (*Guildry*, p. 149).

GODDISKIRK. Andro Goddiskirk in Longfurd is mentioned in an act of the barony court of Calder, Lanark (*Analecta Scotica*, I, p. 399), and Richard Goddiskirk was burgess of Edinburgh, 1423 (*Egidii*, p. 45).

GODFREY. The ON. personal name *Guðröðr*, 'God's peace,' was early borrowed by the Gaels, appearing as *Gofraig* in Middle Gaelic (1467 MS.), in modern Gaelic as *Goraidh*. From it comes MACGORRIE, MACGORRY, q.v.

GODFREYSON, 'son of GODFREY,' q.v. John Godfrason who witnessed a quitclaim on the lands of Gladsmure, 1427, appears again in 1430 as Gothrasoun, sergeant to the sheriff, and also took part in the perambulation of the lands of Gladmor (*James* II, p. 14, 16).

GODRIC. From OE. personal name *Gōdric*, ME. *Godrich*. Dougal fiz Gothrik of the county of Dunfres who rendered homage in 1296 is probably Dougal Gotherykessone of the county of Wyggetone, and Dugall, son of Gotrich, juror on an inquest at Berwick in the same year (*Bain*, II, p. 210, 211, 215).

GODRICSON. 'Son of Gŏdric,' an OE. personal name. Dugall, son of Gotrich, who served on an inquest at Berwick, 1296, is probably the Dougal Gotherykessone of the county of Dumfries and the Dougal fiz Gothrik of Wyggetone who rendered homage in the same year (*Bain*, II, p. 210, 211, 215). Nigel fiz Gothrek of Dumfries also rendered homage at same time (ibid., p. 185). Murdac Gothreson witnessed a sasine in Fife, 1481 (*Laing*, 182).

GODSEL. Sir Thomas Godsel was chaplain of St. Nicholas within the burgh of Lanark at the time of the Reformation (OPS., I, p. 119). Lower, Bardsley, and Harrison derive the name from Godshill, Isle of Wight, but Weekley points out that "it is almost entirely a Gloucestershire and Herefordshire name," and suggests *Godescealc*, 'God's servant,' as one source of the name (p. 21, 42).

GODSMAN. This surname still exists in Aberdeenshire, and GOODSMAN is most probably a variant. James called 'Godisman' was canon of Brechin in 1298 (*Pap. Lett.*, I, p. 575), and John Godisman was juror on an inquisition made at St. Andrews in 1303 (*Bain*, II, 1350). Johnne Goddisman in Tulifour was convicted of spulzie in 1510 (RSCA., I, p. 96–97), James Godsman in Kellie appears in 1633 (ibid., II, p. 371), and in 1644 and 1650 there are entries of payments to 'post' George Goddisman of Aberdeen (SCM., v, p. 163, 174). James Godsman died in Old Deer in 1835, aged 100 years, and Willie Godsman was a well-known 'character' of Aberdeen in the first half of the nineteenth century.

GOGAR. From the lands of Gogar near Edinburgh. Henry de Goger witnessed a charter of the tithes of Baveley (now Bavelaw), c. 1200 (LSC., 57). William Gogar, a Covenanter, was hanged in the Grassmarket of Edinburgh in 1681 (PSAS., XLV, p. 233).

GOGY. William dictus Gogyn was vicar of the church of Inverkethyn, 1314 (RD., 344), and William Gogy or Gugy appears in 1330 as provost and custumar of the same town (ER., I, p. 267, 278, 304, 316). John Gugy was abbot of Neubotle between 1402–09 (*Neubotle*, pref., p. xxiv). John Guge in Aberdeen, 1493 (CRA., p. 49).

GOLD. An OE. personal name, *Gold(a*, from *gold*, the metal (*Redin*). Adam Gold, bailiff of Montrose, rendered homage, 1296 (*Bain*, II, p. 198). The surname is not uncommon in Angus and GOOLD may be a variant of it. Angus Gold in Over Kinmonth, 1582, and eight more of the name around Brechin are in record (*Brechin*).

GOLDER. Robert Golder, indweller in Hamilton, Lanarkshire, 1675 (*Campsie*). Harrison says it is the same as Gilder, from OE. *gold* + the agental suffix *-ere*.

GOLDIE. A diminutive of GOLD, q.v. This surname appears now to have its home in the shires of Ayr and Lanark. William Goldy, servitor to the bishop of Moray, 1567 (REM., p. 400). Edward Goldie of Craigmuie, 1718 (*Kirkcudbright*). Rev. John Goldie (1763–1847) was minister of the parish of Temple, Midlothian, for fifty years. GOUDIE is a variant.

GOLDING. Probably the OE. personal name *Golding*, i.e. Gold(a)'s son. The rashness of a Scots soldier, Ralph Golding, at the bridge of Rokesburgh in 1333 led to Sir Andrew Moray of Bothwell, the Regent, being taken prisoner by the English (*Hailes*, II, p. 197).

GOLDMAN. The name of a family long notable in the mercantile annals of Dundee, and supposed by some to have come from Flanders. Goldman, however, is an Old English personal name. The first of the name mentioned in Dundee records is James Goldman, admitted burgess in 1562. The name is found on tombstones in the Howff Cemetery, Dundee, as early as 1605, and Peter Goldman, a member of the family there commemorated, is author of Latin "Poemata" in the *Delitiae Poetarum Scotorum*, 1637, I, p. 364–376. Fifteen of the name are recorded in the Commissariot records of Brechin. William Goldman, junior, was heir of William Goldman, merchant burgess of Dundee in 1614 (*Inquis.*, 560). Golman 1632. For genealogical notes on various members of the family see *Wedderburn's Account book*, p. 106–107.

GOLDRING. From the old 50 shilling lands of Goldring in the bailiary of Kylestewart. Thomas of Goldringe held a land in Prestwick, 1511 (*Prestwick*, p. 42).

GOLDSMITH. From the occupation of "goldsmith." In early Latin records *Aurifaber*. William Aurifaber witnessed a gift of land to the Hospital of Soltre c. 1250–66 (*Soltre*, p. 32). Ewgenius (Ewen) aurifaber was one of an inquest at Dumbarton in 1271 (RMP., p. 191), and Martin Aurifaber appears as burgess of Aberdeen in 1281 (REA., II, p. 278). Walter Aurifaber, burgess of Roxburgh in 1285 (*Kelso*, 219) is doubtless "Walter the goldsmith, burgess and alderman of Roxburgh," who rendered homage in 1296 (*Bain*, II, p. 197). Rogier le orfeure (Fr. *orfevre*) of Berwick, also rendered homage in 1296 (ibid., II, p. 213). John Goldsmith (aurifaber) was bailie of Edinburgh in 1342 and rendered to

Exchequer the accounts of the city (ER., I, p. 489, 623). Gilbert Goldsmyth held a tenement in Irvine in 1426 (*Irvine*, I, p. 130). Johannes dictus Goldsmyth was prebendary of Crowdan (Cruden) in 1427 (REA., I, p. 228), Micael Goldsmyt was burgess of Dumfries in 1453 (*Edgar*, p. 226), Johannes Goldsmyth or Goldsmyt appears as a notary public in Glasgow in 1472 and 1488 (REG., p. 420, 463), and possessed a land there in 1494. Andrew Goldsmyth was member of a committee in Aberdeen in 1481 (CRA., p. 41). Goldsmicht 1493, Gouldesmyth 1549.

GOLIGHTLY. *See under* GALLETLY.

GOLLACH. A surname current in Caithness. From Gaelic *gallach*, a stranger, a Caithnessman. "The Norsemen were strangers to the Gaelic-speaking inhabitants" (*Beaton*). Henry Golliche was a parishioner of Clyne, 1566 (OPS., II, p. 723).

GOLLAN. From Gollan in Kinross-shire. William de Golin is witness in Fife c. 1216-24 (LAC., 70), and William Gollan was bailie of Linlithgow, 1359 (ER., I, p. 619). John Gollane was 'husband' in vill of Tullibothy, 1437 (SCM., v, p. 261), and William Gollan, a charter witness in Inverness, 1536 (*Laing*, 403). John Gollane was one of the burgesses of Stirling who attacked the cruives and fishings of the abbot and convent of Cambuskenneth, 1366 (*Cambus.*, 55). Gilbert Gollan, burgess of Inverness, 1556 (*Rec. Inv.*, I, p. 4) may be Gilbert Gollan who served on an inquest there in 1591 (OPS., II, p. 670). Alexander Gollane was bailie of Rosmarkie, 1568 (ibid., p. 544), Mungo Gollan and Robert Gollan were bailies there, 1600, and John Golland was 'custumer and uptacker of the toll pennie' in Inverness, 1603 (*Rec. Inv.*, II, p. 14, 15). George Gollon was a writer in Dundee, 1737 (*Brechin*), and John Gollan was a Jacobite prisoner in 1746. The name was liable to be confused in record with GULLANE, q.v.

GOOD. (1) probably from the OE. personal name *Goda* or *Code*. (2) shortened from a personal name, as Goodman, Goodrich, Goodwin. (3) less probably, I think, from the adjective 'good'. George Gude and Mariota Hommyll, his spouse, are mentioned in 1517 (RSS., I, 2946; for many additional references to him see *Inchcolm*, p. 135). Thomas Gude, bailie of Lowdoun, Ayr, 1533 (*Laing*, 390). John Gwid, mason, was builder of the tower of Pollok, 1536 (*Pollok*, I, p. 271), and John Gud held a tenement in Glasgow, 1555 (*Protocols*, I). Herbert Guid was infeft in lands of Auchencairn, 1561 (*Nisbet*, I, p. 219). Magnus

Guid, retoured heir of James Guid in Kirkwall, 1636, may be the Magnus Good, merchant and burgess of the same town, 1648 (*Retours, Orkney*, 23, 55). George Good was author of *Liberton in ancient and modern times*, Edinburgh, 1893. Godde 1564, Gud 1554.

GOODAL, GOODALL. Probably from Goodall (now Gowdale) in Yorkshire. William Gudeal held a carucate of land from the Abbey of Kelso in Witelaw, c. 1290 (*Kelso*, p. 461). John Guidall in Dysart, 1541 (*Dysart*, p. 7). Thomas Goodall was witness in Perth, 1544 (*Rollok*, 24). Payment was made to Andrew Goodeaill's wife, 1650 (SCM., v, p. 177). William Guidaill, burgess of Kirkwall, 1657 (*Retours, Orkney*, 86), John Gottal in Stitchill, 1658 (*Stitchill*, p. 14), Agnes Guiddell in Mure of Kirkbuddo, 1680 (*Brechin*), and John Goodale in Dumfries, 1689 (RPC., 3. ser. XIV, p. 688). Goodaile 1687.

GOODBRAND. A personal name, in ON. *Guðbrand*. James Goodbrang was in Boigtoun, Aberdeen, in 1716 (SCM., IV, p. 172), and John Goodbrand was 'cupar' in Keith, Banffshire, in 1721. Two Goodbrands were among the Jacobites of the '45, and James Goodbrand was member of Huntly Volunteers in 1798 (*Will*, p. 19). About Cullen, Banffshire, this surname is pronounced Gweebran. A family of Brands in the same district and contemporary may have been related.

GOODBURN. Local. Henry Thomas Goodburn of Peebles was married in 1941. There is a Goodsburn in Strathaven, Lanarkshire.

GOODFELLOW. Generally explained as 'good fellow,' 'good companion.' Bardsley records the name Godfelawe in Essex in 1273. John Guydfallo or Gudfallow, vicar of Glenberuy in 1434 and 1435 (REB., I, 60; II, 49), is probably the John Gudefalow who appears as presbyter of St. Andrews and notary public in 1469 (*Laing*, 160). Robert Gudefallow was charged with rescuing a felon in 1529 (*Trials*, I, p. 142*), Richard Gudfallow had a precept of remission in 1536 (RSS., II, 2033), and Robert Gudfallow was an inhabitant of Brechin in 1548 (REB., II, 200). William Guidfellow was heir of James Guidfellow in Leuchares in 1627 (*Inquis.*, 1328), David Goodfellow was servitor to the earl of Southesk in 1683 (*Brechin*), and William Goodfellow in Over Abbingtoun, parish of Craufurdjohn, 1662, and five more of the name are recorded in the Lanark Commissariot Records. The name also occurs in Edinburgh in 1632 (*Edinb. Marr.*), and William Goodfellow was tenant in Swinie, 1800 (*Heirs*, 513). Gudfallo 1592.

GOODHOSE. Robert Goodhose witnessed instrument of resignation of the lands of Wolle, 1474 (*Home*, 22).

GOODLAD. Stodart (II, p. 385) says Goodlet, old Gudlade, is an old surname and occurs in the neighborhood of Stirling in the fourteenth century. It is also an old surname in Fife, James Gudlad, king's sheriff, appears there in 1491 (*Dundas of Dundas*, p. lxvii). John Gudlawid was witness in Linlithgow, 1531 (*Johnsoun*). The name occurs in Perth in 1543 as Gudlat. Robert Guidlett, maryner in Kinghorn, was slain in 1574 when engaged at the fishing on the west coast of Ross-shire (*Coll.*, p. 100–101), and David Guidlaid, who appears as a scribe in St. Andrews, 1585 (*St. Andrews*, p. 556), may be David Gvdlad (1594) whose tombstone appears in St. Andrews churchyard (PSAS., XLV, p. 536, ill.). Joannes Guidlat of Uphall was heir to John Grahame, 1602 (*Inquis.*, 94). John Guidlaw, cordiner in Dysart, 1641 (*Dysart*, p. 51), Henry Guidlat of Abbotishauch appears in 1643 (*Inquis.*, 2832), and David Guidlaid was retoured heir of David Guidlaid, quondam bailie of St. Andrews, his father, 1645 (*Retours, Fife*, 649). Alexander Gudlait in Airth, 1655 (*Bruces of Airth*, p. cx), and in 1671 a criminal charge was made against John Guidlet or Guidlett of Abbotshall (*Just. Rec.*, II, p. 57, 74). Some early sixteenth century 'ferrylouper' (the name given a Scottish settler in Orkney and Shetland) from Fife, carried the name to the Shetland Islands, where it is still found as Goodlat, Goodlet, and Gudlad, and pronounced Goylat or Goalet. Isabella Goodlet died in Edinburgh, 1941. In Shetland the name is confined mainly to "The Ness," Tingwall, and Burra. Goodlate 1624, Goodlatt 1750, Gudlat 1625, Gudlet 1613. Weekley (p. 231) compares this name with Fr. *Bonvillain* and *Bonvalet*.

GOODLAND. Jonet Gudelande held a tenement in Glasgow, 1550 (*Protocols*, I). Bardsley and Harrison say from the OE. personal name *Godland*, and Harrison also as second guess says 'belonging to Go(o)dland.'

GOODLET. See GOODLAD.

GOODMAN. (1) The common OE. personal name *Godmann*, ME. *Godeman*, Latinized *Bonus Homo* and *Homo Dei (Searle)*. (2) In Scotland the designation given to a landowner however large his estate, who held his land not of the Crown but of a subject *(Joseph Bain)*.

GOODSIR. Now a rare Scots surname. Perhaps from Scots *gudsyr*, *gudschir* (pron.

'gutscher'), 'grandfather.' William dictus Godechere was prepositus of Crail, 1343 (ER., I, p. 520). Rev. Robert Wodrow in his *Correspondence* spells the name of Rev. James Goodsir as Gutcher.

GOODSMAN. A rare name in Scotland, most probably a variant of GODSMAN, q.v.

GOODSON. David Gudsoun, canon of Holyrood, 1547 (*Binns*, 40). Explained as = Fr. *Bonifant* (i.e. *bon enfant*) (*Weekley*, p. 247), and as 'son of Good' (*Harrison*).

GOODSWAIN. A family of this name was connected with the Abbey of Dunfermline in the fifteenth century. Andrew Gudswañ was a charter witness apud Dunfermlyn in 1412 (RD., p. 280). John Gudeswane, notary public in St. Andrews diocese in 1422 (*Cambus.*, 103) is probably the John Gudswan, notary public apud Dunfermelyn, who witnessed a charter of the lands of Halis near Edinburgh in 1438 (RD., 409). Andrew Gudsuane was a charter witness in Dunfermline in 1456 (ibid., 448), James Gudswan was 'ourman' in Dunfermline in 1491, vicar of Carnbee, and later dean of Fife (DBR., 34), and Schir Jhone Gudswayne was chaplain in Dunfermline in 1507 (RD., p. 361). Gudsuan 1492, Gudesvane 1504. The name may be for 'good swain,' i.e. good servant.

GOODWILLIE. Michael Gudwillie is recorded in Dempstertoun, Fife, in 1633 (RPC., 2. ser. V, p. 94), Walter Goodwillie in Burtreebush was charged with deforcement in 1680 (RPC., 3. ser. VI, p. 587), and Mitchell Goodwilly appears in Pitlower in 1703 (*Dunblane*). Persons of this name mostly trace their origin to Fife. Weekley (p. 243) compares this name with Pruguillun (i.e. Preux-Guillaume recorded in the English *Feet of Fines*).

GOODWIN. A surname found in the shires of Ayr, Lanark, and Stirling. From the OE. personal name *Gōdwine*, 'God friend.' The spelling Goodwin is due to the fact that the *o* in Godwin was originally pronounced long. Godwin, dapifer, and Godwin, camerarius of the bishop, witnessed a quitclaim by Robert, bishop of St. Andrews, 1127 (*Nat. MSS.*, I, 27). Thomas Goodwyn, brother of the Hospital of St. John of Jerusalem in 1414, appears again in 1426 as Thomas Gudewyne, brother of the order of St. John of Jerusalem (*Bain*, IV, 854; *Egidii*, p. 47).

GOOLD. Most probably a variant of GOLD, q.v.

GORDON. Owing to the fact that place names of this form occur in France it has been customary to trace the Gordons to a continental source. The earliest known home of the Scots family was in Berwickshire, and here we find a place name Gordon, from which the surname may have been derived. There was also a distinguished family named Gurdon in Hampshire, England, with whom it has been suggested they were connected. It has been further suggested that the Gordons were cadets of the Swintons as the coats of arms borne by the two families are the same. "Could this descent be established, the antiquity of the Gordons would be assured by tracing their ancestry through Ernulf of Swinton (the assumed father of Richard and Adam) and Odard of Bamburgh up to Waltheof the Saxon earl of Northumberland in 968, a pedigree which might account for their early traditions" (*Sc. Peer.*, IV, p. 507).

The first Gordon recorded in Scotland is Richer de Gordun, lord of the barony of Gordon in the Merse. Between 1150–60 he granted a piece of land and the church of S. Michael to the monks of Kelso, a grant confirmed by his son, Thomas de Gordun (*Kelso*, 118, 126). Adam de Gordun, probably a brother, along with Richer or Richard witnessed the quitclaim of lands of Swinton by Patrick, first earl of Dunbar (*Raine*, 117). The Gordons are by most writers referred to as a 'clan', but they have not the slightest claim to be considered as such — the relation of their followers to the chief was entirely feudalistic. William Gordon, a Scot, was mate and ice-pilot of the Danish attempt to find the North-West passage in 1619. The Polish family of Gordon now living at Ycon are descended from Nathaniel Gordon who left Scotland in 1707 (*Fischer* I, p. 58). The late Dr. J. M. Bulloch compiled an exhaustive work on the Gordons, *The House of Gordon*, Aberdeen, 1903–12, in 3 v.

Sir Alexander Seton in 1408 married Elizabeth Gordon and became the ancestor of the house of Huntly. "He spent much of his time in Aberdeenshire, where he greatly extended the Gordon lands and laid the foundations of a strong clan following. He is said to have rewarded all who took the name of Gordon, and became his vassals, with a gift of meal, whence certain branches of the clan were called the 'Bow o' Meal' Gordons, just as the 'Jok' and 'Tam' Gordons distinguished the collateral or illegitimate descendants of the original stock. It is only by such a process of adoption that the large number of Gordon families existing as early as the latter half of the fifteenth century can be accounted for" (Watt, *History of Aberdeen and Banff*, Edinburgh, 1900, p. 86). A correspondent in a recent issue (1943) of the London Times has made the absurd suggestion that the name is derived from Gordium in Phrygia and was introduced into Britain by a returned crusader.

GORGIE. From the place of the same name, a suburb of Edinburgh. John Gorgie, maltster, burgess of Edinburgh, is in record in 1628 (*Retours, Edinburgh*, 613).

GORGON. John Gorgon, weaver and burgess of Dumbarton, 1702 (RDB.).

GORME. May be from G. *gorm* 'blue.' Donald Gorme was witness at Lochlevyn, 1546 (*Rollok*, 3). Janet Gorme in Achnafie, 1717 (*Dunkeld*).

GORMLA. G. *Gorm-fhlaith*. A woman's name, well-known in Highland tales, but long obsolete. Gormflaith was the wife of Olaf Cuaran and mother of Earl Siggtrygg, and Gormlath, daughter of Malcolm MacHeth, was second wife of Harald Maddadson, earl of Orkney. Now rendered in Ireland by Barbara!

GORMLEY. Recorded in Argyllshire. It may be from Ir. *MacGormghaile*, 'son Gormghal,' a rare Irish surname (*Woulfe*).

GORMOK. Local, from Gormack near Blairgowrie, Perthshire. Thomas Gormok was minister at Fyvie, Aberdeenshire, 1574 (RMR.). Gilbert Gormak was admitted burgess of Aberdeen, 1604 (NSCM., I, p. 99), and Margaret Gormak appears in Peithill, 1633 (SCM., III, p. 105).

GORN. An Orcadian surname of local origin. There are places of this name in Rendall, Sandwick, and Westray. Walter Gorn Old has written on theosophical subjects.

GORRIE. Curtailed from MACGORRIE, q.v. Eleven persons of this name are recorded in the Commissariot Record of Dunblane in the seventeenth and eighteenth centuries, mainly in the parish of Foulis. The Gorries of Perthshire are said to be descended from some Macgorries who settled about four hundred years ago in the neighborhood of Logie Almond. Andrew Gorry in parish of Caterlinge, 1631 (*Brechin*). William, son of Donald Gorrie in Logiealmond, and others were charged with hamesucken in 1637 (RPC., 2. ser. VI, p. 463). William Gorrie in Culnaclich, tenant of the earl of Tullibardine, was charged in 1642 with the wrongful imprisonment of John McAgo (ibid., 2. ser. VII, p. 298). Thomas Gorrie was captain of the watch at Logiealmond in 1682 (ibid., 3. ser. VII, p. 638). This "Watch" or company was probably the earliest formed on

GORRIE, *continued*

the Highland border; the Black Watch companies were not raised until 1725. The AFM. state under 835 that "Goffraidh, son of Fergus, chief of Oriel, went over to Alba to strengthen the Dalriada at the request of Cinaedh Mac Alpinn," a very early instance of the adoption of Scandinavian names by the Irish, and indicative of intermarriage. Gofraid 989 (*Tighernach*), Gothbrith 917 (AU.), Goithbrith 920 (AU.), etc. The name answers to ON. *Guðfroðr*, a more ancient form of *Guðroðr*. It became a common name in the royal race of the Isle of Man, and in later Manx ballads is corrupted into *Orree*. As forename: Gorre McDonill VcGorre, 1582 (*Poltalloch Writs*, p. 135).

GORTHIE, GORTHY. From the old barony of Gorthie in Perthshire. The founder of this family appears to have been Tristrann or Tristram who witnessed Earl Gilbert's foundation charter of Inchaffray c. 1200. He later granted to Inchaffray a croft in Edardoennech near the pond of the mill of Gortin, c. 1208. His sons, Henry and Tristram, appear as witnesses in later charters in the same chartulary (*Inchaffray*, p. 8, 24, 31, 34, 38, 39, etc.). Another Tristram de Gorty witnessed a charter by Bricius de Ardrossane in favor of the same monastery in 1271 (LIM., p. 22). A later Tristram de Gorty appears in 1365, and a still later Tristram of Gorti or Gorty, who witnessed Atholl charters in 1428 and 1430, is mentioned again in 1432 as Tristram Gorti of that Ilk (*Inchaffray*, p. 128, 147; *Athole*, p. 706, 707). In 1470 we have a bond of manrent by a succeeding Tristrem of Gorte of that Ilk to Laurence, lord Oliphant for two years (*Oliphants*, p. 16). Tristram continued as a personal name in the family of Gorthy for nearly four hundred years. Wille Gorthy, a follower of Campbell of Lundy, appears in 1541 (RSS., II, 3666). The family ended in an heiress who married a Lundie. For an account of the barony see Fittis, *Sketches of olden times in Perthshire*. The surname continued in Dunblane in the sixteenth century (*Dunblane*).

GORTHRICK. John Gorthrick in Enierness in 1701 (*Wigtown*) may have derived his name from Girtrig, near Irvine.

GOSFORD. Most probably from Gosford in the parish of Aberlady, East Lothian. Master William de Goseford, parson of Castlemilke, who rendered homage in 1296 (*Bain*, II, p. 212) is probably the William de Goseford who was charged with holding certain churches in Scotland and England without papal dispensation in 1309 (*Pap. Lett.*, II, p. 53). In 1359 we have record of a remission of double custom to William de Gosseford (ER., I, p. 607), and in the same year a payment to him as William de Gosford (ibid., p. 608).

GOSLENTOWIS. Goslentowis or Gosklentovis, servitor in Cluny, Perthshire (*Rent. Dunk.*, p. 131, 140, 142). The editor says (p. xxvi): "A nickname abbreviated into the less recognisable Sklentovis."

GOSLINTOUN. William Goslintoun, member of Scots parliament for Lanarkshire, 1625 (*Hanna*, II, p. 495), derived his name from the vill and lands of Goslintoune in the shire.

GOSMAN, GOSSMAN, GOZMAN (in Fife). From the occupation, the 'gooseman,' or tender of the geese. Geese filled an important place in the domestic economy of early rural populations. In Anstruther, Fife, it was formerly believed the name was derived from Guzman, a grandee of the Spanish Armada! The name was recorded in Edinburgh, 1939.

GOSPATRIC. See under COSPATRIC, the more common form of the name.

GOSWICK. Walter de Goswyke, bailiff of Berwick in 1297 (*Bain*, II, 967) appears in 1304 as William de Gosewyck, mayor of Berwick on Tweed (ibid., II, 1603). Roger de Goswyc purchased a land in the tenement of Lambirtone in reign of Robert I (RMS., I, 10). From Goswick near Holy Island, Northumberland.

GOTHEWAIT. Of local origin from an obsolete place name near Edinburgh. Robertus Gothewait or Gothewaite witnessed charters by Adam filius Patricii de Crebarrin and Johannes de Crebarrin near the middle of the thirteenth century (RD., p. 103, 105).

GOTT. From the old place of the name in the parish of Tingwall, Shetland. Laurance Got in Funzie, 1627 (*Shetland*).

GOTTERSON. Patrick Gothrason leased part of Cupar Grange c. 1446 (*Cupar-Angus*, I, p. 124). Thomas Gothrasoune, a boy of eight years of age, was publicly flogged for *interfectio* in Legerwood, 1493 (*Trials*, I, p. 16*). John Gotherstoun or Gotterson is recorded in Dunfermline, 1579–86 (*Dunfermline*), and William Gotterstoune was burgess there, 1689 (RPC., 3. ser. XIV, p. 185). Quintiane Gottersoun in Shaws, parish of Dalserf, is recorded in 1601 (*Campsie*), and Alexander Gottersoun in North Berwick, 1623 (*Retours, Haddington*, 447). John Gotterson at Laudermylle, 1638, and three more of the name are recorded near there (*Lauder*). Claims were made against

Robert Guttersone in Stitchill, 1666, and Isabel and Catharine Gotterstone were indwellers there, 1737 (*Stitchill*, p. 39, 194). There is a farm named Gotterston (a contraction of 'Guthrie's town') near Dundee, but the name seems more likely of southern origin.

GOTTERUMSON. Nicoll Gotterumson in Culzevo in Yell recorded in 1613 (*Shetland*), and Swannie Guthrumson in Moull in the parish of Unst in 1625 (*Shetland*).

GOUDIE, GOUDY. Variants of GOLDIE, q.v., of which they are the popular pronunciation, e.g. "Goudie terror o' the Whigs" of Burns. The name appears in Edinburgh from 1598 onwards (*Edinb. Marr.*) in the forms Gowdie, Gaudie, Goddie. Robert Gowdie, writer in Edinburgh, 1643 (*Inquis.*, 2797), and John Gawdie was one of "those who are matriculat in the Companie of Merchands of Edinburgh," 1687 (*Sc. Ant.*, XII, p. 128). William Goodie in Ayr, 1689 (*RPC.*, 3. ser. XIV, p. 674). The surname was early carried to the north, appearing in Shetland first in 1576 in the person of Gawane Gadie of Lougasettar, Dunrossness (*Oppressions*, p. 73, 81; *Goudie*, p. 71). William Gady was servitor to Magnus Loutfute of Fleck, 1603 (*OSR.*, I, p. 226). Gayn (Gavin) Gadie in Clumlie died in 1629 (*Sc. Ant.*, XII, p. 39). There was a town or village of this name and a "Little Goudie Chapel." It existed in the policies of Camperdown (Maxwell, *Old Dundee*, 1891).

GOUDIELOCK. Gilbert Goldelokis was a witness in Shetland, 1623 (*OSS.*, I, 15). D. M. Goudielock was a printer in Glasgow, 1908. A Walter Guldeloc is recorded in co. Oxford, 1273 (*Bardsley*).

GOUINLOCK. See under GOWANLOCK.

GOUK. From the Old West Scandinavian *gaukr*, 'a cuckoo.' The word was often employed as a personal name, not necessarily a nickname, and the surname was not uncommon in Scandinavian England, especially in Lincolnshire (*Lindkvist*, p. 140; *Björkman* II, p. 37). James Gouk in the Cottoun of Over Dvssert, parish of Marytoun, 1631, and two others of the name are in record (*Brechin*). The surname is still to be found in Montrose and its vicinity (*Jervise*, II, p. 390, 391).

GOULD. A form of GOLD, q.v., with intrusive *u*. Eleven Goolds of the seventeenth and eighteenth centuries are recorded in the Commissariot Record of Dunblane.

GOURLAY, GOURLIE. Probably from some place in England. Ingelramus de Gourlay, first of the name recorded in Scotland, held land in Clydesdale and in Lothian c. 1174 (*Caledonia*, I, p. 132). His son, Hugh de Gurley, possessed lands in Fife and Lothians, and some time after 1180 witnessed a charter by Ingelram de Balliol of the church of Inuerkileder to Abbey of Arbroath (*RAA.*, I, p. 39; Jervise, *Angus*, p. 312). A later Ingeramus Gurle was witness, 1244 (*Cambus.*, 171), Hugh Gurle and William Gurle were present at a conference at Roxburgh, 1254 (*ES.*, II, p. 583), and William, son of William Gurlay, made a gift to Abbey of Newbattle, 1293 (*Neubotle*, p. 175). Several of the name rendered homage in 1296, viz. Roger Gourlay, William de Gurleye, Huwe de Gurleghe, and Patrick de Gurleghe, parson of the church of Loghorwurde, all four of the county of Edinburgh (*Bain*, II, p. 208). Adam de Gurle of Roxburghe also rendered homage, and as Adam de Gourlay appears as witness at Roxburgh, 1304 (ibid., p. 209, 376). Sir Patrick Gourlay, rector of the church of Lochorwart, was also witness between 1300 and 1320 (*Hay*, p. 7). Alain de Gourlay and Adam de Gourlay were on inquest at Roxburgh, 1303 (*Bain*, II, 1435). Payment of a debt for sheep was made to Hugh of Gurlay, 1328, and in 1330 Robert Gourlay was provost of Stirling (*ER.*, I, p. 116, 266). Henry Gourlaw in 1380 granted to his son John the lands of Reuelwood in parish of Cavers which lands remained in his family till sold by them after the Reformation (*OPS.*, I, p. 527). John Gourlaw, monk of Arbroath, 1392 (*Cambus.*, 75), and Alexander Gourlay of Kyncraig attested to the marches of Kyrknes and Louchor, 1395 (*RPSA.*, p. 5). John Gourlaw was king's officer, 1529 (*Irvine*, I, p. 36), and Robert Gourlay was a distinguished merchant and citizen of Edinburgh, in latter half of the sixteenth century. Thomas Gurlay was attorney at Perth, 1546 (*Rollok*, 20). The Gourlays of Kincraig, Fife, held those lands for over six hundred years. There is a Gourlaw near Lasswade, Midlothian, but this may have been named after the family. Gorlay 1286, Gowrlaw 1509, Gurla 1689, Gurlaw 1574, Gwrla 1540, Gwyrlay 1532; Goirlay, Gouerlay.

GOURTON. From the old barony of Gorton in Midlothian. Edward de Coyertone (for Gouertone), king's tenant in Edinburghshire, rendered homage, 1296. His seal bears an escallop (?) and legend, S' *Edwardi de Goverty* (*Bain*, II, p. 201, 534). Margaret de Gouiertoun held the lands of Gouiertoun in Loudonia in the reign of David II (*RMS.*, I, App. I, 111).

GOVAN. Of territorial origin from the old lands of Govan in Lanarkshire. Christian, widow of Symon de Govane, held lands in Govan in 1293 (REG., p. 210). Adam of Gouvan was one of an inquest at Peebles, 1304 (*Bain*, II, 1436), and in Peeblesshire a family of the name flourished for centuries. William de Gouane witnessed a charter by William, lord of Douglas, between 1306–29 (RHM., I, p. 13). Sir John de Gowen was rector of the church of Maxtoun in 1326 (*Dryburgh*, p. 247), and in 1325 John de Govan granted seven rigs in Brummelaw to the Friars Preachers of Glasgow (LCD., p. 155). Laurence de Govan was sheriff of Peblys, 1359 (ER., I, p. 566). William Govan or Guvane was canon of Glasgow, 1425–46 (REG., 329, 348). John de Govane was prior of the Predicant Friars of Glasgow, 1451 (Napier, *Partition of Lennox*, p. 19). John Gwuan was a tenant under the bishop of Glasgow, 1511 (*Rental*), William Guvane of Cardno appears as a Peeblesshire laird, 1530 (*Trials*, I, p. 147*), John Govand, fruictman, admitted burgess freeman of Glasgow, 1589 (*Burgesses*), David Gowane, portioner of Schettilstoun, 1606 (*Retours, Lanark*, 58), and Margaret Gooven is in record in Edinburgh, 1634 (*Edinb. Marr.*). From several notices in old records it is evident that the Govans of Peeblesshire were a family of some importance in the fourteenth century. They retained possession of Cardrona until 1685, their ancestral estate, after which they appear only as burgesses of Peebles and owners of certain patches of land in its neighborhood; and as such the family has now disappeared (Chambers, *Peeblesshire*, p. 393). The last of the name was William Govan of Hawkshaw, who died in Edinburgh, 1819 (ibid.). Govean 1536, Goveane 1669, Govans 1684, Guuan 1440.

GOVANLOCK, GOVENLOCK. See under GOWANLOCK.

GOVE. A form of Gow, q. v. Colin Gove was constable of Taruedal, 1278 (*Beauly*, p. 64). There are a few persons of the name recorded in and around Inverness.

GOVERNOUR. Ten persons of this name are recorded in the Commissariot Record of Dunblane in the eighteenth century. Weekley (p. 207) suggests this name may have been "associated especially with the Passion Play."

GOVINLOCK. See under GOWANLOCK.

GOW. From G. *gobha*, 'a smith,' or perhaps a shortening of *Mac gobhann* or *Mac a' ghobhainn*, 'son of the smith.' The smith was a man of importance in most of the clans, so that the name has no particular connection with any one clan. The Gows are usually included in Clan Chattan though there are many of the name in Perthshire, and eleven of the name appear in the Commissariot Record of Dunblane in the seventeenth and eighteenth centuries. George Gow and Henry Gow were burgesses of Dysart, 1580 (*Dysart*, p. 40), and Michael and Robert Gow in Culcoly were among the followers of Stewart of Kinnaird in a raid in 1595 (RPC.). The tradition that the Gows are descended from 'Hal o' the Wynd,' who took part in the clan battle on the Inch of Perth, 1396, is merely a piece of folklore.

GOWAN. Colin Gowin Kenvay in Tiree denounced rebel, 1675 (HP., I) (Kenway his place of residence). The usual genitive form of *gobha*, 'a smith,' is *gobhainn*, but it is often the same as the nominative and made Gowan. (2) Some of this name may be from GOVAN, q.v., as Gowan was a common sixteenth century spelling of the place name (v and w interchanged).

GOWANLOCK, GOVANLOCK, GOVENLOCK, GOVINLOCK, GOUINLOCK, GOWANLOCH. Of local origin from some small place probably in Roxburghshire or Selkirkshire. It is said to be an old surname and place name in Ayrshire, in the fifteenth century spelled Gavenleck, but I have found no record of this. Richard Gowanlok was a charter witness in Edinburgh in 1471 (*Neubotle*, 303), and Patrick Gowanlok was banished the town in 1530 for harboring a woman infected with the pestilence (MCM., II, p. 106). Gilbert Gowanlock appears in Beimersyd in 1637 (*Lauder*), George Gowdelock was a merchant in Legertwood in 1767 (ibid.), and Robert Govanlock became landlord of the old Mosspaul Inn in 1816. Gavinlock's Land was an old tenement in the Lawnmarket of Edinburgh, and in 1837 it housed about 300 persons. Govanlock in Melrose in 1942. Cf. GOUDIELOCK.

GOWANS. A surname recorded in Linlithgow and Perth, and four of the name are in the Commissariot Record of Dunblane in seventeenth and eighteenth centuries. John Govans (v = w) in Middle-house, parish of Carluke, 1701 (*Lanark CR.*). As GOWAN, q.v., with possessive 's. Gowns 1787.

GOWANSON. An Englishing of MACCOW, q.v. In 1578 complaint was made against Alexander Gowansoun, son to umquhile Alexander Gowansoun 'that wes hangit in Dundee' (RPC., III, p. 51).

GOWINSKEY. William of Gowinskey, burgess of Irvine, 1260 (*Irvine*, I, p. 5) may be the William Gobynsckeghe or Gobynskeghe of Ayrshire who rendered homage in 1296, and had his lands restored to him (*Bain*, II, p. 207, 218). William de Gobenskethe held land in Ayrshire in the reign of Robert I (RMS., I, 46). Gobynskeghe and Gobenskethe probably represent modern Cobinshaw in the parish of West Calder.

GOZMAN. See GOSMAN.

GRADEN. From the lands of Graden, near Coldstream, Berwickshire. Peter de Grayden granted to Julian, his eldest daughter, two bovates of land, with pertinents, in the town and territory of Graydene, c. 1288 (*Edmonstone*, p. 76). Among the witnesses are Walter de Grayden and Herbert de Graydene. Wautier de Greydene of the county of Berewyke rendered homage in 1296. His seal bears a crown of thorns (?) and S' *Walt' d' Graydn* (*Bain*, II, p. 202, 557). Robert Graiden is recorded in Graystainerig in 1653 and John Grayden in Earnshaw in 1698 (*Lauder*). A family of this name held the lands of Ernslaw or Erneslaw in the parish of Eccles in the seventeenth century (*Retours, Berwickshire*, 211, 329, 380, 434). Graidin 1673.

GRAEME. See GRAHAM. This spelling is that adopted by George Buchanan in his *History* (bk. v, c. iii) for the name of the legendary leader of the Scots at the breaching of the Antonine Wall, and "there can be little doubt that the pages of the great humanist so long regarded as unquestionable authority are chiefly responsible for this form of the name. It has been used principally by the Inchbrakie and Garvock branches and their cadets Guthrie, Braco, and Graemeshall, Balgowan, and Eskbank" (*Sc. Peer.*, vi, p. 193).

GRAGIN. Local. John of Gragin was one of the witnesses to the gift of Dundas to Helias, son of Huctred (*Arniston Memoirs*, p. xxv). Willelmus de Gragin, a charter witness in Perth in reign of Alexander II (*Scon*, p. 61).

GRAHAM, GRAHAME, GRAEME. The name of an illustrious family of Anglo-Norman origin, which settled in Scotland early in the twelfth century. The name is derived from OE. *grægham*, 'grey home,' from the manor of that name (temp. Domesday Book). The popular derivation from a chief named Grim or Gram who broke through the wall of the emperor Antoninus between the Forth and Clyde in 420 A. D., which afterwards from him became known as 'Graham's Dyke,' is nonsense. This legend, says Freeman the historian of the Nor-

man Conquest, illustrates "the old-fashioned principle which has done so much to discredit genealogy and heraldry in the eyes of sensible men, that any exploded myth, any rubbish in fact, is good enough for family history . . . It is almost incredible that a legend, which would now-a-days raise a laugh even in a Board school, should be gravely offered for the credence of our hard-headed colonial cousins."

The first of the name recorded in Scotland is William de Graham who received from David I the lands of Abercorn and Dalkeith and is witness to several of that king's charters. The earliest in which his name appears is commonly said to be the foundation charter of Holyrood Abbey (LSC., I). This charter, as was usual in those times, is undated, but as the *Chronicle of Melrose* (p. 68) records the foundation of the Abbey in 1128 the charter has been assumed to be of the same date. William de Graham, however, appears in a charter the date of which Sir Archibald Lawrie places c. 1127 (ESC., p. 59). William de Graham next appears in a confirmation by King David of a grant by Gospatric frater Dolfini of Ederham and Nesebit to the monks of St. Cuthbert of Durham (*Raine*, 20), and c. 1141 he was one of the perambulators of the bounds of Clerchetune (now Clerkington) in Haddingtonshire (RPSA., p. 181). Henry de Graham, a great-grandson of this William, married the daughter of Roger Avenel, on whose death in 1243 he became possessed of the Avenel estates in Eskdale. The Grahams or Grahames were very numerous in Liddesdale and the Debateable Land, occupying almost the whole of the southern portion of the latter district, and also a portion of the northern or Scottish side. A sept of the Cumberland Grames, consisting of 124 persons, under their chief, "Walter, the gude man of Netherby," being troublesome on the Scottish Border in 1606 were transplanted from Cumberland to Roscommon in Ireland (*Calendar of State Papers, Ireland*, 1603–1606, p. 554). Sir John de Grahame of Dundaff, the faithful friend of the patriot Wallace, was slain at the battle of Falkirk, 1298. From the War of Independence downwards the Grahams have taken a prominent part in the affairs of Scotland, the two most outstanding individuals of the name being James Graham, first marquess of Montrose, who carried on the war in Scotland for Charles I, and John Graham of Claverhouse, Viscount Dundee, who fell at Killiecrankie in 1689. In the Roll of the Scots Guards in France the name appears as Giresme, and on the Highland Border it was used as an Englishing of M'Gillemhearnaig, a sept name in the Graham country. Graam 1341, Grahavm 1532, Grahem 1561, Graheme 1547, Grahm

324

GRAHAM, Grahame, Graeme, continued

and Grahme 1672, Grahym 1464, Graiham 1591, Grame 1411, Graym 1467, Grayme 1522, Greeme 1716, Grehme 1550, Greme 1778, and (undated) Graem, Gram, Grem, Greym, Greyme. See also Grim.

GRAHAMSLAW. From Grahamslaw in the parish of Eckford, Roxburghshire. John de Grymeslawe of the county of Roxburgh, who rendered homage in 1296 (Bain, II, p. 199), appears to be the first of the name in record. John of Grymslawe, juror on inquisition at Roxburgh, 1361 (Bain, IV, 61). Thomas Grymislaw was juror on an inquest at Jedburgh in 1464 (Cavers, p. 728), may be the Thomas Grymsley, a Scot, who had letters of denization in England, 1480 (Bain, IV, 1465). Adam Grahamslaw of Newton, one of the lairds of Roxburghshire who submitted to the king's will at Jedburgh in 1530, may be the Adam Grameislaw who appears as a witness in Glasgow in 1550 (Protocols, I). William Grahamslaw, servitor to my lord Boyd, was admitted burgess of Glasgow in 1576 (Burgesses). Walter Gremslae in Nether Stitchill is in record in 1677 (Stitchill, p. 80). Graimslaw 1662, Gramislaw 1684, Grymyslaw 1493, Grymslowe 1547.

GRAINGER, Granger. "The farms, which are still found throughout the country in the neighbourhood of old abbeys, named 'The Grange,' were the farm steadings where the monks carried on their farming operations, and where the grain and cattle derived from their more distant possessions were stored and housed. Around 'the grange' were clustered numerous cottages for the labourers and their families, and the whole was under the charge of a monk, or lay brother, named from his office — 'The Granger'" (Laing, Lindores Abbey and its burgh of Newburgh, p. 61). In Latin the name of the office was rendered granatarius, 'manager of the victual,' and appears in Scots as granitar, graintlie-man, or gryntal-man. Gocelin, brother of Hugh Granger, witnessed the grant of the church of Pulloc to the monks of Paisley, c. 1189–99 (RMP., p. 100). Robert de la Graunge of the county of Roxburghe rendered homage in 1296 and in 1303 served as juror on an inquisition made at Roxburgh (Bain, II, p. 199, 376). In 1299 Robert the 'granatorius' of Holyrood took oath to be a true liegeman to the king of England (ibid., p. 268). John Graneter was juror on an inquest at Inverness in 1430 (RMS., II, 179). Grenger 1595.

GRAMISSONE, 'son of Graham,' q.v. Alexander Patrik Gramissone was exhorter at Cannisbie, Caithness, 1567 (OPS., II, p. 792). A double name at this date is rare.

GRANET. This name in the Glasgow Directory may represent the fifteenth century name Graneter (Latin granetarius, the keeper of a granery). Cf. Grainger.

GRANGE. From residence at or beside a grange. Alexander Grange alias Campbell in Achunahainat, 1768 (Durness).

GRANGER. See under GRAINGER.

GRANT. Highland seannachies notwithstanding there is no doubt of the Norman origin of the Grants (i.e. of the chiefs) who were introduced into the North by the Bissets on their return from their exile of 1242. In England the Bissets and the Grants possessed adjoining lands in Nottinghamshire and were intermarried. In 1246 Henry III of England granted Lowdham to Walter Byset till he should recover his lands in Scotland. The adjacent manor of East Bridgeford was then held by William le Grant, husband of Alfreda Byset, the heiress (Stodart, II, p. 308). There was also a famous Norman family of Grants whose motto also was "Stand fast" (Tenons Ferme). The earliest reference to the name Grant connected with Scotland is that of Thomas Grant, merchant of the king of Scotland, who, on 2d of January 1252 was deposed from his office of visor of York Castle. The first Grants recorded in Scotland are Laurentius et Robertus dictus Grant, witnesses in 1258 to an instrument drawn up in the Bishop's Court at Inverness to enable John Byset, the younger, to give the church of Conveth to the Priory of Beauly (Beauly, p. 52–53; REM., p. 134–135). Sir Laurence was sheriff of Inverness and bailie of Inuerchoich in 1266 (ER., I, p. 36), and Robert, his brother (?), held land in Nairnshire. From the marriage of Laurence Grant with the heiress of the Glencharnich family the Grants date their real establishment in the North (Invernessiana, p. 30). The first Grant lands are Stratherrick, where they are found in the fourteenth century, and by the end of that century they are found in most of the later lands held by them. The surname remains preceded by le or the in the fifteenth and even in the sixteenth century (Stodart, II, p. 308). John le Graunt, a Scots prisoner from Dunbar, was warded in Gloucester Castle in 1297 and in the same year was freed on mainprise along with Ralph le Graunte (Bain, II, 938, 940). Thomas le Graunt was plundered of his goods and chattels and one of his hands cut off by thieves maintained by Sir Duncan de Feringdraut in 1305 (ibid., 1735), and Maurice Grant was attorney for the provost of Inverness in 1330 and afterwards sheriff of the same town (ER.,

I, p. 310, 465). Richard Grant was prebendary of Assynt in 1394 (*Pap. Pet.*, I, p. 572). The sixth laird of Freuchie was knighted by James VI, and his grandson had his lands erected into the regality of Grant. Some Achnachs are said to have changed their name to Grant. Grantt 1828.

GRANTHAME. John de Granthame who granted a quitclaim in favor of the Abbey of Kelso c. 1270 (*Kelso*, 36) most probably derived his name from Grantham in Lincolnshire.

GRANTULLY. Perhaps from the lands of Grantully in the parish of Dull, Perthshire. Robert de Grantell' witnessed a confirmation charter by Alexander II at Edinburgh in 1224 (*Neubotle*, 122). Adam de Quarenteley was presented to the church of Colbaynnston (Covington), Lanarkshire, in 1262 (*Bain*, I, 2676). Ellen de Quaranteley who swore fealty to Edward I of England in 1296 (Palgrave, *Illustrations*, p. 300) is doubtless the Ellen de Quarantley to whom Robert I gave the lands of Bellitstan and Grunley in the forest of Maldisley in excambion (RMS., I, 76). See GARTLY.

GRASS. A curtailed form of GRASSIE, from GRASSICK, q.v.

GRASSICK. From G. *greusaich* or *griasaich*, 'shoemaker.' "The term *greasaighe* in the older language meant 'decorator,' 'embroiderer;' the modern 'shoemaker' is a specialized meaning" (*Watson* I, p. 410). The name is of frequent occurrence in Aberdeenshire, particularly in the parishes of Glenbuchat and Strathdon. The local pronunciation is Gracey, whence the softened forms GRASSIE and GRASS, q.v. John Grasse alias Cordonar was one of the tenants of the Kirktoun of Crathe (i.e. Crathienaird) in 1539 (ER., XVII, p. 658). Donald Grasycht is in record in Lochalsh in 1548 (RMS., IV, 204), Elspet Grassiche in Tullochaspak appears in 1612 (RSCA., II, p. 187), and Patrick Gressiche was cordyner in Stron, 1613 (RPC., XIV, p. 644). David Grassiche in Kepache was charged with violence in 1617 (RPC., XI, p. 68), Gillecallum Graysich in Molaii and John M'Gillepatrik Grasich were Glenurquhay's vassals, 1638 (BBT., p. 403). Andrew Greasich appears in Loggies in 1649 (IDR., p. 369), and Alexander Greoschich (Greoshich, or Greishich) in Towie who was accused of curing cattle by charming, 1669 (*Alford*, p. 143, 146) may be the Alexander Greshach who was elder at Strathdone in 1686 (ibid., p. 375). The name was early rendered by Scottish Souter (Patrick Souther in Strathdee in 1527). Graisich 1649, Grasseich 1631,

Grecie 1633, Gresich 1696. See also MAC-GREUSICH.

GRASSIE. A weakened form of GRASSICK, q.v. John Graissie or Grecie in Balchlayvie or Bochlyvie is recorded in 1632 and 1633 (*Dunblane*), and another John Grassie in Ardgeicht appears in 1643 (RSCA., III, p. 17). Alexander Grassie was member of Huntly Volunteers, 1799 (*Will*, p. 8), and James Grassie published his *Legends of the Highlands from oral tradition* in 1843. Graissie 1632.

GRAY, GREY. Perhaps from Gray, a town in the department of Haute-Saône, France. The first of the name recorded in Scotland is Hugo de Gray, witness in a charter by Walter de Lundin, a. 1248 (*Sc. Peer.*, IV, p. 269). The surname is now common all over Scotland. John Gray, mayor of Berwick, witnessed a gift of land to the Hospital of Soltre between 1250–66 (*Soltre*, p. 32). William de Grey witnessed resignation of the lands of Nysebyte by William de Nysebyte, 1255 (*Bain*, I, 2026), and William Gray was a charter witness at Newton of Ayr, c. 1280 (RMP., p. 72). Robert Gray, castellan of Banff in 1291, was probably an Englishman (*Bain*, II, 542). Henry Grey of Fife rendered homage in 1296, and Huwe Grey, juror on an inquest at Berwick, also rendered homage (ibid., p. 198, 204, 215). John Gray was provost of Crail, 1327 (ER., I, p. 65). William dictus Gray witnessed a charter by Muriel, widow of Sir William de Rose, between 1333–63 (*Rose*, p. 117). John Gray of Broxmouth had a charter of the lands of Craigy in le Mernys, 1357 (SCM., V, p. 247), and Laurence Gray was custumar of Montrose, 1359 (ER., I, p. 612). The land of Molyne was leased to Ibbote Gray in 1376 (RHM., I, p. lviii), and John Gray was rector of the church of Ferne in Angus, 1394 (RAA., II, 42). William Graa was one of the prominent men of Orkney in 1427 (*Oppressions*, p. 109), Robert Gray, "chamerlane of Aberbrothoc," 1497 (RAA., II, 383), and John Gra, tenant in Raynstruder, 1531 (*Rental*). See under MAC-GLASHAN.

GREAT. James Great in Kirkpatrick-Irongray, 1755 (*Dumfries*). Bardsley records this name in Lincolnshire in reigns of Edward I and II, and compares it with GRANT, the great, large.

GREATHEAD. Matthew Gretheuith or Greatheued was alderman and provost of Aberdeen between 1271 and 1281 (*Friars*, 13; REA., II, p. 279). In 1271 he appears as Matthew Grossetechte (for Fr. *Grosstête*) and in a charter of c. 1281 (REA., II, p. 281) as Grethenith, an error for Gretheuith. John le

GREATHEAD, *continued*

fiz Walter Gretheuede, burgess of Peebles, rendered homage in 1296 (*Bain*, II, p. 198). John called Gretheuyd was a witness in 1343 (*Melros*, p. 457), and Walter dictus Gretheued was burgess of Aberdeen in 1345 (CAB., p. 318). Anne or Amie Greitheid was a follower of Campbell of Lundy in 1541 (RSS., II, 3666). Cf. G. *Canmore*.

GREEN. From residence near a 'green.' "As every village had its green, it is not surprising that our modern directories teem with the name" (*Bardsley*). Roger del ('of the') Grene in Roxburghshire rendered homage in 1296 (*Bain*, II, p. 206). Master John Grene, chancellor of Moray, 1463 (OPS., II, p. 838).

GREENACRE. A surname recorded in Aberdeen. A modern importation from south of the Border. Bardsley has record of the name from the reign of Edward III (1327-1377).

GREENAN. Of local origin. There is a Greenan near Ayr, another in Bute, and a Grenan (1675) in Argyll *Retours* (no. 85).

GREENFIELD. A common self-explanatory place name. The seal of Master William Greenfield (1289) reads, S' Wil'mi de Grenefevd (*Macdonald*, 1165). Thomas Greinfield, a Scot, had letters of denisation in England, 1480 (*Bain*, IV, 1465). W. Greenfield in Dunbeath, 1816.

GREENGRASS. A surname recorded in Aberdeen. Perhaps of recent introduction from England. Bardsley has the name but can find no early references before 1623.

GREENHEAD. From the lands of Greenhead in the parish of Innerleithen, Peeblesshire. There was also a Grenheid near Kelso in 1567. In 1290 an inquest was held to determine the responsibility for the death of Robert de la Greneheued (*Bain*, II, 407). Cristiane del Grenehevede of the county of Selkirk rendered homage for his lands in 1296 (ibid., p. 208). His seal bears an eight-rayed figure and S' *Cristiane de la Grinay* (ibid., p. 552). Aymer del Greneheued served as juror on an inquisition made at Selkirk anent the sheriffdom of Selkirk in 1305 (ibid., 1681), and Huchoun de la Greneheued was received by the king of England's peace in 1321 (ibid., III, 734). The lands were forfeited by the family in the reign of David II and were bestowed on William Broun (RMS., I, App. II, 1158, 1213). In the same reign Richard Greneheuyd or Greinhuid had a charter of certain lands in Roxburgh by the forfeiture of William Waldefield (ibid., App. II, 952).

GREENHILL. Local, from one or other of the many small places of the name. Bryce of Grenehill in record, 1478 (ALC.). Thomas Grenhil witnessed an appointment by John, earl of Lennox, 1521 (*Pollok*, I, p. 246). James Greinhill was examined for the Test in 1685 (RPC., 3. ser. XI, p. 434).

GREENHILLS. Local. Katherine Greenhills in Hamilton, 1607 (*Campsie*) probably derived her surname from the old twenty-shilling lands of Greinhillis in the barony of Kilbryde, Lanarkshire. A commission was issued in 1558 for the trial of Johne Grenehillis in Lanark (ER., XIX, p. 422). John Greenhills in Brunsie, 1772 (*Dunkeld*).

GREENHORN, GREENHORNE. Local, from some place not known to me, 'at the green corner' (OE. *hyrne*, 'corner').

GREENLAND. Local. There is a Greinlands in Dumfries *Retours*, 173. John Grienland was preacher of the Gospel at Anwoth, 1720.

GREENLAW. The name of an old family in Berwickshire, derived from their lands there. They may have been an offshoot from the Dunbars. William de Grenlawa, c. 1180 (*Kelso*, 333). An agreement between the abbot of Kelso and Roland de Grenelawe regarding the chapel was made c. 1200 (ibid., 145). Magister William de Grenlau, a churchman, witnessed a charter by Walter, bishop of Glasgow, c. 1208-18 (LCD., p. 236), and in 1221 was one of a number appointed to settle a dispute between the churches of Glasgow and Kelso (REG., 116), and c. 1221-31 witnessed the grant of the church of Lympetlaw to Kelso Abbey (*Soltre*, p. 25). In 1233 he witnessed resignation of the lands of Eduluestun to the church of Glasgow (REG., p. 140). William of Greenlaw, son of Roland, son of William, witnessed Melrose documents of 1236-37 (*Melros*, 298, 274), and held lands in Halsington of Robert de Muschamp, part of which he gave to Melrose Abbey before 1247 (ES., II, p. 545n.), in which year he died (*Chron. Mail.*, s.a.). Matheu de Grenlawe fiz William de Grenlawe of Berwickshire and William de Grenlawe of Edinburghshire rendered homage in 1296 (*Bain*, II, p. 206, 198). William de Grenelawe was clerk to Sir John de Mowbray in 1308 (ibid., 1868), and in 1327 and following years there are records of payment of king's alms to Symon de Grenlaw (ER., I, p. 60, 90, etc.). William de Grenlaw was archdeacon of St. Andrews, 1361 (*Cambus.*, 160). Gilbert de Grenlaw or Grynlaw, canon of Aberdeen, 1386, afterwards bishop of Aberdeen and chancellor of Scotland, died in 1422

(REA., I, p. xxxiv-vi, 172). Thomas Grenlaw, archdeacon, had a safe conduct in England, 1424 (Bain, IV, 943), Thomas de Grenelawe was bailie of the Temple, 1426 (Egidii, p. 48), Thomas de Grenlaw, vicar of Conveth, was made burgess of Aberdeen, 1439 (NSCM., I, p. 5), and Thomas Grenlaw was vicar of Erth, 1452 (Pollok, I, p. 172). Nicholas Grenlaw was rector of Eddilstoun, 1503 (Simon, 64). Grenelaw 1531, Greynlaw 1429, Grinlav 1447, Grinlaw 1484.

GREENLEES. Local. Greenlees (East and West) is near Cambuslang, Lanarkshire. Robert Greynleis, son and heir of John Greynleis, was admitted burgess freeman of Glasgow, 1574 (Burgesses). William Greenlies in Paisley, 1689 (RPC., 3. ser. XIV, p. 320). Greinlies 1675, Greneleis 1555.

GREENOCK, GRINOCK. From the town of Greenock in Renfrewshire. Huwe de Grenhok of the county of Lanark rendered homage in 1296 (Bain, II, p. 213). Sir John Grenok was chaplain and curate of Carriden in 1538 (Johnsoun), Robertus Greenock, faber ferrarius, in Bannockburne, 1669 (Inquis. Tut., 943), and the Rev. James Grinock was minister of Gourock from 1780 to 1789 (Fasti, 2. ed., III, p. 196).

GREENRIG. Probably from Greenrig near Lesmahagow, Lanarkshire. William del Grenerige of the county of Lanark rendered homage in 1296 (Bain, II, p. 206).

GREENSHIELDS, GREENSHIELS. From Greenshields in the parish of Liberton, Lanarkshire. There are many of the name in the Commissariot Record of Lanark, 1595–1800. John Greenscheills is recorded in Eister Moderwell in 1624 (Campsie), William Greinscheillis was retoured heir of William Greinscheillis de eodem in 1617 (Retours, Lanark, 111), and William Greenscheills appears in Ormistoun in 1687 (Peebles CR.). Greynchellis 1499, Grenescheill 1602.

GREENYARDS. An individual named Greneyardis, dempster of the barony court of Lenzie, Dumbartonshire, in 1479 (SBR., p. 264), most probably derived his name from Greenyards in the parish of Cumbernauld, in the same shire.

GREER, GRIER. Generally considered to be a shortened form of Macgregor, but in latter half of seventeenth century was commonly equated with Grierson. Gilbert Grier was witness in Dumfriesshire, 1542 (Anderson). George Grier was appointed minister in Aberdeen, 1598 (SCM., V, p. 125), and the name is recorded in Edinburgh, 1599 (Edinb. Marr.). William Greir was retoured heir of William Greir in Dalgoner in the 40/ land of Dalgoner, 1617 (Retours, Dumfries, 95). George Greir is in Ayr, 1656 (Ayr, p. 198), and Gilbert Greir of Chappell is in record in 1676 is mentioned in following year as Gilbert Greirsone of Shappell (Retours, Dumfries, 284, 287). James Grier or Grierson was schoolmaster in Dumfries, 1675; Rosina Greir is in parish of Rerrick, 1684 (RPC., 3. ser. IX, p. 573), and Fergus Grier or Greirsone was an aged prisoner in the Canongate Tolbooth, Edinburgh, 1686 (ibid., 3. ser. XII, p. 207–208). Groir 1667.

GREG, GREGG. Variants of GREIG, q.v.

GREGAN. Perhaps from Ir. O'Gréacháin, descendant of Creachán (dimin. of creach, blind), Anglicized Greaghan, Greahan.

GREGOR. A personal name from the Greek Γρηγόριος, 'watchful,' through Latin Gregorius. It was a favorite ecclesiastical name from the third century. St. Gregory I, 'The Great,' died 604. Gregorius was seneschal of Coldingham Priory in the reign of William the Lion (Raine, 163). Robert, son of Gregor, who witnessed the deed of sale of Adam, son of Thurkill, to the prior of Coldingham, c. 1240, was probably his son (ibid., 337). Sheep were stolen from Marioun Gregour in Spynie, 1595 (SCM., II, p. 128).

The name was borrowed by the Gaels and appears in EIr. (Lat.) as Grigorius, MIr. Grigour, G. Griogair, hence MacGriogair, Macgregor. "When Hector Boece invested the obscure usurper Grig, with the name and attributes of a fictitious king, Gregory, the Great, and connected him with the royal line of kings, the Clan Gregor at once recognised him as their eponymus ancestor, and their descent from him is now implicitly believed in by all the Macgregors" (Skene, CS., III, p. 364).

GREGORSON, 'son of GREGOR,' q.v. An Englishing of MACGREGOR. Grigorussoun (in Shetland) 1624.

GREGORY. From the Greek personal name Γρηγόριος, through Lat. Gregorius, 'watchman.' Several early Scots bishops bore this name, appropriate for the overseer of a church. Gregorius Duncheldensis, episcopus, c. 1150 (REG., 11); Gregorius episcopus de Ros, 1171–84 (REM., 3); Gregorius Moraviensis episcopus, 1150 (RD., 1). Gregory of Rutherford was a charter witness in reign of William the Lion (Melros). William filius Gregorii, provost of Crail, 1330 (ER., I, p. 265). Thomas Gregory was accused of deforcing in 1569

GREGORY, *continued*

(RPC., I, p. 685). John Gregorie was minister of Drumoak in 1633 (SCM., III, p. 94), and Master Alexander Gregorie was retoured heir of Master John Gregorie, sometime minister of Dilmaik, his father, in 1651 (*Retours, Aberdeen*, 308). Greigory 1737.

GREGSON, 'son of GREG,' q.v. Thomas Gregson was tenant at Butterdean Mains, Chirnside, in 1805.

GREIG, GREGG. The first form a common surname especially in Fife and along the east central coast. In old parish records the name is spelled Greag (1689), Greg, Grege (1536), Gregg, Grieg, Grig (1508). Walter Greg witnessed a charter by Malcolm, earl of Fife, c. 1214–26 (RHM., II, p. 1). Patrick Grige was admitted burgess of Aberdeen, 1488 (NSCM., I, p. 33), and John Grige held land there, 1493 (REA., I, p. 334). Johannes Greg was chosen common councillor in Aberdeen, 1502 (*Guildry*, p. 192). David Greg was member of council of Stirling, 1522 (SBR., p. 275), and Paul Grege in Leith accepted the king's coronation, 1567 (RPC., I, p. 563). The Norwegian Griegs are descended from John Grieg of Fraserburgh, whose son Alexander (1739–1803) settled in Bergen, 1779. The father of Edward Grieg (1843–1907), the composer, was British consul at Bergen (*Konversations Leksikon*, Kristiania, 1921). Admiral Greig of the Russian Navy was a Scot. See under GIRIG for origin. Grig 1609.

GRENDON. Most probably from one of several places in England named Grindon or Grendon. The manor of Grindon in Cumberland was originally held of the kings of Scotland by the Grindon family in drengage (Moore, *Lands*, p. 40). William de Grendon rendered homage at Berwick, 1291 (RR.). The land of Reginald de Grendoun in Aberdeen is mentioned, 1317 (SCM., V, p. 7). John of Grendon had a protection in England for a year in 1372 (*Bain*, IV, 202). See GRINTON.

GRENEBURN. Local. John of Greneburn, a Scot, had a safe conduct into England, 1361–2 (CSR., I, p. 137).

GRESOUN. John Gresone was witness in Aberdeen, 1516 (REA., II, p. 313), and another John Gresoun, provincial of the Friars Preachers of St. Andrews, 1545 (*Laing*, 494) is probably the John Gresoun, Gryson, or Gresone, professor of sacred theology in St. Andrews, 1560. Andro Gressoune and Joke Gressoum appear in the Rental of the Abbey of Kelso, 1567 (*Kelso*, p. 520). Cf. GRIERSON.

GREUSACH. A curtailed form of MACGREUSICH, q.v. John Gresich in Delbadie was fined in 1613 for assisting outlawed members of Clan Gregor (RPC., 2. ser. VI, p. 215).

GREWAR, GREWER. Shortened from MACGRUAR, q.v. One of the oldest recorded surnames in Braemar. Persons of this name appear to have been long settled in Kindrocht (now known as Braemar), and on the tombstone of James Gruar in Tominrau, who died in 1807, is the following verse:

"Four hundred years have now wheeled round,
   With half a century more;
Since this has been the burying ground
   Belonging to the Gruers."

John Grewyr was tenant in Fortour c. 1520 (*Cupar-Angus*, I, p. 300), and Thomas Growar, burgess freeman of Glasgow, 1628 (*Burgesses*).

GREY. See *under* GRAY.

GRIER. See *under* GREER.

GRIERSON. The Griersons of Lag, Dumfriesshire, claim descent from Gilbert, second son of Malcolm, dominus de MacGregor, who is said to have died in 1374, but, says Col. Fergusson, "there is no evidence or foundation for the story commonly current that this family was an offshoot of the Highland family of MacGregor" (*Lairds of Lag*, p. 16–17). Gilbert Greresoun who had a grant in 1411 of Mekildaltoun and Dormont from Archibald, earl of Douglas may be the Gilbert Grierson who had a charter of the lands of Drumjoan in the Stewartry of Kirkcudbright from Princess Margaret, daughter of Robert III, widow of the fourth earl of Douglas dated April 1429 (*Celt. Mon.*, VIII, p. 239). William Grerson had a safe conduct into England, 1451 (*Bain*, IV, 1232). Robert Greresoune in Drumfreis had a remission for the slaughter of Sir John Mc brare, chaplain, 1502 (*Trials*, I, p. °39). John Greyson or Grierson, provincial friar of Blackfriars in Perth, c. 1526–59, appears in record as Gresone, Gresoune, Greisoun, Greysoun, and Griersoun, the last his own signature (*Milne*, p. 137, 232, 236). As John Greirsoune he appears as professor of sacred theology, 1557 (*Friars Ayr*, p. 96). Andrew Grierson was factor to the earl of Glencairn in 1671 (*Just. Rec.*, II, p. 59). In a list of papists which was given in to the presbytery of Kincardine O'Neil in 1704 many names are given of the Griersons *alias* M'Gregors of Glengairn (*Jervise*, II, p. 167). Of Sir Robert Grierson of Lag, who figures in Scott's *Redgauntlet*, many tales were told of his severity and bloodthirstiness by the peasantry of Galloway. See GRESOUN.

GRIEVE. From the office of 'grieve,' overseer of a farm, bailiff, or under steward. The name may be the equivalent of mediaeval 'prepos- situs.' Johan Greve of Haytone, Berwickshire, rendered homage, 1296 (*Bain*, II, p. 207). Johannes Grefe in the parish of Fyvy was ex- communicated in 1382 (REA., I, p. 165). John Grefe was one of an inquest in Prestwick, 1470 (*Prestwick*, p. 2). Lawrence Greif witnessed a sasine in Lauderdale, 1493 (*Laing*, 217), Andro Greiff was member of an assize at Cupar, 1521 (SCBF., p. 222), and George Greif witnessed a sasine in 1525 (*Home*, 35). Alex- ander Greif was admitted burgess of Aberdeen, 1528 (NSCM., I, p. 49), and in the same year John Greif was 'rentalit in mylne of Edylstoun' (*Rental*). James Greife was tenant under Kelso Abbey, 1567 (*Kelso*, p. 520), Mathow Greif was 'redar' at the Kirk of Monekyn, 1569 (RPC., I, p. 684), Alexander Greif was school- master in Stirling, 1603 (SBR., p. 103), and Johannes Grieff, burgess of Bruntiland before 1605 (*Inquis.*, 213). John Grieve was a minor Border poet, and another John Grieve, provost of Edinburgh, 1782–83, was publicly horse- whipped by some roughs because he had placed some of their lady friends, ladies of easy virtue, in the pillory. The Greves of Greviston, in Traquair parish, may have been so named from the office which they held. They gave name to Greviston there, spelled Grewiston in 1436, in 1463 Greistoun. Gref 1470, Greiuve 1585, Greyf 1526, Greyve 1296.

GRIFFIN. The English form of the Welsh personal name Griffith (Gruffydd). Robertus Griffin held land in Newtyle before 1226 (LAC., 39), William Griffin was witness to a charter by Andrew, bishop of Moray, 1233 (*Pluscardyn*, p. 203). Griffinus, canon of Mo- ray, witnessed excambion of the lands of Dolays Michel (Dallas), 1232 (REM., p. 88).

GRIG. The king "round whose name, amplified to Gregory by the writers of a later age, a cloud of legendary fiction gathered." See GIRIC.

GRIGOR. A form of GREGOR, q.v. The Grigors of the north are chiefly descendants of some 300 Macgregors whom the earl of Moray transplanted in 1624 to the north, from his estates in Monteith, to oppose the Mackin- toshes (*Scots notes and queries*, II, p. 144).

GRIM. The first reference may be from OE. *grimm* 'grim,' 'fierce.' The later references may be forms of GRAHAM, q.v. Grim, Grym, and Gryme are not uncommon in England in thir- teenth and fourteenth centuries (*Bardsley*). Thomas Grym witnessed a confirmation by Patrick, earl of Dunbar, n.d. (*Neubotle*, p. 81.)

Cuthbert Grym was pledge for Andro Fishar, 1488 (*Lanark*, p. 4), and William Grime was burgess of Montrose, 1635 (*Jervise*, I, p. 161). Sir James Grym was co-notary in Strathmiglo, 1541 (*Gaw*, 63). Isobel Gryme is recorded in Montrose, 1641, and another Isobel Grim in Dundee, 1683 (*Brechin*).

"I'm damned if I will sail with you, Sir Graham,
     Though I may seem uncivil,
But Graham is Graeme, and Graham is Grim,
     And Grim, sir, is the Devil.'" — *Old Ballad.*

GRIMBALD. From *Grimbald*, an OE. and ME. personal name meaning 'fiercely bold.' Robert Grimbal witnessed the charter by David I of the church of S. Marie of Berwic to the monks of S. Cuthbert, c. 1130–33 (*Raine*, 18). Adam fitz Grimbaud (the NF. form of the name) of the county of Are rendered homage in 1296 (*Bain*, II, p. 202). Robert Grimbalde of Ber- wickshire also rendered homage (ibid., p. 207).

GRIMBISTER. An old Orcadian surname de- rived from the lands of Grimbuster in the parish of Firth. The name has now quite dis- appeared. Cobeyne (= Kolbein) Grynbister was roithman in 1509 (REO., p. 81), Anne Grimbuster or Grymbuster granted to her brothers Alexander and Magnus Grimbuster her sister-part of their lands in Firth, 1560–61 (ibid., p. 264), and Andrew Grimbister in Grimbister is recorded in 1688 (*Clouston*, p. 35). The name became lost in Davie, the patronymic of one of the family, and Davies occupy Grimbister at the present day. Gryn- buster 1523.

GRIMKETEL. An old Norse personal name, *Grimketil*, later *Grimkel*, common in Iceland and Norway. A carucate held by Grimketil was given to the Abbey of Paisley between 1165 and 1173 (RMP., p. 5).

GRIMMAN. A variant of GRIMMOND, q.v. W. Grimman in Pitrodie, 1816.

GRIMMOND, GRIMOND. Perthshire surnames. Disguised forms of (MAC)CRIMMON, q.v., with accretional *d*. John Griman was witness in Perth, 1534 (*Rollok*, 1). Anna Grimen in Perth, 1657. John Grimmond in Cottoun of Pitfour, 1665, and Elspeth Grimmon there in 1685 (*Dunblane*). James Grimman apud Newmilne of Nairne, 1698 (*Inquis.*, 8024). William Gryman in Auchtergaven, 1698, and Andrew Grimman in Easter Tullyneydies, 1724, and eight more of the name are in record (*Dunkeld*).

GRINDEGRETH. A family named Grinde- greth or Grindegret was prominent in Dum- friesshire in the thirteenth century. Johannes Grindegret witnessed a charter of a carucate

GRINDEGRETH, *continued*
of land in Langholme c. 1270 to Herbert Maxwell (*Pollok*, I, p. 125; RHM., II, p. 7). The family also made grants to Lanercost and Holmcultran, c. 1280–90, and one of the family was burgess of Dumfries c. 1290 (*Edgar*, p. 7, 220, 222). Grindagret in Holm Cultran Register looks like Norse for 'door-stone,' *grindar-grjot.*

GRINOCK. See under GREENOCK.

GRINTON. This name may be a form of Grindon, from the place of that name in Northumberland. Thom Gryntone was tenant in Stobo, 1633 (*Rental*), Patrick Grintoun, reidare at Lyne, 1574 (RMR.), and Joannes Gryntoun was retoured heir in lands of Fewarislandis, 1578 (*Retours, Linlithgow*, 13). Thomas Grintoun was mealmaker in Portsburgh, Edinburgh, 1667 (*Laing*, 2615), and Elizabeth Grinton is recorded in Strathmilne, 1698 (*Torphichen*). See GRENDON.

GRITHMAN. Johan Grithman of Berwickshire rendered homage, 1296 (*Bain*, II, p. 206). A grithman was one who took grith, or sanctuary, in a church.

GROAT. In 1496 William de St. Clair, earl of Caithness, granted to John Grot, son of Hugh Grot, a charter of one pennyland in Duncansbay, Caithness (Calder, *Sketches of history of Caithness*, 1861, p. 245). The name is also found in Fife, and till within recent years it was common in Dysart, being found there so early as 1545, when Christinn Grott and Walter Grote appear in record, and Henricus Grot in 1571 (*Dysart*, p. 14, 15, 36). Hugo Grot was chaplain in Wick in 1530 (*Trials*, I, p. 149*), and William Grot was retoured heir of Malcolm Grot of Tankernes, his grandfather, in 1632 (*Retours, Orkney*, 18). The name is most probably from Low German or Dutch *groot* (pron. grote), 'great, tall.' Robert Mackay, *History of the house of Mackay*, 1829, has a silly story of the origin of the name. Groit 1630, Grott 1726.

GRONTBACHELAR. Hostyn Grontbachelar de Elgin was juror on the inquest concerning the king's garden there, 1261 (APS., I, p. 99 red).

GROSART, GROSSART. Current surnames but not common. Harrison explains the name as meaning 'big, stout' (OF. *gros*) + the Fr. diminutive suffix -*ard*. In 1711 Alexander Grosert, merchant, in Bo'ness, formerly of Rotterdam, was granted disposition of Logie. In 1714 Alexander Grosert granted the fee of the lands to his grandson, Walter, who was collector of

customs at Alloa, and died in 1760 (Stephens, *Inverkeithing*, p. 203–204). Rev. Alexander Balloch Grosart (1827–1899) was an editor of reprints of rare Elizabethan and Jacobean literature.

GROSKENEHT. Gaffridus Groskeneht, witness in Aberdeen, 1387 (REA., I, p. 177). Probably an Englishman.

GROSS. A descriptive name, from OFr. *gros*, large, fat. Michael Gross is mentioned in an inhibition by the bishop of Glasgow, 1294 (RMP., p. *203). John Gros or Gras forfeited lands in Berwick in the reign of David II (RMS., I, App. II, 846).

GROSSET. A rare current surname, probably a variant of GROSART, q.v.

GROTSETTER. An old Orcadian surname from the lands of Grotsetter in the parish of St. Andrews. James Grosetter is mentioned in 1572 (REO., p. 290).

GROUNDWATER. An old Orcadian surname of local origin from Groundwater in Orphir. Alexander Grundwater in Gyre, Orphir, died in 1686, and Edward Groundwater in Tankerness was captured by the press-gang about 1812 (*Old Lore Misc.*, I, p. 201). "One Groundwater, an Orkney man," was one of those concerned in the horrible murder of Janet Cornfoot, a supposed witch, in Pittenweem, 1705 (*Edinburgh magazine and literary miscellany*, v. 1, p. 206).

GRUAR, GRUER. Curtailed forms of MACCRUER, q.v., from Gaelic *Mac Grudaire*. See also GREWAR.

GRUB. John Gruub was witness in the inquiry concerning the Templars in 1309 (Wilkins, *Concilia*, p. 383). Alan Grub was present at assize on land of Gladmor, 1430 (*James* II, 16). James Grub in Abirsnethock, 1633 (SCM., III, p. 74). George Grub, citiner of Brechin, 1611, and six more of the name in record in the vicinity (*Brechin*). Groob 1646. An OE. personal name *Grubba*, found in compounds, may be the origin of the name. Unlikely to be from MACROBB. One of this name gave origin to GRUBBET, q.v.

GRUBBET. From the old barony of the same name in Roxburghshire. About the year 1180 Symon de Grubbeheued witnessed a charter "super totum halech de territorio de Pronewessete" (now Primside) by Galfridus Ridel (*Kelso*, 368), and c. 1220 he, or perhaps a succeeding Symon, witnessed another charter of land in the territory of Molle (ibid., 169). About 1181 Huctred de Grubbeheued and

Symon, his son and heir, gave the Abbey of Melrose some land in Grubbeheued, called Halkale in Elstaneshaleche (*Melros*, p. 110). Huctred of Grubheued had a convention with the monks of Melrose between 1203 and 1214 (*Melros*, p. 110, 111). Simon de Grubbeheued, knight of Scotland, was one of twelve Scottish knights appointed to meet a similar number of English knights to consider the working of the laws and customs of the marches of the two kingdoms in 1249 (*Bain*, I, 1749). In 1250 and in 1255 John de Grubheued witnessed charters of grazing lands in the district of Molle (*Kelso*, 149, 160), and between 1253 and 1280 as John de Grubeshewed he witnessed a charter by Nicolas Corbet in favor of an hospital in Northumberland (*Laing*, 9). There appears to be no further record of this family. See GRUB.

GRUMANSON. John Grvmansonne in Strathdon, 1494 (ADA., p. 203).

GRUMBAIG. William de Grumbaig, squire of John, earl of Caithness, who had letters of safe conduct in 1291 (Stevenson, *Hist. Docs.*, I, p. 229), probably derived his name from Grumbeg, a township on the northern shore of Loch Naver. There is another Grumbaig in the parish of Kildonan.

GRUMENGRIG. James Grumengrig, notary public in the diocese of Dunkeld, 1527 (*Athole*, p. 712).

GRUNDISTOUN. A brief of inquest was purchased by Thomas Grundistone, 1478 (ADC., p. 5). David Grundistoune de Kingask was juror on inquest at Cupar, 1516, and Thomas Grundistoune sat as sheriff-depute in Cupar in 1518 (SCBF., p. 50, 136). Mirabell Grundieson is in record in Fife in sixteenth century (*Macfarlane*, II, p. 190), and Thomas Grandiston of Kingask and Walter Grandiston of Glaslie were jurors on inquest held at Cupar, 1505 (ibid., II, p. 537). Thomas of Grundystoun witness, 1439, and David Grundistoun, witness, 1516 (*Binns*, 9, 28). Alexander Grundistoun and Thome Grundistoun had precept of remission for slaughter committed on William Lousoun, 1529 (RSS., II, 69). Walter Grundestoun was retoured heir of his brother David Grundestoun, 1544 (*Retours, Fife*, 3), Thomas Grundistoune of Kingask was charged in 1558 with abiding from the raid of Lauder (*Trials*, I, p. °404), and Patrick Grundestoun was constable of the parish of Cults, in Fife, 1633 (RPC., 2. ser. V, p. 94). There is a Grundiston near Hawick.

GRUNDY. Metathetic for Gundry, from the OE. personal name Gundred. Robert Grundy

de Neuton, Roxburghshire, rendered homage, 1296, and Adam Grondy was juror on inquisition made at Roxburgh, 1303 (*Bain*, II, p. 199, 376).

GRUOCH. Munch (*Chron. Man*, p. viii) says that Gróa, granddaughter of Aude, daughter of Ketil Flatneb, was married to Duncan, earl of Caithness. Her name, he says, was rendered *Gruach* (Gruoch) in Gaelic records, and that it is very probable that from this Gruach and her husband, Duncan, the far-famed Macbeth's queen was descended, and had got her name. Gruoch, daughter of Boite or Bodhe (a son of Kenneth III) was married to Gillacomgan, the pretender of the Moray house, killed in 1032. She afterwards married Gillacomgan's cousin Macbeth, who had succeeded to the Moray claim.

GRYCIE. Perhaps from Fr. *gris*, grey, with diminutive -*ie*. Mungo Gryse witnessed an instrument of sasine by the abbot of Sweetheart Abbey, 1555 (*Laing*, 632). The wife of Robert Grycie in Buittle was charged with being a papist, 1684 (RPC., 3. ser. IX, p. 571).

GUDEWARLD. A remission was granted to Johannes Gudewarld in 1489 for his part in holding Dumbarton Castle against the king (APS., XII, p. 34; *Lennox*, II, p. 132).

GUELP. A surname early recorded in Aberdeen. Robert Guelp appears there in 1400 (SCM., V, p. 15), and David Qulep was admitted burgess of the burgh in 1460 (NSCM., I, p. 17; CRA., p. 23, 26). Thomas Guelp or Quelp was burgess there, 1463 (REA., I, p. 286), and William Guelp or Quelp, burgess in 1487 (CRA., p. 43), had "a fischinge of the watter of Done," 1490 (SCM., V, p. 31).

GUFFOCK. An old Galloway name, from MACGUFFOCK, q.v.

GUIDID. The name of an early Pictish king (CPS., p. 25). The name means 'woodman,' from the root seen in Welsh *guid*, *gwydd*, OG. *fid*, now *fiodh* (*Watson* I, p. 115).

GUIDING. Margaret Guiding was set at liberty from the Canongate Tolbooth, Edinburgh, 1684 (BOEC., IX, p. 173). John Gudding, bailie of Kirkintilloch, 1665 (*Sasines*, 1228). See GUIDLING.

GUIDLING. David Gudeling sold part of the mill of Ardett in Fife in 1558 (ER., XIX, p. 77). Malcolm Guidling, portioner of Kirkintilloch, 1661 (*Sasines*, 1008). See GUIDING.

GUIDO. A Norman personal name of Teutonic origin, also commonly spelled Wido. At the time of the Domesday Survey William filius Widonis, i.e. William Wido's son, was a tenant in chief in the counties of Wilts, Gloucester, and Somerset (*Lower*). Widone, father of Robert, sheriff of Roxburgh, c. 1136 (*Raine*, 21). Wydo, Widone, Gwydo, or Guido was abbot of Lundores in time of Radulph, bishop of Brechin (RAA., I, p. 126–128).

GUILD. Alexander Gulde rendered to Exchequer the accounts of the bailies of Stirling, 1421 and 1425 (ER., IV, p. 370, 398), Thomas Gulde and William Guld, 'husbandis,' charter witnesses, 1481 (*Panmure*, II, 252), and Henry Guld is mentioned in a Scone document of 1491 (*Scon*, p. 198). Kath. Guld, spouse of Alexander Boys of Panbryd, 1502 (RAA., II, 427), Thomas Guld, prebendary of Collegiate Church of Holy Trinity, Edinburgh, 1512 (*Soltre*, p. 167), may be Thomas Gulde, monk of Newbattle, 1521 (*Neubotle*, p. 284), and William Gwill was slain in Aberdeen, 1584 (SCM., II, p. 57). Nineteen persons of the name are recorded in the Commissariot Record of Dunblane in seventeenth and eighteenth centuries. Gwild 1581. Probably Goold is a variant. Macbain (v, p. 46) says the name is a curtailed form of *guilder*, i.e. member of a guild, but ?

GUILLE. Lower says an old Jersey family of this name "sent some branches to England, where they altered the orthography to Gill." A family of the name is recorded in Bonnyrig, Midlothian.

GULLAN, GULLANE, GUILLAND, GULLAND, GULLEN. From the old lands now village of Gullane in the parish of Dirleton, East Lothian. R. L. Stevenson in his *Catriona* spells the place name 'Gillan,' and the local pronunciation is 'Gool-an.' William de Colin, whose seal is appended to a renunciation of land and pasturage of Molle to the Abbey of Melrose, 1170 (*Seals*, 188), may be William de Golin, a charter witness in the reign of William the Lion (LSC., p. 38). William de Gulyne witnessed confirmation charters by William, bishop of St. Andrews, 1211–26 (*Soltre*, p. 16, 17) and is probably the William de Colin who renounced the vill of Greater Lummesdene before 1214 (*Raine*, 54). Willelmus de Colin witnessed a charter of the tithes of the church of Kinghorn a. 1200 (LSC., 47), the gift by Philip de Mubray to the monks of Dunfermline c. 1202–14 (RD., p. 95); as senescallus of the bishop of St. Andrews he attested the grant of the church of S. Giles of Ormystoun to the Hospital of Soltre between 1211–26

(*Soltre*, p. 16), and appears as rector of the church of Golyn c. 1224 (*Dryburgh*, p. 33). He is also the William de Colin, witness to several charters by William, bishop of St. Andrews (RAA., I, p. 106–118). Waldevus de Golyn is mentioned c. 1220, and about the same date we have record of a gift by Osmund de Golyn (*Dryburgh*, p. 22, 23). John de Golin was witness to a grant made relative to the church of Scoonie, Fife, c. 1260 (RPSA., p. 160), and Adam de Gulyne, archdeacon of Lothian witnessed gift of the lands of Quhytwel to Soltre after 1228 (*Soltre*, p. 29). Mariot de Golyn of Edinburghshire rendered homage in 1296 (*Bain*, II, p. 198), John de Golyn witnessed a charter of lands of Dauyston c. 1330 (RHM., I, 40), John de Guling held a land in Edinburgh in 1405 (*Egidii*, p. 42), William de Gulyne, charter witness in Dundee, 1430 (HP., II, p. 164), and John Gulyng held a tenement in Northberwyk in 1477 (CMN., 36). Five persons named Gulline are recorded in the Commissariot Record of Wigtownshire in the eighteenth century. Guilland 1678, Gulane 1504, Gulen 1584, Gullen 1697, Gulan 1499, Guillein 1557.

GULLILAND. Of local origin from Guililand near Dundonald, Ayrshire. John Guliland in Cunningham, Ayrshire, 1640. John Guileland was exonerated from rebellion, 1686 (RPC., 3. ser. XII, p. 81). Mr. James Gilliland was minister at Greenlaw, Berwickshire, 1725 (*Lauder*).

GULLINE. Probably from Ir. (*Mac*)*Coilín*, 'son of Coilin,' a variant of *MacCailin*. Recorded in Wigtownshire in eighteenth century (*Wigtown*).

GULLOCH. Recorded in Ross. Probably from (MAC)CULLOCH, with C hardened to G.

GUNION, GUNNION, GUNNYON. From (MAC) CUNNION, q.v. John Gunnion in Cammford, parish of Kirkinner, 1684 (RPC., 3. ser. X, p. 267), Janet Gunnion in Bailliewhirr, 1788 (*Wigtown*). William Gunnyon edited an edition of Burns's complete works with memoir in 1865.

GUNN. This name like Leod in MACLEOD, q.v., is an abridged or pet-form of some such longer Norse name as *Gunn-arr*, *Gunn-björn*, *Gunn-laug*, or *Gunn-olfr*. Gunni is an old West Scandinavian personal name (*Lindkvist*, p. 216). The Norse diminutive is *Gunna*, whence the Gaelic *Guinne*, with adjectival *Gunnach*. The Gunns are of Norse origin, and the first of the name connected with Caithness was Gunni, son of Olaf, a Caithness chief of the twelfth century (*Orkneyinga Saga*, 1873 ed., p. 73). They were a warlike clan and occupied mainly the Highland portions of Caithness. Their connection with the county as a distinct clan ended about 1619 (Henderson, *Caithness family history*, p. 319).

(2) A pension was paid to John, son of Gun or Gune by the provost of Rutherglen, 1327 (ER., I, p. 70, 87, etc.), and two years later John, son of Gvn and nine men were paid for rigging sent to Tarbert (ibid., p. 127). This Gunn may be of a different origin, cf. English name Gunne (1273). Robert Gun was deacon of craft in Stirling, 1565 (SBR., p. 280).

GUPILD. From the OF. *goupil* 'fox,' with accretionary *d*. The word still survives in modern French *goupillon*, a sprinkler, originally made of a fox's tail. A family of this name took a prominent part in the affairs of Edinburgh in the fourteenth and fifteenth centuries. Payments were made to Matthew Gupi or Gupil by the custumar of Cupar and by the custumars of Edinburgh in 1328 (ER., I, p. 95, 100). William Guppylde who had a charter of the lands of Lumlethyn and Cragoc in the sheriffdom of Forfar from his cousin in 1366 (RMS., I, 247; *Macfarlane*, II, p. 465) is doubtless the William Gopeld who with Walter Copeld complained of being plundered by wreckers in England in 1370 (*Bain*, IV, 164). William Guppild is recorded as alderman and burgess of Edinburgh in 1368 and 1380 (*Egidii*, p. 1; *Laing*, 67). The tenement of John Gupilde in Edinburgh is mentioned in 1468 (*Neubotle*, 299, 302). Gupilt 1382.

GURDONE. Adam Gurdone of Stirlingshire rendered homage, 1296. His seal shows a lion or dog's head couped, *S' Ade de Gordwne* (*Bain*, II, p. 208, 557). Cf. GORDON.

GURNAY. Aleyn Gurnay of the county of Roxburghe rendered homage for his lands in 1296. His seal bears a squirrel feeding within two squares interlaced and legend *S' Alani Gorley* (*Bain*, II, p. 199, 533). Of Norman origin, probably from Gournai-en-Brai in the arrondissement of Neufchatel.

GURRAN. From Ir. (*Mag*)*Corráin*, a variant of *MacCorraidhin*, 'son of Corraidhín' (a diminutive of *corradh*, 'spear'). James Gurran in Clauchen of Dalry, 1675 (*Kirkcudbright*).

GUTHRIE. From the barony of the name in Angus. The first of the name recorded is probably the Guthrie sent to France after Sir William Wallace in 1299. In 1348 Adam de Guthrie witnessed a decreet to a burgess of

Dundee, Jon of Guthere was juror on the marches of Woodwrae in 1388 (*Bamff*, p. 22), and Sir David Guthrie of Guthrie was armorbearer to King James III, David Goithry was admitted burgess of Aberdeen in 1460 (NSCM., I, p. 17), John Gothra was tenant in Balmyle in the same year (*Cupar-Angus*, I, p. 142), William of Guthre was alderman of the burgh of Forfar in 1464 (RAA., II, 159), and James de Guthre *de eodem*, a charter witness in 1473 (REG., 400). John Guttere, witness in Linlithgow in 1534 (*Johnsoun*), John Gottraye, burgess of Edinburgh in 1540 (*Irvine*, I, p. 46), Robert Gotray, witness in Glasgow, 1551 (*Protocols*, I), and James Gotthra was miller at the mill of Eyemouth in 1581 (*Home*, 209). John Gotheray had a feu of part of the lands of Kirktoun of Blair in 1584 (*Scon*, 222). The form Gottray was an old spelling of the name in Prestwick, Ayrshire, John Gotrey was burgess there, 1507 (*Prestwick*, p. 10), Peter Gotrav, burgess of Irwene, 1597 (*Inquis. Tut.*, 1263), John Gottray in Eymouth mylne, 1616 (*Inquis.*, 8541), and John Guttraw confest he committed blood [i.e. assaulted to the effusion of blood] upon Richard Gothraw, his younger brother in 1659 (*Stitchill*, p. 18). Peter Gotraye was admitted burgess of Glasgow in 1601 (*Burgesses*), John Goathra is recorded in Broomdykes in 1672, and Adam Goatra in Eist Gordon in 1675 (*Lauder*). Samuel Guthrie (1782–1848) was one of the original discoverers of chloroform.

Although the Guthries of Guthrie were closely connected with the lands belonging to the Abbey of Arbroath yet no one of the name is found in the first volume of the Register of the Abbey. An old rhyme designating the main line and principal branches of the surname names them:

> "Guthrie o' Guthrie,
>   and Guthrie o' Gaigie,
> Guthrie o' Taybank
>   an' Guthrie o' Craigie."

As a forename we have Gothra Morison, c. 1443 (*Cupar-Angus*, I, p. 121).

An Irish patronymic, O'*Laithimh*, now usually Anglicized Lahiff, by some name has been rendered Guthrie from an erroneous notion that it is derived from *lathaigh*, i.e. of the slough or puddle (O'Donovan in AFM.). Gothra 1534, Gothray 1595, Gotrae 1671, Gotrav 1672, Gottraw 1664, Gottray 1551, Gutherie 1624, Guthree 1640, Guthrye 1632, Guthry 1428, Gutrae 1671, Gwtterie 1565; and Gottrae, Gottre, Gutherye, Gutthre, Guttre.

GUTTERSON. *See under* GOTTERSON.

GUYND. John Gynd in Pendriche, parish of Brechin, 1612 (Brechin) derived his surname from the lands of Guind or Goind, now Guynd, in the parish of Carmyllie, Angus. Guynn 1816.

GYLLEMAHAD. 'The gille of Ceti or Coeddi,' bishop of Hi, who died in 712 (Watson II, p. 12). Gyllemahad Macgyllepatric appears in a Moray charter of 1236 (REM., p. 31).

GYLOCH. Ten persons of this name are recorded in Dunblane and parish of Port in the seventeenth century (Dunblane).

GYNES. Ingeram de Gynes held the lands of Lambirtone c. 1315-21 (RMS., I, 6). Ingeramus de Gynys witnessed a charter to the Friars Preachers in Elgyne, 1367 (ibid., 245). Perhaps from Guines, near Calais, early forms of which are Gisnes, Gysnes, and Gynes. Cf. JEANS.

HAB, HABBIE. See under HOB, HOBBIE.

HABBISHAW. A surname recorded in Kirkcudbright, may be from Habbieshowe near Auchinleck, Ayrshire.

HACCHEPETIT. Johannes hacchepetit witnessed a charter by Richard Lupellis, dominus de Hawic, c. 1183 (RPSA., p. 262).

HACKET, HACKETT. Old spellings of HALKETT, q.v., which have become independent surnames.

HACKING. A surname found in Dumfriesshire, probably of late introduction from across the Border. From the place of the name in the township of Billington, parish of Blackburn, Lancashire. There was a family of Del Hacking there in the thirteenth and fourteenth centuries.

HACKNEY. Adam called Hakenay had a charter of lands in Ayr, 1316 (Ayr, p. 21). Johannes Kahew alias Haknay, burgess of Edinburgh, 1467 (Neubotle, p. 265, 268). John Halkney in Buchat, parish of Alyth, 1783 (Dunkeld). John Hackeny at Westhaven of Panbride, 1800 (Brechin). Lower, Bardsley, and Harrison record this name and all derive it from Hackney in Middlesex.

HACKSTON. A curtailment of HALKERSTON, q.v. David Hackston of Rathillet, Covenanting leader, was executed 1680. An old account of the murder of Archbishop Sharpe calls him Haxton (Analecta Scotica, II, p. 388). David Hagstoun in Kippen, 1602 (Dunblane), and William Haikston, tailor in Edinburgh, 1685 (Edin. App.).

HACSMALL. Adam Hacsmall on inquest made at Peebles, 1262 (APS., I, p. 101; Peebles, 5).

HACWRANG. William Hacwrang witnessed a charter by John de Mountfort, c. 1211-14 (RAA., I, p. 47).

HADDEN, HADDON. Variants of HOWDEN, q.v. Silvester Hadden of Kellor witnessed a retour of service at Forfar, 1514 (SCM., v, p. 292), Adam Haddane of Dolphington appears in 1679 (Lanark CR.), and Alexander Haddin was married in Edinburgh, 1696 (Edinb. Marr.). George Haldon was builder in Edinburgh, 1939. A family named Hadden was long identified with the history of Aberdeenshire.

HADDINGTON. From the old burgh of the name in East Lothian. Rannulfus de Hadintun was one of the first to build a house in the new burgh of Glasgow, c. 1177-99 (LCD., p. 235; Innes, Sketches of early Scotch history, p. 120). Malcolmus de Hadingtouna was a burgess of Aberdeen in 1317 (SCM., v, p. 11), and Thomas de Hadington was vicar of Marchinche (Markinch) in 1332 (Pap. Lett., II, p. 508). Sir J. of Hadingtun was prior of St. Andrews in 1269 (RPSA., p. 349), and David de Hadingtone and Johan de Hadyntone both of the county of Fyfe rendered homage in 1296 (Bain, II, p. 204). John Hadyngton, a Scottish merchant, petitioned the English chancellor for redress in 1405, and James of Hadyngton, Scots merchant, had a safe conduct in England in 1422 (Bain, IV, 712, 921). John Haddingtoun was chaplain in St. Andrews diocese in 1456 (CAB., p. 395), Johannes de Hadingtoune was burgess of Perth in 1440 (RD., p. 297), Sir Henry Hadingtoun was vicar of Kincardin-onele and Master of the Hospital of the Trinity College beside Edinburgh in 1511 (Soltre, p. 35), and Jhon Hedingtoune was juror on an inquest in Melrose in 1607 (RRM., I, p. 54). Hadintoun 1517, Headington 1687.

HADDO. See HALDAWACH.

HADDOCK. Probably from Haydock in Lancashire, England, of which Haddock is the local pronunciation. There is, however, a Haddockstone (1626 Haddockstane), near Johnstone, Renfrewshire, with which the name may be connected. Ninane Haddok was rentallit "in xij schilling vi. penny land in Westir Daldowye," 1553 (Riddel, The Salt-foot controversy, p. 61). Janet Haddock in Cauldstreme, parish of Carluke, 1621, and two more of the name (Lanark CR.).

HADDON. See under HADDEN.

HADDOW. A surname found in the shires of Kirkcudbright, Ayr, and Lanark. Not likely to be = HADDO. It may be a form of HADDOCK, as -ck is often dropped in surnames (cf. Nimmo — Nimmock, Rollo — Rollock, etc.). Archibald Haddow in Overquarter in record 1603 (Campsie). The name is a common one in the Commissariot Record of Lanark.

HAFFIE. Curtailed from MACHAFFIE, q.v. William Haffie of Fuffock, Kirkcudbright, is mentioned in 1789 (Kirkcudbright).

HAG. Andrew Hag was prior of Pluscardine, 1454 (Beauly, p. 137). "Schir Wilzame Hag to be chapellane of the chapell of Sanct Rok at the brigend of Stirling," 1500 (RSS., I, 476).

HAGGART. A corruption of MACTAGGART, q.v. The name was not uncommon in Perthshire in the late sixteenth and seventeenth centuries. John Haggart is recorded in Perth in 1595 (RPC., v, p. 651), and — Haggart was portioner of Dulgarthill near Dunkeld in 1598. John Haggart and William Haggart appear in Eister Keppet (Caputh) in 1618 (ibid., XI, p. 368), and William Hagart, called Long William, in Eister Capeth was slain in 1619 (ibid., XII, p. 78).

HAGGARTY, HEGGERTY. Of recent introduction from Ireland. Woulfe explains the name as from O'hÉigcertaigh or O'hÉigeartaigh, 'descendant of Éigceartach' (unjust).

HAGGAS, HAGGIS. Of local origin from Haggis, a common place name occurring in the shires of Berwick, Ayr, Lanark, Renfrew, Aberdeen, and Banff. Gilbert of Haggehouse, a Scots merchant, was arrested at Lynn in England without cause, 1394 (Bain, IV, 162). William Haggus held land in the Almory of Abirbrothoc in 1427 (RAA., II, p. 56), Patrick Hagus (Haghous, or Hagavs), near the Water of Brothoc, is mentioned c. 1457–82 (RAA., II, p. 94, 149, 155, 188), and John Haggous was burgess of Dundee in 1610 (Brechin). Dominus Johannes Haggis was witness at Elgin, 1547 (REM., p. 395).

HAGGER. A claim was pursued against Isobel Hagger in Stitchill, 1723 (Stitchill, p. 185). The name occurs in Suffolk in thirteenth century as Hacgard (Guppy, p. 85). Cf. English surname Haggard.

HAGGERSTON. The seal of Hugo de Hagarstn is appended to a charter of the lands of Ballesdon to the monks of St. Cuthbert of Durham, n.d. (Seals Supp., 461). Probably from Haggerston near Ancroft, Northumberland.

HAGGIE. A different name from HEGGIE, q.v. Alexander Hagy was present at perambulation of the bounds of Kyrknes and Louchor, 1395 (RPSA., p. 3), and Sir Andrew Hagy, chaplain in Stirling, 1556 (SBR., p. 69) may be Andrew Haggie who received payment for the queen's household expenses, 1557 (ER., XIX, p. 389). Symon Hagy appears in Kinglassie, 1615 (Fordell, p. 162). Harrison says it is a double diminutive of one of the Hag(g) names.

HAIG. The first of the name recorded is Petrus del Hage, who witnessed the sale of two serfs, their sons and daughters, and all their progeny between 1162 and 1166 (Diplomata Scotiæ, 75). From the year 1412 the family of Haig of Bemersyde invariably used the form of Haig. Originally the name was in two syllables, Ha-ge, with the g sounded hard as shown by the spelling Hag-he (c. 1185). The name is in OE. haga, an enclosure, yard, from the root hag, to surround. The word also survives in the modern haw (in hawthorn, Hawick for Haw-wick, and in hayward, the hedgewarden). The old prophecy attributed to Thomas the Rhymer referring to the leading family of the name:

"Tide, tide, whate'er betide,
There'll aye be Haigs in Bemersyde,"

proved false in 1867 when the Haigs of Bemersyde died out. It has been said that the true reading of the prophecy is

"Betide, betide, whate'er betide
There'll aye be a hag on Bemersyde,"

alluding to the hag or thicket which covers and clings to the cliff from Bemersyde down to the Tweed. For a history of the family and name see The Haigs of Bemersyde: a family history, Edinburgh, 1881.

Bemersyde was purchased from its owner and presented to Field-Marshal Earl Haig in 1921 as a gift from the nation.

HAILBOTISHED. John Hailbotished held land in Perth under the Abbey of Aberbrothoc, 1330 (RAA., II, p. 8). Cf. under THURBOTHEUED.

HAILES. Most probably from Hailes in the parish of Colinton, Midlothian. There is another Hailes in the parish of Prestonkirk, East Lothian. Magister Wilelmus de Halis witnessed a charter by Roger, bishop elect of St. Andrews, c. 1189–98, relating to the church of Halis, and also witnessed, as de Hales, another charter by the same bishop (RPSA., p. 153; RAA., I, p. 102). John de Halis was abbot of Neubotil in 1398 (LSC., 110), and Daun (= Don) John Hayles, abbot of Balmorenagh (Balmerino) had a safe conduct into England in 1408 (Bain, IV, 744).

HAIN. Recorded in Fife and Kinross-shire. Weekley says it is a contraction of Hagan, Harrison says it is local from Hayne (Somerset, etc.), and Bardsley says it is a personal name.

HAINING, HAINNING, HANING, HANNING, HENNING. Surnames of local origin found around Hawick and in Dumfriesshire. William Hanyng was retoured in lands in the parish and barony of Halywode in 1630 (Retours, Dumfries, 142), and John Hayning, portioner of Glengaber, was retoured heir of George Hayning in Glengaber, 1655 (ibid., 223). Robert Hynnem, bookbinder in Dumfries, 1671. Adam Haining recorded at Clauchan of Girthon, 1771 (Kirkcudbright). There is a Haining near Selkirk, and a Hanyngstoun in Kirkcudbright Retours.

HAIR, HARE. From Ir. O'hIr, 'descendant of Ir.' Both forms are common in Kilbarchan, Ayrshire. William Hare, burgess of Edinburgh, 1366, in the following year made a gift to the altar of the Virgin in St. Giles's church (Egidii, p. 19; RMS., I, 261). Patrick Ahayre, Ahayr, or Ahaire, bailie of Ayr in 1415, 1420 (Ayr, p. 9, 11; ER., IV, p. 327) appears as Patrick Hayre, Hair, or Hare, alderman there in 1430 and 1438 (Ayr, p. 85; Friars Ayr, p. 49). As Patrick Ahar he was a member of the Guild of Ayr, c. 1431 (Coll. AGAA., I, p. 228). Christine Hare appears in Irvine, 1506 (Irvine, I, p. 158), John Hare and Niven Hare were voters in the parish of Qwilton (Coylton), 1513 (Ros, 52). David Hair was 'dompnus' of Neubotle, 1528 (Neubotle, 309), and Nevin Haire was one of an assize in Carrick, 1529 (RMS., III, 849). Sythock Hair was concerned in the slaughter of Donald McEwin in the Cors of Balmaclellane, 1529 (RSS., II, 128). Payment was made in 1563 to the heirs of Andrew Hair in the service of the late queen, who was drowned in Dee Water (ER., XIX, p. 208). John Hair was tenant under the Abbey of Kelso, 1567 (Kelso, p. 526), and one of the keys of the 'common box' of the Canongate of Edinburgh was granted to Johnne Haire in the same year (MCM., II, p. 307). Simon Hair is recorded in Dunfermline, 1576 (Dunfermline), and George Haire was retoured heir of Robert Haire, son of John Haire, gardener to the earl of Mortoun, his father, 1673 (Retours, Edinburgh, 1206).

HAIRHILL. Local. William Hairhill in Barcaipell, 1684 (Kirkcudbright).

HAIRSTAINS. Halbert Hairstanis signed the Band of Dumfries in 1570 (RPC., XIV, p. 66), and James Hairstanis was a witness there in 1576 (Edgar, p. 243). John Hairstanis, senior, burgess of Dumfries, was retoured heir of Matthew Hairstanis of Craigs in lands in the parish of Kirkmahoe, and in the 10 mark lands of Grange in the parish of Ur in 1629 (Retours, Dumfries, 139; Retours, Kirkcudbright, 179). Matthew Harstanes was retoured heir of his father, John Harstanes de Craigs, in 1686 (Retours, Dumfries, 314), and in 1699 William Hairstanes was retoured heir of Matthew Hairstanes de Craigs, his father (ibid., 355). Janet Hairstanes in Cornharrow in 1789 (Kirkcudbright). Of local origin from some small place of the name. There is a Hairstones Height in the parish of Kirkpatrick-Juxta, and a Hairstanes in Linlithgow Retours (237). Harestones in the parish of Kirkurd, Peeblesshire, derives its name from several standing stones near by. By some the name has been changed to Hastings. Hairstens c. 1740.

HAITLIE, HEATLEY, HEATLIE, HEATLY. William de Hatteley, son of Sir Robert dictus de Hatteley and Matilda his wife, with the consent of his wife Emma, about 1230 granted to the monks of Kelso a right of way through his land of Mellerstan and permission to build a bridge over the Blackburn (Kelso, 136). Another Robert de Hetlye, who possessed lands in Faunes and Melockston, is probably Robert de Hattely who in 1270 witnessed a charter by William de Alwentum (Alwinton) to the Abbey of Melrose of the lands of Halsinton. John de Hetlyn and Alexander de Hetlve appear in 1292 (Stodart, II), and Alexander de Hateleye rendered homage at Elgyn en Morreve, 1296. His seal bears a boar's head couped, erect to dexter, and S' Alex' de Hateley (Bain, II, p. 183, 195, 541). Johan de Hatale of Peeblesshire also rendered homage, 1296 (ibid., p. 207). William de Hetley was one of the men-at-arms in the garrison at Roxburgh Castle in 1335–6–7. William Hatle, Scots merchant, had a safe conduct to travel in England, 1412, and David Hatley, Scottish merchant, the same in 1475 (Bain, IV, 829, 1433). John de Hatele rendered his account of receipts of Strathurde in Perthshire, 1453, and Leonard Haitlie was portioner of Haliburtoun in 1631 (Inquis., 1827). In a bond of assurance dated April 1568 the Brownfields bind themselves and their servants under the penalty of £1000 Scots, and assure Alexander Hately in Lembden, John in Broomhill, George in Hordlaw, Laurence in Haliburton, and Leonard, brothers, and Patrick Hately in the Klevis, their children, household, men and servants, that they shall be unharmed and unmolested for three years. Nicollas Heathlie in Bleakuer, 1672 (Lauder). Haitlve 1529, Haittlev 1606, Hatlie 1458, Hatly 1478, Haytli 1447, Heatlie 1659.

HALBERT. Jonet Halbert and Mariota Halbert are recorded in 1643 (*Inquis.*, 2790), John Halbert of Dallblair, 1677 (ibid., 8714), and William Halbert, schoolmaster at Auchinleck, Ayrshire, published *The Practical figurer*, Paisley, 1789. Weekley (p. 161) suggests it is from the name of the weapon, and Miss Yonge suggests it came to Britain "with its Danish invaders." Halbert Glendinning is a character in Scott's *Monastery*.

HALBERTSON, 'son of HALBERT.' William Halbertson, tenant in Drumbankhead, Dalswinton, 1760.

HALCRO, HALCROW. An old Orcadian surname derived from the lands of Halcro in South Ronaldsay, which again were named from Halcro in the parish of Bower, Caithness. The l is an interpolation showing that the preceding vowel is long. A seventeenth-century tradition on record claims that the family were descended from a natural son of King Sverrir of Norway. David Haucrow, tacksman of Qwybrown in Ronaldsay, 1492, appears to be the first of the name recorded (REO., p. 405). The name is not found in Peterkin's Rentals. Sir Nycoll Haucro or Halkraye was parson of Orpher in 1534 and 1539 (ibid., p. 216; *Goudie*, p. 143), and Hew Halcro of that Ilk is mentioned in 1640 (MCM., II, p. 211). Hacra 1575, Hacro 1528, Hawcro 1548. Hacroe also occurs.

HALDANE. (1) The name *Healfdene*, the 'Half-Danes,' an appellation of the Hocingas and the Secgans, who took part in the campaign against Finn in the lay of *Beowulf*, later became a common OE. personal name, *Heal(f)-dane*, Latinized *Haldanus*. Halden filius Eadulf was one of the witnesses to Earl David's *Inquisitio* into the territorial possessions of the church of Glasgow a. 1124 (REG., 1). Halden was steward of Earl Waldeve, 1178 (*Bain*, I, p. 151). In 1255 sixty acres of land outside the castle of Scardeburc were demised by Roger Haldane (ibid., 2030). Halden, a nativus or serf, was gifted to Kelso Abbey by Waldeve the earl (*Kelso*, p. 198). (2) Anderson (*Sc. Nat.*) says a younger son of the Border house of Hadden or Hauden (see under HOWDEN) became possessed of the estate of Gleneagles, Perthshire, by marrying the heiress of that family and that Aylmer de Haldane of Gleneagles rendered homage, 1296. In the thirteenth and fourteenth centuries the family were barons of some consequence in Perthshire, but the name is now rare there. David Hadden, tutor of Glennageis, was one of an assize, 1614 (*Trials*, II, p. 439). Distinguished bearers of this name are: Richard Burdon Haldane (1856–1928), first Viscount Haldane; John Burdon Sanderson Haldane (b. 1892), professor of biometry, University College, London; and Miss Elizabeth Sanderson Haldane (1862–1937), the first woman justice of peace for Scotland (1920). Haddin 1477, Haldan 1816, Haldin 1650.

HALDAWACH. Alanus de Haldawach in the parish of Fyvv, excommunicated in 1382 (REA., I, p. 165) derived his surname from Haddo in the parish of Forgue, Aberdeenshire.

HALE. Michel de Hale del counte de Edeneburk rendered homage, 1296. His seal shows an eight-rayed figure and S' *Micael d' Hail* (*Bain*, II, p. 201, 547). Bardsley has 'Richard de la Hale' in Oxfordshire, 1273; Weekley says Hale is dative of HAUGH; and Harrison says it is for HALL. Cf. HAILES.

HALFKNIGHT. Robert halfchniht was one of those who attested the grant of the church of Tuenham to the Abbey of Holyrood, c. 1230 (LSC., p. 60). Bardsley and Weekley have English examples of this name but both have missed its significance. Bardsley interprets the name as " 'the half knight,' one not in full knighthood," and Weekley (p. 235) says "I take it that a 'half-knight' was a servitor of small efficiency." In the Middle Ages lands were generally held by knight's service — *per servitum militare*, as the formula has it. The unit of this tenure was the service of one knight or fully-armed horseman (*servitium unius militis*) to be done to the king in his army for forty days. Before the end of the twelfth century the appearance of portions of knight's fees shows that payments were accepted in lieu of military service: "When it is said that a man holds the twentieth part of a fee, this cannot mean that he is bound to serve for two days in the army; it must mean that he and others are bound to find a warrior who will serve for forty days, and that some or all of them will really discharge their duty of money payments" (Pollock and Maitland, *History of English law*, I, p. 267). Two charters of King David I afford us instances of this service of half a knight's fee. Alexander de St. Martin had a grant of certain lands between Hadingtoun and Alstanefurd, to be held of the king by the service of half a knight (*servicium dimidii militis*); and the king engages to pay every year from his treasury ten marks of silver until he make up a full knight's fee (*Lawrie*, p. 150). In the same manner Walter de Riddale, c. 1150, had a grant of Whitimes (an error for Whittune), the half of Eschetho and Lilislive (now Lilliesleaf), with the pertinents, to be held in feu by the same service as that of Alexander de St.

HALFKNIGHT, *continued*

Martin as freely as any of the king's barons, de Riddale's neighbors, hold their lands (ibid., p. 180). Henricus Reuel had a grant of Cultrach in Fife from William the Lion "per servicium dimidii militis" (*Balmerino,* App. 2). The name is therefore to be understood as meaning one who rendered the equivalent of a half knight's service, or held half a knight's fee.

HALIBURTON, HALLIBURTON. Of territorial origin from the lands of Haliburton in Berwickshire. Near the end of the twelfth century David filius Tructe (or Truite or Trute) granted the church of his vill of Halyburton "cum tofta et crofta et duabus bouatis terre" to the monks of Kelso (*Kelso,* 268). About the year 1230 this grant was confirmed by Walter, the son of David, son of Truite, and about 1261 Philip de Halyburton again confirmed the gift of the church of Halyburtun and pertinents to the Abbey of Kelso as formerly made by David filius Trute his *proavus* and Walter his *avus* (ibid., 269, 270). Sir Henry de Haliburtoune witnessed a grant of lands in Dunypais, c. 1200 (*Cambus.,* 83), and also appears as witness c. 1242–3 in a charter by Matilda, countess of Angus (RAA., I, p. 332). Adam de Haliburtun witnessed a charter by Matilda, countess of Angus (ibid., 49). Philip de Haliburton, c. 1260, son and heir of William de Haliburton, confirmed the grant of Melocstan to the Abbey of Kelso made sometime previously by his uncle (*avunculus meus*) (*Kelso,* 137), and also witnessed a charter by Patrick, 3. earl of Dunbar to Coldingham (*Raine,* 138). Henry de Haliburtoune rendered homage in 1296. His seal bears a shield charged with a bend and S' *Henrici de Haliburton* (*Bain,* II, 816). In 1300 he witnessed a charter by Adam de Baddeby (*Home,* 225), and in 1309 was a witness in the enquiry concerning the Templars (*Wilkins,* p. 382). Ralph de Halibourton, a degenerate traitor, was enlarged from prison in England to be taken to Scotland to help those Scots seeking to capture William Waleys in 1305 (*Bain,* IV, p. 373). Walter de Halyburtoun appears as a witness in 1362 and 1367 (*Egidii,* p. 11; CAB., p. 540), Walter Haliburton was one of the hostages for the king of Scotland in 1425 (*Bain,* IV, 981, 983), and Patrick Hallyburton, a native of Scotland, had permission to remain in England in 1466 (ibid., IV, 1367). The Hallyburtons of Pitcur were an old family in Angus and Perth, and another old family were the Halyburtons of Foderance in Angus. Halburton 1364, Haliburntoun 1526, Halliburton 1713, Hallyburtoun 1601, Halvborton 1393, Halybourton 1415, Halyburtoune 1667, Healyburton 1679, Heleburtone 1614,

Helibourtone 1650, Helliburton 1698, Hollyburton 1547.

HALIDAY. See under **HALLIDAY.**

HALINTUN. Henricus de Halintun who witnessed a charter by Adam filius Serloni a. 1200 (LSC., p. 29) probably derived his name from Hallington, Northumberland.

HALIVOW. Andrew Halivow, tenant in Bowdene, 1567 (*Kelso,* p. 518).

HALKERSTON, HALKERSTONE. Originally Hawkerton, from lands in the Mearns held by the king's falconer (see under FALCONER). Johan de Haukerstone of Edinburghshire rendered homage, 1296. His seal bears an eagle (rude), S' *Joh' d' Havk'tun* (*Bain,* II, p. 203, 558). The surname was common in Edinburgh in the fifteenth and sixteenth centuries. The principal access at that time from the city to Trinity College and Hospital was a steep alley known as Halkerston's Wynd, so named, it is said, from the builder of Queen's College, John Halkerstoun or Haukirstoun (1462–1463). Others say the wynd was named from David Halkerston who was killed in 1544 when defending the town against the English (Wilson, *Memorials of Edinburgh in the olden time,* II, p. 30, ed. 1891). Robert de Halkerston was rector of Cultir, 1468 (*Neubotle,* 301), and his successor was William Halkerstoun who was presented to the benefice c. 1483 (OPS., I, p. 175), and appears again in 1489 as William Havkerston (REG., 457). Violet Halkartoune in Syde 1581 (*Brechin*), William Halkerstoun, portioner of Hilcairnie (*Inquis.,* 695), and Jeanna Halkistoune was heir to Mr. David Halkistoune in Anstruther, 1646 (ibid., 3128). The name now shortened to HACKSTON and HAXTON. Hakkerstone 1500, Hallcarstoune 1493.

HALKET, HALKETT. This surname may be derived from the lands of Halkhead, Renfrewshire, although a family bearing a different name (Ross) have been long (in record) in possession of the property. As *-et* sometimes represents *-wood* (as Aiket = Oakwood) the place name may have been originally Hawkwood, and there is a Hawkwood near Strathaven, Lanarkshire. Sir Henry Hakette witnessed a charter by Henry de Graham, c. 1230 (HMC., 2. Rep., App., p. 166). Richard Haket was juror on inquisition at Dumfries, 1259 (*Bain,* I, 2176; APS., I, p. 88), and Sir Walter Haket was in the service of Robert de Brus, earl of Carrick, 1298 (ibid., II, 995). Thomas Haket was burgess of Are, 1415–27 (*Ayr,* p. 11, 82), and David Hacat, a Scotsman, had a safe conduct in 1432 (*Bain,* IV, 1051). The Halketts of Pitfirrane in Fife are said to have been settled there as early as the reign of David II, from whom they acquired the lands of Lumphanans and Ballingall. Philip Hagat, lord of Balnagall (Ballingall) is in record, 1390 (*Pitfirrane*, 7). "Daui hacet of lüfennen" made a contract with the abbot of Dunfermline, 1437 (RD., p. 285). Robert Hacat held land in Stirling, 1463 (RD., p. 467), and William Hakket of Petfurane had a remission for slaughter committed by him in 1499 (*Trials*, I, p. °100). John Halket was chosen kirkmaster of Dysart, 1537 (*Dysart*, p. 4), Robert Holkat was a prior in Culross, 1569 (*Laing*, 844), and Archibald Halkhead was an elder in Dysart, 1641 (PBK., p. 209). George Halket (d. 1737) was author of the ballad "Logie of Buchan." Hacate 1437, Hached 1560, Hacheid 1543, Hackat 1515, Hackate 1439, Hackatt 1650, Hackeat 1573, Hacked 1574, Hacket 1372, Hacquett 1599, Hagheid 1545, Hakat 1549, Hakcet 1585, Haket 1670, Hakete 1429, Hakheid 1575, Hakheyd 1545, Hakkat 1500, Hakked 1579, Halkede 1526, Halkeid 1509, Halkeit 1585, Halkhaide 1632, Halkhead 1592, Halkhed 1534, Halkheid 1583, Halkheide 1513, Halkhet 1532, Halkit 1634.

HALL. Local. In Latin documents *de Aula*. Waldeu de Aula witnessed a charter by Walter de Veteri Ponte a. 1200 (LSC., 44). John of the Hall was one of an inquest made at Berwick, 1302 (*Bain*, II, 1313), and c. 1311 Thomas dictus del Halle witnessed resignation by Adam de Dowane of his land of Grenryg in the barony of Lesmahagow (*Kelso*, 195). In 1325 mention is made of Thomas dictus de Aula (LCD., p. 237), and Andreas de Aula held land in Aynstrother c. 1330 (*Dryburgh*, 252). The first Hall of Fulbar in Renfrewshire was Thomas de Aula, surgeon, who for his faithful service obtained from Robert II a grant of land in the tenement of Staneley, barony of Renfrow, 1370 (RMS., I, 407, 540). The direct line of Hall of Fulbar ceased c. 1550. Richard de Aula was tenant in Garvald, 1376 (RHM., I, p. lviii). Nichol del Hall was merchant of the duke of Albany, 1400 (*Bain*, IV, 570). William de Aula was chaplain to Alexander Hume of Dunglass, 1423 (HMC., 12. Rep., App. 8, p. 87), and another William de Hall held a land in Irvine, 1426 (*Irvine*, I, p. 130). John de Hall, witness in Glasgow, 1454 (LCD., p. 176), burgess there in 1456, and mentioned along with Nicholas de Aula, 1463 (REG., 380, 389). Allane of Hall in Sancharmvr was burgess of Prestwick, 1470 (*Prestwick*, 13), and in 1485 there is recorded an indenture between Robyne of Hall of the Fulbare and the Friars of Glasgow (LCD.,

p. 195). Henrie Hall in Perth was charged with participating in 'Idolatrus pastyme' in 1581 (Mill, *Plays*, p. 279). David Hall (c. 1714–1772), born in Edinburgh, became partner with Benjamin Franklin in printing business. Hale 1485, Haw 1497.

HALLAM. Probably a late introduction from England. Janet Hallam in the Carse of Twynholm, 1758 (*Kirkcudbright*). From Upper Hallam, a township in the old parish of Sheffield.

HALLEY, HALLY. William Hally in Perth, 1666 (DPD., I, p. 158), John Hally, portioner of Balbrogo, 1700 (*Dunkeld*). Seventeen persons of this name are recorded in the Dunblane Commissariot Record from 1602. (2) Local, from Halley in Deerness, Orkney. Thomas Halle, tacksman there, 1509 (REO., p. 82, 398, 412). Bardsley has Haley as a Yorkshire family name, and Halley as local from some place of the name which he thinks was in Derbyshire.

HALLIBURTON. *See under* HALIBURTON.

HALLIDAY, HALIDAY. The Hallidays of Hoddom, Dumfriesshire, were an old family there, and probably gave their name to Halliday Hill in the parish of Dalton. Thom Haliday was a nephew of Wallace (Henry the Minstrel, *Wallace*, VI, 535, S. T. S. ed.), and Adam de Halide, juror on inquest at St. Andrews, 1303 (*Bain*, II, 1350). John Halyday, archer of the East March, 1404 (ibid., IV, 669), John Halliday of Hoddom in record, 1439 (PSAS., XXIII, p. 36), Ambrose Halyday and David Halyday, merchants in Edinburgh, 1479 (*Bain*, IV, 1457). William Halliday held a tenement in Dumfries, 1506 (*Edgar*, p. 229), John Halyday, burgess of Dumfries, 1570 (RPC., XIV, p. 66), and another John Hallieday was bailie of Culross in last half of the seventeenth century (BOEC., VIII, p. 120). Grissell Holiday in Corrysholme, 1624 (*Dumfries*). John Holyday, weaver in Polwart, 1668 (*Lauder*). The name was carried by Scots to France and appears there as Halliday, vicomte de Pontaudemer. Haliday 1717, Hallyday 1634. OGer. *Halegdag*, Ger. *Heiligtag*, are family names.

HALLIWELL. Of local origin, perhaps from Halywell mentioned in Berwick Retours. Thomas de Halvwell was supprior of the Abbev of Kelso, 1465 (*Kelso*, 530), and Robert Halywell was notarv public in St. Andrews diocese, 1473 (RHM., II, p. 220). Thomas Halvwell, a Scot born at Grynlawe, in 1480 had letters of denization in England (*Bain*, IV, 1465), John Halywell was killed in 1535

HALLIWELL, *continued*
(RSS., II, 1642), and William Halywell was burgess of Linlithgow, 1537 *(Johnsoun)*. Janet Hallywell is recorded in Dalcove, 1668 *(Lauder)*, Robert Halliwall, portioner of Darnick, 1683 (RRM., III, p. 8), and Arthur Hollivall in Manorhill, 1690 *(Peebles CR.)*. Haliewooll 1651, Halliewooll 1656, Halliwoll 1660, Hallowall 1681, Holiewall 1644.

HALLUM. Most probably a variant of HALLAM, q.v. John Hallum or Hallume was hanged for being a Covenanter, 1685 *(Hanna, II, p. 268)*. His epitaph is given by Dick (p. 97).

HALSON. An English surname. 'Son of Hal,' a diminutive of Harry. Thomas Halson in Burnfoot of Kingkell, 1754 *(Dunblane)*.

HALWARTSOUN. Mans Halwartsoun, witness in Sandwick, 1624 (OSS., I, 57). Perhaps 'son of Alwart' (Alward), a variant of OE. personal name *Ælfweard*.

HAM. A Caithness surname, of local origin from the small place of the name near Dunnet.

HAMILL, HOMILL, HOMMILL. Of Norman territorial origin. William de Hameville witnessed a confirmation charter of the fishery of Torduf between 1194–1211 *(Holm-Cultram, p. 35)*. As William de Heneuile or de Heyneuile he appears as witness in two Annandale charters by William Bruce, between 1194–1214, and in a resignation by Dunegal, son of Udard within the same period *(Annandale, I, p. 2, 3)*. In the reign of William the Lion, Walter de Hamule settled in Lothian where he obtained lands *(Caledonia, I, p. 592)*. He made a grant to the Abbey of Newbattle *(Neubotle, 84)*. Alan Homel perambulated the lands of Rath, c. 1206 (RAA., I, 67). Andreas Homyl was bailie of Roxburgh c. 1338 *(Dryburgh, 314)*, and John Homyl acted as bailie for Sir John Montgomery in 1413. John Homil or Homel was juror in an inquiry respecting right to muir ground at Irvine, 1417 *(Irvine, I, p. 20)*. Another John Homyll was appointed Master of the Grammar School of Aberdeen, 1418 (CRA., p. 5). Robert de Hommyl had a charter of Roughwood, Ayrshire, and confirmation of previous and older grants to his family in 1452 *(Ayr Fam., I, p. 373)*, and Hugh Hammill of Roughwood went to Ireland with Montgomery of Ards. The old Ayrshire family of the name is now extinct. Ada Homyle held a tenement in Glasgow, 1487 (REG., p. 452), Alexander Homil possessed a tenement there in 1497 (ibid., 476), and Hommyle, the king's tailor, was one of the victims executed at Lauder Bridge by the nobles, 1482 (Hume Brown, *Hist. Scot.*, I, p. 277). Alexander Hommyll was on inquest on lands in Gowane (Govan), 1527 *(Pollok, I, p. 258)*, Archibald Hommyle had sasine in Glasgow, 1550 *(Protocols, I)*, Sir John Hummyll was prebendary of Kippane in same year *(Rollok, 64)*, and George Hommill, burgess of Irvine, was heir of Jonet Hommill, daughter of quondam John Hommill in Halkettis, 1606 *(Inquis. Tut., 93)*. Nigel Hommill was merchant burgess in Glasgow, 1648 *(Inquis., 3477)*, and Hew Hamill was called 'ane knave,' 1678 *(Corsehill, p. 145)*. Hammel 1671, Hammyll 1620, Homill 1548, Hommylle 1514.

HAMILTON. The house of Hamilton was represented from 1294–95 to a date something short of 1346 by Walter Fitz Gilbert, the father of David, who styled himself on his seal *David Fitz Walter*, but who was more fully styled Sir David Fitz Walter Fitz Gilbert. Sir David was succeeded by his son of the same baptismal name who, in 1378, was the first of the house to style himself by his territorial title alone, David de Hamilton, although Walter had been described among the lairds of Renfrewshire as "Wauter fiz Gilbert de Hameldone" as early as the Homage Roll of 1296 (J. H. Stevenson, PSAS., LXV, p. 243). A Gilbert de Hameldun, clericus, was one of the witnesses to a charter by Thomas de Cragyn to the monks of Paisley, 1272 (RMP., p. 233). Walter Fitz-Gilbert was witness in 1294–95 to a charter of the manor of Blackhall in Renfrewshire by James the High Steward to the same monks (ibid., p. 96), and in 1296 he rendered homage as Wauter fiz Gilbert de Hameldone (Bain, II, p. 212). The surname is not derived from Hamilton in Lanarkshire, but from some place in England. There are several places named Hambledon or more commonly Hambleton in Yorkshire, Lancashire, Bucks, and elsewhere in England. There was also a place of the name in Northumberland from which the Scots family may more originally be derived, but there is no evidence available to prove the connection. Henrik Albertson Hamilton, Latin poet of Denmark, who flourished in the reign of Christian IV (1588–1648) was of Scottish extraction. In the French archer muster-rolls Ouatte Amiton appears for Watty Hamilton. Hameldon and Hemildon 1424, Hammeltoune 1532, Hammyltoun 1531, Hammyltoune 1547, Hamulthone 1537, Hamyltone 1432, Hamyltoune 1388, Hommyltoun 1426.

HAMPTON. From one of the many Hamptons in England. Bardsley says there are at least thirteen parishes of the name there.

Rogerus de Hamtone witnessed resignation of the lands of Edeluestun to the church of Glasgow, 1233 (REG., p. 141). Margaret Hampton in Inverscandie, 1657 (*Brechin*).

HAMSHAW. Bardsley says this name is local from Hallamshire through the intermediate link Halmshaw, a West Riding form. John Hamshaw in Kirklistoun, 1678 (*Edin. App.*).

HANCE. A curtailed form of *Machans*, one of the forms assumed by MACANGUS, q.v.

HANDASYDE, HANDYSIDE. From a place named Handyside near Berwick. Richard de Hanggandsid, *dominus ejusdem*, in 1398 had an annual pension of two marks out of the ferms of Medilham in the barony of Bolden for his faithful counsel and aid given and in future to be given (*Kelso*, 520). John Hangandsyd witnessed a charter by the same Richard of a land in Lytyl Newton to the Abbey of Kelso, c. 1398, and Adam Hangalsyde also appears as a witness in the same year (ibid., 521; LSC., 110). Patone de Hangaldesyde served on an inquest anent a fishing on the Tweed in 1467 (RD., 461), and in 1469 as Patrick Hangangside he is mentioned in a retour of the lands of Wedderburn (*Sc. Ant.*, VII, p. 25). In 1494 we have mention of the tenement of quondam William Hangitsyde in Glasgow (REG., p. 487), in 1532 there is record of the lawborrowis of Richard Hangandsyde in Litill Newtoun (RSS., II, 1491), and in 1563 Nigel Hangetsyide was a witness in Glasgow (*Protocols*, I). A charter of Richard of Hangansyde of that Ilk to his son, Alexander was confirmed in 1563 (RMS., IV, 1463). Elizabet Hangetsyde and Dandie Hanginsyde were tenants under the Abbey of Kelso, 1567 (*Kelso*, p. 524, 527). James Hangitsyde in Caldstreime appears in 1654, and John Handisyde in Thirlstaine in 1665 (*Lauder*). Lower's explanation of the origin of the name from a personal deformity is erroneous. Some notes on the family are given in the *History of the Berwickshire Naturalists' Club*, XIV, p. 294–295. Handisyd 1685, Hangandsyid 1649.

HANDLEY. A not uncommon name in the Stewartry. From Ir. *Ó hAinle*, 'descendant of Ainle,' with intrusive *d*.

HANESEL. Michael de Hamesl or Hanesel who witnessed charters by King David I to the monks of the church of St. Andrew at Northampton between 1124–30 (*Lawrie*, p. 51, 58) is probably to be identified with Michael de Hanslope who succeeded Winemar the Fleming in all his lands (Lipscomb, *History of Bucks*, IV, p. 349).

HANGINGSHAW. Gilbert de Hanguydeschawe of the county of Rokesburgh rendered homage in 1296 (*Bain*, II, p. 214). Small places of this name appear in the Retours of Roxburgh (Hanganshaw), Selkirk (Hangingschaw), and Lanark (Hangingshaw Over and Nether).

HANGPUDYNG. Odardus filius Ricardi Hangpudyng in Glasgow, 1293 (REG., p. 210). Merely a nickname, not a surname.

HANING. See under HAINING.

HANKIN. From Flemish diminutive of *Johan* + *kin*. As forename: Hankin Criouner in Aberdeen, 1408 (CWA., p. 313).

HANLE. From one or other of the several places of the name in England. Paganus de Hanle witnessed confirmation by Robert de Quinci in the reign of William the Lion (LSC., p. 30).

HANNA, HANNAH, HANNAY. "The very common name Ahannay, now Hannay, may be for *ap Sheanaigh*, 'son of Senach,' rather than for *úa Seanaigh*" (*Watson* III, p. 17). Gilbert de Hannethe of the county of Wiggetone rendered homage, 1296, and in the same year as Gilbert Hahanith was juror on an inquest concerning the succession to Elena la Zuche in Scotland (*Bain*, II, p. 205, 215). John of Hanna was master of a ship of James, king of Scotland, 1424 (ibid., IV, 966). John Hanay, a witness in Glasgow, 1477 (REG., p. 462). Robert Ahannay of Sorbie had precept of office of curatory, 1499 (RSS., I, 319), a 'brew caldron' was stolen from Ellen Hannay, 1514 (*Ros*, 81), James Ahannay was the king's culverner in 1529 (ALHT., V, p. 375), and John Ahannay was baker to the queen, 1566 (ER., XIX, p. 340). The 'knaiffscheipes' of the mills of Melrose were vacant by the death of Mathew Ahanney, 1565 (RRM., III, p. 355), Thomas Hannaye, smith, was made burgess freeman of Glasgow at the request of the archbishop of Glasgow, 1575 (*Burgesses*). David Hanna was tenant in the barony of Mousewall (Mousewald), 1673 (PSAS., XXIII, p. 74). Perhaps the most famous of the name was James Hannay, dean of Edinburgh, who attempted to read the Episcopal liturgy before Jenny Geddes in St. Giles's church, Edinburgh, in 1637. Soon after 1600 a feud broke out between the Hannays of Sorbie and the Murrays of Broughton, which appears to have ended in the ruin of the former family.

HANNAN. In the southwest this name is from Ir. *Ó hAnnain*, 'descendant of Annan.' George Hannan, burgess of Kirkcudbright, 1645 (*Re-*

HANNAN, continued

tours, *Kirkcudbright,* 231), and John Hannan is in the parish of Carsfern, 1684 (RPC., 3. ser. IX, p. 575). (2) John Hanyn was burgess of Berwick, c. 1147 (*Kelso,* 31). It is said there were families or a family of this name in or about North Berwick at the end of the eighteenth century. A Thomas Hannan purchased a number of books at the sale of the library of Wedderburn of Blackness, 1710 (*Sc. Ant.,* VII, p. 46).

HANNING. See under HAINING.

HANTON. Walter Hantoun witnessed a protest in 1500 (*Cawdor,* p. 106). John Hanton, burgess of Montrose, 1600, and five more of the name are in record (*Brechin*). There is a place named Hantestoun (1661) in *Forfar Retours* (379).

HAPPREW. From the lands of the same name near Stobo, Peeblesshire. Robert de Hopprew who appears as a notary public in Paisley in 1426 (RMP., p. 149) is probably the Robert de Hoprew, procurator of the bishop of Brechin in 1435 and notary public there in the following year (REB., I, p. 48; II, p. 52).

HAPPY. Alexander Happy, shoemaker, burgess of Dumbarton, 1762 (RDB.). Lower has the name as English but gives no satisfactory explanation.

HARALD. From the ON. personal name *Haraldr,* naturalized among the Gael as Arailt or Erailt. Harald, chaplain to the bishop of Dunkeld, was the first bishop of the see of Argyll, created c. 1200, because he was acquainted with the language of the people of those parts. As Harald, bishop of Ayrgaythyl, he had a grant from Alexander II in 1228 of three dauachs of Culkessoch, which "the said bishop and his successors "in ecclesia Lysmoriensi' should hold" (REM., p. 25). His name was preserved in Killespeckerrill, i.e. church of bishop Erailt or Harold, at one time the alternative name of the parish of Muckairn.

HARALDSON, 'son of HARALD,' q.v. John Haraldson was surety for the earl of Orkney, 1434, and in 1438 'balye off Kirkwaw' (REO., p. 49, 71). Thomas Harraldsoun, tacksman of Tukquy and Are c. 1500 (ibid., p. 409). (2) Probably an Englishing of MACRAILD, q.v. Angus Haraldi, juror on inquest at Inverness, 1430 (RMS., II, 179). John Heraldsoun, tenant in Kindroch alias Casteltoun, Strathdee, 1539 (ER., XVII, p. 657).

HARBERT. A variant of Herbert, from OE. *Herebeorht.* David Harbert, born at Aberdeen,

had letters of denization in England, 1479–80 (*Bain,* IV, p. 298). Adam Harbart, witness in Ayr, 1611 (*Ayr,* p. 145).

HARCARSE. From the lands of Harcarse in the parish of Fogo, Berwickshire. Adam of Harcarres, cellarer, was elected abbot of Newbottle in 1216 and in 1219 abbot of Melrose (*Neubotle,* pref., p. xvii; *Chron. Melr.*). Alan de Harekare, distrained for debt in 1254 (*Bain,* I, 1968), may be the Sir Alan de Harecares who witnessed a gift of land in Aython to the monks of Coldingham, 1259 (*Raine,* 203), and the Alan de Harecarr' who witnessed a charter by Patrick, 3. earl of Dunbar before 1289 (ibid., 136). As Alan de Harcaris he witnessed a Fife charter c. 1280 (LAC., p. 186). Mariorie de Harkars, Roger de Harkars, and Thomas de Harkars, all of Berwickshire, rendered homage in 1296, and likewise did Alisaundre de Harcars of Fife (*Bain,* II, p. 207, 213). Sir Robert Harcars or Harechas was sheriff of Perth, 1304–5 (*Bain,* II, p. 439), and Alexander de Harcars was sheriff of Forfar in 1306 (*Macdonald,* 1255, 1256). Provision of a canonry and prebend of Moray was made in 1325 for John Harkars, rector of Aldam in the diocese of St. Andrew (*Pap. Lett.,* II, p. 245, 313), and Thomas Harkars was granted a canonry and prebend of Glasgow in 1342 (*Pap. Pet.,* I, p. 255). Robert Harkares had a charter of the barony of Kelour in 1324 from Robert I (RMS., I, App. I, 77), and John de Harkers had a gift from the king, 1329 (ER., I, p. 210). Thomas de Harkars petitioned for a canonry and prebend of Glasgow, 1342 (*Pap. Pet.,* I, p. 1). Gilbert Harcars was a charter witness in the Mearns, 1351 (RAA., II, 25), William de Harcarrys was witness in Glasgow, 1430 (LCD., p. 165), and William Harkes was witness in Linlithgow, 1444 (*Sc. Ant.,* XVII, p. 115). Marjorie Harcarse held lands in the lordship of Hutoun, 1415 (*Home,* 18), and Thomas Harcars was subprior of Arbroath, 1482 (RAA., II, 212). The name was carried to Orkney, and three individuals named Hercas were among those respited for their share in the slaughter of John, erle of Cathnes, 1539 (RSS., II, 3151). Alexander Harkass was canon of Holyrood, 1547 (*Binns,* 40). Janet Arcus in Braquoy, 1668 (*Orkney*), and William Arcas or Orcas was bailie of Kirkwall, 1568 (REO., p. 288). James Harcas was in the Scottish parliament in 1605 (*Stodart,* II, p. 53). The name seems to have at an early period become rare, and is now (1941) more common as Harkess.

HARCUS. The present Orkney spelling of HARCARSE, q.v.

HARDEN. From the lands of Harden in Roxburghshire. John de Hardene of the county of Roxburghe rendered homage in 1296 (*Bain*, II, p. 199), a horse was purchased from Ricardus de Harden, 1312 (*Bain*, III, p. 428), and William of Harden was custumar of Dundee in 1359 (ER., I, p. 614). There is also a place Harden in Yorkshire.

HARDGAT. Local. There are two places named Hardgate in CD. David Hardgat in Aberdeen, 1442 (CRA., p. 397).

HARDGRIP. Renaud de Hardegreypes of Peebles rendered homage, 1296 (*Bain*, II, p. 198). John Hardgrip was admitted burgess of Aberdeen, 1523 (NSCM., I, p. 48). Björkman I (p. 65) compares Old West Scandinavian *Harðgreipr*, Searle has *Ardegrip* as a personal name, and Baring-Gould (p. 187) says "Ardgrip is found several centuries later [than DB.] in Parliamentary writs as *Hardgripe*."

HARDIE, HARDY. From OFr. *hardi*, bold, daring. Hardy is a common French surname. (1) The tale of Malcolm Ceannmor addressing the first Hardy, after he had performed a William Tell exploit, "Hardy thou are and Hardy thou shalt be" (*Celt. Mon.*, VII, 137), is nonsense. William Hardy of Lanarkshire rendered homage, 1296 (*Bain*, II, p. 213). Alexander Hardy is in record in Arbroath, 1505 (RAA., II, 440), and William Herdy of Orkney had a respite for his share in the battle of Summerdale, 1529 (RSS., II, 3151). Robert Hardy, *latimus*, church of Holy Trinity, Edinburgh, 1519 (*Soltre*, p. 183), and William Hardie, unicorn pursuivant, 1566 (RPC., I, p. 480). Alexander Hardie appears in Meikle Tippertie, 1633 (SCM., III, p. 95), and the name is found in Lauderdale from 1643. Several Hardies are recorded in the Commissariot Record of Dunblane in the sixteenth and seventeenth centuries. (2) The Hardies of Crathie and Crathienard, originally MACHARDIES, q.v., were a wild and extravagant race (*Invercauld*, p. 260). Hardye 1586. Magnus Hardie or Hairdy was a witness in Kirkwall, 1613 (OSR., p. 277-278).

HARDKNEIS. Thomas de Hardkneys was juror on inquest made in St. Katherine's Chapel, Bavelay, 1280 (*Bain*, IV, 1762). Sir Thomas Hardkneis, notary public in Peebles, 1448 (*Peebles*, 14).

HARE. See under HAIR.

HARESHAW. Jonet Hairshaw in Meikle Ernock in 1671 (*Campsie*) derived her surname from the small place named Hareshaw in the parish of Avondale, Lanarkshire.

HARESHEFD. A nickname? 'Hare's head.' William Hareshefd received to the king of England's peace, 1321 (*Bain*, III, 724).

HARG. A curtailed form of (MAC)HARG, q.v. Andrew Harg, indweller in Wigtown in 1760 (*Wigtown*).

HARGREAVES. Of recent introduction from England. It is an old Lancashire local name. There are, however, other places of this name in England.

HARKESS. A modern variant of HARCARSE, q.v. Harkass 1547.

HARKINS. A surname in Aberdeen. Probably from Harry, a form of HENRY, q.v., + diminutive -kin, and gen. -s, = son of Harkin.

HARKNESS. Harrison explains this name as "dweller at the Temple-Headland" (from OE. *h(e)arg + ness*), a place name unknown to the author. Up to the end of the sixteenth century the notices of this name connect it with Annandale and subsequently with Nithsdale. In the churchyard of Dalgarnock, near Thornhill, are several tombstones of persons of this name, who were mostly tenants of the farms of Locherben and Mitchellslacks in the parish of Closeburn, and Holestane in that of Durrisdeer. James Harkness of Locherben was leader of the band of Covenanters who rescued some Covenanters from the royal troops in the Pass of Enterkin while being convoyed to Edinburgh for trial, 1684. Thomas Harkness, brother of James, was subsequently executed in the Grassmarket of Edinburgh in 1685 for having taken part in the affair. Jennet Herknesse in Tinwald was examined for the Test in 1685 (RPC., 3. ser. XI, p. 433), and James Harkness was at a conventicle at Polgavin Muir in the following year (ibid., XII, p. 405). Alexander Harkness was schoolmaster at Dumfries, 1820–30. A branch of the family went from Dumfriesshire to Ulster in the seventeenth century, and settled finally in the county of Limerick, where the family of Harkness of Garryfine still possess lands. James Harkness was mason in Hawick, 1809 (*Heirs*, 569). Edward Stephen Harkness (born in Cleveland, Ohio, 1874), founder of the Pilgrim Trust, was descended from Harknesses of Dumfriesshire. He died in 1940.

HARLAW. Of territorial or local origin from some place named Harlaw near the Border. There is a Harlaw Muir in Peeblesshire, and there appears to have been a Harlawbanks

HARLAW, *continued*

there also. A vill and lands of Hairlaw in Midlothian is recorded in 1565 (*Retours*). William de Harlau witnessed a charter in favor of the Abbey of Scone c. 1204–41 (*Scon*, 125), and Richard de Harlau and William de Harlau were on an inquest held at the chapel of St. Katherine, Bavelay, near Edinburgh, in 1280 (*Bain*, IV, 1762). William de Harlau was on an assize at Berwick in 1296, and Matthew de Harlawe rendered homage in the same year (*Bain*, II, 730, 824). William Harlau or Harlow was burgess of Edinburgh in 1566 (*Diur. Occ.*, p. 97; RPC., I, p. 447). William Harlau is recorded in Neubotle in 1528 (*Neubotle*, 309), and John Harlaw was saddler in Edinburgh in 1604 (*Edinb. Marr.*). Nathaniell Harlaw was minister at Ormestoun, 1609 (*Trials*, III, p. 600).

HARLAWBANKS. From the old lands of the name in Peeblesshire. Matho Harlawbanks is in record in 1480 (EBR., p. 39), and John Harlawbanks witnessed an infeftment of date 1547 in the barony of Newlands, Peeblesshire (Buchan, *Peebles*, III, p. 57). Mariot Harlabanks was assaulted in the church of St. Giles 'in the presence of the sacrament,' c. 1554 (*Liber Offic. Sancti Andree*, p. 132).

HARLE. Johannes de Herl who witnessed a confirmation charter by Gilbert de Vmframville to the Abbey of Kelso, c. 1228 (*Kelso*, 325), probably derived his name from Kirkharle (1177, Herle) in Northumberland. The Harles of Kirkharle owned much property in Northumberland (*Guppy*, p. 314). The surname is recorded in Coldstream; in Glasgow 1943.

HARLEY. A surname recorded in Fife and Clackmannanshire. Probably a late incomer from England. Cf. HARLE.

HARPER. From the office of "harper." In early times the harper was a hereditary official in the households of many great families, and the Brehon laws rank the harp as "the one art of music which deserves nobility" (*Brehon laws*, v, p. 107). In some districts lands were attached to the office as shown by the place names Croit a' Chlarsair, "the Harper's Croft," in the parish of Kiltarlity, near Dundonald, Ayrshire, and elsewhere, and the lands of Harperfield in the parish of Lesmahagow are probably of the same origin. "The last hereditary harper appears to have been Murdoch Macdonald, harper to Maclean of Coll, who died at an advanced age in 1739" (*Clan Donald*, III, p. 126). Several individuals named Harper appear in the Ragman Roll as having

rendered homage in 1296: (1) William le Harpur of La Lawe, of the county of Edinburgh. His seal bears a shield charged with a harp (?), *S' Walraun le Harpevr* (*Bain*, II, p. 201, 547). (2) Uctins [= Uchtred] le Harpur of the county of Lanark, a tenant of William of Moravia. His seal carries a crosspatée and the legend *S'Oting le Harp'e* (ibid., II, p. 208, 553). In the same year a writ was issued to the sheriff of Lanark to restore his lands to Ughtred le Harpur (ibid., p. 225). (3) Robert le Harpur of the county of Are, (4) Johan le Harpur of the county of Berewyk, and (5) Rogier le Harpur of Hom', also of the county of Berewyk, are the others named in the record. In 1297 a messuage in Berwick-on-Tweed and a particate of land in the Fyskergate was granted to Ughtred le Harpur and his heirs (ibid., 915). Walter Harper was a tenant of the Douglases in the barony of Buittle in 1376 (RHM., I, p. lix), and Pate Harper, clarsha (G. *clarsair*) had a payment of xiiijs. in 1507 (ALHT., III, p. 392). As this name is fairly common in the Stewartry it is probably a translation of MACCHRUITER, q.v., which in Gaelic has the meaning of "son of the harper."

HARPERFIELD. Of local origin from the lands of Harperfield in the parish of Lesmahagow, Lanarkshire. Elizabeth Harperfield in Bordland, parish of Lesmahago, 1622, and four others of the name are recorded in the Commissariot Record of Lanark, 1595–1800. Erchebaud de Harpenfeld of Lanarkshire who rendered homage in 1296 (*Bain*, II, p. 213) may have derived his name from the same place. In the Bannatyne Club edition of the Ragman Roll (p. 166) the name is spelled Harpenfeud.

HARPERSON. "Son of the Harper." It is most probably a translation of MACCHRUITER, q.v. See under HARPER.

HARRIS, 'son of Harry,' a form of HENRY, q.v. A surname more English than Scottish.

HARRISON, 'son of Harry' (from HENRY through the intermediate form Hanry). Sir Laurence Harryson or Herryson, a native of Scotland, had letters of denization in England, 1497 (*Bain*, IV, 1623, 1629). James Harryson, Scottisheman, was author of "An Exhortacion to the Scottes to conforme themselfes to the honorable, Expedient, & godly Vnion betweene the two Realmes of Englande & Scotland," published in London, 1547. Magnus Harison in Gillisbrek, parish of Lunnasting, 1613 (*Shetland*).

HARROLD. In Orkney a contraction for Harraldson.

HARROW. A surname found in the parish records of Canisbay. Of local origin from Harrow near Mey, Caithness. Johannes Harrow in Aberdeen, 1408 (CWA., p. 314), and Robert Harrow was a member of the corps of Huntly Volunteers in 1798 (Will, p. 19). (2) Local, from another place of the name. Robert Harrow was one of the burgesses of Stirling who attacked the cruives and fishings of the abbot and convent of Cambuskenneth, 1366 (Cambus., 55).

HARROWER. A surname common to Fife and district. "The first of this name [no date?], is described as a Flemish gunner; it may be a form of Harruwijn" (Sc. Ant., IV, p. 114. So Rev. A. W. C. Hallen the editor, who had a penchant for tracing most Fife surnames to a Flemish source). William Harower or Herwart had a charter of the office of keeper of the king's muire and cunningare in Crail in liferent in the reign of David II (RMS., I, App. II, 909). Robert Harwar was burgess of Perth, 1440 (RD., p. 297), and 'Sir' John Harwar who was vicar of Cortochquhay in 1452 (REB., II, 87) may be the John Harwar, chaplain, mentioned in 1455 (RAA., II, 104). James Harwar was vicar of Banchoryterne in 1465 (RAA., II, 161), Thomas Harrowar is in record in Belheluy, 1506 (REA., II, p. 96), and Thomas Harrour appears as vicar pensioner of Arbroath, 1512 and 1524 (RAA., II, 532, 585). Thomas Herrowar was witness in Aberdeen, 1536 (Aboyne, p. 65), and the escheat of William Harrowar was disponed to James Prymrois in 1603 (RD., p. 496). The surname appears several times in Dunfermline between 1561 and 1700 (Dunfermline). The surname is from the occupation, a worker on the land, from ME. harwe, a harrow, with agental suffix -er. Harrowair 1561, Harruar 1535, Harruer 1698, Haruar 1519, Harvar 1464.

HART. There was a manor named Hert in Durham, mentioned in 1288 and again in 1296 when Cristina, widow of R. de Brus, lord of Annandale, was dowered in the same (Bain, II, 556, 826). Hart 'of that Ilk', however, says Stodart, is a mere complimentary addition. Mainprize by Henry Hert, burgess of Lanark, is recorded in 1296 (Bain, II, p. 184). Michael Hart received from Robert I a charter of the lands of Brakysfield (now Braxfield) which Adam Braks resigned (RMS., I, App. II, 603), and in 1316, as Michael Hertt in Lanark, he is in record as a witness (Kelso, p. 159). Nichol Hart was accused of part in the murder of Cardinal Beaton, 1546 (RPC., I, p. 32), Hugh Hert was juror on an inquisition held at Lochmaben in 1347 (Bain, III, 1499), John Hart was bailie of the burgh of Canongate, Edinburgh, in 1561 (MCM., II, p. 285), and another John Hairt or Hert was king's messenger in 1570 (Irvine, I, p. 54, 55). Mr. William Haert or Heart of Livilands was advocate to King James VI, Mr. John Heart was minister at Crail in 1644 (Edinb. Marr.), and Malcolm Heart is recorded in Easter Feodel in 1727 (Dunblane). A family of this name were burgesses of Edinburgh, Edward sitting in parliament for the burgh in 1586, and Andrew, printer to the king, published an edition of the works of Sir David Lyndsay, etc. A pension was paid to Marion Heart in Edinburgh, 1734 (Guildry, p. 148).

HARTLEY, HARTLY. From Hartley (Hartecla 1265, Hartcla 1291, Hartla 1306) a manor in the parish of Kirkby-Stephen, Westmoreland. Michael de Hardcla or Hartcla was deputy sheriff of Westmoreland in 1276 and 1277, and sheriff of Cumberland in part of the year 1285 and then until 1298. On the execution of his brother Andrew de Hardcla, earl of Carlisle, for treason, he fled into Scotland with a number of his friends (Chronicon de Lanercost, ed. Stevenson, p. 250). David Hertley was shipmaster in 1469 (Bain, IV, 1389).

HARTRIG. John Hartrig was member for Dumbarton in the Scots parliament, 1579 (Hanna, II, p. 498). There were lands named Heartrig in Roxburghshire in 1700.

HARTSIDE. From the old barony of the name in the parish of Wandel, Lanarkshire. William de Hertyshed (Hertisheued, Hertishede, or Hertished) witnessed grants of land to Soltre between 1198 and 1250 (Soltre, p. 11, 12, 15, 20, 23, 26, 31), and also witnessed David de Lindeshey's charter of Brothiralewinn to the monks of Neubotle, c. 1230 (Neubotle, p. 106). William de Hertesheuede, sheriff of Lanark, doubtless the same individual, witnessed charters by Alexander II dated at Cadihou in 1225 (REG., p. 111, 113; Levenax, p. 92). Alan de Hertesheued witnessed charters by Cecilia de Molle, c. 1200 (Kelso, p. 116, 120, 127), a charter by David, bishop of St. Andrews, relating to the church of Linton in 1240 (ibid., p. 322), and a charter by John, son of Hugh de Reveden, c. 1250 (ibid., p. 401). Sometime in the latter half of the thirteenth century Richard de Hertishevit witnessed two charters in favor of the house of Soltre (Soltre, p. 28, 29). Aleyn de Herteshede of the county of Berewyke who rendered homage for his lands in the Merse in 1296 (Bain, II, p. 207) is doubtless the Allan de Hertesheued who, c. 1327, granted to Sir Alexander Seton a toft and croft and two oxgates of land in the

346

HARTSIDE, *continued*

territory of Ulkiston. The family appears to
have died out in the direct line in the first
half of the fourteenth century as the barony
of Hertysheuid was in the ward of the Crown
in 1359 (ER., I, p. 582). There are several
entries in 1506-7 of payments to John Hert-
seud "pailzeoun man" (ALHT., III–IV).
Thome Hartsheid held a land in Aberdeen,
c. 1550 (REA., II, p. 226) and Henry Hartsyde
was tenant in Hilton of Rosyth in 1577
(Stephens, *Inverkeithing*, p. 198). The name
of Thomas Herdsed who appears in St. Andrews, 1528 (*Laing*, 370) is probably another
spelling. Other old forms of the surname are:
Harthsyid 1568, Hartsid, Hartsyd, Hertis,
Hertsede, Hertside, Hertseid, Hertsyd, and
Hertisseid.

HARVEY, HARVIE. *See under* HERVEY.

HARVIESTON. From Harvieston near Gorebridge, Midlothian. William de Herviston witnessed charter of land in the tenement of
Ballintrodo, 1300-20 (*Hay*, 7).

HARWOOD. Of local origin, probably from
Harwood near West Calder, Midlothian. Roger
de Hauewod held land of Gouyrton near Edinburgh, 1317 (*Neubotle*, p. 306), and Ada,
daughter of Roger de Harewood or Hauwod, is
mentioned in Aberdeen in same year (SCM.,
v, p. 3). The lands of Trowere in the earldom
of Carrick were resigned by Janet de Hawod,
1430 (RMS., II, 162). William Harwod appears as a witness in Edinburgh in 1464 (*Neubotle*, p. 252), Johnne Harwod was a burgess
of the same city in 1565 (RPC., I, p. 430),
and George Harwod held three husbandlands
of the town of Wester Coitis of the monks
of Neubotle in the first half of the sixteenth
century (*Neubotle*, p. 339). George Harrot
and William Harrot were tenants under Newbattle Abbey in 1563 (ibid., p. 328), and
William Harrat was burgess of the Cannon-
gate of Edinburgh, 1568 (MCM., II, p. 316).
David Harwode was heir of William Harwode,
portioner of Cottis in 1618 (*Inquis.*, 754), and
William Harewood *alias* Wood was grieve to
Lady Drylaw, 1674 (*Just. Rec.*, II, p. 301).
(2) The laird of Harwood who was one of
those appointed to keep order on the Marches
in 1564 doubtless derived his title from Harwood near Hawick in Roxburghshire. Spelled
Harratt in Workman MS.

HASBANE. William Hasbane in Scotfauld,
1594 (SCM., II, p. 126), and James Hesbane
sometime in Burghsea, 1688 (*Moray*). Margaret Hasbein in Moynes was one of the
Auldearn witches, 1662 (*Trials*, III, p. 605).

HASLOP. *See under* HISLOP.

HASSAN. John Hassan, R.A.C.C., was married in Glasgow, 1942. Harrison has Hasson,
which he says is probably for Hal's son, from
Hal, a pet form of Harry.

HASSENDEAN. From the ancient barony of
the name in the parish of Minto, Roxburghshire. There are but few scattered references
to the family of this name who derived their
surname from the lands. Helias de Hadestanden was one of the witnesses to the gift
of the lands of Dundas to Helias, son of
Huctred, in the reign of David I or Malcolm IV
(APS., I, p. 82), and c. 1170 Richard de
Hastenden witnessed the charter confirming
the gift of the church of Kilmaurs to the Abbey
of Kelso (*Kelso*, 286). In the reign of Alexander II (1214–1249) Christina, daughter of
William son of Adam of Astenesdene, granted
to Hugh the brewer of Astenden a charter
of lands in the territory of Astenden (*Melros*,
p. 241). About 1330 Sir Thomas of Hassynden
was warden (*custos*) of the monastery of Kelso
(*Kelso*, p. 381), in 1374 Thomas Hassyndon
was parson of the church of Mynto (*Rot.
Scot.*, I, p. 965), and a third Thomas Hassynden
was one of the archers of the East March
in 1404 (*Bain*, IV, 669). Thomas Hassindaine,
1634 (*Lauder*).

HASTAN. Of local origin from the island of
Hestan in the parish of Rerrick, Kirkcudbright-
shire. John Hastan was resident in the parish
of Borgue, and William Hastine and Thomas
Hastan were residents in the parish of Senneck,
1684 (RPC., 3. ser. IX, p. 567, 569). Janet
Hasten is recorded in Torphichen, 1712
(*Torphichen*).

HASTIE. Robert Hasty and John Hasty were
tenants of Herthornhill in 1376 (RHM., I,
p. lxvii), Thom Hasti witnessed an instrument of sasine dated 1478 (*Home*, 24), and
John Haisty was witness to another instrument of sasine in 1525 (ibid., 35). Henricus
Hastvis was witness in Scone, 1523 (*Scon*,
p. 203), and Thomas Haistie, a monk of
Beauly, was one of those charged with oppression done to Master Gawin Dunbar, treasurer of Ross, in 1543 (*Trials*, I, p. 328).
John Haste was one of the visitors of crafts
in Stirling, 1556 (SBR., p. 278), Sandie Heis-
tie and Robene Haistie were tenants on land
of Kelso Abbey in 1567 (*Kelso*, p. 518, 519),
and Thomas Haistie held the teindscheaves of
the kirkland of Gogar in the same year (*Soltre*,
p. 130). John Hastie in Dyik of Stainebyres
in 1626 and twenty-four more of the name
are recorded in Lanark Commissariot Record,
1595–1800. A family of Hasties are said to

have been hereditary pipers of the burgh of Jedburgh for nearly three hundred years. Heastie 1657, Haiste 1606, Heasty 1686; Haist, Hasty, Heste.

HASTINGS. The old Scottish family of Hastings were a branch of the English family of that name settled in Scotland during the reign of William the Lion, from whom they obtained a grant of the lands of Dun in Angus (*Caledonia*, II, p. 592). Johanne de Hastinge, lord of Dun and sheriff and forester of the Mearns, c. 1178, witnessed a confirmation charter by Turpin, bishop of Brechin, c. 1178-98 (REB., II, 257). He also witnessed a confirmation charter by the king of the church of Aberrotheven to Inchaffray, c. 1199-1200, and was still alive in 1210 (*Inchaffray*, p. 4, 265). As John de Hastinkes he was juror in a dispute regarding the Kirketun of Aberbruthenoth in 1206 (SCM., v, p. 210). His son David de Hastinges married Forflissa or Fernelith, countess of Atholl, and succeeded in her right to the earldom in 1242 (*Inchaffray*, p. 265). Adam de Hastenge witnessed the confirmation of the church of Dunin to Inchaffray c. 1203-4 (ibid., p. 21), and as Adam de Hastinges he witnessed the gift of the land of Okelffas to the canons of Holyrood a. 1214 (LSC., p. 213). He "had from King William a gift of the lands of Kingledoors in Tweeddale, which he afterwards gave to Arbroath Abbey" (*Inchaffray*, p. 271). Johannes de Hasting was one of the witnesses to a charter by William the Lion dated at Forfar, a. 1214, and David de Hasting witnessed a charter by Alexander II of a fishing in the thanage of Scon in 1234 (*Scon*, p. 22, 41). William, son of Robert de Hastings, witnessed the gift of a stone of wax yearly to the church of Glasgow in 1233 (REG., p. 101), and Sir Robert de Hastangg was sheriff of Roxburgh in 1298 (*Bain*, II, 1007). Some Harestanes have changed to Hastings.

HASTINGWAYT. John de Hastingwayt, a Scots prisoner of war from Dunbar Castle, was sent to Castle of Crukyn, 1296 (*Bain*, II, p. 177). Probably from the place near Kendal in Westmoreland, in 1323 Astenthwayt (*Lindkvist*, p. 102).

HASWELL. From Haswell in Durham. Adam de Lambertun granted to Galfridus de Hesswel, his grandson, a third part of his lands of Lambertun, c. 1190-1200 (*Home*, 223; BNCH., XVI, p. 332). William de Hessewelle of Roxburgh rendered homage in 1296. His seal bears a lion rampant on a rose (?) and S' Willel.mi de Heswel (*Bain*, II, p. 198, 548). Peter de Hessewel, juror on inquest at Dumfries, 1304 (*Bain*, II, p. 412). John de Hessewell, dominus de Eddellysheued, who witnessed a charter by Roger de Auldton c. 1354 (*Kelso*, p. 387) may be the John of Hessewelle who was one of an inquest at Roxburgh, 1357 (*Bain*, IV, 1). Thomas Haswele, servitor to the earl of Douglas, 1408 (ibid., IV, 765). Robert of Haswell granted certain lands in the sheriffdom of Peebles in 1436 to his son Patrick Haswele and to his brother William Haswel (OPS., I, p. 521). In 1438 there is record of sasine of the lands of Murefelde to John Haswel, and in 1519 of the same to David Hasthwell (*Laing*, 116, 316). James Haswell or Hasmall, abbot of Newbattle before the Reformation, witnessed the destruction of his monastery by the troops of the earl of Hertford (*Neuboile*, preface, p. xxvii). The surname still exists in Newbattle. Haswellsykes in Manor parish, is from a former owner of this name. Hasswell 1753, Haswall 1662.

HATEWELE. Mr. Hatewele was English master at Dumfries, 1643 (*Dumfriesshire and Galloway Nat. Hist. and Ant. Soc., Trans.*, 3. ser. XXI, p. 127).

HATHAWAY. Perhaps from English place name, Hathaway. Bardsley has de Haythewy in Yorkshire, 1379. Alexander Hathwy appears as a witness in Linlithgow in 1444 and 1465 (*Sc. Ant.*, XVII, p. 115; REA., II, p. 316), and Robert Hadowy was burgess of Lychtcow (Linlithgow), 1460 (*Ayr*, p. 35). Robert Hathwe who witnessed an agreement of 1502 is probably Robert Hathwy, tacksman in Faray, Orkney, 1503 (REO., p. 412, 413.). James Hawthowie was heir of Patrick Hathowie in Blaknes, 1600 (*Retours, Linlithgow*, 22, 23), and John Hathowie was heir of John Hathowie in Heuchheid his father, 1607 (*Inquis.*, 308). Catharine Haddowie was married in Edinburgh, 1622 (*Edinb. Marr.*), Bessie Haddowie is recorded in Hamilton, 1626 (*Campsie*), Cuthbert Hadowy was burgess of Edinburgh, 1646 (*Inquis.*, 3105), and David Hathowie was retoured heir of Cuthbert Hawthowie, burgess of Edinburgh, 1665 (*Retours, Edinburgh*, 1127). John Haddoway in Parkhead of Douglas, 1656, and three more of the name are in Lanark Commissariot Record. Haddowy 1511, Hadoway 1724.

HATHINGTON. John Hathyngton, a Scot, had a safe conduct through England to go on pilgrimage to Seint Jake beyond seas, 1410 (*Bain*, IV, 800). John Hathinton, witness in Edinburgh, 1467 (*Neubotle*, 300). The name may be from Haddington, but does not agree with any of the early spellings of the town's name.

HATHORN. See under HAWTHORN.

HATMAKER. From the occupation of "hat-maker," a now probably obsolete surname. Duncan Hatmaker was admitted burgess of Aberdeen in 1481 (NSCM., I, p. 29), and Thomas Hatmaker was burgess there in 1487 (CRA., p. 44). John Hatmaker appears as witness in Brechin in 1511 (REB., II, 165, 166). Peter Hatmaker was member of assize at Cupar in 1521 (SCBF., p. 223), Henrie Hatmaccar was indweller in Leith in 1561 (MCM., II, p. 286), and Alexander Hat-makker had a "tenementum infra burgagium de Elgyn" in 1565 (REM., p. 436). George Hatmaker was retoured heir of James Hat-maker, portioner of Coutfauld, his father, in 1642 (Retours, Elgin, 78), and in 1684 Jon Hatmaker "for his imprecationes to the stent masters to remaine in prison during the Magistrats pleasure and to be fynd at their pleasure" (Rec. Inv., II, p. 320).

HATRICK, HATTRICK, HETTRICK. A different name from HEADRICK? Harrison under Hattrick says from OE. Heaðoric, "war ruler." James Hatrick appears in Kilmalcolm, 1650, James Hatrig in Thriplie, 1689, and James Hattridge of Houston, 1741 (Kilbarchan). Robert Hattridge was member of the University of Glasgow, 1696 (MCM., III, p. 67). Robert Hetrick, the Dalmellington poet, published his Poems and songs, 1826. Heathricke 1654.

HATT. Andrew Hatmalin, Thomas Hatmalin, and Duncan Hatmalin are recorded in Aberdeen in 1493 (CRA., p. 50). The index gives the name as 'Hatmaker,' for Thomas, but makes no mention of Andrew and Duncan. William Hatt in Brounhill, 1633 (SCM., III, p. 90), and Alexander Hatt, a trade burgess in Aberdeen in 1670, is perhaps Alexander Hatt, maltman there in 1697 (ROA., I, p. 236, 246). Alexander Hatt was a farmer at Haughton of Bieldside, Banchory-Devenick, 1846. Harrison says from a trade name. Perhaps Hatmalin is an error of transcription. Cf. HATMAKER.

HATTON. (1) Local. William de Hatun who witnessed a charter by Matthew, bishop of Aberdeen, c. 1171–99 (RPSA., p. 299) may have been an Englishman. (2) Perhaps from the Hattoun in Forfar Retours (517, 520). Helen Hautoun in Nether Balnakeyth, 1593 (Brechin). (3) A curtailed form of (MACIL-)-HATTON, q.v., current in Kintyre and adjacent parts of Argyllshire.

HATTONRIG. John Hattanrig, witness in Renfrew, 1575 (Laing, 916). From Hattanrig in barony of Dowchall, Renfrewshire.

HATTRICK. See under HATRICK.

HAUEUILLA. Ricardus de Haueuilla witnessed Edgar's grant of Mortun to the church of Kelso, c. 1200 (Kelso, 347).

HAUGH. Local. There are many places of the name in CD. Peter de Halugh who witnessed a charter by Robert de Burneuill to the Abbey of Kelso, c. 1200–14 (Kelso, 323), is probably Sir Peter de Halu or of the Halch, a cleric, burgess of Rokesburc in 1235 and prepositus in 1237 (ibid., 285, 301). John de Hawhe, notary public in Glasgow, 1409 (RMP., p. 57). John Haugh in Callintoyis, 1617. John Haugh in Meikle Daltone, 1685, and three more of the name (Dumfries). "This very puzzling word occurs in an immense number of place names, and consequently in many surnames, but nobody seems to know what it means" (Weekley, p. 61). The name originally possessed an l, and Barbour in his Brus writes halche, from OE. healh.

HAUGHAN. Perhaps from Ir. Ó hEacháin, 'descendant of Eachán,' diminutive of Eochaid (Woulfe, p. 560).

HAUGHIE, HAUGHY. This name may be from Ir. Ó hEochadha, 'descendant of Eochaid,' which is Englished Haughey and Hoey. Thomas Haughey (1826–1870), born in Glasgow, served in the U. S. army during the Civil War, later member of Congress, was assassinated in Alabama. John Newlands Haughy from Turriff was killed in the first Great War (Turriff), and William Haughie died in Edinburgh, 1941. Cf. under OUGHTON.

HAUKERIST. Ricardus de Haukerist was one of the twelve knights appointed in 1249 to meet twelve from England to settle the law of the marches (APS., I, p. 413). Johanne de Haukerist was a charter witness c. 1318 (James II, p. 11).

HAUNCHES. Gilbert Haunches and Thomas de Haunches, both of Roxburghshire, rendered homage in 1296 (Bain, II, p. 202, 209).

HAUNSARD. Johan de Haunsard of Forfarshire who rendered homage in 1296 (Bain, II, p. 199) was most probably a descendant of the Hansards of England.

HAVER. Hardly likely to be from French place name Havre, as suggested by Johnston. Harrison says ME. haver, a buck, a he-goat. Gilbert Heware, chaplain, witnessed an instrument of sasine, 1446 (Irvine, I, p. 137), and Robert Hafere was one of the perambulators of the bounds of Prestwick, in the same year (Prestwick, p. 116). "John Haveris airis" in

Prestwick are mentioned in 1470, "Wille Hewyre was maid burgesse" of the burgh in 1482, and Will Haver "wes our tane for a common seller of pettis" in 1497 (*Prestwick*, p. 6, 29, 33). In the same record the name is also spelled Hafwery and Hauere 1509, Haifry 1514, Haverve 1505, Havery 1499, Hawery 1513.

HAVERYNTON. Sir Robert de Haverynton witnessed resignation of lands in Annandale, a. 1245 (*Bain*, I, 1682). Harrison has the name Haverington, most probably the same, but does not say where the place is. Not in Lower or Bardsley.

HAW. Local, from some place in the Lowlands. John Haw held a land in Glasgow before 1494 (REG., p. 487). Robert Haw was tenant of Fruquhy, 1508 (*Cupar-Angus*, I, p. 267). Alexander Haw was a tenant under the bishop of Glasgow, 1512 (*Rental*). John Haw at Blainslie near Melrose, 1563 (*Lauder*). Perhaps a smoothed down form of HAUGH, q.v.

HAWEY, HAWIE. Forms of HOWIE, q.v., found in Ayrshire. Helen Havie (v = u) in Ladykirk, Berwickshire, 1655 (*Lauder*).

HAWICK. From the town of Hawick, Roxburghshire. Various persons surnamed 'of Hawick,' tenants of the Lovels, lords of the barony of Hawick, or residents and burgesses of the town appear in record as early as 1175–79. Roger, son of John of Hawic, was a charter witness at that date (*Melros*, p. 129), and Hugh de Hauic witnesses a charter by Robert de Lundris (RAA., I, 61). William Hawick was prebendary of Guthrie, 1234 (REB., I, 60). Robert of Hauewyk of Roxburghshire rendered homage, 1296. His seal bears a lion coiled within two squares, interlaced, and S' *Rob'ti de Havwic* (*Bain*, II, p. 200, 532). John de Hawewyk, clerk, had a safe conduct from Richard II to study at Oxford in 1380 (*Rot. Scot.*, II, p. 20). Andrew of Hawyk (Hawic, Hawik), rector of Listoun, was secretary to Robert, duke of Albany, and is frequently mentioned in record. John of Hawike, presbyter and notary public in Glasgow diocese, 1410–30 (LCD., p. 165, 237; RMS., II, 9). Robert de Hawyk was depute collector of customs for the burgh of Edinburgh, 1425 (ER., IV) and juror on an inquisition made there in 1428 (RAA., II, 61). The Hawicks of Skatska, Delting, are referred to in 1575, and appear to have been people of some prominence. Andrew Hawick of Skattiska in Zetland was debtor to the burgesses of Dysart in 1578 (*Dysart*, p. 39).

HAWLEY. Donaldus Hawley and John Hauly his son were two of the killed in the Drummond-Murray feud at Monzievaird, 1490 (*Scot. Rev.*, I, p. 119), and Thomas Hawlie was witness in Perthshire, 1550 (*Gaw*, 14). Lower, Bardsley, and Harrison have Hawley as a surname of local origin.

HAWOC. William filius Hawoc (or Hawok), burgess of Perth, held land in the burgh of the abbot and convent of Scone, c. 1240–45 (*Inchaffray*, p. 62, 63). From OE. *hafoc*, 'a hawk.' The word was also used in OE. as a personal name.

HAWORTH. Most likely from Haworth, a village in Yorkshire. Johannes Hauewrth had a grant of land in the territory of Gouerton, c. 1317 (*Neubotle*, p. 305).

HAWSON. Probably English and a variant of HALSON, q.v. Moris Hawsone was juror on inquest anent a fishing on the Tweed, 1467 (RD., p. 358).

HAWTHORN, HAWTHORNE, HATHORN. An old Galloway surname. The name is local from Hawthorn in the parish of Easington, county Durham. A family of the name were proprietors of Meikle or Over Aires in the parish of Kirkinner. In 1455 the Chamberlain accounts "for 15 bolls farinae avenaticae" (oatmeal) of the escheat of Daude Halthorn (ER., VI, p. 195, 205). Two Hauthornes were summoned to compear before the Lords of Council in Jan. 1484 (ADC., p. * 97). The family became kyndlie tenants on the lands of Airies under the Church, and 'Sir' Mychaell Hathorne was reader in Toskertoun in the first list of Reformed clergy (*Agnew*, I, p. 425; *Laing*, 408). Margaret Hathorn appears in Carstairs, 1602 (*Lanark CR.*), Anna Hauthorne was heir of James Hauthorne, burgess of Stranraer, 1628 (*Inquis.*, 1432), and Esther Halthorn in Pathhouse of Colleum is in record, 1728 (*Kirkcudbright*). Halthoirne 1591, Halthorne 1556, Haulthorne 1587, Hauthorn 1676, Hawthorne 1628.

HAWTHORNDEN. From Hawthornden in the parish of Lasswade, Midlothian. Matheu de Hauthorndene rendered homage in 1296 and had his lands restored to him. The seal attached to his homage bears 2 birds in a bush, and S. *Mathei d' Havthornde* (*Bain*, II, p. 201, 226, 559). He is probably the Mathew de Hauthornden who witnessed the sale of a tenement in Gouertun in 1317 (*Neubotle*, p. 306).

HAXTON. A surname current in Fife, a variant of HACKSTON, q.v.

350

HAY. A considerable number of OHG. words were introduced into Gallo-Roman speech between the eighth and tenth centuries. Among the words then introduced was *haga*, which we find in the Capitularies of Charles the Bald (823–877) spelled *haia*, the modern Fr. *haie*, a hedge. By the middle of the eleventh century or earlier the word had entered into the name of a place in the arrondissement of Coutance — La Haye du Puits, and so gave name to a family *de la Haye*. The first of the name in Scotland was probably William de Haya who obtained the lands of Herrol (Errol) in Gowrie from William the Lion c. 1178–82 (SCM., II, p. 303), and is in record as witnessing charters by Malcolm IV after 1160 and others by William the Lion c. 1170–1200 (REM., 5; LAC., p. 1; and elsewhere). In one of the charters of Malcolm he is styled *pincerna* or cup-bearer to the king. Another William de Haia, a churchman, clerk to Gilbert, earl of Strathern, is in record c. 1206–11 (LIM., xxv; RAA., I, 86). David de Haya was vicecomes of Forfar c. 1200–14 (RAA., I, 64). Thomas de Haya made a gift to the Hospital of Soltre c. 1202–38 (*Soltre*, p. 15). John de Haye witnessed a confirmation charter by Alexander II dated at Muschelbrucht, 1228 (RMP., p. 215), and with Thomas de Haya witnessed a charter of the earldom of Levenax to Maldouen in the same year (*Levenax*, p. 2). Edmund de la Haye and Thomas de la Haye of Perthshire and Huwe de la Haye of Fife rendered homage, 1296 (*Bain*, II, p. 204). Thomas de Hay, lord of Lochorwart, was a charter witness c. 1300–20 (*Hay*, p. 6). Of William Hay, Constable, slain at Dupplin, 1332, Boece tells us that his race would have been extinguished had not his wife been pregnant, "an old fable often repeated in our histories" says Lord Hailes (*Annals*, II, p. 187). Hugo dictus Haiy held land in Ayr before 1320 (RMS., I, 43), and Thomas del Hay was one of the hostages for ransom of King David II, 1363 (*Bain*, IV, 81).

HAYDUF. Hugh de Hayduf, bailie of Bemersyd, 1326 (*Melros*, II, 378).

HAYROCK. A family of this name was early connected with Moray. Hugh Heroc, burgess of Elgin, one of the inquest on the king's garden there in 1261 (APS., I, p. 99 red), is doubtless the Hugh Herock, burgess of Elgin, who granted the lands of Daldeleyt to the church of Holy Trinity, Elgin, in 1286 (REM., p. 283). Archebaldus Heroch, archdiaconus de Moray in 1268 (ibid., p. 279) appears to have been chosen bishop of Caithness in 1273 (*Dowden*, p. 236–237). Patrick Heyrock was provost of Elgin in 1272 (*Innes Familie*, p. 55),

Wauter Herok, dean of Moray, rendered homage, 1296 (*Bain*, II, p. 211). Walter Herok or Herot, a canon of Glasgow, appears as dean of Moray in 1328–29 (*Pap. Lett.*, II, p. 285, 288), and provision of a canonry of Caithness was made to Adam Herok in 1329 (ibid., p. 288), who appears again in 1341 as Adam called Heroch, chancellor of Caithness (*Dowden*, p. 242).

HAYTER. Thomas Hayter of Aberdeen to serve on a ship of war, 1540 (CRA., p. 172). Probably from Haytor, a hundred in county Devon.

HAYTON. From one or other of the two places so named in Cumberland. Johan de Haytone in Dumfriesshire rendered homage in 1296, and in 1304 petitioned against the oppressions of Sir Maheu de Redman, sheriff of Dumfries (*Bain*, II, p. 210, 397). Thomas de Haytone, vicar of the church of Cambosneythan, and Johan de Hayton, warden of the Hospital of St. Leonard of Torrens, Lanarkshire, also rendered homage (ibid., p. 204, 214). Cf. HEITON.

HEADRICK. Perhaps local. Jamieson (*Scottish dictionary*) defines Headrig, Hetherig, or Hidderig as "the ridge of land at the end of a field." Several of the name Hedrig or Hedrick are recorded in Dunblane (*Dunblane*). Rev. James Headrick (1758–1841) was divine, agriculturist, and mineralogist. Thomas Black Hedderick died 1941. Cf. under HEATHERWICK.

HEADRIDGE. A form of HEADRICK, q.v.

HEATHERILL. A surname recorded in Glasgow. Probably local from some place named Heatherhill.

HEATHERWICK, HEDDERICK, HEDDERWICK. (1) From the old lands of Haddirvyk or Hathirvyk in the regality of Arbroath in Angus. Robert Hadowy or Hadowe, servant in Clunie in 1511 and 1515, appears in 1510 as Robert Hadwye, in 1511 as Robert Haderwyk, as Haderwik in 1512, and as Hadervik in 1513 (*Rent. Dunk.*, p. 40, 149, 174, 177, 182, 187). John Hadirvike had a precept of remission in 1536 (RSS., II, 2002), Johnne Hedderwick resigned the quarter lands of the Mains of Clein in 1585 (*Scon*, p. 229), and Andrew Hetherweck (Hethirweck, Hatherwick, or Henderweck) of Pittillo appears as a writer in Edinburgh in 1684 (BOEC., IX, p. 166, 169, 174). (2) John of Hathyrwyk who appears as a juror on an inquisition on the lands of Swinton in 1408 (*Swinton*, p. xviii), however, probably derived his surname from Hedderwick in the parish of Dunbar. Hetherweck 1699. Cf. HEADRICK.

HEATLEY, HEATLIE, HEATLY. *See under* HAITLIE.

HEBBURN. A variant of HEPBURN, q.v.

HEBDEN. A family of this name possessed the island of Eday, Orkney, in the nineteenth century (Smith, *Orkney memorials*, p. 66). Probably from one or other of the villages of the name in the West Riding of Yorkshire. William de Hebden was rector of Burnsall, Yorkshire, in the reign of Edward III (*Guppy*, p. 429).

HEBRON. William Hebrone in Blairsheoch, parish of Blackford, 1681 (*Dunblane*). James Hepbrone of Miltoune of Innerlochtie, a witness, 1661 (*Rec. Elgin*, II, p. 296). From Hebron near Morpeth, Northumberland. The name is not uncommon in Yorkshire.

HECFORD. Alexander de Hecford witnessed a charter by Alan, lord of Galloway to the abbey of Kelso, a. 1208 (*Kelso*, p. 202). Probably from Heckford in England (in *Harrison*).

HECTOR. Most probably from the classical (Homeric) Hector. Hector, medicus, is mentioned in connection with the lands of Balgillachy in sheriffdom of Forfar, 1369 (RMS., I, 333). Master Robert Hector was vicar of Northmewene (Northmavine) in 1525 (*Goudie*, p. 141). James Hector claimed to be principal gunner of Dunbar Castle, 1565 (RPC., I, p. 395). John Hector in the parish of Glendovan, 1673 (*Dunblane*), and David Hector, workman in Aberdeen, 1749 (*Aberdeen CR.*). There was an Aberdeenshire family of this name probably connected with the HECTORSONS, q.v. The name is also used as Englishing of G. *Eachdonn*, a name with which it has no etymological connection. As forename: Ekkie Armstrong took part in the Maxwell raid of Stirling, 1585. Heckie 1569.

HECTORSON. 'Son of HECTOR,' q.v. Ronald Hectorson was bailie of Alexander, bishop of Moray in 1535 (OPS., II, p. 716). John Hectorsoune of Garloch was forfeited in 1547 (ibid., p. 406). Angus Hectorson (in Myllarie) was subject to the jurisdiction of the earl of Caithness in 1565 (RPC., I, p. 424), and William Hectoursone in Langwall had a remission in 1567 (SCM., IV, p. 155).

HEDDERICK, HEDDERWICK. *See under* HEATHERWICK.

HEDDING. Alexander Hedding of Ponderualls, 1690 (*Dunkeld*). Probably of English origin from Headon or Hedon in Yorkshire (*Bardsley*).

HEDDLE, HEDDILL. Of local origin from land of the name in Orkney. The family are said to have held land in Harray and Stenness prior to 1303. William in Hedal was one of the prominent men of Orkney in 1424 (*Oppressions*, p. 107; REO., p. 41). William Haldell was present at deliverance of a decree by the lawman in West Mainland, c. 1500 (REO., p. 75). William Forster Heddle, author of *The Mineralogy of Scotland*, Edinburgh, 1901, was born in Orkney. Haddale 1503, Haddell 1640, Hadell 1558, Haldell c. 1500, Heddell 1513, Hedeill 1509; Haidale.

HEDERSTONE. Local. John de Hederstone, juror on inquisition at Dumfries, 1304 (*Bain*, II, p. 412).

HEDLAM. Johan de Hedlam, "southchantour del eglise de Ros," rendered homage, 1296 (*Bain*, II, p. 204). An Englishman most probably. The name is of local origin from Headlam near Gainford (in 1316 Hedlem).

HEDLEY. Most probably from Hedley in Northumberland. Schero de Hedley witnessed confirmation of grant of Swaynystoun to the Hospital of Soltre c. 1221–40 (*Soltre*, p. 26), and Robert de Hedlye of Edinburghshire rendered homage in 1296 (*Bain*, II, p. 201).

HEDUN. Local. Peter de Hedun, burgess of Aberdeen, c. 1214 (RAA., I, 82). Magister Nicholas de Hedon or Hedun, dean of Moray, witnessed perambulation of the bounds of Conan and Tulloch, 1254 (ibid., 366). Stephen de Hedun, one of the chapter of Scon in the reign of Alexander III (*Scon*, p. 82). Cf. HAYTON and HEITON.

HEFFREN. An Irish name of recent introduction. Probably from Irish Ó hEimhrín (diminutive of Éimhear).

HEGGIE, HIGGIE. A shortened form of MACKEGGIE, q.v. Donald Hegy, 'pvpar,' had a remission from Queen Mary for assisting the English in burning the town of Dunnone and besieging the castle, 1546 (RSS.). Patrick Hegy had sasine of lands in Perthshire, 1567 (ER., XIX, p. 557), Barbara Heagie was heir portioner of James Heagie, merchant burgess of Stirling, 1617 (*Inquis.*, 708), Janet Heggie, witness in Burntisland, 1640 (PBK., p. 167), Andrew Hegie, junior, burgess of Stirling, 1642 (*Inquis.*, 2762), and John Heggie was schoolmaster at Forfar in 1670 (Lamont, *Diary*, p. 222). Three generations of Heggies were employed in succession in the Carron Ironworks (Gibson, *Lairds*, p. 201). Heagy 1599, Heegie 1642.

HEGGIN, Heccins. From Ir. O'hUiginn, descendant of Uige (Woulfe). John Hegyne in Hunterstoun, Ayrshire, 1593 (Hunter, p. 31). Andrew Heggin, wright in Edinburgh, 1692 (Edinb. Marr.). Joannes Hegin, heir of William Hegin, burgess of Queensferrie, 1666 (Inquis., 5000). John Hegin in Elphistoun, 1671 (Edin. App.). Patrick Heggins, sailor in Kincardin, 1697 (Inquis., 7853). See Higgins.

HEITON. From Heiton near Kelso, Roxburghshire. Richard de Hetun appears as a charter witness, c. 1190 and 1214 (Melros, 153, 154). Magister John de Hetun, a churchman, witnessed a grant to Cambuskenneth Abbey, c. 1180 (Cambus., 15), canon of Dunkeld, 1216 (Pap. Lett., I, p. 46), and charter witness, c. 1215-18 (LAC., 33). He also witnessed the gift of Buthyrgasc to the Abbey of Scon before 1214 (Scon, p. 20), and the charter of Maderin (Madderty) to the Abbey of Inchaffray, c. 1215-21 (Inchaffray, p. 31). Adam de Hetune sold to the monks of Melrose the land of Hungerig and the meadow of Holemede c. 1227-38 (Melros, p. 257-258). Nicholas de Hedon, archdeacon of Moray, 1254 (Pap. Lett., I, p. 295). John of Heton of Roxburghshire rendered homage, 1296. His seal bears an eight-leaved figure, and S' Ioh's de Hettvn (Bain, II, p. 199, 532). Thomas de Hetoun or Heton, a charter witness at Lamberton, 1332 (BNCH., XVI, p. 327, 330), and a later Thomas of Heton was a hostage for the security of Berwick-on-Tweed, 1338 (Rot. Scot., I, 522). William Heton, juror in Lanark, 1498 (Lanark, p. 9), Sir Peter Hetoun or Heton, a cleric, witness in Irvine, 1499 (Simon, 23), and Alexander Hettoun, a monk of Cupar, 1500 (REB., I, 220). Andrew Hiettoune, portioner of Darnick, 1682 (RRM., III, p. 7). Heitoun 1299, Hetown 1607. Cf. Hayton.

HELBECK. From Helbeck or Hillbeck in Westmoreland, England. William of Hellebec was one of the witnesses to the gift of the lands of Dundas to Helias, son of Huctred, probably in the reign of Malcolm IV (Nat. MSS., I, 23). William de Hellebeke of the county of Dunfres rendered homage in 1296. His seal bears 3 stars, 2 and 1, not on a shield, S' Wilelmi Helebec (Bain, II, p. 206, 554). He may be the William de Hellebek who in 1316 was imprisoned on suspicion of theft, escaped from the king of Scotland's prison at Penrith, and fled to the churchyard of the parish church, whence he was dragged to the prison at Carlisle. Bishop John of Halton demanded his immediate release, as he had been wrongfully taken out of a sanctuary (Moore, Lands, p. 122).

HELIAS. See under ELIAS.

HELLEWYK. William de Hellewyk witnessed gift of the church of Wemys in Fife to the House of Soltre, c. 1200-40 (Soltre, p. 13).

HELM. Of local origin from the old lands of Helme in the barony of Cavers, Roxburghshire. Hendrie Helm was tenant on the lands of the Abbey of Kelso, 1567 (Kelso, p. 526). Margaret Helme was resident in the parish of Borgue, 1684 (RPC., 3. ser. IX, p. 567), and Henry Helm was portioner of Middlem, 1789 (Heirs, 449). The name of James Kelene, tenant on lands of the Abbey of Kelso, 1567 (Kelso, p. 521), is probably an error for Helme.

HELTERER. Roger Helterer and John Helterer were witnesses in Glasgow, c. 1290 (REG., p. 200).

HEMBRY. Joseph Hembry in Kilbarchan, 1761 (Kilbarchan). Probably from Hembury, now Broad-Hembury in Devonshire. Hembrow is a Somerset surname.

HEMMING. Hemming was one of the witnesses to the charter by King Duncan II to the monks of S. Cuthbert in 1094, the earliest Scottish charter (Nat. MSS., I, 2). Douglas Hemmigar occupied the Cot of Barm in Firth, Orkney, c. 1850 (Old Lore Misc., III, p. 158). ON. or Old West Scandinavian, Hemingr, Hemmingr, very frequent (Lindqvist). Old Dan. Hemming.

HEMPHILL. Probably from Hemphill near Galston, Ayrshire. A debt was due to Robert Hemphill, 1689 (RPC., 3. ser. XIV, p. 672), and another (?) Robert Hemphill appears in Stewartoune, 1704 (Corsehill, p. 205). Hempill 1706.

HEMPSEED. Janet Hempseed in Nether Ardoch, 1611, and John Hempseed in Cambuschiney, 1664 (Dunblane). George Hampseid was member of the Scots parliament for Cullen, 1639 (Hanna, II, p. 497), and Walter Kempseid, sometym minister at Auchterless, 1664 (Alford, p. 57. In Fasti, 2. ed., VI, p. 249, his name is spelled Hempseid). Weekley (p. 196) says: "An uncomplimentary surname," apparently with reference to size. Perhaps a corruption of Hempstead. The name of John Hempseil in Cullen, one of an assize in Aberdeen, 1597 (SCM., I, p. 17) is perhaps another form of the name. John Hempseed died in Edinburgh, 1940.

HENDCHYLD. Richard Hendchyld of Crail, one of those appointed to treat for the ransom of David II in 1357 (CDE., 6; *Fœdera*, III) is doubtless the Richard Hendschyld or Heendchild who appears as bailie and burgess of Crail in 1359 and 1361 (ER., I, p. 653; II, p. 61), whose tenement in the burgh of Carale is mentioned in 1380 (*Neubotle*, p. 236). Hendechylde c. 1380.

HENDEMAN. Adam Hendeman was witness to a grant by Robert de Brus, lord of Annandale, c. 1215–45 (*Bain*, I, 1680).

HENDERSON. The same as HENRYSON, q.v., "son of Henry," with intrusive "d." In course of time this form with intrusive *d* gradually ousted the earlier form Henryson. A small clan or sept of this name held lands in Upper Liddesdale, but are not included among the Border Clans named in the 1594 Act of the Scottish Parliament "For punisement of thift, reif, oppressioun and sorning" (APS., IV, p. 71–72). The Hendersons of Fordell in Fifeshire, the chief Lowland family of the name, are believed to be descended from the old Dumfriesshire family of Henrysons. William Henrison, senior, was chamberlain of Logmabane Castle under Edward III in 1374 and following years (*Bain*, IV, p. 49, etc.). David Hennerson was a tenant of the Casteltoun, Ardmanoch, in 1504 (ER., XII, p. 661). James Hendirsoune had sasine of land as heir of his brother David Henrisoune in Glasgow in 1553 (*Protocols*, I). John Hendrysone witnessed a bond of manrent in 1586 (BBT., p. 237). The name became D'Handresson among descendants of Scots in France. Hendersone, Hendersonne, Hendersoun (1668), Hendirsone, Hendirsoun, Hendirsoune, Hendrisone (1494), Hendrisoune (1549), Henersoun (1603), Hennersoune (1542), Hennryson (1511), Henresoun, Henreysoun, Henriesoun, Henrison, Henrisone, Henrisoune (1511), Henrisoun (1465), Henryesson, Henryson, Henrysone (1486), Henrysoun, Henrysoune.

(2) A branch of the Clan Gunn bears the name Henderson, and the traditional account of their origin is "that they are descended from Henry Gunn, a younger son of George Gunn, who was chief of the clan in the fifteenth century. After the slaughter of their chief and several of his sons in a combat with the Keiths, a family difference led to Henry separating himself from his surviving brothers and settling in the lowlands of Caithness. In 1594 we find mention of a champion of the clan Gunn, named Donald Mac-William *Mac-Hendrie*, who may have had something to say in the matter of the Henderson patronymic; but the popular account is, as has been said, that they

are the descendants of Henry Gunn" (Henderson, *Caithness family history*, p. 283).

(3) The Hendersons of Glencoe have Englished their name from Gaelic *MacEanruig*, and claim a preposterous descent from one Eanruig Mor Mac Righ Neachtan, "Big Henry son of King Nectan," supposed to have been a Pictish king who reigned from A. D. 700 to 720! A more modest and more probable claim is descent from a Dughall MacEanruig, who is believed to have flourished in the first half of the fourteenth century. As a clan or individually they have made no mark on Scottish history.

HENDRIE, HENDRY. See under HENRY.

HENNING. See under HAINING.

HENRICKS, 'son of Henrick,' 'an Anglicization of the Scandinavian Henrik' (*Harrison*). Jane Henricks, residenter in Eyemouth, 1795 (*Lauder*).

HENRY, HENDRIE, HENDRY. These names are common in the districts of Ayr and Fife. The *d* is intrusive after *n*. Henricus, dapifer, was a witness c. 1183–88 (*Scon*, p. 27), and Henricus (Chen) was bishop of Aberdeen, 1282–1328 (ibid., p. 97). William Henry was witness in Perth, 1551 (*Rollok*, 74), Allan Henry, burgess of Irvine, 1552 (*Protocols*, I), Hendyre Hendry, burgess of Stirling, 1562 (SBR., p. 80), John Hendrie was tenant of the marquis of Huntly, 1600 (SCM., IV, p. 261), and William Henrie was member of Huntly Volunteers, 1798 (*Will*, p. 8). As forename: Hendrie Ralstoun (1519) and Hendrie Dwn (1527).

HENRYSON, 'son of HENRY,' q.v. The earliest references to this name locate it in Aberdeen. John filius Henrici appears as burgess of Aberdeen in 1317 (SCM., v, p. 11), and James Henrisson or Henrison, Aberdeen merchant, complained in 1370 of his ship being plundered by English wreckers (*Bain*, IV, 158, 164). John, son of Henry, was admitted burgess of Aberdeen in 1399 (NSCM., I, p. 1). John Henrici witnessed an instrument of resignation in Brechin in 1434 (REB., I, 65), Walter Henrison was 'sergeand' in Edinburgh in 1467 (*Neubotle*, 299), and Thom Henryson was tenant of Milhorn in 1478 (*Cupar-Angus*, I, p. 213). Richard Henrisone witnessed a precept of sasine dated 1479, and John Henrisoun of Pilmure witnessed a retour of special service in 1505 (*Home*, 23, 29). James Henrisone was member of assize at Cupar, 1521 (SCBF., p. 223), and Malcolm Henrysone alias Makandov or Henry Makandov alias Henrysoune is recorded in Glasgow in 1528 (LCD., p. 90, 91). John Henrysone had a charter of parts

HENRYSON, *continued*

of Arlarie in 1607 (RD., p. 500), and Mausia Henrysone, spouse of Magister Henry Charter, writer to the signet, is recorded in 1640 (*Retours, Ayr*, 347). Robert Henryson (1430?–1506), schoolmaster of Dunfermline, has been called the Scottish Chaucer. There was an old Dumfriesshire family of Henryson, of which William Henrison, senior, was chamberlain of Logmabane Castle under Edward III in 1374 and following years. He received from the king of England "an annuity of 20 l., when he was driven by the Scots from his lands in the lordship of Loghmaben, with his children, and had nothing to keep them" (*Bain*, IV, p. 14, 100). He died in 1395. The name is said to have been early carried to France appearing there as D'Arson. It is now merged in HENDERSON. Henerson 1512, Hendriesoun and Henriesone 1627, Hendryson 1510, Henrysonne 1616.

HENSHILWOOD, HENSHELWOOD, HINSHELWOOD. Of local origin from the small place named Henshilwood at Carnwath, Lanarkshire. John Hinschelwood was burgess of Lanark in 1625 (*Lanark CR.*: nine more of the name are recorded here). Agnes Henchelwood recorded in Craigend in 1689 (*Torphichen*), and Sergeant-major Thomas Henshilwood was killed at Salonica in 1917. Hinselwood 1708.

HENWOOD. Probably from Henwood, a tithing in the parish of Cumnor, co. Berks, England.

HEPBURN. Of territorial origin from Hebburn in the parish of Chillingham, Northumberland, where a family of the name flourished from 1271 (their earliest appearance in record) till late in the eighteenth century, when it ended, like so many other old families, in an heiress (*Archaeologia Aeliana*, XIV, p. 302). The Scottish Hepburns have been described as 'an old and powerful race but of uncertain origin and of evil destiny.' The founder of the family was Adam de Hepburne or de Hylburne, said to have been taken prisoner by the earl of March, who afterwards gave him lands in East Lothian, for saving the earl's life from a savage horse. As Adam de Hylburne, he and his spouse Mariote Fourbaire had a charter of Trepprane (now Traprain) and Dumpeldar in the reign of David II, from the earl of March (RMS., I, App. I, 117). He also had other charters of Southauch and Northalls (i.e. South Hales and North Hales) which had been forfeited by Hew Gourlay of Beinstoun (ibid., App. II, 853–855). At one time the Hepburns held great sway in East Lothian, and in the sixteenth century there were Hepburns of Hailes, Waughton, Smeaton, Bolton, Alderston, Bearford, Beanston, Humbie, Keith, Nunraw, and

Monkrigg. Samuel Khebron who commanded a regiment of Scots in Sweden, 1612, was probably a Hepburn. Hopburn 1589.

HEPE. From the lands of Heip or Heap in the old barony of Wilton in Roxburghshire. Adam de Hepe rendered homage for his lands in 1296. His seal bears a rose-bush and S' *Ade de Hepe* (*Bain*, II, 811, p. 531). He may have been ancestor of the Waughs of Heip (OPS., I, p. 326). Henry del Hepe and John del Hepe were two common and notorious robbers in Roxburgh in 1301 (*Bain*, II, 1227).

HERALD. A form of Harald, ON. *Heraldr*. It occurs in med. Latin as Airoldus = OFr. *herolt*, French *Heraut*, which has been substituted for the Norse name. William Herald, schoolmaster in Tannadice, died 1863.

HERBERT. From the OE. personal name *Herebeorht*, 'army bright.' About the year 1200 Herbert filius Herberti de Camera granted a half carucate in Dunipace to the Abbey of Cambuskenneth (*Cambus.*, 79). One or other of these Herberts most probably gave name to Herbertshire near Denny, Stirlingshire. Herbert, third abbot of Selkirk, was bishop of Glasgow, 1147–1164.

HERBERTSON, 'son of Herbert,' from OE. personal name *Herebeorht*, meaning 'army bright.' Archibald Herbertson was burgess of Glasgow in 1525 (REG., 497), and Robert Herbertsoune was notary public there in 1536. The name is common in the Glasgow Protocol books of the sixteenth century as Herbisone (1551), Herbisoune (1550). George Harbertsone is recorded as a witness in Glasgow in 1559 (HP., II, p. 203), William Herbesone of North Berwick is mentioned in 1555 (CMN., p. 70), and Richard Harbertson, son of John Harbertsoun, notary, was burgess of Glasgow in 1605 (*Inquis. Tut.*, 75). Margaret Herbertson is recorded in the parish of Monkland in 1619 (*Campsie*), and Martin Herbertson was tenant in the barony of Mousewall (Mouswald, Dumfriesshire) in 1673 (PSAS., XXIII, p. 74). An action at law against Georg Harbiesone in Hairshaw, 1706 (*Corsehill*, p. 213). Harbersone, Harbertsone, Harbeson, and Harbisone 1706, Herbertsoun 1609.

HERCULES. As forename we have Hercules Dykis in Kelso, 1567 (*Kelso*, p. 524), and Hercules Menteith, 1570.

HERCULESON, HERCULSON. Shetland surnames, found mainly in the parishes of Lunnasting and Tingwall. Other variants are Harcleson and Harkelson. Hercules here is a corruption of ON. *Hakon* or *Haakon*, familiarly *Hakki*.

HERD. From the occupation, a herdsman or shepherd. In the absence of fences herds were very necessary. David Herd (1732–1810), ballad collector and antiquary. See also HIRD.

HERDMAN. From OE. *hiredman*, retainer, follower, one of the *hired* or body of domestic retainers of a great man. Robert hirdmand witnessed a charter by William de Cunynburg c. 1268 (RHM., I, p. 9). Symon Hirdeman was received to the English king's grace in 1321 (*Bain*, III, 724). James Hireman was parishioner of Kinkell, 1473 (*Inverurie*, p. 122), "Sir" Alexander Hyrdman was chaplain in the diocese of Dumblane in 1479 (SBR., p. 265), and "Schir" John Hirdman was a notary public at Slains in 1508 (SCM., II, p. 265). William Hyrdman was hired apprentice at Cupar-Angus Abbey, 1485 (*Cupar-Angus*, I, p. 307). (2) the man who tended a herd, especially cattle.

HERFORD. William de Herford who rendered homage at Berwick, 1291 (RR.), probably derived his name from the city of Hereford, England.

HERINTON'. Perhaps from Herrington near Houghton-le-Spring, co. Durham. Thomas de Herinton' witnessed a charter by Patrick, 3. earl of Dunbar, 1261 (*Raine*, 137).

HERIOT, HERRIOT. From the lands of Heriot in the parish of the same name in Midlothian. Early references to the name are all nearly to the district from which the name is derived. Henry de Heriet witnessed confirmation of the church of Karnewid (Carnwath) to Joceline, bishop of Glasgow, c. 1164–74 (REG., 52), and Laurence de Herryhot witnessed a grant of the lands of Swavnystoun to the Hospital of Soltre c. 1221–38 (*Soltre*, p. 24). The lands of Trabroun in the sheriffdom of Berwick were confirmed to John de Heriot de Trabroun, son and heir of James de Heriot de Nudre Marschele in 1424 (RMS., II, 13). Robert de Hervot was witness in Edinburgh in 1429 (REG., 336), William Heryot or Heryote in Haddington made an annual gift of five shillings to the monks of Neubotle in 1458 (*Neubotle*, p. 244, 247), and John de Heriot was vicar of Soltre in 1468 (ibid., 301). The Heriots who appear in the Glasgow district in the sixteenth century were probably connected with Henry Sinclair, dean of Glasgow, who was of the Roslin family (*Rental*). John Heriot, George Heriot, and Patrick Heriot had special respite and protection in 1504 (*Trials*, I, p. °42, °43). John Hareot and Andrew Hareot were witnesses in Glasgow in 1525 (REG., 497), William Heriot was burgess

there in 1549 (*Protocols*, I), and Walter Heriot was vicar of Linlithgow in 1537 (*Johnsoun*). Buchanan says William, John, and Gilbert Heriot safely conducted Robert the Steward out of reach of his enemies in the time of Edward Balliol. Hereate 1569, Hereot 1543, Hereote 1558, Hereott 1595, Heret 1569, Herioitt and Herrioitt 1595, Heriott 1601, Herote 1544, Herreot 1559.

HERKLESS. Probably of local origin from Erchless in the parish of Kiltarlity, Inverness-shire, old spellings of which are Herkele (a. 1222), Erchelys and Herchelys 1258, Ercles 1403, and Arcles in 1512. Rev. John Herkless published a life of Cardinal Beaton in 1891.

HERLEWINE. An OE. personal name, meaning 'army friend.' Daniel, son of Herelewine, witnessed a charter by Uchtred, son of Fergus, lord of Galloway, c. 1166 (*Coll. AGAA.*, IV, p. 55).

HERMISTON. This surname appears to have sprung from two localities: (1) from the lands of Hermiston (old Hirdemaneston) in the old barony of Lilliesleaf, and (2) from the barony of Herdmanston in East Lothian, but mainly from the former place. Alexander de Hirdmanestun witnessed a charter by Jocelin, bishop of Glasgow confirming the grant of the church of Pulloc to the church of Paisley c. 1177–99 (RMP., p. 99, 101). In 1202 he also witnessed a charter of the land called Schotteschales in the territory of Lilliesleaf (REG., 99). Johan de Hirdmanstone or Hirdmanestone of the county of Berewyke rendered homage in 1296. His seal bears a merlin perched on a gloved hand (?), and S' *Iohis de Hirdmainston* (*Bain*, II, p. 185, 200). Alexander de Hirmanestone of the county of Rokesburk also rendered homage, and in 1305 he was juror on an inquisition made at Selkirk (ibid., 1681 and p. 209). Some years later the lands of Hermiston in Lilliesleaf seem to have passed from possession of the family to William de Stapilton in 1349 (*Rot. Scot.*, I, p. 728). The surname was early carried to the north. Andrew Hirdmanniston, archdeacon of Caithness, witnessed the settlement of a controversy in 1328 (REM., p. 152), and in the following year provision was made of a deanery of Moray to Master Andrew de Hirdmannstron (*Pap. Lett.*, II, p. 298). In 1368 Mariota de Hirdmannystoun, daughter of the deceased Andrew of Hirdmannystoun, quitclaimed 6 marks of vearly revenue of Tarbat Ross (OPS., II, p. 443). David Hermiston was tenant in the toune of Reddene in 1567 (*Kelso*, p. 521), and Marion Hermistone is recorded in Fogoe in 1690 (*Lauder*). Hirdmeston 1566.

356

HERON, Herron. The old family of Heron in the Stewartry claim descent from the Herons of Chipchase who appear in Northumberland in the eleventh century. Jordan Heyrun is in record c. 1150 (REG., 11), and Walterus de Hayroun was clerk to William the Lion c. 1178–80 (RAA., I, p. 27). Robert Hevrun was parson of the church of Forde, 1292 (Rot. Scot., I, p. 14). Roger Heron, a charter witness in 1321, appears in a writ by Roger Corbet of Langton in 1330 as Roger Hayron (Laing, 29, 35), and Thomas le (error for de) Heron, knight, was witness to a demise by Roger Corbet of Langton in 1329 (ibid., 33). David Herroun was elected sergeant of Aberdeen, 1526 (Guildry, p. 196), and John Herrowne was already burgess there, 1505 (NSCM., I, p. 43). Alexander Herowne, cuik, was burgess freeman of Glasgow, 1607 (Burgesses), John Harron is in the parish of Keir, 1680 (Dumfries), and Thomas Herron, wright, burgess of Edinburgh, 1734 (Guildry, p. 148). Some time after the Revolution (1688) the family of Heron had their lands of Kerroughtree in Kirkcudbrightshire consolidated into the barony of Heron, but the name has since reverted to its Gaelic designation. Heirun 1251, Herrone 1675, Herroune 1677, Herroun 1526. In Ulster this is said to be an Anglicized form of M'Ilheron (Mac Giolla Cheardin).

HERONSON. William Heronsone was member of council of burgh of Inverkeithing, 1687 (Inverkeithing, p. 221).

HERRIEGERRIE. A curious local corruption of the name Garioch, q.v. See also Geerie. William Herriegerie, miller of Caden and his family are in the Poll Book of 1696. John Heregerie in Carnehills died in 1795 (Jervise, II, p. 323). Cf. the tale of "Francie Herriegerie's Shargie Laddie" in William Alexander's Sketches of life among my ain folk. Hargegare 1707.

HERRIES. Chalmers says the old family of this name were probably a branch of the Anglo-Norman family of Heriz of Nottinghamshire, and came into Scotland in the train of David I. William de Heriz, first of the name recorded in Scotland, appears as witness to charters by Earl Henry, David I, William the Lion, Walter the Steward, etc. Several other individuals of this name also appear in Scotland in the twelfth century but their relationship is not clear. The first authentic information commences with William de Heriz of the county of Dumfries who took the oath of fealty to England in 1296 (Bain, II, p. 185). Since the middle of the fourteenth century the leading family of this name has been identified with

Galloway. Richard Hereis had a gift from Robert I of the lands of Elstanefurd in the sheriffdom of Edinburgh (RMS., I, App. II, 268). David de Herice de Dery witnessed a confirmation charter of the Mill of Conweth, 1461 (RAA., II, 138), and Donald Heriss, M. A., of St. Andrews diocese, appears in 1464 (REB., II, 106). Harbert of Herys of Tarreglys had a safe conduct into England, 1424 (Bain, IV, 942). Some of this name appear in Banff in the fifteenth century. David Heris was bailie of Finlay Ramsay of Bamff, 1483, Margaret Hirys was one of the heirs of deceased Andrew Heris, 1496, and Robert Herys granted a charter there in 1498 (Bamff, p. 33, 37, 39). Alexander Hereiss of Wester Craig and John Herreiss were witnesses to an instrument by Master Alexander Ramsay, 1534, and Elen Heres was infeft in the one-sixth part of the lands of Owchtyreleth in 1533 (ibid., p. 61, 64). Richard Hereis was apparent of Mabie, 1604 (Retours, Kirkcudbright, 56). Haries 1686, Heris 1262, Herreis 1587, Herreise 1451, Herres 1580, Herrice 1365, Heryce 1405, Heyres 1438.

HERRING. Mawer (p. 112) gives Hering as an OE. personal name. Adam Hereng' witnessed a charter by William the Lion to the Priory of Coldingham (Raine, 50). Petronilla, daughter of Adam Harang of Meinichoch (? Minnigaff), granted to the church of Melrose part of the lands of Bortwic in the parish of Roberton in the reign of Alexander II (Melros, p. 30, 34). An account of the domestic tragedy which nearly brought the family of Herring to ruin in 1371 is described in the Memorie of the Somervills, I, p. 118–121. The tragedy occurred at Gilmerton Grange near Edinburgh. Gilbert Heryng witnessed a charter of the Halgh of Scuny in Fife, 1395 (Wemyss, II, 33), and John Hering, dominus de Glasclune, was present at perambulation of the marches of Kirknes and Louchor in the same year (RPSA., p. 3). Patrick Heryng was juror on a claim to a third part of Cranshaws in 1453 (Swinton, p. xxxix), John Heryng or Herynge held part of Cowbyr, 1457 (Cupar-Angus, I, p. 132), and William Hering was one of several charged with holding Dunbar Castle against the king, 1479 (APS., II, p. 125). Robert Hering was agent for the countess of Huntly, 1483 (CRA., p. 412), and James Hering of Tulybole in record in 1491 (Fordell, p. 89) may be James Heryng who was vicar of Murhus (Murroes) in 1508 (RAA., II, 464). James Herring was appointed provost and parson of Methven, 1574 (Methven, p. 4). Herene 1622.

HERRIOT. A variant of Heriot, q.v. Dauzat (p. 83, 141) gives Herriot as a diminutive of Henri, but this derivation does not apply to Scottish Herriot.

HERTFORD. From the town of Hertford in the county of the same name in the south of England. The family of this name in Renfrewshire were vassals of the Stewarts or Fitz-Alans. Robertus Hertford, precentor Glasguensis, with the consent of Galfridus, his nephew and heir, granted the fishery of Lvnbren in the Lennox to the church of Paisley, a. 1225 (RMP., p. 211–212). Robert Herthford had a charter "de terra illa que dicitur Dalmaunach" from Maldovenus, earl of Levenax, a. 1224 (ibid., p. 217), and in 1228 Duugallus filius Alwyn, earl of Levenax made to Robert Hertford a gift of the land called Dollenlenrach to be held by him and his heirs (ibid., p. 214, 215). William de Hertford granted the church of Neleston to the monastery of Paisley c. 1230 (ibid., p. 104). The name appears to have early died out in Scotland.

HERVEY, HERVIE, HARVEY, HARVIE. From Hervé, a Breton personal name introduced into Britain by the Normans. In Latin records Herueus, Herveius, and Herveus. Herueus, son of Philip Marescall, confirmed the church of Keith to the Abbey of Kelso (Kelso). A donation by John filius Heruei, abb de Varia Capella, is recorded in 1319 (LSC., 91). John Hervy was one of the gustatores vini in Aberdeen, 1398, and bailie in 1400 (CRA., p. 375; SCM., v, p. 14). John Hervi, juror in Edinburgh, 1428 (RAA., II, 61) may be the John Herwy who possessed a tenement there, 1430 (RMS., II, 173). James Hervy received a tenement in Aberdeen, 1470 (CRA., p. 29), John Harvy of the diocese of Aberdeen appears in records of the Scots College of Paris, 1479 (Analecta Scotica, II, p. 36). Andrew Hervy was dean of guild in Edinburgh, 1476 (REG., 411), Thomas Herwy was witness in Aberdeen, 1489 (REA., II, p. 303), and Robert Hervie was member of Huntly Volunteers, 1798 (Will, p. 8). Harve 1550, Harwe 1550, Harwy 1527, Heruie 1577, Herve 1579, Herwie 1633.

HERVINGSTOUN. William de Heruingstoun or Heruyngstoun in Edinburgh, 1400–02 (Egidii, p. 37) probably derived his surname from Harvieston in the parish of Borthwick, Midlothian.

HERWART. From the OE. personal name Hereweard, OWSc. Hervaeðr. Henricus Herwart witnessed donation by Henry de Aynestrother to the Abbey of Dryburgh, c. 1330 (Dryburgh, 252). William Herwart was the earliest known vicar of Fernuale (Farnell) in the diocese of Brechin, 1435 (REB., I, 67; II, 42, 44).

HESLET. Probably an old spelling of Haslett or Hazlitt. John Heslet, waulker, burgess of Glasgow, 1575 (Burgesses).

HESLOP. A variant of HISLOP, the common form of the name, q.v.

HESTWALL. An Orcadian surname derived from the lands of Hestwall in the parish of Sandwick. Cristie Hestwale and Johne Hestwale were tacksmen of 2½d land of Hestwale, South Sandwick, in 1503 (REO., p. 416), James Hestuall was one of the arbiters in a dispute in 1593, and Barnet Hestuall was juror on an assize in 1605 (ibid., p. 168, 179). Hastwall c. 1524.

HETH. For earlier AED, q.v. 'Ed Comes' or 'Head Comes' who appears as witness to King David's charter of confirmation to the Abbey of Dunfermline c. 1128 (RD., 4 — believed to be of doubtful authenticity) and to the same king's charter of confirmation to the same abbey of the 'shire' of Kirkalden (ibid., 16) has been confused by the author of The Complete peerage (s.v. Fife) with Ethelred, third son of Malcolm Canmore and first earl of Fife (Sc. Peer.). Malcolm mac Heth, first earl of Ross, witnessed a charter of Dunfermline Abbey as Malcolm Mac Eth, c. 1157, and as earl of Ross was entrusted with the defense of the Benedictine Priory of Urquhart in Moray, a cell of Dunfermline (RD., p. 25; Skene, Highlanders, p. 417). See also MACKAY. Edh mac Kynnath was slain in battle in Strath Alun (CPS., p. 151). Eth, son of Alwyn, first earl of Lennox is witness to a charter c. 1193 by Duncan, afterwards earl of Carrick (Melros, p. 22). Hath filius Gilbrid occurs c. 1230–40 (LAC., 73).

HETTOFT. Dominus Nicholas de Hettoft witnessed resignation of the lands of Edeluestun to the Church of Glasgow, 1233 (REG., p. 141). The expansion of Hettoft not known.

HETTRICK. A variant of HEADRICK, q.v.

HEUGH, HEUGHS. Local, perhaps a variant of HAUGH, q.v. Heugh and Haugh are old names, now rare, but surviving in the West. Thomas Hewch, 1508. William Heuche, hospitaller, Holy Trinity, Edinburgh, 1543 (Soltre, p. 108).

HEUGHAN. See under HUGHAN.

HEW. The common Scots form of HUGH, q.v., a favorite forename in the family of Dalrymple. Hue de Galbrath, juror on inquisition at Lanark, 1303 (*Bain*, II, p. 345). James Hew was burgess of Glasgow, 1627 *(Burgesses).*

HEWAT, HEWET, HEWETT, HEWIT, HEWITT. From HEW, q.v., the Scots form of Hugh + the French diminutive suffix -*et*. Alisoune Hewat is in Cockburnspath, 1662, and five more of the name in the vicinity *(Lauder).* The French form *Huet* was introduced into Britain and is found in ME. deeds. Meg Huet appears in Aberdeen, 1408 (CWA., p. 316).

HEWATSON, HEWETSON, HEWITSON, 'son of HEWAT,' q.v.

HEWISON. 'Son of little HUGH,' q.v. Mr. Johne Houestoun received payment 'for his fie of the Gramair Schoil,' 1613 (*Rec. Inv.,* II, p. 116). In the same record the name is spelled Heweson, Howeson, Howeston, Howstoun. A tombstone in South Ronaldsay records a Donald Hoeson, 1648, and in Craven's *Church life in South Ronaldsay and Burray* the name occurs as Huison in 1680. The Rev. J. King Hewison (1853–1941) has published a history of Bute and newspaper articles on Scottish ecclesiastical history, etc.

HEWITT. *See under* HEWAT.

HEXTILDESPETHE. Huwe de Hextilde-spethe of the county of Rokesburk rendered homage in 1296. His seal bears a patriarchal cross, S' *Hugonis de Hexteldspehe* (?) (*Bain*, II, p. 208, 552). Cf. Mawer (p. 114) under Hexham-on-Tyne. The name may be connected with OE. *hago-steald*, bachelor, young man. ? now Hexpeth in Berwickshire. Hextilda, wife of Richard Cumyn, witnessed her husband's grant of the church of Lyntunruderic to Kelso Abbey c. 1160 (*Kelso*, 274). She was daughter and heiress of Gothric or Uchtred, son and heir of Donalbane, king of Scots.

HEYSLOP. A variant of HISLOP, q.v.

HIDDLESTON, HIDDLESTONE, HUDDLESTON. Of local origin from Huddleston in the parish of Westerkirk, Dumfriesshire. James Hedilstone was dempster in barony of Carnwath, 1534 (CBBC., p. 158). Thomas Hiddilstoun was a tailor in Edinburgh in 1609 *(Edinb. Marr.),* Roger Hiddelstoun held land in the barony of Dinscoire, 1688 (*Retours, Dumfriesshire,* 323), William Hidleston in St. John's Clachan is in record in 1703 (*Kirkcudbright),* and Robert Huddleston, schoolmaster in Lunan in Angus, edited the Montrose edition of Toland's *Druids,* 1814. There is also a Huddleston in the parish of Sherburn in the West

Riding of Yorkshire from which the Dumfriesshire place name may have been borrowed. Hidlesson 1705.

HIGGIE. *See under* HEGGIE.

HIGGINS. William Higgins was member for Linlithgow in the Scots parliament, 1689 (*Hanna*, II, p. 498). Most probably from Ir. O'hUiginn, descendant of Uige *(Woulfe).*

HIGHET. A phonetic variant of HIGHGATE, q.v.

HIGHGATE. An old surname about Glasgow. Of local origin, perhaps from Highgate, near Beith, Ayrshire. HIGHET is a variant. Johne Hechet was burgess of Glasgow in 1527 (*Pollok*, I, p. 256). William Higait or Hegait, notary in Glasgow, 1547–55 (*Protocols,* I) appears as burgess there in 1562 (RPC., I, p. 214), and as William Highgate, town clerk, was charged with using injurious words to a bailie, 1564 (RPC., I, p. 302). William Hegait or Heched was burgess of Glasgow in 1574 (*Pollok*, I, p. 309, 311), Archibald Highgate or Hiegat was member of Scots parliament for Glasgow, 1586 (*Hanna*, II, p. 498), Archibald Heygait was clerk of the burgh of Glasgow in 1609 (MCM., II, p. 395), and Gilbert Heighat pursued another for debt in 1675 (*Corsehill,* p. 127). Hechat 1540, Heychat 1541, Highet 1706.

HILL. William de la Hyll, son of Waldeve son of Aldewyn, resigned lands in Mydilham in 1271 (*Kelso*, 352), William o' the Hull rendered homage, 1296 (*Bain*, II, p. 198), and in 1321 William de le Hille was received to the king of England's peace (*Bain*, III, 724). It was Richard de Hulle (= Hill), 'a varlette of Scotland,' who 'stikked and killed' Catarine Mortimer, 'a damoisel of London,' one of the inmates of the harem of David II in 1360 (*Neubotle,* pref. p. lxl). William de Hill was tenant of Telny and Coteland, barony of Abirdoure in Fife in 1376 (RHM., I, p. lxiv), and Laurence del Hylle granted a charter in favor of the Carmelites of Aberdeen in 1380 (*Friars,* 19). Johannes de Hyl in the parish of Fyvy was excommunicated in 1382 (REA., I, p. 165), and John of Hille, a native of Scotland, had letters of naturalization in England in 1385 (*Bain*, IV, 345). John de Hyll was chaplain of St. Giles Church in Edinburgh in 1426 (*Egidii,* p. 46), and a family of this name as early as 1450 possessed lands at Niddrie in Midlothian, and had the designation of Hill of that Ilk. Robert de Hyll was a citizen of Brechin in 1447 (REB., II, 68), Adam de Hill, common councillor in Aberdeen, 1435 (*Guildry,* p. 186), Richard of Hill was a wit-

ness in Aberdeen in 1469 (CRA., p. 406),
Ninian Hill, 'fabro lignario,' was burgess of
Montrose in 1592 (REB., II, 229), and another
Ninian Hill was a citizen of Glasgow in 1642
(*Retours, Lanark*, 206). Hyl 1476. The sur-
name is common in the Campsie Commissariot
Record.

HILLHOUSE. Of local origin from one or
other of the half dozen small places of the
name in Ayrshire. William Hillhouse appears
in Irvine, 1689 (RPC., 3. ser. XIV, p. 722).

HILLIE. Local. Euphame Hillie in Mirrieton,
parish of Hamilton, 1638 (*Campsie*).

HILLIS. The nets of Adam Hillis in Aberdeen
were tampered with, 1442 (CRA., p. 7).
Watte Hillis, tenant of part of Cupar Grange,
1514 (*Cupar Angus*, I, p. 296).

HILLOCK. Local. John Hillock, witness in
Glasgow, 1517 (LCD., p. 214). John Hyllok,
witness at Tuliboill, 1546 (*Rollok*, 5). Robert
Hillock in Drumlithie, 1601 (*Brechin*), Isobel
Hillok in Dunblane, 1623 (*Dunblane*), John
Hilloks, maltman in Edinburgh, 1627 (*Edinb.
Marr.*), and James Hillock, merchant in Dum-
fries, 1735 (*Dumfries*).

HILLOW. Of local origin, cf. Hillowtoune in
Kirkcudbright Retours. Archibald Hillo in
Hillotoun witnessed a sasine in Dumfries, 1592
(*Dumfriesshire and Galloway Nat. Hist. and
Ant. Soc., Trans.*, 3. ser. XX, p. 204). Mar-
garet Hillow in Maynie, 1667, and three others
of the name in seventeenth and eighteenth
centuries (*Kirkcudbright*). James Hillow in
Dumfries, 1713 (*Dumfries*).

HILSON. Son of *Hild*, an OE. personal name.
Robert Hildson witnessed a charter of the
barony of Cultir in Lanarkshire, 1367 (RMS.,
I, 270). John Hyldsone or Hildsone was tenant
of the earl of Douglas in the barony of Kylbouho (Kilbucho) in 1376 (RHM., I, p. xlvii; II,
p. 16). James Hillson in Whinkerstanes, 1665,
and Marion Hilston in Lidgertwood, 1668
(*Lauder*).

HILTON. Johan de Hiltone of the county
of Berewyke rendered homage in 1296 (*Bain*,
II, p. 206). John de Hilton sold to the monks
of Melrose a tenement within the town of
Lessydwyn in 1415 commonly called the tenement of William de Hilton (*Melros*, p. 535–
537). From the old barony of Hiltoun in
Berwickshire.

HINSHAW. Most likely from Henshaw,
Northumberland. Kenthigern Hynschaw obtained sasine of a tenement in Glasgow in
1563 (*Protocols*, I), and Robert Heindschaw

was minister at Kilmany, Fife, 1574 (RMR.).
William Hinshaw became burgess freeman of
Glasgow by purchase in 1613 (*Burgesses*),
Thomas Hindshaw appears in Netherton of
Hamilton in 1632 (*Campsie*), James Hyndshaw
was merchant burgess of Glasgow in 1652, and
William Hindshaw, heir of James Hindshaw,
merchant burgess of Glasgow, is recorded in
1680 (*Inquis.*, 3689, 6163). Hindschaw 1626,
Hinschaw 1631.

HINSHELWOOD. See under HENSHIL-
WOOD.

HIRD. A variant of HERD, q.v. Hird is the
Scottish pronunciation of 'herd', a herdsman.

"The gude hird, walkryfe and delygent."
Lyndsay, *The Dreme*, 897.

W. dictus Hyrd was actornatus (attorney)
of Bernard, abbot of Aberbrothoc in 1328
(RAA., I, p. 318). Willie Bryand was 'hyrd'
in Prestwick, 1527 (*Prestwick*, p. 52). John
Hird was a tenant of the Douglas in Louchurde in 1376 (RHM., I, p. xlvii; II, p. 16),
William Hirde was witness in Cupar in 1511
(*Laing*, 279, 280), Henry Hird had precept of sasine of two ninth parts of the lands
of Arlarie in 1605 (RD., p. 502), and Walter
Hird, doctor of medicine in Renes in Britanny
in Francia was retoured heir of William Hird,
his father, in rents of lands in the barony of
East Weymis in 1626 (*Retours, Fife*, 370).

HIRSEL. From The Hirsel near Coldstream,
Berwickshire. Adam de Hereshill witnessed
confirmation of the church of Wiston to the
Abbey of Kelso, c. 1200, and about the same
date he attested the grant by Andrew Mansel
to Kelso (*Kelso*, 337, 507). Alexander de Her-
sille was one of a number appointed to settle
a dispute between the church of Glasgow and
the Abbey of Kelso in 1221 (REG., 116).

HISLOP, HASLOP, HESLOP, HEYSLOP, HYSLOP.
Local, at the hazel-hope. Alexander Heselihope
held a land in Edinburgh in 1425 (RMS.,
II, 22), and William Heslihope or Heslvhop
appears as rector and vicar of the church of
Cortoquhy (or Cortochquhy) in 1429 and
1439 (REB., I, 47; II, 49). Stephen de Hes-
lyhope, presbyter and notary public of Glasgow in 1446, appears again in 1455 as Stephen
Heslop (*Irvine*, I, p. 47, 137). Archibald Hes-
lihop "ytherwais callit Schir Suythe" had remission for reset of outlawed Rutherfurds in
1501 (*Trials*, I, p. 102*), and Thomas Heslop
"pensionario preposito ecclesie parochialis de
Houston," is in record in 1525 (REG., 497).
John Hesilhop was a witness in Glasgow in
1555 (*Protocols*, I), Hobe Heslop was a tenant of the abbot of Kelso in 1567 (*Kelso*,

HISLOP, Haslop, Heslop..., *continued*
p. 520), Williame Hessilhoip, reidare at Stow, 1574 (RMR.), and Alexander Hasillip appears in Carsfern parish in 1684 (RPC., 3. ser. IX, p. 575). Heislope 1643, Heslope 1606, Heslvhoipe 1434, Heslyope 1429, Hyslope 1698.

HISSILHEDE. Adam Hissilhede who possessed a tenement in Glasgow, 1486 (REG., p. 451) probably derived his surname from Hazelhead near Beith, Ayrshire.

HOB, HOBBIE. Persons named Robert were commonly known as Hab, Hob, Habbie, and Hobbie according to the part of the country in which they resided. Hab and Habbie were more common in the west ('Habbie Simpson') and Hob and Hobbie on the Border. Hobe Bald, Hobe Heslop, Hob Hog, and Hobe Petersone were all tenants on lands of the Abbey of Kelso, 1567 (*Kelso*, p. 520–522). Hobbe witnessed resignation of land in Kelso, 1237 (ibid., 355), and Simon Hob was admitted burgess of Aberdeen, 1443 (NSCM., I, p. 8). Habbe Anderson in Dumfriesshire, 1557 (M'Dowell, *Lincluden*, p. 111). Robert Grieve alias Hob Grieve in Lauder, was accused of witchcraft, 1649 (Sinclar, *Satan's invisible world discovered*, 1871, p. 45–56). Edward I in an angry letter (*Nat. MSS.*, II, p. xiii) calls Bruce "King Hobbe." Hobbie, from Hob(b) + diminutive suffix -ie.

HOBART. Patrick Hobart, burgess of Dundee, 1649 (*Inquis.*, 3515). A variant of Hubert, from OE. *Hygebeorht*, meaning 'bright mind.'

HOBBAN. A pet diminutive of ROBERT, through Hob(b).

HOBKIRK. As there does not appear to have been a barony of Hobkirk (OPS., I, p. 351) the name is of local origin from Hobkirk, the local pronunciation of Hopekirk, near Hawick, Roxburghshire. James Hopkirk, reidare at Caringtoun, 1574 (RMR.). James Habkirk, surgeon in Edinburgh, is in record in 1690 (*Edinb. Marr.*). Francis Hopkirk is recorded in the parish of Cranstoun, 1689 (RPC., 3. ser. XIV, p. 206), and William Hopkirk in Melrose, 1690 (RRM., III, p. 109). James Hobkirk from Cavers, exiled Covenanter, was drowned off Orknev, 1679 (*Hanna*, II, p. 254). William Hopkirk, late belt maker in Edinburgh, 1726 (*Guildry*, p. 131).

HOBSON. 'Son of HOB,' a pet diminutive of Robert, and so = Robertson.

HODDAM. From the old lands of Hoddam in the parish of the same name, Dumfriesshire.

Odard de Hodolm witnessed a confirmation charter of a fishery in Torduf, c. 1194–1211 (*Holm Cultram*, p. 35), and as Udard de Hodelma or Hodalmia he, along with Robert de Hodalmia, witnessed between the same dates a resignation of land in Weremundebi and Anant (*Bain*, I, 606; *Annandale*, I, p. 1–3). He may also have been the Hudardus de Hodelma who witnessed the gift by Huctred filius Fergus to the Hospital of S. Peter of York, c. 1158–1164 (*Edgar*, p. 219). Robert de Hodolm of the county of Roxburgh rendered homage in 1296. His seal bears a crow or jackdaw and S' Rob'ti d' Hodolm (*Bain*, II, p. 199, 550). Adam de Hodolm of the county of Dunfres also rendered homage in the same year. His seal bears a rude figure of an animal and S' Ade de Hodvme (ibid., II, p. 203, 555). Adam de Hodholme possessed part of the lands of the town and tenement of Kirkborthwyc, c. 1320 (RMS., I, 20), and Adam de Holdena, rector of the church of Kirkepatrik-domando, witnessed the gift of half of Litel Gouan to the Hospital of Polmade (Polmadie) in 1320 (REG., p. 229). Robert Hoddome was retoured heir of George Hoddome, burgess of Edinburgh in 1632 (*Retours, Edinburgh*, 705), James Hoddom is in record in Svmontoun in 1638 (*Lanark CR.*), and John Hoddam in Burnesvde, 1693 (*Dumfries*).

HODGE. A diminutive of RODGER, q.v. Laurence Hoige, witness in Glasgow, 1550 (*Protocols*, I). Mariota Hodge is recorded in Edinburgh in 1625 (*Retours, Edinburgh*, 545), and Thomas Hodge was merchant burgess there in 1629 (*Retours, Peebles*, 79). Robert Hodge, born in Scotland, emigrated to America in 1770 and established the firm of Hodge and Shober, printers. In England "Hodge was so common a rural name that it became a generic term for a rustic" (*Harrison*).

HODGEN, 'son of Ro(d)ger,' from the pet form HODGE + diminutive ending -en. Adam Hodgeon in Hillaire, parish of Lesmahagow, 1685, and eight more of the name are recorded (*Lanark CR.*). John Hodgen in Hillend, Lanarkshire, 1708 (*Minutes*, p. 35).

HODGES, 'son of HODGE,' q.v. Thomas Hodgis was burgess of Glasgow in 1487 (LCD., p. 202). Hodgs 1573.

HODGKIN. From HODGE, q.v., + English diminutive suffix -kin. Alexander Hogekin had sasine of the lands of Nether Broderstanes in the barony of Soltray in 1583 (*Soltre*, p. 151).

HODGSON, 'son of HODGE,' q.v. Most probably of recent introduction from the south.

HODGTON. From the old lands of Hodgtoun in Angus (*Retours, Forfar*, 352). Christian Hodgstain is in record in Mains of Crage, 1602, William Hodgton in Hedderwick, parish of Montrose, 1641, and William Hodgstoun in Hederwick, 1669 (*Brechin*).

HOEBDYUY. William Hoebdyuy *de eodem* witnessed grant of office of derethy of Tarves in Aberdeenshire, 1463 (RAA., II, p. 129). Hardly likely to be from Abdie in Fife, in 1481 Ibdy.

HOEY. Most probably a variant of Hoy (1). Alexander Hoey in Threipwood, 1644 (RRM., I, p. 106).

HOGARTH, HOGGARTH. Perhaps local, from dial. *hoggarth*, 'an enclosure to fold lambs in.' Cf. HOGGART.

HOGG, HOGGE. This surname is usually explained as a nickname derived from the name of the animal. "This agrees," says the late Professor Skeat, "with the fact that Hogg is a common surname at this day; and with a still more important fact that it was thus used as a surname even in the eleventh century" (*Proceedings, Cambridge Philological Society*, 1902, p. 16). Ailmer Hogg occurs twice in the Ramsay Chartulary, I, p. 188, and III, p. 39, in documents of 1043–79. Philip le Hog appears in the English *Hundred Rolls* in 1274, and Alan le Hogge in a Lancashire Inquisition in 1323. While the surname is thus possibly derived in some instances from the name of the animal there are other undoubted instances pointing to·different origins. About the year 1280 Andrew Fraser gave to the Abbey of Kelso a bondman, Adam the son of Henry del Hoga (i.e. 'of the Hog') "nativo meo cum tota sequela sua" (*Kelso*, p. 95). About the year 1250 mention is made of the croft of Henry de Hoga in Gordun, Berwickshire (ibid., 121, 122), and c. 1270 John de Grantham, son and heir of Emma the daughter and heir of Salomon del Hoga, made a grant from her lands at Berwick, which Radulph de Bernewill held, to the monks of Kelso (ibid., 36). Again about 1280 there is mention of the croft which Adam del Hoga held in the time of Lady Alycie de Gordun (ibid., p. 95). Thurcyl Hoga is one of the witnesses to a charter of Cnut, 1024 (Kemble, *Codex Dipl.*, IV, 741). The spelling of the name here, Hoga, the earliest record of its occurrence, certainly points to OE. *hoga*, 'careful,' 'prudent,' as origin of the name at least in this instance. Turkil Hog, a serf of Bertram son of Adam of Lesser Riston, was sold to the monks of Coldingham along "with his sons and

daughters for three merks of silver, which in my great want they gave me of the money of the house of Coldingham" (*Nat. MSS.*, I, 54). Malmor Hoge is included in the inhibition directed against Malcolm, earl of Levenax and his adherents by the bishop of Glasgow in 1294 (RMP., p. °203). Henry Hogg' of Roxburghshire, and John Hog, burgess of Edinburgh, took the oath of fealty to England in 1296 (*Bain*, II, p. 197, 200). There seems to have been a family of this name of great prominence in Edinburgh in the fourteenth century. Roger Hog was one of the most influential burgesses of the city between 1358 and 1363, and Simon Hog appears as a burgess in 1402 (*Egidii*, p. 5, 39; RMS., I, 164; ER., III, p. 83). Alan Hog, Scottish merchant, complained in 1370 of his goods being carried off by English wreckers (*Bain*, IV, 164), and seven years later Isabelle Hog or Hoge held a tenement in Edinburgh (RMS., I, 650, 684). In 1379 the Castle of Berwick was taken from the English by —— Hog, Lydzetwod, and their companions. John Hog was presbyter and notary public in the diocese of Glasgow, 1462 (*Neubotle*, 290), Archibald Hoge was king's officer in Irvine, 1529 (*Irvine*, I, p. 36), and John Hoge, portioner of Dryburgh, heir of William Hoge, his father, was retoured heir in certain lands in Berwickshire, 1661 (*Retours, Berwick*, 316). Thomas Hog (1628–1692) was a prominent Covenanter, and James Hogg, the Ettrick Shepherd, is the best known bearer of the name. The Hoges and Hoggs of Virginia, U. S., are descended from three brothers who emigrated from Edinburgh, c. 1745. Hogge 1656, Hogh 1496. Hoig 1515, Hoige 1526, Hogis (not pl.) 1519, Howg 1686.

HOGGAN, HOGGON. Andrew Hoggan is recorded in Threapmuir, parish of Fossoway, 1686 (*Dunblane*), John Hogine in Boig, 1717 (*Brechin*), and William Hoggan was provost of Lochmaben, Dumfriesshire, 1776.

HOGGART. From ME. *hogherde*, one in charge of hogs i.e. young sheep. Henry Hoggart witnessed an instrument of sasine, 1525 (*Home*, 35), and Robert Hoghvrd was a witness in Dunfermline, 1555 (*Laing*, 633). A commission was appointed in 1562 for trial of Robert Hoggart (ER., XIX, p. 496). George Hoggart or Huggart was a pensioner of Thirlestane Hospital in 1676 (Thomson, *Lauderdale*, p. 71). The surname was common in Stitchill and neighborhood in the seventeenth century as Haggeard, Hoggart, Hoggeart, Hoggearth, Hoggearthe, and Hoggard (*Stitchill*). Hogard 1676, Hogeard 1666.

HOGSON, 'son of Roger,' through the pet diminutive Hog(g). Thomas Hogisson, bailie of Lanark, 1425 (*Lanark*, p. 377). Reignalt Hoggesson (or Hoggessone) or Reynald Hogsson had safe conducts into England in 1424–25 (*Bain*, IV, 961, 964, 986). John Hogyssoun witnessed a charter of lands in Ayr, 1426 (RMS., II, 65). Quintyne Hogesoun and Johnne Hogesoun, followers of the earl of Cassilis, were respited for murder, 1526 (RSS., I, 3386). James Hogesoun in Halhill, 1624 (*Lanark CR.*).

HOGSYARD. All the early references confine this name to Glasgow. George Hogisvarde, witness in Glasgow 1551 and 1554 (*Protocols*, I). In the Protocols the name also appears as Hogisvairde (1556) and Hogezaird (1568), and in the index all the forms are grouped under Hodgart. William Hoggiszaird was heir of John Hoggiszaird, calcearius, burgess of Glasgow, 1639 (*Inquis.*, 2419), Mr. Hendrie Hogsyard, bursar of theollogie in Glasgow, 1654 (RUG., III, p. 578), and Robert Hogsvard in Quarreltoun, 1759 (*Kilbarchan*). William Hogiszearde, burgess freeman of Glasgow, 1596 (*Burgesses*), and John Hogard (d. 1640) was buried in Fishwick churchyard, parish of Hutton. Annabell Hogsyaird, 1694, reappears in 1707 as Anable Hodge (*Corse-hill*, p. 187, 222). Hoggisyaird 1626, Hoggisyard 1617.

HOLASTONE. Richard de Holastone of Berwickshire who rendered homage, 1296 (*Bain*, II, p. 201) probably derived his surname from Holystone, Northumberland, in 1240 Halistane.

HOLBECH. From Holbeach in Lincolnshire, England. John de Holbech, canon of Moray, 1258 (REM., 122), was no doubt an Englishman.

HOLCOTE. From some place in England. There were lands named Holcote in Northamptonshire held by David I (*Moore, Lands*, p. 36). Guppy (p. 74) mentions an ancient family of Holcott of Buckland, Berkshire, "which seems to have left but few descendants at the present day." Wautier de Holcote of Roxburghshire rendered homage, 1296 (*Bain*, II, p. 199). Robert Holkat was a monk of Culross in the middle of the sixteenth century (PSAS., LX, p. 93). William Alket, burgess of Aberdeen, 1275 (*Fraser*, p. 11) may represent the same name.

HOLDING. Alexander Holding in Dumfries, 1751 (*Dumfries*) probably derived his surname from Holden in Lancashire.

HOLLAND. More likely to be of local origin than from Holland (Netherlands). There are several places named Houlland in Shetland, and there are Hollands in Orkney. Hollandbush is in Stirlingshire, and Holland-Hirst is in the parish of Kirkintilloch. There are also places named Holland in England. Willelmus de Holland, a witness in the reign of Alexander II (*Scon*, p. 53). Richard Holande, vicar of Ronaldsay, 1467 (SCM., V, p. 393) derived his surname from one of the three places so named in Orkney. Thomas de Holande was chaplain in Dundee, 1452 (REB., I, 153), and 'Sir' Andrew Holand was vicar of Eroly, 1469 (*Cupar-Angus*, I, p. 144). Bartholomew Holland, John Holland, and Walter Holland were repledged to liberty of the burgh of Irvine, 1472 (*Irvine*, I, p. 28), and Ralph Holland was a witness in Ayr, 1687 (*Ayr*, p. 211). William Holland and Peter Holland are mentioned in an Orkney witch trial, 1616 (Rogers, *Social life in Scotland*, III, p. 302).

HOLLINS. A surname recorded in the Stewartry. Most probably of local origin from Hollins in Yorkshire.

HOLMES. Johannes Holmys, capellanus, witness in Ayr, 1460 (*Ayr*, p. 35), doubtless derived his name from the lands of Holmes near Dundonald in Kyle Stewart. There were also lands named Holmes in the barony of Inchestuir. James Hoomes in 1668 to find caution that he will not harm any of the inhabitants of Inverness (*Rec. Inv.*, II, p. 233).

HOLTALE. Roger of Holtale witnessed a writ by Roger Corbet at Langtoun, 1330 (*Laing*, 35), and Johannes de Holtale held a land in Edinburgh, 1382 (RMS., I, 732).

HOME, HUME. Of territorial origin from the barony of Home in Berwickshire. "In early times," says Miss Warrander, "the name was spelled indifferently Home or Hume. In later days the Polwarth branch adopted the spelling with a u, while the head of the family, Lord Home, retained the o; but they all spring alike from the same stock" (*Marchmont and the Humes of Polwarth*, Edinburgh, 1894, p. 16n). David Hume, the philosopher and historian, always spelled his name with u, while his brother, John of Ninewells, insisted on spelling the name as 'Home.' There is an amusing note on this dispute by John Home of Ninewells in Kay's *Edinburgh portraits*, ed. 1837, II, p. 72. Of David Hume it is said that to have his name pronounced "as if to rhyme with 'comb'" made him furious, and he explained he was driven to sign himself 'Hume' by 'thae glaekit English bodies, who could not call him aright.'" Hume of Godscroft, the historian of the House of Douglas, is known in the world of letters as *Theagrius*, the Greek translation of his territorial designation, Godscroft. The family of Home is claimed by some to have sprung from the old Saxon earls of Dunbar and Northumbria, but there is no proof that such was the case. Their arms show that they advanced themselves by successful marriages. Sir Thomas Home married Nichola, of the ancient family of Pepdie of Dunglas; Sir Alexander Home, first Lord Home (d. 1491) married Mariota, heiress of Landells of Landells. An heiress of the Lords Halyburton also brought them an increase of their possessions, and the heiress of the Douglases vastly increased their fortunes by bringing to the earl of Home the wide lands of the family of Douglas at Douglas, Bothwell, Bonkle, and in Angus. Ada, daughter of Patrick, fifth earl of Dunbar, is said to have married her father's cousin, William, son of Patrick of Greenlaw, but the marriage is nowhere proved, and the terms of a charter by William of Home, of date 1268 (Kelso, I, 99–101) suggests that she was not his mother (Sc. Peer., III, p. 254). Geffrai de Home of Lanarkshire rendered homage in 1296. His seal bears the device of a crescent enclosing a star of seven rays, S' Galfridi de Hom (Bain, II, p. 186, 204). Adam de Hom served on an inquest held at Berwick in the same year (ibid., p. 216). Alexander de Hume witnessed a charter of the lands of Drumgrev, 1408 (Annandale, I, p. 12), and Alexander Hume and David Hume were conservators of the truce between Scotland and England, 1451 (Bain, IV, 1239). William Hoom, merchant burgess of Glasgow, 1661 (Inquis., 4469). Oliver Wendell Holmes was descended from a David Hume, one of several hundred Scots prisoners sent by Cromwell to America (Finley, The Coming of the Scot, p. 28). Hoome 1498, Houme 1577, Hovme 1517, Howm 1488, Howme 1436, Hoym and Huym 1488, Hoyme 1550, Hum 1464, Hvvm 1544, Hwime c. 1530, Hwm 1442, Hwym 1581; Hewme, Hom, Hoom, Houm, Houmm, Hwme, Hwyme.

HOMETANCARDUS. Frepobaldus filius Hometancardi, witness, c. 1177–99 (RMP., p. 98).

HOMILL, HOMMILL. See under HAMILL.

HONEYMAN. One in charge of the bees. "In old times when mead or metheglin was a favourite beverage, and when sugar was unknown in England, the propagation of bees and the production of honey furnished employment for many persons" (Lower). "We all belong to Fife" has long been a phrase used by the bearers of the name Honey-

man in Scotland. They appear all to hail from between Falkland and St. Andrews, although the name is also met with in the district around Ayr. "The earliest bearer of it yet met with was a Flemish gunner in the Scottish service in the 15th century" (Sc. Ant., IV, p. 113). William Hwnymane and Johne Hwnymane were jurors on an inquest at Cupar in 1522 (SCBF., p. 266). The will of Andrew Hunyman of Over Carnve is dated Feb. 16, 1549, Alexander Huniman of the Convent of Dunfermline is recorded in 1555 (Laing, 633), Jhone Honeman appears in Lindene in 1606 (RRM., I, p. 9), and Robert Hinniman was second minister of Dysart in 1661 (Dysart, p. 52). The Orkney family of Honeyman is descended from Bishop Honeyman who married Mary Stewart, heiress of Graemsey. Hinniman 1654, Honeyman 1550, Honneyman 1586, Honnyman 1679, Honyman 1563, Hunniman 1586, Hunvman 1542, Hwnian 1593, Hwneman 1547, Hynnyman 1650.

HOOD. Huda in OE. is a shortened personal name. The leader of the Surrey men in A. D. 853 was named Huda (Anglo-Saxon Chron., s.a.). A composition between Andrew, bishop of Moray and Robert Hude (or Hod) relating to the manor of Lamanbrid was made in 1225 (REM., p. 459–460). Robertus Hud of Leth (Leith), witness in an Inchcolm charter c. 1220–26 (Inchcolm, p. 12). Robertus Hod received a payment from the sheriff of Aberdeen, 1264 (ER., I, p. 12). Johannes Hode was burgess of the vill of Forays, 1332 (RAA., II, 14). David Hude or Huyd appears as vicar of Luntrathyne or Luntrethyn, 1447–52 (REB., I, 153; II, 67), and John Hude was vicar of Abernyte, 1467 (View, p. 576). Michael Hud was tenant on lands of the Abbey of Kelso, 1567 (Kelso, p. 528). Hwid 1574.

HOOK. Local. William de Huk' was in charge of Thomas Galloway, 1296 (Bain, II, 729). Adam de Huke, tenant in vill of Moffet, 1376 (RHM., I, p. lxii). The name continued in Sanquhar and neighborhood till eighteenth century and is still represented in the place name Heuklands (Dumfriesshire and Galloway Nat. Hist. & Ant. Soc., Trans., 3. ser. XIX, p. 118).

HOPE. Of local origin. John Hope of Peeblesshire rendered homage, 1296, and Symon de la Hope was received to the king of England's peace in 1321 (Bain, II, p. 207; III, 724). Thomas Hope held a tenement in Edinburgh, 1478 (RMS., II). The later earls of Hopetoun are descended from John de Hope, one of the retinue of Queen Magdalen, wife of James V (Wilson, Reminiscences of old Edinburgh, I,

HOPE, *continued*

p. 134). Adam Hoip and William Hoip were witnesses in Parton, 1541. John Hoip was tenant on lands of Kelso Abbey, 1567 (*Kelso*, p. 520). Houp 1607.

HOPKIN, 'son of Hob' (pet form of Robert) + English diminutive suffix -*kin*. Matthew Hopkin, miller, 1609 (*Hunter*, p. 44). John Habkine of Stewartounkirk was pursued for debt, 1675 (*Corsehill*). In the index of Corsehill baron-court book Habkine = Hopbkin = Hopkin, and William Hebkine is recorded in Campbeltown, 1682. Habkin and Hopkine 1682. As forename: Hobkin de Wallinford, a. 1329.

HOPKIRK. A variant of HOBKIRK, q.v.

HOPPER. Lower, Bardsley, Harrison, and Weekley explain this name as 'hopper,' dancer at a fair or festival. Robert Hopper received the acre of land called Stampardesakyr in the territory of Coldingham, and in 1275 witnessed a charter of lands in Raynington to the Abbey of Coldstream (*Raine*, 282, 387). The name of a burgess family of good standing in Edinburgh from beginning of the fifteenth century (*Stodart*). David Hopper held a tenement in the burgh in 1486 (RMS., II, 1655), and Adam Hoppar was a notary public in the diocese of St. Andrews in 1524. Henry Hoppare witnessed a charter by Andrew, abbot of Melrose in 1540 (RRM., III, p. 225), Henry Hoppar was tenant of Westbarns in 1559 (ER., XIX, p. 402), and John Hoppar of Coldingham is recorded in 1593 (*Laing*, 1254). James Hopper of Bourhouss appears in 1628 (*Inquis.*, 1388), Thomas Hopper in Caikilaw in 1668 and Thomas Happer in Calkilaw or Crakilaw, in 1687, perhaps the same person (*Lauder*). Hoppert 1581.

HOPPILAND. Local. Probably from Hoppyland in county Durham, England. William Hoppiland, notary public in St. Andrews diocese, 1455 (*Cambus.*, 97). Eupham Happyland was before the Justice Court of Edinburgh, 1663 (*Just. Rec.*, I, p. 71). Jackson (*Place-names of Durham*, p. 67) takes the name to mean 'Oppa's land,' from Oppa, an old personal name.

HOPPRINGLE. *See* PRINGLE.

HOPRIG. Gairlie de Hoprig who appears in a retour of the lands of Wedderburn in 1469 (*Sc. Ant.*, VII, p. 25) derived his name from Hoprigg near Cockburnspath, Berwickshire.

HORDEN. Johan de Horredene of Lanarkshire rendered homage in 1296 (*Bain*, II, p. 208). John of Hordene, a Scot, had a safe conduct into England, 1408 (*Bain*, IV, 766). The seal of Galfridus de Hordene (undated) is described by Macdonald (1348). From Horden in county Durham, spelled c. 1050 Hore-dene and Hore-tune, and in 1260 Horden.

HORN, HORNE. A well-known OE. personal name, probably of Norse origin. Aluuin Horne in DB. (*Ewen*, p. 88). John Horn was beaten and evil-treated on the Border, 1279 (*Bain*, II, p. 47). In 1328 there is entry of cockets of Lochmaben for Alan Horne (ER., I, p. 99). John Horn apud Furvy, forestaller in Aberdeen, 1402 (CRA., p. 384). David Horne is mentioned in a sasine relating to Cupar, 1456 (*Panmure*, II, 238), and Agnes Horn is recorded in Glasgow, 1487 (REG., 447). John Horne was admitted burgess of Aberdeen, 1497 (NSCM., I, p. 39), and Alexander Horne contributed towards church repairs there in 1508 (CRA., p. 79). William Horn, attorney for Robert, archbishop of Glasgow, 1503 (REG., p. 505), James Horne, bailie of Haddington, 1567 (RPC., I, p. 558), and Alexander Horne, canon of Ross, 1584 (RPC.). Horn of Westhall, an old family in Oyne (AEI., p. 108–111). Hurne 1561.

HORNCASTLE. Sir John de Horncastre, prior of Coldingham, 1278 (*Raine*, 274), derived his name from Horncastle, Lincolnshire, in OE. *Hyrn-castre*, in thirteenth century *Hornecastre*.

HORNDEAN. From the village and ancient parish of Horndean (c. 1120, Horeuordene), Berwickshire. William de Horuirden granted two acres in Horuerden to the Abbey of Kelso between 1160–1200 (*Kelso*, 320). Eufemme, widow of William de Hornedene of the county of Wyggetone, rendered homage in 1296 and had her lands restored to her (*Bain*, II, p. 214, 219). John Hornden had a charter of the lands of Lisclefe in the sheriffdom of Berwick from Robert I (RMS., I, App. II, 274).

HORNER. From the obsolete occupation of "horner," a maker of horn spoons. Nicholas Horner was a leading burgess of Arbroath in the latter half of the fifteenth century (Hay, *Arbroath*, p. 107). It is uncertain if Horner's Wynd (now, since 1860, Commerce street) be named from him or from the Horner's Croft being located there. Thomas Hornar was a burgess of Arbroath in 1452 (RAA., II, 94), and Andrew Hornar or Horner appears as witness to Scone charters in 1544 and 1570 (*Scon*, p. 207, 212). The surname is also found in Glasgow in 1551. Francis Horner (1778–1817), the political economist, was the most prominent bearer of the name. Hornear 1553.

HORRIE. See under HOURIE.

HORSBURGH. Of territorial origin from the old ten pound land of the same name in the parish of Innerleithen, Peeblesshire. *Horsabrōc* occurs in an OE. charter (Kemble, *Codex Diplomaticus*, III, 397). "The first of the race is believed to have been an Anglo-Saxon, designated Horse or Orse, who, settling on lands on the north bank of the Tweed, there reared the castle or burg which communicated the present surname to his descendants" (Chambers, *Peeblesshire*, p. 373). The earliest record of the name, however, is in the reign of Alexander II (1214–49), when Symon de Horsbroc witnessed a charter by William Purveys of Mospennoc to the monks of Melrose (*Melros*, p. 215). William de Horsebroch, "clericus decani et capellani Ecclesie de Glasguensis," is in record in 1283 (REG., 234). William de Horsbroch, probably the same person, was a notary public in 1287 (CMN., 23). Simon de Horsbrok, who entered the foreign service of Edward I of England in 1297, had his lands restored to him in that year (Bain, II, 952). He is mentioned again in the years 1302 and 1304 as holding his lands of the same king (ibid., p. 424, 428). Master Michael de Horsbrok, a priest, witnessed a grant by Sir William of Durem, knight, of certain burgage lands in Peebles between 1306 and 1330 (*Melros*, p. 378), and William de Horsbrok was a bailie of the burgh in 1329 (ER., I, p. 626). Simon Horsbroke was one of the archers of the East March of Scotland in 1404 (Bain, IV, 669), and in 1440 Robert Horsbruk was "tercius prior" of St. Andrews (RD., p. 300). Alexander Horsbruk of that Ilk appears in 1479 (ALA., p. 76, 86), and in 1550 another Alexander Horsbruik was served heir of John Horsbruik, his father, in the lands and mill of Horsbruik of old extent of ten merks (*Retours, Peeblesshire*, 6). An illustration of the old house or castle of Nether Horsburgh is given by Chambers (*Peeblesshire*, p. 374). Other old forms of the surname are Horsbrook 1640, Horsborrough 1686, Horsburche 1620. The local pronunciation is Horsbra.

HORSLEY. Richard de Horsleye of the county of Lanark, who rendered homage in 1296 (Bain, II, p. 214) most probably derived his surname from Horsley in Northumberland. The lands of the Horsselvs in Lanarkshire are recorded as forfeited in 1369 (RMS., I, 330).

HORTON. Pieres de Hortone of Edinburghshire who rendered homage in 1296 derived his name from one of the many places named Horton in England, perhaps from one of the three places of the name in Yorkshire.

HOSACK, HOSSACK, HOSICK. A common northern Scots surname and an old one in the Inverness and Cromarty districts. Alexander Hossack appears in Inverness in 1508, but the origin of the name says Macbain (v, p. 77) is obscure. It may be local. Cf. Hossack, the name given to the east mouth of the Thurso river. John Hossok was a tenant in the Castletoun of Ardmanoch, 1504 (ER., XII, p. 661), and William Hosak and Andreas Hosak were tenants there in 1539 (ibid., XVII, p. 680). William Hossoke was tenant of Akinhede in the barony of Kynnedour in 1565 (REM., p. 438), and sheep were stolen from Robert Hosak in the regality of Spynie, 1595 (SCM., II, p. 129). Cristiane Hosack in the "parochin of Suddi" is mentioned in 1652 (IDR., p. 247), and Alexander Hossack is recorded in Fortrose, 1726 (HP., II, p. 336). John Hosack was author of *Mary Queen of Scots and her accusers*, 2 v., 1869–74.

HOSE. May be from Norman de Hosse, i.e. of Houssaye in Normandy. A family of this name possessed the manor of Craigie in Kyle, during the reigns of Malcolm IV and William the Lion. Walter Hose succeeded his father in the manor in the beginning of the reign of William the Lion. The father of Walter, who is not named in the record, had granted the church of Craigie half a carucate of land and Walter granted it another carucate, and before 1177, for the salvation of the souls of his father and mother he granted the monks of Paisley the church of Craigie with all its lands and pertinents. Johannes Hose, younger brother of Walter, also appears as parson of the church of Craigie. Johannes Ose, probably a son of Walter, witnessed the concession by Gilbert, son of Henry St. Martin, of the land of Fulton to the monks of Paisley, c. 1208–33, and as Johannes Huse witnessed, c. 1210, the gift by Malcolm Loccard of six acres in Svmuntun to the same monks. In 1272 the church of Craigie was confirmed to the monks of Paislev bv Thomas de Cragyn, the son and heir of John Hose, who had assumed his surname from the lands. The family ended in two heiresses, Christian and Matilda, daughters of Sir John Hose, the eldest of whom married Sir William Lvndsav, a younger son of Sir David Lyndsay of Crawford. In 1272 there is a further confirmation of the gift of the church of Craigie to the monks of Paisley by Walter de Lvndsav, miles, "filius et heres quondam Christiane Hose et Matildis soror ejusdem Christiane, heredes quondam domini Johannis Hose militis." The onlv records of the family are contained in the charters in the *Registrum Monasterii de Passelet*, p. 50, 71, 231–233.

HOSEASON. An old Shetland surname of Norse origin. It is a corruption of Aassieson, "the son of Aassi," a form of OSWALD, q.v. In Shetland the name is generally pronounced in accordance with its original spelling, Aassiesen, and less correctly Osison and Hosison, whence the form Hoseason. The name has no connection whatsoever with the biblical Hosea. Elias Hoseason in Stevenson's *Kidnapped* was captain of the trading brig the "Covenant" in which David Balfour was kidnapped. Some notes on the Shetland family of the name are given in F. J. Grant's *Zetland family histories*, 1907.

HOSICK. A variant of HOSACK, q.v.

HOSPITAL. Robert del Hospital del counte de Berewyke rendered homage, 1296 (*Bain*, II, p. 205). Isobel de Hospital was a taxpayer in Yorkshire, 1327 (*Ewen*, p. 167). Cf. SPITTAL.

HOTSON. See under HUDSON.

HOULISTON. From Howliston in Heriot parish, Midlothian (Houlastoun 1653, in *Retours*, 1039). Richard Huliston rendered homage, 1296. His seal reads: S' Ric' de Hvlotistvn (*Macdonald*, 1358). This name was recorded in Hawick, 1941.

HOULSON. John Houlsoun witnessed an instrument of date 1446 (*Prestwick*, p. 114), Huchon Hulson was witness in Ayr, 1471, and Thomas Houlson was bailie of the same burgh in 1491 (*Friars Ayr*, p. 54, 63). Houlsone 1491.

HOUNAM. See under HOWNAM.

HOURIE, HORRIE. Clouston suggests that this Orcadian surname is possibly a corruption of Thoreson, since the Norse *th* frequently becomes *h* in Orkney (*Clouston*, p. 34). Hourston, Horraldshay, Hurtiso, etc., are spelled with *Th* in the early records. There is, however, a place name Hurre or Horrie in the parish of St. Andrews from which the name may have come. Gawane Herre or Hurre is in record in the parish of St. Andrews, 1519. In 1568 Iggagartht (i.e. Ingagarth) Hurrie, daughter of Adam Hurry and lawful heir to John Hurry, sold the half of the place of Hurry to James Irrewing of Sabay (*REO.*, p. 126). In the Shetland rental of 1716 A. Horrie accounts for the skatt of 2 merks land in Sandwick, Unst (*Old Lore Misc.*, VII, p. 59–60). Magnus Horrie, a native of Shetland, and once one of the clerks of Exchequer in Edinburgh, became a resident of Algiers and by 1766 was described as being "so high in favour and confidence with the Dey of that place that he made him one of his principal secretaries" (*Old Lore Misc.*, VII, p. 11–12). Gawane Herre (Hurre), of great age, was resident in the parish of St. Andrews, Orkney (*OSR.*, I, p. 63). George Hourie was tenant of Nistaben, Firth, Orkney, c. 1850.

HOURSTON. A surname of Orkney and Shetland, from the old township of Hourstane in the parish of Sandwick, Orkney. Magnus Hourstoun is recorded in Evie in 1640 (*MCM.*, II, p. 211), and Hew Hourston of that Ilk was lawrikman in North Sandwick in 1678 (*SHR.*, XIV, p. 59). Still current.

HOUSGARTH. An old surname in Orkney, from Housgarth in Sandwick. There is another Housgarth in Sanday, but the former seems to have been the source of the name. William Housgarth was tacksman of How in 1503 (*REO.*, p. 417). Alexander Housgarth, roithman (councillor) in Sandwick was juror on an inquest in 1514, and in 1565 Nicoll Housgair agreed to make payment for the teinds of Housgair of the crop of 1565 (ibid., p. 87, 371). The family patronymic (Nicolson) appears eventually to have prevailed, and Housgarth vanished from Orkney as a surname.

HOUSTON, HOUSTOUN. Of territorial origin from the old barony of the name in Lanarkshire. The ancient family of Houston originally bore the name of Paduinan, from a place of that name in Lanarkshire. In the reign of Malcolm IV Baldwin de Bigre gave the lands of Kilpeter to Hugh de Paduinan, who appears as a witness to the foundation charter of the Abbey of Paisley between 1165–73 (*RMP.*, p. 6). Hugh's son, Reginald, obtained from Robert, son of Waldev, son of Baldwin de Bigre, a confirmation of these lands. Hugh, son of Reginald again, obtained a charter from Walter Fitz-Alan, the High Steward, now become superior of the lands, wherein it is narrated that his father and grandfather held the lands of the family of Bigre (charters cited in OPS., I, p. 83). "The barony had now taken its Saxon name from the settlement of the first of these old lords — Huston or *villa Hugonis*" (loc. cit.). Finlay of Huwitston, witness to a Renfrew charter of late thirteenth century (ibid., I, p. 77) is probably the Fynlawe de Hustone, knight, of Lanarkshire, who rendered homage, 1296 (*Bain*, II, p. 203). His seal bears a fess chequy, with three (indecipherable charges) in chief, S' *Finlay de Hovstvn* (*Macdonald*, 1350). John of Hoston was canon of Cambuskvnel, 1341 (*Pap. Lett.*, II, p. 555), Johannes de Howistone was witness in Paisley, 1406 (RMS., I, 874), and Patrick de Huyston, canon of Glasgow, 1415

(REG., 325). Alan Hawystoune held a tenement in Glasgow, 1435 (LCD., p. 250), Alexander Howstoun was repledged to liberty of burgh of Irvine, 1460 (*Irvine*, I, p. 27), Sir James Howstone was vicar of Estwood in 1525 (REG., 469), and Mungow Hawstoun, burgess of Glasgow, 1527 (*Pollok*, I, p. 256). The tenement of Thomas Hawstoune in Glasgow is mentioned in 1550, and John Hawstoune sold a barn there in same year (*Protocols*, I). (2) People of the name of Houston in the Canisbay district (there pronounced Hougstoun) are descended from Rev. Andrew Ogstoun (see OGSTON), minister of Canisbay, Caithness (1601–1650), and the Houstons of Ross-shire are believed to be descended from Rev. Thomas Houston of Inverness, who died in 1605 (*Sc. Ant.*, VI, p. 94–96). Hawistoune and Hawistoun 1505, Hostan 1517, Hostine 1731, Houstone 1527, Houstown and Houstowne 1672, Howstone 1660, Howstoun and Howstoune 1550, Howvstoun 1425, Huison 1675, Huistone 1670, Huston 1671.

HOW. Local. Matthew de Hou witnessed a charter by Eschina de Lundor to Kelso Abbey, c. 1190 (*Kelso*, 147). John Ho, probably an Englishman, was burgess of Aberdeen, 1273 (*Fraser*, p. 11), and Andrew Howe was witness at Ardlar, 1522 (REA., I, p. 388). Letters were issued against John How for defrauding the king's customs, 1524 (*Irvine*, I, p. 35), George How is in Over Johnstone, 1654 (*Kilbarchan*), and a payment was made to William How, glover, 1735 (*Guildry*, p. 153).

HOWAT, HOWATT. From How, a form of HUGH, q.v., + dimin. -at (-it). Sir Robert Howat, a cleric, witness in Aberdeen, 1469 (REA., I, p. 289), and Alexander Howat was admitted burgess there, 1600 (NSCM., I, p. 95). Henry Howatt, burgess of Dundee, 1622 (*Brechin*), and James Howatt, merchant burgess in Glasgow, 1691 (*Retours, Ayr*, 662).

HOWATSON, HOWITTSON, 'son of HOWAT,' q.v. Caution was found for Jok Howatson, 1569 (RPC., I, p. 660). George Houatsone was dismissed from his regiment in 1689 (RPC., 3. ser. XIV, p. 566). George Howatson in Todstoun, 1725 (*Kirkcudbright*). An old spelling is Hoatson. The place name Howatson (now part of the farm of Grange) in Midlothian was in 1484 Howatstoun, Houatstoun 1585, Howitstoun 1600.

HOWBURN. Probably from Howburn near Carham, or from Holburn near Lowick (in 1278 Houburne). David de Houhburne granted 'piscaria de Orde et piscaria de Blakewel,' 1220 (*Kelso*, 55, 57, 61). James de Houburn is recorded in 1254 as holding a quarter of one knight's fee (*Bain*, I, 372). Thomas de Houburne, evidently an Englishman, canon of St. Andrews, was ousted from the Priory of Pitinweme 'by the Scots,' 1306–7 (*Bain*, II, 1964–1965). John de Howburne is in record in 1387 (*Laing*, 78). Sir Thomas Hoborne was vicar of Fossoquhy, 1510 (*Cupar-Angus*, I, p. 279), Patrick Howbrone and his son had a grant of the fruits of the kirk of Fossoquhy in 1511 (*Cupar-Angus*, I, p. 259), and Andro Howburn, Patrick Howburn, Robert Howburn, and Peter Howburn, had a tack of the fruits of three-quarters of the kirk of Fossoquhy in 1545 (ibid., II, p. 32–33). John Howburne is mentioned as holding land in Hawick also in 1545 (RMS., II, 3107). Andrew Hawburin of Tuliboill and Robert Hawburn were witnesses, 1546 (*Rollok*, 5), and Andrew Hoberne was tenant of Tuliboll, 1561 (PSAS., LX, p. 77). Robert Howbroune is recorded in Newtoune, 1608 (RRM., I, p. 71), and Jeanna Howburne and Sicilia Howburne were heirs portioners of Andrew Howburne in Drochellis, 1610 (*Inquis.*, 484, 485). Holburne 1476. James Holburn, elder in Menstrie, 1675 (*Edin. App.*) and Sir James Holburn was ruling elder in the parish of Logie, 1718 (*Logie*, I, p. 152).

HOWDEN. From the old barony of Hadden or Halden. Bernard, son of Brien, of an Anglo-Norman family, had a grant of the manor of Hauden in Roxburghshire from William the Lion (*Morton*, p. 114). Ulkillus de Hauden witnessed a grant by Bernard filius Brien of a carucate of his land of Haudene to the Abbey of Kelso c. 1165–71 (*Kelso*, 214). Bernard de Hauden made a grant of 'quatuor bollis frumenti' out of Hauden to the Hospital of Soltre in the reign of Alexander II. His gift was witnessed by Hugh de Hauden and William de Hauden (*Soltre*, p. 10). Bernard de Hauden witnessed a charter by Walter filius David filius Tructi in favor of Kelso Abbey, c. 1230 (*Kelso*, 269). Reginald de Havden witnessed grant of church of Lympetlaw to Soltre, c. 1221–31 (*Soltre*, p. 25), and Elmer de Hauden witnessed a charter by Richard Germyn, dominus de Lvmpatlaw, in favor of the same Hospital (ibid., p. 26). Complaint was made against Aymer, son and heir of Bernard de Haudene of the kingdom of Scotland, in 1278, and as Eymer or Avlmer de Haudene of the county of Edneburk he rendered homage, 1296 (*Bain*, II, p. 32, 201). Svmon de Holden and Bernard de Hauden, both of Roxburghshire, also rendered homage (ibid., p. 199, 200). William Hauldyn was bailie in Lanark, 1328 (ER., I, p. 86), and Brouchtaun in Peeblesshire belonged to Edward de Haudene in 1350 (*Stodart*, II, p. 323; RMS., I,

HOWDEN, *continued*

App. II, 771). Johannes de Hawdene, son and heir of William de Hawdene, had a charter of the lands of Hawdene and Yethame in 1407 (RMS., I, 912), and in 1523–24 the same lands were confirmed to William Haldane of that Ilk (ibid., II, 247). Joannes Haddane, heir of William Haddane *de eodem*, was retoured heir in half the lands of the barony of Bruchtoun in 1550 (*Retours, Peebles*, 5), and in 1624 John Halden of Halden was served heir to his father George Halden *de eodem* in the lands and barony of Halden (*Retours, Roxburgh*, 124). Haddon (of that Ilk) 1618, Hadden (of that Ilk) 1627, Hauldene 1633. Cf. HALDANE.

HOWGATE. Local. There is a Howgate near Carluke, and another near Penicuik, and Howgate Easter is near Roslin. The surname is recorded in Troon, 1941.

HOWIE. Local, perhaps from some obsolete place name in Ayrshire. William Howe, witness in Brechin, 1519, appears in 1526 as William Howye, sergeand of the town, and two years later he is William Howie (REB., II, 172, 180–181). Johnne Howy, a follower of the earl of Cassilis, was respited for murder, 1526 (RSS., I, 3386). Dand Howie or Howy was tenant on land under the Abbey of Kelso, 1567 (*Kelso*, p. 522), James Hwi was in Dunfermline, 1569 (*Dunfermline*), and Robert Howe or Howie, principal of Marischal College, Aberdeen, author of *De Aeterna Dei Providentia*, Basel, 1591, Latinized his name *Hovæus*. Archibald Howie was burgess of Glasgow, 1625 (*Burgesses*), John Howie was retoured heir of Andreas Howie in Meikle Warkhill, Oyne, Aberdeenshire, 1634 (*Retours, Aberdeen*, 224), and James Howie in Foggihillock, Ayrshire, 1667, appears again in 1672 as James Hui (*Corsehill*, p. 74, 102). Paterson records a local tradition that the Howies of Ayrshire sprang from a family of Waldenses who took refuge in Scotland (*Ayr*, III, p. 245), but no proof is offered for the belief. The best known of the name in Scottish history is John Howie (1736–1793) of Lochgoin, author of the *Scots worthies*. Cf. How.

HOWIESON. 'Son of Howie,' a diminutive of How, an early form of HUGH, q.v. Hewcysoune, an error for Heweysoune (*Workman MS.*). John Howison, burgess of Edinburgh, 1450. His son had a charter of Cramond Regis, 1465 (Wood, *Parish of Cramond*, 1794). Nicholas Howyson, presbyter of S. Andrew's diocese, 1475 (*Kelso*, 532). John Howison admitted burgess of Aberdeen, 1406 (NSCM., I, p. 2), and another John Howison was member of assize in an

Aberdeen shipping case, 1451 (CRA., p. 19). Martin Howesone, notary public in a Monymusk charter (*View*, p. 180), may be Martin Hoveson, burgess of Inverness, 1546 (CRA., p. 245). Dandie Howisone, tenant on lands of Kelso Abbey, 1567 (*Kelso*, p. 528), John Howisone, cantor in the Collegiate Church of Holy Trinity, Edinburgh, 1519 (*Soltre*, p. 184), and Robert Houissoune, burgess of Dundee, 1628 (*Brechin*). The name of the Rev. Thomas Howieson, minister of Boleskine in the last half of the seventeenth century, is also spelled Huison and Houston. Thomas Houison in Natherton of Mosplat, Lanark, 1711 (*Minutes*, p. 114). Howeson 1709, Howesoune 1602, Howiesoune 1551, Howyson and Howysoun 1570, Huisone 1686.

HOWITSON. *See under* HOWATSON.

HOWITT. Another spelling of HOWATT, q.v.

HOWLATSON. Patrick Howlatson or Howlatsoun was a beidsman in Edinburgh, 1575–80 (*Soltre*, p. 144, 230). John Howlatson in Ersiltoune, 1653, and other three in record (*Lauder*). John Houlatsone, servitor to earl of Rothes, 1665 (*Irvine*, II, p. 193), Bessie Hulletson in Berwickshire, 1674 (*Lauder*), and James Howlatson was married in Edinburgh, 1682 (*Edinb. Marr.*). An old name in Earnscleugh. Howlatsone 1665.

HOWNAM, HOUNAM. From Hounam in Roxburghshire. William de Hunum, son of John son of Orm, built a chapel in honor of S. Mary on his lands of Rasawe and c. 1190 gave the lands to the monks of Melrose on certain conditions (*Melros*, I, p. 122–123). He and his successors appear to have assumed the name of de Laundeles (see OPS., I, p. 393–395). John Hounam in Bridgend, 1642, appears again in 1662 as John Hownhame (RRM., I, p. 92; II, p. 1). Robert McNeill Hounam was married in Edinburgh 1942. Hownham 1662.

HOWSON, 'son of How,' a form of HUGH, q.v. "Howe or Heve (*v* for *u*) propyr name *Hugo*" (*Prompt. Parv.*). Moris Howsone on inquisition anent a fishing on the Tweed, 1467 (RD., 461). Paton Houyson of Cowbyre, 1473, is probably Patrick Houyson, tenant of Balgrescho, 1482 (*Cupar-Angus*, I, p. 172, 232). James Houssoune, bailie of burgh of Prestwick, 1509 (*Prestwick*, p. 39). Housone 1509. Cf. HOWIESON.

HOY. (1) local, from some place of the name near the Border, perhaps now obsolete. Jhone Hoye of Colmesliehill, 1607, and Jasper Hove there in the following year (RRM., I, p. 38,

67). Peter Hoy in Newhouses, 1653 (*Lauder*). (2) The Orkney surname is also of local origin, from the island of Hoy (c. 1225 Haey = high island).

HOYLE. Local. There is a Holl near Kirriemuir and another near Meigle, Perthshire, and there are lands named Holl or Hoyle in *Forfar Retours* (2, 268, 312, etc.). There is also a Holl or Hole in Ayrshire. Jacobus Hoyle, burgess of Anstruther, 1669 (*Inquis. Tut.*, 940), and Agnes Hoill was married in Edinburgh, 1692 (*Edinb. Marr.*).

HOZIER. The surname of a family in Lanarkshire, derived from the occupation of 'hosier' or dealer in hose or other knit goods. The suffix -*er* as in collier, glazier, sawyer, etc., appears as -*ier*, due apparently to assimilation to French derivatives in -*ier*.

HUDDLESTON. *See under* HIDDLESTON.

HUDSON, HUTSON, 'son of RICHARD,' q.v., from Hud(d), formerly a common pet form of the name. James Hudson, charter witness, 1466 (*Kelso*, 531). John Hudsone and Willie Hutson were tenants on land of the Abbey of Kelso, 1567 (*Kelso*, p. 524, 530), and in the same year William Hutson in Leith acknowledged the king and regent (RPC., I, p. 562). In 1660 there is record of payment to William Huteson in Stitchill (*Stitchill*, p. 20), and Adam Hutson is recorded in Smailholme, 1637 (*Lauder*). Hutson is common in Dunblane from 1612 (*Dunblane*). Hutsone 1591. (2) Hutson and Hudsone were also spellings of Huchon, a diminutive of Hugh. In 1524 and 1527 Hugh Ross of Kilravock appears as Hutson and Hudsone Ross (*Cawdor*, p. 125, 148, 149).

HUGAN, HUGGAN, HUGGIN. Diminutives of HUGH, q.v. Andrew Hugoun, latimus, 1519 (*Soltre*, p. 185). Robert Huggou (perhaps a miscopying of Huggon) in Glasmount, 1540 (*Dysart Rec.*, p. 6), and John Huggoun had sasine of lands of Neddyr Pitgrugny, 1545 (*Gaw*, 41). John Huggon in Dunfermline, 1579 (*Dunfermline*), and Agnes Hugan in Auchencraw, 1628 (*Lauder*). Janet Huggin or Hugin was witness in Bute, 1662 (HP., III, p. 4, 13), and David Hugin appears in Rind, Aberdeenshire, 1685 (CRA.). Huggin (in Rothesay) 1689. John Huggan in Kirktoun, 1721 (*Dumfries*).

HUGH. (1) An early Teutonic personal name, from OHG. *hugu* (OSax. *hugi*, MHG. *huge*), mind, spirit, thought. In OFr. the name became *Hugue* and *Hugues* (the -*s* paragogic), with diminutives *Hugot*, *Huguet*, *Hugon*, *Huot*,

Huet, *Huon*, *Hue*, and *Huc*. In DB. the name is common as *Hugo*, and later it became a favorite personal name in England as *Hugh(e*, *Hew(e*, *Huw(e*. In Scots the most common form was HEW, q.v., with affectionate diminutive *Hughie*. Howioun off ffodyrgame (Fotheringham) is mentioned in a vernacular writ dated 1391 (*Roxburghe*, p. 13), and in a Latin writ of later date the same person is mentioned as Hugo de Fothyrngham. Hve de Simpring appears in the reign of David I (*Kelso*, 272). William, son of Hugh, burgess of Aberdeen, was one of the witnesses to a charter by Fergus, earl of Buchan, c. 1189–99 (RAA., I, p. 57). (2) Hugh is the accepted English equivalent of G. *Aodh* although there is no connection between the words either in origin or meaning. (3) In Argyllshire Hugh is recognized as the English equivalent of EOCHANN, q.v. (4) In the north and northwest Hugh is used as an Englishing of UISDEANN, q.v.

HUGHAN. Diminutive of HUGH, q.v. Alexander Hughan, merchant in Creetown, Kirkcudbrightshire, 1773 (*Kirkcudbright*).

HUGHES, 'son of HUGH,' q.v. It is not very common.

HUGHSON, 'son of HUGH,' q.v. John filius Hugonis, burgess of Aberdeen, 1317 (SCM., V, p. 10), Johannes filius Hugonis, dean of Christianity in Elgin, 1375 (RAA., II, p. 33), and Colynus filius Hugonis, tenant in vill of Butyll, 1376 (RHM., I, p. lx). Thomas Hugonis was a forestaller in Aberdeen in 1402 (CRA., p. 384), William Hugosoun, bailie of Glasgow in 1433 (LCD., p. 248), and Andrew Hughson, forester general of the lands of Camsy, 1471 (*Cupar-Angus*, I, p. 220). Hughsone 1483.

HUIE. An Argyllshire surname, an abridged form of MACILGHUIE, q.v., or *Macilguie*, which again is from *Mac Gille dhuibh*, 'son of the black lad.' Individuals of this name are found in Aberdeenshire in the latter end of the sixteenth century, and Arthur and William Huie were tenants of the marquess of Huntlie in 1605 (SCM., IV, p. 280). Andrew M'Ahoy in Seater, Caithness, was put to the horn in 1670 and two years later the Privy Council ordered that Andrew McHui in Moy and John and Donald McAhuies in Seater were not to be reset or intercommuned with (RPC., 3. ser. III, p. 194, 492).

HULDIE. Patrick Hulde, a charter witness in 1552, had sasine of two tenements in Emocht in 1557 (*Home*, 205, 206), Alexander Huldie held the fishings at Eyemouth, 1576,

HULDIE, *continued*

and Robert Huldie was one of a number who attested the boundaries of Huttsonis Croft in 1651 (*Home,* 208, 220). Helen Huldie in Coldingham accused of witchcraft, 1629 (RPC., 2. ser. III, p. 270), a ship of George Holdie in Eymouth was sunk by witchcraft before 1634, and another George Huldie is in record in Aytoune, 1669 (*Lauder*). Huildie 1581.

HULK. Thomas Halc mentioned in Aberdeen, 1398, appears again in 1402 as a forestaller along with John Hulk (CRA., p. 377, 393). Mathew Hulk also in Aberdeen, 1400 (SCM., v, p. 14). Probably Englishmen. Weekley says (p. 64) from *Hulk,* a hut or shed, and mentions Agnes atte Holk in *Patent Rolls,* 1202–1338.

HUMBLE. A pension was paid to Schir John Hummill c. 1562 (*Cupar-Angus,* p. 362). Thomas Humble in Auchinchrie, 1633 (*Inquis.,* 1982), William Humbill retoured heir of Jean Humbill, 1650 (*Retours, Edinburgh,* 1023), and Isobel Humble is recorded in Bawfield of Clochie, 1750 (*Brechin*). Lower suggests this name comes from the manor of West Humble in Surrey, and Bardsley agrees. Harrison derives it from the moral characteristic.

HUME. *See under* HOME.

HUMPER. Walter Humper, exiled Covenanter from Damellington, was drowned in shipwreck off Orkney, 1679 (*Hanna,* II, p. 253). The name is a variant of English Hamper, a maker of hanapers (OFr. *hanapier*), baskets or hampers in which writs were deposited in Court of Chancery.

HUMPHRAY, HUMPHREY. Hum- appears to point to the personal name *Hum-friđ,* 'great for peace,' but the older Teutonic seems to point to the tribal name 'Hun,' *Hunfriđ,* 'Hun peace.' The Scots form is usually UM-PHRAY, q.v. As forename: Umfried Campbell, 1514 (*Ros,* 98).

HUNDLESHOPE. From Hundleshope near Peebles. Archibaldus of Hundewulchopp or Hundwaluchishope was juror on inquests on the lands of Hopkelchoc in 1259 and 1262 (APS., I, pref. p. 98, 101 red; Bain, I, 2162).

HUNT. From OE. *hunta,* ME. *hunte,* 'huntsman,' 'hunter.' Hence the same as HUNTER.

HUNTER. A surname derived from the chase, in early charters Latinized *venator.* As the surname early appears in widely different parts of the kingdom there is no reason to think that all bearing the name have a common

ancestor. William venator, who was one of the witnesses to the Inquisition of Earl David, before 1124 (REG., p. 5), is apparently the first of the name recorded in Scotland. Yone Venatore was one of the witnesses to a Beauly charter of 1231 (*Beauly,* p. 33). Adam Hunter was granted the hereditary office of sergeantry in all causes touching life and limb throughout the abbey land of Crauford belonging to the Abbey of Newbattle before 1259 (*Neubotle,* p. 121). John the hunter (venator) was one of the jurors on an inquisition made on the lands of Hopkelchoc (now Kailzie) in 1259 (Bain, I, 2162; APS., I, p. 88). Aylmer le Hunter of the county of Are, Johan Hunter of the forest of Passelay, Huwe the Hunter of Stragrife, and Richard the Hunter of Stragryfe, rendered homage for their possessions in 1296 (*Bain,* II, p. 205, 212, 213), as also did Thomas le Huntere (ibid., 730). Maurice Hunter was provost of Striuelyn in 1327 (ER., I, p. 67), Aymon Hunter was bailie of the burgh of Culan (Cullen) in 1328 (ibid., I, p. 91), and Thomas Hunter was a tenant of the Douglas in the parish of Morton in 1376 (RHM., I, p. lvi).

Hunter of Hunterston, Ayrshire, is apparently the oldest family of the name. The Hunters of Polmood contested the honor of precedence with Hunter of Hunterston, but as Burke says (*Landed gentry*) it is noteworthy that the house of Hunter of Polmood was never styled "of that Ilk," a distinction accorded to the Ayrshire family. A "Pedigree of Hunter of Abbotshall and Barjarg, and cadet families: Hunter of Bonnytoun and Doonholm, Hunter-Blair of Blairquhan, Hunter of Auchterarder, Hunter of Thurston," was published in London in 1905. An account of the Ayrshire family is in Paterson (2. ed., III). The old Orcadian surname of Hunto, of quite different origin, is now merged in Hunter. Huntair 1530, Huntayr 1565, Huntter 1527, Hwntar 1535, Hwntare 1454, Hounttar, Hountter, and Hunttar in 1528.

HUNTINGDON. From the Honour of Huntingdon in England which came into the hands of the royal family of Scotland through the marriage of David, brother of Alexander I, to Matilda, daughter of the Countess Judith, niece of William the Conqueror, and Waltheof, earl of Northumberland. John de Huntedun witnessed grant by Gillemor filius Gilleconel to the church of Lesmahag, a. 1144 (*Kelso,* 187). Johannes de Huntendun witnessed the gift by Peter filius Fulberti of the church of Pulloc to the Monastery of Passelet c. 1189–99 (RMP., p. 100). John de Huntedun, rector of the church of Duresdere, a. 1200, is doubtless John de Huntedun who witnessed an agreement between the abbot of Kelso and Bernard de Hauden, c. 1202–11 (*Kelso*, 28, 211).

HUNTLY, HUNTLEY. From the ancient hamlet of Huntlie in Berwickshire, now extinct. Robert de Hunteleghe of the county of Roxburghe rendered homage in 1296 (*Bain*, II, p. 199). The name Huntly in Aberdeenshire was borrowed from Huntlie in Berwickshire, the old barony of Gordon, including Huntlie, being owned by the earls of Huntly down to 1638.

HUNTO. An old surname in Orkney derived from the lands of Hunto in the isle of Stronsay. Oliver Hunto was juror on an assize in Birsay in 1574 (REO., p. 135). The surname is now merged in HUNTER.

HUNTRES. John Huntres witnessed a bond of manrent, 1508 (*Panmure*, II, 276). Bardsley and Harrison have this name and explain it as 'huntress,' feminine of Hunter. In the English Hundred Rolls the name appears in Latin, *Venatrix*.

HURD. A variant of HERD, q.v. Allan Hurd in Mekill Cadderwood, 1610 (*Campsie*).

HURL, HURLE, HURLL. Rare current surnames. Possibly weak forms of Hurrell, Fr. *Hurel*. David Hurl had a safe conduct into England, 1424 (*Bain*, IV, 970).

HURRAY, HURRY, HURRIE. Variants of URIE, q.v. Captain John Horie, a man of "approved value and experience in warres" is mentioned in the *Ruthven correspondence* (Roxburghe Club), p. 151. Sir John Hurry, a prominent officer in the civil wars of the seventeenth century, came from the family of Urrie of Pitfichie, Aberdeenshire. William Hurry, a minor poet of the nineteenth century.

HUSBAND. 'Husband' probably corresponded to English 'yeoman,' one owning and himself cultivating a piece of land. According to Cosmo Innes (*Legal antiquities*, p. 242) a husband was the farmer of a husbandland of 26 acres. In 1437 we have mention of John Parvus, *husband*, in the vill of Tullibothy (SCM., v, p. 261). Alexander Husband was prepositus of Invernairn in 1291 (*Bain*, II, p. 543), and in 1295 he was one of those who attested to the valuation of Kylrauoc and Estirgedeys (*Cawdor*, p. 3; *Rose*, p. 30). Andrew Husband was a weaver in Perth in 1506. Andrew Husband, portioner of Nether Kincairdney, had sasine as heir of his father John Husband, of an annual rent from lands of Stralochie in the parish of Capeth, 1679 (DPD., I, p. 262). John Husband in Snaigo, Kirkcudbright, 1689 (RPC., 3. ser. XIV, p. 778). James Husband

in Craigend, 1695, and eight more of the name are in Commissariot Record of Dunkeld.

HUTCHEON, HUTCHON. From Fr. *Huchon*, diminutive of HUGH, q.v. *Huchon* was used in AF. of the thirteenth century instead of Huon as the regular oblique case of Hue. In Scotland during the fourteenth, fifteenth, and sixteenth centuries Hutcheoun (*ch* sibilant) regularly appears as a Christian name, the equivalent of Hugh or Hew in the vernacular. Hucheon Fraser, lord of the Lovet is mentioned in 1422, and in 1510 a succeeding Lord Lowat is named Heow (*Beauly*, p. 305, 323). Huchon Ker appears in 1467 (RD., p. 359), and Huchown the Ross, 1481. Sandy Huchose appears in Aberdeen, 1497 (CRA., p. 425). 'John Hutching wyfe' was a 'kaik-bakster' in Stirling, 1525, and Helen Huchown was amerciat there in 1547 (SBR., p. 25, 47). James and Robert Huchone or Huchoun were tenants of the vill of Raffort, 1565 (REM., p. 444), and David Hutcheon was gardener in Fyweis Wallis, 1596 (SCM., I, p. 92). John Hucheon, burgess of Aberdeen, 1598 (NSCM., I, p. 93). Patrick Hutcheoun, 'quhytfischer' in Futtie, 1602, is probably Patrick Hutchone, ferryman at Aberdeen, 1612 (CRA., p. 226; SCM., v, p. 94). Harie Hutson was witness in Kirkcaldie, 1639, and John Hutchen, elder, in parochine of Kirkcaldie, 1641 (PBK., p. 141, 210). George Huchone, trade burgess of Aberdeen, 1642 (ROA., I, p. 232). William Hutcheon from Auchterless was killed in the first Great War (*Turriff*). The name was early borrowed into Gaelic and became there *Huisdean* or *Uisdean* (pronounced like 'ocean'). This spelling is due to the fact that Gaelic lacks the sound of *ch* in church, so that in names borrowed from English it renders it *sd* pron. *sht*), thus Fletcher becomes Fleisdeir and Richard becomes Risdeart. In the *Book of Lecan*, compiled c. 1400, Clandonald of Sleat is referred to as *Clann Uisdinn*, and in the description of the Isles of Scotland prepared for the use of James VI (c. 1577–95), the same clan is called "Scheall Hutcheoun, that is to say, the offspring of that man callit Hutcheoun" (Skene, CS., III, p. 432). As a Gaelic forename: Husceoun M'Inclerich, 1548 (RMS., IV, 204). As forename: Huchon Hulson in Ayr, 1471 (*Friars Ayr*, p. 54); Hugh *alias* Hucheoun Monro, 1628 (*Retours, Ross*, 183). Houcheon 1589, Hucheoun 1563, Hutchone 1616.

HUTCHESON, HUTCHIESON, HUTCHISON. From Hutcheon, Fr. *Huchon*, diminutive of HUGH, q.v. James Huchonsone held a land in Glasgow, 1454 (LCD., p. 175), John Huchonson was admitted burgess of Aberdeen, 1466 (NSCM., I, p. 19), George

HUTCHESON, HUTCHIESON..., continued
Huchunson, burgess of Glasgow in 1471 reappears as George Hucheson in following year (REG., 395; *Sc. Ant.*, XVII, p. 119). Thom Huchonson had a precept of remission for his share in burning Lochfergus, 1488 (RSS., I, 3), and Robert Huchonsone, 'sangster and master of the organis' in Aberdeen is referred to again in 1496 as Huchosone and Huchonsoun (SCM., v, p. 30, 32, 34). John Huchonsoun had a remission for slaughter committed by him, 1497 (*Rose*, p. 164), William Huchison was tenant of Uthircloy, Ardmanoch, 1504 (ER., XII, p. 661), and Peter and James Huchonsone were members of assize at Cupar, 1521 (SCBF., p. 223). John Hutchesone was retoured heir of Hugh *alias* Hutcheoun Alistersoun in certain lands in the sheriffdom of Inverness, 1624. George and Thomas Hutcheson, brothers, founded the hospital in Glasgow which bears their name in 1639–41. Howchesoun 1519, Huchesoune 1550, Huchisone 1505, Huchwsone 1515, Hwchwson 1525, Hwchesoun 1513, Hwtchwson 1525.

HUTTON. Symon de Hotun was juror on an inquest held before the sheriff of Lanark, 1263 (*Bain*, I, 2677). John Hudton was abbot of Cupar in 1460. George Hutone had a charter of the croft "vulgo vocato le ackorne waird," 1605 (RD., p. 498), and Alexander Huttoun was "deacone of the skinneris" of Stirling, 1614 (SBR., p. 137). Thomas Huttoun was retoured heir in lands in the parish of Kellis, 1621 (*Retours, Kirkcudbright*, 150), Patrick Huttoune was burgess of Dundee, 1649 (*Inquis.*, 3516), and Christian Huittoun was retoured heir of Hendrie Huitoune, portioner of Newbiggings, her brother, 1654 (*Retours, Fife*, 833). Hutoun 1641, Hutoun 1529, Huttyne 1562. A common surname in Dunblane Commissariot Record. The Huttons of Cumberland were an old family, 'de Hoton.'

HYND. From the occupation, a 'hind,' peasant, ME. *hine*, the *d* being excrescent. The earliest references to the name connect it with Glasgow. David Hyne or Hynde appears as burgess there between 1454 and 1460 (LCD., p. 179, 252; REG., p. 412), and Robert Hyne in 1456 (REG., p. 406). George Hynd or Hynde was citizen of Glasgow, 1472, and Patrick Hyne was burgess of Linlithgow in the same year (*Sc. Ant.*, XVII, p. 116, 118). William Hynd held a land in Glasgow, 1496, and Christine Hynd held a tenement there in 1500 (REG., p. 493, 501). Thomas Hynd and David Hynd, followers of the earl of Cassilis, were respited for murder in 1526 (RSS., I, 3386), and Riche Hynd appears in Dunfermline, 1577 (*Dunfermline*).

HYNDFORD. The lands of Hyndford in Lanarkshire were held before 1249 by Gamellus de Hindeford (*Bain*, I, 2175), who evidently derived his name from them.

HYNDMAN. Weekley and Harrison say from ME. *hende*, courteous, and Harrison further suggests (2) keeper of the hinds. The family of Hyndman of Springside was originally of Lunderstown in Renfrewshire which they possessed as far back as the days of James V (Robertson, *Ayrshire families*, II, p. 346). The name is found in Bute in 1649 (*Hewison*, II, p. 267), John Hyndman appears there in 1662 (HP., III, p. 12). John Hynman appears in Kilcattane, 1662 (*Isles*), and John Hyndman was merchant in Largs, 1749 (*Hunter*, p. 73). The name of Annie Heyman who was at a meeting of witches in Bute in 1662 is perhaps intended for Hyndman (HP., III, p. 8, 28).

HYSLOP. A variant of HISLOP, q.v.

IAIN. G. for John, older *Eoin*. Pronounced e-an. In compound *Seathain* as *Mac Gille Sheathain*, now *M'Illeathainn*.

IBIOT. Perhaps from Ibb, diminutive of Isabel + Fr. dimin. *-ot*. John Ibiot, burgess of Aberdeen, 1443 (NSCM., I, p. 8). William Abote in Mekill Gourdes, 1584 (RSCA., I, p. 305).

ICENER. Said to be a phonetic attempt at pronunciation of Elshener in Fife and Clackmannan.

IDDINGTON. A Border surname, a variant of EDINGTON, q.v.

IDILL. Bardsley says from Idle in Yorkshire, but our earliest reference points to a personal name as the origin. Idellus was chaplain in Glasgow, c. 1202–07 (RMP., p. 110). At a later date the surname is found chiefly in Aberdeenshire and in Angus. William Ydil was one of the temporary bailies of Elgyn, 1343, and in 1363 was burgess (REM., p. 290, 313) William Ydil, a man of the duke of Albany, had a safe conduct in England, 1401 (*Bain*, IV, 584). William Ydill, charter witness, 1407, appears again in 1410 as William Idille de Murebrakis, when he received a charter of part of Balcalv and Kyngerrok in Fife (RMS., I, 896, 927). John Ydill, notary-public in Dundee, 1421, appears in 1425–34 as Ydile and Idill (REB., I, 62; II, 42, 44; HP., p. 177; *Panmure*, II, 190). Master Walter Ydill, vicar of Inverurie, 1428, is doubtless Master Watt Ydill recorded in Aberdeen, 1442, mentioned again in 1455 as Walter Idill, canon of Aberdeen (CRA., p. 7; RAA., II, 104). Walter de Idil who was directed to resign the rectory of Logy in Buchan, 1437 (*Pap. Lett.*, VIII,

p. 645–6) and Walter Ydil de Tal, canon of Aberdeen, 1464 (RAA., II, 153), is probably the same person. Andrew Ydill was witness at Dudhope, 1572 (*Poltalloch Writs*, p. 144). Allexr. Ydle, cordiner and deacon conveiner of the trades in Aberdeen, 1681 (ROA., I, p. 239), and William Idill, clerk of the Exercise of Alford, 1686 (*Alford*, p. 372). This surname in some instances has been merged in YULE, q.v. Ydyll 1445.

IDVIE. From Idvies in the parish of Kirkden in Angus. The *s* in the place name is English plural and modern. Malcolm de Edivin was one of the jurors in a dispute regarding the Kirktun of Aberbuthenoth in 1206 (SCM., V, p. 213). Malys de Ediuyn witnessed the perambulation of the lands of Conan and Tulloch in 1254 (RAA., I, p. 325), and Schir Jon of Ydwy was "parson of that Ilke" in 1388 (*Bamff*, p. 22). David de Idwy or Yduy who appears as archdeacon of the cathedral of Brechin in 1410 and 1450 is probably the David de Idwy who witnessed a charter in favor of William Lam in Brechin in 1420 (REB., I, 27, 131; II, 273). Thomas Eduein to remain in ward, 1561 (SBR., p. 78).

ILBAREN. Johannes Ylbaren of Perth sold a toft to the monks of Scone, 1219 (*Scon*, 51).

ILCHATTAN. Several of this name are recorded in Argyll (*Argyll*) in seventeenth century. Shortened from (MAC)ILHATTAN, q.v.

ILE. Alisaundre del Ile (Ille) of Perthshire, and Johan del Ile, burgess de Ennerkethin, rendered homage, 1296 (RR.). See also LYLE.

ILIFF. A surname in Fife. Robert filius Ylif witnessed a quit-claim to the lands of Drumkerauch, 1260 (RPSA., p. 346). Adam filius Ilif de Aldengraue witnessed a quit-claim by Henry de Prendirgast, and as Ada filius Ylif witnessed a charter by Thomas filius D. de Quikiswde, c. 1240 (*Raine*, 187, 333). Eilaf and Ailef are recorded in Northumberland, 1166 and 1176 (Hodgson, *History of Northumberland*, p. 10, 25). From earlier OE. *Aethelwulf*.

ILLINGWORTH. This surname found in Caithness is doubtless from Illingworth in the parish of Halifax, in the West Riding of Yorkshire.

IMBART. From the OE. personal name *Imbeorht (Searle)*. In 1265 there is an entry of hides given to Imbartus at Roxburgh Castle (ER., I, p. 30), and Master Imbert was directed to inspect the walls of Jedburgh Castle, 1288 (ibid., p. 44).

IMBRIE. Same as IMRIE with epenthetic b.

IMLACH, IMLAH. Thomas Imlach apud Logabussis was charged with being a forestaller in Aberdeen in 1402 (CRA., p. 383). John Imlach was admitted burgess of the same burgh in 1440, Thomas Imlach in 1449, and John Imlaw in 1479 (NSCM., I, p. 6, 12, 28). Robert Emlach was schoolmaster at Abercherdour in 1636 (*Strathbogie*, p. 8), Thomas Imloch appears in Nigg, Ross-shire, in 1607 (RPC., VIII, p. 342), and George Imlach was a square-wright in Keith, Banffshire. John Imlacke, Mill of Pettie, a tenant of Gordon of Gight, was prosecuted for riot in 1678 (RPC., 3. ser. v, p. 340). John Imlah (1799–1846), minor poet, born in Aberdeen, was author of "O gin I were where Gadie runs." Imbloch 1637.

IMLAY. A softened form of IMLACH, q.v. Agnes Imelie was burnt for witchcraft in Aberdeen in 1597 (SCM., v, p. 68).

IMPETRANY. Peter de Impetrany of Innerkethene to have his lands restored to him, 1296 (*Bain*, II, 832).

IMRAY, IMRIE. Shortened forms of the old personal name *Amalric*. The first of the name recorded in Scotland appears to have been Emeric, a Lombard of Flanders, who was spoiled by John Crabbe of Berwick in 1329, and indemnified by the chamberlain (ER., I, p. 213). The escheat and forfeiture of Ade Emry, burgess of Dunblane, is recorded in 1424 (RMS., II, 16). Walter Ymery and Thomas Ymery were tenants of Conlony alias Condland in 1513 (*Cambus.*, 9), and James Immerie in Dunfermline, 1563, appears also as Immerri (1567) and Immerrie (1569) (*Dunfermline*). John Imry was portioner of Fordell, 1579 (*Inquis. Tut.*, 1200). John Imbrie (with intrusive *b*), burgess freeman of Glasgow, 1611 (*Burgesses*), Thomas Imbrie was constable of the parish of Ferrie, 1633 (RPC., 2. ser. v, p. 93), and John Imbrie, coalgreive apud Kincardine, 1697 (*Inquis.*, 7802). The name also occurs in the kirk-session records of Gask in the seventeenth century. John Imrie in Abernethie, 1618, and several others named Imrie and Imbrie are recorded in the neighborhood (*Dunblane*). Payment was made to David Imbrie in St. Andrews, c. 1688 (PSAS., LIV, p. 238), and James Imbrie took the oath at Strickmartine, 1689 (RPC., 3. ser. XIV, p. 231). Imre 1548, Ymre 1547.

INCH. There are places of this name in Angus and in Perthshire from which this surname may be derived. John del Inche, burgess of Inverkeithing, rendered homage in 1296 (*Bain*,

INCH, *continued*

II, 880). John de Inche witnessed a charter by John Ramsay, burgess of Montros in 1430 (REB., II, 34), and William de Inche, 'husband' in the ville de Tullibothy, is in record in 1437 (SCM., V, p. 261). Thomas Insche witnessed an instrument of sasine in the barony of Banff in 1507 (*Bamff*, p. 45), and Duncan Insche was burgess of Culross, 1652 (*Dunblane*). George Inch, late burgess of Edinburgh, 1734 (*Guildry*, p. 147).

INCHAFFRAY. Fergus de Insula Missarum and Michael de Insula Missarum (the 'Isle of Masses,' the Latin form of Inchaffray) rendered homage at Perth, 1291 (RR.).

INCHBAIKIE. Muriele de Inchebeky of Perthshire rendered homage, 1296 (*Bain*, II, p. 213).

INCHEEN. Richard Incheen recorded in Aberdeen, 1402 (CRA., p. 383), and in a list of thieves in the same burgh, 1411, is the entry "John Inchouen est communis fur" (ibid., p. 4).

INCHES. Local. The family of Inches of Perthshire were a sept of Clann Donnchaidh or Robertsons. One of the Inches in the Tay at Perth was the scene of the Clan battle in 1396.

INCHMARTIN. From the place of the same name in Perthshire. Sir Henry de Inche Martin was one of the Scottish prisoners taken in Dunbar Castle in 1296, and in August of the same year agreed to serve the English king in France or abroad (*Bain*, II, 742, 942). In the following year John de Inchemartin had a protection granted him to go to Scotland on the king's business (ibid., 961). Sir David de Inchemartyn, a Scottish prisoner of war was hanged in 1306 (ibid., II, 811), Sir John of Inchmartyn, c. 1310, granted the Abbey of Cupar-Angus his lands of Murthuil in Mar (*Cupar-Angus*, I, p. 349–350), and in 1331 a charter of the lands of Wardroperisthon was granted to John de Inchemartyn (SCM., V, p. 10). Gilbert de Inchemartin was among those killed at the battle of Durham in 1346 (Hailes, *Annals*, II, p. 386). John de Inchmartin witnessed a Brechin document in 1364 (REB., I, 20), another John de Inchemartyn appears in Aberdeen in 1412 (CRA., p. 388) who may be the same with John de Inchmartyn, secretary to Alexander Stewart, earl of Mar in 1420 (SCM., IV, p. 117), and possibly with John de Inchmartyn who was archdeacon of Ross in 1426 (RMS., II, 56). Andrew de Inchemartyne or Inchmartin, burgess of Perth in 1432 appears as bailie of the burgh in 1458 (HP., II, p. 170; RAA., II,

114), and John de Inchemertan appears as a witness in Brechin in 1448 (REB., I, 117). The seal of John of Inchmartin, 1320, reads S' *Iohannis de Hincmartin* (*Macdonald*, 1412).

INCHMETHAN. Local. Richard Inchmethane held land in Aberdeen, 1396, and as Richard de Inchethane was burgess there, 1441 (REA., II, p. 293; I, p. 204).

INCHMURDO. Symone de Ynchemurthac who witnessed the gift of fifteen acres of Balmulinauch (Balmerino) to the church of St. Andrews before 1225 (RPSA., p. 272) derived his name from Inchmurdo near Boarhills in Fife. Inchemurthach was one of the manors of the bishop of St. Andrews.

INCHTURE. From Inchture in the Carse of Gowrie, Perthshire. Robert de Inchetorn' or Inchethor performed homage to England in 1296, and in May of the same year appears as a prisoner in Fotheringay Castle (*Bain*, II, p. 169, 177). In August following he agrees to serve in the English king's service in France or elsewhere abroad (ibid., p. 243).

INCHYRA. From Inchyra in the parish of Kinnoull, Perthshire. An agreement was made by Duncan de Inchesireth and the prior of May c. 1250 (*May*, 38), and Johannes de Inchesyrith filius Duncani filii Jacobi de Pert appears in the reign of Alexander III (*Scon*, p. 82). Aly Inchera occurs in a list of Aberdeen criminals in 1411 (CRA., p. 4), and Andrew de Inchsera was bailie of Stirling in 1429 (ER., IV, p. 486).

INDULF. The Pictish Chronicle records that in the reign of Indulfus (*Indolb*) 'oppidum Eden' (Edinburgh) was evacuated by the Angles and left to the Scots (Skene, CS., I, p. 365). Anderson (ES., I, p. 475) says Indulf seems to be Scandinavian, = Dan. Hildulf.

INFIRMITORIO. Thomas de Infirmitorio, a charter witness in Ayrshire before 1357 (RMS., I, 182). John de Infirmitorio was perpetual vicar of the church of Innerkelor, 1394 (RAA., II, 42).

INGEBALD. Hugh, son of Ingebald, witnessed the resignation of land in Weremundebi and Anant to William de Brus and his heirs c. 1194–1214 (*Bain*, I, 606; *Annandale*, I, p. 1), and one Ingebald held land in Kelso, c. 1200 (*Kelso*, 354).

INGERAMISMAN. The 'man' or 'servant of Ingeram.' See INGRAM. Willelmus dictus Ingeramisman held land in the barony of Strathekyn before 1366 (RMS., I, 213). Ingeram de Wenton is one of the witnesses to the charter.

INGHEAN. G. 'daughter,' corruptly *nighean*, OIr. *ingen*, cognate with Latin *indigena*. The word occurs in the bilingual inscription of Eglwys Cymmun, Wales: *Inigena Cunigni Avittoriges — Avittoria filia Cunigni* (Thurneysen, *Handbuch des alt-Irischen*, p. 180). The word means 'the inborn.' In the public records it appears as *nean, nein, nin*. See Nɪɴ.

INGHSTER. See under INKSTER.

INGLESTON. Local, from Ingleston near Meigle, Perthshire. John Ingletoun in Kirkintilloch, 1666 (*Sasines*, 1305). James Inglestoun, portioner of Kirkintullock, 1696 (RPC., 3. ser. xɪɪ, p. 133).

INGLIS. A surname from Northern English and Scots *Englis* (OE. *Englisc*), meaning the English(man), in Latin documents *Anglicus*. Richard Anglicus witnessed David's great charter to Melrose, a. 1153 (*Melros*, 1). Adam le Englis witnessed a confirmation charter of the fishery in Torduff, c. 1194–1211 (*Holm-Cultram*, p. 35), and Walter Anglicus witnessed a charter by Alan, lord of Galloway to the Abbey of Kelso, a. 1208 (*Kelso*, p. 202). In 1296 Rauf le Engleys was commanded "to answer at law as a man at the king's faith and peace to all having claims against him" (*Bain*, ɪɪ, 805). Several individuals of the name rendered homage in 1296: Johan le Engleys of Berwickshire, Phellipe le Engleys, Wautier le Engleys, and Richard le Engleys, all three of Lanarkshire, and Mawcolum le Engleys of Perthshire (ibid., p. 204, 206, 209, 212). Nisbet says that from Philip le Engleys descended the Ingleses of Branksholm and Manor, and that the Inglises of Tarvet may be descended from Johan le Engleys. In 1296 Malcolm le fiz Lenglevs claimed Kentyre as his heritage, and in 1300 he had a safe conduct by land or sea, with his men and galleys to harass the Scots (ibid., p. 225, 294). Before 1321 Robert ɪ granted to Ade Barbitonsoris the toft in Moffat with two bovates of land adjacent "que quondam Willelmus dictus Ingles ad firmam tenuit in villa de Moffet de domino Vallis Anandie avo nostro" (RMS., ɪ, 37). John Inglis was a forestaller in Aberdeen, 1402 (CRA., p. 385). Thomas Ynglis witnessed a renunciation by Walter Scott of Bukcleuch, 1449 (*Soltre*, p. 319). James Ynglis appears as canon of Glasgow, 1452 (REG., 373), and the name of Master Alexander Lenglis, archdeacon of St. Andrews, appears also as Inglys and English (*Bain*, ɪv, 1564). Alexander Inglvssh, ambassador of the king of Scotland, 1478, is probably the same person (ibid., 1454). The name was early carried to France and there appeared as D'Anglars. In Scotland the name also occurs as Angel. Ingleis 1574, Inglish 1686, Inglisse 1680.

INGLISTRICHSTON. John Inglistrichston appears in Tofts in Yell, 1613 (*Shetland*).

INGRAM. From the OE. personal name *Ingelram*, later *Ingeram*, also ʍE. *Ingelram, Ingeram*, Latinized *Ingelramus*. Hyngelrom, clericus, witnessed a charter by David ɪ to the Abbey of Neubotle, c. 1142 (*Neubotle*, p. 14). Engelram (Engellram, Ingelleran, Hingelram, Engeram), rector of Peebles, archdeacon of Glasgow, became chancellor of Scotland in the reign of Malcolm ɪv (*Lawrie*, p. 364). Hyngelramus de Monte acuto was a witness in Dumbarton, 1271 (RMP., p. 192). John Ingeram held a land of the abbot of Arbroath, 1330 (RAA., ɪɪ, p. 8). Sir William Ingelram was chaplain of Stirling, 1476 (SBR., p. 259), and William Ingrim in Tullobeg is mentioned in 1716 (SCM., ɪv, p. 170). As a forename it appears as Imgrie in 1580. Engram 1249, Ingrm 1541.

INGSAY. Edward Ingissay and Johne Ingissay were jurors on assize at Birsay, 1574 (REO., p. 136), and John Ingsay in Bea appears in 1640 (MCM., ɪɪ, p. 211). William Ingsay, a witness in Shetland, 1623 (OSS., ɪ, 23). From the land of Ingsay in Birsay, near Swannay Loch.

INGSON, Iɴᴋsoɴ. Probably for Ingo-son, 'son of Ingo.' Inkson is the Moray pronunciation of the name. Thomas Inkson in Corgyle, 1777 (*Moray*).

INKSTER, Iɴɢʜsᴛᴇʀ. These names occur in Orkney and Shetland, and are corruptions of *Ingsgar* (Clouston). William Inkseter, tacksman of Skelbustir, and Huchown Inksettir, tacksman of Gryndale, are in record in 1492 (REO., p. 406). Magnus Ingsitter (Ingseter, or Inkster) appears as bailie-depute of Orphir between 1570 and 1584 (REO., p. 150, 292, 400), and Edward Ingsetter or Inksetter was a witness in 1589 and 1600 (ibid., p. 260, 316). Duncane Inksetter in the parish of Brassay is recorded in 1576 (*Oppressions*, p. 20), James Ingsetter appears in Sandwick in Burray in 1615 (*Shetland*), Edward Ingsetter of Leogar and Hucheon Ingsetter in Orakirk are mentioned in 1619 (OSS., p. 51), and Edward Inksetter was retoured heir of Alexander Inksetter in Bowrester in 1648 (*Retours, Orkney and Shetland* 57). Inksitter 1579, Insitter 1581, Yngsetter 1586.

INNERARITY. See under INVERARITY.

INNERDALE. Local. Janet Innerdale recorded in the parish of Lochlee, 1758 (*Brechin*).

INNERLEVEN. From Innerleven in the parish of Wemyss in Fifeshire. William de Enerlevyn and John de Enerlevyn, sons of Robert de Enerlevyn, acquired a charter of the Halgh in the barony of Scuny (Scoonie) in 1395 (*Wemyss*, II, 32).

INNERLOCHTY. Reginaldus de Innerlochty who served as juror on an inquest held in the episcopal lands of Aldrochty in 1393 (REM., p. 205) doubtless derived his name from Inverlochty in Moray near the town of Elgin.

INNERLUNAN. David de Innerlunan who, with the will and consent of Gillicrist Macgilliduffie, granted to the monks of Beauly all his land of Ouchter-Tarradale in 1275 (*Beauly*, p. 60) probably derived his name from Inverlunan in Angus, the old name for the parish of Lunan. Sir David de Ynverlunan, a cleric, probably the same person, was witness at Dornoch, 1275 (CSR., I, p. 46). Nicholas de Inverlounan, a Scots prisoner from Dunbar, was sent to Ledes Castle in 1296 (*Bain*, II, p. 177).

INNERRAN. Local. Patrick Innerran in Terbert fined for reset of Clan Gregor, 1613 (RPC., XIV, p. 644). There is an Inveran in the parish of Gairloch and another in Sutherland (in 1608 Innerane), but these places seem too far north.

INNERWICK. From Innerwick in East Lothian. A family of this name, vassals of the Stewarts, obtained their lands from their superiors in the latter part of the twelfth century. Roland de Inuerwič witnessed a charter of two parts of land in the territory of Inuerwyc by Robert de Kent to Kelso c. 1190 (*Kelso*, 255). William de Innerwic witnessed a grant of the church of Cragyn (Craigie in Ayrshire) to the monks of Paisley by Thomas de Cragyn in 1272 (RMP., p. 233). Robert Inderwick or Innerwick in Chirnsyde in 1652 and six more of the name are recorded in the Lauder Commissariot Record. James Inderwick and John Innerweik were indwellers in Chirnside, 1656 and 1666 (*Craw*, p. 16, 17).

INNES. Of territorial origin from the barony of the same name in the parish of Urquhart, Moray. Part of the barony is an island formed by two branches of a stream running through it, hence the name (from Gaelic *innis*, 'island'). The first of the name in record was a Fleming named Berowald ('Berowaldus Flandrensis'), who obtained from Malcolm IV a charter of the lands of Ineess et Etherurecard (Easter Urquhart) in the province of Elgin (REM.,

p. 453–454). The existence of this Berowald is confirmed by a charter to his grandson, Walter de Ineys, granted in 1226: "Alexander Dei gratia Rex Scotorum, etc. sciant non concessisse et hae charto confirmasse Waltero filio Johannis filii Berowaldi Flandrensis Inees" (*Innes Familie*, p. 53). Berowald or Beroald continued a favorite name in the family. Beroald Innes of Knokorth is recorded in 1633 (SCM., III, p. 83), and Beroald Innes was appointed schoolmaster of Bellie, 1664 (*Strathbogie*, p. 146). This Walter de Ineys, who appears to have been the first to assume the territorial designation, witnessed a composition between the bishop of Moray and W. de Petyn relating to the lands of Ardtrillen, Duldavy, Lunnin, etc., in 1226 (REM., p. 25), and another agreement between the bishop and David de Strathbolgyn in 1232 (ibid., p. 30). William de Inays swore fealty at Aberdeen in 1296. The device on his seal is a star of six points, S' Will'i de Ynays (*Bain*, II, 785). Robertus de Innes, juror on inquest in 1389 regarding the mill lands of Quarelwode (REM., p. 171). A branch of the family of Innes of Innes is found in Caithness, 1507. Innice 1685.

INNINTHOME. G. *inghean Thòmaidh*, 'Tommie's daughter.' Gradach Ynnythome, tenant in Strathdee, 1527 (*Grant*, III, p. 71n).

INRIG. A surname in Keiss, Caithness, locally pronounced Enrig. John Inrick appears in Canisbay Parish Register c. 1620. (1) doubtfully explained as "tenant of the home or enclosed patch of land"; (2) from (Mac)Enrick or (Mac)Eanrick, from G. *MacEanruig*, "son of Henry;" (3) probably a corruption of Dutch "Hendrik." Cf. Groat, a name of Dutch origin.

INSHAW. Local. James Inshaw held a tenement in Glasgow, 1548 (LCD., p. 111).

INSTABILLIE. An old surname in Orkney, from Instabillie in the parish of St. Ola. Burne Instabele was juror on an assize in Sandwick in 1553, and a family of the name held land in Tronston in Sandwick in 1601 (REO., p. 106, 371).

INVERARITY, INNERARITY. From Inverarity in the parish of the same name in Angus. A David Enererity is mentioned in 1675. James Inverarity was a nephew of Robert Fergusson the poet. Eliza Inverarity was a celebrated singer in the thirties of last century (SN&Q., II. ser. VIII, p. 65–66), and William Inverarity was minister of Caputh in 1832. Inverarity is entirely distinct from Inverharity and Inverquharity (locally pronounced Inverwharity) both in the same county.

INVERBERVIE. Symone de Inuerberuyn who witnessed a charter by Umfridus de Berkeley, c. 1204–11 (RAA., I, 89) derived his name from Inverbervie in Kincardineshire, now usually Bervie.

INVERDOVAT. Gregoire de Inredovet of Fifeshire who rendered homage for his lands in 1296 (Bain, II, p. 204), derived his name from Inverdovat in the parish of Forgan, Fife.

INVERESK. From Inveresk near Edinburgh. Radulphus de Inueresk was juror on an inquest apud Muskylburg, 1359 (RD., p. 267).

INVERKEILOR. From Inverkeilor, a village and parish in Angus. Robert de Inuerkileder witnessed a charter by Earl David, c. 1198 (LAC., 8), and p. 1180 a charter by Ingelramus de Balliol of the church of Inverkileder to the monks of Arbroath (RAA., I, p. 39). Robertus de Inuerkeledī, charter witness in Perth a. 1214, appears as sheriff of Moernes (Mearns) c. 1225 (ibid., p. 91, 149).

INVERKEITHING. Michael de Inverkethin was prior of Coldingham before 1389 (Pap. Pet., I, p. 573). John de Innerkeithin is recorded as burgess of Edinburgh in 1423 (LSC., p. 229). Of local origin from the town of Inverkeithing in Fife.

INVERLEITHEN. From Inverleithen, now Innerleithen in East Peeblesshire. Willelmus [persona] de Inverlethan witnessed William de Moreuille's charter of Gillemoristun to Edulfus filius Uctredi before 1196 (REG., p. 40).

INVERLOCHTY. Andrew of Inverlochtyn, one of an inquest concerning the king's garden at Elgin in 1261 (APS., I, p. 99 red), derived his name from Inverlochty near Elgin in Moray. William de Inuerlochty, son and heir of Thomas de Inuerlochty, had a charter from the bishop of Moray, c. 1299–1325 (REM., p. 147).

INVERNAIRN. From Invernairn, the old name for the town of Nairn. Magister Rogerus de Innernarryn witnessed a gift by Hugh Herock, burgess of Elgin, to the church of Elgin in 1286 (REM., p. 284). Adam de Invernary was perpetual vicar of Elgin in 1329 (Pap. Lett., II, p. 288).

INVERNESS. From the town of Inverness. John de Inuernys held a land in Inuernys, 1361 (REM., p. 305).

INVERNOCHTY. Of local origin from Invernochty, the former name of the parish of Strathdon, Aberdeenshire. Galfridus Innernochty in Aberdeen, 1408 (CWA., p. 312).

INVERPEFFER. From Inverpeffer in the parish of Panbride in Angus. The first of the name recorded is Walkelinus braciator ('the brewer') who had a charter of the lands of Inuerpefir from William the Lion, c. 1178–80 (RAA., I, p. 165). Nicholas de Inuirpefer, perhaps his son, witnessed a confirmation charter by Adam de Morham sometime about 1220 (ibid., I, p. 21), and is probably Nicholas de Inuerpeffvn or Inuerpephin, who witnessed other charters between 1219–40 (LAC., 15, 18; RAA., I, p. 265). Adam de Inrepeffre or Inverpeffree rendered homage in 1296 and had his lands restored to him (Bain, II, 730, 832, and p. 199). David de Enrepeffre of the county of Anegos also rendered homage in the same year (ibid., II, p. 207). Malcolm de Innerpeffer, sheriff of Clackmannan and Auchterarder in 1305, was sent as a prisoner of war to the Tower of London the following year for rebelling with Robert de Brus (ibid., II, 1691, 1858), and a later Malcum de Inverpeffri was canon of Dunblane in 1332 (Pap. Lett., II, p. 508). David de Inverpefer, juror in Angus in 1322 (RMS., I, App. I, 29), is probably David de Innerpefir "tunc locum tenente vicecomitis de Forfar" in 1333 (RAA., II, p. 13). A third part of the lands of Cragy were confirmed to Patric de Innerpefir in 1378 (Charters and writs of Dundee, p. 12). William de Enuerpeffir appears as prebendary of Lethnot in 1435 (REB., I, 76), and in 1456 there is reference to the land of Katherine Ennerphefyr in Glasgow (REG., 380). Others of the name are to be found in fourteenth century records in Banff, Clackmannan, Ross, and East Lothian. Now extinct?

INVERURIE. From Inverurie in the Garioch, Aberdeenshire. Thomas de Inuerowry was charter witness in Aberdeen, 1297 (REA., I, p. 38), J. Inuerory was admitted burgess there in 1400 (NSCM., I, p. 1), and W. Innerrory is recorded there, 1408 (CWA., p. 313).

IONGANTACH. A name given Cailin Maith or good Colin Campbell, a fourteenth-century worthy "because he was singular and odd in his Conceipts," (HP., II, p. 91). Giongantach, surprising, wonderful.

IRELAND. A family of this name is in record in Scotland in the last quarter of the thirteenth century. John Yberniens de Frertun was a witness in 1288 (RPSA., p. 346), and Patrick of Ireland, accused of housebreaking at Forfar, was hanged in 1296 (Bain, II, p. 190). David de Ireland was one of the Scots prisoners taken at Dunbar Castle in 1296; cattle belonging to Walter de Ibernia were driven

IRELAND, *continued*

off from a moor near Aberdeen in the same year; Robert de Irland of Stirlingshire rendered homage, 1296; and John de Irland (Hibernia) agreed to serve the king of England in France and elsewhere outwith England (ibid., II, p. 176, 192, 205, 243). Duncan, earl of Fife in 1336 granted a charter of the barony of Murthly, Perthshire, to John de Yrelande as held by his ancestors. The family, often called "de Hibernia," held Murthly till about 1440 (*Stodart*, II, p. 394). John de Irlande who held a land in Perth, 1424 (RMS., II; 18) may be the John Irland (without 'de') who was burgess there in 1437 (SCM., v, p. 261). Andrew Irland was a witness in Perth, 1478 (RAA., II, 202), and Walter Irland bailie there, 1488 (*Methven*, p. 31). Andrew Erland or de Ireland was a Scots merchant, 1450-51 (*Bain*, IV, 1230, 1240), Schyr Andro Irlande was vicar of Torreff (Turriff), 1489 (SCM., II, p. 259), William Yrlande, notary in Arbroath, 1502 (RAA., II, 438), Johannes Irland, vicar of Perth, 1524 (*Scon*, p. 205), Cuthbert Irland a follower of Campbell of Lundy, 1529 (RSS., II, 59), and Henry Airland in Strathconkie, 1602, is doubtless Henry Irland in Strahenrie, 1614 (*Fordell*, p. 160, 162). (2) In Roxburgh a family named Ireland held lands called Ireland's land in the barony of Wilton. In 1454 John of Irelandys of that Ilk, "in his urgent and known necessity" sold the lands to David Scott. Mathew Ireland was appointed doomster in Berwick and Roxburgh in 1524 (*Home*, 34). (3) The Irlands of Orkney are of local origin from Ireland (ON. *eyrr-land*, a gravelly beach), the largest township in the West Mainland. Thomas Arland appears in an agreement drawn up at Kirkwall in 1369 (*Diplomatarium Norvegicum*, I, p. 308). Master John Irland was chaplain in Wick, Caithness, 1530 (OPS., II, p. 752). A pedigree of the family of Ireland of Ireland is given in REO (p. 452-453). By the middle of the seventeenth century the family seems to have disposed of all their land, and the name is now believed to be extinct in the islands. For Ireland as a place name in Scotland see *Watson* I, p. 232-233.

IRNHOSE. Simon Irnhose was bailie of Lanark, 1410 (*Lanark*, p. 377). John de Irnhos was prebendary of Kambuslang, 1458 (REG., p. 408).

IRONGRAY. Henry Irngrey was charged at Carlisle in 1279 with having sold cloths *contra assisam* (*Bain*, II, p. 36). From Irongray, Dumfriesshire.

IRONPURSE. Alexander Irynpurs held land in Inuernys, 1361-65 (REM., p. 305, 317).

Lower says several individuals bore this surname in the reign of Edward I. In the English Hundred Rolls it is spelled Irenpurs, Irenpurse, etc.

IRONS. A surname confined mainly to Angus. Part of the vill of Baldovy was leased to David Yrnis or Irnys and Agnes his spouse 1485 and 1500 (RAA., II, p. 220, 407). William Irnis was tenant under the Abbey of Arbroath, 1506 (ibid., 452). Johannes Irnys, his wife and son, Jacobus Irnys, had a lease of part of the vill of Kynclune, 1535 (ibid., p. 526), and Sir James Irnis was notary public in Perth, 1546 (*Rollok*, 44). Eufamie Yrnis was spouse to John Farie in Dundee, 1586 (REB., II, 354), and Elizabeth Irons appears in Myresyde of Cannedy, parish of Meigle, 1690 (*Dunkeld*). Irones 1695, Yrnes 1526. See under THORNTON.

IRONSIDE. There is a place Ironside at New Deer, Aberdeenshire, and a farm called Earnside in Moray. At Black Ironside, or Earnside, near Newburgh, Fife, Wallace is said to have gained a victory over the English and drove them out of Fife. The surname most probably originated from the Aberdeenshire place. In the eighteenth century the surname was very common in the district of New Deer. Mage Irynsyd was banished from Aberdeen in 1570 (CRA., p. 368), Patrick Irnesyde in Tarnehill was a victim of the Aberdeen witches in 1597 (SCM., I, p. 133), and James Irnesyde, at the old mill of Foveran, was accused in 1627 of being an "idle and masterless man" (RPC.). Edmund Yrinsyde who witnessed a quit-claim of the land of Drumkarauch in 1260 (RPSA., p. 346) may have derived his name from Earnside near Newburgh. Thomas Ironside was a minor poet of the nineteenth century. Andrew Jamieson Ironside was a land surveyor in 1870, and four men named Ironside from Turriff and New Byth served in the first Great War (*Turriff*). Dr. G. E. Ironside, a native of Aberdeen, published the first Greek book printed in New York, the *Institutio Græcæ grammaticis*, 1817.

IRVINE, IRVING. Erewine and Erwinne are OE. personal names (*Searle*), and a Gilchrist filius Eruini witnessed a grant by Ranulfus filius Dunegal in Galloway between 1124-65. The surname, however, is of territorial origin: (1) from Irving, the name of an old parish in Dumfriesshire. There are many Irvings (or Irvines as most of the Dumfriesshire families spell the name) here. (2) from Irvine in Ayrshire. The Dumfriesshire parish however was the chief source of the name. Robert de Hirewine, a charter witness in 1226, is first of the name recorded. A charter by Gamelin, bishop of St. Andrews, c. 1260, is witnessed by Robert de Iruwyn (*Stodart*, II). John de Herwyne was a tenant under the Douglases in the barony of Buittle, 1376, and Gilchrist Herwynd was tenant in the parish of Morton in same year (RHM., I, p. lvii, lix). William de Irwyne, Clerk of Register, obtained the Forest of Drum, Aberdeenshire, in free barony from Robert I, 1324 (*Illus.*, III, p. 292), and was thus ancestor of the Irvines of Drum. In 1331 he had another charter of lands from Alexander, bishop of Aberdeen (REA., I, p. 52), and in 1332 provision was made of a canonry and prebend of Dunkeld to John de Irwyn (*Pap. Lett.*, II, p. 385).

"Gude Sir Alexander Irvine,
The much renownit Laird of Drum,"

fell in the battle of Harlaw in 1411. An offshoot of the Aberdeenshire family appears in Shetland in the middle of the sixteenth century. James Vrowing (as his name is spelled) was fined in 1602 "for bleiding of Jhone Leisk" in Dunrossness (Mill, *Diary*, p. 185). Adam Irvine, burgess of Irvine in 1455, doubtless derived his surname from residence there. The Boneshaw family of Irvine was considered by Act of Parliament in 1587 as chief family of the name. Washington Irving (1783–1859), the American author, was son of William Irving, a native of Shapinsay, Orkney. In the North of Ireland the name has become confused with Ir. Erwin from *OhEireamhoin.* Eirryn, Erevein 1587, Erwine 1432, Erwing, Erwyn 1445, Erwyne 1438, Hurven, Irewing, Irewyne 1519, Irrewin 1550, Irrewine 1568, Irrewing 1572, Irruwing, Irrwin, Irrwing, Iruin 1602, Iruyn 1514, Iruyne 1493, Irvein 1534, Irveing 1679, Irveyn, Irvin, Irving, Irvinge 1641, Irvinn, Irvying 1596, Irvyn 1500, Irwan, Irwen, Irwing, Irwyng 1593, Irwynn, Urwen 1547, Urwin, Urwing 1576, Urwyng 1571, Vruing 1624, Vruving 1568, Vrwin 1567, Wrwing 1566, Yirewing 1576, Yrewing 1586, Yrwen 1592, Yrwin, Yrwing 1424. *Plural*: Eurwings, Irrewings, Irrwingis, Ivyerins, Irwaynes, Irwenis, Irwingis, Irwynnis, Urewens, Yrwens, Yrwins. There are many spellings in index to REO.

IRVINGSON, 'son of IRVINE,' q.v. Erasmus Irvingson in Middaill, parish of Waiss, 1613, and other two of the name *(Shetland).* Bartill Irwingsone in Gewing, a charter witness, 1623 (OSS., I, 8). An offshoot of the Aberdeen family of Irvine appears in Shetland in the middle of the sixteenth century.

ISAAC. From the Hebrew *yishāq*, 'he laugheth,' the name given to the son of Abraham and Sarah from the circumstances of his birth.

"A well-known personal name in the surname period, but no more confined to the Jews than Adam or Abel. Hundreds of English people bear one or other of these surnames in whose veins there flows not a single drop of Jewish blood" (*Bardsley*). The name was not uncommon among ecclesiastics in the twelfth and thirteenth centuries. Isaac was prior of Scone from 1154 till 1162 (*Annals*, p. 68), and Magister Isaac was a cleric of St. Andrews, 1201 (ibid., p. 334). Ysaac of Brechin was a charter witness there c. 1178–98 (REB., II, 257), and Ysaac de Banevin (Benvie) was one of a jury regarding the Kirketun of Aberbuthenoth, 1205 (SCM., v, p. 210). Isaac, son of Samuel, was one of the witnesses to the gift by Walter, son of Alan, to the monks of Scon, c. 1214 (*Scon*, p. 91), and Isaac, burgess of Aberbrothoc, witnessed a charter by Matilda, countess of Anegus c. 1242–43 (RAA., I, p. 82). Isaac of Scone witnessed a quit-claim of the land of Drumkarauch in 1260 (RPSA., p. 346), and Gillandes Macysac witnessed a charter in favor of the priory of Beauly in 1231 (*Beauly*, p. 33). 'Sir' Thomas Isaac was a witness in Edinburgh in 1358 (*Bain*, IV, 17), Andrew Isak of Scotland had a safe conduct into England in 1405, John Ysaac had a safe conduct to pass to France in 1447 (ibid., 687, 1203), and Thomas Esok was canon of a church of Argyll in 1448 (HP., II, p. 182). Thomas Esak was messenger-at-arms for Dunbartane in 1569 (RPC., I, p. 659). Jonet Isack was a witch in Kilwinning, 1662 (HP., III, p. 25), and in 1671 a charge of usury was brought against Robert Isack in Kirkcaldy (*Just. Rec.*, II, p. 55). "A certain squire named Thomas Isaac" married Matilda, daughter of King Robert Bruce (Fordun, *Annals*, clxix). Concerning this singular mésalliance the late eminent genealogist, Mr. Alexander Sinclair, writes: "The name was not so low as it seemed. It was disguised into Ysac, Ysaac, and de Ysaac to make it appear noble . . . This individual not long after had his name borne by gentry bearing the same name with coat armour, in the south of England. In Devonshire there were Isaacs of Buriat, temp. Henry III, who bore Sable, a bend or, on a canton argent a leopard's face gules. In 1460 there was also John Isaac of Bekesbourne, sheriff of Kent, who had the same arms, but the leopard's face or. Probably Thomas, the lucky adventurer, was connected with one of these old families" (*Herald and genealogist*, VI, p. 594). Isaac, clericus, was bailie and burgess of Aberdeen in 1332 (ER., I, p. 427). Eizack 1694.

ISAACSON, 'son of ISAAC,' q.v. Henry Isakisone in Huie in Unst, 1648 *(Shetland).*

ISABELSON, 'son of Isabel.' Geoffray Isabel-sone of Berwickshire, rendered homage, 1296 (*Bain*, II, p. 207).

ISBISTER. An Orcadian surname of local origin. There is an Isbister in the parish of Rendall, another in Birsay, a third in South Ronaldsay, and still other two in Northmavine and Whalsay in Shetland. The surname, however, comes "from none of these, but from a portion of the large township of Grimeston in Harray, once known (though not in the rentals) as the town of Isbister" (*Old Lore Misc.*, v, p. 32). Robert Ysbuster, who was a witness in Harray in 1557, appears again in 1565 as Robert Ysbister of that Ilk, Malkom Eysbuster was bailie of Harray in 1607, and Huchoun Isbister and Adam Isbister were witnesses in Kirkwall in 1610 (REO., p. 108, 120, 178, 184). Four persons named Ysebuster were members of the bailie court of Stenness, 1576, and Malcolm Yisbuster was bailie of Harray, 1605 (OSR., I, p. 269, 275).

ISDAILE. *See under* EASDAILE.

ISETT. *See under* IZAT.

ITERSON. *See under* OUTERSON.

ITHANE. William de Ithane, witness in an Aberdeen document of 1439 (CRA., p. 6) derived his name from Ythan in Aberdeenshire.

ITHARNAN. Tighernach records that Itharnan died among the Picts, A. D. 669. He is not mentioned in the Irish Calendars. He gave name to Killearnan in Ross-shire, and there was a chapel of his in the old monastic church on the Isle of May.

IVAR. In Gaelic spelling *Imhaer* and *Iomhar*, a borrowing of the ON. personal name *Ivarr*. It was a favorite forename with the Camp-bells of Strachur, and the name of Ivar Camp-bell of Strachur (in the first half of the sixteenth century) appears in contemporary documents as Evar, Euer, Evir, Ewar, Iver, Ure, Urie, Yvar, Yvir (HP., IV, index). Other recorded spellings are: Euar 1349, Ever 1478, Iwur 1326, Ywar 1359. It has been also erroneously rendered Eugenius (HP., IV, p. 11). Ivar or Ivarr was a favorite name of the Danish kings of Dublin in the ninth and tenth centuries. See MACIVER.

IVERACH. From the adjectival form of Mac-iver (*Iamharach*). Jonet Ivirach appears in Rangak, Caithness, in 1661 (*Caithness*), and Lachlan McKivirrich is in record in 1682 (IDR., p. 106). Rev. James Iverach (1839–1922), D.D., born in Caithness, was Principal

of the Aberdeen Free Church College. See also IVORY.

IVET. From Ive or Ivo, q.v. + diminutive -*et*. Adam filius Iuette witnessed gift of the church of Cupre by Richard, bishop of St. Andrews, a. 1173 (RPSA., p. 137). Johannes Juet (J = I) witnessed a charter by Alan, the sacrist, of land in Glasgow, c. 1300 (REG., p. 216). Malt was bought from William, son of Iuete, 1329 (ER., I, p. 189), and Patrick Yvat was slain in Tane (Tain), 1583 (HMC., 2. *Rep.*, *App.*, p. 179).

IVISON. Son of Ivo, q.v., a common early personal name. Found in England in 1273 (*Bardsley*).

IVO. A common personal name in the Middle Ages, in ME. *Ive*, *Ivo*, *Yvo* (in DB. *Ivo*). It means 'yew' (the tree which was formerly used for making bows). Ivo, a vassal of the Bruces, received a grant of the lands of Kirk-patrick in Dumfriesshire, and took his name from them. In another charter, slightly later in date, he appears as Ivo de Kirkpatrick (see KIRKPATRICK). He may have been the Iuone (= Ivone) who witnessed a charter by Eschina domina de Molle, c. 1165–77. Iuo or Hyuo was a clerk of Morebattle between 1201–05 (*Melros*, p. 105, 107, 109), and Ivo was the name of a Friar Preacher of Ayr, 1261–66 (*Pap. Lett.*, I, p. 385, 423).

IVORY. From Gaelic *Iamharach* (Iverach), the adjectival form of *MacIamhair*, i.e. MAC-IVER, q.v. The name has also reached Orkney. Sir James Ivory (1765–1842), mathematician, and James Ivory (1792–1866), Lord Ivory, judge, were two distinguished bearers of the name.

IZAT, IZATT, ISETT. Alexander Ezat was witness in Culross, 1569 (*Laing*, 845), and Thomas Essat, messenger in Kilwinning, 1577 (*Irvine*, I, p. 221). Jeanna Easet was retoured heir portioner of Thomas Easet in Kilwinning, 1599 (*Retours*, *Ayr*, 20), and George Izat was admitted burgess of Glasgow, 1630 (*Burgesses*). George Izat, shipmaster in Kincardine, 1785 (*Dunblane*). Seven persons of the name Ezat or Eizat are recorded in the neighborhood of Culross and Tulliallan in the seventeenth and eighteenth centuries (ibid.). The name is explained as later forms of Isoud, Ysolde (Ysoude), or Iseult, daughter of the duke of Brittany and wife of Tristram of the Arthurian legend. Esat 1621, Eyzatt and Ezatt 1644.

JACK. Now considered a variant of John, but more correctly of James, from French Jacques, pronounced 'zhak.' As a forename we have Jak Donaldson in Cowpar Grange, 1453 and

Jak Richardson in 1469 (*Cupar-Angus*, I, p. 129, 154). Wil. Jak was tenant of the mill of Kethek in 1473 (ibid., I, p. 178), and Duncan Jak appears as a charter witness in Dundee in 1480 (HP., II, p. 187). Gilbert Jak was a resident of Vddynston in 1498 (REG., 478–479), John Jak held a tenement in Glasgow before 1498 (ibid., p. 500), and Katherine Jak in Stirling was charged with assault in 1545 (SBR., p. 40). Richard Jak in Auld Roxburghe was beheaded for slaughter in 1502 (*Trials*, I, p. 27*), and Robert Jack, merchant and burgess of Dundee was "hangit and quarterit for false coin called Hardheads whilk he had brought out of Flanders" in December, 1567 (Birrel, *Diary*). William Jak who was admitted burgess of Aberdeen in 1554 (NSCM., I, p. 64) may be the William Jak who was "admittit maister of Saint Thomas Hospitall" there in 1580 (CRA., p. 39), and possibly the Wilyem Jaik who was elected deacon of the kirk of Aberdeen in the same year (SCM., II, p. 54). Thomas Jack, who was master of the Grammar School of Glasgow before 1574, Latinized his name Jacchaeus. The ship of Andro Jaik of Aberdeen was lost in 1577 (SCM., II, p. 47). Peter Jak held a feu in Scone in 1586 (*Scon*, p. 232), and Jonet Jak is in record in Kyndrochat in 1589 (REB., II, 227). The surname was not uncommon in Aberdeen in the seventeenth century (*Retours, Aberdeen*, 303, 304). Cf. JACQUE.

JACKSON, 'son of JACK,' q.v. This surname is more English than Scottish, as it has never been popular in Scotland. In the Middle Ages Jack was more often used as a diminutive of James than of John, so that really the name is correctly 'son of James,' the Latin form of which is *Jacobus*, in French *Jacques* (pron. zhak). William Jacson was admitted burgess of Aberdeen in 1409 (NSCM., I, p. 3), and William Jaksone, burgess of Glasgow in 1447, is mentioned again in 1454 as Wylly Jaksone (LCD., p. 168, 178), and perhaps again in 1467 as William Jacsoun, sergeand (*Scots Lore*, p. 105). Thomas Jaksoun was tenant in Grange of Balbrogy, 1468, Ranald Jakson, tenant of Kersegrange, 1478 (*Cupar-Angus*, I, p. 143, 212), and David Jaksone was summoned in 1479 to answer to parliament for treason and other crimes (APS., II, p. 129). Henry Jacsone was a brother of the order of Friars Preachers of Aberdeen in 1486 (REA., II, p. 300), Thomas Jackson is in record in Dysart in 1540 (*Dysart*, p. 6), and Nicholas Jaxsone rendered to Exchequer the accounts of the bailie of the burgh of Renfrew in 1558 (ER., XIX, p. 42). Jacksone 1600, Jackstoin 1689.

JACOB. From the Hebrew personal name *Ya' kob-el*, said to mean 'God watches over' (*Montgomery*). The name was popular on the continent in the Middle Ages. Alan Jacob was burgess of Dundee, 1321 (HP., II, p. 225), and William Jacob was bailie there in 1348 (RAA., II, 22).

JACQUE. Gideon Jacque was admitted to charge at Liberton near Edinburgh, 1692 (*Fasti*, I, p. 172; VII, p. 530). From *Jacque(s)*, the French form of Jacobus. Cf. JACK.

JAFFRAY, JAFFREY, JAFFERY, JEFFRAY, JEFFREY, JEFFEREY, JEFFRY, JEFFREYS. From *Geoffroi*, the NF. form of OE. *Godfrith*. Jaffray was an old family name in Aberdeen. Symon le fiz Geffrai and Piers le fiz Geffray, burgesses of Peebles, rendered homage in 1296 (*Bain*, II, p. 198). Payment was made to David Geoffrey, Scottish merchant, for injuries and trespasses committed on him in 1474 (*Bain*, IV, 1412), John Joffray appears as witness, 1511 (*Soltre*, p. 84), and a later John Jofra was witness in Brechin in 1552 (REB., I, 233). William Joffra held a tenement in Linlithgow in 1536 (*Johnsoun*), Alexander Joffray was bailie of Edinburgh, 1596, and Alexander Jaffray, bailie of Aberdeen, purchased the estate of Kingswells in 1587. Robert Japhra, smith in Windiege, parish of Monkland, 1605 (*Campsie*). Alexander Jaffray was chosen provost of Aberdeen in January, 1636, on which Spalding says: "Many lichtleit both the man and the election," he "not being of the old blood of the toun, but the oy (grandson) of ane baxter, and therefor was set doun in the Prouest's deass befor his entering, ane baken pye, to sermon. This was done diverse times; but he miskend all and never quarreled the samen" (*Memorials*, Bann. Club ed., I, p. 40). Rev. John Jaffray was first Episcopal minister of Lonmay, Aberdeenshire, after the establishment of Presbyterianism (AEI., p. 64). Jafra 1629, Jafrey 1687, Jafrai c. 1613, Jalfray 1652, Japhrae 1718, Japhray 1618, Jofray 1583.

JAFFRAYSON. "Son of JAFFRAY," q.v. An old Aberdeen surname. Richard le fiz Geffrai de Ekford, Roxburghshire, rendered homage in 1296 (*Bain*, II, p. 203), and Jon Joffrayson of Turyne was one of the surveyors of the marches of Woodwrae, 1388 (*Bamff*, p. 22). James Jaffraysoun appears as a forestaller in Aberdeen in 1402 (CRA., p. 383), and James Jaffrason, John Joffraison, and James Jofrasone were admitted burgesses of Aberdeen in 1409, 1445, and 1488 (NSCM., I, p. 4, 10, 33). John Jaffraison is mentioned in connection with burgh affairs in Aberdeen in 1448 (CRA., p. 17). Alexander Galfridi in Brechin, 1435,

JAFFRAYSON, *continued*
and John Galfridi there 1450 (REB., I, 79, 159). Alexander Joffrasoun was a witness in Brechin in 1476 (REB., I, p. 199), and another Alexander Joffrason was burgess of Stirling in 1481 (*Cambus.*, 211). Robert Jofrasone had a lease of part of the vill of Grangie [i.e. Grange] de Connane, 1501 (RAA., II, p. 338). Jofrasoun 1512, Joffrayson 1408.

JAGGER. Finlay Jager, son of quondam Radulphus Jager, and Andreas, his son, were burgesses of Glasgow, c. 1290 (REG., p. 198–200). Dr. Jagger of Pencaitland was married, 1939. The name is not uncommon in Yorkshire (West Riding). "A North English and Scots word for a peddler, carter, teamster."

JAMES. From the personal name. Three persons named James took an active part in the foundation of the early Christian church: (1) James the Elder, (2) James the Younger, or the Little, and (3) James the Great. St. James was the patron saint of the Fitzalans, hence doubtless the popularity of the name among the Stewart kings, and Gaelic SEUMAS, q.v. The current surname probably of recent introduction from England.

JAMESON. *See under* JAMIESON.

JAMIE. A current surname in Aberdeen. A diminutive of JAMES, q.v. Robert Jame, burgess of Linlithgow, 1537 (*Johnsoun*). Elizabeth Jamie in Scheills, parish of Kilbryde, 1623 (*Campsie*), and Gilbert Jamie in Crawfurdjohn, 1623 (*Lanark CR.*).

JAMIESON, JAMESON, 'son of JAMES.' A family named Jamieson or Neilson held the office of Crowner of Bute from the beginning of the fourteenth century or earlier to the seventeenth century. Alexander Jemison had a safe conduct to trade with England in 1445 (*Bain*, IV, 1178), William Jamyson was tenant of Pollock, 1472 (*Cupar-Angus*, I, p. 221), and John Jamesone was repledged to liberty of the burgh of Irvine in the same year (*Irvine*, I, p. 28). Robert Jacobi was citizen of Brechin, 1493 (REB., II, 138), and Schir Symond Jameson was 'wiccar pencionar of Mathy' in 1497 (*Cupar-Angus*, I, p. 251). Fergus Jacobi, 'coronator de But' (Bute) in 1501, is mentioned in the same document as Fergus Jamisone (LCD., p. 205). John Jamvson was admitted burgess of Aberdeen, 1465 (NSCM., I, p. 19), David Jameson was dompnus of Newbattle Abbey, 1528 (*Neubotle*, p. 309), John Jamezing was respited for his share in the slaughter of John, erle of Cathnes, 1539 (RSS., II, 3151), and c. 1550 William Jamesoune in Aberdeen was paid 'to mend the

keyheid' (SCM., v, p. 51). Jamysone 1477, Jimessone 1631.

JAPP. David Yeap (Jape, Yape) was a charter witness in Perth in the reign of Alexander II (*Scon*, p. 52, 55, 58). As David Yep he witnessed a charter by William de Lavcestria, 1240 (*Inchaffray*, p. 62). John Jape was a skinner and burgess of Glasgow, 1584 (*Burgesses*); Alexander Jaip was a feltmaker in Edinburgh, 1672 (*Edinb. Marr.*); and Walter Jap is recorded in Fordell, 1699 (*Inquis.*, 8107). Collin Jap and John Jap appear in the parish of Dumbennan, 1716 (SCM., IV, p. 170); and Mathew Jaap, merchant in Stewarton, 1707, appears again in the same year as Jop (*Corsehill*). Cf. JOB and JOPP.

JAPPIE, JAPPY. Believed to be modern diminutives of JAPP, q.v. In Buchan, east of the Burn, there were in one small community of fisherfolk twenty-nine Jappys (Barclay, *Banffshire*, p. 68).

JARDIN, JARDINE, 'Of the garden,' from residence bv one. The first of the name in Scotland is Winfredus (*sic*, Wmfredus) de Jardine who flourished before 1153, and witnessed charters by David I to the abbevs of Kelso and Arbroath (*Dumfries and Galloway Nat. Hist. and Ant. Soc., Trans.*, 1891–92, p. 48). Umfrid de Jardin witnessed a charter by Robert de Bruvs to the Abbey of Arbroath, c. 1178–80 (RAA., I, 37), and as Humphrey del Gardin witnessed confirmation of a fishery in Torduf c. 1194–1211 (*Holm Cultram*, p. 35). Patrick de Gardinus was cleric to the bishop of Glasgow c. 1200 (*Kelso*, 148), and Sir Humphrey de Gardino witnessed a resignation of lands in Annandale a. 1245 (*Bain*, I, 1682). Jordan del Orchard of the county of Linlescu (Linlithgow) rendered homage, 1296. His seal bears a tree, S' *Jordani d' Gardino* (*Bain*, II, p. 201, 218, 533). William de Gardino had a grant of the lands and barony of Hertishuvde (Hartside) in Lanark from David II (RMS., I, App. II, 1014). John Jardin or Jarding of Applegarth granted a charter to George Hume of Wedderburn in 1476 (*Home*, 23). William Jarden was master of a family in the parish of Buittle, 1684 (RPC., 3. ser. IX, p. 569), Jean Gerdain was servitrix to the marchioness of Douglas, 1712 (*Lanark CR.*), and Mr. Andrew Gerden, minister in Annandale, 1777 (*Dumfries*). Sir William Jardine (b. 1800) wrote several works on natural history. See also GARDYNE. Jardane 1609, Jardein 1643, Jerden 1698.

JARGOUN(?). Robertus Jargun witnessed a sale of land in Glasgow, c. 1280–90 (REG., p. 98). Jhone Jargowne, tenant in barony of

Glasgow, 1515 (*Rental*) may be the John Jargoune in the parish of Govane, 1524 (LCD., p. 80). Jargawnne 1564 (in Glasgow).

JARRATT. A late form of GERARD, q.v.

JARROW. A current surname. From Jarrow-on-Tyne. Bede (IV, 6, 19) mentions a tribe or people (*Gyruii*) between Mercia and East Anglia. See under JARUM.

JARUM. From Jarrow-on-Tyne, old spellings of which are: In Gyruum (c. 750, Bede), Gyruum (1125), Jarou (1345), Jarrow (1396). Walter de Jarum witnessed a confirmation charter by Symon Loccard to the Abbey of Kelso c. 1180 (*Kelso*, 333). William de Jarum of Roxburghshire and Peres de Jarum, parson of Killos in Dumfriesshire, rendered homage, 1296 (*Bain*, II, p. 202, 212). Rogier de Jar' [Jarum] del counte de Lanark, and Thomas de Jar', provender del eglise de Ros, also rendered homage, 1296 (ibid., p. 204, 214).

JARVIE. A diminutive of Jarvis for Gervas (Gervase), a ME. personal name. Thom Jarva appears in Stirling, 1527 (SBR., p. 31), Edward Jarvey in Powhous, 1633 (*Inquis.*, 1983), Robert Jarvie, workman in Lessuden, 1693 (*Peebles CR.*), and John Jervie in Falkirk, 1689 (RPC., 3. ser. XIV, p. 226). In Scott's *Rob Roy* Bailie Nicol Jarvie was a Glasgow tradesman and magistrate.

JASSIMINE. A variant of JESSIEMAN, q.v.

JEANS. A surname recorded in Moray, and perhaps the same as Janes formerly current in Aberdeenshire. Macbain (v, p. 31) suggests it is a metronymic form from Jean = John. Agnes Jenis, spouse to William Tullo in Kynclune, is in record, 1510 (RAA., II, p. 395). It might be local from the place name Geanies, the earliest recorded form of which was Genes. Ingeramous de Genes appears as witness at Berwick, 1275, and he probably derived his name from Guines near Calais, an old spelling of which was Gynes. See GYNES.

JEDBURGH. Of local origin from the town of the name in Roxburghshire. Several individuals or families of the name appear in the thirteenth and fourteenth centuries. Robert de Giwrth was one of the witnesses to a charter of the lands of Molle, c. 1225–35 (RMP., p 77). Robert de Jeddeworthe, parson of the church of Kermyghkel (Carmichael) of the county of Lanark rendered homage in 1296. His seal bears a priest robed holding the sacrament(?), and S' Rob'ti de[g]edewrd cl'ic(?) (*Bain*, II, p. 210, 558.). About the year 1300 Vedastus de Jeddeword

held lands off the monks of Melrose (*Melros*, p. 684), and in 1343 Thomas de Jedworth was a monk in the Abbey of Melrose (ibid., p. 424). In 1358 Robert of Jedworth received a safe conduct to travel in England for a year (*Rot. Scot.*, I, p. 823), and Hugh of Jedworth was *actornatus* (attorney) of the prior of St. Andrews in 1390. The seal of Patrick Jedworth of Gamvlschelis, 1464, is described by Macdonald (1434).

JEFFRAY, JEFFREY, JEFFEREY, JEFFRY, JEFFREYS. Assimilated forms of Geoffrey. See under JAFFRAY.

JELLIE, JELLY. Thomas Jelle held a tenement in Ayr, 1518 (*Friars Ayr*, p. 81), and William Jellie is recorded in Cruikens, parish of Carnwath, 1673 (*Lanark CR.*). Andrew Jellie and his wife were residents in the parish of Borgue, 1684 (RPC., 3. ser. IX, p. 567), and William Jelly a mariner in Creetown, 1798 (*Kirkcudbright*).

JELLYBRAND. *See under* GELLIBRAND.

JENKIN. This surname may be of Flemish origin as we know that many people of that race entered Scotland. John Junkin or Junkyn, senior and junior, were tenants in Birnie, Moray, 1565 (REM., p. 441), John Jenkin, maltman, was burgess of Glasgow, 1584 (*Burgesses*), and Bartholomew Junkyne was admitted burgess of Aberdeen, 1607 (NSCM., I, p. 104). David Jonkene in Balbarny was juror on inquest, 1617, concerning the extent of the boundaries of Brechin and of Navar (*Inquis. Valorum*, 10), Archibald Jenking or Jeinking, tailor in Hamilton, 1637 (*Campsie*), Robert Jeynkene retoured heir in tenement in Hamilton, 1646 (*Retours, Lanark*, 222), and Agnes Junkine in Kingorne, 1648 (PBK., p. 322). John Junkein, son of David Junkein, merchant burgess of Edinburgh, 1650 (*Inquis.*, 3610), George Jinkin in Aberdeen, 1653 (*Strathbogie*, p. 244), John Juncken in Pettindreich, 1688 (*Moray*), and Mr. Robert Junkine was minister at Abernethy, 1689 (RPC., 3. ser. XIV, p. 289).

JENNER. An aphetic form of ME. *engynour*, 'engineer,' one who operated engines of war. Early forms of the name in England are L'Ingenieur, Le Geneur, Gynner, etc. Anneys la Gynnere del counte de Berewyk rendered homage, 1296 (*Bain*, II, p. 212). In 1392 there is reference to the tenement of Alan Gynowr in Edinburgh (*Egidii*, p. 27), Patrik Genour held lands in Inverness in 1452 (*Invernessiana*, p. 122), umquhile Thomas Genor is referred to in 1492 (RSS., I), Donald Jenor, 'legislator,' is mentioned in 1499 (*Cawdor*, p. 101), William Genour was tenant of the

JENNER, *continued*

Casteltoun, Ardmanoch in 1504 (ER., XII, p. 661), and John Jenour had sasine of his father's lands in the lordship of Ardmanacht in 1564 (ibid., XIX, p. 523). The spelling JUNOR occurs in Inverness.

JERDAN. A variant of JARDINE, q.v. Jon Jerdein was tenant on land of Neubotle Abbey, 1563 (*Neubotle*, p. 326). Andrew Jerdon was burgess of Jedburgh, 1659 (RRM., I, p. 244), Andrew Jerdan was gardener at Paston, 1770 (*Heirs*, 353), and William Jerdan (1782–1869), journalist, was born at Kelso, Roxburghshire. David Jerdan printed in Dalkeith 1850 and 1852 the gospel of St. John and the Book of Jonah translated into the Efik language of Old Calabar.

JEROMSON, 'son of Jerome.' A Shetland surname. S. Jerome (Lat. *Hieronymus*), one of the four great Latin Fathers, prepared the Vulgate version of the Bible.

JERVIS, JERVISE. Forms of the personal name Gervase. William dictus Geruavs, clerk, 1287 (CMN., 23) may be William fiz Gervays who rendered homage, 1296 (*Bain*, II, p. 205). William Jarves, witness, 1565 (RPC., I, p. 329), and another William Jarves was cottar in Wundishor, 1583 (*Brechin*), and Thomas Jarves appears in Baldutho, 1670 (*Inquis.*, 5315). Andrew Jervise (1820–1878) was a distinguished local antiquary and historian. Gerwes. Cf. JARVIE.

JESSIEMAN, JESSIMAN, JASSIMINE, JESSAMINE. Perhaps local from Jesmond, Newcastle-on-Tyne, spelled Gesmond in 1414, Jessemond in 1449, and Jasemond in 1772. John Jesseman and William Jessieman are recorded in the lordship of Huntly, 1600 (SCM., IV, p. 262, 265). James Jessimen in Westertoun, 1654 (*Strathbogie*, p. 254), John Jessieman in Drumdelgie, parish of Bollerie, 1710 (*Moray*), James Jessyman and John Jessyman in the parish of Dumbennan, 1716 (SCM., IV, p. 171), Ann Jessamin appears in Aberdeen, 1770 (*Aberdeen CR.*), and John Jessiman and Thomas Jessiman were members of the Huntly Volunteers, 1798 (*Will*, p. 7). Alexander Jessamine of Gretna died 1937.

JOASS. See under JOSS.

JOB. A common personal name in England in the Middle Ages, which does not necessarily point to Semitic origin. It was early softened to Jopp in the north of England and in Scotland.

JOBSON, 'son of Job.' Janet Jobsone in Edinburgh, 1618 (*Edinb. Marr.*), Andrew Jobson

was portioner of Wolfclyde, parish of Culter, 1650 (*Lanark CR.*), and David Jobson was writer in Dundee, 1791 (*Brechin*).

JOCELIN. A double diminutive from Josse, for the Breton saint-name *Jodoc* or *Judoc* (from Breton *jud*, 'fighter'; Latinized *Jodocus*). Jodocus (†669), an Armorican prince of Welsh extraction, became a hermit at Ponthieu, where he is still remembered as S. Josse. In Cornwall he is commemorated as S. Just. Jocelin or Goscelin was elected bishop of Glasgow in 1174 and died 1199 (*Dowden*, p. 298–299). Gocelinus, archdeacon of Dunkeld, c. 1188 (*Scon*, p. 27; RAA., I, p. 141). Gilbert, son of Jocelinus or Goscelinus, burgess of Aberdeen, c. 1189–99 (RAA., I, p. 57, 136). Jocelin hostiarius to King William the Lion, a. 1214 (RAA., I, p. 260). Gocelin de Balliol, brother of John Balliol, in record, 1260 (LAC., p. 152). William Gocelyn of Scotland rendered homage, 1296 (*Bain*, II, p. 203). GOCELYN is a variant spelling of the name.

JOEL. From the OF. personal name *Johel*, well evidenced in ME. records. William and Alexander, sons of Joel (Johel, Juhel, or Yuel), were burgesses of Perth in the reign of Alexander II (*Scon*, p. 52, 58, 62). Cf. YELL.

JOHALDSTOUN. Local. Thomas of Johaldstoun witnessed an instrument of sasine, 1476 (*Home*, 22).

JOHN. From Heb. *Jehohhan* through Greek *Iōannes*, Lat. *Ioannes*, is in G. *Iain*.

JOHNMAN. A surname recorded in central Scotland may be intended as an Englishing of MACIAN, q.v.

JOHNSON, 'son of JOHN,' q.v. Wautier Jonessone of Berwickshire rendered homage in 1296 (*Bain*, II, p. 207), and William Jonessone, merchant of Aberdeen, complained that his goods shipped in a Flemish vessel had been arrested at Grymesby in 1368 (*ibid.*, IV, 146). John Johnson (filz Johan), a Scot going abroad, had protection through England in 1371, Adam Jonesson, a Scots prisoner of war, was discharged from Newgate prison in 1375, Richard Johanson, servant of the duke of Albany had safe conduct into England in 1401, and Johan Joneson the same in 1422 (ibid., 195, 227, 584, 914). Malcolm Jonis was one of the prominent men of Orkney in 1427 (*Oppressions*, p. 108), and William Johannis (the Latin genitive) witnessed a Montrose charter of 1430 (REB., II, 34). The garden of Paulus Johannis in Glasgow is referred to in 1454 (LCD., p. 176), Alexander Johnson of Aberdeen received letters of denisation in England, 1480

(*Bain*, IV, 1465), Sir Nicholays Johannis, perpetual chaplain of the altar of Holy Cross, Brechin, 1493, appears in the same document as Sir Nicholas Johnson (REB., II, 137), and Thomas Jonsoun was burgess of Ayr in 1503 (*Friars Ayr*, p. 70). Some MACIANS, q.v., have Englished their name Johnson. The northern (Caithness) Johnsons are descended from John, third son of George Gunn, the Crowner. Johnnesson 1424, Johnnessone 1530, Johnseun 1565, Jonson 1422, Jonsone 1510.

JOHNSTON, JOHNSTONE. Shortly after 1174 John the founder of the family of Johnstone, gave his name to his lands in Annandale, Dumfriesshire, whence his son Gilbert took his surname. "Who John, the father of Gilbert, was it is now perhaps impossible to determine. He may have been a native settler who, when the Bruces were made lords of Annandale, elected to hold his lands from them, or, as seems most likely, he followed his overlords from their Yorkshire, or more southern, estates, and was gifted with the lands to which he gave his name, and which, later, formed the parish and barony of Johnstone" (*Sc. Peer.*, I, p. 231). Gilbert, son of John, appears in charters granted by William, lord of Annandale, 1195–1215. Within the same period he is also styled Gilbertus de Jonistoune, "thus in a brief space showing both the patronymic and the territorial surname" (ibid., p. 230). Gilbert, son of John, witnessed a charter by William Bruce to Adam de Carlyle between 1194 and 1214, and as Gillebertus de Jonistune he witnessed a charter of the lands of Pennersaughs within the same period (*Annandale*, I, p. 2, 3). Robertus de Jonistoun witnessed a charter by Gilbert of Glencarny to Duncan of Feryndrawcht, c. 1281–98 (*Grant*, III, p. 7). Johan de Jonestone, knight of the county of Dunfrys, Gilbert de Jonestone of Dumfriesshire, and Thomas de Jonestone of Roxburghshire, rendered homage, 1296. The seal of Johan shows a shield with two garbs (?) and a canton dexter over a third; charges indistinct, S' *Iohis de Ionestone militis*, while the seal of Gilbert is a gem bearing a head in profile, S' *Gilberti de Ionestovn* (*Bain*, II, p. 185, 200, 202, 549). Stephen de Johnston, called the Clerk, said to have been a younger brother of the laird of Annandale, was secretary to Thomas, earl of Mar who died in 1377 (*Inverurie*, p. 453). Aye (= Adam) Jonson was present at the perambulation of the bounds of Kyrknes and Louchor, 1395 (RPSA., p. 3), and William Jonson of Mourthull was one of the assizors on the marches of Woodwrae, 1388 (*Bamff*, p. 22). Andrew Johnson (? for Johnston) called "Schaklok" was admitted burgess of Aberdeen, 1436 (NSCM., I, p. 4), and Adam

of Jonstoun was one of the conservators of the truce between Scotland and England, 1451 (*Bain*, IV, 1239). John Johnston alias Jonston, a native of the vill of Jonstone in Scotland, received letters of denization in England, 1463, and Adam of Johnston, Robin of Johnston, Gilbert of Johnston, and Mathewe of Johnstone, who petitioned for safe conducts to travel in England in the same year (*Bain*, IV, 1335, 1340), probably derived their surnames from Perth which was often named Johnstoun or St. Johnstoun in record. Another territorial family of Johnstones took their name from the lands of Jonystoun, now Johnstonburn, an estate in the parish of Humbie, East Lothian. Hugh de Jonystoun witnessed a charter of these lands to the House of Soltre (Soutra), c. 1250 (*Soltre*, p. 31). Between 1296 and 1324 John de Jonystoun "quondam filius Hugonis de Jonystoun" resigned to Soltre "totam terram meam de Jonystoun cum omnibus libertatibus et aysiamentis" (ibid., p. 40). Robert Johnston alias "Ding the Devill" in record, 1609 (RPC., VIII, p. 778). In former days the Johnstones formed one of the most powerful and turbulent clans of the West Border, and were at constant feud with their neighbors, especially the Maxwells, hence probably their ironical description, "the gentle Johnstones." Jhonestowne 1609, Jhonstoun 1616, Johanstoun 1450, Johnestoun 1493, Johnestoune 1530, Johngston 1736, Johnnesone 1530, Johnnestoun 1608, Johnnestoune 1558, Johnnstoun 1503, Johnstounne 1575, Joneston 1245, Jonhesone 1491, Jonhstone 1499, Joniston 1329, Jonstoun 1683.

JOINER. A variant of JENNER, q.v., influenced by the occupative name 'joiner.' Alexander Joyner in Aberdeen, 1798 (*Aberdeen CR.*).

JOINSON. A north English form of Johnson. Donald Joinson was married in December, 1941. See JOYNSON.

JOLLIE, JOLLY. Alan Joyly apud Bervy had a precept of remission in 1492 (RSS., I, 17), and James Joly was vicar of Dalry in 1541 (*Anderson*). Janet Jolly in Leslie, 1646 (PBK., p. 294), George Jollie was retoured heir of his brother, Robert Jollie, burgess of Edinburgh, 1677 (*Retours, Edinburgh*, 1243), and Janet Jolly appears at Custitoun, 1681 (*Kirkcudbright*). Charles Jolly or Jollie was prisoner in Canongate Tolbooth, Edinburgh, 1684 (BOEC., IX, p. 121, 123), and Mr. George Jollie was minister in Cockenzie, 1689 (RPC., 3. ser. XIV, p. 325). Rev. James Jollie was senior chaplain of Church of Scotland and chaplain of St. Andrew's Church, Madras. Weekley says from older Joliffe (p. 289), and Harrison says from ME. *joly, joli*, merry, gay.

JONKIESON. A diminutive of JOHN + son. James Jonkiesone was married in Edinburgh, 1647 (*Edinb. Marr.*). James Jonkison, indweller in Edinburgh, 1670 (*Edin. App.*), and David Jonksone in West Lumbinne, 1671 (*Dunblane*). James Jonkison in Biggar, 1679 (*Lanark CR.*).

JOPP. An early sharpened form of Job. Robert Jop was burgess of Perth, 1353 (*Scon*, p. 128). John Joip was a tenant under the earl of Huntly in Tollebeig, Strathbogie, 1600 (SCM., IV, p. 265). James Jopp was merchant and stamper in Huntly, 1747 (*Moray*), and there was a burgess family of Jopp in Aberdeen, one of which was provost at the time of the visit of Johnson and Boswell. John Jopp was one of the Huntly Volunteers in 1801 (*Will*, p. 8). Jop 1622. Jupp may be a variant spelling. Canon Jupp was founder of Aberlour (Banffshire) Orphanage.

JOPSON, 'son of JOP(P),' an early sharpened form of Job. John Joppison and Alan Jopsone were tenants of Gramptoun in the valley of Moffat, Dumfriesshire, 1376 (RHM., I, p. lxii). Joppison is perhaps a diminutive form.

JORDAN. A common personal name in the last half of the twelfth century, "derived from the river Jordan, which became popular in crusading times throughout western Europe, and nowhere more than in England, owing to flasks of Jordan water being brought home to be used for baptismal purposes" (*Woulfe*, p. 672). Jordan the Fleming was chancellor to David I in 1142–43, in a charter of Adam son of Swain, c. 1136–53 (*Register of St. Bees*, p. 70–71). Jordan de Wodford, charter witness in Angus, c. 1170 (RAA., I, p. 38). Jordanus Brac granted a piece of land to the church of S. Mary and S. Kentigern of Lanark, c. 1214 (*Dryburgh*, p. 156). Magister William Jordanus witnessed confirmation charter by Gilbert, bishop of Aberdeen between 1228–39 (RPSA., p. 302). Jurdane 1473.

JORIE. A surname found in Wigtownshire. For origin see under MACGEORGE.

JOSS, JOASS. Perhaps from Fr. *Josse*, from *Jodoc* or *Judoc* (a derivative of Breton *jud* 'battle'), the name of a famous Breton saint of the seventh century. A family named Joass were of considerable importance in Banffshire in the eighteenth century, and possessed the lands of Colleonard. William Joos was chaplain to King Robert III, 1402 (RMS., I, p. 651). Thomas Joce was bailie of Inverkeithing, 1359 (ER., I, p. 621). William Joss was tenant of Westhall, Aberdeenshire, 1513 (REA., I, p. 355). Agnes Joas was rebuked in church "for having ane excommunicate persone at

her marriage," 1661 (*Rec. Elgin*, II, p. 301). Rev. James Maxwell Joass of Golspie was a well-known antiquary. Joasse 1669, Joiss 1662.

JOSSY. Thomas Jowsy was burgess of Glasgow, 1433 (LCD., p. 248), and James Jousie "merchand in Lintonis Cloiss," Edinburgh, 1572 (*Diur. Occ.*, p. 303). The seal of Robert Jossie, 1512, is described in Macdonald (1445). John Joicie, burgess of Edinburgh, made burgess of Dumbarton, 1636 (RDB.). John Jousie, chirurgeon in Edinburgh, 1686 (RPC., 3. ser. XII, p. 200), Edward Jossev, skipper in Boness, 1689 (ibid., 3. ser. XIV, p. 258), and John Joussie was burgess of Edinburgh, 1692 (*Inquis.*, 7222). Jossy was an eighteenth-century surname in Musselburgh but is now extinct there. Alexander Jovsie, late burgess of Edinburgh, 1736 (*Guildry*, p. 158).

JOY. Robert Joi or Joy, burgess of Perth, had a charter of land there forfeited by Adam Foustoune, an Englishman, from David II (RMS., I, App. II, 924). Land in vico Sellatorum of Perth was held by Robertus dictus Joy in 1332 (*Scon*, 163), probably the same person. Probably a Norman personal name, Joie, Joye — "corresponding to Lat. Letitia; but possible merely a descriptive epithet bestowed on one of a joyous disposition" (*Woulfe*, p. 670).

JOYNER. A variant of JOINER, q.v.

JOYNSON. A form of JOHNSON, q.v., probably of recent introduction from England. See also JOINSON.

JUBB. An old surname in Yorkshire. It is the northern English form of Job. In the reign of Edward Langshanks (1273) the name is represented as Jubbe in the wapentake of Osgoldcross (*Hundred Rolls*).

JUDGE. From the office of 'judge,' in Latin charters rendered *judex*. Kineth, judex, witnessed a charter by Earl David, c. 1202–07 (LAC., p. 11, 38, 88). Keraldus judex witnessed a charter by Randulf de Strathphetham, c. 1222 (REB., II, 3). Gilbert, judex, witnessed a charter by Maldoweny, earl of Levenax to the Abbey of Kelso between 1225 and 1246 (*Kelso*, 220), and Walter, judex, witnessed a quit-claim of the land of Drumkarauch in 1260 (RPSA., p. 346). Ewayn Judex was present at pleas held at Dull in Atholl in 1264 (RPSA., p. 349), and Andrew le Jugeor or le Jugger rendered homage in 1296 (*Bain*, II, 730, 816). His seal bears a head within tracery, and S' *Andree Jvdicis* (ibid., p. 554).

JUDSON. William Judison, Thomas Judison, and other Scottish merchants complained that their vessel was captured and sunk by the English during a truce, 1359 (*Bain*, IV, 23). Andrew Yutsoun was provost of Edinburgh, 1387 (Nisbet, *Plates*, p. 10). Guppy says this is a contracted form of Jordanson from Jourdain, but more probably "son of Jud," for Jude.

JUNOR. A surname found in Inverness, said by Macbain (V, p. 47) to be a form of JENNER, q.v.

JUPP. A variant of JOPP, q.v.

JUSTICE. From the office of magistrate. Patrick Justice, priest, witnessed instrument of sasine in Perthshire, 1474 (*Athole*, p. 709), and another Patrick Justyce was tenant of the mill of Kerso, 1472 (*Cupar-Angus*, I, p. 163). The lands of James Justeis and Thome Justeis in Scone are mentioned in 1491, and Gilbert Justeis witnessed a charter by the abbot of Scone to William Peblis in the same year (*Scon*, p. 200, 201). The surname is not infrequent in registers relating to the midland counties during the sixteenth century (Nisbet, *Plates*, p. 152). Adam Justice, portioner of Newbigging, 1624, and seven more are recorded in Lanark Commissariot Record between 1595–1800. Patrick Justice was towncouncillor of Perth, 1567 (RPC., I, p. 505), Gavin Justice was indweller in Stirling, 1648 (*Inquis.*, 3483), and Robert Justice was merchant in Glasgow, 1673 (ibid., 5678).

KAILZIE. From the old lands afterwards the parish of Kailzie (now suppressed) in Peeblesshire. Patrick de Hopekeliou was one of the witnesses to the perambulation of the marches of Stobo, c. 1190 (REG., 104; APS., I, p. 88). Robert de Hopkelchoc is mentioned in 1259 as present at an inquest held at Peebles regarding the land of Hopkelchoc (APS., I, p. 99 *red*), and Archibald de Hopkelioc and Clemens de Hopkelioc appear in 1262 on an inquest regarding the moss of Waltamshope (ibid., I, p. 101 *red*; *Peebles*, 5). Erchebald of Hopkelioch witnessed a deed by Malcolm, son of David Dunne of Conestablestoune, between 1260 and 1268 (REG., p. 176). William de Hopkelioghe of Peeblesshire rendered homage in 1296. His seal bears a lion passant to sinister, S' *Willelmi de Hopcailhou* (*Bain*, II, p. 205, 533). William of Hoppekelyok served on an inquest at Peebles regarding the lands of the late William Malevile (ibid., II, 1436), and in 1305 it is recorded that the land of William de Opkeliok in the county of Poebles 'cannot be laboured for William's poverty' (ibid., IV, p. 373.)

KAMES. Local. There are several places named Kaims and Kames. Andrew Kames, burgess of Glasgow, 1621 (*Burgesses*). Mareon Kaims, resident in the parish of Borgue, 1684 (RPC., 3. ser. IX, p. 568).

KARR. A "genteel" pronunciation of KERR, q.v.

KATHEL. *See under* CATHAL.

KAY, KEAY. There was an old family of this name (Kay) in Yorkshire, and Kay and Kaye are recorded in Lincolnshire, Hunts, and Cambridgeshire, as far back as the thirteenth century (*Guppy*, p. 430). The Middle Welsh personal name *Kei* is a borrowing from Latin *Caius* (J. Morris Jones, *A Welsh grammar*, p. 102). (2) Some of the later records of the name may derive from *Macaoidh* (Mackav), as in the Isle of Man the omission of 'Mac' is recorded there as early as 1610 (Kee), 1617 (Kay), Key (1616), Kie (1618), etc. In Scotland the 'Mac' may have been dropped earlier. Kae of Corslats were an old family of West Lothian, and Keay was common in Perthshire. Phillip Qua appears in Aberdeen, 1317 (SCM., v, p. 9), and Donald Ka there in 1399 (CRA., p. 3). Thomas Kaa on an inquest taken at Berwick-on-Tweed, 1370 (*Bain*, IV, 175). Patrick Ka, burgess of Linlithgow, died 1445 (*Anal. Scot.*, I, p. 174), and Henry Ka appears as bailie of the same burgh, 1461 and 1472 (RAA., II, 137; *Scot. Ant.*, XVII, p. 117). Ranald Cay, priest, witnessed an instrument of sasine in Perthshire, 1474 (*Athole*, p. 709). James Ka, who held two perticates of land in Linlithgow in 1549 (*Laing*, 552), may be the James Kaa who rendered to Exchequer the accounts of the same burgh in 1563 (ER., XIX, p. 223). Alexander Ka was burgess of Edinburgh, 1536 (*Johnsoun*), Thom Kay, witness in Brechin, 1552 (REB., I, 233), and William Kav, tenant under the Abbey of Newbattle, 1563 (*Neubotle*, p. 327). Margaret Ka in Methven, 1587 (*Methven*, p. 67), Robert Kaa retoured heir of Robert Kaa, in burgh of Kirkwall, 1647 (*Retours, Orkney*, 49), John Cay in Quhitefield, 1653 (*Dunblane*), and Alexander Kae, bailie of the Canongate, Edinburgh, 1677 (*Edinb. Marr.*). John Kae recorded in Cavertoune, 1683 (*Peebles CR.*), and Alexander Kae at Coldingham-law, 1742 (*Lauder*). Key 1641.

KEAN, KEAND. From (MAC)KEAN, q.v. As *n* in vulgar speech strengthens itself by taking *d* we have Keand. John Kene was writer to the signet, 1609 (*Retours, Peebles*, 42). James Kewne appears in the parish of Borgue, 1684 and Barbara Kwen, resident there in the same year (RPC., 3. ser. IX, p. 568). Mary Keand in Kirkcudbright in 1689 (ibid., XIV, p. 758).

KEAY. *See under* KAY.

KEDDER. Probably from the village of Cadder, Lanarkshire. Andrew Kedder in St. John's Kirk, 1598 (*Lanark CR.*). James Crescent or Keder in the parish of Cairnwaith, 1686 (RPC., 3. ser. xii, p. 369). William Kedder, late deacon of the ffleshers, 1728 (*Guildry*, p. 135).

KEDDIE, Kedie, Keddy, Kiddie, Kiddy. The ship of John Kede, a Scotsman, was wrecked at Holkham, Norfolk, England, in 1388 (*Bain*, iv, 381). John Kady in record in Dysart, 1577 (*Dysart*, p. 38), Margaret Keddie in Falsyde, parish of Roberton, 1623 (*Lanark CR.*), Dorathia Kadie, heir of Alexander Kadie, tailor in Edinburgh, 1616 (*Inquis.*, 629), and James Keadie, hatmaker there in 1635 (*Edinb. Marr.*). David Kedie in Weyms, 1630, James Keddie was bewitched there in 1639, and Robert Keddie was elder in Dysart, 1641 (PBK., p. 14, 141, 209). Alexander Ceddy was fined for "straicks and ryot" in 1664 (*Stitchill*, p. 31), and Donald Kedde in Moy, Caithness, to be apprehended as a rebel in 1670 (RPC., 3. ser. iii, p. 194). From (Mac)keddie, q.v. The name of John Kede (1388) probably from another source.

KEENAN. A Galloway surname, also recorded in Aberdeen. Perhaps from Ir. *MacCianáin* or *O'Cianáin*, 'son or descendant of Cianán.' The O'Cianains were a literary family in Ulster, hereditary historians to the Maguires (*Woulfe*).

KEIL, Keill. John Keill, chirurgian in Dundee, 1615 (*Beats*, p. 251), Thomas Kyill, burgess of Dundee, 1624, and David Keill in record in Haughmuer, 1774 (*Brechin*). John Keill, an eminent astronomer, was born in Edinburgh, 1671, and James, his brother, born 1673, was an eminent physician. James Keel was member of the Huntly Company of Volunteers, 1805 (*Will*, p. 30).

KEILLER, Keillor. *See under* KELLAR.

KEIR, Kier. (1) Local, from Keir in Stirlingshire. Patrick Ker was one of the jurors on the marches of Westere Fedale, 1242 (LAC., p. 26). Alexander del Keire had a gift of money from the king (ER., i, p. 115), and Andrew del Ker of Stirlingshire rendered homage in 1296 (*Bain*, ii, p. 210). William Ker was one of the burgesses of Stirling who attacked the cruives and fishings of the abbot and convent of Cambuskenneth, 1366 (*Cambus.*, 55). John Kere, burgess of Strivelyne and Mariota his wife had a charter of land in Aberdeen, 1366 (RMS., i, 229), and William of Keir witnessed a deed at Cluny, 1462 (SCM., v, p. 286). Robert Kar, a monk of Inchaffray,

1544–64 (*Inchaffray*, intro., p. xcviii–ix). Thomas Kar was deacon of craft in Stirling, 1555 (SBR., p. 278), and Thomas Kere rendered to Exchequer the accounts of the burgh of Forfar, 1558 (ER., xix, p. 40). Kire 1686. (2) A personal name, from G. *ciar*, swarthy. Donald McDonche W'Alexander Keir and Malcolm M'Neill V'Alexander Keire were witnesses to a seisin of lands in Ayrshire, 1553 (OPS., ii, p. 86).

KEITH. Of territorial origin from the lands of Keith in East Lothian. Fraser (*History of Laurencekirk*, p. 28) would have us believe the Keiths to be descended from the Catti, a Germanic tribe, who in the early centuries of the Christian era inhabited what is now Hesse in southwest Germany! A section of the tribe emigrated to Scotland at the beginning of the eleventh century under a leader named Robert, who helped defeat the Danes under Camus at Barry in 1010! Malcolm de Keth witnessed Eschina de Londonis's gift of the church of Molle to the Abbey of Kelso, 1185 (*Kelso*, 146), witnessed a gift of lands in Inuerwyc to the same abbey c. 1190 (ibid., 255), and is in record again as witness to the confirmation of the church of Lundoris to the Abbey of Lundoris in 1202 (LAC., 107). Bernard de Keth witnessed a charter by Hugh rydale, dominus de Craneston, a. 1200 (*Neubotle*, 12). Magister John de Keth, a cleric, witnessed the gift of Swaynystoun (Swanston) to the Hospital of Soltre, between 1238–70 (*Soltre*, p. 28). Johannes de Keth in Perth, 1289 (ER., i, p. 49), and Bernard de Keht was juror on an inquest at Berwick in 1296 (*Bain*, ii, p. 210). Andrew Kethe of Enyrrugy was one of the hostages for King James i in 1425 (*Bain*, iv, 983). Antoun of Keth, a witness in Aberdeen, 1484 (CRA., p. 414). "The Keith of 1455 was first made Lord Keith, and then the first Earl Mairschall. There was a line of ten earls between 1455 and 1715, and there is hardly a Scotch noble family who have not the blood of the Keiths in their veins" (SHR., ii, p 390). Moysie (*Memoirs*, p. 47–48) under 1584, mentions one Andreas Keathe, a Scotsman and councellor to the "King of Suaddan" (Sweden) came to Scotland to visit the King and friends. "Albeit of meane parentis, vit throw his guid behauiour promouit to great honour, and promotioun;" and by the king was (15 March) "maid lord Dingvall." John Ket was admitted burgess of Aberdeen, 1534 (NSCM., i, p. 53). In Germany in the eighteenth century the name was transformed into Kite, and in the United States it has become Cate. Kayt 1542, Keyth 1626, Keythe 1621, Keytht 1590. (2) In Caithness this surname is in Gaelic *Càidh*. "That it represents a short form of *MacDha'idh*," says Prof. Watson, "is phonetically possible but otherwise unlikely" (I, p. 382). In the fourteenth century one of the Keiths of the Earls Marischal family married one of the heiresses of the Cheynes of Akergill, and settled in the North, hence their North of Scotland connection. Thomas Keith, a Scottish soldier in the British army serving in Egypt, was taken prisoner by the Turks in 1807, embraced Islamism, and after many adventures became governor of El-Medina where Mohammed is buried.

KELBURN. From the lands of Kelburne or Kelliburne in the parish of Largs, Ayrshire. John Kailborne was witness in Bute in 1502 (LCD., p. 206), John Kelburne was burgess of Rothesay in 1667 *(Isles)*, John and Ninian Kelburn appear in Rothesay in 1689, and several other Kelburnes appear in Bute at end of the seventeenth century (*Hewison*, II, p. 207).

KELDAY, KILDAY. An old surname in Orkney derived from the place named Keldall in Holm. Andro Keldall or Caldell was juror on an assize in 1565 and in 1605 (REO., p. 120, 179). Dauid Keldell, burgess of Kirkwall in 1597 (ibid., p. 321), may be the David Keldall who had wadset of land in Clouston, Orkney, in 1616 to which his brother Andro Keldall was witness (OSRec., I, p. 240, 241). Walter Keldall of that Ilk appears in record in 1617 (REO., p. 398), and Elspeth Kelday died in 1687 *(Orkney)*.

KELDELETH. Robert de Keldeleth, the first mitred abbot of Dunfermline, became abbot of Melrose, 1268 (*Chron. Mail.* in ann.). Keldeleth appears to have become Kinleith or Kenleith (near Currie). Cf. Kellet (pron. Kelt) in Lancashire (Wyld and Hirst, *Place names of Lancashire*, p. 166, in 1227 spelled Keldelith).

KELEBEUHOC. Adam de Kelebeuhoc who witnessed a charter by Walter, son of Alan the son of Walter the Steward, between 1202 and 1213 (*Melros*, p. 63) derived his name from Kilbucho in Peeblesshire.

KELLAR, KELLER, KEILLER, KEILLOR. From the lands of (Easter and Wester) Keilor in the adjoining parishes of Newtyle and Kettins in Angus. The names are still common in the district. Stephen de Cellar, burgess of Roxburgh, 1262 (*Melros*, p. 294). Duncan de Cellario, burgess of Perth, 1292 (*Milne*, p. 5) is doubtless Dunkan del Celer, burgess of Perth, who rendered homage in 1296 (*Bain*, II, 814 and p. 197). Ranulph de Kelor swore fealty at Kyndromyn (Kildrummy) in Mar

in same year. His seal bears a cross crosslet fitche, cantoned with four pellets, S' *Ranulphi d' Kelor* (ibid., 800). Thomas de Cellar, burgess of Perth, 1345 (*Scon*, p. 127), and Stephen de Cellario, archdeacon of Brechin, 1372 (REB., I, 20). John de Kelore in 1383 granted to John de Ardlere an annual of six merks out of the two vills of Kelore (RMS., I, 727). This John appears to have been the last of his family who held lands in Angus, but the surname, as already mentioned, is by no means rare. Johannes de Kelor, juror on a trial in Moray, 1398 (REM., p. 212), Agnes Kelour or Kellor had a charter from David II of Kepnemade and the new park of Stirling (RMS., I, 179, •225). Kelour was a personal name in Moray as well as a place name in Angus (*Sc. Ant.*, xv, p. 68). Keloure 1296.

KELLAS. Of local origin from the lands of Kellas (now a village) in the parish of Dallas, Moray. In 1562 the lands of Ester and Wester Kelles and of Corcoponoch were granted by the bishop of Moray with consent of the Chapter to William Farquharsone (REM., p. 409). David Kellas from Marnoch served in the first Great War *(Turriff)*. There is also a hamlet of the same name in the parish of Murroes in Angus.

KELLER. See under KELLAR.

KELLET. A surname of recent introduction in Scotland from across the Border. Of local origin from Kellet, a village in north Lancashire.

KELLO, KELLOE, KELLOW. From the old lands of Kelloe in the barony of Hume, Berwickshire. Kelloe is also a place name in Durham and there is a Kellah in Northumberland. The surname was formerly common around Coldingham. William de Kellawe was bailiff of the king of Scotland in 1278 (*Bain*, II, p. 29). Richard de Kellow was a charter witness in Roxburgh, c. 1338 (BNCH., xxiv, p. 226), Patrick Kellow witnessed a notarial instrument dated 1442 (*Home*, 21), and John de Kello or Kellow was witness to a claim to a third part of Cranshaws in 1453 (*Swinton*, p. xxxix). Andrew Kelaw was admitted burgess of Aberdeen in 1484, and a later Andrew Kelo in 1542 (NSCM., I, p. 31, 58). John Kello, merchant of Edinburgh, and William Kello, shipmaster, probably a relative, are in record in 1490 (*Bain*, IV, 1565). Bartholomew Kello, collector of tax in 1545 (RPC., I, p. 15) was probably the Bartholomew Kello who was clerk of the diocese of St. Andrews in 1549 (*Laing*, 552), John Kelo was town bellman in Aberdeen, 1562 (Mill, *Plays*, p. 152), and Gilbert Kello was reidare at Balhelvy, 1574

KELLO, KELLOE, KELLOW, continued

(RMR.). Robert Kelo was burgess of Aberdeen in 1595 (CRA., p. 121), John Kello was retoured heir of John Kello, inhabitant of Biggar in 1618 (Inquis., 779), Charles Keillo in Aberdeen received payment for beer in 1639 (SCM., v, p. 154), and John Kello was servitor to the earl of Eglintoun, 1665 (Irvine, II, p. 194). James Kiloh served in the first Great War, and three men named Killoh from Gamrie and Alexander Keilloh from Auchterless were killed (Turriff). The surname was also formerly current in Shetland (1602) but is not now found there (Mill, Diary, p. lxxxix, 182).

KELLOCH (in Argyll), KELLOUGH (in Inverness). From old spellings of G. MacCeallaigh. See MACKELLY.

KELLOCK. There is a Keiloch in Braemar, Aberdeenshire, but it is not certain that this is the place of origin. The references, with exception of the first, point to a source further south. Robert de Kellok [? in Aberdeenshire] received money from the Lord Chamberlain in 1343 (ER., I, p. 530). Anna de Keloche appears in Stirling, 1372 (RMS., I, 380, 430), and David Kellocht witnessed a Fife deed in 1495 (Laing, 221). An annual rent of 6 bolls of oats from the land of Primrose was payable to Giles Kellock, 1567 (Pitfirrane, 161). Alexander Kellock was burgess of Dunfermline, 1581 (ibid., 269). Nicholas Kellok and William Kellok had each a charter of the third part of the mill of Lassodie or Lassody in 1606 (RD., p. 499). Archibald Kellok was burgess of Kirkaldie, 1650 (Inquis. Tut., 772), Robert Killocke was schoolmaster at Fawckland (Falkland), 1662 (Lamont, Diary, p. 127), and Robert Kellock was heir of James Kellock, portioner of Maistertoun, 1666 (Retours, Fife, 999). John Killoch, sometime in Pollmach, appears in 1688 (Moray), and several Kelloks are recorded in the parish register of Dunfermline, 1561–1700. The name appears in Edinburgh, 1941. Cf. KILLOCK.

KELLOE, KELLOW. See under KELLO.

KELLOUGH. See under KELLOCH.

KELLS. Local. Oppression and hamesucken was done to John Kells in Wigtune, 1513 (Trials, I, p. 93*). Alestr Kells in Torrisheich, and Arthur Kelles in Glencarvie, both in 1682 (Invercauld, p. 263, 264). The first derived his surname from Kells in Kirkcudbrightshire.

KELLY. From the lands of Kelly, near Arbroath, Angus. There is another Kellie near Pittenweem, Fife, but the references point to the former locality as the source of the surname. John de Kelly was abbot of Arbroath,

1373 (APS., I, p. 197). Waulter of Kylle coming to the Scots hostages in England had a safe conduct in 1424 (Bain, IV, 961). David Celle was nineteenth abbot of Cambuskenneth, 1445–63. William Kelle held land in Kyntor, Aberdeenshire, 1498 (REA., I, p. 340), and James Kelle was notary public in diocese of St. Andrew, 1526 (CMN., 36). (2) A family named Kelle, long resident at Dunbar, apparently derived their name from an old spelling of KELLO, q.v., which hardened into a separate surname. Cudbert Kelle was tenant of Eistbarnis of Dunbar, 1559 (ER., XIX, p. 401), and rendered to Exchequer the accounts of the burgh of Dunbar, 1563 (ibid., p. 223). In 1590 Alexander Kellie was bailie of Dunbar (RPC., IV, p. 481). Captain John Kellie was retoured heir in certain lands in Berwickshire, 1659 (Retours, Berwick, 310), and Nicol Kellie was burgess of Dunbar, 1688 (RPC., 3. ser. XII, p. 253). (3) Convallus de Kelle, who witnessed an instrument of sasine of the lands of Mernys and Netherpollok, 1454 (Pollok, I, p. 176), most probably derived his name from the lands of Kelly in the parish of Innerkip, Renfrewshire (mentioned in the reign of James III). (4) A surname found in Galloway. For origin see under MACKELLY.

KELMAN, KILMAN. Of local origin from a place in Aberdeenshire. There is a Kelman Hill in the Cabrach. Kelman is a common surname in the shire, and several of the name are buried in Mortlach churchyard. William Kelman, admitted burgess of Aberdeen in 1591 (NSCM., I, p. 81) is probably the merchant burgess there in 1605 (ROA., I, p. 231). Alexander Kelman was admitted burgess of Dundee in 1589 (Wedd., p. 189), and James Kelman appears in Aberdeen in the same year (CRA., p. 64). Barbara Kilmaine is recorded in Edinburgh, 1603 (Edinb. Marr.), Isobel Kelmane in Auld Aberdeen, 1621 (RSCA., II, p. 247), and James Kelman, against whom a charge was made in 1633, is probably Jams Kelmane in Belchirrie against whom there was an action for debt in 1636 (RSCA., II, p. 375, 413). William Kelman appears in Balnamoon, 1747 (Moray), James Kelman was member of Gartly Company of Volunteers in 1798 and John Kelman member of the Huntly Company (Will, p. 18, 24), and James Kelman from Alvah was killed in the first Great War (Turriff). Kelmann 1596.

KELSO. From the town of the name in Roxburghshire. About the year 1200 Arnald, son of Peter de Kelso, gave the messuage of Kelso to the monks of the abbey (Kelso, 354). Richard of Kelchow was clerk to the Lord Chancellor, c. 1220 (Athole, p. 704), and witnessed a charter by Elena, daughter of Alan, lord of Galloway, in favor of the bishop of Glasgow, 1233 (REG., p. 138). John de Kalchou who witnessed a charter in favor of the Hospital of Soltre, c. 1214–19, is probably John de Kelcov who witnessed a grant of the lands of Jonystoun to the same house in 1250 (Soltre, p. 19, 31). Humphrev de Kalchou witnessed a resignation by Alan de Sarcino in favor of the church of S. Mary of Kelso, 1260 (Kelso, I, p. 219; II, p. 283). Huwe de Kelshowe of Ayrshire, who rendered homage in 1296 (Bain, II, p. 199, 551), is supposed to have been ancestor of the Kelsos of Kelsoland, an old family (now extinct) in the parish of Largs. The legend on his seal reads, Sigill' Hvgonis de Calcovia. In 1403 Johannes de Kelsou, "filius domini de Kelsouland," quitclaimed the land called Langlebank in the parish of Largyss to the monks of Paisley, and in 1432 pledged himself to give the monks there half a stone of wax yearly at the feast of S. Mirinus, from the ferms of Kelsowland (RMP., p. 244, 369–372). The name of the Kelsos of Sannox in Arran, an old family there (offshoot from Ayrshire), has been Gaelicized Caolisten. The name is also recorded in Bute in 1541 (RMS., III, 2583). Kelsoland was sold in 1671 to John Brisbane of Bishopton, who changed the name from Kelsoland to Brisbane. Kelsow 1624.

KELT. Of local origin from Kelt (Easter and Wester) near Denny, Stirlingshire. Vilelmus Kelt who witnessed a lease by Alexander, commendator of Inchaffray, 1521, is witness to another lease by Gauine, archbishop of Glasgow, 1544 (Inchaffray, p. xcviii). Robert Keld appears in Dunblane, 1669 (Dunblane), and Janet Kelt is recorded in Whitefield, 1744 (Dunkeld). Recorded in Edinburgh, 1942.

KELTIE, KELTY. From the old lands of Keltie near Callander, Perthshire. James Keltie was heir of John Keltie, burgess of Edinburgh, in 1616 (Inquis., 662), and Adam Keltie, servitor to the chancellor of Scotland in 1628 (REB., II, 244), appears in 1631 as one of the clerks to the Exchequer (Burgesses). The surname is also recorded in Edinburgh in 1647 (Edinb. Marr.), and is common in Dunblane Commissariot Record in the seventeenth and eighteenth centuries.

KELTON. Of local origin from the village of Kelton in the parish of the same name, Kirkcudbrightshire. John Keltone in Bordland, 1685 (Dumfries).

KELVEY, KELVIE. Shortened from (MAC)KELVIE, q.v. David Kelvie is recorded in Campbeltown, 1686. William Kelvie of Upper Crae recorded in 1769 (Kirkcudbright).

KELWINY. Isaac de Kelwiny of Perthshire rendered homage, 1296 (Bain, II, p. 200).

KEMBACK. From Kemback in Fife. Thomas de Kenmake witnessed a charter by Hugo de Nidin of lands in Fife, c. 1204–28 (SHSM., IV, p. 312). The local pronunciation of Kemback is still Kemmak.

KEMIE. See under KEMY.

KEMLO. Local. Walter Kemblock witnessed a charter of the division of the lands of the domus de Passelet and William de Sanchar, 1280 (RMP., p. 228). Nicholas Kemloc in Ayr, 1348 (Friars, Ayr, p. 17). John Kemlok, presbyter and notary in Brechin, 1472–75–77 (SCM., IV, p. 136, 183; Cawdor, p. 56).

KEMMY. See under KEMY.

KEMNIE. Local, probably from Kemnay, a village in Aberdeenshire. James Kemnie in the parish of Glass, 1716, and George Kemny in the parish of Dumbennan in same year (SCM., IV, p. 168, 171). Joseph Kemno of Old Machar, a Jacobite of the '45.

KEMP. This surname is usually explained as from ON. kempa, OE. cempa, ME. kempe, 'warrior, champion.' William Kemp, burgess of Edinburgh, 1423 (Egidii, p. 45). Donald Kemp, burgess of Dingwall, 1563 (RMS., IV, 1455), and William Kemp in Dingwall, 1613, a Macgregor resetter (RPC., XIV, p. 648). See KEMPT.

KEMPT. This surname found mainly in Aberdeenshire appears to be of different origin from KEMP, q.v. Duncan Kembdie, burgess of Aberdeen, had a charter of the lands of Arduthie, 1330 (HMC., 8. rep., p. 301). Peter Kempdv held a land in Aberdeen, 1362 (REA., I, p. 104), Thomas Kymdv was one of an assize held at Artrowquhir, 1436 (CAB., p. 394), Johannes Kympdy witnessed a charter by Duncan Kymdy, constable of Aberdeen, 1449 (REA., I, p. 254), Andrew Kempty was admitted burgess of Aberdeen in 1477 (NSCM., I, p. 27), and William Kimpty was constable of Aberdeen, 1484 (CRA., p. 42). James Kympte, witness in Forres, 1529 (Rose, p. 201), and John Kympty of Carnmuck who held lands in Ellon, 1543, appears again in 1562 as Kemp of Cormuck (Mair, p. 37). John Kempty was retoured heir of William Kemptie de Carnuick vel Carmuk, 1552 (Retours, Aberdeen, 12). Thomas Kempt retoured heir of Alexander Kempt, burgess of Aberdeen, 1636 (ibid., 234), Gilbert Kemtie appears as "regis muntion" in Brechin in 1605 (REB., II, 235), and George Kempty is apud molendinum de Gordes in 1642 (Inquis., 2628).

KEMY, KEMIE, KEMMY. From (MAC)KEM-
MIE, q.v. James Kemy was one of the peti-
tioners for the formation of the Corps of Huntly
Volunteers in 1798 (*Will*, p. 5).

KENDILLOWY. Duncan Kendillowy, witness
in St. Andrews, 1545 (*Laing*, 494).

KENDRICK. A shortened form of MACKEN-
DRICK, q.v.

KENE. A family of this name seems to have
acquired the lands of Reveden (Redden) prob-
ably at end of the thirteenth century, and had
possession of them till after the Reformation
(OPS., I, p. 442). They also possessed lands
in the shires of Berwick and Dumfries. 'Sir'
John Kene was a priest in Edinburgh, 1513
(*Stodart*, II), and Patrick Kene in Selkirk was
fined £500 [Scots] in 1590 (RPC., IV, p. 481).
Richard Kene was served heir to his father
John Kene, writer to the signet, in the lands
of Redden, 1609 (*Retours, Roxburgh*, 52).
Patrick Keine was burgess of Selkirk, 1642
(RRM., I, p. 97), Janet Kein is in parish of
Borgue, 1684 (RPC., 3. ser. IX, p. 566), and
James Kein, late bailie of Selkirk, 1698
(*Peebles CR.*).

KENILWORTH. David de Kenilworth in Berwick rendered homage, 1291 (RR.). From
Kenilworth in Warwickshire.

KENISON. A form of CUNIESON, q.v.

KENNA, KENNEY, KINNA. From (MAC)KENNA,
q.v. J. G. Kinna wrote and published a *History
of the parish of Minnigaff*.

KENNAN. Shortened from (MAC)KENNAN,
q.v. Richard Kennan witnessed a sasine by
the abbot of Sweetheart, 1555 (*Laing*, 632).
Eight of the name are in local record between
1663–1800 (*Kirkcudbright*). John Kennan appears in Kirkbryde, 1675 (*Kirkcudbright*), and
James Kennan was bailie of Dumfries, 1695
(*Inquis.*, 7646).

KENNARDY. Of local origin from Kennerty
(in 1548 Kennarty, 1486 Kennardy) in the
parish of Peterculter, Aberdeenshire. James
Kennardy was admitted burgess of Aberdeen
in 1467, James Kennarty in 1486, Robert
Kennerti in 1504, and Thomas Kennerty in
1516 (NSCM., I, p. 21, 32, 46). Johannes
Kennerty, cleric in Aberdeen, 1497, and Andreas Kennerty held a land in the burgh, 1499
(REA., I, p. 339, 345).

KENNAWAY. See under KENNOWAY.

KENNEDY. Sir Andrew Agnew says (I, p. 33)
that the "first appearance of a Kennedy in
Galloway" is in 1034, when "Suibhne mac

Cinaeda ri Gallgaidhel" is mentioned in the
Annals of Ulster. This, however, is an error.
MacCinaeda is not MacKennedy but Mac-
Kenna. The earliest Kennedy recorded in Scotland appears to be Gilbert mac Kenedi, who
witnessed a charter by Raderic Mac Gillescop
of lands in Carric to the Abbey of Melrose
early in the reign of King William the Lion
(*Melros*, I, p. 29). Henry Kennedy or Mac-
Kenede is named in 1185 as one of the leaders
and instigators of rebellion in Galloway, and
is stated to have fallen in battle (Fordun,
Annals, xvi). Gillescop MacKenedi, senescallus
de Karric, is twice in record in the reign of
Alexander II (*Melros*, I, p. 171), and Gillecrist
filius Kenedi witnessed a grant of lands in the
same district within the same period (ibid.,
p. 172). Maldouen Macenedy or Mackenedi
appears as charter witness in the Lennox
c. 1240–8 (*Lennox*, II, p. 7). Hugh and Murdoch Mackenedy served as jurors on an inquest made at Gerwan (Girvan) in 1260 (*Bain*,
I, 2674), and the latter, as Murthan Mac-
Kenede, witnessed a charter of the church of
Maybothel in Carrick before 1250 (CMN.,
p. 15). Fergus Makenedy who rendered to
Exchequer the accounts of the sheriff of Ayr,
1266 (ER., I, p. 34), may be the ffergus mac
Kenedi who witnessed John Cumyne's grant of
a right of way by his wood and the bridge of
the black ford called in Scots Athebethy to
the monastery of Inchaffray in 1278 (*Inchaffray*, p. 100), and c. 1285 witnessed another
charter by Alexander de Dunhon of the land
of Arachor to Sir Patrick de Graham (*Montrose*,
p. 166). Alexander MacKennedy who appears
as a charter witness between 1230–70 (RMP.,
p. 134, 137, 138) is probably Master Alexander Kenedi (without 'Mac'), canon of Glasgow, c. 1272–83 (ibid., p. 53, 127), and as
Magister Alexander Kenedy, charter witness in
Glasgow, c. 1290 (REG., p. 200). As dominus
Alexander Kennedy, canon of Glasgow, he
rendered homage, 1296 (*Bain*, II, p. 194).
Sir Hugh Kennedy possessed lands in Lanarkshire in 1296 (*Rot. Scot.*, I, p. 29b), and as
Huwe Kenedy rendered homage for them in
the same year. His seal bears a garb, four
pellets on either side, S' *Hugonis Kinnedi*
(*Bain*, II, p. 203, 544). Sir Malcolm Kenedy
was camerarius Scocie in 1338 (SCM., v,
p. 244), and Gilbert McKenedy witnessed a
charter by John, earl of Carrick of lands in the
lordship of Kyle in the reign of Robert II (*Melros*, II, p. 453). John Kennedy of Dunure was
captain of the clan Muintircasduff about 1346
(RMS., I, p. 574). John Kennedye witnessed
a charter by Robert II to Duncan, earl of
Leuenax in 1384 (*Levenax*, p. 8), and in 1393
there is confirmation of the lands of Buch-
monyn in the earldom of Levenax to John

Kennyde, son of Fergus Kennyde (ibid., p. 44). Donald Kenedi attested a charter by Stephen Flemyng, master of the Hospital of Soltre, 1426 (Soltre, p. 52). Gilbert Kennedy of Bargany in 1464 had a charter of the 25s. land of Coffe, and the lands of Kellolie in the parish of Sanct Michaelis Muntercasduff, etc., from Gilbert Kennedy of Cullean (Culzean) (Paterson, Ayr, II, p. 347). This charter is interesting as showing that the lands of Kirkmichael belonged of old to the clan Muntercasduff.

The name early made its way to the northeast. Duncan Kennedy was provost of Aberdeen, 1321-2, Peter Kyneidy was burgess there, 1333-42 (REA., I, p. 54, 72), David Kynidy, bailie in 1376 (ER., II, p. 542), and Thomas Kennedy was infeft in the ownership of Auchorthies, 1390 (Banchory-Devenick, p. 158). A family of Kennedys held the lands of Kermuck in Aberdeenshire for several generations. The Moray Kennedys, it is believed, came north with the possession of the earldom of Moray by Janet Kennedy and her son by James IV. This branch is known as Ceannaideach. In Arran the Kennedys are in the Gaelic of the island M'Cnusachainn or possibly M'Rusachainn, "a name which awaits explanation." The Kennedys of Lochaber are the ones known as M'WALRICK (G. MacUalraig), q.v.

Symson in his Large description of Galloway (written c. 1660) gives an old rhyme descriptive of the power of the Kennedys:

" 'Twixt Wigton and the toun of Air,
Portpatrick and the Cruives of Cree,
No man needs think for to bide there,
Unless he court with Kennedie."

The modern G. form of the name is Ceannaideach, Ir. Cinnéididh, from earlier Cinnéide or Cinneidigh, Mid. Ir. Cendétig (Book of Leinster, fol. 150b20), literally "ugly headed" (Kuno Meyer) or "grim headed" (Watson I, p. 409). Cf. the Gaelic name of Loch Etive, Loch Eitigh, "ugly, horrid loch," (from name of the goddess of the loch) Watson I, p. 46. Canedie 1420, Kanide 1526, Kanvdi 1521, Kenadie 1558, Kenate 1575, Kendy 1439, Kendye 1562, Keneby and Kenedy 1462, Keneidy 1342, Kenide 1535, Kennadee 1450, Kennatie and Kennaty 1567, Kennerty 1487, Kennetie and Kennety 1583, Kennetye 1566, Kennide 1500, Kennite 1538, Kennyde 1520, Kennydy and Kinydy 1486, Kenyde 1477, Kinnerty 1493, and among the Scots Guards in France Camede.

KENNETH. G. Coinneach, MG. Coinndech, Coinnidh, OG. Cainnech. The name of S. Cainnech, contemporary of S. Columba, recorded by Adamnan (V. C., III, 17) in Irish-Latin as Cainnechus, comes from * cannico-s, 'fair one.' From it again comes MacCoinnich, MACKENZIE, q.v. Simeon of Durham mentions a king of the Picts named Cynoth and Cynoht. This is the king whose death is recorded in AU. under A. D. 774: Mors Cinadhon regis Pictorum. Kyned thainus de Katel is a witness a. 1177 (CMN., 3). Kineth, Kyneth, or Kinef appears as witness in Lindores charters, c. 1200 (LAC., p. 11, 38, 88). Kennauch mac aht (ht here, as often, written for th) mentioned in the Chronicle of Melrose (1215) was probably a relative, possibly a son, of Malcolm Macheth (d. 1168). The patronymic Macheth seems to have become a family name. Kennauch Makyny was present at pleas held at Dull in Atholl, 1264 (RPSA., p. 349). Kenachv, brother of Bethan le Doul, was juror at Perth, 1305 (Bain, II, p. 456). One named Kineth held part of Sipland, Kirkcudbright, c. 1210-14 (BNCH., XVI, p. 263). Rorie Mc Eane VcKyniche and Gillespick VcEane VcKynnich in Torlosk, Mull, were put to the horn (declared outlaws), 1629 (RPC., 2. ser. III, p. 46). Gillespick also appears in same record (II, p. 341) as Archibald McEane VcKynyts. (2) The name which appears in English as Kenneth is of different origin. It is the old Scots Gaelic king's name Cinaed, found in the Book of Deer as Cinatha. It means 'firesprung,' the aed being the same as aed in Mackay. In early record it appears as Cinaed, Ciniod, Cionaodh, Cinaet, Cinaeth, Ciniath, Cinioch, Kinat, Kinath, Kinet, and Kineth.

KENNETHSON, 'son of KENNETH,' q.v., and so = MACKENZIE. Alexander Kennethson on an inquest at Inverness, 1430 (RMS., II, 179). Thomas Kenyeochsone, juror on inquest made at Dornoch in 1545 (OPS., II, p. 641). John Kennochsen, clerk of the diocese of Ross, 1444 (Pap. Lett., IX, p. 426), is probably John Kennachtsoun (perhaps is the same as John Kennati) who was chantor of Caithness in 1455 and 1497 (OPS., II, p. 617). Kenneochson or Kenndochson is found in Caithness 1663 (Caithness).

KENNIESON. William Kennieson in Jordieston, 1745 (Dunkeld). Here most probably a variant of CUNIESON, q.v.

KENNOWAY, KENNAWAY. From the lands of that name now forming the parish of Kennoway in Fife. Peter Kennaway in the parish of Torphichen is in record in 1684, and Peter Kennaway in Cathlaw in 1687 (Torphichen). David Kennaway, apothecary, burgess of Lithgow, 1687 (Inquis., 6866), Peter Kennoway was retoured heir of James Kennoway of Kettlestone in 1693 (Retours, Linlithgow, 276), and

KENNOWAY, Kennaway, *continued*

John Kennawie of Adieweill, in the parish of West Calder, appears in 1647 (*Inquis.*, 3344). R. Kennewie, Loch-house, 1816.

KENT. A family of this name, evidently English vassals of the Stewards, were settled at Innerwick in East Lothian, in the middle of the twelfth century. Radulfus de Kent received some lands in Ennyrwic from Walter the Steward c. 1165 (RMP., p. 5), and before 1177 he witnessed the gift of the church of Cragin (Craigie) in Kyle to the monks of Paisley (ibid., p. 232). Robert de Kent gave a territory in Inneruic to the monks of Melrose in the reign of William the Lion (*Melros*, p. 59), and a grant to the Abbey of Kelso c. 1190 (*Kelso*, p. 213). Thomas de Kent witnessed a charter by Alan Ronald's son, c. 1200–33 (*Melros*, p. 227), and as Thomas de Cantia (the Latin form of his name) witnessed a charter by John, son of Michael de Methkil, to Melrose, c. 1230 (*Wemyss*, II, p. xlvi). Robert de Kent of the county of Lanark rendered homage in 1296 (*Bain*, II, p. 204), William de Kent was admitted burgess of Aberdeen in 1408 (NSCM., I, p. 3), another William Kent had a lease of the auchtene part of Maistertoun in Fife, c. 1570 (RD., p. 487), and Robert Kent was a burgess of Burntisland in 1612 (*Laing*, 1639).

KENTIGERN. The name of Glasgow's patron saint. The sanctity attached to Kentigern was probably due to his having inherited the position of a priestly king (*Folklore*, XVII, p. 330). His name in Welsh is *Cyndeyrn* (in *Achau'r Saint*, 'Pedigrees of the Saints'), from *Cyn* + *Teyrn*, in composition *Deyrn*, 'chief lord' (*Anwyl*). In the *Annales Cambriae* (c. 612) the name appears as *Conthigirnus*. The Gaelic is *Ceanntighern*. It was a favorite forename in the sixteenth and seventeenth centuries, and, as we might naturally expect, most of the examples are from in and around Glasgow. Kentigern Tennant mentioned in Edinburgh, 1523 (*Soltre*, p. 267) may be the Kenthigern Tenende who granted letters of reversion of the lands of Lany and Aldirstoun in 1555 (*Protocols*). Kentigern Monypennie, prebendary of Spynie, 1534 (REM., intro., p. xxiii) is referred to in 1546 as dean and vicar-general of Ross (RMS.), and again in 1573 as deacon of Ross (*Seals Supp.*, 741). Kentigern Mortoune in Glasgow, 1537 (LCD., p. 101) is probably Kenthigern Mortoun, owner of a tenement there in 1557 (*Protocols*). Quintigern Huntar of Huntarstoun was killed at the battle of Fawsyde in 1548 (*Retours, Ayr*, 8); and the relict of quondam Kentigern McCrynnill is in record in 1557 (ER., XIX, p. 416). Kenthi-

gern Hynschaw obtained sasine of a tenement in Glasgow, 1563 (*Protocols*). Quintigernus Reid was 'horreareus' of Trinity College, Edinburgh, 1584 (*Soltre*, p. 152). Quintigernus Rig had a charter of the lands of Carberrie in 1600 (RD., p. 495). Quintigern Makcall was one of the bailies of Edinburgh, 1610 (*Laing*, 1597). Quintigernus Dalgleis in Mynto, Roxburghshire, 1616 (*Retours, Roxburgh*, 85). Quintigern Gibb was retoured heir in the lands of Achmilling, Ayrshire, in 1611 (*Retours, Ayr*, 513). Kentigern Henry and Kentigern M'Farlane were students at St. Andrews University in 1773–75.

KEPPAR. Kennach filius Keppar, juror on inquisition made at Banff, 1342 (REA., I, p. 73). William Keppar had a precept of remission for offences committed by him, 1536 (RSS., II, 2114).

KEPPIE. See KIPPIE.

KER, Kerr. An old Border surname of local or territorial origin. The Lothian branch of the family spells the name Kerr, and the Roxburgh branch Ker. In the fifteenth and sixteenth centuries often spelled CARR. The Lancashire place name Carr is from ON. *kjarr*, 'copsewood, brushwood.' Johannes Ker, *venator* (i.e. 'hunter') aput Swhynhope (now Soonhope near Peebles), one of the witnesses to the Diuise de Stobbo, c. 1190 (REG., 104), is the first of the name recorded in Border history. William Ker was witness to an agreement between the burgh of Irvine and Brice of Eglunstone (Eglinton) in 1205 (*Irvine*, I, p. 3). Richard Ker held the lands of Ylifistun (now Eliston) in Roxburghshire, in the reign of Alexander II, and Thomas Kaurr was sheriff of Roxburgh, 1264. The ship of Thomas Ker, merchant of Aberdeen, was plundered at sea by the English in 1273, and Richard Ker was summoned to answer to a charge of trespass at Fenewicke, 1279 (*Bain*, II, 9, 10, 149). Thomas Kevr or Kayr swore fealty at Kyngorne, 1291, and in 1296 was juror on an inquisition anent the lands of Disarde (Dysart) (ibid., II, p. 124, 204, 216). William Kerre of Avrshire, Henry Ker of Edinburghshire, and Nicol Kerre of Peeblesshire rendered homage in 1296 (ibid., p. 199, 203, 207), and Wvlliam Ker was one of an inquest on the lands of Lady Elena la Zuche in Conyngham, Ayrshire, 1296 (ibid., p. 216). John Kerr obtained a charter of all the lands and tenements in Auldtounburn resigned by John de Copeland, dated Monday after the Feast of the Purification of the Blessed Virgin, 1357, and another to him and his wife Mariot of part of the lands of Molle and Auldtounburn in the regality of Sproustoun resigned by William de Blackdene in 1358 (*Roxburghe*, p. 8). John Keor of Culter was juror in Lanark, 1432 (RAA., II, 65), and Huchon Ker witnessed sealing of an inquest anent a fishing on the Tweed, 1467 (RD., p. 359). Walter Carr of Sesseford was one of the ambassadors of James, king of Scotland, 1491 (*Bain*, IV, 1577). Car 1515, Kar 1680, Karre 1422, Kere 1493; Cer. The name of the family of Ker of Graden appears in 1686 as Care, Kare, Karr, and Kerr. See under CARR.

KERLIE. From (MAC)KERLIE, q.v. As Kearle it was an old surname in the parish of Ballantrae, Ayrshire (*Paterson*, II, p. 87). Kerle was the name of one of Sir William Wallace's 'speciall men' (Henry's *Wallace*, IV, 194).

KERMATH. See under KERMUCK.

KERMUCK. Generally supposed to be a form of CORMACK, but really of local origin, from Kermuck near Ellon. Willilmus dictus Kermaghe held lands in Aberdeenshire, 1382 (RMS., I, 682), and in 1552 we have mention of William Kempt "de Carmuick vel Carmuk" (*Retours, Aberdeen*, 12). In 1562 the name is spelled Cormuk (*Mair*, p. 37), and a family of Kennedys held the lands of Kermuck in Aberdeenshire for several generations. The name of James Kermay who leased Campsie in Angus in 1448 (*Cupar-Angus*, I, p. 127), may be a softened form of the name. Cf. Kermath, a current Fife surname. In 1655 there is mention of the Hill-faulds of Carmuck (*Retours, Aberdeen*, 331), and an Andrew Kermuck was a white-fisher in Montrose in 1685 (*Brechin*).

KERNEIL. Local. Willelmus de Kerneil, persona de Dunde, a witness, c. 1202–14 (RAA., I, 189). Perhaps the Willelmus de la Karnayll who witnessed a charter of the land of Neutyl (Newtyle) before 1226 (LAC., 39). From Carneil in the parish of Carnock, Fife.

KERON. See under KERRON.

KERR. See under KER.

KERRACHER. From (MAC)KERRACHER, for which see under MACERCHAR.

KERSE, KERSS. David Kerse was made burgess of Linlithqw in 1472 (*Sc. Ant.*, XVII, p. 120). Of local origin from Kerse near Grangemouth. Agnes Kerse in Chamerstoun, 1664 (*Dunblane*). (2) Now a rare Border surname. Doncan of Keryss witnessed an Ayrshire charter, c. 1370–80 (*Laing*, 64). Gilbert de Keris, witness, c. 1344 (*Melros*, 460). In 1513 James IV granted a charter to Alexander Kers of the lands of Ballincrieff, East Lothian. Rab Kerse o' the Trows, a famous fisherman of the time

of Scott, is called "that prince of water men" by the late Sir Herbert Maxwell.

KERSEN. Thomas Kersen, cooper in Edinburgh, 1653 (*Edinb. Marr.*), may have derived his name from Kersie near Alloa, the early form of which was Carsin. Robert Kersson (Kairsson or Kersein), minister at Neutoune near Edinburgh, 1661.

KERTMEL. From Cartmel, a parish in Lancashire. William de Kertmel witnessed confirmation by Christianus, bishop of Candida Casa, of the church of S. Marie and S. Bruoc of Dunrod to the monks of Holyrood in the reign of Malcolm IV (LSC., p. 20).

KESSAN, KESSEN, KESSON. From *Cessán*, a side form of *Cessóg*. See KESSOG. Kessan filius Senane witnessed a confirmation charter by Duncan filius Gillemichel Makedolf, c. 1270 (*Levenax*, p. 85). Earl Malcolm granted the lands of Blarvotych and Drumfynvoich with court of bloodwits, "which is called in Scots (que scotice dicitur) *fuilrath*," to Kessan Young for the yearly reddendo of twenty stones of cheese (ibid., p. 45). Evgenius filius Kessani witnessed confirmation charter by Bruce to Sir John Colquhoun, 1308 (*Lennox*, II, p. 407). Kessanus, clericus, witnessed a charter by Douenaldus, earl of Lennox, sometime after 1334 (*Levenax*, p. 93). Kessanus dictus McGhillecharrik is in record, 1360 (*Red. Bk. Menteith*, II, p. 241). Kessan de Nentbolg witnessed a charter of land of Blarechos in Strathblane by Duncan, earl of Levenax, 1398 (*Levenax*, p. 74). George Kessane was clerk of the diocese of Glasgow, 1562 (*Laing*, 748), and William Kessane and George Kessane were burgesses of Air, 1562 (RMS., III, 1421). As forename: Kessane Williamsoun, servant to Alexander Hamilton, laird of Auchinhowy, 1530 (*Trials*, I, p. 150 *). Kessen in Bathgate 1942.

KESSANSON. An early Englishing of MACKESSON, q.v. Alan Kessaneson was burgess of Stirling in 1481 (*Cambus.*, 211). John Kessanson of Nyngbog is mentioned in 1499 as being pursued in an action at law by John, lord Drummond before the Lords of the Privy Council for the spoliation of his lands of Dromond (now Drummond) (*Strathendrick*, p. 248).

KESSOG. S. Kessog, a bishop and martyr of the sixth century, is specially connected with Luss on Loch Lomond. His name in old Gaelic, *Cessóc, Ceaság*, is probably the same as *Cessán*, "who is styled 'son of the king of Alba, and a chaplain of Patrick.' His name is a reduced form of some compound beginning with *cess*, a spear" (*Watson* I, p. 277, 278). His

KESSOG, *continued*

bell is mentioned as still in existence in 1566 (RMS., IV). The endearing prefix *mo* 'my' is sometimes attached to his name, as Mechesseoc (1200) and Mahessoc (1211), and later misunderstood as Mac, in Mackessoc. He is commemorated in several place names. As forename: Kessog Findlauson, one of an inquest held at Dunipace, 1426 (*Cambus.*, 87).

KESWICK. A surname found in Dumfries, of local origin from the town of Keswick, north of Derwentwater, Cumberland.

KETTINS. An old surname in Angus derived from the old barony of the name, now the village and parish of Kettins. See under CAITHNESS.

KETTLE, KETTLES. Ketill is an ON. personal name (Old West Scand. *Ketill*, Old Dan. *Ketil*), and until recently was one of the four commonest surnames in Iceland. The surname Kettle though not so common as it once was in Fife is still met with there. "Kettles were weavers at Muthill, Perthshire, and gun-makers at Doune in the same county" in the eighteenth century (*Sc. Ant.*, IV, p. 113). The name of the gun-makers is spelled Kettell and Caddell, and they were probably relations of the Kettells, weavers in Muthill (ibid., VIII, p. 187). Ketell de Perth was burgess there in the reign of Alexander II (*Scon*, p. 62). James filius Ketel witnessed a composition between the Priory of May and Duncan de Inchesireth (now Inchyra), c. 1250 (*May*, 38). Gelis Kettill appears in parish of Nesting, Shetland, 1576 (*Oppressions*, p. 21), and James Kettle in Noorhead of Cultmalindie, 1689 (*Dunkeld*).

KETTLESTONE. Either from the lands of Kettilstoun (1605) in West Lothian, or from the lands of Kettilstoun (1635) in Stirlingshire. William de Ketlistoun made a quitclaim of the land of Ketlistoun in 1244 (*Cambus.*, 171), and William dictus de Ketilistoune is mentioned in 1282 (ibid., 49).

KEVAN. A Kirkcudbrightshire surname. A form of CAVENS, q.v. John Kevan, tenant in Barbershall, Parton, 1792 (*Kirkcudbright*), and five Kevands are recorded in the Commissariot Record of Wigtown in the eighteenth century. Agnes Kevand in Caumford, parish of Kirkinner, 1684 (RPC., 3. ser. X, p. 267).

KEVITT. James Kevitt and Martin Kevit were residents in the parish of Senneck, 1684 (RPC., 3. ser. IX, p. 568). From (Mac)Kevitt from Ir. *MacDhaibheid*, son of Davet, diminutive of David.

KEW. From the occupation of "cook," AF. *keu*, OF. *queux* (from Latin *coquus*). John le Keu, a Scots prisoner taken at the capture of Dunbar Castle, was sent to Montgomery Castle in 1296 (*Bain*, II, p. 177). William le Keu of Knolle in the county of Lanark and Richard le Keu of the county of Fife, rendered homage for their lands in the same year (ibid., p. 205), and Cristin le Cu of Stratherne was a Scots prisoner in Carlisle Castle in 1305 (ibid., p. 449). The seal of William of Knolle bears a raven (?) and S' *Will' Coci de Knol* (ibid., p. 553). Hugh Kew de Den was a notary public in Aberdeen in 1451 (SCM., V, p. 21).

KIBBLE. Perhaps from OE. *Ceo(l)bald*, 'nautically bold.' Alwinus Kybbel held land in Totenham, Middlesex, c. 1120 (*Lawrie*, p. 48). A payment was made to "the wife Kibbile" in Dunkeld, 1512 (*Rent. Dunk.*, p. 231). Jean Kibbil was one of a trio of strenuous viragos in Paisley, 1628 (Lees, *Abbey of Paisley*, p. 266), James Kible in Knock was burgess of Glasgow, 1666 (*Campsie*), and John Kible took the Test in Paisley, 1686 (RPC., 3. ser. XI, p. 496). William Kebble, 1742 (*Kilbarchan*).

KID, KIDD, KYD, KYDD. An old Angus surname in Dundee and Arbroath. (1) It *may* be from OE. *Cydd(a)* or *Cydd(i)*. Cf. Gilchrist Kide who held land near river Nethan, 1180–1203 (*Kelso*, 110). (2) The name, however, is more probably a diminutive of Christopher. Robertus Kyd de Dunde is mentioned in 1357 (CDE., 6). The seal of Andrew Kyde is appended to instrument of 1473 (*Seals Supp.*, 590). Sande Kid and Thome Kyd 'callit Balty Kid' were summoned to attend an inquest at Forfar, 1450, and John Kyd and Nychol Kyd appear in Brechin in same year (REB., I, 147, 152). Cristiane Kydde, son and heir of Roger Cissor, held part of the land of Langforgrunde in the sheriffdom of Perth, 1470 (RMS., II, 452). Alexander Kyd held a land in Aberdeen, 1492 (REA., I, p. 331). The Kyd family appears repeatedly in the burgh records of Dundee from 1520 up to the present day (*Wedd.*, p. 195). Alexander Kid was 'chanoun of our Soueran Lordis chappell' in Stirling, 1530 (SBR., p. 39, 266), William Kyd was burgess of Perth, 1563 (*Methven*, p. 66), Robert Kyd was portioner of Nethermains, 1571 (*Retours, Ayr*, 708), and William Kyd was retoured heir of Robert Kyd, son of Master James Kyd of Craigie, in lands in the parish of Alloa (*Inquis.*).

KIDDIE, KIDDY. See under KEDDIE.

KIDLAW. From Kidlaw in the parish of Yester, East Lothian. Henry de Kidelowe of the county of Edinburgh rendered homage in 1296. His seal bears S' Henr' de Kidlav (Bain, II, p. 201, 546). Robert de Kydlawe, friar preacher in Edinburgh in 1309 (Wilkins, *Concilia*, p. 382) is doubtless Robert de Kydlau who appears as rector of the church of Penchatland, c. 1320 (*Neubotle*, p. 297).

KIDSTON. From the lands of Kidston in the parish of Peebles. The 'tún' of Kide or Kyde. Gilcrist Kide held land near the river Nethan, c. 1180–1203 (*Kelso*, 110). Roger de Kydeston was juror on an inquest touching the lands of Hopkelchoc in 1259 (*Bain*, I, 2162; APS., I, pref. p. 88). As Roger de Kedistun he was also juror on an inquest along with Michael of Kedistun regarding the moss of Walthamshope in 1262 (*Peebles*, p. 5; APS., pref. p. 91). Kidstone 1687, Kidstoun 1733, Kidstoune 1652.

KIER. A variant of KEIR, q.v.

KILBOWIE. From Kilbowie near Glasgow. Andrew Kilbowie or Kilbowy was chosen "extraordiner persone of counsell" in Stirling in 1604 (SBR., p. 112).

KILBRIDE. From the town of (East) Kilbride in the Middle Ward of Lanarkshire. John de Kilbrid witnessed a charter by Florence, bishop elect of Glasgow, c. 1202–07 (RMP., p. 110), Reginald de Kelbride was appointed an attorney in 1277 (*Bain*, I, 89), and Gilbert de Kilbride of the county of Lanark rendered homage in 1296 (*Bain*, II, p. 204). Druwet de Kilbryde of the county of Are, who also rendered homage in 1296 (ibid., p. 213), may have derived his name from the small town of (West) Kilbride in the district of Cunninghame, Ayrshire.

KILCONQUHAR. From Kilconquhar('Church of S. Conquhar,' commemorated 3 May) in Fife. Duncan de Kilkuncwauch witnessed the gift of 15 acres of Balmulinach (Balmerino) to the church of St. Andrews before 1225 (RPSA., p. 272). Adam de Kilconcath, who was killed in the 'Holy War' in 1270 (*Chron. Mail.*, s.a.), is Adam de Kilconquhar who became earl of Carrick in right of his wife, Marjory, daughter of Nigel, second earl (*Macdonald*, 1497). A petition was made on behalf of Thomas de Kilconkar for a canonry in Moray, 1380 (*Pap. Pet.*, 1557).

KILCULLEN. This surname, recorded in Oban and neighborhood, is of Irish origin, from Ir. *Mac Giolla Chaillin*, 'son of the servant of S. Caillin.' The g of *giolla* being hardened through the influence of the c of *Mac* which has been rejected.

KILDAY. *See under* KELDAY.

KILDUNCAN. From the old lands of Kilduncan near Kingsbarns, in Fife. Bartholomeu de Kyldunham of Fife rendered homage in 1296 (*Bain*, II, p. 204). His seal bears a star of six points and S' *Bartholom'i* (?) *de Kil* . . . (ibid., p. 549). Kyldunham must, I think, he meant for Kilduncan. John de Kylduncane possessed a land in Crale in 1421 (RAA., II, 56).

KILGOUR. From Kilgour near Falkland, Fife. The surname is found all over Fife and is also common in Aberdeenshire. It is also found in North Australia, and has given name to a river there. Sir Thomas Kilgour, who appears in 1528 as chaplain of St. Thomas in the palace of Falkland (RSS., I, 4018), is probably the same "Sir" Thomas Kilgoure to whom several entries of payments of ten bolls of bear occur in 1563, 1566, 1567, etc. (ER., XIX, p. 243, 343, 385). In 1567 there is also an entry of an annual pension of 45 shillings to Sir Thomas Kingoure (ibid., p. 393). John Kilgour of Aberdeen was ordered to serve on a ship of war in 1540 (CRA., p. 172), Richard Kilgour appears twice as a witness in 1550 and 1551 (RMS., IV, 455, 645), David Kilgour of Lathrisk was one of an assize in Fife in 1555 (ibid., 1006), and there is mention of a debt due to Henry Kilgor in 1572 (*Dysart*, p. 37). David Kylgour was retoured heir of Alexander Kylgour de Nethill, his father, in 1600 (*Retours, Fife*, 86), John Kilgour was "sacristar of the cathedrall kirk of Aberdene" in 1607 (SCM., V, p. 134), and Henry Kilgour was retoured heir of his grandfather, Andrew Kilgour, in 1644 (*Retours, Aberdeen*, 274). Hamilton Kilgour, minister of Collace, died in 1777. Kilgor 1572, Kilgowre 1665.

KILHAM. Peter de Killum who witnessed a charter by Roger Maule and Godit, his spouse, to the church of St. Cuthbert of Carram, c. 1200 (SHSM., IV, p. 310), derived his name from Kilham in the parish of Kirk Newton, in Cumberland.

KILLAN. John Killan in Cleckaime, parish of Lesmahago, 1677, and Robert Killand in Deidwatters, parish of Lesmahago, 1678 (*Lanark CR.*). This name in Irish is O'Cilleáin, descendant of Cillean, a diminutive of Ceallach, an ancient and once very common name.

KILLOCK. From the old forty-shilling lands of Killoch (1624), Ayrshire, of old extent. John Killock witnessed the tack of Little Mains of Caldwell, 1649 (*Caldwell*, I, p. 287). Mungo Kelloch was recorded in the parish of Kilmalcome, 1657 (*Kilbarchan*), and Hellin Kellock was examined for the Test in Tinwald, 1685 (RPC., 3. ser. XI, p. 434). John Kellock was

KILLOCK, *continued*
a cordiner in Sanquhar, 1659, and three more are recorded near there (*Dumfries*). Cf. KEL-LOCK.

KILLRIE. William Killrie in Edinburgh, 1682 (*Edin. App.*), may have derived his surname from Kilry in Perthshire.

KILMAIRS. Thomas Kilmairs alias Wischett, burgess freeman of Glasgow, 1600 (*Burgesses*), derived his surname from the burgh of Kilmaurs (Kilmareis 1600, Kilmaris 1601) Ayrshire.

KILMAN. A variant of KELMAN, q.v.

KILMARNOCK. From the town of Kilmarnock in Ayrshire. Johannes de Kylmernoc who held land in Ayrshire in the reign of Robert I (RMS., I, 46) is probably the Johannes de Kylmernock who appears as burgess of Ayr in 1348 (*Friars Ayr*, p. 16). See KILMERNOU.

KILMARON. From the lands of Kilmaron in the parish of Cupar, Fife. Several individuals of this name appear as witnesses in charters by Malcolm, earl of Fife, c. 1204–28 (SHSM., IV, p. 311). Thomas de Kilmaron witnessed a charter by Earl Malcolm of the church of Abercrumbin to Dunfermline Abbey (RD., p. 83), and as dominus Thomas de Kilmaron was a witness, c. 1239, to a charter to the Hospital of Soltre (*Soltre*, p. 13). About 1220 he witnessed a grant by Thomas de Lundin to the nuns of North Berwick (CMN., 11), and, as Thomas de Kilmeron, witnessed the charter by Malcolm, earl of Fife, a. 1228 (ibid., 9). He is probably the Thomas de Kimmalron who witnessed a charter by Fergus, earl of Buchan before 1214 (CAB., p. 408). A later Thomas de Kylmeron in 1293 granted a tack of the lands of Torer in Fife in favor of Alexander called Schyrmeschur, son of Colin son of Carun (SHR., XVII, p. 157). Sir Peter de Kilmaron, knight, witnessed a charter by David de Strathbolgy, earl of Atholl, c. 1284 (*Cupar-Angus*, I, p. 349). William of Kilmaron who held the land of Levingston and the land of Hirdmanston before they were granted to Archibald of Douglas by Malcolm, earl of Fife, in the beginning of the thirteenth century, may be the William of Kilmaron who witnessed a charter by Malcolm, earl of Fife to Alexander of Blar, c. 1250 (*Rothes*, p. 503).

KILMARTIN. An Irish surname recorded in Fife. Ir. (*Mac*) *Giolla Mhartain*, 'son of (S.) Martin's servant.'

KILMERNOU. Reynaud de Kilmernou of Ayrshire, who rendered homage, 1296 (*Bain*, II,

p. 205), probably derived his surname from the burgh of Kilmarnock. His seal shows an eight-rayed figure, *S' Regnal d' Kilmernoc* (ibid., p. 556). See KILMARNOCK.

KILMINSTER. Lower and his successors record this as a Scottish surname, from Kilminster near Wick, Caithness. I have never come across the surname in record. The local pronunciation of the place name is Kilmster, which points to a Norse ending -*ster*. Bardsley's surnames Kilminster, Killmaster, Kilmister, certainly did not derive from the Caithness place name.

KILOH. *See under* KILLOH.

KILPATRICK. Of local origin from one or other of places so named. Stevene de Kilpatric del counte de Dunfres rendered homage, 1296. His seal shows a saltire and chief, *S' Jehan de Kirkpatrik* (*Bain*, II, p. 198, 545). Nigel Kilpatrick was a Scots prisoner of war in Kenilworth Castle, 1302 (*Bain*, II, p. 341). Thomas de Kylpatrik, rector of Suthek, 1468 (REG., 393); and Marion Kilpatrick in Kildonane 1700 (*Wigtown*), probably derived their surnames from Kilpatrick in the parish of Closeburn, Dumfriesshire. John Kylpatryk, bailie of Thomas, abbot of St. Colm's Inch, 1495 (*Laing*, 221), and Thomas Kilpatrick of Easter Calder, 1669 (*Campsie*), may have derived their name from (East or West) Kilpatrick in Dumbartonshire.

KILROS. Local. Malcolm de Kilros, a Scots prisoner of war in Rochester Castle, 1297 (*Bain*, II, 939).

KILRUIFF. Local. John Kilruiff in Carntrodleane was charged with wrongeous intromission of sheep from James Kilruiff in Tofthillis, 1608 (RSCA., II, p. 111). Another James Kilruiff in Auldfauld is mentioned in the same year (ibid., II, p. 137).

KILSPINDIE. From the village of Kilspindie in the parish of the same name, Perthshire. The Register of the Priory of St. Andrews contained: "53. Carta terrarum de Knispinethyn, et Finegally, et Dundinauch, facta per Davidem episcopum Malcolmo de Knispineth, 1247" (from the contents as printed by Pinkerton, *Enquiry*, new ed., Edinburgh, 1814, I, p. 454). Malcolmus de Kinspinithin and Margeria his wife with consent of William, their eldest son, granted part of a toft in Perth to the monks of Lundors, c. 1200 (LAC., p. 80). This Malcolm also held land in St. Andrews (RPSA., p. 285). Maucolum de Kynspinedv, tenant of the bishop of St. Andrews in Fife rendered homage, 1296. His seal bears a rabbit

(?) eating the root of a tree, S' *Malcolmi de Kimspinod* (?) (*Bain*, II, p. 205, 544).

KILVINTOUN. Mr. Richard Kilvintoun or Kilwyntoune who had a pension granted him in reign of David II (RMS., I, App. II, 1267) derived his name from Kilvington in North Riding of Yorkshire.

KILWHISS. From the lands of Kilwhiss in Fife. Alexander de Kylwos was promoted from the chancellorship to the deanery of Ross in 1350 (*Pap. Lett.*, I, p. 204). He is the person mentioned in the Calendar of Fearn as bishop of Ross under the name of Alexander Frylquhous. His name is also spelled Kylquhous and de Culchws (*Beauly*, p. 202). The death of Sir Thomas Kilqwhous, chaplain of Tallatry, in the parish of Tain, is recorded in 1503 (RSS., I, 981).

KIMMERGHAME. From Kimmerghame near Duns, Berwickshire. Robert de Kynbriggeham, Johan fitz Wautier de Kymbregam, and Johan de Kymbrigham, all three of the county of Berewyke, rendered homage in 1296 (*Bain*, II, p. 205–207), and David de Kynbridgeham was attorney for the custumars of Berwick in 1330 (ER., I, p. 278). John of Kymbrigeham, son of David of Kymbrigeham, held a tenement in Berwick-on-Tweed in 1367 (*Bain*, IV, 135).

KINBUCK. From the lands of Kinbuck, a few miles north from Dunblane. Ricardus miles de Kenbuc witnessed a confirmation charter by Tristram to Inchaffray, c. 1208 (*Inchaffray*, p. 25), and he also appears in other Inchaffray charters between 1211 and 1234 (ibid., p. 25, 47, 48). In a charter by Robert, earl of Stratheryn the earl calls him "Dominus R. filius Lugan miles meus" (ibid., p. 50). He was brother of the Countess Ysenda, Earl Gilbert's second wife (ibid., p. 40). "The proof of the identity of 'Ricardus de Kenbuc' with 'R. filius Lugan' is found in a charter granted to the Abbey of Cambuskenneth by Malcolm de Dromond, lord of Mar, in 1395, ratifying gifts of parts of the lands of Cambushinnie, made to the Abbey by his predecessors, 'Richard son of Luguen' and 'Joachim de Kynbute'" (*Inchaffray*, p. 273). Joachim de Kenbuc (Kynbuc or Kinbucche) was one of the witnesses to a grant of the church of S. Mordac of Kellemurthe (i.e. Kilmorich in Argyllshire) to Inchaffray, c. 1246, and also appears in other charters in the same record between 1247–66 (ibid., p. 64–65, 68, 77, 85). Sir Joachim was the first of the family of Kinbuck of that Ilk, who held the lands of Kinbuck for several generations (LAC., p. 243). Alan de Kynbuk or Kynbuc witnessed the settlement of a dispute regarding the patronage of the vicarage of

Strugeth in 1287 (*Inchaffray*, p. 111), and is a witness in other charters between 1285 and 1290 (HMC., 2. Rep., App., p. 166; *Athole*, p. 705). Maucolum de Kynbuk of the county of Perth rendered homage in 1296 (*Bain*, II, p. 200), Nicholas de Kynbuk appears as archdeacon of Dunblane in 1358 (LIM., p. 31), and William of Kinbuk was one of the inquest on the lands of Aldy in 1432 (*Athole*, p. 707). The seal of Archibald de Kenbucke is appended to a charter of the lands of Classmigall in Strathern in 1455 (*Seals. Supp.*, 556; *Macdonald*, 1498), and in 1471 Malcolm of Kynbuk resigned the lands of Glassingal into the king's hands (SBR., p. 255).

KINCAID, KINKAID. Of territorial origin from the lands of Kincaid in the parish of Campsie, Stirlingshire. Robert de Kyncade *de eodem* appears as witness in 1450 (LSC., 125) and 1451 (REG., 365). Patrick de Kynkad and George de Kynkad witnessed charters of lands in St. Leonard's, Edinburgh, in 1457 (*Neubotle*, 284), and David de Kyncade was bailie of Edinburgh in 1467 and again in 1493 (ibid., 299). Thomas Kyncavd *de eodem* witnessed foundation charters of the Collegiate Church of Biggar in 1545 (SCM., v, p. 308), and appears again in 1550 as Thomas Kyncaide of that Ilk (*Protocols*, I). James Kincaid, notary at Kilchoan, and his servitor Alexander Kincaid, appear in 1609 (*Poltalloch Writs*, p. 78). Kinkaid 1547, Kyncaid 1510, Kynked 1493.

KINCAVEL. From the old lands of Kincavel, now Kingscavil, in the parish of Linlithgow, West Lothian. Hugo de Kyncavil was juror on an inquest made apud Rane in 1413 (REA., I, p. 214). Henrie Kyncauile who received possession of a land in Dunfermline in 1488 (DBR., 1) appears in the same record as Kyncauill and Kyncawill. James Kincavell was burgess of Monrois (Montrose) in 1589 (RPC., IV, p. 401), and Henri Kinkevill, a sailor, is recorded in Burntiland in 1642 (PBK., p. 221).

KINCORTH. Gilbert, Arthur, and Andreas de Kyncorth, vassals of the abbot of Arbroath, had a lease of a passage boat from the abbot of Arbroath, 1435 (RAA., II, p. 69). Local, but not likely to be from Kincorth in Moray.

KINCRAIGIE. Of local origin from a place of the name. There are places named Kincraigie in Fife, Perthshire and Aberdeenshire. Sir James Kincragi was dean of Aberdeen, 1520 (*Macdonald*, 1504), and Magister John Kyncragy is recorded there in 1537 (REA., II, p. 112). Sir Andrew Kincragy was vicar of Parton, Kirkcudbright, 1541 (*Anderson*). Nisbet says "of that Ilk," but does not say where. Kincrage 1502 (CDE., 58), Kyncraigye and Kyncragye 1549.

KINDNESS. An Aberdeenshire surname. Androw Kyndnes is recorded in Banff, 1615 (*Rec. Elgin,* I, p. 142). Frederick Kindness of Turriff served in the first Great War and George Kindness was killed (*Turriff*).

KINFAUNS. From the old lands of Kinfauns in the parish of the same name in Perthshire. John de Kinfaunes, burgess of Perth, is in record in 1324 (*Milne,* p. 19).

KING. A surname of some antiquity and still met with in many parts of the country, Berwick, Fife, and Aberdeen. The first of the name recorded in Aberdeenshire is "Robertus dictus King" who bequeathed to the prior and convent of St. Andrews land in that shire which was the subject of a convention in 1247 between his brother's daughter, Goda, and the prior and convent (*Sc. Peer.,* III, p. 588). A family of this name were in possession of Barra or Barrocht in the parish of Bourtie from an early period, and in 1493 parted with a portion of the land (*Inverurie,* p. 103). John Kyng was burgess of Perth in 1421 (RAA., II, 56), James Kynge witnessed sealing of an inquest anent a fishing on the Tweed in 1467 (RD., p. 359), John King witnessed a sasine in 1495 and Patrick King the same in 1525 (*Home,* 26, 35). Adam King (d. 1620), a Scottish scholar Latinized his name Adamus Regius. Some of the proscribed Macgregors are said to have adopted this name.

KINGAN. Alexander Kingarn, burgess of Kirkcudbright, 1679 (*Kirkcudbright*), John Kinging, resident in the parish of Senneck, 1684 (RPC., 3. ser. IX, p. 568), Andrew Kingan in Large, Kirkcudbright, 1689 (ibid., XIV, p. 738), and Ann Kingan in Craiglemine, 1787 (*Wigtown*). From Ir. *O'Cuineáin,* descendant of Culinean (an attenuated form of Conán).

KINGARTH. Thomas de Kyngarth of Perthshire who rendered homage, 1296 (*Bain,* II, p. 200, 532), derived his surname from the lands of Kingarth in the stewartry of Strathern. His seal bears a goat leaping, a serpent (?) below, S' *Thomae de Kyngerth* (?).

KINGHORN. Of territorial origin from the old barony of the same name in Fife. Adam de Kyngorn, clericus regis, witnessed a charter by Roger de St. Michaele between 1204–11 (RAA., I, 81), and William de Kyngorn was constable of Edinburgh in 1292 (*Neubotle,* p. 292). Two clerics of this name rendered homage in 1296: (1) Mestre William de Kyngorn persone of Lystone in the county of Linlescu. His seal bears an eagle displayed, and S' *Wilʼi dʼ Kyngorn clerici* (*Bain,* II, p. 194, 211, 543). (2) The other William de Kyn-

gorne who rendered homage was persone of the church of Kyltierne in the county of Inthernesse, i.e. Inverness (*Bain,* II, p. 210). Johannes de Kingorn, fistularius regis, had a uniform of striped cloth, 1303–4 (*Bain,* IV, p. 474). Adam de Kyngorn, a notary public in 1343 (*Melros,* II, 457) may be the Adam de Kynghorn who was rector of Karn in 1357 (*Neubotle,* p. 309). Gilbert de Kyngorn was a burgess of Glasgow in 1428 (LCD., p. 244), Robert Kingorn was a monk of Paisley in 1432 (RMP., p. 370), and in 1454 Emmote de Kyngorn held a land in Glasgow (LCD., p. 175). Laurence Kyngorne had warrant to import Scottish goods and export English merchandise in 1495 (*Bain,* IV, 1613), and James Kinghorne who had a charter of the lands of Morpheisfauld in 1597 may be the James Kingorne who had a "tak of the greit custumes of Dumfermling" in 1605 (RD., p. 494, 502). Alexander Kinghorn, a Scot, was physician-in-ordinary to King Christian II of Denmark (1513–1523).

KINGLASS. From the lands of Kinglass, near Bo'ness, West Lothian. Matthew de Kynglas, burgess of Linlithgowshire, rendered homage in 1296, and in 1312 a horse was purchased from him (*Bain,* II, p. 198; III, p. 421). An indenture was made between Matthew filius quondam William de Kynglas and the Hospital of Soltre in 1306 (*Soltre,* p. 43, 44). Andrew de Kynglas was burgess of Glasgow, 1413 (REG., 323), and mention was made of the *ortus* of John Kynglasse in Perth, 1497 (RAA., II, 382).

KINGLASSIE. From the vill of Kinglassie in the parish of the same name in Fife. Mirable Kinglassie possessed a twelfth part of the lands of Caldsvde, Inverkeithing, in the latter part of the fifteenth century (William Stephen, *History of Inverkeithing and Rosyth,* p. 101, 122). Isobella Kynglassy, daughter of John Kynglassy, burgess of Perth, sold an annual rent in that burgh, and Patrick Kynglassy was one of the witnesses (*Rollok,* 26). John Kynglassy was a mason at the querrell of Cragy, 1551 (ibid., 108).

KINGLEDORES. From the place of this name in the parish of Drummelzier, Peeblesshire. David Kyndilduris witnessed an instrument of sasine in 1525 (*Home,* p. 35), and George Kenultours is recorded in Quhitsome in 1665 (*Lauder*).

KINGO. Margt. Kingow "captivat for witchcraft," 1643 (Cook, *Annals of Pittenweem,* p. 49). Besseta King3eo (3 here = guttural *y*), heir of Thomas King3eo olim burgess of Pettinweim, 1650 (*Retours, Fife,* 1586). Denmark's greatest hymnographer, Bishop Thomas

Hansen Kingo (1634–1707), was of Scottish extraction, grandson of a Scottish tapestry weaver who settled in Slangerup.

KINGSON. John Kingsoun (Kyngsone or Kyngsoun) appears as witness in Kirkwall, Orkney, 1532–1560–1575 (REO., p. 137, 264, 337). The surname is recorded in England in 1379. Bardsley says "the son of the man who acted as king in the local festivals," but?

KINGSTOUN. John Kingstoun, minister at Sandwik, 1574 (RMR.). Probably from one of the twenty-four or more places of the name in England.

KINHILT. A surname from the old lands and barony of the name in Wigtownshire, now spelled Kilhilt. Now obsolete. Thomas de Kithehilt of Wigtownshire, who rendered homage in 1296 (Bain, ii, p. 205), may have derived his name from this place.

KININMONT, KININMONTH, KININMONTH. Of territorial origin from lands of the name in Fife. There are two Kininmonths in Fife, one in the parish of Monimail, the other near Pitscottie. Kinmont in Annandale was Kynmund in 1529. Kyninmonthe now Kinmouth is in Banffshire. Among the witnesses to a charter granted by Ernald, bishop of St. Andrews (1160–62), is Odo marescallus, 'Odo the marshal' (RPSA., p. 127). In later charters this Odo appears as the dapifer (ibid., p. 45, 134, 175, etc.; Scon, 40), or senescald (ibid., p. 135, 141, etc.) of Bishop Richard (1188–1202). About 1189–99 William the Lion confirmed to him a charter of the lands of Kynninmonth which had been granted by the prior of St. Andrews (Macfarlane, ii, p. 531, 533). His son Adam frequently appears as a charter witness simply as Ada or Adam filius Odonis (RPSA., p. 154, 157, 260, etc.; Scon, 84). Between 1250–60 Adam filius Odonis with consent of his wife and John his heir, made a sale and granted a charter to the prior of St. Andrews of his land "in villa Sancti Andree cum edificiis in ea constructis" (RPSA., p. 281). "John's charter is not recorded; but his original deed of consent, executed at the same time, and before the same witnesses, with the charter of his father, is still extant; and on his seal we find the family surname for the first time: S' Iohannis de Kininmvnd" (ibid., preface, p. xviii). Matthew, brother of Odo, was bishop of Aberdeen, 1172–99 (REA., i, preface, p. xx–xxi). Elias de Kinindmund witnessed a Fife charter granted in 1228 (Laing, 6), and c. 1290 another Helva de Kynninmond witnessed a charter of lands "Johanni filio Willelmi filii Lambini" (ibid., 15). William de Kynemuthe of Edinburghshire rendered

homage, 1296. His seal reads: Sigill. Willi de Kinmonet (Bain, ii, p. 201, 551). Alexander de Kinnemunt, canon of Brechin in 1322 (Pap. Lett., ii, p. 223), archdeacon of Lothian, 1327 (LSC., 88; RAA., i, p. 339) was elected bishop of Aberdeen, 1329 (Dowden, p. 110), and a later Alexander de Kyninmund was elected to the same bishopric in 1356 (REA., i, preface, p. xxx). Provision was made in 1329 of a canonry and prebend of Aberdeen to Malisius de Kinninmont (Pap. Lett., ii, p. 297), and another Malisius de Kynynmonde was juror on lands in Fife, 1390 (RMS., i, 854). Jamvs of Kyninmond of that Ilke in 1438 asserted his right to the office of bailie, steward, and marischel under the prior of St. Andrews, which his remote ancestors held under the early bishops (RPSA., preface, p. xix). In an old French chronicle mention is made of several Scots who fought at the battle of Liége, 14 September, 1407, among whom is Helis de Guenemont. Other Kininmonts who settled in Burgundy and Touraine, and acquired large estates there, appear in French records as Quinemonts (Burton, Scot abroad, i, p. 66, 82). Others of the name (Kinnemond, Kinninmundt) settled in Sweden, but the family there has now died out. In Scotland the old family of the name terminated early in the eighteenth century in an heiress, Grissel, who married Sir William Murray of Melgund. Kennemuthe 1296, Keyninmonth 1639, Kinemunthe 1291, Kinenmont 1653, Kinindmund c. 1228, Kininmund 1303, Kinninmont 1714, Kinninmonthe and Kinnynmonthe 1651, Kinninmunth 1298, Kyninmond 1438, Kynnemunth 1296, Kynnynmonde 1427, Kynvnmoncht 1536. The name of Janet Kinugmont in Wester Balnabriche, 1621 (Brechin) is probably a misspelling. There was a D. Kinninmont in Anstruther, 1816.

KINKAID. See under KINCAID.

KINKELL. From the hamlet and ancient parish of the name in Strathearn district of Perthshire. Walter Kynkell was "marifeodus vnius partis senescallatus de Stratherne" in 1488 (REG., p. 464, 503). Jon Kinkel gave evidence in a witch trial in Brechin in 1650 (Extracts, records Presbytery of Brechin, p. 46).

KINLOCH, KINLOCK. From the lands or barony of Kinloch at the head of Rossie Loch, parish of Collessie, Fife. Murinus de Kindelouc or Kindelouch and Maurice de Kindelouch witnessed grants by Roger de Quincy and Henry de Winton, c. 1202–52 (RPSA., p. 256, 257, 272). Galfridus de Keldelach was a charter witness, c. 1237 (LAC., 78), and John de Kyndelouch and his heirs had a confirmation of the privilege of a mill-pool in Fife, c. 1250

KINLOCH, KINLOCK, *continued*

(SHR., II, p. 173). William de Kyndelloche of Fifeshire rendered homage in 1296. His seal bears a rabbit below foliage, S' *Will'i de Kinlhoi*, and in the same year as William de Kindelow he was one of an inquest on the lands of Disarde (Dysart) (*Bain*, II, p. 204, 216, 545). Johannes de Kyndelouch, *miles*, attested a confirmation charter by David II to Ysabella de Fyf in 1365 (RMS., I, 221), Sir John Kyndeloch was chaplain to friar Andrew Meldrum, brother of the Hospital of St. John of Jerusalem in Scotland, 1438 (*Bain*, IV, 1117). The Kinlochs have had a long and honorable connection with Dundee, and George Kinloch was elected the first M. P. for Dundee in the Reformed Parliament of 1832. Kynloche 1615, Kynloicht and Kynloycht 1555.

KINLOCHIE. The seal of Johannes de Kenlochy is appended to a charter of an annual rent from a tenement in St. Andrews dated 1438 (*Seals. Supp.*, 557), George Kenloquhy was bailie of Crail, 1513 (*Crail*, p. 40), and Robert Kenloquhy was 'baxter and citiner' of St. Andrews in 1557 (*Laing*, 666).

KINLOSS. Andrew Kynloss, friar preacher in Aberdeen, 1486 (REA., II, p. 300), derived his surname from the hamlet of Kinloss in the parish of the same name in Moray.

KINMAN. This surname is most probably a shortened form of KINNINMONTH, q.v. John Ky(n)man witnessed a quitclaim of the land of Drumkarauch in 1260 (RPSA., p. 346). Johannes Kynman was senescallus to Sir Gilbert de Haya (*Cupar-Angus*, I, p. 339). The S' *Nicolaii Kynman* is appended to a resignation of the lands of Megginch, 1461 (*Seals Supp.*, 591). William Kinmond of Hill, 1652, appears again in 1665 as William Kinman of Hill when he granted a bond in favor of Mr. Henry Malcome (DPD., I, p. 107; II, p. 454). Andrew Kinmann was burgess of Dundee in 1651 (*Brechin*), and Sophie Kinman had letters of alienation of the lands of Mureaidge in the lordship of Errol in 1664 (DPD., I, p. 151). Kynman 1658.

KINMONT. Local, from Kinmont in the lordship of Methven, Perthshire. Robert de Kinmont was vicar of the parish church of Cupar, 1440 (RD., p. 300), Robert Kynmont in Dundee was charged with aiding the English, 1552 (*Beats*, p. 327), and Andrew Kinmont was burgess of Dundee, 1634 (*Brechin*). Recorded in Errol, 1941.

KINNA. From (MAC)KENNA, q.v.

KINNACH. A form of KENNETH, q.v.

KINNAIRD. From the barony of the same name in Perthshire. The first of the name in record is Radulphus Ruffus, who received a charter of the lands from William the Lion, c. 1180 (*Macfarlane*, I, p. 52). Between 1204 and 1214 there is record of a royal confirmation of a grant by Richard of Kinnard, grandson of Radulf "Ruffus". (*Laing*, 3). Rauf de Kynnard swore fealty to Edward I at Kincardine in 1296. The seal attached to his homage bears a shield charged with a saltire, cantoned with four crosses, S' *Radulf de Kynard* (*Bain*, II, p. 184, 214). Richard de Kynnard of the county of Fyfe also rendered homage in the same year (ibid., p. 214). Reginald de Kynnard was one of the witnesses to a charter by John de Wardroperisthon, c. 1330 (SCM., v, p. 10). William de Kynard was burgess of Perth in 1428 (RMS., II, 109), another (?) William de Kynnarde was a notary of St. Andrews diocese in 1430 (*Irvine*, I, p. 24), Thomas de Kynnarde, a charter witness in 1431 (HP., II, p. 169), Andrew de Kynharde, a charter witness in Dundee in 1435 (ibid., II, p. 177), Alan de Kynnarde granted a charter of the lands of Hill, 1449 (RMS., II,), and William Kynnard of that Ilk is mentioned in 1546 (SCM., IV, p. 217). Erche (i.e. Archie = Archibald) Kinȝerd was a tenant of the Abbey of Kelso in 1567 (*Kelso*, p. 524). Kynnaird 1618, Kynnerd 1591, Keneris (pl.) 1603. Other forms are Kinard (1643), Kynarde, Kynnart.

KINNAIRDSLIE. Sometime between 1177 and 1199 Stephen de Kinardesleia or Kinardeslec appears as witness to a charter to Robert Croc and to one to Henry de Nes granting them permission to build chapels for their private use (RMP., p. 78), and is also witness to a grant of the church of Polloc to the Abbey of Paisley within the same period (ibid., p. 98, 100). Sometime between 1218 and 1222, as Stephen de Kinnardesley, he sold his land of Drumsleed to Gregory, bishop of Brechin (REB., II, 271, 272). Walter de Kinardley was juror on an inquest at Gerwan (Girvan) in 1260 on the marriage contracted between Hector, son of Sir Hector, and Samuel Mackan's daughter (*Bain*, I, 2674).

KINNEAR, KYNNIER. From the lands of Kinnear near Wormit, Fife. Symon, son of Michael, gave a carucate of land of Cathelai to the church of St. Andrews. His grant was confirmed by King Malcolm IV (RPSA., p. 195), and King William confirmed the grant of Chathelach, with common pasture for twenty-four beasts, and eighty sheep, which Symon, son of Michael gave, and his son Alan confirmed (ibid., p. 212). The descendants of Symon took the name of Kinnear, and were the vassals of the Priory of St. Andrews in the lands of Kathlac, etc., which they held till the beginning of the eighteenth century (*Lawrie*, p. 448). Reginald de Kener witnessed gift of one mark of silver annually by Alexander, earl of Buchan to the Abbey of Arbroath, c. 1250 (RAA., I, p. 266). Simon, son of Simon de Kyner, made a grant of part of the lands of Kathlac to the church of St. Andrew which was confirmed by Alexander II, 1216 (RPSA., p. 292, 294). Sir John de Kyner rendered homage, 1296 (*Bain*, II, p. 169), Petrus Kynior was elected common councillor of Aberdeen, 1477 (*Guildry*, p. 189), John de Kynor was admitted burgess of Aberdeen, 1439, and Adam Kynnor in 1457 (NSCM., I, p. 5, 15). John Kynnier was retoured heir of David Kynnier *de eodem*, his father, 1543 (*Retours, Fife*, 2), and Joanne Kingzow in Brechin, 1600, appears again in 1602 as John Keingzer (REB., II, 231, 232). John Kenyr, charter witness in Inverness, 1536 (*Laing*, 403). Henry Kinneir of Kinneir was appointed commendator of Balmerino Abbey, 1574, and John Kinneir of that Ilk was bailie of the abbey (Campbell, *Balmerino and its abbey*). Kenneir 1613, Kinner 1601, Kynnair 1598, Kynner 1527, Kynnier 1662.

KINNEIL, KINNELL. Margaret Kynnell in Inverkeithing was accused of witchcraft in 1623 (RPC., XIII, p. 181). Perhaps from the village of Kinneil near Bo'ness in West Lothian, rather than from Kinneil in Angus. William de Kynell, however, who was custumar of Montrose in 1359, more probably derived his surname from Kinneil near Montrose.

KINNERIS. Of local origin from Kinneris near Letham, Angus. James Kineris was admitted burgess of Dundee, 1602 (*Wedd.*, p. 101). Andrew Kinneress, burgess of Dundee, 1622, and six others of the name are in record (*Brechin*). John Kynneries was member of Scots parliament for Inverness-shire, 1647 (*Hanna*, II, p. 501).

KINNERNIE. John of Kynnernny, a "masoun of the luge" in Aberdeen in 1483 (SCM., v, p. 26), most probably derived his name from Kinnernie near Dunecht, Aberdeenshire.

KINNES. A reduced form of MACINNES, q.v., current in Argyllshire.

KINNIBURGH. From Conisborough in Yorkshire. Galfridus de Coningesburg witnessed a confirmation charter by Malcolm IV in favor of the Abbey of Scone, 1164 (*Scon*, p. 8). William de Cuniggeburc or Cunigburc, who possessed the manor of Stapelgorton in the twelfth century, granted to the monks of Kelso the chapel of Stapelgortune sometime after 1153 (*Kelso*, 35). Sir William de Cuningburcht, knight, witnessed a charter of lands in Egilfechan c. 1249 (*Annandale*, I, p. 7), and Thomas de Cunyngburgh witnessed a charter by Alan hostiarius, 1261 (REA., II, p. 275). Gilbert de Coningesburghe who was outlawed in 1278 for the slaughter of Richard Bullok in the field of Cambok (*Bain*, II, p. 34) may be Gilbert de Cuningysburg', who witnessed an agreement in 1284 and a Renfrew charter in 1294 (RMP., p. 66, 96; OPS., I, p. 77). Sir William de Conynsburghe or Conyngesburgh of Lanarkshire rendered homage, 1296. His seal bears a rabbit, S' *Willi' Konisbovrg* (*Bain*, II, p. 203, 226, 555). Duncan de Coningesburghe of the county of Dunfres, and Gilbert de Conyburke of county of Are also rendered homage, 1296 (*Bain*, II). William of Cunigburgh and Fynlaw Spens were appointed in 1468 to make the inquisitions or values of Bute, and William Cunnyburgh was retoured heir in certain lands there in 1554 (*Retours, Bute*, 1). John Cunninbure was bailie of the 'burght of Kirkintulloch,' 1563 (OPS., I, p. 505), and Isobel Cunyburch is recorded in Auchinloich, 1605 (*Campsie*). Katharine Cunyngbrucht had sasine of land in Bute, 1618, and in 1643 the marquis of Argyll acquired sasine of their lands in Bute from Ninian Cunningham alias Cuniburgh, elder, and from John Cunningham alias Cuniburgh, younger (*Sasines*, I, p. 13; II, p. 239). Over 250 different spellings of the name have been noted from official sources by Mr. T. C. Kinniburgh, of Folkestone, Kent, who is compiling a history of his family. Some of these are Ciniburgh, Cwinnigbrughe, Kinnebrew, Kennybrew, Kimbrough, and Kinnebroch (this last at the beginning of the nineteenth century).

KINNIESON. A sept of Macfarlane (*Buchanan*, p. 92). A form of CUNIESON, q.v.

KINNOCH, KINNACH, KYNOCH. From the G. personal name *Coinneach*, Old G. *Cainnech*, now Kenneth. William Kinzeoch, officer in Methven, 1588 (*Methven*, p. 73). William Kanauch in Ardune, Patrick Kanauch in Auld Rein, and John Kanauch in Bonitoune, are mentioned in 1610 (RSCA., II, p. 164). Duncan Kynnoch in Dalcroane was fined for reset of Clan Gregor, 1613 (RPC., XIV, p. 639). Thomas Kinnock in Scotston, parish of Renfrew, 1617 (*Campsie*). William Kanzeauch in Ledinturk was concerned in an action of spulzie, 1633 (RSCA., II, p. 372), and Helen Kenoch is recorded in Tiubeg, 1663 (*Caithness*). Thomas Kinnoch alias Robertson in Dalmungell, 1742 (*Dunkeld*), and William Kynoch in Longhillock, 1752 (*Moray*). As a forename we have Kennach in 1342 (REA., I, p. 73).

404

KINNON. Most probably from (Mac)KINNON, q.v.

KINPONT. Of local origin from Kilpunt near Broxburn, West Lothian. John de Kilpuc [sic], king's tenant in Linlithgowshire, rendered homage, 1296. His seal bears a stag's head cabossed between a star and crescent, a human head between the antlers, S' Iohis de Kenpvnt cl'ici (?). In the same year a writ was directed to the sheriff of Linlithgow on behalf of John de Kynpunte (Bain, II, p. 201, 218, 533). John Kynpont, monk of Culross, middle of the sixteenth century (PSAS., LX, p. 93).

KINROSS. From the lands, afterwards parish of Kinross in Kinross-shire. Gillebertus de Kinros attests a St. Andrews charter, c. 1170 (RPSA., p. 216). Henry de Kynros witnessed grants to the Abbey of Arbroath, c. 1204–11 (RAA., I, 33) and to the Abbey of Cambuskenneth, c. 1214 (Cambus., 18). He also witnessed a confirmation charter by William the Lion, c. 1201 (Inchaffray, p. 18), and is doubtless the Henricus de Kinros who attests other charters about the same period (RAA., I, 64). Johannes de Kinros granted a charter to Alexander de Oggoluin (Ogilvie) of lands of Belaucht before 1232 (SHSM., IV, p. 314). John de Kynros who witnessed a quitclaim of the land of Drumkarauch, 1260 (RPSA., p. 364), is probably John de Kynros who was sheriff of Kinros in 1266 (ER., I, p. 34). Gilbert de Kynros had the lands of Cuthylgrudyn given him for life, 1263 (ER., I, p. 34), and Thomas de Kynros was empowered in 1275 to appoint and remove attorneys at pleasure (Bain, II, 48). Master Aco [Azo] de Kynross rendered homage, 1291 (RR.). Gilbert de Kynros was elected a lineator in Aberdeen, 1398 (CRA., p. 374), Robert Kynros was heir of James Kynros, procurator and burgess of Edinburgh, 1597 (Inquis., 6), and a plaid and sword were stolen from William Kynross in Menteath by Macgregors in 1635.

KINTIE. Colin Kintie was servitor to Janet Stephen in Kineddar, 1699 (Moray), and Thomas Kintie is recorded in Dreadlein, 1702 (Banff Rec., p. 237).

KINTILLO. William Kintillo in Cassindewglie, who is in record in 1649 (Fordell, p. 34), derived his surname from the lands of Kintillo in Angus (in 1668 Kintillok).

KINTOCHER. Alanus de Kyntocher, mentioned in a charter of c. 1226–34 (Inchaffray, p. 49), probably derived his name from Kintocher near Crieff. There is, however, another Kintocher in Aberdeenshire.

KINTORE. From the town of Kintore in central Aberdeenshire. Johan de Kintowar and Wautier de Kyntowhar, both of the county of Perth, rendered homage in 1296. The seal of the former bears an eight-rayed figure and the legend S' Joh' de Kintoy. The seal of Walter bears a pair of open shears in pale, points up, and S' Walt' de Kintoyir (?) (Bain, II, p. 200, 532, 533). William de Kyntor, 'magister ecclesie' in Aberdeen in 1407 is probably the William de Kentor who is in record as a witness in 1410 (SCM., V, p. 19; REA., II, p. 296). Richard of Kyntore, merchant of Aberdeen, who had a safe conduct into England in 1438, is most probably the Richard Kyntor, merchant of Scotland, who had a similar safe conduct in 1451 (Bain, IV, 1114, 1451) and the Richard de Kentor, pro tem. provost of Aberdeen in 1463 (REA., I, p. 286). Alexander Kenturr (without the 'de'), another Aberdeen merchant, who had a safe conduct into England in 1439 (Bain, IV, 1130), may be the Alexander de Kyntor who was elected bailie of the burgh in 1440 (CRA., p. 6). John de Kyntor was bailie of Aberdeen in 1464 (RAA., II, 155), William and David Kintor are recorded there in 1493 (CRA., p. 50), and Christen Kyntoir in 1594 (ibid., p. 93). Alexander Kintire was servant to the earl of Dunfermling, 1684 (Edinb. App.). Kintoir 1602, Kyntour 1556.

KINTRAE, KINTREA. Of local origin from the lands of Kintrae in the parish of Spynie in Moray. The first form is found in Moray and Banff, and the second in Glasgow.

KINZEAN. John Kynzean witnessed an instrument of sasine at Bordland of Laik in Kirkcudbright, 1552 (Laing, 598). Perhaps from Ir. MacCoinín, son of Coinín, an old personal name.

KIPP. Of local origin from a small place named Kype in the parish of Avondale, Lanarkshire. William de Kype witnessed resignation of claim by Adam de Dowane of all his lands in the vill of Douane in the barony of Lesmahagow, 1301 (Kelso, 193). Janet Kype appears in Goislingtoun, parish of Stanehous, 1622 (Lanark CR.), and William Kype in Kirkton of Kilbryde is recorded in 1677 (Campsie).

KIPPEN. Of local origin from Kippen near Stirling. Thomas Kippen in Machanie is mentioned in 1630 (LIM., 110). Hary (i.e. Harry) Kipen in Dunning complains against his minister, 1689 (RPC., 3. ser. XIV, p. 188). Andrew Kippin, residenter in St. Johnstown (Perth), 1693 (Edin. App.), and Andrew Kippen was chamberlain to the laird of Grandtully, 1717 (Dunkeld).

KIPPIE, KEPPIE. Fife surnames. Keppie is also found in Shetland (introduced there probably by some ferry-louper from Fife). There were lands of Kippo in Fife (*Retours*, 136, 251, etc.). Margaret Kepie in Edinburgh, 1697 (*Edinb. Marr.*). Kippie appears in 1942.

KIRBISTER. Probably from Kirkbuster in Orphir, of which it is a softened pronunciation. An old surname in Orkney which has vanished from the islands. Kirbister *alias* Hutcheson was an old name in Orphir, but Kirbister has gone and Hutcheson remains (*Clouston*). There is also a Kirkbuster in Deerness and another in the parish of Walls. Johne Kirkbuster, juror on assize, 1573, appears as Kirbister in the following year (REO., p. 134, 292).

KIRBY. A surname recorded in Aberdeen. Most probably of recent introduction from England. There is a Kirby in the North Riding of Yorkshire.

KIRK, KIRKE. Of local origin from residence near a kirk. Sir Patrick Kyrk, chaplain of the altar of S. Mary, Perth, 1456 (RAA., II, 107), Andrew Kyrk, witness at Arbroath, 1459 (ibid., 127), and Alexander Kirk, bailie of St. Andrews, 1520 (*Stodart*, II, p. 416). James Kirk, charter witness at Inveraray, 1608 (*Poltalloch Writs*, p. 143). The old Dumfriesshire surname of KIRKHOE is now merged in this name.

KIRKBRECK. Of local origin from Kirkbreck in Orkney. Pettir Kirkbreke was one of a court of arbiters in Holm, Orkney, in 1605 (REO., p. 179), and Bernard Kirkbrek in Kirkbrek is in record in 1640 (MCM., II, p. 211).

KIRKBRIDE. Of local origin from a place of the name. Richard de Kirkbride was heir portioner of Helewysa de Levintone, Cumberland, 1274 (*Bain*, II, 21, 28, 50). For the old family of Kirkbride of Kirkbride, Cumberland, see *Cumberland and Westmorland Antiquarian and Archaeological Society Transactions*, new series xv, p. 63–75.

KIRKBY. From one of the many Kirkbys in the north of England. Adam Kirkby of Berwickshire rendered homage, 1296, and had his lands restored to him (*Bain*, II, p. 207, 226).

KIRKCALDY, KIRKCALDIE. From the town of Kirkcaldy in Fife. Willilmus de Kyrcaudi, cleric in Stirling, 1299 (RAA., I, p. 277). In 1331 we have record of money paid to John de Kirkcaldy (ER., I, p. 370), and Andreas de Kirkaldy, capellanus S. Marie de Anderistona (= St. Andrews), was granted a pension of five merks a year by King David II in 1363

(RMS., I, 167). The land of Simon de Kyrcaldy in Edynburgche is mentioned in 1366 (RMS., I, 261; *Egidii*, p. 19), and perhaps the same Simon appears as a burgess there in 1392 (*Egidii*, p. 28). John of Kirkaldy, Scots merchant, had a safe conduct into England in 1426 (*Bain*, IV, 999), Andrew Kirkcaldy was scribe of the town council of Dysart in 1535 (*Dysart*, p. 3), and in 1540 mention is made of "veneranda mulier Agnes Karcalde" in the same town (ibid., p. 6). Marjory Kirkcaldy was a resident in Dysart in 1572 (ibid., p. 37), and David Kirkaldie was a tenant of the abbot of Newbattle in 1563 (*Neubotle*, p. 327). Sir William Kirkcaldy of Grange took a prominent part in the murder of Cardinal Beaton in 1546, and was himself executed in 1573. An old family of Kirkcaldy of Inchture ended in an heiress, Marjorie, who was married to Reginald Kinnaird and got the lands confirmed to him by a charter of Robert III (RMS., I, App. II, 1866). Kircade 1646.

KIRKCONNEL. Of territorial origin from the lands of Kirkconnel in the parish of Troqueer, Kirkcudbrightshire. William, son of Michael de Kirkeconeual, granted to Holmcultran for the souls of himself and his wife half of all the land between Polleychos and Grenesiche from Polleroth to the Water of Nid, c. 1235–53 (*Holm Cultram*, p. 47). Thomas, son of Andrew de Kyrconeuel, granted to the same abbey half of the land with the moss lying between Polchos and Grenescych in Kyrconeuel within certain bounds described, c. 1280–90 (ibid., p. 48). One of the witnesses is Andrew de Kirkoneuill. Thomas de Kirconnel of the county of Dumfries rendered homage in 1296 and later had his lands restored to him (*Bain*, II, 832, and p. 198). Andrew and Thomas de Kirk Coneval were jurors on an inquisition concerning the lands of John de Hirdmanstone made at Dumfries in 1304 (ibid., 1619). Agnes Kirkconnell in Drumme, 1675, and two more (*Dumfries*). Watson Kirkconnell was author of *International aspects of unemployment*, London, 1923.

KIRKCUDBRIGHT. From the burgh of the same name in Kirkcudbrightshire. Gilbert de Kircudbrich is in record in 1257 (LSC., p. 80), and Adam de Kirkuchbrich, rector of Bolton in the diocese of Glasgow, was made a papal chaplain in 1264 (*Pap. Lett.*, I, p. 408). William of Kirkudbrid slew William Tixtor with a staff in 1278, and was otherwise "of ill repute" (*Bain*, II, p. 35). Adam of Kirkcudbright appears as physician to Alexander, eldest son of the king of Scotland, 1284, and restored him to health "contrarily to the opinion of other physicians." See a note on him (ES.,

KIRKCUDBRIGHT, *continued*

п, p. 682). Thomas de Kirkcudbright was consecrated bishop of Galloway in 1294 (*Dowden*, p. 359). William of Kirkuthbright, master of the Hospital of Turrithe [Turriff] of Banffshire rendered homage, 1296 (*Bain*, п, p. 211).

KIRKDALE. Of local origin from Kirkdale in Kirkcudbrightshire. Michael de Kirkedale was juror on an inquisition made at Berwick on lands in Dumfriesshire in August, 1296 (*Bain*, п, p. 216). The family of de Kirkdale held the lands about Kirkclaugh Mote from 1296 to 1457.

KIRKHAM. A surname recorded in Fife. Probably a recent incomer from England. There is a parish of this name in Lancashire. Alexander Kircum in parish of Birsav, 1640 (MCM., п, p. 211) may be of local Orcadian origin.

KIRKHAUGH. Of local origin. Kirkhaugh in Cumberland was held by the Viponts in thirteenth century and subinfeoffed to William of Kirkhaugh in 1258 (*Moore, Lands*, p. 44). A payment was made to Anabelle, widow of William de Kyrkhalch, 1364 (ER., п, p. 124), and Jonet de Kirchalche had a charter from Andreas de Moravia of the lands of Tuchadam with pertinents, 1392 (RMS., i, 844). William de Kyrkhalch witnessed a confirmation charter bv David, earl of Carrick in Edinburgh, 1394 (SCM., v, p. 252), and John Kirkhauch de Glenesland is in record, 1677 (*Retours, Dumfries*, 287). Cf. KIRKHOE.

KIRKHOE. An old Dumfriesshire surname formerly common about Dunscore, and now curtailed to KIRK. Elizabeth Kirko was retoured heir portioner of John Kirko of Chapell of lands in the barony of Dunscore, etc., 1615 (*Retours, Dumfries*, 86). John Kirkco of Smidaywoll, 1643, and eight more of the name (*Dumfries*). Marie Kirko was resident in the parish of Borgue, 1684, and John Kirko, Alexander Kirko, and James Kirko were residents in the parish of Buittle in the same year (RPC., 3. ser. ix, p. 567, 570). James Kirko or Kirkoe, a Covenanter, was shot at Dumfries, 1685 (*The Gallovidian*, 1921, p. 30; *Hanna*, п, 256, 265). John Kirkoe was portioner of Glengaber in the barony of Holywood, 1692 (*Retours, Dumfries*, 335), and John Kirkow was tenant in Auchlane, 1732 (*Kirkcudbright*). The Kirkos, Kirkhaughs, or Kirk, intermarried with Grierson of Barjarg, M'Naught of Culford, etc. (*Stodart*, п, p. 416). Cf. KIRKHAUGH.

KIRKHOPE. A surname recorded in Aberdeen, but most probably introduced there from the south. There is a Kirkhope in Selkirkshire.

KIRKHOUSE. Of local origin from a place of the name in Shetland. The farm of Kirckehuusz in the parish of Delting is mentioned in 1597 (Goudie, *Celtic and Scandinavian antiquities of Shetland*, p. 117). Margaret Kirkhouse in Moo, Shetland, 1648 (*Sc. Ant.*, xII, p. 90).

KIRKINTILLOCH. From the old burgh of barony of the same name in Dumbartonshire. Alisaundre de Kircontolaghe or Kyrkyntolaghe of the county of Lanark rendered homage in 1296 and had his lands restored to him (*Bain*, п, p. 204, 224). John de Kirkentolaw granted to William of Douglas his land of Qwytfeld in the barony of West Linton in the sheriffdom of Peebles in 1323 (RHM., п, p. 11, 23). Michael de Kyrkintowlach witnessed a donation by Henry de Aynestrother to the Abbev of Dryburgh, c. 1330 (*Dryburgh*, 252), and in 1367 William de Kirkyntulach was constituted Master of the Hospital of St. John of Polmade (REG., p. 278).

KIRKLAND. There are many places of this name in the shires of Dumfries, Ayr, Lanark, Stirling, etc., from one or other of which the surname may have been derived. Johannes fil. Joh. de Kyrkeland held land in the territory of Gordon, c. 1280 (*Kelso*, 124). William de Kyrkland was burgess of Glasgow, 1424 (LCD., p. 242), and in 1463 and 1471 we have mention of Alan de Kvrklande and John de Kirkland there (REG., 389, 395). George Kirkleane, burgess freeman of Glasgow, 1599 (*Burgesses*), and James Kirkland was appointed constable in Lanark, 1709 (*Minutes*, p. 55).

KIRKMAN. Probably from office, one in charge of a church. The name is recorded in England from the fourteenth century, but is less common in Scotland.

KIRKMICHAEL. From the village of Kirkmichael in Perthshire. Michael de Kirkmichael witnessed an obligation of 1336 (*Scon*, 166).

KIRKNESS. Of local origin from Kirkness in Orkney. There is also a Kirkness in Shetland. Sir Thomas de Kirknes, knight, witnessed a charter by Henry de St. Clair, earl of Orknev, at Kirkwaw in 1391 (RMS., i, 824; *Diplomatarium Norvegicum*, p. 402). Angus of Kirkness appears as archdeacon of Hjaetland (i.e. Shetland) in 1426 (*Dipl. Norv.*, п, p. 512), John of Kirknes was lawman of Orkney in 1438 (SCM., v, p. 391), and John Kirkness of that Ilk was lawrikman in North Sandwick in 1678 (SHR., xiv, p. 59). William M. Kirkness was a bank official in Edinburgh before 1940.

KIRKPATRICK. From a chapel formerly dedicated to S. Patrick which gave name to the farm in the parish of Closeburn. The first of this name in record appears to have been Roger de Kirkpatrick who attested a charter by one of the Bruces who died 1141 (Nisbet, *Plates*, p. 42), "but neither his office, location, or 'place,' if he had one, is otherwise mentioned." Ivo [de Kirkpatrick] and his heirs had a charter from Robert Bruce of a place between the fishings of Blawad [Blawatwood] and the Water of Esk, c. 1190 (*Annandale*, I, 1), and a charter from William Bruce of lands in the fee of Pennersaughs, c. 1194–1214 (ibid., p. 3). Roger de Kirkpatrick and Robert de Kirkpatrick witnessed confirmation of a fishery in Torduff between 1194–1211 (*Holm Cultram*, p. 35). Humfridus de Kirkpatric who witnessed a charter by Henry de Grahame before 1200 (RHM., 3), is probably Sir Humfridus de Kirkepatric who witnessed along with Sir Roger de Kirkepatric a quitclaim by Richard de Bancori to Robert de Brus of the whole land of Loverwode (Locharwood) before 1245 (*Bain*, I, 1684). Ivone de Kirkpatrick had a charter of the whole land of Kelosbern from Alexander II in 1232, which remained in possession of the family till 1783 "when an improvident heir found it necessary to dispose of the ancient patrimony" (*Old statistical account*, XIII, p. 232). John de Kirkepatrike of Dumfriesshire rendered homage, 1296 (*Bain*, II, p. 206). Roger de Kirkpatric, knight, also of Dumfriesshire, swore fealty to England in the same year. His seal bears in a trefoil compartment three shields meeting at base, each shield charged with a saltire and chief, S' *Rogeri de Kirpatric* (ibid., p. 185, 531; *Macdonald*, 1523). A Roger de Kirkpatric is traditionally said to have stabbed Cumyn, but the papal bull of excommunication designates the homicide Robert. In the burial place of the Kirkpatricks of Kirkmuchael in Garrell (vernacular pronunciation of Garvald) old churchyard is the monument of the ancestor of the late empress Marie Eugenie of France. Near the end of the eighteenth century William, son of William Kirkpatrick of Conheath, became a wine merchant in Malaga, and married Dona Francesca, daughter of Baron de Grivegnee. One of their daughters, Maria Manuela, married the Count del Montijo, and their daughter, Marie Eugenie, married the Emperor Napoleon III. Sir Bernard Burke, in his *Vicissitudes of families* (p. 46–49, ed. 1859) narrates that this marriage with a Kirkpatrick was being considered a mésalliance in aristocratic circles, whereupon Mr. Charles Kirkpatrick Sharpe of Hoddam, was consulted and produced a Kirkpatrick family-tree showing a root in kings. This was shown to King Ferdinand VII, and so amused him that he exclaimed, "O let the young Montijo marry the daughter of Fingal."

KIRKTON. There are many individuals of this name in the parish of Kirkton, Roxburghshire, but as the name is attached to so many different localities no certain conclusion can be drawn that it took its origin from the land in this parish. This surname appears in several records in different parts of the country and as the place name is common it is possible that persons bearing this surname are of different origin. William de Kirketon appears as witness in Aberdeen in 1243 (LAC., p. 90). Adam de Kirketone of the county of Edneburk rendered homage in 1296. His seal bears a stag's head cabossed, a cross between the antlers, S' *Ade d' Kirketon* (*Bain*, II, p. 213, 554). Another Adam de Kirketone of the county of Berewyk also rendered homage in the same year (ibid., p. 208, 213). Richard of Kirketon served as a juror at Roxburgh in 1361 (ibid., IV, 61), and Thomas de Kirkton was juror on an inquest held in the episcopal lands of Aldrochty in Moray in 1393 (RÉM., p. 205). Adam Kirktoune in Craling-mvlne produced at the aire at Jedworthe in 1493 a remission for certain crimes committed by him (*Trials*, I, p. 18), and William Kvrkton was a notary public in Glasgow in 1498 (REG., 479). Adam Kirktoun held the lands of Stewartfield, Jedburgh, in 1607 (*Retours, Roxburgh*, 46), Mr. John Kirktown was schoolmaster of Jedburgh before 1691 (*Peebles CR.*), and John Kirktoun was portioner of Lilliesleaf, 1748 (*Heirs*, 218).

KIRKWOOD. Of local origin. There are places named Kirkwood in the shires of Ayr, Dumfries, and Lanark. John Kirkwood possessed a tenement in Stirling in 1476 (SBR., p. 260), Alexander Kirkwod, a follower of the earl of Cassilis, was respited for murder in 1526 (RSS., I, 3386), and John Kirkwood was a voter in parish of Qwilton (Coylton), 1513 (*Ros*, 52). James Pugh Kirkwood (1807–1877), hydraulic engineer, builder of one of the largest waterworks in the U. S., was born in Edinburgh. Kirkuod 1574, Kirkvod 1577.

KIRLIE. John Kirlie, wobster, was admitted burgess of Glasgow, 1613 (*Burgesses*), and Cuthbert Kirlie was messenger in Paisley, 1688 (RPC., 3. ser. XIII, p. 244). May be a variant of KERLIE, q.v.

KITCHEN, KITCHIN, KITCHING. The surname Kitchin or Kitching is found in several counties of north England (*Guppy*). Meaning "of the kitchen," it is almost the same as Kitchener, the officer in charge of the monastery kitchen.

KITSON. "The son of Kit," a diminutive or pet form of Christian and Christopher. Payment was made in 1359 to John Ketyson by the bailies of Stirling (ER., I, p. 622), and in the following year he appears as John filius Cristiani, gate-keeper (janitor) of the Castle of Stirling. In 1361 he reappears as Johannus Kytysona and in the following year as Joh. Kytysoun and again in 1365 as Joh. Ketyson (ER., II, p. 28, 61, 206). The name has been probably confused in some instances with Kidston, a name of territorial origin.

KNARSTON. An old Orcadian surname derived from the township of that name in the parish of St. Ola. There was a family of Knarston of that Ilk. William Knarstane was juror on an inquest in 1584 and Gilbert Knarstane was a witness in 1610 (REO., p. 162, 183). Knairstan 1601, Knarstoun 1640.

KNELAND. See under CLELAND.

KNIBET, KNIBIT. These names recorded c. 1258–71 (LIM., XXXIII) are errors for KIN-BUC. See KINBUCK.

KNIBLO. Barbara Niblo is recorded in Edinburgh, 1598, and Helen Knebulo there, 1609 (Edinb. Marr.). William Knublock in Balgray, 1677 (Lanark CR.), Grizel Kniblo in Edinburgh, 1688 (Edinb. Marr.), Jacobus Knibloe or Kniblo was regent of the College of Glasgow, 1693 (Pollok, I, p. 343), and John Kniblo in Inchshanks, 1709, and three others of the name are in record (Wigtown).

KNIGHT. Robert dictus Knycht, burgess of Abirbrothoc, had a charter of a piece of land in Aberbrothoc in 1331 (RAA., II, p. 10). In 1435 John Knycht, canon of Brechin, was rector of Funewyn (Finhaven) (REB., I, p. 196; II, 49, 104). He is probably the John Knycht who appears on an inquest on the lands of Tulloch in 1438 (RAA., II, 83). Katrine Nycht, wife of John Nicholsoun, burgess of Dumfries, is in record in 1544 (Anderson). Alexander Knyt was on an inquest made at Prestwick in 1572 (Prestwick, p. 73). By some erroneously considered a translation of G. Mac Neachtain.

KNIGHTON. Nicol de Knyghton del counte de Edinburgh rendered homage, 1296 (Bain, II, p. 199). From one or other of the several places of the name in England.

KNIGHTSON. William Knightes sone of Eglesham of the county of Lanark rendered homage in 1296 (Bain, II, p. 213). Francis Knythsoun was bailie of Edinburgh in 1464 (Neubotle, p. 252). In the same year Cuthbert Knichtstoun, Scottish merchant, had a safe conduct to travel in England (Bain, IV, 1343), and in 1466, as Cudbert Knythson or Knychtson, he appears as burgess of Edinburgh (Kelso, 531). In 1531 a charter was granted to Thomas Knvchtsoun by John, prior of Pittenweem (May, lviii). The seal of George Cnichson, son and heir to umquhile Alexander Knichtsoun, burgess of Edinburgh, is appended to a charter of 1521 (Macdonald, 1528). Thomas Knvchtsone was juror on a witchcraft trial in Orkney, 1616 (MCM., II, p. 190). There was a family of this name of Mallenv, Midlothian.

KNOCKDOLIAN. From Knockdolian in the parish of Colmonell, Ayrshire. Johan de Knoudolyan of Ayrshire rendered homage, 1296. His seal bears two heads respecting, a lily between, S' Joh'is de Knodolian (Bain, II, p. 205, 557). Dugallus filius Johannis de Knokdolian had a charter of "terris de Avelott (Wellok)" from Robert I (RMS., I, App. II, 341), and Johannes de Cnocdolian, knight, witnessed a confirmation charter by King Robert the Bruce to John de Carlton of the lands of Dalmakeran, c. 1316–1318 (Annandale, I, p. 132). Nicholas Knockdolian was among the Scots prisoners taken at the battle of Durham in 1346 (Hailes, Annals, II, p. 389). He may be the Nicholas de Knocdolian who witnessed a charter of the land of Duppolle to the Friars Preachers of Ayr in 1381 (Friar, Ayr, p. 23). The lands of Knockdolian passed into possession of Fergus M'Cubbin, c. 1660.

KNOKYNBLEW. John Knokvnblew admitted burgess of Aberdeen, 1456 (NSCM., I, p. 15) derived his name from Knockinglew in the parish of Inverurie, spelled Knokvnblewis in 1460.

KNOKYNTYNNANE. William de Knokyntynnane del counte de Innernesse rendered homage, 1296 (Bain, II, p. 210). Knokintinall, Knokyntineal, and Knokintyall occur in Inverness Retours.

KNOUT. A ship of Knut the wealthv, citizen of Berwick, was carried off by Erlind, earl of Orkney, in 1156 (Orkneyinga Saga, Edinburgh, 1873, p. 161). Hugo Cnot granted an annual-rent of two shillings to the Priorv of Inchcolm, c. 1210–29 (Inchcolm, p. 9). The name also occurs in records of Coldingham Priory as Cnovt. Richard Knut witnessed resignation of the lands of Langholm and Brakanwra, 1281 (RHM., I, p. 11). Adam Knout and John Knout were burgesses of Roxburgh, 1296, and rendered homage in that vear (Bain, II, p. 197, 199). Isabele Knout of Roxburghshire also rendered homage (ibid., p. 200). Baring-Gould (p. 338) says the name is common enough in the north of England, and is an English form of Dan. *Knut* or *Knud*, that has been Latinized into *Canute*. Bardsley and Harrison give it also from *Knut* and (2) as local.

KNOWLES. A form of KNOX current in Aberdeen. Knowls 1808.

KNOX. The Renfrewshire family of Knox is derived by Crawfurd (*Macfarlane*, II, p. 276–284) from Adam son of Uchtred, who in the reign of Alexander II received from Walter the Steward the lands of Knock in the barony of Renfrew. The lands were named from the remarkable prominence there called "The Knock." The *s* is English plural. In 1234 the land of Cnoc in Renfrewshire was held under the abbot of Paisley by Duugallus filius Cristini and Matilda his spouse, who claimed lands in Kilpatrick as heirs of Dufgallus, the rector, brother of the earl of Lennox (RMP., p. 178). About 1260 John de Cnoc or Knoc witnessed a charter of the lands of Haldhingleston (Ingliston), Renfrewshire, and in 1272 he witnessed the gift which Sir Antonius Lombardus (Anthony the Lombard) made to Paisley of his right in the lands of Fulton to the Abbey of Paisley (ibid., p. 51, 58). In the following year he witnessed, along with William de Knoc, a grant of lands by Malcolm, earl of Lennox to the same Abbey (*Levenax*, p. 15–17). About 1272 Hugo Cnox gave to the monastery of Inchcolme two shillings yearly (Ross, *Aberdour*, p. 133), William de Knoc witnessed a division between the lands of the house of Paisley and William de Sanchor in 1280 (RMP., p. 228), and Johannes de Knoc witnessed confirmation of the church of Cragin (Craigie) to the same house (ibid., p. 233). In 1328 there are records of payments to Alan del Cnoc or Alan de Knockis (ER., I, p. 113, 115). Uchtrede Knox of the Cragyns and Johne of the Knok of that Ilk were arbiters in a dispute between the burgh of Renfrew and the abbot of Paisley, 1408 (RMP., p. 406). Thomas de Knok held a tenement in Irvine, 1426 (*Irvine*, I, p. 130), George Knox was sergeant in Edinburgh, 1467 (*Neubotle*, 299), and John Knollis was sergeant in Linlithgow, 1549 (*Laing*, 552). William Knollis, custumar of Linlithgow in 1560, appears again in 1565 as William Knowis (ER., XIX, p. 111, 294). William Knocks and John Knoks, indwellers in Cunyngham Baidland, 1662 (*Hunter*, p. 60).

There was another family of Knows, Knox, or Knollis of that Ilk in the parish of Deer, Aberdeenshire, quite distinct from the Knoxs of Renfrew. Marion Nucx in record in Aberdeen, 1408 (CWA., p. 316). John Knowis admitted burgess of Aberdeen, 1460, appears again in 1464 and 1475 as John Knollis or Knollys (NSCM., I, p. 17; RAA., II, 154). Sir William of Knollis, a member of this family appears in 1463 as rector of Quhitsum, preceptor of Torfichen in 1480, and prior of the Order of St. John of Jerusalem, 1493 (CMN., 32; *Peebles*, 27; Bain, IV, 1594). David Knowis was retoured heir of Alexander Knowis, burgess of Aberdeen, his father, 1605 (*Retours, Aberdeen*, 98), and James Knolls was sailor in Aberdeen, 1721 (NSCM., II, p. 108). The surname is now Knowles in Aberdeen. Cnoxe 1558, Knoches 1311, Knoicce 1345, Knokis 1330, Knokkis 1468, Knolles 1463, Knows 1615, Nox 1570.

KRINGILTOUN. Robert Kringiltoun witnessed a gift by Thomas de Hava to the Hospital of Soltre between 1208 and 1238 (*Soltre*, p. 15). There is a Cringletie in the parish of Eddleston with which the name may be connected.

KYD, KYDD. *See under* KID.

KYLE. Of local origin from the district of Kyle in Ayrshire. Walter of Kyle had a safe conduct into England in 1424 (Bain, IV, 970), Margaret Kile possessed a tenement in Glasgow in 1428 (LCD., p. 245), George Kyle appears as burgess of Edinburgh in 1538 (SCM., II, p. 195), and John Kile and Thomas Kile were burgesses of Irvine in 1538 (*Irvine*, I, p. 42). Robert Kyle who appears in record as bailie of Irvine in 1572 and 1590 (ibid., p. 56, 64) is probably the Robert Kyle, burgess of Irwene, who was retoured heir of Andrew Kyle, resident in Glasgow, in 1606 (*Inquis.*, 259). James Kyll was a cooper in Edinburgh in 1662 (*Edinb. Marr.*), and David Kyle, portioner of Lassudden, 1772 (*Heirs*, 363). The Kyles of Laurel Hill, county Derry, are of Scottish descent. Kyile 1556.

KYLL. Mark Kyll, portioner of Lessudden, 1662 (RRM., II, p. 14). Mr. William Kyll preached in a barn at Muckroft, 1687 (RPC., 3. ser. XIII, p. 195). Laurance Kyll, weaver in Perth, 1682 (*Edin. App.*), and another Laurance Kyll was pensioner in Edinburgh, 1734 (*Guildry*, p. 147). Kylle 1701. *See also* KYLE.

KYLMON. From Kilmun in Cowal, Argyllshire. Humfredus de Kylmon is mentioned in an inhibition by Robert, bishop of Glasgow, 1294 (RMP., p. * 203).

KYNGESSELAWE. Adam Kyngesselawe who held land in Thirlestan, c. 1300 (*Dryburgh*, 92–93) derived his name from Kingslaw near Tranent, Midlothian.

KYNGESSYDE. Richard de Kyngessyde of Berwickshire who rendered homage, 1296 (*Bain*, II, p. 206), probably derived his surname from Kingside (c. 1250 Kyngesside) in the parish of Eddleston, Peeblesshire. William Kingesev and his wife who had a grant of lands of Capronystoun (Innerleithen) from Robert I (RMS., I, App. II, 598) probably derived their name from the same source.

KYNNIER. *See under* KINNEAR.

KYNOCH. *See under* KINNOCH.

KYNTESSOC. Henricus de Kyntessoc, witness at Kynlos, 1229 (REM., p. 87), derived his name from Kintessack in the united parish of Dyke-Moy, Moray.

LACHANN. A degraded form of LACHLAN, q.v. From the frequent repetition of the names Eachann, Lachann, Lachann, Eachann, the Maclean pedigree, it has been said, sounded like a dog lapping soup or porridge! "Mar choinn ag òl eanaraich, tha ainmean Chloinn 'Illeathainn: Eachann, Lachann; Eachann, Lachann; Eachann, Lachann; Teàrlach" (Iain Mac Cormaic, *Dùn-Àluinn, no an t-oighre 'na dhìobarach*, Paislig [1912], p. 245).

LACHIE. G. *Lachaidh*, a diminutive of LACHLAN, q.v.

LACHLAN. G. *Lachlann* (dial. *Lachlainn*), the modern form of the still older but now disused *Lochlann* (*Celt. Rev.*, VI, p. 16). That Lochlann means 'Norway' Prof. A. Bugge has abundantly shown (*Royal race of Dublin*, 1900). Lohlan, son of Huddredy, witnessed a charter by Uchtred, son of Fergus, lord of Galloway, to the Hospital of S. Peter at York, c. 1158–64 (*Bain*, II, p. 422). Lochlan, perhaps the same person, was heir of Fergus of Galloway a. 1166 (LSC., p. 19). Eugene fiz Loghlan of the county of Perth rendered homage, 1296 (*Bain*, II, p. 204). Cristin, son of Louchelan, bailiff of Strivelin, made payment of the issues of the town, 1304–5 (ibid., p. 440). Adam Lachlane was juror at Irvine, 1417 (*Irvine*, I, p. 20), and Laccan Doncanson Cambel was charter witness at Perth, 1470 (OPS., II, p. 111). The name of Johnne Lauchland in Mossyde, 1668 (*Corsehill*, p. 81) may be this name with accretionary *d*. The 40 penny lands of Lauchlenstoun in Ayrshire are mentioned in 1674 (*Retours, Ayr*, 598). Lachillan and Lachtillan 1516, Lachlann 1436, Lachlin c. 1431, Lauchlan 1674, Clanlachlane 1452.

LACHLANSON. An early Anglicizing of MACLACHLAN, q.v. "William Lauchlanesone sone of wmquhile Lauchlane M'anetosche of Galowye" gave his bond of manrent in 1497 (SCM., IV, p. 189).

LACHLIESON. A variant of LACHLANSON, q.v.

LACKLAND. Explained as 'landless.' John sine terra witnessed a grant to the Hospital of Soltre, c. 1180–1214 (*Soltre*, p. 5).

LACRAIE. William de Lacraie, c. 1200 (*Cambus.*, p. 73). Roger de Lacrej witnessed a charter by William the Lion, a. 1200 (LSC., 33).

LADYURD. Thomas de Ledyorde of the county of Peebles who rendered homage in 1296 (*Bain*, II, p. 207) derived his surname from Ladyurd in the parish of Kirkurd, Peeblesshire.

LAFFRIES. A payment was made to Johne Lafreis in Inverness, 1616 (*Rec. Inv.*, II, p. 146), James Lafreis was writer in Edinburgh, 1675 (*Argyll Sasines*, I, p. 245), James Laffreis of Barvennan, 1681 (*Inquis.*, 6292), and John Laffries, bailie of Wigtown, 1711 (*Wigtown*). The name is misspelled Lasrieis in 1614 (*Rec. Inv.*, II, p. 122).

LAFOUR. Peter Lafour, late servitor to the marquis of Tweddal, 1698 (*Edin. App.*). ? a Frenchman.

LAG or LAGG. From the old barony of Lag in the parish of Dunscore, Dumfriesshire. Robert de Lage had a charter of lands of Neatherholme, Auldtounayle, etc., in Dumfriesshire from David II (RMS., I, App. II, 1358). The charter is printed in RHM., II, 94, but is undated. There is another Lagg at Irongray, Dumfriesshire, and Lagg near Gatehouse, Kirkcudbrightshire.

LAHORE, LOHOAR. A surname found in Glasgow is most probably from the lands of Locher (c. 1208–32, Louhere and Louuhir) in the lordship of Avondale. John of Lochor was juror on an inquisition held in Lanark in 1498 and again in 1501 as Jhon Loquhour (*Lanark*, p. 9, 11). Patrick Laquhoir is recorded in Dalzellis-Kittimure in the parish of Stanehouse, in 1624, and John Lochquhar in Dalzel-Kittimure in 1634 (*Lanark*). Robert Lochore (1762–1852) was author of *Patie and Ralph: an elegiac pastoral on the death of Robert Burns*, Glasgow, n.d. Lawquhoir.

LAIDLAW. A Border surname confined mainly to Selkirkshire and the vales of Ettrick and Yarrow. There is a Laidlawstiel near Galashiels. There is a tradition that the Laidlaws had their origin in England, and the name has been traced over the Border down to the south of England under the variants Laidlaw, Laidley, Laidler, Ladly, and Ludlow. William of Lodelawe was charged in 1296 with concealing a horse from the English (*Bain*, II, 822). William Ladlaw was portioner of Newtoune, 1650 (RRM., I, p. 127), John Laidlaw appears in Blackchester, parish of Lauder, 1674 (*Lauder*), and Thomas Laidlaw in Haugh, 1682 (*Peebles CR.*). A family of Laidlaw (Ladylye, Laidley, or Laidlaw) of Mosfennan, Peeblesshire, was seated there during part of the seventeenth and eighteenth centuries (*Stodart*, II, p. 308). William Laidlaw (1780–1845) was confidential friend of Sir Walter Scott and also his steward at Abbotsford. Laidla 1644.

LAIDLER. Guppy (p. 315) says this is the Northumberland form of LAIDLAW.

LAIDLEY, LAIDLIE. A variant of LAIDLAW, q.v. Margaret Laidlie in Thirlstane in record, 1685 (*Lauder*). Ladla 1738, Ladly 1739.

LAING. A form of OE. *lang*, 'long,' 'tall.' Thomas Laing engaged in 1357 that Dumfries shall pay part of the ransom of King David II. Thomas Layng, notary public in Edinburgh in 1461 (LSC., p. 151), appears again in 1467 as Thomas Laing, burgess and notary public (*Neubotle*, p. 261, 263). John Layng was rector of Newlands in 1472 (REG., 398), treasurer to King James III (*Nisbet*, I, p. 202), and bishop of Glasgow, 1473–74 (REG., p. 422). The surname is common in the Glasgow Protocol books of the sixteenth century, Archibald Layng was priest and notary public in St. Andrews diocese in 1502 (*Bain*, IV, 1691), and John Laying appears in Tolhoip, Shetland, in 1623. David Laing (1790–1878) was a distinguished antiquary. Laing, like Lang, is sometimes used in Kintyre as a curtailed form of LOYNACHAN (from O'Loynachan), q.v. Lainge 1556, Laynge 1673, Leang 1597.

LAIPER. *See under* LEAPER.

LAIRD. Perhaps = laird, a landlord, owner of land or houses, ME. *laverd*. Roger Lawird or Lauird of Berwick made an agreement with the Abbey of Kelso relating to his land of Waldefgat, Berwick, 1257 (*Kelso*, 35). Thomas le louerd of Peeblesshire rendered homage, 1296 (*Bain*, II, p. 207). Thomas Lairde, witness in Glasgow, 1552 (*Protocols*, I). David Laird, reidare at Fovern, 1574 (RMR.).

LAKIE. A surname in Angus, evidently a variant of LECKIE, q.v.

LAMB. *Lamb* is an ON. personal name, ODan. *Lam*. Adam Lamb of Sympering (Simprim) witnessed a charter of lands in Grayden (Graden), c. 1288 (*Edmonstone*, p. 76). Adam Lamb, persone of the church of Foulisworthe, Berwickshire, and Lambe fiz Austyn de Nibreim, rendered homage, 1296 (*Bain*, II, p. 205, 212). Thomas Lambe, tenant in Thornhill, Dumfriesshire, 1376 (RHM., I, p. lvi). Willelmus Lambe was juror at a court held at "Le Ballocis Hill" near Inverness, 1376–7 (*Family of Innes*, p. 63). John Lambe, esquire of Scotland, received from Richard II of England in 1379 the sum of 20L for killing Oweyn of Wales, the king's enemy in France (*Bain*, IV, 273). Duncan Lam held a tenement in Edinburgh, 1392 (*Egidii*, p. 27). Simon Lamb was bailie of Aberdeen, 1391 (RAA., II, 41) and in 1398 was elected common councillor (CRA., p. 374). William Lamb had a charter of two tenements in Brechin, 1420 (REB., II, 273). Richard Lamb was a 'baylye' of Edinburgh, 1423 (LSC., 113). Master Archibald Lame was appointed to teach young monks and novices in the Abbey of Arbroath, 1486 (RAA., II, p. 245). John Lame was admitted burgess of Aberdeen, 1487 (NSCM., I, p. 33), and Alexander and David Lam were burgesses of Arbroath, 1505 (RAA., II, p. 358). John Lam was presbyter in Abernethy, 1547 (*Gaw*, 9, 22), and Marcus Lamb appears in Petculane, 1550 (*Rollok*, 69). Marcus Lambe was prebendary of Holy Trinity College, Edinburgh, 1554 (*Soltre*, p. 200). Lamme 1551; Lame. The descendants of a prominent family of this name connected with Leith from the days of Bruce emigrated to Australia about the beginning of the nineteenth century.

LAMBDEN. From the lands of Lambden (Lambden *alias* Hassingtoun, 1633) in Berwickshire. Roland de Lambeden witnessed confirmation charter by Philip de Halyburton to the Abbey of Kelso, c. 1261 (*Kelso*, 270). Henry of Lambden was chamberlain of the monastery of Kelso, 1260 (*Chron. Mail.*, s.a.)

LAMBEKIN. From LAMB, q.v., + diminutive ending -*kin*. Lambekin, dapifer, witnessed a charter by Earl Gospatric to Priory of Coldingham, a. 1166 (CCPC., p. 8).

LAMBERT. An OE. personal name, *Landbeorht*, meaning 'landbright.' Lambert, dapifer, witnessed Earl Gospatric's grant of Ederham and Nesebite to the monks of S. Cuthbert, a. 1153 (*Nat. MSS.*, I, 25). He is probably the individual who had a controversy with the abbot of Kelso in 1177 concerning the "terra de Berewyc que fuit Dodini" (*Kelso*, p. 343). Lambard, vicar of Caral in the county of Fife,

LAMBERT, *continued*

rendered homage in 1296 (*Bain*, II, p. 204). Robert Lambert was indweller in Kingorn in 1630 (PBK., p. 14).

LAMBERTON. Of territorial origin from the old barony of the name in Berwickshire. William de Lamberton witnessed a charter by David I to the church of Dunfermline of a fishing in the Tweed and a toft in Berwick, c. 1136 (RD., 10), and also witnessed another charter by the same king (1147) confirming Earl Gospatric's gift of the villages of Ederham and Nisbet to the monks of S. Cuthbert at Coldingham. Adam de Lamberton granted c. 1190–1200 to his nephew a third part of his land of Lambertun, and within the same dates he granted ، ، Galfrid de Hessewel, his grandson, a third part of the same lands (BNCH., XVI, p. 332). John de Lambertoune witnessed a grant of land in Dunypais, c. 1200 (*Cambus.*, 83), and attested the letters of protection to the prior and monks of Lesmahagow granted by Alexander II in 1230 (*Kelso*, 185). Ade de Lambirtoun was steward to the prior of Coldingham, c. 1270 (BNCH., XVI, p. 334), and several individuals of the name holding lands in the counties of Berwick, Lanark, Edinburgh, Fife, Forfar, and Stirling, rendered homage in 1296 for their possessions (*Bain*, II). William de Lambirtoun granted the church of Deruisyn (Dairsie) to the prior and convent of St. Andrews in 1300 (RPSA., p. 120), John of Lamerton was burgess of Innerkethyne in 1395 (*Laing*, 82), and David Limbertoune is recorded in Watersyde, 1658 (*Kilbarchan*). "From this ancient family, which has been long extinct, probably sprung the famous William Lamberton, bishop of St. Andrews, the most distinguished person of the name, by whose advice and assistance the immortal Bruce was encouraged in his efforts to deliver Scotland from the English yoke" (*Scot. Nat.*, II, p. 628).

LAMBIE, LAMBY, L'AMI, LAMMIE. Diminutives of LAMB, q.v. "A name once of good repute as a native name in Angus, though those who bear it in modern times have sought a French origin, and spell it L'Ami" (*Innes*, p. 31). Henry Lambi was a charter witness in Dundee, 1281 (HP., II, p. 223). Gilbert Lamby and John Lamby were members of inquest made at St. Andrews in 1302–3 (*Bain*, II, 1350), and John Lamby was witness in Brechin, 1364 (REB., I, 20). Alexander Lambie had a charter from David II of the lands of Bernes in the barony of Crail, Fife (RMS., I, App. II, 932), and Liolph and Nigel Lamby were customars of Montrose, 1372–79 (ER., II, p. 381, 406, 561, etc.). Liulph Lambie in 1401 witnessed a wadset in favor of Duthac Carnegy.

'Mariora Lammeis dothyr' and 'Thome Lammeis wif' were king's tenants in Strathdee, 1527 (*Grant*, III, p. 70). There were Lamies or Lammies of Dunkenny as early as 1542, and George Lammie of Dunkenny was a charter witness in 1628 (REB., II, 244). Andrew Lamby was one of those accused of part in the murder of Riccio in 1565 (RPC., I, p. 437), Silvester Lammie was laureated at University of St. Andrews, 1617, Lammie is recorded in Wester Futhie in 1613, Silvester Lammy in Montrose, 1730 (*Brechin*), and Robert Lambie, maltman at Deanfield, is recorded in 1772 (*Campsie*). The L'Amys who succeeded the Lambies of Dunkenny are merely akin to the old family in name. Lamme 1500, Lammee 1603, L'Amy 1401. There is also an old ballad of 'Andrew Lammie.'

LAMBIN. Diminutive of LAMBERT, q.v. Lambyn Asa had a grant of the lands of Draffan and Dardarach, c. 1147–60 (*Kelso*, 102). He gave name to the manor of Lamington in Lanarkshire. William, son of Lambyn, held a toft in Perth, c. 1200 (LAC., p. 80).

LAMBINSON, 'son of LAMBIN,' q.v. William filius Lambini witnessed charters by Christina Corbet and her husband in favor of the Priory of St. Andrews, c. 1241 (RPSA., p. 263, 278).

LAMBISTON. Of local origin. Richard de Lambiston ('the tūn of Lambi') was a charter witness in Dundee, 1281 (HP., II, p. 223).

LAMBY. See under LAMBIE.

L'AMI. See LAMBIE.

LAMINGTON. From the manor of the same name in the parish of Lamington, Lanarkshire. Lambin Asa, from whom the manor derives its name, flourished in the reigns of David I and Malcolm IV. Between 1147 and 1160 he received a grant of the lands of Draffane and Dardarach in Lesmahagow from Arnold, abbot of Kelso (*Kelso*, 102), and at about the same period James, the son of Lambin, obtained the lands of Loudin and others in Ayrshire (OPS., I, p. 173). "The descent of the manor from Lambin, its first lord known to record, cannot be traced with any precision" (ibid., p. 174), as there seems to be a break in the possession of the property in the latter half of the thirteenth century. William de Lamygton rendered homage in 1296, in the same year William de Lambyngestone was committed prisoner to the castle of Hardelaghe, and William, son of William de Lambingestone, was committed to Fotheringay Castle (*Bain*, II, p. 169, 177). Their possessions were doubtless forfeited, as in 1329 the lands of Lamington were in possession of Alexander de Seton, and since 1387 have been in possession of the family of Bailie of Lamington (RMS., I, App. I, 126). John Lambyngtoun or Lambynton is in record in Aberdeen in 1400 and 1408 (SCM., v, p. 15; CWA., p. 314), Thomas Lambynton was admitted burgess of the burgh in 1406, John and Duncan Lammyton in 1467, and Andrew Lamytoun in 1579 (NSCM., I, p. 2, 20, 74). John of Lammyntoñ and Andro Lammyntoñ were fined for absence "fra ye offerand on Candilmesday" in Aberdeen, 1483 (Mill, *Plays*, p. 117), and William Lammyntone held a croft in Aberdeen, 1492 (REA., I, p. 329). Lammyngtone 1505, Lammyntoune 1477, Lamyntone 1490.

LAMLEY. From Lambley near Knaresdale, Northumberland, in 1201 Lambeley and in 1542 Lamlev. Robert de Lambeley witnessed charter by Patrick, second earl of Dunbar of the vill and church of Ederham to the Priory of Coldingham, a. 1248 (*Raine*, 135). Radulphus de Lamblev or Lamley, abbot of Arbroath became bishop of Aberdeen, 1239 (RAA., I, p. xiii; *Dowden*, p. 103–104).

LAMMAS. Recorded in Annan 1801. Of English origin from Lammas, a parish in the diocese of Norwich.

LAMMIE. *See under* LAMBIE.

LAMMIESON, 'son of LAMMIE.' See under LAMBIE. Johannes Lammeson, Donald Lammeson, and Ago Lammesone, were tenants on lands in Strathdee, 1527 (*Grant*, III, p. 70). Thomas Lameasoun in Rerwick, Shetland, 1624 (OSS., I, 89). Lameasoune 1624.

LAMMOK. William Lammok held land in Irvine, 1426 (*Irvine*, I, p. 130), and another William Lammock was burgess there, 1499 (*Simon*, 29).

LAMMOND. Form of LAMOND, q.v.

LAMOND, LAMMOND, LAMONT. The name of an important family in Argyllshire in early thirteenth century, derived from ON. *lögmaðr*, 'lawman, lawyer.' The Gaelic name of the family was MACERCHAR, q.v., and Lawman may have been adopted in consequence of their chief having been invested with some judicial powers. Lamond also occurs as a surname in the rural districts of Scandinavian England, especiallv in Lancashire. The *Lancashire Assize Rolls* for 1247 mention Adam, son of Laghman and Adam Laweman, probablv the same person (Record Soc. ed., 1904, p. 28, 39). Ladhmunn, son of Donald, son of Malcolm III was killed bv the man of Moray in 1116 (ES., II, p. 160: his name "may be considered

an indication of his mother's nationality"). Between 1230 and 1246 "Duncanus filius Ferchar et Laumannus filius Malcolmi nepos ejusdem Duncani" granted the church of S. Finan or Kilfinnan to the monks of Paisley (RMP., p. 132). Malcolm, the son of Lauman, and Malmore, the son of Laumun (the latter is also mentioned as Malmory Maklaweman of Argyll), are mentioned again between 1270 and 1290 (RMP.; Palgrave, *Documents*, I, p. 300). In 1290 a dispensation was granted Molmure, son of Lagman, knight, and Christina, daughter of Alexander called of Ergadia, who intermarried in ignorance that they were connected in the fourth degree of affinity (*Pap. Lett.*, I, p. 518). About the same date John, the son of Lagman, son of Gilcom M'Ferchar, granted certain lands in heritage to Sir Colin Kambel (OPS., II, p. 53). Lawemund McGreghere (error for McEreghere) was summoned in 1292 to render homage to King John Balliol (APS., I, p. 448a), and in 1296 John Laumansone of the county of Perth rendered homage for his lands (*Bain*, II, p. 204). Duncan filius Laumanni witnessed a charter by Robert II in 1384 to Duncan, earl of Lennox (*Levenax*, p. 8). John Lawmwnd was bailie of Cowale in 1456 (LCD., p. 179), and in 1466 the monks of Paisley had a dispute with John Lawmond of that Ilk regarding the church of Kilfinan, which was settled in their favor on production of the charters granted to them by his ancestors (RMP., p. 145–151). The Lamonts are said to have been formerly verv powerful in Cowal, the chief being described as Maclamond of all Cowal ("MacLaomuinn mor Chomhal uile"). The clan was at one time persecuted by the Campbells, and a savage massacre of Lamonds was one of the charges against the marquess of Argyll in 1661. There was also a Gillebride filius Lamund witness to a charter bv Fergus, earl of Buchan before 1214 (CAB., p. 408). Johann von Lamont, the distinguished Bavarian astronomer and magnetician, was born John Lamont, son of the earl of Fife's forester at Braemar, in 1805 and died in 1879. His portrait is in *Fischer* II, pl. opp. p. 170. Ladmann 1467, Lagmane 1410, Lamand 1708, Lamann 1431, Lamentht 1586, Lamount 1673, Lawmond 1529, Lawmonth 1583, Lawmonthe 1649, Lawmound 1597. In the belief that the name is of French origin it is commonly mispronounced Lamont' in the United States. Lam'ont is the correct wav. See MACLAMOND.

LAMONDSON. 'Son of LAMOND,' q.v. See also MACLAMOND. Laumondsoune 1465, Lawmanson 1402, Lawmansone 1449, Lawmondson 1445, Lawmondsone 1451, Lawmondsoune 1455.

LAMONT. *See under* LAMOND.

LANARK. Of local origin from the town of the same name in Lanarkshire. Individuals bearing the name occur in record as charter witnesses as early as the second half of the twelfth century. William de Lannarch witnessed a charter by Eschina, wife of Walter (the Steward) before 1177 (RMP., p. 74). In 1279 Robert de Lanarc was one of the witnesses to a settlement regarding the tithes of the church of Roberton (*Kelso*, 346), and two years later Richard de Lanark appears as a witness in the Chartulary of Cambuskenneth (*Cambus.*, 1). William of Lanark occurs in a list of the garrison of Stirling Castle, probably at its surrender to the Scots in the end of the year 1299 (*Bain*, II, 119). Ninian Lanarik was a cordiner in Edinburgh in 1605 (*Edinb. Marr.*).

LANCFORD. John de Lancford was archdeacon of Caithness, 1358 (CSR., I, p. 131). Most probably an Englishman, from one or other of the eight places named Langford in England.

LANDALE, LANDEL, LANDELLS, LANDELS, LANDLES. Robert de Landeles confirmed a grant of six bovates of Brochesmuth to the Abbey of Kelso a. 1174, which was witnessed by Hugh de Landeles and Sequard de Landeles (*Kelso*, 322). William de Laundeles, who died 1227 (*Chron. Mail.*, s.a.), was son of John, son of Orm, lord of Hunum (Hownam), who appears in record, 1164–74 (*Melros*, p. 141). Robertus de Landeles witnessed gift of Herol (Errol) to Willelmus de Haia by William the Lion (SCM., II, p. 303, 305). Walter de Laundells was prisoner of war taken at Dunbar, 1296, and Freskums [*sic*, Freskinus] de Laundeles of Roxburghshire rendered homage in the same year. His seal bears a stag's head cabossed, within an orle, S' *Freskin de Landeles* (*Bain*, II, p. 177, 200, 532). William de Landallis (Landel, Landells, Laundels, Laundelvs) was bishop of St. Andrews, 1341–85 (Dowden, *Bishops*, p. 25–27). William Landallis had a charter of lands of Oxenhame, 1390–91 (RMS., I, App. II, 1678), and as de Laundelis had a charter of the lands of Swynset about the same time (ibid., 813). Simon Landailis was a monk of Cupar Abbey, 1456 (*Panmure*, II, 236), William Landalis leased part of Cowbyr, 1457, and Wil Landal, probably the same person, was tenant in Kemphill, 1474 (*Cupar-Angus*, I, p. 132, 193). The family ended in direct line in an heiress who was married to Sir Alexander Home, first lord Home. Ebenezer Landells, projector of *Punch*, was a native of Berwick-on-Tweed. Landaill 1606, Landallys 1448.

LANDES. David Landes, witness in Glasgow, 1550 (*Protocols*, I). James Landass was bailie of Ranfrew, 1650 (*Pollok*, I, p. 251), Robert Landass was ordered imprisoned for performing worship in a private house, 1670 (*Fasti*, III, p. 228), Robert Landes, maltman, took the Test in Paisley, 1686 (RPC., 3. ser. XI, p. 496), and Robert Landes was portioner of Robriestoun, 1743 (*Campsie*). About the year 1400 some Lamonts had to fly to escape the king's displeasure, and one of them went to Paisley where he was settled by the abbot as a 'Land(l)ess' man (McKechnie, *The Lamont Clan*, 1938, p. 4, 65). There is a place named Landis in New Abbey parish. Landess 1779.

LANDLES. *See under* LANDALE.

LANDON. Local. Gavin Landoune, writer, in parish of Hamilton, 1679 (*Campsie*). Perhaps a syncopated form of Langdon, an English place name.

LANDRETH. George Landreth, son of Patrick Landreth, feuar in Calstrem (Coldstream), died in 1690, and James Landreth, 'wiver,' in Hume, died in 1717. William Landreth was tenant in Sweethope, 1777 (*Stitchill*, p. 207), and Mr. James Landreth was minister at Simprin, Berwickshire, 1756 (*Lauder*).

LANDROK. John Lanorok was murdered in Stirling, 1546 (SBR., p. 43). Patrick Landrok in Wemyss accused of witchcraft, 1626 (RPC., 2. ser. I, p. 275). Lanerok 1546.

LANDSBOROUGH. An Anglicized form of MACCLANSBURGH, q.v. David Landsborough published *Arran: a poem*, Edinburgh, 1826. His son wrote on botanical subjects. Current as Landsburgh in Kirkcudbrightshire, 1942.

LANDSMAN. Surname in Fife. Probably from the occupation, one who looked after the open wood. "For through this laund anon the deer will come." 3 Henry VI, III. Nichol Landesman or Launsman had safe conduct into England, 1424 (*Bain*, IV, 961, 963).

LANE. Local. David Laine, tenant in Balledy, 1510 (*Cupar-Angus*, I, p. 278). William Lain admitted burgess of Aberdeen, 1539 (NSCM., I, p. 56).

LANEMALBRIDE. From Lhanbryde in Moray. Abraham de Lanemalbride witnessed a confirmation charter by Richard, bishop of Moray, between 1187–1203 (REM., p. 456).

LANG. From OE. *lang*, "long," i.e. "tall." As a byname this occurs in OE. charters as early as

972–92, e.g. "Aetheric thes langa" (*Cartularium Saxonicum*, 1130), and "Eadweard se langa" (*Battle of Maldon*, 1. 273). William Lange of the county of Berewyke rendered homage in 1296 (*Bain*, II, p. 207). Adam Lang was one of an inquest on lands in Aberdeen in 1341 (REA., I, p. 69), and Walter Lang appears as a burgess of Edinburgh in 1381 and 1392 (*Egidii*, p. 22, 28). Willelmus Lange witnessed an instrument of concord between the bishop of Aberdeen and John de Forbes dominus ejusdem in 1391 (REA., I, p. 189). Robert Lang was chaplain to Duncan, earl of Lennox between 1394–98 (*Levenax*, p. 60, 65, 74), and William Lang was rector of the church of Turreve (Turriff) in 1408 (AAB.). Thomas Lang was bailie of the abbot of Holyrood in 1457 (*Neubotle*, 284), a William Lang appears in Brechin in 1435 (REB., I, 79), and Thomas Lange in Elenehall was a charter witness in 1580 (*Laing*, 1002). A burgess family of this name long maintained a position of influence in the town affairs of Selkirk, and John Lang was freeman of the Craft of Taylors there in 1650. Andrew Lang, classical scholar and folklorist, and Cosmo Gordon Lang, archbishop of Canterbury, are perhaps the two most prominent bearers of the surname. The Loynachans, an old family in Kintyre, changed their name to Lang.

LANGCHESTER. Sir Adam de Langchestre, canon of Jeddeworth, 1297 (*Bain*, II, 969), derived his name from Lanchester (1345 Langechestre) in county Durham.

LANGLAND, LANGLANDS. The old family of Langlands of that Ilk derived their name from a small property of the name in Peeblesshire. The family were also lords of half the barony of Wilton in Roxburghshire, and sometimes took their designation from that property. The family ended in heirs female with the death at Hawick in 1814 of Miss Langlands, who was buried in Wilton Church. Marion Cumyne, widow of quondam Johannes de Langland, had a charter of the lands of Milsallystoun and Ochtirheuyd in 1364 (RMS., I, 151). Charles Langlandis was vicar of Dryvisdall, 1531 (*Soltre*, p. 107), and Jemie Langland was tenant on the Abbey lands of Kelso, 1567 (*Kelso*, p. 524). James Langlands was called to account in 1576 as surety for Will Robson and decreed to pay 20 marks as assythment on behalf of the latter (RPC., II, p. 571). Gawan Langlandis appears in the Register of Cupar Abbey c. 1550, and John Langlandis is recorded in Dunfermline, 1561 (*Dunfermline*). James Langlands, younger in the Queinsferrie, 1653 (*Inquis.*, 3857), and Robert Langlands in Wiltoune burne, 1696 (*Peebles CR.*).

LANGMORE, LANGMUIR, LONGMOOR, LONGMORE, LONGMUIR. Local, from one or more of the places so named. There is Longmore near Ayr, and Langmuir near Kirkintilloch. Elice de la Longmore and Robert de Langemore of county of Edinburgh, and Johan de Langemore of Ayrshire rendered homage, 1296 (*Bain*, II, p. 199, 201, 205, 210). John de Langmure de eodem, juror in Irvine, 1417 (*Irvine*, I, p. 20), probably derived from Longmuir near Kilmaurs. John of Langmuir is in record in 1424, and Robert Langomwire in 1524 (Irving, *Dumbartonshire*, p. 573, 575). John Langmour, presbyter, witnessed a deed regarding the Collegiate Church of Dalkeith, 1477 (RHM.). George Langmur was on assize at Kirkcudbright, 1508 (*Trials*, I, p. 55*). Henry Langmuir, burgess of Renfrew, 1574 (*Campsie*). Robert Langmure was heir of Isabella Langmure, his sister, in the 40s. land of Kirkland, 1609 (*Retours, Ayr*, 111). Jane Longmoor died in Birkenbog, 1854 (*Fordyce*, p. 90). Langmuire 1649.

LANGRIG. Local. Robert Lanrig, burgess freeman of Glasgow, 1584 (*Burgesses*). John Langrig in Fleurs, 1632 (*Campsie*). See also LANRICK.

LANGSIDE. From Langside, the scene of Queen Mary's defeat in May, 1568, now a suburb of Glasgow. Andrew Langsyde held a tenement in Glasgow before 1487 (REG., p. 454), and another tenement in the same city belonged to Archibald Langside in 1548 (LCD., p. 111). The name also occurs in the Glasgow Protocol books as Langsyide (1560).

LANGSKAILL. An Orcadian surname of local origin from Langskaill in the parish of St. Andrews. Andro Langskaill in Lanksckell was one of the jurors on an assize at Tankerness in St. Andrews parish in 1559, and Johne Langskaill was one of the "jugis arbitratouris" in a dispute in 1571 (REO., p. 111, 130). David Langskaill or Laneskaill is in record in Kirkwall in 1640 (MCM., II, p. 211). George Langskail was witness in an Orkney witch trial in 1708 (Low, *Tour through Orkney and Shetland*, p. 202). Langskeall 1701.

LANGTON. From the lands of Langton in the parish of the same name in Berwickshire. Aleyn de Langetone of Berwickshire rendered homage, 1296. His seal, a gem, S' *Alain de Langtwne* (*Bain*, II, p. 211, 557). Patrick of Langeton was juror on an inquisition held before the sheriff of Berwick in 1300 (*Bain*, II, 1178). William Langton was appointed by Henry VII "maister of our ordenances" in Berwick in 1504 (ibid., IV, 1738). Gulielmus Langtoun of Earlehaugh, 1693 (*Retours, Peebles*, 198).

LANGWILL. Local. John Langwill was admitted burgess freeman of Glasgow in 1608 (Burgesses). John Languill held land in Brechin, 1613 (REB., II, 240) and in 1622 is recorded as citiner there (Brechin). John Langwill, flesher in Edinburgh, 1637 (Edinb. Marr.), Allane Langwill in Hillhouse, Ayrshire, 1666 and 1680 (Corsehill, p. 16, 152), and John Langwill in parish of Kilkerran, 1676 (Argyll). Langwell and Langwill in Campbeltown, 1686. Lingwil 1682.

LANRICK. From the old five-pound lands of Langrigs in the Stewartry of Annandale (1607, Langriggs). John Lanrick was town clerk of Dumfries, 1754 (Dumfries). Drumlanrig is on the end of a drum (G. druim) or long ridge of a hill. See also LANRIG.

LAPRAIK. From the lands of Lapraik, of old Lekprevik. The old castle of Lekprevik is about a mile and a half from Kilbride in Lanarkshire. The family of Lapraik are said to have had a grant of the heritable office of sergeant and coroner of the lordship of Kilbride in the reign of Robert III confirmed to them by several charters of the Jameses (OPS., I, p. 101). Jacobus de Lekprewyk had a royal charter of the lands of Polkarne in Kyle regis in 1365 (RMS., I, 204), and Alexander de Lekprewikk de eadem is in record as a charter witness in 1450 (ibid., II, 408). Alexander de Lekprewyk witnessed an instrument of sasine of the superiority of Pollok in 1486 (Pollok, I, p. 192), Jame Lekprewik was "fylit of pycry" (i.e. pilfering) in 1488 (Lanark, p. 1), John Loparx possessed a tenement in Glasgow in 1498 (REG., p. 500), and Alexander Likprivik appears in 1509 (REG., 488). James Lekprywyk who was made perpetual vicar of the parish church of Inverness in 1521 is probably James Lekprewik, vicar of Arbirlot in 1522 (RAA., II, 559, 575). John Lekpreuik is in record in Dalquharn in 1575, and another John Lekpreuik in Grenoktoun appears as a witness in the same year (RRM., III, p. 265, 281), and still another John Likprevik was burgess of Edinburgh in 1583 (Soltre, p. 150). Robert Lekprevik introduced printing into St. Andrews in 1572, and Alexander Lecprevik was one of those tried for the murder of George Hamilton in 1509 (Trials, I, p. 62*, 110*). In 1607 Gavin Lekprevik was ordered put "in the joggis" for "dinging of Marioun Maxwell his stepmother" (MCM., I, p. 408). John Lapraik (1737–1807), a minor poet, was a friend of Robert Burns. Lekprevek 1478, Likprevik 1610, Leikprivick 1622, Lekpriuick 1562, Lekprivik 1594, Lekpreuik 1509.

LAPSLEY. Colene Lapslie was treasurer and master of work in Stirling, 1642 (SBR., p. 291).

Robert Lapslay, clerk of the weighhouse in Edinburgh, 1646 (Edinb. Marr.), George Lapslie, merchant in Stirling, 1661 (SBR., p. 236), and William Lapslie in Glenmvlne, parish of Campsie, 1669 (Campsie). Coline Lapsley appears in Logie, 1686 (Logie, I, p. 130).

LARDNER. A surname derived from the occupation of lardiner, one who had charge of the larder, AF. lardiner, OF. lardier. William, son of Ralph the lardener, quitclaimed lands in Anant to Robert de Brus, 1218 (Annandale, I, p. 4; Bain, I, 704). Alan le larderer was a charter witness in 1250 (LAC., 57). Michael le Lardiner of Linlithgowshire and William le Lardyner, burgess of Stirling, rendered homage in 1296 (Bain, II, p. 197, 198). John Lardnar was burgess of Stirling, c. 1300 (Cambus., 222), payment was made to Walter de lardario for expenses of the queen, 1328, and in 1343 herrings from Inverness were delivered to Malcolm de lardario (ER., I, p. 116, 516).

LARG, LARGUE. Either from Largue in the parish of Forgue, Aberdeenshire, or from Largue in the parish of Cabrach, Banffshire, more probably the former. Peter Larg in the parish of Dunbennan appears in 1716 (SCM., IV, p. 169), and Isobel Largoe or Largue in Aberdeen, 1742. G. Largue in Haddo, 1816. Jonathan Largue from King Edward served in the first Great War (Turriff).

LARGIE. From Largie in the parish of Insch, Aberdeenshire. Alexander Largie at Kirktoun of Fetteresso, 1656 (Brechin).

LARNACH, LARNACK. The first form is current in Caithness and the second in Atholl. Latharnach means a Lorne man or man from Lorne, the th in Gaelic is used to divide syllables. It may also be the adjectival form of Maclaren. William Larnach in Stralovh was fined for reset of Clan Gregor, 1613 (RPC., XIV, p. 636). Alexander Miller Larnach, retired postmaster of Huntlv, Aberdeenshire, died 1941. The name of William Lurnach, an outlaw of Scotland, in record in 1204 (Annals, p. 345) not likely to be of same origin.

LASPUR. Edmund Laspur resident in Aberdeen, 1723 (NSCM., II, p. 147).

LASSWADE. From the old barony of Lasswade in Midlothian. Gaufridus de Laswade who witnessed a charter of the church of Karreden to the monks of Holyrood before 1153 is probably Gaufridus, presbyter de Laswade of the reign of Malcolm IV (LSC., p. 10, 13, 15). An indulgence was granted in 1215 to Richard de Lassewade to receive an additional benefice (Pap. Lett., I, p. 63). William de Lessewade, tenant of the bishop of St. Andrews in the county of Edneburk, rendered homage for his lands in 1296 (*Bain*, II, p. 205).

LATHANGIE. A variant of LETHANGIE, q.v., recorded in Markinch, Fife.

LATHDUGIE. A Fife surname, of local origin from some place of the name in the shire. Several place names there begin with Lath-.

LATHRISK. From the old barony of Lathrisk in Fife. The first of the name in record appears to be William de Laskreske of the county of Fyfe who rendered homage for his lands in 1296 (*Bain*, II, p. 204). George de llothreisk, son and apparent heir of Alexander de llothreisk, obtained the lands of Spittalefeld beside Inverkeithing in 1477 and resigned them in the same year (RD., 478, 479). John Lathreisk was bailie of Dysart in 1525, and another John Lathrisk, elder, was chosen "Kirk master" of St. Serfs in 1534 (*Dysart*, p. 3, 33). Walter Lathrisc appears as salt collector in 1575 (RPC., II, p. 726), and James Laithrik was a notary public in Cupar in 1581 (*Soltre*, p. 145). The surname early reached the Orkney Islands and is in record there in 1511 as Laithreis (*Laing*, 282). Michell Lathreish in Dysart was father of Alexander Lathrice, a captive among the Turks in 1632 (PBK., p. 36, 37). The surname is or was pronounced Larisse. Laithresk 1547, Lathreis 1562, Lawchresk 1510.

LATIMER, LATTIMER, LATTEMORE. From OF. *latinier*, ME. *latymer*, an interpreter, literally one knowing Latin. The form Latimer is of easier pronunciation. The Latimeris were included among the unruly clans of the West Marche in 1587 (APS., III, p. 467). See also LOTTIMER.

LATTA, LATTO. A form of LAWTIE, q.v. James Lattay in Lochwinnoch in 1677, and James Lata in Midtoun, parish of Lochwinnoch in 1709 (*Kilbarchan*). Several of this name recorded in Dumbarton in the eighteenth century (RDB.). The second form is found in Aberdeen.

LATTEMORE, LATTIMER. See LATIMER.

LATTOUN. John Lattoun elected common councillor, Aberdeen, 1398 (CRA., p. 374).

LAUCHARRIT. Janet Laucharrit recorded in Edrem in 1670 (*Lauder*) most probably derived her surname from Lochquharret (now Vogrie) in Midlothian.

LAUCHT. Of local origin, perhaps from Laught near Thornhill. There is another Laucht near Saltcoats. John Laucht appears in the parish of Cadder, 1567 (*Campsie*).

LAUDER. From Lauder in Berwickshire. Robert de Lavedre is said [erroneously] to have obtained lands in Berwickshire from Malcolm Canmore (*Thomson*, p. 6). Sir Robert de Lauedre witnessed a charter by John de Mautelent to the Abbey of Dryburgh (*Dryburgh*), and William de Lawedre appears as sheriff of Perthshire in reign of Alexander III. As early as 1297 the Lauders were possessors of the Bass Rock in the Firth of Forth. Robert de Lauueder, who had a charter of the lands of Colden in barony of Dalkeith, 1316 (RHM., I, p. 17), may be Robert de Loweder, justiciar of Lothian, 1327–31 (*Raine*, 141; RHM., I, p. 38). Another Robert de Lawdre was one of the borowis for the earl of Douglas's bounds on the Middle March, 1398 (*Bain*, IV, 510). Robert de Lawedre and Thomas of Lawedre were merchants and burgesses of Edinburgh, 1425 (ibid., 976), and Alan of Lawadyr witnessed a charter by Stephen Fleming, master of the Hospital of Soltre, 1426 (*Soltre*, p. 52). William Lawedre was one of the conservators of truce between Scotland and England, 1451 (*Bain*, IV, 1239), and Robert of Lawdir was one of those sent to conduct the envoys with the Princess Cecilia's dower to Edinburgh, 1477 (ibid., 1445). Sandiris of Lawdyr witnessed a sasine, 1478 (*Home*, 24), and James Lawdre had letters of denization in England, 1480 (*Bain*, IV, 1465). William Lauder, literary forger and classical scholar, died 1771. Ladar 1550, Laudor 1498, Laudre 1388, Lauedre 1425, Laueeder 1315, Lauther 1699, Lavedier 1333, Lawadir 1426, Laweadre 1425, Lawedire 1420, Lawedre 1413; Laweddir. The name became Lawther and Leather in Ulster.

LAUDERDALE. From the name of the western district of Berwickshire. Johannes Lathirdale, notary public, witnessed a confirmation charter by Andrew, bishop of Glasgow, 1472 (REG., p. 420). Sir David Luthirdale or Luthiredale appears as archdeacon of Dunkeld, 1477–78 (*Bain*, IV, 1444, 1449). Cf. Lidderdale and Lutherdale.

LAUGHLAN, LAUGHLAND. Forms of LACHLAN, q.v., current in Ayrshire. Robert Laughland, cook in Edinburgh, 1642 (*Edinb. Marr.*), and — Lauchlein in Aberdeen, 1643 (SCM., v, p. 106).

LAUMANSON. 'Son of LAMOND,' q.v. See also MACLAMONT.

LAURENCE, LAWRANCE, LAWRENCE. From the Latin personal name *Laurentius* through French *Laurence*. The church of Edzell was

LAURENCE, LAWRANCE. . . , continued

dedicated to S. Laurentius the Deacon, who was martyred under Valerian by being roasted on a gridiron, A. D. 258. The saint's well is near by the churchyard. Magister Laurentius, a cleric, was a charter witness, c. 1150 (REG., 11), and Laurentius was archdeacon of Brechin in 1368 (RMS., I, 236). John Lourens was admitted burgess of Aberdeen in 1541 (NSCM., I, p. 57), and John Lourance was notary in Duns in 1663 (Lauder). Lauraince 1608, Laurence 1644, Lauritan 1665, Lawrence 1629, Lorrance 1716, Lourence 1574, Lourens 1541, Lowrance 1446, Lowrence 1584, Lowrens 1569.

LAURENCESON, 'son of LAURENCE,' q.v. Walter Laurenceson alias Lauranceson, a Scot, had letters of denization in England, 1480 (Bain, IV, 1471).

LAURENSON, 'son of LAURENCE,' q.v. John Laurentii, licentiate of decrees and vicar of Culessy, 1443 (REB., I, 90), and Andro Louranstoun had a precept of remission in 1491 (RSS., I, 10). Arthur Laurenson, Shetland antiquary. In old Shetland documents within the Norse period (c. 1600) this name appears as Lauritzon (Goudie, p. 110, 130).

LAURIE, LAWRIE. Diminutives of LAURENCE, q.v. Innes (p. 21) says Laurie is another shape of Laurenceson, but this is unlikely. The church of Edzell was dedicated to S. Laurence the Martyr, and his well is near by the church-yard. The name has been also explained, with still less probability, as from Scots lowrie, 'foxy.' The name of Gavin Lawrie, governor of New Jersey during the colonial period, is spelled in a letter quoted in The Haigs of Bemersyde as Lowry. In old records (barony court book of Stitchell, kirk-session records, tombstones, etc.) the surname is found spelled Lauri (1655), Laurie, Laurri, Laury (1665), Lawrie, Lawry, Larrie, Larry, Lowry, Lourie, Loury, and Lowrry.

LAVEROCK. Generally explained as a nickname from the lark, but perhaps more likely a corruption of the OE. personal name Leofric. Alexander Laverock had a charter from Robert III of a tenement in Perth (RMS., I, App. II, 1781). John Laverok who petitioned for a benefice in gift of abbot of Dunfermline, 1403 (Pap. Pet., I, p. 627), may be John Lauerok who was rector of the parish church of Cambuslang in 1427 (HMC., 12. Rep., App. 8, p. 122). Laurence Lauerok was a presbyter of Scone in 1471 (Scon, p. 195), and Henry Lawerok witnessed a charter to William Peblis in Scone in 1491 (ibid., p. 201). Thomas Laverok obtained a respite for slaughter committed by him in 1515 (RSS., I, 2650), James Laverok was burgess of Linlithqw in 1529, and Elizabeth Laverok in the same town had sasine in her favor in 1536 (Johnsoun). William Laverok was commissioner from the earl of Weyms, 1638, and David Laverock was elder in Auchterdirran, 1640 (PBK., p. 126, 173). Agnes Laverock is recorded in the parish of Torphichen, 1713, and Jean Leveruck in the parish of Bathgate, 1674 (Torphichen.) Laverack or Laverick was common in Yorkshire in the eighteenth century and found in Notts in reign of Edward I (Guppy, p. 415). See also LEVERICK.

LAVEROCKSTONES. Local. The gift of the ward of William Laverokstanis, portioner of part of Purveshill, Peeblesshire, and his daughters was made in 1541 (RSS., 4434). Agnes Lariestaines in Purveshill, 1579 (Retours, Peebles, 13).

LAW. There are ten or more places named Law in Scotland from which this name may have been derived. It was a common surname in Glasgow in the sixteenth century. In 1428 Robert de Lawe had a safe conduct to pass through England on his return from Spain. James of Law compeared in court with an accusation against another in 1488 (Prestwick, p. 32), and Quintigernus Law is in record in 1644 (Inquis., 2991). John Law (1671–1729), the financier and projector of commercial schemes, was born in Edinburgh.

LAWMANSON. An Englishing of MACLAMOND, q.v. John Laumanson of Perthshire rendered homage, 1296 (Bain, II, p. 204). Celestine Lawmanni (= Lawmanson), son and heir of Robert Lawmanni, and Cristin Lawmanni are charter witnesses in 1402 (RMS., II, 3138). Patrick Lawmondson was crowner (coronator) of Cowale from 1445 to 1450 (Accounts of Great Chamberlains, v. 3), and in 1481 John Lawmanson de Inuervn witnessed a Cowal charter (LCD., p. 192).

LAWRANCE, LAWRENCE. See under LAURENCE.

LAWRIE. See under LAURIE.

LAWSIDE. About 1855 an infant was found by the side of a road leading past Lawside Farm, Dundee, by the farmer's sister, Miss Leslie, and its parentage was never traced. The child was brought up by the farmer people and named after its finder and the place of discovery — Mary Ann Lawside.

LAWSON. 'Son of LAWRENCE,' q.v., through the diminutive 'Law.' Richard Laurence of

Byker (i.e. Biggar) of Lanarkshire rendered homage, 1296 (*Bain*, II, p. 213). Richard Lawson was canon of St. Giles', Edinburgh, and laird of Grothill, 1370. John Lawson de Lyntoun was tenant under Douglas in Linton, 1376 (RHM., I, p. lii; II, p. 16). Ady Lawsoun was a forestaller in Aberdeen, 1402 (CRA., p. 384), John Lauson held a land there, 1436 (REA., I, p. 234), and the house of another John Lawsone in Leyth is referred to, 1462 (*Soltre*, p. 65). Richard Lawson was town clerk of Edinburgh, 1482, clerk of justiciary, 1490, and clerk to the ambassadors of James, king of Scots, 1495 (*Bain*, IV, 1484, 1564, 1612). He may be the Richard Lausoun of Edinburgh who gave his bond of manrent in 1508 (SCM., II, p. 278). Richard Lawson, laird of Hariggs (where George Heriot's Hospital in Edinburgh now stands) was appointed Lord Justice Clerk c. 1488. His wife's name is commemorated in "Lady Lawson's Wynd" near by. Alexander Lawson (1773–1846), born in Lanarkshire, died in Philadelphia, engraved the best plates in Alexander Wilson's *Ornithology* chiefly "for the honor of his old country," and for a financial return not exceeding one dollar a day. The name was early carried to France, and is said to appear there at the present day as De Lauzun. It became Loson in Posen, 1593. Lason 1599, Lasone 1681, Lasoun 1640, Lausone 1540, Laweson 1480, Lawsoune 1607, Losone 1544, Losoun 1532.

LAWTHER. A variant of LAUDER, q.v. John Lawther, bricklayer in Dumbarton, 1792 (RDB.).

LAWTIE. This surname takes the form 'Laitties of yᵗ Ilk' in Workman's MS. (a heraldic MS. dated 1623), but generally takes the form of Lautie or Lawtie in MSS. The lands of Laithis in Ayrshire, from which the surname is taken, were granted to the Fullartons on the resignation of Thomas Laithis of that Ilk, c. 1350 (*Stodart*, II, p. 190; RMS., I, 397). William del Lathes was juror on an inquisition at Lochmaben in 1347 (*Bain*, III, 1449), and William Lathis and Adam Lathis were witnesses in AYR in 1476 (*Friars Ayr*, p. 55). Thomas Laysse and Andrew Layse, sons of Adam Lavse in Ayr, are in record in 1509, and Friar Andrew Lathis, son of Adam Lathis, resigned a tenement in Woodgate, Ayr, in 1518 (ibid., p. 75, 81). Adam Lawte witnessed a precept of clare constat at Coldingham in 1525 (*Home*, 35), John Lawta witnessed a notarial transumpt in Haddington in 1537 (*James II*, 21), James Lawtie was member of Scots parliament for Cullen, 1628 (*Hanna*, II, p. 502), and Mr. James Lautie was minister at Chirnside in 1695 (*Lauder*).

LAYCOCK, LEACOCK. Evidently from Laycock in the West Riding of Yorkshire. William Laicok was vicar of Retre (Rattray) in 1492 (RAA., II, 338). John Lacok, canon of Dunkeld, was auditor of accounts of the bishopric between 1505–17 (*Rent. Dunk.*). Sara Lacok in Edinburgh, 1602 (*Edinb. Marr.*). Jean Leacock in Fordie, 1695, and three more of the name are in record (*Dunkeld*).

LEACH, LEITCH. From OE. *læce*, 'doctor.' The medicus regis is often mentioned in old charters. Henry Leche held a tenement in Glasgow, 1325 (LCD., p. 157). Henry Leche, 'vallettus' to David de Bruys (*Rot. Scot.*, p. 724, 797), is later referred to in a safe conduct by Edward III of England in 1348 as "Hector medicus David de Bruys." From another reference to him in 1369 (RMS., I, 333) he turns out to be a MacBeth, perhaps one of the family of hereditary doctors of that name so famous in West Highland history. William de (an error for 'le') Lech' or Leche was burgess of Aberdeen, 1362 (REA., I, p. 105, 106). He may be William Leche, merchant of Aberdeen, whose goods were plundered in England, 1370, when his ship was driven ashore in Kirklee Rode, Suffolk (*Bain*, IV, 158). John Leitch, canon of Glasgow, appears in 1363 as Leche, and in 1372 as Lithe (for Liche) or Leche. Robert Leche, seneschal to the earl of March and Moray, 1367 (RMS., I, 265). Ferchard Leche had a grant of lands in Assynt in 1386 to be held for the services of old due and wont (OPS., II, p. 695, 704). The land of Thomas Leyche is mentioned in 1421 (RAA., II, 56). Patrick Leiche (Lech, Leich, Leche) appears several times as a canon of Glasgow between 1440–82, and built and endowed S. Mauchan's altar in the church there (REG.). John Leche had a garden in the same city in 1487 (LCD., p. 200). Gilbert Leiche was made burgess of Aberdeen, 1452 (NSCM., I, p. 13), and Alexander Leche, chaplain, a Scotsman, received letters of denization in England in 1484 (*Bain*, IV, 1500). Sir Archibald Lech, chaplain at Lismore, 1511 (*Poltalloch Writs*, p. 183), is Sir Archibald Leycthe, provost of Kilmun in 1520 (*Cawdor*, p. 135). Leatch 1779, Leeche 1638, Leiche 1550, Liech 1767, Litch 1639.

There was an old family of this name (Lech, Leech, Leich, Leitch) in Menteith in the sixteenth century who gave name to Leitchtown there, and the Leitches of Logie-Almond are said to have been a family of doctors. Andrew Leiche, preceptor of the grammar school of Brechin in 1580 is probably Andrew Leitche who was minister of Maritoun (Maryton), Montrose, 1587 (REB., 216, 329). A tombstone in Maryton reads: "Heir lyis Villame

LEACH, LEITCH, continued

Lietch and David Lieth tvoe briether soum tyme in Old Montrois" who died in 1666 (Jervise, I, p. 368). John Leech of Aberdeen, author of Rudimenta Grammaticæ Latinæ, London, 1624, Latinized his name Leochaeus.

In the fifteenth century the lands of Kildavanan in Bute were held by a family named Lech for a "yearly reddendo of two pennies or a pair of gloves within the parish church of Bute." John Lech, son of deceased Gilzequhome or Gilquhome, had a grant of these lands in June, 1429 (RMS., II, 129), which had belonged by heritage to the same Gilzequhome. In 1466 or earlier Gilchrist Leiche, lord of Kilmavanane, granted to his son and heir, David Leiche, these same lands, except two acres called the Clours. See MACINLEICH.

LEACOCK. See under LAYCOCK.

LEAD. Of local origin. There is a place named Lead at Cartmore, Stirlingshire. Andrew Lead or Load in the parish of Kilbarchan, 1659, and William Led in Weitlands, 1655 (Kilbarchan). Hew Load, town officer in Paisley, took the Test in 1686 (RPC., 3. ser. XI, p. 496; ibid., XII, p. 383).

LEADBEATER, LEADBETTER, LEADBITTER. From the obsolete occupation of 'leadbeater' (ME. ledbetere), maker of leaden vessels and sheet lead for roofs. Walter Ledbeter of Heydon was before an assize at Newcastle-on-Tyne on suspicion of robbery in Scotland in 1256 (Bain, I, 2047, m. 15). Thomas Ledbeter was custumar and provost of Linlithgow in 1328 and following years (ER., I). Alexander Leadbetter, merchant in Kelso, 1831 (Heirs, 739). Leadbetter in Glasgow, 1942.

LEADHOUSE. Local. Simon of Ledehouse assisted Sir James of Douglas in his capture of Roxburgh Castle, 1313 (Barbour, Brus). Adam de Ledhuss who held a land "in vico de Futy," Aberdeen, in 1363 (REA., II, p. 283), is probably Adam de Ledhovs, burgess of Aberdeen, 1391 (RAA., II, p. 40). William Leedhous of Scotland was unjustly imprisoned in Oxford in violation of the truce of 1392 (Bain, IV, 448). Sir John Ledhous, chaplain at Cragy, 1499 (Simon, 2). Jhone of Leidhows or Lydhowsse was tenant in Ranstrudyr, 1525–30 (Rental), James Leidhous and William Leidhous were tenants on lands of Kelso Abbey, 1567 (Kelso, p. 523, 528). Thomas Leadhouse, tenant in Drygrange, 1682 (RRM., III, p. 35), and Agnes Leadhouse in Carchesters, 1690 (Peebles CR.).

LEAL. Andrew Leal, treasurer of the church of Aberdeen, 1479 (REG., p. 440). William

Leal, shoemaker in Forres, 1765 (Moray). Kenneth Leal, for robbing the mail, was executed and hung in chains between Elgin and Fochabers, 1773 (Thomson, Public records of Scotland, p. 131).

LEAN. A shortened form of (MAC)LEAN, q.v.

LEAPER, LEIPER, LAIPER. From OE. lēapere, a basket-maker. A lēap was a basket made of rush or sedge. Johannes Leper was a burgess of Edinburgh in 1189 (Nisbet, I, p. 304). Walter Lippre witnessed a charter of Turriff in 1272 (REA., I, p. 34), Patrick Leper was a burgess of Edinburgh in 1368 (Egidii, p. 1), and Andrew Lepar witnessed an instrument of concord between the bishop of Aberdeen and John de Forbes, dominus ejusdem, in 1391 (REA., I, p. 189). Alexander Lepar was admitted burgess of Aberdeen in 1408 and William Lepar in 1487 (NSCM., I, p. 3, 32), and Alan Leppar and Adam Leppayr were burgesses of Prestwick in 1507 (Prestwick, p. 10). An illustration of the Lepar tomb in St. Andrews is in Proceed. Soc. Ant. Scot., XLV, p. 508–509. The name has nothing to do with leper, one affected with leprosy (ME. and AF. lepre). Leiper 1711, Leipper 1608.

LEARMONTH, LEARMONT, LEARMOND, LEIRMONTH. An old surname in the Merse, derived from the lands of Learmonth, Berwickshire. William de Leirmontht was juror on an inquisition at Swinton in 1408 (Swinton, p. xviii). Andrea de Lermwth in Edinburgh in record, 1413 (CDE., 21), appears again in 1426 as Lermonth (Egidii, p. 46). Alexander Leyremonthe or Leremonthe was clerk of works of the town and castle of Berwick, 1434 (Bain, IV, 1080). Jacobus Lermonth was presbyter of Glasgow diocese and notary public, 1454 (Pollok, I, p. 176). William of Lermonth, summoned in 1479 to answer to Parliament for treason and other crimes (APS., II, p. 129), may be the William of Lewrmonth who witnessed a declaration by John of Roule in the same year (Home, 25). Sir James Learmonth of Dairsie, master of the household to James V, was provost of St. Andrews in 1546. William Lermonth witnessed a precept of sasine at Coldingham, 1557 (Home, 195), and persons named Leirmount, Leirmontt, and Lermont appear in the list of tenants on lands of the Abbey of Kelso, 1567 (Kelso). The family of Leirmonth of Balcomy is now extinct. The Lermontoff family of Russia claim descent from Learmont of Scotland. The claim seems well attested. Laremonth 1676, Larmont 1671, Larmonth 1698, Learmonthe 1628, Leirmontht 1548, Lermond 1685, Lermound 1566, Levrmount 1525. Michael Lermontoff, one of the greatest Russian poets in the nineteenth century was descended from a Scots emigrant of the seventeenth century. John Learmont published a volume of *Poems* in Edinburgh, 1791.

LEASK, LEISK. From the old lands of Leask, now Pitlurg, in the parish of Slains, Aberdeenshire. William of Lask, *dominus ejusdem*, in 1380, granted a pound of wax yearly to the church of S. Mary of Logy iuxta Elone (REA., I, p. 134). Thomas de Lask or Laysk was bailie of the barony of Fyndon, 1390 (CAB., p. 272), and in the following year he witnessed a charter by Henry St. Clair, earl of Orkney (RMS., I, 824; REO., p. 28). Amy Lowsk apud Kyngudy was accused of being a forestaller in 1402 (CRA., p. 385), Henry de Laske witnessed a grant by Robert III to the Blackfriars of Perth in 1405 (*Milne*, p. 39), and Johannes de Louask was juror on an inquest apud Rane, 1413 (REA., I, p. 214). William de Lowask was burgess of Aberdeen, 1445 (NSCM., I, p. 10), and Umfra Laysk of that Ilk in 1461 granted a charter of a piece of land called Brinthous in Aberdeenshire (CAB., p. 364). People of this name early migrated to the Orkneys, and James of Lask is recorded there as 'Lawman' in 1438 (SCM., v, p. 391). Laisk c. 1524, Lesk 1490.

LECKIE, LECKY. An old surname common in the shires of Dumbarton and Stirling, derived from the barony of Leckie in the parish of Gargunnock, Stirlingshire. Murdoch Leckie received a grant of two fourth parts of Bathewnn and Altremony from Robert III (RMS., I, app. II, 1819). David Lekky was denounced rebel in 1537 (*Trials*, I, p. *178), Janet Laiky appears in Cammok, parish of Glenylla, 1599, and Euphemia Laikie in Carneleithe, 1694 (*Brechin*). The surname appears as Lecque among the Scots Guards in France, and the Leckies of Antrim and Carlow in Ireland are of Scottish descent. In Forman's heraldic MS. the name is spelled Leuke. The individual who had a charter of the lands of Leckie in the reign of David II was a descendant of Corc, brother of Maldouen, third earl of Lennox (*Sc. Peer.*, p. 330).

LEDDERKIN. Alexander Ledderkin of Aberdeen, a Jacobite of the '45, probably derived his surname from Ledekin near Insch, Aberdeenshire.

LEDGERWOOD. *See under* LIGERTWOOD.

LEDINGHAM. A surname found in Aberdeenshire. George Ledinghame is recorded in Auchinlek in 1574 (RSCA., I, p. 217). John Liddinghame in Cheppiltoune was charged to underlie the law for assault in 1603 (ibid., II, p. 45), and George Ledingham was a member of the Gartly Company of Volunteers in 1798 (*Will*, p. 24). Ledigan was the form of the surname in Mar in the seventeenth century. There is a place Ledikin in Culsalmond which was spelled Lethinghame in 1644 and Ledinghame in 1600 (Macdonald, *Place-names of west Aberdeenshire*), and Prof. Mackinnon compared it with Leideag, pl. Leideagan, "a common name for fields, especially those on outskirts of farms, in the West Highlands" (loc. cit.). Andrew Ledingham from Turriff was killed in the first Great War (*Turriff*).

LEE, LEY. Local. The earlier references point to an English origin. Alan de Leia witnessed a charter by Eschina uxor Walteri a. 1177, and a later Alan de Leya witnessed a charter by Alexander, son of Walter, senescallus, 1246 (RMP., p. 75, 89). Phelippe de la Leye rendered homage, 1296 (*Bain*, II, p. 196). Robertus de Lee, 1436 (*Home*, 6). John Lie in Snook-miln, 1718 (*Lauder*).

LEES. In the Highlands this name derives from M'Illiosa (*Mac Gill'Iosa*), 'son of the gillie of Jesus,' corrupted to M'A'Lios and Lios, whence *Lees*.

LEGAT, LEGGAT, LEGGATE, LEGGATT, LEGGET, LIGGAT, LYGATE. Two origins are offered for this name: (1) Probably from OE. personal name *Leodgeard*, "of which *Leggett* is the regular diminutive" (*Weekley*); (2) from the office, "the legate," an ambassador, a delegate, ME. *legat*, *legate*. This, I think, is the chief or only parent of the name. Adam Legate who rendered to Exchequer the accounts of the bailies of Stirling in 1406 (ER., IV, p. 59) appears again in 1412 as burgess of the town (*Cambus.*, p. 63). Walter Leget or Legat of Scotland had safe conducts into England in 1421–2, and Master John Legat had a safe conduct to pass to Rome in 1448 (*Bain*, IV, 911, 915, 1206). Thomas Legat of Tayn witnessed a notarial instrument, 1477 (*Cawdor*, p. 63), Laurence Legat possessed a tenement in Irvine, 1540 (*Irvine*, I, p. 166), and Archibald Legate was burgess freeman of Glasgow, 1574 (*Burgesses*). John Leggat was "baxter and burges" of Stirling, 1591 (*Sc. Ant.*, VI, p. 166), and Thomas Ligat is recorded at the kirk of Steuartoune, 1670 (*Corsehill*, p. 94). Six brothers named Leggat from King Edward served in the first Great War (*Turriff*). Probably confused with LIDGATE, q.v. Liegait 1611, Liegatt 1603, Liggaitt 1696.

LEGERTWOOD, LEGERWOOD. *See under* LIGERTWOOD.

LEGG, Legge. The earliest reference to this surname in old records of Banffshire is c. 1588, when William Leg in Newmyll gave his son "his portione naturall." In 1648 Patrick Leg "was indyttit and accusit haldin and reput as ane commoun theiff and ane notorious theiff without fang and in fang," etc. (SN&Q., I, p. 45–46). Margaret Leg in Stracathrow, 1627 (Brechin). Gilbert Leg, weaver in Invereichnie, 1702 (Banff Rec., p. 237), and Walter Leg was member of the Gartly Company of Volunteers, 1798 (Will, p. 23). James Legge (1815–1897), one of the most distinguished Sinologists, was born at Huntly, Aberdeenshire. The name has been derived from Old West Norse Leggr (Jónsson, Aarbøger for nordisk Old-kyndighed, 1907, p. 221), but in Scotland is more likely to be of local origin, from ledge, dative case of OE. leáh, 'at the lea.' Matheu de Leghe of Dumfriesshire rendered homage, 1296 (Bain, II, p. 198). Lyg 1598.

LEGGAT, Leggate, Leggatt, Legget. See under LEGAT.

LEGHENDY. Probably from Lethenty in the parish of Alford, Aberdeenshire. Richard de Leghendy of Aberdeenshire rendered homage, 1296 (Bain, II, p. 203).

LEGIDEN. An old surname in Inverurie, Aberdeenshire. Probably from the croft of Legisden (Retours, Aberdeen, 1683), now Leggetsden near Pitcaple.

LEGROW. Of local origin from Legrow in Holm, Orkney. Elizabeth Legrow and Margaret Legrow, daughters of Patrick Legrow or Legrov, sold the three merkland of Legrow in 1552 (REO., p. 248–249).

LEICESTER. From Leicester, the chief town in Leicestershire, England. Magister John de Leicestria and Richard de Leicestria appear as witnesses to a charter by Roger de Beaumont, bishop elect of St. Andrews, c. 1189–98 (RPSA., p. 153). John de Leicester, archdeacon of Lothian, was elected bishop of Dunkeld in 1211 and died in 1214 (Dowden, p. 52–53). Robert de Laycester witnessed a charter by his cousin Richard de Levcestria in the reign of Alexander II (Scon, p. 56). William of Leicester, burgess of Edinburgh, rendered homage, 1296 (Bain, II, p. 197). This surname does not appear to have lasted more than three or four generations in Scotland.

LEIDHOPE. David Leidhope witnessed charter of sale of two tenements in St. Andrews, 1519 (Crail, p. 29). Isabel Leddop, 1584. Ladhope is a quoad sacra parish in Melrose parish.

LEIGHTON. From the barony of Leighton in Bedfordshire, England. Robert de Lectun and Symon de Lectun, his brother, witnessed a charter by Peter de Pulloc, c. 1177–99, granting the church of Mernes, Renfrewshire, to the church of S. James of Passelet (Paisley) (RMP., p. 98). William de Lechton witnessed a charter to Walter de Rossy of Rossy in Angus, c. 1260 (RAA., I, p. 337) may be William de Lectona who attested a charter by John de Moravia of lands in Strathbolgy, c. 1284 (REM., p. 462). William de Leghtone, knight, swore fealty at Kyngorne, Fife, 1291 (Bain, II, 508), Sir Thomas de Lighton, deputy chamberlain, 1340 (ER., I, p. 455), and Duncan de Lychtoun became sheriff locum tenens of Angus, 1391 (ER., III, p. 268). Alexander of Lyghton was one of the brothers of the Hospital of St. John of Jerusalem, 1414 (Bain, IV, 854), Alexander of Lichtoune was landowner in Angus, 1415 (REB., I, 37), Walter de Lychtoun was rector of Edzell, 1435 (Jervise, LL., p. 4), and Duncan de Lichtoune was vicar of Brechin, 1457 (REB., II, 274). Johan Lichton of Ullishaven emigrated to Sweden before 1633. His son became governor of Reval and Esthonia in 1681 and president of the superior court of justice in Åbo, 1687. Alexander Leighton, M.D., a cadet of Usan, is celebrated for the severity of treatment he received from the Court of Star Chamber. Lechtone and Lechtoun 1485, Leghtowne 1651, Lichtone 1502, Lichtoun 1514, Lightoun 1670, Lychten 1567, Lychtone 1463.

LEIPER. See under LEAPER.

LEIRMONTH. See under LEARMONTH.

LEISHMAN. The chief cradle of the Leishmans is around Falkirk, "where the name occurs with a frequency bewildering to the record searcher." Among the Border clergy in pre-Reformation days Leishman was no uncommon surname. Thomas Lescheman or Leisman, burgess of Glasgow, 1435–43 (LCD., p. 242, 251). William Leischman or Leschman was prior of Fogo, 1465–66 (Kelso, 530–531). Mychell Leisman in Carnwath, 1529 (CBBC., p. 108), and John Leishman, burgess of Stirling, 1550 (Sc. Ant., VI, p. 178), may be John Lecheman or Lescheman who was bailie and custumar of Stirling, 1559–60 (ER., XIX, p. 83; SBR., p. 73, 279). Duncan Leishman of Hiltoun and Middlethird, Stirling, and others were fined in 1622 for destroying wood in Torwood Forest. James Leischmanis dochter in Lanark, is mentioned in 1644 (RPC., 2. ser. VIII, p. 153). James Leisman in Dunsyre, 1708 (Minutes, p. 37). Six of the name are recorded in the Commissariot Record of Dunblane from 1554. Leischeman 1561.

LEISING. A common personal name in the northern counties of England in mediaeval times. From Old West Scandinavian *Loysingi* (<*loysingr*, 'a freedman'). Laysinge, Cumbrensis judex, was one of the witnesses to Earl David's *Inquisitio* of Glasgow, c. 1124 (REG., p. 7). Leising attested King David's great charter to Holyrood, c. 1128 (LSC., p. 6). Alexander filius Leysing is mentioned in the first half of the thirteenth century (*Dryburgh*, 46). One of this name may have given origin to Leisington, mentioned in 1283 (*Oliphants*, p. 3).

LEISK. *See under* LEASK.

LEITCH. *See under* LEACH.

LEITH. From the town or territory of Leith, Midlothian. There are three fables in circulation, says Stodart, as to the history of the Leiths. (1) That they held the barony of Restalrig, and that that property was carried by an heiress to an ancestor of the Logans of Restalrig. (2) Restalrig gave a surname to its early owners, and it is not till the fifteenth century that Leiths are to be found holding some lands there; they were burgesses of Edinburgh and gave their name to Leith Wynd. (3) The founder of the family of Leith of Harthill in the parish of Oyne, was William de Lethe, burgess of Aberdeen, which he represented in parliament, 1367 (*Stodart*, II). William Leythe, burgess of Aberdeen, 1342 (*St. Nicholas Chartulary*, p. 12), is mentioned again in 1363 as William de Leth (REA., II, p. 283). Laurence de Leth was alderman of Aberdeen, 1388 (CAB., p. 380). Gilbert of Leth was custumar of Edinburgh, 1327, and John de Lethe was provost of Linlithgow, 1330 (ER., I, p. 81, 273). Thomas of Leth appears as witness in Kirkwaw (Kirkwall), 1391 (*Dipl. Norv.*, II, p. 402). Robert de Leitht was admitted burgess of Aberdeen, 1406 (NSCM., I, p. 2), and John of Lethe had safe conduct in England for one month, 1420 (*Bain*, IV, 899). Leithe 1641, Leyth 1601, Leytht 1584.

LEITHEAD, LEITHHEAD. Of local origin from the lands of Leithhead in the parish of Kirknewton, Midlothian (Leithesheid 1610, Leithheid 1621). The name occurs several times in the Edinburgh Marriage Records: John Leythead, weaver, 1646, John Leigtheid, stabler, 1657, and William Leithead, indweller, 1676. John Leathheid, burgess of Selkirk, 1663, and another John Lithhead, portioner of Melrose, 1664 (RRM., II, p. 54; III, p. 73). Walter Liethead died 1712 and was buried in Eccles churchyard, and William Leithhead is recorded in Whitelaw, parish of Hawick, 1764 (*Heirs*, 324). Litheheid 1667.

LEKATHY. Laurence Leckatha received the sum of 30 l sterling in 1292 as part of his wages for keeping the castles of Forfar and Dundee (*Bain*, II, 567). William and Laurence de Lekathy of Forfarshire rendered homage, 1296 (ibid., p. 208). Places in the parishes of Kinnettles and Inverarity and in the district of Glenprosen are respectively called Leckoway, Labothy, and Lednathy.

LEMETONE. Patricius de Lemetone, clericus de liberacione, 1278 (RD., p. 52), probably derived his surname from the Northumberland Lemmington (in 1157 Lemetun, 1395 Lematon). Henry de Lematone, parson of the church of Douns, Perthshire, rendered homage, 1296 (*Bain*, II, p. 212).

LEMHALE. Thomas de Lemhale witnessed gift of two bovates of land of Dunypas to the Abbey of Cambuskenneth, by Gilbert de Vmframuilla, c. 1190 (*Cambus.*, p. 108).

LEMMON. A form of LAMONT, q.v. William Lemmon or Lemmont, writer in Edinburgh, 1686 (RPC., 3. ser. XII, p. 535, 539). William Lemmon, feuar in Newmill, 1796 (*Moray*).

LEMPITLAW. From the lands of Lempitlaw in the parish of Sprouston, Roxburghshire. Galfridus de Lempedlawe or Lempedlav appears c. 1190 as clericus regis and camerarius regis (*Kelso*, p. 128, 142). A later Galfridus de Limpedlaue had a charter witness, c. 1258 (ibid., p. 243). William Francis had a charter from Robert the Bruce of the 20 lib. land of Sproustoun which was in the king's hand through forfeiture of Hugo Limpetlaw and others (RMS., I, App. II, 285). William Lempatelaw was bailie of Lanark, 1464 (*Lanark*, p. 377), and John of Lempitlaw in Lanark in 1488 is mentioned again in 1501 as John Lempatlaw (*Lanark*, p. 4, 11). The lands of Andrew Lympetlaw in the burgh of Lanark are mentioned as a boundary in 1580, and in 1587 the lands belonged to William Lempitlaw (RMS., v, 79, 1450). Individuals named Lempetlaw and Lvmpetlaw are recorded in Edinburgh in 1605 and 1610 (*Edinb. Marr.*), and Robert Lympitlaw, skinner, was a burgess there in 1652 (*Inquis.*, 3685). Limpetlaw 1625.

LENDRUM. Of local origin from Lendrum near Turriff, Aberdeenshire. Rev. J. Lendrum was F. C. Missionary at Nagpur, India, 1892–99. Lendrome 1656.

LENG. A variant of LANG, q.v. Properly it is the comparative of lang.

LENNAN. A shortened form of (MAC)LENNAN, q.v.

LENNIE, LENNY, LENY. From the old lands of Leny in the parish of Callander, Perthshire. "In a curious document among the Stirling of Keir charters, giving an account of the families of Leny of Leny, and Buchanan of Leny . . . about 1560, the Laird of Leny says of his family: 'I find in the beginning the Lanyis of that Ilk hes bruikit (possessed) that leving without ony infeftment, except ane litill auld sourd gauin to Gillesiemvir be the King, and ane auld relict callit Sant Fillanis twithe (tooth), quhilk servit thaim for thar chartour quhile (until) Alexander his dayis.'" The little sword is mentioned in a charter by Alexander II, 1227, in favor of Alan of Lany and Margaret of Lany of the lands of Lany on the resignation of the said Margaret: "To be held and possessed by them and their heirs as freely and quietly as the said Margaret held them before this resignation, by virtue of a little sword which King Culen formerly gave by way of symbol to Gillespie Moir [c. 965–970] her predecessor" (Red Book of Menteith, I, p. lxxv). "Our critical age," says Cosmo Innes, "will not receive a charter of Alexander II as proof of a feudal investure by King Culen. We have many instances where the patriotic forger has escaped some of the readiest modes of detection by ascribing the deed which was to dignify his family or burgh to some traditional king of high antiquity, the falsity of whose charter it may not be so easy to expose" (Legal antiquities, p. 87). John de Leny, son of Alan de Leny, who had a charter of the lands of Drumchastell, c. 1270 (Levenax, p. 48), may be magister John de Lena or Lenna, a witness in 1267 (REG., p. 177, 181). A later John de Lanyn of Perth, who rendered homage, 1296, may be John de Lany, juror in Perth, 1304 (Bain, II, p. 200, 414). John de Lany was constable of Tarbert, 1325–26 (ER., I, p. 52). Robertus de Lanyn, M. A., petitioned for a canonry of Dunkeld, notwithstanding he has the church of Conveth, 1381 (Pap. Pet., I, p. 559; see also Inchcolm, p. 159–160). As Master Robert of Lany or Lanyne, provost of the church of St. Andrews, he appears 1408–14 (Bain, IV, 780, 801; Pollok, I, p. 463), Donald Lany witnessed an Atholl charter, 1455 (Athole, p. 708), Patrick Lany was witness at Lany, Perthshire, 1545 (Rollok, 40), and Bartilmo Lanye was a beidman in Edinburgh, 1575 (Soltre, p. 230). Patrick Lany in Lany and John Lanie in Monbrachie were fined for reset of Clan Gregor, 1613 (RPC., XIV, p. 640, 643). Leane c. 1350.

(2) Lennie or Linay, an Orkney surname, from Linay which once formed part of the township of Beneath-the-Dykes in Grimeston, Harray; "but it is possible that North Isles Lennies may have come originally from Linay in North Ronaldsay" (Clouston, p. 33). Mawnis Lenay was a witness in Harray in 1557 (REO., p. 108), Rob Lenay was juror on an assize in 1576, William Lena, witness in 1553, Henry Lene, witness in 1545, and Magnus Lyne, tacksman in Grymestath c. 1500 (ibid., p. 138, 227, 249, 408).

LENNOX, LENOX. Of local origin from the district of the name. John of Levenax, the duke of Albany's man, had a safe conduct into England, 1400 (Bain, IV, 570), and John de Lenox witnessed sale of a tenement in Glasgow, 1428 (LCD., p. 244). William Levinax, younger, of Caly, was accused of forethought felony and oppression in Kirkcudbright, 1508 (Trials, I, p. 54*), and Donald Levenax, a follower of the earl of Casillis, was respited for murder in 1526 (RSS., I, 3386). George Lennox, bailie depute of earl of Cassilis at Glenluce, 1543 (Dumfriesshire and Galloway Nat. Hist. and Ant. Soc., Trans., 3. ser. XXI, p. 293). William Levenax was retoured heir in lands in the parish of Girtoun, etc., 1572 (Retours, Kirkcudbright, 31), and Patrick Levenax was merchant burgess of Glasgow, 1598 (Burgesses). John Lenox of Calie appears in 1647 (Retours, Kirkcudbright, 245), and Walter Lennox in Balcorroch, parish of Campsie, 1669 (Campsie.) James Lennox (1800–1880), son of Robert Lenox, a Scots merchant who emigrated to New York in 1784, was founder of the Lenox Library, now incorporated in The New York Public Library. Levynnax 1556.

LENNY. See under LENNIE.

LENTRON. There was an old family of this name in St. Andrews. Thomas Lentroun was bailie there in 1582, and another Thomas Lentroun was skipper in Leith, 1612 (MCM., II, p. 166). Christine Lentron, native of St. Andrews, died 1647 (Epitaphs, p. 150), and James Lenthrone was retoured heir of Robert Lenthrone, provost of St. Andrews, his father, 1672 (Retours, Fife, 1118). Thomas Lentron was a wright in St. Andrews, 1690 (PSAS., LIV, p. 247), and Elizabeth Lenthorne or Lentron was heir of Patrick Lentron, once merchant of St. Andrews, her father, 1691, 1695 (Retours, Fife, 1311, 1376). Lentrone 1692. Perhaps from Lentram, Bridge of Allan, or a variant of LENDRUM.

LENY. See under LENNIE.

LENZEIS. Local, probably from Lenzie, Dumbartonshire. In 1621 Lenzie was divided into Easter and Wester Lenzie, and later these places were renamed Cümbernauld and Kirkintilloch. Archibald Lenzeis, cordiner, burgess freeman of Glasgow, 1574 (Burgesses).

LEOD. The Leod of MACLEOD, q.v., is explained as from Old West Norse *Liótr*, a name identical with the adjective *liótr*, ugly. Leod dux is mentioned in an OE. charter of A. D. 958 (Birch, *Cartularium Saxonicum*, 1044). The name of earlier Leods may or may not be from the same origin. The oldest copy of the Pictish Chronicle (tenth century) mentions one Leot who made a journey to Rome, c. 966–971 (CPS., p. 10). Léot, abbot of Brechin witnessed a grant by Gartnait and Ete to the Abbey of Deer, c. 1131–32 (*Bk. Deer*, III, 6). As Leod, abbot of Brechin he witnessed King David's grant of Nithbren and Balcristin to the Abbey of Dunfermline, c. 1150 (RD., p. 8). As Led, and Lyed, abbot, he attests two other charters by the same king (RPSA., p. 185, 187). Leod de Brechin witnessed King David's grant of Rindelgros to the Abbey of Reading, c. 1143–47 (*May*, 2), and also the gift of Clerchitune in Midlothian to the church of S. Marie of Hadintune, c. 1148 (RPSA., p. 182).

LESLIE, LESSLIE. Of territorial origin from the lands or barony of the name. Earl David, brother of William the Lion, granted c. 1171–99 the lands of Lesslyn in the Garioch to Malcolm, son of Bartholf (CAB., p. 547), a Fleming. Robert de Leslie was rector of the church of Slains, 1272 (REA., I, p. 34), and Symone de Lescelye or Lesellyn witnessed a quitclaim of Beeth Waldef in Fife, 1278 (RD., p. 52–53). Sir Norman de Lechelyn of Aberdeenshire rendered homage in 1296. His seal bears six shields in a circle conjoined in base, each charged with 3 round buckles on a bend, S' *Normanni de Lecelin, militis* (*Bain*, II, p. 195, 205, 539). Norman of Lesley was a hostage for the king of Scotland in 1425 (*Bain*, IV, 983). The name was early carried to France, and appears there as De Lisle, the family name of the viscounts de Fussy. William Leslie, younger, of Wartle, became bishop of Laibach, Carniola, and metropolitan in the first quarter of the eighteenth century. Old: Leslei, Lesli, Lesly, Lessely, Loussily.

LESMAHAGOW. Of local origin from Lesmahagow in the parish of the same name, Lanarkshire. William de Lesmahagow, burgess of Aberbrothoc, 1423 (RAA., II, 58).

LESSELS. The old family of this name were of Anglo-Norman origin, and possessed the lands of Forgrund in Fife. The old name (Lascelles) is derived from AF. *la celle* (Lat. *illa cella*), 'at the (hermit's) cell.' Alan de Lascels witnessed the gift of the church of Cupre by Richard, bishop of St. Andrews, to the church of St. Andrews, a. 1173 (RPSA.,

p. 137). W. de Laceles witnessed concession of the churches of Forres and Dyke to the bishop of Moray, c. 1189–99 (REM., 12), and before 1203 he witnessed a charter by William the Lion (*Panmure*, II, 81). Radulph Lesselis witnessed Alexander Comyn's charter of the hospital in his new burgh of Buchan, 1261 (REA., II, p. 277), and as Ralph de Lasceles he rendered to Exchequer the accounts of the bailie of Dingwall, 1266 (ER., I, p. 19). In 1288 there is recorded a memorandum of a transaction between Serlo de Lascelis and the prior of St. Andrews (RPSA., p. 346). Johan de Lasceles of Fife, Richard de Lasceles also of Fife, and Rauf de Lasceles of Edinburghshire rendered homage in 1296 (*Bain*, II, p. 205, 213, 204). The seal of Johan reads, S' *Joannis de la schel*, and that of Rauf, S' *Radu . . . e Lascelles* (ibid., p. 552, 539). John de Lascel was one of an inquest made at St. Andrews, 1302–03 (ibid., 1350). John Lassols who witnessed a charter by Robert, earl of Fife, c. 1390 (*Athole*, p. 706), was one of an inquest on the marches of Kyrknes and Louchor in 1395 (RPSA., p. 3). David Lessellis had sasine of the lands of Inverdovet, 1560 (ER., XIX, p. 454). Lassal 1294, Lasselis 1494, Lescellis 1589.

LESSLIE. See *under* LESLIE.

LESSUDEN. From Lessuden or Lessudden, the old name of St. Boswells, Roxburghshire. Gamellus de Lessedewyn and Ever' de Lessedewyn appear as charter witnesses, c. 1203 (*Dryburgh*, 160), and in 1271 mention is made of the land of *quondam* Thomas de Lessedwyn in the vill of Fortun in Athelstaneford (PSAS., XXII, p. 28).

LESTALRIC. See *under* RESTALRIG.

LETHAM, LETHEM. There appears to have been two old families of this name of different origin. (1) From the manor of Letham, now Leitholm, in the parish of Eccles, Berwickshire. Several of these Lethams appear in charters of Coldingham Priory (CCPC.), among the earliest being Ketell de Letham and his son Ketell, witnesses to a charter by Walthevus, earl of Dunbar (*Raine*, p. 26). Ketell's name is believed to be preserved in a corrupt form in Cattleshill in the parish of Polwarth. Robert de Letheham was one of the Scots prisoners of war taken at Dunbar Castle, 1296 (*Bain*, II, 742). Edward de Letham, one of the Scots hostages when Berwick was surrendered to Edward III in 1333, may be Edward de Letham who witnessed a confirmation charter of Snowdon to Dryburgh Abbey, c. 1350 (*Dryburgh*, 232). John Letham in the reign of Robert III obtained the lands of Letham by the forfaultrie

LETHAM, Letham, *continued*
of Patrick, earl of March (RMS., I, App. II, 1949). Robert Leithame held land in Glasgow, 1507 (LCD., p. 260), and in 1553 an annual rent in Glasgow was sold by Margaret Leithame (*Protocols*, I). James Leitham appears in Galtonside (Gattonside), 1663 (RRM., II, p. 75), Andrew Leitem in Avtoun, 1665 (*Lauder*), and John Lethom was miller at the Mylne of Minigaff, 1773 (*Wigtown*). (2) From the lands of Letham in the parish of Dunnichen, Angus. John de Letham witnessed a Fife charter, c. 1210 (SHR., II, p. 175), and Thomas Lethame was witness at Ester Moncreif, 1551 (*Rollok*, 73).

LETHANGIE, Lathangie. From Lethangie near Kinross. William Lethangy was married in Perth in 1561 (*Sc. Ant.*, I, p. 101). Henry Lathangie, heir of Henry Lathangie, portioner of Bennegall, was retoured heir in the third part of the vill and lands of Bennagall in the barony of Drumduff in 1619 (*Retours, Kinross*, 5). The name is still current in Kinross-shire.

LETHEM. *See under* LETHAM.

LETHENTY. Richard de Lethindy of Aberdeenshire rendered homage 1296 (RR.). Hugh de Lethendi was juror on an inquest on the lands of Ledvntosach and Rotmas in 1336 (REA., I, p. 61). From Lethenty near Tullynessle, Aberdeenshire.

LETTRICK. Of local origin from Lettrick near Cambuslang, Lanarkshire. This surname is common in the Protocol books of Glasgow in the middle of the sixteenth century as Letrig and Letrige (1555), Letterik (1553), and Lettrig (1567). David Lettrick was witness in Glasgow, 1572 (LCD., p. 88), and Robert Lettrik was messenger of the laird of Pollok, 1583 (*Pollok*, I, p. 316). James Litterick, born in Glasgow, was elected member of the Manitoba Legislature, 1936.

LEUCHARS. Of territorial origin from Leuchars in the parish of the same name in Fife, the old spelling of which was Locres (1300). Patrick de Locrys (Lochrys, Lochris, or Leuchars) was appointed bishop of Brechin in 1351 (*Dowden*, p. 182), and Schir Thomas of Luchers was parson of Kynnettyllis in 1388 (*Bamff*, p. 22). John de Lucris was elected bailie of Aberdeen in 1398 (CRA., p. 374), a later John de lluchris was a charter witness in Dundee in 1430, as likewise was Richard de Lluchris in 1434 (HP., II, p. 164, 175). Thomas de Luthris, prebendary of Guthry in 1435, appears later as de Lochrys, de Lathress, and de Luchris (REB., I, 20, 75, 130; II, 77). Helen

Leuchars in Hiltoun of Watterstoun is in record in 1597 (*Brechin*), and Katerine Lewchars died in 1749 (*Jervise*, II, p. 115). In Edinburgh, 1942.

LEUGACH. A descriptive name, from G. *lugach*, bandy-legged. Janet Leugach, "comonly so callit," was banished from Inverness, 1681 (*Inv. Rec.*, II, p. 294).

LEVACK. A surname found in Aberdeenshire and Caithness. Margaret Levack in Strathmoir, 1661 (*Caithness*), John Leavock, lieutenant 78th Highlanders, c. 1810. Leavack 1738 (in Caithness).

LEVEN. Local. Perhaps from Leven in Scoonie parish, Fife. There is another Leven in Innerkip parish, Renfrewshire.

LEVERICK. From the OE. personal name *Léofric*. William filius Leveric held land in Galweia, c. 1218–58 (*Holm Cultram*, p. 51). William Lewyryke was clerk of the diocese of Brechin, 1371 (REM., p. 174). See also Laverock.

LEVINGTON. From the barony of Levington in Cumberland. Robert de Levingtona witnessed resignation of land in Weremundebi and Anant between 1194–1214 (*Bain*, I, 606), and Sir Richard de Levington witnessed resignation of additional land in Anan to Robert Brus, c. 1218 (*Annandale*, I, p. 4). John of Leuynton or Lewyntoun was alderman and provost of Edinburgh, 1423 and 1428 (LSC., 113; RMS., II, 116), and was witness there, c. 1426 (*Egidii*, p. 49). Thomas de Levington, erstwhile abbot of Dundrennan, was provided to the rectory of Kirkinner, 1449 (*Pap. Lett.*, X, p. 196). John Lewinton, Scottish merchant, had a safe conduct to travel in England, 1484 (*Bain*, IV, 1503).

LEWARS. Probably a softened form of Leuchars, q.v. Thomas Leweris in Lairdlauch was witness in Kirkcudbrightshire in 1618 (*Laing*, 1798), and Mathew Lewers was 'beucher' in Newtoune, 1640 (*Hunter*, p. 80). David Lewers appears in Fokertoune, parish of Lesmahago in 1680, and ten more of the name are recorded in the Commissariot Record of Lanark between 1680–1800. John Lewars in Barre, 1657, and five more of the name (*Dumfries*). Jessy Lewars (1778–1855) was a friend of Robert Burns.

LEYBURN. Local. There is a Leyburn in Strathbogie, but the surname is more probably from Layburn in the North Riding of Yorkshire.

LEYDEN. A rare surname if still in existence. It is perhaps of local origin from Leithen in Peeblesshire. John Lethane witnessed a notarial instrument in 1517 (*Soltre*, p. 89), and Andro Lethane was appointed 'maister saidler to the king,' 1526 (RSS., I, 3405). Jonet Lethane, a tenant near Melrose, 1546 (RRM., III, p. 148), may be Janet Lithen who was tenant under the Abbey of Kelso, 1567 (*Kelso*, p. 524). James Lethen appears in Lessuddane, 1606 (RRM., I, p. 6). James Leidon from the parish of Cavers, taken at Bothwell Brig, 1679, was banished to America, and drowned in the wreck of the ship off Orkney (*Hanna*, II, p. 254). James Leidden in Earlside appears in 1688, another James Leidden is in Edgerstounshiells, 1690, and a third James Leidden is in Estloidge, 1698 (*Peebles CR.*). John Leyden (1775–1811) was physician, poet, and a great Orientalist.

LEYDYNTOSACH. Hugo de Leydyntosach, son of Adam de Rane, 1335 (REA., I, p. 62) derived his surname from the lands of Lentush (1333 Ledintosaich, 1509 Ledintosche) in the parish of Rayne, Aberdeenshire.

LEYNHALE. Ricardus de Leynhale who witnessed a charter by Patrick, first earl of Dunbar (*Raine*, 27) derived his name from the ancient parish of Lennel, Berwickshire.

LEYS. Of local origin. Thomas de Leys, bailie of Sawlton, c. 1300 (*Dryburgh*, 251). John de Leys appears as perpetual vicar of Abernethy in the diocese of Dunblane, 1327, and in 1332 he had provision of a canonry of Glasgow (*Pap. Lett.*, II, p. 271, 356). Robert Leis, chaplain, witnessed a charter by the earl of Huntlie, 1367 (*Aboyne*, p. 13). John de Levis held a tenement in Edinburgh, 1381 (*Egidii*, p. 21). John Leis was sergeand in Edinburgh, 1423 (ibid., p. 46), Thomas de Leis held a tenement in Dundee, 1443 (REB., I, 92), and John Leis was admitted burgess of Aberdeen, 1451 (NSCM., I, p. 13). Robert Leis, notary public in Aberdeen, 1463, may be the Robert Leis, witness there in 1489 (REA., I, p. 286; II, p. 303). Thomas Leis was vicar of Ellon, 1484 (*Illus.*, III, p. 328). Thomas Leis was subdean of Dunblane and perpetual vicar of Dreghorn (RUG., p. 49).

LIBERTON, LIBBERTON. From Liberton, the name of a village and parish in Midlothian. Aleyn de Lyberton and David de Lyberton, king's tenants in the county of Edinburgh, rendered homage in 1296 (*Bain*, II, p. 199, 201), and in 1311 a jury was named to inquire into the value of the land of (among others) Alland de Liberton and David de

Liberton. The same Alan and David de Libertone appear in 1312 as jurors on forfeited lands in Lothian (*Bain*, III, 245). John de Libertoun held land in Edinburgh in 1405 (*Egidii*, p. 42), William de Lebirtoun or Libertone was provost of Edinburgh in 1425–26–29 (RMS., II, 34; *Egidii*, p. 47; REG., 336), and a benefactor of Newbattle Abbey in 1429 *(Neubotle).* William Libertoune *de eodem* was a witness in 1455 (*Cambus.*, 97), Henry Leberton of the Lainy petitioned for a safe conduct into England in 1464 (*Bain*, IV, 1346), Henry Libertone *de eodem* appears as witness in Edinburgh in 1476 (REG., 411), and James Libbertoune was admitted burgess of Aberdeen in 1483 (NSCM., I, p. 30). Thomas Libertoun was a beidman in Edinburgh in 1575 (*Soltre*, p. 230), James Libertoun was heir of William Libertoun, baker in Edinburgh, 1547 (*Retours, Edinburgh*, 1406), and David Libbertoun or Libbertone, burgess of Edinburgh, had his lands bewitched by a warlock in 1603 (*Trials*, II, p. 422). With the Forresters the Libbertons were the most eminent representatives of burgher nobility in Edinburgh (Wilson, *Reminiscences of Edinburgh*, I, p. 107). Lybertoun 1426.

LIDDEL, LIDDELL, LIDDALL, LIDDLE. Of territorial origin probably from Liddel in Roxburghshire. There is, however, an old manor of Liddel in Cumberland from which the name may also have been derived. Persons named Lidel or Lidale appear in various records of the reigns of David II, Robert II, and Robert III, and James I, but none of them seem to have had lands in Liddesdale (OPS., I, p. 359). Richard de Lidel witnessed a charter of the church of Largs between 1202–34 (CMN., 8). Galfridus Liddal in Roxburghshire is in record 1266 (ER., I, p. 28). Others of the name early migrated northwards and became prominent in Aberdeen. In 1321 Nicholas Lyddal (Leddall or de Lyddal), burgess of Aberdeen, had grant of a charter (REA., I, p. 46), and was provost in 1327. John of Lydel was merchant in Aberdeen, 1358 (*Bain*, IV, 26), and William de Lydell, sheriff there in same year (ER., I, p. 551). John of Ledalle, esquire of Scotland, had safe conduct into England, 1426 (*Bain*, IV, 994). John de Ledail, juror at Lanark, 1432 (RAA., I, 65), George of Ledale, rector of Foresta, was secretary of James III (*Lennox*, II, p. 74). James de Ledale of Halcarstone witnessed a sasine, 1459 (REG., p. 412), and Quintin Liddale of that Ilk served on an inquest held at Jedburgh, 1464 (HMC., 7 Rep., App., p. 728). Ledal 1456, Leddale 1396, Ledelh 1494, Lidel 1497, Lithill 1669, Lydale 1362, Lyddaile 1562, Lyddale 1470; Ledel.

LIDDERDAINE. Local. Isobel Lidderdain in Ersiltoune, 1653 (*Lauder*). James Lidderdain in Kaidslie, 1660, and John Lidderdaine also in Kaidslie, 1664 (RRM., I, p. 260; II, p. 94).

LIDDERDALE. A Galloway pronunciation of the place name Lauderdale (Berwickshire). The Lidderdales were an old landed family in Galloway. Thomas de Lydderdaill or Lutherdale is in record as doctor of decrees and in laws in the diocese of St. Andrews between 1463–69 (CMN., 29, 32; REB., II, 104). Robert Luthirdale, witness in St. Andrews, 1466 (*Laing*, 15), David Luthirdal appears as archdeacon of Dunkeld and Snawdone herald, 1478 (*Lennox*, II, p. 117). Andrew Lidderdale was abbot of Dryburgh, 1489–1506 (*Dryburgh*, p. xix). Stephen Lidderdaill had charter of part of the lands of the Priory of St. Mary's Isle, 1558 (*Stodart*, II, p. 308). John Lidderdale was burgess of Selkirk, 1590 (RPC., IV, p. 481), and James Lidderdaill was retoured heir in three merk lands in Kaidslie and Haggis, Berwickshire, 1625 (*Retours, Berwick*, 140). The name is also found in Edinburgh, 1630 (*Edinb. Marr.*). Thomas Lidderdale and James Lidderdale of Sanct Mary Ile, his son, appear in 1698 (*Inquis.*, 8774). James Liddesdale or Lidderdale was collector of the excise in Aberdeen, 1741–43 (NSCM., II, p. 148, 150). See also LUTHERDALE.

LIDDESS. Thomas Liddis in Craiksfuird, 1646 (RRM., I, p. 136). Andres Liddess in Cruikfoord, 1653, and Thomas Liddess in Mellistaines, 1688 (*Lauder*).

LIDDLE. See under LIDDEL.

LIDGATE, LIDDIATT. Local, "at the lidgate," OE. *hlidgeat*, ME. *lidyate*, *lidgget*, a gate between ploughed land and meadow. A Lidgate near Lauder, Berwickshire, is recorded c. 1170, there is a Ludgate near Coldingham, and there is a Lugat in the lordship of Stow (*Edinburgh Retours*, 1606; Lugget 1648). John Letgate appears as a forestaller in Aberdeen, 1402 (CRA., p. 384). Wilzame Ludgat and Gilbert Ludgat were declared innocent of part in the detention of King James III in Edinburgh Castle in 1482 (*The Lennox*, II, p. 123). Henry Lidgaite and Kentigern Lidgait had precept of remission in 1536 (RSS., II, 2033). James Lidgait in Stitchill was assaulted in 1667 (*Stitchill*, p. 47), John Luggatt in Dundee, 1709 (*Brechin*), and Robert Ludgate, shoemaker in Coldingham, 1795 (*Lauder*). Probably confused with LEGAT, q.v. Ledgait 1609, Lugit 1665. Liddiatt recorded in Corstorphine, 1941.

LIGERTWOOD, LIDGERTWOOD, LIGTERWOOD, LEDGERWOOD, LEGERTWOOD, LEGERWOOD. From the hamlet of Legerwood in the parish of the same name in Berwickshire. The surname early made its way north, and the first form is now quite common in the district of Buchan. Symon de Lichardeswode of Berwickshire rendered homage in 1296, and likewise did Nicol de Lychardeswode, chaplain and warden of the Hospital of Lychardeswode (*Bain*, II, p. 208, 211). The goods of John of Lichardeswode, merchant of Aberdeen, were plundered in England, 1370 (*Bain*, IV, 158), John Leidgerwood, wright in Spittill bounds of Aberdeen is in record, 1655, John Leidgartwood was 'fremane' of the same city, 1656 (ROA., I, p. 233), and William Lidgertwood appears in Crealling hall, 1682 (*Peebles CR.*). Lichardwod 1408, Lidgertwood 1597, Liedgervod 1638, Ligetwod 1612, Liggertwode 1597; Ligarwood.

LIGGAT. See under LEGAT.

LIGHTBODY. William Leichtbody in Dalernok, 1552 (*Protocols*, I). Johne Lychtbodie, reidare at Lanell, 1574 (RMR.). Margaret Lychtbodie retoured heir 'in tenemento in burgo de Lawder,' 1602 (*Retours, Berwick*, 31). Marion Lichtbodie in Mudisburne, parish of Monkland, 1620 (*Campsie*), and William Lytbodie was admitted burgess and guild brother in Glasgow, 1621 (*Burgesses*). John Lightbody in Torphichen, 1678 (*Torphichen*), Marion Lightbody in Dumfries, 1689 (RPC., 3. ser. XIV, p. 694), and James Lightbody in Meadowland, 1709 (*Minutes*, p. 57). Six of the name are recorded in the Torphichen Commissariot Record. Lechtbodye and Leichtbodye 1552, Lychtbody 1688.

LIGHTBURN. Of recent introduction from across the Border, probably from Lightbourn in Lancashire.

LIGHTERNESS. George Lighterness, juror on inquest at Coldingham, 1561 (*Coldingham*, App. v) is probably George Lichtarnes in the Law of Coldingham, charter witness, 1581 (*Home*, 209). John Lightarnes, portioner of Coldingham-law, 1653, and three others of the name are in record (*Lauder*).

LIGHTFOOT. Duncan Lightfot, messenger from Dunfermline, is recorded in 1303 (*Bain*, II, p. 372).

LIGTERWOOD. See under LIGERTWOOD.

LIKLY. Hendrie Liklie was fined for quarrelling in Aberdeen in 1612 (SCM., V, p. 87), and Patrick Licklie is mentioned in 1689 (RPC., 3. ser. XIV, p. 647). Rev. Henry Likly, Rev. John Likly, his son, and Rev. James Likly, his grandson, were successively ministers of Meldrum, Aberdeenshire, from 1706 to 1817

(AEI., p. 50). William Lickly at Gallowgatehead, Aberdeen, 1790 (*Aberdeen CR.*). There is a rare English name, Likely, with which it may be connected. There was a Licklyhead Castle in Premnay, Aberdeenshire.

LILBURN. Probably from Lilbourne in Warwickshire. William Lilburn was admitted burgess of Aberdeen in 1443 (NSCM., I, p. 8), and Angus Lilburn, burgess of Aberdeen, was a charter witness in 1464 (RAA., II, p. 136). Sir Henricus Lylburn, cleric, was charter witness in Aberdeen, 1477 (REA., I, p. 312), Alexander Libburn or Lilburn was curate of Kilmaronok in 1522, and James Lylburne or Lyllburne was liberated from the Canongate Tolbooth of Edinburgh in 1682 (BOEC., VIII, p. 137). James Lilburn from Kinross, exiled Covenanter, was drowned off Orkney, 1679 (*Hanna*, II, p. 253). Lilburne 1470, Lillburn 1668.

LILIENGREEN. Charles Liliengreen was married in Edinburgh, 1700 (*Edinb. Marr.*).

LILLICO. David Lillico in Bairerse and Richard Lillico in Yetholm, 1686 (*Peebles CR.*). William Lillico, R.A.O.C., was killed in the war, June, 1940.

LILLIE, LILLEY. Not a common name anywhere in Scotland. From an *Inquisitio* of 1517 there appears to have been lands named Lillock in the barony of Ballinbreich, Fife (Sibbald, *Fife and Kinross*, p. 83). Liddall (*Place names of Fife and Kinross*) spells the name Lillioche. Wautier Lillok and Thomas Lillok of Peeblesshire rendered homage in 1296. The seal of Thomas bears a six-leaved figure, S' *Thome Lillog* (Bain, II, p. 204, 534). As Walter Lilley and Thomas Lilley they appear as jurors on an inquest at Peebles, 1304 (ibid., II, p. 377). Thomas de Lyllay was a Scots prisoner of war in Bristol, 1305 (ibid., p. 448). John Lillai witnessed a charter of lands of Lintonrothirrik, c. 1316 (RHM., I, 19), and in 1327 it was proposed to bring water through the lands of Thomas de Lillay to the mill of Peebles (ER., I, p. 71). George Lely had remission in 1359 (ER., I, p. 591), William Lillie is recorded in Redden, 1682 (*Peebles CR.*), Issobell Lilie and Thomas Lilie were in the toune of Bowdene, 1567 (*Kelso*, p. 519), and Alexander Lillie in Gatehouse, 1795 (*Kirkcudbright*). Leillei (in Workman MS.), Lyllie 1632. Alexander Lilie was inhabitant of Old Aberdeen, 1651 (*Retours, Aberdeen*, 594), and Robert Lillev, Orientalist, went to Japan in 1875, and after acquiring the language assisted in perfecting the system of printing for the blind now in use there; came to United States in 1881 and was one of the editors of the *Century dictionary*. Also an ancient Lincolnshire surname (*Guppy*, p. 275).

LILLIESLEAF. From the old barony of the name in Roxburghshire, now the parish of Lilliesleaf. The surname is now extinct. In various charters of the reigns of William the Lion and Alexander II, we have mention of a family 'of Lilliesclive.' In the former reign John, Walter, Walleve, Gaufrid, and Alexander appear in the chartularies of Melrose and Kelso, and in the latter Alexander, Gaufrid, William, and Ada appear in the chartulary of Melrose. Roger de Lalescreie (Lilliesleaf) witnessed a charter by William de Veteri Ponte, c. 1198–1214 (*Kelso*, 139), and Magister Stephen de Lilliscliue witnessed gift by Philip de Mubray to the monks of Dunfermline, c. 1202–14 (RD., p. 95). Magister Stephen de Lilliesclive (Lilleliue or Lilliscleue), the principal personage of the name, was several times a witness in both the above reigns between 1209–33, and was one of the arbiters in a dispute between the chapters of Glasgow and Jedburgh. In 1296 Walter of Lillesclif, parson of the church of Kirkebride, John de Lillesclyfe of Roxburghshire, and Johan de Lillesclyve of Peeblesshire rendered homage. The seal of the latter bears an eight-rayed figure and S' *Iohis d' Lelisd* (Bain, II, p. 199, 208, 532). Master Alexander de Lillescliffe, a churchman, had a safe conduct through England from France in 1408 (Bain, IV, 754). As Alexander de Lilliscliff he petitioned for an archdeaconry of Dunkeld in the same year (*Pap. Pet.*, I, p. 638).

LIMOND, LIMONT. Variants of LAMONT, q.v., found in the shires of Ayr, Wigtown, and Renfrew.

LIND. A surname in the parish of Tarves, Aberdeenshire. Norman Lind, parochiner of Botryphnie, appears in 1648 (*Strathbogie*, p. 84), and Alexander Lind in Seaton of Cairnbulg in 1785 (*Aberdeen CR.*). Perhaps same as LINN with accretionary d.

LINDORES. From Lindores in the parish of Abdie, Fife, old spellings of which are Lundoris and Lundors. Duncan de Lundoris was admitted burgess of Aberdeen in 1443, and John Lundoris in 1459 (NSCM., I, p. 7, 16), and John of Lundoris is recorded burgess of the same burgh in 1487 (CRA., p. 44). Thomas Lundoris held land in Scone in 1491 (*Scon*, p. 200), William Lindoor died in 1683 and was buried in Fogo churchyard, Margaret Lindores is recorded in Blaickburn in 1684 (*Lauder*), and payment was made to John Lindores in Home in 1713 (*Stitchill*, p. 167). Walterina Lindores was married in 1939.

LINDSAY. The name is territorial. Said to be of Norman origin, from De Limesay, Pays de Caux near Pavilly, north of Rouen. It is also said to be from Lindsay, a division of Lincolnshire (in AS. Chron.: Lindisse, A. D. 627; Lindissi, 678; Lindesse, 838; Lindesige, 993). Wyntoun (v. 5, p. 259, S.T.S. ed.) referring to the origin of the family expresses a prudent uncertainty:

"Off Inglande coyme þe Lynddissay
Mare of þaim I can noucht say."

The first of the name in Scotland is Sir Walter de Lindeseya, who appears as one of the witnesses in the Inquisitio of Earl David concerning the possessions and rights of the see of Glasgow, a. 1124 (REG., 1). His great-grandson, Sir William de Lindeseia, was one of the hostages for King William the Lion, 1174 (Annals, p. 194). There have been nearly 200 variations in the spelling of the name (Sc. Peer., III, p. 1), and Lord Lindsay (Family of Lindsay, v. 1, p. 3) gives eighty-four spellings. See under MACLINTOCK.

LINEN, LINING. Thomas Linning is recorded in Blaikwood, parish of Lesmahago, 1623 (Lanark CR.), Thomas Lining, parish minister of Lesmahagow, died 1733, and George Linin was appointed clerk to the Baron Court of Stitchill, 1749 (Stitchill, p. 199). James Linen published his Poetical and prose writings in 1865, and James Alexander Linen, born in the United States (1840) of Scottish descent, has written largely on finance.

LINGOCH. Vlfus de Lingoch who witnessed a charter by Eggou Ruffus to the Priory of May early in the thirteenth century (RPSA., p. 383), derived his surname from the lands of Lingoch, now Lingo, in the parish of Carnbee, Fife.

LINKLATER. The true form of this surname is Linklet, derived from one or other of the places of the name in Orkney. Linklater in South Ronaldsay was in 1500 Linclet, in 1596 Linklet; Linklater in North Sandwick was Lynkclet in 1500, and there is a Linklet in North Ronaldsay. The terminal -er is simply the nominative ending (-r) of the Old Norse place name (Lyngklettr), and the Æ at the beginning of the earliest spelling of the name = English 'at,' and was joined to the name by mistake. Criste Ælingeklæt is referred to in the complaint by the Commons of Orkney in 1424 as a 'goodman' (i.e. a gentleman, man of good position) (REO., p. 37). Andro Lynclater (Lincletter, or Linclet) appears as a roithman (councillor) in 1504 and 1514 (ibid., p. 76, 78, 87). Helen Linklet is recorded in Under Failze, Fetlar, in 1613 (Shetland),

Thomas Linkletter in Laxfuird in 1634 (ibid.), and William Linckletter was heir of John Linckletter of Housbie in 1649 (Inquis., 3423). Andrew Linklater of that Ilk was lawrikman (delegate of the people) in North Sandwick in 1678 (SHR., XIV, p. 59), — Clinkclatter appears as a skipper in Kirkcaldy in 1687 (RPC., 3. ser. XIII, p. 131), and Peter Linkletter was one of the quartermasters of the "Bounty" in 1789, and stood by Captain Bligh during the mutiny (Voyage, London, 1792, p. 159). Some persons of this name have migrated south to Aberdeenshire and to Edinburgh. Linklittar 1625.

LINLEY. Most probably from Linley or Lindley, a parish in Yorkshire. Andrew Linley, a procurator, appears in 1561 (RPC., I, p. 187).

LINTON. Of local origin from one or other of the following places: (1) Linton, now West Linton, a village and parish of Peeblesshire, (2) Linton, a parish of Roxburghshire, (3) East Linton, a small burgh in the parish of Prestonkirk, East Lothian. Gamel de Lintun witnessed a charter by Ernaldus, bishop of St. Andrews, c. 1160–62 (RPSA., p. 128), and Magister Robert de Linton was vicar of Kvlelan (Killilan), a. 1214 (Levenax, p. 14; RMP., p. 209). Philip de Lynton, constable of Berewyc, witnessed a Coldingham charter of 1285 (Raine, 262), and in 1296 rendered homage (Bain, II, p. 213). Two Adam de Lyntons of Edinburghshire also rendered homage in the same year (ibid., p. 201). Thomas Lynton was provost of Aberdeen, 1348–49, William de Lyntoun was tenant of the fulling-mill of Scralyne, 1376 (RHM., I, p. lxvii), James de Lintoune was bailie of Edinburgh, 1411 (Cambus., 94), and John Linton is recorded in Balgreddan, 1677 (Kirkcudbright). Lyntoune 1599.

LINWOOD. Of local origin, perhaps from Linwood (1621, Linwoode) in the parish of Kilbarchan, Renfrewshire.

LIPP, LIPPE. An old Aberdeenshire surname. William Lipp to render an account of the eels of Cluny, Perthshire, in 1264 (ER., I, p. 2). Walter Lippe was one of the witnesses to the "carta fundacionis domus elemosinarie apud Turreth" (Turriff) by Alexander Cummyn, earl of Buchan, 1273 (CAB., p. 470). John Lyp or Lyppe of the county of Aberdene rendered homage in 1296. The seal attached to his homage shows a lean dog coiled gnawing a bone, and S' Johanis Lipe (Bain, II, p. 203, 208, 552). Thomas Lipp or de Lipp had a charter from David II of the lands of Netherdull, Drumbeth, and Pettinbruynache, with office of constabulary of Culan in sheriffdom of Aberdeen (RMS., I, App. II, 988). Thomas de Lippes was among the Scots prisoners taken at the battle of Durham in 1346 (Hailes, II, p. 390, who adds: "If he was not a foreigner, I know not who he was"). John Lip was admitted burgess of Aberdeen, 1452 (NSCM., I, p. 13). A family of this name is said to have succeeded to the property of Schivas through marriage with the heiress of Schivas of that Ilk (CAB., p. 334). They were succeeded by Maitlands in the fifteenth century. Rev. Robert Lippe edited selections from Wodrow's Biographical collections, 1890. Two brothers named Lipp from Forglen served in the first Great War (Turriff). The name may be Frisian. Lippe is said to be a pet form of Philip (Winkler, Friesche naamlijst, s.v.).

LISTER, LITSTER. From ME. littester, a dyer. In Latin documents the name is rendered tinctor. Theodoric tinctor of Perth purchased a toft there c. 1200, and Arnald tinctor was one of the witnesses (LAC., p. 73). Richard tinctor was burgess of Kelso in 1237 (Kelso, 335), and Ralph tinctor who was custumar of Linlithgow in 1327 appears in 1329 as provost of the burgh (ER., I, p. 82, 166). Pieres le litstere of the county of Berwyke and Aleyn le Littester of Edinburghshire rendered homage in 1296 (Bain, II, pp. 202, 207). The seal of Aleyn bears a lion rampant, S' Alani tinctoris (ibid., p. 556). Stephen Tinctor was provost of Banff in 1340 (ER., I, p. 458). William tinctor was burgess of Dunfermline in 1316 (RD., p. 236), and Galfridus Lyttistar was chaplain of the chapel of S. Margaret in the Castle of Edinburgh in 1390 (RMS., I, 826; CDE., p. 16). John Litstar, professor of canon law in the newly founded University of St. Andrews, 1410 (Tytler, History of Scotland, II, p. 43). Malcolm Lytstare possessed a tenement in Glasgow in 1428 (LCD., p. 244), and Symon Littystar had a tenement in Dundee in 1449 (REB., I, p. 126). John Litstar was assizar in Aberdeen in 1463 (CRA., p. 26), James Litstar was sergeant of the burgh of Glasgow in 1468 (LCD., p. 182, 184), Robert Litstar or Lytstar appears as citizen of Brechin in 1472 and 1493 (REB., II, p. 138, 276), Vincent Tinctor was prior of the preaching friars of Stirling in 1521 (Cambus., 92). John Littstar was admitted burgess of Aberdeen in 1442 and another John Litstar in 1452 (NSCM., I, p. 7, 13), Sir William Litstar, priest and notary public at Stirling in 1555 (Poltalloch Writs, p. 142), Mathew Litstare, reidare at Tingwall, 1574 (RMR.), George Littister is recorded in Spittelmylne in 1580 (Soltre, p. 144), and Patrick Lister in Tinwald was examined for the Test in 1685 (RPC., 3. ser. XI, p. 434). Letister 1365, Lutster

c. 1431. Pension to Margaret Letstare, 1731 (Guildry, p. 140).

LISTON. From the old barony of Liston, now included in the parish of Kirkliston. Roger de Liston witnessed a charter by Richard, bishop of St. Andrews, 1163–85 (RPSA., p. 179), and again, before 1173, he witnessed the gift of the church of Hadintona by the same bishop (ibid., p. 135). About 1260 Robert de Liston was chaplain of William, bishop of St. Andrews (ibid., p. 158), and Symone de Listone of Linlithgowshire rendered homage, 1296 (Bain, II, p. 205). Thomas de Lystoune witnessed grant to the Blackfriars' Monastery, Perth, 1334 (Milne, p. 27), John Listone was professor of theology in S. Salvator College, St. Andrews, 1501 (RAA., II, 420), and David Liston was a monk of Neubotle, 1482 (Neubotle, p. 276).

LISTUNSCHELIS. Arnold de Listunschelis, juror on inquest held in the chapel of S. Katherine, Bauelay, in 1280 (Bain, IV, 1762), derived his name from Listonshiels near Balerno, Midlothian.

LITHGOW. This surname is a popular abridgment of the name of the royal burgh of Linlithgow, an abridgment found as early as 1311. Magister Symon de Lynlithcu witnessed an instrument at the church of Cargil, 1225, and Petrus de Linlithqw was a canon of the priory of St. Andrews, 1245 (RPSA., p. 307). Peter Linlithku, son of deceased John, son of Alice Linlithku, granted a charter on the sale of a tenement in Berwick-on-Tweed, 1280 and 1290, the charter showing possession by three generations prior to the period mentioned. John de Lithcu rendered to Exchequer the account of his disbursements in connection with the obsequies of King Robert I (ER., I, p. 150). Robert Lithcw, a native of Scotland, had a safe conduct into England, 1440 (Bain, IV, 1143), and William Lithqw was chaplain in Scone, 1480 (Scon, p. 197). Jonete de Linlithgow was spouse of Robert Dicson, 1472 (BNCH., XXIV, p. 89). James Lithgo in Dundee was charged in 1552 with aiding the English (Beats, p. 327), and Robert Lynlytgow was merchant burgess of Glasgow, 1599 (Burgesses). Perhaps the best-known individual of the name was the celebrated traveller William Lithgow of Lanark, whose Rare adventures and painefull peregrinations...in Europe, Asia, and Affrica, was published in 1640. Leythquow 1556, Leythqw 1558, Linlighgow 1642, Lithgou 1678, Lithgouw 1631, Lithquow 1631, Lvihtgow 1433, Lynlithu 1225, Lynlythqw 1565, Lvthcow 1569, Lvthcu 1329, Lythcw 1452, Lvthgw 1513, Lythqu 1341, Lythquow 1555, Lythtgow 1608.

LITSTER. The older spelling of the surname. See under LISTER.

LITTLE. A descriptive name, in Latin documents rendered *parvus*, 'little, small.' Fr. *petit* (of unknown origin) is also used in old documents as an equivalent. Hugo parvus, clericus regis, in reign of William the Lion (*Melros*, p. 32). Hugo parvus, burgess of Dundee, c. 1202 (RAA., I, p. 96). R. parvus, chaplain, witnessed a charter in favor of the Hospital of Soltre, between 1214–40 (*Soltre*, p. 19). John Litill served on an inquest at Lanark, 1313 (*Bain*, III, 1420). An agreement was made between the abbot of Scone and Robertus dictus Lytil, 1332 (CSR., I, p. 105). In 1351 Martin Litill, who witnessed a charter by William, dominus vallis de Ledell, of the lands of Abirdowyr in Fife (RHM., II, p. 56), is probably Martin Lytill who in 1358 possessed the land of Cardvyn (ER., I, p. 563). Nichol Litil was one of the 'borowis' for the earl of Douglas's bounds of the West March, 1368 (*Bain*, IV, 512). Adam Lityll was a tenant of the Douglas in the barony of Kilbucho, 1376 (RHM., II, p. 16). Duncan Petit was chancellor of the church of Aberdeen, 1426 (RMS., II, 54), and Johannes Petit, vicar of Lestalrig, 1448, appears also as J. Litill (*Soltre*, intro., p. xliv). The bequest of Clemens Litill in 1580 was the foundation of the library of Edinburgh University. The Littles occupied the lower part of Upper Eskdale and a portion of Ewesdale, and were recorded in 1587 as one of the unruly clans in the West March (APS., III, p. 466). Armstrong (*Liddesdale*, p. 184) gives the following additional forms of the name from public records: Litle, Littell, Littill, Lytil, Lytle, Lyttille; *plural:* Litillis, Litles, Littilles, Lytills, Lytils, Lytles. See also PETTY. Probably in some instances altered from LIDDELL, q.v.

LITTLEJOHN. Thomas Litilejonhe was admitted burgess of Aberdeen in 1489 (NSCM., I, p. 34), and Robert Litilihon possessed a tenement in Glasgow in 1494 (REG., 469). Arthur Litiljohnne was in 1536 appointed "cordinar to oure soverane lord for all the dais of his life" (RSS., II, 2124), John Litiliohne was burgess of Hamilton in 1541 (LCD., p. 223), and James Litle Johne was a "notar publict and sherefe clerk of Fyiffe" in 1648 (*Fordell*, p. 173). Bartholomew Litilljohne witnessed a Sutherland charter of 1562 (OPS., II, p. 633). Litilihonne 1581, Litiliohoun 1584, Litiliohune 1583, Litilione 1542, Litiljohen 1521, Litiljohne 1530, Litilljohne 1633, Litlejohne 1687, Litljohn 1676, Littiljohnne 1601, Lytiljohne 1619; Littlejohne, Litiljohn, Lytiljohn. Cf. MEIKLEJOHN.

LITTLEMILNE. Of local origin from some small place of the name. James Littlemilne in Mangertoune Milne, 1683 (*Peebles CR.*).

LITTLESON. In some cases perhaps an Anglicized form of MACFIGAN, q.v., current in Argyllshire. James Littleson, 1550 (RPC., I, p. 102).

LITTLEWOOD. A surname recorded in Ayrshire. There is a Littlewood near Pollokshaws, Lanarkshire.

LIULF. From OE. personal name *Ligulf* from OWSc. *Hliolfr* or *Lifulfr*, first evidenced in the Orkneys, c. 1100 (*Orkneyinga Saga*, p. 193, 194). Ligulf de Bebbanburch was one of the witnesses to the charter granting Swintun to the monks of S. Cuthbert, c. 1100 (*Lawrie*, p. 18). Lyulf filius Uchtredi witnessed Earl David's charter founding the Abbey of Selkirk, A. D. 1120 (*Kelso*, 1). He is probably the Liulf son of Uctred who held land near Coldingham before 1136 (Stevenson, *Illustrations*, p. 13). Uctredus filius Liolfi made a grant of the church of Molle to the Abbey of Kelso between 1147–64 (*Kelso*, 416). Uchtred's daughter and heiress, the Lady Aeschine of Molle, became the wife of Walter, son of Alan the first Steward of Scotland.

LIVERANCE. A surname derived from a court office which consisted in delivering food, drink, etc., in the king's household, and specially clothes, hence called liveries (Innes, *Legal antiquities*, p. 224). The Clerk of the Liverance "shall deal with the king's provisions and make the liverance in the hall and outside to each according to his due" (quotation in Mackinnon, *Constitutional history of Scotland*, p. 126). Galfridus de Liberatione was elected bishop of Dunkeld, 1236 (*Dowden*, p. 54). An inquest was held in 1259 to inquire into the tenure by which Adam of Liverance held Padvinian (APS., I, p. 98), and Edward of the Liberatione appears in the same document. John Loverans was a witness in Linlithgow in 1531 (*Johnsoun*, 5), and Alexander Leferans was master of works in Stirling Castle in 1560 (ER., XIX, p. 132–133). Johnne Leverance was minister at Douglas, Lanarkshire, 1574 (RMR.), and another John Liverance was minister at Robbertoun, Lanarkshire, in 1624 (*Lanark CR.*). The surname is now lost in LAWRENCE.

LIVINGSTON, LIVINGSTONE. Of territorial origin from the lands, now parish, of the same name in West Lothian. A Saxon named Leving or Leuing appears to have settled in Scotland under David I. He certainly possessed a grant of the above-mentioned lands, which he called

Levingestūn (in Latin charters, *villa Leuing*). Turstanus filius Leuig (for Leuïg = Leving) in the reign of Malcolm IV granted to the monks of Holyrood the church of Leuiggestun, with a half carucate of land and a toft (LSC., p. 15). Two sons of Turstan, Alexander and William, are mentioned as witnesses to two charters between the years 1165 and 1214, and as Turstan himself is also a witness to one of these charters he must have lived to a good old age (LSC., p. 29; RPSA., p. 180). William Levystone, c. 1290, witnessed a grant by Malcolm, earl of Levenax to Patrick Galbraith (*Levenax*, p. 33). Sir Archibald de Levingestoune of Edinburgh rendered homage in 1296 (*Bain*, II, p. 194, 211), and James of Leyffingstoun was great chamberlain of Scotland in 1456 (*Bain*, IV, 1276). John Levistone in Octofad, Islay, 1747 (*Isles*).

The MacLeays of Appin, a small sept of the Stewarts of Appin, sometimes Englished their name as Livingstone, of whom was the celebrated missionary and traveller, David Livingstone. "There is, of course, no etymological connection between Livingston and M'Leay; it is the slight resemblance of the initial part of the names, together with the fact of the Livingstons having land on the Highland frontier, that caused the equation of the one name with the other" (*Macbain*). This name is used by Pennsylvania Germans as an Englishing of Loewenstein. Leuingstowne 1449, Leuiyngston 1424, Levingston 1561, Levingstoun 1627, Levingstoune 1413, Levinston 1501, Levnstoun and Levyngstoun 1528, Levyngistoun 1296, Levyngstoun 1552, Levynsthon 1429, Levynston 1443, Levynstoune 1472, Lewingstoune 1503, Lewinston 1432, Lewyngstoun 1531, Lewynston 1510, Lewynstone 1550, Lewynstoun 1465, Lewynstoune 1450, Liuiston 1660, Liuistone 1650, Livistoun 1693.

LIZARS. Baring-Gould says, p. 237, from the Lisiere or verge of the Forest of Lyons, *de Lisoriis* in Latin. Hugh de Lysures witnessed a charter by William de Vyerpont to the Abbey of Kelso, c. 1160 (*Kelso*, 319). David de Lysurs, dominus de Gourton, granted a petarie to Neubotle during the incumbency of Abbot Constantine, 1233–36 (*Neubotle*, 27). Sir William de Lisures witnessed a charter of the lands of Athmor, 1245 (RPSA., p. 44), and in 1253 a gift of the land of Cragmilor (Craigmillar) to the monks of Dunfermline (RD., p. 114), and c. 1260–65 an Elphinstone charter (*Elphinstone*, I, 2). Henry de Lysours and Pyeres de Lysours of Edinburghshire rendered homage, 1296 (*Bain*, II, p. 201). The seal of the former bears a scallop shell(?) and S' *Henrici*..., and that of Pyeres an eight-raved figure and S' *Petri Lesuris* (ibid., p. 546, 551).

William Lysurs who witnessed the sale of a tenement in Gouyrton, 1317 (*Neubotle*, p. 306) may be Sir William de Lysur "tunc constabularius castrum Puellarum," 1328 (LSC., 87). John Lysours, a native of Scotland, had letters of denization in England, 1469 (*Bain*, IV, 1384). William Home Lizars, a distinguished Edinburgh engraver, middle of nineteenth century. Lesouris 1553, Lysuris 1328.

LOACHEAD. *See under* LOCHHEAD.

LOARN. "The personal name Loarn, older Loern, pronounced as two syllables, stands for an older *Lovernos*, 'fox' " (*Watson* I, p. 121). From it comes the name of the district of Lorne, Argyllshire. "In modern Gaelic Lorne is *Latharn* or *Latharna*, the *th* serving merely to separate the syllables" (*Watson*, loc. cit.).

LOBAN, LOBBAN, LOBBANS. A Moray surname; a belt of a few miles along the Moray Firth it is said holds most of them. The name is explained as from G. *loban* or *lopan*, and "was given to the progenitor, who is said to have been a Maclennan, from his having hidden under a peat-cart or sledge" (*Henderson*, NI., p. 120). The date is about 1400. The legendary story of the origin of the name was first published by David Carey, the first editor of the *Inverness Journal*, in his novel *Lochiel, or the Field of Culloden*, London, 1820. Sir Charles Lowbane, a cleric, was witness to a submission anent the lands of Strathnarne, 1542 (*Cawdor*, p. 166), William Lobane in 1560 was tenant in Drumderfit (Macbain, *Inverness names*, p. 76), and John Loban was a tenant under the marquis of Huntlie, 1600 (SCM., IV, p. 288). Jonat Lobane and others were accused in 1614 of 'crewel vnmerceifull murther' in Inverness (*Rec. Inv.*, II, p. 121), and Robert Lobein in Deir was charged in 1627 with being an 'idle and masterless man' (RPC.). George Lobban in Bodylair, parish of Glass, is mentioned, 1716 (SCM., IV, p. 168); John Lobon appears in Ternemnie, 1703 (*Banff Rec.*, p. 244); and Elspat Lobban was the maiden name of the mother of James Fergusson, the astronomer. Alexander Lobban in Garland, parish of Dundurcas, 1773 (*Moray*), and John Lobban was member of Huntly Volunteers, 1798 (*Will*, p. 7).

LOCH. Perhaps from the loch now known as Portmore Loch in the parish of Eddleston. Some time before 1230 Walterus de Lacu witnessed a charter by Thomas Masculus, dominus de Louchogov, confirming a grant by his grandfather (*avus*) Radulphus Masculus to the monks of Newbattle (*Neubotle*, p. 24, 26). Reginald of the Loch renounced his marriage portion and all his prospects in the lands of

LOCH, *continued*

Eddleston between 1214–33 (REG., p. 143), but the family lingered about Peeblesshire at least two hundred years longer. This Reginald of the Lake had acquired possession of Eddleston by his marriage with the daughter of Constantine, who was the son of Adam who was the son of Edulph, the son of Utred (*Neubotle,* p. 18). Edulfus filius Vtredi obtained the grant of the lands of Gillemorestun, earlier known as Penteiacob, from Ricardus de Moreville, a. 1189 (REG., p. 39). By him the lands were renamed Edulfstun, now Eddleston. His descendants held other lands on the Esk in Lothian under the heirs of the Morevilles (*Neubotle,* p. 18–24). In 1231 Gillecrist de Lacu was present at perambulation of the boundaries of the lands of Dunduf (RD., p. 111). Monies were allowed Malise de Loghys, a Scots prisoner of war taken at Dunbar Castle in 1296–97 (*Bain,* II, 742, 938), Johannes de Lacu is mentioned in 1317, Ade del Louche was provost of the burgh of Peebles, 1330 (ER., I, p. 274), Thomas de Louch was burgess there in 1448 (*Peebles,* 6, 14), and John Loch was sergeand of the burgh of Edinburgh, 1473 (REG., 400). Michael de Lacu, prebendary and deacon of the College of Holy Trinity, Edinburgh, 1505–08–11, appears also as Michael Loch (*Soltre,* p. 84, 158, 161). Robert Loche was a notary-public in Edinburgh, 1557 (*Laing,* 665), and in 1564 a grant of a land near the market-cross of Edinburgh was made to Archibald Loch. David Loch was hanged by the Regent Murray in the raid on Brechin Castle, 1570. John Loch was treasurer of Edinburgh, 1632–33, and George Loch was made a burgess of the burgh in 1729 by right of his father, George Loch of Drylaw (*Roll of Edinburgh Burgesses*). Mark Loch was provost of burgh of Annan, 1698 (*Dumfries*), and James Loch published a work on agriculture in 1820. Some of the Lochs who removed to Midlothian acquired there the lands of Drylaw, and others of the name acquired Rachan from the Geddeses in the latter half of the eighteenth century (Buchan, *Peeblesshire,* II, p. 446).

LOCHARMOSS. The great waste of Locharmoss in Dumfriesshire gave name to a family. Robertus Loghirmoss, mercator de Scotia, had a safe conduct to travel in England in 1373 (*Rot. Scot.,* I, p. 960), and in 1426 King James I confirmed a charter granted by Archibald, earl of Douglas in 1419 to Michael Ramsav of Ramarskalis and Grenelandis and to Christian his spouse of the lands of "Harthuat in foresta de Daltoun et dominio Vallis Anandie, — que fuerunt Rogeri de Lochirmos" (RMS., II, 71).

LOCHERY. A rare current surname of local origin. Perhaps from Lochrie, near Dailly, Ayrshire, but I know of no references in record.

LOCHHEAD, LOCHEAD, LOACHEAD. Of local origin from lands situated at the head of a loch, and so = Kinloch. The first form is common in the shires of Lanark, Renfrew, and Dumfries. Gilbert de Lakenheued of Lanarkshire and Wautier de Lagenheuede of Aberdeenshire rendered homage in 1296 (*Bain,* II, p. 200, 214). James Lochheid, burgess and guild-brother of Glasgow, 1626 (*Burgesses*). Locheid 1648, Loichtheid 1550.

LOCHKOTTIS. Local, from Lochcote (1607 Lochquott) in West Lothian. John Lochkottis, witness, 1497 (*Binns,* 25).

LOCHMABEN. Nicholas de Lacmaban, a cleric in record c. 1300 (*Cambus.,* 222), derived his name from Lochmaben in Annandale, Dumfriesshire. Adam de Louchmaban witnessed an instrument of sasine of lands of Kylmor, 1270 (RMP., p. 138).

LOCHMALONY. From the lands of Lochmalony in the parish of Kilmany, Fifeshire. William de Laghmanoveny of Fifeshire rendered homage in 1296 (*Bain,* II, p. 204). Alanus de Lochmalony and Willelmus de Lochmalony were jurors on an inquisition on lands in Fife, 1391 (RMS., I, 854). Thomas de Lochmaloni, canon of Caithness, 1436–7 (*Pap. Lett.,* VIII, p. 578) is the Magister Thomas Lochmalony who was "cancellarius ecclesie Rossensis" in 1449 (*Cawdor,* p. 17; *Invernessiana,* p. 116). Alexander Lochmalonie or Louchmalony *de eodem* served as juror on inquests at Cupar in 1517 and 1520 (Sibbald, *Fife,* 1803, p. 201; SCBF., p. 187), and Thomas Lethnalony witnessed a tack by the abbot of Cupar in 1521 (SCM., V, p. 294). James Lochmalony of that Ilk was charged in 1558 with abiding from the raid of Lauder (*Trials,* I, p. 404), and in 1580 William Lochmalony, mariner, was admitted burgess of Dundee (*Wedd.,* p. 88). Andrew Lochmalony, 'marinell,' burgess of the broche of Dundee in 1576 (*Brechin*), and Margaret Lochmalowinie also in Dundee in 1609 (ibid.). Lechmalony 1522, Lochmalowny 1612.

LOCHMILL. Local. Schir David Lochmill or Lochmyll, parson of Stronsay, 1507–13 (REO., p. 79, 335). Michall Lochmyll was kirkmaster of the Baxter Craft of Edinburgh, 1522.

LOCHORE. From Lochore in the parish of Ballingry, Fife. The family of Lochore had their seat on an island in the loch (now drained), and the fact that this site was also known as 'Inchgall,' island of the foreigners, indicates a Gaelic-speaking population in the vicinity at the time of its occupation by new lords in the second half of the tweflth century (*Royal Commission on Ancient and Historical Monuments*, Eleventh report, p. xliii). Constantine de Lochor witnessed a gift by Duncan, earl of Fife, to the nuns of North Berwick before 1177 (CMN., 6), and as Costentin (for Côstentin) de Lochor he witnessed a charter by Ernaldus, bishop of St. Andrews, between 1160–62 (RPSA., p. 128). Philip de Lochor was one of the assize of marches in Fife, 1230 (RD., 196). Constantinus de Lochor acknowledged in 1235 that he had no right to the lands of Kinglassin (Kinglassie) and Pethbokin (Petbachly) near Dunfermline (ibid., p. 101). Andreas de Lochor, his uncle, and Philip de Lochor, his brother, are named as witnesses in the charter. David de Lochor witnessed a gift of 10s. annually to the monks of Dunfermline, 1231 (ibid., p. 108), and in 1242 he witnessed a confirmation charter of Alexander II (REA., II, p. 273). He is probably the David de Louchor mentioned in a quitclaim of the lands of Drumkarauch, 1260 (RPSA., p. 346), and is in record as sheriff of Fife in 1264–66 (ER., I, p. 4, 31, 34). David de Louchor witnessed a charter by Gamelin, bishop of St. Andrews, 1269 (RPSA., p. 174), and as David de Lothar (for Lochar, *c* misread as *t*) he is mentioned in a mandate by the bishops of St. Andrews and Aberdeen in 1264 (*Pap. Lett.*, I, p. 408). David de Louchoř witnessed a charter by Alexander III at Rokesburg, 1279 (RD., p. 53; see more on this David in *Inchcolm*, p. 143–144). Constantine de Logher, sheriff of Fife, who swore fealty to Edward I in 1291, was in 1296, along with Hugh de Loghore, among the Scots prisoners taken in Dunbar Castle (*Bain*, II, 508, 742). In 1305 Constantin de Loghore was juror on an inquisition made at Perth (ibid., 1670), and Hugh de Locwor, probably the above-mentioned Hugh, was witness to the homage of Duncan, twelfth earl of Fife to the abbot of Dunfermline, 1316 (RD., 349). David de Louhore appears in 1328 (ER., I, p. 84), and again c. 1328–32 as David de Louchqwore among the witnesses to a charter by Michael de Wemys (*Soltre*, p. 48). Philip de Lowchqwor umquhile lord of the third part of Pitfirrane is in record, 1435 (*Pitfirrane*, 21). Jonet Lochequoir in St. Andrews was juror for witchcraft, 1595 (*St. Andrews*, p. 800). Margaret Lochoir was retoured heir of her father, William Lochoir, burgess of Kinghorne, 1608 (*Retours, Fife*, 195), and the Rev. Charles Lochore was minister of Drymen from 1824 to 1877. In the *Dunfermline Burgh Records*

(ed. Beveridge) the name occurs as Lochor, Lochquhor, Lochtquor, Locquhor, Lokquhor, and Lokqwhor.

LOCHRIE. A surname recorded by M'Kerlie, may be of local origin from Lochree in the parish of Inch, or from Lochrie in Ayrshire.

LOCHRIG. Of local origin from Lochridge near Stewarton, Ayrshire. In Scots place names *rig* and *ridge* are interchangeable. In 1607 Lochrig is referred to as the 11 merc lands of Lochrig, and in 1690 as the 11 merc lands of Lochridge (*Retours, Ayr*, 95, 661). John Lochrig was witness in Kilwinning, 1559 (*Laing*, 708). The surname appears in the Glasgow Protocol books as Loicherige (1552) and Loichtrige (1562). Irish pronunciation tends to broaden the *o* in *loch* and in print this pronunciation is represented by *lough*, whence Loughridge, the form used by the Scots descendants of the name in Ulster.

LOCHTIE. A surname found in Fife. From Lochty near Thornton in the parish of Markinch. Recorded in Aberdour, 1941.

LOCKART. A form of LOCKHART, q.v.

LOCKE. John Lock of Roxburghshire who rendered homage in 1296 is probably the John Lok' who was juror on an inquest at Roxburgh in 1303 (*Bain*, II, p. 199, 376, 548.) His seal bears an eight-rayed figure and S' Joh'is Log. John Lock, professor of sacred theology in the University of St. Andrews in 1464 (SCM., v, p. 288), is probably the John Lok who appears in the same year and in 1474 as rector of the church of Fynnewyn or Futhnewyn (Finhaven) (REB., I, 196; II, 104), and in 1475 as professor of sacred theology and canon of Brechin (*Soltre*, p. 71). Johannes Lok, witness in Glasgow, 1504 (*Simon*, 68), George Lowk, tenant under the bishop of Glasgow in 1510 (*Rental*), Katherine Lok sold houses in Glasgow in 1544 (*Protocols*, I), and John Lock was burgess there in 1641 (*Inquis.*, 2598). Cf. LUKE.

LOCKERBIE. A surname current in Dumfriesshire, derived from the small town of the name in the parish of Dryfesdale. John Lockerby in Lochmaben, 1790. The lands of Lockerby of that Ilk were long possessed by Johnstons (*Nisbet*, I).

LOCKESTRE. William de Lockestre who witnessed a charter by John, bishop of Dunkeld, c. 1199 (*Inchaffray*, p. 5), "perhaps derived his surname from Logiastre in Perthshire (*Bain*, II, 1108) which I cannot identify" (J. Maitland Thomson, in *Inchaffray*, p. 266).

LOCKFORD. Johannes de Lokforde was juror on inquest apud Rane, 1398, and Adam de Loukforde witnessed a sasine in Aberdeen, 1455 (REA., I, p. 202, 277).

LOCKHART. From OFr. personal name Locard<Teut. Lochard. Stephen and Simon were settled in Lanarkshire and in Ayrshire in the twelfth century. They both acquired large territories and held important offices, and the former gave name to Stevenston in Cunningham. Symon Locard witnessed c. 1153–65 the grant of the church of Wicestun (now Wiston) and its two chapels to the Abbey of Kelso (Kelso, 336). He also attested charters by William the Lion, c. 1165–87 (RMP., p. 76; REG., p. 65), and a charter by Alan filius Walteri, dapifer regis, c. 1190 (Kelso, 260). Symon Loccard (Lochard or Locchard) filius Malcolmi Locard confirmed the church of Symondeston with all its pertinents to Kelso, c. 1180, and about same date confirmed the grant of the church of Wudeschirche (now Thankerston) to the same abbey (ibid., 333, 338). He also claimed the patronage of the 'capella ville ipsius Symone' (ibid., 335). Malcolm Loccard witnessed resignation of land in Weremundebi and Anant, c. 1194–1214 (Bain, I, 606; Annandale, I, p. 3). About 1210 Malcolm Loccard granted six acres of land 'in villa Simonis de Kyil' to the Abbey of Paisley (RMP., p. 70), and in 1228 witnessed a grant by Hugh de Bygris (Kelso, 186). Jordan Locard witnessed an obligation by Duncanus de Carric, 1225 (REG., p. 117). A later Symon Locarde witnessed grant of the church of Wicestun to Kelso between 1247–64, and in 1273 he revived the old claim to the patronage of the church of Symondston and kept back the greater part of the tithes (Kelso, 336, 334). William Locard witnessed confirmation of the church of Cragyn to Paisley, c. 1272 (RMP., p. 233), and Maucolum Lockare of Ayrshire rendered homage, 1296 (Bain, II, p. 206). Sir George Lockhart, President of the Court of Session, was murdered by Chiesley of Dalry, 1689. The Rosses of Balnagown, Ross-shire, are really Lockharts by name. The myth about an ancestor of the Lockharts securing the heart of Bruce which Douglas perilled in the fight with the Saracens in Spain led to the spelling of the name Lockhart, and the alteration of the coat of arms either to perpetuate the belief, or as Nisbet says 'to make their arms more univocal to the name.' Locarde 1291, Locart 1424, Loccard 1296, Loccart 1684, Lokart 1452, Lokarte 1467, Lokcart 1408, Lockhartt 1637, Lockheart 1672, Lokert 1547, Lokhart 1488, Lokharte 1593, Lokhartt 1614, Lokheart 1432, Lokhert 1621, Lokkard 1585, Lokkart 1507, Lokkert 1503,

Lokwert 1591. Andrew Lang (History, I, p. 236) erroneously says the name is territorial, 'de Loch Ard'!

LOCKHEAD. A surname found in Ayrshire, a variant of LOCHHEAD, q.v.

LOCKIE. William Lokky was chaplain in Glasgow, 1503 (Simon, 55), and John Loky is recorded in Strafrank in 1531 (Rental). David Lokkv was "ane of the maris generall of the sheriffdome" of Forfar in 1535 (REB., II, 186), Quhintene Lokkie was burgess of Edinburgh in 1583 (REB., II, 344), and John Lockie was retoured heir in the three mark lands of Martoune in the bailliary of Lauderdaill in 1670 (Retours, Berwick, 365). Laurence Lockie in Lyntoun, Ronald Lockie, and Thomas Lockie are recorded in 1623 (Inquis., 1087). Andrew Lockie appears in Nether Lethnot, 1609 (Brechin). William Lockie who died 1720, Thomas Locky died 1741, and Isabell Locie, are buried in Mertoun churchyard. A writer in the Edinburgh Weekly Scotsman says there are two 'tribes' of this name, one hailing from Peebles, who derive their name from Loch, a place name; the second derivation is from Luckie, from Lucas or Maclucas, but? The name is recorded in Melrose, 1942.

LOCKSMITH. From the occupation of locksmith or maker of locks. Robert lokessmyth in Dumfries in mentioned before 1214 as holding land there (Kelso, 11). In two charters of grants to the Abbey of Holm Cultram of c. 1280 mention is made in one of the lands of Henricus Loker (i.e. Locker) and in the other of Henricus le lokesmyth (Edgar, p. 220–221).

LOCKWOOD. Most probably from Lockwood in Yorkshire. John Locwode, witness in Edinburgh, 1426 (Egidii, p. 48).

LODDER, LODER. A rare surname in Scotland. Perhaps from provincial English loder, a carrier.

LOFTUS. "A Yorkshire surname and several places in the county are so termed" (Bardsley). Robert Lofthous in Lyndene was convicted of concealing certain 'paise penneis," probably English gold coins, 1502 (Trials, I, p. 32*). A contraction of Lofthouse.

LOGAN. There are several places named Logan in Scotland, but the surname has probably been derived from Logan in Ayrshire. Robert Logan witnessed resignation of the lands of Ingilbristoun in 1204 (Dryburgh, 163), and other royal charters in the reign of William the Lion. Adam de Logan witnessed charter of land in Gowrie, 1226 (Scon,

p. 41). Walter de Logan who was on assize of marches in Fife, 1230, and witnessed a charter by Constantine of Lochow, 1235 (RD., p. 102, 196), may be Walter de Logane who witnessed the gift of the mill of Wystoun to the Hospital of Soltre, 1249 (*Soltre*, p. 30). William Logan, cleric, witnessed confirmation of a charter of Cragin (Craigie) in Kyle to the monks of Paisley, 1272 (RMP., p. 233). Thurbrand de Logan was baron of Grougar in Cunninghame in the same year. Thom de Logy or Logyn witnessed a quitclaim of Beeth-Waldef in Fife, 1278 (RD., p. 52–3). Philippe de Logyn, burgess of Montrose, and Thurbrand de Logyn of Dumfriesshire, rendered homage in 1296 (*Bain*, II, p. 198, 211). Wautier Logan of Lanarkshire and Andreu de Logan of Wigtownshire also rendered homage (ibid., p. 198). The seal of the former bears a stag's head cabossed, between the antlers a shield with three piles in point, *Sigillvm Walteri Logan* (*Macdonald*, 1738). The seal of Andreu bears a figure of S. Andrew, *S' Andree de Logen* (*Bain*, II, p. 552). William de Loghyn, a Scots prisoner of war from Dunbar, 1296–7 (ibid., 742, 953). John de Logan who held the land of Grugar in Ayrshire, 1304, may be John Logan, one of the king of England's enemies mentioned in 1307 (ibid., p. 425, 505). John called Logan had a grant of 18 oxgangs of land, etc., in Lyntounrothryk, 1316 (RHM., I, p. 18). John Logan or de Logan appears as clerk of the royal kitchen, 1328–9 (ER., I, p. 89, 95). Donald Logane was "reidar in the Irische toung" at Creich, Sutherland, in 1569 (OPS., II, p. 685). The last of the Ayrshire family of the name was the witty laird of Logan who sold the estate, and died unmarried in 1802. Loggan 1746, Loghane 1511, Lowgane 1646.

LOGDONE. Wautier de Logdone, one of the king's tenants in Edinburghshire, rendered homage, 1296 (*Bain*, II, p. 201). William Lugdon, fiar in Aberdeen, c. 1550 (REA., II, p. 233). Cf. LUGTON.

LOGGAN. Most probably a variant of LOGAN, q.v.

LOGIE, LOGGIE. Of territorial origin from one or more of the many Logie place names. Master John de Logy, canon of Dunkeld, appears in 1271 (LIM., 22). William de Logyn [under Logy in Bain's index] and Malise de Loghis were Scots prisoners of war taken at Dunbar, 1296 (*Bain*, II, p. 177, 178, 244). Wauter de Logy of Fife rendered homage, 1296 (ibid., p. 204), and John of Logy, a Scot, was illegally arrested at Lowestoft, 1405 (ibid., IV, 690). The earliest notice of the family

of Logy of Logy is in 1320, when Sir John of Logy is mentioned as one of the conspirators against Robert the Bruce (*Hailes*, II, p. 119). Philipp de Logy was charter witness in Dundee, 1321 (HP., II, p. 225), and in 1328–9 there is record of payments to Philip de Logy, burgess of Dundee (ER., I, p. 116, 159). Duncan of Logy was arrested in Norwich in violation of the truce, 1396 (*Bain*, IV, 483). John Logge complained against being illegally imprisoned in Orkney, 1424 (REO., p. 39). Alexander Logy was admitted burgess of Aberdeen, 1457 (NSCM., I, p. 16). Robert Loggie, squarewright in Newmiln of Strathisla, 1765 (*Moray*). Loggy 1667.

LOHOAR. A variant of LAHORE, q.v.

LOMBARD. "A native of Lombardy." Antony, a Lombard physician, obtained a grant of the lands of Fulton, Renfrewshire, from Alan, son of Walter, the Steward, a. 1204 (RMP., p. 53). His posterity held these lands under the Stewarts and were surnamed Lombard. In 1272 Sir Antony Lumbard quitclaimed the lands to the monastery of Paisley (ibid., p. 50–51). Lumbard, a layman, was one of those concerned in the mutilation of John, bishop of Caithness, 1202 (CSR., I, p. 3).

LOMMESTONE. Local. Adam de Lomokestun was buried in Melrose, 1247 (*Chron. Mail.*, s.a.). Roger de West Lommestone of Berwickshire rendered homage, 1296 (*Bain*, II, p. 206). Cf. LUMSDEN.

LONCARTE. Probably from Luncarty, Perthshire, or from Luncarty, Aberdeenshire. John Loncardy was witness in Scone, 1544 (*Rollok*, 17), and John Loncarte to be exempt from service in the army, 1552 (RPC., I, p. 136).

LONG. A surname descriptive of the stature of the original bearer. Johannes Longus who witnessed a grant to the Hospital of Soltre, c. 1180–1214 (*Soltre*, p. 5) is doubtless the Johannes Longus who witnessed the grant of Gillemoristun by Richard de Morevil, a. 1189 (REG., p. 39), and c. 1180 a charter by Euerard de Pencathlan to Kelso (*Kelso*, 370). William Longus held land near Lyntonrothrik (?c. 1200) (RHM., I, 3), Adam Long appears in Dumfriesshire, c. 1259 (*Bain*, I, 2176; APS., I, p. 88), Gregory le Long was a burgess of Dundee in 1268 (*Balmerinoch*, p. 25), and c. 1350 William Long witnessed confirmation of Snawdoun to Dryburgh (*Dryburgh*, 232).

LONGAIR. An Aberdeenshire variant of LUMGAIR, q.v.

LONGFORGAN. From Longforgan in the Carse of Gowrie. Sir William de Longfordy, canon of Moray, charter witness 1359 and 1388 (REM., p. 351, 368), as Sir William de Lonkfordyn or Lonkfordy, was chancellor of Caithness, 1390 (ibid., p. 202, 224).

LONGHILL. Local. Gervays de Longhil of Linlithgowshire rendered homage, 1296 (Bain, II, p. 205).

LONGMOOR, LONGMORE, LONGMUIR. See under LANGMORE.

LONGOFEIDDILL. Local, from some place, doubtless in Aberdeenshire. George Longofeiddill in Torrieleyth who renounced his occupancy of the half lands of Torrieleyth in Udny, 1629, may be the George Longowaill in Kynmundie mentioned in 1634 (RSCA., II, p. 311, 396).

LONGSANDIE. Isobel Langsandie in Lochead in Cottoun of Ballandein, 1601 (Brechin), and Jean Longsandie in Brechin (ibid).

LONGTON. Territorial. A different name from LANGTON, q.v. Symon de Longetona witnessed homage of Duncan, earl of Fife to the abbot of Dunfermline, 1316, and John of Loktone was charter witness in Dunfermline, 1456 (RD., 348, 448). Wautier de Longeton of Edinburghshire rendered homage, 1296 (Bain, II, p. 199).

LOOKUP. Of local origin from some place name ending in -hope. In the trial of Agnes Sympson, 1590, the name is misprinted Lenchop and as Linkup in the trial of Dr. Feane (Trials, I, p. 211, 236). There is a Lauchope in Lanarkshire from which the name might be derived, but none of the references point that way. Patrick Luikup in Melrose, 1605, Thomas Lookupe there in 1657, Andrew Lukup or Lukupe in Danyielton, 1662, and Thomas Lukupe in Melrose, 1663 (RRM., I, p. 3, 141; II, p. 33, 65). Janet Lukup was resident in Edinburgh, 1623 (Edinb. Marr.), William Lukup was master of works in Drumlanrig Castle, 1685, George Loukup, wright in Maxwelheugh, 1683 (Peebles CR.), John Lookup, advocate in Edinburgh, 1734 (SCM., III, p. 240), and Andrew Lookup was bailie of Jedburgh before 1771 (Heirs, 358). William Luckup or Lukup, smith in Thornhill, Dumfriesshire, c. 1745. Loukwp 1649, Lowkwp 1651, Lucup 1682.

LORAIN. A variant of LORRAIN, q.v.

LORIMER, LORRIMER. From ME. lorimer, lorymer, OF. lor(i)mier, lorinier, a maker of bits, spurs, stirrup-irons, and generally of all metal articles of horse-furniture. In Latin charters loremarius. Hugh Lorimarius and his heirs had a grant of lands near Perth from William the Lion for services performed by him. Matthew Lorimer, a descendant of Hugh, sold the lands to William de Len, burgess of Perth, by whom they were gifted to the Abbey of Scone in the reign of Alexander II (Scon, p. 60). The name is found in Midlothian in the fifteenth century, in Stirlingshire in the sixteenth, and in Dumfriesshire it is a not uncommon surname. In Edinburgh the Loriners were united with the Hammermen (Maitland, History of Edinburgh, 1753, p. 317). Loremar 1525, Loremer 1667, Loremur 1558, Lorimuire 1688, Lorymar 1445, Lorymare and Lorymere 1510, Lorymer 1530, Lorymayr 1490, Lorymeir 1574, Lourimer 1689.

LORNE. Angus Lorn in Aberdeen, 1408 (CWA., p. 314). Robert Lorne, bailie of Edinburgh, 1423 (Egidii, p. 45), is doubtless Robert de Lorne, a charter witness there in 1425 (RMS., II, 34). Alan de Lorn, canon of the church of Dunkeld, 1433 (REB., I, 59). George Lorn, presbyter of the diocese of Glasgow, 1485, is also referred to at the same time as "Schir George of Lorne, Notar" (LCD., p. 198). Henry Lorne was admitted burgess of Aberdeen, 1488 (NSCM., I, p. 34). John of Lorn had a tenement in Lanark, 1490, and Recherd of Lorn had a tenement there in 1501 (Lanark, p. 8, 11). Donald Lorne is in record in Methven, Perthshire, 1588 (Methven, p. 73), and Archibald Lorne, maltman, was admitted burgess freeman of Glasgow as husband of the daughter of a burgess, 1600 (Burgesses). From Lorn in Argyllshire.

LORNIE. A common surname in the parish of Errol, Perthshire. From Lornie (of old Lornyn), a small place about one and one-half miles from Errol. Balduinus de Lornyn witnessed a charter of "unum rete super matricem aquam de Thei" by David de Haya to the monks of Cupar, c. 1214–49 (SCM., II, p. 307). Sir Duncan de Lornyn, a churchman, witnessed a charter by David de Strathbolgy, earl of Atholl, c. 1284 (Cupar-Angus, I, p. 349). Helen Lornie appears in Dundee in 1609 (Brechin).

LORRAIN, LORRAINE, LORAIN. From Lorraine, a province of France. Roger Loren, the first of the name in Scotland, witnessed an agreement between the Chapter of Moray and Sir Alan Durward, 1233 (REM., p. 97). Dominus Roger de Loranger witnessed a charter by Morgrund, son of Abbe, c. 1239 (SHSM., IV, p. 316). The -er is merely a flourish over the g mistaken by the copyist for -er.

Roger Lohering was juror on an inquest, 1244, concerning the behavior of certain Scottish knights charged with being accomplices of William de Marisco and other enemies of the king of England, accused of piracy in the Irish sea. Eustache de Lorreyne and others were in 1333 directed by Edward III to survey the Castle of Berwick. In 1358 the king of England granted the barony of Coverton to James de Loreyns or de Loreygne, a Scotsman (Bain, IV, 12; OPS., I, p. 399), and in the following year for his "services and steady obedience" he had an annuity in recompense for the loss of his lands (Bain, IV, 24, 28). James de Lorreyn or Lorreyne witnessed a charter by Roger de Auldton, c. 1354 (Kelso, p. 287, 391), and in 1358 he witnessed the grant of the forest of Eteryk to John Kerre (Roxburghe, p. 8). Robert de Lorrevne, juror on inquest made at Roxburgh, 1361 (Bain, IV, 62). Bessie Lorne in Blainslie, parish of Melrose, 1563 (Lauder), Alexander Lorain, notary in Dunse, 1699, and John Lorain, merchant there, 1710 (ibid.). William Lorne in Stitchel, 1689 (RPC., 3. ser. XIV, p. 108). David Lorain died at Grantshouse, Berwickshire, 1940.

LORRIMER. *See under* LORIMER.

LOTHIAN. This surname formerly not uncommon in northwest Perthshire, appears in Gaelic as Loudin, an adaptation of the vernacular Scots pronunciation. John de Loudonia was custumar of Berwick, 1327 (ER., I, p. 80). Patrick Louthyan was burgess of Linlithgow, 1445, and William of Louthiane was witness there, 1472 (Sc. Ant., XVII, p. 116, 118). John of Lowthiane, chaplain in Brechin, 1457, is mentioned in 1476 as John Lowdaine (REB., I, 184, 198). John Lowdyan was tenant of Balgreschach, 1467 (Cupar-Angus, I, p. 149), and another John of Lowdiane was tenant of Auchloch in 1520 (Rental). Wylzem of Lowheane was assizer on lands of Gowane (Govan), 1527 (Pollok, I, p. 258), Walter Lodoune, witness in Linlithgow, 1536 (Johnsoun), and in 1546 Robert Lowdean was member of council of Stirling 'for tailyouris' (SBR., p. 277). William Lowthyane held land in Nether Carmyile, 1552 (Protocols, I), William Lowthiane was portioner of Arlarie, 1642 (Retours, Kinross, 12), William Lotheane was in Auchinairne, 1647 (Inquis., 3388), and Mr. John Lothian was minister of the word of God in the church of Levingstoun, 1665 (Retours, Lanark, 295). Ten of the name, some spelled Louchtheane, are in Dunblane Commissariot Record. "Tradition claims that the surname Lothian, at one time quite common in Glenlyon, originated from [a refugee] — a

Covenanter who came from East Lothian during the persecution and settled in Glenlyon. His original name has not come down to us, but the people of the Glen called him Loudach or the Lothian man, and his descendants are said to have adopted this name and so were called Lothians" (Stewart, A Highland parish, p. 213–14). This tradition is erroneous, as the name appears in the neighborhood much earlier. Lauthiane 1639, Lothean 1546, Loudian 1692, Loudiane 1473, Loudvan 1460, Loutheane 1674, Lowdeane 1549, Lowthiane 1625, Lowthyane 1549.

LOTTIMER. This surname, an early form of LATIMER, q.v., is found in the Glasgow Directory. Adam Lotimer was one of an inquest held at Lochmaben, Dumfriesshire, 1347 (Bain, III, 1499), and John Lottimer in the parish of Tundergarth, 1732, and three more are recorded in Dumfries Commissariot Record.

LOTTO. A variant of LATTA, from LAWTIE, q.v. The family of Lotto in Ayrshire are said to be descended from a survivor of the Spanish Armada (1588)! (SN&Q., III, p. 31). Lato 1715.

LOUDON, LOUDEN, LOWDEN, LOWDON. (1) From Loudoun in the district of Cunningham, Ayrshire. Sir James Dalrymple states (Collections, p. lxv) that he had seen a charter by Richard Moreville, Constable, Jacobo filio Lambini of the lands of Loudoun and others [c. 1189], also another charter by William Morevile Jacobo de Loudun terram de Laudun. "I doubt not," he says, "but Jacobus filius Lambini in the first Charter, was of Clidesdale, and Son of that Lambinus, who gave the name to Lambintoun, and in the second Charter took the proper Sirname of Loudoun from his Lands." Margaret, the only child of James, was married to Reginald de Crawford, sheriff of Ayr, and carried the lands into his family (Caledonia, I, p. 551). John de Lowden was perpetual vicar of Kilpatrick, 1418 (LCD., p. 239). Nicholas de Loudoun or Lowdon held a tenement in Irvine, 1418–26 (Irvine, I, p. 126, 130), and Thomas Lowdain was burgess there, 1499 (Simon, 1). James Lowden of Culmain, 1793 (Dumfries). (2) The surname Louden, current in Fife, is perhaps a spelling of LOTHIAN, q.v. John Loudone and Thomas Loudain are recorded in Dunfermline, 1582 (Dunfermline). Cf. R. L. Stevenson's 'Lowden Sabbath Morn.'

LOUEPRUD. William Loueprud or Laueprud, burgess of Perth, charter witness in the reign of Alexander II, and Serlo, talbator, son of William Loueprud, was burgess there, 1219 (Scon, p. 52, 58).

LOUMGAIR. *See under* LUMGAIR.

LOUNAN, LUNAN, LUNNAN. From the barony of Lunan near Montrose in Angus. Richard de Lounane or Lownan held land in Aberdeen in 1382 (RMS., I, 682) and was elected common councillor of Aberdeen in 1398 (CRA., p. 374), Robert Lownan was admitted burgess of the same burgh in 1411 (NSCM., I, p. 4), and Laurence Lownane is mentioned in 1434 (REB., I, p. 63). Thom Lownan appears in Aberdeen 1408 (CWA., p. 312); Waultier Lowenan, clerk of Scotland, had a safe conduct into England, 1439 (Bain, IV, 1126). John Lownane held land in the Appilgate of Arbroath in 1450 (RAA., II, p. 77), Dominus Laurencius Lownane had built a new school in Dundee in 1435, another John Lounane was a chaplain in Brechin in 1468 (REB., II, 111). Thomas Lunane was proprietor of Mongallie in 1480, and the Rev. William Lunan was minister of Daviot in 1663–77. Several members of a family of this name appear in the Aberdeen Poll Book of 1696, and Robert Lounnan resided in Guild's Hillock in 1732 *(Brechin)*. Lonnane 1662, Lunaine 1632.

LOUR. From Lour, which formed part of the parish of Meathielour united with Inverarity c. 1612. James of Lour witnessed a deed of 1250, and as Jacobus de Lur was a juror in 1257 (RAA., I, p. 90). Laurentius de Lure, juror on inquest in Angus, 1321 (RMS., I, App. I, 29). William Lowar was burgess of Arbroath in 1458 (RAA., II, 115). Jervise says a family of Lur or Lour of that Ilk were councillors of the earls of Crawford in the fifteenth century; and John de Lowre of that Ilk is mentioned in 1466 (Lives, I, p. 117). Adam filius Habha de Lur appears as a charter witness, n. d. (Cupar-Angus, I, p. 344), and John Lovre appears in St. Andrews, 1528 (Laing, 370).

LOURANSTON. Local. Robert Louranston, burgess of Aberdeen, 1591 (SCM., III, p. 155), and William Lowrenstoun was admitted burgess there, 1615 (NSCM., I, p. 115). Lowrenstoune 1597.

LOUSON, LOWSON. Variants of LAWSON, q.v. T. Lowson was admitted burgess of Aberdeen in 1400 and Thomas Louson in 1444 (NSCM., I, p. 1, 8). Fynlay Lowvyson held part of Calady in 1406 (Cupar-Angus, I, p. 130), Hugh Louson, Scots prisoner of war in England, had a safe conduct home in 1423 (Bain, IV, 930), and Andrew Lousone is recorded in Aberdeen in 1493 (CRA., p. 49). Lowsoune and Lausoune 1555.

LOUTHRIE. Probably from Luthrie, parish of Creich, Fife. David de Louthre attested a charter by William de Brechin of lands of Rathmuryel, 1245 (View, p. 625).

LOUTTET, LOUTTIT, LOUTIT, LOUTTITT. From Levetot or Luvetot in Normandy. Sir Roger de Luuetoft witnessed two charters of 1226–34 (Inchaffray, p. 47, 49), and William de louetoft witnessed another charter of 1258 (ibid., p. 78). William de luuetot, probably the same individual, was one of a number appointed to determine the right marches of Westir Fedale, 1246 (LAC., 23). Roger de leuuethot appears as witness, a. 1244 (ibid., 24). These individuals were most probably offshoots of the Louetofts of Nottingham in England, the first recorded of whom in Scotland was Nigel, who acquired the lands of Dolpatrick before 1200. As Nigellus de Dolpatric he was one of the witnesses to Earl Gilbert's great charter founding the monastery of Inchaffray (Inchaffray, p. 8). Adam Loutfute witnessed a retour of service at Harelaw, 1432, and also served on an inquest on the lands of Aldy (Athole, p. 707). David de Loutfuete, brother of Malcolm Loutfute, held the lands of Urchilmany in Strathern, 1450 (Oliphants, p. 10), and in 1459 Malcolm Lowtoit appears as vicar of Tibirmwir (REB., I, 193). John Loutfute held the lands of Balmaclone, 1579 (LIM., 132), and another John Loutfoote or Lutefute, tailor, was burgess of Edinburgh, 1634–40 (Edinb. Marr.). Thomas Loutfutt, aquavitie maker in Brechin, 1612 (Brechin), and Laurence Lutefoot in Rallieloan, 1747 (Dunkeld). In the complaint of the Orcadian Commons in 1426 there is reference to Piris Lwtfut (Piers Loutfoot), and in 1456 Maurice Lowtefute had to do with the fermes of Stratherne. In the Orkney Rentals c. 1500 there is notice of Louttits, and thereafter the name is found in continuous connection with Lyking (perhaps Clumlie is meant) in Sandwick (Old Lore Misc., I, p. 306). Olay Loutfut was tacksman of Sandisend in the parish of Deerness, 1502 (REO., p. 412). The name early spread to Shetland, appearing there in 1427 as Lutzit (z = guttural y) (in Torfaeus, Orcades, 1697), but is said now to be extinct there (Mill, Diary, p. lxxxix). Lowthitt, Lowthytt, and Lowthit in Orkney 1509, Loottfootte 1631, Lowtit 1602, Luttit 1580, Loutfuit, Loutfute, Loutfwit, and Lowitfuit 1557.

LOVANE. Andrew Lovane, king's tenant in lands in Ardmanoch, 1504, and Robert Lovane, tenant of the Castletoun, Ardmanoch, in the same year (ER., XII, p. 660, 661).

LOVAT. Lord Lovat is known in Gaelic as *MacShimidh mor na Mormhoich* (Watson I, p. 501).

LOVE. A common surname in Kilbarchan Commissariot Record, 1649–1772, and still a common surname in Monkland. There seems little doubt that this surname is derived from OFr. *love*, 'a wolf,' the diminutive of which, *lovell*, has also given origin to a surname. In England the name appears in Latin documents as Lupus (Wright, *Courthand restored*), and Walter Lupus was burgess in Dundee, c. 1200 (RAA., I, p. 96). Thomas Lufe appears as witness in Glasgow, 1472 (*Sc. Ant.*, XVII, p. 119), and Jhone Luyff was a tenant in the barony of Glasgow, 1521 (*Rental*). William Lufe and Ranald Lufe were rebels at the horn in 1534 (*Trials*, I, p. 166*), and John Lufe rendered to Exchequer the accounts of the bailies of the burgh of Renfrew in 1567 (ER., XIX, p. 369). John Luiff, skinner, was burgess freeman of Glasgow, 1595, and another John Luif, skinner, was admitted burgess freeman as eldest son of a burgess in 1607 (*Burgesses*). James Love was heir of Robert Love, portioner of Threipwoode, his father, in 1649 (*Retours, Ayr*, 439), and James Love took the Test in Paisley, 1686 (RPC., 3. ser. IX, p. 496). Loove 1658, Loue 1652, Lowe 1657, Luife 1560, Luive c. 1613, Lwyf c. 1541. The name is also used as a translation of the popular etymology of the name Mackinnon (wrongly supposed to be from *MacIonmhuinn*). Lovestone near Girvan derived its name from one of this name.

LOVELL. From NF. *Lovel*<Lat. *lupellus*, little wolf. Louvel and Louveau are not uncommon names in France, and in the romance of *Guillaume d'Angleterre*, one of the 'babes in the wood' is christened Lovel, 'Lovel por le lo l'apelerent' (*Weekley*). A family of this name, a branch of the Lovels, barons of Castle Cary in county Somerset, held lands in Roxburghshire from time immemorial, being seated there long before the Douglases. They afterwards changed their residence to Angus, appearing there about the middle of the thirteenth century, and becoming one of the most influential families. They were of considerable importance in the early annals of Dundee, but became extinct in the male line in 1607 (*Wedd.*, p. 26). Henry Lupellus granted to the canons of St. Andrews two oxgangs of land in Brancheulle (Branxholm) in 1183 (RPSA., p. 261). Later his son Richard, lord of Hauwic, made an exchange with the canons for these lands (ibid., p. 261–262). Hugh Luuel witnessed a charter by Florentius, bishop elect of Glasgow, c. 1202–7 (LCD., p. 236), and about the same date Maurice Luvell was clerk to the same bishop (RMP., p. 110). Maurice Lupellus or Luuel witnessed resignation of the lands of Edeluestun to the church of Glasgow, 1233 (REG.,

p. 138–139). Laurence Lovel was groom of Adam de Liberatione, 1259 (APS., I, p. 98; *Bain*, I, 2175), and Thomas Lovel was a charter witness in Brechin, 1267 (REB., I, p. 8). Sir Richard Lovel was one of the procurators of Alexander III in negotiating the marriage of his daughter with Eric of Norway (APS., I, p. 81). Patrick de Louwel witnessed a charter by James the Steward of Scotland, 1294 (RMP., p. 96). Morice Lovel, parson of the church of Petyt Cares (= Little Cavers) of Roxburghshire, rendered homage, 1296 (*Bain*, II, p. 212). During the War of Independence the family took the English side (*Bain*, II, 891, 1849), and for that cause their lands were forfeited by Bruce. Robertus dictus Lupellus witnessed a charter by Reginald Chen in the reign of Robert I (*Scon*, p. 107). In the reign of David II the lands of James Louell in the valleys of the Esk and Ewes, forfeited by him as an enemy, were granted to William, Lord Douglas (RMS., I, App. II, 803). Richard Lovale, dominus de Ballumby, was juror at Carnconane, 1409 (RAA., II, 490), as de Lufell was a charter witness, 1428 (RMS., II, 109), and as Richard Luwel was juror on an inquisition on lands of Tulloch, 1438 (RAA., II, 83). Isobella Lowell held land in Perth, 1545 (*Rollok*, 4), and James Lowell, custumar of Dundee, 1565, appears in following years as Lovell and Luvell (ER., XIX, p. 291, 323, 370). James Luvell, reidare at Monyfuith, 1574 (RMR.). Lovell 1546, Lowel 1427, Lowele 1427, Luvale 1464, Luvall 1494, Luvhylle 1526, Luwale 1467.

LOVESON, 'son of Love,' q.v. William Lovesone in the parish of Lochwinnoch, 1673, and John Loveson there, 1674 (*Kilbarchan*).

LOW. Of local origin. Furnishing for the king's hall at Scone was delivered to Nicholas Loue in 1331 (ER., I, p. 389). William Low was tenant of Welton of Balbrogi, 1473 (*Cupar-Angus*, I, p. 184). Robert Low was servant to James Meldrum of Segie, 1586, and John Low and Robert Low were witnesses in Brechin, 1583, 1589 (REB., II, 228, 344, 357).

LOWDEN, LOWDON. See LOUDON.

LOWERBURY. Local. Johannes Lowerbury, notary public in Ayrshire, 1632 (*Caldwell*, I, p. 279).

LOWES, LOWIS. From old lands of the name near the Loch of Lowes in Selkirkshire. Lowys, Lowis, Lowes, is a Lowland surname the first record of which appears to be in 1318. In that year Walter Lowys witnessed a charter to lands in the earldom of Dunbar (*Laing*, 22). Patrick de Lowis appears as burgess of Edin-

LOWES, Lowis, *continued*

burgh, 1447 (*Egidii*, p. 77, 114), and in 1449 as Patrick Lowis (without 'de') attested a renunciation by Walter Scott of Bukcleuch (*Soltre*, p. 319). There was a family of Lowis of Mener in Peeblesshire in record 1463–64 (RMS., II, 781), and the family is to be traced beyond the year 1622 (*Retours, Peebles*, 58). Thomas of Lowis in record, 1473 (*Peebles*, 20). Families of the name were also long tenants under the see of Glasgow in Eddleston parish (Buchan, *Peeblesshire*, II, p. 454). Margaret Lowyss held half the lands of Burnetland, Peeblesshire, 1557. Ninian Lowis was member of Scots parliament for Peebles, 1603 (*Hanna*, II, p. 503), and John Lowis of Maner was heir of Thomas of Maner, 1607 (*Inquis.*, 331). There was also a family of Lowis of Merchiston, Edinburgh. Patrick Lowis, notary public, witnessed at Edinburgh, a charter dated 1517 (RMS., III, 173), and in 1524 Stephen Lowvss was witness in Glasgow (LCD., p. 221). James Lowes of Merchistoun was retoured in lands and barony of Hornden, parish of Ladiekirk, 1680 (*Retours, Berwick*, 379, 404). Ninian Lowes was an apothecary in Edinburgh, 1689 (*Inquis.*, 6972). John Lowse in Carnwath, 1601, and Ninian Lowis in Carstairs, 1790 (*Lanark CR.*). John Lous in Scotstoun, 1694 (*Peebles CR.*). The Merchiston family spelled their name Lows in 1689.

LOWRIE. A variant of LAURIE, q.v. We find it as a forename in 1467 in which year Lowry Smith was juror on an inquisition anent fishing in the Tweed (RD., 461), and in 1567 Lourie Quhyt was a tenant of the abbot of Kelso (*Kelso*, p. 524). Gilbert Lowrie in Coldingham witnessed a retour of special service in 1497 (*Home*, 28), David Lowry appears in Irvine as king's officer in 1529 (*Irvine*, II, p. 36), and Robert Lowry possessed land there in 1540 (ibid., 169). Thomas Loure, a charter witness at Doune, 1540 (RMS., III, 2278). John Lourv was officer of the lordship of Ballincreiff in 1557 (ER., XIX, p. 23), and Joseph Lowrye was minister at the kirk of Lenzie in 1620 (SBR., p. 152). James Lowrey was admitted burgess freeman of Glasgow in 1600 (*Burgesses*), John Lourie is recorded in Melrose in 1641, and Thomas Lourie was a Quaker in the same burgh in 1684 (RRM., I, p. 89; III, p. 43). The kirk bell given to S. Nicholas church, Aberdeen, by Provost Levth in 1351, was called the 'Lourie.' Additional evidence that Lowrie is merely a variant of Laurie is shown bv the entry in the Dumfries Retours in 1672 where mention is made of "Robertus Lowrie de Maxweltoun haeres Joannis Lowrie de Maxweltoun," where, of course, the persons named

are members of the old and well-known family of "Annie Laurie."

LOWRIESON, 'son of LOWRIE,' q.v. Robert Lowryson was charter witness in Edinburgh, 1471 (*Neubotle*, p. 274). Robert Lowreson alias Carvour was burgess of Edinburgh in 1511 (*Soltre*, p. 262), Thomas Lorisoun was witness in Perth, 1551 (*Rollok*, 102), and Patrick Lowristoun (with epenthetic *t*) was armourer there in 1612 (*Edinb. Marr.*). Lowrison 1512.

LOWSON. See *under* LOUSON.

LOYNACHAN. Shortened from O'LOYNACHAN, q.v. Lauchlan Loynachan was herd in Ballinatunie, Argyllshire, 1811.

LUCAS. From the Latin personal name *Lucius* <Gr. Λουκᾶς. James Leuches in Torieleithe, 1608, and William Luches there, 1611 (RSCA., II, p. 137, 175).

LUCASSON, 'son of LUCAS,' q.v. Patrick Lucassone and Angus Lucassone were members of the garrison of Stirling, 1339–40 (*Bain*, III, p. 241). Cf. MACLUCAS.

LUCKIE. A diminutive of LUKE, q.v. John Luckie in Spittell, Aberdeenshire, 1724 (*Aberdeen CR.*). Cf. MACLUCKIE.

LUCKIESON, 'son of LUCKIE,' diminutive of LUKE, q.v., or perhaps an Englishing of MACLUCKIE, q.v. John Lukiesoune in M'Williamstoune, 1623 (*Dunblane*), and another John Luckisone was burgess of Stirling, 1669 (*Inquis.*, 5246).

LUCKLAW. Of local origin from Lucklaw in the parish of Leuchars, Fife. William Luklaw appears as one of the bailies of Cupar in 1458 (ER., VI, p. 400), Andrew Luklaw was member of an assize at Cupar in 1521 (SCBF., p. 222), and Svmon Luklawe had a precept of remission for offences committed by him in 1536 (RSS., II, 2114). Alexander Lucklaw was a burgess of Cupar in 1648 (*Fordell*, 170), and Margaret Lucklaw is recorded at Kinnaird in 1739 (*Brechin*). Luiklaw 1654.

LUDDALE. The name of an old Orkney family derived from the land of Luddale in the parish of St. Andrews, Orkney. Mawnus of Luddal, son and heir of Androw of Luddall, sold a half-penny land in Tanskerness in 1455 (REO., p. 190).

LUDDES. Helen Luddes in Craikfurde was accused of witchcraft, 1629 (RPC., 2. ser. III, p. 98).

LUDOVIC. For some reason unknown this was a favorite forename with the Grants, and was used by them as an Anglicizing of Gaelic MAOLDOMHNUICH, q.v. The name is from old Frankish *Hlúd-wig*, 'famed warrior,' Latinized as *Chlodovisus* and *Ludovicus*, now represented by modern German *Ludwig*. Louis and Lewis are doublets.

LUFITHOLT. Malcolm Lufitholt, presbyter in diocese of Dunblane, 1437 (SCM., v, p. 259; *Panmure*, II, 229).

LUFRENT. John Lufferand in Perth, 1568 (*Sc. Ant.*, I, p. 169). Andrew Lufrent, burgess of Perth, heir of James Lufrent, 1607 (*Inquis.*, 315). Perhaps the modern Lovering.

LUGGESPICK. Robert Luggespick, burgess of Dumfries, c. 1290 (Edgar, *Dumfries*, p. 220).

LUGGIE. Of local origin from a small place of the name probably in Lanarkshire. The Luggie is a small stream in Lanarkshire and Luggiebank is near Cumbernauld Station. John Luggie in Lochtwood, 1587 (*Protocols*, x), Thomas Lugy was burgess freeman of Glasgow, 1606, and John Luggie was admitted burgess freeman as married to the daughter of a burgess, 1608 (*Burgesses*). Thomas Luggie in Lochwood, heir of William Luggie, burgess of Glasgow, 1646 (*Inquis.*, 3115).

LUGTON. Probably from the lands of Lugton (an old barony — *Retours*) in Midlothian. Thomas Logtoun in Dunfermline, 1562 (*Dunfermline*), William Lugtoun, tenant in East Barns, Fife, is mentioned in a Dunfermline charter of 1632, and H. Lugtoun of the Committee of the Army signed a letter in the General Assembly at Cupar in April, 1651.

LUKE. Families of this name long had connection with Berwickshire, more particularly with the estates of Spottiswoode and Marchmont. The name is also found early in Glasgow. Adam (p. 138) says the habitat of the Lukes was the shores of Lochfyne, and that they are an offshoot of the Lamonts. Some Maclucases Englished their name as Luke (*Buchanan of Auchmar*). Henry Louk was curate in Linlithgow, 1530 (*Johnsoun*), John Luke or Louk rendered to Exchequer the accounts of the bailies of the burgh of Rutherglen, 1564–67 (ER., XIX, p. 277, 370). John Louk was made burgess of Glasgow as burgess heir, 1582, and a later John Louke received the same privilege in 1691 (*Burgesses*). John Lowk is recorded in Eister Dalbeth, 1587 (*Protocols*, x), Daniel Luck in Little Dalganross was fined for reset of Clan Gregor, 1613

(RPC., XIV, p. 639), William Luck or Luik was member of Scots parliament for Forfar, 1650 (*Hanna*, II, p. 503), and Alexander Luke was dyer in Milntoun of Cluny, 1763 (*Dunkeld*). Lowik 1549. (2) Luke is now used as a shortened (English) form of *MacGille Moluaig*.

LULACH. The name of the unfortunate son of Gillacomgan, mormaer of Moray, king of Scots for seven months, and killed in 1057/8. The name is perhaps from OG. *lu + laogh*, 'little calf' (*Stokes*). Gives MACLULLICH.

LUMBENNIE. Adam de Lumbyny of the county of Fife rendered homage in 1296 (*Bain*, II, p. 204), and in 1312 horses were purchased from Philip de Lumbeny and Malcolm de Lumbeny (ibid., III, p. 429). From Lumbennie or Lumbenny in the parish of Newburgh, Fife.

LUMGAIR, LOUMGAIR. From Lumgair in Dunnottar parish, Kincardineshire. Walter de Lunkyrr (an old spelling of Lumgair) witnessed a deed of vendition of the lands of Drumsleed, c. 1218–22 (REB., II, 272; RAA., I, p. 185). Still prevalent among the fisher folk.

LUMLEY. From Lumley in county Durham. Patrick de Lumley witnessed a Lanark charter of 1367 (RMS., I, 270). He is probably the Patrick of Lumle or Lumley, bailie of Lanark in 1381 (*Lanark*, p. 376), and the Patrick of Lumle, one of the Scots commissioners to arrange a truce with England in 1397 (*Bain*, IV, 491). William Lumlye, witness in West Lothian, 1497 (*Binns*, 23).

LUMSDAINE. *See under* LUMSDEN.

LUMSDALE. From an old pronunciation and spelling of LUMSDEN, q.v., which has become a fixed surname. John Lummisdaill was tacksman of a 1½d land in Trymland, Orkney, in 1503 (REO., p. 418). Robert Lumsdaile is recorded in Aberdeen in 1558 (SCM., IV, p. 58), and payment was made to bailie Lumsdaill in the same burgh in 1643 (ibid., v, p. 107). John Lumsdale was residenter in Lauder in 1760 (*Lauder*). Lumsdall and Lumsdell are also common pronunciations of Lumsden.

LUMSDEN, LUMSDAINE. From the old manor of that name in the parish of Coldingham, Berwickshire. The earliest record of the name is between 1166–82, when Gillem (i.e. William) and Cren de Lumisden witnessed a charter by Earl Waldeve of Dunbar to the Priory of Coldingham (*Raine*, 115). Edward de Aldecambus was accused before William

LUMSDEN, LUMSDAINE, *continued*

the Lion in 1188 of being a wrecker and was sentenced to death, but pardoned in consideration of a large money payment. To raise the necessary sum he was compelled to exchange Aldecambus for Lumsden Major (= West Lumsden, now Dowlaw) and eighty merks of silver with Bertram, prior of Coldingham (*Raine*, 648). Adam de Lummesdene and Roger de Lummesdene of Berwickshire rendered homage, 1296 (*Bain*, II, p. 206). An offshoot of the Lumsdens of Lumsden acquired lands in Fife in the first half of the fourteenth century, and about the same time acquired other lands in Aberdeenshire to which they gave their family name. John de Lummysden witnessed a charter by Duncan, earl of Fife, c. 1335 (REA., I, p. 65). In the muster-rolls of the Archers of the Scots Guard in France, 1498–99, the name appears as Alomesden and Lomesdel (*Forbes-Leith*, I, p. 172, 175), and Lunsten, Le Musten, and Lumesten in the same record doubtless also represent the name. Lummisdane 1497, Lummisden 1495, Lummysdane 1547, Lummysden 1496, Lummysdeyn 1512, Lumsdean 1688, Lumysden 1442, Loummysden 1431, Lumbsdene 1630, Lumisdane 1546, Lumisdayn 1512, Lumisdeane 1557, Lumisdeyn 1548, Lummdane 1497, Lummisdane 1497. Cf. LAMMESTONE.

LUN, LUNN. John Lun or Lwn, charter witness in Coldingham, 1548 and 1557 (*Home*, 195). Mark Lun of the convent of Dunfermline, 1555 (*Laing*, 633), David Lund, notary public in Forfarshire, 1559 (REB., II, 205). William Lun in Craigmilne, 1696 (*Inquis.*, 7687). Lower, under Lunn, says this is a corruption of Lund, and that there are several places of the name in Lancashire and Yorkshire.

LUNAN. *See under* LOUNAN.

LUNCART. A surname found in Strathdon in the seventeenth century. Of local origin from Lunchart, pronounced Lunkart, in the parish of Tullynessle. The place is now included in Muckletown. John Loncarte was exempted from process while in French service (RPC., VIII, p. 136). Tobias Lonkaird in Kinbothok was charged with violence in 1607 (RPC., VII, p. 393). Helen Luncard in Balzordie, 1656 (*Brechin*).

LUNDIE. Local, probably from Lundie near Doune, Perthshire. John Lundie had a remission for his part in burning the town of Dunbertane, 1489 (*Lennox*, II, p. 133). William Lundie of that Ilk, sheriff of Fife, 1491 (*Pitfirrane*, 41). George Lundye, min-

ister of Dummany, 1574 (RMR.). William Lundie in Lundymylne, 1676 (*Edin. App.*). See also under LUNDIN.

LUNDIN. The name Robert de Lundyn, Lundin, Londen, or Lundris appears several times in record about the end of the twelfth and in the early years of the thirteenth century. Some writers have thought they were distinct persons deriving their surnames from Lundie in Angus, or from Lundie in Fife, or perhaps from both places. The editors of the Charters of the Abbey of Inchcolm have shown that this opinion cannot be accepted. "There was only one Robert de London — although his name appears in more than one form — and he appears most frequently before the accession of Alexander II. His mother was evidently Matilda Ferrers, who was married to Richard de Londonia, and Robert seems to have adopted his step-father's name." The evidence adduced in support of their opinion seems conclusive (p. 109). John de Lundoniis witnessed King William's grant of Kinbethach to Gilbert, earl of Strathern, c. 1178–80 (LIM., p. xxii). John de Lundin witnessed a charter by Roger, bishop elect of St. Andrews, concerning the church of Hadintun, c. 1189–98 (RPSA., p. 153), and John de Lundoniis witnessed a grant to Arbroath Abbey, c. 1200 (RAA., I, 10). Philippus de Lundin was a witness to many royal charters from before 1195 to 1204. "Presumed to have been son of Walter son of Philip the Chamberlain, who had a charter of Lundin in Fife from William the Lion early in his reign, and took his surname from the lands. The Lundin family ended in an heiress in the seventeenth century; she married a Maitland, and the heiress of the Maitlands of Lundin carried the estate to her husband, John Drummond, created earl of Melfort" (*Inchaffray*, p. 270).

Walter de Lundy was juror at Perth, 1305 (*Bain*, II, 1670), and John Lundy was a witness in 1458 and 1462 (*Neubotle*, 245, 289). Another John Lundy "of that Ilk" was one of the conservators of the three years' truce in 1484 (*Bain*, IV, 1505). John Lundy had remission for his part in burning the town of Dunbertane, 1489 (*Lennox*, II, p. 133), Jhone of Lundy had precept of a charter of feuferme of lands in Fife, 1499 (RSS., I, 419), and Katherine Lundy was wife of Patrick Culess in Fife, 1517 (ALHT., V, p. 102). Walter Lundye had a charter of the lands of Schanvell with rabbit warren, etc., in 1546 (RD., p. 395). Andrew Lundy was charged in 1558 with abiding from the raid of Lauder (*Trials*, I, p. *404), David Lundy had a charter of the land of Lathalland in 1596 (RD., p. 494), and John Lundy was retoured heir of Master William Lundy *de eodem* his father, 1600 (*Retours, Fife*, 83). James Lundie, heritable proprietor of the town and lands of Skeddoway, resigned the same in 1637 (*Dysart*, p. 50). Issobella Lundie was retoured heir portioner of William Lundie in Sutherfauldfeild, 1620 (*Retours, Fife*, 304). Robert Lunder, laird of Balgonie, was admitted burgess of Glasgow, 1618 (*Burgesses*), and George Lundie, was church elder in Dysart, 1641 (PBK., p. 209). James Lundie of Spittle, 1711, and four more of the name in the neighborhood are in record (*Lauder*), and Rev. John Lundie, minister of Lonmay for 54 years, died in 1807.

LUNING. Engelbert Luning, canon of Caithness, 1329 (CSR., I, p. 91). Searle records two of this name, both moneyers.

LUNNAN. *See under* LOUNAN.

LUSK. A surname recorded in the shires of Kirkcudbright, Wigtown, and Lanark, may be of local origin from Lusk in Dublin.

LUSS. From Luss in the parish of the same name, Dumbartonshire. Maurice de Lus witnessed a charter by Gillemichell filius Edolf, and in 1274 a confirmation charter by Malcolm, fourth earl of Levenax (*Levenax*). Before 1290 Malcolm de Luss witnessed a grant by Malcolm, earl of Levenax to Patrick Galbraith (ibid., p. 33), and about the same time John de Luss witnessed a charter by the same earl (ibid., p. 81), and the grant by Thomas de Cremennane to Murechauch filius Kork (ibid., p. 80). Malcolm de Lus had a payment out of the king's tenth penny in 1329 (ER., I, p. 257), and c. 1350 he witnessed the grant by Donald, earl of Levenax to William de Galbraith (*Levenax*, p. 34). The family merged in that of Colquhoun through the marriage of the heiress, the "Fair Maid of Luss," daughter of Godfrey, sixth of Luss, with Sir Robert of Colquhoun.

LUTAR. From the occupation, one who plays a lute. At the rustic dance of "Christis Kirk of the Grene,"

" Tam Lutar wes thair menstral meit,
He playit sa schill, and sang sa sweit."

William Lutar admitted burgess of Aberdeen, 1463 (NSCM., I, p. 18) is probably the William Lutair recorded in 1468 (RAA., II, 169). John Lutare was hired for the common work of the monastery, 1484 (*Cupar-Angus*, I, p. 306). Johannes Lutare, witness in Irwin, 1499 (*Simon*, 35).

LUTHERDALE. Thomas Lutherdale, canon of collegiate church of Abernethy, c. 1290

(*Laing*, 15). John Luthirdale, rector of Durris, 1477 (*Binns*, 14). Cf. LAUDERDALE and LIDDERDALE.

LYAL, LYALL, LYELL. From OE. *Liulf* (*Ligulf*). Johannes filius Lyelli was park-keeper of Plater, 1329 (ER., I, p. 145, 147), and John Liel or Lyel was treasurer of the church of Brechin, 1411–34 (REB., I, 34, 62). William Lvell had a tenement in Edinburgh, 1414 (REG., 324), and Gilbert Lyell was juror on inquisition at Arbroath, 1452 (RAA., II, 93). Master Andrew Liolle was treasurer of Aberdeen, 1468 (*Bain*, IV, p. 280), and Alexander Liel was admitted burgess there, 1484 (NSCM., I, p. 31). Three sons of Patrick Lyell, bailie of Aberbrothock, went to Sweden in 1638, and became prominent manufacturers there. A son of one of them was ennobled in 1717 and died in 1729. Sir Charles Lyell (1797–1875) was one of the founders of scientific geology. Liale 1442, Liell 1517, Lile 1561, Lyale 1435, Lyll 1646.

LYBURN. Perhaps a syncopated form of LYMBURN, q.v. John Liburne, visitor of the maltmen of Glasgow, 1686 (RDB.).

LYDER. Adam Lyder, burgess of Aberdeen, had a safe conduct into England, 1304, and in the same year he was imprisoned for shipping goods "designed for the Scottish rebels" (*Bain*, II, p. 385, 407).

LYDIARD. A rare surname in Scotland. If not a variant of LADYURD, q.v., then most probably from Liddiard in Wiltshire.

LYELL. *See under* LYAL.

LYFFE. Petrus de Lyffe, canon in the monastery of Scone, 1374 (*Scon*, p. 145) derived his surname from the village or parish of Liff near Dundee.

LYGATE. *See under* LEGAT.

LYLE. A family of this name were barons of Duchal in Renfrewshire as early as the beginning of the thirteenth century. The statement in Wood's edition of Douglas's *Peerage* that "the surname of L'Isle or Lyle was first assumed by the proprietors of some of the western isles in the reign of Malcolm Canmore" is erroneous. They were of the same stock as the Northumberland family of 'de Insula' (as the name appears in Latin) or 'Lisle' (de Lisle, Delisle in French). The first of the name in Scotland appears to have been Radulphus or Ralph de Insula, a follower of the Steward, who witnessed the gift by Baldwin de Bigre, sheriff of Lanharc (Lanark), of the church of Innerkyp to the monks of

LYLE, *continued*

Paisley, c. 1170 (RMP., p. 112), and also, about the same period, witnessed the gift of the ferms of his mill at Paisley by Walter Fitz-Alan for the soul of Sir Robert de Brus (ibid., p. 87). Before 1177 he witnessed the gift of the church of Cragyn (Craigie in Kyle) by Walter Hose to the monks of Paisley (ibid., p. 232), and a. 1189 he attested a charter by Richard de Morevil (REG., p. 39). William de Ylle, witness to a charter by Walter Fitz-Alan, c. 1208–18, is the William de Lile who witnessed a resignation by Roger, prior of Paisley, of certain lands, c. 1222–33 (RMP., p. 20). Sometime before 1228 Peter de Insula appears as witness to a donation to the Abbey of Kelso by Gilbert de Vmfravill (*Kelso*, 325). Alan de Insula, one of the knights of Alexander Fitz-Walter the High Steward, witnessed a number of his charters before 1252 (RMP., p. 21, 87, 91, 113), and Robert de Insula was a cleric of the diocese of St. Andrews about the same time (RPSA., p. 157, 169). Ralph de Insula, lord of Duchyl, witnessed the sale of Aldhingleston to the Abbey of Paisley, c. 1260 (RMP., p. 58), and Peter de Insula witnessed two charters of lands in Lennox to the Abbey of Paisley by Malcolm, earl of Lennox in 1273 (RMP., p. 204, 201*; *Levenax*, p. 15, 17). John del Ille of Berwickshire and Richard del Isle of Edinburghshire rendered homage in 1296 (*Bain*, II, p. 201, 207), and Cristinus de Insula appears c. 1340 as 'tunc vicecomite de Perth' (*Scon*, 167). Payment was made to Robert de Lyle in 1358 for furs for the chamberlain (ER., I, p. 595), and a precept by Robert, dominus de Lyle, dated 1452, is witnessed by Alexander Lyle and William Lyle 'patruis meis carissimis' (RMP., p. 250). In the same year William de Lyle granted the monastery of Paisley 'tertiam partem totius piscarie de le Crukyshot' (ibid.). John Lile of Stanypethe was charged with assisting thieves, 1530 (*Trials*, I, p. 144*), William Leill is recorded in Lumloch, 1671 (*Campsie*), and the surname is common in Kilbarchan Commissariot Record. In the middle of the sixteenth century the family ended in the direct line in an heiress, and the lands of Duchal passed from the Lyles to Porter of Porterfield. Patrick de Lyle was juror on inquisition at Swinton, 1408 (*Swinton*, p. xviii). Some Lyles still exist in the parish of Whittinghame, probably descendants of the old Lylls of Staneypath. See also ILE.

LYLESTON. Local from Lyleston (*Liulf's tûn*) near Hawick. Loel de Liollestone of the county of Berewike rendered homage, 1296 (*Bain*, II, p. 207). Margaret Lylestone, wife of Thomas

Hardie, was the heroine of the story of 'Midside Maggie' (PSAS., XXXII, p. 196).

LYMBURN. Metonymic for LYMBURNER, q.v. Captain Lymburn was an engager on the royalist side, 1648 (PBK., p. 328).

LYMBURNER. From the occupation of 'limeburner,' one who burned limestone to form lime. Thomas Lymburnar, witness in Glasgow, 1552 (*Protocols*, I), Peter Lymeburner, goldsmith there, 1588 (ibid., x), Thomas Lymburner, burgess freeman of Glasgow, 1601 (*Burgesses*), and Alexander Lymburner, merchant burgess of Glasgow, 1641 (*Inquis.*, 2573). Liburnar c. 1540, Lymeburnear 1555.

LYNE. From the old manor of the same name in Peeblesshire. David de Lyne, son of Robert de Lyne, granted to Neubotle "totam peteram de locqueruard que vocatur Wluesstrother," c. 1165–1214, a grant increased by his son Robert within the same period (*Neubotle*, 13, 14). Robert de Scrogges having lost his life in the service of this David, his son received a grant of the lands of Scrogges c. 1208 (REG., p. 73). About the year 1208 Robert of Line, son of David, had a dispute with Gregory, the parson of Stobehe (Stobo), regarding the chapel of Line (ibid., p. 72). The family appears to have ended in an heiress late in the thirteenth century who carried the lands to the Hays of Yester, as at about the same period there is mention of Robert filius David quondam dominus de Lochuerwerd (*Neubotle*, 16).

LYNE or LYNN. The family of Lin or Lynn of that Ilk in the parish of Dalry, Ayrshire, took their name from the cascade on the Water of Caaf, near which stood the ancient castle of Lin (*Paterson*, III, p. 184). The family is now extinct. Another family of the same name possessed the property of Larg in the parish of Inch, Wigtownshire, in the seventeenth century, and M'Kerlie (I, p. 166) thinks they were a branch of Lynes or Lynns of that Ilk. William Lyne was juror on inquisition held by sheriff of Lanark, 1263 (*Bain*, I, 2677). Wautier de Lynne of Ayrshire rendered homage, 1296, and in same year was juror on inquest on lands of Lady Elena la Zuche in Conyngham (*Bain*, II, p. 206, 216). Andrew Linn of that Ilk gave sasine of the lands of Highlees to the laird of Hunterston, 1452, Jhone of Leyn witnessed execution of a summons, 1495 (*Dobie-Pont*, p. 353), and Elizabeth *alias* Bessie Lyn was heiress of David Lyn, shoemaker of Eister Brigend, Kilwinning, 1628 (*Retours, Ayr*, 254).

(2) Another old family of the name of Lyne or Len long resided in Perth. Johannes

filius Lene and Ricardus de Lenna are witnesses there in the reign of Alexander II (*Scon*, p. 55). Martin de Lene witnessed a charter by William filius hawoc, burgess of Perth, c. 1245 (*Inchaffray*, p. 63). William de Len or Lyn who held a land there in 1246 is again referred to in 1258 as William de Lenn (*Scon*, p. 50, 72). Johannes de Lena witnessed a gift to the church of Glasgow c. 1260, and as Johannes de Lenna appears as charter witness in 1267 (REG., p. 177, 181). Simon de Lenna, Cecilia his wife, and John his son and heir occur in Drummond charters, and John de Lenna did homage in 1291 (*Inchaffray*, p. 283). Adam de Lyn in 1343 rendered to Exchequer the accounts of the provost of Perth at Dundee (ER., I, p. 523). Thomas of Lyne was burgess of Perth in 1421, and Malcolm of Lyn witnessed a charter by Malcolm of Crombeth in Strathearn, 1428 (*Athole*, p. 706). Philip de Lyn held land in Arbroath, 1438 (RAA., II, 84), Patrick Lin or de Lyn was burgess of Edinburgh, 1468 (*Neubotle*, 301, 302), James Lyne was prebendary of Abirlade, 1524 (RAA., II, 583), and John Line was trade burgess of Aberdeen, 1656 (ROA., I, p. 233). James Line, fermourer in Kirknewtoune, 1680 (*Edin. App.*), James Len, late deacon of the Hammermen of Edinburgh, 1720 (*Guildry*, p. 123).

LYON. "According to the family tradition the Lyons came to Scotland from France, by way of England, in the course of the twelfth century" (Ross, *The Lyons of Cossins*, Edinburgh, 1901). The name was not uncommon in England in the twelfth and thirteenth centuries, and landowners of the name were in occupation in several of the English shires in the reigns of Edward I and Edward II. The first of the name recorded in Scotland, probably an English soldier, was Thomas Lyon, crossbowman, who formed one of the garrison of Linlithgow peel in the pay of Edward II, in 1311–12 (*Bain*, III, 412). The first known Scots of the name recorded are John the son of Lyon and Hugo the son of Lyon (Johannes filius Leonis, Hugo filius Leonis), members of an inquest on the lands of Rostinot in 1321–22 (RMS., I, App. I, 29). John Lyon had a charter of the lands of Forteviot and Forgundenmy, Perthshire, c. 1342–43 from David II. John Lyon or Lyoun, clerk and secretary to David II, had a charter from Robert II in 1371–72 of the thanage of Glaumysse (Glamis) as a free barony (RMS., I, 411, 549). He had other charters from the same king in which he is described as 'carissimus filius noster' and 'dilectus filius noster' (ibid., 679, 693). James Lvoune was vicar of St. Giles, Edinburgh, 1393 (*Egidii*, p. 29), John Lyon was chaplain to the Lord of the Isles in 1411 (*Bain*, IV,

806), and Patrick Lyon, one of the hostages for King James I in 1425 (ibid., IV, 947, 981, 983) was ennobled as Baron Glamis in 1445. David Lioun had a precept of the Hospital of Balgonyesse with the lands and mill in 1499 (RSS., I, 418), Patrick Lione was bailie of Glasgow, 1525 (LCD., p. 103), and David Lvoune was a witness there, 1550 (*Protocols*). Cosmo Innes says (p. 24): "I have seen petitions of some small clans of the Braes of Angus to be allowed to take the name of Lyon, and to be counted clansmen of the Strathmores." Queen Elizabeth is a daughter of the 14th Earl of Strathmore. Leon (of Glamis) 1646. Lyona, Lyowne.

MABEN, MABON. Probably from the Old British name Maban or Mabon seen in ClachMabanestone on Gretna Mains, Dumfriesshire. Mabon, son of Mellt, and Mabon, son of Modron, occur in the Welsh *Mabinogion* (ed. Nutt, London, 1904, p. 139, 162, etc.). William Maben in Galloscheills, 1657 (RRM., I, p. 149) and John Mabane or Mabone in Coblehouse, 1662 (ibid., II, p. 5, 15). Margaret Meben appears in Bromdykes, 1673 (*Lauder*), and Thomas Mabone was ordained minister of Gordon, 1685 (Thomson, *Lauder*, p. 238). William Maebine in Kirkcudbright signed the Test in 1684 (RPC., 3. ser. x, p. 248), John Maban in Conhaith, parish of Carlaverock, 1639, and David Maban, tanner in Dumfries, 1785 (*Dumfries*), and William Maiben is recorded in Stirling, 1717 (*Sc. Ant.*, VI, p. 87). Sir John A. Maybin of the Ayrshire family, governor of Northern Rhodesia, died 1941. Maebone 1684.

MABIE. From the land of Mabie in the parish of Troqueer, Kirkcudbrightshire. The land of Mayby was confirmed to Durand filius Christin by Alan filius Roland, constable of Scotland, c. 1200–34 (*Holm Cultram*, p. 56). Rev. John Mabie was minister of Kirkmabreck in 1674 (*Kirkcudbright*).

MAC (wrongly contracted M', Mc) is a Gaelic prefix occurring in Scottish names of Gaelic origin, as Macdonald, Maclean, Macphie, and the like, meaning "son." The word corresponds to *son* in names of Teutonic origin, as Anderson, Johnson, Watson; to the *Fitz* (<Lat. *filius*) in Norman-French names, as Fitzgerald, Fitzpatrick; and to Welsh *map* (etymologically akin to *Mac*), shortened to '*ap* or '*p*, as in Ap Richard, whence Prichard (nearly all Welsh names beginning with P, or its mutation B, incorporate *ap*). It corresponds partly to Irish O, though this rightly means "descendant," Irish *Ua*. O or *Ua* is represented in Scots Gaelic

MAC, continued

by ogha, 'grandchild,' which in the combination iar ogha, was borrowed by Lowland Scots as ieroe, a 'great-grandchild.' As O is a complete word it should not be followed by the apostrophe as in the English spelling of Irish names. It represents ua, OIr. aue for a prehistoric * auas or * avas, where an original p is lost, * pavios, which compare with Latin puer for pov-er, Greek pais (for patis), a boy or son. Ui, the nominative plural of Ua, is used in Irish Gaelic to denote a tribe or territory. In Anglo-Irish books this syllable is frequently written Hua, Hui, and more commonly Hy, as in Hy Many for Ui Maine, Hy Fiachrach for Ui Fiachrach, etc. There is only one instance on Scottish ground of this form: Huasuibne for Uasuibne, in 1355 (HP., II, p. 139). (Irish O'Brien, etc., should properly be written without the apostrophe as O Brien, etc.).

In the island of Arran, prefixed to surnames, Mac is always pronounced 'ac. Macnicol, now shortened there to Nicol in English, is still 'Ac Riocail in Gaelic (N at the beginning of Gaelic words is almost if not quite pronounced as r). MacMhuirich (Macvurich) is pronounced in Arran 'Ac Uiri; at Shiskine as 'Ac Fuiri, and is still further curtailed in the English form of the name, Currie. (The Dumfriesshire surname Currie is, however, of territorial origin.) Macintyre suffers at the Southend of Arran much greater curtailment: Iain Mac an-t-Saoir, for example, is shortened to Iain t-Saoir (Tyre). Elsewhere in the West and South Highlands, bordering on the Lowlands, Mac also suffers great abbreviation, the ma disappears and only the c, as the dominant sound, remains. This is of course the case with the Gaelic first. For instance in Argyllshire Iain Mac Comhan (John M'Gille-Comgan really) becomes Iain Comhan in Gaelic, while its English equivalent is Cowan. Similarly Iain Cui'ne stands for Iain Mac Shuibne, Iain Clabhruinn for John Maclaren, Iain Caidh for John Mackay (where kay contains all that remains of David), Iain Clugais for Maclucas, Iain Coinneach for Mackenzie, Iain Clachuinn for Maclachlan, Iain Ciarmaid for Macdermid, and Anna Cheacharna for Maceachearn (Macbain in Northern Chronicle).

In Irish Gaelic Mac regularly becomes Mag (gen. Meig) before a vowel, l and r (O'Maille, Annals of Ulster, p. 51n). When part of a surname both Mac and Mag are treated alike; fully stressed when no Christian name preceded, unstressed when coming between Christian name and surname. This change of Mac to Mag does not occur in Scots Gaelic with the exception of the dialect of Argyllshire, where Macgee or Magee is from Irish Mag

Aodha and not from Scots Gaelic MacAoidh. We have also MagLeod and MagLachlan.

"In most of the Gaelic area of Scotland," says the late Sir John Rhys, "mac, mic, are pronounced at the present day machc, mikhk, with ch and kh like ch in German doch and ich respectively" (PSAS., XXXII, p. 390). This pronunciation is ancient and appears in early Scots records written mach, as Mach gilherve, 1266 (Inchaffray, p. 85). It is also often so written in the Register of the Priory of St. Andrews (Mach Adam, Machgilish, Mach imbethi, etc.), and was common in Galloway in 1684: Machburny, Machgie, Machknight, etc. (RPS., 3. ser. IX). The ch sound of c is also found preserved in the Aberdeenshire surname Machray (for Macrae).

In Irish Gaelic mac sometimes means 'boy,' as in Maelcoisne mac dall, 'Maelcoisne the blind boy.' As a prefix it also means 'young,' goes adjectively before many nouns: MacNia, 'young champion' (Macbain), and in Scots Gaelic it often renders an abstract noun into a material one: Mac mollachd, 'son of curse,' 'cursed one;' and the well-known Mac-talla, 'son of the rock,' i.e. 'echo.'

In Mac c is the dominant sound and tends to thrust itself over on to the beginning of the following syllable, hence Mac(k)ay for Mac-Aoidh, Maccaulay for Macaulay, etc. Mac was also assumed by Norsemen and by some Lowland peoples, e.g. MacLeod, MacRerick, and dropped again in some instances, e.g. Cloud (from Macleod), Rerick (from Macrerick), etc. In the Middle Ages, again, the prefix does not in every case prove, where other evidence is wanting, that its bearer is the son of a Gael, for the word has been taken by, or given to some who were of non-Gaelic origin, as Mac-Thorfinn, MacThore, in Cumberland, etc. Noteworthy are the many 'Mac' towns in Ayrshire in the Retours, M'Clogstoune, M'Clanochanstoun, M'Ewinstoun, M'Ileristoun, M'Roriestoun, M'Wilkingstoun, etc., attesting to a strong Gaelic strain in the population.

MACABHRIUIN, MACBRIOUN, 'son of Brión.' Patrick M'Abhriuin is one of the witnesses in the unique Gaelic charter of 1408 (Bk. Islay, p. 17). This represents Mac úi Bhriuin, which may be for older Moccu Briuin. In the time of S. Columba there was a youth in Iona, Columbanus nepos Briuini, and Molus nepos Briuini was a brother of the Community (Adamnan, II, 16, 29). In the Táin Bó Fráich Dunolly is named Dún Ollaich maic Briuin, 'the fort of Ollach son of Brion' (ZCP., IV, p. 47). John McBryon or McBryoun was tenant of Kilkyne, Tiree, 1541, and Fynnane Mc-Bryon or McBryoun was tenant of Ballemanoch, Tiree, in the same year (ER., XVII, p. 614, 641). Andrew McBrwin was burgess of Dumfries, 1557 (Edgar, p. 242–243). In 1618 the clanbreghoun gave their band to the laird of Calder by Patrick Breghoun in Lagan, Islay, for himself, his son, for Gillecreist Mc breghoun, Gormyk Mc breghoun and others (Cawdor, p. 242). Donald M'Vrion and Iain M'Vrion were among those murdered at Dunavertv, 1647 (HP., II, 257). Four persons named M'Brion are in record, 1675–95 (Argyll). Niall M'Abrioune was servitor to the laird of Lochness, 1658, and Donald Mc abrionne was tenant of Leckabowie, 1669 (HP., IV, p. 222). Ard: McIvrion or Mc vrian, fencible-man in Nether Lorn, 1692 (Commons, p. 34, 35). Eouine M'Brun in Lochibuv, 1702, may have been a relative of Malcolm M'Bryan recorded there in 1693 (Argyll Inv.), and Duncan M'Urion or Vrion was tenant of Ardlussa, Jura, 1729 (Isles). Mcbruin and McBrun, 1684 (Parish). MacBrioun, McBrihon. See Amendments and additions.

MACACHIN. See under MACEACHAN.

MACAD. Johnne McAd was a follower of Walter Ross of Morange, 1596 (RPC., v, p. 304).

MACADAM. G. MacAdaim, 'son of Adam,' from the unaspirated form of the name. Dolfinus mach Adam witnessed a charter by Ernaldus, bishop of St. Andrews, c. 1160–62 (RPSA., p. 128). Nel mᵏKadan, Donald mᵏKadam, and Fynlay McKadem held part of the lands of Calady in 1460, and Neyl mᵏKeden appears again in Calady in 1474 (Cupar-Angus, I, p. 130, 198). John M'Cadame was retoured heir of Duncan M'Caddame, burgess of Avr, his father, 1609 (Retours, Ayr, 115). The Macadams of Waterhead, Ayrshire, of whom John Loudon Macadam the famous roadbuilder was a member, claim to be descended from a Macgregor of the first half of the sixteenth century who fled to Ayrshire. Recently Mr. Roy Devereux, great-grandson of the roadbuilder, in a letter to the press says: "During mv researches for the biography of my ancestor which I am now writing I have found no evidence whatever in support of the tradition that the McAdams are descended from the McGregors." Peter M'Caddame had sasine of lands of Craiglure in the earldom of Carrick, 1615 (Laing, 1742). M'Addam and M'Caddam 1581, M'Adame and M'Addame 1605, Maccadam 1604, M'Caddim 1684, McCadamus (Latin) 1671, Makadam and Mackadam 1592, Makadame 1621, Makcaddam 1569, M'Kadam 1647. An extraordinary spelling in 1714 is Mackadadam (its bearer evidently stuttered in pronouncing his name). See also MACCAW.

MACADIE, MACADDIE, MACCADIE. Anglicized forms of G. MacAda, better MacÁdaidh, from Adaidh, the G. dialectal form of Lowland Scots ADIE, q.v. Gillemichel M'Ade and his son Cearmec are famous in Strathardle tradition. Duncan, son of Gillemychel Mᶜath, excambed a davoch of land of Petcarene in Strathardol for the lands of Dolavs Mychel, 1232 (REM., p. 88). John McChaddy and others in Fearn were denounced for oppression in 1596 (RPC., v, p. 304). Robert M'Kadie in Toldaguhill, 1730 (Aberdeen CR.). The Fergusons of Balmacruchie, by a custom common in the Highlands, were known as MacAdies, and even after the families of this sept left Strathardle and settled in the Vale of Atholl they were always known as MacAdies. These MacAdie Fergusons have been identified with the "Clan Aid" of the 1467 MS. whose eponymus Gillamithil son of Aidh falls about the same time as the above Gillemychel Mᶜath. Mac-Ádaidh, an Easter Ross surname, is also an alternative surname for Munro in certain families.

MACAFEE. See under MACFEE.

MACAFFER. See under MACCAFFER.

MACAFILLICHE. ? for Mac an Mhileadha. Thomas McAphiliche in Gawlariche and James McCaphiliche in Wester Gawlairge were charged with murder, 1615 (RPC., x, p. 404). James McAfilliche or McAfillichie in Gerliche or Gearlaig was denounced rebel and prosecuted for carrying arms, 1619 (RPC., XI, p. 574; XII, p. 132).

MACAGOWNE. John McAgoune in Auchinbreck-Glendaruel, a charter witness, 1609 (Poltalloch Writs, p. 136). Allester McEan Riauche VcAgowne in Foirtirlettir was fined for resetting Clan Gregor, 1613 (RPC., XIV, p. 631). John Moir McAgowne in Inruglas was denounced rebel, 1619 (ibid., XI, p. 574), John M'Donachie V'Agoune in Polloch, 1675 (Argyll Sasines, I, p. 245), Archibald Mc agowne, tenant of Ballichoan in Seill, 1669 (HP., IV, p. 224), and Archibald M'Aghoun in Overfairnoch, 1677 (Argyll).

MACAINSH. A form of MACANGUS, q.v. Not very common.

MACAITCHEN. Perhaps a form of Mac Aichan, from MACEACHAN.

MACALASTER, MACALESTER, MACALISTER, MACALLASTER, MACALLISTER, MACCALISTER. G. MacAlasdair, 'son of ALEXANDER,' q.v. Ranald Makalestyr, who obtained a lease of lands in Arran, 1455, is afterwards referred to as Ranald Alexandri, Reginald McAlestir

MACALASTER, Macalester..., continued

(or McAlestere, or McAlestre) (ER., vi, p. 45, 47, 328–329, 419). Alexander Makalester appears in the Black Isle, 1500 (Rose, p. 169). John Makalester had a precept of remission in 1542 (RSS., ii, 4454). Africk McQuhollastar is mentioned in a charter of wadset, 1571 (Scrymgeour Family Docs., p. 71), and Angus McAlester was a follower of Murdow McCloyd in the attack on the galley of the laird of Balcomie, 1600 (RPC., xiv, p. cxxiii). Ferquhar Mackallister in Dunzean Croy, 1603 (Rec. Inv., ii, p. 6). In 1614 the earl of Dunfermline described one Ihone dow Mcalaster as "the greatest limmer and brokin man in all the north" (HP., iii, p. 172). Mac 'Ic Alasdair is the patronymic of the chief of Glengarry. McAlestare 1540, Makalester 1506, Makeallyster 1585, Makallastair 1576, M'Allester 1632, M'Alstar 1548, McAllestyr 1519, Mcillaistrie 1569, Makallestir 1524, McCalister 1682, McCallaster 1686; McAllestar, McAllestair, McAlestar.

MACALBEA. People of this name were tenants on the estate of Balnespick in the latter half of the eighteenth century. The name has entirely died out or become merged with that of Macbean (Grant, An Old Highland farm). It was at one time the common local name in Badenoch of a small sept of Macbains known as Clann 'ac' Albheatha, probably a form of Maelbeth. Popular tradition, ignorant of the true meaning of the name, made the sept of Macbain the descendant of a foundling child left in the retreat of the Young Pretender's army on Alvie Moor, under a birch bush, where some countrymen found the fair-haired boy and brought him up as M'Geal-bheithe, 'White son of the Birch' (Macbain).

MACALDONICH. G. M'Mhaol-domhnaich, from older Mael-Domhnach, 'servant of Sunday,' or 'Sunday's servant.' In Latin the name is rendered Calvus Dominicus. In 1723 Buchanan ranked the M'Aldonichs as a sept of the Buchanans, and stated that many of the name were assuming the surname of Buchanan "so that the old name of Macaldonich will in a short time turn into desuetude" (p. 107). Duncan and Andrew M'Yldonich were tenants of Culcarne in Easter Ross, 1504 (ER., xii, p. 665). The name of another tenant here at the same time, Andrew M'Gilledonich, shows the Gille-form. Henry Makmuldonych is in Strathmore in Caithness, 1540 (RSS., ii, 3715), and Michael Muldonycht was tenant of Brairnahay in the barony of Birnie, 1565 (RMS., iv, p. 443). Donald M'Ildoniche in the barony of Glenlyoun was fined for reset of Clan Gregor,

1613, and John Dow M'Coldnich in Innernuik was prosecuted for illegally carrying arms, 1618 (RPC., xiv, p. 633; xi, p. 415). John M'Aldenych appears in Inveraray, 1629 (Sasines, 286). Hew M'Oldonich in Nether Rudill is in record, 1672, Donald M'Oldonich or MacIldonich was a Seaforth tenant in 1721, and John M'Uildonich appears in North Galston in 1726 (HP., ii, p. 209, 299, 300, 318). Iuldonycht (1510), and V'Oldouvcht (for V'Oldonycht) appear in the Black Book of Taymouth (p. 179), and several M'Oldonichs are there recorded as vassals of Campbell of Glenurquhay (p. 403). As forename: Muldonich McInriauch in Glenlyoun, 1613 (RPC., xiv, p. 633), Meldonich Makilmichael in Bute, 1646 (Hewison, ii, p. 333), and Mildonich M'Ilmanus, 1673 (HP., i, p. 260).

MACALDOWIE, Macaldowy. Current forms of Maclldowie, q.v.

MACALEAR. A variant of Macclure, q.v., current in Galloway. John Macalier signed the Band of Dumfries, 1570 (RPC., xiv, p. 66).

MACALESTER, Macalister. See under MACALASTER.

M'A'LEVECHEL. See under MACMICHAEL.

MACALEWIN. Ewine Macalewin witnessed a confirmation charter by Dunekan, earl of Karic of a charter by Roger de Scallebroc of lands in Carrik in the reign of William the Lion (Melros, i, p. 26). As Ewein MacAlewi he witnessed a charter by Raderic Mac Gillescop of lands in Carric to the Abbey of Melrose in the same reign (ibid., p. 29), and he appears again as witness in the reign of Alexander ii as Iwan filius Alewain (ibid., p. 172).

MACALEXANDER, 'son of Alexander,' q.v. Raynald Mac Alyschandir had a gift of the lands of Upper Kinmylies from Alasdair Carrach in 1398 (REM., p. 211). Tarlach Makalexander had a grant for life of the stewardry of the lands of Kyntyr in 1481 (RMS., ii.). Macalexander had become a patronymic in Carrick by the end of the fifteenth century. John Alexandri, laird of Dalcopene, Ayrshire, is in record c. 1370–80 (Laing, 64). John Alexandersoun and Alexander M'Alexander 'his bruthir' took part in the second hership of Petty in 1513 (Rose, p. 190). John Makalexander was deacon of craft of Stirling in 1555 (SBR., p. 278), and George M'Alexander de Corsclavis was retoured heir of Thomas M'Alexander de Corsclavis, his father, in 1603 (Retours, Ayr, 64). Mckalexander 1689. Probably in some cases Englished ALEXANDERSON, q.v. In Ulster pronounced or rather mispronounced Mac-Kal-shander.

MACALISTER, MACALLISTER. *See under* MACALASTER.

MACALL, MACCALL, MACCAULL, MACKALL. G. *MacCathail*, 'son of CATHAL,' q.v. The M'Calls of Guffokland were an old Nithsdale family. Robert M'Kawele, lord of Karsnelohe, c. 1370–80 (*Laing*, 64). The Maccalls of Ayrshire and the Lowlands have no connection with the Maccolls. The Maccalls of Dumfriesshire were settled there as early as 1500, and are said to be descended from the Macaulays (*Clan Maccoll journal*, IV, p. 37). John M'Call is recorded in Cumbray, 1583 (*Hunter*, p. 31). Matthew McCall in Maybole, charged with reset of rebels in 1607, appears a few days later as McEall (RPC., XIV, p. 507). Quintigern Makcall, bailie of Edinburgh, 1610 (*Laing*, 1597). John M'Call was retoured heir of Patrick M'Call of Guffokland, his father, 1629 (*Retours, Dumfries*, 138). Robert M'Kaal in the parish of Carsfern was charged with being a disorderly person, 1684 (RPC., 3. ser. IX, p. 574). William McAull, merchant councillor of Haddington, 1686 (ibid., XII, p. 544), and John McCaull, bailie of Maybole, 1688 (ibid., XIII, p. 208). William McAall in Auchintgart and Robert McAll gave their bond in the same year (op. cit., p. 318). M'Aull 1667, McCaule, McCawell, and McGal 1684 (*Parish*), Mackall 1672, Makcale and M'Kall 1663; M'Auld, Maccail, McCale, M'Gale, Magall, Megall.

MACALLAN. G. *MacAilin* or *MacAilein*, 'son of ALLAN,' q.v. Dungall M'Alayne was tenant in barony of Buittle, 1376 (RHM., I, p. lx). Gilfelan M'Allan was one of a number who were accused at Stirling assizes, 1477, of the slaughter of Gillaspy MacClery. John McCallane was tenant of Drumnamark, Ardmanoch, 1504 (ER., XII, p. 661). Alexander roy McAllane McReynald and Innes McAllane McRenald had remission for offences, 1541 (ALHT., VIII, p. 19). Robert M'Allane was retoured heir of Allan M'Allane of Langilwinax, his father, 1555 (*Retours, Bute*, 2). Finlay Macallan appears in the Chanonry of Ross, 1578. William McAllan was a follower of Murdow McCloyd in the attack on the galley of the laird of Balcomie, 1600 (RPC., XIV, p. cxxiii). The Aberdeenshire Macallans are said to be descended from an Allan Macfarlane who settled there "several centuries ago" says Buchanan (*Inquiry*, p. 78), and his son instead of calling himself MacFarlane adopted the name MacAllan. The Sutherland MacAllans are really Mackays, the former surname being merely a patronymic (*Old Lore Misc.*, III, p. 179). George McKallan, servitor to Jannet Moir in Aberdeen, 1700 (ROA., I, p. 247).

Mac Mhic Ailein is patronymic of chief of Clanranald. M'Callane, Makcallane, Makallane. Sometimes (as in Bute) Englished ALLAN. M'Callan and M'Calloun 1663. There is M'Allanestoun in Ayrshire, 1622 (*Retours*).

MACALLASTER, MACALLISTER. *See under* MACALASTER.

MACALLAY, MACALLEY. *See under* MACAULAY.

MACALLUM. A form of MACCALLUM, q.v. Here, contrary to the usual rule, the *c* of Callum has been absorbed by the *c* of Mac.

MACALMAN. A form of MACCALMAN, q.v. For loss of second *c* cf. MACALLUM.

MACALONIE. From G. *Mac gill' onfhaidh*, 'servant of storm.' I saw this name on a shop sign in 1925. William Baine Mc Olonie was tenant of Skarrabollis in Islay in 1686, and Duncan McAloney held a 5/- land there in the same year (*Bk. Islay*, p. 492, 516). See MACGILLONIE.

MACALOWNE. Celestine Mac Alowne received a grant of Balemakinrain (now Ballikinrain) in the earldom of Lennox from his kinsman Donald, earl of Lennox, c. 1333–64 (*Strathendrick*, p. 191). John Macalowne on inquest at Narn, 1431 (*Rose*, p. 127). This was an old name of the Napiers in Strathendrick, but does not appear to have been hereditary (*Strathendrick*, p. 194).

MACALPIN, MACALPINE. G. *MacAilpein*, 'son of Ailpean' (see ALPINE). John MacAlpyne witnessed a charter by Malise, earl of Stratherne of the lands of Cultenacloche and others in Glenalmond, c. 1260 (*Grandtully*, I, p. 126). Monach filius Alpini witnessed a charter by Bricius de Ardrossane to Insula Missarum (Inchaffray) in 1271 (LIM., p. 22). As Monauche Macalpin he witnessed a charter by Thomas of Munimuske, c. 1285 (HMC., 2. Rep., p. 166), and as Monach mac Alpy he is a witness to several AthToll charters between 1284 and 1290 (REM., p. 466, 467, 469, 470; Athole, p. 705). He appears again in a memorandum of 1295 as Monathe Macalpy (*Cambus.*, p. 7). In 1296 as Monaghe fiz Alpyn of the county of Perth he rendered homage. His seal bears a fox carrying a dead goose, S' . . . *Macalpyn*(?) (*Bain*, II, p. 200, 532). Duncan Alpynsone of Augh[in]tulus, of Dunbretan also rendered homage, 1296. His seal bears a rabbit, S' *Dvcani F' Alfini* [sic] (ibid., p. 205, 557). Malcolm Macalpyne witnessed a charter by Duncan, earl of Levenax in 1395 (*Levenax*, p. 65); and Sir John Macalpyn or McCalpy, chaplain, was escheat for his part in the re-

MACALPIN, MACALPINE, *continued*

bellion of the late James Stewart, youngest
son of the Regent Albany (ER., IV, p. 493,
524). Mordac Makcalpy of Scotland at the
special request of his cousin Mordak of Fyfe
had permission from the king of England to
attend the schools of Oxford and Cambridge,
1405 (*Bain*, IV, 699). Robert McAlpy was
clerk of justiciary, 1457 (ER., VI, p. 333). A
contract of marriage between Duncan Aquhonam and Agnes Malcalpyn of Camquhil is
recorded, 1475 (SBR., p. 256). In 1507 there
is an entry of marts to Malcolm Makcalpy
in Bute (ER., XII, p. 512). In 1526 Thomas
M'Calpy was found by an assize to have 'faltit
to the bailye of Stirling,' and two years later,
as Thom M'Calpy, he appears as member of
the town council (SBR., p. 26, 276). John
McAlpyn or M'Calpin, prior of the Friar
Preachers of Perth, appears in record between
1531 and 1534 as M'Cappe and McCawpyn
(ER., XVI, p. 60, 358, 369). During his residence in Wittenberg he received from Me-
lancthon the surname of Machabaeus, by which
he is better known. In 1548 payment was made
"to ane hieland officiar of the Levinax callit
Macalpyne" or "Macalpye" (ALHT., IX,
p. 247). A charge was made against a man
in 1671 for mutilating Adam Mccapen (*Just.
Rec.*, II, p. 66); Robert McCalpie was the
king's cook in 1618 (RPC., XI, p. 388), and
James McAlpie was sheriff-clerk of Renfrew,
1688 (ibid., XIII, p. 290). M'Calppin 1591,
M'Calpyne 1569, M'Cavpy 1507, Mackalpe
1509, Makalpe 1511, Makcaply 1519, M'Kal-
pie 1663, Makcalpyn 1421, MkKalpy 1519,
MacKalpin 1534, McKelpin 1507.

In some of the Gaelic poems in the Dean
of Lismore's book S. Patrick is always called
Macalpine (*Padruig mac Alpain*). The Irish
form of this is *Arpluinn*, which represents Latin
Calphurnius or *Calpurnius*.

The appellation "Clan Alpine" has been
given to a number of clans situated at considerable distances from each other, who have
hitherto been supposed to possess a common
descent from Kenneth Macalpine, the ancestor
of a long line of Scottish kings. These clans
are Clan Gregor, the Grants, Mackinnons, Macquarries, Macnabs, and Macaulays. This combination, however, is unknown to the compiler of the MS. of 1467, and is nothing more
than tradition made into pseudo-history by Sir
Walter Scott.

MACALSHONER. A variant of MACALEX-
ANDER, q.v., from the common pronunciation
of Alexander. M'Alshonair 1607.

MACAMHAOIR. Buchanan mentions a surname, *MacAmhaoirs* (pl.), formerly current

in Buchanan parish, but extinct in his day,
which he said meant 'Officer's sons.' The name
evidently has been *Mac a' mhaoir*, 'son of the
officer.' It was probably the source of the
Dumbartonshire surname WEIR.

MACANALLY, MACANNALLY, MACINALLY.
The third spelling is that of a Macfarlane sept
in Dumbartonshire, doubtfully said to be from
Mac Con Ulaidh, 'son of Cu-Uladh' (hound
of Ulidia, East Ulster). In the original text
of the Book of the Dean of Lismore (p. 34)
is Gilcallum m'ynnolaig, rendered in modern
Gaelic text *M'an olave*, and in English 'son of
the chief bard or physician.' It is still found
in the form M'Inally (p. 50n). On p. 34 it
is spelled *M'yn noollew*, which is rendered
on p. 148 as *Mac an ollave*. A footnote on
p. 148, referring to a poem there, says "the
present composition would indicate the author
as being one of the celebrated Beatons, physicians and sennachies to Lords of the Isles.
There are several of the family whose names
were Gilliecallum."

MACANARGUS. Gillepatric Macanargus was
a charter witness in Dumfries between 1214–
59 (LSC., 70). Neum Anargus is also a witness in the same document.

MACANDIE, MACANDY, MACCANDIE, M'KAN-
DY (1816). Of twofold origin. (1) A Highland
border name, *Mac(Sh)anndai*, from Lowland
Scottish 'Sandy.' (2) A small sept in the island
of Bernera, Sound of Harris, is known in Gaelic
as *Clann 'Ic Anndaidh* or *'Ic Anndai*. The sept,
according to the late Dr. Alexander Carmichael, consists of only a few families (*Carmina
Gadelica*, II, p. 313). The name here is from
the Old Norse personal name *Andi*. In the
local folklore the long-tailed ducks are held
to be enchanted Macandies. John McHandie
was tenant under Andro Monro of Newmore,
1580 (RPC., III, p. 319), and perhaps
M'Chandwe in Inverness, 1556 (*Laing*, 638),
is the same name. Johnne McKande was a
follower of Walter Ross of Morange, 1596
(RPC., V, p. 304), and Gilcallum McSagart
Makcandy and Jhone Murdowsone Makcandie
were followers of Murdow McCloyd in the
attack on the galley of the laird of Balcomie in
1600 (RPC., XIV, p. cxxiii).

MACANDO. Allester McAndo Tossoche in
Perthshire was fined for reset of members of
Clan Gregor, 1613 (RPC., XIV, p. 532).

MACANDREW, 'son of ANDREW,' q.v. G. *Mac-
Aindreis*, for earlier *MacGill'Andreis*. The record spellings however have evidently been
taken from the Lowland pronunciation of the
name. There was a small sept of this name

included in Clan Chattan, who were settled at Connage in Petty. Donald Makandro was one of the sufferers from the first hership of Petty, 1502 (*Rose*, p. 176–177). Makallum MacAndro in Murthlac, 1550 (*Illus.*, II, p. 262). Dowgall McAndro Vuyear in Stuckvullige was fined for reset of Clan Gregor, 1613 (RPC., XIV, p. 645). Thomas McAndrew vic William Guy (= Thomas son of Andrew son of Black William), 1618 (*Rec. Inv.*, II, p. 151). John M'Andrie in Blachaig was denounced rebel in 1675 (HP., I, p. 300). McKandrew 1683.

MACANDY. See under MACANDIE.

MACANECOL. Anechol "theinus de Dunine" witnessed the great charter of Earl Gilbert to the Abbey of Inchaffray, c. 1200 (*Inchaffray*, p. 8), and is also witness to other charters relating to the abbey of about the same date (ibid., p. 3, 12, 14). Dovenaldus filius Macynel who had a charter of land in Gleanfreone, "que dicitur Kealbride," c. 1250, is doubtless Donald filius Anecol, seneschallus of Malcolm, 4th earl of Levenax, who appears as charter witness, c. 1285 (*Levenax*, p. 91, 87), and the Dovenaldus MacAnecol who is included in an inhibition by the bishop of Glasgow against the earl of Lennox, 1294 (RMP., p. * 203). As Donald le fiz Ancol of the county of Dunbretan he rendered homage, 1296. His seal bears a hunting horn stringed, rabbit above: S' *Dovenadi Macancol* (*Bain*, II, p. 203, 544). See also ANECOL.

MACANEDUFF. The goods of Dougal Mackaneduff (i.e. son of black John) were distrained in 1498 (OPS., II, p. 527).

MACANELWHEITHE. Ewin Mc Anelwheithe Cameron in Lochaber was one of those who assisted the Macgregors at Glenfruin and Glenfinlas (Irving, *Dumbartonshire*, p. 277).

MACANEMOYLL. George M'Anemoyll or M'Anemoill in Glenlion in 1512–14 (*Rent. Dunk.*, p. 130, 266). Finlay M'Anevoill witnessed a bond of manrent in Glenurquhay, 1559 (BBT., p. 203). Not patronymics, simply 'son of bald John.'

MACANFIRLEGIND. See under MACNERLIN.

MACANGUS, 'son of ANGUS,' q.v. This form of the name is not common, as it seems early to have passed over to MACINNES, q.v. Duncan Makangus had a remission in 1492 (*Cawdor*, p. 80). Duncan McKinwas in Inveraray, 1535 (HP., IV, p. 26). Gilbert M'Kinshe, cordiner, at the Brigend of Dumfries, 1628 (*Dum-*

fries). "Obiit Joannes Dow M'Enos Vc Condoquhy apud Bonrannoch quinto die Nouembris et sepultus in choro de Fortyrgall MVc sexte fowr yeiris" (*Chron. Fort.*, p. 132–133). "Obitus Duncani M'Cowyll [= MacDougal], qui interfectus fuit per Collinum M'Enos de Barbrek in mense Mai anno Domini MVcxij" (ibid., p. 116). Christian M'Canish in Easter Dumfallandie, 1689 (*Dunkeld*). McKinish 1718, Makanys, McKinwis, McYnwiss. Cf. MACCANISH.

MACANN. Current in the Highlands. Probably Ir. *MacAnna*, 'son of Annadh.'

MACANNALLY. See under MACANALLY.

MACANSH. Disguised form of MACANGUS, q.v. James M'Ance was a merchant burgess of Dumfries before 1678 (*Dumfries*).

MACAOMLINN. "The personal name Aomlinn or Amalyn is rare; it appears first in Highland history as the name of a brother of the earl of Lennox in 1224 — Hamelan, Hamelin, and Amelec or Ameleus, evidently a mixture of the Gaelic name Amalgaid and the English Hammelin or Hamblin, the latter prevailing in the end" (*Macbain*). See under AULAY. In Arran M'Amelyne, M'Omelyne, M'Emlinn is the Gaelic patronymic of the Bannatynes of Kames. See also MACEMLINN. G. D. P. in the Weekly Scotsman says it also occurs as MacCiomlain, MacAmlain, MacEamailain, MacMaoljain, and MacAmelyne. Hamelin is a double diminutive of Hamo(n).

MACARA, MACCARRA, 'son of the charioteer,' from OG. *ara*, 'charioteer' (*Pedersen*, II, p. 101). The surname is still current in Perthshire. Macaras were classed as a sept of Macgregor, and were settled in Perthshire mainly in Balquhidder and on the Braes of Monzie near Crieff. They appear as portioners of Drymmie in Stratheam during the seventeenth and eighteenth centuries, and several individuals of the name appear around Dunblane within that period (*Dunblane*). Dowgall McCarres 'tennent to the Laird of Weyme' and John McCarres Leich in Easter Innervaik were fined for reset of Clan Gregor, 1613 (RPC., XIV, p. 634, 636). John M'Ara, officer at Ayr, 1614 (*Ayr*, p. 149). Donald M'Array was portioner of Drumny, Perthshire, in 1667 (RMS., XI, 1078). The Baron McAra was a Perthshire heritor in 1688 (RPC., 3. ser. XIII, p. 332). Rev. John M'Cara was ordained minister of the Burgher meeting house at Burntshels near Kilbarchan, c. 1745, and one M'Carro was concerned in the Rebellion in the same year. Donald M'Ara is recorded in Dalmore, Glenalmond, 1749 (*Dunkeld*); James M'Cara of Crieff matriculated at Glasgow University in

MACARA, MACCARRA, *continued*

1769, as also did John Macara of the parish of Buchanan in 1771; John M'Caira was a private in the Reay Fencibles in 1795 (*Scobie*, p. 374); and Sir Robert Macara, colonel of the Black Watch, was killed at Quatre Bras in 1815. Balmacarra in Lochalsh appears to be "village of Macara."

MACARDLE, MACCARDLE, MACARDELL. From Ir. *Macárdghail*, son of Árdghal, 'super valor.'

MACAREE. A variant of MACARA, q.v. Twelve persons of this name are in the Dunblane Commissariot Record from 1680, and the name was common in Muthill district. The name is believed by some to mean 'son of the king' (*Mac a' righ*), and in Balquhidder it was sometimes Englished 'King' (*Celt. Mon.*, VIII). John Mcaree in Braco, 1698 (*Muthill*).

MACARLY. An Anglicized form of MACCARLICH, q.v. Allaster Mc arliche was hanged for treason, 1615 (*Trials*, III, p. 364). John Mc airlie appears in Monaltrie, 1682 (*Invercauld*, p. 264).

MACARTAIN. A dialectal form of MACARTHUR current in Skye. Hector M'Cartane was one of M'Nachtane's soldiers shipped to France at Lochkerran, 1627 (*Archaeologia Scotica*, III, p. 257).

MACARTHUR, MACCAIRTER, MACCARTER. G. *MacArtair*, 'son of ARTHUR,' q.v. As a clan the Macarthurs were at the height of their power in the middle of the fourteenth century. They received large grants of lands in Lorne and the keepership of the Castle of Dunstaffnage from Robert the Bruce, whose cause they espoused in the War of Independence (RMS., I, App. II, 353, 368, 372, 620, 621). Early in the fifteenth century their power was broken when their chief John MacArthur was beheaded by James I and most of the estates forfeited. The seat of the clan was Strachur, and a sept of the name were hereditary pipers to the Macdonalds of the Isles. A Gaelic saying current in Islay in connection with the antiquity of the Macarthurs is:

"Cnoic is uillt, is Ailpeinich,
  Ach cuin' a thanaig Artaraich?"
(Hills and streams and Alpinites,
  But whence came the Arthurites?)

Carlich Makkerthyre, witness to an obligation by the earl of Ross in 1439 (*Cawdor*, p. 16) is probably the Tarleto M'Erthir mentioned in 1440 (*Rose*, p. 129). Duncan Makarturicht witnessed a charter of lands in Stratherne, 1529 (RMS., III, 861), Gyllemechall M'Carthair is in record, 1569 (*Moray MSS.*, p. 645), and

Dougall M'Airthour was sheriff-clerk of Argyll in 1595 (HP., I). Another Dougall M'Arthour was notary at Glenurquhay in 1580 (BBT., p. 224), and John Dow McNeill VcHarther of Torvadithe, who had a tack of the teinds of Inschald in 1618, appears again in 1630 as Patrick McKairtour of Tullierodiche (LIM., p. 116, 137). Mc harter 1549. Some individuals of this name have dropped the 'Mac' and become Arthurs (but not all Arthurs were originally Macarthurs), and the name has been also translated Arthurson, a form appearing as early as 1427 (HP., II, p. 159). M'Arthor 1589, McArtour 1516, M'Cairtter 1688, M'Carthour 1580, M'Carthur 1529, Makcairter 1640, Mackartar 1690, Makarthour 1518, Makarthure 1507, Makkerthvre 1439, Mc Cartur 1662, Mcerter 1776. General Arthur MacArthur (1845–1912) of Scottish parentage, served in the Philippines, became Lieutenant-General (1906), being the twelfth officer in the history of the U. S. Army to attain that rank. His son, Douglas MacArthur, is equally famous.

MACARTNAY (Fife). *See under* MACCARTNEY.

MACASBAIG. A side form of MACUSBAIG, q.v.

MACASGILL, MACASKILL, MACCASKELL, MACCASKIL, MACCASKILL, MACKASKIL, MACKASKILL. The Gaelic is *MacAsgaill*, derived from the ON. personal name *Askell* (for * *Asketill*, 'the kettle or sacrificial vessel of the Anses,' i.e. gods). Rob Donn (ed. Morrison, p. 443) spells the name MacCasguill. It was a William MacAskill, probably a member of the family of MacCaskill of Ebost, who led the Clan Macleod against the fleet of Clanranald at Eynot, west of Skye, in the sixteenth century (*Henderson*, p. 54). Donald M'Askle was a corporal in the Reay Fencibles in 1795 (*Scobie*, p. 370), and Calum MacAsguill is author of "Bearnaraidh na h-Earradh" (in *Alba*, I, no. 4, 1920). Angus McAskill, born in Lewis, died in Cape Breton August 8th, 1863, in his thirty-eighth year. He was 7 feet 9 inches in height, and was known as the Cape Breton Giant. (One of his boots, 16 inches in length, is preserved in the Provincial Museum, Halifax.) A ridiculous bombastic work by James D. Gillis, purporting to be an account of his life, was published in Halifax, Nova Scotia, in 1919, under the title, *The Cape Breton Giant: a truthful memoir*. The Macasgills are known as *Clann t-Asgaill*, and the euphonic *t* has given rise to a forename, *Taskill*, Taskel M'Rory, 1745. Macaiskill 1790, Mackaiscail 1766. Mackaiscal (in Crosple) 1769, Mackaiskill 1783, Mackascal 1769.

MACASH. An uncommon form of MACCASH, q.v.

MACASKIE, MACCASKIE. A Galloway surname. G. *MacAscaidh*, 'son of Ascaidh,' a pet form of Askell (see MACASGILL). Thom McKasky was one of the workmen engaged in "the byggen of the kyngis rowbarge byggyte in Dunbretane" in 1494 (ALHT., I, p. 245). Thomas Makcasky was reidare at Clasfurde, 1574 (RMR.), and another Thomas M'Caskie was admitted burgess freeman of Glasgow, 1588 (*Burgesses*).

MACASKILL. See MACASGILL.

MACASKIN. This name is akin to if not the same as Macaskill. There is a Loch Mhic Chaiscin (better Mhic Ascain) in Lorne (*Gillies*, p. 61). See MACASGILL.

MACASLAN, MACASLAND, MACASLIN. Forms of MACAUSLAN, q.v.

MACATH. Kenneth mac aht (*ht* here, as often, written for *th*), an enemy of the king of Scotland, 1215, "was probably a relative, possibly a son of Malcolm Macheth († 1168)" (ES., II, p. 404). Duncan M'Ath had a grant of two quarters of land together with the office of serjeandrie from King Robert I (RMS.). In 1232 the lands of Dolays Mychel were granted in excambion to Duncanus filius Gillemychel M'ath (REM., p. 87–88). The patronymic Macheth seems to have become a family name. See HETH and MACHETH.

MACAUGHTRIE. A Galloway surname. 'Rollant MacUchtraigh ri gallgaidhel in pace, quiaevit' (AU., 1199), 'Roland MacUchtraigh leader of the Gall-Gaidil died in peace.' John Macuchtrie witnessed a charter of coronator of Lennox, 1400 (*Levenax*, p. 95). Janet M'Cuchtrie at Milburn, 1685, and William M'Ouchtrie in Flularg, 1687 (*Kirkcudbright*). The name appears in Anglicized form in 1522, in which year Fergus Uthresoun purchased the lands of Strongassail in the Stewartry of Kirkcudbright (RMS., III, 1094). See COUGHTREY. The duke of Argyll says that "a race called MacUchtre, who are designated as of 'Garvie,' long held these lands which are in Glendaruel of the earls of Argyll in the Middle Ages" (*Celt. Rev.*, IX, p. 347). He adds that they "gradually Anglicised their name to Ochiltree (Argyll Charters, *passim*)."

MACAULAY, MACAULEY, MACALLAY, MACALLEY, MACAULLAY, MACAULLY, MACCALLY, MACCAULAY, MACCAULY. (1) G. *MacAmhalghaidh*, 'son of Amalghaidh,' an old Irish personal name, pronounced almost as Macaulay or Macowley. From this comes the name of the Dumbartonshire Macaulays. (2) G. *MacAmhlaibh* or *MacAmhlaidh*, 'son of Amlaib,' the old Gaelic form of N. *Olafr*. From this comes the Hebridean name Macaulay. Duncan filius Auleth witnessed a charter by Malcolm, earl of Levenax, c. 1285 (*Levenax*, p. 87). As Duncan Macameleth he witnessed a grant to his cousin Murechauch filius Kork by Thomas de Cremennane c. 1290 (ibid., p. 80). In 1326 there is entry of a payment of cheese to two men of Iwar McAulay in Lennox (ER., I, p. 57). Awla McAwla of Ardencapill appears in 1536 (RSS., II, 2152), and we have McCalla of Ardincapill in 1592. Another Awla McAwla was clerk of the watch of Queen Mary's guard, 1566 (MCM., I, p. 35). Duncan M'Auihlay was minister of Fortingall, 1581 (BBT., p. 226). John Makalley was indweller in Inverness, 1602 (*Rec. Inv.*, II, p. 3), and John Dow McAwla and Awla McAwla, his son, in Gairlochhead, were fined for reset of clan Gregor, 1613 (RPC., XIV, p. 643). John M'Kauley, merchant burgess of Edinburgh, was heir of Thomas M'Cauley there, 1623 (*Inquis.*, 1100), and Thomas Makcaulay, writer to the signet in Edinburgh, 1638, appears in 1647 as M'Callow and in 1648 as M'Calley (ibid., 829, 988, 1000). John Dow M'Aule appears in Glenfalloch in 1638 (BBT., p. 401), John Mackalla was armourer and sword-sliper in Edinburgh, 1684 (BOEC., IX, p. 133), and George Makallay was retoured heir of Patrick M'Kalla, apothecary in Cupar, 1688 (*Retours, Fife*, 1298). Hume of Crossrig (*Diary*, p. 127) mentions a controverted election in Haddington, 1703, between Provost McCalla and Edgar the late provost. M'Ala 1582, M'Alay 1546, M'Aula 1717, M'Aulla 1740, McAullay 1721, Macawlay 1591, M'Cala 1582, McCalius (in Latin doc.) 1622, M'Calla and Makcalla 1606, McCallay 1528, McCalley 1598, M'Callie and Mackaula 1663, McCally 1707, McCaula 1589, McCaulaw 1541, McCaulay 1603, McKaula 1686, Makkalay 1454, M'Kallay 1604.

MACAULD. Not a surname but a careless phonetic rendering of *MacChathail*, a name with which it has no connection etymological or otherwise. See MACALL.

MACAULLY. See under MACAULAY.

MACAUSLAN, MACAUSLAND, MACAUSELAN, MACAUSLANE, MACAUSLIN, MACCASLANE, MACCAUSLAND, MACASLAN, MACASLAND, MACCASLAND, MACASLIN, MACCASLINE, 'son of Absalon.' The first of the name recorded appears to be Absalon, son of Macbed (or Macbethe), a churchman, to whom a charter of the island called Clarines (Clarinch in Loch Lomond, later the gathering place of Clan Buchanan)

MACAUSLAN, Macausland..., continued
was granted by Maldoun or Maldouen, third
earl of Lennox, in 1225 (*Lennox*, II, p. 4).
Between 1208–14 as Absalon or Absalone,
'clericus meus,' he witnessed the gift by Ale-
win, second earl of Lennox of the church of
Kamsi (Campsie) to God and S. Kentigern,
and also witnessed the gift of the church of
Cadinros or Cardinros (now Cardross) by
Maldouen, son and heir of Alwin, to the same
(REG., p. 87, 88, 93). As dominus Absalone
de Buchkanan he witnessed Earl Maldowen's
charter to Sir Robert Herthford, precentor of
Glasgow, before 1224 (RMP., p. 217). Absalone, 'senescallus meus' or 'clericus meus',
probably son of Absalon son of Macbed, appears several times as a charter witness between
1238 and c. 1240 (*Levenax*, p. 13, 91, 96, 98).
Absalone, son of Absalone, probably the third
of the name, along with his brothers Gilbert
and Mathew, appear as witnesses between
1273 and 1315 (ibid., p. 15, 16, 20, 85, 99),
and Gilbert filius Absalon served on an inquisition in Dumbartonshire, 1271 (RMP.,
p. 191). Malcolm Macabsolon witnessed a
confirmation charter by Robert I to Sir John
Colquhoun, 1308 (*Lennox*, II, p. 407), and
"Anslan Macgilespie de Lany" (c. 1330) is
mentioned in an old genealogical tree of the
Lanys of that Ilk compiled probably before
1540 (*Strathendrick*, p. 292). It may have
been a Macauslan who killed the duke of
Clarence, brother of Henry V of England, at
the battle of Beaugé in 1421, as the duke's
circlet of gold was brought into camp by
Alexander Macausland (*Book of Pluscardyn*).
Patrick McCaslane of Caldanacht and Donald
McCaslane his brother were followers of the
earl of Argyll in 1536 (RSS., II, 2152), and
the death of Katherine N'Chastyllan at Slattych
in Glenlyon is recorded in 1542 (*Chr. Fort.*,
p. 121). John McAslen in Auchingech and
Patrik More McCaslen in Auchingyle, were
fined for aiding outlawed Clan Gregor, 1613
(RPC., XIV, p. 644). The McCauslands of
Drenagh, county Londonderry, are descended
from the Macauslans of Dumbartonshire.
Makaslane 1478.

MACAVERY. Donald McAverry, 1607
(RPC.). John M'Avyr or M'Awyre appears
as witness in Glenurquhav, 1566 and 1573
(BBT., p. 211, 220). Laran M'Avyre in
Cranich, a Glenorchy vassal, 1638, and John
M'Avyre appears in Craig in same year (ibid.,
p. 401, 402). The name is recorded in Gallo-
way after 1700 (*Dudgeon*).

MACAVI. Iain Mc avi, tenant in Loyng, 1669
(HP., IV, p. 222). Perhaps from Ir. *Mac an
bheathadh*, "son of life," or from Ir. *Mac*

Dháibhidh, a variant of *Mac Dáibhidh*, "son
of David."

MACAVISH, Maccause, Maccavish, Mac-
cawis, Maccaws. In G. *MacThàmhais*, 'son
of Tammas,' the Scottish form of Thomas. John
Gorum Mactawvs was a charter witness in
Glasgow in 1456 (LCD., p. 179). Duncan
Makcawvs acquired the five mark land of
Ardequhlg in Weem in 1475 (SBR., p. 256).
Donald McCawis was tenant of Eglisdisdane
and Balnegregane in 1480 (ER., IX, p. 561),
and Donald M'Awis, son and heir of the late
Duncan M'Awis is in record in 1482 (*Scot.
Ant.*, XI, p. 30). Duncan M'Cause and Allan
M'Cause, bailies on the lands of Glastre in
Argyllshire belonging to James Scrimgeour,
constable of Dundee, in 1490, appear in the
following year as Makavhis (HP., II, p. 188,
190). The death of Donald M'Cawis is recorded in the Chronicle of Fortirgall in 1494;
Henry M'Cawis was a witness in Avrshire in
1485, and Thomas M'Cawis, a member of the
same family, held land there in 1505 (RMS.,
II, 1639, 2899). Lauchlan M'Cawis was vicar
of Lochgoyle in 1528, and Roland or Ronald
Makawis was vicar of Inchalt in 1542–45
(RMS., III, 556, 2909, 3132). John M'Caws
appears as juror on an assize in Ayrshire, 1532
(ibid., 1196), and in the same year a pre-
cept of legitimation was issued to Lauchlan
Makcawis, natural son of Eugene Makcaus
(RSS., II, 1188). John McPhadrick VcAlves
in Auchingyle, and Duncan Ger McAves in
Little Ballernick were fined for reset of Clan
Gregor, 1613 (RPC., XIV, p. 644). Thomas
M'Cawis was served heir to John M'Cawis, his
granduncle's son, in two marks and a half
of the lands of Leanach in the barony of
Strathlaffin 1627 (*Retours, Argyllshire*, 28).
Donald McGillechallum VcEane Dow Vc-
Cavves was charged with fire-raising in 1628
(RPC., 2. ser. II, p. 517); Donald McCaweis
was servitor to Campbell of Inverlevir, 1655
(*Poltalloch Writs*, p. 75); and Duncan Mc-
Caueis in Ardphuir Castell witnessed a testament in 1676 (*Genealogist*, new ser., XXXII,
p. 24). Duncan McAvis was tacksman of Kep-
progane in 1684, and Donald Moir McAvish,
tacksman of Corpleyne in the same year (RPC.,
3. ser. VIII, p. 569). Tavish Mc cavish was
rebel in Killean, Kintyre, 1685 (*Commons*,
p. 3), and Tais Mcavish, elder of Kenmore
Kirk, 1729 (FB., p. 359). McAwis 1483,
M'Awishe 1595, M'Cavss 1618, M'Cauish 1694,
M'Cavish 1693, Makcawis 1545, McKawes
1651, VcKaviss 1533, M'Avish, M'Cavis, Mak-
caws.

MACAVOY, Macevoy. These names are of
Irish origin, found mainly on the West coast

about Glasgow and in Ayrshire, and appear in Galloway only after 1700. From Ir. *Mac a' bhuidhe*, a shortened form of *Mac giolla bhuidhe*, son of *Giolla buidhe*, 'yellow (haired) lad.' Macavy in the '45.

MACAWUTHONE. David McAwuthone was tenant in Strathdee in 1527 (*Grant*, III, p. 68). The *u* is most probably for *n* and the name = Mac Antony, 'son of Anthony.'

MACAYG. Makeg filius Kyin witnessed a grant of lands in Carric in the reign of Alexander II (*Melros*, p. 172). Angus Eyg de Strathnawir received a charter in 1415 (ADC.), and Odo Macayg was rector of S. Conanus in Yle before 1427 (*Pap. Lett.*, VIII, p. 24). In 1456 we have record of Aytho Faurcharsone (*Bann. Misc.*, III, p. 93). Cf. AYG and see under MAC-KAY.

MACBAIN, MACVAIN. G. *Mac a' ghille bhain.* Patrick M'Vaine in Tullich and John M'Vaine in Teray were Glenurquhay vassals in 1638 (BBT., p. 399). Alexander Macbain (1855–1907) was one of Scotland's foremost Celtic scholars. The names are sometimes confused with MACBEAN.

MACBARDIE. John Mackbardie in Crathinaird, 1634 (SCM., II, p. 139).

MACBARNET. Son of Barnet. Donaldus Mac Barnat recorded in Murthlac, 1650 (*Illus.*, II, p. 261). See BARNET.

MACBARRON, 'son of the baron.' It was a Gaelic custom to call small landed proprietors a baron. Finlaw Macawaran, who consented to his mother's surrender of her share of the lands of Glenserw in 1403 (OPS., II, p. 86), was a Maccorquodale. John Rose, first of Wester Drakies, third son of Hugh the ninth laird of Kilravock, was called Mac-a-Bharon (*Rose*, p. 526). The name occurs in Inverness in the sixteenth century as M'Barroun. The 'Mac' is now dropped, and Barron is a well-known surname there. Robert Makwarrane witnessed a charter of lands in the barony of Duntreith, 1531 (RMS., III, 1000), and Malcolme Makwarron was a follower of the earl of Argyll, 1536 (RSS., II, 2152). The name of Donald Makvarraniche, servitor in Inverness (*Laing*, 1399), is from the adjectival form of the name in *-ach*. James Steuart alias McVarroun was free burgess and guild brother of Inverness, 1607 (*Rec. Inv.*, II, p. 52). John and Donald McBarroun are mentioned in the same document as McCarroun in 1619, and Duncan McAvarrane Vc-Clauchlane and Robert Awarrane VcLauchlane in Innerchuirie were also punished in 1619

for illegally carrying firearms (RPC., XII, p. 112–113, 134). Robert M'Barron was a charter witness in Dunblane, 1539 (RMS., III, 1974), and James M'Barroun was a witness in Inverness, 1586 (*Laing*, 1111). Thomas McWarron in Bunchrwe, 1672 (IDR., p. 28). Old: McKvarran, McVarroun. See also BARRON.

MACBAXTER. A Highland border name meaning 'son of the baker' (Scots *baxter*). Donald M'Baxtar witnessed an instrument of sasine of Craginche in 1493 (OPS., II, p. 97). The escheat of William Macbaxtar is recorded in 1543 (ALHT., VIII, p. 214), Donald Makbaxstar was one of the 'boyis' of John, bishop of the Isles in 1585 (*Cawdor*, p. 187), and John McVaxter held a kerrowran in Islay in 1686 (*Bk. Islay*, p. 503). A 'kerrowran' is probably an old local measure of land equivalent to a 'groatland.'

MACBAY, MACBEY. G. *MacBeatha (Bheatha).* John M'Bay gave his bond to John Campbell of Glenurquhay in 1547 (BBT., p. 184). Patrick M'Ba was admitted burgess of Glasgow, 1601 (*Burgesses*), and Callome McBee and Donald McBee in Brockland were fined for reset of outlawed Macgregors, 1613 (RPC., XIV, p. 640). Archibald Reoche Bea or McBea in Torsarie, Mull, was put to horn in 1629 (RPC., 2. ser. II, p. 341; III, p. 45). Janet M'Bae in Brockland, 1665 (*Dunblane*). See also under MACVAY.

MACBEAN. G. *Macbheathain*, 'son of Beathan.' See BEAN. Ferquhar M'Bane took part in the second hership of Petty, 1513 (*Rose*, p. 190). Duncan mc behan in Dunmakglass was bailie of James, earl of Murray, 1539, and Malcolm Makbahing, servant of John, bishop of the Isles to get payment from the lord of Calder, 1585 (*Cawdor*, p. 163, 187). Jonet M'Bend (*d* accretionary) appears in Stirling, 1617 (MCM., I, p. 454), and Alexander McBen in Balquhidder was to be tried for theft, 1621 (RPC., XII, p. 412). In 1621 Angusius M'Beane M'Robert M'Key de Tardarroche was declared heir Avui alia Ay M'Beane M'Robert, fratris germani, "in terris dimidietatis davatae villae et terrarum de Tordarroche in baronia de Castellends de Innerness, pro principali; — terris dimidietatis villae et terrarum de Tulliche, in baronia de Tulliche et Ellerk, in warrentum" (*Retours*, *Inverness*, 39). Farquhar McBean alias McCoilbea had a tack of the half-auchten part of Leald, 1725. His father is mentioned in 1727 as John McAllvia. Alexander MacBean was one of the compilers of Dr. Samuel Johnson's Dictionary of the English language. The Macbeans in Alvie were known as *Clann 'ac al bheatha* for fuller *MacMaolbheatha*, 'son of

MACBEAN, *continued*

the servant of life.' There was also a *Gille*-form as shown by M'Illbea (1773) for *M'Gille-beatha.* See also MACALBEA and MACVEAN.

MACBEATH, MACBEITH. Current forms of MACBETH, q.v. Gillemechell M'Bathe held a tenement in Dornoch, 1504 (OPS., II, p. 639). Robert Mackbayth in the parish of Nesting, Shetland, 1576 (*Oppressions*, p. 21). John M'Beath, heir of Fergus M'Beath of Ballinab, 1628 (*Retours, Argyll*, 33). M'Baith 1663.

MACBEHAIG. The form of Macbeth in Wester Ross. G. *M'Bheathaig*. John McBehaig and Duncane M'Behaig were servants to John Campbell, prior of Ardchattan, 1622 (RPC., XII, p. 665). It also occurs in Ross as *M'Pheathaig*, and is spelled in the Fernaig MS. (1688) M'Pehaig (*Rel. Celt.*, II, p. 90).

MACBELE. Aulon Macbele, a "nativus" (serf), was gifted to the bishop of Moray, a. 1184 (REM., p. 5).

MACBETH. A personal name like Macrae, not a patronymic. It was common in Scotland in early times from the eleventh to the fourteenth century. In old Gaelic it was spelled *Macc bethad*, and means 'son of life,' 'a religious person,' 'man of religion,' or 'one of the elect.' In modern Gaelic the name would be spelled *Macbeatha*. A twelfth-century variant, Mal-beth, is found in record as Malbet, Melbeth, Malbeod, Melbec (with *t* misread as *c*), Malbij, Melbe and Melbeht. Macbeth (1005–1057), mormaer of Moray, became king of Scots after having murdered King Duncan I at Bothnagowan near Elgin, 14th August 1040. "The use he made of his acquired power so far as authentic records show, was generally for the good of his country; while his character, far from being irresolute, was marked by vigour and ability. He was the friend of the poor, the protector of the monks, and the first Scottish king whose name appears in ecclesiastical record as the benefactor of the Church" (Mackenzie, *A short history of the Scottish Highlands and Isles*, 1906, p. 39).

MACBETHSON. Thomas Macbethson was bailie of Forfar, 1361 (ER., II, p. 62). Donald McBeithson and John McBeithsoun took part in the slaughter of William Suthirland of Duffus, 1531.

MACBEY. *See under* MACBAY.

MACBHEATRAIS. One MacBheatrais or Mac-Beathaig in the middle of the seventeenth century was hereditary bard of the Macdonalds of Sleat. He is mentioned in Maccodrum's

'Dimoladh piob Dhomhnuill Bhain' (*Poems and songs*, Glasgow, 1894, p. 53). Forbes says a family named MacBheattrais, MacBheatrais, or MacBeathaig were bards in Skye (*Place-names of Skye*, p. 26).

MACBIRNIE, MACBURNIE, MACBURNEY. The first form occurs often in the Acts of Parliament of Scotland in the early seventeenth century. The name is of Norse origin, from the personal name *Bjarni* (= bear, N. *björn*, a bear), and is therefore parallel to the name Matheson (in Gaelic *M'Mhathain*) and Irish Macmahon (*MacMathghamhain*). David M'Birny was a witness in Kirkcudbright in 1466 (RMS., II, 907), and in 1494 mention is made of the spouse of John Makbirny (ALA., II, p. 356). Cuthbert McBurnie was appointed "Brigmaistre" of Dumfries in 1520 (*Edgar*, p. 203–204). John Makbirny had sasine of lands in Dunscoir in 1591 (ER., XXII, p. 538), and a later John M'Burnie was retoured heir of John M'Burnie of Row in 1680 (*Retours, Dumfries*, 302). William McBurney in the parish of Balmaghie, 1684 (RPC., 3. ser. IX, p. 573). Machburny 1684, Mackbirnie and Mackbirnye 1607. See also BURNIE.

MACBLACKIE. Recorded in Dufftown, seventeenth century. A partial rendering of G. *Mac Gille Dhuibh*, 'son of the black lad.' Alexander Makblaky had a remission for being absent from the army at Solway, 1527 (*Grant*, III, p. 72). Willelmus Mac Blake or Mac Blakke in Murthlac, 1550 (*Illus.*, II, p. 261, 262).

MACBLAIN, MACBLANE. These names are found mainly in the shires of Ayr and Wigtown. The full form was *Mac Gille Bláán*, as shown by the name Gilcomgal mac Gilblaan, who witnessed a grant by Ranulfus filius Dunegal, c. 1124–65, of his heritage in Dumfries to the Hospital of S. Peter of York (*Bain*, II, 1606; *Edgar*, p. 217). Forbes (*Kalendars of Scottish saints*) says S. Blaan or Blane was son of Etha, sister of S. Cathan. His day is August 10, A. D. 590. In the life of the saint compiled by George Newton, archdeacon of Dunblane, he is said to have been son of a daughter of Aidan, king of the Scots Dalriads. There is a notice of the amerciament of one M'Blane in 1473 (ALHT., I, p. 11), and Patrick M'Blayne or M'Blane was a witness in Wigtownshire in 1484 (RMS., II, 1623). John McBlaine, witness in Irvine, 1500 (*Simon*, 7), John M'Blayne or M'Blane and Nic. M'Blane appear as burgesses of Wigtown in 1536 and 1539 (*Laing*, 408; RMS., III, 1971), and Gilbert M'Blayne was burgess there in 1527 (*M'Kerlie II*, II, p. 161). Thomas M'Blane was clerk of Glasgow diocese and notary public in 1618 (*Laing*, 1793), and Andrew M'Blaine in Kilkerran, Ayrshire, was charged with molestation in 1628 (RPC., 2. ser. II, p. 543). McBlean 1649, Mackblayne 1690. Recorded in Edinburgh 1942. The Mac seems to have been dropped by some of the name early in the eighteenth century.

MACBLAIR. Nigel MacBlare had a charter from Donald, earl of Lennox of the lands of Fynwyk (Finnick) c. 1333–4 (*Strathendrick*, p. 212; *Levenax*, p. 55). Ensign Thomas Mac-Blair is mentioned in 1585 (APS., III, p. 394a).

MACBLAIRTICH. Muldonych Makblairtych witnessed a sasine at Forlyngis, 1546 (HP., IV, p. 30).

MACBLANE. See under MACBLAIN.

MACBLAREN. Swene McBlarene, a charter witness at Ellanrie, 1582 (*Poltalloch Writs*, p. 135), and John McBlaren in Dundorne was fined for resetting Clan Gregor, 1613 (RPC., XIV, p. 638). Donald M'Blaren in Dunnamuke and Duncan M'Blaren in Over Scherewaine appear in 1672 (HP., II, p. 207, 209), and Gilbert Mcblaren was a rebel in Kilmichell-Glassarie, 1685 (*Commons*, p. 7).

MACBRABNER. 'Son of Brabner.' See under BREMNER. Complaint was made against Alester McBrabnar in Caddell, 1578 (RPC., III, p. 51). John Makbrebar alias Ochan (? = O'Cain) was concerned in an action of spulzie, 1603 (RSCA., II, p. 35).

MACBRADDEN. Recorded in Argyllshire in 1746. G. *MacBraddin*, 'son of Bradan,' a name meaning 'salmon.' Faelán ('Wolfie') mac Bradán ('salmon') mac Breac ('trout,' 'speckled') was killed in the Daimhliag (church) of Lismor-Mochuda, by Maelseachlainn, son of Muircheartach, son of Breac (AFM., 1051). See BRADEN.

MACBRAID. See under MACBRIDE.

MACBRAIR, MACBRAIRE, MACBRIAR. "Of all the families springing from Dumfries the Mac-Brairs have the longest and most honourable connection, having been virtually hereditary provosts of the burgh for nigh 150 years" (*Edgar*, p. 197). Andrew McBrair was bailie of Dumfries in 1384 (ER., III, p. 125), and in 1473 a remission was granted to Herbert M'Brare (ALHT., I, p. 5). Alexander M'Bair (for M'Brair) and John Dominik M'Bair were witnesses in Bute, 1491 (ADC., p. 203). Robert McBrayr, provost of Dumfries, and Nicholas McBravr, his son, are mentioned in 1481 (*Dumfriesshire and Galloway Nat. Hist. and Ant. Soc., Trans.*, 3. ser. XXI, p. 106). Nicholaus

McBraer was alderman of Dumfries, 1503 (*Simon*, 59). Mention is made in 1499 of the 'movable gudis and money' of umquhile Cuthbert McBrar in Dumfries (RSS., I, 411), Sir John Mc brare, chaplain, was murdered in 1502 (*Trials*, I, p. *39), and John M'Brair was a canon of Glenluce in 1548. "The name of M'Brair," says Sir Herbert Maxwell, "contains in itself a reproach to a celibate order — *Mac brathair* (braher) the friar's son" (*History of Dumfries*, p. 191). Macbraar 1533, Makbraar 1557, McBraare 1494, M'Braier 1667, Makbrair 1510, Makbraire 1506, McBrar 1500, McBrayr 1444, M'Brayre 1573, McBraver and McKbrair 1684, Makbrayre 1667, Makbriar 1579.

MACBRATNEY, MACBRATNIE. An old Galloway surname. G. *Mac Breatnaigh*, 'son of the Briton' (of Strathclyde). Cf. GALBRAITH. The fermes of Clontag and Knockane in Galloway were granted to Martin Birtny or Macbirtny, 'chiteriste,' in 1471 (ER., VIII, p. 89). Elsewhere in the same record Martin appears as Makbrechne (1473, p. 163), McBartny (1474, p. 215), Makbretny (1475, p. 287), Vertue (1477, without 'Mac,' p. 420), and M'Berkny (1479, p. 605). During the years 1502–07 he still enjoyed the fermes of Knokan for his fee, and during these years his name is given variously as Makbretny, Makbarkny, Makbretne, and McBertny. John McBretny was burgess of Quhithern in 1532 (RMS., III). Gillinveine M'Vretny in Killmaluag in Kelislate is in record in 1723 (*Campbell*, I, p. 188). In Galloway the spellings McBraten, McBretnie, and Malbratnie are found in 1684 (*Parish*). Lauchlan Mcbretnach was a rebel in Kilberrie, 1685 (*Commons*, p. 4). McVrettny 1685.

MACBRAYNE. G. *Mac a' Bhriuthainn*, 'son of the judge.' Writing in 1630 Sir Robert Gordon describes the breive as "a kynd of judge amongst the ilanders, who hath an absolute judicatorie, vnto whose authoritie and censure they willinglie submitt...betuein partie and partie" (*A Genealogical history of the earldom of Sutherland*, Edinburgh, 1813, p. 268). As the office was hereditary it placed great power for good or evil in the hands of men "whose qualifications, as arbitrators, must have been of an unequal nature; and whose judgments can hardly have been free from bias" (Mackenzie, *Outer Hebrides*, p. 62). The "chapellanry of Sanct Colme and Sanct Finlagane situat in the isle of Ilaa...vacand be the deces of schir Angus Macbreochane" in 1503 (RSS., I, 911). Eugenius Makbrehin was a student at St. Andrews, 1525 (ERUS., p. 220). Duncan M'Breyane in Cnocknalelit and Anna

MACBRAYNE, continued

M'Breyne in Gortenagor appear in 1672 (HP., II, p. 207, 209), and Donald McBrayan held a *kerroran* (probably equivalent to a 'groatland') in Islay, 1686 (*Bk. Islay*, p. 518). Duncan Mcbrain and Archibald Mcbrain were rebels in Argyllshire, 1685 (*Commons*, p. 4, 6). One MacBraine, an employee in Mackintosh's 'secret work' for the manufacture of cudbear, sold the secret of manufacture to a company in England at the end of the eighteenth century.

MACBRE. One, McBre, a Moray 'proditor,' was hanged in Edinburgh in 1468 (ER., VII, p. 544), and a later M'Bre was keeper of the cattle of the bishop of Dunkeld in the summer of 1512 (*Rent. Dunk.*, p. 187). Perhaps = MACBREW.

MACBREBITER. In Gaelic *breabadair* means "one who kicks," and was applied to a weaver from his kicking the beam of his loom in the process of weaving, and later was understood in a general way as equivalent to "weaver." John and Androw MacInbrebiter were charged with oppression of Grissell Dunbar of Little Rany in 1596 (RPC., v, p. 305). John Mc-Brebair Glas in Glencoinges was denounced as a rebel in 1619 (RPC., XI, p. 574), Finlay M'Inbrebiter of Leadlie took the Test in Rossshire, 1685 (RPC., 3. ser. XI, p. 417), and John McVrebider in Nether Shadir was tenant on the Seaforth estate in 1726 (HP., II, p. 315).

MACBRECK. Sir Andrew M'Brek (M'Brec, Makbrek), who appears frequently in the Lord High Treasurer's Accounts at the end of the fifteenth century, was almoner to King James IV. In 1504 there was a petition in his favor of collation of the provostry of Lincloudane (RSS., I, 1017). Alexander M'Brek appears as burgess of Perth, 1522 and 1531 (SCM., IV, p. 198; *Methven*, p. 45). Sir Archibald M'Brak was a pope's knight of Cambuskenneth Abbey, 1546 (*Laing*, 505), Alexander Makbrek was witness in Edinburgh, 1552 (*Aboyne*, p. 55), Henry M'Brek had feu of quarterlands of Lurg from Abbey of Culross, 1587 (PSAS., LX, p. 82), and Alexander McBrek was heir of Robert Merser, 1608 (*Retours, Perth*, 1090). As the church of Dunrod in Kirkcudbrightshire, not far from Kirkmabreck, was dedicated to S. Mary and S. Brioc, the latter a disciple of S. Germanus of Auxerre, the name is probably connected with him. Symson (*Description of Galloway*, p. 46) states that about thirty years previous to the time of his writing (i.e. c. 1650) part of a statue in wood of S. M'Breck, as he calls him, was to be seen in a chapel at Ferrietown, a little clachan upon the Cree.

MACBRENYN. G. and Ir. *MacBranain*, son of Bran, an Old Gaelic personal name. John Macbrenyn, priest of diocese of Glasgow and perpetual chaplain of Dumfries, petitioned the Pope for the living of Botyl (Buittle) in the diocese of Whithorn, 1381 (*Pap. Pet.*, I, p. 556). As Sir John McBreny he rendered to Exchequer the accounts of the bailies of Dumfries, 1398–99 (ER., III, p. 446, 476).

MACBREW. An old Strathblane surname possibly derived from 'Gilcolmun filius Dovenaldi Macbref' mentioned in an inhibition by the bishop of Glasgow directed against Malcolm, earl of Lennox and his adherents in 1294 (RMP., p. * 203). The name means 'son of the judge,' from *britheimh*, the genitive of *britheamh*. Alexander Makbreif, a follower of Donald Gorme of Sleat, had a remission for his part in the hership of Kenlochew and Trouternes in 1541 (RSS., II, 3943), and Angus McBref, John Dow McBreif, and Angus Mc-Keane Bref were followers of Murdow Mc-Cloyd of Codzauch in Lewis in his attack on the galley of the laird of Balcomie, one of the Fife adventurers, in 1600 (RPC., XIV, p. cxxiii). Mikbrew 1681. See also MACBRE.

MACBRIAR. *See under* MACBRAIR.

MACBRIDAN. A pet or diminutive form of MACBRIDE, q.v., in Gaelic *M'Bhridein*. At Shiskine in Arran the name is occasionally pronounced *MacFrideinn*, and at Southend the *bh* is elided and the name may be heard pronounced as 'Ac 'Rideinn (TGSI., XXI, p. 245). Margarite McBridin had a precept of remission "pro murthuro unius viri inventi [? iuventi] in domo de Barlokert" in 1529 (RSS., II, 448). Gilbert M'Bridan in Bracklev, parish of Killean, is in record in 1686 (*Argyll*), and Mary M'Briden in Brenquhillinie in 1692 (*Argyll Inv.*).

MACBRIDE, MACBRYDE, MACBRAID. G. *Mac Brighde* for earlier *Mac GilleBrighde*, 'son of the servant of Bride,' virgin abbess of Kildare who died 525 A.D. Cristinus McBryd, a man of Thomas de Moravia, had remission of a fine in 1329 (ER., I, p. 592). Giolla Calluim mc ilebhride mhic Phersoin chille-comain (*Rel. Celt.*, I, p. 136). John McGilbride was captain of Bute, 1370–75, and Macbride is an old name in Arran. In 1684 the name appears as McBryd, McBrid, and McKbrid (*Parish*). The form Macilbride was much used in olden time in the lordship of Doune: Makilbred, Makgilbred, M'Gilbrid, 1489–90. M'Ilvreid 1612. The archdeacon of the Isles in 1476 was M'Ylwvrd, made clearer in 1480 by Makkilbreid. See also MACBRIDAN and MACILVRIDE. Mc ilbryd 1685.

MACBRIOUN. See under MACABHRIUIN.

McBROLACHAN. See under O'BROLA-CHAIN.

MACBROOM. Andro McBrome, burgess of Kirkcudbright, was charged with intromitting with pirates, 1576 (RPC., II, p. 603). Joannes McBromius appears in 1655 with his name in Latin form (RUG., III, p. 31). Margaret McKbroome in the parish of Stonykirk, 1684 (Parish). Probably a variant of MACBRAYNE, q.v.

MACBRYDE. See under MACBRIDE.

MACBRYNE. Ir. MacBroin, 'son of Bran.' A variant of MACBYRNE. Hew M'Bryne in Ducharnan, Glassary, 1672 (HP., II, p. 209).

MACBURIE. A variant of Macvurie. See MAC-VURICH.

MACBURNEY, MACBURNIE. See under MAC-BIRNIE.

MACBYRNE. From Ir. MacBroin, 'son of Bran.' John M'Byrne was burgess of Wigtown, 1471 (RMS., II, 1674), and Cuthbert Makbyrn was burgess of Dumfries, 1508 (ibid., 3335; Edgar, p. 231).

MACCAA. A form of MACCAW, q.v., current in Galloway.

MACCABE. G. M'Caibe. In the Book of the Dean of Lismore (p. 90) the name appears as M'Caybba, and the editor says 'the name is a rare one though still existing in the Highlands.' John McKape (McCabe or McRebb, as his name is also spelled) was sent prisoner to Edinburgh, 1689 (RPC., 3. ser. XIII, p. 407, 430, 439). Angus filius M'Kabei, 1349 (REA., I, p. 80) is probably a miswriting for genitive of Maccabeus. "The family of MacCabe are now widely spread through the midland counties of Ireland, especially through Leitrim, Cavan, Monaghan, and Meath, where they are remarkable for their xanthous complexions, their vivacity and vigour. They are evidently a branch of the Macleods of Arran, and would appear to have migrated to Ireland in the fourteenth century" (O'Donovan). The earliest mention of the name in the Irish annals is in the year 1368, when Hugh MacCabe was slain. "The MacCabas first appear in Irish history in the fourteenth century as leaders of galloglachs, i.e. mercenaries of Norse-Hebridean origin, under the Irish princes of Breffny and Oriel. They followed the profession of condottieri for two centuries or more, their chiefs being known by the titles of Constable of Oriel, Constable of Breffny, and Constable

of the two Breffnys, Fermanagh and Oriel. The tradition of their Norse origin is still known in East Breffny (Co. Cavan). Distinctive Hebridean forenames, such as Alan (Aleinn), Somhairle (Sumarlidi), were formerly frequent in their families" (MacNeill, p. 39).

MACCADDELL. Donald Mc Caddell in Drumcassell was fined in 1613 for reset of outlawed Macgregors (RPC., XIV, p. 631). From CADDELL, q.v.

MACCADIE. See under MACADIE. John MacChaddy in Fearn, a follower of Ross of Morange, 1596 (RPC., V).

MACCADU. Donald McCado, bailie at the Logy, charged with interfering with burgesses engaged in the fisheries in the North Isles, 1586 (Coll., p. 103). Dudgeon records M'Cadu in Galloway a. 1700. Probably Ir. MacConduibh, 'son of Cú-dubh' ('black hound').

MACCAFFER, MACCAFFIR, MACAFFER. Ir. Mac Cathbharra, 'son of Cathbharr.' Donald MacCaffer was schoolmaster in Kilchoman, Islay, and receiver of letters sent from the post office in 1807 (Stent Book of Islay, p. 177). Archibald Macaffer, a native of Islay, was author of the comic song 'Oran a' Bhaloon.'

MACCAFFIE, MACHAFFIE. The fuller form of this name is given in a list of Wigtown men (Wodrow, Analecta, IV, p. 22) as Mackilhaffy. This represents Mac Gille Chathbhaidh, 'son of the servant of S. Cathbad.' The name is also preserved in the place name Craig Caffie, parish of Inch, which appears in a charter of the time of Robert I as Kellechaffe or Kellechaffy (RMS., I, App. II, 616). John McCaffe was king's messenger in 1540 (ALHT., VII, p. 440). The name is confined mainly to the Stewartry, and M'Hivey of 1578 (M'Kerlie, I, p. 239) is probably an old spelling of the name. Mc Chaffie 1689. The following forms are all recorded in 1684 (Parish): McHaffine, McIlhaffie, Mahaffie, Mahalfie, Milhaffie. In Stranraer 1940.

MACCAFFRAE, MACCAFFREY. From Ir. Mac-Cafraidh for MacGafraidh, 'son of Godfrey,' a Norse personal name early adopted by the Gaels.

MACCAGIE, MACCAGY. See under MACKEG-GIE. McCagie in Edinburgh, 1943.

MACCAIG, MACKAIG. G. MacThaoig, Ir. Mac-Thaidhg, 'son of Tadhg,' E. Ir. Tadc, Tadg, usually rendered 'poet' or 'philosopher.' The name is confined mainly to Ayrshire and Galloway. Maccaigs are also found in Arran, Car-

MACCAIG, Mackaig, continued

rick, Kintyre, Lismore, Kerrara, Islay, and elsewhere in Argyll, and in Dumfriesshire. The
name also appears as Mackeeg, Mackeig, Mack-
egg, and as Caig in Galloway and Ulster. In
Irish sometimes pronounced MacCaog. Donald
M'Coage is in Irvine, 1681. Kneen (Manx
names) however says that MacCoag in the
Isle of Man is from G. MacDhabhóg, 'son of
Dabhoc,' a diminutive of David. Payment was
made to John Makhaig in Wigtownshire, 1486
(ER., ix, p. 409). Andrew McAige or McCaig
was killed in the blowing up of Kirk of Field
in 1567 (APS., iii, p. 305). Jennat Mackcaige
was examined for the Test in 1685 (RPC., 3.
ser. xi, p. 434), and Archibald McKeag was
a rebel in Kilcheran parish, Kintyre, in same
year (Commons, p. 1). Ir. Tadg appears in
Norse record as Tand or Taðkr, and the Shetland name Tanderson is = Ir. MacThaidhg.
1667 M'Aig, and in 1684 (Parish) the name is
spelled: McCaig, McKaig, McKaige, McKaigh,
Makaig, and McKigg.

MAC CAILEIN. The Gaelic designation of
the duke of Argyll. In older poetry the form
Mac Mhic Cailein also occurs. Sir Walter
Scott's 'MacCallum More' has no authority in
Gaelic. Scott got a good deal of his Gaelic
from Highland chairmen, and, of course, it was
not quite literary. In the first edition of John
Major's Historia, published in Paris, 1521, he
says that the people of Argyll swear by the
hand of Alan the Great ("per manum Alani
Magni"), as if he understood Argyll's patronymic to have been Mac Ailein and not
Mac Cailein Mhóir. Mac Chailein is 'Colin's
son.' MacCalin and MacCallin 1555.

MACCAINSH. A form of Macangus, q.v.

MACCAIRBRE, 'son of Cairbre' (the 'charioteer'). Stevin M'Kerbrycht was charged in
1484 with the offence of "lichtlying and con-
tempcioun done to our Souerane Lordis
Hienes" (ALA., p. 89,* 90 *). Archibald Mak-
harbri (Makharbry, or M'Herbre) was a
student at St. Andrews University, 1508–11
(ERUS., p. 98, 100). The obit of Patrick
M'Carbe is given under the year 1517 (Chr.
Fort., p. 116). In 1527 there is entry of the
gift on the nonentres of the two mark land
of Little Murlogane, etc., to Archibald Mc-
Carbre (RSS., i, 3720), doubtless the Archibald above mentioned. As Makcarbre he witnessed a Glenurquhay bond of manrent, 1538
(BBT., p. 183). A letter of safeguard was
issued to Archibald Makarby in 1529, who
appears again as rector of Kilquhoman in
Ila, 1542 (RSS., ii, 59, 4739). Finlay Mc-
Carbre, Donald McCarbare, John McCarbre,

and Duncan McCarbare were followers of
the earl of Argyll, 1536 (ibid., 2152) John
Dow M'Arbrie witnessed a bond in 1586, and
Patrick Makarbrie in 1597 bound himself if
he shall marry and have children to dispone to
Sir Duncan Campbell of Glenurquhay and his
heirs "a bairn's part of gear" (BBT., p. 240,
225). John M'Carber was a weaver in Inveraray, 1694 (Campbell, i, p. 11), and Elspeth
M'Harbrae is recorded in Little Houm, 1712
(Dunkeld). From the fifteenth to the seventeenth century "there were twenty-four small
landed proprietors (or wadsetters, as they were
called), of the name of Macairbre in Breadalbane; but not a man of that name is now to
be found, nor is there even a tradition of
one of them having ever been extirpated, or
their lands taken from them by force. All
became extinct by natural causes. One of these
M'Cairbres, probably their chief, possessed
Finlarig Castle, afterwards one of the principal
seats of the family of Glenorchy... In the
former editions M'Cairbre was by mistake spelt
M'Rabie. Great antiquity is given by tradition
to the M'Cairbres; they are said to be descended from Cairbre Rua, frequently mentioned by Ossian. Archibald Fletcher, Esq.,
Advocate, is descended from the M'Cairbres
in the female line, and in failure of the male
line, may be considered as their representative" (Stewart, i, p. 26).

MACCAIRTER. See under MACARTHUR.

MACCAISH (curr.). See under MACCASH.

MACCALDRET. Finlay Mc Caldret was tenant of Stromneis Mor, Islay, 1686, and Gillecalum Mc Caldret held a kerrowane there at
same time (Bk. Islay, p. 497).

MACCALDROME. Ivar Mc caldrome was tenant of Leckamore, 1669 (HP., iv, p. 222).

MACCALE. See under MACKAIL. Ane
M'Cale was amerced in 1473 (ALHT., i,
p. 11).

MACCALISTER. See under MACALASTER.

MACCALL, Maccaull. See under MACALL.

MACCALLA. A form of Macaulay, q.v.

MACCALLAM. See under MACCALLUM.

MACCALLAN. A form of Macallan, q.v.,
current in Bute and Argyll. Gybbon M'Callan
or M'Callane had a tenement in Ayr in 1476
(Friars Ayr, p. 54), and Thomas MacCallan
is recorded in Murthlac, 1550 (Illus., ii,
p. 261). John M'Callan in Ayr, 1656 (Ayr,
p. 197).

MACCALLIEN, MACCALLION, MACCULLION. Argyllshire names. From G. *MacCailin*, 'son of Cailin' (*Watson* I, p. 325). Three persons named M'Kallione are mentioned in Aberdeen, 1556 (RSCA., I, p. 125). John McKallone is in record in Innerernanis, 1559 (ER., XIX, p. 442). McCalein 1683.

MACCALLUM. G. *MacCaluim* or *MacC(h)aluim*, for earlier *Mac GilleChaluim*, 'son of the gillie of Calum.' Gilbert MacCalme, merchant in Ayr, 1631 (*Ayr*, p. 64). Iain M'Callum vc Raldounoch was one of those murdered at Dunaverty, 1647 (HP., II, p. 257), and in 1661 Archibald M'Callome was minister at Glassary (Scott, *Fasti*, III, p. 7). Zacharie M'Callan, "a hieland boy in St. Androis," mentioned in 1650 (PBK., p. 365) was most probably a Maccallum. Donald McCallum was sasine witness, 1659 (*Poltalloch Writs*, p. 76). A precept of sasine was addressed to Zacharie McCallum of Poltalloch, 1661 (ibid., p. 137). In 1662 Donald McGillespie vic O'Challum was seized in the lands of Poltalloch and was the lineal ancestor of Neill Malcolm of Poltalloch, who succeeded his cousin Dugald in 1787 and died in 1802. John Wingfield Malcolm of Poltalloch was created Lord Malcolm in 1896 and died in 1902. In 1667 Archibald, ninth earl of Argyll granted a charter to Zachary M'Callum of Poltalloch and the heirs male of his body, 'quibus deficientibus heredibus suis masculis quibuscunque cognominis de Clan Callum' (HP., II, p. 92). Duncan Glass M'Callum or M'Allum was charged with cattle-lifting in the regality of Lennox, 1687 (Irving, *Dumbartonshire*, p. 334). Sometime before 1850 the head of the family of Poltalloch changed the name from Maccallum to Malcolm 'for aesthetic reasons.' An old Highland prophecy that Maccallum should sit in MacCailein Mor's chair was held to be accomplished by Malcolm of Poltalloch becoming possessor of the castle which formed the principal messuage of Lochow (Smith, *Tartans*, p. 145). For the folklegend 'MacCallums offspring of the sixty fools' see Lord Archibald Campbell's *Argyllshire*, p. 304–305. John McHallom appears in the parish of Kirkinner, 1684, and John Mahallum in Barmore, parish of Kirkcowan in the same year. M'Allom 18c., McCalim 1692, M'Callome 1648, McCallwme 1546, McCalume 1686. See also MACCILLECHALLUM.

MACCALLY. *See under* MACAULAY.

MACCALMAN, MACCALMON. G. *MacCalmáin*, 'son of Calman.' A variant of MACCOLMAN, q.v. It is also translated DOVE, q.v., and it often represents MURCHISON, q.v. Mr. Alexander McAlman, dean of Argyll, was allowed to take the Test, 1682 (RPC., 3. ser. VII, p. 343), Jon McCalmin was a fencible-man in Nether Lorn, 1692 (*Commons*, p. 35), and Archibald M'Calman was schoolmaster at Dull, 1765 (*Dunkeld*). McCallman 1746. In 1684 (*Parish*): McCalmon, McCammon, and McCamon.

MACCALMONT. Same as MACCALMAN with accretionary *t*. Gilbert M'Calmont in Ayr, 1581. George M'Calmont, thesaurer of burgh of Air, 1611 (*Ayr*, p. 143). John McCalmond in the Milltown of Kirkcum (Kirkcolm), Wigtownshire, 1618 (RPC., XI, p. 331), and Goarg (George) Mc almont was merchant in Ayr, 1681 (*Hunter*, p. 67). M'Calmount 1630.

MACCALVYN. In *Retours* (*Perth*, no. 68) under the year 1601 is the entry: "Alexander Robertsoun, *haeres* Duncani Robertsoun alias Jacobi M'Calvyn." This is not a patronymic but is derived from the property, the lands of Calvine, forming part of the estate of Faskally.

MACCALZEAN. Adam Makcalveane, member of Skinners' Craft in Edinburgh, 1533 (*Guildry*, p. 81). Ewfame Makcalzane was burned alive for witchcraft in Edinburgh, 1591 (*Trials*, I, p. 247–257). Jean M'Callion in Edinburgh, 1696 (*Edinb. Marr.*). Makcalyane 1564, McCalyean 1561.

MACCAMBIE. A different name from MACCAMIE. Current in Banff. Gillescop MacCamby was present at perambulation of lands of Kinblathmund, 1227 (APS., I, p. 91; RAA., I, p. 163).

MACCAMBIL. A variant of MACCAVELL (from Ir. *Cathmhaoil*). Gilbert M'Cambil, burgess of Innermessan, 1426 (RMS., II, 185). John Mc Cammell in Galloway, 1684 (*Parish*). The name of course has nothing to do with Campbell.

MACCAMBRIDGE. A corruption of G. *Mac Ambróis*, 'son of Ambrose.' This name was formerly current in the Mull of Kintyre. Flora MacCambridge escaped with the infant son of Archibald Macdonald to a remote cave near the Mull of Kintyre in 1647 (*Celt. Mon.*, III, p. 25). William Ambrois obtained letters of horning against the earl of Argyll in 1604 (RPC., XIV, p. 413), Neill M'Camrois is in record in South Kintyre in 1605 (HP., III, p. 80), and John Ambros or Ambrois, man to Neill Stewart, was due fines for resetters of Clan Gregor in 1614 (RPC., XIV, p. 657–658). John Ban M'Camridge is in record in Forline, parish of Kilcalmkill, 1693 (*Argyll Inv.*), and Donald McCambrois was tenant in Killoane, Islay, 1686 (*Bk. Islay*, p. 497). The sur-

MACCAMBRIDGE, *continued*
name has spread to the British colonies, Queensland, Tasmania, and New Zealand. In Antrim the name has become Cambridge and Chambers.

MACCAMIE, 'son of Jamie,' a diminutive of JAMES, q.v. Nigel McCamie witnessed sasine of lands in Arran, 1538 (*Macfarlane*, II, p. 343). In 1547 Robert Makkamy of Maknaucht or Manach in Bute sold his lands to Ninian Stewart (RMS., III, 166). In 1557 John M'Came 'vel M'Caine' was retoured heir of Nigel M'Came, his father, in the lands of Barnauld, Bute (*Retours, Bute*, 3), and in 1560 we have record of sasine of lands in Bute to John McCamie (ER., XIX, p. 460). "Jamieson and McCamie are the Same Sir Name and were both Originally Fullartons... James went to the Isle of Bute and was called McCamie or Jamieson and acquired Lands there and was made Crowner of Bute, as appears by his Designation in May 1538: 'Robertus Jamieson Coronator de Bute.' His Successors remained in that Iseland till within these few Years that they are now Extinct" (*Macfarlane*, II, p. 343). M'Kame 1601, Makcomye 1597, M'Kymmie 1609. See also MACKIMMIE.

MACCAMLEY, MACCAMLY. Current surnames. Woulfe says from * *MacCamlaoich*, son of *Camlaoch*, 'bent hero.'

MACCAMMON, MACCAMMOND, MACCAMON. Woulfe says MacAmoinn, son of Amundr, a Norse personal name. M'Clure (*British placenames*, p. 228) says M'Cammond — son of Oman (from *Amund-r*). William McCamen was warded in the Canongate Tolbooth, Edinburgh, in 1684 (BOEC., IX, p. 168). Recorded in Galloway, 1684.

MACCANCE, MACCANCH. A variant of MACANGUS, q.v. The name appears in Wigtownshire and Minnigaff in 1684 as McCans, McCance, McCanse, McKance, and McKants (*Parish*).

MACCANCHIE. A variant of MACCANCH, with diminutive -*ie*. Alexander M'Canchie in Craichmore, 1658 (*Dumfries*). James M'Canchie in Glengepock, 1681 (*Kirkcudbright*).

MACCANDIE. See under MACANDIE.

MACCANDLISH. Eight of this name appear in Wigtownshire in eighteenth century (*Wigtown*). William M'Candlish in Balmangan, 1794 (*Kirkcudbright*). In 1684 the name appears as Makkanless, McCandlish, McAndlish, M'Canleis, and M'Caunles (*Parish*). The spelling with Mac is probably now extinct. From Ir. *Mac-*

Cuindlis or *MacCuindilis*, son of *Cuindleas* (an old Irish name — *Woulfe*). See CANDLISH.

MACCANDYCHT. John M'Gillendreis Candycht, John Glas M'Candycht, and Gillendris M'Incandycht in Lochalsh, 1548 (RMS., IV, 204). Cf. CANDYTH under CANYCHT. ? = Jacobus Mac Chandyt in Murthlac, 1550 (*Illus.*, II, p. 261).

MACCANISH. Thomas MacKanyss was burgess of Glasgow, 1524 (LCD., p. 261). John M'Caniss in Ballechragan in record, 1664 (BBT., p. 261), and Alexander M'Canish of Garvalt in record, 1698 (*Campbell*, I, p. 29). "It is very probable that the present day MacAnish, MacAinish, and MacAinsh families of Perthshire are descended from the old MacCanish sept of Atholl, and also that they were not of MacInnes or MacAngus origin, but really a branch of the MacNish stock in Atholl" (*Macnish*, p. 50). But cf. MACANGUS.

MACCANNEL, MACCANNELL. Variants of MACCONNEL, q.v. Septs in Tiree (J. G. Campbell, *Witchcraft*, p. 173). Duncan Baine Mccanell, rebel in Knapdeall, 1685 (*Commons*, p. 5). Malcolm M'Cannell in Fernock, 1692 (*Argyll Inv.*), and Donald M'Cannell in Ballimore of Knap, 1712 (*Argyll*). Maccannell is current in Islay.

MACCANQUELL. John Makcanquell, witness in Dunblane, 1523 (RMS., III, 242). James M'Canquall in Easter Feddall, parish of Muthill, 1683 (*Dunblane*). For BALCANQUHALL, q.v.

MACCANSH. A form of MACANGUS, q.v.

MACCAPPIN. A variant of MACALPINE, q.v. Umphra McCapen was charged with tumult in Glasgow, 1606 (RPC., VII, p. 244). Robert McCapie in Duntreath was unrelaxed from horning, 1618 (RPC., XI, p. 300). Donald McApie or McCapie appears in 1667 (ibid., 2. ser. II, p. 115). Malcolm McCapine in Balinoe, parish of Ardskeodnish, was fined in 1686 for being a rebel (ibid., 3. ser. XII, p. 236), and John McCapy was town-clerk of Dunbartane, 1689 (ibid., XIV, p. 318).

MACCARAN. Ir. *MacCiaráin*, 'son of Ciaran,' a diminutive of *ciar*, 'dark brown.' Neill McCarren in Torsavie, Mull, was put to the horn, 1629 (RPC., 2. ser. III, p. 45). Duncan M'Carran appears in Arskornish, Argyll, 1684 (*Argyll Inv.*), and Duncan Mccarren was rebel in Kilmichael-Glassarie, 1685 (*Commons*, p. 7).

MACCARDIE. Johannes McHardy, burgess of Are, 1499 (*Simon*, 37), may be John McCarde, burgess of Prestwick, 1507, who appears again in 1514 as McCardy (*Prestwick*, p. 11, 46). Cf. MACHARDY.

MACCARDLE, MACCARDELL. See *under* MACARDLE.

MACCARGO. A Galloway surname. The escheat of——Makargo in the court of the Steward of Annandale is recorded, 1465 (ER., VII, p. 309). William M'Kergue at Blairquhanmiln was shot for being a Covenanter, 1685 (*Hanna*, II, p. 258). McCarge 1684.

MACCARLICH. G. *MacThearlaich*, 'son of Charles.' Alexander Terleti was rector of the parish church of Kilchoman, 1455, and appears again in the same record in 1463 as Terneciolini (*Pap. Lett.*, XI, p. 262, 480). John Makarlich appears in Ayrshire in 1535 (RMS., III, 1536), and Donald McCarlycht was a 'fugitive fra the law' in 1538 (RSS., II, 2606). Tarlocht M'Ene V'Carlycht, a witness in 1573, appears again in the same year as Charles M'Ane V'Tarlych and as Therlycht M'Ain W'Therlycht (BBT., p. 216, 218, 220). Hector McCarliche in Innerbruoche and Auchinroy McCarliche in Lyne were fined for reset of members of Clan Gregor in 1613 (RPC., XIV, p. 630). Alester McKerlich in Keandamonie in 1618 appears in the same record as McKarlich, McTarlach, and McCarlach (RPC., XI, p. 372–373). Archibald M'Kerlich in Finlarg was a vassal of Campbell of Glenurquhay in 1638 (BBT., p. 402), and Alexander McHerlich appears in Blainabie, 1726 (HP., II, p. 334). M'Harleyth (in Islay). See also under MACARLY, MACCHARLES and MACTARLICH.

MACCARMICK. A form of MACCORMACK, q.v. Malcolm Makcarmych, bailie and burgess of Rothesay, 1503 (LCD., p. 208). John Barne *alias* Makcarmich, sheriff-messenger in Perth, 1528 (*Milne*, p. 193), appears in 1530 as Joh. Makcarmich "unum marorum vic de Perth" (RMS., III, 975). Duncan McCarmik and Patrick McCarmik were tenants in Ochterneid, Kynnarde, 1539 (ER., XVII, p. 672), Duncan Makarmeich was charter witness at Balquhidder, 1549 (HP., IV, p. 32), Cristina Mykcarmy appears in Glasgow, 1552 (*Protocols*, I), John M'Armick in Botary, 1633, and Ketve Mackarmich there, 1636 (*Presb. Bk. Strathbogie*, p. 7, 11). Duncan M'Carmick in Kilbryde, 1675 (*Argyll*), and Robert M'Carmick, tailor, in High Corquhie, 1732 (*Wigtown*).

MACCARNEY, MACCARNIE. Ir. *MacCearnaigh*, 'son of Cearnach,' 'victorious.' Patrick Makcarny was one of an assize in Carrik in 1529 (RMS., III, 849). Duncan Makkarny was one of the tenants on the king's farm of Lawse,

Strathdee, in 1539 (ER., XVII, p. 660). Jac. M'Carny was witness in Edinburgh, 1543 (RMS., III, 2968: in the index his name is equated (wrongly?) with M'Carmich).

MACCARNOCHAN. Gilcrist Mac Karnachan was present at the fixing of the bounds of the Grange of Kircwynin, 1289 (*Holm Cultram*, p. 88). McKernachan 1684 (in Galloway). Woulfe has *O'Cearnachan*, 'descendant of Cearnach' (victorious). Cf. CARNOCHAN.

MACCARRA. See *under* MACARA.

MACCARRACH. Finlay M'Carrach in Achyle, Perthshire, 1630 (*Laing*, 2051).

MACCARRICK. Cuthbert McCarik in Dumfriesshire had a precept of remission in 1535 (RSS., II, 1838), and John M'Carrick appears in parish of Monzie, 1683 (*Dunblane*). Perhaps from Ir. *MacConcharraige* 'son of Cu-charraige' (a personal name meaning 'hound of the rock' — *Woulfe*).

MACCARSON. A composition with Thomas Makcarsane in Kirkcudbright, 1473 (ALHT., I, p. 8). Andrew M'Carsane, witness in Wigtownshire, 1546 (RMS., III, 3309). From CARSON, q.v.

MACCART. 'Son of Art,' an ancient Gaelic personal name, from *Arto-s*, a bear. Art enters into composition of several early names — *Artbran*, *Artgus*, etc. Maccart is also a shortening of MACARTHUR. Donald McAne McCart was tenant of Daweskkir, Islay, 1541 (ER., XVII, p. 616).

MACCARTAIR, MACCARTER. Variants of MACARTHUR, q.v. Gyllemechall McCarthair is in record in 1569 (HMC., 6. Rep., App., p. 645). John M'Cairter in Edinburgh in 1682 (*Edinb. Marr.*), and Androw McKerter was warded in the Canongate Tolbooth, Edinburgh, in 1684 (BOEC., IX, p. 168). Mc Cartur 1662.

MACCARTNEY, MACARTNAY (Fife). Ir. *MacCartaine*, a variant of *MacArtain*, 'son of Artan,' a diminutive of the old personal name Art. It was formerly a common surname in the Stewartry from the early sixteenth century onwards. Gilbert McCartnay in Galloway had a respite for 'tressonable intercommonyng with Inglismen,' 1529 (RSS., II, 431). Thomas McCartnay or Makartnay in Wigtownshire, 1562 (RPC., I, p. 214, 224), and Helen Macartnev is mentioned in 1588 in connection with lands in Dumfries (*Edgar*, p. 247). The Macartneys of Auchinleck are an old family in Ayrshire, and the Macartneys of Lissanoure, county Antrim, are descended from Captain

MACCARTNEY, Macartnay, *continued*

George Macartney of this family. James Mc-Cartnay held 'tua croftis of land liand in the manis [Mains] of Prestoun' in the first half of the sixteenth century (*Neubotle*, p. 339). William Mackartnay, burgess of Aberdeen, 1603 (NSCM., I, p. 97). Ewin McIllecreist Vc-Cartna or VcCartney in Oskalmull was put to the horn, 1629 (RPC., 2. ser. II, p. 341; III, p. 45), and the obit of Rinalda M'Artna apud Rannoch is recorded in 1564 (*Chr. Fort.*, p. 132). George McKertney of Blaikit, 1681, appears in following year as McAirtnay (RPC., 3. ser. VII, p. 217, 488), and John McCartney was officer at Bridgend, 1681 (ibid., p. 34). Donald M'Artna or M'Cartna in Ballacholis, parish of Kilmaluage, 1686–94 (*Argyll; Argyll Inv.*). Mareon Mackertnah and Girsel Mackernah were charged with being disorderly persons in the parish of Crossmichael, 1684 (RPC., 3. ser. IX, p. 574). M'Cairtney, Mackartane, Mackcartane, M'Kairtney, all 1667; Macatnay (in Lauder) 1676.

MACCASH, Macash, Maccaish. Perthshire surnames, probably contracted forms of Mac-tavish, q.v. John M'Ash, sheriff mair in Crieff, b. c. 1700, was son of Duncan M'Ash in Mony-vaird. Marion M'Cash died in 1598. Hector McCaishe was one of those holding the castle of Dunivaig against Bishop Knox, 1616 (or 1614) (*Cawdor*, p. 232). Finlay McCaish in Auchnafrie, Glenalmond, 1662, and Donald M'Caish in East Lethendee, Glenalmon, 1682. Andrew M'Cais in Tombae, parish of Callender, 1666 (*Dunblane*).

MACCASKELL, Maccaskil, Maccaskill, Mackaskil, Mackaskill See under MACAS-GILL.

MACCASKIE. See under MACASKIE.

MACCASLAND, Maccasline. See MACAUS-LAN.

MACCASSANE. *Cassán*, a diminutive of *Cass*, was the name of a saint (*Watson* I, p. 313). William M'Cassane was tenant in town and barony of Prestoun, 1376 (RHM., I, p. lxi). McCassen 1684.

MACCATHAIL, 'son of Cathal,' q.v. Payment of cheese to Gilmor Mc Kathail in Tarbert, 1326 (ER., I, p. 55). Pronounced Mackail, and in old records the name often occurs as McCail. See under MACALL.

MACCATHAY. An old Galloway surname. Gilbert Makcathy was tenant of Grange of Ballyndune super Cree, 1481 (ER., IX, p. 583). Donald M'Cathen (= Maccathie) in Rothesay,

Bute, 1689. Balmacaan in Glen Urquhart is from *Baile MacCathain*, stead of the sons of Cathan.

MACCAULAY, Maccauly. See under MA-CAULAY.

MACCAUP. Archibald McCaup in Lykuarie, in the parish of Glassary, granted a bond, 1686 (RPC., 3. ser. XII, p. 234).

MACCAUSE. See under MACAVISH.

MACCAUSLAND. See under MACAUSLAN.

MACCAVAT. Ir. *MacDhaibhéid*, 'son of David,' q.v. Thomas M'Cabet, a witness, appears in 1527 and Joh. M'Cavethe was burgess of Ayr, 1529 (RMS., III, 500, 786). Letters of legitimation were granted to Michael M'Cavett, natural son of Thomas M'Cavett in Mekill Sonnetes, barony of Glenluce, 1543 (ibid., 2872). Also Englished Cavet and Kevvitt.

MACCAVELL. Donald M'Cawill, witness at Gerrey, 1513 (*Ros*, 60), John M'Cavell was reidare at Kirk Oswald, 1574 (RMR.), and Donald McCavill in Dalclathik was fined for reset of Clan Gregor, 1613 (RPC., XIV, p. 639). Perhaps from Ir. *MacCathmhaoil*, 'son of Cathmhaol.'

MACCAVISH. See under MACAVISH.

MACCAVOR. A kerrowan of Killoane in Islay was set to Gilnive McCavor in 1686, and Donald McCavor was tenant in Gartcharr, Islay, in same year (*Bk. Islay*, p. 497, 501).

MACCAW, Maccaw. The same as Macadam, but from an earlier Gaelic form of the personal name, G. M'Adhaimh, 'son of Adam.' Adam in Gaelic is *Adhamh*, and in the phonetically written Fernaig Manuscript (1688) it is written *Ahu* (*Rel. Celt.*, II, p. 38), and in the still earlier Dean of Lismore's MS. (c. 1512) *Aw3oe* (3 here = *y*). Drumboy was let to Donald McCawe or Makkaw in 1481, and in 1487 he is recorded as dead (ER., IX, p. 585, 637). Patrick and John Makcaw had precept of remission 'pro interfectione quondam Johannis Makcornok" (RSS., I, 1487). John Makcaw was familiar servitor to King James V (SBR., p. 267), and archdeacon of the cathedral church of Lismore, 1547 (*Laing*, 528; Patrick, *Statutes Scot. Church*, p. 88). Donald McCaw Voyll was fined for reset of members of Clan Gregor, 1613 (RPC., XIV, p. 634), and in 1662 Alison Makca is in record in Edinburgh (*Edinb. Marr.*). There was an old family of this name in Bute. In 1506 Gillenow M'Kaw had a grant of the lands of North Garrochach, Gilpatrick MakKaw had half of the lands of South Garrochach, and John MakKaw the other half (RMS., II, 2987). Gilpatrick Makcoe of Dwngull, Bute, is in record, 1534 (ibid., III, 1378). Patrick McKaw and Isobell More McKaw his wife were charged with witchcraft in Bute in 1662 (HP., III, p. 10, 11). In 1696 Gildow MacCaw was Commissioner of Supply for Bute (APS., x, p. 29). James Brown McCaw (1772–1846), of Scots parentage and educated in Edinburgh, ranked as the leading surgeon of eastern Virginia. By the beginning of the nineteenth century the name of the Bute family had become Mackay. "Mac" has been also dropped and CAW, q.v., is a present-day surname. M'Aw 1675, M'Call 1649, M'Cawe 1636, Maccawe 1607, M'Kau, Mackaw, and Makkcae 1506, Mackawe 1625, Makaw 1534. MACCAA is a current spelling of the name in Galloway. (2) A money allowance was made for Johannes filius Donecani Makehou, 'obsidis,' in 1300 (Hist. Docs., II, p. 427), and shortly after his death in Carlisle prison is noted (Bain, II, 1179). This name is probably from the same source as the above.

MACCAWIS, MACCAWS. See under MACAVISH.

MACCAY. See under MACKAY.

MACCEACHAN. See under MACEACHAN.

MACCHANANAICH. G., 'son of the canon.' The Gaelic name of the Buchanans, collectively Na Cananaich. A sept of Macphersons in Skye are also known in Gaelic as Na Cananaich; and John Macpherson, the Glendale 'martyr,' was known to his neighbors as Iain Cananach. Alexander M'Caneny was one of the earl of Moray's tenants in 1389 (REM., p. 200). Kenneth Makchannacht, rector of Kilmonawag, died in 1515 (RSS., I). Ewyn Dow Mc Kananich made supplication against John Campbell of Caldor, 1525 (D. Murray Rose). Dowgall McThannainche who was ordered to be apprehended for violence in 1619 may be Dougall McCannaniche (McChannaniche, or VcChannainche) who was servant to Mr. Donald Campbell of Barbreck, 1622 (RPC., XI, p. 643; XII, p. 635; XIII, p. 11). Gillespick Geir McChannanaiche in Skallashillbeg and John Dow McChannanaiche were charged with assault and illegal warding, 1635 (ibid., 2. ser. v, p. 511). Neill McChananaich in Achitangan, was a rebel in 1685 (Commons, p. 13), Neill mc Cananaich, a fencible-man in Kilmore, 1692 (ibid., p. 29) and Donald M'Ochananaich was feuar of Auchadacheronbeg, parish of Kilmodan, 1695 (Argyll). John M'Ochannanich was tenant of Ardoran in 1730 (ibid.), Donald MacHannanich is in record in Auchtekerrenbeg in 1753, and Donald MacChananich was an elder in the same place in 1843 (Adam, p. 463). Five Maccananichs in Stewart of Appin's regiment in the '45 were killed and one wounded (Coll., p. 199). MacGiolla-Domhnaigh (Some Anglicised surnames in Ireland, p. 7) says that in Ulster and in Scotland Buchanan is known as M'Whannan and Mawhannan.

MACCHANTOR, 'son of the Chanter' (Lat., cantor). Robert Cantoris witnessed a protest by the bishop of Moray, 1398 (REM., p. 210), and caution was found for Johnne McKantour in 1585 (RPC., III, p. 740).

MACCHAPMAN. 'Son of the chapman.' Gilfillan Mcchapman Buy in Kenmore, 1579 (FB., p. 360). See CHAPMAN.

MACCHARLES, 'son of Charles.' Either simply the English Charles or Anglicized from MACCARLICH, q.v. Lauchlan McCharles was tenant of Calgorie and Fladd in Mull in 1674 (HP., I, p. 279).

MACCHARLIE. Duncan McCharlie of Innistreinzie witnessed a bond of maintenance by Archibald, earl of Argyll to Ninian Bennachtin of the Cammis (Kames in Bute), 1538 (Coll., p. 88). Cf. also MACCARLICH and MACKERLIE.

MACCHARMAIG. The Clan MacCharmaig = Argyllshire Shaws. M'Charmaig in '45. Cf. MACCARMICK.

MACCHEACHAN. A form of MACEACHAN, q.v., current in Glasgow.

MACCHESNEY. A surname formerly recorded in Galloway. John MacChessnyes in Little Park, 1638. Richard Makchesnie petitioned against the Service Book, 1637 (RPC., 2. ser. VI, p. 711). William McChesney in Creoch granted a bond, 1679 (ibid., 3. ser. VI, p. 665). Agnes McChesnie was charged with being a disorderly person in the parish of Kirkcudbright, 1684, and John MacChesney was resident in parish of Borgue in same year (ibid., 3. ser. IX, p. 568, 573). Alexander McChesney in Blairs of Kirkmabreck, 1741 (Kirkcudbright). In 1684: McChestnie and McHestnie, and shortened to Chesney and Chestnut (Parish, p. 28, 41, 69, etc.). Perhaps from Chesne (Chesney), the fuller form of CHEYNE, q.v.

MACCHEYNE. Ir. Mac Seaghdin, 'son of Jean,' the Norman-French form of John. Thomas McChyne appears in Blackwood, 1657 (Dumfries). McChain 1768, McChiney 1684, Makine 1772. There is a McCheyneston in the Stewartry. (2) G. Mac Gille Seathdin, 'son of the servant of (S.) John'. Archibald M'Ilchean in Kilmun parish, 1676 (Argyll). Old: MacIlcheyne.

MACCHLERY, Maccleary, Macclery. G. M'a'Chleirich, 'son of the clerk,' i.e. cleric. M'Cleri is found in 1376 (RHM., п, p. 16), and John Clerici (i.e. Macclerich) had a remission from James I for offenses committed by him in 1428 (Rose, p. 126). Malcolm M'Cleriche who was one of an inquest to determine the rights of pasturage which the Temple lands had over the adjoining town and territory of Letter in 1461 (Strathendrick, p. 222) may be the Malcolm M'Clery who appears as witness in Stirling, 1475 (SBR., p. 256). Dugall Clerk (without Mac) had a royal remission for slaughter committed by him in 1497 (Rose, p. 164), Duncan McInclerycht witnessed an instrument of sasine at Duthil, 1537 (Grant, III, p. 270), Husceoun M'Clerich and Husceoun M'Inclerich were tenants in Lochalsh, 1549 (RMS., IV, 204), Donald Gaw McClerich in Morlagane and Duncan McCleriche in Glenlyoun were fined for reset of members of outlawed Clan Gregor, 1613 (RPC., XIV, p. 631, 633). George Makclearie, tailor in Edinburgh, 1648, and Catharine M'Clirie, resident there, 1674 (Edinb. Marr.). Hew M'Lerich and Donald M'Lerich were tenants of Barquhill, 1672 (HP., II, p. 209), and Finlay M'Aclerich appears in Auchlyne, 1638 (BBT., p. 402). The form M'Aclerycht is also common in BBT. in the sixteenth century, and in Islay in 1733 we have M'Inclerie. Of the Clarks of Clan Chattan Mr. Mackintosh says: "This sept was always a small one, and as its heads do not appear to have had any particular holding or lands the traces of it in documents of old date are few" (Clan Chattan, p. 592). M'Clerie 1715, McKleiry 1707.

MACCHOMBICH. See under MACCOMBICH.

MACCHRISTIE, Macchristy, Mackirsty. 'Son of Christie,' diminutive of Christian, q.v. Recorded in Galloway, 1684, as McChristie, McChristin, McChrystine (Parish).

MACCHROYNE. Alester McEwin Vc Chroyne in Auliche was fined for resetting outlawed Macgregors, 1613 (RPC., XIV, p. 633).

MACCHRUITER. From the occupation or profession of cruiteir or harper, often hereditary in the Highlands in past times. In 1346 King David II granted a charter of the land of Dalelachane in the earldom of Carrick to Patrick, son of the late Michael, harper of Carrick ('Patricio filio quondam Michaelis Cithariste de Carryk'). In 1385 we find this same Patrick referred to by the Gaelic form of his name. In this year Duncan M'Churteer, son and heir of the late Patrick M'Churteer, alienated to Sir Thomas Kenedy, lord of Dalmortoun, the whole land of Dalelachane (Laing, 40, 69). Gilbert Makrutur and Andro McRutur, followers of the earl of Cassilis, were respited for murder in 1526 (RSS., I, 3386). Donald Makcruteracht was a witness in the Stewartry of Kirkcudbright in 1531 (RMS., III, 1094), and Andrew Makrutour was juror on an assize in the bailliary of Carrick in the following year (ibid., 1196). William McInchruter was servant to John Grant, fourth of Freuchie, 1568 (Grant, I, p. 140). John M'Chruytor in Auchaharse and Archibald M'Chrytor in Craillmorrull appear in 1672 (HP., II, p. 209). Archibald M'Chritter in Monjudnean, parish of Kilmichell, appears in 1676, and Malcolm M'Chruter in Auchindarroch, parish of Knapdale, 1686 (Argyll). Duncan M'Chruter was one of the buyers of the crop of the 20 shilling land of Mulindra in 1711 (Campbell, I, 102). The name appears in old records: Mc Chruitar, 1686; McQuhartoune and McQuhirtoure, 1686; M'Quhirtour, MacQuhorter, and M'Quhriter, 1592; M'Quirtour, 1636; M'Hruter, M'Hruter, M'Qherter, McWhrurter, McWhurter, M'Whyrter, and McWirter, 1684; M'Heurtter, M'Qharter, M'Quhirtir, 1685; McWhirtour, 1685. The modern form of the name is Macwhirter, q.v. One of the towers of Blairquhan Castle (removed in 1824) bore the name of McQuirter's Tower. The name was also once common in the upper part of the parishes of Buchanan and Callander, and in part of Argyllshire. The Gaelic origin of individuals of the name is disguised by its being frequently translated Harper and Harperson, the former a not uncommon surname in Galloway. The cruit (W. crwth) was an old Welsh stringed instrument, four of its six strings played with a bow, two twitched by the thumb.

MACCHRYSTAL. See under MACCRISTAL.

MACCITHICH. A surname not uncommon in Argyllshire. See under MacKeich.

MACCLACHARTY. See under MACLAVERTY.

MACCLACHER. 'Son of the mason,' from G. clachair, a mason. Fergus Maklaucher held the 10sh. land of Makclauchereistoun ('town of the son of the mason') in Carrick in 1538 (RMS., III, 1849). Thomas Begg Mc chlachar and Thomas Moir Mc chlachar were charged with being 'engagers' in Urray in 1649 (IDR., p. 159, 368). John McClacher was 'tounes officer' of Inverness in 1671 (More Culloden papers, I, p. 170), and another John McClacher appears as a wright in Comrie in 1681 (RPC., 3. ser. VII, p. 47). See also Clachar.

MACCLANE. A current form of MACLEAN, q.v.

MACCLANNACHAN, MACCLANACHAN, MAC-LANACHAN, MACCLANAGHAN, MACLANAGHAN, MACCLENAGHAN. In G. *Mac Gille Onchon*, 'son of the gillie of Onchu,' an Irish saint whose name means 'mighty hound' (*Watson*). The name is or was common in Galloway. Dugall and Patrick MakClennochquhen were convicted of hereschip in Carrick in 1513 (*Trials*, I, p. 88 *). Gilbert M'Clannochane appears in 1544-5 as occupant of the five mark lands of Craggis in the parish of Mochrum (RMS., III, 3163), and in 1546 there is entry of the escheat of Michael McClannochane (ALHT., IX, p. 12). Niniane M'Clennoquhan was reidare at Partoun, and John M'Clanochane reidare at Vchiltrie, Ayrshire, 1574 (RMR.). Decreet against Andro McClennoquhen in Clairend, 1577 (RPC., II, p. 647). Elizabeth McClannochane was retoured heir of John McClannochane in Keremanoche, her father, 1585 (*Retours, Ayr*, 736), and James M'Clanoquhen was heir of Alexander M'Clannoquhen in Ballinglah, 1645 (*Inquis.*, 3061). James M'Lanoquhen in Culinan was a follower of Wchtrid McDougall of Frewche, 1635 (RPC., 2. ser. v, p. 524-525). The name has many forms in the old records: M'Clanachan, M'Clanochan, M'Clennagan, M'Clinighan, M'Cleneghan, M'Clenaghan, M'Clenahan, M'Clenaghen, M'Clenighan, MacClenachan, MacClanahan, McClanaquhen, MacClennochan, MacClannochan, McClunochen, McKlanachen, M'Lanaghan, M'Lannachen, McLanochen, M'Lanoquhen, M'Lenechen, M'Lenochan, McLonachin, and M'Glenaghan (this last form is also found in Ulster, from Mag-). The name is also found in several forms without 'Mac.' Gave name to Balmacclannoquhen in Kyle (1553, RMS.), Balmaclanoquhan in Carrick (1653), and M'Clanochanstoun (1600), M'Clannochanstoun (1627), or M'Clonachstoune (1691) in Ayrshire. Onchu was the name of one of the victors in the battle of Cuil Corra, 649 (*Chron. Scot.*).

MACCLANSBURGH. Patrick Makglamrouth held a half merk of the land of Largmore in the parish of Kells, Galloway, 1473 (RMS., II, 1128), and in 1500 he appears again as M'Clanrauch, tenant of Largmoir, Glenken (ER., XI, p. 453). A man named Macclanarch or Makclanrik deforced the chamberlain of Galloway when collecting ferms in 1486 (ibid., IX, p. 380, 460). Robert McKlamroch was charged with being a disorderly person in the parish of Carsfern, 1684 (RPC., 3. ser. IX, p. 575), and Robert Inclamerock (for M'Clamerock) appears in Airdmiln, 1695 (*Dumfries*).

James McGlainroche (a misreading of McGlamroche) in Leyis petitioned against the church service book in 1637 (RPC., 2. ser. VI, p. 713). Samuel McClamroh, student in the University of Glasgow, 1696, appears again in 1703 as McLanburgh (RUG.). Robert M'Lamroch, son of James M'Clamroch in the parish of Glencairn, matriculated at Glasgow University in 1738, and Robert M'Lemburgh appears in Drumruck, Kirkcudbright, 1763, and seven McClamerochs are recorded in the district in the seventeenth and eighteenth centuries (*Kirkcudbright*). M'Glamroche 1596, MacGlanroch 1637, M'Clannerach 1677, and Dudgeon (*Macs*) gives the additional spellings: M'Clamburgh, M'Lambroch, M'Lambrok. M'Clamoroch is also found, and a modern current form is LANDSBOROUGH, q.v.

MACCLARSAIR, 'son of the harper,' G. *clàrsair*. Andrew McClairscher in Galloway had a respite for "tressonable intercommonyng with Inglismen" in 1529 (RMS., III, 431). Cf. MACCHRUITER.

MACCLATCHIE, MACCLATCHY. See under MACLATCHIE.

MACCLAY. A form of MACLAE, q.v.

MACCLEAN, MACCLEANE. Forms of MACLEAN, q.v., current in Ayrshire. John M'Cleane, merchant burgess, Irvine, 1666 (*Irvine*, II, p. 200).

MACCLEARY. A variant of MACCHLERY, q.v.

MACCLEAVE. Alexander M'Cleave was shoemaker in Minnigaff, 1737 (*Wigtown*). In 1684 (*Parish*) the name is spelled McCleave, McClave, McCleve, and shortened to Cleave. Woulfe has *MacLaithimh*, a variant of *MacFhlaithimh*, 'son of *Flaitheamh*'.

MACCLEE. Ewen M'Clee witnessed an instrument of sasine of the lands of Tollard begg, 1478 (*Lamont*, p. 24). Perhaps from Ir. *Mac Laoidhigh*, 'son of *Laoidheach*,' the name of an old family in Leix (*Woulfe*).

MACCLEIR. Robert McCleir, son and heir of Malcolm McClery in Stirling, 1541 (RSS., II, 4142). John McCleir, cordiner in Dumfries, 1619 (RPC., XI, p. 98), and Thomas McClair, son of George McClair of Prestonpans, 1663. Gottrav M'Leir was accused of forgery in 1664 (*Just. Rec.*, I, p. 83).

MACCLEISH. G. *M'A 'Liòs* for fuller *Mac Gill' Iosa*, 'son of the servant of Jesus.' Mychael M'Cleish or M'Cleisch was tenant of the 'Brewland cum le stallage' in Dumfriesshire in 1376 (RHM., I, p. liii; II, p. 16). Thomas M'Cleche

MACCLEISH, *continued*

was a voter in parish of Qwilton (Coylton), 1514, and Michaile M'Cleys, witness in Carrik, 1514 (*Ros.*, 52, 84). Duncan M'Cleish was servant to Dwgall M'Dugall in Deweldik, 1588 (*Sc. Ant.*, VI, p. 163), another Duncan M'Cleiche was admitted burgess of Glasgow, 1589, and a third Duncan M'Cleishe, burgess freeman in 1627 (*Burgesses*). Robert M'Gleish, burgess of Irvine, 1686, and John M'Cleish, burgess, 1745 (*Irvine* II, p. 309, 324). McCleisich 1704, M'Cliesh 1703.

MACCLELLAN, Macclelland, Macleland, Maclalland, Macllellan, and Maclelland. G. *Mac Gill'* *Fhaolain* (the Gillafaelan of the genealogical MS. of 1467), 'son of the servant of (S.)Fillan.' Fillan, EIr. *Faelan*, OIr. *Failan*, is a reduced form of *faelchu*, from *fail*, now *faol*, 'a wolf.' Maclellans were numerous in Galloway in the latter end of the fourteenth century, and they gave name to Balmaclellan (i.e. Maclellan's town) in the Stewartry. M'Kerlie (III, p. 62) says the lands were granted to John Maclellan by James III in February, 1466, when his name was given to the lands on his bestowing a site for a new church, but I have found no record of this. The lands are mentioned in 1457, in which year Sir Alexander Boyd had sasine of them (ER., VI, p. 347). John M'Lelane filius Dungalli Johnsone had a charter of the lands of Balmaclelane from Vedastus Greresone, dominus de Lag, which received the royal confirmation in August, 1466 (RMS., II, 907). The earliest record of the surname is in 1305–6 when Patrick, son of Gilbert M'Lolane, with several others, took the Castle of Dumfries from followers of Bruce (*Bain*, IV, 389). In the reign of David II, Gilbert McGillolane appears as Captain of Clenconnan in Galloway (RMS., I, App. II, 912), a clan of which there is no other record. As Gylbert Mclolane he appears as juror on an inquisition at Dumfrese in 1367 (RHM., II, p. 64). Gillebertus MacLelan Galvediensis (i.e. of Galloway) was elected bishop of Man and the Sudreys (i.e. the South Isles) before 1325 and held the see for two and a half years (*Chronica Regum Manniae*, 1860, p. 30). Matthew McLolan, knight, and Gilbert, son of Gilbert McLolan, were witnesses, 1347 (*Pap. Lett.*, III, p. 396). Cane McGillolane witnessed the foundation charter of Sweetheart Abbey in 1359 (*Genealogist*, new ser. XVI, p. 218). In 1381 John Maklolayn petitioned for a benefice in the gift of the abbot and convent of Glenluce (Gleynluis) in the diocese of Whitehorne (*Pap. Pet.*, I, p. 559, 561). Ingeram M'Gillelan held lands in Forfarshire in 1372 (RMS., I, 515), and about the same

period or a little later he also held the lands of Dalecarne in the upper half of the barony of Glenstanchere (*Crossraguel*, I, p. 40). Donald Maklellane appears as Steward of Kirkcudbright in 1457 (ER., VI, p. 352), and a later Donald Mclalan witnessed a bond of manrent by Malcolm Moir Makesaig to Ronald Campbell of Barchibayan in 1592 (*Coll.*, p. 198). A number of persons are also recorded in Morar, Inverness-shire, about 1670, the clan Illeulan of the Wardlaw Manuscript (*Wardlaw*, p. 185). Henry M'Lelann held land in Inverness in 1457 (*Invernessiana*, p. 135). Estir Cammis and Cammislittill were let to Thome McFulain (i.e. Maclellan without the 'Gille') in 1480 (ER., VIII, p. 564). Peter McLellan was one of the first to receive from the Crown a grant of land which remained after the expulsion of the Acadians (1755) in Nova Scotia. Some Maclellans in the Aberfeldy district of Perthshire are regarded as a sept of the Macnabs who were the lay abbots of Glendochart. John Mac Donoquhy Mac Lelandis in Muckairn is mentioned under 1596 in connection with a raid (RPC., V). Duncan M'Illewlane in Soccoth was a Glenurquhay vassal, 1638 (BBT., p. 403), Duncan M'Ilelan in Faranbock, parish of Kilbride, 1699 (*Argyll*), Donald Bane M'Illeland in Brawallich, 1717 (*Campbell*, I, p. 159), and Duncan M'Ileolan in Miggerney, 1725 (*Dunkeld*). The name is also current without Mac and with gille preserved. M'Cleallane 1605, McCleilane 1522, McClelan 1509, Maclelane 1424, Maghellen 1478, Maklellan 1653, McKlellan 1684, Maklellane 1512, M'Lelen 1484, M'Lellane 1471, Makellane 1512.

MACCLEMENT, Macclements, Macclemont. Forms of Maclamond, q.v.

MACCLENAGHAN. See MACCLANNACHAN.

MACCLENNAN. See under MACLENNAN.

MACCLERY. A variant of Macchlery, q.v.

MACCLETCHIE. See under MACLATCHIE.

MACCLEW, Macclue, Macclute. Variants found mainly in Ayrshire, Arran, and Glasgow. John M'Clew recorded in Buchlyvie, 1661 (*Dunblane*). See also under Maclae, and for origin see Dunsleve.

MACCLIBARN. Ysaac Macclibarn, father of Andrew de Dalrewach, is mentioned c. 1290 (*Athole*, p. 705).

MACCLIMENTS. A variant of Maclamond, q.v.

MACCLINGAN. A Galloway surname. Alexander M'Clingan in Carsewalloch, parish of Kirkmabreck, 1716 (*Kirkcudbright*). McClingen and M'Clengen 1684 (*Parish*). With omission of 'Mac' gives CLINGAN, CLINGEN, q.v.

MACCLINIE. Letters were raised against Donald McClino, an accomplice of Shaw of Halie, 1569 (RPC., II, p. 570). William, Alexander, and Agnes McClinie appear in Kurckeume (Kirkcolm), and Geo. and Joh. McLinyie in Mochrum parochin, 1684 (*Parish*, p. 19). From Ir. *Mac Giolla Choinnigh*, 'son of the servant of (S.) Canice' (Cainnech — Kenneth). McClinnie 1684.

MACCLINTOCK, MACLINTOCK. G. *Mac Ghill Fhionndaig*, commonly *MacGilliondaig* (for *M'Ill'Fhionndaig*), 'son of (S.) Findan's gillie.' S. Findan was founder of the monastery of Clonard. *Fintan, Fintoc* (whence later *Fionndoc*), are diminutives of *Finn*, later *Fionn*. M'Gillindak is author of a poem in the Dean of Lismore's Book. The Maclintocks belong to Luss and thereabouts and in the district of Lorn around Lochaweside from 1500. Duncan Mc gellentak, witness in Balquhidder, 1549 (HP., IV, p. 32). The name also occurs in the Kirk-Session records of Kenmore, Aberfeldy, in 1757 as M'Ilandick, M'Illandag, M'Illandick, M'Lentick (these four the same person). Another form in the same record is M'Illendaig (*Christie*, p. 16–18). MacIlliuntaig, MacIllintog. Some Maclintocks as early as 1611 are said to have Englished their name as Lindsay. On this Ailean Dall, in his poem to the Lochaber Volunteers in 1795, referring to a warrior from Glenara says:

"Ciamar théid na h-uaislean cruinn
Gun Lindsay 'bhith san airimh
Ga 'n ainm Cailean MacIlliuntaig
Le thionndadh an Gaidhlig."

John M'Inlaintaig in Colgine, Kilbride 1693 (*Argyll Inv.*). James Mcillandaig was the last of the Breadalbane smugglers (FB., p. 364). M'Clintoch 1684, McInlintak 1692. The name of John Macilluntud, priest, of the diocese of Whiteherne, who petitioned for a benefice in the gift of the abbot and monastery of Paisley, 1394 (*Pap. Pet.*, I, p. 619) is probably an error for Macclintock.

MACCLINTON. A variant of MACLINTOCK, q.v., from the form *Fintán*. William McClintoun was messenger in Kyle in 1569 (RMS.). Finlay Macklintoun appears in the parish of Torphichen in 1676 (*Torphichen*).

MACCLONE. A Galloway surname recorded there in 1684. From Ir. *Mac giolla Eóin*, 'son of (S.) John's gillie.' Cf. MACLEAN.

MACCLOOR. A current form of MACCLURE, q.v.

MACCLORGAN. John M'Clorgan was shot at Drummelian (? Drumellan, Maybole) for the crime of being a Covenanter, 1685 (*Hanna*, II, p. 258).

MACCLORY. A surname found in Galloway and in Ulster, derived from Ir. *Mac Labhradha*, 'son of Labhraidh,' whence also Macglory, Lavery, etc.

MACCLOY. G. *MacLughaidh*, 'son of Lewie' (pet form of Lewis). The Maccloys of Bute and Arran are offshoots of the family of Fullarton of Fullarton in Ayrshire. "Two sons went out of the house of Fullarton, one of the name of Lewis and the other James. Lewis went to Arran and was called McLewis or Mccloy he Acquired Lands in Arran holding of the Croun and was made Crouner of Arran" (*Macfarlane*, II, p. 343), and Martin says that the most ancient family in Arran "is by the Natives reckoned to be Mack Lowis" whose "surname in English is Fullarton" (W. I., p. 223). The name appears in 1472 as Maclow, in 1511 as M'Lowe, and in 1526 as M'Loy (Reid, *Bute*, p. 205). Donald Clowie or Makcloye was a witness in Cowell, 1537 and 1540 (RMS., III, 1677, 2146), and Gilbert MacLoy in Glendaruel was slain along with the Lamonts in the massacre at Toward, 1646. Rev. Donald M'Cloy was minister at Kilmodan, 1609, and his grandson was consecrated bishop of the non-jurant church in Edinburgh, 1705, and elected Primus of the Scottish Episcopal Church, 1720. The name is sometimes Englished Maclewis (G. *Luthais*). Some Gaelic writers thinking that Fullarton meant "fuller's town" render the name "son of fulling" (G. *luaidh*).

MACCLUE, MACCLUIE. See MACCLEW.

MACCLUMPHA, MACLUMFA, MACLUMPHA. G. *Mac Gille Iomchadha*, 'son of the servant of (S.) Imchad.' Imchad was the name of an ancestor of S. Senán of Inis Cathaigh, and another Imchad Uallach (i.e. the proud) was ancestor of S. Cronán of Roscrea. Joneta Makgillumquha had a charter of the lands of Closerath and Drumdowle in the barony of Clogstoune, sheriffdom of Wigtoun, from her cousin Alexander Fraser, lord of Philorth, in 1406 (*Illus.*, IV, p. 642). Fergus M'Lymphquhay witnessed an instrument of sasine of the lands of Mureth (Monreith) in 1483 (*Ramage*, p. 187). John Maklunfaw, one of the two occupiers of the 40s. lands of Blarebov in the barony of Mureith in 1509 is probably the John Maklumphaire who was convicted of

MACCLUMPHA, Maclumfa..., continued
stouthrieff of the wood of Garthlone in 1510
(RMS., II, 3394; Agnew, I, p. 330). The late
Dr. Trotter stated (Galloway gossip: Wigtownshire, Bedlington, 1877, p. 66) that the family
of McLumfa, from motives of 'gentility,' had
changed their name to McClew; and that the
old chapel of Killumpha in Kirkmaiden was
"dug up to the foundations about fifty years
since because it spoiled a corner of a turnip
field" (ibid., p. 377). Killumpha in the parish
of Kirkmaiden was known in 1545 as Killum-
quhay-Agnew (RMS., III, 3112) and in 1618
as Kilumpha-Agnew (Retours, Wigtown, 48,
135, 191). The surname M'Cluma, found in
Kellistoune, Dumfriesshire, in 1657 (Dumfries)
is possibly a variant. McClumfa 1636. In 1684
the forms McClunpha, McKClumpha and Mc-
Lumpha are recorded (Parish), and also the
shortened form Clumphae. See also. Maclumfa.

MACCLUNE. Ir. Mac Giolla Eóin, 'son of the
servant of (S.) John,' and so same as Maclean,
q.v. Donald Makclune had sasine of the lands
of Barneill in Ayrshire, 1514 (ER., XIV, p. 563;
Ros, 84). Sir Andree McClune was vicar pensioner of Suthik, 1539 (RSS., II, 3213). William
McClun in Ballairdis was charged in 1621 with
refusing to give instruction in his trade of
tanning (RPC., XII, p. 432). Robert Macclone
of Holmes appears in the same document as
McClune, 1624 (Hunter, p. 51). Robert
M'Clune was retoured heir of Robert M'Clune
of Holmes, his father, 1647, and David M'Clean
(this spelling represents MacGiolla Eóin) was
retoured heir of Robert M'Clane of Holmes,
1673 (Retours, Ayr, 409, 590). Samuel
M'Clune in Mulloch, 1786 (Kirkcudbright).
McClun 1635, M'Clwn 1514, McClwne 1624.

MACCLUNG, Maclung. A rare Galloway surname still current in Ayrshire and Kirkcudbrightshire. G. Mac Luinge, 'son of the ship,'
a seaman. Cf. the name of S. Columba's grandfather, in Latin Filius Nauis, 'Scotica vero
lingua Mac Naue.' The name seems wrongly
equated with Maclurg, q.v., by the editor of
the Parish lists of Wigtownshire and Minnigaff, 1684 (Scot. Rec. Soc.). McClunge 1684.

MACCLURE, Maclure, Maccloor, Mac-
leur. G. M'Ill'uidhir, 'son of Odhar's servant.'
A common surname in Galloway of old as it is
to-day. John McLur, Robert McLure, and
Robert McClure, followers of the earl of Cassilis, were respited for murder, 1526 (RSS.,
I, 3386), and Tho. Maklure was sergeant of
assize in Carrick, 1532 (RMS., III, 1196).
Johnne McLoir signed the Band of Dumfries,
1570 (RPC., XIV, p. 67). Andrew McLuir in

Bugane and three others of the name were
charged with assault, 1607 (ibid., p. 518),
and Fergus McLur in Craigfine was charged
with usury, 1617 (ibid., XI, p. 142). Gilleane
MacIloure was bowman to the laird of Parbrek,
1618 (ibid., p. 464), and John M'Clour appears in Apyn, 1684 (Dunblane). Elizabeth
M'Cloor or M'Clwre is in record in Barley,
Galloway, 1684, and as Elizabeth M'Whore
(!) in Barley, she and Mary M'Whore were
sentenced to be banished to the plantations
for resetting of rebels and other offences in the
same year (RPC., 3. ser. x, p. 257, 604, 615).
Andrew McKluire in the parish of Carsfern
was reckoned a disorderly person (i.e. a non-
conformist) in the same year (ibid., IX, p. 578).
William MacClure (1763–1840), born in Ayr,
was called "Father of American geology."
There are a number of families in Sleat named
in English Maclure, but whose name is spelled
in G. M'Leòra (for MacGille dheòradha), a
side form of Dewar, q.v. The earliest documentary evidence of a clan piper is a reference
to Robert MacLure, piper to the chief of the
Buchanans, in 1600, who got into trouble a
few years later as appears from the Stirling
Kirk-Session Register, under May 28th, 1604.
McCluir and McCluire 1684, Makcluir 1637.
See also Macalear.

MACCLURICH. A surname recorded in Argyllshire. Probably a variant of Macclerich.
See Macchlery.

MACCLUSKY, Macluskie, Maclusky, Mac-
closkey, Macluskey. An Irish name found
in Galloway and Glasgow. Ir. Mac (Bh)loscaidh,
son of Bloscadh, a personal name among the
O'Kanes (Woulfe).

MACCLYMOND, Macclymont, Maccly-
mount. Galloway forms of Maclamond, q.v.
The following spellings all occur in 1684
(Parish): MacClymont, McClamont, McClamot,
McClemen, McClement, McClemin, McCly-
mon, McClymond, and McLymond, and Cly-
mont. McClymonts are mentioned as farmers
in Ayrshire in 1613 (McKechnie, The Lamont
Clan, p. 129). James McClymont, witness in
Carrick, 1687 (RPC., 3. ser. XIII, p. 197).

MACCOAN. See under MACILCHOMH-
GHAIN and MACCOWAN.

MACCOARD, Maccord, Maccourt. Maccord
is an old surname in the parish of Ballantrae
(Paterson, II, p. 87). Woulfe says same as
MacCuarta, MacCuairt, "not improbably a
corruption of MacMhuircheartaigh." Cf. Mac-
kirdy. Nigel M'Corde resigned the lands of
Skeich in the sheriffdom of Wigtoune, 1471
(RMS., II, 1025), and Gilbert Makcorde ap-

pears in Wigtownshire, 1473 (ALHT., I, p. 9). John M'Cord and George M'Cord were occupiers of Nether Barnele in Carrick, 1544 (RMS., III, 3025), and William M'Cord was admitted burgess of Glasgow, 1627 (*Burgesses*).

MACCODRUM. G. *MacCodrum*, not *Mac-Còdruim* as sometimes spelled (*Celt. Rev.*, IX, p. 262). A Hebridean surname having its origin in the Old Norse personal name *Guttorm-r* or *Goðorm-r*, meaning 'good' or 'god serpent.' The Norse name was at one time common in the Western Isles. Among the Hebrideans the Maccodrums are known as the *Clann 'ic Codrum nan ròn*, 'Maccodrums of the seals.' A number of curious stories are told of this sept, some account of which will be found in Gregorson Campbell's *Superstitions of the Highlands and Islands*, p. 284. "All the MacCodrums of North Uist," says Fiona Macleod (William Sharp), "had been brown-skinned, and brown-haired, and brown-eyed; and herein may have lain the reason why, in by-gone days, this small clan in Uist was known throughout the Western Isles as *Sliochd nan Ron*, i.e., 'Race of the Seals' " (*Sin eater and other tales*, p. 156–157). The sept name was *Clann Mhic Codrum*. A celebrated individual of this name was John M'Codrum (1710–1796), a North Uist bard. He was an excellent poet of the modern school and bard to Sir James Macdonald of Sleat. He "had a croft rent-free for life, together with five bolls of meal, five stones of cheese, and £2.5s. of money" (TGSI., XXIX, p. 197). The form *Macodrum* is also in use. Many of the name have made themselves Macdonalds. In Gaelic folklore seals are said to be human beings *fo gheasan*, "under a spell."

MACCOEL. A family named McCoel, McCeol, or McKoel, seem to have pronounced their name McCoal. "This name and its varied spellings occur extensively in the Lochgoilhead Parish Records from 1695 to 1770, when it ceases altogether. It was at one time common in Kilmorich Parish. This family are said to have been a branch of the MacNaughtans" (*Clan McColl journal*, IV, p. 38).

MACCOHENANE. Thomas McCohenane in Rowdill, Argyll, is mentioned in 1541 (RSS., II, 4337). Ane (= Ian) McCohynnoquhen or McConvnnoquhen was tenant of Saligo, Islav, 1541 (ER., XVII, p. 619). Gilleis M'Cochennan was part occupier of the two merk-land of Machribeg, Kintyre, 1596 (HP., III, p. 77).

MACCOILIRE. Murdo McCoilire in Keppoch Mickles in 1726 (HP., II, p. 328) = *Mac Dhomhnuill odhar*, 'son of dun Donald.' Not a patronymic.

MACCOILVAYNE. Duncan Mc Coilvayne was fined for reset of Clan Gregor in 1613 (RPC., XIV, p. 632) = *Mac Dhomhnuill bhain*, 'son of Donald the fair.' Not a patronymic.

MACCOLE. A current form of MACCOLL, q.v.

MACCOLL. G. *MacColla*, 'son of COLL,' q.v. Maccolls have been long settled in Appin and around Ballachulish, and though said to be of Macdonald race they followed the Stewarts of Appin, being native men to the latter. Eighteen Maccolls in Stewart of Appin's regiment in the '45 were killed and fifteen wounded (*Coll.*, p. 199). Historical references to the name are very meagre, and though the etymology of the name from the personal name Coll might infer a connection with the Macdonalds the precise meaning of the name is not quite clear. One of the most distinguished of the name was Evan McColl (1808–98), author of *Clarsach nam Beann* ('The Mountain minstrel'). The earliest known Maccoll of those who held charters of the lands in Glasdrum was Paul MacColl, who must have lived about the year 1500 (*Clan MacColl journal*, III, p. 53). A payment of £25 Scots was made to Mathew M'Koll, merchant burgess of Edinburgh, 1720 (*Guildry*, p. 123). Two men named MacColl, were servants to James Stewart of the Glen. "Although cited in the trial as MacColls, they do not seem to have been MacColls at all. At least the writer of the tale [the Gaelic tale given in TGSI., V, 35] writes, for the most part, MacSholla and Clan Sholla. In Campbell's MS. *Tales* they are said to be descended from a certain Solla, who lived near Oban, and eventually settled at Innseag in Appin (MS. *West Highland tales*, V, 1, p. 210). They are said to have been once Barons of Bealach (bràigh Dhail na Tràgha), but that during the Wars of Montrose they sold their lands and went to live in Lettermore at the foot of Beinn a' Bheithir. It is apparent that the name of Solomon was in the family, for one of the Crown witnesses cited was Solomon MacColl, merchant in Auchindarroch" (TGSI., XXXV, p. 399).

MACCOLLAE. A common surname in Inveraven parish records and in Inveraven kirk-session records in seventeenth and eighteenth centuries. McAllea 1757, Mcalea 1727, McKlea 1750, McKoilae 1704, Mackole 1632, McKollie 1631, McLea 1745, McOlea 1743.

MACCOLMAN. G. *MacColmáin*, 'son of COLMAN,' q.v. The spellings of this name are badly mangled in the early records. Gillenem mac Coleman witnessed charters by Duncan, son of Gilbert son of Fergus of Galloway, of lands in Carric, c. 1200 or earlier (*Melros*,

474

MACCOLMAN, *continued*

I, p. 22, 24). As Gillenem Accoueltan he is witness to a charter by Roger de Scalebroc of lands in Carrik in the reign of William the Lion (ibid., p. 25). As Gillenem Maccolem he witnessed a charter by Raderic Mac Gillescop of lands in the same territory to the Abbey of Melrose in the same reign (ibid., p. 29). As Gillenef Okeueltal he again appears as witness to a grant of lands in the same territory in the reign of Alexander II (ibid., p. 172). See MACCALMAN.

MACCOMB, MACCOMBE. From G. *Mac Thóm*, 'son of Tom,' now often Englished THOM. The *b* is accretionary. Gilchrist Makcome, a follower of the earl of Cassilis, was respited for murder in 1526 (RSS., I, 3386). Roger M'Com appears in Netherglen, 1679 *(Kirkcudbright),* and Robert McKome was charged with being a disorderly person in the parish of Carsfern, 1684 (RPC., 3. ser. IX, p. 574). In the Parish Lists of Wigtownshire and Minnigaff, 1684, the name also appears as McColm, McComb, McCome, and McKComb.

MACCOMBICH, MACCHOMBICH. G. *Mac-Thomaidh*, 'son of Tommie' (diminutive of Thomas). A common name in Breadalbane two hundred years ago (SN&Q., III, p. 172), and still found in Argyllshire. Somerled MacCombich c. 1442 (TGSI., XXII, p. 61). Archibald M'Combich in Coull in Appin, 1690 *(Argyll Inv.).* John Bwy McComiche in the barony of Glenlyoun was fined for reset of outlawed Macgregors, 1613 (RPC., XIV, p. 633). Malcolm M'Chomich in Wuroch, parish of Inshall, 1685 *(Argyll),* and Duncan M'Comick in Euill of Duror, 1686 (ibid.). Duncan Dow M'Chombeich of Achosrigan was in the Rebellion of 1745, and five Maccombichs in Stewart of Appin's regiment in the '45 were killed and three wounded *(Coll.,* p. 199).

MACCOMBIE, MACCOMBE, MACCOMIE, MACOMIE. G. *MacComaidh,* a contracted form of *MacThomaidh,* 'son of Tommie or Tommy.' In Perthshire frequently Englished Thomson. The *b* was introduced into the name about the end of the eighteenth century. MacComy was a common surname in Breadalbane 250 and more years ago. The Glenshee MacComies date their rise from the latter half of the fourteenth century. They appear as a distinct family in Glenshee in the sixteenth century, and in a feu-charter of the lands of Finnegand and Glenbeg granted in 1571 to John M'Comy Moir they are described as being *ab antiquo* tenants and possessors of these lands. Thom Makcome (three syllables), natural son of

Johannes Makcome de Castelmylk, had a precept of legitimation "in debita form," 1508 (RSS., I, 1760). Ewin M'Comie is author of a short poem containing allusions to several individuals famous in Gaelic mythology (*Book Dean of Lismore,* p. 102). Margaret MacColmy was appointed lauendar (laundress) to the prince, 1540, and James M'Comy had 'ane respitt' in 1542 for the slaughter of Alane McRowie (RSS., II, 3557, 4953). An assize upon Ferquhair McCombquhy was summoned at Elgin in 1556 (ALHT., X, p. 318). John Makthomy Makgillewie and William Makthomy Makgilleweyi's son gave their band to Duncan Campbell of Glenurquhay, 1586 (BBT., p. 240). In the "Roll of Clans," 1587, the Maccomies appear as "Clan M'Thomas in Glensche." Kaithren M'Comey, relict of umquhile Ewin M'Ewin, was "convict of blooding of the Lairdis ky" in December, 1623 (BBT., p. 379), which appears to point to a local famine. John McColmie was forfeited for assisting the marquis of Montrose, 1645 (APS.), and Patrick McKommie had a bad reputation as a charmer at Kildrummie, 1663 *(Alford Rec.,* p. 8, 9, 12, etc.). John M'Omie in Creitmoran, 1638 (BBT., p. 401). Mackomie and M'Komy 1696, M'Colmy 1644, McColme 1595, M'Come 1644; McChomay, M'Homie.

MACCOMISH. *See under* MACOMISH.

MACCOMISKEY. This Polish looking name, found in Glasgow, is Irish, *MacCumascaigh,* 'son of Cumascach.'

MACCONACHER, MACCONNACHER. Neil McConquhar or M'Conoquhair was tenant of Calmissary, Islay, 1541 (ER., XVII, p. 618, 639).

MACCONACHIE, MACCONACHY, MACCONACHY, MACCONCHIE, MACCONCHY, MACCONECHIE, MACCONECHY, MACCONKEY, MACCONNACHIE, MACCONNECHIE, MACCONNOCHIE, MACCONOCHIE, MACCONOUGHEY, MACONACHIE, MACONACHIE, MACONECHY, MACKONOCHIE. G. *MacDhonnchaidh,* 'son of DUNCAN,' q.v. The Clan Donnachie *(Clann Donnchaidh),* better known as Clan Robertson of Atholl, are so named from 'Fat Duncan' *(Donncha Reamhar)* de Atholia, who lived in the time of Robert the Bruce. There was an old sept of Macconochies in Bute, and of seventy-five persons holding lands there in 1506 six were of this name. In addition to *the* Clan Donnachie or Robertsons there are three Argyllshire families that were known as MacDhonnachie: (1) MacConchie of Inverawe, an old sept of the Campbells. The Macconnachies of Meadowbank in Midlothian were descended from them. (2) MacDhonnachie Mhor or Campbell of Duntroon. (3) MacDhonnachie or Campbell of Glenfeochan. The Campbells of Kilmartin are of uncertain origin. They may have been originally Campbells or a sept of the MacDhonnachies. The Macconochie Campbells of Inverawe are descended from Duncan (Donachie) Campbell, son of Sir Neil Campbell who died before 1316. Angus M'Conchie witnessed a sasine of Cragniche to Archibald, earl of Argyll, 1493 (OPS., II, p. 97). Huchon McConzochquhy was part tenant of Kynnarde Ross, 1505 (ER., XII, p. 664). Archibald Machonzie de Leragis appears as one of an inquest in 1510. Others named on the inquest are Iain Makchonze in Stronchormaig and Gillespuig McCual McChonzie in the Kneppach, his near kindred. These three were Macconochie Campbells. Fynlaw McAndoche witnessed sasine of the lands of Balnacard, 1514 (Grandtully, I, p. 48), and Donald Dow McDouil McConche is in record, 1518 (Cawdor, p. 129). Gilbert Makonoquhy, a follower of the earl of Cassilis was respited for murder, 1526 (RSS., I, 3386). Duncan M'Condoquhy and John M'Condoquhy witnessed a Glenurquhay bond of manrent, 1528 (BBT., p. 179). Patrick M'Conquhy appears as witness at Kingarth, Bute, 1534, and Joh. M'Conquy de Culwyne was also witness in Bute, 1540 (RMS., III, 1378, 2583), and Eugene McConquhie had sasine of lands there, 1560 (ER., XIX, p. 460). Swyne M'Conquhie and William M'Ane Makconquhye gave their bonds of manrent to George, earl of Huntlie, 1543 (SCM., IV, p. 260), and John M'Conachyw appears as witness in Glenurquhay, 1552 (BBT., p. 197). Thomas Makcongwe, a witness at the monastery of Sweetheart, 1550, and William M'Condoquhy in Drumboe was a witness, 1566 (Laing, 559, 808). Matho McAndochie in Clunes, 1578 (RPC., III, p. 51), Johnne Campbell alias M'Conquhie, tutor of Inverawe, gave his bond in 1585 (BBT., p. 235) and David McConnoquhy or McConoquhy was concerned in the burning and spoiling of Moyness, 1602 (Rose, p. 292). John M'Conche was retoured heir of Allan M'Conechie in Bute, in 1602 (Retours, Bute, 12). Duncan M'Ondoquhy Vane of Kildovie appears in record, 1605 (HP., III, p. 85), and Gillechrist M'Ondochie Voir in Drimcroy, 1638 (BBT., p. 401). Alexander M'Ronache (vel M'Conachie) was retoured heir of Eugene M'Cronachie of Ambrisbeg, Bute, 1632 (Retours, Bute, 42). John McConchei, burgess of Inverness, 1652 (More Cull. Pap., p. 121). Donald M'Onochie in Kilvicewn and Thomas M'Onohie vic Avish in Icolmkill were denounced rebels in 1675 (HP., I, p. 297, 298). Alexander Mc honichv, Gilbert mc khonachy, John Mc chonachv, Archibald mc kihonochy, and Duncan Mc kihonchy were enrolled among

the fencible men of Argyll, 1682 (Commons, p. 58–60). Thomas McConchie was schoolmaster at Corstorphine, 1688 (RPC., 3. ser. XIII, p. 202), Colin M'Conachie Mholaich was one of the duke of Atholl's Fencible men in Glenlyon, 1706 (HMon., III, p. 215), and John McOnachy was a Seaforth tenant, 1721 (HP., II, p. 298). M'Condachie and M'Condachy 1674, M'Condochie 1588, M'Condoquhy 1532, M'Conchrie 1684, M'Conquhie 1586, Makconoch 1506, Mackchonchie 1603, McKondachy 1791, Makchonachv 1576, M'Kunuchie 1597; MacConochey, Makconchie, Makconqwe, M'Onoghuy, Vᶜonchie. McConnchye 1692.

MACCONCHER. A small sept in Lorn. The name is a shortened form of MACCONNACHER, q.v.

MACCONDOCHIE. A form of MACCONACHIE, q.v. A sept of Macgregors were known by the name of M'Condochy or M'Condoquhy, through their descent from a Duncan Leonach (15th century). John Dow Macquhondoquhy was minister of the parish of Laggan in 1575. The name is corrupted into Vᶜ onche, and in 1606 McDonche.

MACCONE. Eugene Makcone and David Makcone in record in Inverness, 1497 (Invernessiana, p. 165). Woulfe gives MacCone as an Englishing of MacEoghain, and says the Anglicized forms of the latter and those of MacEóin "are pronounced so nearly alike that it is impossible to distinguish them" (p. 359).

MACCONECHIE, MACCONECHY. Forms of MACCONACHIE, q.v.

MAC CONELLVICINISH, 1718 = Mac Dhomhnuill mhic Aonghais, not a patronymic.

MACCONICA. This appears to be an English corruption of MACCONACHIE, q.v.

MACCONICH. A name recorded in Atholl from fifteenth to seventeenth century. John McCoynich, witness at Balquhidder, 1549 (HP., IV, p. 32). See under the Anglicized form CUNIESON.

MACCONKEY. A form of MACCONACHIE, q.v.

MACCONNACHER. See under MACCONACHER.

MACCONNACHIE. See under MACCONACHIE.

MACCONNAL, MACCONNEL, MACCONNELL. G. MacDhomhnuill, pronounced Maak oonil. These spellings are simply variants of MACDONNEL, q.v., through assimilation of the initial

MACCONNAL, Macconnel..., *continued*

D. They occur mainly in the shires of Argyll, Ayr, and Wigtown. William Mc conill vayne vic ean vreick in the parish of Urray was charged with being an engager on the royalist side, 1649 (IDR., p. 367). In 1684 (*Parish*) spelled McConnal,. McConnele, McKconnell, McKonnell. (2) MacConnel or MacConnell, Ir. *MacConnaill*, son of Conall, is a name of different origin. Conall here is for an ancient personal name meaning 'high powerful,' in Old Celtic * *Kuno-valo-s.*

MACCONNECHIE, Macconnechy, Macconnochie, Macconochie. Forms of Macconachie, q.v.

MACCONOQUHAR. *See under* MACCONNACHER.

MACCOO. This name appears in the Glasgow Directory, and is most probably from Ir. *MacAodha*, 'son of *Aodh*' (= Hugh), a very common Irish name.

MACCOOISH. *See under* MACCUISH.

MACCOOK. An old surname in Kintyre and Arran, but usually simply COOK in English. (1) From Ir. *MacCúg*, son of Hugh, a branch of the Burkes (*Joyce*). John M'Cuk, Andrew M'Cuk, and Richard M'Cuk were tenants under the Douglases in Garvald, 1376 (RHM., I, p. lviii), and William Mokcok (a papal spelling), priest, petitioned for the perpetual vicarage of Crosmichaells in the diocese of Whitehern, 1381 (*Pap. Pet.*, I, p. 556). (2) from Ir. *Mac Dhabhuc* (in the spoken language *MacCuag*), son of Davuc, a diminutive of David. John M'Coug in Killean parish, 1686, and Kath. M'Coick in Lergiemore, 1695 (*Argyll*). McCoacke 1786, McCock 1762, M'Cook 1774, Mack Cook 1787, Mc couk 1770, M'couke 1728, McCuk 1768; M'Couck, MacCoaig. The name has been popularly explained by a bit of folklore, from "cubhag (pron. k'uh'ak) which is formed directly from -*coo* of 'cuckoo,' by the addition of the native suffix" (Prof. Fraser, SGS., I, p. 207). Two persons named Mc Cick and one named Mc Kick are in Lismore, 1692, several persons named Mc Kyek appear in Kilbride in same year (*Commons*, p. 29).

MACCOOL. One of the many corrupt forms of MacDougal, q.v.

MACCORC. About 1290 Malcolm, earl of Levenax confirmed the grant by Thomas de Cremennane of the quarter lands of Croyne to Murdach MacKork (*Levenax*, p. 80). As Morthan MacKorc he is mentioned in the in-

hibition by the bishop of Glasgow directed against Malcolm, earl of Lennox and his adherents in 1294 (RMP., p. * 203). In other documents of the same period he is referred to as Murechauch or Murechanich (the latter evidently a misprint) filius Kork (*Levenax*, p. 79, 81). Kork or Corc was one of the sons of Alwyn, second earl of Levenax (ibid., p. 98). *Corc* is an old Irish personal name (in gen. in LL., 349a as *Cuirc*: from *corc*, 'heart'). It also occurs as *Curc-* in an ogham inscription found at Rathmalade, Ireland (Macalister, *Studies*, I, p. 72). See also MACCURK.

MACCORD. *See under* MACCOARD.

MACCORKIE. An abbreviated form of MacCorkill, q.v.

MACCORKILL, Maccorkle. G. *MacThorcuill*, 'son of Thorcull,' from a shortened form of Thorketill (see MACCORQUODALE). Jannet M'Korkyll 'qwlk wes slaine' in 1561 is again referred to as Jannet Nvk Kerkyll and Jannet M'Corker (*Dallas*, p. 90). Isaack McCorquell in Drumnacarrie was fined for resetting outlawed Macgregors, 1613 (RPC., XIV, p. 632). Lachlan McOrkill in Cames, Mull, was put to the horn, 1629 (RPC., 2. ser. III, p. 45). M'Thurkill and M'Kurkull occur in 1661 and 1663 (*Argyll; Caithness*).

MACCORKINDALE. A form of Maccorquodale, q.v.

MACCORKLE. *See under* MACCORKILL.

MACCORLEY. Most probably a corruption of Macaulay, q.v.

MACCORMACK, Maccormick. G. *MacCormaig*, *MacCormaic*, or *MacC(h)ormaig*, 'son of Cormac' (see CORMACK). Gillecrist mac Córmaic is one of the witnesses to grant to the Abbey of Deer, 1132 (*Bk. Deer*, III, 8–9). Gilbert McCormok, 1478 (ALC.). Hester M'Gormock was retoured heir of Gilbert M'Cormock of Barley, 1696 (*Retours, Kirkcudbright*, 382). John M'Comok in Path, 1774 (*Wigtown*) is a mis-spelling. John M'Cormick in Broach, 1797 (*Kirkcudbright*). Maccormick is more common in the Highlands. In 1684 (*Parish*): McArmick, McCarmick, McCarmike, McCormick, McKermick, Makarmik, McCornick, McCornock, McCornok, McKornock> Cormack, Cornick, Cramick. Elsewhere: Makcormok, M'Kernok, M'Kornok.

MACCORMYLL. Sir Andrew Mackormvll, vicar of Stratoun and notary public, 1487 (*Prestwick*, p. 117). He is the Andrew M'Cormill, presbyter and notary public of the diocese of Glasgow, 1488 (*Friars Ayr*, p. 61), and

Andrew Makcormyl or Makcormyll, notary in Ayr, 1490, and vicar of Stratoun, 1502 (*Ayr*, p. 94, 96). Cf. Ir. *MacGormghail.*

MACCORNACK, MACCORNOCK. Current variants of MACCORMACK, q. v. Mirabella McCornak had sasine of the lands of Stronegassill, Kirkcudbrightshire, 1516 (ER., XIV, p. 587), and Robert Makcornak de Strongassil confirmed a charter in 1530 (RMS., III, 985). Catharine M'Cornock was married in Edinburgh, 1682 (*Edinb. Marr.*), and in 1684 Margaret McCornock is recorded in the parish of Carsfern (RPC., 3. ser. IX, p. 575), Hew McCornick was bailie of Maybole, Ayrshire, 1688 (ibid., XIII, p. 208), and William M'Cornock appears in Dumfries, 1732 (*Dumfries*). The name of John M'Cronock an exiled Covenanter from Colmonell, drowned in shipwreck off Orkney, 1679 (*Hanna*, II, p. 253) is probably a misspelling. Makcornik 1527.

MACCORQUODALE, MACCORKINDALE. G. *MacCorcadail.* From the ON. personal name *Thorketill*, 'Thor's kettle.' The G. is also given as *MacC(h)orcadail* and *MacThorcadail.* But little is known of the early history of the clan, and the account in Buchanan (who spells the name M'Orquodale) is untrustworthy. Ewen Mactorquedil or Ewgyne M'Corquheddell was summoned to appear before the sheriff in Perth in 1430, and to bring his charters and evidents with him (HP., II, p. 162; *Invent. Scrymgeour family docs.*, 20). In 1434 there is record of a charter to Ewen, son of Ewen Makcorquydill, lord of Maintelan (properly Phantelan) (OPS., II, p. 96, 124). In 1495 Ewen Mikcorcadill granted his lands of Edderlin, etc., to Archibald, earl of Argyll, in exchange for other lands (RMS., II, 2352), and in 1509 his son, Ewen Maccorquodill was retoured heir of his father in lands in Argyll (OPS., II, p. 87). Effric neyn Corgitill is authoress of a poem in the Book of the Dean of Lismore, and John Macrocadill (!) or Makcrocadill was minister of Strathfillan, 1569–85 (Scott, *Fasti*, III, p. 826; RMR.). Lauchlane McQuorquordill, brother to Duncan McQuorquordill of Phantellane, and Johnne Dow McQuorquordill or McQuorquhordell were in 1612 called "notorious thieves and assisters of Clan Gregour" (RPC., IX, p. 510). John M'Orquidill in Port of Lochtay was a Glenorchy vassal in 1638 (BBT., p. 400). The patronymic is still fairly common in Kintyre. The shortened forms MACCORKILL, q.v., and MACCORKLE are also in current use. The Maccorquodales are classed as a sept of Macleod but there is no evidence of any relationship between them. M'Corcadill 1573, M'Cordadill 1666, M'Corqudill 1686, M'Corquidle 1692, M'Corquidill 1470, M'Cor-

quydill 1543, M'Korkitill 1547, McQuorcadaill 1614, Macquorquodale 1648, Makcorcadell 1509, Makcorquidill 1543.

MACCORRAN. Forsith McCorane (or McCoren or M'Quarrane) was tenant of Sessintuly, 1480 (ER., IX, p. 566, 599). As Forsith Mcquharrane he appears as tenant there in 1502 along with Thomas McQuhorrane (ibid., XII, p. 632). A purchase of cloth was made for Katheryne Makcoran, 'lavendar in the court,' 1509 (ALHT., IV, p. 175). Patrick McCorane, clerk of St. Andrews diocese, notary at Ellanrie, 1609 (*Poltalloch Writs*, p. 136), may be Patrick M'Coran, notary, 1617 (*Sasines*, II, 3). Janet M'Corrane in Vnschenoche, parish of Port, 1661 (*Dunblane*), and Dugald M'Corran in Fernoch, parish of Kilmelford, 1698 (*Argyll Inv.*). On the lands of Inchanoch 'there is still to be seen a mound, which the people of the country know as the grave of the McCorrans' (Campbell, *Supplement*, p. 80). The name may be from *MacOdhrain* or fuller *MacGilleOdhrain*, 'son of the gillie of (S.) Odhran.' See also MACQUORN.

MACCORVIE. A Kintyre surname, a variant of MACCORWIS, q.v. Malcolm MacKervaie was a retainer at Inveraray Castle in 1678 (*Celt. Mon.*, XXIII, p. 125), and John M'Kervey appears in Overbancrosh in 1713 (*Kirkcudbright*).

MACCORWIS. A Kintyre spelling of MACKERRAS, q.v. John Makcorwis was a witness at Mayboill, Ayrshire, 1485 (RMS., II). Iain McCorwis was juror on an inquest held at Inveraray, 1525 (HP., IV, p. 26), and in a sasine of the same year he appears as Mccarwvs (ibid., p. 27), bailie for the sheriff of Perth.

MACCOSH. G. *Mac coise*, 'son of the footman,' or 'courier.' The home of the name is in Ayrshire. Erard mac Coisse, 'primeices Eirenn,' died 990 (AU.). John M'Cosh, Patrick M'Cosch, and Donald M'Cosch were voters in the parish of Qwilton (Coylton) in 1513 (*Ros*, 52), and Jo. Makcosche was tenant in lands of Hoilmark in barony of Uchiltrie, 1586 (RMS., V, 1135). Dr. James McCosh (1811–94), born in Scotland, was principal of Princeton College, New Jersey.

MACCOSHAM, MACCOSHIM, MACCOSHEN, MACCOSHIN. G. *MacCòiseam.* The name in fuller form is represented by Gilleostentin of 1230 in the *Registrum de Dunfermelyn* (p. 111). There is a small sept of Macdonalds near Dunvegan known as MacCòiseam, and in the seventeenth century there were Macintyres in Craignish who believed "that the sur-

MACCOSHAM, Maccoshim..., continued
name of Clanntyre VcCoshem were of auld
native men, servandis and dependaris to the
house and surename of Clandule Cregnis alias
Campbellis in Cregnis." In 1612 they gave a
bond of manrent to Ronald Campbell of Barrichibyan, their chief being called in the bond
Gillecallum McDonchie VcIntyre VcCoshem
(Coll., p. 206-207). James Makcosshen, a
follower of the earl of Cassilis, was respited
for murder in 1526 (RSS., I, 3386). Duncan
Roy M'Osham or McCosham was declared a
rebel by the Privy Council in 1671 (RPC., 3.
ser. III, p. 371), decree was pronounced against
Duncan McCoshin in Wruchill for spoliation in
1684 (ibid., 3. ser. IX, p. 579), and Niall Mc-
Coshan witnessed a decreit by Niall Campbell
of Inveraray in 1671 (Genealogist, new ser.
xxxv, p. 40). John M'Cosham in Caolchurilan
in Kilchrenan parish is in record in 1685
(Argyll), Donald M'Cosham in Crouashan in
1699 (Argyll Inv.), John M'Cosham in Keames,
parish of Kilchrennan, in 1702 (Argyll), Duncan M'Cosham in Ederlinemore in 1706
(Campbell, I, p. 63), and Archibald M'Coshim
from Inveraray graduated at the University of
Glasgow in 1852. A small loch in Colonsay is
(or rather was) known as Lochan Moine nic
Coiseam (M'Neill, Colonsay, p. 30). The
name occurs in Islay as Maccoshin, and is there
etymologized as MacOisein, 'son of Ossian.'
Duncan Ban MacIntyre, the Gaelic poet, made
the name famous by calling the gun he used
in stalking Nic Còiseam, 'Cosham's daughter.'
Mc Coasam 1692, Mc Osham 1724.

MACCOSKER, Maccusker. These names are
probably Irish, the second form being found
in Glasgow. Ir. Mac Oscair, 'son of Oscar,' or
of the 'champion.' Ir. Oscar, the personal name,
also meaning 'a champion.'

MACCOSKRIE, Maccoskery, Maccoskry. G.
MacChosgrach, 'son of Coscrach' or 'Coscarach'
(victorious, from coscur, victory). The name
occurs in the Book of Deer in the genitive
as Cosgreg. An individual named Coscrach,
of some importance in early time, gave name
to Fearann Coscraigh in Sutherland. Duuene
MacCoscrach witnessed a charter by Maldouen, third earl of Levenax to Malcolm, the
son of Duncan, of the whole of Glaskell, c. 1217
(Lennox, II, p. 402). There was an old Galloway family of this name. Many references to
them occur in the Register of the Privy Council
between 1540-1640, under MacCoskerie, Mac-
Coskry, and MacCoskery. William Macoscrie
was charged with being a disorderly person in
the parish of Kirkmabreck, 1684 (RPC., 3. ser.
IX, p. 573). Donald M'Coscrich in Inverin,
parish of Kilfinan, 1686 (Argyll), and John

M'Coskrie was miller at Ferrytoun, 1771 (Kirkcudbright). In 1684 the name appears in
record (Parish) as McCorsquey, McCroscre,
McCroscrie, McCroskrie, McKorscra, and
McKoscry.

MACCOSTRICK. John M'Costrick in Burnbank, parish of Kincardine, 1727 (Dunblane).
See under Macostrich.

MACCOTTER. G. Mac Oitir, 'son of Ottar,'
a Norse personal name. The c of Mac has
been attracted to the second part of the name.
'Mac mic Oitir. i. Ottir do lucht Insi Gall,'
Mac Oitir one of the people of the Hebrides,
is mentioned in 1142 (AFM., II, p. 1069).
Hugh Macdonald, the Sleat seanachaidh, mentions a Murdo MacCotter who took part in an
expedition against Orkney c. 1460 (HP., I,
p. 37). John McCotter possessed the particate
of land called Erleseat, Aberdeenshire, 1667
(RMS.). John M'Coatter of Knocknapark,
Ross-shire, took the Test, 1685 (Sc. Ant., XIII,
p. 39; RPC., 3. ser. XI, p. 418).

MACCOUBREY, Maccoubrie. G. Mac Cuith-
breith, 'son of Cuthbert,' q.v. Henry Mc-
Cowthry in Galloway, 1539 (RSS., II, 2967).
The Isle of Man has Coobragh from MacGiolla
Cobraght, 'son of Cuthbert's servant.' The
name of John Makcopery, witness in Bute, 1513
(RMS., III, 1321), is perhaps another spelling.

MACCOUL, Maccoull. A form of Macdougall, q.v. In 1497 we have mention of the
tenement of Nigel Makcowl in Glasgow (REG.,
p. 476). John Makcoule held lands in Dur-
roure in 1500 (RMS., II, 2565). Allan M'Cowle
of Rogary was admitted burgess freeman of
Glasgow, 1579 (Burgesses). Thomas Mackcoul
was burgess of Inverness, 1603 (Rec. Inv., II,
p. 10), and Donald McConeill VcCoull in
Craigdarg was fined for reset of Clan Gregor
in 1613 (RPC., XIV, p. 629). In 1630 Mac-
coulls were included among "brokin and law-
lesse lymmars of the clan Gregour and other
brokin clans" (RPC., 2. ser. IV, p. 100). M'Coul
of Raray is an old branch of the Macdougalls
of Dunolly. Lapis M'Coull or M'Dougall is
the name given an ancient stone weight in
1578 (Coll., p. 165, 172). MacCouil 1594,
McCoule 1684.

MACCOULIE. A form of Maccullie, q.v.

MACCOURT. See under Maccoard.

MACCOWAN. For origin of name see under
Macilchomhghain. John M'Coan in Duchre,
parish of Kilbrandon, 1691 (Argyll Inv.). Perhaps also David M'Kowne, notary in Glasgow,

1550, whose name is also spelled M'Kownne and M'Kowin (*Protocols*, I). M'Kowyne 1558.

MACCOWELL. A form of MACDOUALL, q.v. John McCowill was burgess of Dumfries in 1554 (*Edgar*, p. 237).

MACCOYLE. A form of MACDOUGALL, q.v., current in Perthshire.

MACCRABIT. Andrew M'Crabit in Galloway was shot for being a Covenanter, 1685 (*Hanna*, II, p. 258).

MACCRACH. Nisbet (*Heraldry*, I, p. 98) gives their arms but no particulars: "Argent, a fesse between three mullets in chief, and a lion rampant in base, gules." Mart. McCraich in Alderickinair, 1684 (*Parish*, p. 24); Agnes M'Craich in Kissokdin, 1684 (*Kirkcudbright*); and Robert M'Craich in parish of Fossoway, 1742 (*Dunblane*). Perhaps same as Maccreight, one of the many "Mac" names common in Galloway before 1700. Thomas M'Creigh in Millthird, 1686 (*Kirkcudbright*).

MACCRACHEN. See under MACCRACKAN.

MACCRACKAN, MACCRACKEN, MACCRACHEN, MACCRAKEN. An old Galloway surname. Various explanations have been given of the origin of this name, the most likely of which is that it is "nothing but a variant owing to the action of two well-known dialectal processes of the name MACNAUGHTON," q.v. Settlements from Argyll into Galloway were made about the middle of the eighth century and later, and Watson has pointed out that with regard to dedications in Galloway that there was a close connection between this region and Kintyre. Bláán, Donnán, Faolán, Mochoe, Brigid, Columkille, are common to both districts and he adds "this is likely to be more than a coincidence" (I, p. 171, 179). Michael Makcraken was a follower of the earl of Cassilis respited for murder, 1526 (RSS., I, 3386). Gilbert M'Crekane was burgess of Wigtown, and Michael M'Crekane notary public there, 1536, and burgess, 1546 (*Laing*, 408; RMS., IV, 80). John M'Crekane was vicar of Sorbie, 1536, notary public in Wigtown, 1539 (RMS., III, 1970), and commissary of Farnes and Rennys, 1542–45 (ibid., 3163). John Makcrakane in Wigtoun had a respite for art and part of the breking of Adam Ahannay, 1540 (RSS., II, 3299). Neil Dow McCraikane in Achonacone was town officer of Wigtown, 1628 (RPC., II, p. 283). Dr. Henry Noble McCracken is president of Vassar College, Poughkeepsie, New York State. McCraccan, McKraken, and McKeracken 1684 (*Parish*), Makcarkan 1500, McCrekan 1564, McKrachin 1607; M'Craken,

M'Crokane, M'Krekane. Macfarlane (*Am Briathrachan beag*) explains the name as from G. *MacFhraingein*, 'son of Franklin.'

MACCRAE, MACCREA, MACCREE, MACCRIE, MACRIE. Ayrshire forms of MACRAE, q.v. A common old form of the name in Ayrshire was Makcrie (1586), and Makreith. (Cumnock, 1538). John Makcra was messenger in Ayr, 1621 (*Ayr*, p. 61). Robert McCrie was charged with being a disorderly person (i.e. non-conforming) in parish of Carsfern, 1684 (RPC., 3. ser. IX, p. 575), and William McKrie was flesher in Dunbar, 1688 (ibid., XIII, p. 248). Allan McKree, 'surgan' in Ayr, was admitted burgess of Prestwick, 1733 (*Prestwick*, p. 91). Macra 1631, McKra 1699, and in 1684: McCraie, McCrea, McCree, McKrae, McKrie, McRae (*Parish*).

MACCRAICH. See under MACCRACH.

MACCRAIN, MACCRANE. G. *Mac Crain*, 'son of the pig.' The name of a long-lived family in Jura. The name also occurred in Islay in the seventeenth century, Murdoch M'Rayne held a kerrowran there in 1686 (*Bk. Islay*, p. 504). With the secondary genitive in -*ich* we have John M'Ranich gorme M'Kay in 1642, and Donald gorme M'Ranie choll of the same date and place, Ballinicill. Martin (WI., p. 234) mentions one Gillouir Mack Crain in Jura who "liv'd to have kept one hundred and eighty Christmasses in his own house;" and a stone in the old burying ground of Inver-Lussa is inscribed: "Mary Mac Crain, died 1856, aged 128. Descendant of Gillour Mac Crain, who kept 180 Christmases in his own house, and who died in the reign of Charles I." Cf. the Border surnames SWINE and SWINTON.

MACCRAITH, MACCREATH. Forms of MACRAE, q.v., now current in the shires of Ayr and Lanark. Adam M'Creich witnessed a charter in Ayr, 1438 (*Friars Ayr*, p. 49). John Makmekrathe (= son of Macrath), chaplain, appears as witness in Ayr, 1477 (RMS., II, 1370), and William McAge McRethe, parishioner of Duthil, is recorded in 1537 (*Grant*, III, p. 269). John Makcreith in the barony of Cumnok, 1535 (RMS., III, 1887). Sir Robert McCraith, vicar of Kilmalie (Golspie), 1545 (OPS., II, p. 648). Agnes M'Kravth, liferenter in Dornoch, 1584, Alexander M'Kraith, burgess there, 1603, and Alexander M'Craithe and James M'Raith, his son, mentioned 1630 (ibid., p. 640, 644). William Macreth in Brualand, witness in 1625, appears in the following year as McCreiff and McCreith (OSS., I, 132, 143).

MACCRAKEN. See under MACCRACKAN.

MACCRANE. A variant of MACCRAIN, q.v.

MACCRATH. A form of MACRAE, q.v.

MACCRAW, MACCRAY, MACCREA. Variants of MACRAE, q.v.

MACCREADIE, MACCREADDIE, MACCREDIE. Variants of MACREDIE, q.v. The name is found in Galloway, 1684 (Parish): McCreedie, McKredy, McRadie, McReadie, McReady, McReddie, McRedie, and shortened to Credie. Andrew M'Creddy was provost of Stranraer before the middle of the eighteenth century.

MACCREATH. See under MACCRAITH.

MACCREDDAN. A diminutive form of MACREADIE, q.v.

MACCREDIE. See under MACCREADIE.

MACCREE. See under MACCRAE.

MACCRERY. A form of MACCRIRIE. John McCrery, a follower of the earl of Cassilis, was respited for murder, 1526 (RSS., I, 3386). Another John M'Crery was "the kyngis fule" at the Scottish Court between 1526–40 (Lindsay's Works, ed. Laing, I, p. 252–253). MacCreery in North of Ireland.

MACCREVEY. A form of MACREVIE, q.v.

MACCRIE. See under MACCRAE.

MACCRIMMON. G. MacCruimein. The name is from ON. Hrōmund (Hrō(þ)-mundr, 'famed protector'). The name is found on one of the rune-inscribed crosses at Kirk Michael, Isle of Man, as Rumun. "Sir" Jhone Mcchrummen was a witness at Inverness, 1533 (Cawdor, p. 159). Hector M'Crimmon signed a deed on behalf of Isabella, wife of Sir Rory Mor, who succeeded to the chiefship of Dunvegan in 1595 (Macleod, The Maccrimmons of Skye, p. 4), and Macleod of Dunvegan was complainer against two men named M'Grymmen in 1599 (RPC.). A family of the name were hereditary pipers to Macleod of Macleod, the last of whom, Lieut. MacCrimmon, had a farm in Glenelg in the first quarter of the nineteenth century. The late Dr. Alexander Carmichael, who gives the Gaelic form of the name· as Maccriomthain, says that a woman of the name in St. Kilda recited some of the island songs to him (CG., II, p. 380). Colin McCrimthain is in the Calendar of Oengus the Culdee under 13 December, but this is a different name. Crimthann means 'fox.' The story of the Maccrimmons being of Italian origin is too silly for belief. McCrumen 1717, McGrimmon and McGrinnan 1635.

MACCRINDELL. See under MACCRINDLE.

MACCRINDLE, MACCRINDELL. This surname, found in Ayrshire and Galloway, is a form of MACRANALD, q.v. Dungall M'Kyrnele de Barnele witnessed a charter of the lands of Burghjarg in the sheriffdom of Wigtown in 1489 (RMS., II, 1884), and in 1505 we find recorded a precept of remission to Dougall Makrynnyll de Barneill (RSS., I, 1090), the same individual probably. Sir Duncan M'Krenele was chaplain in Crossraguel Abbey in 1523 (Crossraguel, I, p. 72), and about 1526–28, as Duncan Makrinnyll, he figures in a trial of Kennedys for the slaughter of Robert Campbell and others. Malcome McRyndill, James McCrynnell, William McCrunnell, and Andro Makcrunnell, followers of the earl of Cassilis, were respited for murder committed by them in 1526 (RSS., I, 3386), and in 1530 Malcolme McCrendill was included with others in a letter of protection by King James V (ibid., II, 642). James McCrynnill of Barneile appears in record in 1541 (ibid., II, 3889) and Kentigern McCrynnill in Carrick in 1557 (ER., XIX, p. 416). James M'Crynnill of Barnele granted a charter in favor of his son, Kentigern M'Crynnill of the lands of Barnele and Drummurchie in Carrick in 1544 (RMS., III, 3025), and Robert Boyd of Trochrig was served heir in 1608 of the lands of Trochrig and the five mark lands of Berneile, M'Cryndill, and Snaid (Retours, Ayr, 99). In 1616 Sir John Kennedy of Barneolin was served heir of his father's lands of Baltersane and Knockrinnellis (i.e. M'Crindle's hill), and forty years later John Kennedy of Culzeone was served heir of his father in the same lands of Beltersone and Knokronald (ibid., 134, 483). The place called M'Cryndle (1608), Knockrinnellis (1616), and Knokronald (1656) is now known as M'Crindleston or Macrindleston. The early forms of the name are evidence that long previous to 1608 the M'Crindles lived there and gave their name to the place. The spelling of 1656 points to Ronald or Ranald being the origin of the name, and we know that there were Rannalsounes in Ayrshire who may have come from a common stock — Clanranald Bane of Largie in Kintyre. The Ronalds of the Bennals, near Tarbolton, were probably connected. Loch Inch Crindle in Galloway may have received its name from one of this family. M'Crindill 1542, M'Crynnell 1544, M'Crynnoll 1545. MacCrynell, MacCrynill, MacChrynnell, MacGrindal, MacGrundle.

MACCRIRICK, MACCRIRRICK. Galloway names. Andrew McRerik was hanged at Kirkcudbright, 1457 (ER., VI, p. 353). M'Rerik occurs in Edinburgh, 1462 (Laing, 148), Margaret Makrerik was spouse to Stephen Borthwik, burgess there, 1490 (RMS., II, 2011), and Tho. Makrerik, burgess of Edinburgh, was witness, 1523 (RMS., III, 239). Gilbert M'Crurik in Irvine, Ayrshire, had sasine in his favor, 1536 (*Laing*, 353), and Patrick M'Crerik was burgess of Wigtown, 1579 (RPC., III). Makrerik and M'Rerik 1490; M'Cririck. The Mac- was early dropped: Jo. Rerik de Dalbaty 1469 and 1488, Henry Rerik in Kirkcudbright, 1501. There appears to have been early confusion with RIDDICK, q.v. See also MACCRIRIE.

MACCRIRIE, MACCRIRE, MACCREIRIE. An old Galloway surname. From *Mac Ruidhri*, a dialectal variant of *Mac Ruaidhri*, 'son of Ruaidhri,' from the ON. personal name *Hróðrekr*. Thomas McCrery held half a tenement in Dumfries, 1444 (*Edgar*, p. 225), Luke Makririe was a cook in Edinburgh, 1624 (*Edinb. Marr.*), and another Lucke McCrerie in Annand was charged in 1628 with resetting a rebel (RPC., 2. ser. II, p. 599). John M'Creery, a north of Ireland man of Scottish extraction, was one of the publishers of the Works of Robert Burns, 1806. McCreerie and McCrery 1684; MacCreirie, MacCrire, MakCririe. See MACCRIRICK.

MACCRISTAL, MACCHRYSTAL, 'son of Cristal' or 'Chrystal' (Lowland Scots diminutive of Christopher). Macchrystal is a current Galloway form of the name. Decreet against Neil M'Cristell or Mcristall in Gortnagower for rent, 1672 (HP., II, p. 207, 217).

MACCRISTIE, MACCRISTIN. Galwegian surnames, from Christie or Cristie, diminutives of CHRISTIAN, q.v. In the end of the thirteenth century the earl of Levenax transferred to Sir John of Luss the homage and service of Gillechrist Mac crystine and his heirs (*Levenax*, p. 20). John McCristyne or Makcristyne was bailie of Wigtown in 1459 and provost in 1471 (ER.). Symon Makcristen had a charter of the lands of Mwnkhill granted him in 1484 by the provost and bailies of Wigtown (RMS., II, 1623). He appears again in 1503 as Symon Makcristi, bailie of Wigtown (ER., XII, p. 168), and he is doubtless the Symon M'Cristine or McCristin, sheriff-depute of Wigtown, who was chased by a man "with a drawn quhinzeare" in 1511 (*Agnew*, p. 142; *Trials*, I, p. *89). William Makcrystyn had sasine of lands in Wigtownshire in 1513 (ER., XIV, p. 539), John Makcristyne was burgess of Dumfries in 1506 (*Edgar*, p. 229), and Gilbert M'Cristin held land in the same town, 1544 (Anderson, *Prot. Book*). Sir Donald McCristyn was chaplain of S. Arane (i.e. S. Oran) in Iona, 1542 (RSS., II, 4779). John M'Criste of Clonsche, juror on assize in Wigtown, 1544, appears again in the following

year as Joh. Makcristine (RMS., III, 3032, 3214), and Gilfernan M'Cristin witnessed an Inveryne charter of 1468 (*Lamont*, p. 22). McChristan 1684, M'Chrystine 1503, M'Crastyne 1532, Macrystane 1543, Makcriste 1529, Makcristin 1539.

MACCROBIE. A form of MACROBIE, q.v.

MACCROBIN. A form of MACROBIN, q.v. McCrobine 1684.

MACCROCKETT. In Stirling in 1717 we have William McCrockett (*Sc. Ant.*, VI, p. 87), and Gabriel McCroket is recorded in Gorbels, 1718 (*Minutes*, p. 190). George M'Crockat, coppersmith in Dundee, 1777–83 (*Brechin*). MacCrocart 1590. Other old forms are MacCrochart and MacCrocket.

MACCROM. From G. *crom*, swarthy. John Makcrome had a respite for his rebellion and fire-raising in 1526 (RSS., I, 3640). Several individuals named M'Crom and M'Cron subscribed a bond of manrent to Campbell of Glenurquhay, 1573 (BBT., p. 218). Cf. MACCRUM.

MACCRONE, MACRONE. John McCrone in Galloway had a precept of remission for intercommuning with rebels, 1535 (RSS., II, 1842). Thomas McCron witnessed a Dumfries instrument of sasine, 1566 (*Edgar*, p. 117), and another Thomas M'Crone in Maibie appears in 1657 (*Dumfries*). Jonet M'Rone and Maroun M'Rone are in record, 1618 (*Trials*). Margaret McCron was prisoner in Ayr, 1688 (RPC., 3. ser. XIII, p. 326), John McCrone was recorded at the Kirk, 1668 (*Corsehill*, p. 77), and George McCron was 'burrow officer and town drummer' of Dumfries prior to July 1719 (*Edgar*, p. 205). There is no evidence to support the statement that General Cronje of Boer War fame was of Scottish parentage or descent. ? 'Son of Crón,' an old Irish personal name meaning 'swarthy.' See CRON.

MACCRORIE, MACCRORY. Ir. *Mac Ruaidhri*, son of *Ruaidhri*, 'red king.' John McCrore was tenant of Drumnamark, Ardmanoch, in 1504 (ER., XII, p. 661), and John Mc Crorie was bailie of Maybole, 1688 (RPC., 3. ser. XIII, p. 208). John Mc Crory and John Oig Mc Crory were tenants on Chisholm lands of Inverchanich, 1721 (HP., II, p. 301). Cf. MACRORY.

MACCROSKIE. Alan MacCroskie was a tenant in the parish of Sennick, 1684 (RPC., 3. ser. IX, p. 569).

MACCROSSAN. Common to Scotland and Ireland (Joyce, *Old Celtic romances*, p. 409n). Ir. *Mac an Chrosáin*, son of the rhymer, Ir. *crosán*.

MACCROTTER. Patrick McCrotter Vc Brebee in Achnachyle was charged with violence, 1617 (RPC., xi, p. 68). John M'Cruter in Kilcherne, Ardnamurchan, in record, 1694 (*Argyll Inv.*). A variant of MACCHRUITER.

MACCROW. One of the many variants of MACRAE, q.v. Hew Mackcrow and his brother were murdered by the Campbells at Dunoon, 1646 (*Lamont*, 786; *Hewison*, II, p. 334). Recorded in Edinburgh, 1942.

MACCROWTHER. A form of MACGRUER, q.v.

MACCRUAR. A current form of MACGRUAR, q.v. The slaughter of Malcolme McCrewir in 1542 mentioned (RSS., II, 4906). Janet M'Crewer in parish of Kilmadock, 1674 (*Dunblane*).

MACCRUDDEN. This name, recorded in Glasgow, is Ir. *MacRodain*, 'son of Rodan,' a diminutive of *rod*, spirited.

MACCRUM. Soirll (Sorley) McCrume was one of those who held Dunivaig in Islay against Bishop Knox, 1616 (*Cawdor*, p. 232). In 1684: McCrumb, McKcrumb,> Crome, Crum, Crumb (*Parish*). The name means 'son of the bent one,' G. *Mac a' chruim*, an unidiomatic expression in Gaelic, but found in Glenetive in 1610 as M'Chruimb. Cf. MACILCHRUM. Cromm is a personal name in the Book of Leinster, 350a.

MACCUAIG. G. *MacDhubhaig*, 'son of Blackie.' Two centuries and more ago this name was common in Islay as M'Cuaig, or M'Cowag (1686). In the *Book of Islay* it is spelled M'Cuaig, M'Cowag, M'Crivag, M'Crwag. John McCowig was tenant of Ardochy, 1733 (*Bk. Islay*, p. 549). A different name from MACCOOK, q.v.

MACCUAIL. MACCUAILL. For MACTHUATHAIL, q.v. The name of a few persons in Glenurchy who now pass under the name of Macdonald. In 1630 they were called Macgregors (RPC., 2. ser. IV, p. 100).

MACCUALASKIE, MACCULLASKY. Surnames recorded in Kintyre. Forms of Ir. Macluskie (from *Mac Bloscaidh*, 'son of Bloscadh'). Johnston (*Macs*, p. 42) suggests from *Mac glèoisg*, 'son of the silly woman'!!

MACCUARAIG. A form of MACUARAIG or MACUALRAIG (Kennedy), q.v. J. Maccuaraig is author of the song 'Linn an Aigh.'

MACCUBBIN, MACCUBBING. An old Dumfriesshire surname and a common one in the Stewartry. The family gave name to M'Cub-

binstone in Dumfriesshire. Martin M'Cubyn or M'Cubyne was tenant in the mill of Dalfubill, 1376 (RHM., I, p. lvii). Brice Macobyn, Scottish merchant, had a safe conduct to exercise his trade in England, 1398 (*Bain*, IV, 504). John Makcubeyn held the ten shilling land of Trudonag in 1404 (*Crossraguel*, I, p. 38). Fergus Makcubyn and Johne Makcubyn his son, followers of the earl of Cassilis, were respited for murder, 1526 (RSS., I, 3386). John Makcubyng had a booth in Dumfries, 1567 (*Edgar*, p. 242). William McCuben in Ardlachie was fined for reset of Clan Gregor, 1613 (RPC., xiv, p. 630). Fergus M'Cubein was retoured heir of Fergus M'Cubein of Knockdollian in Carrick, 1677 (*Retours, Ayr*, 611), and Anne McUbein was spouse to Mr. Antony Shaw, minister at Commonell, 1662. Fergus McAbin of Knockdolian contributed to repairs of St. Andrews University, 1681 (PSAS., LIV, p. 229). Alexander MacUbine or M'Ubine in Irongray was hanged for being a Covenanter, 1685 (*Hanna*, II, p. 256, 265). James M'Cubyne was provost of Jedburgh before 1693 (*Peebles CR.*). McCowbyn 1530, M'Cubbin 1675, M'Cubbine 1643, McCubeine 1637, M'Cubene and M'Cubine 1602, Makcubyn 1535, M'Cwbene 1515; MacCubben, M'Ubin. 'Son of Cubbin,' a mutation of Gibbon.

MACCUBIE, MACCUBBIE. James MacCubie, member of parliament for Jedburgh, 1678 (*Hanna*, II, p. 503) may be James M'Cubyne, provost of Jedburgh before 1693 (*Peebles CR.*). Isobell M'Cubbie in record in Newbigging, parish of Carnwath, 1679 (*Lanark CR.*). Diminutive of MacGibbon through the form Cubbon.

MACCUCHEON, MACCUTCHEN, MACCUTCHEON. Forms of MACHUTCHEN, q.v., current in Wigtownshire. James McCutchone in Damelingtoune, 1686 (RPC., 3. ser. XII, p. 151). In 1684: McCutchon, McCutchin, McCutchion.

MACCUDDEN. Ir. *MacAdain*, a diminutive of Adam, 'son of Adam.' (2) or, less probable, from *MacCadáin*, 'son of Cadán,' a rare Ulster surname.

MACCUDIE. A surname found in Wigtownshire. It means 'son of (S.) Cuthbert,' from the diminutive *Cuddie* or *Cuddy*. John M'Cuddy was cook to Bishop Gawin Douglas, and is mentioned in the bishop's will (*Works*, ed. Small, I, p. cxxiv). Cuddv [Cuthbert] Rigg, "fethelar" in Dumfries in 1506 (*Edgar*, p. 103) is the "Cuddy Rig the Drumfress fuill" of Dunbar's "Complaint to the King aganis Mure" (1.24).

MACCUFFIE. See under MACGUFFIE.

MACCUGAN. From Ir. *MacEochagain*, 'son of Eochaidh.'

MACCUIDHEAN or MACCUITHEIN. A minor Macdonald sept near Storr in Skye, *Clann 'ic Cuthain* (or *Cuithen*). They have not borne a good reputation if any value is to be attached to a line of rhyme concerning them:

"Clann 'ic Cuithein chuir an t-sodail."
(Clan MacQuithen, expert in base flattery).

Ruaraidh Duadh Maccuithean was story-teller to Lord Macdonald, from whom he had free lands for his services (CG., 2. ed., II, p. 375), and Campbell obtained one of his West Highland tales from Donald MacCuidhean (*West Highland tales*, IV, p. 456). In Kilmuir there is Baile Mhic Cuithein, 'Macqueen's township,' (Forbes, *Place names of Skye*, p. 57), and in North Uist there is Cnoc Cuithein. See MACQUEEN and MACQUEIN.

MACCUIMRID. A Gaelicizing of the territorial surname Montgomery in Galloway.

MACCUISH, MACCOOISH. MacCuis (a Uist name), otherwise known there as a sept of the Macmhannains, McMannain (Henderson, NI.). The name is also found in the north of Skye. In Harris the form is MacChuthais (Henderson, *Leabhar nan Gleann*, p. 85). In 1718 the following names appear in the rent-roll of Sir Donald Macdonald's estate of North Uist: Donald M'Cowis of Clachan, Neill M'Kuish of Vallakuy, and Donald McChowis of Ulleray. Mr. D. J. McCuish in *Oban Times* says his name is from *Macdubhsidh* (see under MACFEE). In the Isle of Man we have Kewish 1618 (pron. Keouish), Kewsh (1683), from *MacUais* according to Moore, *Manx names*, p. 46. Cf. *MacCoise* (*Woulfe*, p. 334). Mr. D. J. McCuish says that several hundred years ago some Macphees "found their way into North Uist and other neighbouring islands and according to old Rent books, the North Uist sept of the clan spelt their name Macowis, modernised as MacCuish. I, myself am a great-grandson of one of the clan named 'Dubsith' " (in Oban Times, January, 1935). "A family in North Uist is known as 'Dubh-sith,' Black fairy, from a tradition that the family have been familiar with the fairies in their fairy flights and secret migrations" (*Carmina Gadelica*, ed. II, v. 2, p. 354).

MACCULBERT. Found in 1672 as McCulbert (IDR). Considering its provenance most probably meant for MacCuthbert. Charles Colbert de Croissy (1625–1696) claimed descent from the Cuthberts of Castlehill, Inverness. See CUTHBERT.

MACCULLAN. From Ir. *MacCoilin*, 'son of Coilin,' a variant of Cailin. Donald Makcullayn was reidare at Sannyk (Senwick, Kirkcudbrightshire), 1574 (RMR.). In 1684 the name appears as McCullan, McCulland, McKullon, and with omission of 'Mac' as Cullane and Cullen (*Parish*).

MACCULLASKY. A Kintyre corruption of Ir. Macluskie. See under MACCUALASKIE.

MACCULLIE, MACCULLY, MACOULIE. Softened forms of MACCULLOCH, q.v. Martin McColy in Moray had remission in 1363 (REM., p. 164). Maccullie appears in 1607 (RPC.). Gilbert M'Cullie was retoured heir of John M'Cullie in Whitrow in the bailiary of Carrick, his father, 1672 (*Retours, Ayr*, 575). Thomas M'Cullie in Plean, parish of St. Ninians, 1679 (*Stirling*). Gilbert McUllie appears in parish of Caminell, 1686, and James McHullie was prisoner in Canongate Tolbooth, Edinburgh, in same year (RPC., 3. ser. XII, p. 232, 337). Patrick McCullie in Corsehill of Kildies is in record, 1698 (*Muthill*). McColly and McCuley 1686. Christine NcColly in 1706. (2) Maccullie is also a variant of MacWilliam (Macwillie) in Strathaven and Glenlivet.

MACCULLION. See under MACCALIEN.

MACCULLOCH. Much obscurity enshrouds the origin of this old Galwegian name, and no satisfactory pedigree of the family exists. They are said to be described in one of their charters as having their origin "ultra memoriam hominum." The name may be G. *Mac Cullaich* or *Mac C(h)ullach*, 'son of (the) boar.' The name first appears in 1296 when Thomas Maculagh del counte de Wyggetone rendered homage. His seal bears a squirrel, and S' *Thome Maccoli* (?). He appears again in the same year as juror on inquest at Berwick along with his brother Michal, and is probably the Thomas Makhulagh, sheriff of Wigtown, 1305 (*Bain*, II, 198, 215, 458, 550). Michel Maculagh and William Maculaghe also rendered homage (ibid., p. 209, 211). Sir Patrick McCoulagh and Gilbert McCoulaghe were charter witnesses in Galloway, 1354 (ibid., III, 1578). Sir Patrick Macologhe had an annuity of 100 marks "in recompense of his sufferings, and loss of his lands in Scotland for his allegiance" to the king of England, 1360 (ibid., IV, 58), and in 1363 as Sir Patrick M'Owlache had restoration of his lands (*Stodart*, II). Helise Makcoulach was married in 1478 (*Sc. Ant.*, III, p. 105), and Patrick Makcowloch, presbyter and notary of Candidecase, 1480 (*Scon*, 225), may be Patrick Mackullouch, vicar of Arbroath, 1482 (RAA., II, 212). Symon McKowloch of Galloway had a letter of gift, 1500

MACCULLOCH, *continued*

(RSS., I, 555), and David M'Ulloch of Gutters was one of the Committee of War, August 1643 (APS.). The Maccullochs of Tarrel, Plaids, Kindeace, and Glastulich were followers of the earls of Ross (*Northern N. & Q.*, V, p. 58–62; XII, p. 170–174). The Argyllshire Maccullochs are really MACLULICHS, q.v. Makawllauch 1414, McCoulach 1410, M'Coulaghe 1352, M'Cowlach 1476, Makcowllach 1482, M'Cullauch 1439, Maccullo 1550, Makcullo 1642, M'Cullocht 1556, Makcullocht 1546, M'Cullogh 1685, M'Kowloche 1495; in 1684 (*Parish*) McColloch, McCullie, McCullo, McCulloh, McCully, McKculloch, McKulloch; Undated forms: M'Alach, Mackculloch, Makculloch, M'Hulagh, M'Kulagh; and in a papal document (1444) Malrcowlach.

MACCULLONY. The name by which the Young Pretender permitted the Seven Men of Glenmoriston to address him. More correctly it is *Mac'Ill Domhnaich*, "son of the servant of the Lord." The surname was at one time common in the parishes of Urquhart and Kiltarlity. Mackay, *Urquhart and Glenmoriston*, 2. ed., p. 315n.

MACCUNE, MACCUNN. G. *MacEoghain*, 'son of EWEN,' q.v., an old surname in Galloway. Gilcrist McKwnne granted a charter to Roland Kenedy c. 1370–80 (*Laing*, 64). Donald Makcvne had a royal remission for slaughter committed by him, 1497 (*Rose*, p. 164), and John Makcune in Auchincheand, Galloway, had a precept of remission, 1535 (RSS., II, 1862). Another John Makcune was occupier of the 20s. land of Balleballoch, Carrick, 1538 (RMS., III, 1804), and John M'Cune or M'Cunn appears in Craignesten, 1627 (*Dumfries*). See also under MACKEON and MACKUENN. Old: M'Cwne.

MACCURDY. A current form of MACKIRDIE, q.v.

MACCURE. A form of MACIVER, q.v., current in Galloway. Muldouy McCure and Donald Roy McCowir were tenants of Drumglust in 1504, and John McKewvr was tenant of Braune in the same year (ER., XII, p. 663, 664). Vyr MacCuir was officer of the earl of Argyll at Strathache in 1558 (LCD., p. 231), and Ewin M'Kewer of Largothene witnessed Argyll's letters of fire and sword against Clangregor in 1565 (BBT., p. 212). A debt was due to Robert McCuir in 1572 (RPC., II, p. 167), Robert M'Cuir was burgess of Edinburgh, 1577 (RPC., II, p. 728), Joannes Mackure was burgess of Edinburgh, 1614 (*Retours, Edinburgh*,

1485), Katherine M'Cur, spouse of Dougall Campbell of Brichen, also appears in Edinburgh, 1619 (*Retours, Edinburgh*, 418), John McCuir, writer in Glasgow, took the Test in 1682 (RPC., 3. ser. VII, p. 811), and John M'Cuir was indweller in Lanark, 1690 (*Lanark CR.*). See also MACURE.

MACCURRACH, MACCURRAGH. Variants of MACMURRICH, q.v. John McKeane McCourich in Glenlyoune and Duncan McCallum McKeane McCurich in Lawers were denounced as thieves, 1682 (RPC., 3. ser. VII, p. 638). Archibald M'Curich (McKurrich or McUrich), herd in McClay's land in the parish of Dunoon, was transported to New England in 1685 (RPC., 3. ser. XI, p. 94, 312, 315). Another Archibald M'Currich is recorded in Dunoon parish, 1695 (*Argyll*). Shortened to CURRIE, q.v.

MACCURRIE, MACCURRY. A form of MACVURICH, q.v. John Makcurrie was witness in Dumfries, 1569 (*Edgar*, p. 243). Murdoch M'Whirrie (or M'Currie) was minister of Saddell at the erection of the Synod there in April, 1639 (*Fasti*, new ed., IV, p. 64). John M'Curry was tenant at the miln of Pitcairn, 1746 (*Dunkeld*).

MACCURTAIN. *See under* MACKEURTAN.

MACCUS. Maccus and MAGNUS, q.v., are common names in the royal race of Isle of Man and the Hebrides. "Maccus plurimarum rex insularum" one of the eight "subreguli" who are said to have followed King Eadgar to Chester, is Magnus, son of Aralt, who with "the Lagmanns of the Islands" plundered Inis Cathaigh [Scattery island at the mouth of the Shannon], A. D. 974. Maccus defended a bridge with two companions at the battle of Maldon, 991 (Sweet, *Anglo-Saxon reader*, 7. ed., p. 123). Maccus filius Undewyn, witness in Earl David's *Inquisitio*, c. 1124 (REG., p. 5). "It is likely that Longformacus in Berwickshire means the encampment or residence of Maccus" (*Watson* I, p. 495). Robert filius Machus was one of a number appointed to settle a dispute between the abbeys of Glasgow and Kelso, 1221 (REG., 116). From this name we have MAXTON and MAXWELL.

MACCUSKER. *See under* MACCOSKER.

MACCUSPIC. A variant of MACUSBAIG, q.v. The form Maccusbic was also found in Harris in 1900.

MACCUTCHEN, MACCUTCHEON. *See under* MACHUTCHEN.

MACCUTHAN. A minor sept of Macdonalds in Skye, distinct from MACCUIDHEAN, q.v. Like the latter named they appear not to have had a good reputation among their neighbors:

"Clann 'ic Cuthain chuir nam briag."

(The M'Cuthan, expert in lies).

Allaster McUthan in the Larg, Inverness-shire, was put to horn, 1607 (RPC., xiv, p. 459).

MACDADE, MACDAID. These names found mostly in Glasgow are forms of Irish Mac-Daibhéid, 'son of Davet,' diminutive form of David.

MAC DAFRETH. Yrgalac mac dafreth or mac dafrech witnessed two charters by Orabilis, daughter and heiress of Nessus, before 1199 (RPSA., p. 290–291).

MACDAIR. Three individuals named McDair were charged with trespass at Graitney (Gretna), 1622 (RPC., xii, p. 493). Domnall mac Daire. Cf. under MACDOIR.

MACDAIRMID, MACDARMID, MACDEARMID, MACDERMAID, MACDERMID, MACDIARMID, MACDEARMONT, MACDAIRMOND, MACDERMAND, MACDIARMOND, MACDERMONT. All current spellings of the name, the last five with intrusive n. G. MacDhiarmaid, 'son of DERMID,' q.v. The name is a comparatively rare one in record, and when it does appear it is sometimes corrupted into M'Kermit, etc. The Macdiarmids of Glenlyon claim or claimed to be the oldest if not the aboriginal race of the district. Nemeas Mactarmayt was rector of St. Conganus de Duybrinis (Durinish) and afterwards vicar of Kilchoman in Islay, 1427 (Pap. Lett., viii, p. 23). John Makeyrmit was a sufferer from the hership of Petty, 1502 (Rose, p. 176), and another John McKeremyt was tenant of Pollouchquhy, 1504 (ER., xii, p. 667). Jhone McChormeit of Menyenis was partner to a bond of manrent, 1533 (Cawdor, p. 159). Jhone Makhermyk, one of the 'mairs and officiaris of the schirefdome of Pertht,' 1529 (Grandtully, i, p. 68). Finlay Dow McKermeid in Glenlyoun was fined for reset of Clan Gregor in 1613 (RPC., xiv, p. 633). Gillemertene M'Kermit in Soccoth, a Glenurquhay vassal, 1638 (BBT., p. 403). Archibald McDiarmott was a charter witness at Inverlevirmore, 1659 (Poltalloch Writs, p. 76), and Robert Mac-Dermit was liberated from the Tolbooth of Elgin, 1685 (Elgin, i, p. 336). John Dow McDearmeid was tenant of Bols in Islay, 1686 (Bk. Islay, p. 518), John McKermet, rebel in parish of Kilbrandan, 1685 (Commons, p. 11), and Alexander M'Dermite was 'toun clerk deput of Air,' 1687 (Ayr, p. 211). John

McDermeit was a student at Glasgow University in 1698, as was also Patrick M'Dermant of St. Quivox, Ayrshire, in 1811. Several M'Diarmids were among the duke of Atholl's Fencible men enrolled in Glenlyon in 1706 (HMon., iii, p. 215–216), and Isabel M'Kearmet is recorded in Ground of Ballachin, 1700 (Dunkeld). In the Kirk session record of the entry relating to Colin Macdiarmid, the Reay country bard, drowned in 1799, his name is spelled Macdermot. Jon McKiarmid appears in Nether Lorn, 1692 (Commons, p. 34). Mc-Diarmoid 1669, Macdermant 1816, McDiarmoid 1669, McKirrmiad (in Kilmelford) 1692. See also MACTARMAYT.

MACDANIEL, MACDANIELL. Incorrect Anglicizings of MACDONALD, due to the faint assonance between Donald and Daniel. There is no etymological connection between the names.

MACDARMID. See under MACDAIRMID.

MACDAVID. MacDavid is found in Dornoch in 1562. Johnston gives "a 1547 Mich. M'Cade, Gart (Dunblane)."

MACDAWY. Maldoveny MacDawy was one of the inquest which found that the daughters of the late Finlai de Campsi were the lawful heirs of the deceased Dufgall, brother of Maldowen, earl of Levenax, 1271 (Red Bk. Menteith, ii, p. 218; RMP., p. 191). Gilleglass M'Dawy was 'mair' of Petty, 1462 (ER., vii, p. 130).

MACDEARMID, MACDERMAID, MACDERMID, MACDERMAND, MACDEARMONT, MACDEARMONT (this form found in Galloway). The n in the last three names is intrusive. See under MAC-DAIRMID.

MAC DHOMHNUILL DHUIBH. Patronymic of Cameron of Lochiel. Commonly spelled in records MacCoildwy.

MACDIARMOND. See under MACDAIR-MID.

MACDICK. 'Son of Dick,' pet form of Richard. Thomas MacDik is in the list of those exempt from process, 1552 (RPC., i, p. 136).

MACDICKEN. 'Son of Dicken,' a diminutive of RICHARD, and so = DICKINSON. "Ane wob of cammes" (canvas) was stolen from John Makdikin in Stirling, 1555, and in 1564 Patrick M'Dicoun was "ressavit to the fredome of burgesrie and gilt, gratis," for services rendered the burgh (SBR., p. 64, 81). Janet M'Dickon in Easter Kep, 1619 (Dunblane).

MACDILL. One of the many old spellings of MACDOWALL, q.v., which has become a fixed surname. John McDill and Michael Mc-Dill, followers of the earl of Cassilis, were respited for murder, 1526 (RSS., I, 3386). William M'Dill, son of Andrew M'Dill, burgess of Perth, was charged with playing at the Butts in Perth in time of preaching, 1589 (*Spottiswoode Miscellany*, II, p. 266). David M'Dill and Johnne M'Dill were witnesses in Keiris, 1619 (RPC., XI, p. 570), and Andrew M'Dill was witness in the earldom of Carrick, 1615 (*Laing*, 1742). John M'Dill is in Largs, parish of Urr, 1641 (*Dumfries*), and Andrew McDill was charged with being a disorderly person (nonconforming) in the parish of Carsfern, 1684 (RPC., 3. ser. IX, p. 575).

MAC DOBARCON. Cainnech mac meic Dobarcon made a gift to the monastery of Deer, c. 1130 (*Bk. Deer*, II, 20). *Dobarcu* means literally 'water-dog,' and is a name applied to the otter; its modern Gaelic form is *dobhran*, a 'pet' reduction of the longer name as Zimmer points out (Kuhn's *Zeitschrift*, XXXII, p. 163–164). The O'Dobarchon of Thomond are descendants of a man named Dobarchú, who was turned into an otter by S. Brendan as punishment for killing the saint's oxen. The Irish text of the legend is printed by Henri Gaidoz from the Book of Lismore in *Mélusine*, IV, col. 298–299, with English translation by Standish Hayes O'Grady. *Maoldobharchon*, 'slave of the otter,' bishop of Cille Dara is in record in 706 (AFM., I, p. 308).

MACDOIR, MACDOR. Forms of MACINDEOR (?). Bridan McDor in Moray had a remission in 1363 (REM., p. 164). John M'Doir was accused of drunkenness and fighting in the church of Kiltearn, 1672 (IDR., intro., p. xxv). Cf. MACDAIR.

MACDONACH, MACDONNACH. From G. *Mac-Donnchaidh*, 'son of Duncan.' See MACCONACHIE.

MACDONACHIE, MACDONACHY. G. *Mac-Donnchaidh*, 'son of Duncan.' Sometimes translated Duncanson. Finlay McDonchy VcKerris apparent of Glenselche, witness 1582 (*Poltalloch Writs*, p. 135). Duncan Garve M'Donquhy, servitor to the earl of Argyll, 1596 (HP., I, p. 193). Ewin M'Donochie in Balliwilling denounced rebel, 1675 (ibid., I, p. 296).

MACDONALD. G. *Mac Dhòmhnuill* (pron. Maak oonil), 'son of DONALD,' q.v. Properly speaking there is no such surname as Macdonald. *MacDhomhnuill* means 'son of (a particular) Donald': all others of the name are simply *Domhnullach*, 'one of the Donalds' (Henderson, ZCP., IV, p. 244). The chiefs of the clan in the direct line are descended from Donald, eldest son of Reginald, second son of Somerled, Regulus of the Isles. Collectively the clan is known as *Clann Dòmhnuill*, and, due to the absorption of many small septs and 'broken men,' it is therefore the most numerous and widespread of all the clans. It should therefore be borne in mind that all persons named Macdonald are not by any means son of a particular Donald any more than all Campbells are sib to the duke of Argyll. Sir Eneas Macpherson rather spitefully accuses the Macdonalds of vanity in that they "would have all the families descended of theirs in which there is ane (M) or any other letter of their name" (*Loyall Dissuasive*, SHS. ed., p. 108). In *MacDhomhnuill* the d by aspiration is often omitted in pronunciation thus giving rise to the form MacConnell, a spelling common in Ulster. In '*A Chònuill*' for '*A Dhòmhnuill*' ('A' here is all that remains of 'Mac') the sounds of broad *dh* and broad *ch* are liable to confusion, hence MacChonuill for *MacDhòmhnuill* and MacConachie for *Mac-Dhonnchaidh*. In *Waifs and strays*, II, and in Rev. J. G. Campbell's *Witchcraft*, p. 23, are the forms MacConnuill and Ma-Conuill. The attempts in record to render the name from Gaelic pronunciation has resulted in a great variety of forms from which the following is a selection: Makconehill 1479, 1564, Maconhale (of Dunivaig) 1588, McConile 1571, M'Conill 1580, McConnaill 1581, M'Connel 1627, McConnell 1633, McConnil 1564, M'Connill 1597, M'Connyll 1545, VcConull 1613, MakDonald 1571, M'Donnyle 1326, McDonol 1769, McDonoll 1771, McDonyll 1521, M'Douny 1329, M'Kconil 1597, MacKonald 1586, Mackoneye 1571, M'Konnell, M'Oneill, VcONeill 1576, M'Onele (all four of Donnawik = Dunivaig) 1626, McOnill (of Sleat) 1628, Mc orronald (of Eyellanttirrem) 1645, M'zonil 1531, Makconeill 1571, Makconell 1521, Makconnele and Makconell 1571, Mach-Onales and Mac-Coneales (pl.) 1646. Sir James Melville spells the name Machonel. The M'Douny of 1329 above appears three years earlier as John M'Donnyle, bailie of Ile (Islav) (ER., I, p. 52, 196), and Therthelnac Makdonenalde was a charter witness at Lesmore, 1251 (RMS., II, 3126). MACDONELL and MACDONNELL are also recognized spellings of the name at the present time.

MACDONART. A shortened from of M'ILLE DHONGART, q.v. Janet Makdonart in the Stewartry, 1550 (*Laing*, 559).

MACDONELL. The spelling of the name MAC-DONALD, q.v., used by the families of Glengarry and Keppoch.

MACDONLEAVY. See under MACLAE.

MACDOOL. A current form of MACDOUAL, q.v.

M'DORMOND. Not a patronymic, simply = MacDrummond, 'son of (a man named) Drummond.' Also spelled VcDormound. John M'Dormond in Roro in Glenlyon, 1709 (Dunkeld).

MACDOUAL, MACDOUALL, MACDOWALL, MACDOWELL. G. MacDhùghaill, 'son of DOUGAL (DOUGALL)', q.v. The claim of the Macdowells of Galloway to be descended from the ancient native lords of Galloway can neither be disproved nor can it be satisfactorily established (Maxwell, Dumfries, p. 103–105). Mactheuel witnessed a charter by Uchtredus filius Fergusi of the church of Colmanele in the reign of Malcolm IV (LSC., p. 19). Fergus McDuhile in Wigton was juror on inquest at Berwick, 1296, and in same year as Fergus MacDowilt rendered homage (Bain, II, p. 198, 215). He is probably the Fergus MacDowile who witnessed a charter by William, lord of Douglas, 1306–29 (RHM., I, p. 13). In 1307 a pardon was granted Elyas de Vaus at the request of Duncan MacDuel (Bain, II, p. 510), and in same year Dungall MacDouyl, senior, for services rendered, requested for his son Dungal, junior, the marriage of the daughter and heiress of Hugh de Champaigne, deceased, a tenant in capite (ibid., p. 507). Sir Duugal M'Douuille, sheriff of Dumfries and constable of the castle, and his brother, Fergus M'Douuille, are mentioned in 1312 (ibid., III, 278). Dugald McDowille, knight, was witness in Galloway, 1347 and 1354 (Pap. Lett., III, p. 396; Bain, III, 1578), Master Patrick Macduoel was archdeacon of Whitehorne before 1390 (Pap. Pet., I, p. 575), and Gilbert Macduyl was archdeacon of Sodor before 1416 (ibid., p. 605). Vhtred Mcduwell de Dalquheane, notary public, 1515, appears in Inchturing year as Wthred Mcduuyll de Dalhowane (REG., 491, 492). John McCoull in Overgarrell is mentioned in connection with Douglas of Drumlanrig, 1609, his name in one instance being spelled McOull (RPC., VIII, p. 701). John McQuhoull in Arbrak was summoned to appear before the Privy Council, 1621 (RPC., XII, p. 533). Margaret M'Dull and Janet Makdull appear in Edinburgh, 1602 and 1677 (Edinb. Marr.), and Patrick McDull was skipper in Leith, 1675 (Edin. App.). The late Dr. Trotter in his Galloway gossip: Kirkcudbright-

shire (p. 218) gives successive changes of this name:

REAL NAME	PRONOUNCED	FAMILIAR USE	GENTEEL
Mac Dugald (McDoughal)	McDoual McDowall	Dole Dowell	
Mac Dugald McDhugal	McCoull	Cole Coles, Coull	

M'Douell 1547, Makdoval 1590, M'Dovele 1474, M'Dowele and Makdovele 1473, Makdowale 1545, Makdowelle 1391, M'Dule 1615, M'Gowall 1571. The following spellings are also given in RMS.: McDowale, McDowalle, McDowelle, McDowylle, McDowill, McDoville, McDovylle; and in 1684 (Parish) we have McDole, McDoll, McDouell, McDoul, McDowal, McDual, McDuall, M'Kdowall. In north of Ireland it became Madole.

MACDOUGAL, MACDOUGALL. G. MacDhùghaill, 'son of DOUGAL,' q.v. The family of Macdougall of Dunollie is descended from Dugall, eldest son of Somerled of the Isles. The late Dr. Alexander Carmichael described this family as "one of the most unobtrusive and honoured families in Scotland." Duncan MacKowle founded the Priory of Ardchattan, Argyllshire, c. 1230. Robert M'Kowele, lord of Karsnelohe, was witness in Ayrshire, c. 1370–80 (Laing, 64). Fergus Macdowylle had a confirmation charter of the barony of Malkerston, Yetholm and Clifton in 1374 (Stodart, II). In 1443 there is record of the death of Malcolm Mc Dubailwigh aicu, vicar of Kilcalmonell (Pap. Lett., VIII, p. 470), probably a blundering attempt at MacDougall vic Ago. The obit of Duncan M'Cowyll is recorded in 1517 (Chr. Fort.), and Johne MacCoull of Dunnollycht (Dunollie) had a license from Archibald, earl of Argyll, 1557 (BBT., p. 201). Duncan MacCoull of Lorn appears as justice of the peace for Argyllshire, 1610 (RPC., VIII, p. 78), and John McInnes vc Cwill Roy is named rebel, 1625 (ibid., XIII, p. 655). Iain M'duill vc Kemlach and Dougall M'duill vc Ewin alias M'Dougall were among those murdered at Dunaverty, 1647 (HP., II, p. 256), and John M'Dull was burgess of Edinburgh, 1682 (Inquis., 6410). In a list dated 1704 giving the names of clans and the numbers in each to be raised for the elder Pretender the entry 'Mac Dulothes 500 men,' is probably meant for Macdougall. Descendants of a sixteenth-century Macdougal still flourish in Sweden as Duvall and Duwall, and George Julian Gordon Macdougall (1824–94) rose to be a rear-admiral in the Danish service. In Lord Archibald Campbell's Records of

MACDOUGAL, Macdougall, continued

Argyll Macchaill is given as a spelling of Macdougall, and Bane M'Chale and Malcolm M'Hale were tenants in Auchinchgalden in 1594 (BBT., p. 287). In Kintyre Macdougall is pronounced 'Ac 'ughaill, the Dean of Lismore (c. 1512) spells it MacKowle, and in BBT. it appears as M'Cowle. M'Awell 1510, VcCoule 1530, McCoull 1556, McCouyll 1519, McCowell 1520, McCowil 1516, McCuile 1548, Mackdugl 1736, Makquhole 1552; MacCoyle, MacDogall, M'Houl, MacHowell, McKoull, M'Oul, M'Owl, etc.

MACDOUGLE. Another form of Macdougal, q.v.

MACDOWAL, Macdowall. *See under* MACDOUALL.

MACDRAIN. *See under* DRAIN.

MACDUFF. (1) Macduff, 'Thane of Fife,' 'a half or wholly mythical personage,' was really a creation of Fordun, and his story was embellished by Wyntoun, Boece, and Buchanan. Of his existence there is not a particle of proof. Had such a person existed some record of him would surely be found in RPSA. The opponent of Macbeth was Siward, earl of Northumberland, as all historical records show. Moreover MacDuff was not a surname at that time. "The earls of Fife of the race of Macduf," says Skene, "first appear in the reign of David I. In the memoranda of old grants in the Chartulary of St. Andrews is a donation to the Culdees of Lochleven by 'Edelradus vir venerandae memoriae filius Malcolmi regis Scotiae, abbas de Dunkelden et insuper comes de Fyf,' who is the first earl on record. On the narrative that it was granted 'in juvenile aetate,' it is confirmed by his two brothers David and Alexander, in presence, among others, 'Constantini comitis de Fyf,' probably in the reign of Edgar. The charter by King David I remodelling the monastery of Dunfermline (RD., 1) is witnessed, among others, by 'Constantinus comes,' and 'Gillemichel mac duf,' and a later charter to Dunfermline is witnessed by 'Gillemichel comes de Fife.' If Constantine had been of the race of Macduf, and Gillemichel was his son, as many writers affirm, they could hardly appear together thus, 'Constantinus comes, Gillemichel mac duf,' without any mention of their connection; and Gillemichel seems to have been the first earl of the race of Macduff" (*Fordun*, p. 422–423).

(2) *Mac Dhuibh*, ('son of Dubh,' an old Gaelic personal name, 'a curtailment of some longer or double-stemmed name'). Malisius mc Duf witnessed a confirmation charter by Henry,

son of Malise, seneschal of Stratherne, 1284 (REM., p. 467). A bond by David M'Duif of Fandowie, James Makduf in Thannagarne, and others to Sir Duncan Campbell of Glenurquhay is recorded in 1594 (BBT., p. 251). John Roy M'Duff was retoured heir of Gilbert M'Duff, merchant burgess of Dundee, 1626 (*Retours, Forfar,* 158). See also DUFF and MACILDUF.

MACDUFFIE. G. *MacDuibhshithe,* 'son of Dubhshithe' (the black man of peace), the name of an old Colonsay family. See MACFEE. The lands of Glenscharway in Arane were leased to Neil M'Duffy, 1460 (ER., VII, p. 13). Sir Malcolm Macduffy, vicar of Kilmarew (i.e. Killarow in Islay) died 1554 (OPS., II, p. 261). In 1592 the king confirmed a charter of feudifirme by Malcolm M'Duphe, commendator of Ormesav, with consent of the brethren to Archibald Campbell M'Duthie Vekdonill and his heirs masculine of certain lands in the lordship of Knapdale (RMS., v, 2166).

MACDUFFSON, 'son of MACDUFF,' q.v. The goods and lands of Alexander Makdufsone in the Bray of Ros were ordered to be distrained in 1498 (OPS., II, p. 527).

MAC DUNAC. Anegus mac Dunac perambulated the boundaries of Balfeth in Angus c. 1204–1214 (RAA., I, 89). Gillemich mac Dunec who witnessed a charter by William the Lion c. 1178–80 to Gilbert, earl of Strathern, of the lands of Kinbethach (LIM., p. xxiii) is probably Gillemichael McDuncan of c. 1184 (*Athole*, p. 704).

MACDUNCAN. Gillemichel McDuncan witnessed an Atholl charter, c. 1184 (*Athole*, p. 704), and Nicholaus Makdunkan was present at pleas held at Dull in Atholl, 1264 (RPSA., p. 349). See under MAC DUNAC.

MACEACHAN, MACEACHAIN, MACEACHEN, MACEACHIN, MACACHIN, MACECHAN, MACCEACHAN. G. *MacEachainn* 'son of EACHAN,' q.v. The Maceachans of the present day are said to be Macdonalds, but many of them in Arisaig and Uist so long used their patronymic as their surname that the practice has become settled. The late Allan R. Macdonald of Waternish says it is very doubtful if the MacEachens are really Macdonalds, and that there is good reason to believe that they are really Macleans (*The Truth about Flora Macdonald*, p. 14n). Gillecrist Mecachin witnessed a charter by Roger de Scallebroc of lands in Carrik in the reign of William the Lion (*Melros*, I, p. 26). In 1505 'a respit was maid to J. Makachyn and to Donald Moyl Macachane for all crimes, etc., done in ony tyme bigane' (RSS., I, 1174). Andrew M'Cachin was rector of Ardmuchy, 1506 (ER., XII, p. 709), and Archibald McCachin was a tenant in Colonsay in same year (ibid.). Neill Makachyn and Malcolme Makachyn, 'his bruder,' were killed in 1508 (RSS., I, 1709). Alexander M'Quuichin of Dalquhat was outlawed in 1528. Satisfaction was to be rendered the kin of Donald Ballo McAuchin, 1532 (RSS., II, 1525). John M'Gauchane was burgess of Edinburgh, 1540 (ibid., 3773), and William Reoch M'Aychin gave his bond of manrent to the earl of Huntlie, 1543 (SCM., IV, p. 260). Gillespik M'Kouchane was in Mergmonogach, Kintyre, 1605 (HP., III, p. 81), Angus McAchane alias McAllaster is in Islay, 1614 (Cawdor, p. 232), Ard McKukan appears in Nether Lorn, 1692 (Commons, p. 33), and Ewan McEachan or McAihan was a tenant under Chisholm of Erchles, 1721 (HP., II, p. 297). Many Maceachans emigrated to Nova Scotia and to Prince Edward Island and their descendants are now numerous there. McAchine 1635, Makcachane 1605, McEchan 1718, M'Eachine 1705, MacIkin (in Polloundowie) 1662, M'Kiachan 1724. Also Englished Auchaneson. See also MACGEACHAN.

MACEACHERN, MACEACHEARN, MACECHERN, MACEACHRAN. G. MacEach-thighearna, 'son of the horse-lord.' The name goes back to OIr. when it appears as Ech-tigern. On the shaft of the cross at Kilkerran near Campbeltown, Kintyre, is the inscription: Hec est: crvx: Coleni: Mc: Heachyrna: et Katirine: uxoris: eivs (Drummond, Sculptured monuments of Iona, pl. lxxxi). This is probably Colin MacEachern who was chief of the Maceachern in 1499. Charles M'Caichrane held lands in Kintyre, 1605 (HP., III, p. 84). N'Achieran appears in Kenmore, 1682 (DPD., I, p. 486). The name Anna Cheacharna is for Ann Maceachearn and Iain Ceachairne is for John Maceachearn. MacAcharn and McAcherne 1506, McAchern 1505, Makauchern 1507, M'Caichrane 1605, Makcacherne 1515, M'Caikorn 1694, McCauchquharn 1541, M'Caychirn c. 1512, McCochran 1684, M'Eacharin 1647, M'Eacharne 1662, Makeacharne 1659, Makgacharne 1596; M'Gacharne, M'Kecherane, McKechern, M'Kechran, M'Kechrane, and M'Kechren all 1605. Epidion Akron is the name of the Mull of Kintyre in the Geography of Ptolemy, c. 140 A.D. The root of the name is epos, horse; the Epidii, a British tribe, were the 'horse folk,' and it is interesting to note that Kintyre in historic times has always been claimed as the home of the Maceacherns or Maceacherns.

MACEAGH. The Clan Vic Cearch or Each, 'children of the mist,' is a mistranslation of MACGHITTICH, q.v., for MacShithich, 'son of the wolf.' (See under SHAW.) There is little doubt that the name which Sir Walter Scott makes Mac Eagh in A Legend of Montrose, and 'son of the mist,' as if it were from ceathach, is MacShithich (Bàrdachd Ghàidhlig, p. 294).

MACEAN. See under MACIAN.

MACEANLAIG. This is said to be a local (Knapdale) form of MACNEILAGE, q.v. (Gillies, p. 38).

MAC EDA. Comgeall mac eda, c. 1100, made a grant to the Abbey of Deer (Bk. Deer, II, 1). He was probably mormaer of Buchan. In modern Gaelic MacAoidh. See MACKAY.

MACEDDIE. A form of MACKEDDIE, q.v., current in Inverness.

MACEDOLF, 'son of Edolf,' i.e. Eadulf from Eadwulf, an OE. personal name. Gillmychel Makedolf witnessed a grant by Maldouenv, earl of Lennox to Stephen de Blantyr c. 1248 (Levenax, p. 36). Michael, the son of Edolf, doubtless the same person, served on an inquest at Dunbretan in 1259 (APS., I, p. 89 after the preface), and in 1271 as Gilmychel MacHedolf he served on another inquest in Dumbarton (RMP., p. 191). Gillemichel MacEdolf and Donecan MacEdolf were jurors on an inquisition regarding the lands of Stephen de Blantthyre in 1263 (Bain, I, 2338). Donecan is probably the Duncan Maggadelfe of Cambroun, Stirlingshire, who rendered homage in 1296 (ibid., II, p. 205). Duncan Macedolfe witnessed a confirmation by Bruce to Sir John Colquhoun in 1308 (Lennox, II, p. 407), and Duncan Macedolf was juror on an inquisition re the lands of Thomas de Cremennane in 1320 (Levenax, p. 82).

MACEDWARD. G. M'Eideard (G. Eideard, dial. Eudard, from English Edward), 'son of Edward.' A Highland border name. John Red McEdwart was a king's tenant in Strathdee in 1527 (Grant, III, p. 70), and Edward M'Edward is in record in Corran, parish of Lochgoyle in 1697 (Argyll Inv.).

MACELATYN. John Makelatyn or Maklatvne had a safe conduct to travel into England in 1424 (Bain, IV, 961, 964). Prof. Watson says this name appears to represent Mac Gille Etáin, 'son of Etáin's servant.' Etáin is the saint from whom Kirkmaiden in Wigtownshire derives its name. M'Etáin for Mo-Etáin, the virgin of Tuam Noa, was Latinized Medana (Watson I, p. 163).

MACELFRISH, Macelfrisk. A Hebridean surname. Probably from *M'Gille Bhris*, 'son of the servant of (S.) Bricius.' Bricius was a Gaulish saint of the fifth century, and his name was a favorite personal name from 1100 to 1300. There was a Culdee of this name, and a later Bricius (Brice) was bishop of Moray (1203–1222). Donald MacIleresch in Ullerav, North Uist, is recorded in 1718, and probably M'Illfrice of the Edinburgh Marriage records (1669) is same name. Janet M'Lefrish in the parish of Shotts, 1710, and Isable M'Ilfreish in Torphichen in same year *(Torphichen)*.

MACELHINNEY. Of recent introduction from Ireland. From Ir. *Mac Giolla Choinnigh*, 'son of the servant of Kenneth.'

MACELLAR, Maceller. Felanus Ylarii witnessed a charter by Duncan Campbell, lord of Lochow, 1432. This is the Latinized form of Felan Mac Ellar, "it being imagined that Ellar a purely Celtic name was equivalent to Latin Hilarius or Hilary. The MacEllars held the lands of Cruachan on Lochaw, and also Maam and Kilblaan near Inveraray for many centuries and frequently appear as witnesses to Argyll charters" (Duke of Argyll, *Oban Times,* 27 Nov. 1926). I venture to think the Duke is in error and that the name is the same as **Mackellar, q.v.**

MACELLIGATT. This name, found in Galloway after 1700, is a form of Irish M'Elligott, from *MacUileagóid*, 'son of Wilecot,' i.e. little Ulick. Ulick itself is a diminutive of William.

MACELMAIL, Macelmeel, Macelmoyle. G. *Mac Gille mhaoil*. Rev. John MacElmail was appointed Catholic priest in Knoydart, 1884 (Blundell, *Catholic Highlands*, 1917, p. 82). Rev. John McElmoyle (d. 1938), born in Scotland, was known as the "marrying parson" of America's Gretna Green (Elkton, Maryland). Mc illemayll 1636. Mary NcIlvoil, 1704, appears in 1706 as Mor NcIllimoile. See under **Macmillan.**

MACELMOYLE. *See under* MACMOIL.

MACELROY. *See under* MACILROY.

MACELVIE, Macelwee. Current forms of **Mackelvie, q.v.** Found in Bute in 1656 as M'Ilwee (*Hewison*, II, p. 270).

MACELWAIN. *See under* MACILVAIN.

MACEMLINN. A surname recorded in Arran, and Englished **Bannatyne**, a name with which it has no connection. The late Rev. C. M. Robertson, an able Gaelic scholar, gives the correct Arran form as *Maic Eamailinn.* See under **Macaomlinn.**

MACEOCHAGAIN, 'son of Eochagán,' a diminutive of *Eochaidh*, q.v. Gillascoppe Mahohegen appears in the reign of Alexander II in a trial in Edinburgh because he had not given the hostages he had undertaken to deliver into the king's hands (APS., I, p. 68). He appears again in 1223 as Gillescop Macihacian, witness in a charter by Thomas de Colvile of lands in Galloway to the Abbey of Melrose (*Melros*, p. 172).

MACERARD. Nigellus M'Herarde or M'Horrard had a charter of the lands of Kirkanders in the sheriffdom of Dumfries in the reign of Robert I (RMS., I, App. II, 613). Gaelic *Mac Eraird*, Erard's son, Erard being a compound of *air* and *ard*, meaning 'very tall;' in this position *air* becomes *er, ir, or, ur* (*Watson* III, p. 21).

MACERCHAR, Macfarquhar, Mackercher, Mackercher, Mackeracher, Mackerracher, Mackerichar, Mackerichar, Mackerricher. G. *Mac Fhearchair*, 'son of Farquhar,' q.v. Farquharson is the English rendering of the name. Malmur Mac hercar appears in the reign of William the Lion (*Scon*, p. 37). The lands of Lochman M'Kilcolim M'Erewer, Enegus McErewar, and others in Kintyre were erected into the sheriffdom of Kintyre in 1292 (APS., I, p. 91, 447). Lawemund McGreghare (error for McEregere) and Annees (= Angus) son of Duncan McGregere (= McEregere) were summoned to do homage to King John Baliol, 1292 (ibid., p. 448). Macbain says (Skene, *Highlanders*, p. 413) Angus has been claimed as chief of Mackintosh though really head of the Lamonts. John filius Lagmanni filii Aecolmi (for Malcolmi) M'Ferchar, c. 1295. Yvar McFarchard, to whom a payment was made from the fermes of Inverness in 1327, appears in the following year as Eugene McErchar (ER., I, p. 59, 93). In 1337 payment was made to Thomas, son of Ewary McFerchary in Moray (ibid., p. 440). Malcolm Makkarocher was tenant under the earl of Lennox, 1472. Donald McFarquhar, tenant of Drumnamark, Ardmanoch, 1504 (ER., XII, p. 661). Ferquhardus McOwne McArchare and Moricus McOwne McArchare were parishioners of Duthil, 1537 (*Grant*, III, p. 269). Gillechreist M'Kerracher in the Port of Lochtay was a Glenurquhay vassal, 1638 (BBT., p. 400). Alexander M'Kerquhar in Dinra, 1662 *(Caithness)*, and Donald M'Archer in the parish of Callander in the same year *(Dunblane)*. Angus M'Kerrichare and Paul M'Ean vic Errochar in Sheba were denounced rebels, 1675 (HP., I). John M'Erichar in Dale, 1677, and Gilbert M'Archer in Esdale, 1672 *(Argyll)*. Several M'Kerchars or M'Kerchers were among the duke of Atholl's fencible men enrolled in Glenlyon, 1706 (*HMon.*, III, p. 215–216). The Perthshire M'Kerachers are descended from Donald Farquharson who married a daughter of Patrick Duncanson or Robertson, first of Lude. The name also appears in old records as M'Carracher (M'Caraher) and M'Carrower, abbreviated to M'Arar and M'Erar. Patrick M'Carquhar in Drungy, 1547 (*Dunblane*). M'Arequhare 1540, Mc Arquhar 1504, McFerqhrr 1582, McFerquhare 1656, Vic Erqr 1721.

MACERLANE. Current in Ayrshire and Dumbartonshire. See under MACNERLAN.

MACERLICH. *See under* MACKERLEY.

MACETTERICK. *See under* MACKETTRICK.

MACEUR, MACEURE. Galwegian forms of MACIVER, q.v. McEuer in Cullicuddin in 1607 (RPC.).

MACEVOY. *See under* MACAVOY. Christopher MacEvoy (1760–1838), a rich planter in Danish West Indies, later settled in Copenhagen.

MACEWAN, MACEWEN, MACEWING, MACEUEN. G. *MacEoghainn*, 'son of EWEN,' q.v. Gilpatrik mac Ewen was one of the perambulators of the lands of Kynblathmund, 1219 (RAA., I, p. 162). Malcolm mac Ewen is witness to a charter by Malcolm, second earl of Atholl of the church of Dul to St. Andrews a. 1174 (RPSA., p. 246). Patrick McEwyn was provost of Wygtoun, 1331 (ER., I, p. 358). Johannes M'Eogan was cited in 1355 to give evidence regarding the lands of Glasrie in Argyllshire (HP., II, p. 139). George Makewin, a follower of the earl of Cassilis, was respited for murder, 1526 (RSS., I, 3386). Donald Dow M'Coull VcQuhewin in 1574 was 'heddyt' (beheaded) at Kenmore by Campbell of Glenurquhay. John Makewin in Ediramuikie and James Makevin in Kayndknok, his brother, are in record, 1580 (BBT., p. 224). John McEroune, merchant burgess of Glasgow, 1633 (*Sasines*, II, 471), is an error for Macewen. John M'Eun *alias* Fleger in Icolumkill, was denounced rebel, 1675 (HP., I, p. 298). Buchanan says the Macewens "for divers ages have been seneciones or genealogists of the" Campbells (*Enquiry*, p. 23), but apparently the Campbell *seanachaidhean* were really Macdougals. Duncan M'Ewin V'Neill V'Arn, witness at Dunstaffnage, 1597 (N&Q., 11 July 1931, p. 23). This Duncan "was clearly a member of the family of hereditary bards to the Campbell chieftains. They held Barmolloch in Lorne as such,

the property descending to the nearest heirs male that happened to be 'rhymers.' They were Macdougals by origin" (Henry Campbell, *loc. cit.*). Some Macewens in Breadalbane were Macdougalls and a few were Maclarens (FB., p. 362). Complaint was made against Allester Ma Kewin or McEwin, servant to Lord Drummond, 1581 (RPC., III, p. 350, 355). Eouin M'Eouin in Slignish, Ardnamurchan, in record, 1696 (*Argyll Inv.*). The name is still common in Lennox and Galloway. McAine 1691, M'Evine 1528, McEvin 1677, M'Ewine 1638, Mackewin 1603, McKewyne 1546, McEwn 1724. In Galloway (1684): McKewn, McKewan, McKuinn, McYewin. Makewn (*Parish*). Other old spellings are: M'Eun, M'Kevin, M'Kewin, and M'Yowin. There was a M'Ewinstoun in Ayrshire, 1622 (*Retours, Ayr*, 212).

MACFADE. *See under* MACFEAT.

MACFADIN, MACFADION (current in Galloway), MACFADWYN, MACFADYEAN, MACFADZEAN, MACFADZEIN, MACFADZEON. Forms of MACFADYEN, q.v.

MACFADYEN, MACFADIN, MACFADION, MACFADWYN, MACFADYEAN, MACFADYON, MACFADZAN, MACFADZEAN, MACFADZEON, MACFADZEIN, MACFAYDEN, MACFEYDEN, MACPHADEN, and MACPHAIDEN. All from G. *Macphaidein* (or *Macphaidin*), 'son of *Paidean* or little Pat,' and so = Patonson. The late Rev. J. G. Campbell says: "MacFadyens were said to have been the first possessors of Lochbuie, and when expelled they became a race of wandering artificers, *Sliochd nan òr-cheard* — the race of goldsmiths in Mull." (*Clan traditions and popular tales*, p. 41). The earliest record of the name is in 1304 when Malcolm Macpadene appears as a charter witness at Achichendone in Kintyre (RMS., II, 3136). Conghan MacPaden petitioned for the archdeaconry of Argyll in 1390 (*Pap. Pet.*, I, p. 575). John McFadveane is in record in Edinburgh in 1457 (ER., VI, p. 306), and in 1473 a composition was made with Donald M'Fadzeane in Kirkcudbright (ALHT., I, p. 8). Hugh McFattin was tenant of Mydcoule, Petty, in 1499 (ER., XI, p. 444), and Donald Macfadzane, precentor in Lismore in 1507, appears again in 1511 as 'Sir' Donald McFaden (*Poltalloch Writs*, p. 183). He was probably the Sir Donald McFadzeane, chaplain of Tibbirmore in the diocese of Sodor, whose death is recorded in 1540 (RSS., II, 3397). Another M'Faden is in record in Iona in 1532. Finlaius M'Fedden, canon of the Isles, was witness to a charter of Muckairn also in 1532 (*Cawdor*, p. 158), and William M'Fadzean in Dellongfurd witnessed an in-

MACFADYEN, MACFADIN..., *continued*

strument of sasine at Blairquhan, Ayrshire, in 1618 (*Laing*, 1794). William Makfadieane in Beirwell was prosecuted for shooting game in 1620 (RPC., XII, p. 391), and another William Makfadzane in Lyneburne was retoured heir of William Makfadzane in 1643 (*Retours, Dumfries*, 183). The 20s. land of Balmacfadzeane in Wigtownshire is mentioned in 1628 (*Retours, Wigtown*, 70), and John McPhaden was a witness at Leppenmor, 1641 (*Poltalloch Writs*, p. 73). Duncan M'Phadden and Lachlan M'Phadden appear in Uleveiffe in 1672 (HP., II, p. 208), Malcolm M'Faden and Donald M'Phaden both in Auchadabeg were declared rebels in 1675 (HP., I), Janet M'Faggaine or M'Fadzeon was banished for refusing the Test in 1684 (RPC., 3. ser. x, p. 377, 590), and Finlay McPhadan and Angus McPhaiden were tenant farmers in Islay in 1733. They occur again in 1741 as Angus and Finlay McFadzen (*Bk. Islay*, p. 545, 549, 556). Dugald McPhaden was a witness in Islay in 1737 and Katherine McPhyden a witness in 1769 (ibid., p. 430, 472). The M'Fadzeans of Over Killelago are mentioned in 1681 (*Retours, Dumfries*, 305), and Macfadyens are still numerous in Mull and Tiree. An absurd explanation of the name is Mac Fad Ian, 'son of long (or tall) John!' Galloway forms of the name in 1684 are McFaddan, McFydeane, McKfadyean, McPhaddion, and McPhadzen (*Parish*); M'Fedden.

Blind Harry, in the seventh book of his *Schir William Wallace*, records the doings of a Macfadzan, leader of a band of Irish mercenaries in the service of the king of England. Nothing is known of him in Scottish record outside of the pages of Harry. He was eventually slain by Gylmichall, an attendant of Duncan of Lorn, but local tradition says he was hanged from a projecting tree on the summit of Creag-an-uni (Creag an aonaidh). The Macfadyens, whether they deserved it or not, had a reputation for parsimony, as in the following bitter little satire current in Mull, Tiree, and Islay (SGS., I, p. 80):

> MacPhàidein na circe
> Am baile na h-airce:
> Ged dh' fhan e r'a bruithe,
> Cha d' fhan e r'a h-ithe —
> air eagal a pàigheadh."

(Macfadyen of the hen, in the homestead of penury: though he stayed till she was boiled, he stayed not till she was eaten — for fear of paying for her).

MACFAGAN. Probably a form of MACFIGAN, q.v. Thomas M'Fegan in Lauchentyre, 1784 (*Kirkcudbright*).

MACFAIL. *See under* MACPHAIL.

MACFAIT. *See under* MACFEAT.

MACFALL. A current form of MACPHAIL, q.v.

MACFARLAN, MACFARLANE, MACFARLAND, MACFARLIN, MACPARLAN, MACPARLAND, MACPARLANE, MACPARLIN, MACPHARLAIN. G. *MacPharlain*, 'son of Parlan,' from O.Ir. *Partholon* (see BARTHOLOMEW). Malcolm Mcpharlane was one of the witnesses to a charter by Ywar Cambell of Strachur to Duncan, earl of Leuenax c. 1385 (HP., IV, p. 18), and in 1395 Duncan filius Malcolm Makfarlane had a charter from Duncan, earl of Levenax (*Levenax*, p. 64). Andrew M'Farlane of Aracher was admitted burgess freeman of Glasgow gratis in 1577 (*Burgesses*). "The ancestor of the Macfarlanes of Kirkton was George Macfarlane of Markinch, second son to Andrew Macfarlane of that Ilk, in the reign of King James V. George having sold the foirsaid lands of Markinch, went afterwards and settled in the north Highlands amongst his namesakes the Macfarlanes, promiscuously called in the Irish [i.e. Gaelic] language, M'Allans, Allanach, or Clan Allan — i.e. the posterity of Allan, because of their descent from Allan Macfarlane, younger son to one of the lairds of Macfarlane, who settled in Strathdonn, Aberdeenshire, several centuries ago. From him are descended the families of Auchorrachan, Balnengown, Lismurdie, &c., as also several others in Braemar and Strathspey" (Nimmo, *History of Stirlingshire*, 3. ed., 1880, p. 100). Robert Macfarlane (1815–1883), born in Rutherglen, was for seventeen years editor of the *Scientific American*. Makfarland and Makferlande 1546, M'Farlen 1603, Mcfarling 1668, M'Farling 1663, Makferlan 1529, McKfarlen 1728, McFerlane 1612, MacPharheline 1610.

MACFARQUHAR, 'son of FARQUHAR,' q.v., from the unaspirated form of the name. Fergus MacFerchar held lands near Glasgow in the reign of Malcolm IV (*Neubotle*, p. xxxvi). Macbeth Macferkar witnessed the grant of the church of Inuerhouen, c. 1187–1203 (REM., p. 38). Fynlaw Makferchar and Donald Makferchar held part of Murthly in Atholl, 1466 (*Cupar-Angus*, I, p. 145, 153), and Patrick M'Arquhar held the mill of Wester Boquhopill, Menteith, 1534 (RMS., III, 1548). John McFerquhar was concerned in the slaughter of John McAlester, 1538 (RSS., II, 2550), and Finlay M'Farquhersoun, a follower of Donald Gorme of Sleat, had remission in 1541 for his part in laying waste Trouterness in Skye and Kenlochew in Ross (ibid., 3943). John McFarcor was 'cuik to the 30ung laird of Balnagown,' 1590 (*Trials*, I, p. 196), and Donald McFerquhair in Tullichgrein and Allaster Mc-Farquher there were denounced rebels, 1619 (RPC., XI, p. 574). Caution was found for John McWilliam VcPherquhair in Cullclachie, 1627 (RPC., 2. ser. II, p. 5). Makferquhair 1555, McPharquhar 1671. See also MACERCHAR.

MACFATER. See under MACPHATER.

MACFAUL. A current form of MACPHAIL, q.v.

MACFAYDEN. A form of MACFADYEN, q.v.

MACFEAT, MACFEATE, MACFADE (formerly in Galloway), MACFAIT, MACPHADE, MACPHAID, MACPHATE. G. *Mac Phaid*, 'son of Pate,' diminutive of Patrick. In S. Michael's aisle of the church of Fearn is an effigy of Abbot Finlay M'Fead or M'Faid with the inscription: *Hic jacet Finlaius M'Fead Abbas de Fern qui obiit anno mcccclxxxv* (*New statistical account, Ross*, p. 41). "The king esteemed him so highly that he and his descendants were allowed to bear the name of Fearn as their family name" (Gordon, *Monasticon*, Glasgow, 1868, p. 351). Gilcrist McPaid, tenant in Dalmoloak, Kynnarde, in 1539 (ER., XVII, p. 671), Robert M'Faitt at the Mill of Inchrie, witness in 1596 (*Laing*, 1312), Duncan M'Phoid, an engager on royalist side, 1649 (IDR., p. 367), George M'Feat in Achmar, parish of Port, 1674 (*Dunblane*), John Macfeat was a messenger in Stirling in 1729, and Ebenezer M'Feat was mathematical tutor to Sir Walter Scott.

MACFEDRIES, MACFEDRIS. See under MACFETRIDGE.

MACFEE, MACFIE, MACPHEE, MACPHIE. G. *MacDhubhshith*, one of the oldest and most interesting Gaelic personal names we possess. "Its plan and concept," says Dr. Gillies, "go far away beyond those of even our old names" (*Place-names of Argyllshire*, p. 82). Johannes Macdufthi appears as charter witness in Dumfriesshire in the reign of Alexander II (*Melros*, p. 182), and a Thomas Macdoffy rendered homage, 1296 (*Bain*, II, p. 169). The AFM. record Dubside (mod. G. *Dubhsidhe*) as ferleiginn or reader of Iona in 1164, and Skene suggests (CS., III, p. 363) that the clan may have derived this name from him. The island of Colonsay appears to have been the home of the clan, but later a number of the name were located in Lochaber, and were followers of Cameron of Locheil. Archibald McKofee was a tenant in Islay in 1506 and Malcolm Makcofee tenant in Colonsay in same year (ER., XII, p. 709). Morphe mcphe de Colwinsay was cited for treason in 1531 (APS., II, p. 333a),

and Dusey [= Dubhsith] McFee was tenant of Bar in Islay, 1541 (ER., XVII, p. 616). Ewin McAphie *alias* Vic Condachie was one of those ordered to appear either before the Privy Council or before the sheriff and give bond in 1681 (RPC., 3. ser. VII, p. 82), and a notorious freebooter named Macphee about 1845–50 gave name to Eilean Mhic Phee in Loch Quoich, where he established himself with his family, recognizing no law and no landowner. There is an account of him, with portrait, in Ellice's *Place-names in Glengarry and Glenquoich*. John M'Affie appears in Meikle Kildy, parish of Dron, 1747 (*Dunblane*). The name means 'Black (one) of peace,' from *dubh* and *sith* (OIr. *dub* + *sith*), and parallel names are *Cusithe*, 'hound of peace,' and *Fearsithe*, 'man of peace.' A family in North Uist is (or was) known as 'Dubh-sidh,' 'Black fairy,' from a tradition that the family have been familiar with the fairies in their fairy flights and secret migrations (CG., 2. ed., II, p. 354). M'affeith c. 1512, McAffie 1595, M'aphie 1723, M'duffe 1532, Mc duffie 1626, McDuphie 1703, Makfeithe 1605, McFeye 1585, Mc iphie 1609. MACHAFFIE is another current form of the name. McAchopich 1569.

MACFEGGANS. See under MACFIGAN.

MACFEND. A surname confined apparently to Caithness. George M'Fend and David M'Phend in Braibster, 1655 and 1665; Donald M'Fend in Canisbay, 1656; and Margaret M'Fend in Freswick, 1663 (*Canisbay*, p. 4, 6, 14).

MACFERGUS, 'son of FERGUS,' q.v., from the unaspirated form of the name. Johannes filius Fergusii witnessed a royal charter of the lands of Dalmakeran c. 1316–18 (*Annandale*, I, p. 132). A charter granted in 1485 to the abbot of Iona by consent of the Lord of the Isles and his council is witnessed by . . . Colinus Fergusii [i.e. Cailean Mac Fhearghuis], domini cancellarius (*Bardachd Ghaidhlig*, p. 300). Morice Macgillafuirgy, 1455, = Moricius Fergussi (HP., IV, p. 181, 184). M'Fargus 1575.

MACFERRIES. G. *MacFhearghuis (Fear'uis)*, 'son of FERGUS,' q.v. Andreas McFeris, one of the king's tenants in Crethnard, Strathdee, 1527–39 (*Grant*, III, p. 68; ER., XVII, p. 658). Patrick McFers, tenant in Easter Micras (Estir Mecra), 1539 (ER., XVII, p. 659). Katherine M'Ferries, who was accused of witchcraft in Aberdeen, 1597, also appears in record without 'Mac' (SCM., I, p. 182, 184). Thomas McPhereis in Crathinhard is mentioned in 1603, and John Bane McPhires in the same

MACFERRIES, *continued*

place, 1643 (RSCA., II, p. 31; III, p. 14). The name also occurs in seventeenth-century records as M'Pheires, Feres, Phires, Pheres, and Ferries.

MACFERY. Martin McFery, one of an inquest on lands of Dunmaglass, 1414 (*Cawdor*, p. 5). In 1456 Cristina Makfery of Inverness sold the town a piece of ground at corner of Bridge and Church streets (*Invernessiana*, p. 108).

MACFETRIDGE, MACFEDRIES, MACFEDRIS, MACPHETRISH. G. *MacPhetruis* and *MacPheadruis* 'son of Peadrus' (Peter). Gilbert Makfedderis is mentioned in 1503 (RSS., I, 937), Donald McPeteris was tenant of Kilkyne, Tiree, 1541, and Gillecallum McFinlay McFetheris in Howfe (ER., XVII, p. 614). Remission was granted in the same year to Gillecallum M'Federis and his brother Peter M'Federis for their part in the burning of Allane donnand (Eilean Donnain) and other crimes (RSS., II, 3943). Gilbert M'Fedreis in Knokyn and Thomas M'Fedreis in Corspoui were jurors on an inquisition in the bailiary of Kyle-Stewart, 1587 (RMS., v, 1437). M'Phedreis in Luiffistoun witnessed an instrument of sasine in 1618 (*Laing*, 1793). McPhedrice is an old form of the name in Galloway, and MacPhedderis in the parish of Ballantrae (*Paterson*, II, p. 87). It appears as Macfatridge in Nova Scotia. As the name is = Paterson, some of this latter name may have been originally Macfetridge. McPhetrus 1704. M'Fatridge (in Halifax, Nova Scotia).

MACFEY. A form of MACFEE, q.v.

MACFEYDEN. See *under* MACFADYEN.

MACFIE. See *under* MACFEE.

MACFIGAN, MACFIGGANS, MACFEGGANS, MACFIGGIN. A Kintyre surname. In Gaelic *MacFigeinn*, which in the Gaelic of Kintyre represents the surname LITTLESON. The true form is obviously *MacBhigein*, from *beag*, 'little' (Rev. C. M. Robertson). John M'Phigan in Crossag, parish of Kilcalmonell, is in record in 1678 (*Argyll*).

MACFILLAN. Donald McFillane was tenant in Dowart, Stragartnaa, 1499 (ER., XI, p. 417). Gillane M'Phillane M'Kellar, a sasine witness on lands in Argyllshire, 1537 (*Notes and Queries*, 11 July 1931, p. 22). Allester McFolan and Donald McFolan in Wester Cluny were fined for reset of Clan Gregor, 1613 (RPC., XIV, p. 637).

MACFINLAY, 'son of FINLAY,' q.v., from the unaspirated form of the name. Finlay Mc-

Finlay witnessed an instrument of sasine, 1539 (*Poltalloch Writs*), and John McFinlay was a follower of Murdow McCloyd in the attack on the galley of the laird of Balcomie, 1600 (RPC., XIV, p. cxxiii). Hucheoun M'Finla Corikid in Sandside, Caithness, 1663 (*Caithness*), and Dod McFinlay na loigh in the parish of Urray was charged with being an engager in 1649 (IDR., p. 368).

MACFOD. James Macfod, burgess of Dundee, 1623, and Barbara MacFod, relict of James Roger of Dundee, 1632 (*Brechin*). Cf. FOD and MACGILFUD.

MACFORSYTH. See *under* FORSYTHSON.

MACFREDERICK. In Galloway. From MACFETRIDGE through the form MACFEDRIES. McFredricke 1684.

MACFRIZZLE. A surname found in Galloway before the year 1700 (*Dudgeon*). 'Son of Fraser' or 'Fraser's son,' from Frissell, the old spelling of Fraser.

MACFUKTUR. G. *MacFùcadair*, 'son of the fuller,' or in Scots 'waulker.' Johannes McFuktur, tenant in Strathdee, 1527 (*Grant*, III, p. 70). This is an interesting form of the name. It was once not uncommon in the Highlands, and is still occasionally found. See also FUKTOR and MACNUCATOR.

MACFUN, MACFUNN. Current forms of MACPHUN, q.v.

MACFYALL. A Fifeshire form of MACPHAIL, q.v.

MACGAA. A form of MACKAY, q.v., current in Galloway. Patrick McGaie was charged with being at a conventicle in 1686 (RPC., 3. ser. XII, p. 565). McGa and McKga 1684. Shortened to GAA.

MACGACHAN, MACGACHEN. See *under* MACGEACHAN.

MACGACHEY. See *under* MACGEACHIE.

MACGALL. G. *Mac goill*, or *Mac an ghoill*, 'stranger's son,' 'Lowlander.' Andrew Macgall in Pitcog, parish of St. Madois, 1652 (*Dunblane*). M'Gal (in Wigtownshire) 1684. It may also represent MACCALL. See also MACGILL. McGhoill 1704.

MACGANNET. See *under* MACJANET.

MACGARADH. This name was an invention of John Hay Allan who later blossomed forth as John Sobieski Stuart, joint author of the *Vestiarium Scoticum*, the great clan tartan fabri-cation. *Garadh,* he says, in Gaelic signifies 'a dike or barrier,' and is thus nearly synonymous with French *haie,* whence the surname Hay. In his *The Bridal of Caolchairn and other poems,* London and Edinburgh, 1822, he spins a picturesque tale of the heroic deeds of the first recorded of the family who at Luncarty 'stood between the flying Scots and the victorious Danes like a wall or barrier of defence,' and the later adventures of his descendants in Normandy and Britain (p. 334–336).

MACGARMORY. A corruption of MONTGOMERY, q.v. Michael Makgarmory acquired the lands of Plumtoun in the Stewartry in 1512 (RMS., II, 3776). Janet M'Germorie is recorded in Bar of Spottis in 1629 (*Dumfries),* and another Janet M'Garmorie in Kirkcudbright in 1667 (*Kirkcudbright).* See also MACGOMERY.

MACGARRIGLE. An Irish name occurring in the Glasgow Directory. From Irish *Mag Fheargail* 'son of Fearghal,' meaning 'super valour.'

MACGARROW. G. *garbh* gives two forms or pronunciations — -*garrow* and -*garrif* (-*garrav*). One McGillegarrow was tenant of Feryst in 1504 (ER., XII, p. 664), and one M'Illegirf was tenant in Ediravemach, 1594 (BBT., p. 282). Donald Dow McGillegariff in Glenlochie was charged in 1618 with illegal carrying of arms (RPC., XI, p. 373). Donald Glas M'Illegariff in Ardewnaig and several others of the same name gave their bond of manrent to Campbell of Glenurquhay, 1608. The name was common in Breadalbane two centuries and more ago, and the last of the Breadalbane Mcilleghorives left the Ardtalnaig district at the beginning of this century (FB., p. 364). Probably now represented by GARROW, q.v.

MACGARVA, MACGARVEY, MACGARVIE, MACHARVIE. The name of an old family in Galloway. Ir. *MacGairbheith,* 'son of Gairbhith.' William M'Garwe or Makgerwe, notary public in Wigtoun, 1484 and 1488, is probably William Makgarwe, vicar of Pennygham, 1490 (RMS., II, 1623, 1769, 2056). Sir Nicholas M'Garve was chaplain in Wigtown, 1536 (*Laing,* 408).

MACGARVEY, MACGARVIE. *See under* MACGARVA.

MACGAUGHRIN. A form of MACEACHERN, q.v., current in Galloway.

MACGAVIN. Same as MACGOWAN, q.v. Found in Elgin and in Galloway. John Riauch McGawin in Auchanichyle was fined for reset of Clan Gregor, 1613 (RPC., XIV, p. 631), and

Willielmus M'Gawyne is recorded in Hauch, 1643 (*Inquis. Tut.,* 651). M'Gawyn 1643.

MACGAW. A form of MACCAW, q.v.

MACGEACHAN, MACGEACHEN, MACGACHAN, MACGACHEN, MACGECHAN, MACGEACHIN, MACGAUCHANE. Variants of MACEACHAN, q.v. Roland MacGaghen of Wyggeton rendered homage, 1296 (*Bain,* II, p. 198). In 1377 Morice M'Gaychin and others had a safe conduct at request of Archibald Douglas, lord of Galloway (*Stodart,* II). The lands of Callones in Galloway were pledged to Fergus M'Gachyn, 1460 (ER., VII, p. 7), and Fergus Makgachyn appears as witness in Wigtown, 1490 (RMS., II, 2056). Johnne McGachyn was witness in St. Andrews, 1463 (CMN., 34), and Johannes McGaichan, witness in Irwin, 1499 (*Simon,* 35). "Sir" James M'Gauchane was presented to the rectory of Kilblane, 1538 (RMS., III), and D[ominus] Joh. M'Gachand appears as witness in Ayrshire, 1536, and as chaplain and notary, 1540 (RMS., III, 1562, 2280). As Sir John M'Gathan, notary public in Irvine, 1540, he appears again in 1542 as Makgaithane, and in the same year as Makgathane and MacGaithan he is described as rector of Kilblane (*Irvine,* I, p. 173, 183, 196, 201). Janet M'Gathewn in Middle Dalguss, 1701 (*Dunkeld).* William M'Gauchin in record in Newton Stewart, 1792 (*Wigtown).* MakGachane 1544, M'Gaudine [*sic*] 1494, Makgechine 1596.

MACGEACHIE, MACGEACHY, MACKEACHIE. From Ir. *Mag Eachaidh,* an Ulster variant of *Mag Eochadha.* M'Gachie in Bordland, 1684. Neil M'Gechie in Portadow, Kilchenzie parish, 1686 (*Argyll).* Robert M'Keachie in Darnow, 1711 (*Wigtown).*

MACGEE. *See under* MACGHIE.

MACGENN, MACGINN. Irish names in Glasgow Directory. Ir. *Magfhinn,* a variant of *Macfhinn,* 'son of Fionn' (the fair) (*Woulfe).* Recorded in Edinburgh, 1942.

MACGEOCH. Ir. *Mag Eochadha,* 'son of Eochaidh.' A Galloway surname. There is record in 1473 of a composition with John Makgeouch in Wigtownshire (ALHT., I, p. 9). The name is fairly common in the West of Scotland as well as in Ireland. McGeouch and McGooch 1684 (*Parish).*

MACGEORAIDH. Some Macdonalds are known under this name which is unexplained.

MACGEORGE. A late form of MACJARROW, q.v.

MACGHIE, Macghee, Maccee. Ir. *Mag-Aoidh*, 'son of Aodh,' and so same as Mackay. Gilmighel Mac Ethe of Dumfries rendered homage, 1296 (*Bain*, II, p. 198). In the following year, as Gille Michel MacGethe, he was thanked by Edward I for putting down evildoers and for other services (*Hist. Docs.*, II, p. 197; *Bain*, II, p. 234). Neel McEthe, Gillecryst McEthe, Hoen [= Welsh Owen = G. Eoghan] McEthe, Cuthbert his brother, and all of the lineage of Clenafren, made submission to Edward I in 1298 (*Bain*, II, p. 253). Michael Macgethe was juror on an inquisition in Annandale, 1304 (ibid., p. 412). Gilbert McGeth was custumar or collector of customs in the burgh of Kirkcudbrith, 1331 (ER., I, p. 374), and Michael Macge or Mageth, landholder in Galloway, was admitted to the king's peace by Edward III in 1339 (*Rot. Scot.*). Michael Magy, a kinsman of the tyrant David Menzies in Orkney, is mentioned, 1424 (REO., p. 39), and John Makkv, a retainer of Menzies (Menyas), had a safe conduct in England in the same year (*Bain*, IV, 963). Gilbert M'Gy is styled lord of Balmage in 1426 (RMS., II). Robert Macgye (M'Gy, Macge, or Magy) was the king's mime, 1444–49 (ER., III, p. 150, 274, 378). John Makke made oblation by procurator in 1463 for the vicarage of St. Michael's, Dumfries (*Edgar*, p. 135). A composition was made with William Makgey *de eodem* in Dumfries, 1473 (ALHT., I, p. 6), and Schir Ihone Mcgy, persone of Ronaldsay, is recorded in 1480 (OSR., I, p. 53). George McGe or Makge appears in Irvine, 1500, 1508 (*Simon*, 6; *Irvine*, I, p. 159). Mungo Makghe was reidare at Holywod, 1574 (RMR.), and Ion M'Ghey was vicar and minister of Kildalton, 1595. Alexander M'Ghie, heir of Hugh M'Ghie son of Hugh M'Ghie of Atrochie, 1673 (*Retours, Aberdeen*, 416), and Margaret M'Gigh is in Auchtergaven, 1682 (DPD., I, p. 486). The Galwegian family of Macghie gave name to Balmaghie ("Macghie's town"). M'Ge 1555, M'Gey 1473, M'Ghye 1648, M'Gye 1482, Machgie 1684, Makge 1550, Makgee 1527, Makghie 1617; M'Eth, McGie, McGhie, Mackghie, Makgie. In old Galloway documents M'Ghie and M'Kie are used indiscriminately.

MACGHILLECHALUIM. See MACGILLE-CHALLUM.

MACGHILLEGHUIRM. 'Son of the blue lad.' An Argyllshire surname and formerly also in Arran. Gillegorm was a hero of the Maclennans, ancestor of the Lobans. Malcolm M'Ilghuirm in Laggan, parish of Kilchuslan, and Nicoll M'Ilghurn or M'Ilghuirn in Over Kintra are in record, 1675–76 (*Argyll*). Malcolm M'Il-

guirme is in Auchmagarricke, parish of Inshaill, 1691 (*Argyll Inv.*). A small cave adjoining the Preaching Cove at Kilpatrick, Arran, is named Uamh nic-ille-Ghuirm. Duncan Gorm was procurator for James Scrymgeour in Argyll, 1500 (HP., II, p. 199), and Finlay Makane Makgilzorune witnessed a charter of lands in barony of Phantalane, Argyllshire, 1543 (RMS., III, 2902). The name is now Englished Blue, q.v. Gorm, it may be mentioned, is also explained by O'Clery in his Glossary by *dearg* 'red.'

MACGHILLESHEATHANAICH. Englished Shaw in Argyllshire (Jura). Duncan M'Gillehaanich was a tenant in Islay in 1506 (ER., XII, p. 709). Gillecalum McIlleheanich was tenant of Leckamore, and Niall McIlleheanich, tenant of Ballichoan in Seill, 1669 (HP., IV, p. 222, 224). The late Hector Maclean of Islay (*Personal and tribal names among the Gaels*, p. 11) gave the modern form as M'*Ghillesheaghanaidh*, 'son of the servant of the hunter.' (2) It may be for *Mac Gille Sheaghaine*, 'S. Seghine's slave.' Seghine or Segineus was fifth abbot of Hí (623–652). (3) On the other hand the name may be a development of *Mac Gille Seathain*, 'son of the servant of (S.) John.'

MACGHITTICH. A corruption of *MacShitich*, 'son of the wolf,' for which see under Shaw. There was formerly a lawless family or sept of this name in Harris. "About 1664 they attacked the house of Macdonald of Keppoch, and murdered MacDonald himself. For this crime they were extirpated by Sir James MacDonald" (*The Macleods of Dunvegan*, p. 55). See also Maceach.

MACGIBBIE, 'son of Gibbie,' diminutive of Gilbert. A Highland Border name. John McGibby was a tenant of Fraser of Kilbockie in 1681 (RPC., 3. ser. VII, p. 173).

MACGIBBON, Mackibbon, 'son of Gibbon,' q.v. Gebon is written several times for Gilbert in a document of 1455 (*M'Kerlie*, I, p. 99). Donald McAne Gibsoun in Ballemuling, Tiree, 1541, appears in another place as McAneegibboun (ER., XVII, p. 614, 647). Donald M'Gvbbon was sheriff to Duncan, lord of Inneryn, 1511 (*Lamont*, p. 31), and an instrument of sasine by Duncan M'Gybbon of Auchnegarryn in 1525 is in record (ibid., p. 36). Adam McGibbone, parishioner of Duthil, 1527 (*Grant*, III, p. 269), Thomas Makgibboun, minister at Monydie, 1574 (RMR.), and Duncan M'Gibbon was one of the duke of Atholl's fencible men enrolled in Glenlyon, 1706 (HMon., III, p. 215). Robert Finla McGibbonesoun was fined for aiding Clan Gregor, 1613 (RPC., xiv, p. 643). M'Gibon 1685, M'Giboun, Makgeboun.

MACGIBSON. Finlay Macgibsone in Inverness, 1603 (*Rec. Inv.*, ii, p. 6). The meaning is clear.

MACGILBERT, 'son of GILBERT,' q.v. Gilchrist Macgilbert was juror on an inquest in Lennox, 1320 (*Levenax*, p. 82). The Buchanans of Sallochy were known as Gilberts or Gilbertsons, from Gilbert, a member of the Buchanan family. The name is now extinct. John Dow M'Gilbert in Bracklay, a Glenurquhay tenant in 1638 (BBT., p. 403).

MACGILBOYTHIN. In G. *Mac gille Baoithein*, 'son of (S.) Baithene's servant.' Baithene was Columba's successor in Iona, and died in 660. Patrick McGilboytin or Magilboythin witnessed a quitclaim by Michael, son of Durand, to Holmcoltram, c. 1276–78, and was also present (along with his brother Thomas) at drawing the bounds of the grange of Kircwynni (Kirkgunzeon) in 1289 (*Holmcultram*, p. 58, 88). As Patrick de Botyl (= Buittle) of Dumfriesshire he rendered homage in 1296. The seal attached to his homage reads, *S' Patricii d' Gilboithin* or *Makg[ilboian]* (*Bain*, ii, p. 198, 541, 545). In 1296 he also as McGilbochyn served as juror on an inquest made at Berwick concerning the lands of Lady Elena la Zuche in Dumfres, and appears again as Magylboythyn in an inquiry held at Dumfries as to the privileges claimed by Robert de Brus, earl of Carrick in Annandale, 1304 (ibid., p. 216, 412). The last reference to him is in 1324 when mention is made of the lands of Patrick M'Gilbothyn in the "parochia de Botill" (RHM., ii, 23; *Douglas Book*, iii, p. 12).

MACGILCHRIST. G. *MacIlleChriosd* for fuller *MacGilleChriosd*, 'son of the servant of Christ.' Gillascop Mac Gilcrist had a charter of the five pennylands of Fyncharne and others in 1243 from King Alexander ii. This charter is probably the oldest in existence dealing with lands in Argyllshire, and for that reason it has been reproduced in facsimile (HP., ii, pl. opp. p. 227). Alun mac Gillecrist was one of the witnesses to a charter by Moregrund, earl of Mar (RPSA., p. 247). Duncan MacGilchrist of Leuenaghes (i.e. Lennox) rendered homage in 1296 at Berwick-on-Tweed (*Bain*, ii, p. 204). The seal attached to his homage bears an eight-rayed figure and *S' Duncan McGhilc.* At the same date Johan Ewynsone MacGilcrist, one of the king's tenants in Perthshire also rendered homage (ibid., p. 202). Douenaldus Makgilkriste, dominus de Tarbard,

granted to the monks of Paisley the right of cutting wood within all his territory for the building and repair of their monastery (RMP., p. 157). The charter is undated but probably of the end of the thirteenth century. From this Donald, according to Crawford, are descended the M'Gilchrists of North Bar, etc. Merquhir McIlcrist was tenant in Cornekmoir, Tiree, 1541 (ER., xvi, p. 614). Gillechreiste McIlchreist and Donald Beg McIlchreist in Glenlyon were fined for reset of fugitive members of Clan Gregor in 1613 (RPC., xiv, p. 633). John M'Lechreist, John M'Lecgreist in Edderamukie, Euire M'Ean V'Lechreist in Ardchalzie Water, and Gillechreist M'Ean V'Illechreist in Auchnchalden were tenants of the laird of Glenurquhay in 1638 (BBT., p. 339, 399, 402, 403). Archibald M'Gilcreist in Sallum, Tiree, was denounced rebel in 1675 (HP., i, p. 296), John Macklechreist appears in Edinburgh in 1659, and James McIll-Crist was warded in the Canongate Tolbooth there in 1684 (BOEC., ix, p. 193). John McGilchrist was clerk depute to justices of peace of district of Glasgow, 1709 (*Minutes*, p. 53). The name is said to be Englished Christison and Christie. M'Yllecrist 1536.

MACGILFUD. Patrick M'Gilqwhud and Gilbert M'Gilfud were tenants of the Douglas in the barony of Buittle, 1376 (RHM., i, p. lix). Eugenius Makqwhyad, a charter witness at Mayboill, 1485 (RMS., ii, 2656). Cf. FUD and MACFOD.

MACGILGUYN. 'Son of Gwyn's gillie.' Gwyn is Welsh form of Finn. Cudbert Mac Gilguyn, juror on inquest on lands in Dumfriesshire, 1296 (*Bain*, ii, p. 216). John de Maghilgoyny, 'Scotsman and late rebel,' to have his lands restored to him, 1305 (ibid., 1696). 'De' is wrong here, due to the ignorance or carelessness of the English scribe to whom such names were a constant stumbling block. Mag = Mac. The same individual appears in 1296 as M'Gilguyn, and in 1303 as M'Kilguiny (*Bain*, ii). See also MACGILLEGUNNIN.

MACGILL. G. *Mac an ghoill*, "son of the Lowlander or stranger" (*gall*). Macgill early became a surname in Galloway, and is now common in the district (*M'Kerlie*, i, p. 110). Maurice Macgeil witnessed a charter by Maldouen, earl of Leuenach to the church of St. Thomas the Martyr in Arbroath, 1231 (RAA., i, p. 94). James M'Gile or M'Gill, burgess of Edinburgh, 1550 (*Protocols*, i), may be James M'Gill or Makgill of Rankelour-Nether, afterwards Clerk of Register, 1572 (*Irvine*, i, 69). Janet Mack Gil was charged with being a disorderly person (i.e. non-conforming) in the

498

MACGILL, *continued*

parish of Cross-Michal, 1684 (RPC., 3. ser. IX, p. 574). There were Macgills in Jura in 1702, where they were known as *Clann a' ghoill*. Hugh MacGill there, who died c. 1845–50, was known as *Eoghan Mac a' ghoill*. It is said that the name may in some cases be a curtailment of *Mac Ghille mhaoil* = Macmillan. Cf. MACGALL and M'IGHEILL.

MACGILLANDERS. G. *Mac Gill' Andrais* (or *Aindreis*), 'son of the servant of (S.) Andrew.' Gilleasald mac Gilleandris witnessed a charter by Roger de Scalebroc of lands in Carric in the reign of William the Lion (*Melros*, p. 25). Dungal Mac Gilendres was juror on an inquest held at Gerwan (Girvan) in 1260 (*Bain*, I, 2674), and Isaac Macgillendres witnessed a Beauly charter c. 1275 (*Beauly*, p. 57). Patrick and Duncan Makgillandris were tenants under the bishop of Aberdeen, 1511 (REA., I, p. 368, 369). William McGillanderis took part in the second hership of Petty, 1513 (*Rose*, p. 190), Donald McInnenderis was tenant of Glennagadale, Islay, 1541 (ER., XVII, p. 613), John Makgillendris is recorded in Lochalsh, 1548 (RMS., IV, 204), and Muldonych M^cgillandreist was witness at Balquhidder, 1549 (HP., IV, p. 32). Letters were raised against John McClanders and others in Ballachan, 1605 (RPC., VII, p. 72), and Allester McIldreist in Drumnacarrie was fined for reset of Clan Gregor in 1613 (ibid., XIV, p. 632). Ewen M'Ilendrish and Duncan M'Ilendrish in Liddisdaill (Lidistill in Morvern) were denounced rebel, 1675 (HP., I, p. 301). William Mc-Gilandrice appears in 1683 (IDR., p. 114), and John M'Ilandrist is in record in Feorline, parish of Kilmodan, 1696 (*Arg. Inv.*), Isabel M'Illanderous in Tombae in Glenshee, 1726 (*Dunkeld*). In the north the name is believed to have been changed to Ross. In Islay it is Englished Anderson. MacGillendrish 1745, Mc-Ilontris 1736; M'Ilendrish and M'Illandarish (in Islay). See also GILLANDERS.

MACGILLAUENAN. G. *Mac Gille Adhamhnain*, 'son of the servant of (S.) Adamnan.' Duncan M'Gillauenan was one of the "chief men (greinours) of the lineage of Clenafren" in 1298 (*Bain*, II, p. 253).

MACGILLAVERY. See *under* MACGILLIVRAY.

MACGILLECANNICHE. Dominic Macgillakannyth was rector of the parish church of S. Connanus, Waternys, before 1428 (*Pap. Lett.*, VIII, p. 9), John M'Gillekynych VcNeill witnessed a sasine of Skyppynche, 1511 (*Lamont*, p. 32), and John M'Illechanzich was rector of Craginche in 1570 (OPS., II, p. 96, 99). Neill

Makilhannych of Dallilongart was one of an inquest at Donone in 1583 (*Lamont*, p. 416). Niall Og Mc Neill, son of deceased Niall Mc-Gillecanniche, had a charter of the lands of Glentarsen in Cowall, 1602 (*Genealogist*, new ser. XXXVI, p. 80). 'Son of the servant of (S.) Cainnech,' contemporary of S. Columba.

MACGILLECARRACH. John Macgillendris Makgillecarryth was a victim of the first hership of Petty, 1502 (*Rose*, p. 176). Ghillaspic et Kessanus dicti McGhillecharrick are in record, 1360 (*Red Book of Menteith*, II, p. 241). Mc illcharrich 1698. See MACGILLEGARRICH.

MACGILLECHALLUM, in G. *Mac Gille Chaluim*, 'son of Calum's gillie.' Robert Macgillequhaillum or Macgillecq[h]ualum, rector of Lundeffe [Kinloch] to have collation of a canonry and prebend of Dunkeld in 1432 and 1437 (*Pap. Lett.*, VIII, p. 426, 620). Murchard M'Gillecaloune was juror on inquest made at the head court of John, earl of Suthirland, 1471 (OPS., II, p. 673), John M'Yllecallum witnessed a precept of sasine in 1511 (*Lamont*, p. 31), and Dowgall McIlfe McIlchallum was tenant of Skarbols, Islay, in 1541 (ER., XVII, p. 616). Three individuals named Macgillecallum had letters of composition in their favor for their part in aiding the king's rebels in 1510 (*Grant*, III, p. 57). Johne Makgille challum Vikclarich gave his bond to Duncan Campbell of Glenurquhay in 1586 (BBT., p. 240). Jo^n McConill vic gillichalm and Duncan Mc gillichalme were engagers on the royalist side in 1649 from the parish of Alness (IDR., p. 368, 369). Johannes M'Gillechallum was 'interfectus' (slayer) of Lochlan M'Intosh, captain of Clan Chattan (*Chr. Fort.*), Ewin M'Ilchallum and Finlay M'Ilchallum in Kirkipoyle, Tiree, were denounced rebel in 1675 (HP., I), Patrick M'Ilchallume appears in Drumlych, parish of Balquhidder in the same year (*Dunblane*), Duncan Mc Ichallom in Achengarrich is in record in 1701 (*Muthill*), and several McIllichallums or McGillichallums in Shawbost are mentioned in 1726 (HP., II, p. 314). See also MACCALLUM and MALCOLMSON. Mac Gille Challuim 1718, McGillichalloum 1622, M'Illechallum 1592, VcIllichallome 1630. Mac-ille-Challum is' the patronymic of the Macleods of Raasay.

MACGILLECHATTAN. G. *Mac Gille Chatáin*, 'son of the servant of (S.) Catan.' Bavne M'Ylle Cattane, a sasine witness, 1540 (*Lamont*, p. 50). See CATTANACH and GILLECHATTAN.

MACGILLECHIAR, 'son of the dusky lad,' from G. *ciar*, dusky. Malcolm McGileker or

McGilleker was priest of Lismore diocese in 1496 and 1502 (*Poltalloch Writs*, p. 71, 183). M'Gillekeyrs were a sept under Campbell of Glenorchy to whom they gave a bond of manrent in 1547 owning him as their 'ken-kynie' (BBT., p. 185–186). The name also appears in the same record in the same year as VcIllekevr, and James M'Lecheir in Ballemanauchtan was a Glenurquhay vassal in 1638 (ibid., p. 400). John Makgillekeir in Dulshane had a precept of remission for offences committed by him, 1503 (RSS., I, 956), Ferquhard Mc-Gillikeir appears as tenant in Strathdee, 1527 (*Grant*, III, p. 68), and Alane McGillespik McCondochy of Ballemanoch had a respite in 1539 for the slaughter of vmqle Johne Mckilzichzere-sone (*Trials*, I, p. * 253). John McIllchear or M'Illcheare in Ballechragan in Strabane, 1664 (BBT., p. 261). Donald M'Ilcher in Killean parish is in record, 1686 (*Argyll*), Malcolm M'Ilchire in Altbe, parish of Kilcalmanell, 1684, and John M'Ilchurr in Auchacrassanbeg, parish of Kilfinan, 1697 (*Argyll Inv.*). Gilleker M'Mulich occurs in Strathtay, 1480. As MacGilker and MacKilgir it was an old Arran surname, now probably shortened in the island and elsewhere to KERR. Ken-kynie, in Gaelic *ceann cinnidh*, means 'head of the race,' Latin *caput progeni*.

MACGILLECONGALL. 'Son of Congall's servant,' probably S. Congall or Congual who gave name to Dercongal, later Holywood, in Dumfriesshire. S. Congall is also commemorated in Kilwhannel in the parish of Ballantrae. Gilleconel was father of the Gillemor who granted a half mark of silver to the church of S. Machute in Lesmahagow before 1144 (*Kelso*, 187). Adam McGilleconil, one of 'the chief men of the lineage of Clenafren' in Galloway, made submission to Edward I in 1298 (*Bain*, II, p. 253). Andrew M'Gilquhonel in Kirkcudbright who had his fine remitted, 1460 (ER., VII, p. 5), is probably Andrew Makkynquhonale in Wigtown, 1473 (ALHT., I, p. 9). Gilbert Makgilchonil appears as a charter witness in Wigtown, 1498 (RMS., II, 2487), Donald Makgilchonill was a witness in Bute, 1533 (RMS., III, 1321), and Duncan M'Gillespill Vc Illechonvll was a witness in Glenurquhay, 1580 (BBT., 224). Patrick M'Gillichoneill was a chirurgeon in Edinburgh, 1611 (*Edinb. Marr.*). Donald M'illchonnell and Archibald M'illchonnell were among those murdered at Dunaverty, 1647 (HP., II, p. 257). Gregory (p. 18) mentions Mac Ilechonils, the son of Donald's servant, patronymically styled Macruari. M'Gilchonil 1499, M'Gillechonell 1696, M'Gillechonile 1638, Mc ilhonill 1592, Macillichonell 1657; MacIlchonal and MacIlchonel formerly in Kilbrandon.

MACGILLEFEDDELL. Complaint was made against Nicoll McGillefeddell in Clunes, 1578 (RPC., III, p. 51). Agnes M'Gillapheddill appears in Ardclach parish, 1651 (*Dallas*, p. 477).

MACGILLEGARRICH. G. *Macgillecharraich*. John M'Gillegarrich was witness in Inverness, 1536 (*Laing*, 403). John Makgillendris Makgillecarryth appears in Dalcross, 1502. Malcolme Mackgillicharrich in Kinardie, parish of Dingwall, 1685, and Mcgillicharich and Mc gillicharrich in Kincardine parish, 1686 (IDR., p. 360). Macillcary in the Western Isles is the same name. See MACGILLECARRACH.

MACGILLEGLAS. From G. *Mac Ghille ghlais*, 'son of the grey (or sallow) lad.' A very common surname. Duncan M'Gilleglas had a remission from James I in 1498 for various offences committed by him (*Rose*, p. 126). Dowgall m'ille zlass is recorded as author of one of the poems in the Dean of Lismore's Book (p. 98). Thomas McGilliglas was a tenant in Strathdee in 1527 (*Grant*, III, p. 68), and Donald McGilleglas was tenant of Estir Mecra (Easter Micras) in 1539 (ER., XVII, p. 659). John Bane M'Gilleglas appears in Lochalsh in 1548 (RMS., IV, 204), Johnne Mckene Mc ilglas was charged with violence and robbery in lands of Drumquhassil, 1592 (RPC., V, p. 28), Donald Mc Gilliglaish was an 'engager' on the royalist side in 1649 (IDR., p. 367), Evar M'Illoglashe appears in Keirmichellbeg in 1672 (HP., II, p. 210), and Donald M'Ilglash and Gilbert M'Ilglass in Clachaig, parish of Killean, in 1699 (*Argyll Inv.*). Donald Roy M'Gillie glass in Pittherrinine, 1704 (*Dunkeld*). The name is now most probably represented by GLASS. See also MACGLASHAN. McIlliglaish 1724.

MACGILLEGUNNIN. Bran, son of Macgillegunni, witnessed confirmation by Christian, bishop of Candida Casa, of the church of S. Marie and S. Bruoc of Dunrod to the church of Holyrood in the reign of Malcolm IV (LSC., p. 20). Here -gunnin is the Welsh form of *Finnén*, a diminutive of the name of S. Findbarr of Moyville, whose death is recorded in 579 (AU.). The saint's name appears also in its Cymric form in the place name Kirkgunzeon. See also MACGILGUYN and MACGILLEWINNIN.

MACGILLEHELICHY. Ewine McGillehelichy and Duncan McGillehelich his brother were charged with slaughter and other 'haynous' crimes, 1563–64 (*Hist. Clan Gregor*, I, p. 135). John Dow McGilehilich in Trinafour and William McGillechelich his brother were charged with illegally carrying hagbuts and

MACGILLEHELICHY, *continued*

pistollets in 1618 (RPC., xi, p. 373). William M'Gillieheliche in Calvein to be prosecuted for carrying firearms, 1622 (RPC., xiii, p. 105).

MACGILLELANE. Gilbert McGillelane or McGillolane was captain of Clan Connan of Galloway in the reign of David ii (RMS., i, App. ii, 912), and Ingeram M'Gillelan made an assedation (lease) of land in the barony of Redcastle, near Lunan, 1372 (RMS., i, 515). Gilbert Dow McGillalane lived in Bute in 1552 (RMS.), and Angus Mcgilelan was a rebel in Kilberrie paroch, 1685 (*Commons*, p. 4). See also Macclellan.

MACGILLEMICHAEL. See *under* MAC-MICHAEL.

MACGILLEMORISONE. Finlay McGillemorison, tenant of Gargiston, Ardmanoch, William McGillemorisone, tenant of "Brasina de Sudy vocata le Alehous" are in record, 1504 (ER., xii, p. 660, 681).

MACGILLEQUHANGZHE. Duncan Dow Mc GilleQuhangzhe in Wester Dovne was concerned in the slaughter of Johnne McAwlay, 1536 (RSS., ii, 2037).

MACGILLERY. Charles M'Gillery, kinsman of Allan M'Ochtry, chief of the Camerons, 14c., was ancestor of that tribe of Camerons called the Clan M'Gillery. This is the family of the Gilbertsons or Gibsons. (Author's intro. to *Memoirs of Locheill*, p. 10.)

MACGILLESE. See *under* MACGILLIES.

MACGILLESPIE. G. *Mac Gill' easpuig*, 'son of the bishop.' Raderic MacGillescop made a grant of lands in Carrik to the Abbey of Melrose in the reign of William the Lion (*Melros*, p. 28). Dimedall Makgillascop was witness in Lesmor, Argyllshire, in 1251 (RMS., ii, 3136). Ferquhar Makgillespy was a sufferer from the hership of Petty in 1502 (*Rose*, p. 176), Donald McIllaspy was tenant of Ellenynegane, Islay, in 1541 (ER., xvii, p. 615), John M'Lespy was officer at Glenurquhay in 1549 (BBT., p. 187), and Donald Macgillespek in Bute had sasine in 1565 (ER., xix, p. 542). Huistone Macgillespic clervch (i.e. 'cleric') is mentioned in 1585 (*Cawdor*, p. 187), and John Dow M'Ean V'Illespik in Arrechastellan and Archibald M'Ean V'Gillespik in Knokinty were Glenurquhay vassals in 1638 (BBT., p. 403). Donald M'Glespick and Charles M'Ilespick in Breve, and John M'Ilespie in Ardunaig were denounced rebels in 1675 (HP., i). Duncan M'Ilespeck in Arintiber, Kilcolmkill, and Gillespig M'Ilespick in Lochannan, parish of Oilanfinan, appear in 1686 (*Argyll*), Duncan

M'Alespick in Kindrochit in 1696 (*Poll Book*), and Colin McIllespick was a Seaforth tenant in 1721 (HP., ii, p. 304). The name was early Anglicized, John Gilaspison tenant of Crunyhatoun in 1376 (RHM., i, p. lviii). M'Allespick 1696, Mc allisbit 1615, Makgillespi 1538, Makillespik 1591.

MACGILLEURAS. Dungal McGilleuras, one of "the chief men (*greinours*) of the lineage of Clenafren," in Galloway, made submission to Edward i of England in 1298 (*Bain*, ii, p. 253). Prof. Watson suggests that the name may be for *Mac Gille Labhrais*, 'son of (S.) Laurence's servant' (*Watson* iii, p. 20).

MACGILLEVARQUHANE. 'Son of the gillie of (S.) Barchan.' Nigel McGillevarquhane witnessed sasine of the lands of Obbirfeally (Aberfeldy) in Appin, 1525 (*Grandtully*, i, p. 56). Duncan MacGillevarchan was concerned in a raid on Ardencaple in 1600, and Duncan Dow M'Gillevarthane (*c* misread *t*) in Soccoth was a Glenurquhay vassal, 1638 (BBT., p. 403). The parish of Kilbarchan is named from the saint. M'Illevarchan 1594.

MACGILLEVERNAN. Ysaac mac elibarn mentioned in a charter of the lands of Dalrewach, c. 1290 (REM., p. 469). John Dow M'Gillevernan, elder, and Johne Dow M'Gillevernan, his son, take Colyne Campbell of Glenurquhay as 'filium adoptium,' 1563 (BBT., p. 209).

MACGILLEWARNOCH. The Mac-gille-Warnochs, who gave name to Gaitgillmacgillewarnoch in the parish of Borgue, Kirkcudbrightshire, long since shortened their name to Warnock. For the origin of the name see under Macilvernock.

MACGILLEWIE. G. *Mac Ghille dhuibh*, 'son of the black lad.' Macgilleweys are believed to have once held East Allanaquoich and Inverey, and in the middle of the seventeenth century the name is the commonest in the district. They considered themselves to be Lamonts, and in the eighteenth century dropped the name Macgillewey and called themselves Lamont. Sir James Lamont in his "Declaration of the true extraction of the MacIlldowies *alias* Lamont," dated 1661, says that "John MacIlldowie in Castleton in the Brae of Mar and all the MacIlldowies are my true native kindly people and kinsmen." Elsewhere in the Declaration he spells the name MacIlzegowie, MacGilligowie, MacGilledow, MacIlzegui. Whether this relationship is imaginary, or how representatives of this west country clan found their way to the heart of the Grampians is unknown (Stirton, *Crathie*, p. 416). John

M'Gillizvie appears in Crathie, 1633 (SCM., III, p. 139), and John Laman *alias* McGillivi was godfather to a child in Castletoune of Braemar, 1710 (Stirton, *Crathie*, p. 310). John Makgillewie and Malcolm Makgillewe were tenants under the bishop of Aberdeen, 1511 (REA., I, p. 368). The first recorded burgess of Inverness is Donald McGillewe, who is in record, 1521 (TGSI., xxvIII, p. 230), and John Makgillevye, bailie of the same burgh in 1546 (RMS., III, 3233), appears again in 1556–57 as McGillewe, McIlleve, and McGilliwie (*Rec. Inv.*). Forms of the name in Glenurquhay are Macgillewie (1586) and M'Illewie (1638) (BBT.). Donald Monech McGilligowy and Johnne Monech his son, servitor to the provost of Kilmun, were charged in 1596 with violence to Dame Jeane, Lady of Ardkinglas (RPC., v, p. 322). Finlay McGilliewie in Correbroch refused instruction in his craft of tanning, 1621 (RPC., xII, p. 491). M'Gillewie is now a rare name in Perthshire, and the bearers of it there are believed locally to be descended from the only survivor of the Macnishes of Loch Earn slain by the Macnabs in the beginning of the seventeenth century. M'Gilavie, M'Gilevie, and M'Gilvie in 1696. In Inverness other old spellings are: McGilewe, M'Gillewve, MacGilliue, McIlewe, MacYelewe (*Rec. Inv.*). In Edinburgh, 1942. See also MACILDOWIE, MACILDUE, and MACILCHUIE.

MACGILLEWINNIN. In the reign of Malcolm IV Gillecrist mac Gillewinin witnessed a charter by Uchtred, son of Fergus of Galloway, of the church of Colmanele to the church of Holyrood (LSC., p. 19), and about 1250 Nigellus Macgilwynin was witness to a charter by Duncan, earl of Carrick (CMN., 13). Gilwewel McKilguiny was one of an inquisition in 1303 on the lands of John de Hirdmanstone (*Bain*, II, 1619), Gilmor Macwynnyn was witness to an inquest at Kirkwynnin in 1329 (*Holm-Cultram*, p. 56), and Sir John Makilwynzane, a cleric, appears as a notary public in Ayr, 1498, and as witness at Blairquhan, Ayrshire, 1508 (RMS., II, 2433, 3245). The name means 'son of the servant of (S.) Winnin,' the Cymric or Welsh form of Ir. Finnén. The Welsh form of the saint's name is preserved in the place name Kilwinning and the Irish form in Kilfinan. See also MACGILLEGUNNIN.

MACGILLIES, MACGILLEIS, MACGILLESE, MACGILLIS. G. *Mac Gill' Iosa*, 'son of the servant of Jesus.' Malcolm Machgilish witnessed a charter by William the Lion at Perth before 1184 (RPSA., p. 225), and is doubtless the Malcolm Mac Gillis who at-

tested the same king's charter of Kinbethach to Gilbert, earl of Strathearn c. 1178–80 (LIM., p. xxiii; *Athole*, p. 704; *Grant*, III, p. 1). In 1262 an inquisition made at Inverness found that the lands of Mefth (now Meft) had been granted to Eugenius, son of Angus son of Eugenius son of Yothre MacGilhys, thane of Rathven, hereditarily for the service of one serving man and for doing military service at home (APS., I, p. 101; *Bain*, I, 2323). Tawis M'Gillese was tenant of Dobtoun, Dumfriesshire, 1376 (RHM., I, p. lvi). The hereyeld of one M'Gilhois in Strathern was granted to Richard Broustar, 1507 (ER., xII, p. 498), and stouthreif was made of goods of Donald M'Gillis in Wigtown, 1513 (*Trials*, I, p. 96 *). Gilleis McGilleis was concerned in the slaughter of John McAlester, 1538 (RSS., II, 2550), Donald M'Illeis was tenant of Balleclauchane, Islay, 1541, and Doule McIlleis was tenant of Ligin, Islay, in same year (ER., xvII, p. 616, 617, 637). William M'Gilleis gave his bond of manrent to George, earl of Huntlie, 1543 (SCM., iv, p. 260), and John M'Gilleis is in township of Dulsanch, Lochalsh, 1548 (RMS., iv, 204). George Macgilleische was reader at Kilmaronock, 1574 (*Strathendrick*, p. 129; RMR.). The name of Andrew M'Geleis, who appears in regality of Spynie, 1595 (SCM., II, p. 131), is probably another spelling of the name. McIlchallum Vc illische was charged with violence to Dame Jeane, lady of Ardkinglas, 1596 (RPC., v, p. 322), and John McAndro VcIlleis in Inverness district was fined for reset of Clan Gregor, 1613 (ibid., xiv, p. 629). McGillish 1686, M'Ileish 1657, M'Illeish 1688, VcIllesa 1530.

MACGILLIFEDDER. 'Gillie of (S.) Peter.' Gilmory McIlpedder was tenant of Howe, Islay, 1541 (ER., xvII, p. 619, 640). Thomas Moir McGillifedder is in record, 1607 (RPC.). Malcolm McIllephedder was tenant in Aros, Islay, 1664 (*Bk. Islay*, p. 411). Dod: McIliphedir in Nether Lorn, 1692 (*Commons*, p. 34). As forename: Gillepeddir McCallome, 1669 (HP., iv, p. 222).

MACGILLIGIN. *See under* MACKILLICAN.

MACGILLIS. *See under* MACGILLIES.

MACGILLIVANTIC. *Mac Gille mhanntaich*, from G. *manntach*, 'stammering,' 'stuttering.' Patrick filius Gillemanthach was chaplain to Bishop Jonathan of Dunblane, c. 1200 (*Cambus.*, 217). Dr. Macbain gives Donald Macgillivantic in Crathie, Laggan, 1806, and says the Clann Mhic Ghill Mhanntaich were a sept of the Brae Lochaber Macdonalds. See also MANTACH.

502

MACGILLIVRAY, Macgillavery (Aberdeen), Macgillivrie, Macgillivry, Macgillvary, Macgillvray, Macgilvary, Macgilvery, Macgilvra, Macgilvray. G. Mac Gille-bhrath, 'son of the servant of judgment' (doom), from brath, 'judgment.' The name originally may have been Maolbhrath, the Maol- later being displaced by Gille-, as in other instances. The Macgillivrays were an old Argyllshire clan or sept, but they do not appear in the 1467 MS. They are, however, early found in association with the Macleans in Mull, which probably was their original home. Archibald Makillewray was presented to the rectory of the parish church of S. Columba in Beandmovll (Benbecula), 1535 (RSS., II, 1181), as Archibald McIluray he resigned the rectory of Ewist in 1542 (ibid., 4880), and in 1542 as McIlwray he was presented to the chaplaincy of Ellen, Finlagan and S. Columba in Isla (ibid., 4566). Ronald McAllen McIlvery or McIlverie was tenant on lands in Ardnamurchan, 1541 (ER., XVII, p. 645), and Duncan M'Gillewra, witness at Glenurquhay, 1549 (BBT., p. 187). Rev. Martin Mc illura (or McIlvora, M'Ilvra, M'Ilwra) had several ups and downs during his incumbency of different churches in Argyllshire between 1626–50. Farquhar MacGillivray had a feu of the lands of Dunmaglas from Campbell of Cawdor, 1622 (Cawdor, p. 258), and a later Farquhar M'Gillevray of Dunmaglas was one of the signers of the letter to George I in 1715. Donald Moir McGilwrev granted to James Grant of Freuchie in 1646 that he had been engaged in spoilzering (plundering) (Grant, III, p. 240). Macgillivrays took a prominent part in the rebellion of '45, and their chief is said to have been killed in the battle of Culloden, beside the Well of the Dead. VcGillevorie 1609, McGillavrach 1638, McGillievraid 1713, McGillivray 1672, M'Gillowray 1745, M'Gwillwrav 1685, McIlra 1616, McIlvrach 1618, M'Ilvrav 1674, McIlwray 1542; MacGillevoray, M'Gillewra, McGilvra, McIlvrae, MacIloray.

MACGILLONIE, Macgillony. G. Mac Ghill' onfhaidh, 'son of the servant of storm.' The name of an old sept of Clan Cameron. The name is sometimes given wrongly as from G. Gill' an fhaidh, from faidh, 'prophet.' Maurice M'Gillonie had a remission from James I in 1428 for certain crimes committed by him (Rose, p. 126). Alasdair Mor Mac a Lonabhidh was one of the famous M'Gillony Camerons of Strone, Lochaber (TGSI., XXI, p. 223). Buchanan (p. 97) spells the name M'Lonvie. See Macalonie, Maclonvie, and Maelanfaid.

MACGILLREICK, Macilbrick. Variant of Macilriach, q.v. Macfarlane (II, p. 91) says Lord Alexander Fraser of Lovat, served heir to his father in 1350, was never married, had a son born to him called "John nick-named Giellreach, of whom McGillreicks a numerous Clan in the North and South Clan vic ill Reich vic Himi." Donaldus More MacGillereacht in Murthlac, 1550 (Illus., II, p. 261).

MACGILLWHINNICH. G. Mac GilleChoinnich, 'son of Cainnech's gillie,' i.e. Cainnech of Achadh Bó. There was an old Bute family of this name. John Makgylquhinnych was infeft in the lands of Cawnoche there in 1506 (RMS., II, 2987). The name is now Macwhinnie, q.v. Donald McGilquhinye or Makgilquhinye was tenant of Westirend of Eddirgolly, 1480 (ER.). There is record of a discharge by Donald McKilchyniche VcDonell VcKyniche alias McCallum, only son of Gilechyniche VcDonnell in Craigdow, 1615 (HP., IV, p. 46). John Roy McKillichinich was charged with horse-stealing, 1750 (Historical papers of Jacobite period, II, p. 569). Old spellings: McGilquhenyie, Makguylquhynne, Makilhannich. See also Macolchynich.

MACGILMOTHA. Michael M'Gilmocha and Achmacath M'Gilmotha, two of "the chief men (greinours) of the lineage of Clenafren," in Galloway, made their submission to Edward I of England in 1298 (Bain, II, p. 253). Prof. Watson suggests that these names represent Macgille mo-Chai, 'son of Mo-Choe's servant' (Watson III, p. 20).

MACGILNEW. G. Mac Gille nan Naomh, 'son of the saints' gillie.' Patin McGillenef witnessed a charter by Edgar filius Dofnaldi of the church of Dalgarnoc in the reign of William the Lion (LSC., p. 214). Archibald Makgilleneif Tailyour had sasine of land in Bute, 1517 (ER., XIV, p. 596). Ninian Makgilnevis Talzour of Langulbrunag granted a 20s. land in Bute to Allan Makallane, 1546 (OPS., II, p. 216). See also Macilna and Macilneive.

MACGILP. A shortened form of Mackillop, q.v. This form of the patronymic is found mainly in Argyllshire. Miss Lamont of Knockdow suggests that the sons of Ilpin mentioned in Iam Lom's Soiridh do 'n Ghreumach may be the McGilps or McKillops of Glencoe (quoted in McKechnie, The Lamont Clan, 1938, p. 525).

MACGILVANE, Macilvain, Macilvaine, Macilvane, Macilvean, Macilwaine, Mackilvain. G. Mac Gille Bheatháin, 'son of the servant of S. Beathán' (Bean). Thomas Makgilvane was a tenant under Douglas in the barony of Buittle, 1376 (RHM., I, p. lix). John Mcilmeyne was a witness in Dumfries, 1477 (*Edgar*, p. 227). Gilbert Makilmeyn de Grummat, 1503 (RSS., I, 947). Allan McYlveine de Grumet who appears as bailie of the Abbey of Crossraguel in 1523 (*Crossraguel*, I, p. 71) is Alan Makilwene, juror on assize in the bailliary of Carrick, 1532 (RMS., III, 1196). Alane Makilvane, follower of the earl of Cassilis, was respited for murder, 1526 (RSS., I, 3386). Gilbert Macywene and Allan Macywene of Grumett are in record, 1546 (ALHT., VIII, p. 202), and Patrick M'Ilvayne was heir of Gilbert M'Ilvayne of Grummet who was killed in battle of Fawsyde, 1547 (*Retours, Ayr*, 1). Mr. Rollo Makylmenaeus who translated the *Logike* of Peter Ramus, published in London, 1574, may have been Ronald MacIlmeine who appears as a student at St. Andrews University in 1566 as Rolandus M'Kilwein, in 1569 as Renaldus Makilmain, and as Rollandus Machilmane in 1570 (ERUS.). He was probably a member of the family Macilvain of Grumet or Grummet in Carrick. John M'Kilvane and John M'Kilven were two of M'Nachtane's soldiers shipped at Lochkerran, 1627 (*Archæologia Scotica*, III, p. 254). Gilbert M'Ilwyand had sasine of two merklands of Multouns, Galloway, 1674 (*M'Kerlie*, I, p. 171). Margaret M'Ilmeane appears at Carsbratt in 1628 (*Dumfries*), and Alexander Milmine in Sautcroft, 1790 (*Wigtown*). Makilvene, M'Gilweane, McIlveane, Makilwyane, Mekilwaine; in 1684 the name is spelled McIllvain, McElvain, McIllveyan, McIlweian, McIlweine, McIlwain, McKelvain, McKilweyan, McKilwyan (*Parish*).

MACGILVAR. Probably from M'Gille Bhar, 'gillie of (S.) Barre of Cork.' Nevinus Makgilvar, burgess of Invermessan on Loch Ryan, 1430 (RMS., II, 185). MacIlvar another spelling. ? current.

MACGILVARY, MACGILVERY. Shortened forms of MACGILLIVRAY, q.v.

MACGILVEIL. Macgilveil a sept of Cameron (Buchanan, p. 97). — McGilveill, a follower of Murdow McCloyd in his attack on the galley of the laird of Balcomie, 1600 (RPC., XIV, p. cxxiii). Lauchlane M'Ilveolf alias M'Dougall was among those murdered at Dunaverty, 1647 (HP., II, p. 257). Duncan M'Ilvoyle in Dunstaffnage, 1618 (*Sasines*, II, p. 23). David M'Ilwoyll, merchant burgess in Dumfries, 1661 (*Dumfries*). Donald M'Ulvovll in Knockulligan denounced rebel, 1675 (HP., I). Archibald M'Ilveile in Bararack, parish of Glenary, 1689 (*Argyll Inv.*), and Margaret N'ilveil in Killin, 1686 (PDP., I, p. 489). There were MacGilveils of Marlagan, Caillie, and Glenfrean.

MACGILVERNOCK. *See under* MACILVERNOCK.

MACGILVRA, MACGILVRAY. Shortened forms of MACGILLIVRAY, q.v. M'Gilwra (in Cames) 1816.

MACGIMPSY. Ir. *MacDhiomasaigh*, 'son of Diomasach,' from *diomaach*, proud. Gilbert Makgympseis was concerned in the slaughter of Donald McEwin in the Cors of Balmaclellane in 1529 (RSS., II, 128). Thomas M'Gympsy was witness at Bordland of Laik, Kirkcudbright, in 1552 (*Laing*, 598). Alexander McGymphee (probably a miscopying) and John MacGymphee were residents in the parish of Borgue, 1684 (RPC., 3. ser. IX, p. 567). McGimsie, McJampse, MaJamsie 1684, McGympsier 1701, M'Gympsor a. 1700.

MACGINLEY. An Irish name found in Glasgow, Ir. *Meg. Fhionnghaile*, 'son of Fionnghal' (fair foreigner or Norseman). Not a variant of MACKINLAY.

MACGINN. An Irish name. See under MACGENN.

MACGINNIS. In Galloway this is a variant of MACINNES, which again is a side form of MACANGUS, q.v. Patrick McGinnies in Baidlan Mylne, 1669 (*Hunter*, p. 62). Around Glasgow it is most probably a modern Irish importation.

MACGINTY. An Irish name found in Glasgow. Ir. *Mag Fhionnachtaigh*, 'son of Fionnachta' (fair snow) (*Woulfe*).

MACGIRR. Robert M'Girre was in Dalbaitty, 1658 (*Dumfries*), and Andrew McGirr and James McGirr were residents in the parish of Buittle, 1684 (RPC., 3. ser. IX, p. 571). *Mac an gheairr*, 'son of the short, or low-sized man,' and the name was common in Armagh and Tyrone. "The family is supposed to be of Scottish origin, but is, more probably an offshoot of some native family" (*Woulfe*, p. 314). There was formerly a McGhirrston in the Stewartry.

MACGIVERN. A Galloway name of Irish origin, *Mag Uidhrín*, 'son of Uidhrín' (a diminutive of *odhar*, dun-colored), an old Ulster name (*Woulfe*).

MACGLADRIE. This surname, recorded in Edinburgh, is according to Woulfe, Ir. *Mac Gleadra*, 'son of Gleadra,' an Ulster surname. Tho. Mc gledrie appears in the barronie of Machremore, and Patrick Mc gledrie in Yetton (Yettoun, parish of Sorbie), 1684 (*Parish*, p. 40, 55). Pronounced Macglethery in Galloway.

504

MACGLAGAN. A current form of Mac-LAGAN, q.v.

MACGLASHAN, MACGLASHEN, MACGLASSON. From G. M'Glaisein, a diminutive form of M'Ghille ghlais, 'son of the grey lad.' Mulmory M'Glassen in the Black Isle, 1500 (Rose, p. 169). Iain McGalssan or McGlassane was witness at Ardgartene, 1515 (HP., IV, p. 24, 25). John M'Glassan witnessed an instrument of sasine in 1519 (Lamont, p. 34), as also did Cristin M'Gillecallum M'Glassen in 1525 (ibid., p. 36), and Paul M'Glassen is in record in Lochalsh in 1548 (RMS., IV, 204). Several M'Glassanes were among those massacred at Dunavertie in 1647 (HP., II, p. 257). David McKglashen was reported to the presbytery of Inverness in 1681 as a "Saboth braker in the parochin of Croy" (IDR., p. 102), and John McGlassone was burgess of Banff in 1710. Several Macglashans who settled in the Lowlands are said to have Anglicized their name into Gray. The name is also current in the curtailed form GLASHEN. See also MACGILLEGLAS. McGlassin 1692, Mackglesson 1650.

MACGLASRICH, MACGLASSRICH. Donald M'Aglescheryct in Foss gave his bond of manrent to Campbell of Glenurquhay, 1560 (BBT., p. 204), and John Mc Ane Vc Aglassre to answer before the Justice in Edinburgh at the accusation of the earl of Argyle, 1576 (RPC., II, p. 547). John Mc 3lassich was kirk officer of Dingwall, 1653 (IDR., p. 249). McGlasserig was a former Breadalbane surname. The family died out on Lochtayside, the result of a curse laid upon them by a witch (FB., p. 362). John McGlasserig published a book of Gaelic songs and poems about 1780.

MACGLASSON. See under MACGLASHAN.

MACGLENNAN, MACGLENNON. Galwegian variants of MACLENNAN, q.v.

MACGLEW. An old Galloway name. Woulfe suggests that it is perhaps from Mac Dhuinnshléibhe, a variant of Mac Duinnshléibhe, 'son of Donnshléibhe,' an Irish personal name meaning 'Donn of the mountain.' Cf. under DUNSLEVE.

MACGLONE. A Galloway name of Irish origin, Mac Giolla Eóin, 'son of the servant of (S.) John.' See MACLOON.

MACGOLDRICK. A name found in Glasgow and neighborhood of Irish origin, Mag Ualghairg, 'son of Ualgharg' (high temper). An old Galloway form was MACCORLICK.

MACGOLOIGLACHE. Moldonych McGoloiglache appears as a charter witness in 1581 (Poltalloch Writs, p. 72). The name is from Ir. Mac(an)Ghallóglaighe, 'son of the galloglas.' Galloglasses were a body of heavily armed Irish soldiers.

"The mercilesse Macdonnell
    from the Westerne Isles
  of Kernes and Gallow glasses is supply'd."

Macbeth, 1632 ed., Act i, scene 2.

MACCOMERY. A corrupt form of the Norman name Montgomery, current in Galloway.

MACGORLICK. A Galloway name of Irish origin, from Mag Ualghairg, 'son of Ualgharg,' a name meaning 'high temper.' See also MACGOLDRICK and MACWALRICK.

MACGORRIE, MACGORRY. G. MacGoraidh, 'son of Goraidh.' Goraidh, earlier Gofraidh is a borrowing from ON. Guðröðr (for earlier Guðfrøðr). Goraidh or Gorrie is a common name in the West Highlands, especially among the Macdonalds of Skye and the Macleods. The family of Macgorrie is descended from Goraidh or Godfrey, youngest son of "the good John of Isla," Lord of the Isles, who died in 1380. Duncan M'Goffry, a knight of John de Ergadia (Argyll) in 1315 appears in the following year as Donekan de Makoury and in 1319 he appears again as Sir Dungan Mac Gofferri (Bain, III, 479, 521). (2) The Macgorrie Lamonts of Knockdow are descended from Goire an tighearn ruadh, Godfrey the red baron, lord of Inverchaolain, who flourished c. 1430 (McKechnie, The Lamont Clan, p. 418). Archibald, earl of Argyll granted a charter to his servitor John Makgorre of Knokdwff, 1540 (Lamont Inv., p. 49), and Parlane McGorrie in Ardes was fined for aiding Clan Gregor, 1613 (RPC., XIV, p. 644). Allaster M'Gorrie and Allane M'Gorrie appear in the muster roll of the laird of Glenurquhay, 1638 (BBT., p. 398-399). M'Gorie 1611, McGorre 1540.

MACGORTH. In the reign of David II Michael McGorth had a charter 'de parentala de Kenclanen,' otherwise 'Kenelman' (RMS., I, App. II, 913). Prof. Watson says Kenclanen is meaningless, but that Kenelman "may be for Cenél Maine, Maine's sept, which was the name of a sept in Ireland." McGorth may be for mac Dorcha, 'son of dark' (Watson III, p. 21).

MACGOUGAN. See under MACGUGAN.

MACGOUN, MACGOUNE. See under MACGOWAN.

MACGOW. G. *Mac gobha*, now usually *Mac ghobhainn* or *Mac a'ghobhainn*, 'son of the smith.' See also MACGOWAN. The smith in olden times was a very important personage in the clan as being the maker of arms and armor, and as this trade descended from father to son its designation soon became a surname. The land of Drwmfolatvn was leased to Donald M'Gow in 1444, to Glaschen MkGow in 1473, and in 1512 Robert M'Gou was tenant of Drumfallantin (*Cupar-Angus*, I, p. 128, 205, 283). Alexander MacGow in Murthlac, 1550 (*Illus.*, II, p. 261). Also Englished GOWAN-SON, q.v. Makgow 1460.

MACGOWAN, MACGOUN, MACGOWN, MAC-GOUNE. G. *Mac a' ghobhainn* or *Mac Ghobhainn*, 'son of the smith.' MacGowan is the name of an old Stirling family. Forms two to four, found in the Glasgow directory, may be Irish. Gilcallum McGoun had a precept of remission for rapine and other crimes on the lands of the abbot of Cupar, 1503 (RSS., I, 953). Gilbert Makgowin, a follower of the earl of Cassilis, was respited for murder in 1526 (ibid., 3386). William McGown in Pitcalnv, a follower of Ross of Pitcalny, 1592 (RPC., v, p. 31). Murchie McGowy or Murthie McGowne in Fanmoir, Mull, was put to horn in 1629 (RPC., 2 ser. II, p. 341; III, p. 45). Alister McGhowin, an engager on royalist side, in parish of Urray, 1649 (IDR., p. 368). Alexander M'Gowne was retoured heir in the lands of Langlandes of Lochanes in the territory of Dumfries, 1672 (*Retours, Dumfries*, 270), Margaret M'Goune was retoured heir of Alexander M'Goune, merchant in Dumfries, 1682 (*Retours, Kirkcudbright*, 344), and Alexander McGowne and Abraham McGoune were residents in the parish of Borgue, 1684 (RPC., 3. ser. IX, p. 566–567). Macgoun 1703; M'Gouan, Makgowane, M'Govin.

(2) In the reign of David II there was a clan M'Gowan, probably located somewhere on the river Nith, whose chiefship was adjudged to Donald Edzear (RMS., I, App. II, 982). This Edzear was a descendant of Dunegal of Stranith (Nithsdale), whose seat was at Morton, Dumfriesshire, about the beginning of the twelfth century. The name here may indicate descent from Owen the Bald (the Eugenius Calvin of Simeon of Durham), king of the Strathclyde Britons, who was killed in 1018.

MACGRAIL. An Irish name of recent introduction. It is the colloquial form of Macneill in the dialect of Ulster and Connacht. Before vowels and liquids Mac- becomes Mag- in Irish. In Antrim gn becomes gr, hence the sequence Macneill>Magneill>Magreill.

MACGRANAHAN. An old Galloway name, Ir. *Mag Reannacháin*, 'son of Reannachán,' diminutive of *reannach*, sharp, pointed (*Woulfe*).

MACGRANE. An old Galloway surname. Ir. *Mag Raighne*, 'son of Rayny,' a pet form of Raghnall or Reginald (*Woulfe*).

MACGRATH. An Irish form of Gaelic *Macrath* (Macrae).

MACGREEN. A criminal charge was made against Cuthbert McGreen in Gremen, 1671 (*Just. Rec.*, II, p. 57). Woulfe has MacGrean and MacGreen from *Mag Raighne*, a pet form of Raghnall.

MACGREGOR, MACGREIGOR, MACGRIGOR. G. *MacGriogair*, 'son of Gregory.' Gregory, the name of several early popes, was a favorite name in the middle ages. The name of Giric or Gyric, fourth in succession from Kenneth I, was elaborated by Fordun (*Chron.*, IV, 16) into Gregorius, and is the 'Gregory the Great' of feudal fabulists. *He* is the legendary ancestor of the Macgregors. See under GIRIC. "The Macgregors," says R. H. Bruce Lockhart, "had the redeeming merit of picturesqueness, and for that reason they occupy a larger place in Scottish literature than any other Highland clan" (*A Son of Scotland*, 1938, p. 131). On account of the many lawless deeds justly or unjustly laid to their charge, the name of Macgregor was proscribed in 1603 by Act of Parliament. Many of the clan in 1606 in obedience to an Act of the Privy Council renounced the name and adopted the surnames of Stewart, Grant, Dougall, Ramsay, and Cunninghame (*Coll.*, p. 130, 131, 135). The Rev. James MacGregor, one of the founders and first pastor of Londonderry, New Hampshire, was of Scottish origin. The proscription of the name was rescinded in 1661 but revived in 1693, and not finally abolished until the year 1784, after it had been for several years in practical desuetude. Though the name is quite widespread today it is doubtless not borne by all who are entitled to it. A list of those who were fined for resetting outlawed members of the clan in 1613 is printed in RPC., v, p. 629–663. In New York state in 1689 we have mention in a Dutch document of "Macgrigerie uit Schotlandt," and in 1697 of one Patrick Macgrigari. M'Gregare 1500, M'Gregur 1600, McGreigor 1682, M'Grigar 1711, Griger McGriger 1696, McGrigour 1586, Makriggour 1600. See also under GREGOR.

An act anent the Clan Gregor passed in 1617 refers to the earlier act of April 1603 whereby "It wes ordanit that þe name of

MACGREGOR, Macgreicor..., *continued*

m^c gregoure sulde be altogidder abolisched And þat the haill persounes of thatt clan suld renunce thair name and tak thame sum vther name And that They nor nane of thair posteritie suld call þame selffis gregor or m^c gregoure thairefter vnder payne of deade." The act of 1617 referring to the many children of the clan now "ryiseing vp and approcheing to the yearis of maioritie" approves of the earlier act and another of 1613 referring to the clan, further declares and ordains "that gif onie persoun or persounes of þe said Clane who hes alreddie renunceit thair names or heirefter sall renunce and cheinge thair names Or gif onye of thair bairnes and posteritie sall at ony time heirefter Assume or tak to thame selffis the name of gregoure or M^c gregoure ...That everie sick persoun or persones assomeing and taking to thame selffis the said name...sall Incurre the payne of Deathe qlk payne salbe execute vpoun thame vithout fauoure" (APS., IV, p. 550–551).

MACGREUSAICH, 'son of the shoemaker' (G. *greusaich*). Buchanan (p. 141) says the Macgreusichs are originally Buchanans descended from a Buchanan who went to Argyllshire with the laird of Ardkinglass's lady in the reign of James III. In his *Enquiry* (p. 78) he claims them as a sept of Macfarlane. Murquhow M'Grasycht, John McGrassych, and Donald M'Grassycht were residents of Inverness in 1557 and in 1563 (*Rec. Inv.*, p. 6, 7, 103). The 'Challar' M'Grasaych Awyllych (= Atholl-man) was slain at Fortyrgall in 1575 (*Chr. Fort.*, p. 140). William McGrasych in Achachrome witnessed an instrument of sasine at Kilchoan in 1585 (*Genealogist*, new ser. XXXVI, p. 79). Agnes McGressiche in Achonacone and Donald Moir M'Gresche in Tombretherlik were charged with murder in 1617 (RPC., XI, p. 187), Finlay Bayne McGressiche in Collonsa was put to the horn in 1629 (ibid., 2. ser. III, p. 46), and Donald M'Gressich is in record in Girgidell, Ardnamurchan, in 1693 (*Argyll Inv.*). A partial translation of the name is found in 1527, in which year Malcolm Callum Grassichsone had a remission for offences committed by him (RSS., I, 3776). McGreische 1607. See also under GRASSICK.

MACGREWER. See *under* MACGRUAR.

MACGRIGOR. See *under* MACGREGOR.

MACGRIMEN. Donald Owir McGrumen was put to the horn for violence committed on the lands of Campbell of Glenorchy, 1607 (RPC., XIV, p. 473), and in 1613 Finla McGromovne in Foirlettir, who was fined for reset of Clan Gregor, is doubtless Finla Mc-

Grymmen or McGryment in Fettirlettir, denounced as rebel in 1619 (RPC., XIV, p. 631; XI, p. 574; XII, p. 132). Finla McGrymmen in Ballenyden, perhaps the same person, was charged with murder, 1615 (ibid., X, p. 404), and another Finlay McGrimen was accused of being one of the murderers of John Grant of Carron, c. 1630 (*Grant*, III, p. 225). Cf. MACGURMAN.

MACGROARY, Maccrory. These two names, found in Glasgow, are modern Irish importations. Ir. *Mag Ruaidhri* for *Mac Ruaidhri*. See under MACRORY.

MACGROUTHER, Macgrowther. See *under* MACGRUAR.

MACGRUAR, Maccruer, Maccrouther, Maccrowther, Maccruder, Maccrudder, Maccruthar, Maccruther, Maccrouder, Maccrewer, Macrither. G. *Macgrudaire*, 'brewer's son.' Now shortened to Grewar and Grewer. The name is found principally in the south of Perthshire, about Glenartney, and was common in Dunblane and Doune in the seventeenth and eighteenth centuries. The Macgruers of the North as a sept are merged mostly in the Frasers and adjoining clans. The earliest recorded of the name is Gilawmane McCrouder, witness in a charter to John de Cumre, 1447 (RMS., II, 640), and Gilbert McGrevar (ev = eu), tenant of Dowart, Stragartna, 1499 (ER., XI, p. 417). Donald McGruer witnessed a sasine in favor of Thomas Stewart of Grantully, 1494 (*Grandtully*, I, p. 38), Johannes moir Mcgrwdder was parishioner of Duthil, 1537 (*Grant*, III, p. 268), Duncan M'Rudder, witness in Perth, 1547 (*Rollok*, 16), Thomas McGrowder was witness in Lovat, 1550 (REM., p. 410), and Alexander M'Gruder held the parsonage of Lochals (Loch Alsh) and Lochcarron, then apparently united, before 1582 (OPS., II, p. 395, 396; RPC., III). John Makgruder, son of James Makgruder, was a retainer of Lord Drummond, 1580–81 (*Geneal. House of Drummond*, p. 126; RPC., III), and Robert Makrudder was reidare at Kintallartie, 1574 (RMR.). John McGrader, Phledgeour (arrow-maker) in Blairnrowar near Comrie, fined in 1613 for reset of Clan Gregor, is mentioned in the following year as John Grudgear, Phledgeour, in Barnrowar (RPC., XIV, p. 639, 660). Alexander McGruther was younger of Meigar in 1704 (*Muthill*). The name was early Englished, e.g. Gillecrist Brouster, a victim of the first hership of Petty, 1502 (*Rose*, p. 176). Old: Mchrudder and Mchruder.

MACGRUDDER. Macgruder, Maccruthar, Maccruther. See *under* MACGRUAR.

MACGUBB. For Macgibb, 'son of Gibb.' Cf. MACGIBBON. Sir Thomas M'Gub (a cleric) who received payment for custody of the king's provisions in Linlithgow, 1464 (ER., VII, p. 288) is probably Sir Thomas M'Gub or M'Gube recorded as priest in Glasgow, 1472 and 1477 (*Sc. Ant.*, XVII, p. 119; REG., p. 436). Dr. Trotter (*Galloway gossip: Kirkcudbrightshire*, p. 2) says it has been changed to Gibson, for 'gentility.'

MACGUCKIN. A variant of MACGUGAN, q.v., current in Kirkcudbrightshire.

MACGUFFIE, MACCUFFIE. Col. John M'Guffie of Cubbicks in the Stewartry was killed at Flodden, 1513. The foundation stone of the monument to the Wigtown Martyrs was laid by Provost M'Guffie of Wigtown. John M'Kuffie was a councillor in Kirkcudbright, 1570. James M'Cuffie of the Crockes of Sonnik, 1688 (*Kirkcudbright*). William Holmes McGuffey (1800–1873), American Presbyterian clergyman and compiler of McGuffey's 'Readers,' was son of Alexander McGuffey, born in Scotland. A weakened form of MACGUFFOG?

MACGUFFOG. The name of an ancient and once powerful family that at one time possessed lands in central and western Galloway. Patrik McGuffok who made a proclamation at Botil (Buittle) on behalf of Sir Robert Bruce in 1291 (Palgrave, *Documents*, p. 42), is probably Patrick Maccoffoc who appears as witness in 1289 (*Holm Cultram*, p. 88–89). Thomas Macoffoke appears in Berwick, 1297 (*Hist. Docs.*, II, p. 156). Maucolum MacCuffok of the county of Dumfries rendered homage, 1296 (*Bain*, II, p. 206). King Robert Bruce confirmed to Richard Mc cuffok, for his homage and service, "octo bovates terre de Kelinsture et Cloentes in parochia de Soureby" in 1329 (RMS., I, App. I, 101). The name of John McCoffot, rector of Gewilston, witness in Galloway, 1347 (*Pap. Lett.*, III, p. 396) is probably a misspelling (common in papal records of Scottish names). Gilbert M'Guffok was a tenant under the Douglas in Mikilbrekauch in the parish of Buittle, 1376 (RHM., I, p. lix), and Elene Mcguffok appears in Aberdeenshire, 1369 (RMS., I, 342). Thomas M'Guffok who was secretary to Margaret, countess of Douglas, 1429 (RMS., II, 123), may be Thomas Mcguffok who held the church of Glencarn in 1450 (REG., 358). Letters were raised against Johanne McGuffoc, servant of Shaw of Halie, 1569 (RPC., II, p. 70). M'Guffoch 1669, Macgufog 1689; McGuffock, McGuffocke, McGuffog, McGuffolk, Guffock (without 'Mac') all in 1684 (*Parish*). Perhaps the name of Grizzel M'Guffach, apprehended for child murder in Fordyce, 1746 (*Fordyce*, p. 61) is the same. There is a farm in the Stewartry called Guffokland. ? G. MacDabhog, 'son of Davuc,' a diminutive of David.

MACGUGAN, MACGUIGAN, MACGOUGAN. From Mac Guagáin, a corrupt form of Mac Eochagáin, diminutive of EOGAN or EWAN, q.v. John McGowgane and Duncan McGowgane were tenants in Kintyre, in 1541 (ER., XVII, p. 630). Gilcallum M'Gowgane was occupier of Kilcobenache, South Kintyre, 1650 (HP., III, p. 82). Catharine M'Gugane in Clachindunan, parish of Kilcalmonell, 1684 (*Argyll*), and Angus M'Gugan in Auchnacoirle, parish of Killean, 1693 (*Argyll Inv.*). Another current form is MACGUCKIN.

MACGUIGAN. See under MACGUGAN.

MACGUIRE. A personal name. Ir. *Mag uidhir*, G. *Mac uidhir*, 'son of the pale(-faced) man.' In Ayrshire, c. 1740, the name occurs in the forms M'Queir and M'Quyre (*Paterson*, I, p. 596–597). M'Quire of Drumdow, Ayrshire, changed their name to Macrae on succeeding to the Houston estates of James Macrae, Governor of Bombay, in the middle of the eighteenth century.

MACGUNNION. This surname, found in the Stewartry, is a curtailed form of MAC(GILLE)-GUNNIN, q.v.

MACGURK. 'Son of Corc,' with *Mag-* for *Mac-*. Suny (= Suibhne) Magurke held lands in Knapdale and Glenarewyle in 1314 (*Bain*, III, 423), and Arthur M'Gurghe appears in record as bailie depute of Carrik in 1542 (RMS., III, 2684). Macgurkych is author of a poem in the Book of the Dean of Lismore (p. 116). For meaning see under MACCORC.

MACGURMAN, MACGURMEN. A charge was made against John McGurman, tenant in Kirdells, by the laird of Grant, 1681 (RPC., 3. ser. VII, p. 186). Donald M'Guirinan in Nether Fernoch, 1685, appears again as M'Guirman (*Argyll*, p. 21, 39). John McGurman of Wester Gaulrig was a Jacobite of the '45. The name of the piper in the royalist army, 1651, is spelled Macgurmen (Fraser, *Wardlaw* MS., p. 379). There is an Airidh Mhic Guirmen in Jura. Cf. MACGRIMEN.

MACHAFFERY. An Irish name recorded in Greenock. A variant of MACCAFFERY, q.v.

MACHAFFIE. See under MACCAFFIE.

MACHAN. There was a tenement of this name in Vale of Clyde. Adam Machan witnessed two charters by Orabile who died c. 1203. Thomas, son of John of Machan, was juror on an inquest made by Sir Alexander Uviet, sheriff of Lanark, 1262–63.

MACHANS. A rare form of MACANGUS, q.v. John MacHans in Wigtown was fined £600 [Scots] in 1662 (APS., vii, p. 428).

MACHAR. A rather scarce surname found in Aberdeenshire, Angus and Mearns. Isobel Macher in Glenmyllay, 1610 (Brechin).

MACHARDY, MACHARDAY, MACHARDIE. G. MacC(h)ardaidh, 'son of the sloe,' from older G. cardi. The h is intrusive, and silent in the vernacular. The home county of the Mac-Hardies is the Highlands of Aberdeenshire and the immediate neighborhood north and south, but with some few unimportant exceptions they did not own land on Deeside. They were, however, numerous and influential. The Strathdon branch counted themselves of the Clan Chattan and followed Mac-Intosh as their chief (Stirton, Crathie, p. 413–414). Dr. Macbain suggested that the name came from Pictish Gartnaigh, pronounced Gratney, a well-known name of old in Mar. (There was an earl of Mar called Gartney or Gratney about 1300.) He thinks it was developed to MacCardney or MacCarday, and ultimately before 1587 to MacHardy. A commission for the trial of persons accused of the 'crewall slawchter of Thomas McChardy' in Brakmar, was issued in 1560 (Rose, p. 233). John Mackhardie in Crathinaird, 1633 (SCM., iii, p. 139). Donald Fleming alias McQhardies [= M'Hardy] was officer of the baron-bailie's court of Braemar, 1676 (Stirton, Crathie, p. 420), and John M'Ardie and Alexander M'Kardie appear in Invercauld, 1696 (Poll Book).

MACHARG. In the fifteenth and sixteenth centuries this name was common in Carrick and in the mountainous part of Galloway adjoining, and today is common in Glasgow. There were two branches of the family — Mac-hargs of Shalloch in the parish of Kirkpatrick-Irongray, and the Machargs of Cardorkan in the parish of Minnigaff. The Machargs or M'Quhargs of Cardorkan seem to have been of a turbulent character. Finlay M'Quharg and others of the name were charged with fire raising, burning of houses belonging to Stewart of Fintillauch in 1581 (RPC., iii). Eleven years later they took an active part in a feud between the M'Kies and other Galloway families and the Kennedys. Marion M'Quharge was married in 1493 (Sc. Ant., iii, p. 107).

Thomas McQuharg was heir of Thomas Mc-Quharg in lands in Barchclye, 1572 (Retours, Kirkcudbright, 401). Martin M'Quharg was burgess of Kirkcudbright, 1597 (RMS., vi, 579), John M'Quharg petitioned against the Service Book in 1637 (RPC., 2. ser. vi, p. 711), and James M'Quharg was bailie of Minigaff, 1715 (Wigtown). Margaret Mach-harge was charged with being a disorderly person (i.e. non-conforming) in the parish of Cross-Michael, 1684 (RPC., 3. ser. ix, p. 574). Jean M'Harg in Troquhan, 1713 (Kirkcudbright). McGarg, Maharg, McQu-harg>Harge, all 1684 (Parish). M'Carg.

MACHAROLD, 'son of Harold' (ON. Haraldr). A Macleod sept surname. John Makherrald was one of the victims of the her-ship of Petty by the earl of Huntly in 1502 (Invernessiana, p. 181). His name is given as Makherrad in Rose, p. 177. See MACRAILD.

MACHARRIE, MACHARRY. Galloway names, from Ir. Mac Fhearadhaigh, a variant form of Mac Fearadhaigh, 'son of Fearadhaigh,' an old personal name, OIr. Feradach. Hogs Mc-Charry, yhounger, Jhon McCharry and Edwart McCharry were guild brethren of Ayr in 1428 (Coll. AGAA., i, p. 228–229). In the following year Edward M'Harry had a charter of the lands of Knockinnschoch in the earl-dom of Carrick (RMS., ii, 138). In 1449 the name again appears in Carrick as M'Carry (ibid., ii, 371), and in 1455 there is entry of sasine of Knoknunscheach in Carric to Patric Macquarry (ER., vi, p. 74). Maurice M'Carry had sasine of Knockinfeith in Carrik, 1468 (ER., vii, p. 675). Colin McQuharry is in record in Ayrshire in 1480 (ADC., ii, p. 70). John M'Harie, an exiled Covenanter, was drowned on the voyage to the colonies off Orkney, 1679 (Hanna, ii, p. 253). Anglicized CARRIE and perhaps HENRY. McChar-rie and McHarrie 1684.

MACHARVIE. A Galloway surname. See MACGARVA.

MACHATTON. From MAC(IL)HATTON, q.v. Neil McHatton was transported to New England in 1685 (RPC., 3. ser. xi, p. 94). See also HATTON.

MACHAY, MACHEE. Rather from Ir. Mac-Aodha than G. MacAoidh, 'son of Hugh.' Michael M'Hay, a Douglas tenant in Brek-auchlug, 1376 (RHM., i, p. lix).

MACHECTOR. William M'Hector was session clerk in the parish of Ardclach, 1685 (RPC., 3. ser. x, p. 430). See HECTOR and HECTORSON.

MACHEE. *See under* MACHAY.

MACHENDRIE, MACHENDRICK, MACHEN-DRY, MACHENRY, MACKENDRICK, MACKEN-RICK. These are Highland border names meaning 'son of Henry,' in Gaelic *MacEanruig*. The *d* is intrusive as in HENDERSON, which has the same meaning and is used as an Englishing of the name. John M'Henri [Henrici], lord of Koylyan, charter witness, c. 1370–80 (*Laing*, 64). Gilcrist Makhenry, tenant of Hidderbrigende and Drumquharagan in 1480 appears again in 1483 as M'Henri (ER., IX, p. 561, 594). John McKanrig, probably his son, was tenant of Coschamby, Stragartna, in 1499, and appears again as John McCanrig or McCanrik, tenant of Drumquhargane, Strathgartney, in 1502 (ibid., XII, p. 416, 634). Euar Makanry held a merkland of John Culquhone of Lus in Kilmun in 1497 (RMS., II, 2385), and Gilbert Makcanryk, a follower of the earl of Cassilis, was respited for murder in 1526 (RSS., I, 3386). Duncan McKinriche was tenant on lands in Strathdee in 1527 (*Grant*, III, p. 68), and Johnne M'Henry had a remission from Queen Mary for his part in assisting the English in burning the town of Dunnone and besieging the castle in 1546 (RSS.). In 1695 the earl of Argyll was retoured heir in a 'mercata terræ ab antiquo per Iver M'Canrie possessa' (*Retours, Argyll*, 93). Donald McCandrie and John McCandrie in Glaick and Duncan McHenrie in Knockbaine of Strathbren are in record in 1726 (HP., II, p. 332, 338). The Henrys of Argyll and Bute are most probably originally Mackendricks. The names are also Englished HENRY. McHenrik 1590, M'Kendrig 1669.

MACHETH. G. *Macc Aeda*, 'son of Aed.' See under HETH and MACATH.

MACHINCH. A rare form of MACANGUS, q.v.

MACHOLM, MACHOLME. John Makhome, clerk of the diocese of Glasgow, 1477 (*Edgar*, p. 227), appears in 1480 as notary in Dumfriesshire (RMS., II, 1471), and is doubtless the John Makhome, rector of Castillmylk, 1508 (ibid., 3335).

MACHOUL, MACHOWELL. Forms of MACDOWALL, q.v. William Dow M'Houle in Glenkengie, prisoner in the '45 (*Prisoners*, III, p. 98).

MACHOUSTON. A variant of MACHUTCHEN, q.v. The obit of Joannes Mallych M'Huston apud Tullychgamin is recorded in 1523 (*Chr. Fort.*, p. 118). Donald M'Houston in Balnaskeag, a Glenorchy vassal, 1638 (BBT.,

p. 400). Angus McHuiston in Rowrach, Kintail, 1726 (HP., II, p. 328), and Donald M'Houston in Caithness was a prisoner of the '45 (*Prisoners*, III, p. 98). Nein Donle Vick Huiston in Thurso (*Thurso KSR.*).

MACHRAY. A not uncommon surname in Aberdeenshire. "The name Machray is a variant of the Gaelic word, which is most generally but not perhaps most accurately Anglicised as Macrae... These Aberdeenshire members of the sept appear to have spelled themselves Machray for generations; the *ch* was pronounced soft like the *ch* in *loch*, not hard as *k*. It is uncertain when they first migrated from the clan country which lies round the shoulders of Loch Duich, under the shadow of Ben Attow, in the county of Ross, eastward of Skye. They first settled in the neighbourhood of Inverness, and then moved south into Aberdeenshire" (Robert Machray, *Life of Robert Machray, archbishop of Ruperts Land, primate of all Canada*, London, 1909, p. 2). The primate was born in Aberdeen in 1831 and died in 1904. Old forms of the surname in Aberdeenshire records are: McChray 1775, Mackray 1649, McCraw 1763, McKray 1748, McRay, 1773. "Some Machray notes," by Robert Murdoch Lawrance are published in the *Celtic monthly*, v. 24, p. 39.

MACHUDRI. John Machudri is mentioned in a charter by King Alexander III, 1253 (*Lennox*, II, p. 14). Dogal Mac Houtre was juror on inquest regarding the lands of Stephen de Blantthyre (Blantyre), 1263 (*Bain*, I, 2338; APS., I, p. 102). Maldovenus Mc Hudy (evidently the same name) is included in an inhibition by the bishop of Glasgow directed against the earl of Levenax and his adherents, 1294 (RMP., p. * 203).

MACHUGH. A surname in Edinburgh probably of Irish origin. More likely an Englishing of Ir. *MacAodha* than of G. *Aoidh*.

MACHUTCHEN, MACHUTCHEON, MACHUTCHIN, MACHUTCHON, 'son of HUTCHEON,' q.v. The Macdonalds of Sleat are descended from Hugh, younger son of Alexander, earl of Ross and lord of the Isles, whence the clan designation *Clann Uisdein* or *Clann Uisdeann*. John Roy Makhuchone committed slaughter in Ross, 1494–5 (OPS., II, p. 572; *Invernessiana*, p. 165), and John Huchonsoun, the English form of his name is given in 1497 (*Rose*, p. 164). Adam MacHutchoun is recorded in Murthlac, 1550 (*Illus.*, II, p. 262), and Murdow McHuchone, a follower of Murdow McCloyd, was concerned in the attack on the galley of the laird of Balcomie, one

MACHUTCHEN, Machutcheon..., *cont'd*
of the Fife Adventurers, 1600 (RPC., xiv,
p. cxxiii). Hew MacHutcheon in Ayr was
fined £360 in 1662 (APS., vii, p. 425), and
in the previous year Eric Jimen Rore M'Hus-
seon appears in Brawelbie or Brawelbine,
Caithness. Donald McHuiston, tenant on forfeited estates of Seaforth, 1726 (HP., ii,
p. 314), John M'Huitcheon in Inverness, a
Jacobite prisoner of the '45 (*Prisoners*, iii,
p. 98), and Hugh M'Hutcheon of Changue,
1799 (*Wigtown*). M'Hucheoun 1607, M'Hutchon 1740.

MACIAN, Macane, Macean, Mackain,
Mackane. G. *Maclain*, 'son of John.' John,
not Donald, is the commonest forename in the
Highlands. The Macians of Ardnamurchan are
descended from Eoin Sprangach, son of Angus
Mor, lord of the Isles, in beginning of fourteenth century. 'Several families of the name
who have in recent times come to Coll from
Ardnamurchan call themselves wrongly Johnstones' (*Clan traditions*, p. 27). Johnstone
is (1) territorial from Johnstone in Dumfriesshire, and (2) John's town or S. John's town
is an old name for Perth. Many others have
translated their name as 'Johnson', as did the
ancestors of Andrew Johnson, seventeenth president of the United States. The first record of
the name is in 1296, in which year Sir Dovenald
fitz Can (i.e. Donald MacIain) was one of
an inquisition made at Berwick (*Bain*; ii,
p. 195). John Crom Mc kane, a witness in
1433 (HP., iv, p. 202). Andro Makayn was
a sufferer from the first hership of Petty, 1502
(*Rose*, p. 176). McAan and McAyn 1519,
McAne 1607, M'Cane 1538, M'Cayne 1580,
M'Ean 1538, Mackane 1541, Makane 1494,
Makcane 1515, Makcayne 1519, Makkane
1505, Makkean 1647, Mceane 1656, McMak-
kane (evidently a duplication of 'Mac') 1515;
MacEoin, MacJeane, MakCoin. See Mackean.

MACIASGAIR. See MACINESKER.

MAC 'IC DHUGHAIL, the patronymic of
Macdonald of Morar.

MACIGHEILL. A family of this name are
said to have been barons of Barrichebean,
Craignish, before the Campbells. The Whytes
of Argyll are perhaps descended from them.
The name is still remembered in Argyllshire
and in Islay. Dowgall McGeyll was tenant
in Dunvveg and Keanchyllan, and Malcolme
McGeyil was tenant in Kilnachtane, Islay,
1686 (*Book of Islay*, p. 492, 496). John mc
yeall is recorded in Kilmore, 1692 (*Commons*,
p. 28). Islay was one of the havens of refuge

to which the outlawed Macgregors fled, and
the name has been explained as *Clann a'
gheill*, "clan of the yielding." It may be a
variant of *Mac a' ghoill*, "son of the Lowlander." Many Lowlanders from Ayrshire
settled in Kintyre in the seventeenth century
from 1640 onwards. Calum McIgheill in
Nether Lorn, 1692 (*Commons*, p. 33), Katharine M'Iveil appears in Kilchevan, 1772
(*Campbell*, i, p. 183), Mary M'Igheill in
Ardyurd in Mull, 1743 (*Isles*), John M'Ighaill
in Torosav was a prisoner of the '45 (*Prisoners*,
iii, p. 98), and Alexander M'Igheill is in
Nether Fincharn, 1751 (*Argyll*). Cf. Macgill.

MACILARAITH, Macilarith. See *under*
MACILRIACH.

MACILBOWIE. G. *M'Ille bhuidhe* (for
M'Gille bhuidhe), 'son of the yellow-haired
lad.' Donald M'Ghille Buie was one of the
duke of Atholl's Fencible men enrolled in
Glenlyon, 1706 (*HMon.*, iii, p. 215). Mary
M'Ilbowie, tenant of Machrie, Islay, 1733
(*Bk. Islay*, p. 547). The name is now short-
ened (in Argyllshire) to Bowie and Buie.

MACILBRA. ? a shortened form of Macgillivray. Donald McIlbra, tenant of Kinegarry,
Islay, 1733 (*Bk. Islay*, p. 549).

MACILCHOMHGHAIN. G. *Mac Gille
Chomghain*, 'son of the servant of (S.) Comgan.' S. Comgan resided in Lochalsh in last
half of seventh century, and planted several
churches along the west coast. The M'Il-
chomhghains were an ancient race or sept of
untraced origin, and a family of the name
seems to have been early possessors of Inveraray. The large market cross there bears
the following inscription: *Hec est crux: no-
bilivm virorvm: videlicet Dondcani meic
Gyllichomghan: Patrici filii: eivs: et Mael-
more: filii Patrici: qvi hanc crvcem fieri facie-
bat*. Gillacomgan, son of Maelbrigde, mormaer of Murebe (Moray), and fifty of his
men were burned to death, 1032 (AU.). Roderic and Yuar, sons of M'Gillecoan, are among
the witnesses to a charter by John Cambel,
lord of Ardsceodanich, Argyllshire, undated,
but about 1355 (HP., ii, p. 141). Hector
Bui M'Coan was a notorious "robber from
the north," in the beginning of the fifteenth
century (*Memoirs of Ewan Cameron*, p. 18).
Donald McGillequhoane was tenant of part
of Culcarne in Ross, 1507 (ER., xii, p. 665).
John Makynquhone or Mackilquhone in Kilmaronock is mentioned in 1528 (*Cambus.*,
158). Alexander M'Gillvcoan was burgess of
Dingwall, 1537 (RMS., iii, 1721), and John
Makgillechoan, burgess of Dingwall, 1582

(ibid., v, 508), is doubtless John MacGillichoan, parliamentary representative of Dingwall, 1587 (APS., III, p. 428). A bond by Donald M'Gillequhoan and his sons to Colin Campbell of Glenurquhay is recorded in 1552 (BBT., p. 197). John McGillichoane was member of Scots parliament for Dingwall, 1587 (Hanna, II, p. 503). In 1595 Donald McIllichoan for himself and his succession, as one of the native men of Craignish, entered into an obligation of manrent to his chief, Ranald Campbell of Barrichibyan, as representative of the old Campbells of Craignish (Coll., p. 198). Johane Makgillichoan was a notary in Inverness, 1606 (Grant, III, p. 202, 298). Janet McGillichoan in Channonrie was put on trial for witchcraft, 1630 (RPC., 2. ser. IV, p. 13), Patrick M'Lehoan appears in the Glenurquhay Muster Roll, 1638 (BBT., p. 398), and Donald M'ilchoen, Iain M'ilchoen, and Gilchrist M'ilchoin were among those massacred at Dunavertie in 1647 (HP., II, p. 257). Agnes Nick Killichoan is in record in 1669 (IDR., p. 322), John M'Ilchoan appears in Barnacary, parish of Kilmory, 1675 (Argyll), and Gilbert M'Ilchoane in Gelins, parish of Kilbryde, 1697 (Argyll Inv.). In the South Highlands, bordering on the Lowlands, 'Mac' entirely disappears from the name, and e.g. in Argyllshire Iain MacCòmhan becomes Iain Còmhan in Gaelic while its English equivalent is Cowan; and Mr. J. S. Howson says he once saw in possession of one of the parish school children of Inveraray a paper in which the name was turned into Cunningham (Trans. Cambridge Camden Soc., p. 170). S. Comgan was the special patron of the old Glengarry family. "The author of the Letterfearn MS.," says Gregory (p. 303n), "informs us that, in the discussions before the Privy Council, the Mackenzies proved Glengarry 'to have been a worshipper of the Coan, which image was afterwards brought to Edinburgh and burnt at the Cross.'" In Edinburgh it was called "Glengarry's God." M'Gillochoaine 1587, M'Killichoan 1587, Makillichoan 1579.

MACILCHOMIE. Angus M'Ilchomy in Kilmackacharmik parish, 1675, and Mary M'Ilchombie in Strontoller, Muckairn (Argyll). Donald M'Ilchomie in Srondeilliar, parish of Kilmore, 1693, and Archibald M'Ilchomich in Auchnacroish in Lismore, 1699 (Argyll Inv.).

MACILCHRUM. G. Mac Gille chruim, 'son of the bent one,' 'an unidiomatic expression in Gaelic' (Macbain). A family of Macdonalds settled in Benderloch, parish of Ardchattan, for upwards of 300 years were known as Clann-a-Chruim. They appear to have died

out within recent years. They were known variously as McIlchrum, McIlchrumie, McCrumie, and McCrum. Finlay McGillegrum was tenant of Kenmarre in Tiree, 1541 (ER., XVII, p. 614). Malcolm M'Ilchrum in Ledaig, parish of Ardchattan, 1677 (Argyll), and Dugald M'Ilchrumie in Culcharan, 1695 (Argyll Inv.). M'Ilchrom (in Monteith) 1612. M'Chruimb 1610.

MACILDOWIE, MACILDOWY. G. Mac Gille dhuibh, 'son of the black lad.' Macgilladubh the hermit (disertach) of Iona is in record, 1164 (AU.). Nigel Mackegilduf, a charter witness in Carric in the reign of Alexander II (Melros, I, p. 172). Sometime between 1275 and 1294 Gillicrist Macgilliduffi consented to a quit-claim of the lands of Auchterwaddale to the Priory of Beauly (Beauly, p. 61). This early form of the name is preserved in the name of Doull [= Donald] Mac Gilleduf, a victim of the first hership of Petty, 1502 (Rose, p. 176). Gilbert McIlduf possessed a tenement in Dumfries, 1461 (Edgar, p. 226). McKeldowie is recorded in Lochaber, 1616, and the same form is found in Edinburgh, 1697 (Edinb. Marr.). John M'Ilduff was tenant in Bordland, 1642 (Dumfries), and Duncan M'Ildoui in Larichvain, parish of Inshaell, 1686 (Argyll). John Macgildhui in Casteltoune, Kindrochit, was appointed an elder in the church, 1701, and four years later he became an "apostate to popery" (Stirton, Crathie, p. 198–199). Buchanan says the MacAlduies or Blacks are a sept of Lamond, and the name has been sometimes so Englished. Mcgildui 1682, McIllezuie 1684. See also MACGILLEWIE, MACILDUE, and MACILGHUIE.

MACILDOWNIE. G. Mac Gille Domhnaich, 'son of the Lord's gillie.' Robert Mackildowny was admitted burgess freeman of Glasgow, 1573, and William M'Ildownie, burgess by purchase, 1624 (Burgesses). Mr. Robert M'Ildownie was minister at Cumertrees, 1624 (Dumfries), and Robert McIldowny is in Muckcroft, Stirlingshire, 1636. The form M'Gildowny is recorded in CD. as current in Peebles. Said to be shortened to DOWNIE.

MACILDUE, MACILDUY. From G. Mac Gille dhuibh, for which see under MACILDOWIE. Six M'Ildeus from Appin are included in the list of those engaged in the '45. The form Macilduy is not uncommon in the southwest of Perthshire, where there is still a small group of Macilduys known as Clandaindouey (Clann an duibh). The name also occurred in the island of Gometra. McKeldowie 1616, McIlliduy 1715.

512

MACILDUF. G. *Mac Gille dhuidh*, 'son of
DUBH,' q.v. David de Innerlunan, with the
will and consent of Gillicrist Macgilliduffi,
granted the monks of Beauly all his lands of
Ouchter-Tarradale, 1275 (*Beauly*, p. 60).
Gilbert Mc ilduf held a tenement in Dumfries, 1461 (*Edgar*, p. 226). Three individuals named Meikilduff were residents in the
parish of Buittle, 1684 (RPC., 3. ser. IX,
p. 570), and John McKledulfe and Margaret
his wife were listed as papists in the parish
of Urr, 1705 (MCM., III, p. 413). The name
is also recorded in Galloway in 1684 as M'Ilduff, Mickellduff, and M'Malduff (*Parish*).

MACILDUIN. G. *Mac 'Ille dhuinn* (*Mac
Ghille dhuinn*), 'son of the brown lad.' John
Makilduon, burgess freeman of Glasgow, 1608
(*Burgesses*), may be John M'Ildyn, merchant
burgess there, 1631 (*Retours, Lanark*, 170).
Mildonie M'Ilduin in Steligmor, Inverchellan,
1686 (*Argyll*).

MACILDUY. See under MACILDUE.

MACILFERSANE. 'Son of the parson's gillie
or servant.' John M'Eane Vc Ilfersane in
Cawdor. Malcolme Mc Ilfersane was one of
those who aided Angus Oig Maconaill in holding Dunivaig Castle against Bishop Knox,
1616 (*Cawdor*, p. 232). Alexander M'Ilfersane
was minister of Kinloss, in 1618 (RPC., XI,
p. 323).

MACILGHUIE. A phonetic rendering of *Mac
Gille dhuibh*, for which see under MACIL-
DOWIE. This form of the name was not uncommon in Argyllshire in the seventeenth
century. Archibald M'Ilguie in Auchindoune
in Lismore in 1694 (*Argyll Inv.*). Finlay
M'Illhuy and Jonet M'Beith of Canisbay were
married in 1665 (*Canisbay*, p. 19). M'Ilguy
is also found in the seventeenth century. Mc-
Ilhoy (*Parish*) 1684. The name is now Anglicized BLACK.

MACILHAGGA. Most probably for 'son of
the gillie of Mochuda.' See GILMAGU. Michael
Macylhaggow appears as witness at Colmon-
ell, Ayrshire, 1527 (*Laing*, 359). Patricius
McIlhagon (*n* wrongly written for *u*) wit-
nessed a charter to Kennedy of Bargaltoun
at Balmacclannoquhen in Kyle, 1553 (RMS.,
IV, 875), Robert M'Ilhago in Tradidnell, 1597
(*Gallovidian*), and Robert M'Ilhage, fisher in
Ayr, appears in 1715 (*Ayr*, p. 215).

MACILHATTON. G. *Mac Gille Chatain*,
'son of (S.) Catan's servant.' Catan, a saint
of whom little is known, was honored on the
West Coast from Bute to Skye. We have
Kilcattan in Bute and in Colonsay, Kilchattan

in Luing and Gigha, Ardchattan, and in Skye
a cell of the Abbey of Inchaffray was said
to have been previously a residence of S.
Catan. Ewen M'Gillecattan and Neil M'Gil-
hecattan witnessed a Lamont charter in 1465
(*Lamont Inv.*, p. 19). Donald McIlchattan in
Clonarie, 1620 (*Sasines*, II, 81). Patrick Mc-
Ilhatten or McHilhattin was mortally wounded
in Arran, 1672 (*Just. Rec.*, II, p. 85), and
John M'Ilhatton is in record in Foulis, 1670
(*Dunblane*). Lachlan Mc ilchatan, rebel in
Saddell paroch, Kintyre, 1685 (*Commons*,
p. 3). Jannet McIlchattan in Inveraray, 1758.
The surnames HATTON, HEATON, and HUT-
TON, as current in Kintyre and other parts
of Argyllshire, are abridged forms of this
name. Makilhattane 1579.

MACILHAUCH, MACILHAUGH. From
Eochaidh (*Macbain*, p. 64). Hugh Makgilhauche was burgess of Drumfreese, 1425,
and John M'Gilhauche or Magilhauch, rector
of Kirkandris in Portoun, 1426 (RMS., II).
As John de ['de' here an error] Makgilhauth
[*c* misread *t*] or Maucilhaue he appears in
1434 as provost of Lincluden (*Pap. Lett.*,
VIII, p. 493, 630). Finlay Makgilhauche, bailie
of Drumfries, 1434, appears again in 1454 as
McYlhauch (ER., IV, p. 630, V, p. 632), and
John McIlhauch was a notary public in diocese of Glasgow, 1453 (*Edgar*, p. 225, 226).
Thomas Magilhauche or M'Yllauch who appears as rector of Tynwald, 1463 (RMS., II,
765, 815), may be Thomas McYlhauche,
vicar of Gerwane (Girvan) in 1490 (*Crossraguel*, I, p. 49). Johnne McGilhauche was
gude brother to Johnne Campbell of Lundy,
1540 (RSS., II, 3660), John McKilhauche in
Wigtoun was cited to appear before the Privy
Council, 1562 (RPC., I, p. 214) and John
M'Ilheuch was burgess of Wigtown, 1700
(*Wigtown*). Macgilhauch 1426, Makgilhauch
1471, M'Gilhauch 1429, Makkilauche 1495,
M'Gilhauche 1440, M'Gilhauk 1459, McIl-
haush 1453, McKilhauche 1459, Makilhauche
1562, Makclouch 1500; Makgillhauch, Mak-
killauche, Makylhauche, Magilhauch.

MACILHENCH. A Wigtownshire surname.
In 1684: McIlhench, McIlhaunch, Malhensh,
Malhinch. With omission of the apostrophe
(M'Ilhench) it gives Milhench.

MACILHERAN, MACILHERRAN. This was
once a common name, particularly in Bute,
but is now extinct. Of the McIlherans or
Mac-gill-chiarans of Bute the Rev. Dr. Hewison says: "Last century [i.e. eighteenth] that
ancient family lived in every farm and cot
in the district of the Neils, and had their own
burial-ground at Clachieran (*Claodh Chia-*

rain), near Glechnabae. Now they prefer the common name of Sharp" (i, p. 139). (This was probably due to the faint resemblance of *-heran* or *-herran* to *gearan,* diminutive of *gear,* 'sharp'). The full form of the name is *Mac Gille Chiarain,* 'son of the servant of (S.) Ciaran.' There were several saints named Ciaran, the most famous of whom were Ciarán of Clonmacnois and Ciarán of Saighir (Seir-Kieran, Kings co., Ireland). The name means 'little black.' The names of the brothers of the first were *Donnán* ('little brown'), *Odrán* ('little grey'), and *Cronán* ('little tawny'). These names indicate that his family were dark complexioned, and therefore probably of pre-Celtic descent. The saint having left Ireland to labor in Cornwall, his name re-appears there with the regular Brythonic change of Q(C) to P, in the form Pieran or Pirran. John Makilkeranne held half of the land of Scalpsy in Bute in 1506 (RMS., II, 2987), in 1563 John Makgilcharane granted the south half of Scalpsav to James Stewart, son of William Stewart of Ambrismor (OPS., II, p. 235), and Donald Bacach ('cripple, lame') Mc ikkerane in Glenscoradill, Arran, was charged with fire-raising in 1576 (RPC., II, p. 552). In 1633 John M'Ilcherane was retoured heir of John M'Ilcherane of Ard-scapsie, his father, in the lands of Ardscapsie, (*Retours, Bute,* 45), and Robert McIlcheran was portioner of the same lands in 1676 (*Inquis.,* 103). Donald M'Gilcherrane in Cowgach is in record in 1662 (*Isles*). MacIlcheran 1696, MacIlcherrane 1696, M'Ilherran 1689, McKerran 1521. See also MACKERRON. S. Ciaran is the patron saint of Campbeltown.

MACILLEBHAIN. G. *Macgillebáin,* 'son of the fair gillie.' Englished WHITE and WHYTE.

MACILLEDHONAGART. 'Devotee of S. Domangart' of Rath Muirbuilg, co. Antrim. There was a small sept named M'Ille Dhona-ghart at Benderloch, who "now call themselves Macdonalds." Donald M'Illedongart was servitor to the laird of Lochnell, 1658. Janet Makdonart in the Stewartry, 1550 (*Laing,* 559).

MACILLERIACH. See MACILRIACH.

MACILLEVOLLICH, 'son of the rough or hairy lad,' from G. *molach,* hairy, rough. Gillemorie Makillevollich granted to Duncan Campbell of Glenurquhay and his heirs a bairn's part of his gear in 1535, and Duncane M'Illevollvcht, his brother, is witness to the grant (BBT., p. 233).

MACILLEVORIE. See *under* MACGILLI-VRAY.

MACILLRICK, MACILLURICK. Variants of MACILRIACH, q.v., current in Ayrshire.

MACILMALUAG, 'son of the Gille of Mo-Luóc.' (See under GILLEMELOOC and MOL-UAG.) John M'Ilmolnaage (read-uaage) or M'Illmolnadge (*u* misread as *n*) was tenant in Crare, 1672 (HP., II, p. 208, 215), and Donald Mc ilmaluag was charged with being a rebel in Killean parish, Kintyre, 1685 (*Commons,* 5), and another Donald McIlmaluag appears in Inveraray, 1746.

MACILMICHELL. See *under* MAC-MICHAEL.

MACILMORIE. ? Ir. *MacGiolla Mhuire.* John M'Ilmorow, a follower of the earl of Cassilis, was respited for murder, 1526 (RSS., I, 3386). Donald M'Ilmorie or M'Kilmorie, A.M., was translated from Rothesay to Kilmalieu or Glenaray, 1594 (Hewison, *Bute,* II, p. 297). Macilmorrow was an old name in Ballantrae parish (*Paterson,* II, p. 87). 1684: McIlmorrow, McElmurro, McElmurre, McIlmorron, McIlmurran (*Parish*).

MACILNA, MACILNAE. The fermes of Kiddisdale and Arborg were paid to Gilbert Makilna in 1487 (ER., IX, p. 461), and in 1501 the same individual appears as a charter witness in Dumfriesshire (RMS., III, 834). David McIllnave and Marion McKillnae, both in the parish of Carsfern, were charged with being disorderly in 1684 (RPC., 3. ser. IX, p. 575, 578). David M'Ilnae was retoured heir of David M'Ilnae, his father, in the lands of Locheid, 1687 (*Retours, Kirkcudbright,* 357). Andrew Miklenae in Compstone, Kirkcudbright, 1689 (RPC., 3. ser. XIV, p. 737), and James M'Ilnae in Polmerdow and Ninian Miklenae in Bishoptoune, 1696 (*Kirkcudbright*). Makillnae 1637. See also MACGILNEW and MACILNEIVE.

MACILNEIVE, MACILNEW. John M'Ilneive in Ardneach and John M'Iloreive (? for M'Il-neive) in Assoboll were denounced rebel in 1675 (HP., I). Donald M'Ilnew or McKilnew was tenant of Killegane, Islay, 1541 (ER., XVII, p. 617, 638). See also MACGILNEW and MACILNA.

MACILQUHAM. See *under* MACILWHAM.

MACILRAVIE, MACILREAVIE, MACILREVIE = MACILRIACH, q.v. ? = John Makilreve, custodian and administrator of the chapel of the Blessed Virgin at Casteldikis, Dumfries, 1537 (RMS., III, 2083; *Edgar,* p. 8).

MACILRIACH, Macilreach, Macilraith, Macilaraith, Macilarith, Macilwraith, Macgillreich, Macilleriach, Macillrick (Ayrshire), Macilurick (Ayrshire), Macilwrick (Galloway). In G. *Mac 'Ille riabhaich,* 'son of (the) brindled lad.' This is the commonest patronymic or surname compounded with *gille-.* It is common in Galloway and throughout the Highlands, and was a common personal name in Breadalbane 200 and more years ago. A money allowance was granted for Andrew, son of John Make Gille Reue, a Scots hostage who died in Carlisle prison in 1300 (*Hist. Docs.,* II, p. 426; *Bain,* II, 1179). Thomas M'Gilrewy was a Douglas tenant in the barony of Buittle, 1376 (RHM., I, p. lx), and David McKilwirk (i.e. Mcilwrick) was bailie of Dumfries, 1476 (ER., VIII, p. 393). Donald Makgillereoch or Makgillereacht appears as witness in 1485 and 1497 (*Cawdor,* p. 69, 87), and Robert Makgillereach was concerned in the 'spulyie of Kilravock,' 1497 (*Rose,* p. 166). Duncan McGillereach in Fandownyach had a precept of remission for offences committed by him, 1503 (RSS., I, 957), and the obit of Johannes M'Gillerawyth in Glenloquhacy is recorded in 1506 (*Chr. Fort.*). Michael Dow Mᶜal-zerache, an aged Highlander, was convicted of common theft and 'pikry' (petty theft) in Kirkcudbright in 1508 and banished the town (*Trials,* I, p. *53). Nele M'Ilwraith, a follower of the earl of Cassilis, was respited for murder, 1526 (RSS., I, 3386). Patrick M'Gillewriche or Gillevrich was a tenant under the marquis of Huntlie in the Cabrach, 1607 (SCM., IV, p. 282), Neil McIllereoche or McKillereoch in Carnakalliche and John Dow McIllereoche in Ballezartna were put to the horn, 1629 (RPC., 2. ser. II, p. 341; III, p. 46). John M'Ilwraithe was a notary in Mayboill, 1641 (*Retours, Ayr,* 354), Matthew Micklewrath and Donald or Daniel Miklewrock in the parish of Colmonel, were shot for being Covenanters in 1685 (*Hanna,* II, p. 256, 257, 272), and John Mc ilrivich in Achadlarie was a rebel in the same year (*Commons,* p. 12). Donald and Patrick M'Ghille-Reoch were among the duke of Atholl's fencible men in Glenlyon, 1708 (*HMon.,* III, p. 215), Adam Maklewreach was married in Edinburgh, 1614 (*Edinb. Marr.*), and Andrew M'Alwraith was a soldier of the city guard, 1734 (*Guildry,* p. 149). Macilvraith is an old name in the parish of Ballantrae (*Paterson,* II, p. 87), and it is and was a common surname in Kintyre and Islay, appearing on old tombstones there as Macilriach, now shortened to Revie, q.v. The name also exists in Uist and Skye, but is there mostly swallowed up in English by Macdon-

ald. Buchanan records M'Ilrevies as a sept under Clanranald. In Kilmuir, Skye, there is a place called Baile Mhic Illeriabhaich, 'township of the Macgilleriabhachs.' "According to Dr. M'Laren M'Ilwraith of Sheffield, the M'Ilwraiths belonged to these lands, and a bond of manrent between them and the lord of the Isles (or Macdonald of the Isles) was signed at Castle Camus (Knock), Sleat, Skye, on August 13, 1632... Their patronymic was 'Clann Ileirich,' and when asked to write, they always wrote 'MacDonald.' 'Clann Domhnull Riabhaich' were hereditary bards to Macleod of Dunvegan, then to Macdonald of Sleat" (*Celt. Rev.,* IX, p. 80; see also Forbes, *Place-names of Skye,* p. 55–56). A usual written form of the name is M'Gillereoch, but Mackilwraith is found in Carrick in 1538, Makilreve in Dumfries, 1539, and M'Iluraick in Galloway, 1588, M'Illereoch (in Auchlochinluy, 1594), Mackilwraith (Edinburgh, 1596), M'Ilerith (Luss, 1610), M'Gillirick (Abertarff, 1634), M'Gillereith (Benbecula, 1622), M'Illreave (Kirktoun, Kirkmichael, 1672), M'Ilreave (in Cnockalloway, 1672), M'Gillerewyche 1502, McIlwrith and McIllwrick 1687, McKilwrath (1681), M'Gillereach and M'Ilwrathe (1682), M'Ilroych (Kilmore, Argyll, 1687), and in Wigtownshire and Minnigaff in 1684 as McIllvrike, McElvrick, McIllrie, Meiklevrick, and McKilwrath. Sir Walter gave the name Habbakuk Mucklewrath to the fanatical leader of the Covenanters in his *Old Mortality.* One of the Gaelic names of the Devil, it may be mentioned, is *An Riabhach Mòr,* the great brindled or singed one!

MACILRIE. Thomas Makilbrie (an error), servitor to Ninian Neven in Shetland, 1624, appears in the same year as Machilrie, and Thomas McChillrie, chapman, was a witness at Skallowaybankis, 1626 (OSS., I, 52, 96, 152). Duncan M'Illrie in Kartaren, parish of Balquhidder, 1704 *(Dunblane).* Janet M'Ilrae in Drimilling, 1628 *(Dumfries).* Donald M'Ilraw in Balliwilling denounced rebel, 1675 (HP., I, p. 296). Another current form of Macilriach.

MACILROY, Macelroy. G. *Mac 'Illeruaidh (MacGhille ruaidh),* 'son of the red haired lad.' An old surname in the parish of Ballantrae, Ayrshire (*Paterson,* II, p. 87). Michael M'Gilrey was a tenant in Thornhill, Dumfriesshire, 1376 (RHM., I, p. lvi). Donald M'Gilleroi was a notary public in 1465 (*Lamont,* p. 19), and Ade M'Gilroy was tenant of Eglisdisdane and Balnegregane, 1480 (ER., IX, p. 564). Michael Mak Gilrov, bailie of Are, 1488, appears in 1500 as M'Ylroye, and there was a mass for the soul of Nicholas M'Ylroy in Ayr, 1500 (*Ayr*, p. 92, 95, 96). Donald Makgilroy, witness in Rothesay, 1529, is probably Donald Makgilroy or M'Gilroye, witness in Bute, 1545 and 1548 (RMS., III, 820; IV, 49, 273), and John M'Gilroy was attorney in Perth, 1545 (*Rollok*, 40). Elleis Makilrow signed the Band of Dumfries, 1570 (RPC., XIV, p. 66). Gilleis M'Ilroy in Kincardin, Inverness, was fined for resetting Clan Gregor, 1613 (RPC., XIV, p. 629). James M'Ilroy was retoured heir of Walter M'Ilroy in Kincardine, 1636 (*Retours, Clackmannan*, 16). The *Black Book of Taymouth* has the form M'Oulroy under the year 1638, but this is more probably for earlier *Mac Mhaoil ruaidh*. With omission of the apostrophe we have the current surname MILROY, q.v. It is also shortened to Rov according to Trotter (*Galloway gossip — Kirkcudbrightshire*, p. 213). The following spellings are all recorded in 1684 (*Parish*): McElroy, McIllory, McIlrie, McKelrae, McKilrae, McKilrea, McKilroy, McLeroy, McLroy, Meikleroy, and Micklroy.

MACILSCHENOCH, 'son of the gillie of (S.) Seanach.' One McIlschannoch or McIlschanoch was tenant of Maucherybeg in Kintyre, 1541 (ER., XVII, p. 632). Douncane More Makchennach, tenant on lands in Kintyre, 1596, is doubtless Duncan McSchenoch or M'Ilshenoch of 1605 (HP., III, p. 78, 84). Hew M'Schenoch, Gilbert M'Schenoache, and Gilchreist M'Ilshannoch were also tenants in Kintyre in 1605 (ibid., p. 82, 83).

MACILURICK. A form of MACILRIACH, q.v., current in Ayrshire.

MACILVAIN, MACILVAINE, MACILVANE, MACILWAINE, MACELWAIN. See under MAC-GILVANE.

MACILVENNA. Woulfe has the form Mac-Elvenna, from Ir. *Mac Giolla Mheana*, 'son of Giolla Mheana' (servant of Meana), an Antrim surname. William F. McIlvenna was married in Edinburgh, 1939.

MACILVERNOCK, MACGILVERNOCK. G. *Mac Gille Mhearnaig*, 'son of the servant of (S.) Ernan.' A sept name in the Graham country. Gillemernoch, brother of Gilleasald M'Gilleandris in Ayrshire, witnessed a charter by Roger de Scalebroc in favor of Melrose Abbey, c. 1185 (*Melros*, I, p. 25). He was probably ancestor of the Mac-gille-Warnocks who gave their name to Gaitgillewarnoch (in 1464 Gaitgillmakkilwernock) in the parish of Borgue, Kirkcudbrightshire. Malcolm Gilmornaike or Gilmernaykie had a charter of the lands in the reign of Robert I (RMS.,

I, App. II, 682). The family long ago shortened their name to WARNOCK. McKylwernok was one of the wrights engaged by Sir George Calbrathe in 1494 (ALHT., I, p. 246). John M'Ilvarnak or McIlnarinoch (for Iluarinoch) was tenant under Campbell of Ardkinglas, 1579 (RPC., III, p. 235). Thomas M'Ilvernok was tenant of the lands of Hoilmark in the barony of Uchiltrie, 1586 (RMS., V, 1135). Duncan M'Illevernak in Brakley, a Glenurquhav vassal, 1635 (BBT., p. 403). The Rev. Archibald Graham alias M'Ilvernock of the family of Obbe, minister of Rothesay, 1667, was the last bishop of the Isles, 1680–88 (Scott, *Fasti*, III, p. 30, 449–450). Duncan M'Illvernoche in Kirktoun Kirmichell, 1672, appears again in 1694 as M'Ilvenoch (HP., II, p. 208, 213). John McIlvernock of Oib granted a bond of caution, 1684 (RPC., 3. ser. IX, p. 327). In Argyllshire, says Macbain, "M'Gille Mhearnaig is the Gaelic for Graham, popularly explained as from *Gille-bhearnaig*, 'servant of the bite,' or 'greim,' that is Graham!" Mackewernock and Mackehoernock 1661.

MACILVIE. ? = Mackelvie. Gilcallumour McIlve or Gilcallummor McIlvie was tenant of Drumhalden, Islay, 1541, and Doule or Dougall Mc Ilfee, tenant of Ballaharvy, Islay, in same year (ER., XVII, p. 616, 617, 637). Finla McIlvie was fined for aiding Clan Gregor, 1613 (RPC., XIV, p. 632).

MACILVORA, MACILVORAY. ? = MACGILLIVRAY. Archibald McIlvoray, tenant and servant of James Campbell of Ardkinglas, 1579 (RPC., III, p. 235). Donald Macolvorie or Malcovorie in Glasgow University, 1590–1593 (RUG., III). Margaret M'Ilworrie in Carren, 1672 (HP., II, p. 208). John M'Ilvorrie in Isle of Erraie and Malcolm M'Ilvorrie in Forwachlie were denounced rebels, 1675 (HP., I, p. 298, 299). Angus McOulvorie in Neather Bible, 1726 (ibid., II, p. 323).

MACILVRAY. A form of MACGILLIVRAY, q.v.

MACILVRENENICH. Probably G. *Mac Gille Bhriananich*, 'son of the Bute lad.' Gilbert MacIlvrenenich, tenant in Corsyn, South Kintyre, 1568 (HP., III, p. 77). Duncan M'Gilwrindie or M'Ilwrindie, tenant of Garnageroche, Kintyre, 1605 (HP., III, p. 83).

MACILVRIDE, MACILVREED. This name, which occurs mainly in Perthshire, is from G. M'Ilbhrid, an old form of Macbride, the full form of which is *Mac Gille Brighde*, 'son of the servant of (S.) Bride.' Colanus McGilbride in Moray had a remission in 1363 (REM., p. 164), and Columba Mac Gilla-

MACILVRIDE, Macilvreed, *continued*

bridi was rector of Srathwatardail in 1429 (*Pap. Lett.*, viii, p. 100). The archdeacon of the Isles in 1476 was Nigel M'Ylwyrd, and in 1478 as Nigel Makkilbreid he appears as archdeacon of Sodor (RMS., ii, 1277, 1449). The name occurs in the lordship of Doune, c. 1489–90, as Makilbred, Makgilbred, and M'Gilbrid. Muldone McIlbreid was tenant in Tiree, 1541 (ER., xvii, p. 614), Duncan M'Gillebreid is in record in Lochalsh, 1548 (RMS., iv, 204), Gillecallum Mc olvrad, tenant of Leckamore, 1669 (HP., iv, p. 222), John M'Illbrevd in Barnakill, 1672 (HP., ii, p. 209), and Donald M'Ilbreid in Campbeltoun, 1689 (*Argyll Inv.*). Mc ilbryd 1685, Mc ylbride 1513.

MACILWAINE. *See under* MACGILVANE.

MACILWHAM, Macilwhom, Macilwhan, Macilquham. A sept of Lamont. 'Son of the servant of (S.) Thomas.' Thomas Makilquhone and Donald Makilquhone witnessed sasine in favor of Thomas Buchquhanan of Moss, 1505 (*George Buchanan quatercentenary studies*, 1906, p. 530). Ago McGillequhome appears in Strathdee in 1527 (*Grant*, iii, p. 70). Marion M'Ilquhan received a legacy, 1530 (CAC., i, p. 94). Gilcrist McIlhame or McIlhane was tenant of Galtak in Islay, 1541 (ER., xvii, p. 617, 637). James Gilqwham in Dunfermline, 1574 (*Dunfermline*). Duncan Mcilquhome in Straquhar, a sasine witness in 1598 (HP., iv, p. 43). Donald Dow McGillewhome at the Kirk of Drymmen was fined for aiding Clan Gregor, 1613 (RPC., xiv, p. 645). Macilquham also occurs in the barony of Mugdock in the eighteenth century and in Finnick in 1780 as M'Ilquham. Buchanan includes MacIlwhoms as a sept of Lamond, and the name has been Scotticized as Meikleham, Meiklam, and Meiklem. McGilliquhome 1607. Johnston (*Macs*, p. 31) suggests for meaning "*Macghill' chama*, 'son of the bold one's servant'" (!!).

MACILWHANNELL. Recorded in Perthshire. An attempt at a phonetic spelling of Macgillecongall, q.v. Sir Malcum M'Gillequhonill was curate of Straphillan (Strathfillan), 1547, and a witness there in 1561 (BBT., p.185, 204). Duncan M'Lehoniell was a Glenurquhay vassal, 1638 (ibid., p. 400). Thomas MacIlwhannell, farmer, Glaslarich, and Peter M'Ilwhannell, wright, Comrie, Perthshire, 1832 (*Perthshire voter's list*, 1832).

MACILWRICK. A form of Macilriach, q.v.

MACILWRITH. A form of Macilriach, q.v.

MACILYAR. James Damond McIlyar, a U. S. airman, claims to be Scots on both sides for several generations.

MACIMMEY, Macimmie. From G. *Mac Shimidh*, 'son of Simon' (Simmie). See under Mackimmie.

MAC IMPETHIN. Gillepatric Mac Impethin witnessed a charter by David i confirming earlier grants to Dunfermline Abbey, c. 1128 (RD., p. 4; APS., i, p. 358a). Gillecolme Mackthumpethin was a witness to the foundation charter of Dryburgh Abbey, c. 1150–1152 (*Dryburgh*, p. lxix). As Gillecolm mac chimpethin he witnessed a confirmation by David i, c. 1150, and as Gilcolm mac chimbethin he attested the gift of Nithbren and Balecristin to Dunfermline Abbey (RD., p. 7, 8). As Gillecolm Macchinbethin he perambulated the bounds of Balegallin (*May*, 2; *Bain*, ii, p. 527), and as Gillecolmi mach imbethi he witnessed a charter by Ernaldus, bishop of St. Andrews, between 1160–62 (RPSA., p. 128).

MACINALLY. *See under* MACANALLY.

MACINDENE. *See under* DENSON.

MACINDEOR, Mackindewar, Mackinder. G. *Macindeoir*, 'son of the Dewar,' q.v. The Macandeoirs were a sept formerly in Glassrie and now in Lochow. Their ancestor, says Buchanan, went to Argyllshire with Walter, laird of Buchanan's daughter, who, in the reign of James iii was married to Campbell of Ardkinglas. 'In regard there was no other of his Surname in that Country Argyllshire, was thence termed *Deoir*, or a Sojourner, whence his Posterity were termed M'Andeoirs' (*Buchanan*, p. 140). Perhaps so, but Buchanan cannot always be depended upon. Colin Macindoyr was juror on an inquisition on the lands of Inchesturphyn in the thirteenth century (RD., p. 222). Gillaspy McIndewir was tenant of Ardtalloch, Islay, 1541 (ER., xvii, p. 635). John Makindewer (Makeandewer, Makindeora, or M'Indeora) in Portbane, witness to bonds of manrent, 1576–86 (BBT., p. 221–237). Allaster Moir M'Indeir, servant to Alexander Steuart in Auldverik, to answer to charge of violence and robbery, 1592 (RPC., v, p. 28). Sir H. J. Mackinder was author of *Britain and the British seas*, 1914. The M'Indeors or Dewars of Islay often call themselves Macarthurs. M'Doir (with omission of the article) 1672, McInder 1613, McInddeor 1686, Mc Indoer 1692, M'Indoir 1684, M'Yndoir 1560.

MACINDOE, MACKINDEW. The Macindoes of Carbeth were an old family in Strathblane, and James M'Indoe was fiar of a fourth part of Carbeth in 1631 (*Strathblane*, p. 35, 46). Andreas MacYndow in Murthlac, Aberdeenshire, 1550 (*Illus.*, II, p. 261). Donald Makindoye was chamberlain of Petty, Brachlie, and Stratherne, 1558 (ER., XIX, p. 64). William M'Indowie was amerciat in the royal court of Spynie, 1597 (SCM., II, p. 135), and Donald McIndoue in Carnferich was charged with illegally carrying arms, 1618 (RPC., XI, p. 372). Alexander Maciandui in Taymouth, 1698 (FB., p. 364). George M'Indoe (1771–1848) published his *Poems and songs*, 1805. Walter Duncan McIndoe (1819–1872), born in Dumbartonshire, was representative in U. S. Congress, 1863–67. Makaneduy 1526, Makindoy 1561, McIndue 1698. Macindoes are classed as a sept of the Buchanans, and said to be descendants of a Buchanan who migrated to Argyllshire (*Buchanan*, p. 140). Perhaps G. *Mac Iain duibh*, 'son of black John.' See under MACINDEOR.

MACINESKER. G. *Mac an iasgair*, 'son of the fisher.' A common name in the Black Book of Taymouth, and found in Braemar in the seventeenth century as Mac Innesker. One Mc Neskar received payment for 'xv kne hedis' for the king's 'rowbarge' in 1494 (ALHT., I, p. 246). Christiane Neinfinlay Vikeanesker (i.e. Christian the daughter of Finlay son of John the fisher) gave to Duncan Campbell of Glenurquhay and his heir a half of all the gear pertaining to her at her death in 1585 (BBT., p. 233). Niall McInneskar witnessed the sale of the six shilling and eightpence land of Torramore in 1586 (*Poltalloch Writs*, p. 75). Gillow Cam or Gillinewcam McInyeskar in Lochgoilhead was a follower of Neill Campbell of Drumsynnie in 1602 (RPC., VI, p. 484, 507). Gromich McIneskair in Glenlochie and Patrik McNesker in Daldravag were prosecuted in 1618 for illegal carrying of arms (ibid., XI, p. 415, 486). Archibald M'Kinneskar in Lochgoilhead, 1619 (*Sasines*, II, 82). Duncane M'Kinyesker in Kynaldie and Archibald M'Inyeskar in Auchlyne appear in the Glenurchy musterrolls of 1638 (BBT., p. 402), and Alexander M'Inisker appears in the parish of Dumbennan in 1716 (SCM., IV, p. 171). The name was rendered FISHER as early as 1509 (ADC., 21 July). McInzeskar 1633. Now known only as FISHER, q.v.

MACINESPIK, 'son of the bishop,' *easbuig.* Duncan M'Inespik alias Campbell was a witness at Ilanran in 1579 (BBT., p. 223). This Duncan was a natural son of John Campbell, bishop of the Isles (FB., p. 353).

MACINFUTTIR. Among the western Bunloit sufferers in the great Raid of 1545 was John McGillechrist Mor Mc infuttir — John son of big Christopher, son of the Fuidir or stranger bondsman (Mackay, *Urquhart*, 2. ed., p. 442). He is mentioned again in 1548 as John M'Gillicrist Moir M'Infuttir (RMS., IV, 204).

MACINLEICH, 'son of the doctor' (G. *lèigh*). John M'Inleich, a descendant of one of the Beaton doctors who had settled in the Aird, "who kept Lord Lovat's flocks, got into trouble by helping himself to his master's muttons, and was saved from punishment by his wit and archery" (*Wardlaw*, intro., p. xxxviii). Angus McInleich was witness in 1547 (*Poltalloch Writs*, p. 139). Dugall M'Donachie VcInleich (*Mac an lighiche*) of Darrenaneranach, 1622 (*Sasines*, 130). Guarie McInleich was charged in 1686 with intercommuning with rebels (RPC., 3. ser. XII, p. 234). Archibald M'Inlaich is in record in Dunemuick in Glassrie, 1694, and another Archibald M'Inlich in Airluge in Knapdale is in record, 1685 (*Argyll Inv.*). John M'Inlitch is in Craigintervebeg, Ardskornish, 1692.

MACINLESTER, MACINLISTER. See under MACLEISTER.

MACINNES, MACKINNES, MACKINNESS. G. *MacAonghuis,* 'son of ANGUS,' q.v. Donald McKynes was tenant in part of the Elryk in 1514 (*Cupar-Angus*, I, p. 295), Duncan M'Kynnes appears in Lochalsh in 1548 (RMS., IV, 204), and John M'Kynnes witnessed an instrument of sasine in 1530 (*Lamont*, p. 39; *Laing*, 381). Allester M'Callen M'Aneiss and John dow M'Aneiss had assignation of maills, fermes, etc., at Dunoon, 1574 (*Notes and Queries*, 11 July 1931, p. 220). Johnne Dow Mc Inoss in Glenlyon, 1583 (RPC., III, p. 589). Ewin M'Inish in Collicheles was denounced rebel in 1675 (HP., I, p. 300), and four Macinisches in Stewart of Appin's regiment in the '45 were killed and two wounded (*Coll.*, p. 199). Miles MacInnes, a director of the London and North-Western Railway, was also M. P. for Hexham. McInnisch 1692, Mcynwiss 1525, McGinnis and M'Guenis 1745, MacInnish 1745, V'Invische 1587.

MACINNON. A form of MACKINNON, q.v., current in Skye.

MACINREOCH. G. *An riabhach*, 'the brindled one.' Malcolm M'Anreoch was tenant·on lands in the lordship of Menteith, 1530 (RMS., III, 933). Donald McInreoch, 1607 (RPC.). John Dow McInriache in Tomachlagane and Muldonich McInriauch in Glen-

518

MACINREOCH, *continued*

lyoun were fined in 1613 for reset of Clan Gregor (RPC., xiv, p. 631, 633). Duncan Dow McInrioch in Megerney was charged with illegal carrying of firearms, 1618 (ibid., xi, p. 372, 415). Duncan M'Inroich in Drumora, parish of Killean, 1694 *(Argyll Inv.)*. An *Riabhach* is also a common name for the Devil.

MACINRIVER. Donald M'Inriver in Sallachie, 1657 *(Sasines, 937)*. Donald Mc Inriver in Kentra, witness at Kilmartin, Argyll, 1683 *(Genealogist, new ser. xxxv, p. 183)*. Archibald M'Inriver in Barbreck, parish of Craignish, 1684 *(Argyll Inv.)*, and Archibald M'Inriver in Torranbeg, 1708 *(Campbell, i, p. 81)*.

MACINROY. G. *Mac Ian ruaidh*, 'son of John Roy' *(ruadh)*. Makeanroy 1556. The Macinroys were a sept of *Clann Donnchaidh* or Robertson.

MACINSTALKER. See MACSTALKER.

MACINSTRIE, MACINSTRAY. Wigtownshire surnames, explained by Woulfe as *Mac an Astrigh*, 'son of the traveller.' He says it is an Ulster surname probably of Scots origin. Thomas Mackinnistre had sasine of Tanedolane in Kirkcudbrightshire, 1499 (ER., xi, p. 462). Martin Makeynsterre of that Ilk was juror on an assize, 1537 (RMS., iii, p. 1921), and Elizabeth McKynnestrie in the parish of Monygof had sasine, 1535 (ER., xix, p. 543). Marion M'Instrie in Borland of Borgue, 1674 *(Kirkcudbright)*, and another Marion M'Kinister appears in Barlochan, 1747 (ibid.). McKinstrie 1684.

MACINTAYLOR. G. *Mac an tàilleir*, 'son of the tailor.' The English word 'tailor' was early borrowed into Gaelic as *tàillear*. Alexander McKyntalyhur and John Mckyntalyhur were put to the horn in 1392 for their part in the raid of Angus and murder of Sir Walter Ogilvy the sheriff in the same year (APS., i, p. 579). Hugh Makintalyour, a witness, 1495 *(Cawdor, p. 84)*. John Makyntailzour had grant of half the lands of Langilwenach, Bute, 1506 (RMS., ii, 2987), and the name is also found in Bute as M'Intylor in 1707. John Makintailzour had a respite for his part in fire-raising in Arrouchquhir (Arrochar), 1526 (RSS., i, 3640). James McIntailyeour and Janet McIntailyeour, his sister, were tenants of Balnacochane, 1539 (ER., xvii, p. 658). Gillecrist M'Yntalluour witnessed a bond of manrent in Glenurquhay, 1559 (BBT., p. 203), and several McIntailyeours were fined in 1613 for reset of members of the outlawed Clan Gregor (RPC., xiv). The Fine Book of the

Macgregors gives their habitat in 1613 as entirely in Perthshire — at Glenbrerochan (Cluny), Ardache (Menteith), Tullybannocher (near Comrie), Glenlyon, etc. Neel M'Intavleor in Gortenbouie was denounced rebel, 1675 (HP., i), and Archibald M'Intyller and John M'Intyllor in Barnakill appear in 1672 (ibid., ii, p. 207, 217). Gillecrist Talzvr (without 'Mac') is author of a poem in the Book of the Dean of Lismore, and Gillepatrick Tailzeour was sergeant of Dornoch, 1552 (OPS., ii, p. 637). Mceantailyeour 1627, Mcintalveor 1599, M'Intalyeour 1638; McCewntailor, McKintaylzeor. The name is now Englished TAYLOR.

MACINTOSH, MACKINTOSH (the *k* is intrusive). G. *Mac an toisich*. In OG. *toisech* had the meaning 'chief, leader, or front man.' The word occurs in a Welsh ogham inscription as a proper name — *Tovisaci*, from early G. * *to-uess-acos*. The modern Welsh is *tywysog*, 'prince.' The Perthshire Mackintoshes have no connection with those of Inverness beyond the name. Both Mackintoshes are descended from different toschachs — those of Glentilt, who afterwards settled at Dalmunzie in Glenshee, are descended from Ewen (Eugenius or Hugh), son of 'Good John of Islay,' to whom a charter of the thanage was granted by Robert the Steward and lord of Atholl, afterwards Robert ii, about 1345–47 (Skene, CS., iii, p. 272). In 1382 the king issued a mandate to the lord of Badenoch to call Farchard Mctoschy to his presence and to exact from him security that Adam, bishop of Aberdeen and his men on the bishop's lands of Brass (Birse) shall be free from persecution and trouble by Mctoschy and his adherents (APS., xii, p. 18; REA., i, p. 136). A similar mandate was issued to John, earl of Carrick and Steward of Scotland to enforce the same (loc. cit.). Alexander Kevr Makyntosh had a carta feodifirmae from the bishop of Moray with consent of the chapter 'terrarum ecclesiasticarum de Rothymurchus' (REM., p. 415). Eight years later in his bond of manrent to William, earl of Errol, he is described as Alexander Mackintoche, thane of Rathamurchus (SCM., ii, p. 252). Laichlan Mackyntoich witnessed a charter by Alexander, earl of Huntlie to Alexander Stewart of Granetulv, 1468 *(Grandtully, i, p. 21)*. Duncan Mc intosh was captain of Clancattan, 1492 (REM., p. 238–239). Jhone Machvntovs was tenant of Envrvak in Atholl, 1500 *(Cupar-Angus, i, p. 252)*. The 'obitus Dougalli M'Gvnthossuc et Farchardi eius filii cum suis complicibus, vbi interfecti fuerunt apud castrum de Innernvs per Lachlanum M'Inthosse anno &c. v^cxxj' *(Chron. Fort., p. 117)*, and the 'obit

Lawchlan M'Gynthossych, capitani de Clanchatten,' MVᶜxxiiij (ibid., p. 118). In 1528 James v issued a mandate to the earl of Moray and the sheriffs of the bordering counties to leave 'na creatur levand of that clann Macintosh except priests, wemen, and barnis,' but the women and children were to be driven to the coast for transportation to the shores of the opposite continent (SCM., II, p. 84). Angus M'Cuintosych had a charter of the lands of Loppen with mill in the barony of Duris, 1557 (RMS., IV, 1234). Charles Macintosh (1766–1843) was inventor of the waterproofing of cloth by treating with a solution of rubber, whence the garment, 'a macintosh.' Some old spellings of the name show the influence of the old genitive in -gh. McComtosh 1710, Mackantoiss 1591, Mackentase 1652, M'kiltosche 1627, McKintishie 1682, M'Intoch 1532, Makintoch 1597, McKintoch 1477, McKintoche 1644, Mackintoche 1472, Makintoche 1593, McIntoich 1684, Makintoische 1591, Mackintoisch and Mackintoische 1476, Mackintorss 1600, M'Intoschecht 1543, M'Intoschie 1536, Mackintose 1550, Makintoset 1589, M'jntosche, Makjntosche, and M'Intoschve 1684, McKuntosche 1468, M'Kyntossche 1462, M'Kyntoys 1465, McKyntovss 1464, Mactoiche, Maktoiche, Macyntoiche, and Makintoiche (all in same document) 1481, MacYnthogyche (Rec. Inv., I, p. 33), Makynthois and Makintows 1499, M'Ynthosche and M'Ynthose 1569, McYnthosse 1562, MacYntoch 1528, Makyntoice 1473, McYntoisch 1476, Makyntoische 1478, Mc yntose 1524, Mc yntosse 1557, M'yntossich 1482, M'Yntoysche 1582, Malcomtoische 1609, Malcumtosche 1468, Makintoshe 1544, M'Kintoisch 1516, Makkintoische 1466. The chief of the clan is Tighearna na Moighe.

MACINTURNER. G. Mac an tuairneir, 'son of the turner.' G. tuairnear is a loan from Eng. 'turner.' See TURNER. According to Buchanan (p. 117) the Macinturners are (or were) a sept of Clan Lamont. The family of Turner (formerly M'Inturner) of Drimlee, Glenshira or Glen Shiray, are said to have been lairds there for centuries. Gillecrist Makintournour Makgillogoye is recorded in the Black Isle, 1500 (Rose, p. 169). Complaint was made against Duncan Roy McIlturnour (for McInturnour), tenant and servant of James Campbell of Arkinglas, 1579 (RPC., III, p. 235). John McIntowarner in Curichirach and Duncan Roy McIntowarnar in Glenlochie were charged with illegal carrying of arms in 1618 (RPC., XI, p. 372). The editor of "Extracts from the Duntroon Papers" (Genealogist, XXXV, p. 231) suggests that the name (and also TURNER) was originally Makan-

torrunn, 'son of the thunder' or 'son of the thunderer' (G. torrunn), which is etymology run mad. Mc kinturnor 1692.

MACINTYRE. G. Mac an t-saoir, 'son of the carpenter' or 'wright.' Glenoe, near Bunawe, Nether Lorn, was the country of this sept. General Stewart (Sketches, II, p. 82n) states, without giving his authority, that they possessed the farm of Glenoe from 1380 to 1810, a statement constantly repeated without any evidence being offered in its support. By some careless writers, again, Glenoe has been changed to the more familiar Glencoe. Traditionally the Macintyres are given as a sept of Macdonald, but historically they appear always to have been subordinate to the chiefs of Upper Lorn, and they are included among the "native men" of the Stewarts of Appin. Five Macintyres in Appin's regiment in the '45 were killed and five wounded (Coll., p. 199). They are also said to have been hereditary foresters to the Stewarts of Lorn and later to the Campbells of Lorn. The name appears in the Memorials of the Montgomeries (II, p. 49) under date 1490, when Gillechrist M'Yntir witnessed a letter of reversion by the rector of the church of St. Mary at Rothesay, and Christinus M'Yntir witnessed a sasine in favor of the same priest. The ferry of Conane was leased to Ferquhard McYnter in 1504 (ER., XII, p. 664), and Gildow Makintare had a Crown grant of a third of Dunallirde, Bute, 1506 (RMS., II, 2987). Duncan M'Kintier took part in the second "hership of Petty," 1513 (Rose, p. 190). Duncan M'Olcallum and others of the Clan Teir [Macintyre] gave their bond of manrent to Campbell of Glenurquhay, 1556, and several individuals named Makintyr bound themselves to deliver Mwlcallum Makintyr to Duncan Campbell of Glenurchy in 1590 (BBT., p. 200–201, 246). Johnne Mcinteir in Grotik to answer to a charge of violence and robbery, 1592 (RPC., v, p. 28), and another Johnne M'Intheir was prosecuted in 1623 "for latting of umquhile Finlay M'Keissik's bairnis die for hunger and haifing thair geir to sustene tham thairwith" (BBT., p. 379). Duncan Mc anteir was an "engager" on the royalist side in the parish of Urray, 1649 (IDR., p. 368). Hugh Macdonald's story of the origin of the name is too silly for belief. Makintare 1506, McIntyir, McIntyr 1686, M'Kintyre 1690, McYntyre 1540. Several of the name have changed to WRIGHT, q.v.

MACINVALLOCH. A Macgregor sept which Anglicized their name MALLOCH, q.v. The relict of Donald Mc Ynvallich was tenant of Eddirallekach, Strogartnay, in 1480 (ER.,

MACINVALLOCH, *continued*

IX, p. 562). Malcum M'Aynmallycht and others bound themselves to Colin Campbell of Glenurquhay in 1552 (BBT., p. 195). Duncan Maceanvallich in Comrie with his brother Donald appear in the list of Macgregors proscribed after the death of Drummondernoch, dated February, 1590. In 1599 he appears again as Duncan Makinvallich alias M'Gregor of the parish of Comrie (Mason, *Protocol book*). M'Invalich 1483, Mc invalycht 1564.

MACINWILL. Alexander McInwill was one of the tenants of Wester Micras (Mecrav), 1539 (ER., XVII, p. 659), and Gilcallum McEwin McInvill or McInveill was tenant of Cartequhossin, Islay, 1541 (ibid., p. 616, 637).

MACIRVINE, i.e. son of a man named Irvine. An Aberdeenshire surname. William de Irwyne, Clerk of Register, obtained the Forest of Drum in free barony from Robert I in 1324 (*Illus.*, III, p. 292), and was thus ancestor of the Irvines of Drum.

MACISAAC. G. *Mac Isaac* or *Mac Iosaig*, 'son of ISAAC,' q.v. Gillanders Macysac witnessed a Beauly charter of 1231 (*Beauly*, p. 33). John mac ysaac who witnessed a charter by Donald, earl of Lennox in or before 1364 (HP., IV, p. 16) may be John Makysaac who witnessed a charter by Duncan, earl of Lennox, 1395 (*Levenax*, p. 79). Esaig M'Thome V'Esaig witnessed sasine of lands of Craginche to Archibald, earl of Argyll, 1510 (OPS., II, p. 97). Murdoch McIsack to be transported to New England, 1685 (RPC., 3. ser. XI, p. 94). Ann Maciosaig in Ceannlangavat, South Uist, was one of the late Dr. Carmichael's reciters (*Carm. Gadel.*, II, p. 374). In Mackay's *Book of Mackay* (p.5n) the wild suggestion is made that Macisaac "may be a corrupt form of Mackay"! Mc Isaick 1745, M'Isak 1676, Makesaig 1592, M'Iseik and M'Kiseck 1731.

MACIVER, MACIVOR, MAKIVER, MACCURE, MACEUR. G. *MacIomhair*, 'son of Ivar,' from the Norse personal name *Ivarr*. In the Gaelic MS. of 1467 the spelling is *M'Imhair*. Imhair, a Norse chief, joined with Olaf the White, king of Dublin, in his siege and sack of Alclyde (i.e. Dumbarton) in 870-71 (AU.); and another Imhair Ualmhair was slain by the men of Fortrenn in 904 (ibid.). Douenaldus filius Makbeth mac Ywar was one of the perambulators of the boundary between the lands of Arbroath Abbey and the barony of Kynblathmund, 1219 (RAA., I, p. 163;

APS., I, p. 91). In 1292 the lands of Malcolm McIuyr and others in Lorn were erected into the sheriffdom of Lorne (APS., I, p. 91). The relict of Eugenius M'Yuar is mentioned in 1371 (HP., II, p. 147), and in 1427 a royal remission was granted Duncan Yvari, i.e. MacIver (*Rose*, p. 127). Terlach McEuar was charter witness at Carnasserie, 1436 (*Poltalloch Writs*, p. 71). Archibald Makevire of Pennymoure appears as attorney for James Scrimgeoure, constable of Dundee, 1479 (HP., II, p. 184-85), and his sons Archibalde Makewor and Eware Makewore appear as witnesses in the same document. Donald M'Kywyr was charter witness at Sonnachan, Argyllshire, 1488 (*Notes and Queries*, 11 July, 1931, p. 21). Donald McUvyr and Andree McUvyr were tenants of Ballegregane in the barony of Doune, 1499 (ER., XI, p. 415), and John McEvir or McEueyr was tenant of Bairrepoill, Tiree, 1541 (ibid., XVII, p. 614, 647). Duncan Campbell or M'Keuir of Stroneschero had a grant of the lands of Killeane and Lealt in the Stewartry of Glenyray, 1562 (OPS., II, p. 86). Dowgall Makeuir and Alexander Makeuir were jurors on inquisition at Inverara, 1563 (HP., II, p. 204). Eiure M'Onochie VcEiure and John M'Eiure in Cloichran, John M'Euiure in Kendmoir (Kenmore) and Archibald M'Cuiure were vassals of Campbell of Glenurquhay, 1638 (BBT., p. 398-400), and Evander McKiver was a shoemaker in Elgin, 1745 (*Rec. Elgin*, I, p. 452). The Craignish MS. says that the Macivers are descended from Iver Crom, illegitimate son of Gillespick son of Callen maol math, 'good bald Coline,' who married a niece of King Alexander I (SHSM., IV, p. 199). "The Clan Iver lands were forfeited in the seventeenth century and were restored on condition that the heir should take the name of Campbell" (*Henderson*, p. 58). The form Macivor is due to its occurrence in Scott's *Waverley*, "and was never adopted by any family of position in the Clan in Scotland." As Iver was such a common Christian forename it would be impossible to name the particular Iver from whom the Macivers take their name. McEiver 1726, M'Euir 1533, M'Evar 1672, Makewer 1572, Euar M'Ewir 1529, M'Ewyre 1548. See also MACCURE and MACKEEVER.

MACJAMES, 'son of James.' A Highland border surname. Some of this name are probably descended from James Robertson of Strowan, who flourished early in the sixteenth century. About the same date the Robertsons of Pittagowan were called M'William. Alexander McJames was member of an assize on the lands of Garntulie in 1529 (*Grandtully*,

I, p. 69), Johannes McJamis doy was a parishioner of Duthil in 1537 (*Grant*, III, p. 268), and William McJames was a 'teilzeour in Innernes' in 1602 (*Rec. Inv.*, II, p. 2). — McJames, son to Johnne McJames in Kandlocht, was declared rebel in 1619 (RPC., XII, p. 78), Doncan McKjames is in record in 1682 (IDR., p. 106), and John McJames alias McHenish in the regality of Kildrummie was fined in 1686 (RPC., 3. ser. XII, p. 439).

MACJANET, MACJANNET, MACGANNET. Surnames recorded in Ayrshire and Wigtownshire. Alexander M'Jonat lived in Kirkmichael, Ayrshire, 1676.

MACJARROW, MACJERROW, 'son of DEWAR,' q.v. Anderson (*Scot. Nat.*) says that on a tombstone in the churchyard of Urr it is recorded that John Macjore in Cartine died in 1691; also John M'George of Cocklick, his son, died 1726. "There were two other branches," says Anderson, "believed to be of the same family, in the county of Ayr... These branches originally spelled the name MacJarrow, and it so appears in the statute of William and Mary restoring the memory, fame, and worldly honours of above 400 victims of oppression during the twenty-three preceding years." Robert McJarrow in Hoilhous, 1607 (RPC., XIV, p. 518). John McJorrie or McJarrow of Bangeroch (or Penjarrow) and Henry McJorrie or McJarrow of Altrawarie, Ayrshire, were prosecuted for rebellion, 1681 (ibid., 3. ser. VII, p. 7, 217). James McJore was resident in the parish of Borgue, 1684 (ibid., 3. ser. XII, p. 220, 450). Hendry McJerrow was a "merchand in Air," 1704 (*Corsehill*, p. 203) and John McJorrow of Pingerroch, "chirugeon aporie" in Ayr was admitted burgess of Prestwick, 1732 (*Prestwick*, p. 91). M'Joir 1565, M'Joyr 1601, McJury. In 1684 (*Parish*): McJory, McJorrie> Jorie. Makgeore 1662.

MACJASPART. 'Son of Jasper.' Donald McJaspart in the parish of Kiltearn was charged with being an 'ingadger' in 1649 (IDR., p. 160). Jasper appears to have been a not uncommon name in the north in the early seventeenth century. We have Jasparde Dempster, burgess of Inverness, 1582 (*Macdonald*, 636), Jaspert Cuminge in record in Inverness in 1603 and a Jaspert Cuithbert in 1621 (*Rec. Inv.*, II, p. 18, 157).

MACJERROW. See under MACJARROW.

MACJILTROCH. A surname formerly current in Galloway, sometimes spelled McQuiltroch. Gilchrist is now used in its place (Trotter, *Galloway gossip: Stewartry*, p. 60).

MACJOCK. A Highland border name from Lowland Scots 'Jock,' i.e. John. M'Yocks were a sept famous in Glenshee in the seventeenth century (*Macbain*). William Mac Jokke in Murthlac, 1550 (*Illus.*, II, p. 262). Alexander Makiok, servitor to Colin M'Kenzie of Kintail, 1575 (RMS., IV, 2465). Robert McJock in Straloche fined for reset of Clan Gregor, 1613 (RPC., XIV, p. 636). Jon roy McJock, Rorie McJock, and William McJock were charged with being 'engagers' on the royalist side from the parish of Urray in 1649 (IDR., p. 368), and Archibald M'Jock appears in Ballemor in 1672 (HP., I, p. 210). Buchanan (p. 92) claims the Macjocks as a sept of Macfarlane. They have now become Macdonalds.

MACJOKKIE. A Highland border name from Lowland Scots 'Jockie,' diminutive of Jock, i.e. John. John Grant, sone to Petre Grant alias McJokkie in Tulliche was fined in 1613 for reset of outlawed members of Clan Gregor (RPC., XIV, p. 631), and James McEan McJackie in Dalcharne is in record in 1615 (*Grant*, III, p. 315). Patrik McJokie is in record in Wester Tulloche in 1619 (RPC., XI, p. 565), John McPatrick VᶜYockye in Culloch (Tulloch) and Duncane McPatrik VᶜYockye there were prosecuted for carrying firearms in the same year (ibid., XII, p. 132), and several McJokies or MacJokkies were charged with being rebels or for resetting rebels in 1636 (ibid., 2. ser. V, p. 6).

MACK. The surname of an old Berwickshire family. Lindkvist (p. 201) gives *Makr* (or *Maki*) as an Old West Scandinavian man's name from which he derives the old place name Macwra in Yorkshire. John Makke had a safe conduct into England in 1424 (*Bain*, IV, 963), and a later John Mak witnessed an instrument of sasine of a husbandland in Ayton, 1470 (*Home*). William Make appears in Lanark, 1503 (*Lanark*, p. 13), and Jhone Make was tenant of the bishop of Glasgow, 1510 (*Rental*). Robert Mak witnessed sasine of lands in the territory of Quhitsumlawis, 1525 (*Home*, p. 35), and John Mak appears as witness in Linlithgow, 1538 (*Johnsoun*). Bessie Make in Saltoun was accused of witchcraft, 1629 (RPC., 2. ser. III, p. 16). John Mack was one of the nine witnesses who attested to the boundaries of the "thrie aikeres of land called Huttsonis Croft" in 1651 (*Home*, p. 220). John Mack was tenant in Gordon's Mains, 1713 (*Stitchill*, p. 167), and Marion Mack appears in Kirkcudbright, 1800 (*Kirkcudbright*). James Logan Mack was author of *The Border line from the Solway Firth to the North Sea*, Edinburgh, 1924.

MACKAIG. See under MACCAIG.

MACKAIL, MACKALE, MACKELL, MACCALE. G. *MacCathail*, 'son of CATHAL,' q.v. The MacCaills or MacCalls were an old Bute family. Finlay Macchaell was bailie of Rothesay in 1501. In 1506 Finlay Makcaill was recorded as of Dunawhunt, Bute, and John M'Kaill was retoured heir to his grand-uncle's son, Gilnow M'Kaill, in the third part of Ballecaule, Bute, 1575 (*Retours, Bute*, 7). Stephen Makaill appears in 1513 as servitor of the abbot of Arbroath (RAA., II, p. 541), and Svdoc McCaill is in record, 1540 (RSS., II, 3334). Johnne M'Caill was reidare at Sorby, 1574 (RMR.). Donald McCael witnessed sasine of lands at Duntrune, 1651 (*Genealogist*, new ser. XXXV, p. 230). William M'Quhaill in Ayr is doubtless an aspirated form of the name. Hugh M'Kail the martyr, 1640. A family of the name gave name to McKaill's land and Fauld Kaill in Rothesay. M'Caell 1663. See also MACALL.

MACKALL. See *under* MACALL.

MACKAIN, MACKANE. Current forms of MACIAN, q.v., the *c* of mac being repeated in pronunciation as in Mackay, Mackinlay, etc. Andrew M'Kaine (*vel* M'Kame) was retoured heir of John M'Kaine de Barnall, 1601 (*Retours, Bute*, 11).

MACKANDY. See *under* MACANDIE.

MACKANE. See *under* MACIAN.

MACKASKILL, MACKASKIL. Skye spellings of MACASGILL, q.v.

MACKAY, MACKIE, MACCAY. G. *MacAoidh*, 'son of AODH,' q.v. Nothing certain is known of the origin of the northern Mackays beyond the fact that they were early connected with Moray, and may have been a part of the ancient *Clann Morgunn*. The Inverness-shire Mackays are usually called in Gaelic *Mac Ái*, that is, MacDhài, or Davidson; they formed a branch of Clan Chattan (Skene, *Highlanders*, p. 421). In 1326 there is entry of a payment by Gilchrist M'Ay, progenitor of the Mackays of Ugadale, to the constable of Tarbert (ER., I, p. 53, and intro., p. lxxiv). Gilchrist Mac ymar McAy had a confirmation from Robert I of certain lands in Kintyre, to be held by him and his son, a minor, also named Gillichreist or Gilcrist, granted at Mayreth (Monreith) in Galwida, a. 1329 (RMS., I, App. I, 99). Odo Macidh was canon of Argyll, 1433 (*Pap. Lett.*, VIII, p. 468). Several payments were made to Robert Makgye (Macgye, Macye, M'Gy, Makgy, Magy), the king's jester between 1441–50 (ER., V). Gilnew McCay was tenant of Arskynnel Beg in

Kintyre, 1506 (ER., XII, p. 707), and Niniane Makke and George McKe of Myretoun are mentioned in 1538 (RSS., II, 642). Patrick McKe was burgess of Wigtown, 1575 (RPC., II, p. 503), and Daniel M'Cav was retoured heir of Iver M'Cay of Arnagiæ in the lands of Arnagiæ and Ughaddell and in the office of coronator 'insulae et limitum de North Kintyre,' 1662 (*Retours, Argyll*, 71). Percy Wallace MacKaye (b. 1875), an American dramatist and poet. The unique Gaelic charter of 1408 was granted by Donald, lord of the Isles, to Brian Vicar Mackay of Islay (facsimile in *Clan Donald*, I, opp. p. 1). In Islav and in a lesser degree in Kintyre the *a* of Mac is prolonged, the *c* becoming prefixed to the surname, thus MacAoidh becomes MacCaidh on the east side of the island next to Kintyre, MacCaoidh in the middle as at Laggan. It is MacAoidh in the Rhinns. M'Akie 1559, McCa, McCaa, McKa, and McKaa all 1684, MacCey 1719, MacIye 1781, Mackai 1619, Maickie 1600, McKeiy 1618, Makhe 1538, Makie 1558, Mackkye 1588, Makkcee 1506, Makkie 1600, M'Ky 1663, Maky 1513, Makky 1567, Meikkie c. 1649; Makcawe, Mc-Cei, Mackaw, Makay, M'Kee, McKev, Mc-Keve, Makkay, Makkaye, Makkey, Makee, Makkee, Macky, McKy, McKye.

MACKEACHAN. See *under* MACEACHAN.

MACKEACHIE. G. *MacEachaidh*. Robert M'Keachie in Darnow, 1711 (*Wigtown*). In 1684 the name appears as McCeachie, Mc-Cheachie, McKeachie, McKeachy (and without 'Mac' as Keachy, Cachie, Ceachie, Kaachie, Kachie, Kechie) (*Parish*). See also MAC-GEACHIE.

MACKEAMISH. G. *MacSheumais*, 'son of James.' A patronymic almost exclusively confined to descendants of Clan Gunn.

MACKEAN, MACKEAND. Forms of MACIAN, q.v., with the *k* sound carried over from mac and with accretional *d*. Johannes filius Gilberti filius Dovenaldi Mackane had a charter from Robert I of the land of Suthaych in 1329 (RMS., I, App. I, 100). Half of Estir Lanerky and Caschdrapane was leased to Donald McCane or M'Kane, 1480 (ER., IX, p. 561, 594). Andrew Makaynd "for railling on the magistrats...is ordained to the joges ane hour" and on the following sabbath to go "to the pillar foot in sackcloath," 1651 (*Rec. Elgin*, II, p. 278). The name occurs as M'Kaane and Makkaane in Strathardill in 1570 (*Laing*, 851). Nigel McCane was tenant in Islav, 1506 (ER., XII, p. 709), and Johne McKeane, a follower of Murdow M'Cloyd in the attack on the laird of Balcomie's galley in 1600 (RPC., xiv, p. cxxiii). When the Macians (Macdonalds) of Ardnamurchan were driven out of their native territory in the first half of the seventeenth century some settled on the east coast, and several became merchant burgesses of Elgin. The name (in its newer home) was variously spelled Mackean and Mackeand (*Clan Donald*, iii, p. 553–554). James M'Keand, burgess of Kirkcudbright, 1682 (*Kirkcudbright*), and Robert M'Keune, indweller in Edinburgh, 1661 (*Edinb. Marr.*). Six M'Keands are recorded in Galloway in eighteenth century (*Wigtown*), where the local pronunciation is M'Kyan. Spellings in the Elgin records are McKain, Makzane, and Makean. McKen 1760.

MACKECHRAN. A variant of MACEACHERN, q.v.

MACKEDDIE, MACKIDDIE. Forms of MACADIE, q.v. Donald M'Keddie, piper in King Edward, was accused in 1647 "for drinking the devills health and pyping to those who drank it" (*Jervise*, ii, p. 225). The form MACEDDIE is found in Inverness. McKeddey 1684, MacKedy 1647.

MACKEE. A variant form of MACKAY, q.v. John M'Kee was servant to John de Crauforde in 1460 (*Friars Ayr*, p. 50), and Patrick Makkee had a grant of half the lands of Dunguild, Bute, in 1506 (*RMS.*, ii, 2987). A man named Lang Mc ke was taken furth of the 'stokkis' wherein he had been placed by Simon McCristin, sheriff-depute in Wigtoun, 1513 (*Trials*, i, p. *89).

MACKEEGAN. North Uist surname. See under MACKIEGAN.

MACKEEKINE. A form of MACEACHAN, q.v., recorded in Glasgow.

MACKEEVER, MACKEEVOR. Variants of MACIVER, q.v. Old record spellings are: Mac Aver, Mac Geever, Mac Giver, Mac Iver, Mac Ivers, Mac Keaver, Mac Keever, Mac Keeves, Mac Keevor, Mac Keiver, Mac Keur, Mac Kever, Mac Kevors, Mac Kevor, Mac Kivers, Mac Ure, Ewers, Evers, Ivers, Keevers, Keeves, Ure.

MACKEGGIE, MACKAGGIE, MACCAGY. G. M'Adhamh or M'Edhamh, 'son of ADAM,' q.v. Gillemur Mac egu was witness to a convention between the Abbey of Scon and Adam, son of Odo, in the reign of Alexander ii (*Scon*, p. 53). Padmund Macego was juror on an inquisition concerning the lands of Thomas de Cremennan, 1320 (*Levenax*, p. 82). (It should be mentioned that Prof. Watson, i, p. 197, thinks the name in these two entries is perhaps for *M'Égu*, from *Mo'fhécu*, the reduced affectionate form of the name Fechin of Fobhar or Fore). Maldonyth Macego was witness to a Beauly document in 1532 (*Beauly*, p. 208, 210). William McAge McRethe and Johannes McAge Wikurlmor were parishioners of Duthil in 1537, and William McAgow witnessed letters of reversion at Tullochchro in the same year (*Grant*, iii, p. 268–269, 271). William MacAgo in Murthlac, 1550 (*Illus.*, ii, p. 261). Maldonyth M'Ego is cited to Fortrose Cathedral, 1532. Complaint was made against Alexander M'Agie in Caddell, 1578 (RPC., iii, p. 51). William McConeill VcAgow in Lagane and Alester McEan Riauche VcAgawne in Foirtirletter were fined for reset of Clan Gregor, 1613 (RPC., xiv, p. 630, 631). John McWilliam VcAge in Wester Inirrurie and others of the same name were charged with murder in 1615 (ibid., x, p. 404). James M'Aga in 1617 was one of Clan Cameron, and a M'Ago in 1602 was a follower of Macdonald of Keppoch. John Rioche McAgie in Achurrachen and John Thomas VcAgie in Innerrowie were denounced rebel, 1619 (RPC., xi, p. 574). John McAgo in Meikle Trochrie complained of wrongful imprisonment, 1642 (ibid., 2. ser. vii, p. 298), and Dougall M'Kygo appears in Kerara, 1686 (*Argyll*). M'Egie 1635, M'Cagi and M'Cagie 1641.

MACKEICH. A patronymic recorded in the shires of Perth, Stirling, and Argyll. It represents G. MacShithich, 'son of the wolf,' from * sithech, an old Gaelic name for the animal. The initial s is lost by aspiration and the sound of k carried over from the c of Mac. The name is sometimes spelled in Gaelic M'Ithich and M'Cithich. Donald Beg M'Keich and Duncane Rov M'Keich were tenants in Callelocquhane, 1594, and Donald Ammonach M'Keich was tenant in Clagane in the same year. Finlay Kyill McKiech in Branachyle was fined for aiding Clan Gregor, 1613 (RPC., xiv, p. 642), and the name is recorded in Tulloche in 1629 as M'Kevoche (RPC., 2. ser. iii, p. 236). Shiach M'Keich in Eister Ledchrosk in 1638 (BBT., p. 401). John M'Keich in Lix had two horses stolen from him in 1682 (RPC., 3. ser. vii, p. 637), and Duncan M'Keich appears in Kinlochkeilsport, 1698 (*Argyll*). A sailor of this name, a native of Glen Etive, composed to a local beauty the popular song 'Màire Bhàn Dhail-an-eas' (Sinclair, *Oranaiche*, p. 252), and an earlier poet of the name, John Mackeich, was author of the hymn 'Laoidh Mhic Cithich.'

MACKEITH. A form of MACKEICH, q.v. Donald McKethe was a crown tenant in Ed-

MACKEITH, *continued*

dirgolle, 1480 (ER., IX, p. 574). John M'Cayth was servant to James Kayth in 1592 (*Sc. Ant.*, VI, p. 167). John McKeith in Glenfinlas was charged with violence and robbery in the same year (RPC., V, p. 28). Sheep and oxen were stolen from Nauchtane McKeith in Kyllinane, Islav, 1629 (*Cawdor*, p. 271), and Iain M'Keith and Donald M'Keith, his brother, were among those massacred at Dunavertie in 1647 (HP., II, p. 257).

MACKELERAN. A corruption of MACIL-HERAN, q.v.

MACKELLAICH, MACKELLAIG, MACKELLAIGH. In South Uist. See under MACKELLY.

MACKELL. *See under* MACKAIL.

MACKELLAR, MACKELLER, MACELLAR, MACELLER. G. *Mac Ealair*, 'son of Ealair,' the Gaelic form of Latin Hilarius, the name of the bishop of Poitiers, commemorated in the *Felire* of Oengus at 13 January. Hilarius was one of the jury in the trial in 1233 concerning the lands of Monachkeneran (RMP., p. 167). Patrick McKellar was a charter witness at Carnasserie in 1436 (*Poltalloch Writs*, p. 71). A precept of sasine was addressed in 1470 by the earl of Argyll to Cristin M'Callar of Ardare (OPS., II, p. 47), and in 1476 James III granted to Gilchrist Makalere the lands of Ardare and Cragmurgile in the barony of Glastray (RMS.). Archibald Makelar of Argile, 'Scottyshman,' had a safe conduct to travel in England, 1488 (*Bain*, IV, 1550), and Michael M'Kalar witnessed seizin of Cragniche to Archibald, earl of Argyll, 1493 (OPS., II, p. 97). Gilbert McKellar of Ardare and Patrick McKellar are in record, 1496, at Kilmun (*Poltalloch Writs*, p. 183). Duncan McCallar or Makcaller was a charter witness at Dumbarton, 1500 (HP., IV, p. 22, 23). Martin M'Caller attested a Lamont instrument of sasine, 1525 (*Lamont Inv.*, p. 36), and Patrick M'Keller witnessed a Glenurquhay bond of manrent in 1528 (BBT., p. 179). Duncan Makkellar of Ardare was depute of Colin, earl of Argyll in 1518 and in 1538 Gilleane M'Callar was one of the bailies of Earl Archibald (OPS., II, p. 47). Thomas M'Callar was procurator in Perth, 1550 (*Rollok*, 113), Duncan M'Ilpatrik VcKellart was a charter witness in 1553 (OPS., II, p. 47), and Gilmertine M'Eller or MacEllere was concerned in the murder of the laird of Calder, 1594 (HP., I, p. 181). Ellar McKellar in Arinaughton, a witness in 1688 (RPC., 3. ser. XIII, p. 303). Angus McKellor was ordered to be transported to New England, 1685 (ibid., XI, p. 94). Goods were

plundered from Ellar McEllar and Duncan McEllar in Stukskardan, Glenshire, 1679, by Macdonalds and Camerons (*Argyll MSS.*, p. 629). Archibald McKellar (1844-1901), born in Paisley, won national fame as a sculptor in the United States. McAlar 1525, Mc allar 1515, MacCeller 1600, McKelar 1686, McKellayr 1520; old Mackillor.

MACKELLY. G. *Mac Ceallaigh*, 'son of Cellach,' i.e. the 'warlike' one. The Mackellies or Mackailes of Gaitgill were no doubt descended from Gilmalgon (read Gilmahagon) MacKelli who witnessed Abbot Arnald's gift of the lands of Duueglas to Theobald the Fleming (Theobaldus Flamaticus), c. 1150 (*Kelso*, 107). Kalman McKelli and Michael, his brother, were two of the 'chief men of Clenafren,' in Galloway, in 1298 (*Bain*, II, p. 253). Payments were made to Roger McKelli in Culane, Inverness, in 1340 (ER., I, p. 458, 462). John McCelly, witness in Abercorn in 1363, is probably John M'Kelli or M'Kelly, clerk of liverance to Queen Euphemia, who appears in record in 1364 and succeeding years (ER., II; RMS.). Oswald Mackelly was bailie of Edinburgh in 1392 (*Egidii*, p. 28), and Andrew M'Kelli appears as a witness in Wigtownshire in 1426 (RMS., II, 185). Thomas M'Kelle who acquired the lands of Gaitgill, Dumfries, in 1476, and had sasine of the lands of Gategilmakilvernak in 1493 and 1498 (*Edgar*, p. 196; ER.) is doubtless the umquhile Thomas McKelle of Gategill, father of Duncan McKelle, mentioned in 1503 (RSS., I, 998). Thomas Makelly, a follower of the earl of Cassilis, was respited for murder in 1526 (RSS., I, 3386). The name still exists in Wigtownshire as Kelly, and some of the family have changed to Macculloch. The Mackellys (*Mackellaig* or *Mackellaigh*) of Mull have changed their name to Macdonald. In 1684 the name was spelled McKeallie and also appeared in that year without the 'Mac' as Kellie, Kail, Kaill, Kailzie, Kale, and Kalie (*Parish*). (2) There was also a family of this name of some importance in Perthshire in the fourteenth century. Robert II confirmed the charter by which Andrew de Valoniis, knight, granted John McKelly or M'Kelli, son of quondam Galfridus McKelly, all the lands of Byniane with pertinents in the barony of Methfen, 1374 (RMS., I, 613, 707). John McKelly had a confirmation charter of "quatuor acris terre infra vicecomitatum de Strivelyne" in 1376 (ibid., 565).

MACKELVIE, MACKELVEY, MACKELVY, MACKILVIE. G. *Mac Shealbhaigh*, 'Selbach's son.' Sealbhach mac Shealbhaich is the hero in the tale of the Balieveolan Glassrig (Macdougall, *Folk tales and fairy lore*, 1910, p. 216). Morice Macsalny of Dumfriesshire rendered homage, 1296. His seal bears a hunting horn stringed, S' *Morici f' salni* (*Bain*, II, p. 210, 557). In 1300 we have record of an allowance to Mathew, son of Maurice Make Salui, a Galloway hostage (ibid., 1179; *Hist. Docs.*, II, p. 426). Robert M'Kelvie in officecroft in Tongueland, 1736 (*Kirkcudbright*), and Andrew M'Kelvie was barn-officer of the earl of Stair, 1744 (*Wigtown*). In 1684 the name appears (*Parish*) as McKelvie, McIlvey, McIwie, McKelway, Kelvie (Kelvy).

MACKEMMIE. A form of MACKIMMIE, q.v. Francis Makemie, "Founder of American Presbyterianism," was born in county Donegal, Ireland, c. 1658, of Scots parentage. James M'Kemy in Horswood, 1679 (*Kilbarchan*). McKemie 1662.

MACKENABRY. Dean Monro in his "Description of the Westerne Iles" (1549) says that the island of Rum "appertained to Mac-Kenabry of Coll" (Macfarlane, *Geographical collections*, III, p. 280). This is merely an English rendering of Gaelic *Mac Iain Abraich*, 'son of John of Lochaber.'

MACKENDRICK, MACKENRICK. See under MACHENDRIE. John M'Inrig in Mennockmiln, 1601, denounced to the Privy Council. M'Cenrick c. 1740.

MACKENECHOW. McKenechow or Mc-Kinchow was the original name of the Dewars of Kilchoan. A person of this name was beadle of Inveraray parish church, 1660 (*Poltalloch Writs*, p. 77). Duncan M'Kenechow in Inveraray, 1689 (*Campbell*, I, p. 1).

MACKENNA, MACKINNA, MACKINNEY, MAC-KINNIE. Galwegian surnames. G. *MacCionaodha*, 'son of Cionaodh.' Nevin M'Kenze in Wigtown, 1473 (ALHT., I, p. 9). William M'Kinnav, charter witness in Wigtownshire, 1544 (RMS., III, 3063), and John Mackvnnav in Crav, Kirkcudbrightshire, is recorded in 1546 (ALHT., VIII, p. 200). Alexander M'Kinnie was retoured heir of Normand M'Kinnie of Knokdorie in the lands of Rosnevth, 1609 (*Retours, Dumbarton*, 13). Ferquhard M'Kynnie of Levinchullein was retoured heir of Ferquhard M'Kynnie, his father, in lands of Levinchullein in Bute, 1662 (*Retours, Bute*, 65). John M'Hynnie appears in Tarehillis in 1667 (*Dunblane*), and John M'Kennay late at Miln of Bootle (Buittle), 1753 (*Kirkcudbright*). In the south end of Arran the natives "genteelly narrowed the more open vowel sounds by crimping the lips," hence Arranese M'Kinyie and Galwegian M'Kinnie. Mackena,

McKennah, McKeney, McKenney and Kinney filius are recorded in 1684 (*Parish*). M'Kenie 1663. Kennauch Makvny was present at pleas held at Dull, in Atholl, 1264 (RPSA., p. 349).

MACKENNAN. Malcolm McKenyn was juror on an inquest held at Drumfrese (Dumfries), 1367 (RHM., II, p. 64). A discharge in favor of William M'Kennane is recorded in 1542 (*Anderson*), and Andrew M'Kenen, shoemaker, is in Kirkcudbright, 1771 (*Kirkcudbright*). McKennand 1585.

MACKENRICK. *See under* MACKEN-DRICK.

MACKENSEN, the name of the Austrian general in the first Great War has been explained by some as of Scottish origin from Mackenzie. It, however, is German, derived from the vill of Mackensen (from Mackanhusen) in Hildesheim, which takes its origin from the Old High German personal name *Macco*.

MACKENZIE. Pronounced Mackaingye. G. *MacCoinnich* or *MacC(h)oinnich*, 'son of Coinneach.' In Adamnan the name is *Cainnechus*, which is an adjective from the root *cann*, 'fair, bright.' The English form of the name is interesting as preserving the mediæval Gaelic pronunciation of the genitive, which in early Irish is *Cainnigh*, pronounced 'cainny.' Makbeth Makkyneth was present at pleas held at Dull in Angus, 1264 (RPSA., p. 349). Kenzocht (*z* here = guttural *y*) M'Kenzocht of Kintail is recorded in 1491 (SCM., IV, p. 191; *Beauly*, p. 307), and Canoth Makcanehe and Kanoth Makkanehy in 1499 (*Rose*), perhaps the same person. Ewin Makkenye was 'sone and air' to Kenyeoch Maksorle in the Black Isle, 1500 (ibid., p. 169), and Alan McConze was tenant of Culcowe, Ardmanoch, 1504 (ER., XII, p. 662). Donald M'Kenve and Sorle M'Kenve took part in the second hership of Petty, 1513 (*Rose*, p. 190). Gilcrist Makkingze in Wigtownshire was charged with forethought felony, 1513 (*Trials*, I, p. 93*). Kannich oig McKannych Vc ane reoch was fiar of Calzenuchane, 1581 (*Poltalloch Writs*, p. 72), and Johannes M'Kenzie, apparent of Apilcroce, had a charter of the lands of Kildin with the mill in 1606 (RD., p. 498). Makcainze 1570, Makcanze 1571, M'Canzeoch 1551, M'Cenzie 1560, MkEnzi 1678, M'Einzie 1566, MacEnzie 1549, Mc-Hinzie, McHingzie, M'Hunzie, and McKinzie all 1684, M'Kainzie and M'Kenzoch 1586, McKanve 1590, McKanvee 1629, M'Kanze 1544, Mackeanche and Makkanchy 1499, M'Keanzie 1662, Makeinny 1629, Makeinzie 1597, McKenyee 1642, McKenvie 1650, Makenze 1528, Makkangze and McKangzie

MACKENZIE, *continued*

1569, Makkanze 1573, Makkeeinzev 1649, M'Kenezie and M'Keinezie 1620, M'Keinzie 1633, M'Kenich 1532, Makkenv 1663, Makkenvch 1567, Makkennych 1545, Makkenze 1509, M'Kenzocht 1546, McKenzv 1721, M'Kinze 1530, Makkinze 1513, M'Kynich 1718. The adventures of Donald Mackenzie (c. 1783-1851), fur-trader and governor of the Hudson's Bay Company, are recorded in Washington Irving's *Astoria*. "He weighed over 300 pounds, but was so active that he was called 'perpetual motion.'"

MACKEOCHAN. *See under* MACEACHAN.

MACKEON, MACKEOWN, MACKEOWAN, MACKEWAN, MACKEWN, MACKOUN, MACKUENN, MACKUNE. All current variants of MACCUNN, q.v. Woulfe (p. 359) also suggests that these names may also be from *MacEoin*, 'son of John,' as their Anglicized forms "are pronounced so nearly alike that it is impossible to distinguish them." Ninian M'Keun was witness in Lanarkshire, 1513 (*Ros*, 41). David M'Kowne or M'Kownne, notary in Glasgow (*Protocols*). John M'Kewne was retoured heir of John M'Kewne, portioner of Durisdeir, *avi*, 1643 (*Retours, Dumfries*, 180). Andrew M'Keun, shoemaker in Kirkcudbright, 1750 (*Kirkcudbright*). Some Mackeowns in Galloway have changed to Macewing. Old: M'Keun, M'Kounne.

MACKERACHER, MACERCHAR, MACKERCHER, MACKERICHER. *See* MACERCHAR.

MACKERLEY, MACKERLIE, MACERLICH. From G. *Mac Thearlaich*, 'son of Charles.' A common surname in Breadalbane from two to three hundred years ago. Neil M'Ewin M'Kerlich, an accomplice of Donald Gorme of Slate, had remission for his share in laying waste Trouterness in Skye, 1541 (RSS., II, 3943). Decreet against William McCairlie in Quhitherne (Whithorn), 1577 (RPC., II, p. 646). Archibald M'Carlie was occupier of the two mark land of Grenen, Kintyre, 1596 (HP., III, p. 74), and Vᶜ Herloch, 'grandson of Charles,' appears in 1584 (*Poltalloch Writs*, p. 185). Donald Makerliche possessed the seven markland of Ardewnak in 1591 (BBT., p. 248). John McKerlich in Finlarg was fined for reset of Clan Gregor, 1613 (RPC., XIV, p. 635), and Callum M'Kerlich was one of the laird of Glenurquhav's tenants, 1638 (BBT., p. 399). M'Cairlich and Charlieson in BBT., appear to have been Campbells originally, and in Argyllshire they appear under the old name of M'Kerliche (Rev. P. J. Campbell in *Celt. Mon.*, September, 1907).

McCarlie, McCairly, M'Carole, McKairlie, McKairly, McKcairlv, McKearlie, and McKearly, all in 1684 (*Parish*).

MACKERN. A variant of MACKERRON, q.v.

MACKERRACHER. *See under* MACERCHAR.

MACKERRAL, MACKERREL. Ir. *MacFhearghail*, 'son of Fearghal,' a name which means 'super choice.' An old surname in Ayrshire. According to Paterson the first of the name in record is Sir John M'Kirel who distinguished himself at the battle of Otterburne, 1388. The name, however, is found earlier. Recherus Mecmaccharil witnessed confirmation by Dunekan, earl of Karic of a charter by Roger de Scallebroc of lands in Carrik in the reign of William the Lion (*Melros*, p. 26), and as Radulfus Makerel witnessed a charter by Richard de Moreville of lands in Roxburgh to the Abbey of Melrose in the same reign (ibid., p. 95). Gilbert M'Corrill was a tenant under Douglas in the barony of Buittle, 1376 (RHM., I, p. lx). Gilbert Makcarole was tenant of the Grange of Ballyndune super Cree, 1481 (ER., IX, p. 583). Another Gilbert M'Carole, witness in Dumfries, 1534, appears again in 1541 as M'Carrule (RMS., III, 1418, 2603), and in same year as Makcarrell, servant to William McGe of Balmage (RSS., II, 4155). William Makcarole, tenant of Balcrag, Wigtownshire, 1563 (ER., XIX, p. 512). William McKeirell, sheriffclerk of Ayr, 1595, appears in two following years as McCarrell and McKerrell (ER.). William M'Kerrell was retoured heir of William M'Kerrell in Hilhous, his father, in the parish of Dundonald, 1630 (*Retours, Ayr*, 264). Neell McKerll, tenant of Nosbrig, Islay, 1686 (*Bk. Islay*, p. 501). M'Carole 1583, M'Kerell 1602, M'Kirrell 1659, Makerrell 1643; Makcarall.

MACKERRAS. From G. *M'Fhear'us* for fuller *MacFhearghuis*, 'son of FERGUS,' q.v. Duncan M'Karas or M'Keras, tenant of Kernach or Kerynach, Strogartnay, in 1483, appears again in 1499 as McKervis (ER., IX, p. 594, 621; XI, p. 416). John McKerris of Kentyr is mentioned in 1519 (*Cawdor*, p. 130). Willelmus McRobert McKerwyss and Finlaius McRobert McKerwyss were parishioners of Duthil, 1537 (*Grant*, III, p. 269). In 1547 the lands of Stronechreiffiche in the bailliary of Cowell were granted to Makane V'Kerris and Gillebarchane his son, and four years later Gillebarchane was seised in the same lands (OPS., II, p. 78). Johne M'Kearrois appears in Inverness, 1575 (Mill, *Plays*, p. 257), and Finlay McDonchy McKerris apparent of Glenselche, a charter witness in 1582 (*Poltalloch Writs*, p. 135). John Roy Mcfergus appears in Balloch, 1585 (FB., p. 357, 365). Alexander M'Kerras in Bollimenoch was denounced rebel in 1675 (HP., I, p. 297), Callum McKerreis held a kerrowrane in Islay, 1686 (*Bk. Islay*, p. 492), and John McKerrois and Donald McKerrois were tenants in Carabollis in the same year (ibid., p. 517). Donald Mackeroes of Glenselloch was one of those charged with part in the massacre of Lamonts at Dunoon, 1646 (*Lamont*, 786). Duncan M'Kerres in Dalmadie, a Glenurquhay vassal, 1638 (BBT., p. 403), John Bain Mc erras and Patrick Mc erras, rebels in parish of Strachur, 1685 (*Commons*, p. 11). Catharine M'Karras appears in Edinburgh, 1688 (*Edinb. Marr.*), and Donald M'Kerash was tenant in Corspollan, 1730 (*Isles*). Sir Walter Scott, referring to his friend Captain (afterwards Sir) Adam Ferguson, described him as a Highlander whose forbears were known as 'M'Erries.' The Mackerras's or Fergussons of Glensellich and adjacent parts about Strachur were an old race, and are numerous in that parish to this day (HP., IV, p. 26–27). Daniel Fergusson the last of the family who held the lands died in 1805. M'Carish 1671, M'Herreis 1677, MacHerries 1661, McHerres 1608, McKaras and McKearass 1692, Mc Keraish 1662.

MACKERREL. See under MACKERRAL.

MACKERRICHER. See under MACER-CHAR.

MACKERRON, MACKERN. A shortened form of MACILHERAN or MACILHERRAN, q.v., a once common name, particularly in Bute. Gillepatrik Mc Kerin or Makerin held land in Lanarkshire in reign of Malcolm IV (*Neubotle*, p. xxxvi). M'Kerin is given as the name of the blacksmith traditionally credited with the construction of the celebrated cannon "Mons Meg" at Kirkcudbright in 1452. Joh. Makcherane, witness in Bute, 1519 (RMS., III, 1321). Grissel M'Kerron is in record in Chappeltown, Moray, in 1688.

MACKERROW. A surname in Ayrshire, Dumfriesshire, and Galloway. It has been explained in WScot. as G. *Mac Cearrach*, Ir. *Mac Cearrbhaich*, 'son of the gamester.' Woulfe says = G. *Mac Ciothruadha*, 'son of Ciothruaidh,' a name of Norse origin. A writer in WScot. says probably for MacJerrow, the *j* being lost.

MACKESSAN, MACKESSON, 'son of KESSAN,' q.v. Gillecrist Mackessan was juror on an inquest in Lanarkshire, 1263 (APS., I, p. 102; *Bain*, I, 2338). Newyn Mackessan was one of the inquest which found that the daughters of the late Finlay of Campsie were the lawful heirs of deceased Dufgall, brother of Maldowen, earl of Lennox, 1271 (*Red Bk. Menteith*, II, p. 218). Finlay, son of Kessan the clerk, had a grant from Donald, earl of Levenax, c. 1350, of an annual payment from the lands of Ladlewin, in the parish of Killearn (*Levenax*, p. 60). Donald McKessane had a lease of half of Branoquhalve, 1480 (ER., VIII, p. 562). Gilbert Makesayne in Cowall, 1631 (*Sasines*, II, 383). McKesone 1480, McKison 1717, M'Kysone 1663, Makkessane 1486.

MACKESSIE. Donald Mackessie witnessed a charter by John of Ila, Dominus Insularum, 1486 (CAB., p. 458).

MACKESSOCK, MACKESSACK, MACKISSACK, MACKISSOCK, MACKISSEK. From G. *Mac Iosaig*, 'son of ISAAC,' q.v. In 1476 the lands of Ardere in the barony of Glastray were resigned by Mariot, daughter of Molmoria M'Kesek (RMS., II), and Donald Makessaig recorded at Kilmun, 1496, is probably the Donald McEsayg of 1511 (*Poltalloch Writs*, p. 183). John M'Intheir was convicted in 1623 for letting M'Keissik's bairnis die for hunger in Breadalbane (BBT., p. 379 — there was probably a famine). Marion MacKissock was resident in the parish of Boyne, 1684 (RPC., 3. ser. IX, p. 567), Elspet M'Kissick in Belliclone, parish of Madertie, 1688 (*Dunkeld*), and Duncan M'Kissoch or M'Kessogg was a Jacobite prisoner of the '45 (*Prisoners*, III). Cadrain MacCisaig was resident in South Uist, 1871. There is a sept of Mackissocks on the coast of the Moray Firth who probably came there with Colin, earl of Argyll, who married the daughter of the Regent Moray. Makesaig 1592, Makkessake 1591, McKisack 1684.

MACKESTER. A tenant of this name is recorded in 1480 (ER.). Mackeistair was a common surname in Breadalbane two hundred and more years ago (SN&Q., III, p. 172). "The Hays of Kenmore district are said to have come originally from the parish of Yester, and were therefore called 'MacYester' locally" (FB., p. 358). Duncan Mceister in Portbane, 1698 (FB., p. 358). Finlay M'Kester in Kenmore, 1685 (DPD., I, p. 488), and Patrick M'Keaster in Miltoun of Strathbrain, 1748 (*Dunkeld*).

MACKETTRICK, MACETTERICK, MACKETTERICK, MACKITTERICK, MACKITTRICK. Variant forms of the same name all in current use in Galloway. In Gaelic the name is spelled *Mac Shitrig*, 'son of Sitric' or 'Sitrig,' from the ON. personal name *Sigtryggr*, 'true vic-

MACKETTRICK, MACETTERICK..., cont'd
tory.' The name being in the genitive in Gaelic causes the initial S to be lost by aspiration, and the k-sound of c carried over from Mac. The *Annals of Ulster* under the year 892 record great confusion among the Norsemen under the son of Imhar (= Ivar) and Sichfrith, and three years later is the entry: "Sitriucc son of Imhar was slain by other Norsemen." John M'Kethirrvke appears as tenant in "villa de Prestoun" in 1376 (RHM., I, p. lxi). In 1460 the fine of John M'Kittrick in Kirkcudbright was remitted (ER., VII, p. 5), and Thomas Makettrik and his heirs had a charter of the lands of Kelauch in Galloway in 1476 (RMS., II, 1256). John Mc Quhitrig witnessed a charter of amortization by Alexander Gillert, rector of Newlands, 1504 (*Soltre*, p. 325), and Patrick Makketrig in Galloway in 1529 had a respite for his "tressonable intercommonyng with Inglismen" (RSS., II, 431). Robert M'Quhittroche in Culquha (Kirkcudbright) was a charter witness in 1643 (*Laing*, 2330), and John MacKittrick and John Kittrick (without the 'mac') were residents in the parish of Borgue in 1684 (RPC., 3. ser. IX, p. 567). John M'Whitrock appears in Raentone, 1687 (*Kirkcudbright*). The name is also current under the form MUNKITTRICK. Some of this name have changed to Ketteridge as 'more genteel' (*Trotter*). McKitrick 1641.

MACKEURTAN, MACCURTAIN. G. *MacArtáin*, 'son of Artan,' a diminutive of Art, an ancient Irish personal name. Donald Makcurtane who witnessed a · charter by Francis Bothwell, dated at Kirkwall and Halyrudehous in 1572 (RMS., III, 2389), appears two years later as servitor to M. Francis Bothwell, treasurer (REO., p. 350). A family of the name were for generations gardeners in the Isle of Menteith to the Grahams, earls of Menteith (Hutchison, *The Lake of Menteith*). John M'Cartein in Lanevstein, parish of Port, 1666. McCourtoune 1701, M'Keurtane 1692, M'Uretoune 1705, M'Cartein.

MACKEWAN, MACKEWN. See *under* MACKEON.

MACKIACHAN. Formerly an Islay surname. A variant of MACKICHAN, q.v.

MACKIBBON. A form of MACGIBBON, q.v.

MACKICHAN. The same as MACKEICH, q.v., with diminutive -an. Current in Argyllshire. Popularly explained as from *Mac Fhitheachain*, 'son of the little raven' (*Celt. Mon.*, IX, p. 179). "Once upon a time" it is said, when taking a child to be baptized it was customary to give it the name of the first living thing that was met on the way. When the ancestor of the Mackichans was being taken to church a raven met the procession, and accordingly the child was named *Mac Fhitheachain*. Mitchell's suggestion (*History of the Highlands*), possibly derived from Sir Walter Scott, that this name and Mackeith are from *ceathach*, 'mist,' is erroneous. Patrick M'Finlay fyan V'Kiachan, bailie of earl of Argyll, 1576 (*Notes and queries*, 11 July, 1931, p. 22). MACKIACHAN is another form of the name.

MACKIDDIE. See *under* MACKEDDIE.

MACKIE. This name is of considerable antiquity in Stirlingshire, and can be traced in Stirling to the fifteenth century. William Makke, charter witness in a Scone charter, 1491 (*Scon*, p. 199). John Make was 'factour and inbringar of all anualis pertenyn' to Sir John Patonsoun in Stirling, 1520 (SBR.). Andrew Makky was burgess of Stirling, 1574 (RPC., II, p. 418). Donald McCay in Porte of Locharne to answer to charge of violence and robbery, 1592 (RPC., v, p. 27). The Mackies of Mid Galloway, a powerful and prosperous family of the sixteenth and first half of the seventeenth century, were enthusiastic supporters of the Covenanters. Vthreid McKie in Innermessene was accused of slaughter, 1606 (*Trials*, II, p. 515). Alexander Makkie of Stranord, 1628 (*Retours, Kirkcudbright*, 173). McKie, McKee, McKey, Makie > Kie, all 1684 (*Parish*). Cf. MACKAY and MACKIESON.

MACKIEGAN, MACKEEGAN, MACKEGGAN. G. *MacAodhagain*, 'son of Aodhagan,' a diminutive of Aodh. Mackiegans or Mackeegans are an old North Uist family, said to have come from Ireland c. 1600, but the name is found domiciled in the western Highlands before that date. Hew M'Kegane in Coill had a lease in 1567 of certain lands in this island for nineteen years (OPS., II, p. 834, 836).

MACKIESON, MACKISON. Pronounced Meekison. The name of an old family in Stirlingshire and in Perthshire and also of an old family in Inverurie, Aberdeenshire. Thomas filius Mackyson held land in Elgin, 1398 (REM., p. 325). Thomas Makysoun, 'tannator,' in Newburgh, 1402 (CRA., p. 385). Nicolle Makkesson or Makyssone was servant to Gilbert le Haye, one of the Scots hostages in England, 1424–25 (*Bain*, IV, 963, 986). John Makyson was a member of the Guild of Ayr, c. 1431 (Coll. AGAA., I, p. 229). Nicholas Makyson or Mackyson was tenant of part of Kethyk, 1467–73 (*Cupar-Angus*, I, p. 88, 147), and William Makison was admitted burgess of Aberdeen, 1477, Symon

Makeson in 1488, and William Makhesone in 1521 (NSCM., I, p. 26, 33, 47). Letters of custumary of Perth were granted to Andro Mackisoun, 1500 (RSS., I, 484), George Makesoun was notary public in Edinburgh, 1576 (Soltre, p. 138), and John Mackison sat in Scottish parliament as representative of Crail, 1612 (APS., IV). Makesone 1507, Makisone 1486. Cf. MACKESSAN, MACKIE.

MACKILL. A Galloway surname. Patrick M'Kille witnessed resignation of a tenement in Wigtownshire, 1475 (M'Kerlie, I, p. 339), and Gilcrist M'Kille witnessed sasine of Cragniche to Archibald, earl of Argyll, 1493 (OPS., II, p. 97). Cuthbert Makkill was concerned in the slaughter of Donald McEwin at the Cors of Balmaclellane, 1529 (RSS., II, 128). Hugh M'Kill, the Covenanter martyr, executed 22 December 1666, was son of Mathew M'Kill (Coltness Collections, p. 40, 41). Elizon M'Kill is recorded in Craigend, 1676 (Kirkcudbright), and Marion Maccill in Causiend was charged with being disorderly (i.e. nonconforming) in 1684 (RPC., 3. ser. IX, p. 571).

MACKILLAIG. A name still found in the Western Isles. It comes from the Norse personal name Kjallak-r (-r silent), which again was a loan from O. Ir. cellach, 'warrior,' a diminutive of cell, 'war.' See also MACKELLY.

MACKILLIAM. A form of MACWILLIAM, q.v. Robert McKilliam was a graduate of Aberdeen University in 1852.

MACKILLICAN, MACKILLIGAN, MACKILLIGIN, MACKILLICANE, MACGILLIGIN. G. Mac Gill' Fhaolagain, 'son of the servant of (S.) Faolagan.' Faolagan is a diminutive of Faolan, itself a diminutive. Cf. MACLELLAN. The surname, not now common, is confined mainly to Ross and Moray. Thomas McKelegan, who was charged with having 'crewkit' his master's 'hors in yokis, quhar throw he may nocht gang ane fyt' in 1561, is probably Thom or Thomas McKelecan who pleaded guilty in 1565 to having 'cassin dewattis (divots) vpon the ground betwix the schip and the cheppall yard wall' in Inverness (Rec. Inv., I, p. 59, 127). John McGilligaaie in Ardosier and Andro McGilligain there, followers of William McIntosche of Borland, and some others were to be apprehended for slaughter, 'open reifs, herships, fireraisings, and other crimes,' 1613 (RPC., IX, p. 558). John McGillican in Ardinscheir refused instruction in his craft of tanning, 1621 (RPC., XII, p. 491). The famous Covenanting minister of Fodderty, Rev. John M'Killican (d. 1689) is mentioned in the Brodie Diaries published by the Spalding Club in 1863 under the spellings M'Culican, M'Culi-

cam, M'Culikam, M'Culigan, M'Culigin, M'Culikan, M'Culiken, M'Gulican, M'Kelican, M'Kilican, M'Kilikin, McKillicane, M'Kulikan, and Makulikin. Elsewhere he is mentioned as M'Giligan and M'Clagine. Andro McKillican and others were ordered to find caution that none of them 'sall doe harme or skaith to any of the inhabitants' of Inverness, 1688 (Rec. Inv., II, p. 233–234). George H. D. M'Killigin from Forgue was killed in the first Great War (Turriff). M'Culligane 1631, McKillichane and McKilligane 1619, MacKilligin 1721.

MACKILLOP. G. Mac Fhilib, 'son of Philip,' but who the Philip was who first gave name is not known. The aspiration of the f in the genitive case causes it to disappear. Philip is originally a Greek personal name (Philippos) meaning 'horse-lover.' Some of this name are said to have been standard-bearers to the Campbells of Dunstaffnage, others are included as septs of Macdonald of Glencoe and of Macdonells of Keppoch, and Mackillop also occurs as a surname in Arran. Finlaius Macpilibh, priest of the diocese of Argyll, is in record in 1433 (Pap. Lett., VIII, p. 470), and in 1437 John, son of Fynlaius Prioris Macphilib, appears as perpetual vicar of Kilcalmonell (Sancti Colmaneli) in Cnapdul (ibid., p. 625). William Makillop, a follower of the earl of Cassilis, was respited for murder in 1526 (RSS., I, 3386). Donald M'Gillip is mentioned in 1532 (Macgregor, I, p. 87), Robert Makillip was a witness at Penkill, Ayrshire, in 1545 (RMS., III, 3160), Malcum M'Killib witnessed a Glenurquhay bond of manrent in 1547, Tharlocht M'Killib was a witness at 'Iill of Lochtay' in 1649 (BBT., p. 185, 189), and Duncan M'gillop in the Kirktone of Weeme is in record in 1692. Makellop 1509. The name is also current in the abbreviated form MACGILP. A family of this name took the name Macdonald on their intermarrying with the Keppoch family (Blundell, The Catholic Highlands, 1909, p. 139). The Gaelic "motto" of the family, Cadal cha'n aom air fear faire, is of twentieth century origin. McKillip and McKyllap 1692. See also MACGILP.

MACKILVAIN. A form of MACGILVANE, q.v., current in Galloway.

MACKILVIE. See under MACKELVIE.

MACKIM. Gaelic MacShim, 'son of Sim,' diminutive of Simon. Ranald McKym was tenant in part of Cullychmoir, Delny, in 1539 (ER., XVII, p. 667).

MACKIMMIE, MACIMMEY, MACIMMIE. G. MacShimidh, 'son of Simon' (Simmie), of

MACKIMMIE, Macimmey . . ., *continued*
old Mack Himy. Lord Lovat, chief of the ·
Frasers, was so styled patronymically by the
Gaels. Fraser narrating the birth of Simon
Fraser (1570) says of the name Simon: "A
name pretty rare in Scotland, south or north,
although kindly to this famely, being the first
name it had, and hence the Lord Lovat is called
M'Khimy" (*Wardlaw*, p. 160). The patronymic
is probably derived from the Simon Fraser
killed at Halidon Hill in 1333. In 1506 King
James iv granted in heritage to Ewin Mak-
kymme the half of Lepinquhillin in Bute and
to John Makkymmie the other half (RMS., ii,
2987). These Makkymmes may have been the
sons of Symon M'Watt who is in record in
1499. (RMS. wrongly spells the name M'Ky-
nine and Makkynine.) Sym Mak hymme is
recorded as one of the assize concerning the
lands of Garntulie in 1529 (*Grandtully*, i,
p. 69). The name also occurs as Mak Kymmy
in the remarkable letter addressed to Henry
viii of England by John Elder, 'Reddschancke,'
in 1542 or 1543 (*Coll.*, p. 28). Johannes
MacKymmey appears in Murthlac in 1550
(*Illus.*, ii, p. 262). Duncan Makymmie and
James Macfinlay Makemy gave their bond
to Duncan Campbell of Glenurquhay in 1586
(BBT., p. 240). Farquhard M'Kymmie was
retoured heir of Archibald M'Kimmie in the
lands of Levinchulling in Bute in 1609, and
in 1662 his son was retoured heir in the same
lands as Ferquhard M'Kynnie (*Retours, Bute*,
19, 63). Andrew McKimmie and John Mc-
Kimmie were fined in 1641 for reset of outlawed members of Clan Gregor (RPC., 2. ser.
vii, p. 489). John M'Kimmy appears in Iner-
marky, 1716 (SCM., iv, p. 169). Mackimmie
may have been in some instances Englished
as Simson or Simpson. See Maccamie.

MACKINCARDY. Gilbert M'Kincardy was
vicar of Kilmertyne, 1498 (RMS., ii, 2461).
He appears to be the same person as Gilbert
Duncanson who is mentioned as vicar in 1510-
11 (OPS., ii, p. 92). Perhaps *Mac-an-ceirde*,
'the smith's son.' Cf. John M'Kean M'William
M'Ago M'Kincairn in Strathspey, 1616.

MACKINDEW. A current form of Macindoe,
q.v.

MACKINDLAY. A form of Mackinlay, q.v.,
current in Fife.

MACKINLACKOUR. James McKinlackour
recorded in Strathdee in 1527 (*Grant*, iii,
p. 71n). This is not a patronymic but represents *Mac Fhionnlaidh odhair*, 'son of dun
Finlay.'

MACKINLAY, Mackinley. This name is the
Gaelic form of Finlayson, both meaning 'son
of Finlay,' q.v. In Gaelic orthography the
name is *MacFhionnlaigh*. The name is dis-
tinctively a Scottish one, but is found also
in the north of Ireland (Antrim) among the
descendants of the settlers of the Scots Plan-
tation of Ulster. Unlike most other Scottish
surnames beginning with Mac this name is not
a common one, occurring but sparingly in the
public records of the sixteenth and seventeenth centuries as M'Finlay (1663), McInd-
lay (1667), Macinle (1605), M'Kandlay and
M'Keandlay (1627), M'Kinla and Makkinla
(1528), McUinlay and McUnlay (1718), Mc-
Enlea 1706. The name occurs most commonly
in record in Glenlyon and in Balquhidder.
Gillaspyk M'Kynlay witnessed an instrument of
sasine of Cragniche (Craignish) to Archibald,
earl of Argyll in 1493 (OPS., ii, p. 97). Sir
John Finlosoun alias McAlan McKewilla (the
attempt of a non-Gaelic scribe to write Mac-
Fhionnlaigh) was vicar of Kilmorich in 1511
(RMS., ii). John M'Ynla attested a bond of
manrent in Glenurquhay in 1561 (BBT.,
p. 204), Malcolm M'Inley in Balliwilling was
denounced as a rebel in 1675 (HP., i), and
Donald M'Kindlay appears in Innerchocheill
in 1696 (*Dunkeld*), and six others of the name
are in the same record. John M'Keandla appears in Daill in 1661 (*Caithness*). William
McKinley, twenty-fifth president of the United
States, was descended from David McKinley,
an Ulster Scot, born about 1730, and his wife
Rachel Stewart. The Mackintoshes of Cams
(on R. Shee), are also known as "alias Mac-
inlies." McInlie here is = Mac Fhionnlaidh,
though it occurs in RPC., xi, as McLeith, Mc-
Cleich, McKinleiche, McIlleich (Mackintosh,
Mackintosh families in Glenshee and Glenisla,
p. 75-76).

MACKINNA. See under MACKENNA.

MACKINNEL, Mackinnell. Malcolm, earl of
Levenax granted to Dovenaldus Macynel
"unam terram in Glenfreone (Glenfruin) que
dicitur Kealbride que pro quarta parte unius
harathor tenentur," c. 1250 (*Levenax*, p. 91).
Robert M'Kynnell was retoured heir of Robert
M'Kynnell, his father, in the 40d lands of old
extent of Auchincreiche, Dumfriesshire, 1638
(*Retours, Dumfries*, 167). "The McKinnells
and MacKinnons of Dumfriesshire come of an
Highland Clan," and a family named Mc-
Kynnell were tenants of the conventual lands
of Bruntscairth prior to the Reformation, and
there was quite a colony of them in the neighborhood (*Edgar*, p. 77, 194). In 1684 (*Parish*)
the name appears as: McKinnell, McKindell,
McKindle, and shortened to Kinnell and Kin-
dell.

MACKINNES (Fife), MACKINNESS (Glasgow). Forms of MACINNES, q.v.

MACKINNEY, MACKINNIE. *See under* MACKENNA.

MACKINNON. G. *MacFhionghuin* or *MacFhionnghain*, in 1601 McFionguine (*Coll.*, p. 202). The old Gaelic personal name occurs in the Book of Deer in the genitive as *Finguni*. The middle Irish forms are *Finghin* and *Finnguine*, EIr. *Finguine*, and modern Irish *Findgaine*. These forms point to prehistoric Gaelic * *Vindo-gonio-s*, 'fair-born.' Finguine mac Drostain was killed in a civil war among the Picts at Monticarno in 728 (AU.). The Mackinnons, says Skene, were "closely connected with the abbacy of Iona, and repeatedly furnished abbots to that monastery" (CS., III, p. 363). Their connection with the affairs of Iona, however, as the editor of *Highland Papers* remarks, was "not always apparently to the advantage of the church" (HP., IV, p. 171; see also I, p. 83–84). In the old burial ground known as Cladh Beg at Kirkapoll, Tiree, is the tombstone of a prior of this name: *Fingonius. prior. de. Y. me. dedid. Philippo. Iohannis. et. svis filiis. Anno. Domini. M^oCCCC^oXCV^o* (Beveridge, *Coll and Tiree*, p. 150). Lachlann Makfingane witnessed a charter by Donald de Ile, dominus Insularum, to Hector Macgilleone, dominus de Doward, 1 November 1409 (recited in confirmation charter of 1495, RMS., II, 2264). A later Lachlann M'Fvnwyn de Myschenys witnessed a charter by the lord of the Isles in 1467 (*Cawdor*, p. 50). John, son of Lachlann, was abbot of Iona in the end of the fifteenth century. In 1489 he erected a cross in memory of his father and himself: *Hec: est: crvx: meic: Lacclanni: Fingone: et: eivs: filii: Iohannis: X: abbatis de Hy: facta: anno: domini: m^occcc^olxxx^oix^o* (Drummond, *Sculptured monuments in Iona*, pl. xxxvi). He died in 1500, and on the edge of his own monument is inscribed: *[Ioh]annes Macfingone abbas de Y qvi obiit anno dni millesimo qvin[gentesimo]* (ibid., pl. xlv). William Makfingoun who was reader in Paisley shortly after the Reformation, 1560 (RMR.; Lees, *Paisley*, p. 240) may be William Makkynnane who was presented to the parsonage and vicarage of Dingwall, 1587 (RSS.). Archibald M'Fingan and Neil M'Fingan in Sallum, Tiree, were denounced rebels in 1675 (HP., I, p. 296). In Kintyre and in Arran the local Gaelic pronunciation is MacEanain, and in Skye a current form of the name is Mac innon. A popular etymology is *MacIonmhuinn*, from *ionmhuinn*, 'dear' 'beloved,' which has led some Mackinnons to Anglicize their name 'Love' or 'Low,' but all

bearers of these names are not disguised Mackinnons. See LOVE. M'Fingon 1664, McFyngoun 1557, McGinowne 1662, Makenone and Makkynnon 1536, M'Kinin 1745, M'Kinnen 1673, M'Kinoun 1675, Mackiynnan 1545, Makkynine 1506, McKynnoun 1621, McKynnand 1586, McKynnowne 1609, McPhingone 1681, McYnun 1577. In the north of Ireland it has become McKennan, M'Cannon.

MACKINSTRY. Formerly a Galloway surname. M'Kinstrie 1593, M'Kynnistrie 1574. Woulfe says Ir. *Mac an Astrigh*, 'son of the traveller' (Ir. *aistrightheach*), an Ulster surname, probably of Scottish origin.

MACKINTOSH. *See under* MACINTOSH.

MACKINTY. Recorded in Aberdeen. From Ir. *Mac an tSaoi*, 'son of the scholar,' Ir. *saoi* (*Woulfe*, p. 318).

MACKINVEN. A surname at one time common in the west side of Kintyre. It is popularly but mistakenly believed to be a form of Mackinnon, but is really a Gaelic rendering of the well-known Ayrshire family name LOVE, introduced into Kintyre by persecuted Covenanters, to whom the peninsula was a haven of refuge. The Gaelic is *MacIonmhuinn* (in Kintyre *'AcIonmhuinn*), which may be rendered 'beloved son.' Donald M'Invine in Mull was a Jacobite prisoner of the '45 (*Prisoners*, III, p. 106).

MACKIOCK. Gilpatrick M'Keoick and Iain M'Keoick, his brother, were among those murdered at Dunavertie in 1647 (HP., II, p. 257). Alexander McKiock was tenant on the Chisholm estate in 1721 (HP., II, p. 301). John M'Coick in Auchachrossan in parish of Kilfinan 1697 (Argyll Inv.). Cf. M'COOK.

MACKIRDIE, MACKIRDY, MACCURDY. These surnames are common in the islands of Arran and Bute. In 1506 Gilcrist Makwrerdy held the lands of Bransar in Bute (*Hewison*, II, p. 174), and Finlay Makvreirdy had sasine of Brothok there in the same year (ER., XII, p. 720). Donald Makwrarty of Birgadulknok appears in 1534 (RMS., III, 1376); several M'Urartys appear as witnesses in Bute in 1540 (ibid., 2583); and Sir James M'Wartve, a Pope's knight, appears as vicar of Kingarth in Bute, 1554 and 1556. The latter's name, according to Hewison, is also spelled M'Verrit. James Makilveritie, chaplain in the chapel of S. Michael the Archangel in Rothesav Castle, between 1590–1600, appears in the *Exchequer Rolls* as McQuhirertie, McQuhirirtie, McQuheritie (these three spellings in 1596), McIllquharartie (1598), and Makquhirrirtie

MACKIRDIE, Mackirdy..., continued

(1600). Patrick M'Varthie was portioner of Stravanan, Bute, 1622 (Retours, Bute, 29); and Donald M'Urarthie in Kelspok is in record, 1662 (Isles). Donald M'Vurarthy sold his portion of Bruchog (the Brothok above) in 1708 (Hewison, II, p. 174). Donald M'Curthy appears in South Garrachty in 1663 (Isles), and Mr. James Currie or M'Curdie (1790–1887) was minister of Kilbride in Arran (Fasti). Flaithbertach mac Murcertaigh, 'princeps Duincaillden' (i.e. Dunkeld) obiit 873 (AU., s.a.). The name is occasionally cited in the Icelandic Sagas as Myrkjartan, the name of an Irish king (Landnámabók, 2, 18); more correctly as Myrkjartag in the Norwegian codex Fagrskinna (p. 158). As Myrjartak it occurs in the Agrip (Compendium) af Nóregs Konunga Sögum (li. 7, ed. 1929). The modern Gaelic is M'Urardaigh, from early muircheartach, 'sea-ruler,' or 'sea-director' (muir, sea, and ceartach, ruler, director). McKerdie (Bute) 1662, Makilwedy and Makwerich 1506, Makmurrarty 1547, M'Quiritei 1626, M'Vararty 1541, M'Verrathie and M'Verrachie 1600, Makvirrartie 1562, M'Vrathie 1623, MacVurarthie 1520, Makwararthe 1566, Makwarrarty 1517, Makweraith 1517, M'Werarche 1568, Makweraty 1539, M'Werarthie 1564, McWerarthe 1561, Makweriche 1506, M'Weyorauchtie 1566, M'Wrarthie 1642, M'Wrathie 1623, M'Wyrartie 1555; M'Vararthy, Mackwarrathy, Makwarartie, M'Wrerdie, M'Quartie.

MACKIRSTY. See under MACCHRISTIE.

MACKIRVAIL. See under MACKERVAIL.

MACKISON. See under MACKIESON.

MACKISSACK, Mackissock, Mackissek. See under MACKESSOCK.

MACKISTON. Perhaps a variant of Mackieston, recorded in Stirling.

MACKITCHEN. A variant of Machutcheon, q.v., recorded in Fife.

MACKITTERICK, Mackittrick. See under MACKETTRICK.

MACKIVER (in Renfrew). See under MACIVER.

MACKLEY. One of the many modern variants of Gaelic Mac Donnshleibhe. See MACLAE.

MACKLINNAN. A current variant of Maclennan, q.v., recorded in Aberdeen.

MACKNIGHT. A variant of Macnaught, q.v. Jonet Maknacht held the lands of Barskeauch before 1531 (ER., XIV, p. 484), and Gilbert M'Nacht appears as witness in the parish of Partoun, Kirkcudbrightshire, 1541 (Anderson). Jonet Mackneicht who held a charter of Kilquhyndry, Kirkcudbright, 1546 (ALHT., VIII, p. 200), may be the Jonet above mentioned. John McNeight was charged with being a disorderly person (i.e. non-conformist) in the parish of Kirkmabreck, 1684, James Machnight is in the parish of Cross-Michael, and William MacNaight, parish of Borgue, in same year (RPC., 3. ser. X, p. 567, 573, 582). Alexander M'Naight at the new milns, 1743 (Wigtown). The Macknights of Ayrshire and Galloway are said to be a branch of the Macnaughts of Carrick. McKnicht 1585, McKnaicht 1637, Makknacht 1535, M'Knaycht 1641. In 1684 (Parish): McKnaight, McKnaught, McNaight, and McNeight.

MACKNOCATER. McKnocater formerly a personal name in Banffshire. The name occurs in the Kirk-Session Records of Boharm in 1677 as McKnuketer. On Tayside the name occurred as MacNuckater and McNuchter. "This name has not been the proper patronymic of the bearers, but has been applied for the sake of distinction, to the particular branch of the clan to which they belonged. These distinctive names are still to be met with in the Highlands at the present day" (SN&Q., III, p. 158). Isobel M'Nocatter in Kilmarnock, 1603 (Glasgow). See under MACNUCATOR.

MACKNOCKITER. See under MACNUCATOR.

MACKONOCHIE. See under MACCONACHIE.

MACKOUN. See under MACKEON.

MACKRAY. See under MACRAE.

MACKUENN, Mackune. See under MACKEON. Originally perhaps from the Lochfyneside clan Macewan. This clan about 1450 was "broken" and shortly after a branch settled near Leswalt as retainers of the Agnews of Lochnaw. Thence they spread through Galloway and Kirkcudbrightshire.

MACKURY. A Barra form of the name MACRORY, q.v.

MACKYE. A current form of MACKAY, q.v., in Galloway.

MACLACHIE. A form of MACLACHLAN, q.v. Pronounced Maclach-ie (ch guttural). Patrick

M'Lachie, one of M'Nachtane's bowmen, shipped at Lochkerran for service in France, 1627, "stole away be nycht out of ye Ship" (HP., I, p. 114).

MACLACHLAN, MACLACHLANE, MAC-LAUCHLAN, MACLAUCHLANE, MACLAUCHLIN, MACLAUCHAN. G. *MacLachlainn*, 'son of LACHLANN,' q.v. In Irish record is entry under 1060 'Lochlainn Mac Lochlainn' (AFM.). In 1292 the lands of Gileskel Mclachlan and others in Lorn were erected into the sheriff-dom of Lorn (APS., I, p. 91). Gillaspy Mac-Lachlan was present at the parliament held at St. Andrews, 16 March 1308. His name occurs on the seal tag but not in the body of the document. It however may have occurred in the document where it is imperfect, causing a gap in the text (ibid., p. 99). There is an entry in 1327 of payment for maintenance of the son of Reginald son of Lauchlan (ER., I, p. 63). Richard Louchlani (Lat. gen.) was custumar of Stirling, 1328, and in the following year he appears as Ricardus filius Lochlane, sheriff of Stirling (ibid., p. 86, 179). Some time before 1425 Celestine Maclachlane had grant of the lands of Blarindess, Auchintroig, and Garthclachach in the earldom of Lennox (*Levenax*, p. 75). Lachlan Maclachlan of that Ilk witnessed a charter by Lord Home at Stirling, 1555–6 (*Poltalloch Writs*, p. 142). Dougall M'Ean V' Clauchtlan was a Glenurquhay vassal, 1638 (BBT., p. 403). The chief seat of the clan is in Cowal, Argyllshire, the lands of which were acquired by Gilleskel Maclachlan in 1292, and as early as 1314 we find their stronghold there referred to as 'Castellachlan,' i.e. Castle Lachlan. Some Maclachlans were for centuries hereditary captains of Innischonnel to the Argylls. They were probably originally Campbells as it is highly unlikely the custody of the chief fortress of Lochow would have been entrusted to members of another clan (HP., IV, p. 26). M'Clachlane 1643, M'Claichlane 1647, M'Clauchlane 1619, McClauchlan 1622, Makclachlane 1553, M'Clachlene 1590, Makclauchlane 1591, McLauchlane 1625, M'Lauchan 1621, McLauchleine 1692, Macklawchlane 1661, Maklawchlane 1548, M'Lawchtlane 1558, M'Llauchland 1699, M'Laughland 1667, McLawhlan 1704, Maclouchlan 1314, Vclauchlayne 1585. In 1684 (*Parish*): McClauchlin, McGlauchlin, McLaughlane, McLauchlen, Machlachlin. Maclachlan of that Ilk is mentioned in 1555 (*Poltalloch Writs*, p. 142). The name of Andreas Makclotan or Makclowden, student at St. Andrews University, 1467–69 (ERUS., p. 45, 48) is probably the same.

MACLAE, MACLAY, MACCLAY, MACLEA, MACLEAY. These names are commonly but in-correctly explained as from G. *Mac an leigh*. This is merely popular etymology due to the belief that the name means 'son of the physician,' and that the Macleays of western Sutherland are descended from Ferchard Leche, who had a grant of lands in Assvnt, 1386. The full form of the name is *Mac-Dhunnshleibhe*, 'son of Donnshleibhe,' as ex-plained under DUNSLEVE, q.v. In a royal com-mission of 1498 King James III directed certain persons to distrain the lands and goods of Kenyoch M'Conleif and Donald M'Conleif, co-raiders with Chisholm of Comar of the lands of Huchone Ros of Kilrawok (OPS., II, p. 527). Kenzoch or Kennitus M'Coleif held the king's lands of Cumree (Comrie) in Strathconon in 1504 (ER., XII, p. 663), behind Tor Achilty, where tradition placed the seat of the clan. John M'Ewin V' Dunslef appears at Sonnachan, Argyllshire, in 1502 (*Notes and queries*, 11 July, 1931, p. 21), and Finla Mak-gillecallum Makcolluf and John Roy M'Culloiff were tenants under Stewart of Appin in 1509 (*Stewarts of Appin*, p. 193). In 1518 the "clane McDowleanis" (an error for M'Dow-leavis) gave their bond of manrent to Sir John Campbell of Caldor (*Cawdor*, p. 129). The names given in the bond are: Duncan Brec McDunlane, and Jhone Mcdoulane 'his broder.' Dunslane McNeill is one of the parties to the bond, and in all three instances -laue has been misread -lane. John McYndayn Mc-Collef is mentioned in 1519 (ibid., p. 131). Odoni Makdouill Makdunlane [i.e. Makdun-laue] had a remission in 1524, and a son of Duncan M'Dunlewe was appointed minister of the two parishes of Killespic-Kerrill and Kilmaronock in 1541 (HMC., 2 Rep., p. 193). The northern Macleays were known to Sir Robert Gordon as the clan Leajwe; while thereafter they are known in record as Makley (in Alness 1651), M'Ley (in Contin 1677). Macleays were numerous in early times in Easter and Wester Ross and in Argyll. Of the southern Macleays was Jo. M'Ey V'Dunlaif in North Argyll, 1570 (*Cawdor*, p. 177). A cautioner was found for John McClay in Ayr-shire, 1584 (RPC., III, p. 714), and Donald M'Collea was one of Dunolly's men in 1588 (RPC., IV, p. 265), and Duncan M'Collea appears in same year (ibid., p. 333). Patrik M'Conlea in Finran was fined for reset of members of Clan Gregor in 1613 (ibid., XIV, p. 631), and Donald M'Onleif was servitor to Allan Cameron of Locheil in same year (RMS., VII, 871). Donald M'Clae was burgess of Glas-gow by purchase, 1617 (*Burgesses*), and Dun-can Dow McDonochie Brec *alias* McDonnslae and John McEane Dow VcDonochie Brec

MACLAE, MACLAY, MACCLAY..., *continued*
alias McDonnslae were charged with assault
and cattle-stealing, 1623 (RPC., XIII, pp. 270–
271). Mc onlea is a common record spelling
of the name, and its derivation is clearly shown
by the name of Dounslea M^conlea, tenant
of Schewnay, 1669 (HP., IV, p. 222). Donald
roy M'Onlay appears in Lunga, 1633 (*Notes
and queries*, 18 July, 1931, p. 44). Findlay
McClay and Malcolm McClay appear in Drakies in 1646 (*More Culloden Papers*, p. 50),
and Dunsla M'ein Vc onlea and Iain M'onlea,
his brother, were among those massacred at
Dunaverty, 1649 (HP., II, p. 257). Duncan
Mc onlea was bailie of Rothesay, 1662 (ibid.,
III, p. 12), and another Duncan M'Onlea was
burgess of Paisley, 1667 (*Isles*). Iain Mc onlew
was tenant of Torisay, Mull, 1669 (HP., IV,
p. 223), and Duncan M'Onlea, Duncan
M'Dunslea, and Neill M'Dimslea (an error
for Dunslea) appear in Islay, 1686 (*Bk. Islay*,
p. 508, 511). William Livingston, the Islay
bard, always wrote his name in Gaelic
M'Dhunleibhe, and Dr. David Livingstone,
the African traveller, was a Macdonleavy of
Ulva. Allan Dall gives another popular etymology of the name, which he makes to mean
'son of John the grey-haired,'

"Thagrainn cairdeas Mhic-Iain-Léithe
'S gur dìleas do m' chinneadh féin e,
Sheasadh air gach cnoc le chéile,
Nuair a dh' éireadh iad gu strì."

MACLAFFERTY. *See under* MACLAVERTY.

MACLAGAN, MACLAGGAN, MACLAGAIN. G.
M'Gill' Adhagain, 'servant of Adocan,' a
diminutive of ADAMNAN, q.v. In Strathtay the
G. spelling is *MacLathagain*. Donald Mak-
claagan was one of an assize concerning the
lands of Garntulie, 1529 (*Grandtully*, I, p. 69).
This spelling shows that the first *a* was long.
In 1556 there is recorded a renewal of a bond
of manrent for 'sythment and recompens' of
slaughter of John M'Gillenlag (BBT., p. 200).
George M'Lagane is in Dunkeld, 1587. William
McGlagane and John McIlglegane were fined
for reset of Clan Gregor, 1613 (RPC., XIV,
p. 632), and Duncan M'Clagane was minister
of Logierait, 1632.

MACLAINE. *See under* MACLEAN.

MACLAIRISH. This is one of the oldest sept
names of Macdonalds of the north (*Adam*,
p. 145).

MACLALLAND. *See under* MACCLELLAN.

MACLAMMIE. A form of MACLAMOND, q.v.
It is further shortened to LAMMIE. McLemme
1527.

MACLAMOND, MACLAMONT, MACLEMAN,
MACLEMON, MACLIMONT, MACCLEMENT,
MACCLEMONT, MACCLYMOND, MACCLYMONT,
MACCLYMOUNT, MACCLEMENTS, MACCLI-
MENTS. From G. *MacLaomuinn*, 'son of LA-
MONT,' q.v. In the Dean of Lismore's Book
we find VcClymont along with Clynelvmyn
(i.e. Clan Lamont). M'Lagmanid 1358, Mac-
Lagmayn 1410, Mc Laiman 1802, M'Lawmane
c. 1353, Mc Limont 1820.

MACLANACHAN, MACLANAGHAN. *See under*
MACCLANNACHAN.

MACLANE. *See under* MACLEAN.

MACLARDIE, MACLARDY, MACLARTY. *See
under* MACLAVERTY.

MACLAREN, MACLARAN, MACLAUREN, MAC-
LAURIN, MACLAWRIN. In G. *Mac Labhruinn*,
'son of Laurence' (G. *Labhruinn*, MG. (1467)
Labhran). The name has nothing to do with
the old personal name Loarn (from *Lovernos*, 'fox'). The first recorded of the name
appears to be Lorin Mak Gilserf, a witness
in 1258, who appears again in 1266 as Lorne
Mach gilherve (*Inchaffray*, p. 77, 85). Lorn
de Ardebethey of Perthshire rendered homage
in 1296 (*Bain*, II, p. 200). Johannes M'Lern,
capellanus, witnessed a charter of the lands
of Balmaclelane in 1466 (RMS., II, 907).
Donald Maklaurene in Dalbeyich and Finlay
Makneill Vc Laurent were witnesses in 1586,
Laurent M'Laurent, son to Laurent M'Laurent
in Craigruv in Buchquhedir, was witness to
a bond of 1587, and several individuals named
M'Laurent are named in a bond to Sir Duncan
Campbell of Glenurquhay in 1606 (BBT.,
p. 237, 241, 257). Laran McLaran was
charged with robbery and violence in the
lands of Drumquhassil, etc., in 1592 (RPC.,
V, p. 28), and Robert McClawrane in Balquhidder and his son were charged with wearing
hagbuts and killing deer in the royal forest
of Glenfinlas, 1612 (RPC., IX, p. 457). A
decreet against Archibald M'kleren in Acha-
gyll for rent and teinds, 1672 (HP., II, p. 218).
Daniel M'Cleron is in record in Sound of
Yell, 1742 (Mill, *Diary*), and thirteen Maclarens in Stewart of Appin's regiment in the '45
were killed and fourteen wounded (*Coll.*,
p. 199). An epitaph on the south side of the
old chapel of Balquhidder sets forth at great
length the gross heresy of a nameless individual who first suppressed the letter "u" in
the time-honored name: "This ancient patronymic evidently derived from the Dalriadic
chief Laurin of Laurin, in Argyle, whose descendants and kindred at an early period of
our Scottish history were numerous and powerful in the districts of Menteith, Lennox,

Strathern, and Balquhidder, has of late (by Scoto-Saxon transcribers, ignorant alike of Gaelic orthography and its proper pronunciation) been corrupted to MacLaren and Mac-Larin, and thus by the mere omission of the single vowel υ, equivalent to BH in the Gaelic found in the original spelling of the proper name the identity of this modern name with the ancient and euphonick name of Maclaurin is almost entirely destroyed to the mere Gael. This modern corruption of an old clan name is entirely unknown, where the proper name is well-known and never pronounced otherwise in the Gaelic than 'MacLabhrain,' and in the English 'MacLaurin'" (*Stirling antiquary*, I, p. 204). Dr. Richard Cockburn Maclaurin (1870–1920), president of the Massachusetts Institute of Technology, was born in Lindean, Roxburghshire. MacClaran 1698, M'Clarene and M'Clearen 1663, M'Claring, M'Laring, and M'Leran 1745, Macklarain 1574, M'Lairen 1683, McLaurine 1746, Mc-Lawran 1715, McLawrine 1724, Mc leron 1753, M'Larin 1816.

MACLATCHIE, MACLATCHY, MACLETCHIE, MACCLATCHIE, MACCLATCHY. MIr. *Mac Gilla Eidich*, 'son of Eidich's gillie.' There is a Mac Gilla Eidich in AU. (s.a. 1197). Surnames recorded in Ayrshire and Galloway. George McClechie was the king's sergeant within the sheriffdom of Are, 1519 (*Ros*). John M'Cletchie appears in Ayr, 1656 (*Ayr*, p. 197). George M'Clatchy, a native of Ireland, joined the Church of Scotland in 1840, and died in London, 1857 (*Fasti*). Thomas M'Clatchie, missionary in China, in latter half of nineteenth century, was apparently living in 1876, and Thomas Russell Hillier MacClatchie, of H. M. Consular Service and member of the Asiatic Society of Japan, who died in 1886, may have been his son.

MACLAUCHAN, MACLAUCHLAN, MACLAUCHLANE, MACLAUCHLIN. *See under* MACLACHLAN.

MACLAUREN, MACLAURIN. *See under* MACLAREN.

MACLAVERTY, MACLAFFERTY, MACLARDIE, MACLARDY, MACLARTY, MACLEVERTY, MACCLACHARTY (this last a Galwegian spelling). The authors of *The Clan Donald* tell us in grandiloquent language that "The progenitor of the family from whom they take their name was known as 'Fear Labhairt an Righ,' or the King's Speaker, who received this distinction from the circumstance of his being employed by the King of the Isles as special ambassador to hostile tribes at feud with that potentate . . . The office" they add, "appears to have become hereditary in the family" (*Clan Donald*, III, p. 550). The proper Gaelic form of the name is, of course, *MacFhlaithbheartaich* (with omission of *Fh* due to aspiration), 'son of the dominion bearing' or 'ruler.' The name is the same as the common Irish *Flaithbheartach*, now Flaherty, a name which occurs frequently in the *Annals of the Four Masters* and elsewhere. As an adjective modern Irish *flaithbheartach* has the meaning of generous, hospitable (*Dinneen*). Flaithbertach princeps (superior) Duinchaillden died in 872 (AU.), and Flaithbheartach ua Flaithbheartaigh was slain in 1133, a not uncommon ending for Gaels in the Middle Ages. The authors of *The Clan Donald* also state, without offering any proof of their assertion, that the Maclavertys "are descended from the Family of the Isles (i.e. the Macdonalds), and had their original habitat in Kintyre. They broke out early from the main stem, and claim descent from the founder of the Monastery of Saddell." The earliest of the name however in Scottish record is John M'Claffirdy, who filled the subordinate position of tenant under the Douglases in the lands of Mikilbrekauch in the barony of Buittle, 1376 (RHM., I, p. lx). John Macgillecrist Maklafferdich was one of those included in the remission granted Sir John Campbell of Cawdor and others in 1524 for the burning of the lands of Colonsay and the murder of Lachlan Maclean of Dowart in Edinburgh (*Cawdor*, p. 147). Gilcrist Malaverty held the lands of Langulchulchoich in Bute, 1540 (RSS., II, 3704). Alexander McLartych of Gartcharran is recorded in 1609 (*Poltalloch Writs*, p. 135), Archibald M'Clartie was one of M'Nachtane's soldiers shipped at Lochkerran in 1627 (*Archaeologia Scotica*, III, p. 254), Dowgall McLairtie held a sixshilling land in Islay, 1686 (*Bk. Islay*, p. 518), Donald Roy M'Clorty is in Lergihony, parish of Craignish, 1686 (*Argyll*), and Angus M'Clairtick of Gartcharran, parish of Craignish, is in record, 1693 (*Argyll Inv.*). Alexander M'Laertike is in record in Dunnamuke, 1672 (HP., II, p. 207), John M'Laertich was a merchant in Kilchoan, 1713; and Mrs. MacClarty has been immortalized in Mrs. Hamilton's *The Cottagers of Glenburnie*, first published in 1808. The Maclartys gave name to Eilean Mhic Labhartaich or MacLarty's Island (opposite Gartcharran) and to Sgeir Dubh Mhic Labhartaich or MacLarty's Black Rock (MacDougall, *Craignish tales*, p. 39). McClairty 1684, McLartie 1655.

MACLAWRIN. *See under* MACLAREN.

MACLEA. A current form of MACLAE, q.v. In Banffshire the name was spelled Mc o Lea or

MACLEA, *continued*

M^c o Lei, and an old spelling of a branch of the family in Glasgow was McCloo (HP., IV, p. 97).

MACLEAN, MACCLEAN, MACLAINE, MAC-LANE, MACCLEANE (Ayrshire). G. *Mac Gille Eoin*, earlier *Mac Ghill' Eathain*, 'son of the servant of (S.) John.' In the Gaelic genealogical MS. of 1467 the name is spelled Gilleain, and in the M'Vurich MS. Giolla-eoin (*Rel. Celt.*, II, p. 174). Eoin is the classic form of John in Gaelic, but Iain is now more commonly used. The *l* is all that remains of *gille*. The derivation of the name (*Legends*, p. 306) from *Leth-aoin* 'twin,' in allusion to the double origin of the clan, and the translation of the name by Lachlan Maclean (author of *Adhamh agus Eubh*, Edinburgh, 1837), as 'son of a lion,' are instances of 'the Gaelic itch for etymologising.' Collectively the clan is *Clann 'ic 'ill Eathain*. Gilmore Maclyn of the county of Perth rendered homage, 1296. The seal attached to his homage bears a stag's head cabossed, S' *Gilmore Macgylecho* (*Bain*, II, p. 200, 532). In 1326 there is entry of a payment of eight codri of cheese to eight men of John and Neil, sons of Gilhon, and mention is also made of the ship of Dofnald M'Gilhon (misprinted M'Gilbon) which made the circuit of 'le Mole' (Mull) (ER., I, p. 57). In the preface to ER. (I, p. lxxiii) mention is made of Dofnald, Neil, and John, the three sons of Gilhon — the youngest of them the ancestor of the Macleans of Duart. Nigel M'Gillon, custodian of the Castle of Scraburgh, 1329 (ER., I, p. 238). Lachlan M'Gilleon was dominus de Duvayrd, 1436 (*Cawdor*, p. 13), and John M'Gilleoin, dominus de Lochbuye, witnessed a charter by Angus, Master of the Isles, 1485. Lauchlan M'Leand was fiar of Torloisk, 1674 (HP., I). Walter Malynne (= Maclean), abbot of Glenluce, 1517–45 (Rusk, *History of parish and abbey of Glenluce*, Edinburgh, 1930, p. 140). In Tiree this surname outnumbers all others in the island. An old spelling in Perthshire was M'Olaine. John M'Inlay Roy V'Oleane in Kirktoun, a Glenurquhav vassal, 1638 (BBT., p. 403). Donald M'Olloine in Sunniboil, Mull, 1674 (HP., I, p. 279). Alexander McKlane, resident in parish of Borgue, 1684 (RPC., 3. ser. IX, p. 568), and William M'Klin is recorded in Mains, Sanquhar, 1697. Macleans are numerous in Prussia, where some call themselves 'of Coll' (*Fischer*, II, p. 151), and John Maclean, son of the laird of Dowart, who made a large fortune in Sweden and greatly aided in the building of the city of Gothenburg, was ennobled by Queen Christina in 1649 under the name of Makeleen

(SHR., xxv, p. 290). John Maclean (1787–1848), the Tiree bard, spells his name Mac-Illeain in the 1818 edition of his Poems, and in the Antigonish edition of 1856 it appears as MacGilleathain. Mackcline, MackCleiden, Mackelein, Macclen and Makclen 1588; Macklayne, Maklayne, and Makelyne 1536; Macklen 1680; Macgillane 1527; Macgillelane 1500; M'Claine and M'Clean 1674; M'Clane 1514; M'Clayne 1603; M'Cleane 1615; Maclein 1585; M'Gillayne 1549; M'Gilleon 1522, M'Gilleoun 1548, M'Killeane 1603, Maclane 1545, M'Gilleoin 1449; M'Gilleone 1475; Mcgilleoune 1539; M'Gillichean 1656; McIllaine and Mc illaine 1595; Mc illayn 1516; Mc illon 1603; Makclayne 1573; Makclean 1657; Makcleane 1615; Makgilleon 1390; Makgilleone 1496; Makclane, M'Clan, Mclen and Mc Lene 1662; Macklan, Maklane, and M'Klane all 1591; M'Leane 1662; Mcoleane 1561; (undated) Makclane, Makgillane, Makgilleoin, Makgilleon, Makgilleoun. The following additional spellings are all recorded in the *Book of Islay*: Macklain, M'Gleane, M'Illclayne, M'Len, Macklane, M'Gillyane, Makllane, M'Klayne, M'Layne, and M'Gilloyne. Andrew McLean (1848–1922), born in Dumbartonshire, was founder and editor of the *Brooklyn Citizen*, Brooklyn, New York; and John McLane (1852–1911), governor of New Hampshire (1905–1906) and host at the Russo-Japanese conference at Portsmouth, August, 1905, was born in Lennoxtown, Stirlingshire.

MACLEARNAN. G. *MacGill'Ernán*, 'servant of (S.) Ernan.' Ernan is a diminutive of OIr. *iarn*, 'iron,' now written *iarann*. The name means 'little iron one,' and is Latinized by Adamnan (*Vita*, III, 33) as *Ferreolus*, 'cuius nomen etiam potest dici Ferreolus, Scottice vero Ernene.' The parish of Marnock (Banffshire), Kilmarnock, and Inchmarnock (Bute) are named from this saint.

MACLEAY. *See under* MACLAE.

MACLEERIE, MACLERIE (this in Glasgow). Current surnames, probably variants of MAC-CHLERY, q.v. William M'Lerry was a writer (lawyer) in Killearn, 1771.

MACLEES. *See under* MACLESE.

MACLEHOSE. From G. *Mac Gille Thamhais*, 'son of the gillie of Tammas,' the Scots form of Thomas. Gilles Makgilhoise had custody of the royal park and garden of Stirling in 1479 (ER., VIII, p. 563), and Joh. Makgilhewous, probably a relative, was charter witness in same burgh in 1465 (RMS., II, 844; Sc. Ant., VI, p. 163). Patrick Makgilhois witnessed a notarial instrument in Kippen, 1510

(*Cambus.*, 128). John McGilhosche was a victim of oppression in Wigtown, 1513 (*Trials*, I, p. 96*). Duncan McIlhois in Glenlyoun was fined for reset of Clan Gregor, 1613 (RPC., XIV, p. 633). Thomas Macklehois was tailor in Edinburgh, 1612, Thomas Maclehose, cordiner there, 1638, and Catharine Mackilhoise there, 1630 (*Edinb. Marr.*). John McIlhoise in Kilmainane was charged with refusing the authorized instruction of his craft of tanner, 1622 (RPC., XII, p. 670). Duncan McIlhaos was servant to Sir John MacDugall of Dunnoldich (Dunollie), 1623, and sheep were stolen from Thomas McIlhoise in Gargunnock in same year (ibid., XIII, p. 271, 325). John M'Gilchois appears in parish of Logierait and John M'Gillhois in Brae of Tullimet, 1658 (*Dunblane*), and William M'Illhos was an elder in Killearn in same year (*Strathendrick*, p. 55). Seven of the name M'Ilhose are recorded in Dunblane vicinity in eighteenth century (*Dunblane*). By some changed to HOSIER. Now called by some MUCKLEHOSE (Editor, *Trials*, I, p. 96*). M'Ilhoise 1588, M'Llchois (Perthshire) 1611, M'Ilhose or Micklehose (Kippen) 1683, M'Ilhouse 1698, Mcillhose and McKillhose 1681.

MACLEISH, MACLISH. G. *M'A'Lìos,* a shortened form of *Mac Gill' Iosa,* 'son of the servant of Jesus.' It is hard, however, to say, from the old forms (M'Coleis, M'Ilishe) whether the original form was Maoliosa or Gilliosa, for *m* (of Maol) becomes *mh* or *v* and disappears and *g* (of Gille) becomes *gh* and disappears also, leaving stumps like 'aol and 'ill (*Macbain*). In 1542 the name appears as Makleis in Muthill, which points to M'Gilliosa, as does the modern form itself. In 1613 Malleis McColleis in North Perthshire was fined for reset of Clan Gregor (RPC., XIV, p. 634), and Duncane M'Coleis in Muyeirnolycht was one of the laird of Glenurquhay's vassals in 1638 (BBT., p. 339). In the Iona charter of 1580 Gillecrist Og M'Culeis in Ardnahow. Donald don Mc-Leich, 1665 (IDR., p. 310). See also MACCLEISH and MACLESE.

MACLEISTER. The Scottish *fledgear* (from Old French *flechier*), 'arrow-maker,' was early borrowed by Gaelic as *fleisdear* and *leisdear,* and gave origin to the name *Mac an (fh)leisdeir,* 'son of the arrow-maker.' Gillepatrik Makfleger had a royal remission in 1497 for slaughter committed by him in Ross (*Rose*, p. 164; OPS., II, p. 572); and Bauchane McFleger took part in the invasion of the Black Isle in 1499 (*Rose*, p. 169). The Mac-an-Leisdeirs of Argyllshire are now mostly Englished as Fletchers, and Buchanan of Auchmar (p. 107) made them a sept of Macgregor. Several individuals named M'Inlester in Auchalladour

gave their bond of manrent to Duncan Campbell of Glenurquhay in 1587 (BBT., p. 242). Malcolm McInlister witnessed an instrument of sasine in 1588 (*Poltalloch Writs*, p. 75), and Gillepatrik M'Inlestar in Brackley appears as a Glenurquhay tenant in 1638 (BBT., p. 403). Johnne McClester was tenant of Clagenauch in Islay in 1541 (ER., XVII, p. 618), and Duncan M'Inleister is in record in Drynlea in 1672 (HP., II, p. 207). Among the "articles concludit vpone be the barrones and gentlmen of the Shirefdome of Argyle" in 1638 was the following: "Item, that everie baillie, barone, and heretour be cairfull with all diligence to enter fledgeris in all pairtis of the cuntre for making of arrowes, and smythis for making of arrow-heidis" (BBT., p. 395). Donald McInleister and John McInleister in Balquhidder were fined for reset of Clan Gregor, 1613 (RPC., XIV, p. 638). A company of two hundred Highland bowmen was raised in 1627 for service in the war with France (*Archaeologica Scotica*, III; HP., I, p. 114–116). McInleaster 1686, McInlester 1553, Makinlestar 1559.

MACLEITH. McLeith (in Drymen parish) or McIlleich. Patrick McLeith or McIlleich in Tamis of Glenshie was prosecuted for illegal carrying of arms, 1618 (RPC., XI, p. 364–365).

MACLELLAN, MACLELLAND. *See under* MACCLELLAN.

MACLEMAN, MACLEMON. Variants of MACLAMOND, q.v. John Mackleman appears in Edinburgh in 1644 (*Edinb. Marr.*).

MACLENNAN. G. *MacGill'innein* for fuller *MacGill-Fhinnein,* 'son of Finnan's servant.' S. Finnan was founder of the school of Maghbile (now Moville) at the head of Strangford Lough, county Down. Kessanus Macclenane was one of the witnesses to a charter of the lands of Cartonvenach in the Lennox to Maurice, son of Galbraith, c. 1250 (*Levenax*, p. 27). Gilmory Makynnane, tenant of Eddirallekach in 1480, appears in 1483 as Gilmory M'Lenane (ER., IX, p. 562, 595). John M'Clynvne was witness in Are, 1529 (RMS., III, 896), and Adam M'Clenane held property in Culross, 1586 (ibid., V, 1103). James Makclennand in Hoilhous, 1594 (*Hunter*, p. 36). The name occurs in 1592 as M'Clanan, and John M'Linein in Over Law, Kirkcudbrightshire, is in record, 1678 (*Kirkcudbright*). Alexander M'Lennan or M'Glenan in Lochbroom was made prisoner in the '45. John McIllenane or McKillenane in Torloisk, Mull, was put to the horn in 1629 (RPC., 2. ser. II, p. 341; III, p. 46). Rob Donn spells the name Mac-an-Linnein (ed. Morrison, p. 449).

MACLEOD. G. *MacLeòid*, 'son of Leòd,' from a Norse name *Ljótr* (*r* silent) or *Ljót*, 'ugly,' but evidently a curtailed form of some double-stemmed name of which *Ljotr* was the first element, probably *Ljót-ulf*, 'ugly wolf.' There was a Ljótr, a companion of Arnfinn, brother of Anakoll, a viking of the Hebrides (*Ork. Saga*, c. 101). The fact that the Macleods of Cadboll and the Macleods of Lewis quarter the three legs of Man (*trie cassyn* in Manx) and use the same motto, *Quocunque jeceris stabit*, does not necessarily point to a connection between them and the Norwegian kings of Man. Such heraldic assumptions were by no means uncommon in the seventeenth and eighteenth centuries. "The Macleods," as Stodart says, "have a pretension to descend from the old Lords of the Isle of Man, and began apparently early in the eighteenth century to add the arms of Man to their coat" (*Stodart*, II, p. 41). Gillandres MacLeod on a perambulation of marches, 1227 (APS., I, p. 91). Torquil M'Leoid de Leohus witnessed a grant of lands in Badenoch, 1338 (SCM., IV, p. 126). Gilbert or Gilbreid McGloid, tenant in Tiree, 1541 (ER., XVII, p. 614). Murdow McCloyd made an attack on the galley of the laird of Balcomie, one of the Fife adventurers in the Hebrides in 1600 (RPC., XIV, p. cxxiii). There are three branches of Macleod: Macleod of Macleod, in G. *MacLeòid*; Macleod of Dunvegan, G. *Sìol Thormaid*; Macleod of the Lewis, G. *Sìol Thorcuil*. The Rev. Alexander Macleod (1774–1838), preacher and author in New York, born in Mull, was son of Rev. Neil Macleod who entertained Dr. Samuel Johnson during his visit to the island. Thomas Gordon Macleod (1868–1932), governor of South Carolina, was Scottish on both sides. Among Scots descendants in Poland the name has become Machlejd. The following spellings are recorded in 1663: M'Cleod, M'Cloid, M'Glaud, M'Kleod, M'Leud, M'Lewd, M'Loid; Mccleoyd 1633, McCleud 1762, McCloaud 1779, M'Cloide 1559, Macleoad 1655, Maclode 1343, Makkloud 1770, Ma Keloid (of Harris) 1623, M'Loyd 1443, M'Loyde 1436, M'clode 1539, Makcloid 1515. See Amendments and additions.

MACLERGAN. An Islay surname. For *Mac Gille Fheargáin*, 'son of (S.) Fergna's servant.' The fourth abbot of Hi was named Fergna. Donald McLergan is recorded in Tormistell, 1733, John M'Illergin in Buist was denounced rebel, 1675 (HP., I, p. 296), John McIllergan was tenant of Nerebie, Islay, 1733, and John McLergan in Craigfad, 1741 (*Bk. Islay*, p. 548, 552, 558). Neill M'Lergan was changekeeper in Machry Coul before 1755 (*Isles*). Many of this name in Islay now call themselves Maclean.

MACLERIE. *See under* MACLEERIE.

MACLEROY. A current form of MACILROY, q.v. In Strathendrick, 1840. Patrick Macklroy and his wife were residents in the parish of Borgue, 1686 (RPC., 3. ser. IX, p. 567).

MACLESE, MACLEES, MACLISE. G. *Mac Gill Iosa*, 'son of servant of Jesus.' John M'Lese was tenant of Auchinbreck, 1376 (RHM., I, p. liv), and Alexander Macless was witness in Dumbarton, 1500 (LCD., p. 204). Margaret McLiss appears in Fortingall, 1683 (DPD., I, p. 487), and Mary McLise was in Coustone, Cowal, 1762 (*Clan Lamont journal*, II, p. 154). MacAliece has been given as an old spelling in Galloway. See also MACLEISH.

MACLETCHIE. *See under* MACLATCHIE.

MACLEUR. *See under* MACCLURE.

MACLEVERTY. *See under* MACLAVERTY.

MACLIMONT. *See under* MACLAMOND.

MACLINDEN. A form of MACCLINTON, q.v.

MACLINLAGAN. G. *M'Gill' Fhinnlagan*, 'gillie of (S.) Fionnlagan.' Fionnlagan is for earlier Findlucan, diminutive of Findlug. There is a dedication to S. Finnlagan in the island in Loch Finlagan, Islay. The real name of the loch is Loch Bhiollagain, where *bh* is due to eclipsis of initial *f* by *loch*, which was once neuter. The loch is named from the saint (*Watson* I, p. 429, 519). Archibald M'Linlagan was tenant of Stremnish in Islay, 1686 (*Bk. Islay*). See FINDLUGAN.

MACLINTOCK. *See under* MACCLINTOCK.

MACLISE. A current form of MACLESE, q.v.

MACLISH. A variant of MACLEISH, q.v.

MACLITSTER. A Highland Border name meaning 'son of the dyer' (from Scots *litster*, dyer). John Maklitstare, chaplain in Cowal, 1507 (RMS., II, 3133). The tenement of John Maklitstare in Glasgow is mentioned in 1524 (LCD., p. 260), and in 1563 there is reference to Ninian M'Litster, owner of a tenement in the same city (*Protocols*, I).

MACLIVER. An Islay surname. The old pronunciation was Macleever, the modern is Macliver. Probably G. *Mac Gill' Ibhair*, 'son of (S.) Ibhar's gillie.' A commission was granted Campbell of Auchinbreck and others in 1619 to apprehend Ewne M' Finla VcGillevir in Kilchoane, and John McEwne VcIlliver, who had been denounced rebels by Campbell of Barbreck (RPC., II, p. 643). John Roy M'Gilliver in Islay, 1686. Sometimes confused with MACCLURE, q.v. M'Ileur (in Islay) 1733. The above seems to give the line of descent of Colin, Lord Clyde: Colin, son of John, son of John, grandson of John Roy, son of John, son of Ewen, son of Finlav, son of Gillour. The derivation of the name from *Mac a liomhair*, modernized *Mac illimheir*, is an instance of popular but unscientific etymology.

MACLOEN. Malpeder MacLoen, mormaer of the Mearns, slew King Duncan II at Monacheden (now Mondvnes in the Mearns), 1094. In the chronicles his name is spelled Malpeder Makcolm, Malpedre mac Loern, Malpedir filius Lorin, Malpedir mac Loren (CPS., p. 175, 206, 289, 303).

MACLONVIE. Now obsolete, having been merged in Cameron. The Maclonvies or Maclouvies (as the name is sometimes spelled) were one of the four leading branches of the Clan Cameron. In Maclagan MS. the name is spelled *MacLonabhaidh*. See MACGILLONIE.

MACLOON. A Galloway name of Irish origin, *Mac Giolla Eóin*, 'son of the servant of (S.) John.' A variant of MACLEAN, q.v.

MACLOUVIE. Of Strone. See MACLONVIE.

MACLUCAS, MACLUGAISH, MACLUGASH, MACLUGISH. G. *Mac Lùcais*, 'son of Lucas.' Fergus M'Lucas was one of an inquisition held at Inverness on the lands of Dunmaglass in 1414 (*Cawdor*, p. 5), and a remission was granted to John Maklucas in 1524 (ibid., p. 147). Fynlay M'Lowkas witnessed an instrument of sasine of Craginche in 1493 (OPS., II, p. 97), and Donald Maclugash was a charter witness at Castle Lachlan in 1502 (*Poltalloch Writs*, p. 71). Gillepatric McLugas acquired the hill steading of Garrachoran in Glen Lean, 1618 (McKechnie, *Lamont*, p. 140). Iain M'Cluglashe was one of those murdered at Dunavertie in 1647 (HP., II, p. 257), and the name is also found in Bute in 1656 (Hewison, II, p. 270). Patrick M'Clugeis was tenant of Over Ardrosketill in 1664 (*Isles*), and Donald Roy M'Lugas in Ardtounishever was denounced rebel in 1675 (HP., I). John McClugass in Kilchrenan and Ard: McLeougas in Nether Lorn appear in 1692 (*Commons*, p. 32, 34), Finlay M'Clugash in Knockimily, parish of Dunoon, is in record in 1696 (*Argyll Inv.*), and John M'Lougas in Nether Fairnoch, parish of Kilchrenan, in 1698 (ibid.). The latter appears again in 1702 as M'Laugas (*Argyll*). MacLucas and MacClucas are found in Cowal in the eighteenth century. Prof. Watson informs me that the duke of Argyll assures him that the old personal name *Mac Gille mo Luaig*

has also become Lucas in Argyllshire. Many persons have dropped their name Maclucas and have become Macdougalls in the north and Douglases in the south, and in Coll Lucas and MacLugais are now Macdougall. In the Isle of Man the name is current as Clucas. Maclagan's etymology (*Perth incident*, p. 329–330) of the name from *luath* (swift) and *cas* (foot) is erroneous. The Cowal Maclucases are reckoned a sept of the Clan Lamond. McGlugas 1692, McLucase 1609.

MACLUCKIE, MACLUCKY. Corrupt forms of MACLUCAS, q.v. The name appears as McLockie in the parish of Glastoun (= Glasserton), Galloway, 1684 (*Parish*, p. 7, 9). George Macluckie in Kippen, 1726. Cf. Donald Mcluke in Shenlarich, 1644 (FB., p. 366). McLokie 1684.

MACLUGASH, MACLUGAISH, MACLUGISH (in Lorn). Current forms of MACLUCAS, q.v.

MACLULICH, MACLULLICH, MACLULLICK. G. *Mac Lulaich*, 'son of LULACH,' q.v. The name is sometimes wrongly Englished Macculloch, a name of quite different origin. The Argyllshire Macullochs around Lochaweside are really Maclullichs, and are referred to in Gaelic as 'cloinn Lullaich o thulaich Mhaodain' (*Records*, p. 320). A son of Ywar Mac Lulli was one of the hostages to be given by John of Isla, 1350 (*Clan Donald*, I, p. 113). ffinlay McLuiloig is in Nether Lorn, and Dun: mc Clullich in Innishail, 1692 (*Commons*, p. 30, 33). Duncan Maclullich matriculated at the University of Glasgow, 1824. The surname is not common. Hugh Macdonald tells us that Reginald, son of Somerled, was married to MacRandel's daughter or as some say, to a sister of Thomas Randel, earl of Moray, and by her had Angus, of whom are descended the MacLulichs 'who are now called in the low country Pittullichs' (HP., I, p. 13). This is erroneous, the surname Pattullo (and its variants) is of local or territorial origin. See under PATILLO.

MACLUMFA, MACLUMPHA. See MACCLUMPHA. "Another highly respectable and ancient Galloway family, the McLumfas, has become extinct from the same disease [gentility], and a set of people with the low Irish Downshire name of McClew has stepped into their stockings" (Trotter, *Galloway gossip sixty years ago*, Wigtownshire, Bedlington, 1877, p. 66).

MACLUNG (Galloway). See under MACCLUNG.

MACLURE. See under MACCLURE. In Glenelg and in Skye this name is sometimes supposed to be *Mac a leora*, sometimes *Mac an leabhair*, 'devotee of the book.'

MACLURG. G. *MacLuirg*, 'son of Lurg.' Lurg has been explained as G. *lurg*, 'footman.' Loíg(u)ire Lorc, an early king of Ireland, was father of Aillil Á(i)ne. Gilbert Maklurke of the county of Are rendered homage, 1296. His seal bears a squirrel leaping, S' *Gilb'ti Maclurc* (*Bain*, II, p. 205, 554). Andrew Maclurg held land 'in vico fori,' St. Andrews, 1476 (RMS., II, 1228). A precept of remission was granted Donald Maklurg 'apud Are,' 1503 (RSS., I, 944). William McLurg, a follower of the earl of Cassilis, was respited for murder, 1526 (ibid., 3386). Patrick Maklurgh of Kilmore was one of an assize in Carrick, 1529 (RMS., III, 829). Alexander McLurg and Johnne M'Lurg in Ducherie are in record, 1592, and Patrick M'Lurg was servitor to Johnne Wallace of Dundonald, 1598 (RPC., v, p. 574, 704). John McLurg issued a seditious gazette from his coffeehouse in Edinburgh, 1681 (RPC., 3. ser. VII, p. 1), and Claverhouse's 'great villain Mkclorg the smith of Menegaff' is mentioned in 1682 (*Red Book of Menteith*, I, p. xxxix). Sir James M'Lurg of Vogrie, a wealthy Edinburgh merchant, was a large shareholder in the ill-fated Darien scheme. M'Lurge 1686, M'Lurgg 1689.

MACLUSKEY. See under MACCLUSKY.

MACLYN. Thomas Mclyn witnessed a Douglas charter in Dumfries, 1432 (*Douglas Book*, III, p. 418). Donald McLyn, a follower of the earl of Cassilis, was respited for murder, 1526 (RSS., I, 3386). Woulfe says from Ir. *MacFhloinn*, a variant of *MacFloinn*, 'son of Flann,' ruddy.

MACMADETHYN, 'son of MATADIN,' q.v. The lands of Stratheyn et Kyndrochet with their mill were granted to Cospatric Macmadethyn by William Cumyn, earl of Buchan (who died in 1233) (REA., I, p. 14, 15). Cospatric Macmadethyn would appear to be the Cospatrick filius Moded, who, together with his brother Malothen, is witness to a charter by Fergus, earl of Buchan (granted before 1214) to John, the son of Uthred, of the lands of Fedreth and Ardindrach (CAB., p. 408–409). Malotheny mac Madethy was witness to a document relating to the church of Inuerhouen in Banffshire, c. 1210 (REM., p. 15).

MACMAELBRIDE, 'son of the shaveling or devotee of S. BRIDE,' q.v. Gilpatrick Mac Molbrid witnessed a retour of inquest made at Dumbarton, 1271 (RMP., p. 192; *Red Book of Menteith*, II, p. 219). Gilcrist Mac Molbrid is included in the inhibition by Robert, bishop of Glasgow directed against Malcolm, earl of Levenax and his adherents, 1294 (RMP., p. *203). Donald McOlbreid was servitor to

Campbell of Duntroon, 1659 (*Poltalloch Writs*, p. 77), and Gillecallum Mc olvraid, tenant of Leckamore, 1669 (HP., IV, p. 222). Archibald M'Olbryd in Carnbeg, 1684 *(Argyll)*, John Mc olbreed, rebel in Kilberrie paroch, 1685 (*Commons*, 4), and Alexander M'Olbreid at the Ford of Anacra, 1713 (*Campbell*, I, p. 119). McIlbreid 1692.

MACMAELMICHEIL. See under MACMICHAEL.

MACMAGGNIS. 'Son of MAGNUS,' q.v. From the unaspirated form of the name. Ewin Mc Maggnis, baxter, in Inverness, to pay four pounds 'for vsing his craft' in 1609 (*Rec. Inv.*, II, p. 73). Cf. MACMANNAS and MACMANUS.

MACMAIBEN, 'son of MAIBEN,' q.v. Recorded in Galloway and Carrick.

MACMALMUR. 'Son of Malmur,' from G. *Mael Muire*, 'shaveling of (V.) Mary'. Ronald Macmalmur appears in the time of William the Lion (*Scon*, p. 57), and Constantinus Macmalmori witnessed a confirmation by Thomas de Galweta of a charter by William Oliphant, c. 1230 (*Oliphants*, p. 2). Donald McMalmorie in Ardnastaynk was ordered to be apprehended in 1619 (RPC., XI, p. 643). See MALMURE.

MACMAN, MACMANN. From G. *MacMhathain*, 'son of Matthew.' Finlay mc rorie vic Mathon in Urray was charged with being an engager on the royalist side, 1649 (IDR., p. 368), and John M'Man appears in Ballemeanaich, 1678. There are said to be a few Macmanns still in Mortlach parish.

MACMANAMNY. A Galloway name of Irish origin, *Mac Meanmna* (for *Mac Meanma*). See MACMENAMIN.

MACMANAWAY. A Galloway name of Irish origin, most probably a corruption of MACMENAMIN, q.v.

MACMANECHIN. 'Descendant of Manachan' (diminutive of *manach*, a monk). Gillepatric mac Manechin was one of the assessors of the lands of Dunduff in 1231 (RD., p. 111). Ewen (p. 277–278) derives the name from English Mannekin, but this seems unlikely. There was a Manachan, a famous warrior mentioned in AFM. at 866.

MACMANNANDE. Cuthbert McMannande witnessed a sasine in Dumfries, 1532, and in 1549 there is mention of the tenement of the late Nicolas Makmannide there (*Edgar*, p. 235–36). Richard M'Mannady appears in Irvine, 1537 (*Irvine*, I, p. 40).

MACMANNAS (in Elgin), MACMANNES (in Aberdeen). A form of MACMANUS, q.v. One Macmannes and Angus M'Magnus in Stemster, Caithness, 1663. Finlay M'Manis in Mekill Allan, 1668 (*Laing*, 2636), M'Manes 1663.

MACMANUS. From *MacMaghnuis*, 'son of MAGNUS,' q.v. John M'Manis was charter witness at Dunbretane, 1506 (*Lennox*, II, p. 182). Muldonich M'Ilmanus in Penniemore, barony of Dowart, 1673, was denounced a rebel under the name of Callich Frigadell M'Ildonich M'Maines in Pennienmoir (HP., I, p. 260, 301). Buchanan (p. 114) says the MacMainesses were a sept of Colquhouns.

MACMARK. 'Son of Mark.' Gilmonale Mc-Mark was tenant of Cowelche in Tiree, 1541 (ER., XVII, p. 648). Cf. MARK and MACMAR-QUIS.

MACMARQUIS. An Argyllshire surname, now rare. Gaelic *MacMarcuis*, 'son of Mark,' from the Latin form of the name, *Marcus*. Marcus MacDonald, slain in 1397, is recorded in Irish annals as "Constable of gallowglasses" for the O'Connors (*Celt. Mon.*, VIII, p. 181). He was one of the sons of John, lord of the Isles, and Margaret, daughter of King Robert II. From him, according to M'Vurich (*Rel. Celt.*, II, p. 159), are descended the Macdonalds of Cnoicanchluith in Tyrone. Cristinus Macmarkys was rector of the church of St. Moluog de Trentornys (Trotternish) in the diocese of Sodor in 1428 (*Pap. Lett.*, VIII, p. 14). John MacMarkisch was tenant of Kyram Mor in Kintyre in 1506, and Gilnow McMarkische or McMarcus, tenant of Laggan and Keranemore, Kintyre, in 1541 (ER., XII, p. 708; XVII, p. 626, 632), was probably a descendant of his, as also was Donald Makmarkie, occupier of the three merk land of Laggan, Kintyre, in 1596 (HP., III, p. 73). Donald M'Marqueis in Oiban, parish of Seall, is in record in 1676, Neil M'Marcus in Kylipoll, parish of Kilmichell, in 1686 (*Argyll*), Archibald M'Varquise in Catenish is in record in 1691, and Finlay M'Varquies in Airechastelan in 1695 (*Argyll Inv.*). John Macmarquis married Margaret, daughter of Angus MacDonald, fourth of Milton, South Uist, about 1793. William McMarquis, barrack sergeant at Vizagapatam, Madras, died there in 1838. The name is now shortened to MARQUIS, a form found in Inverness as early as 1631. Mac Marc Uis in 1597, MacMarkes 1692, McMarquish 1669, McVarques 1692. There is a promontory in Lorn called Rudha Mhic Mharcuis. Peter M'Varquish was name of the man who blasted M'Fadyen's stone (*Clach Mhic Phadain*) in river Awe.

MACMARTIN. G. *MacMhàrtainn* or *Mac-Mhàrtuinn* for earlier *MacGille Mhartainn*, 'son

of the servant of (S.) Martin.' The saint is Martinus (dimin. of Martius, 'little Mars'), "who was widely reverenced in Scotland, doubtless because of his connection with Ninian's church of Whithorn, which was dedicated to him." Murdac mac Gillemartin witnessed a charter by Roger de Scalebroc of lands in Carric, c. 1185 (*Melros*, I, p. 25; RMS., II, 142). Feruware Macgilmartine or Mackilmartine granted a half carucate of land in Strathblane to Sir David de Grahame, c. 1240 (HMC., 3. Rep., App., p. 386). Adam filius Gilmur Makmartin held the lands of Lethin and Kyinnis before 1290 (*Laing*, 15), and in 1329 there is entry of payment of the king's debt to Fergus McMartin in Gallowav (ER., I, p. 152). Gillaspic mac Marten held land in Loryne, c. 1364 (HP., IV, p. 16). Angus Mertini and Duncan Mertini witnessed a charter by Celestine of the Isles to Alan Donald Duff, captain of Clan Camroun, 1495 (RMS., II, 2281). Ewn M'Gillemertvn and Finlaw M'Mertin took part in the second hership of Petty, 1513 (*Rose*, p. 190). Gilbert McMartyne, a follower of the earl of Cassilis, was respited for murder, 1526 (RSS., I, 3386). M'Gillemertyne appears in Trotternish, 1536, and the name is common in the *Black Book of Taymouth*. In 1613 John McGillemertene in Geche and Finla McMertene were fined for reset of members of Clan Gregor (RPC., XIV, p. 629, 633). The Clann Mhic Mhartainn of Letterfinlay are a sept of the Camerons, and the name has all but disappeared from the Highlands, having been merged into Cameron. This change of name began early, as in 1617 three individuals are designated "Cambroun *alias* M'Martene" (RPC., IX). Makgillemertyn 1495, M'Ilmartine 1675, McIlmartun 1541, M'Ilmertin 1670, M'Mertein 1672, McMertene 1617. A M'Mertinestoun in Ayrshire, 1622 (*Retours, Ayr*, 212).

MACMASTER. G. *Mac a' Mhaighstir*, 'son of the Master,' i.e. a cleric. The word is a borrowing from Latin *magister*, MG. *magisder*. This surname is now found mainly in the shires of Dumfries and Wigtown, but was also the name of a sept in Ardgour traditionally said to have been dispossessed by Macleans in the fifteenth century. Colin, son of John Macmagistir, appears as a canon of Argyll in 1433 (*Pap. Lett.*, VIII, p. 468), and John M'Master is in record in Lanark 1498 (*Lanark*, p. 10). Another John McMaster had a tenement in Dumfries in 1582 (*Edgar*, p. 245). McKmaster 1684.

MACMATH. G. *Mac Mhatha*, 'son of MAT-THEW,' q.v. Alexander M'Math of Dalpeder resigned the office of coronator of Nythisdale

MACMATH, continued

in 1468 (RMS., II, 974). Dalpedder in Dumfriesshire is recorded in 1538 as the seat of the family (*Bucc. MSS.*, 16), which ended in an heiress, Bessy M'Math, who married John Johnstone of Esbyshields. Thomas McMath witnessed an instrument of sasine in Dumfries, 1506 (*Edgar*, p. 228), and M'Math of that Ilk appears in the list of freeholders of Dumfriesshire in 1597. Edward M'Mathe appears as merchant in Edinburgh, 1600 (*Edinb. Marr.*). John M'Mayth was retoured heir of Roger M'Mayth, his father, in lands in barony of Sanquhar, 1601 (*Retours, Dumfries,* 12). William Mckmath was "boxmaster to ye Incorporation of the Walkers" in Edinburgh, 1684 (BOEC., IX, p. 121). "In the seventeenth century a family of merchant burgesses of the name of Macmath flourished in Edinburgh, and the arms assigned to them in Funeral Escutcheons . . . are certainly founded on M'Naught" (*Stodart*, II, p. 187).

MACMAURICE, 'son of MAURICE,' q.v. According to Buchanan of Auchmar the name is derived from an illegitimate son of Maurice, second of that name, laird of Buchanan, in the reign of Robert I. Another sept of Macmaurices, from Maurice, illegitimate son of Walter, fourth of that name, laird of Buchanan, in the reign of James III. Descendants of the latter are now Morreises or Morisons in Perthshire. In Buchanan's time a few Macmaurices in Buchanan parish still retained their ancient name (*Buchanan*, p. 138–139). Arthur filius Mauritii witnessed a charter by Eugen M'Kessan in favor of Celestin M'Lachlan of part of the estate of Garchel in the reign of Robert III (*Levenax*, p. 76). See also MACMORICE and MACVARISH.

MACMAY. Ir. *MacMaighe*, 'son of May,' a diminutive for MATTHEW, q.v. Gilnewland McMay, tenant of Synnerland, Islay, 1541, and Gillonane McMoy, tenant of Corpolan, Islay, in same year (ER., XVII, p. 617, 638, 641). John McMa was tenant of Stromneis Mor in Islay, 1686 (*Bk. Islay*, p. 497). The name of Gilnewland McInay, tenant of Mealand, Islay, 1541 (ER., XVII, p. 620) is a miscopying of Macmay.

MACMEEKEN, MACMEEKAN, MACMEEKIN, MACMEIKAN, MACMEICKAN, MACMEEKING, MACMECKAN, MACMICHAN, MACMICKAN, MACMICKEN, MACMICKING, MACMIKAN, MACMIKEN, MACMIKIN, MACMYCHEN, and MACMEECHAM. All Galloway surnames. Probably from Ir. *MacMiadhachain* ('son of Miadhachan'), which Woulfe (p. 392) Englishes MacMeechan, MacMeekan, MacMeekin, etc. Gille-

crist Mak Makin or M'Mavkin witnessed a charter by Roger de Scalebroc of lands in Carric, c. 1185 (*Melros*, I, p. 25; RMS., II, 142), and Gillebride Macmehin witnessed confirmation of the charter by Dunekan, earl of Karic (*Melros*, I, p. 26). Duncan M'Mavcan appears as witness in Wigtownshire, 1426 (RMS., II, 185), and the escheat of Finiai Makmakyn or M'Makin in le Rendis (Rhinns) is recorded in 1456 (ER., VI, p. 195, 208). Jenetta filia Makmechum sold a six markland of Kirkdale in the parish of Kirkmabreck in 1496 (*M'Kerlie*, IV, p. 249). Alexander Mc-Mychin was charged with preventing the sheriff from holding court in Wigtownshire in 1513 (*Trials*, I, p. *91), and in the same year as Alexander Makmechane he had a remission for mutilation committed by him (ibid., p. 92*). Michell Makmakin in Ardeveill is in record, 1540 (RSS., II, 3666), and Thomas M'Meikin in Killentringane, 1671 (*Inquis.*, 5409). John McMiken charged with being a disorderly person (i.e. non-conforming) in the parish of Rerrick, 1684 (RPC., 3. ser. IX, p. 573). In 1684 the name appears (*Parish*) as: McMeikin, McKmacken, McKmaken, Mc-Mecan, McMeckan, McMeikine, McMeikeine, McMeken, McMichan, McMickan, McMicken, McMickin, McMiken, and Mamiken.

MACMENAMIN. A Galloway name of Irish origin, *Mac Meanman*, 'son of Meanma,' from *meanma*, mind, courage, spirit.

MACMENAMY, MACMENAMIE, MACMENEMY. Surnames recorded in Glasgow. Ir. *MacMeanma*. Variants of MACMENAMIN, q.v.

MACMENZIES, 'son of MENZIES,' q.v. Alexander de Meyneris or Meinzeis had a charter of the lands of Durisdeer, Dumfriesshire, from Robert I (RMS., I, App. II, 146), and in 1376 Johannes de Meigners had a grant of the barony of Enache (Enoch) in the valley of the Nithe which his father had resigned into the king's hands (RMS., I, 585). The family possessed the barony till 1704.

MACMICHAEL. G. *MacMicheil*, for earlier *Mac Gille Mhicheil*, 'son of the servant of (S.) Michael.' Earlier and rarer forms with *Mael-* (*Maol-*) are also found. There were several families named Mac Gill-Mhichell in Bute at the end of the eighteenth century, and the name was not uncommon in the north, appearing in the Inverness-Dingwall Records as McGillimichall (1649), McKilmichel and McKillmichaell (1682). Malmur Mac Gillemichel was one of the perambulators of the lands of Balfeth in Angus between 1204 and 1211 (RAA., I, p. 60). Gillecolme Makgillemichell and Kennathe Makgillemichell were charter witnesses in Lesmore, Argyllshire, 1251 (RMS., II, 3126), and Makbeth Makgilmichel was present at pleas held at Dull in 1264 (RPSA., p. 349). In the end of the thirteenth century Malcolm, earl of Lennox, transferred to Sir John of Luss the homage and service of Maldofen Macgillemychmore and his heirs (Levenax, p. 20). Celestine Macgillemichaell was a cleric of the diocese of Argyll, 1411 (Lennox, II, p. 60), and another Celestine McGilmichel witnessed an Atholl charter in 1453 (Athole, p. 707). Macgillmichell was a crown tenant of Eddergoll, 1480 (Christie, Lairds and lands, p. 84). Muldony Makgillemichell and Finlay Makgillemichell had Crown grants of the lands of Dunallirde-Macgillemichell in Bute, 1506 (RMS., II, 2987). Meldonich Mackillimichael is in record in the same island in 1646 (Hewison, II, p. 333). John Makmychell was burgess of Prestwick, 1507 (Prestwick, p. 10). Johannes McMichell, king's tenant in Strathdee, 1527 (Grant, III, p. 70). Peter McIlmichell appears in Ballichquhaill, 1532 (RSS., II, 1334); and Mans McGillmichell was "jugit in amerciament for the wranguse drawin of ane dowrk," 1557 (Rec. Inv., I, p. 9). Sheep were stolen from William M'Gillemithel in the regality of Spynie, 1597 (SCM., II, p. 137). John McGillemitchell in Foirtitlettir or Foirlettir was fined for resetting members of Clan Gregor, 1613 (RPC., XIV, p. 631, 656), and John McIlvichill, servant of the captain of Clanranald, committed outrage on Mr. Donald Omey in Ardnamurchane, 1624 (ibid., XIII, p. 427–8). David M'Ilvichall appears in Kingcart, parish of Comrie, 1632 (Dunblane). Ewin Bean M'Ilmichell alias M'Illenish in Ardochoyle in Dowart and Ewin M'Ilmichell in Ardjura were denounced rebel, 1675 (HP., I, p. 300); and Donald McIlmichall in Appin was hanged in 1677 for theft and consulting with evil spirits (HP., III, p. 36–38). Janet nein vc Gillmichael was proclaimed a fugitive from Inverness, 1677, and in the following year Anne Ninick gillivichell swerved from the path of moral rectitude (IDR., p. 87, 340). Angus McIllevitchell and Donald McIllevitchell were tenants in Borve, 1726 (HP., II, p. 317). Mary McGilmichal appears in Kilmichal, Cowal, in 1764. Of forms in Maol- (earlier Mael-) we have Dugald McMolmicheyl called McBernaurs, clerk of the diocese of Argyll, who was charged in 1433 with having unduly retained possession of the rectory of the parish church of S. Mary (Kilmory) in Arand (Arran) (Pap. Lett., VIII, p. 473). In 1436 John, son of Dougall (Johannes Dugalli) Macmaelmichaell, clerk of the diocese of Argyll, is also in record (ibid., p. 597). Gilbert McOlmichaell had sasine of lands in Bute, 1564 (ER., XIX,

p. 533). Macmichael is the source of many of our Mitchells, and the Lowland territorial name Carmichael (1180 Kermichel) is often used as the English rendering of it. The McIlmichells of Lismore and Appin and the M'A'Levechels of Kintyre have changed their name to Carmichael. McGillimichaell 1649, M'Ilmichael 1577, McKillmichaell and McKilmichael 1682, Macmitchel 1661, McMitchell 1667, McMichael 1684, McMychel and McMychele 1490; M'killvichel.

MACMICHIE, 'son of MICHIE,' q.v. Gilbrede M'Michy was one of the inquisition retouring Donald, thane of Cawdor, in the lands of Dunmaglass in 1414 (Cawdor, p. 5).

MACMILLAN. G. MacMhaolain or MacGhilleMhaoil, 'son of the bald or tonsured one.' The -an is diminutive ending. Mac-na-maoile, 'son of baldness,' is a side form of the name. Gillemor MacMolan was juror on inquest in Lanarkshire, 1263 (APS., I, p. 102). John Macmulan (Makmilane, or Makmylan) appears as bailie of Glasgow, 1454–55–68–57 (LCD., p. 178, 180, 252; REG., 368, 476). Sir Duncan Macmolane, a Pope's knight, was chaplain of the collegiate church of Kilmone, 1452 (OPS., II, p. 71), and payment was made to "McMwlane the barbour for the leichcraft done be him to the litil boys of the chalmire," 1473 (ALHT., I, p. 68). In 1488 there is record of the "refe of certane gudis" from Walter Makmylane and Mychel McMyllane (RSS., I, 1). Huchone Makgillemuil and others were arbitrators in a dispute anent the marches of the church lands of Croy, 1492 (Rose, p. 156). Gilbert M'Mulane held a tenement in Ayr, 1505 (Friars Ayr, p. 71), and in 1506 the following were tenants on lands in Kintyre: Duncan McMulan (Teyrargis), Lauchlan Makmulane (Glaknahall), Nigel Makmyllan (Coililongport) (ER., XII, p. 707–708). Cuthbert McMilane and John Makmullane, followers of the earl of Cassilis, were respited for murder, 1526 (RSS., I, 3386). Sir Fingon Makmulane was presented in 1540 to the chaplainry of Tibbermore in the diocese of Sodor (RSS., II, 3397), and Robert Makmyllen, burgess of Ayr, 1555 (Ayr, p. 101) is probably the Robert Makmyllane who rendered to Exchequer the accounts of the burgh in 1559 (ER., XIX, p. 88). The name is not uncommon in Galloway and several Macmillans in the parish of Carsfern were charged with being disorderly persons (i.e. non-conformists) in 1684 (RPC., 3. ser. IX, p. 574). Macillemhaoel, according to the Sleat historian, formed one of the council of Macdonald of the Isles at Finlaggan in Isla (HP., I, p. 24). The clan had possessions near Knap, Loch Suibne, and a boulder on the shore

MACMILLAN, *continued*

is said to have had engraved on it in Gaelic their claim or charter to the lands:

"Coir Mhic-Mhaoilein air a Chnap,
Fhad's a bhuaileas tonn air creig."

(Macmillan's right to Knap while wave strikes rock.)

If so "all vestige of it is worn away. This is believed to be not entirely owing to wind and weather, but to the effacing chisels of Clan Campbell, who ere long acquired the lands of their hereditary foes" (*Celt. Rev.*, IV, p. 244). A bailie Macmillan of Partick, Glasgow, a few years ago 'patented' a tartan which he has registered as Breacanseilgmhicgillemheoill Makmillen 1644, McMolland 1606; in 1684 (*Parish*): McKmillan, McMilland, McMullan. MacMylan and MacMyllan 1745. In the *Records of Inverness* the name appears as McGillemeill, McGilleneill, McIlneyll, and McGillymoyll.

MACMILLAR, 'son of (the) miller,' or of a man named Millar. William M'Miller was a witness at Hammyltoune, 1551 (*Protocols, 1*). Donald McMillar to pay the town a certain sum for "the libertie of ane stallinger" in 1609 (*Rec. Inv.*, II, p. 73). A "stallinger" is defined as "one who pays rent for a market-stall; a person, not a freeman, who, for a consideration to his corporation, is allowed to carry on business for a year." Callum M'Myllar was a vassal of Glenurquhay in 1638 (BBT., p. 403).

MACMIN, MACMINN, MACMYN, 'son of MENZIES' (G. *Mèinn*), q.v. Patrick M'Men olim abbate de Dundrenane, 1426 (RMS., II, 185). John Mcmyane or Makmyane in Wigtoun was murdered in 1509 (*Trials*, I, p. 63*, 92*). John McMyne was servitor to Sir Adam Cunninghame of Woodhall, 1658 (*Inquis.*, 4355). Margaret M'Min resided at Netherthird, 1668, and Agnes M'Min at the Milne of Glentow, 1680 (*Kirkcudbright*). Issobel McMinne and Mareon MacMinne were residents in the parish of Borgue, 1684 (RPC., 3. ser. IX, p. 566, 568). M'Mine 1663.

MACMIRRIE. Moreis McMirrie of Culteoun, 1593, in the same year signs his name Morris McMurrie (*Ayr*, p. 122, 126). John Dow McMirrie and Patrick Galt McMirrie in Ausland were fined for reset of Clan Gregor, 1613 (RPC., XIV, p. 638). Janet Makmarrie in Edinburgh, 1624 (*Edinb. Marr.*).

MACMOIL. For older *M'Ilmoil* (*M'Gille Mhaoil*). An Islay surname now sometimes rendered Bell (*Celt. Mon.*, IX). Donald M'Gillemoyll was a sufferer from the hership of

Petty in 1502 (*Rose*, p. 176), and John Makmul was bowman in Lochalsh, 1548 (RMS., IV, 204). See MACMILLAN.

MACMONHACH, otherwise Macmath the name of a former small clan of Kintyre wrongly spelled Macmonhath. Gilbert Macmonhathe, juror on inquisition made in Annandale in 1304 (*Bain*, II, p. 412). Gyllespy McMonauch, juror on inquisition held at Drumfrese in 1367 (RHM., II, p. 64). Monach, Moannach, are variants of G. *Mathanach* (Matheson), pron. Ma'anach.

MACMONIES, MACMONNIES. This surname which occurs in the Stewartry, is a form of MACMENZIES, q.v. "The careless way in which names were written and pronounced in early times makes the change of the vowel more than probable" (*Dudgeon*, p. 24). Thomas Makmynnes was burgess of Dumfries, 1567 (*Edgar*, p. 242; RPC., 1. ser. I, p. 567). James Makmunish and John Mack Munish were classed as disorderly persons in the parish of Cross Michael, 1684 (RPC., 3. ser. IX, p. 574). John M'Monies in record in Carlingwark, 1789, appears again in 1791 as M'Minnies (*Kirkcudbright*). McMynneis 1558.

MACMONNIES. *See under* MACMONIES.

MACMOREHERTHACH. An error for Morcherthach or *Muircheartach*, 'sea-ruler' or 'sea-director.' Gillecrist Macmoreherthach was one of an inquisition to determine the right marches of Westere Fedale in 1246 (LAC., p. 26). Cf. under MACKIRDIE.

MACMORGON, 'son of MORGAN,' q.v. Johannes MacMorgon or Johne Morgin was one of the tenants on the Clan Grant lands in Strathdee in 1527 (*Grant*, III, p. 68, 70). Andrew McMorgoun was one of the tenants in the king's lands of Estir Mecra (Easter Micras) in 1539 (ER., XVII, p. 659). See MORGAN.

MACMORICE, 'son of MAURICE (or MORRIS)', q.v. Sir John Makmoris was rector of Kilmolrov in Arisaig before 1517 (OPS., II, p. 200). His name appears also as Makmwrich on the same page. Finlay McMoris in Auchynnar was a follower of the earl of Argyll in 1536 (RSS., II, 2152). Grissell Macmorice in Petdrichie, parish of Glenbervie is recorded in 1601 (*Brechin*), and John M'Mories in Over Rerrick in 1715 (*Kirkcudbright*). See also MACMAURICE and MACVARISH.

MACMORLAND, MACMORELAND (this latter form recorded in Glasgow and Greenock). Woulfe explains this name, which occurs in

Ulster (and there "apparently of Scottish origin"), as *MacMurghaláin*, 'son of Murghal,' sea valor. Alexander Macmorland, perukemaker in Leith, 1749 (*Lyon in mourning*, II, p. 254). The name is recorded in Minnigaff in 1684 (*Parish*), and in Haddington, 1695. Dr. Macbain (Dictionary, s.v. *Bòrlanachd*) explains the name, erroneously I think, as a derivative from *bòrlanachd, mòrlanachd* (from Eng. *bordland*), compulsory labor for the proprietor.

MACMORRAN (Argyllshire), MACMORRIN (Stewartry). From Old Gaelic *mugh-ròn* 'seal's slave,' from *mug* 'slave' (Zeuss, *Grammatica Celtica*, 2. ed., p. 270), and *ron* 'seal.' Mugron, comharb of Columcille in Ireland and Scotland, died in 979 (AFM.). John McMoryne witnessed a charter by Robert de Graham of lands in Kyle to Melrose Abbey, c. 1344 (*Melros*, p. 427), and Alan McMoryn witnessed the resignation by Sir David de Wemyss of certain lands in 1373 (*Wemyss*, II, p. 15). William M'Moryne was tenant under the Douglas in the barony of Buittle, 1376 (RHM., I, p. lx), and Maurice Macmoryn who was rector there, died in 1381 (*Pap. Pet.*, I, p. 556). William MacMorin (wrongly 'de' MacMorin in the record), lately papal nuncio to the king and realm of Scotland, petitioned in 1395 for the canonry and first prebend of Glasgow (*Pap. Pet.*, I, p. 585). In 1394 his name is recorded as Matuorin (*c* misread as *t*), and in 1408 his death is recorded as M'Moyn (ibid., p. 579, 636). John M'Moryn appears as witness in Kirkcudbright, 1466 (RMS., II, 907), Herbert McMorane had a remission for certain acts committed by him, 1495 (ALHT., I, p. 215), and Alexander McMoren in Galloway had a respite for "tressonable intercommonyng with Inglismen" in 1529 (RSS., II, 43). William Makmorame, merchant burgess in Edinburgh, 1565 (RPC., I, p. 431), Johnne McMorame was messenger at arms, 1575 (RPC., II, p. 503), Edward Makmorane was retoured heir of Margaret Gordoun, his mother, in the lands of Blakat, 1576 (*Retours, Kirkcudbright*, 36), and John Macmorane appears in Cottoun of Dulleward, 1627 (*Brechin*). Gillepatrik McMorane appears in Saligo, 1636 (*Cawdor*, p. 280), MacMorran of Glaspen was Commissioner of Supply for Lanark, 1696 (APS., x, p. 29), and John M'Morin, writer in Dumfries, 1780. The Macmorrans of Mull have nearly all changed to Mackinnon. McKmorran and McMurrin 1684, M'Morine 1758, M'Morran 1667, M'Morrane 1592, M'Morrione 1794.

MACMORTEN, son of (a Lowlander named) Morton. Donald M'Morten in Keirmichelbeg, 1672 (HP., II, p. 210). Cf. MACMILLAR.

MACMULRON. Donaldus M'Mulron, student of St. Andrews University, 1425 (ERUS., p. 8) is most probably Master Donald Macvinnoun [or Macmulroun] who had a safe conduct in England for a year, and the Donald Macmulron, clerk, who had a safe conduct for six months in 1444 (*Rot. Scot.*, II, 320, 325; *Bain*, IV, 1151, 1172). He appears again before 1447 as Donald Maconolron, rector of Kyrkben (Kirkbean), Kirkcudbrightshire (*Pap. Lett.*, x, p. 280). Nevinus Makmulron also appears as a student of St. Andrews, 1472 (ERUS., p. 52). Duncan McMulron, a follower of the earl of Cassilis, was respited for murder, 1526 (RSS., I, 3386).

MACMUNAGLE, MACMENIGALL. From Ir. *MacMaongail*, 'son of Maonghal,' an old Donegal surname.

MACMUNN. G. *Mac Gille Mhunna*, 'son of the servant of (S.) Munn.' Munnu or Mundu is the hypocoristic form of Mo-Fhindu, an affectionate form of Fintán or Fintén Mocumoie, who died in 635. He is commemorated in Kilmun near Inveraray, and a half merkland of the territory of Inverquhapill was occupied in 1497 by a certain procurator with the staff of S. Mund (*cum baculo Sancte Munde*), called in Scots (i.e. Gaelic) Deawray (RMS., II). Members of this old sept of unknown origin are often found mentioned in writs connected with Cowal, the scene of the saint's labors. Cuthbert Makelemwyn of the county of Lanark rendered homage, 1296. His seal bears a mullet and S' Cudb' Machlivini (?) (*Bain*, II, p. 210, 531). In another entry of his homage his name is mangled into Makeleinwra. A family of this name was early settled in Bute, and in 1506 Fynlai Makilmune appears as rentaller of half of the lands of Keremanache (RMS., II, 2987). John Makgillemon had sasine of the same lands in 1517 (ER., XIV, p. 597), and in 1608 Finlay M'Ilmune was served heir to them (*Retours, Bute*, 16). William McKilmoun and Johne Makmun, followers of the earl of Cassilis, were respited for murder, 1526 (RSS., I, 3386). John McYlmun was sergeant of Air, 1562 (RMS., III, 1421), and William Makilmun was messenger there, 1587. Thomas McKilmun was burgess of Kirkcudbright, 1593 (RMS.). Archibald Mc illenaif Vic a fwne, a witness, 1606 (HP., IV, p. 46). Joanne McDonche VcIlmund witnessed sasine of Glasver and Arnfad in the barony of Glasrie, 1608 (*Genealogist*, new ser. XXXII, p. 20). John McIlmune, tanner in Port of Roisdo (? Rossdhu), was declared a rebel for refusing the authorized instruction in tanning of leather, 1621 (RPC., XII, p. 491). James M'Ilmowne, formerly in Auchneische,

MACMUNN, *continued*

was heir of Matthew M'Ilmowne in Mayboill, 1624 (*Inquis.*, 1148), Donald M'Gilmin is in Soccochnasmodan, 1630 (*Sasines*, II, 327), and Kathrine Ncillmoon is recorded in Bute, 1662 (HP., III, p. 10). Angus Mackilmune was one of those massacred by the Campbells at Dunoon, 1646 (*Lamont*, 786). Archibald M'Illmunie was portioner of Succoth, 1672 (HP., II, p. 214). M'Illnumes in record in 1668 (HP., II, p. 219) is probably an error for M'Illmunes, and Angus M'Illmund appears in Fincharne Nedder, 1672 (ibid., p. 208). M'Ilmun 1689, M'Ilmwn 1553, Makilmun 1587, Makilmune 1646, Makylmoun 1543, and in 1684 (*Parish*) McIlmvn, Mcilmin, and McKminne. Mcilphoune, M'ilwhynne. The Macmunns may have been of Lamont origin.

MACMURCHIE, MACMURCHY. The *ch* is guttural. G. *MacMhurchaidh*, 'son of Murdo,' or 'MURDOCH,' q.v. A sept known as *Siolachadh Mhurchaidh*, said to have been descended from one Murdoch, a natural son of Angus Mor of Islay, was formerly numerous in North Uist (*Clan Donald*, III, p. 366). In Kintyre and at Shisken in Arran *MacMhurchaidh* becomes '*Ac Furchaidh* (*f* taking the sound of *mh*), and at Southend in Arran '*Ac 'Urchaidh* (TGSI., XXI, p. 238). Kathel Macmurchy was one of an inquest at Dumbarton, on the lands of Polnegulan, 1259 (*Bain*, I, 2174; APS., I, p. 89). Evyne Makmurche was procurator for Janet Ogilvy of Dundee, 1492, and in 1500, as Owin M'Murquhe, he filled the same office for James Scrymgeour (HP., II, p. 190, 199). In 1498 the goods of Rury Gar Makteir Makmurquhy were distrained (OPS., II, p. 527). John McMurchie was tenant of Kildallag, Kintyre, 1506 (ER., XII, p. 707), Andreas McMorthy was one of the king's tenants in Strathdee, 1527, and Gillecrist Makworricht or Makmoriche was charter witness in Stratherne, Perthshire, 1529–30 (RMS., III, 861, 931). William McMurthe and John McMurthe were tenants of Feris, 1539 (ER., XVII, p. 668). In 1541 Sir Murdoch McMoroquhy (a cleric) was tenant of Arealach or Arealaith, Islay, Neil McMurkka tenant of Kilcavane, there, and Nicholl McMurroquhy, tenant of Bairrepoill, Tiree (ibid., XVII, p. 614, 620, 641). John McDonald McMurquhe is in record in Dornoch, 1568, and John Oig McMurquhie was a 'leiche' or 'doctour of medicine' in Islay, 1615 (*Cawdor*, p. 234). The tombstone of the famous old cateran Donald MacMurchie (who was really a Macleod) is in the old churchyard near Balmakill, parish of Durness, Sutherland. It reads: *Donald Mackmurchou hier lyis lo was*

il to his freind var to his fo true to his maister in veird and vo, 1623, that is "Donald Macmurchou here lies low, was ill to his friend, worse to his foe, true to his master in weird and woe." Gillicallum McWorthie or McVorchie in Abose was put to the horn (outlawed), 1629 (RPC., 2. ser. II, p. 341; III, p. 46). Kenneth McCurchie and Dod McConill roy vic Curchie were engagers on the rovalist side from the parish of Urquhart, 1649 (IDR., p. 368). Angus McCurchie and Normand McWurchie in North Galson, Normand McOil Vic Urchy in Comernihawn, John McUrchie Ken Roy in Shabost, Malcolm McUrchy in Neather Bible, and Finlav McVurchie in Eroble are in record, 1726–27 (HP., II). VcErichie 1655, VcMurrochie and VicWurchie 1649, WicWurchie 1651. In Kintyre pronounced Macmurchie (*ch* gutt.) and as Macmurtchie (*ch* as in church), and without 'Mac' as Murchie or Murtchie. A Domhnull MacMhurchaidh in Islay Englished his name Donald Murdoch.

MACMURDO. A modification of MacMurdoch, in G. *Mac Mhurchaidh*, for which see under MURDOCH. The name appears originally in Kintyre and Arran, and in late sixteenth century in Dumfriesshire. Evarus (Ivar) Makmurthe was a tenant in Kintyre, 1506 (ER., XII, p. 699). Robert Makmurdie was retoured heir of John Makmurdie in Dunscoir, his father, in the lands of Cubbentoun and Ferdene-Makcrerie, "nunc vulgo vocatis Makmurdestoun," 1602 (*Retours, Dumfries*, 15). M'Murdie of Killilego in the parish of Dunskoir is in record, 1675 (ibid., 276). M'Murday 1565. The name is also Englished MURDOCHSON and MURDOSON. "The family of M'Murdo can be traced back for a considerable period, being connected with the parish of Dunscore, and giving name to the property of M'Murdiston . . . There is a charter from the commendator of Melrose, dated 25th July 1565, to William M'Murday and his heirs, of the lands of M'Cubbingstoun and Ferdin-Makrary (possibly Farding-Makrary)" (*Ramage*, p. 66).

MACMURRAY. A Galloway surname. Ir. *MacMuireadhaigh*, 'son of Muireadhach,' a common Irish personal name in the Annals of the Four Masters. Fergus M'Mury and John M'Mury are mentioned in the will of Egidia Blair, Lady Row, 1530 (CAC., I, p. 95). Sir Fergus M'Murre, chaplain in Glasgow, 1553 (*Protocols*, I). Moldone McMurrve in Bute had sasine in 1560 (ER., XIX, p. 464). John M'Murrie in Blackfoord, 1678 (*Kirkcudbright*). Thomas MacMurree and Janet MacMurrie were residents in the parish of

Borgue, 1684 (RPC., 3. ser. IX, p. 567). John McMurrie in Auchentibbert, 1763 (*Wigtown*). In 1684 the name is also recorded (*Parish*) as McKlemuray, McKmurrie, McMurry, Mulmuray, Mulmury>Murray (Mirrey, Moray, Morray, Muray, Murra). There is a Balmurrie (i.e. Murray's town) in the parish of New Luce.

MACMURRICH. A variant form of MAC-VURICH, q.v. Macmurich was a well-known name in Jura, and is at present, in the form of Currie, not unusual in some of the adjoining isles. Cristin M'Murrich of Garharf was bailie of Cowell, 1535 (*Lamont*, p. 53), and Alexander M'Murrich, Gylcrist M'Murrich, Finlay M'Murrich, and Donald M'Murrich were witnesses in the same document. Donald Makmurriche in Killage, 1597. Murdoch Roy M'Murrich was one of those murdered by the Covenanters at Dunaverty, 1647 (HP., II, p. 257). M'Murriche 1663, M'Murrycht 1570.

MACMURTCHIE. A form of MACMURCHIE, q.v. The *ch* is pronounced as in church.

MACMURTRIE, MACMUTRIE. Forms of MAC-KIRDIE, q.v. The first form is current in Ayrshire and Lanarkshire, the second shows metathesis of *t*. Gilbert Makmurtye was a witness in Edinburgh, 1508 (RMS., II, 3217), and William M'Mowtrie was a soldier in Edinburgh, 1684 (*Edinb. Marr.*).

MACMUTRIE. See under MACMURTRIE.

MACMYN. A Galloway surname. See under MACMIN.

MACNAB. G. *Mac an Aba*, 'son of the abbot.' The early chiefs of the Clan Macnab were probably lay abbots of Glendochart, in which glen lay the lands of the clan, and in which there was formerly a great Celtic monastery. In the seventh century St. Fillan founded a monastery in the glen, the upper part of which took its name of Strathfillan from him, and in the reign of William the Lion we find that the abbot of Glendochart ranked as an equal with the earls of Atholl and of Menteath (APS., I, p. 372). In a genealogy of the Macnabs compiled in 1467 we find a Gillafaelan ("servant of St. Fillan") named as one of the early chiefs (*Coll.*, p. 52). A bond of manrent dated 1606 declaring a connection between the Macnabs and the Mackinnons seems mere fancy. A Mathew M'Nab was a tenant of the earl of Douglas in Brekauchbeg in the barony of Buittle in 1376, and Maurice M'Nab was a tenant in Glenwaldy in the barony of Prestoune in the same year (RHM., I, p. lix, lxi). Robert Gynab, a Scots prisoner

of war, was released from prison in Colchester, 1396 (*Bain*, IV, 483). The obit of Patrick M'Gynnab of Bovan is recorded in 1488 (*Chr. Fort.*), and Finlav M'ynnab, author of a satire on lazy bards, preserved in the collection of Gaelic poetry known as the "Book of the Dean of Lismore" (c. 1512), is probably the Finlai M'Genab de Bowayn whose obit is placed in 1525 (*Chr. Fort.*, p. 119). John Makinnab was servitor to James Grant of Freuquhye in 1647 (*Grant*, III, p. 342). M'Knab 1598, M'Knabe and Maknabe 1591, McNap 1692, Milnab (*Just. Rec.*, II, p. 126) 1643.

In the early Celtic Church the abbot of a monastery usually belonged to a leading family of the tribe or *tuath*, and in that family the office was hereditary. "In course of time this system gave rise to great abuses; the monastery grew rich in lands, and the energies of the abbot, or some other leading officer, were directed to temporal rather than spiritual management. In fact, latterly he became a mere layman, holding the abbacy in his family by direct descent, and, delegating his clerical duties to a monk, he himself took to rearing a family in which the monastic lands were hereditary. Crinan, lay abbot of Dunkeld, for example, was a king's son-in-law, and also a king's father — father of the unfortunate King Duncan" (Macbain, *Scoto-Celtic studies*, p. 69). The Abernethies are also descended from lay abbots.

MACNACHTAN, MACNAUGHTAN, MAC-NAUCHTON, MACNAGHTEN, MACNAUGHTAN, MACNAUGHTEN, MACNAUGHTON, MACNAUTON. In G. *Mac Neachdainn*, 'son of Neachdain,' the Pictish NECHTAN, q.v. Gillecrist Mac Nachtan granted the church of Kelmurkhe (Kilmorich) in 1247 to the Abbey of Inchaffray (*Inchaffray*, p. 65). Donald Macnachtane, son of an unmarried nobleman and an unmarried woman, was dean of Dunkeld in 1431 (*Pap. Lett.*, VIII, p. 368, 628). Sir Duncan McNachtan was dean of Dunkeld in 1438 (*Athole*, p. 707), and Donald McNachtan, crown tenant of Eddergoll, 1480 (*Christie*, p. 84). Schir Maureis McNauchtane was vicar of Inchedin in 1510 (*Macgregor*, I, p. 84). Donald Macnachtane, rector of Weem (*Pap. Lett.*, IX). Alexander Maknachtan of Dounderaw signed the earl of Argyll's letters of fire and sword against Clan Gregor in 1565 (BBT., p. 212), and was a witness at Garvie, 1569 (*Poltalloch Writs*, p. 184). John McNauchtane of Dundarrow and Duncan McNauchtane, his brother, were charged in 1596 with violence to Dame Jeane, Lady Ardkinglas (RPC., V, p. 322). John MacNachtan of Dunderaw witnessed a com-

MACNACHTAN, Macnauchtan..., cont'd
mission by the earl of Argyll, 1598 (Poltalloch Writs, p. 75), and Alister M'Nachtane
of Dindaraw was admitted burgess of Glasgow gratis in 1614 (Burgesses). As late as
1627 Colonel Alexander MacNaughten raised
a company of two hundred Highland bowmen for service in the expedition to France
for the relief of La Rochelle. They were,
however, recruited too late for that purpose
(HP., I, p. 113). MacNachtin 1563, Mac-
Naghtane 1513, Macneacain 17c., MacNeac-
den and M'Neachden 1403, MacNaichtane
1618, Macknaughtane 1630. See NACHTYSON.

MACNAE. Surname in M'Kerlie. In 1684
spelled also McNea and Maknae (Parish).
Archibald M'Nae in Blairinnea, 1751 (Kirkcudbright). See under MACNEE.

MACNAGHTEN. See under MACNACH-
TAN.

MACNAIR, Macnayer, Macneir, Macnuir,
Macnuyer. This surname is generally considered to have at least three different origins:
(1) The Macnairs of Ross-shire (Gairloch)
are supposed to derive their name from a
Mac-Iain-uidhir, 'son of dun (odhar) John,'
through Mac-an-uidhir, condensed into
M'In-nir. (2) The Perthshire sept appear in
documents as early as 1370 as Macnayre, in
1468 M'Inayr, explained as M'an-oighre, 'son
of the heir.' A story more or less apocryphal
is told to account for this origin of the name.
(3) The late Prof. Mackinnon suggested Mac-
an-fhuibhir, 'son of the smith;' and Dr. Macbain added another possible derivation from
Mac-an-fhuidhir, 'the stranger's son.' The latter
two names are pronounced Mac-an-ewar, with
dh and fh mute. The Macnairs of Lennox,
some of whom go by the name of Weir, are
reckoned a sept of Marfarlane; the Argyllshire (Cowal) sept are connected with the
Macnaughtons; and the Perthshire Macnairs
are probably a branch of the Macnabs. The
lands of Foss in Perthshire formed part of the
extensive abthania of Dull, which was co-
extensive with the parishes of Dull and Fortingall. When the lands of the Abbey of Dull
came to be secularized the earliest name
found in connection with Foss is Christian Hair
(? error for Nair), who got a charter of the
lands of Wester Fosseiche from Robert I
(RMS., I, App. II, 484). Andrew Mcnayr and
Angus Mcnayr were put to the horn in 1392
as art and part in the slaughter of Walter de
Ogilvy, sheriff of Angus (APS., I, p. 579).
Sir Simone M'Nar, rector of Arddewnane, and
Sir Robert M'Nar witnessed a sasine in favor
of Thomas of Abbyrcromby of that Ilk of the

lands of Murthly and Nether Eskyndi in 1445
(Grandtully, I, p. 10). The obit of Rinalde
N'Gynnayr in 1452 is recorded in the Chron-
icle of Fortingall (p. 112), Malcolm McNov-
are appears as 'mair' of Menteth in 1454 and
1456 (ER., v, vi), and twenty years later
Robert Maknare witnessed a charter by John
of Muncreff of that Ilk (Athole, p. 709).
Duncan M'Kynnayr of Lettyrmarclovne, charter witness, 1457 (Lennox, II, p. 73). Finla
M'Nar or Fynlay M'Nare was witness to a
sasine of the lands of Tollard begg in 1478
(Lamont, p. 24). The tenement of Umfridus
Maknayr in Glasgow is mentioned in 1487
(LCD., p. 200), and Jhoannes Maknavr was
tenant of the lands of Mykil Gwffane (Govan)
in 1521 (Rental). Robert Macnare was a wit-
ness in Perth in 1495 (RMS., II, 896), Donald Maknoyar was respited in 1526 for re-
bellion and fire raising (RSS., I, 3640), and
John Maknewar had a remission from Queen
Mary for assisting the English in burning
the town of Dunnone (Dunoon) and be-
sieging the castle in 1546 (RSS.). Robert
Makynnair, rector of Assint in 1548 (RMS.,
IV, 259) appears again in 1565 as Dominus
Robertus M'Genayr in his obit recorded
in the Chronicle of Fortingall (p. 133).
Patrick McNair in Darquhalliche was fined
for resetting members of the outlawed Clan
Gregor in 1613 (RPC., XIV, p. 634), John
M'Nure from the parish of S. Ninians, a
Covenanter, was drowned off Orkney, 1679
(Hanna, II, p. 253). John M'Nair was 'the-
saurer' of the burgh of Stirling in 1654
(SBR., p. 214), John McKnaire was ap-
pointed bailie there in 1686 (RPC., 3. ser.
XII, p. 493), Donald M'Inuire was tenant in
Danamore, Knapdale, in 1689 (Argyll Inv.),
Finlav M'Nuer was a merchant at Inveraray
in 1720 (Campbell, I, p. 180), and Archibald
M'Inuar, merchant tailor in Rothesay, died in
1784 (Isles). Andrew McNare was the official
bell-ringer of the State-House bell in Phila-
delphia from 1759 to 1776, and may have
rung the Liberty Bell on July 4, 1776, and
also four days later when the Declaration of
Independence was first publicly proclaimed in
Philadelphia. Mc inair 1592, M'Innyeir and
M'Inuyer 1672, Mc Inuair 1746, McKnaer
1527, M'Knair 1608, Maknair 1573, M'Kyn-
nair 1575, Macknair 1664, McNavair 1665,
M'Nare 1456, McNeir 1592, M'Newer 1574,
M'Nuir (Cowal) 1685, Mac Nuire 1746,
M'Nuyer (Inverness) 1681, M'Nvyr 1492,
McNwyar (Kilbride) 1665, and (undated)
M'Innar, M'Innuer, M'Innuier, McNoyar, Mc-
Noyiar.

MACNAIRN, Macnarin. Galwegian sur-
names, the first of which is evidently a metath-

esized form of the second, its form having been influenced by the name of the northern county. Cuthbert M'Narne was tenant on the lands of Auchirdilakdy in Dumfriesshire, 1376 (RHM., I, p. liv; II, p. 16). Malcolm M'Nerane is mentioned in 1509 (ALC., 21 July), and Gillecrist Maknerrane was tenant under Stewart of Appin in the same year (*Appin Stewarts*, p. 193). William M'Nairn had sasine of the Know of Fintalloch in 1767. In Galloway in 1684 the name appears as McKnarin, McKnarrine, McKnrrin, McKnarrie, McNaren, McNarien, McNarin, McNarrine, McNarron, McNearie, and McNearin.

MACNAKILL. Sir John of Argyll was authorized in 1306 to receive to the king's peace (among others) Johan M'Nakyld (*Bain*, IV, 1822). Jacobus Maknakill had remission for his share in burning the town of Dunbertane, 1489 (APS., XII, p. 34; *Lennox*, II, p. 133). John McNakill, chaplain, appears in record, 1493 (*Cambus.*, p. 186), and Martin M'Knakyll held a tenement in Ayr, 1505 (*Friars Ayr*, p. 71). The escheat of John McAknakill is recorded in 1537 (ALHT., VI, p. 324).

MACNAMARA. This stands for the form *Mac con-mara*, 'son of the hound of the sea.' In *Cu-mara*, 'hound of the sea,' *mara* is already in the genitive, so that when *Cu-mara* had to be put in the possessive case, as after *mac*, the *Cú* had to be inflected, hence the form *Mac-con-mara*, now MACNAMARA.

MACNAMIL. G. *Mac na maoile*, 'son of baldness.' It is a side form of MACMILLAN, q.v. McNomoille 1707.

MACNARGID. G. *Mac an airgid*, 'son of silver.' The original may have been a worker in silver, a silversmith. Formerly a surname in Arran. Gilcrist Mc Narkade or McNarkede was tenant of Bray in Islay, 1541 (ER., XVII, p. 619, 640). M'Inurignach 1702, M'Nargenach and M'Nargid 1719. See under SILLARS.

MACNARIN. See under MACNAIRN.

MACNAUCHTAN, MACNAUCHTON, MACNAUGHTAN, MACNAUGHTEN, MACNAUGHTON, MACNAUTON. See under MACNACHTAN.

MACNAUGHT, MACNEIGHT. Gilbert Makenaght of Dumfriesshire rendered homage, 1296 (*Bain*, II, p. 185). Cristinus McNawyche witnessed a charter by John de Meneteeche, lord of Arran and Knapdale, for the monastery of Kilwinning, 1357 (RMS., I, 182; Coll. AGAA., I, p. 169). Fergus M'Nauch of Culconnody and John M'Nauch of Craigow were on assize, 1448. A composition was made with Gilbert M'Nauth in Kirkcudbright, 1473

(ALHT., I, p. 7). Martyne M'Nacht witnessed letters of reversion, 1519 (*Pollok*, I, p. 241). Gillie Genach MacNicht in the Lewis was put to the horn in 1606. John McKnawcht, burgess of Edinburgh, 1612, may be John M'Nacht, merchant burgess there, retoured in lands of Larglach, parish of Kirkpatrick-Durham, 1617, Roger M'Naught was retoured heir in ten mark lands of Killquhannatie, 1634, and Nicola M'Naught retoured in same lands, 1646 (*Retours, Kirkcudbright*, 132, 209, 243). Andrew M'Nauche in Blaccader, 1664 (*Lauder*). The Macneights were an old family in Ayrshire (*Paterson*, I, p. 131). In the index to Laing the name appears as: M'Knacht, Macknaicht, Makknaicht, M'Naycht. M'Nacht 1474, Maknath 1496, Maknacht 1471, M'Knach 1521, MakNauch 1526, Maknaucht 1598, M'Naucht 1498, M'Nauth 1473, McKnaught 1725, Mcknayt 1585, Makenaght 1296, Maknech 1582; MacNaght. In Ulster this name was corrupted to Macnutt, and in the United States it also became McNitt.

MACNAYER. A form of MACNAIR, q.v.

MACNEA. See under MACNEE.

MACNEAL, MACNEALE, MACNEALL. See under MACNEIL.

MACNEE, MACNAY, MACNEY, MACNEA, MACNEIGH, MACNIA. Ir. *Mac niadh*, a variant of *Mac neidhe*, 'son of Nia,' i.e. the champion. Macnia, king of Ard of the Ui Echadh, a district in the baronies of Upper and Lower Iveagh, county Down, d. 702. Macnia comarb of Buite, quievit 1037 (*Chron. Scot.*). Maknee is recorded in 1594 (BBT., p. 285). Donald McNie and Gillemoire McNie in Balquhidder were fined for reset of Clan Gregor, 1613 (RPC., XIV, p. 638). The Dean of Lismore has M'onee; M'Knie 1594; M'Kne 1480 (Menteith and Breadalbane). ? = 1667 M'Ilnaey and M'Knae. In fifteenth-century documents as ER. we have M'Knee.

MACNEEL. See under MACNEIL.

MACNEID. A variant of MACNAUGHT, q.v. The same as McNeit (a sept of Macnauchtan according to Buchanan, p. 102). A small sept of Macneids lived on the northern shore of Dumbartonshire during the sixteenth and seventeenth centuries. Donald McKnett in Easter Ardincaple, 1607 (RPC., VII, p. 669). Robert McNait in Stron of Luss in 1614 was fined for reset of Clan Gregor (RPC., XIV, p. 644). Patrick McNeid in Meikle Innerlawren and Robert McNeid in Over Innerlawren, native tanners, were declared rebels for refusing the authorized instruction in their craft of tan-

MACNEID, *continued*

ning, 1621 (ibid., XII, p. 491). D. Maknod was notary public in Kenmore, Kirkcudbright, 1501 (RMS., II, 2634).

MACNEIGH. *See under* MACNEE.

MACNEIGHT. *See under* MACNAUGHT.

MACNEIL, MACNEILL, MACNEILLE, MAC-NEAL, MACNEALE, MACNEALL, MACNEEL, MACNIEL. G. *MacNèill*, 'son of NEIL,' q.v. With the common dialectic change of initial *n* to *r* we have *MacRèill* (*Watson* I, p. 238). Robert the Bruce confirmed to John, son of Gilbert McNeill, five pennylands of Larglanfeild in 'le Rennys Galwia,' 1329 (RMS., I, App. I, 102), and Nigel M'Nele, laird of Blarekanne (Blairquhan) is mentioned c. 1370-80 (*Laing*, 64). Alexander Maknevll was a notary public in Edinburgh, 1526 (*Soltre*, p. 95). Hector MacNeill of Taynish witnessed a feu charter by Lord Lorne to Niall Campbell of Oib, 1633 (*Poltalloch Writs*, p. 189). The Norsemen early adopted the name, and it appears among them as Njal. It appears to have sometimes been Englished NEILSON, q.v. There are two clans of this name: (1) of Barra, (2) of Gigha. McNaill 1541, McNeall 1675, McNeel 1663, Makneill 1427, McNeyll 1518; M'Nele, Makneyll, Maknill.

MACNEILAGE, MACNEILEDGE. A corruption of *M'Nelis* or *M'Nelus*, from *MacNiallghuis*, 'son of Niallghus,' i.e. 'champion choice' (*niall* + *gus*). A Dumbartonshire name mostly. Cristin M'Nelos witnessed a Lamont charter in 1465 (*Lamont*, p. 19). – McNellus was one of the 'wrychtis' engaged by Sir George Calbrathe in 1494 (ALHT., I p. 246), and in 1500 a trial was held for the slaughter of Gillaspy McNelus or M'Neluse (RSS., I, 480; *Trials*, I, p. *100). Archibald McNelluss witnessed sasine at Larichlvssagnicht, 1515, and Milmore Mc nelos was charter witness at Ferlings, 1525 (HP., IV, p. 25). Archibald Mc-Nelus was miller at Campsaill in 1598 (RPC., v, p. 452), Donald M'Nilladge in Kilfinan parish is in record in 1695 (*Argyll*), Gilbert M'Neilladge was burgess of Rothesav in 1663 (*Isles*), and Daniel M'Nilage is recorded in Paisley, 1749 (*Kilbarchan*). M'Neilas 1663, McNeillas 1678, Macneilledge 1816.

MACNEILLIE, MACNILLIE, MACNEILLY, MACNELLY. A Galloway surname. Probably from Ir. *Mac an Fhileadh* or *Mac an Fhilidh*, 'son of the poet,' *file*, a name almost peculiar to N. E. Ulster — (*Woulfe*). Duncan M'Nelv was a witness in Wigtownshire, 1426 (RMS., II, 185). A composition was made with Ranald

Maknelv in Galloway, 1473 (ALHT., I, p. 9). James M'Neillie was retoured heir of Adam M'Neillie of Auchairne in Carrick, 1671 (*Retours, Ayr*, 572), and Thomas McNeillie appears in Ayr, 1689 (RPC., 3. ser. XIV, p. 672). McKneillie 1686. In 1684 (*Parish*) spelled: McNielie, McKnilie, McKnily, Mc-Naall, McNeelie, McNili, McNilli, McNillie, McNilv, and McNyly. Now often shortened to NEIL in Galloway.

MACNEIR. A form of MACNAIR, q.v.

MACNEISH, MACNISH, MACNEICE, MACNESS, MACKNESS. G. *MacNeis* from *MacNaois*. As Naos is merely a dialectal form of *Aonghus*, 'Angus,' the name has therefore the same meaning as MACANGUS and MACINNES. The Clan Macnish once possessed much of the upper parts of Strathearn, but were nearly exterminated by the Macnabs in a battle fought at Glenboltachan in the year 1522. The lands of Knocbane, Dumfriesshire, were held by Gilmor Macnesche in 1376 (RHM., II, 16). John Dow Macneische witnessed a Grantully charter in 1494. Jonete Maknes was tenant of Drumgy, Menteith, in 1495, and in the following year Mariote Macneis received sasine of the same lands (ER., x). The name of Jonete appears in January and June, 1500, as Jonete Nete or Neis (RMS.). Mariot Makneisch had sasine of the fourth part of Gadgill, Kirkcudbrightshire, in 1517 (ER., XIV, p. 603), and two years later there is on record confirmation of four charters by Mariot, Jonet, Katherine and Elena Makneissche, daughters of quondam Duncan Makneissche de Gaitgill-Makillwarnok in the Stewartry of Kirkcudbright (RMS., III, 191). Donald McNysche and John McNysche, followers of the earl of Cassilis, were respited for murder, 1526 (RSS., I, 3386), and mention is made in 1552 of "a venerable and learned man, Mr. James Makneis, deserving well of the city," i.e. of Glasgow (*Protocols*, I, 152). Thomas McNaoise or McNoaise "confest his malicious imprecaones against the minister" in 1650 (IDR., p. 176, 180), and Marion Maknish was charged with being a disorderly person (i.e. non-conforming) in the parish of Kirkmabreck, 1684 (RPC., 3. ser. IX, p. 573). McKneach and McKnish 1684, M'Kneis 1576, McKneische 1629, McKneishe 1477, Makneisch and Makneische 1508, Makneiss and Makneissche 1520, McNeiss 1550, McNeische 1574, McNische 1622, McNish 1718.

MACNELLAN. James M'Nellane, servant, St. Ninian's parish, Stirling (*Sc. Ant.*, VI, p. 165). John Maknellen, burgess and guild brother, Stirling, 1560 (SBR., p. 75). Spelled M'Knellane and Macknellan in Laing's *Calendar.* McNilland 1590.

MACNERLIN, MACERLANE. From Ir. *Mac an Fhirleighinn*, 'son of the lector,' or 'man of reading.' The firleighinn or ferleighinn was the head of a monastic school both in Scotland and in Ireland. In Iona in 1164 (Reeves, *Adamnan,* p. 407) we find Ferleighinn Dubside as one of the officials of the monastery, and in the following century the name is still preserved in connection with the church of St. Andrews (Skene, CS., II, p. 446). The name occurs as Virolecus in Adamnan (VC., III, 14) as that of a man in Airchartdan (Glen Urquhart) baptized by the saint during his visit there. About 1211 Laurence, archdeacon and ferlan, head of the schools of St. Andrews, appears in connection with a dispute with the prior and canons; his title is Latinized Ferlanus and Ferleynus (RPSA., p. 317–318). Morice Macinnirlegin obtained possession of the perpetual vicarage of S. Comanus's in Ila after he had become excommunicate (*Pap. Lett.,* VII, p. 597). In 1443 Donald, son of Dominic Macnafirlegind, perpetual vicar of S. Comanus's (Kilchoman), evidently a relative, was accused of being "a notorious fornicator" (ibid., IX, p. 404). On the Kilchoman Cross is the inscription: *Hec est crux fac(ta) pro animabus Doncani mec Innirlegin et Mari et Michaelis,* "This is a cross made for the souls of Duncan, son of the lector and Mary and Michael." Its date may be about 1420 or 1430.

MACNESS. *See under* MACNEISH.

MACNEUR. *See under* MACNAIR.

MACNEY, MACNIA. *See under* MACNEE.

MACNICOL, MACNICOLL, MACNICHOL. G. *Mac Neacail,* Middle Gaelic *M'Nicail,* 'son of Nicol.' Nicol is from Latin Nicolas, which again is borrowed from Greek Νικολάς, 'conquering people.' A small sept of Macnicols in Wester Sutherland and in Skye are now generally called Nicolson. The Glenorchy Macnicols are in local tradition said to have sprung from one Nicol M'Phee who left Lochaber in the sixteenth century; they are properly therefore M'Phees (*Henderson,* p. 52). The popular etymology of the name from an ancestor Krycul and the suggestion of the late Capt. Thomas that the name comes from the thirteenth century island chieftain Ottar Snaekollson are both inaccurate. In Arran Mac Neacail is pronounced 'Ac Riocail. MacNicoll in Portree in Skye, according to Hugh Macdonald, formed one of the council of Macdonald of the Isles at Island Finlaggan in Islay (HP., I, p. 24). A half part of the land of Fortar

in Angus was let to one Maknychol in 1470 (*Cupar-Angus,* I, p. 157). Gilbert McNicol was a charter witness in 1533 (*Poltalloch Writs,* p. 137), and Thomas Maknicoll was a witness in Glasgow in 1553 (*Protocols,* I). Malcolmuill McNicoll is in record in 1585 (*Cawdor,* p. 187), John M'Nicoll in Glenfalloch in 1638 (BBT., p. 401), and Nicoll M'Nicoll in Galdanach in 1672 (HP., II, p. 207). The Highland Macneacails may be of Norse origin, but not from Andrew Nicolson the Norwegian baron who distinguished himself at Largs in 1263. M'Nychol 1561, M'Nycholl 1557, M'Nychole 1546, M'Niccoll 1695. Other forms in the Rental Book of Cupar-Angus are: M'Nichole, M'Nicholl, M'Nicoll, Maknichol, Maknicoll, Maknychoil. Other current forms of the surname are MAC-NICHOL and MACNICKLE.

MACNIDER, MACNIDDER, MACNITER. G. *Mac an fhigheadair,* 'son of the weaver.' Matho M'Nedyr was burgess of Ayr, 1471 (*Friars Ayr,* p. 53), and John Makneddar resigned certain annual rents to the Friars Preachers of Ayr, 1515 (ibid., p. 78). Three Maknedars, followers of the earl of Cassilis, were respited for murder in 1526 (RSS., I, 3386). John McNettar, fisherman in Inverness, 1557 (*Rec. Inv.,* p. 8), John M'Knedar, clerk of Glasgow diocese, 1567 (*Friars Ayr,* p. 106); and John McKnedar, notary in Prestwick, 1575 (*Prestwick,* p. 77), may be the John McKnedar, burgess of Ayr in 1585, who appears as cautioner for Oswald McKnedar in £200 (RPC., III, p. 723, 732). A McNoder in Strogarne was summoned to answer a charge of violence and robbery in 1592 (RPC., V, p. 28). Mc-Coull VcNeter in Strathfellen was one of a number who aided the Macgregors at Glenfruin and Glenfinlas (Irving, *Dumbartonshire,* p. 227). John McNedar in Maybole, 1604, and Alexander McNedar in Drumnoir, Ayrshire, 1608 (RPC., VII, p. 548; VIII, p. 671). The name is probably extinct in Scotland, but it occurs in Canada and the United States. Hanford McNider was unsuccessful nominee for the Presidency of the United States in 1932. In some cases the surname has probably been changed to its English equivalent, WEAVER. M'Nedair 1589.

MACNIE. *See under* MACNEE.

MACNIEL. *See under* MACNEIL.

MACNIFF. Most probably from Ir. *MacConduibh,* 'son of *Cu-dub*' ('black hound'), which gives MacAnuff, MacAniff, MacKniff, etc. John M'Kniff in Lochones, 1674 (*Kirkcudbright*), and Donel McKnivr was inhabitant of Stirling, 1717 (*Sc. Ant.,* VI, p. 88). Recorded in Loanhead, 1942.

MACNIGHT. *See under* MACKNIGHT.

MACNILLIE. *See under* MACNEILLIE.

MACNINCH. From *MacAonghus*, 'son of ANGUS,' q.v. Thomas McNinch held the lands of Blarawart in Carrick, 1658 (RMS., x). The name is still in record in Ayrshire.

MACNISH. *See under* MACNEISH.

MACNISHIE. A complaint was made by William Ros of Kilraik (Kilravock) in 1602 against Macdonalds for taking Nesie Mc Nesie's horses, goods and plenishing (RPC., VI). This is the last use of Nes or Nesie as a Christian name. The descendants of this Nesie probably adopted the surname of Mac-Nishie, which occurred in that district in the early part of the nineteenth century (*Macnish*).

MACNITER. *See under* MACNIDER.

MACNIVEN, MACNEVIN. G. *MacNaoimhin*, 'son of the holy one,' a diminutive of *naomh*. In Iona the name is pronounced *MacRaoi'in* (*Watson* I, p. 519), and in Kintyre '*AcRiomhainn*. The Macnivens were connected with the Macnaughtons, and had several farms and places about Lochawe. There is also a Macniven island in Loch Mor, Craignish. They were later dependents of the Campbells. Duncan M'Nicoll V'Nevin was one of Campbell of Barbreck's followers in 1623. John M'Ni-vaine appears in the muster-roll of the laird of Glenurquhay, 1638 (BBT., p. 398). Mc-Newan 1684; McNeiving.

MACNOAH. A Galloway surname now rare. Naoi is the older Gaelic form of Noah (*Watson*). Noah, abbot of Kingarth in Bute, died 789–90 (AU.). John M'Noe was indweller at Bridgend, parish of Troqueer, 1658 (*Dumfries*), and James M'Knoe was "burrow officer in Drumfries," 1687 (RPC., 3. ser. XIII, p. 169). Marion McNoe was registered 'papist' in the bounds of the Presbytery of Dumfries, 1705 (MCM., III, p. 419), Jean M'Noe appears in Dumfries, 1715 (*Dumfries*), and James M'Noah appears in Barsalloch, 1790 (*Wigtown*).

MACNOBLE. A once common surname in Ross though now only NOBLE, q.v. In G. *Mac Nobuill*. There is a place called Coire Mhic Nobuill in the parish of Applecross.

MACNOKARD. G. *Mac na cearda*, 'son of the smith.' In old G. *cerd* meant a worker in brass, and in early times the *ceard* was the craftsman *par excellence*, held in the highest respect, but in later times, through the decay of native industries in metals, the term was degraded and applied to the poorest class of itinerant artificers, patchers of pots and pans, and equated with Scots tinkler. In Burns's time the word seems still to have retained its meaning of a worker in brass, as the caird in the "Jolly Beggars" says of himself:

"My bonie lass, I work in brass,
A tinker is my station."

Macnokard was a common name in the six-teenth and seventeenth centuries and occurs often in old Scots records and documents of that period. Gregor Makenkerd agreed to serve Edward I of England in France, 1297 (*Bain*, II, p. 242). Iain Mc nocerdych was charter witness in Lismore, 1525 (HP., IV, p. 27). Gillecreist M'Conoquhy Duy Vc Nocarde in record in Argyll, 1574 (OPS., II, p. 127), appears again in 1580 as Gillecreist Makonchy Duff V'Nokerd, native servant to Campbell of Glenurquhy (BBT., p. 223). John M'Ne-caird was tenant in Evich, 1594 (ibid., p. 283). Archibald M'Nokaird was portioner of Drumurk, 1629 (*Sasines*, 286), and Myl-doniche or Moldonyt McNoheardie or Mc-Nokeardie in Carnakalliche was put to the horn in the same year (RPC., 2. ser. II, p. 341, III, p. 46). Patrick Dow M'Nokerd in Auchin-chalden and Angus M'Nokerd in Braklead appear in 1638 (BBT., p. 403), Finlay Mc nakaird was an 'engager' on the royalist side from Urquhart, 1649 (IDR., p. 368), and Dun-can M'Knokaird is in Monienirnach, 1672 (HP., II, p. 208). John Dow M'Nockard and Malcolm M'Nockard in Kilvicewn, and Dun-can M'Norcard in Scur were denounced rebels, 1675 (HP., I). Archibald M'Nokaird was mer-chant burgess of Inveraray, 1695 (*Campbell* I, p. 13), and Dond McNougard is recorded in Gerrich, Islay, 1741 (*Bk. Islay*, p. 559). In Argyllshire the name is now rendered Sin-clair. McNikord and McNokord 1699, Mc-Nekard 1724. See also CAIRD.

MACNORANCE. Thomas Maknorance was a charter witness at Balquhidder, 1549 (HP., IV, p. 32).

MACNORAVAICH. In G. *Mac an fhoirbhich*, 'son of the *foirbheach*,' more com-monly *foirfeach* being the Gaelic for '(church) elder.' Donald M'Noravaich of Stuckagoy is in record in 1677. The Inveraray Munros for-merly called themselves McNorvaich. McNore-vick.

MACNORTON. A rare surname, probably a corruption of MACNAUGHTON, q.v.

MACNOTHAC. Duncan Maknothac wit-nessed instrument of sasine of lands of Garn-tullie in 1533 (*Grandtully*, I, p. 72).

MACNUCATOR, MACKNOCKATER, MAC-
KNOCKITER, MACKNOCKER, MACUCHADAIR,
NUCATOR. From G. *Mac an fhucadair*, 'son of
the fuller (of cloth),' Scots 'wauker.' To judge
from the innumerable forms of this name in
the public records its proper spelling has been
a puzzle for the scribes. In 1508 half of Auchinlech Nethyr was leased for five years to John
Makinnocater (*Cupar-Angus*, I, p. 266).
Johannes McFuktor (without the article) and
Elspet Innyfuktour (i.e. *inghean fucadair*,
'the fuller's daughter') are in record in Strathdee in 1527 (*Grant*, III, p. 70), and Donald
rove McInocader witnessed an instrument of
sasine of lands in Knapdale in 1547 (*Poltalloch Writs*, p. 139). Donald M'Ynnocater appears in Balloch in 1560 (BBT., p. 203), John
McInhugater in Airochmore, Stirling, in 1592,
and Patrick McInhuggutir in Glenleidnoch in
1602 (RPC., XIV, p. 396). John Mcincutour
was tenant of Cunningham of Drumquhassil
in Lennox in 1602, and Margaret Nicuncater,
tenant in Kilbride, Lennox, in 1610. Ewne
or Ewin McInnugatour in Ballinacall (or Bal-
limakill), Donald McMungatour or M'Muga-
tour, and John McMigatour in Coull of Balquhidder, Patrick McMuckater in Balledmont,
and Donald McInmugatour in Ballichandie
were fined in 1613 and 1614 for reset of members of the outlawed Clan Gregor (RPC.,
XIV, p. 630, 637, 638, 656, 661; X, p. 122;
IX, p. 228, 483). John Dow McInnow Catter
or McNucatter in Carnakalliche was one of a
number charged with spoliation of a ship
called *The Providence of Dumbarton* in 1629
(ibid., 2. ser. II, p. 341; III, p. 45, 46). Patrick
and William McMuncatter, in Mortlach, followers of Alastair Cumming of Pettiwaich,
were charged in 1642 with carrying prohibited weapons (RPC., 2. ser. VII, p. 286).
Donald Roy M'Nugattar is in record in Dadin,
parish of Comrie, in 1653 (*Dunblane*), and
Donald M'Nawcater in Toweruthan, parish of
Muthill, about the same period (ibid.). Patrick McNowcatter was procurator-fiscal of
Argyll in 1665 and Martine McNaucater, who
held the same office in 1667, is perhaps the
Martin McNucater who was sheriff-officer in
1649 (RPC., 3. ser. II, p. 116, 346; *Genealogist*, n.s. XXXV, p. 42). John M'Enugator was
in the parish of a doctor in 1666 (*Strathendrick*, p. 107). Donald McNowcater was servitor of John Yuill in Inveraray in 1659 (*Genealogist*, n.s. XXXV, p. 230), another Donald
M'Inugator was resident in Dallogane, parish
of Balquhidder, in 1677, and a third Donald
Mcinucter in Bellivillinvege, witnessed an instrument of sasine in 1679 (*Dunblane; Laing*,
2787). John M'Noucater in Auchavyll, parish
of Glasrie, appears in record in 1684, and
in 1694 Maolmorrie M'Innuccater in Kilislet,

parish of Kilberry (*Argyll Inv.*). In the Register of Testaments of Argyll, 1674–1800, we
have John M'Nuccater in Auchadamillan, who
died in May, 1693; Katharine N'Nuccatri in
Stronchurmore, 1695; Margaret N'Nuccater in
Bargaragane, parish of Kelislet, in 1698. Some
Macuchkaders were followers of the Stewarts of Appin in the '45 (*Coll.*, p. 199). Mc-
Knockiter is an uncommon Moray form of the
name, and the Nucators of Dundee are descended from a MacNucator (1830). The
name also occurs in record without the 'Mac'.
Finlay Fuccatour appears in Strowane in 1601
(*Dunblane*), and in 1614 Gibboun Fugatour
in Ferlingbrek, Dumbarton, was fined twenty
marks for reset of outlawed members of the
Clan Gregor (RPC., X, p. 225). The name
is now Englished WALKER, and doubtless most
of our Highland Walkers were originally *Mac
an fhucadairs*. McInukidar 1692.

MACNUIR. See under MACNAIR.

MACNUTT. A variant of MACNAUGHT (of
Kilquhanite, Galloway), q.v. The Macnutts of
Londonderry (now Manchester, New Hamp-
shire, U. S.) are descended from William
McNaught who settled there in 1718. (2)
The Irish Macnutts are said to be MacNuadat,
from *Nuadha*, an early Irish personal name.
Nuadu Argatlam (of the Silver Hand) was
the name of an ancient Irish deity.

MACNUYER. See under MACNAIR.

MACOBNACH. Donald M'Obnach in Sluma-
boll was denounced rebel in 1675 (HP., I,
p. 301).

MACODRUM. A variant of MACCODRUM,
q.v.

MACOISEIN. In Islay this name was Anglicized Mackay. See MACCOSHAM.

MACOLCHALLUM. An obsolete patronymic, originally G. *M'Mhaoil Chaluim*. Gillereoch Makolcallum in the Black Isle, 1500
(*Rose*, p. 169). The obit of Duncan M'Olchallum VcKerlych apud Drumcharre in 1522 is
recorded in the Chronicle of Fortingall, and
likewise the death of the wife of Alexander
McOlchallum in 1542 (*Chr. Fort.*, p. 117,
121). Gilbert M'Olchallum, notary public,
1533 (*Poltalloch Writs*, p. 72), as Makol-
challin was vicar of Lochgoyll in 1540 (*Lamont*, 50), and reappears in 1543 as Gilbert
Makolcallum, rector of Craginche (RMS., III,
2902). John McOlcallum was tenant of land
in Tiree, 1541 (ER., XVII, p. 614). William
M'Olcallum in Rannocht, Malcum his son,
and Donald Roy M'Olchallum Glass, "thair
airis barnis and posterite" gave their band of

MACOLCHALLUM, *continued*

manrent to Colyne Campbell of Glenurquhay in 1552 to be his "afald seruantis . . . renunciand M'Gregour their auld cheif" (BBT., p. 194, 195). Several M'Laurans were known as M'Olcallums in 1559, and Duncan M'Olcallum "and utheris of the Clan Teir" [Macintyre] also gave their band to Glenurquhav in 1556 (ibid., p. 200–202). Gregour Makolchallum in Inuerbar gave his band in 1585 (ibid., p. 232). William McColchollum and Malcolme and George McColchollum, his sons, were charged with slaughter and other "havnous" crimes in 1564, and Malcum MacWolchallum is in record in 1581 (*Macgregor*, I, p. 135, 172.)

MACOLCHYNICH. G. *MacMaolChoinnich,* 'son of the shaveling of Kenneth.' Now rendered Mackenneth or Mackenny, and Englished **MACKENZIE,** q.v. The name of an ancient race of small barons of Chappel Verna in Strachur (HP., IV, p. 46–47). They may have been connected with the ancient church of Kilmalasch. In 1617 we have record of a charter in favor of Archibald McEan rov McOlcheinich, son of Iain rov McOlcheinich, son of Gillespie McGillecheinich of Chappelverna (ibid., p. 47), and in 1632 sasine was made to Iain McIllespie VcEan rov Vcolchynich (ibid., p. 49). John Moir M'Olchynich Taylour is mentioned in 1678, and Duncan rov M'Olchynich in the following year. The *Gille-* form also occurs. See **MACGILLEWHINNICH.**

MACOLEAN. From *Mac a Leathainn,* a common pronunciation of *Mac Gill' Sheathainn,* i.e. Maclean. Patrick M'olane was a witness in Glenurquhav in 1551, Donald M'Olean is in record in Wester Ledchrosk in 1638, and John M'Inlay V'Oleane in Kirktoun was a Glenurquhav vassal in the same year (BBT., p. 205, 401, 403). The name now probably extinct.

MACOLVORIE. Donald Mc Olvorie, rector of Kilmalew, 1618 (*Sasines*, II, 17), appears as Master Donald Makolvorich, parson of Kilmalew, 1629 (OPS., II, p. 85). Donald McOlvorie, provost and burgess of Inverarav, 1649, 1654 (*Poltalloch Writs*, p. 73, 145). Margaret McOlvorie, tenant of Kilchatten, 1669 (HP., IV, p. 222).

MACOMIE. See under **MACCOMIE** and **MACTHOMAS.** Descended from Thomas, a younger son of the sixth Mackintosh. Robert Mac-Homie in the Burn of Glenshee is one of the parties to the Farquharson bond of 1595 granted to Mackintosh as their chief (Mackintosh, *Minor septs of Clan Chattan*, p. 149–150). A different name from **OMAY,** q.v.

MACOMISH, MACCOMISH. G. *Mac Thomais,* 'son of Thomas.' Jo. M'Comes is recorded in Fowlis, 1618 *(Dunblane),* and Donald McHomas was boatman at Inverbreakie, 1688 (RPC., 3. ser. XIII, p. 241). Archibald M'Comash in Inralegan, parish of Innerchelan, 1696, is probably Alexander M'Hamish in Knockdoue, in the same parish, 1699 *(Argyll Inv.).* Donald M'Comash, a Seaforth tenant, 1721 (HP., II, p. 297), Duncan M'Homash in Callander, 1728 *(Dunkeld),* and John Makcomius died in 1777 and was buried in Lennel churchyard. McKomash 1662.

MACONILGLAS. James Macintosche M'onilglas was tenant of Ettras, c. 1603 (SCM., IV, p. 301). Not a patronymic but a phonetic spelling of *MacDhomhnuill glas.*

MACORISH. From Ir. *Mac Fheóruis,* 'son of Piers,' a Norman form of Peter. There is a Macorriston near Thornhill, Dumfriesshire, possibly derived from one of the name.

MACOSHAN. A variant of **MACCOSHEN,** q.v.

MACO'SHANNIG. Formerly Macoseanag in Kilbrandon. See under **O'SHANNAIG.**

MACOSTER, 'son of the door-keeper' (G. *òsdair*). In the old Gaelic monasteries the doorkeeper was called *òsdair,* a loan from Latin *ostiarius.* The word now means innkeeper. Martin (p. 263–264), writing of Iona, says: "There was a Tribe here call'd *Clan vic n'oster,* from *Ostiarii;* for they are said to have been Porters. The Tradition of these is, that before *Columbus* died, thirty of this Family lived then in *Iona,* and that upon some provocation, *Columbus* entail'd a Curse upon them; which was, That they might all perish to the Number of five, and that they might never exceed that Number, to which they were accordingly reduc'd: and ever since, when any Woman of that Family was in Labour, both she and the other four were afraid of Death; for if the Child that was to be then born, did not die, they sav one of the five was sure to die: and this they affirm to have been verify'd on every such occasion successively to this day. I found one only of this Tribe living in the Isle, and both he and the Natives of this and of all the Western Isles, unanimously declare that this Observation never fail'd; and all this little Family is now extinct, except this one poor Man." About 1770 there died in Iona a woman, the last of the race styled *Clan-na-oister,* "who were believed to be the lineal descendants of an individual appointed by Columba doorkeeper of the monastery — an office more likely to have existed in the subsequent Cluniac establishment" (OPS., II, p. 301). A curse similar to that of Columba on the doorkeeper is recorded in the life of Adamnan (CR., v, p. 102; see also p. 98).

MACOUAL, MACOUL, MACOWL. Phonetic forms of MACDOUGAL, q.v. Three persons named M'Oul were tenants of the Kirklands of Strathblane in 1726 (Strathblane, p. 316). Variations "of this type are due to Gaels living in non-Celtic localities, where the unskilled natives fell upon Highlanders by lip and pen till they hardly knew their own address" (Long, Personal and family names, p. 286).

MACOUAT, MACOWAT. Forms of MACWATT, q.v. John Machouat in Gartness in 1729.

MACOULIE. See under MACCULLIE.

MACOULROY. G. Mac mhaoil ruaidh. John M'Oulrov appears in the muster-roll of the laird of Glenurquhay in 1638 (BBT., p. 398). The name is now extinct or merged in MACIL-ROY.

MACOUSTRA. Probably a variant of MAC-OSTER, q.v.

MACPAKE. A rare name from Ir. Mac Péice, 'son of Péic (a variant of the OE. personal name Pic). Lance-corporal Douglas MacPake of Kinlochleven died of wounds, 1940. The name MacPike, now apparently unkown in Scotland and Ireland, may be a variant. James M'Pike, supposed to have been born in Edinburgh, c. 1750, migrated to Baltimore, U. S., about 1772, and a few M'Pikes are mentioned in the third series of Pennsylvania Archives. MacPike occurs in a list of about 300 Galloway 'Macs' (SN&Q., 2. ser. VIII, p. 27). John McPake of Edinburgh was killed in North Africa in April, 1943.

MACPARLAN, MACPARLAND, MACPARLANE, MACPARLIN. See under MACFARLAN.

MACPARTLAND, MACPARTLING. A Galloway name of Irish origin, Mac Pártláin, 'son of Parthalon' (OIr. Partholón). The name is usually equated with Bartholomew, with which, of course, it has no etymological connection. Partholón in Irish legend was the first invader of Ireland 278 years after Noah's flood. Cf. MACFARLAN.

MACPATRICK, MACPHADRICK, MACPHAT-RICK. G. MacPhadruig for earlier MacGille-Phadruig, 'son of the gillie of (S.) Patrick.' Macgyllepatric occurs in a Moray charter of 1236 (REM., p. 31). The form with Maol-occurs, but is less common. A stone in Iona bears the inscription: Or do Mailfataric, 'pray for Mail Patric;' and Malcolm filius Malpatric

witnessed a convention between the prior and canons of St. Andrews and the Culdees there in 1199 (RPSA., p. 319). The obit of Gregory M'Phatryk apud Innerkelthe in Fortyrgall is recorded in 1510 (Chr. Fort., p. 115). Sir Thomas M'Ilpatrick was curate of the church of Drymen, 1511 (Strathendrick, p. 75). Alexander Makfatrik and Elfric Makfatrik had sasine of Killenane, Cowal, in 1504 and 1515 (ER., XII, p. 717, 719), and Affrica Makpatrik, daughter and heiress of Duncan Makpatric, resigned the three mark lands of old extent of Killenane, 1525 (RMS., III). Gilcreis McGilfatrik is in record in Lossit, 1540 (RSS., II, 3666). John Moir M'Gillefatrik and Donald M'Gillefatrik appear in Lochalsh, 1548 (RMS., IV, 204), and Johannes Mac Gille Patrik in Murthlac, 1550 (Illus., II, p. 262). John Dow McPhadrick Moir in Bordling and John McPhatrick Vean were fined in 1613 for aiding Clan Gregor (RPC., XIV, p. 632, 635). Alexander MacPhadrig witnessed a charter of the lands of Dochnacraig, 1620 (TGSI., XXII, p. 257). Angus McIlfatrik, a follower of Murdow McCloyd, took part in the attack on the galley of the laird of Balcomie, one of the Fife adventurers in the Lewis, 1600 (RPC., XIV, p. cxxiii), and John Mcffadrik was accessory to the burning of Barnehill pertaining to Colene Campbell of Lawers, 1612 (Trials, III, p. 223). Allester McPatrick Bwy (Buidhe) and Duncan McPhadrick were fined for reset of Clan Gregor, 1613 (RPC., XIV, p. 637). Finlay McGillifudricke was one of a number charged in 1656 with superstitious "sacrificeing at certaine tymes at the Loch of Mourie" (IDR., p. 280). Patrick M'Ean V'Lephadrik is in record in Glenfalloch, 1638, and Gillepatrik M'Gillepatrik in Ardtattell was a Glenurquhay vassal in the same year (BBT., p. 401, 403). John M'Ilpadrick in Sandlaig was denounced rebel, 1675 (HP., I), and Katharine M'Olphatrick appears in Rawer, 1697 (Dunkeld). Margaret Meiklfatrick in the parish of Kirkcudbright was charged with being disorderly (i.e. non-conforming) in 1684 (RPC., 3. ser. IX, p. 573), and two milk cows were stolen from Archibald M'ilfadrich, tenant on lands of Inverhea, 1685 (Lamont, p. 290). Duncan McIliphadrick and Murdo McIllephadrick in Shabost appear, 1726 (HP., II, p. 314), and Colin M'Phadraig was one of the duke of Atholl's fencible men in Glenlyon, 1708 (HMon., III, p. 216). Macpatrick is one of the aliases of the Lamonts descended from baron MacPatrick, who was ancestor of the Lamonts of Coustone. Mcfaddrik 1598: McGilpharick, McGilparick, and Mcpharick are found in Cowal, 1761 (Clan Lamont journal, II, p. 154). McGilephatrik 1618, McGillepatrick 1536, McGille-

MACPATRICK, Macphadrick..., *continued*

phadrick 1718, McGilliphatrik 1629, McGilphadrick 1746, M'Illepatrick 1566, Mc illephudrick 1617, Mc illfatrik 1637, M'Kilpatrick 1568, Machpatrick 1661, McPhadruck 1771, McPhatricke 1673; McPhadrik, McPhadryk. The name has been Englished PATERSON and PATTERSON.

MACPAYE. Gildow McPaye in Perth, 1471 (ER., VIII, p. 37). Sowtar Makpaa in Litill Treuchare, 1503 (RSS., I, 954). Andrew M'Pe in Obnie, Perthshire, 1688 (*Dunkeld*).

MACPEETERS. See MACPHATER.

MACPERSON. A current form of MACPHERSON, q.v.

MACPETER, 'son of PETER,' q.v. Donald M'Petir, resident in Drumcryne, Ayrshire, 1621 (*Laing*, 1867). See also MACPETRIE.

MACPETRIE, Macpetre. Same as MACPETER, q.v. Ayg' Mac Petri was perpetual vicar of the parish church of S. Columba of Kerepol, 1375 (*Chron. Man*, p. 186). Patricius moir McPatre McWilliam, parishioner of Duthil, 1537 (*Grant*, III, p. 269). The name is still in record.

MACPHADE. See *under* MACFEAT.

MACPHADRICK, Macphatrick. See *under* MACPATRICK.

MACPHAID. See *under* MACFEAT.

MACPHAIL, Macphial, Macphiel, Macfail, Macfall, Macfaul, Macvail. In G. M'Phàil 'son of Paul.' Gillemore M'Phale was one of an inquest at Inverness, 1414 (*Cawdor*, p. 5). Niven M'Phaill was a charter witness at Sonnachan, Argyll, 1488 (*Notes and Queries*, 11 July, 1931, p. 21). Donald M'Pawle witnessed an indenture between Doncan Makyntosche and Huchone the Rois, baron of Kylraok, 1490 (*Rose*, p. 153), and Donald Makfaill and Gylleis Makfaill were witnesses to a contract of friendship between Dunbar of Westfield and the Clanchattan, 1492 (*Coll.*, p. 86). Finlay MacChaell, bailie of Rothesay, 1501, appears in 1503 as Macfaill (LCD., p. 205, 207), and again in 1506 as Makcaill, under which name he received a grant of a third of the lands of Dunallirde in Bute (RMS.). The lands of Dulatyr in the lordship of Petty were let to Gilleis McFale in 1504 (ER., XII, p. 667). Sir John Mcfaell, a Pope's knight, who witnessed a bond of manrent in 1533 (*Cawdor*, p. 159), is possibly D[ominus] Joh. M'Fale who witnessed a charter relating to the church of Lindichty, 1535, and in 1538 appears as rector of the church (RMS.,

III, 1525, 1830). Mare Vykfaill (= mhicFaill) or W'Faill gave band to Campbell of Glenurquhay, 1547 (BBT., p. 184), and Maria M'Kane M'Fale is in record in Lochalsh, 1548 (RMS., IV, 204). William Dow McPhayll was a 'brebner' in Inverness, 1557 (*Rec. Inv.*, I, p. 10); in 1578 complaint was made against Donald McFail in Archindoun (RPC., III, p. 51); John Dow McPaule was in Kenmore, 1579 (FB., p. 371), Angus M'Phaill was vicar of Killespickerell in Mukcarne before 1583 (OPS., II, p. 827). Makphaile, a 'reformed incumbent,' held the parsonage of Farnway [Farnua] in 1589 (*Wardlaw MS.*, p. 185); Donald McPhaull or McFoill in Edinampell was prosecuted in 1618 for illegal carrying of arms (RPC., XI, p. 415–416); Neill McFoill held a lewirheis [a local term for a parcel of land] in Islay, 1686 (*Bk. Islay*, p. 511); and Donald M'Fveill was tenant in Kilmun, 1711 (*Argyll*). The author of the *Book of Mackay* (p. 51) maintains that a section at least of the Macphails sprang from the Mackays, and the list of tenants on the Reay estates about 1678 certainly shows that a number of Macphails were among them. The Seil-Phaill of Sir Robert Gordon appear to have been Mackays descended from Paul, son of Neil MacNeil Mackay, the latter a brother of Angus Dubh of 1411. Katherine N'Phael in Fortingall, 1684 (DPD., I, p. 488). The name is a common one around Ardchattan, and several Macphails were among the fencible men enrolled in Glenlyon by the duke of Atholl in 1706 (*HMon.*, III, p. 216). John M'Phell, taylor burgess of Edinburgh, 1736 (*Guildry*, p. 158). Some Macphails now write their name Macfall and Macfyall. It is also sometimes Englished POLSON, q.v. Mackphaill 1603, M'Fal 1502, Makfaill 1481, Mcffaill 1692, Makfale 1588, Makfele 1510, M'Fveill 1711, Macfauld 1583, M'Kaill 1575, McPaill 1692, McPhaell 1684, McPhale and McPhaile 1699, Nickphaile and Niphail (both fem.) 1670–1671. Latinized Macphalius.

MACPHALLAIN. A form of Macpharlain in western Ross, with assimilation of *r* to *l*.

MACPHARLAIN. See *under* MACFARLAN.

MACPHATE. See *under* MACFEAT.

MACPHATER, Macpeeters, Macfater. G. *Mac Pheadair* for earlier *Mac Gille Pheadair*, 'son of (S.) Peter's gillie.' The name of an old Argyllshire family. Gillipetair mac Donnchaidh is a witness in the *Book of Deer*. Thomas Moir McGillifedder is in record in 1607 (RPC.), and Duncan M'Fater appears in Deochaig, parish of Kilblaan, 1694 (*Argyll Inv.*). McIllepheder and McIllephedrin 1704,

McIllephedder 1706. The name is probably sometimes Anglicized PETERS. See also MAL-PETER.

MACPHATRICK. *See under* MACPATRICK.

MACPHEDRAN, MACPHEDRON, MACPHEI-DRAN. G. *MacPheadarain*, 'Son of little Peter,' or 'Peterkin' from G. *Peadair*, with diminutive -*an*. "The M'Pheidirans of Argyle-shire own themselves to be originally" Macaulays (*Enquiry*, p. 100). The native home of the Clan Pheadirean (Patersons) was on the north side of Lochfyne, where they were formerly numerous (CG., II, p. 359). Dominicus (i.e. Maeldonich) M'Fedran and his heirs male had charter of the one mark land of Sonnachan, Argyllshire, 1349, as attested by a notarial copy made in 1488 (*Notes and Queries*, 11 July, 1931, p. 21). Duncan glas M'Pheddrein held land of Port Sonnachan, 1629, and Gilpatrick M'Pheddrin was sasine witness, 1650 (ibid., p. 44, 47). John M'Federan in Finisharne, parish of Glassrie, 1707 (*Argyll*).

MACPHEE. *See under* MACFEE.

MACPHEELY. This name, found in the Glasgow Directory, is a modern Irish importation. Said by Woulfe to be *Mac Fithcheallaigh*, 'son of the chess-player.'

MACPHEIDRAN. *See* MACPHEDRAN.

MACPHERSON, MACPERSON. G. *Mac a' Phearsain* or *Mac a Phearsoin*, 'son of the parson.' In the Book of the Dean of Lismore the name is spelled M'apharsone. Alexander Makfersan was bailie to the bishop of Aberdeen, c. 1447 (REA., I, p. 250). Bean Makimpersone witnessed a bond between William of Rose and Duncan Makintosche, captain of Clancattane, 1490 (*Cawdor*, p. 74), and in the same year, as Beane Makynparsone, he witnessed an indenture between Doncan Makyntosche and Huchone the Rois, baron of Kylraok (*Rose*, p. 153). Payment was made to David Makfassane "for twa gunnis of matel," 1538 (ALHT., VII, p. 25), Donald Makphersone, prior of Strathphillane, appears as witness, 1585 (BBT., p. 233, 234), and the Badenoch Makfersones made a bond of manrent with the earl of Huntly, 1591 (SCM., IV, p. 246). Duncan Dow M' a Persoun in Kinchraikin was a Glenurquhay vassal, 1638 (BBT., p. 403). A small sept of Campbells in the neighborhood of Glassary, Argyllshire, in the fourteenth and fifteenth century bore the name Macpherson. Donaldus M'Inpersuyn was one of a number cited in 1355 to give evidence regarding the lands of Glassre (HP., II, p. 139). As Donald McMcpersun he witnessed a charter by John Campbell, lord

of Ardsceodanich, undated, but about 1355 (ibid., p. 141). Another Donald Macpherson, evidently of the same family, was rector of St. Columba, Glassrie, 1420, "showing that the name was not a mere patronymic." Donald McKinfarsoun was tenant of Teris Balcony, 1531, and Neill McForsoun, tenant in Arrefeill, Islay, 1541 (ER., XVII, p. 620, 640, 668). Malcolm Makfersoun obtained the heritage of Kerrytonlia in Bute, 1506 (*Hewison*, II. p. 173). "It is known that a number of families of the Badenoch Macphersons settled in the Hebrides; and it is a modern mistake to suppose that nearly all who bear the name in those parts are really Murdochsons, who have no connection with 'Clann Mhuirich bho Bhinnein'" (Sinton, *Poetry of Badenoch*, p. 84). Malcolm McPhersone was "parsoune of Herreis," 1556 (*Coll.*, p. 146). Tormot M'Farsane, vicar of Snizort, 1526. Dun: mc appersone and Gilbert mc persone are in Clachandysart, 1692 (*Commons*, p. 30). Mc-Epersoun 1559, Makfarson 1481, M'Ferson 1685, McFersoune 1662, Makferssoun 1530, M'Inphersonis (pl.) 1594, M'Inferson 1611, NcKherson (fem.) 1682, McKilferson 1506, Mackperson 1646, Mackpharsone 1637; Mc-Person, McPhersen.

MACPHETIE. Some Macleas in Perthshire in seventeenth century called themselves Mc-Phetie, from an ancestor named either Peter or Patrick who went to Appin and was servant to the laird of Weem (HP., IV, p. 98). Cf. MACFEAT and MACPHATER.

MACPHETRISH. *See under* MACFET-RIDGE.

MACPHIAL, MACPHIEL. *See under* MAC-PHAIL.

MACPHILIP, 'son of PHILIP,' q.v. Philip, a son of Fingonius, prior of Iona, is commemorated on a tombstone in Cladh Beg, Kirkapoll, Tiree, 1495 (Beveridge, *Coll and Tiree*, p. 150). Andrew Makphilp was reidare at Ra, Caithness, 1574 (RMR.). Cf. MACKILLOP.

MACPHILLOPSONE. Malcolm M'Phillopsone, heir of Alexander M'Phillop of Inschmernock, *proavi*, 1662 (*Inquis.*, 4607).

MACPHUN, MACFUN, MACFUNN. Variants of MACMUNN, q.v. Neill M'Phune or M'Phuney and Archibald M'Phunie or M'Phuny appear in Dunnamuke, 1672 (HP., II. p. 207, 216). Duncan M'Ilfun in Polfuill, Kilfinan, 1686 (*Argyll*). John M'Fun in Soccoth in Strachur, 1694 (*Argyll Inv.*), John M'Funie in Strachur parish, 1695 (*Argyll*), and Adam M'Phunn in the parish of Inveray, 1762 (*Kilbarchan*). The name of Andrew Mac-

MACPHUN, Macfun, Macfunn..., cont'd

puhan, an exiled Covenanter from Kirkcudbright, 1679 (*Hanna*, II, p. 254), may be an error for Macphun. W. R. M'Phun was the Glasgow publisher of Macleod and Dewar's *Gaelic dictionary*, 1853.

MACPIKE. See under MACPAKE.

MACPOKE. Hugh Macdonald records that a hermit named McPoke killed Godfrey Du or the Black, in the twelfth century (HP., I, p. 7).

MACPREIST. Johnne Brysoun alias McPreist was burgess of Perth, 1618 (RPC., XI, p. 461). Cf. PRIEST.

MACPRIOR, 'son of the prior.' Dougall Makchonochy V'Prior, servitor of Colin Campbell of Glenvrquhay, had a lease of three marks of Balleveolayne in 1576 (OPS., II, p. 166), and in 1587 he appears as Dougall M'Conoquhie V'apriour in Balliewewlane in Lismoir (BBT., p. 241). Mention is made in 1599 of the son of John M'Ewin VcDougall V'Aprioure (OPS., II, p. 115), and the widow of Ewin M'Coull VcDonchie V'Prior in Balleveolan was contracted in marriage in 1633 (*Notes and Queries*, July 18, 1931).

MACQUAKER. Absurdly derived by Johnston (*Scottish Macs*) from Gaelic *Mac chuagaire*, 'son of the awkward, slovenly man,' but simply a form of MACVICAR, q.v. Andrew Macquaker in the parish of Penninghame is in record in 1684 (*Parish*), John Mc Qwaker and Gilbert Mc Quaker were witnesses in Carrick, 1687 (RPC., 3. ser. XIII, p. 197), and John M'Quaker, excise officer at Dumfries, was a friend of the poet Burns.

MACQUALTER. A form of MACWALTER, q.v.

MACQUARRIE, Macquarrey, Macquarie, Macqurrie, Macwharrie, 'the son of Guaire,' an old Gaelic personal name meaning 'proud' or 'noble,' from early Gaelic *gaurio-s*, akin to Gr. γαῦρος, 'proud.' John M'Govre of Wlua witnessed a charter by John of Yle, earl of Ross, in 1463 (*Clan Donald*, I, p. 540). In the royal confirmation of this charter his name appears as M'Geir de Ulva (RMS., II, 801). In the Gaelic genealogical manuscript of 1467 the name appears correctly as M'Guaire. Donald McGillecallum McGorre or McQuhorre was tenant of Kyllewane in Kintyre, 1506, and Gillecallum McNeill McQuhore was also a tenant in Kintyre in the same year (ER., XII, p. 698, 699, 707). Dunslavy M'Worich or M'Vorich of Wlwav is mentioned in 1509 (ALC., 21 July). Dulleis Makwidy of Ulva had a precept of remission for offences com

mitted by him in 1517 (RSS., I, 2878); and in 1581 complaint was made against Johnne Makquharie '*alias* callit the Bent Wowar' (RPC., III, p. 382). Cathell M'Quhorie and Archibald M'Quhoire were two of M'Nachtane's bowmen shipped at Lochkerran in 1627 for service in France (*Archaeol. Scot.*, III, p. 254; HP., I, p. 115). Donaid Makquovrie was retoured heir of Hector Makquovrie in Ulvay, 1630 (*Retours, Argyll*, 36), and in 1673 decreet was pronounced against John and Donald M'Gourie of Ulva (HP., I, p. 260). Hector M'Gourie or MacQuorrie was tenant of Gometra and Oskamul in 1674 (ibid., p. 280, 301), and John M'Warie of Ulva is mentioned in the same year (ibid., p. 265). John M'Quarrie in Lagan was denounced rebel in 1674, and in the following year Hector M'Gourie in Ostamull and Lauchlan M'Gowry, tacksman of Ulva, were similarly denounced (ibid., p. 262, 271). Calum MacQewry in Tongue, 1745 (*Oban Times*). J. H. Macquarrie was attorney-general of Nova Scotia in 1934. A side form of the name is MACWHARRIE, and this shortened to WHARRIE is also in current use. In the Isle of Man the name has become Quarry, and in Ireland it is Gorey (from UaGuaire). M'Coirry 1540, Makcory 1531, M'Corry 1538, Makcorry 1504, Maccurre 1517, McQuharrie 1573, Makquhary 1513, Makquharry 1475, Macquhirrie 1598, Makquhory 1553, Macquore 1545, M'Quorie 1683, Makquyre 1589, M'Rore 1546.

MACQUAT. See under MACWATT.

MACQUATTIE. A form of MACWATTIE, q.v. John M'Quhattie and Bessie M'Quhattie held land in the bailliary of Kyle-Stewart in 1607 (RMS., VI, 1929), and Donald McQuhatti is recorded tenant of Mekill Brinqualis, Moray, in 1504 (ER., XII, p. 670). M'Quatty 1584. Recorded in Edinburgh, 1943.

MACQUAY, Macque, Macquey, Macquie. G. and Ir. *MacAoidh*, 'son of AODH,' q.v. Common in Galloway. M'Qha and McQui 1684.

MACQUEEN. (1) From *Mac Shuibhne*, 'son of Suibhne,' OIr. *Subne*, in Adamnan's Latin-Irish *Suibneus*. In the Gaelic genealogical MS. of 1467 it occurs in the gen. *Suibne* (in the Mackintosh genealogy), and in the Dean of Lismore's MS. (c. 1512–20) it is *M'Soenith*. An old Gaelic personal name which appears to mean 'good-going' or 'well-going.' The aspiration of the S causes the name when preceded by 'Mac' to be pronounced like MacHuin, or MacWheen, and so we have in record the forms M'Quhyne, M'Quhan (now Macwhan), M'Queyn, M'Quhen, M'Quheen, Maquhon, McQuhenne, Mauchquhen,

M'Kquyne (1594). The Q is a continuation of the sound of *c* of Mac. The name has nothing to do with Ir. *MacCuinn*, 'son of Conn,' with which it has been confused through the similarity of sound. Hector Mac Souhyn was one of an inquest held at Dumbarton in 1271 which found that the daughters of the late Finlay of Campsie were the lawful heirs of the deceased Dufgall, brother of Maldouen, earl of Lennox (RMP., p. 191; *Red Bk. Menteith*, II, p. 218). (2) The Skye surname Macqueen is of Norse origin from the personal name *Sveinn*. According to the Kinrara MS. (written in 1690) the Clan Chattan Macqueens came out of Moidart about 1410. Mylmore Makquean was one of the victims of the first hership of Petty, 1502 (*Rose*, p. 176), and in another document relating to the same affair we have mention of Soyne (= Sween) Makrevan (ibid., p. 177). Finlay M'Quene and Gillereoch M'Queane, followers of Donald Gorme of Sleat, had remission in 1541 for their part in laying waste Trouterness in Skye and Kenlochew in Ross (RSS., II, 3943). William Makqueine, rector of Assint from 1577 to 1580 (OPS., II, p. 693) is William M'Quevne, 'subden of Ros,' in 1581 (*Cawdor*, p. 183). Rory Macquein, subdicavne of Ross, witnessed a contract of friendship between Macdonald of Slate and Lauchlan Macintosh, captain of Clanchattan in 1587 (*Coll.*, p. 99). Elyzabeth M'Quen amerciat in 1597 in the regality court of Spynie (SCM., II, p. 135). By 1609 these Macqueens had risen to the dignity of a minor clan, and the chief signs the Clan Chattan Band of that year "for himself and taking the full burden in and upon him of John Macqueen in Little Corrybrough, Sween Macqueen in Raigbeg, and remanent his kin of that race" (Mackintosh, *Clan Chattan*). Donald McQuene in Corribroche and Swein McQuene of Raik (Roag) were denounced rebels, 1619 (RPC., XI, p. 565), Isobell Macquine appears in 1680 (IDR., p. 99), and Suin McSuin of Roag was one of the signers of a letter to President Forbes of Culloden, 1746 (MCP., IV, p. 179). M'Quan, M'Quam, and M'Quain in the Register of births, etc., for the parish of Kilmuir, Skye (Forbes, *Place-names of Skye*, p. 57) are probably variant spellings. M'Quene, M'Quein, and M'Queine, all three in Perth 1653, M'Queyn 1519, M'quevne (of Corrybrough) 1570, Mackqueane 1658. See also **Macquien**.

MACQUEIL. Said to be a phonetic spelling of G. *MacDhughaill* (so Mr. Alexander Mackintosh Mackintosh). Donald Makqueil was tenant of Nethir-Mewane in the lordship of Apnadull, 1500 (RMS., II, 2566). A child of William M'Quell was buried in Greyfriars,

Edinburgh, 1662 (*Greyfriars Burying-ground reg. of interments, 1658–1700*, p. 424). There seems to have been a family of this name in Edinburgh in the seventeenth century whose name appears in record as M'Qweill 1610, M'Quell, M'Qwhal, and Makquall.

MACQUEY, Macquie. *See under* **MACQUAY**.

MACQUHAE. Ir. *MacAodha*, 'son of Aodh,' Anglicized Hugh. Gilbert M'Quha was heir of William M'Quha, 1638 (*Inquis.*, 2391). Janet M'Quhae is in record in Wigtownshire, 1656 (*M'Kerlie*, I, p. 225). Robert McQuha was resident in the parish of Buittle, 1684 (RPC., 3. ser. IX, p. 570), and James M'Quhae appears in Glenmalloch, 1757 (*Wigtown*). William M'Quhae was minister of S. Quivox, 1764–1824 (*Fasti*, III, p. 137), and was succeeded by his son, Stair M'Quhae. See also **Macwha**.

MACQUHAT. A current form of **Macwatt**, q.v. Cuthbert M'Quhat witnessed a notarial instrument of 1506 (*Edgar*, p. 228).

MACQUHENZIE. This is the form which **Mackenzie** takes in Galloway with z pronounced as y. Hector M'Quhynzie in Thornhill is mentioned in 1618 (*Trials*). See also **Macwhinnie**.

MACQUHIR. *See under* **MACWHIR**.

MACQUHIRK. Ir. *MacCuirc*, 'son of Corc.' Cf. **Maccorc**. Patrick M'Chaquhirky was abbot of Tungland, 1458 (RMS., II, 651). David M'Quhirk was bailie of Dumfries, 1487 (ER., IX, p. 556), and his son Thomas Makquhirk is in record as burgess there, 1508 (*Edgar*, p. 230). David Makquhirk was burgess of Dumfries, 1608 (RMS., VI, 3335). McKwhirk, McUhirk, and McWhirkin in 1684 (*Parish*).

MACQUHIRR. A current form of **Macwhir**, q.v. This form is found early. Jo. M'Quhir was a charter witness in Kirkcudbright in 1595 (RMS., VI, 330).

MACQUHIRRIE. John McQuhirrie who was resident in Edinburgh, 1584 (RPC., III, p. 678), is possibly the M'Quhirrie, M'Quhyrrv, M'Qwhyrrcht, Makquhirrie, burgess of Edinburgh in 1574 (*Laing*, 889, etc.). Gilchreist M'Quhury, fisher, burgess freeman of Glasgow, 1600 (*Burgesses*), and the name also occurs in Glasgow in 1618 as McQuhurrie and in 1707 as McCwerie (RUG.). Lachland M'Quhurie was tenant of part of Glenharrie, Kintyre, in 1605 (HP., III, p. 83), and John M'Quhirrich appears in Killmichellbeg, 1672 (ibid., II, p. 214).

MACQUIEN. A Skye surname. G. *MacAoidh-ean*, 'son of little Hugh,' or Hughie. Sometimes erroneously rendered MACQUEEN, q.v.

MACQUIGGAN, MACWIGGAN. Names recorded in Galloway. From Ir. *MacGuagain*, a corrupt form of *MacEochaidhin*, diminutive of *Eochaid*, a common Gaelic personal name in early Scots records.

MACQUILKAN, MACQUILKEN. There was a sept of this name in Kintyre, and the name is still not uncommon in Argyllshire. The Gaelic is *MacCuilcein*, Ir. *MacUilcin*, 'son of Wilkin' (= Scot. Wilkie), a diminutive or pet form of William. John Dow McWilkane had a precept of remission in 1542 (RSS., II, 4454), Neil M'Quilkan in Ardphadrick, parish of Kilberry, is in record in 1676 (*Argyll*), and Ard Mc ulken was rebel in Kilberrie parish, 1685 (*Commons*, p. 4). The name occurs in Islay in 1741 as M'Kouilkan (*Bk. Islay*, p. 555), and Malcolm MacQuilkan was appointed receiver at Bowmore, Islay, in 1815 (*Stent Book*, p. 202). The name is also Englished Wilkinson and Wilkieson. Mcqueelken 1685. Lands named M'Wilkingstoun in Kyleregis are mentioned in 1608 (*Retours, Ayr*, 103).

MACQUILLAN. From Ir. *MacCoilin*, a variant of *MacCailin*, Scots Gaelic *MacCailein*, 'son of COLIN,' q.v. "The family of fighting men brought over from Scotland by the O'Donnells of Tirconnell in the fifteenth century, were sometimes called MacCailin, sometimes MacAilin, and it is impossible to say which form is correct" (*Woulfe*, p. 325).

MACQUILLIAM. A form of MACWILLIAM, q.v., current in Galloway.

MACQUILLY. Probably Ir. *MacCoiligh*, a short form of *Mac an Choiligh*, 'son of the cock' (*coileach*). A commission for the trial of a man named McQuhillie was issued in 1558 (ER., XIX, p. 451). Helen M'Quhillie appears in Edinburgh, 1675 (*Edinb. Marr.*), and Donald M'Quilly of Eigg was a Jacobite prisoner of the '45 (*Prisoners*, III, p. 180).

MACQUILTROCH. See under MACJILTROCH.

MACQUINNES. An odd form of MACINNES, q.v., found in Glasgow.

MACQUISTAN, MACQUISTEN, MACQUISTIN, MACQUISTON, MACQUESTON, MACWHISTON. G. *Mac Uisdein*. In the Fernaig MS. (1688) spelled M'Cuistan. Spelled M'Uisthon in Argyll (*Celt. Mon.*, XII). Mrs. M'Guistan was housekeeper at Dunlop House, the residence of Mrs. Dunlop, the friend of Burns. Mac Queiston 1662. See MACHUTCHEN.

MACQUORN. A variant of MACCORRAN, q.v. John M'Corne, minister at Stratoun, 1574 (RMR.), may be John M'Quorne, minister of Stratoun, who was a witness in 1618 (*Laing*). A later John M'Quorn was minister at Dalmellington, Ayrshire, 1686 (RPC., 3. ser. XII, p. 137). David M'Quorn contributed xx merks towards building the library in the College of Glasgow, 1636 (Scott, *Fasti*, III, p. 95), and Joseph Makquorne appears as a litster in Edinburgh in the same year (*Edinb. Marr.*).

MACQURRIE. See under MACQUARRIE.

MACRA. A form of MACRAE, q.v., current in Stornoway.

MACRAE, MACRAY. This name is a personal one like Macbeth, not a patronymic like Macdonald. It is probably the same as *Maqi Rati* of the ogham inscription found at Keenrath, county Cork, Ireland. The Gaelic is *Macrath*, 'son of grace' or 'prosperity.' *Rat*, 'favour, grace,' is a common element in old Breton names, as *Ratfrid*, *Ratlouuen*, etc. (*Loth*, p. 111, 139, 147). Like many other old personal names Macrath originated quite independently in more than one place and date, and was given to individuals in no way connected with each other. Macraith de Ospitali witnessed gift of the church of S. Marie and S. Bruoc of Dunrod to the canons of Holyrood in the reign of Malcolm IV (LSC., p. 20). Macraht decanus de Carric, c. 1202–07 (RMP., p. 110) may be the same person. Alexander Macrad witnessed a charter of lands of Lus to Maldoun, son of Gillemore, by Maldouen, third earl of Lennox, c. 1225 (*Levenax*, p. 96). Another Makrath, sacerdos, was present at pleas held at Dull in Atholl, 1264 (RPSA., p. 349). Macrath ap Molegan of Dumfriesshire rendered homage, 1296 (*Bain*, II, p. 198). As Makerathe Molegan he had his lands restored to him in the same year. Patrick M'Re or M'Rey was tenant in Tybris (Tibbers), parish of Penpont, 1376 (RHM., I, p. liv; II, p. 16), and Dugall McRay was witness at Kilmun, 1476 (*Poltalloch Writs*, p. 183). A contract of friendship between Macraes and Campbell of Craignish in 1702 is signed by Farquar M'Ra, Donald M'Rah, John MacRah, and D. M'Kra (HP., I, p. 208). Miles McCra or McRaw was tenant under the earl of Seafield, 1721 (ibid., II, p. 297, 310), and Donald M'Raw of Ross, Donald M'Raw or M'Rau of Perth, and Rory M'Raw or M'Rars were among the Jacobite prisoners taken in the '45 (*Prisoners*, III). The late Col. Macrae-Gilstrap restored Eilandonan Castle, the old stronghold of the Macraes. Mackcra, Mackra, and Mackcrae, all 1650, McCrav 1664, McKra 1511, Makraa 1538, Macraw 1816. See also under MACCRAE and MACCRAITH.

MACRAILD. G. *MacRaild* or *M'Ra'ilt*, from G. *Harailt*, M. Ir. *Aralt*, from N. *Harald-r*, whence Harold, Herold. There are some families of this name on the Macleod estates who are popularly supposed to be descended or named from Mac Raild Armuinn, a Danish knight of the reign of Alexander III (Mackenzie, *Macleods*, p. 6). The widow of McRalte, a tenant, appears in Strathdee, 1527 (*Grant*, III, p. 68). The MacRailds of Clan Tarralaich were associated with Petty, near Inverness. Daniel M'Raill was resident in Edinburgh, 1700 (*Edinb. Marr.*). Dr. George Henderson says that "when the name appears as in *Cladh an Easbuig Eraild*, the old name of Muckairn burying-ground, the long vowel form *Räild* does not occur, so that *Raild* possibly may be from *Ragnall*, *Rä'uill*, with epithetic [*sic*, epenthetic] *t*, — in either case Norse" (*Norse influence*, p. 54). The derivation from N. *Harald-r* seems to be more probable.

MACRAINE. A form of MACCRAIN, q.v.

MACRANALD (now a rare surname), MACRONALD. G. *Macraonuill*, 'son of Raonull.' See RANALD. John M'Rynald or Makrynnild was part tenant of Eddirallekach, Strogartnay, 1483 (ER., IX, p. 592, 622). Donald McRanald Vaan (Bhan) appears several times in record as tenant of lands in Kintyre, 1506 (ibid., XII, p. 701, 707). His name is variously spelled in record Mckilrannaldvane, McRynald Waan, McRynald Baan, and McRynall Waan. Allan McRynild was witness at Gawrie, 1569 (*Poltalloch Writs*, p. 139), and Alexander roy McAllane McReynald and Innes McAllane McRenald had royal remissions in 1541 (ALHT., VIII, p. 19). Rannald M'Rannald M'Couilglas of Cappycht appears in 1563 (BBT., p. 206). Complaint was made by Coline Campbell of Glenlyoun against Alexander McAne Dow McKrenald and Johnne Dow McConneill McCrenild, 1583 (RPC., III, p. 589). Mac Mhic Raonuill or its translation, MacRanald (*not* Clan Ranald) is the patronymic form of the name of Keppoch Macdonells. MacRannal, MacRannald, MacRenold, MacReynold, MacRevnvlt, MacRinnell, MacRindle, MacRinnyl, MacRonall.

MACRANDELL. A variant of MACRANALD, q.v. Silwester M'Randell in Gargavache, 1600, and Allester M'Randell of Gargareache, witness, 1603 (SCM., IV, p. 254, 293).

MACRANKIN (1) 'son of Rankin or RANKEN,' q.v. Once a common surname in Ayrshire. Henry M'Rankyne in Glengirvane by Mayboll was a charter witness in Carrick, 1563 (RMS., III, 1421). Neil M'Rankyne in Glengovane, a tenant under Kennedy of Culzeane in 1608 appears in 1610 as Neil Ranking or M'Ranking of Blairquhan (RPC., VIII, p. 426, 671). Margaret M'Rankein in Knoksaith was retoured heir of John M'Rankein in Pynblaid, her father, 1621 (*Retours*, Ayr, 199), and William McKrenkine subscribed to the Test in Edinburgh, 1681 (RPC., 3. ser. VII, p. 724). (2) A once common name in Glencoe and neighborhood. G. *MacFhraing*, 'son of Francis.' This origin is supported by the old Rannoch form found in the name of John Oig Mac Frankeine, 'servitor to the Clandoindouev Vc Alester' in Dounane, who was charged with illegally carrying arms, 1618 (RPC., 2. ser. VII, p. 372). Duncan M'Donchie VcCrankine in Glencoe was one of several to be apprehended for the murder of Duncan and James Stewart, 1617 (ibid., p. 187). Duncan McCraing in Nether Lorn, 1692 (*Commons*, p. 34). The Rankins or Macrankins of Coll were hereditary pipers to Macleans of Duart, and later to Macleans of Coll. They were earlier known as Clan Duille, from Cuduilligh. They had a 'college' at Kilbrennan, Mull, and the last 'professor' was Eoghan Mac Eachain 'ic Chonduilgh, who died c. 1754. They have no connection with Lowland Rankins. The resemblance of the name Rankin with old Gaelic Raingce of c. 1100–50 is most probably fortuitous.

MACRAW, MACRAY. Variants of MACRAE, q.v.

MACREDIE (Ayrshire), MACREADIE (Galloway), MACREADY, MACCREDIE. The Macredies of Peirceton, Ayrshire, are originally from Ireland (in 1720) says Robertson (*Ayr Fam.*, II, p. 70). The first of the family connected with Peirceton was Andrew Macredie, provost of Stranrawer, and originally from Ireland, who purchased the estate from Sir Robert Barclay, last of the family of Peirceton, in 1720 (ibid.). Woulfe explains the name as *MacRiada*, 'son of Riada.'

MACRENNIE. Alexander Macreinny or M'Rennie was hanged for aiding in the insurrection of Alexander, lord of the Isles in 1425.

MACRIE. *See under* MACCRAE.

MACRIMMON. A current variant of MACCRIMMON, q.v.

MACRITCHIE. A Highland border name, 'son of RITCHIE,' q.v. Robert McRichie or Makryche 'of Dalmunzie' and 'in Glenshee' appears in 1571–83–84–89, and his son Duncan McCreiche in Glenshee in 1594. This Duncan is also found in record as Duncan Mcintosche alias McCreitche of Dalmungy in 1584 (RPC., III), and in the Clan Chattan Band of 1595 he is recorded as Duncan Mcrvche of Dulmonaye. The Macritchies are really Macintoshes descended from a Richard Macintosh, and some Macritchies have been connected with the parishes of Clunie and Caputh in Perthshire since 1683 (TGSI., XI, p. 286). John M'Ritchy was tenant in Craigend, 1782 (Dunkeld). Mackritchy 1765, McKreiche 1586, McRiche 1620, McRichie 1647.

MACRITHER. A current form of Macgruther. See MACGRUAR.

MACROBB, 'son of Robb,' from the Scots diminutive of Robert. Some of this name are ranked as a sept of Stewarts, descended from a natural son of Robert, son of Dugald, first of Appin (Sliochd Ailein 'ic Rob'). The lands occupied by them were Glenduror, Lettermore, and Acharn in Duror (Appin Stewarts, p. 184–185). Buchanan has a sept of the name descended from Robert, a member of the family of Buchanan of Leny, and residing mainly in the parishes of Callander and Kilmadock (Buchanan, p. 107). Henry McRob was 'mair' of Menteith in 1458 (ER., VI, p. 423), Andrew M'Robe, witness at Lochlevyn, 1546 (Rollok, 3), Patrick Makrob was admitted burgess of Aberdeen in 1551 (NSCM., I, p. 63), caution was found for John McRob in Ayrshire in 1584 (RPC., III, p. 714), and John McRob is recorded in Brahan in 1726 (HP., II, p. 338). Some Macrobs formerly in Ardeonaig who assumed the name Macdonald are now in Aberfeldy (FB., p. 371). The surname GRUB is possibly a shortened form. McRobe.

MACROBBIE. A Highland border name from Scottish Robbie, diminutive of Robert. A remission was given Maldowny McRobi in Moray in 1363 (REM., p. 164), and James Makroby was tenant in Blalok, Cromar, in 1539 (ER., XVII, p. 66). Francis McRobie and George McRobie in Kinbothok were charged with violence in 1607 (RPC., VII, p. 393). Allister Cain McRobbie, sometime in Urchine, is in record in 1614 (Cawdor, p. 227), Donald McRobie and John McRobie in Kilvean appear in 1646 (Culloden, I, p. 48), and John MacRobbie was a residenter in Huntly in 1797 (Moray). MACCROBIE and MACROBIE are current forms of the name.

MACROBERT, 'son of Robert,' a Highland border name, G. Mac Roibeirt. Angus M'Robert gave his bond of manrent to George, earl of Huntlie in 1543 (SCM., IV, p. 260). Donald M'Aye M'Robert held land at Castlehill, Inverness, in 1586 (Laing, 1111), and Donald Makrobert in Candroquhat witnessed a bond of manrent in the same year (BBT., p. 237). Molchallum M'Robert appears in Craig in 1606 (BBT., p. 257), John M'Robert was in possession of the oxganglands of Brigend, Nigg, in 1659 (Laing, 2540), and another Johne McRobert in the parish of Balmaghie, and Andrew McCrobert in the parish of Tungland were charged with being disorderly persons in 1684 (RPC., 3. ser. IX, p. 572). McRypert is an old spelling.

MACROBIN. In Gaelic MacRoibin, 'son of Robin.' A Highland border name from Robin, Scots diminutive of Robert, and cf. Dunrobin (= fort of Robin), perhaps so named from Robert, earl of Sutherland, in one of whose charters the name first appears (1401). A remission was granted to Patrick McRobin, one of those holding the Castle of Dunbertane against the king in 1489 (APS., XII, p. 34; Lennox, II, p. 133). John Dow McRobyn in Dysart and John McRobyn in Knockyle were fined for aiding Clan Gregor, 1613 (RPC., XIV, p. 636, 644), Margrat MacRobin and Marion MacRobin were residents in the parish of Borgue in 1684 (RPC., 3. ser. IX, p. 567), and Janet M'Robine in Grange of Balmaghie in 1752 (Kirkcudbright). M'Robbine 1663.

MACRONALD. See under MACRANALD.

MACRONE. See under MACCRONE.

MACRORY, MACRORIE, MACRURY. G. Mac-Ruairidh, 'son of Ruadhri.' See RORY. John filius Rothri was present at pleas held at Dull in Atholl, 1264 (RPSA., p. 349). Rouland fiz Aleyn Mac Rotherik of the counte of Innernvs rendered homage, 1296 (Bain, II, p. 210). Report was made in 1297 of lawless proceedings on the part of Lochlan and Rodric Macrogri (of Garmoran) in the West Highlands in ravaging Skye and Lewis and burning ships of Edward I of England commanded by Alexander of Islay, Edward's admiral in the Isles (Bain, II, 903). Ninian, son of Thomas Make Rori, and Gillepatrike, son of Brice Make Rori, Galwegian hostages, died in Carlisle prison, 1298 (ibid., p. 301; Hist. Docs., II, p. 426). Alexander Makrore Mc Kilferson was tenant of Kilkewane, Kintvre, 1506 (ER., XII, p. 707). Gillechallome McRorie in Abirnethie was fined for resetting Clan Gregor, 1613 (RPC., XIV, p. 629). Donald Dow M'Rorie and John M'Rorie in Ballinoo, and

John M'Rourie in Ardtounishever were denounced rebels in 1675 (HP., 1) and Taskel M'Rory of Inverness was a Jacobite prisoner of the '45 (Prisoners, III, p. 184). Macrury is said today to be the oldest clan name in Uist. MacRuaraidh and MacIlliruaidh, Islay surnames, are sometimes Anglicized Reid (Celt. Mon., x), and Mackury is a Barra form of the name. Makreury 1427, McKrory 1682, McRorie 1675, Mc royre c. 1520, Mc royri 1522.

MACRORYVICEANVAN, 1718, not a surname, = Mac Ruairdh mhic Iain bhain.

MACROSTIE, MACROSTY, MACCROSTIE. These names are confined mainly to Perthshire, and may be from DROSTAN, q.v., 'under Lowland influence,' as Macbain suggests. S. Drostan for a time is said to have lived as a hermit near Glenesk in Angus, and he is still commemorated there at Edzell and Lochlee. Alester M'Rostie in Corecharmik made Duncane Campbell of Glenurquhay and Molchallum M'Rostie in Corquhine sole legatees to all his property in 1585 (BBT., p. 231).

MACROWATT. The sheriff of Wigtoune found surety to compound for the hereschip of a 'jument' (an ox used for tillage) from John Makrowat in the forest of Buchan, 1513 (Trials, I, p. * 89). Cf. ROWAT.

MACROWTALGAR. Gillemichin Mc Rowtalgear or Mc Rowtalgar in Arindoch, Atholl, charged with cattle-lifting, 1622 (RPC., XII, p. 669).

MACRUER. Probably a form of MACCRUAR. Dr. Daniel McRuer (1802–1873), born in Knapdale, Argyllshire, "a typical Scotsman with a 'burr' in his talk," performed great service in the U. S. Civil War as an army surgeon.

MACRURY. See MACRORY.

MACRYRIE. Macryries were a sept of Macdonald but the name is now rare. Roithridh is a personal name still in use, and stories are told of Coinnech mac Roithridh (Watson, Place-names of Ross and Cromarty, p. 226). Cf. Donachig mc ryrie for Donnchadh Mac-Riridh in the Fernaig MS. It is doubtful whether ryrie is meant for Riridh, Raoiridh, or Ruaraidh. The name is also current with omission of Mac as Ririe and Ryrie.

MACSAGART. 'Son of the priest,' G. sagart. Gilcallum McSagart Makcandy was a follower of Murdow McCloyd in 1600 (RPC., XIV, p. cxxiii). See MACTAGGART.

MACSCAMBLE. John M'Scamble in Norrach, parish of Whithorn, 1707 (Wigtown). McSkamble 1684.

MACSCHENOCH. See MACILSCHENOCH.

MACSCILLING. Some time before 1326 Patrick MacScilling, evidently a person of some importance in Kintyre, and Finlach his wife, gifted the church of S. Columkill in Kintyre to the Priory of Candida Casa (Whithorn) in Galloway. The gift was confirmed by King Robert Bruce in the twentieth year of his reign, i.e. 1326 (RMS., I, App. I, 20). Macvurich mentions (Rel. Celt., II, p. 156–157) a "Gall mac Sgillin," contemporary with Dugal and Ranald, the sons of Somerled. The Annals of the Four Masters at 1154 mentions fleets of Gallgaedal (Galloway), Arran, Cintyre, Mann, and the Centair Alban, or seaboard of Alban, under the command of Macscelling, a Norwegian. The name is perhaps OE. Scilling, a personal name found in the seventh century poem Widsith (103), and also in an OE. charter of King Cynewulf (A. D. 778). Redin suggests the name may be from the stem *skell- 'to resound, ring,' in OE. scyl, 'sonorous' (Redin, p. 23).

MACSCOLANE. Gillespic MacScolane led a rebellion in the north in 1203–22 against the king of Scots, and was slain along with his sons (Hailes, I, p. 180). He claimed the rights of the ancient mormaers from whom he was descended (TGSI., VI, p. 159).

MACSCOLOC, 'son of SCOLOC,' q.v. Mac sloclac (an error for Mac scoloc) is mentioned in a Dunfermline charter of Malcolm IV (RD., p. 25).

MACSHAND. A surname recorded in Aberdeen is evidently a variant of the North of Ireland name MacShane, from MacSeaghain, 'son of Jean,' the NF. form of John. The Macshands are said to have come originally from Ireland. The spelling has been influenced by the better known Scots name Shand.

MACSHERRY, MACSHIRIE, MACSHIRRIE. G. MacSiridh. There is or was a small sept of this name in Skye, but the name is now seldom met with. In Mull a branch of the Mackinnons went by the same name, but have now become either Macdonalds or Mackinnons. The late Dr. Macbain derived the name from Norse Sigfrid or Sigurd (IV, p. 67), which Henderson thinks is phonetically doubtful, and prefers to derive the name from the feminine Sigriðr (Norse influence, p. 57, 351). Woulfe derives the Irish MacSherry and MacSharry from Mac Searraigh, 'son of Searrach' ('foal, flighty'). John McDonnald VcShirrie and

MACSHERRY, MACSHIRIE..., *continued*

Duncan McEane Glas VcShirie in Oskamull were put to horn for plundering the ship *The Providence of Dumbarton*, 1629 (RPC., 2. ser. III, p. 45). Archibald McShirrie in Leattir was charged with assault and illegal warding, 1635 (ibid., 2. ser. v, p. 511). John M'Sherrie (MacScherie or M'Shirie) in Dowart and Ferquhar M'Sheri in Derryvyll were denounced rebel in 1675 (HP., I, p. 262, 301, 302). Donald M'Shirrie was merchant in Inverarav, 1677 (*Argyll*), and Archibald M'Sherie was chapman in Gortenbuy in Mull, 1702 (*Campbell*, I, p. 44).

MACSIMON, MACSYMON, 'son of SIMON,' q.v. The chiefs of the Frasers are MACKIM-MIES, q.v. *MacShiomoun*, a sept of the Macarthurs (*Gregorson-Campbell*, p. 2).

MACSKELLY. From Ir. *MacScalaighe*, 'son of Scalaighe,' i.e. crier (*Woulfe*). Alexander Maxskelly had remission for his part in burning the town of Dunbertane, 1489 (APS., XII, p. 34; *The Lennox*, II, p. 132). Wattie Makskele witnessed a Kirkcudbrightshire charter of 1569 (RMS., IV, 2745). The name occurs in Galloway in 1684 as McSkellie, McKskelly, and McSkaule.

MACSKIMMING. Thomas Mackskimming in Auchneicht, 1684. The name occurs in Galloway in 1684 as McScumin, McSimyn, and McSkiming (*Parish*). David M'Skimming in Cairndirrie, 1757 (*Wigtown*).

MACSLOY. A Galloway name of Irish origin, *Mac Sluaghadhaigh*, explained by Woulfe as "one of a host, or hosting expedition."

MACSORLEY. G. *MacSomhairle*, 'son of Somhairle,' or SOMERLED, q.v. Alexander M'Sommarrli was cited in 1355 to give evidence regarding the lands of Glassrie in Argyllshire (HP., II, p. 139). He was probably a Lamont of Monydrain in Glassrie as some of this family used the name Macsorley for several generations, but eventually resumed the name Lamont. The lands of Donald Machorle in the sheriffdom of Argyll were in ward, 1488 (ER., v, p. 330). Other spellings of this Donald's name are McChorle, 1449, and Mc-Cowirlee, 1451. In 1511 Angus Lawmont *alias* M'Quorle was infeft in the three merk lands of Achynchoys (*Lamont*, p. 31). The Mac-Soirles of Letterfinlav in Lochaber, later called a sept of Clan Cameron, descended from Somerled, *armiger* to John of Yla, earl of Ross and lord of the Isles. In 1456 Somerled, the son of John, son of Somerled the armiger, received from the lord of the Isles a davoch of the lands of Glennyves along with the office of toscheachdeora (crowner) of all the lands of John of Yla, except the lands pertaining to his foster-child, Lachlan Maclean of Doward (Innes, *Legal antiquities*, p. 81). Some writers on clan history make the Macsorleys a sept of Clan Cameron, but this Somerled had received his charter thirty-six years before the Camerons of Lochiel are known to have had any connection with the district. John Maksorlye had a remission in 1524 (*Cawdor*, p. 147), and similar remissions were granted to Duncan and Angus McSorbe (an error for McSorle) (RSS., I, 4454). Duncan McCourle and his son Alexander witnessed a sasine at Kirnan, 1571, and Gilbert McDonill VcSouerlie and John McDonchie VcSouerlie attested a sasine of 1577 (*Poltalloch Writs*, p. 143, 190). Gillechallum M'Soirll was tenant of Kyngusie Moir in the lordship of Huntlie, 1603 (SCM., IV, p. 298). Ronnald McSoirle was one of those charged with holding the castle of Dunivaig against Bishop Knox, 1616 (*Cawdor*, p. 232), and Allane M'Sorrle and Sorll M'Sorll were among those killed by the Covenanters at Dunaverty, 1647 (HP., II, p. 256). Dod McSoirle in Bellvraid was charged with being an 'engager' on the royalist side in 1649 (IDR., p. 368). Hew M'Sorrill in Domiolgyne is mentioned in 1672 (HP., II, p. 210), Finlay M'Sorle and John M'Sorle in Balliwilling were denounced rebels in 1675 (ibid., I, p. 296), and Donald M'Hoirle was one of the Jacobite prisoners taken at Preston, 1716. McCorle 1563, M'Korle 1530, McKsoirle 1682, M'Sorlle 1647, McSorrill 1672, McSouarl 1577, VcSouerlie 1577. Other old spellings are: M'Coirl, M'Cordlie, Makcorly, M'Couerle, M'Coull, M'Coullie, M'Soirl, M'Souarl.

MACSPADDAN, MACSPADDEN. John M'Speddan in Air, 1531, acknowledged himself in debt to Sir Gavin Fullarton (*Ros*, 1141). John Downlop to make payment to Katerene Mcspadane for 'þe wrangus putten away of hyr dochtyr,' 1564 (*Prestwick*, p. 68). Complaint was made against John McSpedene in Ayrshire, 1578 (RPC., III, p. 43), John Mc Spading appears in Knockindale in 1588 (RPC., IV, p. 328), and Archibald Maxspadane was merchant of the toune of Avre, 1590 (CSPS., x, p. 237). William McSpiddane in Windeehill, prosecuted for usury in 1615 (RPC., x, p. 411), may be William Mc Speddane, maltman in Hafflour prosecuted for overcharge in malting, 1620 (ibid., XII, p. 352). Hew Makspeaden was a merchant in Edinburgh, 1658 (*Edinb. Marr.*), Thomas M'Speddan was a writer (lawyer) there, 1688 (*Inquis.*, 6897), and John McSpadden was a graduate of the University of Glasgow, 1818. Samuel Mc-

Spadden (1756–1834), a Scots Presbyterian emigrant to Virginia and Tennessee, became a soldier in the Revolutionary Army, and made the powder used by the American army in the battle of New Orleans, 1815. In the U. S. the name is also current as MacSpaden and Mac Spedon.

MACSPORRAN. G. *Mac-an-sporain*, 'son of the purse.' In popular tradition the Macsporrans are said to have been hereditary purse-bearers to the lords of the Isles. Martin (W. I., p. 262), when mentioning the tombs in Iona, says: "In the West-end is the Tombs of Gilbrid and Paul Sporran, antient tribes of the Mack Donalds." Duncan M'Sparren was one of M'Nachtane's soldiers shipped at Lochkilche-rane for service in France, 1627 (HP., II, p. 115). Donald M'Sporran in Auchnagairoch, parish of Knapdaill, 1677, and Gormla N'Sporran, spouse to Donald M'Ilcher in Muastill, parish of Killean, appear in the following year (*Argyll*). The late Rev. C. M. Robertson said that Macsporain is merely a Gaelic rendering of the imported name Purcell, but on the other hand it has been recently said (*Weekly Scotsman*, Jan. 1, 1938) that when clan names were proscribed after the '45 the name Mac-sporran was Anglicized Pursell. The Irish form of the name is Macsparran. King Malcolm II (1005–34) is credited in tradition with having a treasurer called Paul na Sporan or Paul of the Purse.

MACSTALKER. G. *Mac an stalcair*, 'son of the (deer-) stalker.' King James IV presented Sir James Makstalkare to the rectory of Ila-moun (Elanmunde) in 1510 (RSS., I, 2045). Duncan McStokker and Gilpatrik McStokker had precepts of remission in 1542 (RSS., II, 4454). James Mac an Stalkair or Robertson was a fierce enemy of the Macgregors. He appears in the Chronicle of Fortirgall (p. 133) as M'Gestalcar, and is there described as a very wicked wretch and an oppressor of the poor ("Fuit nequissimus et oppressor pau-perum unde dicitur malificos ne patiaris viuere super terram"). He was put to death in 1565. Finlay M'Ynstalker appears as witness in Glenurquhay, 1559, and John Roy M'Stalker or Makinstalker in Cranduycht at Ileanran in 1579 and 1586 (BBT., p. 202, 223, 237). Gilbert Makstoker who was occupier of the two merkland of Scotodaill, Kintyre, in 1596, is the Gilchrvst M'Stoquhor who was tenant in 1605 (HP., III, p. 74, 81). Niall M'In-stucker appears in Harnagyll, 1665 (*Sasines*, II, 1236), and Neill M'Instokir in Barmolich, parish of Sadell, in 1692 (*Argyll Inv.*). Some Macinstalkers appear to have been Mac-gregors (*Macgregor*, II, p. 52), and Buchanan claims them as a sept of Macfarlane. Mc-

Istalkir 1716, M'Staker 1627. The castle on Eilean-an-stalcaire in Lismore-Appin is said to have been built by Duncan Stewart of Appin for the accommodation of King James IV on his hunting expeditions, and appears to have been erected subsequently to the year 1501 (OPS., II, p. 169).

MACSTEVIN, 'son of STEVEN,' q.v. William McSteffan and Matho McSteffan, followers of the earl of Cassilis, were respited for murder, 1526 (RSS., I, 3386). Andrew MacStevin in Calararie, a follower of Ross of Pitcalny, 1592 (RPC.).

MACSWAN. A Skye patronymic, in G. *Mac-Suain*, 'son of Swan,' from ON. personal name Sveinn, from *sveinn*, a boy, North English Swevn, akin to English *swain*. John McSwain in Back in 1726 (HP., II, p. 322). Angus M'Swane of Ross was one of the Jacobite prisoners of the '45. The name has no con-nection with MACSWEEN, which is of quite different origin.

MACSWEEN. G. *Mac Suibhne*, 'son of Suibhne' (pron. Sween). Suibhne was lord of Knapdale about the beginning of the thirteenth century. See under MACQUEEN (1).

MACSWIGGIN. A Galloway name of Irish origin. Woulfe says 'son of Swegen' or 'Swen,' a common personal name in Domesday Book. Searle has recorded fourteen of the name.

MACSYMON. *See under* MACSIMON.

MACTAGGART, MACTAGGERT. G. *Mac-an-t-sagairt*, 'son of the priest.' The marriage of clerics in minor orders was permissible, but the marriage of priests had been declared illegal and invalid in the twelfth century. Ferchar Machentagar or Mackinsagart, son of the red priest of Applecross, was knighted by Alexander II in 1215 for his services in quelling an insurrection in Moray (*Chron. Mail.*, s.a.). Though first earl of Ross of the line he was not *the* first earl of Ross. Donald McKyntagart of Dumfries had remission of his fine, 1459 (ER., VI, p. 553), and William Maktygar "ora-tour and beidman" of "the kingis hospitaile of the trinite college besyd" Edinburgh, is in record, 1504 (*Laing*, 248). Thomas McKyn-taggart was tenant in Strathdee, 1527 (*Grant*, III, p. 68), and John Makintalgart in Bocastell made complaint against certain individuals in 1581 (RPC., III, p. 350). Walter McTagart in Glenloy and two other McTagarts were charged with fire-raising and burning houses belonging to Steuart in Fintaillauch, 1583 (ibid., p. 577). Cathrin M'Target or M'Tar-gett in Dunbar was accused of witchcraft in 1688 (RPC., 3. ser. XIII, p. 245). McIntagart

MACTAGGART, Mactaggert, *continued*

1614, M'Intagerit 1541, McIntargart 1615, Mckintaggart 1623, Myketagart 1433, and Mc-Taggard, McTaggate, and McTaggit in Galloway 1684.

MACTALDRACH. A rare Galloway surname recorded there in 1684 as McTaldroch, Mc-Taler, McTalero, McTaleroch, McTaleroh, McTalleroch, McTalerock, McTalzeouch, and McKtaldroch *(Parish)*. The testament of William M'Talleroch in Kilstav was registered in 1684, and likewise that of Finlav M'Talere in Myroch, parish of Kirkmaiden in the same year. James M'Taldrach, a Galloway poet, published his *The Story of Orpheus*, 1774. The name appears in Ulster as Mactaldridge, and some of the name have changed to Taylor, from the assonance *Taldroch — Taylor*. The name has been connected with Pictish TALORG, q.v., but this seems rather far-fetched.

MACTARLICH. G. *MacThearlaich*, 'son of Charles.' Duncan McTerlach, a charter witness at Carnasserie, 1436 (*Poltalloch Writs*, p. 71). Gillespy Maktarliche was servant to Alexander John Canochsone, 1535 (*Trials*, I, p. 170 *). Angus McAne VcTerlych was fiar of Glasvar, 1570–71 (*Poltalloch Writs*, p. 143). McHerloch 1584. See also MACCARLICH.

MACTAVISH. From G. *Mac Támhais*, a form of *MacThamhais*, 'son of Tammas,' the Lowland Scots form of Thomas. Mactavishes are numerous in Argyllshire. The Craignish MS. says the MacTavishes or Clan Tavish of Dunardarie descend from Tavis Corr, second illegitimate son of Gillespick, son of Callen moir math, 'good bald Coline' (SHSM., IV, p. 207). Doncan M'Thamais was one of those cited in 1355 to give evidence regarding the lands of Glassre in Argyllshire (HP., II, p. 139). Duncan McTawisch was tenant of half of Kernach, Strogartnay, 1480 (ER., IX, p. 564). Donald duin Mc tawvs made reversion to Evar Campbell of Strouquhour, 1488 (HP., IV, p. 20). Thomas McTaevis, charter witness at Kenaach, 1515 (HP., IV, p. 24). Alexander M'ktaus in 1589 had custody of Ellanwirrich as constable (*Wardlaw*, p. 184). The Mactavishes of Stratherrick are considered a sept of the Frasers. M'Taveis 1672, McThavish 1676.

MACTEAR, Macteir, Mactier. Shortened forms of MACINTYRE, q.v. Mactyr, a priest in Iona, is in record in 1372. John Makter in Pennvghame was convicted of stouthreif, 1513 (*Trials*, I, p. 92 *), and another John McTeir was tenant in Movmore, Kynnarde, 1539 (ER., XVII, p. 672). Andro Makteir was

'servand to the maister clerk' in 1546 (ALHT., VIII, p. 488). John McTeyr, notary in Prestwick, 1551, may be John McTer who was made burgess in 1559 (*Prestwick*, p. 12, 61). Gilbert Maktyre had sasine of land in Bute in 1564 (ER., XIX, p. 533), and another Gilbert Mactyre was portioner of Ballintail there in 1615 (*Retours, Bute*, 21). Catherine M'Teir was 'demit of witchcrait' in Dundonald, Avrshire, 1602 (*Paterson*, I, p. 425), and John Mc tyre, tailor in Bute, was charmed by a witch for 'ane sore shoulder,' 1662 (HP., III, p. 6). John M'Tire, exiled Covenanter from parish of Kirkmichael, drowned off Orknev, 1679 (*Hanna*, II, p. 253). McTere, McTire, Mteir.

MACTHOM. G. *MacThom*, 'son of Tom,' a diminutive of Thomas. Angus Makthome was a sufferer from the first hership of Pettv, 1502 (*Rose*, p. 176). John Dow McThome in Strathgarrie was fined for reset of Clan Gregor, 1613 (RPC., XIV, p. 636). See also MACCOMA.

MACTHOMAS. G. *Mac Tómais*, 'son of Thomas.' The branch of the Clan Mackintosh which came afterwards to be known by the surname Macthomas was descended from Adam M'William of Garvamore, in Badenoch, a natural son of William, the seventh chief of the clan Mackintosh. The descendants of this Adam settled in Glenshee, Strathardle, and Glenisla. They appear in the roll of clans of 1587 as "clan mᶜ thomas in Glensche;" and in the roll of broken clans of 1594 they are included in the class of "mony brokin men" (APS., III, p. 467; IV, p. 71). Andrew McThomas was parishioner of Duthil in 1537 (*Grant*, III, p. 269). Ave M'Ane M'Thomas is one of the signers in the Clan Chattan band of 1543 (SCM., IV, p. 260). William Mac-Thomas in Murthlac, 1550 (*Illus.*, II, p. 261), Alexander McThomas alias Thomsoune was burgess of Tayne in 1590 (*Trials*, I, p. 204), and William McThomas in Tulliche was fined for resetting Clan Gregor, 1613 (RPC., XIV, p. 629). John McThomas in Erchles, a Chisholm tenant in 1721, appears in the same record as John McComas (HP., II, p. 296, 297), and Donald McThomas in Inverchanich in 1721 appears again in the same record as Donald McComa (ibid., p. 298). The aspirated form, *Mac Thómais*, gives *Macomish*. Mac Homas 1718 (in Lewis).

MACTHORE. Thorfvnn MacThore, a great landowner in Allerdale, in Cumberland, was granted certain rights by Gospatric in the eleventh century. Gospatric was probably the individual who purchased the earldom of Northumberland from William the Conqueror at Christmas in 1067. This is the only certain example of *Mac-* in Cumberland. Thorfynn (*Thorfinnr*) is an old West Scandinavian personal name. Thore (*Thor*) is also Scandinavian.

MACTHORMOID, 'son of TORMOD,' q.v. John McChormeit of Menvenis (Minginish) is mentioned in 1533 (*Cawdor*, p. 159). John Dow McTormoit was a follower of Murdow McCloyd in the attack on the laird of Balcomie's galley in 1600 (RPC., XIV, p. cxxiii), and Neil McTormont and Rory McTormont were entered as pledges for Clan Leane in 1619 (RPC., XIV, p. 583). Dod Mctormoid and Jon Mctoirmoid in the parish of Urray were charged with being engagers in 1649 (IDR., p. 368). Rorie McHormoid was delated for profaning the Sabbath in 1697 (MacRae, *Dingwall*, 1923, p. 325), and several individuals named McHormoid or McCormoid were Seaforth tenants in 1726 (HP., II, p. 314–319). Mc ilichrist vic Coilvic Cormoid (1718) = MacGille-Chriosd mhic Dhomhnuill mhic Thormoid. McTormett 1718.

MACTHORSTEYN. Alexander MacThorsteyn was one of an inquisition held at Gerwan (Girvan) in Karnik, c. 1260 (*Bain*, I, 2674). The name is Old Norse *Thorsteinn*, OE. *Thurstan*.

MACTIER. A form of MACTEAR, q.v.

MACTORFIN. Macbet Mac Torfin witnessed King David's gift of Petnewem et Inerrin (Pittenweem and Invery) to the Priory of May (*May*, p. 3), and as Machet Mac Torfin he perambulated the bounds of the lands of Ballegallin (ibid., p. 2). As Macktorphin he appears as witness in a charter of David I to the Abbey of Dryburgh, c. 1150–52 (RD., p. lxix; *Veitch*, I, p. 253). He was most probably a son of the great Scandinavian magnate, Thorfynn Mac Thore, who held land in Allerdale, Cumberland, in the last quarter of the eleventh century. Thorfynn is an old West Scandinavian personal name, and Thore (= Thor) is also Scandinavian.

MACTURK. A Galwegian surname. Gaelic *MacTuirc*, 'son of Torc,' from *torc*, a boar. John Makturk in Mekle Ariewland in the barony of Mochrum, is in record in 1538 (RMS., III, 1912). Bessie Makturck was married in Edinburgh in 1621 (*Edinb. Marr.*), John Makturke, servitor of George Stewart of Robertoun appears in 1624 (*Laing*, 1938), and John M'Turk is recorded in the parish of Carsphairn in 1674 (*Kirkcudbright*). Several persons of this name were charged with being disorderly (i.e. non-conforming) in the parish of Carsfern, 1684 (RPC., 3. ser. IX, p. 574,

576). John Macturk, parish schoolmaster of Tillicoultry nearly a century ago, was a man of wide culture.

MACTYRE. Ir. *mac tíre*, 'son of the soil (wolf).' Paul MacTyre, a noted Ross-shire chieftain, flourished c. 1360. He has been claimed (wrongly) as ancestor of the Polsons. Mackenzie (*History of the Mackenzies*, p. 39) makes the wild statement that Mactire is from G. *Mac-an-oighre*, 'son of the heir.' This name has no connection with MACINTYRE, q.v.

MACUCHADAIR. See *under* MACNUCATOR.

MACURE. A form of MACIVER, q.v. John M'Ure, the earliest historian of Glasgow, was a Maciver. His grandfather Latinized his name 'M'Iverus,' and then into 'Ure' (Dunlop, *Notes on Dunoon*, 1886, p. 28). The form McUir occurs in 1671, and in the Edinburgh Marriage Register the name is spelled M'Ure, M'Uir, M'Cur, M'Cure, Makcure, Mackuir. John M'Ure was a writer in Glasgow, 1708 (*Minutes*, p. 31).

MACUSBAIG. Henderson (p. 57) gives this as a Harris name (Scalpa, Bernera). "It was extant on the male side in 1900, but is now represented in the family I know of only on the female side." The name is without doubt from Norse *Ospakr* or *Uspakr*, a personal name meaning one who is 'a disturber of the peace,' or one who is 'violent in his conduct' (Fritzner, *Ordbog over det gamle norske Sprog*). The Norse *Konunga Sögur* records under the year 1209–1210 that "Uspak the Hebridean went on piracy into the Hebrides." Dugal, the son of Somerled, had a son named Ospac, and slightly disguised as Aspuig the name occurs in the Macleod pedigree in the genealogical MS. of 1467 (*Coll.*, p. 361). An individual of this name gave name to Buaile Mhic Uspaig in Skye (*Forbes*, p. 94). MACASBAIG is a side form.

MACVADDER. Donald M'Vadder was one of Macnachtane's soldiers shipped in 1627 for service in France (HP., I, p. 114).

MACVAIL. A form of MACPHAIL, q.v.

MACVAIN. See *under* MACBAIN.

MACVANISH, MACVENISH, MACVINISH. In Gaelic *MacMhanuis*, 'son of Mānus,' a personal name among the Macdonalds and the Macleans. The name is from the Norse *Magnúss*, which again is from Latin *magnus*, 'great,' as in Carolus Magnus (= Charlemagne). The first persons in record who bore this name in the Western Isles are Magnus mac

MACVANISH, MACVENISH..., continued

Arailt, a chieftain from the Hebrides in 972, and Magnus Berna from Limerick (Bugge, The Royal race of Dublin, p. 16). The name is found mainly in the shires of Ross and Inverness. Ewin Johne Makvanis in the Black Isle, 1500 (Rose, p. 169). Donald McWeynish, witness in Inverness, 1686 (Rec. Inv., II, p. 343), Malcolm MacVinish of Kerameanach, North Uist, is in record in 1718. The Laoidh Mhanuis, 'Lay of Magnus,' according to the late Dr. George Henderson (Norse influence, p. 51), is the framework of Macpherson's Fingal.

MACVANNAN, MACVANNIN. G. Mac Mhannain, 'son of Buchanan.' The name of a small sept in Skye. They have not a good reputation if there is any truth in the Gaelic saying quoted by Gregorson Campbell (Superstitions, p. 305, 309):

"Clann 'ic Mhannain chuir na braide"
(Clan M'Vannan, expert as thieves).

John M'Vannan was a prisoner of the '45 (Prisoners, III, p. 186). Forbes (Skye place-names, p. 39) says = BUCHANAN, q.v.

MACVARISH, MACVARRAIS. G. MacBharrais (and MacBhairis) or MacMharais, 'son of Maurice.' The name occurs in Alexander Macdonald's poem, the 'Bark of Clanranald,' and is not uncommon among the Macdonalds of Moidart. Findla McVirriche and John Makvirriche were burgesses of Inverness, 1602 (Rec. Inv., II, p. 3), and William M'Wirrich or M'veirrich was burgess there, 1655 (Laing, 2460). Dr. John McWarish, from Drumley, Moidart, was a surgeon in the army of the Young Pretender in the '45 (Albemarle Papers, II, p. 394). Malcolm M'Vurrish or M'Ourich or M'Warish of Tiree, and Lachlan V'Vurich or M'Warish of Moidart were rebels of the '45 (Prisoners, III, p. 186). McVirrist 1607, MacVarish, MacVarrich, and MacVorich in 1745. See also MACMORICE and MACVOREIS.

MACVARQUIS, MACVARQUISH. See under MACMARQUIS.

MACVAY, MACVEY, MACVEAGH, MACVEIGH. G. MacBheatha. John Macvay was tenant of Gargiston, Ardmanoch, 1504 (ER., XII, p. 661). Farquhar M'Vay in Balnakok, Easter Ross, 1507. Fergus M'Veagh, 'habitantis Peanagross' (Pennycross in Mull), was formerly possessor of a Gaelic medical MS. now in the library of Edinburgh University.

MACVEAGH. See under MACVAY.

MACVEAN. G. Mac Bheathain. John M'Wayein witnessed a sasine in favor of Thomas Stewart of Grantully, 1494 (Grandtully, I, p. 38). William McWeane was tenant in the Four Glakkis, Kynnarde, 1539 (ER., XVII, p. 670). The name is common in BBT.: Sorle M'Conill M'Allane M'Baine for whom Glenorchy went cautioner at Balloch, 1564; Patrick Roy M'Veane, cattle farmer in Glenlochy, 1594, may be Patrick Roy M'Bean in Boithworny in same year; John and Finlay M'Vaine in Balloch, 1626; and John and Patrick M'Vaine, Inchadden, 1638. John M'Vane or M'Wean of Inverness, a Jacobite prisoner of the '45 (Prisoners, III, p. 184). See also BEAN and MACBEAN.

MACVEIGH. See under MACVAY.

MACVENISH. See under MACVANISH.

MACVICAR. A not uncommon name in Argyllshire, in G. M'Bhiocair or Mac a' Bhiocair, 'son of the vicar.' James Makuecar was burgess of Glasgow in 1488 (LCD., p. 257). Donald owyr Makfikar was one of the victims of the hership of Petty in 1502 (Rose, p. 176). Mr. Archibald M'Yvicare who appears as provost of the Collegiate Church of Kilmond (Kilmun) in 1529–41-48 (RMS., III, 861, and Argyll charters) afterwards became a monk of Cupar Abbey (Poltalloch Writs, p. 139; Cupar-Angus, I, p. xxiii). The Chronicle of Fortingall records (p. 121) the death in 1542 of the wife of John M'Ayn Rawych V'Gewycar (i.e. John the grizzled son of the vicar); and in 1543 Nevin Makvicar witnessed a charter of lands in the barony of Phantelane, Argyllshire (RMS., III, 2902). Sir Niall McVicar was rector of Lochawe, 1555 (Poltalloch Writs, p. 142), and in 1561 one Makvicar had lands near Inveraray given to him. Schir Newyne M'Vicar was "commissar of Ergile" in 1580 (Coll., p. 17), Patrick McVicar was servitor of George Campbell of Inveraray in 1654 (Poltalloch Writs, p. 73), and Duncan McViccar was ordered to be transported to New England in 1685 (RPC., 3. ser. XI, p. 94). The Macvicars appear first as a small clan dependent on the Macnaughtons, and after the dispersion of that clan they appear to have followed the Campbells of Argyll. The Breadalbane Macvicars appear to have descended from Maurice McNaughton and Duncan McNaughton, who were vicars of Inchadney from 1480 to 1523 (FB., p. 369). A standing-stone formerly on the lawn of the castle of Inveraray was said to mark the old march between the Macvicars and the Macivers (OPS., II, p. 90). Macquaker appears to be a corrupt form of this name. M'Weckare 1663, M'Wicare 1556, McWiccar 1684, Makwicar 1530.

MACVICHIE. A Perthshire surname, a variant of MACMICHIE, q.v. It was a common personal name in Breadalbane one hundred and fifty and more years ago (SN&Q., III, p. 172). John M'Vichie in Balinlauchinduin, parish of Dull, 1774 (*Dunkeld*).

MACVILLIE. Recorded in Langholm. G. *Mac Bhuillie*, 'son of Willie' (G. *Bhuillie*, 'Wullie'). Thomas M'Villie appears in Lanrick, 1629 (*Dunblane*). Mac Vullie is an old spelling.

MACVINISH. *See under* MACVANISH.

MACVINNIE, MACVENNIE. Galloway surnames, variants of MACWHINNIE, q.v. John M'Vinie was author of *The uncertainty of human life described*, Dumfries, 1775.

MACVITIE, MACVITTIE, MACVITTAE, MACWITTIE. Surnames of Ayrshire and Galloway. Thomas M'Vcthee, a witness in Galloway, 1566 (*Laing*, 807). Robert Makvetie and John Makvetie were witnesses in Lanark, 1574 (RPC., II, p. 385). William McVite in Hawick was described in 1627 as a masterless person fit for the wars (ibid., 2. ser. II, p. 85). Margaret McVittie and Gavin McVittie were examined for the Test in Tinwald, 1685 (ibid., 3. ser. XI, p. 433, 434), and William McVittie in Hartbush was charged in 1686 with attending conventicles (ibid., XII, p. 407). Woulfe says the name is from Ir. *Mac an bhiadhthaigh*, 'son of the hospitaller,' but this does not seem likely.

MACVOREIS. John McVurist who was summoned in 1604 "to flit and remoiv him selff out and fra ane ruid burru biggit land" may be the Johne McVarrist, broustar, "bewest the wattir of Niss" referred to in 1613 (*Rec. Inv.*, II, p. 23, 115). Allester McVoreis in Dalchossane and Patrik McVoreist in Lany were fined for reset of Clan Gregor, 1613 (RPC., XIV, p. 631, 643). Callum M'Voreist or M'Vorist was domestic servant to the laird of Glenurquhay in 1638 and Johnne M'Voreiss in Ochtermalie was a vassal of the laird in same year (BBT., p. 399, 403). John and Patrick M'Voris raised an action against Donald M'Niccoll for slaughter committed by him, 1662 (*Just. Rec.*, I, p. 57), Callum M'Vorish in Tombea is mentioned, 1664 (ibid., p. 113), and Duncan McVorist in Drumondernoch recovered decree for stolen goods, 1684 (RPC., 3. ser. VIII, p. 576). Janet M'Vurist in Dalnabo, 1694 (*Dunkeld*). See also MACMORICE, MACVARISH and MACVURICH.

MACVRACHTER. This name, common in Breadalbane in the eighteenth century, is now probably extinct. The name means 'son of the maltman' (G. *brachadair*). Findlay M'Wrack-ater, in Easter Moir, was charged with riot and malicious damage in 1681 (RPC., 3. ser. VII, p. 46). Finlay, Donald, and John M'Brachadair were enrolled among the duke of Atholl's fencible men in Glenlyon in 1706 (*HMon.*, III, p. 215–216); and John M'Vraugheter in More of Glenlyon is in record in 1724 (*Dunblane*). Finlay McVrachadair in Auchlyne, 1770 (FB., p. 372). Cf. MALTMAN.

MACVURICH. G. *M'Mhuirich*, MG. *M'Mhuireadhaigh*. See under MURDOCH. The bardic family of M'Vurich claimed descent from the famous Irish poet Muireach Albannach of first half of thirteenth century. Some of them now call themselves Macphersons by confusion with the Badenoch *Clann Mhuirich*. Gillecolaim mac Muredig is one of the witnesses to a grant to the Abbey of Deer, 1132 (*Bk. Deer*, III, 10). Lacclann M'Murghaich, 'archipoeta,' witnessed a charter granted in 1485 to the abbot of Iona by the lord of the Isles (*Bardachd Gaidhlig*, p. 300), and Donald McMurich and John McMurich were witnesses at Kirnan, 1573 (*Poltalloch Writs*, p. 144). Malcolme McVoriche in Glenlvoun was fined for reset of Clan Gregor, 1613 (RPC., XIV, p. 633), Donald Mc wirrich was tenant of Ballichoan in Seill, 1669 (HP., IV, p. 224) and Patrick M'Mhourich was enrolled in the Duke of Atholl's fencible men in Glenlyon, 1706 (*HMon.*, III, p. 215). Jonet M'Vorich is in Cablea, parish of Little Dunkeld, 1702, and Marjorie M'Vourich in Botwarniebeg, 1728 (*Dunkeld*). In Arran M'Mhuirich is spelled *MacFuirigh* or *AcFuirigh*, and Englished *Currie*. At Southend of Arran it is spelled *Mac uirigh*. Angus McWurie, Lachlane McWurie, and John McWurie were tenants in Islay, 1686 (*Bk. Islay*, p. 507, 509). McVoerich 1682; McVarraich, McVirrich, McVurriche, Makvirriche, McWirriche. In *Rel. Celt.* spelled McMuirigh, McMuiredhaigh, McMuiredhuigh (II, p. 224, 286, 297). See also MACVARISH and MACVOREIS.

MACWALRICK. In Gaelic *MacUalraig* and *MacUaraig*, and sometimes *MacCuaraig*. The name is said to be derived from one Ulrick or Walrick Kennedy, a scion of the Kennedys of Dunure, Ayrshire, who fled to Lochaber early in the sixteenth century and founded the sept of M'Walrick of Leaneachan. In Galloway and in Carrick the old Gaelic personal name *Ualgarg* or *Ualgharg*, 'high temper,' was confused with Teutonic Ulrick, now Ulrich (from Old High German *Uadalrich*, Latinized *Oudalricus*, explained by a Latin gloss as "paterna hereditate dives," patrimonially rich, Foerstemann, *Altdeutsches Namenbuch*, I, col. 981). Sir Duncan McOl-

MACWALRICK, *continued*
rig or Makolrik possessed the chaplainry of St. Ninians, in the parish of Urquhart, before 1556 (*Grant*, III, p. 121). An individual of this name has given rise to Lochan Mhic Cuaraig in Lorne.

MACWALSTOUN. Recorded in Breadalbane, 1579 (FB., p. 372). Cf. WALESTUN.

MACWALTER, MACQUALTER. G. *MacBhàltair*, 'son of WALTER,' q.v. John Makwatter and Ewin McWalter, followers of the earl of Cassilis, were respited for murder in 1526 (RSS., I, 3386). John Graham McWalter in Duchry was fined for reset of outlawed Macgregors, 1613 (RPC., XIV, p. 640), Parlan M'Walter of Auchinvennell, 1619 (*Sasines*, II, 66), David M'Waltir in Mayboill, a witness in 1621 (*Laing*, 1879), and William McWattir in Kilkerrane, Ayr, charged with molestation in 1628 (RPC., 2. ser. II, p. 543). William M'Walter, 'teughter' in Ferne, a witness there, 1675, George M'Watter, witness in Ayr, 1665 (*Laing*, 2745, 2595), and Margaret McWater in the parish of Portpatrick, 1684 (*Parish*). M'Qualter 1667, M'Quatter 1663, McVater 1684. An old form of the name in Galloway was Macquhalter.

MACWARD. G. *Mac a' bhaird*, 'son of the bard.' Fergus Mackabard made a gift of the church of Dunsyer with all its pertinents to the Abbey of Kelso between 1165 and 1214 (*Kelso*, p. 16, 316, 319). Cosmo Innes's suggestion that he was "perhaps of the family of Baird, in which Fergus was of old an accustomed name" (OPS., I, p. 129), I think unlikely. Sir Patrick Makbard was granted the chaplainry of S. Columba in Bute, 1516 (RSS., I, 2775). Robert Makewarde, a servant, who became professor of Humanitie in the old college of St. Andrews in 1560 (Lamont, *Diary*, p. 16), was afterwards minister of the Scots Congregation in Rotterdam. The name is now probably merged in BAIRD. McCuard and McCward 1653.

MACWATER. G. *Mac Bhàtair*, 'son of Walter,' from Water (Watter), an old Scots pronunciation of Walter. See MACWALTER.

MACWATT. A Highland border and Moray and Black Isle name formed from Wat or Watt the Lowland diminutive of Walter. Donald and Gilbert Makwat were the king's couriers in 1455, and the former appears again as king's courier in 1462 as MacVat (ER., VI, p. 105; VII, p. 155). Symon M'Wat is in record in Bute in 1491 (ALA., p. 204). Cuthbert McQuhat, witness in Dumfries, 1506 (*Edgar*, p. 228). John Makwete was tenant

of the lands of Burnokheid, Ayrshire, 1638 (RMS., III, 1807), and Patrick M'Wete was tenant of Brokelhill, Ayrshire, 1533 (ibid., 1319). The name appears in Dornoch in 1603 as M'Kwatt, and there is reference in 1694 to the murder of David Rose alias M'Watt (*Rose*, p. 386). William McWat in Broomesyde, Lanark, 1711 (*Minutes*, p. 114). The name is also in current use under the forms M'Ouat, M'Owat, M'Quat, and M'Quhat, and is also Englished WATSON. M'Huat 1597.

MACWATTERS. A surname confined more or less to Caithness. 'Son of WALTER,' q.v.

MACWATTIE. A Highland Border name, in G. *MacBhàididh*, 'son of Wattie' or 'Watty,' a shortened or pet form of WALTER, q.v. Buchanan says the MacWatties were a sept of the Buchanans of Leny (from Walter, son of John, second of that name, laird of Leny early in the sixteenth century), some of whom found their way to Argyll and elsewhere, but the name occurs much earlier. One fourth of the lands of Parcy was let to John Makwatty in 1446 (*Cupar-Angus*, I, p. 128). Robert Lany alias Buchquhannane M'Watte is a charter witness in 1557 (RMS., IV, 1214). Several individuals of this name were concerned in the burning and spoiling of the lands of Moyness in 1602 (*Rose*, p. 292). Gilbert McWattie in Innerrane was fined for reset of Clan Gregor in 1613 (RPC., XIV, p. 644), and James McWatty was fined 6s.8d. for 'playing at the futeball on the Sabboth nicht' in 1630 (*Elgin*, II, p. 215). The name is also current in the form MACQUATTIE, q.v.

MACWERICH. MacWerich or MacMorich was name of an old Bute family. Gilcrist Makwerich of Achamor held part of the crown lands of Baroun, etc., in Bute, 1506 (RMS., II, 2987), and John Makweriche held half of the lands of Nethir-Dunallirde there in 1533 (RMS., III, 1321). John M'Werycht in Auchinchalden was a vassal of Glenurquhay, 1688 (BBT., p. 403). Gilcrist Makquhirrycht appears as charter witness, 1530 (*Lamont Inv.*, p. 39), and John M'Patrik M'Vyrricht subscribed a bond of manrent to Colin Campbell of Glenurquhay, 1573 (BBT., p. 217). Finlay Dow M'Quherich, tenant of Auchmoir, 1582, is probably Finlay Dow M'Worriche, tenant in Ediravernach, 1594 (ibid., p. 267, 282). Thomas McWorich and Johnne McWorich and others in Dunkeld were charged with armed convocation and assault, 1609 (RPC., VIII, p. 242). John Dow McVirich in Glenlvoun and Allester McViriche in Kirktoun of Blair and Donald McVorich in Balquhidder were fined for reset of Clan Gregor, 1613 (RPC., XIV, p. 633, 638). McVerriche 1607,

McVarraich and MckVurriche 1605, McVurrichie, McWirriche, Makvirriche 1602, Mackvirriche 1603, M'Wrich 1663.

MACWHA, MACWHAE. William M'Why was a witness in 1436 (*Cawdor*, p. 13). Margaret MacWhae was resident in parish of Borgue, 1684 (RPC., 3. ser. IX, p. 567). John M'Whae, shoemaker in Kirkcudbright, 1763 (*Kirkcudbright*). M'Whey and M'Why 1784. See MACQUHAE.

MACWHAN, MACWHIN. Side forms of MACQUEEN, q.v., from G. *M'Shuibhne*. The aspiration of the *s* causes the name to be pronounced like MacHuin. Michael Macqueen, burgess of Edinburgh and re-founder of Magdalen Chapel in the Cowgate of Edinburgh (PSAS., XXI, p. 267), appears in the Accounts of the Lord High Treasurer (V, VI) between 1516 and 1536 as Makquhen, Makquhane, McQuhenne, McQuhenn, McQuhan, Machquhan, McQuheen, Manthquhen, Maquhon, Mauchquhen, and Makquhan. Malcolm Macquhyn is in record in Bute in 1501 (LCD., p. 205), John Makquhon witnessed an instrument of sasine at Bordland of Laik, Kirkcudbrightshire, 1552 (*Laing*, 598), and Duncan M'Quhyn was a witness in Glasgow in 1557 (*Protocols*). Agnes McWhan was charged with being a disorderly person in the parish of Kirkcudbright in 1685 (RPC., 3. ser. IX, p. 573), and Adam or Andrew M'Whan or M'Quhan was shot in the same year for adhering to the Covenant (Mackenzie, *History of Scotland*, p. 626). The inscription on his tombstone in Kells churchyard is given by Dick (p. 454). M'Quheyne 1563, M'Kquyne 1594, M'Whanne 1682, MacWhinn 1684. The name is also curtailed to WHAN and WHIN.

MACWHANNEL, MACWHANNELL. From MACILWHANNELL (in Perthshire), q.v. A composition made with Thom M'Quhonale for remission for crimes in 1473 (ALHT., I, p. 4). John Macquhonnell, a follower of the earl of Cassilis, was respited for murder, 1526 (RSS., I, 3386), and William McQuonneill had sasine of lands in Kylismure, Ayr, 1591 (ER., XXII, p. 533). John Mclhonel and James Mclhonel in Blainror and Patrick Mclwannell in Craigneich are in record in 1698 (*Muthill*). Janet Mclhonell is in record in Blainror, 1700, and Cristian Mclwhannel in Glenlichorn, 1701 (ibid.). John M'Whonnell in Bargrenan, parish of Minigaff, 1719 (*Wigtown*). The form Nclwhannell (for nighean mhic Whannell) is found in 1712. The following spellings of this name are found in Wigtownshire in 1684 (*Parish*): McCwhanelle, McQuhandle, McWeennell, Mcquhannil, McVhomel, McWhanell, McWhaneall, McWhan-

nil, McWhanrall, McWhanle, and McWhanlie. The name also occurs in the same district without 'Mac.'

MACWHARRIE. See *under* MACQUHARRIE.

MACWHIN. See *under* MACWHAN.

MACWHINNIE, MACWHINNEY, MACWINNEY, MAWHINNEY, MEWHINNEY, MACQUHENZIE, Forms of MACKENZIE, q.v., current in Galloway. M'Whunye is still the common Galloway pronunciation of the name. In the Buccleuch MSS. the name occurs as Makquhynze and M'Quhynze (1526), and Makkynnay (1593). Thomas M'Quhinze was chaplain in Ayr in 1502 (*Ayr*, p. 101), and Donald Makquhinze, a follower of the earl of Cassilis, was respited for murder in 1526 (RSS., I, 3386). William McQuhinny in parish of Carsfern was charged with being a disorderly person, 1684 (RPC., 3. ser. IX, p. 575). Alexander M'Whinnie in Cairnfield in 1739 (*Wigtown*). In 1684 the name appears in record as McKwhinney, McQuhine, and McWhynie (*Parish*). See also under MACGILLWHINNICH.

MACWHIR, MACWHIRR, MACQUHIR. William Makwir was deacon of the curriers in Dumfries, 1600 (*Edgar*, p. 248). A charge was made against Robert McWheir in Grange, 1671 (*Just. Rec.*, II, p. 60). Callum M'Ouhir appears in Kenmore, 1684 (DPD., I, p. 488), and John McWhir was minister of St. Andrew's church, Dunfermline, 1810–13 (*Fasti*, III, p. 573). M'Kerlie has the name as MacQuhir or MacQhuir.

MACWHIRRIE. It may be a form of MACCURRIE, q.v.

MACWHIRTER. A form of MACCHRUITER, q.v., current in Ayrshire, the original home of the name. Andrew M'Whirter in Kirkhobble in record in 1749 (*Wigtown*). Rev. Alexander McWhorter (1734–1807), of Scottish parentage, took an active part in the American Revolution and was a trustee of the College of New Jersey, now Princeton University. McWhorter Street in Newark, New Jersey, is named in his honor. The name has become Mewhirter in the North of Ireland. Macquarter 1684.

MACWHISTON. A current form of MACQUISTAN, q.v.

MACWIGGAN. A spelling of MACQUIGGAN, q.v.

MACWILKIE, MACWILKANE. See *under* MACQUILKAN.

MACWILL, 'son of WILL,' q.v. Gilbert Makwille or M'Wille was one of an assize in Carrick, 1532 (RMS., III, 1183, 1196). Donald McUill in Comer Kirktown in 1721 (HP., II, p. 302). John M'Wille in Lochalsh, 1548 (RMS., IV, 204). Patrick MacWill, cautioner for James Gordoun of Pranny, 1607 (RSCA., II, p. 109).

MACWILLIAM. G. *Mac Uilleim*, 'son of William.' The Teutonic name William was early planted in the Highlands, the MacWilliams being powerful Gaelic claimants for the Scottish throne against King William the Lion. The relationship of the MacWilliams to William the Lion is shown in the following table:

Malcolm III

David I, ninth and youngest son of Malcolm III	Duncan II, eldest son of Malcolm III
Henry the earl, younger son of David I, died in lifetime of his father	William fitz Duncan
William the Lion, second son of Henry the earl	Duncan Ban MacWilliam, slain in battle of Mam Garvia in Moray, 1187

Dovenald Ban, slain in Moray, 1215	Guthred, beheaded at Kincardine, 1211

The Clan Mac Mhic Uilleim are descended from William, son of William fifth chief of Macleod (Alexander Mackenzie, TGSI., XXII, p. 58). Duncan Williamson who was concerned in the "spulzie of Kilravock" in 1497 (*Rose*, p. 166) may have been a Macwilliam. Gillecrist Makwilliam in the Black Isle, 1500 (*Rose*, p. 169). Henry Makwilliam or Makwillzam was appointed to a stall in Croudan in 1506, and is mentioned again in 1521 as vicar of Logymar (REA., I, p. 387; II, p. 96). Thome McWilzeme, tenant in Strathdee, 1527 (*Grant*, III, p. 68). The Robertsons of Pittagowan early in the sixteenth century were also known as M'William. John M'Eane M'Williame is recorded in Lochalsh in 1548 (RMS., XIV, 204), and Allester Roy McWilliame in Auchmahechinche and Parlene McWilliame in Ardes were fined for resetting outlawed members of Clan Gregor in 1613 (RPC., XIV, p. 629, 644). Patrick M'William in Ardunaig was denounced rebel in 1678 (HP., I), Callum McQuilliam in Glenlyoun was denounced as "a brokine man" in 1682 (RPC., 3. ser.

VII, p. 638), and Alexander McWilliam was a Seaforth tenant in 1721 (HP., II, p. 295). A family of this name are said to have been established in the parish of Mortlach in 1550, and many of the name have now changed their name to Williamson. Many MacWilliams or MacWillies existed in Glenlivet and the name is found there in old records as McKullie (1637), McCullie (1645), McVillie (1693), M'Quhilzeame (1616), etc. The spellings McCulliam, McCulziame, McCulzian, and McKWilliam occur in Wigtownshire in 1684 (*Parish*). Macuilam 1791. MACQUILLIAM, MACKILLIAM and MACWILLIAMS are also current forms.

MACWILLIE. A Highland border surname from 'Willie,' a diminutive or pet form of WILLIAM, q.v. It is now usually spelled Macwilliam. Richard McWilly was tenant of Camusbeg in the barony of Doune in 1499 (ER., XI, p. 415), and complaint was made against "tailyeour Makwillie, houshald man to the Lard of Tullebragane" in 1581 (RPC., III, p. 350). In Glenlivet, in the parish of Inveravon, Banffshire, in the seventeenth and eighteenth centuries there were many families of this name, and in the records of the middle of the former century the name usually occurs spelled McCullie and McKullie (*Celt. Mon.*). It is thus confused with MACCULLIE, a form of Macculloch occurring in the north. William M'Willie was a member of the Huntly Volunteers in 1798. MACWYLLIE is another form in current use.

MACWILNANE. For G. *MacIlle-bhàin*, son of the fair(-haired) lad.

MACWINNEY. *See under* MACWHINNEY.

MACWYLLIE. A form of MACWILLIE, q.v.

MACYOCK. *See under* MACJOCK.

MACYOCKIE. *See under* MACJOKKIE.

MACZEWNIE. (3 here = Scot. *y*). Finlay M'Zewnie in Darcholar, 1621 (*Dunblane*). Donald Mc Zowne in Auchnafoile was charged with repudiating his wife, 1654 (IDR., p. 260).

MADDAD. This name represents OG. *matad*, *maddad*, G. *madadh*, 'mastiff.' The name of the first known earl of Angus (fl. 1120–60), a witness to several charters in the reign of David I. He appears as Madeth comes (in RD., 1, 29), as Maddoc comes (ibid., 9), and as Maduc consul (*Nat. MSS.*, I, 21; *Raine*, 12). In the *Orkneyinga Saga* it is written *Modadr*, *Moddadr*, and *Moddan*. A later Madeth appears in 1330 as 'prepositus' of

Perth (ER., I, p. 263), and Johannes Madith was *locum tenens* of the sheriff of Banff, 1342 (REA., I, p. 73).

MADUC. A common Welsh personal name, *Madawc, Madog*. The meaning is uncertain, either the 'fox' (obs. Welsh *madog*) or the 'goodly' (from *mad* = G. *maith*). Maduc, consule (earl), witnessed King David's charter of Swintun to Hernulf, a. 1153 (*Nat. MSS.*, I, 21). There is some confusion in the charters between this name and Maddad. cf. *Lawrie*, p. 284, 326, 343, 425.

MÁEL-, MÁIL-, (later MAOL-). The use of this word signifying "cropped," "shaveling," "slave," goes back to pagan times, and it is found in the ogham inscriptions, though rarely. Among the early Gaels close cropped hair was a mark of servile position — the nobles of the tribe always wore their hair long. Though later translated as 'servant,' 'devotee,' "the notion of servitude is for the most part at least, in abeyance. What is indicated is some relation more or less vague to us, between the generic term *maol* and the specific term following in the genitive case." After the conversion of the Gaels to Christianity the names of the leading Gaelic saints were used as personal names with the addition of *máel-*. Examples of this are *Mael-Coluim, Mael-Patraic, Mael-Micheil*, etc. The addition of *Máel* implied that the person so-named was under the saint's charge, or born on his day. At a later date the *Máel-* form gave place to *Gille-*, 'lad,' 'youth,' 'servant,' and still later in most cases we have the simple Callum, Patrick, Michael. Máel in Irish Gaelic names is rarely found separate, and in such a case would most likely be a hypocoristic shortening of one of the many names beginning with Máel-. The many names with *Máel* (Maol) and *Gille* prefixed are of great value as preserving historical evidence "as to the religious cult and ways of thinking, and also in certain cases of the utmost importance as regards the language in use at a particular period in a particular district." "Once the names became established they might be applied without reference to the original circumstances that gave rise to them." In Breton *maol* (*moel*, 1380), 'bald,' enters into the composition of innumerable Breton names, as *Kermaol*, etc. When *maol* and *gille* are aspirated the resultant pronunciation is apt to become confused to non-Gaelic ears, and the same result occurs when these words are in the genitive: (Mh)*aoile*, (Gh)*ille*.

MAELANFAID. In the Gaelic genealogical MS. of 1467 this name is given as that of the father of Donald Du, ancestor and eponymus of Cameron of Lochiel, and also as that of his ancestor six generations further back (*Coll.*, p. 53, 357). The name means 'servant of storm' (*onfaidh*) and not 'servant of the prophet' (*faidh*) as it is sometimes rendered. The old name of Clan Cameron was *Clann Mael-anfaidh*, 'children of the chief of storm.' The name appears later as *Gillonfhaidh*. An Irish saint, Maelanfaid, abbot of Dairinis, is commemorated on 31 January (*Mart. Gorm.*). Angus, Maelanfaid's son, was slaughtered in Skye in 710 (AU.). The name appears again in the same Annals under c. 725 as *Maelanfaidh*. See under MACALONIE and MACGILLONIE. Allan, son of Millony, was known as Ailein Mac Mhaolonfhaidh, which in course of time was pronounced Ailein Mac Olonai, and was pronounced in English Allan Mac Olony. By blundering of some scribe this was converted to Allan Mac Ochtery, "a name which never existed among the Macgillonies or any other Highland clan."

MAELDUN. For earlier Maelduin, 'fort chief.' Maldunus or Maelduin, bishop of St. Andrews, granted the church of Marchinke (Markinch) to the Culdees of the island of Lochleven (RPSA., p. 116), died in 1055 (*Tighernach*). Maledonni mac meic Bead witnessed the grant by Gartnait and Ete of Pet-meic-Cobroig to the church of Deer, c. 1131–32 (*Bk. Deer*, III, 7). In 1507 Maldone Farquharsone appears in Rainy of Easter Ross, and Muldone in Urray (*Macbain* I, p. 160).

MAGALL, MEGALL. Forms of MACCALL, q.v., current in Galloway.

MAGLAGAN. A variant of MACLAGAN, q.v., recorded in Glasgow.

MAGNUS. An ON. personal name, *Magnúss*, the source of MACVANISH, q.v. In Shetland Magnus as a font name is tenth in order of frequency, and eleventh as a surname in the form MANSON (= Magnus's son). There are also seventeen MAGNUSSONS (*Scotsman*, Edinburgh, 16 October, 1886). As a forename we have Magnus Caddenheid in Cortance, Aberdeen, 1633 (SCM., III, p. 116). In the form Mànus it was a common name among the Macleans and Macdonalds, and gave origin to MACMANUIS. See MANSON and MANUS.

MAGNUSSON. See MAGNUS.

MAGUS. John Magus, witness, 1549 (*Gaw*, 15). Perhaps local; there is Magus (Upper and Nether) near St. Andrews, Fife.

MAIDER. Thomas Madoure was present at perambulation of the marches of Kyrknes and Louchor in 1395 (RPSA., p. 3). James Madour was a charter witness in 1466 (Kelso, 531), and Robert Madour and Alan Madour were charter witnesses in Newbattle in 1464 and 1468 (Neubotle, p. 252, 273). James Mador was prior of Lesmahagoo in 1467 (ibid., p. 263), and Patrick Mador, licenciate in theology, a witness in Haddington in 1458, appears in 1462 as Patrick Madowre, abbot of Newbotle (ibid., p. 246, 250). Robert Mador was bailie of Sir Alan Lokarte of Lee in 1477 (ibid., p. 313). Robert Madour and Thomas Madour witnessed a charter to Neubotle Abbey in 1462 (ibid., p. 250), and William Madur or Mader appears as auditor in Lanark in 1488 and 1503 (Lanark, p. 1, 12). The surname also occurs in Arbroath in 1485 as Maddyr (RAA., II, 261). John Madour was witness in Peebles in 1473 (Peebles CR.), and John Mader in Balsanno was a follower of Campbell of Lundy in 1541 (RSS., II, 3666). Sir Richard Mader, cleric and notary public in Ferne, 1545 (Laing, 495), is doubtless Sir Richard Maddir who was granted the chaplainry of St. Andrew of Golspie in 1556 (OPS., II, p. 650, 651), and Bessie Mader is recorded in Brechin in 1577 (Brechin). John Maider was burgess of Irwing in 1642 (Inquis., 2629), Thomas Maydder is recorded in Hardenes in 1652 (Lauder). James Medder was sheriff officer of Roxburgh in 1666 (RRM., III, p. 75), Andrew Madder was burgess of Jedburgh in 1690 (Peebles CR.), and in 1723 a claim was pursued against Agnes Madder in Stitchill (Stitchill, p. 185). Cf. MATHER and MATTERS.

MAIDUS. William filius Maidi perambulated the boundaries of Moniabrok and Stragrif, c. 1202 (RMP., p. 13, 14). Between 1202–07 William and George, sons of Meidus, witnessed a confirmation charter by the Chapter of Glasgow (ibid., p. 110).

MAILER, MAILLER. An old Strathearn surname still found in the shires of Stirling, Perth, and Fife. From the lands of Mailer in the parish of Forteviot, Perthshire. Johan de Malere, the king's tenant in the county of Perth, rendered homage in 1296 (Bain, II, p. 202), and Symon de Maller witnessed confirmation of a charter by Malise, earl of Strathern in 1360 (Scon, p. 136). Robert Meyler is recorded in Perth in 1557. "John Malar son and air of vmquhill Lyonas Maler, burgess of Ochtirardour" is in record in 1615 (Reid, Auchterarder). Mollar, near Touch, Stirlingshire, was formerly spelled Malar, but the Perthshire place seems the more likely source of the surname. The English surname Mailer is of quite different origin.

MAIMUNDE. A variant of Maymond. Robertus Maimunde witnessed an Inchcolm charter, c. 1178–1214 (Inchcolm, p. 5).

MAIN. (1) A surname borne by many fishermen families at Nairn and neighboring villages is simply the Norse MACNUS, q.v., and is probably a survival from the old Viking days in the Moray Firth. Some years ago there were thirty John Mains in the town of Nairn, and a tee-name had to be given each to distinguish them from one another. There are also many of the name in Aberdeenshire. (2) In the southern counties the name is probably another spelling of MAYNE, q.v. William Mane was keeper of the guard of the king (architenens garde), 1477 (SBR., p. 262). William Mane was citinar in Sanctandrois, 1551 (Rollok, 94), and John Mane, tenant on lands of Kelso Abbey, 1567 (Kelso, p. 523). Patrick Mane and James Mane were beidmen in Edinburgh, 1584. James Main of Westerhouse was retoured in lands, 1699 (Retours, Lanark, 452).

MAINLAND. A surname found in Orkney and Shetland, derived from Mainland, the principal island of the Shetland group. Manus Mainland appears as a witness at Kirkwall in 1550 (REO., p. 242). Thomas Mainland was schoolmaster of Bressay, Shetland, in 1907.

MAINS. Perhaps local. Mains was the name given to the principal or home farm on an estate, and the word is common as a place name.

MAIR. "Mair was the designation of an officer who executed summonses and other legal writs. Those who held hereditary appointments being termed 'mairs of fee'" (Protocols, III, p. 28n). Skene (De verborum significatione) adds that the mair was otherwise called Praeco Regis, the king's crier or herald. In the Act of 1426 (APS., II, c. 99) the mair is described as the "king's sergeant" and entitled to bear a "horn and wand." It was "however, a common term denoting any deligated office. It might, for instance, denote a head forester" (Mackinnon, Const. hist. of Scotland, p. 76). In 1606 Robert Dumbar, heir of George Dumbar, in Litle Tarie, was retoured heir of his father "in officio mari vulgo vocato the office of Mairschip of the erledome of Murray and Westschyre of the samin" (Retours, Moray, 22). Abraham marus held land in the Garuach in the reign of William the Lion (LAC., p. 167), Robert le Mare witnessed a charter to the Priory of May by Eggou ruffus early in the thirteenth century (RPSA., p. 383), and Alexander Marus was witness in a Maule charter, 1261 (*Panmure*, II, 85). Symon le Mare of Perthshire rendered homage in 1296 (*Bain*, II, p. 200). Eustace Marr or Mare was collector of contributions of the sheriffdom of Perth 'super Ileff' in 1360 and 1367 (ER., II, p. 41, 423). John Mair, Scottish merchant, had a safe conduct to trade between Scotland and England in 1453 (*Bain*, IV, 1253), Andreas Mayr, witness in Aberdeen, 1477 (REA., I, p. 312), James Mayr, witness in Dumfries, 1544 (*Anderson*), and John Major or Mair (1469–1550), born in Haddington, was "the last of the schoolmen." John Mair, "apostle of temperance," in North America, was born in Aberdeen, 1788.

MAIRGHEAD. The local pronunciation of the Gaelic for Margaret shows that the form Mairghead exists as well as Mairead and Mairearad. The spelling Marghred occurs in the *Book of Clanranald* (*Rel. Celt.*, I, p. 158), and Macfarlane (BB., p. 150) gives it as Mairghread. The first person of distinction in Europe to bear the name was the sister of Edgar Atheling. She received the name in Hungary, where she was born in 1040. The esteem in which she was held as Queen of Malcolm III doubtless made the name popular in Scotland.

MAISLETT. John Maslatt was tenant of Eist Barnis of Dunbar, 1559 (ER., XIX, p. 401), and in 1561 William Maislait rendered to Exchequer the accounts of the bailies of the burgh of Dunbar (ibid., XIX, p. 178). Alexander Maislet was a resident of Edinburgh in 1612 (*Edinb. Marr.*). William Maislet in Haddington gave allegiance to the king's coronation, 1567 (RPC., I, p. 558), Elspeth Maislett is recorded in Eyemouth, 1669 (*Lauder*), and Isobel Mislett in Saltpreston, 1698 (*Edinb. Marr.*). Meslet 1629.

MAITLAND. Perhaps a nickname, but explained without proof or much probability as 'Little wit' or to be more exact, 'Bad wit' (*Baring-Gould*, p. 376). The name occurs frequently in Northumberland in the twelfth and thirteenth centuries as Maltalent (1170) and Mautalent (1230) (*Bain*, I, 123, 1114). The first of the name in Scotland was Thomas de Matulant who appears as witness to a charter by John de Landeles of Hownan in 1227 (*Melros*, I, 247). Gillebertus de Maltalent was a charter witness, c. 1215 (*Panmure*, II, 124). W. Mautalent was one of a number appointed to settle a dispute between the churches of Glasgow and Kelso in 1221 (REG., 116), and William Matalent, perhaps the same person, witnessed

a grant by Hugh de Bygris, 1228 (*Kelso*, 186). Between 1220 and 1240 William Matalent or Mautalent appears as witness in other Kelso charters in which he and others are designed as 'servientes abbatis' (ibid., 153, 194, 242). Sir Richard de Mauteland obtained the lands of Thirlastane by marriage with Avicia, daughter and heiress of Thomas de Thirlestane, in the reign of Alexander II. William de Mautlent confirmed to Dryburgh various grants by his father, d. 1315 (*Dryburgh*). William Maltalent, witness, 1357 (*Neubotle*, p. 309). Robert Matilland or Matillande, dominus de Schewes, present at perambulation of lands of Tarwas and Wldny, 1417 (RAA., II, 53), is probably Robert Maitland, one of the hostages for the ransom of James I in 1424. Maitlands have distinguished themselves as lawyers and statesmen, and also in the naval and military services of Britain. Maltland 1686, Mateland 1489, Matelande 1476, Matlain 1646, Matland 1493, Mautelande 1334, Mautelent 1368, Mawtelande 1424, Metlan 1633; Matheland, Metellan. For local pronunciation of name cf. 'Auld Baby Mettlin that was housekeeper to the first laird o' Tushilaw' of the Ettrick Shepherd's mother.

MAKEPEACE. John Makpesse was witness to a disposition by John de Glasleter in 1361 (*Panmure*, II, p. 177). Joan Makepeace was the name given to the sister of Edward III, when the war with the Bruces was partly pacified by her marriage with David II in 1328. Bardsley's earliest example is dated 1379.

MAKERSTON (or -TOUN). From the lands of Makerstoun near Kelso, Roxburghshire. Master Adam de Malcarristoun, a cleric, was a prominent personage in the first half of the thirteenth century. He was witness to the gift of the church of Wemys in Fife to the Hospital of Soltre and to a gift of lands in Langton to the same house before 1240 (*Soltre*, p. 13, 14; see also p. 19). As Adam de Malkaruiston he witnessed the grant of Dolbethoc to Monvmusk, c. 1233–35 (RPSA., p. 369). In 1245 he is witness to a composition (ibid., p. 330), and in other records, c. 1250, he appears as clericus domini episcopi (ibid., p. 169, 281). In 1259 he was official of Gamelin, bishop of St. Andrews, and later appears as rector of Collessie, and in 1263 as rector of Syreys (Ceres) (*Pap. Lett.*, I, p. 391). John de Malkarestone of the county of Roxburghe rendered homage in 1296. The seal attached to his homage bears a falcon in a gloved left hand and arm, and S' *Ihoannis de Malkerst* (*Bain*, II, p. 199, 532). William de Mulkarriston received payment of an annuity in 1328 (ER., I, p. 114).

MAKGILMORICE. Angus Makgilmorice, tenant of part of Estir Lanerky and Caschdrapane, Strogartnay in 1480, appears again in 1483 as M'Gilmore, and in 1486 as Makgilmor (ER., IX, p. 561, 594, 622). Donald McGilmorische (or Mc ilmorische) was minister at Innerrarae, 1634 (SCM., II, p. 405). See MacGilmour.

MAKILVRENENICH. Gilbert Makilvrenenich was occupier of the two merkland of Corsyn and Bairfairne, Kintyre, in 1596 (HP., III, p. 77). For Mac Gille Bhriananaich, which is probably "really 'son of the Bute lad'" (Watson).

MAKIVER. See under MACIVER.

MÁL. Mál (from * maglo-s), 'noble,' 'prince' (poetical), was early confused with mael, 'shaveling,' 'slave,' rendering it difficult at times to say whether Mael-dub means 'black prince' or 'black slave.' Maglus is a common element in Gaulish names, as Conomaglus, Senamaglus, Vinnemaglus, etc. It is also common in Old Breton names as Mael-scuet, Maelgon, Melveu, etc. (Loth, p. 218).

MALAECHIN. Malaechín is one of the witnesses to the gift by Colban, mormaer of Buchan and Eva, his wife, to the Abbey of Deer (Bk. Deer, VI, 32). The full form of the name is Máel (Fh)échín 'servant of Fechin' of the monastery of Fore (Fobhar) in Westmeath, who died c. 665. In a marginal note to the Feilire in the Leabhar Breac (fol. 80) at January 20 is the entry: "This now is how he was called Fechin: he happened to be picking a bone in his mother's presence, when a child, and his mother said (to him) this is my little Fiachan (or little raven)." The name is also Latinized Corvulus, diminutive of corvus. Malechi which also occurs in the Book of Deer (v) is probably intended for the fuller Malaechin. The saint may have given name to Pitmachie in the parish of Oyne, Aberdeenshire, in 1362 Pethmalachy.

MALBETH. See under MACBETH.

MALBRIDE. OIr. Mael Brighde, 'servant of Brigit.' In a runic inscription in the Isle of Man the name occurs as Mailbrikti, and on the Hunterston brooch now in the Scottish National Museum of Antiquities in Edinburgh, it occurs as Malbritha. Malbrigte, son of Cathal, gave Pett-in-mulenn (i.e. the mill town) to the Abbey of Deer (Bk. Deer, II, 7). Mallebride, sacerdos, witnessed a grant to S. Serf and the Culdees of Lochleven, c. 1107 (RPSA., p. 116). The old church of Panbride in the diocese of Brechin was dedicated to S. Bride. Malbridus (Malbryd, Malle-

bryd), 'priore Kelledeorum de Brechyn,' appears as witness in numerous charters by Radulph and Gregory, bishops of Brechin, between 1202-22 (REB., II; RAA., I). Malbryd Mallod was one of the perambulators of the boundaries of the lands of Balfeth or Belphe in Angus, c. 1204-11 (RAA., I, p. 60). Gillepatric Macmalbride, who witnessed a confirmation charter of land in the Lennox, c. 1270, appears again as Patrick filius Malbrid (Levenax, p. 20, 85). Gilcrist MacMolbrid was included in an inhibition by the bishop of Glasgow, 1294 (RMP., p. * 203). The Mael- form early gave way to Gille- in this name.

MALCOLM. EG. Mael Coluimb, 'devotee' or 'shaveling of Columba,' the particular saint meant being S. Columba of Iona. The later G. is Maol Chaluim. Four kings bore this name. Malcolumb is one of the witnesses to the earliest known Scottish charter, that of King Duncan to the monks of S. Cuthbert, 1094 (Nat. MSS., I, 2). Malcolmus, capellanus Episcopi Dunblanensis (c. 1198) is witness to a confirmation by Simeon, bishop of Dunkeld. Five persons of the name are mentioned in the Gaelic entries in the Book of Deer: (1) Malcolm mac Culeón, who 'gave Bidbin (now Biffie) to God and to Drostan;' (2) Malcoloum mac Cinathá who 'gave the share of the king in Bidbin and in Pet-mecc-Gobrig and two davochs of Upper Rosabard;' (3) Malcolum mac Moilbrigte who gave the 'Delerc'; (4) Dubni mac Málcolaim, a witness to the grant by Gartnait, son of Cannech, and Ete, his wife; (5) Malcoluim mac Molíní, witness to the grant by Donchad, son of MacBead. Between 1189 and 1214 the spelling Malcholom occurs (Kelso, 139), and between 1247-64 the name of Malcolm IV is recorded in the genitive as Malcholoni (ibid., 336), and the name of Malcolm I appears as Maelcolaim in one of the MS. of the Pictish Chronicle (CPS., p. 10). Malcolm, pincerna regis, is a charter witness between 1204-11 (RVA., I, 81 bis), and Malcolm, judex, witnessed an agreement relating to the lands of Sconin et de Gariad, c. 1205 (RPSA., p. 329). Melcalmus canonicus et sacerdos Candidae Casae is in record in 1235 (Forbes, St. Ninian, p. lii). In 1256 Malcolumb, 'natus de Scocia,' charged before an assize at Newcastle-on-Tyne for murder and robbery, sadly belied his name (Northumberland Assize Rolls, p. 90), and in the same year another Maculum, also 'of Scotland,' was murdered (Bain, I, 2047, m 19). Aleyn fitz Maucolum of Berwickshire, Maucolum fiz Maucolum of Perth, Huwe le fiz Maucolum, burgess of Montrose, and several others of the name rendered homage, 1296 (*Bain*, II, p. 198, 200, 207). In the *Orkneyinga Saga* the name of Scottish kings is spelled Melkolmr, and Melkolfr was the name of two thralls in Iceland (*Njal*, 47, and *Rykdaela Saga*, c. 13). The full form Maolchaluim for modern Malcolm or Calum (Callum) was in use till the seventeenth century, but eventually gave way to Gillecaluim and both now appear as Calum and Callum. Molchallum occurs in the *Black Book of Taymouth*, and the patronymic M'Olchallum is quite common there. In the form Maiklum it was an old surname in Strathblane, and in the Lowlands it has become Maecom. In the Vale of Leven, on the border of the Gaelic Highlands, the pet form of Malcolm is Maik (Malcolm Macfarlane, TGSI., XXXI, p. 189–190). Three spellings of the name in 1768 are: Malkam, Malkem, and Malkom. John Malcum was baker in Perth, 1545 (*Rollok*, 4). As forename we have Macan and Macum in 1519, and Malcolmuill McNicoll is recorded in 1585 (*Cawdor*, p. 131, 187). Makallum MacAndro in Murthlac, 1550 (*Illus.*, II, p. 262), and Molcallum McCaldie in Carnakalliche, 1629 (RPC., 2. ser. III, p. 46). As a surname its use is comparatively modern. Makime 1597, Makum 1304, Mallcollum 1692.

MALCOLMSON, 'son of MALCOLM,' q.v. This name is found early, as Symon Malcomesson of Berwickshire rendered homage for his lands in 1296 (*Bain*, II, p. 207). Rogy Malcolmsoun "apud Corthill," is in record in 1402 (CRA., p. 385), Robert Malcolmson was burgess of Stirling, 1437 (SCM., V, p. 260), Thom Malcolmsoun was tenant of Esterdrume in 1474 (*Cupar-Angus*, I, p. 202), and Alexander Malcomson was tenant there in 1489 (ibid., p. 240). In a Latin document of 1467 the name is given in the Latin genitive form, John Malcolmi, burgess of Edinburgh (*Neubotle*, p. 314). Master Gilbert Makelchallum officiated as chaplain in the parish church of St. Martin in Ardskodinche in 1546 (OPS., II, p. 92, 94). As Master Gilbert Malcolm (Malcolmsoun, or Makolchallum) he appears as rector of Craginche (Craignish) in 1542, 1543, 1546, and 1561 (RMS.). Malcomeson, Malcumson, Malcumsone.

MALDER. Arthur Malder at the mylne of Syde, 1629, and three more of the name in Brechin (*Brechin*).

MALDUBH. Old G. 'black prince.' The share of Maldub (*pett Malduib*) was given to the Abbey of Deer by Malsnecte, the son of Lulog (*Bk. Deer*, II). The ancient name of the parish of Inveraray (in 1304) was Kvlmalduff (OPS., II, p. 85). A Gaelic saint, Meildulph,

whom the English called Mailduff, founded a hermitage at Malmesbury, and from him it was known as Maldulfesburh, now Malmesbury.

MALGIRG, 'devotee of (S.) Cyricus.' See GIRIG. Malgirc mac Tralin witnessed the grant by Gartnait and the daughter of Gillemicel to the Abbey of Deer (*Bk. Deer*, 2). Malgirhe the canon, probably of Dunblane, witnessed the grant by Symon, bishop of Dunblane, of the church of S. John to Inchaffray c. 1190 (*Inchaffray*, p. 1; see also p. 263). He is most probably the Malgirk de Mothel (Muthill) who witnessed charters by Earl Gilbert of Strathearn, c. 1198–1200 (ibid., p. 3, 13), and probably the Malkirg, prior of the Culdees of Mothle, who appears as charter witness, c. 1214 (CMN., p. 12). His name is wrongly spelled Malgegill in the *Registrum de Cambuskenneth* (p. 217). A Maelgiricc is mentioned in the Annals of Ulster under 931, and Gyric, a 'mass-priest' (*maessepreost*) in England, was of sufficient prominence to have his death recorded in the *Anglo-Saxon Chronicle* under 963.

MALHERBE. A family of this name settled in Scotland about the middle of the twelfth century. John de Malherb and Adam de Malherb obtained the manor of Morham in East Lothian, and from it they assumed the surname of MORHAM, q.v. The Register of Newbattle Abbey contains several charters to the abbey by Johannes de Morham, Adam Malherb, lord of Morham, and Thomas de Morham (*Neubotle*, 65–67, 75, 77–79). Hugh Malherb, another of the family, acquired the lands of Rossie in the Carse of Gowrie about the same time. He was succeeded by his son Hugh Malherb, who lived under William the Lion. This Hugh made a grant of two bovates of land in the territory of Rossyn (Rossie) to the monks of Arbroath which was confirmed by King William (RAA., I, p. 42, 43). William de Malherb, brother of the first Hugh, obtained a grant of lands also about the same time and granted in insubinfeudation the lands of Balenaus to his brother Ewyn Malherb for his service (ibid., I, p. 69). William was succeeded by his son Thomas who gave (c. 1205) to the monks of Arbroath a donation of two shillings yearly for ever, witnessed by his uncle Ewyn, his cousin Richard, and Hugh, son of Hugh Malherb (ibid., I, p. 68–69). The name probably long extinct.

MALINGSIDE. Andrew Malingside, against whom an action of removal was raised in 1584 (RSCA., I, p. 300), probably derived his name from Mellenside, Culsalmond, Aberdeenshire.

MALISE. Gaelic *Maol Iosa*, Early Irish *Maelisu*, 'shaveling' or 'tonsured servant of Jesus.' This was a favorite name with the old earls of Strathearn, being borne by no less than four of them in succession. Malis or Malisius, parson of Dunblane, is in record c. 1190 and c. 1210 (*Cambus.*, 122), and Malisius, presbyter and hermit, was the first prior of 'Inche Affren,' i.e. Inchaffray, c. 1200 (*Inchaffray*, p. 7; *Cambus.*, p. 313). Another Malisius appears as parson of Cref, c. 1235 (LSC., 66b). Malise, a vassal of the earl of Lennox, gave his name to the lands of Finnick-Malice (*Strathendrick*, p. 211). Malise, a tanist of the Macleans, is said to have had this name given him as an *ainm rathaid* or 'road name.' As a surname it is still with us as MELLIS, q.v., and its allied forms.

MALISON, MALLISON. A common surname in Aberdeen from the fifteenth century. John Malison possessed a tenement in Dunde in 1427 (RMS., II, 95), Thomas Malisone was admitted burgess of Aberdeen in 1445 (NSCM., I, p. 9), and payment was made to Wyll Malisoun there in 1453 (SCM., v, p. 51). Thomas Malitesoun and William Malitesoun appear as witnesses in Aberdeen in 1469 (CRA., p. 406), Willmus Mallyson elected common councillor in Aberdeen, 1475 (*Guildry*, p. 189), John Malisonne was priest there in 1506 (REA., II, p. 96), and John Maleson of Aberdeen was slain at Pinkie in 1547 (SCM., II, p. 34). Alexander Malysonne admitted burgess of Aberdeen in 1556 (NSCM., I, p. 66) may be the Alexander Malysone who was "fermorar of the tounis tak" in 1574 (CRA., p. 20). Malisson 1484, Mallaison 1729, Mallysone 1509, Malyson 1549, Malysone c. 1450, Malyssone 1640, Molison 1816, Molleson and Mollesoun 1649. Male (= Malie) was a common forename for women in Edinburgh in the sixteenth century.

MALLACE, MALLIS. Of local origin from the lands 'de Malles infra Gowry,' 1414 (*Scon*, p. 164). Donald Mallas *de eodem* was witness in 1454 (ibid., p. 184), and Gilcrist of Mallas was tenant of Wester Drumme, 1474 (*Cupar-Angus*, I, p. 197). Brice Malles was surety for James Malles in Caledy, 1456, James Mallase held part of the same land, 1460, and Andrew Malice was tenant of the Walk Mill of Belgrescho, 1482 (ibid., p. 137, 130, 233). William Malice, blacksmith in Stirling, 1546, appears again in 1561 as deacon of craft (SBR., p. 50, 279). Constantene Malice was bailie of Perth in 1619, and in the same year William Malice, merchant of the same town, was charged with smuggling tobacco (RPC., XII, p. 31). Andrew Malice is re-

corded in Soutarhouses, 1713 (*Dunkeld*). Mallice 1771.

MALLENY. From Malleny in the parish of Currie, Midlothian, formerly an old barony. Alexander de Maleny was one of the jurors on an inquest made at St. Katherine's Chapel, Bavelay, in 1280 (*Bain*, IV, 1762). Donald Malynny was king's runner in 1488 (*Trials*, I, p. 5). William Malynnie was burgess freeman of Glasgow in 1575, Patrick Mailyinnie was admitted burgess freeman as married to daughter of a burgess, 1584 (*Burgesses*), and a later Patrick Malynnie became burgess freeman in 1629 (ibid).

MALLIS. See under MALLACE.

MALLISON. See under MALISON.

MALLOCH. The Macgregors of Balhaldie are known as Macian Mhallich or Vallich, that is son of John with the bushy eyebrows (d. 1523) (*Macgregor*, I, p. 121), so named on account of his large shaggy eyebrows. John Malyoch was tenant of the lands of Parcyis, 1473 (*Cupar-Angus*, I, p. 201). In 1589 caution was found for John Maloche in Blakrithven (RPC., IV, p. 350), and in 1613 Duncan McEan Malloche, John Mulloche McEan Graniche, officer in Urquhart, and Duncan McConeill VcEac Mallighe in Clune were fined for reset of members of Clan Gregor (RPC., XIV, p. 626, 630). Helen Malloche, spouse of Robert Livingstoun merchant burgess of Edinburgh, 1628 (*Inquis.*, 1406), and Andro Malloch was schoolmaster in Auchterdirran, 1648 (PBK., p. 318). From Niel Mac Ean Vallich, a son of the John who died in 1523, the poet Mallet was descended. John Wilkes in his *The North Briton*, no. 34, p. 201, refers sarcastically to "the great Mr. Mallet alias Mallock, that ingenious Scot." Maloch 1693, Maylloch 1702.

MALMICHAEL. G. *Mael Micheil*, 'shaveling of Michael.' Modach filius Malmykel episcopus Sancti Andree, 1059–93 (RPSA., p. 117). Modach probably an error for Fothadh. John filius Malmichell on inquest on lands in Aberdeen, 1341 (REA., I, p. 69).

MALMODAN. See under GILMODAN.

MALMORAN. Malmoran de Glencharny had a charter of two davochs in Badenoch from William, earl of Ross, c. 1340 (SCM., IV, p. 125; *Invernessiana*, p. 56).

MALMURE, MALMUIR. G. *Maol Muire*, earlier *Mael Muire*, 'shaveling of (V.) Mary.' Malmure Thein (thane) de Chellin perambulated the bounds of Ballegallin, c. 1150 (*May*,

2). Chellin (now Kelly) is an old 'shire' in Fife. A serf named Malmur belonged to the Abbey of Scon (*Scon*, 37). Malmur mac Hercar and Ronald Macmalmur appear in Scon between 1165–1214 (*Scon*, 37). Malmore, parson of Taruas, witnessed a charter by Mathew Kynninmond, bishop of Aberdeen, c. 1180 (REA., I, p. 13); and Malmure, capellanus episcopi (de Strathern) was a witness c. 1198 (*Inchaffray*, p. 3). Malmure mac Gillemichel was one of the perambulators of the boundaries of Balfeth or Belphe in Angus, c. 1204–11 (RAA., I, p. 60). A dispensation was granted Molmure, son of Lagmann, knight, and Christina, daughter of Alexander called of Ergadia in 1290, who intermarried in ignorance that they were connected in the fourth degree of affinity (*Pap. Lett.*, I, p. 518). Malmor Hoge (? = G. *og*) is included in an inhibition by the bishop of Glasgow against the earl of Levenax and others in 1294 (RMP., p. *203). A son of John Mac Molmari was one of the hostages given by John of Lorn to John of Isla, c. 1350 (*Clan Donald*, I, p. 113). Christy Makmullmory had a royal remission for slaughter committed by him in Ross, 1494–5 (*Rose*, p. 164; OPS., II, p. 572). Malmure (accus.) occurs as a woman's name in a runic inscription at Kirk Michael, Isle of Man. The Latin correlative is Marianus, and in Ireland the name is Englished Myles. M'Wlmoir 1543.

MALOTHENY. Probably 'the shaveling of Eithne' (mother of S. Columba). Maloden marescal witnessed grant of the lands of Perdeyc (Partick) to the church of S. Kentegern, c. 1136 (REG., p. 9), and as Malothen le mareschald witnessed a confirmation by Earl Henry, c. 1144 (RPSA., p. 193). In the reign of Alexander I another Malothen appears as the first known *vice-comes* of Scone, and the old family of *de Scone* were probably descendants of the hereditary sheriff (Robertson, *Scotland under her early kings*, II, p. 491). Duncan, son of Michael son of Malotheny, granted the lands of Kernes to the church of St. Andrews in the time of Malcolm, seventh earl of Fife (RPSA., p. 309). Malotheny macmadethy was witness to a document relating to the church of Inuerhouen in Banffshire, c. 1210 (REM., p. 15). Mallethny and Mallehny were native men (serfs) of the Abbey of Dunfermline in the thirteenth century (RD., p. 221). The later form with Gille- is also found. Gille ethueny who was one of the jurors on the boundaries of Westere fedale, 1246 (LAC., p. 26) may be the Gylehtheny, father of Gillecrist Rothe, who with his issue, born or to be born, were quitclaimed to the abbot and convent of Inch-

affray, 1278 (*Inchaffray*, p. 101). See under GILLE ETHUENY.

MALOTISHOK. Gilbert de Malotishok witnessed a donation by Herbert de Maxwell to the church of Paisley, c. 1300 (RMP., p. 104).

MALPATRIC, 'shaveling of (S.) Patrick,' Latinized *Calvus Patricii* in the S. Gall Codex Priscian, 157a. Malpatricius witnessed the gift of the church of Cupre to the church of St. Andrews and canons of the same by Richard, bishop of St. Andrews, a. 1173 (RPSA., p. 137).

MALPETER. G. *Maelpetair*, 'shaveling of (S.) Peter.' Malpeder, earl of Merns treacherously killed King Duncan II at Monacheden, now Mondynes, on 12th November 1094 (CPS., p. 175; ES., II, p. 90–91). Malpetir mac Domnall witnessed the gift by Gartnait and Ete to the Abbey of Deer, 1132 (*Bk. Deer*, III, 11). The name early gave way to the *Gille*-form, as shown by the name of the Gillipeter who witnessed the gift by Colban, mormaer of Mar, and Eva his wife to the same abbey (ibid., VI). See MACPHATER.

MALPOL. 'Shaveling (or servant) of S. Paul.' Malpol priore Keledeorum de Mothel (Muthill) witnessed a confirmation by Simone, bishop of Dunblane, c. 1178 (CMN., p. 7). We probably have him again, c. 1210, as Cormac Malpole, prior of the Kuldees and persona de Mothell (*Cambus.*, 122).

MALSNECTE. OIr. *Máel Snechta*, 'servant of snow.' "Such names were given doubtless from some connection of birth or childhood" (*Watson* I, p. 288). Maelschnechtai mac Lulaigh ri Muireb died 1085 (AU.). As Málsnecte, son of Lúlóg (Málsnecte mac Lulóig) he gave the share of Maldúib to the Abbey of Deer (*Bk. Deer*, II). The name also occurs in the last quarter of the tenth century as Melsnati, the name of a Scottish earl killed in Caithness (*Ork. Saga*, cc. 84, 85). Sometime between 1093 and 1107 Malnethe son of Beollanus sacerdos witnessed a grant by Ethelred, son of Malcolm III, to the Keledei of Lochleven (RPSA., p. 116). In an undated charter by Richard, bishop of St. Andrews (but between 1163 and 1177), the lands held by a man named Malsnacth were granted to the canons of the Church of St. Andrews (ibid., p. 179). In other charters in the same record, between 1178–83, his name appears as Malsnacht (p. 59), Malsuahit (p. 146, for Malsnahit), and as Malsuaucht (p. 152, for Malsnaucht).

MALTMAN. From the occupation of 'maltman,' a maltster. Alexander Maltman was admitted burgess of Aberdeen in 1527 (NSCM., I, p. 50). The surname is recorded in Botary in 1640 and 1642 as Maltman and Matman (the same individual) (Strathbogie, p. 24, 29). Margaret Maltman is recorded in Coldinghame in 1671 (Lauder). John Maltman in Balnasuim, Kenmore, 1698 (FB., p. 372). See MACVRACHTER.

MALVOISINE. William Malevoisine, a Frenchman, was made chancellor of Scotland 8 September 1199, elected bishop of Glasgow in following month, and bishop of St. Andrews on 20 September 1202 (Dowden, p. 300). His name appears in record as Malevicinus and the current form was Mauvaysin. In the thirteenth century, it is spelled Maleveisin, and Wyntoun spells it Mallvycyne. The name means 'bad neighbour.' As William Mauueisyn, clericus regis, he witnessed a charter by Richard de Friuill to Arbroath Abbey, c. 1178–80 (RAA., I, 90).

MALYNNE. Walter Malynne was abbot of Glenluce, 1517. His real name was Walter Malumy, and in 1533 he renounced a tenement in Edinburgh which he had inherited from his deceased sister, Katharine Malumy (Dumfriesshire and Galloway Nat. Hist. & Ant. Soc., Trans., 3. ser. XXI, p. 230, 290).

MAN. (1) referring to occupation, e.g. woolman, a wool-buyer, dealer in wool; (2) 'man' or servant; (3) in combination with a place name denoting a man from that place, e.g. Blythman; (4) for MANN, q.v. Walterus dictus Man held land in Inuernys, 1361 (REM., p. 305). Thomas Man, a 'man' of the bishop of Moray, had a remission and protection, 1364 (ibid., p. 164).

MANCLARK. An early corruption of Mauclerk (Malclerk), the 'bad clerk.' The opposite is Beauclerk. Peter Mauclerc de Dreux was count of Brittany in 1216 (ES., II, p. 412). The two forms Mauclerk and Malclerk are recorded in Nichol's History of Leicestershire.

MANDERSTON. From the lands of Manderston near Duns, Berwickshire. Archibald of Manderstoune and Wat of Manderstoune were jurors on an inquisition anent a fishing on the Tweed in 1467 (RD., p. 358), and William of Mandirstoun of that Ilk witnessed a notarial instrument in 1478 (Home, 24). William Manderstoune in Hertside had a special respite in 1504, and Robert Manderstoune was accused of part in the murder of the abbot of Culross in 1530 (Trials, I, p. *42, *151). Bertholomew Manderstoun

had a precept of remission in 1536 (RSS., II, 2033), and Grissell Manderston is in record in 1682 (Lauder). Robert Manderston, merchant in Edinburgh, 1724 (Guildry, p. 128). Mawndirstoun 1478.

MANN. Another form of MAIN, shortened from MAGNUS, q.v. John Man was admitted burgess of Aberdeen, 1399 (NSCM., I, p. 1). Christina Man in Aberdeen was described in 1411 as "communis receptor meretricium et furium" (CRA., p. 4). Nicolaus Man was juror on inquest for ascertaining the former tenure of the lands of Kilrawakys et Geddes in 1431 (Rose, p. 129). Andrew Man, resident in Brechin, 1472 (REB., II, 276), William Man admitted burgess of Dundee, 1553 (Wedd., p. 37), and Andro Man was executed in Aberdeen, 1597, for witchcraft (SCM., I, p. 117). Finla Man appears in Dingwall, 1606; Alexander Man, attorney in Ollnafirth, 1625 (OSS., I, 111), William Man in Rames was fined in 1641 for resetting outlawed Macgregors (RPC.), and John Mann was bailie of New Galloway before 1790 (Kirkcudbright).

MANNIE. The mill of Cowpar Grange was leased to William Manny, 1447 (Cupar-Angus, I, p. 125). John Many had a lease of a croft called Croft Ellone, 1549, and Andro Many a lease of the toun of Auld Rayne in the same year (REA., I, p. 442, 444). Robert Mannie was witness in Brechin, 1589 (REB., II, 227), and several individuals named Mani are mentioned in the barony of Skene in 1627 (SCM., V, p. 219). James Meny was tailor in Edinburgh, 1672 (Edinb. Marr.).

MANSELL. OF. Mancel (le manceau, inhabitant of Maine or le Mans). This name first appears in connection with the Abbey of Kelso and shortly afterwards with the Abbey of Arbroath. About 1180 Andrew Maunsel or Mansel witnessed a charter of the church of Pencathlan to Kelso (Kelso, 369). Willelmus Manselmus witnessed William de Moreuille's charter of Gillemoristun to Edulfus filius Uctredi before 1196 (REG., p. 40). Between 1198 and 1222 we find Andrew Maunsel witnessing charters by William de Veteri Ponte and Bernard de Haudene in favor of Kelso Abbey and also witnessing the charter of the church of Brennath (Birnie in Moray) to the same abbey (Kelso, 139, 213, 371). About 1200 he granted liberty to the Abbey of Kelso to build a weir upon part of his ground "in le halech ex orientali parte ville de Roxburgh" (ibid., 507). (This is the dam-head or cauld popularly believed to have been constructed by Michael Scot, through the agency of an infernal spirit. See Scott, *Lay of the last minstrel*, II, 13). Andrew Maunsel was vicar of St. James's Church at Roxburgh in 1226 (*Morton*, p. 110). Robert Mansel or Maunsel between 1200–11 witnessed charters by Philip de Malevill, Vmfridus de Berkeley, Douenald Abbe de Brechin and others in favor of the Abbey of Arbroath (RAA., I, 74, 74 *bis*, 89, 93, 94). Agnes called Maunsell held a burgage in Roxburgh in 1338 (*Dryburgh*, 315).

MANSON. This name was common in Caithness in the sixteenth century and is very common in Shetland (where it is eleventh in order of frequency). It is an assimilated form of MAGNUSSON, 'son of Magnus.' *Magnus* (Latin, 'great') was a popular name among the Norsemen and was borrowed by them in admiration of Charlemagne (in Latin, *Carolus Magnus*). "It is worth remembering," says Dr. Alexander Bugge, "that long before the birth of Magnus the Good [King of Norway, 1035–47] the name Magnus was used among Norse kings of Man and the Hebrides. The first persons who bear this name are *Magnus mac Arailt*, a chieftain from the Hebrides, in 972, and *Magnus Berna* (i.e. Magnus son of Bjorn) from Limerick, who probably was akin to the chieftains from the Hebrides. When Sighvat Skald named the new-born son of St. Olav Magnus after Charlemagne, it was probably not his own invention. He had most likely heard the name in the British Isles, and knew that it was derived from the great Emperor" (*Contributions to the history of the Norsemen in Ireland*, I, p. 16). Jonas filius Magni was one of those who laid charges against David Meyner of Weem in 1427 (*Oppressions*, p. 110). Angus Mangson in Kirkwall in 1446 appears again in 1455 as Anguss Magniss, balʒhe of Kyrkwaw (REO., p. 51, 191). David Manson was tenant of Petconnouchty, Ardmanoch, in 1504 (ER., XII, p. 661), Thomas Mainsoun appears in Dunrossness, Shetland, in 1602 (Mill, *Diary*, p. 182), Robert Mansone was burgess of Dornoch, 1669 (OPS., II, p. 645), and John Mansone, 'dene of gild,' and three other Mansones took the Test in the burgh of Tain in 1685 (RPC., 3. ser. XI, p. 418). William Manswn was burgess of Lanark in 1490 (*Lanark*, p. 6), Finlay Mansoun, reader at Nig, was presented to the vicarage of that church in 1569 (RPC.), and Andrew Mansioun was member of council of the Canongate of Edinburgh in 1568 (MCM., II, p. 312). Joseph Manson was carpenter to Mary queen of Scots and to King James VI (Nisbet, I). Niels Monson was a native of Shetland, 1567 (*Goudie*, p. 129), Finlaw Mansoun was minister at Tayn, 1574 (RMR.). Robert Manson

is recorded in Glen in 1674 and Robert Manson in Fomenoch in 1732 (*Kirkcudbright*). Mans Magnussonn is recorded in Dunrossness in 1602 (Mill, *Diary*, p. 183). Mansons were a branch of Clan Gunn, and spread from Caithness through Sutherland to Ross prior to 1582. Mansson and Manssoun 1625, Maunsone and Maunusone c. 1524.

MANSPETHE. Henry de Manspethe of Lanarkshire rendered homage, 1296. As the legend on his seal reads: S' *Henrici de Mansfelt* (Bain, II, p. 204, 555) he may have derived his name from Mansfield near Thankerton, Lanarkshire.

MANTACH. From G. *manntach*, 'stammering,' Ir. 'toothless,' 'stammering.' Gilcrist Mantauch filius Gilgrewer, a native man of the Abbey of Dunfermline, is recorded in the thirteenth century (RD., p. 221). Thomas Mantach was one of an inquest on the lands of Ledyntoschach and Rotmase, 1398, and was also one of an inquest on the lands of Glak in 1418 (REA., I, p. 201, 216). A protection was granted John Mantache in Ballindallach, 1629 (RPC., 2. ser. III, p. 14). Iain Lom, the Gaelic bard, was sometimes known as Iain Manntach because he had an impediment in his speech. Andrew Mantach in Urquhart, 1792 (*Moray*). A tribe of Keppoch Macdonalds in early sixteenth century were known as *Sliochd Gillemhantich*, or the race of the stutterer (*Gregory*, p. 109n).

MANTHAC. Gillekonel Manthac, brother of the earl of Carrick, was one of the witnesses in 1233 in the dispute between the monks of Paisley and Samuel of Renfrew concerning the lands of Monachkeneran (RMP., p. 168; Innes, *Legal antiquities*, p. 219).

MANTOCHSON. 'Son of MANTACH.' Roderic Mantochson had remission in 1541 for his share in laying waste Trouterness in Skye (RSS., II, 3943).

MANUEL, MANWELL. From Manuel in the parish of Muiravonside, Stirlingshire. The priory of Manuel or Emmanuel here was founded by Malcolm IV for ladies of rank. John Manuel of Stirlingshire rendered homage in 1296 (*Bain*, II, p. 208), and Alexander of Manuel was a monk of Holyrood in 1299 (ibid., II, 1052). David de Manuel is mentioned in a lease of land in Angus in 1329 (RAA., II, p. 1; RMS., I, App. I, 29). William Manuel or de Manuel was abbot of Neubotle from 1413 to 1419 (*Neubotle*, p. xxv), John Manvell was serjeant of the barony of Inverleith in 1610 (*Laing*, 1585), another John Manuell is recorded in Huttoune in 1653,

MANUEL, MANWELL, *continued*

and William Manual was merchant in Lilliesleaf, 1781 (*Heirs*, 407). Sir Michael de Mauwel, monk of Aberbrothok, 1361 (*Panmure*, II, 177) may be meant for Manwel (Manuel).

MANUS. Mànus, a common personal name among Macleans and Macdonalds comes from ON. *Magnúss* through the form *Maghnus*. See MAGNUS.

MANZIES. A form of MENZIES, q.v.

MAOLDOMHNAICH. For earlier *Maeldòmhnaich*, 'Sunday's lad,' literally 'Sunday's servant,' Latinized *Calvus Dominicus*. Meldoinneth filius Machedath, 'judex bonus et discretus,' who appears in the record of a complaint by the monks of St. Serf's Island, Loch Leven, against Sir Robert Burgonensis, c. 1128 (RPSA., p. 117–118), is the Maldouenus mac ocbeth who witnessed King David's foundation charter of the Abbey of Dunfermline in the same year (RD., p. 4), and the Maldouenus judex who witnessed the king's grant to the same abbey of three serfs, Ragewin, Gillepatric, and Ulchil, c. 1126 (ibid., p. 13). Maldouenus de Scona, another witness to King David's charter to Dunfermline (RD., p. 4), as Malothenus vicecomes de Scona, witnessed confirmation by the king of the shire of Kircaldin to Dunfermline Abbey, c. 1130 (ibid., p. 16), and as Malodenus de Scona he also witnessed the gift of Perdeyc (Partick) to the Church of Glasgow, c. 1136 (REG., p. 9). Malodenus marescal and Malduuenus mac Murdac are also witnesses in this last charter. Malduueny, Rex scolarum de Mothel, is in record c. 1214–23 (LAC., p. 50). It was a favorite personal name with the early earls of Levenax, and was also a favorite forename with the Macgillemichaels of Bute. Maldovenus filius Alwinus, earl of Levenax, had a charter of the earldom from Alexander II in 1238 (*Levenax*, p. 1). Thomas filius Maldoueny witnessed the perambulation of the lands of Kynggesside in the parish of Eddleston, c. 1250 (*Neubotle*, 34). Maldovenus mac Hudy is mentioned in an inhibition by the bishop of Glasgow directed against the earl of Levenax and his adherents in 1294 (RMP., p. *203). Maldofeni M'Gillemychelmor appears in Luss in 1300. Donald, earl of Levenax made a grant to Gillaspic filius Macmaldoueny between 1333–64 (*Levenax*, p. 53). Maldowny Beg, Maldowny McMarticam, Maldowny McRobi, and Maldowny McEney were among a number who received royal remissions 'pro homicidiis, combustionibus, rapinis et furtis,' etc., in 1364 (REM., p. 164). 'Muldonych Mowlane fuktoris sone and air' is in record in the Black Isle,

1530 (*Rose*, p. 169), and Muldonich Mc-Crawald appears in Tiree, 1541 (ER., XVII, p. 614). Spelled M'Aldonich in 1723, M'Oldonych in BBT., and as Gilledonich and M'Yldonich in Easter Ross, 1504 (*Macbain* I, p. 160). Meil-dwnyth was author of one of the Gaelic poems in the Book of the Dean of Lismore. Meldonich Mackilimichael and Meldonich Macmow were slain with the Bute militia in 1646 (*Hewison*, II, p. 333). Mildonich M'Ilmanus in Penniemore, 1673, is Meldonich M'Muns, tenant of Peinmore and Aird in 1674 (HP., I, p. 260, 279). Mildonie M'Ilchrist appears in Killurin, 1684, and Mildonie M'Ilduin in Steligmor, 1686 (*Argyll*). "In Skye this name was given to a boy whose maintenance was provided for by the Sunday's collection" (*Watson* I, p. 238). For some unknown reason the name was Englished LUDOVIC, q.v., by the Grants. Macfarlane gives modern Gaelic also as Maol-Domhnuich (BB.).

MAON. An old Gaelic personal name, from *maon*, dumb. It appears in Ard Mac Maon near Loch Katrine (*Watson* I, p. 238). See also MANTACH.

MARCH. Of local origin. Peter Marche or de Marche, burgess of Edinburgh, 1473 (REG., 398, 400), appears as notary public, 1501 (*Cawdor*, p. 112). Peter Marche held a land in Glasgow, 1485 (REG., p. 448). John March in Sware, parish of Craufurdjohn, 1624 (*Lanark* CR.).

MARCHANT. A variant of MERCHANT, q.v.

MARCHBANK, MARCHBANKS. Forms of MARJORIBANKS, q.v. James Marchbank in Blackburne, parish of Crawford-Douglas, 1664 (*Lanark CR.*).

MARCHER. Thomas Marcher, Scottish merchant, complained of being plundered by wreckers off the coast of Suffolk, 1370 (*Bain*, IV, 164).

MARCUS. This, the Latin form of Mark, is still used as a forename in Scotland. Marcus Flukar was warden of the Friary of Inner-keithing, 1564 (ALHT., XI, p. 314). See MACMARQUIS and MARQUIS.

MARCUSSON, 'son of Marcus (Mark).' Thomas Markesoun was tenant of Scralyne, 1376 (RHM., I, p. lxvii). Andrew Marcyson was admitted burgess of Aberdeen, 1411 (NSCM., I, p. 4). Antonius Marcussone in Coliesetter, Unst, 1629 (*Shetland*).

MARESOUN. Probably 'son of the mair.' Payment was made for Alexander Maresoun in Aberdeen, 1599 (CRA., p. 202). See MAIR.

MARGACH. A Moray surname, perhaps a form of MOGGACH, q.v. William Margoch in Rothes, 1799 (*Moray*), and Alexander Margach, a native of Banffshire, was a graduate of Aberdeen University in the sixties of last century.

MARGERIE. William, son of Margerie, and Gilbert, son of Margerie, were bailiffs of Crail, 1297 (*Bain*, II, p. 231). Bardsley says 'son of Margaret, from the popular pet form Margery or Marjory,' and records John Margerie in co. Suffolk, 1273.

MARGREUE. Duncan Margreue held land in Aberdeen, 1383 (REA., II, p. 283).

MARJORIBANKS, MAJORIBANKS. From the lands of Ratho-Marjorie, Renfrewshire, so named from their having been bestowed on the Princess Marjorie, daughter of Robert the Bruce, on her marriage in 1316 with Walter the High Steward. The lands subsequently called "terre de Ratho-Marjoribankis" came into possession of a family of the name of Johnston, who from them assumed the name of Marjoribanks, though they continued to bear in part the Johnston arms (Anderson, *Scot. Nat.*). Also said to be from barony of same name which formerly comprised the greater part of the eastern division of West Calder parish. Also from their lands in Dumfriesshire. Thomas Marjoribankis, clerk of rolls (RMS., I, App. I, 1). A payment was made to Thomas Meriory Banks in Aberdeen, c. 1548 (SCM., v, p. 51). John Mairjoribanks, attorney in Glasgow, 1550 (*Protocols*, I), and in the same year Mr. John Marjorybankis was retoured heir of John Marjoribanks his father (*Retours, Kirkcudbright*, 4). Thomas Marjorybankis in Glasgow had a precept of sasine in 1554 (*Protocols*, I), James Marjoribanks was notary public in Edinburgh in the same year (ibid.), and Mr. Thomas Marioribankis of Ratho was witness, 1557 (*Ayr*, p. 42). Marioribankis 1552, Mariorybankis 1538, Merioribankis 1547, Meriorybankis 1612.

MARK. From the personal name 'Mark,' unless it be (probably) a hardened form of MARCH, q.v. Job Merk was tenant in the towne of Midlyme, 1567 (*Kelso*, p. 520). Peter Marke in Lessudden, 1684 (RRM., III, p. 42). The Border between Scotland and England was divided into the East March, Middle March, and West March. Mark, a Galwegian by race, bishop of Man and the Hebrides, who died 1303 (ES., II, p. 673) derived from the personal name.

MARKINCH. From Markinch in Fife. Symone de Markinc witnessed a grant by Bernard de Hauden to the House of Soltre between 1193–1230 (*Soltre*, p. 10). William Markynch held a tenement in Edinburgh of the Abbey of Newbattle in 1413 (*Neubotle*, p. 237).

MARKLE. From the lands of Markill or Markle in the parish of Prestonkirk, East Lothian. Alan de Merkshulle was one of the archers serving Peter de Lubaud in Livingstone Peel in 1312 (*Bain*, III, p. 411). William Merkyll witnessed an instrument of sasine in 1496 (*Home*, 28).

MARNIE. A surname current in Angus, most probably a weakened form of MARNOCH>Marnoh>Marno>Marnie. Lindkvist says (p. 72) there was a Norman family named Marinny (so in 1265), which yields modern Marny in place names. Above however is most likely source of the Scottish surname.

MARNOCH, MARNOE, MARNO. Of local origin from Marnoch, Huntly, Aberdeenshire. John Mernath was admitted burgess of Aberdeen in 1447, Robert Marnach in 1467, Alexander Marnagh in 1474, and Gilbert Marnoche in 1498 (NSCM., I, p. 11, 21, 24, 39). William Marnach, fermorer, Aberdeen, 1684 (ROA., I, p. 240), and John Marnoch and William Marnoke appear as kirk elders in 1687 (*Alford*, p. 382, 383). Christian Marno was "delate" for running out of church before "closour of divine worship" (ibid., p. 223). Alexander Marnoch was resident in Findhorn in 1701 (*Moray*). The tombstone of William Marnoh, who died in 1706, is in Nigg churchyard (*Jervise*, II, p. 16). The form Marnoe is current in the parish of Laurencekirk. Marnach 1684.

MARNOCK. Gilbert Marnock, lord of the chapmen in Fife and Kinross, 1678 (*Sc. Ant.*, IX, p. 156). Probably from Marnock in the parish of the same name, Banffshire.

MARQUIS. A shortened form of the West Highland name (MAC)MARQUIS, q.v. Elspet Marquis, brouster in Inverness, 1613 (*Rec. Inv.*, II, p. 103), and Finlay Marquis was a refractory tanner there in 1631 (RPC., 2. ser. IV, p. 295), and Alexander Marcus, packer, is recorded there in 1645 (MCM., I, p. 47). Alexander Marquis for fifty-seven years farmer of Farskane died in 1848.

MARR. (1) In describing the parish of Mar, Aberdeenshire, the author of the *View of the diocese of Aberdeen* (1732) says (p. 81): 'There are to this day some people in this country of the surname of Mar, but of no account.' The name is of local or territorial origin from the district in Aberdeenshire so named. (2) Probably also from Marr in Yorkshire. In the Yorkshire dialect *mar* is used of 'marshy land, sodden or reedy ground.' Nicolas

MARR, *continued*

de Mair, attorney for custumars of Berwick, 1328, and in 1330 Colin de Maire was appointed to the same office there (ER., I, p. 97, 278). In 1235 William de Mar, perhaps the earliest of the name in record, witnessed a grant by Radulf Manus to the Abbey of Kelso (*Kelso*, 392). Gilberd or Gilbert de Mar of Fifeshire, John of Mar, bailiff of Linlithgow, and James de Mar of Aberdeenshire, all rendered homage in 1296 (*Bain*, II, p. 195, 198, 200, 209). Richard Mar was present at inquest made at St. Andrews, 1302-3 (ibid., II, 1350), John de Marr, c. 1316, witnessed a charter of the lands of Linton-Rothirrik (RHM., I, 19), and David de Marre was king's messenger in 1327 (ER., I, p. 60). A canonry of Glasgow was granted to John de Mair, chaplain to Joan, queen of Scotland, 1346 (*Pap. Pet.*, I, p. 116). Roger dictus Mar held land of the Abbey of Arbroath in 1329 (RAA., II, 1), Donald de Marre is mentioned in 1353 as late archdeacon of Brechin (REB., II, 394), Master David of Mar was treasurer of Moray, 1358 (*Bain*, IV, 17), and Alexander de Marr was custumar of Dundee in 1359 (ER., I, p. 614). John de Marre, canon of Aberdeen, 1366 (REA., II, p. 58), Andrew de Marr burgess there, 1403 (*Friars*, 24), Thomas de Mar witnessed instrument of concord between the bishop of Aberdeen and John de Forbes, *dominus ejusdem*, 1391 (REA., I, p. 189), and John Marre, merchant of Aberdeen, had a safe conduct into England in 1439 (*Bain*, IV, 1130). Duncanus de Mar was common councillor of Aberdeen, 1408, John de Marr is recorded as holding the same office, 1439, and Alexander de Marr the same in 1475 (*Guildry*, p. 185, 186, 189). George Marr is recorded as late keeper of the city bells in Edinburgh, 1734 (ibid., p. 149). Jonhne of Mar and Dauid Mar to be 'abbat and priour of bonacord,' in Aberdeen, 1501 (*Mill, Plays*, p. 134).

MARSHALL. This word means literally 'horse-servant,' in which sense it is still used in France (*maréchal*, meaning a 'farrier'). The word is OHG. *maraschalh* borrowed through LL. *mariscalcus* into OF. as *mareschal*, and introduced into Britain at the Norman Conquest. In time the position, like that of Constable and Steward, became one of great dignity; but there is little doubt that most of the Marshalls in Scotland derive their surname from the humbler occupation of horse-servant or groom. A very common surname in Torphichen Commissariot Record. Maledoni Marescal is witness to gift of the lands of Perdeyc (Partick) to the church of Glasgow, 1136 (REG., p. 9). About 1170 Symon Marescall witnessed a charter by Walter de Berk-

eley (RAA., I, 56), and between 1178-80 Gillecolm Marescald witnessed a charter by William the Lion of Kinbethach to Gilbert, earl of Strathern (LIM., p. xxiii). Guidone marescaldus witnessed a charter by Robert, bishop of St. Andrews before 1173 (RPSA., p. 135), and Robert Marescaldus de Molle witnessed Eschina de London's gift of the church of Molle to Kelso, c. 1185-1190 (*Kelso*, 146, 147). Philip Marescallus, a charter witness between 1187-c. 1202 (REM., 5; *Inchaffray*, p. 18), married the heiress of Keith-Humbie, and thus became ancestor of the Keiths, Earls Marischal. Adam, marescallus of the bishop of Glasgow, witnessed sale of lands of Scrogges to the church of Glasgow, c. 1208-13 (REG., p. 76), Walter Marescallus witnessed sale of the lands of Drumsleed by Stephen de Kinnardsley, c. 1218-22 (REB., II, 272), and William Marescalls was temporary provost of Aberdeen, 1281 (REA., II, p. 279). Richard, son of David Marshal of Nudref, and Agnes, daughter of Richard Siwart, knight, had a dispensation in 1290 to intermarry in the fourth degree (*Pap. Lett.*, I, p. 510). Several Marschals are among those who rendered homage in 1296 (*Bain*, II). Mairschaell 1590, Mairschell 1652, Marchael, Marschel, and Marschale 1458, Marchell 1605, Marschal 1411, Marschale 1458, Marechall 1448, Marschale 1430, Marscheall 1511, Marschell 1698, Martiall 1684, Merchel c. 1470, Merchell 1567, Mercial 1511, Merschaell 1478, Merschale 1499, Merschell 1643, Merschiall 1548, Mershael 1590, Mershell 1692, Mersell.

MARSHALSON, 'son of MARSHALL,' q.v. Thomas Marschelsoun, burgess of Edinburgh, 1572 (*Diur. Occ.*, p. 300).

MARTIN. This surname is perhaps from three sources: (1) from the personal name; (2) a shortened form of ST. MARTIN, q.v., the name of a once great family in East Lothian; and (3) possibly a curtailed form of MACMARTIN, q.v. Martin, clerk to the chancellor of William the Lion, appears in Angus, c. 1189-99 (RAA., I, 80), and Martin, medicus Willelmi regis, is mentioned within the same period (ibid., I, 8). Walter Martyn was burgess of Edinburgh, 1386 (*Egidii*, p. 23), and Laurence Martyn, a native of Jedeworth, had letters of denisation in England, 1463 (*Bain*, IV, 1335). Robert Martyne was vicar of Garwok, 1497 (RAA., II, 377), Florentyne Martyn of Gyblestoune was juror on assize at Cupar, 1520 (SCBF., p. 187), and there was an old family of the name in St. Andrews in the fifteenth and sixteenth centuries (*Macfarlane*, II, p. 183-198), of which was George Martine (1635-1712), secretary to Archbishop Sharp. The

Martins of Marshadder are descended from Martin, eldest son of Aonghas na Gaoithe (*Clan Donald*, III, p. 567). Abraham Martin "dit l'Ecossais" (d. 1664), was the first king's pilot on the St. Lawrence river, Canada; the Plains of Abraham, the scene of the battle in 1759, are named from the grant of the land which he received in 1617. Mairtein and Martein 1585, Mairtene 1646, Mairtin 1650, Mairton 1663, Marttine 1660, Mertaune and Mertoune 1607, Merteine 1592, Mertene 1604, Merting 1509, Mertn 1687, Mertyne 1537, Mirtine 1688.

MARTINSON, 'son of MARTIN,' q.v. John Martini was burgess of Edinburgh, c. 1360 (REG., 277), John Martynson was burgess of Glasgow in 1463 (ibid., 389), and William Martini was also burgess there in 1480 (LCD., p. 255). Merteinsoun 1624.

MARTYNHOLME. Local. William Martynholme, witness in Avondale, Lanarkshire, 1503 (*Simon*, 63). There is a Martinside in Avondale (*Atlas*).

MARTYSON, 'son of Marty,' diminutive of MARTIN, q.v. Andrew Martyson in Aberdeen, 1408 (CWA., p. 317).

MARWICK. An Orcadian surname of local origin from Marwick ('sea-mew bay') in the parish of Birsay. Sir James David Marwick (1826–1908) was a distinguished antiquary.

MARYKIRK. "1745. A female child, found by two gentlemen on horseback, taken charge of by the session, given out by them to nurse, and baptized Joanna Carolina Marykirk" (Henderson, *Banchory-Devenick*, p. 250). (2) Alexander Marekirk, witness in Birsay, Orkney, 1534 (REO., p. 217), derived his surname from Marykirk in Sanday.

MASAR. From the office of 'macer,' an officer who kept order in law courts, etc., Scots *masar*. James Masar and Lourens Masar contravened Aberdeen town ordinances, 1565 (*Analecta Scotica*, II, p. 315).

MASCULUS. A Latinization "without consideration" of the sound of Maule "caught the ear of the scribe, and he Latinized it without consideration" (Raine, *North Durham*, App., p. 78). William Masculus witnessed a charter granted at Trauequayr (Traquair) c. 1147 to the church of S. John in the Castle of Rokesburg (REG., p. 10). He also acquired the lands of Foulis in Perthshire, and between 1162 and 1186 he granted to his nephew Thomas the cleric the church and church lands of Foulis by a charter which is witnessed by another nephew, Richard, and also by Michael Masculus (RPSA., p. 40, 41). This William is supposed to be the ancestor of the Maules (*Lawrie*, p. 372). Roger Masculus witnessed grant of Gillemoristun to Edulf filius Vtredi before 1189 (REG., p. 39). William Masculus granted a quit-claim to the fishery of Redehouh, 1220 (*Kelso*, 55, 62, 63). Ricardus Masculus witnessed charter of a toft in the ville of Inchesyrith in the reign of Alexander III (*Scon*, p. 83). See also under MAULE.

MASON. There is no evidence in Scotland that this surname had any other origin than from the occupation, OF. *masson*, Fr. *maçon*, a mason. In the Middle Ages we find it Latinized *cementarius*. About 1180 or later Magister Roger cementarius de Forfar witnessed a charter by Ingelram de Balliol (RAA., I, p. 39). He was probably the chief builder or superintendent of the royal palace at Forfar. Gregory, cementarius, who witnessed a charter by Andrew, bishop of Moray, in 1237 (REM., 121) was, says Cosmo Innes, in all probability one of the persons employed in the building of the cathedral church of Elgin (ibid., pref., p. xiii). Richard the Mason was burgess of Aberdeen in 1271 (*Fraser*, p. 9). John le Massun (or le Macune) of Gascony had a claim against the bishop of St. Andrews in 1288 (*Bain*, II, 359). William dictus Masceon who had a charter of land in the burgh of Berwick in 1307 (*Kelso*, 43) is probably William Maceoun de Berwick who received a payment from Exchequer in 1327 (ER.; I, p. 80). William Maceoun had a charter of land in the tenement of Mertone (Morton) near Edinburgh in 1315 (RMS., I, 15), William dictus Maceon was burgess of Peebles in 1317 (*Peebles*, 6), and William Macone was witness in Roxburgh, c. 1338 (*Dryburgh*, 313). Nicholas cementarius, custumar of Stirling, 1360, appears in the following year as Nicholas Masoun (ER., II, p. 14, 60). He is probably the individual who did the sculpture work of the tomb of Robert II, 1377 (ER., II, p. 585). Thomas Mason or Masson, a kinsman of Robert, earl of Fife, claimed the office of prior of Lochleven in 1388 (*Pap. Pet.*, I, p. 575, 576). The surname appears in Edinburgh in 1392 as Masoun (*Egidii*, p. 27), Adam Massovn was burgess of Glasgow in 1413 (REG., 323), Sir John Mason was vicar of Crawfurde Lyndyssay in 1435 (LSC., 114), Peter Masoune was canon of Dunkeld in 1436 (REB., I, 85), David Mavssone was a presbyter of Glasgow in 1463 (REG., 389), Mychell or Michaele Mason was witness in Ayr, 1471 (*Friars Ayr*, p. 54; *Ayr*, p. 91), and William Mason, 'breuer,' a native of Scotland, received letters of denization in England in 1480 (*Bain*, IV, 1462). There was a family named Mason (Meason, Maison, Massoun) prominent in Orkney in the sixteenth

MASON, *continued*

century (REO.). Maissone 1593, Masone 1592, Masoune 1559, Measone 1647, Measoun 1646, Measoune 1608, Meassone 1662, Meassoune 1628, Maissoun 1604.

MASSIE. Perhaps from Fr. *Massé*, a pet name for Matthew, *Mathé*. The Rev. A. B. Scott (*Rise and relations of the Church of Scotland*, p. 300) erroneously says that in Northern Britain 'Vass' and 'Massie' are formed from Brit. *gwas*, a servant. William Massie, Brig of Don, received payment in 1607 for 'drink silver' (SCM., v, p. 80), and George Massie is recorded in Stevinsburne, 1633 (ibid., III, p. 72).

MASSON. This name is derived by some from Maçon and Machon, but in Scotland it is simply a form of MASON, q.v. In the north it may be from MA(N)SON, q.v. Francis Masson, pioneer of botanical science in South Africa, was born in Aberdeen, 1741, died 1805.

MASTER. In Scotland the eldest sons of barons are designed 'Masters,' and the uncles of lords were also called Masters, "which occasioned afterwards the word master to be given to persons whose names were not known" (*Nisbet*, II, pt. IV, p. 191). It was also the title of the individual who had charge of an hospital, as, e.g. Radulphus, magister Hospitalis de Soltre, who swore fealty in 1291. Robert Maister was treasurer of the burgh of Canongate, Edinburgh, in 1568 (MCM., II, p. 312). See also under MASTERTON.

MASTERSON, 'son of the master,' probably a cleric. Robert called Maistersone was a Galloway hostage in 1300 (*Bain*, II, p. 301). Cf. MACMASTER.

MASTERTON. King Malcolm IV (1153–1165) granted the lands of Ledmacdunegil (Ledmacduuegil, or Lethmachduuegil) afterwards called Masterton as formerly held by Magister (= Master) Ailricus, cementarius, to the Abbey church of Dunfermline (RD., p. 21, 30, 42). This Ailricus may be the magister or 'master' after whom the lands took their later name. The first appearance of the surname is in 1296 when William de Mastertone or de Meystertone of the county of Fife rendered homage for his possessions. His seal bears a lion rampant, a rose in front, and S' *Will'i de Maisterton* (*Bain*, II, p. 188, 201). Duncan de Maysterton witnessed the homage of Duncan, earl of Fife to the abbot of Dunfermline in 1316 (RD., p. 235, 236), Svmon de Maysterton, rector, was a witness in 1357 (*Neuboile*, p. 309), and Sir Thomas Masterton was a canon regular of Cambuskenneth in 1476 (SBR., p. 261). The

Mastertons were a family of note in the Dunfermline district before the Reformation, and their genealogy, by Victor A. Noël Paton, is published in the *Miscellany* of the Scottish History Society (I, p. 457–466). Maistertoun 1617, Maistertoune 1642, Maistertown 1550, Maystirton 1434.

MATADIN. A diminutive of MADDAD, q.v. Matadin is one of the witnesses to the grant of Pet-mec-Cobrig to the Abbey of Deer by Gartnait and Ete, his wife, in the eighth year of the reign of King David (*Bk. Deer*). Madechin or Madethin mac Mathusalem witnessed charters by Duncan, fifth earl of Fife, between 1154–1204 (RPSA., p. 242–244). See MACMADETHYN.

MATCHES. "A name common in and peculiar to Orkney" (*Old Lore Misc.*, I, p. 259). "Matches is once or twice found as a Christian name, evidently the same as Mattis or Mattias, the old Norwegian form of Matthew" (REO., p. 252n). James Maches was juror on assize at Stenness, 1576 (ibid., p.139). In Shetland we find Matchesdochter (1615) and Matcheson, 1630 and 1633 (*Shetland*).

MATESON. William Matesone, tenant of the bishop of Aberdeen, 1511 (REA., I, p. 365), and Robert Matisone, 'travellour' in Stirling, 1652 (SBR., p. 298), probably derived their name from Matty or Mattie, diminutive of Matthew + son.

MATHER. (1) a form of MAIDER, q.v. Andrew Mather took 'assurance' of Protector Somerset at Kelso, 1548 (Patten, *Expidicion into Scotlande*, 1548, in *Haigs of Bemersyde*, p. 465). (2) The name is very common in Laurencekirk and neighborhood, and may there be from the place name. Mathers with final -*s* dropped. Cf. MATTERS.

MATHESON, MATHIESON, MATHISON, 'son of MATTHEW,' q.v. Robertus filius Mathei witnessed a charter by Walter filius Alani, a. 1177 (RMP., p. 49). John Mathyson and Michael Mathowson were outlawed as part guilty of the slaughter of Walter de Ogilvy, sheriff of Angus, in 1392 (APS., I, p. 579), and Andrew Mathysoun was a forestaller in Aberdeen in 1402 (CRA., p. 384). William Mathison, witness in Aberdeen, 1446 (REA., I, p. 245). James Methosoun was sub-prior of Tungland, 1566 (*Laing*, 801). *The Green family and its branches from A. D. 861 to A. D. 1904*, New York, 1905, traces (p. 266) the Mathesons to the Maeataea, an ancient tribe inhabiting the country between the Firths of Forth and Tay in the second century! Mathesone 1633, Mathoson 1474, Mathouson 1444.

MATHESON, MATHOWSON. II. (1) The Mathesons of the North are known in Gaelic as M'Mhathain, collectively as Mathanach. In the genealogical MS. of 1467 the name is spelled Mac Matgamna, the full form of which is Mac Mhathghamhuin, 'son of the bear.' (The Scottish bear is mentioned by Martial, Epig., VII, 3, 4). The earliest record of the name is in 1264, in which year Kermac Macmaghan in Inverness received twenty cows of the fine of the earl of Ross for services rendered (ER., I, p. 19). In the Norse Saga he is called Kjarmak son of Makamal = Cormac Macmathan. The Siol Mhathain, a sept of Matheson, in an old Gaelic song appears as Siol Mhothan, and in Sir Robert Gordon's History of the earldom of Sutherland as Seil-Wohan or Seil-Wogan. Matheson has been adopted as the English form of the name simply on account of the similarity of sound. (2) Matheson, Matthewson, Mathieson, meaning 'son of MATTHEW,' q.v., is rendered in Gaelic by M'Mhatha, now MACMATH or Macma, once more or less common in Perthshire, Kintyre, Ayrshire, Galloway, and Dumfriesshire. Some Macmaths have Englished their name Matheson. George Mathesone was tenant in town of Midlyme, 1567 (Kelso, p. 521). The names of John Mathonson, burgess of Aberdeen, 1444 (NSCM., I, p. 8), and David Mathonson, common councillor there, 1475 (Guildry, p. 189), are probably for Mathouson with u misread as n. Sir John Matthyson was rector of Blair, 1546 (Rollok, 14).

MATHEWSON, 'son of MATTHEW,' q.v.

MATHIE. This surname is most probably derived from the name of the old parish of Meathie or Mathie, united to that of Inverarity in 1612 and suppressed in June, 1667 (Scott, Fasti, III, p. 774). (2) It may also be a diminutive of Matthew, but I think the local derivation more probable in Scotland. John Mathei or Mathy was juror on an assize at Liston in 1459 (Edmonstone, 80), William Mathe, witness in Brechin, 1497 (REB., I, 216), and Andro Mathy was tenant of the Grange of Abirbothry in 1506 (Cupar-Angus, I, p. 257). Andrew Mathe deponed to the right boundaries of the Monks Myre in 1546 (ibid., II, p. 4), and a barn and pertinents in Glasgow were sold to David Mathy in 1550 (Protocols, I). Thomas Mathy, witness in Monkland, 1518 (Simon, 47). George Mathie, burgess of Brechin, 1652 (Inquis. Tut., 783). John Mathie, skipper in the Panns, 1689 (RPC., 3. ser. XIV, p. 405), and George Mathie, merchant in Edinburgh, 1724 (Guildry, p. 128). Meathie.

MATTERS. Local, from Mathers near Montrose. Andrew Materis witnessed instrument of resignation in Brechin, 1446 (REB., I, 109). Robert Matters was trade burgess of Aberdeen, 1662 (ROA., I, p. 234). Cf. MATHER.

MATTHEW. From the Hebrew personal name Mattithyah, 'gift of Yahweh,' through Gr. Mattathias, Latin Matthaeus. Matheus, son of Dufsyth the Celtic lord of Conan or Cairnconan (RAA., I, p. 40), Matheus, chancellor to Alexander II, 1229, and Matheus, burgess of Aberbrothock, 1242 (ibid., p. 79, 82, 86). John Mathow in Balhoussy, 1614 (Trials, III, p. 265). Robert Mathow, burgess freeman of Glasgow, 1661 (Burgesses), and Patrick Mathew, late town officer in Edinburgh, 1721 (Guildry, p. 124).

MATTHEWS, 'son of MATTHEW,' q.v.

MATTHEWSON, 'son of MATTHEW,' q.v.

MATUSSAL. Matussale decanus Brechinensis, 1178–98 (RAA., I, 193). Sir Robert Matussal, sub-prior of Dundrennan, became abbot there in 1223 (Chron. Mail., s.a.).

MAUCHAN. From Machan, an old parish in Lanarkshire, now called Dalserf. In ancient Hamilton charters the barony is called Machanshire, and there is still a small estate called Machan within the parish. David de Machan appears as a charter witness in the reign of Alexander II (REG., p. 145), and Thomas, son of John de Machan, was juror on an inquisition held by the sheriff of Lanark, 1263 (Bain, I, 2677). William de Maghan and Patrick de Maghan of Lanarkshire rendered homage, 1296 (ibid., II, p. 213). Sir Adam de Mauchan was archdeacon of St. Andrews, 1300 (RPSA., p. 120), and David, son of Walter de Machane, and John his brother are witnesses at Cadiou (Cadyow), 1367–68 (REG., p. 281, 282). John Mauchan, bailie of Edinburgh, sat in the Scots parliament, 1548, John Mawchtane held a land in Glasgow, 1550 (Protocols, I), Mr. Alexander Mauchane was advocate and sheriff-depute of the county of Edinburgh in the sixteenth century, and Jonet Mawhane was resident in the parish of Colwend, 1684 (RPC., 3. ser. IX, p. 582). The surname appears as M'Han in Timothy Pont's MS. Machanne 1556, Machen 1597, Mauchquhan c. 1523, Mawchane 1550; Mauchain, Mauthane.

MAUCHLINE, MAUCHLEN. From Mauchline in the parish of the same name in Ayrshire. William Maghlyn, Scotsman, and Richard Maughlyn or Maugelyn, esquire of Scotland, had letters of safe conduct into England between 1407–09 (Bain, IV, 749, 766, 785). Sir Patrick Mawchtlyne who witnessed Crail documents of 1512 (Crail) may be Schir Patrick Machlyne who was witness in Edinburgh, 1530

MAUCHLINE, Mauchlen, continued

(Soltre, p. 99). Hugh Machline in Crosshall, 1711 (Minutes, p. 115). John Mauchline of the 78th Highlanders was a composer of light-music tunes.

MAUDUIT. The lands in England of Gilbert Mauduyt, a "Scotsman and traitor" (to England) were forfeited and he himself hanged for rebelling with Robert de Brus, 1306 (Bain, II, 1838, 1856). Weekley (p. 288) says the name is from Lat. male doctus, 'ill taught,' by which it is commonly rendered in mediaeval documents, and Baring-Gould says 'from Mauduit near Nantes' (p. 230). Bardsley (under Mawditt) believes in a local origin for the name.

MAULDSLIE. From the lands or barony of the same name in the parish of Carluke, Lanarkshire. There is a Mauldslie or Maudslie, a moorland farm adjoining Kingside and East Loch.

MAULDSON, 'son of Maud,' diminutive of Matilda. Ricardus filius Maud, who appears in Perth in the reign of Alexander II, is most probably the Ricardus filius Matildis, recorded in the following reign (Scon, p. 61, 83). Matilda, wife of Johannes Furbur of Perth, is mentioned about the same time as Ricardus filius Maud (ibid., p. 61), and another Matilda, daughter of Henricus Wyth of Perth is mentioned in reign of David II (ibid., p. 124). John Mauldsone, tenant in Telny in barony of Abirdoure, Fife, 1376 (RHM., I, p. lxiv). John Maldsone, 1514 (Home, 37). Robert Maldsone, servitor to earl of Eglintoun, 1665 (Irvine, II, p. 194). Maldsoune 1605.

MAULE. The de Maules were descended from the de Maules who possessed the seigneurie of that name in the department of Seine-et-Oise. The first of the name in Scotland appears to have been Robert, who probably came in the train of David I. He appears as witness in a charter by Henry, earl of Northumberland, David's younger son, granting lands in Northumberland to Eustace Fitzjohn (Panmure, II, 67). He seems to have had grants of land in the Lothians, and may have given name to Mauldslie in Temple parish. William, son of Robert, took part in the battle of the Standard, 1138, and obtained the lands of Easter Fowlis in Perthshire (Jervise LL., p. 143). He witnessed c. 1141 confirmation of a charter by Earl Henry to the church of S. Mary of Haddington of the lands of Clerchetune, now Clerkington (RPSA., p. 191). He also had grants of tofts in Selkirk and Clackmannan from Malcolm IV (ibid., p. 80). By the marriage of Peter de Maule with Christina de Valoniis before 1215 he acquired the large baronies of Panmure and Bervie. Sir William de Maul swore fealty to Edward I at St. Andrews, 1291 (Bain, II, 508). Sir Michael de Mauwel, a monk of Aberbrothok, 1361 (Panmure, II, 177) may be Maule or Manuel. Thomas Mauld was maister of the Grammar Schole in Elgin, 1600 (Mill, Plays, p. 236). James Maule, factor to the earl of Moray, 1756 (Dunkeld). Mauld and Maulde 1641, Mauil and Mauill 1526, Male 1649, Maull 1348, Mauul 1286, Mawll 1574, Mawyll 1527. An individual of this name entered the Swedish service in 1654 and was known as Mel. See also under Masculus.

MAULVERER. Of territorial origin from Maulévrier in the arrondissement of Yvetot, Normandy. Hugh Maleverer witnessed resignation of land in Weremundebi and Anant, c. 1194–1214 (Bain, I, 606), and c. 1194–1211 he witnessed a confirmation charter of a fishery in Torduf (Holm Cultram, p. 35). Robert Maleverer had a grant of a ploughgate in the parish of Molle from the monks of Paisley, c. 1225–35, to which Simon Maleverer was a witness (RMP., p. 76–77). Hugh de Maulverer was witness to a grant by Robert de Dundovenald to Sir Robert de Brus of two carucates of land in the fee of Egilfechan, c. 1249 (Bain, I, 1793; Annandale, I, p. 7). Sir Humphrey de Mauleverer witnessed a quit claim of lands in Annan, a. 1245 (Annandale, I, p. 6). Huwe Mauleverer of Dumfriesshire and Rauf Mauleverer of Lanarkshire rendered homage in 1296 (Bain, II, p. 185, 198), and in 1329 an annuity was paid to John Mauleverer (ER., I, p. 208).

MAUNDELL. A form of Mundell, q.v., current in Fife.

MAVER, Mavor, Mawer. From G. maor, a subordinate officer in various capacities, a steward. The Scots pronunciation is Mawr. Mavor is a Speyside surname. Wille Mawar and Johnne Mawar were declared innocent of any part in the detention of King James III in Edinburgh Castle, 1482 (Lennox, II, p. 123). Walter Mawer witnessed a bond of caution in 1564 (ER., XIX, p. 530). John Mawar in Urquhart was warned to appear before the Lord Regent, 1574, and David Mawer of the Loch (Lochs near Urquhart) was slain by some Inneses, 1576. Thomas Maueris is witness in Aberdeen, 1577 (SCM., II, p. 45), and Mark Mawar was member of Scots parliament for Elgin, 1593 (Hanna, II, p. 505). Michael Mawar was portioner of Urquhart, 1587, and John Mawer was a portioner there, 1595 (SCM., II, p. 129). Alexander Mawer was tenant under the marquis of Huntly, 1600 (ibid., IV, p. 287), and another Alexander Mawer was mair-depute in Aberdeen, 1688 (RPC., 3. ser. XIII, p. 263). Mark Mawer of Mawerstoun (the town or tûn of the *maor*) is in record, 1608 (*Cawdor*, p. 222), and Magister Walter Mawer was heir of Walter Mawer of Mawerstoun in lands in Fife, 1608 (*Sc. Ant.*, VI, p. 40; *Retours, Fife*, 193). Mark Mavers was prisoner in the tolbooth of Elgin, 1686 (RPC., 3. ser. XII, p. 258), and John Maver of Overmest was indweller in Garmouth, parish of Urquhart, 1697 (*Moray*). William Maver in Banff (b. 1775) edited an edition of Dr. Johnson's *Dictionary* in 1809 with several thousand additions. In Anglicized spelling of Gaelic names *w* was often used for *v*. English MAWER, from *mawer*, 'a mower,' is of different origin.

MAW. A local surname of English origin. John Maw, smith in Horndine, 1672 (*Lauder*). Gave name to Mawisaiker and Mawisbalk in *Berwick Retours*. 'Schir Maw of the Rede Mayn in Wyntoun's *Original Chronicle* (v. 6, p. 330) is Sir Mathew de Redman, an English knight well known on the marches in the reign of Robert II.

MAWHINNEY. See under MACWHINNEY.

MAWSON. Usually explained as 'son of Matilda,' through the popular form Maud. It is an old Yorkshire name. Baring-Gould gives it as a derivative of Maurice. Robert Mawson was witness in Perth, 1550 (*Rollok*, 67).

MAXPOFFLE. From the lands of Maxpoffle in the parish of St. Boswells, Roxburghshire. Adam de Maxpoffel of the county of Roxburgh rendered homage for his lands in 1296 and had them restored to him. His seal bears a fox carrying off a goose, a man shooting an arrow, star above, S' *Ade de Machispoffil* (*Bain*, II, 832, p. 199, 545). He appears to have afterwards resigned his lands to King Robert Bruce. Mackyspoffil 1320.

MAXTON, MAXTONE. Of territorial origin from the barony of the same name in Roxburghshire. Maxton, the "tun" of Maccus, may have obtained its name from Maccus, the son of Undewyn, who in the reign of David I obtained lands in the neighborhood. The barony passed out of the possession of the family by the end of the twelfth century, being acquired by Robert de Berkeley and later by the de Normanvilles. About the year 1250 Adam de Makuston witnessed a charter by John de Normanvile (*Melros*, p. 223), and about the same period John, son of Philip de Mackuston, quitclaimed to the monks of Melrose the right of pasture in his territory (ibid., p. 226, 227). Adam de Maxton was elected abbot of Melrose

in 1261 (*Morton*, p. 225). Alexander de Maxston, constable of Rokisburg in 1285 (*Kelso*, 219) is probably the same who rendered homage in 1296 (*Bain*, II, p. 209). The Hungarian family of Maxon is descended from an individual of this name who emigrated to that country several generations ago. A family of Maxtons have been settled for six centuries at Cultoquey in Perthshire, and the celebrated Maxton "litany" was the composition of one of its members about the year 1725. The satire was aimed at certain powerful neighbors of his and embodied the popular characteristics of certain Scottish families:

"From the greed of the Campbells,
From the ire of the Drummonds,
From the pride of the Grahams,
From the wind of the Murrays,
Good Lord, deliver us."

MAXWELL. This surname, from the form (Maccusville) in which it appears in records of the twelfth and thirteenth centuries, is commonly thought to be of Norman origin. The name, however, is Old English, and derived from a salmon pool on the Tweed, near Kelso Bridge, still locally known as "Maxwheel." Maccus, son of Undewyn, a Saxon lord, in the reign of David I, obtained a grant of land (now called Springwood) on the Tweed before 1150 (*Morton*, p. 16), and from the fishery attached thereto, called Maccus's Wiel (OE. *wael*, a pool, whirlpool), the lands obtained their name. (Camden, *Britannia*, ed. 1695, p. 909, says the inhabitants of Galloway follow fishing, and that about September they caught "an incredible number of eels in their Weeles," *excipulus*). The place name Maxton in Roxburghshire may be named from the same Maccus. Maccus filius Undwain witnessed David's great charter to Melrose, a. 1153 (*Nat. MSS.*, I, 17). Herbert granted a charter of Macchuswel to the Abbey of Kelso before 1159 (*Kelso*, 2), and witnessed several charters by William the Lion. John de Maccuswell filius Herbert, vicecomes, witnessed a charter by Bernard de Haudene to Kelso, c. 1210 (*Kelso*, 213), charters by William the Lion (RAA., I, 71, 83bis), and a Moray charter of 1225 (REM., p. 461). In 1226 Johannes de Makeswell witnessed a charter by Alexander II concerning the levying of tolls at the cross of Schedenestun, now Shettleston (REG., p. 114). Eymer de Mackisuuell was sheriff of Peebles, 1262 (*Peebles*, p. 4), and is recorded as camerarius to Alexander III in 1260 (REA., I, p. 27). The Maxwells first appear as landowners in Wigtownshire about 1481 (*Agnew*, I, p. 284). Perhaps the best known of the name was the late Sir Herbert Eustace Maxwell. Lawrence Maxwell (1853–1927), solici-

MAXWELL, *continued*

tor-general of the United States, 1893–1895, was born in Glasgow. Mackeswal 1223, Makiswel 1409, Makiswell 1414, Makkiswell 1265, Maligussol (in a papal doc.) 1431, Maxuel 1424 and 1701, Maxvall 1583, Maxvile 1407, Maxwaile and Maxwale 1452, Maxweell 1661.

MAY. Might be from OE. *mæg*, male kinsman (*Redin*), and warrior (*Harrison*). Lower says Le May is common in the English Hundred Rolls. William May rendered homage at Berwick, 1291 (RR.). David May had a feu of the lands of Chapeltoun of Both from the Abbey of Culross, 1587 (PSAS., LX, p. 81). Alexander May appears in Bourhillis, Aberdeenshire, 1597 (SCM., I) and John Maii in Harvestoun in Tillycultrie, 1638 (*Inquis.*, 2347), and Robert Maii in Dunglas, 1640 (ibid., 2529). (2) Associated with Clan Macdonald it is a form of OMAY, q.v.

MAYBIN. A variant of MABEN, q.v.

MAYNARD. A personal name from OHG. *Maginhard* through Fr. *Maynard*. When Bishop Robert was about to set the municipal machinery of St. Andrews in motion (c. 1144) he obtained from the king the services of Mainard, a burgess of Berwick: "Be it known that with the licence of David our king, I have constituted St. Andrews a burgh and that with the king's consent I have made Mainard the Fleming (Mainardum Flandrensem) provost of this burgh" (APS., I, p. 75). Robert Mainard was one of the witnesses to a charter by John de Dundemor to the Priory of May in 1260 (RPSA., p. 385; *May*, 29).

MAYNE. (1) Perhaps from the old personal name Mayne, or (2) from Maine, the French province so named. Our references are not early enough to guide us. Jasper Mayne was clerk of the diocese of St. Andrews in 1505 (*Hunter*, p. 7), and Jhones Mayne rented the land of Gartinwyne in 1520 (*Rental*). John Mayne was burgess of Glasgow in 1549 (*Protocols*, I), Nicolas Mayne was admitted burgess of Aberdeen in 1603 (NSCM., I, p. 98). John Mayne in Touchhill and Robert Mayne in Airth are in record in 1622. John Mayne was burgess of Edinburgh in 1648 (*Inquis.*, 3394), and Thomas Mayne was merchant burgess of Kirkwall, 1655 (*Retours, Orkney*, 72). John Mayne (1759–1846), minor poet and journalist, was author of *The Siller Gun*. Mane 1567.

MEAL. (1) Alexander Meill in Brechin killed by a stroke of a golf-club, 1508 (*Trials*, I, p. 108 *). John Meall, milner at the miln of Pitcoirmick, 1720 (*Dunkeld*). (2) This is also a rare Orcadian surname derived from one of several places of the name in Orkney or Shetland (ON. *melr*, a sandbank). In Peterkin's *Rentals* it is said that the place called Male [now Græmeshall] in 1595 "pertained to William Male," now escheat for theft. Barnard Meall in Aith, witness, 1627 (OSS., I, 186), and William Meall in Fetlar is in record in 1716. It is not certain that the Shetland bearers of the name are of Shetland origin as the name there is confined to Dunrossness, and it appears that a number of Orkney families settled in that district about the beginning of the seventeenth century. In recent times the name has been dropped for (presumably more aristocratic) Melville.

MEALMAKER, MILLMAKER. From the occupation. Mealmaker according to the *English dialect dictionary* is an obsolete name for a 'miller.' William Melmaker held part of the vill of Portyncrag in 1453, and John Melmaker was perpetual vicar of the parish church of Aythin in 1489 (RAA., II, p. 82, 261). George Mealmaker, a Dundee weaver, received a sentence of fourteen years transportation on a charge of sedition.

MEALMAN. From the occupation of mealmonger, one who deals in meal. In Germany the Mahlmann was the miller's assistant (Gehilfe des Müllers).

MEANIE, MENNIE. A surname in Banchory-Devenick and elsewhere in Aberdeenshire. From the lands of Mennie, near Belhelvie, Aberdeenshire. The place name is found in 1696 as Menie. William Meanie was sergeant in the city guard of Edinburgh at the execution of Andrew Wilson the Pittenweem smuggler, 1736. Robert Meanie, chapman in Aberdeen, 1726, and Robert Mennie, burgess in Old Aberdeen, 1797 (*Aberdeen CR.*). William Minie was a member of the Gartly Company of Volunteers in 1798, and Alexander Mennie was a member of the Huntly Company in 1805 (*Will*, p. 24, 30).

MEANIES. A surname current in Aberdeen may be a form of MENZIES, q.v.

MEARNS. This surname probably originated from the two places so named: (1) from Mearns in Renfrewshire (An Mhaoirne, "the Stewartry"). Rodlannus or Rothland de Mernes appears as a witness in Paisley, c. 1177 (RMP., p. 49, 74). He is probably the Roland de Mernis who is in record as a witness before 1204 (ibid., p. 15). Margaret Mearns appears in Eyemouth in 1653 (*Lauder*). (2) from the district of The Mearns, the old name of Kincardineshire. Alexander de Mernys appears in Aberdeen in 1401 (SCM., v, p. 17), and John de Mernys was admitted burgess there in 1408 (NSCM., I, p. 3). Robert de Mernys was chaplain of the parish of Brechin in 1435 (REB., II, 48), in 1466 there is recorded a charter by Alexander de Meirnis, son and heir of William de Meirnis (REA., I, p. 297), and Will of Mernys was a baxter in Aberdeen in 1469 (CRA., p. 405). In 1476 there is mention of the land of Robert Mernis (without 'de') in Inuerowry (REA., I, p. 311), John de Mernys was admitted burgess of Aberdeen in 1464, Alexander Meirnys in 1472, and William Mernis in 1473 (NSCM., I, p. 18, 23, 24). Patrick Myrnis, witness at Kyncragy, 1540 (Aboyne, p. 70), Alexander Mernys, reidare at Weik (Wick), 1574 (RMR.), and John Mernis, burgess of Kyntor, 1597 (SCM., I, p. 116). James Mairnes of Sheriffhall, 1670 (Edin. App.).

MEARSE. Recorded in Aberdeen, and most probably of English origin from residence by a marsh. There are places in England named Mearse (perhaps from ME. *mersche* <OE. *mersc*, a marsh).

MEARSON. Perhaps a variant of MERSON, q.v.

MEASON. Perhaps a variant of MASON, q.v.

MECHIE. A rare current variant of MICHIE, q.v.

MECPHIN. From the old lands of Mecphin near Methven, Perthshire. Robert de Meggefen granted two tofts and four acres in Dolpatrick (otherwise Kenandheni) between 1226 and 1234 (*Inchaffray*, p. 48–49). Roger Mekfen witnessed the charter of Abercairny by Earl Malise of Strathern to John of Moravia (LIM., App., XLII). Roger de Mekfin, *miles*, witnessed the charter by Robert the Steward to Thomas Simple of the land of Cragrossy with pertinents in Stratherne, c. 1360 (REG., p. 275), and as Roger de Mekfen, *dominus de eadem*, he granted the lands of Cambo, c. 1370, to the Abbey of Inchaffray (*Inchaffray*, p. 130). Robert de Mekven, *dominus eiusdem*, granted his brewland with pasture for cows, sheep, and horses, to the same abbey in 1443–44 (ibid., p. 138). This Robert appears to have been the last of his family as in 1450 the lands of the Mekvens had passed to the Toschachs of Monzievaird, who possessed them for two centuries after that date (ibid., p. lxxxv).

MEEK. A family of this name held lands from the abbots of Cupar from the middle of the fifteenth century. William Mek had a tack of part of Cowbyr in 1457, Will Meyk was tenant of Coupergrange in 1468, and William Meyk was tenant of Balmyl in 1485 (*Cupar-Angus*, I, p. 132, 142, 237). Robert Meik was made burgess of Perth, 1545 (Mill, *Plays*, p. 265), John Meyk was a Blackfriar of Perth in 1549, and Susanna Meik is recorded in Dunfermline in 1584 (*Dunfermline*). John Meik in Blairmuckhill appears in 1676 (*Retours, Linlithgow*, 242), Margrat Meike was resident in the parish of Borgue in 1684 (RPC., 3. ser. IX, p. 567), and John Meik in Grange of Aberbothrie, 1695, and five more are recorded in the Commissariot Record of Dunkeld. Meik of Ledcassie (now Carsie) in Perthshire is reckoned an old family.

MEFF. A rare surname found in Aberdeen may be of local origin from Meft in Moray. There was a lord-provost of this name in Aberdeen some years ago.

MEFFAN. A variant of METHVEN, q.v.

MEFFATT. A variant of MOFFAT, q.v.

MEFFEN. A variant of METHVEN, q.v.

MEFFET. See under MOFFAT.

MEGALL. See under MAGALL.

MEGGAT, MEGGET. From the lands of Megget in the parish of Yarrow, Selkirkshire. Randulf de Meggate, who was one of the witnesses to the perambulation of the marches of Stobo, c. 1190 (REG., 104), is the earliest of the name in record. George Meggot, who was "dompnus" of Neubotle in 1528 may be the George Megot who appears as a tenant of the same abbey in 1563 (*Neubotle*, p. 284, 325). The name is also found in Edinburgh in 1633 and 1659 as Miggot and Megget (*Edinb. Marr.*). Alexander Megit in Tineroin (Tynron), 1662 (*Dumfries*). At Cramalt, on the Crammel, near the middle of the glen, are the remains of an old tower, which, according to the tradition of the country, was the seat of Megget of Megget (Pennecuik, *Description of Tweeddale*, p. 248).

MEGGINCH. From the old barony of Melginch, now Megginch, in the parish of Errol, Perthshire. Philippus de Melkinh witnessed the confirmation of Tristram's gift of a croft to the monastery of Inchaffray, c. 1208 (*Inchaffray*, p. 25). The church of Melginch (St. Martin's) was granted to Holyrood Abbey by David Huviet (misprinted Huniet), Alexander and Philip his sons being witnesses (LSC., p. 52, 53). The last named may be the foregoing Philip, and the same with Philip Vvieth who witnessed a grant by Swan, son of Thor, to the monastery of Scone, c. 1211–14 (*Scon,*

MEGGINCH, *continued*

p. 18). The surname was borne later by Duncan de Melginch, who quitclaimed half of the land of Drumkroc in the parish of Melginch to Inchaffray in 1237 (*Inchaffray*, p. 54), and by Stephen de Melginch (*Scon*, 116). Stephen of Melginche also witnessed a charter by Malcolm, seventh earl of Fife, c. 1228 (*Laing*, 6). If Balursin, a place name in the Scone charter "is Balhousie (in 1422 Balulsi) we may infer that the family later on dropped their local surname and, resuming their original patronymic, became the Eviots of Balhousie who subsisted down to the close of the sixteenth century" (*Inchaffray*, p. 273).

MEIGLE. Of territorial origin from the old barony of Meigle in Perthshire. In the time of William the Lion, Simon de Meigle gifted the advowson of the kirk and adjoining chapel to the prior and canons of St. Andrews (Lyon, *St. Andrews*, II, p. 305). Michael de Mygill witnessed the gift by Eufemie, lady of Duffus, to the bishop of Moray in 1263 (REM., p. 278), and as de Migell he bestowed the marsh of Migell on the Abbey of Cupar (*Cupar-Angus*, I, p. 343–344). Roger de Miggel of Perthshire rendered homage in 1296, and Michael de Miggyl who also rendered homage appears in 1299 as a prisoner of war from Dunbar Castle (*Bain*, II, p. 177, 200, 278). In 1305 the king of England directed that an inquiry be made into the dealings of Sir Michael de Miggel with Sir William Wallace, when evidence was produced to show the latter's harsh treatment of him when trying to escape (ibid., II, p. 456). John de Migghil, son of William de Migghil, had a confirmation charter of the barony of Mygghil and pertinents in the sheriff-dom of Perth in 1378 (RMS., I, 690, 778), and in 1381 he resigned the third part of Kintulach (*Cambus.*, 179). William de Megill resigned the barony to David, first earl of Crawford during the reign of Robert III (RMS., I, App. II, 1829). Robert Miggle was under miller at the miln of Birney in 1757 (*Moray*). Mygille 1382.

MEIKLAM, MEIKLEHAM, MEIKLEIM, MEIKLEM. Scotticized forms of MACILWHAM, q.v. William Meikleham was a member of the Maitland Club. Adam (p. 137) says erroneously that MacIlwhom is a corruption of this name.

MEIKLE, MICKEL, MICKLE. A name descriptive perhaps of its first bearer, from Middle Scots *meikill, meikle, mekill*, 'big, large.' Cf. Mekle John Burne in Branxhelm, 1495, and Mekill Henry Nikson, 1516 (*Liddesdale*, p. 188, 207). There is no evidence to support the suggestion that the name is a form of

Michael. Willelmus Mykyl in the parish of Fyvy was excommunicated in 1382 (REA., I, p. 166), and Robertus Mykyl was juror on assize in 1389 regarding the mill-lands of Quarelwode, Moray (REM., p. 171). Willelmus Baxter Mykil was elected a 'lineator' in Aberdeen, 1398 (CRA., p. 374). William Mikil or Mykill was juror on inquest at Narn, 1431, for ascertaining the former tenure of the lands of Kilrawkis and Geddes (*Rose*, p. 127, 129). Richard Mekill, notary public, 1501 (*Cawdor*, p. 110). Elizabeth *alias* Bessie Mekill was retoured heir portioner of John Mekill, burgess of Lynlythgow, 1609 (*Retours, Linlithgow*, 66), William Meikill was retoured heir of Thomas Meikill of Clokisland, his father, 1616 (*Retours, Ayr*, 141), and John Muckle was bellfounder in Glasgow, 1693 (RUG., III, p. 583).

MEIKLEJOHN, MEIKLEJON. A name descriptive of personal appearance of original bearer. Cf. Mekle Johne Burne in Branxhelm, 1495 (*Liddesdale*, p. 188). William Meiklejohne appears in the muster roll of the laird of Glenurquhay in 1638 (BBT., p. 398), and Thomas Meiklejohn was a baxter in Dysart in 1678 (*Dysart*, p. 53). Meakiljohne 1662, Meaklejohne 1646, Meaklejohnne 1626, Mecklijohn 1696, Meikiljohn 1663, Meikiljone 1637, Mickiljohne 1575, Meklejohne 1647, Meicklejohne 1647, Mikiljone 1563, Mikiljon 1565, Mikiljhone 1585. The name is fairly numerous on the northern side of Firth of Forth from Stirling to Dunfermline.

MEIKLEJONES. A variant of MEIKLEJOHN, q.v.

MEIKLEMAN. John Meiklemean in Drumoir, 1677, and Andrew Meiklemean in Gill of Newlaw, 1749 (*Kirkcudbright*). Andrew Miklemein and John Miklemen in Grange, Kirkcudbright, 1689 (RPC., 3. ser. XIV, p. 741, 742).

MEIKLERIGGS. Of local origin from the old lands of Meikleriggs near Paisley, Renfrewshire. Andro Mekleriggis appears as a witness in Paisley in 1504 (RMP., p. 63).

MEILKE. Payment to John Meilke in Mellerstayn, 1705 (*Stitchill*, p. 154). Cf. Frisian Milcke, diminutive of Myle (Winkler, *Friesche naamlijst*, p. 260).

MEIN, MIEN. Adam Mene, juror on inquisition at Roxburgh, 1361 (*Bain*, IV, 62). Adam Mene, scutifer, Glasgow diocese, 1397 (LSC., 111). Berne Mein or Bernard Meyne appears in Melrose, 1608 (RRM., I, p. 61, 64). Robert Meine, mason in Newsteid, 1657, James Meane, mason there, 1662, and Andrew Mein, mason there, 1668 (ibid., I, p. 164; II, p. 7, 203).

Robert Mein or Mean was postmaster of Edinburgh, 1665, 1686 (RPC., 3. ser. XII, p. 404; SBR., p. 249), Andrew Mein was retoured heir in 1687 in lands in East Moristoun, parish of Ligertvvood (Retours, Berwick, 427). James Mein, portioner of Lessudden, 1776 (Heirs, 383), John Mein in St. John's Clachan, 1788, and Isobel Mean in Kempleton, 1746 (Kirkcudbright). Mèinn, the local Gaelic form of Menzies, may be the origin in some instances but cannot be the source of all. Recorded in Duns, 1941. Meen 1689.

MELBURNE. Perhaps from Milburne near Ponteland, Northumberland, old spellings of which are Meleburna (1202) and Melleburn (1255). Magister H. de Melleburne who was one of the witnesses to a charter by John de Morham, c. 1219–46 (RAA., I, 24) may be the Hugh de Melburne who witnessed a confirmation charter by David, bishop of St. Andrews re the church of Wemyss, c. 1233–55 (Soltre, p. 26), and in 1240, as H. de Melleburne, witnessed a charter to Holyrood Abbey (LSC., 76; RD., p. 71).

MELDON. William de Meldun, juror on inquisition on the lands of Hopkelchoc, 1259 (Bain, I, 2162; APS., I, p. 88). John of Meldone was juror on inquest at Peebles, 1304 (Bain, II, 1436), and John de Meldon appears as perpetual vicar of Lothresk, 1366 (REA., II, p. 61).

MELDRUM. Of territorial origin from the old barony of Meldrum (Melgedrum) in Aberdeenshire. Philip de Melgedrum and his son William de Melgedrum were witnesses to the charter by Alexander Cumyn, earl of Buchan, founding the hospital of Turriff. This Philip, or his father, seems to have been earlier known as 'de Fedarg.' Alexander de Melgedrom or Melgedrum witnessed a quitclaim of Beeth Waldef in Fife in 1278 (RD., p. 52, 53). David de Melkedrum of the county of Fife and William de Melkedrom, sheriff of Aberdeen in 1292, rendered homage in 1296 (Bain, II, p. 140, 209). In 1306–7 Thomas, son and heir of William de Melkedrum, a minor, petitioned that he may have reasonable sustenance, etc. (ibid., p. 527). William de Melgedrum was one of the "burgenses rure manentes" in Aberdeen in 1317 (SCM., v, p. 10), and Philip de Meldrome witnessed the grant of the barony of Dalkeith to William de Douglas in 1341 (RHM., II, 45). William de Meldrwm witnessed charters of confirmation by Robert the Steward in 1358 (Inchaffray, p. 126), and a later Willelmus de Meldrom was present at perambulation of the boundaries of Kyrknes and Louchor in 1395 (RPSA., p. 3). William Myldrum, Scots prisoner of war, was beheaded in 1402 (Bain, IV, 646). Meldrum of that Ilk failed in an heiress, Elizabeth de Meldrum, who married William de Seton (son of Sir Alexander de Seton) who fell at the battle of Brechin in 1452 (AEI., p. 52). Floremundus Meldrum was juror on assize at Liston in 1459 (Edmonstone, 80), Thomas de Meldrum was admitted burgess of Aberdeen in 1477 (NSCM., I, p. 26), and John Meldrum, Scottish merchant, had a safe conduct to travel in England in 1486 (Bain, IV, 1517). Meldrome 1348, Meldroom 1681, Meldroum 1344, Meldrowm 1488, Melerum 1434.

MELISS, MELLES. See under MELLIS.

MELLERSTANES. From Mellerstain in the parish of Earlston, Berwickshire (1625 Millerstanis, 1627 Millerstanes). Alexander Mellerstanes was clerk of regality of Melrose, 1608 (RRM., I, p. 68).

MELLING. Probably from Melling in Lancashire. Magister Walter de Melling witnessed the confirmation charter of the church of Wiscytun (Wiston) to the Abbey of Kelso, c. 1260 (Kelso, 339). Walter de Melling, probably the same person, witnessed resignation of the patronage of the church of Killosbern, 1278 (ibid., 341). Walter Mealing was dwelling in the Castleget of Aberdeen, 1597 (SCM., I, p. 89), John Meling was admitted burgess there in 1611 (NSCM., I, p. 110), and James Meling in Denmyln is in record in 1633 (SCM., III, p. 113). David Melline, witness in Elgin, 1661 (Rec. Elgin, II, p. 298). Mealine 1661. (2) In Shetland this surname may represent MELVILLE.

MELLIS, MELLISH, MELISS, MELLES. Forms of MALISE, q.v. Gillemycell Malys, 'tailvour,' is in record in 1481 (Rose, p. 146), and John Males was tenant in Strathdee in 1527 (Grant, III, p. 70). Robert Malies was tenant of Hiltoun of Birneth (Birnie) in 1565 (REM., p. 440), and in 1643 there is entry of payment for ale to John Malleis in Aberdeen (SCM., v, p. 161). The northern surname LEES is probably a curtailed form of this name. Elspet Malice was trade burgess of Aberdeen, 1655 (ROA., I, p. 233). George Malice in Tillieangus, 1730 (Aberdeen CR.), John Melish (1771–1822), geographer, was born in Perthshire, and David Meliss appears in Coupar of Angus, 1773 (Dunkeld). Maleis and Malis 1647, Melis 1751, Mellis 1657.

MELROSE. From the town of the same name in Roxburghshire. In the common speech of the district the place name is pronounced Meuros or Meuwress (Murray, Dialect of the southern counties of Scotland, p. 123).

MELROSE, *continued*

William Melros, a native of Scotland, had licence to enjoy any benefice in England under the dignity of a deanery in 1468 (*Bain,* IV, 1378). David Melros held a land in Edinburgh in 1531 (*Soltre,* p. 269), William Melross appears as a monk of Inchaffray in 1554 and 1564 (*Inchaffray,* p. xcix), and John Melros was burgess of Selkirk in 1590 (RPC., IV, p. 481).

MELVEEN. A surname in Wigtownshire, probably a variant of MILVAIN, q.v.

MELVEN. See *under* MELVIN.

MELVILLE. From the barony of Malaville or Malleville in the Pays de Caux, Normandy. Galfridus de Malveill first appears as witness in a charter by Malcolm IV (LSC., p. 209), and also appears as witness in charters in the following reign of William the Lion. He is among the witnesses to the grant of the church of Tarland to the church of St. Andrews, c. 1165–71 (*Illus.,* II, p. 14, 15), and is also a witness to the earliest existing royal charter to the burgh of Aberdeen (*Aberdeen Charters,* ed. by P. J. Anderson, p. 3–4). Richard Maluvell was taken prisoner at Alnwick along with King William in 1174 (*Bain,* II, p. 117), and appears as a charter witness in 1178 (RAA., I, 2). Persons of the name possessed Kinblethmont as early as 1189 (ibid., I, p. 99). Hugh de Malleville witnessed a charter by Alan filius Walteri, c. 1202 (RMP., p. 14), and Henricus de Malevill witnessed the sale of the land of Drumsleed to Gregory, bishop of Brechin, between 1218–22 (REB., II, 272). Philip de Maleuille, the justiciary of Scotland, witnessed the charter by Alexander II preserving the rights of the burgesses of Glasgow to trade through Argyll and Lennox, 1242 (REG., p. 149), and Gregory de Malville in 1264 granted the monks of Newbattle free passage through his lands of Retrevyn to their Clydesdale possessions (*Neubotle,* p. 161). Eight or nine Melvilles or Malevilles rendered homage to England in 1296 (*Bain,* II). The lands of Melville in Midlothian were one of the earliest possessions of the family and received their name from their first possessor, and so likewise did the lands of Melville in Fife. James Melville, the Reformer, in his *Diary* (Bannatyne Club ed.) spells his own name Melville and Melvin even on the same page (e.g. p. 87, 238), and among older people in the country districts the name is still commonly pronounced Melvin, and it is frequently written Melvin, Mellin, and Melling. Rear Admiral George W. Melville (1841–1912), U. S. N., Arctic explorer, was grandson of a Scot from Stirling. Mailueil 1468, Mailuil 1526, Mailuile 1559, Mailuill 1519, Mailuille 1539, Mailvene 1500, Mailveyne 1491, Mailvil 1525, Mailvile 1527, Mailvin 1504, Mailvyll 1548, Mailvyne 1502, Mailwill 1583, Mailwyn 1456, Mailwyne 1530, Maleuile 1516, Maleuyll 1264, Maluill 1502, Malevil 1468, Malevyle 1400, Malevvn 1470, Malevyne 1467, Malewile 1436, Mallwill 1574, Maluel 1457, Maluile 1510, Maluivll 1509, Malveyn 1457, Malvil 1484, Malvile 1540, Malvyle and Malvyn 1425, Malvyne 1474, Malwill 1456, Malwvle 1428, Malwyn and Malwyne 1447, Meiluill 1520, Mellwell 1610, Melving 1633, Melwene 1543, Melwill 1595, Melwin 1550, Melwyn 1583, Melwyne 1524; Maling, Malling, Meluile, Meluill, Melvyne, Melwing.

MELVIN, MELVEN. Vulgarized forms of MELVILLE, q.v. On the northeast coast pronounced Mellon (*Innes,* p. 50). James Melville, the Reformer, in his *Diary* spells his own name indifferently Melville and Melvin, even on the same page (e.g. p. 87, 238). The variant spelling is also found as early as the twelfth century. Galfridus Malevin witnessed a confirmation charter by William the Lion to Ralph Frebern, c. 1161–63 (SCM., IV, p. 242), and c. 1165 Galfridus de Maleuin is mentioned in another charter (LSC., 27). Andrew Malvyn was burgess of Abirbrothoc, 1387 (RAA., II, 39), John the Malewyn was one of assize on the marches of Woodwrae, 1388 (*Bamff,* p. 22). Alexander Malvyn witnessed resignation of the lands of Wolle, 1474, and John Malewyn witnessed a charter by Archibald, earl of Douglas, in same year (*Home,* 22). Thomas Malwyn was tenant of Balgrescho, 1482 (*Cupar-Angus,* I, p. 232). David Melvill, Aberdeen printer in the seventeenth century, appears in record as David Mailing, and Barbara Mailling was married in Edinburgh, 1633 (*Edinb. Marr.*). The old name of Mailingsland (Traquair) was Meluinsland, from one or other of the Melvilles who rendered homage in 1296. Melwine 1637.

MEMES. From the lands of Memus (1622 Memas) in the parish of Tannadyce, Angus. Jak of Mames was a witness in Lethnott in 1435 (REB., II, 53), and Schir Donald Mamess was chaplain in Brechin in 1446 (ibid., I, 107). John Memise was married in Edinburgh in 1649 (*Edinb. Marr.*), and Rev. Robert Memes, Episcopal clergyman in Stonehaven, died in 1818. Other old spellings: Memess, Memis, Memmis, Miemes.

MENAR. Local from Manor in Peeblesshire. Eustace de Vesci granted Walter of Maner two oxgangs of land in Lium (Lyham), c. 1207 (*Laing,* 4). William Menar or de Menar was a tenant under the earl of Douglas in Liston, 1376 (RHM., I, p. li; II, p. 16).

MENELAW, MENELAWS. Variants of MONILAW, MONILAWS, q.v.

MENMUIR. Local, from Menmuir near Brechin, in Angus. The surname is very uncommon. William Menmuir, witness in a witchcraft trial in Brechin, 1650 (Records, Presbytery of Brechin, p. 28). Charles Menmuir has contributed occasional articles on Scottish subjects to present-day periodicals.

MENNIE. See under MEANIE.

MENTEATH, MENTEITH. Forms of MONTEATH, q.v.

MENTION. John Mentione was "wryter in the Burgh of Edinburgh," 1590 (Sc. Ant., VI, p. 165).

MENTIPLAY, MENTUPLAY. The first form is a Fife corruption of the surname MONYPENNY, and Mentuplay is a form found in the Presbytery records of Caithness in 1709. In the Kirk Session records of Canisbay it is recorded that Helene Mendtheplay was "delate of superstitious goeing or kneeling about the Chappell" of St. Modan, Freswick, in 1652 (Old Lore Misc., V, p. 59).

MENZIES. This name is of Norman origin, being originally de Meyners. In England it assumed the form MANNERS. An Arketill de Mannvers witnessed a charter by William de Veteri Ponte to the Abbey of Holyrood before 1214 (LSC., p. 213). Robert de Meyners, who was created Great Chamberlain of Scotland, is generally considered first of the name in Scotland. He witnessed charters by Alexander II in 1224 (LSC., 63) and 1246 (Scon, p. 51), and the confirmation by the same king of a charter which William, earl of Mar, made to Gilbert de Haya of the lands of Drunlav, 1217 (SCM., II, p. 308). He is probably the Robertus de Meyneiss who witnessed a charter by Alexander II relating to the fugitive serfs in 1248 (Cupar-Angus, I, p. 326). David de Meynness, knight, was one of the queen of Scotland's retinue in 1248 (Bain, I, 1748). Robert de Mesneres, a Scot, an adherent of Henry III of England in 1255 (ibid., I, 1987), is probably Robert de Miners of the diocese of Dunkeld to whom an indult was granted in 1256 (Pap. Lett., I, p. 331). Letters patent were granted by Edward I in 1297 to Alexander de Meygners (Bain, II, 942), probably the Alexander de Meigners who witnessed grant of the office of Constable of Scotland to Sir Gilbert the Hay in 1314 (SCM., II, p. 211), and between 1306–29

witnessed a charter by Robert I to the earl of Ross (REM., 264; Rose, p. 113). Thomas de Meineris was one of the signers of the Barons' letter to the Pope in 1320. Alexander de Meyneris or Meinzeis had a charter of the lands of Durisdeer from Robert I (RMS., I, App. II, 146), and Robert Maynhers had a charter of half the barony of Culter from Robert II in 1385, which his father had resigned (OPS., I, p. 176). John of Menzhers was notary in Perth, 1421 (Athole, p. 706), David Meygnes or Meignes was one of the hostages for King James I in 1425 (Bain, IV, 981, 983), and another David Meyner of Weem was a tyrant and oppressor of the people of Orkney in 1424 (REO., p. 37). The "Red and White" Book of Menzies: the history of Clan Menzies and its chiefs, by D. P. Menzies, F. S. A. Scot., Glasgow, 1894, is one of the most extraordinary family histories ever published. Compiled by a man ignorant of the most elementary principles of historical and genealogical research, the work professes to trace the history of the family from Mannus, second son of King Fergus, B. C. 333! In Gaelic the Menzies's are known collectively as Méinnearach, and there is a local Gaelic form Meinn, whence comes the surnames MEIN and MEINE, both in current use. The name is now pronounced Meeng-us. Mainzeis 1675, Megnies 1447, Meignees 1421, Meigneis 1448, Meignes 1419, Meignez 1424, Meingnes 1460, Meingzes 1651, Meingzeis 1641, Meinyeis 1630, Meinzeis 1658, Meinzies 1677, Mengues 1487, Mengyeis 1591, Mengzeis 1574, Mengzes 1572, Mengzies 1634, Mennes 1349, Menyas 1424, Menyeis 1500, Menyheis 1431, Menyhes 1428, Menzas, Menzes, Menzeis and Menzeys 1550, Menzheis 1503, Menzis 1446, Moygne 1369.

MERCENER. From LL. mercenarius = mercator. Duncanus Mercenar, witness in Aberdeen, 1281 (REA., II, p. 279).

MERCER. From the occupation, ME. mercer <LL. mercerius, Fr. mercier, a mercer, draper, dealer. The word still exists in English in the sense of a dealer in silks. William Mercer or le Mercer witnessed two charters in favor of the Abbey of Kelso, c. 1200 (Kelso, 354, 507). Aleumnus Mercer was party with twenty-three others to a bond given by Alexander II to Henry III in 1244 to keep the peace. He had a grant of Tillicoultry from Walter, son of Alan. His son and successor of the same name resigned his lands into the king's hands in 1261 (Stodart, II, p. 124. Stodart spells Alcunus). A curious story of two Mercers appears in English records, which throws an interesting sidelight on the law of the period. In 1279 "a man unknown was housed

MERCER, *continued*

at Morpathe (Morpeth) with Geoffrey and William, the mercers of Scotland. The stranger rose through the night and stole their goods to the value of 30s., and instantly fled to Cotinwode, followed by William, who slew him in his flight. Both withdrew themselves and are not discredited. They may return if they will, but their chattels are confiscated for flight" (*Bain*, II, p. 42). (Apparently it was lawful to pursue a thief with hue and cry and do summary justice on him if found with the goods in his possession. The Mercers erred in not pursuing the thief in the recognized way.) Duncan Mersar, witness in Aberdeen, 1272, is probably Duncan Mercener, who witnessed a charter by Martin Aurifaber (Goldsmith) there in 1281 (REA., I, p. 37; II, p. 279). Austyn le Mercer, burgess of Roxburgh, Bernard le Mercer, burgess of Perth, and Wauter le Mercer, burgess of Montrose, rendered homage, 1296 (*Bain*, II, p. 197, 198). Thomas dictus Mercer held land "in vico Sellatorum" (Saddlers' street) of Perth, 1332 (*Scon*, 163). There are two old families of this name — the Mercers of Aldie and those of Innerpeffry in Strathearn. The former were intimately connected with the history and prosperity of Perth. The founder of this branch appears to have been Thomas. He had an order from Edward III in 1341 on the coast of Bordeaux for money due for raising men and horses for service in Aquitania. John Mercer, a wealthy burgess of Perth, who flourished in latter half of fourteenth century, was provost of the town in 1357, 1369, 1374, and in 1355 commissioner for Perth to arrange for the liberation of David II (APS., I, p. 517). He was taken prisoner by the English during a truce in 1376, and shortly afterwards released without ransom, much to the chagrin of Walsingham, who mentions his "inestimable wealth." An old rhyme referring to the antiquity of the Mercers of Perth says:

"So sicker 'tis as anything on earth,
The Mercers aye are older than old Perth."

Another rhyme referring to them punningly records that:

"Folk say the Mercers tried the town to cheat
When for two Inches they did win six feet."

This alludes to the exchange of the two Inches of Perth (where the famous clan battle was fought in 1396) for the right of sepulture in St. John's Church, Perth. Marcer 1527, Marsar 1497, Mersare 1428, Marser 1574, Merssar 1618, Mersour 1515, Mersher 1591, Mersser 1607.

MERCHANT, MARCHANT. From ME. *marchaunt*, AF. *marchant*, a 'merchant,' Latinized

mercator in early charters. Radulph Mercator held land in Dunfermline a. 1214 (*Kelso*, 11), and a later Radulph Mercator was a charter witness in Dundee in 1281 (HP., II, p. 223). Thomas called Marchand was a canon of Brechin in 1298 (*Pap. Lett.*, I, p. 576). Morice Merchande was barber of the burgh of Dumbarton in 1456 (*Strathendrick*, p. 192), and in 1495 there is mention of the tenement of Elizabeth Merchand there (REG., 471). Isobella Merchand was retoured heir of Alexander Merchand, burgess of Kilmareis (Kilmaurs) in 1600 (*Retours, Ayr*, 31), and presumptions of witchcraft were given in against Marat Merchant in Brechin in 1650 (*Extracts, Records of Presbytery of Brechin, 1639–1660*). Other old spellings are Merchan, Mertchand.

MERCHISTON. Of local origin from Merchiston, Edinburgh, which in 1494 appears as Merchanistoun. Thomas Merchisoun was "mair of ye quarter of Brechine," 1450 (REB., I, 151). John Merchamestoun in record, 1505. James Merchamston was provost of the Collegiate Church of Corstorphine, 1512 (ALHT., IV, p. 144), and Oliver Merchinstoun was baker in Edinburgh, 1658 (*Edinb. Marr.*). The place name may be derived from Mercheh, father of one of the perambulators of the lands of Clerchetune (now Clerkington near Edinburgh), c. 1141 (RPSA., p. 181). Merchistoune 1663.

MEREWIN. From either of the OE. personal names, (1) *Merewine*, or (2) *Maerwine*. Mereuin filius Colbain witnessed King David's confirmation charter to Dunfermline between 1146–53 (RD., p 7). Meruin seruiens Eggou Rufi, a witness early in thirteenth century (RPSA., p. 383).

MERGIE. A Kincardineshire surname, from Mergie near Stonehaven. Thomas Mergy witnessed the inventory of the estate of Sir John Erskine of Dun, 1513 (SCM., IV, p. 16).

MERGTON. Local. Payment to Agnes Mergton, daughter of late Thomas Mergton of Edinburgh, 1736 (*Guildry*, p. 157).

MERKSHULLE. Alan of Merkshulle, an archer serving in Livingstone Peel, 1312 (*Bain*, III, p. 411). There was a chapel at Markle, Prestonkirk parish, dedicated to S. Maria de Merkill (APS., 1581, III, p. 256). The church was burned in Hertford's invasion.

MERKYNTONE. Simone de Merkyntone witnessed a grant by Andrew Mansel to the Abbey of Kelso, c. 1200 (*Kelso*, 507). Probably from Markington near Harrogate, Yorkshire.

MERLAY. Randulphus de Merlai witnessed a charter by Prince Henry in favor of Eustace FitzJohn, granted at Seleschirche (Hartshorne, *Feudal and military antiquities of Northumberland*, 1858, II, App., p. cxv). Kok de Merlev, a cleric, appears a. 1200 (RHM., I, 3). William de Merlay, a Norman, received the site on which he built Morpeth Castle, in return for his aid in crushing the Northumbrian rebellion against William the Conqueror. Roger de Merlay witnessed the gift by Philip de Pethcox of meadowland in Pitcox to the monks of Melrose in the reign of Alexander II (*Melros*, p. 221, 222). Ricardus de Merlay or de Merlei witnessed confirmation of the gift of the church of Cragyn (Craigie in Kyle) to the monks of Paisley, c. 1272 (RMP., p. 232). Robert de Merleye 'persone del eglise de Westerker,' of the county of Rokesburk, rendered homage in 1296. His seal bears for device, a monster (?), and S' *Roberti de Herlei* [sic] (*Bain*, II, p. 209, 555). Rogier de Merleye of the county of Lanark and Wauter de Merlegh of the county of Rokesburk also rendered homage in 1296 (ibid., p. 211, 213). Alexander Merle, an esquire of Scotland, had an annuity for his good service to King Edward of England in the wars, 1378–79 (*Bain*, IV, 257, 273).

MERLIENE. Walter Merlyoune, mason in Edinburgh, 1496 (ALHT., I, p. cclxv), is probably the Wat Merlzoun, mason, who received a pension for life in 1499 (RSS., I, 399). Walter Merlioun was one of the masons employed on new hall of Holyrood in 1502 (ALHT., II), and Thomas Merliene or Marelzoune was tenant of Hilton of Rosyth in 1577 (Stephens, *Inverkeithing*, p. 198). Several persons of this family appear to have been masons in the king's service. Henry Merlion was employed in building Ravenscraig Castle in 1462–3. "They gave name to Marlin's Wynd in Edinburgh, a close which led from the High Street to the Cowgate, where the South Bridge now is" (ALHT., I, p. cclxv). Under the name Marlzone, Marlzeone, or Merlzone, individuals of this family were employed as masons in Dunkeld between 1505–17 (*Rent. Dunk.*), Dauid Merleon, tenant in Balmyle, 1473 (*Cupar-Angus*, I, p. 182), Isobel Marlioun, liferenter in Rosemarkie, 1585 (OPS., II, p. 579) and Tom Marlzeon is recorded in Dunfermline in 1564 (*Dunfermline*). The name is spelled Merlin in Maitland's *History of Edinburgh*.

MERPYM. Wautier Merpym of Roxburghshire rendered homage, 1296. His seal bears an eight-rayed figure and S' *Walteri Marpin* (*Bain*, II, p. 199, 533).

MERRICKS. Of local origin, probably from Merrick, in the parish of Minnigaff, Kirkcudbright, with genitive -s.

MERRILEES, MERRILES, MERRYLEES, MIREYLEES, MIRYLEES, MIRRLEES. From Merrilees, the name of an estate and hamlet now merged in the estate of Binns, West Lothian. In the Retours the place name is spelled Mureleyis (1602), Murryleyis (1618), and Mirrieleyis (1683). There was also a Mureleyis in Renfrew, 1604 (*Retours*, 18). Thomas Mereleys or Mureleis who was permitted during the pest "till cum in to his awin house of the Mure" in Edinburgh in 1529 (MCM., II, p. 93), may be Thomas Mureleyis "dekin for the time of the Cordinare Craft" in Edinburgh, 1533 (*Guildry*, p. 103). Richard Mereleis was "expellit and banist" from Stirling in 1545 (SBR., p. 41), and Meg Merrilies is the name of the old gypsy woman in Scott's *Guy Mannering*. William Hope Merriles died in Leith, 1941. Mirrilies 1665.

MERRY. Thomas Mirrie was bailie of Ayr, 1607 (*Ayr*, p. 141), Elizabeth Mirrie is recorded there, 1656 (ibid., p. 197), and William Mirrie was "execut in ye grassmercat for murder" in 1682 (BOEC., VIII, p. 132). John Mirrie was writer in Edinburgh, 1686 (RPC., 3. ser. XII, p. 315), and Mr. Thomas Mirrey was schoolmaster at Wandel, 1712 (*Lanark CR.*).

MERRYMONTH. William Merimontht witnessed a testament inventory of Catharine Lauder, 1515 (*Swinton*, p. xci). Perhaps a misreading of Merrymouth, a name recorded by Lower and Bardsley. There is a Merrymouth near Dunlop, Ayrshire.

MERSON, MEARSON. Peter Merson is in record in the parish of Dumbennan, 1716 (SCM., IV, p. 170), Patrick Merson was gunsmith to the Gartly Company of Volunteers, 1798 (*Will*, p. 25), and George Merson from King Edward served in the first Great War (*Turriff*).

MERSTON. Richard Merstoun, seaman in Dunbar, 1688 (RPC., 3. ser. XIII, p. 264). Mary Merstoun in Edinburgh, 1699 (*Edinb. Marr.*).

MERSYNTON. Perhaps from Mersington, Berwickshire. Willelmus Mersynton, witness in Auchleuyn, 1454 (REA., I, p. 274).

MERTON. From Mertoun near St. Boswells, Roxburghshire. Adam de Merton was juror on an inquisition on the lands of Hopkelchoc (now Kailzie) in 1259 (*Bain*, I, 2162; APS., I, p. 88). Nicholas de Merton was rector of

MERTON, *continued*

the church of Kynetlys (Kinnettles in Angus) in 1300 (RPSA., p. 120), and Master John de Merton was rector of Camyslang in 1394 (RMP., p. 107).

MESCHIN. This word means 'younger,' and was used much as our 'junior' to distinguish from an older person of the name. Meschins were great landowners in England in the twelfth and early thirteenth centuries. The lands of Randulf Meschin are mentioned a. 1153 (*Nat. MSS.*, I, 19). Robert le Machun of Strathavan, Lanarkshire, rendered homage, 1296 (*Bain*, II, p. 213).

MESFENNON. Eyr de Mesfennon of Peeblesshire, who rendered homage, 1296 (*Bain*, II, p. 207), derived his name from Mossfennan, Peeblesshire.

MESSENGER. From ME. and AF. *messager*, a messenger, with epenthetic *n*. Gilbert le Messager and Michael le Messager, both king's tenants in the county of Edneburk, rendered homage in 1296. The seal of the latter bears a cross cantoned with 5 stars, and S' *Michael le Messag* (*Bain*, II, p. 205, 210, 549). Rauf le Messager of the county of Berewyk also rendered homage in the same year (ibid., p. 210), and Ivo le Messager of the county of Dumfries (ibid., p. 203). Robert Messynger of Orkenay in Scotland received a safe conduct to travel in England in 1405 (*Bain*, IV, 679), and Alan Messengere, a native of Scotland, was owner of a tenement in Smythefeld, London, in 1482 (ibid., IV, 1485).

MESSER. Most probably from Fr. *messier* (<L. *messarius*,* derivative of *messis*), keeper of a standing crop. A rare surname. Thomas le Messer, a "Scot by nation," was described in 1296 as long resident in Benyngton, England (*Bain*, II, p. 173). John Messor was a notary public in 1461 (*Strathendrick*, p. 222), Robert Messour is recorded in Ellene market, 1643 (SCM., v, p. 107), George Messer in Melrose, 1648 (RRM., I, p. 119), and Thomas Messer, "lait Deane of Gild" of Aberdeen, 1663 (SCM., v, p. 342). Masar 1565, Meisser 1551, Mersser 1650.

MESTON. An Aberdeenshire surname. William Meston (d. 1745), poet. James Mestine, merchant in Aberdeen, 1764.

METHEREL. Joseph Metherel, resident in Aberdeen, 1727 (NSCM., II, p. 118). There is a Metherell in Cornwall.

METHKIL. John, son of Michael de Methkil, who granted to the church of S. Marie de Melros his land of Penshiel in the Lammermuir Hills, East Lothian, c. 1230 (*Wemyss*, II, p. xlv), is the Johannes de Methkill who witnessed the gift of fifteen acres of Balmulinauch (Balmerino) to the church of St. Andrews before 1225 (RPSA., p. 272). He may have been an ancestor of the family of Wemyss of Wemyss. John de Methkil granted the church of Wemys in Fife to the House of Soltre sometime between 1200 and 1240 (*Soltre*, p. 13), and c. 1228 he witnessed a charter by Malcolm, 7th earl of Fife (*Laing*, 6). The name is derived from the lands of the same name, now Methil, in Fife.

METHUEN. A variant of METHVEN, q.v.

METHVEN, METHUEN, MEFFAN, MEFFEN. From Methven in Perthshire. Robert de Methven witnessed a confirmation charter of David, bishop of St. Andrews, concerning the church of Wemyss, c. 1233–55 (*Soltre*, p. 28). Roger de Methfenn of the county of Perth rendered homage in 1296 (*Bain*, II, p. 199). Dominus Roger Meffen was witness to a grant by John Moncreiff before 1320 (*Milne*, p. 6), and Thomas de Methfen held the office of chamberlain in Aberdeen in 1340 (ER., I, p. 456). John of Meffen, doctor of decrees, one of the commissioners for concluding peace between Scotland and England in 1451 (*Bain*, IV, 1239) may be the John Methfen, vicar of Edinburgh, who had a safe conduct into England in 1454 (ibid., 1267). Paul Methuen was an early Scottish Reformer, and the founder of the London publishing house of Methuen and Co. was of Scottish origin. Mathven 1449, Meffane 1444, Meffon 1559, Methvine 1670.

MEWERS. Katherine Mewares appears in the parish of Dolphington, 1624, and two more of the name are in same record (*Lanark CR.*). John Mewers in Newmiln, barony of St. Martins, 1713 (*Dunkeld*).

MEWHINNEY. *See under* MACWHINNIE.

MEY. Local, from Mey near Thurso, Caithness. Margaret Mey in Mey (*Caithness*).

MIBBIE. Perhaps a variant of MABIE, q.v. John Mibbie in Mains of Crossmichael, 1721 (*Kirkcudbright*).

MICHAEL. From the Hebrew personal name meaning 'who is like God.' It is synonymous with Miciah or Micah (Numbers XIII, 13; I Chron. v, 13). Michael was first recorded bishop of Glasgow (*Dowden*, p. 294). Magister Michael witnessed a charter by William, bishop of St. Andrews before 1214 (*Scon*, p. 35), and Michael was abbot of Cambuskenneth in 1307 (*Dowden*, p. 201). This name is the source of MITCHELL and Gaelic *MacgilleMichael*. Part of Belady in Glenyleff was leased to Robert Mychael, 1476 (*Cupar-Angus*, I, p. 223). See also ST. MICHAEL.

MICHALBEGSON. Gaelic-English, 'son of little Michael.' Donald Michalbegson was tenant in part of Petlochry, 1465 (*Cupar-Angus*, I, p. 152).

MICHELSON. 'Son of MICHAEL,' q.v. Gilbertus Michelson or Michaelis was prebend of Kinkell, 1483 (REA., I, p. 315, 316). Mathew Michelsoune in Hundolee was herried in 1493 (*Trials*, I, p. 17*). Andreas Mechilsone had land in Aberdeen in the first half of the sixteenth century (REA., II, p. 234). John Michaelson was murdered by the Campbells in 1646 (*Lamont Inv.*, 786). See MITCHELSON.

MICHIE. An Aberdeenshire surname found mainly in Strathdon, Glengairn, and Crathie. "The name," says the late Dr. Alexander Fraser of Toronto, "is a local diminutive of Michael, and the family is a sept of the Macdonalds of Keppoch, descending from a Michael Macdonald of that branch. A fairly exhaustive enquiry establishes this fact. In the Aberdeen registers the name and its variants are traced to 1570, before which date Michael MacDonald settled in Aberdeenshire. The chiefship of this sept was in the family of Corryhoul, a place occupied for more than 200 years by them, and now represented by Lieut.-Col. John Forbes Michie, Toronto, who, only three years ago, disposed of the last of his ancestral rights in the old home" (*Celt. Mon.*, XXII, p. 159). John Mychy was tenant of part of Morton, 1473 (*Cupar-Angus*, I, p. 170). David Mihie had a son baptized in 1606 (*Aberdeen Jour. N. & Q.*, I, p. 99). As forename we have Michy Nycholson, 1446 (*Cupar-Angus*, I, p. 128).

MICHIESON. An Englishing of MACMICHIE, q.v. Tawis Michison appears in Scon in 1415 (*Scon*, p. 168). John Mechyson was burgess of Aberdeen, 1467 (NSCM., I, p. 21), and another John Mechysone was burgess of Forres in 1482 (*Cawdor*, p. 67).

MICKEL, MICKLE. See under MEIKLE.

MIDDLEMAS, MIDDLEMASS, MIDDLEMISS. The Middlemasses were vassals and tenants of the district around Kelso, and derived their surname from "lie Middlemestlands in villa et territorio de Calco," mentioned in 1629 (*Retours, Roxburgh*, 137). William de Meldiemast who petitioned for a benefice in the gift of the abbot of Kelso, 1406 (*Pap. Pet.*, I, p. 624) was probably Schir Wilyeam Myddilmast, the "lwvit chapellain" of Archibald de Douglas, earl of Wigtoun, vicar of Selkirk in the first quarter of the fifteenth century (RMS., II, 59). King James II confirmed a charter by William Myddilmast, vicar of Lynton, of certain tenements in the town of Peblis, 1439 (*Peebles*, p. 207–208). Thomas Myddilmast is recorded in Ploro, 1495 (*Trials*, I, p. 20*), and John Myddilmest witnessed a charter by Robert, abbot of Kelso, 1497 (*Kelso*, p. 429). Thomas Myddilmaist of Grestoune, a Peeblesshire laird, 1530 (*Trials*, I, p. 147*). Thomas Middlemast was retoured heir in 1566 in the lands of Middilmast as "Middlemast of Middlemast," and Mege and Malie Middilmest were tenants under the Abbey of Kelso in 1567 (*Kelso*, p. 520, 525). David Midlmest is in record in Mairbotle (Morebattle) in 1652 (*Inquis.*, 3701), and Luckie Middlemist kept a famous oyster-cellar in Edinburgh in latter half of eighteenth century. This surname has been recently absurdly explained as from "middlemast," obsolete English for "mainmast," and so a nickname for a very tall man! Medillmest 1537, Medilmaste and Middilmaste 1425, Middelmest 1611, Middlemist 1742, Midelmest 1610, Midilmest 1611, Midlemes 1612, Midlemiss 1685, Midlemist 1670, Midlmess 1674, Mydilmest 1513.

MIDDLEMORE. Local. John Middlemore of Donavourd, 1799 (*Dunkeld*).

MIDDLER. An Aberdeenshire surname of local origin from Midlar in the parish of Leochel-Cushnie. Marjorie Midlar in Raneistoune in record in 1613 (RSCA., II, p. 189). William Mudlert was tenant of the Mill of Carunhill in 1696 (*Poll Book*), and William Medler was tenant in Newtyle about the same date.

MIDDLETON. From the lands of Middleton or Middletown of Conveth, in the parish of Laurencekirk, Kincardineshire. The lands were so named to distinguish them from Conveth Mill and lands on one side and Westerton of Conveth on the other. For about three centuries the family here bore the designation of Middleton of that Ilk. The first of the name recorded appears to have been Umfridus de Midilton who witnessed a grant of the lands of Petmengartenach to the Abbey of Arbroath in 1221, named also a charter of 1238 (RAA., I, 242, 261). Humfrey de Middiltone of the county of Kincardyn rendered homage in 1296 (*Bain*, II, p. 209), and Robert de Middleton was a Scot taken at Dunbar Castle in the same year (ibid., 742). Andrew de Midleton witnessed a charter of the lands of Craigy in the Mernys in 1357 (SCM., v, p. 248), and William Mydiltoune was admitted burgess of Aberdeen in 1488 (NSCM., I, p. 34). William

MIDDLETON, *continued*

Mediltoune appears in Glentanner in 1503 (*Aboyne*, p. 33). Mideltowne 1642, Midiltoun 1430, Midltoun 1652, Myddiltoun 1508, Myddiltoune 1471, Mydilton 1500.

MIDHOPE. Local, from some place of the name, probably near the Border. Simon of Midhope was one of the garrison of Stirling Castle, 1339–40 (*Bain*, III, p. 241). There is a Midghop vel Midhop in Roxburgh Retours (172), 1640.

MIDHOUSE. Of local origin from Midhouse, Evie, Orkney. Magnus Midhous was one of those respited for the slaughter of John, erle of Cathnes, 1529 (RSS., II, 3151; REO., p. 61).

MIDHUNST. John Midhunst in Caiphop and Robert Midhunst in Hownam, 1685 (*Peebles CR.*).

MIDILBURGH. Roger de Midilburgh of Roxburghshire rendered homage, 1296 (*Bain*, II, p. 199). Probably from Middlesborough in the North Riding of Yorkshire, in 1273 Middelburgh.

MIEN. *See under* MEIN.

MILDS. Thome Myldis, tenant near Melrose, 1564 (RRM., III, p. 148), and Thomas Mylds, indweller in Maxpoffle, 1642 (ibid., I, p. 99).

MILFREDERICK. A surname in Galloway. From Macgillepatrick through the forms M'Ilfadrich and Milfadrick. John Milfadrick appears in Minnigaff parish, 1684 (*Parish*), and John Miklefatrick in Kirkcudbright signed the Test in same year (RPC., 3. ser. X, p. 248).

MILHENCH. From M'ILHENCH, q.v., with omission of the apostrophe. John Milhench was bailie of Wigtown in 1775 (*Wigtown*).

MILL. A corruption for ease of pronunciation of MILN or MILNE, q.v., the form still in use provincially. Alexander Myll was tenant of the girnal mill of Kincrech, 1483 (*Cupar-Angus*, I, p. 236), John Myl, carpenter in Arbroath in 1510 (RAA., II, 509), and Thomas Myll, reader in Dyce, 1567 (AEI., 1). Anapill Myll in the lordship of Huntlie, 1600 (SCM., IV, p. 284). James Mill, father of John Stuart Mill (1806–1873), was born in Angus.

MILLAN, MILLEN. Names recorded in the Glasgow Directory are most probably from Ir. *O'Maoldin*, descendant of Maolan (diminutive of *maol*, bald). Cf. MACMILLAN.

MILLAR, MILLER. A surname derived from the occupation of miller, ME. *millere*. It ap-

pears in all parts of the country as every burgh had its miller at whose mill the corn of the neighborhood was ground. Millar is the more common Scottish form of the name. An inquest was held in the castle of Dumfries in the reign of Alexander III on the death of Adam Molendinarius, but probably Millar or Miller did not become a hereditary surname till a much later period (*Stodart*, II, p. 388). Ade molendinarius, a 'man' of the bishop of Moray, had a remission and protection, 1364 (REM., p. 164). Henricus Molendinam ('of the mill' was witness to a document of 1401 (*Cambus.*, p. 21), John and Henry Millare were jurors on an inquest anent fishing on the Tweed in 1467 (RD., p. 461), and James Molendinarius held a tenement in Glasgow in 1481 (LCD., p. 193). Margaret Myllar was tenant of the bishop of Glasgow in 1509 (*Rental*), and in 1540 Robert Millare held land in Irvine (*Irvine*, I, p. 167). Mydlar 1551, Melir 1745, Mylar 1513, Myllair 1511, Myllare.

MILLARD. A form of MILLAR with accretionary *d*. This seems more probable than that the name is a survival of OE. *mylenweard*, the official in charge of my lord's mill.

MILLERT. The local northeast pronunciation of MILLER, q.v. Isobel Millart sometime in Dollas, 1686 (*Moray*). Cf. MILLHARD.

MILLHARD. Most probably a form of MILLAR with accretionary *d*. The tombstone of a family named Goodbrand have their father's occupation so spelled. Cf. MILLERT.

MILLIGAN, MILLIKEN, MILLIKIN, MILLICAN, MULLIKIN. These names are in G. *Maolagan*, OIr. *Maelecan*, a double diminutive of *mael* (-oc-an), 'the little bald or shaven one,' probably in allusion to the ancient Gaelic tonsure. The first form is common in Galloway. Macrath ap Molegan of Wyggetone, who rendered homage in 1296 (*Bain*, II, p. 198) is apparently the first of the name recorded in Scotland. As Makerathe Molgan he had his lands restored to him in the same year (ibid., p. 218). Cymric 'ap,' afterwards reduced to 'A,' is possibly due to Cymric influence. Thomas Ameligane, a witness in Dumfries, 1477 (*Edgar*, p. 227), may be Thomas Amuligane, chaplain and notary public at Wigtown, 1485 (RMS., II, 1624). The name also appears in Perth in 1468 as Milikvn (*Milne*, p. 58). George Amuligane was burgess of Dumfries, 1510 (RMS., II, 3513), and a Schir William Amuligan, a cleric, is mentioned in the same year (*Bucc. MSS.*, p. 14). Thomas Amuligane, a follower of the earl of Cassilis, had a respite for murder committed by him in 1526 (RSS., I, 3386), Cuthbert Amullekyne of Dempstartoune was "dilaitit of the cryme of adulterie" in 1578 (*Trials*, I, p. 78), and John Amiligane witnessed a sasine in Dumfries, 1595 (RRM., III, p. 394). John Myllikin, a 'vabster ald and puir,' was buried in Dysart, Fife, at public expense, 1593 (*Dysart*, p. 41), another Johnne Amulliekin was hanged in 1612 (*Trials*, III, p. 223), and John Mulligane, polentarius (i.e. maltster), burgess of Dumfries, was retoured heir in lands in regality of Lyncluden, 1630 (*Retours, Kirkcudbright*, 183). James Myllighame of Blakmyre was retoured heir of his father in lands in parish of Balmaclellane and Dalry, 1633 (ibid., 200). Robert Mulligane, 'ludimagister' (i.e. master of the play), burgess of Edinburgh, 1649 (*Inquis.*, 3556) is most probably Robert Mulligin designated vulgar (i.e. public) schoolmaster who was married in 1656 (*Edinb. Marr.*). Thomas Mulliken in Cargat was charged with hamesucken in 1672 (*Just. Rec.*, II, p. 84). Major James Milliken purchased part of the ancient barony of Johnstone, Renfrewshire, in 1733, and gave the estate the name of Milliken (*Stodart*, II, p. 260). Robert Andrews Milliken, the American scientist, is of Scottish descent. Millagain 1684, Milligain 1694, Mulikyn 1480, Mulligine 1668, Mullikine 1662. There is a name (Mulekyn) in the *Exchequer Rolls* which might be thought a variant of this. The bearers of it, however, were Italians. In 1364 there is an entry of payment to Donatus Mulekyn for ornaments for the king (ER., II, p. 160), and in the thirty-second year of David II (1361–62) James or Jacobus Mulekyn "of Florence," probably a relative, was master moneyer (*monetarius*) in Edinburgh (ibid., II, p. xciii).

MILLMAKER. *See under* MEALMAKER.

MILLOY. The Milloys of Argyll and Bute are descended from the Macloys of Glendaruel, a branch of the MacLouies or Fullartons of Arran (*Celt. Mon.*). For change of Mac to Mil cf. MILFREDERICK.

MILN, MILNE, MYLNE. A very common surname in Aberdeenshire. Of local origin from residence at or near a corn-mill. This is the more correct form of the surname, OE. *myln* from Lat. *molina*. Hugh de molendino and Johannes de Molendino in the parish of Fyvy were excommunicated in 1382 (REA., I, p. 165, 166). A family of this name were farmers at the Mill of Boyndie for generations (*Jervise*, I, p. 199–200). In 1492 we have record of "Johne of Myll, duelland at the Justice Mvll" (CRA., p. 420), and in 1503 John of Myle at the Myle of Pitcapile was

"accusit for strublance" (ibid., p. 429). Robert Myll was a witness in Arbroath in 1528 (*Laing*, 369), Gilbert Milne had a grant of the chaplainry of Golspe in 1575 (OPS., II, p. 651), and John Miln was servitor of John Scrimgeour of Glaswall in 1610 (*Laing*, 1583). James Millin in Cowie was ordered to pay "ane stein of creischie" in 1617 (*Urie*, p. 25). In the following year his name is spelled Miln and Milne. A family named Mill in Inverurie in the seventeenth century changed the spelling of their name to Milne (*Inverurie*, p. 161). Other forms of the surname in record are Myll, Myln, Millen, Milln, Mylen, etc. (2) A second possible origin for the name in one or two instances is Gaelic *maol*, "bald." John Myill in Petty in 1502 certainly means "John the bald." Mac Giolla-Domhnaigh (*Some Anglicised surnames in Ireland*, p. 42) is in error in stating that Aberdeenshire Miln is an Anglicized form of Macmillan. A family of Mylnes were for centuries master masons to the kings of Scotland. Milln 1721, Millne 1688.

MILNEKNAVE. Adam Milneknave of Carfrae witnessed a charter c. 1380 of the mill of Ulkeston to the Abbey of Dryburgh (*Dryburgh*, 312). Milneknave here probably not a surname as he is styled 'of Carfrae.' The millknave was the under miller. Knave signified originally 'a boy,' later 'a servant.'

MILNER. This is the earlier form of the more common MILLAR, ME. *milnere, mylnere*, a miller. Andrew Mylnar leased part of the Grange of Abirbothry, 1454 (*Cupar-Angus*, I, p. 129). Paton Mylnar, tenant of Westhorn of Grange of Kerso, 1478 (ibid., I, p. 210).

MILROY. A surname current in the shires of Ayr and Wigtown, from M'Ilroy with omission of the apostrophe. The forms Malrie, Malroy, Milrie, Milroy, and Mulroy are all recorded in Wigtownshire and Minnigaff in 1684 (*Parish*). John Milroy in Fintalloch, Penninghame, a Covenanter, was hanged at Wigtown, 1685, and others of the name were obliged to flee from religious persecution. William Milrae was member of the Kirk Session of Twynholm in 1703. See MACILROY.

MILVAIN, MILWAIN. From M'Ilvain with omission of the apostrophe. The name appears in Edinburgh in 1644 (*Edinb. Marr.*), and Alexander Milwaven in Carsduchan is in record in 1765 (*Wigtown*). See MACILVAIN.

MILWEE. A Galloway surname. From M'Ilwee with omission of the apostrophe. For origin see under MACKELVIE.

MINDRUM. Adam of Myndrum, burgess of Roxburgh, rendered homage in 1296 (*Bain*, II, 820). In the same year Giles de Myndrom petitioned the king of England's justices at Berwick for return of the fishings which had been leased to him by the Carmelite Friars of Rosteneth (?) and taken from him on the surrender of the town (ibid., p. 228). Certain lands and burgages which had belonged to quondam Ade de Mindrome in the vills of Roxburghe, Kerton, etc., were granted to Hugh de le Vikeres, c. 1315 (*RMS.*, I, 14), Egidus de Mundrum, perhaps the Giles de Myndrom mentioned above, was bailie of Berwick in 1324 (*Cambus.*, p. 39, 40), and Alan de Mindrome, burgess of Roxburgh, appears as a witness, c. 1330 (*Kelso*, p. 369). John of Mindrom and Alan of Myndrom were jurors on an inquest taken at Roxburgh in 1357 (*Bain*, IV, 1). From Mindrim or Mindrum in Northumberland, near Yetholm.

MINIMAN. Mathew Mynnyman in 1536 had a precept of remission for certain offences committed by him (RSS., II, 2114), and Johannes Menomane had a feu charter of part of lands of the vill of Balcrystie, Fife, c. 1570 (*RD.*, p. 472). The tombstones of John Miniman (1657), melmaker, and of two daughters of Alexander Miniman (1672) are in St. Andrews' churchyard (*PSAS.*, XLV, p. 520, 526; LXX, p. 55). Mr. John Miniman or Niniman was minister of the word of God apud Abernethie (or Abernyt), 1693–97 (*Inquis.*, 7360, 7924). Christian Minniman in Edinburgh had a pension in 1734 (*Guildry*, p. 148).

MINN. Most probably a shortened form of (MAC)MINN, q.v.

MINNOCH. Local, probably from Minnock in Cunningham (*Retours, Ayr*: Mynnok 1622, Monok 1626).

MINTO. From the old village of Minto in Roxburghshire. James Minto in Oxnam in record in 1690 (*Peebles CR.*). Walter Minto (1753–1796), born in Coldingham, became professor of mathematics in the College of New Jersey in 1787.

MINTY. Andrew Myntie was accused of the "slaughter of umquhill Walter Mathie" in 1609 (RSCA., II, p. 151). William Myntie was assignee to the escheat of the late William Craig in Craigstoun in 1632 (ibid., II, p. 351). Margaret Mintie of Towy was excommunicated for breaking the seventh commandment in 1663 (*Alford*, p. 8). George Minty from Inverkeithny was killed at Cambrai in 1917 (*Turriff*).

MIREYLEES. *See under* MERRILEES.

MIRK. George Mirk possessed a tenement in Glasgow, 1458 (REG., p. 392). Jok Merk and Hobe Merk were tenants on lands of the Abbey of Kelso, 1567 (*Kelso*, p. 520, 521), James Merk was tenant under the marquis of Huntlie, 1600 (SCM., IV, p. 269), and Anna Mirk, daughter of Mr. James Mirk, minister, is in record, 1689 (RPC., 3. ser. XIV, p. 271). John Mirk, marine engineer, died in Edinburgh, 1941.

MIRKMYRE. Local. Ade Merkmyre had a remission for his part in burning the town of Dunbartane, 1489 (*Lennox*, II, p. 133).

MIRRILAW. Local, perhaps from Merrylee near Cathcart. George Mirrilaw in Tofts of Douglas, 1656, and four more of the name (*Lanark CR.*).

MIRRLEES. A variant of MERRILEES, q.v.

MIRTLE. A surname recorded in Galashiels. Perhaps a form of Martel, diminutive of Martin. The name is found in England in 1273 as Mertel, Martyll in 1379, and Martill in 1574.

MIRYLEES. *See under* MERRILEES.

MISCAMPBELL. Now a rare surname. It has been suggested that it may be "an Irish (Ulster) corruption of MACCAMPBELL." The Maccampbells of Ulster came from Galloway. It may be an error for M'Scamble recorded in the parish of Whithorn in 1707.

MISSONE. William Missone, trade burgess of Aberdeen, 1640 (ROA., I, p. 292), may have derived his name from Misson, a parish in co. Notts, England.

MITCHELL. From the Hebrew name Michael through the softened French form Michel. Michael was a very common baptismal name in many countries, and its introduction into Scotland was probably due to French influence. Robert Michael de Hyrmanston was a charter witness in 1438 (RD., p. 288), John Michell had a remission granted him in 1489 for his part in holding Dumbarton Castle against the king (APS., XII, p. 34), and John Mitsell held a land in Glasgow in 1496 (REG., p. 493). Andro Mitschell, cagger in Carnwath, Lanarkshire, 1524 (CBBC., p. 19). John Mytschell was a resident in Langside in 1555 (*Protocols*, I), and Thomas Michell had a charter of eight parts of the lands of Muirtoune in 1611 (RD., p. 504). Brodie (*Diary*, p. 294) refers to David Mitchell, bishop of Aberdeen, as "the Bishop, Michel of Aberdeen," and early instances of

Mitchell for Michael as forename are Mitchell M'Brair in Galloway, 1490, and Mitchell Marjoriebankis in 1572 (*Diur. Occ.*, p. 295). Michell is the regular spelling of the name in the Compt Book of David Wedderburne of Dundee. In Orkney Michael as a forename is pronounced Mitchell, and S. Michael's Church in Harray is locally "St. Mitchell's Church." Among descendants of Scots emigrants in Norway the name appears as Mitzel, and Andrew Mitchell, a Scot, introduced the steam-engine into Denmark, 1790. Mechell 1597, Meitchel 1661, Michell 1643, Michill 1567, Mitchol 1552, Mitschaell 1645, Mitschal 1521, Mittchell 1688, Mychell 1556, Mytchell 1602.

MITCHELLHILL. This was long a surname of consequence in Selkirk. Its first recorded holder was Sir John Mitchellhill, a "Pope's knight," chaplain and notary public in 1512. George Mitchellhill was bailie of 'Selkirk in 1590 (RPC., IV, p. 480). Jonet Mitchellhill or Michelhill was the wife of Andro Hart, the Edinburgh printer. Her will (dated 17 March 1606) is printed in the *Bannatyne Club Miscellany*, II, p. 238–241. Three of this name were members of the Scottish parliament for Selkirk between 1579–1667 (*Hanna*, II, p. 506). The name still recorded in Edinburgh (1942). The surname is derived from the small estate of Mitchellhill (= Michael's Hill) in Peeblesshire.

MITCHELSON, MITCHELLSON. This surname, meaning "son of Michael," was common in Newburgh in Fife in the middle of the sixteenth century as Michelson (Laing, *Newburgh*, p. 524). In Latin documents it usually appears in the Latin genitive form, e.g. in 1395 William Michaelis is mentioned as owner of a tenement in Innerkethyn (RAA., II, 44), Johne Michelsone had a safe conduct in England, 1398, Donald Michaelis was vicar of Lethnot in 1435 (REB., II, 48), and in 1439 we have mention of Robert Mechelson whose name is Latinized in the same document as Robertus Michaelis (CDE., 26). Henry Michaelis was a notary in Glasgow in 1454 (LCD., p. 176), in the following year John Michaelis appears as vicar of Kilbride (ibid., p. 253), and (another?) John Michaelis was chaplain in Brechin in 1464 (REB., II, 103). John Michelson was servitor of the earl of Douglas in 1408 (*Bain*, IV, 765), another John Michelson was granted a letter of safe conduct to travel in England in 1433 (ibid., IV, 1061), John Mychelson, a native of Aberdeen, obtained letters of denization in England in 1463 (ibid., IV, 1336), and Sir John Michelsone, a Pope's knight, was parson of Nether Ewes in 1474 (*Liddesdale*, p. 104).

Master John Mychtyson (cf. Michieson), notary public, witnessed a bond of manrent in 1475 (*Oliphants*, p. 20), Andrew Michelson was admitted burgess of Aberdeen in 1484 (NSCM., I, p. 31), John Michelsoun was burgess of Inverness in 1499 (*Cawdor*, p. 102), Andrew Michelson contributed towards buying lead for S. Nicholas Church, Aberdeen, in 1500 (CRA., p. 69), John Mitchelson was minister of Burntisland in 1617 (*Dysart*, p. 45), and Magnus Mitchaelson resided in Northmaven in 1633 (*Shetland*). Mechealsoun 1575, Mechelsonn 1541, Micchelson 1539, Mitchelsone 1683, Michaelsone 1640, Mitchellsoune 1654.

MITHYNGBY. Local. Robertus de Mithyngby sold his land in Glasgow, c. 1280–90 (REG., p. 197). His brother Walter and his daughter are mentioned in the charter.

MOANNACH. Simply a variant of the G. surname *Mathanach* (Matheson), which is pronounced Ma'anach. The interchange of *o* for *a* is quite common in Gaelic. In the parish of Creich, Sutherland, there is Moannach House occupied by a Matheson.

MOAR. A surname apparently confined to Orkney and Shetland. Probably from Mowir, "an old alternative name for the land usually styled Mobisland (anciently Mobisyord) in the rentals, lying in North Dyke" (*Clouston*, p. 33), or perhaps simply a variant of MOIR, q.v. Thomas Mor, tacksman of Marwick, 1492, and Alexander More, tacksman of Quvis in the same year (REO., p. 406, 411). Stewin Moir was juror on an assize at Housgarth, Sandwick, in 1553; and John Moir, juror on assize in Birsay in 1574 (ibid., p. 106, 136). William John Moar died in Edinburgh, 1939.

MOAT. Of local origin. There are two places named Moat in Dumfriesshire, one near Auldgirth, and the other near Lochfoot, Dumfries. James Moat was baxter in Dumfries, 1714, and Thomas Moat, wigmaker there in 1741 (*Dumfries*).

MOBRAY. A form of MOUBRAY, q.v.

MOCHRIE. Of local origin from some small place of the name. There is a Mochriesinch near Airdrie. A correspondent of the *Oban Times*, sometime ago writing from Larbert, said that so far as he knew, those who spell their name this way are related to one another. George Mochry is recorded in the parish of Slamannan, 1699 (*Torphichen*), and Robert Mochrie, portioner of Kirkintilloch, appears in 1663 and 1686 (RPC., 3. ser. XII, p. 133). James Mochrie, maltman, Edinburgh, 1666 (*Edin. App.*). George Mochrie was killed in action, June, 1941.

MODAN. A different name from MODDAN, q.v. It stands for M'Aodhán, i.e. Mo Aodhán (earlier M'Aedán), 'my Aedan.' In genitive it occurs in the name GILMODAN, q.v. See under AEDAN.

MODANE. William Moday or Modane, witness in Aberdeen, 1387, 1400 (REA., I, p. 177, 202); Johane Modane in record there, 1408 (CWA., p. 313); and Alexander Modane admitted burgess, 1443 (NSCM., I, p. 8).

MODDAN. This name appears in old records as Muddan, Mudan, and Muadan. It was the name of the Pictish ruler of Caithness slain by Thorkell Fostri (Ork. Saga, c. 5). The name occurs in an ogham inscription as Moddagni. The name of William Modan, who appears in Aberdeen in 1462 (SCM., V, p. 22) is probably of different origin. Cf. MODAN.

MOFFAT, MOFFATT, MOFFETT, MEFFATT, MEFFET. Of local origin from the town of Moffat in Annandale, Dumfriesshire. Nicholas de Mufet, a cleric, witnessed a charter by Walter, bishop of Glasgow, before 1232 (LSC., p. 55), and c. 1250–51 he appears as archdeacon of Theuidale (Kelso, 148, 149). In 1268 he was elected bishop of Glasgow, but died unconsecrated in 1270 (Dowden, p. 305). Robert de Muffet and Thomas Moffet, both of Dumfriesshire, rendered homage in 1296, and Robert was also one of an inquest on the lands of John de Hirdmanstone in 1303 (Bain, II, p. 198, 206, 431). Walter de Moffat was archdeacon of Lothian in 1348 (SCM., V, p. 246), and Robert de Moffethe was treasurer of the church of Glasgow in 1467 (REG., 391). In 1587 the Moffettis of the West Marche were included among the unruly Border clans (APS., III, p. 467). Robert Moffat (1795–1883), missionary in Bechuanaland, was father-in-law of Dr. David Livingstone. Maffit and Moffit 1686, Moffot 1520, Muffett 1583, Mwffett 1593.

MOGERISLAND. Of local origin from a small place of the name in Ayrshire. Ninian Mogerisland appears as a witness in Ayr in 1590 (Ayr, p. 116). Mongarslandburne is mentioned in 1691 (Retours, Ayr, 663).

MOGGACH, MOYGACH, MUGGACH, MUGGOCH. An uncommon Banffshire surname, from G. mùgach, 'surly.' James Mougache and James Mougache, elder, in Balnabruiche, Strathspey, and Patrik Mougache in Knocken [Knockan, near Botriphnie], were fined in 1641 for resetting outlawed members of Clan Gregor (RPC., 2. ser. VII, p. 489, 494). Thomas Mugah in Strathbogie, 1648 (Strathbogie, p. 86). Alexander Muggach, tenant in land of Grant,

1695 (Banff Rec., p. 173). Margaret Mougach in Drumuir is recorded in 1691 and Grissell Mougach in Belnatomb in 1707 (Moray). The name was found in Halifax, Nova Scotia, 1934, as Muggah.

MOIGNE. From OF. moigne, 'monk.' Marjory Moigne, a widow in Berwick, raised proceedings in a lawsuit in Edinburgh, 1291 (Burton, History of Scotland, II, p. 158), and Wautier le Moigne of Berwickshire rendered homage, 1296 (Bain, II, p. 206). Complaint was made in 1345 that the church of Kynneff had been given to Robert Moyne "then under twenty years of age" (Pap. Pet., I, p. 85). Walter Moygne, knight, witnessed a charter by David II in 1361 (REA., I, p. 90). The lands of Drum which belonged to John Moigne were granted to Alexander de Irwyne, 1389 (RMS., I, 774). Thomas Movgne was 'seriand' of Edinburgh, 1411 (Cambus., 94), and Walter Moyngne was charter witness in Aberdeen, 1426 (RMS., II, 55).

MOIR. A descriptive name from G. mòr, 'big.' The surname is an Aberdonian one, and in Aberdeen it is pronounced More, a spelling also found in early record. Robertus More was one of the burgesses in Aberden, 1317 (SCM., V, p. 10). Reginald More witnessed an Elphinstone charter, c. 1341 (Elphinstone, I, p. 6), and John More was a canon of Aberdeen, 1366 (REA., II, p. 58). Simon More was charged with being a forestaller in Aberdeen, 1402 (CRA., p. 383), and William More was tenant of Uthircloy, Ardmanoch, 1504 (ER., XII, p. 661). The name of the family of Moir of Stonywood was in the eighteenth century spelled Moer, More, and Moore. Mayr and Moyr 1538. Cf. also MOAR.

MOLESWORTH. Anneys de Mollesworthe del counte de Berewyk rendered homage 1296. The seal shows a parrot and another bird and S' Angn. . s. Emol (?) (Bain, II, p. 203, 544). Perhaps from Molesworth in Huntingdonshire.

MOLISON. See under MOLLISON.

MOLK. Adam filius Molk attested a deed between the abbot and monastery of Neubotle and Alexander de Drochil in the middle of the thirteenth century (Neubotle, p. 27). The father, Molk, is probably the individual who gave name to Molkiston now Milkieston near Eddleston, Peeblesshire.

MOLLE. Various individuals named "de Molle" appear in the twelfth and thirteenth centuries but their relationship is uncertain. They took their name from the territory of Molle, now Mow in the upper half of the parish of Morebattle, Roxburghshire. Liulf of

Molle appears to have lived in the reigns of Alexander I and David I, and his son Uctred had the town of Molle and the patronage of the church sometime before the year 1152 (*Kelso*, p. vi after Tabula, and 14, 144, 320). About the same date Vctred, the son of Liulf, granted to the monks of Kelso the church of Molle with its adjacent land and the common pasture of the town of Molle (ibid., p. 144), a grant confirmed by Herbert, bishop of Glasgow (ibid., p. 320) and by King Malcolm IV in 1159 (ibid., p. vi after Tabula). Anselm de Molle, who was also known as Anselm de Wittun, sometime between 1165 and 1190 made a gift of territory in Molle to the Abbey of Kelso (ibid., 13). About 1170 King William the Lion confirmed the earlier grant by Vctred de Molle of the church of Molle to Kelso (ibid., 12), and about 1180 Henry de Molle witnessed a gift by Galfrid Ridel to the same abbey (ibid., 368). Eschina de Londoniis, also known as Lady Eschina de Molle, seems to have inherited the possessions of Uctred sometime before 1177 (RMP., p. 74–76; *Melros; Kelso*). She married, secondly, Henry of Molle (*Kelso*, p. 114, 135, 146), and had four daughters, Margaret, Eschina, Avicia, and Cecilia. On the death of the last named the family appears to have become extinct in the direct line. In 1185 Gillem' de Molle witnessed Eschina de London's gift of the church of Molle, "as far as it belonged to her," to Kelso (ibid., 146). Alexander de Molle witnessed resignation of the patronage of the church of Killosbern (Closeburn) in 1278, and in the following year Radulf de Molle witnessed settlement of a dispute regarding the tithes of the church of Roberton (ibid., 34, 346). In 1490 Robert Mow resigned his lands into the king's hands, who, in the same year, regranted them to John Mow, Robert's brother (RMS.). Robert Mow was admitted burgess of Aberdeen in 1534 (NSCM., I, p. 53). In the sixteenth century the Mows of that Ilk figure in criminal trials (*Trials*, I, p. * 176, * 230, * 256, etc.), and in 1575 the laird of Mow was slain at the battle of Redeswire (*Border Minstrelsy*). Alexander Mow of the convent of Dunfermline is in record in 1555 (*Laing*, 633). James Mow in Dalkeith was summoned before the Privy Council in 1566 (RPC., I, p. 444), Robert Mow was a tenant of the Abbey of Kelso in 1567 (*Kelso*, p. 528), and in 1603 John Mow appears as a burgess of the town of Elgin and master of the sang (II, p. 447). Mr. John Mow was "maister of the Music Scule" in Dundee in 1628 (SCM., II, p. 44). Mr. William Mow, W. S., and his brother Mr. John Mow of Mains, obtained authority upon application to the Court of Session, 11th August, 1789, to alter the spelling of their surname from Mow to Molle, the original form of the name (*Nisbet*, I, p. 319).

MOLLESHOPE. A toft and croft in "moris, juxta exitum versus Wytelawe," held by William de Molleshope, was granted to the Abbey of Kelso, c. 1200–02 (*Kelso*, 148). Molleshope is "the piece of enclosed land (OE. *hop*) in the midst of a marsh" belonging to MOLLE, q.v.

MOLLINS. A Dumfriesshire surname of local origin from Mollance near Castle Douglas (Millance 1628, Mollance 1635, Mollandis 1678, Mollans 1698). There were also lands of the same name in Lanarkshire (Mollans 1617, Molence 1655).

MOLLISON, MOLISON, MOLLYSON, MOLYSON. The earliest references to this name, as with Malison, confine it to Aberdeen. Thomas Mollysone was town clerk of Aberdeen in 1589 (CAB., p. 355). Walter Molvsoun was retoured heir of John Mollysoun of Lachintullie, his father, in 1617 (*Retours, Aberdeen*, 152), Francis Mollison was member of parliament for Brechin, 1685 (*Hanna*, II, p. 506), and Mr. Mollyson was master of the Music School of Old Aberdeen, 1736. David Molvson (1789–1834), poet, was born in Fife. Mollisoun 1599, Molliesone.

MOLUAG. S. Moluag or Mo-Luag, a contemporary of Columba, was founder and patron saint of the church of Lismore, afterwards the see of Argyll. His *bachul* or crozier, now in possession of the duke of Argyll, was long preserved in the island of Lismore. The saint's name originally was *Lughaidh* (pron. Lua), and with the endearing suffix -*oc* and the honorific *mo*- it became Moluag (Latinized *Molocus*), i.e. 'my dear little Lua.' In 1249 a mandate was directed to the bishops of Glasgow and Dunblane to transfer the see of Argyll from the island on which it now is to some more secure and accessible place, the king of Scotland having offered to contribute to the expenses (*Pap. Lett.*, I, p. 251). Malooc filius comitis was one of the witnesses to a charter to Gyllethomas, 1199 (RAA., I, p. 262). In a contract made c. 1224–33 between the bishop of Moray and Lord Walter Cumyn regarding certain lands in Badenoch, mention is made of Gyllemallouock Macnakeeigelle, *nativus*, i.e. a bondman (REM., p. 84). The name of the dean of Lismore in 1251 was appropriately Gillemeluoc. John M'Ilmolnaage (read – uaage) in Crare (Crarare on Loch Fyne) is in record in 1672 (HP., II, p. 208), and Barbara M'Ilmoluag in Clengert, parish of Killean, is in record, 1693 (*Argyll Inv.*). Alexander Gilmaleoch appears in Newmyll, Perthshire, 1530 (RMS., III, 975).

MOLYSON. A variant of MOLLISON, q.v. David Molyson (1789–1834), a minor poet and journalist, was born in Monimail, Fife.

MONACH. Surname in Perthshire. G. *manach,* a monk, used as a personal name. Buchanan makes the Monachs a sept of the Macfarlanes (p. 92). Monach or Moynache filius Alpini witnessed a deed by Bricius de Ardrossane to Insula Missarum, 1271, and is witness to other Inchaffray charters, and also witness to one Montrose and four Atholl charters of the same epoch (*Inchaffray,* p. 92, 111, 289). Donald Monech McGilligowy and Johnne Monach his son, servitor to provost of Kilmun, were charged with violence to Dame Jeane, lady of Ardkinglas, 1596 (RPC., v, p. 322). A family of this name possessed the lands of Wester Finnick-Tennant after 1780.

MONCRIEF, MONCREIFF, MONCREIFFE. From the lands of Moncreiff in the parish of Dunbarny, Perthshire. The three forms are in use by different old families of the name. Matthew Moncrieff obtained a charter from Sir Roger de Mowbray of the lands of Moncrieff and Balconachin, which were erected into a free barony by a subsequent charter from Alexander II in 1248 (Seton, *House of Moncrieff*). John de Moncreif had a charter of the lands of Moncreif from Alexander III (*Nisbet*, II, App., p. 30). William de Monncrefe of Angus and John de Moncref of Perthshire rendered homage, 1296 (*Bain*, II, p. 199, 207), and Thomas de Mouncref was Scots prisoner of war taken at Dunbar Castle in same year (ibid., p. 177). John de Moncrefe, *dominus ejusdem,* is recorded a. 1320 (*Milne,* p. 5). In the middle of the sixteenth century the surname was prominent in Orkney records, and in the nineteenth century individuals of the name were distinguished in the church and in law. Monchrvf 1546, Moncref, Muncreiff, and Muncreiffe 1551, Moncrefe and Moncreif 1565, Moncreife 1456, Moncriefe and Moncrife 1650, Moncrif 1704, Monkreff 1616, Monkreth and Munkrethe 1542 (in English documents), Montcreffe 1456, Mouncref 1305, Muncrefe 1449, Muncreff 1488, Muncreif 1544, Muncrevfe 1432, Muncrif 1688, Muncrife 1555; Moncrief, Moncreiffe, Montcreif, Montcrif, Muncrefe.

MONCUR. Michael de Muncur, miles, witnessed a charter by Ysabella de Brus, c. 1237–48 (LAC., 40). Andrew de Muncurr, retainer of James the Steward, who had his lands restored to him in 1296 (*Bain*, II, 853), may be the Andrew de Monctour who rendered homage in the same year at Berwick-on-Tweed (ibid., p. 196). Robert de Muntcurt (? Moncur) was one of the Scottish prisoners taken in Dunbar Castle in 1296 (ibid., 873), Mariota de Moncur was domina de Rossy in 1302 (SCM., II, p. 316), the lands of Adam de Muncurre in Fife are mentioned in 1365 (RMS., I, 218), and Michael de Munkure held land in Angus in 1398 (*Strathmore,* p. 182). James of Mankorre had a safe conduct into England in 1424 (*Bain,* IV, 963), William Moncure, chaplain, "a native of Scotland," had license to remain there in 1465 (ibid., 1359), David Monquer was a frater of Cupar, 1500 (REB., I, 220), and Andrew Moncur of that Ilk gave his bond of manrent to the earl of Errol in 1541 (SCM., II, p. 268). The family of Muncur of Dundee "for several generations enjoyed a high reputation as armourers" (ALHT., I, p. clxxx), and in the *Exchequer Rolls* between the years 1444 and 1473 are many references to arms made by them, and an annual fee of xx lib. was paid to them as armour makers to the Court. Mancur 1614, Mancwr 1615, Mancurr 1667, Mowncur 1530.

MONEYDIE. From Moneydie in the parish of the same name, Perthshire. Magister J. de Monedy was rector scolarum of St. Andrews, 1285 (*Neubotle,* p. 49). Fynlaus de Monedy was present at perambulation of the bounds of Yochry and Achbrady, 1493 (RAA., II, p. 275), and as Finlai Monedy was one of assize of the lands of Aberkerdor, 1492 (REM., p. 246).

MONFODE. An extinct surname of territorial origin from the lands of that name on Montfode Burn, parish of Ardrossan, Ayrshire. The early generations of the family were vassals of the De Morvilles. The first of the name recorded appears to be John de Monfoit who witnessed a donation by Humphrey de Berkley de Mathers to the monks of Arbroath, c. 1158 (*Nisbet,* II, p. 246). John de Monfode had a charter from Robert I, c. 1320, of part of the barony of Trauirnent formerly belonging to William de Ferrars (RMS., I, 58), and also a grant of the barony of Skrauelyne and the lands of Robertstoun in Lanarkshire from the same king (RMS., I, App. II, 600). Agnes de Munfode had a charter of a piece of land called Hawthornesyk in the barony of Abercorn in 1340 (RHM., II, p. 40, 41) and David II confirmed a charter by Margaret de Monfoode in 1362 establishing a chapel in the church of Dunnanyne. Finlai de Monfode *de eodem* was juror in Irvine, 1417 (*Irvine,* I, p. 20), James Montfovd was killed in the battle of Fawsyde (Pinkie) in 1547 (*Retours, Ayr,* 3), and John Montfode of Montfode, said to have been the last of his line, appears in the list of Commissioners of Supply for Ayrshire in 1661. John Manfood, sometime in Donachadie, appears at Kirkcudbright, 1677 (*Kirkcudbright*). Robertson, writing in 1823 says: "Their memory has perished, nor is there a person now of the name known to exist, nor any name that bears a resemblance to it" (III, p. 294). Monfoad 1816, Monfood 1672, Monfoyde 1470, Montfoid 1600, Montfoyd 1547, Montfood 1669.

MONFRIES. A rare surname of local origin from some place unknown to me. Alexander Monfries was author of *Memorials of J. D. Carmichael of Arthurstone*, c. 1881.

MONIFUTH. Local, from Monifieth in Angus. Michael de Monifuth, hereditary lord of the Abthein lands of Monifuth, 1310 (RAA., I, p. 278).

MONIKIE. Matheus Monukye, witness in Aberdeen, 1491 (REA., I, p. 329), derived his surname from Monikie, a hamlet and parish in Angus.

MONILAW, MONILAWS. From Moneylaws near Branxton, Northumberland (in 1261 spelled Monilawe). Adam Monilaw appears as abbot of Nova Fernia (Fearn) in Ross between 1398–1407 (*Beauly*, p. 313; OPS., II, p. 436). In 1426 mention is made of the land of William de Monilaw in Lauder (*Soltre*, p. 51). Andrew and John Monelaw witnessed an instrument of recognition in 1456 (RAA., II, 106), and in 1477 Thomas Monelaw witnessed a notarial instrument (*Cawdor*, p. 63). George Monnilaws was tenant of Blackburn and Millands, 1763 (Craw, *Chirnside Common*, p. 18). A man named Mangelous (probably an error for Manzelaus (3 = guttural *y*) was charged with destroying salmon fishings on the river Dee, 1533 (*Trials*, I, p. 163).

MONIMAIL. From the town of the same name in the parish of Monimail in Fife. Henry de Monimel del counte de Fyfe rendered homage, 1296 (*Bain*, II, p. 204). A royal pardon was granted to John Monymelle alias Manymelle, 1407 (*Bain*, IV, 734), and Sir Alexander Monimeil was vicar of Premetht (Premnay), 1483 (REA., I, p. 316). Sir Alexander Monymele, "chapellane cessionare and assignay of executtouris of vmquhile Schyr George Andersone" in 1494 (ADC., p. 36), is probably Sir Alexander Monemeill, parson of Forbes in 1506 (CRA., p. 434). The obit of Alexander Monymell, rector of Forbes, is recorded c. 1550 (REA., II, p. 223). If the same person as the preceding he evidently died at a great age.

MONK. There are a number of Gaelic speaking families of this name in Benbecula and North Uist, and it would be interesting to know how long they have been settled in the Outer Isles (*Celt. Mon.*). The name is an Anglicizing of MACMANACHAN, q.v. Domhnall of Ile had a son, a monk, and it was in his time that Baile-an-Mhanuidh in Uist was given to the Church, i.e. in 1440 (M'Vurich, *Rel. Celt.*, II, p. 211). John Monachus rendered homage at Berwick, 1291 (RR.), John Mounk was admitted burgess of Aberdeen, 1486 (NSCM., I, p. 32), and Annas Munk or Munke in Dysart was suspect of witchcraft, 1626 (RPC., 2. ser. I, p. 425).

MONKLAND. Local, from Monkland in the Middle Ward of Lanarkshire. John del Munklond was employed as a woodcutter in 1302 at Linlithgow (*Bain*, IV, p. 366). Monkland was a possession of the monks of Newbattle Abbey.

MONKMAN. William Munkman, Scotsman, and others, complained in 1357 that their ships wrecked in a storm were plundered in Bamburgh and Tynemouth (*Bain*, IV, 10). Explained by Bardsley, Harrison, and Weekley as 'monk's man' (servant).

MONKTON. From a place of the name, now probably Monktonhall in the parish of Inveresk, Midlothian. Robertus de Munketun and Reginaldus, his brother, witnessed a charter by Adam filius Patricii de Crebarrin (now Carbery) in the thirteenth century (RD., p. 104).

MONORGUND. From the old lands of the name now the farm of Monorgan at Longforgan in the Carse of Gowrie, Perthshire. Perhaps now merged in MORGAN. Norrinus de Monnorgund laid claim to the lands of Monachkenneran in Kilpatrick, Dumbartonshire, c. 1270 (RMP., p. 184–203). He married Forveleth, daughter and co-heir of Finlay de Campsie, son of Robert de Redheuch (*Stodart*, II, p. 408). Gilbert de Monorgunde witnessed a charter by William, earl of Errol in 1452 (*Milne*, p. 22), and in the following year mention is made of the land of William Monorgound in Forfar (RAA., II, 101). A charter by Katharine Monorgounde of Balcasky is recorded in 1470 (*Pitfirrane*, 32). Robert Monnorgund who witnessed a confirmation charter to John Blare of Balgilloquhy in 1512 (RMS., III, 3798) may be Maister Robert Monnorgund who was parson of Banquhory in 1519 (SCM., IV, p. 197). Gilbert Monorgound of that Ilk was juror on an inquest in Perth in 1525 (*Athole*, p. 712), Thomas Monorgound was admitted burgess of Dundee in 1538 (*Wedd.*, p. 2), and Elizabeth Monorgund, spouse of James Henrisoun in Balquhormok, is in record

MONORGUND, *continued*

in 1585 (*Scon*, p. 230). William Monorgan was married in Perth in 1568 (*Sc. Ant.*, I, p. 169). Monorgand 1552.

MONREITH. John de Maynreht, one of the inquisition held at Berwick in 1296 which found that Lady Elena la Zuche held *in capite* certain lands in the sheriffdom of Dumfries, is doubtless the John de Meynrethe who rendered homage for his lands in the same year (*Bain*, II, p. 198, 216). W. Munreith was a witness in Ayr in 1647 (*Ayr*, p. 167). From the lands of Monreith in Wigtownshire.

MONRO, MONROE. *See under* MUNRO.

MONTEATH, MONTEITH. From Monteith in southwest Perthshire. Malcolm de Manetheth appears as a witness in 1237 (CMN., 17), Colin de Mentaghe, juror on inquisition at Perth, 1305 (*Bain*, II, p. 456) may be the Kilinus de Mineteth who was perpetual vicar of Kaledrach in the diocese of Dunblane in 1322 (*Pap. Lett.*, II, p. 222), and Johannes de Menetech is recorded in 1333 (*Theiner*, 253). William of Mentethe was arrested in Norwich in violation of the truce, 1396 (*Bain*, IV, 483). Thomas Mentheith held a land in Glasgow in 1496 (REG., p. 493), Johen of Mentecht was juror on an assize in Stirling in 1525 (SBR., p. 24), David Munteitht held a land in Glasgow in 1550 (*Protocols*, I), William Mwntheicht was a witness there in 1553 (ibid.), and Patrick Mynteith was a burgess freeman of the same town in 1611 (*Burgesses*). Manteeth 1653, Mentayth 1585, Menthet 1448, Mentheth 1495, Menynteth 1343, Montecht 1527, Munteith 1613, Muntethe 1605, Mwnteitht 1551, Mynteth 1475, Myntethe 1487.

MONTEIR. David Montier or Monteir was member of the Edinburgh Merchant Company, 1687 (RPC., 3. ser. XIII, p. 135), and Margaret Monteir is recorded in Edinburgh, 1698 (*Edinb. Marr.*). The name of Robert de Mountour who agreed to serve Edward I in France in 1297 (*Bain*, II, p. 242) is perhaps the same.

MONTFORD. Probably from Montfort on the Rille near Brionne, department of Eure. William de Mountfort witnessed a confirmation charter by William the Lion at Munros (Montrose) between 1178–98 (RAA., I, 76), and also witnessed a charter by Turpin, bishop of Brechin, within the same period (REB., II, 257). He appears again at the end of the century as de Munford and de Muntfort (LAC., 75). John de Muntfort witnessed a charter by Rodulph, bishop of Brechin, between 1198–1218 (REB., II, 258), and be-

tween 1211–14 he granted the lands of Glasker to the Abbey of Arbroath (RAA., I, 67). William de Mountfort was parson of Kynef, c. 1211–14 (ibid., I, 70). John de Montford, lord of Elstanford, granted half a stone of wax annually to the Abbey of Neubotle (*Neubotle*, p. 157), and Robertus de Munfort witnessed a gift of a stone of wax yearly to the church of Glasgow, a. 1233 (REG., p. 101). In 1252 John de Monteforti granted to Alexander de Monteforti, his brother, fifty acres of land in the territory of Elstaneford, called Dremmesfeld (*Laing*, 7). Alexander de Monteforti was sheriff of Elgin in 1266 (ER., I, p. 13, 33), Pieres de Montfort of Aberdeenshire, John de Montfort of Edinburghshire, and Robert de Montfort of Kincardineshire, rendered homage in 1296 (*Bain*, II, p. 210, 211), and Robert de Monteforti was rector of the church of Kynef, 1300 (RPSA., p. 120). A family of the name held land in the parish of Lonmay, Aberdeenshire, in the fourteenth century.

MONTGOMERY. The *Memorables of the Montgomeries, a narrative in rhyme* (Glasgow, 1770) referring to the origin of this name says:

"A noble Roman was the root
    From which Montgomeries came,
Who brought his legions from the war,
    And settled the same
Upon an hill 'twixt Rome and Spain,
    Gomericus by name;
From which he and his offspring do
    Their sir-name still retain."

The name is, however, of territorial origin from the ancient castle of Sainte Foi de Montgomery in the diocese of Lisieux in Normandy. "The name of this castle," says Freeman (*Norman conquest*, 1873 ed., II, p. 128) "enjoys a peculiar privilege above all others in Norman geography. Other spots in Normandy have given their names to Norman houses and these Norman houses have transferred these names to English castles and English towns and villages. But there is only one shire [Montgomeryshire in Wales] in Great Britain which has had the name of a Norman lordship impressed upon it forever." The first of the name in Scotland appears to have been Robert de Mundegumri who obtained a grant of the manor of Eaglesham in Renfrewshire. He appears as witness in a charter by Walter Fitz-Alan, c. 1165, endowing the monastery of Paisley (RMP., p. 5). He also appears as witnessing many charters to the abbeys of Paisley, Kelso, and Melrose between 1165 and 1177, as recorded in their chartularies. In 1354 an indulgence was granted John de Mongombro (REB., II, 395). MacCuimrid (in Gaelic),

Makgarmory 1512, Montegomorry 1437, Montegoumeri c. 1180, Montgomrie 1684, Montgomry 1557, Montgumery 1559, Montgumre 1529, Montgumry 1501, Montgumrie 1687, Montgumrye 1509, Montgurie (probably for Montgúrie) 1653, Monthgumry and Monthtgumry 1548, Mountgomrie 1661, Mowngumry 1482, Mundgumri 1170, Mundgumbry 1519, Mungumre 1521, Mungumri 1487, Mungumry 1559, Mungumbry 1500, Muntgomery 1672, Mwngwmry 1562, Mongumre 1592, Mongumrie 1574, and in an old version of the ballad of Chevy Chase Monggombyrry. In local pronunciation corrupted to M'Girmory.

MONTROSE. From the town of Montrose in Angus. Henry de Monros, chaplain, witnessed confirmation charters by Gregory, bishop of Brechin, c. 1218–22 (REB., II, 256, 270, 271), and Mestre Matheu de Monros, clerk, in Perth, rendered homage in 1296 (Bain, II, p. 200). John de Monros appears as perpetual vicar of the church of Tarwais (Tarves) in 1342 (RAA., II, p. 14), Nicholas of Munroos, a Scots prisoner of war, was discharged from Newgate prison in 1375 (Bain, IV, 237), Robert of Montrose, prior of Saint Serf's, was elected prior of St. Andrews in 1385, and another Robert de Monros was rector of Quylk or Quylt in 1392 (Cambus., 76, 77). Robert of Montrose, prior of St. Andrews, was stabbed to death by one of the brethren (Bower, ed. Goodall, I, c. 54).

MONYMUSK. From Monymusk in the parish of the same name in Aberdeenshire. A family of this name appears towards the end of the thirteenth century holding its lands from the prior of Monymusk as overlord. Its last male representative was Sir John Monymusk of that Ilk who died before 1400 (SN&Q., I, p. 187). Thomas of Munimuske granted a charter of the lands of Cuyle, c. 1285 (HMC., 2. Rep., App., p. 166). Malcolm de Munimusk was granted the hereditary custody of the Brecbennoch, one of the most precious relics of the early Celtic Church in Scotland, by the abbot and convent of Aberbrothock, 18 January, 1315 (RAA., I, p. 296). Henry Monimusk forfeited his lands in the reign of David II, but some time later in the same reign he had a charter of remission and a new gift of all his lands within the sheriffdom of Banff and Aberdeen (RMS., I, App. 2, nos. 1103, 1246). Michael de Monymusk petitioned for a canonry and prebend of Aberdeen, 1366 (Pap. Pet., I, p. 527). William of Monymosk had protection for a year in England in 1374 (Bain, IV, 218).

MONYPENNY, MONEYPENNY. "One thing is very certain, this surname has nothing to do with money generally, nor a penny specifically" (Bardsley); and Nisbet says: "Some conjecture that, upon the similitude of arms, the Monypennies are originally from the dauphinates in France." According to the author of The Norman people a Roger Magnepeine is in record in Normandy, c. 1180–95. The name Manipeni and Manipenyn occurs in the English Hundred Rolls (c. 1272). Thomas, prior of St. Andrews, c. 1200–11, gave Richard Monipenie "terram de Putmullin [Pitmilly] quam Malisius tenuit" (Sibbald, Fife, 1803, p. 348). This is probably the first record of the name in Scotland. In 1263 John, son and heir of Richard Monipennie, granted a charter of Mirton to Nichol of Milton (Stephens, Inverkeithing, p. 125). John Manipeny of Fife who rendered homage, 1296, is probably John Monipeny who served on an inquest at St. Andrews, 1303 (Bain, II, p. 209, 346). John Monypeny, who witnessed donation of the land of Quilt in the sheriffdom of Peebles, 1328 (RHM., I, p. 36), is probably John de Monypeny who had (c. 1347) a charter of the lands of Petmolin, which had pertained to the said John's ancestors (RPSA., p. 404–405). William Monypeny, rector of the church of Cambuslang, founded a chaplainry in the chapel of S. Mary of Cambuslang, 1380 (RMS., I, 646). John de Monypenny, dominus de Petmuly, was juror on inquest at Carnconane, 1409 (RAA., II, 49), John Monypeny, a Scotsman, is mentioned in England, 1447, and in the same year William of Menypeny had a safe conduct to travel there (Bain, IV, 1199, 2000). Nicol Monypenny was vicar of Murhous (Murrees) in 1470 (RAA., II, 189), and in the same year William Manypeny, prior of the priory of Portencok (Portmoak in Kinrossshire), had safe conduct into England (Bain, IV, 1390). Kentigern Monepenny was dean of Ross, 1546 (OPS., II, p. 616). Isabel, a daughter of the house of Pitmilly, was mother of Cardinal Beaton (Herkless, Cardinal Beaton, p. 59). Dr. Joseph Robertson informed Lower (Patronymica Britannica) that "about the year 1450 certain lands in Stirlingshire were erected into the barony of Monypenny, and their owner began to style himself 'de eodem' or 'of that Ilk.'" Moniepennie 1662, Monipenni 1490, Moniepennve 1611, Monupenne 1637, Mony Peny 1562. Monepennye.

MONZIEVAIRD. From Monzievaird in Perthshire. Andrew of Moneyvard was one of the jurors on an inquest on the lands of Aldy in 1432 (Athole, p. 707).

MOODIE, MOODY, MUDIE. Perhaps from OE. modig, courageous. Johannes Modi served on an inquest made at Peebles in 1262 (APS., I,

MOODIE, MOODY, MUDIE, *continued*

p. 101; *Peebles*, 5). William Mudy, merchant, had a safe conduct to visit England in 1365 with four companions, and William Mudy, armiger, with two horsemen in 1367-8 (*Rot. Scot.*, I, p. 893, 919). Sorlet, rector of Assend (Assynt) witnessed the charter of Bishop William (Mudy) to his brother-german Gilbert Mudy in 1455 (RMS., II, 1404). Thome Mwdy and Robert Mwdy appear in Brechin in 1450, the former held land there in 1461, and in 1496 John Mwdy held land there (REB., I, 158; II, 139, 274). Mudy occurs in Perth in 1499 (*Methven*, p. 33), William Mwdye was chamberlain of Orkney in 1563 (ER., XIX, p. 231), and Robert Mudie had a charter of part of the lands of Maistertoun in 1600 (RD., p. 496). The direct line in Forfarshire ended on the death of John Mudie of Pitmuies in 1876 (*Stodart*, II, p. 216). George Mudy was enrolled burgess of Dundee in 1576 (*Wedd.*, p. 22), and a burial place for Mudies was erected there in 1602 (Thomson, *Dundee*, p. 395). Muddie 1622, Mwddie 1552, Mude 1569, Mowdie 1575.

MOON. From NF. *(de) Mohun*, an ancient barony near St. Lo in Normandy. The *Itinéraire de la Normandie*, speaking of the place whence the Mohuns derived their name, says: "Masseville appelle ce bourg Moon." In the Roll of Carlaverock (A. D. 1300) John de Mohun is called John de Mooun (Nicholas's ed., p. 18). George Moon, changekeeper in Kilspindie, and James Moon, his son, are mentioned in 1711 (DPD., II, p. 280), and Henry Moon in Fordie, 1722 (*Dunkeld*).

MOONLIGHT. Most probably of local origin from Munlichty in Angus. Thomas Moonlight (1833-1899), sixth territorial governor of Wyoming, U. S., was born in Angus. The surname is very rare if not now extinct.

MOOR, MOORE. See under MUIR.

MOORMAN. From the occupation, an officer in charge of a moor. Thomas Mureman, younger in Kirkbryderig, "dilatit of the schutting and slaughter of deir," 1576 (*Trials*, I, p. 48). 1687: "Every man that keeps cattle upon the More, shall bring his cattle to the Moor-man to be branded" (*New Eng. dict.*).

MORAM. This surname found in the parish of Barry, in Angus, is a variant of MORHAM, q.v.

MORDINGTON, MORTHINGTON. Of territorial origin from the old barony of the same name in Berwickshire, the 'tun' of a Saxon named Mordyn, Mording, or Morthing. William de Mordington, the first recorded of the name, appears soon after 1200 as a vassal of the prior of Durham (*Raine*). William de Morthinton held part of the vill of Lamberton, c. 1235, was chancellor of Scotland in the reign of Alexander II, and witnessed the deed of sale of Adam, son of Thurkill, to the prior of Coldingham, c. 1240 (*Raine*, 337). He bestowed a fishing-water in the Tweed called Schipwel upon the Priory of Coldingham, and in 1249 was one of the twelve knights appointed to ascertain the laws of the marches between the two kingdoms (APS., I, p. 413). He and his son, Sir Peter de Mordingtoun, are frequent witnesses to Coldingham charters (*Raine, App.*). Petrus de Morthington, miles, filius quondam domini Willelmi de Morthington, who granted to Simon de Baddeby a toft and croft in the town of Lambirtoun, c. 1270 (BNCH., XVI, p. 334) is probably the Petrus de Mordington who rendered homage in 1291 (*Bain*, II, 508). Agnes de Morthingtone resigned the lands of Gillandristone in the Garuiache in 1321 (RMS., I, 84). Walter de Morthingtoun had a charter of the barony of Crossebie in the sheriffdom of Berwick from Robert I (RMS., I, App. II, 273). The family appears to have ended in an heiress, the afore-mentioned Agnes, daughter of Sir Peter de Mordingtoun, who married Henry de Halyburton (BNCH., XVI, p. 317-318). Morthingstone 1271, Murthynton.

MORE. A variant of MUIR, q.v.

MOREBATTLE. From the village of Morebattle in the parish of the same name in Roxburghshire. Hugh de Merbotyl and Roger de Merbotele witnessed the grant of the church of Kilmaurs to the Abbey of Kelso, c. 1170 (*Kelso*, 283).

MOREHEAD. A variant of MUIRHEAD, q.v.

MORELAND, MORLAND. Local. There are places named Moreland (Kinross), Morland (Skelmorlie), and Moorland (Gretna).

MOREVILLE. The name of a great Anglo-Norman family which acquired vast possessions in Tweeddale, most of Lauderdale, and other lands in Lothian and Cunningham. Curiously enough, of their place of residence in Scotland, there is no record. Hugh de Moreville, the first recorded of the name in Scotland, was a lifelong friend of King David I, which probably accounts for the great territorial possessions of the family. Hugh became Constable of Scotland before 1140, founded Dryburgh Abbey and the monastery of Kilwinning, and died at an advanced age in 1162 (*Chron. Mail.*, s.a.). The name has been extinct in Scotland since the thirteenth century.

MORGAN. "It is remarkable that the name Morgan exists, or in historic times existed in Scotland nowhere else than in Aberdeenshire and among the Sutherland Mackays" (*Macbain*). "Clan Morgan was long the designation of the Mackays of the Reay country, and it is probable, though perhaps not demonstrable, that there was a close connection between them and the Aberdeenshire Morgans" (Watson, *Rosg Gaidhlig*, p. 246). The Pictish form of the name is *Morgunn*, with gen. *Morcunn* and *Morcunt*. The name exists also in Old British, Old Breton, and Cornish as *Morcant*, Welsh *Morgan*, and the *Morken* of Jocelin's *Life of Kentigern* (c. xxi) is a form of it. It comes from early Celtic * *mori-canto-s* 'sea-bright.' The founder of the Pelagian heresy was a British monk named Morgan whose name was Graecized as Pelagius. Morgrun, comes de Mar, 1214–49 (RPSA., p. 363). Morgund, son of John Abbe, 1204–11 (RAA., I, 72) appears c. 1239 as Morgund filius Abbe, a lay abbot (*Panmure*, I, p. cliv). Morgund de Glenesk, of county of Forfare, rendered homage, 1296 (*Bain*, II, p. 199). John Morgane was burgess of Glasgow, 1419 (LCD., p. 241), and John Murgounis, one of the tenants of Wester Micras (Mecray), 1539 (ER., XVII, p. 659). James Morgound in Gay was fined for resetting Clan Gregor, 1613 (RPC., XIV, p. 636). The name still exists in Aberdeenshire, and John Murgan was one of the Huntly Volunteers, 1798 (*Will*, p. 7). The Morgans appear to have spread down the East Coast as far as Fife, where the place name Ramornie (*Rath Morganaich*) means 'rath (of the) Morganach' (*Watson* I, p. 239).

MORGUND. *See under* MORGAN. As forename: Morgund Mathowson, tenant in Strathdee, 1527 (*Grant*, III, p. 70).

MORHAM. John de Malherb and Adam de Malherb obtained the manor of Morham in East Lothian about the middle of the twelfth century, and the family assumed their surname from it. Adam de Moreham had a charter, c. 1200, of the mill of Stanehous (*Neubotle*, p. 75), and Thomas de Moram witnessed grant of Balnebucht to the monks of Neubotle about the same date (ibid., p. 6). John de Morham filius John Malherb made an amicable agreement with the same monks regarding the watercourses of their respective mills, c. 1220 (ibid., p. 67). Sir John Moreham had as wife Ada de Coluyl and their son Adam de Morham confirmed his mother's gift to Neubotle Abbey, 1249 (*Neubotle*, p. 170). Herbert de Morham, Scots prisoner of war, was sent to Rockingham Castle, 1296 (*Bain*, II, p. 177). Thomas de Morham, senior, held

the lands of Kymbrigham (Kimmerghame), Berwickshire, c. 1315–21 (RMS., I, 5). The family ended in the direct line in an heiress, Eufemia, who married John Giffard of Yester in the reign of Robert I (RMS., I, App. I, 39; *Dalrymple*, p. xxxviii). John de Morham obtained the lands of Pannebrid in Angus from William the Lion, and the surname of Morham or Moram survived in the Barry district till within recent years. The tombstone of David Moram, dated 1656, is in the kirkyard of Monikie. Morham is also an old surname in the joint parishes of Larbert and Dunipace (*Jervise LL*, p. 382). About 1200 this John de Morham witnessed a grant to Cambuskenneth Abbey (*Cambus.*, 79), and c. 1220 he confirmed to the monks of Arbroath the patronage of the church of Pannebrid (RAA., I, p. 19). This John de Morham appears to have died without issue and was succeeded by his brother, Adam de Morham, who confirmed the grant of Pannebrid to Arbroath (ibid., p. 20–21). Adam de Morham was one of twelve knights appointed in 1249 to meet twelve from England to settle the law of the marches (APS., I, p. 413). Henry de Moreham witnessed a charter by Randulf de Strathphetham, c. 1222 (REB., II, 3), and John de Morame, clericus meus, witnessed the gift by Robert de Lundris, one of the illegitimate sons of William the Lion, of the church of Rothuen to Arbroath Abbey (RAA., I., p. 41). See MALHERB.

MORICE. *See under* MORRIS.

MORIN. *See under* MORRAN.

MORISON. *See under* MORRISON.

MORLAND. *See under* MORELAND.

MORNINGTON. Patrick de Morningtone of Lanarkshire rendered homage in 1296 (*Bain*, II, p. 206). There is a Morningtown near Abernethy, Perthshire, but this name may be of recent origin. The name of Peter de Mornington who rendered homage at Berwick, 1291 (RR.), appears as Mornigcon in Bain (II, 508, but in index it is under Morningtone).

MORPAT. Probably from Morpeth (c. 1210 Morpat') in Northumberland. Walter Murpac (perhaps miswritten or misread for Murpat) witnessed a charter of the church of Mernes to the church of St. James of Passelet by Peter de Polloc, c. 1177–99 (RMP., p. 98). Euphan Morpat appears in Biggar in 1643 (*Lanark CR.*).

MORPHIE. Of local origin, most probably from Morphie in the parish of St. Cyrus, Kincardineshire. Walterus de Morfy or Morffy

MORPHIE, *continued*

held land in Dundee, 1381 (RMS., I, 691, 779), Findelaus Morffy was witness in Auchleuyn, 1454 (REA., I, p. 274), and Effie Morphi appears in Dunfermline, 1562 *(Dunfermline)*.

MORRAN, MORREN, MORIN. Shortened from (MAC)MORRAN, q.v. Twelve persons named Morine or Moring are recorded in the Dumfries Commissariot Record (1624–1800), and John Morring of Morringtoune appears in 1630. Hew Morrane in Newbigging of Carnwath is recorded in 1667 *(Lanark CR.)*, and Nathaniel Morren was minister of North Church, Greenock *(Fasti,* v, p. 378). The name also appears in record as Morren, Morin, and Murren.

MORREHAT. Morrehat, juror in an arbitration in Fife, c. 1128, "vir venerande senectutis et Hiberniensis" (RPSA., p. 118). Reeves says probably = Muircheartach. The episcopal residence of Inchmurthach in the southern extremity of St. Andrews parish is called in an instrument Inchmurahat (RPSA., p. 179; Reeves, *Culdees,* p. 248n). Cf. Monehat, *n* for *rr.*

MORRELL. An old Yorkshire family name, represented in other parts of England in the thirteenth century *(Guppy,* p. 430). It is territorial, from Morel in Normandy. Symon Morellus witnessed gift of the church of Molle to the Abbey of Kelso, c. 1190 *(Kelso,* 147).

MORRICH. Andrew Morrich in Kiltearn, 1672, derived his name from G. *Moireach* or *Moirreach* (for *Moireabhach),* a Moray man.

MORRIESON. A form of MORRISON, q.v.

MORRIS, MORICE, MORRICE. Forms of Maurice (from Lat. *Mauricius,* 'moorish,' the name of a saint martyred in 286 A. D.). The name was introduced into Britain by the Normans among whom it was popular. Arthur Mauricius witnessed a charter by the earl of Levenax, 1364 (HP., IV, p. 16). Gilbert Morice or Moris held a tenement in Irvine, 1540 *(Irvine,* I, p. 167, 168), and in 1565 Robert Morese was a tenant on lands of the bishop of Moray (REM., p. 433). James Morriss was a charter witness in Brechin, 1512, and John Moreiss is recorded in 1548 (REB., II, 169, 200). Malcum Moreis was admitted burgess of Aberdeen, 1559 (NSCM., I, p. 66), and John Moreis is recorded in Wester Innergowry, 1585 *(Scon,* p. 229). John Moreis was retoured heir of John Dotchoun, portioner of Corshill, Kilwinning, 1633 *(Retours, Ayr,* 291), and David Moreis appears as coal grieve in Bogie in 1680 (RPC., 3. ser. VI, p. 587). Alexander

Morrice was appointed schoolmaster of Fettercairn in 1674, and David Mores died there in 1696 *(Jervise,* I, p. 251). James Morrice from Monquhitter, Aberdeenshire, was killed in the first Great War *(Turriff).* Moreis 1656, Moress 1552, Morise 1511, Morries 1670, Morys 1497, Moryse 1508.

MORRISON, MORISON, 'son of Maurice.' See MORRIS. In Latin documents the name appears in the genitive *Mauricii* or *Moricii,* e.g. Andrew Mauricii, notary public, 1450 (REB., I, 133), and John Moricii, burgess of Glasgow, 1480 (LCD., p. 255). Andreas Morison, licenciate in law in St. Andrews, 1463 (REB., II, 106). Nicol Morysone witnessed sasine in favor of Adam Crechtoun of Ruchtven (i.e. Ruthven), 1501 *(Bamff,* p. 39). Alan Morsoun held land in Glasgow, 1503 *(Simon,* 53), Wyl Morison was tenant of land of Barrachine, 1520 *(Rental),* Patrick Morisone was a priest in Aberdeen 1522 *(Home,* 45) and Thomas Moresoun was witness in Scone, 1570 *(Scon,* p. 212). Phillane Morieson was burgess freeman of Glasgow *(Burgesses).* George Moreson was bailie of Aberdeen, 1639, and payment was made to Patrick Moorson there in same year (SCM., v, p. 153, 155). William Alaster Moirson in Substerbraell, Caithness, is recorded in 1662 *(Caithness).* In the records of the Scots Guard in France in sixteenth century the name is spelled Maurieon. Moorisone 1682, Moresone (in Kirkcaldy) 1540, Moresoune 1595, Moriesone 1665, Moriesoun 1612, Morisoune 1562. See also MURISON. (2) In Lewis and elsewhere in the West Highlands this name is said to have displaced G. *Mac Gille Mhuire,* 'son of the servant of (the Virgin) Mary.' From this comes Macgillimore, Macgilmore, Macgilvory, MacIlvory, and Mackilmore. John Morrison was the author of *Dain spioradail,* 1828, and Iain Morrison, the poetic blacksmith of Rodel, died in 1852. See under O'MUIRGHEASAIN.

MORTHINGTON. A variant of MORDINGTON, q.v.

MORTHLAND. Of local origin from a place of the name probably in Ayrshire. I have not been able to find it. It may be the Merchland near Eglinton of Timothy Pont's map of Cvninghamia. Joannes Murthlane in Cavenmylne is in record, 1662 *(Inquis. Tut.,* 874), and Joneta Murchland and Agneta Murchland were retoured heirs of John Murchland in Caven Milne, their grandfather, in lands in the parish of Kilwinning, 1671 *(Retours, Ayr,* 574). Archibald Murchland and Johne Murchland in Cutswray, 1666 *(Corsehill,* p. 69), Robert Murchland, surveyor in Irvine, 1689 (RPC., 3. ser. XIV, p. 445), and Archibald

Murchland in Little Corshill, 1704 (*Corsehill*, p. 202). Charles Morthland was first professor of Semitic languages in Glasgow University (1709). Agnes Murkland in Sanquhar, 1798 (*Dumfries*). The name Martland, recorded in Girvan, 1734, is probably another spelling. Murchlan 1686, Murchlane 1678.

MORTIMER. This surname is derived from the barony of Mortemer (Latinized *Mortuum Mare*) in the arrondissement of Neufchatel-en-Bray, Normandy, which name again is a modified form of the name given to the North Sea (*Oceanus septentrionalis*) by the Cimbri. Pliny in his *Historia Naturalis* (IV, c. 27) mentions that Philemon (a geographer of whom nothing is known), who may have derived his knowledge from traders, says the Cimbri call the North Sea *Morimarusa*, that is the "dead sea," as far as the promontory of Rubeas (*Philemon Morimarusam a Cimbris vocari, hoc est mortuum mare, usque ad promontorium Rubeas*). The name is Celtic. The first part is *mori*, a neuter i-stem (Stokes, *Urkeltischer Sprachschatz*, p. 217), Old Irish *muir*, found also in the latter part of the name of the Aremorici ("those who live by the sea"), the old name of the inhabitants of Brittany. The second part of the name is *marvo-s*, "dead," (ibid., p. 203), Irish and Gaelic *marbh*.

The first of the name recorded in Scotland is probably William de Mortimer who sometime after 1165 witnessed King William the Lion's confirmation of the charter of Philip de Euermel to Neubotel (*Neubotle*, 126), and as William de Mortuo Mari witnessed Radulf de Clere's gift of the church of Caledoure to the Abbey of Kelso, c. 1170 (*Kelso*, 348). He was taken prisoner in 1174 at Alnwick along with the king (*Bain*, II, p. 117), but apparently soon afterwards released as he appears as witness in a charter of King William to the Abbey of Arbroath, c. 1178–82 (RAA., II, 535), and c. 1200 he witnessed the gift of the churches of Camsi (Campsie) and Altermunin to the Abbey of Kelso (*Kelso*, 226). About the year 1210 Roger de Mortuo Mari witnessed the confirmation charter by William the Lion of the church of Trauernent (Tranent) to the monks of Holyrood (LSC., 38), and between 1200 and 1214 he witnessed a confirmation by the same king in favor of Arbroath (RAA., I, 93 *bis*). About 1225 this Roger also witnessed the confirmation by Alexander II of his father's grant of right of a fair, etc., to the bishop of Glasgow (REG., p. 113). Walter de Mortuo Mari is mentioned c. 1200 as "tunc decanus ecclesie Glasguensis" (*Kelso*, 148), Hugo de Mortuo mari, prior of May, before 1214 (*Melros*, 53) witnessed a

gift of five acres of land called "elwaldescaleslonigge" in the territory of Stainthon to the Abbey of Melrose, John Mortymar was burgess of Dundee in 1406 (REB., II, 12), and George Mortimuir was retoured heir of Captain John Mortimuir of Glencat, Aberdeenshire, in 1695 (*Retours, Aberdeen*, 496). The Mortimers disappeared as landlords in Aberdeenshire in the first half of the seventeenth century, and the last in direct line of Mortimer of Auchinbady, an old Banffshire family, died in 1716 leaving two heiresses.

"Mortimer's Deep" is the name given to the passage between the mainland and St. Colm's Inch in the Firth of Forth. The legend told to account for the name relates that Alan Mortimer, lord of Aberdour, bequeathed a tract of land near Aberdour to the monks on condition of his body being buried within the hallowed precincts of Inchcolm. "The monks carrying his corps," says Sibbald, "in a coffin of lead, by barge, in the night time, to be interred within their church, some wicked monks did throw the samen in a great deep, betwixt the land and the monastery, which to this day by the neighbouring fishing-men and salters is called Mortimers Deep" (*History of the sheriffdoms of Fife and Kinross*, 1803, p. 92). Mertimer 1702, Mortymer 1471.

MORTON. (1) Of local origin from Morton in Dumfriesshire. Hugh de Mortuñ, prior of May, c. 1204–11 (RAA., I, 47). William de Mortun who witnessed a grant of the churches of Trauerflat and Dungray to the Abbey of Kelso in 1266 (*Kelso*, 345), may be W. de Mortuñ, rector of the church of Dunbenauch, 1269 (RPSA., p. 174). Thomas de Mortoun held the mill of Mortoun, Dumfriesshire, 1376 (RHM., I, p. lvii), and John de Mortoun was provost of the Collegiate Church of Bothevile, 1413 (REG., 323). (2) Of territorial origin from the lands of Myrton or Myretoun, afterwards Morton, in the parish of Kemback, Fife. The Myretons, Myretouns, or Mortons of Cambo were an old and considerable family in Fife, who took their surname from these lands (*Stodart*, II). The family "are said to have derived their name from an ancestor in the fourteenth century, who held office as *mair* of the barony of Crail, and whose own lands were designated Mairtoun. But it is more probable that the family were named from the character or condition of their lands — Myretoun being a corrupt form of Muirtown" (*Crail*, p. 9). William de Myrton, *dominus ejusdem*, appears in record in 1361. Malcolm de Myrtoun witnessed resignation by Sir David de Wemyss of land in Fife, 1373 (*Wemyss*, II, 15). Master Thomas of Mirton, chaplain of the king of Scots, 1422 (*Bain*, IV, 912, 922),

MORTON, *continued*

is doubtless Thomas de Myrtone (Myretoun, or Myrton) who appears between 1429 and 1446 (*Soltre*, p. 298; REB., I, 56, II, 23; REG., 348, 349; *Bain*, IV, 1051). Thomas Myrtone was archdeacon of Aberdeen, 1514 (REA., II, p. 310), and Hector Myrtoune "cheplan of the Magdalin altar," Aberdeen, 1559 (CRA., p. 324). Alexander Morton (1820–1869), inventor of machinery for pointing, tempering and grinding steel pens, was born in Darvel, Ayrshire. Mireton 1431, Mortein and Martein 1694, Mortown 1598, Myrtoun 1584, Myrtoune 1544.

MOSCROP, MOSCROPP. John dictus Moscrop was witness to "instrumentum de creatione abbatis" in 1326 (RMP., p. 10). John Moscrop was burgess of Jedworth in 1426 (*Melros*, p. 533), Patrick Moscrop, witness at Crunzeltoun, 1461 (*Laing*, 145), and Andrew Moscrop was provost of the town in 1558 and sheriff of Roxburgh "in hac parte" (ER., XIX, p. 439). John Moscrop was bailie and burgess of Jedburgh in 1647 (*Inquis.*, 331), and juror on a retour of special service in Duns in 1672 (*Home*, p. 194). John Mosscropt is recorded in Blaiklaw in 1696 (*Peebles CR.*), and Alexander Moscrop in Bartelshill in 1730 (*Lauder*). Moscrope 1658.

MOSES. A form of MOYSES, q.v.

MOSLIE. Most probably a variant of Moseley, of local origin from Mossley in Yorkshire. Thomas Moslie, indweller in Leith, 1698 (*Edinb. Marr.*). David Moslie is recorded in the parish of Sanquhar, 1719.

MOSS. Of local origin from residence beside a moss or marsh. Gregory de Moss was tenant of the earl of Douglas in Louchurde, 1376 (RHM., I, p. xlvii, II, p. 16). James Mose in Kelso, 1567 (*Kelso*, p. 525), James Moss, mealmaker in Ridpeth, and John Mosse, in Darnick, 1662 (RRM., II, p. 7, 39). (2) The Orcadian surname of Moss is derived from the farm of Moss in the parish of Holm.

MOSSMAN, MOSMAN, MOSSMANN. Thomas Mosman witnessed a charter by Stephen Flemyng, Master of the Hospital of Soltre, in 1426 (*Soltre*, p. 52), and Andrew Mossman was tenant of Stobo in 1534 (*Rental*). John Mossman was clerk of the diocese of Glasgow in 1541 (*Home*, p. 252), Patrick Mosman was notary and burgess freeman of Glasgow in 1601 (*Burgesses*), and John Mossman was burgess of Paisley in 1550 (*Protocols*, I). Allan Mosman was a landowner in the county of Roxburgh in 1532, and in the sixteenth century there were burgesses, notaries, and gold-

smiths of the name in Edinburgh (*Stodart*, II, p. 354). William Mosman was beheaded for manslaughter of Ralph Weir in 1532 (*Trials*, I, p. * 159).

MOSYN. Gilbert Mosyn in Roxburghshire who rendered homage in 1296 (RR.) probably derived his name from Mousen near Bamburgh, Northumberland.

MOTHERWELL. Of local origin from Motherwell in Lanarkshire. John de Motherwell was one of the witnesses to the agreement between Alexander II and Henry III of England in 1244 (*Sc. Ann.*, p. 356). Adam de Modervale of the county of Lanark rendered homage in 1296 (*Bain*, II, p. 212). Valter de Modirwall was clerk of the diocese of Glasgow and notary public in 1415 (*Lennox*, II, p. 61), Aristotle Moderwell witnessed an instrument of sasine in 1540 (*Lamont*, p. 50), and Alester Modrell was burgess of Renfrew in 1596 (*Protocols*, x). Joannes Modderwell faber ferrarius in Rutherglen, 1681 (*Inquis.*, 6288). The grandfather of William Motherwell, the poet, spelled his name Moderel. Moderall 1586, Modervell 1607.

MOTTO. John Motto or Mutto, clerk of St. Andrews, 1557 (*Laing*, 666), was compiler of the Black Book of St. Andrews (*Lawrie*, p. 394).

MOUATT, MOWAT, MOWATT. Of Norman origin from NF. *Mont Hault*, Latinized *Monte Alto*, 'of the high mount.' The Monte Altos first settled in Wales, where Mold is a much reduced form of their territorial name. The first of the family in Scotland was Robert de Montealto who appears in the reign of David I, and is understood to have come from Wales. The family early rose to power and position in their new home, and in the reign of William the Lion they had acquired lands in Angus, including the lordship of Fern or Ferne (*Chalmers*, I, p. 531; *Cupar-Angus*, I, p. xvii). Robert de Muhaut and Michaele de Muhaut were witnesses to a charter by William Cumin, earl of Buchan, of half a mark of silver of the ferm of Inuermer, c. 1210–33 (RPSA., p. 231). William de Monte Alto witnessed a perambulation of the marches of the Abbey of Arbroath and those of Kynblathmund in 1219 (RAA., I, p. 163). Alexander de Mohaut, Mouhat, Mouhaut, Muhaut, or Muhauth, as his name was variously spelled, "clericus episcopi Brechinensis," appears frequently in the chartularies of Arbroath and Brechin as a charter witness between 1198–1218. Michael de Monte Alto, as sheriff of Inverness in 1234, witnessed a composition between the bishop of Moray and Walter Cumyn, earl of Mynynteth, concerning the lands of Kynkardyn (REM., p. 99), and in 1242 he witnessed a charter by Alexander II to Gylandris MacLod (REB., I, 4), and in 1248 he witnessed a composition between Freskyn de Moravia, lord of Duffus, and Simon, bishop of Moray, "super usuario nemoris et mores de Spyny et de Fynrossy" (REM., p. 114). William de Monte Alto was sheriff of Crumbathyn (Cromarty) in 1263, and in 1275 attested an agreement between Archibald, bishop of Caithness and William, earl of Sutherland (Bann. Misc., III, p. 24). Bernard de Monte Alto, miles, along with the abbot of Balmurinach (Balmerino) and several knights and nobles accompanied Princess Margaret to Norway, and on his return he with the abbot and many others were drowned in the wreck of their ship (Fordun, Annals, lxiv). In 1289 William de Muhaut was one of the signers of the letter to Edward I of England regarding the projected marriage of his eldest son with the Princess Margaret. In 1296 he rendered homage to the king of England (Bain, II, p. 169, 179, 195), and in 1305 he is referred to as "heritable sheriff" of Crombathyn (ibid., p. 458). Bernard de Mohaut of Peeblesshire, for bearing arms against the king of England at Methven (Meffen), "and feloniously slaying some of the king's liegemen there and taken on the field, and slaying Roger de Tany the king's vallet, in Selkirk forest, and burning and destroying churches in Scotland, was sentenced to be drawn and hanged" (ibid., p. 486). William de Monte-alto, one of the signers of the Scottish Declaration of Independence in 1320, was killed at the siege of Norham Castle in 1327 (Fordun, Annals, cxli). Mowats were settled in Ayrshire as early as c. 1400, and in the seventeenth century we find them in Edinburghshire. The name still exists in the three forms, and in Caithness and the Orkneys it is still not uncommon. In these last places it is pronounced 'Mode,' and to this local pronunciation is due the spelling Maath (Anders Maath of Houkeland, Shetland, 1597 — Goudie, p. 117). John Mowet was prebendary of the church of Guthrie in 1410 (Jervise LL., p. 371), but the name is now almost unknown in Angus, their first home in Scotland, but is still preserved in Mowat's Seat or Mowat's Cairn on Bruff Shank Hill (ibid., p. 278). Axel Mowat (1593–1661), one of the richest men in Norway and an admiral in the Norwegian-Danish fleet, was descended from the Mowats of Balquhally, Aberdeenshire, Meuatt 1578, Mohuat c. 1218, Mout 1624, Movat 1525, Mowait 1494, Mowaite 1545, Mowit 1686, Mwat 1521.

MOUBRAY, MOBRAY. A surname of Norman origin from the ancient barony of Mombray in Calvados. The first of the name in Scotland was probably Robert de Moubray who witnessed the gift of Staplegortoun to Kelso Abbey, probably in the reign of Malcolm IV (Kelso, 350). Philip de Moubray who sat in curia regis, 1208, was probably his son. Philip de Mubraj (j = i) appears as witness to a charter of the church of Boeltun before 1200 (LSC., 33), and about the same date witnessed charters by William the Lion (ibid., 30, 39, 44; Kelso, 412). Between 1204–14 he witnessed two charters in favor of the Abbey of Arbroath by Roger de St. Michaele and Umfridus de Berkelay (RAA., I, 81, 89), and a charter by William the Lion to Galfrid, steward of Kingorn (Laing, 3). With Galiena, his wife, he gifted the church of Muirkethin to the monks of Dunfermline, c. 1202–14 (RD., 94). He also attested King William's grant of right of a fair and his "firm peace" to the bishop of Glasgow, c. 1211 (REG., p. 38), and also witnessed the grant of Lympetlaw to the Hospital of Soltre, c. 1221–31 (Soltre, p. 25). Roger de Mubray sat in council, c. 1225, and was sheriff of Edinburgh, Linlithgow, and Haddington. For the adherence of the family to Baliol and the English interests a large part of their lands were forfeited (RMS., I, 590; App. II, 502, 835, 1098, 1127). William and Andrew Mobrey were merchants in Edinburgh, 1490 (Bain, IV, 1565). On the marriage of Robert Bertoun of Overbertoun with the daughter and heiress of John Mowbray in 1528 he was permitted by the Estates of Parliament to "be callit moubray and haue and bier þat surñem" (APS., II, p. 321a). Mowbra 1532, Mubbray 1428, Mvbrav 1648.

MOULTRIE. See under MOUTRAY.

MOUNSIE, MOUNCEY. A NF. family name meaning "at the Mount," OF. Monceaus < Lat. de Moncels (Zachrisson, Anglo-Norman influence on English place-names, p. 12). Thomas Monsy rendered homage at Berwick, 1291 (RR.), Maut de Mounceaus of Roxburghshire rendered homage, 1296, and William Monceux was juror on an inquest at Lochmaben, 1347 (Bain, II, p. 213; III, 1499). William Monceux, son of William Henryson of Loghmaben, was expelled from his lands for adhering to the English side before 1395 (ibid., IV, 464). Amand Mounceaux was warden of the Castle of Lochmaben in the end of the fourteenth century (ibid., IV, 260). James Monse near Lochmaben came in the king's will for destroying the woods of Lochmabane, etc., 1504 (Trials, I, p. 40*). James Muncie in Garrok to be examined for the Test, 1684 (RPC., 3. ser. IX, p. 579). Dr. Mounsey who sprung from the lowest origin in the vicinity

616

MOUNSIE, MOUNCEY, *continued*

of Lochmabane lived to become proprietor of the estate of Rammerscales (*Trials*, I, p. 40* n). James Muncie, tailor in Dumfries, 1686 (*Dumfries*).

MOUNT. Of local origin. There is a Mount near Dolphington, Peeblesshire, near Cupar in Fife, and near Strathaven, Lanarkshire. Roger of the Mount was juror on an inquest made at Traqueyr, 1272 (*Bain*, II, 34), and Alexander del Monthe rendered homage at Perth, 1291 (RR.). James Mounth was re-toured heir of James Mounth of Poffill of Strakynnes, his father, in the lands of Poffil of Strakynnes vulgariter nuncupatis Sawgreiff-islandis of Strakynnes, 1643 (*Retours, Fife*, 638). Marion Mount is recorded in Braidwood, 1622, and David Mount, burgess of Lanark, 1661 (*Lanark CR.*).

MOUREN. OIr. *Muirgen*, 'sea begotten, a mermaid,' OW. *Morgen*, 'sea-born.' Daughter of Hungus, king of the Picts. According to the Legend of St. Andrew she was the first person buried at Kylrimont (St. Andrews), and a chapel was built there in her honor (CPS., p. 185, 187).

MOUSWALD. From the village of Mouswald in the parish of the same name in Dumfriesshire. John Musfald, who appears as presbyter and notary public in 1440, is probably the Sir John Mousfald, chaplain, who had a dispute regarding a tenement in the Ratonraw in Glasgow in 1447–48 (REG., 344, 351). He appears again in 1468 as John Moussalde, vicar of the parish church of Kilmawaris. William Mowsfald, witness in Glasgow, 1504 (*Simon*, 96).

MOUTRAY, MOULTRIE, MUTRIE. The first of this name in Scotland was probably Adam de Multreve, burgess of Berwick, who swore fealty to England there in 1292 (*Fœdera*, I, p. 772). Adam de Multreve witnessed a charter of Grothill (now Greenhill, a suburb of Edinburgh) in the reign of David II, along with Henry Multrar, burgess of Edinburgh, who had the lands from Henry Braid of that Ilk (*Egidii*, p. 3–15). George Mutrich in Edinburgh was ordered to be burnt on the cheek and banished the city, 1530 (MCM., II, p. 105), and Henricus Moultray had a lease of lands of Gouillis and Lochhillis, 1543 (REA., I, p. 422). Wynnin Multray held a tenement in Irvine, 1542 (*Irvine*, I, p. 199). The General Register House, Edinburgh, is built on the site of the Moutray estate as shown on Gordon of Rothiemay's map of Edinburgh, 1647. General William Moultrie, gover-

nor of South Carolina, 1785–87, 1794–96, was son of a Scottish physician, Dr. John Moultrie.

MOW. *See under* MOLLE.

MOWAT, MOWATT. *See under* MOUATT.

MOYES. From ME. *Moise*, Fr. *Moïse*, 'Moses.' Moisy or Moyse the tailor held land in Brechin, 1267 (REB., I, 5). Henry Mowse, vicar ministrant in Glasgow, 1475 (LCD., p. 254), and Michael Mowse or Mous was merchant in Glasgow, 1591 (*Protocols*, X). Archibald Moysie in Westshiell, parish of Carnwath, 1624, and John Mosie, merchant in Lanark, 1690 (*Lanark CR.*). David Moysie was author of *Memoirs of the affairs of Scotland*, 1577–1603. Robert Mosie, hammerman in the Caltone, Edinburgh, c. 1685 (PSAS., LIV, p. 243), and the name of George Moos in Johnheaven, 1678 (*Edin. App.*), is perhaps another spelling. Recorded in Edinburgh, 1940. Cf. MOYSES.

MOYGACH. A variant of MOGGACH, q.v.

MOYHOUSE. From Moyhouse near Wester Kinghorn (Burntisland) in Fife (RD., p. 429). The land of David Movs is mentioned in 1517 (DBR., p. 56), and in the following year he appears as a witness under the name of David Mius (DBR., p. 56, 299). Eufamie Myhous, spouse of Thomas Westuod, is in record in 1549 (ibid., p. 257).

MOYLE. A descriptive name, from G. *maol*, "bald." Richard Moill was tenant of Uthircloy, Ardmanoch, 1504 (ER., XII, p. 661). Perhaps now merged in MILN and MILNE.

MOYNESS. From Moyness in the parish of Auldearn, Nairnshire, an early spelling of which was Motheys. William, thane of Motheys, was one of an inquest in 1295 (*Rose*, p. 30), and Alan de Mutheys is mentioned in 1360 (REM., p. 304).

MOYSES. A ME. form of Moses (in Chaucer, *Moises*). "Moyses," says Bardsley, "represents an English as distinct from a Jewish descent, and stands to Moses as Salmon does to Solomon." Nicholas dictus Moyses de Bondyngton made a grant to the Abbey of Kelso in 1307 (*Kelso*, 42), and as Nicholaus dictus Moyses, son and heir of quondam Ade dictus Moyses, resigned land and pertinents in the vill and territory of Bondyngtone into the king's hands c. 1318 (RMS., I, 9). William Moyses held land in Irvine, 1323 (*Irvine*, I, p. 123), William Moyses was witness in Aberdeen, 1483 and 1491 (CRA., p. 413; REA., I, p. 329), and Alexander Movses was admitted burgess there, 1440 (NSCM., I, p. 6). The surname is found through a long tract of time among the burgesses of Aberdeen, and is still current as Moses. Cf. MOYES.

MUCKART, MUCKHART. Of local origin from Muckhart near Dollar, Clackmannanshire. P(atrick) de Mukard, cleric, appears as a charter witness in 1250 (RPSA., p. 281). Adam Mukcart was juror on an assize in Stirling in 1521 (SBR., p. 11), and in 1545 Elspeth Mukkart was assaulted in the same town (ibid., p. 40). John Muckart was admitted burgess of Aberdeen in 1569 (NSCM., I, p. 69), and William Muckart was burgess there in 1596 (CRA., p. 133).

MUCKERSIE. From Muckersie, the name of an old parish now part of Forteviot near Perth. Henry Mukcarsie was a merchant in Edinburgh in 1655 (Edinb. Marr.). Recorded in Dollar, 1941.

MUDIE. See under MOODIE.

MUFFORD. Richard Mufford, esquire to the earl of Sutherland, 1366 (Rot. Scot., I, p. 902 b). Probably an Englishman.

MUGGACH, MUGGOCH. Variants of MOGGACH, q.v.

MUGY. Donald Mugy in Edinburgh, 1485 (REG., p. 447, 448).

MUIL, MUILL. Richard Mul attested the valuation of Kilrauoc and Estirgedeys (Easter Geddes) in 1295 (Cawdor, p. 3; Rose, p. 30). The name of John Muild, bookbinder in Edinburgh, 1638 (Edinb. Marr.), is probably the same name with accretionary d. There is a place Muil in the parish of Kirkpatrick-Durham, but there is no evidence of its being the source of the surname.

MUIR, MURE, MOOR, MOORE, MORE. From residence beside a moor or heath, ME. mor(e, moore. Thomas de la More was executor of the will of Dervorguilla de Balliol, 1291 (Bain, II, 535). Several of the name rendered homage in 1296: (1) Dovenal le fiz Michel More de Levenaghes. His seal bears a demon with man's head and cock's feet and spurs, S' Dovenaldi fil Michael. (2) Adam de la More and (3) Renaud del More both of the county of Are. The seal of Adam bears an eight-leaved flower, S' Ade de Lemor. The seals of Renaud bear (a) a hawk, and S' Reginald More, (b) a fleur-de-lys and S' Reginaldi More. (4) Gilcrist More of Ayrshire, whose seal shows a right arm with hawk on perch, . . . ilcrist Mor. (5) Reynaud Mor of Cragg' of Lanarkshire, and (6) Symon de la More of Thangarstone (Thankerton). Adam de la More and William de la More were jurors on the lands of Lady Elena la Zuche in Conyngham, 1296 (Bain, II, p. 216). Ade More who held lands

of Beltone in Berwickshire, in 1315–21 (RMS., I, 4) may be Adam More or Moire, knight, who witnessed charters by Bruce in 1328–29 (RHM., I, 35, 37). Elizabeth Mure, daughter of Sir Adam Mure of Rowallan, became queen of King Robert II, 1347. Adam of Mwre was juror on inquest in Kirkwall, 1369 (REO., p. 16). John Mvr of Enerothyll was witness, 1460 (Ayr, p. 35), and John Mur or Muyr was vicar general of the Predicant Order in Scotland, 1469–70 (Friars Ayr, p. 52; LCD., p. 183). Johannes Mur held a tenement in Glasgow, 1458 (REG., p. 392). Patrick Mur of Cloncard, a follower of the earl of Cassilis, was respited for murder, 1526 (RSS., I, 3386), Mathow Myrre was forspekar (advocate) for John Myrre in 1541 (Prestwick, p. 58), Malleta Mur, tenant in Oswaldesdevn, Dunbar, 1559 (ER., XIX, p. 404), and Isobell Moor of Carleton is recorded in 1760 (Kirkcudbright). The family of Mure of Rowallan became extinct in the male line in 1700. Sir William Mure, poet, John Muir, Sanskrit scholar, his brother Sir William Muir, Arabic scholar and biographer of Mohammed, and Sir John Moore were distinguished bearers of the name. Innes (p. 34) says: "The author of Zeluco and Sir John Moore added an e to the name 'for a difference.'" Moare 1650, Mur 1508, Muyr 1539, Mwir and Mwyr 1525, Mwr 1513, Mwre 1546, Mwyre 1538, Myre 1424, and in Sweden it became Myhr (Fischer III).

MUIRBURN. Of local origin from a place of the name. There is a Muirburn near Strathavon and another near Skirling. John Muirburne in Butterdaine, 1653, and James Murburne in Eymouth, 1674 (Lauder). John Muirburne in Fairneysyde, 1689 (RPC., 3. ser. XIV, p. 260).

MUIRDEN. From Muirden near Turriff, Aberdeenshire. James Muirden was member of the Huntly Corps of Volunteers in 1798, and James Morden was member of the Gartly Company of Volunteers in the same year (Will, p. 19, 24).

MUIRHEAD, MOREHEAD. From one or other of the many localities of the name in the southern counties, perhaps from Muirhead in the barony of Bothwell. The lands and town of Mureheid in the diocese of Ross are mentioned in 1576 (RPC.), but the surname is not likely to have originated there. The first of the name in record is said to have been Sir William Muirhead of Lachope, end of fourteenth century. Probably the same person as William de Murehede who witnessed a charter of lands of Cranshaws in 1401 (Swinton, p. xvii). Andrew Morheid was assizer at Lanark in 1432 (RAA., II, 65), David de Murhed, cleric

MUIRHEAD, MOREHEAD, *continued*
in diocese of Glasgow, is recorded in 1471
(REG., 395), Ricardus Mwreheid, canon of
Dunkeld, 1484 (RAA., II, p. 211) may be
Richard Murhede, dean of Glasgow in 1491
(APS., II, p. 270), Wilyame of Murehede is
recorded in 1484 (*Peebles*, 31), and Thomas
Murhede was parson of Lyne in 1504 (*Trials*,
I, p. *43). Thomas Mureheid, quarryman at
Dunkeld, 1507–15, appears in record as Moir-
hed, Moirheid, and Mored (*Rent. Dunk.*),
David Muirheyd was assizer in Gowane (Go-
van) in 1527 (*Pollok*, I, p. 258), and David
Mourheid was merchant burgess of Dumfries,
1668 (*Inquis.*, 938). In common speech pro-
nounced Murheed. Mooreheid 1624, Morheid
1691, Mureheid 1620, Muirhed 1513, Mure-
hed 1503, Muyrheid 1498, Mwirheid 1577,
Mwreheid 1484, Mwrhed 1493, Mwrheid,
Mwrhied, and Mwrheyd 1522.

MUIRHOUSE. John de Murhouse, dominus
ejusdem, witnessed a confirmation charter at
Lesmahagow in 1427 (RMS., II, 88), and in
1454 and 1487 George de Murhouse or Mur-
houss appears as witness in Glasgow (LCD.,
p. 176; REG., p. 453). John Meurhouis was
burgess of Glasgow in 1629 (*Burgesses*). Perhaps from Muirhouse in Dalry parish, Ayrshire.
Cf. also MURROES.

MUIRY. *See under* MURIE.

MULDONICH. G. *Maol* (earlier *Mael*)
Domhnaich, 'Sunday's servant.' John Muldoniche was tenant on lands in Menteith in 1534
(RMS., III, 1548), and Michaell Muldonycht
was tenant of Brairnahay in the barony of
Birnie in 1565 (REM., p. 443). As a forename we find it in Muldoniche McConochie
and Muldoniche McIlchreist in Glenlyon who
were fined in 1613 for resetting members of
the outlawed Clan Gregor (RPC., XIV, p. 633).
Myldoniche McNokeardie in Carnakalliche
was put to the horn in 1629 (RPC., 2. ser.
III, p. 46). See under MAEL-DOMHNAICH.

MULLIKIN. *See under* MILLIGAN.

MULLION, MULLIONS. Isobel Mullien in
Crieff, 1730, David Mullions, indweller in
Blair Strowie, parish of Arngask, 1753; and
James Mullion in Crieff, 1781 (*Dunkeld*). Cf.
Muling or Mulling in Perth Retours.

MULTRAR. A multurer was one who ground
or had grain ground at a particular mill, (2)
tacksman of a mill. The office was a very un-
popular one in the Middle Ages. Adam Multerer and Henry Multerer were burgesses of
Edinburgh, 1344 (*Egidii*, p. 4), and John

Multrer, bailie in 1360 (ER., II, p. 28). Robert
Multrere or Muterer had charter of lands in
barony of Lastalryk (Restalrig), 1365 (RMS.,
I, 200). Johannes Multrar was one of the
inquest on the marches of Kyrknes and Louchor, 1395 (RPSA., p. 3). Michael Multrer
was chaplain of Colmonell, Ayrshire, 1415
(*Ayr*, p. 9), James Multrar or Multrare was
burgess of Are, 1450 (ibid., p. 26, 28), and
Adam Multrar was burgess of Irvine, 1500
(*Simon*, 9). Mathow Multrar in Irvine was
charged with defrauding the king's customs,
1524 (*Irvine*, I, p. 35). A charter by John
Multrare of Markinch, Fife, is recorded in
1555 (*Pitfirrane*, 129). John Multrare of Sey-
field is recorded in 1514. Richard Multrare
was sheriff of Kinross, 1548 (*Gaw*, 40).

MUNCHES. Of local origin from Munches
in the parish of Buittle, Kirkcudbrightshire.
Margaret Munsies was examined for the Test
in Tinwald in 1685 (RPC., 3. ser. XI, p. 434).

MUNDELL. Of NF. origin. From Norman *de
Magneville*, De Mandeville, Lat. *de Magna-
villa*, "of the great town," a place in Normandy. The de Mandevilles, earls of Essex,
were originally de Magneville. Gilbert Man-
dewel was juror on an inquest held at Traqueyr, 1274 (*Bain*, II, 34). John de Mundeville of Wigtownshire rendered homage, 1296.
His seal shows a figure of a bishop holding
a cross, stars and scallop-shells on either side,
S' *Iohannis de Mondeville cl'ici* (ibid., p. 214,
534). Sir Henry de Mundeville also rendered
homage in 1296, and as Sir Henry de Munde-
wyl was juror on an inquest on the lands of
Lady la Zuche in Wigtownshire in the same
year (ibid., p. 215). Roger de Mandeville was
a competitor for the crown of Scotland in 1291
(Dunbar, *Scottish kings*, 1899, p. 84). Henry
de Mundeville made a gift of three acres
of his territory of Glengelt to the Abbey of
Dryburgh (*Dryburgh*, 186), and in 1297 was
invited by Edward I to go on an expedition to
Flanders (*Bain*, II, p. 232; *Documents illustrative of the history of Scotland*, II, p. 169).
Henry Monwyl witnessed a charter by Nicholas de Drunfres, burgess of the same town,
1394 (SCM., V, p. 251). Robert I gave Fergus
de Monda Willa half of the lands of Stran-
rever in the sheriffdom of Wigtoun (RMS., I,
App. II, 610). Master Simon of Mundeville
or Symon Mundevill (without 'of') had safe
conducts into England in 1407–8 (*Bain*, IV,
728, 761). Henry Mundwell was burgess of
Wigtown, 1498, John Mundville was notary
there in 1610, Robert Mundell was tenant
in the barony of Mousewall, 1673 (PSAS.,
XXIII, p. 74), and James Mundell was examined for the Test in 1685 (RPC., 3. ser.

XI, p. 433). Mundells are still numerous in Dumfriesshire. Mondevyl 1304, Munduail 1486.

MUNDIE, MUNDY. A surname in Longside, Buchan, in eighteenth century. Probably local, from the old lands of Mundy (now Munday near Aberdalgie), in Perthshire. Irish Munday is of different origin.

MUNGALL, MUNGAL, MUNGLE. From Mungall in the parish of Falkirk, Stirlingshire. William de Mongale del counte de Are rendered homage, 1296 (*Bain*, II, p. 210). Thomas de Mungale is in record between 1201–33 (*Soltre*, p. 14), and William of Munghale witnessed Elphinstone charters, c. 1340–41 (*Elphinstone*, I, p. 5; II, 221). Johannes Mungwale appears in Aberdeen, 1408 (CWA., p. 313), Thomas of Moungwele was clerk to Huchone Fraser of the Louete in 1429 (*Wemyss*, II, p. 61), and John Mungalle, a Scot, received letters of denization in England in 1480 (*Bain*, IV, 1465). John Mungwel and Robert Mungale were witnesses in West Lothian, 1485 and 1497 (*Binns*, 20, 25). Alexander Mongall was admitted burgess of Aberdeen in 1587 (NSCM., I, p. 80), James Mungall was a weaver in Edinburgh in 1622 (*Edinb. Marr.*), Robert Mungall is recorded in Dunnider in 1633 (SCM., III, p. 115), and James Mungall in Wester Lenhous in 1638 (*Inquis.*, 2360). The surname also appears corruptly as **MUNGAW**.

MUNGO. The popular name of S. Kentigern. Jocelin in his life of the saint explains it as *carissimus amicus*, 'very dear friend,' but the formation, says Prof. Watson, "is not clear to me" (I, p. 169). It still exists as a forename and surname. Cosmungo appears c. 1190 (REG., p. 89) as one of the witnesses to the *Diuise de Stobbo*, and Mungo appears in Burns's "Tam o' Shanter."

MUNKITTRICK. See *under* MACKETTRICK.

MUNN. From (MAC)MUNN, q.v. Sir John Mwn was procurator-fiscal of vicars of the choir of Glasgow, 1551 (*Protocols*, I). The song *Tho mo rùn air a ghille*, 'O, my love is for the laddie,' was composed by Ceit Mhunna (Catherine Munn, d. 1860), daughter of Hugh Munn of Tobermory, Mull.

MUNNIES. A current corruption of MENZIES, q.v.

MUNNOCH. Surname in Fife. A variant of MONACH, q.v. Robert Munnoch or Monach in Shirgartoune, 1686 (RPC., 3. ser. XII, p. 110, 165). Recorded in Edinburgh, 1941.

MUNNOCK. An old Strathblane surname, a variant of MONACH, q.v.

MUNRO, MUNROE, MONRO, MONROE. G. *Rothach*, 'a man of Ro,' or 'man from Ro.' "According to a tradition which may be substantially correct the ancestors of the Munros came from Ireland, from the foot of the river Roe in Derry, whence the name *Bunrotha*, giving *Mun-rotha* by eclipsis of *b* after the preposition *in*" (*Watson* I, p. 116). In the fourteenth and fifteenth centuries the name appears several times in record as 'de Monro,' showing that it was local or territorial in origin. The family at first were vassals of the earls of Ross. Robert de Monro had a charter from Robert I of Counetis in Strathspey and of the lands of Cupermakcultis (RMS., I, App. II, 60). George de Monro of Foulis witnessed a grant of lands in Badenoch, 1338 (SCM., IV, p. 126), and Robert de Monro was the first assured chief by charter evidence, 1341–72 (Skene, *Highlanders*, p. 417). Joh. de Munro, dominus de Foulis, witnessed a charter of the lands of Usuy in the earldom of Ross, 1463 (RMS., II, 801). Hugh Macdonald, the Skye seanachaidh, tells us that the Monros came into Scotland in the train of Margaret, daughter of Guy O'Kane who was married to Angus Og (HP., I, p. 20), but Dr. Macbain points out that "a clan in the east of Ross, before ever Macdonalds were earls of Ross could hardly have come as attendants on the bride of the lord of Kintyre in west Argyle" (Skene, *Highlanders*, p. 416–17). James Monroe, fifth president of the United States, promoter of the Monroe doctrine (1823), was fifth in descent from Andrew Monroe (d. 1668), one of the Scots prisoners taken at battle of Preston, 1648, and shipped to the colonies. Manro 1538, Monroo 1498, Munroy 1590.

MUNZIE. Of local origin, perhaps from Monzie near Crieff, Perthshire. There is also Moonzie near Cupar. In these names the 3 stands for guttural *y*, but this letter was sometimes pronounced as *s*, as shown by the spelling of Moonzie as Moonsie in the seventeenth century (Mackenzie, *Scottish place-names*, 1931, p. 184–185). Robert Mownzie was admitted burgess of Aberdeen, 1572, and John Munzie in 1592 (NSCM., I, p. 83, 70). Thomas Munzie was tenant in the barony of Leys, Aberdeen, 1640 (SCM., v, p. 228).

MURCHIE. Duncan Murchy, a follower of the earl of Cassilis, was respited for murder in 1526 (RSS., I, 3386). Kath. Murchie recorded in Watten, 1663 (*Caithness*). Robert Murchie, burgess of Irvine, 1664 (*Irvine*, II, p. 165). See MURCHISON, MACMURCHIE, and MURDOCH.

MURCHISON, Murcheson, Murchieson. An Englishing of G. *MacMhurchaidh*, 'son of Murchadh,' Englished Murdoch. Fowill Morthoison was burgess of Inverness, 1452 (*Invernessiana*, p. 122). John Murchosone was witness in Peebles, 1473 (*Peebles*, 24). Findlay Murquhasson and Neill Murquhason or Murquhessoun were tenants in Tiree, 1541 (ER., XVII, p. 614, 647). Alexander Murquhosoun and John, his son, were cruelly slain in Caithness, 1566 (RPC., I, p. 447). Johnne Murchosoun was reidare at Kintail, 1574 (RMR.) and in 1582 Donald Murchesoun was presented to the same church on the demission of John (OPS., II, p. 391). Ewander Murchieson of Octerteir took the Test in Rossshire, 1685 (RPC., 3. ser. XI, p. 417). Duncan Murchison in Achtatoralan and Donald Murchieson in Auchtertite appear in 1726 (HP., II, p. 324, 326).

MURDIE. A rare surname in Sutherland, perhaps connected with Murchison or Murdieson. William Murdie, M.A., M.B., of Stronchrubie, Assynt, died 1941. Perhaps from Murdoch through (Mac)Murdo, q.v.

MURDOCH, Murdock. Two Gaelic names, *Muireach* and *Murchadh*, of different origin, both coalesce and are hopelessly confused in this name. (1) *Muireach* in MG. *Muiredhaigh* (gen., M'Vurich), *Murreich* (Dean of Lismore), *Muireadhaigh* (1467 MS.), Ir. *Muireadhach*, EIr. *Muiredach* (for *Muirfedach*), Ir. Lat. *Muirethac-us*, and in Adamnan (V. C., I, 12) *Muiredachus*, 'belonging to the sea, a mariner.' From this comes Macvurich (*MacMhuirich*), q.v. (2) *Murchadh*, EIr. *Murchad*, from *mori-catus*, 'sea warrior.' From this comes Murchie, Macmurchie, Murchison, and Murphy (formerly in Arran). Murdac and Murdoc are found in DB. as names of landowners in Yorkshire, Sussex, and Oxfordshire. They were either Gaels or Norsemen of Irish descent. Murdac was dean of Appleby, Westmoreland, 1175. Walter Murdac, Morthaich, or Murdoch was a person of prominence in the reign of William the Lion and figures as witness in several charters, and other Murthacs or Murdaks are mentioned about the same time and in the following century. Murdoch, second duke of Albany, executed in 1425, is referred to in English records (in *Bain*, IV) as: Mordac, Mordake, Mordik, Mordoc, Mordok, Mordyk, Moreduc, Mourdac, and Murthak. William Murdoch (1754–1839), inventor of gas-lighting, was proclaimed a deity by Nassred-din, Shah of Persia, who believed him to be a re-incarnation of Merodach or Marduk, 'god of light.' Murdock is a less common spelling of the name.

MURDOCHSON, Murdoson, 'son of Murdoch,' q.v. Gilbert filius Mordaci (Latin gen.) was tenant of the earl of Douglas in the vill of Prestoun, 1376 (RHM., I, p. lxi), and John Murokosone or Murokison appears in the Douglas rental of Kilbochoke (Kilbucho) in the same year (ibid., I, p. xlvii, xlviii; II, p. 16). John filius Murthaci had charter of a tenement in Carale, c. 1380 (*Neubotle*, p. 236). In 1421 mention is made of the land of Gilbert Murdaci (RAA., I, 56), and in 1456 and in 1472 Thomas Murdaci appears as chaplain and presbyter of Brechin (REB., I, 182; II, 276). Malcolm Murthosoun had sasine of the lands of Camlongan-Murthosoun in 1468 (*Gallovidian*). The widow of Finlay Murthawsone was tenant of Auchinbard in 1480 (ER., IX, p. 592), and three years later Patrick Murdachsone was half tenant of the same lands (ibid., p. 595; RMS., II, 1623). Another Patrick Murdesone was burgess of Perth, 1539. Donald Murdowsone, a follower of Murdow McCloyd, was one of those who took part in the attack on the galley of the laird of Balcomie in 1600 (RPC., XIV, p. cxxiii). John Murthesoun in Otterswick, Shetland, witness, 1624 (OSS., I, 64). Murdosone 1546, Murthoson 1483, Murthosoun 1468, Murdachsone 1484, Murdachsoun 1500.

MURDOSTOUN. Katherine Mordourstoun recorded in Quodquen in 1624 (*Lanark*) most probably derived her surname from Murdostoun near Newmains, Lanarkshire.

MURDY. Andrew Murdy, servitor to the miller of Stitchill, 1694 (*Stitchill*, p. 114). Margaret Murdy in Chirnside, 1754 (BNCH). Cf. Murdie.

MURE. See under MUIR.

MUREHALL. Local, perhaps from Muirhall, Carnwath, Lanarkshire. Henrie Muirhall or Murehall in Leith accepted the king's coronation, 1567 (RPC., I, p. 563).

MURGANE. James Murgane in Drumtuthill, 1637 (*Pitfirrane*, 560). Arthur Murgane took the oath, 1689 (RPC., 3. ser. XIV, p. 618). Cf. Morgan.

MURIE, Muiry. Local, from Murie in the parish of Errol, Perthshire. John Murie and Andrew Murie from Glendevon, exiled Covenanters, were drowned off Orkney, 1679 (*Hanna*, II, p. 253). John Muirie of Path of Strouiehill, 1757 (*Dunkeld*).

MURIEL. Ir. *Muirgheal*, earlier *Muirgel*, 'seawhite.' A favorite name for women in the twelfth and thirteenth centuries. (1) Muriel, spouse of Robert de Landeles, a. 1174 (*Kelso*,

322). (2) Muriel de Polloc, daughter of Peter de Polloc, was married to Walter Murdac or Murthac. She and her husband made grants to the Abbey of Kinloss, 1225 (REM., p. 458). (3) Muriel, wife of David de Graham, 1279 (Bain, II, 163). (4) Muriella filia Coneval, 1284 (LIM., xxxv). (5) Muriel Calder or Cawdor was heiress of the thanedom of Cawdor in the sixteenth century. The name appears in Icelandic as Mýrgjol, daughter of Gljómal, an Irish king (Landnámabók, II, 16). From a woman of this name comes Rathmuriel, now Murriel, in Inch parish, Aberdeenshire (Watson I, p. 238).

MURIESON, MURISON, MURRISON. This surname is not common, and seems to be connected more with Aberdeenshire than elsewhere. Simon Mwryson was husbandman of the Grange of Abirbothry, 1448 (Cupar-Angus, I, p. 126), and Johannes Murysone was burgess of Kircaldy in the same year (RD., p. 305). Sir William Mureson, a cleric, was admitted burgess of Aberdeen, 1491 (NSCM., I, p. 35). Tvbbe Mwrisone, tenant of part of Kethik, 1504 (Cupar-Angus, I, p. 256). Archibald Murson was bailie for Arbroath Abbey in Banff, 1528 (RAA., II, 705). John Muresoun was a follower of Campbell of Lundy, 1529 (RSS., II, 59), William Muresoun was reidare at Crouden, 1574 (RMR.), and George Muirsoun in Ferne, a follower of Walter Ross of Morange, 1596 (RPC., v, p. 304). Duncan Murieson was on inquisition in Stirling, 1598 (SBR., p. 89). Murchow Mursone in Gerstone, Caithness, 1664 (Caithness). In Officers and graduates of Aberdeen (New Spalding Club) mention is made of several Murisons who graduated from the university from 1670 onward. Prof. Alexander Falconer Murison, and his son, James William Murison, Judge of the British High Court, Zanzibar, are two of the most prominent of the name. Muirsone 1640, Murisone 1686. George Muirson or Murison (d. 1709), a graduate of King's College, Aberdeen, was missionary for propagation of the gospel at Rye, New Hampshire, U. S.

MURISON. See under MURIESON.

MURRAY. Of territorial origin from the province of Moray. William de Moravia (lord of Petty) was witness to a royal charter to the Abbey of Holyrood, 1203 (LSC., p. 36). A little earlier he appears as William, son of Freskin (Inchaffray, p. 269). Hucting de Moravia witnessed confirmation of the sale of the land of Scrogges, c. 1208–13 (REG., p. 76), and Malcolm de Moravia witnessed gift of a mark of silver annually to the Abbey of Arbroath,

c. 1250 (RAA., I, p. 266), and also attested a charter by Malise, earl of Strathern, c. 1258–71 (LIM., xxxiii). William de Morreve rendered homage, 1296. His seal bears on a triangular shield three stars of six points, with a label of five points, S' Willelmi: de: Morevia (Bain, II, 784; Macdonald, 2050). Sir Andrew de Moravia, Hugh de Morreve, William de Morref of Ramsirgard, and Alan de Morref also rendered homage. Ricardus Murref was burgess of Aberdeen, 1317 (SCM., v, p. 10), and Sir Andrew Moray was designated 'panetarius Scotiae' in 1327. Emma de Moravia was spouse of John Schairp in Aberdeen, 1405 (Friars, 25), John de Murrefe de Ogylface in record, 1424 (LSC., p. 233), and Alexander de Moreff, juror on inquisition on lands of Tulloch, 1438 (RAA., II, 83). Harbard de Murraf held part of Easter Drumy, 1470 (Cupar-Angus, I, p. 156), John of Murrafe was steward to Alexander, duke of Albany, 1476 (Home, 23), Sir Patrick Morra was a monk of Beauly in 1480, and Stephen Murreff was witness in Brechin, 1496 (REB., II, 139). Morray 1591, Murra 1491, Murrafe 1476, Murrai 1444, Murraue 1457, Murraue 1469, Mvry 1546, Mwrey 1732, Mwrray 1555; Mowrrey, Muref, Murref, Murrefe, Murreff, Murry, Mwry. The name Murray in Galloway is most likely from MACMURRAY, q.v.

MURRAYTHWAITE. From the old lands of Murraythwaite in the parish of Cummertrees, Dumfriesshire. Walter Muirthuat (Morgequhat or Maurthuat) was a charter witness in Dumfries in 1453 (Edgar, p. 225, 226).

MURRIE. A Perthshire surname, a form of MURRAY, q.v.

MURRISON. See under MURIESON.

MURROES. Soland de Mureus who witnessed a charter by Ernaldus, bishop of St. Andrews, c. 1160–62 (RPSA., p. 128), derived his name from Murroes in the parish of the same name in Angus. James Mueros, bookseller in Kilmarnock, died 1796 (Scots Magazine). Miss Jessie Meuros Peat of Dunblane died 1933. The placename is now spelled Muirhouse. See MUIRHOUSE.

MURTCHIE. Shortened from (MAC)MURTCHIE, q.v.

MUSARD. A byname from OF. musard, an absent-minded stupid person (Littré). Alan Musarde of Rievaulx was appointed abbot of Glenluce, 1244 (Chron. Mail., s.a.).

MUSCHAMP. "A great name of old in Teviotdale," says Innes (p. 56), "now I suppose extinct." In early documents the name is

MUSCHAMP, *continued*

Latinized *de Campo muscarum*, 'of the field of flies.' A family of this name, most probably of Norman origin, held the barony of Muschamp (somewhere in the north of England) in the latter end of the twelfth century. Sir Engram de Musseus (a misspelling) or de Muscens, a variant, appears as a witness c. 1215–45 (*Bain*, I, 1684, 1685). Although the de Muscamps appear in the Ragman Roll the name early died out — in the direct line it seems to have ended in co-heiresses, c. 1255. Stephen de Muscamp was the 'familiar' of William Fraser, bishop of St. Andrews in 1291 (*Bain*, II, 510). Robert de Muschance or Muscaumpe of the county of Edeneburk rendered homage in 1296. His seal bears an eight-rayed figure and S' *Rob'ti d'Moscocamp* (ibid., II, 193, 210, 546). Thomas de Muscampe of the county of Lanark also rendered homage for his lands in the same year (ibid., p. 206). Marjory, daughter and one of the co-heiresses of Sir Robert de Muscamp, was married to Malisse or Maelissa, fifth earl of Strathearn, c. 1244–45, and was dead in 1255.

MUSHET. From Montfiguet or Montfiquet in the department of Calvados, Normandy. In Scots Latin charters the name is rendered *Monte Fixo*. The first of the name in Scotland appears to have been William de Munfiehet (for Munfichet) who witnessed a charter by Eschina, lady of Molle, wife of Walter the Steward, c. 1165–67 (RMP., p. 75). Richard de Munfichet witnessed a charter by William the Lion confirming the earldom of Lennox to David, the king's brother, c. 1178–82 (LAC., p. 2), and about the year 1200 he witnessed the grant by the same king to the Abbey of Arbroath (RAA., I, p. 13). He is also witness to a Panmure charter a. 1214 (*Panmure*, II, 126). William de Munfichet witnessed confirmation by Alexander II of the final accord between the abbot and convent of Holyrood and Ingeram de Balliol regarding the boundaries of Kircostintyn and Kirkebrid, 1228 (LSC., p. 69), and the same king's charter for sustentation of two chaplains in the church of the Castle of Rokesburg (REG., p. 146). He also appears as vicecomes de Perth, 1241 (*Scon*, p. 46). Hugh Muset, a merchant of the king of Scotland, had letters of protection in England, 1242–43 (*Bain*, I, 1607). William de Munificheth made a gift of lands of Leisington to Bernard de Kergylle in 1283 (*Oliphants*, p. 3). Richard Muschet and David Muschet of Angus rendered homage, 1296, and David de Moschet also appears on inquest at Perth, 1304 (*Bain*, II, p. 207, 211, 414). William de Monte Fvchet held Dundee for Edward II in 1312 (*Charters and*

writs, Dundee, p. 4), and William de Monte-fixo, perhaps the same person, was one of the signers of the Scottish Declaration of Independence, 1320. The family failed in the direct line in middle of the fourteenth century, and John de Drummond, lord of Concrag, is said to have got Stobhall, Cargill, and Kincardine in Perth by marriage with the Munfichet heiress. George Muschate was heir of James Muschate of Burnebank, his father, 1546 (*Retours, Perth*, 1052). A family of Mushet possessed a considerable estate in Menteith. Mr. George Muschet was minister at Donyng, 1619 (*Fordell*, p. 112). Nicol Muschet of Boghall, who was hanged for the murder of his wife in the King's Park, Edinburgh, October, 1720, gave the surname an unenviable notoriety. The supposed site of the crime was long marked by "Muschet's Cairn." Muschett 1816.

MUSSELBURGH. From the town of Musselburgh in the parish of Inveresk, Midlothian. John de Muskilburgh was official of Tevidalie, c. 1190–1220 (*Soltre*, p. 9), and Ranulph de Muskilburg witnessed a grant of the multures of Preston to the Abbey of Kelso about the year 1200 (*Kelso*, 318). A later John de Muskylburg witnessed a charter by Malcolm de Moravia in favor of the Abbey of Dunfermline in 1274 (RD., 207). Magister Johannes de Muskylburg or Muxilburg was clericus de perbenda in 1278 (RD., p. 52, 53). John de Moskelburgh received payment of 10s. in 1304 for guiding the English leaders to the retreat of Sir Simon Fraser and other Scots in the expedition against Sir William Waleys in Lothian (*Bain*, IV, p. 475). Baudrikesland in the tenement of Dregerne (Dreghorn) was forfeited by William de Muskelburgh in 1336 (*Bain*, III, p. 335, 381). Johannes Mussilburgh, doctor in sacred theology, was vicar-general of Friars Preachers, 1459 (RAA., II, p. 110). "The dochtyr of Adam Mussilburchtg" held a land in Dunfermline in 1489 (DBR., 10), and in 1507 mention is made of the "land of the airris of wmquhill Madde Mussilburcht" (ibid., 351).

MUSTARD. This surname is not uncommon in Fife and Perthshire. Alexander Mustard held land in Arbroath, 1521 (RAA., II, 573). William Mustard appears in Balnamoone, 1689 (RPC., 3. ser. XIV, p. 709). Alexander Mustard appears in Alyth, 1688, and five others are recorded in the vicinity. The name of Henricus van Mouster in record, 1414 (ER., IV, p. 296) points to a Flemish origin, and Mustaert is a well-known Flemish surname (*Sc. Ant.*, IV, p. 114). Mustarder (from Fr. *moutardier*), Mustardmaker, and Mustardman are extinct English surnames.

MUTCH. William Mouch, burgess of Stirling, 1520 (SBR., p. 4). George Mutch and John Mutch were in the Jacobite army of the '45. John Lowrie Mutch from Monquhitter served in the first Great War (*Turriff*).

MUTER, MUTTER. Forms of MULTRAR, q.v., with omission of *l*. Thomas Mutter in Weistoun, parish of Stanehouse, 1626, and five more of the name (*Lanark CR.*). Mutar 1606.

MUTRIE. A variant of MOUTRAY, q.v.

MYLES. Gaelic *Mael-Moire*, one of the commonest *mael* (*maol*)-names, has survived till the present day in the Isles especially as Miles or Myles. The names have nothing in common, and the relationship may be due to the assonance of Mael with English miles. Thomas Myles, indweller in Maxpople, 1641 (RRM., I, p. 87). Margaret Myles, a victim of superstition, was hanged in Edinburgh for witchcraft, 1702 (Chambers, *Domestic annals*, III, p. 217). David Myles in Coular of Angus, 1731 (*Dunkeld*).

MYLNE. See under MILN. A family of Mylnes were for centuries master masons to the kings of Scotland.

MYRE. Local, from residence near a bog or mire. David in the Mire, one of the Scots prisoners taken at Dunbar Castle, 1296, obtained his freedom in following year to serve the English king abroad (*Bain*, II, 742, 939). Alexander Myr witnessed a lease by George, abbot of Inchaffray, 1491 (*Inchaffray*, p. xcvii), and James Myr held land in Brechin, 1508 (REB., II, 159).

MYRES. From the lands of Myres in the parish of Auchtermuchty, Fifeshire. The family so named held the office of hereditary macers and sergeants at arms of Falkland Palace (SN&Q., X, p. 25).

MYRETON, MYRTON. See under MORTON.

NACHTYSON. William Nachtyson was admitted burgess of Aberdeen, 1409 (NSCM., I, p. 3). Cf. NAUGHTY.

NAESMITH, NAISMITH, NAISMYTH, NASMITH, NAYSMITH, NESMYTH. From the trade or occupation of 'knife-smith,' a maker of knives. "It has been stated," says Bardsley, "as beyond need of evidence that Nasmith and Neasmith are corrupted forms of Nailsmith, a maker of nails [so Lower explains the name]. The earlier and complete form is found in the *Valor Ecclesiasticus*, viz. Henry Knyfesmythe." The form Knysmithe survived in England till the sixteenth century (*Week-*

ley, p. 228). Adam Nasmith, owner of lands at Brechin, died before 1420. The Nasmyths were an old family of burgesses at Hamilton (*Stodart*, II, p. 317). James Nasmytht, witness in Glasgow, 1543 (LCD., p. 128). George Nasmyth was one of those hanged for holding Paisley against the king and his regent, 1565 (*Diur. Occ.*, p. 201), and John Nesmyt is mentioned by Moysie as one of those concerned in a conspiracy in Holyrood, 27 December 1591 (*Memoirs*, p. 87). There was a resignation of property in favor of Robert Nasmyth in Glasgow, 1552 (*Protocols*, I), Gawin Nasmytht was commissioner of Irvin, 1579 (*Irvine*, I, p. 72), and John Naismith was servitor to countess of Abercorne, 1626 (Lees, *Paisley*, p. 268). "James Nasmith de Coldounknowis Armiger lie Esquyre S. D. N. Regis" was retoured heir in certain lands in Berwickshire, 1630 (*Retours, Berwick*, 168). Naismeth 1816, Nasemith 1687, Neasmyth 1654, Nesmith 1693.

NAIRN, NAIRNE. Of local origin from the burgh of the same name. "A family of the name of 'Nairne' flits across the pages of the old chartulary of Moray between the town of Nairn and a possession in Cromdale, but personal details are wanting" (Bain, *Nairnshire*, 2. ed., 1928, p. 169). The first Nairn recorded appears to be Adam de Narryn who was chaplain of the altar of the Blessed Virgin at Inverness in 1361 (REM., p. 307). Michael de Narne, armiger, witnessed a Perth charter in 1406 (RMS., I, 886). John of Narn, laird of Ardmuthach, and his son, Sir John of Narn, sheriff of Forres, appear in an Atholl charter of 1414 (*Athole*, p. 706). Alexander de Narn appears in Glasgow in 1440 (REG., 344), and another Alexander de Narne of Sandfurde [in Fife] witnessed a Perthshire charter in 1450 (*Oliphants*, p. 10), and still another Alexander Narne, a Scots messenger, received a gift in 1451 (*Bain*, IV, 1231). John of Narn served on an inquest in 1431 (*Rose*, p. 127), Robert Narne was provost of Stirling in 1457 (SBR., p. 399), and Thomas Narne, perhaps a relative, was a witness there in 1481 (*Cambus.*, 212). Duncan Neorne, a follower of the earl of Mar, was charged with resetting outlawed Macgregors in 1636 (RPC., 2. ser. VI, p. 215). The family of Nairn, linoleum manufacturers, have been great benefactors of the town of Kirkcaldy. Charles Murray Nairne (1808–1882), born in Perth, was professor of moral philosophy and literature in Columbia University, New York. Naerne and Naern 1520.

NAISMITH, NAISMYTH. See under NAESMITH.

624

NAOISE. Naoise, the lover of Deirdre, and one of the Red Branch heroes. Also *Naois, Naos* (*MacNaos* — MacNeece). (Dinneen, *Foclóir Gaedhilge agus Béarla*, s.v.)

NAPIER. This surname comes from an office attached to the royal court. In England, in the reign of Henry I, William de Hastings held the manor of Ashele in Norfolk by the service of taking charge of the napery, i.e. tablecloths and linen at the coronation of the English kings. The first record of the name in Scotland is c. 1290 when John Naper obtained from Malcolm, earl of Lennox, a charter of the quarter-land called Kylmethew (Irving, *History of Dumbartonshire*, p. 328). This John Naper is included in the inhibition by the bishop of Glasgow directed against Malcolm, earl of Lennox, and his adherents in 1294 (RMP., p. *203) and is doubtless the John le Naper of the county of Dunbretan who rendered homage in 1296 (*Bain*, II, p. 202). Matheu le Naper of Agheleke (i.e. Affleck in Angus) took the oath of fealty at the same time (ibid., p. 200). Alexander Naper was one of the commissioners for concluding a peace between Scotland and England in 1451 (*Bain*, IV, 1239), and John Napier (1550-1617), the famous mathematician, was the inventor of logarithms. There have been also several other distinguished bearers of the name within the last two hundred years. For the intrusion of *i* in the modern form of the name compare Sawyer (Sawer), Bowyer (Bower), etc. Innes (p. 45) says: "There are Napiers in the North vulgarly called Lepers — *euphoniae causa*." Naiper 1679, Napare 1455, Neaper 1625, Neper 1651, and Napar, Nepare.

NAPPER. A variant of NAPIER, q.v. Adam Napparius witnessed ratification of gift of the church of Lescelyn to the Abbey of Lindores, 1243 (LAC., p. 90). Robert Napper, baker and feuar in Kelso, 1783 (*Heirs*, 423). Recorded in Edinburgh, 1941.

NAR. Nar 'homo abbatis de Scone,' 1163–85 (*Scon*, p. 24), and Thomas filius Nār, a charter witness in the reign of Alexander II (ibid., p. 71).

NASMITH. See under NAESMITH.

NATHALAN. A British saint commemorated in Aberdeenshire and in Kincardineshire. In the Scottish Calendars his name appears as "Nothlan, Nathalan, or Nethalen, in the vernacular Nauchlan or Nachlan... His name is a compound, the first part of which is E. Celt. *nectos*, pure; the second may be the not uncommon *launos*, joyful: *Necto-launos*,

'pure-rejoicing' or possibly 'rejoicing in purity'" (*Watson* I, p. 329–30).

NAUGHTON. See NECHTAN and under MACNACHTAN.

NAUGHTY. An Aberdeenshire surname, probably of local origin from Nochty in Strath Don. John Nachty, witness in Aberdeen, 1450 (REA., II, p. 296). Alexander Nathy was admitted burgess of Aberdeen, 1466, and Andrew Nathty in 1471 (NSCM., I, p. 9, 22). Alexander Nachti, juror on assize in Aberdeen, 1480, appears as Alexander Nathty, citizen there, 1493 (CRA., p. 410, 48). John Nauchty, notary public in diocese of Brechin, 1513 (SCM., IV, p. 12; REB., II, 170). Walter Nawthy was presented to the parish church of Barre in the diocese of St. Andrews, 1533 (RAA., II, 783). Henry Nauchtie was burgess of Kirkwall, Orkney, 1567 (RPC., I, p. 517), and William Nauchtie was servant to Patrick Maule of Panmure, 1576 (*Panmure*, II, 315). Mr. Andro Naughtie was minister at Stow, 1689 (RPC., 3. ser. XIV, p. 133), James Naughtie, miller at Gilcolmstone, 1777 (*Aberdeen CR.*), and Alexander Naughty was resident in Keith, 1792 (*Moray*). By some this name is considered to be a form of NAUGHTON, q.v., but local origin seems more probable. See NACHTYSON. Nauchti 1513.

NAYSMITH. See under NAESMITH.

NEAL. See under NEIL. John Neale was builder of the first house on Princes Street, Edinburgh.

NEAVE. A rare surname recorded in Perthshire. It may be from OF. neve, 'nephew,' but is probably a variant of NEVAY, q.v., but cf. NEAVES. Jean Neave is recorded in Edinburgh, 1661 (*Edinb. Marr.*).

NEAVES. A rare surname. 'Nephew' (from OF. neve, with gen -s) has been suggested as the meaning, but it is, in Scotland, most probably a shortening of BALNEAVES, q.v. — *de villa nativorum*, 'the town of the serfs.' The father of Lord Neaves (1800–76) added the s to the family name of Neave.

NECBOG. Bartholomew Necbog of that Ilk was witness to a sasine given by Alexander Campbell, sergeant of the earldom of Lennox, 1480 (*Strathendrick*, p. 193).

NECGREGOR. This represents Gaelic Nicgriogair, 'daughter of GREGOR.'

NECHTAN. G. *Nechtán* or *Neachdán*, from earlier Nectan or Necton, the OG. form of Pictish Naiton. The name comes from *necht* 'pure one' (from the root *nig* 'wash'), and seems to appear in the ogham inscription found at Lunnasting, Shetland, now in the National Museum of Antiquities, Edinburgh, as *Nehhtonn*. Nectan was the name of the king who expelled the Columban clergy 'across the ridge of Britain' because they refused to accept some of his reforms (*Tighernach*). 'Nectan escob Abberdeen' is one of the witnesses to a grant to the Abbey of Deer, 1132 (*Bk. Deer*, III, 6), and a later Nechten was rector of the church of Killinan, c. 1230 (RMP., p. 132).

NECTOVELIUS. The monument of a Brigantian soldier in the Roman army found near Mumrills, Stirlingshire, reads: *Dis M(anibvs) Nectovelivs f(ilivs) Vindicis an(norvm) xxx stip(endiorvm) viiii nationis Brigans militavit in coh II Thr(acvm)*, "To the Divine Manes. Nectovelius, son of Vindex. Aged thirty. A Brigantian by birth, he served for nine years in the Second Cohort of Thracians" (Macdonald, *The Roman Wall in Scotland*, 1911, p. 352). The Brigantes were a powerful tribe who occupied the north of England and the south of Scotland.

NEESON, NEISON, NEISSON. Anglicized forms of MACNEISH, q.v. F. G. P. Neisson (d. 1876), statistical writer, was born in Kilmarnock. Neyssoune 1467.

NEIL, NEILL, NEAL. G. *Niall*, EG. *Niáll*, Latinized (gen.) by Adamnan (VC., I, 49) *Nellis*, is a diminutive of Ir. *Nia*, 'champion.' Niall was borrowed by the Norsemen and appears in their language as *Njáll* and *Njal*. Among the Normans in France the name became *Nesle* or *Néle*, and by them it was introduced into England and appears in Domesday Book. In England the name was Latinized *Nigellus* on the supposition that it meant 'black,' and in this form is the source of Scottish *Nigel*. Achyne mac Nele attested the bounds of the Grange of Kircwynni and land of Culwen in Kirkgunzeon, 1289 (*Holm Cultram*, p. 88). John Nele was witness in Irvine, 1455 (*Irvine*, I, p. 147), and Thomas Nele was bailie of burgh of Are, 1507 (*Ayr*, p. 37). The family of Neill of Barnwell, Ayrshire, claim descent from a cadet of Macneil of Barra, c. 1550, who is said to have settled in Ayrshire. In Galloway, Neil, it is said, was sometimes used as a shortening of MACNEILLIE, q.v. As forename: Nile Hog, member of council of Stirling, 1557 (SBR., p. 378).

NEILSON, NIELSON, NILSON, 'son of NEIL,' q.v. There were at least two families of this name of independent origin — Neilson of Craigcaffie, Ayrshire, and Neilson of Caithness. (1) The Neilsons of Craigcaffie are said to have traced their descent from Neil, earl of Carrick, husband of Margaret Stewart, who died in 1256. Instead of the usual Gaelic prefix *mac* they added the word *son* to Neil, hence Neilson (*M'Kerlie*, I, p. 136; *Agnew*, I, p. 83). Sometime after 1314 the lands of Craigcaffie were granted by royal charter to John, son of Neil Carrick, who took the name of Neilson as his patronymic (*Dumfries and Galloway Nat. Hist. & Ant. Soc., Trans.*, 3. ser. XVII, p. 184). John filius Nigelli appears in Berwickshire in reign of Robert I (RMS., I, 18), and Nigellus Nelsoun had charter of the lands of Cragcathy from James III in 1474 (*M'Kerlie*, I, p. 136). Neilsons in the reign of James V are said to have been at that time hereditary crowners of Bute for two hundred years (Dobie, *Pont*, p. 225). Craigcaffie was erected into a barony in the sixteenth century and remained in possession of the family till well on into the eighteenth. Morys Neelsoun had a safe conduct into England in 1424, and Henry Nelsone, merchant in Edinburgh, is recorded in 1438 (*Bain*, IV, 964, 1115). John Neilsone witnessed promulgation of a papal bull at Linlithgow, 1461 (*Soltre*, p. 63), another John Neylsone was tenant under the bishop of Glasgow, 1510 (*Rental*). Andrew Neleson was 'dekin of baxsteris' in Stirling, 1546 (SBR., p. 277), and John Neilsoun was a baker in Glasgow, 1554 (*Protocols*, I). Gilbert Neilsoun appears in Meikfas, 1607 (*Retours, Kirkcudbright*, 76), and John Nilsoune of Corsock was retoured heir of Robert Neilsoune of Corsock, his father, 1654 (ibid., 263). John Nilsone in Tinwald was examined for the Test, 1685 (RPC., 3. ser. XI, p. 434), and Jean Nilson is recorded in parish of Tuynhame, 1684 (ibid., IX, p. 473). (2) Nele Nelsoun had grant of lands in Creich, Gerloch, and others in the sheriffdom of Innernys in 1429 for his homage and service in the capture of his brother, Thomas Nelesoun, a rebel (OPS., II, p. 686). William Allan Neilson (b. 1869), president-emeritus of Smith College, Northampton, Massachusetts, was born in Doune, Perthshire. Neillsone 1706, Neilstoun 1707, Neylsone 1558, Nylson 1555; Nelsonne.

NEISH, NIESH. Sir William Neische, presbyter and witness, 1470 (*Laing*, 163). Toppe Neis was in amerciament "for strublans" in Dunfermline, 1492 (DBR., 32). Walter Neasch, master of the royal lardner, 1589 (SCM., II, p. 114), may be Walter Neische who was bailie of Stirling and commissioner "of the tounes rychtis" in Edinburgh, 1598 (SBR., p. 87, 282). John Neis was owner of tenements in Cupar, 1510 (RMS., II, 3491), and David Nes was burgess there, 1608 (ibid., VI, 2157). Naische 1529, Nas 1520, Nech 1543, Neis 1488, Neisch 1592, Neish 1631, Neische 1590, Nesche 1497, Nies 1730, Niesh 1732. See MACNEISH.

NENTHORN. From the lands of Nenthorn in the parish of Nenthorn, Berwickshire. Symone de Naythanthirn appears as a charter witness, c. 1203 (*Dryburgh*, p. 160), and as Simund de Neitanestirn (misread by Anderson Heicanestirn) witnessed a charter by Ricardus de Morville, the constable (Anderson, *Selectus diplomatum*, pl. 75). Henry de Neythantherne of the county of Berewyke rendered homage in 1296 (*Bain*, ɪɪ, p. 207). William de Nethenthyrn, a Scots prisoner taken at the capture of Dunbar Castle in 1296, was sent to St. Briavell's Castle, and was still a prisoner in 1299 (ibid., p. 177, 278).

NESBET, Nᴇsʙɪᴛ. *See under* NISBET.

NESGASK. From an obsolete place name in Perthshire. Colminus de Nesgask had a lease of certain lands and of the parsonage of Nesgask in 1263 (*Inchaffray*, p. 306–307).

NESMYTH. *See under* NAESMITH.

NESS. A current surname, but its connection with the old Gaelic personal name Ness is not certain. Several persons of this name are in record in the twelfth and thirteenth centuries, a few of whom may here be noted. (1) Nesse, member of the religious house of Abernethy, c. 1093–1107 (RPSA., p. 116). (2) Nessius filius Willelmi Lineth was sheriff of Perth in the reign of Malcolm ɪᴠ (*Scon*, p. 8). Nesus or Nessyus filius Willelmi appears as witness between 1178–1200 (RAA., ɪ, 4; *Cambus.*, 70. *The Report on ancient monuments of Fife* says he was "apparently of Norman stock"), and as Neis filius Chilū (Chiluni, Chilunus — errors for Willelmi) he attested a charter by Thor of the church of Tranent to Holyrood, c. 1155 (LSC., p. 11). His daughter Orabilis was married to Robert de Quincy. (3) Ness of Linton witnessed a charter by Robert, bishop of St. Andrews who died in 1158–59 (*Genealogist*, xvɪ, p. 132). (4) Nessus de Dalginge, a witness a. 1177 (CMN., p. 6). (5) Nesus de London (perhaps Lundie in Fife) granted half the village of Smeatoun to his cousin Alan in the reign of William the Lion (*Genealogist*, xvɪ, p. 132). (6) Nes, the son of John of Lundres, gave the monks of Newbattle some land in Forton in East Lothian (*Neubotle*, p. 80), and (7) Nesius filius Nesii made them an additional gift (ibid., p. 81–82). (7a) Nesis of Ramsay and Big Peter, his son, witnessed a charter by Malcolm, earl of Fife, 1217 (PSAS., ʟx, p. 71). (8) Mathew filius Nesse witnessed a quit-claim of the land of Drumkarauch in Fife, 1260 (RPSA., p. 346), and (9) Nessus, medicus domini regis (Alexander ɪɪ), granted the abbey of Cupar-Angus

a charter of the lands of Dunfolenthyn (*Cupar-Angus*, ɪ, p. 348). (10) Nes Fraser, a relative of no. 6, was juror on inquisition on the lands of Hopkelchoc (now Kailzie), 1259 (APS., ɪ, p. 98 red). Thomas Ness was chaplain of Brechin, 1450 (REB., ɪ, 138), and complaint was made upon Christian Ness in Dysart, 1697 (*Dysart*, p. 56).

NESS. (2) Henry de Nes, a retainer of the Stewards, in 1180 received permission to construct a chapel for the use of his own family (RMP., p. 78). He also witnessed the gift of the church of Pollok to the monastery of Paisley by Peter filius Fulberti, c. 1177–99, and about the same date his brother Adam also appears as a witness (ibid., p. 98, 100). About 1202 Henry was one of the perambulators of the boundaries of Moniabroc, and c. 1210 he attested a charter by Malcolm Loccard (ibid., p. 13, 91).

NESSAN. Diminutive of Nᴇss, q.v. Adamnan (V. C., ɪɪ, 20) blessed the cattle of a poor man in Lochaber, named Nesan. His name is from early Celtic * *Nesagnos*, 'sprung from Ness.' The name also occurs in an ogham inscription at Kelgrovane: *Nisigni mac Ercogni* (Macallister, *Oghams*, ɪɪɪ, p. 201). Nessanus, a cleric, was a charter witness, 1359 (HP., ɪᴠ, p. 14).

NETERAULDE. Duncan Neteraulde was outlawed as part guilty of the slaughter of Walter Ogilvy, sheriff of Angus, 1392 (APS., ɪ, p. 579).

NETHERWOOD. Local. There are places of this name in the shires of Dumfries, Ayr, and Renfrew. Descendants of a sixteenth century Scottish emigrant, William Netherwood, still exist in Sweden.

NEUALL, Nᴇᴡᴀʟʟ. An old surname in Galloway. Radulf Nuuel witnessed King David's charter of Swinton to Hernulf (*Raine*, 12). Gardein de Nouel leu de Seneware rendered homage, 1296. Laurence Newale was tenant in Dobtoun, Dumfries, 1376 (RHM., ɪ, p. lvi), Herbert Newell witnessed a notarial deed in Dumfries, 1453 (*Edgar*, p. 225), Nichol Nowale and Thomas Newall signed the Band of Dumfries, 1570 (RPC., xɪᴠ, p. 66, 67). John Newall was witness in Glasgow, 1553 (*Protocols*, ɪ), Thomas Newall, heir of Archibald Newall, burgess of Drumfreis, 1601 (*Retours*, Dumfries, 11), John Newall, heir of Martin Newall of Barnbachall, 1635 (*Retours, Kirkcudbright*, 211), and Andrew Newall in Burnesyde-croft of Endrig, 1680 (*Kirkcudbright*).

NEUBOTLE. Adam de Neubotle who witnessed a charter by Peter de Pulloc, c. 1177–79 (RMP., p. 98) derived his name from Newbattle in Midlothian.

NEUDOSC. Cormac de Neudoesc was juror in a dispute regarding the Kirketun of Aberbothenoth (Arbuthnott), 1206 (SCM., v, p. 213). There was an old church of Neudos in the Mearns (RAA., I, p. 240).

NEUHAM. William de Neuham, templarius, witnessed the gift by Duncan, earl of Fife, to the nuns of North Berwick, a. 1177 (CMN., 6). Probably from Newham near Bamburgh, Northumberland.

NEURS. Probably from Noyers in Eure, a department in northwestern France. H. de Noiers or Henricus de Neurs, clerk to the earl, witnessed charters by Earl David, brother of William the Lion, between 1198–1207 (LAC., 5, 12). Walchelinus Nuerres or Walkelinus de Nuers also appears as witness in charters by the same earl (ibid., 4, 11, 12).

NEVAY. Of territorial origin from Nevay, a former parish in Angus now united to Essie. In 1219 Adam de Neveth was present at the perambulation of the bounds between the lands of the Abbey of Arbroath and the barony of Kinblethmont (RAA., I, p. 162). Alexander de Neve, a Scots prisoner of war in England, had a safe conduct to return to Scotland in 1422 (Bain, IV, 914). Thomas Nevay who witnessed the transumpt of a charter in 1450 is doubtless the Thomas Neiff, chaplain in Brechin in 1453 (REB., I, 146; II, 96). Alexander Nefoy witnessed a commission of bailiary in 1511 (Panmure, II, 279), John Nevay of that Ilk served on an inquest in Angus in 1558 (Southesk, p. 721), and in 1637 another John Neway appears as a charter witness (Laing, 2209). James Nevay went to Sweden in 1579, became governor of Westmanland and Dalarne and was killed by the peasantry (Fischer III, p. 67–68). His name appears in Swedish records as Neafve and Näf, and his epitaph commences: 'Jacob Näif, en Skottskerman af adlig ätt och börde...' (Marryat, One year in Sweden, I, p. 420). John Naiphe of Mathie recorded in 1597 (Fordell, p. 116). Rev. John Nevoy or Nave was accused of being the instigator of the massacre of the garrison of Dunaverty in 1647 (HP., II, p. 249–253). David Nevay of that Ilk is mentioned in 1666 (Laing), and John Nevay (1792–1870), an Angus poet of some merit, is now forgotten. A poor weaver living in Forfar about 1850 claimed descent from the family of Nevoy, which ended in the direct line. Miss G. M. Nevay died in Moffat, 1940. Nauee 1661, Navay 1574, Neafve.

NEVILLE. Perhaps from Néville in Normandy, or Neuville, a common place name in France. Thomas de Neovilla witnessed a charter by Roger, bishop-elect of St. Andrews, c. 1189–98 (RPSA., p. 153). Jacobus de Neuilla witnessed a confirmation by Roger de Quinci of the gift by William de Len to the Abbey of Scon in the reign of Alexander II (Scon, p. 49). Richard de Neville of Perth rendered homage, 1296 (Bain, II, p. 186, 197). Janet Nevill was married in Perth, 1568 (Northern Notes and Queries, I, p. 169).

NEVIN, NEVINS. See under NIVEN.

NEVISON, NIVESON, NIVISON. 'Son of NIVEN,' q.v. Recorded in Dunfermline. Sir Angus de Novynesone persone of Tillydak, 1536 (SCM., IV, p. 202). 'De' here an error.

NEWALL. See under NEUALL.

NEWBERY. Local. Perhaps a form of Newbury. William Newbery, indweller in Leith, 1675 (Edin. App.), and Joseph Newberrie was married in Edinburgh, 1677 (Edinb. Marr.).

NEWBIE. James Newbie, tailor in Edinburgh, 1676 (Edinb. Marr.) may have derived his surname from Newby near Peebles, Peeblesshire.

NEWBIGGING, NEWBIGIN. A surname of territorial origin from one or more of the many farm-steadings so named. Eustace de Newbigging sold to the prior of Coldingham the freedom of William of Newbigging and Burunild (Brunhild) his wife, and Walter and Mabel their children, and all their issue, for the sum of fifteen shillings (Raine, 341). The vill and lands of Newbigging in the parish of Carnwath, Lanarkshire, passed into possession of the Somervilles through marriage with the daughter and heiress of Walter of Newbigging about middle of thirteenth century (Memorie of the Somervilles, I, p. 65). Alan de Neubigging was one of twelve knights appointed in 1249 to meet twelve from England to settle the law of the marches (APS., I, p. 413). Michael de Neubigging rendered account for John de Swyneburn in Cumberland, 1278 (Bain, II, 143), and William de Neubiggyn, dominus ejusdem, was a witness in 1354 (Kelso, p. 384). William de Newbygging, lord of Dunsyar, had a charter of lands in the barony of Cultir from Walter Byset confirmed by David II in 1367 (RMS., I, 243, 270). He derived his name from Newbigging in the parish of Carnwath, Lanarkshire. William de Newbiging was a tenant of the earl of Douglas in the parish of Linton, 1376 (RHM., II, p. 16), and another William de Neubygyng witnessed a charter of lands of Quyltis, Aberdeen, 1387 (CAB., p. 274). Newbiggan 1737.

NEWBURN. Local. There are places of this name in Fife and near Stirling. John Newburn in Barend of Parton, 1724 (*Kirkcudbright*).

NEWCASTLE. John Newcastle, cooper in Edinburgh, 1682 (*Edinb. Marr.*). Most probably from Newcastle-on-Tyne, England.

NEWLANDS, NIELANDS. There was an old barony of Newlands in the sheriffdom of Kincardine, and a parish of the name in Peeblesshire, from either of which the surname may have been derived. The name was common in Glasgow in the sixteenth century, and common in the parish of Dalswinton till recent times. Jasper Newlands of that Ilk in record, 1469. Duncan Newlandis, bailie of the burgh of Linlithgow, 1493 (*Cambus.*, 186), Peter Newlandis, witness there in 1537 (*Johnstoun*), and Kentigern Newlandis, witness in 1542 (*Anderson*). Joneta Neulands was retoured heir in lands in the barony of Monkland, 1675 (*Retours, Lanark*, 331). Robert Newlands, late glover, burgess of Edinburgh, 1726 (*Guildry*, p. 132).

NEWTIBBER. From the old manor of the name formerly in the parish of Newtyle, probably now represented by the hamlet of Newbigging. Richard de Neutebere or de Neucobyry of the county of Forfar rendered homage in 1296 at Kincardine "sur Nele" (Kincardine-O'Neil) (*Bain*, II, p. 196, 205), and Angos de Neucober of the same county rendered homage about the same time (ibid., p. 205). No later notice of this family is on record.

NEWTON. Of local origin from places of the name. The first three persons here named derived their name from the old parish of Newton in Midlothian. James de Neutone and Huwe de Neutone of Edinburghshire rendered homage in 1296 (*Bain*, II, p. 201, 213). Alexander de Newtoun *de eodem* was one of assize on the perambulation of the bounds of Gladmor, 1430 (*James* II, 16). James de Newton, parson of Bedrule, 1479 (*Morton*, p. 53), most probably derived his name from the lands of Newton in the parish of Bedrule. John de Newton is recorded in Glasgow, 1446 (REG., 348), and another John Neuton, 'Scotsman,' had a safe conduct into England in 1463 (*Bain*, IV, 1338).

NIALLGUS, 'choice champion,' a derivative of Niall, 'champion,' gives Ir. M'Nelis and Lowland Scots M'Neilage. (For the termination -age see Westergaard, *Studies in prefixes and suffixes in Middle Scottish*, p. 107–108). Niallgus occurs in the early legendary genealogy of the Macdonalds, seventh in succession from Colla Uais. Duncan le fitz Nelgos of Dunbretan rendered homage, 1296 (*Bain*, II, p. 202). *Niall*, gen. *Néill*, a champion. The name of several early Irish kings. Gives pr. n. *Neil, Njal*, and diminutives *Néillín, Niallán*, and *Niallagán (Dinneen)*.

NIBREIM. Lambe fiz Austyn de Nibreim, tenant under the bishop of St. Andrews in Fife, rendered homage in 1296 (*Bain*, II, p. 205). Nibreim is for Nithbren, the old name of Newburn, Fife.

NIC. An abbreviated form of Gaelic *nighean mhic*, 'daughter of *Mac*,' used after forenames of women.

NICHOL, NICHOLL. *See under* NICOL.

NICHOLAS. Middle Latin *Nicolas* (from Gr. Νικόλας) or late Latin *Nicolaus*, from Gr. Νικόλαος. The name came into mediaeval and modern use in honor of legendary S. Nicholas (Nicolaus), who is said to have lived in the fourth century. Nicholaus medicus Willelmi regis, 1201–07 (RAA., I, p. 27).

NICHOLSON, NICOLSON, 'son of NIC(H)OL,' q. v. Maucolum fiz Nicol rendered homage in 1296 (*Bain*, II, 816). William Nicholai (Lat. genitive) or Nycholayi was burgess of Glasgow, 1419–21 (LCD., p. 241), Gilbert Nicholai was vicar of Aufurde (Alford) in 1435 (REB., II, 52), and Patrick Nicholai, presbyter of Brechin, 1436, appears in 1446 as Patrik Nicholsone, perpetual chaplain of Caldhame (ibid., I, 82, 106). Michael Nycholson leased part of Parcy (Persie), 1443, and Gylbryd Nycholay in 1446 (*Cupar-Angus*, I, p. 120, 128), Matthew Nicholay, witness in Aberdeen, 1489 (REA., II, p. 303), and John Nicholsoun was burgess of Dumfries, 1544 (*Anderson*). Ailleis Neclasson had remission in 1547 for his share in taking and holding the Castle of Akirgill, Caithness (OPS., II, p. 778), and Mallie Niclasson is recorded in the Boigis, 1663 (*Caithness*). The Nicolsons of Lasswade are an old family, knighted in seventeenth century. Sir William Nicolson (d. 1766), four times married, was father of twenty-three children. The Nicholsons of Skye have Englished their name from MACNICOL, q.v. Necolson 1474, Nicollsoun 1624, Nucolsone 1655, Nycholsoun 1483.

NICKLE. A current form of NICOL, q.v.

NICOL, NICOLL, NICHOL, NICHOLL. Diminutives of Nicolas or Nicholas, a personal name introduced into Britain by the Normans. The surname is derived from Greek Νικόλαος, meaning 'victorious people.' David Nycholl was a frater of Cambuskenneth Abbey in 1546 (*Laing*, 505), and John Nuckall and Alexander

Nuckall were 'quhyt fischeris' in Futtie in 1592 (CRA., p. 74). Alexander Nicol was 'gladiator civis Glasguensis' in 1603 (*Retours, Lanark,* 42), William Nuccol was tenant in the barony of Cannegleroch in 1640 (SCM., v, p. 228), and in 1650 James Nickle, upon Mt. Tasker, petitioned the Kirk Session of Auchterhouse to protect him against his mother who had abused him by banning, swearing, and cursing, and calling him a 'lie-and limer' (*Jervise,* II, p. 4). George Nuckle was admitted deacon of Alyth in 1671 (DPD., II, p. 86), William Nuckoll was a tailzeor in Aberdeen in 1684, and David Nuckoll was maltman there in 1697 (ROA., I, p. 240, 246). Nycholl 1537. In some instances Nicol may be a curtailed form of MACNICOL, q.v. (2) Probably from Lincoln in England. Weekley (p. 308) says "the Normans transformed Lincoln into Nicol, of very common occurrence in mediaeval chronicles." Richard de Nicole witnessed a charter by Eschina domina de Molle, c. 1165-75 (RMP., p. 75), and Richard de Nicol, most probably son of the preceding, witnessed another charter of the lands of Molle, c. 1225-35 (ibid., p. 77). Richard de Lincoln granted a portion of land in the territory of Molle, c. 1190, to the Abbey of Kelso, and in another charter of the same land he is mentioned as Richard de Nichole (*Kelso,* 161, 165).

NICOLSON. *See under* NICHOLSON.

NIDDRY, NIDDRIE, NIDRAY. From the lands of Nodref (now Niddry) in the parish of Liberton, Midlothian. Alexander de Nodref witnessed an agreement between Adam Malherb and the Abbey of Neubotle, c. 1214-30 (*Neubotle,* p. 67). A family of the name of Nudre preceded the Wauchopes at Niddry, the date of their last charter of confirmation being dated 1364 (RMS., I, 143). In 1426 the lands of le Quhyne in the barony of North Berwick were confirmed to David Nudre (RMS., II, 69). John de Nudre exchanged his tower and lands in Cramond with the bishop of Dunkeld for the lands of Cammo in the same parish. Thomas Nowddri, Scottish merchant, had warrant for safe conduct to travel in England in 1446 (*Bain,* IV, 1186), Gavin Newdere of Luthin appears as witness in Dirleton in 1519 (*Laing,* 318), and in 1526 David Nudry, burgess of Montrose, had a precept of remission (RSS., I, 3608). John Niddry was tanner in Elgin in 1736 (*Moray*).

NIELANDS. A form of NEWLANDS, q.v.

NIELSON. *See under* NEILSON.

NIESH. *See under* NEISH.

NIGEL, NIGELL. *Nigell-us* is (1) a diminutive of Latin *niger,* 'black,' and (2) a Latinized form of *Neil,* from Ir. *niall,* 'champion.' Here (1) is most likely origin. Robertus filius Nigelli witnessed a grant by Earl David to the church of Glasgow, c. 1123 (REG., p. 8). Nigell, sacerdos, was a witness, c. 1153-66 (*Kelso,* 287), and Nigellus, cancellarius, witnessed charter of a toft in Forfar, c. 1189-99 (RAA., I, p. 53).

NILSON. *See under* NEILSON.

NIMLET. A rare surname recorded in Paisley, 1840.

NIMMO. This surname is sometimes spelled Nemmock (*Nisbet,* I, p. 244). The attempt (*Narrative of Mr. James Nimmo, 1654-1709,* p. xxix) to provide a French origin, from *Ne Mot* is too fanciful. The Nimmos are also traditionally said to be descended from French Protestants who fled from the massacre of St. Bartholomew in 1572, but the name is found in Scotland much earlier. An early form of the name is found in that of Johannes Newmoch, juror on assize at Liston, 1459 (*Edmonstone,* 80). Agnes Nemoch was married in 1490 (*Sc. Ant.,* III, p. 108), and Alexander Nemok was witness in Glasgow, 1587 (*Protocols,* X). Alexander Nemo was retoured heir of John Nemo de Mydilmount in the bailiary of Kylestewart, 1616 (*Retours, Ayr,* 136, 139). Marion Nimoke was married in Edinburgh, 1618 (*Edinb. Marr.*). James Nimmo, the Covenanter, fought at Bothwell Bridge, 1679, and Rev. William Nimmo was historian of Stirlingshire. Nemoche 1598, Nimo 1623.

NIN. In Gaelic, *nin,* a contraction of *nighean* (a corruption of *inghean,* q.v.), daughter, is used in the names of women, corresponding to *mac* in names of men, but the usage is now obsolete outside of Gaelic speech. In Scots records the word appears spelled *nean, nein, neyn, nin, nyn, nyne,* and is often prefixed to the name, e.g. Neinwirrichy = *nighean Mhurachaidh,* Neindonachy = *nighean Dhonnchaidh.* See also NIC.

NINIAN. S. "Ninian appears in the Scottish Calendar at Sept. 16. In Bede he is Nynia (ablative); Alcuin in a letter to the monks of Whithorn written before A. D. 804 calls him Nyniga (genitive); in the same document the Latinized form Ninianus appears for the first time. Nynia, Nyniga probably represent the British name Nynnyaw [recorded in the *Mabinogion: Kulwch and Olwen*]. Later we have in vernacular Scots Ringan, and in Gaelic Truinnean. An early instance of the former is Rineyan in 1301 (*Bain,* II, p. 311); still

NINIAN, *continued*

earlier is the Norse Rinan, if Rinansey, now North Ronaldsay in the Orkneys, is rightly explained as Ninian's Isle" (*Watson* I, p. 293–294). In Shetland we have S. Ninian's Isle in Timothy Pont's map (1608) named "S. Tronon's Yle." This "may be read either as a misprint for St. Ronon's Isle, or possibly as St. Tronon's, seeing that St. Ninian has been known in some other districts as St. Trinyon" (*Goudie*, p. 32). The name appears in Rabelais as S. Treignan. David Rinyhiane, witness in St. Andrews, 1504 (*Soltre*, p. 78) is probably Sir David Ringane, presbyter in Dunfermline, 1512 (*Laing*, 289). David Niniane was reidare at Scony, Fife, 1574 (RMR.). Vernacular Scots Ringan was a common forename in the sixteenth century and later: Ringan or Ringean Armstrong was brother-german to Will of Kinmont, and Rinion Armstrong was executed in 1624. Thomas Ninian was servitor to George Chrystie, 1683 (BOEC., VIII, p. 146), and a complaint was made by Margaret Ninian in Dysart, 1690 (*Dysart*, p. 54–55). Rowie's Ninian, i.e. Ninian son of Robert was a sixteenth century Borderer. Renzion (z = y) 1574, Rynyon 1592.

NINIANSONE. 'Son of NINIAN,' q.v. A sasine was given by Manse Niniansone at Skallowaybankis, 1624 (OSS., I, 50).

NISBET, NISBETT, NESBIT, NESBET. From the old barony of Nesbit in the parish of Edrom, Berwickshire. William de Nesebite witnessed a confirmation of the town lands of Nesbite to the Priory of Coldingham by Patrick, first earl of Dunbar (*Raine*, 116), Dominus Robert de Nesbit, miles, witnessed a charter by William de Horuirden to the Abbey of Kelso, c. 1160–1200 (*Kelso*, 320), and Walter de Nesebyte resigned his rights in the manor of Nesebyte in 1255 (*Bain*, I, 2026). Jone de Nesbyt and Thomas de Nesbyte, both of Berwickshire, rendered homage in 1296 (*Bain*, II, p. 206, 207), and several other Nisbets or Nesbits appear as charter witnesses in the thirteenth and fourteenth centuries. Robert de Nesbit was one of the hostages for Berwickshire in 1340, Philip of Nesbit of that Ilk acted as sheriff in 1493 (*Home*, 21, 26), and Thomas of Nisbet was prior of Coldingham from 1446–56. John Nechisbet, vestiarius, was burgess of Glasgow in 1649 (*Inquis.*, 3503). The name was carried to Sweden in the sixteenth century, and there are many descendants of these settlers now existing in the country. One of the best known of the name was Alexander Nisbet (1657–1725), the heraldic writer. Neisbit 1468, Nesbeth 1574, Nesbut 1450, Nesbuth 1452, Nesbyth 1360, Neisbayt 1574,

Nesebite 1139, Nesebith 1368, Nesebeht 1498, Nesebyte 1255, Nesdret 1544, Nezebet 1507, Nezebeth 1537, Nisbert 1554, Nisbite 1616, Nizbet 1655, Nysbet 1546, Nysbit 1467, Nyzbet 1660. James Nesbit, the translator of the New Testament into Scots, spells his name Neisbit, Neisbitt, and Nesbeit. See also EAST-NISBET.

NIVEN, NEVIN, NEVINS. From *Naomhín*, 'little saint, saintlet.' Latinized *Nevinus*. Formerly a favorite personal name in Galloway and Ayrshire. Nevinus, parson of Neveth, witnessed grant of a saltpan in Rosneath to the monks of Paisley, c. 1230 (RMP., p. 211), and Patrick filius Nevyn mentioned in 1284 (*ibid.*, p. 64) is doubtless Patrick fiz John Nevyn or Neivin of Lanarkshire who rendered homage, 1296 (*Bain*, II, p. 213). Thomas filius Neuini served on an inquest in 1295 (*Rose*, p. 30), another Thomas filius Nyuini or Niuini was a tenant in Garvalde, 1376, and Crunyhatoun was leased to Robert fil. Niuini in the same year (RHM., I, p. lvii–lviii). Thomas Nevin was king's messenger in 1538, and Hew Neving was burgess of Irvine, 1590 (*Irvine*, I, p. 42, 64). James Nevein, heir of John Nivein of Kirkwood, his grandfather, in 2½ merkland of Kirkwood, 1635 (*Retours, Ayr*, 297), John Nivine appears in Corslat, 1675 (*Kilbarchan*), and Patrick Niven or Knevan was a laborer at Castle Stewart, 1793 (*Wigtown*). The Nivens or Nevins of Monkredding were an old family in Ayrshire, found there in 1539 when they had charter of these lands from the Abbey of Kilwinning (*Ayr Fam.*, III, p. 253: Robertson says, "from whence they were derived, or what became of them after leaving this place, are alike to me unknown"). Thomas Newing, younger of Monkridding is in record, 1594 (*Hunter*, p. 33), and Thomas Nevin, heir of Thomas Nevin of Monkredding, his father, succeeded 1680 (*Retours, Ayr*, 617). As forename: Neuen Donaldson from Logy, 1392 (*Grandtully*, I, p. 143), Nevin Makgilvar, burgess of Inverness, 1430 (RMS., II), Nevinus Makmulron in St. Andrews, 1472 (ERUS., p. 52). Nevane 1683, Nevein 1623, Neveine 1603, Nevene 1598, Nevyne 1561, Nevyng 1560, Newein 1602, Newin 1610; Neiven, Nifin, Niving.

NIVESON, NIVISON. *See under* NEVISON.

NIXON. The "son of Nicholas," from the diminutive form "Nick." "The name was common on both sides of the Border, perhaps most so in Bewcastle in Cumberland; but as early as 1376 we find a William Nycson occupying lands in the district of Ermyldoune in Liddesdale" (*Liddesdale*, p. 181). William Nykson was one of the "borowis" for the earl of Douglas's bounds of the West March in 1398 (*Bain*, IV, 512). The following forms of this name are given by Armstrong: Singular: Nekson, Nexson, Nexsoune, Nicksoune, Nicson, Nikson, Niksoun, Niksown, Nixon, Nixoun, Nixson, Nixsone, Nixsoun, Nixsoune, Nycson, Nykson, Nyksone, Nyksoun, Nyksown, Nysson; Plural: Nekesonis, Nekesouns, Neksons, Nexsones, Nexsounes, Nicksons, Nicsons, Niksonis, Niksons, Nixones, Nixons, Nixsonis, Nixsons, Nycsons, Nyksons, Nysons, Nyxons, Nyxsonnes, Nyxsons (op. cit., p. 180).

NOBLE. An English family of this name settled in East Lothian as subvassals of the family of de Vallibus (Vaux) at the end of the twelfth century. William Nobilis held part of the lands of Garmilton under William de Vallibus (*Neubotle*, 117). He was succeeded by his son Radulph who confirmed his father's grants (ibid., 118). Radulphus Nobilis witnessed a grant by Vinianus de Mulineys to the Hospital of Soltre, 1198–1234 (*Soltre*, p. 11), and between 1214–30 he witnessed an agreement between the monks of Neubotle and Adam Malherb, lord of Morham (*Neubotle*, p. 67). A charter by Radolphus le Noble and Thomas le Noble, his son, of the lands of Ylviston, i.e. Eliston, in Edinburghshire, to Sir David Graham, was confirmed by Alexander III, 1253 (Nisbet on RR.). Thomas le Noble and Patrick le Noble of Edinburghshire rendered homage, 1296 (*Bain*, II, p. 199). In 1337 the lands of Garleton-Noble were forfeited. John Nobil appears as a religious of Neubotle in 1398 (LSC., 110). Vilyam Nobile was chamberlain and procurator of the abbot of Arbroath at Inverness in 1464 (RAA., II. 156), and the Nobles of that town may be descended from him. In 1467 the Nobles of Ferm had a charter of the lands of Ferm, now called Coates, near Rutherglen (*Nisbet*). Alexander Nobill and John Nobill were murdered in Inverness in 1497 (Mackintosh, *Invernessiana*, p. 165), and William Nobill was tenant of Culcowe, Ardmanoch, 1504 (ER., XII., p. 662). Patrick Nobill had a remission for his share in holding Dumbarton Castle against the king, 1489 (APS., XII, p. 34). Robert Nobill who witnessed a sasine in favor of Mathew Stewart, son of the earl of Lennox, 1490 (*Lennox*, II, p. 140), is probably Robert Nobill in the burgh of Dunbertane mentioned in 1495 (REG., p. 492). A family of the name held land in Dumbartonshire in the seventeenth century (*Retours, Dumbarton*). Alan Nobill was tenant in barony of Stobo, 1512 (*Rental*). See MACNOBLE.

NOE. A Kirkcudbrightshire surname. From (MAC)NOAH, q.v. Noah, abbot of Kingarth,

died 790 (AU.). William Nae in Galtway, Kirkcudbrightshire, 1689 (RPC., 3. ser. XIV, p. 745).

NOITH. Perhaps local from lands of the name (Noth) in parish of Rhynie, Aberdeenshire. David Noith admitted burgess of Aberdeen, 1456 (NSCM., I, p. 15). Andrew Noysthe admitted burgess there, 1508 (ibid., p. 44), may be a misspelling of the name.

NONTHANK. John Nonthank witnessed a lease by George, abbot of Inchaffray, 1491 (*Inchaffray*, p. xcvii).

NOON. A surname early associated with Aberdeen. John Nvne was admitted burgess of the burgh in 1514, William None admitted in 1559, and Patrick Nown in 1567 (NSCM., I, p. 45, 67, 69). Margaret Nune recorded there, 1585 (CRA., p. 57), and Alexander Nune, textor, was burgess in 1646 (*Inquis.*, 3138).

NORHAM. From Norhan-on-Tweed, England. Magister Henry de Norham, official of Gregory, bishop of Brechin, c. 1218–22 (RAA., I, p. 52; REB., II, p. 256, 262). Thomas de Norham, a charter witness, c. 1260–67 (RPSA., p. 108, 313), and John de Norham, younger, canon of St. Andrews, witnessed homage of Andrew, son of Gilmur, to the prior of St. Andrews, 1269 (ibid., p. 349). Provision of a canonry was made for Thomas de Norham or Noram in 1329 (*Pap. Lett.*, II, p. 294, 297).

NORIE, NORRIE, NORRY. Thomas Nory who held the land of Corchrony in 1360 (REA., I, p. 87), may be Thomas Nory "locum tenentis vicecomites de Aberden," 1388 (CAB., p. 380). William Nory, subprior of St. Andrews, c. 1400 (*Wyntoun*, bk. ix. c. xx) is probably William Nory, canon of St. Andrews cathedral, 1415. Anny Nory is recorded in Aberdeen, 1408 (CWA., p. 314), and William Nory leased Ledcassy in Angus, 1443 (*Cupar-Angus*, I, p. 119). John Nory was the king's chaplain in Kirkwall, 1460 (*Diplomatarium Norvegicum*, V, p. 599), and Walter Nore, notary in Strathendrick, 1480 (*Strathendrick*, p. 194). Thomas Nory and James Nory were burgesses of Edinburgh, 1482 (*Neubotle*, 304). Patrick Nory had remission in 1489 for his part in holding Dumbarton Castle against the king (APS., XII, p. 34), Arthur Norye, witness in Perth, 1547 (*Rollok* 16), and Alexander Noray was rector of Ferne, 1589 (REB., II, 228). Four brothers Norrie from Monquhitter served in the first Great War (*Turriff*). A family of Norrie gave name to Norriston near Thornhill, Perthshire. Old, Norre. See NORN and NORY.

NORMAN, NORMAND. From OE. Norðmann, 'a Northman, Dane.' Normannus, uicecomes, witnessed David's great charter to Holyrood, c. 1128 (LSC., p. 6). Normannus, constapularius de Enneroury (Inverurie), was charter witness, c. 1180 (REA., I, p. 11). William, son of Norman, burgess of Aberdeen, was one of the witnesses to a charter by Fergus, earl of Buchan, c. 1189–99 (RAA., I, p. 57). Norman filius Bertouf or Bertulfi appears c. 1200–14, as charter witness (RAA., I, 83, 93; Neubotle, p. 7). John Normand, juror on inquisition in Roxburgh, 1303 (Bain, II, 1435), is probably John Normand, bailie of Berwick, 1324 (Cambus., 39). There was 'trublance' betwixt Robert Normand and another in Dysart, 1600 (Dysart, p. 26). Norman was also a surname in Dumfriesshire in thirteenth century. It is also used as an Englishing of TORMOD, q.v.

NORMAND. As NORMAN, q.v., with accretionary d. There is a tendency to add a d to names ending in an and on.

NORMANVILLE. The Itinéraire de la Normandie shows two places named Normanville, one near Yvetot and the other in the arrondissement of Evreux, from either of which this name may have been derived. John de Normanville witnessed a grant by Bernard de Hauden to the Hospital of Soltre between 1190–1230, and between 1221–31 he witnessed the grant of the church of Lympetlaw to the same house (Soltre, p. 10, 25). He also gave part of Maxtone to Melrose Abbey (Inchaffray, p. 275). Hugh de Normanville and Alicia, his wife, exchanged some land with the monks of Melrose in the reign of William the Lion (Melros, p. 79–81), and in 1200 he made a similar exchange with the monks of Dryburgh (Dryburgh, p. 144). Dominus Thomas de Normaniuill and dominus Johannes de Normaniuill witnessed quit claim to the lands of Eduluestun to the church of Glasgow, 1233 (REG., p. 140). Sir Walran of Normanville had a grant in 1242 of the lands of Correncrare, Tulichule, and others. Several Normanvilles in the reign of Alexander II, younger sons, filled the office of secular rectors of churches. Wydo (Guido) de Normanuilla was charter witness, 1250 (RAA., I, p. 190), William de Normanville was rector of the church of Mackistun, c. 1250 (Melros, I, p. 305), Sir Waleran de Normanville was buried at Melrose, 1256 (ES., II, p. 585), and Thomas de Normanville presided at an inquest on the lands of Hopkelchoc, 1259 (APS., I, p. 98 red). Alexander de Normanville witnessed a charter by James the Seneschal of Scotland, 1294 (RMP., p. 96), and Walranus

de Normanuilla, miles, was charter witness at Arbroath, 1299 (RAA., I, p. 165). Robert de Normanville of Stirlingshire rendered homage, 1296. His seal bears a coronation of a kneeling figure (the Virgin?), and Robertt . . . Normavil (Bain, II, p. 202, 548). Johan de Normanville and others also rendered homage in same year (ibid.). Descendants of Robert became barons of Gargunnock, and the name was shortened to Norval (Nisbet). See NORVAL.

NORN. A surname formerly in use in Orkney, from ON. Norræna, 'Norse' (language). It was apparently used as an alternative for NORY, q.v. Stevin Norne in Woy (Voy) in Sandwick in 1601 (REO., p. 325). John Norie in Howbister in Orphir in 1612 reappears in 1627 as John Norne. The old family of Norne of Voy, Stromness, are more than once called Norie thus proving the identity of the names.

NORQUOY, NORQUAY. Old Orcadian surnames from one or other of the places named Norquoy in the islands. QN. nord kví, 'north fold.'

NORREYS. From OF. (le)Noreis, Noreys, 'Northman,' 'Northerner.' In Latin record, Norrensis. Robert le Norreis witnessed a charter by Earl Gospatric to the Priory of Coldingham, a. 1166 (CCPC., p. 8). William Norrensis witnessed a charter by Malcolm, earl of Fife, a. 1228 (CMN., 9), Malcolm Norhais was a witness in 1237 (ibid., 17), and Gilbert Noreis, a charter witness, c. 1250 (RPSA., p. 388–9). John 'le Norreys' was one of an inquisition to inquire if Walter Biset was seized in the manor of Ulvington at his death, 1251 (Bain, I, 1836). Richard Norreys of Berwickshire rendered homage, 1296 (Bain, II, p. 206). John dictus Nurys, burgess of Dundee, 1321 (HP., II, p. 225), and John Noreys, a Scot born at Montrose, had letters of denization in England, 1480 (Bain, IV, 1465).

NORRIS. The modern form of NORREYS, q.v.

NORSK. Icel. Norskr, Danish and Norwegian Norsk, 'Norse.' Mans Norsk was minister of Yell, Shetland, 1586 (OSR., I, p. 207). Magnus Norsk was minister in Unst, 1633 (Shetland).

NORTHINCHETON. Local. Nicol de Northincheton, burgess of Peebles, rendered homage, 1296 (Bain, II, p. 197).

NORVAL. A curtailed form of NORMANVILLE, q.v. Robert Norvyle witnessed resignation by Sir David de Wemyss of lands in Fife in 1373 (Wemyss, II, p. 15). Johannes Norwald (with accretionary d), dominus de Cardownalde

(Cardonald near Paisley), was witness to a notarial instrument in 1413 (*Pollok*, I, p. 146). John Norvaile and George Norvil are recorded in Stirling in 1471 (*Sc. Ant.*, x, p. 59, 60). Adam Norwald, witness in Perth, 1547 (*Rollok*, 16), William Norwell who was amerciat in Stirling in 1549 may be the William Norvell 'thesaurar of the burght of Striviling' in 1561 (*SBR.*, p. 55, 77). William Norwell, perhaps the same person, represented Stirling in the Scottish parliament, 1568–86 (*Foster*, p. 275). John Norvell, burgess of Stirling, 1596 (*Logie*, I, p. 17). Gilbert Norvell was admitted burgess of Aberdeen in 1605 (*NSCM.*, I, p. 100), Jon Norwall was merchant burgess there in 1611 (*ROA.*, I, p. 231), William Norwell was burgess and guild brother of Glasgow in 1619 (*Burgesses*), and Alexander Norvall was notary at Carluke in 1656 (*Lanark CR.*). Norowell 1579, Noruell 1555, Norval and Norvel of that Ilk (*Nisbet*).

NORWAY. From the country, 'Norway.' John de Norwagia held land in vill de Berewyc, p. 1147 (*Kelso*, 34), and Patrick Norroway was mayor (mair) of regality of Arbroath, 1528 (*RAA.*, II, 694). See NORN and NORY.

NORY. An Orcadian surname, from ON. *Norge* (pronounced Norre), 'Norway.' "Evidently given originally to a family which came from Norway towards the close of the Norse régime" (*Old Lore Misc.*, v, p. 63). John Nory is described in 1460 as chaplain to King Christian of Norway (*Diplomatarium Norveg.*, II, p. 599). Nicolas Norre was tacksman of Evirbustir and Howie in 1492, John Nory or Nore was a roithman in 1495–1507, Wat Nore a witness in Kirkwall, 1590 (*REO.*, p. 79–81, 90, 199, etc.). Andrew Nory, David Nory, and William Nory, possibly all three from Orkney, were admitted burgesses of Aberdeen in 1457, 1475, and 1478 (*NSCM.*, I, p. 16, 25, 27). Beatrix Nory was retoured heir of John Nory, portioner of Fynnairsie, her father, in 1556 (*Retours, Aberdeen*, 22), and Maister Duncane Nory was Regent of the College of Auld Abirdene in 1569 (*RPC.*, I, p. 675). Cf. also NORIE, NORN and NORREYS.

NOTHINGHAM. Henricus de Nothingham, canon of Caithness, who witnessed a charter of Johannes Fraser de Glenwyn in 1272 (*Scon*, p. 85), probably derived his name from Nothingham (in 1408 Nothigane) in the parish of Latheron, Caithness, now Nottingham.

NOTMAN. A surname almost localized in East Lothian, and can there be traced back for four centuries or more. John Noteman is mentioned in 1297 as on the king of England's service in Scotland (*Bain*, II, 881).

Thomas Notman in Mosshouses, 1662, and Andrew Noteman there in 1690 (*RRM.*, II, p. 12, III, p. 112). Janet Notman in Dryburg, 1669, and Andrew Notman in Roxburgh, 1683 (*Peebles CR.*). C. Notman was town-clerk of Dunbar, and his father was chief-constable of Peeblesshire. 1641 Noltman. There is a Notman Law in Manor parish, Peeblesshire. The name has been explained as a form of 'Nutman,' a dealer in nuts, but?

NUCATOR. See under MACNUCATOR.

NUDIE. Norman Nudie a witness in Linlithgow, 1472 (*Sc. Ant.*, XVII, p. 118). Perhaps from Nydie in regality of St. Andrews, Fife. See also NYDIE.

NUDRE. Robert de Nudre was charter witness in Edinburgh, 1425 (*RMS.*, II, 34), John Nuddre or Nudry was bailie of Montrose, 1431, 1435 (*REB.*, II, 36, 46), and William Nudrie was 'mair of fee' in Brechin, 1450 (*ibid.*, 127). William of Nudry was proctor of Hugo Cuminche, a hermit in the forest of Kilgerie in the barony of Menmuir, in the reign of James II (*ibid.*, II, p. 382). William Nudere was burgess of Montrose, 1524 (*RAA.*, II, 583), prayers were offered in the same year for the soul of Thomas Nudere, archdeacon of Moray (*ibid.*,), and another Thomas Nudry was tenant in the barony of Edilstoun, 1539 (*Rental*). Nudrye 1507, Nwdry 1552, Nwdrye 1509.

NUG. Cormac de Nug perambulated the lands of Balfeth in Angus, c. 1204–11 (*RAA.*, I, 89). He probably derived his name from Nigg in Kincardineshire.

NUISI. Symon de Nuissi or Nuisi witnessed resignation of the lands of Edeluestun to the church of Glasgow, 1233 (*REG.*, p. 138, 139). As Simon de Novsi, persona de Ormestun (in East Lothian) he witnessed a charter of the tithes of Petneweue, 1238 (*Inchaffray*, p. 56).

NUTSHILL. From the old lands of Nutishill or Nuttishill now the village of Nitshill in the parish of Abbey-Paisley, Renfrewshire. John Nuttishill appears as burgess of Glasgow in 1478 and 1494 (*REG.*, 453, 469). As John Nutsyll or Nuttischill he appears again as a charter witness in 1481 and 1483 (*LCD.*, p. 194, 195). Jonet Nutishill is also in record in Glasgow in 1528 (*ibid.*, p. 90).

NYDIE. From Nydie in the parish of St. Andrews, Fifeshire. Hugh de Nidin granted to Alexander de Blar on his marriage with the daughter of Hugh, c. 1204–28, one-half of the lands of Konakin in Fife (*SHSM.*, IV,

NYDIE, *continued*

p. 312). Hugh de Nidun was accused of laying violent hands on the property of the prior and convent of St. Andrews in 1220 (*Pap. Lett.*, I, p. 74), and about the same date he appears as a witness in two writs (RD., p. 67, 142). William de Nidin witnessed the grant of the church of Neleston to Paisley, c. 1230 (RMP., p. 105). As Willelmus de Nydin, clericus regis, he appears as charter witness in 1231 (*Scon*, p. 62; RAA., I, 84). See also NUDIE.

NYMMILL. David Nymmill and William Nymmill in Dalkeith were summoned before the Privy Council, 1566 (RPC., I, p. 444). John Nimbill recorded in Haddington, 1589 (Mill, *Plays*, p. 254). Alexander Nimbill was retoured heir of James Nimbill, lawful son of Mr. John Nimbill minister of the word of God at Cranstoun, 1637 (*Retours, Edinburgh*, 813). Nymbill 1642.

OAG. A form of OGG, q.v.

O'BEOLLAN. The family name of Ferchar Mac-in-tagart, first earl of the line of Ross. The name seems to belong to the herenachs of St. Maelrubha in Applecross (Reeves, *Adamnan*, p. 400). It was a common name in early times, and was borrowed by the Norsemen as *Bjolan* in *Landnámabók*.

OBERVILLE. John de Oberville was on assize of marches in Fife, 1230, and as John de Obiruil he witnessed a gift of 10s. annually to the monks of Dunfermline by Gilbert de Cles (RD., p. 108, 111). In 1291 William de Obervill granted to the abbot and convent of Dunfermline permission to work one coalpit on any part of his property except arable ground, and when one was exhausted to open another (ibid., p. 218). As William Doberville del counte de Fyfe he rendered homage in 1296 (*Bain*, II, p. 204). From one or other of the half-dozen places in Normandy named Auberville. In Domesday Book the name appears as Odburvill and Oburvilla.

O'BROLACHAIN. Flaithbheartach Ua Brolchain was offered the abbacy of Colum-cille in Iona in 1164 (AFM., s.a.) but declined it. Domhnall Ua Brolchain, prior of Derry, perhaps a relative of Flaithbheartach, became abbot of Iona and was builder of the Bell Tower there, or at least of the lower part of it. He died in 1203 (AU.). The mutilated inscription in Lombardic letters on the southeast pier of the cathedral reads: *Donaldus O'Brolchan fecit hoc opus*. Abbot Donald came of a famous family of masons of whom the earliest recorded is Maelbrighde Ua Brolchan, styled

prim saer Erann, i.e. 'chief mason of Ireland' (Adamnan, VC., p. 405). He died in 1029 (AU., s.a.). The rectory of S. John the Evangelist at Kildaltane, Islay, was vacant in 1549 by the decease of Sir John Obrolchan (OPS., II, p. 269). Archibald McBrolachin was one of the tenants in Iona, 1677, and Lauchlan duy McBrolachan appears as merchant in Campbeltown, 1778 (*Argyll*). The name has been Englished Bradley and Brodie (Brody), although these names have no connection with it either in root or meaning.

OCHILTREE, OCHILTRIE. John de Vchiltre was a notary public in Linlithgow in 1399 (LSC., 108), and a tenement in Perth was confirmed to Michael Wchyltre, dean of Dunblane, in 1424 (RMS., II, 18). Archibald Wchiltre witnessed an instrument of sasine of Cragniche to Archibald, earl of Argyll in 1493 (OPS., II, p. 97), Alanus Wchiltre was juror on an assize at Liston in 1459 (*Edmonstone*, p. 80), John Ukiltre of Kildalvan, witness, 1547 (*Poltalloch Writs*, p. 139), and John Uchiltrie was a clerk of St. Andrews diocese in 1576 (*Home*, p. 231). A race of MacUchtres who held lands in Glendaruel of the earls of Argyll "gradually Anglicised their name to Ochiltrie (Argyll charters *passim*)" (*Celt. Rev.*, IX, p. 348). Ouchiltre 1550, Uchiltre 1501, Uchiltree 1576, Vcgiltrie 1567. The name is most probably derived from Ochiltree in the parish of Linlithgow, West Lothian. Oghillrie 1629.

OCHTERLONIE, OCHTERLONY. *See under* AUCHTERLONIE.

OCONOCHAR. Ir. *O'Conchobhair* or *O'Conchubhair*, 'descendant of Conchobar,' an ancient Irish personal name. Duncan Oconochar, mediciner in Lorne, 1622 (*Sasines*, II, 135). Kenneth Oconchar, servitor of Donald Oconchar, mediciner in Lorne, 1636 (*Poltalloch Writs*, p. 192). Dr. Donald Ochonocher the famous mediciner attended the Thane of Cawdor in his last illness in Irvine, c. 1650. John Oconochar in Bravalich, 1672 (HP., II, p. 208). John O'Conocher of Ardeoran, witness, 1668 (*Sasines*, 1405), appears again in 1686 as John Occonicher in Ardoran (RPC., 3. ser. XII, p. 441). James O'Conochar was schoolmaster of Kingarth, Bute, 1699 (*Hewison*, II, p. 285). The O'Conochers were leeches to the Macdougalls of Dunolly and the Campbells of Lochow. Several of the Oconochers in Lorne called themselves Leotch — and as likely as not they were really Macdougalls (*Henry Campbell*). O'Conoher (in Bute 1686).

O'DOCHARTY. Ir. *O'Dochartaigh*, 'descendant of Dochartach' (*Woulfe*). There were a number of people of this name in Islay in early seventeenth century under the Campbells of Cawdor. Donald O'Dochartie in Islay, 1629 (*Cawdor*). James Odocherty and William Odocherty in Tormistell, Islay, 1733 (*Bk. Islay*, p. 552).

ODRAN (ODHRAN). Diminutive of *odhar*, 'dun coloured, sallow.' Skene suggested (PSAS., IV, p. 318) that Adrian, an Irish missionary who arrived in Pictland about the time of the accession of Kenneth Macalpin, was really named Odran, "as the name of the patron saint always enters largely into those of the clergy of the place with the usual prefix of *Gilla* or *Maol; and we find a subsequent bishop of St. Andrews called Macgilla Odran, son of the servant of Odran." A Saint Odran is mentioned in an old life of St. Columba, and tradition has it that he was the first person to be buried in Iona, in Reilig Orain (*Reilic Odhrain*). He is also commemorated in Cladh Odhrain in Tiree, in Kiloran in Colonsay, and elsewhere. A Mailodranus is mentioned by Adamnan (VC., I, 20).

O'DUIBHNE. See under DUBNI. The O'Duibhnes were the ancestors of the Campbells as attested by an early charter. Diarmuid O'Duinn and Diarmaid O'Duibhne are used indifferently. A possible source or perhaps result of confusion is seen in the name of another member of the Fian, viz., Diarmaid mac Duinn meic Donnchadha, of the Erna of Munster, of whom very little seems to be known.

OFFICER. An old surname in Glenbervie. From the office of 'Officer' or official, usually a layman, who presided at the Bishop's Court. Walterus officialis witnessed a charter by Earl David, 1202–3 (LAC., 3). Master Baldred officialis of prior of St. Andrews, 1285 (*Neubotle*, 59).

OGG, OAG. Both these names are from the Gaelic adjective *og*, "young." Donald Oge was one of an inquisition in Aberdeen in 1457 (RAA., II, 108). Finla McJames Uig in Abirnethie was fined in 1613 for reset of members of outlawed Clan Gregor (RPC., XIV, p. 629). Oage 1688.

OGGA. A diminutive of some OE. double-stemmed name. Ogga was one of the witnesses to King Eadgar's charter of Swintun to the monks of S. Cuthbert of Coldingham, 1097–1107 (*Nat. MSS.*, I, 4). As Oggo, Cumbrensis judex, he was one of the jurors who gave evidence regarding the lands of the Church of Glasgow, c. 1124 (REG., p. 5), and as Oggu he witnessed David's great charter of Holyrood, c. 1128 (LSC., p. 6). He may have

been the Oggu, father of Gillandris, one of the perambulators of the boundaries of Clerchetune, c. 1141 (RPSA., p. 181, 191).

OGILL. See under OGLE.

OGILVIE, OGILVY. Of territorial origin from the barony of Ogilvie in the parish of Glamis in Angus. Gilbert, son of Gillebride, first earl of Angus, and younger brother of Gilcrist, third earl of Angus, obtained a charter between 1172–77 of the lands of Purin, Ogguluin, and Kynmethan (*Douglas*, III, 349). This charter exists only in a transumpt made in 1577, as the original was then "werray auld, warne and consumit, and skantlie may be weill red." This Gilbert is also witness to a grant by his brother Gilchrist of the church of Monyfode to the Abbey of Aberbrothok between 1201–4 (RAA., I, 29). Alexander de Oggoluin had a charter of the lands of Belauht and others before 1232 (SHSM., IV, p. 315). Patrick de Oggiluill occurs as witness to a mortification by Roger de Quincy, earl of Winchester, Constable of Scotland, of the church of Losrech (Lathrisk) to the Priory of St. Andrews about 1267 (RPSA., p. 337). He also, as Oggelville and Eggilvyn, took the oath of fealty in 1296. His seal bears a dog (?) at foot of tree, between 2 cinquefoils, and S' *Patricii de Oggilvile* (*Bain*, II, p. 195, 550). Walter de Ogilby was appointed High Treasurer of Scotland in 1425, and about the same date Patrick de Ogilby was Justiciar of Scotland benorth the Forth (*The Lennox*, II, p. 62). David of Ogilby was hostage for the king of Scotland in 1425 and Thomas of Oglevy of Clova had a safe conduct in 1466 (*Bain*, IV, 981, 983, 1366). A long-standing feud between the Campbells and the Ogilvies culminated in 1645 when the latter had their revenge for the burning of "The Bonnie House of Airlie" by setting fire to Castle Campbell near Dollar. An old rhyme referring to some Ogilvie of the past runs:

"Ugly you lived, and Ugly you die,
And now in an ugly place you lie."

"Ugly" here, of course, is a pun on the surname. Old forms of the name in addition to those already noted are: Ogelbe 1531, Ogglebie 1665, Ogiluy 1501, Ogillwe 1533, Ogiluill 1250, Ogilwe 1533, Ogilwill 1348, Ogilwye 1685, Ogilvile 1425, Ogilvo 1516, Ogliwv 1545, Oglevie 1661, Ogvlui and Ogvlvi 1483, Ogyluy 1526, Ogyluyll 1359, Ogylvil 1425, Ogylvy 1452, Ogvllwe 1534, Ogylwe 1492, Ogylwy 1509, Ogylwye 1456, and among the Scots Guards in the service of France it appeared as Ohilby. Other forms (undated) are Ogelvy, Ogiilvy, Ogilbe, Ogilbie, Ogilvi, Ogilwie, Ogivlle, Ogylbe, Ougelby.

OGLACH. Henry Oglach was one of an inquest at Roustenot (Restennet) in 1321 (RMS., I, App. I, 29). William Oglach was burgess of Glasgow, 1447 (LCD., p. 168), and John Oglaucht in the Munktoun was burgess of Prestwick, 1559 (*Prestwick*, p. 13).

OGLAY. William Oglav was admitted burgess of Aberdeen, 1570 (NSCM., I, p. 69). Perhaps from Ogley in Staffordshire.

OGLE, OGILL. Of local origin from the place named Ogle in Northumberland. Robert de Ogle before his death in 1362 held half the barony of the Hospital in Northumberland (*Bain*, IV, 73). Henry de Ogle witnessed a charter of lands in Fife, 1395 (*Wemyss*, II, 33), and Patrick Ogyll witnessed a papal dispensation by the bishop of Dunblane in 1422 (*Hay*, 10). Alexander de Ogil de Popil was one of an assize on the lands of Gladmor, 1430 (*James* II, 16), and Patrick Ogyl (Ogyll or Ogill) held a tenement in Haddington in 1458 and was witness there in same year (*Neubotle*, p. 244, 246–248). John Ogyll witnessed an instrument of sasine in favor of Adam Crechtoun of Ruchtven (Ruthven) in 1501 (*Bamff*, p. 39), the seal of Patrick Ogil is appended to a retour of 1538 (*Seals Supp.*, 787), William Ogill was a witness in Argyll, 1563 (HP., II, p. 206), payment was made to William Ogill, writer in chancery, in 1561 (ER., XIX, p. 136), and Henry Ogle is recorded at Hirsell in 1727 (*Lauder*).

OGSTON, OGSTONE. From the lands of Hogeston in Moray. There was a place Hogyston in the parish of Innerkelour in 1528 (RAA., II, 710), also lands of Ugistoun in the lordship of Lauder in 1557 (ER., XIX, p. 415). The first of the name recorded is Symon de Hogeston who appears in a deed (between 1224–42) settling a controversy between himself and Andrew, bishop of Moray, concerning some portions of the lands of Hogeston, ceded for the sake of peace and in pure and perpetual alms on behalf of his father and mother and all his ancestors, showing that the family possessed the lands anterior to this date (REM., p. 110–111). John de Oguston who witnessed a grant in favor of the chaplain of St. Peter at Duffus in 1240 (ibid., p. 275) may be the John de Oggiston, one of the inquisition concerning the lands of Mefth in 1262 (APS., I, p. 101). He also appears twice as a charter witness within the same period (REM., p. 111, 112). Alexander de Hogeston rendered homage for his lands at Elgin in 1296 (*Bain*, II, p. 195). Reginald de Oggynston, scholar of civil law of the diocese of Moray, was appointed to the chancellorship of the church of Glasgow in

1343 (*Pap. Pet.*, I, p. 14), in 1362, as de Ogghistoun, he paid the arrears of tenth penny of the see of Aberdeen (ER., I, p. 110), and in 1366, as de Oggistone, he is recorded as a canon of Aberdeen (REA., II, p. 58). John de Ogystoun or Ogistoun, *dominus ejusdem*, was present at the perambulation of the bounds of Tarwas and Wldny in 1417 (RAA., II, 53). In 1473 Alexander Ogstoun of that Ilk had licence under the Privy Seal of James III to sell his lands of Ogstoun in the lordship of Moray (*Innes familie*, p. 80, 81). John Hugstoun or Ogstoun was charter witness at Inveraray, 1575 (*Notes and Queries*, 11 July, 1931, p. 22). "The name Ogstone which appears in the Registers of Caithness is evidently that borne by some of the descendants of the Rev. Andrew Ogstone, minister of Canisbay (1601–1650). The name has been changed in modern times into Houston, but its old connection with Hogstown in Strathbogie, from which the name originates, has been persistently maintained through the centuries in the Caithness folk pronunciation of Houston as 'Hougston'" (Rev. D. Beaton in his preface to *Canisbay Records*). The Ogstons of the parish of Slains are said to have assumed their name from the farm of the same name in the south end of the parish. Howgstown 1496, Ogistone 1487, Ogistoun 1545, Ogistoune 1483, Oigsone 1663, Oigstone 1664, Ogstone 1509, Ogystovn 1468, Ugstoun 1574, Ugstoune 1632.

O'HANLEY. Ir. *Ua h-Ainle*, 'descendant of Ainle,' from *ainle*, 'beauty,' also 'a hero or warrior' (*Woulfe*). There are still some people of this name in South and North Uist, who probably came to South Uist about 1600 when Ranald MacRanald, first of Benbecula, married Fionnsgoth Burke, of the Burkes of Connaught. There are also several families of the name in different parts of Canada, descendants of emigrants from the Highlands. See *Oban Times*, 22 July, 1933.

OKILSETTER. From the lands of the same name in Paplay, Orkney. Riche Okkelsetter was tacksman of Okkilsetter in Paplay in 1492 (REO., p. 407). William Oglessetter, who was juror in dispute in 1593, may be the William Okilsettir who was under bailye of Sainct Androis parrochin in 1596 (ibid., p. 168, 172). Nicoll Okilsitter was a juror in 1605 (ibid., p. 179). Ockilsetter 1643.

OLD. The English form of AULD, q.v. William Old, cooper in Coldstream, 1752 (*Lauder*). Walter Gorn Old has written on theosophical subjects. Allan W. Old, H. M. Exchequer Office, Edinburgh, died 1942.

OLDCAMBUS. From Oldcambus near Cockburnspath, Berwickshire. Thomas de Aldecambus witnessed a charter by Adam de Lamberton of the third part of Lambertun, c. 1190–1200 (*Home*, p. 224). Edward de Aldecambus was accused before King William the Lion of 'wrecking,' c. 1198. For this he was condemned to death, but escaped by making a money payment. To raise this he exchanged with the prior and convent of St. Cuthbert, Durham, the lands of Auldcambus for Lumsden Major and his family thereafter are known as de Lumsdens (*Raine*, 648). The seal attached to his excambion bears the legend *Sigill Eduardti de Aldecambus* (*Seals Supp.*, 31).

OLDMAN. Jon Oldman was a trade burgess of Aberdeen, 1668 (ROA., I, p. 235). Lower thinks this might be a corruption of Holman.

OLDOWE. Fergus Oldowe was tenant of Ballenab, Islay, 1541 (ER., XVII, p. 620, 640). See also ALDOWY.

OLIPHANT. Of Norman origin. The family continued to hold land in Northamptonshire long after the principal branch had removed to Scotland. They were close friends of David I, when as earl of Huntingdon he was "getting the Scottish rust rubbed off" by residence in England. David Holifard saved David I at the rout of Winchester, 1141, and was rewarded by a grant of land in Scotland. The name has undergone a curious change due to popular etymology. The earliest forms are uniformly Olifard and Olyfard (Latin *Olifardus*). It seems to have been sometimes pronounced Olifat, as in 1296 (*Bain*, II, p. 176), and later, in some instances in public record, changed to Oliver. The gradual softening of the name was first into Holifarth and Olifarth, then into Olifart or Olyfart, and lastly into Olyfant or Olyfaunt which gave rise to the canting arms borne by the family. "This change was doubtless facilitated if not actually suggested, by the growing popularity of the word Olifaunt, as the name of the 'huge earth-shaking beast,' of which the crusaders brought home such marvellous stories" (Anderson, *Oliphants*, p. xxii). Andrew Oliphant, John Knox's "servant of Sathan," Latinized his name 'Elephantus.' David Olifard, first of the name in Scotland, godson of David I, acquired from the king lands in Roxburghshire, probably after 1141, and appears as witness to several charters of that king, and to later ones by Prince Henry and Malcolm IV. He made grants from his lands to the abbeys of Dryburgh and Jedburgh, and a grant of *vnam thravam de blado* to the Hospital of Soltre, c. 1153–57 (*Soltre*, p. 4). By

Malcolm IV he appears to have been created 'Justiciarius Laudonie.' An Osbert Olifard held land in the Mearns in first half of the reign of William the Lion. Fulcone Olifard witnessed a charter by Jocelin, bishop of Glasgow, 1175–99 (RMP., p. 109). William Olyfat was a Scots prisoner of war in Rochester, 1296 (*Bain*, II, p. 359). William Holifarth or Holyfarth held land of the Abbey of Arbroath, 1300 (RAA., II, 9). Aeneas Eliphant was writer to the signet in Edinburgh, 1711. Olephant 1605, Olifant 1459, Olifard 1283, Olifaunt 1317, Oliphand 1607, Olvfant 1326, Olyfaunt 1363, Olyfawnt 1454, Olyphaint 1582, Olyphard a. 1249, and (in Rhymer's *Foedera*) Elifend. See also OLIVER.

OLIVER. Walter Olifer [Justiciar Laudonie] witnessed William the Lion's gift of the serf Gillemachoi de Conglud with his children and all his descendants to the bishop of Glasgow, c. 1180 (REG., p. 33). Olyver, son of Kyluert, was one of the followers of the earl of March at end of twelfth century (*Neubotle*, p. 57, etc.). He was probably ancestor of the Frasers. Oliverius capellanus Willelmi regis, c. 1204–11 (RAA., I, p. 48; *Inchaffray*, p. 273). John Oliuer, prepositus of Berwick, witnessed a gift of land to the Hospital of Soltre, c. 1250–66 (*Soltre*, p. 32). William Holifarth or Holyfarth held land in Perth, c. 1330 (RAA., II, p. 8), and Thomas Olyver de Swyne witnessed a declaration dated 1436 (*Home*, 20). Wille Olipher in Petarno, a follower of Campbell of Lundy, 1541 (RSS., II, 3666), and William Olover was burgess of Dumfries, 1542 (*Anderson*). Robert Olifeir, burgess of Northberwyk, 1546 (CMN., 73), and Robert Olyphere or Oliphir was bailie of the burgh of North Berwick and of Haddington in 1557 (ER., XIX, p. 71; *Laing*, 664). John Olifer, burgess of Jedburgh, 1680 (RRM., III, p. 100), and John Olipher appears in Bermanie, parish of Elyth, 1688 (*Dunkeld*). In Shetland the Norse name Olaf (ON. *Oleifr*) has been merged in Oliver. Boece tells a picturesque story that the fall of Acre was due to a Scotsman named Oliver (or Olifer or Olifard) who from circumstances over which he had no control was obliged to fight on the side of the Saracens. On recognizing an old acquaintance in the train of David, earl of Huntingdon, and finding means to make himself known, he agreed to open a postern gate to the Scots on the following night (Stewart, *Croniclis*, III, p. 50). The name is probably from OFr. *Olivier*, 'fabricant ou marchant d'olive.' The Norse name *Olaf-r* (-r silent) has had some influence on the great vogue of the name. Oleuer 1527, Oleveir 1521, Oliphar 1517, Olipheir 1590, Olyar 1472, Olywer 1512. Symon le Olaver appears in English Hundred Rolls (1273). Cf. under OLIPHANT.

OLIVERSON, 'son of OLIVER,' q.v. Isaach Oliveri was canon of Aberdeen in 1366 (REA., II, p. 58).

OLLASON. A Shetland surname. Edward Ollasoun had a remission in 1547 for his share in taking and holding the castle of Akirgill in Caithness (OPS., II, p. 778), and Henry Ollasoun was portioner of Gord, 1625 (OSS., I, 114). Flight-lieutenant William Cowan Ollason, R. A. F., was awarded the D. F. C. in 1941. Olasone 1623.

OLLAY, OLLEY. Probably from Ouilly-le-Basset in Calvados, Normandy. The name appears in DB. (1086) as de Oilgi and in 1100 as d'Oilli. Fred Olley and Edward Olley from Turriff served in the first Great War (Turriff). Robert Gillies Ollay died in Edinburgh, 1940.

O'LOYNACHAN. A surname found in Kintyre. The O was sometimes dropped, the name appearing as Loynachan, and some bearers of the name further shortened it to Laing and Lang. According to Woulfe it is Ir. O'Luingeachain, 'descendant of Longachan,' diminutive of Longach.

OMAN, OMAND, OMOND. The first is the common form in Orkney. In Shetland the forms Omand and Omond are more common, mostly confined to the island of Yell. The ON. form of the name was either Hámundr ('high gift') or Amund, Amundi being an old personal name among the Norsemen. In Orkney records we have Edduard Homondsone of Onston (1546), Edward Omand or Omandson (1576), and in 1605 Rychert Ewmendsone (REO., p. 138, 178, 211, 233). Robert Omond was resident in Kirkwall, 1647 (Inquis., 3237). Thome Omond or Omound appears in Kirkbuster, 1530, and Richard Eumound in Cloustoun, 1602 (OSR., I, p. 256, 272).

OMAY, OMEY. This surname is simply O'Mey or O'May with omission of the apostrophe. A family of this name were lairds of Keil in Kintyre, and most of those of the name in record were connected with the church. A letter was directed to Mr. Duncane Omay in 1536 "makand him principall churgiane to the king, etc., and gifand him xl lib" (RSS., II, 3416). James May, son of Mr. Duncan May, was in 1542 presented to the rectory of Kilquhomen (Kilchoman) in Ila, vacant by the death of Mr. Archibald McEarbry [rightly McCarbry] (ibid., 4939). Master Cornelius Omeych was connected with the cathedral of Lismore, 1556 (OPS., II, p. 162). Duncan Omev, a layman apparently, held the three merks eight shillings and four pence land of Kilquhowane (Kilchoman) in Kintyre, 1605

(HP., III, p. 82). Mr. Alexander Omey, who was appointed minister at Monydie in 1608, was ordered by the Privy Council in 1612 to underlie punishment as an "ockerer," i.e. usurer (RPC., IX, p. 425). Mr. Donald Omey, "ane learned, modest, and goode teatcheour at the Kirk of Ardnamurchine," suffered outrage at the hands of John McIlmichill, a servant of the captain of Clanranald, in his kirk, 1624 (ibid., XIII, p. 427–428). The Rev. Duncan Omay was minister of Keil as well as laird in 1638, and his brother Rev. Donald O'Mey, was minister of Kilkeran in the same year. In Irish the name is O'Miadhaigh, and in Lorn it is Gaelicized M'A'Mhiadhaich. Miadhach, a personal name, from miadh, O. Ir. miad, honor, esteem, is parallel to Latin Honorius. The O'May tradition "is that they came to the country [Kilbrandon] to teach and practice weaving" (TGSI., XXXV, p. 269).

OMER. Magister Omerus clericus episcopi Aberdonensis, 1201–07, appears also as archdeacon of Aberdeen, c. 1204–11 (RAA., I, 39, 81 bis).

OMMUNDSEN. 'Son of Amund.' Edward Owmond, Ewmondsone, or Omond appears in Kirkwall, 1616 (OSR., I, p. 274–275). Sergeant Ommundsen of the Queen's Edinburgh Volunteers was four times winner of the Caledonian shield in latter half of nineteenth century. See under OMAN.

OMOND. See under OMAN.

O'MUIRGHEASAIN. 'Descendant of Muirgheas,' sea choice. A surname in Inishowen, county Donegal. At some uncertained date a branch of the family migrated from Inishowen to Scotland and settled in Lewis and Harris. Some of them became bards to the Macleods of Dunvegan. "In 1614 Toirdelbhach O'Murgheasa witnessed the contract of fosterage whereby Sir Rory Macleod gives his son Norman in fosterage to Mackenzie" (Nat. MSS., III, 84). This Norman was Sir Norman of Bernera, who died in 1705, and his elegy was composed by Donnchadh O'Murghesan (TGSI., XXIX, p. 197). Torzeallach O'Murrisane, servant to Sir Rory M'Cleud of Hereis, the Toirdelbach O'Murgheasa mentioned above, was one of a number charged with murder and piracy in 1616 (RPC., X, p. 634). Later the name became O'Morrisone and O'Morison. When the literary tradition with Ireland was broken the O' fell out and Muirgheasain was corrupted to Morrison. Their chief resided at Habost Ness in Lewis and became hereditary brieve or judge of Lewis. Hucheon Morrison was brieve in 1551 and John Morrison in 1596. Little has been preserved of the early history of the family, which practically came to an end about 1600. John Morison, "indweller" of Lewis, writing about 1680, says that the Morrisons descended from one of the "ancient inhabitants" of Lewis named "Mores the son of Kennanus whom the historians call Makurich, whom they make to be the natural son to one of the kings of Norovay" (quoted in PSAS., XII, p. 504). Equally baseless is the modern idea that "Morison" interpreted as "Mary's son," represents Gaelic *Mac Gille Mhuire*. Alexander Morison (*Heraldry of the Clan MacGhille-mhuire*) makes the wild statement that the name is from ancestors who were vassals or adherents of the jarls of More or Moeri in Norway!

ONTHEHULLE. i.e. 'on the Hill.' William Onthehulle of the county of Linlescu (Linlithgow) rendered homage, 1296. His seal bears a cross-bow and bolt in pale, star and crescent in field, S' *Wilelm' de Monte* (*Bain*, II, p. 201, 533). His name also appears as 'Othehille' and 'O' the hull' (ibid., p. 198, 208). There are lands called Hill in the Linlithgow *Retours* (1607). See HILL.

OO. Fergus Oo, a follower of the earl of Cassilis, was respited for murder in 1526 (RSS., I, 3386).

ORABILIS. There were two women so named. (1) Orabilis, daughter and heiress of Nesius, William's son, married Robert de Quincey († before 1200 — *Bower*, I, 515; *Annals*, p. 328). Wrongly called countess of Mar († before 30 June 1203; *Inchaffray*, 21). See much more about her in ES., II, p. 493, 494. (2) Orabilis who married Adam, son of Duncan, earl of Mar, son of Gilchrist, earl of Mar (ES., II, p. 494).

ORANGICH. John M'Ean Orangich held a croft near Tain, 1577. Orangich is a nickname = the 'singer.' Many similar names occur in old Tain charters: e.g. Bragoch, Muldonycht, Rossich, Skianach.

ORCHARD. An old spelling of URQUHART, q.v., which has crystallized into a separate surname. Orchart 1548.

ORCHARDSON. A corruption of URQUHART-SON. In the parish of Fordun the name was variously spelled and pronounced Orcherton or Orchanter, and further corrupted to Orchison. The father of Sir William Quiller Orchardson, the painter, claimed connection with the Highland sept of Urquhartson.

ORCHARDTOUN. "Orchardtoun of that Ilk." No such family ever existed, and "the *Litera prosapiae* under the Great Seal, issued in 1663, in favour of John Orchardton, major of the Guards of the King of Sweden, is one of the best examples of a genealogical fable sanctioned by the highest authority, of which there were many in the seventeenth century" (*Stodart*, II, p. 363). Issobell Orcherton in Aberdeen, 1790 (*Aberdeen CR.*). There is a place Orchardtown in the parish of Udny.

ORD, ORDE. This surname is of twofold origin: (1) from Ord (Orde or Horde), later Kirkurd in Peeblesshire, (2) from the lands of Ord in Banffshire. Adam of Horde of the county of Peebles rendered homage in 1296 (*Bain*, II, p. 197, 207). John Urd was tenant in Spotswood in 1731 and William Ourd, tenant in Ligertwood in 1741 (*Lauder*). Andrew de Ord had the lands of Ord in the parish of Banff from Robert I in the 21st year of the king's reign. Alexander Ord of that Ilk and Walter Ord in Banff wrongfully raised letters against Walter Currour of Inchedrour and others in 1596 (RPC., V). James Ord, wigmaker in Cullen, was a Jacobite of the '45. The surname is now comparatively rare in Banffshire, but appeared in Cullen at end of seventeenth century (SN&Q., I, p. 201). The old family of the name exchanged the lands of Ord for Finachty c. 1590 (ibid.). Laurence Ord was a merchant burgess burgo Vicicanonicorum, Edinburgh, 1696 (*Inquis.*, 7677).

ORE. Perhaps from Oare in Sussex, England. The Ores of Knockoudie, in the shire of Nairn, "were not of great fortune, but occupied a good social standing. The name of Ore existed in Nairn till lately, but the main line has failed in the district" (Bain, *Nairnshire*, 2. ed., 1898, p. 339). James Oare, teacher at Alfoord, 1673, "was approven, but exhorted to study the Hebrew more exactlie" (*Alford*, p. 193). Hew Ore, merchant in Nairn, 1747 (*Moray*). Knockoudie now forms part of farm of Park.

OREM. Perhaps from the English place name Oram or Orem rather than a variant of ORM, q.v. Persons of this name were for a lengthened period tenant farmers in the parish of Kemnay (AEI., p. 22). Henry Owrum was admitted burgess of Aberdeen, 1479 (NSCM., I, p. 28). William Orem recorded in Dullab, 1633 (SCM., III, p. 73), and David Orem in Perth, 1694 (*Inquis.*, 7545). Alexander Orem was bailie of Aberdeen, 1722, and William Orem, town clerk of Aberdeen, wrote a description of the Chanonry, etc., of Old Aberdeen, 1724-5.

ORKIE. Elys de Orky of the county of Fyfe who rendered homage in 1296 (*Bain*, II, p. 204) derived his name from the lands of Orkie in the parish of Kettle, Fife.

ORKNEY. Thomas Orkney of Scotland was illegally arrested at Lowestoff, 1405 (*Bain*, iv, 690). John Orknay held land in Abbirbrothoc in 1457, and in 1478 Thomas Orkynay was witness in Perth (RAA., ii, 111, 202). Another Thomas Orkney was witness in Glenurquhay in 1552 (BBT., p. 197). Robert Orknay was retoured heir of his grandfather in lands in Aytoun, Berwickshire, 1634 (*Retours, Berwick*, 197). The name is also recorded in Edinburgh, 1640 (*Edinb. Marr.*). Orkynnay 1486.

ORM. From *Ormr*, 'serpent,' a favorite ON. personal name (the final *-r* is silent). Orm or Horm was sacerdos of Hume between 1153–56 (*Kelso*, 288). Orm filius Eilaf witnessed King David's great charter to Melrose Abbey, a. 1153 (*Nat. MSS.*, i, 17). John, son of Orm, was one of the witnesses to Waldeve's charter of Dundas to Helias, son of Huctred (ibid., i), and is probably the John filius Horum who witnessed a charter by Eschina uxor Walteri. Orm was father of John, lord of Hunum (Hownam), c. 1164–74 (*Melros*, p. 118), and William filius Orm witnessed a charter by Dovenald, abbe de Brechin, c. 1204–11 (RAA., i, 74 bis). William Orm of Kethe, a Scots prisoner of war captured at Stirling Castle, 1305 (*Bain*, ii, 1644, 1672). David Orme, chamberlain of the Priory of St. Andrews, 1565–70 (RPC., i, p. 403; RHM., i, 50). William Orme was burgess freeman of Glasgow, 1607 (*Burgesses*), and Robert Orum, trade burgess of Aberdeen, 1617 (ROA., i, p. 231). Stodart says (ii, p. 414) that the surname Orme belongs to Fifeshire, particularly to the neighborhood of Newburgh and Lindores Abbey. Henry Orme was abbot of Lindores, 1502, Stephen Orme was procurator to the abbot in the same year (LAC., p. 298), and a later Henry Orme held a tack of land near Lindores, 1564 (RMS., iv, 2666).

ORMISHUK. William de Ormishuk (Ormyshuk, Armishuk, or Hormyshoke), treasurer of the church of Aberdeen, who appears several times as a witness between 1360 and 1392 (REA., i, p. 89, 109, 175, 182, 186), may have derived his name from Ormsheugh now Armsheugh in the upper part of the parish of Irvine, Ayrshire.

ORMISTON. This surname is of two-fold origin: (1) from Ormiston, East Lothian, and (2) from Ormiston in Roxburghshire. Local pronunciation is Wurmston. In a charter granted by Earl Henry between 1147–52 to the canons of Jedburgh, mention is made of a 'toun Orm son of Eylav' (*Morton*, p. 56). In a footnote (p. 49) Morton says there are many families in Scotland of this name, prob-

ably from this Orm, and a family of Ormiston was long settled at Old Melrose. Alan de Ormyston witnessed a charter by Hugh Rydale dominus de Craneston a. 1200 (*Neubotle*, 12), and Walter de Dormeston (i.e. d'Ormeston) was witness to a charter by Walter Olifard junior (SHR., ii, p. 175). Alanus de Hormiston witnessed confirmation by Alexander filius Walteri of his father's gifts to the church of Paisley, 1239 (RMP., p. 225). As Alan de Ormystoun he witnessed the gift of Swaynyston to the House of Soltre between 1238–70, and the gift of Qwhytwel to the same House (*Soltre*, p. 28), and about 1289 he attested a charter by Patrick, earl of Dunbar (*May*, 22). Gilbert of Ormeston was assizer at Traqueyr in 1274 (*Bain*, ii, 34). Henry de Ormestone of Edinburghshire rendered homage in 1296 and was juror on an inquest at Berwick the same year (*Bain*, ii, p. 201, 215). Alice, widow of Aleyn de Ormestone of Edinburghshire, rendered homage, 1296. Her seal bears the legend S' *Agnetis de Ormistvn* (*Bain*, ii, p. 198, 534). John de Ormestone of Roxburghshire also rendered homage, 1296. His seal bears a pelican feeding young on nest, S' *Joh'is de Ormiston* (*Bain*, p. 199, 544). John de Hormiston between 1306–29 granted to the monks of Melrose all the land which he had in the territory of the town of Lessidewyn (*Melros*, p. 379). Andrew de Ormeston, styled 'familiaris David de Bruys' had a safe conduct from the king of England in 1359 (*Rot. Scot.*, i, p. 836), and Andrew de Ormystoun witnessed a charter of land of Longneuton, c. 1377 (RHM., ii, 4), and Alan of Ormyston, a Scots prisoner of war in the Tower of London, was liberated, 1413 (*Bain*, iv, 839). There was deadly feud between Ormestoune of that Ilk and Ker of Cessford in 1564 (*Trials*, iii, p. 393), and several Ormistons were forfeited for treason in 1592. Ormiestone 1662, Ormston 1766, Ormstone 1675; Wormyston, Wyrmyston.

ORMSTON. A curtailed form of ORMISTON, q.v.

ORR. (1) A common Scots surname, and the name of an old Renfrewshire family. "It is a numerous name in the West end of the shire of Renfrew in the parish of Lochwinnoch" (*Nisbet*). Hew Orr rendered homage in 1296. Four persons named Or were summoned to answer charges made against them by the abbot of Paisley, 1503 (RMP., p. 61). John Or was witness in Glasgow, 1550 (SBR., p. 64), Matthew Ore in Paisley, 1654, and James Orre in Barneth, 1678 (*Kilbarchan*. The name is very common in this record). There were also Orrs in Campbeltown, Kintyre, as early as 1640, immigrants most probably from

Renfrewshire. Perhaps from some lost place name. Cf URIE (1). (2) A descriptive name from G. *odhar*, dun, of sallow complexion. Donald Oure, son of Finlay Oure, is mentioned, 1512 (*Athole*, p. 711), and John Or in Moy, a follower of Campbell of Cawdor, 1578 (*Cawdor*, p. 180). Alexander Over *alias* Robertson in Connoch was fined for reset of Clan Gregor, 1613 (RPC., xiv, p. 634), and Alexander Ore was member of Gartly Company of Volunteers, 1798 (*Will*, p. 23). Hugh Orr (1717–1798), born in Lochwinnoch, Ayrshire, emigrated to United States in his twentieth year, took an active part in the Revolutionary War by casting guns and shot for the Continental Army, besides doing much to encourage ropemaking, spinning and manufacture of edge tools.

ORROCK, ORROK, ORRICK. From the lands of Orrock in Fife. Symon de Oroc witnessed a quit claim by Johannes Gallard of the lands of Siwinis Keeth to the Abbey of Dunfermline, 1248 (RD., p. 97). Symon filius Simonis de Oroc with the consent of Robert, his son, and Freskinus, his brother, gave the abbot and convent of Dunfermelyn the lands called Muyoch and Cnokduuy in the tenement of Oroc (ibid., p. 117). Robert de Horock or Horok was juror on an inquisition on the lands of Disarde (now Dysart) in 1296, and was juror again in 1305 along with Simon de Horok (*Bain*, ii, p. 216, 450). Robert de Orrock and Symon de Orrok, both of Fife, rendered homage in 1296 (ibid., p. 204). Robert de Oroc or Orock and Symon, his son, attested the homage of Duncan, twelfth earl of Fife to the abbot of Dunfermline, 1316 (RD., p. 235). In 1513 there is record of a payment by David Arroc in Aberdeen (CRA., p. 83), and John Oraik in Craig Beath is mentioned, 1578 (*Dunfermline*). The lands of Orrock in Fife were sold about 1750 by Robert Orrock, and about 1800 the family bought land in Aberdeenshire which they named Orrock "in memoriam." Several of the name are mentioned in the *Registrum de Dunfermelyn*. Arrok 1536, Orack 1709, Orok 1614, Orrack 1715.

ORTON. Among the witnesses to a charter by Muriel de Polloc, c. 1224–42 (REM., p. 120), is Nicholaus de Urcane. This is evidently a misreading of *c* for *t* in the MS. There is little doubt that the name should be read Urtane, from the land now called Orton near Bridge of Spey.

ORWELL. From the old lands of Orwell in Kinross-shire. Richard de Orewell witnessed confirmation of a charter by Walter, bishop of Glasgow to the Hospital of Soltre, 1231 (*Soltre*, p. 29), and Johannes de Vrwell, one of an inquest in Aberdeen, 1342 (REA., i, 73), may be John of Urwell who had a confirmation of the lands of Drum near Pluscardy, 1343 (HMC., 6. Rep., App., p. 687). Andrew de Urwelle, son of Johannes de Urwelle, had a charter of lands of Samqware, Tulache, and Droni in 1362 (RMS., i, 119), and Johannes de Uruel was juror on assize in 1389 regarding the mill lands of Quarelwode in Moray (REM., p. 171). Andrew de Vrwel, juror on inquest at Narn, 1431 (*Rose*, p. 127), Robert Wrwell, juror on assize at Inverness, 1514 (OPS., ii, p. 663), and James Uruell was 'reidare' at Rhynie, Aberdeenshire, 1576 (Macdonald, *Place names in Strathbogie*, p. 272). Thomas Urrall 'confessit he playit on the trumpt to the gwysars,' 1615, in Elgin (Mill, *Plays*, p. 241). Irruall, Uruel, Wrruell, Wrruwall, Wrwell.

OSBERTUS. From the OE. personal name *Osberht*, 'god bright.' Osbertus was prior de Sancta Cruce, c. 1150 (REG., 11), and Osbert, chaplain in Kelso, c. 1180 (*Kelso*, 368, 369). Osbert Olifard, sheriff of the Mearns, died before 1206. Osbert, prior of Jedburgh, was witness to many charters and died 1174 (*Chron. Mail.*, s.a.; *Annals*, p. 156). Osbertus, brother of Galfridus Redberd, witnessed sale of a tenement in Perth, 1219 (*Scon*, p. 52).

OSBORN, OSBORNE. From the ON. personal name *Ásbjorn*, 'divine bear,' Anglicized Osbeorn and Osbern (OE. *ōs* + *be(o)rn*, 'god warrior'). Osbernus, presbyter, in record 1097–1107 (*Nat. MSS.*, i, 4), and Osbern, capellanus, 1107–24 (ibid., i, 11). Osbernus was abbot of Jaddewurd, c. 1150 (LSC., p. 11), and Osbern, capellanus Glasgow, c. 1180 (*Kelso*, 338). Part of a carucate in the territory of Middilham was granted to Hosbern, a man (*nativus*) of the Abbey of Kelso and to his heirs, c. 1160–80 (*Kelso*, 117). Osbern de Yrnis acquired the land of Thornton in Angus in 1398–9 (*Strathmore*, p. 182), John Osburn was a voter in parish of Qwilton (Coylton), 1513 (*Ros*, 52), and Harie Osburn or Osburne, 'wretter to his majesties signet,' in Ayr, 1648 (*Ayr*, p. 182). John Osburn, dean of guild, Aberdeen, 1730 (*Guildry*, p. 203). Osborne 1656, Oseburne 1596.

O'SHANNAIG. Ir. *O'Seanaigh*, 'descendant of Seanach,' a derivative of *sean*, old, ancient. Murdoch McOsenage or McOsennag was tenant of Macharebeg, Kintyre, 1506 (ER., xii, p. 700). Rev. Malcolm M'Oshenag was minister at Kilcheran, 1622 (*Sasines*, ii, 132), and as M'O'Shanaig was minister at Kilcolumkeil and Kilblaan, 1630. Hew M'Oshenog in Dalbrandan, parish of Kilcolmkill, 1686

O'SHANNAIG, *continued*

(Argyll), and Hugh M'Oshennag of Lepinstra in 1709 *(Campbell, 1)*. The family left Southend, Kintyre, took a farm in Arran, and changed their name to Shannon.

OSLER, OSTLER, OSTLERE, OUSTLER. The "hostler" or "ostler" is the man who takes, or perhaps we should now say took, charge of the horses at an inn, but originally the word meant the inn-keeper himself (OF. *hostelier*). The first form here given is common in Fife. William Ostler or Ostillar was a burgess of Forres in 1430 (RMS., II, 177, 179). Andrew Hostalar, member of an inquest at Nairn in 1431 *(Rose, p. 127)* is probably the Andrew Hostillar in Forres mentioned in 1441 (SCM., v, p. 20), and the Andrew Ostillar who had seizin in the lands of Kynowdie in 1449 *(Cawdor, p. 15)*. Hugh Hostelar was tenant of the land of Bucht in 1456 (RAA., II, 106), and Robert Hoistlair was servitor of Lord Ruthven in 1561 (CMN., 82). Andrew Oistlar, reidare at Rothymurcus, 1574 (RMR.). Ostlar 1552. Ostlere in Kirkcaldy, 1941.

OSOLF. The common OE. personal name *Ōswulf* (Old West Norse *Ásulfr*, Old Swed. and Old Dan. *Asulf*). Osolf filius Eadiue who witnessed Earl David's *Inquisitio*, c. 1124 (REG., 1) is probably the Osulf filius Ediue who with Osolf filius Elfstan witnessed King David's great charter to Melrose, a. 1153 *(Nat. MSS., I, 17)*. The land of Osulf Wittburg was given to the Abbey of Kelso, c. 1140 *(Kelso, 372)*.

OSSIAN. Ir. *Oisin* (pron. Esheen or Usheen), G. *Oisean*, 'little deer,' diminutive of *oss*, 'deer, fawn.' Not from Oswin as formerly maintained by Zimmer. The name occurs as that of a priest in the (Cornish) Bodmin manumissions, where it is written *Osian*, and once *Oysian*. Adamnan (I, 2) mentions Oisseneus, probably an abbot of Clonard, who died 654.

OSTLER, OSTLERE. *See under* OSLER.

O'SUIBHNE. Christinus Huasuibhne was among those cited in 1355 to give evidence regarding the lands of Glassre in Argyllshire (HP., II, p. 139). He was lord either of Otter or of Castle Suine. As Cristinus Huasmabene he also witnessed a charter by John Campbell, lord of Ardsceodanich, undated, but also about the same date (ibid., p. 141). The *hua* is = *ua* or *o* of Irish names, and is rarely found in Scottish names. O'Beolan, the family name of the old earls of Ross, and the Vanduibhne (= O'Duine) in Carswell's dedication of his translation of Knox's Liturgy (1567) are about

the only examples. Cf. MACQUEEN (1), MACSWEEN, and SUIBHNE.

OSWALD. From the OE. personal name *Ōswald*, meaning 'divine power.' The Oswalds of Caithness are descended from James Oswald of Kirkwall, d.c. 1660, and a family of this name has been for more than two centuries resident in Fife. Archibald Oswall, minister of the word of God apud Pankaitland, 1649 *(Inquis., 3581)*. Alexander Oswell of Falkirk, burgess of Glasgow, 1622 *(Burgesses)*. James Oswald was notary in Coldstream, 1665 *(Lauder)*, and David Oswald of Dalders was retoured heir in lands and barony of Skirling, 1683 *(Retours, Lanark, 359)*.

OTTER. From the common ON. personal name *Ottarr*. John Otir witnessed gift of land to the Hospital of Soltre, c. 1250–66 *(Soltre, p. 32)*. Johannes Otyr, witness in Berwick, 1264 *(Neubotle, p. 152)*, may be John Oter, merchant there, who had license to trade by land and sea for two years in 1291, and in 1296 rendered homage *(Bain, II, p. 130, 203)*. His seal shows two chevrons on a shield, a quarrel above, S' *Johannis Otyr* (ibid., p. 554). Gregory Oder also rendered homage in 1296 *(Macdonald, 2174)*. Simon Otyr, burgess of Crail, 1402 *(Royal Hist. Soc. Trans., VI, p. 330)*. Donald Otor was baron of Twlezettyll, 1548 *(Athole, p. 714)*.

OTTERBURN. This surname is derived from Otterburn near Morebattle, Roxburghshire. Alan de Ottyrburne was secretary to Murdoch, duke of Albany in 1426 (RMS., II, 48). William de Ottyrburn, a witness in Glasgow in 1454 (LCD., 176) is most probably the William de Otterburne who is recorded as bailie of Glasgow in 1456 and again in 1463 (REG., 380, 389). John de Ottirburn, rector of the parish church of Liberton in 1456 (LSC., p. 165) may be the John de Otirburne, canon of the church of Glasgow in 1467, and in following years provost of the Collegiate Church of Methven (REG., 391, 392). Master Nicholas Otyrburne or Ottyrburne, Clerk of Rolls in 1456 (Scon, 220), vicar of St. Giles's Church in Edinburgh, and secretary to James II had safe conducts to enter England in 1455, 1456, and 1459 *(Bain, IV, 1271, 1276, 1301)*. Henry Oterburn was a witness in Glasgow in 1468 (REG., 392), Alexander of Otyrburn was bailie of Ayr, 1471 *(Friars Ayr, p. 54)*, Andrew Otterburn had a remission in 1489 for his share as one of the holders of Dumbarton Castle against the king (APS., XII, p. 34), and Gilbert Ottirburn was parson of Slains in Aberdeenshire in 1493 (ADC.). Thomas Otirburne was servitor to the commendator of Arbroath in 1524 (RAA., II, 578),

John Otterburn was tenant in Govan in 1526 (*Rental*), Adam Otterburn was provost of Edinburgh in 1534 (*Seals. Supp.*, 801), and a commission for the trial of John Ottirburne was issued in 1557 (ER., XIX, p. 417). Ottirbyrn 1609.

OTTERSYDE. Of local origin from some small place of the name. James Ottersvde, deacon of the fleshers in Haddington, 1686 (RPC., 3. ser. XII, p. 544).

OUCHTERLONY. See under AUCHTER-LONIE.

OUGHTON. Admiral Oughton (born in Cullen, Banffshire, died there in 1832) was son of John Hawtie or Haughty, shoemaker, in Farskine. The admiral changed his name to Oughton (*Cramond*, p. 119). Lower says probably the same as Houghton, and Harrison says for Aughton which he gives as a form of Acton.

OUSTLER. A form of OSLER, q.v.

OUTERSON, OUTTERSON, UTTERSON, 'son of UCHTRED,' q.v. Surnames recorded in Berwickshire and in Midlothian. The name is found early in Northumberland as Oughtred's or Ughtred's son. William Oughterson in Marscalloch, 1776 (*Kirkcudbright*), and John Oughterson in Milnthird, 1799 (*Dumfries*). Uhtred or Uchtred in place names gives Oughterside and Oughterby. ITERSON is a variant, and see also UTTERSTON.

OUTE WITH THE SWERD. John Oute with the Swerd was a forestaller at Der (Deer), 1402 (CRA., p. 384). A nickname, not a surname. John was perhaps quick to quarrel.

OUTHWAITE. A modern importation from England. Outhwaite was a Yorkshire surname in the seventeenth century. Of local origin from a place of the name in the north of England.

OV. Roger de Ov granted the church of Langetune and its pertinents to the monks of Kelso, c. 1150 (*Kelso*, 138). The charter is witnessed by Hugh de Ov and Thom de Ov, and in King William's confirmation charter Roger's name is spelled de Oy. These persons were connected with a Bedfordshire family which held lands there in 1086. The name is really de Eu (Page, *Victoria hist. of Bedfordshire*, v. 2, p. 11, 211, 223, 261, 263, 267). See Ew.

OVENS. John Ovens in Tranent, 1674 (*Edin. App.*). John Ovens, butcher, Lassuden, 1756 (*Heirs*, 286). Barbara Ovens in Windpath,

1760 (*Lauder*). Adam Ownes in Upsetlingtoun, 1664 (*Lauder*) may be a misspelling.

OVENSTON, OVENSTONE. A Fife surname, from the lands of Ovenston near Pittenweem. John Ovenstone died in St. Monance, 1938.

OVER. Perhaps from one or other of the English places so named. James Our was tenant of Burnside of Stobhall, 1760 (*Dunkeld*). John de Overe appears in the English Hundred Rolls, 1273. Cf. EURE. Perhaps now lost in URE.

OX. Andrew Ox, rector of the church of Inverarity, 1371 (REM., p. 172). Most probably of local origin from residence '(at the) oaks.'

OYKELL. John Ekal alias Calder alias Machustan Macuillam in Arnoboll, 1768 (*Durness*), derived his name from Oykell or Oikell in Sutherland. Rob Donn, the Gaelic poet, was really a Calder from Oikell district, though now called a Mackay. His family registered in the eighteenth century as Makay Calder or Eckel.

PADDOCK. Dugall filius Padock, juror on inquisition in Lennox, 1320 (*Levenax*, p. 82). Lower says Paddoc is the HR. form, to be a personal name, "and to have originated in A-Sax. times, several names of places, such as Paddockswood, Padoxhurst, &c."

PADERUS. Paderus mac Cuning and Gillenbract filius Paderi were charter witnesses in Dumfriesshire in the reign of Alexander II (*Melros*, p. 182).

PADIE. Diminutive of PATRICK, q.v. Padie and Padyne in the Glasgow Protocols and other Glasgow documents are considered as two forms of the same name. John Padie, carter, was admitted burgess freeman of Glasgow because he is a common servant of the town, 1584 (*Burgesses*). James Padie, skinner, admitted burgess freeman, 1606 (ibid.). Mariota Padie, Alison Padie, and Catherine Padie were retoured in lands beside Spittal-Quarter, 1618 (*Retours, Lanark*, 118–120). John Pady, witness in Glasgow, 1542 (LCD., p. 126).

PADKIN. A double diminutive of PATRICK, q.v., through 'Pad' + diminutive -kin.

PADON. A variant of PATON, q.v.

PADSON, 'son of PATRICK,' through the diminutive 'Pad' or 'Padie.' Thomas Padesone, vicar of Kilteirn, 1487 (ADC., p. 236). John Pasdon, burgess of Edinburgh, 1722 (Colston, *Edinburgh Guildry*, p. 126). The same as PATERSON.

PADYN. G. *Paidin,* a pet or diminutive form of *Padruig,* 'little Pat' or 'Paddy.' Padinus (-*us* is Lat. ending) filius Kerkau, 'aput corrukes,' was one of the witnesses to the *Diuise de Stobbo,* c. 1190 (REG., p. 89). Padinus, prepositus, witnessed an undated charter of three acres of Karruderes by Walter del Bois (*Raine,* 166). Patin Mac Gillenef is in record in the reign of William the Lion (LSC., p. 214), and Padyn, a chaplain, who witnessed a charter of confirmation by the Chapter of Dunblane, c. 1235, is doubtless Padin, presbyter of Mothel (Muthill) who appears in 1239 (LAC., 53, 54). Symone filius Padine was pledge for Ingram filius Dungalli in Dumfriesshire in 1376 (RHM., I, p. liii; II, p. 16). Cristofer Paidzeing was repledged to liberty of burgh of Irvine, 1472 (*Irvine,* I, p. 28), and Andrew Pudzane signed the Band of Dumfries, 1570 (RPC., XIV, p. 66). William Padyne, carter, and John Padyne, skinner, were burgesses of Glasgow, 1599 (*Burgesses*). Roger Paidzeane was retoured heir of Thomas Paidzeane of Newtoun in the lands of Huik, Annandale, in 1605 (*Retours, Dumfries,* 30). James Padzean was a writer in Edinburgh, 1666 (*Edinb. Marr.*), and another James Padzean appears in Closeburn parish in 1671 (*Just. Rec.,* II, p. 59). A family of this name in Ayrshire appears frequently in Corsehill Court Book around 1670 as Padzan, Padzean, Pudzein, Puidzan, Puidzane, Puidzean, Puidzeane, Putzan, Putzane, and Puydzean. Alexander Padgen, Janet Padzen, and Andrew Pudgeon appear in the Edinburgh Marriage Records. As forename: Paydene Wilycht and Paedan Oles in Inverness, 1572 (*Rec. Inv.,* I, p. 85, 89).

PADYSMYR. Of local origin from a now forgotten place name in East Lothian. Thomas de Padysmyr held a land in the burgh of Haddington, 1373 (RMS., I, 449).

PAGAN. This surname is described by Bardsley as "one of the most interesting names in our directories." Paganus was a favorite personal name among the Normans (e.g. Paganus de Brausa, 1124, REG., I), and in French was reduced to Payen and Pain and Paine. It is also a pre-Conquest name in England, Ralph Pagan occurring in a document of 1055. The word "originally denoted the inhabitant of a *pagus* or country district. As such people were late in receiving new ideas, the modern notion of *pagan* developed out of the word" (Giles, *A Short manual of comparative philology,* 1901, p. 67). "Either in the sense of habitation or patriotism, Pagano was erected into a Christian name in Italy, and Payen in France; whence England took

Payne or Pain, still one of the most frequent surnames" (*Yonge,* p. 202). Paganus was chaplain in Glasgow, c. 1180 (*Kelso,* 338), Uctred filius Pagani gifted the lands of Carnebro to Paisley before 1265 (RMP., p. 310; *Pap. Lett.,* I, p. 107). The surname is found in the west and southwest of Scotland records for more than three centuries back. Isobel Pagan (c. 1741–1821) was an unfortunate minor poetess, and Theodore Pagan is author of *The Convention of the Royal Burghs of Scotland,* Glasgow, 1926.

PAGANSON, 'son of PAGAN' (Paganus), q.v. Malcolm Pagainson or filius Pagani had the keeping of the gardens of King David II in Edinburgh (RMS., I, App. II, 985).

PAGE. From the office of 'page,' originally a subordinate personal attendant of a knight. John Page was one of the Scots prisoners taken in Dunbar Castle in 1296 and confined in Tunbridge Castle (*Bain,* II, 742, 939). Johannes Page had a charter of a davoch of land in Strathbolgy from Robert I (RMS., I, App. II, 25), and Adam Page, serviens regis, is mentioned in 1363 (RMS., I, 162). John Page was tenant of part of Siokis in 1469 (*Cupar-Angus,* I, p. 154), James Payge was juror on an inquest at Cupar in 1522 (SCBF., p. 266), Thomas Paige was witness in Fife in 1542 (*Laing,* 464), and John Paig is recorded in Paisley in 1749 (*Kilbarchan*).

PAIK. See *under* PEACOCK.

PAIRMAN. Caution was found for Will Pairman and Cristie Pairman of East Teviotdaill, 1569 (RPC., I, p. 661). J. R. Pairman was one of the literary staff of W. & R. Chambers, publishers, Edinburgh.

PAISLEY. Of local origin from the town of Paisley in Renfrewshire. William Passeleue or Passelaw appears as witness in charters by William the Lion, c. 1179–90 (*Kelso,* 260; RMP., p. 8), and c. 1202 as William Passelewe witnessed a charter by Alan filius Walteri (RMP., p. 14). He may have been the William de Passele who witnessed a donation of the church of Kincardin to the Abbey of Cambuskenneth, c. 1199 (*Cambus.,* 121). Dominus Johannes de Passelet, canon of Glasgow, witnessed gift of half of Litel Guvan to the Hospital of Polmade, 1320 (REG., p. 229), and in 1389 the goods of William Passeley, merchant of Scotland, were ordered to be released (*Bain,* IV, 401). Henry Paslaye was burgess freeman of Glasgow, 1600 (*Burgesses*), John Paislie was admitted burgess of Aberdeen, 1616 (NSCM., I, p. 116), Johne Paslay decernit in ane unlaw, 1672 (*Corse-*

hill, p. 107), Hendrie Pasley took the Test in Paisley, 1686 (RPC., 3. ser. XI, p. 496), John Pasly, schoolmaster of Dalmellington, 1689 (RPC., 3. ser. XIV, p. 300), and John Paislay was retoured heir portioner of Thomas Kirkpatrick, 1699 (*Retours, Dumfries*, 356). There was also a Dumfriesshire family named Pasley, several members of which distinguished themselves in public service. William Paislaw, shoemaker in Hawick, 1689 (*Peebles CR.*), and Pasley or Paisley, the notorious 'priest' of Gretna Green, may have derived their name from (How)pasley, originally in the barony of Hawick.

PALDAWY. Local. Alexander Paldawy, witness in Edinburgh, 1514 (*Ros*, 70). Cf. Baldovy in Angus.

PALESTUN. William de Palestun witnessed a charter by Roger Maule and Godit, his spouse, to the church of S. Cuthbert of Carram (Carham), c. 1200 (SHSM., IV, p. 310). He also witnessed a charter to Melrose Abbey (*Melros*, p. 266). Palestun is the old name of Paston, a township in the parish of Kirk Newton, Northumberland.

PALFREYER. A variant of PALFREYMAN. Thomas le Palfreiour was received to the king of England's peace in 1321 (*Bain*, III, 724).

PALFREYMAN. The palfreyman was the person in charge of the saddle-horses of the ladies. Andrew palfridarius received a legacy from the queen in 1328, and in the following year William palfridarius received a similar legacy and at the same time a payment was made to Gilbert palfridarius (ER., I, p. 117, 216, 217). John palframan was juror on an inquest made at Muskylburg in 1359 (RD., p. 267), Simon palframan is mentioned in Aberdeen in 1411 (CRA., p. 388), and Thomas Palframan was admitted burgess of the same city in 1473 (NSCM., I, p. 24). The croft of George Palframan in Kincardine is mentioned in 1490 (SCM., IV, p. 11).

PALLADIUS. The Graeco-Latin translation of S. Patrick's British name *Sucat*, 'good at war.' Obsolete Welsh is *hygad*, 'warlike.'

PALLOCH. John Palloche or Pulloche in Kirktoun Kilmichell, William Pulloche in Ballemor Kirmichell, and John Pollohe in Killmorich, 1672 (HP., II, p. 208, 213, 216).

PALMER. Hugh Palmer witnessed resignation of the lands of Ingilbristoun in 1204 (*Dryburgh*, 163), and in 1253 Ricardus Palmerus de Kingore attested a memorandum of the ornaments of the chapel of Dundemor (LAC.,

p. 72). Alexander Palmer witnessed a sale of land in Glasgow, c. 1280–90 (REG., p. 198), Elye Palmere held a land in Waldeuegate, Berwick, in 1307 (*Kelso*, 43), and Hugh Palmere was "messager" of the earl of Douglas in 1397 (*Bain*, IV, 489). John Palmer was to have the usufruct of the hospital lands of St. James, Stirling, in 1402 (*Cambus.*, 108), Bartholomew Palmer in Glasgow had resignation of a liferent in his favor in 1553 (*Protocols*, I), and Adam Pamer or Palmer was tenant under the abbot of Kelso in 1567 (*Kelso*, p. 524, 525). A palmer originally was one who bore a palm-branch in token of having been to the Holy Land.

PANTER. From OFr. *paneter*, "officer in charge of bread," Med. Lat. *panetarius*. Of the term *Panetarius Scociæ*, the title of one of the officers of the king's household, there are various interpretations. "The late Sir William Fraser, in his courtly style, gives the meaning as 'chief butler;' Mr. Riddell prefers 'master of the household;' the editor of the 'Papal Petitions' translates by the archaic word 'pantler;' while a homely old chronicler calls it 'pantrieman'" (*Sc. Ant.*, XV, p. 56). The office, nevertheless, was regarded as a highly honorable one. It was early confused with 'painter' and so erroneously rendered in Latin documents by *pictor*. John called Payntour, canon and treasurer of Dunkeld, 1328, is also named Pictor (*Pap. Lett.*, II, p. 284–286). Finlaw de Pantre was in the service of David II. The surname was common about Montrose in the fifteenth and sixteenth centuries. William Paneter who held land in Monros, 1350 (REB., II, 7) appears in 1360 as bailie of same burgh (ER., II, p. 27), and Andrew Paneter or Panter was burgess there in 1389 (HMC., 2. Rep., App., p. 167). David Panetar de Monros had a charter in 1407 from the Regent, duke of Albany, of the lands of Cragoth and Ardoch in the barony of Logy in Angus (RMS., I, 896). Andrew Payntour or Pictor, bailie of Edinburgh, 1364, was keeper of the Mint in 1373 (ER., II, p. 149, 430). Walter Paniter was abbot of Arbroath, 1411–33 (RAA., II, p. x). Johannes Pictor, bailie of Are, 1417, appears in 1427 as John Pantour, burgess (*Ayr*, p. 76, 82). John Paniter was one of an inquest in Arbroath, 1452 (RAA., II, 93), and Thomas Payntoure, a witness, 1455 (*Cambus.*, 97). John Panter and David Panter, sons of William Panter, a Scot, a soldier of Roxburgh Castle, are mentioned, 1471 (*Bain*, IV, 1400). Andrew the Painter (Pictor), canon of Orkney, was promoted to the see of Orkney, 1477 (*Dipl. Norv.*, XVII, p. 591); Alexander Panter or Paniter was vicar of Castilstaris (Carstairs), 1505–41

PANTER, *continued*

(*Simon*, 138; *Dowden*, p. 227); and David Paniter was provided bishop of Ross in 1547 (*Dowden*, p. 226–228). Prayers were offered for the soul of David Penneter, burgess of Monthros, 1524 (RAA., II, 583), Patrick Penneter was secretary to the king in 1524 (RAA., II, p. 439), and John Paynteoure was witness in Glasgow, 1554 (*Protocols*, I). The old family of the name was known as Panther of that Ilk.

PANTOK. Radulphus de Pantok witnessed a charter by William Cumyn, earl of Buchan, of the church of Buthelny to the Abbey of Arbroath, 1221 (RAA., I, p. 93).

PANTON. Hugh de Pantona appears as witness, c. 1232–37 (LAC., 90). Alisaundre de Paunton of Lanarkshire rendered homage, 1296. His seal bears a device and S' *Alexand d' Pavntvn* (*Bain*, II, p. 206, 548). David and Oliver de Pantone are in record, 1396-98–1402 (*Stodart*, II, p. 114). William of Panton of Petmedane was juror on assize at Artrowquhi, 1436 (CAB., p. 394), and James Pantone of Pitmeddan and Tulymade died in 1451. John de Pantown, witness in Brechin, 1464 (REB., II, 103), and Alexander Pantone admitted burgess of Aberdeen, 1495 (NSCM., I, p. 38), may be Alexander Pantoune who had remission for forethought felonies there in 1505 (*Trials*, I, p. 104*). Dame Elspeth or Elizabeth Pantone was a religious of North Berwick in 1539–48 (CMN., 56, 65), Jonet Pauntoun was retoured heir of Jonet Sym in Galstoun, her mother, 1606 (*Retours, Ayr*, 81), and Williame Pantoune was heir of James Pantoun of Blackhouse, his father, 1685 (*Retours, Aberdeen*, 473). The name disappeared from among landowners in eighteenth century and is now rare. There is a parish of this name in Lincolnshire.

PANTONSON. Thomas Pantonsoun, a witness in Dumfries, 1641 (*Anderson*).

PAPAY, or PAPPAY. An old Orcadian surname first recorded in 1330 when Pope John XXII allowed Thorwald, the son of Thorwald of Papay, to marry Esa, daughter of Hakon Thorie of the diocese of Orkney (*Diplomatarium Norvegicum*, II, p. 150). In 1391 we find Sir Symone de Papay, knight, one of the witnesses to a charter by Henry St. Clair, earl of Orkney (ibid., II, p. 402).

PAPE. *See under* POPE.

PAPLAY. From the island of the same name in Orkney. Sigurd of Pappley was juror on an inquest held at Kirkwall in 1369, and Peter of Paplay was a citizen of Kirkwaw in 1422 (REO., p. 16, 34). The Paplays "were one of the greatest native families in Orkney till their chief estates passed by marriage to the Irvings, about 1460 . . . and even after that they remained among the leading families in the islands for a considerable period" (PSAS., LII, p. 183). There are many references to individuals of the name in Orkney in the *Records of the earldom of Orkney*. John Papplay was one of those respited for the slaughter of the earl of Caithness in 1529 (RSS., II, 3151), and David Paiplay retoured heir of Patrick Paiplay in Leithe in 1621 (*Inquis.*, 959).

PAPPIL, PAPPLE. From the lands of Pappil near Whittinghame, East Lothian, in old records spelled Pople and Popil, but since 1763 Pappil. Alexander, son and heir of Johannes de Popil, granted several acres of Popil to Gilbert de Chockeburn (Cockburn), c. 1318 (*James*, 9; *Laing*, 22). Patrick, son of Roger de Popill, gifted a toft and garden in the territory of Popill to the Nunnery of Haddington in 1458 (RMS., II, 610).

PARADISE. John Paradice or Paradise appears as servitor to Walter Reid, abbot of Kinloss, 1565, 1581 (*Kinloss*, p. 154; *Laing*, 1028). Paradise was the name given to a pleasure court in front of a monastery or cathedral.

PARAMOUR. Thomas le Peraumer, witness in Berwick, 1284 (*Neubotle*, p. 152). Thomas Paramours, juror on inquisition at Arbroath, 1452 (RAA., II, p. 79). Paramour did not at first imply the illicit sense now attached to it. In the *Cursor Mundi* (E. E. T. S. ed., 11.69–70) the epithet is applied (by men) in a devotional sense to the Virgin Mary:

> "þerfore blesse we þat paramoure
> þat in oure nede doþ us socoure."

PARCLINER. Hugh de Parcliner, perpetual vicar of Kylmacolme after the middle of the thirteenth century (RMP., p. 157).

PARDOVAN. From Pardovan in West Lothian. Alisaundre de Purdevyn of the county of Linlescu rendered homage in 1296. His seal bears a dog and S' *Alexandri de Pvr[devyn]* (*Bain*, II, p. 205, 556). Thomas de Purdevyn of the county of Strivelvn also rendered homage in the same year. His seal bears a fleur-de-lys and *S'Thome de Pv. . .in* (ibid., p. 208, 556). Alexander de Purdouin or Purduwyn in Balhormin, 13th century (*Neubotle*, p. 147–148). Robert de Perduvyn appears in record in 1381 (*Cambus.*, 181), William de Porduvyne was a charter witness in 1415 (RMS.,

II, 158). William de Pordewyn, bailie of Stirling in 1454, may be the William Pardovyn or de Pardovin mentioned in 1462 as clerk to court of the barony of Harbertshire (ER., V, p. 636; Cambus., 91). David Pardewyne was procurator of the Abbey of Arbroath in 1520 (RAA., II, 558), and John Pardovin was a messenger in 1546.

PARGILLS. Payment was made to John Pargillie in 1585 (McCall, Mid Calder, p. 99), Nicol Pargilleis was tailor in Edinburgh, 1629, and Robert Pargilleis was furrier there, 1659 (Edinb. Marr.). Joannes Pargilleis, heir of Abraham Pargilleis of Nether Hendoun, 1667 (Inquis., 5072). Pargilles 1586.

PARGITER. From the occupation of pargiter or pargeter, one who applied rough-cast to the outer walls of houses, a plasterer, from OF. * parjetteur, ME. pargetter, 'a roughmason, or he that trimmeth walls with rough cast' (Nomenclator, 1585).

PARIS, PARRIS. Walter de Paris witnessed a charter by Florentius, bishop elect of Glasgow, 1202–07 (LCD., p. 236). John de Parys of Ayrshire rendered homage, 1296 (Bain, II, p. 199). William de Perys, a charter witness, 1362, may be the William de Perys who witnessed a deed of sale in Aberdeen, 1383 (REA., I, p. 105; II, p. 284). Johnne of Paris was declared innocent of part in the detention of King James III in Edinburgh Castle, 1482 (Lennox, II, p. 123), and Edward Pariss had a remission for his share in burning the toun of Dunbretane, 1489 (APS., XII, p. 34; Lennox, II, p. 133). John of Pares, a charter witness at Dunbertane, 1506 (Lennox, II, p. 182). John Paris was witness in Glasgow, 1513 (Ros, 35), and Elspet Paris in West Lothian was guilty of witchcraft, 1624 (RPC., XIII, p. 422). William Peiris, burgess of Haddington, 1611 (Inquis., 8467), and James Peires, burgess of Linlithgow, 1676 (ibid., 5924). Margaret Parise was married in Edinburgh, 1637 (Edinb. Marr.), and Thomas Pareis was heir of James Stevinstone in Old Listoun, 1686 (Inquis., 6702). The frequency of 'de Paris,' or 'de Parys,' and 'de Parisiis' as English surnames in the thirteenth century, especially in Lincolnshire (Madden, pref. to Matthew Paris, Hist., III) has led Sir J. H. Ramsay (Foundations of England, I, p. 61) to the ingenious inference that the name of the Parisii, who lived near the mouth of the Humber, persisted as that of a district in N. Lincolnshire till that late period. Peiris 1598.

PARK. A family of this name held the lands of Park in the parish of Erskine, from which they derived their name. The family ended in three daughters, co-heiresses, in the reign of James IV (Crawfurd, p. 114). Robert de Parco witnessed a charter by Earl David, c. 1202–07 (LAC., 5), and c. 1210 witnessed another charter by Walter Olifard, junior (SHR., II, p. 175). Sir David de Parco attested a quit-claim by Richard de Bancori to Robert de Brus of the whole land of Loyerwode (Locharwood), a. 1249 (Bain, I, 1684). John of Parc witnessed a mandate by Alexander III in 1266 (Milne, p. 3), and a charter by William de Moravia in favor of the House of Soltre, c. 1278–94 (Soltre, p. 39), and another charter by Willelmus de Morauya, panetarius Scocie, 1292 (REG., p. 202). Sir Johan del Park of Berwickshire rendered homage in 1296 and was juror at Berwick in the same year (Bain, II, p. 206, 215). Walterus de Park in the parish of Fyvie was excommunicated in 1382 (REA., I, p. 165), and Robert II in the fourth year of his reign confirmed a charter of John, earl of Carrick, to John de Park of various lands in the barony of Kilbride. Master Gilbert de Park was rector of the church of Colbwantoun or Colbanton, 1429–30 (REG., p. 322, 326), John of Park was presbyter of Glasgow diocese, 1433 (LCD., p. 248), and James of Park witnessed an instrument of sasine of lands of Aldcathy (Linlithgowshire), 1436 (HMC., 12. Rep. App. 8, p. 109). Thomas de Park held land in Aberdeen, 1445 (CRA., p. 15), Finlaus Park, burgess of Irvine, gave support to a chaplain there, 1455 (Irvine, I, p. 145), George Park had remission for his share in burning the town of Dunbertane, 1489 (Lennox, II, p. 133), and John Park of Dubbs was heir of Alexander Park, his grandfather, 1673 (Retours, Ayr, 588). Mungo Park (1771–1806), African explorer, was born in Selkirkshire. The surname was common in Glasgow in the sixteenth century. (2) There seems to have been a family of this name, Chlann ic Phairce, in South Uist, but they "are nearly extinct here now. I only know one man of that name in the whole of South Uist, where there were many of that name formerly" (Dr. Alexander Carmichael, in J. F. Campbell's Leabhar na Feinne, 1872, p. 200).

PARKER. From the occupation of parkkeeper. William le Parker, parson of Kilmon, Perthshire, rendered homage, 1296 (Bain, II, p. 208, 213). Gilcrist Parker was park-keeper at Cardross in 1329 (ER., I, p. 130), and Matheus Parker, juror on inquest, 1325 (RAA., I, p. 311). Andrew Parkeire, burgess of Dunde in 1368 (RMS., I, 236), appears in same year as Perkerr (Panmure, II, 178). Duncan Parkare was burgess of Dundee, 1429 (RMS., II, 131), and Andrew Parcar witnessed a

PARKER, *continued*

charter by Andrew de Ogilvy of Inchmartin, 1444 (*Milne*, p. 31). Perker 1565. It is difficult for us to form any conception of how important the hunting of game was in the days of feudalism to both the nobles and the vassals. The game preserve, according to its size and character, was known as a 'forest,' a 'chase,' a 'park,' or a 'warren.'

PARKHILL. From the lands of Parkhill in the barony of Torboltoun, Ayrshire. Robert Parkhill, merchant in Glasgow, 1605. —— Parkhill, servitor to Sir George Elphinstone, was admitted burgess of Glasgow in 1631 (*Burgesses*). Patrick Parkhill, son to John Parkhill in Neuckfuit, was a witness in 1657 (*Caldwell,* I, p. 291), and John Parkhill took the Test in Paisley in 1686 (RPC., 3. ser. XI, p. 496). John Parkhill published *The History of Paisley,* 1857.

PARKLEY. From the lands of Parkley in West Lothian. James of Parkley had a safe conduct into England in 1424 (*Bain*, IV, 970), and Sir Patrick of Parkley witnessed a notarial instrument at Dalkeith in 1432 (*Laing*, 110). James of Parkle of that Ilk appears in 1433 (HMC., XIV. Rep., App. III, p. 11) may be the James de Parklye, a witness along with Patrick de Parklee in 1440 (*Cambus.*, 187). James de Parkle *de eodem* is mentioned in 1447–50 (REG., 351; *Scon*, p. 178). James Parklee or Parcle was commissary of Linlithgow and notary public, and in 1439 his seal, *Jacobi de Partele,* is appended to an agreement of that date (*Seals. Supp.*, 805). George Parkle of that Ilk witnessed a notarial instrument at Linlithgow in 1488 (*Laing*, 202).

PARLAN. As forename: Parlane McGorrie in Ardes, 1613. A variant of FARLAN, q.v.

PARRATT, PARROTT, PERRATT, PERRET. From Fr. *Pierre* (Peter) + diminutive ending *-et* (and *-ot*). The surname is common in France as Pierrot, Pierret, Perrot, Perret, etc. (*Dauzat*). Most probably of recent introduction from England.

PARRIS. *See under* PARIS.

PARSON. From the office, a priest or incumbent of a parish. Adam le parson de Souldene of Roxburghshire rendered homage, 1296 (*Bain*, II, p. 199). In mediaeval Latin the phrase *ecclesiae persona* means the person or representative of the church in a parish.

PARTHOLON. *See under* BARTHOLOMEW.

PARTICK. Several individuals of this name appear as charter witnesses at the end of the twelfth and beginning of the thirteenth centuries, and then disappear from record. The name is derived from the old village of Partick in the parish of Govan, Lanarkshire. Walter, the son of Arnald de Parthec, witnessed a charter by Peter de Pulloc, c. 1177–99 (RMP., p. 98). Philip de Perthec witnessed permits to Robert Croc and Henry de Nes to build chapels for their private use, c. 1180 (ibid., p. 78), and c. 1189–99 Ernaldus de Pertec (the Arnald above) witnessed the grant by Helias filius Fulberti of the church of Mernes to the monks of Paisley (ibid., p. 100). Philip de Perthec witnessed a charter by Florence, bishop-elect of Glasgow, c. 1202–07 (ibid., p. 110), and about the same date as Philip de Pertaic he witnessed a charter by Thomas, son of Thancard, in favor of the Abbey of Aberbrothoc (RAA., I, p. 69). William de Perthec witnessed a charter by Walter, son of Alan, c. 1207–14, and as William de Parthik witnessed the gift by Walter the Steward, son of Alan, of churches to Paisley before 1228 (RMP., p. 19, 225). Dominus Jocelin de Perthec witnessed a charter by Maldouen, earl of Lennox, to Robert Herthford, a. 1224 (ibid., p. 217).

PARTON. Of local origin from Parton in Kirkcudbrightshire. Patrick fiz Matheu de Partone of the county of Dunfres rendered homage in 1296 (*Bain*, II, p. 206).

PASLEY. *See under* PAISLEY.

PASSMANDERHULLE. Richard de Passmanderhulle of Edinburghshire rendered homage, 1296 (*Bain*, II, p. 213).

PASTOR. From the office, a 'shepherd,' 'clergyman.' William Pastor and Walter Pastor served on an inquest made at Peebles, 1262 (APS., I, p. 101, red).

PATE. A diminutive of PATRICK, q.v. A surname found in Midlothian and Lanark, and an old name in Fife. Alexander Pate was canon of St. Andrews, 1528 (*Macdonald*, 2185). James Pate in Woodhead, Lanark, to be constable, 1709 (*Minutes*, p. 57). George Paitt in Caingour, 1626, and twenty-three more of the name are recorded in Lanark Commissariot Record. As forename: Pait Quheyt, 1525 (*Rental*), Pait Plumer in Kelso, 1567 (*Kelso*, p. 522). This is an ancient name in Fife, 1587, and later, spelled Pait. At and around this date there were many Patties, Patons, and Patricks in Fife, and Pait may therefore have been a diminutive of one of these names.

PATERNOSTER. About the year 1250 Roger Paternoster, clericus, witnessed a charter by Alexander, earl of Buchan, granting one mark of silver yearly to the Abbey of Arbroath (RAA., I, p. 266). At the end of the charter erecting the Hospital of Turriff in Buchan in 1272 it is recorded that "Rogero dicto Pater noster scriptore dicte carte et multis aliis" (wrote this charter and many more) (REA., I, p. 34), and in the following year he appears as a charter witness (REA., I, p. 470). About the year 1280 he appears again as the cleric or clerk of Alexander Cumyn, earl of Buchan (LAC., p. 157). The last reference to him is in 1296 when he rendered homage at Kildrummy in July (Bain, II, p. 196). This Roger is the only individual of the name I have found in Scottish record. In England, however, the name is not uncommon. It is more correctly Paternosterer, from ME. paternosterer, 'a maker or dealer in rosaries' (paternosters, from the first two words of the Lord's Prayer in Latin). The final -er has been lost by dissimilation. That the name had also another meaning is shown by the following extract from Blount's Tenures (ed. Hazlitt, p. 249–250): "Alice Pater-noster held a land in Pusey in the county of Berks in capite of the king by the service of saying every day five paternosters for the soul of the king and the king's ancestors, and Richard Pater-Noster and John, his brother, performed like service for their relief." It is interesting to note in this connection that an Irish chieftain who commanded at the battle of Clontarf (A. D. 1014) is called in Irish "Maelruanaidh na Paidre," i.e. Mulrooney of the Pater-Noster (AFM.), from which, says Dr. O'Donovan, "we may infer that he had a character for piety." Heintze-Cascorbi (Die deutschen Familien-Namen) record a Cunzinus dictus Paternosterer in Basel in 1304, and a Heinrich Vaderunser in 1565; and Gottschald (Deutsche Namenkunde) records in Breslau Matthias paternoster paternosterer, and notes that the name is also current in Germany as Paternoss and Nusterer. Raymond Paternôtre, a French cabinet under official (1935).

PATERSON, PATTERSON. Scottish forms of 'Patrick's son' or 'Patrickson,' and one of the commonest of Scottish surnames. The native home of the Clan Pheadirean (Patersons) was on the north side of Lochfyne where they were formerly numerous (Carmichael, Carmina Gadelica, II, p. 332). See under MAC-PATRICK. Patterdale in Westmoreland was formerly Patrickdale, 'the dale or valley of Patrick.' William Patrison and John Patonson, 'gentillmen,' witnesses in Aberdeen, 1446 (REA., I, p. 245). Donald Patyrson was ad-

mitted burgess of Aberdeen, 1494 (NSCM., I, p. 37), Ade Patersoun is mentioned in 1499 (RAA., II, 398), and in 1524 letters were issued against Patrik Patersoune for defrauding the king's customs (Irvine, I, p. 35). Robert Patersoun was 'capitane of ane were schip of Dundee,' 1544 (CRA., p. 205), and John Patersoune held land in Glasgow, 1553 (Protocols, I). Fyndlay Patersoun had a tack of the lands of Owar Elrik from the Abbey of Cupar, 1557 (Cupar-Angus, II, p. 170–171), and in the same year John Patersoun, custumar of Cupar, and David Petirsoun rendered to Exchequer the accounts of that burgh (ER., XIX, p. 8). John Patersoune was burgess of Northberwyk, 1562 (CMN., 85), George Paterson, a monk in the monastery of Culross, 1569 (Laing, 844), and Alexander Patersone, burgess of Aberdeen, 1594 (CRA., p. 104). William Paterson (1658–1719) was author of the ill-fated Darien Scheme and originator of the plan of the Bank of England. Patirsone 1497. Ade Patrisoun had a precept of remission in 1536 (RSS., II, 2033). James Patirsone, sheriff-depute of Innernes, 1530, may be James Patirsoun, provost there, 1573 (OPS., II, p. 666, 669). One of the Farquharson genealogies says that "the Patersons in the North" are descended from Patrick, grandson of Ferquhard from whom the clan Farquharson take their name (Farquharsons of Invercauld, p. 4).

PATHHEAD. From the village of Pathhead in the parish of New Cumnock, Ayrshire. Patrick Pethed, notary public in Ayr, 1486, appears again in 1496 as Pathead (RMS., II, 1669; Macfarlane, II, p. 342). Sir William Pethede was rector of Our Lady Kirk, 1485 (Prestwick, p. 30). As Petheid, Pethede, Pethetes, the name is recorded in the Obit Book of Ayr between 1306–1575.

PATHISON. Probably for Patison or Pattison, "son of Pattie," a diminutive of PATRICK. Bessie Pathison at Keir Millne, 1658 (Dumfries).

PATIE. May be the Scots diminutive of PATE, itself a diminutive of PATRICK. John Patie in Pottistoune in record, 1680 (Dumfries). Cf. PATTIE.

PATIENCE. Now a rare surname. Rev. J. Patience is recorded at Ardnamurchan, 1816. Alexander Patience (in 1938) a F. S. A. Scot. Lower says this is a baptismal name for both sexes. A Saint Patient is honored by the Roman Church on 11th September.

PATILLO, PATTILLO, PATULLO, PATTULLO. From either of the two places named Pit-tilloch, (1) near Freuchie, Fife, or (2) in Glenfarg, Perthshire. Ade de Petillok who is

PATILLO, Pattillo, Patullo..., *continued*
mentioned in a memo of 1295 (*Cambus.*, 7)
is probably the Adam de Pethilloch who
appears as an assizer at Perth in 1305 (*Bain*,
II, 1689). William de Pettillok had a charter
of the lands of Gibblotistoun (now Gibliston)
in Fife from Robert I (RMS., I, App. II, 900,
954). John de Pyttyllok held a toft in Portyncrag in 1433 (RAA., II, 68). Robert Pittilloch,
a Dundee man of humble rank, raised recruits
for the French service in the neighborhood
of Dundee in 1423–1424. He accompanied
them to France, entered the French service
becoming commander of the "Hommes d'armes
à la grant paye." In 1452 he obtained letters
of naturalization, was made lord of Sauveterre,
and was known as "le petit roi de Gascoyne."
As Robert Pettillo de Clermont he was one
of the ambassadors accredited by James II to
the kings of France and Castile, and in records
relating to the Scots Guards in France he
appears as Robin Petit Lo. He died in 1460
(*Forbes Leith*, I, p. 63). Robert Pettillo, burgess of Perth in 1567 (RPC., I, p. 505) may be
the Robert Pettullock who held a feu of the
cornemyln of Kynnochtry in 1585 (*Scon*,
p. 224). William Pettillok, reidare at Essie,
1574 (RMR.). Alexander Pattillo was a member of the Huntly Volunteers in 1798 (*Will*,
p. 7), and Robert Pittilloch was author of
Tracts legal and historical, 1827. Hugh Macdonald errs in saying that MacLullichs, descended from Angus, son of Reginald, son of
Somerled, are in the Low Country called Pitul-
lichs (HP., I, p. 13). Pathillok c. 1590, Patillok
1521, Pattillock 1572, Pattullok 1552, Patullow
1557, Pettillow 1524, Petulloch 1558, Petullow
1559, Pitiloch 1681, Pittillocke 1651, Pittilluo
1664, Pittulloch 1600, Pitilloche 1615, Pittillock
1643.

PATISON, Pattison. 'son of Pattie,' q.v., a
diminutive of Patrick. Thomas Patesone in
record, 1488 (*Burnett*, p. 169), and Robert
Patieson took the Test in Paisley, 1686 (RPC.,
3. ser. XI, p. 496). Granville Sharpe Patison
(1791–1851), anatomist and educator, was
born near Glasgow and died in New York
City. Patison 1689, Patisone 1673, Patisoune
1661, Pattison 1767, Pattisoune 1656.

PATON, Patton, Padon. From 'Pat,' diminutive of Patrick, with Fr. diminutive suffix -*on*.
Paton was not uncommon in the western
counties, where in pre-Reformation times Patrick was one of the most popular names. In
Ayrshire pronounced Pauton. Paton is said to
have been the name of a son of Sir Patrick
Herring (fourteenth century). Royal pardons
were granted to Paten Broune alias Broun and
to the servant of Patein or Pateman Broin,

1407 (*Bain*, IV, p. 150). Patone de Hangald-
syde (1467) appears again in 1469 as Patrick
Hangangside. Three persons named Pawton
were voters in the parish of Qwilton (Coylton), 1513, and James Padyne, witness, 1514
(*Ros*, 52, 75). Thomas Pattoun, who was
admitted burgess of Aberdeen in 1538
(NSCM., I, p. 54), may be the Thomas Patton
of Aberdeen slain at Pinkie in 1547 (SCM.,
II, p. 34). Pattoun Gallowey had a tack of
two acres in Carsegrange in 1550 (*Cupar-
Angus*, II, p. 121), and John Pattoun was
admitted burgess of Dundee in 1597 (*Wedd.*,
p. 141). Joneta Pautoun is recorded in Galstoun, 1606 (*Retours, Ayr*, 81), and Ousteane
Paton in Trewin was fined for reset of Clan
Gregor in 1613 (RPC., XIV, p. 639). Alexander Paton of Kinaldie was one of the commissioners appointed for ratifying the valu-
ations of Aberdeenshire, 1662 (AEI., p. 8),
James Patoune was retoured heir in lands in
Tilliecultrie, 1682 (*Retours, Clackmannan*,
49), and James Patone took the Test in Paisley
in 1686 (RPC., 3. ser. IX, p. 496). Paton is
the one prevailing surname in the fishing
village of Usan, the only exception being "one
or two Perts and Coutts...by marriage of
Usan Patons with Ferryden folks" (Edwards,
Among the fisher folks of Usan and Ferryden,
1921). As forename we have Paton Cudbert
1466, Pattoun Millar 1492, Patton Burnkyl
1520, and Pattoun Gallowey mentioned above.
Patoun 1590, Patowne and Pattoun 1686, Pat-
tone 1695, Pattoune 1654, Pawtoun 1529,
Pawtoune 1554.

PATONSON, 'son of Paton,' q.v. A common
surname in the fifteenth century. Nichole
Patenesone was a Scots prisoner of war in
Bamborgh Castle, 1305 (*Bain*, II, p. 449).
Richard Patonson held the land of Newbigging
in 1413 and a tenement in the vill of Edinburgh the same year (*Neubotle*, p. 237, 238).
John Patovnson is in record in Aberdeen in
1444 (CRA., p. 399), and Alexander Patonson
was made burgess there in 1447 (NSCM., I,
p. 11). Donald Patonson served on inquest to
determine the rights of pasturage which the
Temple lands had over the adjoining town and
territory of Letter in 1461 (*Strathendrick*,
p. 222), and Adam Petensen of Scotland had
a safe conduct to travel in England in 1464
(*Bain*, IV, 1343). John Patonson, witness to
an inquisition on a fishing in the Tweed
in 1467 was probably a son of Patone of
Hangaldesvde, one of the jurors on the inquest (RD., p. 359). Matthew Patonsoun
witnessed a charter of the Collegiate Church
of Methven in 1468 (*Methven*, p. 24), and
Alexander Patynson or Patonson, Scottish shipmaster, had safe conducts into England, 1475–

76 (*Bain*, IV, 1433, 1442, 1476). John Patonsoun and David Patonsoun were two "occupatorum carbofodinarum de Gilmertoun" in 1506 (*Soltre*, p. 78). John Pattounsoun was convicted of fishing during prohibited time in Water of Annand, 1504 (*Trials*, I, p. 40*), Schie Lancelote Patonsoun, 'chapellain,' died of the 'grantgor,' 1509 (ibid., I, p. 110*), and Charles Patonsoun was charged with murder, 1512 (ibid., I, p. 81*). John Pawtonsoun was made free burgess of Dumfries in 1536 (Mill, *Plays*, p. 171), and Thomas Pattowsone was admitted burgess of Aberdeen, 1540 (NSCM., I, p. 56).

PATRICK. G. *Pàdruig*, Ir. *Pádraig*, O. Ir. *Patricc*, from Latin *Patricius*, 'a patrician.' The early Latin life of the saint also gives *Cothraige*, the name by which S. Patrick was known during the term of his slavery in Ireland, but this is simply a Gaelicized form of *Pathruig* (with *c* for Latino-British *p*). S. Patrick's full name was probably Patricius Magonus Sucatus. Tirechán, the saint's earliest biographer, assigns him a fourth name, *Cothirthiacus*, which, however, is simply a Latinization of the Cothraige already mentioned. Other early forms of this name, *Qatrige* and *Quadriga*, suggested to Tirechán and others a derivation from *quattuor*, Latin for 'four:' "Cothirthiacus quia seruiuit uii[iu] domibus magorum" (i.e. "because he was a slave in the houses of four magicians"); "many were they whom he served, Cothraige (servant) of a fourfold household" (so in the O. Ir. hymn *Genair Patraicc*). The Tripartite Life (p. 17) states that he received the name Magonus from S. Germanus, and that of Patricius from Pope Celestine, but this is merely monkish tradition. The late Sir John Rhys believed the name Magonus to be a derivation from Goidelic *magus* (whence Irish *mug*, servant), meaning perhaps originally a 'boy,' but it is just as likely to be the Roman cognomen *Magonus*. Muirchu, author of the first formal biography of the saint, says he was also named *Sochet* (the Sucatus above mentioned): "Patricius qui et Sochet uocabatur." The hymn "Genair Patraicc," attributed to S. Fiacc, says: "Sucat his name it was said," and the Tripartite Life adds, this was "his name from his parents" (loc. cit.). A note on the hymn, quoted in the last named work explains this name as "Deus belli uel Fortis belli." The name is etymologically the same as obsolete Welsh *hygad*, 'warlike.'

In modern Scottish Gaelic the name Patrick is found in four forms: (1) *Pàdruig*, with *t* and *c* unaspirated, but reduced to the corresponding mediae. (2) *Pàruig* for *Pàthruig*, in which the *t* has been aspirated and consequently lost and *c* made into medial *g*. (3) *Para*, a pet or curtailed form of the last. (4) *Pàdair* or *Pàtair*, the common form of Patrick in Arran and Kintyre. This last form enters into combination with *cill*, 'a church,' in *Cill-Phadair*, the Gaelic name of Kilpatrick. The name has thus become confused in popular use with Peter and is so Englished. (Per contra, *Ceann+phàdruig* is the Gaelic name of Peterhead in Duncan Macintyre's *Oran na gasaid* (*Songs*, ed. Calder, p. 392). "Pedair as a personal Gaelic name is hardly, if at all, known out of print" (*Celt. Rev.*, II, p. 35). In Scotland not only is Patrick frequently called by the endearing diminutive Peter, but Peter is often called Patrick. In fact, as it has been said, Patrick is the "Sunday name," Peter the everyday one. In the discussion in the House of Lords on the Breadalbane peerage claims (1867) the counsel alluding to a person who had been mentioned in the course of the evidence called him Captain Patrick Campbell. The Chancellor said the captain's name was not Patrick, but Peter. His Lordship was assured they were convertible terms. Lord Robertson (1794–1855), who was christened Patrick, was invariably called Peter (nicknamed "Peter o' the Painch" by Sir Walter Scott because of his rotundity; Maidment, *Pasquils*, p. 222–223); and Patrick Fraser Tytler, the historian, was known to his immediate relatives as "Peter" (Burgon, *Life*, p. 18). Patrick was one of the most popular names in the west of Scotland in pre-Reformation times, and in Ireland only became a popular forename after 1600, due probably to its introduction by the Scots settlers in Ulster. As a surname it is common in Ayrshire, and the old family of that name appear to have been connected with Kilwinning Abbey. Patrick, subprior of Durham, became abbot of Dunfermline, 1201 (*Annals*, p. 333). Patricks of Dunminning, county Antrim, are of Scottish extraction, descendants of the Ayrshire family. John Patric was a notary in 1429 (Robertson, *Ayr Fam.*, II, p. 267). James Patrick, heir of Hew Patrick of Thornedyke his father, 1658 (*Retours, Ayr*, 501). Robert William Cochran-Patrick (1842–1897), a distinguished numismatist, was under-secretary for Scotland. Comes (earl) Patric was a charter witness, c. 1211 (*Kelso*, 403). With *gille-* it gives the common Gaelic personal name *Gillepatrick*, hence *Macphatrick* and *Paterson*.

PATRICKSON, 'son of PATRICK,' q.v. James Patricson and William Patrykson, Scots prisoners of war in the Tower of London, were released from captivity in 1413 (*Bain*, IV, 839), Thomas Patrikson held a tenement in Glasgow in 1422 (LCD., p. 242), and John

PATRICKSON, *continued*

Patrikson was sergeand of Are in 1438 (*Friars Ayr*, p. 49). Robert Patrikson and John Patrikson witnessed an instrument of sasine of the lands of Mernys and Netherpollok in 1454 (*Pollok*, I, p. 176), Richard Patrickson, chaplain, appears in record in 1458 (*Athole*, p. 708), Dauy (Davy = David) Patrickson was burgess of Aberdeen in 1463 (CRA., p. 24), Walter Patricson was a charter witness in Glasgow in 1476 (LCD., p. 190), Henry Patricksone, burgess of Prestwick in 1511 (*Prestwick*, p. 42), Duncan Patrykson leased Enyrvak in Atholl in same year (*Cupar-Angus*, I, p. 225), and William Patrikson, burgess of Inverness in 1514 (OPS., II, p. 663).

PATTENMAKER. From the occupation of "pattiner" or "pattenmaker," a now obsolete trade, AF. *patiner*, OF. *patinier*. The *Promptorium Parvulorum*, 385, defines "Pateyne, of tymbere or yron to walk with, *calopodium*," and the editor adds that pattens were "used by ecclesiastics when treading the cold pavement of a church." They were also in common use by other classes of the people. Pattenmakers is still the name of one of the London City Companies. Henry Patynmakar was proprietor of a tenement in Dundee in 1427 (RMS., II, 95). Specimens of pattens as used until very recent times at Ashford in Derbyshire are in the Scottish National Museum of Antiquities in Edinburgh.

PATTERSON. *See under* PATERSON.

PATTIE. A diminutive or pet form of PATRICK, q.v. 1585 Paty. Cf. Patie in Allan Ramsay's *Gentle shepherd*.

PATTILLO. *See under* PATILLO.

PATTINSON. A variant of PATONSON, q.v.

PATTISON. *See under* PATISON.

PATTON. *See under* PATON.

PATTULLO, PATULLO. *See under* PATILLO.

PAUL, PAULL. This surname is one of considerable antiquity in the parish of Daviot, and occurs in the parish of Fintry in 1654. It is also found in the Lothians and in Fife, where it is considered "by family tradition a Flemish name" (*Sc. Ant.*, IV, p. 114), but is not necessarily so. Robert Paul was member of council of the burgh of Stirling in 1528 (SBR., p. 276), Patrick Paule, witness at Tuliboill, 1546 (*Rollok*, 6), and Janet Paule is recorded in Edinburgh in 1659 (*Edinb. Marr.*). Alexander Paull, mercator in Elgine, 1696 (*Inquis.*, 8769). The Gaelic forms are Pòl (classical) and Pàl (common speech), whence

Polson and Macphail. The name is Latin Paulus, from *paulus*, little. Pawll 1688.

PAULIN. Diminutive of PAUL, q.v. Robert Paulin, surveyor of timber in the wood, apparently at Linlithgow, 1302 (*Bain*, IV, p. 365). Hew Polayn or Polaine acquired a charter of the lands of Fothnevin (Finhaven) in Angus in reign of Robert I (RMS., I, App. II, 583). James Pulane was tenant in Carstairs, 1521 (*Rental*). James Pawlin in parish of Senneck, 1684 (RPC., 3. ser. IX, p. 568). James Paulin in Rendown, 1735 (*Kirkcudbright*).

PAULSON, 'son of PAUL,' q.v. Magnus Paulsoun, tacksman of the Bull ('headhouse,' ON. *ból*, farm) of Halkisnes, 1502 (REO., p. 419). James Palsone was part proprietor of Grindlie and Arie in 1618. "From that time there is no further record of Paulsons in Sanday... It would, therefore, seem that the Paulsons had dropped their patronymic and taken the surname of Fea, probably from the lands of Fea in the near neighbourhood of Stove, which very possibly were at one time their odal property" (REO., p. 206). Sir John Paulson was vicar of Kilmaly in diocese of Lismore, 1559 (*Mackay*, p. 518).

PAXTON. From the lands of Paxton in Berwickshire, the tūn or town of Pac (OE. *Pæcc*). The lands were long owned by the family of Paxton. David de Pakestun was witness to a quitclaim of the land of Swinton by Patrick, first earl of Dunbar (*Raine*, App., p. 27). Walter and Andrew de Paxtun were witnesses to the deed of sale by Adam of Little Reston of Adam, son of Thurkill, a serf, to the prior of Coldingham, c. 1240. Robert de Paxton, prior of St. John of Jerusalem, rendered homage in 1296. Nicol de Paxtone and Robert de Paxton both of the county of Berewyke also rendered homage in 1296, and the latter, in 1304, had the English lands of his grandfather, William de Paxton, restored to him (*Bain*, II, p. 206, 214, 416). Sir John de Paxiston was juror on an inquisition at Berwick on the lands of Lady Elena la Zuche (ibid., p. 215). Patrick de Paxtoun was tenant of Mordyngtoun in 1376 (RHM., I, p. lxiii), and James de Paxtoun was a juror on a claim to the third part of Cranshaws in 1453 (*Swinton*, p. xxxix). Patrick de Paxtoun witnessed a charter of lands in Fife in 1395 (*Wemyss*, II, p. 33). The name is found in Edinburgh in 1400 (*Egidii*, p. 37) and in Aberdeen in the following year (CRA., p. 379).

PAY. Alan Pay was a witness in the enquiry concerning the Templars, 1309 (Wilkins, *Concilia*, p. 383), and William Pa or Pay appears as chaplain in Brechin, 1450–58 (REB., I, 182; II, 83, 97). Bardsley, Harrison, and Weakley say it is a nickname from the peacock (but?).

PAYWELL. Archibald Payweill, tenant under the bishop of Glasgow, 1510 (Rental). Payuell 1511.

PEACE. An Orcadian surname which Mr. Clouston believes to be a nickname. The earliest recorded Orcadian form of the name is Pase or Paise (1402). Anders Pæs, "aff wapu," i.e. armiger, appended his seal to a deed at Copenhagen in June 1433 (Diplomatarium Norvegicum, III, 720). James Pase witnessed a disposition of a land in Wasbister in the parish of Holm in 1483 (REO., p. 195), Magnus Paise owned a tenement in Kirkwall in 1573, and Angus Peace was a witness there in 1553 (ibid., p. 248, 350). William Peace published his Descriptive and historic handbook to the Orkney Islands in 1862.

PEACH. Probably from Pech or Peche in Normandy. Bartholomew Pecche or Peche is recorded in 1239–40 (Bain, I, 1489, 1491). The surname is not a Scottish one. Dr. Benjamin Neeve Peach, the eminent geologist, was son of a Cornishman.

PEACOCK. Pecoc was name of a Domesday tenant, 1086. ME. pecoc, 'peacock.' A gift of six pennies annually was made from the toft of Roger Pacok in Annan in thirteenth century (Reg. Priory St. Bees, p. 354). Andreas Pacok was presbyter and notary public in the diocese of St. Andrews, 1311–21 (RD., p. 251, etc.), and the name appears frequently in the parish register of Dunfermline, 1561–1700, as Paycok (1564) and Paicok (1572). Thomas Pacok had grant of a third part of the land of Quhitfeilde in the barony of Lyntounrothrike in 1378 (RHM., II, p. 129), and another Thomas Pacok was presented to a chaplaincy in 1426 (REG., p. 330). Andrew Pacock was notary public in Dunfermling, 1512 (RD., p. 380), and George Pacok was witness in Linlithgow, 1536 (Johnsoun), George Pacok, admitted burgess of Aberdeen in 1596, may be George Pacok, chirurgian there in 1601 (NSCM., I, p. 89; CRA., p. 218), and a George Pacok was apothecary burgess of the same burgh in 1631 (Inquis., 1843). The name is also found in Edinburgh (Edinb. Marr.) from 1598 as Pacok and Pæcok; Thomas Peacocke, burgess of Edinburgh, 1673 (Inquis., 5640), John Peacocke was heir of John Peacok, scollmaister in Currie, his father, in 1652 (ibid., 3671), and Agnes Peacock is recorded in Westruther, 1652 (Lauder). William Peock (= Peacock), flesher in Stew-

artoune, 1707 (Corsehill, p. 225). In some parts of Scotland the name is said to have been corrupted to Paik.

PEADDIE. See under PEATTIE.

PEARSON. See under PIERSON.

PEART. Katherine Peart in Nather Towie, 1637 (RSCA., II, p. 434). Perhaps from Pert near Stracathro.

PEASTON. From the lands of Peaston near Keith Marischal, East Lothian. Richard fil. Michael de Paystoun granted to Soltre between 1180 and 1214 "quatuor bollas boni frumenti" in pure and perpetual alms, and within the same period he granted the lands of Paistoun to the same church (Soltre, p. 5, 8). Between 1214–49 Michael de Paistoun witnessed a charter in favor of Soltre, and between 1221–24 Helya de Paistoun witnessed a grant by Duncan de Swaynystoun to the same hospital (ibid., p. 19, 23). Alexander Pastone, burgess of Edinburgh, 1380 (Laing, 67). Jonet Paistoun in Dalkeith accused of witchcraft, 1661 (Trials, III, p. 601). John Peastone or Paistoune in Muslburgh, 1689 (RPC., 3. ser. XIV, p. 442, 474).

PEAT. A diminutive of PETER, q.v. John Peet was admitted burgess of Aberdeen, 1485 (NSCM., I, p. 31), Laurence Pete was tenant of Newtoun, 1513 (Cambus., 9), Catherine Peat was warded in the Canongate Tolbooth, Edinburgh, 1682 (BOEC., VIII, p. 121), and Thomas Peat is recorded in Crieff, 1781 (Dunkeld). A Fettercairn surname in the eighteenth century. Peit 1583, Peitt and Pett 1686, Peyt 1521, Piet 1687. See also PATE.

PEATRIE. A surname found in Fife. A form of PETRIE, q.v.

PEATTIE, PEADDIE. Surnames in Fife. Most probably diminutives of PEAT, q.v. Robert Peattie in Quhitswme, 1665, and two more of the name in the neighborhood (Lauder). There is said to be Peattie in Kincardineshire and another in Angus.

PECTIMUR. Hugh de Pectimur witnessed a donation of land in the territory of Kerimor to the Abbey of Arbroath between 1214 and 1226 (RAA., I, 112).

PEDDER. From the occupation, ME. pedder, a packman, pedlar.

'The pirat pressis to peyll the pedder his pak.'
Douglas, Prol. to VIII bk. of Eneados.

John Peddar leased part of Kethyk, c. 1443 and Patrick Pedar held part of the same in 1457 (Cupar-Angus, I, p. 119, 132). John Pedder

PEDDER, *continued*

had a tack of four acres in Betschell haich from the abbot of Cupar in 1558 (ibid., II, p. 172–173), and Sir Alexander Pedder, a Pope's knight, resigned the vicarage of Awoch in the same year (RPC.). Andrew Pedder was a student at the University of Aberdeen in 1627; Lennard Pedder in record in Elgin, 1661 (*Rec. Elgin*, II, p. 299), and John Pedder was a trade burgess in Aberdeen in 1673 (ROA., I, p. 237). The names of Patrick Pettare, witness in Forfarshire, 1479 (*Southesk*, p. 720), and James Petter, W. S., Melrose, 1683 (RRM., III, p. 12) are probably from the same source. John Scott, *pethar*, in Hawick, 1655 (*Annals of Hawick*, 1850, p. 70).

PEDDIE. Probably a form of PEATTIE, q.v. The home of the name seems to have been Perthshire. In West Angus and in East Perthshire intervocalic *tt* becomes *dd*. The surname also occurs frequently in Cromarty parish session records and is found in Angus in fifteenth century. Edward Pedy witnessed resignation of the bell of S. Meddan to Sir John Ogilvy in 1447 (SCM., v, p. 118). Three individuals named Peddy were among those to whom the lands of Kynclwyne (Kinclune) were leased in 1485 (RAA., II, 258). George Pedy was inhabitant of Leith, 1566 (*Soltre*, p. 127). Thomas Baldwin Peddie (1808–1889), manufacturer and philanthropist, "one of the most respected and venerated men" of Newark, New Jersey, was born in Edinburgh. John Peddie, portioner of Kinclune, 1685 (*Retours, Forfar*, 618). Peaddie and Peddy 1516, Pedey 1713.

PEDEN. Pedan, Peden, and Padan were used as diminutives of Patrick in the west of Scotland, where in pre-Reformation times Patrick was one of the most popular personal names. Hugh Pethin was heir of Alexander Pethin in Sorne, 1611, and another Alexander Pethein was retoured heir of Alexander Pethein in Hilheid of Sorn in lands in lordship of Kylismuir, 1648 (*Retours, Ayr*, 418, 776). Marion Pedden appears in South Comerhead, parish of Lesmahagow, 1681 (*Lanark CR.*). Alexander Peden the Covenanter (1626–86) was born in Sorn, Ayrshire. Peathine, Pedin.

PEDROGENY. Johan Pedrogeny of Perthshire rendered homage, 1296 (*Bain*, II, p. 208).

PEEBLES. This surname is of twofold origin, (1) from the town of Peebles in Peeblesshire, and (2) from the old lands of the name near St. Vigeans in Angus. Sir Robert de Peblis, Chamberlain of Scotland in 1328, resigned the vicarship of Ellon in the same year (REA., I,

p. 48–49). Symon de Pebles made a donation of the land of Quilt in the sheriffdom of Peebles, 1328 (RHM., I, p. 36), John de Peblys was master of the Hospital of Peebles in 1362 (*Peebles*, 8), another John de Peblis was burgess of Edinburgh, 1368 (*Egidii*, p. 1), and a third John de Peblys was archdeacon of St. Andrews in 1378 and chancellor of Scotland in 1384 (CAB., p. 233; *Bain*, IV, 322). William of Pebylls, Scottish merchant, had a safe conduct in England, 1446 (*Bain*, IV, 1187), Magister David Peblis was charter witness in Dunfermline, 1483 (RD., p. 372), Johannes Peblis witnessed a charter by the abbot of Scone to William Peblis, 1491 (*Scon*, p. 201), and Henry Pebles alias Peblys of Southampton, late of Edinburgh in Scotland, had a protection in 1495 (*Bain*, IV, 1609). John Peblis was witness in Perth, 1546 (*Rollok*, 12). Sir Bernard Peblis was vicar of Inchynnan in 1555 (*Protocols*, I), John Peblis was procurator to William, master of Ruthven, 1564 (*Scon*, 231), another John Peblis was burgess of Irvine in 1590 (*Irvine*, I, p. 64), and Robert Peiblis was bailie of Irving in 1634 (*Inquis.*, 2054). A family of this name held land of the Abbey of Scone in fifteenth and sixteenth centuries, and the family of Peebles of Broomlands in Cunningham were old landed proprietors. Pebilis 1610, Peeblys 1376, Peibles 1635, Peiblis 1634.

PEEL. John Peil in Dumfries, 1792 (*Dumfries*). A North of England surname, of local origin from residence at or near a *peel* or fortified farm-house.

PEFFERS. Local. Peffer (from Welsh *pefr*, beautiful, pure) is the name of several small streams in Scotland. There are two burns of the name in East Lothian, and there is Peffer Mill near Craigmillar, Midlothian. As a surname it is very uncommon and has been derived from residence on a Peffer burn. There was a David Hay Peffers, antiquarian and fine art dealer in Dunbar some years ago (died 1941). Cf. INVERPEFFER.

PEGLER. Recorded in Aberdeen. Probably of recent introduction from England. Harrison explains the name as 'a gutturalized form of Pedler,' but Guppy says it is an old name in Gloucestershire, formerly Peglour. See PEDDER.

PENANGO. An old surname in Ayrshire, derived from the barony of Pennango in the parish of Cavers, Roxburghshire. Believed now to be extinct. William de Penango had a dispensation in 1332 to be ordained and to hold a benefice (*Pap. Lett.*, II, p. 357), and in 1536 there is record of 'ane singulare fechting betuix' some Johnstons, Moffats, and Gyrie Panago, 'quha was slane' (*Diur. Occ.*, p. 20). James Pennango had a gift of all the goods of James Symontoun in Lekclyok, 1532 (RSS., II, 1414), and Symon Panango had a gift of the nonentres of part of the land of Auchincors and Corsyncon in Ayrshire, 1535-6 (ibid., 1974). Symiune Pannango, 'capitane of Coldinghame,' is mentioned under the year 1543 (*Diur. Occ.*, p. 30), William Penango in Easter Quhytfield witnessed a precept by the commendator of Coldingham in 1557 (*Home*, p. 206), and Hew Pennandgow was one of the followers of the earl of Cassilis at the encounter with the laird of Bargany c. 1600. Robert Penango fermourer in Coberspeth, 1674 (*Edin. App.*). Panango 1535, Pennagow 1607, Pennango 1553.

PENCAITLAND. From the old barony of the name in East Lothian. In the reign of William the Lion we have confirmation of a grant by Euerard de Pencatlan or Pencatheland of the church of Pencatlan to the Abbey of Kelso (*Kelso*, 13, 390), and c. 1180 a confirmation by Walter, son of Euerard de Pencathlan, of the same church (ibid., 389). About the year 1200 Henry de Pencatlet witnessed a charter by Peter de Graham in favor of the Abbey of Neubotle (*Neubotle*, 7), and about 1215 probably the same Henry de Pencatle witnessed a charter concerning the water-course of the mill of Bereford near Morham (ibid., p. 66). Johannes de Pencathlan witnessed the gift by Philip de Mubray to the monks of Dunfermline, c. 1202–14 (RD., p. 95), and also witnessed the grant of the lands of Swaynystoun (now Swanston) to the Hospital of Soltre between 1221–24 (*Soltre*, p. 23). John de Penkatlon was charter witness, c. 1250 (RPSA., p. 388–389). David de Penkatlonde or Pencatland, burgess of Haddington, swore fealty at Berwick on Tweed, 1296, and in the same year was juror on an inquest held at Berwick (*Bain*, II, p. 197, 215). John de Pencatlan was constable of Jeddeworthe Castle when it was surrendered to Edward I in 1299 (ibid., II, 1086), and in the reign of Robert I Thomas de Penkatelande or Pentkatelande was forfeited for adherence to the English cause (RMS., I, 55, 68). Penkatelen and Penketeland 1296.

PENDENAN. Adam Pendenan of Peeblesshire rendered homage, 1296 (*Bain*, II, p. 207).

PENDER. From the office of 'pender' or 'pinder,' impounder of strayed cattle, as defined in the *Promptorium Parvulorum*: "Pyndare of beestys, pynnar, *inclusor*." An old surname in the parish of Mugdock and in Lanark-

shire. William Pender, wobster, burgess-freeman, Glasgow, 1600 (*Burgesses*). David Pender in Carstairs, Lanarkshire, 1644, and eleven more of the name are recorded in the Commissariot Record of Lanark. Robert Pendar of Burne, 1672 (*Inquis. Tut.*, 977), James Pender in Slamannan, 1691 (*Torphichen*), and John Pender in Rindmuir, Lanark, 1711 (*Minutes*, p. 115). Pender and Pinder in many instances in Ireland are said to be shortened forms of Prendergast (*Woulfe*, p. 659). See PENNER.

PENDREIGH, PENDRICH, PENDRIGH. Curtailed forms of PITTENDREIGH, q.v. Pendrich near Bridge of Allan was of old Petendreich. William Pendreicht was one of the brethren of the Abbey of Deer, 1544 (CRA., p. 203). John Pendreych was retoured heir of Robert Pendreych *de eodem* in Maynes of Pendreych, etc., 1547, and in 1604 the same John is referred to as John Pettindreich *de eodem* (*Retours, Banff*, 1, 20). An assessment was made against Alexander Pendriche, 1621 (RSCA., II, p. 250), Alexander Pendrich in Petfoure was charged in 1620 with being an 'idle and masterless man' (RPC., XII, p. 355), and James Pendroch was a merchant in Edinburgh, 1660 (*Edinb. Marr.*).

PENERSAX, PENNERSAX. From the old lands of the name now Pennersaughs in Annandale, Dumfriesshire. Richard de Penresax witnessed resignation of the land of Weremundebi (now Warmanbie) and Anant to William de Brus and his heirs between 1194 and 1214 (*Bain*, I, 606; *Annandale*, I, p. 3). Robert de Perresax (an error for Penresax) of the county of Dumfries rendered homage in 1296 (*Bain*, II, p. 206). John de Penesax possessed Penesax with the mill in the time of Robert I (RMS., I, App. II, 296). The old parish of Penersax was united to Middlebie in 1609, and now forms one parish under the latter name. The surname apparently long extinct.

PENMAN. Of local origin from a small place of the name formerly in Roxburghshire or Selkirkshire. Chalmers (II, p. 971) records a Penmanscore formerly near Minchmoor, and there is a Penmanshiel in Berwickshire, near Cockburnspath. Penman, for Old British *Penmaen*, is rendered 'head of (the) stone' (*Watson* I, p. 354). A pavment was made to Jhon Peneman in 1606 (RRM., I, p. 17), Andrew Penman is recorded in Edmistoun, parish of Biggar in 1638 (*Lanark*), Andrew Penman in Melrose in 1662 (RRM., II, p. 5), and Janet Penman in Lauder, 1654 (*Lauder*). The Reverend Gideon Penman, 'sometime a minister,' was accused in 1678 of being chaplain to the Devil (RPC., 3. ser. V, p. 494). William Pen-

PENMAN, *continued*

man was writer in Edinburgh in 1672 (*Edinb. Marr.*), and John Penman is recorded in Winding-toun-rigg in 1688 (*Peebles CR.*). The names of Agnes Pennane and Issobell Pennane, tenants on the lands of the Abbey of Kelso, 1567 (*Kelso*, p. 526) are probably but another spelling.

PENNECUIK, PENNYCOOK, PENNYCUIK, PENNYCUICK. Of territorial origin from the barony of Penicuik in Midlothian. The first of the family in record is William de Penycook, one of the persons directed to fix the extent of the lands of Lethenhop in the reign of Alexander II, and soon after Sir David de Penicoke is mentioned (*Neubotle*, p. 90, 304). David de Penikok witnessed a charter of the lands of Inuerpefir in 1250 (RAA., I, p. 190). Two persons of the name rendered homage in 1296: Margaret de Penicoke and Huwe de Penicoke, both of Edinburghshire. The seal of the latter bears a griffin passant to dexter, S' *Hvgonis de Penekoi* (?) (*Bain*, II, p. 201, 208, 534). David de Penycuke, *dominus ejusdem*, granted his lands of Burnistoun and Welchetoun to his cousin, William of Creichtoune, 1373 (*Sc. Peer.*, III, p. 55). John de Penykuke, scutifer, is mentioned in 1418 (CMN., 28), Alexander de Penycuyk was master of arts and perpetual curate of the church of Kilconquhar in Fife, 1463 (ibid., 29), and George de Pennicuk (Pennycuk, Penikuke, or Penycuk), bailie and burgess of Edinburgh, appears frequently in record between 1467 and 1473 (*Neubotle*, 299, 300; REG., 398–401). As the ancient charters of the Pennycuicks have long since disappeared it is not possible to ascertain their origin or the exact date of their acquisition of the barony. The lands and barony passed from their possession by sale in 1604. Panecovk 1563, Pencook 1730, Pennycuke 1437, Penycuk 1423.

PENNER. From the office of 'pinner' or 'pinder,' one who impounds stray cattle. George Pennyr was repledged to liberty of the burgh of Irvine, 1460 (*Irvine*, I, p. 27). John Penuyr (for Pennyr) was admitted burgess of Aberdeen, 1461 (NSCM., I, p. 17), and Johannes Pynnir and Robertus Pynnir were witnesses in the same burgh, 1466 (RAA., II, p. 151). See PENDER.

PENNERSAX. See under PENERSAX.

PENNY, PENNEY, PENNIE. Johannes Peny was witness in Elgin in 1343 (REM., p. 290), Mr. John Peny, a Scottish clerk, had a safe conduct in England, 1362 (*Rot. Scot.*, I, p. 867b), and a later John Peny had a grant of the fulling mill of Ballernache in Perthshire in 1375

(RMS., I, 577). George Penny was a writer in Edinburgh in 1433 (REB., I, 59), Alexander Penny held land in Glasgow in 1487 (LCD., p. 256), and John Penny was prior of the order of Preachers in Aberdeen in 1486–7 (REA., II, p. 299; LCD., p. 201). William Peñy held a croft in the sheriffdom of Linlithgow in 1500 (*Neubotle*, p. 281), and in 1529 "Besse Penne oblissis hir neuer to by buttir nor cheise . . . to regrait agane" in Edinburgh (MCM., II, p. 85). Isobel Pennie is recorded in Chirnsyde in 1683 (*Lauder*), and James Penny from Fyvie was killed in the first Great War (*Turriff*). Penney 1470.

PENNYCOOK, PENNYCUICK, PENNYCUIK. See under PENNECUIK.

PENNYSON. 'The son of Penny' (*Bardsley*). John Pennysoun, forestaller in Aberdeen, 1402 (CRA., p. 383).

PENRICE. A surname recorded in the *County Directory* (1876). Ewen (p. 242) gives it as a Welsh local name.

PENSTON. Of local origin from the village of Penston in the parish of Gladsmuir, East Lothian. George Penstoun was a tailor in Edinburgh in 1614 (*Edinb. Marr.*).

PENTLAND. From Pentland, the name of an ancient but suppressed parish in Midlothian. Adam of Pentland was a monk of Holyrood in 1298–9 (*Bain*, II, 1052). Ralph de Penteland was sent to Montrose to arrest a vessel in 1304–5, and at the same date there is entry of a payment to John de Pentland for loading and unloading wool and hides (ibid., II, p. 441, 444). Thomas de Pentland held a land in Edinburgh in 1400 (*Egidii*, p. 37), William Pentland alias Godechild, a Scot, had letters of denization in England in 1480 (*Bain*, IV, 1465), George Paintland, servitor to Sir John Scott of Tarbett, was burgess of Glasgow in 1628 (*Burgesses*), and Robert Paintland was warded in the Canongate Tolbooth of Edinburgh in 1682 (BOEC., VIII, p. 123). Pentlain 1691.

PENTON. Penton, east of Annan, Dumfriesshire, is locally pronounced with the accent on the latter syllable, Pentón. It was originally Pennyton or Penitone. In 1211 "four knights of the county of Lancaster sent to Penitune to see whether the infirmity wherefore Adam de Penitone essoins himself . . . be sickness or not" (*Bain*, I, 505). In the following year Alan de Penigtun acted as witness to a signature on a deed (ibid., 554). In 1295 a summons was issued by Alan de Peniton, and in 1296 it is recorded that Geoffrey de Moubray of Scotland had "10 l. of land in the vill of Raskelf . . . which he gave to Alan de Peningeton, knight, in exchange for land which the late king John gave Alan in Scotland" (ibid., II, p. 173).

PENWEN. Thomas Penwen was perpetual vicar of the church of Wyston, 1406 (*Kelso*, 525). Thomas Penvyn, chaplain to Thomas, bishop of Orcanev (Orkney), 1441 (*Bain*, IV, 1150) is probably Thomas Penven, canon of the church of Glasgow, 1448 (REG., 352). Robert Pendven was rector of Sowdon (Southdean), 1455 (*Melros*, p. 583), and another Thomas Pendwen, canon of Glasgow, and John Pendwen of Sprouston, are charter witnesses in 1475 (*Kelso*, 532).

PENYFADYR. Johannes Penyfadyr, a charter witness at Yester, 1374 (*Yester*, p. 26). Defined of old as a niggard, a miser. 'The idea presumably was that the miser "fathered" or treasured every penny,' or as Congrave, the author of the famous French-English Dictionary says,

'The liberall doth spend his pelfe, The pennyfather wastes himself.'

PEOCK. A surname recorded in Renfrewshire. Most probably a corruption of POLLOK, in common speech pronounced 'Pook.'

PEPDIE. The Pepdies of Dunglass were an old Border family. Stephen Papedi witnessed charters by Waldeve, and by Patrick, fifth earl of Dunbar in 1166 and by Patrick, fifth earl of Dunbar (*Raine*, 114, 116). Eustachius papedi witnessed a grant of land in Haddington to the Abbey of Dunfermline by William the Lion (RD., p. 31), and witnessed a confirmation charter by the same king to Walkelynus, braciator, c. 1200 (RAA., I, p. 166). Eleyne Papede of the county of Berewyk rendered homage in 1296 (*Bain*, II, p. 209), and Ralph Papedi was juror on forfeited lands in Lothian in 1312 (ibid., III, 245). Nichola Pepdie was married in the fourteenth century to Sir Thomas Home, grandfather of Sir Alexander Home who founded in 1403 the Collegiate Church of Dunglass. In 1497 John Papdye who made recognizance not to go ten miles out of London before Easter (ibid., III, 1641) may be the John Papeday mentioned in 1504 as late "maister of oure ordenances" in Berwick (ibid., III, 1738).

PEPPER. Metonymic for 'pepperer,' a dealer in pepper or spices. There was also an OE. personal name seen in Pipernaess. William Peppir, pewderer, burgess freeman of Glasgow, 1608 (*Burgesses*).

PERCY. From the parish and canton of Perci in St. Lo, Normandy. Alanus de Perci is one of the witnesses to David's *Inquisitio* anent the possessions of the church of Glasgow a. 1124 (REG., p. 5). Galfridus de Perci gave a carucate containing five score and four acres in Hetone (now Heiton) to Kelso Abbey, c. 1152 (*Kelso*, 358). Alan de Perci is one of the witnesses to David's grant of Estrahanent (Strath Nith) to Robert de Brus, a. 1153 (*Nat. MSS.*, I, 19). Sara Percie appears in Hiesilsvde, parish of Douglas, 1668 (*Lanark CR.*). There is an article on 'The Percies of Scotland,' by Joseph Bain, in *Archaeological journal*, 1884, XLI, p. 335–341.

PEREGRIM. The name of Alexander Peregrim, Scots prisoner of war in Colchester, 1396 (*Bain*, IV, 483) may be an error for Peregrin, from OF. *pelegrin*, a pilgrim, traveller. St. Peregrinus, bishop of Auxerre, died A. D. 304.

PERISBY. Hugo or Hugh de Perisbi (Perisby or Perysby) appears as charter witness, 1279, 1281, and as vicecomes de Rokisburg, 1285 (*Neubotle*, p. 290; RHM., I, 11, 12; Dryburgh, 13; *Kelso*, 219). Richard de Perysby, Scots prisoner in the castle of Hardelaghe, 1296, had his lands restored to him in the following year (*Bain*, II, p. 177, 244).

PERRATT, PERRET. See under PARRATT.

PERRIE, PERRY. Donald Pery was tenant of Uthircloy, Ardmanoch, in 1504 (ER., XII, p. 661), Robert Pery held part of Kethyk in 1457 (*Cupar-Angus*, I, p. 132), and William Pery had a tack of the eighth part of Kethik, called the Cothill in 1555 (ibid., II, p. 123). Antonius Pery was bailie of the abbot of Scone in 1544 (*Scon*, p. 206), Alexander Perrie was admitted burgess of Aberdeen in 1611 (NSCM., I, p. 110), and John Pierie was skipper in Aberdeen in 1689 (RPC., 3. ser. XIV, p. 649). Cf. PIRIE.

PERTH. From the town of the same name. Robert de Perth witnessed the gift of the church of Hadintona by Richard, bishop of St. Andrews, a. 1173 (RPSA., p. 135). He is probably the Robertus filius Seulfi who sometimes appears as Robertus filius Seulfi de Perth (ibid., p. 132, 136, etc.). Jacobus de Pert and his heirs had a grant of Rosin clerac from William the Lion, and among the witnesses is Samuele de Pert (SCM., II, p. 318). Jacobus de Perth also witnessed a charter by Swan filius Thor, c. 1211–14 (*Scon*, p. 18), and Johannes de Perth witnessed a charter of the lands of Rath in the territory of Kateryn or Katerlyn, c. 1206 (RAA., I, p. 45). Thomas of Perth was one of the garrison of Stirling, 1339–40 (*Bain*, III, p. 241). John de Perth,

PERTH, *continued*

burgess and alderman of the town of Seint Johan de Perthe, and Wadyn de Perth, burgess of the same town, rendered homage in 1296 (*Bain*, II, 814, and p. 197), and a later John of Perth, a Scots merchant, had a safe conduct into England in 1412 (*Bain*, IV, 829).

PERTHAY. Philippe de Perthav of Lanarkshire rendered homage in 1296 (*Bain*, II, p. 213). Walter de Pertehay held the barony of Wiltone in the reign of Robert I (RMS., I, 17).

PESSUN. Richard Pessun of Strivelyn and William Pesshun of Tyninghame, Edinburghshire, rendered homage, 1296. The seal of the latter bears a ten-rayed figure and S' *Roberti* [*sic*] *Peseune* (*Bain*, II, p. 201, 205, 551). Probably same as PEYSON.

PETBACHLY. From the lands of Petbachelin, now Pitbauchley, near Dunfermline, Fife. Marion of Petbachly of that Ilk died in 1456, and her heir sold half of the land to the Abbey of Dunfermline (RD., p. 340–345).

PETCARY. Andrew de Petcary had charter of the lands of Monethin, c. 1368 (*Southesk Book*, p. 18). Probably from Pitcarry near Bervie, Kincardineshire. Richard dictus de Pethkery, witness at Dull, 1264 (RPSA., p. 349) may derive from same place.

PETCON. Petcon of that Ilk was a small ancient family almost unknown to Ayrshire genealogists. Their estate, now Pitcon, near Dalry, Ayrshire, later gave designation to a branch of the family of Boyd. The surname is not now known in the county. Robert de Pictone of the county of Are rendered homage in 1296. His seal bears a crescent, star, and S' *Rob de Pitcon* (*Bain*, II, p. 205, 553). As Robert de Petecon he served as juror on an inquisition at Berwick on the lands of Lady Elena la Zuche in Conyngham in the county of Ayr in the same year (ibid., p. 216). Sir Robert Pitcon was witness to an award in 1488 (RMP., p. 155), and William Pitcon *de eodem* was chamberlain of Kilwinning in 1557. The surname seems never to have prevailed in the district (parish of Dalry), and "probably it was abridged to Conn, of which surname there are several families in the neighbourhood" (Dobie, in *Pont*, p. 356). Petcoun 1563.

PETER. From the personal name Peter, Latin *Petrus*, Greek Πέτρος, from πέτρος, a rock. The surname is not uncommon in Angus and in the shires of Aberdeen and Kincardine. John Peter, follower of the earl of Mar, was charged with resetting outlawed Macgregors

in 1636 (RPC., 2. ser. VI, p. 215), Andro Peiter was witness in Kirkcaldie in 1640 (PBK., p. 157), David Peter was commissary depute of Peebles in 1645, and Alexander Peter was notary public in Melrose in 1648 (RRM., I, p. 121, 126). Petyr 1545.

PETERKIN. From the personal name PETER, q.v., + diminutive -*kin*. Dominus Johannes de ['de' here an error] Petirkyn recorded in 1419 (*Cawdor*, p. 8), Andrew Peterkin was admitted burgess of Aberdeen in 1488, and John Peterkyne in 1537 (NSCM., I, p. 34, 54). Thomas Petirkyn was tenant of the bishop of Moray in 1565 (REM., p. 434), and John Peterkin in Dalbeathe in 1777 (*Dunkeld*). Peiterkin 1685, Pyterkin 1568.

PETERS, 'son of PETER,' q.v.

PETERSON. 'Son of PETER,' q.v. Nigellus filius Petri, one of the burgenses rure manentes, Aberdeen, 1317 (SCM., V, p. 10). See also PATERSON. Pitersoun 1625.

PETLANDY. From the lands of Petlandv near Fowlis, Perthshire. Theobald, son of William, son of Clement, c. 1226–34, granted that part of his land of Petlandi "in agro qui dicitur fitheleres flat" to the Abbey of Inchaffray (*Inchaffray*, p. 48). Luke, son of this Theobald, who granted a croft, c. 1275, to the same House (op. cit., p. 96), appears to have been the first to assume the territorial name of Petlandy.

PETRIE. Diminutive of (1) PETER, q.v., and (2) of PATRICK, q.v. Charles Patre in Balwelow is recorded in 1513 (SCM., IV, p. 14), Mr. Andrew Petre was vicar of Wick, Caithness, 1530 (OPS., II, p. 752; *Trials*, I, p. 149*), and David Petrye was charter witness in Tannadyce, 1603 (REB., II, 233). Payment was made for entertainment in Hendrie Petrie's house in Aberdeen, 1612 (SCM., V, p. 92), and in 1619 he appears as Henry Patrie, burgess (CRA., p. 360). George Paitrie and James Patrie were admitted burgesses of Aberdeen, 1620 (NSCM., I, p. 125), and James Petrie, filius Roberti Petri, was retoured heir of his father, 1688 (*Retours, Aberdeen*, 471). There are several instances in record of Petrie as a forename: Patrick Young, dean of Dunkeld, is mentioned in 1452 as Master Patry Yhong dene of Dunkelden (*Bain*, IV, p. 407), Patry Rede, forspekar in Aberdeen, 1503 (CRA., p. 430), Patry Leslie in 1512, and Patry Walcar in 1517 (ibid., p. 442, 444). Patrick Rov Macgregor, executed in 1667, was commonly known as Petrie Roy Macgregor (Gordon, *Keith*, p. 34, 35). The name is pronounced Paitrie in Aberdeen.

PETTECRUFF. Local. John Pettecruff, voter in Monkland, 1519 (*Simon*, 45). Thomas Petticruff was Lyon King of Arms, 1534 (*Johnsoun*). Cf. Pitcruive in Perthshire.

PETTIE. A variant of PETTY, q.v.

PETTIGREW. This surname is more common in Lanarkshire than elsewhere, and appears many times in the Glasgow Protocol books of the sixteenth century. Thomas Petykren, of the county of Lanark, who rendered homage in 1296 (*Bain*, II, p. 212), appears to be first of the name in record, and there were small landowners of the name in that county long after. John Pettygrew witnessed the promulgation of a papal bull at Linlithgow in 1461 (*Soltre*, p. 63). A booth was leased to John Pedecrw in 1488 for half a mark, and the same year, as John Pethecrew, he was made a burgess of Lanark (*Lanark*, p. 3, 4). Mention is made in 1497 of a tenement of John Pedigrew in Glasgow (REG., 476), and another John Pategrew, tenant in the barony of Glasgow appears in 1515 (*Rental*). Sir Mabut Pedegrew, parish clerk of Monkland, 1518 (*Simon*, 48). John Petticrove of Green, Lanark, 1718 (*Minutes*, p. 190). Petigrw 1447, Pettecro 1548, Pettecru 1551, Pettegrew 1552, Petticrue 1470, Pettiecru 1657, Pettingrew 1605, Pittegrew and Pedegue 1686.

PETTINAIN. The lands of Pettinain in Renfrewshire gave name to three generations of the family of Houston of that Ilk. Hugh de Paduynan and his son Reinaldus or Reginaldus held lands in Rumanoch, c. 1160 (*Neubotle*, p. 93–94). Between 1165 and 1173 Hugh de Pad'inan witnessed a grant of lands to the Abbey of Paisley, and before 1177 as Hugh de Padinnan he witnessed a charter by Walter, son of Alan the Steward (RMP., p. 6, 49). Between 1177 and 1199 as Hugh de Paduine he witnessed a confirmation charter by Jocelin, bishop of Glasgow (LCD., p. 235). In 1455 the lands of Pettinain were bestowed on the ancestor of the house of Johnstone of Westraw or Westerhall in reward for his taking the rebel earl of Douglas at the battle of Arkinholme (OPS., I, p. 140). William Pettinane resided in Cartland in 1684 (*Lanark CR.*).

PETTY, PETTIE. Most probably from ME. *petit* (< AF. *petit*, 'the little'). A local derivation from Petty in the shire of Inverness appears to be the source of the name in at least one instance. Johan Petyt of the Miernes, Lanarkshire, rendered homage in 1296 (*Bain*, II, p. 213). William Petyt was a charter witness in Ayr, c. 1340 (*Friars Ayr*, p. 10), and Master Duncan Petit or Petyt, archdeacon of Glasgow in 1395 (RMP., p. 92; *Egidii*, p. 32),

appears in the same year and in 1400 as chancellor of Moray (REA., I, p. 201, 205). Duncan Petite or Petyt was prebend of the church of Are in 1415 (*Ayr*, p. 9), Richard Petit was vicar of Stewynstoun in 1427 (ibid., p. 82), Robyn Petyt was witness in Ayr in 1471 (*Friars Ayr*, p. 54), and Patrick Pettyt was chaplain in the same town in 1476 (ibid., p. 55). John Pettit is recorded in Edinburgh in 1473 (CDE., p. 48). James Petie, indweller in St. Andrews, 1697 (*Edin. App.*). (2) Fergus de Pety in the parish of Fyvy was excommunicated in 1382 (REA., I, p. 213).

PEUTAN. The Skye form of BEATON, q.v. Iain Peutan, a Skye bard, c. 1700. The name is also spelled PEUDAN and BEUTAN.

PEWTERER, PEUTHERER. From the occupation or trade of 'pewterer,' a worker in pewter. James Pewtherer or Putherer, fermourer in Craigleith, 1667 (*Edin. App.*), James Pewtherer, taylor burgess of Edinburgh, 1732 (*Guildry*, p. 143), and William Peutherer in record at Leslie, 1750 (*Dunkeld*). Andrew Peutherer died in Edinburgh, 1941.

PHAIL. Gaelic genitive of Paul. Domh'll Phail (1798–1875), shepherd poet of Badenoch, was born in Dalnaspidal and died in Kingussie.

PHANES. Of local origin. John Phannis in Kynmundie, 1613, and Alexander Phames in Countiswallis, 1621 (RSCA., II, p. 195, 247). William Phanes, deacon of the Tailor Incorporation of Aberdeen, 1693 (Bain, *Guilds*, p. 189).

PHAUP. A surname now found only in the vicinity of Hawick. Of local origin from a small place named Fawhope on Fawhope Burn, parish of Teviothead, Roxburghshire. The place name appears in record as Fallhope, Phallhope, and Phaehope, and in local speech it is pronounced Phaup. Adam de Fauhope was juror on inquisition as to the rights and privileges claimed by Robert de Brus, earl of Carrick, in Annandale, 1304 (*Bain*, II, p. 412). Ade de Fawhope, perhaps the same person, held the land of Culschogill apparently in the reign of Robert I (RMS., I, App. II, 302n). In 1396 a payment was made to one Fulop, a minstrel (ER., III, p. 431). Archibald Fawup or Fawp was chaplain in the chapel of the Blessed Virgin in Linlithgoe in 1529 (*Johnsoun*), Andrew Phaup or Phaupe appears as notary in Melrose, 1657, 1662 (RRM., I, p. 150; II, p 6), and Thomas Phalp, a Covenanter from the parish of Morrenside (Muiravonside), was drowned off Orkney, 1679 (*Hanna*, II, p. 253). William Phaup is in record in Langtoun in 1686 and Janet Phaup

PHAUP, *continued*

in Ormstoun in 1699 (*Peebles CR.*). Isobel Phaup was a 'cotar' in Stitchill in 1715 (*Stitchill*, p. 171). The Ettrick Shepherd's maternal grandfather, Will o' Phawhope, was, in local tradition, the last man on the Border who had spoken with the fairies.

PHEMISTER. *See under* FEMISTER.

PHENNESONE. A spelling of FINNIESON, q.v. Robert Phennesoune in St. Andrews, 1653 (*Retours, Fife*, 821). Andrew Phenisone in St. Andrews, 1688 (PSAS., LIV, p. 241), appears in following year as Phinisone (RPC., 3. ser. XIV, p. 212).

PHILIP, PHILLIP. Originally a Greek personal name which has the meaning of "fond of horses" (*Philippos*). In old records the name is usually spelled PHILP, which is also a current form. In some cases it may be an Englishing of MACKILLOP, q.v. Walter, son of Philip the chamberlain, had a grant of the lands of Lundin in Fife, c. 1166–71 (SHSM., IV, p. 306), and Walter, son of Philip, granted four bovates in Balcormok to the Abbey of Cambuskenneth (*Cambus.*, 36). Rauf Phelippe of Berewyke rendered homage, 1296 (*Bain*, II, p. 205). Robert Philloppe, sheriff-clerk of Dumfries, 1629 (*Dumfries*). James Philip of Almerieclose was author of the *Grameidos libri sex: an heroic poem on the campaign of 1689*, published by the Scottish History Society.

PHILIPS, PHILLIPS, 'son of PHILIP,' q.v.

PHILIPSHILL. From the lands of Phillipishill (1602) in the parish of Carmunnock, Lanarkshire. James Philipishill had a remission for his share in burning the town of Dunbretane in 1489 (APS., XII, p. 34; *Lennox*, II, p. 133).

PHILIPSON. "Son of PHILIP," q.v. Radulphus Philippi and Roger Philippi of Berwick rendered homage, 1291 (RR.). Henry fitz Phelippe of the county of Lanark rendered homage in 1296. His seal bears a rude device, an eagle (?) displayed, and S' *Henrici fil' Filippi* (*Bain*, II, p. 186, 204). Adam Philipson was a Scots prisoner of war in Newcastle, 1305 (ibid., p. 449). Andrew Philipson was admitted burgess of Aberdeen in 1443 (NSCM., I, p. 7), and the name occurs in Perth in 1485 as Philipsun. Fergusius Philsone, witness in Aberdeen, 1469, is mentioned again in 1499 as quondam Fargus Phipsone (REA., I, p. 304, 346). George Philipsone, merchant in Berwick, 1700 (*Inquis.*, 8260), and Michael Philipson in Dumfries, 1790 (*Dumfries*). Phillipsone 1700, Philpsone sixteenth century.

PHILIPSTONE. John Philipstone, witness in Glasgow, 1505, may have derived his surname from Philpstoun in West Lothian.

PHILP. This name had a considerable extension in Fife, where it is a local pronunciation of PHILIP, q.v. William Filpe, Scottish merchant, was arrested at Lynn in England without cause in 1394 (*Bain*, IV, 462). According to Stodart (II) the name made its appearance in Fife about the middle of the fifteenth century, when Stephen Philp appears as bailie of the burgh of Newburgh in 1473. He appears to have been previously a burgess of Edinburgh (1467). Sir James Philp was curate at Abdie in 1481, Alexander Fylpe was 'servant' of the Abbey of Arbroath in 1501 (RAA., II, 419), John Philp who was curate of Kynnoule in 1521 may be the John Philp who was abbot of Lindores from 1522 to 1566 (LSC., p. lxxvii). Margaret Philp possessed land in St. Andrews in 1557 (*Laing*, 666), Tom Philp is recorded in Dunfermline in 1589 (*Dunfermline*), and William Philp had a charter of the lands of Breryhill in 1594 (RD., p. 493). Filp 1607, Phylp 1656.

PHILPOT, 'son of PHILIP,' q.v., + Fr. diminutive *-ot*. William Phylpot, a native of Scotland, had warrant of denization in England, 1496 (*Bain*, IV, 1630).

PHIMISTER. *See under* FEMISTER.

PHIN. A variant of FIN, FINN, q.v. John Phin in Brountyland, 1597, and David Phin in Quhithill, 1598 (*Pitfirrane*, 367, 380). Walterus Phyne, merchant burgess of Edinburgh, was heir to Margaret Phyn, daughter of quondam William Phyne, 1630 (*Inquis. Tut.*, 465). Magister John Phin was heir to his sister, 1634 (*Inquis.*, 2095). Alexander Phine, one of the elders of Keith, Banffshire, 1648 (*Strathbogie*, p. 88). Mr. George Phinn, minister of Slamannan, 1669 (*Sasines*, 1481), and Henreta Phinn was retoured heir of Mr. George Phinn, minister in the church of St. Laurence, 1696 (*Retours, Fife*, 1392; *Retours, Linlithgow*, 280). Elizabeth Phyn in Achanasie, 1692 (*Moray*). John Phin (1830–1913), American scientist, editor, and publisher, was born in Melrose.

PHIPILL. Andrew Phipel, man of King Alexander and burgess of Innerkethin, 1286 (*Bain*, II, 287). Roger Phipill was member of the Scots parliament for Inverkeithing, 1357 (CDE., 6; *Hanna*, II, p. 509).

PHYFE. *See under* FIFE.

PICARD. This surname probably refers to the province of France from which the early bearers of the name came to Scotland. Hugh

Picard was a canon of Moray in 1266 (*Kelso*, 345), and Stephen Pykard, a knight of Gilbert de Umfraville, earl of Angus, is in record in 1279 (*Bain*, II, p. 45). John Pikard was juror on an inquest held at St. Andrews in 1302–3 (ibid., II, 1350), and Adam le Pycard was a Scottish prisoner of war from Stirling confined in Restormel Castle in 1305 (ibid., p. 449, 451). Sir Patrick Picarde was rector of Torry in 1350 (*Cambus.*, 56), David Piccart was on an inquest at Inverness in 1430 (RMS., II, 179), and also witnessed a charter by Hugh Fraser of Lovat in 1436 (*Athole*, p. 707).

PICKEN. A surname found mainly in Ayrshire. From the NF. personal name *Picon* (*Pi<c>quin*). In England the name is found mainly in Nottinghamshire as Pickin (*Guppy*, p. 535). Andrew Picken was a tailor in Edinburgh, 1621 (*Edinb. Marr.*), and Archibald Picken was heir of Andrew Picken, merchant burgess of Edinburgh, 1624 (*Inquis.*, 1107). John Pikkan appears in Kilbarchan, 1673 (*Kilbarchan*), John Pikin was merchant in Kirktoun, 1682 (*Corsehill*, p. 157), and Thomas Picken, a rebel in Kilblain paroch, Kintyre, 1685 (*Commons*, p. 1). General Andrew Pickens of American Revolutionary fame was the son of a Scots emigrant whose ancestors are said to have been driven out of France by the Revocation of the Edict of Nantes in 1685.

PICKERSGILL. A surname of English origin. Bardsley says from some spot in the North Riding of Yorkshire, which he has failed to find. The name is not included in *The Place-names of the North Riding of Yorkshire*, 1928. Simon Pickersgill, writer in Dumfries, 1722, and two more of the name are recorded in the Dumfries Commissariot Record.

PICKMAN. From the occupation. The pickman or pickieman was a miller's servant whose occupation was to trim the mill-stones by "picking" them when worn smooth by use. 1604, "Sum tennentis . . . wald nocht content thame selffis with the serwice of the peckcaman" (*Urie*, p. 1). In 1520 an acre of land was set to Adam Pikkeman in Arbroath (RAA., II, p. 430). In 1597 there is mention of one Williamson, pickyman, at the miln of Essilmont (SCM., I, p. 133). Janet Pickieman, alias Tappie, 1599, and James Pickieman in Peatie, parish of Bervie, 1686 (*St. Andrews*). Andrew Pickieman, messenger in Kirkaldie, 1689 (RPC., 3. ser. XIV, p. 625). Pickeman 1525.

PICKNOC. Walter Pytnot who witnessed a quitclaim to the land of Fulton in 1272 (RMP., p. 51) is the Walter Pyknoc or Pycknoc who witnessed confirmation of the church of Cragyn (Craigie) to the monks of Paisley, c. 1272 (ibid., p. 233). As Walter Piknoc he witnessed a division between the lands of the church of Paisley and of William de Sanchar in 1280 (ibid., p. 228), and as Walter de Picnoc' witnessed a deed of resignation in 1284 (ibid., p. 65). Teobaud Pictoc of the county of Perth who rendered homage in 1296 (*Bain*, II, p. 202) is probably another of the name. Pycnoch 1270.

PIERS. A ME. proper name, the AF. form of Lat. *Petrus*, Peter. A common personal name with the Normans. Piris Lutfut complained in 1424 that he had been illegally imprisoned (REO., p. 44), and Adam Pers, tacksman in the Nethertown of Grenyng, is recorded in 1492 (ibid., p. 407). A friar, Peter of Kelso, is also referred to as Frere Peres.

PIERSON, PEARSON, 'son of Pierre,' the French form of Peter. The earliest of the name recorded seems to have been Wautier Pieressone of Berwickshire who rendered homage in 1296 (*Bain*, II, p. 206). David Perisone, mercator de Scotia, who had a safe conduct to travel through England in 1369 (ibid., III) may be the David filius Petri, custumar of Haddington, 1373, who appears again in 1375 as David Perysoun (ER., II, p. 399, 469). Johannes Peryson appears in Aberdeen in 1408 (CWA., p. 313), and another John Peresone was bailie of Linlithqw in 1472 (Sc. Ant., XVII, p. 120). John Person leased part of Welton, 1440 (*Cupar-Angus*, I, p. 124), and John Perysoun, tenant in Grange of Balbrogy, 1468, appears again as John Perison or Peryson, tenant of Balbrogi, Chapeltoun, 1473 and 1478 (ibid., I, p. 143, 180, 226). Thom Peirson was servitor of the Abbey of Arbroath in 1506 (RAA., II, 449). Sir Henry Persone, vicar of Halkirk, 1537, appears to have been also known as Sir Henry Patersoun or Petersoun (OPS., II, 756, 757). William Peirsond was one of those respited for the slaughter of John, erle of Cathnes in 1529 (RSS., II, 3151), John Peryson was tenant of Stobo, 1540 (*Rental*), and Johne Persoun and Sandie Peirsoun were tenants on lands of the Abbey of Kelso, 1567 (*Kelso*, p. 524). Robert Piriesoun was burgess of Crail in 1634 (*Inquis.*, 2042), and Archibald Pierson was sheriff substitute of Forfar, 1642 (*Jervise*, I, p. 160). Macpherson was sometimes written M'A'Phearsain, and as the MacA' was dropped, the name (Pearsain) was likely to become merged in Pearson. Pairsone 1648, Pearsone 1688, Peirsonde 1542, Peirsone 1507, Peirsound 1560, Peirsounde 1548, Persone 1614, Peyrsoune 1480, Peyrson.

PIGG, PIGGE. This is probably a nickname, ME. *pigge*, a young swine, a word of doubtful origin. The name is also recorded in England as early as 1273 as Pig and Pigge. The second form is recorded in Aberdeen.

PIGGIE. A surname recorded in Aberdeen, perhaps a diminutive of PIGG, q.v.

PIGOTT. From NF. personal name Picot, diminutive of Pic. Roger Picot was an undertenant in England, 1086 (*Ewen*, p. 89). Donald Piggotis (or Donald Peget) had a charter of lands in the sheriffdoms of Berwick and Aberdeen from David II (RMS., I, App. II, 995). Abraham Pyghot, reidare at Kerymure, 1574 (RMR.). Abraham Pigott, notary in St. Andrews diocese, 1610 (*Laing*, 1583), and Gilbert Piggat was messenger in Edinburgh, 1686 (RPC., 3. ser. XII, p. 233). Payment to Margaret Piggot, in Edinburgh, 1719 (*Guildry*, p. 122). Peggot 1736.

PILCHE. A family of this name were prominent in Inverness in the end of the thirteenth and beginning of the fourteenth century. Patrick Pylche, juror on an inquest in Lanarkshire, 1263, is however, the first of the name recorded in Scotland (*Bain*, I, 2338; APS., I, p. 102). Alexander Pilche, burgess of Inverness, was one of the leading adherents in the North of Wallace and Bruce, and joined the insurrection of Andrew of Moray, 1297 (Barron, *Scottish War of Independence*, passim). Alexander Pylche was prepositus of the burgh of Inuernys in 1327 (ER., I, p. 59), William Pylche held land there in 1361 (REM., p. 306), and William Pylchee, miles, was juror at a court held at "Le Ballovicis Hill," near Inverness, 1376–77 (*Innes Familie*, p. 63). His house in Inverness is mentioned in 1377 (RMS., I, 649, 683). Harrison and Weekley make this a nickname, etymologically = (maker of) pelisse or fur coat. See also *Sc. Ant.*, VI, p. 32.

PILLAN, PILLANS. John Pyllan, tenant in Carstairs, 1525 (*Rental*). William Pillans in Strayfrank, parish of Carstairs, 1624, and six more of the name in the neighborhood (*Lanark CR.*). In Edinburgh in 1644 as Pilons (*Edinb. Marr.*). Pilans 1672, Pillan 1537, Pillane 1541, Pylan 1531.

PILMUIR, PILMORE, PILMER. This surname is most probably of south country origin as there are lands of the name in Berwickshire and Dumfriesshire, and a Pilmoor in the North Riding of Yorkshire. Adam de Pilemor witnessed a charter by Roger, bishop of St. Andrews, c. 1188–1202 (RPSA., p. 270), and Johannes de Pilemour witnessed another by Matilda, countess of Anegus, c. 1242–43

(RAA., I, p. 82). Roger de Pillemuir was freed from obligation of payment to Walter dominus de Venali, 1292 (*Panmure*, II, p. 151). Ade de Pilmure had a confirmation of the lands of Glack, c. 1294 (REA., I, p. 36), and William de Pilmor and Robert de Pylemor, both of county of Edinburgh, rendered homage, 1296 (*Bain*, II, p. 201, 207, 211). John de Pylmor, son of Adam de Pilmore, burgess of Dundee, became bishop of Moray in 1326 (*Dowden*, p. 152–153). He may be the John de Pilmore, monk of Cupar, who had a safe-conduct in 1321 while on a mission from Robert I. The bishop appears to have taken care of his relatives. Richard de Pilmur had provision of the canonry of Aberdeen and prebend of Cruden in 1328 (*Pap. Lett.*, II, p. 286). Thomas de Pylmer, nephew of Bishop John was granted the canonry and prebend of Caithness (*Pap. Pet.*, I, p. 68), and William de Pylmer, another nephew, had the canonry and prebend of Moray (ibid.). William de Pilmur witnessed confirmation of Snawdoun to the Abbey of Dryburgh, c. 1350 (*Dryburgh*, p. 232), Adam de Pilmore was juror on assize regarding the mill-lands of Quarelwode, Moray, and Thomas de Pilmor or Pylmore served as juror in 1393 and 1398 (REM., p. 171, 205, 212). William Pylmoure, merchant of Scotland, had a safe-conduct into England, 1464 (*Bain*, IV, 1347), and William Pilmur was tenant in Milhorn, 1462 (*Cupar-Angus*, I, p. 134). George Pylmuir was witness at Coldingham, Berwickshire, 1557 (*Home*, 195), Thomas Pilmuir appears in Lauder, 1561 (*Lauder*), and William Pilmer in Haltoun of Rattray, 1690 (*Dunkeld*). The name appears to have disappeared from the Garioch after the battle of Harlaw, 1411. Pilmore and Pylmore 1329, Pilmwr 1477, Pylmur 1552, Pylmure 1408, Pylmwre 1468.

PINCHES. Mathew de Pynsach granted a charter in favor of the Carmelites of Aberdeen, 1350 (*Friars*, p. 16). Under 1398 there is an entry "Item, dat. regi de cageris pro ictu sanguineo per Matheum Pynches ad emendam, vis. viii d." (SCM., V, p. 39; CRA., p. 3). Perhaps the Mathew Pynchest who held a land in Aberdeen, 1411 (CRA., p. 387). Pinchast 1405.

PINGLE. A northern way of writing PRINGLE, q.v., though this spelling is also found in the south but less frequently. Roger Pyngille held half of the lands of Withosyme, Berwick, in 1315–21 (RMS., I, 7). Adam Pyngil, burgess of Aberdeen, founded a chapel in the church of S. Mary of Aberdeen in 1376 (REA., I, p. 109), and in 1381 there is record of a charter by him in favor of the Carmelites of the same burgh (*Friars*, 19).

PINKENY. Two brothers, Henry de Pinkeny and Robert de Pinkeny, prominent in Scots affairs on the English side, 1272–1307 (*Bain*, II), derived their name from Pinkney in Norfolk. A Gilo de Pincheni, who lived in the reign of Henry I (1100–35), endowed the monks of St. Lucien in France with lands at Wedon in the county of Northampton (*Lower*). Robert de Pinkeny held the tenement of Balincref before 1296 (*Bain*, II, 857).

PINKERTON. From the old barony of the same name near Dunbar, East Lothian. Nicol de Pynkertone of Haddingtonshire rendered homage in 1296 (*Bain*, II, p. 210). His seal shows a mastiff barking, a rose above, S' Nicolai de Pincriton (ibid., p. 544). Patrick de Penkerton had protection for a year in England in 1396 (ibid., IV, 484). The name was not uncommon on the West Coast in the sixteenth century and earlier. The tenement of John Pinkerton in Glasgow is mentioned in 1494 (REG., 469), and a resignation of property in favor of Felicia Pyncartoun in Glasgow is recorded in 1552 (*Protocols*, I). John Pynkertoun rendered to Exchequer the accounts of the bailies of Rutherglen, 1559, and Malcolm Pincartoun rendered the accounts of the same burgh in 1566 (ER., XIX, p. 89, 325). The barony of Pinkerton was granted to the first earl of Argyll in 1483 on the forfeiture of Albany. John Pinkerton (1758–1826), the historian, is the best known of the name. Allan Pinkerton (1819–1884), the famous American detective, was born in Glasgow. Pincartone 1707, Pincartoune 1540, Pinkartoun 1677, Pinkcartoune 1648, Pinkertoune 1668, Pyncartoune 1533.

PINKIE. From the lands of Pinkie in the parish of Inveresk, Midlothian, the old name of which was Pontekyn (c. 1174–99, *Neubotle*, p. 53). John de Pontkyn witnessed gift of the church of Wemys (Fife) to the Hospital of Soltre, c. 1200–40 (*Soltre*, p. 13), and Peter de Pontekin was one of those who joined his fortunes to those of Bruce (*Bain*, III, 245; Barron, *War of Independence*, p. 414). Adam Pontkyn and Thomas de Pontkyn were members of the garrison of Edinburgh Castle, 1339–40 (*Bain*, III, p. 241).

PINKSTOUN. William Pinkstoun in Kilbarchan, 1765 (*Kilbarchan*), may have derived his name from Pinxton, a parish in co. Derby.

PIPER, PYPER. From the occupation of piper. "Anciently the name of Pyper was very frequent in Perth, and very Considerable Persons are called by that name in the Charters of the Religious Houses. About the time of the Reformation, the principal Families of that

name changed it for Balneaves" (*Sc. Ant.*, I, p. 165). William Pyper held lands of Innerbundy in 1457 (RAA., II, p. 97), Robert Piper contributed to the cost of church repairs in Aberdeen in 1508 (CRA., p. 79), and in the following year Robert Piper and John Piper were "comon menstrallis" in the same burgh (ibid., p. 440). Schir Johne Pipar was chaplain in Dunkeld, 1546 (*Rollok*, 21), and Hugh Pypar in Weik (Wick) had remission in 1547 for his share in taking and holding the castle of Akirgill in Caithness (OPS., II, p. 778). The fishings and annual rent of Kynnoule were sold to John Pypar in 1562 (ER., XIX, p. 489), and the marriage of Alexander Balneaves alias Pyper and Janet Glook is recorded in 1565 (*Sc. Ant.*, I, p. 165). Robert Pyper was a baxter in Inverness in 1609 (*Rec. Inv.*, II, p. 73). Walter Pyper was town councillor of Perth in 1567 (RPC., I, p. 505), Donald Pyper in Fearn was a follower of Ross of Morange in 1596 (RPC., V, p. 304), and William Peper, mylner of Eister Tyrie, 1609 (RPC., VIII, p. 778). Donald Pepar or Pepper was dempster in Inverness, 1610–13 (*Rec. Inv.*, II, p. 76, 116), George Pyper was promoter of the stocking trade in Aberdeen in the Commonwealth and Restoration periods, and a commission of fire and sword was issued against Donald Pyper and John Pyper, sons of Patrick Pyperson, and others, followers of Murray of Aberscorse, Ross, in 1672 (RPC., 3. ser. III, p. 483). A family of this name settled in Goteborg in Sweden, and rendered their name (or had it rendered for them) by the classic Fistulator. Three families of the name are recorded (Marryat, *One year in Sweden*, II, p. 476).

PIRIE, PIRRIE. (1) Most probably from diminutive of Peter through the French form *Pierre*. (2) It might also be local, 'at the pear-tree,' ME. *pirie, atte Pirye*, but first most probable. A common surname in the shires of Aberdeen and Banff. Many generations of Piries have lived at Iriewells in the parish of Udny (AEI., p. 102), and there was an old family of Pyrrie in Paisley dating from the end of the fifteenth century. John Pirre was burgess of Glasgow in 1550 (*Protocols*, I), Adam Peirie, tailzeour in Inverness, 1625 (*Rec. Inv.*, II, p. 165), James Pirie appears in Bogmyln in 1633 (SCM., III, p. 100). William Pirrhie was retoured heir of David Pirrhie in Nuik, 1602 (*Retours, Lanark*, 29), Agnes Pirie was accused of charming in 1664 (*Alford*, p. 56–57), Robert Pirrie, bailie of Paisley, 1686 (RPC., 3. ser. XII, p. 383), and Janet Peirie was retoured heir in a tenement in Glasgow in 1695 (*Retours, Lanark*, 422). William Peirrie is in record in Torres of Luce

PIRIE, PIRRIE, continued

in 1729 (Wigtown), and another William Pirrie was member of the Huntly Volunteers in 1798 (Will, p. 7). Perie 1589, Pirrhy 1674, Pyerie 1601, Peirie, Perry, and Pirrhie 1686, and the spellings Pere, Peiries, Pire, Pirrie, and Pyrie are recorded in Records of the Sheriff Court of Aberdeenshire. Cf. PERRIE.

PIRNIE. Of local origin from Pairney near Auchterarder, Perthshire (1610 Pirney, 1627 Pirnie). Patrick Pirnie was mason in Cargill, 1769 (Dunkeld). There was a family of Pirnie of Moss-side, parish of Redgorton, Perthshire, in the eighteenth and nineteenth centuries.

PIRRET. From Fr. Perret or Pierret, 'little Peter.' James Pirrat, tailor, freeman of Glasgow, 1584 (Burgesses). Walter Pirate in Kirkness, 1640 (PBK., p. 157). Robert Pirret was a "Wet Review" veteran, Edinburgh, 1881.

PITBACHLIE. From Pitbachlie near Dunfermline, Fife. Marjory of Petbachly of that Ilk died and her heir sold half of the land to the Abbey of Dunfermline in 1456 (RD., p. 340).

PITBLADO, PITBLADDO. From the lands of Pitbladdo in the parish of Cupar, Fife. John of Petblatho is mentioned in 1478 (ADC., p. 5), and Peter Pitblado of that Ilk was one of an inquest on the lands of Hough and Pitconnochy in Fife in 1505 (Macfarlane, II, p. 537n). James Pitblawds [Pitblawdo] witnessed a Crail charter of 1517 (Crail, p. 24), Peter Petblatho of that Ilk was juror on assize at Cupar in 1520 (SCBF., p. 187), Peter Potblade in Dundee was charged in 1552 with aiding the English (Beats, p. 326) and Alexander Pitblado of that Ilk is mentioned in 1563 (Laing, 765). James Pitblado was recorded heir of Andro Pitblado de eodem in 1618 (Inquis., 769), and James Pitblado was messenger in Kirkcaldy in 1633 (RPC., 2. ser. V, p. 93). Laurence Pitblado died in Stirling, 1938.

PITCAIRN, PITCAIRNS. Of territorial origin from the lands of Pitcairn in Fife. William de Petkaran was one of an assize at Dunfermline before 1249 (RD., p. 222). John de Petcarn or Pitcairn obtained from his kinsman Sir Hugh de Abernethy in 1250 a charter of the lands of Innernethie (Fife Pitcairns, p. 10). Pieres de Pectarne of the county of Fyfe rendered homage, 1296 (Bain, II, p. 204). Andrew Pitcairn and seven of his sons were killed at Flodden (ibid., p. 27). David Petkarn or Pitcarynn appears as archdeacon of Brechin in 1512 and 1518 (REB., II, p. 169, 173). It was Major John Pitcairn of the Royal Marines who fired the first shot in the American

Revolutionary War. Pitcairn Island in the South Pacific Ocean was discovered by Robert Pitcairn, R.N., in 1767. The last article Sir Walter Scott ever wrote was a notice of Robert Pitcairn's Criminal trials. The Pitcairns still continue as Fifeshire lairds, but they lost heavily in the '15 and '45. Petcairne 1677, Petcarne 1368, Pettcarne 1454, Petkarn 1413, Petkarne 1448, Pitcarne 1489, Pytcarnē 1544.

PITCAITHLY, PITCAITHLEY, PITCEATHLY, PITKAITHLY, PITKEATHLY, PITKETHLEY, PITKETHLY. From Pitcaithly in the parish of Dunbarny, Perthshire. John de Pencathlan (the old form of the name) witnessed a charter of the church of Inverkethyn, c. 1202–14 (RD., p. 95). David Pitcaithly was married in Perth, 1568 (Northern Notes and Queries, I, p. 169), and David Pitcaithlie is recorded in Burnesyde, 1684 (Inquis., 6550).

PITCOX. From Pitcox in the parish of Stenton, East Lothian. Gamellus de Pethcox witnessed a charter by Earl Waldeve to the monks of Melrose of a pasture on Lammermuir, c. 1166–82 (Melros, p. 67; Frasers of Philorth, I, p. inter 12 and 13). Philip de Pethcox gave meadowland in Pethcox to the monks of Melrose in the reign of Alexander II (Melros, 221, 222), permitting them to divert the stream of Pressmennan (Pressmuneburne) from Suinburne eastward. His son Philip is also mentioned (ibid., 220). Philip de Peccokes was buried in Melrose, 1247 (Chron. Mail., s.a.).

PITCULLO. From Pitcullo in the parish of Leuchars, Fife. There was a family of local prominence of this name.

PITFOUR. From Pitfour near Mintlaw, Aberdeenshire. John de Petfur was admitted burgess of the burgh of Aberdeen in 1407 (NSCM., I, p. 2).

PITGLASSIE. Patric de Petglassin appears as a charter witness, c. 1250 (SHR., II, p. 174). Edward de Pethglassyne was charter witness in Fife, c. 1280 (LAC., p. 186). He also witnessed the gift of 10 shillings annually by Gilbert de Cles to the monks of Dunfermline in 1231 (RD., p. 108). Patrick de Pedglassy of the county of Fife rendered homage in 1296 and had his lands restored to him (Bain, II, p. 209, 218). William de Petglassi also rendered homage in the same year (ibid., p. 169).

PITKAITHLY. See under PITCAITHLY.

PITKERRIE. From the lands of Pitkerrie, Anstruther, Fife. John de Petkeri appears as a witness, c. 1280 (May, p. 24), and William de Petkery of the county of Fife rendered homage in 1296 (Bain, II, p. 204).

PITKETHLEY, Pitkethly. *See under* PIT-
CAITHLY.

PITLIVER. From the place of that name
near Dunfermline. William de Petliuer witnessed Fife charters, c. 1230 (RD., p. 98, 99,
105, 112).

PITLOUR. From the place of the same name
in the parish of Strathmiglo, Fife. James Pitlour was a monk of Cupar in 1500 (REB.,
I, 220).

PITMEDDAN. Probably from Pitmeddan in
the parish of Dyce, Aberdeenshire, or Pitmiddan in the parish of Oyne. There is also a Pitmeddan in Fife. John Pytmethane, *dominus
ejusdem*, was one of the perambulators of the
lands of Vldny and Terwas in 1469 (RAA.,
II, p. 160). Pitmiddan in Oyne in common
speech is pronounced Petmathen.

PITSCOTTIE. From the lands of Pitscottie
in the parish of Ceres, Fife. John, son of Ralph
de Petscotyn, rendered homage at Aberdeen
in 1296 (*Bain*, II, p. 195). A horse was purchased from James de Petscoti, 1312 (*Bain*,
III, p. 429). John de Petscoty, burgess of
Perth in 1363 (RMS., I, 146) is probably the
individual who witnessed a Perth charter of
1375 and may be the John Petscoti (without
the 'de') who is mentioned as burgess of Perth
in 1389 (*Milne*, p. 36, 38). Andrew de Petscoty was vicar of Perth in 1403 (*Cambus.*,
167), and Andrew Petscotty witnessed a charter by the abbot of Scone to William Peblis
in 1491 (*Scon*, p. 201). — Petscothy of Con-
cardy, juror on inquisition in sheriffdom of
Perth, 1478 (HP., IV, p. 21). John Petscottye
was bailie at Scone, 1544 (*Rollok*, 17).

PITTECUMBER. Roger de Pittecumber witnessed a charter by Richard Lupellus, dominus de Hawic, c. 1183 (RPSA., p. 262).

PITTENDREIGH, Pittendrich, Pitten-
drigh. There are places named Pittendriech
in Midlothian, Fife, Kinross, Banff, Elgin,
Perth, Kincardine, and Angus. Pittendreigh
in Aberdeenshire, and in Stirlingshire is Pendreich. Pittendreich of that Ilk, an ancient family now extinct (*Nisbet*, I, p. 141). John de
Pethindreich witnessed a charter of the lands
of Lamebryde by Malcolm de Moravia to his
son William de Moray, c. 1278 (REM.,
p. 461). Marion Pettendriech resigned the
lands of Sornfawlache and Greenhill in the
barony of Wigtoun in the reign of Robert III
(RMS., I, App. II,1686), and John of Petyn-
dregh was master of the ship *la Katerine* of
Edinburgh, 1410 (*Bain*, IV, 794). William
Peddendreycht in Inverness, 1568 (*Rec. Inv.*,

I, p. 165). Petindrech 1413, Pettindrecht 1488,
Petyndricht 1576.

PITTENWEEM. Of local origin from the
place of the name in the parish of Pittenweem, Fife. John Pettynwyne is recorded in
Aberdeen in 1448 (CRA., p. 400), and
William Petinwyn was supprior of Aberbrothoc
in 1464 (RAA., II, 160). Johannes de Pettyn-
wvme was vicar of Durris in Moray, 1458
(REA., I, p. 282).

PITTINBROG. From some small place of the
name perhaps in Perthshire. David Pittinbrog
and John Pittinbrog in Perthshire are mentioned in 1550 (*Gaw*, 14).

PLATTER. Of local origin from the old (Forest of) Plater in Angus. Thomas Platter, one
of the brethren of St. Serf's, stabbed to death
Robert of Montrose, prior of St. Andrews
(*Bower*, ed. Goodall, VI, c. 54). The ghost of
Platter haunted a local billiard-marker a few
years ago, and asked him to dig in a certain
spot and give his bones Christian burial. The
bones were found and wrapped in the robe
of an Augustinian friar and were reburied
(Morton, *In Search of Scotland*, 1930, p. 136–
137).

PLAYFAIR. Said to be derived from Old
Scots *playfeire*, a play fellow or companion, but
this perhaps is mere popular etymology. The
older coats of arms of Playfair are said to be
similar to those of the Norfolk Playfords. The
first of the name recorded was William Play-
fayre, the messenger from the earl of Orkney
to Sir John Comyn in 1290 to inform him
of the arrival in Orkney of the "Damsel of
Scotland" (i.e. the Maid of Norway) (*Bain*,
II, p. 107). A citizen of St. Andrews named
Playfair was summoned to appear before the
Privy Council for having taken part in a
demonstration against Melville the Reformer.
David Playfair in Bendochy, 1745 (*Dunkeld*).
Several persons of this name have been dis-
tinguished in the annals of Scotland: Prof.
John Playfair, William H. Playfair the famous
architect, Dr. James Playfair, and Lyon, first
Lord Playfair. Playfeir 1584, Playfer 1585.

PLENAMOUR. John Plenamour, dominus de
Anestoun, attorney of the abbot of Arbroath,
1434 (RAA., II, 69). Andrew Planamouris
held a peat cast on Balnamonismyr, 1495
(ibid., 354).

PLENDERLEITH, Plenderleath. From the
old manor of the same name in the parish of
Oxnam, Roxburghshire. John de Plenderleith
witnessed a charter of lands in Teviotdale in
the reign of King William the Lion (*Melros*,
p. 144), and Nicholas de Prendrelath held the

PLENDERLEITH, PLENDERLEATH, continued
manor of Gilbert de Humfrenvill in socage
before 1291 (Rot. Scot., I, p. 10). John Wishart and Johanna, his wife, daughter and heiress of Nicholas de Prendrelath, are found in
possession of tenements at "Monilawe" (now
Moneylaws in Northumberland) in 1291.
William de Prendrelathe of the county of Roxburgh rendered homage in 1296 (Bain, II,
p. 199). Rev. Patrick Plenderleith (1679–
1715) was minister of Saline in Fife, and
John Plenderleith was provost of Peebles and
member of parliament for that burgh in 1669–
70.

PLEWRIGHT. From the occupation, 'one who
makes or mends ploughs.' In the Promptorium
Parvulorum, c. 1440, plowwryte is defined
'carrucarius.' William Plewryght is recorded
in Thornescheillis in 1649 (Pont). George
Plowright, indweller in Cunyngham Baidland
in 1662 is probably George Plewright, witness
at Ayr in the same year (Hunter, p. 60, 64).

PLOWDEN. An English surname of recent
introduction. The name is local, from Plowden
in Salop.

PLOWMAN. From the occupation of ploughman, a husbandman. Christane Plowman was
charged with superstitious practices in 1653
in the parish of Canisbay, Caithness (Old Lore
Misc., v, p. 61), and William Plewman in
Noiss is in record in 1661 (Caithness).

PLUMER, PLUMMER. From the occupation,
an artisan who worked in lead, originally
applied to a man who also dealt in lead, OF.
plummier>NF. plombier. Wilyam Plumer of
Tweddale, burgess of Andirstoun (i.e. St.
Andrews), was indentured to "theke the mekil
quer [of the Abbey of Aberbrothoc] with lede
and guttir yt al about sufficiandly with lede"
(RAA., II, 43). At the end of the indenture,
which is dated 16th February 1394–5, he is
again mentioned as "Wilyam of Tweddal
plummer." In 1420 there is mention of the
"skalt hows" of Richard Johnson "in the
quhilkis duellis Nichol Plumber" (ibid., 53).
Alexander Plumbar was tenant of Kyncregh
Grange in 1460 (Cupar-Angus, I, p. 133),
Pait Plumer and Dandie Plumer were tenants
of the abbot of Kelso in 1567 (Kelso, p. 523,
529), and in 1642 Andrew alias Dand Plumbar, son of John Plumbar in Kelso, was retoured heir in lands in the bailiary of Lauderdaill (Retours, Berwick, 243). Sir John Plumbar was vicar of Bendochty in 1472 (Bamff,
p. 30), Alexander Plumber was factor to
William, earl of Roxburgh, in 1661 (RRM.,
I, p. 337), and Margaret Plumber is recorded
in Kelso in 1682 (Peebles CR.).

PODEMOR. Doubtless from Podmore in Staffordshire. A horse was purchased from Ricardus de Podemor, 1312 (Bain, III, p. 427).

POET. Till lately said to have been a common
surname in Fife. Said to be a form of the
Flemish name Puijt (Sc. Ant., IV), but more
likely a variant of PATE, q.v.

POILSONE. See POLSON.

POKEBY. William de Pokeby of Edinburghshire rendered homage, 1296 (Bain, II,
p. 201), and Adam de Pokby, capellanus, witnessed gift of Swaynystoun to the Hospital
of Soltre between 1238–70 (Soltre, p. 28).

POLE. A Shetland surname, probably a form
of PAUL, q.v. Patrick Pole in Rerwick, Shetland, was a witness in 1624 (OSS., I, 89).
Cf. POLSON.

POLGOWNY. See under BALGONIE.

POLLARD. William Pollard witnessed a charter by Adam de Lamberton of the third part
of Lamberton, c. 1190–1200 (BNCH., XVI,
p. 332; Home, 224). James Pollart was infeft
in the lands of Costoun in the barony of
Torphichen, 1549 (Laing, 554).

POLLOCK, POLLOK. Peter, son of Fulbert or
Fulburt, had a grant of Upper Pollock in Renfrewshire from the High Steward, and took
his surname from the lands. Between 1177–99
Peter gifted the church of Pulloc and its
pertinents to the monastery of Paisley, a gift
confirmed by Jocelyn, bishop of Glasgow
(RMP., p. 98, 99). Within the same dates
he confirmed the charter of his brother Helias
or Helyas of Perthic (now Partick) to the
same house (ibid., p. 98, 100). Peter de Pollok
or Pulloc also possessed lands in Moray, and
c. 1172–78 he witnessed the charter by William
the Lion granting Burgin (now Burgie) to the
Abbey of Kinlos (REM., p. 454). He also
appears among the witnesses to three other
charters by King William in the same chartulary
between 1187–99 (p. 6, 9, 11). Robert, son
of Fulbert, also appears several times as charter witness between 1165–99, but in no instance is he referred to as 'de Polloc' (RMP.,
p. 6, 7, 12). In another charter of c. 1200 he
appears again as Robert, son of Fulbert, along
with his brother Peter, who appears simply as
"Petrus fratre ejusdem." A daughter of Peter
de Polloc, Muriel, lady of Rothes, married
probably about 1220 Walter Morthach, and
had by him a daughter Eva Morthach, lady
of Rothes. Between 1224–42 Muriel de Polloc
gifted her land of Inuerorkel with all its just
pertinents for the benefit of the house or
hospital erected beside the bridge of Spe

(Spey) for the reception of travellers (REM., p. 120). About 1242 or earlier Eva Morthach, domina de Rothes, confirmed the gift of the church of Rothes which her mother Muriel de Rothes had made to the church of Moray, c. 1235 (ibid., p. 123–124). Among the witnesses appear Robert de Pollok and Adam his son. Thomas de Polloc was witness to a document concerning the land of Cnoc in Renfrewshire, 1234 (RMP., p. 180), and to other charters in same record between 1234 and 1272. In the reign of Alexander II, Robert de Pollok, son of Robert, son of Fulbert, granted in pure alms to the monastery of Paisley twelve pennies yearly from the rents of his land of Pollok, for which he expected in return that he and his heirs be admitted to participation in the spiritual benefit arising from all the pious exercises of the Cluniac Order (ibid., p. 378). Peres de Pollok of Lanarkshire and Johan Pollok of Forfarshire rendered homage, 1296 (Bain, II, p. 211, 212). John Pollok, who was steward of the Abbey of Arbroath, 1299 (RAA., II, p. 164) is John de Pollok, sheriff of Forfar, who was sent with others from Aberdeen to Montrose in 1304 to arrest a vessel of the bishop of Aberdeen reported to be laden with rebel merchants' goods and to bring her to Aberdeen (Bain, II, 439, 441). John Pullok, a Scottish merchant, had safe conduct into England, 1453 (Bain, IV, 1264), Peter de Pollok was one of the witnesses to sale of a tenement in Glasgow to Master Patrick Leiche, canon of Glasgow, 1454 (REG., p. 391), 'Schir' Thomas Pollo witnessed a sasine in 1478 (Home, 24), and John Pollike was a skinner in Edinburgh, 1678 (Edinb. Marr.). The main line of the family of de Polloc disappeared in the War of Succession, "an era of remarkable changes of families and property." The name has become Polk in the United States, the eleventh president of which was James Knox Polk, a great-great-grandson of Robert Polk or Pollok who emigrated from Ayrshire to the American colonies. The place name on Pont's map of Renfrewshire is spelled Pook, and that is the pronunciation in common speech. Nile Pook was servitor to the bishop of Aberdeen, 1549 (REA., I, p. 435), Mariota Pook was wife of John Watsoun in Cannongait, Edinburgh, 1632 (Retours, Edinburgh, 694), and Isabella Pook was spouse of William Orrok in Edinburgh, 1648 (Inquis., 3455). Pollick 1685, Polloch 1225, Poock 1643.

POLMALLET. William de Polmaloc or Polmadoc (now Polmallet in the parish of Sorbie) of the county of Wyggetone rendered homage in 1296 and had his lands restored to him (Bain, II, p. 198, 219). As William de Polmaloche he served as juror on an inquisition

at Berwick in the same year (ibid., p. 215). "His history is lost in oblivion."

POLMOOD. A rare surname, most probably of local origin from Polmood in Peeblesshire. In common speech pronounced Powmood.

POLSON, POLESON, POULSON, POILSONE, PAULSON. 'Son of Paul' (G. Pòl, borrowed from N. Pál). "The name Paul was a favourite one among the Norse, and hence its popularity in Cathanesia" (Macbain III, p. 22). The Polsons are claimed by Clan Mackay historians as belonging to their clan, descended from Paul, son of Neil Neilson, son of Donald (Mackay) who was murdered in Dingwall Castle, 1370. The earliest record of the name is in the will of Alexander Sutherland of Dunbeath, 1456, in which he bequeaths to his daughter Marion "so many ky as she ought to have of William Polsonys ky" (Bannatyne Club Miscellany, III, p. 99). A Hugh Paulson (Lat. Pauli) witnessed a grant of the lands of Thorboll, 1472 (OPS., II, p. 686). Hugh Poilson, perhaps the same person, witnessed a deed of 1497 relating to Torboll, and Schir Johne Poilsone or Poylson appears as chantour of Dornoch in the same year, "chantour of Cataness" in 1500, and in 1506 was presented to the rectory of Ey in Lewis (RSS., I, 138, 539, 1332). Duncan Paulsoun resigned the lands of Ovir Tulleglennis in the baronia de Culbin, 1508–9, and Donald William Poilsoun was occupier of Nether Bulbistar, 1541 (RMS., II, 3298; III, 2450). Hew Poilsoun was reader at the church of Lairg between 1574 and 1578 (OPS., II, p. 698), and Murdo Poilson was burgess of Inverness, 1606–23 (Rec. Inv., II, p. 34, 162). Some Polsons have adopted the name Macphail and others sign themselves Mackay (Book of Mackay, p. 365). Some others of the name on the estate of Balnespik in the latter half of the eighteenth century spelled their name Wilson (Grant, An old Highland farm, p. 158, 176). Cosmo Innes errs in deriving the Polsons from Paul Mactire, lord of Strathcarron, Strathoykell, and Westray in the fourteenth century. The form Poleson occurs in Shetland. Pollsoun 1678, Polsone 1641, Polsoun and Polsun 1456, Poylson 1506, Polysoun 1499.

POLWARTH. From the lands of Polwarth in the parish of the same name, Berwickshire. Adam de Paulwrth witnessed a quitclaim of Suineswde by Patrick, first earl of Dunbar (Raine, 118). Adam de Pauliswithe (error for -wrthe) witnessed another charter by the same earl (ibid., 122), and also one by Patrick the second earl in lifetime of his father (ibid., 125). Ada de Polwrth witnessed a charter by Walter Olifard, c. 1210 (SHR., II, p. 175).

POLWARTH, *continued*

Adam de Paulewurth witnessed a charter by Patrick, earl of Dunbar concerning a grant to Abbey of Melrose, c. 1230–31 (*Wemyss*, II, p. xlviii). Robert de Paulworth and Beatrix his wife made an excambion of lands in 1258 (*Kelso*, 302). Gilbert de Paulwrt, a witness c. 1270 (*May*, 23). Patrick de Poulworth, miles, witnessed donation by Henry de Aynestrother to Dryburgh Abbey, c. 1330 (*Dryburgh*, 253), and as Patrick de Polworche (*t* misread *c*) was a charter witness in Edinburgh, 1364 (*RMS.*, I, 187). William of Polword, a Scot, had letters of protection on going abroad, 1371 (*Bain*, IV, 195). The last of the lairds of Polworth of that name was Sir Patrick Polworth of that Ilk who resigned his lands into the hands of his feudal superior, George, earl of March, who in 1377 bestowed them upon John Sinclair of Herdmanstown (HMC., 14. Rep., App., pt. 3, p. 60). Hennes (Hames or Hauves) Polvoir or Poulvoir, a Scot, at Tours, painted the standard of Joan of Arc. The name is considered by authorities (Francisque Michel, *Les Ecoss. en France*, I, p. 175; John Hill Burton, and Andrew Lang) to be a French attempt at Polworth. George Pollwart witnessed an instrument of sasine, 1495 (*Home*, 26). Grissillda Polwart was heir of Alexander Polwart in Boigcoat, 1668 (*Retours, Linlithgow*, 222).

POMFRET. Of local origin from Pontefract in Yorkshire, of which, says Bardsley, "as everybody knows, Pomfret is the usual pronunciation, and has been for many centuries." Andrew of Ponfret of Lanark was one of those appointed in 1357 to treat for the ransom of David II (CDE., p. 20). Andrew de Pumfrete or Pumfret was juror on an inquest in Edinburgh, c. 1402–05 (*Egidii*, p. 39, 41). John Pontfret, servant of the king of Scotland, had a safe conduct to go from England to Bruges in 1423, and two years later Thomas Pountfrette, servitor of James of Sandilande, had a similar safe conduct (*Bain*, IV, 936, 986).

POMPHRAY, PUMFRAY. From Welsh Ap-Humphrey, 'son of HUMPHREY,' q.v. David Pumfray held a booth in Lanark, 1488, and was admitted burgess of the burgh in the same year (*Lanark*, p. 2, 4). Payment was made to John Pumfray in 1526 (ALHT., V, p. 306), Stephen Pumfray, witness in Glasgow, 1555 (*Protocols*, I), Andrew Pumfra and Alexander Pumfra, witnesses, 1562 (RPC., I, p. 224), James Pumphray is recorded in Abbeygreen, parish of Lesmahago, 1653 (*Lanark CR.*), and John Pumphray in Richartoun, Lanark, 1711 (*Minutes*, p. 114).

PONT. Alanus de Ponte held a toft in Perth in the reign of Alexander II (*Scon*, p. 62). Juliana de Ponte, daughter of Adam de Ponte, burgess of Are, granted an annuity of 21 shillings to the convent of St. Catharine of Ayr, c. 1340 (*Friars Ayr*, p. 10). Patrick Pont was admitted burgess of Aberdeen, 1503 (NSCM., I, p. 41). Robert Pont was provost of Queen's College (S. Trin.), Edinburgh, 1573 (*Soltre*, p. 226), and an assedation of the lands of Cowdennyes baith was made to Helene Pont [Kilpont] before 1585 (RD., p. 488). Magister Robertus Pont, minister of the word of God in St. Cuthbert's Church, Edinburgh, was heir of James Pont, commissary of Dunblane, 1602 (*Inquis.*, 113). Chalmers (*Caledonia*, II, p. 57) says, without giving authority for his statement, that this Robert Pont was "the son of John Pont, a Venetian Protestant who had fled to France, and came into Scotland with James V in the retinue of Queen Magdalene; he obtained lands of Shyres mill, and married Katherine, the daughter of Moray of Tullibardin." Cf. under KINPONT.

PONTON. Wilielmus de Ponton recorded in Ayr, 1305–6 may be William de Ponton who was sent to Ireland by Edward I in 1306–7 to prepare Hugh Byset's expedition from Ireland against Robert de Brus (*Bain*, II, p. 503). Thomas Ponton "wes chosyne abbot of vnresson" in Haddington, 1539 (Mill, *Plays*, p. 251). John Pontoune had charter of a croft of the lands of Muirhall, 1610 (RD., p. 504). Probably from Ponton near Grantham, Lincolnshire. Pontoune and Puntoune 1541. Cf. PANTON and PUNTON.

POOK. A corruption of POLLOCK, q.v. The surname is still current in Scotland, though rare, and is also recorded in Canada.

POOL. Perhaps local, from residence by a pool. William del Pol of Donde granted a charter, 1321 (*Pitfirrane*, 5). William, Adam, and Mathew Pule appear in 1624 (*Inquis.*, 1114, 1115), and John Puill was merchant burgess of Dumfries, 1638 (*Dumfries*). Reservation of the liferent of Blackhills was made to Margaret Puill, 1668 (*Home*, 194). Robert Poill in Inverness to muster the militia, 1684 (*Rec. Inv.*, II, p. 322). William Pool appears in Trailtrow, 1746 (*Dumfries*). The English name Pool, Poole, was written Pull, Poole, and De la Poole in the fourteenth century.

POPE, PAPE. A family of Paips or Papes appear to have belonged originally to Elgin, and some of them were in the legal profession before the Reformation (TGSI., XXVIII, p. 257). In Caithness, Sutherland, and Orkney, the surname is still pronounced Paip. In 1363 William Pop, son and heir of William Pop, burgess of Elgin, made a gift to the altar of the Virgin in the church of S. Giles in Elgin (REM., p. 312), and in 1375 there is mention of Robert Popp of Elgin (RAA., II, 34). Adam Popp and Robertus Popp were jurors on an assize regarding the mill lands of Quarelwode in 1389 (REM., p. 171). David Pap was admitted burgess of Elgin in 1516 (NSCM., I, p. 46), and Sir James Pop, a cleric, was a monk of Beauly in 1540 (Ferrarius, History, p. 49). William Pape, a native of Ross-shire, was appointed schoolmaster in Dornoch in 1585, and chanter of Dornoch in 1602 (OPS., II, p. 618). James Pape was burgess of Kirkwall in 1580 (REO., p. 298), John Pape was a writer in Edinburgh in 1598 (Edinb. Marr.), another John Paip, writer to the signet, is recorded in Aberdeen in 1599 (CRA., p. 206), and Thomas Paip was admitted burgess of Aberdeen in 1622 (NSCM., I, p. 130). Mr. John Paip had a charter of the lands of Kildin in 1606 (RD., p. 498), Magister Robert Paip, advocate, was burgess of Aberdeen in 1624 (Inquis., 1137), and Thomas Pope or Pape is recorded at Cullicudden in 1653 (IDR., p. 249). Paipe 1595.

PORRINGER. Payment to Nicolas Porringer in Edinburgh, 1727 (Guildry, p. 134).

PORTEOUS. A south country surname. The family of Porteous of Hawkshaw, an old family in Peeblesshire. John Pertus of Glenkirk in record 1443, also owned lands in Fife. George Portwis held the lands of Glenkirk in 1478–84 (ALA., p. 81, 140). John Portewis had charter in 1513 of the lands of Glenkirk and Quhitslaid, and Sir William Portus was chaplain in the parish church of S. Bega of Kilbucho, 1550. James Pourtes, glover, in Edinburgh, 1670 (Edinb. App.). Perhaps of local origin from some place near 'Porthouse.' The derivation from Scots porteous, a catalogue or list of persons indicted to appear before the Justice-Ayre, is untenable. Pertuuss 1549, Porteouse 1701, Portews 1479, Portowis 1454, Portows 1561, Portuis 1478, Portuiss 1563, Portuus 1527, Portuuss 1549.

PORTER. From the office of porter, doorkeeper, or janitor of a castle or monastery. The porter was one of the most important officials connected with the castle or monastic institution. Lands and privileges were attached to the office, and in the case of a royal castle the position was often hereditary (see DORWARD). The porter of a religious house was also the distributor of the alms of the convent, for the poor were always supplied "ad portam monasterii," at the gate of the monastery.

He also kept the keys and had power to refuse admission to those whom he deemed unworthy (Innes, Legal antiquities, p. 170). Radulfus the porter witnessed the gift of the church of Cragyn (Craigie) in Kyle to the monastery of Paisley, a. 1177 (RMP., p. 232), and c. 1180 Simon the porter witnessed a charter by William the Lion to Radulph de Graham (HMC., 2. Rep., App., p. 165). Reginaldus janitore witnessed a charter of Skibo between 1203–14, and between 1215–45 Helena, daughter of Roger "sometimes called Porter," sold a grange in Annandale to Robert de Brus, lord of Annandale (Bain, I, 1681). In 1261 Alexander III directed the sheriff and his bailies of Forfar to cause inquiry to be made...whether Margareta, Agnes, Swannoc or Suannoch ('swan neck'), Cristinia, and Mariota, daughters of the late Symon Gatekeeper of Monros (Montrose) are the lawful and nearest heirs of the said Symon in the lands of Inyanev and in the office of gate-keeper of the castle, and if the said deceased Symon died vest and seised as of fee of the said lands and office. The inquest found that a certain man named Crane had and held the foresaid lands hereditarily by gift of King William and died vest and seised of the said lands as of fee. And that the said Simon had the five daughters above named by two wives whom he had married, and that the said Crane, Swayn, and Symon never raised an army, or gave assistance or did anything else in the world for the said lands, except gate-keeper of our lord the king's castle of Montrose ("nec dederunt auxilium nec aliquid aliud in mundo pro dicta terra fecerunt nisi officium Janue Castri domini Regis de Munros"). And the jurors say that the said women are the lawful and nearest heirs of the said Simon (APS., I, p. 100). John the Porter of Linlithgow and Walter the Porter of Lanarkshire rendered homage in 1296 (Bain, II, p. 198, 212). Robert Porter, dominus de Porterfield, in 1399 gave the monks of Paisley an annual rent of sixteen pennies from burgage tenements in Renfrew and also confirmed a former grant of his father, Stephen Porter (RMP., p. 374). John de Janua (doorkeeper), a notary public in diocese of Glasgow, 1418 (CMN., 28), and Donald Portar had remission for his part in burning the town of Dunbertane in 1489 (Lennox, II, p. 133). During the incumbency of Abbot John Schanwell (1480–1509) a charter was granted "with consent of the whole convent, in favour of their lovite servant, John the Portar, whereby in consideration of his faithful service rendered to them in the office of portary of the monastery, which office also his progenitors held successfully and faithfully, and laudably

PORTER, *continued*
guided, they grant to him and his heirs-male for ever, the said office, with all its rights, customs, and emoluments, both within and without the monastery" (*Cupar-Angus*, II, p. 292-293). Gaelic *portair* (from Eng. porter) has also the meaning of 'ferryman.' The *Clann a' Phortair* from whom the Macnaughtons in Glenlyon derive their designation was a ferryman (*Folk tales and fairy lore*, p. 322).

PORTERFIELD. "In several monasteries, a portion of land was appropriated to the Porter. At Paisley this office and land seems to have got into the hands of laymen, and to have become hereditary. The descendants of 'John the Porter,' inheriting the 'porterfield' naturally took the surname from their office, until territorial surnames came into fashion, when they lengthened it into 'Robertus Porterfield *de eodem*,' the founder of a family of consideration in Renfrew" (*Neuboile*, pref. p. xix). John Porterfield of that Ilk obtained from James III a charter of confirmation of his lands of Porterfield in 1460. Some notes on the family are in Crawford's *History of the shire of Renfrew*, p. 30-33. The Rev. John Porterfield (latter half of the sixteenth century) was distinctly a pluralist, holding five churches in Strathendrick in addition to the vicarage of Ardrossan (*Strathendrick*, p. 24, 53). Colin Portfield who was admitted burgess of Aberdeen in 1549 may have been one of the family (NSCM., I, p. 61). The last of the family died in 1815. Portarfelde 1471, Portarfield 1609, Porterfeilde 1555, Portterffeild 1684, Poterfeild 1614.

POTT. Richard Pott in Eskdaill was charged with the theft of four cows in 1513 (*Trials*, I, p. 87*), and Thomas Pot in Reddene and Rafe (Ralph) Pott in Kelso are in record in 1567 (*Kelso*, p. 522, 524). George Pott was merchant burgess of Edinburgh, 1694 (*Inquis.*, 7547). Explained as a shortened form of PHILPOT, which is a diminutive of PHILIP.

POTTER. From the occupation, a maker of pots (rendered "figulus, ollarius, plastes, vrnarius" in the *Catholicon Anglicum*). Simon Potter of Dumbarton was one of those appointed to treat for the ransom of David II in 1357 (CDE., p. 20), Thomas Potter was a tenant of the earl of Douglas in Moffat, 1376 (RHM., I, p. lxiii), and Alexander Potter was admitted burgess of Aberdeen, 1498 (NSCM., I, p. 39). James Pottar witnessed an instrument of sasine in Brechin, 1505 (REB., II, 149), Robert Potter was burgess of Are, 1590 (*Ayr*, p. 116), and Henry Potter was retoured heir in lands in vill of Drumcrostoun, 1630

(*Retours, Linlithgow*, 124). Thomas Potter, a Scot, built a smelting work at Applebys Plads in 1769, thus taking a lead in the Danish iron-foundry industry.

POTTIE. Alexander Pottie, trade burgess of Aberdeen, 1671 (ROA., I, p. 236), George Pottie, gardener at Kirkcudbright, 1787 (*Kirkcudbright*).

POTTINGER. A corruption of *potager*, 'a maker of pottage.' The intrusive n is quite regular, as in 'messenger' and 'passenger,' for 'messager' and 'passager.' The surname appears in Scotland to have been confined mainly to Orkney and Shetland. Alexander Potyngeir and Thome Potyngeir were jurors on an inquest held at Sabay, Orkney, 1522 (REO., p. 95). Alexander Potinger was one of the witnesses to a deed of sale in Orkney, 1552 (*Old Lore Misc.*, IV, p. 66). Peter Pottinger was retoured heir of Agnes Aitkin in lands in Sty, parish of Dunes, 1640 (*Retours, Orkney and Shetland*, 30).

POTTON. Richard de Potton or Poiton (d. 1270), bishop of Aberdeen, was an Englishman. In Boece and later Church books his name is recorded as Pottocht and Pottock (REA., I, p. xxv). Hugh de Potton became archdeacon of Glasgow, 1227 (*Chron. Mail.*), and was a charter witness, c. 1227-35 (RMP., p. 77). John de Potyn, judex, witnessed a quit-claim of the lands of Drumkarauch, 1260 (RPSA., p. 346; see also *Panmure*, II, 83). The name is derived from Potton, a parish and market town in Bedfordshire.

POTTS, 'son of POTT,' q.v. Charles Potts was notary in Kelso, 1727 (*Stitchill*, p. 188).

POULSON. *See* POLSON.

POURIE, POWRIE. From Powrie in Errol, parish of Murroes, Angus. Henry of Pourie was juror on an inquest at Roxburgh in 1361 (*Bain*, IV, 62). William Powry was tried for the murder of the king (Darnley), 1568 (RPC., I, p. 600), and another William Powyre was schoolmaster of Lynlythquow, 1583 (*Sc. Ant.*, XI, p. 131). Isobel Powrie appears in Edinburgh in 1609 (*Edinb. Marr.*), and Johannes Pourie is recorded in Maynes de Erroll in 1670 (*Inquis.*, 5381). Andrew Powrie, mair of the shirieffdome of Perthshire, 1689 (RPC., 3. ser. XIV, p. 769). Nisbet mentions Powrie of Woodcocksholm in Linlithgowshire as an old family of the name.

POW. Thomas Pow was witness in Glasgow, 1553 (*Protocols*, I), Robert Pow, a notary in Eyemouth, 1651 (*Home*, p. 220), Robert Pow, master of the Grammar School of Leith,

1697 (*Inquis.*, 7801), and Mr. John Pow was minister at Coldstream, 1735 (*Lauder*). Gavin Pou, a Scotsman, settled in Orangeburg, South Carolina, in 1740.

POWA. John Powa of Siluerwod, a witness, 1535 (*Hunter*, p. 14), and Thomas Powa held land in Irvine, Ayrshire, 1540 (*Irvine*, I, p. 166). Archibald Poway was admitted burgess freeman of Glasgow, 1577 (*Burgesses*).

POWEK. Charles of Powek was declared innocent of detention of King James III in Edinburgh Castle, 1482 (*Lennox*, II, p. 123); and Hugh and Archibald Powok were charged with murder, 1512 (*Trials*, I, p. 81).

POWER. From OF. *Pohier*, a Picard or native of Picardy, Early Eng. *Poeir*. William Poer was parson of Lemnelar (Lumlair), 1227 (REM.), and a horse was purchased from Thomas Power in 1312 (*Bain*, III, p. 422). William Power, a follower of the earl of Cassilis, was respited for murder, 1526 (RSS., I, 3386). John Powre, witness at Tullyhow, Kynfawnis, 1539 (*Rollok*, 83), and Gilbert Power was burgess of Air, 1586 (*Retours, Ayr*, 740). Margaret Power was retoured heir of Anna Cunninghame, spouse of Hugh Power, merchant burgess of Edinburgh, 1664 (*Retours, Ayr*, 533). William Power recorded in Finick, 1666, and Elizabeth Power in Clonherb, 1679 (*Corsehill*, p. 70, 148). Gilbert Power, merchant burgess of Edinburgh, 1682 (*Inquis.*, 6417).

POWRIE. See under POURIE.

POWTIE. William Powte was master of the ship *Clement* of Aberdeen, 1438 (*Bain*, IV, 1114). David Powte, mason's labourer at Dunkeld, 1515 (*Rent. Dunk.*, p. 294). Mr. John Powtie was minister at Leslie, 1617 (*Dysart*, p. 48), and Mr. Thomas Poutie or Powtie was minister there, 1638 (PBK., p. 1). Probably same as PULTY, q.v.

PRATT. This surname has been derived (1) from OFr. *prat* (<Lat. *pratum*), Fr. *pré*, a meadow, meaning a dweller at or by a meadow, but in no instance in Scottish record does it appear with *de* prefixed. (2) From OE. *praett*, a wile or stratagem. In the *Vita Herewardi* Aelfric Præt, we are told, derived his name from the stratagems with which he continually afflicted the Norman forces. This derivation may be accepted for what it is worth. Prats or Pratts were neighbors of the Grants and Bissets both in the north in early thirteenth century and in their earlier home in Nottinghamshire, and probably came north with the Bissets. William Prat, the first of the name recorded in Scotland, witnessed a charter by William Cumyn, earl of Buchan, before 1200 (REA., I, p. 15), and is also mentioned as sheriff of Invernairne at beginning of thirteenth century (*Illus.*, II, p. 283). William Prat of Fifeshire rendered homage, 1296. His seal bears the Agnus Dei, and S' *Wilelmi Prat* (*Bain*, II, p. 185, 200). Thomas Prat held a land in Aberdeen, 1464 (RAA., II, 155), and as Pret and Pratt he appears as burgess there, 1487–98 (ibid., II, 311). Sir Thomas Prat was presented to the vicarage of Banff in 1497 (ibid., II, 373). David Pratt, an artist of the reign of James IV, had payments made him. George Prat was "toune serjand" of Aberdeen, 1664 (SCM., v, p. 334). Families of the name occur in Fyvie (AEI., I, p. 509). Praitt 1538, Prat, Prath, Proat.

PRATUS. William Pratus or Prathus in Dunfermline, 1579, 1586 (*Dunfermline*) derived his surname from Prathouse near Crossgates, Fife. There is also a Pratis in the parish of Largo, Fife.

PRENDERGAST. From the place of the same name in Pembrokeshire, Wales. The family gave the name of their Welsh home to their new possessions, Prenderguest (now a farm, a. 1152 Prenderghest) near Ayton, Berwickshire. Waldoev de Prendergest witnessed the grant of the church of Kilmaurs to the Abbey of Kelso, c. 1170 (*Kelso*, 283). Helia de Prendregest witnessed a charter by Adam de Lamberton of the third part of Lambertun, c. 1190–1200 (BNCH., XVI, p. 332). Elya de Prendregest and Henry de Prendregest witnessed charters by Patrick, first earl of Dunbar (*Raine*, 116, 117). Adam de Prendergest witnessed the deed of sale of Adam, son of Thurkill, to the prior of Coldingham, c. 1240. Peter de Prendyrgest was juror on inquisition on the lands of Elena la Zuche in the sheriffdom of Berwick, 1296, and in the same year Henry de Prendregast of Berwickshire rendered homage (*Bain*, II, p. 206, 215). Dominus Henricus de Prendergest appears in 1325 as *dominus de eadem* (BNCH., XVI, p. 324), Nicholas de Prendergest was burgess of Glasgow, 1413 and 1424 (REG., 323; LCD., p. 242), and Robert de Prendergest was rector of Glasfurd, 1440 (REG., 344). Plainderghaist 1678, Plendergest 1695.

PRENTICE, PRENTISS. A colloquial apheresis for apprentice, frequently met with in literature.

"A Prentys whilom dwelt in our citee,
And of a craft of vitaillers was he."

Chaucer, C. T. a. 4365–4366.

Henry Prentice, a small merchant in the Canongate of Edinburgh (d. 1788), was the first

PRENTICE, Prentiss, continued

man who introduced into the county of Edinburgh the field culture of the potato. In his lifetime he had his coffin made and his tombstone erected, inscribed: "Henry Prentice, Died..."

"Be not anxious to know how I lived,
But rather how yourself should die."

Chambers, Popular traditions, 1868 ed., p. 344. Prentise 1688.

PRENTY. John Prenty, charter witness, 1481 (Panmure, II, 252). Andrew Prentye or Prente was instructed in 1533 to infeft Elen Heres in the one-sixth part of the lands of Qwchtyreleth (Bamff, p. 61).

PRESCHOUR. Probably from the office of 'preacher,' ME. prechour. John Prechurrys, burgess of Abirbuthoc, 1394 (RAA., II, p. 43), and Thomas Preschour, burgess of Arbroath, 1452 (ibid., p. 80).

PRESFEN. From the township of Pressen (1255 Prestfen, 1309 Presfen, 1428 Pressen). William de Presfen was appointed by Edward III in 1334 to take seisin in his name of the Castle of Jedeworth, and as valettus to the same king he was appointed constable of the castle (Rot. Scot., I, p. 271, 401). William of Presfen and other Scots merchants complained that their ships, wrecked in a storm, were plundered at Bamburgh and Tynemouth in 1357 (Bain, IV, 10).

PRESLIE, Presslie (both in Aberdeen), Presly. Harrison says these are English forms of the name Priestley, a surname of English local origin.

PRESSOCK. An old surname in Glenesk (Jervise II, p. 122). From the lands of Pressock in Angus (1604 Prescheok, 1620 Pressok). Duncan Preshok is recorded in Inerarity, 1686 (RPC., 3. ser. XII, p. 99), and Robert Prescho was burgess of Montrose, 1693 (Inquis., 7371).

PRESTON. From the barony of Preston or Prestoun, afterwards known as Gourtoun and now Craigmillar in Midlothian. Alured de Preston appears as a charter witness in 1222 (LSC., 62), and Lyulph, son of Lyulph de Preston, c. 1240–50, had a charter from John Albus of a piece of land in Linlithgow which he made over to the Abbey of Neubotel (Neubotle, p. 149). Johannes de Prestun witnessed a quitclaim by Johannes Gallard apud Muskilburg in 1248 (RD., p. 97), William de Preston and Henry de Preston appear as charter witnesses in 1292 (Neubotle, p. 292), and William de Prestone and Nicol de Prestone,

both of Edinburghshire, rendered homage in 1296 (Bain, II, p. 201). Nisbet (Heraldry) says that Nicol is Preston of that Ilk and Craigmillar. Philip de Prestoun was a charter witness in 1332 (BNCH., XVI, p. 327), and Sir John de Preston, who was taken prisoner at the battle of Durham in 1346, obtained a charter of the lands of Gourtoun or Gorton in 1342 (Culross and Tulliallan, I, p. 215). Symone de Prestoun was burgess of Edinburgh, 1362 (Egidii, p. 8), and Peter of Preston of Scotland was repaid 13 marks laid out by him in jewels bought for Johanna, late queen of Scotland in 1363 (Bain, IV, 94). William Preston brought from France the arm-bone of S. Giles and gifted it to the church of St. Giles. Alexander Preston, clerk of the realm of Scotland, had a safe conduct into England in 1470 (ibid., IV, 1388), and Will of Preston, charter witness in Ayr, 1491, appears in the same year as Vill of Prestoune (Friars Ayr, p. 63, 64). Sir Simon Preston of Craigmillar, provost of Edinburgh in 1557, gifted the land, etc., of Trinity Hospital. The line became extinct in 1639 with decease of Sir Robert Preston, s.p.

PRESTRE. OF. prestre, a priest. Richard Prestre, burgess of Stirling, rendered homage, 1296 (Bain, II, p. 186, 197). Cf. Priest.

PRESTWICK. From Prestwick in the district of Kyle, Ayrshire. Bartramus de Prestwyc witnessed the confirmation of the church of Cragyn in Kyle to the monastery of Paisley, c. 1272 (RMP., p. 233). John de Presteuuyc, a poor clerk of the diocese of Glasgow, was to have a benefice in the gift of the abbot of Dunfermline in 1344 (Pap. Pet., I, p. 34). In 1375 John of Prestwych, son and heir of Mariot of Garrechel, sold to Colin Cambale half of the island of Insalte (Inishail) in the barony of Lochaw (OPS., II, p. 130). The land of William de Prestwyk "infra burgum nostrum de Hadyngtona" is mentioned in 1373 (RMS., I, 449), and Thomas de Priestwik was a burgess of Glasgow in 1480 (LCD., p. 255).

PRETSELL, Pretswell, Pretcial. From the lands of Pratshill formerly in the parish of Eddleston, Peeblesshire. James Prathill was bailie of William Tweedie of Drummelzier in 1563 (Buchan, Peebles, III, p. 70). Private John Pretswell of Burnetland, Peeblesshire, was killed in the war in 1916.

PRETT. Most probably a variant of Pratt, q.v. John Pret, groom of Adam de Liberatione, 1259 (Bain, I, 2175; APS., I, p. 98). Robert Pret was admitted burgess of Aberdeen, 1462 (NSCM., I, p. 17). George Prett in Baithill, parish of Lesmahago, 1678, and five more of the name in record (*Lanark CR.*). Agnes Prett petitioned for the arrest of her husband's murderer, 1689 (RPC., 3. ser. xiv, p. 587), and William Prett appears in Dykeheads, Lanark, 1711 (*Minutes*, p. 114).

PRIEST. From ME. *prest*, priest. John Prest of Peebles, a Scots prisoner of war, in the Castle of High Peak, 1306 (*Bain*, ii, p. 481). William Preist, shoemaker in Ratanach, 1703 (*Banff Rec.*, p. 244). Andrew Priest from Turriff was killed in the first Great War (*Turriff*). Cf. PRESTRE.

PRIESTHAUGH. From Priesthaugh near Hawick, Roxburghshire. Surety was found in 1569 for Jok Preisthauch and Arche Preisthauch of the Middle March (RPC., i, p. 661).

PRIMROSE, PRIMEROSE. Of local origin from the lands of Primrose in the parish of Dunfermline. The first appearance of the place name is c. 1150, when it occurs in a charter of the Abbey of Dunfermline under the form Primros (RD., p. 5). The exact meaning of the name, which also occurs in Berwickshire, may be "tree of the moor," from Old Welsh or British *prenn*, "tree," and *rhos*, "moor." As a surname Primrose is not common. The first of the name in record appears to have been Jonne Prymros or Primros, mason in Edinburgh, one of the parties who contracted in 1387 for the building of five chapels on the south side of St. Giles's parish church, Edinburgh (CDE., p. 14; *Egidii*, p. 24). Archibald Prymrose was a friar in the monastery of Culross in 1569 (*Laing*, 844), and in 1608 payment was made to a James Prymroiss in Aberdeen (SCM., v, p. 82). Gilbert Prymerose, "clerk of His Maiesties secreit counsaill" in 1631 (ibid., ii, p. 228) was ancestor of Archibald Primrose of Carrington who was created Viscount Primrose in 1700 and earl of Rosebery in 1703. The Primroses first appear on record as owners of lands in and about the middle of the sixteenth century (Nisbet, *Plates*, p. 10). Many Scots emigrated to Sweden in the seventeenth century, and among them was a John Primeroose, afterwards merchant in Stockholm, whose son Henry was ennobled in 1653 and died governor of Johannsborg in 1668. Rev. James Primrose published a history of *Mediaeval Glasgow* in 1913. Prymrois 1587, Prymross 1687.

PRINCE. Magnus Prince was dean of guild in Edinburgh, 1686 (RPC., 3. ser. xii, p. 69), Patrick Prince, merchant in Kirkwall, 1697 (*Inquis.*, 7921), and George Greig Prince and two sons from Turriff served in the first Great War (*Turriff*).

PRINGLE. The old form of this surname was Hoppringle or Hopringle, from the old lands of that name near Stow in Roxburghshire. The earliest notice of the name is in a Soutra charter in which Robert de Hoppryngil is witness to a gift to the Hospital confirmed by Alexander iii (*Soltre*, p. 29). Elys de Obrinkel, tenant of the bishop of St. Andrews in Edinburghshire, rendered homage in 1296. His seal bears a hunting horn and S' Helias de Hoprigkil (*Bain*, ii, p. 205, 544). Thomas de Oppringyl or Hoprynghil occurs in 1368 (RMS., i, 280, 289). John Pryngel in Fife is mentioned in 1406 (RPSA., p. 9), Robert de Hoppringill witnessed a charter by Archibald, 4. earl of Douglas, c. 1413 (*Home*, 18), and William Pringle of Craiglatch had Crown tacks of Craiglatch in 1485 and 1490. Dand Pringill was constable of Cessford in 1515 (*Morton*, p. 30), and in 1573 there is mention of James Hoppryngill, 'beidman' of Edinburgh (*Soltre*, p. 225). Isobell Oppringill was spouse of William Heburne in 1562 (CMN., 83). The pronunciation of the name is now Pring-ill. It has nothing to do with 'pilgrim.' Hoppringeile 1555, Hoppringil 1503, Hoppringill and Hoppringle 1567, Pringel 1470, Pringell 1655.

PRIOR. From ME. *pri(o)ur*, a monastic official next in rank below an abbot. Ricardus Priour was subprior of the Abbey of Dunfermline in 1448 (RD., p. 309). Janet Prior was married in Perth in 1568 (*Sc. Ant.*, i, p. 169). Robert Pryor in Dundee was charged with aiding the English in 1552 (*Beats*, p. 327).

PROCTOR, PROCTER. A contraction of 'procurator,' from ME. *prok(e)tour* (AF. *procuratour*, OF. *procurator*, Vulg. Lat. *procuratorem*), manager, agent, steward.

> "For I make Piers the Plowman
> My procuratour and my reve."
> Piers Plowman.

Gavin Proctor became apprentice in the smithy of the abbey in 1474 (*Cupar-Angus*, i, p. 308), and James Proctor is recorded in Easter Whitewreath, 1688 (*Moray*).

PROFET, PROFAT, PROFEIT. William Propheta was charter witness in Aberdeen in 1281 (REA., ii, p. 279), and John Profite was admitted burgess of the same burgh, 1446 (NSCM., i, p. 10). Thom Prophet appears as "mair of the quarter of Brechin" and sheriff-depute of Forfar in 1473 (SCM., iv, p. 8). Alexander Perfat in Dundee was charged with aiding the English in 1552 (*Beats*, p. 327). Proffeit 1515. Weekley (p. 198) says this name owes its origin to an ancestor who had enacted such a part in mediaeval pageant,

674

PROFET, PROFAT, PROFEIT, *continued*
and the suggestion is not unlikely. On mediaeval pageants see Miss Anna Jean Mills, *Mediaeval plays in Scotland*, Edinburgh, 1927.

PROTT. Walter Prot admitted burgess of Aberdeen, 1445 (NSCM., I, p. 9). Janet Prot in Petty broke the command against adultery, 1683 (IDR., p. 113). William Prott at Portsoy, 1784 *(Aberdeen CR.)*.

PROUD. Perhaps from OE. personal name *Prud*, and perhaps connected with PRYDE, q.v. The lands of John Prowd in Clackmannane are mentioned in 1537 (ER., XVII, p. 737). John Proud in record in Dunfermline, 1583 *(Dunfermline)*.

PROUDFOOT. John Prudfote, 1269 (*Bain*, I, p. 511). Patrick Proudfote was one of an inquest concerning the lands of John de Hirdmanstone, 1303 (ibid., II, 1619). John Prootfoote in Craigie, Perthshire, 1689 (RPC., 3. ser. XIV, p. 770). The spellings Proudfut, Prowdfut, and Prudfut were common in the parish of Carnwath *(Carnwath)*. A treacherous rock in the Bay of Wick, Caithness, is called Proudfoot. Bardsley says the name is common in the HR. — evidently a familiar and colloquial term for a haughty man. Harrison says ME. *Proudfot, Prud(e)-fote*, a nickname for one with an arrogant gait.

PROUDY. Nicholas Proudy or Prowdy, presbyter in Aberdeen, 1449, and notary public, 1463 (REA., I, p. 256, 284, 286). David Prowdi, rector of Tyr, 1462 (ibid., II, p. 91). John Prowdy was accused in 1476 of holding a swine in another's corn (*Prestwick*, p. 27). John Prudie in Blackstoune, 1652 *(Kilbarchan)*.

PROVAN, PROVAND, PROVEN. From the lands of Provan, formerly a possession of the prebendary of Barlanark, one of the canons of Glasgow cathedral. Provand is the vernacular for *prebenda*. A surname around Glasgow and also surname of a family long connected with Strathblane and Killearn. Richard de Prebenda who was clerk to William the Lion *(Cambus.*, 38), is probably Richard de Prebenda, charter witness, c. 1190, 1200, and 1231 (*Home*, 224; *Soltre*, p. 29). Robert surnamed de Prebenda was elected dean of Dunkeld, 1248 (*Chron. Mail.*, s.a.), Adam de Prebenda was clerk to the king, 1263 (*Pap. Lett.*, I, p. 389), and Robert de Prebenda was bishop of Dunblane, 1258–82. John de Prebenda was burgess of Glasgow, 1428 (LCD., p. 245), and Stephen Provand had a remission for his share in burning the town of Dunbretane, 1489 (*Lennox*, II, p. 132). William Prouant (*u* for *v*) was tenant of Achloch, 1521 *(Rental)*, Alexander

Provand was witness in Glasgow, 1552 (*Protocols*, I), and Sir Robert Provane was vicar of Strathblane, 1549, and the surname is found there continuously since (*Strathblane*, p. 36). John Provan, barber burgess of Edinburgh, 1723 (*Guildry*, p. 127).

PROVOST. From the office of 'provost,' chief magistrate of a burgh, in Latin documents rendered *prepositus*. Gilbert, prepositus, witnessed a charter by Henry de St. Martin, p. 1177 (RMP., p. 49).

PRUNTOCH. John Prunto or Pronthoch was minister of Wick, 1580–1607 (Beaton, *Eccles. hist. of Caithness*, p. 297). Agnes Pruntoch was spous to John Clyne in Wick, 1661 (*Caithness*).

PRYDE. John dictus Pride (Prid' or Pryde), burgess of Renfrew, appears several times as a charter witness between 1272 and 1294 (RMP., p. 65, 96, 103; *Levenax*, p. 15, 16). He is probably the Johan of the County of Lanark who rendered homage in 1296. His seal bears a lacertine device and S' *Johanis Prid* (*Bain*, II, p. 186, 204). Alexander Pryd was member of assize at Cupar in 1521 (SCBF., p. 222), Robert Pryde was bailie of Cupar in 1567 (RPC., I, p. 583), and Euphania Pryd was retoured heir of John Pryd, brasiator, citizen of St. Andrews, 1650 (*Retours, Fife*, 793).

PUGGAT. Archibald Puggat and James Puggat were part tenants of Quhitefeld in the barony of Birnie, 1565 (REM., p. 442), and William Puggat was burgess of Elgin, 1689 *(Moray)*.

PUIDREACH, "a Balquhidder man." Gillemichaell Pudroche and Patrick Pudroch were tenants in Clocherane, Glenurquhay, 1594 (BBT., p. 276–277), and John Puderach was a Glenorchy vassal in 1638 (ibid., p. 401). The widow of Ninian Pudrach in Auchintreir was fined for resetting outlawed Macgregors, 1613 (RPC., XIV, p. 638). John Puderach alias Buttar in Crannich, 1638 (FB., p. 354, 372).

PULLAR, PULLER. John de Pulhore of the diocese of Durham is in record, 1339 (*Pap. Lett.*, II, p. 546). This surname is early found in connection with Perth, Henry Pulour being bailie there in 1379 (ER., III, p. 21). Andrew Pullour was tenant in Balmyle, 1473 (*Cupar-Angus*, I, p. 182), and Robert Pullour was tenant of the fishings of Camsy, 1474 (ibid., I, p. 222). Sir Alexander Pouler was chaplain to Sir Alexander Ramsay of Bamff, knight, 1534 (*Bamff*, p. 35), and John Pullour, witness in Perth, 1547 (*Rollok*, 43).

PULLAY. Gilbert Pullay possessed a tenement in Irvine, 1418 (*Irvine*, I, p. 126). Isabella Pullay had sasine in Irvine, 1449 (*Simon*, 1).

PULLO. William Pullo witnessed a charter of a toft by Richard, bishop of St. Andrews, a. 1173 (RPSA., p. 134). Robert Pullo had a grant from the prior of Pittenweem of an acre of land in 1545 (*May*, p. lix), and a later Robert Pullo was retoured heir of John Pullo, burgess of Anstruther Wester, in a tenement in Pettinwem, 1641 (*Retours, Fife*, 603).

PULTY. Andrew Pulty is mentioned in connection with the burgh of Aberdeen, 1448 (CRA., p. 17), and Matthew Pulty was admitted burgess of the same burgh, 1452 (NSCM., I, p. 13).

PUMFRAY. See under POMPHRAY.

PUMPHERSTON. Most probably from Pumpherston, near Mid Calder, Midlothian. John Pumfrastoune, prepositus Glasguensi, 1539 (LCD., p. 60).

PUNDIRACH. A common surname in Breadalbane two hundred years and more ago. From Med. Sc. *pundar*, distrainer, borrowed into Gaelic as *punndair*, one who confines straying cattle.

PUNDLER. From the office of pundler or pound keeper. A pundler was 'a sort of ground officer, whose duty it was to impound stray cattle, and protect plantations and hedges, and generally look after the interests of an estate' (Macdonald, *Place names of west Aberdeenshire*, p. 281).

'I hard ane Pundler blaw ane elrich horne.'
Lichtoun's *Dreme*, 1.59.

David Pundler and James Pundler in Lentibbert are mentioned in 1701 (*Muthill*).

PUNTON. A Lothian surname. Thomas Punton or Povntovn, burgess of Haddington, 1557 (*Laing*, 664), appears as provost there, 1567 (RPC., I, p. 558). John Puntoun was burgess of Queensferrie, 1653 (*Inquis. Tut.*, 794), and James Puntoun appears there in 1676 (*Retours, Linlithgow*, 243), and John Pantone and John Punton are recorded in Dalmeny, 1697 (ibid., 286, 287). Cf. PANTON and PONTON.

PURCELL. Will Pursell was pledge for Wille Broun in Lanark, 1490 (*Lanark*, p. 6). Alexander Pursell in Cousland, 1566 (RPC., I, p. 444). John Pursill or Pursell in Lessudden, 1664 (RRM., II, p. 85, 87), and John Pursell in Melrose, 1692 (ibid., III, p. 115). Pursel 1733. Explained by Lower, Bardsley, and Harrison as a nickname from the young pig,

AFr. *purcell, porcel(l*, diminutive of OFr. *porc*, Lat. *porcus*.

PURDIE. John Purdie was one of an inquest in 1296 which found that Robert de Pinkeny held the tenement of Balincref (*Bain*, II, 857), and David Purdy was a tenant of the earl of Douglas in Linton, 1376 (RHM., I, p. lii). A later David Purde, succentor of Glasgow, 1476–77, appears again in 1491 as Prade (REG., 413, 460), and in the title of his obituary in 1497 his name is given as Prowde (LCD., p. 202). Jonette Purdy in Strafrank is mentioned in 1525 (*Rental*), and in 1585 a grant for life was made to John Purdie of the chaplainry called Nomine Jesu in Brechin (REB., II, 351). James Purdy was Kintyre Herald, 1569 (RPC., I, p. 658). A family of this name were landowners in the parish of St. Vigeans at the end of the sixteenth century. Rev. J. B. Johnston says Purdie is the modern form of OE. name *Purta* or *Purda*, found also in the Border name Purdom. The derivation from Fr. *Par Dieu* is nonsense, and the explanation of the name as a diminutive of Pardovan or Purdevan not much better.

PURDOM, PURDON. From Fr. *Prudhomme*, by metathesis of *r*. Willelmus Prodomme of Scotia, mercator, had a safe-conduct into England, 1373 (*Rot. Scot.*, I, p. 960). John de Purdome held a land in Glasgow, 1454 (LCD., p. 175). As Proudham, Prodham, and Prudom the name is found in the North and East Ridings of Yorkshire, and on the Border it was early found as Prudholm, Purdholm, Purdom, and Purdon. David Purdom was deprived of his lands in Liddesdale by the earl of Angus in 1476. James Purdone was sued for wrongfully occupying certain lands in Middlebie in 1478. In 1487 the tenement of John Purdome in Glasgow is mentioned (REG., p. 454), and in 1494 the lands of David Purdoun in Glasgow are mentioned (ibid., p. 468). William Purdhome was found nearest heir of John Purdhome, his grandfather, in 1509 (Renwick, *Glasgow*). Andrew Purdon was burgess freeman of Glasgow, 1609 (*Burgesses*), Robert Purdon is recorded in Cartarburnfoot, 1686 (*Peebles CR.*), and James Purdon in Newtoun of Partick, 1709 (*Minutes*, p. 58). One of this name gave origin to Purdomston in the parish of Middlebie, Dumfriesshire.

PURROCK. Waryn Purrok, charter witness in Dundee, c. 1204 (RAA., I, p. 96). Robert Purroc, with consent of Walter his son, gave seven acres of land in Ayton to William Scot of Coldingham (*Raine*, 202), Walter, son of Robert Purroch, gave a bovate of land in Aython to the prior and convent of Colding-

PURROCK, *continued*

ham in 1259 (ibid., 203), and in 1276 the same Walter gave all his land 'in superiori Ayton' to the same monks (ibid., 204). In 1283 Johannes dictus purroc, son of William Scot of Coldingham, made a gift of land in the superiority of Ayton to the same monks (ibid., 208). William Purrok who appears as charter witness in Edinburgh, 1425, is doubtless the William Purro, bailie of Edinburgh in 1428 (RMS., II, 25, 116). Andrew Purrok was burgess of Perth, 1468 (*Milne*, p. 58), Richard Purrok appears in Brechin in 1506 (REB., II, 150), and Margaret Purrok is recorded in Dunfermline, 1564 (*Dunfermline*). The name is always without 'de' and the use of 'dictus' would lead one to infer that the name was descriptive. Henry Pyrrok was servant of the parson of Salkeld Regis, Cumberland, 1282 (Moore, *Lands*, p. 121).

PURSE. Adam Purs, secular of Elgin cathedral, 1343 (*Rose*, p. 118). Walter Purse in Dumfries, 1680 (*Dumfries*), and Barbara Purse in Aberdeen, 1769 (*Aberdeen CR.*).

PURTON. A surname recorded in Stranraer, Wigtownshire, is probably a variant of PUR-DOM, q.v.

PURVES. At the parveys (Chaucer, *Prol.*) = at the church porch or portico of St. Paul's, where the lawyers were wont to meet for consultation. Cf. *Parvisum*, the church porch of S. Mary's, Oxford, where the examinations used to be held (Chaucer, *Prol.*, p. 149). A family long settled in Berwickshire, which gave name to Purveshaugh. They were vassals of the earls of March. William Purveys of Mospennoc made a grant along with Sir Archibald of Douglas to the monks of Melrose, c. 1214–49 (*Melros*, p. 215). William Porveys of Peeblesshire rendered homage in 1296. His seal bears a snake nowed and S' Willi' Purvais(?) (*Bain*, II, p. 202, 533). As William Puruys he again appears in 1296 as witness to a charter by William de Billingham relating to lands at Fleurs, near Coldingham (*Raine*). William Pourays of Berwickshire also rendered homage, 1296 (*Bain*, II, p. 206). Alan Purvays de Ercildon witnessed a confirmation charter by Patrick, earl of March in 1318 (*Dryburgh*, 233), William Purwase was one of an inquest at Swinton in 1408 (*Swinton*, p. xviii), and Thomas Purvas had a charter 'de impignoracione terrarum de Swynwode' from Robert, duke of Albany, in 1427 (*Raine*, 145). Andrew Purwas was juror on inquest on lands of Tulloch in 1438 (RAA., II, 83). Jok Purvas or Purwas, a man to 'pitch the pavilions,' and Rob and Wil were yeomen

of the stables in 1474 (ALHT., I, p. 62, 297). Patrick Purwes witnessed a claim to the third part of Cranshaws in 1453 (*Swinton*, p. xxxix), and Andrew Purves was rector of Kynel in 1485 (REG., 439). Saunders Puruose of Erleston took 'assurance' of Protector Somerset at Kelso, 1547 (Patten, *Expidicion into Scotlande*, 1548). John Pureis was witness in Ayr, 1562 (RPC., I, p. 214). The family of Purves of that Ilk were never a leading family, and notices of them are few in the public records. Chambers (*Popular rhymes*, 1892 ed., p. 296) prints a rhyme in connection with the family which reads like a parody of that relating to the Haigs of Bemersyde:

> "Befa', befa', whate'er befa',
> There'll aye be a gowk in Purves-ha.'"

Purvess 1675, Purvose 1547, Purwass 1539, Purwess 1545, Puryes 1627.

PURVEYANCE. Thomas Purvians in Glasgow, 1505 (*Simon*, 112), and Alexander Purveyance, notary in Ayr, 1623 (*Ayr*, p. 155).

PYE. A Fife surname. It is the same as PYOTT, q.v. Kathren Pai in Weyms, 1632 (PBK., p. 36). The tombstone of Eufamie Pye in the Howff, Dundee, carries the arms of Pyot. An old Lancashire name (*Guppy*, p. 253). Cf. Fr. *Lapie*.

PYKAR. A nickname which has not passed into a surname in Scotland. It comes from ME. *pykare*, a petty thief. Thomas Pykar in Aberdeen was described in 1411 as a common 'pikar' (CRA., p. 4).

PYLE. Weekley gives Pile and Pyle as local forms of an English "west-country word for a creek," and cites Robert Attepile and Bennett de la Pylle (p. 69). John Pill held a tenement in Irvine in 1418 (*Irvine*, I, p. 126). Philip Pyle, merchant of the realm of Scotland, had safe conducts to travel in England in 1444 and 1446 (*Bain*, IV, 1161, 1190). Philip Pyle was a notary public in Jedworth in 1454 (*Melros*, p. 569), William Pyle or Pyll appears as burgess of Irvine in 1465 and 1472 (*Irvine*, I, p. 28), and Thomas Pyle was admitted burgess of Aberdeen in 1506 (NSCM., I, p. 43). John Pill was curator for Robert Vaus in Aberdeen in 1533 (CRA., p. 451), six persons of the name are recorded in 1577 (RPC., II, p. 732), Isobel Pylie appears in Edinburgh in 1621 (*Edinb. Marr.*), and George Pyll is recorded in Oxnam nook in 1685 (*Peebles CR.*).

PYOTT. (1) may be a nickname from the diminutive of *pie* or *pye*, a magpie. Cf. PYE. (2) from an inn-sign. J. atte Pye, London, is recorded in 1339 (*Ewen*, p. 230). Brisius Pyot was custumar and burgess of Inverness in 1361 (*Invernessiana*, p. 65). Laurence Pyot or Piote was presbyter and notary public in St. Andrews diocese in 1434, pensioner of Brechin in 1448 (REB., I, 61; II, 72), and in 1441 and 1450 appears as archdeacon of Aberdeen (*Bain*, IV, 1151; *Panmure*, II, 225). Patrick Piot was 'seriandus' in Aberdeen in 1445 (CRA., p. 15), and a sum of money was uplifted for Sir Patrick Pyot in 1475 (SCM., IV, p. 10). John Pyot was a witness in 1455 (*Cambus.*, 97), part of the mill of Craquhy was leased to Thomas Pyot and Patrick Pyot, his son, in 1483 (RAA., II, 217), Thomas Piat was burgess of Aberdeen in 1496 (SCM., V, p. 32), and Malcolm Pyot was admitted burgess there in 1462, and Gilbert Pyot in 1534 (NSCM., I, p. 17, 53). Alexander Piot was feuar of Fofardie in 1564 (*Rent. Dunk.*, p. 346), John Pyet was stabler in Aberdeen in 1596 (SCM., I, p. 88), John Pyett was heir of James Pyet of Overbalmyle, his father, in 1611 (*Inquis.*, 528), and Peter Pyot is recorded in Snaigoe in 1719 (*Dunkeld*). Some individuals named Pyet petitioned the Estates of Parliament in 1707 for permission to change their name to Graham. "Act in favours of William Pyet his Kinsmen and Relations.

"Unto his Grace Her Majesty's high Commissioner, and Right Honourable the Estates of Parliament.

"The Petition of William Pyet for himself, and in name and behalf of his other Kinsmen and Relations of the Nickname of Pyet.

Humbly Sheweth

That your Petitioners Predicessors, were of the Sirname of Graham, and through the unhappy Difference, that in the last Age, did frequently fall out betwixt Clanns; They, by their Neighbours, were forced from their Native Residence, and obliged to Cover themselves under the Sirname of Pyet — And We having by certain Tradition, the True Account of Our Origine, & Sirname of Graham: And We being Earnestly Desirous to be Restored, and make Use of the same in all time coming; which We cannot do, having trade both at Home and Abroad, without a Publick Act, whereby the Traders with Us may be Certiorat.

"May it therefore please your Grace and Lordships to allow Us to Assume and Use Our Ancient Sirname of Graham; and to discharge the Ignominous Nick-name of Pyet, in all time coming. And Your Petitioners shall ever pray.

Edinb: 7 March, 1707.

Her Majestie's high Commissioner and the Estates of Parliament having heard this petitione They grant the desire thereof and alloues the petitioners to assume and use their antient surname of Graham and discharges the nickname of Pyet in all time comeing.

SEAFIELD, Cancellar: I.P.D.P.
(APS., XI, App., p. 111)

The name is the same as PYE as shown by the famous Howff (Dundee) tombstone of Eufamie Pye, which carries the arms of Pyot.

PYPER. *See under* PIPER.

QUARREL. The lands of Carron Hall in the parish of Larbert were formerly called Quarrell (= quarry). They gave name to a family, Quarrel of that Ilk. Thomas de Querle was presented to the church of Ratheu or Ratho in St. Andrews' diocese in 1298 (*Bain*, II, p. 260, 263). William Quarles left Scotland about 1420 and settled in Northamptonshire. The estate appears then to have passed into possession of the family of Reidheuch and afterwards to Bissets. See Gibson, *Lairds and lands of Larbert and Dunipace*, p. 44–45.

QUARRIE, QUARRY. Agnes Quarrie in Bonjedburgh, 1683 (*Peebles CR.*). Quarry recorded in Coldstream, 1942. Cf. QUARREL and QUARRIER.

QUARRIER. Minsheu in his Dictionary defines "Quarrier" as "he that worketh in a Quarrie." John Querreour, quarrier or quarryman to the bishop of Dunkeld, 1507–12, appears in record as Quarreour, Quereour, Querreor, Queryeor, and Quharzeour (*Rent. Dunk.*). Sande Quareour in Kingudie was a follower of Campbell of Lundy in 1541 (RSS., II, 3666). Marion Quarier in Tinwald was examined for the Test in 1685 (RPC., 3. ser. XI, p. 434). John Quarier in Easter Cash, 1732 (*Dunkeld*). Querriour 1596.

QUENDALE. From Quendale in the parish of Dunrossness, Shetland. Jhone of Quendal was "lawrychtman of Dunrossnes" in 1510 (REO., p. 86), and Magnus or Mawnis of Quendaill is in record in 1546 and later years (ibid., p. 126, 128, 230).

QUESCHUTBRIT. Among the witnesses to the *Divise de Stobbo* (the marches or boundaries of Stobo, Peeblesshire), c. 1190, was one named Queschutbrit (REG., p. 89). Prof. Veitch (*History and poetry of the Scottish Border*, I, p. 256) says "Queschutbrit is a puzzle." It is, however, simply a spelling of COSPATRIC, q.v. As his name occurs in an English charter of 1158 as Wescubricht (*Sc. Ant.*, XVII, p. 107) c. 1200, the date usually given for the *Divise* is perhaps too late.

QUILT. Helya de Quilta who appears as a witness in 1237 (CMN., 17) derived his name from Quilt or Quylt in Peeblesshire.

QUIN. Shortened from (Mac)quinn, from Ir. *MacCuinn*, 'son of Conn,' an early Irish personal name. Roger Quin (1850–1925), the 'Tramp Poet,' was born and educated in Dumfries.

QUINCY. The first of this name in record in Scotland is Robert de Quinci, a Northamptonshire baron, who appears c. 1163 (*Melros*, 39), witnessed several charters by William the Lion, and is mentioned as Justiciar, c. 1175 (ibid., 388). The name is territorial from Quinci (now Quinçay) in Maine, France. Robert attested King William's grant of burgh and market to the church of Glasgow, c. 1175 (REG., p. 37), and also the same king's gift of the serf Gillemachoi de Conglud with his children and all his descendants to the bishop of Glasgow, c. 1180 (ibid., p. 33). He also witnessed the gift of carucate of Edenham to the Abbey of Kelso (*Kelso*, 383), the royal donation of the church of Gutherin (Guthrie) to the Abbey of Arbroath (RAA., I, 96), the king's gift of Aulon Macbele, a *nativus* or serf, to the bishop of Moray (REM., 4), and a confirmation of the church of Langtune to Kelso (*Kelso*, 144). He married Orabilis, daughter of Nes, son of William, a great Scottish heiress, and got with her the lands of Locres (Leuchars) and Lathrisk in Fife, fiefs in East Lothian, and elsewhere. He was succeeded by his son, Saher de Quinci, created earl of Winchester in 1207 (*Inchaffray*, p. 270). As Seiher or Seyr de Quenci we find him witnessing charters to the Abbeys of Kelso (*Kelso*, 409) and Arbroath (RAA., I, 93*bis*). Mr. Joseph Bain, the record scholar, in his introduction to the first volume of the *Calendar of documents relating to Scotland* states that the connection of the De Quinceys with Scotland requires illustration. Their rise and decline was equally rapid. Queinci 1246.

QUINTANCE. Lawrie Quintance, quarrior, was admitted burgess freeman of Glasgow, 1585, and Robert Quentance, tailor, the same, 1601 (*Burgesses*). William Quintence appears as a mason in Edinburgh, 1639 (*Edinb. Marr.*).

QUINTIN, QUENTIN. From Lat. *quintus*, 'fifth.' A common Roman praenomen. Formerly a favorite forename in Scotland, but now practically disused. It was also a surname. S. Quintin or Quentin of Amiens, the third century martyr, gave name to many places in France, and was later the patron saint of Kirkmahoe, Dumfriesshire. Florie, relict of Ade Quintinus, made a donation of land in Lempitlaw to the Hospital of Soltre, 1190–1220 (*Soltre*, p. 9). Quentin Agnew was third sheriff of Galloway, 1484–98. Quynting Blak was a witness in Prestwick, 1505 (*Prestwick*, p. 39), Quhintene

Lokkie was burgess of Edinburgh, 1583 (REB., II, 344), Quintine Prestoun was professor of phisick in Aberdeen, 1596 (CRA., p. 144), and Quhinten or Quihintein Thomsone is recorded in Melrose, 1606 (RRM., I, p. 19, 21). Robert Quintene was burgess of Edinburgh (MCM., II, p. 299), and Hesther Quintine was heir of John Quintine, burgess of Hadingtoun, 1605 (*Retours, Edinburgh*, 1446). Quaintein 1606, Quantine 1750.

QUIXWOOD. From the lands of Quixwood near Abbey St. Bathans, Berwickshire. David, son of Ærnald de Quixwood, was a large landowner there in the early years of the thirteenth century and a generous benefactor of the Priory of Coldingham, no less than eight charters of his gifting lands to the Priory being on record (*Raine*, App., 179–186). His gifts were confirmed by his son Thomas de Quikiswde (ibid., 187). David de Quicheswde also, in the reign of William the Lion, endowed a hospital for lepers at Aldecambus (ibid., 59). Richard de Quixwood was prior of Coldingham from 1315 to 1322 (*Coldingham*, p. 121). In the charters the name appears as Quikeswude, Quicheswde, Quiquiswde, Qecheswrth, Quikeswde, Quikiswde, Quicheswode, and once Quichesyd.

QUOTHQUAN. From Quothquan or Quothquhan near Biggar, Lanarkshire. Magister Hund de Cuthquen witnessed a charter by Malcolm Loccard, c. 1210 (RMP., p. 71). James Cuthquen, Edinburgh merchant, who petitioned for the return of his goods captured by the English in the high seas in 1438, is doubtless the James Cuthquen, Scottish merchant, who had a safe conduct to travel in England in 1450 (*Bain*, IV, 1115, 1227). Thomas Quodquen, notary public, 1477, and John Cuthquen, witness in West Lothian, 1487 (*Binns*, 15, 21). Patrick Cuthquhon had a letter of gift in 1500 (RSS., I, 488), and Elizabeth Quytquhen is in record in Linlithgow in 1531 (*Johnsoun*, 5).

QUOYNAMEIKILL. An obsolete Orkney surname from Quoynamekle in Rendall. David Quoynameikill and Manss Quoynameikill were tenants in Rendall, 1629 (Black, *Folklore of Orkney and Shetland*, p. 105, 107).

QUYLTNESS. John de Qwltnys, burgess of Edinburgh, 1362 and 1368 (*Egidii*, p. 1, 8). The name is also spelled Quvltnvs, Qwiltnes, and Quyltnes in 1362, and Qwyltnes in 1381. Most probably from Coltness in parish of Cambusnethan.

RABAN. Edward Raban, said to have been an Englishman, introduced printing into Aberdeen before 1622 (Watt, *Aberdeen and Banff*, p. 226). But the surname was known in the north at a much earlier date. John Rebayn was burgess of Cromarty in 1449, Thomas Ruban was charter witness there, 1467, and Margaret Ribbone had sasine of some land there in 1536 (TGSI., xxxi, p. 299, 322). Rybben 1547.

RABOC. An old spelling of Roebuck, an old West Riding surname (*Guppy*, p. 544). Roger Raboc or Raboch witnessed a charter of the church of Culessin (Colessie), 1262 (LAC., p. 170, 188), and John Rabuk, bailie of Linlithgow, rendered homage, 1296 (*Bain*, II, p. 198).

RADERNIE. William de Retherny was a presbyter and notary public of the diocese of St. Andrews in 1442 (*Panmure*, II, 233). From Radernie in the parish of Cameron, Fife.

RADULF. From the old Teutonic pers. name *Raedwulf* or *Radwolf*. Radulf appointed abbot of Kinloss, 1189, was appointed bishop of Doun in Ireland by the legate John of Salerno. Radulfus, second abbot of Cupar, d. 1189 (*Chron. Mail.*, s.a.). Radulfus, clericus, vicecomes de Perth, in reign of Alexander II (*Scon*, p. 56). Radulph was first abbot of Newbottle (*Neubotle*, pref. p. xiv).

RAE, REA, REE. Rae is an old surname in Dumfriesshire, possibly of local origin, and Raes were numerously represented in Dornock in the fifteenth and sixteenth centuries. "Like other Borderers the Raes seem to have been troublesome and contumacious, so that 'indictati et non comparentes' is in most cases the sole record in answer to the proceedings of the criminal court against them" (PSAS., xxiii, p. 46). Robert Raa, mason, witnessed a charter to the Abbey of Culross, c. 1231 (ibid., LX, p. 72), and Thomas Ra was witness in Glasgow, c. 1290 (REG., p. 200). Robert Ra, burgess of Stirling, witnessed a charter of lands of Dunipas, c. 1296–1300 (*Laing*, 18), and William Raa had a pension in 1329 (*Stodart*, II, p. 368). Robert Raa was juror on inquest at Roxburgh on land in Teuidale, 1360 (*Bain*, IV, 50), William Raa, bishop of Glasgow, died 1367 (REG., p. xxxviii), and Jacobus Ra or Raa held land in Clauchhope, Dumfries, 1376 (RHM., I, p. liii; II, p. 16). Thomas Raa of Scotland petitioned in 1404 for safe conduct to carry away his goods which had been captured at sea by Englishmen (*Bain*, IV, 649), Schir Water Ra was notary and parson of Garuald, 1415–34 (REG., 325; LCD., p. 249), William Raa, presbyter of Glasgow, 1440 (REG., 344), and Wil Ra, myllar of Cruok, 1451 (REB., I, 177). Rany

Ra was on assize in Aberdeen, 1446 (REA., I, p. 245), William Ra or Raa was cellarer of Neubotle Abbey, 1458 (*Neubotle*, p. 245–246), and Alexander Ra had a charter of land in Edinburgh, 1468 (RD., p. 368). James Raa and John Ray were witnesses in Perth, 1546 (*Rollok*, 10, 13). A family of this name were prominent in Edinburgh in the seventeenth and eighteenth centuries and gave name to Rae's Close at head of the Canongate. As Dr. John Rae, Arctic explorer, was a Gael born in Orkney, where his father had settled, he may have been from (MAC)RAE, q.v. See also RAY.

RAEBURN. See under RYBURN.

RAEPER, REPPER. Aberdeen surnames. From the occupation of 'roper' (No. Eng. *raper*), rope-maker or rope-seller. William 'le Ropere' was one of the men sent to Stirling in 1304 to make ropes for the war engines of Edward I (*Bain*, II, p. 412). Alexander Raeper from Turriff was killed in the first Great War (*Turriff*).

RAESIDE, RESIDE. James Rysyid, merchant burgess of Air, heir of Elizabeth alias Bessie Rysyid, lawful daughter of quondam William Rysyid, burgess of Air, 1606 (*Inquis. Tut.*, 94). James Rasyd was occupier of the 20s. land of Brothoklie in 1659, and John Rasyd in Hullerhirst was bailie for Cunynghame in the same year (*Hunter*, p. 68). David Raesyd or Rasyde was servitor to Mr. Robert Huntar of Huntarstoune in 1680 (ibid., p. 62, 64), Robert Rosyde is recorded in Campbeltown in 1682, and David Russide in Hill, 1767 (*Kilbarchan*). William Rawsyde or Rasyde in Irvine, 1700 (*Irvine*, II, p. 316).

RAFFAN, RAFFIN. From Rathven in the parish of the same name, Banffshire, the local pronunciation of which is 'Raffan' or 'Raven.' Three brothers named Raffan from Forglen, Banffshire, served in the first Great War (*Turriff*).

RAFFLES. From Raffles in the parish of Mouswald, Dumfriesshire. John de Refholes witnessed, c. 1215–45, the resignation of the lands of Withstan in the fee of Thonergayth (now Tundergarth) to Robert de Brus (*Bain*, I, 1682). John de Rafhols held the lands of Rafhols in 1361 (Hist. MSS. Com. 6. Rep., App., p. 709). William Raffell in Armini, 1684 (*Kirkcudbright*), William Raphael in the parish of Buittle, 1684 (RPC., 3. ser. IX, p. 570), and William Raffell in Carsethorn, 1793 (*Dumfries*).

RAGEWIN. A serf gifted to the Abbey of Dunfermline by King David, c. 1126 (RD., p. 13).

RAGG. Sir James Rak was chaplain in Edinburgh, 1515 (*Laing,* 311), and Sir Thomas Rag, a cleric, was presented to the chaplainry of the Mount of Ormond, 1546 (RSS). David Rag was appointed minister in Inverness, 1561 (*Rec. Inv.,* I, p. 71), Andrew Rag was reader at Cannisbie, Caithness, 1567 (OPS., II, p. 792), John Rage appears in Stirling, 1682 (*Edin. App.),* Alexander Ragg was bailie of Aberdeen, 1697 (SCM., v, p. 362), and Janet Ragg resident there, 1750 (*Aberdeen CR.).* Ragg and Wragg are typical Yorkshire surnames, probably from ODan. pers. name *Wraghi,* whence the placename Wragbi in the West Riding. Not likely to be a variant of Reoch or Riach as has been suggested.

RAILTON. John Railtoun, burgess of Edinburgh, 1544. Allan Raltoune, burgess freeman of Glasgow, 1607 (*Burgesses*). John Raltoun in Wester Herbourheid, 1684 (*Edin. App.).* Edward Ralton in Kirkcudbright, 1767 (*Kirkcudbright).* Harrison says it looks like an English place name but he can find no trace of it.

RAIN. Sir Thomas Rane, a witness in Irvine, 1260 (*Irvine,* I, p. 5). Janet Rain in M'Narghstoun, 1681 (*Kirkcudbright).* William Raen, resident in parish of Borgue, 1684 (RPC., 3. ser. IX, p. 566). David Rain or Rainey in Galloway charged with being a leveller, 1724. David Rain in Whilliecroft, parish of Borgue, 1757 (*Kirkcudbright).* The name may come from some OE. personal name beginning with *Regen-* (cf. RENTON). But Weekley says "the home of the name is Durham, and in that county *rain* is a dial. word for a strip of land, boundary, etc., which is no doubt the origin of most of the northern *Raynes*" (p. 71).

RAINALDSTON. Probably from Rhenaldstown (now Rennieston on the map) in Upper Crailing, held in the fourteenth century by Robert Bwrelle, and on his forfeiture granted to William of Laundelis and Joneta, his wife, in 1390/91 (RMS., I, 813). Roger de Rainaldstone of the county of Rokesburk rendered homage in 1296 (*Bain,* II, p. 209). Andrew Renneldsone in Darnick, 1664 (RRM., II, p. 86).

RAINING. Halbert Ranyng was burgess of Dumfries, 1567 (RPC., I, p. 568), and several individuals of the name were burgesses there early in the seventeenth century (*Retours, Dumfries,* 116–118), and eight of the name are included in the Commissariot Record of Dumfries from 1638. John Rainnine was examined for the Test in Tinwald, 1685 (RPC., 3. ser. XI, p. 434). Ranying 1573. See also under RAINY.

RAINY, RAINEY, RAINNIE, RENNIE, RENNY. All double diminutives or pet forms of Reynold, a vocalized form of Reginald (see REGINALDUS). The Ranys or Rennys were extensive owners of land in the district of Craig in Angus from the middle of the fifteenth century, and the Rennies of Usan were recognized as an old family. Symon Renny was bailie of Inverkeithing in 1362 (*Stodart,* II, p. 366). John Ravny, pelliparius, was burgess of Stirling, 1436 (*Cambus.,* 209). Andro Renny, a follower of the earl of Cassilis, was respited for murder, 1526 (RSS., I, 3386). Herbert Rainie or Rayning sat in Parliament for Dumfries, 1572, and was provost of the burgh at that time and several times afterwards till 1592 (*Stodart,* II, p. 365). Joseph Rainey was a member of Gartly Company of Volunteers, 1798 (*Will,* p. 23), and John Rennie (1761–1821), the famous engineer, was born in East Lothian. As forename: Rayny de Pethvnstoth, 1402 (CRA., p. 384) and Rayny Voket in Aberdeen, 1409 (NSCM., I, p. 3). See also RANNIE and under RAINALDSTON.

RAIS. William Rase, witness in Glasgow, 1433 (LCD., p. 248). Sir George Rais, presbyter in Hamilton, Lanarkshire, 1528 (*Laing,* 366). Sir John Rais or Raisch, priest and notary public in Glasgow, 1553–55 (*Protocols,* I). Gavin Rauss, burgess freeman of Glasgow, 1577, and John Rass, burgess, 1612 (*Burgesses*).

RAIT, RAITT, RATE. This surname is taken from different localities and was assumed in different parts of the country by persons not related to one another. There are places named Rait in Nairn and in Perth and Raith in Fife and in Ayrshire. The family of Rait of that Ilk took its name from the old castle of Rait beside Geddes, and disappeared from the North, c. 1400. Sir Gervase de Rathe, knight, was constable of Invernairn, 1292, and as Gervays de Rate rendered homage, 1296 (*Bain,* II, 579, 793). In the following year the king of England committed to Andrew Rate all the lands of Gervase Rate, his brother, in Scotland, for which he received a safe conduct to travel in Scotland on the king's business (ibid., 893, 961). In 1299 Andreas de Raath witnessed a charter by the earl of Buchan (RAA., I, p. 165). Several of the name rendered homage, 1296. John de Ratis witnessed lease of property in vill of Glesbany, 1321 (SCM., II, p. 319). John de Rate made an agreement with the abbot and convent of Scon, 1332 (*Scon,* 163), and John Rait, bishop of Aberdeen, died in 1355 after a short episcopate (REA., I, p. xxx). Henry of Rate witnessed instrument of resignation, 1446 (REB., I, 109), and David Rat was citizen of Brechin, 1471 (ibid., I, 193). Gavin Rath was commissary of William Scheves, archdeacon of St. Andrews, 1477 (SBR., p. 261), and Andrew Rayt held a tenement in Glasgow, 1487 (REG., p. 454). Rait of Hallgreen in the Mearns were an old family there. Raitht 1470, Reat 1610, Reyth 1493.

RAITH. An Ayrshire surname. Probably local, from Raith near Monkton. Alexander Raith, burgess of Ayr, 1488–91 (Ayr, p. 93; Friars Ayr, p. 63), and Alexander Recht, junior, witness in Ayr, 1490 (Ayr, p. 94), perhaps son of the former.

RAITIE. See under RETTIE.

RAKSTRA. John Rakstra rendered homage at Perth, 1291 (RR.). This is a Frisian surname of local origin (Winkler).

RALPH. A surname recorded in the town of Nairn. Most probably from Norse *Hrólfr* (from ON. * Hrothuwolfar, 'wolf of fame'), as other names of undoubted Norse origin (Main, Manson) are current in the town. Elsewhere the name may be from the personal name Ralph (from OE. Rædwulf, 'wolf of counsel'). Ralph, abbot of Jedburgh, died 1205 (Chron. Mail.). Magy Rauff appears in Aberdeen, 1400 (CWA., p. 313), Amy Rauff occurs in a list of Aberdeen thieves in 1411, and Henrie Raife was master of a barge there in 1444 (CRA., p. 4, 11). Alexander Rauff was chaplain in Aberdour, Banffshire, 1506 (REA., II, p. 97), John Rauff appears as monk of Inchaffray, 1544 and 1564 (Inchaffray, p. xcviii–xcix), and Wallace Rauff is in record in Edinburgh, 1595 (Edinb. Marr.). John Raif, merchant and burgess of Glasgow, 1607 (Burgesses), George Rauff in Nethermains, 1627 (Craw, Chirnside Common, p. 15), and Thomas Ralph in Partick, 1711 (Minutes, p. 115). As forename: Rafe Pott in Kelso, 1567 (Kelso, p. 524).

RALSTON. From the lands or barony of Ralston near Paisley, Renfrewshire. Crawfurd says Ralph, a younger son of one of the earls of Fife, obtained a grant of the lands from the High Steward, but Nisbet says this is not favored by their arms, for they do not carry the lion rampant, the arms of the old earls of Fife, but three acorns on a bend, intimating that they are of the same stock with those of the surname Muirhead. The first of the family recorded is said to be Nicholas de Ralstoun who witnessed the donation of Fulton by Sir Anthony Lombard to the monks of Paisley in 1272 (RMP., p. 51). Thomas de Raulfestone of Lanarkshire rendered homage in 1296 (Bain, II, p. 204), and

Jacobus de Raulyston, dominus ejusdem, witnessed the election of an abbot of Paisley, 1346 (RMP., p. 10). John Raleston or Raliston of that Ilk was one of the arbiters in a dispute between the burgh of Renfrew and the abbot of Paisley in 1488 (ibid., p. 406–407), Robert Ralston was clerk to the bishop of Caithness in 1504 (OPS., II, p. 623), Hendrie Ralstoun witnessed letters of reversion in 1519 (Pollok, I, p. 241), and Hugh de Ralston of Ralston was killed in the battle of Pinkie, 1547. The estate of Ralston was sold by the family in 1705 to the earl of Dundonald. William Ralston Shedden Ralston (1828–1889) was a distinguished Russian scholar and folklorist. Railstoune 1550, Ralfahstoun c. 1440, Rallstoun 1684, Ralstoune 1656, Raylston (of that Ilk).

RAMAGE. Payment was made in 1304 to Peter Ramage, 'cokinus,' messenger to the sheriff of Perth, for his expenses (Bain, IV, 483). A family of this name long maintained a connection with Stobo in Peeblesshire. Andro Ramage was rentalit in ane oxgang in the West town of Stobo in 1528, and in 1553 Andro Rammage was rentalit in an oxin gang land in the Hilhows of Stobo, "wakand be deces of wmquhil James Rammaige, his fathyr" (Rental). Sir John Rammage was curate of Blanter in 1555 (Protocols, I), John Rammyche in Haddington gave allegiance to the king in 1567 (RPC., I, p. 558), Johnne Rammaige was reidare at Curmannok, 1574 (RMR.), and Edward Rammage was a mason in Edinburgh in 1599 (Edinb. Marr.).

RAMORNIE. From the old barony of Ramornie near Cupar, Fifeshire. John of Remorgun is mentioned in 1381 (Cambus., 181), and again in 1390 when he witnessed a charter by Hugh Fraser of land in the barony of Kinneil (Southesk, p. 718). As Sir John Remorgny, knight of Scotland, he had a safe conduct in England in 1395 (Bain, IV, 472), and as Johannes de Ramorgny, miles, he appears as a charter witness in Edinburgh in 1397 (RMS., I, App. I, 157). Alexander de Ramorgny and Margareta, his wife, had a charter of the lands of Petglassy in 1406 (RMS., I, 887). The family was known as Ramorgney of that Ilk before 1439. Sir John of Ramornie was one of those who arrested the duke of Rothesay, eldest son of Robert III in 1402 and confined him in Falkland Tower.

RAMSAY. The Ramsays are supposed to have come from Huntingdonshire where Ramsey is a local name (Latin de Rameseia). The first of the name recorded in Scotland is Simund de Ramesie who witnessed the charter by Turstan filius Leuingus of the church of Liv-

RAMSAY, *continued*

ingston to the Abbey of Holyrood, c. 1153–65 or at least before 1175 (LSC., 17). He also witnessed a confirmation charter by William de Moreville of the lands of Gillemorestun to Edulfus filius Uctredi before 1196 (REG., I, p. 40). Symone de Ramsay witnessed a charter by Gilbert, earl of Strathern before 1198 (LIM., p. xxiv), and William de Rameshej witnessed a charter by William the Lion before 1200 (LSC., 48). Nessus de Rämisseia or de Ramesia, medicus domini regis, was a charter witness, c. 1220–32 (CMN., 7, 9, 11). William de Ramessay who witnessed a charter by David de Lysurs to the Abbey of Neubotel, c. 1233–36 is the first to appear under the designation 'de Dalwussy' (i.e. Dalhousie) (*Neubotel*, p. 28). William de Rammeseye and several others of the name rendered homage, 1296 (*Bain*, II). Sir Alexander Ramsay of Dalhousie was starved to death in Hermitage Castle, 1342 (Tytler, *History*, I, p. 188). Michael de Ramesay was sheriff of Fife in 1395 (RPSA., p. 2), and Hugo de Ramesay was one of an inquest on the marches of Kyrknes and Louchor in same year (ibid., p. 3). By the middle of the thirteenth century the Ramsays appear as landowners in Angus and in the following century they are divided into several branches. Ramesey 1378, Rameseye 1293, Ramhishay 1328, Ramissay 1320, Ramsa 1510, Ramysey 1261, Remesey 1316.

RAMSDEN. A surname of late introduction from across the Border, from some place of the name probably in the West Riding of Yorkshire. Ramsden is an ancient Yorkshire surname.

RAMSON. Thomas Ramson or Ramsoun, juror on an inquisition in Aberdeen, 1457 (RAA., II, 109) appears in 1462 as "a man of the abbot of Arbroath" (SCM., v, p. 22).

RANALD. The Anglicized form of G. *Raonull*, itself a borrowing from ON. *Rögnvaldr*, 'ruler of (from) the gods,' or 'ruler of counsel.' In MacVurich (*Rel. Celt.*, II, p. 156) it is Raghnall and Ragnall, and in the MS. of 1467 it is Ragnall. The genitive form occurs in a poem in the Dean of Lismore's collection as Rynilt, i.e. Raghnailt. In Easter Ross the name is pronounced Raoghalt (i.e. Ra'olt), and Maccodrum in his *Taladh Iain Mhuideartaich* spells it (Clann) Rà'ull (for Raonall). Ranald Macdonald, son of Alasdair Mhaighistir Alasdair, was known as Ra'oll Dubh. The devocalization of final ll suggested to non-Gaelic ears that a *d* followed (cf. under DONALD). John Rannald was burgess of Glasgow, 1463

(REG., 389), and Patrick Rannald held a tenement in Linlithgow, 1472 (*Sc. Ant.*, XVII, p. 118). Thomas Rawnald was burgess of Dumbarton, 1500 (LCD., p. 204), and Malcolm Ranalde held a tenement in Glasgow, 1506 (REG., 485). The style of Mac Mhic Raghnaill applied to the chiefs of Keppoch is from Raghnall, beheaded at Elgin in 1547. From this comes MACRANALD (G. *M'Raonuill*). See also RAONAILD.

RANALDSON, 'son of RANALD,' q.v. Robert Raynaldi held a tenement in Glasgow, 1433 (LCD., p. 428), and in 1494 mention is made of the lands and garden of Malcolm Renaldi there (REG., 468). In 1511 there is record of a bond of manrent by Doul Ranaldsone, son of wmquhile Ronald Alanson (SCM., IV, p. 195). In the title of the bond his name is given as "Dowill M'Renyll." Cristane Reynaldsone was banished from Edinburgh in 1529 (MCM., II, p. 83), and John Rannaldsoun was witness in Perth, 1551 (*Rollok*, 108). Alexander Ranaldsoun was 'decan to the Baxsteris' in Aberdeen, 1576 (CRA., p. 25); Ellen Ranaldsone is recorded in Dunfermline in 1590 (*Dunfermline*); and Andrew Renneldsone was portioner of Darnick, 1683 (RRM., III, p. 9). Rannaldson 1503.

RANDALL. An apocopated form of OE. Randwulf or Randulf, from *Röndúlfr*, 'shield wolf,' a common ON. personal name. The name "occurs frequently in the Register of Cupar Abbey. Amongst the tenants in Carse Grange are Ranalds, Ranaldsons, Randalsons, and Randalls, or as it is sometimes given, Randal, Randale, Randell, Rendall. There were others about Perth in the days of the Reformation" ("Ancestry of Randall Thomas Davidson, archbishop of Canterbury, 1903," quoted in SHR., I, p. 327). Harry Randell, an Orkneyman, wrote the first communication in the Scots tongue known in Orkney, c. 1436 (*Diplomatarium Norvegicum*, xx, 815). Donald Randale was tenant of Calady, 1464, and Nichol Randale, tenant of Kerse-grange, 1478 (*Cupar-Angus*, I, p. 138, 212).

RANDALSON, 'son of RANDALL,' q.v. Thomas Randalson was tenant of Kersgrange, 1471 (*Cupar-Angus*, I, p. 220).

RANDELSTON. From the old lands of Randelstoun (now Randerston) in the parish of Crail, Fife. Johan de Randolfestone of the county of Fife rendered homage in 1296 (*Bain*, II, p. 204). W. de Rendaliston was juror at perambulation of marches of Melgow, 1306 (RD., p. 409). Nicholas de Randalsthon witnessed a charter of Nether Cameron, c. 1332 (*Wemyss*, II, 12), William Randelstoun held land in Scrabustar, Caithness, in 1557 (OPS., II, p. 610), and John Randelstoune is recorded in Perth in 1654 (DPD., I, p. 153). The lands may have obtained their name from Randolfus who was vicecomes de Scone in the reign of Alexander II (Scon, p. 43).

RANDIE. An old form of RANDALL, q.v. Malie Randie was married in Perth, 1573 (Sc. Ant., III, p. 97).

RANDOLPH. In a paper on "The parentage of Thomas Randolph, earl of Moray," by Prof. D. W. Hunter Marshall (Scottish notes and queries, 3. ser. VIII, p. 2–5) the author suggests that the mother of this Thomas was the legitimate uterine sister of Robert I. This uterine sister, he thinks, was the issue of a previous marriage of the countess Marjorie of which there appears to be some evidence. His father was the Thomas "Randolf" who was chamberlain of Scotland for some years during the reign of Alexander III. The old theory that the mother was Isabel, the full sister of Robert has been found to be inaccurate. Johan fitz Randolfe de Fodiche del counte de Fyfe rendered homage, 1296, and Johan fiz Randolfe del counte de Rokesburk the same (Bain, II, p. 208).

RANISON. 'Son of RAINY,' q.v. An Aberdeenshire surname. Walter Ranyson, juror on inquest apud Rane, 1413 (REA., I, p. 214). Michael Ranison was admitted burgess of Aberdeen, 1462, William Raynison in 1467, and Alexander Ranyson in 1483 (NSCM., I, p. 17, 20, 30). William Ranyson was witness in Coliston, Aberdeen, 1462 (REA., I, p. 285), and Thomas Ranysoun is recorded in Bogfochil, 1463 (RAA., II, 148). William Ranisone was master of the Cordonaris Craft in Aberdeen, 1495 (CRA., p. 424), Andrew Ranisone (misprinted in text, Ramsone) was burgess of Aberdeen, 1496 (REA., I, p. 335), and John Ranison witnessed inventory of the estate of Sir John Erskine, younger of Dun, 1513 (SCM., IV, p. 16).

RANKEILLOR. From the old lands of Rankeillour in the parish of Monimail, Fife. Patrick de Rankeloch in record, 1292 (HP., II, p. 128). David Rankelo, notary public St. Andrews' diocese, 1454 (Scon, p. 184). John Ramkelowr of that Ilk was juror on an assize at Cupar in 1520 (SCBF., p. 187). John Rankello in Vtherogall and William Rankelour also in Vtherogall appear as charter witnesses in 1543 (Soltre, p. 109). In another document of the same date the same persons are referred to as William Rankelo and John Rankelor. Thomas Rinkellow was bailie of the Com-

mendator of Dunfermline in 1555 (Laing, 633), and Alexander Rankelour was retoured heir of William Ramsay, avunculus, in 1605 (Inquis., 193). Rankeillo 1688, Rankeilo 1686.

RANKEN, RANKIN, RANKINE. A pet form of some name like Randolph with diminutive -kin added. The Irish have it as Raincin. The early home of the Rankins was in Ayrshire, where persons of the name were small proprietors before the end of the sixteenth century (Stodart, II, p. 369). John Rankyne, burgess of Glasgow, 1456 (REG., 380), may be John Rankin or Rankyn whose land is mentioned in 1468 (LCD., p. 181, 254). Peter Rankyne of the Scheild appears in 1496 (Bucc. MSS.), and was witness in Kilmarnock, 1504 (Bain, IV, 1737). William Rankin is mentioned in connection with Innerkethin, 1500 (RAA., II, p. 404). Dominus Johannes Rankyn, chaplain, witness in Glasgow, 1503 (RMS., II, 2723; REG., p. 506), may be Schir John Rankin, vicar of Girwane, 1504 (Trials, I, p. * 43). John Rankyn was rector of Hutoune, 1507; another John Rankin was tenant under the bishop of Aberdeen, 1511 (REA., I, p. 363); a third John Rankyn had a house in Irvine, 1533 (Irvine, I, p. 39); and still another John Rankin, a follower of the earl of Cassilis, was respited for murder, 1526 (RSS., I, 3386). Elspet Rankeyne is recorded in Aberdeen, 1570 (CRA., p. 270), John Rinking appears as witness in Glasgow, 1587 (Protocols, X), and William Rankine was a notary in Ayr, 1590 (Ayr, p. 116). As a forename we have it as early as 1429, when Rankin de Fowlartoun is in record in Ayr (Ayr, p. 83), Rankin de Craufurd and Rankin Small in Prestwick, 1446 (Prestwick, p. 144), Rankine de Symontone in Irvine, 1477 (Irvine, I, p. 149), Rankinus Salmone in Glasgow, 1504 (Simon, 111), and Rankyne Davidsoun, reidare at Gawstoun (Galston), 1574 (RMR.). In the records of the Scots Guards in France we have Ranequin Kennedy. Rankein 1678, Rankeine 1638, Rankene 1599, Rankinge 1555; Ranking, Rankini, Renkyn.

RANKINSON. An Anglicizing of MACRANKINE, 'son of Rankin.' Rankin is a diminutive of Reynard or Reginald, and was early borrowed by the Gael. Alan Rankynson was bailie of Glasgow in 1428 (LCD., p. 245), William Rankinson, a chaplain, is mentioned in 1500, and Archibald Rankesoun, a monk of Kilwinning, is in record in 1532 (Ayrshire and Wigtownshire archaeological collections, I, p. 186; LCD., p. 13).

RANNICK. Agnes Rannick in Clerkington was suspect of witchcraft, 1629 (RPC., 2. ser. III, p. 339).

RANNIE. A variant of RAINY, q.v. Walter Rannie held a land in Forfar, 1453, and the name is also found in Arbroath, 1485 (RAA., II, 101, 261). Malcolm Rannie was charter witness in Glasgow, 1473 (LCD., p. 118), Nicholas Rannee was witness in Bute, 1502 (ibid., p. 206), John Rany held an eighth part of the vill of Grangie of Connane, 1510 (RAA., II, 5, 10), and Thomas Ranye had a lease of Mamewlacht in 1549 (REA., I, p. 434). John Rannie was witness in Brechin, 1589 (REB., II, 227), Agnes Reanie is recorded in Edinburgh, 1636 (Edinb. Marr.), Abraham Ranie was a weaver in Melross, Banff, 1702 (Banff Rec., 237), John Rannie, merchant in Edinburgh before 1737 (Guildry, p. 160), and George Ranny, chapman in Elgin, 1798 (Moray). Rane 1545. Variants in index to RSCA. are: Rainy, Rany, Ranye, Raynie, Reny, and Ryne. The name is also variously spelled on tombstones in Old Pitsligo churchyard. As forename: Rany Ra on assize in Aberdeen, 1446 (REA., I, p. 245).

RAONAILD, RAONALT. A woman's name. From ON. Ragnhild. Now erroneously rendered Rachel. Ragnhild was name of the mother of Reginald, son of Somerled. See RANALD.

RAPERLAW. This surname is of territorial origin from the barony of the same name in Roxburghshire. Magister Richard de Raparlaw witnessed a grant to the Abbey of Cambuskenneth, c. 1180 (Cambus., 15), Magister Robertus Raperlu was a charter witness in Scon in 1225 (Scon, p. 53) and as Robertus de Raperes laue witnessed a charter of Madderin (Madderty) to the Abbey of Inchaffray, c. 1215–21 (Inchaffray, p. 31). As Magister Robertus de Rapellis he appears again as charter witness between 1214–29 (LAC., p. 35, 36). In 1279 it was charged against Sir Gilbert de Umphraville, earl of Angus, that he had imprisoned Hugh of Raperslawe, the king's bailiff (Bain, II, p. 45). In 1438 David Raperlawe and others, merchants in Edinburgh, petitioned for the restitution of certain goods taken in vessels on the high seas during the truce (ibid., IV, 1115), William Raperlau appears as curate of the church of St. Peter de Ynchmartin in 1450 (View, p. 575). In 1471 and again in 1511 mention is made of the tenement and lands of William Raperlaw in Edinburgh (Neubotle, 303; Soltre, p. 262). Andrew Raperlaw was burgess of Are in 1491 (Friars Ayr, p. 61).

RASPER. John Rasper in Killilung, 1678 (Dumfries). Thomas Rosper of Glencairn, a Covenanter, was drowned in shipwreck in Orkney, 1679 (Hanna, II, p. 254).

RATE. See under RAIT.

RATHEN. Local, from Rathen, Aberdeenshire. Thomas de Rathen, witness in Elgin, 1262 (APS., I, p. 101).

RATHIE. John Rathie recorded in Melrose, 1646 (RRM., I, p. 112). Recorded in Innerleithen, 1941. The name of Thomas of Raty, servitor of the earl of Murreffe, 1424 (Bain, IV, 963) may be the same.

RATTER. Of local origin from Ratter in the parish of Dunnet, Caithness. Alexander de Ratir who had the perpetual vicarage of Westra, 1443 (Pap. Lett., IX, p. 398), appears as Sir Alexander of Ratir, perpetual chaplain of Saint Andrew the Apostle of Golspi in 1448 (OPS., II, p. 650). Richard Ratter, a Scot born at Hollond [Hollond in either Orkney or Shetland] was granted letters of denization in England in 1480 (Bain, IV, 1465). Master Malcolm Rattar was chaplain of the choir of the cathedral church of Dornoch in 1512 (OPS., II, p. 623), and another (?) Master Malcolm Rotter, natural son of Sir Andrew Rotar, vicar of Halkirk, was legitimated in 1538 (ibid., II, p. 757). John Rattir was mair of Sutherland in 1520 (ibid., p. 665). Alexander Rater in Dornoch who was juror on an inquest made at Inverness in 1542 may be the Alexander Rattar or Ratter, parish clerk of Golspie in 1545 and parish clerk of Kalmaly in the following year (ibid., p. 631, 648, 676). Thomas Ratter who was juror on an inquest made at Dornoch in 1603 may be the Thomas Ratter who held a croft near Dornoch in 1633 (ibid., p. 642, 644). Donald Ratter is recorded in Greenland [in Caithness] in 1662 (Caithness).

RATTRAY. Of territorial origin from the barony of Rattray in Perthshire. In 1253 Sir Thomas de Rettre had a dispute with the abbot of Arbroath regarding the bounds of their properties (Warden, IV, p. 28). Adam de Rethereth witnessed a charter by Cristina de Valoniis, c. 1256 (Panmure, II, 141). Sir Adam de Rotrefe swore fealty to Edward I at St. Andrews in 1291 (Bain, II, 508), and in 1296 Eustace de Rettref was one of the Scots prisoners taken at Dunbar Castle and sent to Wisbeach Castle (ibid., p. 178). Ade de Retref was charter witness at Lochmaben, 1294 (HP., II, p. 130). John de Rettre was collector of contributions in the sheriffdom of Perth 'super Ileff' (Isla) in 1373 (ER., II, p. 423), William Rettre or de Rettre appears as burgess and guild brother of Aberdeen in 1436 and 1438, and David Retre was admitted a burgess there in 1500 (NSCM., I, p. 5, 40; SCM., V, p. 44). Gilbert de Retra leased Tulifergus, a. 1442 (*Cupar Angus*, I, p. 119), Silvester Rettray, a follower of the earl of Cassilis, was respited for murder in 1526 (RSS., I, 3386), and Johnne Ratteray had a feu of the lands of Craigmakeren in 1586 (*Scon*, 234). Catharine Rotray made a gift to the church of Aberdeen, 1549 (REA., II, p. 183). Raittre 1547, Ratre 1550, Ratry 1426, Retrey 1529, Rettra 1490, Retthray 1487, Ruttera 1651.

RAVENESGRAPE. Robert de Ravenesgrape of Lanarkshire rendered homage, 1296 (*Bain*, II, p. 211).

RAVENSMAUGHE. Henry Ravensmaughe, burgess of Peebles, rendered homage, 1296 (*Bain*, II, p. 198).

RAVINSHER. Thomas de Ravinsher sold his land in Waldefgate, Berwick, to the Abbey of Kelso, 1290 (*Kelso*, 44). In later documents his name is spelled Rauenher and Rauenisher (*Neubotle*, p. 154, 155). Of local origin from a place of the name in England.

RAWLIN, RAWLINE, RAWLING. From *Rawlin* (Fr. *Raoulin*), a diminutive of *Rawle* (for Ralph), with accretionary -g. A Dumfriesshire surname. David Rawlynge held a "botha seu opella" in Dumfries, 1588 (*Retours, Dumfries*, 367). Marcus Raulling in Glencapill, 1630, Catherine Ralling in Dumfries, 1642, and Thomas Rawling of Dumfries, 1696, are in the same record (*Dumfries*).

RAWSON, 'son of Raw,' a diminutive of RALPH, q.v. William Rauessone of Berwickshire rendered homage, 1296 (*Bain*, II, p. 206). Andrew Rawsoun, messenger of arms in Banff, 1569 (RPC., I, p. 660). James Rawson, reidare at Raffort, 1574 (RMR.). Robert Rawsoun, witness in Perth, 1595 (*Methven*, p. 99), and Robert Rasoun, writer in Edinburgh, 1626 (*Edinb. Marr*). John Rawsone, writer in Edinburgh, 1655 (*Inquis.*, 4041).

RAY. Thomas filius Ray witnessed confirmation by Alexander, son of Walter, of his father's gift to the church of Paisley, 1239 (RMP., p. 225). John Ray held a tenement in Glasgow in 1487 (REG., p. 454), and William Ray, burgess of Edinburgh, had a safe conduct into England in 1465 (*Bain*, IV, 1361). Sir William Ray is recorded in 1530 as "vmquhyle chaplane to our lady chappell of the brig of Dei" (CRA., p. 129), and William Ray had a charter of six acres of land in the burgh of Kethik from the Abbey of Coupar-Angus, 1558 (*Cupar-Angus*, II, p. 169–170). The surname is also found in Stirling in 1546. See also RAE.

RAYBURN. See under RYBURN. William Rayburn, witness in Gullane, 1579 (*Laing*, 979), and John Reyburn, rebel in Kilchiven paroch, Kintyr, 1685 (*Commons*, p. 1).

RAYNE. From Rayne in the parish of the same name in Aberdeenshire. Robert de Ran' witnessed a charter by Mathew Kynninmond, bishop of Aberdeen, c. 1180 (REA., I, p. 11; RAA., I, p. 136). Adam de Rane and Roginald de Ran were burgesses of Aberdeen in 1317 (SCM., V, p. 10), and Bertillot de Rane was on an assize in same place in 1333 (REA., I, p. 53).

REACH, REIACH (Fife), REOCH, RIACH, RIOCH. From the G. adjective *riabhach*, brindled, greyish. A common descriptive surname. John Reoch was burgess of Inverness, 1452 (*Invernessiana*, p. 153). Part of the lands of Parcy or Parcyis were leased to Alan Reoch or Roeoch in 1463–73 (*Cupar-Angus*, I, p. 136, 201). Robert Reauch and Finlay Reauch were tenants on lands of the bishopric of Aberdeen, 1511 (REA., I, p. 369, 377), and Gilbert Reoch was the king's officer and messenger-of-arms in Irvine, 1514 (*Irvine*, I, p. 33). John Reaucht admitted burgess of Aberdeen in 1530 (NSCM., I, p. 51) may be John Reaucht amerced there in 1539 for "ye non-ganging In corpus criste processioun" (Mill, *Plays*, p. 127). Donald Reach appears as witness in Banff, 1544 (RMS., III, 3062), and Jacobus Reacht in Murthlac, 1550 (*Illus.*, II, p. 262). Complaint was made against John McAwreoch in Litill Urchun and Donald McAwreoch in Caddell, 1578 (RPC., III, p. 51), and John Rioche is recorded in Dunfermline, 1585 (*Dunfermline*), and Kenneth Rioch in Knockdui, 1726 (HP., II, p. 384). Riach was the name of the mate of the brig The Covenant in R. L. Stevenson's *Kidnapped*. Am Fec Reabhaich, 'the brindled or grizzly one, the singed one,' is a popular Gaelic name for the Devil, and *Duncan McCowle voil vic Eayne Rewich* means 'Duncan son of Dougall the bald son of grizzled John.' Reche, Rethe, and Reiach 1541, Reoche 1607, Reuch 1679, Riauch 1597, Rioch 1726.

READ. A form of REID, q.v.

READDIE. See under REDDIE.

READER. From the occupation of 'reeder' or 'thatcher,' ME. *reder(e*. The *Promptorium Parvulorum* has: 'Redare of howsys, *calamator*.' Patrick Reder of Rutherglen was one of those appointed to treat for the ransom of David II in 1357 (CDE., p. 20). Robert Redder, flesher in Edinburgh, 1667 (*Laing*, 2615).

READMAN. A somewhat rare name in Scotland, derived from Redmain in West Cumberland near Cockermouth. The family of Redman or Redmayne was a prominent one in Westmoreland and Cumberland for five centuries, and branches of the family became prominent in Yorkshire. Sir Mathew de Redemaan or Redeman was custodian of the Castle of Dounfres under Edward I in 1304 (*Bain*, IV, p. 470, 471), and a later Matthew de Redmane had a protection for two years for going on the king of England's service beyond seas in 1370 (ibid., IV, 170).

REAVLEY. A surname recorded in Kelso. Local, from Reaveley near Ingram, Northumberland.

REBRON. Robert Rebron in Airthrey, 1690 (*Logie*, II, p. 295).

REBURN. *See under* RYBURN.

RECKITT. A variant of RICKETT, from Rick, diminutive of Rickard (= RICHARD, q.v.) + dimin. suff. -et.

REDBEARD. A by-name. Osbert Redberd witnessed the grant by Robert de Leycestre of his cellar in Perth to the Abbey of Lundors, c. 1200 (LAC., p. 74). Alan Redberd or Rusebarde (OF. *rous*, "red, russet") was a witness in Perth between 1214–49 (*Scon*, p. 56, 57), and Galfridus Redberd or Redbert, burgess of Perth, witnessed a charter of the sale of a toft to the Abbey of Scone in 1219 (ibid., p. 52, 126). Cf. BLACKBEARD, BROWNBEARD, and SMIBERT.

REDDEN. From Redden in the parish of Sprouston, Roxburghshire, formerly a grange of the Abbey of Kelso. Henry de Reueden witnessed a charter of part of Auchynlec to Waldeus filius Boydoni between 1160 and 1180 (*Kelso*, 115), and about 1180 Hugh de Reueden witnessed a grant to the Abbey of Kelso by Radulph de Veir (ibid., 215). About the year 1250 there is recorded a confirmation by John, son of Hugh de Reveden, to Galfridus de Eskford (ibid., 508). In 1258 Hugh de Reueden resigned the lands called Floris (now Floors) to the Abbey of Kelso, and a charter of 1285 establishes the descent of Hugh, son and heir of John son of Hugh de Reuedene (ibid., 215, 218). Frudrick Reddein, baxter burgess of Linlithgow, 1689 (RPC., 3. ser. XIV, p. 622). The wife of Andrew Redden died in Swinton June 1942.

REDDIE, REEDIE, REIDIE, READDIE. Of local origin from Reedie, near Kirriemuir in Angus. James Reddy, witness in Perthshire, 1549 (*Gaw*, 28), David Rady, witness in Dun-

fermline, 1567 (*Laing*, 825), and William Reddie, weaver in St. Andrews, 1580 (ibid., 998). Robert Reddie is in Dunfermline, 1584 (*Dunfermline*), James Reidie, witness in Dysart, 1638 (PBK., p. 132), and John Redie in Lewquheres (Leuchars), 1656 (*Inquis.*, 4149). John Reddie was member of Scots parliament for Dysart, 1681 (*Hanna*, II, p. 510). James Readdie in Anstruther died 1940.

REDDOCH. Stodart says (II, p. 366) the family of Reidheugh took their name from their lands near Comrie, Perthshire. There is also a Redheuch, now Reddoch, in Lanarkshire, and the place name occurs also in other parts of Scotland. John Reidheuche had charter of lands of Lochhouse in sheriffdom of Linlithgow in reign of David II (RMS., I, App. II, 1206), and Andrew Reidheuch of Quarrel, Stirlingshire, is in record, 1462. Robert Redehuch held the altar of Holy Rood of Stirling, 1478 (SBR., p. 264). James Reidheuch, burgess of Stirling, 1481 (*Cambus.*, 211), is probably James Redeheuche, burgess of Stirling, who had a grant of the lands of Tulichiddill, Culturagane, etc., 1502 (RMS., II, 2688). David Reidhuche was charter witness in Dunfermline, 1483 (RD., p. 372), and Patrick Redheuch was bailie of Stirling, 1491 (ER., x). Alexander Reddocht appears as witness in Linlithgow, 1533 (*Johnsoun*), Archibald Reidheuch died on the field of Pynkycleuch, 1547 (ER., XIX, 459), and John Reddocht attested a Glenurquhay bond of manrent in same year (BBT., p. 185). The laird of Cultirbragane, Alexander Reidheuch, appears in the Roll of Landlords, 1587 (APS., III, p. 466). Redeheuche 1502, Redhuche 1637; Redhagh, Reidhaugh, Redhuch.

REDFORD. Of local origin. There are places named Redford in Angus, in the parish of Dysart, Fife, and in the parish of Colinton, Midlothian. Andro Reidfurde, reidare at Pettruthny, 1574 (RMR.). Alexander Reidfurd was admitted burgess of Aberdeen, 1611 (NSCM., I, p. 108), and Andro Reidfurd in Harthoip witnessed a notarial instrument at Raecleuche, 1612 (*Annandale*, I, p. 81). John Reidford was appointed minister at Abercherdour, 1647 (*Strathbogie*, p. 81), Thomas Reidfurde in Melrose, 1662 (RRM., II, p. 21), and William Reidfoord, tenant in Hassendeanbank, 1688 (*Peebles CR.*). Margaret Reidsfoord appears in Langlee, parish of Crawfordjohn, 1675, and Thomas Ridfoord in Crawford, 1728 (*Lanark CR.*). James Rudford was a member of Drumblade Company of Volunteers, 1804 (*Will*). Robert Reidford of Inverkeithny and James Cowie Reidford served in the first Great War

(*Turriff*). Redfoord 1828, Redfurd 1651, Reidfurde 1618; Reidfuird, Reidfuyrd.

REDHEAD. Michael dictus Redhode, burgess of Cupar, witnessed a tack of lands in Fife in 1293 (SHR., xvii, p. 158; HP., ii, p. 128). Fargus Redhede, Scottish merchant, complained in 1358 that goods of great value were carried from the wreck of his ship at Cotum in Clyveland (*Bain*, iv, 26). Richard Reidheid who appears in Aberdeen in 1497 is probably the Rich Redhed who contributed to the church repairs of the same town in 1508 (CRA., i, p. 425), and David Reidheid was admitted burgess there in 1542 (NSCM., i, p. 58). George Reidheid was servitor to Alexander Lillie in Old Aberdeen, 1610, and James Reidheid is recorded in Asleid, 1629 (RSCA., ii, p. 163, 313). Readhead 1660.

REDLAND, Ridland. From Redland in the parish of Stromness, Orkney. Thomas Redland of that Ilk was lawrikman in Stromness, 1678 (SHR., xiv, p. 59). Bessie Redland in Elvister in Walls, 1649 (*Shetland*). Hew Reidland in Sandwick, Orkney, 1675 (*Edin. App.*).

REDPATH, Ridpath. Of local origin from the lands, now village, of Redpath in the parish of Earlston, Berwickshire. The local pronunciation of the name is Rippath, with which compare the spellings of 1545 and 1562 below. William de Redepathe of Berwickshire rendered homage in 1296 (*Bain*, ii, p. 204). Alexander de Redpeth received moiety of the lands of Derington, c. 1329–34. Thomas de Redpethe and Mariota, his spouse, had grant of lands in the vill and territory of Preston in the barony of Bonkylle from Thomas Stewart, earl of Angus, confirmed by Robert ii, 1376 (RMS., i, 667). Walter Redpeth held a land in Edinburgh, 1486 (RMS., ii, 1655), William Rypat appears as a friar preacher at St. Andrews, 1545 (*Laing*, 494), and James Reydpeth of the convent of Dunfermline is recorded in 1555 (ibid., 633). Cristall Redpecht (for Redpethe), witness in Fife, 1548 (*Gaw*, 40). Triamor Reidpeth was feufarmer of Crumrig in 1566 (ER., xix, p. 333), Thomas Reidpeth *de eodem* was retoured heir in lands of Middel Winscheill, etc., in 1602 (*Retours, Berwick*, 28), and David Redpeth was skipper in Borrowstounes in 1655 (*Inquis.*, 4015). Several Redpaths were ministers of local parishes, and George Ridpath, minister of Stitchill, published his *Border history of England and Scotland* in 1776. The surname early made its way north, and Cristal Ridpetht was witness in Kirkwall in 1557, and James Reidpetht was juror on assize there in the following year (OSR., i, p. 264). Readpeth

1654, Redpetht 1516, Ridpeith 1698, Ridpeth 1633, Rippeth 1562.

REDWELL. William de Rubeo Fonte (or Reidwall), canon of Aberdeen in 1366 (REA., ii, p. 58), had a charter of the clerkship of the cockett in Aberdeen in the reign of David ii (RMS., i, App. ii, 794). Cf. Redwalls or Redwells in Fife.

REED. A form of Reid, q.v.

REEDIE. See under REDDIE.

REEKIE. A person of this name in a letter to the "Weekly Scotsman" of Edinburgh some years ago said that in his family Bible under 1731 this name is spelled Rikie; and he adds that he has access to records as far back as 1460 in which the name is spelled Riki and Rikie. James Reky in Dundee was charged with aiding the English, 1552 (*Beats*, p. 327), and John Rekie appears in Leith, 1567 (RPC., i, p. 563). It may be a diminutive of Rickart, q.v., a variant of Richard, and it may also be noted that there is a place named Reikie in the parish of Alford, Aberdeenshire.

REEVE. From the office of bailiff or steward, ME. *reve*. Adam the reeve of Machan was juror on an inquisition by the sheriff of Lanark, 1263 (*Bain*, i, 2677). In this instance the word has not arrived at the surname stage.

REFECTORIO. Robertus de Refectorio, juror on inquisition apud Muskylburg, 1359 (RD., p. 267). The refectorium was the dining hall of a monastery.

REGINALDSON, 'son of Reginald.' Symon Reginaldi in vill de Dalfubill, 1376 (RHM., i, p. lvii) Nicholas Reginaldi held a land in Aberdeen, 1398 (CRA., p. 376).

REGINALDUS. A Latinized form of the OE. personal name *Regenweald*. Reginaldus, a monk of Kelso, was the first abbot of Arbroath, 1178 (RAA., i, p. xii). Reinaldus (the vocalized form of the name) de Muscans was witness to Earl David's *Inquisitio* as to the extent of the lands of the church of Glasgow, c. 1124 (REG., p. 7).

REIACH. See under REACH.

REID, Read, Reed. An epithet surname meaning 'red haired' or 'ruddy complexioned.' "The spelling red is modern, like the pronunciation. The e was originally long, and in Chaucer mss. the form is usually *reed*. In later English it was *reede, read, reade*; in Scottish *reid*" (Skeat, *A Student's pastime*, p. 195). In Latin charters it is rendered *Rufus*. Ade Ruffus witnessed resignation of the lands of Ingilbristoun

REID, READ, REED, continued

in 1204 (*Dryburgh*, p. 163), and William Rufus was juror on an inquest on the lands of Padevinan in 1259 (APS., I, p. 98; *Bain*, I, 2175). Gilbert 'le Rede' of Coul was committed to prison and died there in 1296 (*Bain*, II, p. 192). Red is found as a surname in Aberdeen in 1317 (SCM., v, p. 8), and it is one of the oldest in the parish of Kildrummy. Patrick dictus Rede was on an assize at Rane in 1335 (REA., I, p. 61), John Reed was collector of tithe in the deaneries of Stormonth and Atholl in 1362 (ER., I, p. 110), and James Reed was bailie of the burgh of Stirling in 1364 (ibid., I, p. 146). Reeds were at one period a numerous clan in Kyle. The first of the name there recorded is probably William Rede, son of John Reede, who had a confirmation of the lands and pertinents of Bairskemyn in Kyle in 1375 (RMS., I, 496). John Rede is in record in the parish of Morton in 1376 (RHM., I, p. lvi), William Rede held Wester Pitfoddels in wadset from his cousin Alexander de Moravia in 1389 (*Stodart*, II, p. 367), William Rede, dominus de Ranystoun, was present at the perambulation of the lands of Tarwas and Uldny in 1417 (RAA., II, p. 50), and Wil Red was tenant of Wester Drumme in 1474 (*Cupar-Angus*, I, p. 197). Joseph Reid (1843–1917), born in Ayrshire, was inventor of the Reid oil burner, which did so much to advance the oil industry in the United States. Reid is also used as an Englishing of Gaelic RUADH, q.v. The family of General John Reid (d. 1806–7), composer of the air "The Garb of Old Gaul," and founder of the Chair of Music in Edinburgh University, was descended from Alastair Ruadh of Strathardle (15th cent.). The General was the first of his family to add the letter *i* to his name. In Aberdeenshire this surname has become confused with Rait and Reith. Reede 1477, Reide and Ride 1555, Reyd 1548, Rid 1612.

REIDIE. See under REDDIE.

REIFF. John Reiff in Southeldmyln, Fife, witness, 1598 (*Laing*, 1346). Johannes Reiff, faber ferrarius, burgess of Hamilton, 1646 (*Inquis. Tut.*, 710).

REINARIUS. The Latinized form of OE. *Regenhere*, ODan. *Regnaer*. Reinerius, a monk of Melrose, became second abbot of Kinloss, 1174, abbot of Melrose, 1189, resigned in 1194, and again became abbot of Kinloss, where he died, 1219 (*Chron. Mail.*, s.a.; *Annals*, p. 278).

REINBALDUS. A Latinized form of OE. *Regenbeald*. Reinbaldus or Reimbaldus, third abbot of Scone, was a witness to the foundation charter of Inchaffray, 1200 (*Inchaffray*, p. 8).

REITH. A surname recorded in Aberdeenshire. It may be a shortened form of Macreith, one of the many variants of MACRAE, q.v. Not likely, I think, to be from Raith in Fife. A payment was made to Mary Reith in Edinburgh, 1730 (*Guildry*, p. 136), and Andrew Reith is recorded in Collonoch, Aberdeenshire, 1725 (*Aberdeen CR.*). The name is spelled Raith, Reithe, Rethe, Rethy, and Reyth in RSCA. index.

RELLIE. Heu Reillie was barrowman to Sornbeg, 1686 (RPC., 3. ser. XII, p. 401), and William Rellie was burgess of Prestwick, 1726 (*Prestwick*, p. 88).

RENDALL. From Randall, diminutive of Randolph, or (2) from diminutive of Reynold, i.e. Reginald. Said to be the earliest native Orcadian surname. The earliest mention of it is in 1325–6, when it is recorded that Rechinald (Reginald) de Rayndal's betrothed had been carried to Norway (*Diplomatarium Norvegicum*, VII, p. 125). John Randell or Rendell appears as lawman of Orkney in 1438 and 1446 (REO., p. 10, 51), and James Rendall is recorded in Kirkwall in 1516 (SCM., v, p. 395). Rendaill of that Ilk is mentioned in 1565 (REO., p. 282). The Orkney surname is of local origin from the township of Rendall in the parish of Rendall.

RENFREW. Of local origin from the town of the same name in Renfrewshire. Adam de Reynfru of the county of Edeneburk rendered homage in 1296 (*Bain*, II, p. 201), and Robert Reynfreu or Reynfru, a Scots prisoner of war from Stirling, was incarcerated in the Castle of Old Sarum between 1304–07 (*Bain*, II, 1644, 1668, 1944). Galfridus Renfrew appears in Aberdeen, 1408 (CWA., p. 315). Bartholomew Renfrew appears as a charter witness in Glasgow in 1481 (LCD., p. 194). Robert Renfrew in Abbey parish, Paisley, 1772 (*Kilbarchan*). Andrew Renfrew in Eaglesham died in 1939.

RENIGOD. Renigod Albus who witnessed a charter by Countess Ada of the land of Charel (Crail) is most probably Renigod de Karel, c. 1200 (RPSA., p. 208, 382).

RENILSON, RENNILSON. 'Son of RANDALL,' q.v. John Rendelson in Pestelburne, 1694 (*Edin. App.*). Recorded in Jedburgh, 1941.

RENISON, 'son of RENNIE,' q.v. Several of the name are recorded in the Glasgow Directory.

RENNARIUS. Aluuinus Rennere who was witness to gift of church of Guuen (Govan) to the church of Glasgow, c. 1134, is doubtless Alfwinus Rennere who witnessed the grant of the church of Lohworuora (now Borthwick) to Herbert, bishop of Glasgow, c. 1150 (REG., p. 11, 13). Elwynus Renner, most probably the same person, and Ede, his wife, gifted the church of Neutun in Fife to the Abbey of Dunfermline in the reign of Malcolm IV (RD., p. 25, 55). In the reign of William the Lion Gillexus Rennerius witnessed the gift of "Gill-andreas mac suthen et eius liberos" to the same abbey (ibid., p. 36). "Henrico Rennario meo" appears as witness in several charters by Gilbert, earl of Strathearn in 1199 and following years (LIM., p. xxvi, 5, 8, 12; Inchaffray, p. 4, 8, 31, etc.). In a note on the name the late Prof. Mackinnon says, "Rennarius is manifestly a Latinised form of the Gaelic rannaire, literally 'the divider.' In old Gaelic Saga, the Fled Bricrend for example, the rennairi carved or distributed (or both) the portions of food to individual guests... The correct analysis of the word is rannaim 'I divide' (now roinn) and -aire, cognate with Latin -arius, a suffix indicating personal agent. The word is usually translated 'spencer,' 'but-ler'" (Inchaffray, p. lii).

RENNIE, RENNY. Variants of RAINY, q.v.

RENNIESTON. Local, from Rennieston near Oxnam, Roxburghshire. Nyckoll Renastoun and George Renastroune in the toune of Bow-dene, 1567 (Kelso, p. 518, 519).

RENNOCH. James Rennoch, flesher in Edinburgh, 1628 (Edinb. Marr.). John Rennoch recorded in Kellistoune, near Auldgirth, 1657 (Dumfries).

RENOWOD. John Renothewode, a Scotsman, had a safe conduct into England, 1398 (Bain, IV, 504). John Renowod was witness at Crumzeltoun, 1461 (Laing, 141). Probably = "Ren o' the wood."

RENSHAW. A surname of late introduction from across the Border. It is a Derbyshire surname derived from Renishaw a township in the county (Guppy, p. 137).

RENTON. From Renton in the parish of Coldingham, Berwickshire, the "tūn" or town of Raegen or Rein, a shortened form of the OE. personal name Raegenweald. The Rentons of Renton were hereditary foresters of Coldingham in the reign of William the Lion, and Ricardus forestarius appears in record as Ricardus de Reningtona. In the fourteenth century the Rentons were an influential family of burgesses in Berwick (Home, 13). During

the fifteenth century the family terminated in the direct line in a daughter who married Ellem of Ellemsford. Robert de Rentun witnessed a charter by Herbert, abbot of Kelso, c. 1225 (Kelso, p. 348). Symon of Rennyngton, burgess of Jedburgh, rendered homage in 1296 (Bain, II, p. 197). John de Raynton who had a charter of lands of Over Lamberton in 1323 (original charter quoted in Scots peerage, IV, p. 332) is probably the John de Rainton (Raynton, or Rayneton) who was burgess and customar of Berwick in 1325 and following years and c. 1332 received a charter of lands in Kirclambirton (BNCH., XVI, p. 323, 330). David Rayntoun de Billy, witness in 1473, is probably the David Rantoun who appears in 1479 as attorney for David Hume of Wedderburn (RHM., II, 220; Home, 23). Isobel Renton was a religious of North Berwick in 1548 (CMN., 65), Thomas Rentoun rendered to Exchequer the accounts of the bailies of North Berwick in 1557 (ER., XIX, p. 7), and Archibald Rantoun was a notary public in 1561 (Home, 231). Raintown 1429, Ranton 1464, Rayntoune 1500, Rentoun and Rentoune 1431. Renton in the parish of Cardross, Dumbartonshire, was named from Cecilia Renton of Lammerton who married a Smollett of Bonhill. The town was founded in 1782 by Mrs. Smollett of Bonhill. Simeon of Durham (I, 80) tells us that the father of one of the bearers of the body of S. Cuthbert in its wanderings was Reingualdus "a quo illa quam condiderat villa Reiningtun est appellata" (gu here is Norman French equivalent of w).

RENWICK. From Renwick in Cumberland, old Raveneswic, on the east side of the Eden river. James Renwick, the Covenanter, was the last man executed (1688) for religious principles in Scotland. John Runnick is recorded in Dalzell-Kittimure in 1634, Robert Rinnick in Stanehouse in 1657, John Rennick in Dalzell-Kittimuir in 1686 (Lanark CR.), and Robert Rennick in Newbigging, 1687 (Dumfries).

REOCH. See under REACH.

REOCHTAN. Alexander Reochtan in Chain Bridges of Kirkcudbright, 1667, appears in 1675 as Alexander Reachton, umquhile bailie of Kirkcudbright (Kirkcudbright).

REPPER. See under RAEPER.

RERIK. A shortened form of MACRERIK, q.v. John Rerik had an annuity from the Grange of Spottis, Galloway, in 1460 (ER., VII, p. 7). Master Gilbert Rerik, commissioner of the king of Scots, who had a safe conduct to travel in England, 1471 (Bain, IV, 1395), was arch-

RERIK, *continued*

deacon of Glasgow, 1478 (REG., p. 437), and a charter witness, 1487 (CAC., I, p. 44). William Reryk was a charter witness, 1484 (LCD., p. 202), and a payment was made to Paul Rerik of Dalbety, 1561 (ER., XIX, p. 152). Joannes Rerik was heir in lands of Arnegannoch, 1587 (*Retours, Kirkcudbright*, 408).

RERRICK. *See under* RIDDICK.

RESIDE. *See under* RAESIDE.

RESTALRIG. From the lands, now the village, of Restalrig in the parish of South Leith, Midlothian, anciently Lestalric, and occasionally by some of the older residents pronounced Lestarick. Between 1178 and 1198 Archabaldus filius W. de Duglas resigned the lands of Halis in favor of Thomas filius Edward de Lestalric (RD., 300). Thomas de Lastalric witnessed a charter by William the Lion before 1200 (LSC., 33), between 1211–26, as de Lastalryk, he made a grant to the Hospital of Soltre (*Soltre*, p. 16), and in 1226 a 'concordia' was made between Thomas de Lastalric and Richard, parson of Halis (RD., p. 135). A later Thomas de Lastalrich witnessed a charter by Gamelin, bishop of St. Andrews, in 1258 (RPSA., p. 173), and as Thomas dictus de Lastalric he witnessed the confirmation charter of Trauerflat-Dungray to the Abbey of Kelso in 1266 (*Kelso*, 345). Johannes de Lestalrych, who witnessed an undated donation to Newbattle (*Neubotle*, 235), may be the John de Lestalrike recorded as burgess of Edinburgh in 1362 (*Egidii*, p. 8), and the Johannes de Lestalrik who had a charter of the mill of Instrothire in Fife from David II in 1368 (RMS., I, 235). Johan de Lastalryk of Edinburghshire rendered homage in 1296 (*Bain*, II, p. 198). Simon de Lascalerike del counte de Edeneburk also rendered homage. His seal shows a double-headed eagle displayed, S' *Simoni de Lascalric* (*Bain*, II, p. 201, 546). The family ended in an heiress who married a Logan, in consequence of which the estate passed into possession of that family known afterwards as Logan of Restalrig. 1382 is the last notice of the family of Lestalrig, and Sir Robert Logan is mentioned as lord of Restalrig in 1398 (*Stodart*, II, p. 176).

RESTON. From Reston in the parish of Coldingham, Berwickshire. Adam de Rystona was witness to a quitclaim of the land of Swinton by Patrick, first earl of Dunbar (*Raine*, 117), and Roger de Reston witnessed a deed by Waldeve, earl of Dunbar, in 1166 (*Coldingham*, 178). Oliver de Rystone of the county of Berewyke rendered homage in 1296 (*Bain*,

II, p. 206). The name is early found in Glasgow. John de Restoun was burgess of the city in 1417 (LCD., p. 239). Another John de Restone, who is mentioned as a cleric there in 1440, appears again in 1442 as plain John Restoune (REG., 344, 345), and mention is also made of the tenement of magister John Restown there in 1478 (ibid., 420). Philip de Restoun was vicar of Glasgu in 1450 (ibid., 357). Walter Reston in Shetlestoun, 1711 (*Minutes*, p. 114).

RETSON. A surname recorded in the shires of Dumfries, Ayr, and Dumbarton. A variant of RITSON, q.v.

RETTIE, RAITTIE. Of local origin from the old lands of Reattie or Raittie in the parish of Innerboyndie, Banffshire. Willmus Rettie was common councillor in Aberdeen, 1474 (*Guildry*, p. 187). The name occurs several times in RSCA. as Raittie and Ratie.

REUEL. An old forgotten personal name in England of uncertain origin, but "a common surname in present Yorkshire directories" (*Bardsley*). Rauelin, its diminutive, occurs in DB. (*Searle*). Henry Reuel, whom Chalmers (*Caledonia*, I, p. 590) calls "a foreigner," obtained from William the Lion a grant of the lands of Cultrath in Fife (*Balmerino*, 2). He was one of those taken prisoner with the king at Alnwick, 1174 (*Annals*, p. 181), and married Margaret, a daughter of Orm, son of Hugh of Abernethy. He witnessed the confirmation charter by King William of the church of Aberrotheuen to the Abbey of Inchaffray, c. 1199–1200 (*Inchaffray*, p. 4), and was also witness to several other charters by the same king (LSC., p. 36, 211; RAA., I, 29). Dying without issue he transmitted his lands of Cultrath, Balmerinach, and Ballendard to his nephew Richard, who obtained confirmation of them from Alexander II, and in addition the lands of Esterardent (*Balmerino*, 3). Ricardus Reuel or Reuell witnessed confirmation by King William of the sale of a toft in Coldingham (*Raine*, 57), and also confirmation of a gift of lands in Buthirgasc to the monastery of Scone (*Scon*, p. 20). He also witnessed the gift of Mucraht to the church of Glasgow, c. 1200, and another charter of c. 1208–14 (REG., p. 78, 92). Richard also dying without issue was succeeded by his brother, Adam de Reuel or de Stawell, who, as Adam de Stawelle, gifted fifteen acres of the lands of Balmulinauch (Balmerino) to the church of St. Andrews (RPSA., p. 271–272). In 1225 Adam sold the lands of Cultrath, Ardint, and Balmerinach with its church to Ermengard, the queen dowager, for one thousand merks. Adam went into the king's court at Forfar, before Alexander II himself, and surrendered the whole to Ermengard, and the queen granted the estates thus acquired to the monastery of Balmerinach, which she founded (*Balmerino*, 1, 4, 5, 6). He also witnessed several charters by King William (LSC., 40, 45; *Laing*, II; *Athole*, p. 704; RAA., 69, etc.; RD., p. 32, 38).

REVICH. Of local origin from the old lands of Auchinbothie-Langmure "nunc vocata The Rivoche" (1616, *Retours*, Renfrew, 39). Cuthbert Revoche, witness in Glasgow, 1508 (*Simon*, 86). John Revich, tenant in North Galston, 1726 (HP., II, p. 318). Revoch 1504, Revok 1558.

REVIE. A curtailed form of MACILRIACH, q.v.

REW. A surname now recorded in Laurencekirk. It may be from Row, Dumbartonshire, pronounced Roo. John Rew, rebel in Kilblain paroch, Kintyre, 1685 (*Commons*, p. 1). James Rew in Linlithgow, 1686 (RPC., 3. ser. XII, p. 492).

REWCASTLE. From the place of the name in the parish of Bedrule, Roxburghshire. William de Rucastel of the county of Roxburgh rendered homage in 1296. The seal attached to his homage bears a number of objects and S' Will'i d' Rucastele (*Bain*, II, p. 199, 532). William de Roucastell had a pension of £20 from King Robert Bruce (RMS., I, App. II, 641), Robert Rewcastle, indweller in Hawick, 1674 (*Edinb. App.*), John Rew-Castle is recorded in Edinburgh in 1686 (*Edinb. Marr.*), and Robert Roucastle was a tailor in Hawick in 1688 (*Peebles CR.*). Rewcastell 1614.

REYBURN. See under RYBURN.

RHIND, RHYND, RIND. From the parish of Rhynd in Perthshire. William de Rynd was a charter witness in Aberdeen, 1342 (REA., I, p. 72). Although Rynd or Rhynd is now a somewhat rare name in Angus it is of considerable antiquity in that county. Rinds or Rynds figure in feuds with Ogilvies, Guthries, and other neighbors there (*Stodart*, II, p. 111–112). Murthacus (Murdoch) del Rynde had a gift from David II of four oxgates of land in the royal hunting forest of Plater and four oxgates of Casse in 1366 (RMS., I, 257), and as Muryoch of the Rynde was one of the assizors on the marches of Woodwrae, 1388 (*Bamff*, p. 22). Patrick of Rynd was alderman of Forfar in 1372. William Rinde, witness in Edinburgh, c. 1426 (*Egidii*, p. 49), Henry Rynde was canon of Caithness, 1435 (*Pap. Lett.*, VIII, p. 555), and in 1447 James de

Rynde held a tenement in Brechin (REB., I, 110). James Rynde of Broxmouth was witness in 1470 (*Panmure*, II, 245), and his seal attached to a document dated 1478 reads S' iacobi riende (*Macdonald*, 2275). Sir Laurence Rynd, cleric, was witness at Tuliboill, 1546 (*Rollok*, 5), and a payment was made to Patrik Rynde in Perth, 1614 (Mill, *Plays*, p. 267). William Rynd obtained the rectory and prebend of Arbuthnott in 1548 (SCM., IV, p. 50), and John Rinne or Rind is in record in Elgin, 1661 (*Rec. Elgin*, II, p. 369–370). There is a Rhind in Fife, and Hugh del Rynd, cleric of William de Lamberton, 1300 (RPSA., p. 120) may derive from it. Alexander Henry Rhind (1833–1863), Egyptian explorer, was founder of the Rhind Lectureship in Archæology. The brothers Rhind of Edinburgh were distinguished sculptors. Rhynde 1663, Rind 1655, Rine 1661, Riyin 1645.

RHYDDERCH. The name of Rodercus (gen. Roderco in *Adamnan*, I, 15) filius Tothail, "qui in Petra Cloithe (Dumbarton) regnavit," is better known under the Welsh form of his name, *Rhydderch*. The name appears in Breton as *Rozerch* (1384), old Breton and Old Welsh *Roderch*.

RHYNAS. A Banffshire surname, of local origin from Rannes in the parish of Rathven, Banffshire. John Rynass in Stripeside of Boharm, 1751 (*Moray*).

RHYND. See under RHIND.

RHYNIE. From Rhynie in the parish of the same name, Aberdeenshire. John dictus Ryny appears as capellanus in 1345 (REA., I, p. 78), and Patrick Ryny was admitted burgess of Aberdeen in 1467 (NSCM., I, p. 21).

RIACH. See under REACH.

RICARTON, RICCARTON. There are places of this name in Ayrshire, Lanarkshire, Midlothian, West Lothian, Roxburghshire, Clackmannanshire, and Kincardineshire (Rickarton), "all which names were similarly derived from the appellation of Richard" (*Caledonia*, III, p. 511). Henry Riccarton was burgess of Dysart, 1642 (*Dysart*, p. 51) and John Rickarton was burgess of Selkirk, 1746 (*Heirs*, 211).

RICCALTON. From Riccalton near Oxnam, Jedburgh, Roxburghshire. There is also a Rickleton in Northumberland. Adam de Rukelton of Roxburghshire rendered homage in 1296. His seal bears a figure of eight rays, and S' Ade de Crildvn' (*Bain*, II, p. 199, 533). Alexander de Reclyneton appears as perpetual vicar of Edinburgh between 1296 and 1332

RICCALTON, *continued*

(*Soltre*, p. 42). Alexander de Reclynton had a charter of a tenement "infra burgum de Edynburgche in vico Canonicorum" in 1363, and in 1367, as Alexander Rikklynton or Rykklynton, he appears as constable of Dunbarre (RMS., I, 160, 265; *Raine*, 142). A later Alexander Ryklyngtoun appears as constable to George of Dunbar, earl of March in 1396 (*Wemyss*, II, p. 35). Thomas of Riklintoune was one of an inquest at Jedburgh in 1464 (HMC., 7. Rep., App., p. 728), and in 1550 a fore tenement in Glasgow was sold to Jonet Riklintoune (*Protocols*, I). Robert Rikkletown is recorded in Clyftoun, 1688 (*Peebles CR.*). The following spellings of the name are recorded in the first volume of the Register of the Great Seal: Reclintona, Reclvntona, Reclyntone, Reklintoun, Rekilynton, Rekilyntona, Rickietoun, Ricklintoun, Riclvntone, Rikklvntona, Riklintoun, Ruclintoun, Ryclinton, Ryclintone, Ryclyntona.

RICCARTS. A sharpened form of RICHARDS, q.v.

RICHAN. "Richan is a very puzzling name. It is never, so far as I know, found out of Orkney, and the Richans owned odal land in Ophir in the 15th century; yet the *ch* is not Norse when pronounced as in 'loch' — as it is in this name; and I have never seen it with a *k*, to indicate that it was once hard" (*Clouston*). Mawnis Richen was odaller in Howbuster in 1492 (REO., p. 406). William Richane was one of Lord Robert Stewart's Harmansteine (*hirðmannastefna*, 'a hustings of king's men') in 1574 (OSR., I, p. 267), and William Richane was retoured heir of William Richane, portioner of Howbister in 1657 (*Retours, Orkney and Shetland*, 87). Alexander Richen appears in Brabister, parish of Walls, in 1620 (*Shetland*).

RICHARD. Alan Richert, a follower of the earl of Cassilis, was respited for murder in 1526 (RSS., I, 3386). Thomas Rechard, 1561 (CMN., 80). As forename: Richart Strathern, 1462. An OE. personal name meaning "powerfully rich" (*rice* + *h(e)ard*).

RICHARDS, 'son of RICHARD,' q.v.

RICHARDSON, 'son of RICHARD,' q.v. Thome filius Ricardi had a charter of the barony of Svmundestone in the sheriffdom of Lanark from Robert I, c. 1315–21 (RMS., I, 78). Laurence filius Ricardi was a tenant of the earl of Douglas in Louchurde in 1376 (RHM., II, p. 16). In 1359 Murdac Richardesson, Scottish merchant, and others, complained that their vessel was captured and sunk by the English during a truce (*Bain*, IV, 23). David Richardsone, servant of William Olyfaunt, had a safe conduct into England in 1425 (ibid., 986), John Ricardi held land in Aberdeen in 1451 (REA., II, p. 297), and Robert Richardson of Scotland had a safe conduct into England in 1464 (*Bain*, IV, 1343). Jak Richardson held part of the Grange of Kerso before 1469 (*Cupar-Angus*, I, p. 154). Duncane Richardsone was king's pursuivant in 1529 (*Irvine*, I, p. 36), Master Robert Rychartsone, a cleric, was provost of Sanct Marie Isle and treasurer to Mary, Queen of Scots in 1567 (OPS., II, p. 634), and Thomas Richartson, sailor, was burgess of Dysart in 1640 (*Inquis.*, 2518). Rechartsoun 1553, Rechertson 1540, Rechertsovn 1588, Richartsovn 1556, Richertsoun 1525, Richesoun (in Workman MS.), Richisone 1688.

RICHIESON, 'son of RITCHIE,' q.v. William Rychisone de Nutyntone is mentioned in 1477 (*Irvine*, I, p. 149), John Richeson was tenant of the abbot of Kelso in 1567 (*Kelso*, p. 524), and James Richiesone of Smetoune had a charter of the lands of Smetoune Mill in Mussilburgh in 1594 (RD., p. 493). John Ritchesone appears in Lessuddane in 1608, and James Richeiesone in Hawicksheill in 1662 (RRM., I, p. 71; II, p. 8).

RICHMAN. David Rychman, burgess of Aberdeen, 1499 (REA., I, p. 344). Duncan Richman and John Richman appear in Kintore, Aberdeenshire, 1608 (RSCA., II, p. 112), Janet Richman was married in Edinburgh, 1649 (*Edinb. Marr.*), and Hugh Richman is recorded in the parish of Govan, 1693 (*Kilbarchan*).

RICHMOND. Probably from Richmond, a parish in Yorkshire. John Richmond was retoured heir of John Richmond of Peirisland, his grandfather, in 1616, and Andrew Richmont was heir of John Richmont, portioner of Auchincloich, his brother-german, in 1663 (*Retours, Ayr*, 143, 530). John Richmond (1765–1846) was an early friend of Robert Burns. Ritchmont 1664.

RICKART. A variant of Rickard (= RICHARD, q.v.). A family of this name were landed proprietors in Aberdeen in the seventeenth century. David Rickart was retoured heir of George Rickart, burgess of Aberdeen, 1651 (*Retours, Aberdeen*, 309). George Rickart was laird of Arnage or Arnodge, 1670, 1692 (Mair, *Ellon*, p. 130; *Inquis.*, 7224). David Rickart of Rickartoun, 1746 (*Aberdeen CR.*).

RIDDALL, RIDDEL, RIDDELL, RIDDLE. These surnames have a twofold origin — one personal and the other territorial. The Ridels came from Gascony and the de Rydales from the wapentake of Ryedale in the North Riding of Yorkshire. The two appear almost simultaneously in Scotland, and the names are always distinguished in spelling, a very remarkable thing at that early date. The Ridels never prefixed *de*, and the de Rydales invariably did so because they came from a place so-called. The first Ridel of Craneston (i. e. Cranstoun-Riddell in Midlothian) was probably Gervasius Ridel who appears as a witness in the *Inquisitio* of Earl David as to the extent of the lands of the church of Glasgow, c. 1124, and was most probably a descendant of the Galfridus Ridel de Blaye of 1048 (*The Genealogist*, new ser. VI, p. 1). At this day the name is a strictly personal one in Normandy. Gervasius also appears as a witness to charters in the reigns of Alexander I and David I (REG., 5; *Kelso*, 372; *Melros*, p. 4, 5, etc.). The first of the Riddells of that Ilk was Walter de Ridale or Riddale who received a charter from King David, c. 1150, of the lands of Whitimes (an error for Whittune), Eschetho (to which he transferred the name of his Yorkshire property), and Lilislive (now Lilliesleaf) (*Lawrie*, p. 179–180). He also appears as a witness in many charters in the cartularies of Dryburgh, Holyrood, Glasgow, Newbattle, Cambuskenneth, Dunfermline, etc. He died without issue, c. 1155, and left his property to his brother Anschetil or Ansketil de Riddel by a will which was confirmed by Pope Adrian IV (*Dalrymple*, p. 348). The barony remained in the possession of the descendants of Ansketil for twenty-five generations, till the year 1819. The arms of this family, a chevron between three ears of rye, evidently refer to the old form of their surname, "Rydale," and are therefore what are known as canting arms (*arma cantantia*), the wapentake lying in the valley of the river Rye. Many individuals of the name are in record as holders of lands and as charter witnesses in the thirteenth and fourteenth centuries, and among the more distinguished of the name in later times may be mentioned Robert Riddell of Glenriddell, the friend and early patron of Robert Burns, John Riddell (1785–1862), the peerage lawyer and genealogist, Henry Scott Riddell (1798–1870), etc. Gave name to Riddelstoun in Ayrshire, 1622 (*Retours, Ayr*, 212).

RIDDET. There are families of this name in the parish of Kilbirnie, Ayrshire. As the Ridels had some connection with the district, it has been suggested (*Pont*, p. 168) that the names may be connected, but this seems unlikely. Rithat and Rithet are recorded in Dumfries. Bardsley has Ridout, Rideout, and Riddout (1273 and later) but "can find no satisfactory derivation" of the name.

RIDDICK. From the parish and barony of Rerrick or Rerwick in the Stewartry of Kirkcudbright. The place name is pronounced Riddick, i.e. Red Wick, by the common folk (Trotter, *Galloway gossip—Kirkcudbrightshire*, p. 71). Nicholas de Reraik held a toft and croft in the vill of Treuquer (Troqueer), Kirkcudbrightshire, c. 1280 (*Holm Cultram*, p. 59). Gilbert de Rerik, archdeacon of Glasgow (REG.), sat in the Scottish Parliament in 1467. His seal is described by Macdonald (2274). George Rodyck was witness in Tungland, 1564 (*Laing*, 772), and William Redik of Dalbatye is mentioned in 1577. John Redik was retoured heir in the five merk lands of Barharrow in 1599 (*Retours, Kirkcudbright*, 42), and in 1619 Edward Maxwell was ordered to find caution not to molest James Redick and Hew Redick at the Steppis of Or (Urr) (RPC., XI, p. 589) Agnes Readick was married in Edinburgh, 1630 (*Edinb. Marr.*), and Barbara Reddik was heir portioner of Paul Reddik of Barscheine or Barschein in 1646 (*Retours, Kirkcudbright*, 239). John Reddick or Rodick of Dalbeattie is in record, 1678 and 1699 (ibid., 332; *Inquis.*, 8168). George Riddick is in Littleknox, 1686, and Edward Riddick in Mains of Kelton, 1749 (*Kirkcudbright*). There were Reriks, Reddicks, Rediks, or Redocks of Barnhourie, Dalbeattie, Corbietoun, etc., and the name is still represented in the district.

RIDDLE. See *under* RIDDALL.

RIDDOCH. There was a family of this name in the parish of Fordyce in the eighteenth century. Jonett Riddoche, heir of Hendrie Ridoche of Temptarance, 1657 (*Inquis.*, 4192). Reddoiche 1579, Readdoche 1630, Riddoche 1586. Cf. REDDOCH and RUDDOCH.

RIDLER. From the occupation: (1) a maker of riddles or coarse sieves; or (2) a riddler, a sifter (of grain, etc.). Cf. CRERAR. John Ridlar in Maynis of Eycht, 1617, and Alexander Ridler in Lurg, 1635 (RSCA., II, p. 227, 404). Janet Ridler in Upper Banchory, 1733 (*Aberdeen CR.*).

RIDLEY. From Ridley in Northumberland (in 1279 Rideley). Odard de Rydeley was coroner of Tyndale, 1278 (*Bain*, II, 147).

RIDPATH. See *under* REDPATH.

RIGG. Of local origin from lands of the name near Dunbar, East Lothian, and elsewhere. James Rig or Ryg rendered to Exchequer the accounts of the burgh of Dumfries in 1560 and 1567 (ER., XIX, p. 117, 372), and a family of this name were burgesses of Dumfries and Annan and small landowners in the Stewartry

RIGG, *continued*

of Kirkcudbright. James Rig in Greinmers, Kirkcudbrightshire, 1646 (*Retours, Kirkcudbright*, 239). Robert Rig was burgess of Are in 1503 (*Friars Ayr*, p. 70). Hew Ryg was procurator in St. Andrews, 1548 (*Rollok*, 29), and Quintigernus Rig had a charter of lands of Carberrie in the parish of Inveresk in 1600 (RD., p. 495). James Rigg, poet, died in 1907. A family of this name probably gave name to Rigsland in Fife. Rige 1637.

RILLEWOOD. Local. Thomas de Rillewode of Roxburghshire rendered homage, 1296 (*Bain*, II, p. 209).

RIND. *See under* RHIND.

RINTOUL, Rᴇɴᴛᴏᴜʟ. From the old lands of Rintoul in the parish of Orwell, Kinross-shire. Between 1362–67 there is mention of a *clausum* or enclosed estate bearing the name Rentoule. The surname occurs but rarely in public record, and like the Dalgleishes, the family seems to have "successfully avoided any distinction." There is a family tradition among the Perthshire Rintouls that they are of Huguenot descent, but as here shown, the name is found in Scotland much earlier. Mount Rintoul in New Zealand is called after this family name. Rentowle 1642. The place name appears as Rentowle in Gordon's map of Keanrosse-shyre, 1642.

RIOCH. *See under* REACH.

RIPLEY. Bernardus de Rippeley witnessed the gift by Alexander II of ten marks annually to the Abbey of Arbroath in 1247 (RAA., I, p. 202), and in 1249 he witnessed a charter de Warenna de Muskilburg (Musselburgh) to the monks of Dunfermline (RD., p. 44). He also witnessed confirmation of the gift of the lands of Prendergest to the monks of Coldingham in the reign of Alexander II (*Raine*, 73). Willelmus de Rypeley is mentioned in a charter of 1279 as the progenitor of Sir William de Dolays (Dallas), and as having held the lands of Dolays Mykel under a grant of confirmation of William the Lion (*Dallas*, p. 28). Probably from Ripley, a parish near Ripon in Yorkshire.

RIPON. From the cathedral city of Ripon in the West Riding of Yorkshire. Roger de Ripun was burgess of Aberdeen, 1271 (*Fraser*, p. 9), and Henry de Ripon appears as a charter witness in Dundee, 1281 (HP., II, p. 233). William de Rypun was witness to a renunciation by William Maule of Panmure, c. 1292 (*Panmure*, II, 153), and Walter de Rypon or Rypun was burgess of Edinburgh, 1296 (*Bain*, II, p. 188, 197).

RIRES. From the old barony of Rires in Fife. Gospatricus de Rirais witnessed the gift of the church of Hadintona by Richard, bishop of St. Andrews before 1173 (RPSA., p. 135), and a. 1199 was witness to a charter by Malcolm, son of Earl Duncan, to the nuns of North Berwick (SHSM., IV, p. 309). Ralph de Ronays of Fife who rendered homage in 1296 (*Bain*, II, p. 209) appears as Rereys in RR. Nicholas Reres was prebendary of Renfreu in 1491 (REG., 460). Alexander Rireis in Strathtodla is mentioned in 1606 (RSCA., II, p. 91), Thomas Rires was minister of Lonmay in 1633 (SCM., III, p. 135), and in the same year a delatione was given in against Mr. William Rires, minister of the same parish (*Alford*, p. 28). John Rires in Ratray, 1634 (SCM., III, p. 135).

RIRIE, Rʏʀɪᴇ. From (Mᴀᴄ)ʀʏʀɪᴇ, q.v..

RISCOLOC. *See under* SCOLOC.

RISK. A common surname in the parish of Fintry in the seventeenth century and still not uncommon in Stirlingshire. Most probably derived from the "Risk" of Drymen (G. *riasg*, a morass with sedge). John Reisk appears as a witness in Glasgow in 1552 (*Protocols*, I). Buchanan of Auchmar classes persons of this name as followers of M'Aslan or Buchanan.

RITCHIE. Formerly a common Border surname. From 'Richie,' a diminutive of Richard, with intrusive *t*. In some instances curtailed from (Mᴀᴄ)Rɪᴛᴄʜɪᴇ, q.v. Michael Rechy in Inverness in the fourteenth century (*Macbain* v, p. 11). Duncan Richie was a messenger in Perth, 1505 (*Milne*, p. 14), and John Riche witnessed an instrument of sasine in Brechin in the same year (REB., II, 149). Duncan Riche was the king's sheriff of Inverness in 1512 (OPS., II, p. 661), and there is mention of the lands of Robert Reche in Glasgow, 1550 (*Protocols*, I). The wife of David Reche in Aberdeen was fined for brewing ale, 1538 (CRA., p. 157). William Ritchie founded the *Scotsman* newspaper in Edinburgh in 1817, and Alexander Ritchie was an Edinburgh artist of repute in early half of last century. As forename: Ritsche Criste was 'delatit of lipyr' (leprosy) in Stirling, 1520 (SBR., p. 5), and Riche Hynd is recorded in Dunfermline in 1577. Rechie 1574, Rechtie 1682, Rychy 1474, Rychze (z = y) 1509, Rytchie 1609.

RITSON. Explained by Bardsley as "'son of Richard,' from the N.-Eng. nick. Rich or Ritchie, whence the patronymic Richison, corrupted to Ritson. This is a familiar Cumberland surname." "The Ritson family name was, according to Joseph [Ritson], a corruption of Richardson. In his 'Memoranda' he records the genesis of the word thus: 'Richardson, Richison, Richson, Ricson, Ritson.' But it is highly doubtful if there is any other authority than personal fancy for this evolution" (A. Burd, *Joseph Ritson, a critical biography*, Urbana, Ill., 1916, p. 13).

ROAN. Local. There are places of this name in the shires of Berwick, Roxburgh, and Ayr. Hugh Roan in Glenmids, 1767 (*Dumfries*), and Samuel Roan in Stroanpatrick, 1780 (*Kirkcudbright*).

ROBB. A diminutive of ROBERT, q.v., and a common surname in Scotland. Jok Robb, voter in Monkland, 1519 (*Simon*, 45). Nicholas Rob was a witness in Dumfriesshire in 1542 (*Anderson*), and John Rob appears as citizen and witness in Glasgow in 1551 and 1554 (*Protocols*, I). Entry money was paid by Jonet Rob for the lands of Cornetoun in Stirlingshire in 1563 (*ER.*, XIX, p. 232), and John Rob, vestiarius in Eister Dudingstoun, was retoured heir of John Rob in the West Port of Edinburgh in 1646 (*Retours, Edinburgh*, 950). Rabbe 1686, Robe 1687. See also MACROBB.

ROBBIE, ROBY. Diminutives of ROBERT, q.v. With Mac- gives the Highland Border name MACROBBIE. Beatrix Robbie and Issobell Robie or Robye were witches in Aberdeen, 1597 (*SCM.*, I, p. 152, 184, 189).

ROBBS, 'son of ROBB,' q.v. Less common than ROBB.

ROBERT, ROBBERT. An OE. personal name, *Robert*, meaning 'bright fame' (*hroð + berht*). Alexander Robert, a Scotsman, arrested as a spy, to be liberated, 1402 (*Bain*, IV, 607). Borrowed into Gaelic as RAIBERT, q.v.

ROBERTON. Of territorial origin from the ancient manor of the same name, now the parish of Roberton, Lanarkshire. In the reign of Malcolm IV the manor belonged to Robert (the brother of Lambin who gave name to Lamington), and took its name from him. Robert of Robertstun witnessed a charter by Hugh, son of Robert, son of Waldeve de Bigar, granted at Lesmahago in 1228 (*Kelso*, 186). Steven de Roberton of the county of Lanark rendered homage in 1296 (*Bain*, II, p. 198), and in 1304–5 Master Stephen de Rodberdeston or Roberdestone was clerk of Sir James de Dalilegh (ibid., p. 423, 455). Before 1329 the lands of Robertstoun in Lanarkshire were given by Robert I to John of Monfode (*RMS.*, I, App. II, 600). John of Robardston was witness to a charter by William de Conyng-

hame in 1365 (*RMS.*, I, 204), and in 1390 John de Robertun of Ernoksaunfoy resigned his lands of Auchinleck in the barony of Renfrew (*RMS.*, I, 799). Stephen de Roberton obtained letters of safe conduct from Henry IV of England in 1408 (*Rot. Scot.*, II, p. 187), John de Robertoun was presbyter in Glasgow in 1440 (*LCD.*, p. 252), and in 1487 John of Robertone of that Ilk possessed the lands of Modervile (now Motherwell) (*ADC.*, p. 30). Wishaw (*Description of Lanark*, p. 17) says Roberton of Earnock was reputed chief of the name in his day. The surname is sometimes confused with Robertson. An erroneous form, MacRoberton, occurs in the Register of the Privy Council in 1600. Robertown 1537.

ROBERTS, 'son of ROBERT,' q.v. John Roberts (1768–1803), American painter, mathematician, and scientist, was born in Scotland.

ROBERTSON, 'son of ROBERT,' q.v. William Robertson (fils Robert), a Scot going abroad, had English letters of protection in 1371 (*Bain*, IV, 195). Mauricius filius Roberti elected sergeant in Aberdeen, 1399 (*Guildry*, p. 184). Thomas Roberti (Latin genitive form) was burgess of Montrose, 1435 (*REB.*, II, 47), Thomas Robertson, a Scot, had a safe conduct to travel in England in 1444 (*Bain*, IV, 1175), and in 1464 John Robertsoune was master of the ship *Marie* of Leith (ibid., 1343). John Roberti was witness in Brechin, 1477 (*REB.*, I, 202), in 1511 Andree Roberti was tenant under the bishop of Aberdeen (*REA.*, I, p. 360), and Sir Valter Robertsone was vicar of Abyrdowr in 1556 (*CMN.*, p. 72). In 1456 Rich. Roberti is mentioned in the body of a document and in signature R. Robertsone (*LSC.*, p. 172). Similarly in 1541 an attestation begins "Et Ego Alexr Roberti," while the signature is Alexr Robertsone (ibid., p. 130). David Robertson was provost of Monybole, 1480 (*Friars Ayr*, p. 57). Duncan Robertson of Atholia had a second son, Patrick, from whose eldest son, Donald, descended the Robertsons of Lude; from his second son, Alexander, the Robertsons of Straloch, and from his daughter the Farquharsons of Invercauld. Jacob Robertson of Struan was physician or 'life-medicus' of Gustavus Adolphus and Queen Christina (*SHR.*, XXV, p. 290). Archibald Robertson (1765–1835), born in Monymusk, Aberdeenshire, while a guest of the first president of the United States, painted from life the miniatures on ivory of General and Martha Washington. The English name of *Clann Donnchaidh*, is from Robert, who, upon the murder of James I by the earl of Atholl and his accomplice, Graham, was fortunate enough to arrest Graham, together with the Master of Atholl, after the commission of the deed.

ROBERTSON, *continued*

Donnacha Reamhar, 'Fat Duncan,' the friend of Bruce, was first of the Robertson chiefs, hence their name Clann Donnachie. William became chief of Struan in 1509. "It was this William who first assumed the name of Robertson. During the first half of the 16th century its use became quite general with all the members of the clan, but in Gaelic they still continued to be called Clann Donnacha — Duncan's children — as the result of their descent from Dunan the Fat" (Stewart, *A Highland parish*, p. 131). The earls of Portmore were traditionally descended from the Robertsons of Struan, but their lineage beyond the grandfather of the first peer has not been traced, and it is still doubtful whether Colyear or Robertson was their original patronymic (Buchan, *Peeblesshire*, II, p. 501).

ROBESON, ROBISON, ROBSON, 'son of ROBERT,' from the diminutives ROB and ROB(B)IE. Patrick Robson is in record in 1436 (*Home*, 6), and Donald Robison and Donald Robertson, 1446, are one and the same person (*Cupar-Angus*, I, p. 124, 125). Wylle Robyson witnessed resignation of a feu in Peebles in 1471 (*Scots Lore*, p. 52), John Robison was vicar of Maxwell in 1475 (*Kelso*, 532), and in 1477 David Robisone was prebendary of the Collegiate Church of Menybole (Maybole) (SBR., p. 261). John Robisone and Edward Robisone were charged with defrauding the king's customs in 1524 (*Irvine*, I, p. 35), Dandie Robsone, Rychert Robisone, Thomas Robisone, and Willie Robisone were tenants on the lands of the Abbey of Kelso in 1567 (*Kelso*, p. 520, 521, 524). Andrew Robsone was retoured heir in the forty shilling lands of Glediswode, Lauderdale, in 1604 (*Retours, Berwick*, 42), George Robesoun was retoured heir of his mother, Jonet Wricht, in lands in the parish of Terregles in 1633 (*Retours, Dumfries*, 151), and Thomas Robson was served heir to Thomas Robson, his 'gudser,' in certain tenements in Thurso, 1654 (*Retours, Caithness*, 24). The name became Robsahm in Sweden (*Fischer* III, p. 263). Robesone 1606, Robsoun 1600, Robsoin 1687.

ROBIN, a diminutive of ROBERT, q.v.

"'Twas then a blast o' Janwar win'
Blew hansel in on Robin."

Mareoun Robyn was a tenant in Stobo in 1540 (*Rental*). John Robein, clerk to the town council of Stirling in 1616, appears again in 1618 as Robene and in 1621 as Robeine (SBR., p. 191, 287). Joannes Robein, burgess of Peebles, 1624 (*Retours, Peebles*, 62). Mr. Henry Robin, late minister at Burntisland, 1730 (*Guildry*, p. 137).

ROBINSON. The "son of ROBERT" from ROBIN, a diminutive form of the name. The tenement of John Robynson in Irvine is mentioned in 1426 (*Irvine* I, p. 130), and another John Robynsone was bailie of Glasgow in 1477 (REG., p. 458). Andrew Robersoun witnessed the sale of a tenement in Arbroath in 1450 (RAA., II, 91). The name was common in Glasgow in the sixteenth century (*Protocols*). That Robin was early considered a diminutive of Robert is shown by an entry in 1483 (LCD., p. 195) where the same individual is referred to as Robyne of Hall and Robert of Hall.

ROBISON. *See under* ROBESON.

ROBSON. *See under* ROBESON. The English Robsons formed one of the four principal clans of North Tyne in the sixteenth century. In Bullein's *Dialogue* they are described as "a wight riding sirname, good honest men and true, saving a little shifting for their living." The northern Robsons are said to be descended (1) from Robert, second son of George Gunn the Crowner, or (2) from John Gunn Robson (1616).

ROBY. *See under* ROBBIE.

ROCK. Perhaps from NF. *la Roche*, an old Norman surname. Adam de Roc witnessed a charter by Richard, bishop of St. Andrews, c. 1170 (*Scon*, p. 30), and Waldef de la Roche, burgess of Edinburgh, rendered homage, 1296 (*Bain*, II, p. 197). Johannes Roch, cleric in Aberdeen, 1462 (REA., II, p. 92). David Ruch, a monk of Dunfermline, 1477 (*Cupar-Angus*, I, p. 208), appears two years later as 'Sir' David Ruth (a miscopying of Ruch) (SBR., p. 264). Alexander Rocht held land in Aberdeen, c. 1500 (REA., II, p. 211). Michael Ruch, a follower of the earl of Cassilis, was respited for murder, 1526 (RSS., I, 3386). James Roch was reidare at Cockpen, 1574 (RMR.). A tombstone in the Howff, Dundee, reads: "Here lyis ane godlie and honest man, Jhone Roche, Brabenar and Borges of Dundie, quha depairtit this lyf the 1 of Februar, 1615 yeiris, being of age 43 yeiris, with his spous, Eufiama Pye, quha hes causit this to be made in remberance of him and their 14 bearnes." John Riock, wright in Loanheid, 1693 (*Edin. App.*). The spelling Rock has now been in part superseded by ROUCH. There was a S. Roque's chapel in Dundee, long since removed, and there was also a "chapell of Sanct Rok at the brigend of Stirling," 1500 (RSS., I, 476).

ROCKHALL. From Rockhall, now Rockhallhead, in the parish of Mouswald, Dumfriesshire. Hugh de Rokele to hold the church of

Kilmaurs during his life, c. 1170 (*Kelso*, 286). Hugh de Rowkell was a tenant of the Douglas in Drumcorke in 1376 (RHM., I, p. lvi). John Rokel petitioned for a benefice in the gift of the abbot of Holyrood, 1406 (*Pap. Pet.*, I, p. 624).

ROCNEK. John de Rocnek and his wife are mentioned in the Mearns, 1342 (RAA., II, p. 17).

RODAN, RODDAN, RODEN. A surname recorded in Dumfriesshire. Perhaps connected with Roddam near Ilderton, Northumberland, which in 1135 was Roden and Rodun in 1230. Roddanhall in Dumfriesshire may have derived its name from that of the family.

RODDAM. The family of Roddam of Berwick was an offshoot of the ancient house of Roddam of Roddam in Northumberland. They first appeared in Berwick, c. 1627. John Rodem was tenant in lands of Inchcwnen, Errol, 1548 (*Rollok*, 46).

RODDIE, RODIE. A double diminutive of Roderick. John Rhoddie was tidesman at Garlieston, 1792 (*Wigtown*). The first form is found in Inverness. Roddy is a common Irish family name, from *O'Rodaigh*, and the name in Wigtownshire may be from that source.

RODGER, ROGER. From the OE. personal name *Hróðgár*, 'famous spear.' Rodger is the more common form with Scots. Roger was appointed abbot of Dryburgh in 1152 (*Dryburgh*). Roger, son of Oggou, attested a deed of middle of thirteenth century (*Neubotle*, p. 27). William Roger was tenant of the abbot of Coupar-Angus in 1468 (*Cupar-Angus*, I, p. 142), another William Roger had a safe conduct into England in 1470 (*Bain*, IV, 1388) and the lands of another William Roger in Glasgow are noted in 1551 (*Protocols*, I). John Roger, mason in Dundee in first quarter of sixteenth century, appears in record as Rogy, Rogie, Rogzy, and William Roger about same time appears as Rogze (*Rent. Dunk.*). Alexander Rodger (1784–1846), minor poet. Rogear 1606. Cf. ROGIE.

RODGERS, ROGERS, 'son of Ro(D)GER,' q.v. Rodgers is the more common form with Scots. Rogers, in some parts of central Scotland, is pronounced Rodgie, and some Gaelic-speaking people in Perthshire pronounce it Rougie and sometimes Rovger. John Rodgers, born in Maryland, 1771, son of a Scots colonel of militia, fired with his own hand the first shot in the war with Great Britain in 1812.

RODGERSON, ROGERSON, 'son of RODGER,' q.v. Ade filius Rogeri held land in Aberdeen in 1281 (REA., II, p. 279), and Stephen dictus Rogersone held land in Edinburgh in 1411 (*Cambus.*, 94). Donald Rogerson was a native man (serf) of the bishop of Moray, 1364 (REM., p. 161). John Rogerson had a safe conduct into England in 1424 (*Bain*, IV, 963), Adam Rogeri was a presbyter in Brechin in 1435 (REB., I, 73), William Rogerson was tenant of the abbot of Cupar-Angus in 1479 (*Cupar-Angus*, I, p. 226), and John Rogesoune signed the Band of Dumfries in 1570 (RPC., XIV, p. 66). Thomas Rodgersone, merchant of Dumfries, 1689 (RPC., 3. ser. XIV, p. 160). John Rogerson (1741–1823), M.D., was medical adviser to the emperor and court of Russia. Rodgerson 1552. See also under ROGERSON.

RODGIE. A diminutive of RODGER, q.v. Helen Rogie or Rodgie was burnt for witchcraft in Aberdeen, 1597 (SCM., V, p. 67). David Rodgie was burgess of Perth in 1677 (*Inquis.*, 6051), and George Rodgie appears in Little Burnbean in 1732 (*Dunkeld*).

RODIE. *See under* RODDIE.

RODINGHAME. William Rodinghame or Rodingham, carter to the bishop of Dunkeld, 1510–15 (*Rent. Dunk.*, p. 125, 297). Probably from some place in England.

RODMAN. Mathew Rodman was burgess of Ayr, 1499 (*Simon*, 21). Weekley says from OE. *radman*, one who held land on military service.

ROGER. *See under* RODGER.

ROGERSON, 'son of Roger.' See RODGER. Macrory is sometimes (but wrongly) so rendered. Rory is from G. *Ruadhri* for *Ruadhraigh*, and Roger is from Teutonic *Hrothgar*. See also under RODGERSON.

ROGIE. A now uncommon surname probably derived from Rogie in the parish of Fodderty, Ross-shire. Sir John Roge was presented to the rectory of Kilmorew in 1511 (RSS., I, 2272), and Mr. Patrick Roge, chaplain, had a precept of legitimation in 1526 (ibid., 3377). The surname is now found in Aberdeenshire. Cf. RODGER.

ROKBY. David Rokby of Scotland, who had a safe conduct into England in 1437 (*Bain*, IV, 1106) most probably derived his surname from Rokeby in Yorkshire. He is doubtless the David Rokeby, merchant of Montrose, who had a safe conduct into England for two years in 1439 (ibid., 1124).

ROLAND, ROLLAND. This name is not recorded in OE. but appears in ME. from Fr. Rolland, Roland<Hrodland or Hruotland, a very common Germanic personal name. About 1180 Alan, son of Roland, appears as witness in a charter of William the Lion to the Abbey of Arbroath (RAA., I, p. 14), and between 1189–99 Rolland, son of Ucdred, witnessed another charter by the same king (RMP., p. 101). Gilbert fitz Roland and Johan fiz Roland of Ayrshire, and Gilascope fiz Rouland of Perthshire rendered homage in 1296 (Bain, II, p. 205, 209). Thomas Rollan was admitted burgess of Aberdeen, 1440, Alexander Rolande in 1471, and John Rolland in 1514 (NSCM., I, p. 6, 22, 45). John Rolland was burgess of Are, 1475 (Ayr, p. 91), and another Jhone Rolland rented land in Gwuane (Govan) in 1520 (Rental). William Rolland, burgess of Aberdeen in 1509 appears in the same year as William Rowand (RAA., II, p. 383), and in 1513 as William Rowan (CRA., p. 83). Rollands of Auchmithie, Angus, were an old family, a still older family were the Rollands of Disblair in Aberdeenshire, and a family of Rolland (Rouland in 1545) held land of the commendator of Dunfermline soon after the Reformation (Stodart, II, p. 309). Rowand was the common pronunciation of the name and it has given origin to the surnames ROWAN and ROWAND, q.v. Rollande 1555, Rollane 1522.

ROLLA. An Aberdeen surname, probably a variant of ROLLO, q.v. Meg Rolly of Foty, Aberdeen, was described as a common 'pikar' in 1411 (CRA., p. 4). John Rollie was a trade burgess of Aberdeen, 1617 (ROA., I, p. 231). Recorded in Edinburgh, 1941.

ROLLAND. See under ROLAND.

ROLLO, ROLLOCK. Two forms of the same name, found mainly in Perthshire and Fife. A transformation of the personal name Rudolph. A family named Rollock were long eminent in Dundee. John Rollo, cleric of diocese of Moray and notary public, 1373 (LAC., 101), another John Rollow was burgess of Edinburgh, 1381 (Egidii, p. 22). Duncane Rollo or Rollok, servant of Aleyn of Bollone (? Boulogne) of Edinburgh, 1394 (Bain, IV, 460), in 1396 had a safe conduct to purchase goods in England (ibid., 476, 477). He is doubtless the Duncan Rollok, juror on an inquest in Edinburgh, 1402, (Egidii, p. 38) and the Duncan Rollo, burgess of Edinburgh, 1413 (RMS., I, 947). William Rollock of Findone gave his bond of manrent "to ryd & gang" with Laurence, Lord Oliphant, 1476 (Macfarlane, II, p. 110). Rook, a not uncommon pronunciation of the name accounts

for David Rook in Glasgow, 1552, referred to in the same record as David Rollok (Protocols, I, p. 115, 116), and Jacobus Rollok, provost of Dundee, 1485, appears in the following year as Rwok, and in 1490 as Rook (RAA., II, p. 239, 246, 264). Robert Rouk resigned the lands of Buteland in the sheriffdom of Edinburgh in the reign of Robert III (RMS., I, App. II, 1791). Agnes Ruke held a tenement in Glasgow, 1428 (LCD., p. 245), and in 1486 James Rouk had a lease of the teinds of Clova (RAA., II, p. 246). George Rollog is recorded in 1526 (ibid., p. 461), and Lamont (Diary, p. 37, 49, 84) referring to the Rev. Alexander Rollock, minister of Perth, spells his name Rogge and Roguel Robert II in the eleventh year of his reign confirms a charter of Duncrub and other lands granted to John Rollo by David, earl palatine of Strathearn and earl of Caithness, 1380 (Stodart, II). Rillict 1550, Rolhoc (of Duncrub) 1471, Rolle 1546, Rolloke 1614, Rolly 1530, Rolok 1640.

ROLSON. Adam Rolson and John Rolson were outlawed as part guilty of the slaughter of Walter de Ogilvy, sheriff of Angus, 1392 (APS., I, p. 579).

ROMANES, ROMANIS, ROMANS. From the old manor of Rothmaneic in the parish of Newlands, Peeblesshire, now known as Romanno. Philip de Roumanoch witnessed an agreement anent the marches of Kingside, c. 1250 (Neubotle, p. 27). Johne of Roumanno of that Ilk is mentioned in 1484 (Peebles, p. 31). The last of the name in the direct line is said to have been Janet Romanno or Romannois who carried the property into the family of Murray by her marriage (before 1513) with William Murray, son of Murray of Falahill and Philiphaugh (Chambers, Peeblesshire, p. 480). There are not many instances of the name in record. Sir Alexander Romannois, a priest and notary public between 1508–20, Thomas Romannois in 1542, William Romannois in Duncanlaw in 1562, and Marion and Helen Romannois in Linton, 1575 (Buchan, Peeblesshire, III, p. 11–12). John Romanoss in Haddington consents to the king's coronation, 1567 (RPC., I, p. 558). James Rolmainhous, burgess of Lauder, 1642, signs the register as James Romanis (RRM., I, p. 97), and James Rolmanhous or -house is in Blainslie, 1662 (ibid., II, p. 20). Robert Romaners was cited 'for playing at the bullets on the Sabbath day,' 1649 (MCM., I, p. 438). William Romanis, smith in Kelso, 1826 (Heirs, 708). Sergeant A. L. Romanis of Edinburgh was killed in action, 1941. Rollmanous 1680, Rollmainhouse 1684, Romainis 1607, Romanis 1643, Rowmanhous 1661, Rowmannous 1608,

Rumannis 1642; Rollmannous, Rolmanhous, Romanus, Rowmainhouse.

ROME. The Romes were a small clan living under the protection of the Johnstones in Gretna, in the sixteenth century, but subsequently increased their fortunes and estates. For a time they possessed the Castle of Dalswinton (Johnstone, *Historical families of Dumfriesshire*, p. 76). John Rome was retoured heir of John Rome of Dalswyntoune-Rome, his father, in lands in Dumfriesshire in 1638 (*Retours, Dumfries*, 166). Robertus Roome and Johannes Roome de Dalswinton, 1674 (*Inquis.*, 5701), and George Rome, writer in Dumfries, 1692 (ibid., 7304). The surname still exists in the shires of Dumfries and Kirkcudbright. Room 1730.

ROMEFARE. Cospatricius romefare was one of the witnesses to the right marches between Stobbo and Hoperewe and Orde, a. 1200 (REG., p. 89). Rompharus presbyter is a witness in early Durham charters (*Raine*, 165, 357). Romares were those who had made the pilgrimage to Rome. OF. *romier*, a pilgrim to Rome (*Piers Plowman*, passus IV, 120).

RONALD. A variant of RANALD, q.v. Jean Ronald, heir of John Ronald, portioner of Blaikburne, her father, 1655 (*Retours, Ayr*, 472). Thomas Ronnald, schoolmaster of the "grammer schoole of Linlithgow," 1662 (SBR., p. 238).

RONALDSON. "Son of RONALD," q.v. Current: Most probably an Englishing of MACRONALD, q.v.

RONAN. Diminutive of Ir. *rón*, G. *ron*, 'a seal.' S. Ronan was a companion of S. Modan, the patron saint of Rosneath; his church was probably at Sheneccles (*Strathendrick*, p. 126-127). Ronan was the name of a monk and abbot of the Culdees of Lochleven, who gave the place of their cell to the bishop of St. Andrews in return for food and clothing, a. 985 (RPSA., p. 113).

RONNAY, RONEY (this current in Kirkinner). Most probably from Ir. O'Ruanaidh, descendant of *Ruanaidh*. James Ronnay was tenant of Stobo, 1528 (*Rental*).

RORISON, RORIESON. An Englishing of MAC RUAIRIDH, q.v. Morgownde Ruryson or Roryson took part in the battle of Gasklune in 1391 and in the following year was outlawed as part guilty of the slaughter of Walter de Ogilvy, sheriff of Angus (APS., I, p. 579). Sir Dougall Ruresoun or Rorieson appears as vicar of Logy and Urquhard and prior of Beauly in 1498 (RSS., I, 273; *Beauly*, p. 329).

Thomas Roriesoun or Roreson was retoured heir of Andrew Roriesoun of Bardannoch in lands in the barony of Glencairn, Dumfriesshire in 1563 (*Retours, Dumfries*, 6; ER., XIX, p. 530). Mention is made in Moysie's *Memoirs* of Thomas Rorestoun, forfeited for coining, 1581, and in the edition of 1755 he is mentioned as "Thomas Roresone of Bardamno." Henry Roresoun appears in Newhouse, Orkney, 1616 (OSR., I, p. 239), and John Roriesone in Holm of Borland in 1675 (*Kirkcudbright*). Roresoun 1619.

RORY, RORIE. Anglicized forms of G. *Ruairidh*, MG. (1467 MS.) *Ruaidri*, OG. *Ruadri*, from proto-historic Celtic *Roudo-rix*, 'red king.' The name is sometimes confused with Teutonic Roderick. Ruadri, mormaer of Mar, appears c. 1131-32 as a witness in the *Book of Deer* (III, 7), and is probably the Rothri comes of the foundation charter of Scone (*Scon*, p. 3). He figures similarly in the great charter of David I to the monastery of Dunfermline (1124-27) as 'Rotheri comes' (RD., 1). Cristinus filius Rury witnessed a quitclaim of land of Drumkerauch, 1260 (RPSA., p. 346). Ruadri of Bute was grandson of Somerled (ES., II, p. 620-621). RORIE is a surname in Aberdeen. Old: Rore, Rorye.

ROSE. The family of Rose of Kilravock are believed to be a branch of de Ross, q.v. They did not blossom into a great clan but have kept well to the old acres, and show a remarkably unbroken pedigree, every link being proved by documentary evidence in *A Genealogical deduction of the family of Rose of Kilravock*, 1848. The tradition in *Clan Donald* (I, p. 101) that the family are descended from one of the Irish O'Cathans is worthless. Muriel de Roys granted a charter, 1333 (*Rose*, p. 116), and William Rose was a charter witness in Inverness, c. 1360 (*Grant*, III, p. 12). Andrew de Rose was perpetual vicar of Innerafferayn in the diocese of Ross, 1440 (*Pap. Lett.*, IX, p. 445).

ROSEMARKIE. Provision was made of a canonry of Ross to William de Rosmarkyn in 1329 (*Pap. Lett.*, II, p. 301), and Gilbert de Rosmarkyn, treasurer of Caithness, is mentioned at the same date. Evidently of local origin from Rosemarkie in Ross-shire.

ROSEWELL. Of local origin from the village of Rosewell in the parish of Lasswade, Midlothian. Isobel Rosewell in Edinburgh, 1602 (*Edinb. Marr.*).

ROSIE, ROSEY. It was charged against Alexander Rosie in Freswick, Caithness, in 1653, that he laid "a dead beast's head in the way wher" a woman's beasts (cattle) went in order

ROSIE, ROSEY, continued

to cause them injury (Old Lore Misc., v, p. 62). Walter Rosie appears in Mey, Caithness, 1661 (Caithness), and John Rossie in May was to be apprehended as a rebel, 1670 (RPC., 3. ser. III, p. 194). The form Rosey is found in Orkney. John Rosie died in Edinburgh, 1941.

ROSLIN. From Roslin or Rosslyn in the parish of Lasswade, Midlothian, the old name of which was Rosclyn. Roger de Rosclyn witnessed a Peeblesshire charter of 1214–49 (REG., p. 128). Henry de Roskelyn witnessed inspeximus of a charter by Alexander III in 1261 (Bain, I, 2276), and in 1279 resigned the lands of Roskelyn and Cattekon into the king's hands (Neubotle, p. 290). Sir Thomas of Roslyne, a knight in the service of Edward I, is the first recorded as buried in the churchyard of Dunnottar Castle, 1336 (SHR., II, p. 404; ER., I, p. cxlvii).

ROSS. (1) The first record of this surname in Scotland is in Ayrshire, a considerable portion of the northern part of which in the twelfth century was held by a family of Ros or Ross, that came from Yorkshire. Godfrey de Ros, a vassal of the de Morevilles, obtained from Richard de Moreville the lands of Stewarton in Cunningham (Chalmers I, p. 505). James de Ros, Reginald de Ros, and Peter de Ros appear about the same time as vassals of Richard de Moreville and as witnesses in his charters. Godfrey de Ros witnessed de Moreville's charter of Gillemoristun, "que antiquitus uocabatur peniacob" to Edulfus filius Utredi, a. 1189 (REG., p. 39). Sir Godfrey de Rose, Arthur de Ross, and Fergus de Rosse witnessed an agreement between the burgesses of Irvine and Brice of Eglunstone, 1205 (Irvine, I, p. 3). Several of the name rendered homage, 1296 (Bain, II). Godfrey de Roos in 1363 had a gift for life of the forfeited lands of Sir John Maxwell and of Bernard of Howdene for his services to England (Bain, IV, 88). Robert de Rooss was charter witness in Perth, 1409 (REB., I, 26), Donaldus de Ross witnessed a notarial instrument, 1413 (Pollok, I, p. 146), and John Roosse (Rosse, Roos) of Montgrenane was one of the conservators of the three years truce, 1484–86 (Bain, IV, 1505, 1520, 1521). (2) In the north the surname is derived from the district of Ross. Malcolm, earl of Ross, c. 1150, was of the Gaelic family of O'Beolán. "There never was an earl who bore the surname of Ross, but when the title passed to descendants in the female line, the lairds of Balnagown assumed the name as male representatives of the earls" (Sc. Ant., IV, p. 1). Alexander Ross of Balnagown,

Master William Ross, and William Ross were among those killed in the battle of Aldecharwis, 1486 (Kalendar of Ferne). (3) A descriptive name, from ME. rous(e<OF. rous, red, or red-haired. There was a dispute in 1306 concerning the lands of John 'le Rous' of Macfothel (Bain, II, p. 501). Stevin the Ros was charter witness, 1455 (Scon, 217), and John the Rosse, baxter in Aberdeen, was forbidden to bear arms, 1484 (CRA., p. 40). John Ross (1726–1800), merchant and U. S. Revolutionary patriot, was born in Tain.

ROSSACH. John Rossach held land in Inuernys, 1361 (REM., p. 305). Probably G. Rosach, a Ross-shire man.

ROSSEDAL. Of territorial origin probably from Rosedale in the North Riding of Yorkshire (in 1186, Rossedal). Two brothers of the name, Turgot de Rossedal and Guido de Rossedal, held extensive lands in the lower part of Eskdale in the reign of Malcolm IV. Turgot gave to the Abbey of Jedburgh the religious house of Lidel and the church of Kirkander, and Guido, with the consent of Radulf, his son, gave 42 acres between the Esch (Esk) and Lidel where they meet, and the freedom of the water from the Moat of Lidell to the church of Lidell (RMS., I, App. I, 94). Turgot was succeeded by William de Rossedal.

ROSSIE. Of territorial origin from the lands of Rossie in Fife. The family of Rossy of that Ilk had an early settlement near Montrose as vassals of the Norman de Malherbe. Robertus de Rossyn was present at perambulation of the marches of the lands of the Abbey of Arbroath and the barony of Kynblathmund, 1219 (RAA., I, p. 163), and Thomas de Rossi, son of Robert de Rossi, had a charter of the lands of Rossi from Hugo Malherb, c. 1245 (ibid., I, p. 337). Walter de Rossy, burgess of Montrose, rendered homage, 1296 (Bain, II, p. 169, 198), and Henry Rossie had a charter of the lands of Inrony or Inyoney in the sheriffdom of Forfar from Robert I (RMS., I, App. II, 461), and Bernard Rossie or Rosse had a charter of the barony of Rossie and the lands of Inene in the same sheriffdom from Robert III (ibid., I, App. II, 1801). Johannes Rossy held land in Aberdeen, 1340 (REA., I, p. 68), John de Rossy witnessed a Brechin document in 1364 (REB., I, p. 20), and David Rossy de eodem was juror on an inquest on the lands of Ouchterlowny in 1457 (RAA., II, p. 96). The name recorded in Edinburgh, 1942.

ROSSNETT. Hugh Rossnett who witnessed a charter of Glack in 1272 (Inverurie, p. 50) is most probably Hugo de Rossneto who appears as canon of Aberdeen, c. 1294 (REA., I, p. 37). Ricardus de Rossnyet was a burgess of Aberdeen, 1317 (SCM., v, p. 11).

ROSYTH. From the lands of the same name in the parish of Inverkeithing, Fife. Sir Robert de Rossive appears in 1230 on an assize of marches in Fife (RD., 196), and is also mentioned in three other writs in the same record (113, 176, 204) between 1231 and 1253. He had two daughters only, one of whom, Mariota, married Nigel de Karrik (*Neubotle*, p. 41), and the other, Ada, married Gilbertus de Aytone (RMS., I, 70).

ROTER. From the occupation, a performer on the rote. The *rote, rota*, or *rotta* was a musical instrument of the guitar type, LL. <W. *crwth*, fiddle. Thomas Roter, the king of Scotland's minstrel, had a safe conduct from the port of Dovor with four horses in 1368 (Bain, IV, 141).

ROTHESAY. Of local origin from Rothesay in Bute. Finlay de Rothussay was a notary public in Cumnock in 1426 (RMS., II, 66).

ROTHIE. Of local origin from Rothie in the parish of Fyvie, Aberdeenshire. Alexander de Rothy in the parish of Fyvie was excommunicated in 1382 (REA., I, p. 165), and Johannes de Rothy appears in Aberdeen, 1408 (CWA., p. 315).

ROTHNEY, ROTHNIE. From Rothney (1359, Rotheneyk) in the parish of Premnay, Aberdeenshire. Three persons of this name rendered homage in 1296: (1) Anegos de Rothenek of the county of Elgin (Bain, II, p. 211), (2) William de Rotheneyk or Rothenayke (or Rothenethe) (ibid., p. 169, 195, 209), and (3) Patrick de Rotheney or Rothenayke of the county of Perth. The seal of the last bears a roebuck running, tree in background, S' *Patricii de Rothenai* (ibid., p. 169, 202, 533). Heugenius de Rothenay, juror on assize on the lands of Ledintoscach and Rotmase, 1333 (REA., I, p. 53). George Rothny or Rothnye was 'reidar' in Mar in 1570 (CAB., p. 230), and David Rothnie was tenant of Halsiewells in 1595 (RSCA., I, p. 350). Frank Alexander Rothnie from Gamrie was killed in the first Great War (*Turriff*).

ROTTENHERRING. A Mr. Rottenherring was recorded as an inhabitant of Ayr in the seventeenth century. Ewen (p. 325) has J. Rotenhering in Yorkshire, 1331.

ROUALEYN. From an old spelling of the name of the barony of Rowallan, near Kilmarnock, Ayrshire.

ROUGH. Thomas Rouche held a croft in the barony of Lesmahagow, 1348 (SCM., IV, p. 245), and Andrew Ruch was bailie of Linlithgow in 1472 (Sc. Ant., XVII, p. 119). Henry Rouch appears as procurator for the bishop of Brechin, 1519 (REB., II, 174), and John Rough, a Dominican of the monastery of Stirling, was "the first man from whom John Knox received any taste of the truth." Ewstachius Roch or Rowgh, a Fleming, had a tack of the lands of Newhaven and later was proprietor of a land in Leith, 1588 (EBR., 1578–89. p. 534, 538). David Rouche had a charter of three sixteenth parts of the vill and lands of Newbirneton, 1601 (RD., p. 497). The surname is now not uncommon in Perthshire. For origin see under ROCK.

ROUGHEAD. This surname is found as early as 1295 when Philippus dictus Rocchet is witness to a charter (*Neubotle*, p. 145). Alexander Roched was chaplain in Brechin, 1435 (REB., II, 55). In 1446 mention was made of "Schir Johne Roched beand chaiplene of ye landis of Caldhame fourty zeir and mair" (ibid., I, 106). James Ruchead was retoured heir of Thomas Rucheid, his father, in lands in the earldom of Marche, 1620 (*Retours*, Berwick, 117). Rochede 1448, Rochhead 1668, Rucheid 1666, Ruchhead 1686. There was an old family named Rocheid of Craigleith and Inverleith near Edinburgh.

ROULEY. William de Rouley of Roxburghshire rendered homage, 1296 (Bain, II, p. 214). Perhaps from Rowley, a parish in the East Riding of Yorkshire.

ROUS. From OF. *rous*, russet, red, probably referring to the complexion or hair. Duncan le Rous, burgess of Haddington, and Morice le Rous, burgess of Stirling, rendered homage in 1296 (Bain, II, p. 186, 197). Johannes Rous or Rowse was juror on inquest apud Rane, 1413, 1418 (REA., I, p. 214, 216). Rose, Rouse, Ruse.

ROUSAY, ROWSAY. From the island of the same name in Orkney. Oliver Rowsay in Stronsay in 1640 (MCM., II, p. 211). Patrick Rowsay in Rothisholm, Orkney, 1657 (*Laing*, 2502).

ROUST. See under RUST.

ROUTLEDGE, RUTLEDGE. Lower, Bardsley, and Harrison say this name is from Routledge in Cumberland, but I cannot find the place. It is not in Sedgefield's *Place-names of Cumberland and Westmorland*. The surname is more English than Scottish, though several of the name are early found north of the Border. Several early notices of the name in connec-

ROUTLEDGE, Rutledge, *continued*

tion with Hawick are given in *The Scotts of Buccleuch* (v. 2, p. 35, etc.). Symon Routlage and his son Mathew were charged with spuilzeit of certain goods in 1494 (ADC., p. 338). David Routlesche was bailie to James Douglas of Caver in 1512 (*Cavers*, p. 730). Martin de Rotheluche, a Scot, was procurator of the Scottish Nation in the University of Orleans in 1537, and again, as 'de Rotheluge,' in 1538 (SHSM., II, p. 100). Lancelot Rutlitch in Appiltrielewis, 1643 (RRM., I, p. 102). Armstrong gives the following old forms of this name: Routelych, Routleche (1516), Routlagh, Routlege (1512), Routlisch (1495), Routluge, Rowtlische, Routlug, Rowtledge, Routlugh, Rutlegs, Rouchligis, and Rowteleges (*Liddesdale*, p. 250).

ROW, Rowe. Local, from Row in Dumbartonshire. William de Rowe held land in Dunipais, c. 1200 (*Cambus.*, p. 108). Rev. John Row (1525–1580) was one of the leading Reformers and first Protestant minister in Perth. The *Hebraeae Linguae Institutiones* of Rev. John Row (1598–1672), grandson of the Reformer, was the first work in Hebrew printed in Scotland. (2) A diminutive of Rowland. Rowe Crosier in Liddesdale, 1586 (*Liddesdale*, p. xxxvi); and Rowe Denum in Lanark, 1488 (*Lanark*, p. 4).

ROWAN, Rowand. (1) from *Ruadhán*, diminutive of *Ruadh*, 'red'. (2) From the Scots pronunciation of Rolland, q.v. Thomas de Rolland (de most probably an error) was common councillor of Aberdeen, 1439 (*Guildry*, p. 186). Agnes Rowan was tenant under the bishop of Glasgow, 1511 (*Rental*), and William Rowan in Aberdeen, 1513 (CRA., p. 83), appears in 1509 as Rolland and Rowand (RAA., II, p. 383). Thomas Rowand was witness in Glasgow, 1550 (*Protocols*, I). Edward Rowane appears in Stirling, 1525 (SBR., p. 25), the daughter of Nicol Rowan had sasine, 1573 (*Pitfirrane*, 181), John Rowane was servitor to Robert Pont of Trinity College, Edinburgh, 1575 (*Soltre*, p. 137), and James Rowane was burgess freeman of Glasgow, 1595 (*Burgesses*). John Rowand (*alias* Long John) was portioner of Meiklegovan, 1692 (*Retours, Lanark*, 407). The wife of Dr. William Guild (early seventeenth century) was Catharine Rolland or Rowen (SN&Q., II, p. 139), Bethia Rouand was heir of Andrew Rouand, portioner of Meikle Govan, 1697 (*Retours, Renfrew*, 214), John Rowand is at Broomloan, 1709 (*Minutes*, p. 54), and Mr. John Rouan was minister at Parton, 1750 (*Kirkcudbright*). David Rowane, a Frenchman, engineer to the queen, 1557–8 (ER., XIX,

p. 6, 38, 85, etc.) probably derived his surname from Rouen.

ROWAT, Rowatt, Rowet. A West country surname. Reservation of a liferent was made to Katherine Rowat in Glasgow, 1554 (*Protocols*, I). John Rowett or Rowatt was member of Scots parliament for Glasgow, 1585 (*Hanna*, II, p. 511). Adam Rowat, maltman, was burgess freeman of Glasgow, 1606 (*Burgesses*). Robert Rowat is recorded in the toun of Stanehouse, 1623 (*Lanark CR.*), payment was made to Mr. Alexander Rowatt in Glasgow, 1631 (RUG., III, p. 571), and Mr. James Rowat, minister at Kilmarnock, complained that he could not get the manse, 1689 (RPC., 3. ser. XIV, p. 389). Dr. Rowett founded the institution in Glasgow bearing his name. Harrison has Rowat, Rowatt, from Fr. Rouat, a double diminutive of Rolf, Rodolf. Cf. Macrowat. The 9 shilling lands of Rowatstoune in Ayrshire are mentioned in 1668 (*Retours, Ayr*, 558).

ROWCHESTER. Symon de Ruhcestre witnessed donations by Gilbert de Vmfrauill to the Abbey of Kelso, c. 1228 (*Kelso*, 325, 326). Probably from Rowchester in the parish of Greenlaw, Berwickshire.

ROWE. See *under* ROW.

ROWET. See *under* ROWAT.

ROWSAY. See *under* ROUSAY.

ROXBURGH. From the town of the name in Roxburghshire. Sometime before 1153 Adam de Rogesburg witnessed a charter by David I in favor of Cambuskenneth Abbey (*Cambus.*, 57), and between 1163–85 Walter of Rokeburg witnessed charters by Richard, bishop of St. Andrews (RPSA., p. 179; RD., p. 58). About the same date the "terra abbacie de Munros" was granted by William the Lion to Hugh de Rokesburc, clericus regis (RAA., I, 95). This Hugh de Roxburgh was chancellor of the kingdom and bishop elect of Glasgow (*Dowden*, p. 299). He died in 1199. William of Roxburgh was cellarer of Newbattle Abbey in 1291 (*Bain*, II, 522), and John of Rokesburg was procurator for the monks of Kelso in their dispute with William Folkard in 1295 (*Kelso*, 203). William of Rokesburgh was master of the Maison Dieu (*domus Dei*) of Berwick in 1332 (*Neubotle*, 153, 155), and John Rokesburgh was charged with breaking parole in 1358 (*Bain*, IV, 25). Rokeburgh 1269, Roxbruch 1563, Roxburch 1567, Roxburg 1342.

ROY. A descriptive surname derived from the personal appearance of the first bearer, G.

ruadh, 'red' (cf. 'Rob Roy'). In 1428 we have record of a remission by James I to Donald Ruffus (i.e. *ruadh*) (*Rose*, p. 126). Moritius Roy was witness in Perth in the reign of James II (*Scon*, p. 189), and Donaldus Roye appears in Murthlac, 1550 (*Illus.*, II, p. 261). Hugh, twelfth Lord Fraser of Lovat was surnamed 'Husten Roy' (Red Hugh), from the color of his hair (*Wardlaw*, p. 155). John Roy, sheriff of Inverness *in hac parte*, 1563 (ER., XIX, p. 507). Complaint was made by Patrick Roy in Dysart, 1695 (*Dysart*, p. 55). Reid has nearly always ousted Roy as a rendering of *ruadh*. Hence Macinroy for earlier Macaneroy (1555), i.e. *M'Ian ruadh*, 'red John's son.'

ROYDS. An English surname of local origin current in Fife. Of comparatively recent introduction.

RUCHEP. John Ruchep was witness to a permit to Robert Croc and to Henry de Nes to build chapels for their private use, c. 1180 (RMP., p. 78). Rowhope in Northumberland was in 1233 spelled Ruhope.

RUCHLAW. Probably from the lands of Ruchlaw in the parish of Stenton, East Lothian. Berthin de Ruchelau witnessed the gift by Philip de Pethcox of meadowland in Pitcox to the Abbey of Melrose in the reign of Alexander II (*Melros*, p. 221-222). Timothee Rouchlaw or Ruchlaw was notary in Chirnside in 1607–18 (Craw, *Chirnside Common*, p. 14), and Thomas Rouchlaw, notary in St. Andrews diocese, 1622 (*Laing*, 1906).

RUCKBIE. See RUICKBIE.

RUDDACH. Alexander Ruddach, burgess of Aberdeen, 1591 (SCM., III, p. 155), and William Ruddocht was admitted burgess there in 1621 (NSCM., I, p. 127). Jonet Ruddauch was retoured heir of James Ruddauch, portioner in Millegin, in the lands of Millegin, etc., 1628 (*Retours*, Banff, 55). Adam and David Ruddah are recorded in 1650 (*Strathblane*, p. 122), Adam Rudoch at Mill of Innes, 1689 (*Moray*), and William Ruddoch in ffortrie, 1690 (*Banff Rec.*, p. 92). George Ruddach in Portsoy, 1742 (*Aberdeen CR.*), and a later George Ruddaich in Portsoy died in 1787 (*Fordyce*, p. 105). Cf. REDDOCH and RIDDOCH.

RUDDOCK. A surname recorded in Dumfriesshire. John Ruddack, schoolmaster at Hoddam, died in 1744. Perhaps from OE. personal name Rudd + diminutive *-ock*. Hew Roddick, miller, 1688, and five more of the name in the neighborhood (*Dumfries*). Appears in Annan in 1801 as Rodic.

RUDMAN. William Rudman witnessed a charter in Edinburgh, 1561 (*Soltre*, p. 125). Cf. RODMAN.

RUET. A surname in the parish of Arngask, may be a variant of ROWET, q.v.

RUFFUS, 'red, red-haired,' from Latin *rufus*, red. Rufus and Ruffus are common in the English *Hundred-Rolls*. Radulphus Ruffus witnessed several Angus charters by William the Lion between 1189 and 1199 (RAA., I, p. 17, 23, 26, 27; *Panmure*, II, 84). John Ruffus was shipowner and burgess of Berwick, 1224 (*Bain*, I, 883), early in the thirteenth century Eggou Ruffus made a grant to the Priory of May, and among the witnesses was Robertus Ruffus (RPSA., p. 382; *May*, 26), David Ruffum de Forfar, a charter witness in the reign of Alexander II (*Cupar-Angus*, I, p. 344), and Michael Ruffus was a Culdee of St. Andrews in 1250 (Reeves, *Culdees*, p. 232). Ricardus Ruffus was juror on an inquest made at Traqueyr, 1274 (*Bain*, II, 34), John Ruffo was burgess of Dundee, 1281 (HP., II, p. 223), and Donald Ruffo had a remission in 1427 (*Rose*, p. 126). This last may be a Latinizing of Gaelic *ruadh* (Roy).

RUGBY. William Rugby in Brechin, 1435 (REB., I, 79). Perhaps from Rugby in England.

RUICKBIE, RUCKBIE. From Rokeby in the North Riding of Yorkshire. David Rukby witnessed a charter by John Ramsay, burgess of Montrose, 1430 (REB., II, 33), and Davy Rukby, Scottish merchant, had a safe conduct into England in 1446 (*Bain*, IV, 1186). James Ruickbie, keeper of the Colterscleugh tollbar, was author of *The Way-side cottager*, Hawick, 1807.

RULE. From the lands of Rule, now included in the parish of Hobkirk, Roxburghshire. The territory in turn derives its name from the Water of Rule, an affluent of the Teviot. Between 1214 and 1249 (REG., 148), we find Alan de Rule, Richard de Rule, and Thomas de Rule appearing as witnesses to charters. Adam de Roule and Thomas de Roule, both of the county of Rokesburk, rendered homage in 1296 (*Bain*, II, p. 199, 209). Adam de Roule, c. 1300, made a grant of four acres of land in Molle to the monks of Kelso which is witnessed by Hugh de Roule and William de Roule (*Kelso*, 168). John de Roule witnessed a quitclaim by Robert de Colleuvll in 1328 (ibid., 480), and Walter de Roule, precentor in Glasgow, is mentioned between 1321 and 1333 (REG., 268, 271, 272; *Kelso*, 486; *Pap. Lett.*, II, p. 382). In 1348 Thomas Ruwell was witness in a Justiciary Court case in Dundee (RAA., II, 22), another Thomas de

RULE, *continued*

Rowle was a tenant of the Douglas in Dalfu-bill in 1376 (RHM., I, p. lvii). William of Roule or Roulle witnessed the grant of the forest of Eteryk to John Kerre in 1358 (*Roxburghe*, p. 9), and was juror on an inquisition at Roxburgh in 1361 (*Bain*, IV, 61). Thomas Roule was rector of Cambuslang in 1429 (REG., 335), and John of Roule was steward of Alexander, duke of Albany, in 1479 (*Home*, 25). Towards the end of the fifteenth century the 'de' was dropped and the name is commonly met with in the forms 'Roule' and 'Roull.' Two poets of this name are commemorated by Dunbar in his 'Lament for the Makaris' (1507-8):

"He [i.e. Death] hes tane Rowll of Aberdene,
And gentill Rowll of Corstorphyne;
Two bettir fallowis did no man sie;
Timor Mortis conturbat me."

John Rouil, afterwards Sir John Rowl, prior of Pittenweem before 1526, "was a dignitary but not an ornament of the pre-Reformation church." James Roull was a tenant of the Abbey of Kelso in 1567 (*Kelso*, p. 519), and John Rowll signed the Band of Dumfries in 1570 (RPC., XIV, p. 66). William Rewell, indweller in Brughtoun, 1671 (*Edinb. App.*).

RUMGAY, RUMGIE, RUNGAY. Surnames current in Fife, perhaps local from Rumgay, earlier Rumgally.

RUMUNDEBI. Sir John de Rumundebi witnessed a quitclaim by Roger, son of William French, of lands in Annan, a. 1245 (*Annandale*, I, p. vi, 6).

RUNCIE, RUNCY. Probably abbreviated forms of RUNCIEMAN, q.v. Runcie is one of the surnames of oldest standing in the parish of Cullen, Banffshire (*New Stat. Acct. Banffshire*, p. 331). Alexander Runcie in Briach, Aberdeen, 1786 (*Aberdeen CR.*).

RUNCIEMAN, RUNCIMAN. This name denoted an individual who had charge of the 'rouncies' or hackney-horses (LL. *runcinus*, a saddle-horse). Patrick Runsyman was indweller in Roxburghshire in 1488, and John Runsyman witnessed an instrument of sasine in 1496 (*Laing*, 217; *Home*, 27). James Runsiman and William Runsiman were tenants in Birnie, Elginshire, in 1565 (REM., p. 441), Johnne Runsyman, reidare at Une, Aberdeenshire, 1574 (RMR.). Alexander Rounseman was tenant of the marquis of Huntlie in 1600 (SCM., IV, p. 267), George Runsieman in Newlandis is in record in 1633 (SCM., III, p. 110), and David Runsiman was retoured heir of John Runsiman in Croylet in the regality of Kinross

in 1653. Alexander Runchiman, weaver in Bassiden, 1666 (*Edin. App.*). Runchyman 1751, Runshiman 1686, Runsoman 1506.

RUNEWALD. Galfridus Runeuald, son of quondam Robertus Runeuald, burgess of Aberbrothoc, 1303 (RAA., I, p. 277). Searle has this name from Förstemann.

RUSK. A surname associated with Strathearn in Perthshire. Most probably a variant of RISK, q.v.

RUSKIE, RUSKY. From the lands of Ruskie, now the name of a village in Perthshire. Maucolum de Rosky of Perth rendered homage in 1296. His seal bears a shield, 3 bars wavy, and a label of 4 points: S' *Malcolmi de Ruski* (*Bain*, II, p. 200, 532). William Ruskie, Scotsman, to be hanged for aiding Bruce, 1306 (*Bain*, II, p. 486). Margaret de Rusky had a dispensation to remain in marriage with John de Kyndeloch in 1340 (*Pap. Lett.*, II, p. 549).

RUSKIN. According to the late Dr. Alexander Carmichael there was formerly at Barraglas in Glenlonain a family of Maccalmans who had a tanning business on the bank of the river Neannt. From stripping bark from the trees for the tanning business they were known throughout the district as *na Rusgain, na Rusgairean*, "the peelers," "the bark peelers," and as *Clann Rusgain*, "the bark peeling family." They thus lost their clan name in their occupation name, like others in the Highlands (*Celt. Rev.*, II, p. 344-5). John Thomas Risken, merchant in Edinburgh, 1785, and John Rusken, 1806, are in record (Butler, *The Tron Kirk of Edinburgh*, 1906, p. 341). Weekley suggests (p. 34) that English Ruskin may have come from Rosekin, and quotes Andrew Rosekin from English *Patent Rolls*.

RUSLAND. An old Orcadian surname of local origin from Rusland in Harray. Peter Rusland had a wadset of one merk land of Kirkbuster in the parish of Orphare in 1530 to which Thome Rusland was a witness. In 1574 John Rusland, son and heir of Peter Rusland, is also in record (REO., p. 210, 211). The name has been Englished RUSSELL.

RUSSEL, RUSSELL. As this name in Scots occurs twice with 'dictus' and never with 'de' it is most probably a diminutive of *rous*, 'red,' (cf. *Dauzat*, p. 95). Chaucer (*Nonne Prestes Tale*) calls the fox 'Daun Russel' alluding to his reddish color. Walter Russell witnessed a charter by Walter filius Alani to the Abbey of Paisley, c. 1164-77 (RMP., p. 87). John, son of Robert Russel of Doncanlaw, granted these lands to the Hospital of Soltre in pure and perpetual alms between 1180-1220

(*Soltre*, p. 5). Robert Russel witnessed a composition anent the lands of Threpland, 1259 (REA., I, p. 27), and another Robert Russel of Berwickshire rendered homage in 1296 (*Bain*, II, p. 207). Andreas dictus Russell was bailie of Aberdeen, 1310 (REA., I, p. 40), William dictus Russelle is mentioned, c. 1320 (RMS., I, 26), Adam Rossel was received to the king of England's peace in 1321 (*Bain*, III, 724), and William Russell was tenant in the vill of Dalfubill, 1376 (RHM., I, p. lvii). Jerome Russell, a Greyfriar, was burned at the stake in 1539 for heresy along with John Kennedy in the High street of Glasgow. Rossell 1528, Rousel c. 1250, Rusel 1514, Russale 1537, Russall 1513, Russaule 1529, Rwsall 1521.

RUST, ROUST. A well-known Aberdeenshire surname. A monosyllabized form of *Russet* (from AF. *russet* < OF. *rousset*, red-haired). William Roust was tenant in Auchinanzie, Aberdeenshire, 1511 (REA., I, p. 363). Robert Roust, notary in Aberdeen, 1540 (ibid., II, p. 324). Alexander Roust was witness in Linlithgow, 1538 (*Johnsoun*). Philip Roust admitted burgess of Aberdeen, 1591 (NSCM., I, p. 83), George Roust, flesher there, 1680 (ROA., I, p. 239), and John Roust in Windmill Brae, 1789 (*Aberdeen CR.*). Rev. James Rust (d. 1874) was author of *Druidism exhumed*.

RUTHERFORD. This, the name of an ancient and once powerful Border family, is of territorial origin from the lands of Rutherford in the parish of Maxton, Roxburghshire. In the reigns of William the Lion and Alexander II we meet with the names of Gregory and Nicholas de Rutherford or Rutheford (*Melros*, p. 75, 76 77, etc.). In the reign of Alexander III (1249–1285) several others of the surname appear, among them being Sir Richard, lord of Rotherford (ibid., p. 295, etc.; *Kelso*; REG., 174). William de Rwthirford, a cleric, witnessed a charter by Henry de Grahame, c. 1200 (RHM., p. 3), and c. 1215 Huwe de Ruwerfort witnessed a charter of Philip de Valoniis (*Panmure*, II, 124). Nicolas de Rotherford witnessed a quitclaim by Malcolm de Constabletun and Alicia, his wife, of a carucate of Edulfistun (now Eddleston) to the Church of Glasgow in 1260 (REG., p. 176), and he also appears several times as a charter witness in the Kelso chartulary between 1270 and 1297 (*Kelso*, 174, 305, 308). He is probably the Nicholas de Rothirford, knight, who rendered homage at Montrose in 1296, in which year also Margarete la fielle Nicol de Rotherforde also rendered homage for her lands (*Bain*, II, p. 181, 207). An Aymer de Rother-

ford of the county of Roxburghe also rendered homage for his lands in the same year, as also did Mestre William de Rotherforde, persone of the church of Lillesclyve. The seal of the former bears an eagle displayed and the legend S' *Aimeri de Rotherford*, and that of the latter bears a wild bull's head cabossed, a human head between the horns, and the legend S' *Will'mi de Rothirford* (ibid., p. 199, 202, 532, 538). Eva and Margery de Rotherforde, heirs of "Monsire Nichol de Rotherforde chivaler Descose," their grandfather, petitioned for seisin of the annual rent of the mills of Doddingestone in Northumberland in 1306 (ibid., 1879). Richard de Rotherford witnessed a charter of Sirildis Saddeler, c. 1330 (*Kelso*, 491), and in 1354 William de Rotherford, dominus ejusdem, appears in the same record (496–500). William of Rotherford and Nicholas of Rothersford were jurors on an inquisition held at Roxburgh in 1361 (*Bain*, IV, 61, 62), and Sir Richard of Rotherfurde, knight, was one of the 'borowis' for the earl of Douglas's bounds on the middle march, 1398 (*Bain*, IV, 510). Richard Ritherford was admitted burgess of Aberdeen in 1411 (NSCM., I, p. 4), and George de Rutherfurde witnessed a charter of Archibald, fourth earl of Douglas, c. 1413 (*Home*, 18). James Ruthyrford and Nicholas Ruthyrfurde were two of the thirty Scottish conservators of the truce between Scotland and England in 1451 (*Bain*, IV, 1239). In the edition of Samuel Rutherford's *Examen Arminianismi*, published at Utrecht in 1668, his name is transformed into Rhetorfortis, and by his continental contemporaries further changed to Retorfortis. Among the Scots settlers in Prussia in 1644 the name appears as Ritterfart. Routherfurd 1338, Rudderfoord 1654, Ruderford 1581, Ruderfourd 1530, Ruderfurd 1545, Ruderfurde 1574, Rudirfurd and Ruthyfurd 1544, Rutherfurd 1436, Ruyerfurd 1589, Ruyrfuird 1592, Rwtherforde 1464, Rwtherfurd 1584, Rwthirfurde 1426, Ruddyfurd (in Inverness). Daniel Rutherford (1749–1819), scientist, discoverer of nitrogen, was born in Edinburgh. Much nonsense has been written by amateur philologists about the origin of the place name, which is simply OE. *hrȳthera ford*, cattle ford, the ford of the cattle. In OE. *hrȳther* or *hrither* has the meaning of "horned cattle."

RUTHERGLEN. From the old barony, now town, of Rutherglen in Lanarkshire. Alexander de Rutherglen was a charter witness in 1272 (RMP., p. 51), and Richard de Roglyn and John de Roglyn were canons of Dunblane in the same year (*Cambus.*, 14). Payment was made to Adam of Rosglen (? Rutherglen), a bloccar, in 1302 (*Bain*, IV, 1786), and

RUTHERGLEN, *continued*
William de Rothynglen (a papal misspelling) was student of canon law and canon of Ross in 1332 (*Pap. Lett.*, II, p. 358). The tombstone of William Ruglyn, canon of St. Andrews and master of works, who died in 1502, is figured in PSAS. (XLV, p. 307). John Ruglene or Rugling alias Tomsoun had sasine of a tenement in Brechin in 1506 (REB., II, 153), A. Rutherglen was a publisher in Glasgow in 1837, and Charles Knight Rutherglen wrote on cornmills in 1883. Ruglan 1739.

RUTHVEN. From the old barony of the name in Angus. The early pedigree of the old family is proved mainly from the chartulary of the Abbey of Scone. Four generations are evidenced in a single deed (*Scon*, 78, p. 47–48). Thor, son of Swein, witness to royal charters between 1127–50 (Lawrie, ESC., p. 72, 186), held the lands of Trauernent (Tranent), the church of which he granted to the monks of Holyrood (LSC., p. 11). Swan, son of Thor, held land in Perthshire, and between 1211 and 1214 he granted to the monks of Scone the lands of Ahednepobbel by the same limits as Robert the chaplain held them, and also a toft in Tubermore (*Scon*, 21). Swan, who seems to have been the first to assume the territorial designation of de Ruthven, also held the land of Crawford in Clydesdale with William de Lindsay as his vassal (*Neubotle*, 102, 103). Walter de Rotheuen witnessed a charter by Sir Fergus de Fedal, a. 1244 (LAC., 24) and Sir Gilbert de Rothwin (Rothewen, Rothewane, or Ruthfen) witnessed charters by Malise, earl of Stratherin, between 1247 and c. 1270 (*Inchaffray*, p. 68, 77, 85, 88). William de Rotheuen witnessed a charter by Muriel, daughter of Coneval, 1284 (LIM., xxxvi), and in 1291 rendered homage at Stirling (*Bain*, II, 508). "Their later history comprises in two generations of Earls, more romance and mystery than have fallen to the lot of any other name in the Scotch peerage" (Innes, *Sketches of early Scotch history*, p. 125). After the failure of the treasonable Ruthven or Gowrie Conspiracy of 1600 Parliament enacted "that the surname of Ruthven sall now and in all tyme cumming be extinguischit and aboleissit for euir," and further ordained that those who bear the said surname and are innocent of the crime of treason shall renounce the surname and take to themselves, their bairns and posterity any other honest and undefamed surname and to use the same in all contracts, etc. (APS., IV, p. 213). In 1641 an Act was passed making it lawful for the Ruthvens of Ballindean (Perthshire), their bairns and posterity "to enjoy and assume to themselves the surname

of Ruthven and to use it as if the Act of 1600 had never been made against them" (RPC., VI, p. 511). William Riven in Ochtergaven, 1683 (DPD., I, p. 487). John Ruthven, architect, one of the builders of High Bridge, New York City, and James Alexander Ruthven (1821–1889), scholar, traveller, and author of the battle-hymn "The flag of the free," were born of Scots parentage. Ravin 1438, Ravvn 1485, Riwan 1560, Riuuen 1671, Roduen (in Froissart), Rotheven 1476, Rothiane 1470, Rothevenne 1425, Rothuen 1478, Rothveyn 1389, Rothwen 1461, Ruthen 1646, Ruthuen 1563, Ruthyn 1435, Ruthwein 1624, Rwithtven 1558, Rwthtven 1553.

RUTLEDGE. Variant of ROUTLEDGE, q.v.

RUXTON. There were families of this name in the shires of Aberdeen and Elgin. Harrison says the name is a variant of Roxton, probably from Roxton in Hants.

RY. Rogerus de Ry, witness in Aberdeen, 1281 (REA., II, p. 279). William Rhy, merchant and councillor in Haddington, 1686 (RPC., 3. ser. XII, p. 544). Perhaps from Ry in Seine-Inférieure. There is, however, a town named Rye in Sussex from which the name may have come.

RYBURN, RAEBURN, RAYBURN, REBURN, REYBURN. From the old lands of Ryburn in the parish of Dunlop, Ayrshire. William of Raeburn witnessed a deed of resignation of lands in the barony of Drumelzier, 1331 (*Hay*, 9). Andrew de Raburn, burgess of Glasgow, 1430, and John of Raburn, witness there, 1454 (LCD., p. 178, 247). Thomas Raburn was vicar in the choir of Glasgow, 1468 (REG., 393), Elizabeth Raburn in Lanark was sued in 1488 (*Lanark*, p. 3), and John Raburn held a land and garden in Glasgow before 1494 (REG., p. 487). Robert Ryburn witnessed a Caldwell sasine, 1496 (*Caldwell*, I, p. 50), James Raburn was chosen "Abbot of vnresson" in Haddington, 1540 (Mill, *Plays*, p. 252), and Jonet Ryburne had a liferent in a back tenement in Glasgow, 1587 (*Protocols*, x). The surname early travelled north to Aberdeen, where David Riburn was admitted burgess, 1409 (NSCM., I, p. 3). John de Raburn appears there as burgess and guild brother, 1433–38 (ibid., p. 4; SCM., v, p. 42), Thomas Reburne or Ryburne was goldsmith, 1463 (CRA., p. 26), Gilbert Riburne admitted burgess, 1480, and William Raburne in 1500 (NSCM., I, p. 28, 41). Sir Thomas Raburne was chaplain in the cathedral of Dornoch, 1544 (OPS., II, p. 623). James Rayburn, bonnet-maker in Stewartoune, Ayrshire, 1705 (*Corsehill*). Sir Henry Raeburn

(1756–1823), portrait painter. Raeburn and Ryburn 1707.

RYMOUR. John Rymour, a freeholder of Berwickshire, rendered homage, 1296 (*Bain*, II, p. 212). This seems to show that Rimour was a surname and not a mere form of Rhymer. Thomas Rimor de Ercildon witness (? in *Melros*) (in *Haigs of Bemersyde*, facsim., p. 463). Henry Rymour was retoured heir of John Rymour, portioner of Kingiskettil, his father, 1601 (*Retours, Fife*, 101). Harrie Rymour is recorded in Kirkcaldie in 1643 (PBK., p. 260), Harry Raymoure was minister of Carnebie, 1649 (*Lamont*, p. 5), and David Rymour was retoured heir of David Rymour, portioner of Kettell, 1667 (*Retours, Fife*, 1020). John Rymour or Rymmor, tailor in Edinburgh, 1680 (*Edin. App.*). Raymour 1664, Rymmour 1650.

RYRIE. From (MAC)RYRIE, q.v.

RYSLAND. Of local origin from an old place of the name in Ayrshire. There is today a Rysland villa at Newton-Mearns. Patrick de Rysland witnessed instrument of sasine of lands of Mernys and Netherpollok, 1454 (*Pollok*, I, p. 176).

RYSSIE. William Rysie, burgess of Dundee, 1568 (*RPC.*, I, p. 605). Isobel Ryssie in Edinburgh, 1632 (*Edinb. Marr.*).

RYSTOUN. Sandy Rystoun, voter in Monkland, 1519 (*Simon*, 45). Local. Riston is a parish in East Riding of Yorkshire.

SABISTON. From the udal land of Sabistane in the parish of Birsay, Orkney. Henry Sabistane was retoured heir of Robert Sabistane in part of the lands, 1662 (*Retours, Orkney*, 94). John Sabiston, a Scots piper in New York, 1935.

SADDLER, SADLER, SAIDLER. From the occupation, a maker of saddles. Siridis Saddeler, wife of Michael Saddeler, burgess of Roxburgh, made a grant to the Abbey of Kelso, c. 1330 (*Kelso*, 491). Robert, called Sadler, was lord of Westirsoftelaw in 1354 (ibid., p. 302). Hugh Sellator ['sellarum artifex'], bailie of Avr in 1415, appears in the same year as Hugh Saddeler (*Ayr*, p. 9, 11). John Sadlare was owner of a tenement in Edinburgh in 1425 (RMS., II, 23), and Thomas Sadlare held a land in Irvine in 1426 (*Irvine*, I, p. 130). John Sadillar and Hugh Sadillar were witnesses to a notarial instrument in 1429 (*Cambus.*, 90), Robert Sadelare is recorded as burgess of Perth in 1488 (*Methven*, p. 29), John Sadillare was a witness in Brechin in 1497 (REB., II, p. 143), Nicol Sadillar was a witness in Linlithgow in 1533 (*Johnsoun*), Marion

Sadler in Lauder Walkmylne, 1635 (*Lauder*). SELLAR has the same meaning from a different source. Sadeler 1430, Sadillere 1391, Sadlar 1431, Saidlar 1532, Saidlare 1508.

SAGE. James Sage had precept of remission in 1536 (RSS., II, 2002). John Sage (1652–1711), Episcopal divine, was born in Creich, Fife. Explained as "wise, learned."

SAHER. An early de Quincy name. Found written Secher, Seyer, Saier, and Sair, it is a corruption of Saire, the name of a hermit saint in the diocese of Rouen, whose cult was popular among the Norman nobility. In LSC. spelled Seier, Seiher, and Saberus (for Saherus).

SAIDLER. See under SADDLER.

ST. EDMUND. Walterus de Sancto Edmundo witnessed a charter by Swan filius Thori, c. 1211–14, and with his son, Henry, was again a witness in 1219 (*Scon*, p. 18, 52).

ST. GERMAIN. Probably from St. Germains, East Lothian, an establishment of the Knights Hospitallers, founded in the twelfth century. Robert de St. German witnessed gift by Philip de Mubray to the monks of Dunfermline, 1202–14 (RD., p. 95). Robertus de Sancto Germano clericus Willelmi regis, 1211–14 (RAA., I, p. 8).

ST. MARTIN. "St. Martin, the military saint of France," says Lower, "was greatly honoured in Normandy, no less than twenty-five places bearing his name being given in the Itinéraire de la Norm." Alexander de St. Martin was a vassal of Countess Ada, mother of William the Lion, in her dower lands of Haddington, and appears as a witness in three of her charters (RPSA., p. 207–209). In an undated charter King David I granted him Alstanefurde and the land which Arkil held by the boundaries between Hadingtoun and Alstanefurd, to be held of the king by the service of half a knight (*Lawrie*, p. 149–150). Some time later he received a charter of the same lands from Countess Ada (*Laing*, 2): "Ada the Countess, mother of the King of Scots, grants to Alexander de St. Martin, the lands of Elstaneford, by these same marches by which King David gave the same Elstaneford to him. She, moreover, gave Barowe, Donecaneslaye, Bangelave, and that land which Uhtred son of Gilise held, and that land which is on the east side of Seton, by those marches by which her men walked the lands and delivered them to him: also the site of his mill on the Tyne, and one carucate of land in Carelsira, to wit, in Petollin, and one full toft in Hadintun, and

ST. MARTIN, *continued*

another toft in Carel, all to be held in fee and heritage for the service of one knight, with sake and soke, tol and theam, infandthef and other liberties." He also witnessed the charter by King David granting lands to Walter de Riddale, c. 1150 (*Lawrie*, p. 179–180), and an undated charter by Countess Ada granting a toft in her burgh of Haddingtona (RD., 152). Alexander de St. Martin left a daughter, Ada, who granted half a mark annually to the Abbey of Holyrood from the rent of her mill at Alstanesford (LSC., p. 26). His brother Adulf accidentally killed Malcolm de More-ville when hunting, and the land of Langlaw was given to the Abbey of Dryburgh in reconciliation (*Dryburgh*, p. 68, 69). Magister Alexander de St. Martin was a prominent member of the chapter of St. Andrews in the beginning of the thirteenth century, and witnessed a confirmation by Johannes de Morham relating to the church of Pannebrid, c. 1219–46 (RAA., I, p. 20).

ST. MICHAEL.
Robert de St. Michael, probably a vassal of the earls of Dunbar, was one of the witnesses to the grant of Dundas to Helias, son of Huctred (*Nat. MSS.*, I). William de S. Michael who had a toft in Munros from King William the Lion (LAC., p. 40), witnessed Eschina de London's gift of the church of Molle to the Abbey of Kelso in 1185 (*Kelso*, 146), and c. 1200 he witnessed the grant of the churches of Camsy and Altermunin to the same house (ibid., 226), and the gift of Balnebucth to Newbattle (*Neubotle*, 7). David de St. Michaele granted his father's toft in Munros to the Abbey of Lundors (LAC., p. 40). Roger de St. Michale settled in the Mearns, probably under a grant from William the Lion, and gave to the monks of Arbroath, in pure alms, the lands of Mundurnachin (RAA., I, 54). He was succeeded in the lands by his nephew, Johannes de S. Michaele, who confirmed the grant of his uncle Roger (ibid., I, p. 55), and witnessed a charter by Richard Lupellus, dominus de Hawic, c. 1183 (RPSA., p. 262). Walter de St. Michaele held land in Brancheulla (Branxholm) in 1183 (ibid., p. 261), and William de St. Michael witnessed a quitclaim by Richard de Bancori of the whole land of Loyerwode (i.e. Locharwood), c. 1214–19 (*Bain*, I, 1684). John de S. Michael rendered homage at Elgin in 1296. His seal is vesica-shaped, in two compartments. In the upper S. Michael, armed with lance and shield, slaying the dragon; in the lower, a mounted man with hawk (?) on wrist, addressed by a figure on foot (perhaps the prophet Balaam and the angel: S' *Johanis de Sco Michaele* (*Bain*, II,

796). A later John de Sancto Michaele, procurator-fiscal of the king in 1427, may be the John de St. Mychaele who was appointed legal procurator of the Abbey of Kelso at courts of Edinburgh and elsewhere in 1435 (HP., II, p. 161; *Kelso*, 528). The old family of the name seems to have ended in an heiress who was married to Henry Kerr, sheriff of Roxburghshire, in 1359.

ST. PHILIBERT.
Thomas de St. Philibert held the lands of Cullelaw in the parish of Aberdour, Fife, 1277 (*Inchcolm*, p. 29). The great Anglo-Norman family of this name derived from one or other of the four parishes of this name in Normandy.

ST. QUINTIN.
A surname recorded in Ross-shire. St.-Quentin is a city in the department of Aisne, France. A Hugh de St. Quintin appears as tenant *in capite* in the counties of Dorset and Essex (DB.).

SALCHOP.
Local. There is a Sauchope near Crail, Fife. Nicholas de Salchop, burgess of Aberdeen, 1317 (SCM., V, p. 10). Thomas de Salchop was chancellor of the same burgh in 1340 (REA., I, p. 40). de Salcop 1333. The *l* is silent.

SALMON, SALMOND.
Salamone was an old Scots spelling of Solomon, a once popular forename, and Salmonde (pron. Salmon) is an old surname in Perthshire still existing. The *d* is excrescent. Salomon, chaplain of the bishop of Glasgow, was present *in curia regis* at Roxburgh, 1159 (*Annals*, p. 40). John Sawmond was tenant of the mill of Drwmys, 1494 (*Cupar-Angus*, I, p. 243). Rankinus Salmone, witness in Glasgow, 1504 (*Simon*, 111). George Salmont is recorded in Linlithgow, 1532 (*Johnsoun*). James Salmond was a canon of Aberdeen, 1546 (LSC., p. 266). William Salmond or Salmound was subdean of Holy Trinity, Edinburgh, 1544, and prebendary there, 1565 (*Soltre*, p. 126, 222). Robert Salmonde possessed a tenement in Glasgow, 1553 (*Protocols*, I). Marion Salmond was murdered in Dundee, 1562 (ER., XIX, p. 497), and John Salmain is recorded in Newtoun, 1688 (*Dunkeld*). John Salmond, burgess of Perth, 1584 (*Poltalloch Writs*, p. 185).

SALMONSON,
'son of SALMON,' q.v. Garth Salmonson in Ulstain Zell, 1648 (*Shetland*).

SALTER.
From the occupation, OE. *sealtere*, *saltere*, a dealer in salt (Klump, *Die altenglischen Handwerkernamen*, p. 67). An old surname in the joint parish of Larbert and Dunipace. Richard Salter held a land in Musselburgh in 1437 (*Soltre*, p. 52), and Robe Salter appears in Stirling in 1524 (SBR., p. 20).

SALTON. From Salton in East Lothian. William de Saulton of Linlithgow was one of those appointed to treat for the ransom of David II in 1357 (CDE., p. 20). John Saltoun and James Saltoun were burgesses of Linlithgow in 1536 (*Johnsoun*), Henry Saultoun, baker in Linlithqw, 1547 (*Binns*, 41), James Saltoune was merchant burgis of Edinburghe in 1657 (*Retours, Linlithgow*, 195), and Harie Saltoun, servitor to the widow Hanna, was released from the Canongate Tolbooth, Edinburgh, in 1683 (BOEC., VIII, p. 145).

SALVESEN. A Norwegian surname of recent introduction into Scotland. The Rt. Hon. Edward Theodore Salvesen, Lord Salvesen, born 1857, son of late Christian Salvesen, shipowner, Leith, died in Edinburgh, 1942.

SAMMOK. Adam Sammok of Trebrun, of Berwickshire, rendered homage in 1296 (*Bain*, II, p. 207).

SAMMOKSON, 'son of SAMMOK,' q.v. Aleyn Sammoksone of Berwickshire rendered homage, 1296 (*Bain*, II, p. 207).

SAMSON. A Biblical name among the Anglo-Saxons and the Normans, from Hebrew *Shimshōn*, in the Vulgate *Samson*, and in the Septuagint *Sampson*. A very rare name in Scotland. Samson was the first known bishop of Dunkeld, c. 1150–c. 1178 (*Dowden*, p. 173). In a document cited in RMS. (II, 1791) his name is spelled Sonson. Laurence Samson was witness in Lanarkshire, 1513 (*Ros*, 41), and Nicolas Samson is recorded in Chirnsyde, 1668 (*Lauder*).

SAMUEL. A personal name from Hebrew *Shemū'el*, probably meaning 'name of God.' "Not always Jewish. There are many Samuels of English descent" (*Bardsley*). Isaac filius Samuel, a charter witness at Scone, c. 1200 (*Scon*, 125). George Samuel, burgess of Edinburgh, 1699 (*Inquis.*, 8106). Samuel, for some unknown reason, is used as an Englishing of the Norse-Gaelic name Somerled.

SAND. Perhaps local. Archibald Sande in Dirleton cited 1566 (RPC., I, p. 444).

SANDALL. John de Sandall or de Sandele, who appears as Camerarius Scocie, c. 1361 (*Dryburgh*, p. 229, 230), was an Englishman. The name comes from Sandal, now the parish of Sandal Magna in Yorkshire.

SANDEMAN. The first of the name of whom we have any authentic record is David Sandeman who lived in Alyth, Perthshire, where he was married in 1628. David Sandeman was provost of Perth, 1735–63. William Sandeman in Faulds of Banff, recorded in the parish of Alyth, 1785 (*Dunkeld*). From the Rev. Robert Sandeman (1718–71) the sect of Sandemanians derive their name. The first of the name may have been an incomer from Denmark. In Jutland the *sandemaend* (*sandemand*, sing.) 'men of truth,' were a constant institution, and had in the local parliament to swear about murders, assaults, rapes, and the like (*Prof. Alexander Bugge*).

SANDERS, SAUNDERS. A popular abbreviation of ALEXANDER, q.v. Alex. Sanderis was tenant of Nether Murtoun, 1479 (*Cupar-Angus*, I, p. 230), John Sandris was witness at Innermeth, 1546 (*Rollok*, 41), Thomas Sanderis or Sandirris held land in Glasgow, 1552–55 (*Protocols*, I), William Sanders had a lease of land in Mains of Petfirran, 1557 (*Pitfirrane*, 139), and James Sanderis was admitted burgess of Aberdeen, 1607 (NSCM., I, p. 104). James Sanderis, reider, was admitted burgess and guild brother of Glasgow, 1630, "for service done and to be done and to gyve him the better curage heirefter" (*Burgesses*), and Robert Sanderis was retoured heir of Alexander Winchester, burgess of Banff, 1662 (*Retours, Banff*, 109). William Saunders (1822–1900), horticulturist and landscape gardener, born in St. Andrews, shortly after the battle of Gettysburg was commissioned to lay out the national cemetery on the field of battle. As forename: Saundris of Murray, i.e. Alexander of Moray, 1429 (*Bain*, IV, p. 405), Saundiris of Lawdyr, 1478 (*Home*, 24), and Sanderis Trotter 1479.

SANDERSON, SAUNDERSON, 'Alexander's son,' from the diminutive Sanders or Saunders. Johannes Sandrison was witness in Kyncardvn, 1434 (HP., IV, p. 238). John Sanderson bought the Temple lands of Lethindy in 1472 (*Athole*, p. 709). William Sanderissone and Vmfra Sanderissone were summoned in 1479 to answer to parliament for treason (APS., II, p. 129), Thomas Sandersone was burgess of Linlithgow in 1545 (*Laing*, 493), and William Sanderson was bailie of Dornoch in 1603 (OPS., II, p. 644). William Sandrissoun was minister of Tynninghame, 1574 (RMR.).

SANDESON, SANDISON, 'Sandy's son,' from Sandy or Sandie the diminutive of Alexander (e.g. Sande Fyndlosone). A family of Sandisons have been long resident in Tullich (*Jervise*, II, p. 158). Thomas Sandsond in Shetland, 1491 (*Goudie*, p. 141). Thomas Sandesoun was tenant of the bishop of Moray in 1565 (REM., p. 437), and Jacobus Sandesoune was the bishop's servitor in 1569 (ibid., p. 395), Johnne Sandesounn 'callit Laird Sandersounn' is mentioned in 1572 (CRA., p. 6), and

SANDESON, Sandison, continued

Patrick Sandesoun was tenant of the marquis of Huntlie in 1607 (SCM., IV, p. 282). Alexander Sandeson, reidare at Knokcandoch, 1574 (RMR.). Sandesone 1661, Sandesoune 1506, Sandiesoune 1647.

SANDFORD. From Sandford, now St. Fort in the parish of Forgan, Fife. William de Sandfor witnessed a charter of part of the lands of Carrecros (= Cairncross), c. 1239 (SHSM., IV, p. 316). Thomas Sandfurd was slain in 1538 (Trials, I, p. *251). The form Santford with unvoiced t due to the following f is the source of the popular etymology of the place name from a mythical St. Fort.

SANDILANDS. Of territorial origin from the lands of Sandilands in the Upper Ward of Clydesdale. These lands were held of the Douglasses in the early part of the fourteenth century. The first of the surname of whom there is any notice is James Sandilands, armiger, a vassal of William, first earl of Douglas, who obtained a grant of lands in Peeblesshire from David II in 1336, and in 1348 became possessor of the lands of Sandilands and Redmyre by charter from William, lord of Douglas (SCM., V, p. 245). By his marriage in 1353 with Eleanora, sister of the earl, he received the barony of Calder, near Edinburgh, in free marriage with her (M'Call, Mid-Calder, p. 52–53). James de Sandylandes appears as a witness in 1357 (Neubotle, p. 309), and in 1424 James Sondelond, lord of Calder, had a safe conduct into England (Bain, IV, 970). Sandeland 1477, Sandelandis 1510, Sandielandis 1608, Sandiladys 1399, Sandyland and Sandylandes 1347, Sandylandis 1374.

SANDISON. See under SANDESON.

SANDOK. James Sandoks or Sandoke had a charter of the lands of Craiglockhart and Stonypethe in the sheriffdom of Edinburgh from David II (RMS., I, App. II, 1096). Bessie Sandok in Rawynstrudyr (Ravensruther near Carstairs), 1536 (Rental). Margaret Sandok in Lanark, 1624 (Lanark CR.).

SANDS. From the lands of Sands in the parish of Tulliallan in Fife, which in 1494 were in possession of Thomas Sands and his mother, Isobel Hudson. John Sands was chaplain at Polkelly in 1487 (RMS., II, 1670). Thomas Sandis of that Ilk was tenant in the quarter lands of Lurg near Culross, 1587 (PSAS., LX, p. 83). Patrick Sands was one of the regents in the University of Edinburgh in 1589 and principal in 1620. Andrew Sandis was treasurer and master of work in Stirling in 1618 and bailie in 1624 (SBR., p. 287, 288), and John Sands of that Ilk is in record in 1638 (Stodart, II). Sandis 1629 (Inquis., 49).

SANG. Innes (p. 25) says this is a shortening of SANGSTER, q.v. John Sang was vicar of Panbride in 1566 (Jervise, I, p. 309). The surname also occurs in Aberdeenshire in the latter half of the seventeenth century. Edward Sang (1805–1890), mathematician.

SANGSTER. An Aberdeen surname, from the office of "singer," or "chorister" in the church. James Sankstar, a charter witness in Aberdeen, 1452 (REA., I, p. 273). Andrew Sancster, friar preacher in Aberdeen, 1486 (REA., II, p. 300). In the reign of James IV there is an entry of payment of ten pounds "to Willyeam Sangstare of Lythgow for a sang buke he brocht to the king" (ALHT., I, p. 114).

SANQUHAR. William de Sanchar who held land of the Abbey of Paisley in 1280 (RMP., p. 227) derived his name from Sanchar, the old name of the parish of St. Quivox, Ayrshire. Michael de Schanthare was bailie of the burgh of Are in 1365 (ER., II, p. 210). From Shanquhar, Gartly, Aberdeenshire, the following named persons most probably derived their surnames: Patricius de Sanquhare had a charter of confirmation of the land of Mure Crofte in the barony of Polgowny in 1408 (RMS., I, 907). Alexander de Sanchar was admitted burgess of Aberdeen in 1449 (NSCM., I, p. 11), and another Alexander Sanchar is mentioned there in 1493 (CRA., p. 50). Duncan Schanchar de Murcroft witnessed grant of the office of Derethy of Tarves in 1463 (RAA., II, p. 129), Thomas Sunquhar was vicar of the church of Kirkcaldy, 1475 (Cupar-Angus, I, p. 205), another Thomas Sankar was burgess of Arbroath in 1510 (RAA., II, 507), and in 1527 John Sanchar was canon of the church of Glasgow (Cambus., 142).

SAUCER, Sauser. From the occupation of 'saucer,' maker of sauces, an important occupation in the thirteenth, fourteenth, and fifteenth centuries. Du Cange defines Saucier or Saussier, "officier de cuisine chez le roi, qui a soin des sauces et des epices." In Latin documents rendered salsarius. The word in early records is sometimes misprinted sanser. Walter Salsarius purchased lampreys for William the Lion, 1214 (Annals, p. 394). Thomas Sanser (for Sauser), a clerk, witnessed a charter regarding the hostilage in Stirling, 1299 (RAA., I, p. 277). Alisaundre le Sauser, bailie and burgess of Innerkethyn, rendered homage, 1296. His seal bears a device and S' Alexandri Salsarii (Bain, II, p. 184, 185). William Sauser in Edinburgh, 1357

(CDE., 6), and Thomas Sauchar was admitted burgess of Aberdeen, 1447 (NSCM., I, p. 11).

SAUCHIE. Local. There is a Sauchie near Madderty, Crieff. Mr. Johannes Sawquhy, vicar of Wallistoun, 1505 (*Simon*, 140). Alexander Sauchy was reidare at Kennowy, 1574 (RMR.). John Sachie, indweller in Hunterstoune, 1658 (*Hunter*, p. 60).

SAUNDERS. The Scottish representative of English Sanderson. *See under* SANDERS.

SAUNDERSON. *See under* SANDERSON.

SAUTEMARAYS. Ranulph, son of Patrick Sautemarays de Popil, charter witness, c. 1318 (*James*, 11). Saumarez was Latinized *De Salso Marisco*. Probably English SALTMARSH.

SAVAGE. From OFr. *salvage*, Fr. *sauvage*, 'wild.' "La Sauvage was a sobriquet of early times, both in Normandy and England, which implied, perhaps, a roughness of manners" (*Lower*). John Sauuage, a witness in 1222 (LSC., 62). James Seavage was married in Edinburgh, 1629 (*Edinb. Marr.*), and John Savadge appears in the toun of Sanquhar, 1641 (*Dumfries*).

SAWRIGHT. From the occupation. John Sawright signed the Band of Dumfries, 1570 (RPC., XIV, p. 66).

SAWYER. From the occupation of 'sawer,' one who saws timber. The *y* is intrusive as in lawyer. Alexander Sawer was burgess of Glasgow, 1447 (LCD., p. 167), Andrew Sauer, juror on inquest at Prestwick, 1470 (*Prestwick*, p. 2), Patrick Saware was paid for sawing boards, 1510 (*Rent. Dunk.*, p. 110), and David Sawar was on assize in Carrick in 1529 (RMS., III, 849). Thomas Sawar was friar preacher in St. Andrews, 1545 (*Laing*, 494), and Alexander Sawer was retoured heir of Alexander Sawer, his grandfather, in the 6d. land of Nethirhoillhous, Ayr, 1638 (*Retours, Ayr*, 336).

SAXBY. A surname of recent importation from England. Mrs. J. M. E. Saxby (1842–1940), the Shetland authoress, was born Edmondston. There are places of this name in the counties of Lincoln and Leicester.

SCADLOCK. Probably the same as Scathlock, found in the English Hundred-Rolls (1273) as *Scatheloc*. Scadlock or Scathelok is the name in Old English ballads of a companion of Robin Hood. James Scadlock, a minor poet, was born in Paisley in 1775.

SCALEBROC. Roger de Scalebroc appears as a landed proprietor in Carrick in the reign of William the Lion. He made a grant to the nuns of North Berwick of Kirkbride de Larges (now Largs), a. 1199 (CMN., 4), and a grant of lands in Carrik to the Abbey of Melrose (*Melros*, I, p. 25). Nothing more seems known of him.

SCALES. Local. There are places of this name in Cumberland and Westmorland. Harbert Skaillis of Chubtricknaul, Dumfriesshire, 1626 (*Dumfries*). Nicolas Skailles in Chirnsyde, 1680 (*Lauder*). One of my nurses in the hospital in New York (1934) was a Miss Scales of Scots parentage.

SCALL. This surname appears frequently in Brechin records from fourteenth to sixteenth century. Nicholas Scall, witness in Brechin, 1364, and another Nicholas in 1448 (REB., I, 20, 117). Robert Skal held a land in Montrose, 1431 (ibid., II, 35). The lands of John Scall in Brechin are mentioned in 1485, and again in 1499 (ibid., II, 120, 148). Walter Skall who witnessed a bond of manrent in 1497 (SCM., IV, p. 190) may be Walter Scall who held land in Brechin in 1512 (REB., II, 197). Skeill 1529.

SCALPY. Johannes Scalpy or Schalpi, cleric of Aberdeen, 1386 (REA., I, p. 172, 173), and another of the name recorded there in 1408 (CWA., p. 312). Andrew Scalpy, citizen of Brechin, 1450 (REB., II, p. 80). There is a farm in East Fife called Skelpie.

SCAPA. From Scapa (Scalpay) in the parish of St. Ola, Orkney. Magnus Scalpay who was juror on assize in Kirkwall in 1579–80 (REO., p. 150) appears in the same year as Magnus a Scapa [which "is pure Norse: *a* = *at* was the preposition generally used in such cases; where we would say 'of '"] (ibid., p. 153). Gelis Scapay, burgess of Kirkwall in 1526 is the Gelis Scelpaye, witness to an agreement of 1534–35 (ibid., p. 219, 335). Elizabeth Scalpa occupied part of a tenement in Kirkwall in 1571 (ibid., p. 344).

SCARBOROUGH. Nicholas de Scardbrow witnessed charters by Willelmus de Hawoc, burgess of Perth, c. 1245 (*Inchaffray*, p. 63), and Roger de Scardtheburge was clericus domini regis, c. 1272 (ibid., p. 95). Robert de Scardeburgh was parson of the church of Conington in 1295 (*Bain*, II, 715). From Scarborough in Yorkshire. See also under SCARTHEBURG.

SCARLETT. Lambertus Scarlet de Anandia [Annan] gifted six pennies annually from the toft of Roger Pacok in the same town in the thirteenth century (*Register, Priory of St. Bees*, p. 354). Nicoll (or Richard) Scarlett had a

712

SCARLETT, *continued*

charter from Robert I of the lands of Forgund, Inchmertein, and Velathis (or Velachis) forfeited by John Ballioll (RMS., I, App. II, 478). From the fourteenth to the sixteenth century a family named Scarlat or Scarlet held lands in Caithness. Thomas Scarlet held the lands of Westyrclithe and Nethirgreneland there in 1377 (RMS., I, 666). Patrick Skarlet was tacksman of Negarth in Evy, Orkney, 1492 (REO., p. 411). John Skarlet was servitor of Alexander Keith, captain of the Castle of Akirgill, Caithness, 1547 (OPS., II, p. 779). Caution was found for James Skarlott in Blackruthven in 1589 (RPC., IV, p. 350), and Marion Scarlet in Watten is in record in Caithness, 1664 (*Caithness*).

SCARNILE. William Scarnile (or Scarniclet) in Tuspister, 1663 (*Caithness*), probably derived his name from Scarmclett near Halkirk, Caithness.

SCARTANE. Andro Scartane, who witnessed a disposition of half of Leirquoy in Stromness in 1554 (REO., p. 254), doubtless derived his name from Scartane in Sandwick, Orkney.

SCARTH. An Orcadian surname from Scarth in the parish of Firth. Fene (i.e. Finn or Finne) Skatht was one of the witnesses to a charter of sale in Orkney in 1482 (*Old Lore Miscellany*, IV, p. 66), and Andro Scarth was member of assize of lawting at Kirkwall in 1514 (OSR., I, p. 254). The name of Donald Scoocht, father-in-law of and agent for Elene, Marioun, and Katryne Clouchston (or Clouston) in Orkney in 1528 may be an error for Scatht or Scartht (ibid., p. 108). The name occurs several times in local records (REO., p. 84, 87, 195, 209). Skartht 1510, Scart 1686.

SCARTHEBURG. Nicholaus de Scartheburg, a charter witness in Perth in reign of Alexander II (*Scon*, p. 61). Warinus de Scharcheburgh, witness in Berwick, 1264 (*Neubotle*, p. 153). Probably from Scarborough, Yorkshire, in thirteenth and fourteenth centuries spelled Scardeburgh. See also under SCARBOROUGH.

SCATTERTY. A rare current surname probably of local origin from Scatterty near Cornhill, Banffshire.

SCHACKLOCK. This rare surname, apparently now extinct, is probably of territorial origin from a small land of the same name (Schakelok) near Stirling, which in 1445 belonged to the Abbey of Cambuskenneth (*Cambus.*, 214). The Schacklocks of Annanie were an old family in the parish of Maryton in Angus, and several individuals of the name are mentioned in the fourteenth century. The earliest occurrence of the name appears to be in 1315, in which year Agnes de Montfort granted a half davat of the land of Slains to Symon called Shakloch (HMC., 8. *Rep.*, p. 300). In 1328 Walter Shakloc granted a charter of his lands of Inieney and a third part of the town of the same name near Montrose to Henricus de Rossy (RAA., I, p. 339). This grant was confirmed by King Robert Bruce in September of the same year (ibid., p. 340). In 1367 Christian, relict of John de Montefort, made a donation of the lands of Kinneff, Slains, etc., to Symon Schaklok (RMS., I, 268). Andree Johnsoun dictus Schaklok is mentioned in 1438 (SCM., v, p. 44), and Robert Schaklok was prior of the Friars Preachers of Perth in 1460 (*Milne*, p. 42). This is also an English surname. Guppy (p. 138) records from the *Hundred Rolls* a (13 cent.) Hamo Shakeloc in Cambridgeshire. A shakelock, according to Halliwell, was a turnkey, and as Ewen says (p. 226) such a name might therefore be an occupational description, and cites (p. 319, 320) "Rog. Schakeloc, Gloucester, 1186–7" from the Pipe Roll. The 1315 reference above also points to a descriptive name.

SCHEILTHOMAS. James Scheilthomas was retoured heir of James Scheilthomas, his father, of Howburnheid in the parish of Thurso, 1672 (*Retours, Caithness*, 29). G. siol, 'seed, progeny.'

SCHEROL. Willelmus Schyroll who held land in Logy, 1380 (REA., I, p. 134) may be the William Scherol who held land in Aberdeen, 1398 (CRA., p. 372). Henry Scherale of Balnacassy is named in an Orcadian deed of 1480 (REO., p. 332).

SCHETHIN. From Shethin near Tarves, Aberdeenshire. Thomas de Schethin was admitted burgess of Aberdeen, 1465 (NSCM., I, p. 19), and Thomas Schethyne, probably the same person, held a land in Aberdeen, 1489 (REA., I, p. 322).

SCHETHRUM. Perhaps from the old lands called Sherthum (1603) or Shethume (1627) in the barony of Balgonie (*Retours, Fife*, 129, 384, 1142, etc.). Alexander Schethrum of Caskelpy (? now Skelpie) was summoned to answer a charge made against him, 1521 (SCBF., p. 208). David Schethim of Skelpsey, 1564 (RPC., I, p. 315). Alexander Schethum de Skelpye, 1581 (*Retours, Fife*, 1466). Euphemia Scherthume and Margaret Scherthume were heirs portioners of Andrew Scherthume of Caskelpie, 1621 (ibid., 319, 320). William Schethrume in Torryburn complained against his minister, 1689 (RPC., 3. ser. XIV, p. 425), and John Sethrum was licensed by the Presbytery of St. Andrews, 1700 (Scott, *Fasti*, new ed., I, p. 366).

SCHEVILE. David Schevile and Alexander Schevil witnessed precept of sasine, 1479 (*Home*, 23). Gilbert Schevil had a remission for his share in burning of Mynto, 1494 (*Trials*, I, p. 19 *). Edward Shewill appears as abbot of Newbattle Abbey, 1526 (*Neubotle*, preface, p. xxvi).

SCHOOLBRED, SCHOOLBREAD, SHOOLBRAID, SHOOLBREAD, SHOOLBRED. A surname of rare occurrence, and seemingly to be met with in Fife alone, and there mainly about Auchtermuchty. It is of local origin from "terris de Kilquhiss Wester, quarum terrae, vulgo vocatae *lie Schulbraidis* de Kilquhiss" [1608] (*Sc. Ant.*, VI, p. 40). Thomas Schoolbraids, portioner of Auchtermuchtie, was retoured heir of lands in Fife in 1661 (*Retours, Fife*, 904), and John Shoulbread or Shoolbraid was F. C. minister of Mortlach, 1846–75. Harrison's explanation, at least in so far as the Scottish surname is concerned, is nonsense. Schoolbraid 1663, Schoolbreads and Scholbreads 1664.

SCLATER, SLATER, SLATTER. From the occupation, ME. *sclater(e*, one whose trade is to lay slates on roofs of houses. Henry Sclatur was concerned in a charge of breaking the peace in Aberdeen in 1399 (CRA., p. 377). Robert Sklatare sold his tenement in Glasgow in 1430 (LCD., p. 247), John Sclater was a burgess of Arbroath in 1458 (RAA., II, p. 99), and another John Sclatar witnessed a Forfarshire obligation in 1497 (ibid., p. 308). Payment was made in 1508 to William Sclater for repairs to the roof of the church of Holy Trinity, Edinburgh, for himself and two men "for xii dais dennar and noneschankis v li" (*Soltre*, p. 162), and John Sklaitter was slater of the palace and church of Dunkeld in 1514 (*Rent. Dunk.*, p. 146). The surname appears in Shetland in 1612 and in 1616 in which year Nicoll Sclaitter or Sklaitter in Skallowaybankis appears on assize (MCM., II, p. 166; OSR., I, p. 241). William Sklaitter of Burnes was retoured heir of John Sklaitter of Burnes in 1662 (*Retours, Orkney and Shetland*, 93). Within recent years most bearers of this name in Shetland have adopted the spelling of Slater and Slatter, whereas the majority of the Orcadian bearers of the name still retain the old spelling of Sclater. Sclatter 1683, Sklaiter 1571, Sklaither 1663, Sklaitter 1609, Sklatter 1640, Skleater 1664, Skleatter 1636.

SCOBIE, SCOBBIE. Of local origin from old lands of the name in Perthshire. Andrew Scobie was bailie of Perth, 1369 (*Milne*, p. 29). Moreis Scobie in Balhaldie confessed in 1610 to practicing charming to cure 'seik folks' (Fergusson, *Alexander Hume*). Letters of horning were issued against Andrew Scobie, 1611 (*Pitfirrane*, 459). Jean Scobie, sometime brewer in Coupar-Angus, 1727 (*Dunkeld*). The Sutherland Scobies are said to be descended from Rev. William Scobie who was licensed by the Presbytery of Strathbogie, 1727, and called by the Presbytery of Dornoch, 1728 (*Fasti*, V, 7). Scobbie 1614.

SCOLLAY. A surname of Orkney and Shetland. Derived by Jacobsen from Skali, now the place name Skaill, probably Skaill in Sandwick. William Skollair was cited in 1566 to appear for contumacy (REO., p. 373), David Scola was burgess of Kirkwall in 1574, and Mathew Scolla and his brother sold land in the township of Isbister in 1595 (ibid., p. 293, 373n). James Scollay of Toftis was retoured heir of David Scollay of Tofts, his father, 1617, and Edward Scollay was retoured heir of Duncan Scollay, burgess of Kirkwall, *proavus*, in 1628 (*Retours, Orkney and Shetland*, 5, 11). Edward Skollow appears in Inverbervie, 1589, and Andrew Skolloph held land there in 1616 (*Laing*, 1184, 1749). For *ay = aw* cf. Shirlaw — -lay. Old spellings: Schola, Scollow.

SCOLOC. In the mediaeval Celtic Church the *scolocs* or *scologs* (in Latin record *clerici nativi*) were the lowest members of the order in a monastic community. They occupied the scoloc or scholar lands from which they were bound to supply clerks who could read and sing. At a later date they appear rather in the character of husbandmen or mere tenants of the church lands. In some charters the scolocs appear as bondmen. Thus in the Register of Dunfermline (p. 221) John Scoloc and Adam his son appear as 'native men' of the abbey. The name here is obviously personal or official for although it was borne by two or perhaps three generations of bondmen they neither inherited it from their forefathers nor transmitted it to their descendants. Ricard Scoloc is witness to a transaction between the prior of St. Andrews and Serlo de Lascelles concerning the lands of Rvhinche in the parish of Forgrund in 1288 (RPSA., p. 346). Gillemor Scolgo [? for Scolog] de Tarualont appears in record in 1222 (*Illus.*, II, p. 19). Riscoloc, probably for *Ri Scoloc*, appears on an assize of marches in Fife in 1230 (RD., p. 111). Donald Williamsone *alias* Skallag, mair and officer to the earl of Sutherland, is in record in 1230 (OPS., II, p. 666). Reginald of Durham in his Book of the Miracles of S. Cuthbert has a chapter (85) with the title

714

SCOLOC, *continued*

De Scholastico quodam Pictorum temerario.
It relates to a Pict of Kirkcudbright who in
1164 broke the peace of S. Cuthbert's cemetery
by a bullfight on S. Cuthbert's day, and speaks
of "clerici qui Pictorum lingua Scollofthes cog-
nominantur." Nicholson says a scribe, or else
the editor of the printed text, has misread
f as f. The word is obviously Scollostes and
so (f. 99) reads in the Bodleian мs. Fairfax
6, which was not used by the editor. The word
is borrowed from Latin apparently, however,
not from scholasticus itself, but from a Latinized form of the Greek σχολαστής (KR.,
p. 185). See also under ASKALOK.

SCONCE. A rare surname still current. Robert
Sconce was sheriff-substitute of Stirlingshire
in the early eighteenth century. Perhaps local.
Sconescroft, Sconeshauch and Scones-Lethin-
die are in Perth Retours and Sconescroft and
Scones-Hauch in Forfar Retours.

SCOON, SCOONE. Most probably derived from
the hamlet of Old Scone in the southeast of
Perthshire. Ysaac de Scone witnessed a quitclaim of the land of Drumkarauch in 1260
(RPSA., p. 346), and Symone de Scone appears
as abbot of Inchaffray in 1365 (*Inchaffray,*
p. 127). Jonne de Scone was one of the masons
who contracted for the building of five chapels
on the south side of St. Giles's parish church,
Edinburgh, in 1387 (CDE., p. 14; *Egidii,*
p. 24), and the name is also found in Edinburgh in 1648 as Skune, and in 1691 as
Scoon (*Edinb. Marr.*). Thomas Scone was tenant of the "half towun" of Balgirscho in Perthshire in 1542 (*Cupar-Angus,* п, p. 185). The
old family of de Scone were probably descendants of Malothen, vice-comes de Scone
in the reign of Alexander ɪ. William Scoon
died in Kelso, 1940.

SCORGIE. Several of this name are recorded
in Aberdeen. Perhaps a softened form of
Scorgeak recorded in Badichell, 1633 (SCM.,
ɪɪɪ, p. 90), now Scourgie. George Scorgie from
Turriff served in the first Great War (*Turriff*).

SCORTONE. Henry de Scortone and Laurence
de Scortone, both of Roxburghshire, rendered
homage, 1296 (*Bain,* ɪɪ, p. 209). Probably from
Scorton in the North Riding of Yorkshire.

SCOTCOCK. Elena Scotcock banished from
Aberdeen, 1400 (CRA., p. 379).

SCOTLAND. A surname found in the shires
of Fife and Clackmannan, and more probably
derived from Scotland (-Well) in the parish
of Portmoak, Kinross-shire, than from the national name. The references favor this view.

Richard de Scocia was clericus regis, c. 1178–
80 (RAA., ɪ, p. 12). Payment to John of
Scotland (*Descoce*), esquire of the king, was
made in 1445 (*Bain,* ɪᴠ, 1177). John Scotland
was retoured heir of Thomas Scotland in Dol-
larbeg in part of the lands of Sheardells in
the parish of Dollar in 1675 (*Retours, Clackmannan,* 42), Charles Scotland, councillor in
Burntisland, 1689 (RPC., 3. ser. xɪᴠ, p. 413),
and George Scotland of Kincardine wrote a
testimonial in favor of Lord Dundonald's coal-
tar for ships in 1784.

SCOTSMAN. Roger the Scotsman (*Scoticus*)
is mentioned in an Annandale charter of 1238
(*Bain,* ɪ, 1427).

SCOTT. A surname "commoner in Northumberland than in Scotland" (*Weekley,* p. 287).
"As Scotus as much meant a Gael as Flandrensis meant a Fleming or Galweiensis a native of
Galloway, the great Border clan of Scott must
have been settlers from beyond the Forth"
(Robertson, *Scotland under her early kings,*
ɪ, p. 290). The first of the name recorded,
Uchtred filius Scot, bears however a good
English name (Uhtred). He appears as witness
in an inquisition of Earl David, c. 1124 (REG.,
p. 7), and appears again as witness to the
foundation charter of Selkirk, c. 1120 (*Kelso,*
1). Henricus de (read 'le') Scotte witnessed
a charter by Earl David, c. 1195–8 (LAC.,
11). Magister Isaac Scotus witnessed charters
by Roger, bishop of St. Andrews, a. 1202
(RAA., ɪ, p. 102, 103). On the death of
David, earl of Huntington in 1219, "he was
succeeded by his surviving son, afterwards
known by the name of *John the Scot* Earl
of Chester" (*Hailes,* ɪ, p. 175). Ade le Scot
held a croft in the vill of Golyn, c. 1221
(*Dryburgh,* 22), and John le Escot was burgess of Berwick in 1263 (*Bain,* ɪ, 2337). Alisaundre Scot of Perthayk, Lanarkshire, Henry
le Scot, burgess of Edinburgh, John le Scot,
burgess of Haddington, Michael le Scot of
Linlithgowshire, Wautier le Scot of Peeblesshire, and Wautier le Scot of Edinburghshire,
were among those who rendered homage in
1296 (*Bain,* ɪɪ, p. 197, 199, 204, 205, 213).
Richard le Scot of Murthoxton, who also rendered homage in 1296, appears to have been
the first ancestor of the ducal house of Buccleuch of whom there is any definite record.
Michael Lescot of Fife who agreed to serve
Edward ɪ of England in foreign service in
1297 is mentioned again as Michael le Scot
(ibid., p. 243–244). The Scots became 'of
Balwearie' only by marriage with the heiress
of the estate between 1260–80 (Brown,
Michael Scot, p. 9). Michael Scot, 'the wizard,'
was most likely born somewhere in the valley
of the Tweed (ibid., p. 9). Robert dictus Scot

was bailie of the burgh of Dundee, 1348 (RAA., I, 22), and Willelmus Scot de Balweary attested the marches of Kyrknes and Louchor, 1395 (RPSA., p. 5). Sir John Scot purchased Tarvet from Alexander Inglis in 1611, and in 1612 his lands in Fife were incorporated as the barony of Scotstarvet. Most of the trade of Lithuania in the eighteenth century was in the hands of Scotsmen and in the language of the country *szātas*, the ordinary word for peddler, is derived from 'Scot' through the German *Schotte*. Scoit 1603, Scoitt 1600, Scotte 1641, Scoyt 1623.

SCOUGAL, SCOUGALL. From the lands of the same name in the parish of Tyninghame, East Lothian, now Seacliffe. The surname is still common in the parish and there was an old family of Scougal of that Ilk. Philip de Scughale witnessed a charter by Hugo de Nidin of lands in Fife, c. 1204–28 (SHSM., IV, p. 312). John de Scugall held a tenement in Stirling in 1412 (Cambus., 210), Patrick de Scugale appears as a knight of the Order of St. John of Jerusalem of Torfiching in 1465 (REA., II, p. 315), and William of Scugall, burgess of Berwick, was juror on an inquisition anent a fishing on the Tweed in 1467 (RD., p. 358). Andrew Scowgale and Thomas Scougale were burgesses of Glasgow in 1468 (LCD., p. 182), John Scowgale was sheriff of Perth in 1505 (Milne, p. 14), another John Skowgale was a brewer in Clony in 1512 (Rent. Dunk., p. 182), and Patrick Scougal, of the family of Scougal of that Ilk, was bishop of Aberdeen from 1664 to 1682. One of the charges against the duke of Albany in 1479 was the cruel slaughter of John of Scougal (Stodart, II). Schowgale 1506, Scouggall 1590, Skowgald 1615, Skowgall 1590, Skugall and Skuggall, 1664.

SCOULAR, SCOULLER. Henry Scoular witnessed a sasine in 1525 (Home, 35). George and Ralph Scouller in Huittoun, 1665 (Lauder). William Scular appears in parish of Cambusnethan, 1679 (Hanna, II, p. 252). George Scooler in Lockerbie, 1750 (Dumfries). Scoler 1651, Scowler 1616, Skoullar 1681, Skowler 1556; Schooler.

SCOULE. Perhaps from Scule, an OE. personal name (Searle). Roger Scoyle was burgess of Aberdeen, 1271 (Fraser, p. 9), and Andrea Scoule was burgess of Perth, 1432 (HP., II, p. 170). William Scowle held land there in 1444 (Milne, p. 30; Scon, p. 187), and in 1458 witnessed an instrument of sasine there (RAA., II, p. 103). Scole 1725.

SCREMERSTON. From Scremerston in Northumberland. William, son of Robert de Schrem-

eristun, made a gift of the lands of Prendergest to the Priory of Coldingham in the reign of Alexander II, and as William de Scremerston is twice recorded as a charter witness (Raine, 73, 332, 351). Adam de Scremerston held land in Berwick in 1300, and Thomas Scremerston held land in the same burgh in 1332 (Neubotle, p. 154, 155).

SCRIMGEOUR, SCRYMGEOUR. From ME. *skrymsher, skirmisour* < OF. *eskermisor*, a fencer. "The family would appear to have been of Celtic origin, and to have been settled in Fife long before they had any connection with Dundee" (HP., II, p. 125n). The first of the name is Alexander called Schyrmeschur, described as son of Colyn, son of Carun [of Cupar] who obtained in 1293 a tack or lease of the land of Torr from Thomas de Kylmaron (memorandum of an old charter quoted in Sc. Peer., III, p. 304). Three generations are here named, and the first, Carun, may be the Schir Alexander Carron mentioned by Boece. In 1298 Alexander called 'Skirmeschur' had a charter from Sir William Wallace, Guardian of the Kingdom, of certain lands near Dundee together with the office of Constable of the Castle of Dundee (Nat. MSS., intro., 14). Eight years later Alexander le Skyrmyrshour, knight, prisoner of war, was hanged at Newcastle-on-Tyne with several others by the express orders of Edward I (Bain, II, 1811). Alexander Skrymchur de Abirbrothoc, was senescallus of the Abbey of Abirbrothoc, 1387 (RAA., II, 39). Thomas Skrymshire was accused of using traitorous language in England, 1465 (Bain, IV, 1357).

Hector Boece in his Cronikls in describing how the office of Standard Bearer came to the Scrymgeours says:

"King Malcolme happinnit to cum to Monymusk, and gat advertising, that al the north partis of Scotland and the Ilis wer confiderat with thir Murrayis aganis him. * * * At last. quhen he wes cuming to Spay, and fand his ennimes of greter power than he micht resist, he espyit his baner-man, for feir of ennimes, trimbland, and not passand so pertlie forwart as he desirit. Incontinent, he pullit the baner fra him, and gaif it to Schir Alexander Carron, quhilk gat mony riche landis for that samin office. Bot his name wes turnit, efter, to Skrymgeour; of quhilk is discendit ane nobil hous, perseverand yit, in gret honour, under the samin surname." In the fifteenth chapter of the same book, Boece assigns the event to the reign of Alexander the First, "namit Alexander the Feirs, becaus he dantit thevis with singular manheid." His words here are: "Afore the king was cumin to Spay, thir conspiratouris gaderit all the power thay

SCRIMGEOUR, Scrymgeour, *continued*

micht, to resist his ouircuming. The king seing thame gaderit on this wise, send his baner man. Schir Alexander Carron, with ane cumpany of chosin men, ouir Spay: be quhais cuming, thir conspiratouris war vincust, and mony of thaim tane and punist to the deith... This Alexander Carron, be his singular vassalage, slew sindry of thir conspiratouris, with ane crukit swerd, afore the king, and was callit, thairfore, Skrimgeour; that is to say, ane scharp fechter: and, for his singular vassalage, he gat armis; in quhilkis, is ane lion rampand, with ane crukit swerd. Otheris sayis, that he was callit Skrimgeour becaus he slew ane Inglisman in singular battall. The principall of this surname is Constable of Dunde: and hes in his baner, ane crukit swerd, in maner of ane huke." Of this popular etymology of the surname the late Sir James Balfour Paul says: "Whatever the real truth of this story may be, it has a better foundation than most of the tales found in the old annals, though the incidents alleged are probably placed at too early a date by the historians" (*Sc. Peer.*, III, p. 303). Crymgeour 1634, Schirmethour and Schyrmethour 1361, Scirmechour 1358, Scremger 1715, Scremgeour 1485, Scrimigeor 1503, Scrimgeoure 1502, Scrimger 1652, Scrimiour 1423, Scrimseour 1681, Scrimzeor 1704, Scrimsour 1342, Scrymgeor 1526, Scrymgeoure 1456, Scrymger 1541, Scrymseoure 1688, Scrymsour 1616, Scrymezour 1413, Scrymsour 1684, Scrymsoure 1818, Skermechour 1384, Skirmesur 1317, Skrimagour 1411, Skrimchur 1389, Skrimechour 1371, Skrymechur 1394, Skrymezoure 1410, Skrymgeour 1587, Skrymgeoure 1490, Skrymger 1661, Skrymgior and Skrymgwr 1361, Skrymiour 1396, Skrymour 1554, Skrymsour 1396, Skrymechour 1378, Skymezour 1413.

SCRIPTURE. From the office of writer, secretary (Lat. *scriptor*). Grenton the scriptor was writer of the charter of Duncan II to the monks of St. Cuthbert of Durham, A. D. 1094 (*Nat. MSS.*, I, no. 2). Jacobus Scriptore witnessed a charter by William filius Bernardi of the lands of Rath in the territory of Kateryn or Katerlyn, c. 1206 (RAA., I, p. 45), and John Scriptore was one of the witnesses to a charter of the lands of Kylmor, 1270 (RMP., p. 138).

SCRIVENER. From the occupation, a writer, a copyist. A later form of ME. *scrivein* (<OF. *escrivain*, a scrivener) + the agental suffix *-er*. Reginald Scrivayner held land in Ayr in 1348 (*Friars Ayr*, p. 17). Cf. Scripture.

SCROGGIE, Scrogie. From Scroggie, a village in Perthshire. William Scrogy, curate, was one

of the witnesses to a charter of 1464 (REA., I, p. 287). David Scroghe was one of an inquest held in the Canongate of Edinburgh in 1561 (MCM., II, p. 289), and Alexander Scrogye was minister in Auld Aberdeen in 1533 (SCM., III, p. 93). Letters of horning were sent by Mr. John Schrogie in 1597 (*Pollok*, I, p. 188), and Robert Scroggy and William Scroggie of Aberdeenshire were among the Jacobites of the '45. Scroagie 1647, Scroggy 1630, Scroghie 1572, Schrogie 1600.

SCROGGS. From the lands of Scrogges in the barony of Stobo, Peeblesshire. Robert de Scrogges lost his life in the service of David de Lyne, and because of that his son Simon had a grant of the lands of Scrogges, c. 1208, from David de Line, and a few years later he sold the lands to Walter, bishop of Glasgow (REG., p. 73, 75, 76). Adam of Skrogges, burgess of Haddington, rendered homage in 1296 (*Bain*, II, p. 197), and the name of William del Skogges of Peeblesshire who rendered homage in the same year (ibid., p. 208) is perhaps from the same source. The surname early travelled north to Aberdeen, appearing there in the latter half of the fourteenth century. In 1398 David de Scrogis was elected common councillor of Aberdeen and in the following year he granted a charter in favor of the Carmelites (CRA., p. 374; *Friars*, p. 22). John de Scrogis, "prepositus" of Aberdeen, was a charter witness in 1436 (REA., I, p. 234), and still provost in 1449 (NSCM., I, p. 12). Alexander Scrogges was master of the ship *Nicholas* of Aberdeen in 1439 (*Bain*, IV, 1130). Scrogs 1444, Scroggis 1399.

SCRYMGEOUR. See SCRIMGEOUR.

SCULLION. An Irish name recorded in Aberdeen, from *O'Scallain*, a variant of *O'Sceallain* (*Woulfe*).

SCUNY. From Scoonie in Fife. Magister Henry Scuny was rector of Kinghorn, 1357 (*Neubotle*, p. 309).

SEATER, Seatter. An old Orcadian surname in Walls, probably derived from Setter in Stromness. Gilbert Seater, witness in Kirkwall, 1580, and Thomas Settar on assize in Harray, 1606 (REO., p. 182, 298). The name is recorded in Edinburgh, 1940.

SEATH, Seth. Surnames current in Fife. Forms of Shiach, q.v. The names have no connection with Biblical Seth. Alexander Seath died in Portobello, 1942. Saythe 1597.

SEATON. See *under* SETON.

SEELER. Probably ME. *seler*, (1) a maker of seals, an important occupation in the Middle Ages, or (2) one deputed to affix official seals to documents. Symon le Sealer rendered homage at Perth, 1291 (RR.), and Michael the Seeler of Roxburgh and Andrew le Seeler of the county of Peebles rendered homage, 1296 (*Bain*, II, p. 197, 207).

SEGGAT. Of local origin from the Vicus Maris "qui vocatur Segait" (= Seagait or Seagate) in the burgh of Abberbroth (Arbroath). Patrick de Seygat was one of the jurors on an inquisition made at Arbroath in 1452 (RAA., II, 93). He is also mentioned in the same document without the "de." In 1483 and again in 1505 we have mention of the land of Laurence Segait or Seygait in Arbroath (ibid., II, 223, 448). David Seget was bailie of Brechin in 1585 (REB., II, 220). Thomas Seggat (Latinized *Seghetus*) was author of a Latin poem in the *Delitiae Poetarum Scotorum*, Amsterdam, 1637, II, p. 490–504.

SEGGIE. Of local origin either from Seggie near Leuchars, Fife, or from Seggie in the parish of Orwell, Kinross-shire. Walter junior de Seggin witnessed a charter by Duncan de Lasceles in twelfth century (RPSA., p. 275). John of Segy had sasine of lands in Kinross, 1417 (*Pitfirrane*, 13). John Seggie in Kingorne, 1647 (PBK., p. 306).

SEIVEWRIGHT, SEIVWRIGHT. See under SIEVEWRIGHT.

SEKER. Walter filius Seker witnessed a grant to the Abbey of Kelso, c. 1200 (*Kelso*, 507). Bardsley has Seager, Seeger, Seaker, Segar, and Seger as variants of a personal name Sigar.

SELBACH. Selbach or Sealbach, an old Gaelic personal name, meaning 'rich in possessions' (*Watson* I, p. 239). The Annals of Ulster under 701 mentions the destruction of Dunollie, near Oban, the principal stronghold of the tribe of Loarn, by Selbach: 'distructio Duin Onlaigh apud Sealbach;' and in 714 its reconstruction by him: 'Dun Ollaigh construitur apud Selbacum.' Selbach claimed the chiefship of the tribe of Loarn (719) and also the kingship of Argyll (723). In 723 he relinquished his kingdom and entered the monastic life (ES., I, p. 207, 215, 219, 220).

SELBIE, SELBY. Adam de Seleby of Berwick rendered homage, 1291 (RR.). John Selby in Aberdeen, 1493 (CRA., p. 49). Probably of English origin from Selby in Yorkshire.

SELCRAIG. An Anglified form of SELKIRK, q.v.

SELDEMAN. Patrick Seldeman, one of an inquest on the lands of Hirdmanstone, 1303 (*Bain*, II, 1619).

SELELTOCH. Henry de Seleltoch, juror on inquisition on the lands of Mefth, 1262 (APS., I, p. 101; *Bain*, I, 2323). Perhaps *-toch* should be read *-coth*. A place apparently in the parish of Urquhart in Moray is spelled Sallelcot in 1237, Saltecot in 1248, and Sallescot in 1531 (REM., p. 102, 114, 424).

SELEMAN. Wdardus dictus Selyman was witness at an inquest which found that the daughters of the late Finlai de Camsi (Campsie) were the lawful heirs of deceased Dufgall, brother of Maldoven, earl of Levenax, 1371 (RMP., p. 192). Johannes Seleman held a tenement in Edinburgh, 1468 (*Neubotle*, p. 274).

SELKIRK, SELCRAIG, SELKRIG. Of local origin from the town of Selkirk. Thomas de Selghkirk rendered homage at Berwick, 1291 (RR.). Hugh de Selkyrk was a burgess of Edinburgh in 1368 and following years (RMS., I, 242), and in 1400 mention is made of a land there belonging to Peter de Selkirk (*Egidii*, p. 37). James Selkrig was town officer in Edinburgh in 1567 (MCM., II, p. 303), and another James Selkrig was a tobacco-cutter there in 1684 (BOEC., IX, p. 157). William Selkrig, maltman in Glasgow, 1580 (*Burgesses*). Jhone Selkreg was tenant in the barony of Glasgow in 1515 (*Rental*), and William Selkrigg was minister of Glenholm, 1679–90. John Silkrigg, late in Cairns of Endrigg, 1731 (*Kirkcudbright*). Celcraig 1680, Salkirk 1789.

SELKRIG. See above under SELKIRK.

SELLAR, SELLER, SELLARS. Most probably from ME. *seler*, a saddler. The name has been also derived from AF. *seler*, *celer*, OF. *celier*, one in charge of a cellar or storeroom, but the former is more likely. Colin Sellar held a land in Aberdeen in 1281 (REA., II, p. 278). A family of this name were blacksmiths in the parish of Botriphnie for 400 years (*Jervise*, II, p. 12), John Sellar was admitted burgess of Aberdeen in 1407 (NSCM., I, p. 2), Thomas Sellar was declared innocent of part in detention of King James III in Edinburgh Castle in 1482 (*Lennox*, II, p. 123), and George Sellar, baxter, was burgess of Glasgow in 1577 (*Burgesses*). The surname was common in Glasgow in the sixteenth century (*Protocols*). Patrick Sellar was bailie of Linlithgow, 1590 (*Sc. Ant.*, XI, p. 132). Seller 1549, Cellar 1646.

SELVESTER. See under SILVESTER.

SELVIELAND. From the 20 shilling land of old extent in the barony of Renfrew. The place name contains the old Gaelic personal name *Sealbhach* from which is derived the patronymic Mackelvie. Cristiane Seuelaund of Cadiou and Patrick de Selvenland of the county of Lanark rendered homage in 1296 (*Bain*, II, p. 204, 213). Late in the thirteenth century the lands which formerly belonged to Patrick de Selvinsland in Renfrew were granted to Stephen, son of Nicholas (OPS., I, p. 77), and in 1368 Hugh Seuiland, dominus terre Pomario (known later as 'The Orchard'), near Cadzow, bound himself to supply two candles of a pound each yearly to the church of Cadiou (REG., p. 282).

SEMAN. An OE. personal name (*Ewen*, p. 263). Ughtred Seman of Lanarkshire rendered homage, 1296. His seal bears the legend, S' *Vctredi filii Semanderal* (*Bain*, II, p. 186, 204).

SEMPLE. An old surname in the West of Scotland usually assumed to be a form of St. Paul, a common place name in France, but the evidence for this origin is not satisfactory. Robert de Sempill witnessed a charter by Malcolm, earl of Levenax, c. 1280 (*Levenax*, p. 83). Thomas dictus Sympil had a charter of lands in the vill and tenement of Langnodrvf (Longniddry) between 1315–21 (RMS., I, 69). Robert Sympill witnessed the donation by Walter the High Steward of the church of Largyss to the monks of Paisley, c. 1317 (RMP., p. 327), and c. 1320 he witnessed the gift of Ellenabot in Loch Lomond to Matilda de Arneth (*Levenax*, p. 83). Alexander Simpil or Simple had a house in Blantroddoks, c. 1300–20 (*Hay, 6*), and William Sympil witnessed a charter of ratification by Malcolm, fourth earl of Levenax, 1330 (*Levenax*, p. 19), and a confirmation charter by Robert the Steward, 1358 (*Inchaffray*, p. 126). Thomas Sympyl, dominus de Egliston, witnessed a Paisley charter in 1357 (RMP., p. 31), and William Simpill de Fowlwod also appears as charter witness in 1452 (ibid., p. 250). Henry Sympile had remission for his part in burning the town of Dunbertane, 1489 (*Lennox*, II, p. 132), John Simple or Simpline appears as witness in Cupar, 1511 (*Laing*, 279, 280), spulzie was committed upon John Simple of Fulvoid, 1546 (RPC., I, p. 66), and Ninian Symepile was burgess of Paislev, 1574 (*Pollok*, I, p. 308). Three individuals of this name, James, Robert, and Francis, were famous song writers in sixteenth and seventeenth centuries. Sempell 1691, Sempile 1653, Sempill 1705, Simpil 1409, Simple 1360, Sympille 1549; Sympele, Sympill, Symple.

SENIOR, i.e. 'the senior,' the elder of two persons of the same personal name. Robertus Senior in the parish of Fyvy was excommunicated in 1382 (REA., I, p. 165). Robert Senzour was admitted burgess of Aberdeen in 1475, John Senzour in 1515, and William Sengzeour in 1578 (NSCM., I, p. 25, 46, 73). Thomas Senzeor was resident in Balward (Balvaird) in 1513 (*Cambus.*, 9), John Senzeour was burgess of Aberdeen, 1522 (CRA., p. 100), and William Sinzour, witness in Edinburgh, 1541 (SCM., IV, p. 38). Archibald Senyeoure rendered to Exchequer the accounts of the burgh of Aberdeen, 1565 (ER., XIX, p. 299), Thomas Sennzeor in Lethame, 1581 (*Retours, Fife*, 1467), James Senzour, bailie of burgh of Cupar, 1690 (*Inquis.*, 7064), and John Sunzeour in Pitgornoch, Fife, is in record in 1633 (RPC., 2. ser. v, p. 94). Senzor 1542, Sonzour 1521. There is a Derbyshire estate of this name (*Guppy*).

SERGEANT. From the office. Richard de (error for 'le') Seriant, witness to a confirmation charter by Henry de Graham, c. 1200 (*Neubotle*, p. 7) may be the Richard Sergant who is witness again about the same date (*Cambus.*, 73). Andrew le Serjaunt and Nicol le Serjaunt of Linlithgow rendered homage, 1296 (*Bain*, II, p. 198), and in the same year a writ was issued to the sheriff of Edinburgh on behalf of Nicholas le Sirjaunt (ibid., II, 832). John Sergaunt was a witness in the enquiry concerning the Templars, 1309 (Wilkins, *Concilia*, p. 383).

SERLE. From Serlo, a Norman personal name. Serlo, the clerk who was present in curia regis at Roxburgh, 1159 (*Annals*, p. 40), is perhaps Serlo, clericus regis Scocie, who gave half a ploughgate of Sprouston to the Abbey of Kelso, c. 1165 (*Kelso*, 216). Serlon, incisor, held land in Perth in the reign of William the Lion (*Scon*, p. 30). Serlon the clerk was a charter witness between 1211–39 (RAA., I, p. 42, 87, 263). Serlo, talliator, charter witness in Perth, c. 1200 (LAC., 66), may be Serlo, talbator, son of William Loueprud, burgess of Perth, 1219 (*Scon*, p. 52). Serlone de Seton appears c. 1250 (RAA., I, p. 266), and Serlo of St. Andrews granted a manse at Colessy to Lindores Abbey, c. 1262 (LAC., p. 98). John Serle, burgess of Perth, rendered homage, 1296 (*Bain*, II, p. 187, 197), and Alexander Serle appears in barony of Rate, 1491 (*Scon*, p. 198).

SERVANUS. A British saint, whose work was mainly in the province of Fortriu or Strathearn. He is said to have founded a monastery at Culross in Fife, "where he lived in great veneration on account of his virtues and miracles." His period is uncertain (sixth or eighth century). His name may be compared with that of Seruan, son of Kedic (*Watson* I, p. 332). His conversation with the Devil is reported at length by Wyntoun (*Original Chronicle*, Scot. Text Soc. ed., bk. v). Gilleserf mac Rolf, a bondman *(nativus)*, was one of the witnesses in 1231 to a perambulation between the lands of the Abbey of Dunfermline and those of David Durward (RD., p. 111). See under GILLESERF.

SERVICE. There is an old Stirling family of this name which may be descended from William Servatur (or le Servetur), burgess of Stirling, who rendered homage, 1296. His seal bears Virgin and Child, S' *Will'i Servatoris* (Bain, II, p. 197, 199, 218, 552). Alisaundre Servays of Roxburghshire also rendered homage, 1296 (ibid., p. 199). Robert Service, servant to the notary of Ayr, 1662 (*Hunter*, p. 61). Dorritie Service in Stitchill, 1673 (*Stitchill*, p. 68).

SETON, SEATON. Of territorial origin, from the village of Sai, near Exmes, in Normandy. "Chalmers's assertion (*Caledonia*, I, p. 517) that Seiher de Say got land in East Lothian from David I and called it Sayton, and that his son, Alexander, took the name of de Seton, is unsupported by any evidence" (*Lawrie*, p. 424). The first Seton in Scottish record is Alexander Setone who witnessed a charter by King David I granting lands to Walter de Riddale, c. 1150 (ibid., p. 180). He also witnessed the grant by Gillemor filius Gilleconel to the church of Lesmahagow about the same period (*Kelso*, 187). Adam de Seton witnessed resignation of the lands of Warmanbie in Annandale, c. 1194–1214 (*Annandale*, I, p. 3). Alexander de Seton witnessed a confirmation charter by Alexander II to the Abbey of Kinloss, 1225 (REM., p. 459). John de Setun was witness in an Annandale charter of c. 1215–45 (*Bain*, I, 1681), and Serlone de Seton, knight, witnessed the gift of a mark of silver to the Abbey of Arbroath, c. 1250 (RAA., I, p. 266). A *History of the family of Seton during eight centuries*, by George Seton, was published in Edinburgh, 1896, in two volumes. Of this work Monsignor (afterwards Bishop) Robert Seton, in his *An Old family, or The Setons of Scotland and America*, New York, 1899, says (p. xii): "It contains some things that are important, many things that are useful, and everything that is superflous." Ceatoun 1567, Ceton 1486, Cetone 1437, Saittone 1588, Schethine 1657, Seatone 1616, Seatown 1670, Seitoune 1516, Seittone 1410, Sethun c. 1230, Setoun 1567, Setoune 1474, Setowun 1528, Setton 1328, Settone

1613, Settoun 1590, Setun 1264, Seytoun 1485, Seytoune 1556.

SEUMAS. The Gaelic spelling of James. Often incorrectly Englished Hamish, which is the English pronunciation of the vocative form (G. *Sheumais*).

SHAIRP. *See under* SHARP.

SHAKESHAW. William Schaikschaw and Finlay Schaikschaw were admitted burgesses of Glasgow, 1550 (*Protocols*, I). Fynlay Schakschaw, wobster, was burgess freeman of Glasgow in 1583 (*Burgesses*), John Schakschaw held lands in Glasgow in 1588 (*Protocols*, x), and William Schankschaw, wobster, probably a son of Fynlaw already mentioned, was admitted burgess and guild brother of Glasgow in 1619 (*Burgesses*). A phrase compound of the Shakespeare class. Schaykschaw 1551.

SHAKGOWAN. Payment was made to Alexander Schakgowine 'for gangin to Strbogie, 1584 (SCM., v, p. 56).

SHAKLE. A surname recorded in Aberdeen. As Skakel and Squakell it occurs in local records of Cullen from 1542 (*Cullen*, p. 120). John Shakell, merchant in Elgin in first quarter of the eighteenth century (*Shaw, Moray*, I, p. 116). A place name *Schakelzerdesnoke* is recorded in Northumberland in 1264, but Mawer says there is no such personal name known in OE. He compares ON. *skökull*, pole of a cart or carriage, which Vigfusson says is used as a nickname in the *Landnámabók*. Hellqvist (*Studier öfver de svenska sjönamnen*, 129) has Old Swedish *Skaeklinge*, a patronymic from Old Swed. *Skakli*, Old West Scandinavian *Skokull*.

SHAND. A rare but old surname in Scotland. "The surname of Shand seems originally to have been confined to the north-eastern counties, particularly Aberdeenshire, and in that county more especially to the districts comprising the parishes of Turriff, Forgue, Drumblade, Auchterless, Culsalmond, Fyvie, King-Edward, and Gamrie. In old times it was variously spelled Schawand, Schaand (1696), Schande, Schand (1528), and Shand... We have also Shandscross given to certain lands on the estate of Delgaty" (*Fermartyn*, p. 198–99). Magister Robert Schawnd was prebendary of Arnaldston, 1522 (RAA., II, p. 436). Probably French. "Philibert de Shaunde was created earl of Bath in 1485; but nothing is known of him except that he was a native of Brittany" (*Lower*). Baring-Gould says from Chandai in Orne (p. 265).

SHANK, SHANKS, SCHANK. Shank of that Ilk, an ancient family in Midlothian, derive their name from lands of that name there. Murdoch Shank, an immediate son of Shank of that Ilk, had charter of lands at Kinghorn, Fife, from Robert Bruce, 1319 (*Nisbet*, II, App., p. 219). Thomas Schankis witnessed a charter in the Castle of Cumnock, 1426 (RMS., II, 65), and in 1474 John de Schankis appears as charter witness in Glasgow (LCD., p. 189). Stene Schanx, witness in Lanark, 1488, appears two years later as Stene Synkis (*Lanark*, p. 5, 6), and in 1489 James Schankis had remission for his part in holding Dunbertane Castle against the king (APS., XII, p. 34; *Lennox*, II, p. 133). Ninian Schankis was a provincial prior of the Dominicans in Scotland, 1490 (RMS., II, 2056), and in 1503 there is record of payments to Rowe Shankis or Schankis (*Lanark*, p. 13, 14). Thomas Schankis was witness in 1508 (*Panmure*, II, 275), John Schankis was indweller in Lethe (Leith), 1595 (MCM., II, p. 219), and in 1599 a payment was made to William Schankis in Futtie (CRA., p. 202). Alexander Shank was burgess of Wigtown, 1712 *(Wigtown)*, and Admiral John Schank died in 1823.

SHANKILAW. Local. Alexander Shankilaw, burgess of Lanark, 1671, and other two of the name *(Lanark CR.)*.

SHANKLAND, SHANKLIN. Local. Grissell Shankiland in Cowhill, 1682 *(Dumfries)*, and William Shankiland in Galtuay, Kirkcudbright, 1689 (RPC., 3. ser. XIV, p. 741). Shankland is said to be an Ayrshire place name, but I cannot find it in the Retours. Shanklin is said to be a common name in Stirlingshire.

SHANNAN, SHANNON, SHENNAN. Ir. O'Seandán, diminutive of *sean*, old, wise. In Galloway and in Kintyre the name was formerly current as Aschennan. Gilqwhongill Aschenane was tenant in Duo Knokis, 1376 (RHM., I, p. lx). Dungall Achinyane in Wigtownshire, 1488 (RMS., II, 1769), and John Aschennan was retoured heir of Cuthbert Aschennane of Park, killed at Pinkiecleuch, 1548 (*Retours, Kirkcudbright*, 1). Robert Aschennane in Culquha, 1566 (*Laing*, 801) may be Robert Aschennane, heir of Robert Aschennane of Dunjop, 1581 (*Retours, Wigtown*, 200). Robert Aschennane, perhaps the same person, had sasine of the lands of Torhous McKie, 1582 (ER., XXI, p. 473). John Shennane was master of a family in the parish of Buittle, 1684 (RPC., 3. ser. IX, p. 570). John Shennan in record in Wester Kirkcassale, 1751 *(Kirkcudbright)*. Aschennay 1513.

SHANWELL. From the lands of Shanwell near Milnathort, Kinross-shire. John Schanwall

(Chanwell or Schanwelle) was abbot of Cupar-Angus from 1480 to 1509, and Duncane Schanwel obtained from the abbot of the same house a ferm of the lands of Schanwel in 1496 (*Cupar-Angus*, I, p. 88, 250). Magister Robert Shanvull who witnessed a precept of sasine in 1494 (*Panmure*, II, p. 259) is probably the Mr. Robert Shanwull who obtained a grant of the chaplainry of the church of Kersegrange in 1496 and appears again in 1507 as "Mr. Robert Schamvell vicar of Kyrcawdy" (*Cupar-Angus*, I, p. 250, 262). ffrater Thomas Schauvel appears as "superior" of Cupar-Angus in 1500 (REB., I, p. 220). Schanwell 1496.

SHARP, SHARPE, SHAIRP. There are few early notices of this surname. William Scharp was a tenant of the earl of Douglas in the barony of Kilbucho, 1376 (RHM., I, p. xlix; II, p. 16), Patrick Sharp in Denburn held land in 1439 (CRA., p. 6), John Scharpe was merchant and bailie of Dumfries, 1656 (*Retours, Dumfries*, 229), James Sharp (1618–1679) was archbishop of St. Andrews, and the name is found in Lanarkshire in middle of sixteenth century. Stodart (II, p. 369) adds Robert Sharp, notary public, 1433; Alexander Sharp of Strathey, Perthshire, 1454; and William Sharp, preceptor of Traileou, 1535. The old Gaelic name MACILHERAN, q.v., was Englished SHARP, perhaps from the faint assonance of *geur*, *giar* (sharp) with *ciar*-an. Schairpe 1577, Schearpe 1626; Scherpe.

SHARPER. Andrew Sharper, resident in the parish of Senneck, 1684 (RPC., 3. ser. IX, p. 569). Elspeth Sharper in Kirkcudbright, 1689 (ibid., XIV, p. 758). James Sharper in Creochs of Nether Sennick, 1720 *(Kirkcudbright)*.

SHARPRAW. Quondam Thomas Scharproo held a tenement in Dumfries before 1519, and Sir William Scharpro, a cleric, mentioned in 1561 (*Edgar*, p. 233, 239), is probably William Sharpro, minister at Tongland, 1574 (RMR.). William Scharpro, witness in Galloway, 1566 (*Laing*, 801). A charge was made against John Sharpraw in Closeburn parish in 1671 (*Just. Rec.*, II, p. 59).

SHARPSTONE. John de Sharpestone of Edinburghshire rendered homage in 1296 (*Bain*, II, p. 213).

SHAW. The Lowland surname of Shaw is of territorial origin. John de Schau witnessed the resignation of the lands of Aldhus to the monks of Paisley in 1284 (RMP., p. 65), and in the same year was witness to the gift of land in the vill of Stewardton by Godfridus de Ros to the same monks (ibid., p. 381). In 1294 William de Schaw witnessed a confirmation charter by James the Seneschal of Scotland to the church of Paisley (ibid., p. 96). Symon del Schawe, Fergus del Shawe, and William de Shawe, all three designated "of the county of Lanark," rendered homage in 1296 (Bain, II, p. 203, 206). John de Schawe was a burgess of Dundee in 1331 (HP., I, p. 225), and in 1409 there is record of a payment by the monks of Melrose to James de le Schaw (Melros, p. 535). James Schaw of Salquhi (Sauchie) witnessed a notarial attestation of the 'sponsalia' or marriage-settlement of James, eldest son and heir of the king of Scots, to the Lady Cecilia in 1474 (Bain, IV, 1417). George Schaw of Craiginbae, 1606 (Retours, Kirkcudbright, 69), and James Shau in Castletoun Miln, 1711 (Minutes, p 115). The families of this name, of south country origin, are found mainly in Kirkcudbrightshire, Ayrshire, around Greenock, and in Stirlingshire. Sha 1705.

(2) Northern Shaw (of Aberdeenshire, a branch of Clan Chattan) has nothing to do with Lowland Shaw. Shaw was adopted as being that most nearly resembling the Gaelic name in pronunciation. The first record of the name is in one of the Gaelic entries in the Book of Deer, recording "Donnachac mac Sithig toesech clenni Morgainn" (Duncan mac Sithech, toisech of Clan Morgan), in Buchan. Sithech, a Culdee of Mothel (now Muthill in Perthshire), was one of the witnesses to a charter by Symon or Symeon, bishop of Dunblane, c. 1178, to the nuns of North Berwick (CMN., 5). As Sythakh Kelede he witnessed another charter by the same bishop (Inchaffray, p. 1). Seth mac Lood, a 'native man' of the Abbey of Dunfermline, is witness in a deed of 1230, and Sithaus (in index wrongly, Sithane), son of Ewald, was a native man of the same abbey in the same century (RD., 111, 222). Sythach Macmallon, a lay thrall or bondman in Badenoch, was turned over to the possession of the bishop in 1234 (REM., p. 84). Fercardus filius Sethi, witness in an agreement also dated 1234 (ibid., p. 99), is evidently Fercardus senescallus de Badenoch of the next document, and probably the individual who gave the name Mac-an-toisich to the Mackintoshes. A charter by Alexander de Yla, earl of Ross, dated 1338, of the lands of Dalnafert and Kinrorayth (now Kinrara) reserves an acre of ground near 'le Stychan' of Dalnafert "in qua situm fuit manerium quondam Scayth filii Ferchardi" (SCM., IV, p. 125). In the Exchequer Rolls between 1455 and 1469 there are numerous references (vols. VI and VII) to three individuals designated the king's 'couriers' or 'messengers.' All three bear

the same surname, which is variously spelled Scheo, Scheho, Schetho, Schethou, Schethow, Scheoch, Schethoch, Scheok, and once wrongly de Schetho, as if of territorial origin. Elsewhere in the same volumes the name is further misspelled Macstag and Makstag, manifestly errors for Macscheo. Mention is made in 1532 "de horreis Willelmi Schetho" near Arbroath (RAA., II, 765). John Schetho, clerk of St. Andrews diocese, 1542 (Laing, 464). Thomas Schedow witnessed a tack by the abbot of Cambuskenneth, 1546 (ibid., 505), and Robert Schedo witnessed a charter by William Lundie of that Ilk, 1593 (ibid., 1260). John Schedo was witness in Falkland, 1548 (Gaw, 8). Thomas Scheoch witnessed a procuratory by Elizabeth Stuart, lady of Garnetully (Grandtully, I, p. 58). Hutcheon siache or Shaw in Rothirmurchus was fined for resetting outlawed Macgregors, 1613 (RPC., XIV, p. 630), and William Schetho, minister of Kilgour, Falkland, was deposed for drunkenness in 1635 (Fasti, II, p. 490). The name means (son of the) wolf; from * sithech (Mid. Ir. sidhach), an old Gaelic name for the animal. Without 'Mac' the name has been Englished as SHAW in Argyllshire, as SETH and SEATH in Fife, and it appears as SHIACH and SHEACH in Aberdeen and Elgin. See also under SITHECH and SYTHAG.

SHEACH. See under SHIACH.

SHEARER, SHEARAR, SHERER, SHERAR. From ME. scherare, one who dresses the pile of cloth, a shearer, in Latin charters rendered cissor or scissore. John Cissor was burgess of Dunfermline, 1316 (RD., 349), and William Scherar, bailie of Berwick, 1324 (Cambus., 39). Fremanislande in the barony of Kylbouho was leased to Ade Cissor, 1376 (RHM., I, p. 1.). Johannes Scherar was bailie and burgess of Aberdeen, 1399 (SCM., V, p. 13, 14), John Scherar was chaplain of the altar of S. Ninian in Edinburgh, 1405 (Egidii, p. 43), and Paul Scissore, burgess of Glasgow, 1417 (LCD., p. 239). Eustace Schechare or Schethare appears in 1425 as a burghal proprietor (RMS., II, 35; Soltre, p. 294). William Scherer was proprietor of a tenement in Dundee, 1427 (RMS., II, 95), and another William Sherar was burgess of Aberdeen, 1451 (REA., II, p. 297). Andro Scherare was parishioner of Kinkell, 1473 (Inverurie, p. 122), and Johannes Scherare was archdeacon of Ross, 1503 (REG., p. 506; Trials, I, p. 42 *). A family of the name appeared in Strathblane early in seventeenth century. John Scharrar was "wachman in ye castell of Stirling," 1587 (Sc. Ant., VI, p. 162), and William Cherire was resident in Stirling, 1717 (ibid., p. 88). Scharar 1589,

SHEARER, Shearar, Sherer..., *continued*
Scheirar 1485, Scheirer 1629, Scheirra 1564, Scherar 1450, Scherare 1492, Scherer 1464, Scherhar 1487, Scherrar 1447, Schyire 1550, Sharar 1597, Sharer 1686, Sherar 1435, Sherare 1597, Sherer 1612, Sherrar 1647.

SHEARGOLD. An English surname of rare occurrence. Walter Sheargold was a witness in the trial of Captain Porteous in Edinburgh, 1736. Lower has the name and says "*Shere*, or pure, gold;" Weekley (p. 266) says "*Shargold*, *Shergold*, perhaps a coin-clipper or a worker at the mint," and Bardsley explains it "Bapt. 'the son of Shergold.' Probably a form of Sargood." Elsewhere he explains Sargood as Sigurd (?). I refrain from adding one more guess.

SHEARSMITH. From the occupation, a maker of shears. Andrew Scheirsmyth was admitted burgess of Aberdeen in 1479 for his labors at S. Nicholas kirk-work (NSCM., i, p. 28).

SHEDDAN, Shedden. Surnames current in Ayrshire. Robert Shedden took the Test in Paisley, 1686 (RPC., 3. ser. xi, p. 496), and Charles Sheddan performed work for the burgh of Irvine, 1744 (*Irvine*, ii, p. 331). There is a Sheddens near Cathcart.

SHEED. Local. Margaret Scheid banished from Edinburgh, 1529 (MCM., ii, p. 89).

SHEEPHEARD. *See under* SHEPHERD.

SHEEPSHANK. Thomas Scheipschank (?) was juror on an inquest made at St. Katherine's Chapel, Bauelay, 1280 (*Bain*, iv, 1762). A correspondent in *WScot* says the name is from a place name, and one such he says is in Galloway, Sheepshank, or perhaps Sheep-hank, i.e. an enclosure for sheep. Name corrupted he says and has acquired wrong meaning.

SHEIL, Sheils. *See under* SHIEL.

SHEIRLAW. *See under* SHERLAW.

SHELLAGREEN. The land of Shellagreen (Sheelagreen, or Shellogreen), in the parish of Culsalmond, Aberdeenshire, gave name to a family in old times. Isobel Shilgreene, spouse to David Enererity, died in 1675 (*Jervise*, i, p. 89; ii, p. 325). The surname is now probably extinct.

SHENNAN, *See under* SHANNAN.

SHEPHERD, Sheppard, Shepphard, Sheepheard, Shippert. From the occupation of 'shepherd,' Latinized *pastor* in early charters. William and Walter Pastor were on inquest held at Peebles, 1262 (*Peebles*, 5). Henricus

Scyphard held land in Elgin in 1363 (REM., p. 312), and Thomas Schiphird or Scippart witnessed inventory of the estate of Sir John Erskine of Dun, 1513 (SCM., iv, p. 16, 18). In 1538 the wife of Wille Schiphird was fined for brewing (CRA., p. 157). James and William Schiphird were tenants of Innerlochthe in 1565 (REM., p. 441), and Thomas Schipperd is recorded in Litill Innerlochte, 1594 (SCM., ii, p. 122). John Schiphird was 'post' in Aberdeen in 1650 (ibid., v, p. 173), and Andrew Schippert, baxter burgess of Dundee who died in 1641 is buried in the Howff there. Gulielmus Schippert in Kynnaldie, 1643 (*Inquis. Tut.*, 657), and Jon Shepherd in Midskeith, 1662 (*Banff Rec.*, p. 21).

SHEPLEY. Perhaps a recent importation from England. There is a township of Shepley and a parish named Shipley, both in the West Riding of Yorkshire. Bardsley says both places seem originally to have been spelled Scheplay.

SHEPPARD, Shepphard. *See under* SHEPHERD.

SHERAR, Sherer. Variants of Shearer, q.v.

SHERET, Sherratt, Sherret, Sherrett, Sherit, Sherrit, Sherritt. All these forms are current in Aberdeen. A criminal charge was brought against James Sherrat in Cardross, Dumbartonshire, 1671 (*Just. Rec.*, ii, p. 59). Shortened forms of Sherwood.

SHERIFF, Sherriff, Sherriffs, Shirreff, Shirreffs, Shirrefs, Sheriffs, Shiriff. From the office of shire-reeve, from OE. *scir(ge)refa*. Robert Schirraff recorded in Aberdeen, 1398 (CRA., p. 373) is probably Robertus Schirafe, juror on inquisition there in 1400 (REA., i, p. 202). Andrew Shirrefs published his *Poems, chiefly in the Scottish dialect*, Edinburgh, 1790. Shiref 1634, Shirefe 1656, Sirreff 1688. The forms with *-s* may be genitive = Sheriff's son.

SHERLAW, Sheirlaw, Shirlaw, Shirley. Of English origin, but as here shown the name has had a long sojourn in Scotland. There are places named Shirley in Derbyshire and in Warwickshire, from either of which the name may have come. Walter de Skirlawe and his men had a safe conduct in England for a year, 1370 (*Bain*, iv, 160). Nicol Schirlaw was 'maid commoun herde' of the burgh of Lanark, 1488 (*Lanark*, p. 1). Matho Scherlaw and Alexander Scherlaw, followers of the earl of Cassilis, were respited for murder in 1526 (RSS., i, 3386), and William Schirrilaw was one of those hanged in 1570 for holding Paisley against the king and his regent (*Diur. Occ.*, p. 201). Walter Schirilaw was admitted guild brother of Glasgow, 1610 (*Burgesses*).

Janet Sherrilaw is recorded in Corro-Mylne, parish of Lesmahago, 1673 (*Lanark CR.*), and David Skierlaw appears in Eyemouth, 1792 (*Lauder*).

SHERRET, SHERRETT, SHERRIT, SHERRITT. See under SHERET.

SHERRIFF, SHERRIFFS. See under SHERIFF.

SHERWIN. Anny Scherwyn is recorded in Aberdeen, 1408 (*CWA.*, p. 314). Harrison and Weekley make this a nickname for a fleet runner, 'a shear wind.'

SHERWINGLAW. Sir Wauter de Scherwinglawe (Sherewyndelawe, or Sherwyntlawe) of Roxburghshire rendered homage, 1296, and had his lands restored to him (*Bain*, II, p. 181, 195, 211, 218). Jocetus de Scherwynlaw, knight, a charter witness, c. 1330 (*Kelso*, p. 369). Mareoun Scherynlaw in Ravynstrudir, 1531 (*Rental*).

SHERWOOD. Most probably from Sherwood, Notts, England. Thomas Schervuid was tenant in Auchlyne, 1511 (*REA.*, I, p. 363).

SHEWALTON. From Shewalton in the parish of Dundonald, Ayrshire, in 1670 (*Retours, Ayrshire*, 568) referred to as the five pound lands of old extent of Sewaltoun.

SHEWAN. A surname recorded mainly in the shires of Aberdeen and Kincardine. Mathew Sewane was admitted burgess of Aberdeen, 1444 (*NSCM.*, I, p. 9). William Sewan held land in Forfar in 1509 (*RAA.*, II, 486). John Schewine, tenant of half of part of Glenboy, c. 1520 (*Cupar-Angus*, I, p. 300), and Thomas Sewan, reidare at Farnwell, 1574 (*RMR.*). John Schewane was burgess of Dundee and David Schewane burgess of Brechin, 1589 (*REB.*, II, 227). James Schewan appears as cancellarius of Brechin in 1605, and in 1608 as bailie of Dundee (*ibid.*, II, 236, 238). Patrick or Peter Schewane was admitted burgess of Aberdeen, 1603 (*NSCM.*, I, p. 97), and Robert Shuan is in record in Edzell, 1714. Shuan is the name of the first mate of the brig *Covenant* in Stevenson's *Kidnapped*. Shewan occurs as a 'Ness' name in Shetland, and by some is mistakenly supposed to be from ON. Swein. In Shetland sasines appears the name of Adam Schewan, 1623.

SHEWANSON, 'son of SHEWAN,' q.v. Donald Schewaneson, juror on inquest at Narn, 1431 (*Rose*, p. 127). John Schewynsoun, witness in Dundrennan, 1545 (*Laing*, 497).

SHIACH, SHEACH. Surnames recorded in Aberdeen and in Elgin. From *sithech, an old Gaelic name for the wolf. See under SHAW(2).

James Schioche, merchant burgess of Perth, 1652 (*Inquis. Tut.*, 788), and Patrick Schioch, merchant there, 1711 (*DPD.*, II, p. 231). In patronymic shape we have it as Schiach M'Keich.

SHIEL, SHIELL, SHIELS, SHIELLS, SHEIL, SHEILS, SHIELD, SHIELDS. Originally a Border surname of local origin. ME. *schele*, cognate with ON. *skali*, "used first of a shepherd's summer-hut, and then a small house." Cf. Burns's "The swallow jinkin round my shiel." Thomas of le Schele was juror on an inquisition made at Traqueyr, 1274 (*Bain*, II, 34). William Schelle of the county of Edeneburk rendered homage, 1296 (*ibid.*, p. 201). Symon de Schele was dean of guild in Edinburgh, 1403, and William de Schellis, presbyter and notary public in the diocese of Glasgow, 1448 (*RD.*, p. 309). Gilbert Schell witnessed sasine of lands of Walle, 1469 (*Home*, 22), and John Scheill was citizen of Glasgow, 1527 (*LCD.*, p. 88). Andro Cheill or Cheild was tenant of land of West Scheill, 1515 (*Rental*), and Andro Scheill, tenant in barony of Glasgow in same year (*ibid.*). Alexander Sheilds or Shields (1660–1700), the Covenanter, wrote his name 'Sheils.' John Shiel died 1721 and was buried in Earlston churchyard. Robert Shiels, the amanuensis to Dr. Samuel Johnson in the compilation of his Dictionary, was born in Roxburghshire. Scheill 1661, Scheils 1552, Schelis 1557, Scheills 1686.

SHILLADY. A surname recorded in Kilbarchan, perhaps a variant of SHILLITO, an English surname of uncertain origin.

SHILLINGLAW. Of local origin from the old lands of Shillinglaw in Peeblesshire. William Shillielaw is recorded in Birkensyde in 1670 and John Shillinglaw in Thirlston Mill in 1683 (*Lauder*). William Shillilaw was shot in Tarbolton in 1685 (Thomson, *Martyr graves of Scotland*, p. 315). John Shillinglaw was tenant in Birkenside Mill before 1806 (*Heirs*, 535).

SHINIE, SHINNIE. Alexander Shinie, soapmaker, Aberdeen, 1785 (*Aberdeen CR.*).

SHIPLAW. About the middle of the thirteenth century, Gilcrist de Schopelaus witnessed the agreement between the abbot and monks of Neubotle and Alexander de Drochyl and Alicia, his wife, as to the marches between the lands of Kynggesside and the Abbey lands of Spurland (*Neubotle*, p. 26–27). In 1259 the same Gilcrist of Sipelawes affixed his seal to the inquisition made on the lands of Padevinan (*APS.*, I, p. 98). The surname is derived from the lands of Schopelaus, now Shiplaw, in the parish of Eddleston, Peeblesshire.

SHIPPERT. See under SHEPHERD.

SHIRE. Thomas Schyire held a land in Glasgow, 1550, and Ninian Schyire, witness there, 1552 (*Protocols*, I), may be Ninian Syre, citizen of Glasgow, 1588 (*Protocols*, x).

SHIRER. Most probably a variant of the old trade name of SHEARER, q.v., found in the shires of Aberdeen and Perth. A family of this name "have long been farmers in the coast district of Buchan" (AEI., p. 44).

SHIRIFF. A variant of SHERIFF, q.v.

SHIRLAW, SHIRLEY. See under SHERLAW.

SHIRRA. Shirra or sherra is the Scots pronunciation of sheriff, final f (ff) being absorbed in the preceding vowel. Cf. Turra = Turriff. Elspeth Shirra was married in Edinburgh, 1676 (*Edinb. Marr.*). Gaelic *siorra*, 'sheriff,' may have been borrowed from Lowland Scots form.

SHIRRAS, SHIRRES. The first form is very common in Aberdeen. Gaufridus Scheres served on an inquest in 1431 (*Rose*, p. 129), Coppin Scheres was a notary public in Aberdeen, 1525 (CRA., p. 113), John Scheras was dempster of court there in 1538 (ibid., p. 154), and Andrew Schiras was burgess of the town in 1591 (SCM., III, p. 155). Alexander Shires was a pistol-maker in Old Meldrum, Aberdeenshire, at the beginning of the eighteenth century. George Findlay Shirras (b. 1885), born in Aberdeen, was director of the Department of Statistics in India.

SHIRREFF, SHIRREFFS, SHIRREFS. See under SHERIFF.

SHIVAS, SHIVES, CHIVAS. Of territorial origin from the old barony of the name in the parish of Tarves, Aberdeenshire. John Sheves, 'scholar in Scotland,' had a safe conduct to study in Oxford, 1393 (*Bain*, IV, 455). Thomas apud Scyves is recorded as a tannator (tanner) in 1402 (CRA., p. 384), Andrew Schewas appears in Aberdeen, 1408 (CWA., p. 312), and a payment was made to John Seues for wine in 1453 (SCM., v, p. 48). William Scheues, 'an accomplished physician and astrologer,' ignorant of theology, coadjutor bishop of St. Andrews, became archbishop in 1477 (*Dowden*, p. 35–37). John Scheues de Kilquhouss was juror on an inquest made at Edinburgh, 1506 (RD., 499), and William Scheuez witnessed a bond of manrent in Fife, 1519 (MCM., II, p. 130). John Scheves, a follower of the earl of Cassilis, was respited for murder in 1526 (RSS., I, 3386). Bessie Schives, spouse of Robert Blinschell, 1596 (SCM., I, p. 89).

John Scives, trade burgess of Aberdeen, 1647 (ROA., I, p. 232). Mr. James Shives was professor of philosophy 'Salmurii infra regnum Galliae,' 1648 (*Inquis.*, 3432), and James Chivas, shipmaster, Fraserburgh, 1759 (*Aberdeen CR.*). Cheivies 1685, Chewis 1696, Chivish 1652, Scheauis 1640, Scheeves 1685, Schevies 1672, Schevys 1477, Schewas 1512, Schewess 1476, Schivis 1689, Schiviz 1685, Sevas 1473, Shawes 1521, Sheifas 1768; Chevis, Chives, Civis, Schevaes, Scheviz, Shevas, Sheves, Shivis, Seves, Sivis.

SHONER. Jacob Schoneir was heir of Alexander Schoneir, his brother, in part of the lands of Drone and mill of the same, 1619 (*Retours, Fife*, 286). Robert Shoner, son of Mr. James Shoner, of Caskieberrian, appears in 1659 (*Fordell*, p. 54), and James Shoner appears in Edinburgh record, 1668 (*Edin. App.*). Stodart (II, p. 107–108) says the family was of Danish origin.

SHOOLBRAID, SHOOLBRED, SHOOLBRED. See under SCHOOLBRED.

SHORESWOOD. John of Shoriswode was juror on an inquest held at Berwick-on-Tweed in 1370 (*Bain*, IV, 175). George de Schoriswode who was rector of Cultir in 1450 (LSC., 121) and a frequent witness in the king's writs, later became bishop of Brechin and chancellor of the kingdom (REB., pref. p. xi). His name appears frequently in record as Schoreswode and Schoriswode, and in the *Memorie of the Somervilles* his name is spelled Chorsewood. Dominus Johannes Schorisvode was a witness in Aberdeen in 1498 (REA., I, p. 344). James Schoriswood was a notary in Glasgow in 1525 (REG., 496), Gilbert Schorswod, mariner, was admitted burgess of Dundee in 1585, as also was John Schorswod or Schirriswod in 1592 (*Wedd.*, p. 80, 93). Robert Schorswood was retoured heir in lands in Baitscheill in the lordship of Home in 1635 (*Retours, Berwick*, 213). The name also appears in Stirling in 1717 as Shereswood, and Thomas Shoarswood was taylor burges in Edinburgh, 1734 (*Guildry*, p. 149). Schoirswood 1635, Schoriswodd 1449, Schorswood 1635, Schorysuuod 1452, Shoarswood and Shoarwood 1693, Scoriswoide 1452, Scoriswoyde 1464.

SHORT, SHORTT. Apparently a descriptive name, from the diminutive size of the original bearer or bearers, ME. *s(c)hort*. It is also sometimes used as an Englishing of GAIR, q.v. In Latin documents the name is rendered *parvus*, e.g. c. 1220 William parvus witnessed a charter by Malcolm, earl of Angus (RAA., I, p. 331). John Schort and Roger Schort were vicars ministrant "in choro Glasguensi" in 1410 (LCD., p. 237). John Parvus, 'husband,' in ville de Tullibothy, 1437 (SCM., v, p. 261). Robert Schorte, witness in Glasgow, 1552 (Protocols, I), James Schorte, bailie of Stirling, 1596 (SBR., p. 281). Anderson (Scot. Nat.) says a Dumfriesshire family named Shortt is supposed to have come originally from Holland. Alexander Short in Blackgrange was excommunicated for disobedience in Logie, 1600 (Logie, I, p. 84).

SHORTHALS. Robert Shorthals, fisherman of Scotlandwell (de fonte Scocie) bought a net to catch fish for Edward I of England in 1304 (Bain, IV, p. 459). OE. scort hals, 'snort neck.'

SHORTHORN. Patrick Shorthorn, smith, burgess of Dumbarton, 1680 (RDB.).

SHORTHOUSE. Bardsley, Harrison, and Ewen say this is a nickname from 'short hose' (stockings). John Schurthouse was tenant in Coteland in the barony of Abirdoure, Fife, in 1376 (RHM., I, p. lxiv). Thomas Schorthouss, chaplain, was witness in Inverarite, 1505 (REB., I, 222), Valter Schorthouss was witness in Dunfermline, 1532 (RD., p. 353), and William Schortes is recorded in Lethems, 1561 (Dunfermline). John Shorttus in Steilend had sasine in his favor, 1572 (Pitfirrane, 172). John Shortous is recorded in Kingorne, 1636 (PBK., p. 92), Robert Shortus in Dunfermline was accused of consulting witches, 1643 (Chalmers, Dunfermline, I, p. 436), and the name also appears in Edinburgh in 1655 as Schorthous (Edinb. Marr.). Schurtus 1449, Shortus 1565.

SHORTREED. This surname is said to occur only on the Border, generally in the neighborhood of Kelso. Several of the name served in India in a civil or military capacity. Euphan Shortreid is recorded in Selkirk, 1684 (RPC., 3. ser. x, p. 383), and William Shortreed of Colmslie in 1753 (Heirs, 307). Robert Shortreed was sheriff-substitute of Roxburghshire in beginning of nineteenth century and a great friend of Sir Walter Scott. Lower says 'probably local.' Cf. SHORTRIG.

SHORTRIG, SHORTRIDGE. A Dumfriesshire surname derived from Shortrig near Ecclefechan, Dumfriesshire. John Schortrek signed the Band of Dumfries, 1570 (RPC., XIV, p. 66), and a John Schortrig was burgess of Dumfries, 1592 (Dumfriesshire and Galloway Nat. Hist. and Ant. Soc. Trans., 3. ser. xx, p. 204). John Shortrig of Garneselloche, 1626 (Dumfries). Robert Shortrigg at Bridgend signed the Test in 1684 (RPC., 3. ser. x, p. 226), and Elizabeth

Shortrigg is recorded in Dumfries in 1689 (ibid., XIV, p. 684). Shotrick 1657. Cf. SHORTREED.

SHOTTON. Robert de Schottun witnessed a charter by Galfridus Ridel to the Abbey of Kelso, c. 1180 (Kelso, 368), and Stephen de Scothun witnessed a charter by Cecilia de Molle, c. 1200 (ibid., 148). Huwe de Shottone of Roxburghshire rendered homage in 1296 (Bain, II, p. 209). Probably from Shotton in the county of Durham, England.

SHURIE. In Orkney a contraction for SIGURDSON. Schewrie, Schewartson, and Stewartsone are all, according to the late Dr. Jakobsen, corruptions of SIGURDSON (REO., p. 142n).

SHUTTLEWORTH. This surname, recorded in Dumfriesshire, is most probably of recent introduction from England. It is of local origin from Shuttleworth in the parish of Bury, Lancashire.

SIBBALD. From (1) the OE. personal name Saebeald, 'sea-bold,' or (2) from Sigebeald, 'victoriously bold.' About 1200 Philip de Maleuille married Eva, daughter of Walter, son of Sibald (RAA., I, p. 64). Between 1203–14 Walter filius Sibaldi witnessed charters granted by Thomas de Lundin and John de Mountfort (ibid., p. 44, 47), and c. 1222 he witnessed a charter by Randulf de Strathphetham to Brechin (REB., II, 3). David Sibald who witnessed c. 1250 two charters by Duncan, earl of Carrick (CMN., 13, 14), witnessed another about the same period by Nicholas, son of Duncan, as David Sibaud (ibid., 15). Donatus Sabbaued witnessed a charter by Earl Roger de Quincy, 1246 (Nisbet, I, p. 125), and Duncanus Sibbaued perhaps the same person as Donatus Sybaldi filii Walteri had a charter of the mill of Lundin (Sibbald, Fife, 1803, p. 369). Sir Duncan Sybald in 1286 granted one stone of wax and four shillings for light to monks of Cupar-Angus (Cupar-Angus, I, p. 344). Thomas Sibalde was juror on inquest on lands of Disarde (Dysart) in 1296, and David Sibbald of Augansouthe of the county of Lanark rendered homage in same year (Bain, II, 212, 216). John Seball of Scotland had a safe conduct into England, 1377 (ibid., IV, 254). Thomas Sebalde or Sybald witnessed charters of the lands of Myrecairnie in Fife in 1386 and c. 1390 (Wemyss, II, 19, 27), and as Thomas Sibald was one of those who attested to the marches of Kyrknes and Louchor, 1395 (RPSA., p. 5). The seal of William Sibbald or Sibbett of Cambuskenneth, 1581, is mentioned by Macdonald (2466). Sebald 1440, Sibauld 1446, Sibbal 1619, Sibbauld 1542.

SIBBET. A form of SIBBALD, q.v., from the Norman French pronunciation of the name. Sir Duncan Sibaud or Sibaut appears as a witness in two charters, c. 1250 (SHR., II, p. 174). Archibald Sibbet, witness in Kirkwall, 1545, appears in following year as Arche Sypbet (REO., p. 233, 338), and Alexander Sibbot was procurator in St. Andrews, 1547 (Rollok, 28). John Sibbett was delaited for the slaughter of Archibald Ballingall in 1560 (Trials, I, p. *425). Patrick Sibbat served on an inquest in the Canongate, Edinburgh, in 1561 (MCM., II, p. 97). Sentence of forfeiture was passed against William Sibbat of that Ilk in 1571 (Diur. Occ., p. 244), and Gilbert Sibbet was admitted burgess of Aberdeen in 1575 (NSCM., I, p. 72). Isobell Sibbitt is recorded in Stand the lane in 1672 (Lauder). The surname appears frequently in the parish register of Dunfermline between 1561-1700.

SICKLINHALE. From a place in Yorkshire. William de Siclinhale witnessed a charter by Malcolm, son of Earl Duncan of Fife, to the nuns of North Berwick, a. 1199 (SHSM., IV, p. 309).

SICLING. Thomas Sicling witnessed gift of land in Cragmilor (Craigmillar) to the monks of Dunfermline, c. 1253 (RD., p. 114).

SIDEY, SYDIE. A surname recorded in Fife, Angus, Perth and Moray. Richard de Sudy witnessed the homage of Duncan, earl of Fife, to the abbot of Dunfermline, 1316 (RD., 348). Nicol Syddie was reidare at St. Bothans, 1574 (RMR.). Gasper Siddie was married in Edinburgh, 1627 (Edinb. Marr.). Charles G. Sidey was Lord Provost of Perth, 1842-48, and Dr. James Alexander Sidey, surgeon and poet in Edinburgh. Cf. SYD and SUTTIE.

SIEVEWRIGHT, SEIVEWRIGHT, SEIVWRIGHT, SIVEWRIGHT, SIVRIGHT, SIVWRIGHT. From the occupation of sieve maker (OE. sife- + wryhta). William Suffwricht witnessed an instrument of sasine in Brechin in 1512 (REB., II, p. 170), and in 1567 there is entry of a payment to Andrew Sifwricht, servitor to John Wischart of Pittarro (ER., XIX, p. 271). John Sivwright in the parish of Glass is recorded in 1716 (SCM., IV, p. 168), and George Seivwright was a member of the Huntly Company of Volunteers in 1798 (Will, p. 19). Seifvright 1643, Siffwright 1696. There was formerly a craft of sievewrights in Edinburgh, referred to by Maitland in his History of Edinburgh, 1753, p. 317.

SILKESWORTHE. William de Silkesworthe who swore fealty at Montrose, 1296 (Bain, II,

p. 194) derived his name from Silksworth, county Durham.

SILLARS. The steps of the evolution of this name in Arran "are traceable from the Kilmorie session records, where we have the Gaelic forms M'Inurignach (1702), M'Nargenach and M'Nargid (1719) for 'Mac-an-Airgid' 'son of the Silver'; and the English form in 'Silver' (1718) later on a tombstone and record 'Siller' and so passing to Sillars. The original may have been a silversmith" (Book of Arran, II, p. 116).

SILVANUS. Silvanus was abbot of Dundrennan Abbey, 1167 (Chron. Mail., s.a.). The name was probably adopted when he professed from that of S. Silvanus, bishop of Gaza, the 'martyr,' c. 308. There were other saints of this name more or less legendary.

SILVER. This surname is not uncommon in the Mearns, and is an old one in the parish of Fetteresso. John Syllar was tenant of the garden of the Hospital of Dundee, 1464 (Cupar-Angus, I, p. 147). James Silvir, "succentor Glasguensi," appears as witness in 1497 (REG., p. 496), and may be James Siluer, rector of Durisdere, 1504 (Simon, 92). William Silver de Stobo was a charter witness, 1506 (REG., 485), and another William Siluer or Silwer was a cleric in Aberdeen, 1540, and chaplain of Folaroull, 1546 (REA., II, p. 113; I, p. 431). The name Silver on a tomb in the Calton cemetery, Edinburgh, near the Stevenson 'lair' probably suggested to Robert Louis Stevenson the surname of his 'Long John Silver' in Treasure Island.

SILVERTON. Local. There are places of this name in Fife and Perthshire, and also a Silverton in Derbyshire. Patrick Silvirton was resident in Vddynston, 1498 (REG., 478). Sillirtoune 1557, Silvertoune 1567.

SILVESTER, SELVESTER. From the personal name Silvestre (Lat. 'belonging to a wood'). "About the year 1200, Sylvestro Gozzolini, of Osimo, founded an order of monks, who, probably, are the cause that Sylvester became known in Ireland as a Christian name, and has come to us as a surname" (Yonge, new ed., p. 179). Siluester, a monk of St. Andrews, a. 1199 (RPSA., p. 290), and Silvester, a monk of Hadingtona, c. 1250 (RPSA., p. 389). John Silvestre, parson of Dolfinstone, Lanarkshire, rendered homage in 1296 (Bain, II, p. 212). As a forename we have it in Siluester of Ratra, 1473 (Cupar-Angus, I, p. 172), and Silwester M'Randell in Gargavache, 1600 (SCM., IV, p. 293).

SILVESTERSON, 'son of SILVESTER,' q.v.

SIM, SIME, SYM, SYME. Diminutives of SY-
MON, SIMEON, q.v. In *Symmie and his bruder*,
a satire in the vein of *Peblis to the play*, we
have mention of

"Bayth Sym and his bruder," and
"Nowthir Syme nor his bruder." ll. 10, 20.

Sim is not always representative of Clan *Mac-
Shimidh* as some think — it is a common English name as well. Sym Clerk witnessed an
instrument of resignation in 1446 (REB., I,
109), John Sym de Banchry is recorded in
1503 (*Cambus.*, p. 64), Andrew Sym was
vicar of Cumry (Comrie) in 1530 (ibid.,
p. 182), and William Sym witnessed a precept of clare constat of 1548 (RD., p. 396).
William Sym in Nether Possill is recorded in
1596 (*Retours, Lanark*, 9), Henry Sim was
constable in the parish of Auchtermuchtie in
1633 (RPC., 2. ser. v, p. 94), John Syme
("Stamp-Office Johnnie") was a friend of
Robert Burns, and James Syme (1799–1870),
the eminent surgeon, was born in Fife. As
forename: Sym Carmichall, 1576 (*Trials*, I,
p. 48). Cim 1562.

SIMMERS. *See under* SYMMERS.

SIMMIE. A diminutive of SIM, q.v. Cf. "Symmie and his bruther," in Laing's *Early popular
poetry of Scotland*. Alexander Simmey, flesher
in Aberdeen, 1613 (SCM., v, p. 88).

SIMON. The personal name of the Frasers of
Lovat. In Gaelic with 'Mac' prefixed, *Mac
Shimidh*, it is pronounced MACKIMMIE, q.v.
See also under SYMON.

SIMOND. Recorded in Fife. The OE. personal
name *Sigemund* regularly gives Simund, and
Simond was the common ME. form for Simon:
"Symound, I have sum thing to seye to thee"
(St. Luke, vii.40 — Wyclif's translation).

SIMPKINS, 'the son of Simkin,' from SIM,
q.v., + the double diminutive suffix -*kin*. The
p is intrusive.

SIMPRING. Of territorial origin from the old
manor of the name in Berwickshire. Hve de
Simpring possessed the manor during the reign
of David I, and in the reign of Malcolm IV
he granted to the monks of Kelso the church
of Simpring with a toft and some lands (*Kelso*,
272). Peter de Simpring, his son, confirmed
his father's grants (ibid., 12).

SIMPSON. Same as SIMSON, q.v., with intrusive *p*.

SIMSON, SIMPSON, SYMSON, 'son of SIM,'
q.v. The *p* is intrusive. William Symsoun was
burgess of Edinburgh in 1405 (*Egidii*, p. 41),
Thomas Symesson of Scotland had a safe conduct into England in 1412 (*Bain*, IV, 829), and
John Symson was a merchant in the service of
Archambaud (Archibald), earl of Douglas in
1405 (ibid., 697). Hugh Symson served on
inquest retouring Donald, thane of Cawdor in
1414 (*Cawdor*, p. 5), Robert Symson, the
king of Scots' servant, had a safe conduct into
England in 1422 (*Bain*, IV, 912), John Simson
was witness in Lythgw in 1444 (*Sc. Ant.*,
XVII, p. 15), and David Semsoun was one of
assize in Aberdeen in 1448 (CRA., p. 401).
Thomas Symson, Scottish merchant, had a safe
conduct into England in 1475 (*Bain*, IV,
1433), and five years later John Symson, a
Scot, had letters of denization in England
(ibid., 1465). David Sympsone was elected
common councillor in Aberdeen, 1477
(*Guildry*, p. 189). Andro Semsoun was 'fylit
of pycry' (i.e. pilfering) in Lanark in 1488,
Jok Semsswne was guilty of 'twillye' (disturbance) in the same year in the same town
(*Lanark*, p. 1, 2), Wylzame Symptsun was
declared innocent of part in detention of King
James III in Edinburgh Castle in 1482 (*Lennox*, II, p. 123), and Johannes Symson witnessed a lease by George, abbot of Inchaffray in
1491 (*Inchaffray*, p. xcvii). Weillie Symsone
was a tenant of the abbot of Kelso in 1567
(*Kelso*, p. 524), James Symsone was retoured
heir in the fulling mill in the barony of Coldinghame in 1646 (*Retours, Berwick*, 269), and
Agnes Sympsone was heir of Alexander Sympson, merchant burgess of Ayr, in 1685 (*Retours, Ayr*, 640). Andrew Symson, "Printer to
the King's most excellent Majesty," was an
Episcopal minister prior to the Revolution in
1688, when the bigotry of Presbyterianism
deprived him of his living and he turned
printer. The most eminent of the name was Sir
James Young Simpson (1811–1870) of chloroform fame, whose monument is in Princes
Street gardens, Edinburgh. Dr. Sutherland
Simpson (1863–1926), head of the department of physiology and bio-chemistry in Cornell University, New York State, was born in
Flotta, Orkney. Semsone 1513, Symesone 1660,
Symesoune 1603, Sympsoun 1605, Sympsoune
1661, Symsoune 1548.

SINCLAIR. This Caithness surname is of
territorial origin from St. Clare in the arrondissement of Pont d'Eveque, Normandy. The first
Sinclairs in Scotland appear to have been
vassals of the great territorial magnates, de
Morville. Their first possession in Scotland was
the barony of Roslin, near Edinburgh, which
they held in the reign of David I (1124–
1153). The earliest bearers of the name appear
in charters connected with the abbeys of Dryburgh and Newbattle, the Hospital of Soltre
(now Soutra in Midlothian), the church of

SINCLAIR, *continued*

Glasgow, etc. An early offshoot of the family became all powerful in Caithness and held the earldom there from 1379 to 1542. The frequency of the surname in Caithness and in the Orkneys is due to the tenants on the lands of the earldom adopting the name of their overlord just as we find tenants who possessed no surnames of their own doing likewise elsewhere. The Sinclairs, like the Gordons and some other families, cannot be called a clan in the true sense of the term. They were a powerful territorial family, whose relationship to their dependents was entirely feudal. John Singular held land in Aberdeen, c. 1450 (REA., II, p. 298). Lassæ Saengkaer (Laurence Sinclair) who was burgomaster of Oddevald in 1504, appears again in 1508 as Laffris Saenckeller (*Dipl. Norv.*, III, p. 746, 757). An old rhyme referring to the bickerings between the Sinclairs and their neighbors says:

"Sinclair, Sutherland, Keith, and Clan Gunn, There never was peace when thae four were in."

Sanclar 1493, Santclar 1539, Santclere 1545, Santoclair 1407, Seincler 1261, Seintclere 1445, Seintclerk 1296, Seyntclere 1405, Sincklair 1634, Sincklar 1597, Sincklare 1684, Sinckler 1647, Sinclaire 1598, Sincler 1620, Singlar 1454, Singkler 1491, Sinkaller 1692, Sinkclair 1667, Sinklare 1640, Synclare 1482, Syncleir 1528, Syncler 1544, Synclere 1470, Synklair 1526, Synklar 1529. In Argyllshire the name is used as an Englishing of Gaelic *Mac na cearda*.

SINGER, SINGERS. From the occupation. The second form recorded in Fife. Cf. Sir Robert Bynne, "cheplaine and singar in the quier" in Aberdeen, 1457 (CRA., p. 289).

SINGLETON. This surname, not common in Scotland, is most probably derived from Singleton in Lancashire. Thomas Singiltoun was member of the skinner's craft in Edinburgh in 1533 (*Colston*, p. 81).

SINTON. Of territorial origin from the ancient barony of the same name now included in the parish of Ashkirk, Selkirkshire. An inquisition made at Selkirk, July 23, 1305, found "that William, formerly King of Scotland [1165–1214] gave the sheriffdom of Selkirk to one Andrew de Synton to be held by answering to the King and his heirs for the issues, and being freed of the farm of the castle ward of Roxburgh and suit thereto, which he and his heirs were used to make for the barony of Synton" (*Bain*, II, 1681). Four generations following the first Andrew

are mentioned in the finding, the fourth, also named Andrew de Synton, while holding the sheriffdom, "was taken at the battle of Dunbar, and sent to the Castle of Fodringeye where he died in prison" (loc. cit.). Alexander de Sintun, c. 1200, witnessed a charter by Henry de Graham (RHM., I, p. 3), and c. 1259 a later Alexander de Sinton also appears as witness in the same record (ibid., p. 7). This later Alexander is also a witness, c. 1260–68, to a quitclaim by Malcolm de Constableton and Alicia, his wife, of a carucate in Edulfistune (REG., 216). Andrew de Sintun witnessed charters by John, son of Michael de Methkil, to the Abbey of Melrose, c. 1230–31 (*Wemyss*, II, p. xvi–xvii). Marie de Synton of the county of Roxburghe rendered homage in 1296 for her lands. Her seal bears a figure of eight rays, and S' *Marie de Sintvn* (*Bain*, II, p. 199, 532). She was, however, ordered to deliver up her lands to the king of England, and about the same time Isabella, wife of the sheriff mentioned above, was allowed to receive back a portion of her lands to cover certain expenses (*Rot. Scot.*, I). About the middle of the fifteenth century the lands of Sinton are found in joint possession of the Scots of Sinton and the Veitches of Dawic.

SITHEAG. The feminine form of SITHECH was well known in the late Middle Ages and during the witch persecutions. Sydok McCaill appears in 1540 (RSS., II, 3334). Shivak M'kleud was married to Angus Macky of Strathnaver, c. 1649 (*Wardlaw*, p. 87). Shihag Vrquhart in Delnies was brought up before the Presbytery of Dingwall in 1649 for practicing divination with the sieve and shears. Shiack nein Finlay vic George in the same parish of Urquhart was cited in 1650 for consulting a witch in Tarvie named Shiack nein Dod (= Donald) (IDR., p. 181). Sithag of Lennox was spouse of John of Lorn. Shiag 1678.

SITHECH, SITHACH, an old Gaelic personal name first recorded in the genitive in one of the twelfth century Gaelic entries in the *Book of Deer* as *mac Sithig*. It is the Middle Irish *sidheach* 'wolf.' Sithach, a Culdee of Mothel (now Muthill) was witness to a charter by the bishop of Dunblane, c. 1178 (*Carta de Northberwic*, no. 5). Seth mac Lood, a "native man" of the Abbey of Dunfermline, is one of the witnesses in a deed of perambulation of 1230 (RD., no. 196). Sythach Macmallon, a bondman (*nativus*) in Badenoch, is mentioned in an agreement between the bishop of Moray and Walter Comyn, earl of Menteth, of date between 1224–33 (REM., no. 76). In another agreement between the same persons regarding the lands of Kynkardyn dated

1234 one of the witnesses is Fercardus filius Sethi (ibid., no. 85). A charter by Alexander de Yla, earl of Ross, dated 1338, of the lands of Dalnafert and Kinrorayth (Kinrora) expressly reserved an acre of ground near "le Stychan" of Dalnafert "in qua situm fuit manerium quondam Scayth filii Ferchardii" (SCM., IV, p. 125). Between the years 1455 and 1469 there are numerous references to three individuals designated the king's "couriers" and "messengers" (ER., VI–VIII). All three bear the same surname which is variously spelled Scheo, Scheho, Schetho, Schethou, Schethow, Scheoch, Schethoc, Scheok, and once, wrongly, de Schetho, as if the name were a territorial one. Sythock Hair was concerned in the slaughter of Donald McEwin in the Cors of Balmaclellane, 1529 (RSS., II, 128). See also under SHAW (2).

SITHOWSON. John Sithowsone and Sithow Cant were tenants under Douglas in Dauchy, Aberdour, Fife, 1376 (RHM., I, p. lxiv). Donald Schethsoun from Logy was transferred to the jurisdiction of the regality of Logy, 1392 (Grandtully, I, p. 143 *).

SITLINGTON. John de Schutlyntone of Edinburghshire rendered homage in 1296 (Bain, II, p. 207). John Sitlington of Stanehouse in Galloway was outlawed as rebel in 1528 (Trials, I, p. 140 *), and William Schitlingtoun was witness in Dumfries in 1541 (Anderson). Agnes Shitlington was in Auchinbreck, 1642 (Dumfries), James Sitlington of Dunscore died in New Jersey, 1685. John Shitlintone, merchant in Dumfries, 1689 (RPC., 3. ser. XIV, p. 690), and John Sittlingtown alias Seton in Stroan of Dalry, 1738 (Kirkcudbright). The outlawry of 1528 probably was the cause of the extermination of the old family of the name, at least in Galloway.

SIVEWRIGHT, SIVRIGHT. See under SIEVE-WRIGHT.

SIWARD. From the OE. personal name Sigeweard, 'victorious guard.' Siward is famous in Scottish history as the victor over Macbeth at the battle of Dunsinnan, 1054. Siward Barn, a Saxon noble, in 1070, with several others, took refuge for a few months in Scotland. Chalmers thinks he was no doubt progenitor of a numerous family in Scotland but gives no reasons for his belief. An Edward, son of Siward, witnessed the confirmation charter by David I to the monks of Dunfermline, c. 1128 (RD., p. 3). His name "appears low down in the list of witnesses, and [he] was probably not a man of high rank" (Lawrie, p. 285). About 1219 Richard Syward witnessed a confirmation charter by John, earl of Huntingdoun, in favor of the Abbey of Arbroath (RAA., I, 84). His grandson, also named Richard, was one of the magnates Scotiæ who engaged to recognize Princess Margaret on the death of Alexander III (Fœdera). David Syward, cleric, was witness to a document anent the land of Neuton juxta Are, c. 1280 (RMP., p. 72). The family took the English side in the War of Independence and were in consequence involved in ruin on the success of the national cause. The Scottish line of Siwards ended in a daughter, Helena, who was married to Isaac Maxwell. She held lands in Fife in the reigns of Robert I and David II (RMS., I, App. II, 701, 1372). Suard 1297.

SKADKAILL. George Skadkaill, cordiner in Elgin, 1577 (Rec. Elgin, I, p. 152). George Skadkill, burgess of Banff, 1606 (RPC., VII, p. 631).

SKADUGHY. Richard de Skadughy of the county of Fife who rendered homage in 1296 (Bain, II, p. 204) derived his name from Skeddoway near Dysart in Fife. William Skeddoway in Aberdeen, 1650 (SCM., V, p. 176). The name of Robert Schodowie in Lundy, 1598 (Laing, 3314) may be of the same origin.

SKAE. See under SKEA.

SKAID. Skaid or Scad is recorded as a surname in Braemar and Cromar in the sixteenth and seventeenth centuries. Helene Skayde is recorded in Millades, 1583 (Aboyne, p. 159). James Skaid was tenant of the mylne of Dunatye, 1600 (SCM., IV, p. 315). Alexander Scad, younger in Dawen, was charged with resetting members of the outlawed Clan Gregor, 1636 (RPC., 3. ser. VI, p. 215). See SKED.

SKAILL. A surname found in Caithness and Orkney records, derived from some one of several small places in Orkney so named. Riche Scale who was present at deliverance of a decree by the lawman in West Mainland, c. 1500, is probably the Richard Skaill who held lands in South Sandwick in 1503 (REO., p. 75, 416). Issobell Skeall in Dungasbey, Caithness, was charged in 1659 with putting "ane blew threid about ane oxe foot wt severall knots upon it," etc. (Old Lore Misc., V, p. 62).

SKAITHMUIR. From the old husband lands of Skaithmuir in the parish of Coldstream, Berwickshire. Johannes de Skathmur appears as a witness in Edinburgh in 1477 (CDE., 50), and James Scaitheumure was a surgeon there in 1605 (Edinb. Marr.). Skaithmur 1503.

SKAITSONE. Susanna Skaitsone in Clerkington was accused of witchcraft, 1629 (RPC., 2. ser. III, p. 339). Local from some place of the name. -son and -ston often interchange in local names.

SKALEBY. Nicholas de Skaleby, juror on 'inquisition at Lochmaben, 1347 (Bain, III, 1499), probably derived his surname from Scalby in the North Riding of Yorkshire, early forms of which are Skalebi, Skaleby, and Scalby.

SKATHISBIE. Local. George Skathisbie was one of an inquest in the Canongate of Edinburgh, 1561 (MCM., II, p. 297).

SKEA, SKAE. An Orcadian surname of local origin from the lands of Skea in Deerness. Magnus Sca was witness to the sale of a toft in Kirkwall in 1480, Bernard of Ska purchased a two mark land in Deldaill within Deirnes in 1505, Sir James Scay was chaplain in Orkney, 1523 (OSR., I, p. 104), John Skay in Deirnes was member of an assize in Tankirnes in 1559, and Madie Skae of Tankirness is recorded in a deed dated 1597 (REO., p. 111, 203, 323, 331). Skaye 1562.

SKEBISTER. Bessie Skebister who was strangled and burned for witchcraft in Orkney in 1633 (Black, Folklore of Orkney and Shetland, p. 115), derived her surname from Skeebuster in Brims, South Ronaldsay.

SKED. Payment was made to William Sked in Falsyde (Fawsyde) in 1674 (Stitchill, p. 75). William Sked in Fausyde, 1683 (Lauder). Robert Sked in Belhaven, juror on assize at Dunbar, 1688 (RPC., 3. ser. XIII, p. 252). Still current in Midlothian. Cf. SKAID.

SKEEN, SKEENE. Variants of SKENE, q.v.

SKELDIE. William Skeldie, heir of David Skeldie in Lintlawes, 1630 (Retours, Edinburgh, 666; Inquis., 1734, 1735).

SKELDON. Local, probably from Skeldoun in Kyle-Regis (Retours, Ayr, 277). It may otherwise be from Skeldon in Yorkshire or from Skeldon in Northumberland. Archibald Skeldin, burgess of Edinburgh, 1569 (RPC., I, p. 676).

SKELLIE. Most probably from Ir. (Mac)Scalaighe, 'son of the crier.' William Skellie in Barledʒiew, 1789 (Wigtown).

SKENE, SKEEN, SKEENE. Of territorial origin from the lands of Skene, Aberdeenshire, erected into a barony in 1317 in favor of Robert de Skene. The first record of the name is in 1296 when Johan de Skene of the county of Edneburk and Johan de Skene of the county of

Aberdene rendered homage (Bain, II, p. 203, 208). The seals attached to the homage shows that the two Johns were one and the same person. The seal bears the device of a head of John the Baptist upon a charger with a hand pointing down (figured in Family of Skene, p. 10), and the legend S Ioh'is de Sceyn. Patrick de Skene, also of the county of Aberdene, also rendered homage in the same year. The seal attached to his homage bears three sgians or daggers, paleways as now borne, and S Patricii de Sken cl'ici [clerici]. Probably, like many other old families, the Skenes were hereditary possessors of the church of Skene, a vicarage dependent upon the church of Kinkell, and took their name from it. This supposition is rendered probable by the designation of Patrick as a cleric, and by the fact that in 1358 a Giliane de Skene is mentioned (ER., I, p. 552) who is probably a descendant of the John de Skene who bore the head of John the Baptist on his seal. Giliane, in Gaelic Gilleoin, is an ecclesiastical name meaning 'servant of (S.) John.' The family enjoyed the estate of Skene from father to son, in nearly uninterrupted succession for more than five hundred years, but in 1828 the last direct male descendant died. Schene 13th cent., Skeen 1509, Skeene 1649, Skein 1601, Skeine 1509, Sken 1474, Skevne 1594, Skine 1653, Skyne 1586. Skeyn and Skyen also occur. Some Skenes settled in Posen, and the name there appears as Skin, 1586.

SKEOCH. There are places of this name in the shires of Ayr, Dumfries, and Stirling. As most of the names noted are connected with the West Coast the name may have been derived from Skeoch, near Mauchline, Ayrshire. John Skeoch was chaplain in Kilbirny in 1507, Andrew Skeoch, presbyter in Glasgow, 1522, appears in 1528 as Skeothe (a misreading of t for c). Sir John Skewych or Skeocht was procurator in Glasgow in 1553, and Elizabetht Skewcht is recorded in Glasgow in the same year (Protocols, I). William Skeoch took the Test in Paisley, 1686 (RPC., 3. ser. XI, p. 496).

SKILLING. A rare surname. Catherine Skilling was married in Glasgow, 1939. Scilling is an OE. personal name. Perhaps reduced from (MAC)SCILLING, q.v.

SKIMMING. A common surname in Wigtownshire. From (MAC)SKIMMING, q.v. In 1684 (Parish) as McScumin and McSkiming.

SKINNER. From the occupation of "skinner" or flayer of hides (ME. skynnere). In Latin documents the name is rendered pelliparius. William pelliparius witnessed a charter by William de Lundin in favor of the canons of

St. Andrews, c. 1250 (RPSA., p. 264). The land of Simon Pellipar in Aberdeen is mentioned in 1281 (REA., II, p. 278), and in 1345 mention is made of the heiress of William Pellipar, umquhill burgess of Roxburgh (*Kelso*, 379–380). Stephan Skynnar held land in Inverness in 1361 (REM., p. 305), John Skinner was burgess of the same town, c. 1360 (*Grant*, III, p. 12), and another John Skinner was admitted burgess of Aberdeen in 1470, and Henry Pelliparius in the year following (NSCM., I, p. 22). Bartholomew Skinner was a witness in Glasgow in 1487 (LCD., 256), and a complaint was recorded by Elizabeth Skinner in Dysart in 1696 (*Dysart*, p. 55). Skynar 1556.

SKIPPER. From the occupation, a 'shipmaster.' William Skipper in Aberdeen, 1493 (CRA., p. 50). Marjory Skipper in Edinburgh, 1669 (*Edinb. Marr.*).

SKIRLING. From Skirling (1275 Scravelyn, 1299 Scravillyn), a village and parish in west Peeblesshire. Adam de Scrawelyn was abbot of Culross, c. 1335 (SCM., V, p. 244). William Skyrlyn was witness in Glasgow, 1520 (RAA., II, p. 429), and another William Skirling witnessed a charter to Mariorie Orrok, daughter of Alexander Orrok of Selybalbe, in 1523 (RD., p. 380). William Skraveling had a lease of the eighth part of Grange, c. 1570 (RD., p. 487), John Skirling is recorded in Dunfermline in 1571 (*Dunfermline*), and Balthazair Skirling was burgess of Perth in 1607 (RPC., VII, p. 333).

SKIRVING, SKIRVEN. As Skirvane it was one of the commonest surnames in the parish of Haddington in the eighteenth century (*Archaeologia Scotica*, I, p. 419). 'Black John Skirving' was said to have been the Earl Marischal's standard bearer at Flodden, 1513. Patrick Skirving was heir of Alexander Skirving, burgess of Edinburgh, his father, 1667 (*Inquis.*, 5082). William Skirving, secretary to the Scottish Friends of the People, 1793, was sentenced by the notorious Braxfield to transportation for fourteen years. Adam Skirving, an East Lothian farmer, author of the song "Tranent Muir," was wrongly credited with authorship of the better-known song "Hey, Johnnie Cope." George Skirving, portioner of Melrose, 1813 (*Heirs*, 603). Skirven 1687.

SLACH, SLACK. Surnames recorded in Dumfriesshire. Of local origin, perhaps from the old lands of Slake or Slack in the parish of Roberton, Roxburghshire. Bardsley gives the name as local, "at the slack or slagg," and records Johannes del Slak in Yorkshire, 1379. In Yorkshire slack has the meaning of "a common." See SLAGG.

SLAGG. Recorded in Glasgow. A voiced form of SLACK, q.v., from ON. *slakki*, a shallow valley, or depression between two hills.

SLAINS. From the parish of Slains in Aberdeenshire. William de Slanes, knight, witnessed a charter by Matthew Kyninmond, bishop of Aberdeen, c. 1180 (REA., I, p. 12). Willelmus de Slanys witnessed a charter by William Cumyn, earl of Buchan, of the church of Buthelny to the Abbey of Aberbrothoc in 1221 (RAA., I, p. 93). Nicol de Slanes in the county of Are rendered homage in 1296 (*Bain*, II, p. 202), and Robert of Slains was member of an inquest held at Artrowquhi in 1436 (CAB., p. 394).

SLASSOR, SLESSER, SLESSOR. All recorded in Aberdeenshire. Robert Sleller (perhaps an error for Slesser), burgess of Aberdeen, 1487 (CRA., p. 44). In 1696 several Slessors were recorded in the parish of Peterhead. Mary Slessor (1848–1915) of Dundee was a famous missionary in Old Calabar. James Slessor of Fyvie served in the first Great War (*Turriff*). SLEASTER, a Braemar surname in the seventeenth century, is perhaps a variant. The name may be of Dutch origin.

SLATER. A variant of SCLATER, q.v.

SLATTER. A variant of SCLATER, q.v.

SLAYWROCK. Perhaps for Slaywright, 'a maker of slays,' i.e. the reed guiding the warp-thread of a loom. Metylda Slaywrock 'in vico Camber' (= Cambergate), Ayr, 1348 (*Friars Ayr*, p. 17).

SLEDGER. From occupation. The *New English dictionary* defines sledger as one who drives or draws a sledge. John Slegear, merchant burgess of Glasgow, 1580 (*Burgesses*). Loyrance Sledger, coibler, admitted burgess freeman, gratis, 1601 (ibid). John Abraham Sledger, H. M. 'inventor' for Scotland, burgess of Dumbarton, 1675 (RDB.).

SLEIGH. The earliest references to this name locate it in Aberdeen, and it is possible that the name is of English origin, as many of the burgesses of the town in the thirteenth century were of English nationality. It may be mentioned, however, that there are local place names from which the surname may have come. There is Sliach in Glengairn, Sleach in Strathdon, Slioch in Drumblade, a Sleich in Perthshire, and Slioch in Ross-shire. John called Sleth was burgess of Aberdeen, 1271, and Andrew Sleth the same in 1275 (*Fraser*,

SLEIGH, *continued*

p. 9, 11). Thomas Slech possessed land in Aberdeen, 1317 (SCM., v, p. 11), and there is on record a charter of land there by Andro Sleiche dated 1342 (*Friars*, p. 15). Patrick Slegh witnessed a charter of lands in Fife, 1395 (*Wemyss*, II, p. 33), John Sleigh appears as guild brother in Aberdeen, c. 1438 (SCM., v, p. 45), and William Sleich was burgess of Glasgow, 1440 (LCD., p. 251). Robert Sleich was admitted burgess of Aberdeen, 1481 (NSCM., I, p. 29), and John Slycht witnessed a sasine in the barony of Bamff, 1507 (*Bamff*, p. 45). Ric' Sleyght de Cüleyg was present at perambulation of the marches between Brokhole and Butterden in 1431 (*Raine*, 639), and as Richard Sleich, 'larde of Cumliche,' was one of an assize in 1433 (*Swinton*, p. xxxiv). John Slegh was master of the ship *le Andrewe of Scotland* in 1453 (*Bain*, IV, 1264). Patrick Sleich de Cunliche was juror on inquisitions on lands of West Reston and Swinton, 1495, 1500 (*Home*, 27; *Swinton*, p. lxxii), and Jeanna Sleith was retoured heir in the lands of Cumlege (Cumliche), Berwickshire, 1574 (*Retours, Berwick*, 5). John Sliche appears in Dunse, 1628 (*Lauder*). Sleiche 1569, Sleicht 1549.

SLESSER, SLESSOR. *See under* SLASSOR.

SLIMON, SLIMMON, SLIMAN, SLIMMAN, SLIMMEN, SLIMMAND. A difficult name. It may be the same as English Sloman or Slowman, a variant of Solomon, as has been suggested, but the early spellings do not favor this view. Thomas Sleuthman witnessed a bond of manrent by Andrew Rollo of Duncroub, 1471 (*Oliphants*, p. 17). Patrick Sluthman was a monk of Newbattle, 1474 (*Neubotle*, pref., p. xxv), Benart Slumane was a tenant under the Abbey of Kelso, 1567 (*Kelso*, p. 529), and William Slewman, reidare at Cavers, 1574 (RMR.). Joannes Asleuman or Aslewman was merchant burgess of Edinburgh, 1623 (*Inquis. Tut.*, 368), Margaret Sluman or Slowman held a lease of land there, 1627–28 (BOEC., x, p. 212–214), and Bessie Slewman was married there in 1629 (*Edinb. Marr.*). John Sluman in Flwriswallis, 1637 (*Lauder*), Bessie Sleoman appears in parish of Douglas, 1661 (*Lanark CR.*), and Nicolas Slimman in Dumfries, 1684 (*Dumfries*). There was a Sluthmanhill or Slewmanshill in Renfrewshire, 1504 and 1510 (RMS., II, 2817, 3484).

SLINK. John Slynk was admitted burgess of Aberdeen in 1406 for his labors made in the common service of the burgh (NSCM., I, p. 2), and Agnes Slynk, "filia et heres quondam Johannis Slynk, burgensis de Aberbrothoc," is recorded in 1452 (RAA., II, p. 80).

SLOAN, SLOANE, SLOWAN. From Ir. *O'Sluaghain*, for *O'Sluaghadain*, 'descendant of Sluaghadan,' probably a variant of *O'Sluaghadhaigh*, from the MIr. personal name *Sluagadach*, 'leader of a military expedition.' Cf. SLOGADADH. William Slowane held a tenement near Dalkeith in 1504 (*Soltre*, p. 324), and Johnne Slowane of Garroche was juror on assize at Kirkcudbright, 1508 (*Trials*, I, p. *55). John Asloane of Garroch is mentioned in 1531 (ALHT., v, p. 396), and John Asloan of Garroch appears as a witness in 1542 (*Anderson*). John Aslowane, burgess of Edinburgh, was contractor of the "leid mynis of Glengoner and Wenlok," 1562 (RPC., I, p. 232), and another John Sloane had sasine of land in the parish of Traquair in 1565 (ER., xix, p. 540). John Slowane was tenant under the abbot of Kelso, 1567 (*Kelso*, p. 524), John Aslowane was burgess of Edinburgh in 1568 (MCM., II, p. 311), and a third John Aslowan had sasine of the lands of Auchincreyth, 1590 (ER., xxii, p. 521). George Aslowane, son to the laird of Garroche, was charged in 1613 with taking part in the performance of mass against the Act of Parliament (*Trials*, III, p. 253), Eduard Aslowane is recorded in Fell in 1616 (*Kirkcudbright*), and Alexander Slowen was a baker in Edinburgh, 1659 (*Edinb. Marr.*). Sir Hans Sloane (1660–1753), was born in the north of Ireland of Scots parents. His collections were the foundation of the British Museum. Asloane 1631, Aslowen 1611, Slowan 1684.

SLOGADADH. The M. Ir. personal name *Sluagadach*, 'leader of a military expedition,' appears as Slogadadh, the name of a leader of the bishop of St. Andrews's host, c. 1128 (RPSA., p. 117). As Slugepah he appears as a witness in King David's letter respecting the consecration of Robert, bishop of St. Andrews, at York, 1128 (Haddan and Stubbs, *Councils and ecclesiastical documents relating to Great Britain and Ireland*, v. 2, pt. 1, p. 215). In the charter of Thurstin, archbishop of York, on the same subject, his name is misspelled Slugedt (*loc. cit.*). An earlier Sluagadach went forth to Rome, c. 966–971 (CPS., p. 10).

SLORA, SLORACH. "Slorach appears in the 14th century as Slorah, a member of the enigmatical Clan Qwhevil famed at the North Inch of Perth in 1396" (*Macbain* v, p. 76). Alexander Slorath (*c* misread as *t*) was witness in Elgin, 1562 (REM., p. 421), Duncan Slora was admitted burgess of Aberdeen in 1571 (NSCM., I, p. 70), and James Slorach was church officer in Botary, 1633 (*Strathbogie*, p. 6). Jon Slorach, shoemaker in Achincleich, 1703 (*Banff Rec.*, p. 244), James Slorach in

Bitterwards, 1789 (*Moray*), another James Slorach was one of the petitioners for the formation of the Corps of Huntly Volunteers, 1798 (*Will*, p. 5), and Alexander Slorach was killed near Hooge, Flanders, 1915. See SLURACH.

SLOSS. A curtailed form of AUCHINCLOSS, q.v. James Aslois *de eodem* was retoured heir of Adam Aslois *de eodem*, his father, in the five merkland of Aslois in the barony of Kilmarnock, 1617 (*Retours, Ayr*, 172). Adam Aslos in Kilmarnock, 1643 (*Inquis. Tut.*, 646), James Slooss, confectioner in Edinburgh, 1678 (*Edinb. Marr.*), Richard Sloce appears in Ayr, 1656 (*Ayr*, p. 198), and William Slose in Kilmarnock, 1688 (RPC., 3. ser. XIII, p. 241). Sluch is a spelling recorded in 1668, John Sluch in Bonhard (*Edin. App.*).

SLURACH. "Slurach et frēs ejus et om̄es clanqwhevil" were put to horn in 1392 for their share in the Raid of Angus in the preceding year (APS., I, p. 579). Slurach is generally considered to be a transcriber's error for Sheach. The theory that the combatants at Perth in 1396 were Shaws and Farquharsons is negatived by the fact that neither of these clans was in existence at that date. Lachlan Shaw, the historian of Moray, was of opinion that the combatants were Macphersons and Davidsons, forgetful of the fact that the Macphersons and Davidsons were too insignificant at that date to have caused such a disturbance. The late A. M. Mackintosh, Clan Chattan historian, was of opinion that the combatants were Clan Chattan and Clan Cameron, but, as the eighth duke of Argyll says, nobody to this day can make out with any certainty who the combatants were. Cf. SLORA.

SLYNGYSBY. Ade de Slyngysby in Edinburgh, 1367 (RMS., I, 57), most probably derived his surname from Slingsby in Yorkshire. John Slingisbie forfeited some land in Edinburgh in the reign of David II (RMS., I, App. II, 1568).

SMAIL. Variant of SMALL, q.v.

SMAILHOLM. From Smailholm in Roxburghshire. William de Smalham witnessed a gift by David Olifard to the Hospital of Soltre, c. 1153–77 (*Soltre*, p. 4). Alexander de Smalham witnessed gift of the church of S. Finan to the church of S. James and S. Mirin de Paisley, c. 1230 (RMP., p. 132). Robert de Smalhame was made abbot of Kelso, 1248 (*Morton*, p. 87), and Adam de Smalham "preferring the sweets of Melrose" to "having rule over the hovel of the monks of Deer, whose fervid religion he was never able to test by true experience" laid down the office

of abbot of Dere, 1267 (*Chron. Mail.*, s.a.). Henry of Smalham, archdeacon of Teviotdale, 1358 (*Kelso*, p. 398). Thomas Smalum in Leith accepted the king's coronation in 1567 (RPC., I, p. 563), and the land of Thomas Smelum is mentioned in 1582 (*Soltre*, p. 147). George Smailhome was one of the Scottish undertakers granted an allotment in Ulster in 1612 (RPC., IX, p. 421), Bernard Smaillome was retoured heir of George Smaillome, his father, in Leyth, in 1633 (*Retours, Edinburgh*, 734), another George Smellum was merchant in Edinburgh in 1678 (*Edinb. Marr.*), and Jacobus Smellholme was portioner of Prestan, 1692 (*Retours, Orkney*, 142). Smaillum 1633, Smealholm 1723, Smellem 1625, Smellholme 1692, Smellum 1687.

SMALER. John Smaler was vicar of Kyngowdrum (Kingoldrum), 1475 (CRA., p. 33).

SMALL, SMALE. Richard Smale or Small, canon of Glasgow, a. 1329, 1337 (RHM., II, p. 10; *Pap. Lett.*, II, p. 540) may be Richard Small, rector of the church of Rachou, 1348 (SCM., v, p. 246). Thomas Smale appears as witness in Roxburgh, c. 1338 (*Dryburgh*, 313), and Cristiana, widow of Thomas Small, held the vill of Estir Softlawe in Teuidalle, 1360 (*Bain*, IV, 50). William Small was a tenant of the Douglas in Linton, 1376 (RHM., II, p. 18). Simo Smale was a forestaller in Ellon, Aberdeenshire, 1402; and John Smale was admitted burgess of Aberdeen, 1407 (NSCM., I, p. 2). Rankin Small was witness in Prestwick, 1446 (*Prestwick*, p. 114), and John Smalle had a safe conduct to trade in England with Scottish merchandise, 1447 (*Bain*, IV, 1190). David Smal of Jedburgh is in record 1450 (RAA., II, 91), and Alexander Small, a native of Scotland, received letters of denization in England, 1503 (*Bain*, IV, 1731). Thomas Sma was tenant under Abbey of Kelso, 1567 (*Kelso*, p. 520), and Henry Smaill is recorded in Lessuden, 1657 (RRM., I, p. 141). Smaw 1565.

SMALLEY. There is a Smalley in Derbyshire. A deed of 1283 runs in the name of "Oliverus et Ricardus Smally prepositi et ceteri prepositi ac cives Glasguenses congregati in placitis burgi que tenebantur apud Glasgu" (REG., p. 210). Ricardus Smaley witnessed a sale of land in Glasgow, c. 1280–90 (ibid., p. 198). John Smalee appears in Aberdeen, 1440 (CRA., p. 395), Thomas Smalle and William Smalle were merchants in Edinburgh, 1438 (*Bain*, IV, 1115), Johannes Smaly, perpetual vicar of Kencoldroun, 1458 (REA., I, p. 282), and David Smalie, notary public of Glasgow diocese, 1530 (*Lamont*, p. 39). John Smaillie in Irvine, 1665 (*Irvine*, II, p. 195).

SMALLWOOD. Of local origin from some small place of the name. John of Smalwod, burgess of Renfrew, received from the monks of Paisley £3 for the lands in the burgh of Renfrew called Beltonland (RMP., p. 375).

SMART. From the OE. personal name *Smert,* found in Suffolk, 1066. Smert is still the common pronunciation of the name in Scotland. John Smert, a Scot, was charged with breaking his parole in 1358 (*Bain,* IV, 25), and William Smert was tenant in Telny in the barony of Abirdoure, Fife, in 1376 (RHM., I, p. lxiv). Henry Smert, Scotsman, prisoner of war, was released to find ransom for himself and others in 1422 (*Bain,* IV, 914). John Smert was a citizen of Brechin in 1452 (REB., II, p. 88), another John Smert, 'husband,' was witness in 1481 (*Panmure,* II, 252), and Johannes Smert held land in Kintore in 1488 (REA., I, p. 341). William Smart, burgess of Tain, was fined for reset of members of outlawed Clan Gregor, 1612 (RPC., IX, p. 520). There were families of this name at Muresk and Tollochin in sixteenth century, native tanners.

SMEAL, SMEALL. Variants of SMALL, q.v.

SMEATON, SMETON, SMIETON, SMITTON, SMITON. From the lands of Smytheton or Smythetun, now Smeaton, near Musselburgh, Midlothian. Henry de Smithetone of the county of Edneburk rendered homage in 1296 (*Bain,* II, p. 210). Henricus de Smeihtone, juror on an inquisition at Muskylburn in 1359 (RD., p. 267). Alexander Smeythtone had a gift of 12 marks land in Eistrud, Shetland, in 1506 (BM., III, p. 108), and Erasmus Smittoune in Snarravo, Unst, is in record in 1613 (*Shetland*). Thomas Smeton or Smeaton (1536-83) was principal of Glasgow University. Smeetoun 1646, Smeiton 1680, Smeton and Smetoun 1584, Smettoun 1624, Smeytone 1678, Smitton 1745.

SMELLIE, SMILLIE, SMILEY. Thomas Smelie, merchant and guild-brother in Glasgow, 1612 (*Burgesses*). James Smillie in Strafrank, parish of Carstairs, 1754 (*Lanark CR.*). William Smellie (1740-1795), printer and naturalist in Edinburgh. Smeallie 1647, Smyllie 1697. Smillie recorded in Edinburgh, 1942. Harrison derives the name as a variant of Smalley, from the name of a place in Derbyshire, but I feel doubtful of this.

SMERLES. Nicholas Smerles, burgess of Dumfries, 1372 (RMS., I, 507). John Smerles held a tenement in Drumfreese before 1425 (ibid., II, 22). Probably an early spelling of SUMMERLEES.

SMETON. A variant of SMEATON, q.v.

SMIBERT. This uncommon surname, found mainly in Edinburgh and the southeast of Scotland, appears to be simply a corruption of "smooth beard." John Smetheberde, monk of Neubotle, was witness to a charter by Alan Lokart, laird of Lee, in 1467 (*Neubotle,* p. 263; see also p. 261, 314). William Smeberd appears as witness to an instrument of lands near Gullane in 1519, and another (?) William Smeithberd was a member of the Edinburgh town council in 1530 (MCM., II, p. 107). William Smeithberd or Smeithberde appointed "Maister armorar" to the king in 1526 (RSS., 3402) appears again between 1538-40 as William Smeberd or Smythberd, armourer to the king (ER., XVII, p. 170, 283). Alexander Smethberd was canon of Holyrood, 1547 (*Binns,* 40), Jhone Smeberd possessed a house in North Berwick in 1555 (CMN., p. 70), and in the following year Sir Alexander Smeberd appears as vicar of the parish church of Wr (Urr) (LSC., p. 298). William Smeberde who appears on an inquest held in the burgh of the Canongate, Edinburgh, in 1561 (MCM., II, p. 289) is probably the same individual who had trouble with the kirk-session over the baptizing of his bairn in 1564 (Kirk session records of the Canongate quoted in Chambers, *Dom. Ann. Scot.,* I). James Smithbaird in parish of Crichton, 1689 (RPC., 3. ser. XIV, p. 145).

SMIDDIE. Local. Robert Smyddie was occupier of "ane maillis mailling of land...in Smiddie in Grymnes within the Yle of South Ronaldsay," 1603 (REO., p. 176).

SMIETON. See under SMEATON.

SMILLIE, SMILEY. See under SMELLIE.

SMITH, SMYTH, SMYTHE. From the occupation.

"For, since the birth of time, throughout all ages and nations,
Has the craft of the smith been held in repute by the people."
— Longfellow, *Evangeline.*

"For more than 400 years a family of Smith, first as kindly tenants, and afterwards as lairds, were settled in the parish of Strathblane at Craigend... The tradition of the family is that when surnames came into use they took their name from their occupation of the smiths and armourers of the Barony of Mugdock" (*Strathendrick,* p. xvii). In Latin documents the name is rendered by *Faber* and *Ferro.* Adam Faber held a croft on the lands of Swaynystoun, c. 1221-34 (*Soltre,* p. 23), and William faber de Karel was a witness, c. 1250 (*May,* p. 38). Robert the smith (*ferro*) witnessed a charter by John, bishop of Dunkeld, c. 1199 (*Inchaffray*, p. 5). William the Smith was juror on an inquest made at Traquair, 1274 (*Bain*, II, 34), Alan Smyth was one of the 'Gustatores Ceruisie' in Aberdeen, 1398 (CRA., p. 375), Thomas Smyth, Scotsman, had safe conduct into England in same year, and Patrick Smyth of Scotland was to be kept in custody in the Tower of London, 1401 (*Bain*, IV, 504, 594). John Smyth was tenant of the 'Fabrile [Smithy] de Inveryalder,' 1539 (ER., XVII, p. 660), and Elizabeth Smythe and Margaret Smythe were heirs portioners of Alexander Smythe in Greinholme, 1621 (*Retours, Ayr*, 209, 210). Prof. Alexander Smith (b. 1865), head of the department of chemistry in Columbia University, New York City, was born in Edinburgh. Smeayth 1661, Smyith 1453, Smyithe 1607, Smytht 1511.

SMITHSON, 'Smith's son.' See SMITH. John Smythson was admitted burgess of Aberdeen in 1406 (NSCM., I, p. 2), and a payment was made to William Smethissone in Cromarty in 1492 (ADC., p. 273).

SMITON, SMITTON. Variants of SMEATON, q.v. John Smiton, musician in Edinburgh (1774), was a cousin of John Smeaton, builder of the Eddystone Lighthouse.

SMOLLETT. John Smolet was one of the sheriffs of King James V in the Lennox, 1513 (*Lennox*, II, p. 208). Martin (p. 253) says that one of the ships of the Spanish Armada in Tobermory Bay was "blown up by one Smallet of Dumbarton, in the year 1588." Harrison derives the name from OE. *smælheafod*, 'small head.' In connection with this etymology he cites an anonymous writer of 1760 who referred to Tobias Smollett, the novelist, as "Sawney Mac Smallhead," but of course we are not to take that as proof of Harrison's etymology. Baring-Gould says it comes from Samuel. John Smollert was suspected of being a fellow conspirator of the earl of Bothwell, 1591 (Moysie, *Memoirs*, p. 88). John Smolate was witness to a notarial instrument of sale of land of Temple of Ballakenrane, 1457 (*Strathendrick*, p. 192). Tobias Smallet, bailie of Dumbarton, was murdered by the Macgregors in 1604 (*Trials*, II, p. 432). Tobias George Smollett (1721–1771), novelist, was born in Dumbartonshire. Smallat 1690, Smallot 1700, Smolet 1506, Smollat 1500, Smollatt 1647, Smollot 1705, Smollote 1587.

SMOLT. Ade Smot had lease of part of vill of Lyntoune in barony of Kylbouho (Kilbucho), 1376 (RHM., I, p. li; II, p. 16). Syd Smolt in Aberdeen, 1493 (CRA., p. 50), and Thomas Smowt was admitted burgess there, 1551

(NSCM., I, p. 63). Patrick Smolts in Ellon, Aberdeenshire, c. 1604. Thomas Smowte in Aberdeenshire, 1634 (*Laing*, 2152).

SMYTH, SMYTHE. *See under* SMITH.

SNADDEN. Perhaps from the lands of Snawdone (1637) or Snawdoune (1649) in the bailliary of Lawderdaill (*Retours, Berwick*, 221, 281). John Snadoune in Wormanbie, Dumfriesshire, 1659 (*Dumfries*). Davina Snadden, schoolmistress, Townhill, Fife, died 1942.

SNAIL. Isobell Snaill had a lease of the lands of Balbuchty, 1585, and John Snaill of Lempottis is mentioned in the same year (*Scon*, p. 224). Perhaps a variant of SNELL, q.v.

SNAPE. An old surname in Inverurie. Probably from Snape near Coulter, Lanarkshire. James Snape on inquest, 1526 (*Carnwath*, p. 56). William Snape in Gledstaines, 1638 (*Lanark CR.*). Snaip 1523; Snyp.

SNAWIE. An Aberdeen surname. William Snawey was admitted burgess of Aberdeen in 1572, and John Snawie in 1613 (NSCM., I, p. 70, 111). George Snowie in record in Aberdeen, 1728 (NSCM., II), and William Snawie at Maryculter, 1768 (*Aberdeen CR.*).

SNELL. An OE. personal name found as Snel, Snel(l), and Sneil, from OE. *snell*, strong, bold, smart. It is also a very common Scandinavian personal name (*Björkman* I). William Snelle was master of the ship *Seinte Marie* of Dundee in 1390 (*Bain*, IV, 410). William Snell, presbyter Glasguensis, was a notary public in 1449 (RMP., p. 83), and Schire William Snell, chaplain, was burgess of Prestwick in 1470 (*Prestwick*, p. 13). John Snell (c. 1629–1679), founder of the Snell scholarships in Oxford for students of Glasgow University, was son of a blacksmith of Colmonell, Ayrshire.

SNOD. William Snod possessed a tenement in the regality of Arbroath, 1535 (RAA., II, 820).

SNODDIE. Andrew Snoddie in Papigo, Caithness, 1661 (*Caithness*), and John Snoddie in Lochlairne, 1686 (RPC., 3. ser. XII, p. 379).

SNODGRASS. An Ayrshire surname derived from the twenty shilling lands of old extent of Snodgers or Snodgrasse in the parish of Irvine and bailliary of Cunningham. Adam Snorgyrs appears as bailie of Are in 1372 (ER., II, p. 486), and Patrick Snodgrass was admitted burgess freeman of Glasgow in 1578 (*Burgesses*). The name occurs in the Glasgow Protocol Books as Snodgers (1556), and Margaret Snodgers was recorded heir of John Snodgers, maltman and burgess of Glasgow,

SNODGRASS, *continued*

in 1621 (*Inquis.*, 972). Andrew Snodgrasse in the Bridgeend of Glasgow was released from imprisonment in 1679 on signing a bond not to take up arms (RPC., 3. ser. VI, p. 296), Neil Snodgras appears as notary in Paisley in 1684 (ibid., IX, p. 321), and Hew Snodgrass, William Snodgrass and John Snodgrass took the Test in the same town in 1686 (ibid., XI, p. 496). Snodgrass 1679, Snodgerss 1608, Snodgrase 1652.

SNYPE. William Snype, witness in Linlithgow, 1534 (*Johnsoun*) may be William Snype who witnessed a precept by Hugh, earl of Eglintoun in 1541 (*Hunter*, p. 19). John Snype had a lease of the customs of Glasgow Bridge, 1575 (*Council Records*, I, p. 37), and Adam Snype was admitted burgess of Glasgow as a burgess heir in 1578 (*Burgesses*). Phillan Snype was cooper and citizen of Glasgow, 1588, and another Phillane Snype, cooper, probably his son, was burgess there, 1657 (*Protocols*, X; *Inquis.*, 4235). Andrew Snype was admitted burgess of the same city in 1610 (*Burgesses*) and Mr. Andrew Snype was librarian of the College of Glasgow in 1642 (RUG., III, p. 573). Agnes Snype was married in Edinburgh, 1638 (*Edinb. Marr.*), and James Snype was officer at Kilmalcome Church, 1700 (*Laing*, 2986). Perhaps local from Snipe in Northumberland.

SOFFLEY. A lazy pronunciation of SOFTLAW, q.v., which has become a separate surname. James Softly was a weaver in Edinburgh, 1638 (*Edinb. Marr.*). Roger Safely was charged with having purchased the wife of John Gilkers, indweller in the College of Nithsdale, for a groat in 1663 (RPS., 3. ser. I, p. 405). William Soflay of Holme in record, 1680 (*Inquis.*, 6232), and Roger Saflay of Holme, who signed the Test in 1684 (RPC., 3. ser. X, p. 226) is probably the Roger Sofflaw of Holm, 1701 (*Dumfries*). Margaret Saffley in Crossmeikle, 1701 (*Kirkcudbright*), Thomas Sofflaw in Woodhouse of Colvend, 1736, and George Soffley of Fell, 1800 (*Dumfries*).

SOFTLAW. From Softlaw in Roxburghshire. Robert de Softlaw witnessed the grant by Richard Germyn to the Hospital of Soltre, c. 1235–58 (*Soltre*, p. 26). Master Aimer de Softlawe resigned the church of S. Marie of Farmainishop in the diocese of Glasgow, 1292 (*Rot. Scot.*), and in 1296 as Aylmer de Softlawe, parson of the church of Douglas in Lanarkshire, he rendered homage (*Bain*, II, p. 210). Adam de Softlawe of Roxburghshire also rendered homage in 1296 (ibid., p. 210), and a John de Softelaw was burgess of Aberdeen, 1363 (REA., II, p. 283). Thomas Softlaw witnessed an instrument of infeftment in the parish of Newlands, Peeblesshire, 1547 (Buchan, *Peebles*, III, p. 57), another Thomas Softlaw was servitor to the earl of Nithsdale, 1622 (RPC., XII, p. 645), and James Softlaw was a merchant in Wigtown, 1741 (*Wigtown*).

SOLAM, SOLAMH. Gaelic bye-forms of Biblical Solomon. The Old Irish *Salemón*, a loan from Latin *Salomō-*, is due to the influence of native names in *-em-ón*, like *Éremón*, from *Ériu*, Ireland. The name was introduced by the Normans.

SOLOMON. From the Hebrew personal name *Shelōmō*. Dominus Salomone de Cupir, a cleric, was charter witness, 1245 (RPSA., p. 44, 282, 293). Salomon Frebern is in record, c. 1270 (BNCH., XVI, p. 334), and a Salomon del Hoga is mentioned about the same time (*Kelso*, 36). Patrick Saulemane appears in 1491 (*Fordell*, p. 89). See SALMOND.

SOMERLED. G. *Somhairle*, MG. *Somuirle*, and in the Gaelic MS. of 1467 *Somairle*, a borrowing from ON. *Sumarliði*, 'mariner, viking, summer wanderer or sailor.' Originally it "was not a personal name, but only signified a viking who used to come to the British Isles in the summer, a pirate, not a settler. The Pictish Chronicle, for instance, speaks of 'the fleets of the Somerleds' (*classis Somarlidiorum*)" (Bugge, *History of the Northmen in Ireland*, 1900, p. 17). Somewhat akin to this was the old Border custom of 'summering,' that is, making excursions into England during the summer season. "For the parentage of Somerled, the 'Regulus' of Ergadia, we have nothing but a traditional Irish genealogy, deducing his descent from the Irish tribe which possessed the district of Oirgialla or Oriel in Ulster, and the strange epithet of Citebi or Cicebi in the contemporary poems" (Skene, in *Fordun*, II, p. 430). Sumerled, sacerdos, first of the name recorded in Scotland apart from Somerled of the Isles, witnessed a confirmation of the church of the Holy Trinity of Dunkeld to the Abbey of Dunfermline, a. 1169 (RD., p. 74). He is probably the Sumerlethus, capellanus, of an Inchcolm charter of c. 1162–69 (*Inchcolm*, p. 1). Sumerleith de Fetherhesan was juror in a dispute regarding the Kirketun of Aberbuthenoth in 1206 (SCM., V, p. 213). Ysaac, capellanus Sumerledi, witnessed a charter by Maldouen, earl of Lennox, 1238 (*Levenax*, p. 13; RMP., p. 161). There is in record an attestation by a Lennox jury that one Somerlet gave his son Thomas sasine of Darlet, now Darleith, c. 1238–80 (*Bain*, IV, 1755). Sumerleht who witnessed two charters by Duncan, earl of Carrik c. 1250 (CMN.,

13, 14), may be Sumerled de Dalcru who witnessed a confirmation charter by Maldovenus, earl of Lennox of lands in Lennox, 1252 (RMP., p. 172), and perhaps the Summerleith Lyen who witnessed a charter of the land of Ouchencloich, c. 1250 (*Levenax*, p. 27). Murdach, son of Sumerleth, was juror on an inquisition held at Gerwan (Girvan) in 1260 (*Bain*, I, 2674). Thomas filius Somerledy was one of an inquest made at Dumbarton in 1271 which found that the daughters of the late Finlay of Campsie were the lawful heirs of deceased Dufgall, brother of Maldouen, earl of Lennox (RMP., p. 191; *Red Bk. Menteith*, II, p. 218), and two years later he witnessed the charter by Earl Malcolm of Lennox granting the church of Kilpatrick to Paisley (*Levenax*, p. 15). John Sommerledi (= son of Sommerled) had a charter of lands in earldom of Carrik from David II (RMS., I, App. II, 1109), and Mordach Somirlyny witnessed a charter of land of Duffale to the Friars Preachers of Ayr, 1381 (*Friars Ayr*, p. 23). Somerled MacCombich is in record, c. 1442 (TGSI., XXII, p. 61), and Sorlet, rector of Assend (Assynt), attests a charter of Bishop William to his brother-german Gilbert Mudy in 1455 (RMS., II, 1404). From a Lamont of this name comes Clan Sorley of Cowal. The name has been corrupted by chroniclers into Sorli Marlady, Surle Maderdy, Sowrdy Madurdy, Surle Muderdi, and Mac Illurdy. Other forms of the name are Sourle, Serle, Simorledy, Somerledy, Somerleti, Surly, Surley, Sorlet (this Latinized Sorletus, 1427), Sorll, Sorlle, and Surleus Camrone was included in a letter of remission 12 March 1631 (RMS., VIII, 1753). Sorrie appears to be a shortening of it, and it has been equated with Samuel, "an instance of the tendency to equate what we do not know with something which at any rate we consider ourselves familiar" (Maclagan, *Perth incident*, p. 307). In the Arthurian romance of *Fergus*, formerly attributed to Guillaume le Clerc (c. 1170 – c. 1230), the name of Somerled of Argyll appears as Saumilloit, and in Wyntoun (bk. VII, 1. 1491) the great Somerled appears as Sowelle. Of the early history of this Somerled, grandson of Gilleadomnan, all we know is derived exclusively from tradition written down only c. 1680 (*Clan Donald*, I, p. 38) by Hugh Macdonald, the Sleat historian.

SOMERVILLE, Somervile, Sommerville, Somervail, Summervail. From a town near Caen in Normandy, Sumar's or Somer's estate. William de Somerville, first of the name in Scotland, came in the train of David I, and received lands in Lanarkshire. There were five Williams in succession, the last dying in 1282.

They appear as witnesses to charters to the religious houses of Melrose, Kelso, Coldingham, Glasgow, Newbattle, and Paisley during the reigns of David I, Malcolm IV, and William the Lion (see their chartularies). One of these Williams in the reign of William is said to have slain a monstrous animal or serpent which greatly devastated the district of Linton, Roxburghshire, and obtained the lands of Linton as a reward. A rude sculpture on one of the walls of the church represents a horseman in complete armor in the act of driving his lance down the animal's throat. An inscription is affirmed to have run thus:

'The wode laird of Lariston
Slew the worm of Wormes glen,
And wan all Lintoun parochine.'

Robert de Sumeruilla witnessed a charter by Duncan, earl of Fife, to the nuns of North Berwick, a. 1177 (CMN., 3). Ralph de Sumervilla, acolyte, was promoted to the church of Linton, 1255. Johan de Lynton of the county of Rokesburk, who rendered homage, 1296 (*Bain*, II, p. 202), was most probably a Somerville as Lynton at that time was a possession of that family. William Somerwele of the Plane, a charter witness in Edinburgh, 1492 (HP., II, p. 193). John Semrell, tenant under the Abbey of Kelso, 1567 (*Kelso*, p. 530), and John Symmerwell was burgessfreeman of Glasgow, 1614 (*Burgesses*). Scumervaill 1521, Semervaile 1525, Simerwell 1689, Someruell 1567, Someruyle 1511, Somervaill 1628, Somervel 1679, Somervele 1451, Somervell 1599, Somervol 1724, Somerwale 1517, Somerwele 1544, Somerwell 1611, Sommerveale 1681, Sommervell and Sommerwall 1600, Sommerwell 1539, Somyruyle 1448, Summyrvil 1424, Summyrvyle 1424, Summyrwil 1493; Sommeruill, Sommerweil, Somyruille, Somyrville, Symmervaill 1544, Symmervell 1650; Somerviel.

SOMMERS. *See under* SYMMERS.

SOMMERVILLE. *See under* SOMERVILLE.

SOONHOPE. Robert de Soynhope was received to the English king's peace in 1321 (*Bain*, III, 724). From the lands of Soonhope in Peeblesshire.

SOONHOUSE. Local. Thomas Suinhouse, fewar in Blainslevis, 1608, James Sunhous in Blainslie, 1660, and John Sownhous, portioner of Blainslie, 1662 (RRM., I, p. 67, 264; II, 11, 21). Thomas Sounhouse, pensioner of Thirlstane Hospital, 1676 (Thomson, *Lauderdale*, p. 71). Sownehous and Sownhouse 1662. Cf. Souness.

738

SOOTIE. An old variant of SUTTIE (of Balgone), q.v.

SORBIE, SORBY. The surname of an ancient family in Galloway who owned the lands of Sorby, which now form the parish of Sorbie, Wigtownshire. Gilbert de Sowreby witnessed a charter by William de Cunynburg, c. 1268 (RHM., I, p. 9). Peter Sorby in Dundee charged with aiding the English, 1552 (*Beats*, p. 326). William Sorbie in Stanehouse, 1626, and three more are in record (*Lanark CR.*). John Sorbie in Upper Achie, 1748, and John Sorbie in Upper Aichie, 1764 (*Kirkcudbright*).

SORLEY, A late form of SOMERLED, q.v. John Soirlie, chapman, mentioned in 1590 (*Sc. Ant.*, VI, p. 166). Custom set to William Soirlie in the Quhynnis, 1598 (SBR., p. 91), and Archibald Soirlie was town officer in Stirling, 1606 (ibid., p. 117). Patrick Sorley in Easter Lethendy, parish of Crieff, 1769 (*Dunkeld*). Sorill 1536.

SORLEYSON. An Englishing of MACSORLEY, q.v. Andrew, son of Somerledy, a charter witness, 1387, appears again c. 1390 as Andrew Sowyrlyson (*Laing*, 72, 74). Thomas Souirlyson who witnessed a charter of lands in Ayr, 1401 (*Friars Ayr*, p. 37) may be Thom Sourlesoun, member of Ayr Guild, c. 1431 (*Coll. AGAA.*, I, p. 228).

SOROULES. William Soroules held the lands of Sorulesfeld in 1208, and gave his name to them (*Melros*, I, p. 90). William Soreweles, citizen of London, complained in 1305 that the 'meir' and bailiffs of Berwick-on-Tweed took 'tolune' from him (*Bain*, II, 1739). The lands still bear the name Sorrowlessfield Mains.

SOUDIE. Thomas Soudie, cordiner in Inverness, 1609 (*Rec. Inv.*, II, p. 73), may have derived his surname from Suddie near Munlochy, Ross-shire.

SOUNESS, SOUNNESS. There were people named Sownes in Aberdeenshire, 1696. Adam Souness died in Ormiston, 1939. The -ss seems to preclude the name being considered as Sones ('son of Sone'). More probably a variant of SOONHOUSE, q.v.

SOUPER. Perhaps from the occupation of soapmaker, ME. *soper(e)*. William Super or Souper, carpenter, was paid for work done, 1689 (RPC., 3. ser. XIV, p. 649-650). William Souper was retoured heir of John Souper, merchant of Aberdeen, his father, 1698 (*Retours, Aberdeen*, 507). William Soupar in Collonoch, mentioned in 1716 (SCM., IV, p. 171), and Patrick Souper in Aberdeen, 1732 (NSCM.,

II). The name still exists in Aberdeen. Soap was first manufactured in Scotland in 1619.

SOUTER, SOUTAR, SOUTTAR, SOUTTER, SUTER, SUTER. From the occupation of shoemaker, cobbler (ME. *soutere* from ON. *sútare*).

"Of that surname I neid nocht be aschamit
For I can mak schone, butekins and buittis:
Gif me the coppie of the king's cuittis,
And ye sall se, richt sune, quhat I can do."
Lindsay, *Ane Satyre of the Thrie Estaites*, 3143-6.

Roger Sutor held land in Dumfries, a. 1214 (*Kelso*, 11), and Kolin, son of Anegus the Souter, was present at the pleas held at Dull in Angus in 1264 (RPSA., p. 349). Bernard called Sutor had a charter of a house in the tenement of Drumelzier, c. 1300-20 (*Hay*, 7), Fynlai sutor was prepositus of Stirling, 1327, and in 1330 Symon sutor was prepositus of the burgh of Culan (ER., I, p. 67, 271). Henry dictus Sutor held a land in Perth, 1375 (*Milne*, p. 35), Moricius Sutar and Simo Sutar de Der (Deer) were charged with being forestallers in Aberdeen, 1402, and several other persons of the name are mentioned there about the same time (CRA., p. 382-385; CWA., p. 312; NSCM., I, p. 3). Reginald Sowtar was burgess of Glasgow, 1422 (LCD., p. 242), Thomas Suteur, a Scots ship owner, had a safe conduct into England in 1438 (*Bain*, IV, 1110), and Thomas Soutar obtained from the abbot of Cupar the lease of a portion of the land of Muirton in 1457 (*Cupar-Angus*, I, p. 235; II, p. 64). Duncan Seutter was tenant in Auchlyne under the bishop of Aberdeen, 1511 (REA., I, p. 363), and Johnne Soutare of Mont had a feu of part of the lands of Wester Banchreis in 1586 (*Scon*, p. 232). In 1460 some members of the house of Johnstone in Annandale assumed the name of Souter, in consequence of "some discontent," and settled in Perthshire. In August, 1663, by Act of Parliament, they were allowed to resume their ancient surname (APS., VII, p. 467). John Suitor, laborer in Ellon, and John Sutter, joiner there, were among the Jacobites of the '45. In some instances Souter is probably a translation of GRASSICK, q.v. Patrick Southar in Strathdee in 1527 (*Grant*, III, p. 70). Sowtare 1464, Suttar 1633. Sir Thomas Urquhart relates as a tradition in his time (he died in 1660) that the two promontories of Cromarty, the "Soutars," were the work stools of two giants who supplied their comrades with shoes and buskins.

SOUTHGATE. Rossi de Southgate and Wadinus [Wady] de Southgate rendered homage at Perth, 1291 (RR.). A wide street in the older part of the town of Perth named South Street was formerly known as the Southgate.

SOUTHHOUSE. Local, 'at the south house,' with reference to its position in relation to another. Southhous in sheriffdom of Edinburgh is mentioned in 1554. Thomas de Southehous was juror on forfeited lands in Lothian, 1312 (*Bain*, III, 243). Thomas Suithhous was voter in Edinburgh, 1580 (*Laing*, 1006).

SOUTHLYNTONE. Local. Johan de Southlyntone of Berwickshire rendered homage, 1296 (*Bain*, II, p. 206).

SOUTHREN. John Southren rendered homage at Perth, 1291 (RR.). A Southerner, one from the South.

SOUTHWICK. From Southwick in Kirkcudbrightshire. Gilbert de Southaic, son of Gospatric [son of Orm], was witness in 1210 to a grant by Alan, son of Roland, to Roger de Lascy (*Bain*, I, 553). The share of Patric de Sutheyk or Sutheyc, heir portioner of Helewisa de Levintone, was retained in the king's hands in 1274 (*Bain*, II, 21, 27). In 1292 an inquisition made at Carlisle in April as to the age of Gilbert, son and heir of Patrick de Suthaik, found that he was born in Tinwald in Scotland and was 21 years of age (ibid., II, 585). On his rendering homage the escheator *ultra* Trent was commanded to give him seisin of his father's lands (ibid., 592). In the same year (1292) he, along with others, sued Robert de Brus senior and Christina, his wife, for the sixth part of the half of the manor of Glassanby (ibid., p. 150). In 1296 Gilbert de Suthayck is recorded as holding lands in Skelton and Kirkeandres, paying 75s. at Easter; in August he rendered homage for his lands and shortly after was juror on an inquisition made at Berwick on lands in Dumfriesshire (ibid., p. 172, 185, 215). At the Michaelmas term, 1296, the sheriff of Cumberland charged himself 67s. 2½d. for the lands of Gilbert de Sothehack in Skelton, and 23s. 4d. for his lands in Kirkeandres, and in December, 1298, the same sheriff was directed to take without delay the land of Gilbert Sotheayk in the vill of Skeldon and Kirkeandres (ibid., 841, 1042). In June, 1300, a sixth part of the lands held in dower by the late Sarra, widow of Richard de Levynton, were ordered to be delivered to Gilbert de Southeyk (ibid., 1140). Thomas de Sutheyche of Dumfriesshire also rendered homage in 1296 (ibid., 810). Walter de Southuyk was rector of the church of Kirkpatrick-Croe in 1320 (REG., p. 229), and Gilbert de Southevk or Sutheg is mentioned as chancellor of Glasgow Cathedral in 1337 and again in 1343 (*Pap. Lett.*, II, p. 540; *Pap. Pet.*, I, p. 15).

SOUTRA. From Soutra, an ancient parish in East Lothian, the old spelling of which was Soltre. Sir John de Seltre or Soltre was chaplain to the bishop of Aberdeen and a charter witness, c. 1240 (REA., I, p. 16; II, p. 272). In 1243 he witnessed ratification of the church of Lescelyn to the Abbey of Lindores (LAC., p. 90). Walter de Soltre, burgess of Berwick, made a grant of land to the Hospital of Soltre, c. 1250–66 (*Soltre*, p. 31). William Soltre, cellerarius, and magister John Soltre witnessed the gift by William Heryote to the Abbey of Newbotvll in 1458 (*Neubotle*, p. 245, 246). William Soltre or Soltree, a monk of the same house, appears as witness in charters by Alan Lokart, laird of Lee, 1467 (ibid., p. 263, 314). Perhaps now lost in SOUTER.

SOUTTAR, SOUTTER. *See under* SOUTER.

SOWDAN, SOWDEN. Of local origin from Southdean, Roxburghshire. James Sowdan in Lauder, no date (*Lauder*). Charles Suddane was burgess of Lauder in 1635 and other three of the name are in the Lauder Commissariot Record. Thomas Suddane was retoured heir in lands in Jedburgh in 1648 (*Retours, Berwick*, 276), and Thomas Soudden is recorded in Melrose, 1682 (RRM., III, p. 35). James Souden died in Stirling, 1940 (*WScot*). The place name was Sovdon in 1296, and it gave name to Soudoun Law.

SOWLUG. John Sowlug or Soulug, stableman to the bishop of Dunkeld in 1506 and following years (*Rent. Dunk.*, p. 86, 89, 115, etc.). A nickname evidently, not a surname.

SPADE. Gilbert Spade and Thomas Spade were burgesses of Linlithgow, 1536 (*Johnsoun*).

SPADEN. Perhaps local pronunciation of SPALDING, q.v. John Spadine, mariner of Aberdeen, 1599 (CRA., p. 201). William Spaden, tenant in barony of Canneglerloch, 1640 (SCM., v, p. 228).

SPAIN. A native of Spain. It may also be a descriptive name given to a Scot who had returned from a residence in Spain. Walterus nepos Willelmi de Spaine witnessed a charter of three acres of Karruderes (Carruthers) by Walter del Bois, n. d. (*Raine*, 166). William Spayne, servant to the king and queen of Scotland, 1424, is doubtless the William Spaigne of Scotland who had a safe conduct into England in 1426 (*Bain*, IV, 969, 992). Malcolm Spainze was witness at Kyncragy, 1540 (*Aboyne*, p. 70), and Cristeane Spanyie or Spainve was spouse of John Widder in Brighous, 1585 (*Scon*, p. 223, 225).

SPALDING. From the town of Spalding in Lincolnshire. Radulphus de Spalding who witnessed a charter of the mill of Caterline in Kincardineshire in 1225 (RAA., I, p. 90) is probably the first of the name recorded in Scotland. Magister John de Spaldyn witnessed a grant of lands in Aberdeen, c. 1294 (REA., I, p. 37). As Johan Despanyding (= De Spanyding) he is mentioned as canon of Elgin, c. 1300 (Rec. Elgin, p. 10), and is probably the Johan de Spauyding who petitioned Edward I in 1304 to give him 20 oaks from his forest of Laund Morgund to build his church of Duffus (Bain, II, 1629, 1708). Symon de Spalding, parson of the church of Ogheltre in Ayrshire rendered homage in 1296 (ibid., p. 206). Tytler mentions in his History of Scotland (I, p. 133, ed. of 1864) that at the siege of Berwick by Bruce in 1318, one of the burgesses of the town named Peter de Spalding, disgusted with the severity of the governor, resolved to aid the besiegers. In reward for his services he received from Bruce in May, 1319, in exchange for his lands and tenements at Berwick, the lands of Ballourthy (Balzeordie) and Petmethey (Pitmachie) in Angus (Carnegies, Earls of Southesk, p. 482) together with the keepership of the royal forest of Kylgerry. William Spaldyng was elected a lineator of Aberdeen, 1398 (CRA., p. 374), Thomas de Spalding and David de Spalding held a tenement in Dundee in 1442 (Charters and writs, Dundee, p. 20), David Spaldeng of Dundee had a safe conduct into England, 1453 (Bain, IV, 1254), John de Spaldynge was deacon in Brechin, 1456 (REB., I, p. 182), in 1479 George Spalding appears as provost of Dundee (Panmure, II, 251). The Spaldings are included in "The roll of the clannis that hes capitanes, cheiffis and chiftanes quhome on thai depend," 1587 (APS., III, p. 467). Spaldene 1684.

SPANG. A family of this name were prominent burgesses of Glasgow in the sixteenth century (Macfarlane, II, p. 283–284). William Spang, son of Thomas Spang, burgess freeman there, 1576 (Burgesses). Spange 1555.

SPANKIE. Walter Spankye held a land in Dundee before 1443 (REB., I, 93), and Alexander Spanky was tenant of Drumdranfurde, Ardmanoch, in 1504 (ER., XII, p. 662). Frequent mention is made (c. 1512–14) in the Rental of Dunkeld of Master Robert Spanke or Spankȝe, steward to the bishop and afterwards dean of Fife (Rent. Dunk., p. 148, 225, etc.). David Spankie was enrolled burgess of Dundee in 1590 (Wedd., p. 151), and James Spankie was minister at Coupar-Angus in 1779 (Dunkeld). Still a surname in the parish

of St. Cyrus, Kincardineshire. Spangy and Spanky 1461.

SPANKIN. Gilbert Spankin was admitted burgess of Aberdeen, 1606 (NSCM., I, p. 103), and in 1629 there is an entry in the local records of a sum "debursit to Gilbert Spankine for makeing the tounes armes in brass" (SCM., v, p. 146).

SPANSWICK. A rare surname in Shetland, of local origin from a small place of the name.

SPARK. William Sperk in Aberdeen, 1408 (CWA., p. 316). John Sperk was tenant of Lytyl Perth in 1472 (Cupar-Angus, I, p. 164). John Sperk was admitted burgess of Aberdeen in 1407 and James Spark in 1539 (NSCM., I, p. 2, 56). Adam Spark is recorded as a monk of Kilwinning in 1532 (LCD., p. 12), and Andrew Spark was a merchant in Irvine in 1698 (Irvine, I, p. 66).

SPARKELYN. Sir Hugh de Sparkelyn, vicar of the church of Kylmacolm, 1303, appears again in 1313 as Hugh de Sparchynge (RMP., p. 376, 381), and Richard de Sperkeling was a monk in the monastery of Paisley, 1368 (ibid., p. 328). Probably Englishmen.

SPEDDING. Goods were stolen from John Spedane in Blakhalche, 1502 (Trials, I, p. * 27). William Speiding, smith in Galloscheills, 1600 (RRM., I, p. 263). John Speddin, writer in Edinburgh, 1692 (Edin. App.). Thomas Speeding in Harlaw, 1733 (Lauder). Thomas Speedin, portioner of Bowden, 1793, and Janet Speeden alias Spiden in Newtoun, 1813 (Heirs, 471, 600).

SPEED, SPEID. Nicholas Speid occupied part of the lands of Cuikstone or Quygstone in Angus, 1410 (REB., I, 84), and Cuthbert Speid was witness in Forfar (Southesk, p. 720). Rev. George Speed, minister of Aberlour, Banffshire, died 1688, and Mr. William Speed, minister at Botraphennie, residenter at Netherbyre, parish of Aytoun, 1706 (Lauder), is probably Mr. William Speed, minister at Ednam, who was deposed in 1689 (RPC., 3. ser. XIV, p. 168).

SPEEDIE, SPEEDY, SPEIDIE. Thomas Spedy, witness in Edinburgh, 1553 (Laing, 614), John Spidie in Dunfermline, 1571 (Dunfermline), and Tom Speedy, game-keeper and naturalist, died 1924. Spathie, Speddie, Spethy.

SPEEDIMAN. David Speediman, glover in Aberdeen, 1721 (NSCM., II, p. 109), and another David Speediman was burgess there, 1756 (Aberdeen CR.).

SPEIR, SPIER. It may be an official name, the 'spyer,' i.e. watchman, from OFr. *espier*. The first is a common surname in Kilbarchan. Willelmus Sper, witness in Perth in the reign of Alexander II (*Scon*, p. 55). Gilbert Spere was a juror in Irvine, 1417, and mention is made in 1418 of the tenement of Roger Spere there (*Irvine*, I, p. 20, 126). David Spere was burgess of Glasgow in 1475 (*LCD.*, p. 254), and in the following year Alexander Speir of Pettincrefe was depute of James, earl of Buchan (*SBR.*, p. 256). John Speire was a witness in Glasgow in 1516 (*REG.*, 492), Thomas Speir was a merchant burgess in Edinburgh, 1626 (*Inquis.*, 1281), and David Speir was bailie of Irvine, 1664 (*Irvine*, II, p. 166).

SPEIRS, SPIERS. Probably from SPEIR, with genitive -*s*, 'son of Speir.' George Speris is recorded in Stirling, 1548 (*SBR.*, p. 51), Janet Speirs appears in Farniknowes, 1679 (*Lauder*), and Thomas Speirs in Torrieburne complained against his minister, 1689 (*RPC.*, 3. ser. XIV, p. 425).

SPENCE, SPENS. From the office of custodian of the larder or provision-room, ME. *spence, spens(e* <OF. *despense*. In the Chartulary of Inchaffray the dispensario appears in each case along with the rennarius, q.v., to whom he was perhaps subordinate (*Inchaffray*, p. 4, 34, 264). From the thirteenth century downwards several persons named Spensa, Dispensa, are mentioned as government officials, and in 1529 we have entry in the royal accounts of livery for 'John Spens at the cupboard' (*ALHT.*, v, p. 383). Roger dispensator witnessed a charter by the bishop of Moray granting the church of Deveth to Spyny between 1202–22, and Thomas dispensator witnessed excambion of the lands of Dolays Mychel (Dallas) in 1232 (*REM.*, p. 61, 88). John Spens was bailie of Irvine, 1260 (*Irvine*, I, p. 5). Between 1296 and 1324 Thomas de Spensa witnessed a charter by John of Jonystoun in favor of the Hospital of Soltre (*Soltre*, p. 41). Nicholaus de Dispensa forfeited land in the vill and tenement of Langnodryf (Langniddry) between 1315–21 (*RMS.*, I, 69). The ship belonging to Laurence de Spense and other Scottish merchants was wrecked at Whitbernes near Newcastle-on-Tyne, 1365 (*Bain*, IV, 114), and Thomas de Spensa and Laurence de Spensa appear as witnesses in Perth, 1375 (*Milne*, p. 36). Henry of Spens witnessed a charter by Robert, earl of Fife, c. 1390 (*Athole*, p. 704), and Fergus de la Spens held a tenement in Edinburgh, 1392 (*Egidii*, p. 27). William de Spensa was one of the perambulators of the marches of Tarwas and Uldny, 1417 (*RAA.*, II, 53),

Patrick de Spens held land in Lauder, Berwickshire, 1426 (*Soltre*, p. 51), and John de Spensa, burgess of Perth in the same year, had a grant of lands in the earldom of Menteth (*RMS.*, II, 45). John de Spens of Perth was bailie of Glendochirde, 1428, John Spens was custodier of Stocket Forest, 1448 (*CRA.*, p. 18), and another John de Spens was admitted burgess of Aberdeen, 1444 (*NSCM.*, I, p. 9). Thomas Spens, bishop of Aberdeen in the latter half of the fifteenth century was, says Cosmo Innes, "so much mixed up with public affairs that to give the details of his life would be to write the account of Scottish politics for the time" (*REA.*, I, p. xl). The name was early carried to France and appears there as D'Espences (de Nettancourt, de Bettancourt, de Vroil, etc.). There is no proof that the family of Spens is descended from Duncan, fourth earl of Fife, as some contend. Despens 1446, Spenss 1681.

SPENDLOVE. This curious surname is found in Lanarkshire as early as the end of the thirteenth century. OF. *espand-loue* perhaps refers to disembowelling (*Weekley*, p. 260). In 1296 Emme Spendloue of the county of Lanark rendered homage for her lands (*Bain*, II, p. 209). In the same year a writ was issued to the sheriff of Lanark ordering him to restore to Simon Spendelove his lands which probably had been forfeited (ibid., 832). William Spendelove, hobelar in Berwick, is mentioned in 1312 (ibid., p. 398). Dobie Spendluf is in Peebles, 1457 (*Renwick, Peebles*, p. 23). A monk of Dunfermline in 1502 bore the name of John Spendluff (*CDE.*, 58), and Dene Vilyam Spendluf was a monk of the same house in the same year (*DBR.*, 125). Mariote Spendluyff was a tenant in the barony of Stobo in 1514, in 1528 John Spendluyff was "rentillayt in ane ox gang of land" in Stobo, and in 1555 mention is made of Ambrois Spendlaw, late rentaller of the Harro of Stobo (*Rental*). The name is also found in England, and Bardsley's earliest example is dated 1273.

SPENS. *See* SPENCE.

SPERLIN. Michael Sperlin held a burgage in Renfrew in the fourteenth century (*RMP.*, p. 374). Harrison equates the name with Sparling = sparrow + (double) diminutive suffix -*ling*. Bardsley records the name in 1273.

SPERSHOT. John Spershot, esquire, had a safe conduct into England in 1399 (*Bain*, IV, 522). There are parishes named Sparshott in Berks and in Hants.

SPICER. From the occupation, ME. *spicer*, dealer in spices. Rauf le Spicer rendered homage, 1296 (*Bain*, II, p. 197), and Eustace Lespicer and Martin Lespicer rendered homage at Berwick, 1291 (RR.). Le is the French definite article.

SPICK. Inquisition was made at Traqueyr in 1274 whether Agatha Spick had right to a house and pertinents in the vill of Traqueyr, and it was found that the house had been purchased by her brother, Robert Spick (*Bain*, II, 34).

SPIER, SPIERS. See under SPEIR.

SPILEMAN. Robert filius Hugonis filii Spileman held a carucate of land apud Rane, Aberdeenshire, c. 1170 (REA., I, p. 10). Harrison says: *Spill* (Teut.), an old personal name + *man*. Cf. German name Spielman, from Old High German *spilaman*, wandering singer, musician.

SPINK. This was at one time a not uncommon surname around Arbroath. Alexander Spink appears as shoremaster there in 1624 (Hay, *Arbroath*, p. 319). The earliest record of the name in Scotland is in 1261 when an inquest was held to determine the right which the wife of Robert Spinc claimed to have to the king's garden of Elgin (APS., I, p. 99).

SPINY. William Spiny, provost of the collegiate church of Tain, 1514 (*Beauly*, p. 184) derived his name from Spynie near Elgin.

SPITTAL, SPITTEL, SPITTLE. ME. *spital*, an aphetised form of OFr. *hospital*. The old Dumbartonshire family of Spittal derived their name from the lands of Spittal in the parish of Kilmaron, which at an earlier date had belonged to the Knights Hospitallers (*Strathendrick*, p. 252). In or before 1394 Adam de Spydeloch resigned the lands of Ladlewn (*Levenax*, p. 59), and in 1461 Donald of Spytale was one of an inquest to determine the rights of pasturage which the Temple lands had over the adjoining town and territory of Letter (*Strathendrick*, p. 222). The Dumbartonshire Spittals are classed as a sept of Buchanan whose chief they followed. Mathew del Spitel is mentioned in a Coldingham charter of 1285 (*Raine*, 262). Walter del Spetalle alias Walterus de Hospitali received from David II a charter of a tenth part of the lands of Kynynmunthe in the quarter of Fortheryf, 1365 (RMS., I, 218, 220), and these lands were in possession of Johannes de Spitale in 1395 (RPSA., p. 3). John Spitale was burgess of Edinburgh, 1423 (*Egidii*, p. 45), William Spittale de Luquhat had a precept of remission in 1526 (RSS., I, 3596),

and dominus John Spettale was chaplain in Linlithgow, 1531 (*Johnsoun*). Henry Spittle, late bookbinder in Edinburgh, 1732 (*Guildry*, p. 142). Spetal 1493, Spetall 1509, Spettall 1529, Spittele 1634, Spittell 1627.

SPITTELAUT. David Spittelaut was admitted burgess of Aberdeen, 1535 (NSCM., I, p. 53), and in 1538 the wife of David Spilyelaucht was punished for her "hawy and gryt strublens" of David Reid, and eight years later David Spilyelaucht himself was condemned "to be brint on the left hand with ane het irne" (CRA., p. 155, 246). Spellings are as in original, but there is some error in the original transcription.

SPOTT. From the lands of Spott, near Dunbar, East Lothian. Eliz de Spot of the county of Edinburgh and Huwe, son of Moyses de Spot of the county of Berwick, rendered homage in 1296 (*Bain*, II, p. 201, 213). Adam Spot granted a charter of land in the tenement of Blantrodoks (Ballintrodo, now Arniston), c. 1300–20 (*Hay*, p. 6). Adam of Spot, bailie of Edinburgh in 1386 (ER., III, p. 139), is recorded again in 1404 (*Egidii*, p. 41), and Jamys Spott of Scotland petitioned for a safe conduct into England in 1398 (*Bain*, IV, 476), and Walter de Spott was burgess of Edinburgh in 1411 (*Egidii*, p. 44). Ninian Spot witnessed a charter of a tenement in Musselburgh in 1437 (*Soltre*, p. 53), appears as presbyter and prebendar of Menmuir in 1454 (*Southesk*, p. 720), and canon of Dunkeld and comptroller and in parliament in 1458 (*Stodart*, II, p. 375).

SPOTTISWOOD, SPOTTISWOODE. From the barony of Spottiswood in the parish of Gordon, Berwickshire. The first of the name who appears in history is Robert de Spotteswode of the county of Berewyk, who pledged adherence to Edward I in 1296 (*Bain*, p. 203). His seal bears a wild boar passant, S' Rob' de Spottiswod (ibid., p. 544). William de Spottiswod, notary public, verified the proceedings which on 15th December 1309 were adopted in Scotland against the Knights Templars (Wilkins, *Concilia*, II, p. 383). Gavin Spottiswod witnessed an instrument of sasine in 1525 (*Home*, 35). John Spottiswood (1565–1639), archbishop of St. Andrews, wrote a *History of the Church and State of Scotland*, published in 1655. Alexander Spotswood, a scion of that Ilk, was one of the ablest and most popular of the representatives of the Crown authority in the early American colonies (1710–1722), and the principal encourager of the growth of tobacco which laid the foundation of Virginia's wealth and also that of Glasgow's "Tobacco Lords." Spotswode 1642, Spotswood 1688, Spottyswod 1368.

SPOWART. A surname common in Fife for which a Flemish origin has been suggested (*Sc. Ant.*, IV). Andrew Spowart appears in Colliarow of Clackmannan, 1695 (*Inquis. Tut.*, 1366).

SPRAGUE. From English dialectal *sprag*, *sprak* (ON. *spræk-r*, lively active), alert, lively, intelligent.

SPRALL. See under SPREULL.

SPREULL, SPROUL, SPROULE, SPREALL, SPRALL. Spreull was the name of an old Dumbartonshire family. Walter Spreul, steward of Malcolm, earl of Levenax, had a charter from the earl of the land of Dalmuir or Dalmore, c. 1280, and c. 1290 witnessed a charter to Arthur Galbraith (*Levenax*, p. 30, 42). For his homage and service he obtained in the beginning of the reign of Robert I another charter of the lands of Dalquhen (ibid., p. 91). In 1296 Wautier Spreul of Lanarkshire rendered homage. His seal bears a hunting-horn, stringed, between three roses, S' *Walteri Sprevile* (*Bain*, II, p. 204, 549). Walter Sprouill paid to Exchequer the contribution of the Barony of Glasgow in 1366, and in 1368 Thomas Sprowl was receiver of stores for Edinburgh Castle (ER., II, p. 259, 306). Thomas Sprewl of Coldoun was witness, 1460 (*Ayr*, p. 35), and Patrick Spruyle is recorded in Edinburgh, 1580 (*Soltre*, p. 235). John Spreull (1646–1722), merchant of Glasgow, for nonconformity was twice tortured and imprisoned on the Bass Rock for six years. Spreuile 1308, Spreule 1547, Sprewile 1549, Sprewell 1573, Sprewyle 1529, Sproule 1369, Sproult 1372, Spruylle 1574, Sprwl 1488.

SPRING. Perhaps local, 'at the spring.' This name is found early in Aberdeen. Henry Spring in Berwickshire rendered homage, 1291 (RR.). John Spryng witnessed an Aberdeen charter in 1342 (REA., I, p. 72), and Andree Spryng was burgess of the town in 1362 (RMS., I, 104). Thomas Springe who had a charter of land of Gask with pertinents in sheriffdom of Abirdene, 1369 (RMS., I, 342), may be Thomas Spryng or Sprynger who appears as burgess there, 1396–99–1410 (REA., II, p. 293, 296; SCM., v, p. 13), and was concerned in a dispute connected with a piece of waste ground, 1398 (CRA., p. 371). Ro. Sprinct was admitted burgess of Aberdeen, 1400 (NSCM., I, p. 1), and Thomas Sprinct is recorded there in 1408 (CWA., p. 313).

SPRINGER. Thomas Sprynger held a land in Aberdeen, 1396 (REA., II, p. 293). Cf. under SPRING.

SPROAT, SPROT, SPROTT, SPROUT. Perhaps from *Sprot*, an OE. personal name, but more likely to be of Scandinavian origin (*Redin*, p. 8). The tradition of those bearing this name in Scotland is that their ancestors were Saxons who came into Scotland after the Norman Conquest of England. The first recorded of the name in Scotland appears to be Hugh Sprot of Ur who witnessed a charter by Eustace Baliol granting the church and lands of Hur (Urr) in 1262 to the monks of Holyrood (LSC., 81). Adam Sprut or Spr'ut was witness in Glasgow, c. 1290 (REG., p. 200). Richard Sprot of Bryset, Roxburghshire, is recorded in 1307 (*Sc. Ant.*, v, p. 22), and Walter Sprot was tenant of Newtoun in Moffatdale, 1376 (RHM., I, p. lxii). William Sprout and John Sprout were elected lineators of Aberdeen, 1398 (CRA., p. 374), William Sprot was admitted burgess there in 1443, John Sprut in 1457, and William Sprut in 1479 (NSCM., I, p. 8, 15, 28). Robert Sprute, witness at Inuerarite, 1505 (REB., I, 222). Twelve of the name are in the Commissariot Record of Kirkcudbright between 1663–1800.

SPROTTY. William Spruty was admitted burgess of Aberdeen, 1494 (NSCM., I, p. 37). John Sprottie, ironsmith in Edinburgh, 1563 (*Laing*, 758).

SPROUL, SPROULE. See under SPREULL.

SPROULISTON. John of Sprouliston, clerk, witnessed a confirmation by William, bishop of Glasgow, c. 1335–67 (RMP., p. 239). He derived his name from Sproulstone in Renfrewshire, referred to in 1616 as the 9s. 8d. lands of old extent of "Auchinbathie olim nuncupatarum Spreulistoun" (*Retours, Renfrew*, 40).

SPROUNT, SPRUNT. John Sprunte leased part of Kethyk, c. 1443 (*Cupar-Angus*, I, p. 119), Andrew Sprount was tenant of Balgreschach in 1473, the Park of Newbigging was granted to Patrick Sprund in the same year, and an eighth part of Balbrogy was let to Patrick Sprwnt in 1476 (ibid., p. 176, 185, 205). Andrew Sprwnt held a land in Aberdeen in 1447 (CRA., p. 15), John Sprwnt was a witness in Brechin, 1476 (REB., I, 199), and Robert Sprunt is recorded in Easter Caputh, 1690 (*Dunkeld*).

SPROUSTON. Local, from the old village of Sprouston in Roxburghshire. Johannes de Sprouston was witness in Aberdeen, 1392 (REA., I, p. 194).

SPROUT. See under SPROAT.

SPRUNT. See under SPROUNT.

SPURNECURTOYS. William Spurnecurtoys was burgess of Aberdeen, 1274 (*Fraser*, p. 11). Ewen records (p. 226) Spurneturtoys (first *t* for *c*) and Spornecurteys 1287.

SPYNIE. From Spynie in the parish of the same name in Moray. Henricus de Spyny was vicar of Banf, 1323 (RAA., I, p. 223). William de Spyny who appears as canon of the church of Moray in 1363 (REM., p. 313) may be the William de Spyny who was procurator for the abbot of Aberbrothoc in 1375 (RAA., II, 34). John de Spyny petitioned for a canonry and prebend of Neu[er] and Ros[ke]ven in Ros, 1407 (*Pap. Pet.*, I, p. 635). Sir William Spyne or Spynie, provost of Thane or Tayne (Tain) in 1509 (OPS., II, p. 661) was dead before 1545 (*Laing*, 495). Espyny 1394.

SQUAIR, SQUIRE. From 'squire,' a knight's attendant, one who bore the knight's shield.

"A Knight ther was...
With him ther was his sone, a yong Squyer."
Chaucer, *Canterbury Tales*, prol.

Thom Squier witnessed a grant of the lands of Drumkerauch in 1260 (RPSA., p. 347), and Johan le Squier of Whyhope of Edinburghshire rendered homage, 1296 (*Bain*, II, p. 201). Thomas Skayre, juror on inquisition at Perth, 1305 (*Bain*, II, p. 450), William Squier witnessed the homage of Duncan, earl of Fife to the abbot of Dunfermline in 1316, and in the same year appears as burgess of Dunfermline (RD., p. 235, 236). Michael Squier was witness in a dispute between James de Dundas and the abbot of Dunfermline, 1342 (ibid., p. 262), and William dictus Squyer was witness to a Perth charter of 1375 (*Milne*, p. 36). John Squyer or Skuyer was one of the masons who contracted in 1387 for the building of five chapels on the south side of St. Giles's parish church, Edinburgh (CDE., p. 14; Nisbet, *Plates*). Thomas Squiar appears in Aberdeen, 1408 (CWA., p. 315), Gilcrist Sqwier had a safe conduct to enter England in 1424 (*Bain*, IV, 963), William Skyar (Sqwyare, or Square) who gifted "vnum antiphonarium" to the church of Aberdeen, died in 1439 (REA., II, p. 135, 204, 218), and John Squyer, chaplain in Dundee, is in record, 1452 (REB., I, 53). Thomas Squeyar in Inverness was fined in 1606 "for the vrangus trubling of Murdo Poilson," and "drawing of the said Murdois bluid with his steked naiff on his wisag and face" (*Rec. Inv.*, II, p. 34), and Alexander Square was nominated to pass upon an inquest in Inverness, 1686 (ibid., II, p. 342). Thomas Skair is recorded in Balnamoon, 1689 (RPC., 3. ser. XIV, p. 709), and Alexander Skair of Burnside, parish of Men-

muir, d. 1751. John James Squires from Marnoch was killed in the first Great War (*Turriff*). Squear 1613, Skuyer and Sqwyer 1387, Squir 1644, Squyar 1630, Squyre 1628, Sqwyar c. 1500.

STABLE, STABLES. James Stubyl was tenant of Balmyle, 1460, and William Stabyl, tenant in Grange of Abyrbothry, 1468 (*Cupar-Angus*, I, p. 142). The name also appears in the same record in the fifteenth century as Stabil, Stablis, Stibles, Stibull, Stibulis, and Stubil. Robert Stibillis or Stibles, son of the late John Stiblis, was admitted burgess of Dundee in 1593 (*Wedd.*, p. 62), Robert Stibbillis appears as lector of the church of Dundee in 1623 (REB., II, 242), and Alexander Stable is recorded in Forgyside, 1698 (*Moray*). The name also appears in Keith, Banffshire, in 1646 (*Strathbogie*, p. 71). Helen Stables in Charleston of Aboyne, 1755 (*Aberdeen CR.*). Many families of this name appear in the Register of Cupar-Angus Abbey.

STAFFEIN. Perhaps meant for STEVEN, q.v. John Staffein, burgess in Kirkcudbright, 1674 (*Kirkcudbright*), is probably the John Staffine who signed the Test there in 1684 (RPC., 3. ser. X, p. 248). John Staffing, burgess in Kirkcudbright, 1722 (*Kirkcudbright*). St. Stephen in Sweden is known as St. Staffan.

STAIG. The Scots form of English STAGG. John Stag rendered homage at Perth, 1291 (RR.). Henry Staig in the parish of Cheindilkirk, 1564 (*Lauder*). James Staig in Dysart, 1584 (*Dysart*, p. 41). David Staig, provost of Dumfries, died 1826.

STAIN. Of local origin from Stain near Biggar, Lanarkshire. John of Staine near Biggar left two coheirs, Agnes of Staine and Janet (*Stodart*, II, p. 383).

STAINEHILL. Local. There is a Stonehill near Dunblane. Isoble Stainehill, witness in witchcraft trial in Brechin, 1650 (*Records Presb. Brechin*, Dundee, 1877, p. 36).

STAINES, STAINS. See under STEENS.

STAIR. Now a forename, as in Stair Agnew, is from the place Stair in Ayrshire. Stair M'Quhae, minister of St. Quivox in 1820.

STALKER. From the occupation of 'stalker,' one who stalks, as a deerstalker. Patrick Stalcare had a remission in 1427 (*Rose*, p. 126), and twenty years later John Stalcare is in record as burgess of Berwick (RD., 461). Donald Stalkair leased the church of Glenyleff in 1447 (*Cupar-Angus*, I, p. 126), and John Stalcare was one of an inquest anent a fishing on the Tweed in 1467 (RD., p. 358). The name of William Staiker, goldsmith and guild-brother in Glasgow, 1607 (*Burgesses*) is probably to be taken as a spelling of Stalker. Stalkar 1491. The name is also recorded in Aberdeen, 1605 (CRA., p. 277).

STAMPARD. Stephen dictus Stampard, son and heir of William Stampard, gifted an acre of land in Coldingham to the prior and monks of Coldingham, c. 1280 (*Raine*, 273, 282). Stephen de Stampard gave Robert Hopper the piece of land called Stampardesakyr in the territory of Coldingham (ibid., 281).

STANDANDSTANYS. Of local origin from one or other of places of the name in Aberdeenshire. There are places of this name near Dyce, Skene, Echt, and Leochel, each with remains of a prehistoric stone circle. David de Standandstanys admitted burgess of Aberdeen, 1457 (NSCM., I, p. 16), appears in 1477 as David de Stannanstanis (RMS., II, 1311).

STANFIELD. Local, from some place of the name in England. James Stanfield, merchant in Edinburgh, 1673 (*Laing*, 2704). Philip Stanfield was executed in 1688 for the murder of his father, Sir James Stanfield of Newmills (*Trials*, III, p. 196). His guilt was discovered by the body bleeding at his touch.

STANFORD. Of English origin from one or other of several places of the name. Adam de Stanford witnessed the grant by William the Lion of burgh and market to the church of Glasgow, c. 1175 (REG., p. 37), and another charter by same king to the church of Paisley (RMP., p. 89). Robert de Standford witnessed sale of a toft to the canons of Scone in 1219 (*Scon*, p. 52), and Roger de Staunforth was vicar of Banchrytarny in 1262 (RAA., I, p. 193).

STANGER. A surname of local origin in Orkney, probably from the 1/2d land of Stanagar (1503) in the parish of Stromness.

STANHOPE. A surname most probably assumed from Stanhope in Tweeddale, but it does not appear that those lands ever were possessed by persons of the name (*Stodart*). Thomas of Stanhope was a resident near there in 1471, and a family of Stanhope possessed Stanhope's Mylne near Edinburgh at the beginning of the seventeenth century. John of Stanhope appears in that quarter in 1479–88–93. Henry Stanehops is recorded in Edinburgh in 1627 (*Edinb. Marr.*). Stanehop, Stanehope 1606, Stenhop 1607, Stanhopes 1627.

STANHOUSE. A variant of STENHOUSE, q.v.

STANLEY. Most probably an early importation from one or other of the places named Stanley

in England. Alexander Stanlie appears as dean of guild of Edinburgh in 1455 (*Cambus.*, 96), and Mathew Stanley, burgess of Edinburgh, had license in 1495 to import Scottish goods into England (*Bain*, IV, 1619). John Stanelie was burgess of Rutherglen in 1647 (*Inquis.*, 3334). Stainley 1671, Stainlie 1608.

STANNERGILL. Marjory Stannergill was retoured heir portioner of William Stannergill, avi, in tenement in Pittinweim in 1634, and Cristina, Issobella, and Agneta Stannergillis were heirs portioners of William Stannergill olim burgess of Pettinweim in 1650 (*Retours, Fife*, 501, 1585). Probably from Stangergill near Dunnet, Caithness.

STANY. Sir Michael Stany was chaplain of St. Andrews diocese, 1391 (*Wemyss*, II, 29), and Thomas Stanne, magistrate of Aberdeen, 1489 (REA., II, p. 302). The manor of Stanney or Staney in the parish of Stoke near Chester gave origin to an old family of this name (*Lower*).

STAPILTON. William of Stapilton, vallettus to Edward Balliol in 1349 (*Rot. Scot.*, I, p. 728) may have been an Englishman. There are two places named Stapleton in Yorkshire, each of which gave name to a family of some prominence, but quite distinct.

STARK. The lands of Estirbalbretane were leased to Richard Starke in 1376 (RHM., I, p. lxvi). William Stark was tenant in Castalstaris in 1540 (*Rental*), and in 1544 we have record of a sasine to Beatrix Sterk in Glasgow (*Protocols*, I). James Stark was heir of John Stark in Auchinvolie, 1629 (*Retours, Lanark*, 164). Burke (*Landed gentry*) says the family of Stark claims descent from Alexander Robertson of Strowan who died 1506 or 1507. Tradition relates that Alexander, younger son of Paul Robertson, having taken part in the family feuds of the day (who at that time did not?), was found guilty of manslaughter and fled to the Lowlands where he acquired the lands of Ballindean, having changed his name to Stirk or Stark. General John Stark (1728–1822) of the American Revolution was son of Archibald Stark, born in Glasgow, 1677.

STARRACK. A variant of STURROCK, q.v.

STARTIN. A variant of STIRTON, q.v., recorded in Aberdeen.

STATER. Robert Stater, prepositus of Berwick, witnessed gift of land to the Hospital of Soltre, c. 1250–66 (*Soltre*, p. 32), and Laurencius le Stater, son of Robertus le Stater, was burgess of Berwick, 1264 (*Neubotle*, p. 152).

STAVERT. Supposed to have been originally Staward, and one of that name is traditionally said to have carried the Douglas banner at Otterburn, 1388 (White, *History of Otterburn*, 1857, p. 131). James Stavert in Earlsyde, 1682 *(Peebles CR.).* General Thomas Hope Stavert of Hoscote died July, 1936.

STAWELL. Adam de Stawell (who was a Reuel) gifted fifteen acres of land of Balmurinach (Balmerino) to the church of St. Andrews before 1225 (RPSA., p. 271). Probably from Stowell in Gloucestershire. See also under REUEL.

STEDMAN, STEEDMAN, STUIDMAN. From provincial English *stead,* a farmhouse and offices, + *man.* Symon le Stedeman was received to the English king's peace in 1321 (*Bain*, III, 724). Steidman is found in Angus, 1505 (RAA., II, 448). Charles Studeman was "cuik at the Canongait port," Edinburgh, 1572 (*Diur. Occ.*, p. 303), and William Stuidman was reidare at Auchterderay, 1574 (RMR.). Alexander Steidman was retoured heir in croft and toft in vill Kinross, 1621 (*Retours*, Kinross, 6), James Stuidman was heir of Robert Stuidman, servitor S. D. N. Regis charissimæ matris, 1633 (*Inquis.*, 1950), and Janet Stoodman appears in Edinburgh in 1643 *(Edinb. Marr.).* Chalmers (*History of Dunfermline*) has a genealogy of the Stedmans of Baldridge, Fife. John le Stedman is recorded in English *Parliamentary Writs* in 1306. Stidman 1688.

STEEL, STEELE, STEILL. Of local origin. There are places so named in the shires of Ayr, Berwick, and Dumfries. In Berwickshire the old parish of Steill is now Ladykirk. Henry Stel was juror on inquisition on lands of Hopkelchoc, 1259 (*Bain*, I, 2162), and William Stele, burgess of Edinburgh, 1423 (*Egidii*, p. 45). John Steil or Steyll appears as prebendary of Kilmoir, 1434 and 1448 (RĒB., I, 60; II, 74), and another John Stevll was tenant of part of Cowpergrange, 1486 (*Cupar-Angus*, I, p. 239). John Steill *alias* Kempy Steill was hanged for theft, 1524 (*Trials*, I, p. 126 *). George Steyll was the king's familiar servitor, 1530 (RMS., III, 957), and Jok Steill appears in the toune of Bowdene, 1567 (*Kelso*, p. 519). William Steill was piper to one of the two companies of Highland bowmen raised in Argyll, 1627, for service in France. William Steel (1809–1881), noted anti-slavery advocate and one of the organizers of the "underground railroad" (a system of secret co-operation for assisting fugitive slaves to escape to Canada), was born in Biggar, Lanarkshire. Steell 1691, Steile 1453, Steyl 1446, Still 1686.

STEEN, STEIN. Syncopated forms of STEVEN, q.v. Found in Fife, the Lothians, Ayrshire and Roxburghshire. Alan Steyn was a monk of Kilwinning Abbey, 1557. John Steyne was burgess freeman of Glasgow in 1575, and James Stein in 1583 *(Burgesses).* As forename: Steyn Tran in Irvine, 1450 (*Irvine*, I, 45), and Steyne of Wod, voter in Monkland, 1519 (*Simon*, 45). Katie Steven or Stein, who lived a solitary life at Laighpark, parish of Kirkoswald, is thought to have been the 'Cutty-sark' heroine of Burns's 'Tam o' Shanter.'

STEENS, STAINS, STAINES. Syncopated forms of STEVENS, q.v. Master John Stenes, king of Scots' ambassador, had a safe conduct in 1425 (*Bain*, IV, 979). Andrew Stanis, king's bailie in Fife, 1540 *(Gaw).* Robert Stanes, beidman in Edinburgh, 1584 (*Soltre*, p. 239). Henry Stains in Carnmore, parish of Stramiglo, 1696 *(Dunkeld).*

STEILHOUS. Local, perhaps from some place in Aberdeenshire. William Steilhous in Straquhan, 1633 (SCM., III, p. 128), and David Steilhous, tenant in the barony of Leys, 1640 (ibid., v, p. 228).

STEILL. See under STEEL.

STEINSMORE. Local. There is Stenmuir near Kelso. Janet Steinsmore appears in Craixiffoord, Roxburghshire, 1660 (RRM., I, p. 266).

STEINSON. A current surname derived from one of the old spellings of STEVENSON, q.v. John Stenson was burgess of Glasgow in 1455 (LCD., p. 252), Thomas Stensoun was freeman of Prestwick in 1556 (*Prestwick*, p. 11), and Willie Stensone was tenant under the Abbey of Kelso in 1567 (*Kelso*, p. 519). James Steinstoun, merchant burgess of Edinburgh, 1654 (*Inquis. Tut.*, 811). Steenson 1724, Steinson 1655, Steinsone 1672, Steinsoun and Stinsoun 1632, Stenesoun 1580, Stensone 1567, Stenstoun 1661, Steynsone 1511, Steynsoune 1576.

STENBISTER. Stephin Stenbister who was a witness in Kirkwall in 1566 (REO., p. 284) derived his surname from the lands of Stenbister in the parish of St. Andrews, Orkney.

STENHOUSE, STANHOUSE. From the old barony of the name in the parish of Larbert, Stirlingshire. The first of the name recorded appears to be John de Stanhus, who witnessed a grant to the Abbey of Cambuskenneth, c. 1200 (*Cambus.*, 79), and about the same period Adam de Stanus witnessed Gilbert de Umframville's gift of teind of the mill of Dunipais to the same house (ibid., 86). Roben of Stanhus was indicted and arrested for larceny in 1278 (*Bain*, II, 148). Sir Robert

Stanhus, a Pope's knight, was chaplain of Mariton in the diocese of Brechin in 1447 (*Southesk*, p. 720). John Stanis was juror on an inquest held at Cupar in 1522 (SCBF., p. 266), and Johanne Stannus, a witness in Dunfermline in 1525 appears again in 1549 with his name Latinized Johannes Lapideedomus, cleric of St. Andrews diocese and notary public (DBR., 255, 280). John Stainehous was a merchant burgess of Edinburgh in 1636 (*Inquis.*, 2220), and "Alexander Stenos, tailer in Coldstrem," died in 1722. Stainhous 1674, Stannouse 1564, Stenhous 1638, Stennous 1644, Stenous 1567.

STEPHEN. This name was introduced into Britain by the Normans, with whom it was a favorite. Although found occasionally in England before 1066, its use then was due really to Christian tradition, Stephen (*Stephanos*) having been the first Christian martyr after Christ. Stephen, diaconus, witnessed a charter by Bishop Edward, c. 1150–71 (RPSA., p. 297). James Stephen, provost and merchant in Elgin, 1780 (*Moray*). Thomas Stephen published his *History of the Church of Scotland* in 4 v. (1843–45). In Scotland the name exists in the more common form STEVEN, q.v.

STEPHENSON, 'son of STEPHEN,' q.v. Ada filius Stephani was burgess of Elgin in 1286 (REM., 221), Henricus Stephani had a charter of land in Ayr in 1409 (*Friars Ayr*, p. 43), William Stephani appears as rector of the church of Lestalric in 1418 (CMN., 28), John Stephani was burgess of Forfar in 1434 (RAA., II, 71) and witness in Brechin in 1435 (REB., II, 48). Alexander Stephenson was tenant in Grange of Kyncrech in 1446 (*Cupar-Angus*, I, p. 145), and George Stephenson (1781–1848), inventor of the locomotive, was of Scottish parentage. See also STEVENSON.

STEUART. A variant of STEWART, q.v.

STEVEN. A Scots spelling of STEPHEN, q.v. Alexander Stevyn was tenant of Glenboy in 1472 (*Cupar-Angus*, I, p. 221). Thomas Steuen was rentalit in land of Auchinnarne in 1509 (*Rental*), John Steuin was a tenant of the bishop of Aberdeen in 1511 (REA., I, p. 365), and Alexander Stevyn held land in Glasgow in 1549 (*Protocols*, I). Ninian Stiving in Kilbarchan, 1659 (*Kilbarchan*). For some notes on Stiven's 'Totums' see Fraser, *History of Laurencekirk*, p. 207–208. Steine and Steyne 1560, Stene 1551, Stevin 1610, Stewin 1565, Stewyne 1597, Stiven 1698. As forename: Stene Lokart, 1488 (*Lanark*, p. 3).

STEVENDALE. Nicolas Stivandale was a prisoner in Montrose, 1685 (RPC., 3. ser. X, p. 173).

STEVENS, 'son of STEVEN,' q.v. This form is less common than STEVEN.

STEVENSON, 'son of STEVEN,' q.v. Nichol filz Steven, chaplain of Scotland, had license to take shipping at London or Dovorre at pleasure in 1372 (*Bain*, III, 198). John Steywynson was one of the surveyors of the marches of Woodwrae in 1388 (*Bamff*, p. 22), John Stevenson was merchant in Aberdeen in 1454 (*Bain*, IV, 1265), and common councillor, 1477 (*Guildry*, p. 189), and Duncan Stewinson was witness in Brechin in 1479 (REB., I, 202). Henry Stevinsoun in Brechin in 1505 appears in the following year as Henry Steynson (ibid., II, 149, 150). John Stevenson, last Roman Catholic precentor of the metropolitan church of Glasgow in 1548 spelled his name Steinstoune (*Biggar*, p. 197). Thomas Steuynesone had sasine of land in Glasgow in 1550 (*Protocols*, I), Andro Steiuinsoun was treasurer of Edinburgh in 1580 (MCM., I, p. 288), and Quostantyne Steynstoune was burgess freeman of Glasgow in 1594 (*Burgesses*). Bryce Stinstone appears in Irvine, 1686 (*Irvine*, II, p. 310). Steinstoune 1613, Steivinson 1685, Steuinsoun 1573, Stevensone 1557, Stevingstoun 1569, Stevinsone 1507, Stevinstine 1684, Stevisone 1663, Stevynesone and Stevynsoune 1550, Stewinsone 1506, Stewinsoune 1583, Stewinstoun 1625, Stewynsone 1550, Stewynsounne 1577, Sthevinson 1493, Sthevinsone 1503, Stivinson 1686; Stevinstoun, Steavensone, Stevenstoune, Stivenson, Stivensone, Stivenstoune.

STEVENSTON. Of territorial origin from Stevenson (*recte* Stevenston) in the parish of Newlands, Peeblesshire. Stevene de Stevenstone of the county of Peebles rendered homage in 1296 (*Bain*, II, p. 207), as likewise did Johan de Stevenstone of the county of Lanark (ibid., II, p. 212). The fortalice of Stevene stood on a high bank of the Lyne Water on the site now occupied by the farmhouse of Stevenson.

STEWART, STEUART, STUART. In OE. the original sense of the word *stiward* (from older * *stigeweard*, 'sty-warden') was one who looked after the domestic animals; hence, by extension of meaning, one who provides for his master's table. The vowel change of *y* is due to the following *w*, and the earliest instance of the final letter of the name being *t* instead of *d* occurs in the *Armorial de Gelre* (c. 1370–88). By the eleventh century the word had come to mean one who superintended the household affairs of another, and was therefore a title of honor. In Scotland the steward was not only chief of the royal household, but his power extended to the collection and

STEWART, Steuart, Stuart, *continued*

management of the crown revenues, to the administration of justice, and in time of war he took first place in the army next to the king. (For development of meaning compare the names CONSTABLE and MARSHALL.) In early charters and kindred documents steward, seneschal (from a lost Gothic word * *sinaskalks*, meaning 'old servant'), and dapifer ('food bringer') are practically synonymous terms. There are four ways of spelling the surname — *Stewart, Steuart, Stuart,* and *Steward,* besides the borrowed Gaelic form *Stiubhard.* The fame of Mary, queen of Scots (who spelled her name Stuart, after the French manner, there being no *w* in that language) and of the Young Pretender has made the French form more popular. The Scottish royal family of Stewart descended from a family of Breton nobles, who were hereditary seneschals of Dol. The first recorded is Alan Dapifer [Dolensis], who flourished about the middle of the eleventh century. See ALLAN. His son, also named Alan, appears several times in Breton history. A grandson of this second Alan, also named Alan, became lord of Oswestry and appears as witness to a grant by Henry I of England to the monks of Marmoutier, c. 1100–08. Walter, one of the four sons of this Alan, was the first of his family in Scotland. He first appears in 1142 when he attests a charter of David I, the 'soir sanct for the crown' to Melrose Abbey (*Melros*, p. 4). He also appears as witness in other royal charters, and King David before his death in 1153 made a grant to this Walter of the office of Steward of Scotland. No original record of this grant now exists, but its bestowal is proved by a charter of Malcolm IV, granted to Walter in 1157 confirming to him and his heirs the donation which King David gave him, namely, the lands of Renfrew, Paisley, etc., and also gives to him and his heirs the royal stewartry (*senescallia*) as 'King David gave the same.' Walter the sixth Steward fought at Bannockburn, 1314, and in 1319 he successfully defended Berwick against the English led by Edward II in person, and was one of the signers of the Scottish Declaration of Independence in 1320. In 1315 he had married Marjory, daughter of King Robert the Bruce, who bore to him a son, Robert, afterwards Robert II, first of the royal line of Stewart, crowned in 1371. Many people imagine that all persons bearing the name Stewart (or its variants) are of royal descent, but it must be borne in mind that there were stewards and stewards, as King James the Sixth emphasized when he said that all Stewarts were not 'sib' to the king. Every bishop, every earl had his steward, who in his own particular domain was simply 'John the steward.' Thus, for example, in a charter of Richard, bishop of St. Andrews, granted between 1163–73, among the witnesses we find 'Galfridus dapiferus episcopi' and 'Odone senescallus Gospatrici de Rirais' (*Archaeologia Scotica*, I, p. 113). Phelippe Styward of Roxburghshire and William le fiz le Stywarde of the counte of Berewyk rendered homage, 1296 (*Bain*, II, p. 199, 203). John Stywarde was one of an inquest at Roxburgh, 1357, Richard Stiward was in the king of England's service, 1371, and John Stywarde of Ennermethe (Invermeath) was a knight of Scotland (ibid., IV, 1, 191, 771). Steuarde 1442, Steuart 1504, Steuarte 1448, Stevarde 1506, Stevarte 1498, Stiuard 1424, Stuard 1421, Stuarde 1508, Stuerd 1490, Stuart 1429, Stuerd 1490, Stuward 1415, Stwyarde 1328. To the Gaels the Stewarts are known as "The race of kings and tinkers," *Stiubhairtaich cinne nan righ 's nan ceàrd.* Robert Stuart (1785–1848), American explorer and "friend of the Indians," was born in Callander. In the seventeenth century an East Anglia family named Styward put forward a story that they were originally Stewarts. Oliver Cromwell's mother was one of them, and on the strength of this it was claimed that Cromwell was descended from the royal family.

STEWARTON. From the old manor of Stewarton in the parish of Eddleston, Peeblesshire. Reginald Steuardiston witnessed an agreement between the abbot and monks of Neubotle anent the marches of Kynggessyde, c. 1250 (*Neubotle*, p. 27). It is uncertain if the Adam de Stywardestone of the county of Perth, who rendered homage in 1296 (*Bain*, II, p. 211) was of the same family. This Adam appears again in 1304–05 as a Scottish prisoner in Carlisle Castle (ibid., II, 1572, 1668). William de Steuartoun, perpetual vicar of Kylbryde in 1446, appears again in 1451 as William Stewartone without the 'de' (*Irvine*, I, 137, 140).

STEWARTSON. *See under* SHURIE.

STIKLAW. Local. Ricardus de Stikelwe witnessed Adam de Morham's grant of land of Dunypais to the Abbey of Cambuskenneth, c. 1200 (*Cambus.*, p. 109), and another Richard de Styclau was seneschal to Gamelin, bishop of St. Andrews, 1268 (RPSA., p. 173). Master Weyland de Stiklawe or Stykelaw, canon of Dunkeld, and Henry de Stiklawe were envoys of Sir Robert de Brus, earl of Carrick (*Bain*, II, 675). William Stiklaw was a witness in St. Andrews, c. 1290 (in transumpt of 1466) (*Laing*, 15). In 1297 Wayland de Stykelowe was ambassador of Eric, king of Norway (*Bain*, II, 961). A horse was purchased from Ricardus de Stikelawe, 1312 (ibid., III, p. 429), William de Sticlau was a charter witness in Inverness, c. 1360 (*Grant*, III, p. 12).

STILL. Alexander Still was admitted burgess of Aberdeen, 1451, Andrew Stile the same, 1511, and James Still in 1591 (NSCM., I, p. 12, 45, 82). Mage (= Madge) Still is recorded there, 1493 (CRA., p. 51), and Thomas Still in 1650 (SCM., v, p. 175). Another Thomas Still was church elder in Muirmailling, 1659 (Grosart, *Parish of Shotts*, p. 58). William Still from Monquhitter served in the first Great War *(Turriff)*. Perhaps an uncommon form of STEEL.

STILLCART. Meg Stillcart, a witch in East Lothian, 1590 (*Trials*, I, p. 238).

STILLIE. Henry Stylle de Saulton made a donation to Dryburgh Abbey, c. 1300 (*Dryburgh*, 250), and Hew Stillie appears in the town of Douglas, 1674 (*Lanark CR.*).

STIRK. A surname which appears to be confined mainly to Fife. Willelmus Stirk was juror on inquisition on lands in Fife, 1390 (RMS., I, 854). Alexander Stirk, collier in Dysart, who appears in record in 1572 (*Dysart*, p. 37), may be the Alexander Stirk, burgess of Dysart, recorded as nearest heir of George Stirk, merchant and burgess of Dysart in 1604 (*Inquis. Tut.*, 65). Helen Styrk and Jonet Styrk held part of the lands of Ouchtermutky, 1551 (*Gaw*, 42, 59). John Stirk in Dunfermline in 1579, and Sande Stirk in 1588, the latter again referred to in same year as Alexander Stirk *(Dunfermline)*. In 1608 George Stirk was retoured heir of John Stirk, portioner of Auchtermuchtie, his grandfather (*Retours, Fife*, 191), Robert Stirk was messenger in Dunfermline in 1633 (RPC., 2. ser. v, p. 93), and Patrick Stirk was an elder in Dysart in 1641 (PBK., p. 209). Riccardus Stirk, portioner of Auchtermuchtie, was retoured heir of Robert Stirk, his father, in lands of Jerrassland of Auchtermuchtie in 1661 (*Retours, Fife*, 906), and William Stirk in Achtennie, parish of Forgandennie, is recorded in 1719 *(Dunkeld)*.

STIRLING. From the town. Gilbertus de Striuelin witnessed King David's gift of Perdeyc (Partick) to the church of Glasgow, 1136 (REG., 3), and Walter de Striveling witnessed charters granted by King David and Prince Henry (*Lawrie*, p. 138). Peter de Striuelin witnessed gift of the church of Karreden (Carriden) to the Abbey of Holyrood before 1158 (LSC., p. 10). Thomas de Stervlen who witnessed a charter by Alexander II of a *yar* (fish trap) super Leven in 1224 (RMP., p. 214) is probably Thomas de Striuelyn, archdeacon of Glasgow, 1228 (*Soltre*, p. 24).

Peter, son of Walter de Strevelyn, held a ploughgate in Hedinham (now Ednam), c. 1247 (*Dryburgh*, 158), and c. 1250 Sir Gilbert de Striuelyng, a cleric, witnessed a convention between Peter, bishop of Aberdeen, and Alan Hostiarius (REA., I, p. 17). Robert de Streuillyn was deacon of Dunkeld, 1263 (LIM., 77), and Michael de Strivelyn was a witness in St. Andrews, 1285 (*Neubotle*, 59). Sir John Stirling of Moray swore fealty, 1291. His seal bears a shield charged with 6 mullets of 6 points, 3, 2, and 1, and S' Joh'is: de: Strivelyn: de: Mo... (*Bain*, II, 495). Andreu de Strivelyn, burgess of Inverkeithing, and Mestre Henry de Strivelyn of Stirlingshire rendered homage, 1296 (ibid., p. 188, 206). Roger de Strevelyn was burgess of Elgin, 1343 (REM., p. 290), Alexander de Strivelin witnessed a charter by Robert the Steward to Thomas Simple of the lands of Cragrossy in Strathernе, c. 1360 (REG., p. 275), and Johannes de Striuelyn de Kyldeny attested the marches of Kyrknes and Louchor, 1395 (RPSA., p. 5). Walter Strivylyng was admitted burgess of Aberdeen, 1459 (NSCM., I, p. 16). A family of this name was settled at a very early period in the neighborhood of Dunmaglass, Nairnshire (REM., p. 99 — 1234). In the family papers of the Stirlings of Keir between 1160 and 1677 their surname is spelled in no less than sixty-four different ways (*Stirlings of Keir*, p. 548).

STIRRAT, STIRRET, STIRRIT. Starrat or Stirrat was a once common surname in the parish of Dalry, Ayrshire. Of local origin from Stairaird (now Stirie) near Stair, in 1698 described as a 40s. land (*Retours, Ayr*, 696). Andreas Starheved resigned the serjandship of Lanark in reign of David II (RMS., I, App. II, 1341) John Sterhede appears in 1493 (CDE., 56 and Robert Sterhed was witness in Irvine, 149 (*Simon*, 71). James Storrat received a chart. "in breade for ane blaink of ane ill eve," 1650 (*Pollok*, I, p. 354). James Stirrat (1781–1843), poet, was born in Dalry. William Starratt was "deacone of the hamermen" of Stirling, 1656 (SBR., p. 222), Mr. Andrew Stirie was minister at Dalry, 1686, and Dorathie Stirrett is recorded there in the same year (RPC., 3. ser. XII, p. 355). Isobel Stirrat is recorded in Campbeltoun, Argyllshire, 1687. David Stirret in Glassell, 1735 (*Aberdeen CR.*).

STIRT. Euphan Stirt in Torryburn was burned for witchcraft, c. 1703 (Webster, *Tracts on witchcraft*, p. 138).

STIRTON. Perhaps from Stirton near Cupar, Fife. Alexander Sturtone is recorded in Inshtuthell, 1688 *(Dunkeld)*. STARTIN is a variant recorded in Aberdeen.

STITCHEL. From the lands of Stitchel in the parish of the same name in Roxburghshire. Milone de Stichele witnessed the grant of the church of Kilmaurs to Kelso, c. 1170 (*Kelso*, 283). Philip de Stichill appears as a witness between 1195 and 1214 (*Cambus.*, 37), and the Chronicle of Melrose records his death in 1221. Mr. Robert of Stichel, the king's doctor, is witness to a charter by William the Lion, c. 1204–14 (*Laing*, 3). Robert de Stichhulle of the county of Berewyke rendered homage in 1296 (*Bain*, II, p. 207), and William Stichehill was one of the archers of the east March in 1404 (ibid., IV, 669). The surname appears to have travelled north. Thomas Stitchel in Boigtoun, Aberdeenshire, is in record in 1716 (SCM., IV, p. 172), and John Stitchell, member of the Gartly Company of Volunteers in 1798 (*Will*, p. 23), may be the John Stitchel, merchant in Huntly in the same year (*Moray*).

STITT. Margaret Stitt in the parish of Twynhame, 1684 (RPC., 3. ser. IX, p. 573). Agnes Stutt in Berncleuch, 1658, and James Stitt in Snaid, 1686 (*Dumfries*). J. D. Stitt, structural engineer, Edinburgh, 1939.

STIÙBHARD. The Gaelic spelling of the surname STEWART. Macvurich spells the name *Sdiuord*.

STIVEN. A variant form of STEVEN, q.v. Charles Stiven (b. 1753), maker of snuffboxes in Laurencekirk, was called 'Prince of snuff-box makers.'

STIVENTON. Perhaps from Steventon or Stevington in (1) Berks or (2) Hants. Willelmus de Stiventona witnessed a charter by Thomas Malherbe of the lands of Balenaus to Abbey of Aberbrothoc, c. 1205 (RAA., I, p. 69).

STOB. Local. Andrew Stob was bailie of Perth, 1365 (ER., II, p. 205). Thomas Stob witnessed a charter of land in Scone, 1491 (*Scon*, p. 199). A payment of alms was made to Andrew Stob in 1506, and David Stob had a respite "at my Lord's mandate" in the same year (*Rent. Dunk.*, p. 88, 91).

STOBA. Most probably a variant of STOBO. Recorded in Dumfries, 1941.

STOBART, STOBERT. A Northumberland surname current north of the Border. Perhaps same as Robert Stobbat in Monaltrie, 1682 (*Invercauld*, p. 264).

STOBHILL. Thomas de Stubhyl was burgess of Irvine, 1260 (*Irvine*, I, p. 5). Payment was made to Maurice de Stubhil in 1292, and as Moriz de Esttubbille of Dumfriesshire

he rendered homage, 1296 (*Bain*, II, 580, 810). His seal bears a shield with three eagles displayed and S' *Mauricii de Stobil* (*Macdonald*, 2712). As Maurice de Stubhille he is thanked by Edward I of England for putting down evildoers in his country (*Bain*, II, 894). He is probably the Maurice de Stubhil who was one of the fermers of Cyplaunde [Sypland near Kirkcudbright] in 1291 (*Hist. docs.*, I, 284). His lands may have been at Barstibly, near Castle Douglas, or his name may be derived from Stobhill or Stubhill.

STOBIE. It may be a form of STOBO, q.v. William Stobbe was burgess of Berwick-on-Tweede in 1318 (*Bain*, III, p. 87). Master Henry Stoby, clerk at Perth, 1356 (*Bain*, III, p. 293). Dand Stobe was tenant on the lands of the Abbey of Kelso, 1567 (*Kelso*, p. 523). Henry Stobie is recorded in Dunfermline, 1587 (*Dunfermline*), and John Stobie had a charter of the lands of Waster Luscoir in 1605 (RD., p. 498). The surname is found in Methven, 1674 (*Methven*, p. 104), and John Stobbie was merchant in Crieff, 1787 (*Dunkeld*). Matthew Stobie was land surveyor in Edinburgh, in the beginning of the eighteenth century.

STOBO. Of local origin from the old barony of Stobo in Peeblesshire. David de Stubhou or Stobhou witnessed charters by Jocelin, bishop of Glasgow, c. 1177–99 (RMP., p. 99, 101). Adam de Stobhou was juror on an inquest held at Peebles in 1262 (*Peebles*, 5; APS., I, p. 101 red). John Stobo was servant to the king in 1583 (MCM., II, p. 351), William Stobo was charged with tumult in Glasgow in 1606 (RPC., VII, p. 244), Mathew Stobo in Kittimure, parish of Stanehaven, 1630, and five more of the name (*Lanark CR.*), and Major Robert Stobo, a native of Glasgow, guided the Fraser Highlanders up the Heights of Abraham at Quebec in 1759. John Stobbo, late taylor burges in Edinburgh, 1730 (*Guildry*, p. 136).

STOCK, STOCKS. English names of local origin. Adam and William of Stokis (in England), 1264 (*Bain*, I, 2363).

STODDARD, STODDART, STODART, STODHARD, STOTHART, STOTHERT. Stothart is the most common pronunciation. From the office of 'stot-hird,' one who tended the stots, i.e. bullocks. The earliest mention of this surname in Scotland is in 1376 when David Stodhirde, John Studehird, and William Studhirde are recorded as tenants of Douglas in barony of Buittle (RHM., I, p. lx, lxxi). Sir James Stodart was presented to a chaplaincy in the Collegiate Church of Methven, 1516 (*Methven*,

p. 40). John Stothart alias Stoddard, weaver at Ashieburn, 1802 (*Heirs*, 519). Lower says "the pronunciation Stoth-erd, Stoth-ard, are a 'genteel' innovation." Stodert 1574, Stodhird 1567. See *Herald and genealogist*, III, p. 552.

STODEGARTH. Local. William del Stodegarth held land in Irvine, Ayrshire, 1323 (*Irvine*, I, p. 124).

STOESIE. Richard Stoesie, printer in Edinburgh, 1644 (*Edinb. Marr.*).

STOKAR. From occupation. In the west of England stokers were "persons employed to fell or grub up trees" (Halliwell, *Dictionary of archaic and provincial words*, s.v.). John Stokar admitted burgess of Aberdeen, 1446 (NSCM., I, p. 11).

STONE. Local, from some place of the name. Probably of English origin. Thomas de Stone of Roxburghshire rendered homage, 1296 (*Bain*, II, p. 209). Thomas de Stone was common councillor of Aberdeen, 1435 (*Guildry*, p. 185), and Jerome Stone (1727–1756), schoolmaster in Dunkeld, "was the real discoverer to modern knowledge of the ancient Ossianic ballads."

STONEYPATH. Robertus de Stampeth or de Stampet, canon of Glasgow, c. 1290–99, appears in 1321 as Robertus de Stannepet, and again in 1325 as Robertus de Stanipeth (REG., p. 200, 228, 234; RMP., p. 131). He most probably derived his name from the lands of Stoneypath (1690 Staniepath) in the old barony of Dunsyre, Lanarkshire.

STONYER. From the occupation, a 'stonehewer,' a quarryman, and so = QUARRIER. Master David Stonyer, hermit of the Chapel of Side, Kilmalcolm, is in record, 1555 (*Crawfurd*, p. 21).

STOOPSHILL. Of local origin from the lands of Stoupishill, now Stoopshill near Dalry, Ayrshire. William de Stoupishill held a tenement in Irvine in 1455, and Margaret Stupqhill is in record in the same town in 1465 (*Irvine*, I, p. 28, 145). Alexander Stoupishill, also in Irvine, is mentioned in 1506 (ibid., p. 158). Stouphill 1542.

STORER. *See under* STORRAR.

STORIE, STORRIE, STOREY, STORY, STORRY. William Stori was charter witness in Dundee, 1281 (HP., II, p. 223). Walter Stori, canon of Aberdeen, 1320 (*Pap. Lett.*, II, p. 208), and Valdus Story was official 'curie Aberdonensis,' 1325 (RAA., I, p. 311). Adam Story was one of 'burgenses rure manentes' in Aberdeen, 1317 (SCM., V, p. 11). Joneta Stury relicta quondam

Johannis Stury, burgess of Edinburgh, 1389 (*Egidii*, p. 22; CDE., 15). John Story in Dundranane was accused of theft, 1511 (*Trials*, I, p. *75), and Nicholas Store was witness in Dundrennan, 1545 (*Laing*, 497). Thomas Storye, burgess of Northberwyk, 1545 (CMN., 65), and James Storie, polentarius in Letha (Leith), 1646 (*Inquis.*, 3106).

STORM. A rare current surname recorded in Nairn. Thomas Storme occupied the tack of Dowalye in 1507 (*Rent. Dunk.*, p. 28). William Storm appears in Tanzie of Boharm, 1784 (*Moray*). Recorded in English *Hundred Rolls*, 1273, and Harrison gives it as a personal name.

STORMONT, STORMONTH. From Stormont, a district in Perthshire. The name is a rare one. Richard Stormonth witnessed an instrument of sasine in the barony of Banff, 1507 (*Bamff*, p. 45). Agnes Starmount in Overlangriggs, 1658 (*Dumfries*). James Stormonth (1825–1882), philologist and lexicographer.

STORRAR, STORER. Weekley says (p. 105) this name means 'the convent treasurer,' but the Scottish name is from the office of 'storour,' one who has charge of the flocks and herds, as described in Douglas's *Eneados* (bk. VII, c. IX, 21–23):

"Tirrheus thair fader was fee maister, and gyde
of studis, flokis, bowis, and heyrdis wyde,
As *storoure* to the king."

The tenant of a sheep farm in Scotland was called a 'storemaster.' William Sturror witnessed sasine by Master Alexander Ramsay in 1534 (*Bamff*, p. 64), and Bessie Storrar is recorded in Easter Cash, 1732 (*Dunkeld*).

STORRIE, STORRY, STORY. *See under* STORIE.

STOTEYLLINGTON. Local. John of Stoteyllington, juror on inquisition on lands in Berwick, 1296 (*Bain*, II, p. 215).

STOTHART, STOTHERT. *See under* STODDARD.

STOTT. Stott, Northern English for steer and also for a heifer, was sometimes used as a nickname (*Mawer*, p. 191). Andrew Stott was admitted burgess of Aberdeen, 1490 (NSCM., I, p. 35). Margaret Stote in Dolphingtoune, 1675 (*Lanark CR.*). Alexander Stote in Maynes of Balyeordie, 1689 (RPC., 3. ser. XIV, p. 709). (2) Ewen (p. 178, 342) with probability suggests that this name is a variant of 'Stout,' and that 'Stout' is of local origin from *steorte* 'a tongue of land.' He cites 'atte stout' in Devonshire, 1327, and 'Rog. de Stote, Northants, 1230.' Cf. STUTE.

STOURTON. Of recent introduction from across the Border. There are several parishes and townships named Sturton in England.

STOVE. Laurence Stove in Garth in 1648 (*Shetland*) derived his name from the small place named Stove in Sanday, Orkney. Gilbert Stove and John Stove are recorded in Deirnes, Orkney, in 1686 (*OS Misc.*, II, p. 55). William Stove was secretary of Glasgow Orkney and Shetland Benevolent Society, 1940.

STOW. Local. There is a parish of this name in Midlothian. Johan de Stowe, persone of the church of Gleinkerny in the Meirnes, rendered homage, 1296 (*Bain*, II, p. 203). Adam Stowe was one of an inquest in Dundee, 1321 (RMS., I, App. I, 29). Janet Stow at Kirkcormok, 1618 (*Kirkcudbright*).

STOYLL. Duncan de Stoyll mentioned in an Aberdeen charter of 1340 (REA., I, p. 18). Johannes Stovll held a land in Aberdeen, 1382 (RMS., I, 682). Perhaps from Stowell in England.

STRABOLGY. From Strathbogie, Huntly, Aberdeenshire. Johannes de Strabolgy, tenant in Auchinanze, 1511 (REA., I, p. 363). In 1916 Mr. Cuthbert Matthias Kenworthy became Lord Strabolgi in the peerage of England (HP., IV, p. 191).

STRACHAN, STRACHEN, STRAUGHAN. Territorial, from the lands of Strachan (pron. Strawn) in Kincardineshire. Waldeuus de Stratheihan with consent of Ranulfus, his son and heir, granted the lands of Blarkerocch to the church of St. Andrew, c. 1200 (RPSA., p. 276-277). Ranulph de Stratheuchin witnessed a charter granted by Thomas de Lundin between 1203-14 (RAA., I, 65). Waldeuus de Strahechen witnessed an undated (but c. 1220) charter of Dunfermline (RD., 202). Ranulph de Straueyhin and Michael de Strathekan were in 1268 appointed attorneys by Alexander, earl of Buchan, to receive the purparty of himself and his wife (*Bain*, I, 2509, 2513). John de Strathechyn de Beeth Waldef, son and heir of late Ranulph de Strathechyn, resigned his lands of Beth Waldef to the abbot and convent of Dunfermline in 1278 (RD., 86). Thomas de Strathechyn who served on an inquest in 1333 (REA., I, p. 54) may be Thomas de Strathawyn who had a lease from the Abbey of Abirbrothoc of lands in the Mearns, 1342, and Thomas de Stradeqwhyn designed "dominus de Knokkis in le Mernys," 1351 (RAA., II, p. 16, 25). Henry de Strathekyn had a charter in 1346, and in 1361 Alexander de Strathechyne had a grant of the lands of Skryne in the barony of Panmure

(*Panmure*, II, p. 166, 174). Abraham Stratheykyn is recorded in Aberdeen, 1408 (CWA., p. 314), Geffray Sterthaughyn had a safe conduct to travel in England, 1424, and John of Straachyn and Alexander (without 'of') the same, 1431 (*Bain*, IV, 963, 1051). William Stradachin became burgess of Aberdeen, 1463, and Donald de Strachauchin in 1465 (NSCM., I, p. 18, 19). James Straithauchin claimed the benefice of Culter, 1489 (OPS., I, p. 175), Sir John Stradachyn, a cleric, was witness in Aberdeen in same year (REA., II, p. 303), and David Straughin was procurator of the Scottish "Nation" in the University of Orleans, 1512 (SHSM., II, p. 97). Strachoun 1624, Strachquhen 1605, Stracquhan 1655, Stradaquhin 1527, Stragham 1537, Strahaquhen 1487, Strahin 1494, Straichane 1675, Straiquhen 1578, Straithin 1525, Strakekvn 1429, Straquahan 1684, Straquhane 1646, Straquhen 1665, Straquhone 1600, Straquhyn 1524, Straquhyne 1554, Straqwhane 1682, Straqwhin 1565, Stratauchin 1560, Strathachin 1459, Strathachine 1483, Strathachtin 1427, Strathachvn 1470, Strathaquhin 1490, Strathaquhine 1504, Strathaquhyn 1498, Strathaqwhyne 1485, Strathauchin 1566, Strathauchine 1445, Strathawchin 1617, Strathawin 1585, Strathechin 1443, Strathzaqwyn (*z* as guttural *y*) 1445, Strauchen 1663, Strauachin and Strauauchin 1541, Strauchquhen 1528, Strauthauchin 1481, Strautquhyne 1597, Strayachin 1406, Strayquhen 1578, Straythauchtin 1469, Straywham 1537; Strachin, Stradachin, Strahan, Straithachin, Straithauchquhyn, Straquhin, Strathachane, Strathaiching, Strathauchinquhyn, Strathechny, Stratheyhan, Strathin, Strethachin.

STRADE. Local. There is a Straid near Comrie, Perthshire, and there are two places named Straid in Ayrshire. William de Strade concerned in a lawsuit in Aberdeen, 1401 (CRA., p. 379) is probably the William Strade or de Strade who appears as burgess there in 1404 and 1408 (*Macdonald*, 2724; CWA., p. 313). Another William de Stradee was admitted burgess of Aberdeen, 1445 (NSCM., I, p. 9), and Thomas Strat was admitted burgess in 1475 (RAA., II, 194).

STRADHELM. Andrea de Stradhelm, witness, 1195-1214 (*Cambus.*, 37).

STRADLEUENE. Auiel de Stradleuene who witnessed a gift by Duncan, earl of Fife, to the nuns of North Berwick, a. 1177 (CMN., 6) derived his name from Strathleven in Fife.

STRAGETH. Local, from Strageath near Muthill, Perthshire. John Strogeth of that Ilk witnessed an instrument of sasine, 1465 (*Athole*,

p. 708), and in 1495 we have a charter by John Strogeith *de eodem* (*Oliphant*, p. 36). William Strageth was sheriff depute in Cupar, 1518 (SCBF., p. 136). Nicol Stregath was witness in Perth in 1541, and Robert Strogeiche the same in 1547 (*Rollok*, 16, 38).

STRAITON. See under STRATTON.

STRALOCH. From the place of the same name in the parish of New Machar, Aberdeenshire. Duncan Straloch who was admitted burgess of Aberdeen in 1460 (NSCM., I, p. 17) is probably the Duncan Straloch who appears as "sergeand" of the burgh in 1475 and in 1489 (REA., II, p. 302; *Guildry*, p. 187). Thomas Straloche was witness in the same town in 1507 (CRA., p. 76).

STRANACK. A not very common surname. As a bearer of the surname says in the 'Weekly Scotsman' that his ancestors came from Aberdeen four generations ago it is probably a corruption of STRONACH, q.v.

STRANG, STRANGE. Probably from OFr. *estrange*, foreign. Later the name through popular etymology was derived from Scots and N. Eng. *strang*, strong. Home le Estraunge was intentive in the king's service in Scotland, 1255 (*Bain*, I, 1999). William Strange, burgess of Montrose, rendered homage, 1296 (ibid., II, p. 199). Thomas de (? for le) Strang held land in Aberdeen, 1340 (REA., I, p. 68), and John Strang was elected common councillor there in 1398 (CRA., p. 374). Walter Strang was one of an inquest at Forfar, 1438 (RAA., II, p. 546). William Strangh, a Scottish merchant, had license to import Scottish goods into England, 1495 (*Bain*, IV, 1619). Sir George Strang, a cleric, was notary in Orkney, 1542 (OSR., I, p. 77). Henry Strang is the earliest mentioned schoolmaster in Dysart, 1579 (*Dysart*, p. 39). Richard Strange, advocate in Edinburgh, 1555 (*Protocols*, I). Strang of Balcaskie, an old family in the East Neuk of Fife. Sir Robert Strange was a distinguished eighteenth-century engraver. An old surname in Orkney. There is also an old West Norse personal name *Strangi*, but the origin is most likely as given above.

STRANGSUNE, 'son of STRANG,' q.v. William Strangsune witnessed a charter to the Abbey of Balmerino, c. 1230 (*Southesk*, p. 717).

STRATH. Local. This surname is common in the shires of Aberdeen, Banff, and Fife. Patrick de Strath (erroneously spelled Strach in *Theiner*, no. 398) was one of the canons deputed to elect the bishop of Dunkeld in 1312 (*Pap. Lett.*, II, p. 96), and c. 1333–36 Adam del Strath was vicar of Elgin (*Rose*,

p. 116). Thomas Strath was admitted burgess of Aberdeen, 1479 (NSCM., I, p. 28). William Strath, reidare at Culsamond, 1574 (RMR.), and Alexander Straith is recorded in Hornden, 1680 (*Lauder*).

STRATHALUETH. Local, from Strath of Alvah, Banffshire. Patricius de Strathalueth held land in sheriffdom of Bamf, 1425 (REA., I, p. 222).

STRATHAVEN. From the place of the same name in the parish of Avondale, Lanarkshire. William fiz Roger de Strathavenyn, William fiz Peres de Strathafayn, and Wauter de Strathawan, all of the county of Lanark, rendered homage for their lands in 1296. The seal of the first named bears an ornament of eight rays and S' *Walt'i f' Rogeri* (*Bain*, II, p. 210–213, 531). Johannes de Strathavane was a charter witness in 1397 (RMS., I, App. I, 157), and John Streatheavn is recorded in Easter Caputh in 1688 (*Dunkeld*).

STRATHBROCK. There is a Strathbrock in West Lothian. Arkanbaldus de Strethbroć witnessed a grant by Hugh de Bygris, 1228 (*Kelso*, 186). There was a burgess family of this name in Aberdeenshire in the fourteenth century. William Strabock (for Strabrock) was provost of Aberdeen, 1329–32. William de Strabrok had a charter from the king of lands of Foveran, Ardache, and three parts of Auchmacoy, 1340 (*Illus.*, I, p. 364., REA., I, p. 67). Henry Strabrok resigned the barony of Foverane in favor of William Toryn or Toring in the reign of David II (RMS., I, App. II, 1247). William de Strabroc petitioned for provision to him of the church of Dunlop in Ayrshire, 1404 (*Pap. Pet.*, I, p. 626), Robert Strabrok, priest of the diocese of St. Andrews, became bishop of Caithness, 1444 (*Dowden*, p. 245), and Richeard Strobrok was tenant of half the links of Sanday, Orkney, 1502 (REO., p. 419). Strabroch 1343.

STRATHDEE. Local. From the Strath of the river Dee.

STRATHEARN. From the old stewartry of Strathearn in Perthshire. "Several persons, male and female, are called de Stratherne, who may have been sons and daughters of the earls, but probably many others were styled de Stratherne merely because they came from the district" (*Inchaffray*, p. lxxii). Maucolum de Stratherne and Robert de Stratherne rendered homage in 1296 (*Bain*, II, p. 200), and Patrick de Strathern was witness to a resignation of lands in the barony of Drumelzier in 1331 (*Hay*, p. 9). Walter Stradher or Stratherne was familiar to the earl of Murref, 1390 (*Bain*, IV, 412). Thom of Strathern or

STRATHEARN, *continued*

Strethern was tenant in Chapeltoun of Kethyk, 1474 (*Cupar-Angus*, I, p. 188, 196). An assignation of the lands of Tulibaglis by Thomas Strathern, heir of umquhile Richart Strathern, is recorded in 1462 (SCM., v, p. 285), and Mungo Stratherne was a witness in Linlithgow in 1538 (*Johnsoun*). Strethern 1695.

STRATHENDRY. The lands of Strathendry in the parish of Leslie, in Fife, gave name to the family of Strathenrie of that Ilk. Roger de Quenci made a gift to Roderick, son of Gillecrist, of the lands of Strathanret, 1226 (SHSM., IV, p. 314). Walter de Strathanry, cleric, witnessed a charter of Alexander Comine, earl of Bochone, c. 1263 (*Inchcolm*, p. 26), and Hervi de Strathanry had his lands restored to him by Edward I, 1304 (*Bain*, II, 1538). Thomas Strathenry had a precept of remission in 1536 (RSS., II, 2002), and Sir Henry Strathenry was presented to the chaplainry in the Collegiate Church of Methven in 1541 (*Methven*, p. 49). John Straehendrie was retoured heir of John Strahendrie in lands in Wester Lochgellie in 1661 (*Retours, Fife*, 887).

STRATHGARTNEY. Andrew de Strugartney agreed to serve Edward I of England in France or elsewhere in 1297 (*Bain*, II, p. 243).

STRATHGRYFE. William fiz Nicol de Stragryfe and Perez fiz Gerard de Stragrife of the county of Lanark who rendered homage in 1296 (*Bain*, II, p. 212), derived their surname from Strathgryfe in Renfrewshire.

STRATHIE. Of local origin from one of several small places of this name in the shires of Aberdeen, Ross, Cromarty, and Caithness. Symon de Strathy rendered homage at Perth, 1291 (RR.). Elizabeth Strathie in Rashiehill, parish of Crieff, 1785 (*Dunkeld*).

STRATHMIGLO. Of local origin from the village of Strathmiglo in the parish of the same name in Fife. John de Stramiglaw was abbot of Dunfermline in latter half of the fourteenth century (RD., p. xiv), and Jacobus de Stramiglaw was licenciate in decrees, 1434 (RPSA., p. 411). Thomas of Stramvglo was official of Laudonie in 1409 (LSC., 117). Johnne Strameglo was burgess of Perth in 1567 (RPC., I, p. 505), and Laurence Strathmiglo was married in Perth in 1574 (*Sc. Ant.*, III, p. 100).

STRATON, STRATTON, STRAITON. From the barony of Straiton in the parish of Liberton, Midlothian. There is also a barony of Straiton in Ayrshire, and a barony of Stratton in Fife.

Richard de Stratun, messenger of Alexander III, 1285 (*Bain*, II, 272), may be Richard de Straton, charter witness, 1292 (*Neubotle*, p. 292). Thomas de Straton or Stratone of Edinburghshire, one of an inquest at Berwick, 1296, also rendered homage in the same year (*Bain*, II, p. 201, 215). Alisaundre de Stratton and James de Stratton, both of Edinburghshire, also rendered homage (ibid., p. 169, 198). Alexander de Straton who signed the baron's letter to the Pope in 1320, may be Alexander de Straton 'consanguineo nostro' who had a charter of property at Inverbervy from David II (RMS., I, 234). John de Stratton, *dominus ejusdem*, witnessed a charter of lands of Wester Mathrys, 1351 (SCM., v, p. 249), and James of Stratton was valet of the earl of Sutherland, 1364 (*Rot. Scot.*, I, p. 889b). John de Stratoun witnessed a quitclaim on lands of Gladsmure, Midlothian, 1427 (*James* II, p. 14), and another John de Stratoun was burgess of Montrose, 1431 (REB., II, 36). There were also Straitons or Strattons in Aberdeenshire. Cristina de Stratone granted a charter in 1451 in favor of the Friars Preachers in Aberdeen (*Friars*, p. 33), and Brice Strayton, a Scot born at Berwick, had letters of denization in England, 1480 (*Bain*, IV, 1465). Walter Stratone was rector of Dunnotter, 1502 (RAA., II, 431), and Arthur Stratoun had charter of the lands of Muretoun in sheriffdom of Forfar, 1593 (REB., II, 368).

STRAUGHAN. A form of STRACHAN, q.v.

STRAWHORN. A surname current in shires of Ayr and Dumfries. Perhaps of local origin. There are lands named Strowarrane (1662) and Strawarrane (1668) in Ayr *Retours* (525, 559).

STREMISTONE. Local. Thomas Stremistone owned a land in Berwick, 1324 (*Cambus.*, p. 39).

STRENGTHIE. Janet Strengthie in Kirkcaldy couldn't agree with her husband, 1633 (PBK., p. 64). James Stuart, a Border Gypsy who died in his 115th year, was known as 'Jamie Strength' (Brockie, *Gypsies of Yetholm*, 1884).

STRICHEN. Of local origin from the lands of Strichen in the parish of the same name in Aberdeenshire.

STRIKLAND. From Strickland (originally Stirkland) in Westmorland. Robert de Strikland witnessed confirmation by Alexander filius Walteri of his father's gifts to the church of Paisley, 1239 (RMP., p. 225). Robert de Stirkeland had protection for two years for going on the king of England's service beyond seas, 1370 (*Bain*, IV, 170). Henry Strickland in Kilbarchan, 1771 (*Kilbarchan*).

STRINGER. From the occupation,. "one who makes strings for bows." Laurence Stringhar admitted burgess of Aberdeen, 1486 (NSCM., I, p. 32).

STROMA. A surname in Canisbay (Caithness) records. Of local origin from the island of Stroma in the Pentland Firth.

STRONACH. An epithet surname from G. *sronach*, 'nosey,' "but from what special feature of that organ the name is derived it seems impossible in our day to determine." The surname seems to be confined mainly to Aberdeenshire. Duncan Stronoch witnessed resignation of the bell of S. Meddan in 1447 (SCM., IV, p. 118), James Stronach was chaplain at Kilrawok in 1524 (*Rose*, p. 199), Andro Stronoch was reidare at Dippill, 1574 (RMR.), John Stronoche was tenant of the marquis of Huntlie in 1586, and justice was administered on Andrew Stronocht in Scotfauld, Spynie, in 1594 (SCM., IV, p. 284; II, p. 126). Agnes Stronach in Kingsgate, 1688, and seven more are recorded in the Commissariot Record of Moray.

STRONO. Perhaps for STRONACH. Cf. TULLO for TULLOCH, etc. Adam Strono of Scotland was illegally arrested at Lowestoff, 1405 (*Bain*, IV, 690). Elene Strono, 1524.

STROTHER. From Strother in Northumberland. William of Strother and other Scots merchants complained that their ships, wrecked in a storm, were plundered at Bamburgh and Tynemouth in 1357 (*Bain*, IV, 10).

STROYAN. A surname in the shires of Dumfries, Wigtown, and Renfrew, is probably from Ir. *O'Sruitheain* or *O'Sruthain*, 'descendant of Sruthan.' Nevin Astrowane, a follower of the earl of Cassilis, was respited for murder, 1526 (RSS., I, 3386). Mylne mentions an insolent person (in sixteenth century) named "William M'Patrik M'Alister M'Robert M'Donoquhy called by other William Strowan" (quoted in *Rent. Dunk.*, p. 317). The surname, which is also recorded in Perthshire, may be of local origin there from Strowan or Struan. John Stroyan, J.P., D.L., died at Lanrick Castle, Doune, 1941, in his eighty-sixth year.

STRUTHERS. The ME. element *strother*, a marsh or swamp, is in common use in northern England and in Scotland. There is a Struther near Stonehouse, Lanarkshire, and a Struthers in Fife, but the references point to an origin further south, perhaps from Strother in Northumberland. The ancient Northumberland family of Strothers were lords of the manor of Kirk-Newton in the barony of Wark on the Tweed. John Strwtheris was witness in Glasgow, 1555 (*Protocols*, I), and Thomas Stroeheris appears in Kelso, 1567 (*Kelso*, p. 526). Strwthiris and Strowdyr 1560.

STRUTT. Probably of recent introduction from England. An old and distinguished surname in Essex, from the fifteenth century. Explained by Harrison as 'stiff, pompous,' but?

STUART. A variant of STEWART, q.v.

STUD. A surname now scarcely known in Scotland. It was early carried to France, appearing there as Estud (Burton, *Scot abroad*, v. 1, p. 85). Alnod Stud appears in *Liber Wintoniensis*, A. D. 1066 (*Ewen*, p. 85).

STUDGEON. Probably a variant of STURGEON, q.v.

STUPERT. An Ayrshire surname. Robert Stawpart who held part of the lands of Owyr Possil, 1513 (*Rental*), appears in 1522 as Robert Stalpart, tenant in Nether Possill (ibid.). One of this name gave name to Stawpartislandis (1504) or Stalparlandis (1510) (RMS., II, 2817, 3484). Andrew Stouphart was boxmaster of Trinity Hospital, Leith, 1759 (*Laing*, 3208), and John Stupart appears in Grange, parish of Logie, 1794 (*Logie*, I, p. 196).

STURDY. From ME. *sturdi*, obstinate, rash <OFr. *estourdi*, rash, careless, heedless. Robert Sturdy, servant of Nicholas Dunbarre, servant of the earl of Marche, 1407 (*Bain*, IV, p. 151).

STURGEON. A surname confined mainly to the shires of Dumfries and Kirkcudbright. Andrew Sturgioun and John Sturgioun were witnesses in Dumfries in 1544 (*Anderson*). Charles Strugeoun (with metathesis of *r*), sheathmaker in Edinburgh in 1608 (*Edinb. Marr.*), appears again in 1610 as Strudgeon (*Laing*, 1584). William Strudgeoun was reidare at Borg (Borgue) in Galloway, 1574 (RMR.). James Sturgeon in Wraithis is recorded in 1611, and Adam Sturgeone was heir of Clement Sturgeoun of Wraithes in 1636 (*Retours, Kirkcudbright*, 102, 213). Margaret Sturgeon appears in Over Carntorsk in 1677 (*Kirkcudbright*), and Agnes Sturgeon was examined for the Test in Tinwald in 1685 (RPC., 3. ser. XI, p. 434). The surname is also recorded in New Abbey parish in 1705 (MCM., III, p. 414, 417). Samuel Sturgeon wrote the *Galloway herds, a lampoon*, published in 1909. Strugeone 1648, Sturgione 1689.

STURROCK. Laurentius Sturrok, chaplain in Aberdeen, 1448 (REA., I, p. 253) is probably Laurence Sturrok, perpetual vicar of the parish church of Covil, 1453 (RAA., II, 96). Alexander Storrok held a fourth part of the vill

STURROCK, *continued*

of Craquhy near Dunnichen, 1509 (ibid., 491). John Storrock in Dundee was charged in 1676 with being a "schismatik and a disorderly person" (DPD., II, p. 443). Storach, Storrack, Storek, Sturrock are the same name originating in the pastoral districts of Angus, and said to mean literally sheep farmers or store-masters (farmers).

STUTE. Gilbert Stute, burgess of Aberdeen, made a gift of land to the abbot and convent of Arbroath, c. 1212 (RAA., I, p. 98). Thomas Stute witnessed a resignation of date 1265 (RMP., p. 64). John Stut leased part of the vill of Dalfubill, 1376 (RHM., I, p. lvii). Cf. STOTE.

STUTEVILLE. Of territorial origin from Estouteville, now Etoutteville in the arrondissement of Yvetot in Normandy. Magister Robert de Stutevil witnessed a confirmation charter by Symon Loccard to the Abbey of Kelso, c. 1180 (*Kelso*, 333). Eustace de Stuteuil granted "duas sceppas farine auene" from his granary apud Lydel to the House of Soltre between 1180–1249 (*Soltre*, p. 6). Robert de Stutevilla witnessed a confirmation charter by Alan Hostiarius of date 1233 (REA., II, p. 268; REM., 83), and in 1276 an inquest was held concerning the lands held by the deceased Johanne de Stuteville (*Bain*, II, 71). Robert de Stuteville, or D'Estotville, dean of Dunkeld, was elected bishop of St. Andrews, *per viam compromissi*, June, 1253, and in 1273 bishop of Dunkeld (*Dowden*, p. 15, 58). Lower says the name is now STOUTWELL.

SUIBHNE. A name of uncertain meaning. *Su* means 'good,' but the meaning of the second part of the name is not clear. The opposite of *Suibhne* is *Duibhne*, where the first syllable has the meaning 'ill, bad.' The Rev. J. G. Campbell half a century ago drew attention to the fact that in Gaelic "*s* begins words denoting ease and motion, or gentle flow, while *d* denotes what is hard, stiff, stubborn, and difficult to move; thus *soirbh* means calm, gentle, quiet, affable, pliant, easily moved, while *doirbh* means rough, fierce, hard, difficult in manner or temper" (*The Fians*, 1891, p. 88). For purposes of comparison between *s* and *d* he gives a list of examples. The same difference extends to other languages besides Gaelic, e.g. Pali *Sukha* and *Dukha* — well-fare and ill-fare. Suibhne, Cuirtre's son, sixth abbot of Iona, died in 657 (*Tighernach*), and another Suibhne, sixteenth abbot, died in 772 (AU.). The death of Suibhne mac Cinaeda, ri Gall-gaidhel (Suibhne, son of Kenneth, king of the Gall-Gaidil) is recorded in AU. under 1034.

John, son of Suffne, complained in 1301 to Edward I of England that his lands had been taken from him by John of Ergadia on behalf of John de Menteth, the king's enemy, and concludes by asking redress (*Bain*, II, 1255; DIS., II, p. 437). Suny (i.e. Suibhne) Magurke held land in Knapdale and Glenarewyle before 1314 (*Bain*, III, p. 80), and Suffne or Swene, son of Ewen (Sunicus or Suffinis Eugenii), lord of Oittyr, granted certain of his lands to Duncan, son of Alexander, in 1431 (OPS., II, p. 54). From *Suibhne* comes Ir. Sweeney. The name has nothing to do with N. *Sveinn*, which became *Suain* in Gaelic.

SULBY. William de Sulby of the county of Lanark rendered homage, 1296 (*Bain*, II, p. 213). There is a place, Sulby in the Isle of Man, from ON. *Sölva-byr*, 'Solvi's farm.'

SUMERSWAIN. Adam Sumerswain held land in Dumfries, a. 1214 (*Kelso*, 11; Edgar, *Dumfries*, p. 134).

SUMMER, SUMMERS. See under SYMMERS.

SUMMERHILL. Of local origin. There is a place of this name in the parish of New Machar, Aberdeenshire, and another in the parish of Ayton, Berwickshire.

SUMMERLAND. Local from a place of the name probably in Caithness. Patrick Summerland in Sandside, 1663 (*Caithness*).

SUMMERVAIL. See under SOMERVILLE.

SUNTER. A corruption of *Sumpter*, a horse or mule that carries burdens, and by extension, the driver of such an animal. David Suntar, constable in the parish of Achtermonsie, 1633 (RPC., 2. ser. v, p. 94).

SURRY. Probably from Surrey in England. Walter Sury or de Sury, first recorded prebendary of Balhelvy, appears as witness in 1321 (REA., I, p. 47). Thom Surry was tenant of the east half of Grange of Balbrogi, 1473 (*Cupar-Angus*, I, p. 185).

SUTHERLAN, SUTHERLAND. From the name of the shire. David de Sothirlandae was partner to an agreement in 1332 (*Scon*, p. 120). Nicolas of Sothyrland had a charter from his brother, the earl of Sothyrland of sixteen davachs called Thorbol in 1360 (OPS., II, p. 725). Maurice de Sotherland had a safe conduct in 1364 (CSR., I, p. 147), and Nicholaus de Suthirlandia was juror on assize in 1389 regarding the mill lands of Quarelwode in Moray (REM., p. 171). Alexander Sutherland was vicar of Westray, 1441 (*Old Lore Misc.*, IV, p. 13), and Master Alexander Suthirland was vicar of Inuernis, 1480 (*Cawdor*,

p. 440). Safe conducts were issued for Margaret of Sutherlande, Robert of Sutherlande, and Alexander of Sutherlande, "Escottz," 1444 (*Bain*, IV, 1175). James de Suthirlande was admitted burgess of Aberdeen, 1447 (NSCM., I, p. 11). Several persons of this name had remissions for their share in taking and holding the Castle of Akirgill in Caithness, 1547 (OPS., II, p. 778). James Suddirland was "onderfold" (= underfoud, i.e. under bailiff) of Fetlar, 1558 (OSR., I, p. 79). Patrick Suddirland, witness in Culross, 1569 (*Laing*, 845), and Alexander Suderland was retoured heir in certain lands in the sheriffdom of Caithness, 1602 (*Retours, Caithness*, 4). Forbes Sutherland, an Aberdeenshire sailor, was the first Briton buried in Australian soil, May, 1770. Suyrland 1665.

SUTHERLINE. Maurice Sutherline or Suthern was a native man of the Abbey of Dunfermline in thirteenth century (RD., 326).

SUTHERNE. The southerner, one from the south. Thomas le Sutherne was received to the English king's peace in 1321 (*Bain*, III, 724). Still current in England as SOTHERN and SOTHERAN.

SUTHSTANES. Local. Alayn de Suthstanes of Edinburghshire rendered homage, 1296 (*Bain*, II, p. 209).

SUTTER. *See under* SOUTER.

SUTTIE. There is a place named Suddy or Suddie in the parish of Knockbain, but the name is more likely to be from the Suthie recorded in Perth Retours. James Suttie was member of Scots parliament for Forfar, 1617 (*Hanna*, II, p. 515). George Sutie in Edinburgh, 1609 (*Edinb. Marr.*), and another George Suttie was collector in Dysart, 1632 (PBK., p. 39). George Swittie was dean of guild in Aberdeen, 1643 (*Guildry*, p. 202). George Sutie, nuper bailie of Edinburgh, 1676 (*Inquis.*, 5873), another George Suittie was heir of James Suttie, his father, burgess of Edinburgh, 1679 (ibid., 6148). Alexander Suite in Belliwin, 1690, and David Suttie in Balgirscho, 1697 (*Dunkeld*). It is also the name of an East Lothian family possessing a baronetcy of Nova Scotia, 1702. Old: Suithe and Suittie. *See also* SIDEY.

SUTTON. From one of the many places named Sutton in England. Mariot de Sutton of Dumfriesshire rendered homage in 1296 (*Bain*, II, p. 198).

SWAFFHAM. From Swaffham in England. Richard de Suafham who witnessed a charter by the abbot and convent of Kelso in 1178

(RAA., I, p. 9), appears again in 1185 as witness to Eschina de Londonis' gift of the church of Molle to the Abbey of Kelso (*Kelso*, 146). Nicol de Swafham, parson of Great Daltone, rendered homage in 1296 (*Bain*, II, p. 214).

SWAIN, SWAYNE. From ME. *Swein* (<ON. *Sveinn*). "*Sveinn* was one of the most usual Scandinavian names in England during Old and Middle English times." Swein Ulfkills sune is a witness in King Edgar's charter granting Swintun to the monks of S. Cuthbert, c. 1100 (*Nat. MSS.*, I, 4). Sweing, presbyter of Fihswic (Fishwick) witnessed grant of a toft at Ednam to the church of S. Cuthbert at Coldingham, 1136 (*Raine*, 22). Elyas Sweyn, constable at Locres (Leuchars, Fife), appears as witness in two charters, c. 1250 (SHR., II, p. 174). James Swayne was tenant of Bordland in the barony of Kylbouho, 1376 (RHM., I, p. lix; II, 16), and Patrick Swane, charter witness in Glasgow, 1474 (LCD., p. 189). The editor of *Dysart Records* says under the year 1546: 'In a deed of this year I find for the first time Swyn (Swayne), a name that still exists in Dysart' (p. 15). Peter Swayne was tenant in Hylle of Mossplat, 1533 (*Rental*), George Swayne was tenant of Newtounleis, 1559 (ER., XIX, p. 403), George Swayne was rector of Methill, 1592 (*Dysart*, p. 42), and John Swane and Bessie Swane were examined for the Test in Tinwald, 1685 (RPC., 3. ser. XI, p. 433). Robert Swyne in Langriche, 1653, and five more are recorded in the neighborhood before 1800 (*Lauder*). Svan 1668, Swen 1591. *See also* SWAN.

SWAINSON, SWANSON, 'son of SWAN,' q.v. The latter form occurs mostly in Caithness. Alanus filius Swani and Walterus filius Swani witnessed a charter of land of Tubermor, 1298 (*Scon*, p. 91).

SWAIP. William Swape admitted burgess of Aberdeen, 1595 (NSCM., I, p. 88), is also in record in the following year (CRA., p. 174). Patrick Suap, indweller and creimer (stall-keeper) in Aberdeen, 1688 (RPC., 3. ser. XIII, p. 262), may be Patrick Swap, merchant there, 1722 (*Aberdeen CR.*). John Swaipe, brother to William Swaipe, merchant burgess of Aberdeen, 1701 (ROA., I, p. 247).

SWAN, SWANN. A variant of SWAIN, q.v. The name does not appear in OE. before 1033. At a later date *Suain* (Swain) and *Swan* are often used for the same person. Swan filius Thore and William filius Thore were witnesses to a charter of the lands of Maddyrnyn (Madderty) a. 1189 (LIM., 6). This Swan was ancestor of the Ruthvens. In the reign of

SWAN, SWANN, continued

William the Lion the greater part of the territory of Crawford parish in Lanarkshire was held by Swein or Swan, son of Thor son of Swein (*Neubotle*, p. 102–104). Henry, son of Alan son of Swan, and Walter, son of Swan, were charter witnesses, c. 1200 (*Scon*, 125). Henricus filius Swani was witness to a concord, c. 1147–50 (RD., p. 9). Suuenus prepositus regis, c. 1130 (ibid., p. 13). Thorus filius Swani, witness at Perth, c. 1130 to a mandate regarding ships trading at Inviresc (ibid., p. 12). William Swyne had charter of eighth part of Gaitmilk before 1583 (ibid., p. 468). David Swan had a letter of tack of the lands and town of Murdocarny, 1499 (RSS., I, 408), Alexander Swan to underlie the law in Fife, 1531 (*Trials*, I, p. 157*), William Suan was witness in Glasgow, 1550 (*Protocols*, I), and half the myln of Dundaff was leased to John Swan in 1585 (*Scon*, p. 226). See also SWAIN.

SWANNAY, SWANNEY, SWANIE. Agnes Swanne was "delate of superstitious goeing or kneeling about the chappell" of St. Modan's in Freswick in 1652 (*Old Lore Misc.*, v, p. 59). Mr. J. S. Clouston says that in looking for a landed origin for an Orkney name "this caution must always be remembered, that in almost every case the family at some time or another can be found on or near the land in question; so that if careful search shows no trace of such a connection, we had better look for some other derivation. On these grounds," he says, "I do not think that Swannay is derived from either Swona or from Swannay in Birsay, but is a truncated form of Swaneson (Swein frequently lingers in old deeds as Swane). The surname is found in many parts of Orkney, but never — so far as I have discovered — in either of these places" (ibid., v, p. 64–65). By some bearers of the name in Orkney the name is shortened to Swan (*Weekly Scotsman*, January, 1936). As forename: Swannie Guthrumson in Moull, Unst, Shetland, 1625 (*Shetland*).

SWANSTON. From Swanston near Colinton, Midlothian. Duncan de Swaynystoun and Mariota, his wife, made grants of portions of their lands of Swaynystoun to the Hospital of Soltre, c. 1221–38 (*Soltre*, p. 23, 24, 26). Jennet Suanstone was a tenant under the Abbey of Kelso in Bowdene in 1567 (*Kelso*, p. 519), John Suanstoune in Bouden, 1641 (RRM., I, p. 86), and Bessie Swenstoune is recorded in Crealling in 1684 (*Peebles CR.*). Swanstone 1699.

SWANTON. William Suantoun, saidler in Irvine, 1666 (*Irvine*, II, p. 205). Perhaps of English origin from Swanton in county Norfolk, England.

SWAYNE. See under SWAIN.

SWESONE. William Suesone or Swesone confessed to breaking the statutes of the town of Inverness, 1605 and 1607, and Thomas Sueson confessed the same, 1613 (*Rec. Inv.*, II, p. 29, 54, 113).

SWIFT. A family of this name were burgesses of Edinburgh, and the chartulary of St. Giles contains frequent notices of them in the time of James II (*Stodart*, II, p. 122). John Swyft was burgess of Edinburgh in 1427 (RMS., II, 92). Swift was the name of a tenth-century landowner in England (*Ewen*, p. 335).

SWINBURNE. Perhaps from the township of Swinburne in Northumberland. There appears, however, to have been a place named Swinburne near Stenton in the reign of Alexander II. William de Swineburne, the king's clerk, was granted a dispensation to hold an additional benefice in 1253 (*Pap. Lett.*, I, p. 283; ES., II, p. 572n). Sir W. de Swyneburne witnessed a charter to the Priory of May by Alexander Comyn, earl of Buchan (RPSA., p. 383). An annuity paid to John de Swyneburne, 1291 (*Bain*, II, 490).

SWINE. "There has long existed in the village of Swinton a family of Swines, the head of which, towards the end of the eighteenth century, asked and obtained permission from the lord of the manor to change the name to Swinton, 'on account of the nastiness of the beast.' The permission was never acted on" (*Swinton*, p. 1n). In connection with this name a story in a Renton charter is worth relating. The charter records that Roger de Riston hired John 'porcarius' (i.e. swineherd) as his substitute in a wager of battle. The swineherd was the victor, and received a toft and croft and three acres of Great Reston as his fee, which he then granted to the Priory of Durham (*Raine*, 397 *et seq.*). Laurence Swyn, burgess of Aberdeen, 1294 (REA., I, p. 35). Adam Swyn of Rystone, Berwickshire, rendered homage, 1296 (*Bain*, II, p. 206). Crispinie Swyne in Dunfermline, 1581 (*Dunfermline*), and Margaret Swyne in St. Andrews, 1589 (*St. Andrews*, p. 645). David Swyne, baker in Edinburgh, 1620 (*Edinb. Marr.*), and Crispine or Crispinion Swyne was church elder in Dysart, 1641 (PBK., p. 209). Perhaps a shortened form of OE. *Sigewine* ('wise friend') through the form *Siwine*.

SWINEFORD. Local. William de Svineford, cleric of the bishop of Glasgow, 1255–6 (*Soltre*, p. 34), witnessed a gift to the church of Glasgow, c. 1260 (REG., p. 177). William of Swineford witnessed grant to the Abbey of Kilwinning, 1286 (*Pap. Lett.*, I, p. 383). From one or other of the English places of the name.

SWINEWOOD. Local. There is a Swinewood near Reston, Berwickshire. Patrick de Svinewde witnessed a charter relating to Fife, c. 1210 (SHR., II, p. 175).

SWINHOUSE. Local. George Swynhouse and James Swynhouse in Over Blainslie witnessed an instrument of sasine, 1575 (RRM., III, p. 342).

SWINTON. The old family of Swinton may be of Anglian origin, as a charter of David I shows the lands of Swinton (Swintun) in possession of (1) Edolf, (2) Liulf son of Edolf, and (3) Udard, his grandson (*Nat. MSS.*, I, 21). Alanus de Svint' witnessed a charter by Patrick, first earl of Dunbar (*Raine*, 116). Sir Alan de Swynton was one of the witnesses to the deed of sale of Adam, son of Thurkill, to the prior of Coldingham, c. 1240 (ibid., 337). Cospatric de Swinton and Hugh, his son, witnessed a charter by Duncan, earl of Fife, to the nuns of North Berwick (CMN., 5). Hugh of Swinton and his son Duncan, who acquired the "thanedom" of Arbuthnot from Walter Olifard, and ejected the Scolocs from their portion of the property most unceremoniously, were the first known members of the Arbuthnot family (Robertson, *Scotland under her early kings*, II, p. 493n). Henry de Swyntone of Berwickshire rendered homage, 1296 (*Bain*, II, p. 206). John, lord of Swyngton, had a safe conduct into England, 1377 (ibid., IV, 254). John Swyntoune of that Ilk, a Berwickshire laird in 1530 (*Trials*, I, p. 147 *). John Swontoun was retoured heir of Robert Swontoun *de eodem* in the lands of Swontoun, etc., in Berwickshire, 1628 (*Retours, Berwick*, 157). Thomas Swentoun, minister at Kirkwall, 1603 (OSR., I, p. 226). The name was carried to France in the fifteenth or early sixteenth century by emigrant adventurers, and appears there as Vincton. In the Berry armorial the name is given as "Sancton." Suentoun 1512, Suyntoune 1637, Sweintoun 1624, Swenton 1539, Swentoun 1549, Swentoune 1655, Swintonne 1658, Swyintoune 1656, Swyntoune 1633.

SWITHIN. From the OE. personal name *Swiþhun*. Donald Swyithne, one of the chaplains of the choir of the cathedral church of Dornoch, 1512 (OPS., II, p. 623).

SWORD. This surname is a corrupt form of the old personal name SIWARD, q.v., famous

in early Scottish history from its having been borne by the victor over Macbeth at the battle of Dunsinnan in 1054. John Swerd, Scotsman, who had a safe conduct into England in 1398, may be the John Swerde, master of a ship of Archambaud (Archibald), earl of Douglas, in 1405 (*Bain*, IV, 504, 697). Alexander Suerd was burgess of Linlithgow in 1536 (*Johnsoun*), Malcolm Sword, son of umquhile Christopher Sword, appears in Stirling in 1628, and Patrick Sword was treasurer of that burgh in 1631 (SBR., p. 162, 165, 289), and burgess in 1646 (*Inquis.*, 3122). Decree was obtained against James Suerd in 1531 (*Cambus.*, 203), James Sourd or Suord was chosen Commissioner of the Kingdom for St. Andrews in 1653 (John Lamont, *Diary*, p. 46), and three individuals named Sword were residents in the parish of Borgue in 1684 (RPC., 3. ser. IX, p. 567). Suorde 1641.

SWORDSLIPPER. From the occupation. A swordslipper was one who made sword-slips or sheaths. In 1574 there is record of payment received from John Johnnestoune, sword sleper, for his burgessship (MCM., II, p. 334). Thomas Swerdsleper was bailie of the burgh of Stirling between 1364 and 1390 (SBR., p. 146 *seqq.*), and Maurice Suerdslep was elected lineator in Aberdeen in 1398 (CRA., p. 374). Johannes Suerdsleper in Aberdeen, 1408 (CWA., p. 316).

SYARE. Thomas Syar and Jonet Syar were tenants in the parish of Kilbride, 1535 (*Hunter*, p. 15). Thomas Scyir (apparently the same name) is recorded in Corsbie, 1583 (ibid., p. 32), and David Syare was admitted burgess of Glasgow, 1598 (*Burgesses*).

SYD. John Syd, peuterer in Edinburgh, 1666, and James Syde, peuterer there, 1681 (*Edinb. Marr.*). Perhaps of local origin. There is a Syde and Mill of Syde in Aberdeenshire, a Syde near Stracathro in Angus, and Syde in Lanarkshire. A family named Syd or Syde was resident in the burgh of Methil, Fife, 1690 (*Laing*, 2882).

SYDSERF, SYDSERFF. From the lands of the same name in the barony of North Berwick. Nisbet, apparently on the strength of the fleur-de-lys in the arms of the family, says they originally came from France. Mariorie de Sydeserfe of the county of Edneburgh rendered homage in 1296 (*Bain*, II, p. 211). William de Sideserfe or Sytserf' of the county of Edeneburk also rendered homage in the same year (ibid., p. 201), and served as juror on an inquest at Berwick. William Sydeserf or William of Sideserff had a safe conduct to pass through England in 1446 and in 1448

SYDSERF, SYDSERFF, continued

(Bain, IV, 1187, 1207). In 1577 the old family of the name is referred to as Sydserf of that Ilk (RPC., II, p. 736). William Sydserff of Rouchlaw was admitted burgess of Stirling in 1617 (SBR., p. 148). Thomas Sydserf (d. 1663) was successively bishop of Brechin, Galloway, and Orkney. Another Thomas Sideserf was editor of the *Mercurius Caledonius*, the earliest Scottish newspaper, published in 1661. Sidserfe 1658, Sinserff 1656, Svdsarfe 1614, Svdserffe 1373, Syidserf 1590, Synserff 1648, Sideserwe (of that Ilk) 1508; also Saidserf and Sadsarf.

SYM, SYME. Variants of SIM, SIME, q.v., the more common forms of the name.

SYMAN. Recorded in CD. Probably a variant of SYMON, q.v.

SYMERS. See under SYMMERS.

SYMINGTON. There is a village and parish of Symington in the Kyle district of Ayrshire, but the old family of Symington derive from Symington in the Upper Ward of Lanarkshire. Symon Loccard, ancestor of the Lockharts of Lee, held both places in the latter half of the twelfth century under the Stewards. Between 1315–21 Robert I confirmed to Thomas filius Ricardi all the barony of Symundestone in the sheriffdom of Lanark (RMS., I, 78). This Thomas son of Richard (Thomas Dickson) was progenitor of the family of Symington of that Ilk. The family held the barony till towards the middle of the seventeenth century. John of Symonton of that Ilk appears as sheriff-depute of Lanark in 1478 and 1490 (ALA., p. 44, 72, 148). John of Symenton was juror in Lanark, 1501 (*Lanark*, p. 11). John Symontoun *de eodem* was served heir to his father in the barony of Symontoun (except 26 oxgates in the town) with the office of bailie of the barony of Dowglas and the captaincy of the castle thereof, and other lands, in 1612 (*Retours, Lanark*, 478). The first real steamship built in the United Kingdom was constructed by William Symington, and launched on the river Carron in 1789. Symmentoun 1578, Symmontone 1682, Symmontoune and Symingtoune 1684, Symontou 1537, Symontoune 1561, Symontown 1687, Symountoun 1632. *See also* under DICKSON.

SYMMERS, SYMERS, SIMMERS, SOMERS, SUMMER, SUMMERS. Metcalf-Jamieson (*Scottish dictionary*) has: Somer, a sumpter, applied to both men and horses, OF. *somier, sommier*. William Sumer witnessed a grant by Richard de Paynstoun to the Hospital of Soltre between 1180–1214 (*Soltre*, p. 5). In 1326

David II granted to William Somyr for life an annual rent of 40s. (*Stodart*, II, p. 375), Johannes Sovmer was burgess of Perth in 1365 (RMS., I, 196), and in 1376 the lands of Scralyve were leased to William Sumer (RHM., I, p. lxvii). George Somyr was one of a number chosen "to inquire and knaw vppone the landis and guidis pertaining to Walter Ogilvy of Owres" in 1478 (ALA., June, 1478), and a later George Svmmer was charged with oppression, 1529 (*Trials*, I, p. 141 *). Adam Summer had sasine in 1550 as heir of Barthillomew Summyr in Glasgow (*Protocols*, I), and Andrew Symmer, quarrior, admitted burgess freeman of Glasgow gratis in 1584, "becaus he is ane calsay maker and hes promised to mak twa rude of calsay, gratis" (*Burgesses*). David Sommer appears in Ancrum in 1633 (*Retours, Roxburgh*, 152), John Svmer was trade burgess of Aberdeen, 1641 (ROA., I, p. 232), John Simmer was fiar of Brathinsch in 1646 (Jervise, *Land of Lindsays*, p. 433), and Elizabeth Simmer is recorded in Stank, parish of Stonehouse, 1687 (*Lanark CR.*). Symmer or Somyr of Balzeordie, an old Angus family of whom nothing much is known. They possessed Balzordie in 1450. In 1682 Symmer of Baljordie were described as "ane ancient familie and chief of the name" (Account of shire of Forfar, *Spottiswoode Miscellany*, I, p. 335). They continued to be considered "chief of the name" till about the middle of the eighteenth century when the male branch failed (Jervise, *Land of Lindsays*, p. 310–311). They took a prominent part in local affairs. At least one member of the family changed the spelling in last century to Seymour. Simer and Simers 1686, Summyr 1550, Sumyer 1454, Symer 1633, Symir 1551, Symmeir 1530, Symour 1688. In the Edinburgh Marriage Records, 1595–1800, the name occurs as: Symmer, Simmer, Symers, Summer, Summers, Somer, Somers, and Sommer; and in Greyfriars Burial Register, 1658–1700: Somers, Simers, Simeres, Sommers, and Summers.

SYMON. A form of SIMON, which in the N. T. represents O. T. Simeòn (and Symeòn). The Hebrew is Shim'ōn, a name of doubtful meaning. Explained by some as meaning "offspring of hyena and wolf" (*Encyclopaedia Biblica*, IV, p. 4531), by others as from the verb *shame* "hear." The N. T. form appears to be due to confusion with a Greek nickname, *Simòn* "flat-nosed." (2) It may also represent the common OE. personal name Sigemund which later became Simon and Sumond. Svmon, capellanus, witnessed a charter by William Bruce to Adam Carlyle, c. 1194–1214 (*Annandale*, I, p. 2), and Symon or Simon, archidiaconus of Aberdeen, was a charter witness,

1172, c. 1189–99 (RAA., I, p. 57). Symon filius Ade Leving, 1298 (*Scon*, p. 92). George Svmon is recorded in the lordship of Huntly, 1600 (SCM., IV, p. 283), and John Symon in Cairnmore, parish of Glass, is recorded in 1743 (*Moray*). Symount 1605.

SYMONS, 'son of SYMON,' q.v. Andreas filius Simonis and Jacobus filius Simonis in Paert (Perth) in reign of William the Lion (*Scon*, p. 29). William filius Svmon, witness, 1178 (RAA., I, 2), Walterus filius Symonis, tenant in vill de Moffat, 1376 (RHM., I, p. lxii), and Henry Symonis, witness in 1499 (*Cawdor*, p. 101). Mr. Andrew Symonis, vicar of Abirdene, was admitted burgess of the town in 1479 (NSCM., I, p. 2).

SYMONSON, 'son of SYMON,' q.v. David Simonson, tenant of part of Couper-Grange, 1471 (*Cupar-Angus*, I, p. 159), and Donald Symonson is recorded in Inverness, 1481 (*Invernessiana*, p. 154). George Symonson appears as a charter witness in Inverness in 1536 (*Laing*, 403). Symonsoun 1624.

SYMSON. See *under* SIMSON.

SYNMERDSBURN. Perhaps for Symmerdsburn (? = Summersburn). Radulfus dominus de Synmerdsburn was rector of the church of Arryngrosk (Arngask), 1282 (*Cambus.*, 2). Perhaps an Englishman.

TABURNER. A player on the tabor, from ME. *taburner*. In Middle English vocabularies *taberner* is glossed "*timpanista, timpanizator*." 1467, "giffin to the tawbronar that playit to the king" (ALHT., I, p. 322). Andrew Taberner was one of the jurors on an inquisition in Edinburgh, 1428 (RAA., II, 61), and a later Andrew Tabowrnar witnessed an instrument of sasine of the lands and castle of Temptalloune in 1475 (*Douglas*, III, p. 106).

TACKET. From Tecket in North Tvndale. Andrea Teket witnessed a charter by Willelmus filius hawoc, burgess of Perth, c. 1245 (*Inchaffray*, p. 63). John de Teket was bailiff of Tyndale, 1279 (*Bain*, II, p. 51). Gilbert Teket, burgess of Stirling, and Phelippe or Philip Taket, burgess of Perth, rendered homage in 1296 (ibid., p. 186, 187). Matthew Tacket, a monk of Culross, had much to do with the laying out of the garden at Stirling for King James IV. Arthur Tacket was tortured for taking part with insurgents at Bothwell Bridge and after (Dalyell, *Darker superstitions*, p. 657). Arthur Taikit was clerk of sasines in Edinburgh in middle of seventeenth century. Robert Taket died in Galashiels, December 1939, and Nettie Mitchell Taket died there in 1942.

TAGGART. A shortening of (MAC)TAGGART, q.v. "*Honi soit qui mal y pense*," says the late Sir Herbert Maxwell, "the rule of celibacy was not strictly enforced upon the clergy of the primitive church" (*Scottish land names*, p. 177). Patrick Taggart was a witness in Dumfries, 1544 (*Anderson*), Christian Taggart is in Inglistoun, 1678 (*Kirkcudbright*), Andrew Tagart appears in the parish of Borgue, 1684 (RPC., 3. ser. IX, p. 567), and William Tagart in Underwood in the same year (*Dumfries*).

TAIS. A surname recorded in Mar in the seventeenth century, probably a variant of TAWS, q.v. John Tais, burgess of Stirling, 1481 (*Cambus.*, 211). Beak Taiss at the Burne syd of Logie accused of being a witch, 1597 (SCM., I, p. 183). John Tais in Torgudland, and William Tais in Mylntoun of Arschine, 1633 (SCM., III, p. 88). Thomas and William Tais, followers of the earl of Mar, were charged with resetting outlawed Macgregors, 1636 (RPC., 2. ser. VI, p. 215). James Tais, son of William Tais, tailor in Dunkeld, 1674 (DPD., I, p. 262). David Taish in Culcrieff, parish of Crieff, 1716, and Grissall Tais in Newbigging, 1721 (*Dunkeld*). James Taes in Belnascough, 1767 (*Moray*), and John Taes, merchant in Banff, 1783 (*Aberdeen CR.*).

TAIT. Originally a nickname. Bede (*Hist. Eccles.*, II, 9) tells us that Ethelberga, daughter of Ethelbert, king of Kent, was otherwise called 'Tate' (fem.), and nine individuals named 'Tata' (masc.) are recorded in Birch's *Cartularium Saxonicum*. The word, meaning 'glad,' 'cheerful,' occurs in ON. as *teitr*, and as a proper name, Teitr, occurs several times in the Icelandic *Landnámabok*. A debt due by the king is recorded paid to Thomas dictus Tayt in 1329 (ER., I, p. 211). Between 1362–70 there are a number of entries of payment of pension to John Tayt, clerk, who appears to have been connected with the hospital of Montrose (ibid., II, p. 115, 359, etc.). Alexander Tayt was burgess of Edinburgh, 1381 (*Egidii*, p. 22). Adam Tayte who had a safe conduct to travel in England in 1424, may be the Adam Tayt, scutifer, a charter witness in Paisley, 1432 (*Bain*, III, 970; RMP., p. 370). Andrew Tait was Master of the Flesher Craft of Edinburgh, 1490 (Colston, *Incorporated trades*, p. 54), and another Andrew Tayt was one of the perambulators of the boundaries of Yochry and Achbrady, 1492 (RAA., II, 339). Robert Tait was tenant of the land of Wydsyd in 1531 (*Rental*), Christie Tett and Dand Taitt were tenants under the Abbey of Kelso, 1567 (*Kelso*, p. 528). The name also appears in Orkney in 1575 (*Oppressions*, p. 7). A family of the name were proprietors of the barony of

TAIT, *continued*

Cherrytrees in 1605 (*Trials*, II, p. 475), and Tait of Pirn, an ancient family in Tweeddale, ended in two heiresses, Margaret and Anne, one of whom married a Horsburgh of that Ilk. Archibald Campbell Tait (1811–1882), born in Edinburgh, became archbishop of Canterbury.

TALBERT. Formerly a surname in Aberdeenshire, and perhaps so still. Malcolmus Tabert was tenant in Auchlyne, Aberdeenshire, 1511 (REA., I, p. 363). David Talbert in Rescobye, 1592 (*Retours, Fife*, 1506).

TALFER. See *under* TELFER.

TALLEY. John Talley, heir of James Talley, *calcearius*, burgess of Edinburgh, 1693 (*Inquis.*, 8754). James Tallie or Taillie, cordiner, burgess of Edinburgh, 1724, 1734 (*Guildry*, p. 128, 147).

TALORCAN. Talorcan is a diminutive of Talorc or TALORG, q.v., with which it is freely interchanged (ES., I, p. 253). Talarican or Talorgan, a Pict, a disciple of S. Donnan, labored mainly in the north and died A.D. 616 or 617. The parish of Kiltarlity derives its name from him. The name under different forms (Talarg, Talore, Tollarg, Talorggan, Tallorcen, Talorgen, etc.) occurs frequently in early Scottish history.

TALORG. The Gaulish personal name *Argiotalus* in reverse. It means 'silver brow,' 'bright browed' — *talo-s*, 'forehead, brow,' OIr. *talas*, W. *tal*; and *arg*, 'silver, white,' seen in G. *airgiod*, 'silver.' Adamnan (I, 20) mentions *Baitanus gente nepos Niath Taloirc*, 'Baetan descendant of Nia Taloirc,' i.e. of Talorc's champion. Talorc here "probably the name of a divinity" (*Watson* I, p. 299). Talorgg filius Drostain was put in chains by his brother Nechtain, 713 (AU.).

TAME. Marjory Tame in Edinburgh, 1687 (*Edinb. Marr.*). Gilbert Tame in the parish of Hailes complained against his minister, 1689 (RPC., 3. ser. XIV, p. 78). Lower, Bardsley, and Harrison say this name is local (Oxfordshire), from residence by the river Tame, but the surname in Scotland is more probably from the Tame in the North Riding of Yorkshire.

TAMSON. "Son of Tam," Scots form of Thom-(as). Margaret Tamsone in Elgin was cited for charming, 1664 (*Rec. Elgin*, II, p. 303).

TANCRED. From the OE. personal name Thancred. Thomas Thancard who witnessed a charter by William the Lion granted at Lan-

narc between 1187–89 (REG., p. 65) gave name to the parish of Thankerton, Lanarkshire. He was one of the witnesses to a confirmation charter by William the Lion to David de Haia, son of William de Haia of Herol (SCM., II, p. 305). Between 1204–11 he gave to the monks of Arbroath the land between Ethkar and Chaledouer which King Malcolm had given Thankard his father (RAA., I, p. 69, 70), and also gave some land at Moydirual (= Motherwell) to the monks of Paisley (RMP., p. 310, 412). Robert, son of Thancard, witnessed a charter by William of Cunnigeburc to the monks of Kelso (*Kelso*, p. 281).

TANDERSON. Shetland surname. As Ir. *Tadg* appears in Norse as *Tandr* or *Tadkr*, Tanderson is probably = Ir. *MacThaidhg*, Maccaig.

TANNACH, TANNOCH. Local. Perhaps from Tannach near Wick, Caithness. There is also a Tannach near Cumbernauld, Dumbartonshire, and a Tannoch in West Lothian.

TANNAHILL. A common surname in Ayrshire, from Tannahill near Kilmaurs. In 1547 there were seven families of the name in Kilmarnock. Archibald Tannahill was sued in the baron court of Corsehill in 1668 (*Corsehill*, p. 78). Robert Tannahill (1774–1810), poet and songwriter. Tanohill 1689.

TANNER. From the occupation, 'tanner of leather.' Thomas le Tannour rendered homage at Berwick, 1291 (RR.).

TANNOCK. From Tannock in the parish of Kilbride, Ayrshire. James Tannock and William Tannock, painters, were born in Kilmarnock.

TARAN. Tarainus was the name of a Pictish noble (*Adamnan*, V. C., II, 23), and Taran, son of Entefidich, a Pictish king, was expelled in 997 (CPS., p. cxxi). The name is equated with Taranis, the Gaulish thunder god, W. *tarann*, Ir. *torann*, G. *torrunn*, thunder.

TARBERT. Local. Walterus de Tarbard, witness to a charter "de bladis terrarum de Cathboll," 1375 (REM., p. 181) most probably derived his name from Tarbat in Easter Ross. John Tarbatt, notary public in Perth, 1421 (*Athole*, p. 706). John Terbert, witness in Kilwinning, Ayrshire, 1559 (*Laing*, 708). Allan Terbert in Achinames, 1654 (*Kilbarchan*), and Robert Tarbert in Campbeltown, 1682. Tarbert for G. *tairbeart*, an isthmus, portage, sometimes appears in place names as Tarbet. Terbart 1517.

TARBET. A form of TARBERT, q.v. James Tarbet, merchant burgess of Edinburgh, 1681 (*Inquis.*, 6308).

TARLACHSON, 'son of Charles,' a partial translation of the Gaelic name. Tearlach is the Gaelic equivalent of Charles. Hector Tarlachson was seneschal of Urchard, 1440 (*Rose*, p. 131). John Tarlasoun was fined for reset of members of Clan Gregor, 1613 (RPC., XIV, p. 635).

TARN. Recorded in Banffshire. Perhaps a variant of TORN, q.v.

TARNEL. The Tarnels of Voe, Delting, Shetland, an old family, are referred to by a 'poet' in 1700:

"...But whence they arose
We neither read in verse nor prose."

TARRAS, TERRAS, TERRIS, TERRACE. Local, from Tarras in the parish of Rafford, Moray. Adam de Tarays, monk, and John de Tarays, notary public, are in record, 1375 (RAA., II, 34). Jacobus Terras, succentor of Moray, 1569 (REM., p. 395). Anna Tarres was retoured heir of James Tarres, formerly bailie of Elgin, in a tenement in Abirdene, 1669 (*Retours, Aberdeen*, 396). A pension was paid to Elizabeth Tarras in Edinburgh, 1732 (*Guildry*, p. 144), and David Tarras appears in Peterhead, 1783 (*Aberdeen CR.*). The name of John Turras of Old Meldrum, a Jacobite of the '45, may be a misspelling.

TARREL. From the old lands of the name in Tarbat, Ross. The old family of the name, now extinct, were followers of the earls of Ross. In the sixteenth century the lands were in possession of the Maccullochs. Johannes de Tarale witnessed confirmation of a charter by the earl of Ross to Paul McTyre in 1362 (RMS., I, 423), and in the following year William, earl of Sutherland granted to John of Tarale six davachs of Ruchy (or Ruthy) in Straflete (OPS., II, p. 719). William Tarraill was juror on inquisition at Inverness, 1430 (RMS., II, 179). Thomas of Terraile was juror on an inquest made at the head court of John, earl of Sutherland in 1471 (OPS., II, p. 693). Angus de Terrel, Alexander de Terrel, and others, were killed in a clan battle "in die scti barnabi apli, año dñi Mᵒccccᵒlxxxvi, apud aldecharwis" (*Kalendar of Fearn*). Jonet Terrell who had a precept of *clare constat* as heir of her grandfather, Hugh Terrell, of the lands of Strathfleit in 1494 (OPS., II, p. 719) is doubtless the Jonet Terrell who had a grant of the lands of Innerbreky and Balnegall in the earldom of Ross to herself and heirs in 1512 (RMS., II), and the Jonet Terroll of Innerbreky who resigned her lands of Petintreill in the earldom of Suderland in 1529 (OPS., II, p. 630). Sir William Tarall, a cleric, held the chancellary of Caithness, 1497 (RSS., I),

and John Taroll of Doill and David Taroll in Doill were participants in the siege of Dunrobin Castle, 27 June 1519 (*Sutherland*, p. 177). Alexander Terrell or Tarrell, son and heir of deceased John Terrell of Doill, who had seisin in half the lands of Doill and Carrell [Tarrell] in 1546, is recorded as bailie of Master William Hepburne, dean of Caithness, 1562, and as bailie of Golspie, 1566 (OPS., II, p. 667, 678, 723, 727). In the early part of last century the remaining members of the clan took the name of Mackintosh.

TARVES. Of local origin from the village of Tarves in Buchan, Aberdeenshire. Thomas Tarwas, abbot of Paisley, died in 1459 (RMP., pref., p. vi). Thomas Tarvass was admitted burgess of Aberdeen in 1502 and Alexander Tarvass in 1504 (NSCM., I, p. 41). Symsoun Terwes was accused of assault in the same burgh in 1544 (CRA., p. 212).

TARVIT, TERVET, TERVIT. Of local origin from the lands of Tarvit in the parish of Cupar, Fife. Henry de Taruethe, tenant of the bishop of St. Andrews in the county of Fife, rendered homage in 1296. In the same year he was juror on an inquest on the lands of Disarde (Dysart). His seal bears an eight-rayed figure and S' *Henrici d' Tarven* (Bain, II, p. 205, 216, 553). There was a family of Tarvit of that Ilk in Fife. Alexander Teruat *de eodem* appears as juror on an inquisition at Cupar in 1516 (SCBF., p. 49). John Tervet of that Ilk and Elias Tervett, his uncle, had remission in 1509 (*Trials*, I, p. 110 *). John Tarvett was tenant of Newbigging in Lothian in 1636 (RPC., 2. ser. VI, p. 592). James Tarvet, wright in St. Andrews, 1683 (PSAS., LIV, p. 239). John Tervett in Newbigging, 1652, and Christian Tervett in Thankerton, 1673, and Janet Tarvett in Edmiston, parish of Biggar, 1681 (*Lanark CR.*).

TASKER. A Perthshire surname. From ME. *tasker*, a thrasher, reaper. William Tasker, sergeant of the guard in Dundee, 1643 (*Beats*, p. 255). James Tasker is recorded in Ardler in 1668 (DPD., I, p. 341).

TASKILL. A forename derived from *Askill*. For its origin see under MACASGILL.

TASSIE. A rare Scots surname, probably a diminutive of Fr. *taisson*, a badger. The modern Fr. surname is Tesson or Teysson. Cf. Tassin de Neubaut, 1296 (Bain, II, 742) and Tassyn de Loran, 1323. John Tassy was admitted burgess of Glasgow, 1594 (*Burgesses*). Margaret Tassie or Tasi and others were charged with committing assault at Gartnavell, 1634 (RPC., 2. ser. V, p. 323, 643). James Tassie (1735–1799) was a celebrated gem-engraver.

TASTARD. *See under* TESTARD.

TATE. *See under* TAIT.

TATENEL. An English name probably from Tattenhall in the county of Chester. About 1180 William de Tatenhill witnessed a charter by Matthew Kyninmond, bishop of Aberdeen (REA., I, p. 12), and about the same date a charter was granted him by the same bishop in which Tatenhill is described as 'homini nostro' (ibid., p. 13). Willelmus de Brenneth dictus Tatenel who witnessed a charter by Hugh Herock, burgess of Elgin, in 1286 (REM., p. 284), is probably the William de Tattenel who rendered homage in 1296 (Bain, II, p. 195).

TAVERNER. From AF. *taverner* (Fr. *tavernier*, from Latin *tabernarium*), an "innkeeper." Henry le Taverner, a crossbowman, was one of the English garrison of Linlithgow Castle in 1305 (Bain, II, p. 464). William Tauernere or Tauerner made a gift of land in Inuernys in 1361 (REM., p. 306, 317), and Joh. Tauernare was burgess in Edinburgh in 1486 (RMS., II, 1655).

TAWESON, TAWESSON. An Englishing of MACTAVISH, q.v. William Tawson appears as bailie of Inverness, 1450 (Invernessiana, p. 119).

TAWS, TAWSE. A phonetic spelling of Gaelic *Tamhas*, 'Thomas.' Tawus M'Gillese was a tenant under the earl of Douglas in 1376 (RHM., I, p. lvi). In 1415 Tawis Michison appears as a charter witness (Scon, p. 205), and Taus ffrasser of Littlegarth is mentioned in 1632 (IDR., p. 25). William Taus (here a surname), tailor in Dunkeld, died in 1667. John Taws in Ordie, 1733 (Aberdeen CR.). The surname TAISE, found in Mar in the seventeenth century, is probably another form of the name. See MACTAVISH.

TAYLER, TAYLEUR. *See under* TAYLOR.

TAYLOR, TAYLER, TAYLEUR. From the occupation of 'tailor,' a cutter-out of cloth, ME. *taillour*<AF. *taillour*, OF. *tailleur*, 'the cutter,' from OF. *tailler*, 'to cut.' In Latin documents rendered *cissor*. A very common name in early Scots records. Alexander le Tayllur was valet of Alexander III in 1276 (Bain, II, 76). John le Taillur held the mill of Selkirk as firmar, 1292 (Rot. Scot., I, p. 80), and Brice le Taillur was one of the Scottish prisoners taken at the capture of Dunbar Castle, 1296 (Bain, II, 742). Six persons of this name in the counties of Roxburgh, Dumfries, Edinburgh, Lanark, and Angus rendered homage, 1296 (Bain, II). John Cissor was tenant of Balgirdane in the barony of Buittle, Adam

Cissor in barony of Newlands, and Andrew Cissor in the vill of Preston, 1376 (RHM., I, p. lx, lxi; II, p. 16). Johannes Cissor in the parish of Fyvy was excommunicated, 1384 (REA., I, p. 165). William Scissor held a tenement in Edinburgh, 1392 (Egidii, p. 27), and Walter Cissor had grant of half the land of Glorat from David II (RMS., I, App. II, 1137, 1183). Alexander Scissorus, 'armigerus meus,' 1344 (REA., I, p. 75). Donald Scissor and Bricius Scissor were witnesses in Inverness, 1462 (Invernessiana, p. 141), and Arthur Scissor in Perth, 1463, is mentioned in same year as Arthur Tailzoure (Milne, p. 52, 53). A grave slab in Dundee records "hic iacet Joannes filivs Philippi Cissoris," with a pair of scissors and a bodkin (Jervise, Memorials, p. * 29). The Taillear dubh na tuaighe (Black tailor of the battle-axe) is a semi-legendary figure in Cameron traditions. Tailer 1649, Tailleur 1296, Taillir 1408, Tailliovr 1608, Tailliour 1588, Taillur 1296, Taillyer and Taillyeor 1655, Taillzier 1660, Tailveour 1593, Tailzieor and Tailzieour 1662, Talyeor 1694, Talyhour 1453, Talyowr 1430, Talzeor 1655, Talzeour 1493, Talzior 1494, Talzour 1540, Talzoure 1467, Tayliour 1661, Tayllur 1296, Taylyhour 1430, Taylyour 1419, Tavlowre 1688, Taylzowr 1525, Telvour 1534, Thailzor 1472, Thalzeour 1484, Tyllour 1720. In many instances an Anglicizing of MACINTAYLOR, q.v.

TEACHER. Now a rare surname. William Teacher introduced a blended whisky in 1830 which he named 'Highland Cream.' Ilgerius Pedagogus is recorded in England, c. 1066 (Ewen, p. 83).

TEALING. John Telyn, tenant under the abbot of Cupar-Angus, 1456, and John Telyng, tenant of Ballgyrco, 1457 (Cupar-Angus, I, p. 137, 138). The tenement of quondam Agnes Telyng in Arbroath is mentioned in 1483 (RAA., II, 223). From Tealing near Dundee.

TEARLACH. Teàrlach is the Gaelic name with which Charles has been equated. There is no connection between the two names, it being simply a case of adopting a name like or nearly like in sound to the Gaelic. The older Gaelic form of Teàrlach is Toirrdhealbhach, E. Ir. Toirdelbach (Toirrdelbach in Book of Ballymote, 1086), "well-shaped." Charles Maclean, the ancestor of the Macleans of Dochgarroch, was known to Highlanders as Toirrdhealbhach. In Irish as a forename it has been Anglicized TURLOUGH and TERENCE (!). See also CHARLES.

TELFER, TALFER. From NF. *taillefer*, 'cut iron,' perhaps a trade name. The name Taillefer was common about the tenth and eleventh centuries. It is most familiar to us as the name of the *jongleur* who sang the Song of Roland at the opening of the battle of Hastings (Wace, *Le Roman de Rou*, 1827 ed., p. 214–215). "In Latin deeds and chronicles it is usually rendered as *Sector-Ferri*, but in other cases as *Ferrum-Sector*, or *Scindens-Ferrum*, or *Incisor-Ferri*" (*Folk-lore*, VII, p. 256). Willelmus Tailfer witnessed a charter by Margaret, countess of Buchan, in favor of the Abbey of Arbroath, c. 1210 (RAA., I, p. 94). William Tailfere had confirmation of a charter of the land of Hareclouche in the sheriffdom of Lanark in 1369 (RMS., I, 322), and the Tailfairs of Haircleugh are in record for more than three hundred years. Andrea Taillefere, 'clericus cancellarie,' was a charter witness at Inverkeithing in 1413 (RMS., I, 947), John Talzefir was scutifer to Sir William Bothwell in 1450 (LSC., 124), and Lourence Talliefere, Scottish merchant, had a safe conduct into England in 1464 (*Bain*, IV, 1343). Thomas Tailyefair was burgess of Stirling in 1476 (SBR., p. 257), John Tailfeyr and Laurence Taillefere were burgesses of Edinburgh in 1484 (REG., 433, 435), and Arthur Talliefere had a pension from the great customs of Edinburgh in 1527 (RSS., I, 3665). Sir Alexander Talifar was prebendary of Holy Trinity of Edinburgh in 1529 (*Soltre*, p. 211), and Laurence Talliefeire was treasurer of Dunkeld in 1539 (SCM., IV, p. 32). Arthur Taillefere de Crechmond, a witness in 1547, may be the Master Arthur Talzefere, canon of Aberdeen in 1549 (REA., II, p. 319; *Statutes Scot. Church*, p. 88). Cuthbert Tailliefeir was servant to Tuedy of Dreva in 1592 (RPC., IV, p. 743), William Tailyeffer was banished from Stirling in 1611 (SBR., p. 129), Alexander Tailliepheir was heir of Bethia Oliphant in 1643 (*Inquis.*, 2849), and Charles Teilfeire was master of a family in the parish of Borgue in 1684 (RPC., 3. ser. IX, p. 569). Tailefeir 1551, Tailfair 1676, Taillefere 1558, Tailliefeir 1632, Tailyefeir 1653, Tailvhefair, 1531, Tailyiefeir 1632, Tailzefair 1621, Tailzefeir 1567, Tailzefeir 1482, Tailziefeir 1657, Talfeir 1599, Talliefer 1550, Talliefere 1526, Talyefer 1512, Talzefer 1403, Tyllefer 1525, Telferr 1689, Telfier 1686, Telfure 1688, Telpher 1599; Telzepher.

TELFORD. From TELFER with accretionary *d*. Margaret Telfuird in Ponfeich, parish of Carmichael, 1674 (*Lanark CR.*). Thomas Telford (1757–1834), the engineer, when he first attended school was registered as Telfer. Tellfoord 1728.

TEMPLE. From the village of Temple in the parish of the same name in Midlothian, formerly the principal place of residence of the Knights Templars in Scotland. "The precep-

tories or priories of the Knights-Templars were often called Temples, and even manorial residences and estates belonging to them obtained the same appellation. The name consequently passed to tenant or bailiff of such a property" (Lower, *Patronymica Britannica*). Agnes de Tempill held a land in the vill and territory of Elstanfurd in the constabulary of Haddington in 1429 (RMS., II, 124). Johannes Tempill had a remission for his share in burning the town of Dunbertane in 1489 (*Lennox*, II, p. 133). William Tempill, canon of the Collegiate Church of Holy Trinity, Edinburgh, appears frequently in record in the first half of the sixteenth century (*Soltre*).

TEMPLEAND. A surname found in Dumfriesshire, derived from the village of Templand in the parish of Lochmaben. There is also a Templand in the parish of Rhynie, Aberdeenshire, and another in Ayrshire. The Knights Templars were extensive owners of land, and "Tempill lands" are frequently mentioned in old charters. There are three places named Templand in Aberdeenshire and three in Ayrshire.

TEMPLEMAN. An official who had charge of the lands or buildings belonging to the Knights-Templars. Robert Templeman witnessed a resignation by Thomas Strachan of Glenkindy, 1406 (SCM., V, p. 254). Thomas Templeman was sergeant for the sheriffdom of Edinburgh in 1450 (ER., V, p. 396), payment was made to David Tempilman in 1503 (*Lanark*, p. 12), and another David Templeman, messenger within the shirefdome of Wigtoun, is mentioned in 1505 and 1517 (*Milne*, p. 14; RSS., I, 2924). John Tempilman had 'ane respet' for slaughter in 1527 (RSS., I, 3852), David Tempilman is recorded in Irvine, 1537 (*Irvine*, I, p. 40), and in 1565 mention is made of the heir of the late Annibill Tempilman, one of the portioners of the temple-lands of Ardersier (*Cawdor*, p. 267). Andrew Templeman, heir of Richard Templeman, portioner of Pitfar, 1685 (*Retours, Perth*, 1127).

TEMPLETON. A surname found mainly in the shires of Ayr and Lanark, and probably derived from Templeton near Dundonald, Ayrshire. Gilbertus de Tempilton, rector of the church of Rothir' (Rothesay) in 1295 (RMP., p. 139) is probably Mestre (Master) Gilbert de Templeton of the county of Are who rendered homage for his possessions in 1296. His seal bears the Virgin and child, a monk at prayer below, and S' Gilb'ti de Temp[leton cl]'ici (*Bain*, II, p. 199, 548). Jacobus de Templetone held land in Ayrshire in the reign of Robert the Bruce (RMS., I, 46), and Johne Tempiltoun, in Are, had a precept of remission for certain

TEMPLETON, *continued*

acts of his in 1491 (RSS., I, 9), and David Tempiltone was sergiand of the burgh of Irvine, 1499 (*Simon*, 31). Jonet Tempiltoun was retoured heir of Hugh Tempiltoun, 'fabriferrarius' and portioner of Corsehill-Kilwinning in 1676 (*Retours, Ayr*, 601).

TENANT, TENNANT, TENNENT. William tenant of Crestone of county of Linlescu, 1296. His seal shows a large dog and S' *Will'i Tenavnt* (*Bain*, II, p. 202, 551). Thomas Tenaunt was one of the witnesses in the inquiry concerning the Templars in 1309 (*Wilkins, Concilia*, p. 383), and John Tenant was one of the garrison of Edinburgh Castle, 1339–40 (*Bain*, III, p. 241). John Tennand was one of the burgesses of Stirling who attacked the cruives and fishings of the abbot and convent of Cambuskenneth, 1366 (*Cambus.*, 55). Andro Tenand was charter witness in Ayr, 1500 (*Friars Ayr*, p. 68), and Andro Tenand and Bob Tenand were voters in Monkland, 1519 (*Simon*, 45). Andrew Tennend was burgess of Are, 1539 (RMS., III, 849), and another Andrew Tennand is mentioned in Dysart, 1542 (*Dysart*, p. 7). Robert Tenent was witness in Glasgow, 1550, and reversion was granted to Kenthigern Tenende in Glasgow, 1555 (*Protocols*, I).

TENDEMAN. Henricus Tenteman witnessed a charter by William filius Hawoc, burgess of Perth, c. 1245 (*Inchaffray*, p. 63). Ralf Tendman, burgess of Perth, was granted freedom from distraint in England, 1290, and in 1296, as Rauf Tundeman, he rendered homage (*Bain*, II, p. 102, 186, 197). Duncan Tendman resigned his share of the lands of Ledyntosach, 1335 (REA., I, p. 60).

TENDER. Alexander Teyndar held a tenement in Arbroath, 1506 and David Tendir was a monk in Arbroath Abbey, 1511 (RAA., II, p. 367, 410). James Teyndar was a charter witness, 1544 (ibid., pref., p. xxxiii), and Jacobus Teinder appears in Edinburgh, 1646 (*Inquis. Tut.*, 701).

TEODBOLD. A form of the OE. personal name *Theobald*, 'people bold.' Teodbold was one of the witnesses to the charter by King Duncan II to the monks of S. Cuthbert, 1094 (*Lawrie*, p. 10). Tebaldus de Norham held a half carucate in Hedinham (Ednam), c. 1147 (*Dryburgh*, 158).

TERBRAX. From the old lands of Tarbrex (1669) in the barony of Dunsyre, Lanarkshire. George Terbrax was member of Scots parliament for Lanark, 1656 (*Hanna*, II, p. 516).

TERNY. Robert de Terny, cleric, in diocese of St. Andrews, 1415 (REG., 325). John Terny, one of an assize at Cupar, 1521 (SCBF., p. 223).

TERRAS, TERRIS, TERRACE. See under TARRAS.

TERREGLES. Makum or Malcolm of Terregles had an agreement of champerty with the sheriff of Dumfries, 1304 (*Bain*, II, p. 397). From Terregles in Kirkcudbrightshire.

TERRY. A diminutive of Theodoric. David filius Terri occurs as donor of a Galloway church to Holyrood in a confirmation of the gift by John, bishop of Whiterne and in the confirmation by William the Lion (LSC., p. 39, 40). The name is found in Arbroath in 1485 (RAA., II, 261).

TERSIE. Local, from some small place probably in Aberdeenshire. William Terse, witness in Awford, 1549, and John Tarsy, charter witness at Dornocht, 1562 (*Aboyne*, p. 74, 79). George Tersie in Old Meldrum, 1732 (*Aberdeen CR.*), and William Tersie in Smithstown, 1792 (*Moray*).

TERVET, TERVIT. See under TARVIT.

TESTARD, TASTARD. Apparently a nickname from Fr., = *la grosse tête*, great head. James Testard in Luidmuic of Glenmuick, 1800 (*Aberdeen CR.*). "Testard is a fairly common name in France; but the mod. form *Tétard* is more frequent" (*Harrison*). Cf. TESTER.

TESTER. A family of this name in Ballater, Aberdeenshire, are said to be descended from a Frenchman who was 'taster' to Mary, queen of Scots, whom he accompanied from France. If this is correct the name may be from AF. *tester, testar*, assayer. More likely, however, the name is same as TESTARD, q.v., with loss of final *d*.

TEUNION, TEUNON, TEWNION, TINNION. Five men named Teunion from Turriff and four brothers named Tewnion from Marnoch served in the first Great War, and William Duguid Teunon and James M. Teunon of Turriff were killed (*Turriff*). These names are corruptions of the name of (St.) Adamnan. Under the effect of aspiration *Adhamh*, 'Adam,' loses the force of its consonants, and with the diminutive termination added, becomes *Aunan, Eunan*, etc. In the northeast, as in Aberdeen and Banff, "there is a tendency to prefix certain consonants to saints' names, either as an equivalent for St., or to facilitate the pronunciation. Thus St. Rule becomes *Trowel*, and St. Anthony *Tantan;* and hence Eunan becomes *Theunan*, as in the parish of Aboyne, where a fresh change takes place, and Adamnan's Well and Tree become *Skeulan Well* and *Skeulan Tree*" (*Adamnan*, p. 256).

TEVIOTDALE. From the district of the same name in Roxburghshire. Archibaldus Teuidall (an old spelling of the place name) witnessed a quitclaim of the lands of Eduluestun to the church of Glasgow in 1233 (REG., p. 140). Archibald Theuidalie witnessed a process of relaxation, c. 1328 (*Kelso*, p. 370), John Tevidale, a Scotsman, was murdered in England, 1419 (*Bain*, IV, 795), and Robert Tiviedaill was warded for murder in the Canongate Tolbooth, Edinburgh, in 1683 (BOEC., VIII, p. 151). Sergeant Teviotdale, R. A. F., was killed in action, 1940.

THACKER. The Scottish form of English Thatcher. A surname derived from the occupation of thacker (ME. *thacker*, from OE. *þaca*, *þæc*, a roof, thatch + personal suffix -*ere*), one who covers a roof with straw, reeds, etc., perhaps now an obsolete craft. A few years ago there was an illustration in the *Scotsman* newspaper of a thacker at work on the roof of Livingstone Tollhouse on the Edinburgh-Glasgow road near Midcalder. Thomas Thekar is mentioned in a list of Aberdeen criminals in 1411 (CRA., p. 4), Cudbert Thekar was a witness in Edinburgh in 1426 (*Egidii*, p. 48), and John Thekar is recorded in St. Andrews in 1525 (SHR., II, p. 266).

THAIN, THAINE, THANE, THAYNE, THEYNE. Now a somewhat uncommon surname but one of some antiquity in the district of Aberchirder. Kyned thainus de Katel witnessed the gift by Duncan, earl of Fife to the nuns of North Berwick, a. 1177 (CMN., 6). Duncan thane of Streuelin (Stirling) witnessed a charter by Gilbert, earl of Strathern, a. 1198 (LIM., p. xxiv), Lorne Theine de Ures witnessed a charter by Randulf de Strathpetham, c. 1222 (REB., II, 3), and William Theynus de Kintor appears as charter witness in 1253 (LAC., 84). Patone Thane, "the ald wycar of Innerkethni" was in 1493 one of the perambulators of the boundary of Yochry and Achbrady (RAA., II, p. 276), and David Thane in Strikmartyne was a follower of Campbell of Lundy in 1541 (RSS., II, 3666). Richard and James Thayn were admitted burgesses of Dundee in 1563 (*Wedd.*, p. 118), Alexander Thaine had a feu of part of the lands of Kynnochtry in 1585 (*Scon*, p. 225), and Patrick Thain received payment in 1608 "for setting up the jebett" (gibbet) in Aberdeen (SCM., V, p. 84). Harrison says from ME. *þeg(e)n*, "thane." The name of the town of Tain is spelled Tene 1237, Thayne 1255, Thane 1483, Tayne and Tane 1487.

THALLON. A surname apparently now confined to Fife. William Thalland, reidare at Auchtertuill, 1574 (RMR.). Robert Thalland in Burntisland, 1612 (*Laing*, 1639) may be Robert Thalland, ruling elder in Burntisland, 1644 (PBK., p. 276). David Thalland in Flockhouse of Dowhill, 1698 (*Inquis.*, 8012). Recorded in 1942.

THAW, THOW. I take these two rare Scots surnames to be the same. James Thaw in Tillyfroskie is recorded in 1789 (*Aberdeen CR.*). I can offer no explanation of the name. The English name *Thew* is explained as ME. *theow*, servant, bondsman.

THAYNSTOUN. W. Thaynstoun, forestaller in Aberdeen in 1402 (CRA., p. 382), probably derived his surname from Thainston near Kintore, Aberdeenshire. The wife of — Thaynston in Aberdeen is recorded in 1408 (CWA., p. 316).

THEMAN. Davy Theman, who was paid by the town council of Aberdeen "for the kepin of thar common horologe and knok" in 1504, appears in 1506 as David Cheman, goldsmith and burgess of the town (CRA., p. 73, 434), and appears again in following year as Theman.

THEMDAILE. In 1487 payment was made to Robert Themdale in Aberdeen for a horse, and ten years later the same Robert Themdaile, probably, was fined for "failzeit in the waching (watching) of the tone" (CRA., p. 60, 415).

THEWLESS. A corruption of THOWLESS, q.v.

THIN. Đynne occurs as name of a witness in an OE. charter of A. D. 808 (Birch, *Cartularium Saxonicum*, 326). Adam Thyn was a charter witness in Glasgow, 1456 (LCD., p. 180). Gilbert Thyne was one of the indwellers of the Ouertoune of Blannyslie, 1547 (RRM., III, p. xxxvii). William Thin in Haddington owns the king, 1567 (RPC., I, p. 558), Alexander Thin, one of assize in Aberdeen, 1596 (SCM., I, p. 116), Andrew Thinne was litster in Edinburgh, 1647 (*Edinb. Marr.*), John Thin was portioner of Blainslie, 1662 (RRM., II, p. 4), and Leonard Thinn is recorded in Blyth, 1668 (*Lauder*). Messrs. Thin, an old established firm of booksellers in Edinburgh.

THIRD. Local. Third was a name often given to a farm, which according to old custom was divided among three tenants. There are more than a dozen places in Scotland called Third, Thirds, and Thirdpart. Thrid near Bemersyde is now spelled Third, but locally spoken of as 'The Thrid.' Adam Third was burgess of Aberdeen, 1596 (CRA., p. 133).

THIRLSTANE. From the lands of Thirlstane in Berwickshire. The Thirlstane family were vassals of the Morvilles. Hugh de Morville granted the lands of Thirlstane to Elsi, the son of Winter. Elsi was succeeded by his son Alan, who assumed the local surname of Thirlstane (*Caledonia*, I, p. 504). Alan de Thirlestan witnessed a charter by Richard de Moruilla to the brethren of the Hospital of Lauder, c. 1170 (*Dryburgh*, p. 269), and c. 1200 he witnessed a charter by Roland of Galloway, son of Uchtred (*Kelso*, 254). As Alanus de Tirlestan he witnessed William de Moreuille's charter of Gillemoristun to Edulfus filius Uchtredi before 1196 (REG., p. 40). Alan was succeeded by his son Thomas who flourished in the reign of Alexander II. The only daughter and heiress of Thomas married Richard de Mautelant and carried the estate to the Maitlands. Willelmus de Thyrlstane in the parish of Fyvy was excommunicated in 1382 (REA., I, p. 165). Bower (*Scotichronicon*, IX, c. 47) tells us that in 1228 the men of Moray revolted and slew a certain brigand *(latronem)*, Thomas de Thirlestan, whose fort they captured by surprise at night. This is doubtless Thomas de Thirlestan who appears in 1225 in possession of the lands of Abyrtarf (REM., p. 20). Lord Hailes says: "It is a pleasant mistake of the transcriber, who wrote latronem instead of baronem" (*Annals*, I, p. 179n).

THOIRS. Andrew Thoris, burgess of Aberdeen, 1595 (CRA., p. 121; NSCM., I, p. 90). Mr. Thomas Thoiris, minister at Udny, 1623–35 (AEI., I, p. 94; SCM., III, p. 77; RSCA., II, p. 404). William Thoirs retoured heir of his mother, Issobell Andersoune, spouse to Thomas Thoirs of Auchorthies, 1658 (*Retours, Aberdeen*, 340). David Thoirs, advocate, Edinburgh, 1671 (*Just. Rec., passim*). Sir David Thoires was imprisoned in 1689 for defaming the Master of Forbes (RPC., 3. ser. XIV, p. 449).

THOM. A diminutive of THOMAS, q.v. Alexander Thome appears as vicar of Stracathro in 1433 and 1447 (REB., I, 60; II, 69), Jok Tom was tenant in Balgreschac, 1473 (*Cupar-Angus*, I, p. 176), Andree Thome held a tenement in Glasgow before 1487, and reference is made in 1497 to the tenement of quondam Walter Thome there (REG., p. 453, 476). A fourth part of the vill of Westirparsy was leased to Alexander Thome and his son Alexander Thome in 1485 (RAA., II, 259). William Thom was witness in Dundrennan in 1545 (*Laing*, 497), Alexander Thome had a tack of a fourth part of Cotzardis in 1555, and Johne Thome a tack of an eighth part of the lands of Wester Balbrogy at the same time (*Cupar-Angus*, II, p. 121, 122). James Thome to stand

in sackcloth for quarrelling in time of divine service, 1661 (*Rec. Elgin*, II, p. 293). Patrick Thome was merchant burgess of Edinburgh, 1673 (*Retours, Edinburgh*, 1205). In 1561 we have an instance of Thom as a forename in Thom Arnot, member of council of Stirling (SBR., p. 279). The founder of the Dublin printing house of Alexander Thom and Co. was a native of Aberdeen. Thom is also used as an Anglicized form of MACTHÓM, q.v. Tom 1685.

THOMAS. A common Anglo-Norman personal name. It is from the Syriac *t⁗omā*, Heb. *to'ām*, 'twin,' rendered by Greek *Didymus* in St. John, XI: 16. In Gaelic it assumes the forms *Tómas*, *Támhus*, hence the Gaelic patronymics MACTAVISH, MACCOMBIE, and MACOMIE, q.v. As a surname in Scotland it is of late introduction from England. Thomas filius Maldoueny attested a deed of middle of thirteenth century (*Neubotle*, p. 27).

THOMASON, THOMASSON, 'son of THOMAS,' q.v. Both forms are current in Shetland. Allan Thomason and Donald Thomassone were summoned as witnesses in Golspie in 1546 (OPS., II, p. 676), and in 1548 the goods of three brothers named Thomassoun in the barony of Skebo were escheated for slaughter committed by them (ibid., II, p. 609). 1537 Tamesone (*Goudie*, p. 114). Thomessone.

THOMLING. From THOM, q.v., + diminutive suffix -*ling*. William Thomling in Heavisyd in 1686 (*Peebles CR.*), and Alexander Thomline, slater in Hawick, 1824 (*Heirs*, 700).

THOMPSON, 'son of THOM,' q.v., with intrusive p. This spelling is more commonly found in England.

THOMS. 'Son of THOMAS,' from the diminutive THOM. It is also an Anglicizing of MACTHOMAS, q.v. "Adam M'Intosh, son of William, the seventh chief of the Clan M'Intosh, was the founder of that branch of the clan which afterwards came to be known by the surname of M'Thomas, son of Thomas, which in time became corrupted to M'Thomie, M'Homie, M'Omie, M'Comie, and latterly M'Combie and Thoms" (*Memoirs of the families of M'Combie and Thoms*, p. 5). Robert M'Thomas, cousin to Robert M'Combie, became plain Robert Thomas; George Thomas, his grandson, was father of Patrick Hunter Thoms, which is the form now used by that branch of the family (ibid., p. 170, 171). Thowmis, Thowms, Thownis.

THOMSON, 'son of THOM,' q.v. A fairly numerous surname in Scotland. John Thomson, "a man of low birth, but approved valour," was leader of the men of Carrick in Edward

Bruce's war in Ireland in 1318 (*Hailes*, II, p. 102, 206). Adam Thomson appears as lord of Kylnekylle, Ayrshire, c. 1370–80 (*Laing*, 64). Johannes filius Thome was elected bailie of Aberdeen in 1398 (CRA., p. 374), and John Tomson witnessed a grant in Ayr in 1401 (*Friars Ayr*, p. 37). Donald Thomson was one of an inquest to determine the rights of pasturage which the Temple lands had over the adjoining town and territory of Letter in 1461 (*Strathendrick*, p. 222). John Thomsoun was juror on an inquest at Dunipace in 1426 (*Cambus.*, 87), Duncan Thomsone of Auchinhampteris witnessed a bond of manrent in 1491 (SCM., IV, p. 189), Cuthbert Thomsoun witnessed a notarial instrument of 1517 (*Soltre*, p. 89), James Tomsone was tenant of the bishop of Glasgow in 1511 (*Rental*), and Peter Thomsone was Ilay Herald in 1561 (ER., XIX, p. 150). "The most conspicuous family of the name were the Thomsons who possessed Duddingston, near Edinburgh, for five generations till sold by Sir Patrick about 1668; his father had been created a baronet in 1636" (*Stodart*, II, p. 140). Many individuals of this name in Perthshire and Argyllshire are really Mactavishes. The surname in these districts is an Anglicized form of Gaelic *Mac Thòmais*, 'son of Thomas,' or of *Mac Thòmaidh*, 'son of Tommie.' The name is usually spelled MaKcome (3 syllables) in the early records, and was formerly common in Upper Deeside. Alexander Thomeson appears in Strathdee in 1527 (*Grant*, III, p. 70). John Dow Thomasson in Perthshire fined for resetting Clan Gregor, 1613 (RPC., XIV, p. 632). Tamson 1654, Thomeson 1504, Thomesoune 1477, Thompesoune 1665, Thomsoune 1535, Tomsoun 1567. In some instances it is also an Englishing of MACCOMIE, q.v. See also THOMASON.

THOR. From the ON. personal name *Thórir* from *Thórr*, the name of the god of thunder. Sometime before 1105 King Eadgar bestowed upon Thor longus, 'the long,' the land of Ædenham (now Ednam), 'unsettled' (*desertam*), who by his own money cultivated and settled it, built a church and gave it and a ploughgate of land to the monks of St. Cuthbert for the weal of the souls of the king's father, his mother, and brothers and sisters, and for the redemption of his own beloved brother Leswin, and for the weal of his own soul and body (*Nat. MSS.*, I, 14). Thor's expression 'by his own money' (*mea propria pecunia*) is perhaps 'the first record of the application of capital to land in Scotland.' Thor filius Swan or Suein, ancestor of the old family of Ruthven, appears between 1130–50, as charter witness and as donor of the church

of Treuernent (Tranent) to the Abbey of Holyrood (RD., p. 12; LSC., p. 11; REG., p. 13). Thor de Trauernent, charter witness and vicecomes, appears about the same time (LSC., p. 8, 9; *Kelso*, 375; RD., p. 11). Thor the archdeacon was a charter witness, c. 1150 (LSC., p. 11). Under the name Horo the death of the archdeacon is recorded in 1163 (*Chron. Holyrood*). Willelmus filius Thore witnessed the gift by William de Haya of the land of Ederpoles to the monks of Cupar in the reign of William the Lion (SCM., II, p. 304). Alexander filius Thore was "witness to several royal charters for a short time before 1200. Nothing more seems to be known of him" (*Inchaffray*, p. 18, 269). Stephen filius Thor' witnessed a document concerning the land of Cnoc in Renfrew, 1234 (RMP., p. 180), and in 1273 Stephen filius Ricardi Thor witnessed grants of land by Malcolm, earl of Lennox to the Abbey of Paisley (*Levenax*, p. 15, 16). Adam Thore, burgess of Edinburgh, 1380 (*Laing*, 67), may be Ade Thor who held land there in 1400 (*Egidii*, p. 37).

THORALD. From the ON. personal name *Thorualdr*, 'Thor ruler.' Early English forms of the name are *Thurweald* and *Turold*. Thoraldus, archdeacon of Lothian, died 1163 (*Annals*, p. 73). His name also appears as Thorandus for Thoraudus (RPSA., p. 191). William Torreld witnessed a charter by Robert, bishop of St. Andrews, c. 1144 (*Lawrie*, p. 133). He is probably the William, son of Thorald, who was witness to a charter by Waldeve, son of Gospatric (RD., p. 94). Alexander filius Thor (= Thorald) witnessed a charter of the church of Kinernyn by William the Lion, c. 1201–7 (RAA., I, p. 40). A remission was granted Andrew Thorrall in Duffus, 1567 (SCM., IV, p. 155). As forename: Thorall (1546).

THORBURN, THURBURN. From the OE. personal name *Thurbrand*, as shown by the ending -brand in the early spellings of the name. Ricardus Torbrand was provost of Aberdeen, 1330 (ER., I, p. 308). Thomas Thurbrande was a notary public in the diocese of Glasgow, 1456 (*Laing*, 142), and Thomas Thurbrandson, also a notary in the same document, may have been his son. John Thorbrand was fined in 1478 for cutting green wood in the forest of Selkirk (ER., VIII, p. 480). John Thornbrand appears in Peebles, 1505 (*Peebles*, 33), and Robert Thornebraid (? *i* an error for *n*) is in record in Glenholm, Peeblesshire, 1544 (RMS., III, 3023). John Thorbrand was tenant in Stobo, 1533 (*Rental*), Robert Thurbrand, tenant on lands of Newbattle Abbey, 1563 (*Neubotle*, p. 325), and George Thurbrand appears in Kelso Abbey rental in 1567 (*Kelso*,

THORBURN, THURBURN, continued
p. 521). Walter Thorbrand in Lessuddane, 1605, and William Thorebrand in Greenhead, 1664 (RRM., I, p. 2; II, p. 95). William Thorbrane, mason in Edinburgh, 1615 (Edinb. Marr.). Archibald Thoirbrand in Dolphington, 1624 (Lanark CR.), and Catharine Thornbrand and Helena Thornebrand were retoured heirs of Magister Thomas Hog 'apud La Rochefort in Regno Galliae,' 1627 (Inquis., 1322-23). John Thorebrand, tailor in Edinburgh, 1643 (Edinb. Marr.), William Thorbran in Schort cleuch, parish of Crawford-Lindsay, 1655, and David Thorburne in Staine, parish of Biggar, 1670 (Lanark CR.). James Thoreburne, Nethertoun of Dallsible, and Mathew Thornebrand, merchant in Dumfries, appear in 1679 (Dumfries), George Torburn, tenant in West Loch, parish of Edhilstane, 1675 (Edin. App.), William Torbrane, provost of Stranraer, 1715 (Wigtown), and Thomas Torburn in Blainderry is in record, 1743 (Wigtown). There are families of the name in Sweden, descended from William Thorburn of Leith, who in 1823 migrated to that country. Grant Thorburn (1773-1863), merchant and publicist, New York, was born in Dalkeith. His great-grandson, S. Grant Thorburn, was mayor of Clifton, New Jersey, 1927.

THORMOND. From the ON. personal name Thormund, 'Thor's protection.' John Thormond one of an inquest to determine rights of pasturage which the Temple lands had over the town and land of Letter, 1461 (Strathendrick, p. 222). See also TORMOND.

THORNEYCROFT. Recorded in CD. Of recent introduction. From Thornycroft in the parish of Prestbury, east Cheshire. Bardsley says: "The family that rose here has spread its roots all over England."

THORNHILL. John de Thornhille who had a protection while serving in Galloway in 1296 (Bain, II, 845) may have derived his name from Thornhill on the Nith in Dumfriesshire.

THORNSYDE. Local, perhaps from some obsolete place of the name in Berwickshire. Ninian Thornsyde of East Nesbet, a Berwickshire laird, 1530 (Trials, I, p. 147 *).

THORNTON. From the lands of Thornton in the Mearns. The first of the name to appear is Laurence de Thorneton, witness in a deed by Henry, abbot of Arbroath, c. 1204-11 (RAA., I, p. 117). John of Thornton, burgess of Montrose, and Johan de Thorntone of the county of Kincardyn en Miernes, rendered homage in 1296 (Bain, II, p. 198, 209). In 1299 Walter de Thorneton, a Scots prisoner of war, who was exchanged for an esquire of Sir

William de Cathecart (ibid., II, 1062), is probably Walter de Thornetone, executor of Marie, countess of Stratherne in the same year (ibid., 1117). Valentine de Thorntoun or Thornetoun had a charter of the lands of Thorntoun in lie Kincardin-Mernes from Robert I (RMS., I, App. II, 18). In 1398-9 Osbern styled de Yrnis ('of the Irons'), evidently from his trade of barber, acquired the land of Thornton (in Angus), and was then styled Osbern of the Irons, laird of Thornton ('Osbernus de Yrnis, dominus de Thornton'). By 1425 his son had dropped the style "of Irons" and became simply "John of Thornton" (Strathmore, p. 182). Alexander de Thorntoun was a notary public in 1455 (RAA., II, 104), John Thorntoun was vicar of Glasgow in 1491 (REG., 460), and James Thornetoun was canon there in 1554 (Protocols, I). Among Scots settled in Prussia in 1644 the name became Dornthon. Thorntowne 1609.

THORSKAILL. Andro Thorskaill and Thomas Thorskaill acted parts in mediaeval plays in Perth, 1553 and 1557 (Mill, Plays, p. 273, 275).

THOW. Probably a variant of THAW, q.v.

THOWLESS. The early references to this name confine it to Brechin and neighborhood. William Thowlas was witness in Brechin, 1464 (REB., II, 103), and five years later Robert Thoulace made a resignation with consent of his father, William Thoulace (ibid., II, 111). In 1493 William Thowless de Conansith witnessed an instrument of resignation (ibid., II, 137), John Thowless in Brechin had a remission for slaughter committed by him, 1508 (Trials, I, p. 108 *), and in 1512 reference is made to the lands of quondam Katherine Thoules in Edinburgh (Soltre, p. 262). Thoulas 1548, Thouless 1537, Thowlace 1508, Thowles 1583. Thowless, thewless, is applied in Scots to bodily qualities, in ME. to mental, but I do not venture to say if there is any connection between the surname and the adjective. Wyntoun describes a man named Lawrisson as 'thowlace,' i.e., wanton, heedless (v. 5, p. 397, S. T. S. ed.).

THREEPLAND. A variant of THRIEPLAND, q.v.

THRESKE. Walter de Threske witnessed a charter by Alexander filius Walteri, senescallus, 1246 (RMP., p. 87). From Thirsk in North Riding, Yorkshire, spelled Threske (1243) and Thriske (1473).

THRIEPLAND, THRIPLAND, THREEPLAND. A rare surname in Scotland, derived from 'The Threipland,' a vale in the parish of Kilbucho, Peeblesshire. Robert de Threpeland of the county of Peebles rendered homage in 1296 (*Bain*, II, p. 207). In 1374 the lands of Threpeland were renounced to James of Douglas, the overlord, by Alicia of Threplande, daughter and heiress of Henry of Threpland (RHM., II, p. 120). The surname is found domiciled in Perthshire in the beginning of the seventeenth century, Andrew Threipland was admitted burgess of Perth in 1628, and George Threapland was a merchant there in 1711. Sir Patrick Threaplane was 'Prowest of Pearth' in 1676 (*Rec. Inv.*, II, p. 268), John Threepland was a bookbinder in Edinburgh in 1643 (*Edinb. Marr.*), and John Thrippland is recorded in Spittell, 1708 (*Minutes*, p. 37). The Thrieplands of Fingask were a family distinguished by a passionate loyalty to the Stewarts in exile. About the beginning of the nineteenth century the laird of Fingask died without direct heir and the family possessions passed to a kinsman, Scott-Kerr, who assumed the name of the old Perthshire family.

THRIFT. A current though rare surname. Weekley (p. 220) derives it from the noun 'thrift.' James Thrift was reidare at Culles (Collace), 1574 (RMR.), and Mr. James Thrift was reader at Auchtooll, 1671 (*Edin. App.*).

THRIST. The land which had belonged to David filius Thrist was given to the Abbey of Kelso, c. 1174–78 (*Kelso*, 383). Johnne Thrist was declared innocent of part in detention of King James III in Edinburgh, 1482 (*Lennox*, II, p. 123), and in 1489 had a remission for his share in burning the town of Dunbertane and holding the castle against the king (APS., XII, p. 34; *Lennox*, II, p. 133). Sir James Thrist, a cleric, was witness in Perth, 1547 (*Rollok*, 44). Harrison explains the name 'bold, brave,' from OE. *þrist*.

THROKTOUN. Johnne Throktoun, reidare at Kirkmaho, 1574 (RMR.). Probably from Troughton near Ulverston, north Lancashire. Bardsley gives Throughton as a 1747 spelling of the surname.

THURBOTHEUED. Adam Thurbotheued in record, 1269 (*Bain*, I, p. 511). Cf. HAILBOTISHED.

THURBURN. A variant of THORBURN, q.v.

THURKIN. Thurkin, 'ventusator' (leech, blood-letter), held land in the burgh of Hadyngton, c. 1210 (*Inchcolm*, p. 9). Perhaps a variant of Thurkil, with interchange of suffix -in for -il(l), as in Askin — Askil, Asketin — Asketil, Roskinn — Roskil.

THURSETTER. Jedein or Gedein Thursetter who was retoured heir of James Thursettar of Wasdaill, his guidser, in 1657 (*Retours, Orkney and Shetland*, 81), derived his name from "the 3 penny land of King's-land called Thursetter."

TIBBERMORE. Evirardus de Tubermor who witnessed a confirmation charter by Robertus de Bruys of the church of Hautwysill (Haltwhistle) in Tyndal to the Abbey of Arbroath, c. 1178–80 (RAA., I, p. 28) derived his name from Tibbermore or Tippermuir in Perthshire. The names of Symon Takmore or Tobbemor and of William Tallemor, both of whom rendered homage at Perth in 1291 (RR.), are probably corruptly spelled forms of this name.

TIERNAN, TIERNANN. From Ir. *MacTighearnáin*, 'son of *Tighernán* (diminutive of *Tighearna*, a lord), with omission of Mac.

TIGERNE. OIr. *tigerne*, 'lord, master.' Tigerne was the name of one of the witnesses to a charter by King Eadgar, c. 1097–1107 (*Nat. MSS.*, I, 4).

TIGRIM. Nicholas Tigrim held a land in Glasgow, 1325 (LCD., p. 237), and Mariota Tygrym had a pension of four pounds sterling per annum, 1376 (RMS., I, 588).

TILLERY. From Tilliery in the parish of Orwell, Kinross-shire. Thomas Tilliery was a tailor in Aberdeen in 1657 (ROA., I, p. 233), Andrew Tilleray, horse-hirer in Aberdeen, took part in the rising of the '45, and William Tillery was a weaver in Aberdeen in 1770.

TILLIE. Probably from Tilly in the department of Calvados, Normandy, or Tilly in the department of Eure (*Lower*). Between 1165 and 1196 Otho de Tilli confirmed to the canons of Dryburgh the toft and croft which William the Lion had given them in Padynnane (Pettinain) (*Dryburgh*, p. 158). David Tillie, portioner of Kynmonth, 1614 (*Inquis. Tut.*, 1319). The name is recorded in Edinburgh, 1940.

TILLIEDAFF. From the old barony of that name in Aberdeenshire. John de Tolidef was bailie of Aberdeen in 1317 (SCM., V, p. 13), and a William de Tulliedaff was among the slain in the battle of Harlaw in 1411. A charter of sale by Andrew de Tullydeffe of that Ilk is recorded in 1450 (*Friars*, 33), and in the same year as Andrew Tulydefe (without 'de') he appears as a charter witness (*Illus.*, III, p. 272). This Andrew appears to have been the first designated 'of that ilk.' John Tulydeff was sergeant of the burgh of Aberdeen in 1469 (CRA., p. 406), Alexander Tulidef of that Ilk witnessed a bond of manrent in 1484,

TILLIEDAFF, *continued*

and an Andro Tuledeff of that Ilk is mentioned in 1504 (SCM., II, p. cxxiv, 255). Andrew Tulydaf (misprinted Culydaf) was on the assize of wheat in Edinburgh in 1495 (EBR., p. 69). Christina Tullidaff was retoured heir of Andrew Tullidaff *de eodem* in 1558 (*Retours, Aberdeen*, 27). William Tullidaff or Tillidaff was appointed minister of Kilbirnie in 1670. In 1535 an individual is referred to as Dillidaff, Dilledaf, and Dvllidaff (RAA., II, 523). The old family ended in the direct line in 1588 in three daughters. Tallydaff 1595, Tilliedaff 1640, Tilliedaffe 1593, Tilliedeff 1597, Tuledeff 1504, Tulidaph 1682, Tulidef 1452, Tulidefe 1572, Tulidif 1509, Tullidaff 1641, Tulliedaffe 1690, Tulliedelph 1691, Twlidef 1523, Twlydeff 1444, Tyllideaphe 1628, Tullideph, and in a MS. of a 1716 the name is spelled Dillidasse (*ff* misread *ss*). See also DILLIDAFF.

TILLOCH. A variant of TULLOCH, q.v.

TILLOL. Master Peres de Tillol, persone of Cultre, Lanarkshire, and Master William Tylliol, canon of Dunkeld, rendered homage, 1296 (*Bain*, II, p. 212). From residence beside a lime-tree, OFr. *tiliol*, mod. Fr. *tilleul.*

TILLYANGUS. From the place of the same name in the parish of Clatt, Aberdeenshire. Cristinus Tulianguse was a tenant of the bishop of Aberdeen in 1511 (REA., I, p. 362). He may have been a descendant of one of the early vassals of the bishopric.

TILLYBOY. Local, from Tillyboy in the parish of Echt (in 1610, Tulliboy). John Tulibo in Aberdeen, /1493 (CRA., p. 49). John de Tulibo was admitted burgess of Aberdeen, 1483, and Andrew Tuliboy in 1493 (NSCM., I, p. 30, 36).

TIMMS. An English surname of recent introduction. From Tim(m), a diminutive of Timothy, with genitive -*s*.

TINDALL, TINDAL, TINDALE. In 1279 the district of Tyndale is described as "outside the kingdom of England in the Kingdom of Scotland" (*Northumberland Assize Rolls*, p. 365). William de Tindal witnessed sale of land of Scrogges to the church of Glasgow, c. 1208–13 (REG., p. 76). R. Thyndal, thesaurarius Glasguensis, 1225 (RMP., p. 212). At various periods we have record of several families of this name in Angus apparently unconnected with each other, but the name has now almost disappeared from the district. One family was long connected with the civic history of Dundee and gave name to Tendal's Wynd there.

The first of the name recorded in Dundee was John Tendall, admitted burgess in 1525 (*Wedd.*, p. 26n, 27). Robert de Tyndale, parson of the church of Graunt Daltone in the county of Dumfries rendered homage in 1296 (*Bain*, II, p. 208). Walter Tyndell or Tindell held a tenement in Brechin in 1493, and John Tendale was a witness there in 1552 (REB., I, 233; II, 136). Patrick Tindaill resigned part of the lands of Craigmakeren in 1586 (*Scon*, 234), David Tindall appears as burgess of Lanark in 1587 (RPC., IV, p. 239), and Cathraine Tindaill was resident in Edinburgh in 1638 (*Inquis.*, 2341). Tendaill 1508, Tendel 1505, Tyndail 1497, Tyndaill 1515.

TINKLER. A northern form of English *tinker*, 'a mender of metal objects, as kettles, pots, and pans.' Jacobus Tinckler held land in Perth in the reign of William the Lion (*Scon*, p. 30). James Tynkler and others were charged with deforcing a messenger in Ednem, 1510 (*Trials*, I, p. *71). Robert Tinker was tenant on the Abbey lands of Kelso, 1567 (*Kelso*, p. 524), John Tinklar and John Tynklar, jr., appear in Nether Mains, Renfrew, 1575 (*Laing*, 916), John Tinker was admitted burgess of Glasgow, 1617 (*Burgesses*), and Allan Tinckler in Stitchill made a claim in 1665 (*Stitchill*, p. 38).

TINLINE, TINLIN. A Roxburghshire surname, probably local. Thomas Tinling in Nether Ancrum, 1711 (*Heirs*, 158). Helen Tinline in Hawick was married, 1939. A feat of archery by one Watt Tinlinn, a retainer of the Buccleuch family, is described in a note to Scott's *Lay of the last minstrel*, IV, 4.

TINNING. Local. A surname recorded in Dumfriesshire. There is a Tininghill or Tynninghill in Dumfriesshire Retours (40, 212). John Tinding of Holles, Dumfriesshire, 1657 (*Dumfries*). "Tyning" is not uncommon in English field names, from OE. *tynen*, to hedge in.

TINNION. *See under* TEUNION.

TINNISWOOD. A surname recorded in Roxburghshire. Bardsley has Tenniswood (from Yorkshire) which he thinks is a sharpened form of Denniswood, i.e. 'the wood belonging to Dennis.' There is an old castle named Tinnies in Peeblesshire.

TINNOCK. A variant of TANNOCK, q.v. Agnes Tinnock in Glespine of Douglas, 1736 (*Lanark CR.*). Nanse Tinnock kept the change-house in Mauchline frequented by Burns.

TINSLEY. Local, from Tinsley in the parish of Rotherham, in the West Riding of Yorkshire. Of recent introduction into Scotland.

TINTO. From Tinto in Lanarkshire. There was a family of Tynto of Crympcramp in the barony of Crawford-Douglas in 1528 (APS., II, p. 328), and Cristina Tynto was retoured heir of Robert Tinto of Crimpcramp, her father, in the lands of Murehouss, in the barony of Thankertoun, in 1623 (Retours, Lanark, 141). John of Tyntow rendered to Exchequer the accounts of the bailies of Stirling in 1402 (ER., III, p. 579). Bessie Tinto was a tenant of the Abbey of Kelso in 1567 (Kelso, p. 527), Beatrix Tinto is recorded as heir of James Tinto, "wrytter to the signett" in 1655 (Retours, Edinburgh, 1049), and Elizabeth Tynto was heir portioner of Bernard Tynto in Oversyidwod in 1608 (Inquis., 353). James Tinto from the parish of Temple was drowned off Orkney, 1679 (Hanna, II, p. 254). Captain William Tinto, Old Monkland, recorded 1942.

TIVERTON. This surname, recorded in Fife, is most probably of late introduction from England. There is a Tiverton in Cheshire and another in Devon.

TOCHER. A surname of the shires of Aberdeen and Banff, of local origin from Tocher (Upper and Nether), near Meikle Wartle, in the parish of Rayne, Aberdeenshire. Tocher, obsolete Gaelic for a causeway, appears several times in our place names. Charles Tocher from Turriff was killed, and several others of the name from the same district served in the first Great War (Turriff).

TOCK. This name was established in England before the Norman Conquest, for "Askyl Tokes sune" (Askyl son of Toke) signs a charter of Edward the Confessor, 1060. Tocca is mentioned as holding the land of Perdeyc (Partick) in a charter by David I to the church of Glasgow before 1136 (REG., 3). Bernardus filius Tocce witnessed the gift by Thor, son of Swan, of the church of Trauernent (Tranent) to the monks of Holyrood, c. 1150 (LSC., p. 11), and before 1200 witnessed a confirmation charter by Rodbertus de Quinci (ibid., p. 30). Tocce, the father of Bernard, is probably the man who gave name to Toxside near Gladsmuir, Midlothian (c. 1142 Thoccheshewyd, p. 1165 Tockesheued, 1608 Toksyd). Sometime between 1235 and 1258 Alan filius Tock, a native man (a serf) was gifted to the Hospital of Soltre, and between 1238 and 1300 there is mention of land held by Tyhoc de Monte Laudonie (Mount Lothian, a small parish now incorporated in Penicuik parish, 1635) in Temple (Soltre, p. 29, 30). Symone Tok was a charter witness in Aberdeen, 1281 (REA., II, p. 279). The S' Joannis Tok is appended to charter of a tenement in Leith, 1601 (Seals Supp., 953), and Isobel Tock is

recorded in Edinburgh, 1649, and Thomas Tock, painter there, 1686 (Edinb. Marr.). Tyock uxor Andrei in villa Bondyngton is in record 1307 (Kelso, 42). This is perhaps the origin of the surname TUKE, q.v.

TOD, TODD. Explained by Bardsley and Harrison as a nickname from provincial name of the fox. With two or three exceptions the second d appears to be no older than the eighteenth century. Baldwin Tod held land in Lambirtoun, c. 1270 (BNCH., XVI, p. 334), and the croft of Robert Tod in the vill of Gordune is mentioned, c. 1280 (Kelso, 124). A reservation of the archdeaconry of Caithness was made to Master John Todd in 1329 (Pap. Lett., II, p. 302), doubtless the Mr. John Tod to whom in 1330 a payment was made to enable him to redeem his books which had been carried off by the English to England (ER., I, p. 311). Nicholas, son of John Tod, was a hostage in England soon after 1330. Several persons of this name were connected with Berwick or Berwickshire later than 1330, one of them giving an annual rent for the maintenance of the bridge over the Tweed, and the name appears in Stirlingshire in 1339 (Bain, III, p. 241), in Perthshire in 1361, and in Ayrshire, 1571. Thomas dictus Todde was canon of Glasgow and rector of Old Roxburgh in the reign of David II (Stodart, II, p. 394). Hugo Tod was pricer of flesh in Edinburgh, 1403 (Guildry, p. 114), John Tode was admitted burgess of Aberdeen, 1445 (NSCM., I, p. 9), John Tode, burgess of Brechin in record 1450 (REB., II, 80), Robert Tod, notary in Perth, 1458 (RAA., II, 114), and Elizabeth Tode, daughter of Alexander Tode, burgess of Edinburgh, 1467 (Neubotle, 299). William Tode witnessed sasine of the lands of Wolle, 1469 (Home, 22), and Johannes Tod witnessed a charter of the monastery of Scone to William Peblis, 1491 (Scon, p. 201). Thomas Tode, burgess of Edinburgh, who had a charter of the lands of Sherefhaul in 1483 (RD., p. 372), was the Sir Thomas Todde or Tod of Serefehaw (Sheriff-Hall) who guaranteed a loan from Henry VII of England to James, earl of Boughan and to himself, and with accomplices undertook to deliver "the K. of Scottis now reyning and his brother the Duke of Roos" to Henry in 1491 (Bain, IV, 1571). John Tod had a remission in 1536 for offences committed by him (RSS., II, 2002). George Tod had a charter of the office of serjeant of the 'shire' of Kinglassie, 1607 (RD., p. 502), and Hew Tod is in record as a 'browdenster' (embroiderer) in Edinburgh, 1611 (Edinb. Marr.). The family of Tod of Kirklands originally came from Musselburgh. Thomas Tod was clerk there in the early

774

TOD, Todd, *continued*

part of the seventeenth century (*Fordell,* p. 191). David Tood appointed councillor of Corsehill, 1710 (*Corsehill,* p. 245). At the present day most of the Tods are found on the West Coast, and the Todds in Edinburgh. William Todd first introduced printing into Thurso, Caithness, in 1825. Robert Elliot Tod, retired banker and yachtsman, appointed commissioner of emigration at New York, 1921, was born in Glasgow.

TODDY. Ade Tody held land in Irvine, Ayrshire, 1426 (*Irvine,* I, p. 130). Simon Tody was burgess of Arbroath, 1476, and Sir John Toddi or Tody was chaplain of S. Ninian, Arbroath, in 1492 (RAA., II, 196, 334). Thomas Toddie was heir of Thomas Todie in Polduff, his father, 1679 (*Inquis.,* 6131).

TODLAW. Local. Galfridus Thodlauch or Todlau was canon of Moray, 1311 (RAA., I, p. 280, 287).

TODRICK. Local. There is or was a place named Todrick or Todderick in Selkirkshire (*Retours, Selkirk,* 22). William Tothrik held a land in Edinburgh, 1428 (RMS., II, 116). Thomas Tothric was notary in a case concerning the third part of Cranshaws in 1453 (*Swinton,* p. xxxix). Archibald Todryk was burgess of Edinburgh in 1464 (*Neubotle,* p. 252), and five years later safe conducts were granted Archibald Todryk, Scottish merchant, and to William Todryk (*Bain,* IV, 1389). William Todrik, merchant and burgess of Edinburgh (d. 1507) married a daughter of Lady Margaret (second daughter of King James II) and Lord Crichton. His name is still preserved in Todrick's Wynd, Edinburgh. Archibald Tothrik (Todrig, or Tothrick) appears as burgess of Edinburgh, 1482 and 1504 (CDE., 52, 54; *Soltre,* p. 324). Sir William Tochryk (for Tothryk), chaplain at Yester, 1491 (*Laing,* 379), and Robert Toddryk witness in Linlithgow, 1536 (*Johnsoun*). George Toddrick or Dodrig is in record as burgess of Edinburgh, 1558–66 (ER., XIX, p. 428; RPC., I, p. 445), and Archibald Toithryke, burgess in 1577 (RHM., II, p. 235). John Toddrick, A. M., of St. Andrews diocese in record, 1580 (*Laing,* 1002), and John Todrick was heir portioner of land in the burgh of Dundee, 1634 (*Retours, Forfar,* 224). Old: Toddrik, Todrick, Todryg, Torryk.

TOENI. From the commune of this name in the arrondissement of Louviers in Normandy. The family of de Toeni was connected with the royal family of Scotland (ES., II, p. 276n). Radulfus de Tounei or de Thonnei witnessed resignation of Cultrach in Fife by Adam de

Stowel and also the agreement between him and Queen Ermengard (LIM., p. 6, 7). Simon de Toeni (Toeny, Toney), a monk of Melrose, became abbot of Kogeshala (Coggeshall in Essex), returned to Melrose in 1168, and was consecrated bishop of Moray, 1172 (*Dowden,* p. 146).

TOFTS. From the old lands or barony of Tofts in the parish of Kirkton, Roxburghshire. Ingram de Toftes, Robert de Toftes, and William de Toftes, all three of the county of Roxburghshire, rendered homage for their possessions in 1296. The seal of Ingram bears a large fleur-de-lys and S' *Ingrami d'Toftis,* and that of Robert an eight-rayed figure and S' *Roberti d'Toftis* (*Bain,* II, p. 199, 200, 532). William of Toftys was rector of the church of Great Cauerys (Cavers) in 1363 (*Melros,* p. 434, 435), Robert Toftis had a precept of remission for the slaughter of Cristiane Forfar in 1499 (RSS., I, 361), and John Tofts in Cribbis is in record in 1637 (*Lauder*). Gavin Toftis, resident in the vill of Saltoun, 1641 (*Inquis. Tut.,* 617).

TOLLER. Probably from ME. *toller(e,* OE. *tollere,* taxgatherer, publican. Hugh Toller, Ambrose Toller, and Nicholas Toller witnessed sale of land in Glasgow, c. 1280–90 (REG., p. 198). Elene Tollare, wife of Willelmus Dubrelle in Inverkethine, is in record, 1392 (RMS., I, 846), and Forsythe Toller was collector of petty customs of Dumbarton in 1428 (ER., IV, p. 462). Tollar 1431.

TOLLOUS. Sir Robert Tolouse, rector of the church of Scraling, 1422 (*Hay,* 10). Henry Tollous, one of assize in Edinburgh, 1529 (MCM., II, p. 96). More likely to be of local origin, 'at the toll-house' than from Toulouse, France. There is a farm named Tullos in Lauderdale.

TOLMIE, Tolme. Of local origin. John Tolmach took part in a conflict between Macleods and Mackenzies in 1611 (Mackenzie, *The Western Isles,* p. 119). Androw Tolmi was 'burra officiar' of Inverness, 1612–16 (*Rec. Inv.,* II, p. 96, 149). The Tolmies of the Hebrides are called Clann Talvaich (*Henderson,* p. 56).

TOMLINE. From Tom, diminutive of Thomas, q.v., + diminutive suffix -*lin(g)*. Thomelinus Hervs was juror on an inquest in Badenoch, 1380 (REM., p. 187).

TONERGARTH. John de Tonergarth, parson of Durnock, Dumfriesshire, who obtained a safe conduct into England, 1366 (Rymer, *Foedera,* VI, p. 535) derived his name from Tundergarth, near Lockerbie. Adam de Tornergeyth had a presentation to the church of Egglesmauhy, St. Andrews' diocese, 1296 (Bain, II, p. 221).

TONNOCH, TONNOCHY. Adam says (p. 174) this form of the name of Clan Donnachie "was adopted by some of its members in order to conceal their identity after the events of 1745." Colonel V. C. Tonnochy was commander of 53rd Sikhs.

TONSON. John Tonson, tenant in Balgreschac, 1473 (Cupar-Angus, I, p. 176). John Tonson witnessed instrument of sasine, 1496 (Bamff, p. 37). Lower, Bardsley, and Harrison say this name is 'Tony's son,' son of Anthony, and Bardsley and Harrison also suggest it may be (2) a corruption of Tomson.

TOPP. Edward Top admitted burgess of Aberdeen, 1486 (NSCM., I, p. 32) is doubtless the Edward Top who was fined in 1497 for "failzeit in the waching of the tone" (CRA., p. 60). Ernest Gillian Topp from Turriff was killed in the first Great War (Turriff).

TORBAIN, TORBANE. Local. There is a Torbain near Kirkcaldy, Fife, another near Parton, Galloway, and a Torbane near Bathgate. George Turbane is recorded in St. Andrews, 1525 (SHR., II, p. 266).

TORBET. A Fife surname. Most probably a variant of TARVET, q.v.

TORLAN. A diminutive of Torlaoch (Turlough). It was not long ago a proper name in Kilmuir, Skye (Forbes, Place-names of Skye, p. 28).

TORMOD. From ON. Þormóðr, 'Thor minded.' A favorite name with the Macleods. It is also spelled Tormoid and is Englished as Norman because of the faint assonance of the first syllables. Tarmot Ger had a remission in 1541 for his part in the hership of Kenlochow and Trouternes (RSS., II, 3943). Tormot 1535 (RSS., II, 1881), Turmode 1343.

TORMOND. From ON. Þormundr, 'Thor's protection.' Also a favorite name with the Macleods. It alternates with TORMOD, q.v., and is the source of the Gaelic dialectal Tormailt (with intrusive l). Tormund 1585. Englished NORMAN simply because of the like sound.

TORMONTSON, 'son of Tormont or TORMOND,' q.v. Thomas Tormontson, tenant of Culcowe, Ardmanoch, 1504 (ER., XII, p. 662).

TORN. A variant spelling of TURING, q.v., which has become a separate surname. Gillanders de Torrin on assize of marches in Fife, 1231 (RD., 196). William Torne admitted

burgess of Aberdeen, 1493 (NSCM., I, p. 37; CRA., p. 50). James Torn in Old Meldrum, 1749 (Aberdeen CR.).

TORPHICHEN. From Torphichen in West Lothian. Simon de Torfekin witnessed a charter by Malcolm, son of Earl Duncan of Fife to the nuns of North Berwick, a. 1199 (SHSM., IV, p. 309). In 1345 Duncan Thorphicheyn wrongly possessed the vicarage of Inchemacbany in the diocese of Aberdeen (Pap. Pet., I, p. 94). Anderson (Scot. Nat.) says that "among the favourites of James III hanged by the incensed nobles over Lauder bridge in 1478 was one Torphichen, a dancing-master."

TORQUIL. A favorite forename among the Macleods. It also occurs as Torcail. In Gaelic it is Torcull or Torcall (gen. Thorcaill or Torcaill), from Norse Thorkell, the shorter form of Thorketill. The genitive Turcaill occurs in the Annals of Ulster under 1124. The name has been also rendered by the Latin Tarquin (!) which it was supposed to resemble (HP., II, p. 288). From the fuller form Thorketill comes MACCORQUODALE. Torculane Makcloide of Lewis was forfeited in 1504 for assisting Donald of the Isles in fire-raising and herships in Badenoch (Trials, I, p. 45 *–48 *). Tairqueill 1600.

TORR. There were old lands named Torr which formed part of the barony of Ballinbreich, Fife, in 1517 (Sibbald, Fife and Kinross, p. 83). Matthew de Torre de Inuerdouet witnessed a transaction between Serlo de Lascelis and the prior of St. Andrews, 1288 (RPSA., p. 346). Thomas de la Tour of Ayrshire rendered homage in 1296. His seal bears a castle with 3 towers (?) . . . Thom. de Tu[rri] (Bain, II, p. 199, 548). Adam Tore was one of those appointed to treat for the ransom of David II in 1357 (Foedera, III, p. 363). James Torre was made town's 'Lord of Bonaccord' in Aberdeen, 1545 (CRA., p. 221).

TORRANCE, TORRENCE. Of local origin from (1) Torrance in Stirlingshire, or (2) from Torrance, East Kilbride, Lanarkshire. John Torrance is recorded in Nethir Cloychtquharne in 1555 (Protocols, I), and John Torrance was a tenant of Newbattle Abbey in 1563 (Neubotle, p. 327). The name also occurs in Edinburgh in 1561 as Torrens (Edinb. Marr.). David Torrance (1840–1906), chief justice of the Supreme Court of Connecticut, U. S., was born in Edinburgh.

TORRIE, TORRY. There are places of this name in Kincardineshire and in Fife, but Torrie of that Ilk was seated in Dumfriesshire till their forfeiture in the reign of James III, who re-

TORRIE, TORRY, *continued*

granted to Thomas Carruthers the lands and church of Torry, etc., "quae ad Georgium Tory de eodem, nostrum felonem et proditorem pertinuerunt, ratione ejus forfeituræ" (*Nisbet,* I, p. 306). Dan Johan de Torry l'abbe de Dounfermelyn had a safe conduct in 1405 (*Bain,* IV, 715). Alexander Torrie in Cockburnespethe-toure, 1653 (*Lauder*). (2) Probably from Torry near Aberdeen. David Torry, burgess of Elgin, 1590 (RPC., IV, p. 498), and William Torie, bailie there, 1638, and Robert Torrie, mason there, 1691 (*Moray*). There were many Torries in Islay, Kerrera, etc., probably followers of Campbell of Cawdor when Campbell acquired Islay. George Torrie in Cawdor, witness to a bond in 1639 (*Cawdor,* p. 285). George Torrie, servitor to John Campbell, fiar of Calder (Cawdor), 1626 (*Bk. Islay,* p. 374). James and John Torrie, tenants in Islay. Robert Torie appears as late taylor burges of Edinburgh, 1732 (*Guildry,* p. 143).

TORTHORALD. From Torthorwald in Dumfriesshire. David de Torthorald was witness in an Annandale charter, c. 1215–45 (*Bain,* I, 1680). Thomas de Torthorald and James, his brother, witnessed a charter by the earl of Carrick of land in Newby after 1271 (*Annandale,* I, p. 8), and in 1278 Sir David de Torthorald was accused with others of having amerced freemen in their lord's courts without their peers and contrary to statute (*Bain,* II, p. 39). Between 1280–90 Sir David witnessed the grant by Thomas, son of Andrew de Kyrconeuel, to Holmcoltran Abbey of half his land (*Holm Cultram,* p. 48), and in 1291 he swore fealty to England at Berwick (*Bain,* II, p. 125). The main line of the house of Torthorald terminated on the death in 1296 of Sir David, whose only daughter married Humphrey de Kirkpatrick. Thomas de Torthorald and James de Torthorald of Dumfriesshire rendered homage in 1296, and in 1298 the bay horse of the latter at the battle of Falkirk was valued at £10 (*Bain,* II, p. 182, 203, 259). The family sided with the English in the War for Independence. Sir Thomas de Torthorald took part in a foray in Nithsdale, 1303–4, and there is evidence that Sir Thomas was at Lochmaben Castle in 1313 as one of the English garrison, and later took part in raids on Pennersax, etc. Sir James de Torthorald was killed fighting for the English at Bannockburn, and his son Sir John 'after an unavailing visit in 1328, to claim his lands in Scotland, was compensated two years later for the loss of them by Edward III' (*Bain,* III).

TORULL. A Harris name from Norse *Thorald.* "'s mór iarguin Nic Thoruill ort" (*Henderson,* p. 57).

TOSCHACH, TOSHACH, TOSHAK. G. *toiseach,* EG. *toisech,* 'chief,' 'leader,' or 'front man.' An ancient Gaelic dignity ranking next to the mormaer. The word is found on a Welsh ogham-inscribed stone as *tovisaci,* in Welsh *tywysog,* and on several of the early British coins it appears under the Latin form of *Tascio.* Symon Tuschech or Tuschecce witnessed two charters by John, earl of Huntingdon in favor of the Abbey of Arbroath, 1219–37 (RAA., I, p. 57, 97). The family of Toschach of Monivaird or Monzievaird in Atholl, now extinct, derived their name from this title, the equivalent of Saxon 'thane.' Robert Steward, afterwards Robert II, before 1371 granted to Ewen Thane of Glentilt, brother of Reginald of the Isles, the whole thanedom of Glentilt in return for faithful service and an annual money payment. Andrew Toische resigned into the king's hands his lands of Brewland of Mekven in the county of Perth, 1450, who granted them to the Abbey of Inchaffray (*Inchaffray,* p. 143–144). About 1502 Finlay, son of Andrew, thane of Glentilt, is mentioned as Finlay Toschach, thane of Glentilt, "and the descendants of this Finlay having, like him, turned their Saxon title of Thane into a Gaelic family designation of Toschach, founded a family called Toschach of Monivaird" (Innes, *Legal antiquities,* p. 80–81). Finlay Tosscheach of Pitteinze appears on an inquest in Atholl, 1516 (*Athole,* p. 711), William Toscheoch of Monyvarde was a follower of the earl of Argyll, 1536 (RSS., II, 2152), James Toscheoch witnessed a confirmation charter in favor of David Toscheoch de Monyvaird, 1544 (RMS., III, 3064), and David Toscheocht was witness at Ile of Lochtay, 1552 (BBT., p. 193). Alester McAndro Tossoche was fined for reset of members of outlawed Clan Gregor, 1613 (RPC., XIV, p. 632), David Tosoch apparent of Monivaird witnessed a tack of property in Strathphilane, 1607 (*Laing,* 1526), and Duncan and James Toscheach appear in the muster roll of the laird of Glenurquhay, 1638 (BBT., p. 398). Alexander Toscheoch was schoolmaster at Moffet, 1699 (*Edin. App.*).

TOSH. A shortened form of (MACIN)TOSH, q.v. Alexander Tosche admitted burgess of Aberdeen in 1606 (NSCM., I, p. 102). Margaret Toash in Aberdeen, 1794 (*Aberdeen CR.*). John Tosh died in Alloa, 1939.

TOUGH, TOUCH. From the parish of Tough (Gaelic *tulach,* a knoll), near Alford, Aberdeenshire. The *ch* and *gh* have the guttural pronunciation of *ch* in loch. In a roll of missing charters of David II is one to Isabel Toulch, sister to Henry Toulch, of the lands of Toulch in the sheriffdom of Abirdene (RMS., I, App. II, 1361). Sande Towcht in Aberdeen was ordered in 1538 to find caution for "strubbling" others (CRA., p. 158). Sir James Toucht was a notary in Fife, 1549 (Gaw, 27), Thomas Tucht was keeper of the inner door of Exchequer in 1561 (ER., XIX, p. 137), one Touch is recorded as burgess of Dysart in 1568 (Dysart, p. 36), and John Towichte was a "baixter" in Aberdeen in 1581 (SCM., II, p. 54). John Touch, trade burgess in Aberdeen, 1611 (ROA., I, p. 231). The surname is most common on tombstones in the churchyard of Kearn (Jervise, II, p. 217). George Touch, skipper in Dysart, was retoured heir of William Touch in Leaven, in ane tenement of land in Pettinweim in 1653 (Retours, Fife, 823). William Touch in Kirktoun of Inch, 1748 (Aberdeen CR.). George Gray Tough of Ythan Wells was killed in the first Great War (Turriff).

TOUNG. Magnus Toung, witness in Toung, 1613 (OSR., I, p. 278) derived his name from Toung in Ireland, Orkney.

TOUX. From the small place named Toux near Cornhill, Banffshire. James Tuickis or Towx in 1650 was "delat to have given away a fauld to ye guidman," i.e. the Devil (Jervise, II, p. 425).

TOWARD, TOWART. From Toward in the parish of Dunoon, Argyllshire. A legend states that in the reign of Robert III two sons of the chief of the Lamonts changed their name to Toward (Dunlop, Dunoon, p. 14), and Buchanan (p. 117) says people of this name are considered a sept of Clan Lamond. Patrick Towart, burgess freeman of Glasgow, 1600 (Burgesses), Agnes Towart in Croftingaw, 1654 (Sasines, 856), and Margaret Towart in 1720 (Dunkeld). Several of the name recorded in Dumbarton in eighteenth and nineteenth centuries (RDB.). Malcolm Toir or Toward, reader in Logie, was "deposed in 1610 for consulting the Egyptians," and Walter Towar was bedell of Logie, 1690 (Logie, I, p. 20, 69; II, p. 296). The name probably confused with TOWER, q.v.

TOWER. The surname of a noted Aberdeen family. The name seems originally De Tour (PSAS., XLVI, p. 442). Patrick Towar in the Cabrach to be apprehended, 1625 (RPC., 2. ser. I, p. 97). William Towar in Auchmunzie, 1633 (SCM., III, p. 119). The name is also found in the Aberdeen Poll Book. Cf. TOWARD.

TOWERS. Nisbet says the family of Towers of Inverleith descended from Walter Towers,

a Frenchman, merchant in Edinburgh in the reign of David II (I, p. 99). William de Tours, vallet of Scotland, was made prisoner in a battle on the March of Scotland, 1359 (Bain, IV, 40). Johannes de Turribus, charter witness in Edinburgh, 1397 (RMS., I, App. I, 157); and John of Touris had a safe conduct in England, 1423 (Bain, IV, 940). John de Turribus was witness in Edinburgh, 1426 (Egidii, p. 47), and David de Turribus is recorded dominus de Blakburne in the same year (LSC., 119). William de Turribus de Crawmond, 1413 (CDE., 21), William de Towris witnessed a St. Leonard's charter, 1457, and Peter de Towris was witness in Edinburgh, 1462 (Neubotle, 284, 290). Thomas Touris, bailie of the barony of Dunkeld within Auchtertool, 1508–13, appears as Towris, Thouris, Towres (Rent. Dunk.). "Schir Alexander Towris off Innerleyth" in record, 1522 (Rental). Dame Jeene or Jonet Towris, a religious of North Berwick, 1539–48 (CMN., 56, 65). George Towris had sasine of land in Haddington, 1558 (ER.), and Sir George Touris was retoured heir of his father, John Touris of Innerleyth, 1605 (Retours, Edinburgh, 153). Toures 1610, Towres 1630, Towrys 1522.

TOWIE. Of local origin from Towie in Aberdeenshire. Alexander Towy was admitted burgess of Aberdeen, 1480 (NSCM., I, p. 29). David Towie, bailie of Elgin, 1593 (Laing, 1259).

TOWNS. Andrew Tovnis was burgess of Edinburgh, 1423 (Egidii, p. 45), and Robert Touneis or Tounnis was sheriff-clerk of Linlithgow in 1531 (Johnsoun). Sir Robert of Toynge, treasurer of the queen's household in 1329, is the most conspicuous of the name (Stodart, II, p. 122). Townis of that Ilk in Workman's MS. Nicol Townis, notary in Linlithgow, 1581, also appears as Thownis (Sc. Ant., XI, p. 131).

TRABROUN. Most probably from Trabroun in Berwickshire, although there is another Trabroun in East Lothian. Three individuals of this name rendered homage for their possessions in 1296, all residents in the county of Berewyke, namely Rauf de Trebrun, William le fiz William de Trebrun, and Alan de Trebrun (Bain, II, p. 207). In the same year Alan de Trebrun was one of the jury on the inquest made at Berwick concerning the lands of Lady Elena la Zuche in the sheriffdom of Berwick (ibid., p. 215). A later Alan de Trebrune witnessed the confirmation of Snawdoun to the monastery of Dryburgh, c. 1350 (Dryburgh, 232). Andrew de Trebrine, priest of St. Andrews diocese, is in record in 1378 (Cambus., 165), and may be Andrew de Trebrun, rector of Kinnoul, 1394 (Pap. Pet.,

TRABROUN, *continued*

I, p. 620). David de Trebrun, cleric and notary public in Moray, is in record in 1398 (LSC., 110). (He also signs without the "de"). Andrew Trebrun was prebendary of Buthirgil in 1450 (REB., I, 131).

TRAGOSE. Jean Tragose in Lie, parish of Lanark, 1682 *(Lanark CR.)*, may have derived her surname from Tregose or Tregoose in Cornwall.

TRAIL, TRAILL. Probably from some place in the north. There is an Abhainn Traill emptying into Upper Loch Torridon. Hardly likely to be a form of Thrale as suggested by Harrison. Thomas Trayle was canon of Aberdeen, 1366 (REA., II, p. 58). Walter Trail (Trayl, or Treyl, or Treyle), of the family of Traill of Blebo in Fife, was provided bishop of St. Andrews in 1385 *(Dowden, p. 27)*, and Magister Thomas Travl was a friar of St. Andrews, 1395 (RPSA., p. 5). Sir Thomas Traell, knight of Scotland, had safe conduct into England, 1395 *(Bain, IV, 497)*. Johannes Trayle was elected sergeant in Aberdeen, 1408 (*Guildry, p. 185*). Thomas Trail was treasurer of Glasgow, 1424 (LCD., p. 242). Thomas Traile was admitted burgess of Aberdeen, 1443 (NSCM., I, p. 7), and James Trayll de Malgask was a witness, 1448 (REB., I, 118). Thomas Travll was appointed a procurator to appear in the Roman curia in 1526 (RAA., II, 633), and Thomas Trel was burgess of Dundee, 1576 *(Wedd., p. 27)*. The Traills of Orkney and Shetland are descended from the family of Traill of Blebo, an ancient family of Fife. Their first appearance in Orkney is in 1523 when David Traile appears as witness in Kirkwall (REO., p. 207). The Traills of Castlehill and Rattar, Caithness, are also of Fife origin. Traell 1583, Trayle 1545; Treil. There were lands named Petintreill in the earldom of Sutherland in 1529 (OPS., II, p. 630), in 1616 Pentraill or Pitentrail (*Retours, Sutherland, 3*).

TRAIN. A different name from Drain (from Ir. O'Dreáin). The first records of this surname are all associated with the burgh of Irvine. Stevn (= Stephen or Steven) Tran was bailie of Irvine, 1540, Thomas Tran was charter witness there, 1455, Mariot Trane was repledged to liberty of the burgh in 1460 (*Irvine, I, p. 45, 147, 27*), and Bartholomeu Trane was witness there, 1499 (*Simon*, 24). Stevin Tran, William Tran, and Hew Tran were burgesses of Irvine, 1590 (*Irvine, I, p. 64*), William Travne, shipowner in Irvine is mentioned. 1557 (CRA., p. 305), and another William Trane in Irrwine, 1583 (*Hunter, p. 31*). Patrick Trane, merchant burgess of Glasgow, 1653 (*Inquis.*, 3825), and

in 1657 Alexander Trayne was heir of Mr. Alexander Trane, late minister at Lochruitoune (ibid., 4197). Johannes Trane was regent in the College of Glasgow, 1693 (*Pollok, I, p. 343*), and Joseph Train was correspondent of Sir Walter Scott.

TRAINER. Recorded in Fife. From Ir. personal name *Tréanfhear*, 'strong man.' Ir. *Mac Treinfhir*.

TRANENT. From the old barony of the name in East Lothian. Thor de Trauernent (the old British form of the place name) witnessed the charter by King David I to the church of S. Cuthbert in Edinburgh, c. 1127, and c. 1144 he witnessed the gift of 52 acres of the land of Dolchet (Dalkeith) to the Abbey of Holyrood (LSC., p. 8, 9). William de Trauernent witnessed a grant by Peter de Grame to the House of Soltre, c. 1190–1238 (*Soltre*, p. 11), and a later William de Trauernent was "rector scolarum" of Haddington in 1374 (*Yester*, p. 26).

TRAQUAIR. From the lands of Traquair in the parish of the same name in Peeblesshire. The surname is and apparently always has been a rare one. Magister Alan de Tracquare witnessed a gift of land in the Hospital of Soltre, c. 1250–70 (*Soltre*, p. 33), and Thomas de Treuequer or Trouequer was decanus de Anegus in 1265 (RAA., I, p. 187, 269). Johannes de Traquair had a charter of lands of Edirdye and Henderstoun in the reign of Robert I (RMS., I, App. II, 11). Alexander Traquair, brother german of quondam Thomas Traquair, ypothecarius, burgess of Edinburgh, 1618 (*Inquis. Tut.*, 271). Dr. Ramsey Heatley Traquair (1840–1912) was a distinguished palæontologist in Edinburgh.

TRAVALOUR. John Travalour received a payment in 1509 (*Rent. Dunk.*, p. 65).

TREMBLAY. Walter de Trembley occupied the lands of Delany in the Mearns, 1263 (*Chamberlain's Rolls*, I, p. * 20), and Robert de Tremblay witnessed a charter of lands in Fife by Sir Alexander de Moray, 1281 (RPSA., p. 342). Robert de Tremblee who rendered homage in 1296 is probably Robert de Tremblay or Trembleye of Elgin en Moreve whose homage is recorded in the same year (*Bain*, II, p. 169, 183, 209). From either of these individuals may have descended some or all of the Trimbills, Trombills, and Trumbles in Fife; but it is certain, says Stodart (II, p. 48), that the Angus family of Turnbull of Strickathrow was founded by a cadet of the Turnbulls of Bedrule. In the thirty-fourth year of his reign David II confirmed a charter of lands in Inverdovat, Fife, formerly held by the deceased

Robert Trymblay, and resigned by his daughter and heir Cicilia (RMS., I, 186). John de Trumbeley witnessed lease of a toft and croft and pertinents in the vill of Glesbany, 1321 (SCM., II, p. 319). Trymlay 1584.

TRENANT. Of local origin from the town of Tranent in East Lothian.

TRENCH. This surname is said to be of French origin and introduced into Scotland after the revocation of the Edict of Nantes, October, 1684. The name is found much earlier in Scotland, and there are places named Trench in England. James Tryncche, witness in 1557 and Helen Trynsche in 1558 (Home, 206). Andrew Trinche is recorded in Dunfermline, 1586 (Dunfermline), John Trinche appears in Eyemouth, 1629 (RPC., 2. ser. III, p. 41), and David Trinsche was fleschear and burgess of Edinburgh, 1658 (Inquis., 4403).

TRENT. Perhaps from Trent, a parish in the county of Somerset, England. This more likely than that the name is a curtailed form of Tranent. Some of the local references, however, point rather to the latter origin. William Trent was a monk of Cupar Abbey in 1456 (Panmure, II, p. 236), and in 1521 Petrus Trent witnessed a tack by the abbot of the same house (SCM., v, p. 294). John Trent was tenant of the Abbey of Neubotle in 1563 (Neubotle, p. 326), a later John Trent was retoured heir of James Trent in Newbottell, his father, in 1638, and in 1661 William Trent was retoured heir of John Trent, his father (Retours, Edinburgh, 834, 1089). Alexander Trent recorded in Hardeismyllne, 1672 (Lauder), and Mr. Patrick Trent, minister at Linlithgow, was deprived of his benefice, 1689 (RPC., 3. ser. XIV, p. 50). William Trent (c. 1655–1724), born in Inverness, became chief justice of the state of New Jersey, and the capital of the state (Trenton) was named in his honor. His son, also named William, built the first fort on the site of Pittsburgh.

TREISDENERIS. Malisius treisdeneris, burgess of Perth, a charter witness, c. 1245 (Inchaffray, p. 63). Michael Troisdeneris in Perth rendered homage, 1296 (RR.). This name is recorded in England in 1258. From Fr. trois deniers, 'three pence.'

TREWEMAN. William Treweman witnessed a charter by William, bishop of Glasgow, 1258 (REG., p. 165). Lower, Bardsley, and Harrison give meaning 'a true man.'

TREWNOT. John Trewnot, a monk of Kelso Abbey, 1435 (Kelso, 528).

TRIMBLE. A metathetic form of TURNBULL, q.v. Janet Trumble in Crosiereige appears in 1674, and John Trimble in Elsrigle, parish of Libbertoun, 1689 (Lanark CR.).

TRIPNAY. Richard de Trippeneth was witness to a grant of the church of S. Servan to Cambuskenneth Abbey in 1273, and ten years later there is mention of Nicholas de Tripena (Cambus., p. 14, 49). Nicol de Trippeneye of the county of Linlescu rendered homage in 1296. His seal bears the Agnus Dei to dexter and S' Nicolai de Tripanei (Bain, II, p. 202, 534). Thomas de Trypnav was dominus de Scotyston in 1381, and in 1402 Patrick de Tripnay, grandson and heir of umquhill Thomas de Tripnay of Scotstoun, confirmed the disposition made by his grandfather to Alan de Laudre (Neubotle, p. xxiv–xxv). "This family and name of Tripnay are now lost" (ibid., p. xxv). John Tripnay, clericus Sanctiandree diocesis, 1413 (CDE., p. 21).

TRISTRAM. Tristram or Tristran continued as a name in the family of Gorthy for nearly 400 years. Tristrannus witnessed Earl Gilbert's great charter to the Abbey of Inchaffray in 1200 (Inchaffray, p. 8). Between 1200 and 1220 Trestram or Tristram filius Trestram witnessed charters by the same earl (LIM., p. xxiv, xxvii, 8, 12, 64). In 1266 an agreement was made between Trestram de Gortyn and Alan, abbot of Inchaffray respecting the right of the former to have a chapel of his own at Gorthy (ibid., p. 46).

TRODY. Johannes Trodi was one of the assessors of the lands of Dunduff, 1231 (RD., p. 111). Henry de Trody was juror on an inquest at Perth, 1305 (Bain, II, p. 456).

TROLLOPE. There was a prominent family of this name in the north of England. The name may be of local origin as suggested by Lower, "although the place from which it was assumed has been forgotten." John Trollop had charter from Robert I of the lands of Forteviot in the county of Perth (RMS., I, App. II, 482). Richard Trolhope, claviger, had charter of lands in Neubotel, 1564.

TROTTER, TROTER. From OF. trotier, mod. Fr. trotteur, a runner, messenger. There was a Border clan of this name the head of which was Trotter of Prentannan, Berwickshire, and the name appears also in the north of England, particularly in the county of Durham, where it is common. The Trotters of Mortonhall near Edinburgh are an old family said to date back to the reign of Robert II (1370–1390). John Trottir served on an inquisition taken at Berwick-on-Tweed, 1370 (Bain, IV, 175). John

TROTTER, Troter, *continued*

Trottar of Fluriswall is mentioned in 1478, and George Trottar and Sanderis Trottar witnessed a declaration by John of Roull in 1479 (*Home*, 24, 25). John Trottare and Alexander Trottare were summoned in 1479 to answer to Parliament for treason and other crimes (APS., II, p. 129). John Trotter, son and heir of quondam Ninian Trotter, had a charter of a carucate called Waringzes land in Coldingham, 1512 (RD., p. 379). Peter Trotar in Reidpeth, 1630 (*Inquis.*, 8606). The name is common in the Commissariot Record of Lauder, 1561–1800.

TROUP. From the manor of Troup in the parish of Gamrie, Banffshire. Nisbet says that Troup of that Ilk ended in an heiress who married a younger son of Keith, Earl Marischal. There appears also to have been land of this name in Ayrshire, as there is mention of the half-lands of John of Trowpe there in a charter of c. 1370–80 (*Laing*, 64). Hamund de Troup of Lanarkshire rendered homage in 1296. The seal attached to his homage bears a hawk (pigeon) on ground; crescent and star, and S' *Hamiln de Trvp* (*Bain*, II, p. 198, 550). In 1304–5 Hamelyn de Trup 'le fiz' complained to Edward I against attacks of Sir Duncan de Feringdraute (ibid., 1734–5). Hamelin de Troupe was one of those accused of treason in the 'Black Parliament' held at Scone in 1320 (*Hailes*, II, p. 120). A succeeding Hamelin de Troupe or Truppe had provision of a canonry and prebend of Aberdeen in 1332 (*Pap. Lett.*, II, p. 385), and in 1345 his petition for the church of Inchebrioc in the diocese of St. Andrews was granted (*Pap. Pet.*, I, p. 86). William de Troup, son and heir of quondam John de Troup, granted the lands of Craigy in the Mearns to John Gray of Broxmouth in 1357 (SCM., v, p. 247), Finlay Troupe in Kincardineshire is in record, 1481 (RMS., II, 1468), Thomas Troup was burgess of Linlithgow, 1538 (*Johnsoun*), and Richard Troup, macer, is in record in 1561 (ER., XIX, p. 135). Normond Trupt was admitted burgess of Aberdeen, 1611 (NSCM., I, p. 108). Gordon of Rothiemay, who was his contemporary, (erroneously) affirms that "Martin Harperson Trumpe, the admirall of Hollande, was the son of a Scottish father, one Harper, borne at Peeterheade in Buchaine" (*History of Scots affairs*, III, p, 84). Trowpe 1565, Trupe 1581.

TROWLUF. Thomas Trowluf was tacksman of Howbister land in Inner Stromness, 1492 (REO., p. 410). Bardsley and Harrison under Truelove explain the name as "faithful love."

TRUMLAND. An old surname in Orkney, from the land of the name in the parish of Rousay. Jannet Trumland and Anna Trumbland are recorded in Orkney in 1684 (*Old Lore Misc.*, II, p. 53).

TRUMPAT. From Fr. *trompette*, a trumpeter. ME. *trompete* was also used with the same meaning. Between 1446–50 pavments were made to Marc Trumpat (Trumpate, Trumpet), the king's jester (ER., v, p. 263, 302, 339). Andrew Trumpat, witness in Perth, 1547 (*Rollok*, 28), and Alexander Trompet was a witness apud Elgin, 1566 (REM., p. 395).

TRUMPENTON. John de Trumpenton witnessed an agreement between the abbot of Holyrood and Roger de Quinci, 1222 (LSC., p. 49). Euerardus [de] Trumpotone witnessed a charter by Alexander II confirming the church of Gasc to the Abbey of Inchaffray, c. 1215–20 (*Inchaffray*, p. 158). He "took his surname from 'Trompyngtoun not fer fro Cantebrigge,' where he held a knight's fee. The Brackley charters shew that he was a retainer of Earl Saher and of his son Roger; and his presence in the Scottish Court must have been either as messenger or as representative of one of them" (Maitland Thomson in *Inchaffray*, p. 307).

TRUMPOURE. Adam le Trompour rendered homage at Perth, 1291 (RR.), and Johannes Trumpoure 'nunc dicte Carric heraldo,' had a charter of lands in Dumfriesshire, 1365 (RMS., I, 206). From the occupation, the 'trumpeter.'

TRUSTRIE. Thomas Trustrie was heir of Thomas Truistrie, his father, burgess of Dumfries, 1600 (*Retours, Kirkcudbright*, 43). Thomas Trustrie, arcurarius, burgess of Edinburgh, 1646 (*Inquis.*, 3135).

TUACH. A scarce surname in Ross. Macbain v (p. 72) says this is evidently from G. *tuathach*, 'northern,' but I doubt this. In 1598 Ewen Mac Ian Tuich and John Mac Ian Tuich were assisters of the Roses of Kilravock in acts of reif and 'briggancie' (RPC., v, p. 498). John Tuach of Logiereich took the Test in 1685 (ibid., 3. ser. XI, p. 418). There is a Touch in Kintore parish, Aberdeenshire.

TUATHAL. In OIr. *Tóthal*, Welsh and Old Breton *Tutgual*, from original *Touto-uallos*, 'folk-ruler' or 'people mighty.' "Tuathal mac Artgusso, prim epscop Fortrenn acas abbas Duin caillenn dormiuit," A. D. 864 (AU.) (Tuathal son of Artgus, chief bishop of Fortrenn and abbot of Dunkeld). Tuadal, episcopus Sancti Andree (1055–59), granted to the Keledei of Lochleven the church of Scoonie (RPSA., p. 116), and Thuadhel, sacerdos Keldeorum, witnessed a grant of lands to S. Serf and the Culdees of Lochleven by Edelradus (Ethelred), son of Malcolm III (loc. cit.). Tvethel or Twothel held the lands of Eth in Moray between 1187–1203 (REM., p. 455, 457). Tothal is mentioned by Adamnan (I, c. 15) as father of Roderc (in Welsh Rhydderch), king of Petra Cloithe (Dumbarton).

TUBIRTHACH. Local, from a place name now probably obsolete (in 1341 Tubertach), perhaps Tipperty near Ellon, Aberdeenshire. Michael de Tubirthach in the parish of Tarwas was excommunicated in 1382 (REA., I, p. 166).

TUDHOPE. Of local origin from Tudhope, near Jedburgh, Roxburghshire, "Tuda's enclosure." Tuda or Tudda are common personal names in Searle. Alexander Tutope in Crocefuird, 1622, and William Tuttup in Nether Affleck, 1665 (Lanark CR.). James Towdop in Hawick was to be exhibited before the Privy Council in 1627 as a masterless person fit for the wars (RPC., 2. ser. II, p. 85). John Tutop was murdered in Leith in 1641 (SCM., II, p. 235). George Tuthop is in record in Stanebyres in 1642, and William Tutop in Stanebyrewood was heir of Arthur Tutop in Leyth in 1647 (Inquis., 2738, 3227). John Tuittup in Auchmedden, parish of Lesmahagow is recorded in 1653 (Lanark CR.), James Tudhope was burgess of Jedburgh, 1703 (RRM., III, p. 131), and Thomas Tudhope, of a Peeblesshire family, was killed at Loos in the first Great War in 1915.

TUKE. Most probably a derivative of TOCK, q.v. John Tuk, 'of Scotland borne,' had license in 1495 to import Scottish goods into England (Bain, IV, 1619). Anna Teuk was married in Edinburgh, 1676 (Edinb. Marr.).

TULGONE. Local from Tulquhon in the parish of Tarves, Aberdeenshire. Gilbertus de Tulgone in Tarwas was excommunicated, 1382 (REA., I, p. 166).

TULLIALLAN. From Tulliallan in southeast Perthshire. Thomas de Tulileliane was one of an inquest at Striuelyn, 1411 (Scon, p. 162). Robert Tulialan in Perth in 1654 (DPD., I, p. 153).

TULLIE, TULLY. Local. There are places named Tullo in Angus, Kincardine, and Aberdeenshire. Thomas of Tillow, a priest, and Andrew of Tullowe had safe conducts into England, 1424 (Bain, IV, 961, 963). David Tullie, portioner of Kynmonth, 1588 (RPC., IV, p. 351).

TULLIS. Spelled Tullas in Wardlaw MS. Francis Tullois was retoured heir of Michael Tulloiss of Hilcairny, his brother, 1555 (Retours, Fife, 27). Mr. James Tullus, minister of Burntisland, is mentioned in 1598 (Dysart, p. 26), Janet Tullous was married in Edinburgh, 1618 (Edinb. Marr.), Mr. John Tullis was minister at Weyms, 1631 (PBK., p. 14), and Alexander Tullis, hammerman in St. Andrews, 1688 (PSAS., LIV, p. 243). Robert Tullis introduced printing into Cupar-Fife in 1803.

TULLOCH, TULLO, TULLOH. From Tulloch in the parish of Dingwall. Nicholas de Tolach was witness in Brechin, 1364 (REB., I, 21). Fergus de Tulache was precentor in Brechin, 1372, an office held by another Fergus de Tulath in 1450 (ibid., I, 20, 130). Walter de Tulache had charter of lands of Bondyngton in sheriffdom of Forfar, 1376 (RMS., I, 570), and David de Tulach had charter of lands of Cragnachtoun and Ednelstoun in Kyncardyn, 1380 (Laing, 65). Walterus de Tolacht, witness in Aberdeen, 1387 (REA., I, p. 177). Wat of Tulloch was one of assize on marches of Woodwrae, 1388 (Bamff, p. 22). John de Tulach was elected a lineator in Aberdeen, 1398 (CRA., p. 374), and John, son of William of Toullocht, was appointed keeper of the Muir of Montrewmonth, 1399 (HMC., 7. Rep., App., p. 718). David de Tolauch who was juror on inquest at Carnconane, 1409 (RAA., II, 49) may be David de Tulach, attorney and depute for Alexander Stewart, earl of Mar, 1423 (SCM., IV, p. 127). John Tulch or Tulach was admitted burgess of Aberdeen, 1411, and Donald de Tulche in 1466 (NSCM., I, p. 4, 20). Thomas Tholak, bishop of Orkney, obtained the Castle of Kirkqwaw (Kirkwall) in feoff, 1422 (Dipl. Norv., II, p. 498). Two Tullochs held the bishopric from 1418 to 1477, and Hector de Tullach was canon there in 1467 (SCM., V, p. 394). A inquest was made in 1438 regarding the land of Walter de Tullawch (RAA., II, 83). Thomas Tullo 'duelland in the chanoure of Ross' had a precept of remission, 1492 (RSS., I, 13). David Tullow, member of assize, 1506, appears as David Tullo of Hylcarny, 1520 (SCBF., p. 187). Tholach and Tolach 1422, Tullauch 1520, Tullocht 1600, Tulloich 1511, Tulloicht 1558, Tulloiss 1529, Tullous 1510, Tulloycht 1560, Tulous 1436.

TUMASON. Henderson (N. I., p. 57) gives this as a Highland name from Norse Tumason (Tumi, Thomas).

TUNNA, TUNNO. Forms of TUNNOCK, q.v. Margaret Tunnow had a tenement in Peebles, 1439 (Peebles, p. 207). Robert Tunno was a tenant under the abbot and convent of Melrose, 1504 (Simon, 126). Thomas Tunno had a

TUNNA, TUNNO, continued

precept of remission in 1536 (RSS., II, 2033), and a payment was made to George Tunno, macer, 1561 (ER., XIX, p. 135). William Tuno was retoured heir of John Tuno "in mercata terrae de Mylneburne in domino de Kylismure," 1595 (Retours, Ayr, 17). Andrew Tuno, portioner of Melrose, 1641, 1663 (RRM., I, p. 88; II. p. 55). Adam Tunno was retoured heir of Alexander Tunno in lands of Hairheuch in the barony of Home, 1617 (Retours, Berwick, 108). Barbara Tunno in Fairknowes, 1682 (Lauder). Tunny, Twnne, Twnno.

TUNNOCK. William Tunnoč witnessed a charter by William de Horuirden to the Abbev of Kelso between 1160–1200, and c. 1237 Adam Tunnoc witnessed a charter of resignation of land in Kelso (Kelso, 320, 355). Thomas Tunnok, juror on inquest in Aberdeen, 1400 (REA., I, p. 203). Nycholaus Tonnok, presbyter in St. Andrews diocese, 1414 (REM., p. 217) appears as Nicholas Tunnok or Tunoh, canon of Ross, 1421 (CSR., I, p. 202–203). John Tunnock was retoured heir of William Tunnock of Milneburne in lands in the barony of Kylestewart, 1663 (Retours, Ayr, 528). There is a Tunnoch near Maybole, Ayrshire. See also TUNNA.

TURBETT. From ON. personal name Thorbiartr. Adam Turbett, messenger at arms for Dumbartane, 1569 (RPC., I, p. 659). William Turbet is recorded in Greenock, 1816.

TURCAN, TURCANE. John Turcane in Kincardine, 1644 (Inquis., 2978), George Turcan there in 1647 (Inquis. Tut., 742). John Turcane in Wester Kincairne, 1658 (Inquis., 4373). John Turkine in Tulliallan, 1689 (RPC., 3. ser. XIV, p. 208). Lieutenant Ronald Somerville Turcan died from wounds in war, 1940.

TURFUS. An Orcadian surname contracted from Torfason (for fuller Thorfinnson). William Thurphinsone witnessed a disposition of part of Garth in Stromness in 1483 (REO., p. 196). The name also appears in Sanday in 1601 as Turphison (ibid.). (2) Local, from some place near Glasgow. Mariot Turfhous in Glasgow, 1488 (REG., 452). John Turfus, cordiner, admitted burgess of Glasgow as burgess heir, 1579 (Burgesses). Recorded in Earlston, Berwickshire, 1940.

TURGOT. From the Old West Norse personal name Thorgaut-r. Turgot, the confessor of Queen Margaret, wrote the Vita S. Margarete, and became bishop of St. Andrews in 1107. Turgot is still an English surname under the forms Thorogood, Thurgod, Toogood, etc.

TURING. An Aberdeenshire surname first found in 1323 in the person of Adam Turin, who is mentioned in a deed regarding the park of Fyvin (Illus., I, p. 198). Two years later he served on inquest to determine the marches between Ardlogie and Fyvie (ibid., III, p. 549). The family was originally of Norman origin, and is said to have first settled in Angus in a barony of the same name, moving from there to Aberdeenshire about beginning of fourteenth century (Fermartyn, p. 565–572). Adam Turim was juror on inquest in 1325 (RAA., I, p. 311). William Toryn received the barony of Foveran in Aberdeenshire in the reign of David II by recognition from Henry Strabrok (RMS., I, App. II, 1247). William de Turyne was a charter witness, 1362 (REA., I, p. 105). Andrew de Turyne, dominus de Fowern, was one of the perambulators of the lands of Tarwas and Wldny, 1417 (RAA., II, 53). Thomas Toryne had safe conduct in 1424 (Bain, IV, 963); and John Turyn was admitted burgess of Aberdeen, 1440 (NSCA., I, p. 6). John Turing was bailie of Edinburgh, 1467 (Neubotle, 299). Thomas Turyn, merchant of Scotland, had safe conduct into England, 1473 (Bain, IV, 1407). William Turin, bailie to John, lord of Glamis, 1498 (CAB., p. 396). Robert Turing held land in Brechin, 1505 (REB., I, 222), William Turing of Fouerane is mentioned, 1550 (REA., I, p. 450), and Thomas Turing was tenant on lands of Newbattle Abbey, 1563 (Neubotle, p. 327). The name is from Turin in the parish of Aberlemno, in Angus. Thurin, Thuring.

TURK. Probably from (MAC)TURK, q.v. John Turk, burgess of Glasgow, 1629 (Burgesses). Martha L. Turk, L.R.C.P., died in Edinburgh, 1942.

TURNBULL. This is one of the many Scottish family names for which popular etymology of an early date has supplied a romantic origin. According to tradition the name is derived from a man named Rule who saved the life of King Robert the Bruce by 'turning' a ferocious bull which had threatened to gore the king. For this timely service Rule obtained a grant of the lands of Bedrule and a new name. Hector Boece (1526), to whom we are indebted for a number of picturesque tales relating to our early history, appears to have been the authority for the bull-baiting story. "Doubtless like many other similar tales," says Ewen, "the story is made to fit the name rather than the reverse" (p. 226–227). Notwithstanding the spelling of 1315 the name is probably from OE. Trumbald, 'strongly bold,' and in Teviotdale it is commonly pronounced Trumell or Trummell. In 1315 Robert I granted a charter of land in the west of Fulhophalche (now Philiphaugh) to William called Turnebule (Willelmo dicto turnebule) (RMS., I, 22). Sometime during his reign David II granted the lands of Humdallwalschop (now Hundleshope) in the barony of Mener to John Trumble (RMS., I, App. II, 917), and c. 1354 Walter Tornebole was witness to a charter by Adam de Roule of the lands of Altonburn (HMC., 14. Rep., App., pt. 3, p. 8). Patrick Turnbull was bailie of Edinburgh, 1388 (ER., III, p. 197), Thomas Tornebule was one of the borowis for the earl of Douglas's bounds on the Middle March, 1398 (Bain, IV, 510), and John Tournebulle, nicknamed "out with swerd," was a Scots prisoner of war in England, 1400 (ibid., 565). Thomas Turnbule witnessed a charter of the lands of Drumgrein in 1408 (Annandale, I, p. 12). William Turnbull was 'cubicular' of his holiness the Pope, 1433 (Bain, IV, 1062), and William Trubul (perhaps for Trübul = Trumbul) was canon of Glasgow, 1452 (REG., p. 395). Maister Jhone Trimbill was vicar of Cleigh (Cleish), 1507 (RD., p. 361), and in the same year Stephen Tournebulle was procurator of the Scottish 'nation' in the University of Orleans (SHSM., II, p. 96). Thomas Trumble appears in Dunfermline, 1586 (Dunfermline), John Trumble in Edinburgh, 1649 (Inquis., 3578), and John Trimble in Clunie, 1725 (Dunkeld). Mark Turnbull was provost of Jedburgh, 1561 (ER., XIX, p. 178), and Mathow Trumble was bailie in Glasgow, 1609 (RUG., III, p. 561). The Turnbulls were among the most turbulent of the Border clans as attested by the frequency of their name in Pitcairn's Criminal trials. The earliest Turnbull arms, those of Agnes Trombel, 1497, are: Ermine, three bars, the center bar being charged with a star flanked by two ermine spots (Macdonald, 2792). William Trumbul in Dalkeith, 1603, bears a bull's head erased (ibid., 2793), but that is possibly canting arms. Persons of the name settled in France bore argent, three bulls' heads, couped sable, armed and langued gules, but the Tournebu or Turnebu family in Normandy, who have been claimed as of Scottish origin, had for arms argent, a bend azure. In Berry a family of Tourneboeuf bore, azure, three bulls' heads (Stodart, II, p. 50), and "les Tournebulle de Champagne portent d'azure à trois têtes de buffle" (Larchey, p. 466). William Paterson Turnbull (1830–1871), American ornithologist, was born in Fala, Midlothian, and Frederick Turnbull (1847–1909), born in Glasgow, introduced turkey-red dveing into the United States. The name of William Turnbull, bishop of Glasgow (1448–54) also appears as Turnbol and Trumbil. Durnbule 1423 (in papal doc.), Trimbulle 1531, Trombill c. 1570,

Tromboul 1547, Troumbull 1510, Trumbell 1654, Trumbill 1567, Trumbyll 1544, Trumpbill 1556, Trymbille 1367, Turmbill 1550, Turnbill 1608, Turnble 1669, Turnebile 1553, Turneble 1646, Turnebule 1528, Turnebulle and Turnbul 1390, Turnibul 1485. See also TREMBLAY.

TURNEBERY. Johannes de Turnebery who possessed land in Carric in 1363 (RMS., I, 135) derived his surname from Turnberry in the parish of Kirkoswald, Ayrshire.

TURNER. From the occupation of 'turner,' a lathe-worker, once a familiar and skilled occupation. A family of this name had possession of the estate of Ardwall in the parish of New Abbey for many generations. Thomas dictus Turnour held land in Aberdeen in 1382 (RMS., I, 682), and John Turnoure held land in Irvine in 1426 (Irvine, I, p. 130). William Turnour, merchant of Scotland, had a safe conduct in England, 1473 (Bain, IV, 1411), and William Turnoure is recorded in Edinburgh, 1482 (CDE., 54). Johannes Turnour, tenant in Kynmonty, 1511 (REA., I, p. 372). Bartholomew Turnor appears in Dysart, 1554 (Dysart, p. 23), and Patrick Turner of Tullinaucht was heir of conquest of Alexander Turner of Kindroght, 1657 (Retours, Ayr, 495). An old surname in Aberdeenshire (seventeenth century) and common in Cowal in the eighteenth century. See MACINTURNER. Turneour 1659.

TURNET. George Turnet and James Turnatt were tenants under the Abbey of Kelso, 1567 (Kelso, p. 526, 529). Thomas Turnet, reidare at Zettame (Yetham), 1574 (RMR.). John Turnet, flesher in Edinburgh, 1660 (Edinb. Marr.).

TURPIE. Diminutive of ON. Thorfinnr (through TURPIN). John Turpy was retoured heir of William Turpy, portioner of Ballomylne, avi, in 1607 in part of Bellomiln, and William Turpie was retoured heir of John Turpie, portioner of Bellomylne, 1610 (Retours, Fife, 180, 217). William Turpie in parochine of Kirkcaldie, 1641 (PBK., p. 211), William Turpie, maltman, Edinburgh, 1672 (Edinb. Marr.) is recorded as brewer in 1688 (Edinb. App.), and Alexander Turpie in Leven, 1688 (Inquis., 6917). David McCalman Turpie published his Chaldee manual in 1879.

TURPIN. From ON. Thorfinnr through Fr. Turpin. Turpin was the name of the second known bishop of Brechin (1178–98). Magister Turpinus witnessed a charter by William the Lion of the church of Foregrund, c. 1165–71 (RPSA., p. 223), and Walter, son of Turpin,

TURPIN, *continued*
exchanged his lands of Kenny for those of Othirlony, c. 1226–39 (RAA., I, p. 262–263). William, son of Turpun, juror on an inquisition concerning the lands of Mefth, 1262 (*Bain*, I, 2323), may have been a relative of Richard Turpin who witnessed a charter by Bernard de Rippelai in the twelfth century (*Dallas*, p. 26). The name appears as Turphin and Turfin in *Liber Ecclesie de Scon* (p. 37).

TURREFF. Of local origin from the town of the name in northwest Aberdeenshire. The local pronunciation of the place name is Turra' or Tirra'. David Turreff was a maltman in Aberdeen in 1682 (ROA., I, p. 240), and Francis Turreff from Fyvie served in the first Great War (*Turriff*). Gaven Turreff edited *Antiquarian gleanings from Aberdeenshire records*, 1859.

TURSTAN. From the OE. personal name *Thurstan*, ON. *Thorsteinn*, 'Thur's stone,' Normanized *Turstan*. Turstan de Crectune (Crichton) who witnessed David's great charter to Holyrood, c. 1128 (LSC., p. 6) may be Turstan filius Levingi, a. 1158 (ibid., p. 7). Radulf filius Turstain was witness to David's great charter to Melrose, a. 1153 (*Nat. MSS.*, I, 17). Malcolm filius Malcolmi Thurstan, c. 1330, is again referred to at same date as Malcolmus filius Malcolmi filii Thurstan (RHM., I, p. 39, 40).

TUSCHET. Henricus Tuschet was witness to a charter by John, earl of Huntedun, c. 1219–32 (LAC., p. 19), and Symon Tuschech, probably a relative, witnessed a confirmation charter by the same earl to the Abbey of Arbroath, c. 1219 (RAA., I, p. 57). As Symon Tuschecce he witnessed gift of a toft in Dundee to the same abbey (ibid., p. 97).

TWADDELL, Twaddle. *See under* TWEEDDALE.

TWATT. A surname common to both Orkney and Shetland. The Twatts of Orkney may derive their surname from Twatt in Birsay, and the Twatts of Shetland from Twatt in the parish of Aithsting. John Twatt or Tuait raised an action at law against the rest of the heirs of Twat in 1563, and in 1580 there is recorded a wadset by Magnus Tuait (REO., p. 119–121, 300). Peter in Twatt was underfoud (underbailiff) of Aithsting in 1624 (ibid., p. 431), and Joneta Tuatt was retoured heir of John Tuatt, dyer in Kirkwall, in 1677 (*Retours, Orkney and Shetland*, 117). Twait 1588.

TWEDDELL, Tweddle. *See under* TWEEDDALE.

TWEED. Local, from residence beside river Tweed. George Tweed in Milntoun of Fishery, 1741 (*Aberdeen CR.*). John Tweed (1816–1886) was a prominent publisher in Glasgow.

TWEEDDALE, Tweedale, Tweedle, Tweeddell, Tweddle, Twaddell, Twaddle, Tweddel. The form Tweeddell is also found in Northumberland, Cumberland, Westmoreland, and the northern part of Yorkshire. John de Tweddale was tenant of the earl of Douglas in the barony of Kylbouho (Kilbucho), 1376 (RHM., I, p. xlvii; II, p. 16). John Twedale and William Twedale were archers of the East March of Scotland, 1404 (*Bain*, IV, 669), and Andrew of Twedale was a charter witness in Dundee, 1434 (HP., II, p. 175). Besse Tuodall in Lanark was heard in 1566 to "call the minister a commoun theiff" (Mill, *Plays*, p. 262), David Tweddell in Pettinane, 1671, and several more of the name occur in the Lanark Commissariot Record. John Tueeddaill is recorded in Contland, Lanark, 1711 (*Minutes*, p. 114), and James Tweeddale was minister at Glenluce in 1791 (*Wigtown*). William Tweedale (born 1828), civil engineer and bridge-builder was born in Beith, Ayrshire. Tueddall 1684, Tweddaill 1696. Other old forms are Toudell, Tueddaill, Tuedell, Tuodell, Twadal, Twaddall, Twidale and Twiddle, Twodell. The modern pronunciation is Tweed'al.

TWEEDHOPE. Local, from a place in the valley of the Tweed.

TWEEDIE. The Tweedies were an old Peeblesshire family, and, according to a favorite mythic story, the first of the name was the child of a species of water spirit or genius of the Tweed, hence their name (Chambers, *Picture of Scotland*, I, p. 190). Unfortunately for the truth of this story the name is derived from the lands of Tweedie in the parish of Stonehouse, Lanarkshire. Finlay de Twydvn of Lanarkshire rendered homage in 1296 (*Bain*, II, p. 202), and Watere de Twydi was juror on an inquest at Lanark, 1303 (*Bain*, II, p. 345). Roger, son of Finlay of Twydyn, had a charter of the house and lands of Drumelzier, c. 1320 (*Hay*, 8). After possessing the lands and barony for fully three hundred years the family lost them in the reign of Charles I. William Tuedin received a gift from Robert I of some tenements in Stirling [*sic*, Skirling] which had been forfeited by Gilbert Lindsay (RMS., I, App. II, 674). In 1362 there is mention of payment of nine merks yearly due from the lands of Hopkelloche by James of Tuedi and his heirs (RMS., I, 130). William de Twidy, a charter witness, 1370 (RHM., II, p. 89). James of Twedy, deputy for Joneta de Graham, lady of Walchtone, 1389 (ibid., II, 189), is doubtless the James of Twedy who witnessed a charter at Dalkeith in 1390 (*Edmonstone*, p. 78). Walter of Twedy granted an annual rent from the lands of Drumelzier, 1426 (*Hay*, 10), Thomas Twedye held a tenement in Irvine, 1542 (*Irvine*, I, p. 191). Elizabeth Twedy held a tenement in Glasgow, 1550 (*Protocols*, I), and Magister Thomas Tueadie was commissary of Aberdeen, 1583 (*Aboyne*, p. 159). The Tweedies had the reputation of being a savage race and at the close of 1592 they reverted to their true character. "We learn from an entry in the Record that they had perpetrated quite as deliberate a murder as that committed by them less than two years previously near the castle of Neidpath. Their victim...was one of the Geddesses, with whom they were at feud, and the scene of the atrocity was at a blacksmith's door in the Cowgate of Edinburgh... The complaint states that 'it is not unknawne how mony slauchters have been committit upon them by James Twedy of Drummelzeair and his friends' ...and now he has committed the barbarous murder of the said James Geddes within the burgh of Edinburgh...having by means of spies, watched the said Laird of Glenhegdon, near his lodgings, found he was in the Cowgait at David Lindsay's buith shoeing his horse, on the 29th of December" (Chambers, *History of Peeblesshire*, p. 119). Pennecuik in 1715 described the Tweedies of Drummelzier as "a powerful and domineering family now quite extinct" (*Description of Tweeddale*, p. 253–254). Tuedy 1560, Tuedye 1627, Tueidie and Tweeddy 1684, Tuevdie 1631, Twedie 1608, Tweedy 1455, Tweiddy 1682; Tuedie, Tuedv, Tueedie, Twyddie.

TWINDAILL. David Twindaill or Tivindaill took the Test in Paisley, 1686 (RPC., 3. ser. XI, p. 496).

TWIZEL. From Twizel in Northumberland, near Coldstream. Agnes de Twysel of the county of Berewyk rendered homage in 1296 and had her lands restored to her (*Bain*, II, 853, p. 212).

TWYNHOLM. From the old lands and barony of the name in Kirkcudbrightshire. Walter de Twynham who witnessed a charter of a carucate of land in Langholme to Herbert Maxwell, c. 1270 (RHM., I, 7; *Pollok*, I, p. 125) may be the Walter de Twynham who held the barony of Levingtone in 1279 (*Bain*, II, p. 37). An inquisition was made before Sir Walter de Tuinan in 1296 (ibid., II, p. 215), and in the same year a writ to the sheriff of Dumfries was issued in favor of Walter

de Twynham (ibid., p. 219). Sir Walter de Tuinan was keeper of the sheriffdom of Wigtoun in 1296, and Walter, son of Richard de Twynham, juror on inquest on lands in Dumfries in same year (ibid., p. 215, 216). William de Twynham, parson of the church of S. Brigid in Ayr. appears between 1296–1307 (ibid., p. 523). Walter de Twinham who was chancellor to King Robert Bruce in 1329 (*Panmure*, II, 164; RHM., I, 37) was probably Walter de Twinam, canon of Glasgow, 1337 (*Pap. Lett.*, II, p. 543), and the Walter of Twynhame who witnessed a charter of Sweetheart Abbey (*Laing*, 46). John Twynholme in Speddoche, 1658 (*Dumfries*). James Tuyman was resident in the parish of Colwend, 1684 (RPC., 3. ser. IX, p. 582). Marion Twynholm in Crofts of Crossmichael, 1748, and John Twiname in Balgerran, 1800 (*Kirkcudbright*).

TYBALD. A form of OE. personal name *Theobald*, 'people bold.' The death of a daughter of Robertus Tybald in Arbroath is recorded, c. 1261–6 (RAA., I, p. 209). See TEODBOLD.

TYNEMOUTH. Magister Thomas de Tinmut who witnessed a charter by William, bishop of St. Andrews, c. 1209–33 (RMP., p. 118) is probably Thomas de Tynemue who witnessed a confirmation charter of the church of Hathyn to the Abbey of Aberbroth, c. 1219–26 (RAA., I, p. 105). The name derived from the mouth of the Tyne in Lothian or from the Tyne in England.

TYNINGHAME. From the old barony of the same name in East Lothian. Sometime before 1147 Hugh de Tingheham witnessed a grant by Earl Cospatric to Kelso (*Kelso*, 288), and sometime after 1165 William de Tiningham witnessed a grant by Serlo, clericus regis, to the same abbey (ibid., 216). Gilbert fiz Henry de Tyningham, tenant of the bishop of Seint Andreu of the county of Edneburk rendered homage in 1296 (*Bain*, II, p. 205). Adam de Tyninghame, a canon of St. Andrews, who became dean of Aberdeen and afterwards bishop, died in 1389 (REA., I, p. xxxii–xxxiii). Thomas de Tyningham who witnessed an instrument of concord between the bishop of Aberdeen and John de Forbes, *dominus ejusdem* in 1391 (ibid., I, p. 189), is the Thomas de Quinnynghame of 1392 and Thomas de Tenynghame, canon of Moray, 1400 (REA., I, p. 182, 205) and he may be the Thomas de Tenynghame who was described in 1418 as a discreet man, 'discretus vir' (CMN., 28).

TYRE. From *Taor*, the reduced Gaelic form of Mac an *t-saoir* (Macintyre). A different name from Tyre of (Paul) MACTYRE, q.v.

TYRIE. Formerly a not uncommon surname in Perthshire derived from the place of the name in the shire. Several persons of the name held important public offices in Perth at end of the fifteenth century (*Methven*, p. 3). The Tyries of Drumkilto, Perthshire, were ardent supporters of the royalist cause, and a family of Tyrie long owned the lands of Dunnideer in the Garioch and later were 'gryte Jacobites.' Maurice de Tiri or de Tyrunn witnessed a charter by William Maule of Panmure, c. 1292 (*Panmure*, II, p. 152, 153), and as Morice de Tiry of Perthshire he rendered homage in 1296 (*Bain*, II, p. 200). Thomas de Tyry was burgess of Arbroath, 1433 (RAA., II, 67), John Tyre was rector of the parish church of Balingre, 1475 (*Soltre*, p. 72), and in 1485 Gilbert Tyrye was vicar of Cargill, Perthshire (REB., I, 212). William Tyre or Tyree was a monk of Neubotle, 1467 (*Neubotle*, p. 261, 263). Schir John Tiri (Tyry, Tyrye, Tyre, or Tiry) appears as rector of Torrens, Lanarkshire, 1489–91 (OPS., I, p. 100), provost of the Collegiate Church of Meffane, clerk-depute of the dean of Glasgow, etc. (REG., 457, 461; *Milne*, p. 13; RMP., p. 61). In 1489 he is referred to as 'Jok of Tyre.' John Tayrie, burgess of Perth, mortified some lands in Perth to the Church of Perth in 1511 (*Nisbet*, I, p. 118), and William Tyre rendered to Exchequer the accounts of the burgh of Perth, 1558 (ER., XIX, p. 46). Michael Tiry or Tyre and John Tyre agree to deliver certain victuals, 1550, and William Tirie was burgess of Perth, 1551 (*Rollok*, 67, 77). John Tyrie, vicar of Cramond in first quarter of the sixteenth century, appears in record as Tyri, Tiry, Tyry, and Tyrye (*Rent. Dunk.*). John Tyrie was servitor of Sir James Scrymgeour of Dudhope, 1609 (*Poltalloch Writs*, p. 144).

TYSON. A form of Dyson, from DENNIS, q.v. A common surname in Cumberland, from where it has come into Scotland.

TYTLER. This surname is not very common, but Lower says that it occurs in the English *Hundred Rolls* (1273). It has been derived from ME. *titeler*, a tatler, but this seems most unlikely. Alexander Fraser Tytler (1747–1813), historian and general writer, was born in Edinburgh. His son, Patrick Fraser Tytler (1791–1849), was author of a large history of Scotland and of other works. James Tytler (1747–1805), scholar and eccentric, commonly called "Balloon Tytler" from his having made the first balloon ascension in Scotland, was born in Brechin.

UCHTRED. A common OE. personal name, in OE. meaning "sprite counsel." Borrowed by the Welsh as Uchtryd, the name occurs at least three times in the *Mabinogion*. Vhtred Eilaues sune witnessed King Eadgar's charter granting Swintun to the monks of St. Cuthbert, c. 1100 (*Lawrie*, p. 18). Vcteredus filius Fergus was one of the witnesses to a charter of a salt-pan (*salina*) in Carsach (i.e. Carse of Stirling) to the Abbey of Kelso, c. 1140 (*Kelso*, 375). As Huctred filius Fergus, with the consent of Roland his heir, he granted to Holmcultram Abbey the vill called Kirkgunnin (now Kirkgunzeon in Kirkcudbrightshire) between 1161–74 (*Holm-Cultram*, p. 48). As Utred, lord of Galloway, he was barbarously murdered by his nephew Malcolm (*Sc. ann.*, p. 257). Uchtred, son of Liulf, who held the mill of Scotley under the king of Scots, granted it to the Priory of Wetheral (*Registrum Prioratus de Wetheral*), and as Uctredus filius Liolfi he made a grant of the church of Molle to the Abbey of Kelso between 1147–64 (*Kelso*, 176). He was the father of Eschina de Molle who married Walter, son of Alan, the first Stewart (*Lawrie*, p. 412). Vhtredus de Neuton witnessed a charter of three acres of Karruderes by Walter del Bois, n. d. (*Raine*, 166), and Uhtred was vicecomes of Lynlythcu in the reign of Malcolm IV (*Neubotle*, 267). Hutredus capellanus de Boultoun attested the gift of Okelesfas to the canons of Holyrood in the reign of William the Lion (LSC., 213), and Huctred the baker (*pistor*) was burgess and alderman of Rogesburgh (Roxburgh) in 1329 (*Dryburgh*, p. 255; *Kelso*, p. 372). The name was wrongly considered to be Gaelic, and Mackenzie (*History of the Camerons*) understood it as meaning "eighth," and accordingly he rendered MacOchtery by *Mac Ochdamh Triath*, "son of the eighth chief"!

UDARD, UDWART. From *Udard-us*, an OE. personal name (*Searle*). Vdard, vicecomes, a. 1153 (*Nat. MSS.*, 22), ancestor of the Swintons. Udard, sixth abbot of Cupar Abbey, died in 1207 (*Cupar-Angus*, I, p. xlix), Hudardus witnessed confirmation of the sale of the land of Scrogges to the church of Glasgow, c. 1208–13 (REG., p. 76). A knight of this name, a vassal of the Bruces, lords of Annandale, held the church of Hodelm (Hoddam) in 1202 (ibid., p. 83). Roger filius Vdardi, perhaps his son, witnessed a charter by William Bruce to Adam de Carlyle, c. 1194–1214 (*Annandale*, I, p. 2), and within the same dates Dunegal, son of Udard, resigned a carucate of land in Warmanbie or Weremundebi (ibid., p. 3; *Bain*, I, 606). Adam, son of Vdard, witnessed an agreement between the monks of Neubotel and John de Morham concerning the water-courses of their mills at Morham, c. 1220 (*Neubotel*, p. 68). Udard, son of

Uttu, witnessed a grant by R., son of Dunegal, to the Hospital of S. Peter (*Bain*, II, p. 421). Reginald fil. Vdardi was a charter witness, c. 1240 (*Kelso*, 194), and Wdard dictus Selyman appears as witness in Dumbarton, 1271 (RMP., p. 192). Udward or Udwart was an old surname occurring frequently in the sixteenth century, but was later lost in EDWARD, q.v. Andrew Uddard was burgess of Dumbarton, 1456 (*Strathendrick*, p. 192), and a later Andrew Uddart was burgess of Edinburgh, 1511 (Nisbet, *Plates*, p. 140). Nicholas Udward, dean of guild of Edinburgh, 1584, provost, 1592, and parliamentary representative of the city in 1585 (APS., III, p. 374) appears in 1594 as Nicoll Vduart or Vduard (ibid., IV, p. 85). Nathaniel Uddart in Edinburgh was the first manufacturer of soap in Scotland, 1619 (RPC., XII, p. 106), and Thomas Uddart was retoured heir of James Uddart in Greinoktoun, his father, 1646 (*Retours, Ayr*, 303). A genealogy of Sir John Lauder of Fountainhall mentions Margaret Uthward, "commonlie called Edward," daughter to Nicol Uthward, dean of guild of Edinburgh (*Analecta Scotica*, II, p. 11), and the old name of the family of Edward of Balruddery was Udward (*Baronage of Mearns*). Odard 1208, Uddert 1644, Uduarde 1560, Udward 1555, Vadart 1585, Vdwart 1553.

UDNY. From the barony of the same name in the parish of Udny, Aberdeenshire. The earliest record of the family appears to be in 1406, in which year Ranald de Vldeny, *dominus ejusdem*, granted to a chaplain serving in the chapel of the Holy Trinity, for the soul of Patrick de Vldeny, his father, "omnes terras meas cum pertinenciis vbi antiqua capella de Vldeny fuit situata et omnes terras meas iacentes inter duos torrentes scilicet de Brony et de Couly" (REA., I, p. 209). Alexander de Vldeny was a charter witness in 1450 (ibid., II, p. 296), and in 1457 the bounds of the lands of William de Vldny or Vldeny were perambulated (RAA., II, 109). Andrew Audny was a burgess of Brechin in 1585, and Alexander Udene was a member of council of Stirling in 1608 (REB., II; SBR., p. 285). The Udnys of that Ilk are said to have been the last family in Scotland who kept a fool as part of their establishment. An account of the family of Udny of Udny is given in the *Thanage of Fermartyn*, p. 425–435. Oudnay 1552, Oudne 1511, Oudny 1613, Owdny 1608, Udney 1743, Udnie 1623, Vdnie 1684, Wldny 1417, Wdny 1574.

UDSTON. From Udston in Lanarkshire. Wautier le fiz Roger de Odestone or Oddestone of the county of Lanark rendered homage for his lands in 1296 and in the same year had his lands restored to him (*Bain*, II, p. 198, 218).

UDWART. *See under* UDARD.

UISDEANN. In the North and Northwest Uisdeann is the G. rendering of Hugh. In the Book of Leccan (1400) the name of Clandonald of Sleat is referred to as Clann Uisdinn, and in an English paper prepared for the use of James VI between 1577–97, this Clann Uisdinn is called "Scheall Hutcheoun."

ULBRAND. Wlbrand witnessed the gift of the church of Innyrkyp beyond the moors (*ultra mores*) to the monks of Paisley, c. 1170 (RMP., p. 113), and Ricardus filius Wlbrand witnessed a confirmation charter by Alan, son of Walter the Steward, c. 1179–99 (ibid., p. 12).

ULFKIL. A common personal name in the south of Scotland in the twelfth century. It is a contracted form of OE. *Ulfcytel* (*Anglo-Saxon Chronicle*, 1004). Ulchel filius Alstan was one of the witnesses to the inquisition by Earl David, prince of Cumbria, on the extent of the lands of the church of Glasgow, c. 1124 (REG., 1), and Ulkil was one of three thralls gifted by David I to the Abbey of Dunfermline, c. 1126 (RD., 19). Ulkil filius Maldred was one of the witnesses to the same king's letter respecting the consecration of Robert, bishop of St. Andrews at York in 1128 (Haddon and Stubbs, *Councils and ecclesiastical documents*, v. 2, part 1, p. 215). As Vlkil filius Meld' he witnessed Earl Gospatric's grant of Ederham (now Edrom) and Nesbit to the monks of St. Cuthbert, a. 1138 (*Nat. MSS.*, I, 25), and again as Vlkillus filius Maldredi he was a witness to the grant by Earl Cospatric to the Abbey of Kelso, a. 1147 (*Kelso*, 288). Ulkil filius Morvyn attested King David's letter respecting the consecration of Robert, bishop of St. Andrews at York in 1128 (Haddon and Stubbs, loc. cit.), and as Ulfchil, son of Merewin, he was one of the perambulators of the bounds of the lands of Clerchetune granted by the same king to the church of S. Mary of Haddington, c. 1141 (RPSA., p. 181). Ulfchill filius Ethestan was one of the witnesses to a charter by David I to the Abbey of Melrose, 1143–44 (*Melros*, p. 4), and Hulfchillus, faber, attested the gift by William Masculus of the chapel of Foules to the canons of the church of St. Andrews in the latter half of the twelfth century (RPSA., p. 265).

ULGRIC. The name of one of the leaders of the Galwegians killed at the Battle of the Standard, 1138 (*Sc. Ann.*, p. 204). OG. *Ual-*

ULGRIC, *continued*

garg, 'high temper,' often confused with OE. *Ulric* (Teutonic *Ulric* or *Ulrich*), meaning 'patrimonially rich,' a favorite forename with the Irish Burkes. See MACWALRICK.

ULKILLESTUN. From Ulkillestun, the old name of Oxton in the parish of Channelkirk. William of Ulkillestun, c. 1162–67, witnessed the sale of two families of serfs by Richard de Moreville to Henry de Sinclair (APS., I, p. 94; *Haigs of Bemersyde*, p. 30).

ULRICK. David Ulrick or Uldrich in Burray, Orkney, 1743 (*Donaldson*, p. 86, 135). Probably local from Olrig in Caithness.

UMFRAVILLE, UMPHRAVILLE. From Umfreville in the canton of St. Mère Église, arrondissement of Valognes, department of Manche. For an account of the family see Hodgson, *History of Northumberland*, v. 1, part 2. The first of the name recorded in Scotland is Robertus de Umframville who witnessed the charter by Earl David founding the church of Selkirk (afterwards removed to Kelso), c. 1120 (*Kelso*, 1). He also appears as witness to numerous charters by King David and others in the chartularies of Kelso, Melrose, Glasgow, Dunfermline, etc. His son, Gilbert de Umframville, witnessed the charter to the church of Glasgow (REG., p. 267). He also witnessed King David's gift of a toft in Berwike to the Priory of May between 1147 and 1153 (*May*, 2), and Prince Henry's charter of Swinton to the church of Durham (*Nat. MSS.*, I, p. 13). A Gilbert de Umfraville granted to the Abbey of Cambuskenneth two carucates of land in the manor of Dunipace (*Cambus.*, 85). (The Umphravilles held the superiority of Dunipace until their forfeiture in the reign of Bruce.) An Odenell de Umframvilla appears between 1147 and 1153 as witness in King David's grant of right of forest to Robert de Brus (*Nat. MSS.*, I, p. 12) and to his charter of Annandale to the same, c. 1153 (ibid., p. 20), etc. What relation he was to the other Umphravilles is uncertain. About 1220 Richard de Umfraville confirmed a grant decima pullanorum to the Abbey of Kelso (*Kelso*, 327, 328) and about 1228 Gilbert de Vmfraville confirmed a donation of his grandfather Odenell de Kelso (ibid., p. 325). Gilbert married Matildis, countess of Angus in 1243 (*Chron. Melr.*, s. a.) and in her right became earl of Angus. He died in 1245, leaving a son also named Gilbert. This last Gilbert, the only one of the Scottish nobility who acted with integrity and spirit in the negotiations with England in 1291, died without issue in 1302. By their adherence to the Baliols and to the

English interests during the War of Independence the Umphravilles forfeited their lands in Scotland and were obliged to retire to England. "The last of the De Umphravilles, formerly Lords of Warkworth, died in a small cottage in the hamlet of Aberwic, not far from Alnwick," a pensioner of the Duke of Northumberland (Maidment, in *Carrick*, p. 17), and one of the last of this great Norman family was William Umfraville, keeper of St. Nicholas's Workhouse, Newcastle, who died in indigent circumstances in 1789 (Chambers, *Peeblesshire*, p. 73). Angus Umphraville, an American poet of Scots parentage, published a volume of his pieces in Baltimore, 1817.

UMPHERSTOUN, UMPHERSTON. Local, from some place of the name meaning "Humphrey's town." Katherine Umpherstoun in Nisbetpathhead, 1680 (*Lauder*). Sheriff-substitute Umpherston of Kinross died 1940.

UMPHRAVILLE. See under UMFRAVILLE.

UMPHRAY, UMPHREY. The same as HUMPHRAY, q.v., with omission of the aspirate. Andreas Vmfray, cantor of the church of Dunkeld, 1374 (*Scon*, p. 145). Andrew Umfray (Umfrey, or Vmfrai), burgess and notary public in Perth, appears several times between 1444 and 1448 (RMS., II, 350; RAA., II, 120; *Scon*, 217). William Vmfra was admitted burgess of Aberdeen in 1459 (NSCM., I, p. 16). Sir William Vmfray was chaplain of Dornoch, 1527 (OPS., II, p. 623), and Thomas Vmphray was burgess of Elgyne, 1590 (*Trials*, I, p. 204). The name is also found in Orkney and Shetland (Foula). Jeanna Umphray and Joneta Umphray were heirs of Andrew Umphray, sailor in Scallowaybankis, 1644 (*Retours, Orkney and Shetland*, 46, 47). Mr. John Umphra, minister at Walls, Zetland, 1671 (*Edin. App.*). Umfra is also used as equivalent to Ulfridus as a Christian name in the fifteenth century in an Aberdeen charter (CAB., 394–395). Aumfray 1481, Umphra 1630, Wmfray 1565, Wmphray 1610.

UMPHRAYSON. "Son of HUMPHRAY," q.v., with omission of the aspirate. John Vmfrasoun was a witness in Edinburgh in 1426 (*Egidii*, p. 48). Thomas Umfraisoun appears in Aberdeen in 1433–34 (SCM., v, p. 41; CRA., p. 391), Patrick Umfraisoun was burgess of Kintore in 1437 (CRA., p. 393), and William Vmfrason was admitted burgess of Aberdeen in 1484 (NSCM., I, p. 31).

UNDERWOOD. From the small place named Underwood in the parish of Symington, Ayrshire. John Vndirwode, who served on an inquest made at Prestwick in 1470, is probably the John Vndirvode, burgess of the same burgh in the same year (*Prestwick*, p. 2, 12). Ondirwod 1507, Ondirwodd 1528, Vndirwod and Wndirwod 1470, Vndirwode 1486, Wndirvod 1476.

UNES. George Unes in Lessudden, heir of James Thorbrand, portioner of Lessudden, 1623 (*Inquis.*, 1077). Thomas Unes, collector in Roxburghshire, 1662, and John Uns, tailor in Lessudden, in same year (RRM., ɪɪ, p. 15, 24). Adam Unes appears in Borland, 1627 (*Dumfries*). John Unnes, exiled Covenanter from Castletoun, was drowned off Orkney, 1679 (*Hanna*, ɪɪ, p. 254).

UNIAET. Uniaet thwite, more correctly Uniaett Hwite, was one of the witnesses to the charter by King Eadgar granting the vill of Swinton to the monks of S. Cuthbert, c. 1100 (*Nat. MSS.*, ɪ, 4). As Unyet albus he witnessed King David's grant of three serfs to the church of Dunfermlyn, c. 1126 (RD., p. 13), and at the same time, as Vnyet, he witnessed the same king's mandate regarding fugitive serfs of the same church (ibid., p. 17). As Vnyet albus he was one of the attesters to David's charter to Dunfermline confirming the grants of preceding kings and making increased gifts, c. 1128 (ibid., p. 4). In 1128, as Vniet Albo, he witnessed David's grant of the tithe of his house at Perth to Dunfermline Abbey (ibid., p. 12). About 1134 he appears as Uniet Albus among the witnesses to David's grant of Govan to the church of Glasgow (REG., p. 11). As Vineth Albus he held land near Edinburgh, and gave a part of Craggenemarf to Holyrood Abbey before 1128 (LSC., p. 6). Lawrie (ESC., p. 328) suggests that "He may have been one of the king's household, whose duty it was to give orders to the steward at Perth." If he is the Vinget who attests with a + the charter by King Duncan ɪɪ to the monks of S. Cuthbert in 1094 and the Uniaet thwite of Eadgar's charter he must have been well advanced in age at the date of his last appearance.

UNSPAC. Unspac held a carucate of land in 1215 (*Cambus.*, p. 118). Dugal, son of Somerled, had a son called Ospac, and we have also the Gaelic patronymic Macusbaic, q.v. The name is Norse *Úspakr*, more commonly *Óspakr*, and is an adjective meaning a "disturber of the peace," one who is "violent in his conduct" (Fritzner, *Ordbog over det gamle norske Sprog*). The name of Raoul fils d'Unspac is engraved on the marble tablet at Dive in Normandy as one of the 449 persons of more or less importance who accompanied William the Conqueror to England (Mackerlie, *Galloway*, p. 320).

UNTHANK. This surname appears to have been not uncommon in the fifteenth and sixteenth centuries. Morice Unthanke of the county of Lanark took the oath of fealty in 1296 (*Bain*, ɪɪ, p. 208). James Vnthank was a witness in Edinburgh, c. 1426 (*Egidii*, p. 49), and John Vnthank was juror on an inquisition held in the same burgh two years later (RAA., ɪɪ, 61). Thomas Unthank, clerk and notary public in St. Andrews diocese, appears several times in record between 1462 and 1471 (*Laing*, 148; RMS., ɪɪ, 771, 783, etc.; *Neubotle*, 298–302). Katerina Unthank was spouse of Walter Beltmakare, burgess of Edinburgh, in 1477 (RMS., ɪɪ, 1308). The later Unthanks may derive their name from the small estate of the name on the left bank of the Rule Water, but the first derived from Unthank in Lanarkshire. A worthy Scot of this name was a hotelkeeper in Paris during the Commune in 1871.

UORET. A Pictish name found on the eighth-century sculptured monument at St. Vigeans in Angus (Nicholson, KR., pl. opp. p. 74). It appears also as the name of a Pictish king (c. 839–841) misspelled in the chronicles *Urad, Uurad, Uuroid, Wrad, Wroid, Fereth,* etc. (CPS.). We have probably another form of the name in *Forat*, with whose sons S. Patrick had dealings in Múscraige Tíre (*Vit. Trip.*, p. 210, 351). Cf. also Breton *Uuoret* (*Loth*, p. 179), explained as meaning 'helper.' The root still survives in Gaelic *fòir*, 'help.'

UPSETLINGTON. From the old lands of the name in Berwickshire, now included in the parish of Ladykirk. Robert de Upsetelintun witnessed a charter by Malcolm, son of Duncan, earl of Fife, to the nuns of North Berwick, a. 1199 (CMN., 9; SHSM., ɪv, p. 309). Upsetlington, 'the Kirk of Steel,' was what is now the parish church of Ladykirk. The place name Steil is probably the contracted form of Upsetlington.

URCHILL. James Urquchill alias Galloch in Rotmell, 1690 (*Dunkeld*), doubtless derived his surname from the small place named Urchill or Urquhill in Perth (*Retours*, 350, 936).

URE. Shortened from (Mac)ure, q.v. Dr. Andrew Ure (1787–1857), a distinguished chemist, was born in Glasgow. As forename (for Iver) we have Ure and Urie Campbell of Strachur, 1545 (HP., ɪv, p. 29).

URGEIST. Urgeist or Wurgest, as it is written in an earlier list of the Pictish kings (CPS., p. 5, 324), is the British equivalent of Fergus, q.v. The old Breton, *Uuorgost*, is found in the chartulary of Redon.

URIE. Adam Urri appears as burgess of Irvine in 1260 (*Irvine*, I, p. 5), and Huwe Urry of Ayrshire rendered homage, 1296 (*Bain*, II, p. 210). Reginald Urry held land in Irvine in 1323 (*Irvine*, I, p. 123), William Urri resigned the lands of Fulton in 1409 (RMP., p. 56), and John Vrry purchased a tenement in Glasgow, 1418 (LCD., p. 239). Thomas Urie, maltman, burgess of Glasgow, 1620 (*Burgesses*), is probably Thomas Urie, polentarius, burgess there in 1643 (*Inquis.*, 2819). The above group of entries point to a place of the name as their origin although they are all without 'de.' (2) The following may have derived their surname from Urie in Fetteresso parish, Kincardineshire. Hugh de Urre who swore fealty at St. John of Perth and again (?) as Hugh Urry at Forfar, 1296 (*Bain*, II, p. 178). Duncan Urry or Urri, Scots prisoner of war taken at Dunbar, incarcerated in Gloucester Castle, 1297, escaped in 1302/3 (ibid., 742, 938, 1399). Hugh or Hugo Vrry, burgess of Stirling, was ordered to replace the cruives (wattled hedges built on tidal flats for catching fish) of the abbot of Cambuskenneth which he and his accomplices had destroyed in 1366 (APS., I, p. 527; *Cambus.*, 54), and Gilbert Vrry held the land of Forglen, 1387 (RAA., II, 39). Urrie 1454, Vrrie 1597, Wrre 1530. See HURRAY.

URMSTON. A surname of recent introduction from England. Of local origin from Urmston, Lancashire. Urm is a form of Ōrm, the name therefore being = ORMISTON.

URQUHART. The vernacular pronunciation is 'Orchar.' From the old barony of Urquhart on Loch Ness, Inverness-shire. From their position in the midst of clans the Urquharts, a territorial family, came themselves to be ranked as a clan. The early history of the family is obscure, but they are known to have held hereditarily the sheriffdom of Cromarty. William de Urchard was the first known sheriff. Adam Urquhart had a grant of the sheriffdom of Crombathie in 1358 from David II (RMS., I, App. II, 1254). Alexander of Hurchart petitioned in 1381 for a canonry of Dunkeld notwithstanding that he held canonries and prebends in Moray and Ross (*Pap. Pet.*, I, p. 561). The father of Charles Urquhart (1669–1734), the Aberdeen Jesuit, appears in the records of his order as Urcart and Hurcar, and in his necrology as Urgart (Becker, *Bibliographie de la Compagnie de Jésus*, 1898, VII, p. 350). Sir Thomas Urquhart (1611–1660), translator of Rabelais (1653), and David Urquhart (1805–1877), diplomat and political writer, are the best known bearers of the name. Urcharde 1455, Urchart 1512,

Urqurt 1603, Urwhart 1660, Vrquhartt 1540, Vrquhat 1544, Wrchquhard 1520, Wrghard 1410, Wrquhart 1567, Wrwhart 1662; Vrqrt.

URR. From Urr in Galloway. Hugh de Hur was one of an assize on the marches of the Grange of Kircwynni and the land of Culwen in Galloway in 1289 (*Holm-Cultram*, p. 88). Hugo of Hurr appears as witness to a charter by the Kirkconnel family to Kirkgunzeon, and the name of Thomas, his son, is appended to another. Huwe de Urre or de Orre of Dumfriesshire rendered homage, 1296. His seal bears a boar's head couped contourné, S' Hvgonis d'Hvr (*Bain*, II, p. 183, 203, 531). Hugh de Ur was one of the jurors on an inquest commanding inquiry as to the privileges claimed by Robert de Brus, earl of Carrick, 1304 (*Bain*, II, p. 412). Francis Wr was burgess of Edinburgh, 1557 (*Laing*, 676), and Alexander Ur was in Orkney, 1576 (RPC., II, p. 737). Thomas Wr was declared heir of William Wr, mercator, "infra patrias de Courland et Cenngall," 1600 (*Inquis.*, 47). Bessie Ur in the parish of Linton was tried for witchcraft, 1629 (RPC., 2. ser. III, p. 170).

URRALL. Grissall Urrall in Elgin accused of being a witch, 1622 (*Rec. Elgin*, II, p. 171).

USHER. From the office of 'doorkeeper,' ME. *uschere*<OF. *ussier*. The office of the usher was to keep the door of the king's apartment, and in addition he was required to know the rank and precedence of all sorts of men, how they should be grouped at table, and many other matters. Thomas the Usser mentioned in 1291 (APS., I, p. 112) is referred to in the following year as Thomas the Doorward. Thomas dictus le Ussher or le Usser of Angusshire rendered homage, 1296 (RR.). Williel-mus Usser witnessed a charter at Lamberton, c. 1332 (BNCH., XVI, p. 330), William Ussere 'dominus tertie partis de Estirbalmatuthill' in 1401 (CAB., p. 392), and John Uschar, burgess of Peebles, 1448 (*Peebles*, 14). Husher 1296, Uscher 1660, Ushear 1624, Vschair and Vscher 1567. Cf. DORWARD.

USUFRUCTUAR. "George Usufructuar of Dunfermling to remain in ward within the place of Dury," 1571 (RHM., I, p. 69). A usufructuary was one who held property for use by usufruct, as a tenant.

UTTERSON. See under OUTERSON.

UTTERSTON. A surname recorded in Edinburgh may be of local origin from Outerston near Gorebridge, Midlothian, locally pronounced Ootersun, but it is more probably a variant of OUTERSON, q.v., as -*son* and -*ton* are often interchangeable. Alison Utirstoune is recorded in East Restoune, 1670 (*Lauder*), and Gavin Utterstone in Nether Stitchill, 1677 (*Stitchill*, p. 79).

UTTING. A long forgotten personal name, from OE. *Utting*, i.e. "Utta's son." A man named Utting may have given name to It-tingston near Huntly, Aberdeenshire, in 1534 Uttinstoun. A charter of 1277 was witnessed by Alan, son of Huting, seneschal of Buchan (Macdonald, *Place names of west Aberdeen-shire*, s. v.). Hutting, "marescallus" of the bishop of Moray, witnessed a charter by the bishop confirming the gift of the church of Deveth to the church of the Holy Trinity of Spyny, c. 1202–24 (REM., p. 61). Utting Cachepol held a toft in the vill of Inver-bervyn, now Bervie, c. 1232–37 (LAC., p. 21). "Cachepol" refers to Utting's office, "catch-poll," i.e. bailiff. Vtting the smith of Stirling was a charter witness, c. 1275 (*Inchaffray*, p. 97). William, son of Utting, possessed a tenement in Drumelzier, c. 1300–20 (*Hay*, p. 7), and Robert Vtting appears as witness in a court held at the standing stones of Rayne in the Garioch in 1349 (REA., I, p. 80). Andrew Vtyn was tenant in Grange of Kerse, 1466 (*Cupar-Angus*, I, p. 154). The last record of the name appears to be in 1647, in which year a protection from writ of exe-cution for debts of William Vtting, skipper, burgess of Anstruther, was granted to his widow and children in consequence of his ship hav-ing been taken by one of the king's frigates, and of his having been killed at Kilsyth (APS., VI, pt. I, p. 819).

VAIL. Curtailed from (MAC)VAIL, q.v.

VAIR. Thomas Vair, tenant near Melrose, 1564 (RRM., III, p. 148). Jhone Vaire recorded in Eildoun, 1606 and Thomas Vair, smith in New-ton Mill, 1658 (ibid., p. 8, 183). The name is also recorded in Stitchill, 1656 (*Stitchill*, p. 8). James Vair was merchant in Dumfries, 1741 (*Dumfries*), and another James Vair was merchant in Melrose, 1805 (*Heirs*, 532). Lower says probably the same as Vere, from the parish and chateau of Ver in canton of Guvray, La Manche, Normandy.

VALE. The Northumberland family of Delaval took their name from the Castle of La Val in the Lower Marne Valley (*Mawer*, p. 173). About 1190 Gilbert de la Val witnessed a charter by William de Hauekeristone of cer-tain lands in the territory of Innerwick to the Abbey of Kelso (*Kelso*, 250). About thirty years later the same or a succeeding Gilbert de Lauelle witnessed a charter by Robert de Schottun to the same abbey (ibid., 336). A third Gilbert de Laual, c. 1280 witnessed a

confirmation charter by Walter de Bolbech "quoddam heremitorium quod vocatur Mer-chingleie" (ibid., 265). William de la vale was chancellor and chamberlain of Berwick-on-Tweed, 1364 (*Bain*, III, 105).

VALENTINE, VALLANTINE, VALLENTINE. This Latin name comes from *valens*, the parti-ciple of *valeo*, "to be strong, healthy." Valen-tinian was the name of several Roman em-perors. The Valentines of Fettercairn are said to be descended from Valentine of Thornton, who in the reign of Robert I had a charter of the lands of Thorntoun "in lie Kincardin-Mernes" (RMS., I, App. II, 18). They were "till of late numerous and influential in the parish, but so few are now left that ere long the name will become extinct" (Cameron, *History of Fettercairn*, p. 226). William Valen-tine had a safe conduct into England in 1424 (*Bain*, IV, 970), Thomas Vallantyne, feuar of Drumbov, 1561 (*Rent. Dunk.*, p. 341), and John Wallentyne was admitted burgess of Aberdeen in 1593 (NSCM., I, p. 84). Vallentein 1650, Wallentine 1679. In the form Weland, Wiland, or Wyland, it was a fore-name among the northern Chisholms.

VALLANCE. From one of several places so named in Normandy. The family was prom-inent in Scotland at an early period. Mac-farlane calls them Valouns, Wallouns, or Wal-loun, "now commonly called Vollum and long ago Valence" (II, p. 128–129). Roger, young-est son of Roger of England, came to Scotland and received the lands of Kilbride, which by his daughter and heiress was carried to the Cumins (*Panmure*, I, p. xviii). Philip de Valoniis, the fifth son of Roger of England, also came to Scotland in the time of Malcolm IV, and had from William the Lion a grant of the baronies of Panmure and Bervie (ibid., I, p. xix). In 1174 he was one of the hostages for the observance by William the Lion of the Convention of Falaise (*Lawrie*, p. 174), and was witness to many charters of that king to the abbeys of Kelso, Neubotle, Arbroath, etc. He also held the high office of Camerarius Regis, and died in November, 1215. He was succeeded by his son, William de Wallonis, who witnessed a charter by Malcolm, earl of Fife, 1217 (PSAS., LX, p. 71), and died in 1219 leaving an heiress, Christina de Va-loniis, who married Sir Peter de Maule and carried the baronies to the Maules. Symon Walense was rector of the church of Kyn-spinidi, 1269 (RPSA., p. 174), William de Valoynes of Fife rendered homage, 1296 (*Bain*, II, p. 209), and John, son of Andrew de Valons, was one of the hostages for the ransom of David II in 1357 (APS., I, p. 519). Andrew

792

VALLANCE, *continued*

Valance was bailie of Edinburgh, 1392 (*Egidii*, p. 28). James of Wallance, lord of Inchegalle, 1393 (*Pitfirrane*, 8), may be Jacobus de Valance who witnessed a charter in Fife, 1395 (*Wemyss*, II, 32), Robert Valence held land in Aberdeen, 1451 (REA., II, p. 297), and John Valency was tenant of the bishop of Aberdeen, 1511 (ibid., I, p. 371). William Wallange was member of the Skinner's Craft in Edinburgh, 1533 (*Colston*, p. 81), James Vallance of Postle was overseer for the election of magistrates for Stranraer, 1689 (APS., IX, p. 51), and Luke Vallange was bailie of Biggar, 1718 (*Minutes*, p. 187). Valandis 1439, Valens 1681, Vallandge 1662, Vallange 1682, Valleng 1640, Walinch 1512, Wallanche and Wallenche 1567, Wallance and Wallenis 1686, Wallang 1569, Wallange 1605, Wallangis 1519, Wallence 1567.

VANNAN. Thomas Vannand occupied lands in Angus, 1505 (RAA., II, 441), and Andrew Vannand had a tack of three bovates of *lie* Maynis de Dolor, c. 1570 (RD., p. 486). Robert Vannane, burgess of Edinburgh, was retoured heir of his father, Henry Vannane, 1633 (*Retours, Edinburgh*, 715). Recorded as Vannam in Boness, 1816. Not likely to be from Gaelic *(Mac)Mhannain*.

VANS. An early corruption of VAUS, q.v., due to the simple error of reading *u* as *n*. Robert the Vanss was directed to retour the rents of barons in Wigtownshire, 1467 (APS., II, p. 91). Vance (in Stranraer) 1770. There is (or was) an old family of Vans of Barnbarroch, Wigtownshire. The first of the family was a nephew of William de Vaus of Dirleton who married the heiress of Barnbarroch, c. 1384 (*Agnew*, I, p. 225), but others of the name appear to have had possessions there at an earlier date as witness a pardon granted at the request of Duncan MacDuel to Elvas de Vaus for homicide in 1307 (*Bain*, II, 1919).

VASSAND. From the old lands of Vassand in the parish of St. Andrews, Orkney. Jhone Vassand testified in a sheriff-court trial held in St. Androuis Kirk in Tankirnes in 1559 (REO., p. 111), and in 1596 Thomas Wassene was charged with planning to evade payment of his debts (ibid., p. 172).

VASSYR. A shortened form of VAVASOUR (an under vassal having other vassals under him). John Vazour was a member of the Guild of Ayr, c. 1431 (*Coll. AGAA.*, I, p. 228). Robert Vassyr in Edinburgh, 1482 (CDE., 52).

VAUGHAN. Patrick Vaughan was a bookbinder in Aberdeen, 1673 (*Edin. App.*). From Welsh *Vychan*, a mutation of *bychan*, little,

small. A personal name of considerable antiquity in Wales.

VAUS, VAUSS, VASS, WAUS, WAUSS. From Vaux, a common French place name meaning 'the dales' or 'vallies' (Fr. *vaux*, pl. of *val*, in early Latin charters de *Vallibus*). In 1199 King John of England confirmed to the Abbey of St. Jean de Falaise the "terram et feodum de Vallibus" in Normandy. The family of Vaus was settled at Lanercost in Cumberland, and were also in possession of Ashill, Seavington, and Seaborough at the close of the twelfth century (Bates, *Chartularies of Muchelney and Athelney, Somerset*, London, 1899, p. 79). Wyntoun (v, p. 53) refers to Robertus de Vallibus, lord of Gillesland (A. D. 1210), an individual who fills a large space in legend and history, as

"a wickyt man
callit Robert of þe Dalis."

A branch of the English family settled in Scotland in the twelfth century and became proprietors of the lands and barony of Dirleton in East Lothian. Little is known, however, of the early history of the family though its members possessed Dirleton for more than two hundred years. John de Vallibus who witnessed a charter by Malcolm IV (LSC., 26) is probably J. de Wall[ibus] who witnessed the grant by William the Lion of a carucate of Hedenham (Ednam) to the Abbey of Kelso, c. 1174–78 (*Kelso*, p. 302), and the Johannes de Vans (i.e. Vaus), one of the hostages for the ransom of the king in 1174 (*Annals*, p. 194). Johannes de Vaus or de Vallibus witnessed a charter of the churches of Moffet, etc., to the bishop of Glasgow, c. 1187 (REG., p. 64), and the gift of Herol (Errol) to William de Haia before 1214 (SCM., II, p. 303). In the reign of William the Lion, William de Vas attested a charter by Eschina domina de Molle (RMP., p. 75), and between 1189–99 Everard de Vallibus witnessed a charter by Robert de London (SCM., IV, p. 243). John de Vallibus, sheriff of Edinburgh between 1214–30 (*Neubotle*, p. 67), is probably John de Vallibus who appears as charter witness in the chartularies of Kelso, Neubotle, Cambuskenneth, and Levenax, and the John de Vallibus who gifted a croft in Golyn (Gullane) to the church of St. Andrew of Golyn and the canons of Driburcht there. William de Wallibus, 'persona ecclesiae de Congilton,' made a gift to the same church (*Dryburgh*, p. 20, 22, 23). About 1220 William de Vallibus, lord of Dirleton, gave the island of Elbotle (as Fidra was then called) to the Abbey of Dryburgh, and in 1240 Alexander de Vallibus "considerans immenentia pericula temporum quam presentium quam futurorum" released the Abbey from the obligation of maintaining a chantry on the island (*Dryburgh*). John de Vaus who was present in the convention at Briggeham (Birgham) in 1289 (APS., I, p. 441) is doubtless Sir John de Vaus of Edinburghshire who rendered homage in 1296 and had his lands restored to him for his good conduct in the following year (*Bain*, II, p. 198, 244). His seal shows a bend between two cinquefoils, *S' Ioh'is de Valibus* (*Macdonald*, 2814). The name travelled early to the north, where we find Willelmus Vaws juror on an inquest concerning the episcopal lands of Aldrochty in 1393 (REM., p. 205). The name was also long and honorably connected with Inverness, appearing there for the first time in 1440 (*Invernessiana*, p. 110). It is also an old surname in Aberdeen. Andrew Vase was burgess there in 1410 (REA., II, p. 294), and John Waus, alderman in 1430 (RMS., II, 156). Robert of Vaus was master of the ship *Nicholas of Aberdene*, 1433 (*Bain*, IV, 1061), and John the Vauss was 'familiar til my lord of Aberdene,' 1476 (SCM., V, p. 25). In Orkney the surname appears in the first half of the sixteenth century as Vas, Vaus, Wais, Was, and Wass (REO.). Walls 1445, Wause 1429, Waux 1568. Tobar Alaidh Bhodhsa, 'Sandy Vass's Well,' is in the parish of Nigg, Ross.

VEDA. The Uecla (or Vecla) of the *Pictish Chronicle* (CPS., p. 6) should most probably be read as Ueda (Veda), the *d* having been confused with *cl*, due to the difficulty of distinguishing in an unfamiliar name between a tall *d* and *cl*. Veda occurs on the engraved tablet (c. 222–235 A. D.) found at Colchester, now in the British Museum, the last two lines of which read: *Donvm. Lossio. Veda. de. svo. posvit. nepos. Vepogeni. Caledo*, "This offering has been made at his own expense by Lossio Veda, a Caledonian, grandson of Vepogenos."

VEDAST. With Latin termination, *Vedastus*. A name adopted by ecclesiastics when they professed. The name comes from Vaast or Waast, in Latin Vedastus, the name of a bishop who died in 540. He was born near Limoges, and baptized Clovis the emperor. A life of him was written by Alcuin. Vedastus de Jeddeword held lands under the monks of Melrose in 1300 (*Melros*, p. 684), Vedastus Greresone is in record, 1466 (RMS., II, 907), Vedastus de Murhede was canon of Glasgow, 1476 (REG., 413), and Master Widast Lawsone was burgess of Aberdeen, 1634 (SCM., III, p. 118). Vedast Neilson is recorded in 1518. There is a church of S. Vedast in London.

VEITCH, VETCH. About 1200 Radulphus uacca witnessed a charter by Henry de Graham (*Neubotle*, 8). Alexander la uache who witnessed a charter of the church of Driuesdale between 1214–19 (REG., p. 126) is probably Dominus Alexander de (for le) Vacca, who witnessed a grant by Richard Germyn to the House of Soltre between 1235–58 (*Soltre*, p. 26). William le Wache of Peeblesshire rendered homage, 1296. His seal bears an arm holding a hawk (?), a cross moline in chief, *S' Willelmi Vache* (*Bain*, II, p. 207, 553). William de Vache witnessed a charter of the lands of Lintonrothirrik, c. 1316 (RHM., I, 19), and in 1331 William Veitch witnessed resignation of lands in the barony of Drumelzier (*Hay*, p. 9). The Veitches appear to have obtained Dawick in the fifteenth century, and William the Wache of Dawic appears as frequent suitor before the Lords of Council and Lords Auditors of Parliament between 1474 and 1494 (ALA., ALC.). William Vache of Dawic and William the Vaich and Walter the Vaich are referred to in 1473 and 1484 (*Peebles*, p. 20, 31). John Vache in Dalkeith was summoned before the Privy Council in 1566 (RPC., I, p. 444), and Dandie Vauche was tenant under the abbot of Kelso, 1567 (*Kelso*, p. 526). James Waitche, lawful son of Alexander Waitche of Hamilton, was heir of Andrew Waitche, portioner of Stewartoun, 1628 (*Inquis.*, 1426). Johannes Weatche, burgess of Edinburgh, 1645 (*Inquis. Tut.*, 692). Vaiche 1526, Vaitch 1621, Vaitche 1664, Veache 1629, Veatch 1665, Vetch 1655, Vetche 1627, Veitche 1624, Weatch 1624, Wesche 1561; Veatche, Veche, Waiche, Waitch, Weich, Weitch, Weitche. Harrison's derivation, "belonging to Viche, a common French place name," is most unlikely.

VELZIAN. From Velzian in Harray, Orkney. Stevvne Walzing in Harra, 1552 (REO., p. 248). John Velzian, assizeman, c. 1558–84, Andrew Awelgeing [*a* here = preposition 'at'], witness in Harray, 1571, and Thomas Wailvom on assize at Ireland, Orkney, 1595 (ibid., p. 403, 289, 170). Andrew Welzian on inquest, 1601, may be the Andrew Velzian recorded in Harray, 1631 (ibid., p. 174, 372). Velziam and Vilyean 1610, Walzean 1601, Velzeoun and Velzeone 1579.

VENNAL. From residence in a vennel (Sc. *vennal*, *vennel*<Fr. *venelle*, a small street). Walter dominus de Venali, burgess of Aberdeen, 1292 (*Panmure*, II, 1510). Geoffry de Venali, also of Aberdeen, swore fealty in 1296. His seal bears device a lion rampant, fighting with a horned dragon, both erect, *S' Galfridi de Wenali* (*Bain*, II, p. 181). Symone de Venella appears as charter witness in Perth, 1365 (RMS., I, 196).

VENNISON. The tombstone of John Vennison is in St. Andrews, dated 1654. He was deacon of the Fleshers' Incorporation, and was "fama et integritate vitae" (PSAS., xlv, p. 523; lxx, p. 51).

VENTERS. Current in Fife. Harrison says it is a weak form, "owing to the stress having fallen back to the first syllable of the Norman (Orne) place name La Ventrouse," as was suggested by Lower. Weekley says Venters, Ventress, and Ventris are for 'venturous.' Bardsley finds no trace of this surname in the early rolls, and suggests it is of later and foreign importation. His earliest example is 1586.

VERNER. John Verner was burgess of Edinburgh, 1428 (RAA., ii, 61). William Vernour claimed land in Edinburgh as heir of his brother John Vernour, 1478 (Stodart, ii, p. 376). Thomas Vernour or Vernor of Auchindinny was charged in 1529 with engaging in feud (Trials, i, p. 143 *). Thomas Verner of Auchindinie, who died April, 1618, and Gavin Verner, who died in 1647, are both interred in Glencorse churchyard (Grant, Call of the Pentlands, p. 100). David Vernor is recorded in Divansyde, parish of Carmichael, 1685 (Lanark CR.), Andrew Vernor was merchant in Edinburgh, 1674 (Inquis., 5775), and John Vernor, merchant in Glasgow, 1690 (ibid., 7015). Harrison says a French form of O. Teutonic personal name Warenheri.

VERNON. A rare surname in Scotland, and most probably of late introduction from south of the Border. The name is territorial probably from Vernon ("place of alders") in the arrondissement of Evreux. There are, however, sixty-four places so named in France. Edward Vernon, surveyor at Drumlanrig, Dumfriesshire, 1742.

VERT. Hew Verth, mealmaker in Edinburgh, 1642, and James Vert, merchant there, 1683 (Edinb. Marr.). Patrick Vert was indweller in Leith, 1686 (Edin. App.). The wife of William Verth died in Leith, 1940. Harrison says the name is from (Le) Vert, a common French place name.

VERTY. Thomas Verty witnessed an instrument of sasine of land of Dun, in Angus, 1473 (SCM., iv, p. 9), and William Verty was admitted burgess of Aberdeen, 1485 (NSCM., i, p. 31; CRA., p. 44). Henrie Virtie or Vertie in Kingorne was accused of uttering malicious speeches in 1645 (PBK., pp. 280–281), and Andrew Vertie was feuar in Duns, Berwickshire, 1689 (Lauder). Alexander Vertue, showmaker (shoemaker) in Polwarth, 1758.

VESSIE. Originally de Vesci, from Vessey in Manche, Normandy. Eustace de Vesci founded the chapel of S. Leonards for the soul of Malcolm iv (Newcastle volume of Archaeological Institute, ii, p. 116). Willelmus de Vesci witnessed the charter by Robert, bishop of St. Andrews, granting the church of Lohworuora to the bishop of Glasgow (REG., 11), and appears in other charters towards the end of King David's reign (Lawrie, p. 430). Eustace de Vesci granted to Walter Maner two oxgangs of land in Lium (Lyham), c. 1207 (Laing, 4), and was slain by an arrow when reconnoitering Bernard Castle in company with King Alexander ii in 1216. Willelmus de Vescy witnessed a confirmation charter of the church of Buthelny to Aberbrothoc, 1221 (RAA., i, p. 93). Jhon Wessy was tenant in Castaris (= Carstairs), Lanarkshire, 1525 (Rental). Agnes Vessie in Westscheill, parish of Carnwath, 1629 (Lanark CR.). William Vessie, burgess of Lanark, 1636 (ibid.), and Marion Vessie in Edinburgh, 1647 (Edinb. Marr.).

VETCH. See under VEITCH.

VICARSON. 'Son of the vicar.' Perhaps an Englishing of MACVICAR, q.v. Alexander Vicarson witnessed seisin of certain lands in the parish of Rogart, Sutherlandshire, in 1529 (OPS., ii, p. 674). William Vicarson was tenant in Dawchcarne, Kynnarde, in 1539 (ER., xvii, p. 671).

VICARY. Recorded in Fife. From ME. vicarie, vicary, an early form of vicar.

> "'Sir preest,' qued he, 'artow a vicary?
> Or art a person? sey sooth, by thy fey.'"
>
> Chaucer, The Parson's Prologue, 11.22–23.

VICCIE. James Victie or de Viccie, persone del eglise de Edeuyn (= Idvies), in Angus, rendered homage, 1296 (Bain, ii, p. 211; RR.).

VICKERMAN. The 'vicar's man' or servant. Recorded in Dumfries. Bardsley says the name is found early in Yorkshire, where it is still common.

VICKERS. Nicholas Vigrus was stewart of Tynemouth, c. 1295 (Laing, 17), Richard Vigrous, burgess of Roxburgh, rendered homage, 1296 (Bain, ii, p. 197), and Hugh de le Vikeres had grant of lands and burgages within the vill of Roxburgh, Kerton, etc. from Robert i, c. 1315 (RMS., i, App. ii, 128). Thomas de Vigurws, burgess of Roxburgh, c. 1338, son and heir of umquhile Agnes called Maunsell, is referred to in same year as Thomas dictus Vigurus (Dryburgh, p. 260, 261, 264; BNCH., xxiv, p. 226). He granted a burgage in the town of Roxburgh to Sir William de

Feltoun, sheriff of Roxburgh, c. 1338 (*Dryburgh*, 313). Nothing more is known of this Thomas. He may have given name to Vigurus or Vigrous Flat. Lands called Vigorushalch in the sheriffdom of Roxburgh are mentioned in 1503 (HMC., xii, pt. 8, p. 178), in 1611 Vigoroushauche (*Retours, Roxburgh*, 67). William del Vikers was juror on an inquest at Roxburgh, 1361 (*Bain*, iv, 62). In 1399 the abbot of Kelso granted to Thomas de Vicaria and his heirs a tenement in Westerkelsow, temporarily held by John de Bolden (*Kelso*, p. 412). Willelmus de Vicar' appears as armiger in Kelso, 1396 (REA., ii, p. 292), and James Viccars of Pethhead, parish of Lesmahago, in record, 1662 (*Lanark CR.*).

VINE. William Vyne was elected bailie of Aberdeen, 1509 (*Guildry*, p. 193). Vine is an old surname of local origin in Dorset and in Sussex.

VINT. *See under* WINT.

VIOLER. A player on the viol, a violist. Warinus le Violer rendered homage at Berwick, 1291 (RR.).

VIPOIG. This name, found in the Pictish Chronicle (CPS., p. 6) as the name of one of the early Pictish kings, is a curtailed form of *Vepogenos*, a name which occurs in the genitive in the Colchester tablet already referred to under Veda as *Vepogeni*. The *Vep. Corf*, i.e. *Vep. Cor. F*. of early British coins found in Yorkshire (Evans, *Coins of the ancient Britons*, p. 411–413) might be for *Vep(ogenus) Cor(otici) F(ilius)*. The full name appears to mean 'Raven's offspring.'

VIPONT, Vipond. There are several places in Normandy called Vieupont or Vieuxpont, and the great Anglo-Norman family so designated came from Vipont near Lisieux (*Sussex Archaeological Collections*, ii, p. 77). The name is Latinized *de Veteri Ponte* = "of the old bridge." The Scottish Viponts are descended from William de Ueupunt or Veteri Ponte who gave the church of Horueresdene to the Abbey of Kelso, c. 1165 (*Kelso*, p. 321), and also witnessed a charter by William the Lion, c. 1165–77 (RMP., p. 76). About 1160 as William de Vyerpunt he granted the "eschalingas in Lambremore" to the church of S. Marie of Kelso, a gift witnessed by Fulcone de Vyerpüt (*Kelso*, p. 257). The Veteri Pontes also held the lands of Carriden for some generations, and about the year 1200 W. de Veteri Ponte, first born of the three sons of W. de Veteri Ponte and Emma de Sancto Hylario, as he describes himself in the charter, granted to the Abbey of Holyrood a tithe of his coal

of Kareddin (Carriden) and a tithe of the profits of all ships and boats loading or unloading in his land of Blackenis (Blackness) (LSC., p. 33). Ivo de Veteri Ponte, probably one of the sons mentioned above, gifted the church of S. Foylan "de majore Sowrby" (Sorbie in Wigtownshire) to the Abbey of Dryburgh, c. 1200 (*Dryburgh*, 56). Between 1238 and 1270 Nicholas de Veteri Ponte and his spouse Anabella made a gift of Swaynyston (Swanston) to the Hospital of Soltre which was witnessed by William de Veteri Ponte, dominus de Boulton (*Soltre*, p. 27–28). Dominus Henricus de Veteri Ponte witnessed a charter by Malcolm, 4th earl of Levenax, c. 1285 (*Levenax*, p. 87), and in 1292 Robert de Veteri Ponte renounced the homage which he had done to Alexander iii for the lands of Aldeneston (APS., i, p. 116). Nicol de Veupount of Tyndale (Tynda3), Aline de Veepount and Robert de Weepunt, both of Edinburghshire, rendered homage in 1296 (*Bain*, ii, 816, and p. 201, 203, 213). Peronel de Veupont of Berwickshire also rendered homage. His seal bears two lozenges in pale, S' *Petronille de Veteriponte* (ibid., ii, p. 208, 554). William de Veteri-ponte witnessed grant of the office of sheriff of Clackmannan to Malcolm, earl of Levenax, in 1309 (*Levenax*, p. 2). Barbour describes Sir William de Vepont, the sixth baron, as one of the "two worthy knights" slain on the Scottish side at Bannockburn. On his death the estates passed into the family of Cockburn by the marriage of his only child Mariota to Sir Alexander de Cokburn (*Cockburn*, p. 34). Willelmus Wypponde was bailie in Buchan, c. 1364 (REA., i, p. 107). The Viponts were among the earliest known landowners in Fife. The refrain of an old song sung by fishermen there runs:

"The leal guidman of Aberdour
Sits in Sir Alan Vipont's chair."

The surname is now almost extinct in Scotland, but it is interesting to note that so late as 1904 the Rev. David Avenel Vipont was selected as successor to Rev. Jacob Primmer in Townhill Established Church, Dunfermline. Vvpunt 1296, Wypownt and Wippunde (in Wyntoun). Alan de Vvpont held the castle of Lochleven in 1333 (*Hailes*, ii, p. 206, 217).

VOCAT. William Vocat, a Scots prisoner of war, was released from Colchester prison, 1396 (*Bain*, iv, 483). Alexander Voket and Johannes Voket appear in Aberdeen, 1408 (CWA., p. 312, 316), Ravny Voket was admitted burgess of the burgh in 1409 and Alexander Voket in 1436 (NSCM., i, p. 3, 4). John Vocat (Voket or Woket), burgess and bailie of Aberdeen, appears several times in record between

VOCAT, *continued*

1435 and 1462 (CAB., p. 393; SCM., v, p. 22, 41; *Illus.*, III, p. 272; CRA., p. 17). He may be the John Vooute, Aberdeen merchant, who had a safe conduct into England in 1438 (*Bain*, IV, 1114). William Voket, merchant of Aberdeen, had a safe conduct into England for two years in 1438 (ibid., 1118), and Andrew Voket, merchant of the same burgh, petitioned for restoration of his goods taken at sea by the English in the same year (ibid., 1115). William Wokete was one of an assize in Aberdeen, 1463 (CRA., p. 26), David Vocat was master of the Grammar School of Edinburgh, 1516 (*Soltre*, p. 264), and Walter Vocat was a notary public in Botary, 1633 (*Strathbogie*, p. 6). The name is now extinct in Aberdeen. Vocate 1442.

VOGAN. John Vogane in Fuchhill, 1657 (RRM., I, p. 140). John Vogane, merchant in Selkirk, 1689 (RPC., 3. ser. XIV, p. 294). Lower has this name, from "a tything in the parish of Chippenham, co. Wilts."

VOLLAR. A surname recorded in Aberdeen, of recent introduction from England. It is a form of Vowler, the English west country pronunciation of FOWLER, q.v.

VOLUME. An early corruption of VALLANCE, q.v., through the forms Velham and Welham. John de Velham was on an assize at Brechin, 1364, and in the fourth year of the reign of Robert II John de Welhame resigned lands in the thanage of Alythe into the king's hands (RMS., I, 610). John de Velham was witness in Brechin, 1448 (REB., I, 117), George Wellem was owner of Woodwrae near Brechin, 1454, and in 1453 and 1509 we have mention of the land of Alexander Vellem in Forfar (RAA., II, 101, 486). Alexander Wellem of Wodwray had a remission for treason committed by him, 1502 (*Trials*, I, p. 103 *). Alexander Wellam de Wodura (Woodwrae) appears as witness, 1519 (*Panmure*, II, 292), and in 1527 had a remission granted him (RSS., I, 3658). He may be the Alexander Wallein (Vallene or Vallance) of Woodwra who served on an assize in 1549 (*Trials*, III, p. 347 *). "James Vallem and George Vallem sonis to Dauid Vallem of Woodwrae" were hanged for stouthreif, etc., 1602 (*Trials*, II, p. 385). The family appears to have fallen into a state of indigence, for in 1630 and again in 1638 the Brechin Session Records show that "Alexr. Wellom, sometyme of Woodurae" received charity from that body. The list of "Rebels" for 1745 contains the names of James Volume, surgeon, Peterhead. Thomas Volume at Bowence, Cruden, and of Thomas

Volumn, servant. The surname is now better known in Buchan than it is in Angus (*Jervise*, I, p. 374): Vellem 1544, Vollom and Volume 1689, Volome 1680, Volum 1732, Wellom and Wolum 1636.

VURIST. Abridged from MACVURISH, q.v. John Vurist in Inverness, 1604 (*Rec. Inv.*, II, p. 23).

WADDEL, WADDELL, WADDLE, WEDDEL, WEDDELL, WEDDLE, WODDELL. From Wedale, the old name of the parish of Stow in Midlothian. The earliest known bearer of the name is Adam de Wedale, "an outlaw of the King of Scots land," who appears in 1204 (*Bain*, I, 342). Stephen de Wedale witnessed a charter of the lands of Swaynystoun to the Hospital of Soltre, c. 1221–24 (*Soltre*, 23), and Thomas de Wedal was canon of St. Andrews, 1280 (*Pap. Lett.*, I, p. 462). Laurence de Wedale of Roxburghshire rendered homage in 1296. His seal bears an eight-rayed figure and S' *Lavrenci d' Vedal* (*Bain*, II, p. 210, 555). Symone de Wedale, abbot of Holyrood, Edinburgh, between 1296–1327 (*Soltre*, p. 42), as Symon de Wedehale was consecrated bishop of Galloway in 1327 (*Dowden*, p. 361). Adam de Wedale, monk of Newbotyl, was witness in proceedings against the Knights Templars in 1309 (Wilkins, *Concilia*, II, p. 382), and Roger de Wedale was canon of Dunblane, 1312 (*Pap. Lett.*, II, p. 102), and in 1321 prebendary of Murthlach (REA., I, p. 47). Provision was made for Thomas de Vedayle of the diocese of St. Andrews, 1344 (*Pap. Pet.*, I, p. 80), William Waldale was juror on inquisition at Muskylburg, 1359 (RD., p. 267), and Thomas of Wedale was one of an inquest at Berwick-on-Tweed, 1370 (*Bain*, IV, 175). Sir Thomas of Wedalle, knight of Scotland, had a writ of passage at the Port of London, 1372 (ibid., IV, 194), Henricus de Wedale was a cleric of the diocese of St. Andrews, 1395 (RPSA., p. 5), and Robert Wedalle, esquire of Scotland, had permission to travel in England, 1405 (*Bain*, IV, 695). Henry of Wedale or Wedhale had a safe conduct into England, 1400–01 (ibid., 570, 584), and Robert of Wedal the same in 1424 (ibid., 970). Robert of Wedale, notary public in Perth, 1421 (*Athole*, p. 706), Thomas Wadel of Blakchester witnessed a retour of special service, 1505 (*Home*, 29), and Thomas Vadle, merchant in Edinburgh, 1555 (*Guildry*, p. 120), mav be the Thomas Vedell mentioned in 1557 (CMN., 74). Robert Veddell in Kelso, 1567 (*Kelso*, p. 525), George Vodell in Kirriemuir, 1610 (*Laing*, 1583), Mungo Woddell admitted burgess of Glasgow, 1613 (*Burgesses*), George Woddell, burgess of Jedburgh, 1672 (*Heirs*, 94), Mr. Richard Waddle, parson of Glasgow, 1682 (RUG., III,

p. 394), and William Waddale, residenter in Forres, 1793 (*Moray*). Alexander Weddell, pewtherer, was burgess of Edinburgh, 1725 (*Guildry*, p. 130). A family of Waddels were brewers at Liff for nearly two hundred years (*Jervise*, I, p. 192). Veddal 1515, Veddel 1604, Weddale 1453, Weddell 1525, Woddell 1598, Wooddell 1644, Wydall.

WADDIE, WADDY. Forms of WALDIE, q.v. James Waddie, charter witness in Edinburgh, 1543 (*Soltre*, p. 110). Thomas Watho was notary in Kelso, 1539 (*Laing*, 434), and John Waddo, tenant of the Almerie lands of the Abbey of Kelso, 1567, may be the John Vaddo, tenant on lands of the Abbey in the same year (*Kelso*, p. 529, 530). Elspeth Waddie in Lauder, 1633 (*Lauder*). Robert Wadie in Clashnettles, 1689 (*Edin. App.*).

WADRITHURT. Thomas de Wadrithurt witnessed a charter by Ingelramus de Balliol of the church of Inuerkeleder to the Abbey of Arbroath, p. 1180 (*RAA.*, I, p. 39).

WAFERER. From the occupation of wafercake maker, ME. *wafrere* or *wafrer*. William Wafrarius, formerly the king's sergeant, was juror on an inquest held concerning the lands of Padevinan in 1259 (*APS.*, I, p. 88; *Bain*, I, 2175). William le wafrer and Steven le wafrer of the county of Lanark rendered homage in 1296. The seal of the former bears an eight-rayed figure and S' *Will'i Vafrer* (ibid., II, p. 198, 545). In 1422 Murdoch, duke of Albany, granted to John Ker, burgess of Lanark, the lands called Wafralandis in the territory of the burgh of Lanark, by the tenure of baking certain wafers of bread for the king when he happened to reside at Lanark: "Faciendo domino nostro regi, et heredibus suis dictus Johannes et heredes sui pro dictis terris cum pertinenciis pistarum wafrarum dicti domini nostri regis quociens ipsium dominum regem apud Lanark contigerit residere" (*HMC.*, 5. Rep., App., p. 633).

WAGHORN. A West country surname, evidently of local origin, like Cleghorn, Dreghorn, Whithorn. Peter Waghorne de Dunbretane was one of those appointed to treat for the ransom of David II in 1357 (*Foedera*, III, p. 365). Finlaw Waghorne was declared innocent of part in detention of King James III in Edinburgh Castle, 1482 (*The Lennox*, II, p. 123). Michael Waghorne, witness in Glasgow, 1501 (*Simon*, 16) may be the Mychell Waghorn who contracted to cover the stalls of the queir of Glasgow in 1506 (*REG.*, p. 612). David Waghorne was owner of land in Glasgow, 1551 (*Protocols*, I). Usually explained as "hornblower or trumpeter," but?

WAINEFLET. Walter de Waineflet, a charter witness in Dundee, 1281 (HP., II, p. 223), derived his name from Wainfleet, a town in Lincolnshire, England. John de Wainflet rendered homage at Berwick, 1291 (RR.).

WAIRDS. John Wairds in Neathertoune, Swartaquoy, Orkney, 1687 (*Orkney*). There are places named Wairds in the Mearns and in West Lothian, and there are other places named Wards.

WAIT, WAITE. From the ME. *waite*, a watchman, sentinel, which again is from OF. *waite*, a guard. Adam Wayt, witness in Aberbrothoc, 1312 (*RAA.*, I, p. 289), and Thomas dictus Weyt, chaplain, Inverness, 1361 (*REM.*, p. 305). Huchown the Wate, tacksman in Grenyng and Bankis in Marwek, 1492 (*REO.*, p. 407). Thomas Waith was a witness in Kelso in 1505 (*Kelso*, 535). George Wait witnessed an instrument of sasine in 1525 (*Home*, 35), Robert Waitt is recorded in Stitchill in 1684 (*Stitchill*, p. 97), and George Waitt in Manderstoun in 1665 (*Lauder*).

WAKE. Johannes de Wak or Wake, miles, held the land of Kirkandris in the sheriffdom of Dumfries in the early years of the fourteenth century (RMS., I, 33, 91). The family took the English side in the war of independence and in consequence lost their lands of Kirkandrews and Breccalache after the battle of Bannockburn (ibid., 28, 33). Stephen Wake was burgess of Edinburgh, 1405 (*Egidii*, p. 41), and John Waik was presbyter of St. Andrews diocese, 1475 (*Kelso*, 532). The "de" points to a local origin, but it may be "le", meaning "the watchful." John le Wake occurs in the English Hundred Rolls (1273).

WAKELIN. "Probably a Huntingdon name. The modern form might be Wesley" (LAC., p. 246). In Fife it hardened into Wakelin. William Wacelin (Wascelyn, or Wascelin) appears frequently as a charter witness in the last quarter of the twelfth and early years of the thirteenth century, and about 1210 he had a charter of the land of Neutyl from Earl David (ibid., p. 14). As William Wacell he appears c. 1170 as witness in RPSA. (p. 41), and is often in Earl David's charters between 1198–1214 (LAC., 2, etc.). As Willelmus Vacel' he witnessed a charter by Earl David, brother of the king, of lands in Garuioch, c. 1211–14 (RAA., I, p. 56). William Wacelin was one of the witnesses to Earl David's great charter of the foundation of the monastery of Lundors, 1198–99 (LAC., p. 5), as William Waccele witnessed a grant of the lands of Lessele to Bertolf, c. 1172–90 (*Rothes*, p. 493), and Walkelinus filius Stephani is a witness

WAKELIN, *continued*
to the same charter. Walkelinus filius Stephani appears frequently as witness in charters by Earl David, son of William the Lion (LAC., index). Walkelyn, braciator regis (king's brewer), had a grant of Inverpeffer, c. 1200 (RAA., I, 233). Ernest William Wakelen died at Wellbank, 1942.

WAKERIE. William Wakerie, tailor in Blairgowrie, 1764 (*Logie*, I, p. 164).

WALDASTON. Local. Thomas Waldaston witnessed an instrument of sasine at Haddington, 1458 (*Neubotle*, p. 248).

WALDEGRAVE. An imported name from Walgrave in Northamptonshire. The excrescent -*de*- occurs early, as a 'Ric'us de Waldegrave' occurs in English Charter Rolls in 1383. The Scottish printer's name was spelled Waldgraw in 1597. John Waldgew was admitted burgess of Aberdeen in 1619 (NSCM., I, p. 124). The name today is pronounced Wall'grave.

WALDEVE. From the OE. personal name *Waldþeof*, the meaning of which is a matter of disagreement among scholars. Wallef filius Arnabol made a grant of land to Kelso Abbey, c. 1153–65 (*Kelso*, 27). Waldeuus, son of Matilda, the queen of David I, by her first marriage to Simon de St. Luz, became abbot of Melrose, and died 1159 (*Chron. Mail.*, s. a.). Waldevus, earl of Dunbar, son of earl Gospatric, one of the sureties in 1175 for William the Lion that he would observe the treaty of Falaise, gave charters to the abbeys of Kelso, Melrose, and to the nuns of Coldingham, and died 1183 (*Annals*, p. 249). Waldev filius Boidini or Boydini, a man of the abbot of Kelso, is in record, c. 1160–80 (*Kelso*, 111, 115). Waldef, vicecomes, witnessed confirmation of grant of the church of Kilmaurs to the Abbey of Kelso, a. 1185 (ibid., 284). Waldevus filius Merleswani, who witnessed the gift of fifteen acres of Balmulinauch (Balmerino) to the church of St. Andrews before 1225 (RPSA., p. 272) may be the person who gave name to Beeth-Waldef in Fife (RD., p. 52). Waldevus, vicecomes, and Waldevus filius Baldwini, vicecomes, witnessed grant of the church of Wicestun (now Wiston) to the Abbey of Kelso between 1247–64 (*Kelso*, 336), and Waldev, son of Baldewin, was one of the witnesses to the gift by Waldev, son of Cospatric, of the lands of Dundas to Helias, son of Huctred (Omond, *Arniston memoirs*, p. xxv). As Walthew it survives as a surname in Lancashire.

WALDIE, WALDY. Abbreviated forms of WALDEVE, q.v. Families of this name have been long resident in Roxburghshire, particu-

larly around Kelso. The name occurs in the chartulary of the abbey as Waitho, Watho, and Waltho (Anderson, *Scot. Nat.*). Sir James Waudy or Waldy was presbyter of Gilstoun and master of Trinity Hospital, Edinburgh, 1526–31 (*Soltre*, p. 203, 213). The name early traveled north, as Ad. Waldi was admitted burgess of Aberdeen in 1400, Thomas Waldy, son of John Waldy, in 1439, and Walter Vaudy in 1547 (NSCM., I, p. 1, 5, 60). Duncan Waudy contributed to church repairs there in 1508 (CRA., p. 79). Walldie 1773. See also WADDIE.

WALERAND. A Teutonic personal name found in DB. Old Ger. *Walerand*, 'battle shield' (*Harrison*). Waleranus, chaplain, witnessed David's great charter to Holyrood, c. 1128 (LSC., p. 6). He appears again as Gvalerenna, chaplain, a. 1158 (ibid., p. 7). Walran, abbot of Dere, died 1234, and the Chronicle of Melrose (s. a.) records his death and burial at Melrose as Lord Walleran de Normanvil. Robert Walerand appears in 1255 (*Bain*, I, 1986), and Phelippe Walran of Edinburghshire rendered homage, 1296. His seal bears an eightleaved rose, S' *Philippi de Walran* (*Bain*, II, p. 201, 546.)

WALESTUN. William de Walestun, juror on inquest held in chapel of St. Katherine, Baveley, 1280 (*Bain*, IV, 1762) may have derived his name from Walston near Penicuik. There is also Walston near Kilmarnock, and another near Tarbolton. Cf. MACWALSTOUN.

WALKER. A trade name from OE. *wealcere*, ME. *walker*, a fuller or thickener of woollen cloth, Latin *fullo*. The 'waulk mill' still preserves the name in many parishes. Thomas dictus Walkar in record in Berwick in 1324 (*Cambus.*, 39), William Walkere held land in Inuernvs in 1361 (REM., p. 305), and Andrew and John fulloni were tenants of the Douglas in the barony of Buittle in 1376 (RHM., I, p. lx). Johannes Walker was juror on an inquest held in the episcopal lands of Aldrochty in 1393 (REM., p. 205), Donald Walcare held land in St. Leonards, Edinburgh, in 1457 (*Neubotel*, 284), Johannes Walcar *alias* hatmaker was made burgess of Perth, 1546 (Mill, *Plays*, p. 265), and Alexander Walker had a charter of feu-ferm of the fuller's mill in Burnemouth, c. 1560 (RD., p. 474). The Craft of Walkeris, Wakers, or Waulkers of Edinburgh obtained a seal of cause in August, 1500, from the magistrates of the city (Maitland, *History of Edinburgh*, p. 308). In Glasgow there is mention in 1454 of "The Kyngis strayt the qwhilk is callit the Walcargat" (LCD., p. 177), in Latin documents *Vicus fullonum*. It was the old name of the Saltmarket till about the middle of the seventeenth century. Valcar 1526, Valcer 1522, Valker 1583, Waker 1681, Walcair 1590, Walcar 1511, Walcare 1486, Walcer 1493, Waulcar 1555. In the Highlands Walker is used as a rendering of *Mac an fhucadair*, for which see under MACNUCATOR.

WALKINSHAW, WALKINGSHAW. From the lands of the same name in Renfrewshire. The Walkinshaws of that Ilk were descended from Duugallus filius Cristini, judex de Levenax, who about 1235 made excambion of his lands of Cnoc for the lands of Walkeinschaw (RMP., p. 178). The Walkinshaws were hereditary foresters to the High Stewards for the barony of Renfrew, hence their armorial supporters, "two foresters in long gowns." Robert Walkyngschaw was a witness in Glasgow in 1551 (*Protocols*, I), and in 1562 there is record of sasine to Constantine Walkinschaw (ER., XIX, p. 495). Adam Walkinschaw is recorded in Fogo in 1679 (*Lauder*). Maria Clementina Walkinshaw became mistress of the Young Pretender, but was obliged to leave him because of his brutal ill-usage. Wakensha c. 1770, Wakinshaw 1658, Wakynschaw 1556, Walkingschawe 1603.

WALKLOT. The lands of George Walklot in Edinburgh are mentioned in 1511 (*Soltre*, p. 262). There was a "domus" Wauklet in Edinburgh mentioned in the confirmation of the foundation charter of Holy Trinity, Edinburgh (ibid., p. 65).

WALKSTER. The same as WALKER, q.v., with the feminine agental suffix -*ster*. William Walkster in Scotstownhill, Moray, 1739 (*Moray*).

WALLACE. This surname has been thought by some to show that the original bearer or bearers of the name came from Wales. The earliest of the name in Scotland are said to have been followers of the Stewarts who came from Shropshire where they had large possessions, but a little way from the Welsh border. It was therefore quite naturally thought that some Welshmen might have been among the vassals of the Stewarts when they came into Scotland. On the other hand it has been claimed that Sir William Wallace was not a Welshman, as we understand the term at the present day, but was a descendant of a native of the British kingdom of Strathclyde. Walensis meant a Briton of Strathclyde as we see from charters of the twelfth century to the people of the Glasgow diocese (extending from Clyde to Solway) headed: *Francis et Anglicis, Scotis et Galwiensibus et Walensibus*, "to French and English, Scots (coast of Ayrshire, etc.), Galloway men and Britons (of Strath-

clyde)." Wallace is therefore most probably a native name meaning a Strathclyde Briton. The surname appears in the twelfth century in Ayrshire and Renfrewshire, parts of the old Strathclyde kingdom as already mentioned. Richard Wal[ensis] who attested a charter by Walter, son of Alan, between 1165–73 (RMP., p. 6) appears to be first of the name recorded. As Richard Walency he (c. 1190) witnessed a charter by Richard de Lincoln of a portion of land in the territory of S. Mary of Kelso (*Kelso*, 161), and as Ric. Waleis he witnessed a charter by Richard de Nichole of an acre of land in the territory of Molle (ibid., 165). Adam Walleis witnessed a charter of "vnum rete super matricem aquam de Thei" by David de Hava to the monks of Cupar between 1212–49 (SCM., II, p. 307), and as Ada Walensis witnessed gifts to the church of Paisley before 1228 (RMP., p. 225). Ricardus Waleyss, knight, and Robertus Waleyss witnessed the gift of Cragyn (Craigie) in Kyle to the monastery of Paisley, c. 1272 (RMP., p. 233). Johannes Walensi witnessed a charter by Gilbert of Glencarny to Duncan of Feryndrawcht, c. 1281–98 (*Grant*, III, p. 7). Sir William Wallace the patriot, the "Terror Anglorum" as the author of *Liber Pluscardensis* calls him, was taken prisoner and sent to London where he was tried and unjustly executed as a traitor in August, 1305. He was no traitor to the English king as he had never sworn fealty to him. Robert Wallays, miles, witnessed a grant to Donald, earl of Lennox, c. 1334 (*Levenax*, p. 61), and again witness in 1336 (*Friars Ayr*, p. 6). John Walays had a charter of the land of Tahurrystona in the barony of Innerwyk, 1372 (RMS., I, 420). Sir John Wales, lord of Craigie, had a safe conduct into England in 1444 (*Bain*, IV, 1163). The lands of Elyrislie (Elderslie) were held by Wallaces as late as 1466 (RMP., p. 370). Valace 1589, Wallace 1560, Vallas and Valles (of Craigie) 1497, Walace 1432, Walais 1292, Walas 1403, Walays 1369, Wallas 1497, Wallass 1531, Wallès 1487, Wallis 1518; Vallace, Valleyis, Valeyns, Waless, Waleys, Wallaise, Wallayis, Walleyis, Wallyis, Walois.

WALLACH. Thomas Wallach was member for St. Andrews in the Scottish Parliament, 1572 (*Hanna*, II, p. 517).

WALLET. Weekley says (p. 156) so far as his evidence goes this name 'is an alteration of *valet*, a servant,' and cites Robert le Vallet or le Wallet, from English Close Rolls, but the earliest Scottish reference appears to be against this view. Wallet *avunculus* Stephani de Melginche was a witness in the reign of Alexander III (*Scon*, p. 81). Andrew Wallet is re-

WALLET, *continued*
corded in the parish of Kirkpatrick-Irongray, 1642 *(Dumfries),* another Andrew Wallet, an exiled Covenanter from Irongray, was drowned off Orkney, 1679 (*Hanna,* II, p. 254), and John Wallet in the same parish was prosecuted for conventicles in 1686 (RPC., 3. ser. XII, p. 207). The name still exists in Dumfriesshire.

WALLINGFORD. From Wallingford, Berks, England. Hobkin de Wallingford or Walingfuird forfeited lands in Scotland in the reign of Robert I (RMS., I, App. II, 264).

WALLS. (1) Most probably a form of WALLACE, q.v. Ibbote Wales, a tenant of the Douglas in Drumcorke, 1376 (RHM., I, p. lvi). John Weles, burgess of Dumfries, and William Wallis in Auchinudane are recorded in 1659 *(Dumfries).* George Wellis, chapman in Dumfries, 1682, and Jean Walls in Amisfield-toune, 1687 (ibid.). John Walls and Halbert Walls were examined for the Test in Tinwald, 1685 (RPC., 3. ser. XI, p. 433, 434). (2) An Orcadian surname from the island of the same name. Donald Wawis was tacksman of Manclett, Wawis, in 1492, and John Wales was a witness in Kirkwall in 1565 (REO., p. 282, 409). The name is still current in Orkney.

WALLSEND. From Wallsend - on - Tyne, Northumberland, c. 1125 Wallesende. Adam de Walesende and Helia de Walesende witnessed a charter of the church of Ærcheldun (now Earlston) to the monks of S. Cuthbert, n. d. (*Raine,* 165).

WALLSON. Thomas Wallson in Elgin acted as a drummer in the rebel army, 1745 (Murray Rose, *Historical notes,* p. 146).

WALPOLE. Most probably from Walpole in the county of Norfolk, England. Willelmus de Walepole witnessed confirmation of sale of the land of Scrogges to the Church of Glasgow, c. 1208–13 (REG., p. 76). Magister Adam de Walpol, cleric of the Church of Glasgow, c. 1235 (LSC., p. 56).

WALSH, WELSH. From ME. *walshe,* OE. *welisć,* foreign, from OE. *walh,* foreigner. The spelling Walsh is due to confusion in the early forms between the noun and adjective. John Walshe was juror on an inquest held at Roxburgh, 1360 (*Bain,* IV, 50). John Walch, a tenant of the earl of Douglas in the barony of Kylbouho, 1376 (RHM., II, p. 16). Sir Robert Velche, a cleric, was vicar of Tynron, 1548 *(Anderson),* John Walcht, a witness, 1467 (*Neubotle,* p. 263), and Robert Velsche, burgess of Dumfries, 1567 (*Edgar,* p. 242). Velsch 1686, Welche 1604.

WALTER. A personal name, Teutonic *Walther, Walthar,* OE. *W(e)aldhere,* 'powerful warrior.' *Wealdhere* in AF. became *Wautier,* which when spelled Walter at a later period was long pronounced Water, and so gave name to Wat, Watt, and Wattie. Patrick Walter was a tenant under Douglas in the barony of Buittle, 1376 (RHM., I, p. lix). Valter 1490.

WALTERSMAGHE. Robert Waltersmaghe was juror on an inquisition at Selkirk, 1305 (*Bain,* II, p. 453). In ME. *maugh* was used vaguely for any relative by marriage and in the north of England usually means brother-in-law.

WALTERSON, 'son of WALTER,' q.v. In Latin charters the name appears in the Latin genitive form, Henry Walteri in Innerkethyn, 1391 (RAA., II, 44). Johannes filius Walteri in Aberdeen was charged in 1398 with unlawfully buying fish (CRA., p. 373). Waltersoun 1514. Duncan Walterson witnessed a notarial transumpt in 1465 (*Lamont,* p. 19).

WANDERS. The local (Meigle) pronunciation of Guinevere, the name of King Arthur's unfaithful queen. The old Welsh is *Gwenhwyvar* (Rhys, *Arthurian legend,* p. 46–47). In Anglo-Norman romances the name became Guenièvre, and in English romances it assumed the forms Wannore and Wannour, and even Gonore, Ganor, or Gaynore (ibid., p. 49). According to local legend in Angus she was buried on Barry Hill in the parish of Alyth.

WANDERSON. Symeon Wandersone or Wandersoune was burgess of Pittenweyme in 1646 (*Inquis. Tut.,* 725, 726), William Wandersoune was retoured heir portioner of Alexander Robertsone, burgess of Pittinweyme, in 1648 (*Retours, Fife,* 755), and in 1653 Kathrine Wandersoun was retoured heir of William Wandersoun, burgess of Pittinweyme, her father (ibid., 811).

WANLESS, WANLISS. "Wanlace and Wanless are names peculiar to Northumberland" (*Guppy*), and in record there in 1523. Simon Wanles was a monk of Melrose, 1451 (*Irvine,* I, p. 141). Robert Wanless, witness in Linlithgow, 1538 (*Laing,* 419). Robert Wandles was admitted deacon of Coupar-Angus in 1683, and John Wanles was tenant in Pitrodie, 1711 (DPD., II, p. 86, 280). Wanlass 1691. Of uncertain origin, the usual definitions offered being, I think, improbable.

WANN. Johannes dictus Wan was canon of Holyrood, Edinburgh, 1406 (RMS., I, 875). Robert Wan was admitted burgess of Aberdeen, 1411 (NSCM., I, p. 4), William Wane appears as burgess of Glasgow, 1433 (LCD.,

p. 248), and Schir James Wan was declared innocent of any part in the detention of King James III in Edinburgh Castle in 1482 (*Lennox*, II, p. 123). Martin Wan or Wanne appears as chancellor of the diocese of Glasgow 1473–87–96 (RHM., II, 220, here erroneously spelled Wau; *Crossraguel*, I, p. 44; REG., p. 493). John Wann was bailie of the burgh of Dumbarton, 1500 (LCD., p. 204), Adam Wane held land in Adamhill, Lanarkshire, in same year (*Simon*, 12), William Wane, official of Lothian, 1514 (*Rent. Dunk.*, p. 265), John Wan had a precept of remission in 1536 (RSS., II, 2002), and John Wan or Wann is in record in Glasgow, c. 1548 and 1550 (LCD., p. 43; *Protocols*, I). Recorded in Edinburgh, 1943.

WANS. William Wans was reidare at Loncaster, 1574 (RMR.), and Robert Wands appears in Belhaven, 1688 (RPC., 3. ser. XIII, p. 245). Wanns were described as hereditary doomsters of the bishop of St. Andrews' Court of Regality.

WARD. John de Warde was a tenant of the earl of Douglas in the barony of Kilbucho, 1376 (RHM., I, p. xlix; II, p. 16) (*de* may be an error for *le*, from the occupation of guard or keeper). Robert Waird was burgess of Stirling in 1601 (SBR., p. 99).

WARDEN. (1) From the office of 'warden' (AF. *wardein*, a guardian). (2) More probably from Warden in Northumberland as the surname appears late with us. John Wardein was admitted burgess of Glasgow, 1627, as servitor to the marquis of Hamilton, and David Wardine was admitted burgess and guild brother, 1629 (*Burgesses*). John Warden in Camphill, 1685 (*Dunkeld*). John Wardan was retoured heir of David Warden, portioner of Auchinaitne, his father, 1698 (*Retours, Lanark*, 447). The name is now found mainly in Fife and formerly in Angus and Mearns.

WARDHAUGH. James Wardhaugh died in Jedburgh, 1939. Of local origin from some small place of the name in England.

WARDLAW. "There are in Scotland several places named Wardlaw, from which this surname may have been derived, but there is no evidence of the existence of Wardlaws of that Ilk" (*Stodart*, II, p. 182). The place name Wardlaw, near Beauly, "the hillock where watch and ward was kept by the retainers of the Norman lord of the Aird, John Byset," occurs so early as 1210 (as Wardelaue) and is interesting as showing the early introduction of the English language there. The first of the surname in Scotland appears to have been Henricus de Wardlaw who re-

ceived a charter from Robert I of half the barony of Wiltone in Roxburghshire (RMS., I, 17). Master Walter de Wardlaw, doctor 'sacre pagine,' was canon of Aberdeen in 1358 (*Bain*, IV, 17). Walter de Wardlaw, archdeacon of Lothian in 1363 (*Egidii*, p. 18) was afterwards the celebrated bishop of Glasgow, cardinal, and ambassador to England. Henry of Wardelawe had a safe conduct into England in 1397 (*Bain*, IV, 490). Henry Wardlaw, nephew of the Cardinal, was bishop of St. Andrews (1403–1440), one of the most famous men of his time, a benefactor of his country, and founder of the University of St. Andrews. From his brother William (died 1420) was descended the Wardlaws of Pitreavie. Sir Patrick of Warlaw witnessed a charter by Hugh Fraser of Lovat in 1436 (*Athole*, p. 707), John of Wardlawe of Recardton received a safe conduct into England in 1464 (*Bain*, IV, 1346), and Alexander Wardlaw or Warlaw of Warenston was a witness in Edinburgh in 1467 (*Neubotle*, 299, 300). Vardlaw 1465, Wartlaw 1657; Vardlau.

WARDLE. A surname recorded in Aberdeen. Of local origin, probably from Wartle in the parish of Lumphanan (in 1696, Warthill = Ward-hill). Lower has an English surname Wardle, from Wardle or Wardhill in Cheshire.

WARDROP, WARDROPE. From the office of keeper of the royal wardrobe. The wardrobe was a repository not only for articles of dress, but for furniture not actually in use, and for foreign spices and confections (ER., I, pref. p. 1). Robertus de Warderob witnessed a charter by Margaret, countess of Buchan in favor of the Abbey of Arbroath, c. 1210 (RAA., I, p. 94). John de Wardroba laid claim to certain lands in Kilpatrick, Dumbartonshire, c. 1270 (RMP., p. 180), and Randinus de Warderoba witnessed a quitclaim of Beeth Waldef in Fife, 1278 (RD., p. 52). Alisaundre de la Garderobe of Edinburghshire and David de la Garderobe of Fife rendered homage, 1296 (*Bain*, II, p. 204, 213). John de Gardropa was appointed proluctor in Aberdeen, 1317 (SCM., v, p. 8), and Adam de Gardropa confirmed the transfer of lands to John Crab there in 1351 (*Friars*, 16). Thomas Vardrop de Gothvnys acquired a fourth part of Thenstoun, 1450, and in 1465 as Thomas Wardropare de Gothnys he had a charter of confirmation of the lands of Thanystoune in the thanage of Kintore (*View*, p. 574, 575). Alexander Wardroper and James Wardroper witnessed a charter of lands in Scone, 1491 (*Scon*, p. 199), Archibald Vedderop was bailie of Glasgow, 1525 (REG., 497), and Thomas Wedderop and James Wedderop were jurors on

WARDROP, WARDROPE, continued

assize of lands in Gowane (Govan), 1527 (Pollok, I, p. 258). Thomas Wardroper of Ballatheis granted a charter in favor of John Montcreiff, 1531 (Methven, p. 43), John Wodrop held a land in Glasgow, 1547 (Protocols, I), Gilbert Wedrop was charged with tumult there, 1606 (RPC., VII, p. 244), William Waddrope was admitted burgess of Glasgow, 1608 (Burgesses), and Barbrye Wadrope is recorded in Swyntounhill, 1671 (Lauder). Wairdrob 1658, Wairdrope 1678, Warddrop 1509. Wardraper 1512, Wardrapper 1686, Wardrob 1642, Wardropar 1467, Wardropper 1509, Wardrupper 1582, Wodderop c. 1530, Woddrop 1591, Woodrope (in Aberdeen) 1731; Wardrap.

WARDROPSTON. In 1331 John de Wardroperisthon and David, his brother, sons of the late Andrew de Wardroperisthon, granted a charter in favor of Sir John de Inchemartyn of the lands of Wardroperisthon (SCM., V, p. 10). There is a Wardrapstoun, 1695, in Forfar Retours (525).

WARES. A common Caithness surname, from Wares near Canisbay, the local pronunciation of which is "Waars," and so written in old charters. Ferquhard Warris in Cannast had remission in 1547 for his share in taking and holding the Castle of Akirgill in Caithness (OPS., II, p. 778). Janet Warrs was delate in 1652 "of superstitious goeing or kneeling about the Chappell" of S. Modan in Freswick (Old Lore Misc., V, p. 59). Elspet Warris, spouse to Walter Rosie in Mey, 1661 (Caithness). Donald Warsse and Swann Warsse in Seater, James Warse there, and John Awairse in Gilles, Caithness, to be apprehended as rebels, 1670 (RPC., 3. ser. III, p. 194).

WARIN. From the Fr. personal name Guerin. Henri filius Warin witnessed the charter of Annandale to Brus, a. 1153 (Nat. MSS., I, 19). Warinus, burgess of Dunberthan (Dumbarton), and Warinus, clericus, charter witness, both in 1234 (RMP., p. 160, 176).

WARK. Probably from Wark-on-Tweed in Northumberland. John of Werk had a safe conduct into England in 1424 (Bain, IV, 970). Jhone of Wark, tenant of the land of Carndene in 1520, is probably the Jhone of Werk recorded as tenant of the Estyr quarter of Cheddilstoun (Shettleston) in the following year (Rental). Robert Wark was declared a fugitive from justice, 1686 (RPC., 3. ser. XIII, p. 19).

WARNOCH, WARNOCK. Curtailed forms of MACILVERNOCK, q.v., found mainly in Lanarkshire. Robert Warnot (probably the same name) had a remission for his share in holding Dumbarton Castle against the king in 1489 (APS., XII, p. 34). Andree Warnoche in Lanark had a remission in 1505 (Trials, I, p. 104*), John Warnok recorded in Glasgow. c. 1530 (LCD., p. 27), James Warnok was a witness in Ayrshire in 1562 (Hunter, p. 68), Andrew Warnok was resident in Phippismilne, Glasgow, in 1597 (Protocols, X), John Warnok was retoured heir of John Warnok in Kittoksvid in 1602 (Retours, Lanark, 32), and John Warnok was registered heir of Alexander Warnok in Auldhous in 1620 (Inquis., 914). James Warnock and Agnes Warnock were residents in the parish of Borgue, 1684 (RPC., 3. ser. IX, p. 567).

WARPLAY. Patrick Warplay in Litlcorshill, 1666 (Corsehill, p. 68). Perhaps an error for Wartley. There were 40s. lands of Wartley in 1668 (Retours, Ayr, 558).

WARRACK, WARRICK, WARROCK, WARRICH. Warrack was not uncommon as a personal name in Aberdeenshire, and occasionally appears in the Poll Book [of 1696] (Macdonald, Place names of west Aberdeenshire, s. v. Warrackstone). Andrew Warrak was admitted burgess of Aberdeen in 1481 and John Warrach in 1614 (NSCM., I, p. 29, 112). Dominus Willielmus Werok officiated at the chapel of Nudry-Merschal in 1502 (Good, Liberton, p. 72), and John Werrok was tenant of the bishop of Aberdeen, 1511 (REA., I, p. 373). Alexander Warrak who was witness in an Aberdeen witch trial in 1596 (SCM., I. p. 88) may be the Alexander Varrak who was paid in 1611 for ringing the common bell of the town (SCM., V, p. 85). James Warrack in Tollafine was accused in 1642 of hiding stolen horses (RSCA., III, p. 7), Donald Worrach in Skinene is in record, 1664 (Caithness), and John Werock was farmer in Upper Liberton, 1712 (Good, p. 72). The surname occurs in Edinburgh, 1619, as Warrok (Edinb. Marr.). Warroch 1738. The origin of this name is uncertain. Warrocks was a barbarous form of LL. warectarius, a ploughman. Warroch Hill in Orwell parish is in Blaeu's Atlas Warrock, and in the Retours the name is spelled Warrok, Warrock, Warroke, and Warroch Burn is the boundary between Fossoway and Orwell parishes. Cf. WARWICK.

WARRAND. Surname current in the North. Martha Warrand in Inverness (Rec. Inv., I, p. 241). David Warrand, merchant in Elgin, 1659 (Donaldson, p. 19), and Alexander Warrand, merchant in Forres, 1744 (Moray). Duncan Warrand edited More Culloden papers, 1923.

WARREN. From Varenne (OFr. de Gwarenne) in the district of Dieppe. Reginald de Warenne granted a charter before 1231 to Laurence Oliphant of lands near Forgandenny (*Sc. Peer.*, VI, p. 530). In 1231 he granted a charter to the Abbey of Culross to which Reginald, younger, of Waren, and Malcolm, his brother, are witnesses (PSAS., LX, p. 71–72). (2) Cf. WARRENDER.

WARRENDER, WARRANDER. From the office of warrener (OF. *warrennier* > ME. *warnere*), an officer employed to watch over the game in a park or preserve, later the keeper of a warren. The *d* is excrescent. In 1264 we have record of payment to the keeper of the rabbit warrens of Crail (*custodi warrenarum de Karral* (ER., I, p. 4). John Warrander had a confirmation charter of Balchristie Links in Fife in 1601 (RD., p. 501). George Warrrender was dean of guild in Aberdeen, 1708 (*Guildry*, p. 202).

WARRICH, WARRICK. See under WARRACK.

WARROCK. See WARRACK.

WARTRIA. Nicholas de Wartria witnessed a confirmation charter by John de St. Michael of the gift by his avunculus to Arbroath, 1214 (RAA., I, p. 55), and p. 1218, as prepositus de Aberbrothoc, he witnessed the gift of a half mark of silver by William de Vallibus to the same abbey (ibid., p. 83), and c. 1225 he witnessed the gift of the mill of Kateryn (ibid., p. 91).

WARWICK. Doubtless from Warwick in the county of the same name in England, rather than from Warwick in Cumberland, which represents Warthewic (1120). Some of the Warwicks of today, however, may derive their surname from Warwick in Cumberland. Ricardus de Warewic witnessed William de Moreuille's charter "Edulfo filius Uctredi Gillemoristun que antiquitus vocabatur peniacob," a. 1196 (REG., p. 40). Willelmus de Warewic witnessed a charter by Adam de Hastengis of land of Kengildurs to Aberbrothoc, c. 1214–26 (RAA., I, p. 87). Richard de Warwyk del counte de Are rendered homage, 1296. His seal shows a crescent enclosing a star, S' Ricardi...Werwic (Bain, II, p. 199, 548). Six of this name are recorded in CD., of whom five are in the shires of Dumfries and Kirkcudbright.

WASFORD. From the old lands of Vasfuird (1633) in the bailliary of Kylestewart. Symon of Waschford was a charter witness in Ayr, c. 1340 (*Friars Ayr*, p. 10), and Andrew Wasforde, son of Simon Wasford, made a grant of land to the Friars Preachers in 1401 (ibid., p. 37).

WASON, WASSON. From WATSON through a delicate sounding of *t*. John Cathcart Wason of Ayrshire, M. P., died in 1921.

WATCHMAN. From occupation. Robert Wachman was voter in the parish of Qwilton (Covlton), 1513 (*Ros*, 52). James Watchman in Dunfermline, 1564 (*Dunfermline*). Jhone Watchman, a cottar in Kirkwall, 1595 (REO., p. 359), may have been of Fife origin.

WATER. A form of WALTER, q.v., ME. *Water*, OF. *Wauter*.

"Nout Willam ne Water."

Ancrene Riwle, p. 340.

John Water was tenant of Colthrop in the barony of Newlands, 1376 (RHM., II, p. 16). Patrick Watter in Aberdeen, to whom a payment was made in 1598, may be the Patrick Watter admitted burgess of the burgh, 1604 (SCM., V, p. 125; NSCM., I, p. 99). Adam Watter in Paxtoune, 1667 (*Lauder*). As forename: Schir Water Ra, 1415.

WATERET, WATRET. "Whutterick or Whitteret used to be a tolerably common name in Galloway," but is now turned into Watret and Wateret (Trotter, *Galloway gossip, Wigtownshire*, p. 378). The name is a corruption of MACKETTRICK, q.v. John Wataret and Katherine Wataret were examined for the Test in Tinwald in 1685 (RPC., 3. ser. XI, p. 433).

WATERLEADER. From the occupation of 'water carrier.' Nevin Watirleder held a tenement in Edinburgh, c. 1426 (*Egidii*, p. 48).

WATERS, WATTERS. Forms of 'Walters,' 'son of WALTER,' q.v. Alison Walters in Fishweicke, 1676 (*Lauder*). Sergeant-Major Watters distinguished himself in the first Great War and was promoted to captain.

WATERSON. A surname of territorial origin from more than one place of the name. (1) From lands of the name formerly in the parish of Fearn. These lands probably obtained their name from Walter, uncle and tutor of Dempster, one of the heirs portioners of the lordship of Menmuir. A payment of twenty-five shillings by William de Walteristoun to David Scot, custos of the burgh of Montrose, is recorded in 1329, and David de Walterstoun had eight marks out of the farms in the thanage of Tannadyce, 1359 (ER., I, p. 158, 589). David Walterstoun *de eodem* was one of the assize chosen to perambulate the marches of Brechin and Balzeordie, 1450 (REB., I, 141; II, 79). Hew Vattyrstone or Watterstone of that Ilk who was on assize held at Forfar, 1495 (RAA., II, 354) is probably Hugh Watterstoun *de eodem* who witnessed a re-

WATERSON, *continued*

tour of service at Forfar, 1514 (SCM., v, p. 292). The Angus Watersons, surname and place name, have long since disappeared. (2) In the reign of Robert II William Waterstoun of that Ilk alienated the lands of Waterstoun in the parish of Kilbarchan, Renfrewshire, to Sir William Cunningham of Kilmaurs (Crawford-Semple, *Hist. Renfrew*, pt. II, p. 141; OPS., I, p. 85, says in 1384). The land of quondam Alexander Walterstoune in Glasgow is mentioned, c. 1540 (LCD., p. 39), and Thomas Wattirstoune was burgess of Glasgow, 1552 (*Protocols*, I). (3) There were also Watersons of that Ilk in Midlothian. A family of this name were royal surgeons. Robert I granted in 1317 a charter to William of Watterston "filio et heredi quondam Johannis surgici, dilecto et fideli nostro" (HMC., 2. Rep. App., p. 181). Watherston and Waltherston are old surnames in Lauderdale, and James Waderstone and William Wadderstoun were bedesmen of Thirlstane Hospital, 1676 (Thomson, *Lauder*, p. 71). *See also* WATHERSTON.

WATHERSTON, WEATHERSTON, WEATHERSTONE. Forms of WATERSON, q.v. John Wadderstaine in Swyntoune, 1652 (*Lauder*), Thomas Waderstoune in Clackmae, 1662 (RRM., II, p. 11), Simeon Wadderstoune in Over Howdon, 1674 (*Inquis.*, 5780), Robert Weathirstaines was herd in Over Langshaw, 1682 (RRM., III, p. 36), Adam Woderstoune in the parish of Langton complains against his minister, 1689 (RPC., 3. ser. XIV, p. 164), and Simon Wadderstoun tenant in Colmslie, 1701 (RRM., III, p. 120). James Watherston, portioner of Trabroun in 1746, and Simon Watherstoun of Netherfield 1752 (*Lauder*). James Watherstone recorded in Earlstoun, 1818 (*Heirs*, 651).

WATSON, 'son of Walter,' from the diminutive form Wat or Watt. Sir Donaldus Walteri, a presbyter of the diocese of Moray, 1493, is mentioned in a document of 1612 as Sir Donald Watsone (*Beauly*, p. 104, 167). The full form Walterson also occurs in common use. John Watson held land in Edinburgh in 1392 (*Egidii*, p. 28), Robert Watsoun was accused of being a forestaller in Aberdeen in 1402 (CRA., p. 384), and Thomas Watson of Stanhous was one of an inquest held at Dunipace in 1426 (*Cambus.*, 87). John Watsoun of Garwaswould was juror on an inquest made at Lanark in 1432 (RAA., II, p. 61), and Nicholas Watson of Dalkeith held a land in the Appilgate of Arbroath in 1450 (ibid., p. 77). Walter Watson, burgess of Dumbarton, was a landowner there in 1494, and a long succession of bailies, provosts, and other town

officers descend from him. In the sixteenth and seventeenth centuries the name was common throughout the Lowlands, and is one of the most common surnames in the north-eastern counties. John Watsone was tenant of Uthircloy, Ardmanoch, in 1504 (ER., XII, p. 661). Andreas Watson was elected bailie of Aberdeen, 1509 (*Guildry*, p. 193). Some of the MACWATTS, q.v., on the Highland line have translated their name to Watson. Vatsone 1533, Vatsoun 1573, Wateson 1462, Watsoune 1517, Wattsone 1686.

WATT. A diminutive of Water, a form of WALTER, q.v. In 1446 there is mention of the seal of Wat of Carnegy (REB., I, 108). Walter Wat held land in Brechin in 1586 (ibid., II, 356), and Alexander Wat was witness to a sasine in 1512 (*Panmure*, II, 282). Patrick Wat in Turriff was admitted burgess of Aberdeen in 1609 (NSCM., I, p. 106), and John Wat was retoured heir of Adam Wat, writer to the King's Signet, in lands in the parish of Stewartoun, etc., in 1663 (*Retours, Ayr*, 529). In a fishing village in Banffshire a number of years ago it was stated that of 300 inhabitants 225 answered to the name of Watt, and many Watts are still found in Aberdeenshire. The Watts of Rosehill are descended from John Watt of Rosehill, the blacksmith who distinguished himself on the king's side in the tumult of 17 December 1596, and was shot in revenge on 17 April 1601 (Calderwood, *History*, VI, p. 104). The grandfather of Alexander Watt (1837–1894), author and theatre-manager in Denmark, was a Scot who settled as a linen manufacturer in Copenhagen in 1796. Vatt 1506. As forename: Wat of Tulloch 1388 (*Bamff*, p. 22); Master Watt Ydill, vicar of Inverurie, 1428. Among the Scots Guards in France one named Watty Hamilton had his name spelled Ouatte Amiton.

WATTERS. *See under* WATERS.

WATTIE. A double diminutive of WALTER, q.v. With Mac it gives MACWATTIE.

WATTS, 'son of WATT,' q.v. It is found mainly in Aberdeenshire.

WAUCHOPE. Territorial, from the district of Wauchopedale in the parish of Langholm, Dumfriesshire. The family appears however to have been early settled in Roxburghshire, but their early charters have been destroyed. They are never found as tenants-in-chief (*in capite*) of the Crown, but always as holding the subordinate although honorable position of a vassal or tenant of a baron, and yet had tenants and vassals of their own, in English feudal law a vavasour (Med. Lat. *vassus vassorum*). Ada de Waleuhope witnessed a charter by

Symon de Lyndsay to the Abbey of Melrose in the reign of William the Lion, and dominus Ada de Waleuhope, evidently the same person, witnessed another charter to Melrose in the same reign (*Melros*, p. 132, 149). Alan de Walchope witnessed a charter by Thomas de Lundin granted between 1203–14 (RAA., I, 65). In 1247 Robert de Waluchop, son of Alan de Waluchop, received from Alexander II a charter of lands in Aberdeenshire (*Arch. Scot.*, I, p. 366), and in 1249, as Robert de Walwehope he was one of the twelve knights appointed to meet twelve knights from England to settle the law of the marches (APS., I, p. 413). As Robert de Walhope he witnessed gift of land in Aython (Aytoun) to the monks of Coldingham, 1259 (*Raine*, 203). Alan de Walchop or Walchoup witnessed a quitclaim of Beeth-Waldef in Fife, 1278 (RD., p. 52–53). Robert de Walghope rendered homage at Aberdeen, 1296, and Thomas Walghope in Edinburgh, a tenant under the bishop of St. Andrews. The seal of the latter bears a hawk or raven killing a bird, S' *Thome Walchop* (*Bain*, II, p. 195, 205, 555). Thomas de Walchope was sub vicecomes of Perth, 1379 (*Scon*, p. 144). Meg Walchop is recorded in Aberdeen, 1408 (CWA., p. 316). David Wauchoip was procurator of the Scottish Nation in the University of Orleans, 1502 (SHSM., II, p. 95), and in the records of the Scots men-at-arms in France the name appears as Vaucop and Vulcob. Walichop 1262, Wauhope 1530, Wawchop 1589. In the North of Ireland it is pronounced Wahab.

WAUGH. The author of *The House of Glendinning* (p. 5) says: "The common border name of Waugh is an abbreviation of Wauchope, the Waughs are sprung from the Wauchopes and have the same arms." David de Waughe of Lanarkshire, Robert Walgh' de Hepe [from lands of Heip or Heap in the parish of Wilton] of Roxburghshire, and Thomas Walghe of Peeblesshire rendered homage in 1296 (*Bain*, II, p. 199, 200, 206). William Waugh, shipman, had a safe conduct into England, 1436 (ibid., IV, 999), and John Wach was a notary public in Peebles, 1448 (*Peebles*, 14). John Walcht was a monk of Neubotle in 1467 (*Neubotle*, p. 314), and William Wagh had a safe conduct to trade within England in 1445 (*Bain*, IV, 1178). John Wech witnessed a tack by the abbot of Cupar-Angus, 1521 (SCM., V, p. 294), Edward Wauch, a follower of the earl of Cassilis, was respited for murder, 1526 (RSS., I, 3386), James Waucht, a witness in Linlithgow, 1536 (*Johnsoun*), and Gavin Weiche, hospitaller in Holy Trinity Church, Edinburgh, 1543 (*Soltre*, p. 108). Jonet Wach recorded in Sandyhill,

1585 (*Scon*, p. 230), and Thomas Ratra alias Waich in Kinclaven, 1649 (DPD., II, p. 240). The Waughs of Heip held these lands from the thirteenth to the seventeenth century.

WAUGHTON. Robert de Walughtone, parson of Walughtone chapel, Edinburghshire, who rendered homage, 1296 (*Bain*, II, p. 210, 554), derived his name from Waughton in East Lothian. His seal shows a chalice and hand and S' *Roberti capellani*.

WAUS, WAUSS. See under VAUS.

WAWANE. Wawane of Steinston is recorded in the Workman MS., but no information given. Adam Wawayne held a ploughgate in the barony of Farnydovne, c. 1372 (RMS., I, 421, 548). A later Adam Wawan witnessed a charter by William, Lord Crichton, apud Strivelyn, 1449 (*Annandale*, I, p. 13). William Wawane presented to the prebend of Ellone in 1479 (ADC., p. 93) appears again in 1502 as William Wawne, canon of Aberdeen (*Bain*, IV, 1697). James Wawan, probably a relative, held the prebend of Ellon in 1521, and James Wawane de Oyne is in record in 1537 (REA., II, p. 112). The surname occurs in Tyninghame in 1644 as Wawand (*Waddell*, p. 56). John Wawane was a witness in Linlithgow, 1531 (*Johnsoun*). Wauane 1540. Lower gives Wawn as the provincial pronunciation of Waghen in Yorkshire. Index to RMS., I, compares this name with WAN, and Turnbull, index to Stewart's *Croniclis* equates it with WAUCH.

WAXMAKER. From the occupation, glossed *cerarius* in the *Catholicon Anglicum*. Martin Waxmakare, the king's servitor, was on the king's service in Bute, 1446 (*Chamb. Accts.*, II, p. 438).

WAYGATESHAW. Of local origin from the £10 land of old extent of Wicketshaw or Waygateshaw in the parish of Carluke, Lanarkshire. John Wicketshaw who was charged in 1618 with trafficking in 'tabaca' (RPC., XIV, p. 581) may be John Wickedshaw, merchant in Edinburgh, 1619 (ibid., XII, p. 143). Gavin Wickitschaw in Zuilschell, parish of Carluke, 1623, John Weikitschaw, indweller in Weitschaw, parish of Carluke, 1629, and Thomas Wicketshaw in Collilaw, 1669, are recorded in Lanark Commissariot Record. Euphemia Wickedshaw was retoured heir of John Wickedshaw, burgess of Edinburgh, 1639 (*Retours, Edinburgh*, 836), and James Wicketshau is recorded in Carnwath, 1711 (*Minutes*, p. 114).

WEATHERHEAD. Of local origin from some small place of the name (a hill), probably in Berwickshire. William Wedderat was bur-

WEATHERHEAD, *continued*
gess of Lauder in 1493 (*Laing,* 217), George Wedderheid or Weddirheid had a precept *carte feodifirme* in 1532 and another in 1542 (RSS., II, 1308, 4671), and Robert Wedderat was clerk of the diocese of St. Andrews and notary public in 1547 (RRM., III, p. 342). Payment was made to Robene Wedderate in renunciation of his tacks in 1567 (*Dryburgh,* p. 404). Andrew Wedderheid rendered to Exchequer the accounts of the burgh of Lauder in 1560 (ER., XIX, p. 117), and five years later we have sasine of land in Lauder to Andrew Wedderat (ibid., p. 544). Cuthbert Wedderet witnessed a sasine of 1541 (*Home,* 252), David Wedderhead is recorded in the parish of Makarstoune in 1559 (*Lauder*), Margaret Watherit in Skaithmoor, 1685 (RPC., 3. ser. x, p. 480), and the tenement of George Waderit is mentioned in 1692 (*Retours, Berwick,* 446). George Hume Weatherhead (1790?–1853) was author of several medical works and M. P. for Edinburgh, c. 1850, and T. C. Weatherhead was author of educational works for examination purposes. Wadderat 1632.

WEATHERLY. Local. Probably from Wedderlie near Gordon, Berwickshire. James Weatherly, tenant of Hoprig and Shiells, 1805 (Craw, *Chirnside Common,* p. 6).

WEATHERSPOON. *See under* WOTHERSPOON.

WEATHERSTON, WEATHERSTONE. *See under* WATHERSTON.

WEAVER. From the occupation. In some instances perhaps an Englishing of MACNIDER, q.v. See also the following name.

WEBSTER. From the occupation of cloth-weaver, in Latin documents rendered *textor*. Robert textor de Inuerdoret was a witness in 1288 (RPSA., p. 346). Malcolm Wobstare, burgess of Stirling, 1436 (*Cambus.,* 209). In 1495 there is mention of the tenement of Matheus textor in Dunbertan (REG., 492), and the house of William the weaver (textor) in Lanark is mentioned in the fifteenth century (*Dryburgh,* p. 154). William Webster, baker and burgess of Dundie, 1688 (*Inquis.,* 8292). Vobstar 1562, Vobster 1597, Wobistar and Wobister 1524, Wobstair 1567, Wobstar 1586.

WEDDEL, WEDDELL, WEDDLE. Forms of WADDEL, q.v.

WEDDERBURN. From the lands of Wedderburn in Berwickshire. Wautier de Wederburne of the county of Edeneburk who rendered

homage in 1296 is the first of the name in record. His seal is a star of seven rays, and S' *Walti de Wed'burn* (*Bain,* II, p. 201, 547). (Edinburgh, it may be mentioned, took in part of Berwickshire in the thirteenth century.) Hugo de Wederburne was a charter witness in 1332 (BNCH., XVI, p. 327), and John de Wederborne was assizor on an inquest relating to the vill of Lumsden in 1364. The seal of Willelmus de Wedirburn is appended to a resignation of the lands of Fastforland, Berwickshire, in 1375 (*Douglas,* III). Although designated 'of Wedderburn' the last two appear not to have owned the lands which are in record at least as early as 1341 in possession of the Homes (*Raine,* 565). William Whedyrburn was present at perambulation of the marches between Brokhole and Butterden in 1431 (ibid., 639). The surname became prominent in Dundee history in the fifteenth century, and from 1557 to 1717 Wedderburns were town clerks there and notaries up to 1787. A branch of the Wedderburns settled in Moravia (Hungary) and still flourish under the name of Wetterborn. The place name Wedderburn in Aberdeenshire may be a transplanted name. Vadderbarne 1597, Vadderborne 1574, Vadderburn 1605, Vederburn 1513, Vethirburne 1505, Wadirburn 1496, Watherburne 1506, Wathirburne 1502, Wedderburne 1532, Wetherburn 1537, Wetherburne 1573, Whedirburn 1441, Wodderburne 1634, Woddirburn c. 1530, and Vodderburn, Wadderburne, Weatherburne.

WEDDERLIE. Patrick Wedderlie had sasine of land in Duns in 1560 (ER., XIX, p. 453), and William Wedderly was juror on an inquest at Coldingham in 1561 (*Coldingham,* App. v). The name is derived from Wedderlie near Gordon, Berwickshire.

WEDDERSPOON. *See under* WOTHERSPOON.

WEEMS. A phonetic form of WEMYSS, q.v.

WEIGHTON. Laurence Wichtan, tenant in Balgerscho, c. 1520 (*Cupar-Angus,* I, p. 299). Schir James Wichthand, notary public, 1526 (*Panmure,* II, p. 305). James Weighton of Boghall, 1713 (*Dunkeld*). From Weighton in East Yorkshire.

WEIR, WIER. Of Norman origin from one or other of the places named Vere in Calvados, Manche, Eure-et-Loire, and Oise. The word was introduced into Normandy by the Norsemen from their own *ver,* a station, as in *fiskiver,* a fishing station, a word etymologically akin to OE. *weir, wear,* a dam. Ralph or Radulphus de Ver is perhaps the first of the name recorded in Scotland. As Ralph de Ver he was taken prisoner at Alnwick along with William the Lion in 1174 (*Bain*, I, p. 174). He witnessed a charter by King William "de decimis episcopatus" of Moray between 1174–84 (REM., 2), and as Radulph de Veir or Veyre, within the same period, he gave a bovate of land in Sprowestun, Roxburgh, to the Abbey of Kelso, his brother Robert being one of the witnesses (*Kelso*, p. 177). The same, or perhaps a succeeding Radulph de Ver or de Uer, witnessed a little before 1204 a grant to the Abbey of Arbroath (RAA., I, 11), and before 1214 another charter by King William (*Panmure*, II, 126). The Weirs of Blackwood, Lanarkshire, claim or claimed to be descended from this Radulph though they only appear in record in 1400, when they obtained the lands of Blackwood. Richard Wer of Lanarkshire rendered homage in 1296 (*Bain*, II, p. 206). In the same year a writ was directed to the sheriff of Edinburgh ordering him to restore to Thomas le [*sic*] Wer his forfeited lands (ibid., 832). Between 1398 and 1400 Rothald or Rotaldus de Were, bailie of Lesmahagow, had a charter from Patrick, abbot of Kelso, of the lands of Blackwodd, Mossinyning, and Durgundreston (*Kelso*, 524), and in 1497 Abbot Robert granted Rogerhill and Brownhill to Robert Weyr for services rendered (*Morton*, p. 148). As vassals of the abbots of Kelso the Weirs held extensive lands in Lesmahagow, and George Were and Thomas Were were jurors on an inquisition made at Lanark, 1432 (RAA., II, 65). George Were had a remission for his share in burning the town of Dunbertane in 1489 (*Lennox*, II, p. 132). William Veir, post in Aberdeen, 1612, received payment for his services (SCM., v, p. 92). Some of the Macnairs in Cowal have Englished their name Weir, and the name in Dumbartonshire may be an Englishing of *Mac Amhaoir*, 'son of the officer.' This last name has been extinct for about two hundred years, and the translation into English may have had something to do with its disappearance. Major Weir, the 'Bowhead Saint,' burnt for witchcraft and other crimes, in Edinburgh, 1670, was one of the celebrities of this name, and in 1794 another Weir, also in Edinburgh, had a museum of natural history at 16 Princes Street. The Caithness pronunciation is Whier, and on a tombstone in Temple churchyard, Midlothian, the name is spelled Wire. The names of James Quhair in Scheilgreen, 1638, and Marion Wayre in Littleclyde, parish of Crawford-Douglas (*Lanark CR.*), may be other spellings of the name. Vere 1709, Wair 1660, Ware 1632, Weare 1608, Weer 1650, Weire 1504, Werr 1501, Weyir 1599, Weyr 1528; Uair, Wir.

WELAND. A form of VALENTINE, q.v. Weland de Styklaw in record in thirteenth century (*Dowden*, p. 59). John Welland was charged with aiding the English in Dundee, 1552 (*Beats*, p. 326). Gilbert Weland was tenant in the barony of Rafford in 1565 (REM., p. 445). William Welands was member for Edinburgh in the Scottish Parliament, 1609, and David Welands, member for Cupar in 1693 (*Hanna*, II, p. 517). In the form Weland, Wiland, or Wyland it was a forename among the northern Chisholms.

WELHAM. Perhaps from Welham in East Riding of Yorkshire. Walterus de Wellam witnessed a charter of church of Dalgarnoc by Edgar filius Dofnaldi in reign of William the Lion (LSC., p. 213–214). Walter de Welham witnessed charter of a carucate of land in Langholme, c. 1270, to Herbert Maxwell (*Pollok*, I, p. 125).

WELLS. Most probably of English origin from one or other of the places of the name in England. In Latin documents *de Fontibus*. Willelmus de fontibus witnessed a gift by Philip de Mubray to the monks of Dunfermline, c. 1202–14 (RD., p. 95), and Henricus de Fonte was witness to the gift by Philip de Mubray of a toft in Inuerkethin to the church of St. Thomas of Aberbrothoc, p. 1219 (RAA., I, p. 85). Richard de Welles witnessed a grant in favor of the chaplain of St. Peter at Duffus, 1240 (REM., 213), and Walter de Welles is mentioned in an Aberdeen document of 1277 (*Friars*, 13). Alisaundre de Welles was warden of the Hospital of St. John of Jerusalem in Scotland, 1296. His seal shows a shield, lion rampant, S' *Fris Alexandri de Welles* (*Bain*, II, p. 202, 558). Galfridus de Wellys, chaplain in Aberdeen, 1317 (SCM., v, p. 5) is probably Galfridus de Wellys, perpetual vicar of Tarwas, 1331 (RAA., I, p. 202; II, p. 9). William de Wellis held lands in Aberdeen, 1342 (REA., I, p. 71). Thomas of Welles, a Scot, had a safe conduct to pass to Rome, 1448, and in 1486 Robert Wellys had a similar protection to pass between Scotland and England (*Bain*, IV, 1206, 1522). Patrick of Wellis, a witness in Perth, 1478 (RAA., II, 202), may be Patrick Wells (without the 'de'), canon of Scon, 1491 (*Scon*, p. 198). Gilbert Wellis was admitted burgess of Aberdeen, 1493 (NSCM., I, p. 37). Robert de Fontibus was archdeacon of St. Andrews, 1498 (REA., II, p. 306), and John de Fontibus or John Wellis was presbyter in Brechin diocese, 1528 (*Laing*, 369). Patrick Wellis was provost of Perth, 1501 (LAC., p. lxxxix), and William Vellis held land in the regality of Arbroath, 1535 (RAA., II, 828). James Wols

WELLS, *continued*

or Wels, an inhabitant of Sanquhar, 1684 (RPC., 3. ser. IX). George Wells, merchant in Dumfries, 1711 (*Dumfries*). Local pronunciation in Dumfries is Walls.

WELLWOOD, WELWOOD. From the lands of Wellwood in the parish of Dunfermline, Fife. The first of the name in record is William Walwod who witnessed a notarial instrument in 1422 (*Cambus.*, p. 103). He is probably the Willyhame of Walwod who was in 1437 one of the "Juggis compositouris of the debaitis...mouit betwix a venerabill fadir in crist Androw...Abbot of Dunfermlyn and the convent of that ilke on a part and Daui hacet of lumfennen on the tother part belangand the landis of petfuran" (RD., p. 285). Thomas Walwood was one of the "Commissari Burgorum" in 1578 "pro Sanctandrois" (RHM., I, p. 15), and William Wallatt, portioner of Touch, and several others of the surname are mentioned in 1588 (RPC., IV, p. 317). The family was intimately connected with the burgh of Dunfermline and for two centuries and more Wellwoods were provosts and officers of the regality. William Welwood was author of the earliest treatise on maritime jurisprudence (*The Sea-law of Scotland*, Edinburgh, 1590) published in Great Britain. In the *Dunfermline Burgh Records, 1488–1584*, the name appears as Vallod, Vallot, Vallud, Valuode, Wallaud, Wallet 1575, Wallod, Wallud 1494, Waluode, Walwode 1490, Wollat, etc. Other old forms noted are: Velvod 1594, Waldwod 1558, Wallude 1512, and Walwood.

WELSH. *See under* WALSH.

WELSHOT. Andrew Welschot or Wilschot occupied part of the lands of Lumphoy in the barony of Ballerno, 1525–30 (*Soltre*, p. 92). Sir Thomas Wilschot, witness in Edinburgh, 1530 (ibid., p. 99).

WEMYSS, WEEMS, WEMES. Of territorial origin from the lands of Wemyss in Fife. The first known of the name was Michael de Methkil (q.v.) who was variously called by that title or by that of de Wemys. In the beginning of the thirteenth century Michael de Wemeth witnessed a charter by Thomas filius Thancardi in favor of the Abbey of Arbroath (RAA., I, p. 69). Gamel, bishop of St. Andrews, in 1261 confirmed a charter by Sir John, son of Michael de Wemys, of the church of Wemys to the Hospital of Soltre (*Soltre*, p. 34). Michael de Wemys witnessed gift of the lands of Lamabride to William de Moray, c. 1268 (REM., p. 461). Sir David Wemyss was chosen ambassador to Norway in 1286 partly because he "of the langage weile couth ken" (*Wyntoun*, S. T. S. ed., v, p. 161). Sir Michael Wemyss rendered homage in 1296 (*Bain*, II, p. 187), but ten years later his possessions were singled out by Edward I for special savage treatment, when Aymer de Valence was ordered "to burn, destroy and strip" his lands and gardens because he (Edward) "has found neither good speech nor good service in him" (ibid., 1787). David de Wemes or Wemys, who was juror on an inquisition held at Perth in 1304 (ibid., II, 1592), witnessed the homage of Duncan, earl of Fife, to the abbot of Dunfermline, 1316 (RD., p. 236), and an obligation by Robert, abbot of Dunfermline, 1326 (RHM., I, p. 34). John Wemys of that Ilk was one of the conservators of the three years' truce in 1484 (*Bain*, IV, p. 309), and James Wemysse was general of 'artelerie' in Scotland, 1666 (*Wemyss*, II, p. 247). In the Muster Rolls of the Scots Guards in France the name appears as Oysmes. Vemis 1549, Vemys 1525, Vemyrs 1518, Veymis 1533, Weemes, Weems, and Wemis 1597, Weemyss 1661, Weimes 1596, Weimis 1598, Weims 1591, Weimys 1600, Wemis 1502, Wemise 1586, Wemyes 1436, Weymes 1586, Weymis 1678, Weyms 1619, Wymes 1414, Wymess 1734.

WENTON. Ingeram de Wenton and Thomas de Wenton were jurors at a court held at Le Bellocis Hill near Inverness, 1376–7 (*Innes Family*, p. 63). Thomas Wentoun of Strikmertene, a charter witness at Dudhope, 1609 (*Poltalloch Writs*, p. 144).

WEREGE. William Wezage who forfeited land in Dumfriesshire in the reign of David II (RMS., I, App. II, 1358) is evidently the William dictus Werege who held a cot in Moffat, Dumfriesshire, in the reign of Robert II (RHM., II, p. 94).

WERNEBALD. Wernebald was the earliest known ancestor of the Cunninghams. Robert filius Warnebaldi and his heirs had a grant of the vill of Parva Draffan from John, abbot of Kelso, c. 1160–80 (*Kelso*, 105), and c. 1170 Robert filius Wernebaldi granted the church of Kilmaurs to the Abbey of Kelso, which grant was confirmed a. 1189 by Robert, son of Robert, son of Wernebald (ibid., 284). Robert, son of Warnebald or Werembald, appears several times as charter witness in the first quarter of the thirteenth century (RAA., I, index; REG., p. 65). He witnessed the gift by William the Lion of a toft in Stirling to the church of Glasgow, c. 1189–99 (REG., p. 67). Robert, son of Warnebald, and Richenda, his spouse, in 1238 made a gift of the lands of Tibberty to the Abbey of Arbroath (RAA., I, p. 198).

WEST. A common surname in Gamrie (*Turriff*), and also found in Perthshire and West Lothian. Janet Wast in Biggar, 1670 (*Lanark CR.*), and Isobel West in Little Dunkeld (*Dunkeld*). Pension was paid to Margt. Waste, relict of Robert Cruizean, late deacon of the cordiners, 1723 (*Guildry*, p. 127).

WESTALL, WESTELL. From the lands of Westhall in the parish of Oyne, Aberdeenshire. Archibald de Westhall or Weschell had a charter of lands of Ouyn in the lordship of Garrioch from David II (*RMS.*, I, App. II, 787). A Mr. Westall killed Captain Gourlay in a duel at North Queensferry, October 30, 1824.

WESTGARTH. Local. There is a West Garth near Colinton, Midlothian. John Westgarth, 1770 (*Lauder*).

WESTLAND, WESTLANDS. Probably from Westlandis vocatis The Leyes of Tullochaddie which were retoured to George, marquis of Huntlie, in 1638 (*Retours, Aberdeen*, 242). Alexander Westland was admitted burgess of Aberdeen in 1461 (*NSCM.*, I, p. 17), and a later Alexander Westland was dean of guild in the same city in the first half of the eighteenth century. John Westland leased part of the Grange of Aberbothry in 1443 (*Cupar-Angus*, I, p. 120), Symon Westland was tenant of Kemphill, 1482 (ibid., I, p. 233), and John Westland in the parish of Banchory-Devenick, died in 1826 (*Banchory-Devenick*, p. 298).

WESTON. Local. There are places named Weston and Westoun in Lanarkshire, and a Weston near Dolphinston, Peeblesshire. William de Westone of Wyggetone rendered homage in 1296. His seal bears two squirrels facing each other, a small dog below: S' W. . de *Wesytonam* (*Bain*, II, p. 214, 534). John of Westone was juror on an inquisition at Peebles, 1304 (ibid., 1436), and John de Westone held a ten-pound land in the tenement of Mertone near Edinburgh before 1315 (*RMS.*, I, 15). William of Westone was in the king of England's service in France, 1369 (*Bain*, IV, 165). Thomas Westoun forfeited his lands in the reign of David II (*RMS.*, I, App. II, 811). Thomas Westoun rendered to Exchequer the accounts of the burgh of Selkirk, 1566 (*ER.*, XIX, p. 326). David Wastoun in Faldlav, parish of Carnwath, 1678, and Alexander Wastoune in Faldlaw, 1689 (*Lanark CR.*). Wastoun of that Ilk in Workman's MS.

WESTRAY. From the lands of Westray in the island of Westray, Orkney. Michael de Westray, knight, witnessed a charter by Henry de St. Clair, earl of Orkney, apud Kirkwaw, in 1391 (*RMS.*, I, 824).

WESTWATER. Of local origin from some small place probably in the west of Fife. The place name may now be extinct. John Westwalter, friar of Culross in 1565, appears again in 1569 as John Vestualter, friar and notary of the monastery of Culross (*Laing*, 782, 844, 845), and is doubtless the John Vostuatter, clerk of the diocese of St. Andrew in 1577 (ibid., 953). Andrew Westwater is recorded in Dunfermline in 1584 (*Dunfermline*), William Westwater in Erniesvde in the parish of Glendovan in 1617 and Robert Westwater in Over Mosvde in 1620 (*Dunblane*), Cristian Westwater was on the stool of repentance in Kirkcaldy in 1640 (*PBK.*, 174), and May Westwater recorded in the parish of Torphichen in 1680 (*Torphichen*). Alexander Macdonald Westwater, Church of Scotland missionary in Manchuria, died 1934. Wastwater a. 1587.

WESTWOOD. Probably from Westwood near Newport, Fife. There is also a Westwood in Perthshire, near Stanley, and there are places of the name elsewhere. Robert Westwood witnessed a notarial instrument in Fife in 1495 (*Laing*, 221). Westout 1498, Wostwood 1575; Wastwood.

WETHERHERD. From the occupation of 'wether-herd' or shepherd (OE. *weder* + *hierde*). Thomas dictus Wethyrhyrde held six bovates of land in Neucraneston, c. 1200 (*Neubotle*, p. 168). William Wytherhird of Berwickshire rendered homage, 1296 (*Bain*, II, p. 210).

WHALE. Now a rare surname if it still exists. Of local origin from the place named Le Whele in 1296 (*Bain*, II, p. 191). The Whele was the name of one of the five churches in the parish of Castleton, near the Whele (or Wheel) Causey, a supposed Roman road, from which it got its name. Thomas Whaill is recorded in Yetham, 1684 (*Peebles CR.*), Andrew Whale was schoolmaster in Stitchell, 1722 (*Stitchill*, p. 183), and his son, Lancelot Whale, became rector of the Grammar School of Kelso (*Heirs*, 474), and schoolmaster to Sir Walter Scott. Robert Whale, son of Lancelot, became a surgeon in the army.

WHAMOND, WHYMOND. William Quhoman witnessed a sasine by Gilbert Ramsay of Banff, 1483, and John Quhoman witnessed an instrument by Master Alexander Ramsay in 1534 (*Bamff*, p. 34, 64). The editor, Sir J. Ramsay, suggests Quhoman may be = Whamond. Andrew Quhoman, witness in Kirriemuir, 1610 (*Laing*, 1583). James Whamond is author of the interesting volume *Jamie Tacket*.

WHAN. A shortened form of (MAC)WHAN, q.v. Complaint was made against Robert Whan, flesher in Dysart, 1678 (*Dysart*, p. 53).

WHANNEL, WHANNELL. From (MAC)WHAN-NEL, q.v. Old spellings in Galloway in 1684 (*Parish*) are Whandle, Whannell, and Whonnell.

WHARRIE. A shortened form of (MAC)WHAR-RIE, q.v. Thomas Quharry or Quharrie in Kincadyou prosecuted Lokart of Cleghorne for 'maisterfull reving' and other offences, 1574 (RPC., II, p. 379, 386). William Quherrie in Hill of Kincaidzo, 1597, Janet Wharrie in Cairtland, parish of Lanark, 1621, and James Quharrie in Aultoun, 1643 (*Lanark CR.*). James Wharrie rebel in Kilblain paroch, 1685 (*Commons*, p. 1).

WHEELANS, WHELLANS. *See under* WHIL-LANS.

WHEELWRIGHT. A wright who made wheels and wheel carriages. Johannes Qhwelwrycht or Chwelwricht held land in Inuernys, 1361–65 (REM., p. 305, 317). "This is still a familiar surname in West Riding, Yorkshire" (*Bardsley*). Cognate names are Cartwright and Wainwright.

WHIGGENSHAW. Local. Thomas Quhiggenshall, servant to George French in Stitchill, 1657, appears in the following year as Quhigginshaw (*Stitchill*, p. 9, 11).

WHILLANS, WHILLENS, WHEELANS, WHEL-LANS, WHILLIS. Surnames current in Roxburghshire, and derived from the old lands of Quheillands (1642), Wherland or Whilland (1653), or Quheilland (1661) in the lordship of Liddisdaill. Thomas and William Querland mentioned in 1505 are referred to in the following year as Thomas and William Querlance (*Peebles*, p. 33, 41). James Quhillans appears in Coldingham, 1622 (*Laing*, 1902), and Robert Whillas was notary there, 1675 (ibid., 2747). Thomas Whillas was juror on a retour of special service in Duns, Berwickshire, in 1672 (*Home*, 194). John Whillas in Upsetlington, 1663, and five more of the name are recorded in Lauder Commissariot Record. Robert Whillas, merchant in Duns, 1688 (*Edin. App.*). Recorded in Lauder, Berwickshire, 1940 (*WScot.*). (2) The Argyllshire bearers of this surname are of Irish origin, an offshoot of the MacWhellans or MacQuhillans of the Route (a corruption of the name Dalriada) in Antrim. In Ir. the name is *MacUidhilin* or *MacUidhlin*, apparently a corruption of MacLlewellen, in 1627 spelled McVuellen. The family is believed to have been of Welsh origin and

settled in Antrim soon after the Anglo-Norman invasion of Ireland. The greater part of their lands were forcibly taken from them by the Macdonnells towards the close of the sixteenth century, completely destroying their power and reducing them to a subordinate position. This probably led some of the name to seek a new home on the opposite shore of Argyllshire.

WHIMSTER. A rare current form of FEMISTER, q.v.

WHIN. A shortened Anglicised form of MAC-WHIN, q.v.

WHINCUP. An English surname of local origin from Whincop in Cumberland.

WHINKERSTONES. From Whinkerstones near Duns, Berwickshire. Thomas de Hynkerstane of Berwickshire who rendered homage in 1296 is doubtless the Thomas de Quinquersteynes who with his wife Cecilia in 1296 quitclaimed to Stephen Pessun all Cecilia's dower in the English and Scottish lands of Ingelram Pessun, her former husband, grandfather of the said Stephen (*Bain*, II, p. 171, 210). John de Qwynkyrstanys appears as a canon of Holyrood in 1372 and 1378 (LSC., p. 98, 101).

WHIPPO. Sir Robert Quhippo was a witness in Lanark in 1490 (*Lanark*, p. 8). He is most probably the Sir Robert Quhippo or Quhippup, chaplain, who had a suit in 1495 as to the ferry at Clydesholm. Sir Thomas Quhuppo was a rentaller in Lanark, c. 1505 (*Lanark*, p. 15). William Quhippo of Kydlaw is mentioned in 1583 (*Soltre*, p. 149), and Eupham Quhippo in Edinburgh in 1598 (*Edinb. Marr.*). David Quhippo of Leyhouss was retoured heir of Thomas Quhippo in the lands of Kidlaw in 1614 (*Retours, Haddington*, 64), and Robert Whippo was burgess of Dysart, 1653 (*Inquis. Tut.*, 796). A family of this name in East Lothian figure in the criminal trials, and after the beginning of the seventeenth century they disappear from the district.

WHIRTER. A curtailed form of MACWHIRTER, q.v.

WHITBY. From Whitby in Yorkshire. Johannes de Whitebi, Nicholaus de Whitebi, Ranulphus de Whitebi, and Robert de Whitebi rendered homage at Berwick, 1291 (RR.). Warin de Whiteby, burgess of Perth, rendered homage in 1296 (*Bain*, II, 814 and p. 197), and Henry de Wyteby held land in Waldeugate, Berwick, in 1307 (*Kelso*, 43).

WHITE, WHYTE. *Huita, Huuita,* and *Hwita* occur as personal names in OE. charters, from OE. *hwit,* 'white.' *Hwita* is also found as a byname. In an OE. charter dated before 925 A. D. we find *Wulfnoð hwita (Cartularium Saxonicum).* Whyte is also used as an Englishing of Gaelic *M'Illebhàin (MacGhillebhàin).* In early record the name is Latinized *albus.* Uuiaett Hwite witnessed King Eadgar's charter of Coldingham, c. 1097–1107 (*Nat. MSS.,* I, 4). Adam Albus appears as a charter witness between 1180 and 1214 (RAA., I, 39, 61), and c. 1198 Simone Albus witnessed a charter by Earl David (LAC., 8). Before 1240 William Albus witnessed the grant of Parva Kyp (Little Kyp) to the Abbey of Kelso (*Kelso,* 181). John Albus was senescallus or steward to Matilda, countess of Angus, 1242 (RAA., I, p. 332). Robert I granted to Adam Quhyt a charter of the lands of Stayhar afterwards called Stauquhat or Barskimming in Ayrshire (RMS., I, App. II, 346), and Adam Albus held lands in Kincardineshire in the reign of Robert II. Gilbert Qwhyt was bailie of the burgh of Rutherglen, 1376 (ER., II, p. 537), Thome White held land in Irvine, 1426 (*Irvine,* I, p. 130), Andrew Qwhit was a citizen of Brechin, 1472 (REB., II, 275), and Pait (= Patrick) Quheyt rented the land of Kendy Hvll in 1525 (*Rental*). Robert Whytte was first provost (1658) the town of Kirkekaldie ever had (Lamont, *Diary,* p. 108). Quheit 1587, Quheitt 1588, Quhit 1497, Quhite 1493, Quhvt 1562, Quhyte 1462, Quyt 1606, Qwhyth 1482, Qwite 1407, Qwyt 1471, Whyt 1646, Whytt 1677.

WHITEBROW. The mill of Westerbalbretane was leased to William Qwhitbrow in 1376 (RHM., I, p. lxvi), and John Qwitbrow was charged with being a forestaller in Aberdeen in 1402 (CRA., p. 384). Henry Quhitbrow was admitted burgess of Aberdeen in 1466 and Walter Quhitbrow in 1473 (NSCM., I, p. 19, 24). Cf. the old Pictish name TALORG.

WHITEBURNE. From Whitburn in West Lothian. Adam de Whiteburne and Gilcrist de Whiteburne in Linlithgowshire rendered homage, 1296. The seal of Adam bears a rose and S' Ade de Witbvrn (Bain, II, p. 201, 551). See under WOODBURN.

WHITECORN. John Quhitcorne in Aberdeen was fined for breaking a town ordinance, 1510 (Mill, *Plays,* p. 139).

WHITECROSS. Probably from Whitecross in the parish of Chapel, Aberdeenshire. John Quhitcorse contributed to church repairs in Aberdeen in 1508 (CRA., p. 79), and Alexander Quheitcross is in record in the burgh

in 1573 (ibid., p. 10). Adam Quhytcors was at the Mylne of Kinguiddie in 1617 (RSCA., II, p. 220). The name is recorded in Edinburgh, 1940.

WHITEFIELD. Local. There are several places named Whitefield listed in the County Directory.

WHITEFOORD, WHITEFORD, WHITFORD. From the lands of Whitefoord on the river Cart about three miles above Paisley, Renfrewshire. The first of the Whitefoords of that Ilk is said by Crawfurd (*History of Renfrewshire,* p. 241) to have obtained his lands by grant from the High Steward for his services at the battle of Largs in 1263, but like all such traditionary statements it is very questionable. A Walter Whitefoord, however, witnessed a charter by Alexander III in that year. In 1296 a writ was directed to the sheriff of Lanark to restore his lands to John de Whiteford (Bain, II, 853). Johannes de Quhetfurd *dominus ejusdem* witnessed a notarial instrument in 1413 (*Pollok,* p. 146), and a later Johannes Quhitefurd had remission for his part in burning the town of Dunbertane in 1489 (*Lennox,* II, p. 133; APS., XII, p. 34). Robert Quhytfurd, cellarer of Crossraguel in 1489/90 is the Robert de Quintfort or Quintfurt who was elected abbot in 1491 (*Crossraguel,* I, p. 47, 54). John Whytefurd is mentioned in the will of Egidia Blair, Lady Row, in 1530 (ibid., I, p. 95), John Quhitefurde of that Ilk is a witness in 1553 (*Protocols,* I), and John Quhitefurde of Myltoune was charged with abiding from the raid of Lauder in 1558 (*Trials,* I, p. *404). The elder line failed in Sir John of that Ilk, c. 1688. Before the main branch of the family settled down to 'Whitefoord' the forms Quhitefuird, Quhitfurde, Quhytfuird (1637), Quheitfurd (1503), Quhvtfurde (1605), Quhytefurd, Quhytefurde (1607), and Quhytfurd (1584) occur. Quhitfurd and Quhitfurde 1512, Whytford and Whyteford 1516.

WHITEHALL. Local. There are several places so named in CD. James Quhithall, burgess freeman of Glasgow, 1585 (*Burgesses*).

WHITEHEAD. "Fair or white haired." Adam Whytehevde de Hoton, juror on inquisition before the sheriff of Berwick, 1300 (Bain, II, 1178). Henry Quhitehede, burgess of Edinburgh, 1423 (*Egidii,* p. 46). Andrew Quhytheide was vicar of Lownane in 1485 (RAA., II, 268), and another Andrew Quhithede or Quhittat was rector of Aldcathy, 1523–4 (*Scon,* p. 202–3). Philip Quhithede was fined for disturbance in Aberdeen, 1492 (CRA., I,

812

WHITEHEAD, *continued*

p. 421), and another Philip Quhitehede or Quhithed was chamberlain of Linlithgow and a witness in 1537 (ER., xix, p. 30; *Johnsoun*). A family of Whitehead of Park flourished in West Lothian in 1585, and Philip Whitehead, sheriff depute of Linlithgow, sat in the Scottish Parliament, 1585 (APS., iii, p. 373). Matthew Weitheid or Weitheit, 1575, or Weitheit, 1577, or Weitit, 1581, appears in Dunfermline (*Dunfermline*). John Whythead at Greatcorse of St. Mary's Isle, 1686 (*Kirkcudbright*), and George Whitehead was tenant in Lochrig, 1845 (*Heirs*, 831). Quhitheid 1526, Quhytheid 1585, Quhythed 1466.

WHITEHILL. Of local origin from one or other of the small places of the name in Midlothian, Lanarkshire, or Kincardineshire. Andrew Quhithill was witness in Linlithgow in 1538 (*Johnsoun*). Payment to Johne Quhythill, 1558 (*Rent. Dunk.*, p. 352). John Whitehill witnessed a sasine of 1577 (*Poltalloch Writs*, p. 190). John Whitehill in Keppoch, 1666 (*Sasines*, 1310). Robert Whythill in Horswood, 1675, and Robert Whithill in Kilbarchan, 1758 (*Kilbarchan*).

WHITEHOPE. Of local origin. There are places of this name in Peeblesshire and Selkirkshire, but probably some place in the north is the source of the name. Henry Qwtthope witnessed a wadset of Little Carcore in Angus, 1401 (*Southesk*, p. 719), and in 1586 caution was found for Gilbert Quhithop, sheriff-clerk of Forfar (RPC., iv, p. 93). Jonet Quhytcoipe in Leyth, 1605 (*Inquis.*, 213).

WHITELAW, Whytelaw, Whytlaw. Territorial, from the lands of Whitelaw in the parish of Morebattle. There was also a barony of Whitelaw in the parish of Bowden. John de Wytelowe of the county of Edneburk, who rendered homage, 1296 (*Bain*, ii, p. 203), was ancestor of Whitelaws of that Ilk near Dunbar (Nisbet on RR.). His seal bears a seven-leaved flower and S' *Joh's de Vitlav* (*Bain*, ii, p. 544). John Whitelaw *de eodem*, a juror on inquest on bounds of lands of Gladmor (Gladsmuir), 1430 (*Hadd. Chs. & Writs*, 16). Archibald de Quhitelaw, archdeacon of St. Andrews 'infra partes Laudonie' in 1470 (*Soltre*, p. 319), appears again in 1486–88 as Archibald Quhitelaw and Quhitlau (*Bain*, iv, 1520–1521; RMP., p. 264). He was an eminent prelate and secretary of state to James iii (*Neubotle*, p. 256; *Bain*, iv, 1564). Patrick Quhitlaw was feufarmer of Pettindreich, 1560 (ER., xix, p. 102), and Bartholomew Quhytlaw had an instrument of sasine of land in Paxtoun, 1578 (*Home*, 231). Margaret Quhyt-

law was retoured heir of Patrick Quhytlaw *de eodem*, 1586 (*Retours, Linlithgow*, 15–17). Quhitelau 1467, Quhyetlaw 1564, Quhytelaw 1564, Whitlau 1736, Whitlawe 1457, Whytlaw 1653; Qwhytlawe.

WHITELOCK. Generally explained as having white locks, white haired. There is, however, an OE. personal name, *Wiht-lāc*, from which it could come. Th Quhvteloke, burgess of Edinburgh, 1403 (*Guildry*, p. 44). Robert Quhvtlok was a tenant under the Abbey of Kelso, 1567 (*Kelso*, p. 524), and in 1586 there is mention of "Anne Quhytlokis cotage" in Auchtirmuktie (ER., xxi, p. 423).

WHITENESS. Local. John de Quhitness, provost of Edinburgh, 1376, was the first in Edinburgh to whom the title of provost was given (*Tracts Scot. Hist.*, 1836, p. 31).

WHITESIDE. A surname found in Lanarkshire may be derived from the lands of Whiteside (Quhytesyde 1625, Whytsyid 1649) in Lanark *Retours*.

WHITESMITH. From the occupation, a worker in white metals, as a tinsmith or silversmith, also a finisher or polisher. In the *Roll of Edinburgh burgesses and guild brethren, 1761–1841* (Edinburgh, 1933) it is recorded that John Lockhart or Lochrie, tinplate worker, was made burgess as apprentice to Andrew Cockburn, white-iron smith, showing change of the designation (1781).

WHITESTONE. John Albo Petro de Ferne, charter witness in Angus, 1267 (REB., i, p. 7). Of local origin. There is Whiteston in Perthshire, and a Whitestone near Skene, Aberdeenshire.

WHITEWELL. Local, from some place of the name in the South. In Latin charters de Albo Fonte. Edward de Albo Fonte, rector of the church of Kirkmolvn, made a grant of the lands of Qwhytwel to the House of Soltre between 1238–1300 (*Soltre*, p. 28). Henry Wvtewele, burgess of Dumfries, 1215 (*Kelso*, 332), is probably the Henry Whitewell, burgess of Dumfries, to whom the monks of Kelso granted a lease of their whole lands in the parish of Dumfries for 12sh. yearly (ibid., 330). Roger de Wytewele in Dumfriesshire, c. 1259 (APS., i, p. 88; *Bain*, i, 2176). Edward de Whitewelle of the county of Edinburgh rendered homage, 1296 (*Bain*, ii, p. 199). Whitewell is a Yorkshire surname from a vill and township of the name in the North Riding.

WHITEWRIGHT. William Whitewright (1783–1874), born in Balmaghie, Kirkcudbrightshire, died in New York City. According to Weekley (p. 227) the name expresses the personality of the bearer.

WHITFORD. *See under* WHITEFOORD.

WHITING. From the OE. personal name *Hwiting*, 'the son of *Hwita*.' Andrew Qwityng was burgess of Edinburgh in 1381 (*Egidii*, p. 22), and Robert Quhiting held land in Edinburgh in 1400 (ibid., p. 37). John Quhitvne or Qwitine filius et heres quondam Roberti Quhiting, burgess of Edinburgh, is in record in 1411 (*Cambus.*, 94), and appears again in 1425 and 1433 as burgess there (RMS., II, 25; REO., p. 329). John Whityne was bailie of Stirling in 1428 (ER., IV, p. 454).

WHITLIE. An English surname, most probably of late introduction. There are several places named Whitley, Whiteley, etc., in England. Patrick Whitlie in Creis, 1669 (*Lauder*).

WHITSLADE. Local. There are lands of Whitslade in the parish of Broughton, Peeblesshire, another Whitslade near Hawick, Roxburghshire, and a Whitslaid near Lauder, Berwickshire. There is also a Weedslade in Northumberland. Willelmus de Wideslade witnessed a charter by Steffan, son of Swan de Œtun (Ayton), to the Priory of Coldingham, c. 1170 (*Raine*, 434). Audoenus de Witslede witnessed a confirmation charter, c. 1190 (*Kelso*, 260). William de Wideslad was witness to a charter by Patrick, fifth earl of Dunbar (*Raine*, 123), and Willelmus de Wideslade or Wydeslade witnessed a quitclaim by David de Quikeswude of the wood of Aldecambus to the Priory of Coldingham (ibid., 185).

WHITSON. William Quhitsoun, bailie of Perth in 1369, is doubtless the Willelmus de [wrongly] Qwhithosum, burgess of the same town in 1379 (*Milne*, p. 29; *Scon*, p. 144). John Quhytson who witnessed a charter by Robert Mersar of Inuerpefery, 1454 (LIM., 120), appears in 1456 as John Quhitsoun, burgess of Perth (RAA., II, 107). In 1484 and again in 1498 the lands of le Peblis in Angus were leased to Thomas Quhitsone (ibid., II, 283, 393). James Quhitsoun was witness in Fife, 1547 (*Gaw*, 9), Thomas Whitson was notary and writer in Kirktoun of Ratray, 1688 (DPD., II, p. 265, 268), Janet Whitson appears in Easter Caputh, 1693 (*Dunkeld*), and Thomas Whitson was an important man in Dundee in 1823. Quhytsoun 1458. Harrison suggests (1) White's son as meaning, and (2) for Whitsunday, a name given to one born on that day. This latter to me unlikely. First preferable. The local pronunciation of the name in Roxburghshire is Whutson.

WHITTET. John Wittet is recorded in Dunfermline, 1586 (*Dunfermline*). David Whittiet or Whittite was accused of fornication in 1648 (PBK., p. 327–328), William Whittat, skinner, was burgess of Dundie, 1657 (*Inquis.*, 4300), Andrew Whittet, slater, burgess of Edinburgh, 1617 (*Edinb. Marr.*), and in 1676 the wife of Thomas Whittitt in Dundee was charged with being a "schismatick and disorderlie person" (DPD., II, p. 443). Andrew Wittet in Dunning complained against his minister, 1689 (RPC., 3. ser. XIV, p. 188), William Whittet was tenant in Pitrodie, 1711 (DPD., II, p. 280), and another William Whittet of Easter Buttergask is in record, 1747 (*Dunkeld*).

WHITTINGHAME. From the lands of Whittinghame in East Lothian. Gilbert de Whitingham was one of the witnesses to a charter by Patrick, first earl of Dunbar before 1214 (*Raine*, App., 116). Petrus de Wyttigham was witness to a charter by Constantine, son of Adam, son of Edulf, to the Abbey of Neubotle, c. 1245 (*Neubotle*, p. 19). A pavment was made to David Wattinghame in 1557 (*Guildry*, p. 120).

WHITTON. Several individuals between 1165 and 1306 appear to have derived their surname from the lands of Whitton in Morebattle parish, Roxburghshire (*Melros*, 47, 91–94, 109, 125–129, 132, 140, etc.). Magister R. de Wyttoñ witnessed a charter by John, prior of St. Andrews in 1285 (*Neubotle*, 59). Michael de Witton and Adam de Wytton, both of the county of Selkirk, rendered homage in 1296. The seal of Michael shows a deer running and S' *Michaelis de Wittvn*, and that of Adam, which is defective, reads S' *Ade de Wittona* (*Bain*, II, p. 198, 544). Richard de Wyttone, persone of the church of Hauwyk, also rendered homage in the same year. His seal bears, if it be his, a lion fighting an enormous dragon, and S' *Ricardi de Wynhov* (ibid., p. 202, 553). Michael de Whitton was chief forester of the forest of Selkyrk in 1303 (*Bain*, IV, p. 457), and David Qwitton was juror on an inquest at Roxburgh in 1361 (ibid., 61).

WHOMMES. From the old lands of the name in the barony of Hawick (in 1510 Quhamvs). The land of Ade de Wammes is mentioned in a charter of the lands of Brancheshelm, Roxburghshire, c. 1183 (RPSA., p. 261). Henry de Hommes of Roxburghshire rendered homage, 1296. His seal bears a hunting-horn, stringed, turned to sinister, S' *Henrici de Wovmvs* (*Bain*, II, p. 200, 532). As Henry del Whommes he was a juror at Roxburgh, 1304 (ibid., 1435).

WHYMOND. A variant of WHAMOND, q.v.

WHYNTIE. A rare surname in Aberdeen, of local origin from Whynty or Whyntie in the parish of Boyndie, Banffshire.

WHYTE. See under WHITE.

WHYTELAW, WHYTLAW. See under WHITE-LAW.

WHYTOCH, WHYTOCK. Perhaps of local origin from Whitehauch, anciently Quhithauch, in Liddesdale. There is, however, an OE. personal name, Hwittuc or Hwituc, from which it may be derived. William Quhittok in Edinburgh had a precept of sasine in 1576 (Soltre, p. 138), and Umphredus Quhittak was heir of James Quhittak in Clevage, 1636 (Inquis., 2241).

WICK. A surname in Orkney, of local origin from the town of Wick in Caithness. Sir James of Weik is in record in 1456 (OPS., II, p. 621), and again in 1461 as Wrke (Clan Donald, I, p. 546). (2) Perhaps of local origin from England. Wyke in Yorkshire was Qwyk in 1297 (Ewen, p. 340), and there are three places named Week in Somersetshire indifferently pronounced Week and Wick. A payment was made to William Wik, a mime who played before King James I, 1430 (ER., IV, p. 680).

WICWOD. Local. Robert Wicwod, witness at Lochlevyn, 1546 (Rollok, 3).

WIDOW. Notwithstanding the first entry I think this name is a form Wido or Wydo for Guido. John son of the widow was juror on an inquest at Lanark, 1303 (Bain, II, 1420). Robert Widow had a charter of the lands of Ardkegy in the barony of Inuerlunan from David II (RMS., I, App. II, 918), and Henricus filius Vidue was juror on an inquest apud Muskylburg, 1359 (RD., p. 267). Robert Wedow and Thomas Wedow appear in Arrot, Angus, in 1513 (SCM., IV, p. 14), and William Weddow is recorded in West Cultmalundie, 1670 (DPD., I, p. 293).

WIDOWSON. James Widowson in Fiddesbeg, 1735 (Aberdeen). Lower and Ewen (p. 248) consider this name as "son of Wido, i.e. Guido." See WIDOW. This name may have been earlier spelled Wedonsone or Wedowsoun. Alexander Wedowstoune, admitted burgess of Aberdeen, 1579 (NSCM., I, p. 74) appears again as Wedonsone in 1595 (CRA., p. 127), and James Wedonsoun was admitted burgess of the same town in 1597 (NSCM., I, p. 91).

WIER. A form of WEIR, q.v.

WIGGEIN. Surety was found in 1569 for Rynne Wiggein and Arche Wiggein in East Teviotdaill (RPC., I, p. 661). Perhaps from Wigan in Lancashire.

WIGHAME. This surname occurs occasionally on the Border, but is not mentioned in the Liddesdale rent rolls of 1376 or 1541. Old forms are Wigham, Wighame, Wigholme, and in the Workman MS. it is recorded as Wighoun and Wigum. Rob of Wvgam witnessed resignation of a feu in Peebles, 1471 (Scots Lore, p. 52), Paul Veghum was burgess of Northtberwyk in 1561 (CMN., 80–81), and Thomas Wigholme was burgess of Edinburgh, 1564 (RPC., I, p. 278). James Wigholme was retoured heir of Andrew Wigholme in lands in the barony of Dummany, 1579 (Retours, Linlithgow, 14), Ninian Whighome appears in Edinburgh, 1619 (Edinb. Marr.), and Whigham of Sanquhar was originally (c. 1618) spelled Wigholme. Edward Wigham was overseer at Leadhills, 1749 (Lanark CR.). Harrison says it is a form of Wickham.

WIGHT. Most probably from the OE. personal name Wiht. Thomas Whight, burgois de Seint John de Perth, rendered homage, 1291 (RR.). A family of this name was settled about Ormiston, East Lothian, from the sixteenth to the eighteenth century. James Wicht was prebendary of the Collegiate Church of Holy Trinity in Edinburgh, 1554 (Soltre, p. 200). Alexander Wycht was a monk of Inchaffray, 1555 (Inchaffray, p. xcix), John Weycht is recorded in Auchtinraicht in the same year (Protocols, I), and Hendrie Veycht and Riche Wycht were tenants on lands of the Abbey of Kelso, 1567 (Kelso, p. 519, 520). Weight 1686.

WIGHTMAN. Harrison says from "wight," strong, active, + man, and Bardsley quotes from Piers Plowman (5195), "A wightman of strengthe." Gilbert Wichtmann was rector of Lyne in 1527 (LCD., p. 85), and John Wychtman rendered to Exchequer the accounts of the burgh of Peebles in 1563 (ER., XIX, p. 225). Thomas Vychtman was witness in Perthshire, 1547 (Gaw, 46), John Waichtman appears in Melrose, 1606 (RRM., I, p. 7), Johannes Wichtman, burgess of Peebles, 1631 (Retours, Peebles, 89), Adam Wightman in Meikle-holme-syde, 1680 (Dumfries), Thomas Wightman is recorded in Broxburne in 1688 (RPC., 3. ser. XIII, p. 235), and another Thomas Wightman was tenant of Whiterigg in 1763 (Lauder). John Wightman was dean of guild in Aberdeen, 1716 (Guildry, p. 202). Wichtman 1569.

WIGHTON. An Angus surname. James Wigtoun apud Dunde had a precept of remission in 1492 (RSS., I, 12). William Wichtoun was resident in Brechin, 1548 (REB., II, 200), Robert Vigtoun, witness in Perthshire, 1549 (*Gaw*, 31), Jean Wichtane was heir portioner of Andrew Wichtane, burgess of Aberbrothock, 1631 (*Inquis.*, 1803), William Wigtone in Lyston-mylne, 1655 (*Lauder*), and George Wighton, merchant in Cupar, 1710 (*Dunkeld*). Thomas Wichtane, notary public in Dundee in the beginning of the seventeenth century, appears also as Vichtan (*Wedd.*). Wichtan 1620, Wychtoun 1578. There is a parish of this name in Norfolk, England.

WIGMER or WIGMORE. Most probably from the OE. personal name *Wigmær*, "war renowned." There are also places named Wigmore in England. A family of this name were prominent burgesses of Edinburgh in the thirteenth and fourteenth centuries. John Wyggemore, burgess of Edinburgh, who rendered homage in 1296 (*Bain*, II, 820 and p. 197) may be the John de Wyggemer who was a witness in the inquiry concerning the Templars in Scotland in 1309 (Wilkins, *Concilia*, p. 382), and the John Wigmor, burgess of Edinburgh in 1328 (LSC., 87). John Wigmer, alderman of Edinburgh in 1344, may be the John Wigmor, lord of Over-Liberton in record in 1362, and the John Wygmer who complained in 1357 that his ships, wrecked in a storm, were plundered near Bamburgh and Tynemouth (*Bain*, IV, 10). Sir Roger Wygmer had a grant of land in 1392 from the common good of the town of Edinburgh, and was a charter witness there in 1397 (RMS., I, App. I, 157) as Roger Wigmere. In the sixteenth century the family of this name possessed a mansion in Jedburgh, now called "Queen Mary's House," from a tradition that Mary, Queen of Scots, stayed in it for a few days in 1566. The surname seems now to be extinct.

WILDGOOSE. John Wildguse who was canon of Aberdeen in 1366 (REA., II, p. 58), is probably the Johannes Wylgus in record in Moray, c. 1391 (REM., p. 129). Andro Wilgues occupied the subdean's croft and mains within the canonry of Ross, c. 1560 (OPS., II, p. 415), and John Wilgus in Levtoun was assizor on witch trial in Aberdeen, 1596 (SCM., I, p. 110). Thomas Vilguis was admitted burgess of Aberdeen in 1612 (NSCM., I, p. 110). In 1613 Gilbert Wilguis and Thomas Wilguiss, baxters, "wer convict for baking of eat breid against the statuttis" of the burgh of Aberdeen (SCM., V, p. 8), and Gilbert Wilguis, most probably the person just named, appears as member of council of the same burgh in 1620 (CRA., p. 370). There were tenants of this name in N. Leask and Knapleask in 1696 and "the burriel ground of the Wildgooses" still remains in the parish of Slains. Probably Willgook, which appears at the same time, is another form of the name. It is still known in Buchan, particularly in Peterhead district. Three persons of this name were on an assize at Stable of Slains in 1597 (*Jervise*, II, p. 248). Searle gives *Wilgils* as an OE. personal name, and Barber has *Wildgis* which I cannot find elsewhere.

WILDRIDGE. Recorded in Airdrie. George Wildridge, cabinet maker in Caldtoun, Edinburgh, 1689 (*Edin. App.*).

WILDSMITH. John Wyldesmyth was one of the jurors on inquest on lands of Hopkelchoc, 1259 (*Bain*, I, 2162; APS., I, p. 88). The English authorities differ in their explanation of this name. Lower suggests "probably a corruption of *weld*-smith," a forger of iron; Bardsley says that the surname in England "is almost entirely confined to Yorkshire, the centre of the woollen trade," so the name may have a connection with wool; Harrison says it means a smith dweller at a weald; and Weekley "the smith in the wild." George W. Wildsmith died in Edinburgh, 1939.

WILKIE. This name is a double diminutive of WILLIAM, q.v. A family of this name were seated at Rathobyres in Midlothian from the beginning of the fourteenth century, and the name early found a home in Fife. David Wilke witnessed a notarial instrument at Pitcairn, Fife, in 1495 (*Laing*, 223), William Wilkie was member of an assize in Edinburgh in 1529, James Wilke was bailie of the burgh of the Canongate in 1561, and John Wilky was member of council of Edinburgh in 1580 (MCM., II, p. 96, 285, 288). Catharine Wilkie is recorded in Dysart in 1541 (*Dysart*, p. 7), James Wilkie was tenant of Newbattle Abbey in 1563 (*Neubotle*, p. 330), Mr. James Wilkie was principal of Sanct Saluatour Colleage, St. Andrews, 1574 (Mill, *Plays*, p. 285), and the accounts of the baillies of the burgh of Lanark were rendered to Exchequer by William Wilkie, burgess there, in 1591 (ER., XXII, p. 172). Robert Wilkie was prior of the Isle S. Serf in Lochleven in 1599, Archibald Wilkie was member of an assize in the Cannongait in 1602 (*Trials*, II, p. 397), and Thomas Wilkie was schoolmaster in Selkirk in 1627 (MCM., II, p. 49). Vilke 1515, Weilkey 1654, Weilkie 1649, Vilkey.

WILKIESON, 'son of WILKIE,' q.v. Johannes Wilkyson was juror in a trial in Moray in 1398 (REM., p. 212), John Wilkysoun was

WILKIESON, *continued*
a forestaller in Aberdeen in 1402 (CRA., p. 384), and Walter Wilkison and John Wilkison were jurors on an assize at Liston in 1459 (*Edmonstone,* p. 80). William Wilkison, notary public in Glasgow, 1504 (*Simon,* 107). Alexander Wilkisone was retoured heir of Alexander Wilkiesone, burges and comon clerk of the burgh of Lauder in 1656 (*Retours, Berwick,* 305), and James Vilkesoun was admitted burgess of Aberdeen in 1551 (NSCM., I, p. 63). Alexander Wilkison, writer in Lauder, 1642 (RRM., I, p. 96), and Thomas Wilkiesone, clerk of regality of Melrose, 1682 (ibid., III, p. 1). Wyleson 1505.

WILKIN, WILKEN, like **WILKIE,** a double diminutive of WILLIAM, q.v. Malcolm Quilquen, 1431 (Coll. AGAA., I, p. 227). Mathew Wilking had a respite in 1499 for "forthocht fellony" (RSS., I, 374). William Wylkyn held a land in Glasgow, 1540 (LCD., p. 39). Thomas Wilkin rendered to Exchequer the accounts of the burgh of Rutherglen, 1557–58 (ER., XIX, p. 7, 40), and as Thomas Wilky he performs the same duty in 1563 (ibid., p. 222). Gawine Wilkene was bailie of Selkirk in 1590 (RPC., IV, p. 480), William Wilking, burgess of Lanark, 1604 (*Retours, Lanark,* 49), and James Wilkeine in Slains, Aberdeenshire, 1649 (SN&Q., VII, p. 75). In 1606 there is entry of William alias Wilkin Johnstone of Elshieshields. Borrowed into Gaelic with Mac prefixed it becomes Maccuilcein, in Anglicized spelling Macwilkin. Wilkyn 1558, Wylkyne 1542.

WILKINS, 'son of Wilken or WILKIN,' q.v.

WILKINSON. 'Son of WILKIN,' q.v. John Wylkynson or Wilkinsoune was a resident of Vddynston in 1498 (REG., 478, 479), Schir William Wilkinsone had a special respite and protection in 1504 (*Trials,* I, p. *42), and Robert Wylkynsone was vicar of Ardrossan in 1537 (LCD., p. 100). From this comes MACQUILKAN, a name met with in Kintyre.

WILL. Diminutive of WILLIAM, q.v. Litil Wil, tanner (*tannator*) apud Fovern, 1402 (CRA., p. 384). Robertus Will was common councillor in Aberdeen, 1435 (*Guildry,* p. 185), John Will, dwelling in Partick, was admitted burgess of Glasgow in 1577 (*Burgesses*), and Andro Will was a 'flaischair' in Aberdeen, 1581 (SCM., II, p. 54). Andrew Will, witness in Orkney, 1625 (OSS., I, 124). An action was raised against John Will in Easter Banchry in 1692, and Thomas Will in Coupar-Angus was charged with contempt of the sacraments

in 1693 (DPD., II, p. 76, 219). Alexander Will was member of Huntly Volunteers in 1798 (*Will,* p. 8). As forename: Wyl Morison, 1520 (*Rental*).

WILLIAM. From Old Germ. *Willihelm.* The name, is found in 1317 (*Peebles,* 6). Adam, the Conqueror. For centuries in England it and John have raced for first place in popularity. It has been the source of a vast number of surnames in Britain and on the continent, and gave name to one of Scotland's early kings, William the Lion (1165–1214). In Orphir it is pronounced *Wullock,* in Evie and Rendall *Willo,* and in Stromness *Willa.*

WILLIAMS, 'Son of WILLIAM,' q.v.

WILLIAMSON. 'Son of WILLIAM,' q.v. Johannes filius Wilelmi, the Latin form of the name, is found in 1317 (*Peebles,* 6). Adam, son of William, rendered to Exchequer the accounts of the burgh of Peebles in 1343 (ER., I, p. 517), and John, the son of William, was bailie there in 1365 (ibid., II, p. 207). Ion Willameson of Angus was on assize of the marches of Woodwrae in 1388 (*Bamff,* p. 22), John Willelmi was official of Brechin in 1434 (REB., I, 60), and Alexander Willvamsone, a native of Aberdeen, and John Williamson, born at Euchemartyn [miswritten for Enchemartyn], received letters of denization in England in 1463 and 1480 (*Bain,* IV, 1336, 1465). 'Jhone Williamson and Donald Willeam Allanson his bruder' are witnesses to a bond in 1527 (*Cawdor,* p. 150). The surname is found in Banniskirk, Caithness, in 1665, and some notes on the family there will be found in Henderson's *Caithness family history* (p. 295–298). David Williamson (d. 1706), minister of St. Cuthbert's, Edinburgh, known in Scottish song as "Dainty Davie," married and buried six wives, and married a seventh who buried him. Individuals named Williamson early entered the military service of France, and the name is found in that country as De Villençon, earlier Viellençon. Thomas Williamson was an archer of the guard in the reign of Charles VIII (1485–98). The surname is also spelled in France D'Oillençon, and the families of this name preserve their old motto 'Venture and win.' John Williamson (1826–1885), American landscape painter, was born in Tollcross near Glasgow. Villelmi (Latin gen.) 1467, Vilzemsone 1556, Williamsone and Weleamsoun 1600, Wilyamson 1503, Wilyemsoun 1537, Wilzaimson 1512, Wilzamesoun 1479, Wilzamson 1448, Wilzeamsone 1511, Wilzongson 1500, Wyllyamson 1515, Wylzemson 1522.

WILLICOCK. Another form of WILLOCK, q.v. Adam Willicok was admitted burgess of Aberdeen in 1578 (NSCM., I, p. 73), and Alexander Willicok in Fechill was bewitched in 1597 (SCM., I, p. 132). Patrick Willicok, son of Alexander Willicok, was burgess of Aberdeen, 1603, and Alexander Wilicok is recorded in Ellon in 1606 (RSCA., II, p. 35, 84). Willecok c. 1500.

WILLIS. "Willie's son." Walter filius Wille held lands in Dumfries a. 1214 (Kelso, 11). Henry Willis was editor of Chambers's Edinburgh journal (1844–45).

WILLISON, 'son of Willie,' a diminutive of WILLIAM, q.v. John Williesoun was commissioner to the Convention for Stirling in 1573 (SBR., p. 280), James Willison in Burnefute, parish of Wandell, 1621 (Lanark CR.)., and Thomas Williesone was heir of William Williesone in Camlig in 1627 (Inquis., 1324). There were families of Willison of Cornton, Craigforth, and of Crawford.

WILLOCK. OE. Willoc, diminutive of Willa, 'little Will.' John Willok was party in an action of spulzie in 1506 (RSCA., I, p. 18). John Willok who witnessed the testament of John Erskine of Dun in 1513 may be the John Villok who was vicar of Stracathro in 1525 (SCM., IV, p. 12, 23). Alexander Willok was witness in Kirkwall, 1545 (REO., p. 228), George Willok and his father, John Willok, are in record in Brechin in 1594 (REB., II, 368), and Christina Willoch, daughter of George Willoch, heir of John Willoch of Carleith, 1688 (Retours, Ayr, 651).

WILLOCKS, WILLOX, 'son of WILLOCK,' q.v. Gilbert Willox, 'wricht,' received payment in 1584 "for biging of the keyheid port" of Aberdeen (SCM., V, p. 56), and James Willox was admitted burgess of the burgh in 1611 (NSCM., I, p. 109). John Wiliks in Aberdeen, 1727 (NSCM., II, p. 120). George Willox and William Willox from Alvah were killed in the first Great War (Turriff). Wellox 1823. Willockis, Willokis.

WILLS. 'Son of WILL,' q.v.

WILSON, WILSONE, WILLSON. 'Son of WILL,' q.v. John Wulson was a merchant in the service of Sir John of Mountgomery in 1405 (Bain, IV, 697), Michael Wilsoun was burgess of Irvine in 1418 (Irvine, I, p. 127), and John Wilson was burgess of Berwick in 1467 (RD., 461). Thomas Wolsoun was tenant of Neubotel Abbey in 1563 (Neubotle, p. 328), and Dand Vilsone and Pait Vilsoun were tenants of the

abbot of Kelso in 1567 (Kelso, p. 519, 524). William Willsoun is recorded as indweller in Cunyngham Baidland in 1662 (Hunter, p. 50). The northern Wilsons are ranked as a sept of Clan Gunn, through George Gunn's son William, who flourished in the fifteenth century. The name was very common in Glasgow in the sixteenth century. Peter Wilson (1746–1825), classical scholar and linguist, professor of Greek and Latin in Columbia University, New York, was born in Ordiquhill, Aberdeenshire; and Alexander Wilson (1766–1813), the American ornithologist, was born in Paisley. For the spelling Wulson compare the Rev. Thomas Chalmers's pronunciation of 'filthy' as 'fulthy.' Villsone 1572, Vylsone 1511, Willesoun 1526, Willson 1668, Wilsoine 1586, Wilsowne 1549, Wilsoune 1554, Wulsone 1568 (this is a common broad pronunciation at the present day), Wylson 1506, Wylsoune 1547; Willsone, Wolson, Wyleson.

WILTON. From the lands of Wilton now in the parish of Hawick, Roxburghshire. John de Wilton appears as witness to several charters in the reign of William the Lion (APS., I, p. 67 *; REG., p. 78). Others of the name in the same reign are Roger de Wilton and Robert de Wilton (REG., p. 85, 86; Melros, 126, 129; Kelso, 304). I. de Wiltune witnessed a charter by Earl David, c. 1201–07 (LAC., 5), and in 1204 he appears as Johannes de Wiltun (ibid., 6). John, younger of Wilton, disputed the patronage of the church of Wilton between 1208 and 1211 (REG., p. 85, 86), and Roger de Wiltone witnessed charters by William the Lion between 1180 and 1200 (RAA., I, p. 41, 61, 65, 166).

WIMOND, WYMOND. From the OE. personal name Wigmund (stem Wig = battle). Wimund, pretender to the Scottish crown, c. 1140, "scribe, monk, bishop, pirate, impostor, rebel, vassal, recluse, whose adventures read like a romance" (Bishop Forbes, S. Ninian, p. xlviii). William Wymondes sone rendered homage, 1296. His seal shows a fleur-de-lys, S' Will'i fil' Wimun (Bain, II, p. 207, 558). William Wymond, juror on inquisition at Peebles, 1304 (Bain, II, 1436). John Vymond witnessed deed of resignation of lands in the barony of Drumelzier, 1331 (Hay, 9).

WINCHBURGH. James de Wyncheburghe who had an annual rent of ten shillings from property in Edinburgh in 1377 (RMS., I, 650, 684) doubtless derived his name from Winchburgh in West Lothian.

WINCHELL. From the old lands of Winscheill (1635) or Winscheillis (1579), now Wind-

WINCHELL, *continued*

shiel near Duns, Berwickshire. In 1280 John de Wyncheles claimed a stolen mare bought in open market at Carlisle (*Bain*, II, p. 58), and another John de Wyndesceles was witness to a charter of Patrick, third earl of Dunbar before 1389 (*Raine*, 138).

WINCHESTER. Most probably from Winchester in co. Hants, England. Thomas de Wincestre of the county of Are rendered homage in 1296. His seal bears a lion rampant, tail contourné, and S' *Thome de Wynchese* (*Bain*, II, p. 202, 533). Another (?) Thomas de Wynchester rendered homage in the same year. His seal is rudely executed and bears a lion (?) rampant and S' *Thome de Wynchetre* (ibid., II, 776). Johan de Wincestre and Henry de Wincestre, both of the county of Lanark, also rendered homage (ibid., p. 212). John Wincestir was chancellor of Dunkeld in 1426 (RMS., II, 84), Magister Henricus Wynsister held a tenement in Glasgow in 1498 (REG., p. 500), and John Wynsister was witness to a deed of 1495 (*Laing*, 221). William Winchestre was vicar of Grantuly in 1505 (SCM., IV, p. 138), Jaspar Winchister was a tenant of the bishop of Moray in 1565 (REM., p. 437), Peter Winsister of Ardtrailye is in record in 1569 (RPC., I, p. 674), Androw Wynsister was minister at Fischweik, 1574 (RMR.), and Florie Winsister was exhorter at the churches of Aberchirder and Rothiemay in 1567 (*Illus.*, II, p. 151). — Wincister (Wynsister, or Winchestir) was bailie of St. Andrews, 1579–82 (*St. Andrews*, p. 436, 481, 543), and John Vinstyr of Artrelle was one of an assize at Inverness, 1591 (OPS., II, p. 669). John Vinchister and Henry Vinchister were members of an assize held at Spynie, 1592 (SCM., II, p. 120). James Winschester, bookbinder, was burgess freeman of Glasgow, 1628 (*Burgesses*), and — Wenchester was burgess and bailie of Banff in 1643 (RSCA., III, p. 12). Peter Winster, indweller in the Cannogate, 1694 (*Edin. App.*). In 1803 the name was referred to as Winchester or Winster, which gives the local pronunciation. Vyncestre and Wyncestïr 1471, Winshecester 1686, Vinster, Wyncistre.

WINDCHESLY. William Windchesly was change keeper in the town of Kilspindie, 1711 (DPD., II, p. 280).

WINDGATE, WINGATE. Of territorial origin probably from Wingate in Northumberland. There is a Wingate in the parish of Kelloe, county Durham, and there is a Windygates in Fife. The greater number of references point to the West Coast. Windegaitis of yt

Ilk in Workman' MS. carry a portcullis as relative to the name. Bartholomew de Windegates was one of an inquest as to the lands of Ada de Baylloil in Northumberland, 1251 (*Bain*, I, 1821). "During the first half of the sixteenth century a considerable family of Wynȝets held property in the city of Glasgow, and members of the family were rentallers of lands in Monkland, Dalbeth, Carmylie, which belonged to the Archbishop of Glasgow" (Winzet, *Certain tractates*, edited by Rev. J. King Hewison, I, p. xi). Thomas Wynzat was tenant under the bishop of Glasgow in 1510 and John Vyngayt in 1512 (*Rental*). Johne Wynzet, voter in Monkland, 1519 (*Simon*, 45), Matho Windiyettis appears in Edinburgh, 1530 (MCM., p. 110), John Wynvet, witness in Dunfermline, 1550 (DBR., 269), and William Wynzett was a notary in Glasgow, 1554 (*Protocols*, I). Allan Winzett, wobster, was admitted burgess freeman of Glasgow, 1589 (*Burgesses*), Thomas Vinzeitis is in Dubtoun, Brechin, 1600 (REB., II, 231), and Gilbert Wingzet, notar and burgess of Stirling, 1656 (*Inquis.*, 4169). Unzet 1551, Vindegates 1493, Windigait 1564, Winet and Winett 1650, Wingit 1685, Winyet c. 1530, Winzet 1560, Winzett 1650, Wydgayt 1514, Wyndgayt 1513, Wyngzet 1557, Wynzet 1559; Vinyet, Vinzot, Windegait, Winet, Wingetus, Wingyet, Winietus, Wynyet.

WINDRAM. *See under* WINRAM.

WINDSOR. Probably from Windsor in Berkshire, early spellings of which are Windlesora (1096), Windlesore and Wyndelshore (1297). W[alterus] de Wyndesovere witnessed a grant by Radulph de Veir to the Abbey of Kelso, c. 1180 (*Kelso*, 215), and c. 1178–82, as Walter de Windesouer he witnessed William the Lion's charter to Arbroath (RAA., II, p. 535), and also the same king's confirmation of Neutun to Walter de Berkeley (ibid., I, p. 329). As Walterus de Windleshore he witnessed William the Lion's grant of the forest of Grenewde, etc., to the monks of Coldingham (*Raine*, 45, 46). T. or G. de Windlesouer witnessed a gift by William de Vallibus of a half mark of silver to the church of S. Thomas of Aberbrothoc, p. 1218 (RAA., I, p. 83, 264). William Wyndfor (? error for Wyndsor) was admitted burgess of Aberdeen in 1445 (NSCM., I, p. 9).

WINDWICK. An old Orcadian surname from Windwick in the island of Ronaldsay, Orkney. Johne Wyndwek appears as a witness in Kirkwall in 1509 (REO., p. 84). James Wvndwvk was arbiter in Cara in 1563, Edward Winduik was a witness in 1520, and John of Wvndwvkk is in record in 1524 (ibid., p. 113, 205, 422).

WINEMARUS. Walter, son of Winemarus, a witness to Earl David's *Inquisitio*, c. 1124 (REG., p. 7). He was the son of Winemar the Fleming, a Buckinghamshire landowner of 1086 (Lipscomb, *History of Bucks*, IV, p. 165). See also under HANESEL. Johannes Winemer witnessed the gift of fifteen acres of Balmulinach (Balmerino) to the church of St. Andrews before 1225 (RPSA., p. 272), and a Winemer witnessed a charter by Countess Ada of land of Charel (Crail) (ibid., p. 208).

WINGATE. *See under* WINDGATE

WINK. A rare but still existing surname. Perhaps a shortened form of *Wineca*, diminutive of the common OE. personal name *Wine*. Winkston near Peebles is the *tūn* of Wink or Wynk. William Wynk who held land in Aberdeen in 1281 (REA., II, p. 279), may be the William Wynk who rendered homage at Perth, 1291 (RR.).

WINKSETTER. An old surname in Orkney derived from the two-penny land of that name in Harray. Margaret Winksetter, spouse to John Sinclair in Bruch, in the parish of Harray, is in record in 1625 (*Orkney*).

WINKSTON. The lands of Winkston in the parish of Peebles gave name to possessors in 1262, when Alexander de Wynkistun was on the inquest for ascertaining the rights of burgesses in the moss of Walthamshope (*Peebles*, p. 5; APS., I, pref. p. 101 red). In 1365 the lands of Winkston were in the hands of the Gledstanes (RMS., I, 208, 209). See WINK.

WINLAW. John Wynlaw witnessed an instrument of infeftment of 1547 (Buchan, *Peebles*, III, p. 57), Jonet Winlaw was heir of James Winlaw, burgess of Edinburgh, 1621 (*Inquis.*, 953), Alexander Winlay is in record in Lanark in 1624, and Marion Wyndlaw in Elserigle, parish of Wellstoune, 1675 (*Lanark CR.*). There is a Windlaw near Carmunnock from which the name may have come.

WINLOCH. Reinnald de Winloch witnessed a permit to Robert Croc and to Henry de Nes to build chapels for their private use, c. 1180 (RMP., p. 78). Winlach appears as a surname in Strathbogie, 1631 (*Strathbogie*, p. 5).

WINNERSTOUN. Laurence de Wynnerstoun or Wynmerstoun witnessed donations by Henry de Avnstrother to Dryburgh Abbey, c. 1330 (*Dryburgh*, 252, 253).

WINNING. A curtailed form of (MACGILLE)-WINNIN, q.v. John Wynning, cordiner, was admitted burgess freeman of Glasgow, 1591,

by reason of his marriage with the daughter and heir of a burgess (*Burgesses*), and Robert Wyneing, cordiner, probably his son, was admitted burgess freeman, 1607 (ibid.). Robert Winnie, bookseller and stationer, Dumfries, 1695–1727 (*Dumfriesshire and Galloway Nat. Hist. and Antiquarian Society, Trans.*, 3. ser. XVIII, p. 141). Chalmers (*Caledonia*, III, p. 341) says Winnin and the patronymic MacWinnin appear to have been common names in Galloway. As forename: Wynnin Multray, 1542 (*Irvine*, I, p. 199).

WINRAM, WINDRAM. Winram was the name of an old family in Clydesdale. Wishaw (*Description of Lanark*, p. 63) says Wynrehame of Wyston held the barony of Wiston, but died without male heirs (? in the fifteenth century). George Wynrahame and Johne Wynrahame were summoned in 1479 to answer to Parliament for treason and other crimes (APS., II, p. 129). John Winram, sub prior of St. Andrews, was superintendent of Fife after the Reformation. Robert Winram was burgess of Dunfermline, 1605, Robert Winrahame, witness in Edinburgh, 1609 (*Edinb. Marr.*), and Robert Wynrahame was Islay Herald, 1615 (HP., III, p. 209). Alexander Windrim was couper in Stitchell, 1659 (*Stitchill*, p. 15), James Winrahame was retoured heir in lands and barony of Wistoun, 1659 (*Retours, Lanark*, 271), and John Winderaham had a lease of Sheens Walls, Edinburgh, 1668 (BOEC., X, p. 151). Thomas Windrame was killed at Gillichrankie, 1689 (RPC., 3. ser. XIV, p. 391), William Windram appears at the Waulkmiln of Coupar in Angus, 1740 (*Dunkeld*), and John Winram, wheelwright in Kelso, 1815 (*Heirs*, 619). Vineram and Winrham 1686, Vinerame 1681, Vinram 1642, Vynram 1596, Winrame 1622, Wynrame 1594, Wynrane.

WINSTON. A late importation from England. There is a Winston near Darlington, county Durham.

WINT. John Vint, tenant on abbey lands of Kelso, 1567 (*Kelso*, p. 529). Bessie Vint and Margaret Vint appear in Heittoun, 1685–86 (*Peebles CR.*), and George Wint in Whitle, 1667 (*Edin. App.*). Guppy (p. 364) gives Wint as an ancient name, occurring in Oxfordshire and Cambridgeshire in the thirteenth century. Vint is also recorded as a surname in England. James Vint died in Blairgowrie, 1941.

WINTER. Most probably the OE. personal name *Wintra* (Birch, CS. 101, A.D. 699) and *Uuintra* (ibid., 108, A.D. 704), associated in the popular mind with OE. *winter*, 'winter' (*Redin*, p. 58). Elsi, son of Winter, had a

WINTER, *continued*

grant of the lands of Thirlstane from Hugh de Morville before 1162 (*Caledonia*, I, p. 504). Jop Wyntyr was a charter witness at Yester in 1374 (*Yester*, p. 26), Thomas Wyntir was bailie of Glasgow in 1447 (LCD., p. 168), John Wyntyr, burgess of Arbroath in 1452 (RAA., II, 94), and George Wynter was a charter witness in Kimmerghame in 1474 (*Home*, 27). David Wyntyr or Wynter, a citizen of Glasgow in 1487–88, held land there before 1494 (LCD., p. 256; REG., p. 457, 487). Robert Wynter, monk of Culross in the middle of the sixteenth century (PSAS., LX, p. 93).

WINTHROPE. See *under* WINTRUP.

WINTON. Of territorial origin from the lands of Winton in the parish of Pencaitland, East Lothian. Alan de Wyntoun witnessed a grant by Peter de Grame to the House of Soltre between 1190 and 1238 (*Soltre*, p. 11), and before 1200 Henry de Wynton witnessed a charter by Hugh Rydale, dominus de Cranestun (*Neubotle*, 12). Aleyn de Wyntone and Gode de Wyntone, both of Edinburghshire, and Thomas de Wyntone of Ayrshire rendered homage in 1296 (*Bain*, II, p. 201, 205, 206, 209). The surname is frequently met with in Aberdeenshire, appearing there as early as 1341, in which year Ingeram de Wenton appears as one of an inquest on tithes (REA., I, p. 69). Andrew de Wyntoun, prior of St. Serf's, Lochleven, author of the *Orygynale Cronykil of Scotland*, was probably a member of the Aberdeen branch of the family. In 1395 he was present at perambulation of the bounds of Kyrknes and Louchor (RPSA., p. 3). George de Venton was prebend of Lonmey, Aberdeenshire, 1427 (REA., I, p. 228). James Wentoun was one of an inquest at Aberdeen, 1457 (RAA., I, 108), and Andrew Wentoune was admitted burgess of Aberdeen, 1477 (NSCM., I, p. 26). Robert Winton, a Scot, had letters of denization in England in 1480 (*Bain*, IV, 1465). Elizabeth Wentoune was retoured heir of John Wentoune in Bogny, her father, 1633 (*Retours, Aberdeen*, 223), and William Winton from the parish of King Edward was killed in the first Great War (*Turriff*).

WINTRUP, WINTHROPE. A Roxburghshire surname of local origin from a place named Winterhope. There was a Winterupe in Jedburgh in the eighteenth century, and there is a Winterhope Burn in Middlebie, Dumfriesshire, and a Winterhopehead (in 1622 Winterhoipheid) near Ecclefechan. Brockie (*The Gypsies of Yetholm*, p. 66) says this name was assumed

by gypsies to hide their origin. Walter Winterhoip in Spittell was charged with trespass on the lands of Sir Andrew Ker of Oxenhame in 1619 (RPC., XII, p. 20), and Robert Winterhope and others, servitors to James Ker of Bewlie, were charged with riot and assault in 1622 (ibid., p. 628). Jhone Wintroip in Elestoune in 1608 was probably father of John Winterope in Erlleistoune in 1657 (RRM., I, p. 70, 141). Another John Wintrope took part in field conventicles in 1684 (ibid., III, p. 43), and a third John Wintrop was portioner of Newsteid in 1681 (ibid., III, p. 103). James Wintrop in Pathfoot, 1722 (*Dumfries*).

WIPER, WIPERS. Weekley (p. 103) says from Ypres in Belgium [but ?]. The name is spelled Wyper in Lanarkshire and West Lothian and Weepers in Fife.

WISE, WYSE. Perhaps from ME. *wys(e,* learned, sage. William Wys was a canon of Moray in 1358 (*Bain*, III, 17), Thomas Wyse, canon of Caithness, 1381 (*Pap. Pet.*, I, p. 561–562), and Robertus Wys was canon of the church of Aberdeen in 1386, 1391 (REA., I, p. 172, 189). Johannes Wyss on inquest in Stravelyn, 1411 (*Scon*, p. 162), John Wis or Wiys, stonecutter to bishop of Dunkeld, 1511 (*Rent. Dunk.*), William Wyeis was member of council of Stirling in 1522 (SBR., p. 275), and David Wyse and his wife had a charter of a "saline patella in Kirkcaldrie" in 1603 (RD., p. 497). Wysse in the parish of Laurencekirk in the eighteenth century.

WISEMAN. An old surname in Angus and Moray. Andrea Wysman witnessed excambion of the lands of Dolays Mychel in 1232 (REM., p. 88), and in the following year attested a confirmation charter by Andrew, bishop of Moray (*Pluscardyn*, 203). Thomas Wisman, prepositus of Elgin, was one of an inquest concerning the king's garden there, 1261 (APS., I, p. 99 red; *Elgin*, II, p. 475), and he and William Wisman were jurors on inquest concerning the lands of Mefth, 1262 (*Bain*, I, 2323). William Wysman witnessed a charter by the earl of Ross, 1263 (REM., p. 279), designed 'de Fores' in 1266 (ER., I, p. 34), c. 1278 and 1286 attested charters by Hugh Herock, burgess of Elgin (REM., p. 284, 461). He may be the William Wysman of Elginshire who rendered homage at Elgin, 1295, and was appointed sheriff of Elgin, 1305 (*Bain*, II, p. 183, 209, 458). Adam dictus Wiseman made a grant of lands to Coldingham Priory, 1285 (*Raine*, 262). William Wiseman obtained from David II the barony of Don forfeited by David de Strabolgi (*Stodart*, II, p. 311), and Willelmus Wyseman, senior, and Willelmus Wyseman, junior, were jurors on an inquest held regarding the episcopal lands of Aldrochty, 1393 (REM., p. 205). Patrick Wyisman was admitted burgess of Aberdeen, 1484 (NSCM., I, p. 31), and Marion Wyseman is recorded in Goslingtown, Stanehaven, 1630 (Lanark CR.). Vyseman 1393, Vysman 1601, Wisman 1667.

WISHART. The same as OF. *Guischard*, from OF. *wischard*, 'prudent, sagacious.' William Wischard witnessed grant of the mill teind to the Abbey of Cambuskenneth, c. 1200 (*Cambus.*, 86). John Wischard, witness in 1245, was present at perambulation of bounds of Conon and Tulloch, 1254 (LAC., 55; RAA., I, 366). William Wischard was a Culdee of St. Andrews, 1250 (Reeves, *Culdees*, p. 232). Adam Wiscard had charter of the land of Kenny Murchardyn, 1279 (RAA., I, p. 332). John Wychard of the Miernes rendered homage, 1296. Andrew Wvcchard (Wyschard or Wychard) of Scotland, a prisoner of war in Hereford Castle, 1305–07 (Bain, II, 1668, 1934). George Wischart was burned for heresy at St. Andrews, 1545/6, and a later George Wischart was first bishop of Edinburgh after the Restoration and private chaplain and biographer of the marquess of Montrose. The writer of the inscription on his tomb believed his name to mean "Wise heart:" *Hic recubat celebris doctor Sophocardius alter, entheus ille Σοφοσ καρδιαν Agricola.* In 1549 Queen Mary presented Mr. James Buchart or Buschart (apparently the same as Wischart) to the chaplainry called Towie (or Tolly) in the diocese of Ross (OPS., II, p. 473). Johnnett Wischart in Aberdeen was burnt for witchcraft, 1596 (SCM., I, p. 94). James Wiseheart or Wysehartt was burgess of Montrose, 1649 (REB., II, p. 247), and John Wishit was prisoner in Canongate Tolbooth, Edinburgh, 1686 (RPC., 3. ser. XII, p. 232). Visart 1428, Vischart 1532, Vishert 1646, Vychart 1553, Vyschart 1442, Wischarte 1567, Wischeart 1508, Wiseheart 1676, Wisheart 1651, Wissart 1435, Wisscheart 1510, Wissheart 1692, Wschartt 1588, Wschert 1541, Wyischart 1563, Wyishart 1567, Wyschart 1442, Wysharde 1296, Wvssart 1485, Wythcharde 1490; Vischarge, Wischarge, Whyssard, Wiscaid, Wischarde, Wischarge, Wischat, Wychart, and among the Scots Guards in France Oulchart.

WISHAW. From the town of the same name in Lanarkshire (in 1303, Weteshawe). Archibald Weitschaw witnessed a charter by William Wrythe to the Abbey of Newbattle in 1462 (*Neubotle*, p. 250). Another Archibald Witschaw (Weicschaw, or Weischaw) was a burgess and charter witness in Glasgow in 1477 and 1478 (REG., p. 462; LCD., p. 191). In 1497 there is mention of the tenement of Archibald Witschaw in Glasgow, probably the same individual (REG., p. 496). The surname is also found in the Glasgow protocol books of the sixteenth century.

WISTON. Of territorial origin from the old barony of the name in Lanarkshire. In the reign of Malcolm IV (1153–65) Wice of Wiceston gave to the monks of Kelso "the church of his village of Wicestun, with its two chapels, namely, of the vill of Robert the brother of Lambin, and of the vill of John the stepson of Baldwin," for the weal of his lord the King Malcolm, of William the king's brother, of himself, his wife and heirs, and for the soul's health of his father and mother, and of all his ancestors and successors (*Kelso*, p. 270). Sir Walter, the son of William "de villa Wice," confirmed this grant of his grandfather (*auus meus*) about the year 1200, and about 1260 the grant was again confirmed to the Abbey by Sir Henry Lord of Wyscytun (ibid., p. 271, 272). In 1263 Sir Henry was found by an inquest to have been a minor when he granted these lands (*Bain*, I, 2677). In 1292–93 Edward I of England, as overlord of Scotland for the time being, confirmed to Walter Logan the ward of the lands and heirs of Henry of Wyston deceased (*Rot. Scot.*, I, p. 15), and about the year 1300 Henry de Prendergest made suit to Edward I "pur les terres Wauter de Wyston" (*Palgrave, Docs. Illus. Hist. Scot.*, I, p. 310). From this date the lands appear to have passed entirely from the possession of the descendants of Wice the founder of Wiston. Helyn Wystoun in Strafrank had license to marry in 1538 (*Rental*).

WITHER. This name, which also appears in the English Domesday Book, is for the earlier OE. personal name *Withthere*. A horse was purchased from Roger Wyther, 1312 (*Bain*, III, p. 420), and Eustace Wethir was prepositus of the burgh of Inuernys, 1327 (ER., I. p. 59). Fergus Wither is recorded in Ballochjargan, Wigtownshire, 1745, and James Wither was chapman in Stranraer, 1763 (*Wigtown*).

WITHERSPOON. See *under* WOTHERSPOON.

WITSTE. John Witste was one of the burgesses of Stirling who attacked the cruives and fishings of the abbot and convent of Cambuskenneth, 1366 (*Cambus.*, 55). Perhaps a Dutch or Frisian name.

WITTON. Perhaps of English origin from Witton, a common place name in England. Hardly likely to be from Whitton near Morebattle, Roxburghshire. Michael de Witton and Adam de Wytton of Selkirkshire rendered homage in 1296 (*Bain*, II, p. 198), and Thomas de Wytton had protection for two years for going on the king of England's service beyond seas, 1370 (ibid., IV, 170).

WODDELL. A form of WADDELL, q.v.

WODDROP. The family of Woddrop of Ellsrickle or Elsridge-hill (partly in Peeblesshire and partly in Lanarkshire) may be descended from James Wedderspuine, one of the Peeblesshire gentry charged with complicity in the murder of Rizzio.

WODERLIE. Of local origin, from Wedderlie, Weststruther, Berwickshire.

WODROW. See under WOODROW.

WODSONE. Peter Wodsone in Berwickshire, 1630 (*Lauder*). Harrison has Woodson, a contraction, he says, of Wooderson, from *wooder*, woodman, woodcutter. Bardsley says 'son of Wodard or Odard,' and Weekley says may be 'son of the woodward.'

WOGRELL. An action for relief of John Waggerale, 1510 (RSCA., I, p. 42). William Wogrell concerned in an action for payment of malt, 1617 (ibid., II, p. 218).

WOLF. *Wulf*, 'wolf' was an OE. personal name, and ON. *Ulf* was a very common name with the Norsemen. Ulfus, senescallus, witnessed a charter by Eschina, domina de Molle, c. 1165–77 (RMP., p. 75); Walterus Lupus was burgess of Dundee, 1202 (RAA., I, p. 96), and Willelmus filius Hulf held land in Aberdeen before 1281 (REA., II, p. 278). Alexander Wlfe witnessed grant of part of a toft in Perth to the Abbey of Lundors early in the thirteenth century (LAC., p. 80). A messuage with "bracina" in the villa de Saulton was held by Willelmus dictus Wolf c. 1295 (*Dryburgh*, 253). Willelmus Lupus, a laic of St. Andrews, 1331 (RAA., I, p. 218). Robert Wolfe was juror on an inquest on the lands of Swinton, 1408 (*Swinton*, p. xviii). John Wolf, witness at Tybermello, 1544 (*Rollok*, 39). John Wolff in Dunse, 1634 (*Lauder*).

WOLLER. Robertus de Woller who attested the grant by Andrew Mansel to Kelso Abbey (*Kelso*, 507), derived his name from Wooler in Northumberland.

WOOD. Local, from residence near a wood (OE. *wudu*). The name appears first in record in the Latinized form *de Bosco* (see BOYCE). There is an OE. personal name, *Wuda*, from which the name might be derived. This became in ME. *Wode*, and later Wood, but the local derivation is most probable for the name in Scotland. William Wod was a witness to the valuation of Kilravock and Easter Geddes in 1295 (*Cawdor*, p. 3; *Rose*, p. 30). In 1370 John Wode complained of having been plundered by wreckers (*Bain*, IV, 164). Ade Wood in Garvald and Roger Wode in Louchurde were tenants under Douglas, 1376 (RHM., I, p. lvii; II, p. 16). A horse was stolen from Adam dictus Wode, husbandman of the bishop of Moray, 1398 (REM., p. 212), and Hugo o' the Wode, 'scocheman,' had a royal pardon, 1407 (*Bain*, IV, 734). William de le Wod is in record, 1413 (CDE., 21). Thomas Wod, a witness in Newbattle, 1458 (*Neubotle*, p. 246). Patrick of Wod witnessed an instrument of sasine, 1476, and Thom of Wod witnessed a declaration by John of Roule, 1479 (*Home*, 23, 25). John Vode was a friar preacher in Aberdeen, 1486 (REA., II, p. 300), and Alexander Woyd was a tenant under the bishop of Glasgow, 1513 (*Rental*). Vod and Void 1526, Voud and Voude 1520, Vould 1522, Wodde 1491, Wode (of Largo) 1506, Woid 1567, Woide 1481.

WOODBURN, WOODBURNE. Of local origin. There are places named Woodburn in Ayrshire, Midlothian, and Kincardineshire. Jonete Wodburn in Irvine, 1506 (*Irvine*, I, p. 158). George Woodburn or Whiteburn in Finnick was shot for being a Covenanter, 1685 (*Hanna*, II, p. 257, 270).

WOODCOCK. William Wodcok, burgess of Glasgow, 1488 (LCD., p. 257). Francis Wodcok held land there in 1552 (*Protocols*, 1). Harrison says: "A nickname from the fowl; at one time a common term for a simpleton," OE. *wuducocc*. Lower says: "A term of reproach, applied to a simpleton, in many early plays. Halliwell." The name is found in England in 1273 as Wodecok.

WOODELL. Local. Most probably for Woodwell. *w* is lost medially at the beginning of an unstressed syllable.

WOODFIELD. Roger Wodyfelde who had a charter from David II of lands, tenements, etc., in the burgh of Dumfries, 1365 (RMS., I, 202) probably derived his surname from Woodfield near Annan, Dumfriesshire.

WOODFORD. From the lands of the same name in the parish of St. Boswells, Roxburghshire. Jordan de Wodford witnessed a charter of Walter de Berkeley, c. 1170 (RAA., I, p. 38), and Walterus de Wudeford witnessed a confirmation charter by Alexander II apud Peebles, 1228 (RMP., p. 403). Robert de Wodforde sometime between 1285 and 1306 bestowed his whole property of Wodfordehous in the territory of Lessedewyne upon the monks of Melrose (*Melros*, p. 320), and in 1296 he rendered homage for his possessions (*Bain*, II, p. 199). A later Robert de Woddeford witnessed a charter by Sirildis Saddeler, c. 1330 (*Kelso*, 491), and is also a witness to several other charters in the same record in 1354 (ibid., 496, 498, 499, 500). As Robert de Vodford, *dominus ejusdem*, he was a charter witness in 1338 (*Dryburgh*, 261), and in 1358 he witnessed the grant of the forest of Eteryk to John Kerre (*Roxburghe*, p. 8). Wodeford 1357.

WOODHALL. Local. There are two places named Woodhall in East Lothian and one in Dumfriesshire. John of Wodhaw, witness in Peebles, 1471 (*Scots Lore*, p. 52).

WOODHEAD. Local. A common place name in the County Directory. Self-explanatory.

WOODHOUSE. Of local origin from one or other of several places of the name recorded in CD.

WOODMAN. (1) From the OE. personal name *Wudemann* (in 1070 Wudeman); (2) from the occupation, a woodcutter. An old surname in the parish of Strichen (*Jervise*, II, p. 137). William Wode[man] was juror on an inquest made in St. Katherine's Chapel, Baveley, in 1280 (*Bain*, IV, 1762). Nicholas Wodman became burgess of Aberdeen in 1400, Thomas Wodeman attained the same distinction in 1486 (NSCM., I, p. I, 32), and is mentioned again in 1493 (CRA., p. 50). Andrew Wodman was a forestaller in Aberdeen in 1402 (CRA., p. 384), and John Wodman, prior of May in 1477 (*Cawdor*, p. 62), was in the same year postulate bishop of Ross (*Dowden*, p. 220). Thomas Wodman was servitor in Monletie in 1633 (SCM., III, p. 132). The surname is also common in Northumberland.

WOODROW, WODROW. From the occupation or office of 'wood-reeve' or overseer of a forest (OE. *wudu* + (ge)refa). The land of John Woddroff in Glasgow is mentioned in 1505 (LCD., p. 258), and a piece of land there was sold by William Wodrufe in 1551 (*Protocols*, I). Patrick Wodruif was reidare at Egleshame (Eaglesham), 1574 (RMR.), Thomas Widdrow was merchant and guild burgess of Glasgow, 1610 (*Burgesses*), and Janet Widdrow or Wardrop at Innerkip was accused of being a witch, 1629 (RPC., 2. ser. III, p. 125). The Rev. Robert Wodrow (1679–1734), minister of Eastwood and church historian, was the best known of the name. His eldest son, Andrew, emigrated to Virginia in 1768 and served on the side of the colonists in the Revolution. Widrof 1551, Widrow 1667, Witherow 1702, Withraw 1683, Woodrow 1672, Wodrofe 1551, Wodruf 1507, Woodrowe 1658, Woodruif 1574; Widdrowe. In Ulster it has become Witherow through change of *d* to *th*.

WOODSIDE. Of local origin from some one of the several small places of the name. The Woodsides here noted probably derived their surname from Woodside in the parish of Beith, Ayrshire. James Wodsyid was a witness in Glasgow in 1550 (*Protocols*, I), James Wodsyd appears in Hunterstoun in 1583 (*Hunter*, p. 31), Jonet Woodsyd, daughter of John Woodsyd, was retoured heir in two tenements in the burgh of Irvine in 1658 (*Retours, Ayr*, 503), and James Woodsyd was bailie there, 1667 (*Irvine*, II, p. 210). Woodsyde 1689.

WOODWARD. The officer whose duty it was to guard the woods and verts therein (ME. *wode ward(e*, OE. *wuduweard*).

WOODYARD. A rare surname. Perhaps from OE. *wudigere (wudiere)*, woodcutter or wood carrier, with accretionary *d*.

WOOLDRIGE. A corruption of the OE. personal name *Wulfric*, 'wolf powerful.' Constantine Wooldrige, joiner in Edinburgh, 1644 (*Edinb. Marr.*).

WORDIE. Dene Thomas Wordye was a monk of Cambuskenneth Abbey in 1546 and 1557, and William Wordye was in the same year procurator for the commendator, David, bishop of Ross (*Laing*, 505; *Stodart*, II, p. 379). John Wordie of Torbrex was commissary-depute of Stirling in 1686 (RPC., 3. ser. XII, p. 363), and the name is found in Edinburgh in the same year (*Edinb. Marr.*). John Wordie was dean of guild in Aberdeen, 1780 (*Guildry*, p. 203). Worde and Wordy 1655.

WORK. An old Orcadian surname derived from the lands of Work in the parish of St. Ola. Alexander Work was a witness in Kirkwall in 1509 (REO., p. 85). William Wyrk, burgess of Kirkwall, had a charter of a tenement there in 1526 (OSR., I, p. 104), and appears there again as Weyllem Wyrk (or Wirk) in 1532 and 1535 (REO., p. 219, 255). John Work was also a witness in the same town in 1555 (ibid., p. 336). The surname is

WORK, *continued*
also recorded in Shetland. George Work in Clet in Quhailsay, 1613, and John Work in Skallowaybank, parish of Tingwall, 1628 (*Shetland*). Virk 1567, Wark 1570.

WORKMAN. From occupation, OE. *weorcmann*, workman, laborer. Under English feudal law, a tenant who had to do certain week-work. George Workman is recorded in Dunfermline, 1563 (*Dunfermline*). James Workman was Marchmont Herald and herald painter in 1597.

WORMET. Probably from the lands of Wormet near Balmerino, Fife, though the references to the name link it mainly with Aberdeen. John Wormet who was elected bailie of Aberdeen, 1398 (CRA., p. 374) may be the Johannes Wormot recorded there, 1408 (CWA., p. 315). Several individuals named Wormot, Wormet, and Wormote were elected burgesses of Aberdeen between 1440 and 1488 (NSCM., I, p. 5, 15, 17, 33). Robert Wormot who appears on assizes in Aberdeen, 1462 and 1463 (SCM., v, p. 22; CRA., p. 26) may be Robert Vormet, witness, 1469 (REA., I, p. 289). Sir Henry Wormot was sacrist of the cathedral of Dornoch, 1472 (OPS., II, p. 623). John Wormat who obtained protection to travel in England, 1486 (*Bain*, IV, 1522) may be John Wormet, burgess of Aberdeen, 1487 and 1502 (CRA., p. 43; REA., I, p. 318; RAA., II, 425). William Wormit was concerned in an action of lawburrows in 1511 (RSCA., II, p. 44), and John Wormet held land in Aberdeen, c. 1550 (REA., II, p. 234).

WOTHERSPOON, WEATHERSPOON, WETHERSPOON, WEDDERSPOON, WITHERSPOON. The meaning of this name is uncertain. 'Sheep pasture' has been reasonably suggested from OE. and ME. *weðer*, 'sheep, lamb,' and *spong*, obsolete English for a tongue-shaped piece of land enclosed by or lying next to higher ground. Late in the thirteenth century Roger Wythirspon, clerk, attested a grant by James the High Steward of lands in Renfrew (OPS., I, p. 77). "Widderspone the foulare that tald talis and brocht foulis to the king" received a payment in 1496 (ALHT., I, p. 307; *Trials*, I, p. 116 *). John Wyddirspwn was tenant of Dalbeth in 1518 (*Rental*), and a tenant of Cupar-Angus Abbey, c. 1500, was named Wychthirspone. Maister Nichol Vithirspouyne who witnessed letters of reversion, 1519 (*Pollok*, I, p. 241) may be Nicholas Wethirspwne, witness in Glasgow, 1548 (*Protocols*, I). Sir Thomas Vaddirspoun, a cleric, was witness at Falkland, 1548 (*Gaw*, 8). Thomas Witherspuyn witnessed a tack by the abbot of Cupar,

1521 (SCM., v, p. 294), and Archibald Wetherspune held the vicarage of Karriddèn, 1546 (LSC., p. 261). Robert Wyddirspune was witness in West Lothian, 1547 (*Binns*, 40). The Rev. John Witherspoon (1722–1794), born in Yester, became president of the College of New Jersey (now Princeton University) in 1768, and took an active part in the American Revolution on the side of the colonists. General William Wallace Wotherspoon (1850–1921), head of the state canal system of New York, was of Scottish descent. Uedtherspon 1560, Uthirspwne 1552, Vatherspoone 1637, Wedderspoone 1620, Wetherspone 1614, Wetherspwne 1549, Wethirspune 1590, Wethirspune 1569, Weyhthirspon 1546, Widerspune 1483, Witherspone 1583, Witherspune 1588, Withirspovune c. 1530, Withirspwne 1575, Wodderspoon 1761, Wotherspone 1601, Wyddirspwnn 1485, Wyderspone 1477.

WOUPLAW. Helen Wouplaw in Glasgow in 1588 (*Protocols*, x) derived her name from the old three pounds six shillings and eight pence lands of Wouplaw (Wouplaw, 1606, Woulplawis, 1640, Woulpla, 1645, Wooplaw, 1670) in the barony of Melrose.

WRA. Henry del Wro of Linlithgowshire rendered homage, 1296. His seal bears an ornament of seven rays, and S' *Henrici del Wra* (*Bain*, II, p. 198, 533). There were lands named Wra in the barony of Glenquhym in 1451 (RMS., II, 481), and there is a Wrae near Langholm, Dumfriesshire.

WRANGHAM. Rinȝeain or Rynȝeane (i.e. Ninian) Wranghame and James Wrangham were summoned in 1479 to answer to Parliament for treason and other crimes (APS., II, p. 129). Probably from Wrangholm, the name of an ancient village near Melrose, the supposed birthplace of S. Cuthbert, now an open field. There was also a barony of Newton of Wranghame in the parish of Culsalmond, 1644 (*Retours, Aberdeen*, 275).

WRANOCK. Patrick Wranock, charter witness in Edinburgh, 1471 (*Neubotle*, 303), and Mariota Wrennok in Stirling, in the same year (*Sc. Ant.*, x, p. 59).

WRIGHT. A surname common to the Lowlands and to the north of England, from OE. *wyrhta*, a worker, chiefly in wood, a carpenter. With Scots it has displaced Carpenter, a surname of Latin origin. Rauf le Wrighte, burgess of Stirling, and Thomas le Whright of the Blakehalle of Lanarkshire rendered homage in 1296 (*Bain*, II, p. 197, 213). In 1342 there is mention of the land of Richard Wricht or Richard dictus Wright in Aberdeen, and Malcolm Vrycht was a charter witness there in 1362 (REA., I, p. 71, 105). Robert Wryhyt, a carpenter of Berwick, was employed on the roof of the chapel and hall called "la Blakhalle" of the Castle of Berwick in 1362, and Thomas Wryhvt of Alnewyk, another carpenter, aided him (Bain, IV, p. 17). A wadset by Robert Vrich, burgess of Dunde, is recorded in 1397 (Pitfirrane, 10), and John Wrycht was concerned in a law dispute in Aberdeen in 1398 (CRA., p. 371), and William Wrycht held land in Edinburgh, 1405 (Egidii, p. 43). William Wrycht of Lethnot is mentioned in 1410 (REB., I, 29), Richard Wryth was perpetual chaplain of St. Clement the Martyr in Dundee, 1427 (RMS., II, 95), and in 1435 William Wrycht, dominus de Glenesk, is referred to (REB., I, p. 75). William Wrythe with the consent and assent of his spouse Cristine Wrycht made a grant in favor of the Abbey of Newbattle, 1462 (Neubotle, p. 248). Richard Writht was admitted burgess of Aberdeen, 1492 (NSCM., I, p. 37). Possibly some Macintyres have Englished their name Wright. Vrycht 1558, Wercht 1473, Wrecht 1462, Wreicht 1536, Wreight 1684, Wrych 1435, Wryt 1610, and in the Register of Cupar-Angus Abbey the name is common under the forms Wiricht, Wirrycht, Wirryht, Wirycht, Wrich, and Wryght.

WRIGHTON. Alexander Wratoun was reidare at Dumblane, 1574 (RMR.). Magister Alexander Wryttoun in Kilwyning in 1637 (Inquis., 2277) is mentioned again in 1658 as Wryttoune and Wryttowne (Inquis., 4329; Retours, Ayr, 499). Wreittoun 1578. The surname is common in Northamptonshire.

WYATT. From the AF. personal name Wyot, Fr. Guyot, diminutive of Guy. Maucolum Wvet of county Anegos rendered homage, 1296 (Bain, II, p. 213). Nothing more is known of him. James Vyot, Wyot, or Wyat, burgess of Arbroath, in record 1464–68 (RAA., II, 151, 167, 174).

WYLD. Usually explained as "wild, untamed, violent," but more likely local from residence at a weald or open country. Bardslev says Wild "was a popular sobriquet in Yorkshire judging by the 1379 Poll Tax and the present county directory." Yorkshire is well known for its Wolds and the Weald of Sussex is also called the Wild. Philip Wilde, M.A., of the diocese of Brechin, was granted a canonry of Glasgow in 1342 (Pap. Pet., I, p. 3), and John Wild or Wyld was rector of Logy in 1372 (REB., I, 20; Jervise, Angus and Mearns, II, p. 230). Randulph Wyld was subdeacon of Brechin

in 1372 (REB., I, 20), David Wilde held land in Dundee in 1442 (Charters and writs of Dundee, p. 21), Ingeram Wyld held a land in the Canongate of Edinburgh in 1493 (LSC., p. 236). Ellen Wild, relict of John Gardyner, 1509 (Rent. Dunk., p. 21). Jonet Wyld appears in Wester Baldryk, 1573 (Pitfirrane, 202). James Wyld is recorded in Cleghorne in 1652 (Inquis., 3681), Thomas Wyld in Quhinkerstaine in 1655 (Lauder), and Christian Weild in Coldingham in 1762 (ibid.).

WYLIE, WYLLIE. A diphthongized form of Willie, a diminutive of WILLIAM, q.v. Cf. Wylly Jaksone in Glasgow, 1454 (LCD., p. 178). Donald Wyly, tenant of Thornhill, Dumfriesshire, 1376 (RHM., I, p. lvi). John Wili held a land in Montrose, 1431, and Robert Wylye was vicar of Kilcoldrum, 1434 (REB., II, 35; I, 60). William Wyly, a witness in Prestwick, Ayrshire, 1446 (Prestwick, p. 114), Robert Wyly, charter witness in Glasgow, 1454 (LCD., p. 178), and Richard Wylv, vicar of Dundee, 1458 (REB., I, 182). In 1509 there is an entry of 'heritabill stat and sessing to Wilze Wille, as sone and air to John Willi' (Prestwick, p. 39). John Wily and Edward Wily in Cragy (Craigie) in Carrick, 1529 (RMS., III, 849). John Weyle was tenant of Castalstaris (Carstairs), 1530 (Rental), David Wyle, notary in Glasgow, 1550 (Protocols, I) and Michael Wylie, collier in Dysart, 1563 (Dysart, p. 30). A dittay against James Vylze and Jonnet Vylze is recorded in 1575 (Prestwick, p. 74). Thomas Wyllie retoured heir of John Wyllie in Old Aberdene, his 'father brother,' 1653 (Retours, Aberdeen, 316). David Weillie in Pendyke recorded in 1659 (Kilbarchan), and Thomas Wylie was minister of the gospel at Kirkcudbriam, 1680 (Retours, Kirkcudbright, 338). Vylie 1602, Vyly 1435, Wile 1477.

WYND. From residence in a wynd or narrow street in a town. Cf. VENNAL. In 1296 a pardon was granted for Geoffry del Wende of Dundee for causing the death of Ralph Chepman (Bain, II, 839). John Wynde, 'officium mari nostri' (i.e. mair of fee = chief executor of the sentences passed by the sheriff), had a charter of land of Petmukyston, Aberdeenshire, 1375 (RMS., I, 626). Christiane de Wyne was a tenant of the earl of Douglas in the barony of Kilbucho, 1376 (RHM., II, p. 16), and Robert Wynde in the parish of Fyvv was excommunicated in 1382 (REA., I, p. 165). The surname was common in Dysart in the sixteenth century (Dysart, passim).

WYNES, WYNESS. Surnames recorded in Aberdeen. Of local origin. A town called Wyndis

WYNES, WYNESS, *continued*

was possessed by a person of the name. Alexander Wyndis of that Ilk was convicted of forethought felony in 1502 (*Trials,* I, p. * 37). John Wyness in Oldtown of Balquhyne, 1761, and James Wynhouse in Cortans in the same year (*Aberdeen CR.*). There was also a town called Wyndes in the parish of Hobkirk (OPS., I, p. 353).

WYRFAUT. Roger Wyrfaut (Wyrfaudt, Wyrfaud, or Wyrfruch) appears in Fife before 1216 (RPSA., p. 279–285). Rogerus Wyrfauk had a half davoch from Hugh filius Waldef, 1242 (RAA., I, p. 206). Another Roger Wyrfauch appears between 1255–71 (RPSA., p. 335). These individuals were probably offshoots from a Yorkshire family named Wirfauc or Wirefauc who were of considerable prominence there in the twelfth and early thirteenth centuries. In English records the name also occurs as Wirefrauk, Wirefaud, and Wyrfauk. The name may be Flemish. The final letter in the second element may be either a *t* or a *c* (these two letters being indistinguishable in the calligraphy of the period) or perhaps a *d* with a stroke like a *t*.

WYSE. *See under* WISE.

WYTH. Laurencius filius Wyth, judex de Perth in reign of Alexander II (*Scon,* p. 61). Thomas Wyche or Withe, burgess of Perth, rendered homage, 1296 (*Bain,* II, p. 197). Henry Wyth, burgess of Dunfermline, appears in 1316 and c. 1340 (RD., 349; *Scon,* p. 124). Bricius Wyche, familiaris regis, had an annuity from the king in 1364 (RMS., I: In this record his name is mangled to Dichty, Wacht, Wicht, Wycht, Wighte, Wyght, Wichtis, and Wricht). Malcolm Wyth witnessed a deed of sale in Aberdeen, 1383 (REA., II, p. 284), and John Vytht was a witness in Brechin, 1509 (REB., II, 162).

WYTHAND. Sir James Wythand was presented to the sacristy of the church of S. Duthac, Tayne, 1532 (RSS., II, 1428). Rannald Withand in Montago is in record, 1540 (*Rollok,* 33), and James Wichthand was reidare at Inchesture, 1574 (RMR.). Johnne Wythand had a feu of half the myln of Dundaff, 1585 (*Scon,* p. 231). Wythhand 1539.

WYVILLE. William de Wiuilla witnessed a grant by Thomas de Lundin to the nuns of North Berwick, c. 1220 (CMN., 11), and in 1228 William de Wiwill witnessed a charter by Malcolm, 7th earl of Fife (*Laing,* 6; CMN., 7). Lower mentions an ancient Norman family of Wyvill, long seated at Slingsby, co. York.

YAIR. John de Zare in record, 1394 (*Cambus.,* 17). Sir John Yare, chaplain of the altar of St. Michael in Stirling in 1471, was present at the redemption of the lands of Easter Leckie in the following year (*Sc. Ant.,* X, p. 62; SBR.). Thomas Yar or Yare was a prominent merchant burgess of Edinburgh, 1473 (ALHT., I, p. lviii), and had safe conducts granted him to travel in England in 1473 and 1484 (*Bain,* IV, 1407, 1411, 1503). In 1480–81 there is record of a grant "octo bovatis terrarum de Halys" in the regality of Musselburgh confirmed to Thomas Zhare or Yhar and his wife (RD., p. 371). John of Yair was deacon of craft in Stirling, 1522 (SBR., p. 275), Jacobus Yair, a charter witness in Perth, 1523 (*Scon,* p. 203), John Yair, son to umquhile James Yair, had a feu of the lands of Balquhormok in 1585 (ibid., p. 225), David Zair is recorded as a chapman in 1592 (*Sc. Ant.,* VI, p. 168), and William Zair was burgess and guild brother of Glasgow, 1621 (*Burgesses*). Yhar 1485, Zar and Zayr 1511. From Yair in Selkirk parish, Selkirkshire.

YAIRFA. Jhone Yairfa in Dernes, juror on assize in 1559 (REO., p. 111) derived his name from Yarpha near Deerness in Orkney.

YALLOWER. Katrine Yalloar in record in Dunfermline, 1499 (DBR., 105). John Yallower resigned the vicarage of the church of monyfwyth (Monifieth), 1525 (RAA., II, 599).

YATES, YEATS, YEATTS, YETTS. Of local origin from one or more small places of the name meaning, "at the gate," from OE. *geat,* ME. *yate.* "A final *s* is not uncommon in surnames derived from topographical features, and may be either the plural formation or genitive case ending, but it is not possible to say which from inspection," or, again, it may be "a meaningless excrescence, the addition of a terminal sibilant being not uncommon with uncultured people" (*Ewen,* p. 251). Adam del Yate was juror on an inquisition held at Lochmaben in 1347 (*Bain,* III, 1499). John Yet held a land in Arbroath in 1425 (RAA., II, 93), Johannes ȝett, capellanus de Vasthall, died 1479 (REA., II, p. 218), William Yet appears as church elder for Fortrie in 1607 (*Mair,* p. 61), and Agnas Yatts is recorded in the parish of Falkirk in 1681 (*Torphichen*). An ancient family in Teviotdale were the Yetts of Yetton. John Yetts, wright in Edinburgh, 1722 (*Guildry,* p. 126). Yeatt 1688.

YEAMAN. *See under* YEOMAN.

YEATS, YEATTS. *See under* YATES.

YELL. (1) A Perthshire surname, may be from Yuel, a form of Joel. William filius Yuel was witness in a Perth charter, n.d., but in reign of Alexander II (*Scon*, p. 58). (2) The Shetland surname of Yell is derived from the name of the principal island of the Shetland group. Old Zell in Easter Skeld, parish of Sandsting, is in record, 1615 (*Shetland*). Persons of this name in Shetland have changed to Dalziel, probably from the idea of its being more aristocratic, and spell Deyell or De Yell.

YELLOWLEES. Local. Bessie Yallowleys was ordered to keep the statutes of Edinburgh, 1529 (MCM., II, p. 93), and Agnes Yeallowlies appears in Sproustoun, 1696 (*Peebles CR.*). In 1567 and 1569 the name is spelled Yalloleis, Yollaleis, and Yallowleis in documents relating to Berwickshire (*Home*). Cf. YELLOWLEY.

YELLOWLEY. Of local origin probably from the "Sichetum qui vocatur ylalwleche extendens ad medium marisii de Balnedrum" mentioned in a thirteenth-century charter (RD., p. 223). Balnedrum is now Bandrum in the parish of Saline. Gillelmus Yhalulok was a student in St. Andrews, 1413 (ERUS., p. 1), David Yhaliluk and Thomas Yhaliluk appear as witnesses in 1445 (*Cambus.*, 214), and in 1459 'Sir' Duncan Zhaluloh exchanged the rectory of the church of Ranpatrick for the benefice of Crawfurd-Lindsay (LSC., p. 148). In 1467 he appears again as Duncan Yalulok, vicar of Crawford-Lindsay (*Soltre*, p. cxix), and as Duncan Yhalulok, presbyter of St. Andrews diocese in 1470 (*Wemyss*, II, p. 98). Bardsley gives Yellowley as a northern English surname of local origin, but "cannot find the spot."

YELTOUN. A surname recorded in Lanarkshire. Perhaps a variant of Youlton in the North Riding of Yorkshire. Thomas Zeiltoune in record at Wistoun, 1601, Jean Yuiltoun in Ampherlaw, 1631, John Yeltoun in Westhilles, parish of Dolphingstoune, 1673, and John Zeilloune (? for Zeiltoune), in Carnwath, 1674 (*Lanark CR.*).

YENSTAY. An old Orcadian family deriving their surname from the lands of Yenstay in the parish of St. Andrews, Orkney. Jhone of Yensta was juror on an assize in Orkney in 1509 (OSR., I, p. 252), and Andro Zinsta was juror on assize, Kirkwall, 1573 (ibid., p. 267). Olav Zensta and John Elder of Zensta were roithmen in Kirkwall in 1516 (SCM., v, p. 395; PSAS., LIII, p. 192). A genealogy of the family from 1509 is given by Clouston (REO., p. 470). Yainistane 1572, Yinsta 1573, Yinstall 1591.

YEOMAN, YEAMAN. From ME. *yoman, yeman, ʒeman*, originally a countryman or retainer, but later a freeholder next under the rank of gentleman, a man who owned free land of forty shillings annual value. Yeoman is not found in OE. but occurs in ME. *yēman, yōman*, cognate with Old Frisian *gāmann* 'villager.' The surname is of comparatively late appearance in Scotland. George Zeman appears as tenant of the bishop of Moray in 1565 (REM., 438), and David Yeamen, merchant, was admitted burgess of Dundee in 1592 (*Wedd.*, p. 123). Archibald Yemen was one of a number who attested the boundaries of Huttsonis croft in 1651 (*Home*, 220), and Christina Yemane or Yeman, spouse to David Goldman, burgess of Dundee, is in record in 1632 (*Inquis.*, 1878, 1879). James Zeaman of Eastwalkmiln in 1666 appears again in 1689 as James Yeoman, collector at the Quire door of the church of Rattray (DPD., II, p. 79, 84), Patrick Yemane of Dryburgh is recorded in 1678 (*Inquis.*, 6069), and David Zeaman was burgess of Dundee in 1683 (ibid., 6461). James Yeaman at West Waulkmiln of Rattray is recorded in 1768 (*Dunkeld*), and John Yeoman in Milntown of Invererashie in 1773 (ibid.). Zemane 1610.

YESTER. Of local origin from Yester in East Lothian. Thomas ʒester witnessed an instrument of sasine of the lands and castle of Temptalloune in 1475 (*Douglas*, III, p. 106), and Thom Zestyr was tenant on lands of Cupar Angus Abbey, 1478 (*Cupar-Angus*, I, p. 212). George Yester appears as familiar servitor of Margaret, queen of Scotland in 1529 (SBR., p. 266), Robert Yester was juror on an inquest at Coldingham in 1561 (*Coldingham*, App. v.), James ʒestir dwelling in Gorty is in record in 1563 (*Methven*, p. 55), and Katherine Yester in the parish of Lauder, 1564 (*Lauder*). Zester 1513, Zister 1596.

YETHAM. A surname derived from the old form of the name of Yetholm. Rawenild de Jetham appears in a charter by William the Lion to the nuns of Manual, c. 1165–71 (SHSM., IV, p. 305). His son Adam appears as witness to several charters in the later years of the same king (*Melros*, p. 130, 131, 239; *Kelso*, p. 138). William de Yetham of the county of Roxburgh rendered homage in 1296. The seal attached to his homage bears a stag's head cabossed, the crucifixion between the antlers, and S' *Willelmi de Yetham* (*Bain*, II, p. 199, 533). He may be the Master William de Yetham who witnessed a notarial instrument at St. Andrews in 1305 (*Bain*, IV, 1807), and the William of Yetham who was granted a safe conduct by Edward II in 1320 (*Fœdera*,

YETHAM, *continued*

II, pt. I, p. 189). William de ȝethame witnessed an instrument of relaxation of c. 1328 (*Kelso*, p. 370), and David Yettam is in record in Gramislaw in 1683 (*Peebles CR.*).

YETTS. See under YATES.

YEULO. See under YOULO.

YOOL. See under YULE.

YOOLOW. See under YOULO.

YORK. From the city of York in the north of England. Robertus de Eboraco witnessed a charter by Hugh, bishop of St. Andrews, c. 1183–88 (*Scon*, p. 32), and Adam of York, burgess of Roxburgh, rendered homage, 1296 (*Bain*, II, p. 197). *Eoforwic* is the OE. spelling of York, Latinized *Eboracum*.

YORSTOUN, YORSTON, YOURSTON, YORKSON. An old surname in the parish of Corstorphine, Edinburgh, where a family of this name held the land to the east of the village known as 'Yorkstounis.' William Yorstoun and James Yorkstoun were burgesses and charter witnesses in Edinburgh, 1484 (REG., 433), Thomas Yorstoun was goldsmith in Edinburgh, 1672 (*Edinb. Marr.*), and Edward Yorkstoun was recorded heir of his father, Thomas Yorstoun or Yorston, goldsmith and burgess of Edinburgh, 1685 (*Inquis.*, 6689, 8735). A family of the same name is early found in Orkney. Robert Yorkstoun is recorded as 'quondam' tacksman of the links of Burray in 1492 and 1502 (REO., p. 405, 412), Robartt Yorkstane was on an assize concerning the rights of grazing on the island of Saba, 1509 (OSR., I, p. 252), William Yorgstone was witness in Kirkwall, 1508 (REO., p. 80), and William ȝorstone was one of those respited for the slaughter of John, erle of Cathnes, 1539 (RSS., II, 3151). "An early connection of the Yorstons with Burray is indicated by the old rental, but they can have been no more than tacksmen there. The evidence of the Uthel book points strongly to Rowsay as their home, and is corroborated by later documents, and by the fact of an early marriage with the Craigies of Brough" (REO., p. 401). Herbert G. Yorston died in Fife, 1939. Yorgston 1735.

YOTSOUN. Andrew Yotsoun, burgess and provost of Edinburgh, 1381 and 1387, also appears as Yutsoun, Yhutson, and Youtson (*Egidii*, p. 21, 23, 24; CDE., 14). Is it the later YORSTOUN? Cf. YUT.

YOULL. See under YULE.

YOULO (YOOLOW, YEULO). Warden says a family of this name occupied a place in the parish of Kettins for three hundred years (IV, p. 22), and Jervise says the surname appears in various forms in the session books of the parish of Kettins from the year 1645 (II, p. 95). In 1645 Robert Yullo was ordered to pay 6 sh. 8d. for drinking on the Sabbath in Kettins (*Jervise*, II, p. 420). For an account of the Yoolaws in the parish see Jervise (II, p. 420–422). Yevlo 1727, Yeulo and Youlo 1654, Youllo 1666, Youlou and Youlow 1711.

YOUNG. A personal name the same in meaning with Gaelic *Og*, 'young.' The name was probably applied, as Bardsley suggests, "in the sense of *junior*, to distinguish father and son when both bore the same personal name." Malmor dictus Juvenis and Ade dictus Juvenis were assizers at Dumbarton in 1271 (RMP., p. 191). John Yong de Dyngvale witnessed a charter by the earl of Ross to Reginald, son of Roderick of the Isles, in 1342 (TGSI., VI, p. 165), and Symone Yong was burgess of Elgin in 1343 (REM., p. 290). John Yhung was a tenant of the earl of Douglas in Moffat in 1376 (RHM., I, p. lxiii), Adam Zung witnessed a notarial instrument in 1413 (*Pollok*, I, p. 146), and Walter Young served on an assize at Edinburgh in 1428 (RAA., II, 61). Alexander Yong was chaplain and procurator of the house of the Holy Trinity of Aberdeen in 1439 (CRA., p. 6), John Zung was a presbyter in Glasgow in 1442 (REG., 346), and William Yhonge and Walter Yhonge, Scottish merchants, had safe conducts into England in 1446 (*Bain*, IV, 1187), and so also had Patrick Yunge (Yonge, or Yhong), dean of Dunkeld in 1449 (ibid., 1212, 1218). William Zhong was vicar of Cragy in 1449 (RMP., p. 83), Robert Yhunge held a tenement in Glasgow in 1454 (LCD., p. 174), and John Zoung was bailie of William, earl of Orkney in 1462 (*Cambus.*, 89). Alexander Yonge, a native of Scotland, had letters of denization in England in 1482 (*Bain*, IV, 1473), William Zung is recorded in Newburgh, Fife, in 1479 (LAC., 153), and Mongw Young was tenant in Stobo in 1528 (*Rental*). Yowng 1456, Ywng 1388, Zeung 1617, Zong 1511, Zonge 1493, Zoonge 1525, Zowng 1522. Cf. YOUNGER.

YOUNGCLAUSE. A current surname, though rare, in Shetland. Young Claus to distinguish from one older. Dutch Claus is a diminutive of Nikola(u)s.

YOUNGER. The comparative of YOUNG, signifying the younger of two bearing the same Christian name. In Latin documents rendered *Junior*. A writer in the *Scottish antiquary* (IV,

p. 113) claims the name is a translation from the Flemish. "There seems little doubt," he says, "that this is a form of Joncker, or Youncker, a common Flemish name. In Scotland it occurs in the three districts where Flemish names appear...As the occupation of the Youngers in the Fife district was in early times salt-making, a business then solely carried on by Flemings it is apparent that they must have been of that race." William Yhunger was a tenant of the Douglas in Telny in the barony of Abirdoure in Fife in 1376 (RHM., I, p. lxiv), Fynlaw Ywnger was one of the assize on the marches of Woodwrae in 1388 (Bamff, p. 22), and John Zownger was tenant of Syokis in 1474 (Cupar-Angus, I, p. 200). Jhone Zoungar was tenant of the 'Brewland off Partyk' in 1521 (Rental), David Youngar is recorded as burgess of Glasgow in 1549 (Protocols, I), William Yungar was a cordiner in Edinburgh in 1573 (Soltre, p. 225), and another William Youngar was a beidman there in 1584 (ibid., p. 239). The Youngers of Clackmannan and West Linton are in record from c. 1559. The Youngers are a famous family of Edinburgh brewers. "The name of Younger, it seems, is of the same stock with the Youngs, by their arms" (Nisbet, I, p. 203). Yhownger 1552, Yhungar 1569, Yongar 1551, Yowngar 1559, Zownger 1515, Zunger 1692; Yhoungar, Yhounger, Yhowngar, Ywngar. Cf. YOUNG.

YOUNGSON. 'Son of YOUNG,' q.v., or 'Young's son.' Patrick ʒongsone was tenant of the bishop of Aberdeen in 1511 (REA., I, p. 377), Alexander Yowngsone was notary public in 1549 (View, p. 180, 182), and another (?) Alexander Youngsoun, chamberlain of Strathdee in 1558 appears in the following year as Alexander Youngstoun (ER., XIX, p. 55, 93). Alexander Youngson was minister at Logymar, 1574 (RMR.). Rev. Robert ʒoungson was admitted minister of Aboyne in 1588 (AEI., p. 118), Androw Youngsone in Auld Abirdene is recorded in 1633 (SCM., III, p. 109), and Mr. Alexander Youngsone was minister at Rayne in 1681 (Inquis., 6291). Leslie Youngson from Crudie served in the first Great War (Turriff).

YOUNIE, YUNIE, YUNNIE. An old Moray surname. John Eunie in Netherglen of Rothes, 1692, and John Yunie in Gerbity, 1699 (Moray). As forename: Zewnie Cleroch in Broubister, 1661. From ADAMNAN?

YOURSTON. See under YORSTOUN.

YRGALAC. Yrgalac mac dafreth or mac dafrech witnessed two charters by Orabilis,

daughter and heiress of Nessus, before 1199 (RPSA., p. 290–291).

YUILL, YUILLE. See under YULE.

YUKEFLETE. From Yokefleet in Yorkshire. Nicholas de Yoksflete had a protection in 1291 in connection with the affairs of Scotland (Bain, II, p. 130), and John de Yucflete or Yocflet was clerk of the [English] queen's pantry and buttery, 1303 (ibid., 1376, 1380). A horse was purchased from Johannes de Yukeflete, 1312 (Bain, III, p. 422). The name does not appear to have survived.

YULE, YOULL, YOOL, YOOLE, YUILE, YUILL, YUILLE, YULL, YULLE, ZUILL. The usual explanation of this name as "one given to children born on Christmas day," does not satisfy me, but I am at present unable to offer a satisfactory interpretation in place of it. "It is pretended that the Yuilles are descended of a son of Drumikills, born upon Yuilday. This pretension is adhered to by some of the name of Yuille, by others not" (Buchanan, p. 296). Johannes Yhole was burgess of Haddington in 1374 (Yester, p. 26). Johannes Yhole was chaplain in Aberdeen in 1391 (REA., I, p. 189), and Simon Youle executed a charter of sale in the same city in 1399 (Friars, p. 21). John Yhule one of the 'appretiatores carnium' in Aberdeen in 1398 (CRA., p. 375) appears in 1400 and 1401 as bailie and burgess of the same city (SCM., V, p. 15; Friars, p. 22). John Yule de Garmiltoun witnessed the perambulation of the marches of Gladsmuir in 1430 (James II, 16), Thomas Yhule was admitted burgess of Aberdeen in 1451 (NSCM., I, p. 12), and a quantity of timber was purchased from Jonete Gule in 1494 (ALHT., I p. 252). Sir Robert Yuile and Willie Yuil were tacksmen in Walls, Orkney, in 1500 (REO., p. 413), John Youle was officer i. Stirling in 1525 (SBR., p. 22), Robert Ywle witness in Glasgow in 1551 (Protocols, I), Thomas Zule was maltman there in 1577 (Burgesses), Inza Yowyll held land in Holland in Firth, Orkney, in 1553 (REO., p. 250), and Mr. James Yuill was minister of Dairsie, Fife, in 1595 (Dysart, p. 42). Alexander Zule or Yule, headmaster of the Grammar School of Stirling (1578–1612) Latinized his name Julius, and Archibald Yuill was town drummer of Rutherglen in the first half of the nineteenth century. Robert Zooll was eldest son of Robert Zuill, merchand citiner of St. Andrews in 1655 (Inquis., 4049), Nicol Zuill was servitor to George Campbell in 1659 (Poltalloch Writs, p. 76), and Robert Yule was an elder in Dysart in 1641 (PBK., p. 209). James Yool, a poet in Paisley, middle of nineteenth century. The form Zuill is not uncommon in

YULE, YOULL, YOOL, YOOLE..., *continued*

Stirlingshire. The Yules were classed among the followers of Clan Buchanan. Sir Henry Yule (1820–1889), military engineer and Orientalist, was the most distinguished bearer of the name. The old Aberdeenshire surname of Idill has been absorbed by Yule. Yoole 1686, Yoile 1516, Youle 1816, Zuille 1711, Zwyll 1550. Cf. under YELL (1).

YUNNIE. *See under* YOUNIE.

YUT. Andrew Yhut was bailie in Haddington, 1458 (*Neubotle*, p. 245, 248), and James Yut was a tenant on abbey lands of Newbattle, 1563 (ibid., p. 326). Cf. Anne Yeid, resident in Edinburgh, 1529 (MCM., II, p. 88). Cf. YOTSOUN.

ZOUCH. Elena la Suchis or la Zouche was daughter and coheir with her sisters, Margaret and Isabel, of Helen, eldest daughter and co-heir of Alan the last of the old lords of Galloway, and wife of Roger de Quincy, earl of Winchester. She married Alan la Zouche of Ashley, county Leicester, who died in 1269. Symon de la Souche del counte de Lanark rendered homage, 1296 (*Bain*, II, p. 213). The lands of Sir Alan de la Souche in county of Are were taken into the king's hands for his not doing service, 1304 (ibid., p. 425). The name comes from a place in Huntingdonshire, in Latin record rendered *de stipite sicio*.

ZUILL. There are still some people in Scotland who spell their name this way but pronounce it YULE, q.v.

Amendments and Additions

ALEESE. Robert Aleese died in Greenock, 1945.

BELLMAN. (2) The name is also of local origin from Belman or Bellman in Westmorland. In 1390 there is record of one John Belman holding two houses and six acres of land at a rental of 4/11 from Phillippa, the late wife of Robert de Vere, earl of Oxford. (Westmorland archives). There are still places in Westmorland known as Bellman Ground, Bellman Houses, and Bellman's Landing is on the shore of Lake Windermere.

BOAG. Act in favor of Adam Boig for printing the Edinburgh Courant, Feb. 13, 1705 (MCM., II, p. 241).

BOECE. An obsolete spelling of BOYCE, q.v. Hector Boece's *Scotorum historiæ a prima gentis origine* was first published in Paris [1527].

BROUN. A variant of BROWN, q.v.

BROUNFIELD. See also BURNFIELD.

BROWN (2). Line 3 for M'aBriuin read M'aBhriuin.

BULLIE. See under BULLY.

BULLY. See also BULLIE.

BURNFIELD. A continuation of BROUNFIELD, q.v.

CALLANACH. An uncommon form of ALLANACH recorded in Appin.

CALLUM. CALUM at the present day passes as the Gaelic equivalent of "Malcolm," which was originally Mael-Coluimb, "Columba's devotee." (ES.,i,22)

CAWART. See also under CALVERT.

CLEATOUN. There is a Cleadon near Whitburn, co. Durham, from which the name may have come.

COMIE. There were families of this name in Aberdeen and Edinburgh. Probably shortened from MACCOMBIE or MACCOMIE.

COWGIL. There is a Cowgill southeast from Lamington, Lanarkshire, from which the name may be derived.

CRAVEN. (1) from Craven in the West Riding of Yorkshire; (2) from MACCRAVEN, q.v. James Brown Craven (1850–1924), historian and archdeacon of Orkney.

CRUICKSHANK. Cf. Crukyshot (under Lyle, 1452).

CUMMING. Last line, Read Wyntoun, v, p. 233.

DOULL. As there were lands named Doill in Caithness in 1519 the Doulls of Thurster and later Doulls may have derived therefrom.

DRUMBLEE. Probably old local pronunciation of the place name Drumblade.

DUBNI. An inscription in Gaelic (Irish) letters on the door-lintel of Carnassery Castle, Argyllshire, is read by Rev. Mr. Dewar of Kilmartin: *Dia le un' nDuimhne*, "God be with O'Duibhne" — i.e., Argyll (*Celt. Mag.*, VII, p. 241). Mr. John White of Inverness regarded the inscription as Latin and read it: *Fidem in diis have* (or *habe*), i.e., "Have faith in God — lit., the Gods" (Macgibbon and Ross, *Castellated and domestic architecture of Scotland*, IV, p. 321).

DUILACH. G. *dubhshuileach*, 'dark eyed.' A sept of Stewarts of Garth, so named from their immediate ancestor who was black-eyed (Stewart, *Sketches*, I, p. 27). John Dulich in Pearsie, 1691 (*Inquis.*, 7159). Donald Doulich in Glenfernate, 1697 (*Dunkeld*).

EDDISLAW. From Edgelaw, near Gorebridge, Midlothian. The wife of Thomas Edglaw in Dalkeith was accused of being a witch in 1661.

ERGO, EGGO. Old forms of ARGO, q.v. In 1612 an action was brought against David Ergo in Creichie, Aberdeenshire by Alexander White in Ludquharne.

EURE. See under OVER.

FALL. See under FAA.

FLINT. For *Evans* read *Ewen*.

FORMAN. See under FOREMAN.

GAUDEN. John Gauden, son of Thomas Gadie or Gauden, was minister of Tingwall, 1675–88 (*Fasti*, VII, p. 291). John Gauden of Overland in Fetlar acquired the lands of Swinister in Shetland, 1684. John Gauden was a tailor in Dyke, 1764 (*Moray*). For an account of the Gaudens of Swinister and Overland see Grant, *Zetland family history*, 1907, p. 78–80.

GILIANE. Giliane Brand in Irvine, 1323 (*Irvine*, I, p. 124).

GILLOUR. Omit "and Macliver."

Amendments and Additions, continued

GIRIC. Line 3 for Ciricius read Ciricus.

HADDOCH. An old spelling of HADDO, and see also HALDAWACH.

HARESTANES. *See under* HAIRSTANES.

HASTIE. Robert Hastie, the last of the hereditary pipers of Jedburgh, died c. 1792.

HAWTHORNDEN. Line 4 from end read *Havthorndë.*

HAY. The song "The gathering of the Hays," which has been published more than once as an ancient ballad, was the composition of John Hav Allan (later Sobieski Stuart), who turned the name Hay into Macgaradh thus falsely giving the family of Hay a Gaelic origin. The song was first published in his *The bridal of Caolchuirn,* 1822. The Hays of Errol held the office of Hereditary Constable of Scotland, conferred on them by King Robert the Bruce.

HENRY. Fr. and OFr. *Henri, Henry,* ML. *Henricus,* Ger. *Heinrich,* probably from OHG. *Heimrich* or *Heimreich,* 'ruler of the home.'

HOMLIN. Sir Andrew Hoinlyn (recte Homlyn), vicar of Stobou, 1426 (REG., 329). Thomas Homlvn was tenant in the barony of Stobo, 1513 (*Rental*). Homlyng 1533.

IONGANTACH. For *Giongantach* read G. *iongantach.*

KEMBO. Recorded in Kincardineshire. A variant of CAMBO, q.v.

KER, KERR. A silly popular explanation of this Border name is that the clan were all left-handed, in Scots "carr-handed" or colloquially "carrv-handit." See Hogg the Ettrick Shepherd's ballad "The raid of the Kers."

KERTLAND. Recorded in Edinburgh, 1940. Most probably of local origin from Cartland near Lanark.

KILDONAN. A present-day surname of local origin. There are several places of the name from which it may have been derived: in Wigtownshire, Ayrshire, Arran, etc.

KIRBY. The Irish name O'Ciarmhaic was barbarized into Keerwick, Kerwick, and Kirby.

LACHEY. G. *Lachaidh,* a diminutive of LACHLAN, q.v.

LAIPER. *See under* LEAPER.

LAVEROCK. In Fife this name was pronounced Layrick or Lerrick.

MABON. Perhaps from *Maponos* ("the great youth"), the name of an ancient British god equated with Apollo.

MACABHRIUIN, MACBRIOUN. Unfortunately two different names were confused here. Macabhriuin and its variants are corruptions of *Mac a' bhriuthain,* "judge's son," as under BROWN (2).

MACAFFIE. John M'Affie in Meikle Kildy, parish of Drone, 1747 (*Dunblane*).

MACALLAN. It is more probable that the Aberdeenshire Macallans were really Stewarts. Drummin in Strathaven was long the seat of an illegitimate branch of the royal line of Stewart, and most of them called themselves "Clan Allan."

MACBAIN. There were also families of this name in Argyllshire in the sixteenth century apparently distinct from the Macbains of Clan Chattan. Fouar M'Bayne was a charter witness there in 1525.

MACCLAMROCH. See under MACCLANSBURGH.

MACCLOUNIE. Current in Dumfries. Perhaps from Ir. *Mac Cluanaigh,* "son of Cluanach." Woulfe suggests it is perhaps a nickname meaning "deceitful." Thomas M'Clouny in Ackennaught, 1657 (*Dumfries*).

MACCORN. A variant of MACCORAN, q.v. Dauid M'Corne was a notary in Glasgow, 1549 (*Protocols, 1*). John McCorn, minister of Straiton, had his name spelled M'Crone, M'Kern, and M'Quherne in the Acts and proceedings of the General Assembly of the Kirk of Scotland.

MACCOSTRICK. Probably G. *Mac Osraic,* "son of Osrac," a common OE. personal name.

MACCRAVEN. A rare Scottish surname recorded in the United States, 1945. Neill Keir McCrevin in lie Holm had a precept of remission in 1542 (RSS., II, 4454).

MACINTOSH is the correct form of the name notwithstanding the spelling with intrusive *k* by "The Mackintosh."

MACKNESS. *See under* MACNEISH.

MACLATCHIE. Prof. Watson suggests from the *Mac Gilla Eidich,* "son of Eidich's servant," mentioned in AU., 1197.

MACLAUCHRIE. A Galloway surname. Perhaps Ir. *MacClochaire,* son of the stonecutter or mason. Rodger M'Clauchrie in Beoch, parish of Kirkpatrick-Irongray, 1639, and James M'Clauchrie in Kirkpatrick-Irongray, 1772 (*Dumfries*). See under MACCLACHER.

MACLELAND, MACLALLAND. *See under* MACCLELLAN.

MACLEOD. They are divided into two branches: (1) Macleod of Dunvegan (and Harris), now "Macleod of Macleod," descended from Tormod; and (2) Macleod of the Lewes, of which the principal branches are Assynt and Rasaay, descended from Torquil. Of these, Macleod of Dunvegan alone holds land in Scotland.

MACMANNAIN. Woulfe says Ir. *Mac Manainn* is a shortened form of *Mac Manannain*, son of *Manannan* (the name of an ancient Irish sea-god). See under MACCUISH.

MACMARQUIS. Angus Macmarquis, a fiddler in Argyllshire, was in trouble with the church, c. 1655, and his name appears in the Synod records spelled McMarquesse, mcMarques, mcMarquess, mcMarcus.

MACMENIGALL. *See under* MACMUNGALE.

MAC MHIC AILEIN, "son of the son of Allan," was the name by which the Chief of the Clanranald Macdonalds was known to Highlanders.

MACMICHIN. While in the majority of instances this name is doubtless a form of MACMECKAN, q.v., it may also be from a diminutive of Michael.

MACNORAVAICH. The Duke of Argyll in a letter to the *Oban Times* (June, 1945) says a family of Munros who lived near Glenarav, Argyllshire, were known in Gaelic as Mac *inroich*, which got corrupted in the Rentals to Mac-Noraraich, etc. If His Grace is right this disposes of the etymology of this name from *Mac an fhoirbhaich*.

MACOSTRICH. Probably G. *Mac Osraic*, 'son of Osric,' a common OE. personal name. MacOstrick and MacCostrick are said to occur in early Kilmarnock records (GDP). Bearers of the name are also said to belong to Clan Cameron. See also MACCOSTRICK.

MACPHATER. Mcfattair (in Killean, 1692).

MACQUEEN. Line 2 for OIr. *Subne* read *Suibne*.

MACTHOMAS. See note in *Bulletin of The*

New York Public Library, LXIV No 2 (Feb 1960) 64.

MACVANNYCHT. From G. *manach*, 'monk.' Alexander McRob McVannycht, 'Alexander son of Rob son of the monk' (Mackay, *Celtic element in old Inverness*, p. 16).

MAHADDIE. Recorded in Forres, March, 1942. A rare Connaught surname (in Ir. *O'Moithide*) of unknown origin.

MAKGILMORICE. Cancel. See MAC GILMOUR.

MARNOCK. Gilbert Marnock was "Lord of the Chapmen in Fife and Kinross," 1678 (*Scot. Ant.*, IX, p. 156).

MARTIN. Line 7 from top for denisation read denization.

MIDHOUSE. Line 4 read 1539.

MOONLIGHT. Recorded in Arbroath, 1940.

MUNRO. Hugh Macdonald, the Sleat seanachaidh is the authority for the statement that the Munros were "so called because they came from the Innermost Roe-water in the county of Derry" (HP., I, p. 20). The name as the late Dr. Macbain says (in Skene, *The Highlanders of Scotland*, 1902, p. 417), "is very difficult to unravel." As all the early charter references show, it must however be of local or territorial origin — *de Munro*. Dr. Macbain suggests that Monadh-Ruadh, or even Bun-Ruadh ("Red Mount," "Red-footland"), would phonetically suit — the former especially. Ruadh, or Rodh, is the latter root and the foundation of the Gaelic name, *Rothach*, a Munro. An origin from *Mac-an-Rothaich*, "son of the wheelwright" is absurd.

MURCHIESON. John Morchowson was "abbot of vnrest" in Peebles, 1472 (Mill, *Plays*, p. 263).

NEWTIBBER. Dauit filius Kyneth de Neuticbyr witnessed a charter of ten marks sterling yearly from lands in Buchan between 1273–89 (LAC., p. 157).

NIC. It also appears in 1522 as *Nek* in NekLachlan.

O'BROLACHAIN. Donald Obrolachlan in the Maie (or Mail), parish of Kilkerran, 1693 (*Argyll*).

PAIK. *See under* PEACOCK.

834

Amendments and Additions, continued

PAPLAY. Line 4 from end read 1539.

PIERSON. Line 15 from end read 1539.

PILMER. A variant of PILMOUR, q.v., recorded in Dysart, Fife, 1943.

PITHIE. Recorded in Aberdeen. It may be a variant of the place name Peattie (Pettie 1637, Peattie 1682) near Bervie, Kincardineshire. There is another Peattie near Coupar-Angus. Peter Pithie, shoemaker in Linlithgow, 1938. The name of Isobel Pittie, married in Edinburgh, 1636 (*Edinb. Marr.*) may be an earlier spelling of the surname.

PREACHER. A current surname recorded in Midlothian. From the office of preacher. As the English verb "preach" is derived from OFr. *prechier*, "to preach," so the surname comes from OFr. *Precheur* or *Precheor*. The earliest record of the surname in England is in 1272–73, when two individuals, John le Precheur and John le Prechur are in record (*Bardsley*). See also under PRESCHOUR.

QUINTIN. 1583 Quhintene.

RENNIE, RENNY. See *under* RAINY.

RYRIE. From (MAC)RYRIE. See under RIRIE.

ST. GERMAIN. This name may have come originally from one of the twelve places of the name in the *Itinéraire de la Normandie.*

SANDIE. A current surname. A double diminutive of Sander, and so ultimately of Alexander.

SEWALL. Either OE. *sæ weald*, "sea dominion" or OE. *sige weald*, "victorious dominion." Sewale was one of the perambulators of Clerchetune (Clerkington, Haddingtonshire), c. 1144 (RPSA., p. 81). Robertus filius Sewal' witnessed the grant of Gillemoristun before 1189 (REG., p. 39), and Sewal' seruiens cancellarii was a charter witness between 1214–26 (RAA., I, p. 87).

SHAW (2). William Schedo, charter witness, 1517 (RAA., II, 543).

SHORTREED. Several families of this name from the neighborhood of Hawick emigrated to Guelph, Ontario, early in the nineteenth century.

SIWES. A current form of SCHEVES, q.v. Gulielmus Sives, heir of Jacob Sives, his father, was served heir to a tenement in villa monasteriali (Nungate) de Haddington, 1678 (*Retours, Haddington*, 333). Sivess 1734.

STIRLING. A family of this name were proprietors of Lauriston in the Mearns in 1243, in which year Alexander de Strivelin made a grant of the chapel of Laurenston to the priory and canons of St. Andrews (RPSA., p. 280). Adam of Stirling is in RR. Sterveling 1513.

SYDIE. Of same origin as SUTTIE, q.v., from place name G. *suidhe*, a seat.

TANDERSON. See *under* MACCAIG.

TOPPING. Recorded in CD. and Aberdeen directory, but most probably of English origin. Bardsley says a "variant of Turpin," and Harrison says "dweller at the top meadow."

TWENTYMAN. A rare surname in CD. A modernizing of OE. *twinterman*, the man who had charge of the two-year-old animals. A twinter (OE. *twi-wintre*) was a two-year-old sheep.

UTTERSON. See *under* OUTERSON.

VASSIE. From Vassy in the department of Calvados, Normandy. Thomas Vassie, minister at Torphichen, was commissioner for visiting the University of Edinburgh, 1649 (APS., VI, pt. II., p. 510). Catharine Vassie appears in Glasgow, 1679 (*Inquis.*, 6145).

VEITCH. The English family De la Vache so far as we know, were in no way connected with the Scottish family la Uache (or la Vache). Scottish Veitch is more probably of OE. origin from the personal name Ucca or Uacca. Wulstan Ucca appears as a charter witness, c. 960 (Birch, *Cartularium Saxonicum*, 1131). Radulfus uacca witnessed a confirmation charter by Henricus, son of Peter de Graham, c. 1150 (*Neubotle*, p. 7). Alexander la Uache appears between 1214–49 (REG., 126), and is most probably the Sir Alexander de Vacca of c. 1235–53 (*Soltre*, p. 26), whose name shows the Normanizing of the OE. Uacca or Vacca, later Vache and then Veitch. Archibald, earl of Douglas, who fell at Verneuil in 1424, had granted his friend and armor-bearer, Barnabe la Vache, the lands of North Sinton.

WHIMSTER. A variant of FEMISTER, q.v. Recorded in Giffnock, 1945.

YTHERNBUTHIB. In the fictitious list of Pictish witnesses to a charter in the Legend of St. Andrews (CPS., p. 187) is Talarg filius Ythernbuthib, which probably represents *Talarg mac Ythernbiuthut*, "Talarg son of eternal life."

Glossary of Obsolete or Uncommon Scots Words Occurring in the Dictionary of Names

advowson, the right of patronage or presentation to a church benefice.

amerced, fined, mulcted.

amerciament, a penalty inflicted.

argentier, treasurer.

assizor, a juror.

band, a written agreement or promise.

beddell, inferior officer of a court. See the name in the Dictionary of names.

bedeswoman, an alms woman, a licensed beggar. Cf. *beidman.*

beidman, beidsman, a public almsman or licensed beggar.

blue-gown, one of a class of former privileged mendicants, so named from the blue gown or cloak he had to wear. Same as *beidsman.*

boll, bow, a measure of capacity for grain, malt, etc.

bon-accord, the French motto of the city of Aberdeen, used as the name of the city itself.

bond of manrent, a written agreement whereby a free person becomes follower of a patron or defender.

bore-brieve, a formal certificate of descent given to a person who had settled or intended to settle on the continent, granted under the great seal or seal of a burgh. It secured his social position in his new abode.

borowis, pl., a borow or borrow was one who became surety for another.

bovate, an ancient land measure.

brasiator, brewer.

brew caldron, a large kettle used in brewing.

brieve, a judicial writ or brief.

broche, burgh, town.

burgage, a tenure in royal burghs under nominal service of watching.

burgageship, the status or privileges by which property within a royal burgh is held of the king.

cagger, cadger, a traveling pedler. See also surname *Cadger.*

calcearius (ML.), shoemaker.

calsay, causeway.

carbonarius, charcoal maker.

carucate, originally an amount of land such as one team of oxen could plough in a season.

caution, bail, security.

cautioner, one who stands surety for another.

cellarer, officer in a monastery who looked after the provisions.

clachan, a hamlet, small village.

claré constat (L.), "it is clearly established," the opening words of a precept of seisin granted to an heir by the superior.

coarb, com(h)arb, the successor in an ecclesiastical office. Irish *comharba.*

collation, presentation to a benefice.

comburgess, fellow burgess, a member of the same burgh.

Commissariot record, the record of the commissary court which had jurisdiction over domestic relations.

compear, to appear in court.

composition, an agreement or settlement of a dispute.

conservator, guardian, custodian.

cordiner, cordinar, a worker in cordwain, a shoemaker.

creelman, one who carries goods or wares, or brings them to market, in a creel.

crewkit, lamed.

croft, a small piece of arable land adjoining a dwelling.

cruives, pl., wattled hedges built on tidal flats for catching fish.

Culdee, one of an order of monks in the early Middle Ages.

culveriner, a soldier who fired or used a culverin.

curator, one appointed by law as guardian.

custumar, a collector of customs. See the surname in the Dictionary of names.

dag maker, pistol maker.

dapifer, a steward in a royal or noble house.

davach, davoch, davat, a measure of land. Gael. *dabhach.*

decreet arbitral, the final judgment or pronouncement of a competent judge or arbiter.

deforced, deforce in Scots law is resistance to an officer of the law in the execution of his duty.

Glossary, continued

delated, accused or charged (ecclesiastical term).

dempster, one who pronounced judgment, doomster. See the surname Dempster in the Dictionary of names.

dinging, beating, striking, assaulting.

disorderly person, a non-conformist, one who refused to conform or subscribe to the established church of the period.

disponed, law term, made over or conveyed to another.

distraint, seizure of goods.

dittay, indictment, charge. OF. *ditté*.

dominus, in the pre-Reformation church this was the title of the inferior clergy in Latin, rendered *sir* in English. Many of these minor clergy in the new order found employment as readers and teachers and gradually became known as dominies (cf. "Dominie Sampson" in Scott's *Guy Mannering*). See also *Pope's knight*.

dominus ejusdem = of that ilk.

doomster. See under *dempster*.

engager, a follower in the Engagement between the Scots Presbyterians and Charles I.

escheat, forfeiture.

escheator, an official appointed yearly to take notice of the escheats in the county to which he is appointed, and to certify them into the Exchequer.

excambed, exchanged.

fermourer, Scots form of *firmarius*, q.v.

ferry-louper, the name given in Orkney to a settler or incomer from the mainland.

fethelar, a fiddler.

feu, a possession held on payment of a certain yearly rent in grain or money.

feuar, one who holds a feu.

feu-farme (or *ferme*), a mode of possessing land.

fiar, one who had reversion of property.

firmarius (ML.), a farmer. In Scotland one who farmed the revenue. See *Farmer* in Dictionary of names.

flesher, a butcher.

forespeaker, an advocate, a pleader in court.

forestall, to buy up the whole stock of goods before they are brought to the market (= cornering in U. S.).

forestaller, one who buys up the whole stock of goods before they are brought to market (= cornerer in U. S.)

forethought felony, premeditated serious crime.

fruictman, a man who sold fruit.

gowk (1) cuckoo; (2) fool, stupid person.

groat, a silver English coin, nominally worth 4d., current until 1662.

gudger, *gudser*, grandfather; a corruption of gudsyr.

hamesucken, feloniously assaulting a man in his own house.

harathor for *arathor*, a Gaelic corruption of Latin *aratrum*, a plough, formerly used as a land-measure. The place name Arrochar is a Gaelic adaptation of the Latin term.

herd, a herdsman.

hereyeld, the fine payable to a superior on the death of his tenant. = English "heriot."

heritor, a landholder in a parish.

hership, a foray, a carrying off of cattle by force.

hortulanus, gardener.

husband land, a division of land containing twenty-six acres.

ilk, the same; of that ilk, one whose surname is same as that of his estate.

indweller, an inhabitant.

infeft, to give possession of heritable property.

infeftment, the symbolical giving possession of land, the completion of the title.

inquest, a judicial inquiry before a jury.

inquisition, investigation, judicial enquiry.

instrument, a written document given in proof of any deed of a court; *to ask an instrument*, to demand a legal document with respect to a deed.

intromission, a law term, the assumption of authority to deal with the property of another.

intromitting, (1) intermeddling with goods which belonged to one deceased; (2) intermeddling with the goods of a living party.

joges, an iron neck-ring — the old Scots pillory.

kerrowan, *kerrowrane*, an old local measure of land in Islay.

kirkmaster, a deacon in a church; (2) a deacon of an incorporated trade.

knaiffscheipe, a certain quantity of grain, the due of the under miller.

knok, a clock.

lawborrowis, a writ requiring a person to give security against doing violence to another.

lawman, one with magisterial powers; in Orkney and Shetland formerly the presiding officer in a court.

lawting, formerly the supreme court of judicature in Orkney and Shetland.

letter of horning, a letter directed to a messsenger-at-arms to enforce payment by a debtor of the debt for which he is prosecuted within a limited time.

liferenter, one who enjoyed a tenancy for life on payment of rent.

limmer, a scoundrel, a thief.

lineator, surveyor, measurer.

litster, a dyer.

lykewake, the watching of a dead body.

mair, an official attending a sheriff for arrestment or executions.

mair of fee, a hereditary officer under the Crown holding certain powers.

maltster, one who makes malt.

manrent. See *bond of manrent.*

march, a boundary.

marifeodus, in Scots mair of fee, a hereditary officer whose power resembled that of a sheriff-substitute.

mart, a cow or ox fattened, killed, and salted for winter provision.

messuage, a dwelling and offices with the adjoining lands appropriated to the household.

miles, a knight. LL.

moneyer, one who coins money, a mintmaster.

mortified, bequeathed.

moyane, means.

multure, the fee paid to the miller for grinding grain.

nonentres, the fine payable to a superior on the failure of an heir to renew investure on the death of his ancestor.

noneschankis, afternoon repast.

nonganging, not going, being absent from.

odaller, a holder of land by uninterrupted succession under no feudal superior. See *udal-land.*

opponed, opposed.

orloge, clock, Fr. *horologe.*

ourman, overseer, master.

oxgang, as much land as could be tilled by the use of an ox.

particate, a rood of land.

peaterie, petarie, a peat bog from which peat is dug. LL. *petaria.*

pelliparius, skinner.

perambulator, one who attested the bounds of a land by walking round the boundaries.

pertinent, anything pertaining to land, generally used in the plural.

pikar, piker, a petty thief.

poinded, seized, distrained.

polentarius, a malt maker.

Pope's knight, a title formerly applied to clerics who had not taken the proper academical degree of master of arts, so as to entitle them to use the higher prefix of master or magister.

portioner, one who possesses part of a property which had been originally divided among co-heirs.

precept, an order subscribed by the king or un er his signature.

prepositus, provost, answering to mayor in England.

presentation, the right of presenting to a benefice.

procurator, a lawyer, advocate.

proditor, a traitor (Latin).

purparty, the share of an estate held by co-parceners and allotted to them in partition.

put to the horn, the proclamation of outlawry after the formality of blowing three blasts of a horn at the town cross.

querrell, stone quarry.

quhinzeare, a dirk.

quit-claim, n. a renunciation of all claim; v. to renounce all claim.

reddendo, the clause of a charter which specifies what duty the vassal is to pay to the superior.

reidare, a reader, one in minor orders in the Scottish Church after the Reformation. See *dominus.*

reiver, robber, thief.

remission, a pardon.

resetter, a receiver or concealer of stolen goods.

respite, a prorogation of punishment or of prosecution.

retour, an extract of the service of an heir to his ancestor.

rude, rood(s), land measure.

sasine, the act of giving legal possession of property; 2, the instrument by which such possession is proved.

scatland, in Shetland a land paying a tax for rights of pasture and peat.

sclater, occup., a slater. See the surname in the Dictionary.

Glossary, continued

seisin, same as *sasine*.

seized, given possession of property by legal authority.

sept, a subdivision of a clan.

seriand, a constable, bailiff.

servitor, clerk, secretary, attendant.

sib, related by blood.

sir, see under *dominus*.

socage, a form of tenure of agricultural land.

spuilzeit, laid waste, carried off as prey.

spulzie, spoil, plunder.

squarewright, a worker in the finer kinds of furniture.

stane, a weight of fourteen pounds.

steked naiff, closed fist.

stokkis, an obsolete instrument of punishment in which the ankles of offenders were confined.

stouthreif, theft attended with violence.

strang, urine long kept and smelling strongly.

sword sliper, one who made sword-slips or sheaths.

tack, a lease.

tacksman, one who holds a lease.

tailzeor, tailor.

tannator, tanner.

teind, a tythe.

tenement, in law, that which is held by tenure, the possessor of which is a tenant, hence lands, houses, etc., held of another for a term of years.

Test, The, an act passed in the Scots parliament, 1681, which was practically a repudiation of the Covenant, and an acknowledgement that the king was supreme in all causes "as well ecclesiastical as civil."

theke, n. and v., thatch, to thatch.

tochdoreschip, the office or dignity of a *mair of fee*, q.v. Gael. *toiseadracht* + Eng. *-ship*.

toft, a messuage with right of common.

tolune, toll, custom.

transumpt, a copy, a transcript.

udal-land, land in Orkney and Shetland held solely by uninterrupted succession, under no feudal superior. See *odaller*.

umquhile, deceased, the late.

vabster, wobster, a weaver.

vendition, the act of selling.

vestiarius, keeper of the wardrobe.

wadset, a contract under which the lender got actual possession of certain lands, and continued to occupy them, virtually as proprietor, until the money was repaid, sometimes after generations had passed.

wisag, face.

wrecker, one who lured vessels to destruction that he might share in the plunder; (2) a plunderer of a wreck.

yokis, in yokis = in harness.